Encyclopedia of
AMERICAN
BIOGRAPHY

Encyclopedia of
AMERICAN
BIOGRAPHY

SECOND EDITION

John A. Garraty, editor

Jerome L. Sternstein, editor

HarperCollins*Publishers*

FIRST EDITION

Library of Congress Cataloging-in-Publication Data

   Encyclopedia of American Biography/edited by John A. Garraty, Jerome L.
    Sternstein.—2nd ed.
      p. cm.
    ISBN 0-06-270017-0
    1. United States—Biography—Dictionaries. I. Garraty, John Arthur, 1920–   .
  II. Sternstein, Jerome L.
  CT213.E53   1995
  920.073—dc20   96-76

97 98 99 00 ❖/RRD 10 9 8 7 6 5 4 3 2

Introduction

This encyclopedia brings together within the covers of one book descriptions and evaluations of the lives of more than one thousand persons. Librarians will no doubt classify it as a work of reference, and we have certainly designed it with that function in mind. It is full of facts and dates. But it is more than a storehouse of information organized for the convenience of anyone who wants to look up the date of Herman Melville's birth or the year that Daniel Webster delivered his "Seventh of March" speech. It is also a compendium of informed opinion intended to aid readers who want to know the *whys*, not merely the *whats*, about the significant figures of our history.

The volume, in short, was conceived with *all* the needs of those who turn to biographical encyclopedias in mind, needs which we—as inveterate users of such encyclopedias—believe we understand. It differs in several respects from works which it superficially resembles because most of these fail to fulfill the different purposes of readers.

The most striking innovation in this book is the way entries are constructed. Each is divided into two parts. The first part attempts to be completely objective—to stick, in other words, to facts. It begins with the subject's full name, place and date of birth and death, and principal occupation. There follows a summary of the subject's life arranged chronologically: education, major stages of career (political affiliation and offices held by statesmen, books written by novelists, discoveries of inventors and scientists, and the like) and, finally, for living persons, present activity. These accounts are as concise as possible and confined to the professional experiences of the subjects. They say nothing about parents, husbands and wives, children, quirks of personality, and similar matters unless these details seem directly relevant to the career that led us to include the person in our book. Except in the sense that they are summaries, and thus selective in their use of facts, they are objective.

The second part of each entry attempts to evaluate the total career of the subject, to explain why the individual is important, and to provide some sense of what he or she was like as a human being. Each interpretive essay was written by someone with specialized knowledge of the subject. The authors' names are appended to the essays along with the title of the book or article that, in their opinion, is the most convenient and reliable source for further information on the person in question.

As we have said, we have made this separation of fact from evaluation to accommodate the differing needs of those who consult the volume. Biographical articles in encyclopedias have usually been organized on the model of conventional full-length biographies. To the extent that they provide any interpretation at all, they tend to integrate the evaluative passages within a chronological narrative. This makes sense in a full biography where it can be assumed that readers will have the time and motivation to absorb the work as a whole, but it is our contention that the format is not well suited to the requirements of an encyclopedia. Normally, users of such works are either looking for a particular fact or have come upon a name and want a brief summary of the person's career to put the name in proper context, or else, knowing at least in a general way who the subject was, they are seeking an expert evaluation, or some impression of his or her personality. In the first instances they may have to read through a long article to find the fact or assimilate the summary; in the second they must more often than not make the evaluation for themselves after reading the article and do so on the basis of inadequate, highly condensed evidence. By dividing fact from interpretation, we simplify the task in all instances. The format also makes clear what is fact, and what is opinion, however informed by facts, and offers much more space for interpretation than is usually allocated in works of this type.

The division of the entries in this way leads to still another advantage that we believe adds considerably to the book's value. The factual sections were drafted before we commissioned the authorities to write the evaluations. The research involved was done by graduate students, most of them candidates in history at Columbia University. Thus we could offer our experts the opportunity to concentrate entirely on the significance of each subject's life, sparing them the task of recording a host of details, the building blocks from which the individual's achievement was constructed. (We did ask the experts to check the factual sections for errors or omissions, but as many of them have spontaneously testified, this was a far less tedious assignment than preparing the summaries themselves.) The result of this method was that we found it relatively easy to enlist authorities who might well have refused to write routine brief biographies.

This encyclopedia differs from most others also in that it contains articles on living persons as well as on significant figures of the past. We have rejected the line of reasoning that says it is too soon to evaluate contemporaries or even to know who among them are really important. We have done so on the ground that all historical judgments, not merely those of persons close to our own time, are relatively impermanent, limited by ignorance, and subject to human error. This being the case, why eliminate the living? Judging which of today's celebrities are truly significant is risky, and we have tried to exercise a certain prudence, but we felt the effort should be made. Put differently, if we had established a cut-off date for inclusion in our book, we would have eliminated many persons that readers want to know about, yet assuredly we would not have published the last word about those who remained. In still other words, what we have to offer is an estimation of the major figures of American history as seen from the perspective of the mid–1970s. We expect, indeed we intend, to add names and probably eliminate others in future editions of this work. We do not expect that later generations will agree entirely with either our judgment of who is important or with our contributors' views of *why* they are important, but we are quite sure that this would be equally true if we had confined ourselves to figures of the past.

The interpretations in the following pages are those of the hundreds of experts who wrote the essays. The choice of the persons described and evaluated is our own—although of course we have profited from the advice of many other scholars. Selecting our subjects was a difficult but fascinating task; we dared undertake it only because we recognized at the start that any list, no matter how long, would be subject to legitimate criticism and emendation. The major problem of selection lies not in human ignorance, of which we possess our full share, but in the establishment of criteria. To the question, What determines a person's importance? there are many answers. The major ones are these: *Significance.* Did the person influence his own times or the course of history in a meaningful way? *Achievement.* Did the individual reach a level of performance in career or profession noticeably superior to high competence? *Fame* (or *Notoriety*). Was the subject widely known to contemporaries or, even if not to contemporaries, to later generations? *Typicality.* Does a person merit inclusion because he or she reflects some broad trend or is representative of some large group?

Some subjects satisfy all these criteria, and pose no problems. George Washington influenced the course of history, his achievements were large, he was and is famous, and he was typical of a certain class of Virginians of his age. The difficulties arise when only one of the criteria is met, and particularly when the others are not even approached. Is "mere" significance proper justification for inclusion? The question is not unlike the riddle of whether or not a tree that falls in a deserted forest makes a noise. Since readers, their curiosity aroused by something they have heard or read, seldom turn to an encyclopedia without a particular name in mind, does an obscure person who has had influence deserve inclusion? What should be done about the economist whose analysis shaped the thinking of a generation or more but whose work has been superseded? Or the actor who dominated the stage in his day but whose style is no longer copied? Or, for that matter, the scientist whose discoveries, while still relevant, have become so much a part of accepted knowledge that his name is seldom mentioned even in textbooks? On the other hand, is fame, even current fame, enough? What of the best-selling novelist whose works have no artistic merit, the current film or television star?

We have dealt with this problem by applying different standards to different kinds of people, standards which reflect our own scale of values, which we readily concede may not be those of others. In the broadest terms, we have decided that significance is always enough to merit inclusion, that "mere" achievement is enough in certain fields but not in others, and that fame unaccompanied by significance or achievement must be truly extraordinary to meet our requirements. All the presidents are included on the ground of fame alone—some on no other. (Having been a president, by the way, was the only "occupation" that automatically ensured inclusion of a person.) More specifically, we include relatively obscure persons such as the jurist Thomas Cooley, the microbiologist Theobald Smith, the educator Ida Wells-Barnett, the public health official Charles V. Chapin, the journalist Wilbur Cash, the physician Elizabeth Blackwell, the economist Tench Coxe, the Egyptologist William Foxwell Albright, and reformers like Grace Abbott, John Boyle O'Reilly, and Sophonisba Breckinridge because in one way or another their lives have shaped our culture. As for our subjective evaluation of achievement, we include many artists from John Singleton Copley through George Caleb Bingham and Thomas Eakins, to Edward Hopper, Georgia O'Keeffe, and Adolph Gottlieb simply because they are marvelous painters, but where, say, baseball players are concerned, great performance alone is not enough. We have not included Ted Williams, Walter Johnson, Ty Cobb, or a dozen others of the highest ability. But we have included Babe Ruth, the equal of course of any of these, and Jackie Robinson, a lesser figure when viewed only as a player, because of their impact on the game, on professional sports in general, and on the larger society. We did not include the assassin Lee Harvey Oswald, although his name is certainly better known than hundreds of persons on our list, or the murderers of Presidents Garfield and McKinley, Adam Guiteau and Leon Czolgosz. However, we did add John Wilkes Booth, partly because his killing of Lincoln had great historical significance and partly because of Booth's stature as an actor.

In short, we consider influence more important than achievement, and intellectual and artistic achievement more important than athletic prowess or, for that matter, business ability or political skill, although large numbers of businessmen and politicians are included because of their influence. We have, by the way, defined influence, or significance, without regard for the quality of the achievement that produced it. A lesser novelist like Horatio Alger finds a place in our pages, and so do Spiro T. Agnew, P. T. Barnum, and such robber-baron types as Jim Fisk and Henry M. Flagler, all because they affected their own or later times in important ways.

One further aspect of the selection process requires explanation. In a number of cases it was difficult to decide whether or not a person qualified for an encyclopedia of *American* biography. We have included many foreign-born persons, even some who never became United States citizens. On the other hand, we passed over a number of individuals of the highest distinction and long resident in the United States. The question we asked was, Where did the person's major achievements take place? We tried to look at each career as a whole and to decide if it was an American career. Thus we included the radical propagandist Tom Paine but not the equally radical (and far more distinguished) Joseph Priestley; the Swiss-born biologist Louis Agassiz, but not the German architect Marcel Breuer; the physicist Edward Teller, but not the rocket expert Werner von Braun. Albert Einstein made our list for his role in persuading President Franklin Roosevelt to develop the atomic bomb and for his connection with the Institute for Advanced Study, not for his achievements as a theoretical physicist, which long antedated his coming to America. We left out many foreigners whose activities in the United States were significant, from General Cornwallis to Alexis de Tocqueville and James Bryce to the Beatles, because they were never more than visitors. The major exception—we put aside borderline cases that we admit could have been decided either way, such as Arturo Toscanini (out) and Mies van der Rohe (in)—was Christopher Columbus, who never even realized that America existed but whom we included because his work made this encyclopedia possible!

The story of how, given these standards, we collected our list of subjects is also, we believe, worthy of explanation. We began by establishing occupational categories—nineteen, as it turned out. Then we considered the history of these fields, with their subdivisions. We made lists, checked histories and biographical encyclopedias, and consulted with specialists when in doubt. It quickly became apparent that different standards should be applied in different fields and at different times within fields. There were not only many more important American businessmen than, say, composers, but the businessmen were more outstanding when viewed in a world setting. As everyone knows, America produced no Mozart in the eighteenth century, no Beethoven, Brahms, Berlioz, Wagner, or even a Tchaikovsky in the nineteenth, whereas from John Jacob Astor and Nicholas Biddle to Rockefeller, Carnegie, Morgan, Ford, Woolworth, and Thomas J. Watson the list of American businessmen of international stature was very long. Our decision was to include the most significant American figures in each area without much regard for their places in any larger context. Similarly, one would have to have been a better writer to make our list if one wrote in the 1850s than in the 1790s, but a more important political leader in the 1790s than in the 1950s: the competition was keener.

Thus our list of subjects was really many lists, each constructed with relatively little regard for the others. Some quickly became much longer than others, and in general they remained so. It is as senseless to try to rate philosophers against explorers as to compare the virtues of corn and cucumbers. One may decide that corn is a more useful food or even that it is better tasting, but such conclusions are of no help in comparing cucumbers.

However long the list, there was always the problem of where to cut it off. These marginal decisions were the most interesting, and our reputations as judges will have to stand or fall upon them. We early determined to make them ourselves rather than to rely upon committees or juries of experts. We did so for several reasons, and now that the project has been completed it is hard to say which were the "real" reasons and which rationalizations after the fact. One was that specialists do not always make the best judges; many, when asked to choose between A and B, insist that both are essential and that, furthermore, so are C and D and E. Specialists also tend to disagree about marginally significant persons, which leaves editors where they were in the first place. Finally—at least this was our conclusion—a lack of profound knowledge is in some ways an advantage; a superficial but broad view of a field, one uncluttered too much by nuances and details, may help one to see clearly its really important personalities.

In the last analysis, whatever the scope of a work such as this, the editors have to make choices. For example, we included Betty Friedan because her book, *The Feminine Mystique,* triggered the modern women's movement, and Bob Dylan because of what seemed to us his enormous impact on the attitudes of young people toward the Vietnam war and the fate of the poor, but left out the well-known feminist Gloria Steinem and the comedian Lenny Bruce because we believed they reflected recent changes rather than caused them to occur. We found it more difficult to decide which of the leading contemporary novelists and poets were significant than to pick and choose among painters and sculptors, and when in doubt we usually left them out. Sometimes, however, we included a person as representative of a number of more or less equally significant contemporaries—the criterion of typicality. We are not so vain as to believe that we always made the correct decisions. Every reader will question some of them. But we doubt that a system of selection based on a consensus of specialists would have reduced the number of such complaints. And although, as we have just said, knowing about corn is of no direct aid in comparing cucumbers, we would like to believe that our digging and weeding in so many gardens over a period of years have made us quite expert at our highly specialized occupation.

We do not mean to suggest that we made no use of the opinions of authorities; nothing could be further from the truth. Many of our contributors suggested additional subjects and convinced us of their importance. In the sciences and modern music, where we did not trust our judgment, we sought out experts whose opinions we respected and relied upon their advice. Of these Donald Fleming and Edward Lurie, historians of science; Saul Benison, whose knowledge of the history of American medicine is encyclopedic; and David Ewen and Stanley Dance, experts in modern music, were especially generous of their time.

Of course we were careful not to leave out important women, or blacks and members of other minority groups frequently ignored or slighted in encyclopedias. We rejected the idea of applying different, lower standards to such persons; an encyclopedia should be a record, not a device for righting ancient wrongs. Our special concern was not to compensate for old injuries but to avoid old mistakes. It is notorious that historians until recently neglected the contributions of women and blacks and thus many of our sources (and we ourselves in the sense that we are products of a particular culture) did not pay proper attention to such persons. We hope and believe that we have searched diligently and educated ourselves sufficiently. In deciding upon these subjects we were greatly aided by Gerda Lerner and C. Eric Lincoln.

In seeking authors for the interpretive essays, we looked first for persons who had written biographies of the subjects. When no good modern study existed or when the authors of such works were unavailable, we usually turned to an authority in the subject's field or profession. But we followed no universal rule. Sometimes we asked a scholar in a different field to write the essay; sometimes we knew or learned of a person eager to tackle a subject out of curiosity, and if we respected the potential author's ability we often gave him the assignment. When we received an especially interesting essay, we frequently offered the contributor a wide choice of other subjects. In general, however, we looked first for the best recent authority, the logical choice, and in well over 80 percent of the cases our first choice agreed to take on the assignment. What was particularly encouraging was the tendency of scholars to applaud the format of our project even when they felt unable to participate and their willingness to volunteer the names of other specialists who might accept when they could not.

Aside from describing the format and assigning rough word limits for the essays, we gave our scholars no instructions. How to define significance and organize the presentation, whether to bestow praise or blame or steer a middle course, whether to emphasize personality and whether to describe it explicitly or by implication and demonstration was in each instance the author's responsibility alone. We hoped that our experts would be fair, and when the subjects were more than ordinarily controversial, we looked for a scholar not completely identified with one position or another.

Given this approach, we exercised our editorial pencils very lightly in revising the essays. In a general way the length of an essay is an indication of our judgment of the subject's importance, but not always. In some instances relatively minor individuals take a good deal of explaining. (This is true of the factual summaries as well.) In other cases where our authors exceeded the assigned limits, we found their essays so interesting that we allowed them more space than we had intended. But sometimes we felt obliged to shorten articles that substantially exceeded the length we had asked for.

Occasionally we asked an author to reconsider a judgment, more frequently to take account of some aspects of the subject's life ignored in the essay. Nearly always the author did so cheerfully; if he did not change what he had written, we let the work stand—only once did we finally feel compelled to reject an article. Needless to say we disagreed with any number of the judgments expressed in the following pages, and so will every reader curious enough to go through this book from cover to cover. But these opinions, however wrongheaded they may appear, are informed opinions. We have discovered that many opinions we disagreed with are among the most thought-provoking. And more than once we found our own views changing as we studied essays that at first reading appeared outrageous—Otis Pease's estimation of Bruce Barton, the advertising executive and author of *The Man Nobody Knows*, for example—or, more often, ones that deepened our insights into careers we had thought we understood, such as Walter LaFeber's subtle discussion of the diplomacy of George F. Kennan, and Otis L. Graham, Jr.'s beautifully balanced analysis of J. Edgar Hoover.

We hope that all we have said above will convey some sense of the pleasure, even excitement, that working on this project has brought us. Of course it has had its tedious hours and also its frustrations. But we have—inevitably—learned a great deal about every one of the persons whose lives are described and evaluated in our encyclopedia, and in the process we have also come to know as friends many of the scholars, journalists, and other experts who have made the project possible. Now the time has come to share all this with others. We trust that they, too, will find here pleasure and excitement along with new knowledge, and that they will also feel that they have made new acquaintances among the authors whose wisdom enlightens the following pages.

Many persons aside from the authors of the essays and the scholars already mentioned have contributed importantly to this book. Cass Canfield, Jr., our editor at Harper & Row, first suggested the need for a new one-volume biographical encyclopedia. When the format was developed, he saw its merits at once and agreed to make the large financial commitment that carrying out the project entailed. Throughout, his enthusiasm and optimism have sustained us. His contribution has ranged from suggesting the names of persons we had not thought to include to sending polite but peremptory telegrams to delinquent authors as our deadline approached. Pamela Jelley of Harper & Row has handled the enormous correspondence involved in the project, managed our complex system of record keeping, typed and retyped thousands of pages of manuscript swiftly and efficiently, and has done all this with remarkably good cheer. Our copy editor, Mildred Owen, caught many errors that had slipped through our editorial net and in several instances pointed out important omissions in the entries, which we have hastened to fill in. Our mainstays among the students who drafted the factual sketches were Stephen Katz and Aaron Singer; others who contributed substantially were Wilbur Miller, Daniel Raskin, Bruce Wilkenfeld, and Dov Zakheim. Rand Hoffman, Michael Kazer, Joseph Paranac, and Michael Perry helped maintain our files and ran countless errands to the Columbia University library, checking facts and locating the names and addresses of prospective authors. To all these persons, and to our wives, Gail Garraty and Trina Sternstein, whose encouragement and forbearance have been a constant support, we extend our profound thanks.

John A. Garraty
Jerome L. Sternstein
New York, N.Y.
February 25, 1974

Introduction to
the Second Edition

In this second edition we have adhered as closely as possible to the standards established in the first. Again we were faced with the daunting task of deciding whom to include in a one-volume work focused on the most important and significant historical actors in American history. This has meant selecting people not included in the first edition who in the last two decades have made significant contributions or whose historical significiance has become clearer with the passing of time. After consulting with experts in a variety of fields, we had long discussions in which we debated the merits of numerous candidates. We came up with about 150 new names which we then whittled down to the 93 who made our final list. Many of those who survived this sorting out process, people like Gloria Steinem, Lee Harvey Oswald, and Ty Cobb were considered for inclusion in the first edition but were in the end rejected for what seemed good reasons at the time. We believed in 1974, for example, that Gloria Steinem reflected the modern feminist movement but had not shaped or propelled it as Betty Friedan had. The last two decades have proved us wrong. Similarly, in the first edition we rejected John F. Kennedy's assassin, Lee Harvey Oswald, but included Abraham Lincoln's, John Wilkes Booth, partly because Booth had an important career as an actor but mainly because we believed Lincoln's premature death had a greater impact on the nation than Kennedy's. Again, the passage of time has caused us to reevaluate not Oswald's personal stature—it remains exceedingly minor—but what now seems the significance of Kennedy's death and because of the continuing controversy that surrounds the assassination. As for Ty Cobb, recent research into the history of baseball and new books about him have convinced us that he had a greater influence in shaping America's national pastime than we had originally supposed.

In choosing new names for this edition, we automatically included the American presidents, Gerald R. Ford, Jimmy Carter, George Bush, and Bill Clinton. Though fine entries on Richard Nixon and Ronald Reagan appeared in the first edition, we asked scholars to reevaluate them and write new essays to bring them up to date. But in all other instances the people included were chosen because of their influence on history and not because of their current celebrity. Steve Jobs and William Gates are cases in point. We included Jobs because of his role as a pioneer developer of the personal computer industry. William Gates, the founder of Microsoft, the dominant force in the software industry, is far richer and far more powerful than Jobs, but we are not sure that he is an innovator. He has found a niche in the computer industry and exploited it brilliantly. Perhaps one day we will change our minds, but as of 1995 we have not been convinced.

In the case of the many subjects in the first edition who are still alive or who have died since 1974, we asked the original authors to reconsider their essays and revise them if necessary. Some biographies, such as the one of Averell Harriman, were rewritten by their authors. Others, such as the entry on Rexford Tugwell, were changed only slightly. If the original contributor did not respond to our requests, when necessary we incorporated new information drawn from recently published biographies and other studies. For example, newly available materials in the archives of the former Soviet Union made it clear that the labor leader Harry Bridges was indeed a member of the Communist Party, and we revised the interpretive essay on him accordingly.

As in the first edition, our goal has been to produce a clearly written, accurate, and useful compendium of American biography that can be read for information as well as for enjoyment. We think we have succeeded, and we believe that anyone who reads, for example, Jeff Broadwater's fresh interpretation of Richard Nixon, or Jameson W. Doig's balanced evaluation of Robert Moses, or Susan Cayleff's portrayal of Babe Didrickson Zaharias, or James J. Flink's analysis of Alfred P. Sloan will think so, too.

Again, we are indebted to the many people who have given unselfishly of their time and energy. At the top of the list is Cass Canfield, Jr., who originally suggested the need for a one-volume encyclopedia of this type and who urged us to prepare a second edition. His extraordinary knowledge of people and events proved especially useful as we struggled over whom to include and exclude in our ever changing list of new subjects. Maron Waxman, our original editor, got us off to an excellent start with her enthusiasm and instinting support. So did her assistants, Kathleen McKitty and Sandra Fox. When Maron left HarperCollins to pursue other interests, Robert Wilson undertook the burden of getting us through. He helped in many ways, gently but firmly prodding us forward. Wilson's assistant, Jeremie Ruby-Strauss, handled the large correspondence and interminable phone calls such a project entails with devotion and efficiency. Several students at Brooklyn College, CUNY, also helped us mightily by looking up citations and gathering and checking facts. To Thomas Holmes, now an LLD as well as a BA, Ira Galtman, and Joseph Lemko we want to extend our thanks. Trina and Adria Sternstein and Ava Sternstein McDermott provided irreplaceable help and support. To our great distress, however, Gail Garraty has passed from the scene. If this were an *Encyclopedia of Wonderful People*, she would have been the first person chosen to be included by everyone who knew and loved her. This volume is dedicated to her memory.

John A. Garraty
Jerome L. Sternstein
New York, N.Y.
November 30, 1995

WHEN NAMES OF PERSONS WITHIN THE BIOGRAPHICAL SKETCHES ARE IN **BOLDFACED** TYPE (EXCEPT FOR ALL UNITED STATES PRESIDENTS WHO ARE OF COURSE INCLUDED IN THIS VOLUME), THIS INDICATES THAT THEIR BIOGRAPHIES APPEAR UNDER THE ALPHABETICAL LISTING ELSEWHERE.

ABBOTT, Grace (b. Grand Island, Neb., Nov. 17, 1878; d. Chicago, Ill., June 19, 1939), SOCIAL WORKER, graduated from Grand Island College (1898), taught at Grand Island High School (1899–1907), and received PhM in political science from the University of Chicago (1909). As a resident of Hull House and first director of the Immigrants' Protective League (1908–17), Abbott lobbied for regulation of private employment agencies and for public employment agencies, compulsory education, regulation of immigrant savings associations, and open immigration. She belonged to the Women's Trade Union League and assisted in the formation of the Amalgamated Clothing Workers in 1914. Abbott was executive secretary of the Massachusetts State Immigration Commission (1913–14); as chairwoman of a Chicago municipal court committee on jails (1915–16), she was the author of its report, "What Should Be Done for Chicago's Women Offenders?" In 1915 she served as a delegate to the Women's Peace Conference at The Hague.

In April 1917, Abbott became director of the industrial division of the U.S. Department of Labor's Children's Bureau, and in that post oversaw the enforcement of the 1916 federal child labor law. During 1918–19 she investigated 1229 mines and factories to ensure that the child labor regulations incorporated into wartime government contracts were obeyed. In October 1919, Abbott joined the Illinois State Immigrant Commission and wrote reports on "Educational Needs of Immigrants in Illinois" and "Immigrants in the Coal Mining Communities of Illinois." As chief of the U.S. Children's Bureau (1921–34) she supported the 1921 Sheppard-Towner Act (which provided grants for women's and children's health protection). She advocated

the child labor amendment to the Constitution and directed studies of maternal and child health, infant care, child labor, unemployment, industrial accidents, delinquency, and child neglect. From 1934 until her death she was professor of public welfare at the University of Chicago and managing editor of the *Social Service Review.* In 1934–35 she served on the advisory council of the Committee on Economic Security which drafted the Social Security Act. She was the first U.S. delegate to the International Labor Organization in 1935 and was a member of the industrial committee for textiles created by the Fair Labor Standards Act of 1938. Grace Abbott was the author of *The Immigrant and the Community* (1917), *The Child and the State* (1938), and *From Relief to Social Security* (1941).

A colleague, **Sophonisba P. Breckinridge,** said of Grace Abbott: "She had exact knowledge of law, governmental organization, labor economics, and administrative relationships." Abbott displayed these qualities both as an administrator and as an educator. While executive secretary of the Immigrants' Protective League she directed surveys of immigrant life and problems, particularly those of women and girls, and recommended the adoption of protective legislation by city and state. The federal Children's Bureau, which she headed for nearly fifteen years, was charged by law with investigating and reporting on "all matters pertaining to the welfare of children and child life among all classes of our people." Under Abbott's direction the Children's Bureau continued and expanded research and publication programs inaugurated by the first chief, Julia Lathrop, and administered the first federal grants-in-aid to the states for maternal and child health.

During the 1920s and early depression years Abbott was the nation's official spokesperson for and advocate of the rights of children and youth. With her associates Katharine Lenroot and Martha M. Eliot, Abbott was responsible for inclusion in the Social Security Act of provisions for federal participation in aid to dependent children, maternal and child health programs, services for crippled children, and welfare services for children needing special care.

To her writing and teaching Abbott brought a fund of practical and theoretical knowledge of child welfare administration. As an educator she strove to equip students for research and publication on social problems, promotion of social legislation, and improved administration of social welfare programs. See Grace Abbott, *The Child and the State* (1938).

ROBERT H. BREMNER

ACHESON, Dean Gooderham (b. Middletown, Conn., Apr. 11, 1893; d. Silver Spring, Md., Oct. 12, 1971), DIPLOMAT, attended the Groton School and graduated from Yale in 1915, Phi Beta Kappa. After a tour of duty with the navy during World War I, he graduated from Harvard in 1918. He served as private secretary to Supreme Court Justice **Louis Brandeis** (1919–21) and then entered private law practice in Washington, D.C. President Franklin Roosevelt appointed Acheson undersecretary of the Treasury in 1933; however, Acheson resigned this position the same year over a disagreement on Roosevelt's gold-purchase plan. Returning to private law practice, Acheson headed a committee to study the operation of the administrative bureaus of the federal government (1939–40). He was also a member of the Committee to Defend America by Aiding the Allies, a group favoring vigorous U.S. support for Great Britain in the war with Nazi Germany. Acheson became assistant secretary of state in 1941 and undersecretary of state in 1945.

As undersecretary, Acheson helped plan the United Nations and the Bretton Woods Monetary Agreement. He wrote the Acheson-Lillenthal Report (1946), which suggested international control of atomic energy. Initially favoring a policy of conciliation with the U.S.S.R., Acheson reversed his view and supported containment of Communism. He helped formulate the Truman Doctrine for aid to Greece and Turkey and the Marshall Plan for the economic recovery of Europe.

Acheson returned to his law practice in 1947 but became Truman's secretary of state in 1949. As secretary he was instrumental in creating the North Atlantic Treaty Organization, implemented the Korean War policy, and worked on the Japanese Peace Treaty of 1951. Bitterly criticized by Republicans for his relationship with **Alger Hiss,** he was blamed for the fall of China to the Communists and for the deadlocked Korean conflict. Acheson retired from office in 1953 but served as a foreign policy adviser to John F. Kennedy. He received the Medal of Freedom from President Lyndon B. Johnson in 1964. Acheson wrote many books and won the Pulitzer Prize in history for his memoir, *Present at the Creation* (1970).

⁂

The most creative and successful American foreign policymaker during the 1900–70 era, Dean Acheson combined a brilliant mind, long experience among the legal and political struggles of Washington, and intense commitment to policies he believed Western civilization must follow to survive challenges from without and within. Those policies, the key to Acheson's personality and statecraft, were classically conservative: "In fact," he remarked in 1969, "I was always conservative."

This conservatism consisted of high sensitivity to and distrust of "the built-in rigidities of human nature," which he perhaps learned abstractly as the son of an Episcopalian minister; the restraints and opportunities inherent in private property; and a fear of any government which through unchecked power (as the Soviet) tried to destroy such property or attempted (as the New Deal in 1933) to manipulate unduly the economy. He assumed the North Atlantic community represented the peak of man's social, intellectual, and political development. The nation-state continued, as it had for two thousand years, to determine world affairs; Acheson's original disdain for the United Nations grew into contempt. He cared little about public opinion ("not because the people do not know the facts … but because they do not know the issues exist"), and once expressed thanks for the absence of public opinion polls at Valley Forge. Such insensitivity helped make him an open target for congressmen and journalists, who accused him of favoring radicals within the government and of being too oblivious to Chinese Communist triumphs between 1946 and 1952.

These attacks by the "primitives," as Acheson labeled his accusers, were highly ironic, for no American was more anti-Communist. He attempted to break the Soviet bloc by developing positions of economic and especially military strength from which the West could dictate terms. West Germany held highest priority, for it formed the industrial heartland whose future determined that of all other European nations. NATO was devised not only to blunt a highly improbable Russian invasion, but also to help quiet internal disturbances within Europe and bind West Germany to the alliance. Acheson later observed that American policymakers were "continually haunted by the spectre" of a German-Soviet agreement similar to those of 1922 and 1939. In 1952 he devised a means by which West Germany could be rearmed and integrated into NATO, a policy that began under an altered agreement in 1955.

Asia, possessing no significant industrial base outside of Japan, ranked low among Acheson's concerns. He indicated an understanding of possible differences between Chinese and Russian Communists as early as 1949–50, although recognition of China was never attempted and the Korean conflict ended hopes for a Sino-American settlement. Because he saw nationalism as the mainspring of diplomacy, Acheson recognized nationalistic fervor as the critical force in Southeast Asia's revolt against France. After months of equivocation, Acheson finally supported the French in May 1950, primarily because he needed their help within the NATO alliance. And because he viewed Asia as less significant than Europe, Acheson worked to remove General **Douglas MacArthur** as supreme commander in Korea before MacArthur's policies created an expanded Asian war which would drain resources from rebuilding Western Europe.

Acheson also favored the general's removal because MacArthur threatened the Executive's control of foreign policy. The president's power, to Acheson's mind, was indispensable if the quicksands of public opinion were to be avoided. Although they were unlike in background, personality, and views on domestic policies, no president ever had more confidence in his secretary of state than did Truman in Acheson. Both shared strong anti-Communist sentiment and intense jealousy of the Executive's prerogatives.

With the growing equality of nuclear bombs and missiles in the late 1950s, Acheson's hope of negotiating with the Soviets only from secure positions of strength became less tenable. As a private adviser he successfully urged John F. Kennedy to stand firm in the 1961 Berlin crisis but was overruled when he advocated a direct strike against Cuban missile sites in October 1962. Military and political changes began outdating Acheson's views. Between 1941 and 1961, however, he was a conservative whose times had caught up with his foreign policies. See Gaddis Smith, *Dean Acheson as Secretary of State* (1972).

WALTER LaFEBER

ADAMS, Abigail (b. Weymouth, Mass., Nov. 11, 1744; d. Braintree, Mass., Oct. 28, 1818), FIRST LADY, the daughter of a minister, she had no formal schooling but acquired a rudimentary education from her parents and other relatives. She supplemented their efforts by wide reading of her own.

In October 1764 she married John Adams, then training to be a lawyer. For more than fifty years they enjoyed a close, loving marriage, although political events often kept them apart. They addressed each other in letters as "dearest friend" and "fellow Labourer," and reaffirmed their marital bond over the many miles separating them. When her husband joined the revolution against Great Britain, she became a keen and observant witness to the events. While he was away for nearly a decade in Philadelphia and Europe making a revolution, she stayed behind in Braintree, Massachusetts, to care for their four young children and manage the family farm.

During the Revolutionary War, she organized local women to sew uniforms and prepare supplies for the Continental Army. Shortly before the colonies declared independence in 1776, she sternly admonished her husband to "remember the Ladies." "Do not put such unlimited power into the hands of the Husbands," she wrote John Adams. "If perticuliar [sic] care and attention is not paid to the Ladies we are determined to foment a Rebellion [sic], and will not hold ourselves bound by any Laws in which we have no voice, or Representation."

In 1797, John Adams became the second president of the United States, and he and Abigail moved to Washington, D.C., the new nation's capital. Many years later their son John Quincy Adams also became a president. Though Abigail Adams did not live to see this event, she is the only woman in American history to be the wife and mother of U.S. presidents.

———— ✽ ————

Although Abigail Adams never held public office—for the customs and laws of her day proscribed such opportunities for women—she was passionately absorbed in the historical events of her time. Her voluminous correspondence reveals a keen intellect and spirited understanding of the political concerns and controversies of her day. She took to heart the democratic ideals expressed in the Declaration of Independence, and with asperity and also insight she offered opinions on everyone from King George to Thomas Jefferson, one of her husband's chief political rivals.

Although she had earlier warned her husband to curtail the "unlimited power" of husbands over wives, she was no feminist—she did not call for equal social and political roles for men and women. Instead, she viewed women's role in life as that of wife and mother, and she firmly believed that women should defer to male authority. But she deplored what she perceived to be men's abusive social and political power over women, and she decried the lack of educational opportunities for women. She believed

that women's education was vital to the country's future because only an educated mother was capable of rearing patriotic sons and loyal, virtuous daughters.

Adams accorded a distinct civic role for women—republican motherhood—without challenging their domestic role. She thus proved that women of her day, who had no legal right to vote or hold public office, could still voice their political ideals and serve their country by raising patriotic children. See Phyllis Lee Levin, *Abigail Adams: A Biography* (1987).

HARRIET SIGERMAN

ADAMS, Brooks (b. Quincy, Mass., June 24, 1848; d. Boston, Mass., Feb. 13, 1927), HISTORIAN, great-grandson of John Adams, grandson of John Q. Adams, attended English schools while his father was U.S. minister to Great Britain during the Civil War. He entered Harvard College in 1868 and received a BA in 1870. After a year in Harvard Law School he served as his father's secretary in Geneva during the *Alabama* Claims arbitration (1871–72). Admitted to the bar in 1873, he practiced law in Boston until 1881, when he turned to historical writing.

Adams's first work, *The Emancipation of Massachusetts* (1887), challenged contemporary views of early New England and argued that the Puritan clergy exercised religious and political tyranny over the people. Later he applied this idea to previous ages, viewing Moses as an early theocrat.

In *The Law of Civilization and Decay* (1895) Adams argued that physical laws of force and energy governed history and that different societies possessed varying degrees of energy. His later works reiterated and expanded this theory. *America's Economic Supremacy* (1900) depicted the growth of America's economic energy and developed the thesis that the international center of energy was moving to the New World. *The New Empire* (1902) further elaborated these ideas, and *The Theory of Social Revolutions* (1913) warned that unless America's economic development was accompanied by administrative and governmental flexibility, centralization would lead to social rigidity.

Adams lectured at the Boston University School of Law (1904–11). In a printed brief (1910) he held that railroad monopolies were incompatible with constitutional governments. As a member of the Massachusetts Constitutional Convention of 1917, he supported the initiative and referendum. His "Revolt of Modern Democracy Against Standards of Duty" contended that self-seeking Americans had lost their standards of duty and their ability for collective thought and energy. This was the theme of his extensive preface to **Henry Adams**'s *Letter to American Teachers of History*, printed in 1920 as *The Degradation of the Democratic Dogma*.

———— ∞ ————

The salient principles of Brooks Adams's thought are first systematically discussed in his *Emancipation of Massachusetts*, which challenged the contention that the Puritans had ruled New England in the spirit of democratic virtue. This book foreshadowed later ideas and attitudes, containing Adams's first attempt "to set forth a scientific theory of history" by applying "certain general laws to a particular phase of development." *The Law of Civilization and Decay* was Adams's first full formulation of his philosophy. He propounded a cyclical theory of history in which the stages of development and decline are governed by thermodynamic laws of concentration and loss of energy. The energy-gathering stages occur early in a society's history when the warrior, priest, artist, and farmer dominate the social order. During this era of imagination, war, and conquest, centralization occurs and surplus energy is created and stored in the form of wealth. But the process of ascendance contains the seeds of decay. The accumulation of wealth brings the advent of the capitalist, a parasite who feeds off the energy gathered by others. Eventually the capitalist triumphs over the accumulators, dissipates the supply of energy, and ushers in the stage of deterioration and destruction. The exhaustion of "energy of the race" may result in its conquest by more bellicose societies,

in a more gradual decline that ends in "disintegration," or in "reversion … to a primitive form of organism." Contemplating the depression of the 1890s, Adams became alarmed about America's future and began to apply his theories to developments in his own country. Internecine class warfare and possible defeat in the struggle for Asian markets presented major threats to national survival. His spirits were briefly raised when his friend Theodore Roosevelt became president. Adams hoped that his agitation for American economic domination of the Far East, greater internal cohesion, and a return to the martial spirit would at last bear fruit. But Roosevelt disappointed his expectations, and the last twenty-five years of Adams's life were enveloped in despondency. Democratic capitalism was disintegrating the social system by fomenting materialism and selfishness. Energy was running down, and catastrophe awaited America through defeat in war and class conflict. At the end Adams sought refuge in the ideas and institutions he had once scorned. Condemning the science that he had formerly worshiped, he now found comfort in the discipline, morality, and communal impulses that he discovered in New England's Puritan past.

Adams's thought was rooted in the development of his personality and in his assessment of his individual and class predicament. By the 1870s friends and acquaintances observed a transformation in him: a bitter, quarrelsome adult had replaced the charming, agreeable youth. Some of this acerbity was due to his hairline defeat for the state legislature in 1877. No doubt the decline of Massachusetts Mugwumpery, with which Brooks and Henry Adams and other Boston Brahmins had been closely affiliated, also contributed to his growing bitterness—and there were rumors of a broken romance. The influence of Henry, who shared his views, and the depression of the 1890s, which he saw as a triumph of money-hungry capitalists over the healthy impulses in American life, deepened his saturnine disposition. Like Henry, as the years passed, Adams felt that he and his class were being displaced by a new elite of grubby materialists and unscrupulous demagogues. National developments were perceived as a macrocosm of Brahmin decline and personal redundancy. A growing sense of alienation and feebleness became the perspective through which Adams viewed the future of America—a doomed land that he felt rejected him and his kind. See Arthur F. Beringause, *Brooks Adams: A Biography* (1955), and Frederic Cople Jaher, *Doubters and Dissenters: Cataclysmic Thought in America, 1885–1918* (1964).

FREDERIC C. JAHER

ADAMS, Charles Francis (b. Boston, Mass., Aug. 18, 1807; d. Boston, Mass., Nov. 21, 1886), POLITICAL LEADER, DIPLOMAT, son of John Quincy Adams, graduated from Harvard (1825), and was admitted to the bar in 1829. Besides practicing law and writing articles on American history, he served as a Whig in the Massachusetts legislature (1841–45), where his strong antislavery opinions led him to be opposed by the more conservative Whigs. In 1848 he was the vice-presidential candidate of the antislavery Free Soil party, running with Martin Van Buren. The party did not receive any electoral votes.

During 1859–61, Adams served in the U.S. Congress as a Republican. Just before the Civil War he was chairman of a northern commission in the House that worked for conciliation. He supported **William Henry Seward** for the Republican presidential nomination in 1860, but he accepted President Lincoln's offer to serve as U.S. minister to Great Britain (1861–68). In England, Adams's major task was to keep Great Britain neutral during the Civil War. He helped allay tensions when the U.S.S. *San Jacinto* stopped the British steamer *Trent* (1861) and removed two Confederate emissaries to Great Britain; and he tried to prevent Great Britain from permitting the Confederacy to build ships in British yards.

In 1871, Adams served on the arbitration commission that resolved the *Alabama* Claims dispute, Great Britain agreeing to repay the United States for damages inflicted by British-built ships used by the Confederacy. In 1872 he supported the Liberal Republicans who opposed President Grant.

Adams edited *The Works of John Adams* (10 vols., 1850–56) and *The Memoirs of John Quincy Adams* (12 vols., 1874–77).

———

Charles Francis Adams, the son and grandson of presidents, confronted to an even greater degree than other men of his class and generation the problem of dealing with the politics of an age of industrialism, immigration, and democracy. Some of his relatives, despairing of carrying on the awesome family tradition of public service, retired to private life. Others broke under the strain; an uncle became an alcoholic, a "brute," and a "bully," and an older brother turned into a drunkard, a philanderer, and a suicide. Charles Francis, emulating the self-control and reserve of his Puritan ancestors, and aided by a considerable personal fortune (he married the daughter of Peter Chardon Brooks, a Boston millionaire), survived and went on to lead a dignified and honorable public career.

Adams's father, his sons, his biographer, and the editors of his diary all describe his personality in similar terms: "self-contained," "cold, calculating, and self-possessed." His father noted the "wise face and sober demeanour" of the 13-year-old boy, and Adams himself candidly spoke of his "grave, sober, formal, precise and reserved" nature. These were not qualities that appealed to the brawling, tumultuous nativist and Irish Catholic politics of midcentury Massachusetts, and Adams was defeated most of the time he backed other candidates or ran for office himself. The businessmen and self-made politicians with obscure origins, such as George S. Boutwell, Nathaniel Banks, and Henry Wilson, tolerated Adams for his campaign contributions, his deserved reputation for rectitude, and the glamour of his name but hardly bothered to conceal their contempt for his patrician hauteur; he was, one of them complained, "the greatest iceberg in the Northern Hemisphere."

Given his fear of the "decided anarchy" of democracy and his unappealing personality, it is understandable that Adams's most important service was as an appointed, rather than elected, official. As minister to England during the crucial Civil War years, he served with diligence and distinction. His friendly personal relations with Lord John Russell, the head of the Foreign Office, helped smooth over the *Trent* affair crisis, and while Adams was unable to prevent the sailing of the Confederate commerce raider *Alabama* from Liverpool, he did help persuade Russell to seize the far more dangerous Laird-built rams. (Russell had already decided, however, to stop the rams a few days before the receipt of Adams's famous warning of September 5, 1863: "It would be superfluous in me to point out to your lordship that this is war.") As American arbitrator of the *Alabama* Claims at Geneva in 1871, Adams was unfailingly patient and practical. The final settlement, in which the British agreed to pay $15.5 million in damages, was a personal triumph for Adams and the beginning of the Anglo-American entente that was so important in our own century.

Adams's most enduring literary effort, in addition to editing the *Works* of his ancestors, is his own diary. This massive journal (36 bound notebooks totaling nearly 11,000 pages) is as methodical, meticulous, and unemotional as its author, but it provides interesting insights into hundreds of important events and personalities: the aging former presidents of Adams's youth, the Whig–Free-Soil–Nativist–Republican political struggles in Massachusetts, the desperate efforts at compromise during the winter of 1860–61 when Adams was a congressman and a member of the Committee of Thirty-three attempting to avoid the Civil War, and his wartime service in England when he did as much as any general (and more than most) to ensure the victory of the North. Faithfully reflecting his personality, the *Diary* is a fitting historical monument and an invaluable historical source. See Martin Duberman, *Charles Francis Adams* (1961).

SAMUEL SHAPIRO

ADAMS, Charles Francis, Jr. (b. Boston, Mass., May 27, 1835; d. Washington, D.C., May 20, 1915),

RAILROAD EXECUTIVE, HISTORIAN, graduated from Harvard in 1856, and was admitted to the bar in 1858. When the Civil War broke out he joined the Massachusetts militia. His first commission was in the U.S. cavalry; toward the close of the war he commanded a regiment of black soldiers. He served at Antietam and Gettysburg, and left the army as a brigadier general (1865).

After the war, Adams envisioned "the railroad system as the most developing force and the largest field of the day." When Massachusetts established a board of railroad commissioners in 1869, Adams was made a member (chairman, 1872–79). While serving on the commission he made a detailed study of the railroad system, and his reports and recommendations were substantiated with facts and statistics. He was particularly critical of railroad stock manipulations; in 1869 he had published in the *North American Review* "A Chapter of Erie" denouncing **Jay Gould** and **Cornelius Vanderbilt** for their attempts to gain control of the Erie Railroad by dubious methods. After the competing trunk lines between Midwest shipping points and the Atlantic ports had established a joint executive committee in the seventies, they appointed Adams one of a board of three arbitrators with eventual power to apportion traffic between them. Adams resigned this job in 1884. In 1878 he published *Railroads: Their Origin and Problems*, in which he described the railroad system and argued that railroads should be managed by experts. From 1884 to 1890 he was president of the Union Pacific Railroad.

Adams was also active in civic and literary affairs. He served on a number of reform commissions in Massachusetts, opposed the election of **James G. Blaine** for the presidency in 1884, and was an overseer of Harvard. He was president of the Massachusetts Historical Society from 1895 to 1915. Besides contributing articles to the *Proceedings* of the society, he wrote two major works: *Three Episodes of Massachusetts History* (1892), a history of Quincy, Massachusetts; and *Antinomianism in the Colony of Massachusetts Bay, 1636–38* (1894).

Adams opposed the Spanish-American War

and the annexation of the Philippines, arguing that such actions were contrary to American democratic traditions. His *Autobiography* was published posthumously (1916).

———— ∝∾∾ ————

Perhaps C. F. Adams, Jr., never found to his satisfaction a role for himself. Superficially he fulfilled the stereotype of the Boston Brahmin: he attended the Boston Latin School, belonged to the best clubs, attained a gentlemanly distinction in scholarship at Harvard, was admitted to the Massachusetts bar, and served as a cavalry officer throughout the Civil War. Thereafter he rode horseback, sailed boats, made money, traveled frequently in Europe, read systematically, voted without much regard to party loyalties, stayed away from church, and wrote history. Although for a brief interval he had a town house in the Back Bay and went daily to an office in downtown Boston, he would have been surprised to be called a Bostonian; his home was Quincy, where he immersed himself vigorously in village affairs, attending town meetings and serving as a member of the school board and as one of the trustees of the public library. He brought to these activities not only energy but a talent for polemics and a somewhat unconventional outlook. Some of these local doings attracted national attention. For instance, Adams publicized in addresses and articles the "new departure" in the Quincy schools and antagonized the educational establishment of the Commonwealth. By the time Quincy had become a city in the nineties, Adams had fled to an estate in Lincoln, Massachusetts, and in the winter months to a residence in Washington, D.C. It is best to interpret Adams as a country gentleman or as the "squire."

When he scrutinized the passing scene of American life, Adams's curiosity was often quickened, and he zealously sought a solution for the ills he detected. Thus after the Civil War he had the alertness to perceive the significance of the railroad, and he hitched his wagon to the star of the locomotive. His articles on the railroad situation in Massachusetts in large measure induced the general court to establish a state rail-

road commission, to which Adams sought and obtained an appointment. Even before he became its chairman, he wrote the reports. In short, he now had a forum for his ideas. Since the railroad was comparatively young—and so was Adams—neither could draw upon an accumulated "science" of transportation. Adams proceeded to inform himself and his fellow citizens everywhere. Speculative, self-assured, provocative, he became a railroad expert at a time when there were few others.

The government must regulate the railroads, he thought, but the principles and practices it should compel were limited. The state must not regulate punitively or excitedly; it must proceed systematically and after investigation. It was folly to ignore the experience and interests of railroad officials and investors. In short the Massachusetts Railroad Commission hoped to convince the railroads to cooperate rather than to force compliance. It was thus an alternative to the granger system of railroad regulation currently developing in the Midwest. Another alternative was self-regulation by the railroads; Adams was willing to substitute railroad pooling and consolidation for railroad competition and its evils. When he became bored with his Massachusetts job, as he did by 1879, Adams resigned and served as an arbitrator for the quarrels that arose between the trunk lines running from the Midwest to the Atlantic coast cities. He also continued as a persuasive expositor of his philosophy. Congress was moving in the eighties toward the national regulation of interstate commerce. By this time his own administrative experience had enlarged, for he was the president of the Union Pacific Railroad. His influence as a public official and private capitalist on the national regulatory movement is hard to disentangle. The "success" of the Massachusetts Railroad Commission in that commonwealth and in others where it was imitated was of general importance. On the other hand, the Interstate Commerce Commission frequently displeased him, perhaps because he had not been appointed to it, a possibility he had earlier half-dreamed of.

When Jay Gould's faction on the Union Pacific

turned him out of the presidency in 1890, Adams's railroad career largely came to an end, but not his usefulness as an informed and dedicated person. Massachusetts called upon his abilities to unravel several tangles. He was, for instance, largely responsible for the creation of parks and parkways in the Boston metropolitan district. As an overseer of Harvard College, he continued his pursuit of educational reform and thus was, for the larger share of the time, a supporter of **Charles W. Eliot.** See Edward C. Kirkland, *Charles F. Adams, Jr.: The Patrician at Bay* (1965).

EDWARD C. KIRKLAND

ADAMS, Henry Brooks (b. Boston, Mass., Feb. 16, 1838; d. Washington, D.C., March 27, 1918), HISTORIAN, great-grandson of John Adams, grandson of John Quincy Adams, and son of **Charles Francis Adams,** graduated from Harvard (1858). He briefly studied law in Berlin and traveled in Italy and France (1858–60). Returning to the United States in 1860, he worked for his father, then a member of the House of Representatives. When President Lincoln appointed his father U.S. minister to England, Adams accompanied him to London, serving as his personal secretary (1861–68).

Upon his return to the United States in 1868, Adams worked as a journalist in Washington before he joined the faculty of Harvard as an assistant professor of medieval history (1870–77). While at Harvard he introduced the seminar method of study and tried to teach his students to study history "scientifically." He edited the *North American Review* (1870–76), one of the nation's leading periodicals, and edited *Essays in Anglo-Saxon Law* (1876) and *Documents Relating to New England Federalism, 1800–1815* (1877).

In 1877, Adams resigned from Harvard shortly after accepting a commission from the only surviving son of former Secretary of the Treasury **Albert Gallatin** to write a biography of his famous father and edit his papers. Adams moved to Washington to be near the national archives and became closely associated with some of the

nation's most prominent personalities. In 1879 he published two works on Gallatin: *The Life of Albert Gallatin* and *The Writings of Albert Gallatin* (ed.). In 1880 he published *Democracy* (anonymously), a novel satirizing corruption in politics and questioning the democratic process. He soon returned to history, publishing *John Randolph* (1882), a critical biography of the Virginia politician. In 1884 he published *Esther* (under a pseudonym), a study of a sensitive woman's efforts to find meaning in life. Following the suicide of his wife in 1885, Adams traveled abroad and for many years divided his residence between Washington and Paris.

Adams became a leading figure in Washington society and a close friend of many politicians, including Theodore Roosevelt. In 1904 he published *Mont-Saint-Michel and Chartres*, a study of the concept of unity in the Middle Ages. As this work was "a study of 13th-century unity," his autobiography, *The Education of Henry Adams*, privately printed in 1904 but not released to the general public until 1918, was "a study of twentieth-century multiplicity." In this work his principal theme was that Western civilization was in a state of crisis because man's production of power was outrunning his ability to control it and that in order to meet the emergency, society must train a new class of leaders by entirely scientific methods. In the absence of such leadership the ever accelerating expansion of technology would destroy civilization.

⬦

Henry Adams's career is a study in paradox and irony. From one point of view, that taken in his celebrated *Education*, written when he was 67, it was a failure; from another, the literary point of view, it was a remarkable success attested to by a shelf of books that have established him as a major American writer. Commonly regarded as a leading American historian in professional circles, his greatest fame has come from the autobiographical *Education*, in which he questioned the validity of historical writing, even of his own. In his monumental *History of the United States During the Administrations of Jefferson and Madison* he had aimed at scientific objectivity, yet he could not resist the artistic impulse to rival the urbane and magisterial style of literary historians like Gibbon and Macaulay.

Adams was reared in a patrician New England family in which dedicated public service was a hereditary way of life, and politics and statesmanship were regarded almost as interchangeable terms. In spite of early ambitions to play an active leadership role in American life, Henry Adams found himself cast in the role of philosophic observer. Intellectually he felt the tug of politics and political power; but by temperament he was drawn to art and shared the aesthetic sensibility of his novelist friend **Henry James.** He was irresistibly attracted to study the great scientific movements of his time—Darwinian evolution, scientific sociology, and philosophical materialism—yet his idealist skepticism led him to question the new scientific dogmas. This ambivalence is exhibited in his two novels: in *Democracy* it is the moral dilemma of practical politics; in *Esther* it is the tension between science and religion. His friend in science, Clarence King, called the novels the "Impasse Series."

Even if temperament had not made him unfit for post–Civil War political life, his path to preferment, as he used to say, was blocked by his equally ambitious elder brothers. As a political journalist in President Grant's freewheeling Washington, Henry Adams made a powerful impression as an advocate of reform, but the impression was lost on corrupt politicians. The experience colored all his subsequent thinking about American life. The individual would be increasingly submerged in the democratic mass. In the brilliant overview of American life in 1817 in the concluding section of his *History,* he posed an array of sobering questions, chief of which was whether the unparalleled material progress that followed in the rest of the century would be matched by moral and social progress.

The terrible depression of 1893 seemed to Adams a symptom of the impending decline of Western civilization. For clues to the causes he turned from the history of the American experience to that of the remoter European past. The search took a singular turn. It led to his taking emotional refuge in the Middle Ages of northern France, from whose art, literature, and cathedral architecture he deduced a unity of thought and sensibility that might serve, as he said, as his "anchor in history" by which to measure the modern loss of values. Out of this study came another masterpiece, *Mont-Saint-Michel and Chartres,* an evocation of the spirit of an age that has, if not wholly the truth of history, at least the truth of poetry.

Adams wrote the more famous *Education* as a sequel to *Chartres.* In the earlier book the dominant symbol of the unity of that period was the Virgin Mary. In the sequel, which Adams thought of as "a Study of Twentieth-Century Multiplicity," the central symbol is the dynamo, the source of infinite power, but, unlike the Virgin, inhuman and mindless. In the account of how he reeducated himself to understand the implications of the age of power, Adams offered himself as an object lesson of the need for the revolution of university education. However, the lasting charm of the book has not been the speculative "Dynamic Theory of History" to which it leads but rather the witty and ironic panorama of the world in which he moved as a privileged observer.

The urgency of the need for drastic educational reform grew to be such an obsession with Adams that in 1910 he privately distributed another book, *A Letter to American Teachers of History,* in which he reexamined the question of the nature of power from a more narrowly scientific viewpoint. He argued that all of the physical and psychic energies in the world were subject to "entropy" in accordance with the second law of thermodynamics and were therefore being steadily "degraded" and dissipated into less and less humanly valuable forms—for example, into the prospective mediocrity of state socialism. Universities must therefore produce a new type of mind, "another Newton," to slow down this process. In an intervening essay, published posthumously, Adams illustrated the dangerous acceleration of the social movement with an analogy, also drawn from physics, based on **Willard Gibbs**'s "Rule of Phase." All of these ideas coalesced into Adams's belief that the technological revolution was speeding the world to a final cataclysmic explosion.

Adams's later philosophic speculations have had little if any acceptance except as prophetic metaphors for the deepening social and political crisis of the present age. They are now chiefly interesting as reflections of the enormous intellectuality of the man and of the courage with which he tried to face up to the dilemmas of modern society. If **Emerson** could urge that the solution of the world's ills called for "soul, soul, and more soul," Adams would counter with the plea for "mind, mind, and more mind." See Ernest Samuels, *Henry Adams* (3 vols.; 1948–64).

ERNEST SAMUELS

ADAMS, Henry Carter (b. Davenport, Iowa, Dec. 31, 1851; d. Ann Arbor, Mich., Aug. 11, 1921), ECONOMIST, graduated from Iowa (Grinnell) College in 1874 and enrolled in Andover Theological Seminary but decided against entering the ministry. He won a fellowship to Johns Hopkins and received a PhD in political economy in 1878, the first doctorate in the social sciences awarded by that university. Adams also studied for a short time in Oxford, Heidelberg, Berlin, Paris, and Bonn. After accepting an assistantship at Hopkins in 1879, Adams taught at Cornell and Michigan in 1880. He returned to Cornell in 1882 and from then until 1886 taught at different times at both universities. His appointment at Cornell was allowed to expire in 1887, partly because of ideas concerning the labor question that he had expressed during the 1886 strike on **Jay Gould**'s railroad system. In 1887, Adams became professor of political economy and finance at the University of Michigan, a post he held until his death.

Adams devoted much of his scholarship to work in public finance. His *Public Debts* (1887) and *The Science of Finance* (1898) represented some of the first scholarly attempts to grapple with the peculiar administrative conditions and problems of public finance that existed in the United States. Along with **Richard T. Ely** and other economists Adams was instrumental in leading the attack on laissez-faire economics. He participated in the founding of the American Economic Association in 1885 and later served as its president. Adams was also interested in statistics; he was statistician for the Interstate Commerce Commission from its beginning in 1887 until 1911, and chief of the Division of Statistics and Accounts of the ICC (1906–11). He aided the Michigan Tax Commission in the valuation of the state's railroads, was an adviser to the Chinese Republic on the standardization of railway accounts (1913–16), a subject in which he long had an interest. Some of Adams's major writings include "Relation of the State to Industrial Action" (1887), "Economics and Jurisprudence" (1897), and *American Railway Accounting* (1918).

Adams was one of the band of New School economists who helped to lay the intellectual foundations for the liberal-reformist state of the twentieth century. Concerned with the "principles to which industrial legislation should conform," he made significant contributions in the areas of public control and public finance.

In his analysis of the relationship of government to the economy, Adams contended that, to prevent competitive conditions in any trade from degenerating to the level of practice of the worst man who could maintain himself in that trade, the state must determine the plane upon which competition should operate and below which it should not be permitted to fall, a concept that has been most influential in the area of labor legislation and in the work of the Federal Trade Commission. In industries characterized by "increasing returns" (natural monopolies), the state, Adams argued, must exercise control to ensure that the potential benefits of monopoly are actually realized by society.

Adams urged the revision of the code of social ethics underlying the existing system of jurisprudence so that "the social interest and the rights of individuals in associated industry" might find proper expression. Since he believed that property was essential to liberty, he thought that society should devise a new theory of property that would afford the worker some proprietary right in industry. Adams foresaw that this right would be defined through the collective bargaining process, and he consequently viewed the labor movement as an effort to achieve "industrial liberty."

A pioneer in the study of public finance, Adams helped to make this field an important segment of the discipline of economics. During his long service with the Interstate Commerce Commission, he stressed the importance of uniform railway statistics as the basis for regulation. His views on the subject were embodied in the Hepburn Act (1906), and his "accounting system" was applied to the regulation of public utilities in general.

Adams was an extremely modest man who minimized his own accomplishments. He impressed students and colleagues alike with his high ideals, his ethical principles, his amiability, and his "winsome gentleness." See Joseph Dorfman, "Henry Carter Adams: The Harmonizer of Liberty and Reform," in *Relation of the State to Industrial Action and Economics and Jurisprudence: Two Essays by Henry Carter Adams* (1954).

SIDNEY FINE

ADAMS, Herbert Baxter (b. Shutesbury, Mass., Apr. 16, 1850; d. Amherst, Mass., July 30, 1901), HISTORIAN, graduated from Amherst (1872) and received his PhD from the University of Heidelberg (1876). When Johns Hopkins University was founded in 1876, **Daniel Coit Gilman,** the school's first president, appointed Adams an associate in history. In 1880, Adams began offering seminars on political institutions, modeled on those held in the German universities where he had studied. Believing that political institutions must be traced "scientifically," he referred to his seminars as "laboratories where books are treated like mineralogical specimens."

In 1882, Adams launched the Johns Hopkins Studies in History and Political Science, which consisted of the doctoral dissertations of his many students, including Woodrow Wilson, **Frederick Jackson Turner,** and Charles M. Andrews. In 1883, Adams contributed *Germanic Origins of New England Towns* to this series. In this work he reaffirmed the "germ theory" of political institutions, arguing that democracy was developed in the forests of Germany and brought over to the United States by the Pilgrims and Puritans. In 1884 he helped organize the American Historical Association, serving as its secretary until 1900. From 1891 until his death Adams was a full professor of history at Johns Hopkins. Some of his books include *Maryland's Influence in Founding a National Commonwealth* (1877), *Methods of Historical Study* (1884), and *Life and Writings of Jared Sparks* (1893).

Long before Herbert Baxter Adams was born, Americans returning from Germany had sought in vain to upgrade the quality of academic standards at home. Not until the establishment of Johns Hopkins University in 1876 as a graduate institution were the frustrated hopes of precursors realized. It was history's good fortune that an adult Adams and the infant university appeared on the scene at the same time.

When he returned from his own pilgrimage to Germany, Adams already had plans for instituting the seminar method in historical research. Rigorous examination of source materials was the requisite for "scientific history." The whole range of knowledge was invigorated by Darwinism; principles of relationship and continuity were sought in every subject.

Adams's main interest was institutional history, the evolution of America's political structure from its "primordial cells" in Germany, which, transferred to England, were then exported overseas. "The whole tenor of our researches," said Adams, "is to show the continuity of English institutions in America." Strongly influenced by the English historian Edward A. Freeman, he proudly displayed Freeman's statement:

"History is past politics, politics is present history." This overconcern with politics left critics of Adams dissatisfied. History, they said, should embrace the wider concerns of humanity.

Though Adams inspired others to become distinguished scholars, his own scholarly efforts lacked distinction. He was the academic counterpart of contemporary leaders of America's economic life. His student Woodrow Wilson spoke of him as "a great captain of Industry, a captain in the field of systematic and organized Scholarship." What Adams did achieve was truly notable. He drew to his seminar the best of America's intellect, which eventually transformed the American mind. See *Herbert Baxter Adams: Tributes of Friends* (1902).

MICHAEL KRAUS

ADAMS, John (b. Braintree, Mass., Oct. 19, 1735; d. Braintree [now Quincy], Mass., July 4, 1826), PRESIDENT, graduated from Harvard (1755) and admitted to the bar in 1758. He became a prominent patriot in 1765 when he attacked the Stamp Act; however, he defended the British soldiers accused of murder in the Boston Massacre (1770). He served in the Massachusetts general court and was a delegate to the first and second Continental Congresses (1774–75), where he helped draft the petition of rights to the Crown and the Declaration of Independence. He was commissioner to France in 1778, and in 1780 drafted the Massachusetts constitution. With **Benjamin Franklin** and **John Jay,** he negotiated the Treaty of Paris (1783), ending the Revolutionary War. In 1785–88 he represented the United States in Great Britain. In his *Defence of the Constitutions of Government of the United States of America* (1787–88), Adams argued that the new Constitution would neutralize tensions between the aristocracy and democracy. After serving as Washington's vice president, Adams was elected president in 1796.

In 1797, Adams sent a commission to France to negotiate Franco-American conflicts. When the French representatives demanded bribes (the XYZ Affair), American opinion was outraged.

Many Federalists demanded war, but Adams, while favoring preparedness, resisted their pressures. When the Republicans opposed war, Federalists sought to crush opposition by passing the Sedition Act (1798), which imposed fines and imprisonment on those criticizing the government. Although Adams did not oppose the act, he sent a new commissioner to France (1800) to allay tensions. War was averted, but the split between Adams and the Hamiltonians led to Adams's defeat by Jefferson in the election of 1800. Retiring from politics, Adams conducted an extensive correspondence with many influential Americans, including Jefferson, with whom he was reconciled after the latter's retirement. Among his important political writings are *Thoughts on Government* (1776) and *Discourses on Davila* (1790).

John Adams rose from obscurity to become one of the principal founders of the United States. Between his graduation from Harvard and the Stamp Act crisis, he became a leading Boston lawyer and, under the watchful eye of his distant cousin **Samuel Adams,** one of the inner circle of Massachusetts radicals. When his mentor **James Otis, Jr.,** declined in mental capacity, Adams assumed the role of legal and constitutional counselor to the opponents of prerogative powers and its champion **Thomas Hutchinson.** Adams's learning in British history and law served him well as pamphleteer and politician, and provided the base for his career as statesman and lawgiver. At the first Continental Congress he recognized the Virginia radicals **Patrick Henry** and the Lees as his natural allies in pressing toward independence. In the second Continental Congress he served as chairman of key committees, including the Board of War, and on the committee that drew up the Declaration of Independence. He was the principal spokesman for the 1776 Plan of Treaties which was adopted as the guide for American commercial negotiations, but his most important contribution to independence was his insistence that republican constitutions be adopted by the rebellious colonies. Following his largely fruitless mission to France, Adams was able to give lasting form to his political convictions as architect of the influential constitution adopted by the people of Massachusetts in 1780.

For the next seven years, during his diplomatic service in France, Holland, and Britain, Adams was instrumental in negotiating loans that kept Congress financially alive; and with Franklin and John Jay he negotiated the Treaty of Paris. As the first American minister to Great Britain, he labored vainly to win trade concessions deemed essential to the economic growth of the United States and especially to the prosperity of mercantile New England. Like his fellow diplomatists, Jefferson and Franklin, Adams grew increasingly concerned with the weakness of the Confederation, ably expressed that concern, and upon his return to the United States was selected vice president, an office that he learned to despise but that afforded him the opportunity to strengthen executive authority by casting a score of tiebreaking votes on key administration measures.

As heir apparent to Washington in 1796, Adams stood at the pinnacle of his career. Contemporaries as well as historians ever since have judged him a man of wisdom, honesty, and devotion to the national interest; at the same time his suspicions and theories led him to fall short of attaining the full measure of greatness for which he longed and labored. Given to severe self-analysis, Adams nursed antagonisms that strongly influenced the course of his life. His convictions about statecraft and what he insisted was a science of politics centered on the role of natural aristocrats and, like a good Newtonian, on the institutional checks that historical study would demonstrate were infallibly capable of regulating both the creative and destructive powers of these aristocrats. In his most important writings Adams recognized the ultimate sovereignty of the people, their legitimate right to a role in the lawmaking process, and their right to guarantees as expressed in a bill of rights; but he was opposed to democracy and more influenced by fears of human cupidity than by hopes of disin-

terestedness. The evidence, he insisted, could be found in the study of history as well as in the writings of his favorite political analysts, Cicero, Machiavelli, Harrington, Sidney, Bolingbroke, and DeLolme. Yet in assessing Adams's political thought and conduct, it is difficult to overlook the role that personal animosity played in shaping them, as in the case of Thomas Hutchinson in early life and **Alexander Hamilton** later. Convinced that a monarch (for so he regarded the American president) must throw his influence first to the popular and then to the aristocratic side if a climate of freedom was to be maintained, Adams heaped praise on the British constitution and overlooked the significance of the two American political parties that had developed by 1797. He openly courted his longtime friend but political opponent, Jefferson, as the nation entered the severe crisis with revolutionary France, and in his attempt to steer the state between humiliating concessions and a potentially disastrous war, he played a lone hand that left him isolated from increasingly bewildered and bitter Federalist leaders. His decision to renew peace negotiations after the XYZ Affair, the buildup of armaments, the passage of the Alien and Sedition Acts, and the appointment of Hamilton to command of the army came like an explosion in February 1799. While a majority of Americans were relieved and sympathetic, the Federalist party lay shattered in 1800 on the eve of its decisive conflict with Jeffersonian Republicanism. Adams had made a typically brave and resolute series of decisions for reasons entirely valid given his conception of politics and his understanding of events, but the personal results were twenty-five years of political inactivity at his Massachusetts home. See Zoltan Haraszti, *John Adams and the Prophets of Progress* (1952).

STEPHEN G. KURTZ

ADAMS, John Quincy (b. Braintree [now Quincy], Mass., July 11, 1767; d. Washington, D.C., Feb. 23, 1848), PRESIDENT, was secretary to Francis Dana, minister to Russia (1781), and to his father, John Adams, in England (1782–83). He graduated from Harvard in 1787 and was admitted to the bar in 1790. After serving as minister to the Netherlands (1794–96) and to Prussia (1797–1801), he was elected to the Massachusetts senate in 1802 and to the U.S. Senate in 1803. Although a Federalist, he supported Jefferson's Embargo Act of 1807, hoping that it would preserve American neutrality. The embargo's unpopularity in New England forced him to resign from the Senate (1808). He was again minister to Russia (1809–14), and in 1814 he was chairman of the U.S. Peace Commission at Ghent, which negotiated the treaty ending the War of 1812. From 1815 to 1817 he served as U.S. minister to Great Britain. In 1817 he became President Monroe's secretary of state.

As secretary of state, Adams was an ardent expansionist. He supported Andrew Jackson's invasion of Spanish Florida (1819) and negotiated the transcontinental treaty (1819) with Spain, which obtained Florida and ended Spanish claims to the Pacific Northwest. He also persuaded Russia to surrender its northwestern claims south of latitude 54'40". When British Foreign Secretary Canning suggested an Anglo-American statement banning further European intervention in Latin America, Adams persuaded Monroe to issue such a statement unilaterally. Many sections of this Monroe Doctrine (1823), which stated among other things that the Americas were to be considered closed to further European colonization, were drafted by Adams.

In 1824, Adams ran for the presidency. When none of the candidates received a majority of the electoral votes (Jackson got 99; Adams, 84; **Crawford,** 41; and **Clay,** 37), the election was thrown into the House of Representatives, where Henry Clay's support elected Adams. When Adams made Clay secretary of state, the Jacksonians denounced the appointment as a "corrupt bargain." As president, Adams failed to build a strong political party. Most of his nationalist proposals were rejected by Congress, and his term was marked by bitter partisan squabbling. In the election of 1828, Jackson defeated him by an electoral vote of 178 to 83.

From 1831 to 1848, Adams served in the U.S. House of Representatives. He opposed the annexation of Texas (1836) and took the lead in the fight against the "gag rule," under which antislavery petitions were laid on the table without discussion. He died of a stroke on the floor of the House.

⸺⸺⸺

Beginning at the ripe age of thirteen, when he was secretary to Francis Dana in St. Petersburg, John Quincy Adams spent almost all his long life in public service. Few Americans can have brought to that service a finer mind or a more ungraceful personality. Adams could be pleasing when he allowed himself to relax, but a mixture of pride, suspicion, singularity, and self-doubt compelled him on most occasions to turn an unwelcoming face toward the outer world. His physical appearance in later life—short, stout, bald, belligerent, with rheumy eyes and careless dress—was all of a piece with the rest of him. In his diary he confessed that he was "a man of cold, austere, and forbidding manners; my political adversaries say a gloomy misanthropist; and my personal enemies an unsocial savage." One detects in this admission a curious pleasure, an odd puritanical relish.

Indeed, the key to the inner quiddity of this most perplexing man seems to lie in the fact that he was both a Puritan and an intellectual, one of the few intellectuals ever to reach the presidency; he was a thinker who gorged himself with feelings of superiority, and a moralist who doubted and deplored this kind of indulgence; a statesman who gloried in success and a fatalist who convinced himself that every triumph must, unless one were very fortunate, be followed in due time by a compensating failure.

He had a keen if quarrelsome sense of duty that, combined as it was with a craving for independence, made him anything but a good party man. He was ostracized by the Federalists; he was scarcely *persona grata* to the Republicans, whose leaders began employing him as a diplomat in 1809. "That both the Adamses are monarchists," said **John Taylor** incorrigibly erroneous,

"I never doubted. Whether monarchists, like pagans, can be converted by benefices, is a problem the solution of which I always feared Mr. Madison would attempt."

Such was the man who became Monroe's secretary of state in 1817 and who could claim a wider experience of European politics than any secretary before or, for that matter, after him. Once he had settled down to his new position he began to give form to that singular vision of America's place in the world that made him one of the greatest secretaries of state and one of the more helpless of presidents.

This vision might be described as follows: The United States was to become a self-sufficient continental bastion and a predominant influence in the Western Hemisphere, a vision, in short, of influential neo-mercantilist isolation, where one spoke the language of commercial reciprocity but did not always put it into action. It can be seen taking shape in the following events: the transcontinental treaty with Spain in 1819, which gave America her boundary line to the Pacific; the noncolonization principle (his chief contribution to the Monroe Doctrine), a stern warning to Russia's (but more particularly to Great Britain's) pretensions in the Northwest; the nationalist Navigation Act of 1820, which compelled the British government to make a significant compromise in the matter of the West Indies carrying trade; the extravagant Navigation Act of 1823, which demanded equal trading rights with the British Empire in the West Indies and by implication in all British possessions in the Americas; his first annual message as president; and his secretary of the Treasury's protectionist reports to Congress.

In his first annual message he seemed to be asking for a centralized government, which would finance the nation's system of internal communications through a careful stewardship of the public lands. Nothing could have been less in tune with the spirit of the times, which was mobile, flexible, and centrifugal. His efforts to bring pressure to bear on the British (he told his friend Robert Walsh that this was simply *moral* pressure) merely produced a suspension of all American trade with the West Indies and helped to lose him the election of 1828. His first annual message was mocked. At the Congress of Panama in 1826, the former Spanish colonies would have nothing to do with his lofty neutralist concept of the freedom of the seas. The Treasury reports ended, if anywhere, in that famous hodgepodge known as the Tariff of Abominations. The whole vision, so delectable and rational in Adams's eyes, faded into nothing. He left the presidency believing that he was, in reputation if not in fortune, a ruined man.

But fate had better things in store for this peculiar but great American. Elected to the House of Representatives, much to his pleasure, from the Plymouth district of Massachusetts, he served in eight successive congresses. Always a fighter, except in the presidency where his nerve failed him, he led and endured one of the cruelest of verbal battles in his opposition to the "gag rule" that precluded all action on antislavery petitions. In 1844 the "gag resolution" was at last defeated. As an antislavery man he opposed the annexation of Texas and the Mexican War, and toward the end he was approaching as near to abolitionism as one could get without actually embracing it. He was known as "Old Man Eloquent" and had become a venerable and even, in some quarters, a popular figure. He has left in his *Report on Weights and Measures* (1821), in his public papers, and above all in his twelve-volume diary, or *Memoirs,* a towering monument to the manifold career and character of a devoted, tortured, and extraordinary man. See Samuel F. Bemis, *John Quincy Adams* (1949, 1956).

GEORGE DANGERFIELD

ADAMS, Samuel (b. Boston, Mass., Sept. 27, 1722; d. Boston, Mass., Oct. 2, 1803), POLITICAL LEADER, graduated from Harvard (BA, 1740; MA, 1743) and entered the family brewery business, which failed. He served as tax collector of Boston (1756–64) and as a member of the Massachusetts house of representatives (1765–74;

recording clerk, 1766–74). In 1765 he helped organize the "Sons of Liberty" to oppose the Stamp Act, and his critical attitude toward Parliament immediately established him as a leading patriot. After the Townshend Acts (1767) were passed, he helped form the Non-Importation Association (1768) to boycott British goods and drafted the Massachusetts "Circular Letter" to the legislatures of other colonies, asserting opposition to the new duties.

Although Anglo-American tensions relaxed after the Townshend Acts were repealed (1770), Adams continued his agitation in favor of colonial rights. He objected to the payment of judges' and governors' salaries by the Crown, which reduced local control. In 1772, on Adams's motion, the Boston town meeting created a committee of correspondence to communicate with other towns and to solicit their views. Thereafter he played a major part in the committee's activity until he went to Philadelphia in late 1774. After the British East India Company was granted a monopoly on the sale of tea in the colonies, Adams supported the patriots who dumped the British tea into the Boston Harbor (1773). When Parliament responded to this action by passing the Coercive Acts (1774), Adams was active in organizing nonintercourse measures and a confederation of the colonies.

Adams was a delegate to both Continental Congresses (serving 1774–82). At the second Congress he supported and was a signer of the Declaration of Independence. He was also a delegate to the convention that drafted the Massachusetts constitution (1779–80) and in 1788 served in the convention called to ratify the new U.S. Constitution, which he approved although he believed that it needed a bill of rights.

After running unsuccessfully for the first Congress of the United States, Adams served as lieutenant governor of Massachusetts (1789–94) and became governor after **John Hancock**'s death. In 1794 he was himself elected governor (serving until 1797). As governor he opposed the Federalists and condemned the Anglo-American Jay Treaty (1795).

Samuel Adams, the most important organizer of the Revolutionary movement in Massachusetts and possibly America from the time of the Stamp Act to the Declaration of Independence, was the epitome of an 18th-century New England republican. Austere in manner, sober, and discreet, he revered the idealized conception of New England's founders that flourished among their 18th-century descendants. From the time he graduated from Harvard, where he publicly defended the thesis that it is "lawful to resist the Supreme Magistrate, if the Commonwealth cannot be otherwise preserved," public life was Adams's single lifelong passion.

Adams found his constituency and first became influential in the taverns, clubs, and fire companies of mid-century Boston. Drawing on these sources of support, he became a leader of Boston's town meeting, where his political sensitivity and tactical flexibility made him a powerful figure. Adams's commitment to the provincial Whig view of Massachusetts rights was absolute from the moment issues relating to customs enforcement and the power of the general court crystallized in the early 1760s. Thereafter he fought continuously and strenuously for imperial recognition of constitutional principles approaching autonomy for Massachusetts and the other mainland colonies.

Adams's central strategy in opposing what he believed were British encroachments was first to employ every conventional and legal avenue of redress and only then to resort to extralegal measures—after a broad base of support had been developed that gave such tactics effective legitimacy. This technique was exercised repeatedly in Boston after 1764. As a result Adams stayed close to public opinion, always trying to influence it but always aware of its limits.

Because Adams acted primarily in concert with others and sought to obscure his personal role, it is often impossible to assess his individual achievements. Some scholars and some of his political adversaries have portrayed him as the wire-pulling genius who singlehandedly controlled Boston politics in the years before 1775. But his associates in Boston and the legislature often acted independently of Adams, sometimes contrary to his wishes. His brilliance as a political manager was widely recognized by his peers, but the structure of politics in colonial Boston and Massachusetts was so decentralized that no single individual could dominate. Of all Adams's many activities he was probably most responsible for the creation and operation of the Boston Committee of Correspondence, for the strategy adopted in Boston to oppose the Tea Act that culminated in the Tea Party, and for bringing the Continental Congress to support Massachusetts in late 1774. Typically, he acted in conjunction with other like-minded leaders in each of these enterprises, and much of his individual role remains hidden.

By the time the War for Independence was over, Adams was over 60, and the city and province in which he had risen to eminence had changed significantly. His own ideology, like his earlier political role, was dominated by the defensive imperatives of resisting rather than creating government power, of preserving liberties, not establishing them. Personally, too, Adams was becoming anachronistic; it was said that "our New England Fathers was his theme, and he had their deportment, habits, and customs." Characteristically, psalm singing was his chief recreation. In his last years Adams became the first Republican governor of Massachusetts, but by now his eminence was based on previous connections to Governor Hancock and the legend of his role in the Revolution, not his personal political ability. By the time of his death, Adams was merely an infirm spectator of public affairs. See John C. Miller, *Sam Adams: Pioneer in Propaganda* (1936).

RICHARD D. BROWN

ADDAMS, Jane (b. Cedarville, Ill., Sept. 6, 1860; d. Chicago, Ill., May 21, 1935), REFORMER, was descended from English and German settlers of Pennsylvania, her parents having immigrated to Illinois at their marriage in 1844. She was very close to her father, a prosperous miller, railroad promoter, and eight-term state senator. She was one of the first generation of college women, graduating from Rockford Seminary (later Rockford College) in 1881. After a term at the Women's Medical College, Philadelphia, she dropped out because of poor health and for the next seven years tried to find something useful and important to do. She rejected teaching and charity work, and there was little else that a young woman could do. She traveled twice to Europe, and on her second visit she became interested in the social reform movement and especially the accomplishments of Toynbee Hall, Whitechapel, London, an early settlement house. With Ellen Gates Star, a friend and college classmate, Addams resolved to found a similar institution in America not only to aid the poor but also to provide useful work for college-educated young people. To this end she acquired the old Hull mansion on Chicago's South Halsted Street in 1889, and in a few years she built it into the most important (though not the first) settlement house in America. To it came men, women, and children who found in Addams, her talented and devoted associates, and the varied activities of Hull House sanctuary from their problems and a source of inspiration for the future. Ultimately Hull House came to consist of thirteen buildings and a staff of sixty-five men and women, many of them recent college graduates, offering not only social counseling but also a wide range of activities from bookbinding to little theater, of which Hull House was one of the pioneers.

Jane Addams was not primarily a social theorist. She taught her followers to meet each problem as a new one and to attack it with experience, common sense, and, above all, tact. Her skill in working with children was noteworthy. So was her interest in feminism, though this was not her primary concern, and she also worked effectively in the field of politics, helping to secure passage of the Illinois Factory Act of 1893 and the Child Labor Law of 1903. Her activities are described in *Twenty Years at Hull House,* which she published in 1910; and her philosophy that the basis of democracy is the identification of its leaders with the common lot, in *Democracy and Social Ethics* (1902). Among her other books are *The Spirit of Youth and City Streets* (1909) and *Peace and Bread in Time of War* (1922).

Her experience in an immigrant neighborhood and her reading of Tolstoy had made Jane Addams a pacifist. With the start of World War I she became active in the world peace movement, which occupied most of her time in her remaining years. In 1915 she became chairman of the Women's Peace Party and president of the International Congress of Women at The Hague. She also served as president of the Women's International League for Peace and Freedom. Her pacifist internationalism, however, was not well received during World War I and in the isolationist years following it, and she was expelled from the Daughters of the American Revolution because of her views. Nevertheless in 1931, with **Nicholas Murray Butler,** she was awarded the Nobel Peace Prize.

———— ⚭ ————

Jane Addams played many roles. She was a frequent and effective public speaker, who talked softly and used personal, human illustrations to hold her audience and make her point. She was also a prolific writer; despite her other activities, she found time to write ten books and five hundred articles. She was not an especially original thinker, but she had the ability to see meaning and purpose in the confusing events of her day and to communicate that meaning to a wide audience. She was also a shrewd businesswoman and a talented executive who had few peers as a fund-raiser and who managed Hull House with its $100,000 yearly budget and large staff. Yet she was always more than a manager: she created a sense of unity and purpose. In addition, she was an expert reformer who mastered the art of arousing public opinion as well as the technique of using statistics, persuasion, and pressure to influence elected officials. She was an idealist in a sense, but she usually worked for what was reasonably possible. She was a master at compromise and conciliation, a talent that allowed her to

accomplish much but that often angered her more idealistic colleagues.

Everything Jane Addams did was newsworthy. She was the subject of children's books and many laudatory articles, while thousands of ordinary people wrote to praise her work. Her public image took on a life of its own. She was compared to Joan of Arc and the Virgin Mary; she was "the only saint America has produced," a British visitor announced. Yet she was usually pictured as a special American kind of saint, practical and useful, symbol of the best of American womanhood. She was, according to the legend, a humble, self-sacrificing woman who gave up a life of ease to serve the lowly.

There was, of course, some truth in the myth, but also much that was exaggerated and false. Jane Addams was far from humble; she was a proud, ambitious woman who gloried in publicity and added to the legend in her own writings, especially her autobiography. She had little interest in material things, but her life was hardly one of sacrifice. She stayed in the best hotels and ate in the best restaurants when she traveled, and she was entertained lavishly by her many wealthy friends. Even Hull House, though far from luxurious, provided a genteel and comfortable existence for its residents. The image and the reality diverged, yet the myth of Jane Addams served a useful purpose in an America where many felt worried and guilty over the contrast between wealth and poverty. She seemed to be doing something about the problems of poverty and the city, and doing it in a practical and sensible way that did not threaten or disturb middle- and upper-class Americans. Of course, there was some criticism of her defense of organized labor and her willingness to welcome all people, even anarchists, to Hull House, but before World War I the criticism was overwhelmed by the praise, and the image of Jane Addams loomed larger than life.

The war changed everything. Because she opposed the war even after the United States got involved, and suggested that soldiers were something less than heroes, she turned, in the public eye, from heroine and saint to villain and traitor.

Even after the war she remained a special symbol of Bolshevism and betrayal for groups such as the Daughters of the American Revolution and the American Legion. Late in the twenties she was still denounced as "the most dangerous woman in America" and accused of "strengthening the hands of the Communists." Of course, there was praise as well for her continued efforts to promote world peace and to solve the problems of the cities, but here as in all her career it was difficult to separate what she actually did and what she symbolized. That in itself was a mark of her importance. See Allen F. Davis, *American Heroine: The Life and Legend of Jane Addams* (1973).

ALLEN F. DAVIS

AGASSIZ, Jean Louis Rodolphe (b. Motier-en-Vuly, Switzerland, May 28, 1807; d. Cambridge, Mass., Dec. 14, 1873), SCIENTIST, received his PhD from Erlangen University (1829) and MD from the University of Munich (1830). After acquiring a collection of specimens brought back from an exploratory expedition to Brazil by J. B. Spix and C. P. J. von Martius, he completed the study *The Fishes of Brazil* in 1829. He traveled to Paris in 1831, where he was befriended by the French naturalist George Cuvier whose views on natural history exerted a profound influence on him. He was professor of natural history at the University of Neuchâtel (1832–45), during which period he wrote *Recherches sur les Poissons Fossiles* (6 vols., 1833–43), studies of the fishes of central Europe and of living and fossil mollusks, and *Nomenclator Zoologicus* (1842), a work aimed at producing a better system of zoological classification. In addition, he undertook extensive glacial studies in Europe, which led him to suggest the existence of a universal glacial era, Schimper's so-called Ice Age, as one of the basic geological periods in the development of the earth. He came to America in 1846 to do research and to lecture. In 1849 he accepted a chair in Harvard's newly organized Lawrence Scientific School, which he held until 1873. While at Harvard he established himself as the most prominent American authority on natural history. He founded the Harvard Museum of Comparative Zoology, serving as director from 1859 to 1873. As a lecturer he toured widely to help popularize the study of natural science. He was among the founders of the National Academy of Science and a regent of the Smithsonian Institution.

Agassiz believed in special creationism, the theory that all the world's flora and fauna were divinely created. He rejected any theory that explained change or postulated development through the action of "physical agents" or environmental factors. He asserted that only with the proper metaphysical framework in mind could the scientist rightly proceed to investigate and assess natural phenomena. He was thus a staunch antievolutionist who went so far as to postulate the occurrence of many special creations. He believed, for example, that blacks were separately created and of a different species from Caucasians. Agassiz never abandoned his anti-Darwinian views, most eloquently expressed in his *Essay on Classification* (1857).

Agassiz's life was devoted to the study of nature. Even the year before his death he organized a summer nature study school that was the precursor of the Woods Hole Biological Institute. From his mentor Cuvier he learned comparative anatomy, paleontology, and the concept that "a physical fact is as sacred as a moral principle." Cuvier's philosophy of nature that affirmed the permanence of species and held organic evolution to be scientifically and theologically false was a belief Agassiz always embraced.

Agassiz established his scientific reputation between 1832 and 1845, his most important contributions being *Poissons fossiles*, a study of nearly a thousand ancient fishes, and his advancement of the glacial theory (*Etudes sur les glaciers*, 1840). Such contributions led to his Harvard professorship. Agassiz was determined to make America superior to Europe in science, advanced education, and academic organization. He was instrumental in establishing natural history teaching at the College of Charleston and Cornell University, in the founding of major American scientific institutions, and in the training of a new generation of naturalists, including his son Alexander, Joseph Le Conte, Edward S. Morse, Nathaniel S. Shaler, and Addison E. Verrill.

In Europe Agassiz's main concern had been scholarship. In America he was a teacher, a spokesman for public support for and understanding of science, and an organizer of intellectual life. His major work in American science was his study of marine animals, *Contributions to the Natural History of the United States* (4 vols., 1857–62), and his extension of the glacial theory to North America.

In the years after 1855, Agassiz was deeply involved in the controversy over evolution. His staunchest opponent was his Harvard colleague, the botanist **Asa Gray,** whose arguments were typical of most of the critics who supported Charles Darwin and rejected Agassiz's arguments. Agassiz believed that evolution was "a scientific mistake, untrue in its acts, unscientific in its method, and mischievous in its tendency." He never deviated from this position. It was buttressed by his Protestant pietism, which convinced him that evolution was contrary to his interpretation of religion and Scripture. As a scientist, Agassiz was completely justified in rejecting the evolution doctrine when Darwin announced it in 1859. However, his consistent subsequent opposition reflected his American career, as his extrascientific involvements prevented him from keeping abreast of new discoveries and ideas. Asa Gray, also a theologically inspired naturalist, believed in the argument for a designed universe and saw no conflict between religion and evolution. Agassiz argued that species symbolized a divine plan, were immutable, and had always existed in distinct plans of creation and categories that made common ancestry impossible. Gray argued that species had originated from a single center of creation and a common pair, and that their variations were facts of nature, the result of causes such as climate, geographical isolation, and phenomena such as the same glacial theory Agassiz

had done so much to establish. See Edward Lurie, *Louis Agassiz: A Life in Science* (1960).

EDWARD LURIE

AGNEW, Spiro Theodore (b. Baltimore, Md., Nov. 9, 1918), POLITICAL LEADER, entered Johns Hopkins University in 1937 to study chemistry, but after three years he transferred to the Baltimore Law School, attending night classes while working for an insurance company and managing a supermarket. In World War II he served as a company commander with the Tenth Armored Division in France and Germany, and won a Bronze Star. He received his law degree from the Baltimore School of Law in 1947 and practiced in Towson, Maryland, a Baltimore suburb. Originally a Democrat, he soon became active in Republican politics and local civic affairs. He worked in several Republican campaigns and in 1957 was appointed to the zoning board of appeals of Baltimore County. In 1961 state Democrats successfully blocked his reappointment to the board, and the subsequent furor gave Agnew much publicity. He was elected county executive, or suburban mayor, of Baltimore County in 1962. Agnew ran for governor of Maryland in 1966 and defeated Democrat George Mahoney, a segregationist and fervent opponent of open housing. In 1967 a graduated state income tax, increased aid to antipoverty programs, an open housing law, and a water pollution control law were enacted with the governor's blessing. In his second year, however, Agnew backed the reduction of health and welfare expenditures and criticized the Poor People's March on Washington. After the April 1968 urban riots, which resulted from the assassination of Dr. **Martin Luther King, Jr.,** he personally confronted moderate black leaders and charged them with failure to control militants in Baltimore.

At the 1968 Republican National Convention in Miami, Agnew, originally a supporter of **Nelson A. Rockefeller,** nominated Richard M. Nixon for president. Nixon later chose him to be his running mate. After Nixon's election, Agnew became the administration's "hard-line" spokesman. He became known for his scolding attacks on opponents of the Vietnam War, radicals, the news media, and intellectuals. In a speech in Des Moines, Iowa, on November 13, 1969, he attacked the "self-appointed" news commentators who, in analyzing a Nixon television address, had "expressed in one way or another their hostility to what he had to say." In a speech after the May 1970 invasion of Cambodia, he labeled war protesters "an effete corps of impudent snobs who characterize themselves as intellectuals." During the 1970 congressional campaign he denounced "radicalliberals" and warned against "permissiveness" in American society.

In the 1972 presidential campaign the Nixon-Agnew ticket was elected by a large majority. When the Watergate scandals surfaced in the spring of 1973, Agnew, who was not involved, appeared to profit politically. He seemed to be the leading candidate for the 1976 Republican presidential nomination. During the summer, however, an investigation of corruption in Maryland unearthed evidence that Agnew had received money from engineering firms in return for government contracts. After repeatedly denying all charges, he pleaded *nolo contendere* to a charge of income-tax evasion. He received a heavy fine and was placed on probation for three years. On October 10, 1973, he resigned as vice president, and the government released evidence of his involvement in other corrupt practices. In May 1974 he was disbarred.

In the decades since he was forced from office, Agnew has remained largely out of the public eye. On occasion he has represented business clients, many of them with interests in the Middle East, and has made headlines with scathing comments about the purported influence of Jews on American foreign policy. Many of his former colleagues and speechwriters, Jews themselves, such as William Safire, a columnist of the *New York Times*, have been shocked and deeply disturbed by his seeming anti-Semitism. That aspect of his character, they allege, was well hidden from them during his years in politics. Agnew never forgave Richard Nixon for helping to force him to resign and refused to have any contact with the former

president or even to answer his phone calls when they were both in private life. Agnew, however, did attend Nixon's funeral in 1994.

⸻

In the public mind, Spiro T. Agnew will be remembered as the only vice president who was forced to resign his office because of criminal acts. The irony of his disgrace—that so prominent a supporter of "law and order" should himself be a lawbreaker—is so obvious as to require no elaboration. That journalists and other victims of his coarse attacks should take such relish in his fall is also easy to understand. Agnew remains important, however, for another reason than as an example of hypocrisy exposed and just retribution, one that illustrates an unresolved problem of American politics. His rise rather than his fall reminds us of the danger inherent in the custom of allowing presidential nominees personally to select their running mates and to choose them usually during the last moments of a hectic convention in response to immediate political needs. In 1968 the derisive "Spiro who?" could perhaps be discounted as Democratic partisanship. The nomination served a useful short-term political purpose (winning the votes of southerners and of northerners who were alarmed by liberal efforts to improve the position of urban blacks), but few Republicans seriously argued that Agnew was well qualified for the vice presidency.

Finally, Agnew is unique as the only person ever to occupy so high an office in the United States who deliberately used his position to try to divide rather than unify the country. Others, of course, have been partisans, sought mean advantage by appealing to popular prejudices or class envy. None but Agnew has defamed whole classes of the population: students, foes of the Vietnam War, "intellectual snobs." The function of the president and the vice president as symbols of community totally escaped him. This may explain why he continued to accept secret payments even after 1968. See Richard M. Cohen and Jules Witcover, *A Heartbeat Away* (1974).

JOHN A. GARRATY

ALBEE, Edward Franklin (b. Washington, D.C., Mar. 12, 1928), PLAYWRIGHT, reared by foster parents, Reed and Frances Albee, a wealthy theater owner and a former model. He briefly attended Trinity College before settling in New York City's Greenwich Village in 1949. He worked at such jobs as office boy, salesman, and Western Union messenger while writing fiction, poetry, and plays.

Albee wrote his first one-act play, *The Zoo Story,* in 1958. Presenting the theme of the lack of interpersonal contacts and the difficulties of true involvement, the play consisted entirely of the conversation of two men, Jerry and Peter, on a park bench. It premiered in West Berlin in 1959 and then at Greenwich Village's Provincetown Playhouse in 1960. Albee followed this with two other one-act plays, *The Death of Bessie Smith* (1960), which described the death of blues singer Bessie Smith and the parallel, though spiritual, deterioration of a white nurse, and *The American Dream* (1961), in which Albee examined and attacked the substitution of artificial for real values in contemporary American society. His first full-length play, *Who's Afraid of Virginia Woolf?* (1962), a drama of a middle-aged couple's disintegrating marriage, became an instant success and a topic of controversy because of its harsh, earthy language. *Tiny Alice,* a metaphysical allegory, appeared in 1964, and *A Delicate Balance* (1966), another drama of family life, won the 1967 Pulitzer Prize. In 1968 he completed *Box* and *Quotations from Chairman Mao Tse-tung.* In *Box,* an experimental play, Albee presented a stage empty except for the outline of a large cube; the only sound is a disembodied voice reciting a type of prose poem. The poem itself, rather than presenting a plot, merely meditates on themes suggested by the word "box" itself. Albee used the motif of the cube in *Quotations* as well, although in that play an ocean liner, from which the various actors recite their lines, is not visible. In both of these plays Albee's sense of the movement of mankind toward a holocaust, and the inability of individuals to conceive of this disaster in other than personal terms, was manifest. His other plays include *Malcolm* (1966) and *All Over* (1971).

Albee won another Pulitzer Prize for his play *Seascape* (1975). Although he has continued to present new plays, they have not been received with the critical and popular acclaim of his previous work.

The career of this leading American representative of the Theater of the Absurd in some ways resembles that of **Eugene O'Neill** in the 1920s. Although Albee has always insisted on his originality, he obviously has been influenced by such writers as Beckett, Ionesco, Genet, Pinter, Brecht, Jarry, and Büchner, and by such movements as Dadaism, Surrealism, and Expressionism. His penchant for reworking ideas of other writers (such as **Herman Melville,** Carson McCullers, Truman Capote, James Purdy, and Giles Cooper) has resulted in some conspicuous failures; but at least one of these adaptations, *The Ballad of the Sad Café* (1963), could be defended as an "artistic success." Yet the reception of almost every one of his "successful" plays has also been flawed by strong dissenting opinions from unsympathetic critics. A provoker of controversy, Albee sometimes deliberately offends, and he has been idolized by young activists for opposing the so-called establishment. The label "rich boy makes good" made him vulnerable to critics who did not like his excellent satire and criticism of society (in plays like *The American Dream* and *Bessie Smith*). To critics of his indeterminate or "unsatisfying" endings, he replies, "I'm not interested in the kind of problems that can be tied in a bundle at the third-act curtain." To detractors who find his plays "difficult," he answers, "Art isn't easy—and it demands of its audience the willingness to bring to it some of the intensity and perception its creators put into it."

As a serious artist of great integrity, Albee has made the problem of illusion and reality one of his favorite themes, and he has very effectively dramatized some of the most nightmarish aspects of a heretofore little-imagined world beyond illusion. "How much reality are audiences prepared to face?" he asks. And no matter how much it hurts, he is willing to give them all they can take—and more. See Richard E. Amacher, *Edward Albee* (1969).

RICHARD E. AMACHER

ALBRIGHT, William Foxwell (b. Coquimbo, Chile, May 24, 1891; d. Baltimore, Md., Sept. 19, 1971), ARCHAEOLOGIST, ORIENTALIST, graduated from Upper Iowa University in 1912. He taught high school for a year in Menno, South Dakota, before entering graduate school at Johns Hopkins University's Oriental Seminary in 1913. After receiving his PhD in Semitic languages in 1916, he continued studying at the university on a Johnston scholar fellowship for research.

After brief service in the army in 1918, Albright went to Jerusalem to study modern Hebrew and Arabic at the American School of Oriental Research; he became acting director of the school in 1920 and was director from 1921 to 1929. During this period he directed important excavations at Gibeah of Saul, Bethel in Palestine, and Baluah and Petra in Jordan. *Archaeology of Palestine and the Bible* (1932) described this work and that of others in the field. Albright returned to Johns Hopkins in 1929 as W. W. Spence professor of Semitic languages, a position he held until his retirement in 1958. He was also director of the American School of Oriental Research in Jerusalem (1933–36), during which period he conducted excavations at Tell Beit Mirsim. He published *Archaeology and the Religion of Israel* in 1942. After spending 1946 as a visiting professor at the University of Chicago, Albright became chief archaeologist of the Sinai phase of the University of California African Expedition (1947–48) and chief archaeologist of the South Arabian Expedition of the American Foundation for the Study of Man (1950–51), which excavated at Wadi Bayhan and Hajar Bin Humaid in Arabia. He was perhaps the first expert to recognize the antiquity of the Qumran biblical scrolls, discovered in a cave near the Dead Sea in 1947. His 1953 article in the *American Scholar* titled "The Dead Sea Scrolls" dated the Isaiah scroll at about 100 B.C. He was elected to the National Academy of Sciences in 1955 and was research professor at the Jewish Theological Seminary of America in New York from 1957 to 1959. Some of his books include *From the Stone Age to Christianity* (1940), *Archaeology and Christian Humanism* (1964), *New Horizons in Biblical Research* (1966), and *Yahweh and the Gods of Canaan* (1968).

—⁂—

Albright, because of his diverse training, was an Orientalist in the tradition of the 19th century, a time when scholars were able to encompass the entire spectrum of ancient Near Eastern studies, although he did his work in the twentieth century when increased material and information forced most Orientalists to specialize in a particular discipline. He was an important archaeologist, chronologist, philologian, epigrapher, and biblical scholar. His linguistic ability was his greatest asset. It was supported by a keen memory, which was legend during his lifetime. Together, these assets gave him a self-assurance that was sometimes viewed as arrogance. It was not uncommon for him to give an impromptu lecture immediately following a paper delivered by another scholar. His ability to marshal a vast amount of information from memory would normally sway the audience in favor of the speaker—if Albright agreed with him—or to the contrary if he did not. More than one paper remained unpublished because of this habit.

Albright had a continuing concern for synthesis; however, before such could be done he felt there had to be a proper foundation, and therefore much of his work revolved, directly or indirectly, around chronology. His pottery analysis, based primarily on his work at Tell Beit Mirsim, has influenced all subsequent excavations in Palestine. He stressed the value of the common potsherd for dating the various levels of an excavation and demonstrated how the changes in pottery forms could serve as a basis for sequence dating. Also, his work on the historical development of the ancient Hebrew script was invaluable when the Dead Sea Scrolls were discovered. He was instrumental in recognizing the antiquity of these documents, which were perhaps the most important discovery of this century for biblical studies.

Albright was influenced by his religious background; his interest in the Bible underlay his entire work. At a time when many European scholars questioned its historicity he remained a staunch defender—very much like Schliemann and Troy—and could say, "I have grown more conservative in my attitude to Mosaic tradition." This attitude was criticized by some but well received by other Americans who did not belong to the critical European school. See Frank Moore Cross, "William Foxwell Albright: Orientalist," *Bulletin of the American School of Oriental Research,* 200 (Dec. 1970), 7–11.

JOHN D. SCHMIDT

ALCOTT, Louisa May (b. Germantown, Pa., Nov. 29, 1832; d. Boston, Mass., Mar. 6, 1888), WRITER, was educated at home by her father, Amos Bronson Alcott, a well-known teacher and abolitionist. She then worked as a teacher, domestic worker, and at other jobs, and eventually began to write poems and short stories for children. A collection of fairy stories, *Flower Fables,* was published in 1854, and in 1860 the *Atlantic Monthly* began publishing her work. An ardent abolitionist, Alcott served briefly as a nurse in the Union Hospital at Georgetown during the Civil War. *Hospital Sketches* (1863), a collection of letters dealing with this experience, established her literary reputation. After writing an unsuccessful novel, *Moods* (1864), she spent a year (1865–66) in Europe. She served as editor of *Merry's Museum,* a children's magazine (1867) before writing her best-known work, *Little Women* (1868–69). This largely autobiographical story of New England family life was a great financial success and was translated into several languages. Alcott followed it with *An Old Fashioned Girl* (1870), then *Little Men* (1871), a story based on the experiences of her nephews. Spending most of her time in Boston, she devoted much of her later life to such reforms as temperance and women's rights but also continued her writing. Some of her many books include *Aunt Jo's Scrap Bag* (6 vols., 1872–82), *Work* (1873), *Jack and Jill* (1880), and *Jo's Boys* (1886).

Although Louisa M. Alcott brought happiness to generations of girls through such classics as *Little Women* and *Little Men,* her own life, begun in genteel but bleak poverty, was one of hard work and self-sacrifice. At an early age she discovered that her revered father was incapable of supporting his family, and so she assumed the role of breadwinner. A romantic at heart, she began by writing swashbuckling novels, which were unsuccessful. But when, at the suggestion of a Boston editor, she produced her first book for girls, fame and fortune arrived. At 36 she was able to write in her journal: "Paid up all the debts—thank the lord—and now I could die in peace."

Alcott was one of the new women, breaking with tradition and sponsoring woman suffrage and other causes. It was she, not her father, who volunteered when the Civil War broke out. Serving as a nurse, she contracted a fever and was never in robust health again. She was heroic, not in the manner of her early heroines but on a scale that was much more human. She did not always bear her yoke in silence but complained from time to time in the privacy of her journal. And she could be caustic about her neighbors, such as Mrs. Nathaniel Hawthorne, who came back from Europe with "high falutin' ideas." If she was unhappy at not being married, she never mentioned it. She worked so hard to support her sisters and their children that she had no time to fall in love.

She was a devoted daughter and a courageous woman, but above all she was a portrayer of little girls who remain true to life no matter how superficial customs change. Her books will be enjoyed as long as children still read. See Ednah D. Chaney, ed., *Louisa May Alcott: Her Life, Letters and Journals* (1889).

MARJORIE WORTHINGTON

ALDRICH, Nelson Wilmarth (b. Foster, R.I., Nov. 6, 1841; d. New York, N.Y., Apr. 16, 1915),

POLITICAL LEADER, studied at the East Greenwich Academy before going to work for a wholesale grocer in Providence, R.I. When the Civil War broke out, he served in the Tenth R.I. Volunteers. After an attack of typhoid he left the army and returned to Providence. In 1865 he became a junior partner in the grocery. Later he became president of a Providence bank, president of a local board of trade, and president of the United Traction and Electric Company, which controlled Rhode Island's electric railway lines. Investments in that business, which were facilitated by a $5 million loan from the American Sugar Refining Company, served as the basis of Aldrich's fortune.

In 1869 he entered politics as a Republican. He served in the Providence common council (1869–75), and in the Rhode Island state legislature (1875–76). In 1879 he was elected to the U.S. House of Representatives and in 1881 to the Senate. As a member of the Senate Finance Committee he took an active role in framing the Mongrel Tariff (1883) and quickly established himself as a leading Republican authority on economic questions. His political program was, with little variation, the program of American business in the late 19th and early 20th centuries: a sound currency, a protective tariff, and minimal government interference in private enterprise. During the 1880s and 1890s he worked to weaken the Interstate Commerce Act (1887) and the Sherman Antitrust Act (1890), regarding both as useless, unnecessary political expedients that would do more harm than good. Aldrich was chiefly responsible for framing the Republican "Senate Substitute" for the moderate Democratic Mills Tariff Bill (1888). His report not only served as an important campaign document in the presidential election of that year but also was the model on which the McKinley Tariff of 1890 was patterned. As chairman of the Senate Finance Committee, Aldrich played an important part in structuring the Dingley Tariff (1897). Although he recognized the need for an increase in the money supply and supported the Sherman Silver Purchase Act (1890), he strongly opposed the free coinage of silver and helped draft the Gold Standard Act (1900).

During the Progressive Era, Aldrich stood out as one of the nation's leading conservatives. When Congress increased its control over interstate commerce with the Hepburn Bill (1906), he forced the adoption of changes (known as the Allison amendments) that by indirection enabled the railroads to challenge the decisions of the ICC in the courts. Eventually, however, the courts refused to review the commission's rulings. In 1908 the Aldrich-Vreeland Act was enacted into law under Aldrich's direction; it created a National Monetary Commission (headed by him) to study the banking systems of the United States and Europe and devise a "more elastic currency." In 1909, Aldrich successfully led the fight against revising the tariff downward. The resulting Payne-Aldrich Tariff had a great deal to do with arousing the ire of insurgent Republicans in Congress and Progressives throughout the nation against the administration of William Howard Taft, who relied heavily on Aldrich for advice.

In foreign policy matters Aldrich strove to prevent the Spanish-American War but played a major role in rounding up votes to secure passage of the Treaty of Paris (1898), which provided for the annexation of the Philippines and Puerto Rico. He also helped frame the Platt Amendment (1901), which permitted the United States to intervene in Cuba. Although he supported Theodore Roosevelt's plans to build an Isthmian canal, he was generally critical of what he regarded as the president's free-wheeling interventionist policy in the Caribbean.

Before and after Aldrich's retirement from the Senate in 1911, he concentrated on his "Aldrich Plan," which sought to provide the nation with a modified central banking system and an "elastic currency" by creating fifteen branch banks under private banker auspices. However, Congress refused to consider his proposal. Although the Federal Reserve Act (1913) contained many elements derived from his original plan, Aldrich spoke out against it largely because it gave the president power to appoint the board of governors and permitted the reserve banks to issue notes in a manner that he regarded as inflationary.

⚬⚬⚬

Nelson Aldrich was the brightest clerk in Waldron and Wightman's wholesale grocery, a tireless, eager-to-please young competitor who knew exactly what he wanted from life: "Willingly or forcibly wrested from a selfish world, *Success!* Counted as the mass counts it by dollars and cents!" Aldrich got all he was after, and more. He wound up a millionaire many times over and became a card-playing intimate of Cardinal **Gibbons** and **J. Pierpont Morgan,** father-in-law to John D. Rockefeller, Jr., chairman of the Senate Finance Committee, and the acknowledged leader of the Republican Big Four—that celebrated quadrumvirate of senior senators who dominated the upper house at the turn of the century.

Little about the mature Aldrich suggested his humble origins or the fierce determination with which he pursued power and wealth. Over six feet tall and two hundred pounds, with broad shoulders, a square, handsome full-boned face, piercing brown eyes, white hair, and flowing mustache, he appeared a well-bred, supremely confident man of affairs, untouched by privation or anxiety. Actually, he was not brilliant or well educated or witty, and he suffered from gnawing feelings of inadequacy. His speeches never stimulated and rarely surprised. Instead, crammed with facts and statistics gathered from hundreds of private and public sources, and delivered from memory in a frank, direct way "like one bank director to another at a board meeting," they nearly always informed—and intimidated. Though cool and somewhat forbidding in public, he smiled readily and was the soul of charm, geniality, and courtesy in private. In an age when fiery personal and partisan controversies coursed through national politics, he did not hate or hold grudges. Until the insurgent revolt he had few enemies—the result not only of his temperament but of hundreds of loans, campaign contributions, and legislative favors with which he forged a personal network of reciprocal loyalty and profit on both sides of the congressional aisle.

Politics for him was an art form; as a painter knows his palette he knew whom to flatter, whom to offer a seat on a major committee, and whom to isolate on a minor one. While the beneficiaries of his patronage were never allowed to forget the source of their fortune, his victims seldom realized until too late who was responsible for their discomfiture, for he plotted their downfall quietly and with a smile.

Among contemporary politicians only Theodore Roosevelt approached him as a technician of parliamentary warfare, and even Roosevelt preferred to accommodate him on party and legislative matters. "Aldrich is a great man to me," Roosevelt once told **Lincoln Steffens,** "not personally, but as the leader of the Senate. He is a kingpin in my game. Sure, I bow to Aldrich; I talk to Aldrich; I respect him, as he does not respect me. I'm just a president, and he has seen lots of presidents."

All this made Aldrich the premier powerbroker on Capitol Hill during the McKinley, Roosevelt, and Taft administrations, and in the judgment of many Progressives then and historians since, "the living embodiment of that sordid and corrupt system which has left its ineffaceable brand on the history of the Republican party for three decades." In reality he was the incarnation of triumphant capitalism. Convinced that unfettered business enterprise had infinite capacity to produce the good life, at minimal cost, and thereby persuaded that in providing a hospitable legislative environment for business he was doing an invaluable service for the country, he was the practicing political equivalent of the great captains of industry. Like other self-made men of the era, he was simply true to his experiences and the materialistic ethos of his time. "Of course a man is influenced here," he once said, "by the business he has been in, by the alliances he has formed, and by his environment." And yet the Progressive charge that he used his public position for private gain does have some validity. Aldrich not only represented big business and advanced its interests but also profited from that representation. He was not bought, he was not hired, he was not really corrupted; rather, he was subvented. Loans, stock participations, bonds, business deals, all came his way and enabled him, while remaining in politics, to acquire the means to support the elegant lifestyle he craved—leather-bound books, antique china, medieval tapestries, paintings, annual trips to Europe, and a hundred-acre estate on Narragansett Bay modeled after one he admired in the Loire valley. If the source of most of his wealth ever bothered him, he never showed it. In his view of things the nation was the residual beneficiary of the political aid he rendered business; therefore his conscience was clear. Unfortunately, however, his reputation as an ardent, sincere, even creative agent and manager of the politics of American capitalism will forever remain suspect. See Nathaniel Wright Stephenson, *Nelson W. Aldrich: A Leader in American Politics* (1930).

JEROME L. STERNSTEIN

ALGER, Horatio, Jr. (b. Revere, Mass., Jan. 13, 1834; d. Natick, Mass., July 18, 1899), WRITER, graduated from Harvard in 1852. After a trip to Europe he spent the next three years writing for local newspapers. Under pressure from his father he entered Harvard Divinity School and received his degree in 1860. He spent the next year traveling in Europe and in 1864 was ordained as minister of a Unitarian church in Brewster, Massachusetts. Two years later, however, having written several unnoticed novels, Alger moved to New York City to devote himself to literature. Drawing on his experiences in social work at the Newsboys' Lodging House in New York, he began to write stories for and about young men. His first serial story, *Ragged Dick* (1867), became a best-seller; he followed it with two other serials, *Luck and Pluck* (1869) and *Tattered Tom* (1871).

Growing enormously popular and wealthy, Alger wrote several biographies of self-made American statesmen—including *Abraham Lincoln, the Backwoods Boy* (1883) and *From Canal Boy to President* (1881), the story of James Garfield—illustrating how bright young Americans had conquered poverty to become great figures. This "Alger hero" deeply influenced his generation and sanctioned the business creed of his time. Alger also wrote a collection of poems, *Grand'ther Baldwin's Thanksgiving* (1875). In 1896 he moved to Natick, Massachusetts. A prolific writer, he produced some 119 novels during his lifetime.

⸺⚬⚬⚬⸺

Controversy continues to blur Alger's life, at least among the few scholars and amateur investigators who have taken the time to examine it. Some view him as a quiet, unobtrusive man, a product of his strict New England upbringing, whose life is more or less described in the upright, exemplary young men he wrote about. If one is to believe his diaries and letters, however, which have the ring of authenticity even though most of what is in them is difficult to prove, Alger emerges as a probable psychotic who broke away from his religious upbringing and immediately after his graduation from Harvard discovered sex in Paris through affairs with a café singer and a visiting English girl. In these encounters the biological roles were reversed, and Alger was quite literally, in the old melodramatic phrase, a love captive. After a disastrous trip to San Francisco, which ended in a bizarre, confused retreat to a hill cabin, he returned to Peekskill, New York, and there fell in love with a married woman who was on a trip to America to visit her sister. His incredible, successful pursuit of this lady, during which her love cooled and she at last rejected him, ended in a brief confinement for Alger in a Paris hospital.

During the years he spent in New York he lived most of the time at the Newsboys' Lodging House, from which most of the material for his books came. His relationship with the boys and with his only close friend, Charles O'Connor, their superintendent, has suggested to some researchers that Alger suppressed a homosexuality, which came closest to expression in his love for a young Chinese inmate of the house, Ah Wing, who was accidentally killed, a tragedy that appears to account for much of the writer's subsequent psychotic behavior.

Certainly homosexual elements are present in Alger's books, filled as they are with romanticized boys. Girls make only brief cardboard appearances. As soon as the stories of these boys end, almost always with a single lucky stroke that elevates them from struggle to success, Alger loses interest. The tales end abruptly as the boys approach manhood, with the imminent prospect of a conventional marriage. The only woman in Alger's life with whom he had a successful relationship was his sister Olive, with whom he spent his last three years.

All the while he was achieving fame as a writer of boys' books, Alger's real creative urge was to write a Great Novel. On his last day he tried to struggle from bed to a table where paper and freshly sharpened pencils awaited the beginning of this work, but he had no strength. Olive put him back to bed and pulled the covers up over this strange little man with the wistful mustache and sad eyes (like the famous description of **Andrew Mellon,** he looked like a man just leaving the room), whose appearance was so utterly incongruous with the life he led. "You've written enough, Horatio," Olive told him. A few hours later he was dead.

Alger's popularity in his lifetime and for long afterward (some of his titles were reissued as late as the 1960s) was based much less on the idea of "the American Dream" that his work later came to symbolize than on the fact that his books were adventure tales much loved by growing boys. Their locales (New York, San Francisco, the South Seas, the circus) were also extremely attractive to small-town and country boys everywhere in the late 19th century, boys who longed to break away from farm and village and seek their fortunes in the great cities, as they are still doing today. See John Tebbel, *From Rags to Riches: Horatio Alger and the American Dream* (1963).

JOHN TEBBEL

ALI, Muhammad (b. Louisville, Ky., Jan. 18, 1942), BOXER, born Cassius Marcellus Clay, Jr., learned how to box at age 12. He had more than one hundred amateur bouts and won the 1959 national Golden Gloves and Amateur Athletic Union light-heavyweight championships. In 1960 he won the national Golden Gloves heavyweight and AAU light-heavyweight titles. He represented the United States at the 1960 Olympics in Rome, capturing the light-heavyweight gold medal. Turning professional, Clay won his first pro bout as a heavyweight in 1960 and went on to become the top challenger for the heavyweight crown. Undefeated in all his pro bouts, Clay became known for his boastfulness and outspokenness, and for his humorous poetry in which he often accurately predicted the round in which his opponents would fall. In 1964 he defeated Sonny Liston for the heavyweight championship of the world and subsequently won several title defenses.

Shortly after the Liston fight Clay announced his membership in the Black Muslims, a group advocating black nationalism and the establishment of a separate black state in the United States; he changed his name to Muhammad Ali. In 1966, Ali publicly condemned the Vietnam War. He refused to be inducted into the army the following year on the grounds of his conscientious objector beliefs as a Black Muslim and of his being a minister of the Muslim faith. Ali was convicted of draft evasion by a federal court, sentenced to a $10,000 fine and five years in prison, and stripped of his heavyweight crown by the World Boxing Association. Ali remained inactive in boxing for three and a half years while his case was being appealed. Finally, in 1970, the courts ruled that suspending his license was "arbitrary and unreasonable," and Ali made a successful comeback in boxing. However, he lost his bid to regain the heavyweight title, being defeated by Joe Frazier on March 8, 1971, in a much publicized and highly profitable (each fighter earned approximately $2.5 million) New York fight. A rematch on January 28, 1974, in which Ali defeated Frazier, grossed $16 million. Later in 1974, Ali regained his title by knocking out George Foreman in Zaire, Africa, and defended it ten times before relinquishing it in a fight with Leon Spinks in 1978. Later that same year Ali defeated Spinks and became the first heavyweight to ever regain the championship twice. Ali retired in 1981. He remained in the public eye, traveling and making appearances at charitable events, but in recent years he has slowed down considerably. It was revealed during the 1980s that he was suffering from Parkinson's disease.

———— ⚬ ————

Muhammad Ali, *né* Cassius Marcellus Clay, Jr., likely will be remembered as a black prizefighter who defied white authority and epitomized militant black pride long after his exploits in the ring are forgotten. Ali, conjuring up memories of Jack Johnson and the dream of a "white hope" early in the twentieth century, broke the mold of the black boxing champion set by **Joe Louis** in the thirties of always appearing humble and deferential to whites. As unlike Louis, Joe Walcott, Ezzard Charles, and Floyd Patterson as possible, Ali flaunted his championship and publicly boasted of his prowess. Welcoming controversy, he preached the Black Muslim faith and demanded that boxing officials and sports writers refer to him by the name given him by **Elijah Muhammad.** Most pointedly, Ali eschewed the tradition of black athletes being either superpatriotic or apolitical by denouncing United States intervention in Vietnam and refusing to be inducted into military service.

Symbolically playing the same role acted out by **Adam Clayton Powell, Jr.,** in politics and Stokely Carmichael in the black protest movement, Ali refused to conform to the hat-in-hand, grateful black stereotype demanded of him by many whites. For this "effrontery," law enforcement and boxing officials combined to deny him his livelihood and threaten his liberty. The Illinois Athletic Commission would not permit him to box unless he apologized for his views on the Vietnam War. The World Boxing Association stripped him of his championship title, although his conviction for draft evasion still remained on appeal. And a federal judge in Houston imposed on Ali the harshest possible sentence the law permits for violating the Selective Service Act, despite numerous precedents to the contrary and protests against the racial makeup of the draft board. Such obviously arbitrary and spiteful acts made Ali a more influential black figure than his exploits in the ring alone ever could.

Ali suddenly became another major name on the roster of victims of American racial injustice and a new model of defiance for millions of angry blacks. On TV talk shows, before college audiences, and at rallies in ghettos throughout the country, he popularized Black Muslim teachings and deprecated the values of integration. In less than a decade the Olympics hero to Americans of all races had become another voice in the swelling chorus of discord that would do so much to spark racial disorders, white backlash, and black bitterness. See José Torres, *Sting Like a Bee: The Muhammad Ali Story* (1971).

HARVARD SITKOFF

ALLEN, Richard (b. Philadelphia, Pa., Feb. 14, 1760; d. Philadelphia, Pa., Mar. 26, 1831), RELIGIOUS LEADER, was born a slave, owned by a Quaker lawyer. Soon after his birth he was sold along with his parents to a farmer near Dover, Delaware. Allen joined the Methodist Episcopal Church in 1777. Educating himself, he was licensed to preach in 1782 and conducted services with the permission of his master. In 1784, Allen attended the first general conference of the Methodist Church in Baltimore. In 1786 he purchased freedom for himself and his family and returned to Philadelphia where he preached to blacks at the St. George Methodist Church. Becoming increasingly dissatisfied with racial discrimination in the church, Allen established an independent church, the Bethel Church, in 1787 in Philadelphia. The church prospered so that a new building was dedicated in 1794 by Bishop Francis Asbury, the first Methodist bishop in the United States. In 1799, Allen was ordained a deacon, and in 1816 he became a bishop in the Methodist Episcopal Church.

During the War of 1812, Allen helped recruit blacks for the defense of Philadelphia. In 1816 the expansion of separate black Methodist churches throughout the East offered the opportunity for the founding of the African Methodist Episcopal

Church. Allen was chosen the first bishop and served in this position until his death. The church, one of the strongest black organizations, extended its influence throughout the North and aided the underground railroad in freeing slaves. Allen denounced the American Colonization Society, founded in 1817, which sought to send black Americans back to Africa, but he participated in a movement to resettle blacks in Canada. His autobiography appeared as *The Life, Experience, and Gospel Labors of the Rt. Rev. Richard Allen* (1793).

Critic of slavery, forceful opponent of any derogation of his race, a firm believer in the bright future of black men in the Western Hemisphere, Allen was outstanding among that first generation of black leaders who, emerging soon after the Revolution, thought, spoke, and acted for themselves, preferring to lodge in the hands of black men a major part of the responsibility for determining their place in American society.

Throughout his life Allen was a proponent of—and a man deeply prompted by—the principles of Christian charity. "The love of this world," he remarked in his autobiography, "is a heavy weight upon the soul which chains her down and prevents her flight towards heaven. Habitual acts of charity loose her from it by degrees, and help her in her struggle to disengage herself and mount upwards." This was a philosophy requiring action to right wrongs, especially those done to his "black brethren." Allen might counsel the slave to "put your trust in God" rather than to rebel against bondage; but he was an outspoken foe of the institution of thralldom. He might advise his black brothers to "love our enemies"; but this did not preclude the establishment of organizations peculiar to black men where they might mingle without discrimination, thus initiating the pattern of parallel race institutions for solidarity and self-help that would develop more fully in the latter part of the century. He might exhort the blacks of the nation to demonstrate their capacity for freedom by cultivating the bourgeois virtues of industry, frugality, and thrift; but he was generous in aid to the unfortunate among his people. Central to all these actions was Allen's conviction that black men, though made unequal by the conditions under which they lived, are in no way inferior to other Americans. See Charles H. Wesley, *Richard Allen, Apostle of Freedom* (1935).

JEROME H. WOOD, JR.

ALLEN, Woody (Allen, Stewart Konigsberg) (b. Bronx, N.Y., Dec. 1, 1935), FILMMAKER, graduated Midwood High School (1953) in Brooklyn, N.Y., where he grew up. He attended New York University and City College of New York but dropped out of both to pursue comedy writing. With a new name, "Woody Allen," before he turned 20 years old he had already sold thousands of gags to New York tabloid newspapers. At 23 he landed a job with NBC-TV and began to write for comedians Sid Caesar and Art Carney.

Before 1960 he had signed with talent managers Jack Rollins and Charles Joffe, who would later produce his films, and began performing his own material in a small New York nightclub. Success led to a Grammy-nominated comedy album and then to starring in and directing motion pictures. His first film, as scriptwriter and actor, was *What's New, Pussycat?* (1965). He would soon achieve worldwide fame as a filmmaker, beginning with *Take the Money and Run* (1969) and *Bananas* (1971). His *Annie Hall* (1977) became a hit, and thereafter Allen would make about one film per year as he explored first the comic genre and then more serious venues of filmmaking.

Allen has earned many awards as a filmmaker, including an Academy Award for best picture for *Annie Hall*, and for *Hannah and Her Sisters* (1986). In the early 1990s he also became infamous for a troubled personal life. His marriages and relationships have been many and public, often thinly disguised in plots and autobiographical characterizations in his films.

Allen is the author of two Broadway plays,

both hits, and humorous essays, many of which have appeared in *The New Yorker*. He also plays the clarinet regularly in a New York nightclub.

———— ✲ ————

There have been many paths used to become a notable filmmaker; Woody Allen took one nontraditional approach, becoming a famous comedy writer and then performer. At Greenwich Village's famous coffee house, The Bitter End, Allen developed a now legendary comic persona, the little guy tormented by big philosophical issues and his unfailing hard luck with women. Allen honed the art of comedy in front of a live audience night after night, six nights a week.

Success on stage led to movie roles and then to directing. Since the mid–1970s Woody Allen has become Hollywood's *auteur*, America's answer to Ingmar Bergman and Federico Fellini. His personal films, first comedies and now more and more dramatic fare, deal with subjects that have always obsessed Allen: sex, death, and the meaning of life. Allen makes his movies on modest budgets, by Hollywood standards, shooting his films in and around New York City, where he lives. Despite the growing seriousness of his work, audiences have never lost sight of Allen the performer and the character he created for himself in his days as a comedian: a nerdy neurotic whose only defense against a hostile universe is his sense of the absurd.

Allen made his debut as a director with a film so modest that no one ever thought to tamper with it. Released by a company specializing in low-budget fare, *What's Up, Tiger Lily?* (1966) was a Japanese James Bond spoof, with hip dialogue composed of surreal one-liners. By the early 1970s Woody Allen had developed a cult following.

In 1977, Allen moved toward serious themes with the success of cinematically complex *Annie Hall*. While still a comedy, *Annie Hall* embraces more sophisticated narrative devices where Allen as hero, for instance, addresses the camera. Allen's screen persona in *Annie Hall* reflected his real-life status at the time: a New York Jewish entertainer with a non-Jewish girlfriend (Diane Keaton), an outsider looking in on the exclusive worlds of both Hollywood and the Gentile establishment. For many, *Annie Hall* remains the quintessential Woody Allen movie: personal and thoughtful but at the same time sharply satiric.

Thereafter this very private man has explored his life's work, what it means to make movies: *Stardust Memories* is a self-indulgent but interesting Felliniesque fantasy in which Allen acts as a celebrity struggling with the burden of fame. A *Midsummer Night's Sex Comedy* (1982) was the first Allen film to feature Mia Farrow and is an homage to Ingmar Bergman. *Zelig* (1983) combined Allen's continued fascination with celebrity and his growing interest in cinematic technique, brilliantly dissecting genre by seamlessly merging new footage with vintage newsreels. Allen hit his second peak in 1986 with *Hannah and Her Sisters*, a knowing, Chekhovian look at New York family relationships.

Woody Allen was able to make these and other films because he long had a patron in Arthur Krim of United Artists. When Krim left United Artists to found Orion Pictures, Allen worked off his contract and rejoined him. Orion's bankruptcy in the mid–1990s obliged Allen to switch again, to Tri-Star, and will serve to denote a new period in his moviemaking career.

But Woody Allen is more than just a comic-turned-filmmaker. He plays New Orleans jazz clarinet with his group, the New Orleans Funeral and Ragtime Orchestra, every Monday night at Michael's Pub in New York. In 1991, much to the disappointment of his hard-core fans, he signed a three-million-lire agreement with Italy's National Association of Consumer Cooperatives to direct a series of TV commercials. All in all, Allen is clearly one of the most fascinating, complex, creative minds in American filmmaking in the late twentieth century. See Eric Lax, *Woody Allen: A Biography* (1991)

DOUGLAS GOMERY

ALLISON, William Boyd (b. Perry, Ohio, Mar. 2, 1829; d. Dubuque, Iowa, Aug. 4, 1908), POLITICAL LEADER, graduated from Western Reserve

University in 1849. Admitted to the bar in 1852, he settled in Iowa in 1857 and took an active part in Republican politics. In 1862 he was elected to the U.S. House of Representatives. In Congress he pushed such measures as river improvements and aid to railroads, and began to emerge as a champion of the western developer and as an expert in such fields as transportation, the tariff, and the budget. A staunch radical in his early years, he supported the impeachment of President Andrew Johnson.

In 1872, Allison was elected to the U.S. Senate and soon became one of the most important members of that body, serving as chairman of the Appropriations Committee (1881–1908). He played a major role in the passage of the Bland-Allison Act (1878), which placed a brake on the movement for unlimited free coinage of silver by committing the government to purchase only between $2 million and $4 million of that metal monthly.

As a senior member on the Finance Committee, Allison was prominent in the framing of the "Senate Substitute" to the proposed Mills Tariff Bill of 1888. This Republican protectionist answer to the Democratic attempt to reduce the tariff became the basis for the McKinley Tariff of 1890.

Throughout the 1880s and 1890s, Allison was a quadrennial candidate for the Republican presidential nomination, with some hard-core support in Iowa and among western railroad interests and Wall Street but little elsewhere. Nevertheless, he continued to win reelection to the Senate and increased his already considerable influence there when in 1897 he assumed the chairmanship of the Republican conference and the steering committee. That same year, when Senator **Nelson W. Aldrich** became ill, he took over the management of the Dingley Tariff and steered it through the Senate. During Theodore Roosevelt's administration, Allison generally worked with the other members of the Republican "Big Four"—Aldrich, **John Coit Spooner,** and Orville H. Platt—to moderate and restrain the president's reformist impulses and policies. But, characteristically, he remained always on warm personal terms with the president and functioned in a mediating, nonabrasive fashion. In his last legislative effort, the contest over the Hepburn Railroad Act of 1906, he helped compose the differences between Roosevelt and Aldrich over the question of judicial review of the Interstate Commerce Commission's power to fix railroad rates by getting both sides to accept the so-called Allison Amendments, which left the matter deliberately vague and hence secured its passage.

———— ∞ ————

William Boyd Allison was a politician's politician. His ability to keep his own counsel, to smooth rough edges and soothe heated tempers, to reconcile the seemingly irreconcilable was legendary. Warm and amiable by nature, he was so polite and deferential, without being oleaginous, that he probably had more friends and fewer foes on both sides of the aisle than any man in Washington. Although of only average intelligence, he was considered by many a "wise man" and was termed the "sage old pilot of the Senate." Actually, this spade-bearded, five-foot-eight, two-hundred-pounder had no apparent interests other than the game of politics and seemed to derive no greater joy from life than reporting the annual budget out of the Appropriations Committee, which he headed for more than twenty-five years. On occasion he would take to the floor of the upper house to deliver, in short, pithy sentences, a speech explaining some departmental authorization or to the stump in Iowa to champion the protective system and sound money, but he much preferred working behind closed doors arranging face-saving compromises, such as the mildly inflationist Bland-Allison Act, or scheduling the Senate's business from his seat on the Republican steering committee. Concerned with process rather than policy, committed to party more than principle, he was an ideal negotiator who pursued harmony with the same earnestness and passion that reformers gave to causes. Perhaps no member of the GOP was less doctrinaire, less of an ideologue, or more of an exponent of the credo that to get along one must go along. Indeed, his reputation for reasonableness and flexibility was such that some of the oldest inhabitants on Capitol Hill swore that they could not recall having heard him volunteer an opinion on any subject whatsoever in all his years in Congress. As one Republican senator remarked, "He was so pussy-footed he could walk from New York to San Francisco on the keys of a piano and never strike a note."

Yet his "cautious, foxy manner of talking" could not mask the fact that his voting record invariably reflected the desires of the dominant corporate interests of the nation. Western railroad executives regarded him, correctly, as their "most powerful friend," as did many Wall Street bankers, Pennsylvania steel magnates, and New England textile barons, whose well-being he considered essential to America's prosperity. Still, he was no mere big-business mouthpiece. More than any other member of the Senate's inner circle, he was sensitive to the nuances of public opinion, and he generally kept free of the bribery and graft with which some of his closest colleagues became involved. Whether or not he would have been president, as his friends claimed, "if he had been affirmative, or constructive, positive and creative," is impossible to know, but there is no question that he would have left a larger mark on the history of the country had he possessed those qualities. Instead, his superabundance of caution produced an essentially barren legislative record. He is important largely for what he represents—a forerunner of the modern-day "consensus" politician—not for what he accomplished. See Leland L. Sage, *William Boyd Allison: A Study in Practical Politics* (1956).

JEROME L. STERNSTEIN

ALTGELD, John Peter (b. Nieder Selters, Ger., Dec. 30, 1847; d. Joliet, Ill., Mar. 12, 1902), POLITICAL LEADER, was brought to the United States while still an infant and grew up in Richland County, Ohio. Altgeld worked on his father's farm and received little formal schooling. He

served as a private in the Civil War (1864–65) before becoming a schoolteacher near Mansfield, Ohio. In 1869, Altgeld moved west, working as a laborer, teacher, and law clerk. He was admitted to the Missouri bar in 1871, became city attorney for Savannah, Missouri, in 1872, and was elected state's attorney for Andrew County, Missouri, in 1874. In 1875, however, he resigned this position and opened a law practice in Chicago, where he quickly made a fortune in real estate speculation and building. An unsuccessful Democratic candidate for Congress in 1884, Altgeld was elected judge of the Superior Court of Cook County (Chicago) in 1886 and became chief justice four years later (1890–91).

In 1892, Altgeld was elected the first Democratic governor of Illinois since the Civil War. One of his first acts as governor was to pardon the surviving anarchists of the Haymarket Riots (1886), who, he concluded, had not been given a fair trial. Altgeld initiated state prison reform, a new parole system, humane treatment for prisoners, and a streamlined criminal court procedure. He helped get legislative protection for woman and child labor and modernized the University of Illinois. When the American Railway Union tied up midwestern railroads to protest wage cuts (Pullman strike, 1894), Altgeld opposed President Cleveland's use of federal troops to suppress the strikers. In 1896, at the Democratic presidential convention, he supported **William Jennings Bryan** and the free coinage of silver at a 16:1 ratio with gold. He played an active role in the presidential campaign but lost his own reelection bid for governor. Altgeld returned to his Chicago law practice with his partner **Clarence Darrow** and unsuccessfully ran as an independent candidate for mayor of Chicago in 1899. Some of his major writings include *Our Penal Machinery and Its Victims* (1884), in which he argued that the poor had little equality before the law, and *Live Questions* (1890).

One of Vachel Lindsay's best-known poems, "The Eagle That Is Forgotten," is about Altgeld. It is a moving tribute to a great American—*Fortune* magazine included him, with **Ralph Waldo Emerson,** in its Heroes of America series in 1943—whose stature, unlike that of most political leaders, grows through the years. Lindsay's major theme was that Governor Altgeld in the 1890s had championed, only to be bitterly denounced by the Establishment of the day, the liberal political ideas that by the 1900s had enabled Theodore Roosevelt and Woodrow Wilson, both of whom had attacked him as a "radical," to rise to political glory. With a poet's insight, Lindsay was right in complaining that Altgeld deserved more credit as a pioneer in American social thought than most historians formerly had been inclined to give him.

Altgeld is recalled usually in connection with his pardon of the Haymarket anarchists. He issued it knowing well the risk, not because he sympathized with anarchy but because he believed passionately that even despised anarchists were entitled to justice. But he should be remembered more for urging social reforms—in behalf of labor, exploited women and children, the mentally ill, and other unfortunates; and against corrupt acquisition and use of great wealth. An intellectual, an astute politician, he was to the Democratic Party in his era, by his official acts, his writings, and speeches, what Jefferson was in the founding period and what Franklin D. Roosevelt was in the 1930s, an "eagle" in behalf of the "common man." He was incorruptible, rich when he became Illinois's governor, almost penniless at his death, but undismayed by the penalty he paid for his honesty and his fidelity to democratic principles. Above all, he aggressively defended impoverished immigrant Americans against snobbishness and contempt. See Harry Barnard, *"Eagle Forgotten": The Life of John Peter Altgeld* (1962).

HARRY BARNARD

ANDERSON, Marian (b. Philadelphia, Pa., Feb. 17, 1902; d. Portland, Ore., Apr. 8, 1993), SINGER, sang in her church choir and began to study voice when she was 19. In 1925 she won a competition that led to a contract with the Philadelphia Symphony Orchestra. In 1926 a grant from the National Association of Negro Musicians enabled her to study in Europe until 1929, when she returned to New York to perform at Carnegie Hall. She then won a second scholarship for European study, extending from 1929 to 1933. During 1933–35 Anderson toured Europe, winning the praise of Arturo Toscanini and Jan Sibelius. In 1935 she gave a recital at New York's Town Hall and the following year sang for President and Mrs. Franklin Roosevelt at the White House before touring Europe, Africa, South America, and the United States.

In 1939 the Daughters of the American Revolution refused to allow Miss Anderson to sing in its Constitution Hall, Washington, D.C., and **Eleanor Roosevelt** resigned from the D.A.R. in protest. The government then opened Lincoln Memorial to her, and Anderson sang there before 75,000 people on Easter Sunday, 1939. Her repertoire has included the song literature of Bach, Beethoven, Brahms, Handel, Haydn, Schumann, Schubert, Mahler, and Strauss, and the operatic literature of the French and Italian schools. She is especially noted for her renditions of black spirituals. Late in her career, on January 7, 1955, she made her debut at the Metropolitan Opera House in New York City as Ulrica in Verdi's *Masked Ball*. According to the music critic of the *New York Times*, "men as well as women were dabbing at their eyes" during the tumultuous ovation. In 1957, Anderson performed in India and the Far East under State Department auspices, and in 1958, President Eisenhower appointed her a delegate to the 13th General Assembly of the United Nations. She sang at President John F. Kennedy's inauguration in 1961 and that same year sang for American troops stationed in Berlin. In 1962 she toured Australia and in 1964 began her farewell concert tour at Constitution Hall. She gave her last concert at Carnegie Hall in New York on April 18, 1965.

In the 1970s, Anderson made periodic stage appearances as a reader for Aaron Copland's "Lincoln Portrait." Frequently honored late in life, she received the Presidential Medal of

Freedom in 1963 and in 1978 was in the first group of performers to receive honors from the Kennedy Center of Performing Arts in Washington, D.C. President Ronald Reagan presented her with the National Arts Medal in 1986.

Anderson spent much of her retirement living on her farm, "Marianna," in Danbury, Connecticut, but in 1992, wheelchair-bound in her last years, she moved to Portland, Oregon, to live with her nephew, the conductor James dePreist.

———— ✹✹✹ ————

Marian Anderson was the first black singer to achieve international recognition as a concert artist. Although not as politically controversial as **Paul Robeson** and more directly communicative, both personally and as an artist, than Roland Hayes, Anderson did not achieve renown without the inevitable difficulties and prejudices. Many of the incidents coincident with her struggle had a permanent effect on her career. The less than adequate technical training that she received as a student took its toll earlier than it should have. And again, the strong desire that she had to sing on the stage was not realized until late in her career, when she sang in Verdi's *Masked Ball* at the Metropolitan Opera. Anderson met all these trials with great dignity and quiet modesty. Her career has therefore taken on symbolic meaning and pioneering importance; yet she deserves to be remembered above all as one of the supremely gifted singers of this century.

Her art was a combination of both natural and acquired abilities. She was endowed with a voice of over three octaves in range, dark but rich in sound and capable of unusual agility and coloristic variety. Her ability to communicate was immediate, and its effect was arresting and intense. To these natural endowments was added, by the strength of her intelligence and seriousness of purpose, an unusually keen stylistic awareness and great linguistic skill. Her repertoire was broad and varied, and she brought the same understanding to the whole field of the German *lied* as she did to such operatic heroines as Carmen, Delilah, and Eboli. She was thus in

every sense the universal artist. See Marian Anderson, *My Lord, What a Morning: An Autobiography* (1956).

ALLAN R. KEILER

ANDERSON, Maxwell (b. Atlantic, Pa., Dec. 15, 1888; d. Stamford, Conn., Feb. 28, 1959), PLAYWRIGHT, graduated from the University of North Dakota (1911), where he studied drama under Frederick Koch, and received an MA from Stanford University in 1914. After a year as an English professor at Whittier College, he became a newspaperman with the San Francisco *Bulletin* and later with the *Chronicle*. He arrived in New York City in 1918, where he worked as an editorial writer for the New York *Evening Globe* and the New York *Morning World*, and contributed poems and theater reviews to the *New Republic*. In 1923, *White Desert*, his first play, had a two-week run in New York. The following year saw his first Broadway success, *What Price Glory?*, written in collaboration with Laurence Stallings. This play, based on Stallings's experiences in France during World War I, revolved around the swashbuckling rivalry between a captain and sergeant of a marine company over a local French girl. The robust realism with which war conditions were portrayed caused some furor, but the play—filmed three times—won such acclaim that Anderson was able to resign from the New York *World* and devote his entire time to playwriting. In 1925, again with Stallings, he completed both *First Flight*, a play about the early career of Andrew Jackson, and *The Buccaneer*, concerning the 17th-century pirate Sir Henry Morgan.

In 1930, Anderson, now writing on his own, completed *Elizabeth the Queen*, which enjoyed immediate success in the Theatre Guild production starring Alfred Lunt and Lynn Fontanne. The first of his many historical plays written in loose blank verse, this dramatization of the romance of Elizabeth Tudor of England and the Earl of Essex emphasizes a recurring theme in Anderson's plays: the conflict between the struggle for power and the force of sexual passion. In *Mary of Scotland* (1933), the idealistic but misguided Mary's infatuation with James Hepburn, Earl of Bothwell, is juxtaposed with the unending clash of political creeds. In 1933, Anderson also published the prose drama *Both Your Houses,* an indictment of the U.S. Congress that won a Pulitzer Prize. *Winterset* (1935), probably his best-known play, combines a contemporary gangster milieu with verse dialogue as the Romeo and Juliet romance of Mio and Marianne is played off against the grim background of Mio's struggle to avenge his unjustly executed father. His poetic fantasy *High Tor* won the Critics' Circle Award the following season.

In 1938, Anderson joined Robert Sherwood, Elmer Rice, S. N. Behrman, and Sidney Howard to form the Playwrights' Company. During World War II he produced a series of patriotic idealizations of "victory through faith" that included *Candle in the Wind* (1941), *The Eve of St. Mark* (1942), and *Storm Operation* (1944). After the war he gained success again with *Joan of Lorraine* (1946) and *Anne of the Thousand Days* (1948), the last of his Tudor plays. During the last decade of his life Anderson turned to adaptations, including *Lost in the Stars* (1949, music by Kurt Weill), which is a dramatization of the Alan Paton novel *Cry, the Beloved Country; The Bad Seed,* an adaptation of William March's tale of childhood criminality which became Anderson's last Broadway hit in 1954; and a version of Brendan Gill's novel *The Day the Money Stopped* (1958). Anderson also published a volume of poetry, *You Who Have Dreams* (1925), as well as collections of critical essays.

⊷

Convinced, as he stated in his preface to *Winterset,* that the theater is "essentially a cathedral of the spirit, devoted to the exaltation of man" and that only poetry can lend it sufficient "power to weld and determine what the race dreams into what the race will become," Maxwell Anderson deliberately abandoned the prose of his early successes in quest of a poetic theater. Critical of the drama of the twenties, which in his view conveyed "a low opinion of the race of men" and "rejected the war between good and evil," he demanded an affirmative theater that would demonstrate that "man has a dignity and a destiny," that "man is not perfect, but seeks perfection." From *Elizabeth the Queen* through *Anne of the Thousand Days,* Anderson—succeeding where failure might have seemed inevitable—created a body of verse plays whose popularity constitutes a unique chapter in the history of modern American theater.

Anderson once commented that a playwright must possess "a certain cleverness in striking a compromise between the world about him and the world within." In his choice of subject matter as well as in his free, conversational verse form he displayed a keen sensitivity to the demands of a broad public. An audience, he maintained, goes to the theater for a "vision of what mankind may or should become. Your vision may be faulty, or shallow, or sentimental, but it must conform to some aspiration in the audience, or the audience will reject it." This insistence on moral reaffirmation is related in turn to two other "rules" in Anderson's seminal essay *The Essence of Tragedy* (1938), a document that bears significantly on his practice as a dramatist. Essential to his dramaturgical formula is the recognition scene: "A play should lead up to and away from a central crisis, and this crisis should consist in a discovery by the leading character which has an indelible effect on his thought and emotion and completely alters his course of action." Hence the crisis in *Mary of Scotland* is reached with Mary Stuart's belated recognition of her mistake in having rejected the love of Bothwell. At a comparable juncture in *Winterset,* Mio's realization that he cannot pursue vengeance if "it falls on his beloved" frees his spirit from its "long trauma of hate and fear and death." Anderson's second, related "rule" is: The hero who makes the central discovery must be imperfect and must change for the better. He "must pass through an experience which opens his eyes to an error of his own. He must learn through suffering." Thus, King McCloud, the disillusioned deserter from the Spanish Civil War in *Key Largo* (1939), is made to complete Anderson's tragic blueprint by his (somewhat contrived and sententious) final sacrifice: "A man must die / for what he believes ... and if he won't then he'll end up believing / in nothing at all—and that's death, too."

The academic formality of this tragic pattern of passion, recognition, and reconciliation to fate has led some critics to liken the effect of Anderson's plays to "the conclusion in a Euclidean proposition set up for the purpose." "He is too well aware of its theory for his own creative good," John Mason Brown felt. "He writes of ecstasy by rote rather than by inspiration." Yet this viewpoint tends too readily to overlook the range and prolificity of Anderson's dramatic experimentation as well as the vigor of his quest for an imaginative and literate theater. Even more unjustly, it disregards the importance that his best plays have had in reestablishing a place for poetic drama on the American stage. See Mabel Driscoll Bailey, *Maxwell Anderson: The Playwright as Prophet* (1957).

FREDERICK J. MARKER

ANDROS, Edmund (b. London, Eng., Dec. 6, 1637; d. London, Eng., Feb. 24, 1714), COLONIAL GOVERNOR, entered the English army and fought in the West Indies (1666) against the Dutch. He was commissioned a major in Prince Rupert's Dragoons in 1672 and two years later became bailiff of the island of Guernsey, England. The Duke of York appointed him lieutenant governor of New York in 1674; he served until 1681 when the colonists demanded his recall for his rigid enforcement of revenue laws and alleged attempts to extend his jurisdiction. Knighted in 1681, Andros was made Gentleman of the Privy Chamber to the king in 1683. When James II, the former Duke of York, merged seven northern provinces into the Dominion of New England in 1685, he appointed Andros governor. The king hoped to tighten his control of the colonies, enforce the navigation laws, and provide the colonists with better security against the French and Native Americans.

Arriving in Boston in 1686, Andros had the power to make ordinances, assess taxes, and administer justice, since all colonial charters had been revoked and the colonists no longer had legislative assemblies. The Dominion added New York and New Jersey in 1688, but Andros alienated the merchants by strictly enforcing the navigation acts, the people by raising taxes, and the Puritan clergy by favoring the Anglican Church. Following William of Orange's overthrow of James II, the people of Boston revolted in 1689, seized the Dominion offices, and put Andros in jail. William allowed the Dominion to lapse and restored colonial charters. Andros was sent to England for trial, but charges against him were dropped. He served as governor of Virginia from 1692 to 1698. Returning to England in 1698, Andros served as lieutenant governor of Guernsey (1704–6) before retiring and spending the rest of his life in London.

❦

Andros's career is significant because it coincides with the quarter century when the British Empire acquired the form and character it would keep until 1775. Andros was one of the first colonial career servants of the Crown, with governorships in New York, New England, and Virginia, and his experiences are thus symptomatic of the vicissitudes of Anglo-American change. The problems he faced—governmental organization, religious diversity and conflict, competition for trade and land, strained relations with Native Americans—were the critical ones between 1674 and 1698. Although Andros was not an imaginative statesman, he was a dedicated administrator; the importance of his positions meant that his successes and failures would influence imperial policy and provincial responses.

What shaped his character and assumptions? He came from a royalist family of moderate wealth, learned discipline and the privileges of power from his extensive military training, and absorbed his politics from the intrigues at Charles II's court. Andros emerged from his own laconic papers and those of contemporaries as an aristocratic and loyal soldier who expected obedience from his subordinates and subjects. A colorless man, and increasingly insensitive to popular sentiment, his temperament was ill-suited to the realities he encountered in America. Thus each of his provincial administrations ended (with a trial or inquiry in England) when public problems became personal crises, for Andros did not react well under pressure.

Why, ultimately, did he not succeed? In part because he was neither ruthless enough to cow his provincial subjects into submission nor ingratiating enough to win himself a broad base of local support. In part because he arrived in New England at a critical moment without prior experience of the peculiar religious and political development of that area. And in part, finally, because he was continually caught in a cross fire between imperious assumptions of the Crown and unfamiliar imperatives of colonial life. See Jeanne G. Bloom, "Sir Edmund Andros: A Study in 17th-Century Colonial Administration," unpublished PhD dissertation (Yale University, 1962).

MICHAEL KAMMEN

ANTHONY, Susan Brownell (b. Adams, Mass., Feb. 15, 1820; d. Rochester, N.Y., Mar. 13, 1906), REFORMER, attended the Friends' Boarding School in Philadelphia (1837–38). After teaching at several academies and heading the Female Department of the Canajoharie (N.Y.) Academy (1846–49), she left teaching to work for the temperance movement in Rochester. While a delegate to the 1852 Sons of Temperance meeting in Albany, she was discriminated against because of her sex and organized the Woman's State Temperance Society of New York later that year. She served as an agent for the American Anti-Slavery Society (1856–61) and was active in teachers' organizations, urging equal pay for women teachers. She worked for the passage of the New York law of 1860 giving women equal property rights. During the Civil War she organized the Women's National Loyal League to press for the emancipation of blacks.

After the war Anthony focused her efforts on the woman suffrage movement. She urged an addition to the Fourteenth Amendment that would guarantee women the right to vote. From 1868 to 1870 she published a women's rights periodical, *The Revolution*. Together with her life-long associate **Elizabeth Cady Stanton,** she organized the National Woman Suffrage Association in 1869, serving as chairman of its executive committee. In 1872 she was arrested for registering to vote in Rochester. When fined $100, she refused to pay, and the fine was never collected. In 1888 she helped organize the International Council of Women in London. When the National and the American Woman Suffrage associations merged in 1890, she became vice president, succeeding Stanton as president in 1892 and serving in that post until 1900. In 1904, Anthony joined with **Carrie Chapman Catt** to form the International Woman Suffrage Alliance in Berlin. Together with Stanton and other feminists, Anthony compiled and edited *The History of Woman Suffrage* (4 vols., 1881–1902).

———— ⚬⚬⚬ ————

Susan B. Anthony did not find a fountain of youth, but she found the next best thing: a way to live actively and productively to the age of 86. There was an element of luck, as perhaps there is in all great lives. When she was 30 she met Elizabeth Cady Stanton, with whom she formed one of the most productive intellectual partnerships in American history. Together they stimulated and led one of the major social movements of the 19th century. The movement would have happened anyway, but their contribution of intellectual vigor and broad-ranging concern made it more than it would otherwise have been, and the experience of creating it made *them* more than they would otherwise have been.

Three observations of Anthony at widely separated moments in her life illustrate her growth as a human being. The first describes a young woman in her thirties. "Whenever I saw that stately Quaker girl coming across the lawn," Stanton wrote in her memoirs, "I knew some happy convocation of the sons of Adam was about to be set by the ears." And so it was. Together they shook up legislatures, assailed bastions of male supremacy, battered at the Congress, traveled the backwoods of frontier states promoting woman suffrage, composed the massive *History of Woman Suffrage,* and had a jolly good time to boot.

The second comment came from a male newspaper reporter observing Susan B. Anthony as she returned from her first trip to Europe in 1882. By then she had spent thirty-odd years working for women. "She is sixty-three," he wrote, "but looks just the same as twenty years ago. There is perhaps an extra wrinkle … a little more silver … but her blue eyes are just as bright, her mouth as serious, and her step as active as when she was forty. She would attract attention in any crowd."

After twenty-four years more of hard labor in the cause of women, she went to Baltimore for a meeting in honor of her eighty-sixth birthday. "We literally sat at her feet," wrote Lillian Welsh, a pioneer woman doctor, "and knew we were in the presence of a great soul.... I carried away with me the impression of a woman characterised by great simplicity, strength and dignity, indomitable spirit and infinite patience."

On the average, we in the twentieth century live longer than those in the 19th, and there is a creeping fear, especially among women, of what old age will be. Miss Anthony did not worry much about such things because she knew there was always more work ahead. Her last message was typical: "Failure is impossible!" She was right. Fourteen years later the Nineteenth Amendment was adopted. See Katharine Anthony, *Susan B. Anthony: Her Personal History and Her Era* (1954).

ANNE FIROR SCOTT

ARMSTRONG, Daniel Louis (b. New Orleans, La., July 4, 1900; d. New York, N.Y., July 6, 1971), MUSICIAN, son of a turpentine worker, grew up in an impoverished New Orleans black ghetto. Forced to help support his family, he received little formal education, but after a brush with the law Armstrong spent a year and a half (1914–15) in the New Orleans Colored Waifs' Home where he learned to play the cornet. Following his release he toiled at various jobs and studied music with New Orleans jazz musician Joe

(King) Oliver. In 1918 he replaced Oliver in Kid Ory's band and spent the summers of 1920 and 1921 playing on a Mississippi riverboat. In 1922 he joined King Oliver's band in Chicago as second cornetist and went to New York (1924–25) to work in the Fletcher Henderson band where for the first time he began to play trumpet. Returning to Chicago in 1925, he was featured as a soloist in clubs and theaters, and began to record under his own name for the first time. His virtuosity on trumpet and the novelty of his deep, husky voice in melodic improvisations quickly made him a popular recording star. In 1929 he formed his own band for a New York engagement, and throughout the following decade he usually appeared at the head of a big band. His nickname "Satchelmouth" was abbreviated to "Satchmo" by an English critic during Armstrong's first British tour (1932). He returned the following year for an extensive tour of Europe and appeared in his first movie, *Pennies from Heaven*, in 1936.

During the 1930s, as his popularity continued to grow, Armstrong exerted a strong stylistic influence on what was to become known as the Swing Era, but after World War II he abandoned the big band and returned to an informal sextet that was closer in spirit to that of the original New Orleans groups in which he had played.

He made his first African trip, to Nigeria and Ghana, in 1956 and again toured Africa for the United States Information Agency in 1960. In 1965, Armstrong toured central and eastern Europe, and gave a performance before 100,000 people in Budapest. Armstrong appeared in numerous plays, movies, and television shows, and recorded about 1,500 tunes. His recording of "Hello, Dolly!" (1964) sold 2 million copies.

———— ⌘ ————

Louis Armstrong is generally recognized as the most influential musician in the history of jazz. He gave the music a whole new vocabulary and was the inspiration not only of many trumpet players but also of great musicians—themselves influential—on other instruments, such as pianist **Earl Hines,** saxophonist Johnny Hodges, and trombonist Jack Teagarden. Arrangers were not less impressed: his conceptions were harmonized for brass teams, and entire bands began to phrase in the Armstrong manner.

His virtuosity on trumpet was such that it could not be confined to the original and somewhat restricted New Orleans idiom. The freedom of expression for which jazz is noted, and its emphasis on individualism, primarily resulted from his audacious invention. So prodigal was he of ideas and energy that many mistook his playing in the early thirties for exhibitionism, but any reasonably close study of his records from that period will reveal constant creativity. As he grew older, and owing to the exacting nature of his instrument, his style became more concentrated and less exuberant, but he always remained capable of unexpectedly powerful and poignant variations. Apart from his exceptional imaginative gifts, his tone, vibrato, and inflections gave an instantly recognizable character to his trumpet playing, and these were essentially extensions of qualities found in his singing. The warmth and genial humor in his voice enabled him to communicate readily with people in lands where English was not understood, and in his last years he achieved the biggest successes of his career as a vocalist rather than as an instrumentalist. See Max Jones and John Chilton, *Louis* (1971).

STANLEY DANCE

ARNOLD, Benedict (b. Norwich, Conn., Jan. 14, 1741; d. London, Eng., June 14, 1801), MILITARY LEADER, participated in a march of Connecticut troops against Fort William Henry at age 16, but the fort fell before his detachment arrived. Settling in New Haven, Connecticut, he managed a store and engaged in trade with the West Indies. Arnold became a captain in the Connecticut militia in 1774 and was a colonel when he participated with Ethan Allen and the "Green Mountain Boys" in the capture of Fort Ticonderoga (1775). He was wounded in the assault on Quebec in 1776 and promoted to brigadier general. In 1776, at the battle of Valcour Island on Lake Champlain, he checked a British

invasion of New York. After the battles at Ridgefield and Compo Hill, in which he punished British troops who had raided Danbury, Connecticut (April 1777), Congress made him a major general, later predating his commission to advance his seniority. He led a relieving army that forced the British to end their siege of Fort Stanwix, part of the campaign that ended with the surrender of General Burgoyne at Saratoga, and played a conspicuous though controversial part in the final battles of the campaign (1777).

Arnold took command of Philadelphia in 1778, where he married Margaret Shippen, a socialite. They lived beyond their means, and the Executive Council of Pennsylvania accused Arnold of exploiting his official position for personal speculation and using military personnel for private purposes. He was court-martialed but cleared of the most serious charges and merely reprimanded for the rest (1779–80). It is now known that his misconduct was worse than his accusers believed. After Arnold was given command of West Point in 1780, he entered into a plot to surrender the fort to the British. When a British spy, Major John André, was captured, Arnold's correspondence with British General Henry Clinton revealed that Arnold was a traitor. He escaped to the British lines and later, in British uniform, led expeditions against Richmond, Virginia, and New London, Connecticut. In 1781 he went to England where he remained most of the rest of his life.

On the Bemis Heights battlefield at Saratoga stands a monument to Benedict Arnold's wounded leg. The monument does not mention the traitor general's name but calls him the most brilliant soldier in the Continental Army. The treason and the brilliance together suggest why Arnold will surely remain one of the most written-about figures in American history and historical fiction as long as there is a United States. Those who emphasize Arnold's brilliance—at the head of whom is Kenneth Roberts with his unforgettable portrait in the novels *Arundel* and *Rabble in Arms*—point to Arnold's contribution to the seizure of Fort Ticonderoga in 1775; to his inspiring leadership in the march up the Kennebec River and down the Chaudière in the fall and winter of 1775 for the attack on Quebec (and to the American failure to take the city and the expedition's loss of momentum after Arnold was wounded on New Year's Day); to his winning of a possibly crucial year's stay of the British invasion up Lake Champlain by building a fleet on the lake and forcing the British to fight the naval battle of Valcour Island; and to his reckless gallantry at Freeman's Farm and Bemis Heights before John Burgoyne's surrender at Saratoga. More cautious historians stress that whatever brilliance Arnold possessed was always flawed. At Saratoga, they argue, he not only endangered the unity of the American forces through an unseemly quarrel with Horatio Gates, but his genuinely reckless attacks at Bemis Heights cost unnecessary casualties and jeopardized a victory that the cautious defensive planned by Gates and others had already ensured. Quarreling and recklessness, and financial as well as military gambling and extravagance, in the critics' eyes always damaged Arnold's usefulness to the Revolution and eventuated in the treason in which an unbalanced personality finally entrapped itself. See Willard M. Wallace, *Traitorous Hero: The Life and Fortunes of Benedict Arnold* (1954).

RUSSELL F. WEIGLEY

ARTHUR, Chester Alan (b. Fairfield, Vt., Oct. 5, 1829; d. New York, N.Y., Nov. 18, 1886), PRESIDENT, graduated from Union College (1848) and was admitted to the New York bar in 1854. He was quartermaster general of New York during the Civil War, serving until January 1, 1863, and in 1871, President Grant at the behest of Senator **Roscoe Conkling** of New York appointed Arthur to the lucrative position of collector of the port of New York. President Hayes, however, attacked the Conkling machine and removed Arthur (1878).

A member of the Stalwart faction of the Republican Party, Arthur was elected vice president in 1880 and became president after James Garfield was assassinated in 1881. He cut his ties with Conkling and continued the investigation of post office scandals, in which many Stalwarts were implicated. But while Arthur said he favored civil service reform, he never actively supported it. He questioned most proposals offered by reformers, and he did not trust the validity of competitive exams. In 1883, however, when Congress passed the Pendleton Bill, which set up a Civil Service Commission to administrate competitive exams, "classified" specific jobs, established a system for advancement, and abolished political assessments, Arthur signed it into law. He vetoed the pork barrel 1882 river and harbor appropriation bill, which was little more than a raid on the Treasury surplus (it passed over his veto), and although he signed measures excluding Chinese and regulating other immigration, Arthur insisted on and secured technical improvements in that legislation. He condemned the existing tariff but failed to lead the fight for the 20 to 25 percent reductions proposed by his moderately protectionist tariff commission. When it was finally enacted, the tariff of 1883 bore little resemblance to his commission's recommendations. Arthur also advocated government regulation of railroads and supported appropriations to construct a modern navy. He failed to obtain the Republican presidential nomination in 1884.

⊶⊷

Like the tale of the prodigal son, the regeneration of Collector Chet Arthur into President Chester Arthur has had universal appeal. Although inspirational, Arthur's transformation is bad history. In reality he changed little; both before and after becoming president Arthur was an effective politician, spoilsman, and administrator.

Strongly antislavery, Arthur joined the Republican Party at its inception and became an ardent worker for the party organization. As a reward for his services, Arthur, who was handsome, over six feet, and wore gold braid well, was appointed engineer in chief on the New York governor's military staff. With states recruiting and equipping volunteers during the Civil War, the job became important, and Arthur proved himself so prompt, reliable, discreet, and resourceful that he was awarded ever more responsible positions until he became quartermaster general for the state. While he held these jobs, contracts were let to the lowest responsible bidders, specifications were carefully met, and accounts were rigidly kept, and although the opportunities for favoritism and graft were great, Arthur ignored them.

After the war Arthur applied his administrative prowess to politics and helped Roscoe Conkling build his machine. For his honesty, efficiency, and loyalty to Grant and Conkling, Arthur was appointed collector of New York. With nearly one thousand officials under him, he was responsible for collecting two-thirds of the nation's tariff revenue. Demonstrating an outstanding grasp of the revenue laws, Arthur continued to prove himself an able administrator and within the limits imposed by the spoils system brought a measure of efficiency to the custom house.

Even after President Hayes removed him from the custom house, Arthur remained the dominant Republican in New York City. When anti-Grant forces nominated James A. Garfield for president, they balanced the ticket with Arthur as vice president. Failing to realize that Arthur personified spoils politics at its best rather than at its worst, civil service reformers were dismayed. One of them, however, perceptively noted that "Arthur was a necessity" since "Conkling & Co. were half-ready to knife the candidate, relying upon 1884 for Grant. Arthur is the chairman of the Republican State Committee, & won't commit *hari kari* even for Grant. Many pleasanter things, but not many wiser, have been done."

Although Arthur had remained friendly with Conkling, the fact that the man who assassinated Garfield claimed to be of their political faction made Arthur avoid Conkling after becoming president. Arthur's behavior, however, remained consistent. He continued to desire a partisan, efficient civil service to one selected by open competitive examinations, and only after Republicans suffered defeat in 1882 did he support the Pendleton Bill. Arthur's civil service policy, **John Hay** remarked, was to "gobble all the vacancies for his particular friends and to talk reform at every gobble." As in his earlier career, however, the efficient, experienced administrator frequently rose above the politician.

Not enough of a leader to excite the electorate, too much of a spoils politician to win reformers, and enough of a sound administrator to lose Stalwart support, Arthur's attempt to succeed himself failed. His old antagonist **James G. Blaine** won the 1884 Republican nomination and lost the election when he failed to carry New York, while Arthur, whose prestige, knowledge, and power might have tipped the balance, remained aloof. Having achieved a partisan goal through a nonpartisan stance, Arthur retired from politics and died two years later. See Thomas C. Reeves, *Gentleman Boss: The Life of Chester Alan Arthur* (1975).

ARI HOOGENBOOM

ASHLEY, William Henry (b. Chesterfield, Va., c. 1778; d. Boonville, Mo., Mar. 26, 1838), BUSINESSMAN, POLITICAL LEADER, settled in upper Louisiana in 1802. He mined lead briefly and then formed a company to supply the mining camps with merchandise in exchange for lead. By 1810 he had extended his operations downriver to New Orleans. He also mounted a trading expedition up the Red River, invested in the New Orleans—New York trade, and attempted to set up business in Baltimore, but each of these enterprises failed. He returned to Missouri on the eve of the War of 1812 and began the manufacture of gunpowder. During the war he served as captain, colonel, and finally general of the militia. In 1819 in St. Louis he engaged in real estate speculation. In partnership with Andrew Henry he participated in the upper Missouri fur trade, leading three expeditions to the Rocky Mountains in search of furs and directing a fundamental reorganization of western fur gathering (1822–26). He sold out in 1826 to employees

Smith, Jackson, and Sublette at a substantial profit but continued his association with the trade for another half-dozen years, selling furs on commission in New York and advocating aggressive military and diplomatic policies in the Northwest before congressional committees.

Ashley became the first lieutenant governor of Missouri in 1820, ran unsuccessfully for governor and U.S. senator, and served in the U.S. House of Representatives from 1831 to 1838. Though an early supporter of Andrew Jackson, he defied Jacksonian orthodoxy and party discipline, and accepted designation as a Whig shortly before his death.

Ashley was a striking example of the 19th-century frontier entrepreneur. Attuned from youth to the promise of an emerging commercial capitalism, he achieved success finally by adapting traditional fur trade operations to the distinctive conditions of the Far West. He substituted hired employees for Native American hunters, shifted the harvest from Plains rivers to mountain streams, implemented a system of discipline and organization in his expeditions, and adopted a semiannual rendezvous as a trade fair to replace the fixed trading post. These methods freed his trappers to range over the whole western third of the continent, drawing maps and spurring American territorial ambitions as they went. His accomplishments demonstrated the value of organization, capital, and national marketing in the exploitation of distant western resources. His success hastened as well the exhaustion of those resources, for a combination of international rivalry and intense competition among private companies eliminated the beaver from much of the Northwest within a decade. Western miners, lumbermen, cattlemen, and others of the next generation would imitate Ashley's innovations, often with distressingly similar results.

Ashley's public career illustrated the complexities of early Jacksonian politics. Despite a shortness of stature, an austerity of manner, and an awkwardness in public, he succeeded in projecting the unmistakable qualities of leadership to mountain men, bankers, and frontier farmers alike, and earned broad popular support over a span of nearly twenty years. His political posture defies easy categorization, for he supported the egalitarian qualities of Jackson and the economic program of **Henry Clay**'s American System. St. Louis businessmen, Missouri River planters, and land speculators with whom he associated were slow to support his candidacy for office in the 1820s, and when they finally fell in line, they were forced to tolerate his Jacksonian identity for lack of any viable alternative. Jacksonians such as **Thomas Hart Benton,** seeking to impose discipline with the restoration of the two-party system in the 1830s, managed finally to purge him, thus clarifying party lines and forcing the Whigs into an open minority status in the state for the next generation. But Ashley's departure, though predictable, deprived the Democrats of a successful and vigorous advocate of 19th-century entrepreneurial ambition. See Richard M. Clokey, *William H. Ashley: Enterprise and Politics in the Trans-Missippi West* (1990).

RICHARD M. CLOKEY

ASTOR, John Jacob (b. Waldorf, Ger., July 17, 1763; d. New York, N.Y., Mar. 29, 1848), MERCHANT, emigrated to New York City in 1784 and became assistant to a fur trader, Robert Bowne. In 1786 he began his own fur-gathering expeditions to upper New York, and in 1790 opened a wholesale and retail fur outlet in Manhattan. When the British evacuated the Great Lakes forts in accord with Jay's Treaty (1794), he extended his fur-trading business in the Northwest Territory. By 1800 he was the leading American fur dealer with a fortune estimated at $250,000.

Astor entered the Asian trade in 1800, exchanging furs for silk, tea, and chinaware. Forming the American Fur Co. in 1808, he extended his fur-gathering enterprise into the Louisiana Territory and in 1811 established a trading post at the mouth of the Columbia River. He invested much of his profits in real estate, especially in Manhattan where by 1812 he had purchased more than $500,000 worth of property.

During the War of 1812, Astor invested heavily in federal securities. In April 1813 he and his associates underwrote $2 million in federal bond issues. By abstaining from risky foreign trade ventures and speculating heavily in government securities as peace approached, he emerged from the war with his fortune intact.

Following the Peace of Ghent (1814), Astor extended both his fur business and his Asian commerce. In 1816 he brought his son William into a partnership to help run his burgeoning commercial empire. After accumulating more than $20 million he abruptly liquidated his commercial interests in 1834 and invested his capital in real estate, insurance and banking, railroad bonds, and public securities. Astor founded libraries and donated to colleges throughout his life, and he bequeathed more than $2 million to philanthropic causes. However, he transferred most of his fortune to his son William.

———⟨∞⟩———

Astor's career spans and beautifully illustrates an important period of transition in American economic and business life. This transition was from diversification to specialization in business, and the period in which it occurred with increasing rapidity covered approximately the last quarter of the 18th and the first quarter of the 19th centuries. During these years, as in the colonial period of American history, the dominant business figure was the merchant engaged in foreign trade. He was a jack-of-all-trades rather than a specialist. He imported as well as exported, sold at both wholesale and retail, insured ships and goods, freighted vessels, lent money, and invested in real estate and other business enterprises. He did all these things simply because the demand for any single good or service was not sufficient to permit him to make as good a living. His business behavior aptly illustrates the truth of Adam Smith's famous dictum that the degree of specialization depends on the width of the market—that is, on the quantity of demand.

As the population grew and real incomes per person increased, it became more and more possible to split up the functions of the merchant.

Common carriers made it unnecessary for exporters to ship abroad in their own vessels; merchants specialized as importers or exporters, or as wholesalers or retailers; advertising and credit rating rose as separate occupations; and banking and insurance became functions of corporations organized for those purposes.

While Astor, as both merchant and investor, followed a pattern of diversification throughout his career, he came increasingly to specialize in investments in real estate. Up to 1820 he bought most of his land with profits from the China and fur trades. Between 1820 and 1834, however, income from rentals and sales financed real estate investments amounting to $445,000. Between 1835 and the year of his death (1848) income from rents alone exceeded the amount invested in land ($832,000). He made his most profitable investments in New York City real estate. He could increasingly specialize as "Manhattan's landlord," as he came to be known, because of the phenomenal growth of that city and also because of the care he took to buy land that lay in the path of population advance. The population of America's largest city grew from about 124,000 in 1820 to more than 1 million in 1860, thus "widening the market" for real estate. At the time of his death all agreed that the greatest source of his wealth was to be found in the increased value of his lands in Manhattan. Shortly before he died he is reported to have said, "Could I begin life again, knowing what I now know, and had money to invest, I would buy every foot of land on the Island of Manhattan."

The great wealth that Astor won from real estate, particularly because it enabled him to become the richest American of his day, serves as a conspicuous example of the kind of fortune that was to be bitterly attacked by the late-19th-century social critic **Henry George.** In *Progress and Poverty* George maintained that it was population increase and movement, rather than business acumen, that created such fortunes, and his remedy for what he regarded as a rank injustice was a single tax on land. George overlooked the acumen implied by successful investment, just as he overlooked the investments sunk in wild lands bypassed by arteries of transport and population advance. The widening market in land was only one of an increasing number of widening markets in 19th-century America, and no small part of the reason Astor did well was that he judged well. See Kenneth W. Porter, *John Jacob Astor, Business Man* (1931).

STUART BRUCHEY

AUDUBON, John James (b. Les Cayes, Santo Domingo, Apr. 26, 1785; d. New York, N.Y., Jan. 27, 1851), ARTIST, SCIENTIST, was the son of a French naval officer stationed in the French West Indies. He went to France in 1791 and studied geography, music, fencing, and drawing. In 1803 he arrived in the United States and settled near Philadelphia where he lived the life of a country gentleman and became interested in American birds. In 1804 he made his first bird "banding" experiment in order to study migratory patterns. He spent a year in France (1805–6) but returned to the United States and opened a general store in Louisville, Kentucky (1807). In 1809 he moved to Henderson, Kentucky. Unsuccessful in business, Audubon was jailed for indebtedness in 1819 but was released when he declared himself bankrupt.

Audubon then became a taxidermist for the new Western Museum of Cincinnati (1819–20). In 1820 he took a trip down the Ohio and Mississippi rivers, observing birds and making sketches. After working at various jobs to support his artwork, he went to Philadelphia in 1824 to seek a publisher. He was not successful, however, and after a year in St. Francisville, Louisiana, earning money for the trip, he went to Great Britain in 1826. In London he secured an engraver to publish his *Birds of America* (4 vols., 1827–38), which contained more than one thousand figures of about five hundred species.

When he returned to the United States in 1831, Audubon was acclaimed as one of the greatest American naturalists. He made several trips to Texas, Florida, and Louisiana before returning to Edinburgh in 1834 to continue writing *Ornithological Biography* (5 vols., 1831–38), the text for *Birds of America*. He returned to the United States in 1839 and in 1841 purchased a farm on the Hudson River, which is now Audubon Park, New York City. During 1842–45, Audubon completed the color plates for his *Quadrupeds of North America;* his sons finished the text (1846–54).

❦

John James Audubon, out of embarrassment over his illegitimacy or out of high spirits, invented many tales about his birth, but the one most repeated was that he was a child of the American backwoods. Although raised in France, he liked being called "La Forêt" and affected, especially when in Europe, the fur cap, wolfskin coat, and shoulder-length hair groomed with bear grease of the frontier. Audubon's strikingly American intellectual career gave point to this chosen persona of American backwoodsman.

When he came to the United States, he gaily neglected his financial concerns to pursue his favorite pastimes of hunting and sketching. These interests, along with his fascination with birds and taxidermy, became the foundation of his later achievements, but he only slowly came to realize that his family's well-being depended on making a profit. Failing to interest an American publisher in the bird studies on which he had worked for two decades, Audubon found the British scientific community more hospitable. Aided by a brilliant British engraver, Richard Havell, Jr., he began to publish *The Birds of America* in 1827. For the next eleven years he supervised this work while he constantly sought subscribers for the expensive volumes. The life-sized pictures, drawn both from nature and from stuffed models, were minutely accurate but derived their distinction from the artistically unified compositions where birds were placed in graceful relationship to flora and background. In many cases Audubon also instilled the studies with emotion, ranging from the tenderness of "Passenger Pigeons" to the melodrama of "Barn Owls."

Skeptical of systems and pedants, Audubon made his scientific contributions on the basis of firsthand knowledge and infused his five-volume *Ornithological Biography,* like his pictures, with keen observation and a romantic love of American birds and their environment. At 57, Audubon began a new series of drawings, *Quadrupeds;* his work on this project halted only when debilitating illness overtook him in 1847.

Neither as artist nor as scientist was Audubon a genius, but as a man who united the two cultures he was almost without a peer. In some ways the transplanted Frenchman best met the demand that nationalistic American critics had long made: to create a new kind of art from the physical and emotive realities of the New World. See Alice Ford, *John James Audubon* (1964).

DAVID GRIMSTED

AUSTIN, Stephen Fuller (b. Wythe Co., Va., Nov. 3, 1793; d. Austin, Tex., Dec. 27, 1836), POLITICAL LEADER, spent his childhood in Missouri and attended Transylvania University in Lexington, Kentucky. He returned to Missouri in 1810 and became director of the Bank of St. Louis and a member of the territorial legislature (1814–20). Austin then settled in Arkansas and was appointed judge of the first state judicial circuit (1820). Next he briefly studied law in New Orleans, where he also worked for the Louisiana *Advertiser.*

In 1821, Austin visited Mexican Texas and was granted permission to settle three hundred families there; in January 1822 he founded the first Anglo-American community in Texas. Until 1828 he governed Texas, opposing the abolition of slavery. After Mexico abolished slavery, he came out for a contract labor law whereby slaves could be brought into Texas, technically as indentured servants.

Austin believed that Texas could best prosper as a Mexican state, but at the convention of San Felipe de Austin (1833) the Texans, who chose to separate themselves from Mexico, sent him to Mexico City to present their demands. The Mexican government, however, arrested him as a revolutionary. He was not released until 1835. When he returned to Texas, he opposed a declaration of independence, arguing that Texas did not have the resources either to win or to main-

tain its independence. But when the Texas revolution broke out (1836), he went to Washington to seek aid and recognition for the new republic.

In 1836, Austin was defeated for the presidency of Texas by **Sam Houston.** He became secretary of state under Houston, an office he held until his death.

———

Austin devoted his life to the establishment of a prosperous middle-class Anglo-American group in Texas. He was a man eminently suited to shaping such a mass settlement. Earnest, possessing a powerful sense of duty, hardworking, he persevered in honest and just jurisdiction of his settlements. He was, however, totally unconcerned with the rights of those who were not settlers or Mexican citizens—that is, black slaves and Native Americans.

"My mottoes have been—the redemption of Texas from the wilderness, fidelity and gratitude to my adopted country, and to be inflexibly true to the interests and just rights of my settlers," he wrote in 1831. His total "fidelity and gratitude" to the Mexican government greatly furthered the success of Austin's enterprise. He gladly became a Mexican citizen to secure the permission to be an impresario. During the period he governed Texas, he faithfully administered Mexican law and maintained good relations with Mexico. Indeed, when another not so successful impresario attempted to trigger the Fredonian Rebellion in 1826, Austin threw his entire diplomatic energies into assuring Mexican authorities of the fidelity of the majority of settlers; he even joined an anti-Fredonian military force. Crucial to his fidelity was his determination to have only solid citizens. All immigrants had to apply to him personally, presenting credentials proving good character; those not living up to his standards were ousted.

But Austin's feelings of duty to "the rights and interests of any settlers" also led him to some conflicts with, and ultimately to the great break with, Mexico. The Mexican government was utterly opposed to slavery. Many of Austin's settlers, however, were slaveholders; he also feared that immigration to Texas would cease if Americans heard slavery was prohibited there. Austin ultimately circumvented the Mexican law with a law declaring slaves brought into Texas to be indentured servants for life; slave children would be freed at age 14.

Austin followed the American frontier tradition in his battle for the "rights" of white settlers and his simultaneous inability to envision any kind of rights for the aboriginal occupants of Texas. He did not even consider Texas to have been occupied prior to his settlements: in 1832 he was to recall "the enterprise I undertook in settling an uninhabited country." In point of fact his settlers had to contend with several tribes of Native Americans in the "redemption of Texas from the wilderness." Austin argued against

Mexican suggestions that Native Americans also be granted lands. He wrote of two tribes in 1821 that "there will be no way of subduing them but extermination." He refrained from large-scale attempts at military extermination of the tribes only because he feared news of wars with them would frighten away potential settlers.

In all, Austin created in Mexican territory a frontier society with middle-class American values. He can be remembered positively for his dutiful dedication to the settlers; but it should not be forgotten that he thoroughly institutionalized slavery in Texas and furthered the bloody American practice of Native American genocide. See Eugene C. Barker, *The Life of Stephen F. Austin, Founder of Texas, 1793–1836* (1970).

DOUGLAS T. MILLER

BABBITT, Irving (b. Dayton, Ohio, Aug. 2, 1865; d. Cambridge, Mass., July 15, 1933), PHILOSOPHER, graduated from Harvard in 1889 and taught French at the University of Montana (1889–91) before studying at the Sorbonne in Paris (1891–92) under Sylvain Lévi. In 1893 he received an MA from Harvard in Oriental studies. He taught romance languages at Williams College (1893–94) and became an instructor of French at Harvard in 1894. He was promoted to associate professor in 1902 and to professor of French literature in 1912, a position he held until his death.

A popular lecturer and teacher, Babbitt also wrote extensively on a wide variety of subjects. His *Literature and the American College* (1908) attacked dilettantism in college education and called for a curriculum strictly based on ethical principles. This book also expounded his philosophy of the new humanism, or neohumanism. In works like *The New Laokoön* (1910), *The Masters of Modern French Criticism* (1912), and *Rousseau and Romanticism* (1919), he attacked romanticism and its offshoots, realism and naturalism. Babbitt was

an exchange professor from Harvard to the Sorbonne in 1923 and was elected to the American Academy of Arts and Letters in 1930. Some of his other writings are *Democracy and Leadership* (1924), *On Being Creative and Other Essays* (1932), and a translation of the Dhammapada (1936), which appeared posthumously.

Irving Babbitt is said to have told his students to make use of his ideas, if they liked, but not to quote him by name—for that would discredit them, the critical opposition to Babbitt's writings being fierce. Harold Laski wrote in his *American Democracy* that Babbitt left no disciples.

Yet both Babbitt and Laski were mistaken. Babbitt's most eminent disciple was T. S. Eliot, who—despite a difference with Babbitt on the necessity for a transcendent religion—repeatedly acknowledged his great debt to his old professor at Harvard. University and college presidents like Nathan Pusey and Gordon Chalmers were Babbitt's inheritors, too. And the "American humanism" which Babbitt expounded remains a living force in American thought.

Babbitt was no Brahmin: in his youth he was a newsboy, a reporter, and a cowboy. But he lived with a high dignity that was reflected in his very dress, and loved and hated with a prophetic vehemence; he disdained easy success or popularity, and died with the fortitude that had marked his life.

This mordant critic held the Germanic doctoral degree in a merciless contempt and fought with equal fervor against the degradation of the American college into a luxurious center for dilettantes and against the false specialization of the PhD. For Babbitt the great end of literature and of education was ethical. He found himself in a world that was proceeding to dedicate itself to the study of subhuman relationships, which were mistaken for the whole of life—a culture sinking into a meaningless aestheticism, an arid specialization, a mean vocationalism.

To egoism and appetite, oppressing his age, Babbitt opposed humanism—the study of man's essential nature, with its strict ethical disciplines. Humane studies are those that teach a man his dignity and his rights and his duties. The humanist struggles to develop, by an act of will, the higher nature in man, while the mere humanitarian believes in "outer working and inner *laissez faire*," material gain and emancipation from ethical checks. Several of Babbitt's books remain in print; all in all, his influence has been as wide and as enduring as that of any scholar of his time. See Frederick Manchester and Odell Shepard, eds., *Irving Babbitt, Man and Teacher* (1941).

RUSSELL KIRK

BACON, Nathaniel (b. Friston Hall, Suffolk, Eng., Jan. 2, 1647; d. Gloucester Co., Va., Oct. 26, 1676), POLITICAL LEADER, was a cousin of Francis Bacon. After being indifferently educated at Cambridge and at Gray's Inn, he emigrated to Virginia in 1674, where his family connections won him a seat on the council of state. He early developed a strong sympathy for the settlers' troubles, the most critical of which was the alleged inability of the governor, Sir **William Berkeley,** to provide protection from the Indians. The governor opposed Bacon's insistence on stern military action against the Indians. After Bacon proceeded without Berkeley's permission to head an expedition against the Indians in 1676, he was proclaimed a rebel. His expedition struck a responsive chord in the people, however, and the governor called for elections to a new assembly to consider all grievances. The new assembly met in June and enacted a number of liberal reforms. Although Berkeley severely castigated Bacon for his previous actions, he restored him to his seat on the council soon after the new assembly convened.

But Bacon continued to fight the Indians without authorization from Berkeley. Civil war ensued, the struggle culminating in Bacon's laying siege to Jamestown, which he burned to the ground in 1676. The governor fled to the Eastern Shore, and Bacon, after exacting oaths of fidelity from his followers, continued his expeditions against the Indians and his criticism of the governor's rule. Before he could complete his task (if, in fact, he ever defined one), he died and the rebellion collapsed.

⁂

To describe the career of Nathaniel Bacon is perhaps more a task of psychohistory or mythology than of conventional history. Bacon was described and condemned by the commissioners sent to investigate the causes of the rebellion as "slender, blackhair'd and of an ominous, pensive, melancholly Aspect, of a pestilent and prevalent Logical discourse tending to atheisme in most companyes … of a most imperious and dangerous hidden Pride of heart, despising the wisest of his neighbours for their Ignorance, and very ambitious and arrogant," but his image began to be drawn in a more flattering style following the American Revolution of 1776 when certain historians conceived of the disturbance started by Bacon as a forerunner of the political upheaval that occurred a hundred years later. While the character of Bacon is still in dispute, the most recent scholarship has looked in vain for evidence of Bacon's commitment to democratic reform while exposing more clearly his unsavory as well as unauthorized assaults on Virginia's Indian subjects and Indian neighbors. None of the Indians slaughtered by Bacon was among those denominated "enemy" Indians by the government. All were officially friends and allies of the colony, though charged by Bacon with complicity in the attacks on the frontiersmen by hostile "foreign" Indians. Moreover, though the mild reforms of the June Assembly have been designated "Bacon's Laws" by later historians, the evidence—including that of the laws themselves—suggests that he had no hand or interest in them. Thus, while Bacon will forever figure in American mythology, it will be more appropriately as a model of the Indian hater than of the political reformer. See Wilcomb E. Washburn, *The Governor and the Rebel: A History of Bacon's Rebellion in Virginia* (1957).

WILCOMB E. WASHBURN

BAER, George Frederick (b. Lavansville, Pa., Sept. 26, 1842; d. Philadelphia, Pa., April 26, 1914), FINANCIER, studied at Somerset Institute and Somerset Academy and at the age of 13 became a printer's devil for the Somerset *Democrat*. After working for two years for the Ashtola Lumber Mills near Johnstown, Ohio, where he rose to treasurer and head bookkeeper, he attended Franklin and Marshall College (1860–61). In 1861 he joined his brother Henry as editor of the *Democrat*. At first Baer opposed the Civil War, but in 1862 he helped organize and became captain of the 133d Pennsylvania Volunteers. He fought at Antietam, Fredericksburg, and Chancellorsville, rose to major, and was discharged as adjutant general of the Second Brigade. He returned to Somerset, studied law, and was admitted to the bar in April 1864. Appointed counsel of the Berks County Railroad, he conducted several damage suits successfully against the Philadelphia and Reading Railways Co. He became confidential adviser to John R. Richards, counsel for the Reading Road, and in 1870 succeeded him as the Reading's

counsel. During the Panic of 1873, Baer helped rehabilitate numerous firms, serving as local representative for **J. Pierpont Morgan** and for the Vanderbilt interests in Pennsylvania.

In 1901, with Morgan's aid, Baer was elected president of the Philadelphia and Reading Railways Co. He also became president of the Temple Iron Co., which controlled anthracite coal properties in Pennsylvania. Because Morgan refused to be drawn into the anthracite coal strike of 1902, Baer became the leader of the interests opposing the strike and firmly refused to negotiate with the striking miners. He received national attention when a letter dated July 17, written in response to an appeal to end the strike, was published. However, under pressure from the government and J. P. Morgan, he finally agreed to the arbitration of the strike in October 1902.

⸱⸱⸱

For his achievements in business George Baer would qualify as a typical but commonplace robber baron of the late 19th century; he would now be forgotten except for the remarkable arrogance of his Social Darwinism and the singular insolence of his pronouncements. In the anthracite coal strike of 1902 he refused to bargain with the United Mine Workers. A photographer from Wilkes-Barre, William F. Clark, remonstrated, expressing a hope that "God would send the Holy Spirit of reason" into his heart. Baer's well-publicized reply made him far better known than his position in industry could ever have done.

With magnificent egotism he begged Clark not to be discouraged because the interests of the laboring man would be "protected and cared for—not by the labor agitators, but by the Christian men to whom God has given control of the property rights of the country." In his peroration, which has modern connotations, Baer asked Clark to pray earnestly and to remember "that the Lord God Omnipotent still reigns, and that his reign is one of law and order and not of violence and crime."

In a later meeting at the White House with Baer and **John Mitchell** of the United Mine Workers, President Theodore Roosevelt was impressed by Mitchell and vastly annoyed at the "extraordinary stupidity of the woodenheaded gentry" who operated the mines. He was to confess, in later years, that if it had not been for the dignity of his high office, he would have taken Baer by the seat of his breeches and "chucked him out of the window."

Over the many years there has been general agreement that Baer was a "pious pirate" who believed in the "divine right of plutocrats." For that esoteric reason his reputation could be everlasting. See Elsie Gluck, *John Mitchell, Miner: Labor's Bargain with the Gilded Age* (1929).

C. H. CRAMER

BAKER, James Addison, III (b. Houston, Tex., Apr. 23, 1930), LAWYER, POLITICIAN, graduated Princeton University in 1952 and received a law degree from the University of Texas at Austin in 1957. Before entering law school he spent two years in the Marine Corps. Baker practiced law at Andrews, Kirth, Cambell and Jones, a corporate law firm in Houston, until 1981. A Republican, Baker ran the 1970 Harris County Senate campaign for his close friend George Bush, then a congressman. Bush lost, but Baker demonstrated great organizational ability, which he again displayed in the 1972 presidential election as the leader of the Republican campaign in fourteen Texas counties that year. He was named State Republican finance chairman. In 1975, President Gerald Ford appointed him undersecretary of Commerce. The following year he managed Ford's unsuccessful election campaign; although Ford lost to Jimmy Carter, Baker's formidable skills as campaign tactician were credited with making the election closer than expected. He rejoined his law firm in 1977 but remained very active in politics. In 1978, Baker ran unsuccessfully for Texas attorney general and managed George Bush's primary campaign for the Republican presidential nomination in 1980. When Ronald Reagan gained momentum, Baker persuaded Bush to drop out, and after Reagan's nomination and selection of Bush as his running mate, Baker became the senior adviser to the

Reagan campaign team. Following Reagan's victory over Carter, Baker, regarded now as the ultimate insider, was named White House chief of staff. His responsibilities included managing the White House personnel office, handling legislative affairs, and overseeing and coordinating the Reagan domestic and foreign policy agenda. In 1985, at the start of President Reagan's second term, Baker switched jobs with secretary of the Treasury Don Regan. Baker left the Treasury in 1988 to manage George Bush's presidential campaign. Almost immediately after his victory Bush appointed him secretary of state. Baker resigned in 1992 to take over as Bush's chief of staff and manager of his reelection campaign. Following Bush's defeat, Baker returned to the practice of law in the Washington office of Baker & Botts, the law firm founded by his grandfather.

―◦≈◦―

James A. Baker III represents old Texas money. This is not the new money of the coarse dealmaker but the inherited wealth of families who send their offspring east to preparatory and Ivy League schools. Old money in Texas used to be Democratic because the state's confederate heritage meant that the Republican Party was almost nonexistent in most of the state. After Republican presidential candidate Barry Goldwater campaigned as both a social and economic conservative in 1964, the Republican Party began to grow in Texas. Nevertheless, until the late 1960s, economic elites were usually conservative Democrats. Jim Baker, as he preferred to be called, was a Democrat, too, although inactive politically until asked by Texas Congressman George Bush to help in Bush's 1970 campaign for the U.S. Senate against Democrat Lloyd Bentsen. Baker and Bush had become friends in the 1960s when Bush was a Texas oilman. Although Bush lost, he ran well in Harris County, which includes Houston, where Baker ran the campaign.

Besides old money, the other defining element of Baker is the absence of a political creed or deeply held set of convictions. He got involved in politics because Bush asked him for help. Neither as a youth nor as an adult is there evidence that

Baker sees politics as a means to advance any particular conception of the good society. Baker's family taught that politics could only get in the way of the family business. Baker is a skilled manager and a workaholic, but he has never developed a political vision.

Baker's reputation as a manager and not as an ideologue explains in part the surprise (and, for some, relief) when Reagan appointed him chief of staff in 1981. Baker was a steadying and moderating influence. Much of President Reagan's early success with Congress was attributable to Baker's organizational and persuasive abilities.

As secretary of the Treasury, Baker was credited with innovative work in the international arena. He forged an agreement with Great Britain, France, West Germany, and Japan to make exchange rates more closely reflect underlying market forces. In addition, he advanced efforts toward coordination of international economic policies. On the domestic front, Baker was less successful. He lost control of the debate over the 1986 tax reform legislation and was criticized for not being on top of the savings and loan scandal.

As secretary of state under Bush, Baker was in his element. As the Communist regimes of the Soviet Union and Eastern Europe disintegrated, he worked closely with Congress to push through assistance packages to facilitate transitions to democracy. Nevertheless, there were also charges of shabby ethics and poor judgment during his tenure. One damaging allegation involved his personal intervention in 1989 to support loan guarantees to the government of Saddam Hussein. Later reports showed that Iraq had used the credits to support its nuclear weapons program. Other highly publicized charges involved numerous private trips on military planes in 1989 and 1990. In response Baker reimbursed the government for part of the costs.

Above all, Baker is considered by many to have been the quintessential campaign manager. Pundits attributed Gerald Ford's narrow victory over Reagan at the 1976 Republican National Convention in large part to Baker's shrewd handling of the delegates. When Baker took control of Ford's campaign against Jimmy Carter, Ford trailed by thirty percentage points. Although Ford lost in a very close election, Baker received much credit for closing the gap through the "rose garden" strategy of emphasizing presidential image. Baker's reputation as a campaign genius grew when he ran Bush's successful campaign in 1990 against Michael Dukakis. Rather than focusing on Bush's ideas for the future, Baker developed a relentlessly negative campaign strategy attacking the Democratic candidate. Four years later, in August 1992, Bush again turned to Baker. One columnist wrote: "In comes Baker, out go the issues." Baker's performance angered many Republicans, however, and cost him his reputation of campaign management invincibility.

Out of office, Baker practiced law and tested the presidential waters. In May 1995 he announced that he would not be a candidate for president in 1996. See James A. Baker III, *The Politics of Diplomacy: Revolution, War and Peace, 1989–1992* (1995), and Robert Dallek, *Ronald Reagan and the Politics of Symbolism* (1984).

ROBERT O'CONNOR

BAKER, Josephine (b. St. Louis, Mo., June 3, 1906; d. Paris, France, Apr. 12, 1975), ENTERTAINER, the daughter of a drummer, Eddie Carson, and a washerwoman, Carrie McDonald, she worked while still a child as a live-in maid and a waitress before getting her first job in show business as a chorus girl in 1921 with a traveling black vaudeville troupe. Although she soon became a well-known performer in the United States, starring in the Ziegfeld Follies of 1936, her real fame centered in Paris, France, where she was a headliner in La Revue Megre and the Folies-Bergeres. She also starred in such movies as *La Sirene des Tropiques* (1927), *Zou-Zou* (1934), and *Princesse Tom Tom* (1935). Baker married five times but had no natural children. Instead, she adopted ten children of different races and ethnic backgrounds. During World War II, Baker worked for the French Resistance and was later awarded the Croix de Guerre, the Rosette de la Resistance, and the Legion d'Honneur by her adopted homeland for her contributions. She returned periodically to the United States where she spoke out against segregation and the racisim she often confronted. On August 28, 1963, she walked shoulder to shoulder with **Martin Luther King, Jr.**, in the famous March on Washington. That same year, ill, bankrupt, and evicted from her longtime home in the south of France, she was rescued by the efforts of Princess Grace of Monaco who arranged for Baker and her children to live in a villa in Roquebrune, near Monte Carlo. Beloved to the end by the French, more than twenty thousand attended her funeral in Paris.

Josephine Baker's life was the quintessential rag-to-riches story. At the **Booker T. Washington** Theatre, the black vaudeville house in St. Louis, she went on at the last minute with the Dixie Steppers for an injured chorus girl. Her radiant personality and exuberant antics stole the show. She was only 15.

Opportunites for black performers in the United States were too limited for the irrepressible Baker, and she escaped to Paris. Her "Danse Sauvage," dressed in a very short skirt of feathers and nothing else, was a show stopper, and she immediately won the hearts of the French. In another show she was clad in what became her famous "banana skirt"—and, again, nothing else. With a solid sense of the theatrical, she made spectacular entrances, often carried upside down or lowered from high above the audience. She appeared in public with her pet leopard or strolled with several swans on a leash. But it was not Baker's personal eccentricities or theatrical idiosyncrasies that made her so popular, it was her magnetic personality, a winning combination of sophistication and an honest love for performing and for her audiences. Yet despite Baker's international success she always felt incomplete and dissatisfied. She attempted to fill that personal void with five marriages and her "Rainbow Tribe" of adopted children. In the end the racism she experienced in her mother country and the failure of its people to accord her the respect and

love she found among the French hurt deeply. With that in mind, she once said that the high point of her life was walking with Martin Luther King in the March on Washington. See Phyllis Rose, *Jazz Cleopatra: Josephine Baker in Her Time* (1989).

ROY SORRELS

BAKER, Newton Diehl (b. Martinsburg, W. Va., Dec. 3, 1871; d. Cleveland, Ohio, Dec. 25, 1937), POLITICAL LEADER, graduated in 1892 from Johns Hopkins University, where he concentrated in the social sciences under **Richard T. Ely** and Woodrow Wilson. Gaining a law degree from Washington and Lee University in 1894, Baker practiced in Martinsburg until he was appointed secretary to Cleveland's postmaster general, William L. Wilson, in 1896. Returning from a trip to Europe in 1898, Baker became a clerk in a large Cleveland law firm headed by Martin A. Foran. In 1902, Baker entered municipal politics, first as legal assistant to **Tom L. Johnson,** reform mayor of Cleveland, then (1905) as city solicitor. In that post he fought and won a six-year battle for lower public transit fares. In 1911 he was elected mayor by a record majority. As mayor (1912–16) he secured home rule for the city and municipal ownership of public utilities. Active in Ohio Democratic politics, Baker was an early supporter of Woodrow Wilson for the presidency. He helped to break the unit rule that would have withheld Ohio votes from Wilson at the Democratic national convention of 1912. Offered the post of secretary of the interior, Baker declined, preferring to finish his term as mayor.

When Wilson's secretary of war, Lindley M. Garrison, resigned because he objected to compromise on preparedness, the president appointed Baker to the post (March 6, 1916). Immediately embroiled in military affairs pertaining to Mexico, Baker had little time to give to building up the army. In his subsequent conduct of the war preparation program, however, he accomplished much in a remarkably short time. Nevertheless, he was the target of widespread criticism for his administration of the War

Department, and a Senate investigation in December 1917 laid considerable blame on him for its deficiencies.

Baker's career after 1920 was almost the reverse of his early years. Returning to his law practice he developed a specialization in transportation, public utility, patent, and antitrust cases in a period of great activity and controversy in these fields. Gradually becoming conservative, Baker gave the New Deal only lukewarm support because he considered its vast extension of control as unwise and unconstitutional.

Baker had favored America's joining the League of Nations and served in 1928 as a member of the Permanent Court of Arbitration. Long interested in interfaith friendship, he was a leader of the National Conference of Christians and Jews.

A moderate progressive rather than a social planner, Newton D. Baker shared Woodrow Wilson's admiration of Edmund Burke's philosophy of gradual change and Jefferson's faith in individualism and local self-government. Baker viewed the city as the experimental station of democracy and believed that good government largely involved obtaining good personnel rather than effecting basic structural changes. As mayor he coined the term "civitism" to summarize his philosophy of local patriotism and dedicated service to the commonweal. Although he supported public ownership of utilities, Baker emphatically endorsed the private property free enterprise system. Wartime governmental controls over the economy therefore alarmed him as dangerous precedents for a centralized bureaucratic state; consequently, President Wilson had to turn to others to achieve the degree of federal economic controls required by the war effort. Baker also became greatly distressed at rising social tensions during 1917–20 and called upon businessmen and labor leaders for a revival of a sense of common values and individual responsibility for the public good. Later, during the Depression, Baker feared that New Deal social and regulatory measures would substitute security for private initia-

tive and create a statist society. Yet he did not break with FDR and continued to give the Democratic Party a measure of support. In foreign policy Baker also remained a true Wilsonian, continuing to advocate membership in the League of Nations and World Court, opposing "outlawry of war" as a sentimental abstraction and the neutrality laws as immoral, and condemning Japanese aggression in Asia and totalitarian imperialism in Europe. See C. H. Cramer, *Newton D. Baker, A Biography* (1961).

DANIEL M. SMITH

BAKER, Ray Stannard (b. Lansing, Mich., Apr. 17, 1870; d. Amherst, Mass., July 12, 1946), JOURNALIST, REFORMER, graduated from the Michigan Agricultural College at East Lansing (now Michigan State University) in 1889. He then worked in his father's real estate business and spent a semester in 1892 studying law and literature at the University of Michigan. He moved to Chicago in 1892 to work as a reporter for the Chicago *Record.* He soon became subeditor of the paper and in 1897 was named managing editor of McClure's Syndicate, for which he wrote many articles. He was appointed associate editor of *McClure's* magazine (1899), which soon became a leading muckraking journal. In his articles Baker exposed and attacked malpractices in business and government, including railroad rate discrimination, political corruption, and the efforts of employers to crush unions.

Baker joined **Ida Tarbell, William Allen White,** and other muckrakers in 1906 to purchase the *American* magazine; he remained as an editor of the magazine until 1915. He also traveled widely and wrote several books, including *Following the Color Line* (1908), a pioneering exposé of the race problem in the United States. During this period he wrote many philosophic essays on human nature under the pseudonym David Grayson. These were collected in *Adventures in Contentment* (1907), *Adventures in Friendship* (1910), and seven successive volumes that eventually sold a total of some 2 million copies in America, the British Commonwealth, and in several foreign language translations.

Baker became friendly with Woodrow Wilson around 1910 and supported Wilson's presidential policies after 1912, including the decision to enter World War I. In 1918 he served as special commissioner for the State Department and went on several diplomatic missions to Great Britain, France, and Italy. He was director of the press bureau of the American Committee to Negotiate Peace at Paris during the 1919 Versailles Peace Conference. A supporter of the League of Nations, Baker wrote *What Wilson Did at Paris* (1919) to help win public support; this book later was revised and expanded as *Woodrow Wilson and World Settlement* (3 vols., 1922). Shortly before his death in 1924, Wilson asked Baker to write his official biography. The first volume of *Woodrow Wilson: Life and Letters* appeared in 1927; the eighth and final volume was published in 1939 and won a Pulitzer Prize for biography. Baker also coedited, with W. E. Dodd, the six-volume *Public Papers of Woodrow Wilson* (1925–26). Baker published a two-part autobiography, *Native American* (1941) and *American Chronicle* (1945).

———— ⚮ ————

By temperament and profession, Baker was sensitively attuned to the mood and interests of the middle-class, middle-brow audience for which he wrote. His articles, crisp in detail, balanced in judgment, embodied the canons of the New Journalism and his own belief that the age demanded "facts, facts piled up to the point of dry certitude." Although his refusal to specify remedies frustrated critics on the left, his reports helped introduce the public to the realities of modern America. The Grayson adventures, pastoral idylls exuding an extenuated Emersonianism, mirrored a more tender aspect of progressive thought. Under cover of his pseudonym, Baker-Grayson in effect debated with himself many of the issues that troubled his generation. While the reporter-reformer moved gradually to the left, even flirting for a time with a sort of Fabian socialism, David Grayson preached a cosmic optimism wherein social conflict dissolved in positive thinking. Baker laid no claim to original thought. "That a

man is 'ahead of his time' or 'behind his time,'" he once remarked, "is an admission he is second rate." His success as a reporter and the countless letters David Grayson received from grateful readers are monuments to this conviction.

Mild-mannered, shy before an audience, Baker was drawn to the charismatic leaders of his day. He worked closely with Theodore Roosevelt, even claiming influence in shaping the Hepburn (railroad) Bill, until the president's attack on "muckrakers" blighted the relationship. His deepening devotion to Wilson after 1912 climaxed a lifelong search for a cause. A beacon of liberalism in the interwar years, *Wilson: Life and Letters,* although superseded by recent scholarship, rightly won the admiration of historians and general readers. See Robert C. Bannister, Jr., *Ray Stannard Baker* (1966).

ROBERT C. BANNISTER, JR.

BALANCHINE, George (b. Petrograd, Russia, Jan. 9, 1904; d. New York, N.Y., Apr. 30, 1983), CHOREOGRAPHER, studied at the Imperial Ballet School (1914–17). When the school closed during the Revolution of 1917, he worked for a time as a messenger and as a pianist in movie theaters. The school, however, soon reopened as the Academy of Opera and Ballet, and Balanchine graduated in 1921. He danced in various ballets, becoming a member of the Soviet State Dancers in 1924. In that year the group toured Western Europe; when ordered to return to Russia, Balanchine went to Paris where he joined Diaghilev's Ballet Russe (1924–29). After the Ballet Russe dissolved following Diaghilev's death (1929), Balanchine became director of the Royal Theater of Copenhagen. He was an organizer of the Ballet Russe de Monte Carlo in 1932.

In 1933 he went to the United States at the invitation of Lincoln Kirstein to found the School of American Ballet (1934), and in 1948 he became artistic director of the new New York City Ballet, which employed graduates from the American School. One of its most notable successes was its 1962 tour of the Soviet Union. Balanchine was also a choreographer for the Metropolitan Opera

(1934–37) and for many Broadway musicals, such as *On Your Toes* (1936), for which he created the ballet *Slaughter on Tenth Avenue*. Among his nearly two hundred major ballets were *Pastorale* (1927), *Apollon* (1928), *Cotillion* (1932), and *Orpheus* (1948). From the 1960s through the 1980s Balanchine repeatedly demonstrated his wide range and balletic imagination. During those years he went from the 1966 *Stravinsky Variations*, in which the same music was repeated three times, to his Romantic masterpiece in 1980, *Robert Schumann's Davidsbündlertanze*, to the popular *Vienna Waltzes*. In 1975 he directed a Ravel Festival, followed by a Tchaikovsky Festival (1981) and a Stravinsky Festival in 1982. He also did choreography for many films, including *The Boys from Syracuse* and *I Married an Angel*. He authored *Balanchine's New Complete Stories of the Great Ballets* (1968).

———— ∞ ————

Balanchine was inarguably the single most important influence in America's ballet development over the last half-century. There were other and differing influences at work, but Balanchine's personal prestige in the ballet field was unequaled. His standards derived from the elegant styles of Leningrad rather than the much more flamboyant style of Moscow. Indeed, he was often called the heir to the traditions of Russia's greatest 19th-century choreographer and ballet master, Marius Petipa. He was also influenced, however, by Serge Diaghilev, for it was as Diaghilev's final major ballet discovery that he made his first significant choreographic contributions with such masterpieces as *The Prodigal Son* and *Apollon*.

Almost immediately upon presiding over the establishment of the American Ballet he recognized the differences between American and European dancers, not only in shape and size but also in rhythms, dynamisms, and other characteristics. From then on he adapted traditional ballet to the lean, limber, swift, precise athleticism of his new charges. His choreography for American dancers revealed two major directions: extension of the technique of the *ballet d'école* to include

new areas of virtuosity and movements partly related to modern dance; and, choreographically, the evolvement of a ballet genre that dispensed with story, situation, and even décor—these, to use a term created by the Denishawn dancers of the 1920s, might be described as "music visualizations." Over the years his troupes specialized in such ballets, culminating in *Jewels*, the first full-length (three acts) abstract ballet in history. He did, of course, create ballets with stories and elaborate production (*Orpheus, A Midsummer Night's Dream, Don Quixote,* and his own version of *The Nutcracker*), but the accent was on short ballets.

Balanchine's influence extended beyond his own company and his own school. He gave his ballets freely to many other ballet companies and his influence, therefore, was theatrical and stylistic as well as academic, international as well as national. See Lincoln Kirstein, *Movement & Metaphor* (1970).

WALTER TERRY

BALDWIN, James Arthur (b. New York, N.Y., Aug. 2, 1924; d. St. Paul de Vence, France, Dec. 1, 1987), WRITER, graduated from DeWitt Clinton High School in New York City in 1942. He held a number of odd jobs to support himself while writing during 1942–45. His essays soon began to appear in such periodicals as the *Nation, New Leader,* and *Commentary.* In 1945 he received a Saxton Fellowship and in 1948 a Rosenwald Fellowship.

In 1948, Baldwin moved to Paris, living in Europe until 1956. *Go Tell It on the Mountain* was published in 1953. Partly autobiographical, this book described the religious conversion of a 14-year-old black boy living in Harlem and his relation to his family, especially his father. In 1955 he published *Notes of a Native Son*, a collection of essays in which he expressed his views on racial issues in the United States and abroad. His next work was *Giovanni's Room* (1956), a novel dealing with homosexuality and moral responsibility.

In 1961, Baldwin published *Another Country,* which is set in Harlem and Greenwich Village, and *Nobody Knows My Name,* a collection of articles on diverse topics. *The Fire Next Time* (1963) reviewed the position of the African-American in the United States, discussed the rise of the Black Muslims, and warned Americans that they must face the question of black equality immediately. In 1964, *Blues for Mister Charlie* appeared, a play arguing that discrimination is a disease of white society. Previously Baldwin had written *The Amen Corner,* his most often produced play. *Tell Me How Long the Train's Been Gone* (1968) is a study of a black actor's climb from the streets of Harlem to fame and the moral questions that confront him. Baldwin generally lived abroad, returning periodically to the United States. In 1971 he wrote (with **Margaret Mead**) *A Rap on Race,* and in 1974 the novel *If Beale Street Could Talk. The Evidence of Things Not Seen* (1985), an essay about the murder in the late 1970s and early 1980s of twenty-eight black children in Atlanta, Georgia, was one of his last published works.

James Baldwin's progress toward religious conversion was vividly described in *Go Tell It on the Mountain,* a novel whose deeply religious mood was suggested by its title, the words of a spiritual. This novel, because it was autobiographical and because it probed so deeply into the life and character of its author, described Baldwin the person so well that we can without difficulty trace his subsequent work—essays, fiction, and drama—back to that seminal piece. Baldwin's religious conversion led him ultimately to become a minister at the age of 14. Although he later gave up the ministry, he did not give up his strong belief in Christian values, especially love and most other tenets of Christian morality. Baldwin was by no means an institutional Christian, but he was a great moralist, and his most characteristic tone was of moral indignation, the legacy of his early faith.

In his novels Baldwin consistently explored love relationships among his characters. *Go Tell It on the Mountain* focused on the relation between John, the central character, and his father. There we see John embrace the church in order to fulfill his desperate need for love and a sense of belonging, neither of which his father is willing or able to supply. The implication is that John's whole sense of identity and self-worth is dependent on his involvement in a love relation. The same holds true in the second novel, *Giovanni's Room,* though Baldwin's frank and open treatment of homosexuality there obscured the novel's theme from many critics. At the novel's conclusion one of the characters is about to be executed for a murder, a murder that would not have occurred had his lover, the protagonist, not abandoned him to resume a heterosexual relationship. The novel poses the question of the protagonist's moral responsibility for the fate of the doomed man who is literally about to cease to exist because of the failure of a love relation. *Another Country* explores the same problem in a broader context. People who survive well in the world, Baldwin says, are those able to love and be loved. Those incapable either die (literally) or lead chaotic, shallow, meaningless lives. *Tell Me How Long the Train's Been Gone* suggests something of a shift from Baldwin's earlier preoccupation. Though still concerned with the love relation, Baldwin shifted his focus, exploring the problems confronting a successful, sensitive, socially conscious black artist (an actor but a thinly disguised James Baldwin). In all his fiction Baldwin's major interest was in the individual and in his attempt to come to terms with his existence.

Baldwin's essays intended to be far more directly social in orientation but were nonetheless largely subjective. Most frequently starting from his own private experience, Baldwin generalized about the society at large, especially as this related to racial issues. In the essays (as in the fiction) he was highly moralistic, relying largely on ideal Christian morality as a standard for assessing the attitudes and actions of society. His most famous single essay, "The Fire Next Time," bore out these generalizations. Most critics rate his essays above his fiction or his drama (his weakest genre), and indeed he has been said to be foremost among modern American essayists.

A sensitive, intelligent, honest man, Baldwin revealed in his work intense involvement. Torn between his commitment to art and his social responsibility, he tried desperately to reconcile the two drives. The tension between his aesthetic inclinations and his sense of social responsibility was strongly expressed in his later works, and his early statement that he wanted to be first of all a writer and second a social being (*Nobody Knows My Name*) probably no longer held at the end of his life.

Baldwin's magazine and television interviews revealed something of his strong tendency toward emotionality; underneath all his attempts to persuade ran an emotional current. He was known to be very tough at times, but his tough exterior probably protected a fragile core. All of his fiction contained at least one extremely sensitive character, and one cannot but feel that Baldwin in creating such characters was projecting an essential element of his own psyche. See Edward Margolies, *Native Sons* (1968).

DONALD B. GIBSON

BANCROFT, George (b. Worcester, Mass., Oct. 3, 1800; d. Washington, D.C., Jan. 17, 1891), HISTORIAN, POLITICAL LEADER, graduated from Harvard in 1817. After studying theology at Harvard for a year, he went to the University of Göttingen (MA and PhD, 1820). He then moved to the University of Berlin, where he attended lectures given by Hegel. He returned to the United States in 1822 and briefly taught Greek at Harvard before opening the Round Hill School at Northampton, Massachusetts (1823), with J. G. Cogswell. In 1823 he also published a book of poems. He left Round Hill in 1831 to pursue a writing career. Bancroft was an ardent Jacksonian Democrat, and he supported the president's policies in a number of articles in the *North American Review*.

In 1834, Bancroft published the first book of his ten-volume *History of the United States*, from the discovery of America to the end of the Revolutionary War. In 1834 he also sought election to the Massachusetts general court but was defeated. President Van Buren appointed him collector of the Port of Boston (1837). In 1844 he was an unsuccessful candidate in the Massachusetts gubernatorial election, but President Polk appointed him secretary of the navy (1845–46). Bancroft helped establish the U.S. Naval Academy at Annapolis; sent Captain John D. Sloat, commander of the Pacific Squadron, to seize the California ports if a war with Mexico should erupt; and, as acting secretary of war (May 1846), ordered General Zachary Taylor to cross the Texas frontier, thereby precipitating the Mexican War.

Bancroft was U.S. minister to Great Britain (1846–49), where access to the British archives enabled him to continue work on his *History*. When the Civil War broke out, he at first disapproved of Lincoln's actions but soon became one of the president's staunchest supporters. On February 12, 1866, he delivered a "Memorial Address on the Life and Character of Abraham Lincoln" before the House of Representatives. Bancroft next served as U.S. minister to Berlin (1867–74), where he continued to search the archives for material for his *History*. The *History* was completed in 1874, but in 1876 he brought out a six-volume revised edition. In 1882 he completed his *History of the Formation of the Constitution of the United States* (2 vols.), which was included in the final revision of his *History* (6 vols., 1883–85). Bancroft's other works include *Literary and Historical Miscellanies* (1855) and *Martin Van Buren to the End of His Public Career* (1889).

⁘

Bancroft was a quick-witted, wiry little man with alert, expressive eyes and rapid speech, sporting a long gray beard in his later years. His zest for work, resilience, and bounce prompted **Oliver Wendell Holmes, Sr.,** to wonder if he were not composed of vulcanized india rubber. Despite his arduous work habits, his ten-volume *History* took fifty years to complete, but it was the greatest achievement of his life, which was dotted with early failures. He had failed as a preacher and as a poet. He had failed as a tutor at

Harvard and as a teacher at Round Hill, where he was known among the boys as "the crittur." He succeeded in winning a high place in political circles but never won an election. He was one of the better secretaries of the navy, but as a diplomat he made no mark on history.

It was as a historian that Bancroft won fame in his own time and a place in history. He combined all of the elements necessary in his *History* to make it the most popular literary and scholarly embodiment of the optimistic, democratic faith of 19th-century America. He portrayed history as a cosmic drama of opposing individuals, forces, and nations working out God's plan for the triumph of liberty, justice, and humanity. He saw American history as a steady march from oppression toward liberty, from scattered settlements toward a unified republic. Bancroft's strong democratic bias led to the uncritical discovery of democracy and equality in everything American, and his Fourth of July oratorical style elicited criticism that he had sacrificed "perspicuity to ornamentation." He personalized history in terms of the men whose decisions and actions determined the direction of events, sometimes too much so; although he was an accurate scholar, he did present his own paraphrased condensations from documents as literal quotations. His work was based, however, on thorough research in European and American archives that he helped open to scholars.

He collected many honors for his achievements, including admission to the floor of the Senate and election as second president of the American Historical Association, the organization of a new school of trained historians who would soon turn their critical guns on the "father of American history." Bancroft's work was never as bad as his critics implied, especially after the later revisions. He did not neglect economic issues: he carefully described the effects of British mercantile policy on the revolutionary movement, set American events in American history in the European context, was realistic about the effects of foreign diplomacy on the course and conclusion of the war, and was sophisticated in his discussion of the role of religion and the ideas of the Enlightenment in giving form to the new republic. In fact, Bancroft's star has recently risen anew, and historians have discovered that political issues and ideals such as liberty were as real as, if not more important than, economic issues as causes of the American Revolution. See Russel B. Nye, *George Bancroft, Brahmin Rebel* (1945).

DAVID B. VAN TASSEL

BANNEKER, Benjamin (b. Ellicott Mills, Md., Nov. 9, 1731; d. Baltimore, Md., Oct. 25, 1806), SCIENTIST, the son of a mulatto mother and black father, was born a free man. He attended a private Quaker school near Joppa, Maryland. Always interested in mechanical and scientific problems, Banneker began making astronomical calculations for almanacs in 1773, and in 1789 he accurately predicted an eclipse. In 1789 he sold the large farm he had inherited from his father for an annuity and devoted himself to his studies. From 1792 until 1802 he published an accurate and popular yearly almanac. He also assisted in surveying the lines of the new District of Columbia after 1790. He wrote a dissertation on bees and calculated the recurrent cycle of locust plagues. He maintained an interest in political and social matters. A vigorous opponent of slavery, he attacked notions of black inferiority in a now famous letter to Secretary of State Thomas Jefferson in 1791. Banneker also supported peace movements, advocating the appointment of a secretary of peace as well as a secretary of war to the president's cabinet.

Mild-mannered and retiring, Benjamin Banneker was a bachelor who fit the image of the 18th-century rationalist, dedicated to the exploration and application of natural law for the betterment of mankind. As a black rationalist he broke new ground and suffered conditional acceptance by the scientific elite. Thomas Jefferson credited Banneker's almanacs as "instances of moral eminence," and **David Rittenhouse** called them "a very extraordinary performance, considering the color of the author."

Public notice came late to Banneker, since his self-education as mathematician and scientist did not accelerate until his middle years. As a member of the District of Columbia Survey Commission he was probably the first civilian black public servant of the federal government. His almanacs were widely used in the middle states, and his exchange of letters with Jefferson was published in pamphlet form. Since his private papers were destroyed when his home caught fire on the day of his funeral, only hearsay testifies to a larger correspondence with men of science in the Western world.

Like a good 18th-century intellectual, Banneker had a sphere of interest wider than, but colored by, science. He constructed a clock in 1761 without ever having examined one closely and with wood as his only material. While there is no documentation to verify that he engaged in scientific agriculture, his orchards, farm animals, bees, and fields were productive and well managed. He was not bound by church dogma, but he occasionally attended Quaker meetings and publicly recorded his belief in a supreme being whose laws men transgressed when they killed other creatures.

His proposal for the office of a secretary of peace was brief but prophetic. It contained strong endorsements of free public education, the prohibition of capital punishment, and the abolition of the militia, military dress, and military titles. Banneker related "universal and perpetual peace" to "universal and equal liberty," undergirded by "the principles of Republicanism and Christianity."

Banneker demanded little of life. He enjoyed music and played the violin, mostly by and to himself. He engaged in country store discussions with his Maryland neighbors without record of bitter disputation. More than most of his black contemporaries, he won and deserved recognition as a man and as a scientist. See Henry E. Baker, "Benjamin Banneker, The Negro Mathematician and Astronomer," *Journal of Negro History*, III (April 1918), 99–118.

LESLIE H. FISHEL, JR.

BARLOW, Joel (b. Redding, Conn., Mar. 24, 1754; d. Zarnowiec, Poland, Dec. 24, 1812), POET, briefly attended Dartmouth College before transferring to Yale, where he received a BA in 1778. While a student he took part in the battle of Long Island (1776). After graduation he taught briefly and did postgraduate work at Yale before becoming chaplain of the Fourth Massachusetts Brigade (1780–83). In 1784, with Elisha Babcock, he established a weekly paper, the *American Mercury,* at Hartford, Connecticut, but in 1785 left this post to read law, being admitted to the Connecticut bar in 1786. However, he devoted more time to writing than to law. He contributed poetry (1786–87) to the *Anarchiad,* a publication of the "Hartford Wits," a group of young writers trying to create a distinctive national literature. With the publication of his nine-volume *The Vision of Columbus* (1787), a poetic view of the past and future of the United States, Barlow established his literary reputation and emerged as a leader of the "Wits."

In 1788 Barlow went to Europe as an agent for the Scioto Land company. He met **Thomas Paine,** Joseph Priestley, and other republicans, and he wrote several radical tracts, including *The Conspiracy of Kings* (1792) and *Advice to the Privileged Orders* (1792). As a result of his *A Letter to the National Convention of France, on the Defects in the Constitution of 1791* (1792), he was made a citizen of France. Barlow served as American consul to Algiers (1795–97) and negotiated treaties with Tunis, Algiers, and Tripoli respecting American commerce. His mock-heroic poem of New England, *Hasty Pudding* (1796), enjoyed tremendous popularity. Barlow returned to the United States in 1805 and settled near Washington, D.C., where he remained active in public affairs, serving as a director of the Bank of Washington. He drafted *The Prospectus of a National Institution to Be Established in the U.S.* for promotion of the arts (1805), and he also published an enlarged edition of *Vision of Columbus, The Columbiad* (1807). In 1811, President Madison appointed him minister to France to negotiate a commercial treaty with Napoleon, but before he could do so, Barlow died in Poland during Napoleon's retreat from Moscow.

———⊶⊷———

Before going abroad, Barlow had been a typical Connecticut conservative. Like his fellow "Wits," he dabbled in prophecy verse, such as *The Prospect of Peace* (1778), one of many epic poems written in heroic couplets that flourished in the hothouse atmosphere of optimistic nationalism of these years. It shared a common vision of rising glory for America—for her art, science, and religion—and it predicted that the millennium would first occur in the New World. Little more than a rhymed and mechanical exercise, this poem prepared the way for *The Vision of Columbus*, a more expansive effort along the same lines, equally turgid and heavy-handed, and almost wholly derivative—in its reliance on Pope for style, Milton for structure, and (among others) Lord Kames, Camoëns, de Ercilla, and Voltaire. *The Vision*, too, had a beneficent view of progress, divinely guided and culminating in millennial peace and happiness. It arraigned religious superstition, exalted reason, and found America the last best hope for mankind.

Barlow's European years produced a total transformation in the man; London and Paris were windows on a larger world. His friends were Lafayette, Paine, Jefferson, and the philosophers in the French capital; and Priestley, Godwin, Horn Tooke, and Mary Wollstonecraft in London. Representative of the thought of them all, Barlow's *Advice to the Privileged Orders* appealed to man's intelligence and reasonableness, and displayed an unremitting hatred of institutional religion and of all arbitrary power. The Church, it claimed, corrupted man's nature; the military system was tyrannical; the legal system draconian; the feudal system unjust. The *Advice* stressed the need for education in the largest sense and also a more equitable distribution of the "common stock of the community" in the belief that both were necessary for a complete renovation of society. Barlow's *A Letter to the National Convention* was an aggressively republican endorsement of the French Revolution, the Terror notwithstanding. A statesmanlike document, it warmly praised disestablishment and overthrow of Bourbon rule; and two of its specific recommendations—annual elections and proportional representation—were incorporated in the 1793 French constitution. *The Prospectus of a National Institution*, one of two major works written upon Barlow's return from Europe, again suggests his lifelong interest in education, educational reform, and a national university. *The Columbiad* was another epic in mock-heroic style—much in the tradition of *The Vision* and much like it in the author's desire to eliminate both feudalism and superstition and to guide men toward "habits" of democratic thinking. But it was a completely revised work. Progress, to be sure, occurred along predetermined lines, but now it was nature's, not God's, design.

In almost all his work Barlow finds the church-state alliance egregious, condemns religion as a priestly concoction, affirms deistic belief in the sublime moral teachings of Jesus, reaffirms the Paine-Jefferson conviction that the earth belongs to the living, with its implication of property redistribution, and maintains a consistent hostility toward all forms of political and social injustice. Unlike Paine and Jefferson, however, Barlow constructed no system. His mind was inquiring rather than systematic. Unlike them, too, he grew more radical, more combative, with age. By the early 1790s he was the paradigm of republican man—tolerant, cosmopolitan, pacifist, humanist—with a vigorous and undefeated faith in deism, Lockean empiricism, Baconian experimentation, natural rights, and democratic polity. See Milton Cantor, "The Life of Joel Barlow," unpublished dissertation (Columbia University, 1954).

MILTON CANTOR

BARNARD, Henry (b. Hartford, Conn., Jan. 24, 1811; d. Hartford, Conn., July 5, 1900), EDUCATOR, graduated from Yale in 1830. After teaching for a year in an academy, he studied law and was admitted to the Connecticut bar in 1834. Following a trip through the southern and western states and in Europe, he was elected in 1836 to the Connecticut General Assembly as a Whig, serving from 1837 to 1839. He successfully sponsored legislation for better school supervision and became secretary of a board set up for that purpose.

Long convinced of the necessity for improving America's public schools, Barnard sought to demonstrate to the public that education was of practical value and also that it was the duty of the commonwealth to support education and make it available to everyone. With this in mind he started the *Connecticut Common School Journal* and founded the first teacher training institutes. Moving to Rhode Island in 1842, he secured the establishment of the Rhode Island Institute of Education in 1845. When Connecticut established its first normal school in 1849, Barnard accepted the dual job of principal and superintendent of schools. During these years he published books on school legislation and on the architecture of public school buildings. There followed a period in which Barnard was, briefly, chancellor of the University of Wisconsin and president of St. John's College. In 1867 he became U.S. commissioner of education, but the administrative nature of the duties did not appeal to him, and he resigned, retiring to his home in Hartford in 1870.

For more than twenty years prior to 1882, Barnard published at irregular intervals the *American Journal of Education,* an encyclopedic compendium of information and viewpoints on public education. From it was adapted a fifty-two-volume *American Library of Schools and Education.* Barnard devoted most of his personal fortune to these publications.

———&⊶———

Henry Barnard was one of the two most eminent and influential educational promoters in 19th-century America; the other was **Horace Mann.** Barnard, unlike Mann, spent his entire adult career encouraging the development of public education, both through his own labor in Connecticut and Rhode Island and elsewhere through his example, advice, and publications. The latter, principally his *Journal,* constitute a unique and massive compendium of educational history and literature. Barnard promoted public education zealously and singlemindedly, sometimes using the techniques of the religious revivalist to rouse apathetic communities, always stressing the introduction of professionalism into education through the training of teachers and the organization of public education into a unified, hierarchical, and ultimately national system. Thus he was an especially apt choice as first U.S. commissioner of education. In contrast to many other schoolmen of his day, Barnard did not advocate completely free education. The payment of some fees directly, he felt, encouraged parents to maintain an active interest in their children's schooling. Barnard's belief in the power of education to solve problems of crime, poverty, and social conflict remained another strong commitment throughout his life. A deeply religious, patriotic, fundamentally conservative man, Barnard did not question existing social and economic structures. Rather, he sought to fashion a school system that would concentrate on moral education. Essentially, he hoped for the reform and regulation of an increasingly urban and industrial society through the formation of personality and the shaping of behavior in a mass public educational system. See Michael B. Katz, *Class, Bureaucracy and Schools: The Illusion of Educational Change in America* (1971).

MICHAEL B. KATZ

BARNUM, Phineas Taylor (b. Bethel, Conn., July 5, 1810; d. Bridgeport, Conn., Apr. 7, 1891), IMPRESARIO, after a grammar school education, edited an anticlerical newspaper, *The Herald of Freedom,* in Danbury, Connecticut, in 1831, but had to stop publication when sued for libel. He moved to New York City in 1834 and the following year presented a show featuring Joice Heth, who pretended to be George Washington's 161-year-old black nurse. After varied business efforts Barnum opened a New York museum in 1842 that featured natural history exhibits and "curiosities," freaks, music, and drama. A particularly successful drawing card was Charles Stratton, a midget billed as "General Tom

Thumb," with whom Barnum toured Europe in 1844. In 1850 he promoted a long concert tour in the United States for Swedish singer Jenny Lind, which was a large financial success.

Barnum served two terms in the Connecticut state legislature (1865–69) as a Republican. He was an unsuccessful candidate for Congress in 1867 but later served as mayor of Bridgeport, Connecticut (1875–76). In 1871, Barnum returned to New York to open "The Greatest Show on Earth," which toured the nation successfully. He changed the circus's means of travel from wagon to railroad. Competition forced Barnum to combine with rival James Anthony Bailey in 1881 to form the Barnum & Bailey circus featuring two, three, and even four rings of activity. In 1882, Barnum imported a huge performing elephant, Jumbo, that soon became the star of the show. Barnum wrote many books, including an autobiography, *The Life of P. T. Barnum* (1st ed., 1855) and *The Humbugs of the World* (1865).

———— ∞∞ ————

P. T. Barnum dubbed himself the "Prince of humbugs." As with most of his claims, Barnum stretched the truth a bit, but he saw to it that he was the best-advertised humbug of the 19th century. And his whole life was to point the moral that democratic truth is whatever the public is led to believe.

Historically, Barnum exists as the persona created in his autobiography, first published in 1855 and issued in revised form every few years thereafter until 1888. The book, like Barnum's career, is a combination of piquant reality and genial fraud welded seamlessly into amusing myth. Barnum often considered making a "curiosity," like the Fejee Mermaid he exhibited, that would "show no seams" where the parts of other realities were joined into a more interesting one. He best succeeded in his own life.

Barnum would certainly be delighted with the way his biographers have repeated his more extravagant claims, none of which is true. He did not introduce entertainment to a grimly practical America of the 1830s; he did not initiate in the 1840s the successful "Museums" that joined nat-ural history exhibits, oddities, plays, and low admission rates; he did not make drama respectable for Americans by labeling his theater a "lecture hall"; he did not introduce classical music in 1850 by adding his megaphone to Jenny Lind's voice; he was not principally responsible for the development of the circus; he made no clear contribution to advertising techniques. What Barnum did do was take advantage of practices and tastes others had developed, use them wittily, and always see to it that his name became attached to them. Barnum's genius lay less in the tricks he used to make money than in his insistence on publicizing his tricks so that no one was ever sure when or why he was lying. He provided entertainment for the masses certainly, but no modern literary figure has made more exquisite art out of the uncertainties of appearance and reality. Barnum's main contribution to the circus was to introduce three rings so that, because of the sheer extent of the activity, spectators had little chance to concentrate on, or be bored by, any single act.

He represented perfect commitment to conventional 19th-century values of what he called "go-aheaditiveness"—progress, moneymaking, boosterism—and genial recognition that humbug ruled the world after all in politics, religion, business, and law as well as show business. Yet he knew cynicism was the greatest of humbugs, and he supported several unpopular causes. He briefly ran an anticlerical newspaper in the 1830s; he was a zealous temperance man; in his brief career as a Connecticut legislator he fought the railroad lobby and ringingly supported black equality and the Fourteenth Amendment. Throughout his life he advocated the creed of the Universalists, whose doctrine of universal salvation, he pointed out, made them the only sect that really "believes in success."

Barnum believed in success, but less than he believed that life's pleasure came in variety and in conning and being conned in an amusing way. He was the cracker-barrel philosopher living in proto-Indian and Gothic palaces in Bridgeport, Connecticut, the Yankee democrat hobnobbing equally with midgets and European royalty, the man of the present willing to buy the best of the past, from Shakespeare's home to the ruins of Pompeii—the "Prince of humbugs" perhaps, but certainly a shrewd retailer of American perplexities and humor. See M. R. Werner, *Barnum* (1923).

DAVID GRIMSTED

BARRYMORE, John (b. Philadelphia, Pa., Feb. 15, 1882; d. Hollywood, Calif., May 29, 1942), ACTOR, made his debut in a small role in Hermann Sudermann's play *Magda* in 1903 in Chicago. His first New York City appearance came in December of that year, at the Savoy theater, in *Glad of It*. During the next six years (1903–9) he played in New York and on tour, but his first major success and his achievement of the status of a "matinee idol" came in 1909 when he appeared in *The Fortune Hunter*, a play by Winchell Smith. During 1909–16 he appeared in a variety of plays, including *Princess Zim Zim* (1911) and *Believe Me, Xantippe* (1913), as well as in a number of silent films, including *An American Citizen* (1913). Although at first noted only for his handsome profile and his charming stage personality, he soon acquired an effective satirical humor that broadened his range. In 1916, however, when he appeared in Galsworthy's play *Justice*, he began the remodeling of his image, a process that continued with his appearance in *The Jest* (1919) and that culminated in his performances in *Richard III* (1920) and in *Hamlet* (1922). After a successful New York City engagement in this last role, he toured the United States (1923–24) with his version of the play and then took it to London (1925), where he was once again received with wide acclaim. Soon after these triumphs he began to concentrate on the movies. He starred in a number of silent films, such as *Don Juan* (1926), and then in a wide variety of "talkies," including *Twentieth Century* (1934), *Topaze* (1933), and *Grand Hotel* (1932).

In 1939, Barrymore made a brief return to the theater, starring in *My Dear Children*, a comedy by Catherine Turney and Jerry Horwin, which played in New York City after a nationwide tour. He had long been a heavy drinker and in 1935

had tried a Hindu massage-herb "cure." During the tour of *My Dear Children* he drew large crowds to the theater, but these were spectators intent on the comedy of John Barrymore adlibbing on the stage. This was his last stage appearance, and he returned to Hollywood to play in *The Great Profile* (1940), a film produced by Darryl F. Zanuck, and in a Paramount picture, *The Invisible Woman* (1941).

⊷≫≪≪⊶

Applause for the versatile actor John Barrymore will continue to ring for generations. Whether he was a clown or a meditative sufferer sounding the depths of a troubled heart, his handsome profile, expressive hands, and eloquent voice made him an instrument of beauty.

In early life he tried art and journalism, but the theater, inherent in his blood, soon enticed him. Maurice Barrymore and Georgianna Drew, his parents, faced the footlights while their children, Ethel, Lionel, and John, lived in Philadelphia with their grandmother Louise Drew, who managed the Arch Street theater.

On stage Maurice Barrymore was witty and charming, a dynamic Adonis. His son John was like him. Both father and son seemed forever seeking something; they drove themselves toward perfection. John loved rehearsals as opportunities to grow. Often he went to first rehearsals with all lines perfectly memorized. Supreme success came with his great roles, after years of growth, through portrayal of characters as vastly different as Dr. Jekyll and Mr. Hyde, Sherlock Holmes, Captain Ahab, Peter Ibbetson, Beau Brummell, Don Juan, and Hamlet. And with each part he cut neatly and deeply into the consciousness of the most sluggish audience. After voice training and mind-stretching study he reached his zenith as Hamlet. His Hamlet was different on different nights, yet always meditative, always sincere, always Freudian—and most of all always masterfully portrayed.

His life's work includes parts in at least thirty-two stage plays and fifty-two movies. Hollywood paid him fabulous money. At first he had a reputation for modesty, yet his complex character had shed chameleon colors everywhere. He was a heavy drinker, a wild spender, a marital failure (his wives were Katherine Harris, Michael Strange, Dolores Costello, and Elaine Barrie). Miss Costello, a charming girl and one he loved deeply, tried too hard to entice him away from alcohol. Neither she nor the cure he took from a Hindu doctor completely succeeded. Dissipation and overwork led to cirrhosis of the liver and other complications that caused his death about six years later.

At 53 the great Barrymore was fighting an amnesialike experience that led him to forget his lines. In one picture fifty-six takes were made in one day before this desperate, determined man gave up for the day, only to return the next day to complete the scene. When, partially recovered, he later returned to the stage, to movie parts, and to radio, no one expected him to follow the scripts.

John Barrymore was a paradox, a contradiction—a score of men. One of them was the masterful dramatic actor, portraying the tragic words of great minds. Another was the gay wit, mocking himself, making people laugh and forget their troubles. In this role he concluded his memorable career. See Margot Peters, *The House of Barrymore* (1990).

THOMAS E. CHENEY

BARTON, Bruce (b. Robbins, Tenn., Aug. 5, 1886; d. New York, N.Y., July 5, 1967), ADVERTISING EXECUTIVE, WRITER, attended Berea College and graduated from Amherst in 1907. Between 1910 and 1918 he edited two small family magazines and managed publicity for the United War Work campaign. In 1919 he helped form an advertising agency in New York that in ten years became the firm of Batten, Barton, Durstine, and Osborne. His most famous advertising campaigns were for General Mills (he invented Betty Crocker), Cluett Peabody collars, Gillette shaving cream, U.S. Steel, General Electric, and the Harvard Classics. Barton was generally considered a dominant force in advertising, and at his retirement as the firm's board chairman in 1961 BBD&O was the fourth largest

agency in the nation, with annual billings of $300 million.

Barton also became a popular writer on topics related to the search for personal success. Over a fifty-year period he contributed hundreds of articles and syndicated columns to *Redbook, McCall's, Collier's, American Magazine,* and *Reader's Digest.* Best known were his two books, *The Man Nobody Knows* (1925) and *The Book Nobody Knows* (1926), presenting the ministry of Jesus and the Bible as worth the attention of modern men and women who desire to improve their lives and the effectiveness of their social behavior. For two years *The Man Nobody Knows* headed the best-seller lists; forty years later it was still in print with sales exceeding 700,000 copies. From 1919 through 1940, Barton served as a publicist for and adviser to the Republican Party and its presidential candidates. First appointed, then elected, congressman from New York City (1937–41), he was named in a poll of national correspondents as one of the ten ablest legislators in Washington. He ran as a Republican candidate for senator in 1940, losing to James Mead, a New Deal incumbent from upstate New York. Barton returned to his advertising work until 1961 and continued until his death to write inspirational articles for mass magazines.

In his triple career as advertising man, popular writer, and publicist for the Republican Party Barton came to embody for a generation of historians and social commentators those middle-class values that (they asserted) had dominated America in the twenties but that the depression exposed as obsolete, shallow if not meretricious, and destructive of liberal ideals. But it is possible that Barton's critics have misjudged his politics and his writing and so have missed the significance of his career and the temper of his times. Franklin Roosevelt's speechwriters were pleased at how effectively during the 1940 campaign their famous slogan "Martin, Barton, and Fish!" stamped as a political reactionary a publicist who had once written articles on behalf of Calvin Coolidge and who in 1939 had voted, as did most

Republicans in Congress, against repeal of the arms embargo. The slogan was clever trickery, for Barton, called in as a professional to improve the party's image, had been urging forcefully that Republicans broaden their appeal to reach the workingman and the average voter and try to outdo the Democrats in defending liberal principles. Indeed, in 1940, he helped secure the Republican nomination for **Wendell Willkie.** Sophisticated readers found morally obtuse, even silly, a book which appeared to say that Jesus was at heart an adman and a sales executive. Yet despite a number of ludicrous passages (which Barton omitted or modified in a later edition), *The Man Nobody Knows* was fundamentally critical of the commercial ethos of the day. Its principal thrust was to urge business-minded Americans, concerned with success, to model their lives on a man who, Barton insisted, exemplified humaneness, sociability, service to others, the leadership to inspire ordinary people to rise above themselves, a capacity to love everyone as persons but to tolerate in no one hypocrisy, cruelty, or misuse of power, and the courage to defend one's beliefs and, if necessary, die for them that others might be saved.

This was in a sense the creed of the progressive reformers who were attempting to reshape the American social and political system during Barton's lifetime. Personally charming and urbane, Barton rejected for himself the role of reformer. In an age of mass media and mass persuasion his craft was with words, and he seemed to prefer to persuade others to act on beliefs than to act on them himself; yet few men in business life revealed in writing more of their own values. Barton insisted that advertising and mass media should educate men and women to produce and consume more and so to realize a better life, to perceive so intensively the horror and the cost of hunger, disease, poverty, and war that they would eventually put an end to them. It was characteristic of him to compose a General Electric advertisement in the twenties that stated, "Any woman who does anything which a little electric motor can do is working for 3¢ an hour!" It was a commercially inspired sentence, but it mirrored progressive doctrine. It was equally characteristic that during World War I, Barton volunteered to Evangeline Booth a phrase that became the unofficial slogan for the Salvation Army: "A man may be down, but he's never out," and that looking back much later on the millions of words he wrote, he wanted to think that those were "the most enduring." Barton believed in material progress, in self-improvement, in individualism, and in the Judeo-Christian ethic, and none of the profound crises through which his generation lived appreciably changed the tenor of his writings or their capacity to reflect what masses of Americans, optimists in the progressive tradition, apparently continued to want to hear. See Bruce Barton, *The Man Nobody Knows* (1925).

OTIS PEASE

BARTON, Clara (Clarissa Harlowe) (b. N. Oxford, Mass., Dec. 25, 1821; d. Glen Echo, Md., Apr. 12, 1912), NURSE, REFORMER, began teaching at the age of 16. In 1851, after completing a course at the Liberal Institute (Clinton, N.Y.), she organized and briefly headed a free school in Bordentown, New Jersey. Two years later she became a copyist in the U.S. Patent Office.

At the outset of the Civil War, Barton provided both nursing care and supplies for those in the Sixth Massachusetts Regiment who were wounded during the Baltimore riot (April 1861). She also organized a parcel post service for soldiers that was maintained throughout the war and provided nursing aid and supplies at the battles of Antietam (at her own expense), Fredericksburg, the siege of Charleston, and the Wilderness campaign. She later became superintendent of nurses in General **B. F. Butler**'s army (June 1864). In 1865 she headed a search for missing soldiers and that year identified more than 90 percent of the graves at Andersonville, Georgia, which she helped to establish as a national cemetery.

In the following years Barton served in military hospitals and distributed supplies during the Franco-Prussian War. Returning to America, she successfully campaigned for ratification of the 1864 Geneva Convention, and in 1882, America joined the International Red Cross, Barton herself having founded the American Red Cross Society in 1881; three years later, as American delegate to the Red Cross conference in Geneva, she secured the adoption of an amendment that authorized the provision of Red Cross relief during peacetime calamities. As president of the American Red Cross (1882–1904) she organized and often led relief expeditions to areas devastated by floods and hurricanes. She served as president of both the National First Aid Association (1905–12) and the Children's Star League. She published several books and pamphlets on the history and aims of the Red Cross as well as an autobiography, *The Story of My Childhood* (1907).

Clara Barton literally hewed out her own career from unpromising materials. Although legend made her a founder of the great U.S. Sanitary Commission, which serviced Civil War troops, she had little connection with it. She was essentially a supplier of provisions, which she independently solicited and distributed in the front lines while also ministering to soldiers as occasion permitted. Following the war she helped build her own reputation through public lectures until her voice gave out in 1868. Her need to work and also to lead resulted in crises of illness that she overcame as she made new plans and connections. Need for rest and a change took her to Europe in 1869; the next year she involved herself in the Franco-Prussian War. Her outstanding innovation was to set up work systems in French cities where needy women could sew, producing necessary clothing in exchange for food.

The manner in which she personally directed the American Red Cross was phenomenal. Her *Red Cross in Peace and War* (1898), published when she was close to 80 years old, described travels and administration in the midst of floods, wars, and pestilence that would have been wearing on a much younger body and mind. Barton was naïve in her satisfaction over the many honors and medals accorded her, but there can be no doubt that she brought comfort and hope to numerous people, from Charleston, South Carolina, where in 1882 an earthquake occurred, to Galveston, Texas in 1900 when a tidal wave struck the city; as well as in Russia and Turkey, which endured other disasters.

Nevertheless, by 1900, Barton drew criticism because of her arbitrary rule of the American Red Cross in an increasingly complex society. Reluctantly, she resigned in 1904. However, her worldwide fame continued to underscore the unique quality of her achievement. See Ishbel Ross, *Angel of the Battlefield* (1956).

LOUIS FILLER

BARUCH, Bernard Mannes (b. Camden, S.C., Aug. 19, 1870; d. New York, N.Y., June 20, 1965), FINANCIER, graduated from the City College of New York in 1889. He became an office boy for the brokerage firm of A. A. Housman in 1891, studied law and finance, and became a securities expert. Named a partner in 1896, he profitably invested in the sugar market in 1897 and became one of Wall Street's most successful speculators. A millionaire at 30, Baruch left Housman in 1903 to establish his own industrial development firm. During the next fourteen years he invested for himself and others in rubber plantations in Mexico and other profitable raw material production ventures throughout the world.

An active Democrat, Baruch was a close friend of and adviser to Woodrow Wilson; he frequently visited the White House after Wilson became president. He was appointed to the President's Advisory Commission, Council of National Defense, in 1916. After American entry into World War I, Baruch was chairman of the committee on raw materials, minerals, and metals, and a member of the commission in charge of purchases for the Allies. As chairman of the War Industries Board (1918), Baruch carried out a master plan of industrial mobilization. He accompanied President Wilson to the Versailles Conference as an economic adviser, serving as chairman of the raw materials division, Supreme Economic Council, and as delegate to the committee on economic reparations. He was also a member of the President's Conference on Capital and Labor (Oct. 1919). During the 1920s Baruch became interested in improving agricultural efficiency. He was a member of President Harding's Agricultural Conference in 1922; he advised farm organizations and gave money (1925) to aid cotton-growing areas of South Carolina that had been ravaged by boll weevils. After the Wall Street crash (1929), from which he emerged unscathed, Baruch advised President Hoover on the formation of the Reconstruction Finance Corporation (1932) but refused a position on that body. During the New Deal he was an unofficial adviser to Franklin D. Roosevelt. He turned down the secretaryship of the Treasury and served in an official capacity only in 1933 as vice-chairman of the National Transportation Committee. Having advised preparation for war as early as 1934, Baruch made numerous suggestions for mobilization plans in 1941. In 1942 he was chairman of Roosevelt's special committee investigating the rubber shortage (his "office" was a park bench near the White House). During 1943–45 he was adviser to **James F. Byrnes,** director of mobilization. President Truman appointed Baruch U.S. representative to the United Nations Atomic Energy Commission in March 1946: in December Baruch presented a plan for international control of atomic energy. The Commission approved the Baruch Plan, but the U.S.S.R. vetoed it in the Security Council. Baruch broke with Truman over the president's opposition to price control in 1949, but until his death he continued to advise presidents unofficially, especially Dwight D. Eisenhower, on domestic and foreign policy. He wrote *Baruch: My Own Story* (1957) and *Baruch: The Public Years* (1960) besides various official reports.

Bernard Baruch's success story is the embodiment of a folk myth—a young man who came out of the South to conquer the city and attain all his dreams of wealth and fame. Because of the myth of his great wealth—vastly exaggerated—he amassed the reality of power. Because of the legend that he was the adviser to presidents, he exercised a very real influence on Capitol Hill. He emerged finally as "the Park Bench statesman," a kind of unofficial adviser to middle America. "He does it with mirrors," a bemused contemporary declared.

He was a super-American in an era when patriotism was still fashionable. "Here's this wonderful country," he exclaimed, "and look what it's done for me." Yet he mused, not without bitterness, "I could have been president of the United States if I had not been a Jew." Perhaps. The dream ended when, as the nation's most conspicuous and powerful Jew, he was on the receiving end of **Henry Ford**'s bitter anti-Semitic attacks in the 1920s. Yet, as one who felt himself to be "not primarily a Jew but an American," he affronted many of his fellow Jews. He was too conservative for the liberals, not religious enough for the Orthodox; he preferred sports to books and cast a dubious eye on Israel. He gave as generously to Catholic charities as to Jewish ones. "Aren't you ever going to do anything for your people?" a critic demanded. "You're damned right I am," he responded. "They're the American people."

Baruch's love affair with the public lasted to the end of his long life; in his eighty-first year he was cheered for minutes in a New York theater. Yet as a public man he never held elective office, and his only real experience with responsible power came when he mobilized industrial America while chairman of the War Industries Board under Woodrow Wilson. He rejected a similar post under Franklin Roosevelt, satisfying himself as adviser to the "assistant president," James F. Byrnes. Always, he was too much the egotist to damage his legend by actually exercising official power. See Margaret L. Coit, *Mr. Baruch: The Man, the Myth, the Eighty Years* (1957).

MARGARET L. COIT

BEARD, Charles Austin (b. Knightstown, Ind., Nov. 27, 1874; d. New Haven, Conn., Sept. 1,

1948), HISTORIAN, ran a newspaper in Knightstown, with his older brother Clarence (1891–95) before entering DePauw University. Earning his PhB in 1898, Beard spent the next two years studying at Oxford where he helped found the Labour (later Ruskin) College in 1899. He also made speaking tours on industrial reform for the Labour Party and wrote articles on this topic. After teaching at Cornell (1899–1900) and then spending two more years in England, Beard enrolled in 1902 at Columbia University; he received an MA in 1903 and a PhD in political science in 1904. His dissertation was titled "The Office of Justice of Peace in England in Its Origin and Development." He became adjunct professor of politics at Columbia in 1907, associate professor in 1910, and professor in 1915.

Having previously written eight books on politics and European history, such as *The Industrial Revolution* (1901) and *Introduction to the English Historians* (1906), Beard published *An Economic Interpretation of the Constitution of the United States* in 1913. In this work he attempted to identify and describe those groups that successfully united and overcame opposition to the making of the new Constitution of 1787. Beard followed this work with *Economic Origins of Jeffersonian Democracy* (1915), using similar ideas. Both books were respectfully received in academic circles but strongly criticized by many because of their insistence that the founding fathers were influenced by material gain. Beard resigned his position at Columbia in 1917 in protest over the dismissal of two professors, J. McKeen Cattell and Henry Wadsworth Longfellow Dana, because of their opposition to U.S. entry into World War I. He served as director of New York City's Training School for Public Service (1917–22) and helped organize the New School for Social Research in New York in 1918.

Beard spent the remainder of his life traveling and writing extensively. He wrote for such magazines as the *New Republic, Harper's,* and *Scribner's,* and published numerous books, including the critically acclaimed *Rise of American Civilization* (2 vols., 1927), which he wrote with his wife **Mary**. He rejoined Columbia's faculty in

1939 as a visiting professor of government and became a professor of American history at Johns Hopkins University in 1940. Although he supported most New Deal domestic policies, Beard opposed Roosevelt's foreign policy, especially Lend-Lease, peacetime conscription, and other military-preparedness ideas. He argued for "American continentalism," the belief that the United States could and should stay out of European and Asian affairs; he opposed attempts to revise the Neutrality Acts. After the war Beard published *American Foreign Policy in the Making, 1932–1940* (1946) and *President Roosevelt and the Coming of War, 1941* (1948), which accused Roosevelt of leading the country into war by subterfuge. Some of Beard's other books include *The Idea of National Interest* (1934) and *America in Midpassage* (1939).

Nominally a political scientist, and without academic employment during the years when he was at the height of his powers, Beard may have had more influence on the writing of American history than any other single person. His chief contributions were in three areas: the interpretation of the adoption of the Constitution; the analysis of the Civil War and its causes; and the understanding of twentieth-century American foreign policy.

In *An Economic Interpretation of the Constitution of the United States* (1913), Beard sought a "removal of the Constitution from the realm of pure political ethics and its establishment in the dusty way of earthly strife and common economic endeavor." He had discovered in the records of the U.S. Treasury accounts that showed the personal holdings of government securities by the members of the convention that drafted the Constitution. Listing these findings and recalling that the value of government securities increased considerably when the Constitution was adopted, Beard suggested that the founding fathers had been personally interested in the success of their work. He presented George Washington as a businessman with vast western landholdings in addition to government securities and argued that the fathers generally had "personal posses-sions" which led them to consider the "advan-tages which the beneficiaries expected would accrue to themselves first."

As Beard saw it, the Constitution was promot-ed by well-to-do possessors of liquid capital, which he called "personalty," and opposed by possessors of "realty," or land. Small farmers, although numerically a majority, were no match for the **Hamilton**s, Madisons, or **Jay**s in political management. Moreover, for fear of offending the majority of the voters, the Constitution contained no property qualification for the suffrage; instead it artfully concealed in innocuous verbiage a series of devices intended to keep government firmly in the hands of the rich. Hence an unde-mocratic Constitution was adopted.

In *The Rise of American Civilization* (1927), Beard and his wife presented an essentially simi-lar view of the Civil War. Indeed, they termed the Civil War a "second American Revolution," by means of which northern capitalists (again the holders of "personalty") used the national gov-ernment to establish their supremacy over south-ern plantation owners. Beard had done little research in the Civil War period, but he sketched this conception so convincingly that it has remained the view to be refuted among histori-ans to this day.

During the 1930s and 1940s, as the United States moved into and through World War II, Beard turned his attention to the economic inter-pretation of foreign policy. His attempt to show that President Roosevelt had considerable responsibility for the outbreak of war with Japan earned him a second period of exile and neglect among professional historians. But his broader thesis that American foreign policy is based on the premise that overseas economic expansion is required to prevent domestic economic collapse has been developed by William Appleman Williams and other students, and is the single most challenging critique of recent American for-eign policy.

There can be no doubt that Beard argued for an economic interpretation in a muckraking manner influenced by the pre–World War I Progressive movement. The question posed by his work is whether this too narrow and too per-sonal style of economic interpretation should lead us to broaden an economic interpretation or to abandon it altogether. See Lee Benson, *Turner and Beard: American Historical Writing Reconsidered* (1960).

STAUGHTON LYND

BEARD, Mary Ritter (b. Indianapolis, Ind., Aug. 5, 1876; d. Phoenix, Ariz., Aug. 14, 1958), REFORMER, HISTORIAN, was the third of six children of Eli Foster Ritter, a lawyer, and Narcissa Lockwood, a schoolteacher. She grew up in a comfortable, upper-middle-class, conser-vative community strongly influenced by the Methodist Church. In 1893 at the age of 16, Mary entered DePauw University, her father's alma mater, where she met her future husband, **Charles Beard.** After graduating in 1897, she taught high school in Greencastle, Indiana. In 1900 she and Charles Beard married, and she went with him to England where he was study-ing at Oxford. There, while Charles was involved in establishing Ruskin Hall, a working-class men's college, Mary discovered the militant woman's suffrage movement. They returned to New York in 1902 where Mary started graduate school at Columbia. She dropped out in 1904 before getting a degree to devote most of her energies to being a wife and mother of two chil-dren, a daughter, Miriam (b. 1902), and a son, William (b. 1907). But she also became active in the suffragist and trade union movements. In 1910 she was named editor of the *Woman Voter*, the official voice of the Woman Suffrage Party of New York. Particularly interested in working-class women's concerns, Beard opposed the Equal Rights Amendment then being pushed by some activists in the women's movement. Her opposition to ERA was based on the grounds that its passage would eliminate hard-won protective labor legislation applying to women who worked in factories and other manual jobs.

Beard remained active in a variety of progres-sive causes dealing with women and labor, but around 1915 she began to concentrate on writing and scholarship. Between 1915 and 1933 she published numerous works geared especially to throwing light on the role of women in history. Among her books during this period were *Women's Work in Municipalities* (1915), *A Short History of the American Labor Movement* (1920), *The Rise of American Civilization* (1927), which she co-authored with her husband, *On Understanding Women* (1931), and *America Through Women's Eyes* (1933). In 1936 she was the dominant force in establishing the World Center for Women's Archives in New York, founded for the purpose of preserving women's history. She chose as the Center's motto, "No documents, no history," a saying attributed to the French historian Fustel de Coulanges. This groundbreaking project started well, but because of inadequate funding it disbanded in 1940. In 1946, Beard published perhaps her most important historical work, *Women as Force in History: A Study in Traditions and Realities*.

In all of her writings, but particularly in *Women as Force in History* (1946), Mary Beard prefigured many of the themes and ideas that women's historians and feminists of later generations would take up and focus on. In that pioneering book, written when she was 70 years old, Beard analyzed the influence of *Blackstone's Commentaries* on women's lives. According to Beard, it contained mistaken interpretations based on a misunderstanding of the status of women in English common law. From that starting point Beard outlined in forceful yet dispassionate prose women's impact on history throughout the ages.

Mary Beard devoted her life to the preservation of women's place in history. She believed, as did few others of her time, that women were not absent from history but rather had been "penned out" by historians. She strove through her writings and research to reinsert women into history and to awaken humanity to women's enduring historical role. This is perhaps why her writings have not been more accepted by some modern-day feminists, especially those who favor an oppression versus instrumentality analysis of the role of women in history. Beard rejected the kind of history and feminism that portrayed women as oppressed victims of a male-dominated society. Rather, Beard argued, women were always "a continuous force" in history and not merely objects of oppression. Her life's goal, reflected in *On Understanding Women* (1931), was to make readers and historians aware that "women have always been alive to everything that was going on in the world. They always will be." To Beard, women were ever-present and active throughout history as the essential nurturers and preservers of culture. In her life and her work Mary Beard was living proof of this truth. See Nancy E. Cott, ed., *A Woman Making History: Mary Ritter Beard Through Her Letters* (1991)

AMY MAHONEY

BEAUMONT, William (b. Lebanon, Conn., Nov. 21, 1785; d. St. Louis, Mo., Apr. 25, 1853), PHYSICIAN, taught school and read medicine in Champlain, New York. He became an apprentice to Dr. Benjamin Chandler of St. Albans, Vermont, in 1810 and was licensed to practice medicine in 1812. When the War of 1812 broke out, he was commissioned as a surgeon's mate in the U.S. Sixth Infantry at Plattsburg, New York, and participated in the battles of York (Apr. 1813) and Niagara (July 1814), and in the siege of Plattsburg (Sept. 1814). In 1815, Beaumont established a practice in Plattsburg but reenlisted in 1820 and was sent to Fort Mackinac, Michigan, as post surgeon. There, in June 1822, he treated a young Canadian trapper, Alexis St. Martin, who had been accidentally shot in the stomach. A permanent opening, or fistula, covered by a flap of the inner coat of the stomach, developed; when pushed back, the flap exposed the interior of the stomach. In 1825, Beaumont began using this fistula for a scientific study of the stomach. He carefully observed the chemical nature of digestion, secretions, gastric juices, and various rates of digestion.

After St. Martin returned to Canada,

Beaumont was stationed at Fort Niagara (1825–26), Fort Howard on Green Bay (1826–28), and Fort Crawford on the upper Mississippi (1828–32). Contacting St. Martin again in 1829, he continued his experiments (1829–31) and then obtained a furlough for work in Washington, D.C. (1832–34). He published a scientifically acclaimed book on his work, *Experiments and Observations on the Gastric Juice and the Physiology of Digestion* (1833) after having sent gastric juice samples to leading chemists, including **Benjamin Silliman** of Yale, for analysis. Ordered to the Jefferson Barracks near St. Louis in 1834, Beaumont was later transferred to St. Louis where he also engaged in private practice. He resigned from the army in 1840 and spent the rest of his life in private practice in St. Louis, publishing a second edition of his book in 1847.

—⚬⚬⚬—

The romantic image of Beaumont as a "frontier physiologist" has been somewhat overdrawn, for despite his lack of formal training in physiology and his isolation at various military outposts, he had access to current literature on digestion as well as to advice from men more knowledgeable than himself. As a result his observations on digestion in his patient St. Martin were not merely of a random, common-sense character but were also conceived with a degree of sophistication for the precise purpose of settling some fundamental points of controversy.

The work of Lazzaro Spallanzani in the 18th century had strongly suggested that digestion is carried out largely by the solvent action of the gastric fluids, but there continued to be serious doubts about this theory, largely because of the difficulty of obtaining and identifying physiologically active gastric secretions. Thus through the first third of the 19th century controversy persisted between the proponents of the gastric juice theory and those who held that digestion is due chiefly to the direct and peculiarly vital action of the stomach lining on the food. Once Beaumont had become aware of this dispute, he took full advantage of the fistula in St. Martin to study the powers and properties of the gastric juice, which he was able to obtain quite easily by inserting a tube through the fistula. Most important, he repeatedly demonstrated that the gastric fluids have a solvent effect on food outside the stomach that is identical with the effect of digestion within the stomach. Thus, in the view of Johannes Müller, the leading physiologist of the age, Beaumont's work conclusively established that the gastric juice is indeed the principal agent in gastric digestion. Beaumont also confirmed that the acid secreted by the stomach is the hydrochloric, and he reported many other detailed observations on the action of the stomach.

Beaumont shrewdly recognized not only the scientific importance of his investigations but also their potential for bringing him a certain measure of renown. Thus, although he sought and obtained the advice and assistance of Robley Dunglison, the most eminent American physiologist, he rather bluntly informed him that he wished to avoid too close an association, which might require sharing credit for the work. After the publication of his book he tried, without success, to obtain reimbursement from Congress for his efforts. See Jerome J. Bylebyl, "William Beaumont, Robley Dunglison, and the 'Philadelphia Physiologists,'" *Journal of the History of Medicine and Allied Sciences*, XXV (1970), 3–21.

JEROME J. BYLEBYL

BEAUREGARD, Pierre Gustave Toutant (b. St. Bernard Parish, La., May 28, 1818; d. New Orleans, La., Feb. 20, 1893), MILITARY LEADER, graduated second in his class from West Point in 1838. After serving with the Engineer Corps, primarily in Louisiana, he participated in the Mexican War (1846). As a member of General **Winfield Scott**'s staff, he saw action at Tampico, the siege of Vera Cruz, Cerro Gordo, Contreras, Chapultepec, and Mexico City. He was brevetted for his conduct at Contreras (Aug. 1847) and at Mexico City (Sept. 1847) where he was wounded twice. After the war Beauregard served with the Engineers in New Orleans, Mobile, and other points in the South. He was promoted to captain in 1853 and was named superintendent of the U.S. Military Academy in 1860. He held that post only briefly, however, and resigned from the army in February 1861 to join the Confederate cause. Appointed brigadier general on March 1, 1861, Beauregard launched the first military action of the Civil War when he ordered the successful bombardment of Fort Sumter, April 12, 1861. Beauregard attained the rank of general after he was second in command to **Joseph E. Johnston** at First Bull Run (Manassas) in July 1861. In April 1862 he led the Confederate forces at Shiloh after General A. S. Johnston had been killed. Forced to retreat, he fortified Corinth, Mississippi, but then skillfully retreated again when **H. W. Halleck** advanced on the city. In June 1862 illness forced Beauregard to relinquish his command to General Braxton Bragg, but he returned the following year to command the defense of the Georgia and South Carolina coasts. He successfully withstood the siege of Charleston (1863–64). In the spring of 1864, Beauregard defeated General **Benjamin Butler** at Drury's Bluff. In mid-June he held Petersburg against Grant's strong Federal advance, perhaps preventing the capture of Richmond. In October 1864 he assumed command of the Military Division of the West, largely an advisory post. During the closing months of the war he served on the south Atlantic coast and joined J. E. Johnston as second in command of the Carolina campaign.

After the war Beauregard was president of the New Orleans, Jackson and Great Northern Railroad (1866–67) and later adjutant general of Louisiana and manager of the Louisiana lottery. In 1888 he was appointed commissioner of public works of the city of New Orleans. He wrote several books and articles on Civil War subjects, including *A Report on the Defence of Charleston* (1864) and *A Commentary on the Campaign and Battle of Manassas* (1891).

Known as "Napoleon in Gray" and "the Great Creole," Beauregard brought a Gallic flair to the Confederate corps of generals. From his somewhat diminutive size and extravagant mannerisms to his grandiose plans, he reflected his French idol. But in effect he was a pale shadow of the original Napoleon. Contentious and argumentative, the dashing Beauregard could dream up flamboyant plans for leading victorious Confederates clear to the Ohio River. This often impractical daydreaming undoubtedly lowered his effectiveness as an offensive commander; it was as a defensive general that Beauregard was at his best.

His defense at Corinth in 1862, of the south Atlantic coasts, and especially his masterful campaigns in 1864 at Bermuda Hundred and before Petersburg were his outstanding moments as a general. After containing Butler south of the James River, Beauregard, with a very small force, withstood the heavy assaults of Grant's army in mid-June 1864 until **Robert E. Lee** came south of Richmond with the Army of Northern Virginia. When pressed by the enemy, he rose to the challenge and met the foe with a stubborn desperation that was not to be denied. Some credit him with temporarily saving Petersburg and even the Confederate capital at Richmond.

One of the major deficiencies in Beauregard's character was his inability to get along with his superiors, including Confederate President **Jefferson Davis.** His biographer, T. Harry Williams, maintains he would have developed into a very good field commander if given the chance, but Beauregard cannot be rated with the great captains of the Civil War. He was second echelon but a valuable man to have in command in a tight spot. See T. Harry Williams, *P. G. T. Beauregard: Napoleon in Gray* (1954).

E. B. LONG

BECHET, Sidney (b. New Orleans, La., May 14, 1897[?]; d. Paris, France, May 14, 1959), MUSICIAN, started playing clarinet at 6 and studied with New Orleans clarinetist George Baquet. About 1908 he began performing with New Orleans bands. He toured Texas and other southern states with Clarence Williams's band

(1915–16). Returning to New Orleans in 1916, Bechet joined King Oliver's Olympia Band, toured with it, and then moved to Chicago. Moving to New York City in 1918, he joined Will Marion Cook's Southern Syncopated Orchestra and toured England and the Continent in 1918–19. After playing with Bennie Peyton's band in Paris, Bechet returned to New York in 1921. He played less clarinet and more soprano saxophone in this period, being one of the first jazz musicians to use this instrument extensively and recording such songs as "Wildcat Blues" (1923) and "Kansas City Man Blues" (1923). Bechet briefly played with **Duke Ellington** (1925) before touring Europe and Russia with the Revue Nègre (1925–28). Between 1928 and 1938, Bechet played with Noble Sissle's band in Paris and New York. After 1938 he led several small American groups.

In 1946, Bechet appeared as both an actor and musician in *Hear That Trumpet* on Broadway. He settled in Paris in 1949, returning to the United States only for brief visits in 1951 and 1953. His composition "Petite Fleur" (1952) was popular in both France and the United States, and his ballet score *La Nuit est une Sorcière* (1953) was performed in the Paris Conservatory. He led a sextet at the 1958 Brussels World Fair.

———— ∞ ————

Sidney Bechet was one of the handful of jazz musicians whom Duke Ellington named "the great inimitables," and of the many talented players who came out of New Orleans he was second only to **Louis Armstrong** in terms of virtuosity and invention. Although he was a superb clarinetist, when he discovered the soprano saxophone he found an instrument even better suited to his personality. On it, he produced a big tone that dominated any ensemble as surely as if he had been playing trumpet. From first to last, his style scarcely varied in its drive and sweeping lyricism. Few jazz musicians could keep up with him, and many were overwhelmed by his unbridled power and constant flow of ideas. It is doubtful whether he ever fully subscribed to the doctrine of New Orleans collective improvisation

with its fixed roles for trumpet, trombone, and reed instrument. The broad vibrato, which was a striking and emotionally expressive characteristic of his playing, came to be regarded as old-fashioned during the 1930s, jazz being always subject to unpredictable vagaries of fashion. With the return to favor of the original New Orleans idiom at the end of that decade, Bechet's exceptional gifts were again recognized at their true worth, not least in France where he spent his last years in honor and security. Of musicians inspired by him, the most notable was Johnny Hodges, who played both alto and soprano saxophones in Duke Ellington's band. Bechet wrote many attractive themes, but "Petite Fleur" was his only composition to achieve significant commercial success. See Sidney Bechet, *Treat It Gentle* (1960).

STANLEY DANCE

BEECHER, Henry Ward (b. Litchfield, Conn., June 24, 1813; d. Brooklyn, N.Y., Mar. 8, 1887), RELIGIOUS LEADER, graduated from Amherst College in 1834. He studied at Lane Theological Seminary in Cincinnati, where his father, Lyman, was president, and was ordained in 1837 by the New School Presbytery of Cincinnati. In 1839 he became minister of the Second Presbyterian Church of Indianapolis, and in 1847 he accepted the pulpit of the newly formed Plymouth Church of Brooklyn (Congregationalist) where he remained until his death.

At the Plymouth Church Beecher won fame as one of the greatest orators of his day. His emotional, florid style attracted an average of 2,500 persons a week at the church. He discussed important political and social questions both in the church and in the *Independent*, a Congregational journal he edited, and the *Christian Union*, which he founded. He opposed slavery and counseled disobedience to the fugitive slave law, although he opposed radical abolitionism. He supported **John C. Frémont** for president in 1856 and Abraham Lincoln in 1860. During the Civil War, Beecher urged vigorous prosecution of the military effort against the

South. He made a trip to Great Britain in 1863, arguing the northern point of view. But after the war Beecher supported President Andrew Johnson and a moderate Reconstruction policy toward the South. Joining a number of journalists, intellectuals, and businessmen, Beecher sought to improve the tone of American politics, which he had come to regard as increasingly corrupt. As was the case with the other "best men" he associated with, Beecher firmly believed in laissez-faire economics and disapproved of labor unions, which he considered instruments of despotism. He was a staunch Darwinian and supporter of scientific biblical criticism.

In 1874 scandal marred Beecher's career when a colleague on the *Independent,* Theodore Tilton, accused him of having committed adultery with Tilton's wife. The jury failed to reach a verdict, and the case was dropped. Beecher subsequently was exonerated by his Congregationalist colleagues and continued preaching, traveling, and writing until his death. His major publications include *Evolution and Religion* (1885), *Yale Lectures on Preaching* (1872–74), and *Life of Jesus the Christ* (1871–91), completed by his son W. C. Beecher and his son-in-law Samuel Scoville.

—————◦◦◦—————

Beecher in his lifetime experienced the travails as well as glories of having become a public institution, and later interpreters have tended to evaluate him less as a man and preacher than as a symbol of American Victorianism. Though a theological rebel and on some points a social radical, Beecher did reflect many of the central values of a middle-class culture that he, like most Americans of whatever social level, considered normative. Yet such representativeness was scarcely remarkable in a popular preacher and lecturer, and did not constitute his distinctiveness. What gave Beecher his place in American history were highly unusual oratorical and, in a special way, pastoral abilities.

Photographs of the elderly Beecher suggest physical softness and possibly sanctimoniousness, but the man in his prime had projected quite different qualities: physical strength, robust health, and a temperament marked more by romantic ebullience than by complacent piety or censoriousness. His sermonic style was earthy and humorous, his method of address extemporaneous, his voice noted for effective variation rather than sonority. Unlike Phillips Brooks, Beecher believed ministers should speak out on all public questions, and his sermons and lectures were therefore notably topical. A master of the art of rhetorical illustration, he relied for subject matter on a constantly renewed experience of observing and conversing with ordinary people. Although he shunned the more routine pastoral duties, he achieved many of the same ends through an unusual capacity, on and off the platform, for hearing and responding to individual needs.

Beecher's romantic impetuosity and what he himself called his "hatred of neatness, love of disorder" expressed themselves as much in his ideas as in his general deportment. His thought pretended to little originality or systematic coherence. His central theological and homiletical idea, however—that of a loving rather than a vindictive God—remained powerful and consistent throughout his career. See William G. McLoughlin, *The Meaning of Henry Ward Beecher: An Essay on the Shifting Values of Mid-Victorian American, 1840–1870* (1970).

W. R. HUTCHISON

BELASCO, David (b. San Francisco, Calif., July 25, 1853; d. New York, N.Y., May 14, 1931), THEATRICAL PRODUCER, received his early education in Victoria, British Columbia, and San Francisco. After brief periods as an actor with a California touring company and with Piper's opera house in Virginia City, he became stage manager and resident dramatist with Maguire's theater in San Francisco in 1874. Except for an unsuccessful attempt to produce one of his plays, *Hearts of Oak* (coauthor, James A. Herne), in New York in 1880, Belasco continued working in San Francisco at Maguire's until 1876, then at Lucky Baldwin's Academy of Music. In 1882 he returned to New York as stage manager and dramatist at the Madison Square theater. He moved to the Lyceum theater in 1884 and wrote such plays as *Lord Chumley* (1888) and *The Charity Ball* (1889). Achieving independence in 1895 with *The Heart of Maryland,* he produced plays, including *The Girl of the Golden West, Rose of the Rancho, Men and Women,* and *The Girl I Left Behind Me.* These productions, and especially *Madame Butterfly* (1900), won Belasco the title of "the wizard" for his masterful creation of atmospheric illusions and his spectacular stage settings. He also gained fame as the sponsor of Mrs. Leslie Carter, David Warfield, Ina Claire and other stars. In 1907, having prospered from his theatrical work and spurred by the difficulties he had faced in conflicts with the "Theatre Trust" which had monopolized major houses during the 1890s, Belasco built his own theater, the Stuyvesant (later the Belasco). Although he continued to stage some of his own works, such as *The Return of Peter Grimm* (1911), he worked primarily on building a large stock of players and plays. In 1919 and 1924 his efforts to fight Actors Equity strikes failed, but he remained active in the New York theatrical world.

The most flamboyant impresario of his time, Belasco combined in his life and work both the demonic energy and the Puritan inhibitions of pre–World War I America. Through a long and phenomenally successful career he never violated the taboos of what he termed a "healthy" middle-class taste. As an exponent of "naturalism" in stage settings and scenic effects, he insisted on (and often achieved) a degree of photographic realism unmatched by any of his competitors. Indeed, his experiments with stage lighting and mechanical gimmickry of all sorts contributed to a genuine technical breakthrough for the American theater, as the fruits of advanced technology were applied for the first time on a massive scale to the problems of play production.

Unfortunately, Belasco lavished his inventive skills on second- and third-rate scripts that seldom justified their spectacular trappings. He offered his audiences a steady diet of romantic escapist fare that carefully refrained from any serious criticism of the status quo. His homogenized productions resulted less from a want of courage than from temperament and conviction: to Belasco the theater meant illusion, make-believe, entertainment; he could not conceive of the drama as a vehicle of social protest or clinical psychology. For the little theaters and their controversial playwrights he had only contempt, dismissing their offerings as "dirty, salacious, and brutally sordid." Yet Belasco's own most celebrated efforts, such as *Du Barry,* were merely "sex plays" of a different sort that skirted the scatological without ever quite abandoning conventional middle-class mores—just as, in real life, Belasco himself reveled privately in pornography while affecting in public the garb and demeanor of a cleric. His flawed achievement in the arts was a fit emblem of the "democratic taste" of that larger society whose cultural interests he so devotedly served. See Craig Timberlake, *The Bishop of Broadway* (1954).

MAXWELL BLOOMFIELD

BELL, Alexander Graham (b. Edinburgh, Scot., Mar. 3, 1847; d. Cape Breton Island, Nova Scotia, Aug. 2, 1922), INVENTOR, SCIENTIST, EDUCATOR, was educated at the Royal High School in Edinburgh and privately by his grandfather Alexander Bell, a speech teacher in London. He taught elocution in preparatory schools in Elgin, Scotland, and Bath, England, before becoming an assistant (1867) to his father, Alexander Melville Bell, a leading speech teacher and phonetician. In 1868 the young Bell used his father's system in teaching speech to deaf children at Susanna E. Hull's school in Kensington. In 1870 he emigrated with his parents to Brantford, Ontario.

Beginning in 1871, Bell demonstrated his speech-teaching methods at several New England schools for the deaf, becoming a leader in that field. To train teachers in his methods he established a private school in Boston in 1872 and served as a professor of speech and vocal physiology at Boston University (1873–77). Meanwhile he experimented with a device for transmitting several telegraphic messages at once over a single wire by means of superimposed intermittent currents of different frequencies, and also with devices for the graphic recording of sound waves impinging on diaphragms, so that his deaf pupils might analyze their own speech. In the summer of 1874, Bell fused his two lines of experiment to conceive the basic principle of the telephone. At Boston, on June 2, 1875, he first transmitted vocal sounds, though not intelligible speech. On March 7, 1876, he received a patent for the telephone. Later that month he transmitted intelligible speech by both the variable resistance and the electromagnetic principles. Bell subsequently patented improvements on the telephone but abandoned that field of invention in the early 1880s; he continued at intervals, though, to testify for the Bell Telephone Company and its successors through two decades of invariably successful suits against patent infringers and counter-claimants.

The wealth that came to Bell from his telephone inventions served to support more than forty years of further experiments. His "photophone" of 1880 used a selenium cell as a receiver in the transmission of speech along a beam of light. His electric probe, developed in the vain hope of saving the life of President Garfield in 1881, was used to locate metal fragments in wounds during several wars. His vacuum-jacket respirator of 1881 anticipated the iron lung. His 1902 system of construction with mass-produced, interchangeable, tetrahedral cells was a pioneering type of space frame architecture. He financed other men and collaborated with them in making **Thomas A. Edison**'s phonograph commercially practicable, in improving hydrofoil boats, and in aeronautical experiments, beginning in the early 1890s and culminating in the Aerial Experiment Association of 1907–9. He financed the journal *Science* (1882–94), supported **Albert Michelson**'s early experiments on the speed of light, and made significant contributions in the statistical study of inherited deafness and longevity. He was also influential in shaping the policies of the National Geographic Society and its magazine,

and served as its president (1898–1903). For fifty years Bell crusaded for the integration of the deaf into the hearing world through lip reading and speech, in 1890 founding what is now the Alexander Graham Bell Association for the Deaf. On questionnaires he always recorded his profession as "teacher of the deaf."

⁂

The social and economic significance of the telephone goes without saying. Its inventor, Alexander Graham Bell, might seem at first glance to be one of those who have had greatness thrust upon them. His fine sense of pitch, unusually keen hearing, thorough knowledge of the mechanics of speech and hearing, and expertness in acoustics, telegraphy, and the piano all seem, in conjunction with time and place, to have ordained his place in history. Yet what he endured and overcame to reach that place shows his fame to have been earned, not fortuitous. He needed and had an uncommon array of inner qualities: a bold, sometimes impractically fanciful originality of thought; an invincible optimism and a will to shine that joined in great tenacity of purpose; a brave disdain for the naysaying of experts; and a kindliness that he translated into active and effective humanitarianism. After the telephone success, both pathos and triumph were revealed in his cheerful enthusiasm through decades of experiment along lines that at last proved fruitless, and in the resilience with which he then set to work on new ideas. On the night of his death, as he struggled to dictate his latest thoughts, someone urged him not to hurry. "I have to," he replied.

One key to his character may lie in an editorial comment on a series of "Simple Experiments" that Bell wrote in his old age for deaf children. "Few men," remarked the editor, "possess the gift of seeing things from the viewpoint of a child so clearly as Alexander Graham Bell." In this truth lay Bell's chief weaknesses—scientific naïveté, extravagant enthusiasms, fits of impatience, an absorption in whatever currently occupied him—that sometimes seemed inconsiderate and egocentric. In it also lay his essential strengths.

Bell produced enough in his post-telephone experiments to justify them, at least by normal standards. Nevertheless, the variety of his interests and talents invites speculation as to whether he might have spent his energies more productively. On the evidence of his private notebooks, he had no aptitude for mathematics and therefore none for theoretical physics; his scientific contributions were largely empirical. Might he have become a business leader like **Cyrus McCormick** or **George Westinghouse?** His father-in-law, Gardiner Hubbard, a brilliant promoter of business enterprises (most notably the Bell Telephone Co.), at first scorned Bell's business ability and welcomed Bell's renunciation of such matters. Later, perhaps on the basis of Bell's adroitness in organizing and leading the campaign against sign language, Hubbard conceded that interest, not capacity, was Bell's only lack in that respect. It remained a decisive lack. Mrs. Bell, who inherited her father's business sense as well as his fine intellect, grasped the commercial possibilities of her husband's patent on tetrahedral construction and tried to develop them. But Bell was already absorbed in building a flying machine and gave her little encouragement.

Bell's own keenest regret was, in particular, at having been prevented by the demands of a patent suit from continuing an experimental school for deaf children that he had started during the 1880s, and, overall, at not having an extra lifetime to give to the education of the deaf. What he did helped to ease and enrich their lives. If he had abandoned technology after the telephone and had concentrated on education, whether of the deaf or in general, he might have enjoyed a second career as distinguished, although not as famous, as the first. But if at the end Bell had any consciousness of wasted time or lost opportunities, those regrets must have been tempered by retrospect of a life filled far beyond the lot of most with zestful work, ample fortune, popular acclaim, family love, and unalloyed benefactions to his fellow men. See Robert V. Bruce, *Bell: Alexander Graham Bell and the Conquest of Solitude* (1973).

ROBERT V. BRUCE

BELLAMY, Edward (b. Chicopee Falls, Mass., Mar. 26, 1850; d. Chicopee Falls, Mass., May 22, 1898), REFORMER, WRITER, was educated in local schools and spent one year at Union College, Schenectady, New York (1867–68), before traveling in Europe (1868–69). Upon his return he studied law in Springfield, Massachusetts, and was admitted to the bar in 1871 but never practiced. Bellamy joined the New York *Evening Post* in 1871 but shortly after moved to the Springfield *Union,* where he wrote editorials and book reviews (1872–78). After a trip to Hawaii he joined his brother to found and edit the Springfield *Daily News* (1880). In 1882, however, Bellamy left the newspaper to devote himself to literature. He wrote short stories for magazines, many of which appeared in the posthumous collection *The Blind Man's World and Other Stories* (1898), and also several novels, including *The Duke of Stockbridge* (serialized in 1879), a historical novel of Shays' Rebellion.

Becoming increasingly concerned with the social problems of the day, Bellamy spent two years working on his best-known book, *Looking Backward: 2000–1887* (1888). Set in the year 2000, this romance described a utopian socialist world where people enjoyed a planned economy, security, and peace. Bellamy expounded his "Nationalist" dogma in the book, advocating government ownership of utilities and industry but denouncing Marxian socialism and class warfare. *Looking Backward* sold about a million copies, and Nationalist clubs sprang up throughout the country to discuss the social implications of the novel. Believing he could peacefully change capitalist America into his utopian world, Bellamy moved to Boston and founded a weekly newspaper, the *New Nation,* to advance his ideas (1891). Declining health, however, forced him to limit activities. He gave up the paper in 1894 and spent his last years writing *Equality* (1897), a sequel to *Looking Backward.* His novels include *Six to One: A Nantucket Idyll* (1878), *Dr. Heidenhoff's Process* (1880), and *Miss Ludington's Sister* (1884).

Edward Bellamy's brief reform career—1888–96—reflected as well as directed the growth of a social conscience in the American middle classes who read his *Looking Backward* with such enthusiasm. The appearance of the utopian novel in 1888 marked a transformation in its author's outlook not unlike the conversion experience assigned to his fictional hero, Julian West. As a newspaper editorialist and author of sentimental fantasies, Bellamy had observed American society in the Gilded Age from the outside; disenchanted with commercialism, cutthroat competition, and the rise of monopoly, he was yet disinclined to join those reformers seeking an alternative economic order. *Looking Backward* itself was first designed as a simple fable—"a cloud-palace for an ideal humanity," Bellamy described it—rather than as a model for social reconstruction. Bellamy's discovery of his organizational principle in the Industrial Army, however, convinced him that the ordered and peaceful replacement of American capitalism by a new cooperative system was possible within his lifetime. The writing of *Looking Backward* thus convinced its author of the need for immediate action and launched him on a belated career as a reformer. For the next eight years until his health failed, Bellamy organized Nationalist clubs, founded a newspaper and a magazine to popularize his plan for managing the United States as a giant cooperative trust, and after 1892 supported the Populists, whose proposals he accepted as first steps toward utopian solidarity.

Although the central concept of his utopian scheme was seemingly that of a gigantic regiment of workers dedicated to the service of the state, Bellamy was engaged at a deeper level of reflection with less authoritarian and more genuinely humanitarian concerns: the equitable distribution of a growing American abundance; the creation of a decentralized and ecologically balanced society; the peaceful elimination of capitalism; and the cultivation of true individualism through religious means. It was this ethical vision of American possibilities, rather than his rigid blueprint for the twentieth-century postindustrial state, that caught the imagination of his contemporaries and after his death continued to inform the consciences, if not the methods, of Progressive reformers. See John L. Thomas, *Alternative America: Henry George, Edward Bellamy, Henry Demarest Lloyd and the Adversary Tradition* (1983).

JOHN L. THOMAS

BELLOW, Saul (b. Lachine, Quebec, Can., July 10, 1915), WRITER, grew up in Montreal and Chicago (1924), where he attended public schools. After two years at the University of Chicago, he transferred to Northwestern University (1935) and received a BS in anthropology and sociology in 1937. Bellow briefly attended graduate school in anthropology at the University of Wisconsin but soon turned to literature. After working for the WPA Writers Project, Bellow taught writing at Pestalozzi-Froebel Teachers College in Chicago (1938–42). During World War II he served in the U.S. merchant marine and, upon his discharge, as an editor for the *Encyclopaedia Britannica* (1943–46). During this time Bellow published his first novel, *The Dangling Man* (1944), which was followed by *The Victim* (1947). He taught English at the University of Minnesota (1946) and won a Guggenheim fellowship for study in Paris and Rome (1948–49). In Europe, Bellow wrote *The Adventures of Augie March* (1953), a picaresque story of a young man from the Chicago Jewish community trying to find himself. The book, a best-seller, won the National Book Award and established Bellow's literary reputation.

Bellow taught at Princeton (1952–53) and Bard College (1953–54). He won another Guggenheim fellowship (1955–56). Next he published *Seize the Day* (1956) and *Henderson, the Rain King* (1959), along with numerous stories and essays. In 1962, Bellow became a professor with the Committee on Social Thought at the University of Chicago. His *Herzog* (1964) won the 1964 National Book Award. A Broadway play, *The Last Analysis* (1964), was not successful, but Bellow rewrote *Seize the Day* as a drama and followed this up with *Mosby's Memoirs and Other Stories* (1968) and

Mr. Sammler's Planet (1969), which also won a National Book Award. In 1975, *Humbolt's Gift* won a Pulitzer Prize and firmly established Bellow's reputation as perhaps America's leading postwar novelist. This status was reinforced in 1976 when he was awarded the Nobel Prize for Literature. In subsequent years Bellow continued to demonstrate his breathtaking talent as a writer of fiction and social commentator with such works as *The Dean's December* (1982), *More Die of Heartbreak* (1987), *Him with His Foot in His Mouth* (1984), a collection of short stories, and *The Bellarosa Connection* (1989).

Saul Bellow's novels are characterized by an intense preoccupation on the writer's part with the deeper levels of the experience of the particular individual. From *Dangling Man,* his earliest novel, through *Mr. Sammler's Planet,* to the *Bellarosa Connection,* one of his latest, this orientation has been apparent, each novel focusing carefully and in detail on the subjective elements of the experience of a central character. Bellow deals in the bizarre, the exotic, the unusual, the eccentric. His main characters are intelligent, highly sensitive persons who find themselves in (or put themselves into) situations that force them to come to terms with submerged or otherwise unfamiliar aspects of their psyches. If the situations Bellow writes about are not unusual themselves, then the mind of his central character is likely to be in an anxious, distortion-producing state whose perspective causes severe tension between the character and his world (e.g., Joseph in *Dangling Man* or Leventhal in *The Victim*).

One of Bellow's greatest strengths as a novelist lies in his ability to create memorable, larger-than-life characters (usually eccentrics). One such creation is Einhorn, the crippled yet vitally alive entrepreneur and fatherly counselor to Augie March. Unable to walk, nearly immobile physically, Einhorn yet manages through the strength of his will to function in as many capacities as most men. Henderson (the rain king) is another such creation. A physically large man, wealthy and hence free from ordinary economic burdens,

Henderson has within him a voice that says, "I want, I want," although Henderson has no notion of the object of his inner want. His adventures, which lead him to Africa and to confrontation with primeval forces, result finally in his achievement of the capacity to relate to others in a clumsy, awkward, though nonetheless significant way. Moses Herzog, a third eccentric and memorable character, writes letters to hundreds of people—to the president, his analyst, his former wife's priest, his mistress, his relatives, and friends, to people both dead and alive. He writes down aphorisms, thoughts and half-thoughts, conclusions. By the end of the novel the "spell" has passed and he has "no messages for anyone," implying that he has become comparatively well.

A hallmark of Bellow's work is its humor. *Henderson, the Rain King* is his most humorous work and at the same time the most purely comic in the generic sense. Other works, *Augie March* for example, contain elements of humor, though their tone is generally serious. Seriousness of tone, however, does not preclude the verbal humor of *Herzog* (e.g., "If you are going to be on the knees of your soul, you may as well scrub the floor"), the situational humor of *Henderson* (his interaction, for example, with African tribes), or the humor resulting from Bellow's creation of eccentric characters. See Irving Malin, *Saul Bellow's Fiction* (1969).

Donald B. Gibson

BELLOWS, George Wesley (b. Columbus, Ohio, Aug. 12, 1882; d. New York, N.Y., Jan. 8, 1925), ARTIST, graduated from Ohio State University in 1903 and then studied painting in New York City under **Robert Henri** (founder of the Ashcan school), Kenneth H. Miller, and H. G. Maratta. Bellows was particularly interested in Jay Hambidge's idea of dynamic symmetry, a theory governing the relationships of squares and rectangles within a painting. He carefully studied Goya and Daumier and later El Greco and Renoir, but he soon came to believe that the observation of life as it actually exists was more important than the study of old masters. His fascination with everyday life and the commonplace is apparent in such works as *Forty-Two Kids* (1907, Corcoran Galley, Washington, D.C.), an animated canvas showing boys bathing along a New York riverfront; in his paintings of prizefights, such as *Stag at Sharkey's* (1907, Museum of Art, Cleveland); and in *The Circus* (1912, Addison Gallery of American Art, Phillips Academy, Andover, Massachusetts), which depicts a dancer on horseback before a large crowd.

Bellows's work was immediately acclaimed; in 1909 he was elected an associate member of the National Academy, the youngest painter ever so honored. Between 1910 and 1919 he taught at the Art Students League (New York), and at the Art Institute of Chicago. During World War I he painted *Edith Cavell* (1918, Museum of Fine Arts, Springfield, Massachusetts) and *The Return of the Useless* (1918), depicting a trainload of French peasants repatriated by the Germans because they were unfit for work. In 1916, Bellows began experimenting with lithography, sometimes producing lithographic replicas of his own oils. But most of his lithographs were original works, his *Billy Sunday* (1923) and *Dempsey and Firpo* (1924) being among the best known.

❧

Bellows tried to capture the dynamism of the twentieth century by means of a descriptive realism rather than by evoking abstract processes symbolic of modern society. He responded directly with his senses to the masculine vigor of labor, to the raw physical impact of competitive sports, and to the turbulent life of slum dwellers. He did not think or feel in ways analogous to the electronic, telegraphic, or cinematic methods characteristic of Parisian modernism. For Bellows the twentieth century was a personal adventure; he wanted to feel and to experience intimately the life around him. His vision was concrete, not speculative. As a result he was considered in his lifetime a thoroughly American artist, pragmatic and practical in his outlook and responses, able to communicate easily with his appreciative audience.

Compared to his fellow painters in the Ashcan school, Bellows's approach was the broadest. Although they all painted urban and rural views, Bellows often sought larger contexts. He did not paint the single slum dweller but a street full of people. Instead of a small group at the beach, he painted a vast throng. Rather than show a riverfront promenade, he painted workmen, their horses, and great ships, thus evoking the power and strength of the modern city instead of limiting himself to the pleasantries of a river view.

The least sentimental but the most romantic of the early twentieth-century realists, Bellows was cut in the mold of Theodore Roosevelt, especially because of the aura of action and drive that characterizes his work. See Charles H. Morgan, *George Bellows* (1965).

MATTHEW BAIGELL

BELMONT, August (b. Alzey, Prussia, Dec. 8, 1813; d. New York, N.Y., Nov. 24, 1890), FINANCIER, POLITICAL LEADER, was educated in Frankfurt-am-Main at the Jewish gymnasium. In 1828 he became an apprentice in the Rothschild banking house in Frankfurt. In 1834, as a companion and secretary to one of the partners, he traveled to Naples, the Vatican, and Paris. Sent by his employers to Havana, Cuba, in 1837, Belmont went instead to New York City to look after the Rothschild interests during the financial panic of that year. He opened a banking office, August Belmont and Co., on Wall Street and later became the official Rothschild agent in the United States. Belmont prospered and quickly emerged as one of the leading bankers in the country. He underwrote a large part of the U.S. Treasury loans during the Mexican War. He also served as consul general for Austria in the United States from 1844 to 1850 when he resigned in protest against Austrian oppression in Hungary.

During the 1840s, now a U.S. citizen, Belmont became active in Democratic Party politics. He served as minister to the Netherlands under President Pierce (1853–57). Emerging as a financial backer of the Democratic Party, Belmont supported Senator **Stephen Douglas** of Illinois and the concept of popular sovereignty. After the

1860 Democratic national convention at Charleston, South Carolina, broke up, Belmont played an active role in the Baltimore convention that nominated Douglas for president and was named Democratic national chairman. He campaigned vigorously for Douglas's election, but after Lincoln's victory he backed the president and the Union war effort. Belmont visited London in 1861 and Paris in 1863, pleading the northern cause with European merchants, financiers, and diplomats. His activities were credited with helping to prevent European diplomatic recognition of the South. When some Republican newspapers (after the war) impugned his loyalty to the Union, Belmont published *A Few Letters and Speeches of the Late Civil War* (1870) as proof of his consistent support for the North. He favored President Andrew Johnson's approach to Reconstruction, insisted that the federal government redeem war bonds in specie, and backed hard-money policies as opposed to the issue of greenbacks. Belmont retired as Democratic national chairman in 1872 after its convention backed Liberal Republican candidate **Horace Greeley** for president. He continued to champion hard currency and supported Senator **Thomas F. Bayard** of Delaware for the Democratic presidential nomination in 1876, 1880, and 1884.

Excepting politics, Belmont was a notable success in several fields of endeavor. He was one of the leading private bankers of his time, and his Rothschild connections made him important on the international banking scene as well. He was extremely influential in New York's high society; his contemporaries regarded him as the arbiter of what then constituted good taste in manners, morals, and cuisine. In the world of culture he was a founding patron of the original Metropolitan Opera House, and his private collection of paintings was one of the three largest in the United States. In sports, Belmont introduced thoroughbred racing to America and was a founding member and first president of the New York Jockey Club.

Only in politics did Belmont meet with continual frustration. No one to date has served longer as Democratic national chairman than he, but though he gave unstintingly of his time and money and brought a superior talent for organization to the tasks at hand, he never attained the results or recognition commensurate with the magnitude of his efforts. As a foreign-born Jew in a heyday of nativism and as a wealthy banker in a period of anticapitalist agitation and recurrent economic depression, his motives were often suspect and his activities hampered by unfavorable publicity. His inability to unite key party factions and imbue them with a cohesive vision militated against his success. Even had he been able to surmount the handicaps of personal identity and party divisiveness, it was highly improbable that he (or any other Democrat) could have been the architect of electoral victories. His most significant work coincided with the convulsive years of war and reconstruction when no strategy could have staved off the erosion of loyal leadership and faithful rank and file. See Irving Katz, *August Belmont* (1968).

IRVING KATZ

BENEDICT, Ruth Fulton (b. New York, N.Y., June 5, 1887; d. New York, N.Y., Sept. 17, 1948), ANTHROPOLOGIST, graduated from Vassar College in 1909. After teaching English at the Orton School for Girls, Pasadena, California (1912–13), she returned to New York City in 1914. A number of her poems written in this period were published in the *Nation* and *Poetry* under the name Anne Singleton. Following a year at the New School for Social Research (1918–19), she transferred to Columbia University where she began studying under anthropologist **Franz Boas.**

Awarded a PhD in 1923, she began teaching anthropology at Columbia. *Patterns of Culture,* published in 1934, was based on her fieldwork among the Zuñi Indians of southwestern United States and on her analysis of secondary sources from the Dobu and Kwakiutl Indians of the Pacific Northwest. In 1935 she published *Zuñi*

Mythology (2 vols.), based on her own fieldwork and the analysis of the work of others. *Patterns of Culture,* one of the first attempts to integrate anthropology, sociology, and psychology, also introduced Benedict's concept of cultural relativism. She saw personality structure as comprehensible only in terms of a society's total culture and argued that aspects of different societies could not be understood by removing them from their context and comparing them to each other.

In 1936, Benedict became an associate professor of anthropology at Columbia. During 1936–39 she was acting chairwoman of her department. Using cultural relativism as a guiding concept, she analyzed and attacked racism in *Race: Science and Politics* (1940) and *Races of Mankind* (in collaboration with Gene Weltfish), a 1943 pamphlet on racial equality. On the staff of the Office of War Information during World War II, Benedict studied various cultures important in the war effort. In 1946 she published *The Chrysanthemum and the Sword: Patterns of Japanese Culture.* This book, derived mainly from her work during World War II, was written without her having visited Japan, but Japanese and non-Japanese scholars were impressed by its insights. She was elected president of the American Anthropological Association in 1947 and a year later was promoted to professor of anthropology at Columbia.

━━━ ∞ ━━━

Ruth Benedict was a highly dignified person and physically attractive, with gray swept-back hair in her later years. She was at once distant and yet very interested in, and exceedingly helpful to, the group of graduate students who gathered around her. As a teacher she was not an articulate lecturer, but she had a strong influence on many students who later became productive professional anthropologists, including Marian S. Smith, Buell Quain, Oscar Lewis, Jules Henry, Irving Goldman, Ruth Landes, Carl Withers, Helen Codere, and Charles Wagley. An elegant stylist in her own work, she was always surprised by the awkwardness of her students in presenting their research data and their lack of general cultural background. She rather expected

anthropologists to bring to their profession the rich philosophical and literary background that she herself possessed.

She was for many years partially deaf in one ear. This, combined with her rather distant manner, did not make her an expert field researcher, although she was highly sensitive to people of other cultures. Her career, however, was intricately involved with that of **Margaret Mead,** whose field research was both extensive and highly competent. Often it would seem that Ruth Benedict and Margaret Mead functioned as a team, one working in New Guinea and the other following the progress and using her intuitive insights from a distance. Benedict insisted on field research among her students and followed that research to the smallest detail. Most of her important interpretations were thus based on field research by others. She was not an anthropologist in the tradition of Boas and his early students, nor of the British social anthropologists, but she kept that tradition alive. Her special contribution was theoretical; she wrote articles important to education, to mythology, to culture change, and to other subjects of contemporary relevance. But above all she was a great humanist able to interpret the principal values and themes of various cultures. See Margaret Mead, *An Anthropologist at Work: Writings of Ruth Benedict* (1959).

CHARLES WAGLEY

BENJAMIN, Judah P. (b. St. Croix, V.I., Aug. 6, 1811; d. Paris, France, May 6, 1884), POLITICAL LEADER, was brought to the Carolinas in 1813 by his parents who settled in Charlestown, South Carolina, in 1822. In 1828, after two years at Yale College, he went to New Orleans where he took odd jobs, taught English, and studied law. After admission to the bar he became a highly successful attorney and together with Thomas Slidell published a *Digest* of Louisiana Supreme Court decisions. In 1842 he was elected as a Whig to the state assembly and served in the constitutional convention of 1844–54; in 1852 he won a seat in the U.S. Senate. Reelected as a Democrat in 1859, he delivered a notable secession speech in 1860 and a farewell address in 1861. Upon the establishment of the Confederacy, **Jefferson Davis** appointed him attorney general in 1861, secretary of war later that year, and after the fall of Roanoke Island in 1862, secretary of state. In this position he sought in vain to obtain European recognition for the South, sought to raise money through the Erlanger loan, and finally advocated emancipation to secure troops and induce the British and French to recognize the Confederate states. At the time of the collapse of the southern government he took an open boat to the Bahamas and made his way to England where he rose to the position of Queen's Counsel and established another enviable legal career, especially after the publication of his book *Treatise on the Law of Sale of Personal Property*. After his retirement in 1883 he moved to Paris.

―――⊗∞⊗―――

Judah P. Benjamin's amazing career as the first Jewish cabinet minister in modern times and as the close associate of Jefferson Davis, crowned as it was by renewed fame at the British bar, has made him one of the best-known Confederate officials. His books on commercial law became standard, his orations in the Senate and courts of two continents were widely admired, and his legal reasoning was a model of clarity. Generally believed to have written many of Davis's messages, he suffered in silence the attacks on him, especially after the fall of Roanoke Island, and became the lightning rod for the administration, which could not admit its shortage of resources.

If his diplomatic ventures were not crowned with success, it must be remembered that he faced an impossible situation in view of the Confederacy's lack of international standing. His defense of slavery and his purchase of a plantation, Bellechase, where he engaged in sugar production, mark him as a representative of antebellum southern society, although he had an uncanny ability to adapt to changing surroundings. Optimistic, ever courteous and forthcoming, he was never heard to complain about his unhappy marriage or about the incessant insults to which he was exposed. His fame as a lawyer was unexcelled. See Eli N. Evans, *Judah P. Benjamin: Jewish Confederate* (1988).

HANS TREFOUSSE

BENNETT, James Gordon (b. New Mill, Keith, Banffshire, Scot., Sept. 1, 1795; d. New York, N.Y., June 1, 1872), EDITOR, studied for the priesthood at the Catholic Seminary in Aberdeen before emigrating in 1819 to Halifax, Nova Scotia, where he taught bookkeeping. He worked in Portland, Maine, Boston, and New York before joining the Charleston (S.C.) *Courier* as a translator of French and Spanish-American newspapers. Returning to New York in October 1823 he tried to establish a commercial school but failed. Two years later he joined the staff of the New York *Courier,* which he soon purchased and resold. He then worked for the *National Advocate* (1826) and for two years for the New York *Enquirer.* He became associate editor of the *Morning Courier and New York Enquirer* when the two dailies merged in 1829. In 1832 he left the *Courier and Enquirer* to publish the New York *Globe* but soon moved to Philadelphia, where he purchased a share in the *Pennsylvanian* and became its editor. The following year he returned to New York and on May 6, 1835, produced the first issue of the New York *Herald,* which sold for a penny. This politically independent daily soon featured money market reports and a table of sales on the stock exchange. In 1838, Bennett hired six European correspondents and established a Washington press corps. He introduced the practice of holding interviews at the scene of events, was the first editor to use the telegraph extensively, and established an overland express service in 1844, which during the Mexican War often supplied the *Herald* with battlefield accounts long before they could be secured at government offices in Washington.

In 1860, Bennett supported **Stephen A. Douglas** for president and showed a marked partiality for the southern point of view. But once the Civil War broke out he was staunchly Unionist. During the war Bennett employed sixty-three correspondents who reported from all the battlefronts. In 1867 when Bennett retired from active management of the *Herald* in favor of his son, the paper's daily circulation stood at ninety thousand, and its total advertising revenues were second only to those of *The Times* of London.

A gifted and controversial editor, Bennett transformed the American newspaper. Expanding traditional coverage, the *Herald* provided sports reports, a society page, and advice to the lovelorn, soon permanent features of most metropolitan dailies. Bennett covered murders and sex scandals in delicious detail, faking materials when necessary. He expanded levels of coverage to include local, state, and national news, most dramatically in a successful fight against a rule barring out-of-town correspondents from the Senate floor. His adroit use of telegraph, pony express, and even offshore ships to intercept European dispatches set high standards for rapid news gathering. Asserting independence from advertisers, he demanded cash in advance and required frequent changes in advertisers' copy. Reacting against a series of disappointments with the *Globe* and the *Pennsylvanian,* Bennett disclaimed "all politics." Although the *Herald* generally supported Democratic causes, he thus challenged prevailing assumptions concerning press partisanship. A breezy, often flippant style, bold headlines, woodcuts, and a low price made these innovations attractive and affordable to a mass audience. Some of Bennett's practices, however good for circulation, earned him bitter criticism, even physical assault. Nor could he claim entire credit for all innovations, since many started with Benjamin Day's *Sun* and others were simultaneously developed in the fifteen or more dailies launched in these decades. But Bennett perfected these techniques in a paper that, if sometimes vulgar, offered diversion and perhaps a measure of social cohesion as agrarian, small-town America became urban, industrial, and fragmented.

Combining opportunism and reform, Bennett exposed fraud on Wall Street, attacked the Bank of the United States, and generally joined the Jacksonian assault on privilege. Reflecting a growing nativism, he published excerpts from the anti-Catholic disclosures of "Maria Monk," and he greeted Know-Nothing-ism cordially. Defending labor unions in principle, he assailed much union activity. Unable to condemn slavery outright, he opposed abolitionism. Personally, Bennett could plumb the depths of tastelessness, most notably in a sensationalist announcement of his engagement to the talented and graceful woman he married. In private life, however, his bearing was modest, despite a sturdy six-foot frame and commanding air. A mirror of Jacksonian America, he revealed its creative energies no less than its flaws. See Oliver Carlson, *The Man Who Made News: James Gordon Bennett* (1942).

ROBERT C. BANNISTER

BENNETT, James Gordon, Jr. (b. New York, N.Y., May 10, 1841; d. Beaulieu, France, May 14, 1918), PUBLISHER, was educated privately and at the Ecole Polytechnique in Paris. When the Civil War began (1861), he returned to America to secure a commission as lieutenant in the Union navy. After receiving thorough training in the operation of the New York *Herald,* which his father owned and edited, Bennett became managing editor of the paper in 1866. When the *Evening Telegram* was established the following year, he became executive head of that paper as well. He assumed proprietorship of both dailies after his father's death (1872) and transformed the *Tribune* into a mirror of his own tastes and predilections. The paper excelled in coverage of military, nautical, social, and (after the Mackay-Bennett cable was completed and the Commercial Cable Co. formed) European news. Bennett financed or helped to finance numerous expeditions, notably Henry M. Stanley's search for David Livingstone (1869–72), the *Pandora*'s search for the Northwest Passage (1875), and the *Jeannette* Polar expedition (1879–81). During the financial difficulties of 1873, Bennett opened free kitchens in poor districts of New York City. In 1882 he established the Herald Relief Fund for Irish Sufferers, toward which he donated $100,000.

After 1877, Bennett usually resided in Paris, but he retained almost complete control over his New York papers. He founded a short-lived London edition of the *Herald* and in 1887 established a Paris edition. During the latter years of Bennett's proprietorship, the *Herald's* circulation was hurt by his quarrel with newsdealers (1884), his conviction and $31,000 fine in a lawsuit filed by **W. R. Hearst** (1907), his eccentric treatment of his employees, and competition with other New York dailies.

An avid sportsman, Bennett introduced polo to the United States, competed in the first transatlantic yacht race (1866), and donated cups for balloon (1906), auto, and airplane (1908) competitions.

———— ❦ ————

Bennett's whole life was eccentric. Gifted though he was in many ways, he failed to live up to his potential and left a declining business at his death. Throughout his career he was unpredictable. The young Bennett did not have the start of a typical boy. Taken to Paris by his mother, he received a private education and acquired habits of what in those days was called profligacy. When thrust into full responsibility for the *Herald* at the age of 31, his personal reputation already was the cause of dismay among fellow journalists.

Though erratic, Bennett also was full of confidence and enterprising enough to sustain the *Herald's* qualities as an outstanding journal for two decades. He kept tight control over the management even while spending much of his time abroad. All major decisions were his, and the paper came to reflect his personal tastes. Full attention was devoted to international affairs, sports, and social events. Stunts such as the sending of Henry Stanley to search for David Livingstone added a tone of excitement to the paper.

But in the long run Bennett's egotism and style of living undermined his paper. Conflicts with employees weakened the staff, and his lavish spending drained the paper's financial resources. When other newspapers were expanding in the last decade of the century, the *Herald* did not keep pace. Its strength ebbed with the waning life of a brilliantly eccentric journalist. See Richard O'Connor, *Scandalous Mr. Bennett* (1962).

HAROLD W. CARY

BENTLEY, Arthur Fisher (b. Freeport, Ill., Oct. 16, 1870; d. Paoli, Ind., May 21, 1957), POLITICAL and SOCIAL SCIENTIST, PHILOSOPHER, attended York College, Nebraska, and the University of Denver, and worked in his father's bank before entering Johns Hopkins University in 1890. After Bentley graduated in 1892, he wrote a monograph, *The Condition of the Western Farmer as Illustrated by the Economic History of a Nebraska Township* (1893). He then studied economics and sociology at Johns Hopkins (1892–93) and the University of Berlin (1893–94), and received his PhD (in economics, philosophy, and jurisprudence) at Johns Hopkins in 1895. That same year he published his first theoretical essay, "The Units of Investigation in the Social Sciences," in the American Academy of Political and Social Science *Annals*. He was a docent in sociology at the University of Chicago for the academic year 1895–96 and attended two seminars there with **John Dewey,** who greatly influenced him. From 1896 on, Bentley was first a news reporter and then an editorial writer for the Chicago *Times-Herald* and the *Record-Herald*. His first major work in political science, *The Process of Government* (1908), displayed his actionist or behavioral approach to studying the social sciences: the study of politics should focus on process and overt behavior. The book also contained a keen analysis of group pressures. Declining health caused Bentley to retire in 1911, but he was active in the American Red Cross during World War I and was a leader of the Progressive Party in Indiana in the presidential election of 1924.

Continuing his writing during his long retirement, Bentley's *Relativity in Man and Society* (1926) applied **Alfred Einstein's** theory of relativity to sociology, while *Linguistic Analysis of Mathematics* (1932) suggested clarifying the relationship of ordinary language to mathematics. *Behavior, Knowledge, Fact* (1935) presented his ideas on effective techniques for studying human behavior. Bentley participated in a seminar on language at Columbia in 1941–42 and became a coauthor with John Dewey of *Knowing and the Known* (1949), a critique of various theories of logic and scientific knowledge. Bentley and Dewey's *A Philosophical Correspondence: 1932–1951* (edited by Sidney Ratner and Jules Altman in 1964) contained many of their best interchanges. *Inquiry into Inquiries: Essays in Social Theory* (1954) examined basic theories in the social sciences, and a book about the American business and political scene written after World War I was published posthumously as *Makers, Users, and Masters* (1969), edited by Sidney Ratner.

———— ✺ ————

Arthur F. Bentley was a thinker of great originality and profound understanding of complex problems in many fields of scientific inquiry, ranging from political science to the theory of scientific method and knowledge. He also had the courage to advance challenging hypotheses that went against many dominant views and vested intellectual interests of his time. The vigor of his criticism of established figures and his revolutionary ideas for restructuring whole areas of scientific research prevented Bentley from being accepted in the university world until John Dewey invited him to lecture at Columbia University in 1941–42. For almost forty years he was in an academic wasteland as heartbreaking as that of **C. S. Peirce** or **Thorstein Veblen.** But Bentley carried on his scientific inquiries throughout his long life with intense energy and great gusto. In his personal life he inspired great affection and admiration from many who came to know him. Although a formidable controversialist, he was able to win friends, and he showed deep compassion for the unfortunate.

Among Bentley's many achievements was his establishment in 1908 of the theoretical basis for the study of "pressure groups" or "group pressures." Those he influenced included such notable political scientists as **Charles Beard,** Bertram Gross, David Truman, and Earl Latham. Bentley's tough-minded realism made some critics consider him an extreme relativist and cynical conservative. Actually, he was an idealist, concerned about improving the welfare of all exploited groups and promoting change in society.

Another important contribution was his and Dewey's development of "transactional analysis." In this type of study all the parts or elements of a situation (e.g., a baseball game) are seen as active participants, each element influencing every other in the process or activity. This approach—as against those stressing "self-action" or "interaction" of objects or persons—has inspired creative research in biology, physics, political science, psychology, and sociology. Adelbert Ames, Jr., and Hadley Cantril in psychology are two of many figures who achieved striking results in their field through the application of this new method of analysis. See Sidney Ratner and Jules Altman, eds., *John Dewey and Arthur F. Bentley: A Philosophical Correspondence, 1932–1951* (1964).

SIDNEY RATNER

BENTON, Thomas Hart (b. near Hillsboro, N.C., Mar. 14, 1782; d. Washington, D.C., Apr. 10, 1858), POLITICAL LEADER, studied at the University of North Carolina but was expelled for thefts from his roommates. He moved with his family to a farm near Franklin, Tennessee, in 1801, and was admitted to the bar in 1806. In 1809 he was elected to the Tennessee senate. During the War of 1812 he served as Andrew Jackson's aide-de-camp. He moved to St. Louis in 1815, where he practiced law and edited the Missouri *Enquirer.* Elected to the U.S. Senate from Missouri in 1820, Benton served from 1821 to 1851.

Uncompromisingly opposed to paper currency, Benton advocated "hard money," and he vehemently opposed the Second Bank of the United States. During the controversy over rechartering the Bank in 1832, Benton was the Democratic Senate floor leader, and he later sponsored the resolution that expunged from the Senate journal the resolution to censure Jackson for his actions during the bank crisis. Over the years Benton modified his views on slavery. In 1820 he opposed any restriction of slavery in Missouri; by the late 1840s and the 1850s he was favoring gradual emancipation. He changed because he espoused westward expansion, believed that slavery was hindering the rapid development of the West, and ultimately came to see slavery as a moral evil. He was a lifelong supporter of policies designed to enable poor men to obtain western lands easily. As early as 1824 he introduced a bill providing for "graduation" of the price of land. Public lands that failed to find buyers at the "upset" price of $1.25 an acre were to be offered at gradually reduced rates and, if no purchasers materialized, given away free to actual settlers. However, Benton opposed the annexation of Texas in 1844 on constitutional and other grounds, although he supported the war with Mexico. During the Oregon boundary dispute he favored the compromise that settled the boundary at the 49th parallel.

Although he represented a slave state, Benton was a nationalist and staunch Unionist, opposing all secessionist ideas. He attacked **John C. Calhoun**'s states' rights resolutions of 1847 and opposed the Compromise of 1850 because he felt that it made excessive concessions to slavery interests, particularly in the new fugitive slave law and the Texas boundary settlement. These actions, together with his failure to support the Democrats' presidential candidate, **Lewis Cass,** after Martin Van Buren agreed to run on a Free Soil ticket in 1848, offended his pro-slavery constituents and led to the loss of his Senate seat in 1850. Although he was elected to the House of Representatives in 1852, his opposition to the southern position cost him his seat two years later and destroyed his chances of being elected governor of Missouri in a campaign to vindicate his policies.

After retiring from politics Benton wrote his important *Thirty Years' View* (1854–56), in which he reflected on his long career, and wrote an extended, sharply critical *Examination* (1858) of the **Dred Scott** decision, in which the Supreme Court ruled that Congress could not limit the extension of slavery into the new, western territories. Just before his death he completed his *Abridgement of the Debates of Congress, 1789–1856* (1857–61).

⟶⟵

Big, bull-necked, with a massive head on massive shoulders, Thomas Hart Benton was a picture of physical and intellectual force. As the first man to serve thirty years in the Senate, he gave all of his mental powers and trenchant if often overblown oratory to the political causes he espoused. His lasting significance lay in these commitments and particularly in his affirmation of popular democracy.

His earliest concern was for the West. He condemned the failure to add the Texas area to the United States in the treaty with Spain in 1819 and insisted that the Pacific Northwest was American by right. He supported free access to the mountain fur trade for St. Louis firms and **John Jacob Astor**'s interests. He also envisioned the Missouri and Columbia river lines as a potential trade route to the Pacific and Asia, and supported action to make the long Santa Fe trail safe for traders.

In the second phase of Benton's career his views became more national and more agrarian. His proposals to make public lands easily available to settlers were, of course, "western," but they also expressed his idea of a freeholder's commonwealth. After 1825 he joined the cause of emergent Jacksonian democracy, condemning John Quincy Adams's election over Andrew Jackson by the House of Representatives as a violation of the popular will. He also repeatedly offered a constitutional amendment for the direct popular election of presidents. His attack on the "Monster" Bank of the United States was, for him, also a thrust at speculative enterprise and a defense of an Arcadian republic. He condemned commercial, note-issuing state banks, too: "I did not join in putting down the Bank of the United States to put up a wilderness of local banks," he declared; "I did not strike Caesar to make Antony master of Rome." His alternative was gold and silver currency, "hard money." These questions became the great symbolic issues of the decade, and Benton's long battle for a sound "farmer's" currency won him his nickname, "Old Bullion."

The final, climactic phase of Benton's career was concerned with the Union and slavery. A small slaveholder from a slave state, he at first supported slavery and always feared abolitionist "agitation." With the expansion of the nation to the Pacific in the 1840s, however, he opposed the spread of slavery. He wanted the new territories for his freehold farmers; he feared that the slavery issue might divide the nation; and he ultimately saw black bondage as an evil in itself. He rejected both the Wilmot Proviso and John C. Calhoun's pro-slavery resolutions as unnecessary and dangerous: they were like "two halves of a pair of shears" that could sever the Union. When his opposition to the Compromise of 1850 stirred up a pro-slavery faction against him in Missouri, he valiantly reiterated his "principles" across the state but lost his Senate seat nonetheless. In his last years he condemned the Kansas-Nebraska Bill and the Dred Scott decision, and criticized James Buchanan's administration for being excessively pro-southern. In 1856, however, he refused to support the first Republican presidential candidate, his son-in-law **John Charles Frémont.** He would inevitably be a sectional candidate, Benton thought; and even close family ties must yield to concern for the Union.

In his autobiographical *Thirty Years' View,* Benton reiterated his central convictions: equalitarian democracy, defense of the national Union, and opposition to slavery and its expansion. See William N. Chambers, *Old Bullion Benton: Senator from the New West, 1782–1858* (1956).

WILLIAM N. CHAMBERS

BENTON, Thomas Hart (b. Neosho, Mo., Apr. 15, 1889; d. Kansas City, Mo., Jan. 19, 1973), ARTIST, studied at the Art Institute of Chicago (1906–07), meanwhile working as a cartoonist for the Joplin (Ill.) *American.* From 1908 to 1911 he studied painting in Paris at the *Académie Julien.*

After returning to the United States (1912) he established himself as a painter. During World War I he served as an enlisted man in the navy. After the war he experimented with a kind of semi-abstract style, but in the early 1930s he became a leader among regionalist artists, a largely midwestern group that glorified American energy and argued that contemporary European art was decadent and effete. Benton's work featured contorted, elongated, heavily muscled figures of cowboys, gamblers, Indians, and other "American" types, painted in strident colors. He also painted murals in this style, beginning with a series for the New School for Social Research in New York City (1921). His murals brought him many commissions, among them the Whitney Museum Library (1932), the Indiana Building at the Chicago World's Fair (1933) and the Missouri State Capitol (1935). Typical of his work are the painting *July Hay* (Metropolitan Museum of Art, N.Y.) and the mural *Huck Finn and Nigger Jim* (Missouri State Capitol).

From 1935 to 1940, Benton was director of the department of painting at the Kansas City (Mo.) Art Institute. After Pearl Harbor he executed a series of ten large paintings called *The Year of Peril* as propaganda for the war effort. These were reproduced as posters by Abbot Laboratories and the Associated American Artists and distributed widely by the government. Among other works of this type his *Negro Soldiers* (1942) is typical. After the war he continued to paint; his mural for the Harry S. Truman Library, Independence, Missouri, is a good example of his later style. He published his reminiscences, *An Artist in America* (1937).

Formulated with self-conscious and vigorous opposition to the modernism that had begun to infiltrate American painting, a revival of conventional realism emerged in the decade of the 1930s. This movement found a most articulate and unreserved advocate in Thomas Hart Benton. He championed an art "of and for the American people," seeking to capture both the permanent and the vanishing images of his time. His forte was the depiction of life in middle and agrarian America, sadly neglected in his opinion by the decadent and corrupt art created in New York.

Ironically, Benton began his career in New York painting synchronist abstractions inspired by those of his friend Stanton Macdonald-Wright. After his World War I navy service, however, Benton became disenchanted with the "political and aesthetic doctrines drawn from middle European philosophizing" and denounced his earlier work, complaining that "it took me ten years to get all that modernist dirt out of my system." Freed from his past, he became one of the first Americans to capitalize on the Mexican revival of mural painting; with two sets of well-publicized murals in 1930 and 1932 he achieved national prominence as the painter most responsible for revitalizing a long-neglected art form. In these murals and those that followed, farmers, workers, and bureaucrats were rendered as tense, monumental, and highly plastic figures based on the mannered prototypes of Tintoretto and El Greco. Benton painted with a crude strength and animation that activated even the accompanying machinery, architecture, and industrial smoke. So enormous was the popular appeal of these murals that Benton never again changed his style or his reactionary point of view. His work can therefore be seen not only as a unique and nostalgic record of small-town America but also as a revealing document of depression-era tastes and attitudes, of which Benton was both product and accurate judge. See Thomas Hart Benton, *An Artist in America* (1937).

PATRICIA FAILING

BERENSON, Bernard (b. Bernard Valvrojenski, Lithuania, June 26, 1865; d. Florence, Italy, Oct. 6, 1959), ART CRITIC, was brought to the United States by his parents in 1875. He enrolled in Boston University in 1883 but with the assistance of **Isabella Gardner** he shifted to Harvard, receiving an AB in 1887. He then studied at galleries in Paris, London, Oxford, and Berlin (1887–88). During 1888–1900 he continued to travel, largely supported by commissions for paintings he purchased for Mrs. Gardner's growing collection. Most of this period, however, he spent in Italy, and especially in Florence, where he worked in the city's art galleries. By 1900, Berenson had published *Venetian Painters of the Renaissance* (1894), *Florentine Painters of the Renaissance* (1896), and *Central Italian Painters of the Renaissance* (1897), and had become recognized as the world's leading authority on Italian Renaissance painting. By then he had also moved into his forty-room eighteenth-century villa, I Tatti, outside Florence. Throughout the rest of his career Berenson lavished much attention on this home, adding a formal Italian garden, filling it with his growing collection of Renaissance and Oriental art, and making it a center for visiting scholars and travelers from around the world.

Besides his writing, Berenson was active as an adviser and authenticator for virtually every significant art collection created or expanded during his lifetime. He based his decisions on his library of more than forty thousand books and on his original method of authentication, by which he first isolated the characteristics of the painter in question through a study of all works of undoubted authenticity and then looked for these unique traits in the art object under consideration. He also published numerous works after 1900, including *North Italian Painters of the Renaissance* (1907), *Essays in the History of Sienese Painting* (1918), and *The Study of Critics of Italian Art* (1901, 1902, 1916). During World War II, although he opposed Italy's alliance with Germany, Berenson remained with his art treasures, library, and photographs (which he had bequeathed to Harvard). Until 1943 he was permitted to remain undisturbed at I Tatti. When the Germans took control of Italy, he fled to the Vatican. After the war Berenson gained a reputation as a philosopher and humanist through such works as *Sketch for a Self Portrait* (1949) and *Rumour and Reflection* (1952). Born of Jewish parentage, he was baptized into the Protestant Episcopalian Church as a youth and converted during his twenties to Roman Catholicism, which he called "humanity's grandest and most beautiful achievement."

Berenson will long be remembered as one of the foremost modern scholars, aestheticians, connoisseurs, and critics of Italian painting of the Renaissance. His many books and essays on specific artists and paintings, on the history and psychology of art, and on problems in aesthetics have contributed greatly to the general understanding not only of Italian Renaissance painting but also of the whole Western tradition in art. His concepts of tactile values in art and the sense of a physical response in the viewer to painting and space composition opened up a whole body of discussion on the psychology of art. Just as important was his work as a collector and in deciding attributions. By the early years of the twentieth century Berenson had become the most influential critic, providing attributions particularly to Italian Renaissance painting, as well as becoming the leading agent for the sale of Italian Renaissance pictures in the United States. By and large his attributions have been sustained, and the paintings he selected form an important part of several leading American collections. His significance further extends to the great house and library he established at I Tatti and the intellectual center he created there. His own large collection of paintings and bronzes, the huge library of books on art, history, philosophy, literature, and travel, and the grounds and gardens provided the ambience of I Tatti, but always at the center was the man himself. To his passion for knowledge, his sensitivity, perceptiveness, wit, and humanistic compassion, Berenson added a remarkable hospitality. According to all accounts, he was one of the great conversationalists of the twentieth century. At the heart of his many interests ultimately lay his deep concern for the nature and pleasures of visual experience. See Sylvia Sprigge, *Berenson: A Biography* (1960).

PAUL R. BAKER

BERGER, Victor Louis (b. Nieder-Rehbach, Austria-Hungary, Feb. 28, 1860; d. Milwaukee, Wis., Aug. 7, 1929), NEWSPAPER EDITOR, POLITICAL LEADER, attended government schools and universities in Vienna and Budapest. He came to the United States in 1878 and settled in Milwaukee, where he taught German in the public school system (1881–82). He soon became active in left-wing political circles and in 1892 assumed the editorship of the Wisconsin *Vorwärts*, the Milwaukee German daily of the Socialist Labor Party. In 1901 he became editor of the *Social Democratic Herald*, a socialist weekly which he replaced with a daily, the Milwaukee *Leader*, in 1911. He continued as editor of the *Leader* until his death.

Never prone to be tolerant of divergent socialist views, Berger led a split in the Milwaukee Socialist Labor Party in 1892 in reaction to what he considered its doctrinaire insistence on extreme Marxism to the exclusion of the socialism through reform and public ownership approach which he espoused. He then organized a new Social Democratic Society, which soon joined with local trade unions and the People's Party to advocate his own socialist program. He found an ally in **Eugene V. Debs,** president of the American Railway Union, and together they organized the Social Democracy of America in 1897 and, in 1898, with fellow proponents of political action, the Social Democratic Party. In 1900 the new party merged with a dissident Socialist Labor Party faction led by Morris Hillquit, who had split with party leader **Daniel De Leon** over the issue of dual unionism. The next year a unity convention was held in Indianapolis, where the Socialist Party of America was formed. Berger became a perennial member of the executive board representing the party's right wing. In that capacity he advocated a moderate, evolutionary brand of socialism through the ballot box, a revisionist type of Marxism similar to what was then developing in Germany. Berger believed that American conditions allowed for peaceful change, and therefore he argued that reforms through the political system could lead to a socialist order ushered in by legally enacted nationalization. A virulent racist, Berger felt that socialism could be achieved only in an America controlled by whites, and he frequently decried what he envisioned as the imminent threat of black, yellow, and eastern European ("New Immigrant") domination of the country.

Meanwhile, Berger had built a strong socialist political machine in Milwaukee that, aided by German Americans and organized labor, became the major force in municipal politics. In 1910, Berger became the first Socialist elected to the House of Representatives. In Congress he was an unsuccessful proponent of such measures as child-labor legislation, old-age pensions, and nationalization of major industries. After losing campaigns in 1912, 1914, and 1916, he won reelection to the House in 1918 on a peace platform. He had militantly opposed American entry into World War I, but after intervention he offered only mild criticism of the war effort. Nevertheless, his wartime dissent, his German ancestry, and his party's continuing attacks on the Wilson administration's prosecution of the war resulted in the loss of second-class mailing privileges by his newspaper and his own indictment in 1918 under the Espionage Act. In January 1919 he was convicted of giving aid and comfort to the enemy and sentenced to twenty years in prison. Consequently, he was denied his seat in the House by a vote of 309 to 1. While on bail pending appeal of his conviction, Berger won a special election to fill his vacant seat by an increased margin, but again the House refused to seat him. Finally, in January 1921, the Supreme Court reversed his conviction, and that November he was again elected to Congress and took his seat without opposition. He was reelected two more times but was defeated in 1928 when he supported **Al Smith** for the presidency.

Berger was mercurial in temperament, both aggressive and jovial, good-natured and yet a fierce infighter. Loyal to friends and congenial even to foes, Berger gained respect but seldom real affection. Neither creative nor brilliant, he was a studious, widely read individual. His strength lay in his ability to manipulate and per-

severe as a politician; he was most effective in his role as a party boss. He loved fame, but despite his vanity, he never placed personal ambition before the party to which he dedicated his life.

Berger built the most successful socialist machine ever to dominate an American city. In 1910 the Milwaukee socialists won city hall; later they held the mayor's office from 1916 to 1940. Berger, however, after brief service in the city council, concentrated on national politics. His local prestige enabled him to become one of the most powerful voices in the reformist wing of the national Socialist Party. His commitment to democratic values and the nonviolent socialization of the American system led the party away from revolutionary Marxist dogma. He shaped the party into a force that, while struggling against its own left wing, symbolized participation in the political order to attain social reforms. In 1917, Berger reluctantly supported his party's antiwar position, which violated his pragmatic stress on working within the realities of the system. His fears were borne out by the resultant public hostility and by government persecution.

In the party schism of 1919, Berger opposed allegiance to the emergent Soviet system. His shrunken party echoed his preference for a peaceful, democratic, and gradual transformation to socialism, and thus embodied his life's teachings of party responsiveness to American conditions. See Sally M. Miller, *Victor Berger and the Promise of Constructive Socialism, 1910–1920* (1973).

SALLY M. MILLER

BERKELEY, William (b. London, Eng., 1606; d. Twickenham, Eng., July 9, 1677), COLONIAL GOVERNOR, was a brother of the first Lord Berkeley of Stratton and a member of a family long favored at the court of the Stuart kings. After study at Oxford (BA, 1624; MA, 1629), he had some success as a playwright and was knighted by Charles I in 1639. He went to Virginia as governor in 1642 and, except for a few visits to England, remained there until shortly before his death. His early career, before the onset of the Puritan Revolution, was highly successful; he resolved factional disputes, consented to making the General Assembly a final court of appeal, even over his own judgments, and crushed the Indian uprising of 1644, which was followed by a long period of peace. He experimented with a variety of crops and set a good example for the other colonists by his own regular habits; but he persecuted the Quakers and the few Puritans who had found their way to Virginia, and bragged that there was neither printing press nor free school in his colony. During the English civil wars he made Virginia a haven for Cavaliers and royalist clergy, and stoutly opposed an expedition that the Commonwealth sent in 1652 to depose him. He surrendered when offered terms favorable to the colony and was permitted to retire to his plantation.

Berkeley was reinstated as governor upon the Stuart restoration in 1660 and demonstrated a firm hand in dealing with the House of Burgesses, the Council, and even the vestries of the colonial churches. His administration was challenged in the rebellion led by **Nathaniel Bacon,** who besieged Jamestown, burned it, and forced Berkeley to flee. Charles II, by now impatient with the turbulent conditions in Virginia, sent troops to repress it. The commission of investigation also sent by the king disapproved the policy of severe repression that the governor instituted after Bacon's sudden death, and replaced Berkeley. Returning to England to remonstrate, Berkeley died without having had an audience with the king.

━━━⟨∞⟩━━━

Sir William Berkeley, like his nemesis Nathaniel Bacon, Jr., is the object of continuing controversy among historians. All agree that the governor was haughty and imperious, as befitted one of that breed of well-born poets and soldiers who graced the Tudor-Stuart period of English history. Most agree that he was an outstanding governor for most of his career, fighting for the colonists against burdensome economic and political restrictions imposed by the mother country while ignoring his own self-interest and restricting the tendency to self-aggrandizement on the part of others within the colony. Some historians, however, claim that he became querulous and tyrannical in his old age and that he increasingly flouted the will of the people until they rebelled against him in the incident known as Bacon's Rebellion. Others, however, point out that virtually every accusation made against him before the rebellion has been found to be without merit or without evidence to sustain it, even by the commissioners sent over by Charles II to investigate the causes of the rebellion. Berkeley's reaction to the first stirrings of rebellion was characteristic: he called on the people—even those without property—to elect a new assembly and to examine any faults that he may have committed, promising to join them in requesting a new governor if they found that course appropriate. The newly elected assembly instead begged him to continue as governor. When Bacon turned his volunteers for the Indian war against the governor, Berkeley sought vigorously to destroy those who sought to destroy him. In this he was successful, turning the tables on Bacon by capturing his fleet when it attempted to capture him in his refuge on the Eastern Shore. In this cautious age Berkeley has few champions; but he lived in an imperious age, and as the King's viceregent in Virginia he acted as he had seen his two masters, Charles I and Charles II, act in England in dealing with turmoil and dissent. Unfortunately, he had no chance in 1676, as he had a quarter of a century before, to justify himself to his countrymen, to his king, or to future historians. See Wilcomb E. Washburn, *The Governor and the Rebel: A History of Bacon's Rebellion in Virginia* (1957).

WILCOMB E. WASHBURN

BERLE, Adolf Augustus, Jr. (b. Boston, Mass., Jan. 29, 1895; d. New York, N.Y., Feb. 17, 1971), LAWYER, won three degrees from Harvard, BA (1913), MA (1914), and LLB (1916), becoming at 21 the youngest man ever to have received a law degree from Harvard. He then joined the law office of **Louis D. Brandeis** in Boston, but in 1917 he enlisted in the U.S. army, rising to first lieutenant. He was a member of the American delegation to the peace conference at Versailles. In 1919 he joined the New York law firm of Rounds, Hatch, Dillingham, and Debevoise, and also worked as a volunteer for the Henry Street Settlement House. During 1924–33 he was a member of the firm of Lippitt and Berle, and then founded, with his brother Rudolf, the firm of Berle and Berle, specializing in corporation law and Latin American affairs. In addition to his practice Berle lectured occasionally at the Harvard Graduate School of Business Administration (1925–28). He was a professor of corporate law at Columbia University from 1927 to 1964. He published such books as *Studies in the Law of Corporate Finance* (1928) and *The Modern Corporation and Private Property* (1932, with Gardiner C. Means), a work which argued that the managers of corporations were becoming independent of their stockholders and possessed a power equal to that of the leaders of government. This book brought Berle to the attention of Raymond Moley of Columbia, who recruited him for Franklin D. Roosevelt's New Deal "Brain Trust." Although Berle declined appointment to an official post, he was an active member of the New Deal inner circle, serving as special counsel for the Reconstruction Finance Corporation (1933–38). During this period he was also a close adviser of Mayor **Fiorello H. LaGuardia** of New York and served on the city planning commission. During 1938–44 he was assistant secretary of state for Latin American Affairs, playing an active part in carrying out the Good Neighbor Policy and initiating many programs of economic aid. He attended inter-American conferences in Lima (1938) and Havana (1940), and helped draft the Act of Chapultepec, adopted by twenty Latin American nations in 1945; it called for joint action in repelling aggression anywhere in the Western Hemisphere.

In 1944, Berle returned to his teaching, writing, and law practice but briefly served as U.S. ambassador to Brazil (1945–46). In 1954 he published *The Twentieth Century Capitalist Revolution,* and in 1959, *Power Without Poverty.* He was appointed by President John F. Kennedy to chair two task forces created to study the problems of Latin America and to devise new approaches for the United States there (1960–61). In this capacity he recommended establishing the Alliance for Progress to provide loans and economic aid, and support social reform and lower trade barriers for Latin America.

Of the "service intellectuals" helping to shape modern American government, Adolf Berle was one of the most brilliant, versatile, and influential. Moving in and out of governmental positions, attaching himself to rising men of power, and overwhelming weaker personalities with the sheer force of his intellect and the amazing breadth of his expertise, he helped shape and implement new policies in such diverse areas as corporate taxation, railroad reorganization, trade relations, sugar controls, Latin American affairs, and urban planning. Through his writings, moreover, he became a leading articulator and shaper of what later scholars would call "corporate liberalism." In the *Modern Corporation and Private Property* he not only documented the rise of a managerial elite but set forth the possibility of its becoming a "neutral technocracy" imbued with an overriding sense of social responsibility and public trusteeship. As a New Dealer he attempted to fuse the semisocialism of the left with the Christian and managerial corporatism of the right, arguing as he did so that the best approach to economic reform and direction lay through an enlightened and moralized "partnership" of business and government. In the 1950s he developed the notion of a "revolutionary" corporate capitalism, and in the years that followed he continued to find solutions in a mixture of public and private planning, corporate conscience, and state-enforced pluralism. To latter-day critics he seemed more conservative than liberal, but for those who would understand the ideas shaping the American version of the welfare and managerial state his works are difficult to ignore. See Jordan A. Schwarz, *Liberal: Adolf A. Berle and the Vision of an American Era* (1987).

ELLIS W. HAWLEY

BERLIN, Irving (b. Temun, Russia, May 11, 1888; d. New York, N.Y., Sept. 22, 1989), COMPOSER, was born Israel Baline, one of eight children of a cantor who fled the pogroms for the United States in 1893. Growing up on New York City's Lower East Side, Berlin had only two years of formal education. After his father died he took to the streets as an entertainer. He advanced to singing in saloons and plugged songs for publisher Harry von Tilzer at Tony Pastor's Music Hall for five dollars a week. As a singing waiter in a Bowery restaurant (1905–7) Berlin learned to pick out tunes with one finger on a battered piano. His musical education proceeded no further. He never studied harmony—Victor Herbert warned him it would cramp his style—and picked out tunes only in the key of F sharp, a handicap that he overcame by using a special piano capable of transposing to any desired key. In 1907 he published his first song, "Marie from Sunny Italy," for which he wrote only the lyrics. It earned virtually nothing, but Berlin's talent for Italian dialect proved to be his start. His first real hit was "Sadie Salome, Go Home." Meanwhile ragtime, a distinctive popular musical style, had become a nationwide craze. In 1911, Berlin wrote a piece partly in the new beat, and the result, "Alexander's Ragtime Band," sold a million copies in a few months.

Berlin wrote the complete scores for two Broadway shows before World War I; the first was *Watch Your Step* with Vernon and Irene Castle. He wrote songs for the *Ziegfeld Follies* of 1910, 1911, 1919, and 1920, and in 1927 wrote the entire score. "A Pretty Girl Is Like a Melody," from the *Follies* of 1919, became the theme song of the *Follies*. In 1921 he built, with Sam H. Harris and Joseph Schenck, the Music Box theater for intimate musical revues and wrote "Say It with Music" for the first *Music Box Review* with which it opened. His list of musical comedy hits is long, the most famous being *The Cocoanuts* (for the Marx Brothers, 1925); *Face the Music* (1932); *As Thousands Cheer* (1933), which included a number about lynching; *Louisiana Purchase* (1940); *Annie Get Your Gun* (1946), Berlin's longest-running show; *Miss Liberty* (1949); *Call Me Madam* (1950);

and *Mr. President* (1962). During the Depression, Berlin wrote the songs for some of the most successful musical motion pictures: *Top Hat* (1935) with Fred Astaire and Ginger Rogers; *Follow the Fleet* (1936); and *On the Avenue* (1937). Later Berlin movie musicals include *Holiday Inn* (1942), in which the fabulously successful "White Christmas" was included; *Blue Skies* (1946); *Easter Parade* (1948); and *There's No Business Like Show Business* (1954). Among his more than nine hundred songs are such popular classics as "All Alone," "Remember," "What'll I Do?" "Always," "Blue Skies," and "Someone to Watch Over Me."

Berlin, drafted in 1917, was sent to Camp Upton, Long Island, where he was assigned to write a soldiers' show. The result, which played thirty-two performances at the Century theater, New York, was *Yip, Yip, Yaphank,* in which Berlin brought down the house with his epitome of the agonies of reveille, "Oh, How I Hate to Get Up in the Morning." In World War II, Berlin repeated his feat with the service show *This Is the Army* (1942), which earned $10 million for Army Emergency Relief. It toured for three and a half years, with Berlin doggedly appearing throughout the run in a show-stopping repetition of his greatest 1917 number. One of the most popular of his songs today is the patriotic "God Bless America."

In his last years Berlin lived on Beekman Place in Manhattan and became very reclusive, even refusing to see old friends. His only real link with the outside world seemed to be his telephone. When a party celebrating his one-hundredth birthday was held in Carnegie Hall in May 1988, he gave his reluctant blessing but did not attend.

⁂

No American popular composer produced more song hits, accumulated the kind of sales figures these hits did, or dominated the American popular music scene for as long a span of time as Irving Berlin. For more than half a century he adapted himself resiliently to changing song styles without any diminution in his popularity, productivity, or the quality of his output. He wrote ragtime songs and ballads, show and movie tunes, patriotic and war songs, the kind of rhythmic songs passing off in the 1920s as jazz— and produced enduring classics in each category.

Berlin never initiated trends, just as he never experimented with new forms or idioms. His song structure followed the traditional Tin Pan Alley pattern of a sixteen-measure verse and a thirty-two-measure chorus. His harmonic and rhythmic invention was never personalized. Notwithstanding his technical shortcomings as a musician, which were both obvious and many, he remained a remarkable (if highly intuitive) composer. His strong suit was his lyricism, which at best possessed a charm, freshness, and spontaneity few have equaled. There was an inevitability in the way his melodies flowed from the first measure to the last. The ease and grace of his lyricism and his elementary structure suggested that songs came easily to Berlin. They did not. The process of creation, selection, revision, and refinement was for him a long and painful, as well as painstaking, process. This applied to the words as well as to the music, for Berlin was his own lyricist and an exceptionally competent one, too. The writing of the words usually preceded the melody and dictated the kind of melody Berlin wrote. Once the song was completed, words and music seemed indivisible, as if they had been conceived simultaneously. The finished product never betrayed the anguish with which it was fashioned. Simplicity was its keynote, but it was a simplicity that came only when musical and verbal thought was condensed to its essentials. See Laurence Bergreen, *As Thousands Cheer: The Life of Irving Berlin* (1990).

DAVID EWEN

BERNSTEIN, Leonard (b. Lawrence, Mass., Aug. 25, 1918; d. New York, N.Y., Oct. 14, 1990), MUSICIAN, COMPOSER, studied the piano with Heinrich Gebhard and composition with Walter Piston at Harvard. After graduating in 1939 he attended the Curtis Institute of Music in Philadelphia (1939–41) and studied conducting with Fritz Reiner and piano with Isabelle Vengerova. During the summers of 1940 and 1941 he studied with Serge Koussevitzsky, conductor of the Boston Symphony Orchestra, at the Berkshire Music Center in Tanglewood, Massachusetts. He produced operas for the Boston Institute of Modern Art in 1941–42 and published his first composition, *Clarinet Sonata* (1942). Bernstein was appointed assistant to Koussevitzsky at the Berkshire Music Center in 1942 and went to New York City that same year to direct a "serenade" concert at the Museum of Modern Art. In 1943, Artur Rodzinski named him assistant conductor of the New York Philharmonic Orchestra. He achieved widespread recognition and critical acclaim when he substituted for conductor Bruno Walter of the Philharmonic on November 14, 1943. His symphony *Jeremiah* (1942) won the New York City Music Critics Circle Prize as best new American orchestral work of the 1943–44 season. In 1944 his ballet *Fancy Free* was adapted into the popular Broadway musical *On the Town.*

From 1945 to 1947, Bernstein led the New York City Center Orchestra and in 1948 was guest conductor of the Israel Philharmonic. He was a professor of music at Brandeis University (1951–56) and lectured on music on the television show *Omnibus* (1954–55). Continuing his composing, he wrote a jazz rhythm piece, *Age of Anxiety* (1949), the Broadway musicals *Wonderful Town* (1953), *Candide* (1956), and *West Side Story* (1957), and the musical score of the movie *On the Waterfront* (1954). Bernstein became co-conductor of the New York Philharmonic with Dimitri Mitropoulos in 1957; he became sole conductor the following year. His television series *New York Philharmonic Young People's Concert* gained a 1960 Emmy award. In 1958, Bernstein and the Philharmonic toured Latin America, Europe, and Asia. They played in the Soviet Union (1958–59) and Japan (1961). He published two books, *The Joy of Music* (1959) and *The Infinite Variety of Music* (1966). In 1969, Bernstein retired as conductor of the Philharmonic and toured Europe with the Vienna Philharmonic Orchestra in 1970. He composed *Kaddish* (1963), *Chichester Psalms* (1965), and *Mass* (1971) for the opening of the John F. Kennedy Center for the Performing Arts in

Washington, D.C. In 1972, Bernstein was appointed Charles Eliot Norton professor at Harvard University. In 1976, Bernstein returned to Broadway with *1600 Presidential Avenue*, a work done in collaboration with Allan Jay Lerner. Though awaited with great anticipation, it closed after only seven performances.

Bernstein had been connected with the Israel Philharmonic Orchester for over thirty years, and in the late 1970s they put on a retrospective festival of his music to celebrate his debut with them. In 1988 he was named laureate conductor of that orchestra. That same year, to celebrate his debut with the New York Philharmonic, he conducted the orchestra once more in an all Bernstein program. Bernstein received numerous awards and honors, but in 1989 he turned down a medal from the Bush administration to protest what he regarded as censorship of an AIDS exhibition by the National Endowment of the Arts. He contributed much time in his last years to concerts to benefit AIDS research and counseling.

⸺⸺∞⸺⸺

"It's easy to dislike Lenny, for obvious reasons," said Felicia Bernstein early in her husband's career. "He's been too gifted, too successful, too lucky."

It was luck—being in the right place at the right time—that gave Bernstein his opportunity to take over for the ailing Bruno Walter in 1943. But luck, as Louis Pasteur once observed, favors only those who are prepared for it. Substituting at short notice and scoring a big triumph with the Philharmonic established Bernstein as a musical personality worth watching. On the other hand, Bernstein could have fumbled his big opportunity, with a nationwide audience listening in, making himself ludicrous and giving his career and reputation a setback from which they might have been years in recovering. And as Bernstein moved in his early days from one triumph to another, it became evident that while luck might have launched his career, it was the breadth and versatility of his talent that kept it moving.

The sheer protean variety of Bernstein's doings, in fact, led some observers to feel he had undertaken too many projects to do them all well. Bernstein himself expressed regret that composing, which he regarded as the most personal and profound expression of his musical thought, often had to be done on time borrowed from other things. Perhaps inevitably, his works were of uneven quality as a result. At their best, however, they were outstanding. *West Side Story*, for example, was an immediate triumph, and its revivals suggest it may be of more lasting importance than just another "Broadway musical."

Bernstein's conducting career was relatively brief; he retired at an age when a conductor is often thought of as "one of the promising younger men." Nevertheless, he reached the top within a decade as musical director of one of America's most prestigious orchestras and with guest appearances that took him to most of the great orchestras and opera houses of the world.

Furthermore, in the early stages of his career he was continually breaking new ground. He was the first native-born, wholly American-trained conductor to have a big international career. Today the sight of gifted young Americans leading orchestral concerts and operatic performances abroad is not a novelty, but it was Bernstein, in the 1940s and 1950s, who showed the way. See John Briggs, *Leonard Bernstein, the Man, His Work and His World* (1961).

JOHN BRIGGS

BETHUNE, Mary McLeod (b. Mayesville, S.C., July 10, 1875; d. Daytona Beach, Fla., May 18, 1955), EDUCATOR, studied at the Scotia Seminary (Concord, N.C.), and graduated from the Moody Bible Institute in Chicago in 1895. During 1895–1903 she taught at four southern schools for black children, working longest (1899–1903) at the Palatka, Florida, Mission School. In 1904, Bethune founded the Daytona Normal and Industrial Institute, which in 1923 came under Methodist Episcopal sponsorship and amalgamated with the Cookman Institute to form the Daytona Collegiate Institute. In 1928 it became known as Bethune-Cookman College.

In 1936, President Franklin D. Roosevelt

97

appointed Bethune director of the Division of Negro Affairs of the National Youth Administration and made her a special adviser on minority affairs. Her work in the Division of Negro Affairs was devoted primarily to increasing educational opportunities for black youth. In 1935 she founded the National Council of Negro Women and six years later became a special assistant to the secretary of war to assist in selecting women to attend the Women's Army Corps Officers School. She retired from Bethune-Cookman College in 1947.

First prominent as a founder of a normal and industrial school for blacks, Mary McLeod Bethune became nationally known as a black leader, a presidential adviser, and the first black woman to head a federal office. She was a deeply religious person who originally aspired to be a missionary, and her work as a college president amounted to a crusade for the spiritual and educational improvement of black children. Her school, one of the few open to blacks in Florida, emphasized in its early years religious and cultural objectives and occupational skills rather than a liberal arts curriculum. By the 1940s, however, it had become a four-year liberal arts college. Her work for her school and her service as president of the National Association of Colored Women in the 1920s won her national prominence; her appointment as director of Negro Affairs of the National Youth Administration followed. Upon her insistence, NYA programs were designed to provide educational and occupational training for black youth rather than consisting primarily of "make-work" projects. The NYA supported programs to combat illiteracy and provided financial aid for students seeking high school diplomas and college, graduate, and professional degrees.

Bethune's influence was felt in many circles, partly through personal contacts and partly through her work in a variety of civic organizations. She was instrumental in organizing the Federal Council on Negro Affairs (the so-called Black Cabinet), a group of federal officials attempting to persuade units of the federal government to address themselves to the most urgent problems of black people. On the surface a simple and straightforward woman, Bethune was not only idealistic but also shrewd, strong-willed, and forceful. These qualities enabled her to function as a semireligious inspirational leader who used religious and moral values as rationales for the achievement of specific, practical goals, thereby commanding the cooperation, support, and respect of white philanthropists, liberal leaders, and government officials, and also blacks. See Catherine Owens Peare, *Mary McLeod Bethune* (1951).

DeWitt S. Dykes

BEVERIDGE, Albert Jeremiah (b. Highland Co., Ohio, Oct. 6, 1862; d. Indianapolis, Ind., Apr. 27, 1927), POLITICAL LEADER, HISTORIAN, worked his way through high school and Asbury College (now DePauw University) in part with prize money earned in oratorical contests. After graduating in 1885 he practiced law in Indianapolis (1887–99). In 1899 he was selected as a compromise candidate for the U.S. Senate by the Republican caucus. Elected, he immediately became one of the Senate's chief spokesmen for imperialism. Addressing the Senate during his first year in that body, contrary to custom, he declared, "The Philippines are ours forever ... and just beyond ... are China's illimitable markets. We will not retreat from either.... We will not renounce our part in the mission of our race, trustees under God, of the civilization of the world."

In 1905, Beveridge was renominated for the Senate without opposition and was handily reelected. Thereafter he became increasingly identified with the insurgent, or midwestern Progressive, wing of the party. A firm supporter of President Theodore Roosevelt's policies concerning the regulations of big business, Beveridge substantially aided the passage of the Pure Food and the Meat Inspection acts of 1906. He also took the lead in championing child-labor legislation. Beveridge long advocated a tariff commission and was one of the handful of senators who led the revolt against the Payne-Aldrich Tariff of 1909. He was defeated for reelection in 1910 when conservative Republicans withheld their support. In 1912, Beveridge delivered the keynote speech at the Progressive Party convention that nominated Theodore Roosevelt for president. He ran for governor of Indiana on the Progressive ticket in 1912 but was defeated. Beveridge rejoined the Republican Party in 1916 and supported **Charles Evans Hughes** for the presidency. Although he received the Indiana GOP nomination for the U.S. Senate in 1922, he was again defeated.

Very nationalistic and anti-British, Beveridge wrote a book sympathizing with the Central Powers while serving as war correspondent in Europe in 1915. After April 1917 he supported the war but opposed U.S. participation in the League of Nations. Between 1903 and 1907, Beveridge had written an account of his visit to the Russo-Japanese war zone and several books on religion and preparation for leadership aimed primarily at young adults. After he left the Senate he wrote a biography of Chief Justice **John Marshall,** of which two volumes appeared in 1916 and two more in 1919. At his death Beveridge, a meticulous researcher and writer, had completed two volumes of a life of Abraham Lincoln.

One of the most dynamic American senators of the twentieth century, Albert J. Beveridge threw himself with vigor and unsurpassed assurance into any cause he championed. It is no exaggeration to state that he was the premier orator of imperialism in the United States. Preparing his speeches with exemplary care, memorizing most of them, on the stump he became an eloquent Republican rival of the Democrats' **William Jennings Bryan.**

Relatively young and decidedly brash when he entered Congress, Beveridge had a tendency to offend some older and less brilliant men. His enemies within the Republican Party multiplied in the course of his second Senate term when the Hoosier's reform convictions and devotion to

Theodore Roosevelt led him to oppose standpatism in many of its forms. The reaction in Indiana, which had a strong conservative streak, was Beveridge's defeat in his third-term effort—partly a result of undercutting by the Charles W. Fairbanks Republican faction. It may be that Beveridge believed more wholeheartedly in the "Bull Moose" movement than did Roosevelt himself. Certainly, Beveridge's later political prospects were seriously damaged by his prominence as a Progressive supporter of TR.

An entirely different side of Beveridge's character and personality came into public view when he shifted from the role of statesman to that of scholar. Investing his talents in deep research for biographies of John Marshall and Abraham Lincoln, the delver in primary source materials proved consistently modest and painstaking in his approach to historical judgments. He not only went to great lengths to find facts but consulted numerous academicians, usually weighing their estimates of men and measures before reaching conclusions of his own.

The most remarkable facet of Beveridge's intellectual growth is seen in his evaluation of **Stephen A. Douglas.** Born into a fervid Republican family during the Civil War, and long a zealous Republican partisan equating Douglas with the selfish and the sinister, the biographer of Lincoln now discovered much virtue in the Illinois adversary of the Great Emancipator. Indeed, few residents of ivory towers have attained objectivity more impressive than that of Beveridge in his last years.

Beveridge's is a classic case of able Americans' success in excelling in a second career after being frustrated in the first one. It is possible, even probable, that he will be remembered longer and more favorably for the quality of his books than as a politician. Members of bench and bar have placed a high premium on the Marshall volumes, which were awarded a Pulitzer Prize. Both a statesmanlike approach and scholarship of a lofty order are evident on the pages of the truncated *Lincoln.*

Nor should it be assumed that Beveridge lost all his following in politics. In 1922, at 59, he defeated incumbent Harry S. New for the Indiana Republican senatorial nomination. With a slightly different development of events, he would have beaten the popular Democrat Samuel M. Ralston in the autumn of that year and thus might have gone on to win new congressional prestige. Politics' possible loss was history's undoubted gain as a more mellow Beveridge unobtrusively returned to the scholar's sanctum and to his provocative analyses of movers and shakers of earlier times. See John Braeman, *Albert J. Beveridge: American Nationalist* (1971).

HOLMAN HAMILTON

BEVERLEY, Robert (b. Middlesex County, Va., c. 1673; d. King and Queen County, Va., 1722), HISTORIAN, was educated in England and, on returning to Virginia, became volunteer scrivener to the colony's secretary of state. By 1696 he had held positions as clerk of the General Court, the Council, and the General Assembly. He was elected to the House of Burgesses as representative from Jamestown (1700–2 and 1705–6). While on a trip to England in 1703 to protect his interests in a litigation before the Privy Council, Beverley wrote some letters home to friends in the Assembly that attacked Virginia's Governor Francis Nicholson and the surveyor general of customs for the colony for alleged corruption. Attempts by Beverley's friends to censure the officials failed, however, and the uproar created ruined his political career. He retired to his estate, Beverley Park.

While in England, Beverley had become interested in writing a history of Virginia after reading what he regarded as an inferior one composed by John Oldmixon. He published his *History and Present State of Virginia* in London in 1705 (revised ed., 1722). This book described the colony's history and resources, the Indians, and contemporary political and social conditions, especially plantation life. Beverley condemned prevailing racial prejudices toward Indians and recognized Indian grievances as real. He spent his later years compiling the laws of Virginia, published as *An Abridgement of the Public Laws of Virginia* (1722).

Beverley, though less renowned than the New England historians **William Bradford** and **John Winthrop,** deserves to be remembered as an important chronicler of his native Virginia. For the first years of the colony Beverley's *History* relied on Captain **John Smith**'s *Generall Historie* (1624) as well as on official records. He was particularly enthusiastic over the abundant natural resources of Virginia. He accounted it a mistake that the whites did not accept the Indians' offers of intermarriage and so avoid the violence that undermined relations between the races. He also praised the simplicity of the Indians' life with its abundant leisure. Having little or nothing in the way of material possessions, they were able to enjoy all things, but the English, he noted, "have taken away great part of their Country, and consequently made every thing less plenty amongst them."

Beverley was dubious about many of the changes that the English settlers made in the state of nature. "I can't call them Improvements," he wrote. Yet as a conscientious planter he was annoyed at the want of industry among his fellow Virginians. "They spunge upon the Blessings of a warm Sun, and a fruitful Soil, and almost grutch the Pains of gathering in the Bounties of the Earth." In contrast to those colonials who remained transplanted Englishmen, Beverley wrote and thought as a self-conscious American. His *History* in turn reflects the easy manner and simplicity that also characterized his personal lifestyle. See Louis B. Wright, Introduction to Robert Beverley, *The History and Present State of Virginia* (1947).

ARTHUR A. EKIRCH, JR.

BIDDLE, Nicholas (b. Philadelphia, Pa., Jan. 8, 1786; d. Philadelphia, Pa., Feb. 27, 1844), BANKER, was educated at the University of Pennsylvania and the College of New Jersey (Princeton). He studied law under William Lewis of Philadelphia (1801–4). He spent the next three years in Europe, first as an unpaid secretary to John Armstrong, the American minister in Paris, then as a traveler through Switzerland, Italy, and Greece, and finally as secretary to James Monroe, minister to Great Britain. Returning to Philadelphia in 1807 he began the practice of law but soon was devoting more time to politics and literature. In 1810 he was elected as a Federalist to the lower house of the Pennsylvania legislature and also began to edit the journals of the **Meriwether Lewis** and William Clark expedition. His marriage to Jane Craig, a wealthy heiress, in 1811 enabled him to abandon the law, and he became editor of the *Portfolio,* a literary magazine (1811–14). In 1814 when the British invasion of the Chesapeake area seemed to threaten Philadelphia, he was elected to the Pennsylvania senate, where he introduced a conscription bill and other measures for defense of the state. He also prepared Pennsylvania's rejection and condemnation of the sectionalist proposals of the Hartford Convention. His nationalist sympathies, which led him to abandon the Federalist Party, were unacceptable to many Republicans, and he was defeated in two races for the Congress (1818, 1820).

In 1819, President James Monroe appointed Biddle as one of the five government directors of the Bank of the United States. He was reappointed in 1820 and 1821, and in 1823, after a year's absence from the board of directors, as required by the charter, he was elected president of the Bank. He continued in this office until 1836, leading the unsuccessful effort to obtain a recharter against the opposition of President Andrew Jackson. After the national charter expired, he was elected president of a successor institution, the United States Bank of Pennsylvania. He resigned in March 1839, and in 1841, as a result of pressures engendered in large part by an international financial crisis, the bank failed. Biddle, blamed for the failure, was indicted for fraud and theft, but the court dismissed the charges without argument as being unfounded. He then retired to his country home on the Delaware River, north of Philadelphia.

———∞∞∞———

Nicholas Biddle was a leading defender of a significant constitutional and economic point of view at one of the decisive turning points in American history, and the defeat of his effort to gain a recharter for the Bank of the United States during the administration of Andrew Jackson had momentous consequences for the nation. The state banks, the currency, and the credit structure were left without controls, guidance, and protection, subject to the unrestrained laws of trade, speculative manipulation, and foreign influence. The effects of this defeat were found not only in the financial crises of 1837 and 1839 and the costly depression that followed but also in the disordered and unsatisfactory financial system that hampered the national economy throughout the rest of the 19th century and into the twentieth.

Biddle appreciated and understood what was at stake in the conflict. As a member of the Pennsylvania legislature he had unsuccessfully opposed a resolution hostile to the recharter of the first Bank of the United States and had predicted that if the institution were permitted to die the nation would "cut the main artery" of its resources at a moment when it was preparing for war. The inability of the national treasury and the state banks adequately to provide needed financial support for the War of 1812 confirmed the accuracy of his prediction, and he enthusiastically supported the movement, initiated by President Madison, that led to the chartering of the second Bank of the United States in 1816.

As a government director of the bank, he strongly supported the new president, Langdon Cheves, in the difficult task of recuperation and reform. When he became president himself, he proved an effective manager of the institution; under his administration it faithfully served the government by providing a safe depository for its funds, transferring them from place to place, paying the public creditors, and acting as fiscal agent, all without cost to the Treasury. It was equally useful in the private sector. Its notes constituted a national currency of uniform value in all areas of the country, and through the power to expand or contract money and credit it regulated the rates and supply of domestic and foreign exchange, guided and checked the local state banks in their operations and issues, and protected them and the rest of the economic community from sudden, injurious financial pressures.

So usefully did it operate that all the inherited hostility apparently disappeared, and it was not an issue in the presidential campaigns of 1824 and 1828. Biddle, as a private citizen, voted for Jackson in both elections, confidently believing that no administration would desire "to set the monied concerns of the country afloat" as they had been in the period between the closing of the first Bank of the United States and the rechartering of the second. He proved to be mistaken. Jackson's silence masked a bitter hostility to the bank, credit, and paper money, and in his first message to the Congress raised the question of its recharter some six years before it was to expire. He made the unsubstantiated charge that it had failed to establish "a sound and uniform currency," and also resurrected the contention that the charter was unconstitutional, believing, as he was later to say, that as president he had the right to act on his own view of the Constitution without regard to the actions or statements to the contrary by each of his predecessors, most of the Congresses, and the federal courts.

Biddle, during the next ten years, was an opponent of these views, but not as a partisan until Jackson's veto of the recharter in 1832 and his transfer of the government's funds to state bank depositories freed him from the requirement of political neutrality that he had accepted as president of the nation's bank. Jackson's actions (which he justified on the grounds that the bank was a private and irresponsible monopoly, a conspiracy by a financial oligarchy to dominate the political and economic life of the nation, and a device through which the wealth of the rich and the poverty of the poor were both increased) had the effect that Biddle feared, and the sole result of Jackson's financial policies was the elimination of an institution that had public responsibility for the general welfare and sufficient resources and strength to protect and sustain the national economy.

Within four years, in May 1837, all the banks were forced to suspend specie payments, and Biddle's attempt to prevent this financial crisis from initiating a depression, though temporarily successful, ultimately failed. Throughout 1837 and 1838 he used the resources of the state-chartered United States Bank of Pennsylvania to restore the market prices of stocks and commodities, thus providing the means for payments and collections, and in March 1839, thinking that the danger of depression had been overcome, he resigned as president of this successor to the Bank of the United States. Shortly afterward, however, a renewal of financial pressure from outside the country, compounded by mistakes of those in charge of the institution, brought about its failure in the spring of 1841. A depression ensued that was worldwide in extent, and most of Biddle's contemporaries, including many of those who had supported him in the conflict with Jackson, blamed him and his policies for this economic disaster.

The justice or injustice of this verdict is a matter of only personal concern, but whether just or not, it should not be permitted to obscure the fact that Biddle, anticipating the monetary theories and policies of many twentieth-century economists and central bankers, argued for a controlled system of paper credit and against an unthinking adherence to a purely specie currency. It also should not be forgotten that under his direction, as one of his informed admirers said, "When danger threatened, when credit was trembling, when confidence was shaken, whenever, in a word, a revulsion was threatened with its disastrous train of circumstances, this bank, strong in its power, stronger in its inclination to do good, anticipated and averted the crisis." The nation could have used such an institution in the troubled years that lay ahead. See Thomas P. Govan, *Nicholas Biddle: Nationalist and Public Banker, 1786–1844* (1959).

THOMAS P. GOVAN

BIERCE, Ambrose Gwinnett (b. Horse Cave Creek, Ohio, June 24, 1842; d. Ojinaga [?], Mexico,

Jan. 11, 1914 [?]), WRITER, spent most of his youth in Indiana except for a year of study (1859) at the Kentucky Military Institute. He fought with the Union army during the Civil War and was severely wounded at the Battle of Kenesaw Mountain. Breveted a major in 1867, he then resigned his commission, took up residence in San Francisco, and began a career as a journalist. In 1872 he went to England, where he subsequently published three books of journalistic essays: *The Fiend's Delight* (1872), *Nuggets and Dust* (1872), and *Cobwebs from an Empty Skull* (1874). Ill health and familial obligations forced him to return to California in 1875.

For the next dozen years, though continuing to write, he spent much of his time and effort attempting to gain a fortune, first through mining and then real estate. In 1887, Bierce began an association (which was to last for more than twenty years) as a feature writer for various publications of **William Randolph Hearst,** notably the San Francisco *Examiner* and the New York *Journal.* During these years his fame as a satirist and short-story writer grew with the publication of several collections, including *Tales of Soldiers and Civilians* (1891), *Can Such Things Be?* (1893), and *The Cynic's Word Book* (1906), known today as *The Devil's Dictionary.* His *Collected Works* (twelve volumes) appeared in 1912. In late 1913, Bierce visited Mexico, and although the facts of his death have never been ascertained, it seems probable that he died at the Battle of Ojinaga on January 11, 1914.

"Bitter Bierce," "The Wickedest Man in San Francisco," and "The Devil's Lexicographer" are only a few of the choice epithets that have been given to Ambrose Bierce, one of the nation's most gifted satirists and almost certainly its most caustic one. In his lifetime Bierce achieved considerable fame and more than a little notoriety for the pungent and often perverse quality of his essays, short stories, and sayings. Today, while his *Devil's Dictionary* still remains fairly popular, he is probably best remembered for the mystery surrounding his disappearance in Mexico.

Americans enjoy—even, as in the instance of **Mark Twain,** venerate—their humorists as long as they infuse their wit with convincing touches of sympathy and understanding for human frailty. In the light of an unhappy, poverty-filled childhood, a broken marriage, the death of two of his three children, and persistent ill health, Bierce refused to offer such concessions. An accomplished craftsman, he chose to continue the tradition of vitriolic satire associated with Jonathan Swift. (Indeed, his "Oil of Dog" is highly reminiscent of the misanthropic Swift's "A Modest Proposal.") His is the type of humor that appeals to a select audience. **H. L. Mencken** was charmed by it; contemporary devotees of black humor certainly should be.

In addition to his works of satire, Bierce made genuine contributions to American literature with his tales of horror and a few early examples of the realistic short story. **Edgar Allan Poe**'s excepted, Bierce's sense of the macabre rarely has been surpassed. "The Suitable Surroundings," "One Summer's Night," and "The Death of Halpern Frayser" are particularly fine examples of the horror story. In terms of realism, certain of Bierce's stories—"Chickamauga" and "One of the Missing," for example—antedate and perhaps may have influenced **Stephen Crane** in depicting the grimness of war.

Despite his diverse literary achievements, Bierce's reputation ultimately rests on his work as a humorist. Savage satire may not be palatable in an age that has known firsthand both genocide and nuclear devastation. Yet if an honest and brilliant attempt to portray the dark side of American life provides legitimate cause for remembrance, the general lack of attention paid to Bierce has been unjustifiable. See Richard O'Connor, *Ambrose Bierce* (1967).

ROBERT MUCCIGROSSO

BIERSTADT, Albert (b. Solingen, Germany, Jan. 7, 1830; d. New York, N.Y., Feb. 18, 1902), ARTIST, was taken to America as a child; at 21 he decided to become a painter. He studied for four years (1853–57) in Düsseldorf and Rome.

After returning to the United States in 1857, Bierstadt joined an expedition to survey an overland wagon route to the Pacific coast. His numerous sketches of western scenes made on this trip were the basis for the many large canvases he painted during the rest of his life that brought him fame and a substantial income. *Laramie Peak,* exhibited in 1861, was a striking success among easterners who were longing to get an idea of what the West looked like, two decades before train travel to the region was possible. Rich men and institutions bought eagerly. One of his best-known works, *Valley of the Yosemite,* was purchased by the Lenox Library; **August Belmont** bought *Burning Ship.* But critics during his lifetime did not rate him highly. In 1885 he began to paint animals of North America, and in 1887–88 he traveled to Spain and the West Indies for material for four historical pictures of the discovery of America. One of his last and best-known works is *The Last of the Buffalo* (1890).

———— ∞ ————

Albert Bierstadt was the founder of the Rocky Mountain school of American painting. To him and his followers of the Hudson River persuasion, the Far West was a romantic expanse of untrammeled and happily terrifying nature. He created huge, melodramatic canvases, exploiting the picturesque scenery for maximum effect. During the 1870s and 1880s these slick, inflated paintings moved into the collections of American railroad barons, English noblemen, and Russian princes.

In Europe he had learned a simple, tonal style that is at its best in some of his early, luminous paintings of the untouched wilderness, such as *Thunderstorm in the Rocky Mountains* (1859). The grandeur of the Rockies and other towering mountain ranges rivaled the Alps, and Bierstadt brought to them a manner developed in his birthplace. He typified the paradoxical mentality of the Bismarckian era that wavered between the ancient German attachment to the idyllic and the new spirit of aggression. His mountain scenery of the American hinterland resembled the Bernese Alps, and if no Indians or buffalo were included, many of his pictures could just as well have been paintings of Switzerland.

His painting displayed splendid brilliance if not conscientious accuracy. He steepened declivities, sharpened peaks, and identified a mountain by whatever name might appeal to a potential buyer. He gained international fame for his works, commanding the highest prices ever paid to an American artist up to that time. A gift for publicity also helped, although it did not make him better liked by his fellow artists. When his *Rocky Mountains* was first exhibited in New York, streamers were hung across Broadway announcing the fact. The leading painters of the Rocky Mountain school shared not so much in particulars of painting technique as they did in attitude of mind: all believed that the more unusual and stupendous the scenery, the more exaggerated should be the image. They could appeal to the nation's preoccupation with its dwindling frontier by scenes of wild grandeur that excited the sensibilities. These resemblances between Bierstadt's style and scene painting were sometimes recognized by his contemporaries but were forgiven on the grounds that such was the best way to represent grandiloquent and unspoiled scenery.

Bierstadt's technique in composing popular showpieces was derived from both his training in Düsseldorf and his association with the Hudson River school. However, he avoided the minuscule naturalism and local subtleties of atmosphere and foliage characteristic of the Hudson River manner. He enjoyed dramatic light effects, using cloud and mist to blank out large areas in the middle distance and background of his large western canvases and give greater emphasis to a few sensational passages: blue and green mountains whitened in places by light rays, snowy summits glowing against an unshrouded sky, dazzling waterfalls, fleecy clouds shadowed above, a herd of deer or an encampment of Indians brought boldly into the foreground. His paintings are exaggerated in feeling and often marred by his inability to control the intensified colors of his palette. See Gordon Hendricks,

"Bierstadt and Church at the N.Y. Sanitary Fair," *Antiques* (Nov. 1972), 892–98.

WENDELL D. GARRETT

BILLINGS, John Shaw (b. Switzerland Co., Ind., Apr. 12, 1838; d. New York, N.Y., Mar. 11, 1913), PHYSICIAN, LIBRARIAN, graduated from Miami University, Oxford, Ohio, in 1857, and received an MD from the Medical College of Ohio in 1860. He remained there as a demonstrator of anatomy for a year, then joined the army as a contract surgeon. By the spring of 1862 he was a first lieutenant in the Medical Corps, in charge of Cliffburne Hospital, Washington, D.C., and later that year he served as executive officer of the army hospital in Philadelphia. In March 1863 he reported for duty with the Army of the Potomac and served as a field surgeon at Chancellorsville and Gettysburg. After the New York Draft Riots in July he accompanied the Seventh Infantry to New York and was later assigned to hospital duty on Bedloe's Island. In March 1864 he rejoined the Army of the Potomac and served as medical inspector until the fall when he was assigned to duty at the Surgeon General's Office in Washington, in charge of medical statistics. By 1865 he had assumed charge of the Army Medical Museum and Library.

His major task during 1865–95 was direction of the library of the Surgeon General's Office, which he organized and developed into the foremost medical library in the world. He began publication of the library's *Index-Catalogue* in 1880, along with its subsidiary monthly *Index Medicus* (1879). At the same time he devised a reorganization plan for the U.S. Marine Hospital Service; he prepared voluminous reports on sanitary and hygienic conditions in army barracks and hospitals; he conducted a survey of Memphis following the yellow fever outbreak of 1879. He also served as principal adviser to **Daniel Coit Gilman** in the development of the new Johns Hopkins Medical School, planning the curriculum and influencing the selection of the staff. He was president of the American Public Health Association (1880), consultant to the U.S. Census Bureau—where at his suggestion mechanical methods of tabulation were developed—and treasurer of the National Academy of Sciences (1887–98). He was appointed deputy surgeon general in 1890 and was retired from the army in 1895.

From 1890 on, Billings served as part-time official at the University of Pennsylvania and was director of its Institute of Hygiene in 1895–96. In 1896 he was appointed the first director of the New York Public Library. He planned its new building, completed in 1911, reorganized the staff, and doubled the size of the collections.

In 1902, Billings was chosen president of the American Library Association. He drew up plans for the Peter Bent Brigham Hospital in Boston during 1905–8. From 1903 until his death he was chairman of the board of trustees of the Carnegie Institution of Washington.

Billings achieved much in many fields—in hospital construction, in public health and sanitation, in the development of vital statistics, in medical education, and in librarianship. His forte was organizing genius, managerial adroitness. He had vision, and he had a passion for doing. "There would be no coral islands," he said, "if the first bug sat down and began to wonder how the job was to be done."

His most enduring accomplishments were in the field of librarianship and medical bibliography. He created two great research libraries and endowed them with momentum and with goals that have survived. It is significant that he always thought of the library of the Surgeon General's Office as the National Medical Library and indeed had that rubric printed boldly on letterheads and on the title page of one of his catalogs. In 1956 the name of the institution was changed to the National Library of Medicine.

Living at a time when scientific periodicals were rapidly burgeoning in importance and in numbers, he saw clearly the complicated problems of bibliographical retrieval that derive from floods of print, and he devised technological innovations to cope with those problems. He put the processes of indexing on an assembly-line basis; he inaugurated interlibrary loan procedures to make library services more widely available; he launched massive acquisition programs.

Billings was a skilled public speaker, a master of straightforward language touched with wit and an occasional apt allusion drawn from wide reading—he once said he scanned three thousand books a year. He represented the United States abroad on many occasions, perhaps the best known of which was his delivery of an address, "Our Medical Literature," before the Seventh International Medical Congress in London in 1881. During his lifetime he published some 150 papers and many lengthy reports, reviews, and special bibliographies. His writings on bibliography and librarianship have been collected in *Selected Papers of John Shaw Billings* (1965). See F. H. Garrison, *John Shaw Billings: A Memoir* (1915).

FRANK B. RODGERS

BILLINGS, William (b. Boston, Mass., Oct. 7, 1746; d. Boston, Mass., Sept. 26, 1800), COMPOSER, had little academic and no musical training. He was apprenticed to a tanner at the age of 14. Music interested him more than his trade, however, and he began to study the subject and to memorize all the psalms he could find. Around 1767 he decided to abandon tanning and make music his profession. He started out as a teacher of choir singing in the movement to revive music reading after the long lapse of musical literacy in English-speaking churches. In 1774 he organized a singing class in Stoughton, Massachusetts, that in 1786 became the Stoughton Musical Society, America's oldest musical organization. He led the choirs at the Brattle Street and Old South churches in Boston, and elsewhere. He also originated the use of a pitch pipe and an accompanying cello in choir work, the former to begin properly, the latter to maintain rhythm.

Billings also gained considerable renown as a composer of hymns and fuguing tunes. His first collection of hymns and anthems, *The New England Psalm-Singer,* was published in 1770 and was followed by *The Singing Master's Assistant* (1778). He subsequently published four additional volumes of his religious compositions. His most famous single composition, one of the important songs to come out of the American Revolution, was "Chester," a tune borrowed from *The New England Psalm-Singer* for which he wrote new martial lyrics in 1778. Though Billings was the most popular and influential native musician of his time, his florid but occasionally crude compositions went out of vogue in New England before his death; they achieved a new lease on life in the revivalistic South and on the western frontier, surviving for another generation.

⸺∘∞∘⸺

Although Billings's hymns carry over an archaic medieval sound, and although he tastelessly advocated sliding from note to note and reputedly drowned out the other singers with his stentorian voice, his music exhibits an almost rococo restraint and rollicking gait. His penchant for counterpoint appears in a four-voice round, "Jesus Wept," which he wrote at the age of 22, although not until after the Revolution did he plunge fully into the "fuguing-tune" vogue of contrapuntal songs, greatly influenced by Handel's *Messiah*. Billings outgrew much of the crudity of his first hymnbook, as its revised version of eight years later proves. Yet two of the most remarkable numbers of the latter (*The Singing Master's Assistant*) had appeared in the earlier version with different words: "Chester," reset with the famous "Let tyrants shake their iron rod," and "Methinks I Hear a Heav'nly Host," his favorite melodic invention, which recurs in other guises with other words through all his collections, including the *Continental Harmony* of 1794. Another notable number of the 1778 collection was "Jargon," whose discords seem to spoof his own earlier ineptitudes.

The bravado of his personality and vigor of his strains correlate with the burgeoning new republic. He appealed principally to "middlebrows" (including **Samuel Adams**), even though he did sell concert tickets at his shop and taught choristers in Episcopalian King's Chapel. It would be unfair to deny his native genius or the merit of his best songs, but it would be equally foolish to forget that he composed in the age of Mozart. See W. Thomas Marrocco and Harold Gleason, *Music in America ... 1620–1865* (1964).

CYCLONE COVEY

BINGHAM, George Caleb (b. Augusta Co., Va., Mar. 20, 1811; d. Kansas City, Mo., July 7, 1879), ARTIST, emigrated with his family to the town of Franklin on the Missouri frontier in 1819. Like many other artists brought up on the frontier Bingham was largely self-taught; he copied engravings and painted with homemade pigments. Encouraged by the better-established artist Chester Harding, he concentrated on portraiture (1834–38). As a result of his strength at drawing likenesses, he was fairly successful and in 1835 moved to St. Louis for further study and better patronage. In 1838, while studying briefly at the Pennsylvania Academy of the Fine Arts in Philadelphia (1838), he was exposed to the pictures of **Gilbert Stuart, Thomas Sully,** and John Vanderlyn. His first subject in the genre mold, *Western Boatmen Ashore,* exhibited at the Apollo Gallery in New York in the fall of 1838, was unsuccessful, and Bingham returned to portraits and to Missouri. When he again journeyed east in 1840, this time to Washington, D.C., he showed marked improvement in his portraiture, good examples of which are the portraits *John Quincy Adams* (1844, Collection of James Sidney Rollins II, Columbia, Mo.) and *Jacob Fortney Wyan* (1838/39, Charles W. Leonard, Bunceton, Mo.).

Encouraged by the patronage of the American Art Union, which purchased four of his paintings in 1845, including *Fur Traders Descending the Missouri* (1845, Metropolitan Museum of Art, N.Y.), Bingham thereafter concentrated on genre painting and soon became widely recognized as "The Missouri Artist." In 1846 an engraving of his *Jolly Flatboatmen* (1846, Senator Claiborne Pell, Washington, D.C.) was widely circulated by the American Art Union and brought Bingham fame

and critical praise. Other paintings in his river series include *Raftsmen Playing Cards* (1847, City Art Museum, St. Louis), *Watching the Cargo* (1849, The State Historical Society of Missouri), and *Shooting for the Beef* (1850, Brooklyn Museum, N.Y.). Active in local politics, Bingham ran unsuccessfully for election to the Missouri legislature in 1846 as a Whig; two years later he ran again and was elected. His paintings of this period reflect his interest in politics: *Canvassing for a Vote* (1851/52, William Rockhill Nelson Gallery of Art, Kansas City, Mo.), *County Election* (1851/52, City Art Museum, St. Louis, Mo.), *Stump Speaking* (1853/54, Boatmen's National Bank, St. Louis), and *Verdict of the People* (1854/55, Boatman's National Bank, St. Louis). In 1856 he went to Europe, making his headquarters in Düsseldorf (1856–59). Following his return he again turned to portrait painting, most of his canvases being painted on commission from the State Capitol. His portraits of **Henry Clay** and Andrew Jackson were among those lost in the Capitol fire in 1911. He was state treasurer (1862–65) and was named adjutant general of Missouri in 1875. The Civil War stimulated one of Bingham's most controversial paintings, *Martial Law or Order No. 11* (1865/68, Cincinnati Art Museum), a defense of civil liberty as opposed to militarism. In 1877 he was appointed professor of art at the University of Missouri.

⸎

Bingham's paintings of river scenes and election activities constitute his best work. Although carefully designed compositions, they convey the impression of spontaneity and vitality that his later works lack. These were the paintings that the Art Union found embodied "the spirit—the sentiment of the nation," a phrase that reveals the cultural nationalism influencing his artistic career: his belief that art was "the chief agent in securing national immortality."

As satires, Bingham's election paintings are more comical than caustic. Especially in *The Verdict of the People* and *Stump Speaking,* his characters are presented ideally, as genial and intelligent yeomen rather than as crude frontier churls.

By this time Bingham was beginning to think seriously about art and its social mission. *The Emigration of Daniel Boone* (1851, Washington University) is an unconvincing and theatrical attempt at historical painting on an epic scale. Bingham's tendency to melodrama reached its height in *Order No. 11*, in which he employed unnatural color to heighten emotional effect. Far heavier in treatment and spirit than his earlier works, it is also far less successful. So were Bingham's later paintings, which were conceived under the Düsseldorf influence and reveal the artist's growing self-consciousness with respect to technique and subject matter.

Bingham's place in American art history thus rests on his early scenes of the American frontier of the mid–19th century. Especially when anecdote is combined with landscape, as in *Fur Traders Descending the Missouri*, he communicates the color and mystery—the poetry—of the western experience. See Fern Helen Rusk, *George Caleb Bingham, the Missouri Artist* (1917).

LILLIAN B. MILLER

BIRNEY, James Gillespie (b. Danville, Ky., Feb. 4, 1792; d. Eagleswood, N.J., Nov. 25, 1857), REFORMER, studied at Transylvania University (Lexington, Ky.) and graduated from the College of New Jersey (now Princeton) in 1810. He was admitted to the bar in 1814 and practiced law at Danville. Two years later he was elected to the lower house of the Kentucky legislature as an independent. After moving to Madison County, Alabama (1818), he served as a representative to the first General Assembly of Alabama (1819). Taking up residence in Huntsville in 1823, he was elected mayor the following year, served as public prosecutor until 1826, and for a time was counsel for the Cherokee Indians. Through his efforts the Alabama legislature passed bills prohibiting the importation of slaves to the state (1827, 1832), but they were subsequently repealed. In 1832, Birney became an agent for the American Colonization Society, but he resigned in 1834. In his "Letter on Colonization," first published in the Lexington (Ky.) *Western Luminary*,

he explained his resignation on the grounds that he felt the colonization society condoned slavery as a system, an attitude that was irreconcilable with his notions of justice. That same year Birney freed his six slaves, and in 1835, having moved back to his native state two years previously, he organized the Kentucky Anti-Slavery Society. After encountering great difficulties in publishing an antislavery journal in Kentucky, he moved to New Richmond, Ohio, where the *Philanthropist* first appeared in January 1836. In 1837 he was indicted in Cincinnati for harboring the fugitive slave Matilda Lawrence but was acquitted. As a member and later executive secretary of the American Anti-Slavery Society, Birney strongly opposed **William Lloyd Garrison**'s attacks on the Constitution, feeling that only through political action and voting could slavery be eradicated. As the presidential candidate of the Liberty Party in 1840, Birney polled 7,000 votes. That same year he traveled to England where he served as vice president of the World's Anti-Slavery convention. In 1844, as the Liberty Party presidential candidate, he polled 62,268 votes. Birney published several articles and books on colonization and antislavery themes, including *The American Churches: The Bulwark of American Slavery* (1840).

———— ∞ ————

In many ways James G. Birney fits the stereotype of the southern gentleman planter-slaveholder-lawyer. He was intelligent, proud, often imperious and impatient, and elitist in a paternalistic fashion with a strong sense of civic responsibility. His spirit of noblesse oblige, coupled with a blunt intellectual honesty and reinforced by his conversion to the **Charles G. Finney** revival emphasis on helping one's fellowmen, compelled him to suit action to belief by defending society's underdogs: Indians, slaves, and all who lacked opportunity. Once engaged in reforms he was sustained by pride and stubbornness as well as by a deeply ingrained optimism that people educated to "truth" would act upon it. Consequently, he was disappointed at being always a minority leader and experienced moments of great bitterness and frustration. By the time of his death he foresaw that emancipation would come only through bloodshed and war.

Birney's significance in the antislavery movement lay partly in the fact that he was a southerner with a firsthand knowledge of the "peculiar institution." Second, he was one of the ablest interpreters of antislavery constitutional positions. His tone was moderate, rational, and legalistic rather than emotional or revivalistic. He saw himself as a reformer but was never comfortable with the label of "radical"; steering the movement into political channels was therefore an attempt to keep it within the mainstream of American reform and progress. He was not out to overthrow the basic structure of the social order but only to see that people on the bottom rung had a chance to climb regardless of their race. See Betty Fladeland, *James Gillespie Birney: Slave-holder to Abolitionist* (1955).

BETTY FLADELAND

BLACK, Hugo La Fayette (b. Harlan, Ala., Feb. 27, 1886; d. Bethesda, Md., Sept. 25, 1971), JURIST, POLITICAL LEADER, studied at the Birmingham Medical College (1903–4), then enrolled at the University of Alabama Law School at Tuscaloosa and received his LLB in 1906. He was admitted to the bar in 1906 and practiced briefly in Ashland, Alabama, but soon settled in Birmingham where he specialized in tort, labor, and contract law (1907–14). During 1910–11 he also served as a police court judge in Birmingham. In 1914, Black was elected county prosecutor for Jefferson County, a post he held until he enlisted in the army in 1917. In 1918, after being released from the armed forces (in which he had risen to the rank of captain in the Nineteenth Artillery Brigade), he resumed his practice in Birmingham. During this period Black was briefly (1923–25) a member of the local chapter of the Ku Klux Klan. In 1926 he was elected to the U.S. Senate as a Democrat, serving from 1927 to 1937. In the Senate he was a member of the Judiciary Committee but gained most attention in his role as investigator into Washington lobby-

ists' activities, especially those involving the Muscle Shoals controversy (1930) and the Public Utility Holding Company Act (1935). After the 1932 election he was a staunch supporter of President Franklin D. Roosevelt and the New Deal.

In 1937, Roosevelt named Black associate justice of the Supreme Court. In spite of demands that he be rejected—stirred primarily by the revelation of his earlier ties to the Klan—the Senate confirmed him in October 1937. On the Court he was a member of the "liberal bloc" that supported New Deal economic and social legislation. Later, however, he became especially noted for his defense of the Bill of Rights as absolute guarantee of personal rights (in contrast to the views of such Supreme Court justices as **Felix Frankfurter,** who sought to "balance" individual rights against the needs of government). Thus, in *Kingsley International Pictures Corporation* v. *Regents* (1959), Black maintained that the Court was not the supreme judge of morals and censorship. In *Communist Party* v. *Subversive Activities Control Board* (1961) he contended that outlawing of the Communist Party violated the First Amendment. His greatest importance, however, was in gradually convincing a majority of the Court that the due-process clause of the Fourteenth Amendment applied the first eight amendments to the states as well as to the federal government. In *Gideon* v. *Wainwright* (1963), in which the Court ruled that the Sixth Amendment guarantee of counsel for the accused in all felony prosecutions was to be applied in all state cases, and in *Escobedo* v. *Ill.* (1964), which ruled as inadmissible statements taken by the police when a suspect in a state case was refused the right to see an attorney, Black's positions became major influences on the enforcement of law at the state level throughout the nation. In 1962, in *Engel* v. *Vitale*, Black delivered the decision which ruled that even "nonsectarian" prayers in a public school were illegal because they violated the separation of church and state guaranteed in the First Amendment.

Justice Black was a powerful and influential voice on the Court during his long tenure. Having served for sixteen years before the appointment of Chief Justice Earl Warren, his opinions, frequently in dissent, had pointed directions and laid the foundations for the greater protection that would be given by the Court to civil liberties and civil rights. He was able to join in converting his earlier dissents into the prevailing doctrine of the Court.

It is possible to rationalize this "activist" movement in terms of maintaining the constitutional structure and processes of the society, and thus to differentiate it from the activism of the Court in the decades before Black's appointment when social and economic legislation was invalidated in the name of protecting private property and liberty of contract from deprivation without due process of law. The newer movement focused on such issues as equal voting rights (malapportionment, racial disqualifications, poll taxes), liberty of speech, press, and assembly, and safeguards for the accused in criminal cases. These interests can be viewed as a special responsibility of the judiciary, relating as they do to the maintenance of representative and responsible government, in contrast to the older judicial vetoes on laws regulating wages, prices, and labor relations.

Justice Black would not have adopted this rather abstract formulation. He rejected the labels "activist," "dynamic," and "creative," which some admirers fastened on him. His dissociation of himself from the judicial activists of the past took a different line: they were importing their own social philosophy into the Constitution under the vague rubrics of liberty and due process of law, while he was giving effect to explicit guarantees in the Bill of Rights.

His judicial philosophy in this regard consisted of two elements: one, that the specific provisions of the Bill of Rights, directed against the national government, must be interpreted literally; and second, that the Fourteenth Amendment, directed against the states, by referring to the "privileges and immunities of citizens of the United States" incorporated each and every provision of the Bill of Rights. Thus the First Amendment, mandating "no law abridging the freedom of speech or of the press," meant no law, "without any ifs, buts, or whereases" (*Beauharnais* v. *Illinois*, 1952). The explicit guarantees of a jury trial, the privilege against self-incrimination, the protection against double jeopardy, and the right to counsel were binding on the states no less than on the central government.

Black's constitutional philosophy owed much of its force to its simplicity and absoluteness. Thus he rejected the clear and present danger test because it is a judicial gloss on the unconditional right of speech, and he would have recognized no legal limits even on political defamation or on obscene publications (*Beauharnais*, supra; *N.Y. Times* v. *Sullivan*, 1964; *Ginzburg* v. *United States*, 1966). But even Black was obliged to recognize that speech could be regulated legitimately with respect to its time, its place or manner, or its purpose. Vocal demonstrations could be prohibited, for example, in the courtyard of a jail (*Adderly* v. *Florida,* 1966), and verbal appeals could be enjoined as part of an illegal boycott (*Giboney* v. *Empire Storage Co.,* 1949). His explanation was that in these contexts speech was interlaced with conduct, and the latter could be regulated if there was a compelling public interest requiring it.

Black's literalism, which served generally to maximize the reach of specific constitutional guarantees, could also preclude the recognition of new constitutional rights. Thus when a majority of the Court found in the interstices of the Constitution a protected right of privacy, and thereby invalidated a law prohibiting the use of contraceptives, Black dissented; although he deemed the law patently unsound, he could find nothing in the Constitution to debar a state from enacting it (*Griswold* v. *Connecticut,* 1965).

Beyond particular doctrines, Black's power derived from his firm vision of the American constitutional order and his incisive eloquence in bringing the vision to bear on specific controversies. He held a Jeffersonian image of an individualistic, rational, self-confident people free to think as they will and to speak as they think. He had an exceptional capacity to cut through the legal complexities of a case to the human concerns at its center. On the bench no one was a keener questioner; in conference, by all accounts, he was an intense combatant, who expected the same of his colleagues. His opinions have the power to move because he himself was deeply moved, as when he wrote in a case involving a confession extracted after days of continuous grilling, "Under our constitutional system, courts stand against any winds that blow as havens of refuge for those who might otherwise suffer because they are helpless, weak, outnumbered, or because they are non-conforming victims of prejudice and public incitement" (*Chambers* v. *Florida*, 1940). See John P. Frank, "Hugo L. Black," in L. Friedman and F. L. Israel, eds., *The Justices of the United States Supreme Court*, III (1969), pp. 2321–70.

PAUL A. FREUND

BLACKWELL, Elizabeth (b. Bristol, Eng., Feb. 3, 1821; d. Hastings, Eng., May 31, 1910), PHYSICIAN, emigrated to New York City in 1832 and moved to Cincinnati in 1838, where she taught in her family's boarding school. In 1842 she went to teach in Henderson, Kentucky, and in 1844 to Asheville, North Carolina, where after school hours she began to study medicine by herself. A Charlestown Medical College professor, Dr. Samuel Dickson, tutored her during 1847, and that October she gained admission to Geneva Medical College in New York. In 1849, having become the first woman MD in the U.S., she went to the Hôpital de la Maternité in Paris to study obstetrics. Later she studied in London (1850–51) and then returned to New York to start a medical practice. Patients were slow to come to a woman doctor, and in 1853, Blackwell opened a one-room dispensary. In 1857 she expanded this to a hospital, the New York Infirmary for Women and Children, where later (1868) she established the Women's Medical College. In 1861 she played a leading role in forming the Women's Central Association of Relief to provide military nurses for the Union. Dr. Blackwell returned to England in 1869 to enter private practice. In 1875 she

became a professor of gynecology at the London School of Medicine for Women but lectured only one year before ill health forced her to retire. Thereafter she wrote several books on sex education and moral reform.

Elizabeth Blackwell from childhood lived in a liberal and progressive atmosphere. Her father was a zealous champion of social reform, women's rights, temperance, and the abolition of slavery. One sister became a newspaper correspondent, another an author and artist; her brothers Samuel and Henry married Antoinette Brown, first American woman minister, and Lucy Stone, antislavery and women's rights leader; and her sister Emily became a doctor and joined her in her fight for a place for women in medicine.

Elizabeth Blackwell was a small woman, feminine and diplomatic in implementing her revolutionary ideas but with a strong will, resilience, and courage. She thrived on challenges. Her charm, well-developed sense of humor, and firm, yet unaggressive approach were compelling assets in rallying able young women to her side and in winning the support of influential physicians whose help she needed to combat prejudice against working women, especially in the medical profession. Nor was she content for women merely to enter the door; she set up higher standards of education and training at the hospital and medical school she founded to ensure that its graduates could bear the inevitable close scrutiny of male medical critics.

Having begun sensibly to advocate proper hygiene and physical education to help free women from the stigma of "the weaker sex," she went on, after gaining acceptance for women doctors in America and in her native England, to work for moral reform, writing and lecturing on behalf of sex education for young people and the abolishment of the "double standard" and of prostitution. She continued to urge higher standards of hygiene and sanitation, and criticized what she considered excessive surgery in medicine. Although most of her progressive ideas and reforms were rooted in wisdom and common sense, she opposed two important advances—vaccination (because of the death of a child patient early in her career) and animal experimentation, so basic to the advancement of medical knowledge.

She was a good doctor, but she will live in time more as a pioneer in opening the medical profession to women and in advocating enlightened views toward health and sex. See Elinor Rice Hay, *Those Extraordinary Blackwells: The Story of a Journey to a Better World* (1967).

ELIZABETH H. THOMSON

BLAINE, James Gillespie (b. West Brownsville, Pa., Jan. 31, 1830; d. Washington, D.C., Jan. 27, 1893), POLITICAL LEADER, graduated from Washington College in 1847, then taught school while studying law. After moving to Augusta, Maine, he edited the Kennebec *Journal* (1854–57). He served in the state legislature (1859–62; speaker, 1861–62) and in 1862 was elected to the U.S. House of Representatives as a Republican (serving 1863–76; speaker, 1869–76). In Congress, Blaine took a moderate stand on Reconstruction, supported hard money, and favored international reciprocity agreements.

In 1876, Blaine appeared to be the most likely candidate for the Republican presidential nomination. However, the publication of the "Mulligan Letters," which linked him to the granting of congressional favors to the Little Rock and Fort Smith Railroad, soiled his reputation. He was elected to the U.S. Senate and served until 1881 when President James Garfield named him secretary of state.

As secretary of state Blaine pursued a vigorous foreign policy, particularly toward Latin America. He sought to increase American trade and influence in Latin America by blocking all attempts at European intervention there. However, many of his plans—such as his attempts to hold a Pan-American conference and to modify the Clayton-Bulwer Treaty of 1850 in which the United States and Great Britain agreed not to construct an isthmian canal separately—never came to fruition. After Garfield's assassination, Blaine resigned.

In 1884, Blaine was the Republican presidential nominee. His debatable reputation and his opposition to civil service reform led many "Mugwump" Republicans to support Grover Cleveland, the Democratic nominee, who won the electoral vote 219 to 182. Cleveland received fewer than 25,000 more popular votes than Blaine; a change of 600 votes in New York would have given the election to Blaine.

Blaine served as secretary of state in the Harrison administration (1889–92). He organized the first Pan-American Conference (1889); tried to negotiate a treaty for an isthmian canal with Nicaragua; advocated the annexation of Hawaii; and tried to settle the Bering Sea dispute with the British (1889). Blaine's congressional career is recorded in his *Twenty Years of Congress* (1884–86).

James Gillespie Blaine captivated a whole generation of Republican voters. The words "brilliant" and "magnetic" came easily to newsmen, who treated him like a matinee idol. A compelling speaker with great presence, he was an effective campaigner. He sought to enlarge the GOP's constituency after the 1870s by emphasizing the unifying appeals of tariff protection and nationalistic goals. But the imagination and quick thinking that made him so popular with voters also worked to his disadvantage. His impatience irritated more sober and equally powerful politicians, and Blaine was more successful at suggesting programs and outlining new departures than in achieving them.

Blaine was most prominent as a contender for the presidency. He sought the nomination in 1876, but dispute over the Mulligan Letters and the unresolved question of his personal integrity in office rather quickly weakened his desire for the office. Yet he was unquestionably the choice of most Republicans in 1884 when he narrowly missed being elected after an unprecedented campaign effort. He could have been nominated in 1888, but he early supported the dark horse

Benjamin Harrison rather than wage another divisive and personal campaign.

Blaine enjoyed being secretary of state more than presidential politics. His keen Americanism caused critics incorrectly to label him a jingo, but his attitudes pleased Republican voters and won some important marginal support among the Irish and other immigrants. Blaine strongly supported tariff reciprocity to increase American exports but was not a territorial expansionist. His "Pan-Americanism" rested on the assumption that arbitration procedures, equitable trade, and the exchange of people and ideas would promote hemispheric stability peacefully. Partisan domestic criticism weakened his diplomacy, and like most people, Blaine underestimated the nationalism that animated Latin American countries.

Blaine was a thoroughly political being, and he could discuss the politics of almost every part of the country. Yet after 1876 he did not really expect to win the presidency and often compared himself to **Henry Clay.** He was fond of literature, was an engaging conversationalist, lived well, and traveled extensively. He seldom answered critics, holding simply that "nothing is so weakening as regret." His health declined steadily with age, and a persistent hypochondria reflected a strain of melancholy behind his overt vigor.

Blaine's name was attached to no great law, and his imaginative diplomacy failed to mature, yet his achievements were both subtle and important. He was essentially a party leader rather than a legislator, advancing many ideas and programs that strengthened the GOP. Despite his personal impact on voters, he sincerely preached the virtues of loyalty to national party programs rather than to leaders. Despite the criticism surrounding his career, his very presence added productive determination to the GOP. He was a force for cohesion and a major architect of the Republican majority coalition that finally triumphed in 1896. See David S. Muzzey, *James G. Blaine, a Political Idol of Other Days* (1934).

H. WAYNE MORGAN

BLAIR, Francis Preston (b. Abingdon, Va., Apr. 12, 1791; d. Silver Spring, Md., Oct. 18, 1876), JOURNALIST, graduated from Transylvania University in 1811. He served briefly in the War of 1812 as an aide to his uncle, George Madison, governor of Kentucky. He was admitted to the bar in 1817 but never practiced law.

Ruined financially by the panic of 1819, Blair became one of the leaders of the "New Court" Party, a Kentucky political faction that demanded laws preventing foreclosures for debt. When the "Old Court" Party in power refused to respond to these requests, the legislature created a new court of appeals in defiance of the existing court and named Blair its clerk. Blair also became president of the Commonwealth Bank, which issued loans liberally.

In 1824, Blair supported **Henry Clay** for president as a sectional candidate. Shortly thereafter, however, Blair switched his allegiance to Andrew Jackson, becoming a staunch Jacksonian Democrat and advocating the direct election of the president by the people, legislative control over judicial decisions, cheap land for settlers, and the abolition of imprisonment for debt. Following Jackson's election in 1828, Blair wrote editorials for the Frankfort (Ky.) *Argus of Western America* in which he attacked the Bank of the United States and nullification theory. He believed the tariff should be reduced, although he believed protective tariffs constitutional.

In 1830, Jackson (on the suggestion of **Amos Kendall,** former editor of the *Argus* and a member of Jackson's "kitchen cabinet") called Blair to Washington to edit the *Globe.* This daily newspaper became the leading spokesman for the Democratic Party in general and for Jackson's ideas in particular. Blair also became a member of Jackson's kitchen cabinet. The *Globe* ardently supported Jackson in his fight to destroy the Bank of the United States and to uphold the power of the presidency. In 1834, Blair began publishing the *Congressional Globe,* a record of the daily proceedings in Congress.

Blair supported James K. Polk for the presidency in 1844, but opposed the annexation of Texas, believing that it would lead to a war with

Mexico. Following Polk's election, Blair was asked to sell the *Globe* to Thomas Ritchie, former editor of the Richmond *Enquirer* and a loyal supporter of Polk. The new administration organ was called the *Union*.

In 1848, Blair opposed the further extension of slavery and supported Martin Van Buren, the Free Soil Party's presidential candidate. Hoping to revive the spirit of Jacksonian democracy, he supported Franklin Pierce in 1852. When Congress passed the Kansas-Nebraska Act (1854) establishing the principle of popular sovereignty in the territories, Blair asserted that this act violated the Missouri Compromise of 1820, which banned slavery north of latitude 36'30".

No longer able to support the Democratic Party, Blair was one of the leading organizers of the new Republican Party and presided over its first, organizing convention in Pittsburgh in February 1856. When the Civil War broke out, he supported Lincoln's policies. In 1864 he journeyed to Richmond, the Confederate capital, to discuss with **Jefferson Davis** the possibilities of a cessation of hostilities.

Following the Civil War, Blair's opposition to the harsh reconstruction measures advocated by the Radical Republicans led him to return to the Democratic Party.

⁓

Blair was a slight, skinny, stooped man with a rounded dome at the back of his head: there, Andrew Jackson remarked, he kept his brains. Indeed, Francis Preston Blair had brains in plenty, and he was a tiger at the editorial desk. He put his pen at the service of politics and helped to form a new brand of journalism that was lively, expansively democratic in spirit, and highly partisan.

During the Jacksonian era the United States experienced a media revolution or newspaper explosion. In 1800 the nation had only about 200 newspapers, most of them rather barren weeklies. By 1828 there were 861, and by 1840 there were 1,577, of which 209 were dailies. Newspapers also became larger, more informative, and livelier, although almost all were attached to one political party or another. Blair got his start as an editorial writer on the Frankfort *Argus,* which became one of an informal chain of papers devoted to making Andrew Jackson president in 1828. His great days, however, came with his editorship of the brilliant Washington *Globe* from 1830 to 1845. This daily breathed the democratic (and Democratic) spirit of the Jacksonian persuasion and offered a varied fare of political news spiced with pungent editorials. Lesser presses elsewhere reprinted items from the *Globe,* which thus acted as a feeder and ideological pacesetter for Democratic Party papers across the country: newspaper combines and press associations lay in the future. Thus, in a new era of mass political participation, the *Globe* and other papers played a major role in the development of the second, "democratizing" party system of 1828–54. The newspaper press was its basic communications medium.

In addition to his editorial labors Blair was also an active behind-the-scenes politician. Like many other rising professional politicians of the time, he never ran for elective office. He was an adviser to Jackson, helped to write a number of the president's state papers, and stood with the "Radical" Van Buren—**Thomas Hart Benton— Silas Wright** group in the Democratic Party. His support of the Free Soil ticket in 1848 and his switch to the new Republican Party after 1854, despite his southern origins, were rooted in his growing belief that popular democracy and the extension of slavery to the West were incompatible. Along with other "Radical" Jacksonians, he had opposed abolition; but now he saw slavery extension as an evil and the disruptive issue of the day. He was an influential figure for years, but his monument was the *Globe* and its role in the media revolution of his time. See William E. Smith, *The Francis Preston Blair Family in Politics* (2 vols., 1933).

WILLIAM N. CHAMBERS

BOAS, Franz (b. Minden, Westphalia, July 9, 1858; d. New York, N.Y., Dec. 21, 1942), ANTHROPOLOGIST, attended the universities of Heidelberg, Bonn, and Kiel, receiving his doctorate from Kiel in 1881. Although his main university interest had been in physics and geography, he soon became interested in ethnology. After an expedition to Baffin Island (1883–84) to study the Eskimos, he decided to devote his life to anthropology. In 1886, Boas made his first of many trips to study the tribes of British Columbia, especially the Kwakiutl Indians. German anti-Semitism and Bismarck's antiliberal policies led Boas to become an American citizen in 1887. He became assistant editor of *Science* and an instructor of anthropology at Clark University. In 1896 he moved to Columbia as a lecturer in anthropology and was appointed a professor in 1899, a post he held until his retirement in 1936. He also served as curator of anthropology at the American Museum of Natural History in New York (1901–5). In 1902 he helped found the American Anthropological Association, serving as its president (1907–8). He was also president of the American Association for the Advancement of Science (1931).

Boas was instrumental in laying much of the foundation of modern anthropology in America as an empirical discipline. At Columbia he trained a large number of students, and these, with their students, represented the vast majority of American anthropologists until after World War II. A prolific scholar, he emphasized facts gathered firsthand as the basis for and check on interpretation. He criticized the sweeping deductive theories of cultural evolution so popular in the nineteenth century, rejected all theories of racial inequality, and bitterly attacked Nazi theories of Aryan superiority. Boas helped found the American Folklore Society (1888) and the American Association of Physical Anthropologists (1928). He also contributed to linguistics; he edited the monumental *Handbook of American Indian Languages* (1911–12) and helped establish the *International Journal of American Linguistics* in 1917. Much of his theoretical writing has been collected in *Race, Language and Culture* (1940), *The Mind of Primitive Man* (1911), and *Anthropology and Modern Life* (1928).

Boas was possessed of a consuming personal enthusiasm in building a new science, but his enthusiasm was restrained by exceptional rigor when it came to means and methods. Thus, while bringing new statistical methods to physical anthropology, he warned against an uncritical transfer of such methods to cultural analysis. Insisting on firsthand data gathering in the field and on the importance of penetrating the mental life of different peoples, he also raised the fundamental question for anthropologists of transcending the mental sets of their own culture. He stamped modern American anthropology with these attitudes. Warm with those close to him, Boas was formal in public and uncompromising in ethical and professional matters. To his students he was paternalistic and intensely loyal; he demanded from them personal loyalty and scientific integrity—but not agreement. Thus, Boasian anthropology proliferated in a great variety of directions and theoretical approaches, retaining in the process a notably empirical philosophy. Boas founded no "school"; indeed he considered schools inappropriate in science. Rather he bequeathed a set of attitudes: stress on problems rather than a priori theory; recognition of the complexity of cultural phenomena and rejection of deterministic shortcuts in explaining them; emphasis on evidence and sensitivity to the exceptional case as the critical test in cultural theory; the use of methods appropriate to a given problem rather than the pursuit of method per se at the risk of triviality; and finally awareness of the implications of ethnocentrism in both studying and theorizing about other cultures. In brief, his legacy was scientific rigor without scientism, and empiricism without methodologism. See Walter R. Goldschmidt, ed., *The Anthropology of Franz Boas* (Memoir of the American Anthropological Association, No. 89, 1959).

IGOR KOPYTOFF

BOK, Edward William (b. Helder, Netherlands, Oct. 9, 1863; d. Lake Wales, Fla., Jan. 9, 1930), JOURNALIST, emigrated to the U.S. in 1870 and settled in New York. In 1876 he became an office boy for the Western Union Telegraph Co. Later he was a stenographer for Henry Holt and Co. and for Charles Scribner's Sons. In 1887 he was made advertising manager of *Scribner's* magazine.

In 1886 he founded the Bok Syndicate Press, which marketed a variety of feature articles to newspapers throughout the country. The syndicated "Bok page" was unique in that it featured articles by Ella Wheeler Wilcox and others on women's interests. The success of this enterprise attracted the attention of publisher Cyrus Curtis, who invited Bok to become editor of his *Ladies' Home Journal* in 1889. During his thirty-year tenure in that post, Bok introduced numerous innovations. He maintained high literary standards and pioneered the advice-to-readers format. He took editorial stands in favor of woman suffrage and conservation, and starting in 1892 refused to accept patent medicine advertisements. Enlisting the aid of other editors in this cause, he led a crusade that contributed to the enactment of the Pure Food and Drug Act in 1906. Bok was also the first editor to break the journalistic taboo against publishing articles on venereal disease.

During the final decade of his life Bok devoted much of his time to philanthropic activities. An active member of the post-World War I peace movement, Bok was an ardent supporter of the World Court and offered a $100,000 American Peace Award for the best workable plan to achieve it. His autobiography, *The Americanization of Edward Bok* (1920), was awarded the Pulitzer Prize in 1921.

⁂

In his triumphant progress from rags to riches Bok exemplified in real life that winning combination of middle-class virtues—hard work, thrift, and absolute honesty—so familiar to readers of **Horatio Alger.** There was no such thing as luck, he always maintained; success in America had to be earned, as he had managed through determined effort to overcome the disadvantages of poverty and a meager formal education. Convinced that the business elite of the Gilded Age owed their position to superior talent, he

romanticized their achievement in the pages of the *Journal* and held them out alike as models of competitive struggle and arbiters of "good taste." A thoroughgoing conservative on all moral questions, Bok nevertheless helped to revolutionize magazine publishing by adapting the old-fashioned techniques of personal journalism to the needs of a mass audience. Through the effective use of public opinion polls, reader surveys, and correspondence columns, he gave millions of middle-income wives and mothers a sense of participation in journalistic policymaking and assured that the *Journal's* coverage would keep abreast of changing audience trends. His impact on popular taste was most marked in the 1890s when he published a series of plans for low-cost "dream houses" that soon materialized across the nation, complete with Bok's prescribed furnishings for "tasteful" interior decoration based on photographs taken inside the homes of his wealthy friends. Although he occasionally attacked social as well as aesthetic evils, he was in no sense a muckraking journalist; his appeal to the women of America lay in his close attention to their everyday interests, his safe and sane canons of "scientific" household management, and his comforting reassurance that the Protestant ethic still worked in an industrialized and impersonal society. See Russell Lynes, *The Tastemakers* (1955).

MAXWELL BLOOMFIELD

BOONE, Daniel (b. near Reading, Pa., Nov. 2, 1734; d. near St. Charles, Mo., Sept. 26, 1820), EXPLORER, had little or no formal schooling. In the spring of 1750 his family moved to North Carolina, settling in the Yadkin Valley in 1751. In 1755, during the French and Indian War, he fought in General Braddock's disastrous Pennsylvania campaign. Returning to North Carolina, he worked on his father's farm. In 1767 and again in 1769 he made trips to Kentucky, where he explored the central Kentucky region. Acting as an agent for Colonel Richard Henderson of the Transylvania Co., he led a group of settlers to Kentucky in March 1775, erecting a fort at what was to become

Boonesborough. He spent the next year engaged in hunting, surveying, and Indian fighting. In February 1778 he was captured by the Shawnees but escaped in time to warn Boonesborough of an impending Indian attack. After spending a year in the East he returned to Kentucky in October 1779, bringing with him more settlers.

In 1779, Virginia invalidated Henderson's land grants and made Kentucky a county of Virginia. Boone was made a lieutenant colonel of the Fayette County militia, and in April 1780 he was chosen for the legislature; in 1782 he was appointed sheriff and county lieutenant. He also served as a deputy surveyor.

Although Boone claimed several tracts of land in Kentucky, his claims were invalidated because they were not registered properly. In the fall of 1788 he left Kentucky and traveled to Point Pleasant (now W. Va.). There he was appointed a lieutenant colonel and in 1791 a delegate to the Virginia legislature. In 1798, after all his holdings in Kentucky had been lost, he moved to Missouri where he spent most of his remaining years on land given to him by Congress.

———⁂———

Daniel Boone long ago became one of the most important symbols in American pioneering. Actually he was not one of the frontier's best woodsmen, and it can hardly be said that he was an original trailbreaker. His famous long hunting journey in 1769 was neither a trailblazing adventure nor a land-hunting expedition. He wandered in largely virgin country and gained some knowledge of landmarks, such as the lay of the mountains and the course of streams, in the central part of present-day Kentucky. In 1775 at the head of a party of trailblazers he simply followed the old Warrior's Trace and then the hunters' trail from Cumberland Gap to the south bank of the Kentucky River.

At Boonesborough, Boone proved only a fair organizer of the settling party, and in subsequent months he was definitely a secondary figure in the political wrangling over land claims. Boone's real moment of glory, however, came when he and his companions were captured at the Lower Blue Licks early in 1778. During that spring and summer the pioneer proved himself a clever man and an able and responsible leader. The saving of Boonesborough and the defeat of Black Fish and Dequindre in the extended siege in August and early September 1778 demonstrated Daniel Boone's foresight. Later he became a patriarchal figure in both Kentucky and Missouri. Through his restlessness and adventurous spirit his heart was in the act of pioneering. Hardly a heroic figure in the romantic American sense, standing only five feet seven inches tall, he made up for physical size in a peculiar brand of charisma. He was laconic in manner, but nevertheless he caught the imagination and affection of his contemporaries. To future Americans he became a symbolic figure.

Fortunes of history smiled on this backwoodsman. Lord Byron in a romantic poem gave him almost worldwide notoriety. John Filson, in the so-called *Autobiography*, spoke for him in heroic terms. In this document Boone became a central frontier figure, a position he was to hold for the future. Neither Byron nor Filson came close to the basic historical facts, but they, along with Daniel Bryan in *Muse of the Mountains*, created just the kind of romantic and heroic figure Americans needed to symbolize pioneering on the old frontier. The literary Boone embodied all the capabilities and virtues of a people approaching an endless sea of virgin land filled with adventures behind every sycamore and around every bend of a river. He never sold this adventure short in deed or word. In many ways Daniel Boone, like other American heroes, has become an embodiment of every American's inner hope of escaping it "all" to engage in the great adventure. Chester Harding did Boone's image no harm in the fine full-faced portrait he painted just at the end of the old hunter's life. See John Mack Faragher, *Daniel Boone: The Life and Legend of an American Pioneer* (1993).

THOMAS D. CLARK

BOOTH, John Wilkes (b. Bel Air, Md., May 10, 1838; d. Bowling Green, Va., Apr. 26, 1865),

ACTOR, son of the actor Junius Brutus Booth, made his stage debut in 1855 in Baltimore playing a minor part in *Richard III.* He then played at the Arch Street theater in Philadelphia (1857–58) before joining a Richmond, Virginia, Shakespearean stock company in 1859. Emerging as a star performer, Booth toured the country (1860–61); his repertoire included mostly Shakespearean plays, and he frequently appeared with his brothers, Edwin Thomas Booth and Junius Brutus Booth, Jr. In 1863, Booth briefly retired because of bronchial trouble but returned for successful performances at New York's Winter Garden theater (1864–65).

Unlike the rest of his family, Booth sympathized with the South. (He was a member of the Virginia militia company that captured **John Brown** at Harpers Ferry in 1859.) During the Civil War he developed a deep hatred for President Abraham Lincoln. In 1864 he gathered a band of conspirators and plotted to abduct Lincoln and take him to Richmond. Staged in early 1865, the abduction failed because Lincoln did not appear at the planned spot; the conspirators then decided to assassinate Lincoln and the entire cabinet. Booth himself was assigned to kill Lincoln. On the evening of April 14, 1865, he entered the president's box at Ford's theater (Washington, D.C.), where Lincoln was watching a performance of *Our American Cousin,* and shot him in the head. Booth escaped but was trapped in a barn near Bowling Green, Virginia. After the barn was set on fire, Booth either was shot or shot himself.

The father of John Wilkes Booth, a great Shakespearean actor, and to many observers unsurpassed in portrayal of Richard III, contributed the cultural inheritance of love of Shakespeare and the stage to his sons. His son Edwin, the Hamlet of all Hamlets, became the most noteworthy of the Booth clan. His son John Wilkes, still on the road to actor fame at 27, ended his career, after playing many Shakespearean roles, with a final dramatic act—the murder of President Abraham Lincoln in Ford's theater.

John Wilkes Booth was strikingly handsome, Byronic in his melancholy (a family trait), and possessor of a powerful charisma. In his youth he was a lover of animals, a player of the piano and flute, a wild-brained, quixotic boy; he was athletic, imaginative, romantic, and good-hearted, a reader, spouter of heroic speeches, and dreamer of dreams. But he also had an unsatiated thirst for alcohol and a certain identifiable neurotic vacillation between tenderness and violence.

Beginning his career as an actor at 17, he overacted in youthful exuberance with athletic leaps and bombastic diction. Later as Romeo he melted hearts until fame and income grew. His brother Edwin played Hamlet in depth as a melancholy man precariously balanced on the edge of madness. When John Wilkes played Hamlet, Hamlet was fiery and convincing, though mad throughout. Only months before he died, John Wilkes played Mark Antony in a production in which his brother Junius played Cassius and Edwin played Brutus.

John Wilkes Booth became obsessed with a love for the Confederate cause and with a belief that slavery was a great blessing, this no doubt a result of ego, of his own unfortunate Byronic vanity. At the same time he became conscience-smitten for not having served the South as a soldier, and he resolved to act. First he planned to kidnap the president and hold him for ransom of Confederate prisoners. That plan failed. Then came the grandiose and dastardly plan to assassinate the president, the vice president, and the cabinet. For stimulated as he was by violent hate, he thought it better for the leaders to perish than for a nation to fall into dishonor. It was a time of tense political hatreds, and Booth became the center of violent action. He was in his own eyes God's angry man.

Booth had frequently acted on the Ford theater stage and frequented its every corner; in fact it was Ford's theater where he collected his mail. To make plans was easy. The execution of the murder was worthy of the actor. He fired the fatal shot and leaped from the box to the stage. The plan worked but with one damning flaw. Ironically, the spur his brother Edwin had given him, saying "Wear this with honor," caught in the draped American flag in Lincoln's box as he jumped for the stage about ten feet below, thus distorting the landing and breaking the bone in his leg above the instep. It was related how the assassin, as he fell on the stage, brandished a bloody knife with which he had wounded a guard in Lincoln's box and cried, "Sic semper tyrannus," the Virginia state motto and the words said by Brutus as he buried the knife in Caesar. Then he added, "The South is avenged."

John Wilkes Booth kept a diary during his days of flight before he was caught by the law. An entry there supports the thesis that he murdered Lincoln not for money (he had a $20,000-a-year income), not for personal revenge, but for an espoused concept: "I struck for my country alone." John Wilkes Booth fell to the law, shot through the head as was his victim: "Blood will have blood." See Philip Van Doren Stern, *The Man Who Killed Lincoln* (1955).

THOMAS E. CHENEY

BORAH, William Edgar (b. Fairfield, Ill., June 29, 1865; d. Washington, D.C., Jan. 19, 1940), POLITICAL LEADER, attended the University of Kansas (1885–87) and was admitted to the bar in 1887. In 1890 he moved to Idaho where he established himself as a successful attorney. He ran for the U.S. Congress as a pro-silver Bryanite Republican in 1896 but was defeated; in 1907 he entered the Senate as a Republican. When **Clarence Darrow** defended **William D. Haywood** (and others) on a charge of murdering Idaho's governor Frank Steunenberg, Borah served as a special prosecuting attorney.

In the Senate, where he served until his death, Borah supported the direct election of senators, an income tax, and an eight-hour day, which was granted to railroad workers by the Adamson Act (1916); however, he opposed woman suffrage and a child-labor amendment as an invasion of states' rights. He was also one of the leading prohibitionists in the Senate. Although he agreed with Theodore Roosevelt on many issues, Borah supported Taft, the Republican nominee, in the election of 1912. Borah voted for President Woodrow Wilson's declaration of war, but he opposed a conscription bill that fixed the draft age at 18 (1917) and the Espionage Act (1917), which provided severe penalties for persons found guilty of aiding the enemy.

Following the war Borah was the leading spokesman of the isolationist "irreconcilables" who categorically opposed American entry into the League of Nations. When Wilson toured the country to gain support for the League, Borah followed him, condemning the president's ideas. Although Borah was an isolationist, he believed that the U.S. should try to preserve world comity. In 1920–21 he proposed resolutions that led to the Washington Disarmament Conference (1921), which set limits on the number and tonnage of the capital ships of the major naval powers. In 1924 he became chairman of the Foreign Relations Committee. He opposed America's joining the World Court, which he saw as a "back-door" entrance into the League. Borah also opposed U.S. intervention in Latin American affairs. But in 1927 he urged Secretary of State **Frank Kellogg** to make the Kellogg-Briand Pact outlawing war a multinational rather than just a bilateral pact between the United States and France, and he also believed that the United States should recognize the Soviet Union.

During the New Deal, Borah supported many reform measures, including the Social Security Act (1935) and the Fair Labor Standards Act fixing minimum wages and maximum hours of employment (1938). He also advocated the remonetization of silver. But Borah was one of the leading critics of the National Industrial Recovery Act (1933), because he believed that the NRA codes encouraged monopoly. He also excoriated Franklin D. Roosevelt when the president tried to "pack" the Supreme Court (1937).

In foreign affairs Borah remained a staunch isolationist. He saw the war in Europe as another typical power struggle that the United States must avoid. He opposed the repeal of the neutrality acts and denounced all of Roosevelt's attempts to aid the Allies.

If there was one prime quality of the mind of Borah, it was that he thought like an orator. Borah was essentially a stump speaker in the western tradition. When he commenced his law practice, he began to sense his power with audiences, and after fifteen or so years as a man of eloquence, in the course of which his income rose to a handsome figure for an Idaho lawyer at the beginning of the twentieth century, perhaps $30,000 a year, he found his niche as an individual. Being an orator, he considered himself a master of logic, but one must point out that he was not above making debater's points, such as when before a great audience in Chicago in 1919, arguing against the League of Nations, he paced back and forth on the platform, his thumbs locked in his armpits, hurling such loaded questions as: "Is there an American who wants a foreign nation to say when and where the Monroe Doctrine should apply?" A leather-lunged, leonine figure on the platform, his jowls shaking as he spoke, Borah was exactly the sort of individual to make his way in politics in the United States before the age of amplification, and indeed for twenty years thereafter.

Borah possessed three ideas that came out of his youth and western heritage. One of them was that Europe had a set of primary notions wholly different from those of Americans. The British government, Borah believed, had oppressed the people of Ireland, Egypt, and India, and was not to be trusted. Likewise the other associates of the world war, which were always looking eagerly for ways to do in the people of the United States.

A second idea was that the fathers of the Republic were a group whose wisdom was never to be equaled. Every piece of legislation or of political maneuver, American or foreign, had to be set against the ideas and actions of the founding fathers, and if it did not measure up, it was wanting in merit. This sort of outlook often led Borah into legalism and an intensely personal exegesis of the Constitution, and because the fathers often had much suspicion for the nations of Europe, it followed that Borah, too, was suspecting.

His third major idea was that the American people needed a fierce patriotism, and to this end he constantly spoke in and out of the Senate. It was a mystical patriotism but the sort that had come out of the Union victory in 1865, and that derived also from the conquest of the frontier and the quick rise of the Republic to world power in 1898.

Borah fondly had supported Theodore Roosevelt, who was president during his entrance into Washington politics, and once remarked: "Since Roosevelt left the White House there has been no leader of the Republican party I could cooperate with." He of course shared Roosevelt's opinions, good and bad, and when the nation turned toward other concerns, Borah could only resort to nostalgia and, given his utterly safe Senate seat, oratorial opposition. His moral effervescence proved extremely attractive on the national scene for many years, though in his last days in the Senate time clearly had passed him by.

It is of interest that Borah, though chairman of the Foreign Relations Committee in the latter 1920s, never went abroad. He believed that "I should add little to my knowledge by infrequent brief trips to Europe. It is often wiser to stand off and obtain a clear picture. One might become merely confused by firsthand information." Three times he made tentative plans, but on each occasion he canceled them. See Marian C. McKenna, *Borah* (1961).

ROBERT H. FERRELL

BORLAUG, Norman Ernest (b. Cresco, Iowa, Mar. 25, 1914), SCIENTIST, graduated from the University of Minnesota in 1937 with a BS in forestry. Always fond of outdoor life, he served in the Idaho National Forest in 1937 and with the U.S. Forest Service (1938–39) on various assignments, including that of junior forester in Massachusetts (1939). He returned to the University of Minnesota in 1940 as a research assistant and earned his MS (1940) and PhD (1941) in plant pathology. After working as an instructor at the University of Minnesota in 1941 Borlaug joined the E. I. du Pont de Nemours

Foundation in Delaware in 1942 as a plant pathologist in order to study the effects of various new chemicals on plants.

In 1944, Borlaug, with a team of American scientists, went to Mexico City for the Rockefeller Foundation to explore the possibilities of bringing agricultural technology to underdeveloped nations. Here Borlaug did his most important work in developing high-yield, highly adaptable dwarf wheats, which tremendously increased the world's cereal supply. From 1944 to 1966, while based in Mexico with the Rockefeller Foundation, Borlaug did consulting work and brought his "green revolution" to many nations, including India, West Pakistan, Tunisia, and Morocco. In addition to wheat breeding, Borlaug has experimented with fungicides, weed killers, and plant pathology. In 1966 he became head of the International Maize and Wheat Improvement Center in Mexico City. In October 1970, Borlaug was awarded the Nobel Peace Prize for his work in eliminating famines in underdeveloped countries. He has won numerous other awards, including the Distinguished Service Medal of Pakistan (1968). In 1981, Borlaug became a consultant for the International Maize and Wheat Improvement Center, and in 1984 he was appointed a professor of international agriculture at Texas A & M in Denton, Texas. He has also served as president of the Sasakawa Africa Association (1988) and directed the Global 2000 Agricultural Programs in Africa. His estensive publications include *The Green Revolution, Peace and Humanity* (1971) and *Food Production in a Fertile, Unstable World* (1978).

<hr/>

When Norman Borlaug won the Nobel Peace Prize in 1970, he was not a well-known figure outside international agricultural circles, despite his lifelong dedication to solving the problems of feeding the world's ever-expanding population.

As a scientist he was both ingenious and sophisticated, but he had been working empirically in the unglamorous field of applied agricultural research. The award was therefore recognition of a man who symbolized what had come to

be called the "green revolution"—the rapid increase in food–grain production in developing countries in the 1950s and 1960s, which took a great deal of the sting out of the pressures of uncontrolled population growth.

Borlaug's life embodied the historical forces that produced the vision of an adequate world food supply. He joined the efforts of a private foundation—Rockefeller—to extend the Good Neighbor Policy in Mexico in the 1940s by developing strains of agricultural plants that would produce more output than in the past. Here the American tradition of agricultural research coincided with the American quest for a quick "technological fix" for social problems. Over the years Borlaug spoke aggressively for the need to use and develop scientific knowledge and techniques already available, and his actions suited his words eloquently.

A member of one of the early large-team research efforts almost from the beginning, after twenty years Borlaug had become head of the wheat team and the man credited with the payoff, however modestly he disclaimed his own individual contribution. The team research effort was combined with another American tradition, agricultural extension work, commonplace when he was a boy in rural Iowa. The ethnocentric attempt to impose an American pattern on peoples of very different cultures succeeded. Contrary to prediction, by the post–World War II era innovation was possible in folk agriculture, and Borlaug and his colleagues were able to introduce on a mass scale both new strains and new techniques. The agricultural revolutionaries offered only a "package deal," as Borlaug called it.

A man of great energy and dedication who drove himself and others day and night, Borlaug spoke for the old dream of introducing the American material success story around the world. In an era when ecologists were criticizing agriculture for poisoning the earth with chemicals, Borlaug spoke up on the side of fertilizers and pesticides, of the technical means that helped grain-importing economies almost miraculously to become self-sufficient. See Leonard Bickel,

Facing Starvation: Norman Borlaug and the Fight Against Hunger (1974).

J. C. BURNHAM

BOURNE, Randolph Silliman (b. Bloomfield, N.J., May 30, 1886; d. New York, N.Y., Dec. 22, 1918), WRITER, was born deformed—hunchbacked, with a stunted body and heavy facial features. After graduation from the Bloomfield high school in 1903, Bourne worked intermittently until 1909 when he entered Columbia College. He became editor in chief of the *Columbia Monthly* and also published articles in the *Atlantic Monthly.* After graduating (1912), Bourne received an MA in sociology from Columbia (1913) and published *Youth and Life,* which called upon American youth to spearhead a drive for social progress. He was awarded a Gilder traveling fellowship by Columbia in 1913, which enabled him to study in Germany, England, and France. Upon his return to New York City, Bourne became a contributing editor to the newly founded *New Republic,* writing articles on a variety of cultural topics, notably developments in education and literature. In 1916 he published *The Gary Schools,* a study of educational experimentation in the schools of Gary, Indiana. His main concern soon shifted to pacifism, however, and was reflected in *Towards an Enduring Peace* (1916), a symposium that he edited. In articles published in the *Masses* and the *Seven Arts* he vigorously condemned the entrance of the United States into World War I. After his death two collections of his essays were published, *Untimely Papers* (1919) and *The History of a Literary Radical* (1920).

———⚬⚭⚬———

Bourne was one of two crippled youths who contributed significantly to early twentieth-century thought. But though Homer Lea's (1876–1912) disabilities made him a militant imperialist, they made Bourne an idealist who believed in youth's destiny to right the failures of the old and disillusioned. Bourne was not overly original. His dream of a "trans-national" America

of immigrants derived from the philosopher Horace M. Kallen, and his educational ideals from **John Dewey.** Bourne's literary criticism compounded realism and romantic individualism from a variety of sources, including **Irving Babbitt** (whom he later repudiated) and the impressionist **Joel Spingarn.** Bourne did not rate himself an eclectic, however. He saw himself—and was seen by friends of the "youth movement" of his time—as using all social resources to create a new and dynamic society. Bourne's preoccupation was to break down differences between the normal and the dissident and even abnormal; this turned him against such artists as Thackeray and made him an enthusiast for **Theodore Dreiser** and Dostoevsky. His main concern was culture and society; few had so wide and varied an acquaintanceship as he. However, America's complicity in what was then the European war increasingly divided his associates. The decision of the *New Republic* to become a factor in the war's progress diminished Bourne's status with its editors, and the victory of the party of intervention in the war deprived Bourne of much of his earlier prestige and income. Bourne's optimistic outlook deserted him. With Van Wyck Brooks, Waldo Frank, and other admirers he planned a new approach to literature and politics: satiric in tone, radical in program. His death made him a sentimental memento to friends who ranged in action and ideas between bohemianism and party-line Communism. A Randolph Bourne memorial award for peace in 1940 was erased by the coming of a war to which almost all these friends subscribed. See Louis Filler, *Randolph Bourne* (1966).

LOUIS FILLER

BOWDITCH, Nathaniel (b. Salem, Mass., Mar. 26, 1773; d. Boston, Mass., Mar. 16, 1838), SCIENTIST, left school at the age of 10. Becoming interested in math and science he spent much time reading at the Salem Athenaeum. Between 1795 and 1803 he made five voyages to various places around the world, first as clerk and eventually as a supercargo and part-owner. On each voyage he studied and taught navigation, and in 1799 edited J. H. Moore's *The Practical Navigator,* the leading book on navigation at the time. In 1801, Bowditch rewrote Moore's book and published *The New American Practical Navigator* under his own name. This book improved and corrected Moore's older work, making the text simpler and more accurate. Nine editions were published during Bowditch's lifetime, fifty-six since his death.

In 1804, when Bowditch became president of the Essex Fire and Marine Insurance Co., he began a survey of Salem's harbors and wrote a series of twenty-three papers that were published in the *Memoirs* of the American Academy of Arts and Sciences (1804–20). These dealt mainly with navigation, astronomy, and surveying. Between 1814 and 1817, Bowditch also translated and added commentary to the first four volumes of P. S. de Laplace's *Mécanique céleste* (published 1829–39). Refusing teaching positions at many universities, he accepted a position as actuary for the Massachusetts Hospital Life Insurance Company in Boston (1823) and remained in that post until his death. He also served as president of the American Academy of Arts and Sciences (1829–38).

———— ∞ ————

Nathaniel Bowditch worked at a time when there were few mathematicians in his native country, and his career reveals both the advantages and the limitations of scientific work in the United States. Apprenticed at an early age and completely self-taught in science, he was yet accepted in the highest circles as a scientist of the first rank, and his business career left him ample time to pursue his scientific avocation. In his time the best mathematical minds were generally drawn off into surveying or engineering if in governmental work; or, if employed in the colleges, their time was devoted to elementary instruction. Bowditch, as an extremely well paid insurance executive, was able to devote the bulk of his time to science, and he was also able to finance the publication of his own important

works, for which there was not a sufficient commercial market in this country.

Bowditch mastered French in order to study French mathematics, and as a result he became one of the first men in the United States who could understand continental mathematics, then far advanced over the English, which still clung to an outdated Newtonianism. His great work was, of course, his translation of Laplace's *Mécanique céleste,* an explication of Newtonian mechanics applied to astronomy, which incorporated a hundred years of continental refinements, then practically unknown in the English-speaking world. Although he added no original theoretical work, it was no mere translation; the notes that he added—amounting to nearly as many words as the original text—provided a thorough exposition of the latest mathematical thought and long served as a textbook.

Bowditch had a powerful rather than an original mind. His researches were competent, and they reveal a meticulous mind at work, but with perhaps two exceptions, they were of only minor importance. His prodigious memory, which it is said did not extend to people or their names, aided him in the mastery of a number of modern languages and in the work for which he is best known—correcting, extending, and supplying bibliographical references for the works of others. In this capacity he was without a rival in his own time. See R. E. Berry, *Yankee Stargazer: The Life of Nathaniel Bowditch* (1941).

GEORGE H. DANIELS

BOWERS, Claude Gernade (b. Hamilton County, Ind., Nov. 20, 1878; d. New York, N.Y., Jan. 21, 1958), HISTORIAN, DIPLOMAT, began his journalistic career as an editorial writer for the Indianapolis *Sentinel* in 1900 after briefly reading law. He joined the Terre Haute (Ind.) *Gazette* in 1903 and the *Star* in 1904, and ran for Congress as a Democrat that year but was defeated. He ran again and lost again in 1906. After service on the Terre Haute Board of Public Works, he went to Washington as secretary to Indiana Senator John W. Kern (1911–17). In 1917 he became editor of the Fort Wayne *Journal-Gazette.* He published *The Irish Orators* (1916) and *The Life of John Worth Kern* (1918). These books were followed by *The Party Battles of the Jackson Period* (1922) and *Jefferson and Hamilton* (1925), which were well received by the historical profession despite their obvious Jeffersonian-Jacksonian bias. *The Tragic Era* (1929), which dealt with Reconstruction, was perhaps his most widely read work; *Beveridge and the Progressive Era* (1932), a biography of his youthful political idol Senator **Albert Beveridge** of Indiana, was the book he most enjoyed doing.

In 1923, Bowers became an editorial writer for the New York *Evening World,* moving to the New York *Journal* as a political columnist in 1931. Bowers defended the liberal wing of the Democratic party in his editorials. He delivered the keynote address at the 1928 Democratic national convention in Houston and remained a powerful figure in the Democratic Party. In 1933, President Franklin D. Roosevelt appointed him ambassador to Spain. An advocate of the Loyalist cause, Bowers resigned in 1939 when the United States recognized the victorious regime of Francisco Franco. He became ambassador to Chile in 1939, serving until his retirement in 1953. *My Mission to Spain* (1954) described Bowers's stay in Spain and blamed Western ineptness and fear of Communism for Franco's victory. *Chile Through Embassy Windows* (1958) told of his years as ambassador to that country. *My Life: The Memoirs of Claude Bowers* (1962) was published posthumously. His other books included *Jefferson in Power* (1936), *The Spanish Adventures of Washington Irving* (1940), *The Young Jefferson* (1944), and *Pierre Vergniaud: Voice of the French Revolution* (1951).

Public speaking was the principal interest of the young Claude Bowers. Winning the 1898 Indiana High School Oratorical Contest, he soon was nicknamed by fellow Democrats "the Gatling-Gun Orator of the Wabash." First nominated for Congress when only 25, he made sacrifices in Republican years but won wide popularity as a Democratic spokesman. Almost certainly he would have been a senatorial nominee if he had remained in Indiana.

Already on confidential terms with numerous national Democratic leaders, Bowers in New York became close to **Robert F. Wagner** and Franklin D. Roosevelt. For years no other speaker was more in demand at Democratic meetings in various sections. His highly dramatic books also found favor in Democratic circles, and Bowers did much to hold the party together in the 1920s. He likewise contributed significantly to the "Jefferson revival." In *The Tragic Era* he popularized ideas of the historian William A. Dunning, going beyond the "Dunning school" in denouncing Reconstruction carpetbaggers and in praising President Andrew Johnson.

As ambassador to Spain, Bowers sympathized strongly with the Second Spanish Republic. He believed the 1936 rebellion would have failed quickly without Hitler-Mussolini support and thought the struggle essentially a World War II rehearsal. In Chile fourteen years, the slight, fragile-appearing man with mournful eyes and an omnipresent cigar proved a popular diplomat whose admiration of the Chilean people and their institutions was genuine. Bowers combated Nazi and Communist influence in turn, working vigorously to improve Chile-U.S. relations through the Good Neighbor and Point Four programs. See Claude Bowers, *My Life* (1962).

HOLMAN HAMILTON

BOWLES, Samuel, III (b. Springfield, Mass., Feb. 9, 1826; d. Springfield, Mass., Jan. 16, 1878), JOURNALIST, attended local public schools and entered the newspaper business in 1844 as a general helper on the Springfield (Mass.) *Republican,* a paper founded by his father in 1824. He spent the winter of 1844–45 in Louisiana to recover from an illness, then returned to edit the *Republican.* He won a newspaper "war" with the Springfield *Gazette,* which the *Republican* absorbed in 1848. Upon his father's death in 1851, Bowles took over complete control of the paper. By 1860 it had a circulation of twelve thousand for the weekly edition and six thousand for the daily. Bowles emphasized accurate, concise, and impartial reporting of the news and became known for his vigorous, independent editorials. He supported the Wilmot Proviso (1846) and the Compromise of 1850. Although he disliked slavery, Bowles attacked abolitionists as troublemakers. He opposed the Kansas-Nebraska Act of 1854, however, and urged a constitutional end to slavery. Bowles helped form the Republican Party in Massachusetts (1855) and backed **John C. Frémont's** presidential candidacy in 1856. He supported Abraham Lincoln for president in 1860 and 1864, favored vigorous prosecution of the war, and editorialized in favor of Lincoln's moderate views on Reconstruction.

After the Civil War, Bowles traveled throughout the United States, describing his experiences in *Across the Continent* (1865), *The Switzerland of America* (1865), and *Our New West* (1869). An opponent of radical Reconstruction, Bowles nevertheless favored the impeachment of President Andrew Johnson. He was one of the leading critics of President Ulysses S. Grant's administration and helped promote the 1872 Liberal Republican movement that nominated **Horace Greeley** for president. After he made trips to California (1873) and Europe (1874), Bowles's health failed. He was a semi-invalid in his last years.

―――――∞∞∞―――――

The time was right for Samuel Bowles, and through his initiative, drive, and sensitivity to life about him, he built a national reputation with a small newspaper in a small city. Denied the opportunity for a higher education, he had gone to work with his father who ran a print shop and edited a small weekly paper in Springfield. Within a year the enterprising youth had persuaded a reluctant father to embark upon a daily newspaper, the first in Massachusetts outside of Boston.

His apprenticeship was brief—experience and responsibility came quickly. His ability to make acquaintances easily made him a productive local news gatherer. And broader experience came when he was called upon to report the events of the Whig nominating convention in 1848. Full responsibility for the paper fell upon him at his father's death, when he was only 25. Slowly he broadened the horizons of his paper. Close relationships with Springfield's representatives in the state and national capitals afforded him not only valued news letters but, more significant, deeper insights into politics. At the same time his enterprising spirit brought him into contact with public leaders throughout New England.

By the mid-fifties Bowles and his newspaper had attained national stature. Becoming increasingly liberal politically he broke with the Whigs and led in the establishment of the Republican Party in Massachusetts. Fearless reporting of the secret convention of the Know-Nothing Party in 1855 enhanced his reputation as a critic of the old politics.

While Bowles thus became a national figure, perhaps his most solid achievement was his contribution to news reporting. A familiar figure at popular gatherings such as the agricultural fairs and college commencements in the area (Amherst College made him a trustee), he was ideally suited to direct an active news-gathering service. Insistent, too, on high editorial standards, he sought through recruiting college graduates for his staff to make journalism, in his words, "a profession and not a stepping-stone." Although Bowles seemed to the journalist George Harvey to have failed in not building a strong financial basis for his paper, nevertheless the qualities that he had given it, sustained by a staff he had trained, enabled it to remain prominent for a full forty years beyond his death. See George S. Merriam, *The Life and Times of Samuel Bowles* (1969).

HAROLD W. CARY

BRADFORD, William (b. Austerfield, Yorkshire, Eng., 1590; d. Plymouth Colony [now Mass.], May 19, 1657), RELIGIOUS and POLITICAL LEADER, was a member of a small group of religious nonconformists who met at the home of William Brewster in Scrooby. In 1606 this group separated from the Church of England, believing it beyond redemption. Bradford accompanied the Scrooby congregation to Amsterdam, Holland (1609), and then to Leyden. Calvinist in theology and Congregationalist in polity, this group, now known as the Pilgrims, left Leyden for America in 1620. They landed at Plymouth and first signed the Mayflower Compact, a preliminary plan of government for the new colony.

In 1621, after the death of John Carver, Bradford was elected governor of the Plymouth colony, a position he held for thirty terms (1622–56). As governor, Bradford supervised agriculture and trade, and made annual allotments of land. In 1636 he helped draft a body of laws defining the duties of the different magistrates. Bradford sought to retain fellowship with all reformed churches. He reluctantly helped the Massachusetts Bay colony during the Pequot War (1636–37), joined the New England Confederation (1643), and attended the synod of 1647 at Cambridge.

In about 1630, Bradford began writing his classic *Of Plimmoth Plantation,* a history of the Pilgrims. This work was completed in 1651 but was not published until 1856.

Three things seem to have molded William Bradford's character. First, his parentage—he was born to a prosperous yeoman family and all his life displayed the combination of gentleness and firmness by which the farmer controls his stock. (**Cotton Mather** called Bradford the "shepherd-guardian" of Plymouth and composed a two-line epitaph: "Men are but flocks: Bradford beheld their need,/And long did them at once both rule and feed.") Second, the fact that he was effectively orphaned. His father died when Bradford was but 16 months old, his mother remarried when he was 4, and he was consigned first to the care of his grandfather and then at 7 to his uncles. Third, the influence of the Reverend Richard Clyfton, whose preaching awakened in the teenage boy a deep humility, devoutness, and a commitment to an unpopular religious polity that set him on the road leading through the

Scrooby congregation to Leyden and eventually to Plymouth.

The Plymouth of the Pilgrims and Bradford are inextricably conjoined. Indeed, the Pilgrim story largely rests on the sweeping, magnificent Elizabethan prose of the governor's history, which, although unpublished for more than two centuries, was well known in manuscript and a major source for every local history, beginning with Nathaniel Morton's *New Englands Memoriall* of 1669. And from the first gathering of the Old Colony Club and the celebration of Forefather's Day in 1769, the Pilgrims and Bradford have been an essential starting point for an American mythology.

Yet Plymouth colony was essentially a rural backwater, its origins lying in an attempt to escape the world, its problems, and its sins. Events were thrust upon the settlement and its governor rather than precipitated by them from the very beginning when faulty navigation and accidents of the sea brought the Pilgrims to shore beyond any legitimate jurisdiction and forced them to resort to their own devices by framing the Mayflower Compact. Bradford himself clearly preferred the quiet life. By patent, for example, he and whomever he chose had exclusive proprietary rights to the soil and governance of Plymouth after 1630. But the governor had no love for power and authority; he chose to share these rights with all the freemen of the colony. He could not bring himself to join with the magistrates and ministers of nearby Massachusetts in enforcing a single religious way in New England. And while he was regularly elected to high office, he seems to have accepted it reluctantly, as a duty—in 1633, for example, he "by importunity gat off" from serving a year. All the while he tried desperately to keep life simple and quiet for the settlement as a whole. In the mid–1630s he attempted to keep the colony out of the conflict with the Pequot Indians precipitated by Massachusetts, sending his people to war only in response to great pressure from the larger colony. And he tried to retain the original compact Pilgrim village focused on the church in the face of economic pressure from Massachusetts, which was pushing his people toward materialism and dispersal. Bradford's and the Pilgrims' inability to escape the press of events imparts a sadness to both his life and the Plymouth story, a sadness mirrored in his great history and in a number of poems written late in life for his children, in one of which he lamented: "Love and fervent zeal do seem to sleep,/Security and the world on men do creep." This pathos and an altogether remarkable and likable character, not greatness in the sense of great involvement, mark the man. See Samuel E. Morison, ed., *Of Plymouth Plantation, 1620–1647* (1953), and Bradford Smith, *Bradford of Plymouth* (1951).

DARRETT B. RUTMAN

BRADLEY, Omar Nelson (b. Clark, Mo., Feb. 12, 1893; d. New York, N.Y., Apr. 8, 1981), MILITARY LEADER, graduated from West Point in 1915. Commissioned a second lieutenant in the infantry, he served as captain and temporary major in the northwestern United States during World War I. After the war he was appointed a professor of mathematics and statistics at South Dakota State College (1919–20), and following a four-year stint as a mathematics instructor at West Point, he completed the advanced course at the Infantry School, Fort Benning, Georgia (1925).

Between 1925 and 1938, Bradley served in Hawaii, taught at the Infantry School, graduated from the Army War College, and taught again at West Point. After a two-year tour with the Army General Staff in Washington, he was named commandant of the Infantry School (Feb. 1941) and was given a star. Appointed a major general the following year, he commanded the 82nd and then the 28th Infantry divisions in Louisiana and in February 1943 became field aide to General Dwight D. Eisenhower. He was appointed deputy commander of the II Corps under General **George S. Patton, Jr.,** and in April he assumed command of the II Corps in Tunisia where he led the American troops in the final campaign that swept North Africa clear of Axis forces.

He commanded the II Corps in Sicily, then was given command of the American ground forces preparing in the United Kingdom for the Normandy invasion. On D-Day, June 6, 1944, he was in command of the First Army, which made the landings on Omaha and Utah beaches. After heading the American ground forces in June and July, he took command of the Twelfth Army Group. Eventually he commanded 1.2 million men, the largest single field command in American history. At the war's end Bradley, now a full general, served as administrator of Veterans' Affairs. In 1948 he became army chief of staff and the first chairman of the Joint Chiefs of Staff. He was raised to the rank of General of the Army in 1950.

As chairman of the Joint Chiefs, Bradley opposed **Douglas MacArthur's** Far Eastern policies and advocated a global strategy of containing the Communist forces in Korea and in Europe. Upon his retirement from the army, Bradley became chairman of the board of the Bulova Research and Development Laboratories. In 1956 he headed a presidential commission that reviewed the laws pertaining to veterans' benefits. Bradley also served on the board of the Food Fair Stores and of Metro-Goldwyn Mayer. He lived in El Paso, Texas, beginning in 1977.

⸎

Bradley was known as "the soldier's soldier," for he was plain and homespun in his appearance, speech, and demeanor, completely natural in his manner, without pretension or flamboyance, bereft of glamor. Yet he managed to project with great success and effect a quiet confidence as well as a charismatic image, essentially one of rural middle America, to his superiors, associates, and subordinates alike. The qualities he personified in World War II were those of professional knowledge, technical expertise, and sound judgment. He was one of the most competent field commanders in American military history.

Stationed in the United States during World War I and thus deprived of the opportunity to make a name for himself in combat as did many of his contemporaries, Bradley rose to prominence as the consequence of hard work and dedicated performance. He was fortunate to be at the Infantry School with **George C. Marshall,** who remembered him when Marshall became army chief of staff. Bradley's effectiveness in command of the Infantry School and of the 82d and 28th divisions in training reinforced Marshall's appreciation of him and led to his assignment to North Africa where he impressed Eisenhower. Sensing Bradley's tactical capacities, Eisenhower put him under Patton. When Patton left the II Corps in order to plan the invasion of Sicily, Bradley took the corps command and brilliantly executed the final American campaign in North Africa. He commanded the corps in Sicily, again serving under Patton, who headed the Seventh Army.

Because of Bradley's personal and professional balance, he was selected to command the American ground forces in the United Kingdom and to lead them in the Normandy invasion. He directed the First Army superbly in the landings, in the subsequent battle of the hedgerows, and in the climactic Cobra operation, which precipitated the breakout.

As Twelfth Army Group commander, with the First (Hodges) and Third (Patton) armies under him, Bradley directed the breakout, the response to the German counterattack at Mortain, and the American part of the Allied encirclement at Argentan-Falaise. He liberated Paris, marched to the Siegfried Line, reacted successfully to the Ardennes counteroffensive, crossed the Rhine, and, with three field armies under him (including now Simpson's Ninth), drove across central Germany and into Austria and Czechoslovakia.

His deployment of large units in battle was conspicuously faultless, and Eisenhower called him his best tactical adviser. Bradley functioned on the same organizational level as Jacob L. Devers, the Sixth Army Group commander, and Bernard L. Montgomery, the British 21st Army Group commander.

After the war, as chairman of the Joint Chiefs of Staff, he displayed the same stability of judgment. By his strategic and tactical perceptions he helped prevent the escalation of the Korean War, which he called the wrong war in the wrong place at the wrong time. See Omar N. Bradley, *A Soldier's Story* (1951).

MARTIN BLUMENSON

BRADSTREET, Anne (b. Lincolnshire, Eng., c. 1612; d. Massachusetts, Sept. 16, 1672), POET, lived as a child on the estate of the Puritan Earl of Lincoln where her father, Thomas Dudley, was steward. At the age of 16 she married Simon Bradstreet. In 1630 they joined her parents in the Puritan migration to Massachusetts. Although her father was deputy governor and her husband a future governor, Anne was less than enthusiastic about the move and did not immediately join the Boston church. Childless in the first years of marriage, in 1633 she gave birth to a son, Samuel; seven other children followed. In 1644 the family settled in North Andover, Massachusetts. A busy pioneer wife and mother, she also wrote poetry. A brother-in-law took some of these poems to England where they were published in 1650 as *The Tenth Muse, Lately Sprung up in America,* a publication she neither edited nor sanctioned. She spent her later years writing lyrical meditations on her life in Puritan New England.

———— ∞ ————

Bouts of poor health did not prevent Bradstreet from cultivating a remarkable literary talent that must have been awakened by a good education in Lincolnshire. Her early poems published in *The Tenth Muse,* alluding to political issues of Stuart England and reflecting Renaissance models, suggest the influence of writers such as Philip Sidney and Edmund Spencer. It is her later lyrical works that carry a distinctive voice and make her a notable writer. This mature and highly personal poetry established Anne Bradstreet as America's first genuine poet. Her poems combine the love of husband, family, home, beautiful objects, the natural world, and ordinary daily experiences with a profound faith in God's providence. Bradstreet's work is a window into the life of New England's founding generation. Her sensibility is a powerful illustration that at its best Puritan piety did not require a prudish or sanctimonious rejection of life. Her lyrics were published in Boston posthumously in 1678 as *Several Poems Compiled ... by a Gentlewoman in New England.* See Joseph R. McElrath and Allan P. Robb, eds., *The Complete Works of Anne Bradstreet* (1981), and Rosamond Rosenmeier, *Anne Bradstreet Revisited* (1991).

DONALD F. M. GERARDI

BRADY, Mathew B. (b. Warren County, N.Y., c. 1823; d. New York, N.Y., Jan. 15, 1896), PHOTOGRAPHER, had little formal education. He developed a friendship with William Page, an artist, who encouraged him to take up drawing and who later introduced him to **Samuel F. B. Morse.** Morse taught him to take daguerreotypes, a recently developed (1839) photographic process used primarily for portraits. In 1844, Brady opened his own studio in New York and was soon acclaimed for his mastery of the medium. He won awards at the annual exhibitions of the American Institution from 1844 to 1848 and became the first daguerreotypist to receive a gold medal from this institution in 1849. He gained additional acclaim for his innovation of tinted daguerreotypes made on ivory. As early as 1845 he conceived a plan of taking the portrait photographs of all the famous men and women of his day. In 1850 he held an exhibition and published a book called *Gallery of Illustrious Americans.* He stuck to this plan throughout his career, as evidenced by his collection of presidential portraits ranging from John Quincy Adams to William McKinley. In 1851 he displayed a collection of forty-eight portraits at the Crystal Palace Exhibition in London and won a medal and a commendation for his "beauty of execution." He won a similar medal at New York's World Fair two years later. While in London he first became acquainted with the new wet-plate photographic technique and adopted it soon thereafter.

At the outbreak of the Civil War in 1861, Brady won approval from President Lincoln and others for his proposal to accompany and photograph the Union armies in camp and in battle. He devoted his entire fortune ($100,000) to the hiring and equipping of teams of photographers whose work he directed and coordinated from his office in Washington. Despite cumbersome photographic equipment and often hazardous battle conditions, Brady's team covered virtually every phase of the war and amassed about 3,500 pictures. Not content with playing a purely supervisory role, Brady himself took part in some of the battlefield photographing. He covered, among others, the First Battle of Bull Run in 1861, the battles of Antietam and Fredericksburg in 1862, and the Battle of Petersburg in 1864.

Despite Brady's artistic success the war project led to his financial ruin. Forced to sell his New York studio in 1873 and then his negatives in 1874, he never fully regained his prewar eminence as a portraitist. Only in 1875, through the intercession of **Benjamin F. Butler** and James A. Garfield, did Brady finally receive some remuneration from the government, which purchased about two thousand of his pictures for $25,000. He spent most of his later years in Washington, D.C., managing his sole remaining studio.

⁕

For more than two decades Mathew Brady was the most famous photographer living in the United States. Through a combination of hard work (taking thousands of daguerreotypes and wet plates) and keen business sense (building ever larger, more expensive, and more ornate gallery-studios to attract the Victorian public), Brady gained both international fame and financial success. To some he seemed to be a shy, rather reserved man, but his two major projects— *The Gallery of Illustrious Americans,* filled with his own portrait photographs, and the coverage of the Civil War—suggest enormous ambition and a sense of history. To many of his famous sitters, moreover—from Jenny Lind to **Edgar Allan Poe** and from **Henry Clay** to Abraham Lincoln— Brady could be charming, with an Irishman's gift for storytelling that made the long periods of immobility before the camera more bearable. Not a very tall man, with thick curly hair, a mustache and goatee, and glasses to compensate for deteriorating eyesight, Brady occasionally posed before his own camera wearing the white duster that protected his clothes from darkroom chemicals.

Roger Fenton, the English photographer who went to the Crimea (1855), was the first to cover a war with his camera, but Mathew Brady's attempt—at his own expense—to record the Civil War on every front was a far more extensive project, requiring great courage and perseverance. At first unwanted by the federal government, the Civil War plates made by Brady and his assistants are now a national treasure. See James D. Horan, *Mathew Brady, Historian with a Camera* (1955).

ELLWOOD C. PARRY III

BRANDEIS, Louis Dembitz (b. Louisville, Ky., Nov. 13, 1856; d. Washington, D.C., Oct. 5, 1941), JURIST, studied in Germany (1874–75) and received an LLB from Harvard Law School (1877). After briefly practicing law in St. Louis he moved to Boston. Perceiving that industrialism was transforming American society and that the law was lagging behind economic realities, Brandeis advocated a "living law," arguing that the law had to go beyond precedent and respond to changing reality. In the 1890s, therefore, he decided to become a "people's attorney."

As a counsel for the Massachusetts Board of Trade at the turn of the century, Brandeis fought against gas utility increases. In 1905 he represented the New England Policy-Holders' Protective Committee in its suit against the Equitable Life Assurance Society of New York. After condemning life insurance practices he went on to advocate a system whereby savings banks would offer life insurance policies at economic rates. Such a law was passed by the Massachusetts state legislature in 1907. A year later in the case of *Muller* v. *Oregon* he presented his epoch-making "Brandeis brief" before the Supreme Court, arguing in favor of an Oregon law limiting the working day for women laundry workers to ten hours. Brandeis used sociological and economic evidence to prove that long hours of work were damaging both to the health of individual women and to

society in general. The Court sustained him.

Beginning in 1908, Brandeis worked to prevent the New York, New Haven, and Hartford Railroad from acquiring a monopoly on transportation in New England; in 1910 and 1913 he appeared before the Interstate Commerce Commission to argue against rate increases. In the process he set forth his "efficiency" argument to prove that railroads were being mismanaged. In 1910 he helped mediate a New York garment workers' strike. Of Jewish extraction, Brandeis joined the Zionist movement in 1912, remaining an active Zionist for the remainder of his life.

In 1914, Brandeis published *Other People's Money,* a study based on his own investigations and the hearings of the congressional Pujo Committee (1912–13). In this exposé he attacked monopolies, interlocking directorates, and the so-called money trust. Like President Wilson, he believed that the United States must become a more competitive society, that the "small unit" of business must be preserved; and Brandeis soon became one of Wilson's leading "New Freedom" advisers.

In January 1916, Wilson nominated Brandeis as an associate justice to the Supreme Court. Despite powerful opposition the Senate confirmed Brandeis's nomination by a vote of 47–22, thus making him the first Jewish justice. While on the Court he maintained the same philosophy that he had held as an attorney: that economic and social facts take precedence over legal theory. During his early years on the Court he aligned himself with **Oliver Wendell Holmes, Jr.** In *Schenck* v. *U.S.* (1919) he agreed when Holmes placed limits on free speech, and in *Abrams* v. *U.S.* (1919), in which the Court convicted Russian emigrants who protested American intervention in Russia, he and Holmes dissented. In 1932 he dissented in the Oklahoma ice case (*New State Ice Co.* v. *Liebmann),* arguing that a state should have a right to experiment with economic measures even if they are not a necessity.

During the New Deal, Brandeis was one of President Roosevelt's staunchest supporters on the bench. However, he joined the Court in a unanimous decision when it struck down the

National Industrial Recovery Act (*Schecter* v. *United States*, 1935) on the ground that it sought to regulate intrastate rather than interstate commerce. But when the Court nullified the 1933 Agricultural Adjustment Act (*United States* v. *Butler*, 1936) because the processing tax in the act sought to regulate agricultural production, he joined **Benjamin Cardozo** and Chief Justice **Harlan Fiske Stone** in dissent. Brandeis retired from the bench in February 1939. During his remaining years he urged Americans to boycott German products as a protest against Hitler's policies.

---⊶∞⊷---

Throughout his long public career, Louis D. Brandeis consistently pursued one major ideal: that of a liberal progressive society based on democracy and social justice. Brandeis early became convinced that the gigantic trusts that by 1900 had come to dominate large segments of American business not only were hopelessly inefficient in a narrow economic sense but also menaced the very existence of political democracy itself. In successive campaigns as a "people's advocate" he fought for a Boston subway franchise favorable to the public interest, for equitable Boston gas rates, for savings bank industrial insurance, against the attempts of the Morgan interests to monopolize the New England rail system, and against the extraordinary control exercised over American business by a few great New York banking houses. Thereby he sought to ameliorate what he called "the curse of bigness" and to establish a new industrial democracy based on a partnership between business, organized labor, and the public.

His persistent attacks on big business and his support for organized labor inevitably won Brandeis a reputation in conservative circles as something of a radical. In reality, however, he never challenged the fundamentals of capitalism itself; rather, he looked back with nostalgic longing toward the vanished Jeffersonian notion of a self-regulated economic order characterized by competition among a great variety of small entrepreneurs.

Brandeis's career as an associate justice of the U.S. Supreme Court proved to be a logical extension of his work as a "people's advocate." Already in his celebrated brief in *Muller* v. *Oregon* (1908), he had anticipated more or less precisely the judicial philosophy to which he would adhere on the Court. Above all he sought to infuse constitutional law with the living realities of the social order. He was also an unabashed judicial activist, little interested in narrow legal precedent, who sought to use the Court's decision-making process as an instrument for the evolution of a progressive democratic society. In a day when the dominant constitutional philosophy on the Court very largely reflected the legal interests of conservative American capitalism, Brandeis's stance inevitably thrust him into the role of a "great dissenter." Only in the curious intellectual partnership he formed with Justice Holmes did he find a measure of support for his position, although the social and legal premises from which the two men worked were radically different.

Thus Brandeis joined with Holmes in one dissent after another protesting the Court's resort to the due process clause of the Fifth and Fourteenth amendments to obfuscate federal and state social legislation. His dissenting opinions in the Burns Baking Co. case (1923) and in the New State Ice case (1932) constituted classic appeals to his judicial brethren to allow government some elbow room for social experimentation. Again Brandeis, also for the most part with Holmes's support, dissented from the Court's decisions sanctioning the use of the injunction in labor disputes. Thus in *Duplex Printing Company* v. *Deering* (1921) and in *Bedford Cut Stone Company* v. *Journeymen Stone Cutters' Association* (1927) he objected strenuously to the Court's action in upholding antilabor injunctions under the Sherman Act, pointing out that the Clayton Act presumably prohibited this practice. Finally, it was Brandeis even more than Holmes who objected when the majority justices, beginning with the Abrams case, discarded the "clear and present danger" doctrine in First Amendment free speech cases and resorted instead to the regressive "bad tendency" doctrine so reminiscent of the discredited Sedition Act of 1798.

In his last years on the Court, Brandeis became a fairly consistent judicial protagonist of the New Deal. In only three instances—notably in the celebrated Schecter "Sick Chicken" case of 1935 where a New Deal flirtation with the cartelization of American industry ran head-on into his long-standing opposition to monopoly—did Brandeis join with his more conservative judicial brethren to strike down a New Deal statute. Before his retirement from the Court, Brandeis was rewarded by seeing the majority justices accept not only the major constitutional premises of the New Deal but also his own positions on First Amendment liberties, on labor legislation, and on judicial abuse of the due process clause. Thus Brandeis emerges finally as a lifelong champion of an open libertarian democratic society, a goal in quest of which a majority of the nation's political leaders appear to be engaged even in the late twentieth century. See Alpheus T. Mason, *Brandeis: A Free Man's Life* (1946).

ALFRED H. KELLY

BRECKINRIDGE, John Cabell (b. Lexington, Ky., Jan. 21, 1821; d. Lexington, Ky., May 7, 1875), POLITICAL LEADER, graduated from Centre College, Danville, Kentucky, in 1839. After studying law at Transylvania College (1840–41) he practiced law in Lexington, Kentucky, beginning in 1845. After service in the Mexican War (which he had not at first supported) he was elected to the Kentucky legislature in 1849 and to the U.S. House of Representatives as a Democrat in 1851, serving two terms. In 1856 he was elected vice president of the United States. During this period he was in favor of the preservation of the Union. Breckinridge refused to seek the presidential nomination at the badly divided Charleston convention of the Democratic Party in 1860, but when the southern segment of the party reconvened in Baltimore and nominated him, he accepted. During the campaign he declared himself in favor of preservation of the Union, contending that it could be saved if Congress would not attempt to exclude slavery from the territories. He received the electoral votes of eleven slave states but not Kentucky. In December 1860 he supported the Crittenden Compromise, but after the firing on Fort Sumter he urged Kentucky to call a convention to decide whether to secede or not, placing himself against that state's declaration of neutrality. Military law was declared in Kentucky after both Confederate and Union armies invaded it, and Breckinridge fled south. Entering the Confederate army as a brigadier general, he was promoted to major general in April 1862. He served at Shiloh, Vicksburg, Murfreesboro, Chickamauga, Chattanooga, and Cold Harbor, and became secretary of war of the Confederacy in February 1865. After Appomattox he fled to Cuba, then to Europe, and then Canada in 1868. Allowed to return to Lexington in 1869, Breckinridge became active in railroad building projects, some of which eventually became part of the Louisville and Nashville Railroad.

⁂

John C. Breckinridge was neither a great statesman nor a great soldier, but admirers considered him the personification of Kentucky chivalry. He "is a most noble looking man—a ladies man," wrote a Confederate soldier. "Such piercing blue eyes, I never saw before. His very looks show his superiority over most men." Tall, graceful, and handsome—one girl called him "the handsomest man in the Confederate army"—he had the appearance, cordial manner, pleasing voice, and eloquent address that endeared him to voters, soldiers, and women alike. "Breckinridge, though not much of a military man, is … gallant, chivalrous & generous," announced an officer. Mrs. Mary Chesnut, the famous diarist who liked Breckinridge "better than any," caught him kissing four of the prettiest girls she had ever seen. "They are my cousins," he insisted. Breckinridge was brave, charming, dignified, and devoted to his friends, but he was no intellectual giant. A friend admitted that at times "a strange indolence or apathy" assailed Breckinridge; "he needed to be spurred to action, and without some special incentive was often listless and lethargic."

Sometimes he drank too much. He was charged with being drunk and unfit for duty during the battle of Chattanooga, and one observer claimed that wherever Breckinridge went he "brought the perfume of Kentucky bourbon with him." Yet the Confederacy's ordnance chief called Breckinridge an excellent secretary of war who knew how to "push work off upon others and not involve himself in details." Another contemporary noted: "There is nothing narrow, nothing self-seeking, about Breckinridge." And **Robert E. Lee** considered him "a lofty, pure, strong man." See William C. Davis, "John C. Breckinridge: A Personality Profile," *Civil War Times Illustrated*, VI (1967), 11–18.

GRADY MCWHINEY

BRECKINRIDGE, Sophonisba Preston (b. Lexington, Ky., Apr. 1, 1866; d. Chicago, Ill., July 30, 1948), SOCIAL WORKER, EDUCATOR, graduated from Wellesley College in 1888. After teaching in a Washington, D.C., high school (1888–94) she clerked for a year in her father's Lexington law office before being admitted to the Kentucky bar in 1895, the first woman admitted in that state. She did not practice law, however, but entered the University of Chicago where she received a PhD in 1901 and a JD three years later, the first woman to receive a law degree there. She became an instructor at the University of Chicago in 1903. With Julia Lathrop she founded the Chicago School of Civics and Philanthropy in 1907 (renamed the University of Chicago School of Social Service Administration in 1920). Breckinridge founded the Immigrants' Protective League (1908), became vice president of the National Woman's Suffrage Association (1911), and was named a delegate to the Women's Peace Conference at The Hague (1915). In 1912 she wrote *The Delinquent Child and the Home* (with Edith Abbott) and *The Modern Household* (with Marion Talbot), and in 1917 she completed the report *Truancy and Non-Attendance in the Chicago Schools*. During 1925–29, Breckinridge was a dean and professor of public welfare administration at the University of Chicago School of Social Service Administration; in 1929–33, dean of the College of Arts, Literature, and Science; and in 1933–42, professor emeritus of public welfare. She published *Family Welfare Work in a Metropolitan Community* (1924), *Marriage and the Civil Rights of Women* (1931), *Women in the Twentieth Century* (1933), *The Family and the State*, and *Social Work and the Courts* (1934), and *The Illinois Poor Law and Its Administration* (1939). In 1927 she was one of the founders of the *Social Service Review*, of which she was an editor until her death.

Breckinridge's activities extended through most of the spectrum of reform causes of the early twentieth century. She was an early advocate of economic as well as political equality for women and was active in supporting better working conditions, minimum wage laws, and shorter hours for women working in factories and mills. Her belief in justice for American blacks led to her involvement in the NAACP and Urban League branches in Chicago. She also championed the right of workers to bargain collectively, the abolition of child labor, and world disarmament. She was a strong advocate of "casework" techniques in the professional education of social service workers, and in a period when some of her fellow leaders still harbored doubts about state intervention, she advocated governmental aid and involvement in the welfare process.

———————

Sophonisba Breckinridge's career exemplifies both the dilemmas and the opportunities facing talented women in the opening decades of the twentieth century. Born into an elite Kentucky family (her father served in Congress), with ready means to support her ambitions, Breckinridge quickly accumulated a number of "firsts" as a woman, including a PhD in political science and economics at the University of Chicago. And yet, despite impressive legal and academic credentials, she had difficulty in settling on a career. It took time and a series of coincidences, including a stay at Hull House, to decide the issue; then Breckinridge began to champion various Progressive reforms and focus her energies on social work. In a sense, a traditional concern for women and children occupied her, and yet this choice did not inhibit the scope or innovative character of her activities.

Remarkably energetic, intellectually imaginative, and totally dedicated to her work (students heard time and again that the need for sleep was a weakness to be overcome), Breckinridge brought coherence to a wide range of interests. Her most vital achievement involved the professionalization of social work. Borrowing freely from the "case method" of law schools, she had her students at the University of Chicago analyze relief records. Her PhD training led her to insist on a heavy research element in social work education with impressive publication results. Her legal knowledge prompted her to oversee a major investigation into the evolution of poor relief laws in the United States and the changing nature and position of the family in American society. She had a firm sense in both instances that historical analyses could promote effective policy formation.

Together with other Progressives, Breckinridge had a keen and unshaken faith in the value of state intervention on behalf of the underprivileged. While her predecessors in charity work had insisted on remedial action by private agencies, Breckinridge led the reorientation to government activity. Only public agencies, she insisted, could offer "universal provision … [and] continuous service." And to these ends she supported juvenile court organization, widow pension programs, and protective legislation for women and children.

Today Breckinridge stands as a pioneer figure in the organization of social work and social welfare, one who charted the basic intellectual and administrative dimensions of the field. Some of her accomplishments, it is true, are more controversial now than at the time of her death. Many contemporary critics are not at all certain that the professionalization of social work has benefited either the practitioners or their clients; and the very idea of wholesale state intervention, whether in the guise of the juvenile court judge or the legislator protecting womanhood, is sus-

pect. Still, few would quarrel with the basic premise underlying Breckinridge's activities: that the powerless and the disadvantaged are society's responsibility, and their needs must be met with decency and humanity. See *Social Science Review,* volumes 22, 23, 28, for appreciations of Breckinridge's work.

DAVID J. ROTHMAN

BRENNAN, William Joseph, Jr. (b. Newark, N.J., Apr. 25, 1906), graduated from the Wharton School of Finance of the University of Pennsylvania (BS, 1928) and received a scholarship to Harvard Law School. He studied there under **Felix Frankfurter**, whom he was later to join on the Supreme Court. He graduated Harvard Law School in 1931 among the top ten in his class.

In 1932, Brennan joined the firm of Pitney, Hardin & Skinner in Newark. The son of a trade union leader, he specialized in labor law. At the beginning of World War II he served with the Army General Staff Corps and became director of the civilian personnel division of the army, attaining the rank of colonel. In 1949 he was appointed to the New Jersey Superior Court, and the next year to the Appelate Division. From 1952 to 1956 he served on the New Jersey Supreme Court, where he was influential in procedural reform.

A Republican, Brennan was appointed to the U.S. Supreme Court by President Dwight Eisenhower in 1956. Described as "the Great Conciliator," Brennan was known for his success as a coalition builder. For more than a third of a century he was one of the high court's leading voices for civil rights and civil liberties, consistently opposing the death penalty and taking liberal and expansive positions on issues of abortion, free speech, freedom of the press, affirmative action, and the rights of women, minorities, and criminal defendants. He retired in 1990 following a mild stroke.

It is hard to overestimate the influence Justice William Brennan had on the development of law and politics in the United States. The recipient of a recess appointment by President Eisenhower in 1956, and confirmed by the Senate in 1957, Brennan served under three chief justices—**Earl Warren, Warren Burger, and William Rehnquist.** Brennan wrote an extraordinary number of opinions and helped to shape the contours of the laws governing equal protection, due process, freedom of expression, and criminal procedure.

During Brennan's early years on the Supreme Court he forged a strong friendship with Chief Justice Warren. The two spent hours together discussing the issues before the Court. Under Warren's direction the Court entered an era of unparalleled activism, and William Brennan was a leader in that movement, often helping to mold majority opinions. In *Baker* v. *Carr*, Brennan held that the reapportionment of state legislatures was a justiciable issue, opening the door to a number of cases that virtually revolutionized state government while establishing the principle of "one man, one vote." In *New York Times* v. *Sullivan*, Brennan altered the law governing libel by adding the "malice" requirement, explaining that "debate on public issues should be uninhibited, robust, and wide open." Brennan was influential in shaping the opinion in *Griswold* v. *Connecticut*, the controversial case in which a constitutional "right to privacy" was first articulated. Justice Douglas, the author of the Court's opinion, was going to base his position on "a right to association," but Brennan convinced him that "privacy" was a fundamental constitutional guarantee. In later years Brennan argued that privacy rights are "part and parcel of the Bill of Rights."

As the Supreme Court moved more to the right under Chief Justices Burger and Rehnquist, Justice Brennan found himself defending positions he had taken earlier. He fought hard to extend the reach of equal protection as far as possible to include disadvantaged groups and sought to counter the more conservative jurisprudence of the majority of his fellow justices. By now he was more often than not in the minority on important issues and was forced to write what became a profusion of dissents. But at times his views prevailed. In 1973 he wrote the plurality opinion in *Frontiero* v.*Richardson* that held classifications based on sex are inherently suspect.Three years later the Court decided that classifications by gender had to be held to intermediate scrutiny and had to further important government objectives. Brennan maintained his support for the extension of affirmative action as well. In *Regents of the University of California* v. *Bakke* (1978), Brennan asserted in dissent that the Court "cannot … let color blindness become myopia, which masks the reality that many 'created equal' have been treated within our lifetime as inferior both by law and by their fellow citizens." That same year Brennan wrote the opinion of the Court in *Monnell* v. *New York City Department of Social Services* (1978). It was an important federalism case which held that local government can be sued under Section 1983 of the Civil Rights Act. In one of the last major opinions he wrote for the Court, *Texas* v. *Johnson*, Brennan found flag burning to be an expression protected under the First Amendment.

Few on the Supreme Court have served for as long as William Brennan or have had as much of an influence. His critics assert that he engaged in making law rather than interpreting it, and dealt in moral philosophy rather than constitutional law. His admirers have hailed him as a great defender of the Bill of Rights. He wrote with elegance and force. Looking back on his career he remarked, "I never thought I was wrong." History will judge whether he was right. See Melvin I. Urofsky, *The Continuity of Change: The Supreme Court and Individual Liberties, 1953–1986* (1991).

EUGENE W. HICKOK

BRIDGES, Harry Renton (b. Melbourne, Australia, July 28, 1901; d. San Francisco, Calif., Mar. 30, 1990), LABOR LEADER, born Alfred Bryant Renton Bridges, acquired the nickname Harry while a sailor. He graduated from the St. Brennan's parochial high school in Melbourne in 1917 and then briefly worked in a stationery store before going to sea. He sailed throughout the Pacific and arrived in San Francisco in 1920. After working as an oil rigger he returned to the sea. He took part in a maritime strike in New Orleans in 1921 and settled in San Francisco in 1922, working as a longshoreman. He tried to set up an International Longshoreman's Association local in 1924 and again in 1926 but failed. Bridges took over the militant periodical *Waterfront Worker* in 1932 and finally succeeded in organizing an ILA local in 1933. He led a strike against the Pacific shipowners in 1934 and persuaded teamsters and ship crews to strike in sympathy; he was elected chairman of the Joint Maritime Strike Committee. On July 5, 1934, police charged the picket lines, killing two, and California Governor Frank Merriam declared martial law. This led to a general strike in San Francisco. The longshoremen's strike was finally settled by arbitration. The union won such demands as a thirty-hour work week, higher wages, and time and a half for overtime. Bridges led another successful strike on Pacific ports in 1936–37.

In 1937, Bridges led all Pacific locals of the ILA into the Congress of Industrial Organizations, reorganizing the union as the International Longshoremen's and Warehousemen's Union. He became the first president of the ILWU, regional director of the CIO, and a member of the CIO's executive board. In 1938, Secretary of Labor **Frances Perkins** obtained a warrant for his deportation as a Communist, but at the deportation hearing in 1939, Harvard Law School Judge James Landis acquitted him for lack of evidence. In 1940 the U.S. House of Representatives passed a bill for his deportation, but it died in the Senate Immigration Committee. He was again ordered deported in 1941 by Attorney General Francis Biddle, but the Supreme Court invalidated the order in 1945. He finally became a U.S. citizen in September 1945.

Bridges had opposed selling scrap metal to Japan and vigorously backed the war effort after Pearl Harbor. He wrote a patriotic pamphlet, *Women in the War* (1943), and also began writing a column, "On the Beam," for the *Dispatcher,* the official organ of the ILWU, in 1943. After the war he led a 95-day Pacific maritime strike (1948) and a 178-day Hawaiian strike (1949). In 1949 he was indicted by a federal grand jury for perjury and conspiracy in denying at his citizenship hearing that he had ever been a Communist Party member. He was found guilty in 1950, but the indictment was dismissed by the Supreme Court (1953) because of the statute of limitations. The government reopened the case in 1954, but Bridges was cleared of all charges in 1955. Bridges signed a contract in 1960 in which West Coast longshoremen agreed to accept automation provided their jobs were ensured. He was appointed commissioner of the San Francisco Port Commission and a member of the San Francisco Port Authority in 1970. Bridges led a 134-day strike that closed all West Coast ports in 1971, eventually gaining higher wages and job insurance for union members. He headed the ILWU until 1977.

⎯⎯⎯∞⎯⎯⎯

Raised in impeccably middle-class surroundings—his father was a successful realtor and an Empire Loyalist—Bridges's later left-wing radicalism was the product of three influences: his uncle Renton, an active Australian Laborite; **Jack London,** whose *Sea Wolf* drew him to the sea and whose *Iron Heel* led him to question capitalism; and his observations while a sailor of the effects of British imperialism and of the cruel poverty of the working class in the mother country.

In his early years Bridges was gregarious, an enthusiastic pub crawler, fond of women and attractive to them. "The person Harry Bridges most reminded me of was Jimmy Walker, strange as that might seem," John Gunther's *U.S.A.* stated in 1946. "Lean, boyish, alert, with a hawklike humor and a touch of the dapper— also a touch of city streets—Bridges resembles in several respects the former mayor of New York. He is, however, not a playboy. He hasn't the time."

Historians of American labor have long doubted that Bridges was a member of the Communist Party despite the government's relentless crusade to deport him, for he seemed too much a maverick to endure the disciplined allegiance the party required. That he was so regarded by the government seemed to be based on his unremitting criticism of the exploitative side of capitalism, his admiration for the Soviet experiment, his "premature" opposition to European fascism, and his early opposition to the cold war and Vietnam. Evidence recently unearthed in the archives of the Soviet Communist Party after the collapse of the Soviet Union has revealed, however, that he indeed was a member of the Communist Party as the government claimed but was never able to prove to the satisfaction of the courts.

Bridges's left-wing views kept him from major leadership in the U.S. labor movement, which was a pity because he was personally incorruptible, and largely because of his leadership, the union he led was one that few others could rival for internal democracy, for good working conditions, and for a sense of the role a union can play in the wider struggle for social justice. See Charles P. Larrowe, *Harry Bridges* (1972).

Charles P. Larrowe

BROOKS, Gwendolyn (b. Topeka, Kans., June 7, 1917), POET, graduated from Wilson Junior College (Chicago) in 1936 and then worked in a variety of office, newspaper, and magazine jobs. She won Poetry Workshop awards at the summer Midwestern Writers Conference at Northwestern University in 1943 and 1944 and also won the prize of the annual Writers' Conference in Chicago in 1944. Her first work appeared in *Poetry* magazine in 1945; other poetry followed in such periodicals as *Harper's, Common Ground,* the *Yale Review,* and the *Saturday Review.* Her first collection, *A Street in Bronzeville* (1945), portrayed ghetto life as she had seen it on Chicago's South Side. She won the creative writing award of the American Academy of Arts and Letters in 1946 and Guggenheim fellowships for creative writing in 1946 and 1947. A second collection of poetry, *Annie Allen* (1949), describing the experiences of a woman in Bronzeville, won the 1950 Pulitzer Prize for poetry. She published a novel, *Maud Martha,* in 1953 and more collections of poems: *Bronzeville Boys and Girls* (1956), *The Bean Eaters*

(1960), and *Selected Poems* (1963). Since 1967, Brooks has taught courses on poetry at Northeastern Illinois State College, Elmhurst College, and Columbia College in Chicago. She was named poet laureate for Illinois in 1968, succeeding **Carl Sandburg.** Some of her more recent poetry collections include *In the Mecca* (1968), *Riot* (1969), and *Aloneness* (1971).

Few poets have displayed in their personal lives the same characteristics that they write about so well as Gwendolyn Brooks. She has steadfastly focused her verse on the qualities of strength, endurance, beauty, and dignity. Her poems are distinctly people-centered, frequently portraits in verse of ordinary Chicago African-Americans for whom she has the greatest compassion and empathy. Brooks has insisted that the writer's obligation is to live with eyes and heart open. She is an outstanding example of the poet responding to her climate and connecting herself and her readers to that climate. For young blacks in Chicago, Brooks has sponsored and funded poetry competitions, initiated writing workshops, and encouraged countless neighborhood cultural events.

A fastidious master of form and language, she has been termed a traditionalist because of her regard for the sonnet form, couplets, quatrains, and the Italian terza rima. Nevertheless, her work is also characterized by experiments with free verse and metrical variations. Throughout her career Brooks has believed that the poet's duty is to words, and her verse is sprinkled with puns, allusions, double meanings of words, and internal rhymes. She has turned in her later years to poetry reflecting a keener social awareness. Beginning with *In the Mecca,* her tone has become more committed to the mood of young, nationalist-minded blacks. Her voice has become sterner, her use of satire and irony more pronounced. A signal event of this poetic redirection was her decision in 1969 to publish with the black-owned Broadside Press. See Gwendolyn Brooks, *Report from Part One* (1972).

Barry Beckham

BROWDER, Earl Russell (b. Wichita, Kans., May 20, 1891; d. Princeton, N.J., June 27, 1973), POLITICAL LEADER, left grammar school to work in various clerical jobs to help support his family. He joined the Socialist Party in 1906 and, in 1912, William Z. Foster's Syndicalist League of North America. He organized the Bookkeepers, Stenographers and Accountants Union (AFL), serving as president (1913–17). In 1914 he obtained a college degree by taking correspondence courses. In 1914–15, Browder organized the League for Democratic Control, which sought to submit U.S. entry into World War I to a popular referendum. After American entry he was arrested for organizing protest meetings and evading the draft.

Browder joined the new American Communist party, formed by secession of the Socialist Party's left wing, while still in jail (1919). After his release in 1920 he resumed his career as a labor leader. He attended the Communist International and Red International Labor Unions congresses in Moscow (1921). From 1927 to 1929 he worked in China for the Soviet-supported Pan Pacific Trade Union Secretariat. After his return to the United States he became administrative secretary of the American Communist Party (1930) and then general secretary (1934). In 1934 he proclaimed that "Communism is twentieth-century Americanism," seeking to identify the party with American traditions and institutions. Browder attracted national attention as the leader of the party's "Popular Front" program (1935–39). As the Communist Party's presidential candidate in 1936, Browder polled 80,181 votes. After traveling to Spain in support of anti-Franco Republicans (1937–38), Browder was sentenced (1940) to four years' imprisonment for traveling on a false passport. While appealing his case he ran for president again in 1940, this time receiving 46,251 votes. The decline in the party's strength was due in part to disillusionment with its support of the Hitler-Stalin nonaggression pact of August 1939. Browder entered a federal prison in 1941 but was pardoned by President Franklin D. Roosevelt in 1942.

After Hitler invaded the U.S.S.R. in 1941, Browder's energetic advocacy of unconditional support of Allied war efforts helped the party regain much of the support it had lost. In 1944 it was renamed the Communist Political Education Association. In *Victory—and After* (1942) and *Teheran: Our Path in Peace and War* (1944) Browder called for the postwar cooperation of labor and capital, and the peaceful coexistence of Communism and capitalism.

However, after changes in Soviet policy resulting from the cold war, Browder was criticized by the Communists as a "right deviationist." He was replaced as general secretary of the reestablished CPUSA by William Z. Foster in 1945 and expelled from the party in 1946. From 1946 to 1949 he served as U.S. representative for Soviet publishing houses. He was indicted in 1950 for refusing to answer questions at a Senate investigation but was acquitted in 1951. In 1952 he and his Russian-born wife were indicted for false statements in her 1949 application for U.S. citizenship. The indictment was dropped in 1959. In his later years Browder engaged in lecturing and historical research.

Earl Browder grasped undisputed control of the Communist Party organization in 1934 and for the next eleven years dominated American Communism as no one had done before. This unlikely Marxist, who spoke in the flat accents of his native Kansas, led his party through its period of greatest popularity. But the success of Browder-era Communism proved paradoxical, and his career demonstrated the problems and failures of the Communist effort in the United States.

The twisting ideological line of international Communism bred internecine warfare that weakened the American party in its early years. Browder, who came to radical politics from a home filled with Populist and Socialist literature, obediently followed the dictates of the Kremlin in these struggles. He had learned of Stalin's unchallenged power in several trips to China and Russia and at the appropriate times attacked both "leftist" Trotskyites and "right revisionists," whose theory of "American exceptionalism" argued that conditions in the United States were unique, that Communists must defer revolution here and "Americanize" their cadres in a long struggle for gradual influence.

Ironically, Browder's great achievement came in the Popular Front, a new period of American exceptionalism decreed by the Comintern in 1933. Scrapping the old program of conspiratorial militancy, which had failed to attract support in the dark days of depression, he energetically embraced the new program of moderation. Browder now rejected revolution, claimed America's historic heroes as his forebears, even supported FDR. This new-model Communism prospered in New Deal days because it denied its socialistic heritage and offered potential converts the succor of a mass movement without the liability of an un-American ideology. Earl Browder ignored the unhappy implications of such "success."

While he endured another disastrous change in program dictated by Moscow in 1939, the wartime years of American-Soviet amity offered one more effective period of conciliatory policy. At war's end, however, he was deposed as just another "rightist obstructionist." The shrewd student of changing Comintern fashion had been converted to the one peculiar way his movement could prosper. He had to be purged by a party that had never taken its direction from indigenous American conditions. See Irving Howe and Servic Coser, *American Communist Party* (1962).

DAVID H. BENNETT

BROWN, John (b. Torrington, Conn., May 9, 1800; d. Charlestown, W. Va., Dec. 2, 1859), ABOLITIONIST, worked as a tanner for his father, who was also an abolitionist and an agent for the underground railroad. In 1826, Brown moved to Richmond, Pennsylvania, where he set up a tannery and used his barn as a station for the underground railroad. A succession of business failures forced him to move frequently. Before settling in North Elba, New York, a community for blacks,

he lived in Springfield, Massachusetts, and various places in Ohio.

In 1855 five of Brown's sons moved to Kansas where they hoped to obtain land and help establish Kansas as a free state. John Brown joined them, settling near Pottawatomie Creek where he became active in the free-state movement. After the pro-slavery forces sacked Lawrence (1856), Brown and a group of his followers murdered five pro-slavery settlers at Pottawatomie Creek. Following this incident, Osawatomie was burned and Brown's men were dispersed.

Brown then went to Massachusetts where such leading abolitionists as **Theodore Parker** and Thomas Wentworth Higginson agreed to help him "liberate" southern slaves. He planned to establish a free state in the southern mountains and from there attack slaveowners and liberate blacks. In the summer of 1859 he decided to attack the army arsenal at Harpers Ferry, Virginia. He rented a farm five miles away as a base, and in October 1859 crossed the Potomac and captured the arsenal and the bridge leading to the ferry. During this assault Brown's men killed five people (including a black), while they lost ten men (including two of Brown's sons). Two slaves Brown had liberated also died in the fighting. Brown's force was quickly suppressed by U.S. Horse Marines under Colonel **Robert E. Lee.** Brown was taken to Charlestown, West Virginia, where he was tried and found guilty of murder, treason, and conspiring with slaves to rebel. His execution made him a martyr to the abolitionist cause.

—⁂—

All his adult life Brown was an austere, godly, polygonal man. If he was extremely religious, he could also be dictatorial and self-righteous, with an imperious egotism that made him intolerant and unappreciative of others, especially his own sons. He could become obsessed with a single idea—now slavery, now land speculation, now a wool crusade in Massachusetts, now a black community in upstate New York—and pursue his current project with single-minded zeal. He could be glaringly incompetent as a businessman, with a talent for exaggeration when he was excited. But at other times he could be scrupulously honest. And he could be kind and gentle—extremely gentle. He could stay up several nights caring for a sick child or his ailing father or his afflicted first wife. He could hold children on both knees and sing them the sad, melancholy refrains of his favorite hymn, "Blow Ye the Trumpet, Blow," which celebrated death and man's unification with God. He could stand at the graves of four of his children who had died of dysentery, weeping and praising God in an ecstasy of despair. He could teach his children to fear God and keep the Commandments—and exhibit the most excruciating anxiety when the older ones began questioning the value of religion. All his life he could treat America's "poor, despised Africans" as fellow human beings and hate the way white people oppressed them. He could offer to take a black child into his home and educate him. He could deplore racial discrimination in the North, hide runaways on the underground railroad, and feel an almost paralyzing bitterness toward slavery itself—that "sum of villainies," that "great sin against God"—and toward all the people in the United States who sought to preserve and perpetuate it.

Brown learned most of his beliefs from his father, who taught him "from earliest childhood" to oppose slavery and to fear an all-wise, just, and all-powerful God, a God who demanded the most exacting obedience from the frail, wretched sinners He placed on trial in this world. For the rest of his life Brown was a devout Calvinist who believed in foreordination, providential signs, and man's total dependence on God. In the Kansas civil war, after fifty-six years of unmitigated trial, Brown decided that God had chosen him for a special destiny: he was to liberate the slaves by invading the South and inciting an insurrection. As he gathered a handful of conspirators behind him, he vindicated his war against slavery on several grounds: the institution was "a most barbarous, unprovoked, and unjustifiable War" against blacks, it violated God's Commandments, and it contradicted the cherished ideals of the Declaration of Independence. By the late 1850s, he contended, slavery had become so entrenched in this "so-called Christian land" that only violent revolution could eradicate it. Thus it was not only Brown's volatile, messianic temperament but the racist, slave society in which he lived—a society that claimed to provide liberty and justice for all—that finally brought John Brown to Harpers Ferry. See Stephen B. Oates, *To Purge This Land with Blood: A Biography of John Brown* (1970).

STEPHEN B. OATES

BROWN, Moses (b. Providence, R.I., Sept. 23, 1738; d. Providence, R.I., Sept. 6, 1836), BUSINESSMAN, REFORMER, was a member of the family trading and manufacturing firm of Nicholas Brown and Co. from 1763 to 1773. After the Revolutionary War he was one of the first Americans to take an interest in cotton manufacturing. At the time, England held a monopoly on cotton-manufacturing machinery. Brown, however, in 1789 set up the firm of Almy and Brown and induced the Englishman Samuel Slater, an employee of Richard Arkwright (inventor of the spinning jenny), who had migrated to America, to construct a water-powered cotton-spinning machine modeled after those used by Arkwright. This was the first successful cotton textile factory in America. The cotton manufacturing firm of Almy, Brown, and Slater was formed in 1790 to operate the textile mill in Pawtucket, Rhode Island.

Brown became a member of the Rhode Island General Assembly in 1764, representing Providence for nine years. In 1773 he left the Assembly.

In 1774 he became a Quaker and devoted the remainder of his life largely to philanthropic and educational activities. He joined the antislave trade and antislavery movement, and was the leader in the founding of the Friends School in Portsmouth, Rhode Island, now known as the Moses Brown School. He was also a founder and member of the Providence Athenaeum Library, the Rhode Island Bible Society, and the Rhode Island Peace Society.

Moses Brown's public life is best understood as a response to values inherited from his New England upbringing and to values adopted from the Society of Friends when he became a Quaker in his mid-thirties. From his older brothers, Joseph, John, and Nicholas, from Governor Stephen Hopkins, and from other friends in Rhode Island he acquired a strong sense of public responsibility—that men had a duty to engage in public affairs beyond what was in their own selfish interests. As a young man Brown discharged this responsibility by representing Providence in the General Assembly for almost a decade, where he emerged as a leader in the struggle for supremacy between the northern and southern sections of the colony by supporting the founding of Rhode Island College and by working to have it located in Providence.

Brown's conversion to Quakerism in 1774 gave added meaning to his life and new direction to his public activities. His earlier commitment to public service now became rooted in the religious values of the Society of Friends. Although he was attracted to Quakerism at first because of its otherworldliness and because he thought it would enable him to achieve salvation, he soon realized that there existed within Quakerism a long tradition of social responsibility and that many Quaker leaders had labored courageously and humanely to reform an evil and hostile world. When trouble with England began, he embraced the Quaker doctrine of pacifism and remained neutral during the War for Independence. He was not inactive, however. He saw the war with England as a tragedy because it caused human suffering, and he worked publicly to ameliorate suffering among the victims of war. When he freed his slaves and launched an attack against the slave trade and slavery, he was responding to the humanitarian impulse that had always existed within Quakerism. His long and successful efforts to provide educational opportunity for ex-slaves and for Friends' children were also manifestations of this humanitarian impulse. His suc-cessful promotion of the cotton manufacturing industry is also best understood as an expression of humanitarianism. His main motive was to provide an opportunity for young people to learn a trade so that they could maintain their self-respect and become useful members of society.

Although his success is an important chapter in the economic development of America, its significance lies more in its promise than its immediate achievement. It did not usher into America the Industrial Revolution, and that was not Brown's purpose.

Although Brown acted for most of his life in response to the older traditions of New England and the religious values of the Society of Friends at a time when most people seemed to be shedding traditions and eschewing religious for secular values, he nevertheless had a modern cast of mind. Possessed of a strong historical sense, he read and studied avidly the early Quaker writers, but his purpose was to learn what they had to teach him about the principles of conduct, not to find a program of action. The problems of the 17th century and Friends' answers to them were not, in his opinion, the same as those of his own time. Unlike some people who become conservative in their old age and close their minds to the changes in the world they are about to leave, Brown never lost interest in the events going on about him. His consistent modernity is all the more remarkable when it is remembered that he lived for almost a century and was active for most of that period. When he died in 1836, America was a vastly different country from the one he entered in 1738—it had passed through several eras. Yet he did not belong more to one than to another. See Mack Thompson, *Moses Brown: Reluctant Reformer* (1962).

MACK THOMPSON

BROWN, William Wells (b. Lexington, Ky., c. 1815; d. Chelsea, Mass., Nov. 6, 1884), WRITER, REFORMER, the son of a white slaveholder and a black mother, was taken to St. Louis at the age of 10 and hired out on a Mississippi River steamboat. Next, he was employed by the antislavery editor **Elijah P. Lovejoy** on his St. Louis *Times*. While working again on a steamboat Brown escaped to Ohio in 1834, aided by a Quaker named Wells Brown, whose name he took. He then worked as a steward on Lake Erie steamboats and helped many fugitive slaves get to Canada.

In his spare time Brown read widely. From 1843 to 1849 he was a lecturer for the Western New York Anti-Slavery Society and the Massachusetts Anti-Slavery Society, being associated with the radical abolitionists **William Lloyd Garrison** and **Wendell Phillips.** Brown also became interested in other social reforms and supported such movements as temperance and world peace. In 1849 he visited England and represented the American Peace Society at the Peace Congress in Paris, remaining in Europe until 1854. *Three Years in Europe* (1852) detailed some of his experiences abroad.

He wrote an autobiography and also a play, *The Escape* (1858), and several historical works: *The Black Man* (1863) attacked notions of black inferiority by detailing the lives of blacks who overcame great obstacles, *The Negro in the Rebellion* (1866) described the role of blacks in the Civil War, and *The Rising Sun* (1882) traced black history in Africa and America. Brown also wrote many articles for such periodicals as the *Liberator* and the London *Daily News*.

───── ∞ ─────

William Wells Brown made several significant contributions to the struggle for equality of black Americans. As one who had lived in slavery and had escaped by his own efforts, his vivid descriptions of the "peculiar institution" made a strong impression on those who heard him or read his works. Like other former slaves who spoke for the abolition movement, Brown added an element of authenticity not available to his white colleagues. His presence at antislavery meetings attracted large crowds, and he proved an effective speaker, combining pathos and humor in his lectures. A Vermont newspaper reporter described how Brown held an audience's interest for nearly two hours with his wit and speaking

ability: "His dignity of manner, his propriety of expression were more than we had expected to see in one who had spent the early part of his life as a slave."

It was by providing an example of the self-educated man who fled slavery and became a successful writer that Brown made his major contribution. While some autobiographies of former slaves were largely recorded by white abolitionists, Brown penned his own, a work that eventually sold out four editions in the United States and others in Europe. He was the first American black to write a novel, a play, and a book of black history. His novel, entitled in its first edition *Clotel: or, The President's Daughter,* though flawed, was a pioneer effort that provided an example for later black writers. Brown wrote several plays, which he read to enthusiastic audiences in many northern cities. His three books of history suffer by modern standards, but each of them called attention to the rich heritage shared by black people throughout the world.

Brown's literary works, along with his many contributions to antislavery and other reform movements, testify to his competence and ability to engage in prolonged work. He was a clever, likable person with a pronounced sense of humor. Still, not everything he attempted succeeded. He used a visual panorama of slavery to illustrate his lectures in England, but it was not effective. For several years he urged blacks to emigrate to Haiti, but few responded. He practiced medicine for the last nineteen years of his life with little apparent success. Nevertheless, his legacy included, in addition to his publications, the powerful example of a former slave succeeding as a writer. See William Edward Farrison, *William Wells Brown: Author and Reformer* (1969).

LARRY GARA

BRUCE, Blanche Kelso (b. Farmville, Va., Mar. 1, 1841; d. Washington, D.C., Mar. 17, 1898), POLITICAL LEADER, was the child of a slave mother and a white plantation owner. He was educated by a white half-brother. In 1861, Bruce escaped to Hannibal, Missouri, where he taught school. He attended Oberlin College (1866–68) and then moved to Floreyville, Mississippi, where he became a farmer. He soon accumulated considerable wealth and property. Entering politics, he was appointed conductor of elections for Tallahatchie County in 1869 and served as sergeant-at-arms for the Mississippi state senate in 1870. He became assessor of Bolivar County in 1871 and sheriff the following year. Also in 1872, Bruce obtained a seat on the Board of Levee Commissioners of the Mississippi River. He was elected to the U.S. Senate from Mississippi in 1874 as a Republican and served until 1881.

He opposed Chinese exclusion and favored fair treatment for Indians as well as blacks. He pressed for improved navigation of the Mississippi River and an end to corruption in government. After his term Bruce settled in Washington, D.C., serving as register of the Treasury (1881–85). He was chairman of the black exhibit at the World Cotton Exposition in New Orleans (1884–85) and was later appointed recorder of deeds of the District of Columbia (1889–95). Bruce was a popular public speaker and greatly in demand as a lecturer. He served as a trustee of Howard University in his later years. In 1895, President William McKinley again appointed Bruce register of the Treasury, a position he held until his death.

⁂

Bruce was the only African-American prior to the 1960s to serve a full term in the U.S. Senate. As senator from Mississippi during a period when radical Reconstruction was coming to a close, he performed his duties in a competent, dignified manner so that even many of his opponents gave him credit for probity, affability, and unperturbable good humor.

Bruce's instincts were those of a convinced advocate of civil rights, integration, and the elevation of his race. His own spectacular rise from slavery to affluence—he possessed great business acumen—constituted a model for aspiring blacks. Reconciliation of the races, not hatred, was his theme, and he opposed measures of vengeance against the former slaveholders. He

maintained this stance despite the evident injustices of the post-Reconstruction regime in his adopted state. Yet, unlike his more conservative predecessor, Hiram R. Revels, he always maintained his faith in the radical Republicans.

In a period of general corruption Bruce upheld the better traditions of the Senate. No breath of scandal ever touched him despite his well-known friendship with **Roscoe Conkling,** who was considered one of the leading spoilsmen of the time. Bruce's reputation for reliability and honesty was well deserved.

Bruce's main efforts were devoted to the welfare of the blacks. As chairman of the committee to investigate the causes of the failure of the Freedmen's Bank he benefited the investors. Forcefully though unsuccessfully he advocated the seating of P. B. S. Pinchback, the black claimant for one of Louisiana's Senate seats. He secured pensions for black veterans. But his concerns were by no means limited to black affairs. He supported the construction of railroads, the improvement of navigation of the Mississippi River, and bills furthering the general interests of his state. Consistent in his advocacy of racial equality, he opposed Chinese exclusion and injustices affecting the Indians.

Although Bruce's performance was enviable, the end of Reconstruction brought about his retirement from Congress. Thereafter he continued to give evidence of his administrative talents in the federal offices to which he was appointed. The record that he made served as a refutation of the charges by "redeemers" of black misgovernment during Reconstruction. See Melvin Urofsky, "Blanche K. Bruce: U.S. Senator, 1875–1881," *Journal of Mississippi History,* XXIX (May 1967).

HANS TREFOUSSE

BRYAN, William Jennings (b. Salem, Ill., Mar. 19, 1860; d. Dayton, Tenn., July 26, 1925), POLITICAL LEADER, graduated from Illinois College (1881) and Union College of Law in Chicago (1883). He then practiced law in Jacksonville, Illinois (1883–87). After moving to Lincoln, Nebraska (1887) he was elected to the U.S.

Congress as a Democrat in 1890. He became associated with the silver bloc in Congress and voted against the repeal of the Sherman Silver Purchase Act (1893).

Bryan ran for the U.S. Senate in 1894 but was defeated. He then became editor-in-chief of the Omaha *World-Herald,* a prominent pro-silver paper. In 1896, Bryan rocked the Democratic presidential convention with his "Cross of Gold" speech in which he espoused the virtues of silver and of agrarianism, and he then received the Democratic nomination. The key issue in the 1896 presidential campaign was the free coinage of silver at a ratio of 16:1 with gold, to which William McKinley, the Republican nominee, was categorically opposed. McKinley conducted a "front-porch" campaign at Canton, Ohio, while Bryan toured the country extensively. In an election marked by sharp sectional divisions, McKinley defeated Bryan, 271 electoral votes to 176.

After serving as a colonel during the Spanish-American War, Bryan once again received the Democratic presidential nomination in 1900, running on an anti-imperialist, pro-silver platform. He was again defeated by McKinley, 292 electoral votes to 155. In 1901, Bryan established the *Commoner,* which became the outlet for his views. He ran against William Howard Taft for the presidency in 1908 but once again lost, 321 electoral votes to 162. At the 1912 Democratic presidential convention Bryan gave his support to Woodrow Wilson, who, when elected, appointed Bryan secretary of state.

As secretary of state Bryan promoted a number of international arbitration treaties. Although he was an anti-imperialist theoretically, he tried to preserve American interests in Latin America so as to exclude European powers.

When World War I broke out, Bryan favored a policy of strict neutrality. He opposed American loans to the Allies and questioned Wilson's permitting American citizens to travel on British vessels that might be sunk by submarines. Believing that Wilson's notes to Germany regarding the sinking of the *Lusitania* were too belligerent, he resigned (1915).

Throughout his career Bryan was one of the leading reform politicians in the nation and was often instrumental in keeping the Democratic Party wedded to reformist policies. At different stages of his career he championed (and was often successful in getting his party to sponsor) such reforms as the initiative and referendum; direct election of senators; progressive tax legislation, including a graduated income tax and an excess profits tax; public control and/or ownership of "natural" monopolies; progressive labor legislation, including maximum hours and minimum wages; government guarantee of bank deposits; woman suffrage; and government aid to farmers, including some form of minimum prices for crops.

Bryan in his later years became identified with prohibition, real estate speculation in Florida, the Ku Klux Klan (he opposed denouncing the Klan by name at the 1924 Democratic presidential convention), and the "crusade" against evolution. In 1925 he helped prosecute John Thomas Scopes, a teacher in Dayton, Tennessee, who taught the theory of evolution. Scopes was defended by **Clarence Darrow,** who subjected Bryan to an intense cross-examination during which Bryan stated that he accepted the Bible literally. Bryan died a few days later.

———&—

"You may dispute over whether I have fought a good fight," Bryan told his fellow Democrats in 1904, "you may dispute over whether I have finished my course; but you cannot deny that I have kept the faith." Though much of his career still lay ahead—the third campaign for the presidency, the secretaryship of state, the impassioned crusades for peace, prohibition, fundamentalism, and a myriad of other reforms—Bryan never came closer to defining the essence of his entire life's work.

From his entry into national politics as a congressman in 1890 to his death thirty-five years later, it was Bryan's special role (he would have called it his "destiny") to promulgate and defend the beliefs so carefully inculcated in him during his youth in Illinois and so closely nurtured and guarded by him during his mature years in Nebraska: the belief in an omnipotent God whose Word was embodied in the Bible; the belief that Christianity was a temporal as well as a sacred creed requiring not simply faith but works, and directing man to reform not merely himself but all of society; the belief that collective wisdom was superior to individual wisdom: if every human being was potentially equal to every other, then all men of good will and correct principle were worthy of participating in the governmental process, for what was crucial was not a man's training but his spirit; the belief that progress was assured since mankind, with all its imperfections, was essentially good and therefore capable of approaching perfection and of creating on this earth a richer and more rewarding life; the belief that both spiritually and materially rural America was the heartland of the nation, for under the beneficent influence of Nature man could produce the essentials of life and develop more easily and naturally those instincts with which all men were endowed; the belief that the United States adhered more closely than any other nation to the principles of Christianity and was the instrument by means of which the world would be led into an era of democracy, peace, and brotherhood.

This set of beliefs, which can be summarized as faith in Christianity, majority rule, the primacy of the rural way of life, and the American mission, profoundly shaped all of Bryan's actions. They were responsible for the most noble and the least worthy aspects of his career: his struggles to improve and expand the democratic process as well as his distrust of the expert wherever he was found, especially in the civil service or the university; his campaigns in behalf of the industrial worker as well as his repeated attempts to keep urban America subordinate to the rural West and South; his persistent fight against privilege and inequality as well as his failure to defend the civil liberties of African Americans; his insistence on independence for the Philippines and neutrality in World War I as well as the interventionist and imperialist policies he pursued toward Mexico and the Caribbean as secretary of state; his

supreme faith in man's potentialities as well as his nagging fear that man was always on the verge of succumbing to the internal and external temptations that surrounded him.

If it was Bryan's function to champion the beliefs that informed and shaped the culture in which he was born and lived, it was his fate to do so in a particularly trying age. The farmers and townsfolk, the agrarian democracy, the Protestant fundamentalism, the simplistic and optimistic moral universe which took it for granted that good was rewarded, evil punished, and progress assured, that had flourished throughout most of the 19th century were in a serious state of decline. The growing concentration of economic and political power, the increasing ethnic and religious heterogeneity of the American population, the rise of huge polyglot cities with unfamiliar moral codes and lifestyles—in short, all the changes brought about by industrialization, urbanization, and the new immigration—seemed to be shaping an America alien to Bryan's experience and expectations. Bryan's participation in the struggles of the Populist and Progressive movements was aimed at maintaining and restoring the economic and political power of rural, small-town America in a changing world, just as his later participation in the prohibition and fundamentalist movements was geared to defending its cultural integrity.

To these struggles Bryan brought his great eloquence, his indefatigable energy and sense of purpose, his honesty and sincerity, his genuine love of his fellow citizens, and his delight in speaking to and often for them. He brought also a personality structure that characterized so many American politicians at the turn of the century: a lack of introspection, a compulsive optimism, an inability to question any of his own actions, a propensity to visualize himself as a vessel carrying out God's ends, a devotion to men in the mass rather than men as individuals, an unfailing ability to rationalize all events so that they confirmed his expectations and his fundamental principles. Above all, he brought an unwavering and uncritical defense of his faith; a defense that constituted his most enduring strength and his most tragic weakness. See Paolo Coletta, *William Jennings Bryan* (3 vols., 1964–69).

LAWRENCE W. LEVINE

BRYANT, William Cullen (b. Cummington, Mass., Nov. 3, 1794; d. New York, N.Y., June 12, 1878), WRITER, attended public schools and was tutored in Latin and Greek. In 1808 he wrote *The Embargo,* a political satire, and after briefly attending Williams College (1810) he read law and was admitted to the bar (1815). He practiced first in Plainfield, Massachusetts, and then (1816–25) in Great Barrington, Massachusetts.

In his spare time Bryant wrote poetry. "Thanatopsis," published in the *North American Review* in 1817, and a collection, *Poems* (1821), established his literary reputation for writing serious, simple poetry vividly evoking the beauty of nature. In 1825, Bryant gave up law and moved to New York City where he became coeditor of the *New York Review and Athenaeum* magazine. A year later he became assistant editor of the New York *Evening Post* and, in 1829, editor in chief and part-owner. He remained with the *Post* until his death.

In his editorial columns Bryant defended Jacksonian democracy, supported free trade and workingmen's rights, and spoke out forcefully against slavery. In 1848 he broke with the Democrats by supporting Free Soil candidate Martin Van Buren for the presidency and later participated in the founding of the Republican Party. During the Civil War he urged vigorous prosecution of the struggle and urged Abraham Lincoln to issue the Emancipation Proclamation. After Appomattox, however, Bryant became a critic of radical Reconstruction and backed President Andrew Johnson during his impeachment trial. In his later years Bryant concentrated on translating Homer (completed in 1871) and some Spanish poets. Some of his poetry collections include *The Fountain and Other Poems* (1842), *The White-Footed Deer and Other Poems* (1844), and *Thirty Poems* (1864).

The brightness of Bryant's early fame as a nature poet, "the American Wordsworth," somewhat obscured the importance of his later career as journalist, orator, and critic. His energetic, many-sided life is inadequately expressed in the slender volume of his verse, excellent as much of it is. The 1832 edition of *Poems,* published in England with an introduction by **Washington Irving,** contains the essential Bryant. His achievements, simple and unpretentious as they now seem, were in his day triumphs in the modernization of American prosody. In his "Essay on American Poetry" (1818) he attacked 18th-century formality, saying that it "allows just as much play and freedom to the faculties of the writer as a pair of stilts allows the body." His craftsmanship was remarkably adroit and resourceful (he was the one contemporary **Edgar Allan Poe** thoroughly respected). However, he remained from youth to age a moralizer in blank verse. Though a "romantic" who was influenced by the works of Byron, Cowper, and James Thomson, Bryant was, as man and poet, reserved, even austere, his "coldness" firmly established in literary tradition by **James Russell Lowell**'s humorous lines: "There is Bryant, as quiet, as cool, and as dignified/As a smooth, silent iceberg, that never is ignified." His mind was discursive and enumerative, lacking the imaginative and intellectual voltage found in poets of the first rank. As an editor he took high ground on the controversial issues of the day and defended it firmly. His steadfast championship of the rights of free men, his concern for the public welfare, and his sincerity and fairness elevated the level of 19th-century American journalism and exerted a widespread influence in many areas of national life. The hereditary Federalism (evidenced in his youthful satire *The Embargo*) gave way early in life to an idealistic liberalism and faith in democracy based primarily on the simple belief that individual liberty is the panacea for political ills. See Tremaine McDowell, *William Cullen Bryant* (1935).

WILLIAM McCANN

BUCHANAN, James (b. Mercersburg, Pa., Apr. 23, 1791; d. Lancaster, Pa., June 1, 1868), PRESIDENT, graduated from Dickinson College (1809) and admitted to the Pennsylvania bar in 1812. A state legislator (1815–16), U.S. congressman (1820–31), minister to Russia (1832–33), and U.S. senator (1834–45), he became President James K. Polk's secretary of state in 1845. Buchanan helped settle the Oregon boundary dispute (1846); he was instrumental in Polk's elaboration of the Monroe Doctrine; and he made some effort to purchase Cuba. While he was U.S. minister to Great Britain (1853–56), Buchanan joined Pierre Soulé (U.S. minister to Spain) and John Y. Mason (U.S. minister to France) in drafting the Ostend Manifesto (1854) under orders from President Franklin Pierce; it urged Spain to sell Cuba to the United States and stated that if a slave rebellion in Cuba detonated a counterpart in the United States, the latter would be justified in seizing Cuba.

Buchanan was elected president in 1856, defeating the Republican **John C. Frémont,** 174 electoral votes to 114. Two days after his inauguration the Supreme Court, in the **Dred Scott** case, declared the Missouri Compromise (1820) unconstitutional, thus opening all federal territories to slavery. Buchanan thought slavery a moral evil but maintained that the federal government could not interfere with the institution in the states. Believing that a president could not negate the work of a state constitutional convention, Buchanan reluctantly endorsed the pro-slavery Lecompton Constitution of Kansas (1857), thereby alienating Senator **Stephen A. Douglas** of Illinois. Their disagreement helped to split the Democratic Party.

After Lincoln's election as president in 1860, Buchanan denied the right of secession, called for a constitutional convention to clarify the status of slavery in the territories, and recommended steps to save the Union, which Congress ignored or voted down. When the South attacked Fort Sumter, Buchanan supported Lincoln's war effort.

James Buchanan was often assailed for the personal traits of which he was most proud. Ridiculed as a "friend of the obvious," he was a man of transparent purpose rather than a trickster or role player. Condemned as vacillating by political extremists in the North and South, he held middle ground on principle and insisted that only by compromise and mutual restraint could self-government survive. Self-respect, self-restraint, and a rigorous devotion to public duty were deeply rooted in his nature; as president he brought these qualities to bear on the rising emotional storm over slavery.

Youthful misadventures and years in politics gave Buchanan the self-control to face frustration with outward calm. As a young lawyer he had been conscientious and conventional. Politics made him increasingly cautious and calculating. As a legislator and a diplomat he excelled in finding and ordering the essential facts, but he never dramatized his ideas or aroused public enthusiasm. He rarely exhibited passion, reserving his rare outbursts for party schismatics or for fanatics and extremists. Buchanan rejected all absolute modes of thought and generally advocated middle-of-the-road courses, seeking to minimize political controversy by drawing antagonists to a common higher ground. The avoidance of extreme positions became the trademark of his political credo; he held no brief for non-negotiable principles of morality or ideology.

Beginning his career as a Federalist and ending it as a Jacksonian, Buchanan best fit the original Jeffersonian mold. He possessed a bona fide equalitarian spirit, was personally unpretentious, and acquired a Chesterfieldian gentility. He had a strong partiality for country people and country living, and a dislike of large cities. On the political issues of his day he advocated not a high or a low tariff but moderate specific duties to sustain both factories and farms and bring in some revenue. He wished neither unregulated state banking nor banks controlled by the state but proposed many alternatives between wildcatting and total control. He wished to acquire neither all of Oregon nor all of Mexico but half the former and the portion of the latter actually occupied before 1847. He deplored slavery but accepted the constitutional sanction for it in the states, and as president accepted the Supreme Court dictum that slaves could not be excluded from federal territories.

Buchanan's election as president in 1856 signified the victory of a conservative defender of the Union against a new sectional party, many of whose members called stridently for dissolution of a union with slaveholders. His party split over his endorsement of the pro-slave Lecompton Constitution of Kansas. The antislavery people had refused to vote for convention delegates or against the slavery articles. As president, Buchanan declined to outlaw, by executive edict, the local Kansas elections in which the complainants had refused to exercise their right to vote and had consequently lost. After Lincoln's election and the beginning of secession, Buchanan managed to hold the violent passions of the opposing sections in check and to turn over to Lincoln a people still at peace and with eight of the fifteen slave states still in the Union.

Buchanan never married, partly because of the tragic death of his fiancée in 1819. Despite this, he had a rich family life. His father's death in 1821 left him responsible for his mother, six younger brothers and sisters, and ultimately ten orphaned nephews and nieces. Three of the latter came to live with him, including Harriet Lane, who became mistress of the White House during his term. He provided financial security for the rest during his lifetime. He had acquired a modest fortune from his law practice and through real estate, and was never dependent on political office for a livelihood, a fact which gave him a freedom of action that he relished.

Although he was "antimatrimony," he sought the company of women and was a favorite with them all through his life. Buchanan was a *bon vivant* and an excellent raconteur. His experiences at the courts of Czar Nicholas and of Queen Victoria gave him a large store of anecdotes, and he knew all the prominent U.S. politicians of his era. He cultivated a wide circle of political associates but had few intimates among them. His closest friends remained outside the political arena, mostly his hometown neighbors in Lancaster, Pennsylvania, where he had lived

since 1809 and maintained his country estate, Wheatland. See Philip S. Klein, *President James Buchanan* (1962).

PHILIP S. KLEIN

BUCKLEY, William F., Jr. (b. New York, N.Y., Nov. 24, 1925), WRITER, attended the University of Mexico in 1943 and left to serve in the U.S. Army (1943–46). In 1950 he graduated from Yale University, where he headed the college newspaper and which he skewered in *God and Man at Yale* (1951). Following a stint in the CIA (1951–52), Buckley and L. Brent Bozell coauthored the polemical *McCarthy and His Enemies* (1954). The following year these brothers-in-law launched *National Review*, which rapidly became the leading journal of American conservatism. *Up from Liberalism* (1959) furthered Buckley's position as a preeminent spokesman for the political right. During the 1960s both his prominence and his audience expanded through new media ventures, notably a weekly syndicated newspaper column, *On the Right*, which commenced in 1962, and a weekly television series, *Firing Line*, which began four years later. Buckley ran an unsuccessful but highly publicized campaign for mayor of New York in 1965 as the candidate of the recently organized Conservative Party of New York. In 1973 he served with the U.S. delegation to the United Nations. Although he has not again sought elected or appointed office, he has maintained his position as a guru to conservatives and as a commentator on public affairs. Beginning with *Saving the Queen* (1976), he has also authored, among other works, a series of spy novels set against the cold war.

⸻

William F. Buckley, Jr., was to the manor of conservatism born. His father, a staunch Roman Catholic and self-made oil millionaire, successfully instilled in him the importance of religion and private property, both of which would become pillars of belief. At age 6 young Buckley wrote the King of England demanding that his nation honor its debts from World War I; years later he excoriated his collegiate alma mater for harboring an economics department that scorned free enterprise and a religion department that was insufficiently religious. Like countless others, conservative and not, he deemed Communism an implacable foe of the West's most cherished values and became an outspoken and eloquent cold warrior.

But Buckley was much more than a cold warrior and certainly not a rigid ideologue. Speaking out on numerous controversial issues during a public career that has spanned nearly half a century, he has at times taken positions highly atypical of mainstream conservatives. These have included the impassioned defense of a convicted murderer and the plea for the legalization of drugs. To the surprise of many he also supported the treaty that relinquished American sovereignty over the Panama Canal. This pragmatic quality has persistently characterized his conservatism. Lukewarm toward the civil rights movement of the 1960s, for example, he subsequently strongly endorsed the goal of electing a black president. In his writings but even more so in his public appearances Buckley has both delighted and exasperated audiences with his urbanity and recondite vocabulary, his impish smile and withering sarcasm. As a longtime spokesman for modern Americian conservatism, with its coat of many and frequently clashing colors, Buckley has had few if any peers. See John B. Judis, *William F. Buckley, Jr.: Patron Saint of the Conservatives* (1988).

ROBERT MUCCIGROSSO

BULFINCH, Charles (b. Boston, Mass., Aug. 8, 1763; d. Apr. 15, 1844), ARCHITECT, graduated from Harvard in 1781 and toured Europe in 1785–87. His travels and especially his visit to Rome and Florence greatly stimulated his interest in architecture, which Thomas Jefferson encouraged. Returning to an America where there were few trained architects, Bulfinch designed several churches, notably the Hollis Street Church in Boston (1788) and churches in Taunton and Pittsfield. In 1792 he designed the State House at Hartford and the next year, the Boston theater. His most important structure, and for many years the most imposing public building in America, was the Massachusetts State House in Boston, completed in 1798. Beginning in 1792, Bulfinch designed a series of houses that, in their use of delicate details patterned after the English designer Adam, markedly changed American domestic architecture. He introduced the oval parlor and the curved staircase into the stern, rectilinear colonial New England house.

Bulfinch, who served almost continuously on the Boston board of selectmen for twenty-six years, contributed heavily to the development of the early 19th-century city, encouraging such innovations as free public instruction for both boys and girls, street lighting, better city government, and unified architectural design, as in the blocks of houses that he built at Franklin Place and on the Common. After losing his private fortune in 1795 he turned to professional architecture with considerable success. In the next twenty years he designed a house for Harrison Gray Otis, warehouses on India Wharf, Massachusetts General Hospital, the Maine State House, the Church of the Holy Cross, and the New South Church. When **Benjamin Latrobe** resigned as architect of the Capitol at Washington in 1817, Bulfinch took his place. His chief contribution was the detailed design of the western elevation, which became the actual "front" of the building.

Bulfinch returned to Boston and, at 67, retired, thereafter occasionally making short trips to inspect the many houses in the Federal style that his work had inspired and that, until the advent of the Greek revival in the 1820s, represented the dominant architectural style in America.

———— ✦ ————

Bulfinch's lifestyle and style of architecture alike exemplified the essential conservatism of New England culture in Revolutionary and early Federal times. Compare, for example, Bulfinch's Massachusetts State House (1795–98) with Jefferson's Virginia State Capitol at Richmond (1785–88), and it will be plain that Jefferson understood, as Bulfinch apparently never did, that the Revolution demanded a new kind of architectural metaphor in American public buildings. Jefferson's literal "revival" of specific republican Roman buildings made a visual symbolic statement of conviction that the Revolution had reincarnated the ideal government of antiquity, promising a new quality of life for all. Jefferson thus created not only a new style (his Capitol was the first architectural example in the Western world of the Roman revival proper) but also led the way toward the broad 19th-century "Victorian" principle of eclectically reproducing past styles in order to symbolize literary, political, and religious ideas associated with particular epochs. This whole approach to architecture was foreign to Bulfinch's outlook; he remained in essence an 18th-century colonial gentleman-designer, albeit the greatest in that tradition. But just because Bulfinch was more conservative, his influence on American architecture was more lasting. The Roman revival, with its specific ideological associations, soon dissolved into other revivals as pristine Revolutionary fervor died away. But from the 1870s on, Bulfinch's simpler, solider, broader kind of "colonial classicism" steadily gained in appeal. By the 1960s the Roman revival had long been a dead movement in architecture, but colonial vernacular essentially inspired by Bulfinch still flourished mightily, providing an image of stability to people threatened by precipitous change. See Harold Kirker, *The Architecture of Charles Bulfinch* (1969).

ALAN GOWANS

BUNCHE, Ralph Johnson (b. Detroit, Mich., Aug. 7, 1904; d. New York, N.Y., Dec. 9, 1971), DIPLOMAT, graduated from the University of California at Los Angeles in 1927 and received an MA in government in 1928 from Harvard. He was appointed an instructor of political science at Howard University (1928), became assistant professor and department chairman (1929), and served as special assistant to the president of the university (1931–32). Bunche returned to study at Harvard in 1932. After traveling through Togoland and Dahomey to gather information for his dissertation comparing colonial rule in these two areas, he received a PhD in 1934. While continuing his work at Howard, Bunche did postdoctoral research at the University of Capetown, South Africa (1936), and at the London School of Economics (1937). He was staff member of the Carnegie Corporation's Survey of the Negro in America (1938–40) and assisted Swedish sociologist Gunnar Myrdal from 1938 to 1940 in gathering information for Myrdal's book on race relations, *An American Dilemma* (1944).

In 1941, Bunche became senior social science analyst for the Office of the Coordinator of Information (later the Office of Strategic Services). He was principal research analyst in the Africa and Far East Section of the OSS (1942–43) and chief of its Research and Analysis Branch's Africa section (1943–44) before moving to the State Department in 1944, where he was acting and then permanent (1945) associate chief of the division of Dependent Area Affairs dealing with colonial problems. While with the State Department, Bunche attended the Dumbarton Oaks Conference planning the new United Nations (1944), the San Francisco Conference (1945), where he helped draw up the trusteeship sections of the U.N. Charter, and the first U.N. General Assembly meeting in London (1946). He joined the U.N. Secretariat permanently in 1947 as director of its Trusteeship Division and helped set up guidelines for these territories to achieve independence.

Bunche was appointed special assistant to the Secretary-General's Special Committee on Palestine in 1947. In this post he recommended partition of Palestine into Jewish and Arab states. In 1948, Secretary-General Trygve Lie appointed Bunche head of the U.N.'s Palestine Commission after the original appointee, Count Folke Bernadotte of Sweden, was assassinated by an Arab terrorist in Jerusalem. His negotiation of the dispute between the Arabs and the Israelis led to an armistice in 1949. For this work Bunche won the Spingarn Award of the NAACP in 1949 and the Nobel Peace Prize in 1950. He continued as head of the U.N.'s Trusteeship Division and became undersecretary-general in 1955. Bunche became chief troubleshooter for Secretary-

General Dag Hammarskjold with the title of undersecretary for special political affairs in 1957 and continued in this capacity under Secretary-General U Thant (1967–71). He organized and directed U.N. peacekeeping missions during the Suez crisis (1956), the Congo crisis (1960), and in Cyprus (1964). He received the Presidential Medal of Freedom from John F. Kennedy in 1963. Active in the American civil rights movement, Bunche participated in the march from Selma to Montgomery, Alabama, in the 1960s and served as a member of the board of directors of the NAACP for twenty-two years until his death. Declining health forced him to retire from the U.N. in 1971. *The Political Status of the Negro* (1973), a collection of interviews conducted in the South during the 1930s, appeared posthumously.

The grandson of a former slave, Ralph Bunche began his career as a young militant black critic of American society and concluded it as the very embodiment of the Establishment—a man without color, an international civil servant of the highest rank, and a defender of the U.S. role in Vietnam. Though orphaned at the age of 13 and forced to go through college on an athletic scholarship, Bunche won a Phi Beta Kappa key and became the first African-American to be granted a PhD from Harvard's government department. Among black intellectuals Bunche early established himself as one of the most trenchant opponents of the gradualism and conciliation urged by the NAACP and as the preeminent spokesman for a socialistic America to be forged by an alliance of black and white workers. He envisioned the National Negro Congress, which was organized in his home in 1936, as a superalliance of black groups that would supplant the legalism of the NAACP and press for the class needs of the oppressed black masses. His research memoranda on the political status of African-Americans and the strategies of race betterment organizations, completed at the end of the 1930s for Gunnar Myrdal's *An American Dilemma*, remain classics of their genre and indispensable to any student of African-American history.

During World War II he became the first black desk officer in the history of the State Department and helped author the United Nations Charter. After joining the permanent secretariat of the U.N., his service as Secretary-General Trygve Lie's right-hand man and chief troubleshooter led to his great diplomatic success in negotiating the 1949 armistice between Israel and its Arab neighbors. His work as a peace-seeking mediator and, after 1958, as undersecretary for special political affairs in the U.N. Secretariat earned Bunche the esteem accorded one of the world's first truly international diplomats. However much of a second-class citizen he remained at home, much of the rest of the globe prized him as a preeminent statesman of his age.

Although a distant observer of most of the critical events of the civil rights revolution, and thus a frequent target of the young militant blacks of the 1960s who remained either ignorant of or impervious to the knowledge of the racial battles he had once fought and of the symbolism of his position as the U.N.'s highest-ranking American, Bunche nevertheless deemed it important to participate in the 1963 March on Washington and the march from Selma to Montgomery two years later. He did about as much as any man could to live out his creed: "I have a deep-seated bias against hate and intolerance. I have a bias against racial and religious bigotry. I have a bias against war, a bias for peace. I have a bias which leads me to believe that no problem of human relations is ever insoluble." See Brian Urquhart, *Ralph Bunche: An American Life* (1993).

HARVARD SITKOFF

BUNDY, McGeorge (b. Boston, Mass., Mar. 30, 1919), EDUCATOR, received his AB from Yale in 1940. After an extended tour of South America, he became a junior fellow at Harvard (1941). He ran for the Boston City Council as a Republican that same year but lost. As an army intelligence officer during World War II he participated in planning the invasions of Sicily and France (Operation Overlord). Returning to Boston in

1946, he helped **Henry L. Stimson** write his autobiography, *On Active Service in Peace and War* (1948). In 1948, Bundy went to Washington, D.C., as a consultant to the Economic Cooperation Administration, which administered the Marshall Plan. After serving as a foreign policy adviser to **Thomas E. Dewey** during the presidential campaign of 1948, he became a political analyst for the Council on Foreign Relations. He returned to Harvard in 1949 as a lecturer in government, rising to professor of government in 1954. In 1952, Bundy edited *Patterns of Responsibility,* a study of Secretary of State **Dean Acheson**'s foreign policy. He was appointed dean of the faculty and graduate school at Harvard in 1953.

Although he had supported Dwight D. Eisenhower for president in 1952 and 1956, Bundy worked for Democrat John F. Kennedy in the 1960 presidential campaign. Upon his election Kennedy appointed Bundy special assistant for national security affairs. In this capacity Bundy headed the staffing effort for the National Security Council and coordinated foreign policy and defense matters for Kennedy and, later, Lyndon Johnson. Bundy played an important role in the decisions relating to the Cuban missile crisis (1962) and the dispatch of American troops to the Dominican Republic (1965). He was a major policymaker in planning American intervention in South Vietnam and strongly advocated the beginning of the strategic bombing program of North Vietnam in 1965. In 1966, Bundy left the White House to become president of the Ford Foundation, remaining there until 1977. In 1968 he published *The Strength of Government.* He received the Presidential Medal of Freedom in January 1969. In recent years Bundy has been a history professor at New York University and has written on arms control and matters dealing with international relations.

———— ∞ ————

Bundy is an "Eastern Establishment" educator who achieved limited public prominence in two Democratic administrations. He has been an assertive academic administrator and an aggressive but disciplined presidential adviser who has not established a colorful public presence commensurate with his prominence in public life.

At Harvard, Bundy established himself as a powerful dean. In Washington with Kennedy—in a relationship Bundy likened to his administrative role at Harvard—he also quickly established an influential position in the government, handling his work for the president in a way that was compatible with exercising power over a tenured faculty, a disciplined assertiveness with which he "encouraged and influenced the initiatives of others," as I. L. Destler has put it. Bundy's operating style was less compatible with President Johnson's, and when he left the White House, his successor, **Walt Rostow,** followed quite different practices. On Vietnam, Bundy was less of a hawk than Rostow and, until the spring of 1965, less of a hawk than President Johnson.

At the Ford Foundation, Bundy presented himself briefly as a forceful public personality, and Ford as a conspicuous social innovator. But some foundation actions roused congressional hostility. Perhaps in reaction Bundy became less visible. His lowered public image and direct administrative interactive style, however, remained as characteristic as it had been at Harvard and in the White House. See Joseph Kraft, *Profiles in Power* (1966).

PAUL Y. HAMMOND

BURBANK, Luther (b. Lancaster, Mass., Mar. 7, 1849; d. Santa Rosa, Calif., Apr. 11, 1926), HORTICULTURIST, worked for the Ames Plow Co., Worcester, Massachusetts (1864–67). After attending Lancaster Academy, Lancaster, Massachusetts (1867–68), where he first became acquainted with the work of Darwin, he worked on his family's farm for two years and on his own truck farm in Lunenburg, Massachusetts (1870–75), where he developed the Burbank potato. In 1875 he went to Santa Rosa, California. Following a short stint in a nursery, he bought his own fruit and vegetable farm in 1876. Employing practical experience and Darwinian evolutionary theory, Burbank used such techniques as crossbreeding, hybridization, and grafting to develop new varieties of berries in 1878, stoneless prunes in 1879, thornless blackberries in 1880, new varieties of gladioli in 1882, and pear, quince, peach, chestnut, loquat, and persimmon varieties in 1884. In 1885 he gave up truck farming to devote himself entirely to experimentation, the results of which he sold to local nurseries. Burbank turned to apples and almonds in 1886, to tomatoes in 1887, and plums in 1889. His Van Deman quince won the Wilder Medal in 1891, and his plumcot won the Buffalo Pan American Exposition gold medal in 1901.

During 1893–1901, Burbank published the annual *New Creations* catalog. In 1904 the St. Louis International Exhibition awarded the Burbank rose a gold medal. Never systematic about gathering scientific data, Burbank nevertheless became a famous experimenter, and in 1905 the Carnegie Institution granted him $10,000 a year and an assistant, George H. Shull, to record his work for genetic research. Burbank had little interest in the project, and in 1910 the Carnegie Institution withdrew its support. From 1905 to 1911 he taught a course in plant breeding at Stanford University.

In 1907, Burbank wrote *Training of the Human Plant,* a pamphlet stressing the importance of environment in human development and advocating careful education to rear socially aware and useful children. In 1909 he grew his 136th variety of lily, and in 1911 he produced a thornless raspberry and the Burbank cherry. He then turned to directing the writing of *Luther Burbank: His Methods and Their Practical Application,* the twelve volumes of which were completed in 1915. In 1921 he completed the eight-volume *How Plants Are Trained to Work for Man,* a record of his creations. Among his most famous plants are the Shasta daisy and a spineless cactus that was a valuable cattle food.

Burbank had indefatigable energy and was a tenacious free spirit uninterested in personal profit. A humanist who loved all mankind regardless of station, he was an archetypal **Walt Whitman** whose romanticism was tempered by devotion to practical aims. Burbank was also a controversial figure, seeming to some heretical because of his strong opposition to religious fundamentalism, to others a childlike eccentric, and to still others a wizard whose experiments seemed an impious tampering with nature. His undisciplined character did indeed result in failure to keep records of the thousands of experiments undertaken, thus ending support from the Carnegie Institution.

In terms of science, Burbank's work, as Hugo de Vries affirmed in a special chapter of his 1907 monograph *Plant Breeding,* was entirely unsurpassed and laid the foundation for applied botanical genetics. The mere descriptive record regarding the production of more than one hundred new plant and vegetable varieties reveals Burbank's stature. Among them were the Shasta daisy; plants introduced in North America from Australia, Japan, and South America; breeds of cacti; grains and grasses that vastly improved cattle production; and the production of new varieties of fruits and vegetables of high value to national agriculture, such as corn, plums, peaches, quinces, tomatoes, and berries.

Burbank's methods involved the unique application of Darwinian principles to the American environment. Specimens from other areas of the world were introduced and flourished under new conditions of life. New varieties were produced by crossing two parental forms and recrossing the resultant offspring with a related form so as to grow plants of greatest vigor and yield. Burbank's mastery of his field was evident in his ability to preserve such variations by selecting for preservation those forms best suited to survival and most necessary for permanent improvement of life forms. Hybrid vigor was put to an immediate test by Burbank through his method of grafting variant forms onto a full-grown parent so as to determine in short order the quality of a new and young variety of flower or plum. Burbank thus devoted his life in nature to the personification of the laws of selection and preservation, which evolutionists had identified with controlled and natural organic creation. His account of this endeavor appeared in the posthumous autobiography, written with Wilbur Hall, *The Harvest of the Years* (1927). See W. L. Howard, "Luther Burbank," *Chronica Botanica*, IX (1945), 299–506.

EDWARD LURIE

BURGER, Warren Earl (b. St. Paul, Minn., Sept. 17, 1907; d. Washington, D.C., June 25, 1995), JURIST, attended night school at the University. of Minnesota and in 1931 received his law degree from the St. Paul College of Law where he taught contract law for the next seventeen years. Having passed the bar in 1931, he joined the St. Paul firm of Boyesen, Otis & Faricy, where he practiced until 1953, specializing in corporate, real estate, and probate law. Burger, a Republican, entered the political arena in 1938 when he backed Harold Stassen's successful bid for the Minnesota governorship. In the 1952 Republican national convention he was influential in delivering the Minnesota delegation's votes, pledged to Stassen, to Dwight D. Eisenhower. The next year, following Eisenhower's election, Burger was appointed assistant attorney general in the Justice Department's Civil Division. In 1955, Burger argued the administration's case against John F. Peters, a government employee dismissed for disloyalty. The skill with which he handled this difficult task led to his appointment that year to the U.S. Court of Appeals for the District of Columbia.

As a federal judge Burger aligned himself with the conservative wing of the judiciary. He became an outspoken opponent of what he viewed as the Warren Court's leniency toward criminal defendants. Increasingly, he employed extra-judical means to convey his views on such matters as liberalization of the insanity defense and the Supreme Court's 1966 decision in *Miranda* v. *Arizona* upholding a criminal suspect's rights to remain silent. He also became a public advocate for judicial reform, which he regarded as a related concern: expanded constitutional protections for criminal defendants clogged dockets, contributing to a system that frustrated "decent people."

Owing to lame-duck President Lyndon Johnson's failed attempt to fill the recently vacated seat of Chief Justice **Earl Warren** with a Democrat, when Richard Nixon entered the White House in January 1969, one of his top priorities was the appointment of a strict constructionist to head the court. Burger was his man. On June 23, 1969, he was sworn in as the fifteenth chief justice of the Supreme Court. Burger served for more than seventeen years in this role, retiring on September 26, 1986, to take up President Ronald Reagan's invitation to head the Commission for the Bicentennial of the Constitution.

⸺ ∞ ⸺

Throughout his career as a federal judge Warren Burger made the cause of court reform and modernization his own. On the Supreme Court he introduced new time-saving technologies, such as word processors and photocopiers. Lawyers seeking admission to the Supreme Court bar were permitted to apply by mail rather than undergoing a series of personal interviews. Oral arguments before the Court, previously limited to two hours, were cut in half. The justices themselves ceased their former practice of reading whole opinions from the bench, summarizing them instead. Although he failed to convince Congress to lighten the Supreme Court's workload by creating a temporary national appellate court and increasing the size of the federal judiciary, Burger was successful in introducing streamlining measures into the federal court system. He lobbied for an Institute of Court Management, responsible for training non-judicial court administrators. Established in 1970, the Institute over the next decade helped increase dispositions of cases in federal district and appellate courts by more than 30 percent. Many federal jurisdictions adopted Burger's money-saving proposal to limit juries in civil cases to six individuals, and the Federal Bureau of Prisons accepted his recommendation of dealing with prisoner grievances internally as a means of cutting down habeas corpus petitions in the courts. At the state level many courts went along with

Burger's suggestion for cooperative councils to eliminate parallel state and federal trials of some mass tort cases and agreed to participate in a national center for state courts where they could pool resources.

But if Burger demonstrated great abilities as an advocate for court reform, he was less successful in leading the Court in a conservative direction. Multiple individual opinions in any given case, relatively rare during Earl Warren's tenure, proliferated. Another measure of his inability to mobilize support for his views was that Burger himself dissented more frequently than any chief justice except **Harlan F. Stone**, who presided over the most politically fractured and publicly contentious court in history. Moreover, contrary to the expectations of conservatives who had warmly supported Burger's appointment, during his tenure the Court consolidated rather than cut back the expansion of individual liberties that had taken place during the Warren years. With *Roe v. Wade* (1973) the Burger Court even augmented this expansion by elaborating a right that had previously been little recognized, the right of privacy. Burger himself wrote opinions for the Court majorities in *Miami Herald Publishing Co. v. Tornillo* (1974), upholding First Amendment press freedoms; *Fullilove v. Klutznick* (1980), approving affirmative action programs; and *Swann v. Charlotte-Mecklenburg Board of Education* (1971), permitting school busing in the interests of racial integration. And his opinion for a unanimous Court in *United States v. Nixon* (1974), which led directly to Nixon's resignation under threat of impeachment, lent new meaning to the truism that justices often disappoint the presidents who appoint them. See Bernard Schwartz, *The Ascent of Pragmatism: The Burger Court in Action* (1990).

LISA PADDOCK

BURNHAM, Daniel Hudson (b. Henderson, N.Y., Sept. 4, 1846; d. Heidelberg, Ger., June 1, 1912), ARCHITECT, attended school in Chicago and Waltham, Massachusetts. In 1868 he returned to Chicago to work in a mercantile house, but he soon grew tired of business and entered an architect's office. In 1870 he went to Nevada to prospect unsuccessfully for gold. He returned to Chicago, entering the architectural office of Carter, Drake and Wight in 1872. With draftsman **John W. Root** he formed the firm of Burnham and Root in 1873. It prospered quickly; Burnham designed homes and buildings from Detroit to San Francisco. By effectively using steel skeleton construction in such Chicago structures as the Montauk Building (1881), the Masonic Temple (1890), and the Monadnock Building (1891), he helped inaugurate the skyscraper. In 1890, Burnham was appointed chief of construction for the World's Columbian Exposition, which opened in Chicago in 1893. His efficient coordination of all architecture, building, and artwork for the fair led to his election as president of the American Institute of Architects in 1894.

In 1893, Burnham joined with Charles McKim and others to found the American School of Architecture in Rome (later called the American Academy in Rome). In the decade that followed, D. H. Burnham and Co. designed New York City's first skyscraper, the Flatiron Building (1902), and the Union Station of the Pennsylvania Railroad in Washington (1904). Appointed in 1901 by the U.S. Senate to head a committee to plan the development of the nation's capital, his proposal marked the beginning of the city planning movement in the United States. As the leader of this movement he was consulted by the cities of Cleveland and San Francisco and was asked by Secretary of War William H. Taft to design a plan for Manila in the Philippines in 1904. His "Plan of Chicago," presented in 1909, emphasized "city beautiful" ideas: modern parks, residential sections, and efficient transportation. President Taft appointed him chairman of the National Commission of Fine Arts in 1910, and in this capacity he advised the Lincoln Memorial Commission as to the location of its monument.

Daniel Burnham's concept of what architecture should be was shaped by the manifest need to create convincing images of stability and unity in a country torn apart by civil war. Some of the forces of extreme egalitarianism and romanticism which produced that conflict had been evidenced in the welter of architectural modes jostling during the two decades preceding it, when the original Classical revival images of American revolutionary ideals were superseded by confusing varieties of Gothic, Egyptian, and Italianate revivals. Richardsonian Romanesque, the dominant style of the late 1870s and 1880s, appealed to the postwar mood through its solidity and honesty, and Burnham's early architecture followed that lead. But by the 1890s, overtones of primitivism and medievalism in Richardsonian Romanesque were making it unacceptable, as **Louis H. Sullivan**'s Transportation Building at the 1893 Columbian Exposition showed; his virtuoso display of individual talent had little to do with the Exposition's announced theme, which was to display American growth to greatness over four centuries. By contrast, Burnham and McKim seized the opportunity to revive here the pristine Classical revival image of American ideals and unity, on a much larger scale and with greater archaeological accuracy than ever before. Thus their basic scheme for the Exposition was drawn from Thomas Jefferson's plan for the University of Virginia—a long axis flanked by classical buildings, with a replica of the Pantheon at its head. So exactly did Burnham and McKim gauge the country's need that their "Revival of the Classical Revival" remained the dominant image of American ideals for thirty years, from Washington to Manila. Not until after 1929 did a new kind of American architecture seem called for. See Charles Moore, *D. H. Burnham: Architect, Planner of Cities* (1968).

ALAN GOWANS

BURR, Aaron (b. Newark, N.J., Feb. 6, 1756; d. Port Richmond, N.Y., Sept. 14, 1836), POLITICAL LEADER, graduated from the College of New Jersey (now Princeton) in 1772, studied theology there for a year, and then studied law before joining the Continental army. He participated in **Benedict Arnold**'s expedition to Canada, served on General Washington's staff, and then was transferred to General Putnam's staff, rising to lieutenant colonel (1777).

Burr was admitted to the bar in 1782 and practiced law in New York. In 1789, Governor **George Clinton** appointed him attorney general of New York, and in 1791 he was elected to the U.S. Senate (serving from 1791 to 1797). In 1797 he was elected to the New York State Assembly, where he built a political machine that enabled the Jeffersonian Republicans to gain control of the state legislature in 1800. Burr, however, failed to be reelected to a second term in 1799.

In the presidential election of 1800, Burr ran as Thomas Jefferson's vice presidential candidate. Both men received 73 electoral votes. Since no distinction was then made between presidential and vice presidential candidates, the election was thrown into the House of Representatives. **Alexander Hamilton,** because of his distrust of Burr, persuaded his congressional supporters to throw the balance to Jefferson. Burr therefore became vice president. He ran unsuccessfully for governor of New York in 1804, Hamilton once again campaigning against him. Because Hamilton had attacked Burr's character, Burr challenged him to a duel. They met at Weehawken, New Jersey (July 11, 1804), where Hamilton was mortally wounded. Burr fled southward but returned to Washington to preside in his capacity as vice president over the impeachment proceedings against Supreme Court Justice Samuel Chase.

While vice president, Burr suggested to the British minister in Washington that he would "effect a separation of the western part of the United States" for £110,000. When this offer was rejected, Burr joined General **James Wilkinson,** and in 1806 they organized a force at Blennerhassett Island in the Ohio River. Burr planned either to foment a revolution in Mexico (still a colony of Spain) or to lead the western territories out of the Union (this point has never been clarified). Wilkinson, however, betrayed

Burr, who tried to escape to Spanish Florida. He was captured and tried for treason before the U.S. circuit court in Richmond, Virginia (1807). Presiding Justice **John Marshall** ruled, however, that since it could not be proven that Burr had committed an "overt act" against the United States, he could not be convicted of treason.

Following his trial Burr traveled abroad and did not return to the United States until 1812. He then resumed his law practice in New York.

———∞∞∞———

Aaron Burr's career is a jigsaw whose pieces seem hard to fit together. A member of an austerely Presbyterian family, grandson of the great scholar-preacher **Jonathan Edwards,** Burr was a notorious womanizer, so energetic in amorous intrigue as almost to qualify as the American Casanova. A brave soldier who maintained strict discipline, he was at the same time wayward and insubordinate. Ambitious and guileful, he was also in some ways oddly casual and candid. A well-regarded lawyer, he was apparently unable to apply to himself the shrewd advice he proffered to clients. The ups and downs in his long life were as striking as his own resilience in accepting them. At one stage he was within striking distance of becoming president, but within a few years he was enduring an impoverished and disgraced exile in Paris, living by his wits and nearly starving in the process. Stigmatized as the killer of Alexander Hamilton and widely regarded as a traitor to his country, Burr was yet able to reestablish a substantial law practice in New York. Hardly a model family man, he was nevertheless an adoring and adored father, whose brilliant daughter Theodosia wrote at one of the darkest moments in his life that to her he appeared "so elevated above other men" that "very little superstition would be necessary to make me worship you as a superior being."

We shall never know exactly what went on in his mercurial mind. But it is much too simple to dismiss him as an unscrupulous trickster, an early specimen of the American con man. Perhaps the best way to approach understanding is by comparing Burr with his arch-rival

Hamilton, for the two men had a great deal in common. Small, quick, charming, articulate, restless, sophisticated, both revealed a certain contempt for their more plodding contemporaries. Both evidently had doubts as to the soundness and permanence of their new nation. Both sought a hand in shaping it, through politics and through larger, vaguer dreams of military adventure. While both achieved distinction in the testing profession of the law, neither could quite forget the dramas and dangers of the military life. Neither could remain indifferent to the appeal of a pretty woman. Each had a taste for intrigue, yet neither was a hypocrite. They tended to divide mankind not into the good and the bad but into the clever and the dull, the active and the passive. As a result each earned the devotion of some of his fellows and the distrust of others. Burr's visions were no doubt more inchoate, but he and Hamilton were not alone in nourishing schemes of empire and in being fascinated by the prospects for conquest offered by the crumbling provinces of the old Spanish hegemony. (Andrew Jackson was in some respects a man of similar stamp, as his campaign in Spanish Florida was to show only a few years after Burr's trial.) He never seems to have acted from personal spleen. It is clear from Hamilton's correspondence, however, that at least from 1796 he was obsessively hostile to Burr. Again and again he insisted that Burr was a dangerous villain. Within the code of their own era and their own temperaments, we may feel that Aaron Burr had at last no alternative but to face his spiritual twin, pistol in hand, on the dueling ground in Weehawken. See Milton Lomask, *Aaron Burr* (1983).

MARCUS CUNLIFFE

BUSH, George Herbert Walker (b. Milton, Mass., June 12, 1924), PRESIDENT, graduated from Phillips Academy in 1942 and, after serving as a naval aviator in the South Pacific, graduated from Yale University in 1948 and became an entrepreneur in the West Texas oil patch. Moving to Houston in 1959 as head of the Zapata Offshore Company, he became active in local

Harris County Republican politics. He was elected to Congress in 1966 and reelected in 1968, but lost his seat to Democratic opponent Lloyd Bentsen in 1970.

Bush served in a succession of appointive positions, first under President Richard Nixon as representative to the United Nations (1971–73) and then as chairman of the Republican National Committee (1973–74). President Gerald Ford appointed him to head the U.S. liason office in Beijing, China (1974–75), and he directed the Central Intelligence Agency from 1975 until the inauguration of President Jimmy Carter in January 1976.

After failing to win the 1980 Republican presidential primaries, Bush was chosen by Ronald Reagan as the party's vice presidential candidate. The Reagan-Bush ticket then defeated the opposing Democratic slate of President Jimmy Carter and Vice President Walter Mondale by 489 to 49 electoral votes. As vice president Bush was reelected along with President Reagan in 1984, turning back their Democratic challengers, Mondale and **Geraldine Ferraro,** by 525 electoral votes to 13. When he became the Republican presidential candidate in 1988, he chose Senator J. Danforth Quayle as his vice presidential running mate. They defeated Democrat Michael Dukakis and his running mate, Senator Lloyd Bentsen, 426 electoral votes to 111.

George Bush never did succeed in escaping the patrician New England Yankee stereotype, which was associated with Eisenhower Republicanism of the 1950s and the party's "Eastern Establishment." His affability and salesmanship enabled him to build a political career with the support of loyal friends drawn from each stage of his life. As a transplanted New Englander he had to accommodate to the Texas social and political environment. His inherent fiscal conservatism also had to extend to social views to bring him into line with key constituents within his adopted state. Nevertheless, he increasingly confronted the reality of the party's rightward drift even while serving in appointive offices during the 1970s and as vice president under Reagan.

His own presidency never fully escaped the Reagan shadow, with strong ideological conservatives of the so-called New Right continuously skeptical about his fidelity to their principles. He also lacked his predecessor's charismatic leadership ability, which, combined with the circumstances of his own background, handicapped him with working-class Democratic voters.

Bush, who had accommodated himself with loyalty during his vice presidency, attempted to continue in that mold, especially by upholding high levels of military spending, opposition to abortion, the advocacy of a balanced budget amendment to the Constitution, economic growth over environmental concerns, and appeals to nationalism as well as to "family values."

He was passive at home and active abroad, winning considerable approval for handling the crises caused by the dissolution of the Soviet Union (1989-91), which concluded the cold war. Temporarily, at least, his popularity soared as a result of his leadership of the Persian Gulf crisis (1990-91). The massive deployment of military forces to Saudi Arabia in the fall of 1990, Operation Desert Shield, to keep Middle Eastern oil from Iraqi control, was followed in January by the opening of Operation Desert Storm to force Sadam Hussein out of Kuwait. After a brief ground war with minimal opposition, the United States called off further fighting. The Iraq government was still in place, but Kuwait had been liberated, accomplishing the immediate objective but leaving Bush open to criticism that he had not followed through on his vows to depose the tyrant of Baghdad.

His more controversial actions were in working to maintain normal relations with the People's Republic of China even after the brutal Tiananmen Square massacre of June 1989 and, six months later, on December 20, the launching of Operation Just Cause, the invasion of Panama to oust strongman General Manuel Antonin Noriega.

It was in his approach to domestic policies that

Bush, reputedly a moderate, was under most pressure to preserve the Reagan legacy. Although he continued to deemphasize federal activism and to stress the maintenance of a conservative free market economy, he came under increasing criticism from his party's right wing. They were especially outraged when he retreated from his emphatic 1988 campaign vow that there would be "no new taxes" by agreeing to a Democratic congressional compromise in 1990. He also accepted a civil rights bill in 1991 similar to one he had vetoed earlier. Consequently, he was forced to admit that his administration's regulatory spending exceeded President Carter's. His concessions included compromising the substance of the Clean Air Act that he had supported in 1990. By the summer of 1991 the start of a prolonged downturn in the economy began to erode his newfound popularity. That fall, pressures from the political right became especially visible with the entry into the Republican presidential primaries of conservative commentator Patrick J. Buchanan and the depiction of Bush as a betrayer of their cause.

Bush withstood the right wing, but his renomination came from a convention that was heavily flavored by Buchananite appeals and recognition of the political power of the religious right. Facing additional challenges from the independent candidacy of multibillionaire **H. Ross Perot** of Texas, who stressed the $4 trillion federal deficit as a legacy of the Reagan-Bush years as well as from the Democrats, the Bush-Quayle ticket received only 168 electoral votes to 370 for **Bill Clinton** and vice presidential candidate Al Gore, Jr., with Perot taking 19 percent of the popular vote. See Michael Duffy and Dan Goodgame, *Marching in Place: The Status Quo Presidency of George Bush* (1992).

HERBERT S. PARMET

BUSH, Vannevar (b. Everett, Mass., Mar. 11, 1890; d. Belmost, Mass., June 28, 1974), SCIENTIST, earned his BS and MS degrees from Tufts College in 1913 and taught mathematics there while earning engineering degrees at both Harvard and M.I.T. in 1916. He worked in the test department of the General Electric Co. in 1913, entered the inspection department of the U.S. Navy in 1914, and did research on submarine detection in 1917–18. He joined the faculty of M.I.T. in 1919 and served as vice president and dean of the school of engineering from 1932 to 1938. He headed the Carnegie Institution in Washington, D.C. (1939-55) and was chairman of the National Advisory Committee for Aeronautics (1939-41).

In World War II, Bush held several important administrative posts, including the directorship of the National Defense Research Committee (1940–41) and the Office of Scientific Research and Development (1941–46), the major civilian organization to conduct scientific research on problems related to the war. He coordinated the American scientists' research on many important military developments, including the atomic bomb. In 1945 he prepared a report for President Franklin Roosevelt entitled *Science, the Endless Frontier,* outlining his vision of a peacetime role for scientific research. He remained a scientific administrator and adviser during the postwar era, serving on several presidential commissions on scientific and military affairs, and frequently testifying before congressional committees.

Among Bush's numerous inventions are the differential analyzer for solving complex differential equations with as many as eighteen unknowns, and the network analyzer, designed to test the capacity of power systems to perform under stress. He produced new gaseous conduction devices, modified vacuum tubes, and developed changes in the design of four-engine bombers. He also wrote numerous articles and two books on technical subjects, two collections of essays, *Endless Horizons* (1946) and *Science Is Not Enough* (1967), and a widely read book, *Modern Arms and Free Men* (1949), which stressed his view of the role of science in protecting and strengthening democratic institutions. His autobiography is entitled *Pieces of the Action* (1970).

Although Vannevar Bush made notable contributions to industrial technology and served as an administrative officer of both educational and philanthropic organizations, his greatest mark was made as organizer of and spokesman for the American scientific community. His many advisory and administrative posts gave him close contact with important political leaders in Washington. When, by the spring of 1940, his work as chairman of NACA convinced him that the nation needed a crash program in weapons research, he was in a central position to initiate such an effort.

First in the NDRC and later in the OSRD, Bush was enormously successful in bringing together military, political, and scientific leaders, and focusing their efforts on the development of new weapons and countermeasures. Through the innovative use of grants and contracts his organization gave bold leadership to the nation's wartime scientific effort. In a direct extension of this effort, Bush became a major architect of the postwar relationship between science and government. A spokesman for the elite (rather than democratic) tradition of American science, he sought to insulate science from political responsibility even as he sought to gain federal subsidy for research.

A craggy, plainspoken New Englander, Bush was no reformer. He worked easily with the military, political, industrial, and educational elite of the nation and frequently found himself at odds with scientists less well placed or politically conservative than he. With the unifying effect of the wartime emergency removed after 1945, Bush spoke increasingly for only a segment of American science. He continued, however, to be honored for his three great achievements: his organization of science in wartime, his advocacy of continued federal subsidy after the war, and his championship of the value and importance of basic scientific research. See James Phinney Baxter III, *Scientists Against Time* (1946).

CARROLL PURCELL

BUTLER, Benjamin Franklin (b. Deerfield, N.H., Nov. 5, 1818; d. Washington, D.C., Jan. 11, 1893), POLITICAL and MILITARY LEADER, graduated from Waterville (now Colby) College in 1838. While teaching school in Lowell, Massachusetts, he studied law and after admission to the bar in 1840 established a lucrative practice that he maintained throughout his life, greatly adding to his fortune by shrewd investments in the booming New England cotton textile industry. Butler was elected as a Democrat to a term in the Massachusetts Assembly in 1853 and to the state senate in 1858. A member of the conservative wing of the Democratic Party, Butler supported **John C. Breckinridge** over **Stephen A. Douglas** for the 1860 presidential nomination. However, after secession he was a firm backer of the Union. Entering military service early because of his close association with the Massachusetts militia, Butler received considerable publicity when he relieved Confederate pressure on the capital and then occupied Baltimore.

Butler was in charge of the land forces that occupied New Orleans in May 1862, and in this position he issued an order establishing punishment for New Orleans women who insulted Union soldiers; this earned him the name of "Beast." The corruption that pervaded Butler's administration added to his unsavory reputation. He was relieved from his post in December 1862 and given command of field forces in eastern Virginia and North Carolina.

Butler served in Congress from 1867 to 1875. As a leader of the Radical Republicans, he was one of the House managers during the impeachment proceedings against President Andrew Johnson. Defeated during the Democratic landslide of 1874, Butler was reelected to Congress in 1878 as a Democrat although avowing support for the Greenback cause. In 1878 and 1879 he ran unsuccessfully for governor of Massachusetts, first as an independent with Democratic and Greenback support, and then as a Democrat. He was elected on the Democratic ticket in 1882. His administration accomplished little, largely because the legislature was solidly Republican and violently anti-Butler. Harvard, for the first time in its 250-year history, refused to give an honorary degree to a governor of Massachusetts while Butler held that position. His last political activity was as candidate for president on the Greenback ticket in 1884; he received only 175,370 votes.

———— ❧ ————

Butler was one of the most controversial 19th-century American politicians. Demagogue, speculator, military bungler, and sharp legal practitioner—he was all of these; yet he was also a fearless advocate of justice for the downtrodden, a resourceful military administrator, and an astonishing innovator. He was passionately hated and equally strongly admired, and if the South called him "Beast," his constituents in Massachusetts were fascinated by him. Few ever managed to disregard him.

Detesting the Massachusetts Brahmins, Butler entered politics as a Democrat. Early in his career he perfected the tactics for which he was to become famous, the sensational airing of important grievances. His agitation in favor of the ten-hour workday was followed by a reduction of the working hours of the Lowell mill hands, but Democratic politics in Massachusetts was not a profitable enterprise. The slavery issue irrevocably alienated an important group. Many of the foes of slavery were Brahmins, and Butler decided to stay loyal to the national administration. Like many of the workers whom he championed, he was blind to the horror of the "peculiar institution." But he retained access to federal patronage.

The Civil War brought about a complete change in Butler's position. Left stranded by the collapse of the pro-southern wing of his party, he fell back on his military experience in the Massachusetts militia. As brigadier general of volunteers he rallied the Breckinridge Democrats to the flag and came to the relief of the beleaguered capital. Lincoln knew how to appreciate this contribution to national unity.

Butler's wartime exploits were among the most controversial of his career. Inept as a field commander, he proved himself a vigorous administrator, and the more the South hated him,

the more the North admired him. If tales of corruption followed him everywhere, in New Orleans he nevertheless suppressed disorder, maintained discipline in the midst of a trying situation, and prevented an outbreak of yellow fever. The celebrated "woman order," in which he threatened to treat any refractory female as "a woman of the town plying her avocation," was a skillful device to keep a turbulent populace under control. His failure in 1864 as commander of the Army of the James revealed his weakness as a strategist.

During the Civil War, Butler was converted to a strong antislavery position, and his contributions to the cause of the blacks were considerable. His characterization of runaways employed by the enemy as "contraband of war" laid the foundations for the first Confiscation Act. His reactivation of the Confederate Corps d'Afrique as a Union regiment set a precedent for other black units, and afterward he never abandoned the interests of the freedmen.

As a leading advocate of radical Reconstruction, Butler played an important role in the conflict between president and Congress. His effectiveness was marred by the frequency with which he engaged in personal altercations, and his conduct as one of the principal managers of the impeachment trial of Andrew Johnson was dubious. Nevertheless, he deserves recognition as a persistent critic of southern terrorism and as one of the chief authors of the Civil Rights Act of 1875.

Butler's advocacy of inflation was less impressive; nor was his reputation enhanced by his close collaboration with President Ulysses S. Grant. He became a veritable symbol of Grantism, the spoils policies of the 1870s. "This 'civil service reform' I characterize as a trick," he said. "It is always popular with the outs and never with the ins, except with those who have a strong expectation of soon going out." Constantly harassing the "respectable" wing of the Republican Party, he kept Massachusetts politics in turmoil. But even when he returned to the Democratic Party and became governor in 1883, he maintained his solicitude for immigrants and blacks. In 1884 he seriously marred his record by running for the presidency as a People's Party candidate with secret Republican subsidies. Yet in spite of his faults his record was a positive one. By rallying the Democrats in 1861, by working for the elevation of the blacks, and by championing the rights of immigrants and labor he set a pattern for progress and proved himself far ahead of his time. See H. L. Trefousse, *Ben Butler* (1957).

HANS L. TREFOUSSE

BUTLER, Nicholas Murray (b. Elizabeth, N.J., Apr. 2, 1862; d. New York, N.Y., Dec. 7, 1947), EDUCATOR, received his AB (1882) and PhD (1884) from Columbia University. After study in Berlin and Paris he joined the Columbia faculty in 1885. Within five years he was a full professor and dean of the faculty of philosophy, and in 1901, when **Seth Low** was elected mayor of New York, he succeeded Low as president of the university, a position he occupied for the next forty-four years.

Butler took over the university in the midst of a building program on the new Morningside Heights campus, a move he had strongly influenced. While carrying through an aggressive program of land acquisition and construction, coupled with a successful fund-raising program, Butler improved the faculty by attracting noted scholars from other universities. By the end of his career Columbia had become one of the leading educational institutions in the country.

Butler was also deeply involved in Republican politics. While he never realized his ambition to hold national office—his name was substituted as William Howard Taft's running mate after James S. Sherman, the nominee, died during the campaign of 1912—he exerted some influence in the selection of **Charles Evans Hughes** as Republican presidential candidate in 1916. His own bid for the Republican presidential nomination in 1920 made little progress. In 1928, after several years of denouncing prohibition as a failure, he spoke out against Herbert Hoover's unwillingness to support repeal and for a time considered supporting the Democratic nominee **Alfred E. Smith** who was his close friend.

International relations was Butler's other field of interest. In 1907, 1909, and 1910–12 he acted as chairman of the arbitration conferences that **Andrew Carnegie** sponsored at Lake Mohonk, New York, believing that a way had to be found short of war to settle disputes between nations. Nevertheless, he ardently supported America's entrance into World War I. A member of the Carnegie Endowment for International Peace, Butler succeeded **Elihu Root** as its president (1925–45) and traveled to Rome in 1927 to obtain the pope's endorsement of the Kellogg-Briand Pact. Throughout the 1930s Butler warned that Hitler was a threat to world peace, and beginning in 1940 he favored American intervention on the side of the Allies in World War II. Columbia, he said in a speech more than a year before Pearl Harbor, had entered the war "between beasts and human beings." He invited any faculty member who did not approve of this position to resign; however, he assured professors that their disapproval would not lead to dismissal.

In 1904, Butler almost precipitated a student rebellion at Columbia when he abolished football, a decision that stood for ten years. Although generally a supporter of academic freedom, in two controversial cases Butler ruled that this freedom did not extend to "moral misconduct." In one case he forced an English professor who had been named corespondent in a divorce suit to resign; in the other he forced a pacifist off the faculty.

———— ✤ ————

Characteristically, the two men Nicholas Murray Butler believed to have the greatest minds in American history—**Alexander Hamilton** and Elihu Root—were prototypes of himself. Like Hamilton he rose to power in his adopted New York through administrative capacity and the patronage of the city's financial elite; like Root he was never in as much danger of being drafted to run for elective office as he imagined. If Republican Party leaders correctly doubted his mass appeal, Columbia undergraduates understandably questioned the humanity of "Nicholas the Miraculous." His relations with the Columbia faculty were more ambivalent. Surprisingly tolerant of the varied intellectual labors of his younger scholars, he demonstrated this tolerance in ways that led many to suspect it was grounded in indifference. Yet his reputation as an autocrat must be qualified by the fact that his commitment to *Lehrfreiheit,* the right of the faculty to set academic policy, was genuine. Unlike **Abbott L. Lowell** at Harvard, he made no effort to restrain the research-oriented wing of the faculty in its subordination of the interests of the college to those of the graduate faculties. Not only did he generally let the faculty have its way but his success as a fund-raiser "downtown" provided the money to pay for it. That he was a snob is harder to gainsay. No one who writes in his autobiography "It has been my happy fortune to meet, to talk with, and often to know in warm friendship almost every man of light and learning who has lived in the world during the past half-century" can be charged with false modesty. Deaf and then blind, Butler spent his last years going through the motions until the Columbia trustees mustered the courage to tell him he must resign. But even at the very end he conducted himself in a manner worthy of a man who had once faulted a European monarch because he "was not very kingy." See Nicholas Murray Butler, *Across the Busy Years* (2 vols., 1939–40).

ROBERT A. McCAUGHEY

BYRD, Richard Evelyn (b. Winchester, Va., Oct. 25, 1888; d. Boston, Mass., Mar. 11, 1957), NAVAL OFFICER, EXPLORER, attended Virginia Military Institute (1904–7) and the University of Virginia (1907–8), and graduated from the U.S. Naval Academy in 1912. Four years later he retired from active duty because of a leg injury. Nevertheless, he was permitted to enter the navy's aviation service, and after training in Pensacola, Florida (1917), he commanded the U.S. Naval Air Station at Halifax, Nova Scotia (1918). The following year he was placed in charge of equipping the navy's first transatlantic

flight, and in 1921 he crossed the Atlantic in a dirigible.

In 1925, Byrd commanded the aviation unit of the MacMillan Polar Expedition in Greenland. The following year he commanded the Byrd Arctic Expedition. Operating from Spitzbergen, he made the first flight over the North Pole (Floyd Bennett, copilot) and was awarded the Congressional Medal of Honor. In June 1927 he flew a payload-carrying plane from the United States to France, demonstrating the feasibility of commercial transatlantic aviation.

In 1928, Byrd made his first expedition to the Antarctic. Establishing a base that he named Little America (Dec. 1928), he and three companions flew over the South Pole (Nov. 1929). Returning to the United States in 1930, he was promoted to rear admiral. His book *Little America* (1930) is an account of that expedition.

During 1933–35, Byrd led his second expedition to the Antarctic, again establishing a base at Little America. For five months during the winter of 1934 he lived alone at a weather station 123 miles south of this base. His book *Alone* (1938) is an account of this experience. During this expedition Byrd discovered and named the Edsel Ford Range, the Rockefeller Plateau, and the Marie Byrd Land.

Byrd undertook his third polar expedition as head of a U.S. Antarctic Service team (1939–41). In a series of four flights he discovered five islands, a peninsula, and some mountain ranges. When World War II broke out, Byrd served under Admirals **Ernest J. King** and **Chester W. Nimitz.**

Byrd again traveled to the Antarctic as head of the U.S. Navy's Operation Highjump (1946–47) and made several aerial maps of the continent's coastline. In 1955 he was in charge of Operation Deepfreeze, which was undertaken in conjunction with the International Geophysical Year. His writings include *Skyward* (1928), *Discovery* (1935), and *Exploring with Byrd* (1937).

⸻

Byrd was the most famous American explorer of his generation, but his services to naval aviation as an inventor and as congressional liaison officer during 1919–23 when the naval air arm was in jeopardy were sufficient in themselves to assure him a place in naval annals. However, he found the role of explorer both satisfying and suited to his talents and adventurous spirit. He captured the imagination of the American public through his lecture tours and his radioed reports from Little America. After 1945 he lent his prestige to naval Antarctic projects over which others had actual command.

Byrd's own expeditions were characterized by meticulous organization and advanced scientific programs. He exhibited great concern for his men's safety and welfare, both in his planning and in personal acts of courage. In many respects intensely egalitarian, he followed naval tradition in refraining from fraternization with his men even in the close quarters characteristic of polar exploration.

Better than any other explorer, Byrd represented the transition from the privately financed explorer to the government expedition, and from the dogsled to the airplane and tractor. His most spectacular accomplishment was his first flight to the South Pole, his most enduring his demonstration that a large scientific staff could winter in Antarctica and perform useful work. More than any other individual he was responsible for opening Antarctica to the world of science. See Edwin P. Hoyt, *The Last Explorer: The Adventures of Admiral Byrd* (1968).

JOHN E. CASWELL

BYRD, William (b. near falls of James River, Va., Mar. 28, 1674; d. near falls of James River, Va., Aug. 26, 1744), PLANTER, WRITER, was educated in England where he studied law in the Middle Temple in London and was admitted to the bar in 1692. Returning to Virginia that same year, Byrd was elected to the House of Burgesses. He went back to England in 1697 to defend Sir **Edmund Andros** against charges of hostility to the Anglican Church and as an agent for the colony, but upon his father's death in 1704 he returned to Virginia to manage the family estate. In 1709 he was appointed to the Council of State,

the supreme court of Virginia, and served on it for the rest of his life. During the clash between the Council and Governor **Alexander Spotswood,** Byrd went to England in 1715 to present the colonists' case. Spotswood was removed for usurping the colonists' judicial power, and Byrd remained in London as agent for Virginia.

Byrd returned permanently to Virginia in 1726. He built a large mansion, accumulated the largest private library in the colonies, and enlarged his estate. In 1728 he served as a commissioner to establish the boundary between Virginia and North Carolina, and wrote an account of this adventure, "History of the Dividing Line." This essay, "Journey to the Land of Eden," "A Progress to the Mines," and others were published posthumously in *The Westover Manuscripts* (1841). In 1743–44, Byrd served as president of the Council of State. His intimate diary, discovered and published after his death, provides a revealing picture of southern plantation life.

⸺∞⸺

Although called by his most recent biographer, Pierre Marambaud, "the first Southern writer of real value," Byrd's importance lies in the fact that in an otherwise poorly documented time and place (the South during the first half of the 18th century) his diaries and writings provide an insight into a stratified colonial society in slow transition toward home rule and eventual independence. By virtue of long residence in England and association with the ruling classes there (he spent half his life in England) and as a member of the Council of State of the colony of Virginia, Byrd was sympathetic to the Crown's interest in the colony. Nevertheless, as a proud Virginia landholder (at his death he owned 179,000 acres of land) he was also solicitous of his own and his fellow planters' economic interests. Increasingly during the 18th century the interests of the colonial landed elite conflicted with the maintenance of royal authority. Byrd was effective as the Assembly's agent in England in disputing that authority as expressed in the actions of Lieutenant Governor Spotswood. However, when his persistent opposition to Spotswood threatened to cost him his seat on the Council, he cautiously trimmed his sails in order to maintain his position within the hierarchy. Careful plantation manager, judicious councillor, serious reader, fastidious writer, amateur scientist, and amorous flirt, Byrd was not the stuff of political heroes; perhaps the age—which he so admirably reflected—did not allow it. See Pierre Marambaud, *William Byrd of Westover, 1674–1744* (1971). The best collection of Byrd's writings is Louis B. Wright, ed., *The Prose Works of William Byrd of Westover: Narratives of a Colonial Virginian* (1966).

WILCOMB E. WASHBURN

BYRNES, James Francis (b. Charleston, S.C., May 2, 1879; d. Columbia, S.C., Apr. 9, 1972), POLITICAL LEADER, JURIST, left school early but studied law in his spare time and was admitted to the South Carolina bar in 1903. He then moved to Aiken, South Carolina, where he bought and edited a newspaper, the *Journal and Review*. A Democrat, he was elected solicitor, or district attorney, of the Second Judicial Circuit, South Carolina, in 1908 and two years later to the House of Representatives, serving until 1925. He was defeated for the Senate in 1924, but after practicing law in Spartanburg, South Carolina, he was elected to the Senate in 1930. After the election of Franklin Roosevelt he supported much early New Deal legislation, but after 1936 he joined the Democratic opposition to the New Deal. Byrnes remained personally loyal to Roosevelt, however, and vigorously pushed for the repeal of the Neutrality Laws and for passage of the Lend-Lease Act. In 1941, Roosevelt appointed Byrnes associate justice of the Supreme Court, but the following year persuaded him to become director of the new Office of Economic Stabilization, which was designed to curb wartime inflation. He became director of the Office of War Mobilization, a body to supervise production of war and civilian goods, in 1943.

Byrnes accompanied Roosevelt to the Yalta Conference in 1945, and after Roosevelt's death he was appointed secretary of state by President Harry Truman. Byrnes attended the Potsdam Conference and participated in the Big Three foreign ministers' councils in the fall of 1945. He also attended the United Nations Security Council and General Assembly meetings of 1946–47 and the Paris Peace Conference, which made formal peace treaties with the defeated Axis powers. Byrnes's famous "Stuttgart" speech (1947) urged the formation of an autonomous democratic Germany. Resigning as secretary in 1947, Byrnes returned to law practice in Washington. He was governor of South Carolina from 1951 to 1955. He criticized Truman's "welfare state," supported Dwight Eisenhower for president in 1952, and opposed the integration of public schools. Byrnes retired in 1955 and wrote his autobiography, *All in One Lifetime* (1958).

The only American to serve in prominent positions in the legislative, judicial, and executive branches of the federal government in the twentieth century, James F. Byrnes played a significant role in the development of the New Deal, the winning of World War II, and in the period of the cold war. He was an innately optimistic man, and his greatest talent was his ability to find common ground between men with conflicting ideas and to achieve viable compromises. In the 1930s, Byrnes bridged the gap between Franklin Roosevelt and the powerful southern committee chairmen in the Senate and thus helped secure passage of many key New Deal measures despite his own ideological reservations. During World War II he resigned from the Supreme Court after a brief tenure to become FDR's economic troubleshooter, refereeing disputes between government agencies, setting priorities for scarce commodities, and keeping peace between management and labor. Roosevelt described him as "assistant president on the home front," and it was an accurate label.

Byrnes's most controversial and most important service came as secretary of state in the formative years of the cold war. New Left revisionists have damned him for getting tough with Russia, particularly for recommending dropping the atomic bomb on Japan to frighten the Soviets. On the other hand, President Truman criticized him in his memoirs for "babying" the Russians at the Moscow Foreign Ministers Conference in December 1945. Neither view does justice to Byrnes. Despite his seemingly ideal qualities as a conciliator, he failed because his diplomacy embodied the prevailing popular belief in American beneficence in world affairs. Unable to understand the fears of the Soviets, Byrnes sought a postwar settlement that would deprive Russia of her control over Eastern Europe, an area vital to her security, and would in effect perpetuate the American atomic monopoly by imposing international control over the new weapon in gradual stages while forbidding Russia to build her own bomb. The result was two years of futile negotiations that served only to delay the cold war until 1947. Yet despite his failure, Byrnes made a valiant effort to avoid hostilities with the Soviets and helped restrain President Truman and his more belligerent advisers. See James F. Byrnes, *All in One Lifetime* (1958).

ROBERT A. DIVINE

CAGE, John Milton, Jr. (b. Los Angeles, Calif., Sept. 5, 1912; d. New York, N.Y., Aug. 12, 1992), COMPOSER, attended Pomona College in Claremont, California (1928–30), but left after his sophomore year to travel and study in Europe. After returning to and living in California for two years, he moved to New York to study with composers Adolph Weiss and Henry Cowell and then went back to Los Angeles to study with **Arnold Schoenberg**. From 1936 to 1941 he was active in California and the Northwest as an organizer and composer of percussion concerts. In 1938 he invented the prepared piano in which unusual sounds were generated by the application of various objects, such as nuts and bolts, to the piano strings; his works for this new instrument began with *Bacchanale* (1938) and culminated in the *Sonatas and Interludes* (1946–48). He moved to New York in 1942 and made his debut there in February 1943 with a percussion concert that included *First Construction in Metal* (1939) and *Imaginary Landscape No. 3* (1942).

In 1943, Cage began a long association with the dancer Merce Cunningham and started studying Eastern philosophy and Zen at Columbia University under Gita Sarabhai and Daisetz Suzuki. Partly as a consequence he became interested in the application of chance procedures to composition, notably in the *Music of Changes* (1950–52) and *Williams Mix* (1952), and also began writing music independent of choreography for the Cunningham company. He was associated with Black Mountain College in the summers of 1948 and 1952 and while there worked with David Tudor, **Robert Rauschenberg**, and others to apply his aesthetic of chance procedures to theatrical as well as musical events. From these experiments followed pieces such as *Water Music* (1952), *4' 33"* (1954), and a series of *Variations* (1958–66) that require the performer to choose most of the materials for a given performance.

In 1949, Cage received a National Institute of Arts and Letters award and a Guggenheim fellowship. After teaching at the New School for Social Research from 1955 to 1960, Cage was appointed a fellow of the Center for Advanced Studies at Wesleyan University in Middletown, Connecticut (1960–61). While there he complied his first volume of essays, *Silence* (1961), and began work on a commission for full orchestra, *Atlas Eclipticalis*, performed in 1964 by the New York Philharmonic. He became interested in the writings of **Buckminster Fuller,** Marshall

McLuhan, and Norman O. Brown, and began to investigate problems of quantity and use in compositions such as *HPSCHD* (1968) and *Song Books* (1970). Partly as a result of this broadened activity Cage's work has had significant impact on the arts and humanities outside the field of music. In the 1960s Cage toured the United States and abroad, giving lectures, concerts with David Tudor, and performances with the Cunningham company. In 1966–67 he was composer in residence at the University of Cincinnati; the following two years, an associate of the Center for Advanced Studies at the University of Illinois at Urbana; in 1969, an artist in residence at the University of California at Davis; and in 1970, again a fellow at Wesleyan's Center for Advanced Studies. In March 1974 his work *Empty Words* was performed in New York City, composed of "nonsyntactical mixed phrases, words, syllables and letters obtained by subjecting Thoreau's *Journal* to a series of I Ching chance operations." Cage's later works include *Roaratorio* (1979), an electronic composition containing thousands of sounds and noises referred to in James Joyce's novel *Finnegan's Wake*, many of them recorded at spots mentioned in the book, and five *Europera* pieces, composed between 1987 and 1991. A recipient of numerous awards, Cage was elected to the National Institute of Arts and Letters (1968) and to the American Academy of Arts and Sciences (1978). He also was awarded the French government's highest honor for distinguished contribution to cultural life, Commandeur de L'Ordre des Arts et des Lettres (1982). In addition to *Silence,* other publications include *A Year from Monday* (1967), *Notations* (1969), *M* (1973), *Empty Words* (1979), and *I–IV,* the Charles Eliot Norton lectures he delivered at Harvard University in 1988–89.

※

The crux of John Cage's philosophy was the assertion that opposites must be seen as nonopposites. Throughout his life he argued this position with elegance and humor and from it mounted a vigorous attack on European artistic intentions, distinctions, and value judgments. In the first phase of his career (1938–50), for example, Cage rejected both harmonic and atonal compositional systems because of the distinction they made between musical sounds and noise. He became the champion of noise, writing for percussion instruments alone, incorporating into his ensembles unconventional instruments such as radios, buzzers, and flowerpots, even altering the piano to make it an instrument of noise rather than pitch.

In the early 1950s, under the influence of Zen Buddhism and other Eastern philosophies, Cage rejected a second fundamental distinction, between intended and unintended sounds. In *4' 33"*—possibly his most notorious composition—the performer makes no sounds at all; the music is entirely the result of audience noise, passing cars, and other ambient events. Cage's purpose was to open people's ears to the sounds about them, to awaken them to the life they live, and to make art coextensive with that life. In so doing he rejected yet another category: since the composer has no greater control over events than his audience, the two become functionally the same. In this music all become simply listeners; no one is privileged, no one is talented; hearing is an activity in which all participate as equals.

The position is radically and anarchically egalitarian, and, in fact, since 1960, Cage turned increasingly to its social and political consequences, especially as interpreted by global populists such as Marshall McLuhan and Buckminster Fuller. He evolved a vision of political and artistic anarchic democracy, technologically possible for the first time in history, based on abundance and the consequent rejection of distinctions, and with this vision he joined a long line of American thinkers and musicians that wound backward through the experimentalists of the early 1900s (Henry Cowell, Lou Harrison, Carl Ruggles), past **Charles Ives** and his transcendentalist ancestors, and on to such lesser-known figures as Anthony Philip Heinrich, Benjamin Franklin White, and **William Billings.** Cage's immense stature in 20th-century music—he was with Arnold Schoenberg among the most influential composers of recent times—was both a vindication and a necessary denial of this tradition. See Richard Kostelanitz, *John Cage* (1970).

WILLIAM BROOKS

CALDER, Alexander (b. Lawnton, Pa., July 22, 1898; d. New York, N.Y., Nov. 11, 1976), SCULPTOR, entered the Stevens Institute of Technology in 1915 and was graduated with a master's degree in engineering in 1919. After working for several years as an engineer, seaman, and lumberjack, he went to New York in 1923 to study at the Art Students League and to work as an illustrator for the *National Police Gazette.* In 1926 he began exhibiting his paintings at the Artists' Gallery in New York and published his first book, *Animal Sketching.*

Fascinated by the balance maintained in the course of performance by members of the Ringling Brothers and Barnum and Bailey Circus, which he covered for the *Gazette* in 1925, Calder began to try to embody this blend of balance and motion in his art. He traveled to Paris in 1926, where he organized a miniature circus, consisting of animated three-dimensional toys made of wire, wood, and cork, which attracted wide attention. He also constructed *Fishbowl with Crank* (1929) in which the turning of a small hand crank caused wire fish to "swim."

Inspired by the colorful geometric forms created by Piet Mondrian, Calder turned to abstraction in 1930. In 1932 he became the first to exhibit what Marcel Duchamp labeled "mobiles," abstract sculptures, often consisting of metal discs or globes suspended from wires, which were set in motion either by pulleys or small motors. Soon he began constructing delicately balanced mobiles that were moved by random air currents. As he gained experience and technical facility in this medium, Calder achieved an international reputation. He adapted the mobile to a wide range of environments and functions. During the 1930s he designed mobiles to be used as scenery for performances of **Martha Graham**'s dance troupe. He also created water mobiles for the New York World's Fair (1939–40) and for the General Motors Technological Center in Detroit

(*Water Ballet,* 1954), and a forty-five-foot mobile for what is now New York's Kennedy International Airport (1957).

Though best known for his work with mobiles, Calder produced many other sculptures and much nonsculptural art. In World War II he responded to the scarcity of metal by creating a "constellation," a type of stabile fashioned of pieces of wood fastened to metal rods. In the 1960s and 70s he demonstrated a preference for spacious "see-through" sculptures composed of thin metal sheets, such as his huge *Teodelapio* that stands in a square in Spoleto, Italy; large trucks can pass through its widely spread "legs." He also combined elements of motion and repose in several hybrid "mobile-stabiles," such as the large outdoor *Spiral* (1958) that adorns UNESCO's headquarters in Paris. In 1974, though in poor health, he constructred an enormous mechanized mural for the new Sears Tower in Chicago, a work that seemed to sum up his life's work as it revolved, swung, and turned as if on a giant roasting spit. The comprehensive retrospective exhibition of his works at New York's Guggenheim Museum in 1964–65 also focused attention on his gouaches and on his illustrations for such books as *Aesop's Fables* (1931) and *Selected Fables of La Fontaine* (1948). He published *Calder: An Autobiography with Pictures* in 1966.

Although not the inventor of kinetic object-sculpture—Marcel Duchamp's *The Bicycle Wheel* (1913) was the first work of this type—Alexander Calder is known primarily as the creator of the "mobile." He has also produced other types of art—"stabiles," "mobile-stabiles," wire sculptures, mechanized toys, paintings, drawings, book illustrations, and jewelry—but it remains the mobile that has captured the affection of millions. Early French recognition, by election to membership in the *Abstraction-Création* group in Paris in the 1930s, anticipated recognition in New York and elsewhere. Today he has an international fame because of his mobiles and because of his talent for parody and humor, which permeates all his work.

Calder's biographers have tended to lay stress

on his early training in mechanical engineering, perhaps because it made him seem more authentically American. The artist has consistently discounted this aspect of his experience and has preferred to stress the aesthetic side: his background as the son and grandson of sculptors and his three years at the Art Students League under the painter **John Sloan.** Asked by the critic Katherine Kuh which had influenced him more, nature or modern machinery, he replied with the following Newtonian statement: "Nature. I haven't really touched machinery except for a few elementary mechanisms like levers and balances. You see nature, and then you try to emulate it. But, of course, when I met Mondrian I went home and tried to paint.... The simplest forms in the universe are the sphere and the circle. I represent them by discs and then I vary them. My whole theory about art is the disparity that exists between form, masses, and movements.... Even my triangles are spheres, but they are spheres of a different shape." See his *Calder: An Autobiography with Pictures* (1966), and Barbara Rose, ed., *Readings in American Art Since 1900* (1968).

LAWRENCE CAMPBELL

CALHOUN, John Caldwell (b. Abbeville District, S.C., Mar. 18, 1782; d. Washington, D.C., Mar. 30, 1850), POLITICAL LEADER, graduated from Yale (1804), attended law school in Litchfield, Connecticut, and was admitted to the South Carolina bar in 1807. After serving a term in the South Carolina legislature (1808–9) he was elected to the U.S. Congress as a Democrat (serving 1811–17), where he became one of the leaders of the "War Hawks," an expansionist group of congressmen. Throughout this period Calhoun was an ardent nationalist, supporting a strong navy, a standing army, internal improvements, protective tariffs, and a national bank.

In 1817, President James Monroe appointed Calhoun secretary of war. In this position, which he held until 1825, he supported internal improvements and took a moderate stand on the Missouri Compromise (1820), which banned slavery north of latitude 36'30".

In 1824 and again in 1828, Calhoun was elected vice president. During the 1820s it became increasingly clear that the South's economy would be based chiefly on agriculture rather than manufacturing. It was also a period of declining cotton prices. Calhoun therefore modified his nationalistic views. Following the passage of the high Tariff of 1828 the South Carolina legislature issued his *South Carolina Exposition and Protest* arguing that protective tariffs were unconstitutional and that a state could nullify any "unconstitutional" legislation.

Just as sectional difficulties were becoming accentuated, so personal animosities increased. When President Andrew Jackson learned that Calhoun, while secretary of war, had favored censuring him for his seizure of a Spanish fort while in pursuit of Seminole Indians in Florida (1818), he was furious. When a South Carolina convention "nullified" the Tariff of 1832, Calhoun resigned as vice president and was elected to the U.S. Senate from South Carolina. Jackson threatened to enforce the law with troops, even to hang Calhoun. Tensions were allayed when **Henry Clay** helped negotiate the Compromise Tariff of 1833, which gradually reduced duties. South Carolina then repealed its nullification ordinance.

In 1844–45, Calhoun was President John Tyler's secretary of state. Fearing that Great Britain would induce Texas to end slavery, he sought to annex Texas so as to preserve the sectional balance in the Senate. However, he opposed the war with Mexico that followed annexation. In the controversy over the future of slavery in territory gained in that war, he denounced the Wilmot Proviso (1846), which would have banned slavery from all territory taken from Mexico, and issued his own resolutions (1847). These argued that the federal government was only the trustee of the territories, which were owned jointly by the states, that any law interfering with slavery would be a violation of states' rights, and that the people of a territory had a right to adopt whatever form of state government they desired as long as it was republican in principle. Calhoun hoped to resolve the tariff question by getting the northern manufacturers to join the southern planters in producing for export, thereby eliminating the need for high tariffs. To stop slavery agitation he tried to work out a planter-capitalist coalition against the abolitionists, but his efforts failed.

Calhoun opposed Henry Clay's Compromise of 1850, arguing that it did not contain enough guarantees to protect the South. In his final speech before the Senate (read by Senator James Mason of Virginia), he predicted that the Union could be saved only if the South as a section was given equal rights in the newly acquired western territory. He demanded passage of a constitutional amendment based on the idea of a "concurrent majority." There should be a dual executive representing the two great sections, each with a veto power over acts of Congress.

———— ⁂ ————

With his fine intellect, his New England education, and his strongly national outlook during the War of 1812, Calhoun seemed at the time he entered Monroe's cabinet to have an almost unlimited future ahead of him. Then the growing divergence of interest between North and South brought him at last to a sectional position on such matters as the Tariff of 1824, passed over the united opposition of the slave states, the Missouri Compromise, and a series of landmark decisions by the Supreme Court that strengthened the national government, already controlled by a northern majority in Congress. Yet he never ceased to hope that the differences might be reconciled.

Calhoun sided privately with the planters but took no public stand until 1827 when the prospect of still higher tariffs brought widespread disaffection in the South. The crisis came in 1828 after the "Tariff of Abominations" sent cotton prices plummeting to a new low and brought open talk of secession in South Carolina. Calhoun's carefully reasoned *Exposition and Protest* of that year offered an alternative to withdrawal from the Union: the doctrine of nullification or state interposition, by which a minority interest might protect itself against the power of

the majority within the existing constitutional framework. The Constitution, so his argument ran, was a compact between sovereign and independent states. These states, by mutual agreement, created a general government and delegated to it the exercise of certain specified powers. Should the government overstep its defined limits, any of the contracting parties might interpose to arrest or nullify the unauthorized action. A single state might thus declare an act of Congress unconstitutional and prevent enforcement within its limits. Only an amendment to the Constitution, requiring concurrence of three-fourths of the states, could override such a veto.

The doctrine was put to the test in 1832 when a state convention declared the tariff to be null and void, and forbade its enforcement in South Carolina. For a time civil conflict threatened, but Jackson, while asserting the power to use force, scrupulously avoided doing so. Calhoun resigned the vice presidency to take a seat in the Senate, where he defended nullification against **Daniel Webster** and helped to secure passage of Clay's compromise tariff. He professed to believe that his doctrines had carried the day, but he was well aware that the preponderance of power lay with the national government.

Calhoun also knew that the real issue between North and South was not the power to levy and collect taxes but slavery, which was coming under general attack by reformers everywhere. If the "peculiar institution" of the South was to continue in the face of world opinion against it, it must be established that Congress, with its growing antislavery strength from the northern states, had no power to interfere. This was the task Calhoun now undertook. Too honest to defend a morally indefensible position, he convinced himself that African slavery was indeed a positive good, in the best interest of both races, even though his own logic required that he reject the egalitarian premise of democracy. He then sought to mold the slaveholding states into a single bloc politically powerful enough to resist any encroachment from the North.

In his posthumously published *Disquisition on Government* he developed a reasoned defense of the permanent minority the South had now become. Here he refined the dogma of the concurrent majority, first suggested in the *Exposition.* Government by a numerical majority he pronounced to be as absolute as government by a single dictator. This absolutism, he then reasoned, could be controlled only by giving "to each interest or portion of the community a negative on the others." The will of each major interest group—the agricultural interest, the manufacturing interest, the commercial interest—would be determined by its own majority, which might then interpose to arrest action taken by numbers alone. In an unfinished *Discourse on the Constitution,* to which the *Disquisition* was intended as an introduction, Calhoun then applied his theory to the actualities of government in the United States. The individual states at that time were dominated for the most part by a single economic interest. The Senate therefore represented the concurrent majority while the House spoke for numbers. A few minor changes, to ensure the veto by interest, and the geographical federalism of the founding fathers became a functional federalism of a type more familiar to the twentieth century than to the nineteenth.

However he might rationalize from his experience, Calhoun the practical politician saw safety for the interest he represented only in the power to block hostile legislation. With the balance of strength between North and South in the Senate about to be destroyed by the Compromise of 1850, Calhoun demanded almost with his last breath a sectional veto. He wanted only to *preserve* the Union, but in the contract theory of the constitution he had provided the intellectual basis for its destruction. He provided also a generally applicable defense for minority interests by giving to each segment of the body politic a concurrent voice in legislating for the whole. In his recognition of the pluralistic nature of our society, Calhoun pointed the way to a new and increasingly important area of political analysis.

Intense and dynamic, Calhoun brought the full resources of his extraordinary mind to bear on whatever problem confronted him. He possessed to an unusual degree the ability to generalize from experience and to universalize his judgments. His speeches, even when extemporaneous, were always clearly organized, with conclusions flowing inevitably from premises so compellingly stated as to baffle challenge. He spoke rapidly, in short staccato sentences that led the listener on whether he wished it or not. In person he was tall, lean, austere, with a great crown of wiry brown hair turning iron gray and growing longer with the years. With his gaunt face and brilliant eyes he was an arresting figure, a man to be taken seriously whatever he might say or do, so obvious was his own sincerity. From friend and foe alike he commanded respect, and by the sheer power of his intellect and the magnetism of his personality he wielded an influence far beyond his political due. He was the living embodiment of an idea that he imposed on lesser men by the force of his own conviction. See Charles M. Wiltse, *John C. Calhoun* (3 vols., 1944–51).

CHARLES M. WILTSE

CAMERON, Simon (b. Lancaster Co., Pa., Mar. 8, 1799; d. Donegal Springs, Pa., June 26, 1889), POLITICAL LEADER, served as a printing apprentice on the Northumberland County *Gazette* (1815) and the Harrisburg *Republican* (1816–21). During 1821–27 he owned and edited for brief periods the Bucks County *Democrat* (Doylestown, Pa.), the *Pennsylvania Intelligencer* (Harrisburg), and the Harrisburg *Republican.* In the years that followed he was active in such varied enterprises as the construction of the Pennsylvania Canal, railroad projects, and the operation of the Bank of Middletown, of which he was one of the founders (1832). A Democrat, Cameron was an early partisan of Andrew Jackson. He supported a drive, beginning in 1830, to ensure the renomination of Jackson for president; was active in 1832 in supporting Martin Van Buren for the vice presidency; and worked in 1833 to secure the election of James Buchanan to the U.S. Senate. During the early 1840s Cameron was especially active in support of Buchanan, whose hopes for the presidential nomination he supported in 1844. In 1845, however, Buchanan resigned from the Senate to take a post in the cabinet of President James K. Polk. When Buchanan's candidate to succeed to the Senate, George W. Woodward, announced his support for a tariff policy aimed primarily at revenue, Cameron, long a leading supporter of high protective tariffs to aid growing industry in Pennsylvania, opposed his candidacy. After voicing support for increased periods of probation before foreigners could be naturalized, and for the distribution of the proceeds from land sales to the states, Cameron was elected to the Senate by a coalition of Whigs, Native Americans, and protectionist Democrats. After his election Cameron hoped that his long support for Buchanan would secure favor from the administration. He soon found, however, that he was to be ignored in matters of patronage in the state. In response Cameron began to organize a bloc of supporters based on personal loyalty, which became the nucleus of a powerful Cameron political machine. In the Senate, Cameron opposed the Walker Tariff of 1846, which lowered rates. He also voted for the Wilmot Proviso, although specifically denying any intention to attack slavery in the existing slave states. He was defeated for reelection in 1848 by James Cooper, a Whig. During 1849–55, Cameron concentrated on his business enterprises and the growth of his state machine. His opposition to the Kansas-Nebraska Act, his continued support for protective tariffs, and his advocacy of rivers and harbors legislation kept him from winning Democratic support for another Senate term. In 1855 he was supported by the Know-Nothing Party in an unsuccessful attempt to reenter the Senate, and in 1856 he joined the newly formed Republican party and supported **John C. Frémont** in the presidential campaign.

Cameron served as U.S. senator as a Republican (1857–61). During this term he opposed the Lecompton Constitution and continued to favor high tariffs. In 1860 he supported Abraham Lincoln for president; as a result Lincoln appointed him secretary of war in 1861. But numerous complaints of corruption and favoritism within the department led Lincoln to

transfer Cameron in 1862 to the post of minister to Russia. Cameron returned to the United States in 1863 and ran for the Senate but was defeated. He was elected in 1867 and remained in the Senate until 1877 when he resigned to make room for his son, James Donald Cameron. During these years the Cameron political machine reached the peak of its power. After his retirement, though remaining in touch with the activities of the machine, Cameron was busy primarily as a gentleman farmer in Lancaster County and as a traveler to the West Indies and Europe.

⸎

Cameron was one of the most successful political bosses in 19th-century America. Shrewd, wealthy, and willing to devote his considerable talent and affluence to the cause of building up a powerful organization, he finally became the almost undisputed arbiter of Pennsylvania politics. His success was due partially to his business acumen, partially to his real devotion to the paramount interests of his state, especially the cause of tariff protection, and partially to his knowledge of political management. He knew how to reward friends, punish enemies, and maintain contacts with members of parties other than his own.

From the very beginning Cameron's career was marked by great agility. Acquiring wealth through prudent investments in publishing, banking, industry, and transportation, he deftly manipulated factional differences among Pennsylvania Democrats to his own advantage. In 1845 he succeeded in his bid for election to the Senate by relying on a combination of insurgent Democrats and Whigs. In 1857, following the breakup of the old party system and the rise of the Republicans, he procured election to the Senate by a combination of Republicans, Know-Nothings, and Democratic bolters. Then, in 1860, in spite of an ever widening rift with Governor-elect Andrew G. Curtin, he emerged as his state's favorite son for the Republican presidential nomination. This strategic position enabled him to bargain successfully for a post in Lincoln's cabinet.

Cameron did not distinguish himself as secretary of war. The department was beset with inefficiency and fraud, and the president removed the secretary by appointing him envoy to Russia. Nevertheless, Lincoln, appreciating Cameron's great political ability, continued to work closely with him.

It was after the Civil War that Cameron reached the pinnacle of his influence. Overcoming his rivals, in 1867 he returned to the Senate and perfected the most masterful political machine that Pennsylvania had ever known. With his lieutenants Matthew Quay and Robert W. Mackey, as well as with his son, J. Donald Cameron, he successfully manipulated state and federal patronage. Opposed to Andrew Johnson's Reconstruction policies, he became an intimate adviser of President Ulysses S. Grant. Even Rutherford B. Hayes's lack of sympathy did not diminish the power of the old politician, who was able to hand over intact both his influence and his Senate seat to his son. Personally affable, Cameron was often suspected of using dubious methods, but he was never convicted of enriching himself at the public's expense. His importance lies in his establishment of the Pennsylvania Republican organization. See Erwin Stanley Bradley, *Simon Cameron* (1966).

HANS L. TREFOUSSE

CANNON, Joseph Gurney (b. New Garden, Guilford Co., N.C., May 7, 1836; d. Danville, Ill., Nov. 12, 1926), POLITICAL LEADER, supported his family after his father died by working as a store clerk while studying law in his spare time. He studied at the Cincinnati Law School for six months before setting up a law practice in Shelbyville, Illinois (1858). He soon moved to Tuscola and then Danville, where he lived for the rest of his life. He served as Illinois state attorney for the 27th judicial district (1861–68). After being defeated as a Republican candidate for Congress in 1870, he was elected to the 43d Congress (1873–75) and served until 1891. In Congress he opposed civil service reform, was against conservation, supported the acquisition of the Philippines, and was an ardent protectionist.

Cannon was reelected to the 53d Congress (1893–95) and served in the House until 1913. He was chairman of the Committee on Appropriations (1897–1903), where he made a point of practicing thrift and retrenchment. Elected speaker of the House in 1903, he ran that body in a firm, often arbitrary, manner. Dominating the important Rules Committee, he chose committee members and chairmen on the basis of their personal allegiance to him and his "standpat" policies, a procedure soon called "Cannonism." Cannon was permanent chairman of the 1904 Republican national convention and received 58 first-ballot votes for president at the 1908 convention. In 1910 a combination of Democrats and insurgent Republicans broke Cannon's power by enlarging the Rules Committee, providing for the election of its members by the House, and excluding the speaker from membership. Refusing to make the affair a personal matter, however, the insurgents did not accept Cannon's resignation; he remained speaker until 1911. Cannon was defeated for reelection to the 63d Congress but regained his seat in the 64th (1915–17); he continued as a member of the House until his voluntary retirement in 1923.

⸺≪≫⸺

Joseph Gurney Cannon was an earthy, small-town politician, completely lacking in imagination, who through hard work, much guile, an abundance of favors rendered, and accumulated seniority made it to the top on Capitol Hill. He was razor-thin and of average height, with pink cheeks, clear blue eyes, and a white stubble of a beard. He had a prairie lawyer's gruff informality of dress and manner; his suits, though well made, sober, and dark, always looked slept-in; his gray felt hat, worn indoors and out at a rakish angle, was perpetually stained. On the stump or in the well of the House he was a figure of "immense comic popularity," wrote **John Hay,** but "unspeakably grotesque"; behind the scenes he was a shrewd, calculating partisan—a "strong, hard, narrow old Boeotian," was the way Theodore Roosevelt described him. Whether in public or private, in the company of friends or strangers, presidents or dowagers, he was always blunt, downright "Uncle Joe," as he smoked his two-for-a-nickel cigars, rained tobacco juice into any handy receptacle, swore and cursed, told Lincoln stories, and indulged his taste for whiskey and his passion for poker. Characteristically, he moderated his drinking as he grew older and always played his cards close to the vest, tending to "stand pat" with whatever hand fate dealt him rather than trying for something better.

As in poker so in politics—his philosophy was to "stand by the status," particularly since he believed that the Republican program of high tariffs, economy in government, and a minimum interference with private enterprise had been instrumental in making America "a hell of a success." Claims by Progressives that it would become a greater success if Congress heeded their demands for such things as lower tariffs, minimum-wage and maximum-hours legislation, an income tax, national parks, and measures to curb the abuses of big business struck him as arrant "socialist" nonsense, and he used his powers as House speaker to quash their proposals, whatever the political consequences. The sole purpose of government, he held, was "to afford protection to life, liberty and property ... and when that is done by a wise legislature, then let every tub stand on its own bottom, let every citizen root hog or die." This attitude, combined with his unabashed philistinism ("Not one cent for scenery," he said in dismissing a conservation proposal), his implacable opposition to tariff reform, and his uncompromising resistance to Progressives in his party, eventually provoked the insurgent revolt, helped ruin the Taft administration, weakened the speakership, cost him his seat in Congress, and made his name a byword for power wielded in behalf of special interests. Yet, contrary to his reputation then and since, he was less an ally of Wall Street than a spokesman for the Main Street banker and small businessman on the make, less a conscious defender of the rich and privileged than simply an unreflective son of the Middle Border on the loose. See Blair Bolles, *Tyrant from Illinois* (1951).

JEROME L. STERNSTEIN

CANNON, Walter Bradford (b. Prairie du Chien, Wis., Oct. 19, 1871; d. Franklin, N.H., Oct. 1, 1945), PHYSIOLOGIST, received his BA (1896) and MD (1900) from Harvard University. Appointed an instructor at Harvard upon his graduation, Cannon became professor of physiology at the Harvard Medical School six years later. His research into the process of digestion and its relation to body health continued until 1911 when he published *The Mechanical Factors of Digestion.*

From 1912 to 1942, Cannon was a consulting physiologist to Boston Children's Hospital and Peter Bent Brigham Hospital. His initial work on digestion led him to study emotional effects on digestion, reported in *Bodily Changes in Pain, Hunger, Fear and Rage* (1915). Cannon next turned to the endocrine system, but his work was interrupted by the war. He was commissioned a first lieutenant in the Medical Corps and was assigned to direct the laboratory at the U.S. base hospital, Camiers, France. There he studied surgical shock related to war wounds and published his findings in *Traumatic Shock* (1923).

Following World War I, Cannon resumed his investigations of the thyroid and adrenal glands. He explained the role of the sympathetic nervous system and of the adrenal medulla in maintaining body stability in *The Wisdom of the Body* (1932). In 1929–30 he was Harvard exchange lecturer in France and in 1935 was visiting professor at Peiping Union Medical College. Cannon served as national chairman of the Medical Bureau to Aid Spanish Democracy (1936–38) and in the late 1930s worked with the Medical Aid to China and United China Relief committees. In 1942 he retired from Harvard. During World War II he served as chairman of the National Research Council's Committee on Shock and Transfusion.

⁂

Walter B. Cannon was the most distinguished American physiologist of the first half of the twentieth century and the only one whose ideas had a significant impact outside his own profession. While still a freshman in the Harvard Medical School he made a permanent mark on the history of medicine by introducing in 1897 the bismuth or barium meal to render the organs of the alimentary canal opaque to the newly discovered X rays. This method rapidly spread to every modern hospital in the world as one of the great diagnostic tools—fundamental for detecting tumors of the digestive tract and gastric and duodenal ulcers.

Cannon now became the first man to "see" food at all stages of its passage through the alimentary canal. He observed the frequency of the peristaltic waves by which food was churned and moved along, and determined the duration of the various phases of digestion for different diets. He also demonstrated that the proximate cause of hunger was powerful contractions of the empty stomach. These and other researches made Cannon one of the major contributors to elucidating the physiology of digestion.

Cannon had early been struck by the observation that the peristaltic waves of the stomach in digestion would sometimes cease abruptly. He soon discovered that the animals in question were frightened or angry and that the physiological reverberations of this emotion persisted after the cause had been removed. Cannon's effort to explain these phenomena led to his becoming the world pioneer in studying the physiology of strong emotions. He ranked next to his contemporary Sigmund Freud as the principal student of the nature and function of emotions and made a significant contribution to the ever increasing recognition of their importance in personal and social life.

Cannon's distinctive contribution to the subject lay in his being the first to associate the emotions with the activity of hormones—specifically, adrenaline, the product of the adrenal medulla. The main purport of his celebrated book *Bodily Changes in Pain, Hunger, Fear and Rage,* founded largely on his own research, was that in threatening situations adrenaline put the animal organism on an emergency footing, physiologically geared for "fight or flight." In the second edition of *Bodily Changes,* Cannon acknowledged that in modern urban man, who does not customarily either flee or fight however provoked, the physi-

ological mobilization triggered by the release of adrenaline can be actively harmful by leading, for example, to chronic high blood pressure or cardiac acceleration. Cannon's remarks on this theme made him one of the patron saints of psychosomatic medicine.

Despite his increasing interest in pathological conditions, Cannon's main conclusion from his own researches was overwhelmingly positive— that higher organisms incorporate a variety of self-regulatory mechanisms for maintaining their internal stability in the face of external threats. This idea had already been expressed by the 19th-century French physiologist Claude Bernard, but Cannon in 1926 coined the term "homeostasis" for the stabilizing tendency and marshaled the evidence, much of it from his own laboratory, that he had been accumulating since Bernard's death. With the single exception of evolution through natural selection, homeostasis has proved to be the most influential of all integrating concepts in biology. It has also been invoked, by analogy, in various sociological theories and cited by **Norbert Wiener** as a biological exemplification of cybernetics.

With Sir Henry Dale and Otto Loewi, Cannon was one of the three men who established the chemical nature of neurotransmission in the autonomic ("involuntary") nervous system. Before their time, neurotransmission had generally been regarded as a purely electrical phenomenon. See Walter B. Cannon, *The Way of an Investigator: A Scientist's Experiences in Medical Research* (1945).

DONALD FLEMING

CAPRA, Frank (b. Palermo, Italy, May 18, 1897; d. La Quinta, Calif., Sept. 3, 1991), MOVIE DIRECTOR, emigrated to the United States with his parents in 1906 and received a chemical engineering degree from California Institute of Technology (1918). He worked as a film editor and writer for slapstick comedies before achieving his first great success directing Jean Harlow in *Platinum Blond* (1931). His comedy, *It Happened One Night* (1934), starring Clark Gable and

Claudette Colbert, was a popular and critical success, winning five major Academy Awards. Capra then directed a string of profitable and patriotic pictures: *Mr. Deeds Goes to Town* (1936), *You Can't Take It with You* (1938), *Mr. Smith Goes to Washington* (1939), *Meet John Doe* (1942), and *Arsenic and Old Lace* (1944). Capra made several distinguished documentaries during World War II. His later films did not capture the public's attention, although *It's a Wonderful Life* (1946), a box office failure, has become a perennial favorite on television. His autobiography, *Name Above the Title* (1971), is a revealing reprise of his life and career.

Capra, the son of immigrants, is famous for championing the common man. Nearly all his films have a political thrust, centering on lone individuals who rise to rectify corrupt businesses and governments dominated by dictatorial bosses and politicians. Capra's films are populist, instilling the belief that people know best and that America is constantly threatened by elements that would make it elitist and authoritarian. Capra's appeal is sentimental and melodramatic, skillfully playing on the audience's emotions by always making his heroes the underdogs.

Capra has been criticized for making politics simplistic and for relying on unrealistic plot resolutions in which the hero triumphs against the rich and the powerful. His films celebrate the life of ordinary people and profess a faith in the amateur who can cleanse politics and business of its jaded professionals. Capra endows the idea of citizenship—that American government belongs to everyone—with an integrity unrivaled by any other filmmaker. If he veers toward the naïve and sentimental, he expresses the American faith in individualism and in political rights that flow from the people and not from their governors.

His best films, regardless of their politics, show an exquisite gift for comedy, timing, and character development. He was especially aided by male stars, such as Gary Cooper and James Stewart, who were charming combinations of the morally earnest and the unpretentious, and female stars, such as Jean Arthur and Barbara Stanwyck, who were feisty and alluringly feminine. See Joseph McBride, *Frank Capra: The Catastrophe of Success* (1992).

CARL ROLLYSON

CARDOZO, Benjamin Nathan (b. New York, N.Y., May 24, 1870; d. Port Chester, N.Y., July 9, 1938), JURIST, was graduated with honors from Columbia College in 1889, received an MA in 1890, and attended Columbia Law School until 1891 when he was admitted to the New York bar. In practice Cardozo quickly gained recognition as a "lawyer's lawyer," preparing briefs and arguments for other attorneys to use in actual trials. His work on cases at equity and in the appellate division led to his *Jurisdiction of the New York Court of Appeals* (1903), a standard handbook. In 1913 he was elected justice of the New York supreme court on a fusion ticket, but after only one month, in February 1914, Governor Martin A. Glynn elevated him to one of the temporary positions on the court of appeals, the state's highest court. In 1917 he was elected to a full term as associate justice in that court and in 1926 was a successful candidate for chief justice. In such decisions as *MacPherson* v. *The Buick Company*, in which he established the right of redress against the manufacturer to a person injured by a latent defect in a car, Cardozo helped to shape the common law to meet contemporary conditions. In lectures at the Yale Law School he set forth his views on the role of judges and the relations of law to life. His resulting book, *The Nature of the Judicial Process* (1921), was later extended in works in 1924 (*The Growth of the Law*) and 1928 (*The Paradoxes of Legal Science*).

In 1932, when **Oliver Wendell Holmes, Jr.,** retired from the U.S. Supreme Court, President Herbert Hoover appointed Cardozo to his seat. His Supreme Court career paralleled the New Deal's most innovative domestic reform activities, and Cardozo voted to uphold most of this legislation. His dissent in the Carter Coal case (1936) chastised the majority for its heavy-handed use of inflexible rules to negate the valid use of federal power. However, he voted with the rest of the Court to invalidate the NIRA, which he considered "delegation run riot," and he privately abhorred Roosevelt's Court-packing plan. Following the 1937 "switch," he wrote eloquent opinions upholding the social security program and validating broad use of the federal taxing and spending power to advance the general welfare. He was a strong civil libertarian.

———— ∞ ————

Cardozo's career, some have contended, was shaped by a compelling need to redeem his family name, disgraced by his father, a Tammany judge charged with political corruption in the Boss **Tweed** scandals and forced to resign from the bench. The young Cardozo was a compulsive worker, known as a "walking encyclopedia" of the law, and reputed for candor and honesty. He tried no sensational cases, nor would he appeal to the passions and prejudices of a jury. Never marrying, he cultivated only a few close friends and dispelled his loneliness in intensive legal work and such activities as his vigorous participation in launching the American Law Institute. He was known internationally by the 1920s as an outstanding common law judge; his influence lay in his capacity for perceiving in the particular facts of a private law case the principles that were contending for recognition and elucidating them in such a way as to dramatize their broader and long-range social utility. Often associated with the legal realists, he was less ready than they to depart from precedent and more convinced that there was justice in legal consistency. Litigants, he contended, benefited from a faith that there was even-handed administration of justice in the courts.

His move to the Supreme Court forced him into a new role, the field of public law, statutory and constitutional. In this capacity, although generally liberal, he continued to be concerned principally with judicial rather than political or economic philosophy, differing sharply here with his friend **Louis D. Brandeis.** His Carter Coal dissent was a good example of the common law judge seeking to show the unfortunate social results that the judicial application of unwise doctrine would produce. Similarly, in his famed Palko ruling he sought to evaluate the social effects of further nationalization of the Bill of Rights, concluding that flexibility here was desirable, that courts should decide which rights were "implicit in the concept of ordered liberty" and "so rooted in the traditions and conscience of our people as to be ranked as fundamental." This process, he felt, would properly leave in the judiciary's hands the task of evaluating virtually on a case-to-case basis whether the legislative estimate of contemporary needs properly respected individual rights, as well as the technical means for "modernization" of the Bill of Rights on a careful basis.

Such fine-line drawing did have its limitations, however. And while Cardozo's name stands high in common law jurisprudence and in the area of jurisprudential thought, the simplicity and immediacy of the principles that he laid down were seldom such as to provide broader guidelines for coping with new challenges and dealing with the more complex and subtle problems of subsequent decades. See B. H. Levy, *Cardozo and Frontiers of Legal Thinking* (1969).

PAUL L. MURPHY

CAREY, Mathew (b. Dublin, Ire., Jan. 28, 1760; d. Philadelphia, Pa., Sept. 16, 1839), PUBLISHER, and **CAREY, Henry Charles** (b. Philadelphia, Pa., Dec. 15, 1793; d. Philadelphia, Pa., Oct. 13, 1879), ECONOMIST. Mathew, the father, apprenticed himself to a printer and early wrote pamphlets defending Ireland against British oppression. He was jailed in Newgate for his attack on the House of Commons, and when again threatened with prosecution he fled to Paris where he came under the patronage of **Benjamin Franklin** and formed a friendship with Lafayette. These men encouraged his emigration to Philadelphia in 1785. There he edited a succession of magazines, the *American Museum* of reprinted items being the best remembered. After an arduous start he prospered as publisher and bookseller. Always active in the life of his city, he won wide respect for his services in the yellow fever epidemic of 1793. He founded the Hibernian Society to assist Irish immigrants and helped form the first Sunday School Society in the United States. As a charter member of the Pennsylvania Society for the Promotion of National Industry, he published persuasive pamphlets urging protective tariffs and internal improvements. He was one of few Republicans to support the recharter of the Bank of the United States (1810). His *Olive Branch* (1814) strove to reconcile the Republican and Federalist parties. A devout Catholic, he was the first to publish the Douay Bible in this country.

Henry Charles Carey joined the family publishing firm in 1817 and was later head of Carey, Lea, and Carey. At 42 he retired to devote himself to economic study and writing. His formal works, such as *Principles of Political Economy* (3 vols., 1837–40) and *Principles of Social Science* (3 vols., 1858–59), were widely translated abroad. For years he contributed regularly to **Horace Greeley**'s New York *Tribune*. He was a vehement foe of slavery and in several ways urged the South to add manufactures to agriculture. In his home he held a seminar for local disciples and visiting devotees ("Carey vespers"), which extended his influence as the leading American nationalist economist.

———— ✺ ————

The Careys were inspired by the capacities of richly endowed America, which they wished to develop through the fostering care of government. Their ambitions for this country were intensified by their Irish hostility to Britain, against which nation they would rear a successful competitor. Both were strongly influenced by the example of **Alexander Hamilton,** and (Henry Charles especially) by the advocacies of Friedrich List, the German economist who sojourned in Pennsylvania. Mathew Carey was most notable for the internal improvements he promoted, such as the Chesapeake and Delaware canal and the Pennsylvania System of Public Works, and for national banking and industrial legislation, which he furthered. Command of his own press

assisted the steady flow of his publications, of course, but their currency was due to the force and charm of his writing style.

The son began where the father left off, adding theory to practice. In contrast to the individualist, laissez-faire economists of the classical school of France and Britain, he urged the power of associated effort. For him natural laws supported the harmony of social interests. Instead of European pessimism, exemplified in Carlyle's branding of political economy as the "dismal science," the younger Carey was buoyantly optimistic. Surrounded as he was by the expanding American economy, he denied the desponding rent theory of David Ricardo and the ominous population predictions of Thomas R. Malthus. Cultivation, Carey maintained, did not descend from better to worse soils but began historically with the least fertile, and only as capital and labor accumulated were the richer lands exploited. Correspondingly, he insisted, food supplies tended to increase faster than population. He undertook to refute the classical doctrine of wages tending toward a mere subsistence level. On the contrary, improvements in capital and invention had the effect of increasing the share of labor both absolutely and relatively.

His wide reading, in deciding on works to be published by the firm, supplied him with abundant illustrations for the arguments in his own writings. He assumed a correspondence between natural science and social science that was often more apparent than real. While original and boldly creative in his thought, he lacked the mental discipline that more formal schooling might have furnished. On the other hand, to his benefit, he escaped any sterilizing effects of imbibed authority. He urged the mutual betterment of industry, agriculture, and commerce. Opposing the territorial division of labor, he lamented the costs of transport over great distances and also the proliferation of intermediaries in commerce and credit. Varied economic production in close relationship illustrated, for Carey, the principle that two is more than twice one. He antagonized the followers of the cosmopolitan, free trade system of Adam Smith, discounted the advantage of huge industrial centers, and anticipated the recent movement toward dispersed, relatively self-contained economic communities. His advocacy of industrial development for the cotton states began to be acted upon in his lifetime and has flourished conspicuously since. Henry C. Carey as economic or, more broadly, social theorist illustrates the observation that a thinker in his field is apt to be the product of his particular environment. See Kenneth W. Rowe, *Mathew Carey: A Study in American Economic Development* (1933), and A. D. H. Kaplan, *Henry Charles Carey: A Study in American Economic Thought* (1931).

BROADUS MITCHELL

CARLSON, Chester F. (b. Seattle, Wash., 1906; d. New York, N.Y., Sept. 18, 1968), INVENTOR, completed a two-year cooperative program at Riverside (California) Junior College and earned a BS in physics from the California Institute of Technology in 1930. In 1939 he received a law degree from the New York Law School, New York City. In 1930 he accepted employment with the Bell Telephone Laboratories, working first as a researcher, then in the patent department. Laid off from this post, he spent a short time with a small patent firm before joining the patent department of the P. R. Mallory Company, an electrical manufacturing concern in New York City. He remained there until 1945, ultimately becoming head of the patent department.

Carlson began his search for a simple and inexpensive copying process in 1934. A search of the literature undertaken in 1934–36 led him to center his attention on processes employing photoconductivity. By the end of 1937 he had conceived the basic steps of the process later to be known as xerography. In October 1938 he and Otto Kornei produced the first copy made by the Carlson process. Two years later a partially successful automatic machine was built according to plans Carlson had drawn up. In 1944 the Battelle Memorial Laboratories licensed Carlson's electrophotography (xerography) patents and further improved the process.

Proceeds from the Battelle licensing agree-

ment and from a later sublicense to the Haloid Company (later the Xerox Corporation) allowed Carlson to retire in 1945. He spent the rest of his life as a consultant and independent inventor.

Chester Carlson's main strengths as an inventor were a clear perception of a practical need (the need of a law office for quick, clean copies), a grasp of the basic principles of physics and printing, and the persistence to sustain a long campaign. No mere attic tinkerer, he had a solid grounding in industrial research. His key contribution to xerography was not a mechanism or an experimental result (he was a poor technician and lacked ability as an experimenter) but rather a concept: the use of a high electric voltage to charge a sheet of insulating or semiconducting material in order to make it very sensitive to small amounts of impinging light. His background in patent work probably contributed greatly to his success, allowing him first to avoid repeating previous dead ends and later to file claims controlling electrophotography (especially those in U.S. Pat. 2,297,691, granted in 1942).

Carlson acknowledged that he was motivated by a desire to get rich. Hardship, economic and physical, was a main theme of his career. The son of an arthritic itinerant barber and of a mother who suffered from tuberculosis, he was the main financial support of his family from the age of 12. He left college with debts of $1,400 and was discharged from his first full-time job due to cutbacks occasioned by the Great Depression. In financial difficulties throughout the 1930s and trying to keep up his triple careers—office worker, inventor, and law student—he developed severe spinal arthritis that further handicapped his efforts.

His long campaign did bring eventual rewards. His proceeds from the licensing agreements with Battelle and Haloid eventually made him a multimillionaire. A consultant but never an employee, of Xerox, his later efforts were devoted to more of his own ideas, including a method of electrostatic character printing. He spent his last years in Pittsford, New York, and shared only peripherally in the attention belatedly lavished in the 1960s on the copying technique he had conceived. See John H. Dessauer and Harold E. Clark, *Xerography and Related Processes* (1965).

GEORGE WISE

CARNEGIE, Andrew (b. Dunfermline, Scot., Nov. 25, 1835; d. Lenox, Mass., Aug. 11, 1919), INDUSTRIALIST, emigrated with his family to Allegheny, Pennsylvania, in 1848. After working as a bobbin boy in a textile factory and as an engine tender, in 1849 he became a messenger boy in a Pittsburgh telegraph office and a telegraph operator in 1851. **Thomas A. Scott** of the Pennsylvania Railroad hired Carnegie as a private telegraph operator and personal secretary in 1853, and appointed him superintendent of the western division in 1859. When Scott became assistant secretary of war in 1861, he employed Carnegie as a superintendent of military transportation and director of telegraph communications.

In 1857, with money borrowed from Scott, Carnegie purchased ten shares of Adams Express Co. stock. He helped promote Theodore T. Woodruff's design for a railway sleeping car in 1860. In 1865 he resigned from the Pennsylvania Railroad Co. He managed the Keystone Bridge Co., sold railroad securities in Europe, was instrumental in the expansion of Western Union Telegraph Co., speculated in oil, and invested in iron manufacturing.

During the depression of 1873, Carnegie invested almost all his resources in steel. By adopting the Bessemer process and other technological innovations he raised the quality and reduced the price of Carnegie steel. He transformed his enterprises into a vertically integrated unit controlling raw materials, transportation, manufacturing, distribution, and finance. He moved toward virtual control of the American steel industry during the depression of 1893–97, acquiring massive iron deposits in the Mesabi range and purchasing the Pittsburgh, Shenango and Lake Erie Railroad that connected the steel center with the Northwest water routes. He supported his associate **Henry C. Frick**'s efforts to break the union in the Homestead strike (1894).

Carnegie sold out to the newly formed United States Steel Corporation (1901). He devoted the remainder of his life to philanthropy, creating, among other funds, the Carnegie Corporation of New York, the Carnegie Endowment for International Peace, the Carnegie Foundation for the Advancement of Teaching, and the Carnegie Institution of Washington, D.C. He also financed many public libraries for towns and colleges.

Carnegie wrote numerous essays on business and public affairs. In "The Gospel of Wealth" (*North American Review,* 1889), he endorsed the accumulation of capital as a requirement for human progress, but he also emphasized the moral obligation of the rich to dispense their fortunes in a way "to produce the most beneficial results for the community."

Andrew Carnegie, son of a hand loom weaver and grandson of a cobbler, spent the first years of his life in Dunfermline, Scotland, at a time when all of Britain was embroiled in the Chartist movement. Both his paternal and maternal families provided leaders in Scottish Chartist activities, and one of his earliest memories was that of being awakened in the night by a neighbor shouting through the window to inform his parents that his uncle had been imprisoned for seditious activity. The radicalism of the artisans of Scotland that was directed against the established order of aristocratic privilege was an essential part of Carnegie's heritage. Emigrating to the United States with his parents, the 12-year-old Carnegie believed that in America he had found the Chartist's utopia of equality in political participation and economic opportunity. He was never to lose this faith in the American democratic process.

But there was another part of Carnegie's heritage, bequeathed to him by his mother, which was at least as important as the political dreams of his father. Margaret Morrison Carnegie expected no easy millennium, for she knew that the political hopes of her father and her husband put no bread on the table or any "siller in the sporran." She saw life as it existed around her—

a brutal, ruthless struggle for existence, where those who had any chance for success must take advantage of every opportunity, cut corners at every turn, and use elbows to push to the head of the line. It was she who kept her children out of the soup lines by stitching shoes and selling groceries when her husband's loom was silent for want of orders, and it was she who finally sold off their few possessions, bundled her family together, and forced them "to flit" out of Scotland to America when it was apparent that the day of the hand loom weaver was forever over.

These two contradictory gifts of humanitarian idealism and self-centered realism were to be the sum of Carnegie's inheritance. They were to provide the continuing tensions in his life and make Andrew Carnegie the complex person that he was. Almost from the start, young Carnegie was both spectacularly lucky and spectacularly shrewd in taking full advantage of America's industrial development. He was immensely fortunate in the beginning to make the acquaintance of and become the favorite of one of the country's most able and most daring railroad executives, Thomas A. Scott. It was Scott who gave Carnegie his first lessons in speculation and business manipulation. Although Carnegie was later to popularize the maxim, "Put all your eggs in one basket and then watch that basket," in these early years he subscribed to the more traditional aphorism. For his financial nest eggs he had baskets made of telegraph wires, Pullman sleeping cars, railroad stocks, bridges, and oil derricks, and all of these held golden eggs. By the age of 33, Carnegie had an annual income of nearly $50,000 from his many investments. At that moment he took a hard, unpitying look at himself and the kind of life he had elected to pursue. So far it had been the fulfillment of his mother's ambitions. But the other part of his inheritance could never be totally ignored. On a December evening in 1868 he wrote himself a memorandum of instructions: "By this time two years I can so arrange all my business as to secure at least 50,000 per annum. Beyond this never earn.... The amassing of wealth is one of the worst species of idolitary [*sic*]. No idol more debasing than the worship of money."

Andrew Carnegie did not retire at 35, however. The memorandum was carefully filed in his desk drawer and was disregarded as its author continued to "push inordinately." Entering into the iron business with his younger brother, Tom, he was one of the first of the iron manufacturers to shift his attention to the development of Bessemer steel in 1872. A decade later, "steel was king," and Carnegie was the king's first minister. The Carnegie plants dominated the American steel industry, and leaving Britain far behind, American steel dominated the world.

The secret to Carnegie's entrepreneurial success lay in the old-fashioned, simple partnership organization that Carnegie maintained throughout the twenty-nine years that he was engaged in the manufacture of steel. In an age that saw the development of the modern corporation, owned by a multitude of absentee stockholders, Carnegie's "association" of partners, who were all active managers of the company, had a distinct advantage over its competitors. With no stockholders to worry about, Carnegie could keep both the capitalization of the company and the annual dividends low. Profits made were put back into the company to make it more efficient, more competitive. By owning 58 percent of the company, Carnegie could with equanimity ignore the discontent of his junior partners who wanted more dividends and less expansion. Profits, for Carnegie, were always tangential to and a mere consequence of reduced costs of production. To reduce costs he would quickly scrap a new machine, a new process, or an entire mill in favor of more efficient operations. Labor was simply another item of cost, but if wages were low, so also were the salaries of management. It was his obsession with costs that drove Carnegie into the development of verticality within his manufacturing structure, and by the end of the century the Carnegie Steel Company controlled every ingredient essential in steel manufacturing. What he had effected in a little over a quarter-century was the largest and most successful "empire of business," as he called his association, in the world.

Carnegie, in moments of expansive generosity,

liked to say that he owed his success to the extraordinary group of "young geniuses" that he had managed to collect as his managing partners. "Take from me all the ore mines, railroads, manufacturing plants, but leave me my organization, and in a few years I promise to duplicate the Carnegie company." This simply was not true, and certainly Carnegie, vain as he was, knew it was not true. With the notable exceptions of **Henry Clay Frick** and **Charles M. Schwab,** Carnegie's "young geniuses" were quite ordinary men who could be—and frequently were—easily replaced. The success of the Carnegie empire was almost totally due to Carnegie himself—to his drive, his imagination, his boldness and innovative daring, and, above all, his insatiable appetite for more—more iron, more rails, more customers, more power. Short of stature, mercurial in temperament, Carnegie could easily be compared to another empire builder. John Walker, a close associate of both Carnegie and Frick in many business ventures, did just that when he said that the Carnegie works had both a Napoleon and a von Moltke. "And don't ever forget that Carnegie was the Napoleon."

Carnegie's 1868 memorandum to himself lay in his desk drawer disregarded but not forgotten. The old troublesome questions raised in that self-analysis remained, even though they had in no way retarded his drive to imperial power. He tried to placate the heritage of radical Dunfermline by carrying Chartism back to Britain in the 1880s. He bought a syndicate of newspapers to promote the cause of republicanism in Britain; he entered enthusiastically into British politics, supporting such radicals as Kier Hardie and John Burns for Parliament; he even toyed with the idea of reclaiming his British citizenship and standing himself for Parliament on an antimonarchical ticket. But still the old doubts remained. By accumulating a fortune that ran into the hundreds of millions, had he "degraded himself beyond hope of permanent recovery"? Of even greater importance, what had been done to his beloved, egalitarian America when one man could accumulate as much wealth and power as he had? Not until he pronounced his

"Gospel of Wealth" in 1889 did he, as he himself wrote, "find refuge from self-questioning." With this gospel of stewardship he justified the accumulation of great wealth, for the man who amasses a great fortune will also know best how to distribute it for the benefit of society. He had at last found a way to reconcile to his own satisfaction his two worlds of plutocracy and democracy.

Always something of an intellectual snob, Carnegie found personal pleasure in practicing his own gospel, for it permitted him to associate with poets and artists, philosophers and college presidents. He had always found his business associates and fellow millionaires in America exceedingly dull and limited in intellect. He would dismiss them as men who had "never read any book except a ledger." But in giving away his millions he had ample opportunity to get to know the intelligentsia of the entire Atlantic community. And they discovered, often to their surprise, that he had more to give than dollars. Herbert Spencer, Matthew Arnold, **Mark Twain, Andrew White,** and above all, John Morley became close personal friends.

Carnegie had written a much quoted line: "The man who dies thus rich, dies disgraced." In 1919 there was much speculation in the world press as to whether or not he had died in a state of grace. He had. Of his $350 million in United States Steel first mortgage bonds, not a single bond remained. He had succeeded in giving it all away for what he hopefully believed was "the benefaction of all mankind." With his death most Americans felt that an age had ended because Carnegie had for many years served as a living showpiece for what his countrymen liked to think was the very essence of the American experience—the poor immigrant boy who makes good, the **Horatio Alger** hero, the great benefactor, the missionary for world peace, the democrat who could talk back to kings. The public library was his palace and the steel rail his scepter. Carnegie, in short, was America's own success story of self-fulfillment.

But Carnegie was far more realistic about the meaning of his own life. Long before his death he realized that by his very success he had done more than any socialist to destroy the very system of free enterprise under which he had flourished. In 1909 he had written that the age of competition was over and that in the future the economy would have to be regulated by the national government. He advocated a supreme industrial court that would fix all wages and prices.

Carnegie was never one to weep over change, for being an eternal optimist, he was sustained by the belief that the world moves "ever onward and upward." And with this faith, radical Dunfermline, in spite of Homestead, protective tariffs, and labor spies, might still claim him as its own. See Joseph Frazier Wall, *Andrew Carnegie* (1970).

JOSEPH FRAZIER WALL

CAROTHERS, Wallace Hume (b. Burlington, Iowa, Apr. 27, 1896; d. Philadelphia, Pa., Apr. 29, 1937), SCIENTIST, received his BS from Tarkio College, Missouri, in 1920 and his MS from the University of Illinois in 1921. He was an instructor in chemistry at the University of South Dakota (1921–22) before returning to Illinois where he received his PhD in organic chemistry in 1924. After two years as an instructor at Illinois and two years at Harvard in 1928 he became director of organic chemistry research at a new laboratory at the experimental station of E. I. du Pont de Nemours & Co. in Wilmington, Delaware.

At du Pont, Carothers and his associates investigated high molecular weight structures and the mechanism of their formation by polymerization—the joining of many molecules into one large molecule. They invented the synthesis of chloroprene (marketed as the synthetic "rubber" neoprene) from hydrogen chloride and an acetylene compound. Between 1930 and 1935 they developed nylon and laid the fundamental groundwork for developing most of the rest of today's synthetic fibers (such as Orlon and Dacron). Carothers served as associate editor of the *Journal of the American Chemical Society* (1930) and editor of *Organic Syntheses* (1933). He was elected to the National Academy of Sciences in 1936. He suffered from periods of deep depres-

sion in his last years and committed suicide in 1937.

⚬⚬⚬

Carothers crowded a lifetime's worth of scientific work into the decade 1926–36. His research led directly to the long-sought goal of a synthetic fiber. An intensive, perhaps compulsive worker with a sensitive, withdrawn nature, these most productive years led to a period of increasingly severe depression, nervous illness, and failing health, which led him to take his own life.

His strength as a scientist lay mainly in his ability to combine methodical experimentation with systematic and original analysis. He was uncomfortable as a lecturer, preferring to absorb himself totally in his research. His movement from an academic post to industry gave full play to his unique strengths. The modern equipment, pure reagents, and expert assistance provided at the du Pont central research laboratory allowed him to explore deeply a single basic theme: the preconditions for, and consequences of, the building up of long chains of organic molecules.

His research project, which culminated in the development of nylon, stands as an example of that rarely encountered "ideal type" of industrial research: fundamental scientific investigation leading quickly and directly to a practical product. Carothers's main personal contribution to the effort was the development of a theory of condensation-polymerization and a systematic terminology to describe it. He also helped introduce the use of the molecular still as a means of building extremely heavy "superpolymer" molecules.

In fifty-one scientific papers and fifty-two patents between 1929 and 1937, Carothers outlined not only these results but also fundamental advances in the synthesis of an artificial rubber (neoprene) and in the synthesis of cyclic compounds. A tireless and uncomplaining worker, his few diversions—reading and listening to music—provided little escape from the pressures of his enormous productivity. In the end, body and mind lacked the resilience to sustain the pressures of achievement he had placed on himself. See Roger Adams, *Bibliographic Memoir of Wallace Hume Carothers* (1939).

GEORGE WISE

CARSON, Johnny (b. Corning, Iowa, Oct. 23, 1925), ENTERTAINER, after serving in the U.S. Navy Reserves in World War II, he graduated from the University of Nebraska in 1949. A year earlier he began his career in broadcasting with a job as a radio announcer at KFAB in Lincoln, Nebraska. He moved to WOW radio and WOW-TV in Omaha, and then in 1950 to KNXT in Los Angeles, California. There he also worked as a comedy writer for Red Skelton. He got his own TV show, *Carson's Cellar*, in 1951 and became master of ceremonies of *Earn Your Own Vacation* in 1954. The following year he starred in *The Johnny Carson Show* for CBS, and three years later, in 1958, he became the headliner of *Who Do You Trust?* on ABC.

In 1962, Carson took over as host of *The Tonight Show* on NBC, the leading late-night entertainment and celebrity slot on television, and kept it at the top of the ratings for thirty years before retiring in 1992. He continues to appear as a highly paid nightclub performer, generally in Las Vegas, and is president of Carson Productions.

———

Mort Sahl, the comedian, called Johnny Carson "an anesthetist. He's Prince Valium." But if Sahl was bored, most of the rest of America wasn't. As the host of *The Tonight Show* he became almost an extra member of millions of American families. Sleepy-eyed viewers forced themselves to stay up to at least hear Johnny's monologue. As he put it, Johnny was "giving a party," and everyone was invited.

He became king of the night in a way that would have made even Count Dracula jealous, earning as much as 17 percent of NBC's total revenues and exerting a powerful influence on the careers of performers and writers. A book touted by Carson stood a good chance of being a bestseller; a performer with a gig coming up could always heat up the box office by an appearance with Johnny.

Carson didn't invent late-night television, he didn't even create *The Tonight Show*. It was created in 1954 as a vehicle for comedian Steve Allen. Allen was host until 1957 and was replaced by Jack Paar, who retired from the show in 1962. But if Carson didn't invent the genre he institutionalized it and made it into an American phenonemon.

In the early days the show went on the air at 11:15, but most NBC affiliates didn't pick it up until 11:30. They were thus missing Johnny's monologue, and he was miffed. His strategy, defying the network, was to develop each night a "fifteen-minute virus" and not make his entrance until 11:30, letting his announcer and sidekick Ed McMahon and the band hold forth until then. NBC finally relented and changed the starting time.

Carson always had late-night competition, but he outlasted and outperformed them all. He could always get the big stars. When he was with regulars or felt comfortable with guests, he would trade ad-libs. For the rest, the show was almost always carefully scripted. McMahon would set Carson up for a joke penned by one of the show's many writers, or Johnny would do the same for a guest. A classic example was when Senator **Barry Goldwater** appeared in 1966. Carson intentionally stumbled over a line, then turned to the ex-presidential candidate, saying, "Did that ever happen to you? When you just can't get out what you mean?" Goldwater replied on cue, "Yes, for three and a half months two years ago." Scripted or not, America loved it. Carson's ratings were always high, and his salary grew and his work schedule shrank as the years went by. When he retired from the show, many Americans felt they had lost a member of their family. See Lawrence Leamer, *King of the Night* (1989).

ROY SORRELS

CARSON, Rachel Louise (b. Springdale, Pa., May 27, 1907; d. Silver Spring, Md., Apr. 14, 1964), MARINE BIOLOGIST, REFORMER, graduated from the Pennsylvania College for Women in 1929 and then did graduate work in biology at Johns Hopkins University (MA, 1932). She taught zoology at the University of Maryland from 1931 to 1936, spending summers at the Marine Biological Laboratory in Woods Hole, Massachusetts. In 1936, Carson took a civil service job as aquatic biologist with the U.S. Bureau of Fisheries in Washington, D.C., which became the U.S. Fish and Wildlife Service when it was reorganized with the Department of Interior in 1940.

Carson wrote her first article on the sea in 1937 for *Atlantic Monthly* magazine, and this work was later expanded into a book, *Under the Sea Wind* (1941), which described ocean life in layman's terms. She was editor in chief of the Fish and Wildlife Service's publications (1947–52), and her second book, *The Sea Around Us* (1951), won the 1951 National Book Award for nonfiction. Carson won a Guggenheim fellowship for study in marine biology in 1951–52, and in 1952 she resigned her government job to devote more time to writing. After finishing *The Edge of the Sea* (1955), describing the shoreline of the eastern U.S. and its life, Carson turned to the problem of the increasing use of pesticides. After more than four years of research she published *Silent Spring* (1962), which attacked the indiscriminate use of poisonous chemicals to kill insects. The book sparked a controversy over the use of pesticides. President John F. Kennedy set up a commission to study the problem in 1963; the commission's report substantially supported Carson's position. She testified before a Senate committee on commerce examining the pesticide issue, and after her death in 1964 several regulations were passed requiring stricter labeling of ingredients and other pesticide controls. Her *Sense of Wonder,* originally written in 1956, was published posthumously (1965).

The beginning of the "Age of Ecology" can be traced to the publication of Rachel Carson's book *Silent Spring* in 1962. Before that event, concern for the environment was confined to small, ill-coordinated groups interested in soil, forest, and water management, wilderness preservation, and the protection of certain birds, fish, and mammals. Environmental hazards to man himself were generally thought to have ended with the abatement of the great 19th-century water-borne epidemics.

Rachel Carson jolted America (and much of the world) into reality. It must be said that she was a reluctant crusader. She enjoyed a comfortable income from her best-selling books about the sea. She disliked controversy and notoriety. Exploring the natural world with a few close friends and translating that experience into a resonant yet precise prose were all the joy and excitement she asked from life. Being a scientist does not necessarily alert one to the degradation of the world's environment; many of Carson's colleagues in and out of government missed the signals or chose to ignore them. But her scientific training reinforced her reverence for life, giving her the sort of "ecological conscience" that drove her to speak out against mankind's senseless rush to deprive the world of its loveliness and diversity.

Through her reading and observation it became clear to her that long-lasting chemical pesticides, including DDT, had already caused immense destruction among many kinds of living things. Their impact on man remained cloudy, but the evidence was disturbing enough to suggest that residues of certain pesticides carried by every human being in his tissues might bring about irreversible physiological changes.

Rachel Carson did not call for the abandonment of all chemical pesticides. She did ask that the more insidious compounds be banned and that wise, discriminate use be made of the others. So profound was her investigation into the threatened roots of life and so eloquent her voice that her message carried beyond the specific problem of pesticide use. "There is no question," a government expert on natural resources said following her death, "that *Silent Spring* prompted the federal government to take action against water and air pollution—as well as against persistent pesticides—several years before it otherwise might have moved." She had alerted a whole nation to the environmental perils caused by a runaway technology. See Frank Graham, Jr., *Since Silent Spring* (1970).

FRANK GRAHAM, JR.

CARTER, James Earl (Jimmy) (b. Plains, Ga., Oct. 1, 1924) PRESIDENT, attended Georgia Southwestern University (1941–42) and Georgia Institute of Technology (1942–43) before entering the U.S. Naval Academy. Graduating in 1946, he served for the next seven years aboard battleships and submarines, including a stint in 1951 in the nuclear submarine program under Admiral **Hyman G. Rickover**. In 1953 he received an MA in nuclear physics from Union College. That same year, after rising to lieutenant commander, he resigned from the navy upon the death of his father to join the family peanut farm and warehouse business in Plains.

Entering politics as a Democrat, Carter was elected to the Georgia state senate (1963–66). In 1966 he ran in the Democratic gubernatorial primary but lost. In 1970, however, he won the Democratic nomination and general election. In 1974, after one term as governor, he announced his intention to seek the presidency and presented his ideas in *Why Not the Best?* (1975). Though relatively unknown outside his native state and with little support from the party professionals, Carter captured the Democratic nomination and narrowly defeated the incumbent Republican President Gerald R. Ford in 1976.

Carter confronted multiple economic problems upon taking office, including inflation and a growing trade deficit linked to large increases in oil prices by OPEC. He instituted gasoline price controls in 1977 and two years later proposed a national energy policy stressing conservation and the use of alternative fuels. Carter's other domestic initiatives included the Airline Deregulation Act (1978) and major structural changes in the cabinet. He divided the existing Department of Health, Education and Welfare into the Department of Health and Human Services and the Department of Education, and created a Department of Energy.

In foreign affairs the Carter administration stressed détente with the Soviet Union and human rights, using moral suasion, arms embargoes, and diplomatic pressure to force nations into compliance with Western human rights standards. He withdrew support from Nicaraguan dictator Anastasio Somoza, who was soon overthrown by Sandanista rebels in July 1979. That same year formal diplomatic ties were renewed with China, and Carter signed the SALT II treaty with the Soviet Union, limiting strategic arms, although the Senate later refused to ratify it. Earlier, in 1978, fifteen nations, including the United States and the Soviet Union, signed a treaty designed to halt the proliferation of nuclear weapons. Against formidable opposition his administration won Senate ratification for a treaty handing over control of the Panama Canal to Panama, effective in the year 2000. The high point of Carter's foreign policy initiatives, however, was his success in brokering the Camp David Accords between Israel and Egypt (1978).

The latter part of Carter's presidency was rocked by two major foreign policy crises. First, after the shah of Iran was deposed by Islamic fundamentalists (Jan. 1979), militants stormed the American embassy in Tehran in November, took sixty-six hostages, and demanded the return of the shah from exile in the United States, where he had been given sanctuary to undergo treatment for cancer. The administration refused their demands. Although some hostages were released, fifty-two were held for over a year. A botched rescue attempt by the military in April 1980 severely damaged Carter's already plummeting popularity, and although a deal was eventually reached with Iran whereby the hostages were to be traded for some Iranian assets frozen in the United States, their release did not come until minutes after the end of Carter's presidency.

Carter's second crisis arose when Soviet troops invaded Afghanistan in December 1980. Voicing astonishment over the Soviet action—which to some critics demonstrated his naïveté in foreign affairs—Carter ordered an embargo on high technology and grain sales to the Soviet

Union and organized a boycott of the 1980 Olympic Games in Moscow by nations aligned with the United States.

After winning a bruising battle with Senator Edward Kennedy for renomination, Carter lost in a landslide to Ronald Reagan in the 1980 election. Out of office Carter has kept active in charity work, lecturing, mediating international disputes, writing, and running the Carter Center at Emory University in Atlanta, Georgia. Among his publications are his memoirs, *Keeping Faith: Memoirs of a President* (1982), and *The Blood of Abraham* (1985), a book on the Middle East.

Jimmy Carter ran a very successful two-year campaign for the presidency and emerged as the Democratic nominee in 1976 because he understood the politics of running in state primary elections better than his rivals and was the sole moderate in a field of liberal competitors. He also presented himself as honest and truthful in the wake of the Watergate scandal, repeatedly promising Americans that he would not "lie to them." However, he was more effective as a candidate in the primaries than he was in the general election, which he barely won. This was because Carter was not receptive to the demands of Democratic liberal factions and interest groups for a resumption of a period of Democratic reform. These tensions later became a problem for his presidency in his relations with Congress. Carter identified a number of programmatic reforms that he wanted to initiate: an energy conservation program, welfare reform, and tax reform. And he was cautious in regard to expensive programs such as national health insurance. He did finally succeed in passing a comprehensive energy program, but much of it was dismantled during the Reagan years. The tensions with the liberal wing of his party grew so strong that Senator Edward Kennedy challenged him for the nomination in 1980, thus sowing disunity in the Democratic Party.

But his achievements in foreign policy were considerable: the Panama Canal Treaties, the establishment of diplomatic relations with China, the successful negotiation of the Camp David

agreements with the leaders of Egypt and Israel, and the agreement with the U.S.S.R. on the SALT II arms reduction treaty. Carter's intelligence and mastery of substance permitted him to play to his strengths in foreign policy when the people to be persuaded were a handful of leaders of other nations.

Carter was the prisoner of an economy with simultaneous inflation and unemployment ("stagflation"), a difficult position for a Democratic president. The Keynesian economic theory of his advisers was not well suited for dealing with "stagflation" effectively, and the strength of inflation required more of a recession to cut high prices than a Democratic president could risk. The OPEC cartel's oil price increases of 1979 fed inflation and contributed strongly to his defeat by Reagan, especially when the Iranian hostage crisis and the Soviet invasion of Afghanistan are considered. However, President Bill Clinton was the legatee of Carter's effort to take the Democratic Party to the center of the political spectrum.

Carter was a highly intelligent president who used his knowledge of policy as an instrument of persuasion, but he lacked the intuitive skills of a good politician and his relations with Congress thus suffered. He sent too many proposals to Congress in his first year without making his priorities clear and did not seem to understand the need to husband and conserve his limited political resources. After that first year, relations with Congress were better because the Carter White House, which was not staffed with experienced Washington hands, put together an effective machine for working with the Democratic leadership and members of Congress. But the mistakes of the first year diminished the president's reputation with the media and the public, and he never recovered. The Washington media never really liked Carter, perhaps because his moral earnestness and seeming apolitical style did not match the expectations of journalists about what a politically skillful president should be like. The negative opinions of Washington "insiders" eventually shaped public perceptions. The fact that Carter was not particularly good in molding public opinion added to his woes. His effective campaigning in 1976 had been based on personal rather than policy appeals. He separated campaigning and governing to his own detriment, and he was too much the engineer in government. His great policy achievements were the result of his own efforts, and by the same token, in his dramatic failures, especially the hostage crisis with Iran, he stood alone. He was not a skillful builder of coalitions, but there may have been few coalitions to build in such a period of fragmented parties and splintered and voracious demands on government.

Carter has been one of the most respected ex-presidents in American history because of his work at the Carter Center and his personal contribution of time and effort to charitable enterprises. He has also played a valuable role in international affairs as a negotiator and mediator of disputes. Once out of office, few ex-presidents have demonstrated their intelligence and moral passion in ways as visible and dramatic as the man from Plains. See Erwin C. Hargrove, *Jimmy Carter as President* (1989).

ERWIN C. HARGROVE

CARVER, George Washington (b. near Diamond Grove, Mo., July 12, 1861; d. Tuskegee, Ala., Jan. 5, 1943), SCIENTIST, born of slave parents, graduated from Iowa State College of Agriculture and Mechanical Arts with a BS in agriculture (1894). He then became a member of the faculty and was placed in charge of the greenhouse and bacterial lab working in systematic botany. After obtaining his MS degree in 1896, he was appointed head of the agricultural department and director of agricultural research at Tuskegee Institute in Alabama, positions that he held for the rest of his life.

Carver sought to enable poor southern farmers, especially blacks, to make a better living from the soil. He stressed soil improvement and crop diversification, and did pioneering work in the production of useful synthetic materials from common farm crops and waste materials. When the boll weevil attacked southern cotton and thus devastated the South's one-crop economy, he urged the planting of soil-enriching peanuts and sweet potatoes, from which he was able to develop more than four hundred synthetic materials, including dyes, soap, cheese, and a milk substitute. He also produced synthetic marble from wood shavings, fertilizers from swamp muck and leaves, and other materials from pecans, cowpeas, and wild plums. He developed the so-called Carver's Hybrid, a variety of cotton that yielded fat bolls on stems long enough to provide protection against rain-splashed soil. In 1935 he was made collaborator in the Department of Agriculture's Bureau of Plant Industry, Division of Mycology and Disease Survey. Throughout his career he refused to take financial advantage of his discoveries, despite lucrative offers, and in 1940 he contributed his life's savings to the establishment of the George Washington Carver Foundation for the perpetuation and extension of his research work. He was the recipient of numerous medals and awards, and the plantation on which he was born was declared a national monument in 1953.

⎯⎯⎯⎯∞⎯⎯⎯⎯

Carver's poverty-stricken rural background nourished self-reliance; but it is not so clear what drove him to acquire higher education or what led him to abandon a good position and devote himself altruistically to the improvement of the southern farmers' life and work. In part it may have been a deep religious faith, which imbued his life with humanitarian concern and a sense of purpose and destiny; in part the desire to show others how they, too, could surmount the obstacles he had overcome. His early years did impose a permanent lifestyle: Carver lived in simple, solitary fashion, a plain and modest man. To him such material "necessities" of life as clothing and money were unimportant; what mattered was that his work was provided for. Warm, open, accessible, and well loved, Carver above all dreaded hurting other people; consequently, he evinced his convictions and principles through accommodation rather than belligerence, using his sense of humor to good advantage.

Two traits, frugality and love of nature, strongly shaped the character of his scientific contributions. A youthful fascination with nature developed a keen ability to "see" where others only "looked." His research discoveries reflect that attentiveness to the unobserved within the familiar; they result from a methodology that stressed observation before experiment. Carver's abhorrence of waste, the legacy of early poverty, found expression in his uncanny ability to find overlooked practical and economical uses in common objects. His success depended on this in large part, for it meant that his discoveries could be convincingly demonstrated, their benefits readily appreciated by the uneducated farmers they were designed to aid.

By releasing the potential for progress already present in the environment, Carver's contributions revolutionized southern life. Through example and instruction, including an innovative school on wheels, teaching crop rotation, waste utilization, and the benefits of new crops, he relieved southern agriculture of its one-crop dependency, improved diet and nutrition, and raised poor farmers' hopes and achievements. The overall impact of his work is immeasurable because it caused lasting improvement in the quality of life for millions, an achievement for which Carver well deserves his fame. See Lawrence Elliott, *George Washington Carver: The Man Who Overcame* (1966).

DONALD DE B. BEAVER

CASH, Wilbur Joseph (b. Gaffney, S.C., May 2, 1901; d. Mexico City, Mex., July 1, 1941), WRITER, EDITOR, worked in a variety of shipyards and army posts from Maryland to Florida (1917–18) before studying at Wofford College, South Carolina (1918), and at Valparaiso University (1919). In 1920 he entered Wake Forest College and received his BA in 1922. After a short stint at the Wake Forest Law School (1922–23) he became an instructor of English at Georgetown College in Kentucky (1923–24) and then taught at the Hendersonville School for Boys in North Carolina (1924–25). He worked briefly as a reporter for the Chicago *Post* (1925) and then at the Charlotte (N.C.) *News*, as reporter, assistant to

the editor, and state news editor (1926–27). After a tour of Europe in 1927, Cash became editor of the semiweekly Cleveland *Press* in Shelby, North Carolina (1928). In 1929 he began a career as a freelance writer and journalist. During 1929–37 he had a number of articles accepted by **H. L. Mencken**'s *American Mercury,* including a "Close View of a Calvinist Lhasa" (1933), regarding life in Charlotte, "Buck Duke's University" (1933), and "The Genesis of the Southern Cracker" (1935). In the fall of 1937, however, his freelancing not having produced a satisfactory income, Cash became an editorial writer for the Charlotte *News* (1937–41) where he specialized in international affairs. In 1941, after more than a decade of intermittent work, he published his magnum opus, *The Mind of the South.* In the spring of that year, while living in Mexico City on a Guggenheim fellowship, Cash, expressing concern that "Nazi killers" were following him, committed suicide.

※

Cash's fame rests on a single book, *The Mind of the South,* which emphasizes the unity and continuity of southern thought from its colonial origins through the 19th and into the 20th century. To Cash the typical southerner was proud, brave, individualistic, courteous, honorable, generous, and loyal; but he was also swift to act, violent, intolerant, romantic, narrow in his concept of social responsibility, sentimental, attached to false values, especially racial values, and too likely "to justify cruelty and injustice in the name of those values." Though Cash concentrated on white southerners, a perceptive black writer has pointed out that black southerners were "directly influenced" by many of the forces Cash "so excellently outlined." *The Mind of the South*—often praised as "provocative," "brilliant," and "magisterial"—has become increasingly influential since its publication. No serious attack on the book occurred until 1969 when C. Vann Woodward of Yale charged that Cash—who had tried to write "an unbiased history of the South from the hillbilly point of view"—had ignored evidence that refuted his thesis, failed to recognize the existence of a genuine southern aristocracy, neglected blacks and the significance of slavery, and overemphasized the plain folk and the Piedmont. Woodward contended that Cash's "consensus" thesis of unity and continuity was wrong historically. This view was challenged, however, by Professor **David Herbert Donald.** "In basic matters the South is, and always has been, unchanging," insisted Donald. This scholarly disagreement, which one contemporary reviewer predicted Cash's book would excite, seems likely to continue. See C. Vann Woodward, "W. J. Cash Reconsidered," *New York Review of Books*, XIII, 10 (Dec. 4, 1969), 28–34, and Joseph L. Morrison, *W. J. Cash: Southern Prophet* (1967).

GRADY MCWHINEY

CASS, Lewis (b. Exeter, N.H., Oct. 9, 1782; d. Detroit, Mich., June 17, 1866), POLITICAL LEADER, attended Exeter Academy and taught school for a year before moving in 1801 to the Northwest Territory where he became a lawyer. He was elected prosecuting attorney in 1804 and to the Ohio legislature in 1806, where he was a strong supporter of the policies of Thomas Jefferson. As a colonel in the War of 1812, Cass was serving under General William Hull when Detroit was surrendered on August 16, 1812, and later figured in the victories of General William Henry Harrison, notably over the combined British and Native American forces in the battle of the Thames on October 5, 1813. He left the army with the rank of brigadier general to begin an eighteen-year (1813–31) service as governor of the Michigan Territory. He energetically pushed locally supported improvement projects and negotiated treaties with the Native Americans. As President Andrew Jackson's secretary of war (1831–36) he prosecuted the Black Hawk War of 1832, and then in defiance of a Supreme Court decision upholding treaties with the Cherokees, he implemented Jackson's decision to remove the Cherokees and the other southern tribes west of the Mississippi River.

As minister to France (1836–42), Cass, who was strongly anti-British, complicated the work of Secretary of State **Daniel Webster** who sought to improve relations with England. When Cass denounced a proposed five-power treaty permitting the visiting and searching of suspected slave vessels on the high seas, Webster forced his resignation. Elected to the Senate in 1845, Cass energetically supported the expansionist policies of President James Polk in Oregon, Texas, and Mexico. In 1848 he resigned from the upper house to run for president on the Democratic ticket but lost when a large number of Democratic voters in New York and Pennsylvania defected to the Whig Zachary Taylor. Reelected to the Senate (1849–57), Cass, a strong nationalist, supported the Compromise of 1850. He had in 1847 set forth in the Nicholson Letter his support of the right of the people in a territory to decide whether it should be admitted as a free or slave state. It was the first formulation of the doctrine of "popular sovereignty" in response to the Wilmot Proviso. When **Stephen A. Douglas** introduced the Kansas-Nebraska Act of 1854 to revoke the Missouri Compromise and implement "popular sovereignty," Cass gave his support, believing that slavery would never be adopted. Appointed secretary of state in James Buchanan's cabinet, Cass drifted steadily in the direction of Douglas's position in opposition to a pro-slavery constitution for Kansas and resigned in protest against Buchanan's failure in 1860 to reinforce the Charleston forts after the secession of South Carolina. Convinced that the Democratic Party was irretrievably shattered and Lincoln's election inevitable, Cass withdrew from politics but thereafter supported the Union war effort.

Cass was a typical Jacksonian. Aggressive and convinced that it was America's manifest destiny to rule most of the North American continent and to be dominant in the Western Hemisphere, he consistently supported expansionism. All obstacles to expansion were automatically designated enemy. His anti-British sentiments were rooted in his desire to annex Canada. He dismissed the Native Americans as an impediment to be removed by whatever methods necessary. As

Jackson's secretary of war he was in large measure responsible for the infamous Trail of Tears along which thousands of southern Native Americans were forced to march in the mid–1830s. Like numerous other northern politicians he was concerned that the slavery issue might disrupt the Union. When faced with the **Wilmot** Proviso's call for federal action to close the territories to slavery, he countered the measure with his popular sovereignty doctrine. It left the decision on the admission or rejection of slavery to the residents on the spot. Left with such an option, he believed, no territory would accept slavery. It was his conviction that popular sovereignty would result in the prevalence of free soil but without unnecessarily offending southern feelings. His doctrine was seized upon by Stephen Douglas during the debate over the Compromise of 1850, and Cass was frequently consulted as the final Compromise was hammered out. In 1852, Cass, still hankering after the presidency, came forth as a supporter of the Compromise.

His service in the Buchanan cabinet was typified by his effort to conciliate the deepening antagonisms between the North and the South. Chosen as a compromise candidate for the State Department, he found it more and more difficult to support Buchanan's seeming concessions to the South. His support of Douglas increased as he realized that northern Democrats could not abandon popular sovereignty if they were to maintain themselves against the Republican support of Free Soil. Ironically, it was the Charleston *Mercury* that in 1848 had defined the logic of Cass's doctrine. "He says to the South, you are right," the *Mercury* argued; "such a restriction as is proposed by Mr. Wilmot is unconstitutional, and cannot be adopted. He says to the North, why raise any unnecessary disturbances! When we get new territory it will be free—slavery will have no existence there—it will be impossible to give it being. The end you have in view will certainly be accomplished, and you can afford to give up the triumph of the argument on principle if you are made certain of the triumph in your application of it to new territory." Once the chances for compromise had ended, Cass adopted a Jacksonian stance: the Union had to be preserved. He lived long enough to see it restored. See Frank B. Woodford, *Lewis Cass: The Last Jeffersonian* (1950).

JAMES P. SHENTON

CASSATT, Mary Stevenson (b. Allegheny City, Pa., May 22, 1845; d. Mesnil-Théribus, France, June 14, 1926), ARTIST, was born into a wealthy family. She studied painting at the Pennsylvania Academy of Fine Arts in Philadelphia (1861–65), then went to Europe for further training in 1868. In Parma, Italy, she studied the works of Correggio, and she later studied the works of Velázquez in Spain. She settled permanently in Paris in 1874 and became friendly with Edgar Degas, the renowned French Impressionist. Though much influenced by Degas, Manet, and other Impressionists, she worked out her own personal mode. Cassatt often chose the theme of motherhood and created intimate scenes of mothers and babies amid quiet surroundings. She also painted many pictures of beautiful and interesting women, such as *The Morning Toilet* (1886, National Gallery of Art). Cassatt exhibited with the Impressionists in 1879, 1880, 1881, and 1886. She gave her first independent exhibition in 1891 and in 1893 gave a larger exhibition in the Gallery of Durand-Ruel in Paris. In 1890 she produced a series of colored etchings influenced by a Japanese exhibition in Paris.

Cassatt enjoyed enormous prestige in France; although she was commissioned to do a mural for the Woman's Building in the Chicago Exposition of 1893, she was not as appreciated in the United States as in Europe. Increasingly bad eyesight and declining health caused her to limit her later work, and after 1914 she stopped painting. Some of her most notable canvases include *The Lady at the Tea Table* (1885, Metropolitan Museum, N.Y.) and *Woman Sewing* (1886, Louvre, Paris).

Mary Cassatt is significant not only for having been one of the three or four finest American artists of her day but also for having been America's greatest woman painter. In addition, she exercised a profound influence on collecting in America and more than any other person was responsible for the popularity of French Impressionist paintings in this country. She not only advised the Havemeyer family but also the Whittemores, Mrs. J. Montgomery Sears, and other important collectors.

Once she had completed her studies at the Pennsylvania Academy, she insisted on going to Europe, believing that any artist who wished to succeed must make a long and exhaustive study of European masters. In Paris in the early seventies she came to full maturity in the stimulating environment of the French Impressionists, who gave her encouragement and invited her to participate in their exhibitions.

In the seventies Cassatt used a light-keyed palette and a painterly approach that may be said to be truly Impressionist in style, but in the eighties she developed a more solid method of painting. After 1890, when she was greatly influenced by Japanese prints, a strong linear element entered her work, and she compressed space and altered perspective in order to emphasize design.

She was a superb draftsman, which is especially apparent in her drypoints and color aquatints. She made an intense study of French 18th-century *pastellistes*, and her own contribution in this medium is highly distinguished. Mary Cassatt was a truly individual artist and one who held to the highest standards. Taking no pupils, seldom accepting commissions, she was never in a position of having to compromise. Her work has integrity and honesty totally free of sentimentality. See Frederick A. Sweet, *Miss Mary Cassatt, Impressionist from Pennsylvania* (1966).

FREDERICK A. SWEET

CATHER, Willa Sibert (b. Winchester, Va., Dec. 7, 1873; d. New York, N.Y., Apr. 24, 1947), WRITER, graduated from the University of Nebraska in 1895. After working for a Pittsburgh magazine, the *Home Monthly* (1896–97), she spent three years on the Pittsburgh *Daily Leader* as

assistant telegraph editor and music and drama critic. In 1901, following a period of freelancing, she left journalism to teach Latin and then English in Pittsburgh high schools. Writing in her spare time, she published a book of poems, *April Twilights* (1903), and a collection of stories, *The Troll Garden* (1905). She moved to New York City in 1906 to become a contributing and then managing editor of *McClure's* magazine; she resigned from active editorship in late 1911 after finishing her first novel, *Alexander's Bridge* (1912). Her second novel, *O Pioneers!* (1913), was followed by *The Song of the Lark* (1915) and *My Antonia* (1918). She won a Pulitzer Prize for *One of Ours* (1922), a war novel. Her short novel *A Lost Lady* (1923) continued her use of Midwest settings.

Later in the 1920s, however, Cather made major use of the Southwest for background (foreshadowed in *The Song of the Lark,* 1915) in *The Professor's House* (1925) and most significantly in *Death Comes for the Archbishop* (1927), a historical re-creation of the life of Archbishop Lamy and his vicar in 19th-century New Mexico. Her next work was *Shadows on the Rock* (1931), a story of 17th-century Quebec. Her last novel, *Sapphira and the Slave Girl* (1940), described the Virginia of her ancestors and childhood. Other works include a rather bitter short novel, *My Mortal Enemy* (1926), *Lucy Gayheart* (1935), a collection of stories, *Youth and the Bright Medusa* (1920), and a volume of essays, *Not Under Forty* (1936).

Willa Cather's reputation, which is still growing, rests on meticulous craftsmanship and a skillful blending of realism and romance, of the particular and the universal. Her evocative use of Nebraska roots her work deeply in specific time and place, and her subtle employment of myth and symbol gives her fiction an appeal transcending chronological and geographical limits. Her skill derives from a long apprenticeship that included forty-three published stories, many of which tried out themes and subjects later perfected, before she attempted the novel form.

Later, however, she regarded her first novel as

a false start because its materials were contemporary, urban, and cosmopolitan, and its technique Jamesian. She came to believe that a writer's materials had to tease "the mind over and over for years" before being set to paper. Thus with *O Pioneers!* she "hit the home pasture," creating Alexandra Bergson, a Swedish immigrant in Nebraska who combines Cather's two major topics: the pioneer character and the westering movement. *My Antonia,* Cather's later masterpiece, portrays a Bohemian immigrant (also an earth-mother figure) against the wild land being tamed. Based on a real friend of her youth, this novel embodies all of Cather's affirmative feelings about the immigrants and is a drama of nostalgic memory created from materials well aged before being used. Another Cather conviction was that artists must sacrifice everything to art. This view is rendered dramatically in *The Song of the Lark,* which combines Cather's own western youth with the career of a Wagnerian soprano (Olive Fremstad).

During the 1920s Cather shared the disillusionment of the "lost generation." Her important *nouvelle, A Lost Lady,* besides creating a rounded portrait of Marian Forrester (an Emma Bovary of the prairie), mourns the passing of the pioneer days and indicts encroaching materialism and the coming of the exploiters. It also works out Cather's theories of the "novel *demeublé,*" the unfurnished novel, in which all superfluous description and action are carefully pared away, leaving a work of art brief but richly suggestive. *The Professor's House,* Cather's most autobiographical novel, further reflects its author's disenchantment. It also continues her longtime experimentation with the novel form by inserting within the story the self-contained "Tom Outland's Story." This tale foreshadows Cather's brilliant use of historical materials in *Death Comes for the Archbishop,* a novel that achieves the effect of a series of frescoes. It also signals Cather's retreat into the past, a withdrawal from contemporary life that continued during the rest of her career. See James Woodress, *Willa Cather: Her Life and Art* (1970).

JAMES WOODRESS

CATLIN, George (b. Wilkes-Barre, Pa., July 26, 1796; d. Jersey City, N.J., Dec. 23, 1872), ARTIST, grew up on a farm where he developed an interest in frontier life and Native Americans. After receiving an informal education he studied law at Tapping Reeves's well-known academy in Litchfield, Connecticut (1817–18). He then practiced law in Luzerne County, Pennsylvania, but spent much of his spare time painting. In 1823 he moved to Philadelphia and then to Washington (1824–29), devoting himself to portrait painting. In 1828, Catlin painted three portraits of Governor **DeWitt Clinton** of New York. Later he was commissioned to do a composite picture of the Virginia Constitutional Convention of 1829–30 in Richmond. Unsatisfied with this mode of painting, Catlin decided to depict Native Americans. He spent the next years (1832–37) living with and sketching the Great Plains Native Americans during the summer months and then finishing his pictures in oils during the winter. Catlin painted six hundred portraits of Native Americans, carefully recording their costumes and culture. Although often poor in anatomy and artistic quality, Catlin's portraits were highly realistic and powerfully projected Native American life.

From 1837 to 1852, Catlin exhibited his collection of paintings, examples of Native American crafts, and live Native Americans in the United States, England, France, and Holland. He also wrote many books describing his travels and experiences, including *Letters and Notes on the Manners, Customs, and Conditions of the North American Indians* (1841). After he lost his collection through an unsuccessful business venture in 1852, Catlin spent his later years making several trips to South and Central America, sketching the natives there. The bulk of his collection can be seen in the Smithsonian Institution, Washington, D.C. Some of his other writings include *Life Among the Indians* (1867) and *Last Rambles Amongst the Indians of the Rocky Mountains and the Andes* (1867).

George Catlin was one of a group of artists who, after 1830, made the national experience of the frontier their major theme. Catlin's career was, in particular, the singleminded expression of a profound enthusiasm for nature. The grandeur and tranquility of the American wilderness uncorrupted by man beyond the western frontier, which once seemed hostile and savage, became his inspiration. He had painted vigorous but rather harsh portraits in eastern cities before he caught his first sight of Native Americans passing through Philadelphia on their way to the capital. The "silent and stoic dignity of these lords of the forest" who "strutted about the city … equipped in all their classic beauty with shield and helmet, tunic and manteau—tinted and tasseled off exactly for the painter's palette," made a deep impression on him. He hastened westward to record the still-untrammeled aboriginal life of these Native Americans. The embellished face and picturesque costume of these exotic inhabitants of the New World captured international curiosity, and Catlin set out to become their "historian."

Catlin's first Native American portraits and many of his best scenes of buffalo hunts, Native American dances, and ceremonies were executed during the summer of 1832, a feverish period of activity among the tribes of the upper Missouri. On trips to southwestern Oklahoma in 1834 and to the upper Mississippi in 1835 and 1836, he added substantially to what was to become his famous Indian Gallery. The staccato quality in these works reveals his extraordinary ability to catch a likeness, to grasp the dramatic essence of his subjects, to capture a freshness and vitality of on-the-spot observation in spite of his naïve understanding of perspective and limited ability in drawing the human body. His hundreds of drawings and paintings glorified the Native American, yet seldom at the cost of truth.

Catlin pursued his mission with a grave sense of its importance. The depicter of Native Americans, painting beyond the frontier, felt impelled to work as speedily as possible: having done the face, he would dash in outlines of the figure and details of dress and ornament that he might want to include later in long strokes of paint and pencil. Under these circumstances his art was improvisation; his Native American portraits and genre scenes with all their crudities and unevenness were an achievement of great originality and power. These Native American likenesses, minutely drawn landscapes, and primitive genre scenes excited his contemporaries; in the two decades that followed Catlin's pioneering there was scarcely a village or natural wonder of the West not pictured in one medium or another. Catlin's convincing, strange, exotic renditions were part of a larger impetus in 19th-century American painting to understand and record the vast spectacle of the empire's westward course. See Mary S. Haverstock, *Indian Gallery: The Story of George Catlin* (1973).

WENDELL D. GARRETT

CATT, Carrie Lane Chapman (b. Ripon, Wis., Jan. 9, 1859; d. New Rochelle, N.Y., Mar. 9, 1947), REFORMER, received a BS in 1880 from Iowa State College. From 1881 to 1885 she worked in the school system of Mason City, Iowa, first as principal of the high school (1881–83) and then as superintendent of schools. In 1885 she became coeditor of the Mason City *Republican*. When her husband, Leo Chapman, died in 1886, she moved to San Francisco where she worked as a reporter. In 1887 she returned to Iowa and began a career as a public lecturer. She married George W. Catt in 1890. She soon became involved in the movement for woman suffrage, serving as state organizer and lecturer for the Iowa Woman's Suffrage Association (1890–92). In 1892 she became an organizer of and lecturer for the National American Woman Suffrage Association, then served as its president (1900–4). She resigned that post to assume the presidency (1904–23) of the International Woman Suffrage Alliance, in which capacity she made numerous trips to Europe and a world tour (1911–12). In 1915 she became chairwoman of the Empire State Campaign Committee for woman suffrage in New York and was persuaded to resume the presidency of the American Woman Suffrage Association to lead the fight for ratification of the Nineteenth Amendment. After World War I she helped organize the National League of Women Voters, served as president of Women Citizen Corporation, the publishers of *Women Citizen* magazine, and founded the Committee on the Causes and Cures of War. She was a leading figure at such conferences as the Pan American Women's Conference held in Baltimore in 1922. During the 1930s she worked to aid refugees from Germany and sought to secure U.S. membership in the World Court.

———∞∞∞———

Carrie Lane Chapman Catt, the best organizer woman suffrage ever had, was, with **Elizabeth Cady Stanton** and **Susan B. Anthony,** one of its three greatest leaders. They were chiefly writers, speakers, exhorters; Catt was a master builder who reached the apex of her powers just when they were most needed. She was notable for her ability to subordinate sentiment—and sometimes even principle, her enemies thought—to necessity. She helped found the Woman's Peace Party in 1914 but stayed in the background thereafter so as not to compromise woman suffrage with pacifism. When embarrassed by militant suffragists who picketed the White House in 1917, she did not hesitate to disown them. On taking charge of the NAWSA, Catt immediately replaced the old board with women she could trust to advance her policies. They were mostly rich (though she was egalitarian), for only independent women could work for the movement full-time. Catt opposed racism, but she allowed NAWSA members, especially in the South, to discriminate against blacks; to do otherwise would divide suffragists. She could be sharp and witty, but rarely was in public because such traits did more harm than good. Her grip on reality never faltered. After women got the vote, many were disappointed that equal suffrage did not bring the millennium. Catt never thought it would and proceeded to put her great talents and abundant energy to the service of those interests she had wanted the franchise to advance.

Carrie Catt was not a distinguished writer and intellectual like Elizabeth Cady Stanton, or a powerful speaker like her predecessor Dr. Anna Howard Shaw. Nor did she win the reverence accorded Susan B. Anthony. But she was a supremely gifted politician. Some anti-male suffragists forgot that it would take the votes of men to gain the vote for women. Catt never did. She understood that President Woodrow Wilson would support equal suffrage, and Congress enact it, only if the issue was promoted so as to make the hope of political gain more compelling than the fear of lost face or lost votes. Everything she did was based on that knowledge.

She was not unfeeling or illiberal; quite the contrary. Many leading suffragists had no important desires beyond woman's rights. Catt cared about peace, the condition of immigrants, child welfare, and much else. But she believed that women could not help the powerless until they themselves had power; to gain it she sacrificed whatever stood in the way of enfranchisement, including her own warmest instincts. Critics called her "Boss Catt." Radicals wished that she had done more to change the system rather than only helping women better themselves within it. A few have thought that the whole suffragist emphasis on politics was misplaced, that what harmed women most was not their limited citizenship but rather their roles as wives and mothers, and that what they needed was not political reform but new marital and domestic institutions. These charges and arguments did not trouble Catt. She felt that the world was improved a step at a time, and she had a large part in helping America take one of those steps. She was a great politician and, equally important, a great person, too. In an age notable for its distinguished women Carrie Catt was second to none. See Mary Gray Peck, *Carrie Chapman Catt* (1944).

WILLIAM L. O'NEILL

CHANNING, William Ellery (b. Newport, R.I., Apr. 7, 1780; d. Bennington, Vt., Oct. 2, 1842), RELIGIOUS LEADER, graduated from Harvard College in 1798. After a year and a half tutoring in Richmond, Virginia, he returned to Harvard to study divinity. He was ordained a Congregational minister in 1803 and was installed as pastor of the Federal Street Church in

Boston, remaining there until his death.

The theological controversy that had long been smoldering within the Congregational Church broke out in the open during Channing's lifetime. Taking a liberal, or Arminian, position, Channing opposed Calvinist theology. In 1819 he preached an important sermon in Baltimore that established him as a leader of the Unitarian movement. This denomination (for such it became) emphasized human reason and the dignity of human nature. The supernatural element of Christianity was retained by Unitarians of Channing's day, but the traditional view of Christ as equal to the Father and part of a triune Godhead was denied. Channing organized the Berry Street Conference of liberal ministers in 1820, a precursor of the American Unitarian Association.

Channing's writing and preaching reflected wide interests. His *Remarks on National Literature* (1823) criticized American writers for imitating European modes and called for a truly native literature. Much of the latter part of his life Channing devoted to social reform. He was concerned with poverty, the condition of workers, and public education. He spoke out against American territorial aggrandizement and war. He also devoted considerable attention to the problems of slavery and race relations. His volume *Slavery* (1835) attacked the institution as ethically indefensible. Temperate in tone though it was, the statement came early enough to offend many conservative northerners.

───── ⟨⟩ ─────

Channing drew together two principal strains in Western thought—Protestantism and the Enlightenment. He exemplified a sincere Christian piety and faith in divine revelation; at the same time he was as much a believer in social progress, empirical inquiry, and man's potential greatness as Jefferson. In achieving this synthesis Channing was indebted to the Scottish "commonsense" philosophy of Thomas Reid. He did not possess a genuinely original mind, but he had undeniable integrity and addressed himself with clarity and open-mindedness to the issues

of his day. His graceful style helped make his sermons widely read in this country and abroad; he was universally acknowledged a man of the finest cultivation.

Channing held an image of the clergyman as intellectual and moral leader of the community. He regarded all his activities—religious, literary, and social—as part of a general effort to uplift mankind. His view of life was humanistic, predicated on human dignity and the careful cultivation of all aspects of human nature, especially the conscience. American Unitarianism, with which Channing will always be identified, has remained more important as a cultural and social influence than as a religious sect.

Channing's reformism was of the patrician type. He wanted men to acknowledge their moral duties but desired no essential transformation of society. Most of the abolitionists, like many popular revivalists, seemed to him tasteless, and he was unwilling for a time to be associated with them. Eventually, however, he concluded that he must take a stand against human bondage.

The Transcendentalists owed much to Channing's forthright rejection of the doctrine of original sin and his enthusiasm for belles lettres at a time when imaginative literature was often regarded as corrupting by American clerics. **Ralph Waldo Emerson** admired him but detected a lack of warmth; he called Channing "the nearest that mechanism could get to the flowering of genius." Later generations, too, have found in Channing, along with his many virtues, a somewhat remote and precious quality. See Madeleine Hooke Rice, *Federal Street Pastor* (1961).

DANIEL W. HOWE

CHAPIN, Charles Value (b. Providence, R.I., Jan. 17, 1856; d. Providence, R.I., Jan. 31, 1941), PUBLIC HEALTH OFFICER, graduated from Brown University (AB, 1876) and studied medicine in the office of Dr. George D. Wilcox, Providence (1876–77), at the College of Physicians and Surgeons in New York City (1877–78), and at the Bellevue Hospital Medical College (MD, 1879). Following a one-year tour as house physician at Bellevue (1879–80), he returned to Providence where for a few years he practiced medicine and did charity work for the Providence Dispensary. In 1884 he was appointed Providence's superintendent of health, serving until 1932. During his forty-eight-year tenure, Chapin developed and implemented many new sanitary practices, based on his belief that contact infection was more significant than air transmission in the spread of communicable diseases. Under his leadership, Providence in 1888 established the first municipal public health laboratory in the United States, conducted the first systematic tests of mechanical filtration of water (1889–93), and in 1910 built the first American infectious disease hospital to use aseptic nursing.

As Providence city registrar (1888–1932), Chapin collected the vital statistics that were essential to his studies of disease. His registration methods were widely emulated. Chapin was also active as a teacher, serving as instructor and professor of physiology at Brown (1882–95) and as a lecturer at Harvard Medical School (1909), Harvard-M.I.T. School for Health Officers (1913–22), and Harvard School of Public Health (1922–35). He directed an American Medical Association survey of state public health activities throughout the nation (1913–15), and during World War I he was a member of the council established by the National Red Cross War Council to advise on health needs and work in Europe. An active contributor to and officer of many national and local medical and public health organizations, he ultimately received numerous honors, including the Honor Medal of the National Academy of Sciences.

⁂

Chapin was the epitome both of the New England conscience and of the Progressive-era physician in seeking scientific solutions to the problems brought on by immigration, industrialization, and urbanization. He first of all provided American health officers with a much needed set of reliable principles and then with an administrative methodology. His most important scientific role was as a pioneer in applying the early discoveries of bacteriological research to the practical public health management of American cities. In this work he showed the fallacies of outdated theories of disease based on filth and proved that such time-honored practices as disinfection after infectious diseases were nothing but empty rituals. Simultaneously, he demonstrated that personal contact was the principal means by which the ordinary communicable diseases of American cities were transmitted. Chapin spread these and other doctrines of the "New Public Health" around the world by many writings but notably through his book *The Sources and Modes of Infection* (1910).

Personally modest and lacking in pretense, Chapin was an immensely creative and inspirational force in national public health circles. An efficient administrator, he became a model for 20th-century professional health officers. His great concern was to put public health work on a rational basis. Insisting that smells and dirt per se have little to do with health, he urged ridding health departments of garbage collection and nuisance abatement functions; officials then could concentrate on activities more directly connected with health. Chapin spent much of the latter part of his career delineating the priorities of public health work and evaluating American health departments quantitatively according to these priorities. See James H. Cassedy, *Charles V. Chapin and the Public Health Movement* (1962).

JAMES H. CASSEDY

CHAPLIN, Charles Spencer (b. London, Eng., Apr. 16, 1889; d. Corsier-sur-Vevey, Switzerland, Dec. 25, 1977), ACTOR, grew up in the slums of London. As a youth he held various jobs and played bit parts in vaudeville and the legitimate theater. In 1906 he toured England with the Fred Karno vaudeville troupe. While with a second Karno company touring the United States in 1910, he was discovered in Hollywood by Mack Sennett who signed him to star in his Keystone films in 1913. While with Sennett, Chaplin appeared in such comedies as *The Property Man* (1914) and *Tillie's Punctured Romance* (1914). He next turned to writing and directing. He joined the Essanay Co. in 1915 and made such films as *A Night Out* (1915) and *The Tramp* (1915). Chaplin usually appeared in his "little tramp" role, a sad-looking but humorous vagabond wearing baggy pants and a worn-out derby. He made twelve comedies for the Mutual Film Co. in 1916, including *The Vagabond* and *The Pawnshop*. He signed with a new First National Exhibitors' Circuit in 1917 to make such movies as *Shoulder Arms* (1918), *The Kid* (1920), and *The Pilgrim* (1923). Meanwhile he finished building his own studio in Hollywood in 1918, and in 1919, together with Mary Pickford, **D. W. Griffith,** and Douglas Fairbanks, formed an independent releasing company, United Artists.

After his contract with First National expired in 1923, Chaplin produced only his own films made at his own studio and released through United Artists. Developing stars like Jackie Coogan, Paulette Goddard, and Georgia Hale, Chaplin made (among other films) *The Gold Rush* (1925) and *The Circus* (1928). His first two talking films, *City Lights* (1931) and *Modern Times* (1936), contained ludicrous sound effects aimed at satirizing talking movies. He directed and starred in *The Great Dictator* (1940), a satire on Adolf Hitler. Chaplin was investigated many times in the 1940s by the House Un-American Activities Committee for his alleged pro-Communist leanings but was never prosecuted; he was, however, found guilty in a paternity suit in 1945. After making *Limelight,* an autobiographical story of an aging entertainer, Chaplin left the United States in 1952 and, still an English citizen, was later denied reentry into the United States because of his leftist leanings and his income tax problems. He went to live instead in Vevey, Switzerland, and settled his U.S. income tax case for $500,000 in 1958. *A King in New York* (1956), filmed in England, attacked American anti-Communist hysteria. Chaplin published *Charles Chaplin: My Autobiography* (1964) and directed *A Countess from Hong Kong* (1967) for Universal Pictures. He finally returned to the United States in 1972, an event that triggered an enormous revival of his films. He received a special Oscar from the Motion Picture Academy and many accolades in New York. By that time, however, Chaplin was not the bubbling actor of old. In obvious physical and mental decline, he could do little more than nod his head and smile tightly in response to the applause.

—∞∞—

His peers—Buster Keaton, Mack Sennett, Stan Laurel, W. C. Fields—regarded him as perhaps the greatest comedian who ever lived, certainly the greatest screen artist of them all. The literary world—George Bernard Shaw, **Edmund Wilson,** James Agee, to name just a few of his idolaters—agreed. And the public whose adoration made him a millionaire many times over unquestioningly accepted him as the perfect symbolic representation of what was finest in the spirit of the common man.

The passage of time makes the question of Chaplin's rank as an artist more and more debatable (as we come to comprehend more fully the austere artistry of Keaton, for example). But about another, related point there can be no debate at all: Chaplin was the greatest *celebrity* the movies have ever produced. No artistic "personality" of the twentieth century has so imposed himself on mass consciousness, none has enjoyed greater renown, none suffered so devastating a rejection when, in the 1940s and 1950s, his leftist political views and his private morality—both quite innocent by later standards—were called into violent question.

It all began simply enough when the onetime music hall comedian was struggling to find a place for himself in the rough-and-tumble comic world of the Sennett studio. Needing some gags in a hurry one day, the producer sent Chaplin off to the wardrobe department, where he found the raiment that would forever be identified with him—the too-small bowler, the too-large shoes, the springy bamboo cane. In the very act of finding this outfit, Chaplin found his character as well—or so he would later claim. "You know, this fellow is many-sided," he told Sennett, "a tramp, a gentleman, a poet, a dreamer, a lonely fellow, always hopeful of romance and adventure." But, he added, he was not above picking up cigarette butts, stealing candy from a baby, or giving a lady a kick in the pants. He was, in short, everyman—or at least everyman as he liked to think of himself.

Actually, it took Chaplin a couple of years to refine his characterization, to bring his delicate and subtle pantomime to the peak of perfection he achieved in his Mutual films (1916–17) and the First National group (1918–23). Still ahead of him was his long masterpiece, *The Gold Rush*, as well as *The Circus, Modern Times,* and *City Lights,* works that were less satisfactory as a whole, though they contained, of course, moments of his most inspired comedy. He had reached the peak of his popular success, however, and it seems fair to say that from roughly 1923 onward he started to feel some discomfort with the character he had created, with the direction of the industry in which he was engaged, and, growing more and more obvious from the middle of the 1930s, with the world he inhabited.

One gains a sense, brilliantly noted by Robert Warshow, that the essence of the relationship between the Tramp and his society altered. In the early films their conflicts had been innocent ones; the Tramp had been fundamentally irrelevant to the world's self-important concerns. As the century wore on, however, even so marginal a character could no longer be ignored—not in a statist, often totalitarian world. And so, as Warshow said, the society becomes, in Chaplin's later films, "a living, malevolent organism." A natural sweetness thus disappears from the artist's work, to be replaced far too often by slightly desperate sentimentality and liberal-minded preachment. In the end, alas, the Tramp himself disappeared; the center of Chaplin's creative universe suddenly became vacant. The Little Fellow simply could not survive in the modern world, any more than the Victorian values that formed him could.

Chaplin himself seemed to lose touch with his roots as well as his public. Now, it seemed, when he looked in the mirror, he could see only himself, the world celebrity, a great man of a sort not too different from the kind the Tramp had once plagued with his anarchical ways. The rest was egoism, his last major attempt at an artistic state-

ment being *Limelight,* in which he played a down-at-the-heels comedian about to die. It was, said critic Andrew Sarris, "a conception of sublime egoism, unparalleled in the world cinema," since "to imagine one's own death, one must imagine the death of the world." His triumphant return to the United States to receive a special Academy Award in 1972 was a satisfying, reconciliatory last act to the drama of his celebrity but one which occasioned a degree of sadness at Chaplin's failure ever to make a statement as a mature artist that could match the brilliantly artful optimism of his young manhood. Doubtless, he was the author of some of the misery that led to that odd blend of misanthropy and empty uplift that marred the works of his later years. But what artist, possessing a deep consciousness of the spirit of his century, has actually survived the onslaughts of the modern celebrity system, not to mention the age of total politicization, intact? Few, if any, have given more moments of pure and uncomplicated pleasure than Chaplin did during his years of greatness. See Charles Chaplin, *My Autobiography* (1964).

RICHARD SCHICKEL

CHARLES, Ray (b. Albany, Ga., Sept. 23, 1932), MUSICIAN, born Ray Charles Robinson, later dropped his surname. He became blind at the age of 7 (as a result of glaucoma) and was placed in the St. Augustine (Fla.) School for the Blind where he learned to play the piano and clarinet. He left the school at 15 and began composing and working as a musician, traveling throughout the South. In 1950 he moved to Seattle, Washington, where he formed a trio copying the style of the singer Nat "King" Cole. Charles organized his own band in 1954, and its first job was accompanying singer Ruth Brown. Later that year he began recording for Atlantic Records. His music, a combination of rhythm and blues and gospel music, soon became popular. Later on it was greatly admired by jazz artists as well. In 1960, Charles switched to ABC-Paramount records and recorded his first big hit, "Georgia on My Mind." He gave the first integrated concert in a public auditorium in Memphis, Tennessee, in 1961. His 1962 album *Modern Sounds in Country and Western Music* sold more than a million copies, and one of its selections, "I Can't Stop Loving You," sold over 2.5 million. In 1962, Charles got his own record label under ABC-Paramount called Tangerine Records. He made a world tour of ninety concerts in nine weeks from Japan to Algeria in 1964. Charles has appeared frequently on television and has written the theme songs for such movies as *The Cincinnati Kid* (1965) and Academy Award winner *In the Heat of the Night* (1967). Some of his best-known hits include "Hallelujah I Love Her So" (1956), "Let the Good Times Roll" (1959), "Hit the Road, Jack" (1961), and "Busted" (1963). In recent years Charles has continued to roll out hit recordings, but he has become even more of a public persona than ever because of his role on TV as a singing pitchman for Pepsi-Cola and periodic appearances at political and patriotic events.

A large part of Ray Charles's importance rests with the fact that he began his career trying to sing straight for white audiences and rose to prominence through his passion. It was Ray Charles more than any other single artist who paved the way for rock and for soul; more significant, he brought about a more eclectic appreciation for music in his varied audiences. Charles is currently popular not only with pop audiences but with country/western and rock and soul as well—not merely because of his enormous charisma and versatility but because for him there are no artificial distinctions among the musical forms. If Charles can feel it, he can play it, and if he plays it, everyone feels it. There is nothing cool about the man. He doesn't merely play the piano, the piano is an extension of him. "He ennobled every song he sang," wrote Lillian Roxon, one of the best of the music critics of the 1970s. "They're still talking about what he did to 'You Are My Sunshine.' For rock fans the best example is the Beatles' 'Yesterday,' which he changed from a wistful and nostalgic ditty to a song of monumental despair and regret." Indeed, it is Charles's

projection of ecstasy arising from the pit of tragedy that was and is the core of his appeal. He became during the 1950s and 1960s the next step historically from the Delta blues men. It was he who really started the popularization of blues in the young, white, middle-class communities. It was he who launched the Twist to a far greater extent than Chubby Checker or anyone else. "What'd I Say?" broke the ground for the Beatles. The Twist broke the ground for a more spontaneous type of popular dancing that opened the way for a more intensified, rhythmic, and sexual communion between the partners. It was Charles who upset every conservative in America. And he still sits in the other room, breaking new ground, building bridges to the sensual and the feeling, the expressive. And he is still spawning imitators in the white rock world who "cover" his style; some even rise to prominence. Joe Cocker is one example, but almost every musician doing pop or soul these days has come under Charles's influence. See "Ray Charles" in Lillian Roxon, ed., *Rock Encyclopedia* (1969), pp. 93–100.

JONATHAN EISEN

CHASE, Salmon Portland (b. Cornish, N.H., Jan. 13, 1808; d. New York, N.Y., May 7, 1873), POLITICAL LEADER, JURIST, graduated from Dartmouth College (1826). After teaching in Washington, D.C., he studied law and was admitted to the bar in 1829. Settling in Cincinnati (1830) he became associated with the antislavery movement. He defended fugitive slaves, helped organize the Liberty Party (1840), and was active in the Free Soil Party (1848). In 1848 he was elected to the U.S. Senate by a Free Soil–Democratic coalition.

While in the Senate, Chase opposed the Compromise of 1850 and the Kansas–Nebraska Act (1854) as concessions to slavery. In 1855 he was elected governor of Ohio (reelected 1857). As governor he engaged in many interstate conflicts arising out of the enforcement of the Fugitive Slave Act and reorganized the Ohio militia. In 1860 he was again elected to the Senate as a Republican. He attended the 1861 "Peace

Convention" in Washington that attempted unsuccessfully to allay sectional tensions.

Chase resigned from the Senate to become Abraham Lincoln's secretary of the Treasury (1861–64). When the Civil War broke out, he devoted most of his efforts to war finance. Although he favored hard money, he was forced to agree to the issuance of "greenbacks." Chase was instrumental in creating the national banking system (1863). During the war he took a radical position, urging that General **George McClellan** be discharged and believing that the president's Emancipation Proclamation was too weak. He clashed repeatedly with the moderate secretary of state, **William Seward,** and with the president. He resigned in 1864. In that same year, however, Lincoln appointed him chief justice of the Supreme Court.

As chief justice, Chase supported the Radical Republicans who believed that blacks should be guaranteed their civil rights before the South was readmitted to the Union. He dissented in *Ex parte Milligan* (1866), in which the Court ruled that neither Congress nor the president could permit a military commission to try civilians in areas that were not adjacent to a war zone. He concurred in the cases of *Mississippi* v. *Johnson* and *Georgia* v. *Stanton* (1867), which upheld the Reconstruction Acts of 1867. Chase presided over **Jefferson Davis**'s trial at Richmond (1868), but the case was terminated when President Andrew Johnson pardoned Davis. Although Chase did not approve of the attempt to impeach President Johnson, he presided over the proceedings. Never an active candidate for the presidency, Chase always welcomed support, and in 1868 he almost succeeded in getting the Republican nomination.

In the Legal Tender case of 1870 (*Hepburn* v. *Griswold*), the Chase Court declared greenback money was not legal tender. When the Court reversed this decision in 1871, Chase dissented (*Knox* v. *Lee*; *Parker* v. *Davis*). In the "Slaughterhouse" cases (1873), the Court announced that the Fourteenth Amendment applied to federal, not state, citizenship. Chase dissented, arguing that the amendment should be interpreted broadly.

In face and form Chase was a model for president of the United States. Six feet in height, broad-shouldered, and well built, with a finely shaped head, a handsome face, and a courtly manner, he looked a leader of men. And fine qualities were behind this imposing front. Methodical, hardworking, and efficient, he quickly rose to prominence at the Ohio bar. As a U.S. senator he organized the antislavery forces in Congress. His two terms as governor of Ohio demonstrated his capacity for administration. Successful in law and politics, principled and ambitious, by 1856 he was a leader of the northern opponents of slavery and nursed presidential aspirations.

But if these years brought a considerable measure of achievement, they also disclosed defects of mind and character. As Chase rose to prominence a certainty of opinion, a touch of pomposity, and a tendency to sanctimonious smugness became more and more pronounced. When confronted by the necessity of making great decisions he sometimes showed a distressing tendency to straddle. He lacked a sense of humor, and he lacked charisma. Despite his desire to serve his country and mankind, he had no appeal to the hearts of men.

The limitations that marred Chase's high qualities did not prevent his rendering substantial services to the nation during the years of war and Reconstruction. As secretary of the Treasury he confronted the enormous problem of conducting the financial operations of the wartime government. He made some bad mistakes, especially by his delay in adopting an adequate system of taxation and in the issuance of legal tender notes. But his handling of the patronage was above average, and the establishment of the national banking system was an achievement in which he played a major role.

Distrust of Lincoln as an administrator, together with differences over patronage, cooled relations between Chase and the president. The secretary repeatedly offered his resignation. He did so once too often and in 1864 unexpectedly found himself out of office. But Lincoln still had high respect for his abilities and on the death of Chief Justice **Roger Taney** appointed Chase as Taney's successor.

In his new post Chase endeavored to enhance the Supreme Court's importance in the national government and to restore the balance between state and national power that had existed before the Civil War. His most important judicial opinion, he believed, was that in *Texas* v. *White* (1869), in which he held that Texas, as a state, had never been out of the Union, thus abandoning his earlier adherence to **Charles Sumner**'s theory of state suicide.

But on the bench Chase could not forget the White House. He had hoped to succeed Lincoln in 1864. In 1868 he would have accepted either the Republican or the Democratic nomination, and four years later he would have yielded eagerly to the call of the Democrats or the Liberal Republicans. Outstanding national figure though he was, this unseemly eagerness was a factor in his failure to achieve the post that he most highly prized. See John Niven, *Samuel P. Chase: A Biography* (1995).

GLYNDON G. VAN DEUSEN

CHAVEZ, Cesar (Estrada) (b. Yuma, Ariz., Mar. 31, 1927; d. San Luis, Ariz., Apr. 23, 1993), LABOR LEADER, grew up on a small farm near Yuma. During the depression of the 1930s the farm failed, and Chavez lived in California migrant farm labor camps where his father sought employment. After serving briefly in the U.S. Navy (1944–45), Chavez returned to the life of a migrant farm worker in the cotton fields, vineyards, and orchards of California and Arizona. In 1952 when Saul Alinsky turned his attention to the plight of the Mexican-Americans of the Southwest and helped establish the self-help Community Service Organization, Chavez became a paid staff member, organizing voter registration drives in San Jose, California, founding CSO chapters in Oakland and in the San Joaquin Valley, and assisting Mexican-Americans in their dealings with police, welfare, and immi-

gration officials. By 1958 he had risen to general director of the CSO but was becoming increasingly disenchanted with its growing middle-class perspective and membership. In 1962, after failing to commit the CSO to the organization of a farm workers' union, he resigned.

Moving to Delano, California, Chavez founded the National Farm Workers Association. By the mid–1960s the NFWA had grown to include seventeen hundred families and had won two pay raises in the Delano area vineyards. In September 1965, when eight hundred Filipino grape pickers of the Agricultural Organizing Committee voted to strike, the NFWA joined them, and in 1966 the two unions merged to form the United Farm Workers Organizing Committee.

A long and bitter struggle with the grape growers followed—a struggle that saw the union gain the support not only of politicians such as **Robert Kennedy** but of labor unions such as **Walter Reuther**'s UAW, and of many church organizations. In addition to the traditional union weapons of strike and picketing, Chavez employed church meetings and sit-ins, and he organized a three-hundred-mile march to the capital at Sacramento. When the major table-grape growers refused to settle, even after most wine-grape growers had come to terms, he organized a nationwide boycott of California grapes, sending out two hundred UFWOC workers to mobilize support, particularly in large eastern cities. In July 1970 twenty-six major grape growers, representing 75 percent of California's grape production, severely hurt by the growing success of the boycott, signed contracts recognizing the UFWOC as the workers' union. Chavez then turned to organizing the lettuce growers of California and the migrant farm laborers of the Florida citrus groves. In 1972 he signed a contract with the Minute Maid Division of the Coca-Cola Corporation, which won recognition of his union as the bargaining agent for the citrus pickers. Other successful boycotts and organizing ventures followed, but many of the largest California growers, in an attempt to head off Chavez and his union, invited the International Brotherhood of Teamsters to unionize their workers. Chavez denounced the agreements as "sweetheart contracts" and eventually forced the Teamsters to back down. He was helped by Governor Jerry Brown's effort in 1974 in getting the state to adopt the Agricultural Labor Relations Act, a landmark piece of labor legislation establishing collective bargaining for farm workers and granting the Chavez union concessions. As a result the Teamsters abandoned the struggle with Chavez in 1977, leaving the field to the United Farm Workers. Though the United Farm Workers had some successes, it never obtained the dominance Chavez dreamed about. A decade after the Delano strike, only about 10 percent of the grapes were harvested by members of his union. Chavez, growing increasingly frustrated, charged that "spies" were infiltrating the union and thus weakening it. At one point he purged the union of all non-Latino officials to ensure loyalty. In the 1980s, with the Republican Party in control of the governor's mansion and allied with the growers, Chavez was on the defensive. He revived the use of the boycott to energize his cause, this time against Salinas Valley lettuce growers and non-union grapes. But this tactic failed to attract the enthusiastic backing it had earlier. By the 1990s the United Farm Workers was weakened by growing internal dissent and a perception among some observers that it was no longer a social cause but a conventional union. By 1995, Chavez and the United Farm Workers had been able to organize about 20 percent of California's agricultural workers, or about 200,000 people.

❧

It is not difficult to understand the public adulation Cesar Chavez received as a result of the grape boycott, for his position was and continued to remain a uniquely pure one. He insisted on nonviolence in a period when violence had gained increasing acceptability as a tactic of social change. He made alliances and used white and nonwhite organizers at a time when racial exclusivity was the trend among most Third World groups. He insisted that his salary, like that of all the UFW's organizers, be $5 a week

plus room and board despite the fact that the UFW was established as an organized union.

But it would be a gross underestimation of Chavez to see his primary achievement as that of embodying the moral idealism of the early 1960s, for he did what nearly everyone else—including labor leaders and growers—thought could not be done: organize farm workers. He demonstrated not only that farm workers were ready and able to join unions but, through the largest boycotts ever seen in this country, that there was also a way to make their struggle effective. In accomplishing this Chavez was able to overcome, at least in California, the legal vacuum in which farm workers had been kept (remaining excluded from such basic New Deal legislation as the National Labor Relations Act) and the strategic problems of organizing strikes on farms thousands of acres in size. The result was that in the 1970s the farm worker struggle became a permanent part of America's social landscape. Their struggle is not over by any means, but because of Chavez's efforts they have achieved some significant gains, and the unique union he founded is in no danger of fading from view. See Peter Matthiessen, *Sal Si Puedes: Cesar Chavez and the New American Revolution* (1969).

NICOLAUS MILLS

CHEEVER, John (b. Quincy, Mass., May 27, 1912; d. Ossining, N.Y., June 18, 1982), WRITER, was expelled in 1929 from Thayer Academy in Milton, Massachusetts, for smoking and poor academic performance. He worked as a freelance writer, producing book synopses for Metro-Goldwyn-Mayer before publishing his first story in *The New Yorker* (1935), which became his major venue for satirical stories about modern urban and suburban life. A prolific short story writer, he published several well received collections: *The Way Some People Live* (1943), *The Enormous Radio and Other Stories* (1953), *The Housebreaker of Shady Hill* (1958), and *Collected Stories* (1978). His novels have been highly regarded, especially *The Wapshot Chronicle* (1957), which won the National Book Award, and *The Wapshot Scandal* (1964), which won the Howells Medal of the Academy of Arts and Letters. Later novels, *Bullet Park* (1969) and *Falconer* (1977), were also well received, as were the posthumously published *The Journals of John Cheever* (1991).

Cheever wrote eloquently about the American family, often focusing on affluent New Englanders in a state of moral decline. Sad and sophisticated, often humorous, his stories and novels evoke the peculiar isolation and discontent of suburban living, which seems comfortable and yet leaves his characters uneasy. The stories tend to be more tightly structured than the novels, although *Falconer*, a study of an ex-professor's experiences in a prison, put Cheever in the front rank of contemporary novelists.

Like other *New Yorker* stort story writers, Cheever has been criticized for mannered prose; his facile style has provoked negative criticism. But his sense of form is so exquisite that it usually triumphs over sentences that might seem almost too polished. The best Cheever stories have an exuberance and bizarre humor that make them pulse with life. An element of the fantastic and the baroque enters his fiction in such stories as "The Enormous Radio," a classic and a staple of the college curriculum.

His journals rival his fiction in importance. Not only are they a valuable cultural document, recording his sensitive and candid reaction to his world, but they are an extraordinary revelation of his character and his struggles with marriage, homosexuality, drinking, and with the all-encompassing demands of being a writer. The journals have a heroic, unflinching quality that is perhaps matched only by *Falconer*, Cheever's last novel. See Scott Donaldson, *John Cheever: A Biography* (1988).

CARL ROLLYSON

CHILD, Lydia Maria Francis (b. Medford, Mass., Feb. 11, 1802; d. Wayland, Mass., Oct. 20, 1880), WRITER, received her education in Medford public schools. Her first two books were popular novels: *Hobomok* (1824), about life in early Salem and Plymouth, and *The Rebels, or Boston Before the Revolution* (1825). She ran a private school in Watertown, Massachusetts (1825–28), then married David Lee Child, a lawyer, in 1828. She soon became involved in the abolitionist movement and published *An Appeal in Favor of That Class of Americans Called Africans* (1833), which was followed by *The Oasis* (1834), a collection of antislavery essays, and *An Anti-Slavery Catechism* (1836). From 1840 to 1844 she edited, at times with her husband's help, the *National Anti-Slavery Standard,* a New York City weekly. Though the Childs moved in 1852 to a small farm in Wayland, Massachusetts, Lydia Child retained an active interest in the antislavery movement. In 1859, while **John Brown** lay wounded in a Virginia prison after the attack on Harpers Ferry, Child's offer to help nurse him in prison led to an exchange of letters published as *Correspondence Between Lydia Maria Child, Governor Wise, and Mrs. Mason* (1860). Besides her abolitionist writings, the diversity of Child's interests was reflected in such works as *The (American) Frugal Housewife* (1829), a popular manual on "domestic economy," *Flowers for Children* (1844), *The Progress of Religious Ideas Through Successive Ages* (1855), and *The Right Way, the Safe Way* (1860), based on the history of the emancipation of slaves in the West Indies.

Lydia Child pioneered women's activities in several fields but made her greatest impression by force of character and philanthropic goals. Her early novels made her popular, and *Juvenile Miscellany, The Frugal Housewife,* which appeared in numerous editions between 1829 and 1855, and other books for girls and women brought her funds and brilliant companionship. Her marriage to David Lee Child promised a successful partnership.

Both Child and his wife were impressed by **William Lloyd Garrison**'s abolitionist argument, but it was Mrs. Child who created the sensation with her *Appeal* in 1833. This early expression of "immediatist" abolitionism, demanding a negative attitude toward slavery abettors, harmed her in the eyes of her conservative admirers but converted to positive abolitionist views such influential persons as **William Ellery Channing** and **Charles Sumner.**

Mrs. Child published many antislavery miscellanies and cooperated with other antislavery workers. Although she was no woman's rights advocate, her *History of the Condition of Women in Various Ages and Nations* (1835) broke new ground, as her *Liberal Progress of Religious Ideas Through Successive Ages* did later. When she assumed in New York editorship of the Garrisonian *National Anti-Slavery Standard,* she lived in the home of the Quaker abolitionist Isaac T. Hopper, whose biography she later wrote. In 1844, embittered by abolitionist factional disputes, she retired from active participation in the movement but retained a vital interest in public developments. Her *Letters from New York* (1843, 1845) were among her liveliest and most durable writings.

Lydia Child, freed of her more constricted interests, became one of the most distinguished women of her time. Her correspondence with Governor Henry A. Wise and Mrs. Mason, wife of a Virginia senator, precipitated her again into the public view and furnished evidence of a new respect for abolitionists in the North. Such publications as *The Right Way, the Safe Way,* urging emancipation, contributed judiciously to the contemporary debate. Her *Letters* (1883), published posthumously, rounded out a career of cultural as well as philanthropic importance. See Carolyn L Karcher, *The First Woman of the Republic: A Cultural Biography of Lydia Maria Child* (1995).

LOUIS FILLER

CHOMSKY, Avram Noam (b. Philadelphia, Pa., Dec. 7, 1928), SOCIAL SCIENTIST, graduated from the University of Pennsylvania in 1949, where his interest in linguistics had been developed by Professor Zellig Harris. Chomsky was an assistant instructor of linguistics at the University of Pennsylvania (1950–51) and received his MA degree there in 1951. For the next four years (1951–55) he was a junior fellow at Harvard. He was awarded his PhD in linguistics from the University of Pennsylvania in 1955 and then became assistant professor of modern languages and linguistics at the Massachusetts Institute of Technology. He was promoted to associate professor in 1958, full professor in 1961, and Ferrari P. Ward professor of foreign literature and linguistics at M.I.T. in 1966. Chomsky's first book, *Syntactic Structure* (1957), expounded his view that every individual has an innate ability to learn languages which is put into use once a language is initially heard. This represented a new approach to linguistics as opposed to the prevailing behavioral point of view. He followed up on these and other linguistic ideas with *Current Issues in Linguistic Theory* (1964), *Aspects of the Theory of Syntax* (1965), *Topics in the Theory of Generative Grammar* (1966), *Language and Mind* (1968), and *Sound Patterns of English* (1968, with Morris Hall). A research fellowship at the Harvard Center for Cognitive Studies from 1964 to 1965 led to *Cartesian Linguistics* (1966). He was also Beckman visiting professor at the University of California at Berkeley (1966–67) and delivered the Shearman Lectures at University College in London and the John Locke Lectures at Oxford University (1969).

During the early 1960s Chomsky became an outspoken critic of America's participation in the Vietnam War and soon emerged as a leader of the antiwar movement. He participated in the 1967 protest march on the Pentagon and wrote many articles for *Ramparts, Liberation,* and the *New York Review of Books* attacking the intellectual community for providing the ideological justification for America's interventionist foreign policy. Many of these essays appeared as *American Power and the New Mandarins* (1969). From the 1960s to today he has continued his radical critique of American foreign policy in a host of books and essays. Basically, they argue that an economic, social, and political elite, unmindful of the needs of the great masses of Americans, have conspired to pursue an imperialistic foreign policy hostile to the interests of the Third World but beneficial to their own corporate interests. Just as he opposed American participation in Vietnam, he was a strident critic of the Gulf War in 1990–91 and has ardently criticized American policy in the Mideast generally, especially our intimate relationship with Israel, a country he views with a baleful eye. Books in which he gives his views include *At War with Asia* (1970), *Problems of Knowledge and Freedom* (1971), *Studies on Semantics in Generative Grammar* (1972), and *Human Rights and American Foreign Policy* (1978).

Noam Chomsky, the most celebrated linguist of the last decade, has achieved an international reputation unparalleled for linguists during their lifetimes. He has been widely accepted as having revolutionized the discipline in its goals, boundaries, epistemology, theory, and methodology. He has also dramatically revised scholarly consideration of language among those working in other disciplines, notably in philosophy, psychology, education, and anthropology. While his original and current views are widely challenged by many, the new directions he has set for linguists have left a permanent imprint on the character of the discipline in basic ways. He has not only been an energetic innovator but has also legitimized and revived interest in aspects of linguistics such as universal grammar, semantics, syntax, lexicon, cognitive process and structure, and language acquisition, originating in classical and older European traditions that were seriously neglected by his predecessors in the United States during the preceding quarter of a century.

His system of linguistic analysis, called "transformational-generative," has replaced the earlier American descriptivism (with its emphasis on a scientific skepticism, empiricism, and inductiveness) with a new idealism, largely deductive in approach, and presented within very formalistic rules. He has enriched and stimulated the discipline greatly despite having limited his own work mainly to the areas of epistemology and English. He is virtually unique in the traditions of linguistics as someone whose influence stems rather from the philosophical side than from the experience of working with the data of many languages.

As a moral, gentle, and idealistic scholar he has also involved himself in idealistic politics, taking strongly partisan positions for social justice and against war, especially the Vietnam War, and American foreign policy generally, with the same passion that he has brought to linguistics.

In admitting everyone's freedom to criticize acts by the government, he has warned that violence can also bring on retaliation by that government. In an essay, "On Resistance," Chomsky wrote: "We must not, I believe, thoughtlessly urge others to commit civil disobedience, and we must be careful not to construct situations in which young people will find themselves induced, perhaps in violation of their basic convictions, to commit civil disobedience. Resistance must be freely undertaken." See John Lyons, *Noam Chomsky* (1970), and Mark Achbar, ed., *Manufacturing Consent: Noam Chomsky and the Media* (1995).

HARVEY PITKIN

CHURCH, Frederic Edwin (b. Hartford, Conn., May 4, 1826; d. New York, N.Y., Apr. 7, 1900), ARTIST, studied with **Thomas Cole**, 1844–1846. He began exhibiting at the National Academy of Design, New York, in 1845 and was elected a full member of the NAD in 1849. In 1853 he made his first trip to South America; he returned there in 1857. His painting *Niagara* (1857) received tremendous aclaim in New York and London, where John Ruskin greatly admired it. In 1858 he moved to the Studio Building in New York City. The following year he exhibited his huge *Heart of the Andes*, a painting that stunned contemporaries and that was purchased for $10,000, a record price at that time for a work by a living American painter. In 1859 he also sailed along the coast of Newfoundland and Labrador with the Reverend Louis Legrand Noble, whose book *After Icebergs with a Painter* appeared in 1861 with illustrations by Church. In 1860 the painter moved to Hudson, New York, where a decade later he and the architect Calvert Vaux began constructing his magnificent home, Olana. His traveling continued, to the Middle East in 1868 and Greece and Italy the next year; he wintered in Mexico from 1880 to 1890.

During this period his reputation as America's foremost landscape painter declined (as did interest in the genre itself). Following his death the Metropolitan Museum of Art in New York featured a memorial exhibition of Church's paintings.

———— ∞∞∞ ————

During the middle decades of the 19th century, Frederic E. Church stood as the premier figure in landscape painting, the field of art most esteemed by Americans. Church, who traveled extensively throughout his career, amazed contemporaries with the realistic, exotic, and awe-inspiring character of his often enormous compositions. Church's *Niagara* thrilled American and British audiences with its dramatic point of view, which put the viewer right on the edge of the roaring cataract. Niagara was the first of Church's "Great Pictures," works that appeared as single-picture, paid-admission special exhibitions. Other notable examples include *Heart of the Andes* and *Twilight in the Wilderness* (1860). When *Heart of the Andes* appeared, it was framed by an enormous wooden structure that imitated a window and was flanked by dried tropical plants that Church had brought back from his trips to South America.

Having studied with Thomas Cole, the artist who had introduced Americans to landscape painting as a serious and worthy pursuit, Church inherited and furthered Cole's practice of combining realistic detail and idealistic composition to create landscapes of heroic dimensions and content. Church's paintings offered viewers images that were not only aesthetically pleasing and geographically fascinating but also dynamically evoked nationalistic and religious associations. More than any other of his contemporaries, Church convincingly expressed the power, the beauty, and the richness of nature. See Franklin Kelly, et al., *Frederic Edwin Church* (1989).

MARK THISTLETHWAITE

CLARK, George Rogers (b. Charlottesville, Va., Nov. 19, 1752; d. Louisville, Ky., Feb. 13, 1818), MILITARY LEADER, after some exploring expeditions on the Ohio River, served as a captain of militia in Lord Dunmore's War (1774) against the Shawnee and Ottawa tribes in the Northwest. He later explored Kentucky, surveying land there for the Ohio Company, and was commissioned (by Virginia) a major in charge of the defense of that area.

During the Revolutionary War, Clark attempted to overwhelm the anchor points of British influence north of the Ohio. Although poorly supported by Virginia, he captured Kaskaskia and Cahokia in the Illinois country (1778) and, to the east, Vincennes on the Wabash River (1779). Since he failed to receive substantial reinforcements, he was unable to capture Detroit, the most important British post in the interior.

Despite Cornwallis's surrender at Yorktown (1781), the war in the West continued. In 1782, as a brigadier general for Virginia, Clark led an expedition against the Shawnees, protecting frontier settlements and keeping the British on the defensive around Detroit. He was later a member of a board of commissioners that supervised the allocation of land in Illinois, and he served on a commission to negotiate treaties with the Native Americans of the Northwest. In 1786 he led an unsuccessful expedition against the Wabash tribes in Kentucky and Indiana.

In 1788 Clark sought to establish a colony west of the Mississippi, opposite the mouth of the Ohio River. However, his demands for religious and political freedom for the colonists were not acceptable to the Spanish, who controlled that area. In 1793 the French accepted Clark's plan to conquer Louisiana, but when President Washington issued his "Neutrality Proclamation," the proposal was not implemented. In 1798, however, Clark revived his plan. When the U.S. government ordered him to give up his appointment as a general for the French, he refused and fled to St. Louis.

In 1803 he settled in Clarksville, near the falls of the Ohio River, an area which was given to his Illinois regiment by Virginia. There he served as chairman of a commission to allocate land.

———— ∞∞∞ ————

George Rogers Clark, a sinewy six-footer, was a dynamic leader, popular with his own soldiers and accomplished in dealing with the Native Americans, whose style of high-flown, metaphorical oratory he had mastered and used effectively in pacifying a number of the tribes. A flaming redhead, he possessed a fiery temperament, a restless nature, and a thirst for derring-do that at once brought him bright successes and dismal failures. An extremist, he never leveled off, never contented himself with normal achievements. The pinnacle of his short but spectacular train of Revolutionary War triumphs came in 1778–79 when, with little more than a handful of men, he severely shook Britain's hold on the Illinois country.

Yet it is a myth—too often repeated by reputable historians—to say that Clark "won the West," that his achievements made it possible for American diplomats to secure the Mississippi River as the western boundary of the United States in the peace treaty of 1783. In fact, Clark remained on the defensive during the final years of the conflict when the Native Americans resumed their devastation of the frontier. Moreover, there is little if any evidence to indicate that the American peace commissioners in Paris were aware of the developments in the trans-Appalachian region.

In any case, many Americans did not sufficiently appreciate Clark's hardships and achievements; the state of Virginia hounded him for years about settling accounts that were not all his responsibility. His debts helped drive Clark into various rash, speculative enterprises which combined with other related problems—alcoholism and mental disintegration—to bring him to a pathetic end. See John Bakeless, *Background to Glory* (1957).

DON HIGGINBOTHAM

CLARK, John Bates (b. Providence, R.I., Jan. 26, 1847; d. New York, N.Y., Mar. 21, 1938), ECONOMIST, graduated from Amherst in 1872 and was one of the first Americans to do advanced work in economics, studying for three years in Europe at Heidelberg and Zurich. Returning to the United States in 1875, he began teaching as a pro-

fessor of history and political economy at Carleton College (Northfield, Minn.). He returned to the East to teach economics at Smith (1881–92), concurrently at Amherst and Johns Hopkins (1892–95), and finally at Columbia (1895–1923). In 1885 he joined with **Richard T. Ely,** Simon Patten, and other economists concerned with professionalizing the discipline and opposed to the status quo in economic theory and policy to organize the American Economic Association, serving as president in 1894. He edited the *Political Science Quarterly* (1895–1911), was a member of the American Peace Society, and served as director of the Division of Economics and History of the Carnegie Endowment for International Peace (1911–23).

Clark's early writings present a moderate Christian socialism, influenced by English examples, sharply critical of contemporary business practices. In *The Philosophy of Wealth* (1886) he outlined his vision of a system of "full cooperation" under which industrial strife would be eliminated because laborers, through profit sharing, would become capitalists.

He supplemented this philosophy with a theory of value grounded in an ideal of free competition. He stressed the importance of what he called "effective utility," a measure of the power of a good or service to satisfy the subjective wants of individuals. Individual valuation was constrained by social or market valuation, which was determined by the written and unwritten laws of society. This theory resembled the concepts of marginal utility developed earlier by W. Stanley Jevons in England and the Austrian school of economists, although Clark had no knowledge of Jevons's work at the time.

In his later writings, particularly his major books, *The Distribution of Wealth* (1899) and *The Essentials of Economic Theory* (1907), Clark moved away from his earlier concern with social reform, which he no longer considered within the discipline of economic theory, to concentrate on a reformulation of his theory of value, which he hoped would result in the development of an ethical and scientific validation of the economic foundations of modern society. He developed a theory of marginal, or final, productivity in a stable economy which stated that as long as competition remained free, the returns of both capital and labor would be fixed in the same equitable way.

Because free economic competition was of central importance to his theory, Clark devoted considerable time in his later years to the development of proposals for the correction of monopolistic abuses. These proposals and their theoretical basis were described in *The Control of Trusts* (1901), written in collaboration with his son, John Maurice Clark.

———— ∞∞ ————

John Bates Clark exerted considerable influence on contemporary economists through his warm, tolerant personality and the clarity and persuasiveness of his ideas. A member of the first generation of professional economists in the United States—men trained at universities for careers in research and teaching—he contributed significantly to the development of the institutions and scholarly canons of his profession.

His contributions to social theory and economic policy must be separated from his efforts to formulate answers to several central questions of economic theory—in particular the definition of value and the principles governing the distribution of wealth in a static economy. As a social theorist Clark stimulated discussion of Christian socialism and interventionist alternatives to unregulated conflict between workers and employers. His views on economic policy, especially the control of harmful monopoly, influenced many leading public men, notably his friend Woodrow Wilson, and were reflected in the legislation creating the Federal Trade Commission.

Clark's economic theory, influential and elegant, would have been more important had he fulfilled his ambition to complement his analysis of a static economy with a theory of dynamics. Misunderstanding by later economists and historians of the self-imposed limits on his economic theory has frequently caused them to mislabel him an economic conservative.

Clark's breadth, as scholar and teacher, is best exemplified by his pride in having had a profound influence on two very different and significant American economists: his student (at Carleton) **Thorstein Veblen** and his son John Maurice Clark. See Joseph Dorfman, *The Economic Mind in American Civilization*, Vol. III (1959), ch. 8.

D. M. FOX

CLAY, Cassius. See Ali, Muhammad.

CLAY, Henry (b. Hanover Co., Va., Apr. 12, 1777; d. Washington, D.C., June 29, 1852), POLITICAL LEADER, studied law under **George Wythe** of Virginia and was admitted to the bar in 1797. He moved to Lexington, Kentucky (1797), where he practiced law and was elected to the state legislature (serving 1803–6, 1807–9). Briefly in the U.S. Senate (1806–7, 1810–11), he disapproved of rechartering the Bank of the United States on constitutional grounds and favored federally financed internal improvements as well as higher tariffs on manufactures.

In 1811, Clay entered the U.S. House of Representatives (speaker, 1811–14), where he became one of the leaders of the "War Hawks," an expansionist group of congressmen who favored war with Britain. In 1814 he was a member of the U.S. peace commission at Ghent, which drafted the treaty ending the War of 1812.

Clay was elected to the House four more times, serving as speaker from 1815 to 1820 and from 1823 to 1825. He advanced a nationalistic program, including the building of canals and highways, the rechartering of the U.S. Bank, protective tariffs to stimulate industry, and expenditures for national defense. He disapproved of the Transcontinental Treaty of 1819 with Spain because it surrendered American claims to Texas. When Missouri submitted its constitution for approval, northern congressmen refused to accept it because of a clause barring free blacks and mulattoes from entering the state in violation of the U.S. Constitution. Clay then devised that part of the Missouri Compromise (1819–21) in which Congress accepted the Missouri constitution, but asserted the state could not pass any laws violating the federal Constitution.

By the 1820s Clay had fully developed his "American System," which called for protective tariffs for eastern manufactures and federally financed internal improvements to benefit the West. In 1824 he helped engineer the passage of the highest tariff up to that time. He also then ran for president. None of the candidates (Andrew Jackson, John Quincy Adams, **William H. Crawford,** and Clay) managed to get a majority of the electoral votes, so the election was thrown into the House of Representatives. As Clay had the smallest number of electoral votes (37), he was constitutionally disqualified. He threw his influence to Adams, who was elected. Adams then appointed Clay secretary of state, which enabled the Jacksonians to claim that Clay and Adams had made a "corrupt bargain" to win the election.

In 1831, Clay was again elected to the U.S. Senate. In 1832 he took the lead in seeking congressional recharter of the second Bank of the United States, bringing himself into conflict with Andrew Jackson, who vetoed the recharter bill. The veto became the major issue in the election of 1832 in which Clay, running on the National-Republican ticket, was defeated for president by Jackson, 219 electoral votes to 49. When South Carolina threatened to nullify the Tariff of 1832, Clay and **John C. Calhoun** helped arrange another famous intersectional adjustment. The compromise Tariff of 1833 reduced duties gradually, providing South Carolina with an excuse to back away from nullification.

After the demise of the bank, Clay continued to support the idea of a national bank. He opposed Martin Van Buren's sub-Treasury plan (1837). Clay vainly sought the Whig presidential nomination at the 1839 Whig convention in Harrisburg. After Van Buren's defeat by William Henry Harrison in the election of 1840, Clay pushed through the repeal of the independent Treasury system, but his effort to establish a new Bank of the United States was checked by the veto of President Tyler.

Clay again ran for president in 1844, this time on the Whig ticket, but lost to James Polk who had 170 electoral votes to the Kentuckian's 105. Clay opposed the declaration of war against Mexico and lost the Whig nomination to Zachary Taylor at Philadelphia in 1848. His final major role in politics developed during the Taylor and Millard Fillmore administrations when, as a senator, he was prominent in the debates resulting in the Compromise of 1850. This compromise admitted California into the Union as a free state, dividing the rest of the Mexican cession into the territories of New Mexico and Utah. The Texas debt was paid off and the Texas–New Mexico boundary adjusted. In addition, the slave trade was restricted in the District of Columbia, and a strong Fugitive Slave Act was passed.

———— ✸ ————

From the beginning to the end of his political career, covering half a century, contemporaries saw in Henry Clay qualities they nearly always esteemed whether or not they followed his leadership. At the outset the Kentuckian, transplanted from Virginia, was nothing less than a prodigy. A U.S. senator before he was 30, Clay at 33 became speaker of the House on his first day as a member of that body. From that time forward he was a force to be reckoned with in numerous ways—as an advocate of the War of 1812, as an opponent of the Mexican War, and as one who feared and warned against a civil war and said he would side with the Union against his own state if such a conflagration came.

On the tariff, on internal improvements, on the first and second Banks of the United States, on the questions of slavery and slavery's extension, on foreign affairs, and on party policy, Clay's words were heard early and often. Speaker of the House longer than any other 19th-century figure, secretary of state under John Quincy Adams, Clay was a senator on and off from 1806 to 1852. In the prime of life (unlike **Daniel Webster,** who was essentially a deliverer of set speeches) the gentleman from the Bluegrass was a master parliamentarian who almost certainly would have become prime minister if America had had the British system. Yet, like Webster and Calhoun—those other titans with whom he is frequently compared—Clay never reached the presidency. Five times he tried, and tried valiantly. Perhaps the best opportunity was the earliest. In 1824–25, William H. Crawford edged out Clay for third place in the electoral college by 4 votes (41 to 37). It was entirely conceivable that Clay could have picked up three more electors and Crawford two fewer from the New York General Assembly; if so, the speaker of the House at Washington would have been in contention against Jackson and Adams in a chamber where he was very popular.

On the second occasion, 1832, Clay had no more than an outside chance against the formidable Jackson. But it seems likely that Clay, as well as Harrison, could have beaten Van Buren in 1840 if the Whig nomination had come his way. Clay was his own worst enemy in 1844 when he tried to carry water on both shoulders respecting the Texas annexation issue. Four years later he was denied the nomination the final time; at 71 he was not only old but a chronic loser.

Why all those frustrations, defeats, denials of the willowy and engaging "Prince Hal," the famed "Pacificator"? The answer is that Clay was before the public so long, and identified with so many issues, that voters held things against him as well as for him and eventually tired of his candidacies. From Clay's day well into the twentieth century only one sitting senator was elected president of the United States, and not a single chief executive was chosen wholly because of an outstanding congressional career. The Clay experience, therefore, was more typical than atypical. He was one of the most spectacular victims of what became an American tradition.

Clay's legislative talents were so great that it is no surprise to find them exaggerated here and there. His 1850 contributions illustrate the tendency. So replete with drama was the last appearance together of Clay, Calhoun, and Webster that one might erroneously suppose the three collectively—or Clay individually—wrought the Great Compromise of that year. This certainly was not the case.

Clay was a notable public speaker, of such quality that persons who merely read his words in the *Congressional Globe* can have no notion of his effectiveness. Like **James G. Blaine,** he was magnetic. And Clay's magnetism pervaded varying milieus—as evident in court and in Washington drawing rooms as on Capitol Hill and the Kentucky hustings. Indeed, it is doubtful whether, on a sustained basis, any other American of any generation surpassed the suave yet imperious "Harry of the West" as both a House and a Senate spokesman. See Glydon G. Van Deusen, *The Life of Henry Clay* (1937).

HOLMAN HAMILTON

CLEMENS, Samuel Langhorne (pseudonym, Mark Twain) (b. Florida, Mo., Nov. 30, 1835; d. Redding, Conn., Apr. 21, 1910), WRITER, was raised in Hannibal, Missouri. He left school at the age of 12 and was apprenticed to a printer. After working for a local newspaper he became a journeyman printer, working in St. Louis, New York, Philadelphia, and Iowa (1853–54). In 1857 while traveling to New Orleans he was apprenticed to a riverboat pilot and became a licensed pilot a year and a half later. When the Civil War broke out, he joined a Confederate volunteer company but left after one week to accompany his brother to Carson City, Nevada (1861). After an unsuccessful career as a prospector he became a reporter for the Virginia City (Nev.) *Enterprise* and adopted the pseudonym Mark Twain, a river term meaning two fathoms deep (safe water).

In 1864, Twain went to San Francisco where he worked as a reporter for the *Call.* He came into national prominence the following year when *The Saturday Press* in New York published his short story "The Celebrated Jumping Frog of Calaveras County." This "tall tale" was soon reprinted in newspapers throughout the United States. After serving as a correspondent in the Sandwich Islands, Twain began his long and successful career as a lecturer (1866). In 1867 he published his first book, *The Celebrated Jumping Frog of Calaveras County, and Other Sketches.* Twain then sailed for the Holy Land as a correspondent. The result of this journey was *The Innocents Abroad* (1869) in which he extolled the virtues of the New World as opposed to the Old and satirized American tourists who learned about Europe from guidebooks. In 1869 he moved to Buffalo where he wrote for the *Express* and contributed sketches to the New York *Galaxy,* a literary magazine.

In 1871, Twain moved to Hartford, Connecticut. In 1872 he published *Roughing It,* which was based on his journey to Nevada in 1861 and his experiences on the new frontier. The following year Twain and Charles Dudley Warner wrote *The Gilded Age* in which they satirized the speculative mania and corruption of the Grant era. In their characterization of the optimistic Colonel Beriah Sellers they captured the spirit of the age. *Tom Sawyer,* published in 1876, was based on Twain's recollections of his childhood in Hannibal. *The Prince and the Pauper* (1882), set in Elizabethan England, dealt with the theme of transposed identities. *Life on the Mississippi* (1883) was based on his experiences as a riverboat pilot.

The Adventures of Huckleberry Finn, a study of two characters who are searching for freedom, was published in 1884. Huck, the uneducated but compassionate son of a drunkard, is seeking to escape from "civilization," while Jim, a courageous but naïve black slave, is attempting to gain his freedom from bondage. By his use of "local color," Twain sought to reproduce a distinctive southern dialect and to describe a specific way of life.

In 1889, Twain published *A Connecticut Yankee in King Arthur's Court.* In *Pudd'nhead Wilson* (1894) he touched on the subject of miscegenation. Although he often criticized the money-getting spirit of the Gilded Age, Twain himself was an inveterate speculator. He had been successful as a publisher, but his heavy investments in a typesetting machine ruined him financially, forcing him to turn to H. H. Rogers of the Standard Oil Co. for help. In 1896 he wrote *Joan of Arc,* his favorite book. He then went on an international lecture tour, which he described in *Following the Equator* (1897).

After the Spanish-American War (1898) Twain became an ardent anti-imperialist. His most bit-ing criticism, however, was directed not at the United States but at King Leopold of Belgium for his policy in the Congo (see his "King Leopold's Soliloquy"). During the last years of his life Twain's writings reflected a very pessimistic view of human nature. This attitude is most evident in such works as "The Man That Corrupted Hadleyburg" (1900), a short story depicting greed in a provincial town; *What Is Man?* (1906), a deterministic novel in which he asserts that man is basically selfish; and *The Mysterious Stranger* (1916, posthumously), a story set in 16th-century Austria in which he suggests that perhaps life "is all a dream—a grotesque and foolish dream." *Mark Twain's Autobiography* was published in 1924.

⸺⸺

From the publication of "The Celebrated Jumping Frog" in 1865, Mark Twain has been a living writer, for his unpublished writings continue to appear with sufficient fanfare to make him a vital competitor in the publishing world. Yet for all the popularity and the occasional recognition in literary circles his books have enjoyed, it was not until **Ernest Hemingway**'s now famous observation in *The Green Hills of Africa* (1935) that *Huckleberry Finn* was both the first and the best book in American literature that Mark Twain began to be viewed as a writer's writer. Twenty years later **William Faulkner** told students in Japan that Mark Twain was really the father of American literature and that all subsequent writers were descended from him. Both Hemingway and Faulkner were emphasizing that Mark Twain, by being the first of our major writers to discover an American language, also discovered an American consciousness. The arc of his career discloses both the process and the nature of his discovery.

It is easy to forget that he began as a criminal. Guilty of the capital crimes of treason and desertion, Samuel Clemens entered the Nevada Territory in the midst of the Civil War, but instead of finding the silver he sought, he found the pseudonym that named and freed his genius. Under that pseudonym he reconstructed his life in the form of literature that was to reach and touch and please the world. The sources of his power rested in utter clarity of style, a remarkable command of vernacular, and, most important, a truly universal humor. Significantly enough, *The Innocents Abroad*, which brought him national popularity, was the record of the first organized pleasure excursion from the New World to the Old. Written in a style so clear that it made every style it faced seem somewhat archaic, fusty, and redundant, his humorously irreverent narrative belittled Europe itself as well as his own image of Europe which had previously belittled him. From this establishment of a present perspective Mark Twain invaded the past in *Roughing It* and "Old Times on the Mississippi," recalling his life as a miner and a pilot in the form of tall tales that transformed the failures and humiliations of the past into a greenhorn's encounter with the realities and deceptions of experience. In *Tom Sawyer*, Mark Twain pushed the pleasure principle into the realm of childhood, converting the shame, anxiety, and self-pity of boyhood into triumphs of play and make-believe, disclosing at the same time that the essential lie of the adult world turned upon dressing up play and pleasure as work and high seriousness.

In *Huckleberry Finn* he carried his humor to its limits, taking it to the heart of the tragic history of slavery. By making Huck Finn the hero of his own adventure of helping a runaway slave in the Old South, Mark Twain gained universal moral approval of Huck's "bad" action; and by making Huck the narrator of his own story, he freed Huck's dialect from its traditional literary frame and secured universal indulgence in Huck's "bad" language. Out of this indulgent approval Mark Twain released the instinctive freedoms of childhood that adult civilization suppresses, revealing that the real tyrant in the world was not simply southern slavery, which the Civil War had ostensibly abolished, but the conscience—whether northern or southern—that enables adult civilization to indulge, approve, and enjoy acts of war, murder, and brutality.

If Huck was able to reject this adult civiliza-tion at the end of his book and retire into the territory of childhood, Mark Twain was left to face the disillusion. He did face it—clamorously in *A Connecticut Yankee*, ironically in *Pudd'nhead Wilson*, and satirically in *The Mysterious Stranger*—but never with so good a humor again, for he could never refrain from railing at the conscience, or Moral Sense, that disguises with seriousness and high purpose the pleasure man takes in cruelty.

Whatever disillusion *Huckleberry Finn* left Mark Twain with, it remained to become an American classic—a true novel of Reconstruction—that brought not the old but an entirely new South back into the Union, converted the tragic history of slavery into a boyhood odyssey of humor, pursued the pleasure principle down the great Mississippi into the slavery and repression of civilization, and lifted "low" humor and "low" language into high art. See Justin Kaplan, *Mr. Clemens and Mark Twain* (1966).

JAMES M. COX

CLEVELAND, Stephen Grover (b. Caldwell, N.J., Mar. 18, 1837; d. Princeton, N.J., June 24, 1908), PRESIDENT, was admitted to the New York bar in 1859. Active in Democratic politics, he served as assistant district attorney of Erie County (1863) and as "reform" mayor of Buffalo (1881–82). As governor of New York (1882–84) he vetoed a bill to reduce the fares charged by the New York City elevated railway, maintaining that it was an evident violation of the company's contract with the state.

In 1884, Cleveland defeated **James G. Blaine** for the presidency, 219 electoral votes to 182 (a shift of 600 popular votes in New York would have reversed the result). As the first Democratic president since the Civil War, he appointed a southerner to his cabinet, and he vetoed many veterans' pension bills on the ground that they were draining the national treasury.

Cleveland believed in the principle of "rotation in office" but insisted on honesty and efficiency; he personally studied all applications for patronage. Convinced that the protective tariff aided trusts and increased the cost of living, he devoted his entire 1887 message to tariff reduction. Running for reelection in 1888 on this issue, Cleveland led Benjamin Harrison in the popular vote 5,540,050 to 5,444,337, but Harrison carried the electoral college, 233 to 168. In 1892, however, Cleveland was again elected president, defeating Harrison 227 electoral votes to 145.

A hard-money advocate, Cleveland believed that silver agitation had caused the panic of 1893. He persuaded Congress to repeal the Sherman Silver Purchase Act (1890), which had committed the government to purchase 4,500,000 ounces of silver monthly. In 1895, when the gold reserve fell to $41 million, Cleveland negotiated a loan of $62 million with the financier **J. Pierpont Morgan.** During the Pullman strike (1894), in which the American Railway Union tied up all the midwestern railroads to protest wage cuts, Cleveland called out federal troops to ensure the delivery of mail, thus breaking the strike.

In foreign affairs Cleveland refused to annex Hawaii because he questioned the legality of the provisional government. In 1895 he forced arbitration of the Venezuela-British Guiana boundary dispute on the ground that British policy conflicted with the Monroe Doctrine. After a serious war scare, Britain consented to the creation of a commission to arbitrate the dispute (1896). At the 1896 Democratic convention, Cleveland was repudiated, losing control of the party to the silverites led by **William Jennings Bryan.**

After leaving office Cleveland remained active in public life, lecturing and contributing articles to many periodicals. He was also an important trustee of Princeton University, where he opposed the policies of Woodrow Wilson.

Stephen Grover Cleveland was the son of a penniless, pious, hardworking Presbyterian minister, and much about his public career was redolent of the small-town parsonage. His childhood environment was reflected in his scrupulous attention to detail, devotion to the letter of the law, penchant for efficiency, and uncompromising belief in honesty, duty, and self-reliance. In his private life, on the other hand, he was neither careful nor abstemious. Obese early in life from too much beer and heavy food, he was an inveterate saloon-goer during his twenties and early thirties. He remained unmarried until his middle years and for a while consorted with Maria Halpin, for whose illegitimate child he later admitted responsibility. In these two opposed strains of his personality—the public piety and the private indulgence—Cleveland epitomized the split that ran through the soul of Victorian America.

Cleveland believed in the self-made man, but his rapid rise to the presidency was in some ways a matter of luck. His choice of Buffalo as a place to live and pursue his career was the first happy accident. The city was well established and yet open to newcomers, as a larger and older place was not. At the same time success in Buffalo politics made him a highly visible figure in the largest state in the Union. As an upstate Democrat, moreover, he could well afford to defy the New York City Tammany machine. His two years as governor of New York took place at a time when the public craved honesty and reform, and Cleveland appeared to represent both. When his record as governor is closely examined, however, it becomes clear that his reputation consists largely of vetoing appropriation bills and hurling verbal challenges at Tammany.

He was the only president who served two discontinuous terms. This fact may explain the incredible difference between his reputation after his first four years in office and after the second. In March 1889, Cleveland left the White House a hero, endorsed by the American people, having lost to his opponent only because of the electoral college's idiosyncrasies. In March 1897 he departed from Washington, his name "a hissing and a byword," as his contemporaries would have said. Yet Cleveland, the man and the political leader, had changed little in those eight years; it was the country and the Democratic Party that had.

Cleveland was a political and social conservative. He was a reformer, but a reformer only in the limited mid–19th-century sense of that term.

To Cleveland and to many of the Mugwumps who supported him in 1884 and after, the heart of reform was government impartiality and fiscal honesty, not social justice.

This strain runs straight through his political career. As mayor of Buffalo, Cleveland fought the aldermanic "ring" that was costing the city dearly. But he did little to improve the well-being of the city's poor. As governor of New York he approved a state civil service law, fought special legislation for private claimants, and defied Tammany and the bosses. But he also vetoed a bill to force the elevated railroads of New York City to reduce their fares to five cents, a measure that would have helped the city's wage earners.

But his essential conservatism is best exhibited during his presidency. In his first term Cleveland distinguished himself by fighting to extend the merit system to federal employees and by vetoing special pension legislation, although this latter entailed offending the powerful Union veterans' organization, the GAR. These actions, like his attack on the protective tariff that climaxed his first four years, was based on the Mugwump principle of "a fair field and no favor." It was the moral code of the virtuous American family, and it reflected the values of the small-town parsonage that Cleveland had known as a child. To many Americans it seemed a refreshing change from Grantism, and they largely approved of it.

But between 1889 and the mid-1890s times changed. In that crucial interval the nation entered the shoals of the severe depression of the nineties. In the East the mills and factories slowed and stopped; in the West farms were foreclosed. Labor and agrarian discontent flooded the land. Seldom before in the country's history had class lines been so sharply drawn. Men now wanted something more than honest, impartial government.

Cleveland proved unequal to the new mood. His solution for the depression was "honest money," even if that meant turning to the "Money Power" and accepting the terms of its ruler, J. P. Morgan. His way of dealing with labor discontent, when it exploded as a major railroad strike, was to allow his attorney general, **Richard Olney,** to issue an injunction against the American Railway Union. He then followed Olney's advice and called for federal troops to quell disorders connected with the strike. In effect the federal government won the strike for the railroads' General Managers' Association.

These moves destroyed Cleveland's political influence and severely damaged the Democratic Party. It led to the revolt of the party's western and southern wings, and the repudiation by the Democrats at their 1896 convention of everything Cleveland had stood for. With Bryan's nomination and the 1896 free silver platform, wrote **Allan Nevins,** "the party of Tilden and Cleveland passed out of existence." See Allan Nevins, *Grover Cleveland: A Study in Courage* (1932).

IRWIN UNGER

CLINTON, DeWitt (b. Little Britain, N.Y., Mar. 2, 1769; d. Albany, N.Y., Feb. 11, 1828), POLITICAL LEADER, graduated from Columbia College in 1786. In 1787, in a series of letters signed "A Countryman," he opposed the new Constitution because of its centralizing features. He was admitted to the New York bar in 1788 and served as private secretary to Governor **George Clinton** of New York, his uncle, from 1790 to 1795. He was elected to the New York state assembly in 1797 and to the state senate the following year (serving 1798–1802). Clinton was one of four senators who sat with the governor **(John Jay)** on the Council of Appointment.

Clinton served in the U.S. Senate (1802–3), where he introduced the Twelfth Amendment to separate the voting for president and vice president (adopted 1804). He resigned from the Senate in 1803 to become mayor of New York City, a position he held until 1815 except for 1807–8 and 1810–11. He was the chief organizer of the Public School Society (1805) and a patron of the New York Orphan Asylum and the New York City Hospital. In 1812 the antiwar Republicans nominated Clinton for the presidency, and he was also supported by the Federalists. But he was defeated by James Madison, 128 electoral votes to 89.

After his service as mayor, Clinton devoted his energies to a project for a state canal from Lake Erie to the Hudson (he had been New York canal commissioner since 1810). In 1816 the state legislature adopted his plan, and the Erie Canal was completed in 1825. He was elected governor of New York in 1817 (reelected in 1820) but was hampered by intraparty squabbles. In 1824 the "Albany Regency," a political machine led by Martin Van Buren, obtained the removal of Clinton as canal commissioner. Clinton then ran again for governor and was elected (serving from 1825 to 1828).

So tall, so handsome, so august in bearing, DeWitt Clinton was called the "Magnus Apollo." He rose in the rough school of New York state politics under the tutelage of his uncle, Governor George Clinton. He was given to moderate social reform but was also credited with establishing the spoils system of political appointments in the state. He was in any case a thoroughgoing pragmatist. With New York commercial interests suffering under the restrictions of the War of 1812, Clinton became one of only two presidential candidates to run on a major-party coalition ticket—the other was **Horace Greeley** in 1872. In his bid against James Madison in 1812, Clinton sought the support of the dissident "Peace" Republicans and of all-out, antiwar Federalists. If Clinton had won wavering Pennsylvania as well as his own New York, he would have beaten Madison by 114 electoral votes to 103.

After the war and the breakdown of national parties, Clinton headed a New York state party or faction of his own in opposition to the "Albany Regency" forces of Martin Van Buren. In the end, the Clintonians were bound to lose to the Regency, which emerged as the first full-scale professional state party organization. Meanwhile, always concerned for trade and economic development, Clinton had brought off his great triumph—construction of the Erie Canal, which connected the port of New York and the Hudson River to the Great Lakes and the far-flung trade routes of the West. The completion of "Clinton's Ditch" in 1825 established New York as the nation's major commercial entrepôt, at the expense of Philadelphia, Baltimore, and other would-be rivals. The preeminence of the Empire State was assured for decades to come. See Dorothie Bobbé, *DeWitt Clinton* (1962).

WILLIAM N. CHAMBERS

CLINTON, George (b. Little Britain, N.Y., July 26, 1739; d. Washington, D.C., Apr. 20, 1812), POLITICAL LEADER, was a lieutenant of rangers during the French and Indian War and served in the expedition led by Colonel John Bradstreet against the French at Fort Frontenac on Lake Ontario (1758). After studying law in New York City he practiced in Little Britain, where he became clerk of common pleas (1759) and district attorney (1765). In 1768 he was elected to the New York provincial assembly. In 1774 he served on the New York committee of correspondence, one of several intercolonial organizations that was created to communicate information regarding British violations of American rights. He served as a delegate to the second Continental Congress (1775–76). When the Revolution broke out, Clinton was made a brigadier general of militia. In 1777 he lost Fort Montgomery to the British under Sir Henry Clinton.

Clinton was governor of New York (1777–95). During the war he dealt severely with Loyalists. In 1789 he opposed the federal Constitution, arguing that New York would gain very little under it. However, the state convention over which he presided ratified the Constitution, 30 to 27. In 1791, Clinton helped obtain the election of **Aaron Burr** to the U.S. Senate, thereby gaining the support of the powerful Livingston family. In the gubernatorial election of 1792, **John Jay** apparently received a majority of the votes, but Clinton was reelected when pro-Jay ballots in three counties were invalidated.

Clinton declined to run for governor again in 1795 but returned to politics in 1800 as a member of the state assembly, and in 1801 he was again elected governor. In 1804 he was elected vicepresident, serving under Thomas Jefferson during the latter's second term. He stood as a factional Republican candidate for the presidency in 1808 but was overwhelmed by the "regular" nominee, James Madison, 122 electoral votes to 6. However, Clinton retained the vice presidency, an office he held until his death. In 1811 he broke a tie in the U.S. Senate by casting his vote against the rechartering of the Bank of the United States.

⸺⸺

As suave and dignified as he was shrewd, George Clinton was a transitional figure in politics. The son of an Irish immigrant, he was something of a self-made man who spent fifty-three of his 73 years in public office, twenty-one of them as governor of New York.

When Clinton began his career, the state was largely dominated by cliques of great landowners and old-family connections. Social status conferred political preeminence, and plain men tended to defer to their "betters." As politics became more open during and after the American Revolution, Clinton emerged as a unifying force among a variety of interests, personalities, and factions. In place of a politics of status, he served as a master broker in a game of multiple interests. His vision was commercial, and he hoped to make the Empire State virtually self-sufficient. On this question he differed with **Alexander Hamilton,** his inveterate political foe: Clinton saw no need for the new federal Constitution of 1789 or the Bank of the United States, and Hamilton favored both. Although he allied himself with the established Livingston clan against Hamilton, Clinton also cultivated the new, urban elements associated with Aaron Burr. By judiciously balancing legislation and offices in a manner that held his varied constituency together, he won and held power.

As Hamilton worked to establish the Federalist Party in New York, so Clinton helped to found the Jeffersonian Republicans there. He also helped bring about the New York–Virginia alliance that was the mainstay of the party nationally. Yet, as a transitional figure, Clinton was hardly a disciplined party man in the modern, 19th-century style, and he was frustrated in his ambition to

become president. In his old age he had to settle for the vice presidency instead. See E. W. Spaulding, *His Excellency George Clinton* (1938).

WILLIAM N. CHAMBERS

CLINTON, William (b. Hope, Ark., Aug. 19, 1946), PRESIDENT, was born William Jefferson Blythe IV but as an adolescent took the surname of his stepfather Roger Clinton. (Clinton's biological father had died only months before his son's birth.) Though lacking a stable, happy family life—his stepfather was an alcoholic and wife beater—young Clinton excelled at school as a student and athlete. Passionately interested in politics, he met President John F. Kennedy and Arkansas Senator **J. William Fulbright** in the summer of 1963, just before matriculating at George Washington University. There he served as class president twice and in the summer of 1965 worked for Fulbright and for the unsuccessful Arkansas Democratic gubernatorial candidate. Upon graduation in 1968 he accepted a prestigious Rhodes Scholarship to study at Oxford but passed up a third year there to attend Yale University Law School, where he met his future wife, Hillary Rodham. He received his law degree in 1973 and launched his political career. He lost a race for congressman in 1974 but won election as state attorney general two years later. In 1978 he became Arkansas's youngest governor, only to lose his bid for reelection two years later in large measure because of a highly unpopular tax on gasoline that he had initiated. Repeated success marked Clinton's political fortunes during the 1980s, however. He again won the governorship in 1982, 1984 (the term was now four years), and 1988. These victories and the reforms he brought to the state's educational system gained for him wider political recognition, as did the overlong nominating speech he delivered in 1988 for Governor Michael Dukakis of Massachusetts, the eventual Democratic standard-bearer. Four years later, despite unfavorable personal publicity which included charges that he was a draft dodger during the Vietnam War, Clinton gained his party's presidential nomination. Promising change and benefiting from an economic recession and the third-party candidacy of **H. Ross Perot,** he subsequently defeated incumbent George Bush.

———— ❧ ————

Clinton represents a new-style Democratic centrist in the thrust and tone of his presidency. True to the messages of his campaign, domestic concerns topped the agenda during the first two years of his administration. His first budget, mandating higher taxes on upper-income citizens and cuts in the growth of several programs, all geared to reducing the deficit that had grown alarmingly during the Reagan-Bush years, was pushed through the Democratic-controlled Congress against great opposition. But it appeared to work. The deficit began to shrink and the economy improved, with unemployment diminishing and the gross domestic product accelerating. The recession that marked the last years of George Bush's administration was over. Gun control legislation also emerged. The so-called Brady Bill, which mandated a five-day waiting period for handguns, passed Congress in 1993, as did a measure the following year that outlawed private possession of certain assault weapons. After acrimonious national debate the administration also prevailed upon Congress to ratify the North American Free Trade Agreement in 1993 and, with considerably less acrimony, the General Agreement on Tariffs and Trade the year after. Clinton's biggest failure was his inability to secure passage of a comprehensive health plan that would have provided, among other innovations, universal health coverage and a national health board to oversee and contain spiraling medical costs.

In the area of foreign policy Clinton appeared to be operating crisis by crisis, without a firm overall strategy or direction. He withdrew American forces sent to Somalia by Bush but used troops to restore President Jean-Bertrand Aristide to power in Haiti. Clinton also decided not to couple a most-favored-nation trade status for China with the latter's dismal human rights record even though he had sharply criticized his predecessor for precisely the same policy. Some problems—notably the grisly Bosnian civil conflict and North Korea's possible development of nuclear weapons—remained seemingly intractable, although the United States did reach a shaky accord with North Korea in 1994 and negotiated a tentative cease-fire in the Balkans in the fall of 1995.

During his yet unfinished term in office Bill Clinton could point to some noteworthy successes in both domestic and foreign affairs. Even from the embarrassing defeat of his health care reform program he was able to salvage some gains, notably the stabilization of certain medical costs, the increased number of workers covered by their employers, and the proliferation of cost-conscious health maintenance organizations. Yet continuously dogged by allegations of earlier sexual misconduct and financial impropriety (grouped together under the term Whitewater, a failed real estate venture in which Clinton had invested) while serving as Arkansas governor, of indecisive leadership and of poor appointments, Clinton increasingly lost support as his presidency progressed. He suffered from a widely held perception that he was an irresolute leader. Critics charged that he lacked fundamental principles. Supporters attributed the president's seeming uncertainty to his pragmatic, non-ideological approach to policy. Whatever the reasons, he has changed his position or at least noticeably wavered on issues as diverse as allowing homosexuals in the armed forces, committing weapons and troops to the Bosnian imbroglio, and naming various individuals to high government positions.

As Clinton's first term began to wind down, he was confronted by a problem no Democratic president had faced since Harry Truman: in the off-year congressional elections of 1992, Republicans gained control of both houses for the first time in forty years. Currently the Republican-dominated Congress under Speaker **Newt Gingrich** in the House and Majority Leader **Bob Dole** in the Senate, citing its "Contract with America," is calling for a dramatic rollback of the welfare state. To what extent the chief executive will either accede to or resist this challenge as yet remains unclear.

What does seem clear is that Bill Clinton, despite his demonstrated intelligence, driving ambition, and ability to triumph over the adversities of a damaged childhood, has not provided the leadership many of his supporters had expected. Remarkably, even Clinton has agreed with this critical assessment of his first two years in office. In a remarkable interview he provided a reporter in November 1995, Clinton admitted that he behaved "like a prime minister, not a president." He also observed he was "so anxious to fix the economy" that he "changed philosophically and missed the boat," and he "let Democrats down" by not stressing centrist themes of personal responsibility which he had campaigned on. Whether he will catch "the boat" before his first term ends remains to be seen. See David Maraniss, *First in His Class: A Biography of Bill Clinton* (1995).

ROBERT MUCCIGROSSO

COBB, Tyrus Raymond (b. Narrows, Ga., Dec. 1, 1886; d. Atlanta, Ga., July 17, 1961), ATHLETE. While still a child, Cobb's father, an educator and state senator, was shot to death by his mother, who claimed she mistook him for an intruder. Cobb left home in 1904 at age 17 to play minor league baseball for Augusta of the South Atlantic League. After an undistinguished season his contract was nonetheless purchased by the Detroit Tigers. He had a mediocre rookie year with the Tigers in 1905, seeing only limited action, but the following twenty-three seasons saw him accumulate a .367 lifetime batting average in 3,033 games, the highest average in baseball history.

A left-handed hitting outfielder, Cobb led the American League in batting a total of twelve times, including a series of nine consecutive seasons from 1907–15, and he batted .400 three times. His 892 career stolen bases remained a record until it was broken by Lou Brock in 1977. His 4,172 lifetime hits also was a record until Cincinnati Reds player Pete Rose broke it in 1985. Cobb was a "pure" hitter who made up for a lack of natural ability with intensely hard work and long practice sessions at the plate. Cobb was very

unpopular with opponents as well as with many of his teammates for his temperamental nature and ferocious style of play. He was appointed player-manager of the Tigers for the 1921 season, a position he held until the end of the 1926 season when he was implicated along with Cleveland Indians' manager Tris Speaker in a betting and game-fixing scandal. Although dropped as Detroit's manager, he was cleared by the baseball commissioner, Judge **Kenesaw Mountain Landis**. Cobb then signed with Connie Mack's Philadelphia Athletics in 1927 but retired after the 1928 season.

In 1936, Cobb was the leading vote-getter among the first five players elected to the Baseball Hall of Fame. Having made a fortune in shrewd investments, particularly in the Coca-Cola Company, he lived quietly if somewhat erratically in retirement in California and Nevada. Moving back to Georgia shortly before his death, Cobb helped set up an educational foundation and a medical research center there.

———————

"Shoeless Joe" Jackson called him "a peach of a player," and "the Georgia Peach" was his nickname ever after; sportswriter Paul Gallico considered him the greatest player who ever lived, and many other baseball experts agreed. But Ty Cobb became a baseball legend as much for his abrasive personality as for his superb athletic prowess. Although he accumulated more records on the diamond than any player before or since—123 of them, many still unbroken—he also left behind a reputation for pugnacity unmatched in the history of the game.

That Cobb was a phenomenal ballplayer no one ever disputed. Shrewd, dedicated, and courageous, he won the awe if not the affection of fans and colleagues alike. "Ty," as **Joe DiMaggio** observed, "was too much for everybody." Less well known were his private benefactions. After retiring he counseled players such as Ted Williams, established a scholarship fund and a hospital, and anonymously supported more than three dozen former ballplayers in financial need.

Despite his international fame and private

generosity, however, the truculent ballplayer alienated almost everyone he worked with. A confirmed racist, he refused to play an exhibition game in Cuba against an ethnically mixed team. He was accused of sharpening his spikes and deliberately jabbing opponents with them when he slid into base. It was said that as a manager he intimidated rather than led his players. Twice divorced and at odds with his children, he was no more successful with family relationships. According to journalist Heywood Broun, Cobb was "perhaps … the least popular player who ever lived." When he died, rich and alone, no official representative of the sport to which he contributed such vitality and skill attended his funeral. See Al Stump, *Cobb: The Life and Times of the Meanest Man Who Ever Played Baseball* (1994).

DENNIS WEPMAN

CODY, William Frederick (b. Scott Co., Iowa, Feb. 26, 1846; d. Denver, Colo., Jan. 10, 1917), BUF-FALO HUNTER, ARMY SCOUT, SHOWMAN, apparently received less than a year of formal education. In 1857 he took his first job as a wagoner and messenger for the freighting firm of Russell, Majors, and Waddell, and in the winter of 1857–58 he served with a wagon train dispatched to Utah to supply the troops sent there under Colonel Albert Sidney Johnston to subdue the Mormons. He took part in his first trapping expedition in the winter of 1859–60. In 1860–61 he worked as a stock-tender and rider with the Pony Express. Only 14 years old at the time, he completed one of the longest pony express rides in history—more than 320 miles, at an average speed of fifteen miles an hour. During the Civil War he scouted for the Ninth Kansas Cavalry against the Kiowas and Comanches (1862) and served as an enlisted man in the Seventh Kansas Cavalry in Missouri, Tennessee, and Mississippi (1864–65).

In 1867–68 he provided buffalo meat for the Kansas Pacific Railroad construction camps, earning the nickname "Buffalo Bill" and much of his reputation at this time. He was chief of scouts for the Fifth Cavalry during 1868–72 when he began a lengthy stage career by starring in *The Scouts of the Prairie,* written by his friend Edward Z. C. Judson—better known as "Ned Buntline." Cody returned briefly to the Fifth Cavalry in 1876 to fight the Sioux and Cheyenne. In 1883 he gave up the stage to form what was to become "Buffalo Bill's Wild West," along with Dr. W. F. Carver. When Carver sold out in 1884, he was replaced by Nate Salsbury, with whom Cody was to be associated until Salsbury's death in 1902. The show made extensive tours throughout America and was widely imitated. There were European tours in 1887–88, 1889–90, 1891–92, and 1902–6. During this period he bought land near North Platte, Nebraska, where he built a huge ranch and later helped establish the town of Cody, Wyoming.

Although his show was long very popular, it was increasingly in financial trouble. In 1909, Cody combined it with "Pawnee Bill's Great Far East," but in 1913 he lost his shares in it and became a hired performer in other shows. He also appeared in a number of early movies. An excellent scout and marksman, he retained his tirelessness, sharp eyesight, and skill as a rider to the end of his life.

———— ❧ ————

Buffalo Bill's extraordinary career exemplifies the transition from the real trans-Mississippi West of history and the mythical West of today's movies and television. Teamster, gold miner, trapper, Pony Express rider, guerrilla raider on the Kansas-Missouri border, Civil War cavalry-man, stagecoach driver, buffalo hunter, cattle-man, and for several years one of the most respected army scouts on the Northern Plains, Cody personally experienced every legitimate employment dear to current legend with the pos-sible exception of lawman (a lack partially miti-gated by his friendship with Wild Bill Hickok). Cody's larger contribution was the translation of this authentic knowledge and background into an increasingly "realistic" product palatable to masses hungry for vicarious experience of the "Wild West." Not the originator of frontier melo-drama, he was one of its most successful purvey-ors for a dozen years. Not the innovator of fiction with a western locale, he was probably the writer of at least the first several dime novels attributed to him, and he lent himself as author and/or hero to many more. Most important, although not the creator of the Wild West show, he brought it to its finest form as theater. From today's perspective Cody assumes an equality with figures like **Mark Twain** and **John Ford** in having developed the vernacular through which the world will no doubt long conceptualize a historic time and place. See Don Russell, *The Lives and Legends of Buffalo Bill* (1960).

ROBERT R. DYKSTRA

COHAN, George Michael (b. Providence, R.I., July 3, 1878; d. New York, N.Y., Nov. 5, 1942), ACTOR, COMPOSER, attended public schools briefly but was soon performing with his actor parents as a member of the Four Cohans, who toured the East and Midwest during the 1880s and 1890s. By 1892, George Cohan was also writing songs and sketches for his family's act. In 1901 he expanded one of his works into a full-length musical play, *The Governor's Son.* Although not successful in New York City, it was a hit on tour. In 1903, Cohan completed *Running for Office,* a musical farce, but this play, too, had only a short run in New York. In 1904, however, he joined with Samuel Henry Harris to form a production partnership. During the next decade Cohan produced numerous musicals and had many successes. Among the most famous were *Little Johnny Jones* (1904), which introduced such songs as "Yankee Doodle Boy" and "Give My Regards to Broadway"; *Forty-Five Minutes from Broadway* (1905); *George Washington, Jr.* (1906), which included "You're a Grand Old Flag" and "I Was Born in Virginia"; and *Hello Broadway* (1914). During this period Cohan also continued to act, becoming one of the stars of the Broadway theater. He also wrote a number of nonmusical plays, including *Get-Rich-Quick Wallingford* (1910). In 1917, after the United States entered World War I, Cohan wrote "Over There," which quickly became the most popular war song of that conflict. In 1920, however, after he had led a

losing battle against a strike called by the Actors' Equity Association, he attempted to withdraw from the New York City theatrical world. During the next decade he made a number of trips to Europe, went briefly into "seclusion" in Atlantic City (1924–25), and wrote a number of plays, including *The Tavern* (1920) and *The Song and Dance Man* (1923). During the 1930s he briefly returned to prominence for his widely acclaimed performances in **Eugene O'Neill**'s *Ah, Wilderness!* as Nat Miller (1933) and in *I'd Rather Be Right* (1937), in which he played the role of Franklin D. Roosevelt. He published an autobiography, *Twenty Years on Broadway* (1924–25).

Work, speed, and energy characterized George Michael Cohan from childhood. A prodigy, he played violin at 7, wrote and sold a song at 13, and in his teens became the prime force of his father's vaudeville company, the Four Cohans. Cohan was a songwriter, dancer, actor, playwright, play doctor, stage director, manager, and producer. He became the best-known theater man in America, a mixer and a mingler, who compensated for his small stature with excessive talent, virtuosity, and ambition.

Cohan said that to succeed in the theater one must "think of something to say. Then say it the way the theatergoer wants to hear it said, meaning of course that you must lie like the dickens." His uncanny ability to sound out the public mind and catch the common denominator of taste, to say it the way the people wanted it said, made his career one never surpassed in popular theater. The production company of Irish George M. Cohan and Jewish Samuel H. Harris ran many theaters concurrently both in New York City and on the road—all with phenomenal box-office success.

As a voice of his age Cohan made people laugh or cry. At the beginning of the 20th century, when Victorian tastes survived, he was in the mid-current of its sentimentalism, as judged by the half-hundred plays he wrote, rewrote, or partly wrote, and by the five hundred songs he composed. In these he showed a passionate love for America. His stirring nationalistic spirit rises to highest pitch in "I'm a Yankee Doodle Dandy Born on the Fourth of July" (actually July 3). He likewise moved people to patriotic fervor in many songs, among which are "She's a Grand Old Flag" and "Over There" (for which he received the Congressional Medal).

On his sixty-fourth birthday, four months before his death, his friend John H. Murray presented to him a giant cake done in Yankee Doodle colors, a fitting symbol of his life's work. See Ward Morehouse, *George M. Cohan, Prince of the American Theater* (1943).

THOMAS E. CHENEY

COLDEN, Cadwallader (b. Ireland, Feb. 7, 1688; d. Long Island, N.Y., Sept. 28, 1776), COLONIAL GOVERNOR, SCIENTIST, graduated from the University of Edinburgh in 1705, then studied medicine in London. In 1710 he emigrated to Philadelphia where he became a merchant and a doctor. After moving to New York in 1718 to accept the post of surveyor general, Colden made important contributions to surveying procedures and helped develop a land policy for New York. Living near Newburgh, in Orange County, he pursued his scientific interests in botany, medicine, and physics. His botanical work was recognized and published by Linnaeus, and Colden developed a wide correspondence with botanists on both sides of the Atlantic. He published a few medical pieces, a history of the Iroquois Indians, and an ambitious treatise on gravitation.

Colden became lieutenant governor of New York in 1761 and thereafter discharged the duties of governor except for brief periods. A staunch supporter of the Crown, he endeavored to administer the succession of revenue measures that began with the Stamp Act. For his refusal to oppose enforcement of that unpopular measure, he was burned in effigy in 1765. Ousted from office in 1776, he retired to Long Island.

Colden played a major role in both the government of colonial New York and the advancement of science in colonial America; in each realm he demonstrated qualities of self-confidence, hard work, and an eye for the main chance. Although trained in medicine, he seized the opportunity for preferment by a Scottish governor when he moved to New York and thereafter relied on the Crown for his and his family's advancement. He served long as senior member of the Council and several times held the reins of power. He was positive in his advocacy of policy and unresponsive to adverse, especially to popular, opinion. Of course, he was entirely out of sympathy with the Revolutionary movement.

He cultivated assiduously a variety of sciences, believing that political and economic success should be only a foundation for intellectual attainment. His greatest achievement was in descriptive botany, which brought him to the attention of the European natural history circle and into contact with American groups seeking to promote scientific study. Rather early, he turned over this work to his daughter Jane, and later he turned over his interest in electricity to his son David. Most of his writing in medicine, mathematics, and physics was of a speculative character, not much related to experience or experiment. His greatest effort was to extend Newton by explaining the cause of gravitation. This received wide attention in Europe but was ultimately rejected as a failure. Nevertheless, Colden deserved the scientific recognition he received and in several fields raised the level of understanding in America. See Alice M. Keys, *Cadwallader Colden* (1906), and Brooke Hindle, "Cadwallader Colden's Extension of the Newtonian System," *William and Mary Quarterly,* 3d ser., XXIX (1955), 99–115.

BROOKE HINDLE

COLE, Thomas (b. Bolton-le-Moors, Lancashire, Eng., Feb. 1, 1801; d. Catskill, N.Y., Feb. 8, 1848), ARTIST, emigrated to the United States in 1819. After traveling with a friend to St. Eustatius in the West Indies, he settled in Steubenville, Ohio. While working as a wood block engraver and designing wallpaper patterns in a factory established by his father, Cole began painting portraits. In 1823 he moved to Philadelphia to study at the Pennsylvania Academy of Fine Arts. In 1825 he took the first of many trips through the Hudson River Valley to paint landscapes. *The Clove, Catskills* (1827, New Britain Museum of American Art) and *Romantic Landscape* (1827, New York Historical Society) are examples from this period. *Expulsion from the Garden of Eden* (1828, Museum of Fine Arts, Boston) firmly established his artistic reputation.

Cole visited England (1829–31) and traveled through France and Italy (1831–32) before returning to New York in 1832. He settled in Catskill, New York, in 1836, thereafter producing many landscapes, including *The Voyage of Life* (1840, Munson-Williams-Proctor Institute, Utica), a four-canvas work representing the four ages of man in landscapes. He visited Europe again in 1841–42. He painted religious and allegoric themes in his later years, such as *The Cross and the World—The Pilgrim of the World on His Journey* (1846–47, Albany Institute of History and Art). Some of his other important canvases include *The Course of Empire* (1832, New York Historical Society), *The Titan's Goblet* (1833, Metropolitan Museum of Art, New York), and *In the Catskills* (1837, Metropolitan Museum of Art, New York).

Guided as a man by a profound religiosity and idealism, and as an artist by academic principles that awarded history painting primacy in the subject hierarchy, Thomas Cole became a landscape painter of impressive imaginative depth.

In a period of national self-confidence when the American public was enjoying an increased interest and pride in the beauty of native scenery, Cole accepted the emerging belief that the history of this country was embodied not in crumbling ruins or tales of ancient virtues but in the land itself. His efforts to reconcile his attachment to history painting with this awareness of what constituted "history" in America directed his art. His most characteristic landscapes are composed rather than topographical, poetic rather than dryly descriptive. They frequently include references to a variety of literary sources. Cole's desire to convey philosophic, moral, and religious truths

in these works often led him to exceed the bounds of a single canvas, to design companion pairs or series. For example, *The Course of Empire,* the earliest of the major heroic series, records in five large canvases the cycle of civilization. These scenes reflect Cole's affection for Claude Lorrain, Salvator Rosa, and John Martin, as well as his own great skill as a landscape painter. Subtle changes in time of day and season, as well as more obvious changes in costume, activities, and architecture, are manipulated to evoke contemplation of the perishability of the works of man in contrast to the timelessness of nature. Cole's lofty ambitions in landscape painting often conflicted with the desires of his patrons for straightforward American views. While he decried their lack of "a higher taste," he could answer these patrons' demands with fresh renderings of native scenes. These naturalistic landscapes look forward to the brilliant nature studies of the painters of the 1850s and 1860s, particularly Durand and Kensett.

Cole's art, then, looks back to 18th-century ideals, reflects the most profound philosophical concerns of his own day, and anticipates the best landscape art of the succeeding generation. See Louis Legrand Noble, *The Life and Works of Thomas Cole,* Elliott S. Vesell, ed. (1964).

HELENE BARBARA WEINBERG

COLLIER, John (b. Atlanta, Ga., May 4, 1884; d. Taos, N.M., May 8, 1968), REFORMER, EDUCATOR, attended Columbia University (1902–5) and briefly studied at the Collège de France in Paris. Returning to Atlanta, Georgia, in 1905, he became a social worker among newly arrived immigrants. He then moved to New York City where he continued his social work. After serving as the civic secretary of the People's Institute of New York City, he helped found the National Board of Review for Motion Pictures (1910; secretary to 1914). During 1915–19 he was the director of the National Training School for Community Centers. In 1919 he moved to California to become the state's director of community organizations (1919–20).

Greatly disturbed by the white man's attitudes

and actions toward Native Americans, Collier concluded that the Native American would indeed become the "vanishing American" unless reforms were instituted. In 1920 he traveled throughout the Southwest, living with Native Americans and studying their culture. In 1921 he was appointed director of social service training at State Teachers College in San Francisco (1921–22). In 1923 he became the executive secretary of the American Indian Defense Association, and he was the editor of *American Indian Life* during 1926–33. In these positions he tried to get the federal government to return land it had illegally taken from the Native Americans and to stop the future sale of their lands. He also urged Native Americans to preserve their culture.

In 1933, President Franklin Roosevelt appointed Collier commissioner of Indian Affairs, a post he held until 1945, the longest tenure of any commissioner. In 1934 he helped pass the Indian Reorganization Act (Wheeler-Howard Act), which restored land to the Native Americans, forbade future sale of reservation land by the government, and sought to make the Native American more self-sufficient.

Collier served as director of the National Indian Institute (1941–45). In 1947 he was appointed professor of sociology at the City College in New York. He retired in 1954. Some of his books include *Indians of the Americas* (1947) and *Patterns and Ceremonials of the Indians of the Southwest* (1949).

Collier was the most humane, innovative, and controversial of all U.S. commissioners for Native American affairs. Experience in urban community organization had convinced him that modern man was the dehumanized product of industrialization. During a season of despair he discovered the southwestern Native Americans who had heroically clung to an ancient, vibrant, and ennobling communal way of life. Shocked that these Native Americans, with much to teach modern man, were often despised, exploited, and misunderstood, Collier launched an attack on the policies of the federal government. He rapidly became an expertly informed and feared critic.

By the late 1920s the historic assimilationist policy, which assumed that Native Americans and their culture would ultimately disappear, was undergoing revision. In its place Collier advocated a pluralism that asserted the right of the Native Americans both to continue in their old ways and to participate in white civilization. The key to survival and self-respect was land, and Collier's greatest accomplishment was to reverse the trend of Native American land loss. He also encouraged tribal self-government, Native American arts and crafts, progressive educational objectives and techniques in Native American schools, religious freedom, and the staffing of the federal service with those who understood and respected Native Americans. This sweeping program and his strong advocacy embroiled him in controversy with Congress, vested interests, partisans of assimilation, and even some Native Americans, which finally limited his influence. Toward the end of his term he initiated pioneer anthropological investigations and promoted international cooperation in sustaining and constructively governing indigenous peoples throughout the Americas. His commitment to the way of the Pueblo Indians, evident in his writings and policies, was so deep, pervasive, and mystical that it became a religion. See John Collier, *From Every Zenith: A Memoir* (1963).

JOHN BARNARD

COLUMBUS, Christopher (b. Genoa, Italy, 1451; d. Valladolid, Spain, May 20, 1506), EXPLORER, first went to sea at about age 14. Between 1470 and 1473 he was a corsair in the service of René d'Anjou. In 1474 he sailed to the Greek island of Chios. In a naval battle off Cape St. Vincent in 1476 he was shipwrecked but managed to reach Portugal. Thereafter he made trips into northern waters (1477), sailing either to Iceland or England, to Madeira, and to the Guinea Coast. Hoping to reach the Orient by sailing westward, Columbus sought the backing of King João II of Portugal, but the king refused (1485). In 1486, Columbus tried to interest the Spanish monarchs, Ferdinand and Isabella, in a westward expedition. His proposal was rejected twice, but in 1492, following the Spanish defeat of the Moors at Granada, Ferdinand and Isabella agreed. Columbus was named Admiral of the Ocean Seas, viceroy, and governor-general of all the lands he might discover, and granted one-tenth of all the profits of his voyage.

On August 3, 1492, Columbus sailed from Palos, Spain, commanding a squadron consisting of his flagship *Santa Maria* and two smaller vessels, the *Niña* and *Pinta*. After stopping at the Canary Islands for water and repairs (August), he sailed due west and then southwestward. On October 12, 1492, he reached the island of Guanhani (San Salvador). Believing he had reached "the Indies" (the name used for the islands of eastern Asia), he called the local inhabitants "Indians." He sailed on to Cuba and then to Hispaniola, where he established a fort. When he returned to Spain on March 15, 1493, he was hailed as a hero.

Columbus again set sail for the New World, planning to colonize the region, in September 1493 with seventeen ships. He made a landfall in the Leeward Islands (November) before proceeding to Puerto Rico and then to Hispaniola. Finding that the fort he had built during his first voyage had been destroyed, he constructed a fortified town that he named Isabella (January 1494). After exploring Cuba, sailing to Jamaica, and visiting a number of islands, he returned to Spain in 1496.

Columbus departed on his third journey to the New World in May 1498, sailing from Guadalquivir with seven ships. After stops at Madeira and the Canary Islands (June), where he dispatched three ships to Santo Domingo, he proceeded in a more southerly direction, reaching Trinidad. He sighted South America (August) and then sailed to Hispaniola, where he found the colony in chaos. After the arrival of a new governor, Columbus was arrested and taken to Cadiz in chains (November 1500). He was soon released, but much of his former authority and prestige were gone.

Columbus's final journey to the New World commenced in May 1502. Departing from Cadiz with four ships, he reached Santo Domingo but was denied permission to land. Proceeding to Honduras, he explored southward, going as far as Central Panama (July 1502–April 1503). In June 1503 he reached Jamaica. After spending over a year in Jamaica he returned to Spain on November 7, 1504. The last eighteen months of his life were passed in relative obscurity.

In 1487 the Portuguese Bartholomeu Dias rounded the southern cape of Africa and named it Good Hope, "for the promise it gave of finding India, so desired and for so many years sought after." Columbus's first voyage was a race to India by a rival mariner who intended to serve God and his king, convert idolaters, and get rich by discovering and exploiting an alternative and better route to the spices and legendary treasures of Asia. In the end, the Portuguese reached India first. Vasco da Gama anchored off the Malabar Coast on May 20, 1498. But Columbus, although he died still believing that he, too, had reached India, effectively discovered a new world.

The 15th-century Portuguese and Spanish voyages of discovery mark the beginning of both American history and the European age of world history. Medieval Europe, despite fruitful contact with the Islamic world, brief encounters with East Asia, and the Norsemen's visits to "Vinland the Good," was a closed society. Between 1500 and 1900, Europeans largely displaced the populations of three other continents and settled there themselves. They conquered India, partitioned Africa, and decisively influenced the historical development of China and Japan. The entire earth became Europe's economic hinterland, political satellite, and technological debtor.

These long-term consequences of the discoveries, so clear to us because the epoch of European dominance they initiated is now over, were invisible to Columbus's contemporaries. Most 16th-century intellectuals hardly mention the New World. Ecclesiastics viewed it only as a providential opportunity to convert the heathen to Christianity. Many more books were published about the Turks than about Native Americans or the European settlers in America. Descriptions and maps of the world produced decades after Columbus's voyages do not mention America. Columbus's own posthumous reputation was meager, wholly incommensurate with his present fame.

Contemporaries normally judge the men and events posterity considers epoch-making by narrow standards of immediate personal interest and ambition. What interested most Europeans in America was the discovery—made after Columbus's death and as unforeseen as that of the New World itself—of silver deposits of unparalleled richness at Zacatecas and Guanajuato, north of Mexico City, and the fabulous sugarloaf mountain of silver at Potosí in the present Bolivian highlands. The results in colonial Latin America were a pattern of settlement dictated by the location of silver deposits and an economy in which agriculture, stock farming, manufacture, and trade developed as functions of mining. The result for Europe was the irrigation of its economy by a prodigious flow of silver. The very fleets that followed the routes Columbus had charted across the Atlantic were spoken of as the "fleets going to the Indies to bring back the gold and silver of His Majesty and private individuals."

Europe's vastly increased supply of treasure profoundly affected economic life, the balance of power, and the fortunes of individuals. Europeans paid for the luxuries of the East with silver from the West. The discoveries initiated by Columbus made possible the commercial exploitation of the sea route to Asia pioneered by Dias and Da Gama, while the exchange of American silver for Eastern spices intimately linked the first European colonial empires: the Spanish in the New World, a vast mining community managed by European settlers and worked by Native Americans, and the Portuguese, a loose string of forts and stations around the periphery of the Indian Ocean. The wealth of these empires, united in 1580 under King Philip II of Spain, supported a Spanish ascendancy in Western Europe, provided those sinews of war accurately defined by contemporaries as "money, more money, and again more money," and paid for Philip's campaigns against

England, France, and his rebellious subjects in the Netherlands. Most important of all, the circulation of American silver reinforced the inflationary effects of demographic expansion and rapidly pushed up prices. The "price revolution" seriously penalized wage earners and magnified the revenues of commercial and agricultural entrepreneurs, a profit inflation that accelerated capital accumulation and satisfied one important requirement for the development of capitalism.

In the 1620s imports of American silver began to diminish, prices stabilized or fell, and the English, Dutch, and French prepared to break the Spanish monopoly on the Atlantic economy. Europeans no longer viewed the New World primarily as an obstacle across or around which they must frantically search for a passage to India or as the probable location of still undiscovered deposits of precious metals. Most of North America remained open and unpreempted. It offered not immediate wealth but a refuge. The need was great. After decades of religious upheaval, religious war and persecution, religious minorities had few options and few rights except the *ius emigrandi*, the right to emigrate. Four months before Columbus sailed from Palos, Ferdinand and Isabella expelled all professed Jews from their kingdoms. In November 1620 a group of sectarian Christians landed on the continent Columbus had opened up, the first of the emigrants and refugees who were to populate the United States and Canada.

We know relatively little about Columbus's personality except what we can deduce from his actions. Clearly he was a remarkable sailor. That he possessed the single-minded vision, tenacity, and courage characteristic of genius is equally clear. The imaginative hypothesis that guided his career was in part mistaken. Understandably he had not the remotest idea of what his achievement was to make possible. The achievement was impressive enough. Its extraordinary and unexpected consequences have legitimately given his career and person a world-historical importance. See Samuel E. Morison, *Admiral of the Ocean Sea* (1942).

EUGENE F. RICE, JR.

COMPTON, Arthur Holly (b. Wooster, Ohio, Sept. 10, 1892; d. Berkeley, Calif., Mar. 15, 1962), PHYSICIST, was educated at the College of Wooster (BS, 1913) and Princeton (MA, 1914; PhD, 1916). He served for one academic year (1916–17) as instructor of physics at the University of Minnesota before he went to work for the Westinghouse Lamp Co. at East Pittsburgh, Pennsylvania, as an engineer (1917–19). In 1920, after spending a year as a National Research Council fellow at the Cavendish Laboratory at Cambridge University, Compton returned to teaching. He taught physics at Washington University in St. Louis (1920–23) and at the University of Chicago (1923–45), then served as chancellor of Washington University (1945–53), and later as Distinguished Service professor of natural philosophy (1953–61) at that institution. In his research during the early 1920s into the properties of X rays, Compton discovered that changes in wave length occur when the rays are scattered by substances such as graphite. For the discovery of this phenomenon, known as the "Compton effect," he shared the Nobel Prize for physics in 1927 with the British scientist Charles T. R. Wilson. Compton's major findings were published in *The Physical Review* in May 1923 and later summarized in his *X-Rays and Electrons* (1926). Compton also did important investigations into the nature of cosmic rays. During 1931–33 he directed a worldwide survey into cosmic ray incidence and intensity.

In 1941, Compton was appointed chairman of the National Academy of Sciences' committee to evaluate the military potential of atomic energy. During 1942–45 he directed the Metallurgical Division of the Manhattan Project, where he guided the development of the production of plutonium for the American atomic bomb project.

Arthur H. Compton was, above all, an extraordinarily talented physicist—an experimentalist with an exceptionally firm command of theory—and a gifted educator whose interests extended far beyond the bounds of physics into philosophy, religion, and other humanistic areas of learning. Together with his two brothers Karl and Wilson and his sister Mary, Arthur was reared in a religious and challenging home atmosphere in Wooster, Ohio, where his father taught philosophy at Wooster College before becoming dean. All four children had distinguished adult careers and, together with their parents, earned the title of "America's First Family of Learning."

Arthur Compton's scientific interests first centered on astronomy and on airplanes, and even in these youthful activities his great skill and patience in observation and his thorough love of working with his hands, so characteristic of his later career, were already evident. His interest in X rays dates to his undergraduate days at Wooster College and was greatly deepened through his graduate study at Princeton University and through his year as an instructor in physics at the University of Minnesota. His 1922–23 Nobel Prize-winning researches, in displaying the particlelike behavior of X rays alongside their well-known wavelike behavior, compelled physicists for the first time to take **Albert Einstein's** 1905 light quantum hypothesis seriously, and they formed a key link in the chain of developments that culminated in the discovery of quantum mechanics a few years later. His cosmic ray researches of the 1930s yielded a great deal of information on their nature and behavior. In his later career, after the war, religious and philosophical concerns as well as the moral and political implications of nuclear energy played a larger and larger role in his life. In this connection, just as in his work in physics, he traveled and lectured widely.

Compton's many undergraduate and graduate students, and his numerous colleagues and associates, while not always agreeing with his general religious and philosophical convictions, remember him as an inspiring, dynamic, self-confident, yet fundamentally modest person. See Marjorie Johnston, ed., *The Cosmos of Arthur Holly Compton* (1967).

ROGER H. STUEWER

CONANT, James Bryant (b. Dorchester, Mass., Mar. 26, 1893; d. Hanover, N.H., Feb. 11, 1978), EDUCATOR, whose father had been one of the earliest photoengravers, early developed an interest in chemistry. He received his AB (1913) and PhD (1916) from Harvard where he specialized in chemistry and was an editor of the Harvard *Crimson*. Upon graduation he went into business manufacturing chemicals, but when an explosion killed one of his partners, he returned to the academic world. An instructor at Harvard in 1919, by 1927 he was a full professor of organic chemistry engaged in important research on chlorophyll and hemoglobin.

When **A. Lawrence Lowell** of Harvard retired in 1933, Conant succeeded him as president. Among the changes he instituted was the development of a new MA teaching degree (1936). Conant insisted on both scholarship and successful teaching in granting promotions. Perhaps his most important innovation was to broaden the process for granting tenure by including on the review committee responsible and interested persons outside the university. He secured the endowment of several university professorships and sponsored the endowment of Harvard National scholarships as well as the Nieman fellowships for promising newspaper men. Conant embraced the concept of liberal education that had been developed at Columbia a few years before, introducing a program of broad general education courses for freshmen and sophomores.

Conant has been a strong force in calling for reforms in the public school system, stressing higher standards, fewer educational training courses for teachers, and more emphasis on English, foreign languages, mathematics, and social studies. His *The American High School Today* (1959) sold half a million copies and was widely credited with stimulating a trend toward higher intellectual standards.

Conant had a long history of government service. As a member of the Chemical Warfare Service during World War I he developed a process and a plant for the manufacture of Lewisite gas. As chairman of the National Defense Research Committee during World War II he supported the feasibility of the Manhattan Project that produced the atomic bomb; subsequently he served on the scientific advisory committee of the Atomic Energy Commission.

In 1953 he was appointed U.S. high commissioner to the Federal Republic of Germany, and in 1955 he became the first U.S. ambassador to West Germany, serving until 1957.

Conant published many books on scientific and educational subjects, among them *On Understanding Science* (1947), *Education in a Divided World* (1948), and *The Education of American Teachers* (1963). His autobiography, *My Several Lives: Memoirs of a Social Inventor*, appeared in 1970. That same year President Richard Nixon gave Conant an Atomic Pioneer Award for his contributions in World War II and in postwar development of atomic energy.

─────

Although James B. Conant had gained national recognition by the early 1960s as the "self-appointed critic" of America's public schools, little was known in 1933 about the young chemist who had just become president of Harvard University. Conant liked to think of himself as a "tough-minded idealist," his ideal being Jeffersonian democracy. The United States had become great, he believed, because in it, as in no other country, equality of opportunity and the natural aristocracy of the talented had become near-realities. By the 1930s, however, social stratification threatened to nullify this heritage. Yet there was a corrective—free public education—and it was his commitment to the schools that prompted Conant to try to "Endow the Talented" and promote social mobility through scholarships, testing programs to identify excellence, and the recruitment of eminent scholars and teachers.

Conant's other basic commitment was to the pre-Hitler Germany of outstanding intellectual achievement. Disillusioned, Conant had discovered early that National Socialism was bitterly reactionary and racist; and by 1940, when he felt that Nazism was also a threat to American security, he called for its defeat at all costs, even if this meant war for the United States. Conant was also instrumental in mobilizing civilian scientists for the national defense; and when war came he served as one of the top two advisers to the government on military research and development.

Conant's service did not end in 1945, and by 1947 he had become a self-described "Cold War Warrior." Feeling that postwar Russia was in some ways as menacing as prewar Germany had been, Conant retired from Harvard in 1953 to become U.S. high commissioner to West Germany. Ironically, his job was not to disarm the Germans but to rearm them. Returning to the United States in 1957, Conant also returned to an old concern of his—the public schools—and he did so at a propitious time, coincidentally with Russia's launching of *Sputnik*. He swiftly became one of the best-known and most influential educational reformers in the country. See James G. Hershberg, *James B. Conant: Harvard to Hiroshima and the Making of the Nuclear Age* (1995).

WILLIAM M. TUTTLE, JR.

CONKLING, Roscoe (b. Albany, N.Y., Oct. 30, 1829; d. New York, N.Y., Apr. 18, 1888), POLITICAL LEADER, attended Mount Washington Collegiate Institute, New York City (1842–46), studied law in Utica, and was admitted to the bar in 1850. A popular, flamboyant orator, he figured conspicuously at Whig conventions, and by 1858, after being elected mayor of Utica and then to Congress, he had become a member of the new Republican Party. He served in every Congress except one (1863–65) until 1867 when he was elected to the Senate. A strong supporter of radical Reconstruction, Conkling soon took the lead in New York Republican politics and became a dominant figure nationally as the head of the party's "Stalwart" faction. He was reelected to the Senate in 1873 and 1879.

In 1876, Conkling was defeated for the Republican presidential nomination by Rutherford B. Hayes. Worried about the future of the Ulysses Grant wing and infuriated at the appointment of his enemy, William M. Evarts, as Hayes's secretary of state, Conkling questioned the legitimacy of the president's claim to his office after the "disputed" election. When the new president began an investigation of the operations of the U.S. custom house in New York, traditionally controlled by the New York Republican organization, open warfare broke out between Conkling and the administration. Largely because of Conkling's opposition, Hayes failed to be renominated in 1880. The convention ultimately chose James A. Garfield in what Conkling thought was a compromise. Upon obtaining office, however, Garfield appointed **James G. Blaine,** the head of the "Half-Breed" faction and Conkling's most bitter political enemy, secretary of state, and another enemy, William H. Robertson, collector of the Port of New York. The latter act especially outraged Conkling, who regarded that position as his own personal preserve. As a result, following a long fight over Robertson's confirmation, Conkling and his fellow senator **Thomas C. Platt** resigned and offered themselves to the New York legislature for vindication. They both failed to gain reelection.

In the years that followed, Conkling successfully practiced law in New York City. Arguing a case before the U.S. Supreme Court in 1882, he maintained that the "due process" clause of the Fourteenth Amendment—which he helped write—had been intended to apply to corporations as well as persons, an interpretation the Court eventually accepted.

⸺❧⸺

Roscoe Conkling's fourteen-year career in the U.S. Senate can stand as a symbol not only of the rise and fall of the so-called Senate boss but also of an age when patronage, much more than issues, dominated American politics.

The senator was preeminent during the early 1870s when both President Grant and the Senate agreed to the disposal of federal patronage in New York State according to his wishes. President Hayes tried to challenge Conkling's prerogatives in the later 1870s, but the legislator momentarily prevailed when his Senate colleagues refused to confirm any nominations he opposed. Conkling's power vanished in 1881, as the Senate reversed itself and sustained President Garfield's appointment of a Conkling rival to the most influential patronage job in New York State. Then, after Conkling resigned his Senate seat in a huff, the state legislature failed to reelect him, thereby not only ending his political career but also presaging the demise of the political principles and outlook he represented.

Conkling's precipitate decision revealed at least as much about himself as it did about American national politics. Articulate, handsome, supremely confident of his own rectitude and superiority, he regularly registered savage contempt for anyone who dared challenge or disagree with him. Thus, though he clearly craved the power of public office, in 1881 he preferred to risk it all rather than share it with the resurgent office of the president.

As early as 1866 the vain Conkling became known as the congressman with the "turkey-gobbler strut." Fifteen years later that same strut propelled Senator Conkling away from the center of American political life. See David M. Jordan, *Roscoe Conkling of New York* (1971).

SARA LEE BURLINGAME

COOKE, Jay (b. Sandusky, Ohio, Aug. 10, 1821; d. Ogontz, Pa., Feb. 16, 1905), BANKER, was educated in a village school and became a clerk in a general store in Sandusky in 1835. In 1836 he became a clerk in a wholesale house in St. Louis. Following the collapse of this enterprise during the panic of 1837, Cooke worked as a clerk for the Washington Packet and Transportation Co. in Philadelphia. In 1839 he became a clerk in the banking house of Enoch W. Clark in Philadelphia and in 1843 a junior partner with one-eighth interest in the company. On January 1, 1861, he opened his own banking house, Jay Cooke and Co., in Philadelphia.

Cooke became the leading financier of the Civil War when three months before the fall of Fort Sumter his brother Henry, a close political associate of Secretary of the Treasury **Salmon P. Chase,** helped him secure an option to sell a $2

million bond issue in Pennsylvania. After successfully floating the issue, Jay Cooke was appointed government agent to sell war bonds in 1862. He skillfully utilized patriotic newspaper advertisements to attract the savings of working people and convinced government officials of the efficacy of offering lucrative interest rates (as high as 7.3 percent) to attract the capital of large financiers. In January 1865 he was appointed fiscal agent of the Treasury Department. Cooke received $1.7 million in bond sale commissions and other undisclosed amounts in his various government operations. He also established valuable ties with financiers and government officials.

Following the war, Cooke expanded his operations, opening branches in New York in 1866 and London in 1870. Although he continued to handle government securities, he also financed private business ventures in coal, iron, and railroads. In 1869 he became fiscal agent for the Northern Pacific Railroad. However, overinflated security issues and inefficient management of construction drove the line, and Cooke, into bankruptcy in 1873. This unexpected failure of the nation's leading financial concern precipitated the panic of 1873.

After being discharged from bankruptcy in 1876, Cooke speculated in the Horn Silver Mining Co. in Utah. He reaped $800,000 from this venture in 1880. By utilizing his skill, experience, and connections, he subsequently made profitable investments in mining, public utilities, and real estate. At his death he bequeathed a modest fortune to his family.

***

Cooke's chief significance lies in his contribution to the development of investment banking in America. Investment bankers are middlemen between the suppliers and users of long-term capital funds. Prior to the Civil War the demand for these funds originated mainly in the needs of the railroads, although an increasing number of textile and other manufacturing corporations, especially in the late 1840s and 1850s, were beginning to seek long-term capital by offering their securities (mainly bonds) for sale. Nevertheless, even when the capital needs of state and local governments were included, the total demand was so relatively small as to permit a host of unspecialized middlemen to serve as financial intermediaries. Besides investment bankers, these included commercial banks, stock and exchange brokers, auctioneers, and organizers of lotteries.

The large-scale needs of the federal government for loans during the Civil War had an important impact on this situation. As the "financier of the Civil War" Cooke's bond-selling methods, particularly his appeals to masses of patriotic Americans, exhibited for the first time the potential importance of small pools of savings. The years between 1870 and 1900 witnessed an increasingly voracious demand for capital to refund the government's Civil War debt and to service the needs of a rapidly developing and increasingly corporate business economy. Building on the wartime experience of Cooke, investment banking emerged during these years as a specialized occupation fully able to cope with the financial needs engendered by the massive changes in transport, mechanization, and urbanization that are associated with the term "industrial revolution." See Henrietta M. Larson, *Jay Cooke, Private Banker* (1936).

STUART BRUCHEY

COOLEY, Thomas McIntyre (b. near Attica, N.Y., Jan. 6, 1824; d. Ann Arbor, Mich., Sept. 12, 1898), JURIST, graduated from Attica Academy in 1842. After legal studies in New York and Michigan he was admitted to the bar in 1846. During 1846–56 Cooley practiced law and engaged in business for brief periods in Michigan and Ohio. In 1857 he secured an appointment from the Michigan legislature to compile the state's statutes, and from 1858 to 1865 he was official reporter for the Michigan Supreme Court, editing volumes V–XII of the *Michigan Reports.* In 1864 he was elected a judge on the Michigan Supreme Court, a position he held until 1885. During 1859–84 he also served as a professor of law at the University of Michigan.

Cooley wrote extensively, especially in the field of constitutional law. In 1868 he published his most important work, *A Treatise on the Constitutional Limitations Which Rest upon the Legislative Power of the States of the American Union,* the first important study of the impact of written constitutions on state legislation. Cooley asserted that all legislation was presumed valid unless it violated specific and express provisions of the Constitution. He also argued that the independence of the state executive should be maintained and that courts should not distinguish between ministerial and discretionary aspects of the executive's power. Cooley viewed the existence of coordinate, independent branches of government as the key to the survival of representative government. Among his later works probably the most notable were *The General Principles of Constitutional Law* (1880), a widely used text, *The Law of Taxation* (1876), and *Treatise on the Law of Torts* (1879), which was long considered the authoritative American work on the subject.

After 1885 he became increasingly involved in the affairs of the nation's railroads. In 1887, President Grove Cleveland appointed him to the newly formed Interstate Commerce Commission, on which he served as chairman until 1891.

It is characteristic of Cooley that the *National Union Catalogue* lists ninety-seven editions of his books, but there is little published about him. An unceasing worker, he was described at his death as "possessed by the demon of work." His happiest years came in 1865–85 when he successfully managed three careers—professor of law and usually dean, justice of one of the most distinguished state courts, and author of the preeminent law books of his generation.

Destiny consistently pushed him away from the practice of law, which was his life's ambition and for which his modest and retiring personality and weak voice ill suited him. Fortuitous events directed him into the life of judicature and scholarship for which he was perfectly equipped. For example, when he became a law professor he was *assigned* the task of becoming expert in constitutional law by the two senior professors because the field did not interest them.

Cooley coined the phrase, "A public office is a public trust," and he lived by it. Retired from the bench and the university, he became the first chairman of the Interstate Commerce Commission. He was penman of the ICC as well, writing nearly all of its impressive reports and working himself into a state of exhaustion from which he never really recovered.

The doctrine of judicial restraint permeates Cooley's writings, but that was not the message desired by his age. Instead, his contemporaries overemphasized his references to "liberty of contract" in order to transform him into a patron saint of laissez-faire. See Harry B. Hutchins, "Thomas McIntyre Cooley," in William D. Lewis, ed., *Great American Lawyers*, VII (1909), pp. 431–91.

DONALD O. DEWEY

COOLIDGE, Calvin (b. Plymouth, Vt., July 4, 1872; d. Northampton, Mass., Jan. 5, 1933), PRESIDENT, graduated from Amherst College (1895) and later practiced law in Northampton. He was a Republican member of the Massachusetts general court (1907–8), mayor of Northampton (1910–11), a state senator (1912–15; president, 1914–15), lieutenant governor (1916–18), and governor of Massachusetts (1919–20). Coolidge came into national prominence in 1919 during the Boston police strike when he asserted that no one was permitted to "strike against the public safety."

He was elected vice president of the United States in 1920, and became president when Warren Harding died (1923). Coolidge was himself elected president in 1924, receiving 382 electoral votes to 136 for **John W. Davis** and 13 for **Robert M. La Follette.**

When the scandals of the Harding administration were discovered, Coolidge removed all those who were implicated. Devoted to laissez-faire, Coolidge announced, "The chief business of the American people is business." Like Harding, he appointed pro-business advocates to the government's regulatory agencies. He also retained the conservative **Andrew Mellon** as secretary of the Treasury. In 1924 the Senate passed a bonus bill for the veterans of World War I over Coolidge's veto. Coolidge approved Mellon's Revenue Act of 1926, which reduced personal income and inheritance taxes. In 1927, and again in 1928, Coolidge vetoed the McNary-Haugen bill, which would have authorized government purchase of agricultural surpluses to be sold abroad.

In Coolidge's first annual message to Congress (1923) he urged U.S. participation in the World Court, but he failed to press this matter to a successful conclusion. Nor did he ever support American entry to the League of Nations. Although he opposed cancellation of interallied war debts, he arranged for reduced interest rates. In 1924 he signed under protest an immigration bill that was aimed specifically at excluding Japanese immigrants. The passage of this bill helped exacerbate U.S.-Japanese relations. In 1928, Coolidge supported the multinational Kellogg-Briand Pact, which called for the outlawing of war. Choosing not to seek the Republican presidential nomination in 1928, Coolidge retired in 1929.

⎯⎯⎯⎯

Through faithful service to the Republican Party and his constituents, Calvin Coolidge rose steadily up the political ladder. He was identified with no political creed more exciting than "Do the day's work." He was reserved in personality and unexceptional in intellect and talents. What he offered were reliability, because of his sincere commitment to public service, and availability, because his practice of law was never as promising as his political opportunities. The basis of Coolidge's success was that he was the safe choice in the right place at the right time.

During the 1919 Boston police strike, Coolidge's dictum, "There is no right to strike against the public safety by anybody, anywhere, any time," put him in the limelight. And he was available the next year when the Republican national convention delegates demanded a nonorganization nominee for vice president.

When, after twenty-nine lusterless months as vice president, Coolidge became president upon Warren Harding's death, he moved rapidly to control the party organization, thereby ensuring his nomination for president in 1924. By then he had weathered the political crisis occasioned by revelations of scandal in the Harding administration. Indeed, he had established himself in the public mind as a man of integrity, and one cautious and constitutional in the administration of government. With this image, and aided by an economic upswing, he gained a landslide election victory. Although the taciturn Coolidge was skillful in bidding for public favor, he was also what the voters wanted. He was the essence of stability, and he believed in nurturing the golden goose of big business so that it might produce bountifully for society. After the stresses of the Wilson and Harding administrations, that was what most Americans wanted.

Coolidge was an able administrator, demanding and receiving satisfactory and economical performances from his subordinates. His relations with Congress were another matter. Often the White House and Congress were out of step. Yet the legislators cooperated with Coolidge in keeping down appropriations, reducing taxes, and paring the national debt. The Senate also ratified the Kellogg-Briand treaty. Unfortunately for Coolidge, these grand accomplishments of the 1920s seemed mockeries with the coming of depression and world war during the 1930s. Coolidge must also be credited with, among other things, the improvement of relations with Latin American nations, orderly growth of aviation, regulation of radio broadcasting, encouragement of cooperative solutions to agricultural problems, and successful resistance to the McNary-Haugen bill, which, by encouraging inflation and the dumping of surplus farm products abroad, would have created problems at least as serious as those it might have solved.

Yet it is plain that Coolidge was limited in vision in dealing with emerging problems. He misconceived or ignored, like the vast majority of Americans, the underlying causes of economic, racial, and international discord. Although probably no president could have solved these problems, the attempt might have somewhat reduced their proportions. In balance, Calvin Coolidge was not as great as the 1920s saw him, but he was not as lacking as future decades would view him. See Donald R. McCoy, *Calvin Coolidge: The Quiet President* (1967).

DONALD R. McCOY

COOPER, James Fenimore (b. Burlington, N.J., Sept. 15, 1789; d. Cooperstown, N.Y., Sept. 14, 1851), WRITER, was dismissed from Yale in 1806 and went to sea. In 1807 he was commissioned a midshipman in the U.S. navy, serving until 1810. In 1811 he married Susan Augusta DeLancey, the daughter of a prominent New York family, and settled in Westchester County to lead the life of a country squire.

In 1820, Cooper published his first novel, *Precaution*. Relying on flight and pursuit themes set against the background of the northern frontier or the high seas, he soon became one of the nation's most popular romantic writers of fiction. *The Spy* (1821), a tale of the American Revolution, was based on the adventures of an agent during the British occupation of New York. In 1822, Cooper moved to New York City where he began work on his "Leatherstocking Tales," in which he created the character Natty Bumppo, a moral and resourceful frontiersman who overcomes the rigors of nature and the villainous conduct of man by his superior qualities. In *The Pioneers* (1823), Cooper's hero was an old scout living in a frontier village with his loyal Native American comrade Chingachgook. *The Pilot*, also published in 1823, was a seafaring romance. It was followed by *Lionel Lincoln* (1825), a novel about Boston during the days of Bunker Hill. In *The Last of the Mohicans* (1826), Cooper's hero, now called Hawkeye, participated in the French and Indian War in the Lake George area.

During 1826–33, Cooper traveled abroad. There he wrote *The Prairie* (1826), the third novel in the Leatherstocking series, in which the hero was an "old trapper" on the Great Plains, living among the Pawnee Indians. While in Europe,

Cooper extolled the virtues of American democracy, as is evident in his *Notions of the Americans* (1828), an epistolary novel about an Englishman in America. *The Red Rover* (1828), *The Wept of Wish-ton-Wish* (1829), and *The Water-Witch* (1831) were all romances set in the United States or on the high seas. He also published a number of European romances satirizing feudalism. These works include *The Bravo* (1831), *The Heidenmauer* (1832), and *The Headsman* (1833).

Returning to the United States in 1833, Cooper was disappointed with the society he encountered. Although he was a Democrat in politics and a supporter of political democracy, he opposed the "leveling" process of the Jacksonian era, believing that the concept of the gentleman should be preserved. Criticized for his aristocratic views by the press, he responded in *A Letter to His Countrymen* (1834) and *The American Democrat* (1838). His disillusionment with American society is illustrated in *Homeward Bound* (1838) and *Home as Found* (1838), studies of Americans who have just returned from abroad and are critical of what they see. Cooper's quarrels with the press led him to sue a number of newspapers for libel.

In 1839, Cooper published *The History of the Navy of the United States of America*. *The Pathfinder* (1840), another novel in the Leatherstocking series, was set in the St. Lawrence and Lake Ontario region in 1760. *The Deerslayer* (1841), the final work in the series, was an account of the hero's adventures on the New York frontier during the 1740s. (The adventures of Natty Bumppo can be read in the following chronological order: *The Deerslayer, The Last of the Mohicans, The Pathfinder, The Pioneers,* and *The Prairie.*)

In 1840, Cooper returned to the theme of adventure on the high seas, publishing *Mercedes of Castile* (1840), a novel about **Christopher Columbus**'s first voyage; *The Two Admirals* (1842), an account of the British navy before the American Revolution; *The Wing-and-Wing* (1842), a tale of a French privateer in the Mediterranean toward the end of the 18th century; and *Ned Myers* (1843), a biography of a sailor he once knew. Other works of this period include *Wyandotte* (1843), a study of the effects of the

American Revolution on a small town; *Le Mouchoir* (1843), a discussion of fashionable life in New York; and *Afloat and Ashore* (1844) and *Miles Wallingford* (1844), both of which deal with the evils of impressment.

In 1845 Cooper published *Satanstoe*, the first of three novels in the "Littlepage Manuscripts" series, based on the history of a prosperous upstate New York family. This work was followed by *The Chainbearer* (1845) and *The Redskins* (1846). Taken together the novels trace the history of three generations of Dutch patroon society, culminating with the anti-rent wars of the 1840s. *Lives of Distinguished American Naval Officers* was published in 1846.

Some of Cooper's other works include *The Monikins* (1835), *Sketches of Switzerland* (1836), and *Gleanings in Europe,* issued in five volumes (1836–38).

Cooper was not only American but was always an Americanist. His contribution and its flavor come from that, although to his own time he seemed a liberal in Europe and a conservative in the United States. He studied America and cared for it whether he was expressing his idealism by examinations of European decay in novels like *The Bravo, The Heidenmauer,* and *The Headsman,* or as in *Home as Found* by his dismayed sense of his country's failure to live up to his dream. America was, as **Henry James** would have put it, Cooper's *donnée,* his "given." The mission of American literature, Cooper insisted, was to find its own identity in the expression of its national ideals.

Cooper gave a great deal, as readers are continuing to discover. His pictures of Europe are mirror images of what he hoped for his own country during the seven years he spent abroad, chiefly in Paris, as a self-appointed citizen plenipotentiary. His letters recording the European revolutionary period deserve the attention of any historian of that time. Cooper is not quite an exchange Tocqueville, but he deserves being taken into account.

So do his observations on his fellow countrymen after his return from his residence abroad. Cooper was no Jacksonian. His criticisms of republican abuses are cantankerous but representative. Novels like *Satanstoe* and *The Chainbearer* are unsurpassed as chronicles of pseudobaronial Hudson River manners. His novels of the sea are multifaceted and in their way pioneering. His writings are multiply useful if used. They can be.

His greatest gift was the image of a prototypal American landscape and of prototypes who as free men moved in forests and over lakes and prairies. Not only Americans responded to the Leatherstocking Tales. Goethe, having read *The Prairie*, marveled in his diary at the "rich materials and his ingenious handling of them." He proposed that German writers should themselves use American episodes of history. Balzac, reviewing *The Pathfinder*, wrote, "Leatherstocking is a statue, a magnificent moral hermaphrodite, born of the savage state and of civilization, who will live as long as literatures last. I do not know that the extraordinary work of Walter Scott furnishes a creation as grandiose as that of this hero of the savannas and forests." Italians read Cooper omnivorously from 1828 on, when translations of four of his works appeared simultaneously. Not until **Sinclair Lewis** gave America a Main Street and then a Babbitt did Europe have substitutes for the "matter of America."

Cooper's characters were at best two-dimensional, but his narratives moved with superb élan. Natty Bumppo was an example of what a just-minded, pure, and self-reliant man might be. Chingachgook was the noble savage as good friend. Because Cooper did not really know the forest or a Bumppo, he was not held down by details. Instead he became the voice for the common instinct for adventure. His characters fill out the void in our longings and imagination. In Cooper's accounts of the frontier we have myth rather than miscegenation.

"Rigid adherence to truth," Cooper wrote in his preface to the Leatherstocking Tales, "an indispensable requisite in history and travels, destroys the charm of fiction; for all that is necessary to be conveyed to the mind by the latter had better be done by delineations of principles, and of charac-

ters in their classes, than by too fastidious attention to originals." Yet myth becomes truth when handed down. Cooper's Leatherstocking Tales have become historical data.

As historical data they have increasingly provided material for cultural historians. Books like Henry Nash Smith's *Virgin Land* and Richard Lewis's *The American Adam* have shown a respectable way to reach him. Historians of ethnic attitudes include his fictions, recognizing that Cooper has helped to shape our attitudes even when we have not read his books. His books have in a very real sense become a part of our own "given." John Cawalti's *The Six Gun Mystique* puts it bluntly when he states, "The Western was created in the early 19th century by James Fenimore Cooper." With such a father, the patrimony has once again become worldwide. See Donald A. Ringe, *James Fenimore Cooper* (1962).

NORMAN HOLMES PEARSON

COOPER, Peter (b. New York, N.Y., Feb. 12, 1791; d. New York, N.Y., Apr. 4, 1883), INDUSTRIALIST, INVENTOR, PHILANTHROPIST, received only one year of formal schooling but obtained wide practical experience helping his father in hatmaking, brewing, storekeeping, and brickmaking. At the age of 17 he was apprenticed to a coachmaker. During his apprenticeship he invented a machine for mortising the hubs of carriages, the first of its kind in this country. Cooper next went into the cloth-shearing business. While still in his twenties he bought a glue and isinglass factory that provided the basis for his wealth.

In 1828, Cooper established an ironworks in Baltimore and soon produced *Tom Thumb*, the first steam locomotive built in the United States. "This locomotive," Cooper later recalled, "was built to demonstrate that cars could be drawn around short curves, beyond anything believed at that time to be possible." Its success encouraged confidence in the possibility "of building railroads in a country scarce of capital, and with immense stretches of very rough country to pass ... without the deep cuts, the tunnelling, and the levelling which short curves might avoid." Cooper credited his "contrivance" with saving the Baltimore and Ohio Railroad from bankruptcy.

In 1835, Cooper sold his Baltimore ironworks, taking a large portion of his pay in Baltimore and Ohio Railroad stock. Increase in the market value of the stock (from $44 to $230 per share) greatly enriched Cooper and allowed him to begin a number of other enterprises. These included iron mines, blast furnaces, foundries, a rolling mill, and a wire factory. In 1840 his rolling mill introduced the use of anthracite coal for puddling and in 1854 produced the first iron beams and columns for structural use. In 1856 one of his blast furnaces made the first trial of the Bessemer process in America. In 1879 the Iron and Steel Institute of Great Britain awarded him its Bessemer gold medal.

Cooper was president of the North American Telegraph Co., which controlled half of all American telegraph lines, and also of the New York, Newfoundland and London Telegraph Co., which, after a twelve-year struggle, succeeded in laying the Atlantic cable. He showed his faith in the latter project by making financial advances without which the undertaking could not have been completed.

In 1859, Cooper founded the Cooper Union for the Advancement of Science and Art, designed to provide "free courses of instruction in the application of science and art to the practical business of life." A hard-money Democrat in his youth, opposing the issuance of paper money by private banks, Cooper became a strong supporter of a flexible, nationally controlled paper currency in the 1860s and in 1876 ran for the U.S. presidency on the Greenback Party ticket. He received about 82,000 out of the approximately 8.5 million votes cast. In the early 1880s, when over 90 years of age, he assumed leadership of the National Anti-Monopoly League, which opposed the growth of trusts. During the final third of his life Cooper expounded his opinions on political economy in numerous public statements, letters, and pamphlets. His views were brought together in two volumes: *Political and Financial Opinions of Peter Cooper* (1877) and *Ideas for a Science of Good Government* (1883).

One of the outstanding American businessmen of the 19th century, Cooper was also a devoted public servant, a self-educated political economist, and a generous and innovative philanthropist. As New York City alderman he supported movements for paid police and fire departments, improved water supply, and the establishment of small parks and squares. A long-time member of the New York City Board of Education and an ardent advocate of free public education, he successfully opposed the use of public funds for support of parochial schools. In national affairs he favored a paper currency, civil service reform, and a protective tariff.

Cooper's ideas of political economy, derived in part from the theories of economist **Henry C. Carey,** were influenced by Cooper's business interests and grounded in his allegiance to the common man. He always identified himself as "a mechanic of New York" and thought of himself as the spokesman of "poor toilers and producers." In his business career he demonstrated the economic capabilities of the little man; in his public activities, addresses, and writings he denounced privilege and advocated policies to make economic opportunity available to all. Recognizing the obligation of government to promote the general welfare and to regulate industry and commerce in the national interest, Cooper foreshadowed the major themes of 20th-century reform movements.

As a philanthropist Cooper's importance lies not in the magnitude of his donations but in his publicizing and practice of the doctrine that wealth is a public trust. Long before **Andrew Carnegie,** who attributed his philanthropic activities to Cooper's example, Cooper declared that men of wealth should administer their fortunes as trustees for the benefit of society. "The duty and pleasure of every rich man," he maintained, was "to do something in a public way for the education and uplifting of the common people."

Cooper Union, the unique educational institution he created, continues to flourish as a center for college-level instruction in engineering, art, and architecture, and through its museum, library, and lecture series diffuses knowledge of science and the arts to the general public. Cooper provided the building, its equipment, and a fund to maintain the physical plant. During his lifetime and until about 1900, however, it was necessary to rent space in the building to tenants in order to support the library and instructional programs. Shortly after the turn of the century substantial gifts by the Cooper and Hewitt families and other donors, including Andrew Carnegie, provided an endowment fund permitting the entire building to be devoted to educational purposes.

One of Cooper's associates described him as "a man who was intensely practical yet never commonplace." Cooper's mechanical talent, business acumen, and zeal to improve himself and others made him, in the words of **Allan Nevins,** "as distinctively an American type as Benjamin Franklin, and one as quickly taken to the American heart." See Allan Nevins, *Abram S. Hewitt: With Some Account of Peter Cooper* (1935), and Miriam Gurko, *The Life and Times of Peter Cooper* (1959).

ROBERT H. BREMNER

COPLAND, Aaron (b. Brooklyn, N.Y., Nov. 14, 1900; d. North Tarrytown, N.Y., Dec. 2, 1990), COMPOSER, first received piano lessons from his sister when he was 11. While attending high school in 1916 he decided to become a composer and began to study harmony with Rubin Goldmark. Copland then became the first student to enter the American Conservatory opened after World War I at Fontainebleau, near Paris. He later moved to Paris where he studied with Nadia Boulanger for three years. After returning to the United States in 1924, his *Symphony for Organ and Orchestra* was introduced by the New York Symphony Society. Copland first came to prominence soon after that with two major works employing jazz idioms: *Music for the Theater,* a suite for orchestra (1925), and the *Concerto for Piano and Orchestra* (1927), both first performed by the Boston Symphony under Serge Koussevitzky. From that time on Koussevitzky gave Copland encouragement and performed many of his major works. Copland held a Guggenheim fellowship (1925–27), and in 1930 his *Dance Symphony* won a prize of $5,000 in a contest sponsored by the RCA Victor Company. This and several orchestral and piano works that followed were in a highly complex idiom, the jazz tendencies having been abandoned in 1927.

Convinced by 1934 that he was losing contact with audiences, Copland began assuming a more assimilable style by employing folk themes and popular melodies within the context of serious works. He achieved an outstanding success with the first such work, *El Salón México,* for orchestra (1936), based on popular Mexican melodies. He then used cowboy songs in the ballets *Billy the Kid* (1938) and *Rodeo* (1942), and a Shaker tune in *Appalachian Spring* (1943). The last originated as a ballet for **Martha Graham** but became popular as an orchestral suite after winning the Pulitzer Prize. In *Lincoln Portrait,* for narrator and orchestra (1942), which used excerpts from Lincoln's letters and speeches as text, Copland also quoted **Stephen Foster** and the famous folk ballad "Springfield Mountain." His Third Symphony (1946), though influenced by American folk music, did not resort to quotations; it received the Boston Symphony Award of Merit and the New York Music Critics Circle Award. A pronounced American identity also prevails in his only full-scale opera, *The Tender Land,* first produced by the New York Opera in 1954 and since then extensively revised. Beginning in the middle 1950s, Copland abandoned any traces of folklorism for avant-garde techniques, including serialism.

Copland wrote incidental music for motion pictures, notably *Of Mice and Men* (1939), *Our Town* (1940), *The Red Pony* (1949), and *The Heiress* (1949). With the last he won an Academy Award. He also wrote music for radio, television, and stage, and for children. He also wrote a work designed for performance by young people, a play-opera, *The Second Hurricane* (1937).

Copland, who virtually abandoned composing after 1970, was always actively engaged in teaching and the professional life of music. He organized concerts and festivals of modern American music; chaired the executive board of directors of the League of Composers; headed the department of composition, then chaired the faculty, at the Berkshire Music Center at Tanglewood (1940–65); delivered lectures at Harvard; and was the author of several books, including *Copland on Music* (1960) and *The New Music: 1900–1960* (1968). In 1964 he received the Presidential Medal of Freedom from President Lyndon Johnson and was the recipient of many other honors: the Henry Howland Memorial Prize by Yale University (1970); the Gold Baton from the American Symphony Orchestra (1978); and the Kennedy Center Lifetime Achievement Award (1979). His birthdays—70th, 80th, and 85th—were celebrated by performances of his music in the United States and overseas.

When, in 1924, Walter Damrosch rehearsed the New York Symphony Society in Copland's first major work to get an American hearing—the *Symphony for Organ and Orchestra*—he commented: "If a young man can write a piece like that at the age of twenty-three, in five years he will be ready to commit murder." Damrosch was objecting to Copland's modernism. In his last compositions, in some of which Copland employed the serial technique, he once again became victimized by denunciations for avant-garde tendencies. Thus in the half-century or so that represented Copland's career as composer it had come full circle. He started out and he ended up as a modernist. But in between he worked in styles and idioms that were comparatively conservative in methodology and materials, and that sought to reach out for a wide audience appeal. This first happened in the 1920s when he embraced jazz in *Music for the Theater* and the *Concerto for Piano and Orchestra*. It happened again when he adopted folklorism, the style in which he wrote the works for which he became most famous. It is significant to point out, however, that in consciously striving for greater simplicity and a more popular appeal, Copland made no descent in the quality of his product.

In short, in whatever idiom Copland chose for his compositions he maintained his high integrity besides revealing an extraordinary mastery of technique and articulateness. Whatever he wanted to say he said clearly, skillfully, economically, and with originality. The trenchant intellect that so distinguished him in his lectures, writings, and teachings—and his high-minded purpose as a musician—always governed his compositions. *El Salón México, Appalachian Spring, Billy the Kid, Lincoln Portrait*—for all their excursions into popular or folk areas—were the creations of a major composer: this is why Copland dominated American music and influenced American composers more than any other man for half a century and why he deserved the sobriquet "dean of American music." See Arthur Berger, *Aaron Copland* (1953).

DAVID EWEN

COPLEY, John Singleton (b. prob. Boston, Mass., 1738; d. London, Eng., Sept. 9, 1815), PAINTER, was much influenced during his childhood by his stepfather Peter Pelham, a portrait painter, skilled mezzotint engraver, and schoolteacher. Although the opportunities to see paintings or to learn advanced techniques were limited in pre-Revolutionary America, Copley made the most of them. He studied anatomy books and prepared a book of anatomical drawings for his own use. He published a mezzotint engraving when he was 15 and in the same year, 1753, began his professional career as a portrait painter. As an artist he painted not only oils but pastels and miniatures on ivory and copper as well. Apart from a six-month visit to New York and a brief trip to Philadelphia, he worked primarily in the Boston area. In 1766 he sent a portrait of his half-brother Henry Pelham playing with a pet squirrel to England for exhibition at the Society of Artists and wrote to his countryman in England, the artist **Benjamin West,** for his opinion of the picture and his advice. West and other artists in London, notably Joshua Reynolds, were struck with the considerable talent that the painting revealed. However, repeated encouragement from Reynolds and West failed to induce

Copley to come to England, for he had developed a lucrative practice in America. The increase in civil turmoil on the eve of the Revolution disrupted his patronage, however, and he then decided to go to Europe. Arriving in England in 1774, he immediately set out on a trip to view the art treasures of France and Italy, and when he arrived back in England, he was joined there by his family. He never set foot in America again.

Elected a full member of the Royal Academy in 1783, Copley worked in London until his death. Although he achieved considerable early success in England as a "history" painter, the later years of his life were not altogether happy. Some of his paintings did not sell, and he became involved in political squabbles at the Royal Academy. Financial problems plagued him, and he was fortunate that a daughter married a wealthy Boston merchant whose repeated loans were welcome in his last years. His lawyer son John Singleton Copley, Jr., in later life achieved fame as Lord Lyndhurst, three times lord chancellor under Queen Victoria. Born in Boston before the family left for England, Lyndhurst was the only lord chancellor ever to have been born outside of Great Britain.

Copley's career divides itself into two distinct periods. During the first, lasting until 1774 when he left America for Europe, Copley was the preeminent portrait painter in colonial America. He recorded the likenesses of many who were later to achieve fame during the American Revolution, such as **Samuel Adams, Paul Revere,** and **John Hancock** (Boston Museum of Fine Arts). The primary characteristic of Copley's American portrait style is its realism. He rendered with precision the appearance of his sitters, their costumes, and their surroundings, reproducing form, color, and texture with astounding fidelity, and catching the exact feel of each sitter as a functioning human being with a clearly defined role in his society.

Copley was motivated by strong professional pride and ambition. He was not content to be acknowledged as the best portrait painter in the American colonies. He longed to measure his skills against the great masters of Europe, both old and modern. Although ambition alone would not have been sufficient to induce the pragmatic Copley to leave America, political disruption of his professional career was. Shortly after the Boston Tea Party, in which he played a minor role as the unsuccessful link between radical friends and Loyalist in-laws, he departed for Europe. After studying the old masters on the continent for a year and a half, he settled in England late in 1775 and began the second phase of his career, which lasted forty years until his death.

Although Copley in England continued to paint portraits out of economic necessity, his loftier aspirations were in the direction of history painting. He gained early notice with his dramatic painting *Watson and the Shark* (National Gallery of Art). Pursuing the path opened by Benjamin West in his famous *Death of Wolfe* of 1771, Copley transferred the realism of his American portrait style to a new realism in history painting. In the major historical works that secured his reputation, the *Death of the Earl of Chatham* and the *Death of Major Peirson* (Tate Gallery), he perfected a type of history painting in which he sought absolute verisimilitude of setting, costume, action, and likenesses. He applied this technique not only to great moments of contemporary history but also retroactively to the past, as with his painting *Charles I Demanding the Five Impeached Members of Parliament* (Boston Public Library).

Copley's innovations affected French history painting from David to Meissonier, but are of perhaps greater interest as reflecting new attitudes toward history itself developing in the late 18th century. While his paintings are intellectually notable for their realism, they are visually notable for their color. From the subtle and tasteful palette of his American portraits to the brilliance of his English works, Copley stands forth as a superb colorist. He ranks as one of the greatest of all American artists, certainly the best of the colonial period; an important innovator in history painting; and in sum one of the major artists of the 18th century. See Jules David Prown, *John Singleton Copley* (2 vols., 1966).

JULES DAVID PROWN

CORNING, Erastus (b. Norwich, Conn., Dec. 14, 1794; d. Albany, N.Y., Apr. 9, 1872), MERCHANT, FINANCIER, worked as a boy in his uncle Benjamin Smith's hardware store. Moving to Albany in 1814 he entered into partnership in a hardware business and soon thereafter bought a small foundry and rolling mill. This enterprise eventually became one of the largest manufacturers of hardware in the country. Partly to develop markets for his manufactures, he moved into the newly developing railroad business, investing in the Mohawk and Hudson, between Albany and Schenectady, and joining in the promotion of the Utica and Schenectady in 1833. He served on the original board of directors and became the president of the new line. Several other connecting railroads were soon built to constitute a continuous link between Albany and Buffalo.

In the early 1850s Corning was instrumental in the consolidation of these lines into the New York Central. He served as its president until 1864. He was also a director of the Hudson River Railroad, which became the first link in **Cornelius Vanderbilt**'s railroad empire; the Michigan Central, a connecting link from Buffalo to Chicago; and the Chicago, Burlington and Quincy, an extension through Iowa into Nebraska.

Corning's interests also extended to banking, to investments in state securities, and to land speculation in both New York and the West. He was instrumental in the chartering of the Albany City Bank in 1834 and remained its president until his death. He was also an investor in two Detroit banks. His land speculations included townsite promotions at Corning and Irving, New York, and investments in timber and agricultural lands in Iowa, Michigan, and Wisconsin.

The dovetailing of Corning's interests is illustrated by his participation in the chartering of a railroad to tap the coal fields of Pennsylvania through Corning, New York, to provide traffic for the Central. Even his interest in politics served his business interests. An early member of the Democratic Albany Regency, he used his influence to aid his enterprises. He served four terms as mayor of Albany before 1837 and was a state senator (1842–46) and a congressman (1857–59, 1861–63). He was also a regent of the University of New York from 1833 until his death.

⁂

Erastus Corning was the archetype of the early American capitalist. Beginning as an apprentice and handicapped by a lifelong lameness, he took advantage of every opportunity to parlay his considerable skills as an organizer and opportunist into a sizable fortune, great economic influence, and not inconsiderable political power as well. A hardware merchant, he branched out, first into manufacturing, then into enterprises that provided a market for much of his product, and, as he acquired more wealth and some political prominence, into related enterprises that could both benefit from and be benefited by his other activities. He was the personification of the increasing sophistication of the evolving American economic system. While he is best remembered for his connection with the development of the New York Central Railroad, the essential unity of his hardware, merchandising, railroad, banking, land speculation, and political enterprises—like that of the stage of economic development he personifies—is of far greater importance. Of equal significance for understanding the growth of the system was his complete conviction, held in common with such of his predecessors as William Duer and such of his contemporaries as Patrick Tracy Jackson, that there was no "conflict of interest" between his various roles. That belief would come in the era of corporate giants and product specialization. As his biographer puts it, "The old capitalist, Albany oriented as he was and accustomed to the simpler business organizations of an earlier day, would not have liked and perhaps would not have understood [that era], but it was one which he had done much to help create." See Irene D. Neu, *Erastus Corning, Merchant and Financier, 1794–1872* (1960).

LESLIE E. DECKER

COTTON, John (b. Derby, Eng., Dec. 4, 1584; d. Boston, Mass., Dec. 23, 1652), RELIGIOUS

LEADER, graduated from Cambridge (AB, 1603; AM, 1606), and ordained as an Anglican deacon and priest in 1610. He served as head lecturer and dean of Emmanuel College, Cambridge, and received his divinity degree in 1613. In 1612, Cotton became the vicar of St. Botolph's in Lincolnshire, where his Puritan beliefs led him to change the liturgy of church services. When the **Winthrop** fleet left for America in 1630, Cotton preached the farewell sermon at Southampton.

Cotton's disagreements with the Church of England soon brought him under attack. To avoid a summons requiring him to appear before the Court of High Commission, he emigrated to Massachusetts Bay (1633). He became the "teacher" of the church at Boston and soon established himself as one of the colony's leaders. Cotton was a conservative in politics, arguing that magistrates should have lifetime tenure. However, he did not favor arbitrary or unlimited government. He approved of the banishment of **Roger Williams** (1635), which he suggested was evidence that the Puritans were still loyal Englishmen who accepted the authority of the Crown. In 1626, Cotton drafted a very severe Mosaic law code for the colony, but the General Court rejected it.

Cotton was one of the leading protagonists in the "Antinomian controversy." He believed that a "covenant of works" (salvation through good deeds) was not a reliable sign of "election" (salvation) because it imputed to men powers they did not have. But when **Anne Hutchinson** carried Cotton's theology to its logical conclusions by stating that God's grace was a mystical experience based on personal revelation and precluding any moral effort, Cotton supported her banishment.

Cotton was a prolific writer. Some of his most important works are *The Way of the Churches of Christ in New England* (1645), a study of Congregationalism; *Milk for Babes* (1646), a catechism; and *The Bloody Tenent Washed and Made White* (1649), an answer to Roger Williams's plea for religious liberty.

In 1630 when John Cotton bid a sermonic farewell to the departing Puritans of the great Winthrop fleet, he had been vicar of the prestigious St. Botolph's Church in old Boston in Lincolnshire for eighteen years. A marked man, under pressure from the Laudian establishment, he followed the chosen people to New England in 1633. There he was made teacher of the Boston church and soon became the most able, albeit suave, expositor and defender of the New England way.

The founders of Massachusetts were a peculiar brand of Puritans whose views and practices raised doubts even in the minds of erstwhile friends in England, primarily because their errand into the wilderness to establish a Bible commonwealth required a notable shift in perspective and emphasis. In England cohesion was bolstered by persecution from without. In New England the troublesome threats to solidarity came from deviants within the fold who did not deny the basic principles but, building on them, came to conclusions at odds with the orthodox consensus. Outstanding among them were Roger Williams and Anne Hutchinson.

Cotton's "Bloody Tenent" exchange with Williams took place a decade after Williams's banishment and does not necessarily reflect the views of either around 1635. Williams's theological orthodoxy was never questioned. He as well as Cotton accepted the doctrine of the separation of the realms of nature and spirit. Williams held that in practice this meant the absolute separation of church and civil authorities, and concluded that the state's coercive power should never be used to induce or maintain religious beliefs or practices. Cotton held that when Christians had the opportunity they must first set up true churches and then form a government that would nurture and protect both their doctrine and practice. The coercive power of civil authority might be invoked when the church's authority proved inadequate to keep its house in order. To Cotton, who believed in freedom only for consciences "rightly informed," the use of such coercion was not to force a man's conscience but to enforce it—that is, to induce him to do what his conscience must tell him he ought to do. Williams argued for the freedom even of consciences wrongly informed.

Anne Hutchinson, although excommunicated for persisting in error (heresy), intended only to expound the orthodox views of Cotton, whom she idolized. Cotton emphasized the work of the Spirit, as did all the Puritans; Hutchinson, deducing from his sermons that the Person of the Holy Ghost dwelt in the justified Christian, became an "enthusiast" admitting to direct divine revelations. For that she was excommunicated, Cotton reading the sentence. Further holding that sanctification (a moral life) was no evidence of justification (rightness with God), she was accused of "anti-nomian" views that appeared to sap the foundations of all government. For this she and several of her supporters who formed a political party were banished by civil authority. That it took a delegation of his colleagues to convince Cotton that she was in error suggests that she was probably expounding correctly enough a popularized version of what he preached.

In the history of the vicissitudes of New England Puritanism, John Cotton may be seen on the one hand as the ancestor of those who defended establishment to the bitter end in 1633 and on the other hand as the progenitor of the spiritual and idealistic tradition that flowered in **Ralph Waldo Emerson**'s transcendentalism. See Larzar Ziff, *The Career of John Cotton: Puritanism and the American Experience* (1962).

Sidney E. Mead

COUGHLIN, Charles Edward (b. Hamilton, Ontario, Can., Oct. 25, 1891; d. Bloomfield Hills, Mich., Oct. 27, 1979), RELIGIOUS LEADER, attended parochial schools in Hamilton. After graduating from St. Michael's College of the University of Toronto (1911), Coughlin entered the church and was ordained in 1916. In the years following he was a teacher at Assumption College, Toronto (1916–22) and held pulpits in Kalamazoo and Detroit, Michigan, before he was sent to erect and take over the pastorate of the Shrine of the Little Flower in Royal Oak,

Michigan (1926). In 1926 he began a series of sermons and children's shows on the radio, and he achieved national attention in 1930 when he started to interject his political and economic views into his broadcasts. Under the auspices of the Radio League of the Little Flower, Coughlin bitterly attacked Communism, internationalism, and President Herbert Hoover. At first he came out in favor of the New Deal but soon turned against it because of what he considered its inadequate monetary policies. In 1934, CBS radio removed him from the air, but Coughlin launched his own radio network, the National Union for Social Justice—with a membership in the millions, organized by congressional district "cells"—the magazine *Social Justice* to propagate his views, and a charitable organization, Social Justice Poor Society, Inc.

As Coughlin's criticism of Franklin D. Roosevelt became increasingly harsh and his anti-Semitism more obvious, his popularity began to wane, and the American Catholic hierarchy became increasingly displeased. In 1941, Edward Cardinal Mooney, his direct superior, told Coughlin to halt broadcasting. His association with the Christian Front, a quasi-fascist organization, left him vulnerable to charges that he was a Nazi sympathizer, and in 1942, *Social Justice* was barred from the mails by the attorney general. It soon halted publication. Two years later the National Union for Social Justice was dissolved and Coughlin dropped almost completely from the public view. He continued as pastor of the Royal Oak parish, however, until 1966 when he retired from his pulpit and built a house in Birmingham, Michigan. In retirement he stayed out of the limelight, but he continued to write pamphlets and tracts denouncing Vatican Council II and its reforms of Church liturgy, and "atheistic, godless … Communists." Some of his many books include *The New Deal in Money* (1934), *A Series of Lectures on Social Justice* (1935), and *Am I Anti-Semitic?* (1939).

Articulate, charming, zealous in behalf of the depression-bred poor, Charles Coughlin's appetite for adulation and power soured the movements that brought him prominence. He was a radio pioneer endowed with a magnificent voice who offered a swelling middle- and working-class audience a monetary panacea that was a curious potpourri of populist and papal encyclical ideas. Yet he never rejected the free enterprise system, attacking instead sinister international bankers and brain trusters as the real culprits in the economic crisis. His assaults on the political, economic, and intellectual leadership intensified when he turned against FDR, who had rejected Coughlin's hyperinflationist theories. To an ethnic following formerly victimized by nativists, the radio priest suggested that the real "un-Americans" were the establishment "internationalists" (with capitalist or Communist leanings) who had caused the depression. In 1936, Coughlin wed the National Union for Social Justice—a vast movement completely under his control—to the new Union Party in a flamboyant vendetta against the New Deal. Although he petulantly "retired" from politics after defeat, he reappeared in 1938 at the head of a new group of more militant followers. The increasingly lurid anti-Semitic tone imparted by Coughlin's speeches made the Christian Front less a foreign policy pressure group favoring isolationism than another vehicle for the passions and prejudices of a leader now turning toward fascism.

Coughlin seemed to thrive on controversy during his political career; later he would regret doing much of what had brought him fame in an age of depression and world war. His success underscores many of the tragic dissonances in American social history. See Charles J. Tull, *Father Coughlin and the New Deal* (1965).

DAVID H. BENNETT

COUZENS, James (b. Chatham, Ontario, Can., Aug. 26, 1872; d. Detroit, Mich., Oct. 22, 1936), AUTOMOBILE MANUFACTURER, POLITICAL LEADER, after a public school education and two years of business school, moved to Detroit (1890) where he worked for a railroad until he became a clerk in Alex Y. Malcomson's coal business (1895). When **Henry Ford** sought financial backing for his automobile factory, Malcomson and Couzens aided the venture (1902). Couzens became Ford Motor's business manager in 1903, and after Malcomson broke with Ford, the company became essentially a Ford-Couzens partnership (1905–15). Couzens conducted the firm's financial affairs and was responsible for the famous $5-a-day wage plan of 1914, although Ford received the publicity. He resigned from Ford Co. in 1915.

Seeking a career in public service, Couzens served as chairman of the Detroit Street Railway Commission (1913–15), in which post he favored municipal ownership of the lines. Appointed Detroit police commissioner in 1916, he launched a rigorous law enforcement campaign that helped elect him mayor in 1918 (reelected 1921). As mayor he improved the civil service, carried out a program of public works, brought the streetcars under municipal ownership, and defended the free speech and assembly of radical groups.

In 1922, Governor A. J. Groesbeck appointed Couzens U.S. senator to replace T. H. Newberry, who resigned under charges of corruption. As senator, Couzens joined **Robert M. La Follette**'s Progressive Republican bloc and became a leading advocate of a redistributive income tax, heading an investigation of the Bureau of Internal Revenue in 1924–25. When the government sued Couzens for underpayment of income taxes on Ford Motor stock he had sold in 1919, he proved that he had actually overpaid his taxes (1925). Having been elected in 1924 and reelected in 1930 despite regular Republican opposition, Couzens criticized President Herbert Hoover's economic policies. His opponents charged him with precipitating the banking crisis of February—March 1933 because he opposed a Reconstruction Finance Corporation loan to Detroit banks. He was a supporter of President Franklin Roosevelt's New Deal, although remaining a Republican. In 1933 he was a U.S. delegate to the London Economic Conference. His public support of Roosevelt's reelection in 1936 led to his loss of the Republican nomination for senator.

To stand by himself if need be; to say what he truly thought, regardless of consequences; in short, to be an independent man—such was the outstanding quality of James Couzens. It was a quality that made him, Canadian-born, a remarkable American.

Even without his fourteen years' service in the U.S. Senate he would have been exceptional for his mark on industrial and political history. The mammoth Ford Motor Co., notable for its pioneering in manufacturing techniques and employee relations, as well as for its size, is one of his monuments. Without Couzens it might have gone the way of several hundred other motorcar companies—into extinction. He was its financial genius. He was also its social conscience. He was not only the innovator of its then (1914) revolutionary $5-a-day wage plan but the advocate—long before many sociologists and economists—of a guaranteed annual income for industrial workers.

The Ford company made him his millions, but the millions, instead of separating him from people of ordinary means or no means, made him the vigorous champion of the economic underdog. Thus, when he became mayor of Detroit, he was a "people's mayor," like Tom Johnson of Cleveland, "Golden Rule" Sam Jones of Toledo, and **Fiorello LaGuardia** of New York. Thus, too, when he became a senator, he advocated every measure in behalf of labor, of small farmers, of home owners, and, during the Great Depression, of the jobless millions, standing roaringly meantime against every measure that in his view unjustly favored the privileged rich. His special target was another multimillionaire, Secretary of the Treasury **Andrew W. Mellon,** because Mellon proposed reducing income taxes on the rich as a prosperity measure. Nominally a Republican, Couzens had contempt for all the Republican presidents under whom he served— Warren Harding, Calvin Coolidge, and Herbert Hoover—because he felt they ignored the needs of the masses of Americans. Yet for Franklin D. Roosevelt, Democrat, he had what amounted to love. No one supported Roosevelt's program more ardently than Couzens, the millionaire

Republican. It was said that Couzens "hated all other millionaires." In a sense that was true. But his hate for the overrich was mainly derived from a sense of justice—for fellow human beings who did not share fairly in the profits of American industry. That sense and his streak of independence made him a great political figure, though often misunderstood or misrepresented because of his pugnaciousness. See Harry Barnard, *Independent Man: The Life of Senator James Couzens* (1958).

HARRY BARNARD

COXE, Tench (b. Philadelphia, Pa., May 22, 1755; d. Philadelphia, Pa., July 16, 1824), SOCIAL SCIENTIST, studied law at the College of Philadelphia (now the University of Pennsylvania) but dropped out before graduating to become in 1776 a partner in his father's counting house, Coxe, Furman and Coxe. Having remained neutral during the American Revolution, Coxe was arrested, allegedly for aiding the enemy, after the British evacuated Philadelphia in 1778. He was later paroled when no one appeared to testify against him. He was a member of the Annapolis convention of 1786 and firmly supported adoption of the new Constitution. In 1787 he published *An Enquiry into the Principles on Which a Commercial System for the United States of America Should Be Founded*, in which he expounded the need for the development of American industry, protective tariffs to promote that development, and the encouragement of trade in American bottoms. To this aim he helped found the Pennsylvania Society for the Encouragement of Manufactures and the Useful Arts (1787). Also in 1787 he became secretary of the newly formed Pennsylvania Society for the abolition of slavery and remained active in the antislavery movement all his life. He presented his views on the Constitution, *An Examination of the Constitution for the United States* (1788), in which he argued that the Constitution would provide a sound national commercial and currency policy.

Coxe served as assistant secretary of the

Treasury under **Alexander Hamilton** (1789–92) and as commissioner of the revenue (1792–97); he criticized **John Jay**'s Treaty (1795) and switched allegiance to the Jeffersonian Republicans in the election of 1796. President John Adams removed him from the commissioner's post. Again supporting Jefferson in the presidential election of 1800, Coxe published in the Philadelphia *Aurora* a personal letter he had received from then Vice President John Adams in 1792 in which Adams accused fellow Federalists Thomas and Charles Pinckney of being under British influence while in government employ. The letter caused an immediate sensation, and legal action was taken against the *Aurora*'s editor, William Duane. Coxe found employment in Jefferson's administration as purveyor of public supplies (1803–12). He spent the rest of his life serving in a variety of minor federal and Pennsylvania state government posts: collector and supervisor of the revenue at Philadelphia (1813–15) and clerk of the quarter sessions court of the state of Pennsylvania (1815–18). In such economic writings as *A View of the United States of America* (1794), *An Essay on the Manufacturing Interest of the United States* (1804), and *A Statement of the Arts and Manufactures of the United States of America for the Year 1810* (1814), Coxe called for a balanced economy; the joint pursuit of agriculture, manufacturing, and commerce; and especially development of the cotton industry in the South.

———

Tench Coxe was among the earliest, best-equipped, and most persistent advocates of a balanced economic development for the young American nation. Probably his chief particular contribution was his pioneer promotion of cotton cultivation and manufacture. In this, as contrasted with some others, he was equally solicitous for agriculture and for industry. It was through one of the societies that Coxe fostered that **Samuel Slater** came to this country and introduced the first satisfactory carding and spinning machinery.

As an economist Coxe differed from Hamilton, **Mathew** and **Henry C. Carey**, Friedrich List, Daniel Raymond, and John Rae in two respects that limited his influence. He relied more on furnishing information of profitable opportunities for enterprisers than on invoking and directing governmental policy. Even had he been more inclined toward protective legislation, his wavering political allegiance was a handicap. In the second place Coxe did not incorporate his recommendations in a system of theory challenging the laissez-faire doctrine of Adam Smith and others of the classical school of economic thought.

In that formative period of national progress it was not possible to serve two masters. After diverging from the Federalists he was poorly rewarded for his service to the Republicans. Jefferson and Madison confined him to offices below his capacities. This was a hardship to Coxe personally; more important, it deprived the public of his best efforts. See Harold Hutcheson, *Tench Coxe: A Study in American Economic Development* (1938).

BROADUS MITCHELL

COXEY, Jacob Sechler (b. Selinsgrove, Pa., Apr. 16, 1854; d. Massillon, Ohio, May 18, 1951), REFORMER, left school at the age of 15 to work in an iron mill. After briefly working as a stationary engineer and scrap iron dealer, he moved to Massillon, Ohio, where he opened a sandstone quarrying factory in 1881. He was early interested in monetary reform, believing "that the government should not only coin money but issue it and get it direct to the people without the intervention of banks." In 1885, running on the Greenback Party ticket, he was an unsuccessful candidate for the Ohio state senate.

In 1894 during the depression, Coxey decided to dramatize the suffering of the poor by leading a march on Washington to demand relief through a program of public works set forth in two bills that he wanted Congress to enact: the Good Roads Bill, requiring the secretary of the Treasury to issue $500 million of legal tender currency to be expended by the secretary of war to improve county roads; and the more comprehensive Non-

Interest-Bearing Bond Bill, providing that any state or local unit of government needing public improvements might obtain funds by issuing bonds for a project to an amount not above half the assessed value of property within its limits, to be deposited in the Treasury as security for a loan of legal tender currency. The bonds were to be retired in twenty-five annual installments. Both bills required the employment of any unemployed man who applied, at a wage not less than $1.50 for an eight-hour day. Marching across Ohio, Pennsylvania, and Maryland, Coxey picked up supporters along the way (no more than five hundred), reaching the capital on May 1. When Coxey's "army" proceeded down Pennsylvania Avenue and reached the Capitol grounds, he was arrested for trespassing and his followers were quickly dispersed by the police.

In 1894, Coxey ran for Congress on the Populist Party ticket but was defeated; in 1897, running on a platform (along with his original proposals) supporting pensions for old soldiers, the direct election of the president and U.S. senators, and the initiative and referendum, he was defeated for governor of Ohio.

Always the reformer, Coxey continued to advocate his ideas throughout the early 20th century. In 1914 he again led a march on Washington. This time he was permitted to present his proposals. In that same year he published *Coxey's Own Story*. In 1916 he ran for the U.S. Senate but was defeated. During an interview with President Warren Harding (1922) he urged the president to attack the banking interests and to abolish the Federal Reserve System, which he called a tool of those interests.

During the remainder of his life Coxey ran and was defeated for the following offices: U.S. Congress (1924, 1926), U.S. Senate (1928), and president of the United States (1932, on the Farmer-Labor ticket, receiving 7,309 popular votes). During 1931–33 he was mayor of Massillon.

Coxey in 1894 was a successful self-made businessman, a congenital reformer, and a Populist politician. His deep sympathy for those who suffered most from the depression led him to work out remedies incorporated in the two bills that he wanted Congress to enact. The elements of his plan had all been advocated by Greenbackers, Populists, or labor groups. Coxey's contribution was to assemble them into an ingenious combination that he hoped would relieve suffering and help restore prosperity by providing a more plentiful currency, better transportation for farmers, public improvements for cities, jobs for the unemployed, and the eight-hour day for labor. He came to consider the non-interest-bearing bond idea the final solution of the problem, and he advocated it persistently to the end of his long career.

An army of the unemployed marching to the national capital to petition for relief was then a novel expedient. Coxey, with his flair for publicity, made it as spectacular as possible. His own arguments, delivered with quiet sincerity, appealed to the intellect more than to the emotions, but some picturesque characters combined features of a circus and a revival meeting to stir up enthusiasm. All of this was news, and the press gave it an enormous amount of coverage. A visiting English publicist observed that Coxey, by the unique device of his "petition in boots," had commanded more space for advertising his wares than any millionaire in America could have afforded.

Congress gave no serious consideration to Coxey's bills. They represented a phase of Populism. Many Populist proposals, then regarded as dangerously radical, were later enacted into law, but Coxeyism was not one of these. Majority opinion continued to reject fiat money, and in 1894 it opposed most federal measures appropriate to a welfare state. See Donald L. McMurry, *Coxey's Army: A Study of the Industrial Army Movement of 1894* (1968).

DONALD L. MCMURRY

CRANE, Harold Hart (b. Garretsville, Ohio, July 21, 1899; d. off Fla. coast, Apr. 27, 1932), POET, grew up in Cleveland. In 1916 he left high school to go to New York City to devote himself to poetry. He worked at various jobs to support himself, and after unsuccessfully trying to enlist in the army during World War I, worked in a shipyard on Lake Erie (1918). Following a stint as a clerk in one of his father's stores in Akron, Ohio (1919–20), Crane became a Cleveland advertising writer. Meanwhile, he continued writing poetry, including "Black Tambourine" (1921) and "Praise for an Urn" (1922), publishing his work in such small literary magazines as *Dial.* Returning to New York in 1923, Crane established his literary reputation with such poems as "For the Marriage of Faustus and Helen" (1923), "Voyage I–VI" (1926), and then his first book of poetry, *White Buildings* (1926). He spent the summer of 1926 writing on a plantation on the Isle of Pines off the coast of Cuba and later traveled through California (1927–28) and Europe (1928–29). Crane's long poem *The Bridge* (1930), which utilized the Brooklyn Bridge as the medium for describing American life and destiny, won great critical acclaim for the author. In 1931 he traveled to Mexico on a Guggenheim fellowship to write an epic on Hernando Cortez, Montezuma, and the conquest of Mexico. However, beset by numerous personal problems, including depression brought on by the death of his father and alcoholism, he never did so. While returning to New York by ship, Crane jumped overboard off the Florida coast. His *Collected Poems* (1933) was edited posthumously by his friend, literary critic Waldo Frank, and his *Letters 1916–1932* appeared in 1952.

—⟨∞⟩—

The dramatic disorder of Crane's life has influenced his literary reputation, and not wholly to its detriment. The origins of some of his most impressive passages have been attributed to personal neuroses and to emotional states he induced by deliberate derangement of the senses. Crane said he "was more interested in the so-called illogical impingements of the connotations of words on the consciousness than ... in the preservation of their logically rigid significations." He often achieved an astonishing aptness

of imagery—acute, concrete, mystical, but it was in single passages rather than entire poems that he displayed the range and intensity of his perceptions. His most ambitious work has a fragmentary, "patchy" quality. Critic Elizabeth Drew said the less successful poems were "an exasperating combination of the meretricious and the meritorious." Crane knew thoroughly the works of John Donne, Christopher Marlowe, **Edgar Allan Poe, Walt Whitman,** Jules Laforgue, Arthur Rimbaud, and T. S. Eliot. Eliot's *The Waste Land* affected him profoundly, and he reacted against its assumption that there was little hope for the 20th century. He would move, he said, "toward a more positive, (if I must put it so in a skeptical age) more ecstatic goal." His greatest poem, *The Bridge,* reflects this intention. It is based on an optimistic, Emersonian faith in America's future. But Crane's romantic affirmations were somewhat feverish and at odds with his penetrating awareness of human frailty. His attempts to resolve the conflict (and he sometimes succeeded brilliantly in fusing disparate impressions) vivified the poetic language of the 1930s. Crane's distinction as one of the most important American poets of his time is genuine. See Samuel Hazo, *Hart Crane: An Introduction and an Interpretation* (1963).

WILLIAM McCANN

CRANE, Stephen (b. Newark, N.J., Nov. 1, 1871; d. Badenweiler, Ger., June 5, 1900), WRITER, briefly attended Lafayette College and Syracuse University (1890–91) before moving to New York City where he was a reporter for the New York *Herald* and *Tribune.* In 1893 he published (at his own expense and under a pseudonym) *Maggie: A Girl of the Streets,* a naturalistic novel in which he tried to show the effect of environment on the shaping of life.

In 1895, Crane published *The Red Badge of Courage.* Using the Civil War as his setting, he attacked the romantic illusions of war. He next served as a war correspondent, covering the Greco-Turkish War and the Spanish-American War for **Joseph Pulitzer**'s New York *World.*

Crane's experiences in Cuba led to the publication of *Wounds in the Rain* (1900).

Crane spent his remaining life in Europe where he became friends with such prominent authors as H. G. Wells, **Henry James,** and Joseph Conrad. Some of his other works include the short story collections *The Little Regiment* (1887) and *The Monster* (1899), and the poetry collections *The Black Riders* (1895) and *War Is Kind* (1899).

Born after the Civil War, Stephen Crane grew up in a small-town America in which memories of that war were being transmuted from history into legend. Like many others of his generation Crane became impatient with a mythology to which he felt no adherence but that offered itself as the central feature of his culture, and the remarkable achievement of *The Red Badge of Courage* is compounded of the facts that in it he deflates the mythology and yet presents what was immediately accepted and still is accepted as the definitive fiction of the conflict that stands as the central trauma in American history.

This large achievement is based on an extraordinary literary genius. Crane went beyond the realism of **William Dean Howells** (whom he knew and who always stood ready to assist him), beyond a literary outlook based on acutely observed social details, to a technique closer to—although not the same as—naturalism. In *The Red Badge of Courage,* as in most of Crane's other remarkable fictions, the social fabric has little importance when compared with the psyches of the central characters and the uneasy emotional relationships they have with their social and physical environment. This environment is experienced as an impersonal set of attractions and menaces rather than as separate objects with their own integrity. Fellow human beings or familiar features of the landscape evaporate into the moods they call forth. As John Berryman pointed out, the typical Crane character is marked by pretension and fear, and it is the uneasy shifting of emotions connected with these states rather than any process of thought or mental development that characterizes their careers. In the harsh and frequently violent world of Crane's fiction, what men call thought is exposed as rationalization after the fact; the motives from which they act are prerational and therefore not to be conveyed by abstract or conceptual words.

Accordingly, Stephen Crane developed a remarkable style designed to reflect these views of the human condition. English syntax—especially the ornate late Victorian syntax of his day—designed to show the rational and moral nature of the human condition through complex sentences that organized clauses into neat and balanced dependence on other clauses was distrusted by Crane. He turned instead to simple and compound sentences in which events could be given equal emphasis rather than valued and in which temporal sequence would not be misrepresented as causal. Abstract diction and the vocabulary of thought processes were replaced by images (with a memorable preference for color) so that consciousness was represented by feeling rather than thought.

Most notably in *Maggie,* "The Open Boat," "The Monster," and "The Blue Hotel," as well as *The Red Badge,* Crane achieved a fiction of style, form, and content that moved away from the trustful vision of the institutions of family, church, and state on which so much of 19th-century fiction was based. He presented a world in which shaping forces were starker and more primitive. His distrust of thoughts rather than feelings, his preference for settings in which violence was present as potential if not as fact, and his avoidance of abstract diction and complex syntax all mark him as the first of the 20th-century American writers, albeit he died six months into 1900.

In his career, which included globe-trotting journalistic assignments, front-line presence at wars and experience of shipwreck, bohemian residence on New York's East Side and gentlemanly residence in an English manor house, public disagreement with the police on behalf of a prostitute and marriage with the manager of a house of ill repute, disappearance for a period into the Havana underground, and death before the age of 29, Crane provided a model of the literary life that led a new generation of would-be writers into newspaper work and adventure as the necessary background for novel writing. His career takes its place beside that of **Edgar Allan Poe** as a chapter in the mythology of the American writer misunderstood and misused by his society. See Robert W. Stallman, *Stephen Crane: A Biography* (1968).

LARZAR ZIFF

CREEL, George (b. Lafayette Co., Mo., Dec. 1, 1876; d. San Francisco, Calif., Oct. 3, 1953), JOURNALIST, POLITICAL LEADER, became a newspaper man after graduating from public school. Following an apprenticeship on the New York *World* as a cub reporter in the mid–1890s, he became editor of the Kansas City *Independent* (1899). In 1909 he became editor of the Denver *Post*, and he then headed the *Rocky Mountain News* (1911–13). Active first in Missouri reform politics, Creel for a time displayed much sympathy with socialism but by 1912 was an ardent Wilson Democrat. President Woodrow Wilson appointed him chairman of the Committee on Public Information in April 1917. Until he left that post in March 1919, he conducted an industrious campaign to drum up support for the war effort and the Liberty Loan bond drive. In this post Creel established an informal censorship system that served to minimize the need for a formal censorship law. Even so, Congress subjected him and his office to bitter criticism, and it halved his appropriation requests. After the war Creel turned to magazine writing. He also wrote books on his experiences with the Committee, patriotic biographies, and studies of Ireland and Mexico. He remained a staff writer for *Collier's* magazine until the late 1940s.

In the 1930s Creel served in a variety of public positions: chairman of the San Francisco Regional Labor Board (1933), chairman of the Advisory Board of the Works Projects Administration (1935), and U.S. commissioner at the Golden Gate Exposition (1939). In 1949, **John L. Lewis** appointed him public relations consultant to the United Mine Workers. Originally a supporter of Franklin D. Roosevelt, Creel ultimately broke with him because of the president's alleged encouragement of "the Russian system."

⁂

Creel's moment in history came during 1917–19 when he headed the Wilson administration's Committee on Public Information. All his personal characteristics came to the fore in this position—his predilection for Wilsonian reform abroad as well as at home, his personal magnetism, his taste for controversy, his tendency to attribute evil rather than misjudgment to those who criticized him. Creel's public life reflected both the strengths and the weaknesses of the "progressive mentality" to which historians as diverse as **Hofstadter,** Braeman, and Kolko have given close attention in recent years. The decision to "advertise" Wilsonian ideals reflects a bit of the "boosterism" characteristic of many Progressives, the belief that salesmanship was an entirely appropriate method of attracting support for ideals.

As an administrator Creel was extraordinarily energetic, quick to make decisions, often impulsive. He was capable of inspiring strong devotion even from the academic Guy Stanton Ford who presided over the Committee's stable of scholars charged with preparing the "copy." Wilson seems to have held Creel in high regard, probably because of his unbending personal loyalty to the president as well as his effective methods of purveying administrative dogma. Defending the prewar policies of his chief, Creel wrote in April 1918: "I would rather be an American, killed in the unpreparedness that proved devotion is to declared principles, than a German living as the result of years of lying, sneaking, treacherous preparation, for a wolf's spring at the throat of an unsuspecting world." This kind of attitude, vintage progressivism of a certain sort, proved most appealing to millions during World War I. See George Creel, *Rebel at Large: Recollections of Fifty Crowded Years* (1947).

DAVID F. TRASK

CRITTENDEN, John Jordan (b. Versailles, Ky., Sept. 10, 1787; d. Frankfort, Ky., July 26, 1863),

POLITICAL LEADER, graduated from the College of William and Mary in 1807 and entered the practice of law. In 1809, after moving to western Kentucky, he became attorney general of Illinois Territory. Crittenden was elected to the Kentucky legislature in 1811, served in the army during the War of 1812, and was appointed to an unexpired term in the U.S. Senate in 1817. On the expiration of his term in 1819 he returned to Kentucky. He was U.S. district attorney (1827–29) but was removed by President Andrew Jackson, whom he opposed. A conservative Whig in Kentucky politics, Crittenden supported the "Old Court" faction over the "New Court" faction. He served in the state legislature again (1829–32) and was elected to the U.S. Senate in 1835. Reelected in 1840, he resigned soon thereafter to become attorney general in William Henry Harrison's cabinet. Opposed to the policies of Harrison's successor, John Tyler, he resigned from the cabinet and was reelected to the Senate in 1842.

When Zachary Taylor died in 1850 and was succeeded by Millard Fillmore, Crittenden again became attorney general. But he returned to the Senate in 1854 in time to oppose the Topeka and Lecompton constitutions for Kansas. His chief object was to preserve the Union, and he sought a policy toward slavery which would achieve that end. He supported John Bell for president on the Constitutional Union ticket in 1860. That same year, after the election of Abraham Lincoln, Crittenden introduced resolutions to reestablish the Missouri Compromise and guarantee slavery in the District of Columbia, but both northern and southern radicals opposed this "Crittenden compromise." His proposal for a national referendum on secession also failed, and the Washington Peace Conference he promoted was equally ineffective. Crittenden helped keep Kentucky in the Union, but he opposed a number of federal acts that he felt went beyond the Constitution, such as confiscation of rebel property, the use of black troops, emancipation, and the use of military courts outside war zones. He served in the U.S. Congress from 1861 to 1863.

Crittenden was one of the most representative border-state Whigs of the pre-Civil War period. Although overshadowed by his fellow Kentuckian **Henry Clay,** he performed important services of conciliation for his constituents. His moderation, his kindliness, and his avoidance of personal rancor earned him the respect of friends and opponents alike.

As a good Kentucky Whig, Crittenden firmly believed in the importance of the maintenance of the federal Union. He also generally supported his party's stand in favor of protective tariffs, distribution of the proceeds from land sales, and opposition to Jacksonian banking and Native American policies. But his political course was always marked by prudence and the avoidance of extremes. He was a conservative in act as well as in thought.

Crittenden's conservatism determined his attitude toward slavery. Although himself a slaveholder, he had long been disturbed by the destructive influence of the "peculiar institution." The Union was for him more than a mere political concept; its welfare constituted the essence of his ideology. Consequently, he consistently deplored the sectional animosities engendered by the slavery question. Seeking to assuage the passions of both pro-slavery and antislavery colleagues, he was eager to avoid all measures potentially subversive of sectional harmony. Thus he opposed the annexation of Texas and the war with Mexico, became a fervent advocate of the Compromise of 1850, and considered the Lecompton Constitution in Kansas a fraud. His aim was sectional peace and reconciliation, and he believed abolitionists and fire eaters equally at fault in bringing about strife and discord.

Crittenden's greatest contribution was his effort to preserve the Union when after Abraham Lincoln's election the secession crisis threatened to destroy the national fabric. He sought to avoid disaster by introducing the compromise that bears his name. Although it narrowly failed of adoption, it nevertheless helped its author retain the confidence of his constituents. His counsels of moderation contributed in a large measure to the success of the Union cause in Kentucky. Whether the state could have been kept from seceding without his untiring efforts is dubious, and Lincoln for one considered the retention of his native state essential.

Crittenden's later opposition to emancipation and to the conscription of black troops followed naturally from his conservative prejudices. But he continued to lend his support to the maintenance of the Union, the cause that had been his lifelong goal. See Albert D. Kirwan, *John J. Crittenden, the Struggle for the Union* (1962).

HANS L. TREFOUSSE

CROCKETT, David ("Davy") (b. near Limestone, Tenn., Aug. 17, 1786; d. San Antonio, Tex., Mar. 6, 1836), SOLDIER, EXPLORER, left home in 1799 but returned after three years of wandering to help pay off his father's debts. He served as a scout in the Creek Indian War (1813–14), then moved to western Tennessee where he became a justice of the peace, a colonel of the militia, and, in 1821, a member of the state legislature.

In 1822, Crockett moved to what is now Gibson County, Tennessee, where he became famous for killing, so he claimed, 105 bears. After running unsuccessfully in 1825 for a seat in the U.S. Congress, in 1826 he was elected to Congress as a Democrat (serving 1827–31). As a congressman he supported the interests of the squatters in western Tennessee. Crockett's opposition to President Andrew Jackson's Native American policy cost him reelection in 1830.

In 1832, Crockett was reelected to Congress as a Whig. A colorful personality who could entertain a crowd with his tales of frontier life, Crockett came into national prominence during a much publicized tour of Baltimore, Philadelphia, New York, and Boston (1834). In 1834 he published *A Narrative of the Life of Davy Crockett*.

Failing to win reelection to Congress in 1834, Crockett, in search of further adventure, moved to Texas. He was one of about 187 men who were killed during Santa Anna's siege of the Alamo in 1836.

If he were judged solely on his meager historical accomplishments, Crockett would not deserve a place in this volume. His importance in American history lies in the symbolic and legendary roles he played during and, even more dramatically, after his lifetime. As a representative from the western clearings in the Congress of 1827, Crockett cut a strange figure and sounded a new note among the eastern politicians. Born and raised on the southwestern frontier, he looked and talked the part of the hunter and "Indian fighter," but not in the style of the taciturn, solemn **Daniel Boone.** Rather, Crockett reflected the spirit of the braggart backwoodsman who styled himself half a horse and half an alligator with a touch of the snapping turtle. The newspapers and both political parties, Jacksonian Democrats and Whigs, found good copy in the breezy westerner and developed him into a colorful and outspoken personality, in the process we would today call packaging. How much of a hand Crockett had in the several books written in his name remains conjectural, but he seems to have been more the pawn than the master of his publicity.

In his careful biography *David Crockett, the Man and the Legend,* James Shackford has sought to recapture the historical person. Such verified speeches and letters of Crockett as he unearths reveal a mediocre and limited individual speaking conventionally about the interests and rights of his constituents in the western lands. But the Crockett of the *Sketches and Eccentricities,* of the *Life,* and of the comic almanacs issued in his name from 1835 to 1856 is a lusty epic hero cast in the mold of Jacksonian America—even though he was ultimately adopted by the Whigs as a counterfoil to "Old Hickory." This Crockett, especially in the almanacs, is a chauvinist, a racist despising blacks, Native Americans, and Mexicans, a depredator of game, a violent killer of men and beasts with rifle and hunting knife. He is also a clever raconteur and mimic, a wag and jokester, a ringtailed roarer clad in buckskin breeches and coonskin cap and talking in backwoods imagery. His death-in-action at the Alamo ignited his legend.

With the advent of the Civil War this character ceased to intrigue the American public and faded from the scene. A century later, in the 1950s, Crockett enjoyed a second posthumous wave of popularity, propelled largely by **Walt Disney,** but this latter-day characterization caught neither the historical nor the legendary figure, and Crockett emerged as a wooden version of nature's nobleman. His most positive role—partly historical, partly literary, partly folk—was that of the politician from the hinterland, the man of the people speaking common sense in waggish anecdotes, tilting against the establishment, and expressing the promise of America in the tall-tale rhetoric of the new West. Confronting the emperor of Haiti, in one of the almanac stories, he says, "I am Colonel Davy Crockett, one of the sovereign people of Uncle Sam, that never kneels to any individual this side of sunshine." Then he thrashed all the blacks. This was the figure young America admired. See Richard M. Dorson, *Davy Crockett, American Comic Legend* (1939).

RICHARD M. DORSON

CROGHAN, George (b. near Dublin, Ire. [date unknown]; d. Philadelphia, Pa., Aug. 31, 1782), FRONTIERSMAN, emigrated to Pennsylvania in 1741 and established his home on the frontier near what is now Carlisle. His early success at trading with Native Americans was due in large part to the rapport he achieved with them. By the beginning of the French and Indian War he was operating a string of trading posts throughout the upper Ohio valley. After 1754, his business ruined by the war, he served as a scout for General Edward Braddock in his campaign against the French.

After the war Croghan, on a visit to England, urged a strong department, independent of the colonial governments, to deal with the Native Americans in the territory west of the Appalachians, which the peace treaty had transferred to England. Sent out to help in the settlement of the Illinois country, he was taken prisoner by Native Americans. Later freed, he ultimately helped in making peace with Pontiac. He helped to negotiate the Treaty of Fort Stanwix in 1768, which established a line beyond which settlers were not to go, but his idea of a centralized administration for Native Americans was not adopted. Moving to Pittsburgh, Croghan became heavily involved in land companies, notably the Indiana Land Co., which planned to found a new colony, Vandalia. The Revolution ended these speculations, and he spent his last years in poverty. Although frequently accused of being a Tory, perhaps because his pro–Native American policies were unpopular with settlers, Croghan was actually chairman of the Pittsburgh committee of correspondence. Knowledge of the history of the American frontier in this period is based to a large extent on his journals and correspondence.

———

Competent, ambitious, and suave, Croghan was a significant figure in the early westward expansion of the American people. He was keenly sensitive to the struggle for empire being waged between England and France in North America in his day, and expended every effort to assist the former—often at the expense of his personal financial well-being and even though it frequently caught him up in the maelstrom of imperial and provincial politics, making him at times suspect and unpopular. Croghan viewed himself—and thought that later generations might best remember him—as a peacemaker, "acting the part of a beloved man, with the swan's wing, white paper, and white beads." But the peace he sought was one that would, while promoting to a large extent the territorial integrity of Native Americans and fair dealings between them and the oncoming pioneers, ultimately facilitate European settlement of the West and handsome profits for speculators like himself who coveted the virgin land and launched bold schemes for its development. His motives were both idealistic and materialistic: he was both peacemaker and "King of the Traders"; he would have the Native Americans love the English but stand in awe of their power; sincerity and guile were the polarities of his personality. Ultimately, his life was replete with irony, for even as he sought to protect Indian rights, even as he sought to have their ancestral lands reserved to them (until such time as they could be purchased by land jobbers and settlers), he was abetting the historical process that would culminate in the debilitation of red men and the hegemony of white. See Nicholas B. Wainwright, *George Croghan, Wilderness Diplomat* (1959).

JEROME H. WOOD, JR.

CROLY, Herbert David (b. New York, N.Y., Jan. 23, 1869; d. Santa Barbara, Calif., May 17, 1930), JOURNALIST, studied for a year at the City College of New York and for two years at Harvard before becoming secretary to his father, a journalist, in 1888. In the years that followed he edited the *Record and Guide,* a real estate paper, and worked on the staff of the *Architectural Record.* He returned to Harvard in 1892 but suffered a nervous breakdown in 1893 and spent a year abroad to recover from it. He returned again to Harvard in 1895 to study philosophy.

Leaving Harvard in 1899, still without a degree, he spent a year in Paris before taking up the editorship of the *Architectural Record.* He resigned that position in 1906 to write *The Promise of American Life* (1909), which gained him a reputation as one of the most perceptive and influential American political writers. Though neither it nor its sequel (*Progressive Democracy,* 1914) was a bestseller, Theodore Roosevelt's "New Nationalism" approach to reform was influenced by Croly's work. Championing a vigorous Hamiltonianism in public polity, Croly attacked complacency and argued for the constant reevaluation and revision of America's democratic institutions in the light of ever changing conditions. In 1910 he was awarded his Harvard BA, credited to the class of 1890.

In 1914 when Willard Straight founded the *New Republic,* Croly became its editor. Along with such writers as Walter Weyl and **Walter Lippmann,** he helped mold it into a major, nonpartisan, progressive periodical. After World War I, despite having gained a reputation as a spokesman for President Woodrow Wilson, Croly editorially denounced the Treaty of Versailles, an

act that cost the *New Republic* half its circulation. In his final years he moved leftward. He supported **Robert La Follette** for president in 1924. Thereafter, he lost interest in political affairs and devoted most of his time to studying religious and metaphysical questions.

—◦∞◦—

Despite his shyness, his slight stature, and his quiet voice that often drifted off into inaudibility, Herbert Croly led an active social life that brought him into close relations with leading American politicians and intellectuals. He preferred the written to the spoken word, and his major impact on American life came through his books and his editorship of the *New Republic.*

"The Promise of American Life," according to Croly, consisted of "an improving popular economic condition, guaranteed by democratic political institutions, and resulting in moral and social amelioration." In his book of that title Croly examined at length past attempts to realize that promise and rejected them as inadequate to a present marked by the closing of the frontier, an economy dominated by powerful corporations, organized labor on the rise, a fragmented population, and entry of the United States on the world scene.

The way to fulfill the promise was to revivify American nationalism and to make the state the true servant of the people. Then Hamiltonian methods would serve democratic ends. He hoped to attract the best men to government service, men who could settle national policy by a disinterested consideration of the true national interest. Such a government need not attack large corporations but rather could control and direct them to serve national goals. And such a government would assure that American power on the world scene would be used to preserve international peace. It could redistribute income more equitably among its citizens.

These ideas dominated Croly's later writings. In *Progressive Democracy* he stressed democratic and moral themes more than nationalism, yet all three aspects of his thought remained important. His detailed explication of them in response to changing events while editor of the *New Republic* made him a major influence on intellectuals during the 1920s. See Charles Forcey, *The Crossroads of Liberalism: Croly, Weyl, Lippmann and the Progressive Era, 1900–1925* (1961).

MILTON BERMAN

CUFFE, Paul (b. Cuttyhunk, Mass., Jan. 17, 1759; d. Westport, Mass., Sept. 7, 1817), AFRICAN NATIONALIST, was the son of an ex-slave father and an Indian mother. He turned to the sea at an early age. After several voyages as an ordinary seaman on board whalers and general cargo ships, he went into business for himself and was so successful that eventually he acquired a fleet of six ships. He was the United States' first truly wealthy black. Sailing with a crew composed entirely of blacks and Indians, Cuffe traded in Europe, South America, and the Caribbean.

Cuffe joined the Society of Friends in 1808. Influenced by Quaker teachings, and by English and American Quaker philanthropists, he became interested in African redemption. He sailed to the British colony of Sierra Leone in 1811 to investigate the possibilities for settling skilled free blacks there. He hoped that black American technicians would introduce "civilization" and Christianity to their African brethren and that Sierra Leone converts would spread these principles through black Africa. The War of 1812, however, temporarily prevented him from making additional voyages to Africa. With the return of peace in 1815 he sailed to Sierra Leone with thirty-eight black pioneers. These were to be the advance contingent for the wave of volunteers that he anticipated would enlist in the great missionary task of civilizing Africa. Cuffe intended to make an annual pilgrimage to the colony, carrying a shipload of emigrants and returning home with a cargo of African products to pay for his expenses. He contracted a fever in the summer of 1817 and died before he could further the plan.

—⁂—

Cuffe was the very epitome of the 19th-century American Dream: the successful self-made man. That he achieved wealth, fame, and a par-

tial degree of social acceptability in a thoroughly racist society is testament to his great talents and strength of character.

Thoroughly American in outlook, for most of his life he accepted unquestioningly the basic tenets of the Puritan ethic: that hard work and community service led to salvation. Consequently, his evolving interest in Africa was initially an extension of his efforts to fulfill the doctrine of Good Works. Undertaking the task of "civilizing" Africa was for him a logical progression from his paying for a new Quaker meeting house in Westport, Massachusetts, or his building this town's first schoolhouse.

But gradually his attitude toward Africa and the United States changed. Continuing to experience the sting of racism firsthand even after achieving considerable recognition as a result of his initial African venture, Cuffe despaired of the United States ever being able to cope fairly with its racial problem. Thus, although continuing to hold that black Americans had an obligation to enlist in the cause of civilizing Africa, he became a black nationalist and accepted the notion of a mass black exodus to an African Zion. Tragically, American racism forced him to accept the racist doctrine of separation as the ultimate solution. See Sheldon H. Harris, *Paul Cuffe: Black America and the African Return* (1972).

SHELDON H. HARRIS

CUMMINGS, Edward Estlin (b. Cambridge, Mass., Oct. 14, 1894; d. North Conway, N.H., Sept. 3, 1962), POET, received his BA (1915) and MA (1916) from Harvard before volunteering in the Norton Harjes Ambulance Corps in France as a driver (1917). While in France he was arrested for alleged treason for corresponding with anarchist **Emma Goldman** and placed in an internment camp for several months. Upon his return to the United States in 1918 he was drafted into the U.S. army as a private and stationed at Camp Devens, Massachusetts, until after the armistice. In 1920 he moved to New York City to take up writing and painting, but spent much time in Paris with friends, including **Ezra Pound** and

Archibald MacLeish. His first book, *The Enormous Room* (1922), based on his experiences in the French internment camp, was well received by critics. He published his first collection of poems the following year, *Tulips and Chimneys* (1923). Most of his time after 1923 was spent in Greenwich Village, a farm in New Hampshire, and traveling in Europe.

In his poetry Cummings stressed the theme of individuality over modern conformist living. He innovated and experimented boldly in style, form, and even punctuation and grammar, signing his work "e.e. cummings." Some of his poetry collections included *XLI Poems* (1925), *ViVa* (1931), *No Thanks* (1935), and *Collected Poems* (1938). He also wrote poetic dramas, including *Him* (1927), *Tom* (1935), and *Santa Claus: A Morality* (1946), and a prose journal of his 1931 trip through the Soviet Union titled *Eimi* (1933).

Cummings was also a painter. He had one-man shows at the American British Art Gallery in New York City (1944 and 1948) and the Rochester Memorial Gallery (1950). He was Charles Eliot Norton professor of poetry at Harvard in 1952–53 and published his lectures there as *i: six nonlectures* (1953). Some of his later poetry collections include *Poems, 1923–1954* (1954), *95 Poems* (1958), *A Miscellany* (1958), and *73 Poems* (1963), published posthumously.

⸎

Cummings was the son of a Unitarian minister who was once a Harvard instructor, and the poet's famous unconventionality arose out of a longstanding American tradition. His parents were first introduced by **William James;** Professor Francis James Child baptized him; he studied sonnets with **Josiah Royce;** he graduated from Harvard magna cum laude and delivered the commencement address. All his poetry, idiosyncratic and maverick as it seems at first to be, can be regarded as the working out of a statement his father once made from the pulpit, echoing a familiar theme of **Ralph Waldo Emerson** and **Henry David Thoreau** and **Emily Dickinson:** "The Kingdom of Heaven is no spiritual roof garden: it's inside you." The intense individualism

and moral idealism of Cummings's New England heritage emerged in a lifelong hatred of all social institutions and abstractions, and it pushed him toward a belief in love as the saving grace of all human experience. At odds with this traditional romanticism, or at least qualifying it, was his satiric impulse, which led him throughout his career toward categorical denunciations, the loathing of ordinary people, self-righteous isolation, and an indulgence in private rhetoric. Like **Sinclair Lewis,** another uneasy satirist, Cummings poured his contempt over "the Great American Public" and that "monster, manunkind" even while celebrating the wonder and beauty of natural things and simple instincts. Echoes of Thoreauvian elitism and Swiftian disgust may be heard even in some of Cummings's profoundest efforts to glorify wholeness of feeling and the transcending power of love.

His reputation has always been mixed. In recent years criticism has tended to view him as ranking below the great poets of his age. The standard criticisms, first voiced by R. P. Blackmur's influential essay "Notes on E. E. Cummings' Language" (1931), derive from the sense that "sentimentality, empty convention, and commonplace" rule both his language and ideas. Yvor Winters, **Edmund Wilson,** F. O. Mathiessen, Randall Jarrell, and others have accused Cummings of a too easy sweetness, of a failure to develop beyond adolescent devices (obvious targets, cheap shock tactics), and of an ultimate egocentrism that fatally undercuts his affirmations of love. The standard defenses of Cummings have revolved around the idea that New Criticism has set up false expectations for his poetry, that his simplicity is his strength, that he transcends the impurities of ordinary experience (irony, paradox, ambiguity) through a Platonic or mystical evocation of wholeness. Another defense has been that his poems are not so simple, so naïvely romantic, or so devoid of those complexities that the New Criticism admires. And to the charge that Cummings did not develop or was monotonous, his defenders have asserted that his vision deepened and crystallized, that he abandoned his early prankish and erotic devices and became a far more inward and transcendental poet. Painstaking exegetes have demonstrated how his subtlety of craft increased as his awareness of the human predicament grew. Finally, his reputation has been bolstered by appreciators of *The Enormous Room, Eimi,* and *Him,* who have found in Cummings's narrative skill a responsiveness to humanity which is free of the dogmatism that plagues much of his poetry. See Norman Friedman, *E. E. Cummings: The Art of His Poetry* (1960), and *E. E. Cummings: A Collection of Critical Essays,* ed. by Friedman (1972).

DEAN FLOWER

CURLEY, James Michael (b. Boston, Mass., Nov. 20, 1874; d. Boston, Mass., Nov. 12, 1958), POLITICAL LEADER, after graduating from high school, entered the real estate and insurance business. Elected to the Boston common council in 1899 as a Democrat, he then served in the Massachusetts state legislature (1902–3). In 1904 he was sent to prison for impersonating a friend at a civil service exam. That same year, however, he was elected to the board of aldermen and six years later to the U.S. House of Representatives. Reelected to the House in 1912, Curley resigned in 1914 when elected mayor of Boston. As mayor he spent large amounts of money on Boston parks and hospitals, and was accused of bringing the city to the edge of bankruptcy. Although he rewarded his friends and dealt ruthlessly with his enemies, Curley failed to build an effective political machine. He was defeated for mayor in 1917 but regained the office in 1921 and 1929. Curley supported **Al Smith** for president in 1928 but switched his allegiance to Franklin D. Roosevelt in 1932.

Curley was governor of Massachusetts from 1935 to 1937. He took advantage of New Deal public works and relief programs to build many roads, bridges, and mental hospitals. In 1936 he was defeated in the race for the U.S. Senate by Henry Cabot Lodge, Jr., and in the years following he lost out in bids to become mayor of Boston (1937) and governor of Massachusetts (1938). However, Curley again won election to the House of Representatives in 1942 and 1944; in 1945 he was elected mayor for the fourth time. Curley was convicted in 1947 of using the mails to defraud and influence the granting of government contracts while in the House; he was sentenced to eighteen months in jail. While in prison he remained mayor and even beat off an attempt by some Republicans to call a special election to replace him. He was released by President Harry Truman after serving five months and returned to his Boston office. Defeated for reelection in 1949 and again in 1951, Curley retired from politics. Edwin O'Connor's best-selling novel *The Last Hurrah* (1956) was supposedly based on Curley's life. Curley filed suit for invasion of privacy when the book was made into a motion picture; the case was settled out of court for an undisclosed sum. Curley's last public office was a position on the Massachusetts State Labor Commission in 1957. That same year he published his autobiography, *I'd Do It Again.*

James Michael Curley was among the best-known and most colorful of the big-city, paternalistic bosses. Irish, Catholic, and Democratic, he typified the second-generation immigrant who "made it" in America by making a profession of politics. Capitalizing on Irish-American resentment against the Republican, Harvard-educated Brahmins who dominated Boston's social and economic life, Curley liked to think of himself as "Mayor of the Poor." He appealed most strongly to slum areas like South Boston, Scollay Square, and Roxbury Crossing. Whether as a young leader of Ward 17 or governor of Massachusetts, Curley helped immigrants adjust to urban life by finding them jobs, easing their troubles with the law, building them playgrounds and public baths, and attending their weddings and wakes. In return he unabashedly asked for and expected their support at the polls.

Despite his considerable achievements, Curley's life was marred by loneliness, tragedy, and frustration. Partly because his wife and seven of his nine children died at early ages, he threw himself into politics with uncommon energy. Because his feuds with fellow Irish chieftains such as John (Honey Fitz) Fitzgerald, Patrick Kennedy, and Martin Lomasney were legendary, he tried as mayor to centralize patronage and make the ward heeler obsolete. During the Depression he used federal relief and work projects as a tool of his political ambitions. But Curley never built a really solid organization in Boston and never enjoyed the power or statewide influence of other well-known urban bosses, such as Tom Pendergast in Kansas City, Ed Crump in Memphis, or Frank Hague in Jersey City. His greatest political disappointment came in 1933 when Franklin D. Roosevelt refused to reward his campaign support with an appointment as either secretary of the navy or ambassador to Italy. Curley thought Roosevelt had reneged on a firm commitment, and he never forgave him.

Throughout his long life Curley retained his ebullient spirit and his irrepressible energy. See Jack Beatty, *The Rascal King: The Life and Times of James Michael Curley, 1874–1958* (1992).

KENNETH T. JACKSON

CURTIS, George William (b. Providence, R.I., Feb. 24, 1824; d. Staten Island, N.Y., Aug. 31, 1892), EDITOR, REFORMER, attended school in Massachusetts (1830–35) and Rhode Island (1836–39), and moved with his family in 1839 to New York City where he worked as a clerk for a merchant for a year. As boarders at Brook Farm in West Roxbury, Massachusetts (1842–44), Curtis and his brother were greatly influenced by **Ralph Waldo Emerson** and other Transcendentalists. After two years of study and farm labor at Concord near Walden Pond, Curtis departed in 1846 on a four-year tour that took him to France, Italy, Germany, Egypt, and Syria. His descriptive travel books, *Nile Notes of a Howadji* (1851), *The Howadji in Syria* (1852), and *Lotus–Eating* (1852), were based on letters sent, as a member of the editorial staff, to the New York *Tribune*. From its first issue in 1852 Curtis was an editor of *Putnam's Monthly* in which his *Potiphar Papers* (1853), a satire of New York social life, and *Prue and I* (1856) were first published. His novel *Trumps* (1861) first appeared in *Harper's Weekly*. In 1856 when *Putnam's Monthly* failed, Curtis, as a general partner, assumed a large debt for which he was not legally liable.

As an editor, lyceum lecturer, and political orator, Curtis expressed strong opposition to slavery, beginning in the **John C. Frémont** campaign of 1856. He was also a strong advocate of woman suffrage. In 1853 he began writing the series "The Editor's Easy Chair" for *Harper's Monthly*, and after serving as leading editorial writer of *Harper's Weekly* from 1857 on, he became political editor in 1863. When *Harper's Bazaar* was established in 1867 he began the series "Manners upon the Road," which continued until 1873.

A Republican, Curtis was an unsuccessful congressional candidate in 1864 and a delegate to Republican nominating conventions (1860, 1864, 1876). But in the 1870s and 1880s he became disillusioned with the Republican Party, largely because of the widespread "spoils system." As a leading advocate of civil service reform, Curtis supported selection of officials through examinations rather than partisan politics and was chairman of President Ulysses S. Grant's Civil Service Commission (1871–73). He later served as president of both the New York and the National Civil Service reform associations. In the 1884 presidential election Curtis supported the Democratic candidate Grover Cleveland rather than the Republican **James G. Blaine** on moral grounds. He became a nationally influential Independent or "Mugwump." It was Curtis whom **Roscoe Conkling** bitterly castigated at the 1877 Republican state convention as a "man-milliner," referring to the recent concern of Curtis's magazine with fashion. The epithet implied that reformers, predominantly educated men with cultivated manners, were effeminate and that reform was the proper realm for such types.

In 1864, Curtis was appointed a regent of the State University of New York, becoming chancellor in 1890, and was chairman of the Committee on Education in the New York State constitutional convention (1866–68). Curtis declined numerous offers of public office, including the ministry to Germany and England that President Hayes offered him in 1877. He continued to lecture in his last years.

---❧❧❧---

An editor, author, orator, and professional good citizen of great contemporary prominence, Curtis helped transmit the somewhat battered traditions of antebellum New England individualism to postwar urban America. The serene high-mindedness of his moral principles was perhaps more vital to his reputation than his achievement in either literature or politics. The son of a prosperous merchant, Curtis spent a leisurely youth. Absorbing a liberal education and a certain dreamy idealism from his years at Brook Farm and Concord, he retained many attributes of a cultivated transcendental dandy when he returned from Europe in 1850 to launch his writing career. His travelogues and gentle satires won a broad middle-class audience. **Henry Wadsworth Longfellow** noted "a golden glow in his pages, as if he dipped his pencil in the sun." Slavery inspired a decisive turn to politics in the late fifties, and civil service reform thereafter became his commanding public passion. By the 1870s his quarrel with Roscoe Conkling's brand of politics made him the acknowledged leader of the reform wing of the Republican Party in New York. His participation in the Mugwump bolt of 1884 ended his considerable influence in the councils of the GOP. Meanwhile, as editor for *Harper's Weekly,* Curtis distinguished himself from fellow reformers by his advanced stands on black equality and woman suffrage. Skeptical of laissez-faire abstractions, he was a mild economic nationalist and favored many schemes of federal intervention for the public welfare. Genial, dapper, and engaging, Curtis embodied the Genteel Tradition in its fresher and more open moods. See Gordon Milne, *George William Curtis and the Genteel Tradition* (1956).

GEOFFREY BLODGETT

CUSHING, Harvey Williams (b. Cleveland, Ohio, Apr. 8, 1869; d. New Haven, Conn., Oct. 8, 1939), PHYSICIAN, graduated from Yale in 1891

and received his MA and MD from Harvard in 1895. He spent four years at Johns Hopkins and then studied abroad in Berne and Liverpool. On his return to Baltimore he entered the department of surgery at Johns Hopkins where he eventually became associate professor in charge of surgery of the central nervous system. During 1912–32 he served jointly as associate professor of surgery at Harvard and as surgeon in chief at Peter Bent Brigham Hospital. From 1933 until his retirement in 1937 he was the first Sterling professor of neurology at Yale. During World War I he was the director of a U.S. base hospital in France, and in 1918 he was made senior consultant in neurosurgery to the American Expeditionary Forces. He was awarded the Distinguished Service Medal for these activities.

Cushing was a renowned brain surgeon and wrote numerous books on the subject. He developed the method of performing brain operations with local anesthesia and made important contributions to the classification of brain tumors. He performed the first successful operation for an intracranial hemorrhage in a newborn child in 1905. In 1901 he became the first to introduce the use of blood pressure determinations into the United States, and he later undertook important studies of blood pressure in surgery, culminating in the formulation of Cushing's law, that the increase in pressure on the various parts of the skull causes the blood pressure to increase to a point above the pressure exerted against the medulla. In addition, his work *The Pituitary Body and Its Disorders* (1912) gained him an international reputation. He was also an accomplished writer, renowned not only for his numerous monographs on technical subjects but also for his two-volume *The Life of Sir William Osler,* which won the Pulitzer Prize for biography in 1925.

---❧❧❧---

Historians in recent years have ranked the presidents of the United States in categories from "Great" to "Failure." A similar scale for American physicians probably would place Harvey Cushing with the "Near-Great." In surgical skill and inventiveness he was among the "Great" certainly for his own day. He led in the specialty of neurosurgery but at the same time was critical of overspecialization. This stemmed possibly from his educational background in the classics and literature and his long association with and unbounded admiration for Sir William Osler. Both of these physicians were classicists in the knowledge of language and history, and both believed that physicians along with persons of all other professions needed such an educational background.

The friendship with and adulation for Osler, twenty years his senior, had a tremendous effect on Harvey Cushing. In ideas and writing he imitated and—unwittingly, perhaps—plagiarized Sir William. For example, Osler referred to Drs. **William and Charles Mayo** as St. Cosmos and St. Damian. Cushing in turn used these terms in speaking of various other physicians. As for the Mayos, however, he was less generous than Osler and compared Rochester, Minnesota, with Lourdes, France. Osler and Cushing both pursued the interest of history and medical history. Although they could evaluate historical facts rather well, on the whole physicians were praised as individuals and medicine as a profession, a common tendency of medical historians until recent times.

Cushing stood with American Medical Association President Morris Fishbein in vigorous opposition to compulsory national health insurance. According to one biographer he played a major part in keeping health insurance out of Social Security bills of 1935. He was an individualist in medicine even in his family life, where he insisted on operating on his own children.

To make brain surgery less hazardous was a momentous achievement. Added to this, Cushing was a literary humanist, a factor that brought him a Pulitzer Prize. See Elizabeth H. Thomson, *Harvey Cushing: Surgeon, Author, Artist* (1950).

EUGENE P. LINK

CUSTER, George Armstrong (b. New Rumley, Ohio, Dec. 5, 1839; d. Little Big Horn, Mont., June 25, 1876), MILITARY LEADER, graduated from West Point in 1861. He fought as a second lieu-

tenant in the first battle of Bull Run (July 21, 1861) and served on General **George McClellan**'s staff during the Peninsular campaign (May–June 1862). He saw action at Gettysburg (July 1–3, 1863), and on **Philip Sheridan**'s staff during the Shenandoah Valley campaign (Sept. 1864). He attracted national attention when he relentlessly pursued **Robert E. Lee**'s army from Richmond to Appomattox and accepted the Confederate flag of truce on April 9, 1865. After attaining the rank of major general of volunteers, Custer was mustered out of volunteer service in 1866 and resumed his permanent rank of captain. When the Seventh Cavalry was organized later that year, Custer was promoted to lieutenant colonel and named its commander.

After taking part in General W. S. Hancock's disastrous Indian campaign of 1867, Custer was court-martialed for disobeying orders and suspended from the army for one year. Recalled by Sheridan shortly thereafter, he defeated Chief Black Kettle's Cheyennes in the battle of the Washita River (Okla.) in 1868. He spent the next few years exploring the Yellowstone River and the Black Hills of Dakota, and fighting periodic battles with Indians. He published *My Life on the Plains* (1874), describing these experiences.

Assigned in 1876 to General A. H. Terry's expedition against hostile Sioux and Cheyennes under Chief **Sitting Bull,** Custer first testified before a congressional committee on corruption in the Indian Bureau. His testimony angered President Ulysses Grant, who relieved him of his command. A popular outcry, however, forced Grant to reinstate him. He rejoined the Seventh Cavalry in Montana. While on Terry's expedition against Sitting Bull in 1876, Custer split his forces and then encountered a concentration of about 2,500 to 4,000 Native Americans. In the resulting battle he was killed along with his entire force of more than 260 officers and men.

General George Armstrong Custer was the epitome of the military personality that looks upon war as a game. He possessed raw humor, power to make quick decisions, lust for battle, impetuosity, a massive ego, romanticism, driving ambition, and determination. He believed that "Custer's luck" would lead him to victory and glory.

Yet there were other sides to his character. He was fiercely loyal to his family. His devotion to his wife Libbie was matched only by her love for him. He neither smoked nor drank; he loved dogs and the hunt; he had an eye for pomp, and demanded spit and polish neatness of his troops although he often dressed flamboyantly in non-regulation uniform. Although he led his troops to death, he certainly never planned it that way. When overwhelming numbers of hostiles surrounded Custer and his troops, there is strong evidence that they fought with the courage and discipline expected of military men.

Nevertheless, the sum of his personality, along with the jealousy engendered by his early success, made Custer a man with many enemies. He did take grave risks, disobeyed orders, and indulged in impetuous actions that bordered on irresponsibility. These actions cost the lives of men. Questions were also raised about his honesty and integrity.

He was, then, the incarnation of a certain type of American hero: impetuous, devil-may-care, and successful—until that afternoon of June 25, 1876, on the hills, gullies, and bluffs bordering the Little Big Horn River. See Jay Monaghan, *Custer: The Life of General George Armstrong Custer* (1959).

RICHARD A. BARTLETT

DALEY, Richard Joseph (b. Chicago, Ill., May 15, 1902; d. Chicago, Ill., Dec. 20, 1976), POLITICAL LEADER, worked his way through De Paul University, receiving an LLB in 1933. A Democrat, Daley was elected to the Illinois house of representatives in 1936 and two years later to the state senate. He served as minority leader of the senate from 1941 to 1946. In 1946 he was defeated in the race for Cook County (Chicago) sheriff.

Daley was deputy controller of Cook County when Governor **Adlai E. Stevenson** appointed him director of the Illinois department of finance in 1949; he also served as a legislative consultant to Stevenson. In 1950, Daley was appointed to fill the vacancy of Cook County clerk and won a full four-year term later that year. He became chairman of the Cook County Democratic Party in 1953 and quickly built it into one of the strongest political organizations in the country. Daley was elected mayor of Chicago in 1955 and was reelected handily in 1959, 1963, 1967, 1971, and 1975. During his tenure he reorganized the police department and started a large urban renewal

program. As one of the nation's most powerful old-line urban Democratic politicians, Daley was a frequent adviser to Presidents John Kennedy and Lyndon Johnson on matters pertaining to domestic affairs. He was responsible for bringing the 1968 Democratic convention to Chicago and supported **Hubert H. Humphrey** for the nomination. Many blamed him for precipitating the violence during the convention—the so-called Chicago riot between police and anti–Vietnam War demonstrators—a charge he vigorously denied. While his supporters in Chicago still viewed him with affection, his standing in the national party suffered as a result of his role at the convention. Changes in the national Democratic Party's nomination rules pushed through by Senator George McGovern's supporters further eroded Daley's influence nationally. At the Democratic convention in 1972 an anti-Daley faction led by Jesse Jackson succeeded in unseating his slate of delegates. When Daley went to the Miami convention, he found the doors barred to him. After McGovern's defeat by Nixon in 1972, Daley was once again courted by the party's inner councils, but his influence had clearly waned.

❧

Richard J. Daley was often referred to as the last of the big-city bosses. A second-generation American of Irish stock, he was a self-made man. Like many other urban politicians, he chose politics as his vehicle of mobility. He used the goods of the political world—friendship, favors, patronage, and legislation—to develop his power, and he became a master in the use of political persuasion. Daley capitalized on his personal influence and his efficient political machine to create an informal centralization of power that overcame the formal decentralization of Chicago and Cook County government. Although an Irishman, he successfully transcended ethnic and racial boundaries, and Chicago's major social groups consistently supported him for reelection. Daley developed a citywide machine and a loyal retinue, and he repaid their devotion with access to jobs and contracts. His long survival as boss of his party as well as mayor derived, however, from more than his machine. He backed the projects and goals of the downtown business establishment, he responded to demands for reform when corruption got out of hand, and he occasionally supported liberal candidates for major political office. Daley's difficulties as mayor rose primarily because of his and his machine's inability to adapt to the demographic and economic complexities facing American cities in the 1960s and early 1970s. He resisted demands by Chicago's growing black population for greater control over its political destinies and a larger share of the economic pie. He did not understand and would not tolerate hostility to constituted authority by antiestablishment youth groups. By 1972, Daley had overstayed his term of power, and opposition to the machine and racial tension combined in that year's Democratic primaries to inflict a major defeat on his machine candidates. His inability to comprehend the forces of change buffeting America tarnished his image in later life, but many observers still regarded him as an outstanding urban political leader during a time

of troubles for American cities. See M. Royko, *Boss* (1971).

JOEL A. TARR

DANA, Richard Henry (b. Cambridge, Mass., Aug. 1, 1815; d. Rome, Italy, Jan. 6, 1882), WRITER, LAWYER, REFORMER, entered Harvard in 1831 but was forced to take a leave of absence in 1833 because of an eye injury. In August 1834 he went to sea, sailing around Cape Horn to California. Returning to Boston in 1836, he reentered Harvard and received his degree in 1837. In 1839–40 he was an instructor of elocution at Harvard.

In 1840, Dana was admitted to the bar. Hoping to ameliorate the harsh life of seamen, he published *Two Years Before the Mast* (1840), a graphic account of ship life from the point of view of the sailors. Because of his love for the sea and sympathy for sailors, Dana decided to specialize in admiralty law; his manual *The Seaman's Friend* (1841) soon became the standard work on the subject.

Although Dana was not an abolitionist, he deplored the institution of slavery. In 1848 he was one of the founders of the antislavery Free Soil Party and attended the party convention in Buffalo. Following the passage of the Fugitive Slave Act of 1850, he defended a number of runaway slaves. In 1853 he was a member of the convention that revised the Massachusetts constitution. In 1859 he published *To Cuba and Back,* a travel book.

In the position of U.S. attorney for the district of Massachusetts (1861–66), Dana successfully urged the U.S. Supreme Court to sustain the federal blockade of southern ports. He lectured at Harvard Law School (1866–68). With William M. Evarts, Dana served as U.S. counsel for the prosecution during the proceedings against **Jefferson Davis.** In 1867 and 1868 he served in the state legislature. In 1868, running for Congress as an independent Republican, Dana was defeated by **Benjamin F. Butler;** in 1876 he was appointed minister to England by President Ulysses Grant, but he was not confirmed by the Senate. He represented the United States at the Fisheries Commission in Halifax in 1877.

———∞∞∞———

Dana's life, like that of his friends the Adamses, is a chapter in the decline of patrician political power in the United States. The Danas, stemming from a penniless Puritan immigrant in 1640, rose to an apogee with Francis Dana (1743–1811), member of the Continental Congress, ambassador to Russia, and chief justice of the state supreme judicial court. Richard Henry, the judge's grandson, admired his ancestor's aristocratic hauteur and aloofness. His own similar temperament destroyed his hopes of political power in democratic, industrializing 19th-century Massachusetts. In most of the major events of his public career—helping write a state constitution that was rejected by angry Irish voters, campaigning for Congress against Benjamin F. Butler, a brawling boardinghouse keeper's son, Dana was defeated because he clung to an outmoded and inflexible code of honor. He felt that the minor posts he attained were unworthy of his powers, and he lamented that his life had been a "failure."

Despite his sense of inadequate achievement, at isolated intervals Dana did play a significant role in important events. At considerable personal sacrifice he took part in the Free Soil campaign of 1848 and won a notable antislavery propaganda victory in the Anthony Burns fugitive slave case of 1854. As wartime district attorney, his brief in the Prize cases (1863) won a favorable decision for the government. His book *Two Years Before the Mast* is a classic account of Mexican California and a stirring narrative of life at sea. These and other accomplishments might have been a source of considerable satisfaction to a man with less distinguished ancestry and lesser expectations. See Samuel Shapiro, *Richard Henry Dana, Jr.* (1961).

SAMUEL SHAPIRO

DANIELS, Josephus (b. Washington, N.C., May 18, 1862; d. Raleigh, N.C., Jan. 15, 1948), EDITOR, POLITICAL LEADER, studied at the Wilson (N.C.) Collegiate Institute. Starting newspaper work at the age of 14, Daniels became editor of the Wilson *Advance* when only 18. After briefly attending the University of North Carolina's Law School he was admitted to the bar in 1885 but never practiced law. In 1885 he purchased the Raleigh *State Chronicle* and two years later was elected to the office of printer-to-the-state. After repeated financial difficulties Daniels consolidated the *State Chronicle* and other newspapers (1894) into the Raleigh *News and Observer.* He soon turned the *News and Observer* into a crusading organ for progressive reform. His editorials supported the abolition of child labor and sweatshops, railroad and utility regulation, and collective bargaining. He also backed woman suffrage and Prohibition. He opposed U.S. colonialism after the Spanish-American War but defended white supremacy and "Jim Crow" laws. Always active in the Democratic Party, Daniels served as director of publicity for successive presidential campaigns of **William Jennings Bryan** and Woodrow Wilson. In 1913, Wilson rewarded Daniels by making him secretary of the navy.

Daniels's term as secretary was stormy; he was criticized for prohibiting alcohol on board ships and for attacking the navy's concept of discipline. However, he increased his department's efficiency and provided strong leadership during World War I. After the war Daniels supported naval disarmament and a shipbuilding "holiday." Although he returned to the *News and Observer* in 1921, he remained active in the Democratic Party. In 1932 he campaigned for Franklin Roosevelt, his former assistant secretary of the navy, and became ambassador to Mexico after Roosevelt's election. In this post Daniels worked to implement Roosevelt's Good Neighbor Policy and helped prevent Mexico's expropriation of the properties of U.S. oil companies from disrupting relations between the two nations. In 1941, Daniels once again returned to the *News and Observer.* Between 1939 and 1947 he wrote five volumes of autobiography that were widely acclaimed.

———∞∞∞———

Josephus Daniels epitomized, often simultaneously, much of the best and worst in the post–Civil War South. Lifelong sympathy for the poor and underprivileged led him to champion the causes of public education, organized labor, woman's rights, freedom of the press, religious liberty, and democratic government from the days of Bryan through the New Deal. Yet at the same time he fully shared, even capitalized on, the prejudices of his fellow southern whites, achieving his first journalistic success through using racial demagoguery to help establish one-party Democratic rule in North Carolina in the 1890s. Despite frequent clashes with party conservatives, Daniels never wavered in his southern Democratic loyalty, and although his early Negrophobia mellowed decidedly in later years, he declined to question white supremacy. His political and social views on the national scene followed those of his friend and mentor Bryan, but with greater sophistication and flexibility. Despite sharing the Great Commoner's deep devotion to the values of small-town and rural, white, Protestant, middle-class society, Daniels broke with Bryan in the 1920s over the antievolution crusade and the Ku Klux Klan. Similarly, in spite of a common attachment to peace, the two men split during World War I. In personality and as a public figure Daniels combined two sets of contrasting qualities: gentle amiability and combative controversiality; unaffected simplicity of character and outlook, and shrewd, skillful management of men and affairs. Both combinations served him well in his careers in journalism, politics, government, and diplomacy. On balance, his contributions to the South fell heavily on the side of humanitarianism and progress, and both his newspaper and his sons continued Daniels's example of enlightened, responsible journalism and public service. See Joseph L. Morrison, *Josephus Daniels: The Small-d Democrat* (1966).

JOHN MILTON COOPER, JR.

DARROW, Clarence Seward (b. Kinsman, Ohio, Apr. 18, 1857; d. Chicago, Ill., Mar. 13, 1938), LAWYER, REFORMER, briefly attended Allegheny College and the University of Michigan Law School. After clerking in a Youngstown, Ohio, law office he was admitted to the bar in 1878. For the next nine years he practiced law in several Ohio towns. In 1887 he moved to Chicago where for two years he was a junior law partner of **John Peter Altgeld.** In 1889 he was appointed assistant corporation counsel for Chicago and then chief counsel. In this position he worked to reduce transit fares.

In 1894, Darrow became counsel for the Chicago and North Western Railroad. However, when **Eugene V. Debs** and the American Railway Union were held in contempt of court for striking against the trunk lines running in and out of Chicago, Darrow, sympathizing with the labor movement, quit his job to defend Debs. For the remainder of his life Darrow remained an advocate for the "underdog." During the 1902 Pennsylvania anthracite strike he represented the United Mine Workers, describing their plight to President Theodore Roosevelt's investigating commission. When **William D. ("Big Bill") Haywood** and other members of the Western Federation of Miners were charged with the murder of Frank R. Steunenberg, former governor of Idaho, Darrow successfully defended them and pointed out the connections between the mining industry and the local government (1905–7). However, when James B. and John J. McNamara were charged with bombing the offices of the Los Angeles *Times* and killing twenty people, Darrow entered a plea of guilty (1911). This decision alienated many of his socialist followers. Following this trial he was accused of attempting to bribe jurors but was acquitted.

Returning to Chicago, Darrow again set up a private practice. Opposed to capital punishment, in 1924 he defended Nathan Leopold and Richard Loeb for the murder of 14-year-old Bobbie Franks. By introducing psychiatric evidence he proved that his clients suffered from temporary insanity, thereby winning a commutation of the death sentence. An agnostic, Darrow was one of the defense attorneys in the famous 1925 "Scopes trial" in which he defended a Dayton, Tennessee, schoolteacher who had violated a Tennessee law banning the teaching of evolution. The climax of the trial came when Darrow cross-examined **William Jennings Bryan,** a supposed authority on the Bible and one of the prosecuting attorneys. During Darrow's questioning, Bryan, a staunch fundamentalist, admitted that he accepted the Bible literally.

In the spring of 1934, Darrow was appointed chairman of a National Review Board whose job it was to determine whether or not the National Industrial Recovery Act (1933) was unfair to small businesses. After a four-month investigation Darrow's committee excoriated the NRA. Some of Darrow's published works include *Farmington* (1904), an autobiographical novel, *Crime, Its Cause and Treatment* (1925), and *The Story of My Life* (1932).

❧

Clarence Darrow was in the first instance an extraordinarily successful trial lawyer who lent his impressive talents to the cause of organized labor, black people, the poor, and on occasion even the wealthy social outcast. His powerful forensic skill, his instinct for drama, his uncanny memory for critical detail, and his persuasive abilities with juries gave him a reputation in the courtroom comparable to those enjoyed earlier by Luther Martin, William Pinkney, **Daniel Webster,** and Joseph Choate.

Darrow's sympathetic interest in the cause of the "underdog" arose in considerable part from his pessimistic-ethical insight into the nature of ultimate reality. Hardly a profound social theorist, Darrow had absorbed from Charles Darwin, Herbert Spencer, Ernst Haeckel, Thomas Huxley, and other 19th-century thinkers a philosophy of agnostic mechanistic determinism which convinced him that life itself was probably without ultimate meaning except for man, that criminal law was no more than a product of arbitrary social convention, and that the criminal himself was so completely a product of his biological heritage and social environment that he could not help being what he was. Indeed, Darrow constantly insisted that "we are all criminals" and that only the accident of fate put one man in the docket and another on the bench.

Darrow's intellect, personality, and other natural endowments were such that he might conceivably have emerged as an outstanding national political leader or social reformer. But his corrosive sense of skepticism was too powerful to enable him to identify for very long with any social movement, so he remained a solitary eclectic, lacking either the focus or the emotional commitment that successful reform leadership commonly requires. See Irving Stone, *Clarence Darrow for the Defense* (1941).

ALFRED H. KELLY

DAUGHERTY, Harry Micajah (b. Washington Court House, Ohio, Jan. 26, 1860; d. Columbus, Ohio, Oct. 12, 1941), POLITICAL LEADER, received a law degree from the University of Michigan in 1881 and set up a practice in Washington Court House, Ohio. He served as township clerk and then (1890–94) two terms in the Ohio state legislature as a Republican.

In 1893, Daugherty moved to Columbus and developed a lucrative law practice, representing large corporations. He failed in his attempts to run for state attorney general (1895) and governor (1897) but proved successful in managing the campaigns of his friend Warren G. Harding. It was Daugherty who guided Harding to the 1920 Republican presidential nomination and election. Harding appointed Daugherty attorney general of the United States in 1921. Because of many charges of corruption leveled against Daugherty, in 1922 the House of Representatives attempted to bring impeachment proceedings against him but failed. In 1924 a probe that brought to light the illicit activities of the custodian of Alien Property finally forced President Calvin Coolidge to demand Daugherty's resignation.

Daugherty returned to his Ohio law practice and was tried and acquitted in 1927 of charges of graft and fraud involving the Alien Property custodian. He spent the rest of his life attempting to clear his and Harding's reputation. A book, written in collaboration with Thomas Dixon, *The Inside Story of the Harding Tragedy* (1932), was part of this effort.

Harry Daugherty once said, "Law and politics, you know, go hand in hand." A practitioner of that belief throughout his life, Daugherty was early noted for his success in securing economic advantages for his clients by means of political pull, causing him constantly to be condemned for his unsavory manipulations yet grudgingly admired for his ability to "deliver the goods."

Daugherty's insight into politics and politicians was something of an art. He seemed to know just when to cajole, when to bluster, when to seize the initiative, and when to retreat. Daugherty once claimed that he never met a politician who was unfathomable. His friend Harding clearly fell into this category; and although Daugherty later took too much credit for engineering Harding's nomination and election, he was a major factor in both.

Unlike most men, Daugherty never sought popular acclaim. Bitterly opposed for attorney general, he accepted the appointment as a reward for loyalty and as a sop to his own vanity. He naturally became an immediate focal point for much antiadministration criticism. He filled this role proudly and belligerently; even his strident anti-labor action in securing the repressive Wilkerson injunction in 1922 left him totally unrepentant.

Often characterized by his enemies as "the moral test of the Harding administration," Daugherty remained controversial to the end. His various scrapes with Congress, his alleged connections with the infamous Ohio Gang, and his supposed involvement in irregularities in the Justice Department not only led to his political demise but set the stage for continuing acrimony. Although never convicted of any wrongdoing, Daugherty also never testified under oath or permitted a full investigation of his activities. Instead, he remained sullenly defiant to the day of his death, maintaining that he had "done nothing that prevents my looking the whole world in the face."

Available evidence indicates that Daugherty was not criminally involved in the various scandals that wracked the Harding administration. He was not the "leader" of the Ohio Gang, nor was he connected in any way with **Albert Fall** and Teapot Dome. Daugherty's official silence concerning all these matters stemmed more from a misguided desire to protect Harding's name from possible "woman trouble" than to mask graft and corruption. Still, such action, regardless of motive, did little to preserve his own reputation or that of Warren Harding and his "normalcy" administration. See Robert K. Murray, *The Harding Era* (1969).

ROBERT K. MURRAY

DAVIS, Benjamin Oliver, Sr. (b. Washington, D.C., June 1, 1877; d. North Chicago, Ill., Nov. 26, 1970), MILITARY LEADER, was the grandson of a slave. After studying in Washington, D.C., public schools he attended Howard University (1897–98) before dropping out to enlist in the army during the Spanish-American War. He saw service as a temporary lieutenant on the Mexican border. Although mustered out at the war's conclusion, Davis reenlisted in the regular army as a private and served in the Philippines (1901–2) during the insurrection. In 1901 he was commissioned a second lieutenant in the regular army. Davis became professor of military science at Wilberforce University, Ohio (1905–9). From 1909 to 1917 he was stationed in Liberia, Wyoming, and Arizona. During World War I he served with the all-black cavalry outfit, the Ninth Regiment, in the Philippines, and was promoted to lieutenant colonel in 1920.

After teaching military science at Tuskegee Institute in Alabama (1920–24), Davis became instructor of the 372d Infantry of the Ohio National Guard in Cleveland. Promoted to full colonel in 1929, he alternated teaching assignments between Tuskegee and Wilberforce until 1938 when he became commanding officer of the all-black 369th Harlem Regiment of the New York National Guard. In 1940, Davis was promoted to brigadier general, becoming the first black ever to hold that rank in the U.S. armed forces. Davis briefly retired from the army on July 31, 1941, but was called back to active service the next day. He saw duty in various advisory and inspecting capacities having to do with the use of black troops and on General Dwight Eisenhower's staff as special adviser on the problems of black soldiers. He retired in 1948.

———⁂———

The career of General Davis is significant not for his personal accomplishments, because whatever his abilities might have been the U.S. army gave him only a limited sphere in which to display them, but for its reflection of the slight forward movement the army permitted the black soldier in World War II as compared with the overt racism and discrimination of World War I. Davis's career illustrates also that the forward movement of the black soldier by World War II, though real, was still appallingly slight by the standards of one generation later. When the United States entered World War I, the ranking black officer of the army, Colonel Charles Young, was promptly retired on dubious grounds of physical unfitness. Young's retirement set the keynote for a policy of consigning the black soldier mainly to segregated labor battalions, using him in combat even in the customary all-black units of the day as little as possible (the four old regular army black combat regiments never went to France), and rationalizing everything with pronouncements candidly endorsing the notion of black racial inferiority. In 1940 the changing political climate of the New Deal years led to the promotion of Young's successor as ranking black colonel, Davis, to brigadier general. Also, by 1940 army policies could not be quite so unblushingly discriminatory as in 1917; but little had changed in practice. Although Davis at first received command of a cavalry brigade (containing the black Ninth and Tenth regiments), he spent World War II mostly in troubleshooting assignments trying to ease the lot of the black soldier and make him more useful to the country in a service still embarrassed to have to accept blacks. Davis proposed "the breaking down of the so-called Jim Crow practices within the War Department and on the military reservations," but the practical goals he had to labor for were modest ones, such as securing the right of black officers to command whites junior to them in rank or trying

to eliminate separate black and white facilities in camps staffed mainly by blacks; to the latter request he felt obliged to add that "the disposition and use of these facilities be left to the decision of the local commanders who are most familiar with the racial problems involved." By contributing to the decision to convert black service troops into replacements for white casualties in combat units during the acute manpower shortage after the Battle of the Bulge, he did at last help win a beginning for a place for the black soldier as a fighting man like any other. See Ulysses Lee, *The Employment of Negro Troops (United States Army in World War II: Special Studies)* (1966).

RUSSELL F. WEIGLEY

DAVIS, Elmer Holmes (b. Aurora, Ind., Jan. 13, 1890; d. Washington, D.C., May 18, 1958), JOURNALIST, graduated from Franklin (Ind.) College in 1910 and won a Rhodes scholarship for study at Oxford University in England. He received a BA from Oxford in 1912 and then settled in New York City where he joined the editorial staff of *Adventure* magazine. In 1914, Davis became a reporter for the New York *Times;* he quickly rose to sports writer, foreign correspondent, and editorial writer. He covered the 1915 voyage of **Henry Ford**'s Peace Ship and many national political conventions through the fictitious character of "Godfrey Gloom." He also wrote *History of the New York Times* (1921) and a successful novel, *Times Have Changed* (1923).

In 1924, Davis left the *Times* to become a freelance writer. He wrote numerous novels, short stories, and essays on politics and history, many of which were collected in *Not to Mention the War* (1940). The Columbia Broadcasting System hired him as a radio news commentator in 1939, and he quickly won a large following with his dry humor, perceptive comments, and emphasis on factual detail.

Davis left CBS in 1942 to become director of the U.S. Office of War Information, which coordinated government war news and propaganda. He always fought suppression of facts and clashed with the military on several occasions over this issue, particularly when a military commission failed to release details on a trial of eight Nazi saboteurs. He also clashed in 1945 with President Harry Truman, who had rescinded Davis's order banning all foreign publications in occupied Germany. When the OWI was abolished after the conclusion of the war in 1945, Davis joined the American Broadcasting Co. as a radio commentator and then television commentator. He attacked McCarthyism and irrational fears of a Communist conspiracy, and warned of the danger to civil liberties in America. His collection of essays and speeches on these topics, *But We Were Born Free* (1954), sold nearly 100,000 copies. Davis's last book, *Two Minutes Till Midnight* (1955), was a collection of articles on the danger of thermonuclear war.

In a speech at Harvard during the peak of McCarthyism, Elmer Davis recalled the fears of the Philistines as they prepared for battle with the Israelites. After realizing that nobody was going to save them, they said to one another, "Be strong, and quit yourselves like men; and fight." "And they did fight," observed Davis, "and delivered themselves. So may we; but only if we quit ourselves like men." This homily was one that Davis himself followed throughout his life. He combined political sagacity with the conviction that America had become a great nation because of its freedoms and devotion to truth. As a newscaster he never hesitated to enter the fray in defense of those ideals. Yet his strong beliefs never led him to equate conformity with patriotism or dissent with disloyalty. The very fairness and objectivity that won him so large a radio audience in 1941 did not equip him, however, for the job President Franklin Roosevelt insisted that he fill in 1942—director of the Office of War Information. The nature of this position required its director to be skilled in political nuances enabling him to maximize dissemination of information about the president's war measures without simultaneously appearing to be an administration propagandist and thereby antagonizing a suspicious Congress. As Davis soon learned, his talents were useless here, but he

remained at his post with stoic resignation to serve the man he believed embodied the best interests of the nation. Davis lived his finest hour during the early 1950s when he and his friend **Edward R. Murrow** raised their voices against the forces of **Joe McCarthy,** which they viewed as threatening to the constitutional rights of all Americans. His vigorous defense of freedom of the mind at a time when so few ventured to speak out reveals a man who felt that ethics and principles ought to provide a foundation for political as well as personal life—and who acted on his convictions. See Roger Burlingame, *Don't Let Them Scare You: The Life and Times of Elmer Davis* (1961).

SYDNEY WEINBERG

DAVIS, Jefferson (b. Todd County, Ky., June 3, 1808; d. New Orleans, La., Dec. 6, 1889), POLITICAL LEADER, attended Transylvania University, Lexington, Kentucky (1821–23), before accepting an appointment to West Point, where he was graduated as a second lieutenant in 1828. He served in Wisconsin Territory and in the Black Hawk War (1832) but resigned his commission (1835) to marry a daughter of Zachary Taylor and become a Delta planter. Grief over the death of his bride of three months caused him to become a semirecluse on his plantation for seven years. A staunch Jeffersonian Democrat, he was elected to the U.S. Congress in 1845 but shortly resigned his seat to serve in the Mexican War as commander of the Mississippi Rifles. He participated in the siege of Monterey and the battle of Buena Vista, where he was painfully wounded.

In 1847, Davis entered the U.S. Senate and became chairman of the Committee of Military Affairs. During the debates leading to the Compromise of 1850 he supported the Fugitive Slave Act and the bill creating the Utah Territory. In all measures he advocated a strict construction of the Constitution. He remained in the Senate until 1851 when he ran for governor of Mississippi. Narrowly defeated, he devoted himself to agriculture until President Franklin Pierce made him secretary of war (1853). In this position he greatly strengthened the army and coastal defenses and made numerous reforms at West Point; ordered surveys and reconnaissances of railway routes to the Pacific; and engineered the Gadsden Purchase, by which for $10 million the U.S. acquired from Mexico some thirty thousand square miles of territory in the Southwest. Davis was an expansionist and favored the annexation of Cuba by purchase from Spain. He urged the support of the Kansas-Nebraska Act (1854) opening these territories to slavery.

Davis returned to the Senate in 1857. He was a most reluctant secessionist, speaking for the Union and seeking "to harmonize the views" of his constituents. He preferred to give President-elect Abraham Lincoln a chance to reassure the South. Davis remained in the Senate until twelve days after Mississippi seceded. He then accepted a major-generalship to prepare his state for defense. In February 1861, at Montgomery, against his wishes, he was unanimously chosen president of the Confederacy.

As president, Davis tried first to settle North-South differences over a conference table, but when Lincoln sent armed ships with reinforcements to Fort Sumter in Charleston harbor in April 1861, war resulted. Davis unsuccessfully tried to get Britain and France to support the Confederacy. His approval of conscription laws and his suspension of habeas corpus alienated many southerners. When the Civil War ended in 1865, Davis and his cabinet fled southward. Davis hoped to reach Texas and continue the fight in the trans-Mississippi. He was captured near Irwinville, Georgia, on May 10 and imprisoned at Fort Monroe (1865–67). He was indicted for treason but never brought to trial.

Shattered in health, Davis went to Canada and then to England, but was eventually allowed to return to the United States. For a few years he was president of an insurance company in Memphis. Then he settled in Biloxi, Mississippi, where he completed his *Rise and Fall of the Confederate States* (1881).

Jefferson Davis was first called "the most misunderstood man in history" by his Ohio biographer Landon Knight. Part of this misunderstanding was due to the prejudice of northern historians and defeated southerners, who in their misery needed a scapegoat. During the war Davis was the victim of vituperative fabrications by certain inimical newspaper editors, whom he misguidedly refused to muzzle because of his firm belief in free speech. These false accusations have seeped down the years into the minds of students on both sides of the Mason-Dixon line.

Jefferson Davis was chosen president of the Confederacy because there was no other man in the South whose combined record for leadership, political or military, compared with his, and his position in history as the only president of the Confederacy is unique. He was a president without a precedent; he efficiently had to establish a new nation in the cauldron of a great war and prepare defenses against invasion by a foe with ten times the industrial might and four times the white population of the Confederacy. He also had to contend with rival southern political leaders and with jealous generals such as **Joseph E. Johnston** and **Pierre Beauregard.**

Davis was generally regarded by the North as well as the South as a "virtuous and resolute man." Integrity, probity, and principle were three words repeatedly used in characterizing him in his own time. Others were courage, patience, and charm. But Davis's four years at West Point did not inculcate in him the pliancy and assumed cordiality of the politician. He could not suffer gladly bumptious self-seekers. He was often not conciliatory and thus sometimes appeared obstinate and hypersensitive. Yet the discipline instilled at the military academy gave him a sovereign command in later years when he was almost overwhelmed by the tragedy of defeat.

Whatever his weaknesses, Davis possessed that centralizing force of mind that gives strength and unity to character. His very nature rebelled against anything that savored of the demagogue. He was no provincial; he was nation-minded and world-minded. Yet states' rights was something like a religion to him.

In appearance Davis was tall, slender, and handsome, with chiseled features, fair hair, and blue-gray eyes. His bearing was aristocratic. His manners were impeccable except when he was suffering from blinding facial neuralgia. He possessed a peculiarly sweet, well-modulated, and resonant voice that easily won his audiences.

In his youth Davis was known for his sunny disposition. At college and at West Point he was a party to mischievous pranks. As a young army officer he was praised by his fellows for his expert horsemanship, his dancing, and his ability to handle troops. His chief diversion besides breaking in wild horses was reading. The captured Black Hawk, who was put in Lieutenant Davis's charge along with four other Native American prisoners, paid tribute to his consideration and compassion in his autobiography (1833): "He is a good and brave young chief in whose conduct I was very much pleased." All his life Davis was horrified by anyone who would oppress the weak in an inferior or defenseless position.

Davis never gave up his belief in the southern cause. When almost every important southern figure, military or political, asked for amnesty after Appomattox, Davis steadfastly refused. As the elected head of his government he felt he must uphold the principles for which the South had fought: constitutional liberty, the rights of states, and the consent of the governed. He maintained that the southern states in seceding had done no wrong, that under the Constitution any state had the right to withdraw from the compact of states. Yet in one of his last public appearances he admonished young southerners to "let the past bury its dead, its hopes, and its aspirations, … to lay aside all rancor, all bitter sectional feeling, and to take your places in the ranks of those who will bring about a reunited country." Davis died a man without a country, but he remained a kind of uncrowned King of the South. See Hudson Strode, *Jefferson Davis* (4 vols., 1955–66).

HUDSON STRODE

DAVIS, Stuart (b. Philadelphia, Pa., Dec. 7, 1894; d. New York, N.Y., June 24, 1964), ARTIST, whose father was art director of the Philadelphia *Press* and the Newark *Evening News*, left East Orange

(N.J.) High School (1910) and went to New York City to study with **Robert Henri.** He also worked as a cartoonist for *Harper's Weekly* (1913) and drew covers and drawings for the *Masses* (1913). At 19, Davis displayed five watercolors at the pioneering International Exhibition of Modern Art of 1913 (known as the Armory Show). This exhibition left a deep impression on Davis; he turned from realism toward greater abstraction in his work. After drawing maps for the Army Intelligence Department during World War I, Davis settled down to paint in New York and, in the summers, in Gloucester, Massachusetts. His canvases often incorporated elements of city signs, billboards, calligraphy, and numbers. *Cigarette Papers* (1921, private collection) shows the dominant influence of synthetic cubism, an approach he often employed. Davis's Eggbeater series (1927–28) demonstrates his passion for order, syntax, and discipline. In 1928, Davis went to Paris and painted many abstracts of that city, including *Place Pasdeloup* (1928, Whitney Museum, N.Y.). He painted a huge mural, *Men Without Women*, in New York's Radio City Music Hall in 1932.

Davis joined the Federal Art Project in 1933 and later became an art teacher for the WPA. A leader of the American Artists' Congress (1934–39), which opposed Nazi ideas in the field of culture, he was editor of their publication *Art Front*. Davis painted a mural in the Communications Building in the 1939 New York World's Fair. In 1944 the New York Museum of Modern Art gave Davis a retrospective showing of fifty-three canvases; many awards followed, including a Guggenheim fellowship (1952), two Guggenheim international awards (1958, 1960), and the Gold Medal of the Pennsylvania Academy of Fine Arts (1964). Some of Davis's best-known paintings are *Lucky Strike* (1921, Museum of Modern Art, N.Y.), *Midi* (1954, Wadsworth Atheneum, Hartford), and *Something on the Eight Ball* (1954, Philadelphia Museum of Art).

Spanning half a century of artistic achievement, the painting of Stuart Davis documents the encounter of an unusually analytic, disciplined mind with the speed, force, and dynamism of contemporary urban America. From his study with Robert Henri, Davis acquired a taste for the vernacular as subject matter; out of the 1913 Armory Show grew his determination to become a modern artist; from his dedication to rigorous methodology evolved his completely personal style of painting. In the famous Eggbeater series, for example, Davis nailed an electric fan, a rubber glove, and an eggbeater to a table and for one year painted nothing else.

The effects of this severe exercise can be traced through more than thirty years of subsequent painting in which the impact of manmade America—its architecture, advertising, industrial design, mechanized rhythms, and hectic pace—is abstracted into a series of two-dimensional forms held together as tightly as a jigsaw puzzle, yet active and animate with ribbons of movement and careful contrasts of scale and color.

A wry humorist who had little patience with hesitation and lack of commitment, Stuart Davis, like his paintings, gave the impression of forcefully containing energy. Jazz records and often a television set were played in his studio while he labored over his carefully structured compositions, for, as he explained, "I see the artist as a cool spectator-reporter in an arena of hot events."

Although he championed modernism for fifty years, Davis hated to be categorized as an "abstractionist," maintaining that, since he painted real experiences of real things, he was actually a realist. An independence from movements and fashion always characterized Davis's work, however, an accomplishment that has almost no parallels in 20th-century American art. See Diane Kelder, *Stuart Davis* (1971).

PATRICIA FAILING

DAWES, Charles Gates (b. Marietta, Ohio, Aug. 27, 1865; d. Evanston, Ill., Apr. 23, 1951), DIPLOMAT, BUSINESSMAN, studied at Marietta College (BA, 1884) and Cincinnati Law School. Admitted to the bar in 1886, he practiced law in Lincoln, Nebraska (1887–94). Having acquired interests in midwestern gasworks in 1894, Dawes became president of the firms that supplied LaCrosse, Wisconsin, and Chicago. Long an active Republican, he was midwestern director of William McKinley's 1896 presidential campaign. McKinley appointed Dawes controller of the currency in 1897; in this post he helped reorganize banks that had failed in the panic of 1893 and instituted reforms designed to lessen the impact of future panics. In 1902 he resigned the controllership, unsuccessfully seeking the Illinois senatorial nomination. He then returned to business, organizing the Central Trust Co. of Illinois.

During World War I, Dawes served as lieutenant colonel of the Seventeenth Engineers, rising to brigadier general on General **John Pershing**'s staff. Remaining in France after the armistice, he served on commissions that supervised disposal of army surplus matériel. Returning to the United States in 1919, Dawes advocated American entry into the League of Nations. Upon the creation of the Bureau of the Budget in 1921, President Warren Harding named Dawes its director.

In 1924, Dawes was appointed a member of an international commission that met in Paris to determine how German reparations payments to the Allies could be guaranteed. Dawes prepared a report (the Dawes Plan) with Owen D. Young that provided for stabilization of the German currency, a large foreign loan to bolster the economy, and reduced annual reparations installments on a sliding scale reaching maximum payment in 1930.

In 1924, Dawes was elected vice president under Calvin Coolidge. The next year he received the Nobel Peace Prize for his reparations plan. He was chairman of the financial commission to the Dominican Republic (1929); delegate to the London Naval Conference (1930) and the Geneva Disarmament Conference (1932); and served as ambassador to Great Britain (1929–32). In 1932, President Herbert Hoover appointed him director of the Reconstruction Finance Corporation, which provided loans to depression-threatened industrialists and bankers, but Dawes resigned only a few months later. He was criticized for obtaining an RFC loan for his bank shortly after his resignation. In 1934, the federal government having sued for recovery of the loan, Dawes paid his share of the government's levy on stockholders.

The long private and public career of Charles G. Dawes illustrates what one historian has termed "a quest for order" in an America undergoing a revolutionary industrial and urban transformation in the late 19th and early 20th centuries. Dawes repeatedly joined other successful businessmen in trying to rationalize business organization and practice, and in advocating more efficient governmental machinery to regulate and encourage the economy. During his early years as a lawyer and embryonic businessman in Nebraska, Dawes helped fight discriminatory freight rates. Subsequently he advocated changes in the antitrust law to permit business, labor, and farmer combinations that were in the public interest but to punish unfair and harmful practices. The financial panics of 1893 and 1907 caused him to join others in urging currency reforms. As McKinley's controller of the currency and as first director of the budget under Harding, Dawes implemented a number of reforms to preclude future panics and to bring greater economy and efficiency to governmental expenditures. He also displayed his managerial talents as purchasing director for the AEF in World War I and in 1921 in overhauling what became the Veterans Bureau. During the Great Depression, Dawes directed the Reconstruction Finance Corporation's efforts to shore up the nation's shaky banking system and railroads. These RFC loans were in his view and, as time proved, sound and necessary to avert a national financial and economic debacle harmful to all. But Dawes essentially agreed with Hoover that government must not go beyond regulating and encouraging the economy; he objected to subsequent New Deal programs that transformed the RFC into a broad lending agency and to other measures that directly involved government in the economy.

Dawes was one of the most colorful figures in American public life during the interwar years. Bluff and sharp-spoken, but fair and able to compromise, he was a cartoonist's delight with his outthrust jaw, underslung pipe, and his favorite oath popularly translated as "Hell 'n' Maria." He delighted the public, though not all bureaucrats or senators, when as budget director he pursued economy with evangelical broom-waving fervor and as vice president harangued the Senate on inaugural day about its penchant for verbosity and endless debates. Although a Republican of long standing and repeatedly in government, Dawes was not really fond of politics and preferred his private banking and family life. Far from a conservative standpatter at home or abroad, he must be classified as moderately progressive and internationalist in his views. A courageous man, he denounced the methods of the powerful Ku Klux Klan during the 1924 presidential election; yet, disliking socialism intensely, he helped pin the unfair label of radicalism on the **Robert La Follette** Progressives in that same campaign. His most notable public achievements came in 1924 when he helped formulate the constructive Dawes Plan that temporarily resolved the reparations conundrum and offered hope of reintegrating a peaceful Germany into the world society and economy, and in 1929 when as Hoover's ambassador to Great Britain he held private discussions with Prime Minister Ramsay MacDonald that helped clear the path to the successful London Naval Arms Conference of 1930. Dawes also was one of those behind Hoover's moratorium on intergovernmental debts in 1931. See Bascom N. Timmons, *Portrait of an American: Charles G. Dawes* (1953).

DANIEL M. SMITH

DAY, Dorothy (b. Brooklyn, N.Y., Nov. 8, 1897; d. New York, N.Y., Nov. 29, 1980), WRITER, REFORMER, advocated socialism while a student at the University of Illinois (1914–16). At 18 she became a reporter for the New York *Call*, a socialist daily newspaper. She left the *Call* in 1917 and became assistant editor of *The Masses*, a radical paper, and then went to work for the

Liberator. By 1918 she engaged primarily in freelance writing.

Although a socialist, Day gradually became attracted to the Catholic Church and converted to Catholicism in 1927. In 1933 she began the Catholic Worker Movement with French-born Peter Maurin, an idealogue who wrote in melodic free verse. Day emerged as the Movement's leader, Maurin its conscience. Day spread its message primarily as editor and columnist for its newspaper, the *Catholic Worker.* She visualized love as the means of achieving true human and spiritual fellowship through direct personal action. The *Catholic Worker* supported organized labor and the New Deal, opposed segregation and racism in America, and fascism abroad, and advocated voluntary poverty for its adherents. The Movement established Houses of Hospitality to feed and house the Depression's destitute. Several small collective farms constituted an additional focus of the Movement. Day, a pacifist, opposed the draft and military preparedness during World War II. In the decades after the war, her writings criticized U.S. cold war policies, McCarthyism, nuclear testing, civil defense, government bureaucracy, the Korean and Vietnam wars, and alleged that the government was repressing the Left.

───── ∞ ─────

It is difficult to measure Day's success or failure as an activist during the Great Depression and the decades that followed. Considering the totality of social and economic problems then and since, she had little practical impact in alleviating them. Yet throughout the Depression, Catholic Worker Houses of Hospitality fed thousands daily and sheltered and clothed a significant number. Its other involvements—such as opposing racism, anti-Semitism, and anti-Catholicism in Mexico, aiding alcoholics, holding art classes for slum children, helping settle strikes, and finding housing for the homeless—had some effect.

Yet perhaps Day's greatest impact was her example of personal self-sacrifice and unswerving dedication to social regeneration. Many on the Catholic Left during and after the Depression came out of Day's Catholic Worker Movement. William Callahan organized the Association of Catholic Conscientious Objectors. John Cort founded the Association of Catholic Trade Unionists. Others founded independent labor schools and intrareligious friendship houses. Catholic journalism felt Day's influence. The *Canadian Social Forum,* the first *Christian Front,* the *Catholic Student Digest,* and the *Source* came out of the Movement. So did John Cogley, editor of *Commonweal*; Edward Willock, cofounder of *Integrity*; Edward Marciniak, founder of *Work*; and **Michael Harrington**, whose writings about poverty amid plenty helped fuel the Great Society programs of Lyndon Johnson.

Dorothy Day was the mortar that held the Catholic Worker Movement together. Day was the prime organizer, the first editor of the newspaper, controller of the funds, and the key decision-maker. Her personality, leadership qualities, and labor orientation determined the approach of the Movement. In the 1930s Day, through the Catholic Worker Movement, rekindled American Catholic social reform activities that had lain relatively dormant for over a decade. She began a new antiestablishment tradition in American Catholic activism. See William D. Miller, *A Harsh and Dreadful Love: Dorothy Day and the Catholic Worker Movement* (1973).

NEIL BETTEN

DEANE, Silas (b. Groton, Conn., Dec. 24, 1737; d. Deal, Eng., Sept. 23, 1789), POLITICAL LEADER, graduated from Yale in 1758 (MA, 1763). He was admitted to the Connecticut bar in 1761 and quickly became affluent as a lawyer and merchant. In 1769 he served as chairman of a local committee opposing the Townshend Acts. He became a member of the Connecticut General Assembly in 1772, secretary of the legislative committee of correspondence the following year, and then served as Connecticut's representative to the first and second Continental Congresses (1774–75). After serving on the naval and military procurement committees of the second Congress, he was denied reappointment by the Connecticut assembly, but in March 1776, Congress sent him to France as an unofficial minister.

In France, Deane helped obtain eight shiploads of French supplies, which arrived in America in time to be of value at the battle of Saratoga (1777). He also recruited several able foreign officers including Lafayette, De Kalb, Pulaski, and Steuben. In association with **Benjamin Franklin** and Arthur Lee, Deane helped negotiate treaties of alliance and commerce with France in 1778. While in Europe, Deane earned a fortune dabbling in trade; he was recalled by Congress in 1777 to answer Arthur Lee's insinuations that he was guilty of embezzlement. Unable to reach a settlement with Congress over his accounts, he became disillusioned with the American cause and advocated reconciliation with England. His intercepted letters were published in New York (Oct. 1781) and were reprinted as *Paris Papers; or Mr. Silas Deane's Late Intercepted Letters* (Mar. 1782). Accused of treachery, Deane took up residence in Ghent, Holland, then England. In 1784 he defended his conduct in *An Address to the Free and Independent Citizens of the United States.* In 1842, Congress cleared him of corrupt practices.

———— ∞ ————

Silas Deane's rapid rise into the Connecticut oligarchy demonstrates the opportunities for advancement open in the American colonies to a man with an eye for an opportune marriage and a penchant for commerce. By 1775, Deane's commercial activities and ambitions, his extensive speculation in western lands, and his highly placed and like-minded economic associates prompted him to advocate independence, a course that would best stimulate American enterprise.

In his mission to France, Deane rendered stalwart service in purchasing and forwarding needed supplies, but he made two serious errors. First, he did not appreciate the growing "radical" sentiment in Congress that holders of public office should not take advantage of their position to amass personal profit. If Deane prospered less than his enemies charged, he was certainly indis-

creet in not avoiding the appearance of evil. Second, just as serious for his career, Deane eloquently advocated a political as well as a commercial alliance with France, a measure whose wisdom was disputed sharply in Congress. When Deane was charged with corruption and was subsequently defended by the indiscreet French minister to America, Conrad Alexander Gérard, the issues of corruption and the French alliance were joined. Deane was thus at the center of a policy conflict that stimulated creation of a congressional bloc habitually suspicious of French motives and policies. French intervention to support Deane and to discredit the radical Lee-Adams faction also underscored the problems a small nation encountered when it became the satellite of a great power, a lesson that impressed even the most ardent Francophiles. See G. L. Clark, *Silas Deane* (1913).

MARVIN H. ZAHNISER

DE BOW, James Dunwoody Brownson (b. Charleston, S.C., July 10, 1820; d. Elizabeth, N.J., Feb. 27, 1867), JOURNALIST, worked for a Charleston mercantile house before attending the Cokesbury (S.C.) Institute (1839) and the College of Charleston. After graduating in 1843 he read law and was admitted to the South Carolina bar the following year. He practiced law only briefly, however, and began contributing political articles to Charleston's *Southern Quarterly Review*, including one on the Oregon question in 1844 urging compromise with Great Britain, which received national attention. That same year he became editor of the *Quarterly*. In 1845 he moved to New Orleans. His *Commercial Review of the South and Southwest* first appeared in 1846 but failed in 1849. After receiving financial support from Maunsel White, a wealthy sugar planter and merchant, he revived the magazine in 1849, and within two years it had the largest circulation in the South. He also headed the Louisiana Bureau of Statistics. In this post he made a valuable report to the state legislature on population, industry, and commerce in 1850. President Franklin Pierce appointed De Bow superintendent of the writing of the seventh (1850) U.S. census in 1853. In addition to this work he published *Statistical View of the United States* (1854), a compendium to the 1850 census.

De Bow left his government post in 1855 to devote more time to his magazine, now known as *De Bow's Review.* A longtime friend and admirer of **John C. Calhoun,** he upheld the southern cause, urging southern unity, the continuation of slavery, and (eventually) secession. He wanted to make southern agriculture self-sufficient by establishing a transcontinental railroad between the South and West, and building a Central American canal, and he also advocated the building up of industry in the South using slave labor. De Bow was president of the 1857 Knoxville commercial convention and was active in many similar conventions. He spent the Civil War as chief agent for the purchase and sale of cotton for the Confederate government. Reviving the *Review* in 1865 (it had been suppressed by federal troops during the occupation of New Orleans), De Bow also served as president of the Tennessee Pacific Railroad Co. until his death.

———— ❧ ————

James Dunwoody Brownson De Bow, as editor of the journal finally called *De Bow's Review* and as superintendent of the seventh census of the United States, demonstrated the need for sound statistical data with which to plan economic change, whether on a state, regional, or national basis. He showed that statistics being collected could be greatly improved in both accuracy and usefulness. De Bow's advocacy of slavery and secession have obscured his interest in building a balanced economy in the South. His proposals included agricultural improvement, industrial development, promotion of trade, and railroad and canal construction—plans that might be advocated 125 years later for almost any underdeveloped nation. De Bow used comparative statistical data in advocating his ideas and was continually attempting to improve his material. His greatest achievement as a statistician, however, came with his appointment in 1853 as superintendent of the census. Earlier, he had made many

suggestions, some of which were adopted, as to material needed. His job was to complete the publication of the data collected in 1850. In doing so, and particularly in preparing a *Compendium,* De Bow called upon specialists for assistance, made inquiries to correct obvious errors, rearranged the material to make it more useful on both a national and a regional basis, and carefully explained how the material for this and previous censuses had been collected, with some discussion of possible errors. When he completed the task and returned to his *Review,* he left a landmark—a means by which to evaluate earlier censuses and to improve subsequent ones. See O. C. Skipper, *J. D. B. De Bow: Magazinist of the Old South* (1958).

WAYNE D. RASMUSSEN

DEBS, Eugene Victor (b. Terre Haute, Ind., Nov. 5, 1855; d. Elmhurst, Ill., Oct. 20, 1926), LABOR LEADER, was the son of Alsatian immigrants. Leaving school at 14 he worked in the railroad shops in Terre Haute and then as a locomotive fireman. In 1874 he became a clerk in a wholesale grocery business, helping to found the next year the first local lodge of the Brotherhood of Locomotive Firemen. In 1878 he became associate editor of the *Locomotive Firemen's* magazine, and in 1880 he became the magazine's editor as well as treasurer and grand secretary of the Brotherhood. He was also (1880–84) city clerk of Terre Haute and (1885) a member of the lower house of the Indiana state legislature.

Beginning in the late 1870s as a defender of the status quo and an opponent of the 1877 railroad strikes, Debs soon began to criticize social conditions. Believing that the labor movement served only some workers, he began to view labor's problem as primarily one of class or group solidarity. For this reason he early opposed unionization along craft lines, and he resigned his position with the Locomotive Firemen, sacrificing his $4,000 annual salary, and formed the American Railway Union, a labor organization that opened its doors to all railroad workers, operating or nonoperating, skilled or unskilled. At first the ARU grew rapidly when a major strike it organized against the Great Northern Railroad in April 1894 ended in victory for the union. But later that year, against Debs's better judgment, the organization was drawn into the strike against the Pullman Co. After an outbreak of violence in Chicago and the intervention of the federal government, Debs and several union associates were sentenced to six months in jail for contempt of court. The union was destroyed in the process. Debs later claimed that the reading and reflection he did in jail converted him to socialism.

In 1896, Debs supported **William Jennings Bryan** for president, but the next year he organized the Social Democratic Party of America. In 1901 his followers merged with a faction of the Socialist Labor Party led by Morris Hillquit and Job Harriman to form the Socialist Party of America. Debs, who was to be the Socialist presidential candidate five times, ran in the 1900 presidential election and received 96,000 votes. In 1904, while editing a Kansas Socialist newspaper, the *Appeal to Reason,* and lecturing widely, he polled 400,000 votes. In 1912 he received 901,000 votes, the highest percentage of votes (6 percent of the total) ever gained by a Socialist presidential candidate in America.

Debs opposed the United States' entry into World War I, and his speech to Ohio Socialists in June 1918, in which he denounced the war, led the federal government to indict him under the Espionage Act. He was convicted and sentenced to ten years in prison. While in the penitentiary at Atlanta, Debs received 920,000 votes as the 1920 Socialist candidate for president. On Christmas Day, 1921, President Warren Harding commuted Debs's sentence.

Debs remained a Socialist when the Communists split off from the party in 1919, although he was sympathetic to the Russian Bolsheviks. In the following years he was occasionally vocal in his criticism of American Communists. In 1924 he supported the presidential candidacy of Senator **Robert M. La Follette.**

⚬⚬⚬

Debs's origins were middle class; son of a small storekeeper, he developed only slowly from a fair-

ly conventional, small-city, midwestern Democrat to a Socialist whose radical rhetoric attracted a national following. Although he read such Socialists as **Edward Bellamy, Laurence Gronlund,** and some American Marxists, each of his shifts to the left grew from his personal experience rather than from persuasion by a social theorist. He was an advocate of craft unionism until, in the 1885 strike against the Chicago, Burlington, and Quincy Railroad, it appeared to him that the craft organizational principle was inherently inadequate for railroad labor. He subsequently left the Brotherhood of Locomotive Firemen to found the American Railway Union, which he organized along industrial lines. When federal political power wrecked the ARU and sent Debs to jail after the disastrous Pullman strike, Debs turned to political action. He supported William Jennings Bryan on the Populist ticket in 1896—Bryan ran also as a Democrat—even though it had been a Democratic president, Grover Cleveland, who had headed the administration that crushed the ARU. Only when reconstruction of the Democratic Party seemed hopeless after the election did Debs set about organizing the Social Democratic Party. He was one of the founders of the Industrial Workers of the World in 1905, hoping that the Socialist Party would be the revolutionary political arm and the IWW, "one big union," would be its economic arm. He never fully abandoned this goal as an ideal, although he played no role in the IWW after its earliest years because he was discouraged by its incessant internal fighting. It has been said that Debs's socialism was more from the heart than from the head; it certainly was from the heart, but it would be more accurate to say that his views, while rational, were based on his observations rather than on theory or doctrine.

His political and economic views changed over the years, but many of the values and ways of thinking he learned in his youth persisted. Named for Eugène Sue and Victor Hugo, Debs grew up on the ideals of French romanticism, and he never departed from them. He frequently quoted from Hugo and from French revolutionary songs in his writings and speeches. Similarly, he steadfastly remained a Hoosier culturally; one of his favorite poets was James Whitcomb Riley, who was a close friend and drinking companion. Debs was unusually generous; apparently on several occasions he gave poor men the overcoat off his back. And he was romantically sentimental; he could be moved to tears by a sad story, and even when he was writing passionately revolutionary editorials, he could give beautifully bound volumes of Elbert Hubbard as Christmas gifts. A charismatic and highly effective if old-fashioned and flowery public speaker, Debs was one of the most popular leaders of labor and socialist movements in American history. See Nick Salvatore, *Eugene V. Debs* (1982).

DAVID A. SHANNON

DEERE, John (b. Rutland, Vt., Feb. 7, 1804; d. Moline, Ill., May 17, 1886), INVENTOR, MANUFACTURER, worked as a blacksmith in Vermont until 1837. He then moved to Illinois. Observing that the iron-and-wood plows that local farmers had brought from the East worked poorly in the tough virgin prairie soil, he devised one with a steel share. To this he added a polished wrought iron moldboard (the upper portion of the plow, the curvature of which affects its efficiency) of his own design. He found an ironmaster who could make the steel his plow required, and they began to manufacture plows in quantity.

In 1847, Deere transferred his operations to Moline, Illinois. In 1857 he was turning out ten thousand plows a year. His business, incorporated in 1868 as Deere and Co., added cultivators and related cultivating equipment to the line. Deere was president of the company until his death.

When John Deere constructed his first "steel" plow in 1837, using saw steel for the share and polished wrought iron for the moldboard, a new era began in prairie agriculture. The cast-iron plow, used in the East from the 1820s, would not scour in the heavy, sticky soils of the prairies; the soil clung to the moldboard instead of sliding by and turning over. The smooth-surfaced metals used by Deere cut and turned the soil in furrows with less effort than was required to pull either cast iron or wooden plows. By the beginning of the Civil War the steel plow had largely displaced all other types on the prairies.

The steel plow was a key to the opening up of the prairies. There is evidence that some early farmers, discouraged by the seeming impossibility of handling the sticky prairie soils, abandoned their farms. Deere's plow changed this and helped bring some of the world's most productive farmland into use. In 1850, 5,864,227 acres were under cultivation in Illinois and Iowa, and in 1870 there were 28,726,419 acres.

The steel plow, which could be pulled by horses rather than oxen, was part of the first American agricultural revolution. This change was marked by the adoption of horse-drawn machinery and, in the northern United States, by the move from a self-sufficient to a commercial agriculture. The tools and machines, such as the steel plow, the grain drill, and the grain harvester, were developed before the Civil War and were adopted during and just after the strife.

John Deere's fame rests primarily on his plow even though he manufactured other machines. He believed in the importance of his plow but, so far as the available evidence shows, never realized that a revolutionary change was taking place in agriculture. Deere was representative of the able, aggressive manufacturer of his time, devoted to business, honest, religious, and aggressively moral in following the codes of his era. As a businessman and human being he differed little from many others, but as a persistent man with a practical idea he left his mark on the prairie. See Neil M. Clark, *John Deere: He Gave to the World the Steel Plow* (1937), and Edward C. Kendall, *John Deere's Steel Plow,* Paper 2, U.S. National Museum Bulletin 218, Smithsonian Institution (1959), pp. 15–25.

WAYNE D. RASMUSSEN

DE FOREST, Lee (b. Council Bluffs, Iowa, Aug. 26, 1873; d. Hollywood, Calif., June 30, 1961), INVENTOR, received his PhB (1896) and PhD (1899) from Yale, where he studied with J.

Willard Gibbs. His doctoral dissertation was on Hertzian (radio) waves. In 1899–1900 he worked in the telephone laboratory of the Western Electric Co. in Chicago, and in 1900–1902 he lectured at Chicago's Armour Institute, where he also designed an alternating current transmitter.

In 1902, De Forest established the De Forest (later renamed United) Wireless Telegraph Co. in Jersey City, New Jersey, which installed the first high-powered naval radio stations. Believing that radio reception could be improved by a sensitive detector of radio waves, he developed the audion tube in 1906. This invention (more generally known as the triode vacuum tube), his use of the microphone in radio broadcasting (1907), and his development of the oscillating audion (1913) earned him the sobriquet "the father of radio broadcasting." The audion amplifier also helped pave the way for transcontinental telephony.

In 1934 he established the Lee De Forest Laboratories in Los Angeles, which manufactured shortwave apparatus. The holder of more than three hundred patents, De Forest was also a pioneer in the fields of movie sound recording and television. In 1950 he published his autobiography, *Father of Radio.*

—————✤—————

If necessity is the mother of invention, the need to overcome the deficiencies of the poverty and isolation of De Forest's southern childhood accounts for his independence, self-reliance, and inventiveness. Abundant episodes from his youth testify to a strong desire to achieve, to conquer hardship, and to an early dedication to a career of invention. Because of his education De Forest did not fit the traditional myth of untutored Yankee ingenuity, of inventors developing new technology without benefit of scientific training. Yet, like his contemporaries, he possessed the qualities of the traditional tinkerer-inventor: visionary faith, self-confidence, perseverance, and the capacity for sustained hard work. But though able to inspire a loyal following of assistants, even when short of funds, he failed to secure as loyal or scrupulous a corps of financial backers. Despite the periodic swings in his fortunes, De Forest maintained a deep faith in the system of laissez-faire capitalism. It suited his competitive and fighting nature, his somewhat eccentric individualism.

However, these qualities also frequently led him into patent litigation until late in life when he decided only to invent and let others develop the commercial potential of his inventions. Before his third and last marriage in 1930, his personal life had as many ups and downs as his business career. Music afforded him solace and release; De Forest expressed his lifelong love of it in the choice of opera for his early broadcasts. That choice also fit his utopian vision of radio's potential to unite mankind and upgrade culture; he despised the vulgar commercialization of his "child."

De Forest's studies of amplification and feedback, together with his development of the first commercial talking pictures (1923), represent noteworthy contributions to what have become major technical, economic, and cultural aspects of contemporary life. But his outstanding achievement is the triode, which at first he neither fully understood nor appreciated despite his scientific education. Essential to radio and the electronics industry, it ranks as one of the most important inventions in human history. See Lee De Forest, *Father of Radio* (1950).

DONALD DE B. BEAVER

DE KOONING, Willem (b. Rotterdam, Holland, Apr. 24, 1904), ARTIST, studied at the Rotterdam Academy of Fine Arts and Techniques (1916–24) and emigrated to the United States in 1926 when the only English word he knew was "yes." For the next several years he supported himself as a housepainter and commercial artist, working for decorators and doing murals for speakeasies. In 1935 he spent a year on the Federal Arts Project, for the first time devoting himself solely to painting. In 1937 he designed a mural for the Hall of Pharmacy for the 1939 New York World's Fair.

After sharing a studio with the painter Arshile Gorky in the late 1930s, he began exhibiting in New York group shows early in the 1940s and had his first one-man show at the Egan Gallery in 1948. In the same year he taught at Black Mountain College, with which Joseph Albers, **Buckminster Fuller,** and **John Cage** were also currently associated. He taught at Yale's Art School (1950–51), was invited to exhibit at the Venice Biennale (1950), and won first prize at the Chicago Art Institute's Annual (1951). Exhibitions of his work at the Martha Jackson and Sidney Janis galleries in New York in 1956 resulted in de Kooning's becoming a solid commercial as well as a critical success.

De Kooning's first critically acclaimed paintings were the series of black and white abstractions shown in 1948, their limited palette reflecting the artist's financial state. (An example of these is *Painting,* 1948, Museum of Modern Art, New York). Late in 1951 he began his long series of abstractions based on the theme "woman," of which *Woman I* (1951–52, Museum of Modern Art) is the most well-known example. From 1955 until 1964 his abstractions became associated more with landscape than with the figure, as in *Suburb in Havana* (1958, collection of Lee V. Eastman, New York) and *Door to the River* (1960, Whitney Museum of Art, New York). After 1964, de Kooning again returned to the figure in such works as *Woman Acabonic* (1966, Whitney Museum of Art) and *The Visit* (1967), part of the Knoedler Gallery's extensive collection of de Kooning's work. De Kooning continued painting and exhibiting during the 1970s and the mid-1980s but his work became progressively thinner and more pared down, probably a consequence of Alzheimer's disease. In 1994 a major retrospective of his work opened at the National Gallery of Art, In Washington, D.C., went to the Metropolitan Museum of of Art in New York (1994–95), and traveled to the Tate Gallery in London. In the last decade or so, as de Kooning has slipped into senility, his affairs have been in the hands of his lawyers and family members.

―――∞∞∞―――

By the end of the 1950s, in the opinion of many, the most influential painter at work in the world was the Abstract Expressionist master Willem de Kooning. Although it was 1948 before he was given his first one-man show, de Kooning had previously acquired a formidable underground reputation that served to boost him to prominence, along with **Jackson Pollock,** as the leading exponent of "action painting."

The Abstract Expressionists saw painting as both autobiographical and as an expression of universal themes; for de Kooning it became an event in which the track, force, and direction of brushwork were visual counterparts of the artist's state of mind. Derived originally from the Surrealist concept of psychic automatism, this approach compares the individuality of brushwork with that of handwriting, maintaining that, with its unpremeditated employment, the artist can plumb the depths of the psyche. In de Kooning's case, a painting results from dynamic interchange between hand and mind, its surface being constantly altered by numerous additions and subtractions of pigment. Frequently, these corpulent surfaces reveal the figure of a woman, a demonic creature born from the act of painting itself. The dislocated spatial environment from which these figures leer and recede marks another of de Kooning's obsessions—the spontaneous and impactful recording of his personal confrontation with urban chaos, wherein nothing really belongs, has a place, or remains constant.

Charismatic and eloquent, de Kooning accomplished a reconciliation of radicalism and tradition that attracted record numbers of younger painters, indicating that, above all, his painting was particularly well anchored to the spirit of his time. See Thomas B. Hess, *Willem de Kooning* (1959), and David Sylvester, Richard Shiff, and Marla Prather, *Willem de Kooning, Paintings* (1994).

PATRICIA FAILING

DELANY, Martin Robison (b. Charles Town, Va., now W. Va., May 6, 1812; d. Xenia, Ohio, Jan. 24, 1885), REFORMER, was born a free black. He moved to Chambersburg, Pennsylvania, in 1822 and then to Pittsburgh in 1831, where he studied under the Reverend Lewis Woodson, a man interested in educating young blacks. He also studied medicine in the 1830s under several Pittsburgh doctors. Beginning in 1843 he published a newspaper, *Mystery,* which gained wide appeal in the Pittsburgh area. He assisted **Frederick Douglass** (1847–49) in editing the abolitionist paper *North Star.* Delany published *The Condition, Elevation, Emigration, and Destiny of the Colored People of the United States, Politically Considered* (1852), a book that recommended emigration as a solution to racial discrimination and that anticipated **Booker T. Washington** in its emphasis on practical education for blacks.

Becoming increasingly convinced that blacks could not live decently in white America, Delany assembled the National Emigration Convention in Cleveland in 1854. The convention met again in 1856 and 1858 in Chatham, Ontario. Delany visited the Niger Valley in Africa in 1859 and concluded a treaty with African kings that offered inducements for American blacks to settle in Africa. In 1860 he visited Liverpool, England, and delivered a paper to the International Statistical Conference in London.

Returning to the United States, Delany assisted in recruiting blacks for the northern army and served as an examining surgeon in Chicago. In 1865 he received his commission as a major, the first black major in the history of the U.S. army. Delany served in the Freedmen's Bureau and also as a customhouse inspector in Charleston, South Carolina. He was a trial justice in that city and vigorously fought political corruption. In 1874, Delany was nominated for lieutenant governor on the Independent Republican ticket but was defeated. He spent his later years writing *Principia of Ethnology: The Origin of Races and Color* (1879).

On February 18, 1865, President Abraham Lincoln jotted a one-sentence memorandum to Secretary of War **E. M. Stanton:** "Do not fail to have an interview with this most extraordinary and intelligent black man." The most extraordinary thing about the bearer of this note of introduction, Martin R. Delany, was his deep-seated pride of race and his wide range of activities expressive of this sentiment. Delany has been called "the father of African nationalism," a sobriquet reflecting his pride in his color and ancestry, his insistence that black Americans control their destiny, and his firm belief that black Africa would one day regain its ancient glory. In the main his early career was divided between editing a newspaper in Pittsburgh and touring the antislavery circuit. His abolitionist sympathies brought him into the orbit of **John Brown,** but at the time of Harpers Ferry he was in Africa exploring the Niger River. Before returning home he toured the British Isles to large audiences. Both before and after the Civil War, as if his public activities were not sufficient to bring his fellow blacks to his way of thinking, Delany often turned to his pen, bringing out pamphlets, a novel, and two book-length treatises. By word and deed Delany's pride in blackness and his emotional attachment to Africa struck a responsive vein in the hearts of many black Americans of his day and subsequently. See Dorothy Sterling, *The Making of an Afro-American: Martin Robison Delany, 1812–1885* (1971).

BENJAMIN QUARLES

DE LEON, Daniel (b. Curaçao, Dec. 14, 1852; d. New York, N.Y., May 11, 1914), REFORMER, was the son of a surgeon in the Dutch colonial army in Curaçao. In 1866 he was sent to a gymnasium at Hildesheim, Germany; it is disputed whether he then attended the University of Leyden in Holland. He came to the United States in 1874 and settled in New York City. De Leon edited a newspaper advocating Cuban independence and taught Greek and Latin at the Thomas B. Harrington School in Westchester, New York (1874–76). He entered Columbia Law School in 1876 and received his LLB in 1878. He then went to Texas to practice law but returned to New York in 1886 to lecture on international law and Latin American diplomacy at Columbia.

Meanwhile, De Leon actively supported the candidacy of single-tax advocate **Henry George,** who ran for mayor of New York in 1886. Shortly thereafter he became a Marxist, believing that a socialist trade union movement was necessary to initiate a revolution that would establish a dictatorship of the proletariat. He joined the Knights of Labor in 1888 and became affiliated with **Edward Bellamy's** Nationalist movement the following year. Finding these groups too moderate, De Leon joined the Socialist Labor Party in 1890; he left Columbia in 1891 to become national lecturer of the party and rapidly emerged as its most prominent spokesman. He was the party candidate for governor of New York in 1891 and 1902, and ran for numerous other political offices.

In 1892, De Leon became editor of the official party organ *Weekly People,* which became the *Daily People* in 1900. He attacked the trade union movement and especially the AFL for its failure to adopt socialism. He also criticized the Knights of Labor and led a seceding faction in 1895, the Socialist Trade and Labor Alliance. In 1899 a dissident group of Socialist Labor Party members who resented his control left De Leon's party and formed the Socialist Party of America. De Leon participated in the founding of the Industrial Workers of the World in 1905 and immediately merged his Socialist Trade and Labor Alliance with it. When friction again developed over De Leon's attempts to use the IWW for Socialist Labor political activity, he withdrew from the IWW in 1908 to form the Workers' International Industrial Union.

———— ∞ ————

Personally kind and generous, De Leon of all American socialist leaders came closest to embodying the doctrinaire sectarianism that characterized so many European intellectual leaders of revolutionary movements in the late 19th century. Indeed, in his insistence on ideological purity and the dominance of the Socialist Labor Party over the rank-and-file working-class movement, De Leon in part anticipated and in part followed the Bolshevik model of the austere revolutionary leader. However, he did not possess either Lenin's tactical genius or his opportunities for mass action. Although after the IWW founding convention of 1905 De Leon displayed a belated willingness to compromise his earlier political Marxism by incorporating elements of

anarchosyndicalist thought into his philosophy, his persistent search for doctrinal purity led to splits in the SLP, in the IWW, and indeed in every major movement he participated in.

Although praised by his admirers as one of the few original thinkers among American socialists, recent scholarship has thrown doubt on the originality of his ideas. Beginning in the 1890s as a neo-Lassallean who upheld the ballot box as the only successful way of achieving socialism, De Leon came to advocate revolutionary industrial unionism as the primary means of revolution only after the IWW was founded in 1905, not during the 1890s with his Socialist Trade and Labor Alliance, as is commonly thought. During the last decade of his life he espoused a form of apolitical (but not necessarily antipolitical) syndicalism in which the industrial union movement was to become the main agent of revolutionary change. But this represented a synthesis of previous French and American syndicalist thought rather than De Leon's own. See Don K. McKee, "Daniel De Leon: A Reappraisal," *Labor History,* I, 3 (Fall 1960), 264–97.

JOHN H. M. LASLETT

DeMILLE, Cecil Blount (b. Ashfield, Mass., Aug. 12, 1881; d. Hollywood, Calif., Jan. 21, 1959), MOVIE PRODUCER-DIRECTOR, graduated from the American Academy of Dramatic Arts in New York in 1900. For the next decade he acted in numerous plays, wrote some himself, and managed his mother's play brokerage house. He also organized and played leads in his Standard Opera Company. In 1913, DeMille turned to motion pictures and joined Jesse L. Lasky, Arthur Friend, and Samuel Goldfish (later, Goldwyn) to form the Jesse L. Lasky Feature Play Co. Their first production, *The Squaw Man* (1914), was a tremendous success, and in 1915, DeMille became the director-general of the newly formed Famous Players-Lasky Corporation in Hollywood, California. Under DeMille's direction the company turned out many popular films, including *Joan the Woman* (1916), *The Romance of the Redwoods* (1917) with Mary Pickford, and his first biblical film, *The Ten Commandments* (1923). DeMille organized the Mercury Aviation Co. in 1919, one of the world's first commercial airlines. He served as its president until 1921 when the company was dissolved.

In 1925, after Famous Players-Lasky canceled his contract, DeMille established the Cecil B. DeMille Pictures Corporation. He became known for his extremely expensive productions with huge casts and sets, and for pictures on biblical and historical themes. *The King of Kings* (1927), the story of Jesus, which he produced and directed, epitomized this superspectacular genre. It earned enormous profits. During the years of the silent films DeMille developed such stars as Gloria Swanson, Wallace Reid, Geraldine Farrar, Thomas Meighan, Bebe Daniels, Leatrice Joy, and William Boyd. In 1928 he became a producer-director for MGM, where he made his first all-talking feature, *Dynamite* (1929), In 1932 he joined Paramount as an independent producer, making *The Sign of the Cross* (1932). Other successes followed, including *Cleopatra* (1934), *The Crusades* (1935), *The Plainsman* (1936), and *Union Pacific* (1939). For his talking pictures he preferred to use established stars, as he did with Claudette Colbert, Fredric March, Gary Cooper, Jean Arthur, **John Wayne,** and Charlton Heston. From 1936 to 1945, DeMille served as host for the Lux Radio Theater, which brought plays and screenplays featuring well-known stars into millions of American homes. He was forced to resign when he refused to pay a one-dollar assessment imposed by the American Federation of Radio Artists, which opposed a California initiative vote abolishing the closed shop. In 1953, DeMille won an Academy Award (the Irving G. Thalberg Memorial Award). On that occasion his movie of circus life, *The Greatest Show on Earth* (1952), was also honored by two awards. His new, spectacular version of *The Ten Commandments* appeared in 1956. DeMille finished his *Autobiography* (1959) shortly before his death.

The name Cecil B. DeMille belongs to that day of screen pioneers when there were giants at work in the medium, laying the foundation for a titanic multimillion-dollar industry. Between 1913 and 1956, DeMille personally produced and directed seventy feature films; he also supervised and assisted in the direction, writing, and production of many other pictures at Paramount and Producers Distributing Corporation-Pathé, where he had his own producing unit. The power of other giants in the industry faded and vanished, but DeMille continued, a fighter and filmmaker, to the end of his life.

He knew what the movie public wanted, and he always gave it to them—entertainment! It did not matter whether he was presenting a modern story, a period piece, a biblical spectacle, or a romance of the ancient world. A master showman, he gave his audiences the ultimate in cinematic drama, as **P. T. Barnum** had in the circus, as **David Belasco** did in the theater. He spared no expense, and his name became the most potent of all box-office lures. If it was a DeMille production, it needed no other guarantee for top success. Many critics may have scorned him and his films, but in the end awards were lavished on him and them.

He also helped put Hollywood on the map as the film center of the world, and when he stopped making pictures, Hollywood was in its sad decline. The name DeMille endures because with all the glamour, spectacle, sex, and tense action that highlighted his productions, he had grasped two fundamentals of successful picture-making: characters who would capture and hold an audience's interest; and a straight-line story that constantly moved forward and upward, crashing over barriers on its way to explode in one final dramatic climax where all was resolved—usually, oddly enough, unhappily for all survivors. DeMille characters struggled continually through sin, strife, and silken seduction to realize that he who wins must compromise. Winning itself was always a bitter victory. Every feature he made, from *The Squaw Man* in 1914 to *The Ten Commandments* in 1956, is illustrative of that philosophy. See Donald Hayne, ed., *The Autobiography of Cecil B. DeMille* (1959).

DEWITT BODEEN

DEMPSEY, William Harrison (Jack) (b. Manassa, Colo., June 24, 1895; d. New York, N.Y., May 31, 1983), BOXER, attended the Manassa village school through the eighth grade and then began to work at a variety of jobs including picking fruit, lumbering, mining, and shining shoes. All the while aspiring to a career in the ring, he trained diligently and was a professional boxer by the age of 18. In 1917 fight manager Jack Kearns arranged a series of matches that earned Dempsey a reputation and, in 1919, a title bout with heavyweight champion Jess Willard. Nicknamed the Manassa Mauler, the six-foot-one-inch Dempsey beat the much taller and heavier Willard and became the new champion.

Dempsey successfully defended the title six times before losing it to Gene Tunney in 1926. He lost again in a rematch the following year in which he knocked Tunney down but didn't retire to a neutral corner as required. The resulting delay in starting the referee's count gave Tunney a few extra seconds to recover and possibly cost Dempsey the fight.

As popular in defeat as he was when he was champion, Dempsey remained a celebrity for the rest of his life. He served in the Coast Guard during World War II as a physical training and morale officer. In 1950 an Associated Press poll named him the greatest fighter of the half-century. In his later years the genial ex-champ owned and operated a restaurant in New York City's Times Square and was always available to greet his faithful public and pose for pictures.

During the scant seven years that Jack Dempsey held the world heavyweight title, he set no pugilistic trends, but he established a personal style that enlarged and elevated the audience for boxing. He won seventy-two of his recorded seventy-eight fights, forty-nine by knockouts, but it was neither his technique nor his record in the ring that won and sustained his popularity. Known for his powerful right hand, his fierce aggression, and his dogged resilience in the ring, he was still more admired for his personal generosity and modesty. His gallantry in victory and his grace in defeat made him a symbol of sportsmanship. When his wife asked him what happened the night he lost his title, his rueful response, "Honey, I forgot to duck," became a part of the language, and his insistence on being led back into the ring to shake Tunney's hand after the bout entered boxing legend.

Perhaps the first national superstar among boxers, Dempsey enjoyed unprecedented personal popularity. The 1921 fight in which he defended his title against Georges Carpentier brought the first million-dollar gate in boxing history, and his second bout with Tunney had the largest live audience ever recorded for a fight. The famous "long count" in his 1927 match with Tunney is still a matter of lively controversy. A legendary hero of American sports, Jack Dempsey was known as the Champ until he died, fifty-seven years after he lost the title. See Jack and B. P. Dempsey, *Dempsey* (1977).

DENNIS WEPMAN

DEMUTH, Charles (b. Lancaster, Pa., Nov. 8, 1883; d. Lancaster, Pa., Oct. 23, 1935), ARTIST, studied at the School of Industrial Arts in Philadelphia and also at the Pennsylvania Academy of Fine Arts (1905–8) under Thomas Anshutz and William Chase. He spent 1909 studying independently in Europe; he made return trips in 1911, 1912, and 1913. Influenced by the European Cubists and also by Aubrey Beardsley and Toulouse-Lautrec, Demuth joined the gallery of **Alfred Stieglitz** on his return to New York in 1914 and enjoyed the most productive period of his life. He illustrated the works of his favorite authors, including **Henry James's** *The Turn of the Screw* and **Edgar Allan Poe's** *Masque of the Red Death*. Under the influence of his close friend Marcel Duchamp, he turned to watercolor painting and did a series of illustrations of nightclub performers and vaudeville stars. He later did numerous still lifes. His work was characterized by fluid, graceful lines, delicacy, and a mottled texture that he obtained by carefully blotting his watercolors. In 1920 he began to work in oil and composed several studies of factories and industrial life, and *I Saw the Figure 5 in Gold* (1928, Metropolitan Museum of Art, N.Y.), perhaps his best-known canvas. But increasingly poor health (he developed diabetes in 1920) forced Demuth to retire to Lancaster. He spent his last summers (1930–34) painting in Provincetown, Massachusetts. Some of his most highly regarded watercolors are *In Vaudeville* (1918, private collection, Philadelphia), *Houses* (1918, Columbus Gallery of Fine Arts, N.Y.), and *Acrobats* (1919, Museum of Modern Art, N.Y.).

———∞———

Demuth was one of those artists who in the period between the two world wars managed to strike a balance between European modernism and traditional American realism. These artists—**Charles Sheeler** was another—have been called Precisionists or Immaculates.

Although a painter of still lifes and occasional figure studies, Demuth is best known for his industrial landscapes, which revealed the influence of Cubism and Futurism. But unlike the European exponents of these styles, Demuth seems first to have conceived his subjects realistically and then added an abstract overlay. He recognized the integrity of the object, but he then manipulated it into an abstract pattern.

Although aware of Dadaist developments through his friendship with Marcel Duchamp, Demuth never mocked industrial forms in a Dada manner. (Few American painters, if any, had become that disenchanted with modern life.) However, Demuth did not engage the industrial landscape in a human discourse. With minimal sensuous elaboration of textures or colors, he portrayed an environment emptied of human beings, as if an autonomous precisionism rather than human contexts or sociological observations served as his source of motivation.

These paintings, which of all Demuth's work suggest the frenzied pace of modern life, thus indicate an inner spiritual malaise. His attraction to, but also his rejection of, the American landscape paralleled similar sentiments voiced by writers such as **H. L. Mencken** and **Sinclair Lewis,** thus linking Demuth firmly with the pessimistic intel-

lectuals of the 1920s. See Emily Farnham, *Charles Demuth, Behind a Laughing Mask* (1971).

MATTHEW BAIGGELL

DEWEY, George (b. Montpelier, Vt., Dec. 26, 1837; d. Washington, D.C., Jan. 16, 1917), NAVAL OFFICER, studied at Norwich University and graduated from the U.S. Naval Academy (1858), briefly served in the Mediterranean, and was made the executive officer of the *Mississippi,* which was part of Admiral **David Farragut's** fleet at New Orleans (1862) and Port Hudson (1863). After further Civil War service with the Atlantic blockading squadron and at Fort Fisher, and duty as executive officer of a number of ships, he was given command of the *Narragansett* (1870–71, 1872–75) on which he surveyed the Gulf of California. Promoted to captain (1884), he was appointed chief of the navy's Bureau of Equipment and Recruiting in July 1889; in 1895 he was named president of the Board of Inspection and Survey. In 1896 he received the rank of commodore.

In November 1897, Dewey was given command of the Asiatic Squadron. When the Spanish-American War broke out, Dewey, following the Naval Department's war plan and its order over Assistant Secretary of the Navy Theodore Roosevelt's signature to destroy the Spanish squadron at Manila Bay, sailed from Hong Kong and entered the bay on the night of April 30, 1898. The next morning Dewey attacked, destroying the entire Spanish fleet without losing a ship or a man. For these actions he was made a rear admiral and in 1899 admiral of the navy.

Returning home a national hero, Dewey contemplated running for the presidency, but no party beckoned him. In 1900 he was made president of the general board of the Navy Department, a position he held until his death. In 1913 he published his *Autobiography.*

———∞———

Admiral Dewey became a national hero late in life more through accident than through outstanding ability. In the late 1890s he requested sea duty, and seniority entitled him to a command as important as the Asiatic Squadron. The Navy Department reckoned him to be bold and resolute enough to carry through its plan for that squadron in the increasingly likely event of war with Spain. The navy perceived that Spain was most vulnerable not in Cuba but in the Philippine Islands. There the decrepit Spanish Far Eastern Fleet might be defeated by the stronger American Asiatic Squadron and a sufficient American foothold in the Philippines gained to serve as a makeweight in subsequent peace negotiations. When war broke out, Dewey led his squadron to victory as scheduled in Manila Bay on the glorious first of May 1898. His personal contributions mainly came later. For nearly three months until reinforcements arrived, he held Manila Bay despite an absence of enough troops to give him a firm base ashore and in the face of a truculent intrusion by a stronger German fleet feeling out the possibility of Germany's inheriting Spain's position in the islands. More important, as president of the general board of the navy from 1900 to 1917 and seniority chairman of the army-navy joint board from its creation in 1903 to 1917, Dewey used his prestige and good sense to make a sound if small beginning toward interservice strategic planning. See John A. S. Grenville and George Berkeley Young, *Politics, Strategy, and American Diplomacy: Studies in Foreign Policy, 1873–1917* (1966).

RUSSELL F. WEIGLEY

DEWEY, John (b. Burlington, Vt., Oct. 20, 1859; d. New York, N.Y., June 1, 1952), PHILOSOPHER, graduated from the University of Vermont (1879) and earned a PhD at Johns Hopkins University, where he came under the influence of the pioneer child psychologist G. Stanley Hall. After a year of teaching, Dewey was appointed assistant professor at the University of Michigan in 1884 and professor of philosophy at the University of Minnesota four years later. From 1889 to 1894 he held the same post at Michigan; he then became head of the department of philosophy, psychology, and education at the University of Chicago. There he taught

ethics, logic, and education, and was director of the school of education. In 1904 he joined the faculty at Columbia, where he taught for twenty-six years.

In 1887, Dewey published *Psychology*, in which he claimed that the subject was a natural science, not a branch of metaphysics. Deeply influenced by **William James,** he sought to erase the line between liberal arts and vocational education, teaching that instruction had to be combined with doing and that full development of the child's cultural interests was necessary to a development of his ability to solve problems. In *The School and Society* (1899), a very influential book, Dewey made psychology the basis of pedagogical development, noting that to be successful an educational system had to satisfy four interests of the child: conversation, curiosity, construction, and artistic expression. Out of a laboratory school that Dewey established in Chicago in 1896 grew the modern progressive school. He decried the old concept of education as something not useful in itself but only as preparation for the future. "An activity which does not have worth enough to be carried on for its own sake," he declared, "cannot be very effective as preparation for something else."

Dewey saw philosophy as a practical science. His equalitarian views led him to rebel against the classical idea that the philosopher had access to a higher form of knowledge than did the common man. Such a viewpoint, he declared, was inconsistent with modern society, which had to be classless if it was to succeed. Philosophy, in short, was to be rated by its accomplishments. William James accepted Dewey as a philosophical pragmatist, naming him and his followers the "Chicago School." Another name for Dewey's thought is "instrumentalism."

Dewey's other strong interest, and one in which his equalitarian views were decisive, was politics. A product himself of the Progressive Era of reform, by the end of World War II he had abandoned any faith in the established political parties, which he considered merely "the errand boys" of big business. He tried to help organized labor form a Liberal Party in 1946 to wrest power from what he thought of as the special interests. He also supported such liberal causes as the Civil Liberties Union, the National Association for the Advancement of Colored People, and the New York Teachers' Guild. He was a founder of the New School for Social Research and lectured widely in Asia, Turkey, and Mexico. A member of the Committee for Soviet-American Friendship in the 1930s, he studied educational methods in Russia. In 1937 he went to Mexico as head of a commission that investigated the Stalinist charges against Trotsky, then in exile in that country, and found no basis for them.

———— ∞∞ ————

John Dewey's fame is primarily as an educator, his reputation ranging from that of the foremost theorist of education of our time to that of the chief instigator of the moral breakdown of American civilization. But Dewey was an educator only in the sense that he considered the philosophy of education to be identical with philosophy. When someone asked him if he used his own educational principles in his classroom, he is reported to have replied, "I'm not a teacher. I'm a philosopher." And Dewey *was* a philosopher, first and last. As a result he was and is misunderstood fairly consistently because of his concern for a wide variety of human problems, a concern that is always from a philosophic perspective. For example, when he argued in the early days after the Russian Revolution that we should keep an open mind on what he saw as the most far-reaching social experiment ever tried, he promptly was branded a Bolshevik in some quarters. Similarly, when several years later, after a visit to the Soviet Union, he expressed grave doubts about the direction the experiment was taking, he was labeled a reactionary just as promptly in other quarters.

The irony is that amid the furors swirling about his head throughout his long and vigorous life Dewey remained a quiet, soft-spoken, gentle scholar whose principal interest was in finding out how the world works, certainly not in arousing such contradictory passions. Of course, finding out about the world, for Dewey, is not separable from conduct: what a man believes is what he acts upon; and love of truth requires a man to look his world squarely in the face and to learn from what he sees and does. He also learned willingly and substantially from friends and from critics, but he always measured the contributions of both by what the most careful observation of the world could disclose.

During Dewey's ten years at the University of Chicago, together with his colleagues such as George H. Mead and James R. Angell, he laid the theoretical groundwork for an approach to human problems that has marked indelibly the development of psychology, religion, sociology, economics, and political science—as well as philosophy and education—in this country. Beginning with a biological conception of the interrelations between a living organism and its environment, Dewey developed a method of inquiry that was scientific, humane, and flexible, a method he proposed for application to morals, politics, education, and art. And he himself demonstrated that method in those fields and others in a steady stream of books, essays, and lectures. The result is the most fully expounded philosophy the United States has produced, a body of work expected to run to more than forty volumes in the definitive collected edition now in the process of being published. Dewey wrote for people in every walk of life, his articles appearing in journals of every description—popular, technical, and scholarly. The impact of the ideas he expressed probably has been as great and as widespread as was possible in a nation that is by temper and intent unphilosophical.

Dewey spent his life advocating a new conception of experience and a more intelligent attitude toward experiencing. He saw the function of intellect as that of bringing the accumulated knowledge and experience of the past to bear on the problems of the present so that the future can be richer, more open, and more satisfactory as experience than the past has been. In his words, thought has the task of freeing experience from routine, on the one hand, and from caprice, on the other. He maintained that in every phase of human activity our purposes and the instruments we use to implement them should grow and take form in the very process of the activity, not be taken for granted as given facts in the world or as untested ideas in our minds. Instead of another item for the textbooks to catalog under *American* philosophy (as somehow distinct from European philosophy), Dewey tried to provide an American *philosophy*—a call for organized intelligence to cope with fast-moving corporate societies, of which the United States is the foremost example. See Jo Ann Boydston, ed., *Guide to the Works of John Dewey* (1970).

DARNELL RUCKER

DEWEY, Thomas Edmund (b. Owosso, Mich., Mar. 24, 1902; d. Bal Harbor, Fla., Mar. 16, 1971), POLITICAL LEADER, graduated from the University of Michigan in 1923. After earning his LLB from Columbia (1925) he worked as a member of two prominent New York City law firms and began to engage actively in New York Republican politics. He served as chief assistant to the U.S. attorney for the Southern District of New York (1931–33) and as U.S. attorney for a brief period in 1934. A year later Governor Herbert Lehman appointed Dewey special prosecutor to investigate organized crime. Together with a powerful legal staff he prosecuted leaders of commercialized vice and racketeering in the poultry, trucking, restaurant, and baking businesses, obtaining seventy-two convictions in seventy-three prosecutions. This brought him great renown, and he was easily elected district attorney of New York County in 1937. In this post he continued to enhance his reputation as a "racket buster." Running against Lehman for governor in 1938, Dewey lost in a close election but emerged as a leading candidate for the Republican presidential nomination in 1940, which went, however, to **Wendell Willkie.**

Dewey left the district attorney's office in 1941 and was elected governor of New York a year later. Gaining the Republican presidential nomination in 1944, Dewey campaigned for lower taxes, less government spending, but retention of social security and other parts of the New Deal. He was defeated by Franklin Delano Roosevelt

by an electoral vote of 432 to 99. Reelected governor in 1946, Dewey was nominated for the presidency again in 1948. He ran a conservative campaign on a platform of lower taxes, reduced government spending, and support of the United Nations and the European Recovery Program. Although polls indicated that he was far ahead, he lost to Harry Truman by an electoral vote of 303 to 189 (with 39 electoral votes for J. Strom Thurmond, the States' Rights Party candidate). Dewey was elected governor a third time in 1950 and was influential in gaining the Republican presidential nomination for Dwight D. Eisenhower over **Robert A. Taft** in 1952. He retired from public office after his term as governor expired in 1955 and developed a lucrative Wall Street law practice.

During his twelve years as governor, Dewey developed the State University of New York system, opposed discrimination in employment and housing, and favored expansion of the state's unemployment and welfare system and its highway network. The Governor Dewey Thruway from Buffalo to New York was named in his honor. Dewey's ideas and speeches have been compiled in three books: *The Case Against the New Deal* (1940), *Journey to the Far Pacific* (1952), and *Thomas E. Dewey on the Two Party System* (1966).

―――∞∞∞―――

Dewey was a powerful political figure who dominated the policies and direction of New York State and strongly influenced the Republican Party for two decades. He rose swiftly on the basis of his ability, drive, and careful selection of staff assistants. An extremely hard worker, he was eminently skillful, efficient, inner-directed, and vigorous—qualities that characterized his administrations in New York. His public presentations were similar: proper, calm, disciplined, and self-assured. These traits were significant assets in helping him in three gubernatorial elections, but his impersonal, correct stance was less appealing when contrasted with the charismatic image of Franklin D. Roosevelt and the feisty nature of Harry S. Truman. Unfortunately, he will long be remembered for his loss to Truman in 1948, an election he actually had little chance of winning but that had been heralded as a certain Dewey victory.

Though highly critical of the New Deal, Dewey espoused a moderate political philosophy that included strong support for governmental action in domestic affairs and internationalism in foreign policy, policies that often ran contrary to those espoused by Republican conservatives. As one of the leaders of the eastern wing, he also antagonized conservative and right-wing Republicans when he led the fight for Eisenhower's nomination over Senator Taft in the 1952 convention. Nonetheless, his contacts within the Eisenhower administration enabled him to maintain a degree of influence on national policy. See Thomas E. Dewey, *The Case Against the New Deal* (1940).

JOSEPH BOSKIN

DICKINSON, Emily Elizabeth (b. Amherst, Mass., Dec. 10, 1830; d. Amherst, Mass., May 15, 1886), POET, spent her entire life in Amherst except for a year at South Hadley Female Seminary, now Mount Holyoke College (1847–48), and a few brief trips. In her early thirties she withdrew from the world, ostensibly to devote herself to her father and other members of her family. She lived as a recluse but corresponded with several friends, including Thomas Wentworth Higginson, a noted literary figure who did *not* encourage her to publish her poetry. After her death, nearly 1,800 poems were discovered, of which only 7 had been published. Her verse, marked by verbal economy, rhythmic vitality, sharp imagistic perception, and wit, is written in several popular forms including versions of hymnbook meters. She treated such conventional romantic subjects as nature, love, death, and immortality in a manner that was and still is unconventional, eccentric, and unique. Her works, published posthumously on the basis of manuscripts difficult to decipher, have always been popular. They include three series of *Poems* (1890, 1891, 1896), *The Single Hound* (1914), *Further Poems* (1929), *Unpublished Poems* (1936),

The Poems of Emily Dickinson (3 vols., 1955), and *The Letters of Emily Dickinson* (3 vols., 1958).

Emily Dickinson thought of herself as "small, like the Wren," with hair "bold, like the Chestnut-Bur," and eyes "like the Sherry in the Glass, that the Guest leaves." She was a woman of great emotional intensity and imaginative vitality. "I never was with any one who drained my nerve power so much," wrote Thomas Wentworth Higginson after a visit. The absolute integrity with which she was committed to her family and friends and, above all, to her poetry is hardly evident in the legends of unrequited love and spinsterish queerness that her renunciation of the world inspired. In fact, she used the world and its conventions to help her be a poet. Thus, she took advantage of that social convention of her time which tolerated the withdrawal of an unmarried woman into the bosom of her family to help her conserve her energy for her poetry. In the same way, she used the conventions of the nursery-rhyme-like hymnbook meters, which provided the form for her poems, to help her write to please herself. She was concerned with poetry as a way of expressing felt experience. And she conceived of experience, perhaps because of her religious consciousness, as imbued with meaning. The poet, she wrote, "Distills amazing sense/ From ordinary meanings." She wanted to capture the meaning of experience intensely, in language that was imagistically resonant rather than discursive. For her, poetry was to be powerful rather than sedate. As she put it, "If I read a book [and] it makes my whole body so cold no fire ever can warm me, I know *that* is poetry. If I feel physically as if the top of my head was taken off, I know *that* is poetry." Her several dozen great poems perhaps achieve the effects she wrote about, joining feeling and meaning so intensely and freshly that they appear to be the only ways of realizing their subjects. The accomplishment of those poems outweighs the few dozen sentimentally mediocre poems she wrote and does not lessen the value of those hundreds of her poems which are "only" first rate, not great in absolute terms. In her best work she explored such profound matters as what it means to live in aware-ness of the coming of death ("Because I could not stop for Death/He kindly stopped for me"), the nature of suffering ("After great pain, a formal feeling comes/The Nerves sit ceremonious, like Tombs"), and the possibility of hope in a world that seems threatening and precarious ("The mob within the heart/Police cannot suppress/The riot given at the first/Is authorized as peace"). She expressed herself by using what she could of con-ventional rhymes, rhythms, and grammar, and by discarding the irrelevant. In this way, among oth-ers, she anticipated the development of much 20th-century American poetry, but it is a sign of her distinctiveness that she has had no imitators. See John Cody, *After Great Pain: The Inner Life of Emily Dickinson* (1971).

ELY STOCK

DICKINSON, John (b. Talbot County, Md., Nov. 8, 1732; d. Wilmington, Del., Feb. 14, 1808), POLITICAL LEADER, studied law under John Moland, a leader of the Philadelphia bar, and in London at the Middle Temple (1753–57). After returning to Philadelphia he developed a suc-cessful law practice, but he soon decided to enter politics. In 1760 he was elected to the Delaware assembly. He then served in the Pennsylvania assembly (1762–65; 1770–76), where he defended the Pennsylvania system of proprietary govern-ment, believing that any change would be for the worse. His opposition to **Benjamin Franklin** on this issue (Franklin favored the establishment of a royal government) cost him his seat.

After Parliament passed the Sugar Act (1764) and the Stamp Act (1765), Dickinson published *The Late Regulations Respecting the British Colonies . . . Considered*, arguing that the only way to get these taxes repealed was to show the English merchants that enforcement would be detrimen-tal to their interests. As a delegate to the Stamp Act Congress in New York (1765), he drafted the petition asking Parliament to repeal the tax but opposed violent resistance to the act. After the Townshend Acts were passed (1767), he pub-lished his *Letters from a Farmer in Pennsylvania to the Inhabitants of the British Colonies*, denying Parliament's right to tax the colonies but also arguing that conciliation was possible.

Thanks largely to his authorship of the *Farmer's Letters*, Dickinson became the most prestigious leader among Americans insisting on colonial rights within the framework of empire. In the sec-ond Continental Congress (1775) he drafted the official "Petition to the King" and also wrote the "Olive Branch Petition," the colonists' final plea for redress of grievances before declaring their independence. With Thomas Jefferson he issued in 1775 the "Declaration of the Causes of Taking up Arms," a condemnation of all British actions since 1763. Still he hoped for conciliation, and in 1776 he voted against the Declaration of Independence.

He continued to serve in Congress (represent-ing Delaware in 1776–77 and 1779–80), where he drew up the first draft of the Articles of Confederation (1776). Later he served as presi-dent of the Delaware Supreme Executive Council (1781) and held the same position in Pennsylvania (1782–85). In 1787 he attended the federal convention at Philadelphia as a delegate from Delaware. He signed the new Constitution and supported the charter in his "Fabius" letters.

Although Dickinson maintained his interest in political affairs, he held no public office during the remainder of his life. In 1801 he published two volumes of his writings.

⸎

Dickinson was a leading early spokesman for the conservative tradition in America. Rejecting such radicals as **Thomas Paine** and such manip-ulators as Benjamin Franklin, he believed that political principles and actions not rooted in his-tory and tradition were inherently destructive. He learned to believe in the "rights of Englishmen" as won over the years and incorpo-rated into governmental procedures and the common law, but he remained skeptical of the so-called rights of man. He also rejected Rationalism on the ground that man is an irrational creature, better understood through observation than through logic. "Experience," he said, "must be our only guide. Reason may mislead us."

Between 1765 and 1776, Dickinson's cautious but firm position—maintaining that Parliament was attempting dangerous innovations and that the colonies were seeking only to preserve ancient liberties—won him great support and prestige. In 1776, when the Revolution took a more radical turn, he was left behind. There was, however, another reason for his eclipse, to be found in personal attributes. In public councils his demeanor often cost him the followers that his writings had won. Grave and emaciated, invariably dressed in black, he affected a pontifical manner that regularly alienated others. Almost at the outset of the Constitutional Convention, for example, he proposed the celebrated "Connecticut Compromise" on representation in Congress. Yet because of his lack of tact and sense of political timing, his proposal was ignored—only to be picked up again later when it came from other sources, with the result that history never recognized his contribution. See David L. Jacobson, *John Dickinson and the Revolution in Pennsylvania, 1764–1776* (1965).

FORREST MCDONALD

DiMAGGIO, Joseph Paul (b. Martinez, Calif., Nov. 25, 1914), ATHLETE, one of nine children born to Italian immigrants. DiMaggio demonstrated remarkable natural skills as a teenager playing sandlot baseball on San Francisco's North Beach playgrounds. He began his professional career in 1932 with the San Francisco Seals of the Pacific Coast League. In his first full season DiMaggio hit in sixty-one consecutive games, the longest hitting streak in professional baseball history. In November 1934, Colonel Jacob Ruppert, the owner of the New York Yankees, purchased DiMaggio's contract from the Seals for approximately $50,000 and five minor league players. DiMaggio did not join the Yankees, however, until after the 1935 season, in which he was named the Pacific Coast League's Most Valuable Player.

DiMaggio played for the Yankees from 1936 to 1951 except for a two-year stint in the army (1943–45). Because of an injury he did not make his debut with the Yankees until May 3, 1936, a month after the season had started. The Yankees won the World Series that year, the first of four consecutive titles. As a result DiMaggio became the only player ever to play on World Series winners in each of his first four seasons. Playing center field in the vast reaches of Yankee Stadium, DiMaggio demonstrated tremendous range and a rifle arm. He also shined as a baserunner. But it was as a consistent .300 power hitter that he excelled. His great exploit was a fify-six-game hitting streak that still stands unbroken. It lasted from May 5, 1941, until July 16, 1941, when it was ended by Jim Bagley of the Cleveland Indians.

In 1949, DiMaggio became baseball's first player to earn $100,000 per year. During that season he missed the first sixty-five games because of an injury to his heel. Upon his return to the lineup he went on to hit .346 in 272 at-bats for the season and was instrumental in propelling the Yankees into first place past their hated rivals, the Boston Red Sox, in one of the era's most memorable pennant races.

DiMaggio announced his retirement on December 11, 1951, and his uniform number "5" was also retired. His career statistics included a .325 batting average, 361 home runs, and 1,537 runs batted in. He was named to the American League All-Star team in every year of his career. He played in ten World Series with the Yankees during which they won nine. DiMaggio won the American League's Most Valuable Player Award three times, in 1939, 1941, and 1947, and was elected to the Baseball Hall of Fame in 1955. In January 1954 DiMaggio married movie star **Marilyn Monroe**, but they divorced nine months later.

Following his retirement DiMaggio briefly became a Yankee broadcaster. He continued his association with the Yankees by attending spring training and serving as an instructor. He never had a desire to become a manager but served as vice president and coach for the Oakland Athletics in 1968–69. In recent years DiMaggio appeared in television commercials and in newspaper ads as the spokesman for banks and makers of coffee-brewing machines. Generally, however, he has stayed out of the limelight except for attending Old-Timers' Day events.

———— ✦ ————

Considered the best outfielder and one of the most effective batters of his time, Joe DiMaggio provided professional baseball with a model of dignity and style that elevated the image of the sport. Polished and always well dressed, he succeeded the relatively rough-hewn **Babe Ruth** as the baseball superhero of the 1930s and 40s. He was one of the postwar triumvirate of great hitters, with Ted Williams of the Boston Red Sox and Stan "The Man" Musial of the St. Louis Cardinals, but was regarded as the best all-round athlete of the three.

Known also for the grace and speed of his fielding and his powerful throwing arm—his nickname "Yankee Clipper" is a tribute to both, while "Joltin' Joe" testifies to his power at bat—DiMaggio also represented an extraordinary example of triumph over handicaps. Often playing despite crippling injuries and against medical advice, he racked up record after record. He retired at the age of 37, declining the Yankees' offer of a third $100,000 contract, because he saw his physical powers and reflexes deteriorating.

The poised and taciturn DiMaggio was recognized by his teammates as a natural leader from the beginning of his career. His only significant conflict was with his last manager, Casey Stengel, who resented his charisma. Relations between them remained strained throughout Stengel's tenure but never interfered with DiMaggio's performance on the diamond.

DiMaggio's impressive career and personal presence have left a legacy of professionalism to a generation that knows his supple stride and classic batting stance only from legend and photographic record. See Joseph Durso, *DiMaggio: The Last Knight* (1995).

DENIS WEPMAN

DISNEY, Walter Elias (b. Chicago, Ill., Dec. 5, 1901; d. Los Angeles, Calif., Dec. 15, 1966), FILM ANIMATOR, PRODUCER, attended high school in Chicago and studied at night at the Chicago Academy of Fine Arts. He dropped out of school in 1918 to serve as a Red Cross ambulance driver in France. Returning to the United States in 1919, he worked as a commercial artist in Kansas City, Missouri, before becoming an animator for Kansas City *Film Advertising* (1920–22) and forming his first—and soon bankrupt—production company. Disney moved to Hollywood, California, in 1923 and formed a partnership with his older brother Roy to make cartoon films. The latter managed business affairs, which he was to do throughout their joint careers, while Walt drew the *Alice in Cartoonland* series (1923–26). Disney then directed *Oswald the Rabbit*, a series of animated short subjects, for Universal Studios (1926–28). In 1928 he released the first animated sound film, *Steamboat Willie*, which introduced Mickey Mouse to the American public. After the enormous success of Mickey, Disney introduced more cartoon characters, including Donald Duck, Pluto, and Goofy. He created his "Silly Symphony" cartoon series, including *Skeleton Dance* (1929), *Flowers and Trees* (1932), and *Three Little Pigs* (1933) in color. In 1937 he risked all that he had gained to produce *Snow White and the Seven Dwarfs*, the first full-length animated film, and was rewarded with enormous financial and critical success.

Pinocchio (1940) was Disney's second full-length cartoon. *Fantasia* (1940), an animated interpretation of the music of Bach, Tchaikovsky, Beethoven, and others, conducted by Leopold Stokowski, received wide critical acclaim although it fared poorly with the general public. During World War II, Disney made propaganda and defense training films for the government. Thereafter he continued making full-length animated features such as *Cinderella* (1950) and *Alice in Wonderland* (1951). *Song of the South* (1947) combined live actors with animated figures, while such movies as *Treasure Island* (1950), *Robin Hood* (1952), and *20,000 Leagues Under the Sea* (1954) completed his transition to almost exclusive reliance on actors for his films. His *Seal Island* (1948) pioneered wildlife documentary films for theatrical release, and he followed it with similar films, including *Beaver Valley* (1951), *Nature's Half Acre* (1951), and *The Vanishing Prairie* (1954), which was feature length. In 1954, Disney started his television show *Disneyland* and produced many programs especially for TV, including *Davy Crockett* (1955). His other television shows were the *Mickey Mouse Club* (1954–58), *Zorro* (1957), and, the successor to *Disneyland, Walt Disney's Wonderful World of Color* (1961). In 1955, Disney opened his popular amusement park, Disneyland, at Anaheim, California. He was constructing another park, Disney World, at Orlando, Florida (completed in 1971), at the time of his death. His film *Mary Poppins* (1964), which included animated sequences, grossed more than $50 million. The Disney Studio won thirty-nine Oscars from the Motion Picture Academy during his lifetime.

Walt Disney was the prisoner, and in later life perhaps even the creature, of a largely fictitious public image. When he died, for example, the Los Angeles *Times* speculated editorially that he must have gained his deepest joy "from seeing the flash of delight sweep across a child's face and hearing his sudden laughter at the first sight of Mickey Mouse or Snow White or Pinocchio." It was a theme that echoed and reechoed not only in his obituaries but throughout the media during his lifetime. "Warm," "wonderful," yet withal "a very simple man … that you might not look twice at on the street"—that was his corporation's line, and it was quite uncritically accepted by the media and therefore by the general public as well. There is always a shortage of "nice guys" to profile.

This is not meant to imply that Disney was entirely a misanthrope. He probably had nothing *against* the laughter of children. But this image of him vastly oversimplifies the character and achievements of an ill-educated youth who transformed himself, in a little more than four decades, from a bankrupt and not particularly talented commercial artist into, literally, Hollywood's last tycoon—that is, the last man to exercise absolute and single-handed control not only over a major movie studio but over an endlessly expanding entertainment empire embrac-

ing television, books, records, merchandise for children, and, most important, the famous amusement parks: Disneyland in California, the world's first great experiment in the creation of environments for entertainment purposes; and Disney World in Florida, which he planned but did not live to see completed. One does not achieve any—let alone all—of the things Disney achieved unless one is tougher and more single-minded than the notion of him as a sort of Uncle to the Nation suggests.

In fact, novelist Aubrey Mennen came closer to the truth about him when he described Disney as "a tall, somber man who appeared to be under the lash of some private demon.… I remember him smiling only once." That demon began to form in a childhood that was poverty-stricken and dominated by a mean-spirited father. There seems little doubt that the memory of that hard time fired Disney's powerful acquisitive instinct and also led to his lifelong infatuation with technological advances. He was always among the first in Hollywood to embrace new technologies (sound, improved color processes, special cameras, all manner of devices to enhance the magical elements in moviemaking), and perhaps it is not too fanciful to see these devices as the toys he was denied in boyhood. Certainly Disneyland, that grand orchestration of the latest technologies of entertainment (many of which were patented by the Disney firm itself), was the projection of a child's dream of a super amusement park, a big rock candy mountain. And in his last years Disney fussed over it, worried about it, protected it, as a child might some beloved collection of tin soldiers or bubble gum cards.

Of course, there was more to him than a certain childishness. His faith in progress through technological innovation was very much the faith his generation learned at the knees of **Henry Ford** and **Thomas Edison**—as was the aesthetic these innovations were supposed to serve but very often dominated. At its best, early in its history, the Disney studio turned out work that was full of the most exuberant energy, and the short subjects featuring Mickey Mouse and friends are certainly among the high points in the history of animated film. Disney, however, yearned for finer things without being able to define them in any very sophisticated way. Of the feature films only *Pinocchio* and the charming *Dumbo* recaptured the *brio* of the shorts. For the most part Disney knew no better than to aspire to a certain realism in art and design, while characters and situations were ever reduced to the cute and the sentimental, qualities he carried over into the live-action films that dominated his production schedule from 1950 onward.

His success with the mass audience was based on this reductionism, of course, but the intellectual and artistic community that at the beginning of his career had nominated him the logical successor to **Charlie Chaplin** deserted him. That seemed to embitter him, lower his aspirations. He consoled himself with power (which he exercised compulsively, in nagging detail), with the trappings of celebrity, and with his enormous wealth. Many of his employees—especially the most creative ones—found him grasping and domineering, particularly after a strike in 1941 spoiled his dream of the studio-as-family, Disney as paterfamilias. These qualities began to become visible between the lines of even the most benign interviews, and at the end he seemed to speak of nothing but his desire to order and control his domain, to be beholden to no one. About art he had nothing to say. About politics and the social order his views were as primitive as his appreciation of technology was sophisticated. The laughter of children did not come up much in his conversation. Instead, when asked what his proudest achievement was, he replied, "The whole damn thing. The fact that I was able to build an organization and hold it." Spoken like a **Sinclair Lewis** character. He was, at last, what he had always been—a true son of the middle border, the true son of his father, anything but "Uncle Walt." See Richard Schickel, *The Disney Version* (1968).

RICHARD SCHICKEL

DIX, Dorothea Lynde (b. Hampden, Maine, Apr. 4, 1802; d. Trenton, N.J., July 17, 1887),

REFORMER, started teaching school at the age of 14 in Worcester, Massachusetts. During 1821–35 she ran a girls' school in her grandparents' home in Boston and wrote a number of children's books, including *Hymns for Children* (1825) and *Ten Short Stories for Children* (1827–28).

Poor health forced her to leave teaching and to travel abroad (1835–38), but in 1841 she returned to teaching, holding Sunday school classes in the East Cambridge, Massachusetts, House of Correction. Appalled by conditions in the prison, particularly by the fact that the insane and feeble-minded were treated as criminals, she set out on a crusade to reform the state's prisons, almshouses, and insane asylums. During 1841–44 she visited approximately eighteen state penitentiaries, three hundred county jails and correction houses, and five hundred almshouses. Typical of her findings was a *Memorial to the Legislature of Massachusetts* (1843). Besides describing the physical conditions of the asylums, she asserted in this work that the insane were "chained, naked, beaten with rods, and lashed into obedience!" As a direct result of her work the Massachusetts legislature improved the Worcester asylum.

During the next few years she pursued her reform goals in a number of other states as well as in Canada and England. In 1854 she tried to get Congress to channel the funds it received from the sale of national land into care for the insane. Such a bill was passed by both houses of Congress but was vetoed by President Franklin Pierce. During 1854–57, Dix again traveled abroad.

After the Civil War broke out, the surgeon general of the army appointed her superintendent of women nurses. After the war Dix continued to investigate the conditions of the insane and spent her last years residing, more as guest than patient, at a New Jersey hospital she had helped to found.

⸺⸺⸺

The cult of asylum building that swept Jacksonian America had no more enthusiastic or dedicated advocate than Dorothea Dix. She came to this crusade by an odd route. Her childhood had been a lonely one. Her father, busy eking out a living on a Maine farm or traveling about as a Methodist preacher, could not provide a secure or affectionate household, and Dorothea desperately moved from one relative to another seeking an alternative. Loneliness also typified her youth; then a broken engagement added to her isolation. She spent her early adulthood trying to recover from both a physical and a mental breakdown.

Ostensibly too frail to continue running a girls' school, Dix discovered by way of a casual invitation to visit the local Cambridge jail the miserable lot of the pauper insane. With the frightening energy of one who is filling a void, she took hold of this cause. For well over thirty years she traveled from state to state, over the roughest country roads, to inspect out-of-the-way almshouses and jails.

Dix's first concern was with the comfort and security of the insane. Her memorials to state legislatures invariably began with a recounting of the awful neglect and cruelty that she had discovered. But her avid sponsorship of asylum care had another dimension to it: she was certain that insanity was curable. Reading thoroughly in the writings of America's first psychiatrists, Isaac Ray and Samuel Woodward among others, Dix accepted and popularized their arguments. Insanity, she explained, had its origins in the extraordinary openness and fluidity of American society—men who saw no limits to their opportunities, who tolerated no intellectual or political restraints, often broke under the strain to achieve. The cure for this malady was to place the mentally ill in well-ordered, highly routinized settings, at public expense. Society must make recompense, Dix insisted, "for these disastrous fruits of its social organization." Armed with this formula, she persuaded many state legislatures to found public insane asylums.

There was a heroic quality about Dix's effort. Her ability to overcome personal problems and to labor so steadfastly to realize her conception of the public good was remarkable. Many contemporaries found her a saintly figure: "the most useful and distinguished woman that America has produced," declared one tribute. And there can be no slighting the quality of her humanitarianism. The condition of the pauper insane was all that she claimed it to be; clearly it demanded amelioration. Still, Dix seems too much the advocate of incarceration, unable to reckon with the dangers inherent in this venture. Her unwavering dedication to this innovation led her and most of her contemporaries to put institutionalization first and caution second. Hence, procedural safeguards to protect the insane against involuntary commitment had no part in her program, nor did the systematic regulation of conditions in the asylums themselves. By the 1870s, Dix witnessed the all too rapid and gross deterioration of the asylums, but there was little she could recommend except to start the asylum venture all over again. She was the single-minded reformer—and the fruits of her effort warrant our admiration, and our skepticism, too. See Helen E. Marshall, *Dorothea Dix: Forgotten Samaritan* (1937).

DAVID J. ROTHMAN

DODGE, Grenville Mellen (b. Danvers, Mass., Apr. 12, 1831; d. Council Bluffs, Iowa, Jan. 3, 1916), ENGINEER, graduated from Norwich (Vt.) University in 1851. He then moved to Peru, Illinois, to engage in civil engineering and railroad building. He became an engineer for the Illinois Central Railroad in 1852. Next he surveyed a route from Davenport, Iowa, to Iowa City for the Mississippi and Missouri Railroad. He settled in Council Bluffs, Iowa, and from 1855 to 1861 engaged in banking, business, and railroad construction. At the outbreak of the Civil War, Dodge was commissioned in the Iowa Volunteers and served in Kentucky, Tennessee, Alabama, and Georgia, building bridges and reconstructing and equipping railroads for military use. He attained the rank of major general. After fighting Indians west of Missouri, Dodge left the army in 1866 and became chief engineer of the Union Pacific Railroad, which constructed the first transcontinental line in the United States. He completed that task on May 29, 1869. Dodge, a Republican, also served a term in the U.S. House of

Representatives (1867–69). He remained active in party politics until his death and, among other things, played a vital role in settling the disputed presidential election of 1876.

In 1871, Dodge became chief engineer of the Texas and Pacific Railway and in 1880 joined **Jay Gould** to develop railroads in the Southwest. He also planned and constructed numerous lines for such railroads as the International and Great Northern and the Fort Worth and Denver City. He acquired the Denver, Texas and Gulf (which became the Union Pacific, Denver and Gulf in 1890) and served as its president (1892–93). In 1898, President William McKinley appointed him to his commission studying management of the war with Spain. After the war Dodge organized the Cuba Railroad Co. and completed a line from Santa Clara to Santiago, his last construction. Retiring to his home in Council Bluffs in 1903, Dodge spent his later years writing and participating in such patriotic clubs as the Military Order of the Loyal Legion, serving as commander in chief (1907–8). His books include *How We Built the Union Pacific Railway* (1910) and *Personal Recollections of President Abraham Lincoln, General Ulysses S. Grant, and General William T. Sherman* (1914).

———

Grenville Dodge lived a long, varied, and adventurous life; indeed, few Americans have been so versatile and effective. He was a Civil War general, a congressman, and one of the most powerful state politicians of his generation. Yet he was also a pioneer and an Indian fighter, and a banker and railroad builder. Outdoor men as different in temperament as Jim Bridger, **"Buffalo Bill" Cody,** and Theodore Roosevelt called him their friend. He was proudest of his "glamorous" achievements as a general and western pioneer, but his other work was more important from the modern perspective. In politics he was the leader of Iowa's ruling faction—a man whose persuasive lobbying could ensure passage of legislation. He made and unmade United States senators and congressmen, drafted laws and resolutions, and was the friend and adviser of every Republican president between the Civil War and World War I.

But his most enduring accomplishments were in the field of railroad building and western development. He surveyed and built more than ten thousand miles of track and established such important towns as Dodge City, Cheyenne, and Laramie. As chief engineer of the Union Pacific Railroad he constructed the first transcontinental line across the United States. His contribution to the development of the railroads of the Southwest was perhaps even more significant. Throughout his long life, this nervous, energetic little man enthusiastically completed every task he undertook. His monuments—railroads and cities—dot the plains and mountains of the modern West. See Stanley P. Hirshson, *Grenville M. Dodge: Soldier, Politician, Railroad Pioneer* (1967).

STANLEY P. HIRSHSON

DOLE, Robert Joseph (b. Russell, Kans., July 22, 1923), POLITICAL LEADER, graduated from Russell High School (1941), and attended the University of Kansas, where he was a premedical student and athlete. He enlisted in the U.S. Army in December 1942 but finished his second year at the university before being called to active duty in June 1943. After basic training, Dole trained in the medical corps, studied engineering at Brooklyn College in New York, and graduated from Officer Candidate School at Fort Benning, Georgia (Fall 1944). Less than six months later, Lieutenant Dole was severely wounded leading a Tenth Mountain Division platoon against a German machine gun position in Italy's Po Valley. Despite a prognosis that he might never walk again, Dole regained use of all but his right arm and hand after three years of hospitalization, multiple surgeries, and intensive physical therapy. Returning to school to prepare for the law, he spent a year at the University of Arizona, then enrolled in Washburn Municipal College (later Washburn University) at Topeka, Kansas, in 1949.

While still a student at Washburn, Dole entered politics. In 1950 he won election to the Kansas House of Representatives as a Republican representing Russell County. He served a single term and, after graduating with B.A. and L.L.B. degrees in 1952, returned to Russell to practice law. That same year, Dole was elected county attorney, a post he held for four two-year terms. In 1960, after a hotly contested Republican primary, Dole captured the Sixth Congressional District seat. An aggressive, determined campaigner, he easily won reelection in 1962 although reapportionment had combined his northwest Kansas district with the southwest to make the "Big First." When Kansas voted Democratic in the 1964 Presidential election for the first time since 1936, Dole barely eked out a victory, but in 1966 he overwhelmed his opposition by a better than two to one margin. In 1968 Dole was elected to the U.S. Senate. His only serious challenge in four subsequent senatorial races came in 1974 in the wake of the Watergate scandal. That year, Dole, who had served the Republican Party faithfully as national chairman (1971–73) while managing to avoid implication in the scandals that forced President Richard Nixon to resign, narrowly defeated Democratic Congressman William Roy, a Topeka physician, in a bitter campaign that focused much attention on the abortion issue. In 1976, President Gerald Ford chose Dole as his running mate. In that role, he earned the reputation as the Republican campaign's "hatchet man" in its losing battle with the Carter-Mondale ticket. Subsequently, Dole launched an aborted bid for the 1980 Republican presidential nomination, became chairman of the Senate Finance Committee (1981), and was elected majority leader in 1984. After the GOP lost control of the Senate in 1986, Dole became minority leader, a position he held throughout his second bid for the Republican nomination in 1988 and the administration of George Bush (1989–93).

In the first two years of William J. Clinton's presidency, Dole drew much attention as the titular head of the GOP for his acerbic wit, which attracted journalists and television comics. Some called him "Dr. Gridlock" because under his leadership Republicans defeated much of the administration's program, but he backed the president in the successful fight for the North American Free Trade Agreement (NAFTA) and held a consistent, non-partisan position on Bosnian policy favoring the use of air support and a lifting of the arms embargo. Dole supported President Clinton's commitment of U.S. troops as part of the NATO peacekeeping force in December 1995, despite his personal reservations. When the GOP captured both houses of Congress in 1994, Dole regained the Senate majority leader's position despite his intention to seek the presidency for a third time in 1996.

To say that Bob Dole, the man who would be president, is an enigma, is to state the obvious. He has at times during his career been described in terms of the progressive Republican tradition of former Kansas governor and 1936 presidential candidate **Alfred M. Landon**, the father of Dole's Kansas senatorial colleague during 1979–1997, Nancy Kassebaum. But with few exceptions— mostly at times when the business of legislating made moderation and compromise essential— Dole's record is one of relatively consistent conservatism. He opposed most of Lyndon Johnson's Great Society programs but voted for the Civil Rights Act of 1964 and the Voting Rights Act of 1965. Not surprisingly, in light of his background and geographical roots, Dole has long supported federal programs of assistance to the disabled and to the American farmer. With liberal Democratic senator and former presidential nominee George McGovern of South Dakota, Dole managed to overhaul and expand the food stamp program in the mid–1970s.

Dole first gained a measure of national celebrity with his vigorous, partisan defense of Richard Nixon's Vietnam policy. Since assuming a leadership role in the Senate nearly two decades ago, however, Dole has enjoyed the respect of many of his colleagues, both Republican and Democrat, for his pragmatism. Some even describe him as a statesman, whose greatest contribution has been his ability to work deals, bringing two seemingly disparate sides together, and thus making the legislative process work. Despite his reservations about Ronald Reagan's economic policies,

Dole championed the administration's cornerstone legislation, the Economic Recovery Act of 1981 that included large budget and tax cuts. But the next year, concerned about the growing budget deficit, the senator pulled off a stunning legislative victory with the passage of his Tax Equity and Fiscal Responsibility Act (TEFRA), a reform measure which raised taxes by closing some of the previous measure's loopholes. Dole convinced the administration to support his plan, but many conservative critics accused Dole of "going liberal" and charged that TEFRA was the undoing of Reagonomics. Republican Congressman **Newt Gingrich**, later to become Speaker of the House, would label Dole "the tax collector for the Welfare State."

Although frequently criticized as a man with no firm political principles—a waffler who determined his position with the political winds—Dole's contradictory philosophy makes perfect sense for a man committed to the profession of politics and government. Dole understood that success in American politics is often only attainable through compromise. To govern through a legislative process, compromise is a necessity. And to succeed in politics one must win elections, which often necessitates a modification of one's own positions to meet the demands of the electorate. Unlike many of his Republican colleagues of the mid–1990s, Dole is no ideologue, a fact that had both positive and negative implications for his third drive to gain the White House which he launched on April 10, 1995 in Topeka, Kansas, with a speech defining his "mainstream conservatism."

A "workaholic" with virtually no interests outside politics and government, Dole believed he deserved the presidency. He was consumed by a desire to succeed, and thus was willing to do whatever it took to attain his goals. Measured in terms of political victories, Dole's is a spectacular Kansas success story. He has never lost a state election. Indeed, although some relish the idea, a Kansas political scene without Dole is hard for most to imagine; many cannot remember that landscape before his towering figure appeared. In total congressional service—over 35 years—

Dole set a Kansas record, and, although his margin of victory was not as great as his popular, three-term colleague, Nancy Kassebaum, and he was sometimes criticized for being out of touch with his native state, Dole's base of support has been remarkable over the years. Thus, the senator's place in Kansas political history is assured. How he will fare in the national memory, however, largely depends on the success of his 1996 presidential bid. See Jake H. Thompson, *Bob Dole: The Republicans' Man For All Seasons* (1994).

VIRGIL W. DEAN

DOLE, Sanford Ballard (b. Honolulu, Hawaii, Apr. 23, 1844; d. Honolulu, Hawaii, June 9, 1926), JURIST, POLITICAL LEADER, was the son of missionaries from Maine who directed Punahou School (later Oahu College), a school for mission children. After studying for one year at Williams College he read law for another year in Boston and was admitted to the Massachusetts bar in 1869. He then returned to Honolulu where he practiced law and became active in the political, religious, and cultural life of the community. Elected to the Island legislatures of 1884 and 1886, he pressed the native government for a new constitution giving more power to American residents.

Dole, however, disapproved of the radical action against King Kalakaua proposed by the American-dominated Hawaiian League and resigned from its executive council. But he took the lead in drafting the "Bayonet Constitution" limiting drastically the sovereign's power, which the king was forced to accept in the bloodless revolution of 1887. From 1887 to 1893 Dole was an associate justice of the Hawaiian Supreme Court. Although he played no part in the American-inspired revolution of January 1893, he accepted the presidency of the provisional government, and when the Republic of Hawaii was proclaimed in 1894, he was chosen president, serving until 1898 when the United States annexed the Islands. In 1900 he was named territorial governor of Hawaii, but he resigned in 1903 to become a U.S. district judge, a post he held until 1915.

⬗

Dole was essentially a moderate among American settlers in Hawaii. He believed that the native government did not afford the propertied stable elements of the kingdom political power commensurate with their economic contribution and that it was both corrupt and extravagant. Nevertheless, he was of the opinion that a constitutional monarchy would best serve the interests of the native Hawaiians, and he favored holding the throne in trust under a regency until Queen Liliuokalani's niece, Princess Kaiulani, reached her majority. He was not a director or part-owner of a corporation or a large plantation and not affluent—his tax bill was only $6 in 1892. His influence among the Americans was more a matter of his reputation for integrity than wealth.

Actually, Dole regretted the whole affair of 1893. If his views had prevailed, he would have employed more tactful ways than the treatment rendered Liliuokalani. But he trusted that history "would not be critical.... We are but men, and I but one, and just an opinion, against the destiny of a nation." And his indomitable stand against President Grover Cleveland's proposal to restore "Queen Lil" deterred the use of force and the spilling of blood that would have followed any attempted restoration. He served creditably as governor of Hawaii. He enjoyed the distinction of being the only American to hold the presidency of a foreign state and the governorship of a U.S. territory. Probably no other man in the Islands could have done as well in steering the fragile ship of state through the turbulent waters of 1893–98. See Merze Tate, *The United States and the Hawaiian Kingdom* (1965).

Merze Tate

DONALD, David Herbert (b. Goodman, Miss., Oct. 1, 1920), HISTORIAN, graduated from Millsaps College (1941), and earned an MA (1942) and PhD (1946) from the University of Illinois. He was an instructor of history at Columbia University (1947–1949), an associate professor of history at Smith College (1949–1951), and then returned to Columbia as an assistant professor in its graduate faculty, where he gave his first of many legendary PhD seminars. Donald became a full professor at Columbia in 1957. Specializing in the Civil War era, Donald, a prolific writer, published *Lincoln's Herndon* (1948), wrote the text for *Divided We Fought: A Pictorial History of the War, 1861–1865* (1952), edited *Inside Lincoln's Cabinet: The Civil War Diaries of Salmon P. Chase* (1954), published a collection of essays in *Lincoln Reconsidered* (1956, rev. 1961), and wrote *Charles Sumner and the Coming of the Civil War* (1960), which won a Pulitzer Prize for biography (1960).

From 1959 to 1962 Donald was a professor of history at Princeton University. He spent the 1959–1960 academic year as Harmsworth professor of American history at Oxford University. From 1962 to 1973 he was professor of American history at Johns Hopkins University, and from 1973 until his retirement in 1991 he was the Charles Warren professor of American history and professor of American civilization at Harvard University. While at Princeton, Donald edited *Why the North Won the Civil War* (1960) and rewrote J. G. Randall's *The Civil War and Reconstruction* (1961, rev. 1969), and during the Johns Hopkins years he wrote *The Politics of Reconstruction, 1863–1867* (1965), *The Nation in Crisis, 1861–1877* (1969), and *Charles Sumner and the Rights of Man* (1970). At Harvard, Donald published *Liberty and Union: The Crisis of Popular Government, 1830–1890* (1978) and won his second Pulitzer Prize for biography (1988) with his *Look Homeward: A Life of Thomas Wolfe* (1987). After a lifetime of studying the Civil War and the men involved in it, Donald brought out a biography of *Lincoln* (1995).

⬗

It is fitting that the most outstanding student of James G. Randall—the historians' historian among Abraham Lincoln scholars of an earlier generation—should be David Herbert Donald. He is the biographer of central figures in the nation's crusade against slavery, and he has trained generations of scholars at Columbia, Princeton, Johns Hopkins, and Harvard. A superb lecturer, a brilliant stylist, and an exacting critic, Donald was demanding of his students, but equally demanding of himself in behalf of their training, forging an unusually strong bond with them.

His biographies, written from the perspective of his subjects and in the context of their times, avoid moralizing. Although the Civil War has become the American *Iliad*, he demythologizes without debunking its heroes. Donald is noteworthy for avoiding the common trap of forwarding an agenda by looking to the past.

Donald has written provocatively on a variety of subjects from abolitionists in the 1830s to writers in the 1930s. Although his *Look Homeward: A Life of Thomas Wolfe* won his second Pulitzer Prize, his reputation among historians rests chiefly on three brilliant biographies of three difficult subjects: William H. Herndon, Abraham Lincoln's law partner who became his controversial biographer; **Charles Sumner**, the radical Republican senator from Massachusetts; and Abraham Lincoln. In *Lincoln's Herndon* Donald explained how Herndon, in trying to destroy the myth of Lincoln the demigod, created the myth of Lincoln the western pioneer. Donald's *Sumner* (the first volume of which won Donald's first Pulitzer Prize) is an appreciative yet critical and balanced biography of a man whose constant moralizing and self-righteousness alienated both friends and foes during his lifetime and has tried the patience of all but the most admiring historians since then. Donald's prodigious research enabled him to thrust the reader of his *Sumner* back in time to witness the Civil War and Reconstruction through Sumner's eyes.

Lincoln, however, is probably the most challenging biographical subject in American history. So much evidence that has been piled up by Herndon and others has been used to create mythic Lincolns whose chief value lies not in what they tell one of Lincoln, but in what they reveal of American values. Refusing to play God by making Lincoln into his own image, Donald rigorously tore away the myths, sifted the evidence—with which he is more familiar than his predecessors—and again moved the reader back into the mid-nineteenth century to portray Lincoln as he perceived himself and as he saw the problems he confronted. In the process, Donald has both revived the historic Lincoln and established a benchmark against which to measure future Lincoln biographies. See William J. Cooper, Jr., Michael F. Holt, and John McCardell, eds., *A Master's Due: Essays in Honor of David Herbert Donald* (1985).

ARI HOOGENBOOM

DONNELLY, Ignatius (b. Philadelphia, Pa., Nov. 3, 1831; d. Minneapolis, Minn., Jan. 1, 1901), POLITICAL LEADER, attended public schools in Philadelphia. He was admitted to the bar in 1852 but gave up his practice in 1856 and moved to Nininger, Minnesota, to seek his fortune in land speculation. Wiped out financially by the Panic of 1857, he became a wheat farmer. However, he soon entered politics as a Republican. He served two terms (1859–63) as lieutenant governor of Minnesota and three terms (1863–69) in the U.S. House of Representatives. In the House, Donnelly supported the Radical Republican Reconstruction policies. He also favored federal land grants for railroads. He was defeated for reelection in 1868 and returned to farming in Minnesota.

Convinced that the Republican Party was becoming the instrument of the privileged few, Donnelly left it in 1871 and served in the Minnesota state legislature (1874–78) as an independent. He edited the *Anti-Monopolist* (1874–78), a St. Paul weekly newspaper that supported the demands of the Granger movement for currency and banking reform, railroad rate regulation, and easy credit for farmers. Defeated for Congress as a Greenback-Democrat in 1878, Donnelly temporarily retired from politics and turned to writing such books as *Atlantis: The Antediluvian World* (1882), which supported the lost-continent theory, and *The Great Cryptogram* (1888), which suggested that Francis Bacon actually wrote Shakespeare's plays. His books were quite successful, and he was soon lecturing throughout the United States and Europe. He published an apocalyptic novel, *Caesar's Column* (1891).

Meanwhile he returned to politics. He ran unsuccessfully for Congress in 1884 but was elected to the Minnesota state legislature in 1887 as a leader of the Farmers' Alliance. He helped form the Populist Party and ran as its candidate for governor of Minnesota in 1892 but was defeated. He reluctantly supported **William Jennings Bryan** for president in 1896. Thereafter he remained active in the declining Populist Party. He edited its Minneapolis-based publication, the *Representative,* and ran for vice president on its ticket in 1900.

───

Throughout his life Donnelly was driven by a desire for fame and fortune. His ambitions frustrated within the Republican Party, he moved toward political independence, the Democrats, the Populists, or radical coalitions when his choice held an opportunity for success. Political leaders welcomed his support because he commanded an ethnic and Roman Catholic constituency. Denied instant economic success through speculation and lobbying activity, he was cynical about the economic system but always admired men who attained great wealth. Donnelly had an uncanny ability to identify social problems and an inherent sympathy for the underdog in society. Both in his novels and as a political figure, he dramatized problems of race, religion, poverty, industrialization, and urbanization. But like most 19th-century political reformers, his solutions to social problems were simplistic. He had neither the time nor the inclination to think deeply—he was always harassed by personal financial concerns and political campaigns—and he tended to substitute brilliant and bizarre flashes of insight for careful analysis. The vehemence of his social critique, the nature of his solutions to social problems, and his unusually powerful oral and written rhetoric won him a wide audience. His foes denounced him as a corrupt demagogue, but he was a hero among people who opposed the political, scientific, and literary establishment, for he challenged each in turn with "commonsense" arguments: the politicians with populist government; the scientific community with theories opposing glacial geology; and the literary world with his mathematically sustained contention that Francis Bacon wrote Shakespeare's plays. He remains an important figure in American history partly because of his writings and accomplishments and partly because he serves as a convenient symbol of the popular response to the unrest of an era that witnessed drastic changes and reordering in American life. See Martin Ridge, *Ignatius Donnelly: Portrait of a Politician* (1962).

MARTIN RIDGE

DONOVAN, William Joseph ("Wild Bill") (b. Buffalo, N.Y., Jan. 1, 1883; d. Washington, D.C., Feb. 8, 1959), ATTORNEY, GOVERNMENT OFFICIAL, attended Niagara College and Columbia University, from which he received a BA (1905) and a law degree (1907). After graduation Donovan returned to Buffalo where he practiced law and married. Following service on the Mexican border with the First Cavalry unit of the National Guard, Donovan was appointed major in the 69th "Fighting Irish" Infantry Regiment of New York. In 1918 the Regiment went into combat in Europe, where Donovan distinguished himself. By the war's end he had become a colonel, the most decorated officer of the war, and acquired the nickname "Wild Bill." Following the armistice Donovan traveled to Vladivostok as an official U.S. observer of the Russian civil war. Over the next two decades he made many other trips abroad as an official observer of foreign and military affairs.

In February 1922, Donovan became U.S. district attorney for western New York. In September 1922 he was nominated for lieutenant governor of New York by the Republican Party but lost the election. In 1924, "Wild Bill" was appointed assistant attorney general in the Justice Department. Donovan resigned in 1929 to start a law firm that eventually became highly successful as Donovan Leisure Newton & Irvine. In 1932 he was the Republican gubernatorial candidate and was again defeated.

Donovan remained in private practice until

July 11, 1941, when, with the outbreak of World War II on the horizon, President Franklin Roosevelt appointed him to the newly created post of coordinator of information; his task was to collect intelligence and disseminate propaganda. On June 13, 1942, this became the Office of Strategic Services, which was given responsibility for intelligence gathering and analysis, covert propaganda against the enemy, and unconventional warfare. Donovan headed the OSS throughout World War II. After the war, the OSS was disbanded but was eventually reborn as the Central Intelligence Agency. Following Germany's defeat, Donovan briefly served as assistant prosecutor at the Nuremberg trials but returned to the United States before the trials commenced. Donovan served as ambassador to Thailand in 1953–54 before returning to private life.

In 1940, President Roosevelt sent "Wild Bill" Donovan on a fact-finding trip to Europe. There Donovan met with members of Britain's Secret Intelligence Service, which was the predecessor of the Special Operations Executive, Britain's unconventional warfare unit. SOE specialized in guerrilla tactics, intelligence gathering, and covert propaganda. This trip convinced Donovan that U.S. involvement in World War II was inevitable and that America must develop an unconventional warfare unit like SOE. As a result Donovan coauthored a pamphlet, *Fifth Column Lessons for America,* in which he argued that France collapsed because German agents had undermined its will to resist by using propaganda and subversion. Donovan lobbied Roosevelt to create an intelligence agency to preclude America's falling victim to similar tactics. Accordingly, Roosevelt appointed Donovan to the coordinator post and charged him with collecting intelligence affecting "national security" and conducting "supplementary activities … important for national security." Donovan interpreted the latter phrase to mean unconventional warfare and propaganda. His interpretation put him at odds with the military and other government agencies, particularly the Federal Bureau of Investigation, which believed that Donovan was usurping its powers. The battles over turf continued until Roosevelt created the OSS and placed it under the Joint Chiefs of Staff. As head of the new agency with the rank of brigadier general, Donovan modeled it after the British SOE. It proved very successful in conducting guerrilla warfare, black propaganda, and collecting intelligence behind enemy lines. Donovan received a promotion to major general in November 1944.

Following the war Donovan argued that an intelligence agency like OSS was necessary even in peacetime. Despite his pleas the OSS was disbanded. With the rise of the cold war between the United States and the Soviet Union, however, Donovan's views eventually prevailed. In 1947, President Harry Truman agreed to the creation of the Central Intelligence Agency. See Lawrence Soley, *Radio Warfare* (1989).

LAWRENCE SOLEY

DOS PASSOS, John Roderigo (b. Chicago, Ill., Jan. 14, 1896; d. Baltimore, Md., Sept. 28, 1970), WRITER, graduated from Harvard in 1916. After briefly studying architecture in Spain he volunteered in the ambulance service of the French army during World War I. He also served with the Red Cross in Italy and with the U.S. Medical Corps. After the war he traveled in Spain, Mexico, and the Near East as a freelance writer. His first novel, *One Man's Initiation* (1920), was unsuccessful, but *Three Soldiers* (1921), based on his war experiences, was well received by the critics. *Manhattan Transfer* (1925), a panorama of New York society written in a complex, stream-of-consciousness style, firmly established his reputation. In 1930 he published the first part of his *U.S.A.* trilogy, *The 42nd Parallel;* it was completed with *Nineteen-Nineteen* (1932) and *The Big Money* (1936). By tracing the stories of some thirty fictitious Americans of different social strata, Dos Passos gave a moving, bittersweet appraisal of America from 1900 to 1929. The volumes were sympathetic to the common man and to radical causes.

A strong political activist partial to the left wing, Dos Passos was an early contributor to the radical magazine *New Masses* (1926). He was arrested in Boston for demonstrating in favor of Sacco and Vanzetti (1927) and in 1928 visited the Soviet Union. In 1932 he supported William Z. Foster, the Communist Party candidate for president. However, he stopped writing for the *New Masses* in 1934, and after visiting Spain during its civil war (1937–38) he became deeply disillusioned with Communism and began to move toward the right. A second trilogy, *District of Columbia* (1949), described the failure of the New Deal. In *Midcentury* (1961) he bitterly attacked trade unionism. In his later years Dos Passos became a frequent contributor to the conservative *National Review,* and in 1964 he supported **Barry Goldwater** for president. A prolific writer, Dos Passos produced more than thirty novels and plays, including *Streets of Night* (1923), *The Theme Is Freedom* (1956), and *The Portugal Story* (1969).

———— ∞ ————

Dos Passos's writings have been characterized, in varying degrees of emphasis at various periods in his career, by several social and political themes: an agrarian suspicion of industrialism and urban life; an anarchistic distrust of power; a Jeffersonian skepticism toward institutions that threaten individual moral autonomy; a Veblenian faith in the value of labor and the dignity of workmanship; a personal quest for identity that later led him, the illegitimate son of Portuguese lineage, to turn from fiction to historical study in order to find ideological roots in the American past; and an unswerving intellectual integrity that enabled him to see, long before many of his contemporaries, the perilous promises of the welfare state, mass society, and scientific technology. A humble, soft-spoken, decent human being, Dos Passos commanded the admiration of friend and foe alike—even his political enemies, while criticizing his "deviations," conceded he was "dangerously honest." Where Dos Passos stood politically is not as important as what he stood for personally—individual liberty and human freedom.

Jean Paul Sartre once heralded Dos Passos as "one of the greatest writers of our time." What impressed Sartre and other literary critics was the innovative technique and bold imagination Dos Passos brought to the art of prose fiction. He was the first major American writer to introduce the "collective novel" as a means of capturing the totality of American society by creating characters from a variety of regional and class backgrounds. He was also the first to develop a purposely fragmented narrative style in order to convey the frantic tone and mechanical temper of modern technological society. But this mode of literary naturalism forced Dos Passos to express the thoughts and feelings of his characters through external description of the environment that oppressed them. As a result the characters often emerge as vaguely passive, and the reader learns more about American society than the individuals who compose it. Ironically, although Dos Passos passionately believed in individual freedom, he could never create convincing fictional characters who possessed the will to be free. An optimist himself, Dos Passos's novels always end in defeat. Only in the study of American history could Dos Passos completely overcome his pessimistic view of contemporary American society. See Daniel Aaron, "The Riddle of John Dos Passos," *Harper's,* CCXXIV (Mar. 1962), 55–60.

JACK DIGGINS

DOUGLAS, Stephen Arnold (b. Brandon, Vt., Apr. 23, 1813; d. Chicago, Ill., June 3, 1861), POLITICAL LEADER, grew up in Vermont and New York and settled in Illinois in 1833. Admitted to the bar in 1834, he rose rapidly in Democratic politics, serving as state's attorney (1834); member of the Illinois legislature (1834–37); Illinois secretary of state (1840); judge of the Illinois Supreme Court (1841–43); and member of the U.S. House of Representatives (1843–47). He was elected U.S. senator from Illinois in 1847. In Congress, Douglas supported the Mexican War and, as chairman of the Senate Committee on Territories, played a major role in the passage of the Compromise of 1850, which decided that the future of slavery in the territories gained from Mexico should be determined by actual settlers—the principle known as popular sovereignty. He was prominent in the Young America movement, which called for rapid internal development, moral support for democratic revolutions abroad, and the possible annexation of territories in Latin America. In 1854, Douglas's Kansas-Nebraska Act, repealing the Missouri Compromise prohibition of slavery in land north of 36'30" and opening Kansas and Nebraska territories to slavery under popular sovereignty, precipitated another sectional crisis. The law made Douglas a controversial figure in the North and thus contributed to his failure to win the presidential nomination in 1856. In 1857 he broke with Democratic President James Buchanan over Buchanan's Kansas policy.

Douglas was reelected to the Senate in 1858, defeating Republican Abraham Lincoln. During the debates of this campaign Douglas advanced his "Freeport Doctrine." The Supreme Court's **Dred Scott** decision, guaranteeing the right of slaveholders to bring their human property into any federal territory, was meaningless, he claimed, because under popular sovereignty local residents could keep slavery out by refusing to enact protective police legislation. This Freeport speech helped Douglas win the senatorship but cost him the support of the South. In 1860 the Democrats split over his presidential candidacy, the northern wing nominating him, the southern choosing **John C. Breckinridge.** In the election Douglas received 1,383,000 votes but won only twelve electors, in New Jersey and Missouri. In the secession crisis he offered his support to President Lincoln but died shortly after the outbreak of the Civil War.

Douglas was a man of good if not exceptional intellect, gregarious, an excellent politician, and capable of seeing the United States and its national needs in the broadest perspective. He succeeded at almost everything he attempted; rarely has a man seemed so closely attuned to his time and place in history. His law practice was large and prosperous. He dabbled in Chicago real estate

and made a large fortune. Politics suited him to perfection. Although very short, his appearance was so imposing that men called him the "Little Giant."

The foundations of his politics were expansion and popular sovereignty. That it was proper to let frontier settlers determine their own institutions in a democratic manner was to him axiomatic. He believed arguments over the future of slavery in the territories were a waste of time and energy since natural conditions would keep the institution out of the West. He saw no moral issue in slavery at all, being convinced that blacks were inferior beings. An utter cynic (it was his greatest failing), he cared not, he boasted, whether slavery was voted up or down. As a shrewd politician he could see that the question was interfering with the rapid exploitation of the continent; all he really cared about was that it should be settled so that the country could get on with more important matters: building railroads, acquiring new territory, expanding its trade. This probably accounts for the monumental miscalculation of his life—his sponsorship of the Kansas-Nebraska Act. Blind to the moral implications of repealing the Missouri Compromise, he reasoned that no one could legitimately object because the region west of Missouri, unsuited to plantation agriculture, would surely become free. However, while popular sovereignty presented many practical difficulties, Douglas genuinely believed in the concept.

The contest with Lincoln for the Illinois senatorship was much influenced by Douglas's break with Buchanan, who tried to defeat him. Douglas's whole future was at stake—his Senate seat, his position in the Democratic Party, his hope of being elected president. His strategy in the seven debates was to make Lincoln look like an abolitionist. He accused all Republicans of favoring racial equality. He pictured himself as a heroic defender of democracy, attacked on one side by "black" Republicans and on the other by the Buchananites, but ready to fight to the last breath for popular sovereignty. He forced Lincoln to equivocate and backtrack on the question of black rights, and when Lincoln, in turn, threw the Dred Scott decision in his face, he extricated himself with a brilliant piece of legerdemain, the Freeport Doctrine, which probably won him the election by satisfying Illinois Democrats that popular sovereignty was still a viable solution to the problem of slavery in the territories.

At the 1860 Democratic convention, Douglas broke with the southern wing of his party even though the split destroyed his chances of election. He realized this quickly, accepted his fate, and for the first time in his career rose above ambition and achieved real greatness. "Mr. Lincoln is the next president," he said. "We must try to save the Union. I will go south." In the heart of the Cotton Kingdom he denounced secession, enduring threats, snubs, and an occasional pelting with eggs and vegetables. After election day he worked ceaselessly for some solution to the crisis that might avoid war. Whether he actually held Lincoln's tall hat while the new president delivered his inaugural is one of history's much-debated minor mysteries, but the tale, true or false, testifies to Douglas's ultimate devotion to the United States and the principles of democracy. See R. W. Johannsen, *Stephen A. Douglas* (1973).

JOHN A. GARRATY

DOUGLAS, William Orville (b. Maine, Minn., Oct. 16, 1898; d. Washington, D.C., Jan. 19, 1980), JURIST, graduated from Whitman College in 1920 and received an LLB from Columbia Law School in 1925. He then entered the prominent Wall Street law firm of Cravath, De Gersdorff, Swaine, and Wood, specializing in corporate finance. In 1927 he became an assistant professor at Columbia Law School. Moving to Yale Law School a year later, he taught corporate law and bankruptcy. This led to his appointment (1934) to direct a Securities and Exchange Commission study of the protective committees that reorganize bankrupt corporations. He became a member of the SEC in 1934 and chairman in 1936. A defender of the small investor, Douglas pressed for full disclosure of information about new securities and prodded the New York Stock Exchange to reform its operations. In March 1939, President Franklin D. Roosevelt named him

to the Supreme Court.

On the Court, Douglas quickly established himself as a liberal. Roosevelt considered him a possible vice presidential candidate in 1944. In 1948 he discouraged a presidential boom by liberals and turned down an invitation to be Harry S. Truman's running mate.

In his years on the Supreme Court, Douglas applied his financial expertise to important rate-setting and antitrust cases. In 1947 he dissented in a case in which the Court rejected the Justice Department's charge that the purchase of the Columbia Steel Co. by U.S. Steel subsidiary Consolidated Steel violated antitrust laws. His 1949 opinion invalidated Standard Oil of California's "exclusive dealer" contracts for service stations. But Douglas gained his widest reputation as an outspoken champion of civil liberties and opponent of all forms of censorship. Along with Justice **Hugo Black** he dissented in the 1951 Court decision that upheld the constitutionality of the anti-Communist Smith Alien Registration Act of 1940. A frequent target of conservatives, Douglas was the subject of an abortive impeachment investigation in the 91st Congress. He suffered a stroke in 1974 that confined him to a wheelchair. He retired from the Court in 1975.

⎯⎯⎯∝∾∾⎯⎯⎯

Douglas was one of the most liberal and militant justices of the Supreme Court, early in his career a reforming administrator of the laws governing securities, and throughout a vigorous, controversial writer. Outwardly his life seems to have had the makings of a characteristic American success story: the fatherless child, overcoming an early bout with polio, helping support his widowed mother, working his way through high school and college, riding a freight car across the continent to attend Columbia Law School, graduating into a prestigious New York law firm, sweeping everything before him as he reached the successive rungs of the ladder—law school professor, SEC commissioner, Supreme Court justice—in the eyes of many clearly bent for the presidency.

Yet the real meaning of Douglas's life lay in the opposite direction, not toward conventional single-minded success but toward unconventional many-faceted fulfillment, always challenging whatever establishments he encountered.

As an economic reformer he linked the Populist tradition of the Northwest with the Brandeisian tradition of curbing the financial interests whose power was swollen by the use of "other people's money." He linked that in turn with the economic philosophy of FDR's New Deal, which he did so much himself to formulate. His memorandum on corporate reorganization, submitted in the early days of the Securities and Exchange Commission, was an eight-volume document detailing the ways in which investment bankers involved in reorganizations secured both profits and power from continuing control of the companies, and in his brief tenure as SEC chairman he had a chance to translate this corporate knowledge of his into regulatory rules. Even more important, as a Supreme Court justice (appropriately he succeeded to **Louis D. Brandeis**'s seat) he unswervingly led the struggle to control corporate power when it threatened the worker, the consumer, or the small businessman. He did so, moreover, as an insider who knew the dodges and strategies and how to cope with them.

As a judge, Douglas's strength lay in a forthright liberalism that rarely left any question as to where he would stand, especially on cases involving the Bill of Rights. His judicial career had four phases: as an active leader in the Roosevelt Court, both in dissent and in majority; as dissenter in the Vinson Court, especially in the cold war cases; as a militant member of the majority on the Warren Court; and again as the leader of the liberal minority on the Nixon Court. His reading of the First Amendment was, like Hugo Black's, an absolutist libertarian one. On freedom of religion, on the rights of accused persons, on the one-man-one-vote cases, on the right of access to contraceptive information, on obscenity cases, on school desegregation and other civil rights issues, Douglas sought to protect rights of dissent, privacy, equal access, and freedom of political action, even in cases that seemed extreme to his fellow liberals. He did it partly as a judicial activist who believed that the Court must be sword as well as shield, partly out of a basic personal stance as a rebel, which gave him a strong empathy for other rebels. Douglas's liberalism had a more sustained militancy than other Roosevelt appointees to the Court—Black, **Felix Frankfurter, Robert H. Jackson**—but it had a one-dimensional quality, less brilliantly resourceful in constitutional stratagems than Black's, less learned and tortured than Frankfurter's, with less statesmanlike depth than Jackson's. His judicial style was muscular and combative, very much as in his many books, but not memorable.

His judicial career was only one phase of an almost Jeffersonian many-sidedness, as teacher, naturalist, traveler, explorer, mountain climber, writer, lecturer, political man. He was Faustian in his appetite for life. Both by precept and by example he scorned the traditional view that a judge should lead a gray and neutral life lest he be accused of being a partisan. Douglas gloried in his partisanship as he gloried in an expressive life that included four marriages and three divorces. Inevitably this aroused conservative hostility. Several times enemies sought his impeachment, but after some flutterings and flickerings the attempts sputtered out. See W. O. Douglas, *Go East, Young Man: The Early Years* (1974), and Vern Countryman, *Douglas of the Supreme Court* (1959).

MAX LERNER

DOUGLASS, Frederick (b. Tuckahoe, Md., Feb. 1817; d. Anacostia Heights, near Washington, D.C., Feb. 20, 1895), REFORMER, was born Frederick Augustus Washington Bailey, the son of a black slave and a white father. At the age of 7 he was sent to Baltimore, Maryland, where, while working as a house servant, he learned to read and write. After serving under a number of owners he tried to run away but was captured (1836). In 1838, however, while working as a ship caulker in Baltimore, he escaped to New York City. He then moved to New Bedford,

Massachusetts, changed his name to Douglass, and worked as a common laborer.

In 1841, Douglass attended a convention of the Massachusetts Anti-Slavery Society in Nantucket. In an extemporaneous speech delivered there, he so moved his audience that he was asked to join the society as a lecturer. Although he was often ridiculed and assaulted while he spoke, he continued to lecture. In 1845 he published his *Narrative of the Life of Frederick Douglass.* In 1847, after a visit to Great Britain and Ireland, he began to publish the *North Star* (Rochester, N.Y.); along with **William Lloyd Garrison**'s *Liberator,* it was a leading organ of the abolitionist movement. The *North Star* also supported industrial education for blacks and woman suffrage. Douglass, unlike Garrison, soon came to believe that the abolitionists must use political means to achieve their ends, aligning themselves with parties and accepting the constitutional system. In 1859 he traveled to Canada and England.

When the Civil War broke out, Douglass helped recruit a number of black regiments for the Union army. During the Reconstruction period he continued to work for black equality. During 1871–91 he held a number of government positions, serving as assistant secretary of the Santo Domingo Commission (1871), federal marshal (1877–81), recorder of deeds (1881–86) of the District of Columbia, and U.S. minister to Haiti (1888–91).

———— ∞∞ ————

Frederick Douglass was the preeminent black abolitionist and agitator for equal rights during the 19th century. As editor and journalist he militantly articulated the moral issue of human freedom and equality, and the gap between America's Christian democratic values and its racial prejudice and discrimination. At the same time he was also characterized by a pragmatic temperament that sometimes exasperated the purists among his fellow reformers.

As a youth Douglass experienced slavery in all its variety from its most oppressive forms to its most paternalistic. Escaping from servitude on his second attempt in 1838, Douglass three years later was "discovered" by the abolitionists and entered on his extraordinary career as one of the greatest of the antislavery orators and editors. At first he identified himself with the American Anti-Slavery Society in the principles of Garrisonian abolitionism. By the end of the decade, however, his own quest for leadership and his desire to establish his own antislavery journal, combined with his growing doubts about the practicability of Garrison's exclusive reliance on moral suasion, produced tensions between the two men that culminated in a complete break in 1851. Thereafter Douglass was associated with the cause of the Liberty and Radical Abolition parties, though his pragmatic bent often led him (reluctantly) to endorse Free Soil and Republican candidates. Although white abolitionists tended to exclude blacks from decision-making positions in their movement, Douglass was so Olympian a figure that his positions had to be taken seriously by them.

Douglass was a champion of equal rights for *all*, regardless of sex as well as race. He played a prominent role in the woman's rights Seneca Falls Convention of 1848 and in the Negro Convention movement of the 1840s and 1850s. He counseled blacks both to agitate for their citizenship rights and to elevate themselves morally and economically. Militant though he was, he refused **John Brown**'s plea to join the latter's conspiracy. Douglass felt that armed revolt was not a practical strategy.

During the Civil War, Douglass used the pages of his journal to press for the arming of black troops and the emancipation of the slaves. After Abraham Lincoln issued his noted Proclamation, Douglass personally recruited black soldiers for the Union army. But these activities were, in his view, only a prelude to the larger task of securing full citizenship rights and ending all forms of racial discrimination—a task to which he devoted the remainder of his career.

Although in his later years he functioned as what one historian has called a "Republican wheel horse" (Douglass believed that whatever advancement the black man made came through the Republican Party), he was not uncritical of the party's shortcomings. He continued to protest against the immoral and growing patterns of segregation, disfranchisement, and mob violence. Yet at the same time he kept his faith in the ideal of the ultimately complete assimilation of blacks into American society—a fact symbolized by his second marriage to a white woman in 1881. As Douglass put it a few years before his death: "The real question is whether American justice, American liberty, American civilization, American law, and American Christianity can be made to include and protect alike and forever all American citizens … is whether this great nation shall conquer its prejudices, rise to the dignity of its professions, and proceed in the sublime course of truth and liberty [which Providence] has marked out for it." See William McFeeley, *Frederick Douglass* (1991).

AUGUST MEIER

DOW, Herbert Henry (b. Belleville, Can., Feb. 26, 1866; d. Rochester, Minn., Oct. 15, 1930), CHEMIST, INDUSTRIALIST, graduated from the Case School of Applied Science (BS, 1888). He then traveled throughout Michigan, Pennsylvania, Ohio, and West Virginia doing research on the subject of brines before becoming professor of chemistry and toxicology (1888–89) in Cleveland's Huron Street Hospital College. He patented a method for obtaining bromine by blowing air through slightly electrolyzed brine in 1888 and then organized a small company in Canton, Ohio, to develop this process in 1889. The venture failed, but the Midland (Mich.) Chemical Co. successfully adopted the process in 1890, mainly by employing the new direct-current generator. Dow next began experiments on the electrolysis of brine for the production of chlorine at Navarre, Ohio, in 1895. He moved his operations to Midland the following year, where he founded the Dow Chemical Co. in 1897 to manufacture bleach from chlorine. The new firm prospered, and in 1900, Dow bought out Midland Chemical Co. and took over the bromine market.

As president and general manager of his company, Dow expanded into many new areas. He manufactured insecticides, pharmaceuticals, and in 1916 produced the first synthetic indigo in the United States. By 1918, Dow's technique for the production of magnesium from the electrolysis of magnesium chloride made him a leader in this field; experiments with alloys of magnesium produced Dowmetal. During World War I, Dow served as a member of the advisory committee of the Council of National Defense and helped with American experiments in chemical warfare. In 1923 he developed synthetic phenol, used as an antiseptic, and in the years that followed produced iodine from Louisiana brine and later California petroleum brine. During his lifetime he was granted some one hundred patents.

⸙

Herbert Dow was one of the pioneers of industrial chemistry in the United States. When he was born, the American chemical industry was still in its infancy. By the time of his death in 1930 the United States had become preeminent in many fields of chemical manufactures. In this growth Dow and the Dow Chemical Corporation which he founded and nurtured played significant roles.

Dow's creative genius embraced science and business, innovative chemistry as well as industrial production and management. His blending of chemistry and engineering facilitated the transformation of laboratory theories into profitable everyday consumer products. His capacity for innovation was one of the keys to his success. His policy was not to concentrate on well-known products or processes but to seek out new ones and to generate new demands. His introduction of bromine, cheap phenol, and carbon tetrachloride as well as the manufacture of synthetic indigo reflected this talent. Dow was also extraordinarily adept in developing mass production methods and automation for a wide range of chemicals, including chlorine, iodine, and electrolytic cells. Finally, Dow often pioneered in increasing the efficiency of chemical manufacturing, whether by the utilization of by-products or the use of continuous processes. His methods helped break the monopoly of the German chemical cartel in indigo, bleach, and salicylates, and to make American chemicals competitive in worldwide markets. He was surely one of the most notable creative entrepreneurs of the first half of the 20th century. See Murray Campbell and Harrison Hatton, *Herbert H. Dow: Pioneer in Creative Chemistry* (1951).

GERALD D. NASH

DOW, Neal (b. Portland, Maine, Mar. 20, 1804; d. Portland, Maine, Oct. 2, 1897), REFORMER, had a devout Quaker upbringing. After attending the Friends' Academy in New Bedford, Massachusetts (1817–19), he entered his father's tanning business, becoming a partner in 1826. While active in tanning, banking, and investment, Dow became increasingly concerned with the evils of alcohol and interested in the growing temperance movement. He was the Portland Young Men's Temperance Society's delegate to the 1834 state convention, which established the Maine Temperance Society to fight distilled spirits. In 1837, Dow withdrew from this organization to help form the Maine Temperance Union to work directly for total abstinence and prohibitory legislation. A statewide prohibition law was passed in 1846, but Dow considered it inadequate because of its limited enforcement provisions.

Dow was elected mayor of Portland as a Whig in 1851 and took the lead in seeking stronger prohibitory legislation. Dow's efforts resulted in the "Maine Law" of 1851, which barred the manufacture and sale of liquor and granted search and seizure powers to ensure enforcement. Dow became an international figure, toured the North crusading for temperance, and served as president of the World's Temperance Convention in New York City in 1853. Twelve other states enacted the Maine Law in whole or part. He was reelected mayor of Portland in 1855. A serious anti–Maine Law riot led to repeal of the prohibition law in 1856, but a weakened version was reenacted in 1858. Dow lectured in England in 1857 and then served in the Maine legislature (1858–60) as a Republican.

A fervent antislavery crusader, Dow joined the Thirteenth Regiment of Maine Volunteer Infantry as a colonel when the Civil War broke out in 1861. He was promoted to brigadier general in 1862. Wounded at the battle of Port Hudson (La.), he was captured by the enemy. After a period in Confederate prisons in Mobile and Richmond, he was released in a prisoner exchange.

Dow returned to Portland in 1864 and continued his temperance crusade. He visited Great Britain twice (1866–67, 1873–75) and ran for president of the United States in 1880 on the Prohibition Party ticket, receiving 10,304 votes. In 1884, Dow was active in a successful campaign for a prohibitory amendment to the Maine state constitution. His autobiography, *The Reminiscences of Neal Dow, Recollections of Eighty Years* (1898), was published posthumously by his son.

⸎

Growing up in a family and a society that stressed social controls, Dow learned to prefer the legal compulsion of prohibition to persuasion as a means of advancing temperance. Yet as an orator and a writer he was very effective in persuading part of the electorate to support prohibitory laws. Because of his inability to overcome the remaining opposition to enforced local prohibition in his city, he turned to a statewide law. The realignment of political parties in the early 1850s allowed him to win passage of the Maine Law and to attract a following for it elsewhere, mostly in the North. By his exaggerated reports of the law's easy enforcement and by lecture tours to which he subordinated even his family obligations, he helped temporarily to spread prohibition. The Maine Law movement became part of the coalition that produced the Republican Party, together with antislavery and antiforeignism, which Dow also espoused. An ambitious man, proud of his work, Dow hoped for political advancement. He lost his best opportunity because of his consistent fondness for physical force, which at the Portland Riot of 1855 led him to order militia to fire into a mob. Politicians already disillusioned by the problems of prohibition hastened to disown Dow and his Maine Law. Among Dow's other weaknesses were his reliance on countless verbal attacks on individuals and a streak of avarice that several times served to discredit him as a philanthropist. Nevertheless, he was sincerely dedicated, courageous, and kindly toward co-believers. Dow survived to become a saintly symbol for the revived temperance movement. He was the most important 19th-century prohibitionist. See F. L. Byrne, *Prophet of Prohibition: Neal Dow and His Crusade* (1969).

FRANK L. BYRNE

DRAKE, Daniel (b. near Bound Brook, N.J., Oct. 20, 1785; d. Cincinnati, Ohio, Nov. 5, 1852), PHYSICIAN, SCIENTIST, grew up in Mays Lick, Kentucky, a frontier community. He had only limited education in local schools. In 1800 he began to study medicine in the office of Dr. William Goforth in Fort Washington (later Cincinnati). After completing his apprenticeship he spent brief periods at the Medical College of the University of Pennsylvania (1805–6) and in practice at Mays Lick (1806–7). He then established an office in Cincinnati, where he published *Notices Concerning Cincinnati* (1810–11) and *Natural and Statistical View, or Picture of Cincinnati and the Miami Country* (1815), which included observations on local medicinal plants, meteorological data, and a brief history. In 1815 he returned to Philadelphia to study medicine again at the University of Pennsylvania (MD, 1816). In 1817–18 he taught at Transylvania University but then returned to Cincinnati where he gave public lectures and worked to secure a state charter for a proposed Medical College of Ohio. The institution opened in 1820 with Drake as president and professor of medicine, but disputes with the faculty brought his dismissal in 1822. During 1823–27 he served on the faculty at Transylvania University, but he returned once more to Cincinnati where he served on the faculty of the Ohio Medical College (1831–32) and in a new medical department at the Cincinnati College (1835–39). After the latter's collapse he joined the faculty of the Louisville (Ky.) Medical Institute (1839–49). Drake edited important medical journals almost continuously from 1828 to 1849.

After returning briefly to the Ohio Medical College (1849–50), Drake remained at Louisville until 1852. Here he completed his most famous publication, *A Systematic Treatise, Historical, Etiological, and Practical, on the Principal Diseases of the Interior Valley of North America* (1850–54). This opus included more than 1,800 pages of data on the topography, meteorology, customs, population, and diseases in the interior regions of the nation. In 1852 he returned for the last time to Cincinnati, to head another proposed new medical school. A consistently active booster of the city, Drake was instrumental in securing a state charter (1821) for Cincinnati's Commercial Hospital and Lunatic Asylum. He also sought to improve the city's trade through the development of canals and railroad links.

❦

Drake's *Systematic Treatise* is regarded as a masterpiece of medical geography and sociology. Rejecting a priori medical systems, the work presents systematically the results of a lifetime of correspondence and of Drake's own observations during five journeys, undertaken after the age of 50, ranging from Canada to Florida and from western New York to the Indian Territory. Drake treated the etiology of diseases for which environmental factors seemed to him significant and neglected other ailments. Opposing the then dominant view that miasmas caused cholera and malaria, Drake espoused an animalcular hypothesis.

In this and all matters Drake's method was that of Baconian induction: "acute observation, accurate comparison, judicious arrangement, and logical induction" (1821 lecture). This method, Drake believed, would reveal Nature's secrets by which the universe was governed, permitting man to live by the rules for his own benefit. Lack of knowledge meant being bound. Drake did not deem this mode of inquiry impossibly demanding; even "amateurs" could pursue it after rudimentary instruction. So to enhance popular education Drake sponsored numerous efforts to create schools, museums, and societies, and he enjoined research according to his methods on all the would-be physicians in his classes.

Drake applied his environmental perspectives to the political world, seeking answers to questions of stability in both local and national society. Temperance, which Drake considered sociologically and not morally, he thought an indispensable ingredient of urban tranquility. By induction Drake sought to demonstrate the pivotal role of the Interior Valley in maintaining the integrity of the nation. Thus, while his medical treatise was his stellar achievement, that work formed a consistent pattern with the rest of Drake's active and diversified career. See Daniel Drake, *Physician to the West, Selected Writings ... on Science and Society,* ed. with introductions by Henry D. Shapiro and Zane L. Miller (1970).

JAMES HARVEY YOUNG

DREISER, Theodore (b. Terre Haute, Ind., Aug. 27, 1871; d. Hollywood, Calif., Dec. 28, 1945), WRITER, the son of a German immigrant, he was raised in scrimping poverty. After attending parochial and public schools in Indiana, he briefly attended the University of Indiana (1889–90). For the next few years he held a succession of newspaper jobs in Chicago, St. Louis, Pittsburgh, and New York, where he finally settled in 1894.

Influenced by the writings of Balzac and especially the deterministic philosophy of Herbert Spencer, Dreiser came to view man as a helpless victim of indifferent natural forces. In 1900, with the encouragement of **Frank Norris,** he published his first naturalistic novel, *Sister Carrie,* a study of a young girl who goes to Chicago from a small western town. After having a brief affair with a salesman, she meets Hurstwood, a successful restaurant manager who is married. The story analyzes the gradual degeneration of Hurstwood and Carrie's rise to fame and fortune. Because of the frankness with which Dreiser dealt with sex, his publisher (Doubleday) refused to print more than one thousand copies. After this setback Dreiser earned a living for several years as a surprisingly successful editor of conventional magazines for women. But his creative energies were not stifled. His *Jennie Gerhardt*

(1911), another novel about an apparently amoral woman, was favorably received. *Sister Carrie* was reissued, and Dreiser's career began anew with a succession of long, powerful novels. *The Financier* (1912) introduced the dynamic character Frank Cowperwood, who was patterned after Charles T. Yerkes, a Chicago traction magnate. This was followed by another Cowperwood novel, *The Titan* (1914). In 1915 he issued *The "Genius,"* an account of an artist's inner compulsions. *Free and Other Stories* appeared in 1918, and an autobiography, *A Book about Myself,* was published in 1922.

In 1925, Dreiser published *An American Tragedy,* the most complete statement of his philosophy. Using an actual case as his framework, he shows that the real criminal was not Clyde Griffiths, the killer, but the slum environment in which he grew up. In 1927, Dreiser traveled to Russia. His articles on Russia, written originally for the New York *World,* were published under the title *Dreiser Looks at Russia* (1928). In 1932 he issued *Tragic America* in which he urged Americans to be cognizant of Russia's achievements. *America Is Worth Saving* (1941) is an isolationist tract.

In 1944, Dreiser was awarded the Merit Medal for fiction by the American Academy of Arts and Letters. The following year he joined the Communist Party. His two final works, which were published posthumously, were *The Bulwark* (1946), a study about a Quaker's religious convictions, and *The Stoic* (1947), the final volume in the Cowperwood trilogy. Other writings include *The Hand of the Potter* (1918), a naturalistic play; *Twelve Men* (1919), sketches of acquaintances; and *Hey, Rub-a-Dub-Dub* (1920), a collection of essays.

⸺⸎⸺

There is a perennial division in the arts between the fastidious craftsmen and the creators who pour out their feelings, those who believe in technique and those who believe in emotion. **Henry James,** for instance, liked to think he belonged to the first persuasion. English novelists of the 19th century, he once noted unfavorably, lacked the professional control of their French colleagues: they produced "loose, baggy monsters" of novels. And James would surely have approved of the famous dictum of the architect **Mies van der Rohe** that "less means more." Another writer, the 20th-century American novelist **Thomas Wolfe,** belonged to the second camp. Distinguishing between the "leaver-outers" and the "putter-inners," Wolfe stated the case for the putter-inners: life was too big, too various, too complicated to be rendered in neat aphoristic diagrams—the head denied the heart.

Dreiser, too, was emphatically a putter-inner whose motto might have been "more means more." His critics have complained that he was a clumsy fellow, capable of appalling clichés; that his novels were trundling narratives interspersed with didactic essays, the wooden alternating with the leaden; and that his attitudes remained stuck in the Social Darwinist framework of the period 1900–15 when most of his fiction was written or conceived. Since, on the whole, 20th-century American fiction has revealed a concern for form rather than content, criticism of Dreiser has been severe. Those who place a higher value on his work concede that he lacked the connoisseurship, the formal professionalism of the usual man of letters, but they maintain that this deficiency was an aspect of Dreiser's strength. What he labored to impart was certainly the truth of life in his America; and for him this truth was embraced neither by the intelligentsia nor by the conventional purveyors of polite fiction. Leaver-outers, he felt, were often evaders or people (like James?) who simply did not know the score. In Dreiser's world, as he had discovered from firsthand experience, "fallen" women were quite often nicer and more prosperous than their respectable, unfallen sisters. A phrase like "easy virtue" was meaningless. There was no hard-and-fast line between the criminal and the honest. No one was entirely innocent, and therefore no one was entirely guilty either. Existence was a cruel, blurred, puzzling business. Morality was all very well: people's lives were determined not by what they ought to do but by what they could not help doing. In the struggle for survival the weak went under. The rare few who triumphed over circumstance, like Dreiser's Cowperwood, were endowed with exceptional force. In them the primal drives—for sex, fame, money (each of these an aspect of power)—were so intense that they achieved at least a temporary mastery. They were the men who, in obedience to their "chemisms," made others obey them and shaped the new city-America in their own image. Some people might earn a comfortable intermediate living by catering to popular appetites, as Dreiser did through magazine editing or his brother Paul by writing catchy songs. The rest, the mass, like his sadly ineffectual crippled father, were doomed to remain underdogs.

Dreiser would have said that if his novels were loose, baggy monsters, that was how life was. Though his fascination with the Cowperwood-supermen was sometimes naïve, there is an enduring strength, a stubborn uncensorious honesty in his best books. Dreiser was the counterpart in words to the Ashcan painters of his era. The pictures he painted were not pretty; they were—much more important—real. See W. A. Swanberg, *Dreiser* (1965).

MARCUS CUNLIFFE

DREW, Charles Richard (b. Washington, D.C., June 3, 1904; d. Burlington, N.C., Apr. 1, 1950), PHYSICIAN, graduated from Amherst College in 1926. After briefly coaching basketball and football at Morgan College in Maryland, he entered McGill University's Medical School in Montreal, receiving his MD and Master of Surgery in 1933. He interned at Montreal's Royal Victoria Hospital and the Montreal General Hospital before returning to the United States in 1935 as instructor of pathology at the College of Medicine at Howard University. He became an assistant in surgery at Howard in 1936 and also a resident in surgery at the Freedmen's Hospital in Washington, D.C. Drew gained a General Education Board fellowship to do postgraduate work at Columbia's College of Physicians and Surgeons in 1937, where he investigated the properties of blood plasma. He received his Doctor of Medical Science degree from Columbia in 1940, and his dissertation was published as *Banked Blood: A Study of Blood Preservation* (1940).

In 1940, Dr. John Beattie of the Royal College

of Surgeons, one of Drew's teachers at McGill, asked him to secure new supplies of plasma made necessary by World War II. Working with the Presbyterian Hospital in New York City and the Blood Transfusion Association, Drew devised the blood-bank process to store large amounts of plasma. When the United States entered the war, the American Red Cross appointed him director of its plasma storage program for the U.S. armed forces. Drew bitterly objected to the segregation of plasma supplies for whites and blacks. In 1942 he left the plasma program to become professor and head of the Department of Surgery at the Howard University College of Medicine. He won the Spingarn Medal of the NAACP in 1944 for his work on blood banks. Drew became medical director and chief of staff at the Freedmen's Hospital in 1946. He was killed in an automobile accident while on the way to a medical meeting at Tuskegee Institute in Alabama.

Natural endowments and accidents of fate explain Charles Drew's permanent place in the annals of American medicine. A jovial and amiable personality made him popular wherever he went. The breadth of his interests—he was, for example, a versatile athlete in high school and college, a star in football, basketball, baseball, and track—added to his appeal. In addition, having been nurtured in the strictly segregated atmosphere of Washington, D.C., he was equipped to deal with the problem of competition in the white world. His excellent medical education prepared him for making good use of his abilities. At Howard he developed a first-class surgical training program; at the time of his death, eight of the twenty-one black specialists in surgery in the United States had been his students.

Drew's main contribution was his development of the blood-bank concept for collecting and storing plasma. When World War II suddenly produced the need for enormous amounts of plasma, he was the right man in the right place at the right time, and he solved the problem brilliantly. On the other hand, a different accident of fate—the fact that Drew was black—sharply lim-

ited his usefulness to humanity. When he naturally and rightly objected to the medically absurd policy of segregating black and white blood, he was allowed to leave the plasma program in 1942, just when it was moving into high gear. Back at Howard he continued to do valuable work, but in a color-blind society he would have accomplished more. In this sense his career typifies the social cost of race prejudice. This truth can be illustrated in another ironical way. After the accident that caused his death he was rushed to an all-white hospital in North Carolina. Everything possible was done in an effort to save him. Nevertheless, the myth developed that he had been refused treatment and allowed to die unaided. See W. Montague Cobb, "Charles Richard Drew, M.D.," *Journal of the National Medical Association,* XLII (1950), 238–46.

W. MONTAGUE COBB

DREXEL, Katharine Mary (b. Philadelphia, Pa., Nov. 26, 1858; d. Cornwells Heights, Pa., Mar. 3, 1955), REFORMER, was the daughter of F. A. Drexel, millionaire philanthropist and banker. After being educated by private tutors she decided to devote herself and her income (she controlled a trust fund estimated at $14 million) to the educational needs of Native Americans and blacks. Directed toward a religious vocation by Bishop James O'Connor of Omaha, Nebraska, and personally encouraged by Pope Leo XIII, she retired at the age of 31 to a convent in Pittsburgh in order to reach a final decision. On Lincoln's birthday, 1891, she founded the Sisters of the Blessed Sacrament for Indian and Colored People and became the first superior of a small group destined to reach five hundred by her death 64 years later. Requests for help soon abounded, and Mother Katharine responded, particularly in the South and Southwest, by building more mission schools and by assigning teachers from her own order. Later she extended her foundations to Boston, Chicago, and Harlem, and in 1915 established Xavier University in New Orleans. Conservative estimates indicate she spent and bequeathed more than $12 million to educate

Native Americans and blacks. Today her nuns still staff clinics, social centers, and schools in the United States and abroad.

~~~

In her life and work Drexel mingled deep sensitivity to the needs of others with a willingness to spend and be spent in their service. From both parents she inherited a sense of thrift, personal responsibility, moral stamina, filial fear of God, and love of neighbor. Even in the Gilded Age she believed that blacks and Native Americans "are the direct responsibility of the white people of the United States." Education alone, she felt, could develop in these two minorities the character and ideals of citizenship that had helped to build a nation. With a keen business instinct for the practical combined with otherworldly faith, she became a social and religious pioneer who worked equally well in city ghettos and on Indian reservations. This early devotion to interracial work by 1925 had inspired another Philadelphian, Anna Dengel (founder of the Medical Mission Sisters), to say, "To my mind Mother Katharine saved the reputation of the U.S. as regards the racial question." Publicity-shy and spiritually motivated, Drexel gave herself and her millions without fanfare. The superficial observer appreciated her outward largess, but only intimate friends and associates saw that a heroic detachment from wealth and self-aggrandizement drove her ever onward. This insight prompted Jesuit **John La Farge,** author of the *American Amen,* to salute her as "a great American; a mighty apostle of God's Holy Church; a soul who walked long and fearlessly" as a millionaire in poverty. Contemporaries recalled how "she went long distances, in all kinds of conveyances, and often walking where there was no other way. She went simple, silent, and unknown." Though a New York *Times* obituary noted that "she gave her millions as cheerfully as she devoted her life," it was a black judge in Philadelphia, Theodore Spaulding, who best caught her spirit when he said that her greatest contribution was "the sacrifice of herself." See M. Duffy, *Katharine Drexel* (1966).

HARRY J. SIEVERS

DUBINSKY, David (b. Brest-Litovsk, Poland, Feb. 22, 1892; d. New York, N.Y., Sept. 17, 1982), LABOR LEADER, was educated in Polish Hebrew schools and then worked in his father's bakery in Lodz. Becoming active in the local labor movement, Dubinsky led and won a strike against all the town's bakeries including his father's. In 1908 he led another strike but was arrested and sent to prison. In 1909 he was banished to Siberia by the Russian government, but he escaped to European Russia and eventually made his way to the United States. Arriving in New York City in 1911, he learned the cloak-cutting trade and joined the cutters' union Local 10, a division of the International Ladies' Garment Workers Union, that same year. Gaining quick recognition for his organizational talents, Dubinsky took a seat on Local 10's executive board (1918) and became vice chairman (1919), then chairman (1920). In 1921 he became manager-secretary of the Cutters' Union division of the ILGWU and president of Local 10 in 1922. Elected a vice president of the ILGWU that same year, he bitterly fought Communist and radical infiltration of the union. In 1929 he relinquished all his positions to become general secretary-treasurer of the ILGWU, and upon the death of Benjamin Schlesinger in 1932 he was elected president of the union.

Dubinsky succeeded in enlarging the union's membership, clearing its debt, and starting training programs for members. He was elected vice president of the AFL in 1934 and again in 1935 but resigned a year later to support the efforts of **John L. Lewis** and other dissidents in behalf of industrial unionism. He helped the new Congress of Industrial Organizations to organize iron, steel, and other industrial unions, but his own union never formally joined the CIO. In 1940, Dubinsky rejoined the AFL and worked for its merger with the CIO; when this was accomplished in 1955, he served a year as vice president (1955). Always active in politics, Dubinsky helped found the American Labor Party in New York (1936), the Liberal Party in New York (1944), and the pressure group Americans for Democratic Action (1947). Dubinsky retired as head of the ILGWU in 1966.

Of all American labor leaders, David Dubinsky, in his career as president of the ILGWU between 1932 and 1966, exemplified most successfully the harnessing of Jewish social idealism to the pragmatic philosophy of the American labor tradition. Attaining the office after a prolonged and bitter struggle with the Communists, which had reduced the union's membership to fewer than 50,000 and which in later years made anti-Communism something of an obsession, Dubinsky, short, dynamic, and impishly engaging in his personal manner, continued to develop the progressive social policies that had earlier made the ILGWU a pioneer in civil rights, union education, pension benefits, and health care. He also took advantage of the NIRA and other New Deal labor legislation to rebuild his union so that by 1965 it had more than 440,000 members, Jewish-led but mostly composed of blacks, Italians, and Puerto Ricans (few of whom, however, have so far been advanced to positions of leadership).

Pragmatism, honesty, and a flair for tactical leadership were also among Dubinsky's outstanding characteristics. Politically, this led him to leave the Socialist Party of America in 1936 to help create the American Labor Party (and in 1944 the Liberal Party), enabling New York's garment workers to combine national support for the New Deal with local independent political action. Within the labor movement it led Dubinsky to give strong support to the industrial union and socially progressive ideals of the Committee for Industrial Organization, but to oppose the formal splitting of the AFL that led to the creation of the CIO. As a result, after a brief period outside both organizations, on returning to the AFL in 1940, Dubinsky devoted the rest of his career to reestablishing unity between the two wings of the labor movement, fighting corruption within the ILGWU and in the labor movement generally, and helping build up the International Confederation of Free Trade Unions. See "David Dubinsky, the ILGWU, and the American Labor Movement: Essays in Honor of David Dubinsky," special supplement of *Labor History*, IX (Spring 1968), 5–126.

JOHN H. M. LASLETT

DU BOIS, William Edward Burghardt (b. Great Barrington, Mass., Feb. 23, 1868; d. Accra, Ghana, Aug. 27, 1963), REFORMER, WRITER, HISTORIAN, graduated from Fisk University in 1888 with a BA and from Harvard University with a BA in philosophy in 1890 and a PhD in history in 1895. His dissertation, "The Suppression of the African Slave Trade to the United States, 1638–1870," was the first publication of the Harvard Historical Series.

During 1894–96, Du Bois taught Greek and Latin at Wilberforce University in Ohio. In 1896 he became assistant instructor in sociology at the University of Pennsylvania, where he carried out the research for *The Philadelphia Negro* (1899), a pioneering sociological study of an urban black community. He served as professor of economics and history at Atlanta University (1897–1910), also organizing the annual conferences on African-Americans whose proceedings and research were published as the *Atlanta University Studies* (1896–1914). A founding member of the Niagara movement, an all-black group that agitated for full civil rights for blacks, Du Bois was active in the movement during 1905–9. In 1909 he joined with several other blacks and liberal whites to form the National Association for the Advancement of Colored People (NAACP), taking the posts of director of publicity and research, and editor of *The Crisis*, the organization's monthly paper. In 1934 he left the NAACP after a dispute with the leadership over what course the organization should take to combat the effects of the Depression on the lives of black Americans. He returned to Atlanta University as head of the department of sociology and founded *Phylon*, a journal of social science and culture. In 1944 he rejoined the NAACP as director of special research, a post he held for four years. Du Bois retired from this position in 1948 at the age of 80. In 1950 he was an unsuccessful candidate for the

U.S. Senate on the American Labor Party ticket. He continued his writing and was active in the American left movement in such organizations as the Council of African Affairs and the Peace Information Center. In 1951 he was indicted by the federal government as an agent of a foreign power but was acquitted. In 1961 he joined the American Communist Party, left the United States, and took up residence and citizenship in Ghana. While in Ghana, Du Bois worked as editor in chief of the *Encyclopedia Africana* until his death.

Throughout his life Du Bois was active in the Pan-African movement, attending the First Pan-African Conference in London in 1900 and the First Universal Races Congress in London in 1911. He sponsored Pan-African congresses in 1919, 1921, 1923, and 1927, and served as honorary chairman of the 1945 congress held in Manchester, England.

Among the more significant of Du Bois's twenty-one books are the collections of essays, *The Souls of Black Folks* (1903) and *Darkwater: Voices from Within the Veil* (1920); the historical studies, *Black Reconstruction* (1935) and *The World and Africa* (1947); and the novels, *The Quest of the Silver Fleece* (1911) and *Dark Princess: A Romance* (1928).

Du Bois won numerous commendations and honorary degrees; he was a fellow and life member of the American Association for the Advancement of Science and a member of the National Institute of Arts and Letters. In 1953 the Communist-sponsored World Peace Council at its Budapest meeting awarded him its Peace Prize of $7,000, and in 1959 he accepted the Lenin Peace Prize of the Soviet Union.

───── ⊷∞⊷ ─────

The greatness of Du Bois and perhaps the reason for his impact on American black intellectuals and political leaders in Africa, the Caribbean, and the United States can be grasped if the complexity of his long life and work are viewed from the two complementary perspectives of "double consciousness" and "a life lived experimentally and self-documented." Du Bois himself in *The Souls of Black Folks* (1903) wrote that "the Negro is a sort of seventh son born with a veil, and gifted with second sight in this American world—a world which yields him no true self-consciousness, but only lets him see himself through the revelation of the other world. It is a peculiar sensation, this double consciousness, this sense of always looking at one's self through the eyes of others, of measuring one's soul by the tape of a world that looks on in amused contempt and pity. One ever feels his two-ness—an American, a Negro; two souls, two thoughts, two unreconciled strivings; two warring ideals in one dark body, whose dogged strength alone keeps it from being torn asunder."

St. Clair Drake, the black sociologist, said in 1964, "Du Bois's major contribution to our epoch is not the shelf of books he wrote or the scores of articles, nor even the thirty-odd leadership years with the NAACP, but is rather the contribution of *'a life lived experimentally and self-documented'*—a restless, seeking, ever searching quest.... Du Bois conceived of his life as a continuous probe, touching the sensitive areas along the color line, and considered it his duty to document the results of the probing as well as his own reaction to the situations."

It is through these two prisms that we can view the activities of Du Bois's life. His double consciousness led him to expand his view of the race problem to its worldwide dimensions, to see that "the problem of the 20th century is the problem of the color line—the relation of the darker to the lighter races of men in Asia and Africa, in America and the islands of the sea."

This double consciousness also led him to search along the black side of the color line—both past and present—to consider the importance of Africa to the African-American. From this search stemmed Du Bois's attempts at organizing a Pan-African movement in the 20th century and constant efforts to include the African background or the African dimension to every study of the African-American that he undertook.

The double consciousness also led Du Bois to look with some detachment on the lives and activities of black Americans and to express, often quite sharply, his disagreement or disapproval. His quarrels with **Booker T. Washington** and, later, with **Marcus Garvey** can be viewed in this light, as well as the criticisms of various blacks that appeared in the pages of *The Crisis* from time to time.

Stemming from Drake's view that Du Bois led "a life lived experimentally and self-documented" one gets a greater understanding of the apparent contradictions and inconsistencies in Du Bois's life and work. First, Du Bois used a wide variety of forms and forums to project his ideas. He wrote the history and sociology of the trained scholar; he wrote brilliant polemical and expository essays. In the area of fiction, he wrote poems, plays, and several novels. As an editor he used the pages of *The Crisis* and *Phylon* to great advantage to spread his own ideas as well as the ideas and writings of a number of black authors—young and old. He participated in a number of types of organizations from the NAACP and Niagara movement to the Pan-African congresses to various scholarly conferences. The silent march against lynching that Du Bois led in New York in 1917 was a significant nonviolent protest activity.

In the area of ideologies and politics, Du Bois simultaneously supported both capitalism and socialist economic systems. At the turn of the century he was very much in favor of capitalist development for black Americans, but he also felt that the ideas of Marx and other European socialists should be studied. He joined the Socialist Party in 1911 and left it in 1912. Throughout his life he advocated and gave encouragement to the idea of producer and consumer cooperatives as a possible solution to the economic problems of black people. Only in the years following World War II did Du Bois express his final disillusion with capitalism and committed himself to socialism as the only way to end the poverty and exploitation of the masses.

In his advocacy of various strategies for the liberation of black Americans, Du Bois shifted from his early emphasis on the "talented tenth," a trained, educated elite who would lead the way, to a reliance on the working class of blacks who were not as susceptible to the temptations and corruptions that the United States offered the black elite. Du Bois saw fit to oppose the methods of Booker T. Washington and of Marcus Garvey, while later admitting that he shared much of their views as to ends.

Evaluations as to the ultimate worth of Du Bois's contribution to the worlds of scholarship and to the liberation of blacks throughout the world will vary as the focus shifts from one aspect of his life to another. As a leader, in the common sense of that term, Du Bois was clearly not very successful. He commanded no large following, neither founded nor led any mass movement or organization. But he apparently never wanted to, not seeing that as one of the roles he should play. Professional scholars usually express grudging admiration for Du Bois's obvious talents but lament that he "wasted" so much time engaging in polemics and propaganda when there were so many good books that he could have written, so many scholarly topics that would have benefited from his sustained undivided attention. The ultimate contribution that Du Bois has to make, it seems, is the example of undiminished commitment to and untarnished integrity in the cause of human freedom for a life that exceeded nine decades. That took some doing. As Kwame Nkrumah, late president of Ghana, said at the funeral services in 1963, "Dr. Du Bois is a phenomenon." See Daniel L. Lewis, *W.E.B. Du Bois: Biography of a Race, 1868–1919* (1993).

JOHN H. BRACEY, JR.

DUKE, James Buchanan (b. near Durham, N.C., Dec. 23, 1856; d. New York, N.Y., Oct. 10, 1925), INDUSTRIALIST, worked for his father in the tobacco trade and studied at the Durham Academy. Although he enrolled in Guilford College near Greensboro in 1871, he abandoned his studies after three months to return to the family firm in Durham. He became a partner in Washington Duke and Sons in 1878 and quickly emerged as its dominant figure. After the company began to concentrate on the manufacture of cigarettes in 1881, Duke reduced costs by installing the new Bonsack rolling machines, and he enhanced the popularity of his cigarettes by introducing the crush-proof but easily accessible sliding cardboard box.

Duke began to develop a national market for his tobacco products in 1884. Establishing new headquarters in New York City, he advertised on billboards and in newspapers across the country, and created a national network of sales agents and distributors. He also created a network of warehouses and buyers in the tobacco-growing areas of the South. By 1889 he was producing half the cigarettes manufactured in the United States. Following the "tobacco wars" of the 1880s he combined the four major cigarette producers into the American Tobacco Co. (1890) and consolidated the major plug tobacco manufacturers into the Continental Tobacco Co. in 1898. He gained control over other tobacco products with the formation of the American Snuff Co. in 1900, the American Cigar Co. in 1901, and the American Stogie Co. in 1901. He also consolidated retail outlets with the formation of the United Cigar Stores Co. in 1901. The Supreme Court ordered the dissolution of this "tobacco trust" in 1911.

Duke began to invade foreign markets with the formation of the British-American Co. in 1902. He also invested heavily in hydroelectric utility systems, forming the Southern Power Co. in 1905. An active philanthropist throughout his life, Duke created a $120 million endowment in 1924 for hospitals, colleges, and churches in North Carolina. He granted one-third of the endowment to Trinity College, which was renamed Duke University in 1924. He also donated an additional $24 million to Duke University building funds (1922–25) and bequeathed this institution 10 percent of his residual estate (1925).

A self-made man, Duke was a fervent advocate of the gospel of work. "No man ought to be allowed to live if he will not work," he used to say. "No matter if he has millions or if he has nothing." As head of the great "tobacco trust," he maintained elegantly appointed offices along lower Fifth Avenue in New York, and there, much as in his youth, he toiled at his desk ten to twelve hours a day, six days a week. Prominently displayed on his office wall as a reminder of his humble beginnings was a picture of the small log-house "factory" on the Duke family farm in the "bright leaf" tobacco region of North Carolina.

"Buck" Duke was the son of an impoverished Confederate veteran, Washington Duke, who after the Civil War returned to his farm with total resources of fifty cents and two blind army mules. Young Duke worked in the fields, flailed out tobacco on the floor of an old barn, and frequently set out with his father on journeys by covered wagon to sell the family brand of smoking tobacco in towns and villages. On these trips "Buck" showed an unmistakable knack for shrewd trading, and well before he was out of his teens he was supervising the factory operations of the expanding family concern. He was quick, tirelessly persistent, and had a bold imagination.

The vogue of cigarette smoking in the United States was largely the creation of massive advertising, and no one, with the possible exception of George Washington Hill, did more than Duke to popularize the cigarette through remarkable salesmanship. Duke, however, was more than a huckster. With his detailed knowledge of the product and with his mastery of the intricacies of corporate organization and finance, he was a true captain of industry. In these respects he resembled **John D. Rockefeller,** whom he considered the greatest American and whose Standard Oil empire served as the structural model for the tobacco combine. Later, he recalled having asked himself, "If John D. Rockefeller can do what he is doing in oil, why should I not do it in tobacco?"

Until the late 1870s cigarette consumption in the United States was small. The advent of mechanization opened up new vistas; it also posed urgent problems. The Bonsack machine adopted by Duke could roll 200 cigarettes a minute in contrast to a daily hand production of 2,500 units by a superior workman. Duke grasped the necessity of a market capable of absorbing the immensely enlarged output. He also knew, since machine methods were within reach of other manufacturers, that it would be necessary to consolidate the industry in order to avoid chaotic gluts and destructive price competition. Some of his trade practices were harsh and reprehensible, but he never made the mistake of believing that a product "sells itself." He always directed his merchandising to the masses. "Tobacco is the poor man's luxury," he said. "Where else can he get so much enjoyment for his five or ten cents?"

The ultimate tribute to Duke's organizational brilliance came when the Supreme Court ordered the breakup of the tobacco trust. It developed that only Duke himself had the requisite expertise for presiding over the complex reorganization. Afterward the component companies were able to conduct their business separately as if nothing had happened. Foes of the trust, notably Theodore Roosevelt, were infuriated.

Duke was a powerfully built man. He stood six feet two inches and had red hair and the high color of his Scotch-Irish ancestry. For all of his dynamic business methods, he generally had an air of imperturbable calm. One of the few concessions he made to the dignity of his station as head of American Tobacco was a reduction in his daily consumption of chewing tobacco in favor of strong cigars. He does not seem to have had any personal preference for cigarettes; his statue on the Duke University campus shows him holding a cigar.

For many years Duke discreetly kept a mistress, Mrs. Lillian F. McCredy, a divorcée who shortly after meeting the tobacco magnate established herself in a five-story mansion off Central Park West. He married her in November 1904, but their protracted attachment did not survive a turbulent and short-lived marriage. In September 1905, Duke brought a divorce suit that resulted in a sensational trial, and a divorce was granted in 1906. In 1907, Duke married Mrs. Nanaline Holt Inman, by whom he had one child, Doris Duke. He is buried in an imposing marble mausoleum in the Duke University chapel, alongside his father and his brother Ben. See John W. Jenkins, *James B. Duke* (1927).

WILLIAM GREENLEAF

DULLES, John Foster (b. Washington, D.C., Feb. 25, 1888; d. Washington, D.C., May 24, 1959), DIPLOMAT, graduated from Princeton (1908), studied at the Sorbonne (1908–9), and received an LLB from George Washington Law School (1911). In 1911 he joined the law firm of Sullivan and Cromwell (partner in 1920; head in 1927). Dulles served as a special agent for the Department of State in Central America in 1917. During World War I he worked in the U.S. army intelligence service (1917–18) and was an assistant to the chairman of the War Trade Board (1918). He served on President Woodrow Wilson's staff at the Versailles Peace Conference, was the leading U.S. delegate to the Reparations Commission, and then returned to his law practice.

In 1945, Dulles attended the U.N. Conference on International Organization at San Francisco, which drafted the charter of the U.N. He was the U.S. delegate to the U.N. General Assembly (1946–50). During this period he also served as an adviser to the State Department. In 1949 he was appointed to fill an unexpired term in the U.S Senate but was defeated when he ran as a Republican for a full term in 1950. He then became a consultant for the State Department. In 1950–51 he negotiated the U.S.-Japanese peace treaty, restoring Japan's sovereignty and allowing American bases to remain in Japan.

In 1953, President Dwight Eisenhower appointed Dulles secretary of state. He became the chief architect of American foreign policy. He argued that "containment" of Communism should be replaced by a policy of "liberation" of the captive people in Communist-controlled areas, but "by processes short of war." Dulles believed that peace could be maintained by threats of "massive retaliation" against any Communist aggression.

Dulles was also an advocate of international alliances. Following France's defeat in Vietnam (1954) he organized the South East Asian Treaty Organization (SEATO) to resist armed attack and subversion in the Far East; in 1955 he formed the Central Treaty Organization (CENTO) to meet aggression in the Middle East. When the Chinese Communists threatened to seize the Chinese

Nationalist–occupied "offshore" islands of Quemoy and Matsu (1954–55), Dulles urged Eisenhower to defend the islands, but the president refused.

In July 1956, Dulles announced that the United States would not finance the construction of the Aswan Dam in Egypt. In retaliation Egypt nationalized the Suez Canal. The British and French, aided by the Israelis, then invaded Egypt. However, Dulles and Eisenhower supported an international demand that they withdraw, and the canal remained under Egyptian control.

Dulles then helped draft the "Eisenhower Doctrine" (1957), which asserted that the United States was prepared to use armed force in the Middle East to stop aggression. In 1958 when the Russians threatened the security of West Berlin, Dulles urged that armed force be used to defend the area. In April 1959, his health undermined by cancer, Dulles resigned as secretary of state.

———

Dulles employed sharp cold war rhetoric edged by a grave, indeed dour, public personality. A fellow Wall Street lawyer observed that in court Dulles was not "one of these amiable persons," although in Washington he was more pleasant because there "we were both ... on the side of the United States." Such a personality fitted the anti-Communist atmosphere of the 1950s. Fearing their power and sharing their ideology, Dulles appeased congressional and other public opinion leaders who urged tough policies against Communism. One result was a purging of suspect State Department personnel; the resulting loss crippled the Foreign Service well into the 1960s.

Between 1944 and 1950, however, Dulles was one of the few who urged a more conciliatory approach toward the Soviets. His experience as a renowned international lawyer and his deep religious faith shaped this softer approach, for as a lawyer he conceived of the world as a cohesive system, and as a Presbyterian he believed good and evil struggled for control of the system. Dulles hoped that through conciliation the Iron Curtain might be lifted, allowing beneficent Western influences to reintegrate the Communist

bloc into the world community. This phase of his life closed with the Korean War, the appearance of McCarthyism, and his hope that a Republican victory in 1952 would fulfill his lifelong ambition to become secretary of state. The earlier dream of a non-Communist world community never disappeared, as the "liberation" remark revealed, but his failure to react to the East Berlin uprising of 1953 and the Hungarian revolt of 1956 demonstrated his willingness to work within a divided world.

Dulles was a strong secretary of state, working closely with President Eisenhower and utilizing the president's immense popularity. The two maintained close touch with congressional opinion, thereby carefully working in traditional constitutional channels that were considerably less utilized by administrations before and after. Dulles accepted the Truman administration's policy to build positions of military strength that hopefully, over an extended period of time, would break down the Communist bloc. Accepting Truman's policy of rearming West Germany, Dulles intensified that key commitment in Europe. But his most significant contribution lay in extending such positions of strength to former colonial areas. After World War I he perceived that European colonialism, which he condemned for its exclusivity and nondemocratic practices, was disappearing. He feared the chaotic aftermath would open the areas to Communist influences. Dulles never tired of quoting Stalin's remark, "The road to victory in the West lies through the revolutionary alliance with the ... colonial and dependent countries." This anticolonialism and fear of Communism helps explain Dulles's anti-European policy during the Suez crisis.

The negotiation of the American-Japanese peace treaty in 1951, Dulles's most notable diplomatic achievement before 1953, created a critical position of Western strength. He emphasized the reciprocal relationship required between Japan and Indochina. SEATO further attempted to stabilize the latter area, although Dulles then encouraged the South Vietnamese not to meet with the North Vietnamese, as provided in the

1954 Geneva Agreements, to plan elections for the whole of Vietnam. That decision was the fatal first step toward renewed war in Indochina and the ultimate undermining of SEATO. Here and in similar attempts to extend alliance systems to South Asia and the Middle East, Dulles mistakenly assumed that neutralism (which he thought "immoral") and nationalism could be subordinated to anti-Communism. In Latin America he followed historic American policy by indirectly intervening in Guatemala to overthrow a government that Washington considered dangerous to American interests.

Contrary to his highly publicized rhetoric, Dulles sought to maintain the status quo and extend the diplomacy of the previous administration. Rhetoric and policy further diverged when Dulles bent to Eisenhower's concern over the budget and accepted deep cutbacks in conventional military forces. This prevented extended American conventional commitment to supposed anti-Communist struggles, thereby lessening possibilities of such intervention. Nuclear weapons theoretically remained the important tool, but by 1955, Dulles began to realize their ineffectiveness in most diplomatic situations. Basically, Dulles was a conservative who attempted unsuccessfully to stabilize the non-Communist world through traditional means. See Townshend Hoopes, *The Devil and John Foster Dulles* (1973).

WALTER LaFEBER

DUNCAN, Isadora (b. San Francisco, Calif., May 27, 1878; d. Nice, France, Sept. 14, 1927), DANCER, left public school at 10 to study the dance. While still in her teens she and her older sister Elizabeth taught their "new system" of dance based on natural, improvised movements that interpreted music and poetry. In 1896, with her mother, an accomplished musician, she left San Francisco for the East. She met Augustin Daly in Chicago and then joined his theatrical company in New York. In 1899 the Duncan family traveled to London where Isadora was influenced by Greek art, which she studied in the British Museum. After private appearances in London (1900) and Paris (1902) she scored her first substantial success in Budapest (1903).

Duncan opposed constraining movements, clothing, and morals. She danced in a loosely draped costume resembling a Greek tunic and was the first Western dancer to appear on stage barefoot. Her dances were expressive improvisations with natural movements that were not readily repeatable. She was the first person to dance interpretively to music of master composers. She was innovative also in her attitude toward woman's rights. Considering the marriage contract degrading to women, she refused to marry but had two children, Deirdre (born 1905) and Patrick (born 1910), both of whom died tragically in an accident in 1913.

During the height of her career Duncan toured the United States, South America, and Russia, and established dancing schools in Germany, France, Greece, and the United States. She was an early supporter of the Russian Revolution, and in 1921 she was invited to establish a children's dancing school in Moscow. In 1922 she married the young Russian poet Sergei Essenine, Soviet marriage laws being more favorable to women than those of Western nations. She returned to America with him for a tour but was detained for a short time by U.S. immigration officials because she was suspected of being a Bolshevik. The tour was only partially successful, and she then left the United States for the last time. After 1923 her career was erratic. Facing the decline of her dancing powers and financial difficulties, she wrote her autobiography, *My Life* (1927). She was killed in a freak accident when her long silk scarf caught in the wheels of the automobile in which she was riding. She was pulled out of the car and died instantly.

⸎

Isadora Duncan, iconoclast, keen-minded adventurer, and possessor of undying energy, was made of the stuff of which new art is born. An innovator, a breaker of taboos, she liberated the dance from worn-out formulas; she brought interpretive dance to the world of choreography. Her piano-teacher mother put classical music and dance foremost in her life. She early developed a Shelleyan love of freedom and an obsessive devotion to self-expression, revolting against all superficially restricted movements and the confining costuming of the classic ballet. The dance to her was life; the art of dance had its own reward. She danced because she had to, and in the process transformed her impressions of the sea, winds, clouds, and man's joys and sorrows into graceful movement. She wrapped herself in the loose robes of the Greek goddesses and in every movement presented what could be called postures of perfection in plastic art.

She created more than one hundred dances, interpreting such classics as *Antigone, Oedipus Rex, Omar Khayyám,* and *Acis and Galatea,* and elucidating the music of Bach, Beethoven, Bizet, Chausson, Chopin, Gluck, Mozart, Rimsky-Korsakov, Strauss, Tchaikovsky, Wagner, and other masters. Wherever she performed—in America, France, England, Germany, Hungary, Russia, and South America—she brought audiences to tears with her brilliance. As the novelist **Edith Wharton** put it, "Suddenly I beheld the dance I had always dreamed of, a flowing of movement into movement, an endless interweaving of motion and music satisfying every sense as a flower does or a phrase of Mozart's." In Russia, Michel Fokine, master of ballet, became enchanted by her and was inspired to daring innovations.

But turbulence born of impracticality characterized her life. Being generous to a fault, she fluctuated between poverty and riches. She exulted in the ecstasy of Eros only to sacrifice the human lover for her greatest love, the dance. Despair engulfed her at the drowning of her beautiful children in the Seine. She espoused the Red Russian cause, thus arousing people of her homeland to resentment. When she finally married, it was to a Jekyll and Hyde who vacillated between alcoholic mania and beautiful serenity until he dramatically inked a poem in his own blood just before he hanged himself. See Allan Ross Macdougall, *Isadora: A Revolutionary in Art and Love* (1960).

THOMAS E. CHENEY

DUNNE, Finley Peter (b. Chicago, Ill., July 10, 1867; d. New York, N.Y., Apr. 24, 1936), JOURNALIST, served an apprenticeship on three Chicago newspapers before he became city editor of the Chicago *Times* in 1891. Thereafter he was on the staff of the *Evening Post* and *Times-Herald* (1892–97) and managing editor of the Chicago *Journal* (1897–1900). Using Jim McGarry, Irish owner of a Chicago saloon frequented by reporters and politicians in the 1890s, as his model, Dunne created his famous journalistic character Martin Dooley, the witty, philosophical saloonkeeper of Archey Road who spoke with a rich Irish brogue. Dunne and Dooley rose to national prominence in 1898 with the publication of Dunne's essay "On His Cousin George" about Admiral **George Dewey**'s conquest of the Spanish fleet in the Philippines. From then until 1910, in *Mr. Dooley in Peace and in War* (1898) and five other Dooley books, Dunne's humorous political critiques won him a wide audience. He established such dictums as "the Supreme Court follows the election returns" as parts of American political lore.

In 1900, Dunne moved to New York where he contributed editorials and Dooley articles to *Collier's* and briefly edited the New York *Morning Telegraph.* A close friend of **Lincoln Steffens, Ida Tarbell, Ray Stannard Baker,** and **William Allen White,** he joined them in 1906 to edit the new *American* magazine. In 1911 he undertook a series of articles on politics and literature for *Metropolitan,* a moderate socialist periodical, but he returned to *Collier's* in 1915. Though his Irish dialect writing had become dated, he continued to use it as a vehicle for his political commentary until his death.

Finley Dunne has long had a reputation as an American humorist that in many ways has concealed his real character and importance. His background in a shabby-genteel Irish immigrant's family and his early exposure to the poverty and underworld of Chicago gave him a critical perspective and attitude that the optimistic middle-class American Protestant reformer simply did not have.

In clothes and manner Dunne was extremely conservative; in much the same way the humor of his pieces masked their serious point of view. In fact, Dunne was often cynical and depressed, and his moodiness at times seriously hampered his writing career. His work and friendships associated him in practice and in the popular mind with the muckrakers, but this alliance was somewhat misleading. Dunne's chief interest was in character development, whether in the person of his friend Theodore Roosevelt or in the Irish models for his saloon characterizations. Only while developing characters in print could he express his strong views about social conditions and reform: his hatred of capitalists such as **George F. Baer** during the 1902 coal strike, for example, or his extreme dislike of militarism and imperialism. He was also a contributor to local reform movements in Chicago and Illinois, and was particularly savage in portraying figures like traction magnate Charles T. Yerkes as being rapacious and amoral.

Dunne deserves a small but secure place in American history for his reform journalism, his relationships to several important political and literary figures, such as Roosevelt and **Mark Twain,** and his contributions to ethnic and satirical literature. Indeed, Mr. Dooley is still probably the most quoted humorous commentator on the American scene, and his tolerance, pessimism, and cynicism are a good indication of Dunne's own views. Dunne should also be remembered as one of the first Catholic and Irish writers to establish himself as a national figure in American letters, transcending any sort of ethnic prejudice. See Elmer Ellis, *Mr. Dooley's America* (1941).

ROBERT N. CRUNDEN

DU PONT, Eleuthère Irénée (b. Paris, France, June 24, 1771; d. Philadelphia, Pa., Oct. 31, 1834), BUSINESS LEADER, son of the noted physiocrat, economist, and publicist Pierre Samuel du Pont de Nemours, was educated by private tutors. In 1787 he became an assistant to Antoine Laurent Lavoisier, a chemist in the royal gunpowder works at Essonnes. When Lavoisier was trans-ferred to the Treasury Department (1791), du Pont left Essonnes to help his father operate a new publishing firm in Paris. The du Ponts printed pamphlets advocating a constitutional monarchy and organized a band of sixty irregulars to fight for the Crown. When the monarchy fell, Pierre du Pont left Paris. Irénée, however, remained to serve in the national guard and to operate the family printing company. The Directory arrested both du Ponts in 1797. Following their release, they emigrated to America.

The du Ponts arrived at Newport, Rhode Island, in January 1800. After noticing that American gunpowder was more expensive and inferior to the French, Irénée decided to manufacture gunpowder. In July 1802 he formed a partnership with Peter Bauduy, a Haitian refugee, and established a powder mill on Brandywine Creek near Wilmington, Delaware. One year later E. I. du Pont de Nemours and Co. delivered the first shipment of saltpeter to the U.S. government. The firm quickly emerged as the leading gunpowder producer in the nation; by 1804 it had a network of sales agents and was manufacturing 45,000 pounds of powder. During the War of 1812 it sold 750,000 pounds to the government.

In 1810, with his brother Victor and his partner Bauduy, Irénée founded Du Pont, Bauduy and Co., a woolens manufacturing company. Unable to compete with imported British woolens, the firm failed, causing Irénée to become a high-tariff advocate. In 1815 he joined a group of Wilmington textile manufacturers to support a tariff on British woolen cloth. Thereafter he was a frequent petitioner to Congress for high tariffs.

In 1817, du Pont became vice president of the Society of the State of Delaware for the Promotion of American Manufacturers and a member of its committee to survey the state's economy. In 1820 he was a Delaware delegate and member of the board of managers of the National Institution for the Promotion of Industry, organized in New York. An advocate of internal improvements, in 1811 he invested in the Kennett Turnpike Co. (a Delaware concern), and in 1821 the American Philosophical Society appointed him to a commission to survey a route for a canal between the Chesapeake and Delaware bays. In addition to being a director of the Second Bank of the United States he served as a director of the Farmers Bank of the State of Delaware (1814–22 and 1826–27).

———— ⚮ ————

Eleuthère Irénée du Pont de Nemours is mainly significant as the founder of the E. I. du Pont de Nemours company, which has become one of the most important industrial enterprises in the world. Unlike his father, who was a brilliant philosopher and idealistic dreamer, Irénée had a practical mind.

Irénée, until the du Pont family's migration to America, was dominated by his father's thoughts and actions. It was through his father that Irénée met Lavoisier, who instilled in him a lifelong interest in scientific agriculture and botany. The father encouraged Irénée to train with Lavoisier, who managed the state gunpowder works at Essonnes. When Lavoisier was transferred, Irénée preferred to join his father's newly established printing business. Significantly, although P. S. du Pont founded the press and shaped the editorial policy, Irénée managed the business and despite the tides of revolution and terror made it profitable.

It was P. S. du Pont, in 1797 after his second arrest and incarceration, who decided that the family should migrate to America. He made this decision not primarily to flee from persecution but because his lifelong interest in America led him to believe that the New World offered superior economic opportunity. The elder du Pont planned to found a company to speculate in western lands. There would also be a trading firm to handle imports and exports. Pierre's two sons, Victor and Irénée, would accompany him and participate in the management of the new ventures.

Pierre's ideas were visionary and impractical. Previous failures of French, English, and Dutch land companies had destroyed interest in this type of project. And high prices for western lands further discouraged investors. In the words of

Mack Thompson, the historian of the du Pont family's migration, "P. S. du Pont had a penchant for being in the wrong place at the wrong time with the wrong idea."

Pierre therefore had to abandon his dreams of building a land company and use the little capital he could raise to support the foundation of a trading firm in New York, which Victor managed. At this point Irénée founded his powderworks on Brandywine Creek.

From the first Irénée's venture was a separate company. By 1802 there were three du Pont companies involved with America: Du Pont de Nemours Père et Fils et Compagnie (the father's firm), Victor du Pont de Nemours and Co. (Victor's New York trading firm), and Irénée's E. I. du Pont de Nemours and Co. Irénée's main problem was capital. He started with nothing but the skills he had mastered while working with Lavoisier and his father's encouragement. The powder enterprise cost more than $50,000. Of this the father supplied only about $16,000 through his company, which in turn received two-thirds of the stock in the explosives firm. The rest Irénée raised by taking into full partnership with him Peter Bauduy, who had already established himself as a substantial businessman and who supplied $8,000 in cash, and the credit for borrowing much more. At the start, therefore, Irénée provided the technical knowledge and management while an outsider made available most of the capital. Irénée's partnership with Bauduy proved difficult, however, and his goal became the purchase of Bauduy's interest, which he accomplished in 1815.

Things did not go well for the other du Pont enterprises. Victor's trading company failed in 1805, and in 1811 the father's firm failed with its powder company shares as its only asset.

The senior du Pont's failure left Irénée as the only du Pont financial success. Irénée, loyal to his family above all else, at once pledged to make good his father's debts, which he finally accomplished several years after Pierre's death in 1817.

Irénée emerged as a highly successful businessman, and his heirs inherited a financially strong powderworks. In so doing Irénée firmly established the du Pont family in America. The cost was high. Although he succeeded in his adopted land, he was never really at ease, and he always longed for his native France. As a practical man, however, Irénée realized that he could never return home and that his future and that of his family lay on the Brandywine rather than the Seine. See B. G. du Pont, *Life of Eleuthère Irénée du Pont from Contemporary Correspondence* (11 vols.; 1924).

STEPHEN SALSBURY

DU PONT, Pierre Samuel (b. Wilmington, Del., Jan. 15, 1870; d. Wilmington, Del., Apr. 5, 1954), BUSINESS LEADER, graduated from the Massachusetts Institute of Technology (1890) and entered the family's company as a chemist, helping to develop a smokeless gunpowder. He then engaged in real estate activities in Lorain, Ohio (1899–1902). In 1902, with his cousins Alfred Irénée and Thomas Coleman, he purchased E. I. du Pont de Nemours and Co., becoming its treasurer. In 1915 he organized a syndicate that purchased Coleman's shares, thereby gaining virtual control of the company. This action led Alfred to sue Pierre for breach of trust, but after a four-year court fight the legality of the purchase was upheld. Du Pont served as president of his company (1915–20), and when World War I broke out in Europe, it became one of the Allies' leading American munitions suppliers.

In 1917, du Pont began to purchase General Motors stock. In 1920 he became chairman of the board and president of that company. He was also active in Delaware public life, serving as a member of the state board of education (1919–21) and as tax commissioner (1925–37; 1944–49).

Although du Pont was a Republican in state politics, his opposition to prohibition led him to support **Alfred E. Smith,** the Democratic nominee, for the presidency in 1928. In 1932 he backed Franklin D. Roosevelt. He also continued to maintain his interest in state affairs, serving as state liquor commissioner (1933–38). Following the passage of the National Industrial Recovery Act (1933), which permitted industries to regulate themselves by setting up codes of fair com-

petition, du Pont was appointed to the National Labor Board, whose job it was to mediate disputes arising out of these codes.

In 1934 the Nye committee investigating the munitions industry charged that the Du Pont Co. was one of many armament manufacturers whose economic interests helped influence American intervention on the side of the Allies in 1917. This affair, added to du Pont's growing disenchantment with the New Deal, led him to help organize the American Liberty League (1934). Composed primarily of disaffected businessmen who believed that the New Deal was socialistic and infringing on their capitalistic initiative, this organization soon became one of the leading anti-Roosevelt forces in the 1936 presidential campaign.

In 1940, du Pont again became chairman of the board of the Du Pont Co. In his final years he contributed large sums to school construction projects in Delaware.

⸰⸰⸰

By the time he was 50, Pierre Samuel du Pont personally controlled the largest chemical and the largest automobile companies in the world. The assets of these two firms—E. I. du Pont de Nemours and Co. and the General Motors Corporation—in 1929 exceeded $1.8 billion. Pierre du Pont's achievements, however, differed from those of the best-known American business leaders. Unlike **Cornelius Vanderbilt, Andrew Carnegie, John D. Rockefeller, Gustavus Swift,** or **Henry Ford,** he did not create giant business empires. Instead he transformed existing enterprises into efficient, modern industrial corporations. No American businessman was a more successful corporation builder.

At each company the challenge of transformation was totally different, but in both cases du Pont's background and early training served him well. The grandson of **Eleuthère Irénée du Pont,** the founder of the family explosives firm, Pierre benefited from a tradition of commitment to business and a sizable pool of family capital. His education at M.I.T. provided him with an engineering and scientific background that gave him a rational and systematical approach to business management. In fact, because of his college training he reacted strongly against the technological backwardness of the family firm and left it in 1898 to join his cousin, Coleman du Pont, at the Johnson Co. in Lorain, Ohio. There he received invaluable experience in the technologically and organizationally advanced steel, electric, and traction industries.

In 1902 the death of Eugene du Pont, the president of the family firm, gave Pierre the chance to put his training to use. The older generation of partners willingly turned the company over to three young cousins—Alfred I., Coleman, and Pierre du Pont. The latter two immediately embarked on a strategy of transforming the small firm into a modern industrial enterprise. Since the 1870s the explosives industry, like many other American industries, had been run by a cartel of small family firms. The first step, then, was to bring the companies in the cartel together in a single corporation, the E. I. du Pont de Nemours Powder Co., which in turn was controlled by the three cousins.

Administrative consolidation followed legal combination. Pierre and Coleman placed the many explosives works (they produced more than 70 percent of the industry's output) into three operating departments—black powder, smokeless powder, and dynamite. Sales offices and agencies were brought together in a single geographically organized sales department in which salaried personnel replaced agents and salesmen working on commission. All buying became concentrated in the purchasing department. The traffic department scheduled the flow of materials in and finished goods out of the many plants and distributing warehouses. The new development department was one of the first in American industry to concentrate on scientific research in improving process and product. The financial office, headed by Pierre du Pont as treasurer, developed uniform cost accounting procedures to determine costs and prices and to provide for statistical data for the evaluation of performance of the divisions and the company as a whole. Overall coordination,

appraisal, and planning were carried out by an executive committee made up of the heads of the major departments and chaired by Coleman du Pont, the president.

Once this centralized, functionally departmentalized structure had been completed, Pierre rather than Coleman came to have the most to say about managing the powder company. Pierre made the critical decision that the company should expand by concentrating on the domestic market, leaving international business to European companies. He then worked out the plans for financing the building of new plants and the purchasing of sources of raw and semi-finished materials. After he became acting president in 1909 and president in 1915, he continued to be the guiding force in the executive committee. He was responsible for the handling of the antitrust suit that led in 1912 to the splitting off from Du Pont of two new enterprises, the Hercules and the Atlas powder companies; for the vast expansion of production to meet the demands of the Allied powers and then the United States for explosives in World War I; and finally for the program of diversification into chemicals in order to make the most effective use of resources acquired by the wartime expansion.

In April 1919, Pierre du Pont resigned as president of his company, fully expecting to retire from active business. In December 1920, however, he reluctantly became president of General Motors. Three years before he had agreed, at the urging of John J. Raskob, his most loyal lieutenant and successor as treasurer at Du Pont, and **William C. Durant,** president of General Motors, to have the Du Pont Co. invest $25 million in General Motors. The sharp postwar recession, by causing a precipitous drop in the demand for automobiles, threatened this investment. At the same moment Durant, by attempting to maintain the price of General Motors stock on the New York Stock Exchange, became suddenly caught with debts exceeding $30 million. To prevent Durant's bankruptcy, Pierre and his associates, aided by **J. P. Morgan** and Co., purchased a large block of Durant's General Motors stock. Then at the urging of the bankers and the Du Pont Co.'s executive committee, Pierre took Durant's place as president.

At General Motors, Pierre du Pont's challenge was to transform a loosely knit, promoter's speculation into a rationally organized, effectively managed business enterprise. He began by applying the accounting and statistical controls developed at Du Pont. He also set up a new type of administrative structure. The many divisions and companies acquired by Durant maintained their autonomy and their existing centralized, functionally departmentalized organization. Over them, du Pont placed a general office consisting of general executives who were relieved of all operating duties and a large advisory staff. In this new decentralized structure the autonomous divisions carried on the day-to-day business while the general office coordinated, appraised, and planned for the many autonomous divisions and for the corporation as a whole. Finally, he devised a market strategy of having a line of cars "for every purse and purpose." By the mid–1920s, du Pont's reforms had been achieved, and General Motors had become one of the most profitable industrial firms in the world. Of more importance, General Motors and the Du Pont Co. were already becoming models for corporate reorganizers and builders in many industries in both America and Europe.

In 1924, Pierre turned over his controlling share of both General Motors and Du Pont to members of his family, and in 1929 he retired from business. He then began to devote his energies to improving the educational system of Delaware, to enlarging the magnificent gardens at Longwood, his home north of Wilmington, and to building an impressive library of studies in business, economics, and French history. A strong opponent of prohibition, he became a leader in the movement to repeal the Eighteenth Amendment. Later, he helped found the Liberty League but took little part in its activities against Franklin D. Roosevelt's New Deal. Pierre du Pont's significant work all came before 1929, when as a major innovator in corporate management he helped make the modern industrial enterprise the most powerful private economic institution ever created. See Alfred D. Chandler, Jr., and Stephen Salsbury, *Pierre S. du Pont and the Making of the Modern Corporation* (1970).

ALFRED D. CHANDLER, JR.

DURANT, William Crapo (b. Boston, Mass., Dec. 8, 1861; d. New York, N.Y., Mar. 18, 1947), MANUFACTURER, grew up in Flint, Michigan, where he left high school without graduating to work in his grandfather's grocery store. After engaging in several business ventures, in 1886 he bought a Flint carriage factory; in 1904 he gained control of the Flint Wagon Works and began manufacturing automobiles. The following year he combined this company with the ailing Buick Motor Car Co. and soon built it into a success. In 1908–9 he bought out the Cadillac, Oldsmobile, and Oakland (Pontiac) automobile companies and formed the General Motors Co. In 1910, General Motors suffered losses and was reorganized by creditors who demoted Durant to vice president. He then organized the Chevrolet Motor Co. (1911) and by manufacturing a popularly priced car was able to stage a comeback. In 1915 he bought out General Motors with the support of the du Pont interests and formed the giant General Motors Corporation. During Durant's second administration only the Buick division of General Motors really prospered, and in 1920, when the post–World War I depression hit, he was ousted. He headed Durant Motors, Inc., from 1921 to 1929 when he retired from the auto business to become a stockbroker. Though possessor of a huge personal fortune, Durant, a heavy speculator, was wiped out by the 1929 stock market crash. He filed for bankruptcy in 1936, listing his assets at $250. However, he later regained part of his fortune by investing in the rayon industry and in New Jersey real estate.

"Billy" Durant was a man of vision and enthusiasm. He had outstanding talent as a promoter and salesman. He also had some organizing ability, but he had little interest in routine management. He was therefore very successful in getting enterprises started, but then he would lose interest and his attention would be diverted elsewhere, usually to something more grandiose and speculative. He could be remarkably astute in recognizing the possibilities of a technical device, such as the Buick car and the Frigidaire, but he also made serious mistakes because he was basically ignorant of technology and unwilling to listen to advice about it.

These traits show clearly in Durant's greatest achievement, the founding of General Motors. He had the insight to realize that in what was then a high-risk industry the best way to ensure both stability and growth was to have an organization capable of offering cars in a variety of makes and price ranges, and controlling its suppliers of parts and components. But having made this giant step, Durant expanded the company too fast and burdened it with unwise acquisitions.

The second Durant regime at General Motors was an enlarged repetition of the first except that the involvement of du Pont funds provided a sounder financial base. There was a period of successful expansion, including acquisitions that brought **Alfred P. Sloan, Jr.,** and Charles F. Kettering into General Motors. But then Durant became absorbed in stock market speculation, and his management of General Motors became so erratic that Walter Chrysler left and Sloan was planning to resign when the 1920 depression came along to force Durant out.

Durant's ambitions were far-reaching but fundamentally realistic; in other hands General Motors became the kind of corporation he had envisioned. His own failure was due to excessive enthusiasm that clouded his judgment. It was honest enthusiasm; there never was any suggestion that Durant's promotions were fraudulent or were intended to take advantage of others. His associates and subordinates were personally fond of him even when they disliked his way of doing things. See J. B. Rae, *American Automobile Manufacturers: The First Forty Years* (1959).

JOHN B. RAE

DWIGHT, Timothy (b. Northampton, Mass., May 14, 1752; d. New Haven, Conn., Jan. 11, 1817), WRITER, EDUCATOR, RELIGIOUS LEADER, was the grandson of **Jonathan Edwards.** After graduation from Yale in 1769, Dwight became headmaster of Hopkins Grammar School. In 1771 he returned to Yale as a tutor, studying theology in his spare time. A supporter of the American Revolution, Dwight served as chaplain to the Connecticut Continental Brigade (1777–79). Forced to return to Northampton by his father's death, he spent the next four years farming, preaching, and serving a term in the Massachusetts state legislature. In 1783, Dwight accepted a pulpit at the Congregational Church of Greenfield Hill, Connecticut, where he was ordained. Here he established his reputation. He became associated with a group of writers known as the "Hartford Wits," most of them contemporaries at Yale, who wanted to establish an American literary tradition. Dwight's *The Conquest of Canaan* (1785), the first American epic poem, came out of this school of thought. His later *Greenfield Hill* (1794) was a patriotic description of American scenery, history, and social conditions.

Elected president of Yale in 1795—a post he held until his death—Dwight became recognized as one of the most influential intellectual leaders of his time. A staunch Federalist and Calvinist, he frequently attacked the French Revolution, democracy, and infidelity. Often criticized for his conservatism, he received the title of "Pope" Dwight from his critics. At Yale, however, Dwight abolished many obsolete customs and methods of discipline. He encouraged the teaching of science and established a medical department. Always deeply concerned with the training of clergymen and theological education, he was a founder of the Andover Theological Seminary. Some of his many writings include *Theology, Explained and Defended* (5 vols., 1818–19) and *Travels in New England and New York* (4 vols., 1821–22), both published posthumously.

⸻

Descendant of generations of Puritan ministers, Timothy Dwight was one of the most fascinating and complex personalities of his time.

Spurred by a consuming ambition to succeed, he permanently destroyed his health while a tutor at Yale by a regimen of overwork and dietary self-discipline. Blessed by neither intellectual and creative brilliance nor the emotional ability to relate well to his peers, Dwight succeeded by hard work and mental discipline, which included a phenomenal memory and the ability to perform two or more tasks simultaneously. He was aided by a deep oracular voice and an imposing physical appearance that gave him the look of a leader. Those who knew him well found him curiously insecure and indecisive, particularly about exposing his literary efforts to public criticism. Much of his poetic work was done early in his career, typically published years after it had been written. Both his poetic and his theological work were largely derivative. While subsequent critics have detected some attempts at innovation in his poetry, it was done self-consciously and without real emotional involvement. Dwight did identify strongly with the landscape and history of rural New England, and his best writing was done in those parts of *Greenfield Hill* and the *Travels* that dealt with these themes.

Continually plagued by ill health, particularly deteriorating eyesight and excruciating migraine headaches, Dwight impressed knowledgeable contemporaries with his lack of self-pity and his drive to carry on. He was always torn between the emotional peace of the rural pastor—his happiest years were spent at Greenfield Hill—and the demands of active public life that "duty" and ambition brought him to seek and accept. Dwight's reputation was built on the degree to which he embodied and spoke for the traditional New England establishment of his day. See Leon Howard, *The Connecticut Wits* (1943).

J. M. BUMSTED

DYLAN, Bob (b. Duluth, Minn., May 24, 1941), MUSICIAN, was born Robert Allan Zimmerman. He learned to play piano, guitar, and harmonica while leading several high school rock bands. Graduating from high school in 1960, he briefly attended the University of Minnesota but spent most of his time in the bohemian folk-music circles of Minneapolis. In quick succession he idolized and absorbed the performing styles of various rock, country, blues, and folk performers. The most influential of these was **Woody Guthrie,** the populist balladeer.

Arriving in New York in January 1961, Zimmerman changed his name to Dylan and was quickly accepted into the Greenwich Village folk scene that included Jack Elliott, Pete Seeger, **Allen Ginsberg,** Hugh Romney, Phil Ochs, Joan Baez, Bill Cosby, and Dave Van Ronk. He fabricated an elaborate myth about his past, claiming that he was orphaned, abandoned, and befriended by various legendary performers, had traveled as a carnival freak, and had hoboed around the South and West.

Dylan's first album, *Bob Dylan*, was released by Columbia Records in March 1962. It showed him as a traditional urban folk musician, but by the time of its release he was writing a profusion of protest ballads such as "Masters of War," "Ballad of Emmett Till," "Talking World War III Blues," and "Blowin' in the Wind." This last, recorded by Peter, Paul, and Mary, sold more than a million records and helped make Dylan the darling of the radical folk set. Seeger, Baez, and others performed many of his songs, and he toured widely throughout the United States and the world during 1964–65. One of these tours was made into a film, *Don't Look Back.* Increasingly he substituted an electric rock sound for the simpler acoustical sound of his earlier successes. This alienated his folk following but helped to introduce him to a much larger teenage audience.

Critically injured in a motorcycle accident in 1966, Dylan did not record for two years. The albums released after the accident, from *John Wesley Harding* to *Nashville Skyline,* were recorded in a country style, which again shocked many Dylan "purists." His first book, *Tarantula*, a collection of prose poetry (completed in 1966), was published in 1971. Early in 1974 he successfully returned to the concert stage. He continued to produce rock, country, and even gospel music albums of his own compositions in the 1970s and 1980s, some of them selling into the millions. In

1985 he appeared at concerts to benefit victims of African famines, and in 1986 he toured Japan, Australia, and the United States with rock star Tom Petty. But although he remained active through the 1990s, appearing in concert and other venues, he has not been able to recapture the aura and musical power of the 1960s.

———— ∞ ————

Bob Dylan was central to the countercultural effervescence of the 1960s. Beginning in 1962 he transformed the radical protest ballad into a form able to make more general comments on the human condition. Most of his early "love" songs were hostile or frightened condemnations of demanding females ("It Ain't Me Babe" and "Don't Think Twice, It's All Right"), greatly expanding the range of the popular genre of love songs from the habitual focus on puppy love. The self-aggrandizing myths he fabricated about his past as well as his diffident attitude, unkempt, sickly appearance, and shy but hostile stage presence (reminiscent of James Dean) made him an idol of alienated youth. Courting teen-girl adulation but also fearing crowds and the loss of privacy, Dylan missed his chance to become "bigger than **Elvis Presley,**" one of his professed ambitions, when Beatlemania swept the world's youth in 1964. Trying to change with the times he increasingly returned to a rock-based sound that alienated his Old Left folk following but became a prime model and symbol maker for the youth-ful New Left ("Subterranean Homesick Blues" and "Ballad of a Thin Man").

His motorcycle accident and temporary retirement reenergized the myth-making about Dylan. Rumors suggested that he was incapacitated by drugs or destroyed by agents of the CIA. Many thousands, expecting Dylan to appear, traveled to the 1969 Woodstock Festival held near his rural retreat. His return to recording in a nostalgic country folk style helped to legitimatize the swing of the counterculture to romantic communalism. The *New Morning* album of 1970 showed Dylan still alienated from the larger society but able to enjoy the full range of human relationships and to understand without condemning. Basically content, he no longer spoke to or for youth.

Dylan's enduring impact has been to enrich profoundly the range of topics, symbols, and moods available to popular music lyricists. In a similar way his rough, individualistic delivery of his own material paved the way for other writer-performers to present their music rather than have their material be completely homogenized to fit the fads of the moment. Finally, while all lyrics are condemned as nonpoetry by traditionalists, Dylan's lyrics are being analyzed as poetry in some academic circles. This suggests that in time the standards of aesthetics are likely to change to accommodate the works of Dylan and his followers. See Anthony Scaduto, *Bob Dylan* (1971).

RICHARD A. PETERSON

———— ∞ ————

EADS, James Buchanan (b. Lawrenceburg, Ind., May 23, 1820; d. Nassau, Bahamas, Mar. 8, 1887), INVENTOR, ENGINEER, worked in a St. Louis dry goods store before getting a job as a Mississippi River boat purser (1838–42). During 1842–45 he operated a steamboat salvage business on the Mississippi, using a diving bell he had invented, and in 1845 started a glass factory in St. Louis. It failed three years later. In 1848 he returned to steamboat salvaging, was highly successful, and retired in 1857. He had acquired extensive knowledge of rivers from his work, and in 1861, President Abraham Lincoln sought his advice on the military use of rivers. As a result Eads obtained a government contract to build armored steamboats. During 1861–65 he designed and built fourteen "ironclads," the first ships with steam-operated guns. In 1867 he became the engineer for the Mississippi River steel cantilever bridge at St. Louis (completed in 1874), which necessitated the introduction of new construction techniques. He then undertook, against the recommendation of the Army Corps of Engineers, to cut a channel to deepen the mouth of the Mississippi. Jetties at the South Pass were built during 1875–79 after the federal government agreed to pay Eads upon the successful completion of a channel thirty feet deep. Congress appointed Eads in 1879 to the Mississippi River Commission to plan further navigational improvements and flood control. During 1881–84, Eads designed harbor improvements for Toronto, Veracruz, Mexico, and Liverpool, England. His *Addresses and Papers,* containing his contributions on engineering, hydraulics, and the behavior of rivers, was published in 1884.

———⚙———

Eads's importance in our history revolves around two interrelated activities: engineering and urbanization. The four major projects of his career utilized technological innovation to assure that St. Louis would develop into a national urban center. The design of ironclads during the Civil War was instrumental for victory in the West and secured the dominance of St. Louis as a manufacturing and commercial center. The construction of the first bridge across the Mississippi River south of the Missouri guaranteed the commercial future of St. Louis after the war. Eads's South Pass jetties provided a solution to an impassable delta where sand bars blocked ships exceeding a twelve-foot draft from negotiating the passes between the Gulf of Mexico and the Mississippi. A permanent channel opened St. Louis to lucrative eastern markets. Eads's unfulfilled dream to transport ships across Mexico with a multiple-track railway built without excessive excavation and time-consuming locks would have made St. Louis into a much more important international port than its rival Chicago. His plan, which would have shortened the distance between San Francisco and St. Louis by two thousand miles over the Panama Canal route, was approved by Mexican authorities,

sanctioned by the House of Representatives, but blocked in the U.S. Senate.

Though the exact place of Eads as an innovative engineer is still open to question and a definitive biography is yet to be written, he did attract many capable and imaginative engineers to his staff, and under his direction they tackled some of the most dramatic construction projects of the 19th century. Henry Flad, William M. Roberts, George Morison, Theodore Cooper, and Elmer Corthell were among his assistants who went on to become prominent engineers.

As an independently wealthy citizen prior to the Civil War, Eads could well have afforded to tend his rose garden and pursue his love of poetry; yet he chose to become one of the most controversial individuals of his age. Though often suffering from illness, he worked on the cutting edge of cultural and technological change. He did this with great self-confidence and bold determination, starting each of his large projects with only about one-tenth the needed capital for completion. One has to admire his persistence in the details of fabrication as well as his entrepreneurial initiative in channeling the diverse interests of **Andrew Carnegie,** Senator **Carl Schurz, J. P. Morgan,** and many others into his innovative projects. As a result he secured the future of St. Louis, embarrassed the prestige of military engineers, and exemplified the importance of the engineering technique in the urbanization process. See Charles Van Ravensway, "James B. Eads," in John A. Garraty, ed., *The Unforgettable Americans* (1960).

RAYMOND H. MERRITT

EAKINS, Thomas (b. Philadelphia, Pa., July 25, 1844; d. Philadelphia, Pa., June 25, 1916), ARTIST, studied at the Pennsylvania Academy of Fine Arts and at the Ecole des Beaux-Arts in Paris under Jean Léon Gérôme, whom he deeply admired. Traveling to Spain for his health in 1869, Eakins was also impressed by the Baroque realists Ribera and Velázquez. He attended classes in anatomy at the Jefferson Medical College upon returning from Europe in 1870. First as an instructor in anatomy and then as professor of painting at the Pennsylvania Academy, he insisted that his students gain a thorough knowledge of human and even animal anatomy through dissection in addition to their work in painting and sculpture. Eventually, his revolutionary methods, including the use of an undraped male model in front of a class of female students, engendered bitter criticism, which cost him his position in 1886. Except for the last six years of his life when he ceased to work almost completely, Eakins continued to paint industriously, to lecture on painting and anatomy in Philadelphia and New York, to sculpt at times, and even to take photographs.

Eakins's masterpiece is the large canvas of *The Gross Clinic* (1875, Jefferson Medical College), a scene in the operating theater of Dr. **Samuel D. Gross,** the foremost surgeon in Philadelphia. The tension, drama, and undisguised bloodiness of this unusual subject are portrayed in an uncompromising, realistic style that offended some of his contemporaries. A similar subject, *The Clinic of Dr. Agnew* (1889, University of Pennsylvania School of Medicine), is a later variation on the same scientific theme.

Eakins also painted many single portraits, including *The Concert Singer* (Weda Cook) (1892, Philadelphia Museum). As an active sportsman who enjoyed vigorous outdoor activity, Eakins is perhaps best known for his paintings of oarsmen on the Schuylkill River, hunters and fishermen along the Delaware, and boxers or wrestlers in combat, such as *Max Schmitt in a Single Scull* (1871, Metropolitan Museum of Art, N.Y.), *The Swimming Hole* (1883, Fort Worth Art Center), and *Salutat* (a boxer receiving the ovation of the crowd) (1898, Addison Gallery of American Art).

Scientific as well as artistic interest in the problems of measuring and depicting the human figure in motion led Eakins to experiment with multiple-exposure photography, achieving results that were unique in America at that time (1884). In sculpture Eakins's largest works were the two horses in relief for the Memorial Arch, Prospect Park, Brooklyn, and two battle scenes in bas relief for the Battle Monument in Trenton, New Jersey, in the 1890s.

In an age of international fame for some American artists, namely **James McNeill Whistler** and **John Singer Sargent,** Thomas Eakins was barely known outside of Philadelphia and New York. He annually sent his carefully crafted paintings and watercolors to numerous public exhibitions, including a few to the Salon in Paris in the 1870s, but he never tried to attract attention to himself—probably because his native Quaker reticence frowned on shallow displays. In 1893 when Eakins was asked to provide a personal sketch for a biographical dictionary, he replied by sending only the barest outline of his career with a simple explanatory sentence: "For the public I believe my life is all in my work."

In truth Eakins's private life was relatively uneventful. A more than dutiful only son, he remained extremely close to his father Benjamin, who provided the financial support and the constant encouragement which were needed to launch and sustain a career that was never lucrative. Eakins was also especially fond of his younger sister, Margaret, who posed for many of his early portraits and genre scenes at home; her death in 1882 was profoundly felt. In 1884 he married Susan Hannah Macdowell, who had been one of his most gifted pupils at the Pennsylvania Academy. In effect, she sacrificed her career to support his work, and after his death in 1916 she tried to see that his paintings were placed in important public collections.

As a teacher Eakins inspired lasting devotion and respect. To outsiders his unorthodox methods of art instruction seemed controversial, even heretical, but to insiders they were remarkably honest and thorough—like his art. Instead of drawing endlessly from antique casts, his students were encouraged to start sketching in oils as soon as possible, and every one of them was expected to take part in the smelly, unpleasant, but important task of dissecting a cadaver in order to learn basic human anatomy. The ability to create totally convincing three-dimensional forms was the ultimate product of this part-painterly, part-scientific training. In 1886 when Eakins left the Pennsylvania Academy, so did a number of his loyal students; at the new Art Students League they founded, he continued to serve as their friend and teacher, this time without pay.

In contrast to the dashing brushwork and self-conscious aesthetics of Whistler and Sargent, Eakins's greatest strength was the directness and honesty of his vision. To the refined Victorian sensibilities of the period his style and subject matter often seemed rough, ugly, and uncompromising. Because he refused to flatter his sitters, painting them as they appeared—frail, human, and careworn—he never became a fashionable portraitist. Without many commissions he had to persuade friends and passing acquaintances to sit for him in order to keep working. Official recognition came late in his career, but today Eakins is generally considered the best American painter of the 19th century. See Lloyd Goodrich, *Thomas Eakins: His Life and Work* (1933).

ELLWOOD C. PARRY III

EASTMAN, George (b. Waterville, N.Y., July 12, 1854; d. Rochester, N.Y., Mar. 14, 1932), INVENTOR, INDUSTRIALIST, left school in the seventh grade to work in a bank, and by 21 had saved $3,000. Fascinated with photography, he bought a bulky camera and wet-plate outfit but was unhappy with this tricky, tedious process. He invented a machine for coating rigid dry plates. By 1880 he was engaged full-time in the development, manufacture, and sale of photographic goods. Four years later he invented a flexible, paper-backed film that he sold, first in a roller attachment and later, box camera and all, in 100- and 25-exposure rolls, skillfully promoting it with advertising: "You press the button, we do the rest."

Eastman's objective was a strong, self-supporting film which could be processed by local shops and would be usable in the motion picture camera that **Thomas Edison** had invented. Experiments with nitrocellulose were unsatisfactory until Henry M. Reichenbach, a chemist whom Eastman had hired in 1886, devised a formula that, when processed by a technique and equipment of Eastman's devising, yielded a successful product. An eager market for "snapshot" goods had been created by the earlier film, and Eastman and Reichenbach quickly patented their inventions (1889). Assigned to the Eastman Dry Plate and Film Co., which had been capitalized in 1884 at $20,000, these patents were the basis for a business that after several reorganizations became, in 1901, the Eastman Kodak Co. of New Jersey. By Eastman's death the company, which controlled 75 to 80 percent of the American photographic goods market, had expanded its capitalization nearly seven hundred-fold. A policy of buying up related patents and setting up foreign subsidiaries assured the company's worldwide prominence. In 1914 a federal court ordered payment of $5 million for infringement of the claims of a patent that had been applied for shortly before Eastman's but never exploited. Eastman's domination of the domestic market was broken during the Taft administration when the company agreed to allow retailers to sell competitive goods, and in 1921 the company divested itself of a number of small camera, plate, and paper manufacturers, ending an antitrust action that had been instituted by the Wilson administration.

Eastman gave away about one-half of his wealth during his lifetime to a variety of philanthropies, the most important of which were the Massachusetts Institute of Technology, the University of Rochester, and the Eastman School of Music. Although often surrounded by celebrated guests and eager attendants at his Sunday evening musicales, he remained a lonely bachelor who shunned publicity and was rarely photographed. Less and less able to comprehend the increasingly complex business that he had founded, he was virtually inactive in the company after 1930. In 1932, Eastman committed suicide, leaving a note reading: "To my friends: My work is done; why wait?"

George Eastman laid the foundation of the modern system of photography and built on it the largest and most successful manufacturing company of its kind in the world. He combined in one person three qualities that the rapidly unfolding industrial technology of the late 19th century demanded. At 21 a shy bookkeeper content to bend over his ledger, as he said, for eleven hours a day, he nevertheless resented the advancement of a bank official's relative over him. He then revealed a talent for risk-taking that induced him to strike out on his own in the totally uncharted field of photography. Despite an education that had ended in the seventh grade, he experimented constantly, acquiring a practical grasp of chemistry and mechanics that went straight to the heart of the problem of devising a formula and a practical manufacturing process for a flexible, transparent, self-supporting film. And his own enthusiastic interest in advanced amateur photography did not becloud the remarkable business acumen which enabled him to see that what the public wanted was a simple, fool-proof method of taking and quickly processing "snapshots." From doggedly persisting work in the laboratory to the writing of advertising slogans that turned his early product's disadvantage into a selling point (he invented the name Kodak on nothing more than the feeling that "K" was a "strong" letter and was the first letter of his mother's maiden name), Eastman was the master of every phase of his business.

He never had to share his spectacular success with anyone. Few supported his faith in the feasibility of new films in the early days (Henry A. Strong was an extremely fortunate exception), and even his chemist, Reichenbach, destroyed a bright future by attempting secretly to go into business on his own. Fiercely proud of his company's products, Eastman abominated most of the goods with which others sought, by imitation or innovation, to compete with them. He insisted that he bought up related patents and companies only to keep inferior goods from being substituted for his. Whatever his motives, he succeeded in dominating his industry long after other "monopolies" had given way to competition or been broken up. The basic Eastman-Reichenbach patents expired by 1906, but a policy of plowing a large percentage of net profits back into further product development kept the company in the lead. No

less significant was the company's leadership in the art of continuous production of films and papers, as much a part of Eastman's contribution as the film itself. Neither the patent decision of 1914 nor the antitrust decree of 1921 had any measurable effect on Eastman Kodak's success. Eastman always saw the company primarily as an innovator. At his death it was on the verge of developing color photography. Precision optical goods were then virtually a German monopoly, and Eastman's failure to encourage the growth of a high-quality domestic camera industry must be counted as one of his few oversights.

The handsome profits of Eastman Kodak supported not only aggressive research and development programs, but an employee relations policy that included after 1912 a profit-sharing plan and, by 1928, a pension and life insurance plan as well. Eastman, who had found listening to music one of the few activities that could divert him from care and who believed that the growth of leisure time called for new forms of beneficial diversion, hoped in his bequests to the Eastman School of Music and the Rochester Symphony to make music more widely available. Another aim was to develop an American style of musical composition and performance rather than solely to mirror European musical ideals. His true monument, however, is Eastman Kodak, a model of corporate application of science and technology to business. See C. W. Ackerman, *George Eastman* (1930).

ALBRO MARTIN

ECCLES, Marriner Stoddard (b. Logan, Utah, Sept. 9, 1890; d. Salt Lake City, Utah, Dec. 18, 1977), BUSINESSMAN, BANKER, graduated from Brigham Young College in 1909 and then spent two years (1909–11) as a Mormon missionary in Scotland. Upon his father's death in 1912 he inherited a family estate of several million dollars, with which he organized the Eccles Investment Co. (1916), a holding company. From 1920 to 1934 he acquired numerous banks and businesses, and served on the boards of many corporations. The First Security Corporation, which he founded in 1928, operated twenty-six banks in Utah, Idaho, and Wyoming.

Deeply worried about the Great Depression sweeping the nation during the 1930s, Eccles, in testimony before the Senate Finance Committee in 1933, called upon the federal government to take an active role in managing the economy. In 1934, President Franklin D. Roosevelt appointed him assistant secretary of the Treasury and later that year governor of the Federal Reserve Board (1934–36). Eccles became chairman of the board of governors of the Federal Reserve System in 1936. During World War II he was a member of the Economic Stabilization Board (1942–46) and a delegate to the 1944 Bretton Woods Conference on international currency stabilization and economic reconstruction. He resigned from the Federal Reserve System in 1951 and returned to private business as chairman of The First Security Corporation, a post he held until 1975 when he became honorary chairman. Eccles was one of the first businessmen to oppose the Vietnam War publicly. He also championed world population control and spoke out in favor of closer relations with Communist China long before President Richard Nixon's opening to China. His publications include a collection of papers, *Economic Balance and a Balanced Budget* (1940), and *Beckoning Frontiers* (1951), his memoirs.

Marriner Stoddard Eccles was something of an enigma to many of his contemporaries. A free-wheeling Rocky Mountain entrepreneur, he pyramided a modest family fortune into a formidable western economic empire that included commercial banks, hotels, sugar refineries, lumber companies, and railroads. Eccles was, in short, the very model of the aggressive American capitalist, a shrewd practitioner of the free-enterprise system on the Mormon frontier of Utah. At the same time he became a passionate New Dealer, a firm believer in centralized economic management by the federal government, a tireless if ineffectual spokesman for Keynesian fiscal heresies within the Roosevelt administration, and a perpetual target of verbal abuse by the business establish-

ment between the mid–1930s and the early 1950s.

Eccles represented both an old and a new breed of American businessman. As a westerner he combined the hinterland's traditional resentments against Wall Street control of money, banking, and credit with the concrete political influence to do something about it. He used his position on the Federal Reserve Board and FDR's support to push through Congress the Banking Act of 1935 that gave to the Board and to the Treasury greatly expanded authority over the nation's banking and monetary system. From the perspective of Eccles and other western capitalists, coordinated public management of the money supply was more desirable than private control lodged in New York City. In the midst of depression, a tenacious Utah banker achieved what decades of agrarian protest and Bryanesque rhetoric had not been able to accomplish.

Eccles broke fresh ground even where western businessmen were concerned, however, by becoming a zealous advocate of compensatory fiscal policy during the 1930s. He perceived what few businessmen at the time perceived: deliberate budget deficits by the federal government could quickly counteract depression, restore corporate profits, and save free enterprise without provoking radical structural changes in the economy. Through its spending and taxing policy, Eccles argued, the federal government could become the benign underwriter of last resort, smoothing out the socially disruptive forces of economic booms and busts. Eccles's fiscal ideas were scorned at the time by FDR and his more orthodox economic advisers. They were, nonetheless, a prescient formula for salvaging the American economic system by making capitalist business cycles somewhat more bearable for those forced to endure them. See Marriner Eccles, *Beckoning Frontiers* (1951).

MICHAEL PARRISH

EDDY, Mary Morse Baker (b. Bow, N.H., July 16, 1821; d. Chestnut Hill, Mass., Dec. 3, 1910), RELIGIOUS LEADER, was educated by private tutors. In 1862 poor health caused her to consult an unorthodox doctor in Portland, Maine, Phineas Parkhurst Quimby. Quimby temporarily improved her health by using the unconventional medical device of suggestion. In 1866 she suffered a serious fall on the ice near her home in Lynn, Massachusetts. Crippled, she turned to the New Testament and received a sudden healing. This led eventually to her founding of Christian Science, based on belief in the healing powers of Christ, which she contended modern Christian religions had lost.

After devoting several years to study of the Bible, writing, lecturing, and demonstrating Christian Science in Lynn and elsewhere, she published *Science and Health with Key to the Scriptures* (1875), a book that has sold millions of copies to date. She founded the Christian Scientists' Association in 1876, the Church of Christ, Scientist, in 1879, and the Massachusetts Metaphysical College in 1881, the last two in Boston. In 1889 she retired to Concord, New Hampshire.

From that city she reorganized the Christian Science movement and in 1892 formed the First Church of Christ, Scientist, in Boston, which became the mother church of the denomination. She also wrote numerous books and articles. She founded the periodicals *Christian Science Journal* (1883), the *Christian Science Sentinel* (1898), and the newspaper *Christian Science Monitor* (1908). At her death Mary Baker Eddy left a religious organization of about 100,000 members and an estate appraised at more than $2.5 million.

The only woman in modern world history to found a major religion, Mary Baker Eddy was also single-handedly responsible for the survival and spread of Christian Science. In outline her life seems filled with drama and purpose. But, surprisingly enough, the first half of it was obscure and outwardly aimless. She was 45 years old before she found her life purpose. Not until she was nearly 80 was she a truly famous woman. And only after her death was she widely revered.

In childhood Mary Baker, often loving, bright, and appealing, was subject to ill health and occa-

sional hysterical seizures. Later, when she was a young widow, her health was so poor that her only child was taken away from her, and she did not see him again for nearly thirty years. Much of the first forty-five years of her life was spent in a search for health and for an answer to the riddle of human unhappiness.

Eddy's strong personality was reflected in the organization and doctrines of the religion she developed. From the beginning she firmly controlled the church she created. She was the sole source of the by-laws that still govern the church today. Christian Science doctrine reflected Eddy's strong Bible orientation and her conviction that "Spirit is God, and man is His image and likeness. Therefore, man is not material; he is spiritual." Opposed to this was the doctrine of "malicious animal magnetism," or "mental assassination," the belief that by concentration an enemy could poison or destroy a mentality insufficiently anchored in God. Eddy held that her last husband, whom she dearly loved, had been killed this way. Finally, reflecting its founder's sex, background, and outlook, Christian Science, which substituted readers and practitioners of both sexes for clergymen, appealed principally to women, to members of the middle classes, and to city dwellers.

Mary Baker Eddy had a curved nose, which stood out prominently on a long face marked by a wide mouth and a high forehead. Her most attractive features were her large, deep-set, blue-gray eyes and her exceptionally clear white skin. Her hair, which turned from curly chestnut to white as she grew old, was always perfectly set. She was slightly built but carried herself erect, walked gracefully, and dressed fashionably.

Sometimes visionary, usually giving the impression of gentility, refinement, and kindness, but occasionally blunt and direct, Eddy was imbued with great organizational and managerial ability, energy, unquenchable drive and ambition, together with a sense of destiny and self-assurance that enabled her to survive and to profit from disasters similar to those that swept away other would-be prophets of her day. Creating and saving from numerous critics and enemies an important religion, she has left a lasting and growing heritage. See H. A. Studdert Kennedy, *Mrs. Eddy, Her Life, Her Work and Her Place in History* (1947), and Robert Peel, *Mary Baker Eddy: The Years of Discovery* (1966) and *Mary Baker Eddy: The Years of Trial* (1971).

STANLEY P. HIRSHSON

EDISON, Thomas Alva (b. Milan, Ohio, Feb. 11, 1847; d. West Orange, N.J., Oct. 18, 1931), INVENTOR, had almost no formal education. In 1859 he got a job hawking newspapers and candy on the railroad between Port Huron and Detroit. During his spare time on the runs he set up a chemistry lab in the baggage car. In 1863 he became a telegraph operator.

In 1869, Edison patented his first inventions, a vote recorder and a stock ticker. After moving to New York he helped form Pope, Edison, and Co., the world's first firm of electrical engineers, but in 1870 he sold his interest and began to manufacture stock tickers. Using his office as a workshop he invested in the quadruplex telegraph (1874), which could send four messages simultaneously. In 1876 he devised the carbon telephone transmitter. In the same year he set up the first industrial research laboratory in Menlo Park, New Jersey. There he invented the phonograph (1877) and the carbon filament incandescent lamp (1879). The carbon filament lamp and the system of electrical distribution he devised were key developments in the modern electronics revolution.

Much of his later work was involved in creating and promoting companies to market his many inventions, such as the Edison General Electric Co., which eventually merged with the Thomson-Houston Co. to form the General Electric Co. (1891). He was also involved in extensive litigation to protect his patents. Edison gradually lost control of his companies to capitalists led by **J. P. Morgan.** In 1892 his holdings in G.E. were reduced to 10 percent, and he sold out.

In 1887, Edison moved his laboratory to larger quarters in West Orange, New Jersey. Here he worked more slowly and relied on detailed daily progress reports from his assistants. Countless products of collective invention came out of West Orange. The 1890s saw the development of a fluoroscope, a process for magnetic separation of iron, the development of the storage battery, the invention of a dictating machine, a mimeograph, and a moving picture machine.

During World War I, Edison was president of the Naval Consulting Board and directed research on flame throwers, torpedo mechanisms, and submarine periscopes. After the war he worked with **Henry Ford** and Harvey Firestone in attempting to develop rubber from domestic plants, a project brought to successful completion after his death.

⚬⚬⚬

The plain people of America made Thomas A. Edison one of their most admired folk heroes during his lifetime and after. He was the "smart one," the self-taught Yankee inventor who epitomized the practical genius of our people; his rise to riches from the lowly estate of train boy and tramp telegrapher, moreover, seemed a perfect enactment of the American Dream. Meanwhile, men possessed of formal scientific education tended to belittle him as a mere "mechanic," ignorant of the usages of exact science and addicted to the old cut-and-try method of invention. Later, more informed commentators expressed a more just estimation of his role, with **Norbert Wiener** holding that he was much more than an old-fashioned mechanical inventor and brought about significant advances in the very method of invention. Edison actually carried out a transition in 19th-century science from the old-fashioned individualistic way of invention to that of specialized teams, armed with good tools, engaged in systematic research. Apart from his many and famous inventions, Edison is now regarded as a central figure in the technological revolution of his time.

Curiosity was his ruling trait as boy and man. He learned from a popular book on science how to experiment with chemicals and the electric current of voltaic jars, such games becoming his obsession. The affliction of deafness in boyhood disposed him to work in solitude. He could hear, however, the click of the Morse telegraph and chose to specialize in this field. After some years as a telegrapher and an inveterate contriver of diverse instruments, Edison, at 22, blossomed forth as successful and rich, thanks to his improved stock quotation "ticker."

The turning point in his career came in 1876 when he gave up the manufacture of telegraphic instruments and moved to the village of Menlo Park, New Jersey, there establishing a full-fledged research laboratory in which he proposed to devote his full time to "systematic" inventive work. He equipped his laboratory with good scientific instruments as well as steam engines, furnaces, dynamos, and stores of chemicals and metals. A select team of twenty clock-makers and mechanics and one university-trained mathematician worked with him in what he called his "invention factory," where, he announced, he would be turning out inventions every few days—and even "to order"—then generally made good his boasts. Here was the first industrial research laboratory—only a few universities had such equipment then—which only years afterward was imitated by Bell, General Electric, and Eastman Kodak, and by European industrial concerns. The German scholar Werner Sombart remarked wonderingly that in America Edison had actually made a "business" of invention.

His remarkable powers of observation were soon shown in the making of the phonograph, a beautiful example of inventive work based on a new application of known scientific laws. After the famous hunt for the carbon filament electric lamp, the Edison system of current distribution in parallel circuit made light and power economical, exhibiting, as E. S. Hatfield said, "a wonderful power of going straight to the practical end, like Leonardo da Vinci." On the other hand his two-electrode vacuum bulb, which was his one important scientific discovery (the "Edison effect"), came through serendipity; he did not even understand it, though it led other minds to radio and the advancement of electronic techniques.

Edison had plenty of artistic temperament and was an uninhibited eccentric and an autodidact whose jests at the expense of the scientific fraternity sometimes caused men to regard him as anti-intellectual and reactionary. However, he relied greatly on some eminent mathematical physicists, such as A. E. Kennelly, and showed in his work a fine understanding of the principles of science (in his time) as well as a tremendous faith in the method of scientific experimentation. While he pretended to be only an "empirical inventor" pursuing the "silver dollar," he continued to undertake ever new projects and risked whole fortunes in them—only in order to "invent more." When his long-pursued ore-milling scheme ended as a very costly failure, he said with a laugh: "Well, it's all gone, but we had a hell of a good time spending it!"

In an era when too many Americans were haunted by ideas of acquisition, Edison, prodigy among the world's inventors, forever engaged in "making things," typified the spirit of workmanship. His innovations created new industries and incalculable new wealth. At the time of his funeral President Herbert Hoover desired to have the great dynamos of the country stop for three minutes but learned that it would have been catastrophic to attempt to halt the torrential flow of electrical energy that Edison had helped generate. See Matthew Josephson, *Edison* (1959).

MATTHEW JOSEPHSON

EDWARDS, Jonathan (b. East Windsor, Conn., Oct. 5, 1703; d. Princeton, N.J., Mar. 22, 1758), RELIGIOUS LEADER, graduated from Yale College in 1720. After studying theology for two years he became a Presbyterian minister but returned to Yale as a tutor (1725–26). In 1727 he became assistant to his grandfather, Solomon Stoddard, in the church of Northampton, Massachusetts, and in 1729 he became pastor.

Edwards believed that the Puritans, by adopting good works as a means of salvation, had strayed from the true Calvinist faith; he sought to restore orthodoxy to the Congregational churches. His preaching served as a catalyst for the New England phase of the religious revival known as the Great Awakening. Edwards's hellfire-and-brimstone sermons, the most famous of which was "Sinners in the Hands of an Angry God" (1741), described the omnipotence of God, the depravity of man, and the agony of life without God. He believed that salvation was a spiritual experience in which the effusion of God's beauty and righteousness is imputed to man, independent of effort on the part of the recipient. Among trinitarian Congregationalists his ideas had a powerful influence for nearly a century after his death.

By 1748, Edwards was refusing to admit candidates to full communion unless they could give very persuasive evidence that they had received God's saving grace. He revoked Solomon Stoddard's long-standing practice of admitting to membership and communion all those who professed faith and were not of openly scandalous behavior.

Edwards's congregation dismissed him in 1750, and he settled in Stockbridge, Massachusetts, where he served as a missionary to Native Americans. In 1757 he was appointed president of the College of New Jersey (now Princeton). He assumed the office in January 1758 but died shortly thereafter of complications following a smallpox inoculation. Among his important writings are *The Freedom of the Will* (1754) and *The Great Christian Doctrine of Original Sin Defended* (1758).

—⁂—

Jonathan Edwards came as close as any historical figure we know to living in absolute harmony with his principles. From the day in 1723 that he renewed his baptismal covenant and gave "all that I am and have to God, so that I am not in any respect my own," he seems to have devoted his prodigious intellect rigorously to the service of his intense, uncompromising piety. More than two centuries after his death he commands admiring attention as the exemplary Puritan, striving to think clearly in the world for the glory of God.

Edwards's powerful influence during the Great Awakening owed at least as much to his philosophical and psychological thought as to the few hellfire sermons with which his name has been traditionally associated. For more than a decade before the Great Awakening he had been working out the theological consequences of the Enlightenment, and he explained them in quiet, logical sermons whose explicit titles indicate the unusual lessons he drew from John Locke and Isaac Newton. Edwards contended that the new psychology and physics, far from overthrowing the sovereign God of Calvinist theology, proved man's continuing and absolute dependence on Him. The earth had been created not for man's happiness but for God's glory, and it was only as an expression of God's infinite benevolence that the earth and its inhabitants were even now sustained from moment to moment. Saving grace consisted in "a new sense of the heart," a transformation of one's entire way of perceiving the world. It led the new Christian toward true virtue, a loving consent to Being in general, a love of the largest benevolence, a love of God.

After his dismissal from the Northampton church, Edwards wrote the majestic volumes that established his influence for the next half-century—volumes on original sin, the illusion of free will, the nature of true virtue, and the purpose of creation. Many modern students have valued him even more highly for his brilliant works on the psychology of conversion, pamphlets and books written during and very soon after the religious revivals of the 1730s and 1740s. More than a century before **William James,** he wrote meticulously of the varieties of religious experience, and his efforts to describe the phenomena so that his readers might distinguish the genuine marks of divine grace remain among the best psychological observation and the best American literature of his generation.

We need not choose between those who have called Edwards the last medieval American and those who have called him the first modern one. He is equally in character as an impassioned believer and as a thorough, perceptive analyst; as an uncompromising dogmatist for a sovereign God and as a self-taught thinker insisting that liberal theologians join him in facing the implications of their mutual admiration for Locke and

Newton; as a proud and subtle minister teaching his people the truth and as an explicit defender of the democratic implications of his doctrine that true religion requires no formal learning but chiefly altered affections. His proud belief in the strength of human reason led him to conclude that the intellect was relatively unimportant in the highest human experience, and it led him to the tragic confrontation that ended in his dismissal from a church he had served for nearly twenty-five years. See Ola Elizabeth Winslow, *Jonathan Edwards, 1703–1758: A Biography* (1940).

DAVID LEVIN

EINSTEIN, Albert (b. Ulm, Ger., Mar. 14, 1879; d. Princeton, N.J., Apr. 18, 1955), SCIENTIST, grew up in Munich. He graduated from the Federal Institute of Technology in Zurich in 1900. Failing to obtain a teaching position, Einstein was appointed patent examiner at the Swiss Patent Office in Berne, Switzerland (1902). He continued studying in his spare time and earned a PhD in physics from the University of Zurich in 1905. That year Einstein published five papers, including his papers on his light quantum hypothesis, on his special theory of relativity, on the mass-energy equivalence, and on his theory of Brownian motion. These works brought him wide acclaim, and he was named professor of theoretical physics at the University of Zurich in 1909. He became professor of physics at the German University of Prague in 1911 but returned to teach at the FIT in Zurich in 1912. The following year Einstein was named to a research professorship at the University of Berlin.

Continuing his researches in relativity, Einstein published his general theory of relativity (1915), which interpreted gravitation in a non-Newtonian way. He won the 1921 Nobel Prize in physics for his photoelectric effect equation of 1905. Einstein joined the Intellectual Cooperation organization of the League of Nations in 1922 and traveled extensively; he also worked for the Zionist movement to reestablish a Jewish national homeland in Palestine. In spite of a period of poor health, Einstein published two papers in 1929 describing his unified field theory, which attempted to subsume both gravitational and electromagnetic phenomena under a single field-theoretical umbrella.

Einstein emigrated to the United States in 1933 to escape Nazi anti-Semitism and accepted a professorship of theoretical physics at the Institute for Advanced Study in Princeton. There he continued his researches on his unified field theory and its formidable mathematical and conceptual difficulties, many of which remain to this day unresolved. In 1939 he wrote a letter to President Franklin D. Roosevelt advising him of the potential of atomic warfare, which contributed significantly to the establishment of the Manhattan Project for development of the A-bomb. Einstein acted part-time as an adviser to the navy during World War II. He retired from his position at Princeton in 1945 but continued to work there until his death. He became a leader of the World Government Movement with other scientists and served as chairman of the Emergency Committee of Atomic Scientists to warn of the necessity for nuclear arms control. Some of his many books include *Builders of the Universe* (1932), *The World as I See It* (1934), and *Out of My Later Years* (1950).

Albert Einstein was the only physicist of this century whose achievements rank with those of Copernicus, Galileo, and Newton. No one produced a more profound intellectual revolution in our physical and philosophical conceptions of the nature of radiation, of atomic phenomena, and of space and time. His masterworks of 1905 essentially laid out the major avenues of research in theoretical physics in this century. His light quantum hypothesis, when finally vindicated by **Arthur Holly Compton** in 1922, forced physicists to regard light as corpuscular in nature under certain circumstances and hence to accept the fact that the wave theory is not universally valid. This constituted the deepest revision in our ideas on radiation since the work of Young and Fresnel in the early 19th century. Einstein's theory of Brownian motion, when experimentally confirmed by Jean Perrin in 1908–11, constituted very strong proof for the existence of atoms, and other closely related studies of Einstein established the pervasiveness of the wave-particle duality in microphysical phenomena. Finally, Einstein's special theory of relativity, which is entirely consistent both with experiments that display the nonexistence of ether and with experiments proving the equivalence of mass and energy, entailed the most fundamental change in our ideas on space and time since the days of Newton three centuries ago. Precisely the same statement can be made about the change in our ideas on gravitation precipitated by Einstein's general theory of relativity of 1915, which found its first confirmation through Eddington's solar eclipse experiments of 1919. Einstein's unified field theory, which he regarded as the capstone of the Faraday-Maxwell field-theoretical program, fared less happily, since its immense mathematical and conceptual difficulties prevented its completion. Nevertheless, the entire history of science teaches us that profound physical insights are usually reborn in one guise or another, and future generations can only profit from Einstein's strenuous endeavors.

To all but his very closest colleagues and friends Einstein appeared increasingly aloof and detached, even otherworldly, as he grew older, although his subtle sense of humor seldom failed to endear him to his conversation partners, and his commanding presence universally generated respect and esteem. In general, in spite of an intense concern for humanity and a deep social consciousness, he found less satisfaction in direct personal associations than in religiously contemplating the harmony of the universe. He despised educational authoritarianism, intellectual coercion, regimentation, and militarism in any form, constantly advocating instead intellectual freedom and pacifism. See Philipp Frank, *Einstein: His Life and Times* (1947).

ROGER H. STUEWER

EISENHOWER, Dwight David (b. Denison, Tex., Oct. 14, 1890; d. Washington, D.C., Mar. 28, 1969), PRESIDENT, graduated from the U.S. Military Academy in 1915. He served as a captain in World War I, organizing Camp Colt for the training of tank troops. He later graduated from the Command and General Staff School at Fort Leavenworth, Kansas (1926), the Army War College, Washington, D.C. (1929), and the Army Industrial College (1932). In 1933 he was General **Douglas MacArthur**'s special assistant and then served under MacArthur as assistant military adviser to the Philippine Commonwealth (1935–39), rising to lieutenant colonel in 1936.

After World War II broke out, Eisenhower was named chief of the war plans division in the office of the chief of staff. In June 1942 he assumed command of the U.S. forces in Britain. He led the successful Allied invasion of French North Africa (1942), which culminated in the surrender of General Rommel's Afrika Korps (May 1943). In 1943 he commanded the invasion of Sicily and Italy, and in 1944 became supreme commander of the Allied Expeditionary Force in Western Europe. He organized the D-Day invasion on June 6, 1944. After driving the Germans from France and turning back their last counteroffensive in Belgium at the "Battle of the Bulge" (1944), Eisenhower's armies invaded Germany. After the Germans surrendered (May 8, 1945), he became commander of the U.S. occupation zone in Germany. In November 1945 he succeeded General **George C. Marshall** as chief of staff. Eisenhower's wartime experiences are told in his *Crusade in Europe* (1948).

Eisenhower became president of Columbia University in 1948 but left in 1951 to become supreme commander of NATO forces in Europe. He was the Republican presidential candidate in 1952, defeating **Adlai Stevenson,** 442 electoral votes to 89. His trip to Korea (1953) led to an armistice, ending the Korean War. Elsewhere in Asia, he recognized the South Vietnamese regime of Ngo Dinh Diem (1955) when the French were driven out of that country by Vietnamese Communists. During this time the Chinese Nationalists under Chiang Kai-shek were engaging in an artillery duel with China from the small Nationalist-occupied islands of Quemoy and Matsu. Although Eisenhower had allowed

Chiang to take the offensive, the president, fearing an atomic war, refused to enter the fight. Hoping to allay tensions in the Far East and in Europe, Eisenhower attended a summit conference at Geneva (July 1955) where the major topic of discussion was the disarmament and possible reunification of West and East Germany.

In 1956, after Egypt nationalized the Suez Canal, Great Britain, France, and Israel attacked Egypt. Eisenhower refused to support this action, and with Russia also protesting, these powers were forced to withdraw. Eisenhower then announced the "Eisenhower Doctrine" (Jan. 1957), which asserted that the United States was prepared to use armed force in the Middle East to stop aggression instigated by "international Communism." He sent troops into Lebanon and Jordan when pro-Egyptian elements threatened the governments of those countries (1958).

When the Soviet Union launched its *Sputnik* earth satellite (1957), Eisenhower ordered an intensification of America's space program, and the first satellite was launched in 1958. After Soviet Premier Nikita Khrushchev's visit to America in 1959, a summit conference was scheduled for May 16, 1960. On the eve of this meeting a U-2 reconnaissance plane was shot down over Russia (May 1960). When the pilot confessed to being a spy and Eisenhower refused to apologize to the Soviet Union, Khrushchev canceled the conference.

Domestically, Eisenhower approved the expansion of social security, created a new Department of Health, Education and Welfare, supported federal school and highway construction, and signed the "Soil-Bank Bill" (1956) to compensate farmers for reducing their output. He was reelected in 1956, once again defeating Stevenson, 457 electoral votes to 73. In 1957 when attempts to integrate the public schools in Little Rock, Arkansas, were accompanied by riots and hostility from local and state officials, Eisenhower sent in federal troops to integrate the schools. During his second term Congress also passed a National Defense Education Grant (1959) to expand the study of the sciences; an Atomic Energy Cooperation Bill (1959) to

exchange information with allies; and a Medical Care Bill (1960), a federal-state program to help the needy and the aged.

After retiring in 1961, Eisenhower wrote *Mandate for Change* (1963) and *Waging Peace: The White House Years* (1965), memoirs of his presidency.

General Dwight David Eisenhower occupied a unique place in military history. He commanded air, ground, and sea forces in four invasions, the last of which—Overlord, the invasion of France—was the largest amphibious operation ever undertaken. In addition he was the supreme commander of the Allied Expeditionary Force, which made him the military head of British, Polish, Canadian, Norwegian, French, and other national armed forces in the European campaign of 1944–45. No one before or since has ever had to walk such a slippery tightrope between conflicting national interests and service rivalries, but Eisenhower did so without a misstep. Indeed, his most impressive accomplishment was holding the alliance together in the face of enormous difficulties.

Some called him "the chairman of the board" and dismissed him as a general with a big grin but an empty head, one who did little more than pour oil on troubled waters and insist that his British and American subordinates get along with each other. But in fact Eisenhower was an outstanding strategist. When he served as Chief of Staff George C. Marshall's principal planner, he suggested the use of Australia as a base for a counteroffensive against the Japanese. In June 1942 he selected Normandy as the site for the invasion of Europe. He planned as well as commanded the invasions of North Africa, Sicily, and Italy.

In the final campaigns in France and western Germany, Eisenhower insisted on a broad front approach, attacking the Germans all along the line. That strategic decision has been much criticized, first of all by British Field Marshal Bernard Montgomery who advocated a single narrow thrust toward Berlin. The critics argue that his method, although safe, was unimaginative and prolonged the war. In Eisenhower's view the single thrust was much too risky and might have led to defeat. His last important strategic decision—to leave Berlin to the Russians and concentrate on mopping up the remnants of the German army—remains the subject of bitter dispute. What is clear is that he was a forceful commander who had a tight grip on the battle and saw to it that it was fought the way he wanted it to be fought.

As president, Eisenhower is often regarded as having been weak, a tool of big business, uninspiring, and neglectful of the real needs of the country. In his view, however, the United States needed a period of tranquility and consolidation following the shocks and changes brought about by the Depression, World War II, and the Korean War. That attitude suited the mood of a majority of American citizens. "The bland leading the bland," one humorist called the Eisenhower administration. No real gains were made in reform legislation, and although Eisenhower presided over the initial assault on legal segregation, he did so reluctantly. But as the first Republican president in twenty years he did uphold the gains made during the New Deal and the Fair Deal. If he did not extend reform, neither did he undermine social security, welfare programs, and other measures, although many Republicans wanted him to. His was a stand-still administration, giving the country an opportunity to catch its breath between waves of reform.

In foreign policy Eisenhower certainly compiled an outstanding record. Despite Republican rhetoric about a death struggle with Communism and the need to "liberate" Communist-held territory, from his ending of the Korean War within months of taking office, to his resisting of widespread and insistent demands to invade Vietnam in 1954 to save the French position at Dien Bien Phu, Eisenhower kept the peace. These eight years of peace, in the highly dangerous atmosphere of the cold war, became perhaps his finest achievement. In comparison to his predecessor and his successors, he refused to participate in an arms race with the Soviet Union. His greatest fear was that such a race would lead to intolerable inflation, a military-industrial complex, and force the nation to ignore its domestic responsibilities. "Every gun that is made, every warship launched," he declared, "is a theft from those who hunger and are not fed, those who are cold and are not clothed." Throughout the second half of the 1950s, Eisenhower kept the number of ICBMs level at two hundred while he reduced the size of the army and navy. Within two years of his leaving office the United States had one thousand ICBMs.

Eisenhower was open, honest, friendly. His famous grin and relaxed manner drew people to him. He was a favorite with the troops because he took a deep interest in their well-being. His popularity was reflected by his catchy and universally used nickname, Ike. He had a legendary temper but a remarkable ability to keep it under control, and he worked effectively, if not always easily, with the great men of his age, including such difficult characters as Charles De Gaulle, Winston Churchill, Franklin D. Roosevelt, Montgomery, and **George S. Patton.** A German intelligence analysis of Eisenhower, made on the eve of Overlord, caught his character well: "He manages to inspire his subordinates to supreme efforts through kind understanding and easy discipline. His strongest point is said to be an ability for adjusting personalities to one another and smoothing over opposite viewpoints." But Montgomery, with whom Eisenhower disagreed on numerous occasions, has left the best description: "He has the power of drawing the hearts of men towards him as a magnet attracts the bits of metal. He merely has to smile at you, and you trust him at once." See Stephen E. Ambrose, *Eisenhower* (2 vols.; 1983, 1984), and Eisenhower's own memoirs, *The White House Years* (3 vols.; 1963, 1965).

STEPHEN E. AMBROSE

ELIOT, Charles William (b. Boston, Mass., Mar. 20, 1834; d. Northeast Harbor, Me., Aug. 22, 1926), EDUCATOR, attended the Boston Latin School before entering Harvard at 15. After graduating second in his class, Eliot taught mathematics and chemistry at Harvard, but he did not receive tenure. After a period of further study in Europe, he returned to Cambridge in 1865 as a professor at the Massachusetts Institute of Technology.

In 1869 Eliot published two articles on "The New Education" in the *Atlantic Monthly,* which led, although not without opposition, to his election as president of Harvard. Eliot inaugurated extensive changes at Harvard. He conceived of the university as a college surrounded by a cluster of professional schools, coordinated but with considerable autonomy. He made the recruitment of a faculty of active scholars a primary goal, raising the funds to expand their numbers and increase their salaries, and seeing to it that academic freedom was assured. He developed an elective system, modifying the traditional classical curriculum. After 1894 there were no required courses except for English and modern languages at Harvard (although Eliot's successor reintroduced some).

Eliot aggressively sought the upgrading of graduate training at Harvard. A separate graduate school of arts and sciences was set up in 1890, the first PhD having been conferred in 1872. Eliot's greatest successes were the medical and law schools, in which both the quality and the methods of instruction were fundamentally altered. An undergraduate degree was made a condition of admission to the professional schools.

The preparation of students for college was another of Eliot's primary concerns, and he strongly influenced secondary school curriculums by modifying Harvard's entrance requirements. He believed that the high schools and academies should provide a college preparatory education for all their students so that the individual could defer the decision about college attendance until his last year. Discipline at Harvard was greatly relaxed during Eliot's years, and compulsory chapel attendance was abolished in 1886. Athletics were encouraged, but Eliot never accepted modern college football, which he considered not a sport but a kind of war. His ideas about education and its relationship to life are described in *The Religion of the Future* (1909), *The Happy Life* (1896), and *John Gilley, Farmer and Fisherman* (1899). Eliot was

deeply interested in public affairs. He condemned the restrictive practices of labor unions but spoke favorably of such progressive measures as arbitration and profit sharing. An anti-imperialist at the time of the Spanish-American War, Eliot nevertheless supported enthusiastically President Woodrow Wilson's decision to enter the war against Germany.

⁂

Eliot must be ranked among the great enterprisers of the Gilded Age. He would have made a superb businessman, as the directors of the Merrimack company suspected when they offered him the superintendency of their textile mills just four years before he became president of Harvard University. The qualities he might have brought to Lowell served him well in Cambridge: the ability to capitalize on the ideas of others; enormous energy; a compelling if less than endearing executive presence. By all the quantitative standards of the marketplace (he increased the endowment tenfold and quadrupled the enrollment), his forty years at Harvard were a thumping success.

Yet he was not simply one of **Thorstein Veblen's** "captains of erudition," applying proven business principles to the merchandising of higher education. There was about him, as he acknowledged, something of the "successful Philistine" but also a genuine commitment to the educational process. Though not a profound or original thinker, and indifferent to abstract research, he effectively served the cause of disinterested scholarship within the university walls by acting as its ambassador to the world without. Part mediator and part advocate, he personified for his generation the proposition that these two worlds, however different their ends, were not inimical.

His temperament was bullish, though obscured often by his personal aloofness. Because of a birthmark covering the right side of his face, his childhood had been a trying experience and he learned early that discouraging familiarities, eschewing introspection, and, as he was always advising freshmen, "looking forward and not back," he could more easily live with his disfigurement, if at the cost of appearing "cold as an icicle."

Fortunately, he had less need for the affection his students and faculty withheld than the power (he called it "the increased capacity for useful service") his presidential office afforded. When asked during his first months in office why the medical school was suddenly being told to revise a curriculum that had served for eighty years, Eliot responded, "Because there is a new president." The medical curriculum was revised. Under Eliot parietal rules were relaxed, compulsory chapel abolished, the elective system extended, and a graduate school established. These last two reforms, for which his administration is principally remembered, were the ideas of others. An extensive elective system had earlier existed at Harvard under President Josiah Quincy in the 1840s, and the graduate school idea was pioneered in America at Johns Hopkins before being implemented in Cambridge.

Although unable to secure his elective system against his successor's modifications, to persuade parents of the utility of the three-year AB, or to convince undergraduates that football was brutal and baseball "tricky," Eliot prevailed often enough during his four decades as president to take cheerfully an occasional rebuff. Indeed, by the end of his administration his reputation as an academic statesman caused him to be respectfully solicited on all sorts of public issues. As with his educational views, his politics reflected his almost serene confidence in the perfectibility of mankind.

And why should he have believed otherwise? He had been blessed with opportunities for useful service given to few of his Brahmin contemporaries; in Harvard he left a legacy he believed would endure. "Your changed beliefs are an outcome of your experience in life," Eliot told a despairing **Charles Francis Adams** in 1914, "and my unchanged beliefs are the outcome of my experiences and observations in life." Twelve years later he died, a happy and fulfilled man, yet one certain, in his buttoned-up way, that the best was still to come. See Henry James, *Charles W. Eliot* (2 vols., 1930).

ROBERT A. MCCAUGHEY

ELIOT, John (b. Widford, Hertfordshire, Eng., Aug. 1604; d. Roxbury, Mass., May 21, 1690), RELIGIOUS LEADER, graduated from Jesus College of Cambridge University in 1622. After teaching in a grammar school at Little Baddow, Essex, Eliot went to Boston with a group of Puritans in 1631. He settled in Roxbury, Massachusetts, and the following year became pastor of the local Puritan church, where he remained until his death.

Eliot became interested in converting the local Native Americans to Christianity, and by 1647 he was able to preach to them in their language. An account of his activities, *The Day-Breaking* (1647), was published in England and resulted in the creation of the Society for the Propagation of the Gospel in New-England (1649) to give him financial support. Eliot started a settlement for his "praying Indians" near Natick, Massachusetts, in 1651, and several other villages sprang up shortly after. These settlements of converts maintained their own code of law and schools.

Sponsored by the reorganized Company for the Propagation of the Gospel in New-England, Eliot translated the Bible into the local Indian language, publishing the New Testament in 1661 and the Old Testament in 1663. He also trained the Native Americans to be evangelists and teachers and traveled throughout New England on missionary work. King Philip's War in 1675 ruined many of his settlements, however, as vengeful colonists and Native Americans attacked the Christianized natives. Only four villages were left standing after the war, and these soon collapsed. Eliot nevertheless continued his missionary work. A prolific writer, some of his many books include *The Christian Commonwealth* (1659), *Communion of the Churches* (1665), and *The Harmony of the Gospels* (1678).

Despite the heavy demands of his Roxbury parish and the needs of his own large family, John Eliot found time for more extensive and varied missionary activities than any other clergyman in the English colonies. Almost single-handedly he invented a written version of the Natick dialect, translated the entire Bible and dozens of religious tracts, catechized potential converts, created more than a dozen praying towns, and solicited financial support from correspondents throughout England. In many respects his efforts proved fruitless: the number of converts remained a small minority of the native population; his best efforts at racial harmony crumbled before the passions of war; and despite generous contributions from individuals and organizations in the mother country, his missionary work never enjoyed adequate funding. Yet he persevered until his death. As early as the 1640s he was recognized on both sides of the Atlantic as the embodiment of Puritan efforts to Christianize the Native Americans; no one emerged in the 18th century of comparable stature.

During his long and amazingly active life Eliot participated in most of the major religious events of his day. He took part in the trial of **Anne Hutchinson** and in the drafting of the Cambridge Platform, in both cases on the orthodox side. Because his *Christian Commonwealth,* which proposed that civil governments be reorganized according to strict biblical formula (he had employed such a formula in his praying towns), was burned in public, Eliot has sometimes been considered a theological maverick. The official objection to his pamphlet seems, however, to have been Eliot's chastisement of Charles I rather than his quixotic proposal; at the Restoration such criticism of the Stuarts appeared unwise. Eliot did diverge from most of his fellow Puritans in his determination to pay more than lip service to the oft-stated obligation to proselytize the heathen. In all other respects Eliot was the epitome of New England Puritanism. See Ola Winslow, *John Eliot, "Apostle" to the Indians* (1968).

ALDEN T. VAUGHAN

ELLINGTON, Edward Kennedy ("Duke") (b. Washington, D.C., Apr. 29, 1899; d. New York, N.Y., May 24, 1974), MUSICIAN, studied at public schools in Washington, D.C., and earned a scholarship to Pratt Institute (Brooklyn) but declined it. After briefly studying music with pianist Henry Grant, Ellington played the piano in small nightclubs while taking odd jobs to support himself. His first composition, "Soda Fountain Rag" (1915), was inspired by a job as a soda jerk. In 1918 he formed his own band, the Washingtonians, which moved to New York in 1922. Ellington played at Barron's in Harlem before going to the Kentucky Club in midtown Manhattan. From 1927 to 1932 he played at Harlem's Cotton Club, where his performances brought him national recognition when broadcast over CBS radio. He first toured Europe with his band in 1933, again in 1939, and many times after World War II.

Ellington composed more than a thousand tunes during his career. During the early 1930s he pioneered in extending orchestral jazz compositions beyond the three-minute record with such pieces as "Creole Rhapsody" (1931) and "Reminiscing in Tempo" (1935). He wrote such popular dance numbers as "Mood Indigo" (1930) and "Sophisticated Lady" (1933), and conducted "Black, Brown, and Beige," a musical history of the African-American in the United States, at Carnegie Hall in 1943. During the 1950s Ellington wrote such compositions as "Harlem" (1951), "Satin Doll" (1953), and "Night Creature" (1955). He wrote motion picture scores for *Anatomy of a Murder* (1959), *Paris Blues* (1961), (which gained an Academy Award nomination), *Assault on a Queen* (1966), and *Change of Mind* (1969). Ellington and his band toured the Middle and Far East in 1963 for the U.S. State Department. In 1969, on the occasion of his seventieth birthday, Ellington received the Presidential Medal of Honor and made a round-the-world goodwill trip.

❧

Although widely regarded as its foremost exponent, Duke Ellington considered "jazz" a term both demeaning and restrictive. He once loosely defined it as "music with an African foundation which came out of an American environment," while recognizing that what it primarily stood for was "freedom of expression." The last phrase is the key to the breadth that made him a unique figure in 20th-century music. His dislike of categorization was frequently expressed in words and just as frequently in music. He began to write extended works in the 1930s that went beyond the existing bounds of jazz composition, and he subsequently treated all challenges and problems as opportunities for the fresh deployment of his skills, whether in film or show scores; in concert performances by symphony orchestras or his own band; in music for major Shakespearean or ballet companies; and ultimately in what he, as a religious man, regarded as his greatest achievement the sacred concerts performed before people of all creeds in cathedrals, churches, and temples throughout the United States, Canada, and Europe. Internationally honored, he never lost his sense of proportion or his attachment to his musical roots. The blues are an ever present element in his music, and he always hired musicians capable of maintaining the basic traditions he established in the 1920s. His originality of mind inevitably made him a great innovator, but he was also a conservative who esteemed the best of the past, used it as his foundation, and never bowed to ephemeral fashions. See Stanley Dance, *The World of Duke Ellington* (1970).

STANLEY DANCE

ELLISON, Ralph Waldo (b. Oklahoma City, Okla., Mar. 1, 1914; d. New York, N.Y., Apr. 16, 1994), WRITER, attended Tuskegee Institute in Alabama (1933–36). In 1936 he moved to New York City where he worked with the New Deal Federal Writers Project and began contributing articles to such periodicals as the *New Masses* and *Antioch Review.* During World War II he served in the merchant marine.

In 1945, Ellison was the recipient of a Rosenwald fellowship, thereby enabling him to work on his novel *Invisible Man,* which received the 1952 National Book Award for fiction. Based largely on Ellison's own experiences as a black man in the South and North, the novel retrospectively depicts the frustrations endured by an idealistic young black. Disillusioned by the world he

has encountered and no longer able to endure the mental agony of his shocking experiences, the central character makes himself "invisible" by secluding himself in an apartment house basement on the edge of Harlem, hoping that someday he can return to a better world.

Ellison was a National American Academy Arts and Letters Fellow in Rome (1955–57). In 1958 he joined the faculty of Bard College, where he lectured on Russian and American literature until 1961. Since then he has been a visiting professor at the University of Chicago, Rutgers, and Yale, and has lectured on African culture at numerous other universities. In 1963 he was awarded an honorary PhD from Tuskegee. In 1970 he became the Albert Schweitzer professor of the humanities at New York University until his retirement in 1979. In 1969 he was awarded a Presidential Medal of Freedom. *Shadow and Act,* a collection of twenty essays dealing with his life and work, was published in 1964. In that same year he was also elected to the American Institute of Arts and Letters.

⚬❧⚬

No living American writer received as much critical acclaim and as many honors for such a small body of work as did Ralph Ellison for his one novel *Invisible Man.* A truly remarkable novel, it has spoken to 20th-century Western men in a way that few single literary works have. Its irony, ambiguity, paradox—its multiplicity of levels of meaning—have given the novel a depth and breadth unequaled in modern American fiction. Ellison put forth a particular vision of life, examining it through the course of the novel in intricate detail. That vision of life was one which held that in a complex, industrial age the individual was so terribly overwhelmed and powerless as to be incapable of making decisions affecting the basic directions in which his life moved. Needless to say, others, especially those more politically inclined, do not agree.

The title *Invisible Man* (note that it is not *the* Invisible Man), refers to a tendency that Ellison believed was characteristic of our time, a tendency for the individual in a mass, complex society to lose or have denied him his personal identity. Since the central character of the novel is a black man, the meaning of invisibility has more particular application as well: the black man, because of the assumptions others are likely to make about him based on whatever identifies him as being black, is categorized and defined as though social ideas and attitudes are capable of defining his *essential* self apart from his own special makeup. Hence, invisible man is at once man generally and black man particularly. In this way the novel, written by a black writer about a black character's experience, intends to be universal in scope.

Invisible Man is about a central character (who remains nameless) whose odyssey leads him from the rural South to New York and through a succession of experiences that ultimately result in withdrawal from the world into an underground retreat and, symbolically, into himself. As he progresses he is shorn of naïve illusions about his identity, his potential place in the world, and his relation to the society about him. Stylistically the novel moves from realism, through impressionism, to surrealism as the central character learns that things are not as they seem, that institutions may mask the operation of quite arbitrary forces, and that the apparent orderliness of the society about him only thinly veils impinging chaos. The more he becomes convinced of the irrationality of the society, the more he retreats into himself, becoming, finally, totally dependent on his own instincts and intelligence in order to define himself and reality.

Although there is always danger of error in identifying an author with a character, the similarities between the writer and the character are evident in Ellison's essays and interviews. The idea that the individual cannot be meaningfully defined in sociological terms, that the social conception of an individual can never approach defining the individual's essential self, runs like a red thread through Ellison's thought. Given this assumption, we should not wonder that he refused to be categorized as a black novelist and that he totally rejected the notion that his racial identity was in any way an index of his thought, character, or mode of response to the world. Ellison was strongly individualistic in his

thought, and the source of his individualism he identified as particularly American. The similarities between his own thinking and that of **Ralph Waldo Emerson** did not go unnoticed by Ralph Waldo Ellison. Ellison did not deny his blackness, but he insisted that his heritage and personal identity were within a larger historical and cultural context than racial considerations alone would allow. See Donald B. Gibson, ed., *Five Black Writers* (1970).

DONALD B. GIBSON

ELLSWORTH, Oliver (b. Windsor, Conn., Apr. 29, 1745; d. Windsor, Conn., Nov. 26, 1807), POLITICAL LEADER, JURIST, entered Yale in 1762 but left after two years to attend the College of New Jersey (later Princeton), where he received his BA in 1766. After studying theology for a year he turned to law and was admitted to the Connecticut bar in 1771. He spent a few years farming and practicing law in Windsor, becoming its representative to Connecticut's General Assembly in 1773. Two years later he moved to Hartford where he was appointed to the five-member Committee of the Pay Table, which supervised the colony's military expenditures. He was appointed state attorney for Hartford County in 1777, a member of the Governor's Council in 1780, and a judge of the Connecticut superior court in 1785. As Connecticut's representative in the Continental Congress (1777–83), Ellsworth served on several committees, including the Committee of Appeals, which decided federal-state conflicts over the disposition of ships captured by American vessels. In 1787 he was selected to be one of Connecticut's three delegates to the federal Constitutional Convention. In the debate between small states and large states over representation in the proposed new government, Ellsworth advocated a system that eventually met the demands of both. The Connecticut Compromise established a bicameral legislature with proportionate representation in the House of Representatives and equal representation in the Senate. Ellsworth proposed the name "the government of the United States" to replace "the national government" and was an active member of the committee that dealt with the judiciary. He viewed the Supreme Court as the interpreter of the Constitution. In the slavery debate he supported the three-fifths ratio for counting slaves for both taxation and representation, and opposed abolition of the slave trade.

A Federalist, Ellsworth was elected as one of Connecticut's first two senators (1789–96). As chairman of the committee responsible for the Judiciary Act (1789), he drafted the bill outlining the federal judicial system. He supported **Alexander Hamilton**'s economic policies, took part in devising the economic boycott designed to bring Rhode Island into the union, and, having suggested **John Jay**'s mission to England, influenced the Senate's approval of the Jay Treaty. In 1796 he was appointed by President John Adams to succeed John Jay as chief justice of the Supreme Court. In 1799 he was asked by Adams to participate in negotiations with France in order to avert increasing hostilities. He arrived in Paris in 1800. After directing negotiations with Napoleon and coming to an agreement regarding freedom of commerce between France and the United States, Ellsworth returned to America in 1801. He then resigned from the Supreme Court because of poor health but continued to participate in Connecticut politics.

———— ⊗⊗ ————

Ellsworth was one of the leading members of Connecticut's revolutionary generation, and while only a second-echelon figure on the national level he nonetheless made a number of valuable contributions to the establishment of a viable government under the United States Constitution. At first glance a somewhat eccentric figure who dressed elegantly, indulged in snuff, and frequently talked to himself, he was in reality a forceful leader and effective debater, a man of integrity and ability. Although a firm Federalist, he was not an absolutist or purist like so many of that party. A politician as well as a revolutionary, he engaged in a number of constructive compromises during his career. Although a warm advocate of a strong and active

federal government whose powers would be derived mainly from the people and not from the states as under the Articles of Confederation, he was one of the first members of the Constitutional Convention to reject the extreme nationalist position of the Virginia Plan. "The only chance of supporting a general government lies in grafting it on those of the original states," he argued. As architect of the highly controversial federal judiciary system he shrewdly allowed the state courts to have concurrent jurisdiction in very broad areas. Finally, in 1799, Ellsworth broke with some of his closest associates in the Federalist party to help negotiate peace with France because he felt it was in the best interests of the country. See William Garrott Brown, *The Life of Oliver Ellsworth* (1905).

RICHARD E. ELLIS

ELY, Richard Theodore (b. Ripley, N.Y., Apr. 13, 1854; d. Old Lyme, Conn., Oct. 4, 1943), SOCIAL SCIENTIST, attended Dartmouth, graduated from Columbia in 1876. He then studied philosophy in Europe but soon became interested in political economy. After earning his PhD from the University of Heidelberg in 1879, under economist Karl Knies, Ely accepted a teaching position at Johns Hopkins in 1881. At Johns Hopkins, Ely became increasingly shocked by injustices in the American social order; he spoke out against woman and child labor and attacked the evils of big business and monopolies. Becoming embroiled in the controversy between "old" and "new" economics, Ely participated in the founding of the American Economic Association in 1885, an organization that led the attack on classical and laissez-faire economics. He was the AEA's first secretary and later president (1899–1901). A deeply religious man, Ely believed that churches had a duty to the social order and was active in such organizations as the Christian Social Union. His *Social Aspects of Christianity* (1889) articulately stated his views and was a best-seller.

Ely became chairman of the economics, political science, and history department at the

University of Wisconsin in 1892. He worked closely with **Robert La Follette** and other Progressive leaders in the state to make Wisconsin into the "laboratory" of the Progressive movement. Always interested in organized labor, Ely was the first president of the American Association for Labor Legislation (1907–8). Ely was also a leading proponent of academic freedom. He established the Institute for Research in Land Economics and Public Utilities in 1920 and its *Journal* in 1925. Some of his many scholarly writings include *Monopolies and Trusts* (1900), *Outlines of Economics* (6th ed., 1937), and *Ground Under Our Feet* (1938), his autobiography.

※

In the late 19th century Ely was a leader of a wide-ranging revolt against absolutistic social theory. The classical economists, Ely argued, had conferred the dignity, permanency, and universality of natural law on their economic principles. Ely found their ideas antithetical not only to traditional Christian ethics but also to the findings of modern science. The economic behavior of man, unlike other animals, was shaped by history. Thus an ever changing economic theory should reflect each stage of a society's evolution. This viewpoint would soon prevail in both philosophy and the social sciences in America. The social sciences were also to be normative, that is, as a method of resolving social problems. The goal, to Ely, was simply the practice of the Golden Rule in social relations. He indicted American society for allowing the amoral booster to define the criteria for success and the machine to become ascendant over man. Yet his preaching of brotherhood and his advocacy of a "Golden Mean" between socialism and private enterprise seldom confronted directly the existing power structure of society. For he uneasily shared both the values of a simple Christianity and the values of the American gospel of success. His ambition to be recognized as an original economic theorist seemed to conflict with an equal desire to remake his world. The failure of the public to respond instantly to his mission and of

his fellow professors to perceive both his accomplishments and the righteousness of his cause sometimes led to personal bitterness and an attitude of moral superiority. By confusing criticism of his methods with a personal challenge to his sincerity, he sometimes offended and even abused his closest friends. See Benjamin G. Rader, *The Academic Mind and Reform: The Influence of Richard T. Ely in American Life* (1966).

BENJAMIN G. RADER

EMERSON, Ralph Waldo (b. Boston, Mass., May 25, 1803; d. Concord, Mass., Apr. 27, 1882), WRITER, graduated from Harvard in 1821. During 1821–25 he helped his brother run a finishing school for girls in Boston. In 1825 he entered Harvard's Divinity School, but ill health forced him to leave after only one month of study. After working on a farm in Newton, Massachusetts, he again taught school. In 1826 he was "approbated to preach" as a Unitarian minister by the Middlesex Association of Ministers. He spent the winter of 1826 in Georgia and Florida. After preaching in various New England churches, in 1829 he was elected by the Second Church (Unitarian) of Boston to serve as the Reverend Henry Ware's colleague. A few weeks later he assumed full charge of the church. He resigned in 1832, however, because he could no longer conscientiously administer the Lord's Supper, arguing that the bread and wine sacrament had become a meaningless ritual, too far removed from its original symbolic immediacy. In his *Journals,* which he started to keep while at Harvard, he wrote that the clerical profession was "antiquated."

In 1832–33, Emerson traveled in Europe where he met Samuel T. Coleridge, William Wordsworth, and Thomas Carlyle. With the last he carried on a correspondence lasting almost forty years. Upon his return to the United States he did some preaching but soon abandoned the pulpit for the lecture platform. In 1834 he moved to Concord where he met **Henry David Thoreau** and helped start the Transcendental Club. In 1836, Emerson published *Nature,* the first full expression of American transcendentalism, a mystical and intuitive way of perceiving life which argued that man, a part of "divine" Nature, could transcend reason through faith in himself and in the basic benevolence of the universe, and thus stretch *beyond* his known capacities, which indeed were limitless. In August 1837, Emerson delivered the Phi Beta Kappa oration at Harvard, "The American Scholar," calling on Americans to put aside their concern for European values and seek inspiration in their own culture. In July 1838 he delivered the "Divinity School Address" at Harvard, an attack on the clerical establishment that made him *persona non grata* at Harvard for about thirty years.

In July 1840, Emerson helped found the *Dial*, the transcendentalist magazine that he edited from 1842 to 1844. In this period he published his *Essays* (1st ser., 1841; 2d ser., 1844), some of the best known of which include "Self-Reliance," calling on man to "transcend" his environment in order to make use of his unlimited capacities; the "Over-Soul," a mystical, neo-Platonic statement arguing that the Over-Soul is the reservoir of spiritual power; "Circles," in which the image of the circle is Emerson's symbol of perfection; and "The Poet," who, according to Emerson, is supposed to be the transmitter of the "truth."

In 1847–48 he traveled abroad, lecturing in England and France. In 1847 he published a volume of *Poems*. Long an opponent of slavery, Emerson became more outspoken in his attacks on that institution after the passage of the Fugitive Slave Act (1850). In 1857 he met **John Brown** and sympathized with his attempts to free the southern slaves.

In 1870, Emerson was again asked to lecture at Harvard, but in his last years he was often sick and lost all his mental powers. His essays and other writings were published in *Addresses and Lectures* (1849), *Representative Men* (1850), *English Traits* (1856), *The Conduct of Life* (1860), *Society and Solitude* (1870), and *Letters and Social Aims* (1876). Among his best-known poems are "Concord Hymn" (1837), "Each and All" (1839), "Compensation" (1841), "Hamatreya" (1847), and "Brahma" (1857).

It is good Emersonian doctrine to establish an "original relation" with nature or with minds and artifacts inspired by nature—never to resort to intermediaries. Protean Emerson is best seen in his essays, poems, and journals, where he appears in a variety of guises: iconoclast, prophet, revolutionist, elitist, scholar. The portrait of the bland Concord sage looking serenely on the shambles of the world is as partial as the others. Less familiar is the writer who for all of his affirmations about self-reliance and the integrity of the self conducted throughout most of his literary life a dialogue between his sundered and antithetical selves. Even further in the shadows lurks the troubled husband-father, unsure of his vocation, whose often-quoted apothegms on a kindly destiny and the superficiality of sorrow were uttered in the teeth of personal affliction. The "Orpheus of optimism" experienced the black night that hedged "the facts of our being" and declared that those unacquainted with the House of Pain knew only half of the universe. Evil remained for him an *objective* fact although one that might be *subjectively* dissolved.

Emerson may have been the last American artist of distinction whose own divided loyalties enabled him to mediate between materialists and utilitarians ("men of understanding," he called them, rooted in a pig-led world and unable to translate Nature's hieroglyphics) and radical idealists, whose case he argued before the intolerant majority. He supported all sorts of schemes to unshackle the human spirit, and (more strongly after the 1840s) he came to respect the interdicts of Fate or Necessity that restrained it. As the reformer, agitator for the Party of Hope and the religion of the affections, he discovered useful truths in the claims of cranks, in fads and utopian schemes. But Emerson, the Yankee pragmatist, was also charmed by skeptics and practical doers. He responded to—even identified with—the "bruisers" who demonstrated their superiority over the "agglutinated" masses by converting "the sap and juices of the planet to the incarnation and nutriment of their design."

Whether he spoke for wealth and power or for the exponents of transcendental "wild oats," he did so as a revolutionist of the word. His works are a sustained experiment in language, an effort to cut through dead verbiage to the hardpan of reality and approximate in words the "veracity of angles." The enduring Emerson is not the neo-Platonist or Abolitionist or Propagandist or Yea-Sayer or Maxim-Monger but the poet with a "festal style" who established a bridge between the commonplace world and the supersensible regions and made the ordinary extraordinary. He is the master of paradox brilliantly invalidating his own pronouncements.

Emerson called upon his auditors to disdain the "courtly muses" of Europe, distrust bookworms, and worship nature as the abiding fount of inspiration, yet his own speculations were the fruition of a lifetime of reading, and he was more at home in his study than in the woods. The dominating literary figure of his age, he simultaneously glorified and subverted its assumptions. He inspired a number of disciples, some of whom (most notably Thoreau and **Walt Whitman**) carried his principles beyond the point he had wished to take them and were true to the spirit of his teachings in rejecting his authority. In writing about himself he became the biographer of his countrymen or at least their interpreter by recording America's aspirations as well as its noise and bustle and by articulating for the world what he took to be the happy import of democratic tumult.

Although his auguries seem less valid today than the dark premonitions of **Nathaniel Hawthorne** and **Herman Melville,** the confidence he radiated was shared by his confident generation. On occasion he failed to live up to the exalted standards he set for the American Scholar. His parochialism and prejudices sometimes clouded his vision; his shyness and coldness clashed with the genial salutations he made to his audience. In his best and most typical moments, however, he did not betray the scholar's obligations and met Albert Camus's definition of an intellectual: "someone whose mind

watches itself." Emerson still speaks directly to the private ear, is still the liberating intelligence. Like the poets he celebrated, he "planted the standard of humanity some furlongs forward into Chaos." See Ralph L. Rusk, *The Life of Ralph Waldo Emerson* (1949).

DANIEL AARON

ERIKSON, Erik Homburger (b. Frankfurt-am-Main, Ger., June 15, 1902; d. Harwich, Mass., May 12, 1994), EDUCATOR, PSYCHOANALYST, studied art at art schools in Karlsruhe and Munich (1921–24), traveled in Germany and Italy (1924–27), then returned to Karlsruhe to teach art. In 1927, however, at the invitation of his friend Peter Blos, he became a teacher in an experimental school that Blos ran in Vienna. There he became acquainted with the members of the Vienna Psychoanalytic Society, which had developed around Sigmund Freud. During 1929–33, Erikson studied at the Vienna Psychoanalytic Institute, working especially with Anna Freud. After the Nazi seizure of power in 1933 he left Vienna, traveling first to Denmark and then to the United States where he held positions at the Harvard Medical School (1934–35), the Yale Medical School (1936–39), and the University of California at Berkeley and at San Francisco (1939–51). In 1951, Erikson refused to sign a "loyalty oath" demanded of all faculty by the university regents. Although he was retained, he resigned when others who refused to sign were dismissed. During 1951–60 he served as a senior staff member at the Austen Riggs Center in Stockbridge, Massachusetts, an experimental institute for the treatment of emotionally disturbed adults and adolescents. In 1960 he was appointed professor of human development and lecturer in psychiatry at Harvard.

Erikson first gained widespread fame in 1950 when *Childhood and Society* was published. In this book, as well as in such later theoretical works as *Insight and Responsibility* (1964) and *Identity: Youth and Crisis* (1968), Erikson, though still working within the Freudian tradition, introduced major modifications into that system of analysis. He emphasized the concept of "eight stages of life," ranging from infancy to old age, each associated with a "crisis" that has to be surmounted if the individual is to be free of neuroses. In his theoretical works as well as in his psychohistorical studies, *Young Man Luther* (1958) and *Gandhi's Truth* (1969), Erikson emphasized the interaction of external forces, notably culture, society, and even contemporary history, with the development of the individual psyche.

In 1970, Erikson formally retired from Harvard. Living in Cape Cod, Massachusetts, and Marin County, California, he continued to write essays and books and to lecture. In 1987 he moved back permanently to Cambridge, Massachusetts, because of the establishment there of the Eric Erikson Center for clinicians and scholars. During these years he published studies dealing with the last stage of life, old age: *The Life Cycle Completed* (1982) and *Vital Involvement in Old Age* (1986), coauthored with his wife, Helen Kivnick. A collection of his papers, *A Way of Looking at Things*, edited by Stephen Schlein, came out in 1987.

※

Of all the very talented thinkers who have worked in the psychoanalytic tradition, Erikson was the most creative except for Freud himself. As an artist Erikson was an observer. His first work with children, as one of the pioneers of play therapy, also cast him in an observational role. As a clinician and student of life patterns he continued to be an observer. From psychoanalysis he learned additionally to take account of the passions that distract and distort perception. His work was therefore striking for the rare detachment with which he viewed his fellow humans.

Erikson's most significant substantive contribution was the way he described the epigenetic life stages. Karl Abraham, one of Freud's first followers, had early described a series of types of instinctual gratification necessary for infant survival and development, embodying important and lasting elements of character strength. Freud developed this elaboration of his own work, but it was Erikson who in the World War II era extended the epigenetic and stage model to later childhood and adulthood. Whereas the psychoanalytic stages of development were previously expressed in the evolution of libidinal drives, Erikson applied the idea to the whole life cycle, adding specifically adolescent and adult patterns.

Erikson's epigenetic stages included physical-developmental, learning, drive, and social consciousness, all integrated into the whole of personality and culture. His contacts with anthropologists in the 1930s led him to compare child rearing in various cultures. He then realized that each different culture provided in its own way for each stage and crisis of the developing child—"unconscious attempts at creating out of human raw material that configuration of attitudes which is (or once was) the optimum under the tribe's particular natural conditions and economic-historic necessities," as he put it in an early formulation. This emphasis on external actuality (or each individual's historical-existential reality) put Erikson among the pioneers of ego psychology, those psychoanalysts who emphasized the positive, adaptive, and reality-oriented capabilities of the human psychic apparatus.

Erikson's fame developed just as psychiatry and especially psychoanalysis became broadly popular in post–World War II America. Although his work was appreciated throughout the world, in the United States he became a unique figure. As the analyst became the secular priest, so it was Erikson specifically who came to embody psychiatric wisdom, the priest of the priest and yet a man whose clear formulations of complex processes could be understood by college undergraduates. His synthesis of psychoanalysis, public concern, conservative ethics, personality theory holism, and even existentialism with keen observation, good sense, and an emphasis on the strengths of humankind made him a spokesman for liberal intellectuals of the 1950s and after. Best known for work on troubled youth and the identity crisis of late adolescence/early adulthood, Erikson provided reassuring and constructive formulations for many Americans, especially young Americans who felt the depersonalizing forces of their own increasingly bureaucratized society. See Robert Coles, *Erik H. Erikson: The Growth of His Work* (1970).

J. C. BURNHAM

EVANS, Oliver (b. New Castle County, Del., 1755; d. New York, N.Y., Apr. 15, 1819), INVENTOR, MANUFACTURER, was apprenticed at 14 to a wagon maker. In 1772, learning of the atmospheric steam engine of Thomas Newcomen, he built a road vehicle embodying steam power. Meanwhile he continued to perfect a completely new series of water-powered mechanical devices that, installed together, revolutionized flour milling. In 1786, Pennsylvania granted him a patent on the exclusive use of his milling machinery, and Maryland, which granted the same protection the next year, extended it to the use of steam power. Millers were slow to adopt Evans's machinery, but with his brothers he entered the milling business in Wilmington and installed his system. By 1820 it had all but replaced the traditional equipment. By 1802, Evans had developed a working steam engine. Despite much public ridicule because of his insistence on using high-pressure steam, by the end of his life his Mars Iron Works in Philadelphia had manufactured about fifty engines for use throughout the nation. In 1812 he had also opened a steam engine manufactory in Pittsburgh, which was under the supervision of his son George.

⸎

Oliver Evans belonged to that first great generation of American inventors that included **John Fitch, Eli Whitney,** Robert Fulton, and others. In common with them and with the political leaders of the new Republic, Evans saw the world as imperfect but unfinished. As he wrote in 1807, "We see by daily experience that every art may be improved."

Evans pursued two careers simultaneously. First, he attempted to discover the principles of the arts and then to apply these to making improvements in current practice. His two great triumphs

in this line were the completely automatic flour mill (1782) and the high-pressure steam engine (1802). His second career, which began about 1793 when he moved to Philadelphia, was as a manufacturer and merchant, first of general mill supplies and later of steam engines and ironwork.

Although his manufacturing activities earned him a prosperous living, his inventive efforts were less handsomely rewarded. Late in life he wrote bitterly of the inventor: "It is improbable that his Contemporaries will pay any attention to him." His problem lay both in the inadequate patent laws of the period and in the fact that his inventions were so useful that they were universally adopted. Being indispensable, they in effect became public property. After years of controversy and litigation, in a dramatic renunciation at the age of 54 he burned his drawings and specifications for further inventions. Nothing better illustrated his belligerent sense of society's ingratitude for his monumental contributions to the advance of American technology. See Greville Bathe, *Oliver Evans: A Chronicle of Early American Engineering* (1935).

CARROLL PURSELL

EVANS, Walker (b. St. Louis, Mo., Nov. 3, 1903; d. New Haven, Conn., Apr. 10, 1974), PHOTOGRAPHER, studied literature at Williams College (1923) and the Sorbonne (1926). During his years of apprenticeship in photography a fellow worker at the Wall Street firm of Henry L. Doherty was his friend **Hart Crane.** His first published work appeared in Crane's *The Bridge* (1930). His first exhibition was at the Julien Levy Gallery in New York in 1932. From late 1935 to 1937 he was with the photographic unit of the Farm Security Administration. His *American Photographs* (1938) has become a classic of documentary photography. He collaborated with James Agee in investigating conditions among sharecroppers in the South, which resulted in the book *Let Us Now Praise Famous Men: Three Tenant Families* (1941). He joined *Time* in 1943, transferred to *Fortune* in 1945, and for the next twenty years conceived and executed his own ideas for photo-essays. Since 1965, Evans has been professor of graphic design at Yale University. His photographs are included in the permanent collections of the Metropolitan Museum of Art and the Museum of Modern Art in New York, and the Art Institute of Chicago. He is a fellow of the American Academy of Arts and Sciences and the recipient of a Guggenheim fellowship (1941), a Carnegie Corporation award (1962) and an honorary LittD from Williams College (1968).

—————— ✺ ——————

In the late 1920s, Walker Evans committed himself to photography. Within five years he had established the beginnings of a radical new spirit in American photography characterized by candor, economy, and intellectual precision. Evans photographed subjects that had not been considered relevant for the serious photographer: the signs and symbols of the commercial environment, the monuments of an anonymous architecture, the detritus of the industrial landscape. Perhaps more than any other figure, Evans has defined in his work the essence of the documentary aesthetic, in which the poetic uses of pure fact have been exploited in a new and profoundly challenging way. His work has made its impact not only on subsequent photography but on modern literature, film, and the traditional visual arts.

The concept of photography that he evolved in the years following 1930 was original and exacting. He thought of photography as a way of preserving segments out of time itself, without regard for the conventional structures of picture building. Nothing was to be imposed on experience; the truth was to be discovered, not constructed. It was a formulation that freed Evans's intuitions and saved him from too solicitous a concern for the purely plastic values that were of central importance to modern painters. Evans's style rested on two seemingly contradictory tenets. One was an uncompromising acceptance of precise and literal photographic description. The other was a faith in the validity of his intuitions. It has been supposed that Evans's work is basically concerned with the causes of social reform, presumably because his pictures have often dealt with humble people and their works. But if his subjects are often humble, they are almost never ordinary; it is above all quality that he demands of them. His idea of quality is not a sentimental one and cannot be reduced to hortatory slogans. Individually, the photographs of Walker Evans evoke an incontrovertible sense of specific places. Collectively, they evoke the sense of America. See *Walker Evans,* Introduction by John Szarkowski (1971).

JOHN SZARKOWSKI

—————— ✺ ——————

FALL, Albert Bacon (b. Frankfort, Ky., Nov. 26, 1861; d. El Paso, Tex., Nov. 30, 1944), POLITICAL LEADER, taught school in Kentucky (1879–81) and read law in his spare time before moving to New Mexico to prospect. Admitted to the New Mexico bar in 1889, he was appointed associate justice of the territorial supreme court by President Grover Cleveland in 1893 and later served in the legislature of the New Mexico Territory as a Democrat. During the Spanish-American War, Fall, an infantry captain, struck up a friendship with Theodore Roosevelt. He became a Republican and served as attorney general for the New Mexico Territory before being elected to the U.S. Senate in 1912 when New Mexico became a state. In the Senate he became friendly with Senator Warren G. Harding of Ohio, who, upon taking office as president in 1921, appointed Fall secretary of the interior. Fall resigned from this position two years later and returned to his ranch at Three Rivers, New Mexico. In 1924 a Senate investigation revealed that Fall had accepted gifts and payments from both Harry Sinclair and E. L. Doheny for leasing certain oil reserve tracts in Teapot Dome, Wyoming, and Elk Hills, California, to private oil interests. Prosecution against Fall started in 1926; he was convicted in 1929 and served one year (1931–32) in prison. Fall was the first cabinet member ever to be convicted of a felony committed while in office. After his release he returned to New Mexico and lived in declining health and poverty.

───────────

Until the revelations about him in 1924, Fall's life had seemed a success story similar to that of others from the American West. He was bold, able, and highly ambitious. Seeing the advantages of a second language in the New Mexico Territory, he quickly gained a facility in Spanish. In a time of Republican ascendancy he changed from the Democratic to the Republican Party, enhancing his career. Fall was an outspoken individualist, apparently influenced by his youth in Kentucky as well as his diverse experiences in mining, ranching, and frontier politics. He seemed a personification of the vigorous and violence-prone westerner. He also exhibited a nationalistic attitude on foreign policy, especially regarding Mexico where he had business investments. Fall always maintained that the payments he received as secretary of the interior were "loans." Unfortunately for him, he accepted the money while at the same time giving oil leases to those who supplied it. A longtime lover of horses and "the land," Fall wanted funds for the purpose of improving his ranch. He also struggled under a load of debt. If he had acted more cautiously as secretary and not taken bribes, he might have succeeded in a major change of national policy; certainly he intended to weaken the federal conservation programs. Ideally speaking, in his view, the Department of Interior should sell and otherwise dispose of the public lands and then cease to exist. Aside from his corruption Fall was therefore an anachronism (and a dangerous one) in this office. He did, however, give support to the national park system for reasons that are not entirely clear. See Albert B. Fall, *Memoirs,* ed. by David H. Stratton

(1966), and J. Leonard Bates, *The Origins of Teapot Dome* (1963).

J. LEONARD BATES

FARLEY, James Aloysius (b. Grassy Point, N.Y., May 30, 1888; d. New York, N.Y., June 9, 1976), POLITICAL LEADER, graduated from the Packard Commercial School (1906). He worked as a bookkeeper for the Merlin, Keilholtz Paper Co. before joining the Universal Gypsum Co. as bookkeeper, correspondent, and finally salesman (1911–26). A Democrat, Farley served as township clerk of Stony Point, New York (1912–19). He supported **Al Smith** for governor of New York in 1918 and was rewarded by being made port warden for New York City (1918–19). He was chairman of the Rockland County Democratic Committee (1919–29) and supervisor of Rockland County (1920–23). After serving one term in the New York state assembly (1924), Farley became a member of the New York State Boxing Commission. In 1926 he organized his own lime and concrete company (it became the General Building Supply Corporation in 1929) and was its president from 1929 to 1933 and again in 1949.

In 1928, Farley became secretary of the New York State Democratic Committee and helped manage Franklin D. Roosevelt's first campaign for governor. He managed Roosevelt's campaign for reelection in 1930 and became chairman of the state Democratic committee. He spent the next two years working for Roosevelt's presidential nomination, which was accomplished at the 1932 Democratic convention in Chicago. After the election Farley became U.S. postmaster general as well as national Democratic and New York State Committee chairman, in which posts he was the administration's chief patronage dispenser. He took a leave of absence to manage Roosevelt's 1936 reelection. Harboring presidential ambitions himself, Farley broke with Roosevelt mainly over the latter's decision to run for a third term. At the 1940 Democratic convention Farley received 72 votes for president; shortly afterward he resigned both as National Committee chairman and as postmaster general to become board chairman of the Coca-Cola Export Co., a kind of supersalesman worldwide for the soft-drink giant. He remained in that post until 1973 when he was appointed honorary chairman. Farley was a member of the 1953 Commission on Organization of the Executive Branch of Government. His two autobiographies are *Behind the Ballots* (1938) and *Jim Farley's Story* (1948).

———∞———

Of the political handymen serving 20th-century American presidents, James Farley was probably the best known and most skillful. Although damned by conservatives as a partisan spoilsman and by liberals as a glad-handing Babbitt, Farley repeatedly demonstrated a shrewd mastery of the arts of personal contact and political machine-tending, astounded others with his enormous industry and phenomenal memory, and proved remarkably effective in his roles as campaign manager, party prophet, and provider of the New Deal's political muscle. As Democratic national chairman he ran the party with a sophisticated benignity and dazzling attention to detail that helped bring about one of the major party realignments in American history. Farley had relatively little to do, however, with the larger issues and goals of the New Deal. Loyal chiefly to party and tradition, he saw himself as serving a master politician rather than a liberal reformer. And when the break with Roosevelt came, it was mostly over the president's efforts to remake the party, his violation of the no-third-term tradition, and his insensitivity to Farley's political ambitions rather than over New Deal laws and programs. After 1940, Farley would never find another political winner to serve, nor would his ambitions for higher electoral office ever be realized. But partisan politics rather than his business career remained at the center of his later life. In the words of *Newsweek*, he "could no more retire from politics than a poet could retire from poetry," and until his death he remained not only a party patriarch but an activist involved in party affairs and numerous campaigns. See Alden Whitman, *Come to Judgment* (1980), and John Syrett, "Jim Farley and Carter Glass," *Prologue* (Summer 1983).

ELLIS W. HAWLEY

FARMER, Fanny Merritt (b. Boston, Mass., Mar. 23, 1857; d. Boston, Mass., Jan. 15, 1915), COOKBOOK WRITER, studied at Medford High School in Boston until illness caused her to drop out. In 1889 she graduated from the Boston Cooking School and after a stint as assistant director became director of the School in 1891. During the ensuing years she published three highly successful cookbooks and in 1902 opened her own establishment, Miss Farmer's School of Cookery. In 1903 it became part of Simmons College. While running the school at Simmons she also lectured at hospitals on cooking for invalids, the subject of one of her books, and taught a course on it at the Harvard Medical College. From 1905 until her death she wrote a regular cooking feature in the *Women's Home Companion*. In all, she wrote twelve cookbooks, the best known being her second, *The Boston Cooking-School Cook Book* (1896), which went into twenty-one editions during her lifetime and is still in print.

———∞———

A pioneer in the writing of clear, simple recipes for middle-class housewives, Fannie Farmer had an important influence on 20th-century cookery. Homebound by paralysis early in life, she triumphed over her handicap by making herself expert in the management of the home and especially the kitchen.

The Boston Cooking School that she attended and later directed trained teachers, cooks, and housekeepers. Collecting and editing its recipes for publication, Farmer offered its professional secrets for the first time to the general public, and when she left to found her own school, she carried that principle into her curriculum. Dealing with practical rather than theoretical matters, she specialized in everyday cooking for the small modern family and in invalid cookery for the home. Her audience was the modern housewife rather than the professional.

Farmer wrote some specialized cookbooks, including *Chafing Dish Possibilities* (1898) and *Food and Cookery for the Sick and Convalescent* (1904), but her main subject was always the plain diet of the middle class. Her style was straightforward and as simple as the food she described, though she often did add novelty and frills to basic recipes in order to stimulate interest in food equal to her own. Her greatest innovation and the contribution of which she was personally most proud was the use of precise measurements such as the level teaspoon and cup, which permitted amateurs to follow procedures exactly and produce professional-like results. Her dedication to this concept in her writings and lectures was to gain her the title, "The Mother of Level Measurements." *The Boston Cooking School Cook Book* filled a need for clear, precise recipes that the untrained middle-class housewife devoid of servants could follow without fear of failure. For that reason it remains a seminal text in the field of domestic cookery. See Laura Shapiro, *Perfection Salad: Women and Cooking at the Turn of the Century* (1986).

DENNIS WEPMAN

FARRAGUT, David Glasgow (b. Campbell Station, Tenn., July 5, 1801; d. Portsmouth, N.H., Aug. 14, 1870), NAVAL OFFICER, served as a midshipman on the *Essex* when he was 9 years old, having been appointed by his adopted father, Commodore David Porter. He first saw action against the British sloop *Albert* (April 1812) and in the defeat of the *Essex* at Valparaíso harbor. At 13 he was made master of the captured British sloop *Alexander Barclay.*

After the War of 1812 and following service in the Mediterranean (1815–20), he was commissioned a lieutenant (1825). For the next few years he sailed between stations at Norfolk, Virginia, the West Indies, and Brazil. Commissioned a commander in 1841, Farragut commanded the *Decatur* in the Brazilian squadron and later the sloop-of-war *Saratoga* in Mexican waters (1847). He was assistant inspector of ordnance at Norfolk (1851–53), where he drew up a book of ordnance regulations, *Experiments to Ascertain the Strength of Navy Guns*. He became commander of a new navy yard at Mare Island, California, in 1854 and was promoted to captain in 1856.

At the outbreak of the Civil War, Farragut, a staunch Unionist despite his southern background, was a member of the Naval Retiring Board, but in February 1862 he was put in charge of organizing the West Gulf Blockading squadron. Two months later, disregarding orders, he ran the Confederate forts on the lower Mississippi, defeated the Confederate fleet that guarded the route to New Orleans, and captured the city. In July 1862, after he ran his ships past the Vicksburg, Mississippi, batteries, he was promoted to the new rank of rear admiral. Between October and December 1862, Farragut commanded the naval forces that captured Corpus Christi, Sabine Pass, and Galveston, Texas. In March 1863 he blockaded the Red River and cut off supplies to Vicksburg, which Grant captured that month, and Port Hudson, which fell to Farragut in May. Farragut's decisive victory at Mobile Bay (April 1864) assured Union control of the Gulf area for the duration of the war. In December he was named vice admiral, and in July 1866 he was promoted to admiral, a rank specially created for him. The following year he commanded the European squadron on a triumphant tour of Europe.

⚬⚬⚬

America's first admiral does not fit the image of a Civil War naval hero. There was nothing of the glamorous swashbuckler about Farragut, who grew up in the service and consistently performed his duties with competence and diligence. A quiet family man in private life, he lacked social status and a formal education. He sought neither friend nor favor in Washington, preferring to let his record speak for itself. His unimpressive size and appearance completed the picture of an officer who seemed destined for an obscure berth pending retirement.

Paradoxically, Farragut's southern background operated to his advantage. His declaration of loyalty to the Union attracted the attention of the Navy Department and led to his assignment as commander of the West Gulf Blockading squadron over the heads of thirty-six captains. Under Farragut's bold and imaginative direction, this force split the Confederacy, gained control of Mobile Bay, and in effect served to terminate European thoughts of intervention. Farragut's actions unquestionably shortened the war.

Inspired leadership coupled with a keen perception of strategy and tactics set Farragut apart from his fellows and enabled him to score decisively. He prepared for victory only, in the belief that a good offense was the best defense. He knew how and when to cut his losses, and above all he had faith in himself and his mission. President Abraham Lincoln considered Farragut his best appointment of the war. See A. T. Mahan, *Admiral Farragut* (1892), and Charles L. Lewis, *David Glasgow Farragut* (2 vols., 1941–43).

WALTER R. HERRICK, JR.

FARRELL, James Thomas (b. Chicago, Ill., Feb. 27, 1904; d. New York, N.Y., Aug. 22, 1979), WRITER, was brought up in Chicago's Irish South Side. After attending parochial schools where he excelled in athletics, he studied at the University of Chicago (1925–29) and worked at many odd jobs while he tried to establish himself as a writer. Influenced by Sherwood Anderson, whose small-town descriptions reminded him of his Chicago neighborhood, Farrell published his first novel, *Young Lonigan*, in 1932; it was part of a trilogy completed by *The Young Manhood of Studs Lonigan* (1934) and *Judgment Day* (1935). The Lonigan trilogy, like most of Farrell's writings, dealt with American urban life and the lower-middle-class Irish of Chicago's South Side in realistic fashion.

Farrell won a Guggenheim fellowship in creative writing (1936–37) to complete *A World I Never Made* (1936), the first book in a largely autobiographical pentalogy about a young man named Danny O'Neill. From 1946 to 1952, Farrell wrote the Bernard Carr trilogy that dealt with New York literary life and radical political groups. Farrell wrote many short stories and published such collections as *Calico Shoes and Other Stories* (1942). He established himself as a literary critic with *A Note on Literary Criticism*

(1936), which attacked the Marxist view of literature so popular in the 1930s. Although not an activist in politics, Farrell considered himself a Marxist; however, he opposed the Stalinist dictatorship and purges of the late 1930s. Some of his more recent books include a volume of reminiscences, *Reflections at Fifty* (1954), *Boarding House Blues* (1961), *The Silence of History* (1963), *A Brand New Life* (1968), and *Childhood Is Not Forever* (1969). In his later years Farrell never reached the readership he had earlier. The sale of the nine novels he wrote in the 1960s and 1970s averaged about eight thousand copies each.

───◦∞◦───

No writer has described a specific area of American society so thoroughly and comprehensively as Farrell did in the seven novels of Studs Lonigan and Danny O'Neill (1932–43). A consummate realist in viewpoint and method, he turned repeatedly in his fiction to the subject he knew best: the Irish Catholic neighborhood of Chicago's South Side. Drawing on lacerating personal experience, Farrell wrote about people who were victims of injurious social circumstances and of their own spiritual and intellectual shortcomings. He depicted human frustration, ignorance, cruelty, violence, and moral disintegration with sober, relentless veracity. "Passionately honest and passionately narrow," critic Alfred Kazin observed, "he brought to his novels an autobiographical mission as tortured and complex in its way as Proust's." Despite his Marxist leanings, Farrell's fiction is not that of a reformer or a doctrinaire theorist but rather the patient, humorless representation of ways of life and states of mind he abhors. His passion for particulars often makes his descriptions more prolonged than is essential to his purpose, as though one might arrive at truth by merely accumulating inert facts. And his writing usually lacks warmth and subtlety, privations that Farrell seems deliberately to impose on himself and his readers. His pedantic preoccupation with physical details became a serious, if not ultimately overriding, artistic liability. Farrell's place in American letters, however, as certainly the most industrious and probably the most powerful writer in the naturalistic tradition stemming from **Frank Norris** and **Theodore Dreiser,** was solidly established with the Lonigan-O'Neill series. As a novelist and as a literary critic his stubborn independence of mind and rugged artistic honesty have earned him honor and respect even in critical quarters where his later novels are lamented and ignored. See Edgar M. Branch, *James T. Farrell* (1963).

WILLIAM MCCANN

FAULKNER, William Harrison (b. New Albany, Miss., Sept. 25, 1897; d. Oxford, Miss., July 6, 1962), WRITER, grew up in Oxford, Mississippi. In 1918 he enlisted in the Royal Canadian Flying Corps. After two years of study at the University of Mississippi (1919–21), he served as the university's postmaster (1922–24). After the publication of *The Marble Faun* (1924), a collection of poems, he traveled to New Orleans where he met Sherwood Anderson. Faulkner's first two novels, *Soldier's Pay* (1926) and *Mosquitoes* (1927), were studies of postwar disillusionment.

In 1929, Faulkner published *Sartoris*, the first novel in the series on the Sartoris family, and *The Sound and the Fury*, in which he introduced the Compson family. Both of these works, set in mythical Yoknapatawpha County, Mississippi (in reality Lafayette County), which is intended to be a microcosm of the South, deal with the dissolution of the landed and banking aristocracy as personified by the Sartoris and Compson families and the rise of a materialistic and unscrupulous oligarchy as personified by the Snopes clan. They also portray the life of typical southern farmers: the blacks and the poor whites.

In 1930, Faulkner published *As I Lay Dying*, in which by means of soliloquies he analyzed the psychology behind a family's decision to convey their dead mother's body to Jefferson, Mississippi (which is really Oxford), for burial. This work was followed by *Sanctuary* (1931), an account of southern degeneracy. In *Light in August* (1932), Faulkner dealt with a pregnant country girl's search for her lover and the destruction of Joe Christmas, a mulatto rejected by both races.

During the thirties Faulkner worked intermittently as a screenwriter. In 1936 he published *Absalom, Absalom!,* a study of a poor white's driving ambition to obtain a plantation and found a dynasty. *The Hamlet* (1940) dealt with the Snopes clan's attempts to wrest a village from its legal owners.

In 1950, Faulkner was awarded the Nobel Prize for literature. *Requiem for a Nun* (1951) is a sequel to *Sanctuary*. In 1954 he published *A Fable* (awarded a Pulitzer Prize), an allegorical tale about Christ's passion that is set in France during World War I. *The Town* (1957) and *The Mansion* (1959) completed a trilogy about the Snopes clan begun with *The Hamlet*. Some of Faulkner's other works include *Pylon* (1935), *Intruder in the Dust* (1948) and *The Rievers* (1962).

❧

William Faulkner, widely considered the greatest 20th-century American writer of fiction, continued and reshaped our two chief earlier fictional traditions, the symbolic romance fathered by **Nathaniel Hawthorne** and continued by other writers from **Herman Melville** to Robert Penn Warren, and the realistic and naturalistic tradition practiced by **William Dean Howells, Mark Twain,** the early **Henry James, Stephen Crane,** and **Theodore Dreiser.** Faulkner's best and most typical work, like Hawthorne's, is marked by its feeling for the presentness of the past, its attachment to a particular region, its strong antirationalism, its concentration on the psychological aspects of moral decisionmaking in a world in which moral issues are always complex and good and evil ironically intermixed, and its reliance on mythic and archetypal symbols. At the same time Faulkner's work often reminds us of Mark Twain's in its use of folk humor and the "tall tale" (*The Hamlet* and short stories like "Spotted Horses" and "Was," for instance), of the realists in general in its verisimilitude, and of naturalists like Dreiser in its emphasis on determinism—Faulkner's characters often seem "fated," and "doom" is one of his favorite words. His most sympathetic characters are often portrayed as struggling to break their deterministic chains and achieve free and thus responsible action.

Both fictional traditions incorporated in Faulkner's work were transmuted by another influence on him, that of 20th-century symbolism, particularly as we see it in the work of James Joyce and T. S. Eliot. Joyce's *Ulysses* lies behind Faulkner's technique in much of his best work, particularly in *The Sound and the Fury, As I Lay Dying,* and *Absalom, Absalom!* The influence of Eliot's poems "The Love Song of J. Alfred Prufrock" and *The Waste Land* is pervasive in a veiled way in much of what Faulkner wrote before 1940 and explicit in *Pylon.* From Joyce and Eliot, Faulkner learned to scramble the time sequences of his narratives, since all time is present time to consciousness, the past living in the present and the present becoming past before it can be apprehended and articulated. The humblest, sometimes the most sordid, events may be seen as repeating the archetypes of history and myth. Classical myth and biblical stories, particularly the latter, as in *Absalom, Absalom!,* hover over the realistically presented inhabitants of Yoknapatawpha County, lifting what may seem at first mere "local color" regionalism to universal significance. Much of Faulkner's work may be viewed as a fictional reworking of Eliot's poem "Sweeney Among the Nightingales."

With unequaled vividness and unsurpassed emotional power Faulkner records the passing of an era and the birth pangs of a new, as yet unimagined age. It is not simply "the Old South" that Faulkner records and mourns for; it is the whole agrarian, individualistic, and religiously oriented national past. But although nostalgia is perhaps the dominant emotion in his work, and much of the very best of it, like *The Sound and the Fury,* could be described as elegiac, Faulkner never sentimentalized the past. The yet unborn future might threaten not just the old verities but man's very humanity, but Faulkner was persuaded, as he said in his Nobel Prize acceptance speech, that man will endure. See Michael Millgate, *The Achievement of William Faulkner* (1966).

HYATT H. WAGGONER

FERMI, Enrico (b. Rome, Italy, Sept. 29, 1901; d. Chicago, Ill., Nov. 28, 1954), NUCLEAR PHYSICIST, received a PhD from the University of Pisa in 1922. He taught physics at the universities of Florence and Rome during 1924–38. At Florence he developed the Fermi-Dirac statistics, which made possible the theoretical explanation of phenomena involving the behavior of electrons in solids. In 1930–32 he was the first scientist to make use of the neutron to produce the radioactive conversion of one element to another. He created more than forty artificial radioactive isotopes in the process and was awarded the Nobel Prize for physics in 1938 for his work. Disturbed by Mussolini's Fascist regime, Fermi left Italy in 1939 to become a professor at Columbia University. Meanwhile, two German scientists, Otto Hahn and Fritz Strassmann, had succeeded in correctly identifying the phenomena noted by Fermi while experimentally bombarding uranium atoms with neutrons as the fission or splitting of uranium atoms. Fermi, along with other refugee scientists, including **Albert Einstein,** alarmed at the possibility that the Germans might use this discovery to produce an atomic bomb, successfully persuaded the U.S. government to fund the Manhattan Project to produce an American atomic bomb. He was the leader of a research team at the University of Chicago in 1942 that activated the first atomic pile or nuclear reactor, and he worked on the design of the first atomic bomb at Los Alamos.

After the war Fermi took a position at the Institute of Nuclear Studies at Chicago, where he remained for the rest of his life. In theoretical physics his most important contributions were his explanations of the statistical atomic model and of Beta-ray emission, which became the key to the later study of transuranium elements. He also formulated significant theories of cosmic ray origins and of multiple meson production in the collision of high-energy particles. In experimental physics his accomplishments included the first production (but not the identification) of a transuranium element (neptunium) and the achievement of the world's first self-sustaining chain reaction. Some of his many writings include *Thermodynamics* (1937) and *Elementary Particles* (1951).

⁂

Enrico Fermi was the Italian star in the constellation of European physicists who revolutionized the physical sciences during the first half of the 20th century. Although he did not rank with such innovators in theory as Einstein or Bohr, Fermi had an extraordinary impact on the physics and on the physicists of his own day. His contributions to theoretical physics were significant in elucidating the specifics of nuclear structure from the generalized theory of quantum mechanics.

However, Fermi's greatest contributions to science were as a teacher and personal leader. His ability to separate the basic physical elements from the mathematical formalism of a subject was legendary. He attracted students of exceptional ability and inspired highly creative research groups wherever he worked. This ability made him especially effective in experimental physics. His neutron experiments at Rome and his later work with the nuclear chain reaction at Columbia and Chicago became classics of modern research.

Fermi's career (as he himself recognized) epitomized the transition from "classical" to "modern" physics that occurred during his lifetime. He was among the last giants of the discipline who could presume a mastery of the whole field of physics, both theoretical and experimental. In his later years he lamented the rise of "big" science with its teams of specialists directed to predetermined goals, and he yearned for the kind of intimate, open, and spontaneous atmosphere that characterized scientific research before World War II. Fermi's career also illustrated the changing role of the scientist in society—from that of the academic scholar pursuing esoteric subjects to a busy administrator and adviser to political leaders on the life-or-death issues posed by modern military technology. See Emilio Segre, *Enrico Fermi—Physicist* (1970).

RICHARD G. HEWLETT

FERN, Fanny (pseudonym of Sara Payson Willis Parton) (b. Portland, Maine, July 9, 1811; d. New York, N.Y., Oct. 10, 1872), JOURNALIST, attended Catharine Beecher's Seminary, Hartford, Connecticut, and lived as a housewife in Brighton, Massachusetts, from 1834 until her husband died in 1846. She then worked as a seamstress and teacher. Remarried in 1849, she began to write stories, the first of which appeared in a Boston paper, *The Olive Branch* (1851). In 1853, New York publisher James C. Derby brought out her collection of articles and fiction, *Fern Leaves from Fanny's Portfolio,* which established her reputation. A year later she published a children's collection, *Little Ferns for Fanny's Little Friends,* and in 1855 joined Robert Banner's New York *Ledger.*

Fanny Fern wrote a weekly column for the *Ledger* until she died. Her stories and articles dealt with the family, religion, women's careers, woman's rights, and homosexuality. A strong feminist, she called for woman suffrage and equal pay for equal work. Her tone ranged from moral and sentimental to satirical. *Ruth Hall* (1855), a novel, became a highly popular literary scandal because it was autobiographical and unusually personal. It sold fifty thousand copies in its first eight months. In 1857 she published another novel, *Rose Clark.* Fanny Fern's weekly columns were collected in *Fresh Leaves* (1857), *Folly as It Flies* (1868), *Ginger-Snaps* (1870), and *Caper-Sauce* (1872). Her children's stories were published in the *Play-Day Book* (1869) and *A New Story Book for Children* (1864).

⁂

Nicknamed "Sal Volatile" in her student days, Sara Parton breezed through life with effervescence and verve. A large, argumentative brunette with a florid complexion, an aquiline nose, and sharp blue eyes, she made up in self-assurance for what she lacked in beauty and developed a writing style that admirably reflected her personality: pugnacious, commonsensical, optimistic, and affectionate. Her earliest newspaper pieces— staccato vignettes of family life whose air of breathless urgency was enhanced by a lavish use of dots, dashes, and exclamation points—catered to the sentimentalism and bathos so popular in the "feminine fifties." But she soon broadened her interests to include the serious discussion of major social problems, such as prostitution, divorce, child labor, and slum conditions. Although she championed a wide variety of humanitarian reforms and frequently spoke up for woman's rights, she had little conception of institutional change or of the need for any radical restructuring of domestic relations. Instead, she clung to a utopian faith in the efficacy of individualism and self-help, urging upon downtrodden wives and mothers a strategy of patient "boring from within." Women must first improve their health and their minds, she insisted; then, once they had demonstrated their capacity for self-direction and independent thought, their menfolk would yield to their demands for equality. Such naïveté took much of the sting out of Fanny Fern's incessant scolding, as did her infectious sense of humor, which cropped up even in the midst of her most earnest moralizing. For all her deficiencies as a feminist crusader, however, she set a powerful personal example of mobility and achievement in a man's world that was not lost on her half-million devoted readers. See Florence Bannard Adams, *Fanny Fern* (1966).

MAXWELL BLOOMFIELD

FERRARO, Geraldine Anne (b. Newburgh, N.Y., Aug. 26, 1935), POLITICIAN, attended fashionable New York Catholic schools for girls, earning a BA in English at Manhattan's Marymount College in 1956. While teaching in the public school system, she attended night classes at the Fordham University Law School, receiving her JD in 1960. That same year Ferraro married John Zaccaro, a real estate developer, and for the next fourteen years subordinated her legal career to caring for the couple's three children and working for local Democratic clubs. In 1974 she was appointed assistant district attorney in Queens County, where she acquired a reputation as a tough but fair prosecutor.

Ferraro won the Democratic nomination for Congress from New York's Ninth Congressional District in Queens in 1978, receiving 53 percent of the vote in a three-way race. She easily defeated her Republican opponent in the general elections and was reelected in 1980 and 1982. In 1984, Democratic presidential nominee Walter Mondale asked Ferraro to join him on the ticket, making her the first woman to receive a major party vice presidential nomination. Questions about unpaid taxes and her husband's financial affairs tarnished the luster of Ferraro's candidacy in a campaign that saw the Democratic ticket suffer a landslide defeat at the hands of President Ronald Reagan. In 1992 she ran unsuccessfully in the Democratic primary for a U.S. Senate seat from New York. She reflected on her career in *Ferraro: My Story* (1985).

───※───

Ambitious and pragmatic, Ferraro generally aligned herself with the Democratic Party's liberal wing and acquired a reputation as a strong proponent of woman's rights. She was a shrewd and practical politician who avoided dogmatic posturing and recognized the role of compromise in the political process. Above all she was a loyal party worker whose efforts in a variety of local campaigns resulted in a network of community ties she later used in her electoral contests.

Ferraro's years in the district attorney's office strengthened her commitment to woman's rights and the need to provide a safe and secure environment for children. As a member of a newly organized Special Victims Bureau, she dealt primarily with cases of rape, domestic violence, and child abuse. The experience convinced her that much of the crime and brutality which manifested itself in the courtroom resulted from poverty and social injustice.

Her election to Congress in 1978 provided Ferraro a different political forum, one more congenial to her liberal feminist sympathies. In Congress she observed the proper etiquette expected of freshmen legislators and avoided the confrontational politics that had undermined the effectiveness of some of her feminist predecessors. Instead she faithfully served constituency interests in her district and assiduously cultivated Democratic Party leaders in Congress. Her cooperative attitude and liberal politics soon attracted the favorable attention of Speaker of the House Thomas "Tip" O'Neill. With the Speaker's advice and support she quickly rose through the House leadership ranks, securing increasingly more important committee assignments, winning election in 1980 as secretary of the policy-setting Democratic Caucus, and ultimately being trusted by party leaders to chair the 1984 Democratic platform committee.

Geraldine Ferraro's political stock rose even higher when, under her direction, the platform committee hammered out a document that most elements of her diverse, highly contentious party found acceptable. Consequently, she became a logical vice presidential choice when Walter Mondale, the Democratic nominee, sought a dramatic political stroke which might reverse the momentum that seemed to be carrying the incumbent, Ronald Reagan, into a second term.

The vice presidential nominee's reputation as a "team player" suffered during the campaign. The strain of a national election and continual questions about family finances took their toll as her relationship with Mondale's campaign staff deteriorated. Ultimately, it simply was not a liberal, Democratic year; Ronald Reagan won easily. Post-election analyses indicated that Ferraro's name on the national ticket had not significantly influenced the result. As the first woman ever to be nominated on a major party national ticket, however, she advanced the cause of equality for women. See Frank P. Le Veness and Jane P. Sweeney, *Women Leaders in Contemporary U.S. Politics* (1987); Steven M. Gillon, *The Democrats' Dilemma: Walter F. Mondale and the Liberal Legacy* (1992).

GARY M. FINK

FIELD, Cyrus West (b. Stockbridge, Mass., Nov. 30, 1819; d. New York, N.Y., July 12, 1892), MERCHANT, FINANCIER, was educated at the Stockbridge Academy and became an errand boy in the New York City dry-goods firm of **A. T. Stewart** in 1835. Returning to Massachusetts in 1838, he assisted his brother Matthew in the operation of the paper manufacturing firm of Phelps

and Field, and in 1839 he established his own paper mill. In 1840 he became a junior partner in the wholesale paper firm of E. Root and Co. in New York City. When this enterprise went bankrupt in 1841, he reorganized the firm into Cyrus W. Field and Co. In 1853 he retired from management of this enterprise with an estimated fortune of $250,000.

In 1854, Field began to promote the construction of a transatlantic telegraph cable. Frederick N. Gisborne, a Canadian engineer, aroused his interest in this project. Forming a syndicate in Wall Street, Field raised $1.5 million and enlisted the support of leading telegraph entrepreneurs, including **Samuel F. B. Morse.** On August 5, 1858, the firm completed the laying of a 1,950-mile copper cable connecting Trinity Bay, Newfoundland, with Valentia, Ireland. The cable soon broke down, however, and in 1864, Field organized a project to construct a new line. Securing the *Great Eastern,* then the world's largest ship, he completed the laying of a successful cable in August 1867.

After accumulating more than $6 million from the transatlantic cable, in 1875 Field invested heavily with **Jay Gould** in the Manhattan and the Wabash railroads. He reorganized the New York Elevated Railroad Co. in 1877. In 1881 he purchased a New York newspaper, the *Mail and Express.* In 1887, however, Gould drove him to financial ruin in a struggle to gain control of the Manhattan Railroad. Field thereafter lived on the modest returns from his real estate holdings in New York City and Stockbridge, Massachusetts.

———

Cyrus W. Field was the seventh son of David Dudley Field, a Yale graduate in 1802. The founder of the family in this country seems to have come to America before 1630. The family genealogical tree contained a large number of lawyers, divines, and college graduates. Even so, Cyrus and his brothers constituted an exceptional generation. The oldest, David D., was an independent in politics, an eminent lawyer, and the codifier "of all the law of the state of New York"; another, **Stephen J. Field,** served on the U.S.

Supreme Court. All the Fields strove to excel. As individuals they had great physical resources and a religious upbringing. They were a highly visible product of the village culture of 19th-century America.

After a business career characterized by extreme vicissitudes, Cyrus had paid off his debts and accumulated a sizable fortune. By the mid-fifties he took up the Atlantic cable; on all sides the state of the art seemed to promise technology might annihilate time and distance. The U.S. government was surveying five railroad routes between the Mississippi and the Pacific, and in 1860 voted to subsidize a telegraph line across the same gap—all were "transcontinental" in concept if not in reach. In the East visionaries were planning to organize "the Atlantic Ferry," which would cut down the distance across the Atlantic by swift steamers connecting railroads, an eastern terminus in the Maritime Provinces with one on eastern Ireland, and thence to London. Meanwhile both the British and the American governments embarked on a policy of lavish subsidies to rivals in order to shorten the transit between nations by direct and regular sailings on more traditional routes. Whether a submarine cable between the Maritimes and Ireland was feasible was questionable, for it would be much longer than the cables already operating under water in Europe and would run at a lower depth. The sciences of both oceanography and electricity were rudimentary, but Field was able to get a favorable opinion from **M. F. Maury,** the American oceanographer. Maury thought the proposed route would cross a "Telegraph Plateau" somewhat near the surface and that the bottom of the ocean was "soft" and free from currents. In the varied companies, British and American, that laid the cable, Field confined the subscriptions to a limited number of persons, most of whom attracted as much business confidence as he did. He also depended on government subsidies, a monopoly of the right to land a cable on Newfoundland's shores, and the loan of government vessels to pay out the cable. In all these enterprises national pride and ambition played a part, but an international color suffused

them. Thus the laying of the cable would bring about "the realization of a millennium of love among men."

Seldom has an event been celebrated with as much purple rhetoric as the success of the cable; it was a work "noble," "sacred," and "providential." Field was another **Christopher Columbus.** Like Columbus, he hoped for tangible gains. He relied on rates on communications between governments, "mere social intercourse," as well as the dispatch of news to the highly competitive journals in New York City. Less precisely foreseen was the stimulus to organized international markets. Quotations "by cable" for some securities and for wheat and cotton were now speedy and continuously on hand. Prices set in England ruled at grain elevators in American prairie towns and crossroad stores in the South. In spite of the necessity of high rates—initially set at $100 for ten words—and frequent repetitions, the cable quickly proved profitable, and Field accumulated another fortune out of which he paid back the debts incurred in promoting it. This example, testified **George Peabody,** the Anglo-American banker, was "an act of very high Commercial Integrity and honor."

How would a reputation of this order stand up to the speculative business order in the post–Civil War era when a desire to be rich quickly and with a minimum of scruples governed? Unfortunately the Fields were willing to sup with the devil. Critics questioned the integrity of D. D. Field when he served as counsel to the Erie gang who were looting the Erie Railroad and to **William M. Tweed** who was looting the New York City government. Cyrus at the same time appeared as an accomplice or stalking horse to Jay Gould in the Wabash and other railroad speculations. One of the latter was the Manhattan Railroad, a holding company that merged the New York Elevated Companies. By the end of the 1880s the intricate manipulation of these enterprises on Wall Street and in the courts had resulted in the elimination of Field as a factor in the Manhattan Railroad. The collapse of commodity markets in 1887, in which Field was a heavy speculator, explained his downfall as much as did the unscrupulousness of his associates. Neither his reputation nor his fortune survived these disasters. Wall Street erects no memorials to its "victims," a phrase Field applied to himself. See I. F. Judson, *Cyrus W. Field, His Life and Work* (1896).

EDWARD C. KIRKLAND

FIELD, Marshall (b. Conway, Mass., Aug. 18, 1835; d. New York, N.Y., Jan. 16, 1906), MERCHANT, became a clerk in the dry-goods shop of Deacon H. G. Davis in Pittsfield, Massachusetts, in 1851. Rejecting a partnership offer in the firm, he moved to Chicago in 1856, where he worked as a clerk and traveling salesman in the dry-goods firm of Cooley, Wadsworth and Co., becoming general manager in 1861. He borrowed $100,000 from his employers to buy a partnership in the firm, now called Cooley, Farwell and Co., in 1862, and by 1865 he had paid off his debt and accumulated $260,000 from profits made during the Civil War.

In the company of Levi S. Leiter, who had joined the Cooley, Farwell firm in 1864, Field bought into the dry-goods firm of Potter Palmer in 1865. Palmer largely financed the new partnership under the title of Field, Palmer and Leiter, and when he withdrew from the firm in 1867, it became Field, Leiter and Co., retaining that title until 1881 when Field bought out Leiter and gave the firm its modern name, Marshall Field and Co.

Like **Alexander M. Palmer** in Chicago, **A. T. Stewart** in New York, and **John Wanamaker** in Philadelphia, Field built a massive business in both wholesale and retail dry goods. His business remained principally wholesale, but unlike many of his Chicago competitors, he paid careful attention to the developing retail trade. He always bought for cash, even borrowing on short term at high interest in order to meet his bills. This policy enabled him to buy below his competition, as did his policy of buying ahead of demand and creating it by advertising. His credit policy was rigorous, and because of this he suffered few bad debts. In his retail store he catered primarily to the carriage trade and developed a policy of courteous service, home delivery, and an institutional identity by use of a money-back guarantee and a slogan that promised the store would "give the lady what she wants." By acquiring exclusive agencies for some manufacturers, by the development of his own brands, and by the development of a purchasing organization that imported foreign goods in large volume, he achieved a high degree of product differentiation. He followed the lead of Stewart and Wanamaker in organizing his store internally into departments. His firm increased its annual volume from $12 million in 1868 to $25 million in 1880 to $68 million in 1905, despite the loss of his store to fire in 1871 and again in 1877 and despite the panics of 1873 and 1893. By the time of Field's death the retail store had become a Chicago institution, popularly called a "department store," though Field still insisted on calling it a dry-goods store.

Field invested his excess earnings in Chicago real estate, in transportation and manufacturing companies, and in banks. He donated $1 million for the Columbian Museum at the Chicago World's Fair in 1893 and contributed $8 million to the conversion of that display into the Field Museum of Natural History.

———— ✦ ————

Marshall Field was a pioneer in merchandising, but for a pioneer he was most conservative. He rarely invented any policy or created any basic innovation. His talent lay rather in the application of the innovations of others in imaginative ways in his own organization, an organization that from the first reflected both a genius for picking good subordinates and a set of values that would have pleased Samuel Smiles, the great purveyor of the Victorian values of thrift, honesty, and hard work. A paternalistic employer of the "old school," Field paid the lowest echelons of his workers less than the going rate and exacted from them absolute adherence to his rules of behavior, both in and out of the store. However, his success in making his store a highly respected institution made it certain that he never lacked for applicants to fill these posts. Moreover, when a salesclerk or delivery boy showed promise, he rose rapidly and the rewards were great. John G. Shedd, Harry G. Selfridge, and many more became millionaires in Field's employ.

Beyond his moral values and personnel policies, what made Field a multimillionaire was the growth of Chicago. In fact, he probably made as much from real estate investments as from merchandising, and here again it was his adherence to traditional values and his eagerness to "grow up with the country" that made his enterprise a success. It was often said that Field's "passion was his business," and he had little time for or interest in anything else. His was a quiet, unassuming, and gentlemanly manner. He did not participate in politics or, beyond the bare essentials, in the social life of his city. Except for his success in the founding of a family fortune, he had little family life either. His only public address (at the dedication of the library he gave to Conway in 1900) was a paean to the homely virtues of thrift, honesty, and hard work that had ruled his life. See Robert W. Twyman, *History of Marshall Field & Co., 1852–1906* (1954).

LESLIE E. DECKER

FIELD, Stephen Johnson (b. Haddam, Conn., Nov. 4, 1816; d. Washington, D.C., Apr. 9, 1899), JURIST, graduated from Williams College (1837) and studied law in New York City (1838–41). After being admitted to the New York bar, he practiced law with his brother, David Dudley Field (1841–48). In 1849, Field joined the gold rush to California and in 1850 helped found the town of Marysville where he engaged in real estate speculation and served as the town's first alcalde (mayor). Later that year he was elected to the state legislature as a Democrat. In 1857 he was elected to the state Supreme Court, becoming chief justice in 1859.

In 1863, President Abraham Lincoln appointed Field associate justice of the U.S. Supreme Court. Field believed that it was the role of the judicial branch of the government to draw a line between the spheres of action of the national and state governments. On economic questions he was for hard money and laissez-faire. In the legal tender cases, *Knox* v. *Lee, Parker* v. *Davis* (1871), Field dissented, arguing that it was not mandato-

ry for Congress to make greenbacks legal tender in order to ensure their circulation; therefore Congress, by requiring acceptance of greenbacks for debts, had exceeded its delegated powers. Field viewed the Fourteenth Amendment as a restriction on state economic legislation. Therefore, when the Court upheld a Louisiana state law granting a slaughterhouse monopoly, *Slaughterhouse Cases* (1873), he dissented, arguing that such monopolies deprived persons of property without due process of law and represented an encroachment "upon the liberty of citizens to acquire property and pursue happiness."

In 1877, Field sat on a fifteen-man electoral commission to determine the winner of the disputed presidential election of 1876, voting consistently in favor of the Democrats. In the case of *Munn* v. *Illinois* (1877), in which the Court upheld an Illinois law fixing maximum rates for grain storage, he dissented, insisting that the regulation of railroads and warehouse rates represented a threat to private property. In 1886, however, a majority of the Court accepted Field's reasoning that the states could not regulate interstate commerce (*Wabash* v. *Illinois*). In *Pollock* v. *Farmers' Loan and Trust Co.* (1895) he voted with the majority when the Court invalidated a federal income tax on the ground that it was a direct tax. He retired from the Court in April 1897.

The impact of Stephen J. Field on the Supreme Court and American constitutional law is exceeded by few judges. His length of service (thirty-five years) is surpassed only by Chief Justice **John Marshall** and **W. O. Douglas.** On the Court, Field uncompromisingly espoused an influential doctrine of economic freedom, especially for entrepreneurs and corporate property interests. He believed that America's national greatness depended on the constitutional recognition—to be enforced by the Supreme Court—that both the specific provisions of the Constitution as well as basic "natural law" principles protected individual property from restrictive state and federal regulation. In Field's eyes the privileges and immunities and due process clauses of the Fourteenth Amendment represented the ideal vehicles for the implementation of this economic and constitutional philosophy. Initially, the **Morrison R. Waite** Court majority during the 1870s rejected Field's proposed limitations on legislative authority in such cases as the *Slaughterhouse Cases* (state regulation of butcher shops), the *Granger Cases* (state regulation of grain elevator and railroad rates), and the *Sinking Fund Cases* (federal regulation of interstate public corporations). By the mid–1890s, however, Field's dissenting opinions, particularly those emphasizing the protections to property in the due process clause, had become the law of the land. In part this was a tribute to his articulate and persistent defense of property rights, and in part it was a practical consequence of a new judicial majority more attuned to the interests of business enterprise.

Stephen J. Field's lifestyle and personality were as forceful as his constitutional philosophy. He flirted with Democratic presidential politics, hobnobbed indiscriminately with railroad tycoons, and often made life difficult for his associates on the Court. Not until a later constitutional era, which began with the New Deal, were Field's views finally overruled and the Constitution reinterpreted to permit economic regulation. See Carl B. Swisher, *Stephen J. Field, Craftsman of the Law* (1930).

C. Peter Magrath

FILLMORE, Millard (b. Locke, N.Y., Jan. 7, 1800; d. Buffalo, N.Y., Mar. 8, 1874), PRESIDENT, was admitted to the bar in 1823. He served in the New York state assembly (1829–33) and in the U.S. House of Representatives (1833–35, 1837–43), where he became the Whig floor leader. As chairman of the House Ways and Means Committee, Fillmore helped draft the Tariff of 1842. In 1844 he was the Whig nominee for governor of New York but was defeated by **Silas Wright**. While serving as controller of New York he was elected vice president (1848), becoming president when Zachary Taylor died on July 9, 1850.

Fillmore approved of and signed the bills making up the Compromise of 1850, which admitted California to the Union as a free state; established the territories of New Mexico and Utah; adjusted the Texas—New Mexico boundary; restricted the slave trade in the District of Columbia, and provided for the return of fugitive slaves. In 1856 he ran for the presidency on the Native American (Know-Nothing) Party ticket but was defeated, receiving only 8 electoral votes (James Buchanan got 174; **John C. Frémont,** 114). When the Civil War broke out, Fillmore opposed Abraham Lincoln's policies. During Reconstruction he sympathized with Andrew Johnson's position.

⸺

It is an oddity of Millard Fillmore's career that he entered politics as an Anti-Mason and left it as the defeated standard-bearer of elements hostile to Roman Catholicism. For, throughout nearly all his public life, this upstate New Yorker was a mild and moderate man—bland in manner, loyal to party, and a natural compromiser.

Fillmore first aimed at the Whig vice presidential nomination in connection with the 1844 campaign, when Theodore Frelinghuysen was chosen. Four years later the New York controller (having won an off-year statewide election in 1847) proved a logical person to balance a ticket headed by a southern soldier. In November 1848 the Taylor-Fillmore combination defeated Democrats **Lewis Cass** and William O. Butler with a popular plurality and an electoral majority.

Although Taylor owned slaves, as president he opposed slavery's extension. Aided by three Democratic senators and all northern Whig senators except two, Taylor likewise blocked the Compromise of 1850. When Fillmore became the thirteenth president, he cooperated with Whigs **Henry Clay** and **Daniel Webster** and with Democrat **Stephen A. Douglas** in supporting a sectional adjustment. Fillmore appointed Webster to head the State Department and assisted Douglas's maneuvers to muster bipartisan backing for the Compromise. Success crowned their efforts in September 1850, but Fillmore's Fugitive Slave Law enforcement cost him the 1852 Whig nomination.

The 1856 Know-Nothing candidacy was largely an anticlimax. For the rest of his rather long life Fillmore relaxed and relished his role as Buffalo's first citizen. See Robert J. Rayback, *Millard Fillmore: Biography of a President* (1959).

HOLMAN HAMILTON

FINK, Albert (b. Lauterbach, Ger., Oct. 27, 1827; d. Ossining, N.Y., Apr. 3, 1897), RAILROAD ENGINEER, received a degree in engineering and architecture from a Darmstadt polytechnic school (1848) and settled in the United States in 1849. After working for the Baltimore and Ohio Railroad under the chief engineer **Benjamin H. Latrobe,** he was put in charge of designing and constructing bridges and buildings. He invented the Fink iron bridge truss and designed and supervised the building of the first important iron bridges in the United States. His iron truss was first used in 1852 in the bridge over the Monongahela River at Fairmont, Virginia (now West Virginia), then the longest iron railroad bridge in the United States. After serving as section engineer and later division engineer with the Baltimore and Ohio Railroad, in 1857 he became construction engineer and assistant to the chief engineer George McLoed, of the Louisville and Nashville Railroad. His Green River Bridge (1857) surmounted many engineering difficulties. Fink became superintendent of the machinery department in 1859 and chief engineer in 1860. Subject to attack and destruction by southern armies, the Louisville and Nashville line provided the only link between northern armies and the South. In 1865, Fink became general superintendent of the line and in 1869 was made vice president. After the war he reconstructed the railroad and completed the bridge over the Ohio River at Louisville, Kentucky (1872), whose principal span (four hundred feet long) was the longest truss bridge in the world.

Fink developed consistent, rational relations with other railroad lines (unlike the cutthroat competition of his contemporaries), and after the financial crisis of 1873 the Louisville and Nashville was one of the few roads that remained solvent. In 1874 "The Fink Report on Cost of Transportation" investigated railroad costs and laid the foundation for American railroad economics. The report pointed to the importance of reform in managing freight and passenger departments, and standardized freight and passenger rates on a statistical basis. Intending to retire from railroad affairs, Fink resigned from the Louisville and Nashville in 1875. However, he returned to railroading when offered the post of executive director of the recently formed Southern Railway and Steamship Association. During his two years in this capacity Fink ironed out problems arising from the continuing rate warfare among competing southern railroads. In 1877 he was asked by the executives of the four trunk lines entering New York City to oversee an organization that would avoid rate wars. He organized the Trunk Line Association and as its commissioner (1887–89) established machinery to settle disputes by arbitration.

Albert Fink's principal contribution to American railroad development undoubtedly lay in the field of engineering. The strength and boldness of his bridge designs increased the range and economy of railway operation generally; his reconstruction and extension of the Louisville and Nashville Railroad after the Civil War stimulated industrialization in the New South. But Fink gained greater prominence as a statistician and as champion of a system of self-regulation for the railroad industry. A giant of a man, standing six feet seven inches, with a manner and bearing appropriate to his size, he had a quick, orderly mind and a remarkable command of his adopted language. His penchant for order and administrative efficiency made him an enemy of rate competition and led him to advocate cartelization as the only practicable guarantee against rate discrimination. In repeated appearances before congressional committees he protested the outlawing of pooling, urging instead the legalization of a continent-wide association of transportation companies with a British-style clearinghouse to fix rates. Despite the force of his arguments and the demonstrated effectiveness of the British system of control, his testimony had little impact on the movement for public regulation in the United States. His 1874 report on transportation costs, on the other hand, was a seminal document in railroad economics. Through a comparative study of operating expenses on the different branches of the Louisville and Nashville, Fink was able to give precise definition to the many cost variables in a complex industry. His report provided the foundation for a workable system of railroad accounting. See his obituary in *The Railroad Gazette,* April 9, 1897.

GEORGE H. MILLER

FINNEY, Charles Grandison (b. Warren, Conn., Aug. 29, 1792; d. Oberlin, Ohio, Aug. 16, 1875), RELIGIOUS LEADER, attended the Hamilton Oneida Academy in Clinton, New York. Finney returned to Warren, Connecticut, in 1812 to prepare to enter Yale but decided against it. Instead he taught school in northern New Jersey and in 1818 began to read law in Adams, New York. He was admitted to the bar shortly thereafter but gave up law to become an evangelist. Ordained a Presbyterian minister in 1824, he conducted a series of revival meetings in the middle and eastern states (1824–32), emphasizing the fearful consequences of disobeying God. He stressed the individual's ability to repent and developed such revivalistic devices as the "anxious bench" to encourage converts to come forward and "accept salvation." In 1830 he moved to New York City where he received the financial support of two wealthy merchants, Arthur and Lewis Tappan. In 1832 he became pastor of the Second Free Presbyterian Church in New York, using as his base the Chatham Street theater, which the Tappans had procured for him.

In 1835, Finney was invited to found and head the theology department of the New Oberlin (Ohio) College; he served as president from 1851 to 1866 and remained connected with Oberlin until his death. Dissatisfied with the operations of the system of discipline in the presbytery, he withdrew from the Presbyterian Church in 1836 and accepted the pastorate of the Congregationalist Broadway Tabernacle in New York City. He left this post in 1837, however, in order to devote his time to Oberlin. He was pastor of Oberlin's First Congregational Church (1837–72) and helped found (1839) and became a frequent contributor to the *Oberlin Evangelist.* Finney made two evangelizing tours of Great Britain (1849–50, 1859–60). Always interested in social reform, he supported the antislavery and temperance movements, and favored total abstinence from tobacco and coffee. Some of his many books include two collections of sermons, *Lectures on Revivals* (1835) and *Lectures on Systematic Theology* (2 vols., 1846, 1847), and his *Memoirs* (1876).

⁂

Charles Finney epitomized evangelical Protestantism in America. His public career spanned the years (1820–75) when evangelicalism developed and reached the acme of its influence in America. Trained initially as a lawyer, without formal theological education, Finney departed from the revered traditions of a carefully educated ministry. He began to preach with great power and force in western New York in the 1820s following a deeply felt conversion experience that transformed his desultory career as a small-town lawyer into that of a national Christian leader. His itinerant preaching, his emotional fervor, and his lay status all characterized the institutionalized revivalism and the new religious leaders—roving, popular evangelists—that were at the heart of evangelical Protestantism. Finney's central concern was to "save souls" and to produce the conversion experience in the heart and mind of his hearers. All of his preaching, pulpit activities, and revival services were directed toward that end. This, too, was the basic mission of all evangelicals in America. To achieve his ends Finney devised or emphasized special techniques—"New Measures," they were called—of persuasion. The so-called anxious bench, vehement exhortation, and revivals "prayed up" by men, not prayed down from God, were Finney's trademarks and subsequently those of all evangelicals. Needless to say these tactics were in sharp contrast to the more sedate, less emotional, more aristocratic, less democratic characteristics of most religions in the colonial era.

Finney's theology, forcefully projected in his preaching and in his published writings (his *Lectures on Revivals* were widely read), demonstrated and helped along the shift in religious thought that occurred as American Protestants adjusted their colonial Puritan heritage to the 19th century. Orthodoxy, already under subtle attack by such New England ministers as Nathaniel Taylor and Lyman Beecher, was bludgeoned into full-scale retreat by Finney's popular and much more direct espousal of Arminian doctrines. Stress on man's agency in effecting receipt of God's grace and release from spiritual uncertainty was essential for the implementation of Finney's "New Measures" of revivalism and immediate conversion. By the 1840s both Finney's bluntly stated theology and his preaching techniques were accepted in many of the most important American churches.

Finney also believed in a form of perfectionism and in millennialism. These doctrines provided a theoretical base for the utopian striving that powered the wide-ranging interest in social reforms of Finney and most other evangelicals. His work as professor and president at Oberlin College and the history of that school as a great center of abolitionist agitation symbolized perfectly the social activism that characterized the evangelical movement.

In poor health during his last years, Finney all but retired from the public arena, although he continued his evangelistic preaching without letup to the end. By the time of his death in 1875 the evangelical movement reigned supreme within American Protestantism. Science and the Industrial Revolution would soon bring far-reaching changes to the American churches. Nevertheless, evangelicalism remained at the heart of the American religious experience in the 19th century. This fact, in turn, bespeaks the central historical importance of Charles Finney who did so much to give shape and direction to that

movement. See William G. McLoughlin, *Modern Revivalism: Charles Grandison Finney to Billy Graham* (1959).

JAMES FINDLAY

FISH, Hamilton (b. New York, N.Y., Aug. 3, 1808; d. Garrison, N.Y., Sept. 7, 1893), DIPLOMAT, POLITICAL LEADER, graduated from Columbia University (1827) and was admitted to the bar in 1830. He was a Whig candidate for the New York state assembly in 1834 but was defeated. In 1842 he was elected to the U.S. Congress. In 1846 he ran for lieutenant governor of New York but was defeated. However, he was elected lieutenant governor the following year, and in 1848, governor. During his term (1849–50) the legislature extended the public school system and improved the canal system. Fish then served in the U.S. Senate (1851–57), joining the Republican Party and opposing the extension of slavery. When the Civil War broke out he was a member of the Union Defense Committee of New York State.

In 1869, President Ulysses S. Grant appointed Fish secretary of state. As secretary he helped settle the *Alabama* Claims dispute (1871) in which Great Britain agreed to pay an indemnity for damage done by British-built Confederate ships during the Civil War. In 1873 the Spanish in Cuba captured the *Virginius*, an arms-running ship under American registry that actually belonged to the Cuban revolutionary committee in New York. The Spanish executed fifty-three sailors, including some Americans, as pirates. In the resulting controversy Fish persuaded the Spanish government to pay indemnities to the American families. This episode was the climax of many years of diplomacy aimed at ending the Cuban civil war and preventing that war from causing a more serious conflict between the United States and Spain.

Fish was an expansionist, but he supported President Grant's attempts to annex Santo Domingo (1869–70) with scant enthusiasm. The Senate refused to accept the annexation treaty. In 1875, however, Fish did negotiate a reciprocity treaty with Hawaii. He also supported two unsuccessful attempts to construct an interoceanic canal (1870, 1877). After his retirement (1877) Fish was active in many literary and philanthropic organizations, and served as a trustee of Columbia College.

Irony must have caused one of America's worst presidents to rescue Hamilton Fish from historical obscurity and provide him the opportunity to become one of our finest secretaries of state.

Appointed to Grant's cabinet at 60, Fish had to his credit a respectable but undistinguished political career that seemed already finished. He brought to Washington no diplomatic experience but some personal baggage of special significance: a distaste for war and imperialism, an aristocratic disdain for bunkum and an immunity to overexcitement about almost any subject, a large fund of political tact and the sense to put it aside when necessary in favor of stronger measures, and impressive administrative talents that more brilliant men might have neglected to use but that he employed with patience and pleasure. Important attributes, these, which contributed to Fish's three most striking accomplishments. First, he engineered the Washington Treaty and Geneva arbitration, thus laying to rest those Civil War issues that could have caused war between Great Britain and the United States and establishing the foundations for subsequent years of rapprochement. Second, he prevented Cuba's brutal civil war from sliding into a "premature" Spanish-American War. Third, in what stands as an achievement of note in and by itself, he shrewdly used two of Grant's ruling obsessions for his own large purposes, turning the president's infatuation with Santo Domingo to use in his formulation of a carefully controlled Cuban policy and using the ex-soldier's hatred of the Britain-baiting **Charles Sumner** to keep him from joining the politics of Anglophobia and wrecking the settlement of the *Alabama* Claims.

Fish's interest in Samoa, Hawaii, and Latin America markets and an interoceanic canal marks him in some ways as a prototype of the expansionists of the 1890s. But he was really more a latter-day Federalist than an early McKinley expansionist, more concerned with avoiding unnecessary wars and defending already existing American interests than with looking for new areas of adventure.

His record is difficult to fault. Although he blundered more than once in his dealings with Britain and Spain, he recovered quickly and did not permit transitory complications to divert him from the difficult path toward peace, made thorny at every turn by touchy Englishmen, outrageous and stubborn Castilians, arm-waving American jingoes, and a president to placate and serve who could scarcely contain his deep personal urge to whip both Britisher and Spaniard.

One cannot help but be offended by Fish's indifference to the failure of Reconstruction and the dashing of hopes to bring genuine freedom to the former slaves, but in this attitude he had a lot of company among his contemporaries. He chose not to use his great moral authority with Grant for a crusade to clear the thieves and incompetents from the Augean stables of an administration that has become a byword for corruption in American political history. He must have realized that, had he elected to cross swords with his chief, he would have failed in his mission and lost his office as well. And Grant would have been deprived of the one bright success of his unhappy days as president. See Allan Nevins, *Hamilton Fish: The Inner History of the Grant Administration* (1937).

ROBERT L. BEISNER

FISK, James, Jr. (b. Bennington, Vt., Apr. 1, 1834; d. New York, N.Y., Jan. 7, 1872), FINANCIER, worked throughout his childhood at odd jobs and peddling goods in his father's "traveling emporium." In 1860 he became a commission agent for the Boston wholesale firm of Jordan and Marsh. After successfully speculating in confiscated cotton during the Civil War, he opened a brokerage house in New York City in 1865. The postwar deflation drove his firm into bankruptcy, but he promptly recouped his fortune when he served as agent in the sale of Daniel Drew's Stonington Steamboat Line in 1866. He formed the brokerage firm of Fisk and Belden on Wall Street with Drew's assistance in 1866. There he developed a close association with **Jay Gould.** Drew brought Fisk and Gould onto the board of directors of the Erie Railroad in 1867.

Beginning in March 1868, Drew, Gould, and Fisk engaged in a spectacular conflict with **Cornelius Vanderbilt** for control of the Erie Railroad. The Erie triumvirate issued $8 million in watered stock in spite of a judicial restraining order. When Vanderbilt obtained a contempt-of-court ruling in New York, they established a new home office for the Erie in Jersey City, then dispensed more than $1 million in bribes to obtain a New York law that authorized the stock issue. Although they apparently had won the "Erie War," Drew decided to resolve the dispute amicably by retracting the $8 million of watered stocks in May 1868. However, both Drew and Vanderbilt withdrew from the Erie. In July 1868, Gould became president and treasurer and Fisk general manager and controller of the railroad. The new directors of the Erie issued $23 million in watered stock by October 1868. When Drew and other stockholders secured an injunction, **William M. Tweed,** boss of Tammany Hall, persuaded a judge to place the Erie under the receivership of Gould and Fisk.

Gould and Fisk conspired with the brother-in-law of President Ulysses S. Grant, Abel R. Corbin, to corner the gold market in the autumn of 1869. When Grant belatedly released the federal gold reserves on "Black Friday," September 24, 1869, they sold short, making an estimated profit of $11 million. Fisk and Gould continued to plunder the stock market for two more years. However, Fisk's life ended abruptly when Edward Stokes murdered him in a quarrel over a woman.

<hr>

Showmanship and shrewdness explained the early business success of Jim Fisk (even the press rarely used his full first name), but he did not attain notoriety beyond a local scale until he entered the brokerage business in New York in

1865. An inexorable affinity for rogues seemed to draw him into alliances, business and otherwise, with politicians and financiers such as Daniel Drew and Jay Gould. Whether they used him as an associate, a foil, or a scapegoat was beside the point, for Fisk regarded business as somewhat of a joke. It at least underwrote his lavish expenditures and Lydian tastes.

His exploits as a showoff were legendary. When he became the owner of a boat line to Fall River, it was his pleasure to appear on board at departure time in a uniform carrying as many golden bands and stars as an admiral. He also sported lavender kid gloves and a diamond bosom pin "as large as a cherry." When he purchased the colonelcy of the Ninth Regiment of the New York State National Guard, he equipped it and himself with resplendent uniforms and retained a splendid band to head its parades. He once made a round of New Year's calls in a "gorgeous chariot" drawn by a four-in-hand of high steppers and attended by four footmen in flamboyant livery. "When he stopped before any favored house, his mamelukes descended, unrolled a carpet, laid it from the carriage steps to the door, and stood on either side in attitudes of military salute while their august master passed by."

Nothing became his theatrical life more than his leaving it. He failed to anticipate that his favorite "gay lady," Josie Mansfield, might decide to be "kept" at the same time by two men. One was Fisk. The other, Ned Stokes, shot Fisk in 1872 in a New York hotel. The funeral cortege, unmatched since the burial of Abraham Lincoln, elicited from a conservative and respectable lawyer of New York City an accurate appraisal of an involved situation. The "Fiskicide" should be hanged, albeit with a "silken rope." As for Jim, "What a scamp he was, but what a curious and scientifically interesting scamp!... Let us put generosity down to the credit side of the scamp's account.... His influence on the community was certainly bad in every way, but also it is certain that many people, more or less wise and more or less honest, sorrowed heartily at his funeral." Fisk realized that it was a function of the rich to entertain the poor. He did—and he enjoyed the role. See W. A. Swanberg, *Jim Fisk: The Career of an Improbable Rascal* (1959).

EDWARD C. KIRKLAND

FITCH, John (b. Windsor, Conn., Jan. 21, 1743; d. Bardstown, Ky., July 2, 1798), INVENTOR, worked on his father's farm and held a succession of odd jobs before opening up his own brass shop in East Windsor, Connecticut (1764). Because of bad investments and an unhappy home life, he abandoned his shop in 1769 and settled in Trenton, New Jersey, where he started a brass and silversmith business. At the outbreak of the Revolution, Fitch enlisted in a Trenton company as a lieutenant but soon left the army to take charge of a Trenton gun factory; he also sold supplies to Washington's troops. During the early 1780s Fitch became a western land surveyor, and in 1782 he was captured by the Indians, turned over to the British, and held in Canada. Released at the end of the year, he moved to Bucks County, Pennsylvania, in 1783 and organized a company to acquire land in the Northwest Territory. He made several surveying trips to the Northwest (1783–85).

From 1785 until the end of his life Fitch devoted all his time to building and operating steamboats. In 1786 and 1787 the state legislatures of New Jersey, Pennsylvania, New York, Delaware, and Virginia gave him exclusive rights (for fourteen years) to build and operate steamboats on their waters. With the financial assistance of some wealthy Philadelphians, he began work on a forty-five-foot steamboat. In August 1787 he launched a steamboat, propelled by twelve paddles, on the Delaware River before an audience composed of the delegates to the Constitutional Convention. Shortly thereafter he began to transport passengers between Philadelphia and Burlington, New Jersey, and in 1790 he operated the world's first regularly scheduled steamboat on the Delaware.

His backers soon lost interest in his experiments, however, and in 1793 Fitch traveled to France to seek financial assistance. Failing to get money abroad, he went to New York City. But again failing to gain the necessary support, Fitch moved to Kentucky where he spent his last days.

John Fitch had been an undistinguished silversmith, clockmaker, and surveyor when in 1785 he was struck by the notion that steam might be harnessed to transportation. Like the illustrious Richard Arkwright in England (the hairdresser who invented the machine for spinning cotton thread by water), Fitch knew little of mechanics. A partner later complained that "he was the most deficient in that respect of any man I ever knew that professed it." Lacking capital, political influence, and mechanical ability—everything, in fact, but vision and stubborn persistence—Fitch wore out his life trying to perfect his steamboat.

After wandering, as he said, "into a thousand wrong Rodes," during the summer of 1790 he managed to operate a steamboat on scheduled runs across the Delaware River between Philadelphia and Burlington, New Jersey. The venture was a financial failure, and "Poor Johnny" Fitch, as he came to be called, died by his own hand in Kentucky eight years later.

Fitch was difficult to get along with and stubborn concerning his invention. He drove himself relentlessly, pouring all his energies and talents into his scheme. Unlike Robert Fulton, he had to build his own engine. Only such fanaticism could have persisted in the face of so many discouragements. What he lacked other men could supply—only his own vision and commitment were indispensable. They were, however, not enough. Although he failed commercially, he schooled a number of workmen and capitalists in the possibilities of the steamboat, and paved the way for Fulton's achievement. See Thompson Westcott, *The Life of John Fitch, the Inventor of the Steamboat* (1857).

CARROLL PURSELL

FITZGERALD, Ella (b. Newport News, Va., Apr. 25, 1918), POPULAR SINGER, was reared in Yonkers, New York, by her mother, Temperance Williams, and her stepfather, Joseph DaSilva. When she was 14, her mother died. She ran away from her bullying stepfather, and the authorities sent her to an orphanage in Yonkers where she briefly attended school. She ran away again and worked the streets earning pocket money in the numbers racket and warning prostitutes when the police were in the neighborhood. She danced and sang as a child and told friends she would one day be famous. She listened closely to Bing Crosby and the Boswell Sisters, and especially Louis Armstrong, mimicking their voices and the instruments that accompanied them. In 1935 she won an amateur contest at the Apollo theater in Harlem. This led to a job as a vocalist with Chick Webb, a jazz drummer and bandleader. In 1938 the two wrote and recorded "A-Tisket, A-Tasket," based on an old nursery rhyme. It became a great hit, and Fitzgerald received national attention. When Webb died the following year, she took charge of his band. She began working as a solo performer in 1942. She joined the "Jazz at the Philharmonic" group of musicians and singers in 1948, touring Europe and Japan as well as the United States.

Having previously recorded for Decca records, Fitzgerald changed to the Verve label in 1955. Her rhythmic style and clarity of tone soon made her one of the nation's most popular recording artists and entertainers. She made her movie debut as a singer in *Pete Kelly's Blues* (1955), recorded her first album of show music, *Ella Fitzgerald Sings the Cole Porter Song Book*, in 1956, and gave her own jazz concert at the Hollywood (Calif.) Bowl in 1957. Fitzgerald toured Sweden, Germany, Australia, and South America during the 1960s in addition to appearing on numerous television programs and in nightclubs. She also recorded many albums. Indeed, she recorded nearly every year between 1939 to 1989. Some of her many hits include "Into Each Life Some Rain Must Fall," "He's My Guy," "Put a Little Lover in Your Heart," and "I Heard It Through the Grapevine."

Ella Fitzgerald, like **Frank Sinatra**, was a product of the big-band era of the thirties and forties. She was the first of the girl vocalists featured with jazz orchestras throughout that period

to achieve stardom in her own right, outdistancing in popular appeal the musical entity with which she was first associated and also outdistancing all her counterparts in other bands. She was the forerunner of an era ushered in by World War II when the allure of the big-name bands began to diminish and made stars of singers who had gained their experience with them. Prior to this time, most box office names had come out of vaudeville or Broadway shows. The death of bandleader Chick Webb, her guardian and mentor, terminated Ella Fitzgerald's secondary role and initiated a tremendous development in her style and delivery. She eventually established standards no one else could attain.

Unlike her great contemporary Billie Holiday, whose temperament accounted for an enduring association with heartbreak, Ella Fitzgerald's musical personality was warm and benign. Although she loved to sing ballads, a superb ear and uninhibited spirits enabled her to employ idioms on jazz classics formerly restricted to the best instrumentalists.

She has a remarkable range that is fully utilized and a vibrant rhythmic sense. However, an inimitable sound is her greatest attribute. Tones broad and rich are beautifully matched to a phraseology that never appears labored or false. "Ella Fitzgerald is beyond category," **Duke Ellington** once observed, and perhaps it was precisely because she was so superbly endowed that few among her contemporaries dared emulate her, although many acknowledged her as their inspiration. See Stuart Nicholson, *Ella Fitzgerald: A Biography of the First Lady of Jazz* (1994).

HELEN DANCE

FITZGERALD, Francis Scott Key (b. St. Paul, Minn., Sept. 24, 1896; d. Hollywood, Calif., Dec. 21, 1940), WRITER, entered Princeton in 1913 but left in 1917 to enlist in the army. He served as aide-de-camp to Brigadier General John Ryan but never went overseas. His first novel, *This Side of Paradise* (1920), was largely autobiographical. It served as a rallying cry for the rebellious, alienated youth of the 1920s. Fitzgerald then became a highly successful short story writer. His second novel, *The Beautiful and Damned* (1922), was a financial success, but a play, *The Vegetable* (1923), was a dismal failure. In 1924, Fitzgerald moved to Europe where he finished *The Great Gatsby* (1925), the novel of Jay Gatsby's pursuit of an elusive dream and his resulting destruction.

In 1930, Fitzgerald's wife suffered a mental collapse, and he went to Baltimore. He lived in despair, drinking heavily and unable to write. He finally published *Tender Is the Night* (1934), but its lackluster reception further depressed him. In 1937 he moved to Hollywood to become a movie scriptwriter. He enjoyed some success but soon began to drink heavily again. He died while working on a novel about Hollywood, *The Last Tycoon*, which was published posthumously (1941). Some of his short story collections are *Flappers and Philosophers* (1921), *Tales of the Jazz Age* (1922), and *Taps at Reveille* (1935).

—⁂—

Scott Fitzgerald shared more completely than any other writer of his time the feelings and values of ordinary Americans. Jay Gatsby, the hero of *The Great Gatsby*, is, in the intensity of his commitment, an almost fabulous hero, but his commitments are typically American. His boyhood hero was Hopalong Cassidy, his ambition self-improvement ("Practice elocution, poise and how to attain it"), his dream to be very rich and to spend a lifetime ecstatically in love with the top girl. Fitzgerald was not so naïve an idealist as Gatsby: he could hardly escape acquiring some worldliness at Princeton. But he shared Gatsby's ambitions and dreams of glory. What distinguished Fitzgerald from ordinary Americans was his special gift, what he called, in describing Gatsby, "a heightened sensitivity to the promises of life" that made it possible for him to visualize those promises with unmatchable vividness.

Like most Americans, Fitzgerald lived hard. Like them, he worked to make money, not because he was greedy but because he believed that the circumstances of happiness are expensive. Like them, he played hard, too; he went to far too many parties and drank far too much in an effort to find the joy he could never stop believing was just around the next corner. This way of life, though clearly a consequence of the feelings that were also the motive and purpose of his best work, made it difficult for him to get much work done, both because he spent a great deal of time doing other things and because, when he did work, he often wrote popular short stories for money (he wrote more than 160 short stories in his brief career).

As a result Fitzgerald wrote less serious work than might have been expected—two very fine novels and one that might have been had it not been left unfinished at his death, and perhaps a dozen great short stories. But at his best Fitzgerald did something important that had never been done before in American literature. The combination in his work of his typical American's feelings about life and his great gifts makes his stories at once remarkably intimate and romantically dazzling. Everything that happens in them is almost hypnotically familiar— "But that's just the way it is and just the way I feel," people say—and at the same time enchanted in a way our lives are not. "It was themselves he gave back to [them]," Fitzgerald says of Dick Diver, the hero of *Tender Is the Night*, "blurred by the compromises of how many years." This is the effect on us, too, of the great moments of his novels: the magical moment at Daisy's dinner table the first time Nick Carraway goes there ("There's a bird on the lawn that I think must be a nightingale come over on the Cunard or White Star Line," says Daisy—first class, it goes without her saying); or the moment on the Divers' terrace at Antibes when Dick and Nicole "began suddenly to warm and glow and expand" and for a moment the faces of their incongruously mixed group of guests looked up at them "like the faces of poor children at a Christmas tree." At these moments the people in Fitzgerald's novels are living, despite their personal inadequacies, with the completeness of self-fulfillment, of communion with their fellows, of realized delight that their best selves have always dreamed of. What Fitzgerald's novels make us all—at least all Americans—understand is what the possibilities of our lives are and the poignancy of our failure to realize those possibilities. See Arthur Mizener, *The Far Side of Paradise* (1965).

ARTHUR MIZENER

FITZHUGH, George (b. Prince William Co., Va., Nov. 4, 1806; d. Huntsville, Tex., July 30, 1881), WRITER, was admitted to the Virginia bar (1829) and began to practice at Port Royal. As slavery came under increasing attack from abolitionists, Fitzhugh became a defender of the "peculiar institution." He converted the defense of slavery from a negative rebuttal to northern criticism into a strong positive support of the institution. He published two books, *Sociology for the South* (1854) and *Cannibals All!* (1857), which attacked capitalist, laissez-faire society and condemned the middle class for exploiting the working class. The paternalistic economy of the slave South, Fitzhugh believed, was a better alternative. In 1855 he went on a northern speaking tour and debated **Wendell Phillips,** the abolitionist, in New Haven, Connecticut. A regular contributor to *De Bow's Review* (1857–67), he also wrote for the New York *Day Book* and Richmond *Examiner* in the antebellum period.

Having supported James Buchanan for president in 1856, Fitzhugh became an aide to Attorney General Jeremiah S. Black in 1857. Initially, Fitzhugh opposed secession and urged conciliation, hoping that the North could be converted to his views. But by 1857, convinced that the abolitionists would cause a violent conflict, he supported secession and war. After the Civil War he served as an associate judge of Virginia's Freedmen's Court and opposed radical Reconstruction. He wrote frequently for *Lippincott's* magazine of Philadelphia (1869–70), but failing eyesight caused him to become less active. He moved to Texas in 1880.

Although he was in the vanguard of pro-slavery philosophizing, Fitzhugh was perhaps the Old South's most logical and formidable social theorist. A cranky, clever individual who wrote his compositions in a ramshackle, bat-ridden plantation, Fitzhugh stripped away many of the contradictions that characterized pro-slavery thought and brought a little order and coherency into the ideology—and the world view—of the master class.

He wanted slaveholders to stand before the world as Enlightened Reactionaries who ruled an insulated slave community, family-based, self-sufficient, and proudly provincial. He insisted that southern thinkers stop riding the contradictory horses of Lockean liberalism and Enlightened Reaction. Reject the Age of Reason, he told southern slavemasters, and its preoccupations with science, rationalism, and human liberty. Let southerners boldly admit what they were: backward-looking aristocrats who were trapped in a modern world controlled by Lockean liberalism and a competitive market economy. To free themselves from such a world, southerners must destroy capitalism—or "free society"—and revive the virtues of precapitalist Europe when despots ruled the weak, enfeebled multitudes with paternalistic concern and responsibility. Fitzhugh himself, in trumpeting the glories of this bygone age, mounted an impassioned, often incisive attack against the evils of unbridled capitalism. He deplored competition because it produced a class of cannibals whose obsessions with money eroded stable institutions like the family and caused universal exploitation of the poor and the weak, who, he contended, had been better off as serfs in the halcyon days of feudalism. Once the South destroyed free society, the master class would then enslave all workers—white as well as black—and the world would enjoy supreme order and stability. But Fitzhugh was not without his own contradictions. By his own argument, his ideal slave society—reactionary and paternalistic—would have to develop industry and towns in order to achieve self-sufficiency and thus to free itself from the very capitalism he attacked.

Probably not a great many slaveholders embraced Fitzhugh's ideas. Most of them hadn't the courage or the inclination to be such forthright reactionaries. After the war Fitzhugh's writings for the most part were harsh, desperate polemics; and the man himself became a pathetic figure. A paternal racist before the war, he had renounced a strictly racial defense of slavery. But in the postwar period, penniless, going blind, and deeply embittered because of what had happened to his cherished South, he surrendered himself to Negrophobia. See Eugene D. Genovese, *The World the Slaveholders Made* (1969).

STEPHEN B. OATES

FITZPATRICK, Thomas (b. County Cavan, Ire., c. 1799; d. Washington, D.C., Feb. 7, 1854), TRAPPER, WESTERN GUIDE, emigrated to the United States in his early teens. In 1823 he was one of a group of trappers hired by General **William H. Ashley** for an exploratory voyage up the Missouri River. In September of that year Fitzpatrick was chosen to be second in command of a smaller group that was sent from Fort Kiowa (near present Chamberlain, S.D.) to explore the Wyoming region; in 1824 they discovered the South Pass, which later became a major pathway to Oregon. Fitzpatrick continued to work for government expeditions until 1830 when he formed, with James Bridger and Milton G. Sublette, among others, the Rocky Mountain Fur Co. After the company was disbanded in 1834, he continued in the fur trade as an employee of **John J. Astor**'s American Fur Co. He soon returned to his work as a guide, however, and during the 1840s he led such groups as the John Bidwell—John Bartleson Co., the first Pacific-bound emigrant wagon train (1841), and Colonel Stephen W. Kearny's expedition to South Pass (1845).

In 1846, Fitzpatrick was appointed government Indian Agent for a newly created Indian Agency of the Upper Platte and the Arkansas. In 1851, with Colonel D. D. Mitchell, superintendent of the Central Agency, St. Louis, he organized a conference at Fort Laramie that resulted in treaties establishing boundaries for the Plains tribes north of the Arkansas River. In 1853, at Fort Atkinson, Fitzpatrick secured peace treaties with the Comanches, Kiowas, and Kiowa Apaches.

Fitzpatrick was the prototype of the trapper-explorer-guide who spearheaded American expansion to the Pacific Coast in the second quarter of the 19th century. A man of commanding presence, tireless, aggressive, yet intelligent, introspective, and wide-ranging in interest, he achieved a stature at the time unsurpassed by any of his contemporaries, such as Kit Carson or Jim Bridger, whose fame later grew in legend. He earned a rare kind of respect and admiration not only from colleagues, politicians, army officers, and migrating settlers but from Native Americans he encountered as trapper and government agent. It was as agent to Plains tribes that he played his most significant role, composing reasoned and persuasive reports to the Indian Bureau in the late 1840s that rationalized American challenges to control of the Plains by Native Americans. Although skilled at distinguishing among the traits and characteristics of dozens of western tribes, he generalized readily about the inferiority of their civilization and the inevitability of their demise at the hands of the white man. Fitzpatrick expressed doubt that the tribes could survive American conquest, but he concluded that trade offered the only hope of bolstering their capacity to accommodate and endure. Rather than urging then that the established quarantine be perpetuated to protect the remaining tribes from white contact and influence, he asserted that white and Native American interests both required the extension of commercial and diplomatic relations. With his guidance the government negotiated the treaties of 1851 and 1853 that opened the final generation of Native American independence on American soil. See LeRoy R. Hafen and W. J. Ghent, *Broken Hand: The Life Story of Thomas Fitzpatrick* (1931).

RICHARD M. CLOKEY

FLAGLER, Henry Morrison (b. Hopewell, N.Y., Jan. 2, 1830; d. West Palm Beach, Fla., May 20, 1913), BUSINESSMAN, attended district schools until 1844 when he moved to Sandusky, Ohio. After working (1844–52) in Republic and Bellevue, Ohio, in stores owned by L. G.

Harkness and Co., grain merchants, he became a partner in the firm. He remained in Bellevue until 1862 when he attempted to establish a salt manufacturing business in Saginaw, Michigan. By 1865, however, the business had failed, and Flagler moved to Cleveland where he was again a grain merchant. He renewed his acquaintance with **John D. Rockefeller,** whom he had known in Bellevue, and in 1867 joined as a partner in the oil-refining firm of Rockefeller, Andrews, and Flagler. In 1870 this became the Standard Oil Co., with Flagler as secretary-treasurer, later vice president. Although his influence in the company declined steadily beginning in the early 1880s, Flagler held his post as vice president until 1908, and director until 1911.

Flagler was especially involved in developing Florida as a resort center. During his first visits to Florida in 1878 and 1883, he observed the relative lack of transportation and hotel facilities in the southern section of the state. In 1886 he began to consolidate a number of small railroads into the Florida East Coast Railroad. During 1892–96 he extended his lines south to Miami and constructed a series of luxurious hotels along the route. Among the best known of these were the Ponce de Leon in St. Augustine and the Royal Palm Hotel in Miami. By 1912 he had completed a rail link to Key West and finished the dredging of Miami harbor. He also actively promoted the growth of agriculture, especially fruit growing, in the state.

⁂

Henry M. Flagler might be considered one of the robber barons of the late 19th century. He was a pioneer in the U.S. oil industry and accumulated a great fortune. At one time he was as well known as John D. Rockefeller. As he turned his interests toward his Florida developments, his ingenuity as a shrewd businessman became even more evident.

Flagler, like most men with driving ambition and thirst for wealth, was a controversial figure. People opposed to big businesses thought of him as ruthless and grasping. Many Floridians considered him a Yankee carpetbagger who had come to their state to soak up financial gains at their expense. Realizing that he was widely disliked, he once said that anyone who was successful in life was compelled to pay a price for success, that price being the loss of friends and acquaintances.

To his friends, however, Flagler was a warm and personable man who was interested in the welfare of those around him. Certainly he was a man of vision, and although he did not live to see all his developments in Florida take root and become financially productive, he planted seeds in that state that later produced the rapid and unprecedented growth of Florida's east coast. As a result of these enterprises the eyes of the rest of the nation were turned on a state that had never been fully developed. Flagler therefore deserves credit for being the "second discoverer of Florida." See S. Walter Martin, *Florida's Flagler* (1949).

S. WALTER MARTIN

FLAHERTY, Robert Joseph (b. Iron Mountain, Mich., Feb. 16, 1884; d. Dummerston, Vt., July 23, 1951), FILMMAKER, attended the Upper Canada College preparatory school in Toronto (1898–1900). After briefly studying at the Michigan College of Mines (1900–1901), Flaherty worked on mine explorations. He made four expeditions into the subarctic regions of eastern Canada for Sir William Mackenzie between 1910 and 1916, mapping the Baffin Land, Hudson Bay area, and Belcher Island, while also photographing the Eskimos. Beginning with his second expedition (1913), he lived with the natives and filmed their activities, painstakingly accumulating a record that became *Nanook of the North* (1922), a documentary on Eskimo life. Praised by the critics for his ability to capture native life on film, Flaherty was invited by Jesse Lasky of the Famous Players (later Paramount) to make a similar documentary on Samoan life. After living in Samoa (1923–24), Flaherty released *Moana* (1926). He made *The Story of a Potter* (1925) for the Metropolitan Museum of Art, *Industrial Britain* (1933) with John Grierson, and combined with German director F. W. Murnau on *Tabu* (1932), the story of a boy in Tahiti, which won an Oscar from the Motion Picture Academy in 1932 for photography. His *Man of Aran* (1934), the story of daily life in a group of islands off the Irish coast, gained first prize at the Venice Exposition of 1934. After having been commissioned to make a film of Kipling's "Toomai of the Elephants," he worked in India (1935–37), producing *Elephant Boy* (1937) with Sabu, whom he discovered, in the title role. *The Land* (1941) was a study of soil erosion made for the U.S. Department of Agriculture.

During World War II, Flaherty made a series of educational films, including *What's Happened to Sugar?* (1945) on the wartime sugar shortage. He spent 1946 to 1948 filming *The Louisiana Story* (1948) for Standard Oil, dealing with oil wells in the Louisiana bayous and their impact on the Cajun people. Also in 1948, *Nanook of the North* was released with a sound track. In addition to filmmaking Flaherty wrote two novels and two nonfiction works, *My Eskimo Friends* (1924) and *A Film-Maker's Odyssey* (1939).

Flaherty's achievement in filmmaking was unique. He was a director of genius. Though he was hailed by the disciples of John Grierson as "the father of documentary," only Basil Wright inherited his poetic vision. Flaherty took his material from nature, but what he fashioned from it was a work of art comparable to the form a sculptor discovers within a crude monolith. He began as an explorer, and his masterpiece *Nanook of the North* sprang from his admiration of the Eskimo, his life, his art, and his philosophy. He felt it was as meaningful to the "civilized" world, which had spent the four years of World War I trying to destroy itself, as it was to him, torn between a love of the fleshpots and an admiration for the bare struggle for existence.

Flaherty's genius was complex: a gusto for life and simple people, an innocent eye, an infinite patience. His amateurishness was simple. He could not cut his film according to his budget. He preferred, in fact, making films to finishing them. *Nanook of the North*, because its costs were small, made money. But all his other films ran up against financial snags, whether financed by commercial producers or sponsored by official bodies or industrial organizations. *Moana, Man of Aran, The Land,* and supremely *Louisiana Story* are classics of poetic documentary. But all of them bear the traces of the conflict between his love for making films and his dislike of finishing them. See Arthur Calder-Marshall, *The Innocent Eye: The Life of Robert Flaherty* (1963).

ARTHUR CALDER–MARSHALL

FLEXNER, Abraham (b. Louisville, Ky., Nov. 13, 1866; d. Falls Church, Va., Sept. 21, 1959), EDUCATOR, earned a BA after only two years of study at Johns Hopkins in 1886. After teaching at Louisville High School, he founded a preparatory school (1890), which he directed until 1905. He then studied at Harvard (MA, 1906) and at the Universities of Berlin and Heidelberg.

While in Germany, Flexner wrote *The American College: A Criticism* (1908), which led Henry S. Pritchett of the Carnegie Foundation for the Advancement of Teaching to ask him to make a study of American medical schools. As a result Flexner personally inspected each of the 155 medical schools in the United States and Canada and wrote *Medical Education in the United States and Canada* (1910) and *Medical Education in Europe* (1912), in which he branded American medical schools as generally inferior institutions turning out poorly trained physicians. This work sparked a revolution in American medical education. Scores of schools were closed, many others were consolidated, but the best schools received greatly increased support. Several new medical schools were also started, especially at state universities. Within a few years American physicians were being educated on a more scientific basis than ever before.

Flexner was appointed assistant secretary of the General Education Board of the Rockefeller Foundation in 1913. His study *A Modern School* (1916) embodied a plan that spurred the funding and establishment of the Lincoln Experimental School of Columbia University's Teachers College, which did pioneering work in the field of secondary education for three decades. He became secretary of the General Education Board (1917) and served as the director of its division of studies and medical education (1925–28). In these posts he exhibited great fund-raising abilities, raising about $500 million from such patrons as **George Eastman, Andrew Carnegie,** and **John D. Rockefeller.** In 1952, Flexner published a critical assessment of philanthropic support of education, *Funds and Foundations.* In his Rhodes Trust Memorial Lectures at Oxford (1927–28, published with additions in 1930 as *Universities: American, English, German*) he attacked American universities for purveying "bargain-counter and chain-store education" by introducing large numbers of elective, "non-cultural" courses that had no place in his conception of a proper classical education. He expressed admiration for the free and relaxed academic atmosphere, highly conducive to the pursuit of knowledge, which was characteristic of many European universities, and envisaged the foundation of a small academic center along these lines in America, where scholars could concentrate undisturbed on pure learning. This objective was realized in 1930 with the establishment of the Institute of Advanced Studies at Princeton University, of which he was director from 1930 to 1939.

Flexner's ideas were strongly influenced by Johns Hopkins president **Daniel Coit Gilman.** For his own part, Flexner probably influenced American higher education more than any other man who was not directly involved in the operation of a particular university. His crusade to upgrade medical education and his development of the Institute for Advanced Study were his most progressive innovations. Together with his remarkable ability to persuade men of great wealth to make large contributions to education, they will be remembered as his most significant contributions to American education.

Despite these accomplishments, many educators considered Flexner too conservative. It was not that he wanted to return to the classical curriculum of former generations, for although his own studies had emphasized Greek and Latin, he felt that the knowledge most needed in modern urban-industrial society could best be provided by the sciences and social sciences. But he strongly opposed certain trends that many educators considered essential to the democratization of the universities. He insisted that universities should remain small, elite institutions, devoted to the advancement of knowledge, and he disapproved of the extension and vocational programs (schools of business, library science, social work, and so on) through which many universities were trying to serve more of the public. Professors should work to provide the knowledge that their students could use in solving problems of society, but if they themselves became involved in practical affairs, Flexner said, they would be distracted from their true vocation of research and, in the long run, would deprive society of the leadership their unencumbered creative study would provide. See Michael Harris, *Five Counterrevolutionists in Higher Education* (1970).

MAURICE VANCE

FLEXNER, Simon (b. Louisville, Ky., Mar. 25, 1863; d. New York, N.Y., May 2, 1946), PATHOLOGIST, received MD from the University of Louisville in 1889. After doing postgraduate work at Johns Hopkins University, the universities of Strasbourg, Berlin, and Prague, and the Pasteur Institute in Paris, he was appointed associate professor of pathology at Johns Hopkins Medical School in 1895. Four years later he was made professor of pathological anatomy. After heading a Johns Hopkins University commission to investigate dysentery in the Philippines (1899), Flexner became professor of pathology at the University of Pennsylvania (1900). Concurrently, he served as director of the Ayer Chemical Laboratory (1901–3) and as pathologist of Philadelphia Hospital and the University of Pennsylvania's University Hospital (1900–3). In 1902, on the advice of Dr. **William Henry Welch** of Johns Hopkins, Flexner was named the organizer and first director of laboratories for the new Rockefeller Institute for Medical Research in New York City. He was responsible for organizing and staffing the laboratories. Besides his activities with the Institute, he worked with a New York City commission to investigate a cerebrospinal meningitis epidemic in 1904 and helped to develop a serum to treat the disease in 1907. In 1908 he led a similar investigation of infantile paralysis. Promoted to director of the Rockefeller Institute in 1920, Flexner remained in that post until 1935.

During these years Flexner headed an Institute research team investigating the causes of influenza, encephalitis, meningitis, and infantile paralysis, which was his field of specialization. The viral causes of these diseases had previously eluded scientists because of their minute size, but Flexner's team developed filtration and microscopic techniques that made their identification and study possible. By 1933, Flexner had identified the virus responsible for infantile paralysis and found its mode of afflicting the body. In 1937–38, while in retirement from the Rockefeller Institute, Flexner was Eastman professor of medicine at Oxford University. In 1941 he completed *William Henry Welch and the Heroic Age of American Medicine*, with his son, James Thomas Flexner.

It is often said that modern scientific medicine came to America from Europe through William H. Welch and his pupils and colleagues at the Johns Hopkins University School of Medicine. Flexner belonged to that group and was in the first generation of young American physicians who devoted their careers to the validation and extension of the germ theory of disease. He worked on both practical problems as well as on the basic mechanisms and causes of infectious diseases. This was a typical pattern for the time.

Arriving at Johns Hopkins in 1890, shortly after its hospital opened and three years before the admission of the first medical students, Flexner soon became Welch's principal faculty assistant in pathology. Bacteriological studies were pursued in departments of pathology until bacteriologists separated into their own departments in the first two decades of this century. Flexner's own interests were in the effects on tissues of the infectious diseases, and throughout his career he viewed himself primarily as a pathologist.

Despite the formidable list of scientific discoveries credited to him, Flexner's greatest contribution was his guidance of the Rockefeller Institute from its first days in 1902 until 1935. He early impressed the Rockefellers with administrative skill and his judgment of people and issues, so that they placed increasing confidence in his advice and stewardship and added increasingly to the endowment. Flexner, by astute choice of colleagues and by giving them freedom to pursue their researches, created a stimulating and successful research environment. Fitting is the comment written to Flexner by Alexis Carrel, a Nobel laureate at the Institute, who said, "The Rockefeller Institute is yourself. You are its mind." Because of the Institute's great contributions to American medicine, Simon Flexner, as much as any single individual, has influenced the way we practice and study medicine today. See Peyton Rous, "Simon Flexner, 1863–1946," in *Obituary Notices of Fellows of the Royal Society of London*, VI (1948–49), 409–45.

GERT H. BRIEGER

FOLKS, Homer (b. Hanover, Mich., Feb. 18, 1867; d. New York, N.Y., Feb. 13, 1963), REFORMER, taught school for two years before entering Albion College in 1885. Graduating in 1889, Folks went to Harvard where he earned another AB degree in 1890. That same year he was appointed superintendent of the Children's Aid Society of Pennsylvania. In 1893 he became executive director of the State Charities Aid Association of New York, serving until 1947. Particularly interested in destitute children, Folks organized a children's home in New York in 1894; he also published *History of the Care of Destitute, Neglected and Delinquent Children* (1902). Elected to New York's board of aldermen in 1897, Folks served as commissioner of public charities of New York City (1902–3). He was president of the New York State Probation Commission (1907–17), first vice chairman of the White House

Conference on Dependent Children (1909), and president of the National Conference on Charities and Correction (1911). Elected president of the National Association for the Study and Prevention of Tuberculosis in 1912, a year later he became secretary of the Special Public Health Commission set up to fight TB.

During World War I, Folks organized and directed the civil affairs department of the American Red Cross in France. He headed that body's survey mission to Europe (1918–19), wrote *The Human Cost of the War* (1920), and was an adviser to the American Red Cross in Europe (1921). He was president of the fiftieth anniversary meeting of the National Conference of Social Work in 1923. During the Great Depression, Folks advocated government public welfare expenditures, championing such New Deal programs as social security and unemployment relief. He was vice chairman of the National Child Labor Committee (1935), a member of the New York Governor's Commission on Unemployment Relief (1935–36), and chairman of the Governor's Commission on Illegitimacy (1936). Folks chaired the report committee of the White House Conference on Children in a Democracy (1940) and continued working for reform on the domestic front during World War II. A collection of his papers, *Public Health and Welfare: The Citizen's Responsibility* (1958), was edited by his son-in-law, Savel Zimand.

※※※

In many ways Homer Folks was a textbook example of a Progressive-era social worker. His father James, an English immigrant, settled in a Methodist and abolitionist part of Michigan, and Homer's family life was strictly moral in a typically rural Protestant fashion. In his case this background became internalized as a need always to apply himself to the improvement of social welfare. At the age of 15 he wrote that the greatest source of happiness "is doing good to others," and he apparently never changed this basic ideal. He seriously considered the ministry for a career, but the influence of Francis Peabody and George Herbert Palmer turned him to social work. It proved congenial and religiously satisfy-

ing; he perhaps inadvertently confirmed the religious nature of his vocation by marrying, late in 1891, the daughter of a Methodist minister.

The biographical data available on Folks all come from family sources and seem excessively reverent in their tone. He appears to have been tall, slender, earnest, and a bit priggish; he impressed some as an "old world gentleman public servant," much like an English aristocrat. Those not in the family circle found him superior and aloof, while those within assure posterity that he was good-natured and even merry at times. In his various positions he was an extremely competent bureaucrat, efficient at working behind the scenes, but one who usually had full control of himself and was not the type to let his emotions give him away.

Like most social workers, Folks spent much time working for laws to improve institutions for the socially disabled and to widen governmental responsibility in areas of health and welfare. Like **Lillian Wald** and **Florence Kelley,** his close allies, he was also active at times in politics, holding his commissioner of charities position under reform mayor Seth Low and working actively for Theodore Roosevelt in 1912.

Men like Homer Folks, while rarely exciting in themselves, retain importance because the cumulative effects of their lives have permanently changed American life. Better foster homes, children's courts, health laws; social security and medicare; less diphtheria and venereal disease: Folks's legacy lies in a small but definite role in each of these areas. See Walter I. Trattner, *Homer Folks* (1968).

ROBERT M. CRUNDEN

FORBES, John Murray (b. Bordeaux, France, Feb. 23, 1813; d. Milton, Mass., Oct. 12, 1898), FINANCIER, MERCHANT, was educated at academies in Andover and Northampton, Massachusetts. He began his business apprenticeship at 15 in his uncle's Boston counting house. Two years later, with an older member of the firm, Forbes went to Canton, China, to represent the firm. Returning to America a rich man at the age of

24, Forbes established J. M. Forbes and Co., commission merchants and ship owners, and amassed an even greater fortune over the next nine years.

In 1846, Forbes and a group of Boston capitalists, sensing the opportunities offered by railroad investments, bought the Michigan Central line, rebuilt it, and extended it west to Chicago and east to Buffalo. In 1855, Forbes and his associates secured control of a road southwest of Chicago and extended it (and other lines) across Iowa. These roads and the Hannibal and St. Joseph, which the Forbes interests built across Missouri, ultimately became the Chicago, Burlington, and Quincy Railroad.

During the Civil War, Forbes strongly supported the Union. He helped raise regiments in Massachusetts, particularly of black troops, and worked, unsuccessfully, to prevent the sale to the Confederacy of the British-made Laird rams, which took a heavy toll of northern shipping.

After the panic of 1873 the affairs of western railroads were in disarray, and in 1878, Forbes resumed the presidency of the Burlington roads. With the strong support of Charles E. Perkins, who was to take full charge after 1881, Forbes succeeded in stabilizing the relations of the east—west lines that competed for business between Chicago and St. Louis, and the eastern termini of the new transcontinental railroad. Always wary of uncontrolled competition, Forbes brought to the railroads of the new Middle West during the 1880s a measure of stability that was not achieved by eastern lines until the end of the century. Forbes was active in the Republican Party in the postwar period but refused to support **James G. Blaine** in 1884 and instead voted for Grover Cleveland.

The acknowledged leader of a group of New England investors whose financing of western railroads helped open up the vast trans-Mississippi interior to agricultural settlement, Forbes was an outstanding example of the kind of 19th-century entrepreneurial capitalism that developed the resources of a nation. His career reads like a profile of the American "takeoff" into industrialization between 1840 and 1860, for the decision to shift Boston capital from declining sectors such as the China trade to new fields like western railroading was an important chapter of American economic growth.

In undertaking the development of the Michigan Central, Forbes and his associates provided private investment at a time when state aid and foreign capital, following the panic of 1837, were no longer available for improving transportation. The venture was attended by grave risk, but the rewards were sizable, and the road, like others subsequently developed by the Forbes group, assisted in the creation of the largest internal free market in the world.

To all of his projects Forbes brought a mastery of financial management, Yankee shrewdness, infinite patience, and an active leadership that continued until his retirement in 1881. His decisions had a measurable impact on the rise of towns and cities. His observation (made in 1852) that great economic changes "have been effected by individual men's pointing the way and demonstrating by experiment *how* things may be done" anticipated the view of **Joseph Schumpeter** on the strategic role of the entrepreneur in economic history.

Forbes had an enormous appetite for work and thought nothing of spending an entire day at his desk, writing his business correspondence in his own hand. He sometimes drove himself to exhaustion, and only his habit of outdoor exercise—he was an excellent hunter, horseman, and yachtsman—appears to have saved him from an early grave. His strong-willed personality was tempered by a kindly disposition that drew the praise of **Ralph Waldo Emerson,** who wrote that "this is a good country that can bear such a creature as he is."

During the Civil War, Forbes was a tireless and unswerving supporter of the Union cause, which he identified with freedom, progress, science, and nationalism. In this he epitomized the social viewpoint of middle-class northern Republicanism and its militant defense of what he termed "the rights of free labor." The object of the Civil War, he said, was "the assertion of the democratic principle." In a letter to Abraham Lincoln in 1863 he urged the president "to teach your great audience of plain people that the war is not the North against the South, but the people against the aristocrats." See Henry G. Pearson, *An American Railroad Builder: John Murray Forbes* (1911).

WILLIAM GREENLEAF

FORD, Gerald Rudolph (b. Omaha, Nebr., July 14, 1913), PRESIDENT, originally named Leslie Lynch King, Jr.; when his mother divorced Leslie King and remarried, he was renamed at the age of two by his stepfather. Ford grew up in Grand Rapids, Michigan, and graduated from the University of Michigan in 1935 and Yale Law School in 1941. He enlisted in the navy and served in the Pacific during World War II, mostly aboard the aircraft carrier *Monterey*. Discharged as a lieutenant commander in 1946, he practiced law in Grand Rapids (1945–1948) before winning election to the U.S. House of Representatives in 1948 as a Republican from Michigan's Fifth District. He served in Congress for the next twenty-four years (1949–1973) as a fixture and leader of the House Republican minority. Chosen GOP minority leader in 1965, he teamed with Senate minority leader Everett Dirksen to create the "Ev and Jerry Show," a weekly television broadcast in opposition to President Lyndon Johnson's Great Society programs. Although a supporter of the Vietnam War, Ford was critical of Johnson's management of it. A moderate conservative on domestic issues, a loyal team player in politics, Ford was known by friends as just plain Jerry. He acquired a reputation for integrity, honesty, and civility. As Republican House leader he sought to enact President Richard Nixon's domestic programs and supported the administration's foreign policy. In 1973, Nixon nominated Ford for the vice presidency after the forced resignation of Spiro Agnew. He was confirmed by the Senate on November 27 (92–3) and by the House on December 6 (387–35), thereby becoming the first vice president appointed under the Twenty-fifth Amendment.

On August 9, 1974, when Nixon resigned his office due to the Watergate scandal and the threat of imminent impeachment, Ford became president. He sought to continue Nixon's foreign policy, cut domestic spending, curb inflation, reduce taxes, and alleviate the effects of a slumping economy. The Democratic Congress ignored his programs while legislating their own. But of his sixty-one vetoes, fifty-four were sustained. After a hard-fought primary, Ford defeated Ronald Reagan for the 1976 Republican presidential nomination but met defeat at the hands of Jimmy Carter in the general election by a very slim margin. His popular vote was 39.1 million to Carter's 40.1; Ford carried 241 electoral votes to Carter's 297. Out of office Ford became active in business ventures, lectured at colleges, and supported many charities. He also wrote an autobiography, *A Time to Heal* (1979).

Denied his long-time ambition to become Speaker of the House, Ford's twenty-five-year congressional career culminated in a capriciously unforeseen fashion when he became the thirty-eighth president of the United States—the first in the nation's history not elected. On entering the White House he nominated **Nelson Rockefeller,** the former governor of New York, as the new vice president. Ford kept **Henry Kissinger** as secretary of state but soon replaced most of the other Nixon appointees. To heal the nation's psychic wounds, Ford initiated an earned reentry program for draft evaders and Vietnam War deserters. He also pardoned Nixon in the hope it would end the divisive bitterness engendered by Watergate. Public reaction to the pardon was negative, and it no doubt contributed to Ford's defeat in 1976. When Congress would no longer support the Vietnam War, Ford initiated Operation Frequent Wind to rescue fifty thousand Vietnamese who had fought with the United States. He also ordered retaliatory military strikes against the Khmer Rouge government of Cambodia after it seized an American freighter (*Mayaguez*) in 1975. In pursuing détente with the Soviet Union, Ford met with Leonid Brezhnev at Vladivostok in 1974 to conclude the second phase of the Strategic Arms Limitation Treaty (SALT II). That same year he also signed the Helsinki Agreement, which recognized territorial boundaries in Eastern Europe and committed the Soviets to recognize human rights in the satellites under their dominion. Although Democrats in Congress stymied Ford's attempts to counter Soviet adventurism in Africa (particularly Angola), he employed Kissinger's shuttle diplomacy to end the fighting between Israel and Egypt via the Sinai Accords.

In 1976, Ford waged an energetic campaign for votes. Not being a polished orator, he liked to mingle with the crowds. Two assassination attempts in California, both by disturbed women, limited his style of campaigning. His blunder in the second presidential debate with Carter, claiming Poland was not under Soviet domination, unfortunately reinforced the widespread public perception that he was a bumbler of limited ability. Although he served as president for only 835 days, Ford nonetheless helped restore public confidence in the White House by conducting himself in an honorable manner. See Edward and Frederick Schapsmeier, *Gerald R. Ford's Date with Destiny: A Political Biography* (1989).

EDWARD L. SCHAPSMEIER

FORD, Henry (b. Dearborn, Mich., July 30, 1863; d. Dearborn, Mich., Apr. 7, 1947), MANUFACTURER, after being educated in the local public schools, moved to Detroit (1879), working as an apprentice in a machine shop during the day and as a watch repairman in the evenings. In 1880 he became an apprentice in the Detroit Dry Dock Co., a shipbuilding firm. After he completed his apprenticeship in 1882, he worked seasonally as a traction engine operator for the Westinghouse Engine Co. During layoff periods he assisted his father in farming and lumbering in Dearborn. In 1891 he became an engineer for the Edison Illuminating Co. in Detroit. Beginning to experiment with internal combustion engines in his home workshop as early as 1891, he produced his first automobile in 1896 and formed the Detroit

Automobile Co. in 1899. When this enterprise collapsed in 1901, he was briefly associated with the Henry Ford Co. He designed and manufactured racing cars, notably the "Ford 999," which won nationally publicized contests in 1902. With the formation of the Ford Motor Co. in 1903, he resumed production of commercial vehicles.

Ford revolutionized the automobile industry by introducing his Model T in 1908. By perfecting mass-production assembly-line techniques, he and his associates were able to market a sturdy but inexpensive car, one priced within the reach of a progressively larger mass market. (The price of the Model T dropped from $850 in 1908 to $360 in 1916, while sales boomed from 10,607 to 730,041.) Ford also revolutionized industrial labor policies. In 1914 he introduced the $5 wage for an eight-hour day as an incentive for workers to endure the drudgery of assembly-line production and as a means of providing employees with the money necessary to buy Ford automobiles. However, he also instituted tyrannical discipline in the factory and used spies and armed gangs to prevent unionization.

In 1903, Ford became engaged in a legal battle with the Selden patent interests; the outcome established his reputation as a stubborn foe of monopoly. In 1895, George B. Selden had obtained a U.S. patent covering all types of self-propelled road vehicles powered by an internal combustion engine. In an attempt to control the new industry, a Wall Street syndicate in alliance with a number of motorcar builders formed the Association of Licensed Automobile Manufacturers in 1903 and brought an infringement suit against the Ford Motor Co. A federal district court ruling in 1909 went against Ford, but he appealed the case and in 1911 won a decisive victory.

After the success of the Model T, Ford emerged as an authentic folk hero who fulfilled the American dream of rags to riches. He voiced his views freely on a wide variety of issues ranging from the evils of drink to pacifism, and in December 1915 sent the "Peace Ship" to Europe in a vain effort to end World War I through mediation. In 1918 he ran unsuccessfully for the Senate on the Democratic ticket in Michigan. He published virulent anti-Semitic propaganda in his weekly journal, the Dearborn *Independent*, following World War I. However, he retracted these views in 1927.

The Ford automobile empire declined after 1925 as competitors introduced stylish yet relatively inexpensive cars. In 1927 when Ford finally closed his factories for eighteen months to retool for a new model, General Motors and other rival automobile companies rushed in to fill the vacuum. Although Ford increased sales with the new Model A in 1928 and the V–8 in 1932, he never regained his former position of dominance over the market.

During the New Deal, Ford refused to participate in the automobile industry code under the National Recovery Administration. He also continued to resist unionization in defiance of the National Labor Relations Act (1935), and Ford plant security police at the huge River Rouge works in Dearborn were responsible for some of the bloodiest labor violence of that day. Ford finally signed a contract with the United Automobile Workers in June 1941, following a strike at River Rouge. He fully cooperated with the government during World War II, converting his factories to the production of Liberator bombers, jeeps, tanks, and other military equipment.

Ford accumulated more than $1 billion as owner of the motor company. His contributions to philanthropic causes between 1908 and 1947 exceeded $40 million. By far the largest portions went to the Henry Ford Hospital in Detroit and the Edison Institute in Dearborn. The Ford Foundation, which his son Edsel endowed in 1936 with an initial cash gift of $25,000, later received a substantial share of the family's holdings in the stock of the Ford Motor Co.

———∞∞∞———

Ford belongs to that small company of historical personalities who literally transformed the world of their time. With single-minded purpose he concentrated on the design and manufacture of a standardized, durable, utilitarian, and low-priced motorcar aimed at an ever expanding market sustained by high wages and broadly diffused buying power. From his creation of a car "for the multitude" sprang the technological innovation of the moving assembly line as a governing principle of the total process of manufacture. This was the most important contribution to factory technology since the dawn of the Industrial Revolution, and no other method for the organization of production has exerted such a far-reaching influence on life in the 20th century. Thus Ford's democratization of the automobile not only put America and the world on wheels but it also altered the contours of society as much as it permanently changed the topography of cities and nations.

After the five-dollar day rocketed him to international renown in 1914, Ford was acclaimed as a prophet of the machine age and a herald of the day when abundance for all would liberate mankind from the curse of poverty. In the 1920s, at the height of his fame, Ford was a universal byword. "Fordismus," a term epitomizing the ideas of mass production, technological efficiency, and cheap consumer goods, entered the European lexicon, and Ford, last of the rugged individualists of American capitalism, was hailed in the Soviet Union as a symbol of the modern industrial technique needed to build socialism in an underdeveloped country. In 1927, on the eve of the first Five-Year Plan, an American correspondent in Russia commented on the remarkable popularity of Ford: "Incredible as it may seem, more people have heard of him than of Stalin.... Next to Lenin, Trotsky, and Kalinin, Ford is probably the most widely known personage in Russia." But to writers and artists in the Western world, Ford loomed as a vaguely sinister figure personifying the power of a dehumanizing industrialism to stifle individuality and variety under a grinding weight of uniformity. "Ford runs modern society and not the politicians who are only screens," said **F. Scott Fitzgerald** in 1924; and Aldous Huxley, in his satirical fantasy *Brave New World* (1932), depicted a mechanized totalitarian society of the future in which "Our Ford" was worshiped as a deity.

Behind the symbol and the myth was a complex, contradictory, and unpredictable personality. "Mr. Ford," said one of his associates, "had a twenty-five track mind, and there were trains going out and coming in on all tracks at all times." In the realm of technology he was at home and capable of brilliant insights; but when he strayed afield, his ignorance and prejudices betrayed his better instincts, and his flashes of intuition proved an unreliable guide. His long career, strewn with paradoxes and inconsistencies, is split as by a great geological fault. Up to about 1920, Ford was actuated by a generous humanitarianism that afterward gave way to a cynical disdain for "sentimental idealism" and to paranoid obsessions with perpetuating his industrial despotism. He was, as one observer put it, "the sum of a great number of contradictory things which by their nature cannot be added up."

Through all these vicissitudes Ford nevertheless maintained a hold on the American imagination. He became a legend in his own lifetime partly because in an age of big business, when most corporate managers were depersonalized blurs in the public mind, Ford persistently retained his personal identity. Moreover, his rise to business power owed nothing to the dominant trend of huge corporations controlled by finance capital, for the Ford Motor Co. started with an original investment of only $28,000 and grew entirely by plowing back its profits. This paradigm of the cherished American folk belief of practical success would have been enough to endear Ford to his middle-class countrymen, but there were other and deeper impulses operating to create a Ford legend. Even as head of the largest family-owned industrial empire in the world, Ford never lost the common touch and to the end of his days represented the virtues of an older and simpler agrarian society—hard work, self-reliance, practicality, and thrift—that made his career a testament to the validity of the Puritan ethic. By a happy accident the introduction of the Model T was perfectly timed to enhance the Ford myth. It was in 1908–16, when the national mood of progressive reform shaped by Theodore Roosevelt and Woodrow Wilson reached its crest, that Americans first became aware of Ford, and in him they saw a captain of industry whose aims jibed with the optimism and idealism of the Progressive era: his commitment to open competition in a free marketplace, his fight against monopoly, his dedication to making a socially useful product, his quest for technological efficiency, his insistence on passing along production economies in the form of lower prices, his advanced labor policies, and his opposition to war. Ford, an adept in self-advertising, did not hesitate to make the most of this.

Ford's lesser side may be attributed to his narrow utilitarianism, his limited vision, and his inability to grow after he formulated his basic idea of a car for the masses. "I don't like books," he said. "They muss up my mind." He also said, "I wouldn't give five cents for all the art in the world." Yet such observations did not entirely harm his reputation, for they doubtless struck a chord in the populist anti-intellectualism latent in American life. His most celebrated saying was, "History is more or less bunk." Yet it was Ford who in 1915 offered a substantial prize for a history of war that would "show war in all its horrors, instead of glorifying the slaughter—a history that shall discourage war by telling of the great things of peace."

The tragedy of Ford's life is that he became the prisoner of his own growing isolation and hardening prejudices. His most costly mistake was his failure to establish within his company a management structure assuring rational administrative control. As a result the company became a congeries of warring baronial factions whose internal struggles sent the firm rapidly downhill after the mid–1930s. Only herculean measures taken after 1945 rescued the enterprise from irreversible decay.

Of average height, Ford was lithe and sinewy, had a casual and relaxed manner, and used a spare vocabulary. When he spoke, his hands fluttered restlessly, and he could hardly sit or stand in the same place for more than a few minutes. He conveyed an impression of crackling energy and vitality. He was an enthusiastic walker and runner, often challenging his companions to a race; at 65 he was still running three miles a day.

He had fixed and erratic notions about diet and sometimes ate grass sandwiches. See Allan Nevins and Frank Ernest Hill, *Ford* (3 vols., 1954–63).

WILLIAM GREENLEAF

FORD, Henry, II (b. Detroit, Mich., Sept. 4, 1917; d. Detroit, Mich., Sept. 29, 1987), MANUFACTURER, the grandson of **Henry Ford,** founder of the Ford Motor Co., studied at Hotchkiss School and Yale where he was denied a degree at the end of his senior year because of a plagiarized senior thesis. After working for a year in the Ford plant he enlisted in the navy as an ensign in 1941 but was released to return to the family-owned business after his father, Edsel, its president, died in 1943. Although the original Henry Ford had resumed the presidency, young Ford had the backing of other members of the family and in September 1945 became undisputed head of the concern. He first discharged his grandfather's longtime lieutenant, the tough, unpopular Harry Bennett, and then turned to the company's critical labor problems. Settling quickly with the auto unions late in 1945, he moved rapidly to improve the general management of the company and to revitalize its salesmanship. The Edsel car, introduced in 1957, was a costly failure, but the Falcon and the Mustang, brought out in 1959 and 1964, were unqualified successes. In 1964, Ford sold 2,166,044 cars, the largest number in its history. Equal to 28 percent of total U.S. production, this was slightly more than the share that the company managed to retain in the 1970s. The Maverick, a subcompact car only slightly larger than the Volkswagen, was introduced in 1969.

As he grew older, Ford maintained his close control of the company despite a growing taste for international society. Like his grandfather, he guarded his power jealously, eliminating key aides who came too close to him or seemed too eager to succeed him. Lee A. Iacocca, president of the Ford Motor Company and often mentioned as a possible successor to Ford, was one of those who fell into that pattern and was dismissed in 1978. By 1979, however, Ford was willing to give up some authority and resigned as chief executive. But he remained chairman of the board of directors until 1980 and stayed on as chairman of its powerful finance committee until his death.

———— ❧ ————

The day of the mammoth family-owned manufacturing corporation had long since passed when Henry Ford II assumed the leadership of the Ford Motor Co. in 1945. More than once in the previous four decades his grandfather's stubborn individualism had come close to putting the company on the rocks. During the 1930s the Ford V–8 had saved the company, but a stubborn antiunion labor policy, carried out with the brutal tactics of the hated Harry Bennett, had left deep scars by the time a closed-shop contract was signed with the union on the eve of World War II. The company continued to lumber along without a modern record-keeping and data-reporting system, and without a clear-cut organizational structure, emerging from the war in poor shape for the hectic competition that followed resumption of civilian car manufacturing. Young Henry's release from the navy in 1943 to take his father's place at the head of the company had been almost the only alternative to government ownership of the firm, which was vitally important to the war effort. Confrontation with the senior Ford, who seemed determined to keep his grandson out of the top post (he had been furious when young Henry married a Catholic) came shortly after V-J Day when Edsel's widow, backed by old Henry's wife, threatened to sell her stock unless Henry was made president. Demanding that he be designated chief executive officer in authority as well as in name, Henry swept out the old management and built a new Ford Motor Co.

The labor situation by late 1945 was almost beyond saving. Bennett's demoralizing influence had reduced productivity per worker to the lowest level in the industry, and petty sabotage was common. But Ford boldly became the first to sign a new contract with the United Automobile Workers, which was then threatening an industry-wide strike. His next task was to improve the company's salesmanship, which entailed a revision of the cheap car image that the elder Ford's concentration on the Model T and Model A had given it. At the same time, fully realizing that no one could run the company alone, Ford adopted a policy of bringing in the best men he could find and convincing them that he wanted their "know-how" and that he was willing to follow their advice. Chief among these men were Ernest R. Breech, who was "number two man" for more than a decade, and **Robert S. McNamara,** the management controls expert whom Ford made president of the company in 1960. In a period when many old-line automobile companies became extinct and Chrysler, which had had fewer inherent problems than Ford, stumbled badly, Henry's leadership was repeatedly vindicated, and in 1956 the company successfully converted to public ownership.

Although Ford did not achieve his goal of overtaking Chevrolet for the number one spot, and despite a major market planning failure in the introduction of the Edsel car in 1957, the company was strikingly successful. Product innovation since the Edsel was well directed. The "compact" Falcon and especially the Mustang, a sporty yet utilitarian vehicle, were extremely good sellers, and the Maverick tapped a large market of families who wanted to reduce the importance of the automobile in their budget.

Unlike many business leaders, Ford never showed much interest in a government career and was not a leader in industry associations. He did, however, lend his power and prestige for a time to the cause of equal opportunity for minorities and led the effort to build the Renaissance Center, a major inner-city development in Detroit. He continued to spend considerable time on company affairs, sometimes settling a controversial point by reminding his men, "Don't forget—my name is on the building." His taste in executives settled on men like Lee Iacocca (creator of the philosophy behind the Mustang) who took the trouble to make sure they were right and then matched Ford in bluntness and determination. Ford's Rabelaisian temperament, the basis of numerous stories about his robust ideas of a good time, gave way to a more sedate yet no less

determined participation in international "jet-set" society. His continuing commitment to the company in his last years may have stemmed from the strong interest that his son showed in the business. Whether the company remains in the hands of a Ford into the fourth generation and after, however, is less significant than the fact that young Henry successfully piloted the company into the new era of corporate business practices. See Allan Nevins, *Ford: Decline and Rebirth, 1933–1962* (1963).

ALBRO MARTIN

FORD, John (O'Fearna, Sean Aloysius) (b. Cape Elizabeth, Maine, Feb. 1, 1895; d. Hollywood, Calif., Sept. 1, 1973), FILM DIRECTOR, settled in Hollywood, California, in 1913 and first worked in films as a property man. In 1917 he began to write and direct westerns for Universal Studios. During the 1920s he turned out many of these, the most notable being *The Iron Horse* (1924). He won an international reputation and an Academy Award for *The Informer* (1935), a film about an Irishman's betrayal of both his friend and the Irish Republican Army, starring Victor McLaglen. Other important critical successes followed, especially *Stagecoach* (1939), the beginning of Ford's collaboration with John Wayne; *The Grapes of Wrath* (1940), based on the novel by **John Steinbeck;** and *How Green Was My Valley* (1941).

In World War II, Ford served in the naval reserve, rising to the rank of captain. (In the Korean War he was a rear admiral.) He made several documentaries for the government, including *The Battle of Midway* (1942). Among the most successful of his postwar films were *My Darling Clementine* (1946), his trilogy—*Fort Apache* (1948), *She Wore a Yellow Ribbon* (1949), and *Wagonmaster* (1950)—*The Quiet Man* (1952), *Two Rode Together* (1961), and *The Man Who Shot Liberty Valance* (1962). Over the years he directed more than 125 films, many of them for his primary studio, Twentieth-Century Fox, but also for Metro-Goldwyn-Mayer, RKO, Republic, and United Artists. He received New York Critics Awards in

1935, 1939, 1940, and 1941, and Academy Awards in 1935, 1940, 1941, and 1953.

———∞∞∞———

John Ford was Hollywood's great mythifier of the Old West. For him, America's civilizing of the West fulfilled several cosmological destinies—the manifest destiny of America to people the continent; the metaphysical destiny of Christianity's triumph over paganism and Satan; and the humanistic destiny of law and mildness triumphing over anarchy and savagery. In Ford's most important western films, communal effort and the healthy human spirit triumph over two consistent obstacles to progress: the blindness of those who dwell in darkness (inevitably personified by Native Americans) and the selfish treachery that lurks within the souls of some of the civilized themselves.

In his use of the pagan Native Americans as barbaric villains, Ford remains squarely within the tradition of the Catholic theology in which he was raised (Ford later redressed this insult to the Native Americans in *Cheyenne Autumn*, 1964). But he makes even worse villains of those fallen men within civilization itself, those who use institutions and other human beings to serve their own selfish ends. Liberty Valance is a man who bears one of Ford's most ironic and allegorical names, for Liberty's commitment to his own absolute and anarchic license means the death of everyone else's liberty. Illustrative of Ford's vision is his adaptation of *The Grapes of Wrath*, which shifts Steinbeck's social focus (the condemnation of the capitalistic system itself) to a purely human focus—there are *some* greedy and callous rich folks, but the spirit of the people will ultimately triumph. Ford's other deep concern with the Irish and the Irish in America also produced warmhearted characters struggling against personal rather than societal weaknesses.

Ford's cinematic technique is unobtrusive and unself-conscious. Consistent with the stylistic assumptions of his era, he alternated exciting scenes of physical action with dialogue that develops his characters. Perhaps Ford's favorite recurring image is the vast shot—of distant mountains, desert, or plains—with a single civilized object slicing through it: a train, stagecoach, or truck. Ford was also a master editor (as the climaxes of his films consistently reveal), and his two most distinguished cameramen, Joseph August and Gregg Toland, specialized in far shots and gothic lighting effects with extreme contrasts of dark and light. Both devices were well suited to Ford's allegories of little men conquering vast wastes and figures of light doing battle with the forces of darkness. See Peter Bogdanovich, *John Ford* (1968).

GERALD MAST

FORREST, Edwin (b. Philadelphia, Pa., Mar. 9, 1806; d. Philadelphia, Pa., Dec. 12, 1872), ACTOR, left school in 1819 to help support his family after his father's death. He made his stage debut at Philadelphia's Walnut Street theater in 1820 in James Home's play *Douglas* and for the next few years traveled from place to place, playing in Lexington, Cincinnati, around Ohio, and in New Orleans. In 1825 he played in the company of the English actor Edmund Kean, whose work and technique Forrest later copied to some extent. In 1826, Forrest made his first appearance in New York City at the Park theater as Othello and won critical acclaim. Later that year he opened at the new Bowery theater and won large audiences who admired his handsome, manly physique and style. In 1828, Forrest offered prizes for the best dramas written by Americans, resulting in such plays as *Metamora* (1829) by John Augustus Stone and *The Gladiator* (1831) by Robert M. Bird, in which Forrest established one of his greatest roles as Spartacus. He toured Europe from 1834 to 1836 and was well received in London (1836) playing Spartacus.

Forrest again played in London in 1845 but became involved in a controversy with English actor William Macready. Hissed by a London audience, Forrest blamed Macready and consequently hissed him at an Edinburgh performance. The bitterness between the two carried to America, and in May 1849 a mob of Forrest supporters attempted to attack Macready during a performance at New York's Astor Place opera house. The militia was called out and fired on the crowd, killing thirty-one people. Two years later Forrest became involved in a scandal in which he sued his wife for divorce for her alleged love affair with actor George Jamieson. The trial received tremendous publicity, and Forrest often made speeches to audiences between acts to plead his case. He lost the court battle and had to pay substantial alimony. After 1852 he divided his time between acting and residence in Philadelphia. He performed in New York and Boston in 1860, in Chicago and San Francisco in 1866, and made his last appearance in New York in 1871. He left most of his estate for the establishment of a home for aged actors in Philadelphia.

Edwin Forrest was the first native-born American star actor, and for the middle years of the 19th century he dominated his country's stage. His compelling power derived from his commanding physique, his booming and penetrating voice, from that indefinable "x" quality, personal magnetism, his strenuous realism, and his choice of characters whose driving democratic passions paralleled his own. Although only five feet ten inches tall, on stage his bulky, muscular frame seemed to tower like a giant. Anyone who saw him as Spartacus could never forget the tense muscles, the distended neck, the swollen arteries and veins, the rigid jaws, "the orbs now rolling like the dilated and blazing eyes of a bull, while smothered passion seemed to threaten an actual explosion of the whole frame."

The power of his voice matched the power of his massive torso. When, as Richelieu, he threatened to launch the ecclesiastical curse, Forrest's bellow made the theater walls tremble. Lear's delirious prayer to nature reverberated like a thunderstorm. His articulation was sharp, and he could range from piano to forte, from lowest bass to highest treble, with ease.

Some thought he brought too much nature onto the stage: his painfully clinical death rattles in some roles, the whetstone on which Shylock sharpened his knife, the hollow-bladed dagger filled with red paint that he used in *Virginius.* Yet no one denied that Forrest worked up a part with the greatest care, that he was diligently devoted to his profession. Unlike his tutors, Thomas Abthorpe Cooper, Junius Brutus Booth, and Edmund Kean, he was always steady and predictable. See Richard Moody, *Edwin Forrest: First Star of the American Stage* (1960).

RICHARD MOODY

FORRESTAL, James Vincent (b. Beacon, N.Y., Feb. 15, 1892; d. Bethesda, Md., May 22, 1949), FINANCIER, CABINET OFFICER, became news editor of a Poughkeepsie, New York, paper at the age of 18. He attended Dartmouth (1912) and Princeton (1912–15) but did not graduate, owing to academic difficulties and lack of funds. He was a financial reporter for the New York *World*, a clerk, and a cigarette salesman before becoming a bond salesman for William A. Read and Co. (later Dillon, Read and Co.), an emerging Wall Street firm (1916). He served in the navy (1917–19), attaining the rank of lieutenant. After his discharge he returned to Dillon, Read and Co., becoming a partner (1923), vice president (1926), and president (1938).

After Forrestal testified before a congressional committee investigating stock market practices in 1933, in favor of government regulation of the stock market, he became friendly with President Franklin Roosevelt and his close adviser, **Harry Hopkins.** This led to his appointment as administrative adviser on national defense and undersecretary of the navy (1940).

Forrestal supervised the navy's wartime procurement and production program. Upon the death of Secretary of the Navy Frank Knox in 1944, Forrestal took his place. As secretary of the navy he organized business cooperation with the navy, creating the Navy Industrial Association, which was composed of six hundred of the nation's leading industrialists. After the end of the war in 1945, Forrestal opposed rapid demobilization, advocating the maintenance of strong military forces to deter possible Russian aggression. He worked for unification of the military services under a single cabinet-level department and was appointed America's first secretary of defense by President Harry S. Truman when the Department of Defense was established in 1947. Forrestal advocated a peacetime draft, which was instituted in 1948. He opposed the limits on military spending set by the Truman administration. Severe physical and mental decline preceded Forrestal's death by suicide.

⸺⸰∞⸰⸺

Forrestal's life was one of pathos as well as tragedy. As the youngest of three sons brought up in a rigidly Catholic home more given to discipline than affection, Forrestal as a boy seems to have entertained major doubts about himself, and these doubts were never entirely removed by his later achievements. One emphasis throughout his life was on toughness: physical (he was a compulsive exerciser), mental (he forced himself to read the so-called Great Books), moral (he had no use for those he regarded as shirkers and cowards), and, finally, national, in the sense that he believed in the inevitability of the cold war and the need to negotiate from strength. Unfortunately for Forrestal's political career, the toughness was accompanied by a tight-lipped determination and dedication that alienated hard- and soft-liners alike; toward the end of his life when he was far from a well man, Forrestal was increasingly inclined to regard the latter as either Communists or Zionists. Nor was his career helped when, in 1948, it was widely reported that Forrestal was supporting **Thomas E. Dewey,** the Republican presidential aspirant, rather than Harry S. Truman. The inevitable request from Truman for his resignation as secretary of defense followed soon thereafter. Less than two months after leaving office Forrestal was dead.

Perhaps there was never a time in his entire life when Forrestal was not a driven and conflicted man. Certainly he was unhappy in the parochial world of a Hudson River town which he left at an early age and to which he returned only for funerals. But he was not much happier anywhere else. An agnostic who was never able to free himself entirely from the embrace of Catholicism, Forrestal in Princeton and New York remained something of the outgroup Irish Catholic or "Mick" who was never completely at ease in a WASP environment. The Wall Street Forrestal never quite overcame a suspicion of the rich and well-born, although he envied and emulated them; and the Washington Forrestal profoundly distrusted liberals, although he served in the administrations of two of the most liberal presidents in history. In the end none of these conflicts arising from within or without was resolved. Had they been, Forrestal might have been a much more influential figure in the nation's recent history. Certainly he would have had a longer and more contented life. See Arnold A. Rogow, *James Forrestal: A Study in Personality* (1963).

ARNOLD A. ROGOW

FORTEN, James (b. Philadelphia, Pa., Sept. 2, 1766; d. Philadelphia, Pa., Mar. 4, 1842), REFORMER, was born a free black. He briefly attended the school of Quaker abolitionist Anthony Benezet but left in 1775 to help support his family. In 1780 during the Revolution he entered the colonial navy as a powder boy on the Philadelphia privateer *Royal Louis.* Captured by the British, Forten narrowly missed being sold into slavery but was released. During this time he developed a new device for the handling of sails. After spending a year in Europe he became an apprentice to a Philadelphia sailmaker (1785). By 1786, Forten was foreman of the shop, and after 1798 he operated his own sail loft, employing both blacks and whites. He became one of Philadelphia's wealthiest and most influential citizens.

Forten led a meeting of the African Methodist Church in Philadelphia in 1817 to oppose the designs of the American Colonization Society, which promoted the idea of sending blacks back to Africa. An ardent abolitionist, he helped persuade **William Lloyd Garrison** to abandon support of colonization in favor of abolitionism. He helped to organize the Philadelphia Convention of Free Negroes in 1830 to focus on the plight of free blacks and to oppose colonization. He helped launch the American Anti-Slavery Society in 1833 and served on its board of managers. Forten solicited subscriptions to Garrison's *The Liberator* and often aided the newspaper financially. He also supported the temperance, woman's rights, and peace movements.

When Robert Purvis eulogized his father-in-law in March 1842, he closed with the judgment that James Forten was "a *model,* not … for what are called 'colored men,' but for all men." This peroration was grounded in reality. Forten survived physical and mental travail, tough business competition, and personal attacks to secure a solid financial base on which to fight for his deeply held convictions. Possessed of fortitude, ability, brains, and luck, he could be considered a model for any man.

His most striking characteristic was his commitment to principles. These were shaping forces, not empty phrases, for Forten. His home was a castle but also an open door through which passed all manner of men and women, black and white, well known and unknown. His belief in the barbarism of slavery and the urgency of abolition provoked his public statements and impelled his private charity.

He suffered personal discrimination in silence but lashed out at those acts that restricted the rights of free black men and women. Yet he stood with those who condemned the increase in black crime in Philadelphia. His compassion reached across race and business barriers. **Martin Delany** records Forten's visit to a white man whose firm's failure cost him $9,000. "I came, sir," Forten said, "to express my regret at your misfortune.… If your liabilities were all in my hands, you should never be under the necessity of closing business."

Forten was the first black person to bridge the gap between black and white leaders on a peer basis. No one before him had been able to work with whites with mutual respect and the support of the black community. As a bridge across the racial chasm, Forten anticipated **Frederick Douglass, Booker T. Washington,** and a host of later black leaders. Without Forten, abolitionism and other antebellum reform movements might have been almost lily white—with less black input and less firsthand reference to and knowledge of the needs of black Americans. See Ray Allen Billington, "Introduction," in Billington, ed., *The Journal of Charlotte Forten: A Free Negro in the Slave Era* (1961), pp. 12–20.

LESLIE H. FISHEL, JR.

FORTUNE, Timothy Thomas (b. Mariana, Fla., Oct. 3, 1856; d. New York, N.Y., June 2, 1928), JOURNALIST, was born a slave. After emancipation he moved to Jacksonville, Florida, where he attended high school and worked in local newspaper offices. He held several government jobs, including special inspector of customs for the eastern district of Delaware (1875). He attended Howard University (1876–78), then returned to Florida to teach in the local schools. Moving to New York City in 1879 to work as a newspaper printer, he founded his own paper, the *Rumor,* in 1880; it was renamed the New York *Globe* in 1882. When this paper failed (1884), he established another, the New York *Freeman,* renamed the New York *Age* in 1885. This journal became one of the most militant black newspapers in the country. Through his witty and satirical editorials Fortune attacked racial discrimination and white supremacy, advocating equal civil and economic rights for blacks. He also contributed many articles on civil rights to the New York *Evening Sun* and the Boston *Transcript.*

Fortune participated in the founding of the National Afro-American League in 1890. Although this organization soon collapsed, he helped revive it in 1898 as the Afro-American Council and served as its president until the organization disbanded in 1906. The following year a breakdown forced him to sell the New York *Age.* During the 1920s, after recovering his health, he served as editor of the Garveyite *Negro World.* He wrote two books that supported the economic views of **Henry George** while denouncing racism: *Black and White* (1884) and *The Negro in Politics* (1885).

Fortune was a handsome, magnetic man, hot-tempered, impulsive, sentimental, convivial, but given to fits of depression. His importance lies in the contributions he made to black protest ideology and his efforts to keep the spirit of protest alive in an era when the rights of blacks were steadily deteriorating. He was rightly regarded as the most able black journalist of his age. His editorials and his speeches (his reputation as an orator was second only to his reputation as a writer) were brilliant, often bitter attacks on all forms of white racism. Although sometimes accused of inconsistency, throughout his career he uncompromisingly demanded full political and legal rights for blacks and the elimination of all racial distinctions. He believed in racial integration and ultimate assimilation, but experience convinced him that blacks must fight their own battles. His National Afro-American League was an instrument for carrying out his ideology through a program of litigation, education, and political action. Although the League failed, it anticipated the directions that the civil rights movement was to take in the 20th century.

In spite of his militancy and reputation as "Afro-American Agitator," Fortune was, somewhat paradoxically, for many years intimately associated with **Booker T. Washington.** The two men shared the same goals while differing as to methods. Fortune was adviser, confidant, and ghost writer for Washington, while Washington secretly subsidized the *Age.* Fortune later regretted his entanglement with Washington but was unable to escape. His chronic financial difficulties and his dependence on Washington, coupled with an unhappy marriage and addiction to alcohol, contributed to the mental breakdown in 1907 that incapacitated him for several years. See Emma Lou Thornbrough, *T. Thomas Fortune, Militant Journalist* (1972).

EMMA LOU THORNBROUGH

FOSTER, Stephen Collins (b. Lawrenceville, Pa., July 4, 1826; d. New York, N.Y., Jan. 13, 1864), COMPOSER, published his first song, "Open Thy Lattice Love" (1884) at the age of 18. Spectacular successes with two early songs written for minstrel troupes, "Oh! Susannah" and "Old Uncle Ned" (1848), led Foster to devote himself entirely to songwriting. After his marriage to Jane MacDowell (1850), he continued to produce minstrel songs, notably "Camptown Races" (1850), "Old Folks at Home" (1851), and "Massa's in de Cold Ground" (1852). He also turned his attention increasingly to genteel parlor songs, or "poetic ballads," among them "Jeanie with the Light Brown Hair" (1854) and "Gentle Annie" (1856). In the wake of personal crises in the mid–1850s, Foster's compositional activity decreased. He spent his final years in New York, estranged from his wife; while his compositional output rebounded, few songs from the 1860s, with the exception of "Beautiful Dreamer" (1864), rise to the level of his best early work.

❧

Foster was 19th-century America's preeminent popular songwriter. Although he wrote hymns, instrumental music, and incidental theater music, he is remembered almost exclusively for his songs. The parlor songs united resonant poetic imagery with memorable melody, forging a distinctly American idiom from the most familiar features of 19th-century European songs, particularly English and Irish, Italian opera, and German *Lieder*.

Foster's minstrel songs turned from the offensive, racist lyrics typical of the genre (and of his own early efforts) toward a new, more refined minstrelsy. In works such as "Nelly Was a Lady" (1849), "Old Folks at Home" (1851), and "My Old Kentucky Home, Good-Night" (1853), Foster gradually abandoned the use of dialect, portrayed African-Americans with increasing sympathy, and rendered the music sung by slaves as indistinguishable from that sung by the white protagonists of his parlor songs. Despite Foster's limited contact with the South, it was the African-American characters in these hybrid songs whom Foster used to express his most universal, genuine, and deeply felt sentiments. See Steven Saunders and Deane L. Root, *The Music of Stephen C. Foster* (1990).

STEVEN SAUNDERS

FRANKFURTER, Felix (b. Vienna, Austria, Nov. 15, 1882; d. Washington, D.C., Feb. 22, 1965), JURIST, emigrated to the United States in 1894, settling in New York City. He graduated from the College of the City of New York in 1902, worked briefly for the New York City Tenement House Commission, and received his LLB from Harvard Law School in 1906. During 1906–10 he was an assistant to **Henry Stimson,** the U.S. attorney for the Southern District of New York; and when President William H. Taft named Stimson secretary of war (1911), Frankfurter became a legal counsel in the Bureau of Insular Affairs (1911–14).

In 1914, Frankfurter joined the faculty of Harvard Law School. During World War I he held a succession of administrative posts in Washington: assistant to Secretary of War **Newton D. Baker;** counsel to President Woodrow Wilson's mediation commission; assistant to Secretary of Labor W. B. Wilson; and chairman of the War Labor Policies Board, which set up wages and hours regulations for war industries. At the Paris peace conference of 1919 he represented the American Zionists who sought to win support for the establishment of a Jewish homeland in Palestine.

In 1919, Frankfurter returned to Harvard as Byrne professor of administrative law (to 1939). A staunch advocate of civil liberties (he was one of the founders of the American Civil Liberties Union), he was one of the most outspoken critics of the Sacco-Vanzetti trial. His views on this case are presented in his book *The Case of Sacco and Vanzetti* (1927).

In 1932, Frankfurter supported Franklin D. Roosevelt's campaign for the presidency. Although he held no official post in the Roosevelt administration, he was one of the president's leading advisers and recruiters of personnel. He helped frame a number of important New Deal laws. In January 1939, Roosevelt appointed him associate justice of the Supreme Court. He left the bench in ill health in 1962. Some of his occasional writings are collected in E. F. Prichard and A. MacLeish, *Law and Politics* (1939), and P. Elman, *Of Law and Men* (1956). Among his books are *The Business of the Supreme Court*, with J. M. Landis

(1927); *The Labor Injunction,* with N. Greene (1930); *The Public and Its Government* (1930); *The Commerce Clause Under Marshall, Taney, and Waite* (1937); and *Mr. Justice Holmes and the Supreme Court* (1938).

When Felix Frankfurter left Harvard for the bench in 1939, he was generally considered a liberal (in some quarters a radical). Soon thereafter he was widely "accused" of conservatism. In fact, his basic outlook did not change. He remained in private life one of the great liberals of his day. It was crucial in his philosophy, however, that a judge's private convictions were one thing, his duty on the bench quite another. (See his heartfelt opinion in *West Virginia State Board of Education* v. *Barnette,* 1943.) This was the teaching of **Oliver Wendell Holmes, Jr.** By failing to heed it the "rugged individualists" among the "nine old men" destroyed the old Court—just as some later libertarians might have destroyed the new one, if they had had the votes to do so. Whether as professor or judge, whether with respect to liberty or property, Mr. Justice Frankfurter shunned judicial lawmaking. The judge's job, as he understood it, was to decide cases, not to create a brave new world—the legislative function having been given to others. (See his opinion in *Lincoln Federal Labor Union* v. *American Sash and Door Co.,* 1949.) For him, even in the realm of civil liberty, the essence of government by the people is government by the people (not by a nursemaid who lets the children play if they behave): "As society becomes more and more complicated and individual experience correspondingly narrower, tolerance and humility in passing judgment on the experience and beliefs expressed by those entrusted with the duty of legislating emerge as the decisive factors in … adjudication."

It was not that Frankfurter loved liberty less but that he loved democracy—*in all its aspects*—more. The difficulty is that both individual liberty and majority rule are indispensable in the democratic dream. Neither can fully prevail without destroying the other. To reconcile them is a basic problem of free government. Frankfurter did not believe or pretend that reconciliation is achieved by clichés like "liberty of contract" or "freedom of speech." The single-value, conditioned mental reflex gave him no respite from the painful process of judgment. He was a seeker, not a professor, of truth. And so, recognizing that free speech and press, for example, merit special judicial respect, he could not dismiss the sometimes bitter fruits of popular government with a libertarian *presumption* of invalidity. (See his opinion in *Kovacs v. Cooper.*) He knew with Holmes that one's own "certitude [was] not the test of certainty"—that when he and legislatures disagreed, *they* might be right. It followed that judicial intrusion upon the extrajudicial processes of government was permissible only in accordance with that ancient tradition of restraint that all American judges have professed—but not always followed.

It is ironical that in his later years Frankfurter was condemned by some for the very quality that won him a seat on the bench: respect for what T. V. Smith called the legislative way of life. It is even more ironical that for essentially the same approach that won the (privately) conservative Holmes a liberal reputation, the liberal Frankfurter was deemed by some a conservative. What had changed, of course, was the relative liberalism of Court and legislature. But in the Holmes-Frankfurter view from the bench, government by the people is due the same deference, be its fruits liberal or conservative. Plainly, Frankfurter found the crux of the democratic process not so much in the immediate legislative product as in the educative and tension-relieving role of the process itself. A generation ago he wrote: "In a democracy, politics is a process of popular education—the task of adjusting the conflicting interests of diverse groups ... and bending the hostility and suspicion and ignorance engendered by group interests ... toward mutual understanding."

To frustrate these pragmatic political accommodations by judicial absolutes was, in the Frankfurter view, to impede our chief device for maintaining peace among men who are deeply divided—sometimes even in their perceptions of right and wrong. As he saw it, "holding democracy in judicial tutelage is not the most promising way to foster disciplined responsibility in a free people."

There was of course more in Frankfurter than a judicial philosophy of democracy. "One could read everything he has written," **Dean Acheson** thought, "and still have little more than an inkling, if that, of why this man has evoked in so many such passionate devotion, and exercised for half a century so profound an influence. I can think of no one in our times remotely comparable to him." **Reinhold Niebuhr** spoke for many when he called Frankfurter "the most vital and creative person I have ever known." Archibald MacLeish held that "posterity may or may not take our word for it that Felix Frankfurter had more influence on more lives than any man of his generation." True or false is not the point. How deep a soul, how vast a mind, to have evoked these appraisals by such worldly and gifted observers—one a statesman, one a theologian, and one a poet. See Liva Baker, *Felix Frankfurter* (1969).

WALLACE MENDELSON

FRANKLIN, Benjamin (b. Boston, Mass., Jan. 17, 1706; d. Philadelphia, Pa., Apr. 17, 1790), DIPLOMAT, POLITICAL LEADER, INVENTOR, worked as a youth as an apprentice printer before moving to Philadelphia in 1723 to practice this trade. In partnership with Hugh Meredith he bought the Pennsylvania *Gazette* (1729) and in 1730 became the sole owner. He also published *Poor Richard's Almanack* (1732–58), which became famous for its maxims and proverbs.

During 1736–51 Franklin was the clerk of the Pennsylvania Assembly and a member of that assembly from 1751 to 1764. He served as deputy postmaster of Philadelphia (1737–53), and with William Hunter he was deputy postmaster general for the colonies (1753–74). In 1754 he represented Pennsylvania at the Albany Congress, where he drafted a plan for an intercolonial council for Indian defense. Although the congress approved his proposals, the individual assemblies and the authorities in London rejected them.

During the French and Indian War (1756–63), the proprietors of Pennsylvania refused to permit the governor to pass bills for defense unless their estates were exempt from taxation. Franklin was sent to England to present the colony's case (1757), and he remained there until 1762. When he returned, he helped defend Philadelphia when the "Paxton Boys" marched on the city (winter 1763–64) to protest against the inadequate defense against Indian attacks.

Throughout his career Franklin maintained his passion to improve life and to utilize science toward that end. In 1727 he formed the Junto, a debating club that discussed scientific subjects; it later became the American Philosophical Society (1743). He sponsored a city police force, a fire company, a circulating library, a city hospital, and an Academy for the Education of Youth, forerunner of the University of Pennsylvania. In 1744 he invented the "Franklin stove," a freestanding iron fireplace. He began his experiments with electricity in 1746, and in 1752 he performed his famous kite experiment, proving that lightning and electricity are the same thing.

When Parliament passed the Stamp Act (1765), Franklin attempted to get two of his friends appointed as stampmasters. This action hurt his prestige, but he redeemed himself in 1766 when, before the House of Commons, he attacked the Stamp Act as being without precedence, administratively impractical, and unjust. While in England he served as colonial agent for Pennsylvania, Georgia (1768), New Jersey (1769), and Massachusetts (1770).

Franklin tried to conciliate Anglo-American differences. However, he inadvertently exacerbated tensions when he sent his friends in the colonies a number of antipatriot letters written by Massachusetts governor **Thomas Hutchinson.** These letters, published by **Samuel Adams** (1773), helped intensify anti-British feeling. Franklin, however, continued to work for a rapprochement, but after the "Coercive Acts" were passed (1774), he came to favor American independence.

He returned to America and was a delegate to the Second Continental Congress (1775), where he supported the "Petition to the King" for a redress of grievances, sketched a Plan of Union, organized the post office (becoming the first postmaster general), and served on a committee to advise General Washington on defense measures. He was also a member of the committee that drafted the Declaration of Independence. Franklin was then sent by Congress to Paris where he, **Silas Deane,** and Arthur Lee tried to win French support for America. Following the American victory at Saratoga (1777), an alliance was formed and France declared war on Great Britain.

After the Battle of Yorktown (1781), Franklin, **John Jay,** and John Adams negotiated a peace treaty with the British at Paris, which was signed in 1783.

Franklin returned to Philadelphia, and was chosen president of the Executive Council of Pennsylvania. He was a delegate to the Federal Convention (1787), where he helped draft the compromise that settled the question of representation between the large and the small states. After the convention he retired to his home where he entertained a large number of visitors, carried on extensive correspondence, and completed his famous *Autobiography* (1771–89).

⁂

In a well-chosen phrase, Carl Van Doren once called Franklin "a harmonious human multitude." His life first clearly took this form when at about age 14, in the midst of devouring every book in his brother's printing shop, he read Joseph Addison's *Spectator.* Franklin thus acquired not only the felicitous prose style that served him so well for seventy years but a balanced, detailed view of life that left earnestness and humor in a happy equilibrium. He learned from Addison to eschew both the narrow fanaticism of his Puritan forebears and the cynical degeneracy of Restoration fops. He endeavored with Addison "to enliven Morality with wit, and to temper wit with Morality." Franklin, then, did not so much repudiate his family's Puritanism, as many interpreters argue, as accommodate it to the English version of the Enlightenment of which John Locke, Jonathan Swift, Daniel Defoe, and Isaac Newton, as well as Addison, are representative figures.

Franklin's careers as printer, moralist, civic leader, and scientist all exemplify this earnest urbanity. He worked hard, as he reminds us so smugly in his *Autobiography*, and soon became both a master printer and a successful businessman; he retired at age 42 with a sufficient income to support for the rest of his life his more philanthropic careers. As Poor Richard he taught thousands a prim morality that gave poor, fenced-in laboring men practical hints on how to improve their lives, but he had no notion that adages of hard work and thrift represented a full philosophy of life. Indeed, from his usefulness as a citizen of Philadelphia to his dazzling life amid the philosophes and ladies of Paris when past 70, Franklin showed very well how full and varied human existence could be. His civic projects did have a down-to-earth, perhaps even crassly utilitarian aspect about them. But he viewed such orderly, time-saving, mutual enterprises as lending libraries and fire companies as *techniques* that would allow a community to organize and uplift its life in a way that would expand and release individual talents. Though he personified the Yankee tinkerer in his pleasure at inventing such devices as the Franklin stove, bifocal lenses, and the lightning rod, his scientific work fundamentally advanced man's knowledge of the forces of nature. Far from being D. H. Lawrence's caricature of him as a "middle-sized, sturdy, snuff-colored" prig who put up "barbed-wire moral enclosures" to stifle men's lives, Franklin was a man of disciplined imagination and expansive creativity. There were indeed dimensions of life he shortchanged. He showed little sensitivity for poetry and the arts (his invention of the harmonica arose from his fascination with the logic and gadgetry of music, not from aesthetic gifts), and his religious views have a shallow rationalism about them. Of the ambiguity and profundity of human experience he knew very little. But it makes no sense to ignore commanding talents and creativity in some realms simply because other realms seem underdeveloped. Doubtless mankind needs more, not less, of Franklin's style of genius.

Franklin's political career exhibits a corresponding range and eclecticism. He was at once deeply English in his natural affinities and wholly American in his attitudes and way of life. Thus he began his public career as a defender of the British Empire, and he lived happily for eighteen years in London while trying to sustain his concept of the Empire as a growing family that benefited from the well-being of Philadelphia as much as of London or Bristol. But much as he loved English culture and society, his deeper allegiance was to the opportunity, the expansiveness, the prosperity, the egalitarianism, and the self-reliance of Massachusetts and Pennsylvania. Once the life described in his *Autobiography* became for the common man a viable alternative to the extremes of degradation and splendor that had immemorially characterized human existence, Franklin's signature on the Declaration of Independence becomes quite explicable, perhaps even inevitable.

Franklin's life in France allowed him to dramatize for the rest of the world the meaning, as he saw it, of the new nation. In a remarkable way he managed to show how the simple Quaker of the New World, *le Bonhomme Richard*, was a personification of the hopes and ideals of the highly sophisticated world of the French Enlightenment. At once he seemed to rescue the New World from its mean provinciality and the Old World from its degenerate corruption. He proved himself a master at Old World diplomacy in borrowing millions from the court of Louis XVI to sustain a republican revolution; but he steered American diplomacy toward an independent idealism captured in his dictum: "There never was a good war or a bad peace." Though to stern John Adams, Franklin seemed to be sunk in sloth, lechery, and "a fulsome and sickish" thirst for fame, he was in fact the master of the scene around him, able to be courtly, homespun, or diplomatic as the occasion demanded. All of this enhanced rather than compromised or betrayed his nation's cause, as his enemies charged. Franklin's detachment and skill at assuming a variety of roles is in a way an insincerity, but his perfect awareness of what he was doing and why gave an inner integrity to his life.

In his last important public act Franklin took part in the Constitutional Convention of 1787, urging its members to approve the document despite its imperfections. "Having lived long," he said, "I have experienced many Instances of being obliged, by better Information, or fuller Consideration, to change Opinnions even on Important Subjects, which I once thought right, but found to be otherwise." Each member, he urged, should "doubt a little of his own Infallibility." This endless, openminded quest for improvement characterized Franklin the public figure as much as it did Franklin the moralist or scientist, and is in fact the essence of the status given him in his lifetime and thrust repeatedly upon him ever since, of being, for better or for worse, the archetype American. See Carl Van Doren, *Benjamin Franklin* (1938).

RALPH KETCHAM

FRANKLIN, John Hope (b. Rentiesville, Okla., Jan. 2, 1915), HISTORIAN, was educated in the segregated public schools of Tulsa and at Fisk University (BA, 1935). After receiving a PhD from Harvard (1941), Franklin began his academic career teaching at three predominantly black schools: St. Augustine College, North Carolina College for Negroes, and Howard University (1947–1956). In 1956, two years after *Brown* v. *Board of Education* began the era of educational integration, Franklin became chairman of the history department of Brooklyn College of the City University of New York. He moved to the University of Chicago in 1964 and to Duke University in 1982. He has been president of the American Historical Association, the Organization of American Historians, and the Southern Historical Association. Franklin has published more than a dozen scholarly books and scores of scholarly articles. With more than one hundred honorary degrees, Franklin is perhaps the most honored man in academia.

———— ∞∞∞ ————

Franklin's best-known book, *From Slavery to Freedom* (1947), has sold more than 2 million copies and played an important role in defining the emerging field of African-American history. In addition, Franklin has published a dozen other books on the South and on American race relations. Franklin's first book, *The Free Negro in North Carolina, 1790–1860*, was published in 1943. Another volume, *The Militant South* (1956), described militaristic values and practices in the Old South. Yet another book, *A Southern Odyssey* (1976), told about southern travelers in the antebellum North.

With the exception of *Reconstruction* (1961), which challenged the then-prevailing negative view of the blacks who played leading roles in the southern state governments after the Civil War, Franklin's books tended to steer clear of theories and speculative interpretations. Unlike some other major historians who have built large reputations by making provocative arguments that they believe are relevant to contemporary political and cultural concerns, Franklin has forged ahead by making solid, dispassionate, objective contributions to knowledge.

In one of his essays, "The Dilemma of the American Negro Scholar," Franklin maintained that black scholars could establish their place with "the arbiters in the field" only "by maintaining the highest standards of scholarship." Then he wrote, "It is, of course, asking too much of the Negro scholar to demand that he remain impervious and insensitive to the forces that seek to destroy his dignity and self-respect." However, unlike many postmodern scholars who say that all writing is political and that the historian can be as passionate and polemical as he wants on behalf of a worthy cause, Franklin differentiated between propaganda and objective history. He tried to navigate the shoals "between hard-hitting advocacy on the one hand and the highest standards of scholarship on the other."

This is not to say that Franklin eschewed activism. During the litigation that led to *Brown* he prepared a disingenuous "history" for the use of the NAACP and its black clients, and he later subordinated scholarship to advocacy when he criticized the civil rights policies of Presidents Ronald Reagan and George Bush, and when he opposed the Supreme Court nominations of

Robert Bork and Clarence Thomas. But Franklin distinguished between civil rights activism and scholarly writing. When he took stands on current issues, he was acting "as a layman, not as a historian," Franklin insisted. "That's a dangerous line that I would never want to cross. It is like living two separate lives—one as a historian, carefully guarding the limits that one can go in that area, and another as an activist citizen, trying to change things." The reality is that as a historian, teacher, and public citizen Franklin has changed things profoundly. Through his teaching, his scholarship, and his immense learning he has shaped and deepened the nation's understanding of African-American and southern history, and he has by his personal example and lifelong commitment to truth and justice played a significant role in advancing the cause of civil rights. See John Hope Franklin, *Race and History: Selected Essays, 1938–1988* (1989), and George M. Frederickson, "Pioneer," *New York Review of Books,* (Sept. 23, 1993).

RAYMOND WOLTERS

FRAZIER, Edward Franklin (b. Baltimore, Md., Sept. 24, 1894; d. Washington, D.C., May 17, 1962), SOCIAL SCIENTIST, attended Baltimore's public schools and won a scholarship to Howard University. Graduating cum laude in 1916, he taught at Tuskegee Institute (1916), St. Paul's Normal and Industrial School in Lawrenceville, Virginia (1917), and at a Baltimore high school (1918). He received an MA in sociology from Clark University in 1920. He then became a research fellow at the New York School of Social Work (1920–21) and studied in Denmark on a fellowship (1921–22). Frazier next became an instructor of sociology at Morehouse College (1922–24) and also served as director of the Atlanta School of Social Work (1922–27). He was a research assistant at the University of Chicago (1927–29) and received his PhD in sociology (1931). Frazier joined the faculty of Fisk University in 1929 and then went to Howard in 1934 as professor and head of the sociology department. He retired in 1959.

Frazier's sociological writings deal with the African-American and the problem of race relations in America. In 1939 he published *The Negro Family in the United States,* a history of the black family from slavery to the present. His *Black Bourgeoisie: The Rise of a New Middle Class* (1957) was a critical view of the insecurities of that group. In 1935, Frazier was asked by Mayor **Fiorello LaGuardia** to head the New York City Commission on Conditions in Harlem, examining the causes of the 1935 Harlem race riot. He won a Guggenheim fellowship for study in Brazil and the West Indies (1940–41) and served as president of the American Sociological Association (1948), the first American black to head a national scholarly organization. Active in U.N. affairs, Frazier served as chairman of the commission on race relations for UNESCO in 1949. His other books include *The Negro Family in Chicago* (1932), *The Negro in the United States* (1949), and *The Negro Church in America* (1964), published posthumously.

⸺⧉⸺

Frazier was one of the first thoroughly trained black sociologists in the United States and one of the first social scientists to develop a systematic analysis of black American life. A product of the "Chicago school" of sociology, with its emphasis on the structural and associational aspects of human behavior, Frazier was particularly interested in exploring the impact of racial prejudice on the structure of Afro-American society. In his family studies he stressed the disorganizing effect of slavery, segregation, and ghettoization on the black family and argued that the American racial system destroyed African family patterns and created family instability. His controversial work on the black middle class similarly emphasized the strains created by discrimination and prejudice that led to exaggerated, often grotesque, behavior. Frazier was also interested in the comparative study of race relations and attempted to show how demographic, economic, and political factors created divergent racial systems in different parts of the world. Highly regarded as a sociologist during his lifetime,

Frazier in recent years has come under attack from some critics for his emphasis on the pathology of black life and for his refusal to see African influences on black life in the United States. Others have scored him for his rejection of quantitative techniques at a time when many sociologists were turning increasingly to the quantification of data.

Frazier viewed himself primarily as an intellectual and generally rejected the role of a political or racial activist. Nevertheless he was deeply involved in the struggle for black equality. Much of his work was problem-oriented, and in his later writings he was concerned with the question of desegregation. He believed that integration must be the ultimate goal but that blacks at the same time should develop a sense of pride and racial identity. A man of strong convictions and of intellectual vigor, he was a popular teacher as well as a distinguished and productive scholar. See G. Franklin Edwards, ed., *E. Franklin Frazier on Race Relations* (1968).

ALLAN H. SPEAR

FRÉMONT, John Charles (b. Savannah, Ga., Jan. 21, 1813; d. New York, N.Y., July 13, 1890), EXPLORER, MILITARY and POLITICAL LEADER, entered Charleston College in 1829 but was expelled in 1831 for poor attendance. However, his proficiency in mathematics won him a job as a teacher on a naval training ship that was leaving on a cruise to South America. He then received a commission in the U.S. Topographical Corps and was assigned to the party surveying the route for a railroad from Charleston to Cincinnati.

In 1838, Frémont helped survey the upper Mississippi country under Joseph Nicollet, also contributing to the report of the expedition. About this time he fell in love with the 16-year-old daughter of Missouri senator **Thomas Hart Benton.** The senator sought to break up the romance by sending Frémont to head an expedition into Iowa country. The couple soon married secretly, however, and after a reconciliation Benton became a powerful force behind

Frémont's subsequent explorations. In 1842, Frémont explored the Oregon Trail as far as Wyoming, and his report, which his wife helped write, was a great success. The following year he was sent to explore the West. After reaching the Columbia River he pressed southward through Nevada and over the mountains to California. He did not return to St. Louis until fifteen months later, August 1844. Again his report was well received.

As relations with Mexico began to deteriorate in 1845, Frémont, now an army captain, was dispatched with a well-armed party to seek a central route through the Rocky Mountains. The presence of this American military force in northern California helped precipitate the Bear Flag Revolt (June 1846). On learning that war with Mexico had been declared, Frémont went by ship to San Diego, marched north, and took Los Angeles. The command of American forces in California was in dispute between Robert F. Stockton of the navy and General Stephen W. Kearney. Frémont took Stockton's side and was court-martialed after Kearney's command was confirmed. Although President James K. Polk rescinded the sentence, Frémont resigned his lieutenant colonelcy. For two years afterward he farmed his huge Mariposa estate in California and worked its gold mines.

In 1850, Frémont was elected one of California's first senators but drew the lot for the short term that ended in March 1851. Exploration of a route for a southern transcontinental railroad and a trip to Europe in search of better goldmining equipment occupied him until 1856 when he became the new Republican Party's first candidate for president. James Buchanan defeated him, 174 electoral votes to 114.

At the outbreak of the Civil War, Frémont was appointed major general and placed in charge of Union forces in St. Louis at a time when Missouri's decision to secede or to remain in the Union hung in the balance. Adopting an aggressive antisecessionist policy, he attempted to free the slaves by proclamation and was relieved of his command by President Abraham Lincoln. After holding subordinate commands in Virginia, Frémont played no further role in the Civil War.

The last twenty-five years of his life produced a succession of failures at ranching and railroad promotion.

⎯⎯⎯⎯ ⚬⚬⚬ ⎯⎯⎯⎯

John C. Frémont became a legendary figure in 19th-century America. From the moment of his daring elopement with vivacious young Jessie Benton against the will of her famous father Thomas, Frémont attained a kind of Byronic quality in the eyes of the public. Adventurous, romantic, ruggedly handsome, and touched with just enough scandal to render him appealing to the moralistic Victorian age, he seemed to exemplify the impetuosity of "Young America" in Polk's day. People pictured him planting the flag atop lonely peaks of the Rockies, trailblazing with Kit Carson, consorting with Native Americans and mountain men, pushing his way through buffalo country, across unknown deserts, and into uncharted mountains and river valleys; yet withal a scientist of parts, a professional soldier, a U.S. senator, a candidate for president under freedom's banner, a man known for wisdom and dignity among statesmen, resourcefulness and courage in the untamed wilderness, and robust love and tenderness within the family circle. This idealized version of the man became one face of a public image that persisted during his lifetime although in many ways it did not well fit the actual person.

Possibly because of his illegitimate birth, Frémont never sought or took much pleasure in conventional society; his chief joy lay in the wilderness. He found all the social satisfaction he required within his immediate family. When necessity threw him into social situations, as in Washington while senator or as candidate for president in 1856, he spoke little, and when he did speak, it was simply and frankly. His outright declaration in the campaign of 1856 that he disliked nativism quickly aroused his managers to caution him to silence. His normal avoidance of small talk enhanced his reputation for sagacity, a reputation he ruined in 1861 by his rash effort to free slaves in Missouri by a local military proclamation. He was never a joiner and maintained few personal contacts throughout life. His greatest failures occurred in the realm of personal relationships where the qualities of tact, finesse, and judgment of character counted most—in politics, in military command, and in business.

Frémont was essentially an out-of-doors man. Pitted against raw nature, in storm or drought, on mountain or desert, without resources except his own stamina and will, he gloried in the contest and brought to it remarkable powers of courage, self-discipline, endurance, and a determination to surmount all obstacles. He was often a dreamer and was easily led into difficulties by a soaring imagination, which his impulsiveness projected into action without adequate evaluation of impediments to success. Some of the most serious disasters to his exploring expeditions arose from his failure to examine with care the details of a daring move before committing himself to it. His several business enterprises—ranching, mining, and railroading—failed in part from this cause.

If not a lonely man, Frémont walked zestfully alone. Even while leading exploring expeditions he lived much to himself. He imposed a Spartan regimen on his followers but exacted more of himself than of anyone else. His great joy lay in discovering new things in nature, experiences that gave him gratification beyond any he ever felt as a presidential candidate. He engaged in politics and business partly to please Jessie and partly because others persuaded him of success in these pursuits. Though not of bookish temperament, he wrote a number of books on exploration. He possessed ambition and had visions of wealth and prominence, but his deeper spirit preferred an uncluttered outdoor life to personnel management and desk work.

Frémont died in poverty after a life filled largely with promising beginnings ending in frustrating failures. People associated with his ventures tended to love or to hate him, emotions that often arose from what people imagined him to be rather than from what he really was—a nature-loving wilderness explorer. See Allan Nevins, *Frémont: Pathmarker of the West* (2 vols., 1955).

PHILIP S. KLEIN

FRENEAU, Philip Morin (b. New York, N.Y., Jan. 2, 1752; d. Monmouth County, N.J., Dec. 19, 1832), POET, JOURNALIST, graduated from the College of New Jersey (Princeton) in 1771. He spent the next few years teaching, studying theology, and writing poetry. At the outbreak of the Revolution, Freneau wrote several satires against the British and Tories, including *General Gage's Soliloquy* (1775) and *General Gage's Confession* (1775). He spent two years (1776–78) as secretary to a planter on the island of Santa Cruz in the West Indies, where he wrote such romantic poems as "The Beauties of Santa Cruz" (1776) and "The House of Night" (1776). Returning to the United States in 1778, Freneau joined the New Jersey militia, following which he joined a privateer cruising in the Caribbean. Captured by the British, he was imprisoned on a ship in New York Harbor until 1780. His poem *The British Prison-Ship* (1781) described the brutal conditions and experiences of this imprisonment. Freneau then held a position in the Philadelphia post office and contributed patriotic poetry to the *Freeman's Journal* (1781–84). He went to sea again (1784–89) and during that time wrote the lyrical poem *The Wild Honeysuckle* (1786).

Freneau became editor of the New York *Daily Advertiser* in 1790 but soon moved to the capital at Philadelphia, where he was a clerk-translator for the State Department. In 1791, with President Thomas Jefferson's support, Freneau founded the *National Gazette*, which attacked the domestic and foreign policies of **Alexander Hamilton** while at the same time defending those of Jefferson. He gave up the paper in 1793 because of lack of funds and left the State Department. Freneau edited a weekly Republican newspaper, the *Jersey Chronicle* (1795–96), and a New York journal, *Time-Piece* (1797–1800). In his later years he published two collections, *Poems Written and Published During the American Revolutionary War* (2 vols., 1809) and *A Collection of Poems on American Affairs* (2 vols., 1815).

⁂

Freneau lived in perpetual economic uncertainty. An honest adventurer at sea and in the print shop, he identified himself with the common man and wrote for him, not, like nearly all of his contemporaries, for cultured literary circles. He fought all his life against the tyranny of wealth and special privilege. "[The] Earth," he wrote, "which were it not for the lust of pride and dominion, might be an earthly paradise, is by the ambition and overbearing nature of mankind, rendered an eternal scene of desolation, woe and horror." His dream of a millennial age in America was destroyed by the Revolution, and he sought temporarily a private paradise in the West Indies. His best poems fuse his experience of emotional turmoil during the Revolution with the issues of the larger, national crisis. His anti-British and anti-Federalist satires were vituperative, sometimes unfair, but often effective. The *National Gazette* kept alive the Republican cause in Philadelphia. Freneau, Jefferson said, "has saved our Constitution, which was galloping fast into Monarchy." Freneau poured most of his restless energy into propaganda for American independence and radical democracy. His poems, many of which were written hurriedly in response to events, are largely derivative from English models, though sometimes original in their American subject matter and attitude. His work, however, is a valuable record of a sensitive personality passionately engaged in the life of the Revolutionary period. Freneau was perhaps the earliest writer, after **Jonathan Edwards,** to confront and register the rush and pressure of democratic America. See Jacob Axelrad, *Philip Freneau: Champion of Democracy* (1966).

JOHN F. SEARS

FRICK, Henry Clay (b. West Overton, Pa., Dec. 19, 1849; d. New York, N.Y., Dec. 2, 1919), INDUSTRIALIST, after a succession of clerking jobs became a bookkeeper in his grandfather Overholt's distillery. Realizing that the new Bessemer steelmaking process would mean a greatly increased demand for coke, he and a few associates, backed by the banker Thomas Mellon, bought up coal lands in the vicinity of Connellsville, Pennsylvania. The price of coal lands fell drastically in the depression of 1873–77, and Frick bought heavily, selling a branch railroad to raise cash. By 1879, at the age of 30, he was a millionaire.

Andrew Carnegie, realizing the interdependence between his iron and steel mills and Frick's coke facilities, exchanged shares in his properties for shares in the mines and coke ovens of Frick. The association endured despite personal differences, and by 1889, Frick was head of the Carnegie works. In 1892, while Carnegie was in Scotland, workers at the Homestead, Pennsylvania, plant went on strike. Frick brought in private police to evict the strikers, a fight broke out, and ten men were killed in what was the country's worst labor clash up to that time. Frick himself was nearly assassinated by anarchist Alexander Berkman.

Much of the daring and initiative with which Carnegie has been credited in the growth of the American steel industry appears to have been Frick's. He was a strong influence in the decision to buy large holdings in the Lake Superior iron ore regions, which shortly became the main source of supply for American blast furnaces. He also foresaw the need to integrate the company from raw materials to finished goods. By 1899, Carnegie was ready to retire, but he seems to have been relieved when Frick failed to put through a deal to create a mammoth, vertically integrated steel combine with the Carnegie properties at the center. Two years later **J. P. Morgan** succeeded in doing what Frick had been unable to bring off, but the coke manufacturer had retained his holdings in the Carnegie properties and profited fully from the creation of the United States Steel Corp. As a member of the board of directors of the new corporation, Frick took an active interest in its affairs, as he did those of a number of others on whose boards he also served. His retirement from the leadership of the steel corporation coincided with the start of the aggressive program to greatly expand and improve the Pennsylvania Railroad, a vital step in the modernization of the nation's transportation system to which Frick, as director, contributed. He likewise advised in the reorganiza-

tion of the Equitable Life Assurance Society.

Long interested in art, Frick left at his death an extensive collection which, with the New York mansion that houses it and a generous endowment, were his principal public bequests.

⸺ ❧ ⸺

As a young child Henry Clay Frick lived in poverty but was kin to great wealth. His father was an unambitious "hard-scrabble" farmer, but his grandfather Abraham Overholt owned the best-known distillery in western Pennsylvania and was Westmoreland County's only millionaire. Frick was appropriately named for his grandfather's political hero. Few men were to exemplify with greater triumph the advantages of the Kentucky Whig's American system of governmental subsidy and protection, unhampered by governmental controls and taxation. While Young Clay, as his family called him, watched his father trying to earn a bare subsistence out of the poor land available to him, he could look up to his grandfather's great mansion on the hill, and there was never any question in the boy's mind that it was far better to be rich than poor. His only ambition as a child was to become a millionaire like Grandfather Abraham. At the age of 30, with singleness of purpose and a daring that dazzled his associates, he had achieved his goal. Anticipating the moral from Russell Conwell's celebrated lecture long before it was ever written, Frick had found his "Acres of Diamonds" in his own backyard, in the soft coal that lay just under the top surface of the land along the Youghiogheny River, which his father had frequently cursed when his plow hit a seam of the apparently worthless stuff. But this coal was ideally suited for making coke, and while still working as an accountant in his grandfather's distillery, Frick began to buy up the coal lands and to build coke ovens. Financed by Thomas Mellon, Frick greatly overextended himself, but with the boom in the Bessemer steel industry following the depression of the 1870s, he was in a position to take full advantage of the industry's urgent need for coke. He had control of the best coal fields and the largest number of coke ovens in western Pennsylvania. It was not surprising that he came to the attention of the most ambitious steelmaker in Pennsylvania, Andrew Carnegie. In 1881, Carnegie offered to join forces with the young "Coke King" by providing capital for Frick's company, and soon thereafter Carnegie offered Frick a partnership in Carnegie Brothers. Frick accepted both invitations, and from that moment on, the fortunes of the two men were inextricably joined.

By temperament Frick and Carnegie were so different that few of their associates were greatly surprised when friction later developed between them. Carnegie's gregariousness, volubility, and craving for public attention, and his desire to be loved as a great humanitarian, were qualities of character that Frick found repugnant if not outright hypocritical. By nature reserved and formal in all his business associations, Frick never sought public acclaim or notoriety, had no close friends, and apparently devoted all his waking hours to the pursuit of business. Yet in reality Frick and Carnegie in their business philosophy and methods had much in common, and this compatibility of interests does much to explain their great joint success. Both were empire builders in the field of business. Like Carnegie, and unlike Carnegie's other senior partners, Frick was not interested in immediate profits. He was interested in cutting costs and in putting profits into plant expansion rather than in dividends. Like Carnegie, Frick was quick to take advantage of economic recessions to expand while their competitors were timidly retreating. Frick was unquestionably the ablest business manager of Carnegie's many associates, and Carnegie fully appreciated his talents if not his temperament. The years from 1889 to 1900 during which Frick served first as president and then as chairman of the board of directors, Carnegie Steel grew from a major Pennsylvania industry to the world's paramount producer of steel, and much of the credit for this successful growth belonged to Frick.

One associate compared Carnegie to Napoleon and Frick to von Moltke: "Carnegie, the commander and intuitive genius; Frick, calm,

long-headed, deliberate, a great tactician." It was, by outward appearances, an apt description. Yet Frick was more complex, more daring and mercurial in temperament than many of his closest associates suspected. A man who was cold and reserved in the office, Frick was a devoted husband and an affectionate companion to his children; to his business associate, he had apparently no other interests but coke and steel, but he was an avid art collector who found in the flamboyantly colorful Italian Renaissance canvases a welcome antidote to ledgers and cost accounting reports.

He could also, when aroused, be violently explosive. Ultimately, he was the only one with the courage and the egotism to stand up to Carnegie's 50 percent control of the company, and when the final break between the two men came in 1900, he had the satisfaction of knowing that he alone, of all Carnegie's associates, had battled and won his rights against him. Frick refused to be ejected from the company and be forced to sell his share of the partnership at the grossly undervalued book value. He took his case to court and forced Carnegie to yield. Unlike Carnegie, he never pretended to be other than what he was: a tough employer who exploited labor as he exploited the natural resources of the country, a ruthless competitor, and a superb manager. In his world he not only survived but flourished. See George Harvey, *Henry Clay Frick, the Man* (1936).

JOSEPH FRAZIER WALL

FRIEDAN, Betty Goldstein (b. Peoria, Ill., Feb. 4, 1921), REFORMER, graduated from Smith College in 1942. The next year she was a research fellow at the University of California at Berkeley. After her marriage in 1947 she devoted most of her time to rearing three children, but she also wrote for various women's magazines. In 1957 she took a survey of her Smith classmates; the dissatisfactions expressed by these women led her to become aware of "the problem that has no name." In 1960 she published an article in *Good Housekeeping* called "Women Are People Too!" It brought many letters from readers and convinced her that the malaise she had noted was not confined to graduates of high-prestige eastern colleges. Her book on the subject, *The Feminine Mystique* (1963), an immediate best-seller, made Friedan a celebrity. In it she argued that the women's magazines, other mass media organs, educators, and an outdated interpretation of Freudian psychology had created an image of woman's proper role as being only that of housewife and mother. The effect of this "feminine mystique" was to stifle the creativity and inhibit the intellectual growth of women. Their felt but unconceptualized dissatisfactions (the problem that has no name) were producing massive anxieties and wasting vast amounts of human potential.

After the publication of her book Friedan continued to write articles and also lectured frequently. In 1966 she founded the National Organization for Women and served as president. NOW campaigned especially for an end to job discrimination based on sex. In 1969 she was divorced; the next year she resigned as president of NOW and organized a nationwide Women's Strike for Equality (August 1970). In 1971 she founded the National Women's Political Caucus. She also began writing a column for *McCall's*. During the 1970s and 1980s Friedan continued to lecture and write. Increasingly, as the women's movement expanded, issues of class, race, sexual orientation, and ethnicity began to divide women even as gender united them. Some radical feminists began to attack marriage as no more than an institutionalized form of sexual exploitation and to extoll lesbian relationships. Friedan, disturbed at the direction the women's movement seemed to be taking, wrote *The Second Stage* (1982) in which she called for a less hostile and more balanced approach to the problems still besetting women. In the 1990s, the infirmities of age began to make themselves felt and occupied increasingly more of Friedan's attention. She produced *The Fountain of Age* (1993) in which she related how the elderly, especially women, could continue to lead productive and satisfactory lives until their last breath.

Since its publication in 1963, *The Feminine Mystique* has enjoyed enormous popularity, selling 1.5 million copies within a decade. For a book of such fame it had a rather parochial beginning. Betty Friedan, a 36-year-old New York housewife, examined the responses to a biographical questionnaire by two hundred Smith College alumnae fifteen years after graduation. To her surprise she found pervasive in them the complaint of boredom, unhappiness, and dissatisfaction, a tone of undefined but very real anxiety. Each of the women presented her story in very personal terms, as if the misery that she lived with reflected only on her particular inadequacy. It was some awful defect in a woman's character that led her children to guidance clinics, her husband to marital adjustment sessions, and her to a psychiatrist's couch. Friedan, perceiving in the whole of these responses something more than the separate parts, set out to explore "the problem that has no name."

The result, *The Feminine Mystique*, lacks the conceptual power of such a book as Simone de Beauvoir's *The Second Sex*. Nevertheless, Friedan had a good starting point—"a strange discrepancy between the reality of our lives as women and the image to which we are trying to conform"—and she had little trouble in tracing the roots of the image and the grimmer reality it obscured. She very skillfully took the media to task, particularly the women's magazines and advertisements, for invariably presenting an "empty, narrow" view of women. She went on to argue that women's *acceptance* of this mythology robbed them of self-definition, creating a void that was at the core of their problems. When a woman could think of herself only in terms of the roles of wife and mother, when her response to the question, "Who am I?" was inevitably "Tom's wife … Mary's mother," then she not only condemned herself to minimal satisfactions but to failure in the roles themselves. These women clung to their children and husbands with all the tenacity of someone who is drowning, and, predictably, they often took their families down with them. The suburban mother, insisted Friedan, so smothered her child with attention and affection that she left no breathing space for autonomous growth and development. And she did no better by her husband. When sex was all there was to make her feel alive, she was as overbearing in the bedroom as in the nursery. The message was clear and simply put: women, if you submerge yourself in caretaking, you will not only be unhappy but inadequate.

Friedan's diagnosis and solution had their roots in the 1950s. She was ultimately calling for self-assertion, a personal kind of deliverance, escape into freedom. For all her criticism of the media, of schools, even of Freudian doctrines, she was not constructing, as the women liberationists of the 1970s would, an overarching theory to link the oppression of women to some basic quality of the social order. She did not want to reform the politics of sexism or to improve the delivery of health care. She had far more modest goals: to have women free themselves, cast off the yoke of the feminine mystique, get out of the house and into the workplace. "The only way for a woman, as for a man, to find herself, to know herself as a person, is by creative work of her own." To this end she advocated a kind of GI bill for women who wanted to return to or keep up their education; and later, in helping to found the National Organization for Women, she led the attack against legal obstacles to equal employment.

There can be no question but that Friedan spoke for her times. By the early 1960s an unprecedented number of women were entering the workplace, and to an unusual degree these new working women were mothers. Friedan's writings reflected this change, probably doing little to heighten it. And her book was narrow in scope, addressed essentially to college-educated suburban housewives, hardly the majority of the nation's women. Nevertheless, she accomplished a task of crucial importance. She was the one who helped women begin thinking in structural rather than personal terms about their experiences. She helped them realize that their problems were not character faults but faults in the system. And once that breakthrough had occurred, women could begin to unite for common action and indeed make far more astute and important statements about the nature of their group experience. Women read Friedan in such numbers because she gave them company in their misery and taught them to think about escaping it together. A young Connecticut mother spoke for many of her sisters elsewhere when she told Friedan: "I've got tears in my eyes with sheer relief that my own inner turmoil is shared with other women." For this reason Friedan is properly labeled one of the most important founders of the women's liberation movement. See Betty Friedan, *The Feminine Mystique* (1963).

SHEILA M. ROTHMAN

FRIEDMAN, Milton (b. Brooklyn, N.Y., July 31, 1912), ECONOMIST, graduated from Rutgers University (1932) and received an MA from the University of Chicago (1933). Following two years in Washington, D.C. (1935–37), as an associate economist for the National Resources Committee, Friedman moved to New York City where he studied at Columbia University (PhD, 1946). He lectured part-time at Columbia (1937–40) and worked as a member of the research staff of the National Bureau for Economic Research (1937–46, 1948 on). In 1940–41, Friedman served as visiting professor of economics at the University of Wisconsin. During the next four years he was the principal economist for the division of tax research, U.S. Treasury Department, and then became associate director of research for the statistical research group of the division of war research at Columbia University (1943–45). In 1945, Friedman was appointed associate professor of economics and statistics at the University of Minnesota and a year later moved to the University of Chicago. He was named Paul Snowden Russell Distinguished Service professor of economics at Chicago in 1962. Friedman retired from Chicago in 1979 to become a senior research fellow of the Hoover Institution at Stanford, California.

Among his numerous publications probably the best known are *Studies in the Quantity Theory of Money* (1956), *A Theory of the Consumption Function* (1957), *A Program for Monetary Stability* (1960), and *Dollars and Deficits* (1968). With Rose D. Friedman he published *Capitalism and Freedom* (1962), and with Anna J. Schwartz, *A Monetary History of the United States, 1867–1960* (1963). In these works Friedman has sought to provide theoretical and empirical evidence to support the "quantity" theory of money. In contrast to the dominant Keynesian economics, which emphasizes the manipulation of tax rates and governmental spending to combat recession or inflation, the "quantity" theory views the amount of money in circulation as the key influence on the nation's economy. Thus, Friedman has argued against the Federal Reserve Board's discretionary power regarding the size of banking reserves and has supported legislation that would direct it to increase the supply of money at a steady and constant rate.

The second aspect of Friedman's economic philosophy has been his consistent opposition to what he sees as the dangers of ever increasing governmental regulation. He has advocated abolition of such federal regulatory agencies as the Securities Exchange Commission, and of such programs as the existing welfare system. He proposed instead the development of a "negative income tax" that would provide direct payments by the Internal Revenue Service to those families whose income fell below a certain level. While active in both teaching and writing, he served as an economic adviser to Senator **Barry Goldwater** in 1964 and Richard M. Nixon in 1968. He also served as an advisor to the Reagan administration in the 1980s.

Among Friedman's many activities he was a columnist for *Newsweek* magazine for almost a decade in the 1960s and 1970s, and in the 1980s hosted *Free to Choose*, a television series dedicated to his free market ideas. In 1976, Friedman was awarded the Nobel Prize in economics.

———✖———

Milton Friedman is the outstanding theorist and popular champion of the counterrevolution against Keynesian economics. John Maynard Keynes argued that natural cycles in employment and output could be countered by injections of spending power into the economy: government expenditures could be increased or taxes lowered. His views have dominated the economics profession since the late 1940s and have been accepted as doctrine by most liberal governments in Europe and America.

But the minority view—that other government activities are more effective than fiscal policy in "fine-tuning" national income—has regained followers in business and government circles since the onset of serious inflation in the United States in the late 1960s. By Keynesian logic, expansionary fiscal policy should also work in reverse when the economy overheats. Yet the income tax surcharge of 1968 appeared to have little of the desired effect. Friedman and the so-called Chicago School claim that adjustments in the quantity of money in circulation are more crucial to the process than direct fiscal incentives to spend. Although Friedman's ideas have been much in vogue, it is difficult to trace any Nixon administration policies to his ideas, though there is some evidence they had more resonance in the Reagan administration. Still, Friedman's gadfly status remains intact even under the Republicans.

More recently, Friedman's indictment has been expanded; he argues that no government policy can succeed in permanently pushing unemployment below its "natural" level. The implication is that generous welfare schemes are a more realistic approach to ameliorating the plight of the unemployed than a jobs program that creates employment through the demand for goods. See Milton Friedman and Walter Heller, *Monetary vs. Fiscal Policy* (1969).

PETER PASSELL

FROMM, Erich (b. Frankfurt-am-Main, Ger., Mar. 23, 1900; d. Muralto, Switzerland, Mar. 18, 1980), PSYCHOANALYST, received a PhD in 1922 from the University of Heidelberg, having specialized in philosophy, sociology, and psychology. He studied at the University of Munich and at Berlin's Psychoanalytic Institute (1923–24), and began practicing psychoanalysis in Berlin in 1925. He helped found and became a lecturer at the Frankfurt Psychoanalytic Institute in 1929 while concurrently lecturing at the Institute for Social Research at the University of Frankfurt (1929–32). After a 1933 visit to the United States to speak at Chicago's Psychoanalytical Institute, Fromm decided to leave Nazi Germany. He settled in New York City in 1934, where he began practicing psychoanalysis. From 1934 to 1939 he was a lecturer at Columbia's International Institute for Social Research.

Fromm attempted to apply the theoretical framework of psychoanalysis to problems of society and culture. His *Escape from Freedom* (1941) traced the development of man's freedom from the Middle Ages to the present. This work established his reputation as a leading psychologist and thinker. *Man for Himself* (1947) and *Psychoanalysis and Religion* (1950) were similar attempts to relate psychoanalysis to social and cultural problems. Fromm taught at Bennington College from 1941 to 1950. He also joined the staff of the William Alanson White Institute of Psychiatry (Washington, D.C.) in 1945, becoming faculty chairman in 1947. He was appointed professor in the department of psychoanalysis in the medical school of the National University of Mexico in 1951 and head of the department in 1955, a position he held until his retirement in 1965. At the same time he taught at Michigan State University (1957–61). He became adjunct professor of psychiatry at New York University's Graduate Division of Arts and Sciences in 1962.

Fromm examined alienation in a complex society in *The Sane Society* (1955), the emotional experience of love in *The Art of Loving* (1956), and the cold war in *May Man Prevail?* (1961). He also edited *Marx's Concept of Man* (1961). Some later works include *The Revolution of Hope* (1968), *The Crisis of Psychoanalysis* (1970), and *The Anatomy of Human Destructiveness* (1974). In all, Fromm wrote twenty books and scores of articles.

Only within recent years have large numbers of social scientists come to recognize the need to communicate to society a perspective concerning social issues of vital concern. In a fascinating blend of Marxism, humanism, existentialism, psychoanalysis, and Old Testament wisdom, Erich Fromm engaged in such communication long before it became fashionable to do so. As early as 1941 in *Escape from Freedom*, he demonstrated his ability as both a social-historical analyst and a critic to reach the general public. And in his many later works concerning such fundamental problems as the meaning of love, religion, dreams, self-determinism, and the destructive effects on man of industrialization, he continued to broaden his appeal. And there was also much in Fromm's work that precipitated significant social-psychological research (although this is not emphasized often enough). For example, *The Authoritarian Personality,* a pioneering work that presents a classic research program relating psychoanalytic theory to ideology, includes tests of many hypotheses implicit in Fromm's theories of productive and nonproductive character orientations.

Yet he maintained a strong allegiance to and concern with the practice of individual psychotherapy. He enthusiastically continued to develop his unique approach, which he termed "humanistic psychoanalysis." Toward the end of his life Fromm undertook one of his most ambitious ventures. He fortified his own background in neurophysiological processes in order to make a major empirical examination of the roots of aggression in man. In conclusion, Fromm must be regarded as a significant contributor not only to psychology, psychiatry, and psychoanalysis but to the study of the social thought of man in the broadest sense. See E. S. Tauber and Bernard Landis, eds., *In the Name of Life: Essays in Honor of Erich Fromm* (1971).

RICHARD I. EVANS

FROST, Robert Lee (b. San Francisco, Calif., Mar. 26, 1874; d. Boston, Mass., Jan. 29, 1963), POET, entered Dartmouth College in 1892 but left after only a few months. While writing poetry in his spare time he taught school, worked in a textile factory, and traveled in the South. Finally, in 1894, he published his first "professional" poem, "My Butterfly: An Elegy," in the *Independent*. Frost attended Harvard for two years (1897–99) but left without a degree. His grandfather purchased a farm for him near Derry, New Hampshire (1900), and Frost taught English at Pinkerton Academy in Derry (1905–11). Later, he taught psychology at the State Normal School in Plymouth, New Hampshire (1911–12). In 1912, Frost went to England where he met **Ezra Pound** and other poets. He published a collection of mostly lyrical poems, *A Boy's Will* (1913), and also *North of Boston* (1914). Written in common rural language with a combination of seriousness and humor, the poems were acclaimed by English critics, and when Frost returned to the United States in 1915, his reputation was firmly established.

Frost bought a farm near Franconia, New Hampshire, and became professor of English at Amherst College. In 1920 he bought another farm near South Shaftsbury, Vermont, and cofounded the Bread Loaf School of English at Middlebury College. He taught at the University of Michigan (1921–22), Amherst (1923–25), and again at Michigan (1925–26). He returned to New England in 1926, where he taught at several schools. He won his first of four Pulitzer Prizes in 1924 for his collection of poems *New Hampshire* (1923). His collection *A Further Range* (1937) also won a Pulitzer Prize.

Frost became the poetry consultant to the Library of Congress in 1925 and honorary consultant in the humanities to that library the following year. He read his poem "The Gift Outright" at the inauguration of John F. Kennedy in 1961. Later that year he made a trip to the Soviet Union. Frost's two other Pulitzer Prize works were *Collected Poems* (1931) and *The Witness Tree* (1942).

Robert Frost's poetry is nothing less than the voice of old New England projected into the 20th century. And yet it is much more than a New England voice, for Frost was able to make the regional tone and rhythm the means of extending the whole range of poetry in English. More than any American poet of this century he seems both to inherit and to renew the whole tradition of English poetry—and he does it by remaining authentically from New rather than from Old England. For if he was born in San Francisco, he is not less a true son of New England; and when he returned "into his own," he settled himself so deeply in its northern reaches that he seemed as native to the area as **Ralph Waldo Emerson** and **Henry David Thoreau** had ever been.

They were, after all, his spiritual fathers. Emerson had called for an American voice and got two answers: one from **Walt Whitman,** a poetic voice of union; and one from Thoreau, a prose voice of individual secession. The one led horizontally outward in space, breaking forms as it went. The other led vertically downward into region and even locale. Frost descends from the Thoreau line. Emerson had given the New England voice a spirit; Thoreau gave it a separate life; Frost gave it character and form, and in so doing he probably brought it to an end.

Thus, the old antagonisms that his forebears had expressed toward England are still evident in his work, but they become bent of character and cast of mind; and Frost seems so much at ease in his New England—so secure in it—that Old England yields over its life to him. It is surely no accident that he published his first book of poems in London. That first book—*A Boy's Will*—showed him to be in possession of the traditional lyric forms. The very fact that his title came out of **Henry Wadsworth Longfellow** signaled the extent to which he, like Longfellow, had made himself sure of the whole range of English prosody.

And when in 1914 he published *North of Boston*, he laid claim to the space that he would spend the rest of his life occupying. His act of occupation involved bending English poetry, particularly the blank verse line, to New England character and New England nature. And before he had finished, Frost not only showed complete mastery of sonnet, quatrain, dramatic monologue, and love lyric, he was utterly at home in satiric, pastoral, and philosophical verse. Yet Frost never gave himself to the forms so much as he seemed to use the forms to express himself as poet.

In Frost's hands the language was brought down toward the character who spoke it at the same time the speaker was brought somehow upward out of his rural identity to be not a character in poetry but the character of poetry. The whole imaginative operation involved a reorganization—not a revolution—of language as well as values, and a play of mind that threatens to equalize thought and attitude, character and poet, and tone and intonation. Such equality assumes the proportions of a skepticism so complete that all allusions, traditions, and myths which the poet draws upon seem always at the point of enhancing his character at the cost of their own reality. Thus all myths the poetry appropriates are aggrandized by and subordinated to the Myth of Robert Frost. And thus Frost himself emerged from the long and deep obscurity of his beginning—he was 39 when his first book of poems was published—to become not an American poet so much as the poet as American: a folk hero who could, at the end of his long life, occupy center stage at a presidential inauguration and go to Russia as a special ambassador, a representative and embodiment of the American imagination.

The public image would be little or nothing if the poetry did not sustain it. After all, Edgar Lee Masters, Vachel Lindsay, and **Carl Sandburg** each in his way had vied with Frost in this particular endeavor. But Frost's poetry, more than merely sustaining his image, at once authenticates and redeems it. He took such hold of the English poetry he inherited that the very genius of the language yielded an American poetic identity at last—something that was purely *New* England and American. See Lawrance Thompson, *Robert Frost* (2 vols.; 1966, 1970).

JAMES M. COX

FULBRIGHT, James William (b. Sumner, Mo., Apr. 9, 1905; d. Washington, D.C., Feb. 9, 1995), POLITICAL LEADER, graduated from the University of Arkansas in 1925 and studied at Oxford University as a Rhodes scholar, earning a BA in 1928 and an MA in 1931. Returning to the United States, Fulbright entered George Washington University Law School, receiving his LLB in 1934. He then became a lawyer in the antitrust division of the Justice Department. He left the government to become an instructor of law at George Washington University (1935–36) but then became a lecturer at the University of Arkansas Law School. In 1939 he was appointed president of the University of Arkansas but resigned in 1941 because of differences with Arkansas governor Homer Adkins.

Fulbright was elected as a Democrat to the U.S. House of Representatives in 1942 and became a member of the House Foreign Affairs Committee. He was elected to the Senate in 1944 and reelected in 1950, 1956, 1962, and 1968. He was the sponsor in the Senate of the law (1946) that set up an international educational exchange program for graduate students, which bears his name. He also later fathered the legislation that established the John F. Kennedy Center for the Performing Arts, a measure that he claimed was his proudest legislative achievement.

Fulbright became a member of the Senate Foreign Relations Committee in 1949. In 1954 he co-sponsored the censure resolution against Senator **Joseph McCarthy** of Wisconsin. In 1959, Fulbright, who was then chairman of the Senate Banking and Currency Committee, resigned that post to become chairman of the Foreign Relations Committee. Although he supported the Tonkin Bay Resolution (1965) that gave President Lyndon Johnson almost blanket authority to send American troops into Vietnam, Fulbright soon became one of the leading critics of American involvement in Southeast Asia. As a result of his growing opposition to the Vietnam War, Fulbright became anathema to President Johnson, who barred him from the White House. In 1974, Fulbright lost the Democratic senatorial primary in Arkansas to Dale Bumpers by a margin of two to one, thus ending his career on Capitol Hill. He remained in Washington, joined a law firm, Hogan & Hartson, and represented such clients as the Japanese government and the United Arab Emirates.

One of Fulbright's staff members in 1966 and 1967 was Bill Clinton, who viewed the Senator as a mentor. With Clinton's election to the presidency in 1992, Fulbright returned to the White House in 1993 to be honored by the president on his 88th birthday. Fulbright, who was a thoughtful student of American history, wrote several books on various subjects, including *Prospects for the West* (1963), *Old Myths and New Realities* (1964), and *The Arrogance of Power* (1966).

———— ∞∞ ————

J. William Fulbright, a figure of controversy during much of his public career, became a preeminent symbol of opposition to the Vietnam War in the latter years of Lyndon B. Johnson's administration. That period marked a pinnacle of popular recognition for a man who had previously come to public attention through his collisions with higher authority.

As president of the University of Arkansas, Fulbright fought to raise the academic standing of his alma mater against the resistance of a standpat state government. He made headlines after the Republican sweep of the 1946 congressional elections when, as a comparatively young freshman senator, he proposed that President Harry S. Truman appoint Senator **Arthur H. Vandenberg,** senior Republican of the Senate Foreign Relations Committee, to be secretary of state and then resign himself. The party with current popular support would then have the responsibility of government. Truman rewarded the Arkansan with the sobriquet "Senator Halfbright." Not deterred, Fulbright later led an investigation of dubious practices in the Reconstruction Finance Corporation, a venture that again brought him into conflict with Truman.

Fulbright's principal interest, however, was in foreign affairs, and his unyielding insistence on being added to the Senate Foreign Relations Committee in 1949 compelled Majority Leader Scott Lucas to oblige him, at the cost of embarrass-ing relations with Senator Vandenberg, who was thus deprived of an anticipated Republican seat.

On the Foreign Relations Committee, Fulbright gave steady support to the policy of containing the Communist powers and to related foreign aid programs until he began to question the purposes of American intervention in Vietnam and the means by which that intervention was carried out. He appeared to have become a regular member of the Democratic leadership and was regarded as a likely prospect for secretary of state after John F. Kennedy won the presidency in 1960.

Fulbright may be described as essentially Wilsonian in his belief in the moral destiny of the United States and in his conviction that national policy must follow moral imperatives. Lacking the simple assurance of past generations that any action of the United States was—almost by definition—moral, he came to question both the propriety and usefulness of visiting a small country with unprecedented destruction. Was the abandonment of traditional humane values worth the slight political gains the war might bring? He therefore used his chairmanship of the committee to initiate periodic investigations of the aims and conduct of the war in Vietnam and so provided a major forum for attacking President Johnson's policies in Southeast Asia. This activity won him the acclaim of young liberals and radicals, who proposed him for national office even though his voting record on racial issues was that of a conventional southerner.

As casualties increased, with no end to the fighting in view, the war lost much of the popular support it had once commanded while the antiwar movement, which Fulbright had helped launch, came to represent an ever increasing majority of articulate Americans. This was recompense for the diminution of his own and his committee's influence within the government. In May 1974, Fullbright's bid for a sixth term failed when he was defeated in the Democratic primary by Governor Dale Bumpers. See Haynes B. Johnson, *Fulbright: The Dissenter* (1968).

ALAN D. HARPER

FULLER, Richard Buckminster, Jr. (b. Milton, Mass., July 12, 1895; d. Los Angeles, Calif., July 1, 1983), ARCHITECT, ENGINEER, INVENTOR, attended Harvard University but was expelled in his sophomore year, 1915. For the next two years he worked for an importer of cotton-mill machinery as a fitter's apprentice and in the same capacity for Armour Company. In 1917 he attended the U.S. Naval Academy where he received an ensign's commission. Following his discharge from the navy after the war as a lieutenant (j.g.) he went back to the Armour Company but soon quit to join the Kelly-Springfield Truck Company as export manager and, later, national account sales manager (1919–22). From 1922 to 1927 he was in business with his father-in-law, architect James Monroe Hewlett, in the Stockade Building Systems, a construction firm. During this period, living in Chicago, he began to develop and refine his theories of "comprehensive design."

In 1927, having lost control of Stockade, he founded the 4D Company, a research organization. He invented the Dymaxion house, a relatively inexpensive, easily assembled yet luxurious dwelling suspended from a central pillar; it expressed Fuller's philosophy of "doing more with less" by using modern technology in construction and design. Fuller founded the Dymaxion Corporation of Bridgeport, Connecticut, in 1932 to build and sell his house as well as the other inventions that came from his drawing board: a dye-stamped bathroom unit that could be made operative in minutes and the Dymaxion automobile, a rugged three-wheeled vehicle that could attain speeds of 120 miles an hour. Financial success eluded Dymaxion, however, and it failed in 1935.

From 1936 to 1938, Fuller served as assistant to the director of research and development at the Phelps, Dodge Corp. and continued to work on his inventions. In 1940 he designed the Dymaxion steel igloo and received a patent for the Dymaxion Air-Ocean-World Map, which portrayed the continents in such a way that all visible distortions were eliminated (1943). In 1941, Fuller reorganized the Dymaxion Corp. but suspended operations after the United States entered World War II. From 1942 to 1944, Fuller served with the Board of Economic Warfare and as special assistant to the director of the Foreign Economic Administration. In 1944 he reestablished the Dymaxion (Dwelling Machines) Co., and in 1946 he introduced the Wichita house, a round seven-room aluminum structure that employed aircraft construction techniques and sold for less than $7,000. This dwelling, like the earlier Dymaxion house, was a forerunner of the revolutionary geodesic dome (c. 1947), a lightweight, extremely strong enclosure based on a mathematical system Fuller developed called "energetic synergetic geometry," which is an extension of spherical trigonometry. Consisting of struts of high-strength metal alloys arranged latticelike in the shape of a tetrahedron (a pyramidical form with three sides plus a base), Fuller's domes became commercially viable when he built one to house a plant for the Ford Motor Co. in Dearborn, Michigan, in 1953. Subsequently, under the aegis of Geodesics, Inc., and Synergetics, Inc., companies that Fuller founded in 1955, domes of his design were built to shelter the radar of the distant early warning line in Alaska, the U.S. exhibition in Moscow in 1959, the U.S. pavilion at Expo 67 in Montreal, and numerous factories, restaurants, theaters, and sports arenas throughout the world.

In the late 1950s Fuller achieved wide recognition in both academic and professional circles. Appointed professor of generalized design science exploration by Southern Illinois University in 1959, Fuller taught and lectured at most of the leading American universities, including Harvard (where he gave the Charles Eliot Norton lectures in 1961–62), Cornell, Yale, Princeton, and the Massachusetts Institute of Technology. Well into his eighties he continued to spend much of his time "toing and froing" (words he coined) around the world lecturing. He was the author of many books and articles. Among the most important are *Nine Chains to the Moon* (1938), *Education Automation* (1962), *Ideas and Integrities* (1963), *No More Secondhand God* (1963), *Operating Manual for Spaceship Earth* (1969), *Utopia or Oblivion* (1972), and *Earth Inc.* (1973).

⚬⚬⚬

Buckminster Fuller was the prototypical universal man in an age of specialization. While he appeared to have originated in the old Yankee tradition of inventive tinkering, he nevertheless preached a doctrine of messianic, international technological man. He overcame adversity by sheer willpower. Long considered a crank, he achieved success, ironically enough, when the military-industrial complex recognized the portability and versatility of his geodesic dome structures. Yet he went on to become a hero of the youth culture of the 1960s, in part for the way that he attacked—in his manifestos, poetry, and public lectures—every imaginable aspect of the Establishment and status quo. He was intensely curious and research-oriented, and he felt that language must be redesigned for future efficiency. For instance, his own circumstances were described in the metalanguage of his Research Foundation: "Newcomers that might feed eventually into the main trend of articulation are usually unseen and unrecognized by the main trend until major confluence. The early record of contributory trends is often lost, particularly in those categories wherein an inherent lag of many years intervenes between initial pioneering work and popular assimilation of the new art."

Fuller from the late 1950s on had a powerful impact on the architectural profession and received the Gold Medal of both the British and American Institute of Architects, although his major construction, the Dymaxion house, has rarely been built and his primary structure, the geodesic dome, is simply an envelope with little architectural character, internally or externally. The potential scale of geodesic structures for megastructures and container cities endeared him to the Visionaries, a group active in the 1970s. His concepts of World Map, World Game, and Spaceship Earth caught the attention of both environmentalists and futurists, while his pleas for mass-produced prefabricated houses struck a sympathetic response in all those who felt, rightly or wrongly, that the building trades should

model themselves on automobile manufacturing—to which Fuller also contributed in the 1930s with his ill-fated Dymaxion car.

"Bucky" was perhaps best described by himself: "Born in 1895, I have witnessed enough of the characteristics of acceleratingly-accelerating, evolutionary transformations and reorientation of humanity's know-what and knowhow to be able to sense, think, and act fairly successfully, in realistic anticipation of epochally unfolding events." See Robert W. Marks, *The Dymaxion World of Buckminster Fuller* (1960), and John McHale, *R. Buckminster Fuller* (1962).

GEORGE R. COLLINS

FULLER, Sarah Margaret (b. Cambridgeport, Mass., May 23, 1810; d. off Fire Island, N.Y., July 19, 1850), REFORMER, WRITER, was taught Latin and the classics by her father and attended a boarding school in Groton, Massachusetts, for two years (1823–24). After the death of her father (1835) she supported the family by teaching school in Boston (1836–37) and Providence (1837–39). In 1839 she published a translation of Eckermann's *Conversations with Goethe*. That same year she started her "Conversations" or adult education program with some of the most prominent women in Boston. Discussing such subjects as philosophy, education, and the role of women in society, she established her reputation as a great personality and conversationalist. A strong feminist, she believed in the full intellectual potential of women in modern society as well as political, professional, and educational equality; she expressed these views in a controversial book, *Woman in the Nineteenth Century* (1845).

Friendly with such writers as **Ralph Waldo Emerson** and George Ripley, Fuller joined the *Dial*, a transcendentalist magazine, in 1840 as editor, contributing poetry, reviews, and critiques. Transferring the editorship to Emerson in 1842, she moved to New York City in 1844 to become literary critic for **Horace Greeley**'s New York *Tribune*. She crusaded for social causes, encouraged young American writers, and drew American attention particularly to romantic

German literature. In 1846 she went to Europe and met Thomas Carlyle, William Wordsworth, and the Italian revolutionary Giuseppe Mazzini, who greatly influenced her. She secretly married an impoverished Italian nobleman ten years her junior, Giovanni Ossoli, in 1849, a year after she bore their child. During the Roman revolution she nursed wounded Republicans. When the Republican cause collapsed, she fled to Florence and then decided to return to the United States. Her boat was shipwrecked off Fire Island, New York, in 1850, and she perished with her husband and child and the manuscript of what she judged her great work, a history of the Italian revolution. Some of her many other writings include an account of travel in the West, *Summer on the Lakes* (1844), *Papers on Literature and Art* (1846), and *At Home and Abroad* (1856), her correspondence of her European experiences, published posthumously. *The Memoirs of Margaret Fuller Ossoli* (1852) contains the fullest selection of her letters and journals as well as comments about her character by friends.

In 19th-century America it was not easy to be a woman and an intellectual; to be both with uncompromising honesty and passion was Margaret Fuller's life work. The profoundest analyst of the position of women in her day, Fuller was too sensitive to see woman's problem as one only of oppression or to consider political feminism—which she favored—as more than peripheral to its solution. She partly accepted the genteel division of the heart and the head into men's and women's spheres, but as a transcendentalist she knew the superior wisdom of the heart. The transcendental concept of wholeness also gave vitality to her belief that true manliness and womanliness could come only with the full development of both the masculine and the feminine qualities existent in every person. Intellectually close to both Emerson and Greeley, Fuller was an acute literary and social critic. Yet her hurried and inflated prose seldom did full justice to her ideas. She realized this but was too faithful to transcendental spontaneity to devote herself to calculated literary craftsmanship. Her greatest intellectual success came in a series of "Conversations" with Boston women by which she supported herself for several years and where her immense learning, complex perceptiveness, and personal magnetism could have full play.

Her trip to Europe in 1846 produced her deepest personal and societal experiences. A friend and admirer of Mazzini, she supported the Italian revolution actively and through her letters to the New York *Tribune.* With the collapse of the revolution, she returned to the United States, but in the surf off Fire Island, Fuller's personal and intellectual struggles ended. In the words of Horace Greeley, she was "the most remarkable, and in some respects the greatest, woman America has yet known." Or perhaps not known. See Mason Wade, *Margaret Fuller: Whetstone of Genius* (1940).

DAVID B. GRIMSTED

FULTON, Robert (b. Lancaster County, Pa., Nov. 14, 1765; d. New York, N.Y., Feb. 24, 1815), INVENTOR, grew up in Lancaster, Pennsylvania, then the largest inland population center in America. The atmosphere of Lancaster, then known throughout the colonies for its gunsmiths and artisans, seems to have had an effect on him, for he displayed considerable artistic and mechanical aptitude. At the age of 16 he was apprenticed to a Philadelphia silversmith, but he disliked working for others and in 1785 set himself up as an artist.

Despite his lack of formal training he made enough money to finance a trip to London in 1786. He carried with him a letter of recommendation from **Benjamin Franklin** to the artist **Benjamin West**, who became a close friend. In 1791 two of Fulton's paintings were included in an exhibition of the Royal Academy, and this gained him the patronage of Viscount William Courtenay, who invited Fulton to his castle in Devonshire. There, in 1793, Fulton developed a machine to cut and polish marble. Encouraged by the success of this invention, Fulton next drew up plans for a mechanical device to raise ships on canals. His design was so well received that he immediately embarked on a career as a full-time inventor. Although he continued to paint as a form of relaxation until the end of his life, his main creative energies were increasingly directed toward mechanical engineering.

Fulton's *Treatise on the Improvement of Canal Navigation* (1796) brought him international recognition. In 1797 he moved to France where, along with his canal projects, he also promoted his design for a submarine capable of destroying British shipping using underwater bombs. His *Nautilus* was launched in 1800. The vessel, similar to an earlier design by David Bushnell, performed well but failed to interest the French government.

Fulton next turned his energies to steamboats, having met and formed a partnership with **Robert R. Livingston**, then U.S. minister to France. The two launched a steamboat on the Seine in 1803. But prospects in France remained dim, and Fulton returned to England in 1804 at the invitation of the British government. However, the British lost interest in Fulton's inventions after their victory at Trafalgar, and in 1806, Fulton returned to America hoping to promote his submarine design.

Unsuccessful at this and still in partnership with Livingston, who had also returned to America, Fulton again began experimenting with steamboats. Livingston held a monopoly for steam navigation on the Hudson River, and on August 9, 1807, their first steamboat made its trial runs. Next came the historic trip from New York to Albany, on August 17, 1807. By autumn *The North River Steamboat* was running commercially, and in 1808, after a major rebuilding, the vessel was registered as *The North River Steamboat of Clermont*, shortened by the press to *Clermont*.

Fulton married Livingston's cousin Harriet and established an engine works in New Jersey, but his last years were clouded by litigation related to his steamboat designs, which were derived in large part from earlier work done by others. During the War of 1812 he was called upon to design a floating battery for the defense of New York Harbor. The last of his triumphs, the *Demologus*, also known as *Fulton the First*, was launched shortly before the end of the war, in December 1814.

———— ⚬⚭⚬ ————

Robert Fulton is popularly credited with "inventing" the steamboat, but like **Henry Ford**'s automobile, **Thomas Alva Edison**'s light bulb, and the **Wright** brothers' airplane, his *Clermont* was only the first workable example of its type. In the great American tradition of self-taught tinkerers, he devised practical applications for the original ideas of others. James Ramsey and John Fitch in England and naval engineers in France had done important theoretical work on steam power for nautical vessels before he turned his mind to the subject, but it was Fulton's model that first proved commercially successful.

Fulton showed his inventive imagination while still a boy. He earned a local reputation for such ingenious devices as a paddle-wheel boat created to avoid the work of poling on his fishing expeditions at the age of 14. He also displayed an early talent for drawing and earned money providing local gunsmiths with decorative designs. His impoverished mother made the logical decision to exploit his mechanical and artistic aptitudes by apprenticing him to a silversmith, but at the age of 17 he demonstrated a characteristically independent spirit by going into business for himself as a freelance artist, a career at which he was so successful that he was able to buy his mother a farm four years later and go to Europe.

Equally successful in London, Fulton gradually abandoned his career in art for the more challenging one of inventor, turning his mechanical skills to the development of practical and profitable devices. His numerous patents, for which his applications were expertly illustrated by his own drawings, were invariably as practical and useful as his early labor-saving devices. His famous 1796 publication *A Treatise on the Improvement of Canal Navigation*, the first in which he formally identified himself as a civil engineer, included precise calculations of the costs of construction and operation as well as a lucid discussion of the benefits a network of inland canals would confer on the nation's trade. Many of his mechanisms remained in wide use for many years.

As active an entrepreneur as he was an inventor, Fulton promoted his inventions earnestly, with little regard for national loyalty. While in France he tried to convince Napoleon's government to employ his submarine, the first workable example ever developed, in their conflict with the English; failing that, he cheerfully switched sides and made the same effort in London. An American citizen during the twenty-four years he lived abroad, he always kept the government in Washington informed of his activities.

Fiercely ambitious, Fulton engaged in bitter litigation to protect his patents and the monopoly he enjoyed on the steamboat that made his reputation. He was condemned for his undeniable opportunism and accused of an "avaricious desire" to control "all the waters of the Union." He was also charged with relying on others' scientific ideas for his inventions. But history has vindicated him, crediting his bold imagination and pragmatic ingenuity for helping the United States assume a leading position in the dawning age of technology. See Cynthia Owen Philip, *Robert Fulton* (1985).

DENNIS WEPMAN

GALBRAITH, John Kenneth (b. Iona Station, Ontario, Can., Oct. 15, 1908), ECONOMIST, graduated from the University of Toronto (BS, economics, 1931). He then studied at the University of California (MS, 1933; PhD, 1934). After working as an instructor and tutor at Harvard University (1934–39) and studying as a social science research fellow at Cambridge University (1937–38), he became an assistant professor of economics at Princeton (1939–42). While at Princeton he also served as economic adviser to the National Defense Advisory Committee (1940–41) and in the Price Division of the Office of Price Administration (1941–42). During 1942–43 he was the deputy administrator of the Office of Price Administration. He served on the board of editors of *Fortune* magazine (1943–48), as director of the U.S. Strategic Bombing Survey (1945), and as director of the Office of Economic Security Policy (1946), in which position he dealt with the economic affairs of Germany and Japan.

In 1948, Galbraith returned to Harvard as a lecturer in economics and then as professor (1949–60; 1963 on). A prolific writer, his works have often become the focus for major controversy and disputation. His *American Capitalism* (1951) was a study of the development of the American economy, with particular reference to the post–World War II period. In this work Galbraith argued that the major social protection against the monopoly power of American industry was to be found in the emergence of "countervailing" pressures from other blocs such as labor unions. *The Affluent Society* (1958) argued that America had reached a point when the drive for constantly increasing production actually caused more problems than it solved. In it Galbraith urged a shifting of priorities to the public sector, such as the creation of better public housing, law enforcement, mass transit, education, and welfare. In 1967 he published *The New Industrial State*, wherein he argued that the American economy was largely controlled by five hundred major companies, operated by a "technostructure" of well-trained technicians and managers—men as much concerned with the maintenance of their positions as with the increase of profits. In this work he attacked those who view bigness in industry as being inherently evil, yet, as in *The Affluent Society*, he denounced the minimal concern given by the "technostructure" to considerations of beauty or higher values. Among Galbraith's other works are *The Great Crash* (1955) and *The Liberal Hour*

(1960). He has remained active outside the academic community, serving as economic adviser to **Adlai E. Stevenson** in 1952 and 1956, and to John F. Kennedy in 1960 and **Robert Kennedy** in 1964. During 1961–63 he served as U.S. ambassador to India, an experience he described in his *Ambassador's Journal* (1967). He was chairman of Americans for Democratic Action (1967–70). During the campaign of 1968 he and the ADA endorsed Eugene McCarthy for president. Galbraith, though still a passionate liberal, has not participated in recent politics with the same degree of vigor and activism that marked him earlier. He has confined himself to criticizing the rightward drift that characterized economic policy under both Democratic and Republican administrations since the 1970s. He was especially acerbic in his critique of the "supply side" philosophy that underlined the economic actions of the Reagan presidency, accurately predicting that increasing military spending while cutting taxes would pile up huge deficits well beyond anything usually attributed to liberal free-spenders. But not all of Galbraith's pronouncements have been that accurate. During the early 1980s he asserted that the Soviet Union utilized its resources and manpower much more efficiently than the United States did, an analysis that proved dreadfully inaccurate in light of the stunning collapse of Communism. Now retired from Harvard, Galbraith is devoting most of his time to writing.

***

No American economist is better known or has a wider popular audience than John Galbraith. While few of the ideas expressed in Galbraith's nontechnical writing are totally original, his careful didactic style (rendered palatable by fine wit) has made an impression on liberal audiences and won the grudging respect of academic economists.

The Affluent Society, published at the close of the Eisenhower years, argues that the United States should reassess national priorities and divert a portion of its vast resources to the public sector—more schools at the price of fewer tailfins. Galbraith acknowledged the practical difficulty of raising income taxes to pay the bills and suggested as an alternative a national sales tax. The basic ideas coincided nicely with the rise of welfare statism in Europe and became a focus for liberal discontents that influenced the policies of Democratic administrations. Some even credit *The Affluent Society* with a major role in redirecting the New Deal coalition toward massive federal spending projects for middle-income as well as lower-income families. The national sales tax plan reappeared in the 1970s and afterward was tied to the notion of relieving local property tax burdens.

Galbraith's other major work, *The New Industrial State,* challenged the assumptions at the root of modern economics. Taking a cue from the thoughts of **Thorstein Veblen** and **A. A. Berle** and Gardner Means, he asserted reasons for the failure of the competitive marketplace: instead of consumers who know their own minds versus atomistic sellers, markets are dominated by large corporations that create the need for their products through advertising or political action. Little of the theory of welfare economics (much of which dates from the 18th century) can stand under such attack. The lesson inferred is that, under modern capitalism, the neat textbook interpretations of how resources are channeled and who gets the rewards are simply scholastic fictions. See William Breit and Roger Ransom, *The Academic Scribblers* (1971).

PETER PASSELL

GALLATIN, Abraham Alfonse Albert (b. Geneva, Switzerland, Jan. 29, 1761; d. Astoria, N.Y., Aug. 12, 1849), POLITICAL LEADER, graduated from the Geneva Academy (1779) and in 1780 emigrated to the United States, eventually settling in western Pennsylvania (1784). He opposed the centralizing features of the new Constitution, and in 1788 he was a delegate to a conference held at Harrisburg to consider amending it. He served in the Pennsylvania state legislature (1790–92), where he advocated a system of public education and supported bills to abolish paper money, pay the public debt in specie, and establish a Bank of Pennsylvania.

Gallatin was elected to the U.S. Senate in 1793 but was denied his seat because he had not been a U.S. citizen for nine years. During the Whiskey Rebellion (1794) in western Pennsylvania he urged the farmers to submit to government taxation. He served in the House of Representatives (1795–1801) and in 1797 became the leader of the Republican minority. He insisted that the Treasury Department must be accountable to Congress and was instrumental in creating a standing committee on finance.

Gallatin became Jefferson's secretary of the Treasury in 1801. Before the outbreak of the War of 1812 he was able to reduce the public debt from $80 million to $45 million. When Congress passed the Embargo Act (1807) banning trade with foreign nations, Gallatin was forced to rely on internal taxes (which he had always opposed) as a source of revenue.

Gallatin was sent to Russia by President James Madison in 1813 to discuss the czar's offer to mediate a settlement of the War of 1812, and in 1814 he was a member of the U.S. Peace Commission at Ghent. He was U.S. minister to France (1816–23) and to London (1826–27). As president of the New York branch of the second Bank of the U.S. (1831–39), he opposed protective tariffs and urged a return to specie payments after the Panic of 1837.

———— ✑ ————

By his contemporaries Albert Gallatin was ranked only slightly below George Washington, Thomas Jefferson, and Madison, and as a peer of **Henry Clay, John Calhoun,** and **Daniel Webster.** During sixty years in public life his attainments were great and varied: his leadership in Congress and in party organization that helped bring about the election of Jefferson to the presidency; his application during twelve years as secretary of the Treasury (a length of service still unsurpassed) of financial principles that complemented those of **Alexander Hamilton;** his skill as "the laboring oar" of Jefferson's and Madison's cabinets in handling administrative and policy problems of all departments of the federal government; his tact and intelligence in representing the

United States abroad for more than a decade— service that helped bring the War of 1812 to a satisfactory end and contributed to the maintenance of peaceful relations with France, the Netherlands, Great Britain, and Canada. No less exceptional were his activities after he passed the biblical three-score and ten: his influential role in the financial community during periods of great stress and his contributions to the ethnology of the Native American.

Much of Gallatin's eminence derived from the heritage of his native Geneva, the city of John Calvin; that Americans of the later 20th century know so little about his fame may be attributed to that heritage. Because he was born abroad he was blocked from high elective office, perhaps even the presidency; the pronounced accent he bore to the grave marked him ever as an adopted son. The fact that little Switzerland has provided few immigrants to the United States kept him from becoming an ethnic hero like Casimir Pulaski or Friedrich Steuben or **Christopher Columbus.**

Gallatin's character was in the exemplary Calvinistic mold. His patriotism was sincere and abiding, but he never made a parade of it. He made no cheap bids for popularity by act or word. He appealed to men's reason and intellect. Never was he deflected from his conscientious course by the attractions of wealth, power, or fame.

But Gallatin's most considerable handicap to contemporary fame is the degree to which he exemplified Genevan economic principles. Students of government praise him for his probity in office; but in this post-Keynesian age members of the party he helped never invoke his name or his concern for governmental economy, a balanced budget, and the wiping out of the national debt. Recently a fiscal theorist has faulted Gallatin for lack of "boldness of action, decisiveness, and broadness of scope in an era which marked the birth of a nation." The thesis is provocative, yet it may not take into sufficient consideration the disorderly condition of federal finances that Gallatin inherited from preceding administrations and the political realities with which he had to cope while in office.

In any event, if Hamilton and Jefferson have come to represent the opposite sides of the political and humanitarian coin in the continuing American tradition, Hamilton and Gallatin surely represent the opposite side of the fiscal and economic coin: Hamilton the constructive adventurer, Gallatin the prudent conservator. See Raymond Walters, Jr., *Albert Gallatin: Jeffersonian Financier and Diplomat* (1969).

RAYMOND WALTERS, JR.

GALLOWAY, Joseph (b. West River, Anne Arundel Co., Md., 1731; d. Watford, Eng., Aug. 29, 1803), POLITICAL LEADER, studied law in Philadelphia and became a leading member of the bar. From 1756 to 1776 (except for 1764–65) he served in the Pennsylvania assembly, where he supported **Benjamin Franklin**'s attempts to tax the estates of the proprietors and to substitute a royal for a proprietary government.

Although Galloway disapproved of the Sugar Act (1764) and the Stamp Act (1765), he believed that Parliament had the right to govern the colonies, and he opposed all violent opposition to the new taxes. As chairman of the Pennsylvania assembly's committee to correspond with the colony's agents in London, Galloway worked to conciliate Anglo-American differences. He attended the first Continental Congress (1774), where he proposed that intercolonial affairs be supervised by a Crown-appointed president general and a grand council elected by the colonial assemblies, which would have a veto over parliamentary acts affecting the colonies. His plan was opposed by the more radical elements at the Congress and defeated. Galloway refused to attend the second Continental Congress.

Galloway was a Loyalist during the Revolution, favoring petitions for redress of grievances rather than independence. In the fall of 1776, after the colonists broke with England, he fled to British-occupied territory, and when the British occupied Philadelphia, Galloway became its civil administrator. After the Continental army recaptured the city in 1778, he went to England where he became a major spokesman for the American Loyalists. He sought permission to return to America in 1793, but the Pennsylvania assembly rejected his petition.

⸺

Joseph Galloway was both an ambitious American politician and a fastidious legalist preoccupied with questions of imperial order. For years there appeared to be no inherent contradiction between these facets of his life: his goal of replacing the Penn family proprietorship with a royal government fortuitously aligned him with the popular party at the same time that that end advanced the cause of consistency in the empire through the attempt to eliminate an anomalous, quasi-independent unit. The events of the early 1770s, though, revealed that Galloway's two concerns were in fact irreconcilable. Although he recognized the legitimacy of certain American grievances, his insistence on the necessity for colonial subordination to Parliament led him to reject his fellow countrymen's attempts to work out new conceptions of the imperial relationship. His 1774 plan of union perfectly illustrated the trap into which he had fallen: for all its innovation, it was irrevocably doomed by its adherence to traditional constitutional thought.

Throughout his career Galloway's overweening vanity worked to his detriment. In 1774 he believed that he and he alone accurately discerned a solution to America's problems; his opponents thus had to be either stupid or dishonest. Later, during his exile in England, this same egoism contributed to the insensitivity and inadequacy of his analyses of colonial affairs in such pamphlets as *Historical and Political Reflections on the Rise and Progress of the American Rebellion* (London, 1780). Yet in the end Joseph Galloway realized that he had been mistaken, a fact reflected in his 1793 petition to be readmitted to Pennsylvania. See Robert M. Calhoon, "'I Have Deduced Your Rights': Joseph Galloway's Concept of His Role, 1774–1775," *Pennsylvania History*, XXXV (1968), 356–78.

MARY BETH NORTON

GALLUP, George Horace (b. Jefferson, Iowa, Nov. 18, 1901; d. Tschingel, Switzerland, July 26, 1984), SOCIAL SCIENTIST, graduated from the University of Iowa in 1923 and became an instructor of journalism there while earning his MA (1925) and PhD (1928). His dissertation, "A New Technique for Objective Methods for Measuring Reader Interest in Newspapers," contained many ideas later used in his public opinion work. He was head of the journalism department at Drake University (1929–31) and then became a professor of advertising and journalism at Northwestern (1931–32) before moving to New York City in 1932 to be director of research with the Young and Rubicam advertising firm. He became a vice president in 1937 and remained with the firm until 1947.

In 1933, Gallup began taking experimental polls on social and political issues, based on a selected sampling of the population. He applied these concepts to the congressional elections of 1934, accurately predicting that the Democrats would increase their majority. He founded the American Institute of Public Opinion at Princeton, New Jersey, in 1935. In his first presidential election poll in 1936 he predicted that Franklin D. Roosevelt would win by 55.7 percent of the popular vote; Roosevelt actually won by 62.5 percent. Gallup was visiting professor at the Pulitzer School of Journalism at Columbia University (1935–37). He founded the Audience Research Institute in 1939 to survey opinions on movies and other topics. He helped organize the International Association of Public Opinion Institutes in 1947. In 1948, Gallup predicted that President Harry S. Truman would win only 44.5 percent of the popular vote and lose to Republican **Thomas E. Dewey,** but Truman got 49.9 percent and won the election. This was the only time Gallup predicted the winner of a presidential election incorrectly. Publishers' Syndicate began distributing the results of his polls to newspapers in 1952. Gallup served as president of the National Municipal League from 1954 to 1956. For years Gallup was the largest stockholder and chairman of the Gallup Organization, the corporation he created in 1958 to carry out much of his public opinion sampling. Its original mission was to conduct marketing research, but it broadened its activities in the decades since. Under Gallup's direction, however, the organization stayed out of the business of "private" polls, that is, polling carried out on behalf of particular candidates or parties. To Gallup, such polling by his organization would compromise its independence and objectivity. He always stressed the non-partisan nature of his polling organization. As a result, Gallup himself did not vote for president after 1928 when he cast a ballot for **Al Smith**. Some of his many books include *Public Opinion in a Democracy* (1939), *A Guide to Public Opinion Polls* (1944, 1948), and *The Sophisticated Poll Watcher's Guide* (1972).

⸙

George Gallup took "public opinion" off the shelf of theorists and showed America it had opinions, sometimes foolish but mostly wise, on every topic worth reading about in the morning newspaper. Beginning as an expert on audience reaction to media, Gallup turned his sideline into a career by studying the reactions of the whole audience—the total citizenry—to the whole message: affairs of state, silly items in the news, personal standards, and future behavior. Absentminded, tweedy, professional, and deeply rooted in agrarian America, Gallup was an ardent Jeffersonian. He believed that the unbiased poll—as scientific as Iowa's proud tradition of agricultural statistics—would elevate the will of the people from obscurity and doubt to a clear mandate for government to follow. As personally unbiased as his polls, he refused to vote or be swayed either by the liberalism of stylish Madison Avenue or by the conservatism of his publisher clients.

Although Gallup took his polls to fifty nations, he failed to convert any government to rule by majority opinion. Politicians employed subtler pollsters to learn how to manipulate public opinion behind policies they planned to follow anyway. But purveyors of magazines, movies, automobiles, and detergents voted for Gallup with their budgets, for his polls provided an even better guide to what the people would buy than what the purveyors believed. See *Current Biography: 1952* (1953), 200–202.

RICHARD JENSEN

GARDNER, Isabella Stewart (b. New York, N.Y., Apr. 14, 1840; d. Boston, Mass., July 14, 1924), ART COLLECTOR, grew up in New York City. In 1856 she went with her parents to Paris and then to Italy. Among her friends at a Paris "finishing school" was Julia Gardner of Boston whose brother, John Lowell Gardner, Jr., she married on April 10, 1860. She took up residence in Boston where John Gardner was active in manufacturing and finance.

In the spring of 1867 the Gardners made the first of several trips to Europe where Isabella began collecting art. She and her husband later were among the first Westerners ever to visit Angkor Wat in Cambodia on a trip around the world in 1883. Her interest in art and intellectual pursuits soon led to lasting friendships with **Charles Eliot Norton, Henry James,** and **Henry Adams.** The Gardner music room in Boston was frequented by Ignacy Paderewski and many other celebrated musicians. By the 1890s the Gardner art collection was vast, containing canvases by Old Masters as well as by important contemporary artists. When her husband died in 1898, he left $2.3 million to support their plans for an art museum. Isabella Gardner bought land at Fenway and Worthington streets in Boston in 1899 and supervised the planning and building of the museum (1900–2). Named the Isabella Stewart Gardner Museum in the Fenway, it was opened to the public on February 23, 1903.

An intimate friend and patroness of many writers, painters, and musicians, a renowned hostess, an accomplished traveler, and an inveterate collector, Isabella Stewart Gardner was a leading figure in American social life for many years. In Boston she was endearingly known as the "Queen of the Back Bay."

One of the first Americans to collect Old Masters, she brought together in the Fenway museum a remarkable collection of paintings and other works of art. She was herself chiefly responsible for the design of the museum building, which served in her later years as her own home. The collection remains today largely as she arranged it.

In establishing the collection, Isabella Gardner was particularly helped by her close friend and onetime protégé **Bernard Berenson,** who advised her and acted as an intermediary in the purchase of many masterpieces from European dealers. Berenson helped her acquire Titian's *Rape of Europa* and Rembrandt's *Storm at Sea* and *Gentleman and His Wife.* Although focused on Italian mid-Renaissance and Dutch masters, the collection also includes such outstanding works as Botticelli's *The Tragedy of Lucretia,* Piero della Francesca's *Hercules,* and Vermeer's *The Concert,* as well as portraits of Isabella Gardner by **James McNeill Whistler** and **John Singer Sargent.** See Louise Hall Tharp, *Mrs. Jack* (1965).

PAUL R. BAKER

GARFIELD, James Abram (b. Cuyahoga Co., Ohio, Nov. 19, 1831; d. Elberon, N.J., Sept. 19, 1881), PRESIDENT, graduated from Williams College in 1856. He then taught at the Western Reserve Eclectic Institute (now Hiram College) and served as principal (1857–61). In 1859 he was elected to the Ohio senate and in 1861 was admitted to the Ohio bar. When the Civil War broke out, Garfield helped organize the 42d Ohio Infantry and rose from lieutenant colonel to major general. He fought in the battles of Middle Creek (Ky.), Shiloh, and Chickamauga, where he was chief of staff to General William S. Rosecrans.

In 1862, Garfield was elected to the U.S. House of Representatives as a Republican, serving from 1863 until his election as president in 1880. (He had been elected to the U.S. Senate earlier in 1880 for the term beginning in 1881 but declined after the presidential election and never sat in the Senate.) While in Congress, Garfield supported the Reconstruction policies of the radical Republicans, and although he leaned toward low tariffs, he also voted for protection of the products of Ohio manufacturers. Throughout his political career he opposed inflationary schemes.

As campaign manager for Ohio's Senator **John Sherman** at the 1880 Republican convention, Garfield deprived the leading contender, Ulysses S. Grant, of the presidential nomination by engineering the defeat of the unit rule, which required each state to cast its vote as a unit for the delegation's majority candidate. He also blocked the nomination of the other leading candidate, **James G. Blaine,** but could not secure it for Sherman. The deadlocked convention then nominated Garfield as a "dark horse" on the thirty-sixth ballot. In the election he defeated Democrat Winfield Scott Hancock, 214 electoral votes to 155, although his popular plurality was only 7,368. In office, Garfield was plagued with patronage problems. By appointing James G. Blaine—a "half-breed"—as secretary of state, he angered Senator **Roscoe Conkling** of New York, leader of the "Stalwart" faction. Conkling became enraged after Garfield named an anti-Conkling Republican as collector of the port of New York, and with the other New York senator, Thomas C. Platt, resigned from the Senate in protest. However, on July 2, 1881, Charles J. Guiteau, a mentally unstable Conklingite, shot Garfield in a Washington railroad station.

—————

Intelligent and sensitive, Garfield grasped the problems troubling the post–Civil War United States, but his introspective self-doubting nature and his conservatism inhibited his capacity to act. Ironically, his death, boldly exploited by civil service reformers, produced a more lasting achievement in the Pendleton Civil Service Reform Act (1883) than anything he accomplished as congressman and president.

Although there were distinct differences between the young and the mature Garfield, the young religious zealot clearly influenced the later soldier and politician. While slavery and the Civil War converted Garfield into a man of politics, they did not eradicate his early patterns of thought. Passionately religious, young Garfield was a serious, introspective, guilt-ridden boy who doubted the morality of attending theaters and of reading novels. He believed that Christians "had no right to engage in politics" and should not even vote. Garfield was open to new ideas, however, and to liberalize his mind he completed his education under Mark Hopkins at Williams College. There he discovered and loved Shakespeare but each evening also read from the New Testament the same chapter as did his strong-willed mother back in Ohio. At Williams College Garfield became concerned with outrages in Kansas, which led him to oppose the extension of slavery. Returning to Ohio in 1856, he was an effective teacher and a forceful Disciples of Christ preacher but also was sufficiently involved in politics to stump for **John C. Frémont.** To the consternation of his "best friends in Christ" and his mother, Garfield abandoned evangelism by 1859, studied law, and embraced politics. Within two years the secession crisis led him to embrace war as well, and when it came, he recruited many of his regiment—as he did his political followers—from among his students. Though inexperienced, Garfield served ably in the field, but his most distinguished service was as the well-organized chief of staff of the Army of the Cumberland.

Entering Congress during the war, Garfield again overcame inexperience and became a leader in the House of Representatives. He shrewdly perceived the connection between power and the purse strings, specialized in finance, and ultimately chaired the Appropriations Committee. Rather than dominating the House by force of will, Garfield harmonized that body by skill as a parliamentary tactician, orator, and debater. He was conciliatory, courteous, reasonable, generous, fair, patient, and tolerant. A conservative who disliked extremes, Garfield believed in compromise and tried to keep everybody happy. Though he supported radical Reconstruction, he considered ultra-Radicals fools, supported the impeachment of Johnson only at the last moment, and opposed force bills, which to prevent intimidation of black voters let the executive control federal elections. Garfield recognized and feared the growing power of railroads and other great corporations, yet thought the Granger movement to regulate railroads "may be Communism in disguise," disliked organized labor, and opposed the eight-hour movement as a "blunder" and an "unwarrantable interference with the rights of the laborers." Garfield was a staunch anti-inflationist who flirted with international bimetallism, and though he lacked conviction, he consistently voted for protective tariffs. While he thought that Grant did "much to show with how little personal attention the Government can be run," he supported him for reelection. An occasional backer of civil service reform, Garfield skillfully distributed patronage to his followers. Congressional machinery enthralled him; indeed, his reforming ardor cooled as his power grew. In general he avoided large goals and seemed content to correct minor errors and to gain small victories.

As president, Garfield accomplished little beyond successfully attacking senatorial courtesy, which destroyed Conkling's power but cost Garfield his life. Indeed, by replacing the New York collector, under whom competitive examinations had flourished, with a partisan of Blaine, he temporarily set back civil service reform.

"Garfield," commented Senator Henry L. Dawes, "is a grand, noble fellow, but fickle, unstable, more brains, but no such will as Sherman, brilliant like Blaine but timid and hesitating." Garfield appeared "timid and hesitating" not because of cowardice—as many political friends and foes supposed—but because of lack of confidence. As both he and his wife recognized, he suffered from a deflated ego; despite years of political activity he frequently deferred to others, assumed he was mistaken, changed his mind, and hesitated as a leader. A soul-searching man who time and again convicted himself of mistakes and sins, Garfield never lost his youthful habit of self-examination. See Allan Peskin, *Garfield* (1978).

ARI HOOGEMBOOM

GARLAND, Hannibal Hamlin (b. West Salem, Wis., Sept. 14, 1860; d. Hollywood, Calif., Mar. 4, 1940), WRITER, grew up in Mitchell County, Iowa. He studied briefly at Cedar Valley Seminary (Osage, Iowa) in 1881, then moved with his family to the Dakota Territory. After trying his hand at farming, he taught school in Illinois (1882–83). He moved to Boston in 1884 and became a lecturer at the Boston School of Oratory. In 1887, after a visit to Iowa and the Dakotas, and recalling the ugliness and frustrations of his childhood, he decided to tell the story of frontier life and began writing short stories for *Harper's Weekly* and the *Arena.* He published his first collection of stories, *Main-Travelled Roads,* in 1891 and continued his realistic portrayal of frontier life in a series of novels attacking corruption in government, fraudulent land practices, and rural discontent. Among them was *Rose of Dutcher's Coolley* (1895).

Garland then turned his attention to writing a series of romances. His stories about Native Americans, collected in *The Book of the American Indian* (1923), accurately and sympathetically appraised their lives. In 1916, Garland moved to New York and finished his autobiography, *A Son of the Middle Border* (1917), which won critical acclaim. He spent the next few years writing a series of sequels to the autobiography, one of which, *A Daughter of the Middle Border* (1921), won a Pulitzer Prize. In 1929 he moved to Los Angeles and spent the rest of his life developing his interest in psychic experiences. Some of his other works include *Ulysses Grant* (a biography, 1898), *The Captain of the Gray-Horse Troop* (a novel, 1902), and *Crumbling Idols* (1894), which set out his theories of literary criticism.

In his early stories Garland effectively challenged the prevailing myths of rural midwestern felicity. In somber, realistic detail he depicted the dingy, cheerless struggle for subsistence, the incessant and unrewarding toil of frontier farmers and their wives. "A man like me," one of his farmers said, "is helpless. Just like a fly in a pan of molasses.... The more he tears around the more liable he is to rip his legs off." Essentially a Jeffersonian who had read **Henry George** and Herbert Spencer, Garland found little justice for farmers on the Middle Border. And he sided with the poor and the disadvantaged against bankers, mortgage holders, and railroads. Aware of the economic conditions that made farm life drab and hopeless, he became a literary spokesman for agrarian discontent, a Populist advocate. When dealing with material that he knew thoroughly and that fired his imagination, Garland was able to disguise in his fiction his principal limitation: the tendency to solve complex speculative problems with sentiment rather than reflection. The sentimental strain broadened as he aged. He became unsure whether he was a sponsor of rural revolt or a chronicler of collapse, a reformer or a reporter. In the face of literary success, which he had ambitiously sought, his talent tapered off. The desire to speak out directly on social problems and to be accepted in genteel eastern literary circles impaired his art. Though he continued to achieve memorably "poetic" stretches of prose, his ideas were not imaginatively realized, as he chose less familiar and more romantic subjects for his fiction. He partially recaptured lost distinction with the autobiographical *A Son of the Middle Border,* considered by many readers his best book. The pronouncement of one critic (Granville Hicks) that Garland ended as "a garrulous and complacent chronicler of past glories" is harsh but largely accurate. However, the luminous fidelity with which he recorded the suffering, dignity, and despair of an important part of the nation's population during a pivotal period in its history gives his early stories enduring literary significance, a secure, if minor, place in the history of American fiction. See Jean Holloway, *Hamlin Garland: A Biography* (1960).

WILLIAM McCANN

GARNER, John Nance (b. Blossom Prairie, Tex., Nov. 22, 1868; d. Uvalde, Tex., Nov. 7, 1967), POLITICAL LEADER, received only a limited education before moving to Clarksville, Texas, where he read law and was admitted to the bar in 1890. In 1892 he moved to Uvalde, near the Rio Grande, and became a partner of Judge John H. Clark. Garner was elected Uvalde county judge in 1895. In 1898 he was elected as a Democrat to the Texas House of Representatives, where he quickly became recognized as a major spokesman for west Texas.

Garner was elected to the U.S. House of Representatives in 1902 and was continually reelected until 1932. During his first terms in the House, the Republicans were in the majority, and Garner was unable to secure either significant legislation or important committee posts. His effort in 1905 in favor of a graduated income tax failed. He supported the insurgents in the 1910 House battle that reduced the powers of Speaker **Joseph Cannon.** In 1913, after Woodrow Wilson became president, Garner received a place on the House Ways and Means Committee. In 1917, when Democratic Majority Leader Claude Kitchen refused to support the war resolution, Garner became Woodrow Wilson's chief liaison with the House. In 1924 he led a successful revolt against Secretary of the Treasury **Andrew Mellon**'s tax bill and secured a substitute that provided smaller reductions for the upper tax brackets while increasing those for lower-income groups. In 1928, Garner was elected House minority leader, and in 1931, when the Democrats achieved a majority, he became speaker. In early 1932 he introduced legislation calling for expenditures of more than $1 billion on federal public works projects, to be financed by a gasoline tax, and an increase of $1 billion in the capitalization of the Reconstruction Finance Corporation (RFC). Although this was vetoed by President Herbert Hoover, a substitute bill, embodying much of the proposal's substance, was soon passed. That same year he was a candidate for the Democratic nomination for president but accepted the vice presidential slot on the ticket headed by Franklin D. Roosevelt.

During his first term as vice president, Garner was instrumental in expediting the movement of New Deal legislation through the Senate, although some of that legislation was contrary to his desire for a balanced budget and reduced expenditures. After 1936, however, he opposed President Roosevelt's stands on the Supreme Court reorganization bill, on sit-down strikes, on the continued high level of expenditures, and on the third-term issue. In 1941, Garner retired from public life.

⸺⸺⸺

To his contemporaries Garner was an enigma, being viewed variously as an "evil old man," a "political hack," a "demagogue," a "radical," a "pro-Communist," or as a "master politician," a "conservative," and "one of the truly great men of this generation." He was a legend in his own lifetime, and these seeming contradictions were chiefly reflections of his personal background and the attitudes of his region and constituency.

Two forces encountered in his youth on the farm had lasting effects on him. First was the Protestant ethic of hard work and thrift, which he believed accounted for his own financial success. Likewise, the political philosophy behind the Alliance and Populist movements was reflected in his future actions. With the collapse of these farmer revolts, and at the time when he was becoming politically active, the South made a fetish of Democratic regularity and emphasis on the region's economic interests. For it, the Progressive era meant efficiency and development rather than reform, with government being viewed as an agent of industrial prosperity. To Garner's generation there was no conflict between "business progressivism" and social conservatism.

Given these background factors, his apparent political inconsistencies vanish. Thus he could fight for regulation of big business—the beef and steel trusts, for example, gouged his cattle growers and hampered needed rail construction in his district—yet lead the fight for federal assistance for roads and canals. He was antiprotectionist but insisted that in high tariff measures the South's raw materials be given the same protection as northern manufactures. He could support the New Deal as long as it benefited the South most and cost it least, but he could fight it when it promoted organized labor or liberal social ideas, or raised the specter of federal encroachment and administrative centralization.

"As stubborn as a Texas mustang" when his own political verities were challenged, Garner's greatest political talents were those of persuasion and practical compromise. Few have known parliamentary procedure better or used it more skillfully. He introduced few bills but created his power by procedural manipulation and his ability to debate at close quarters and bargain behind the scene. His loyalties, in descending order, were Texas and the South, the Democratic Party, and the legislative branch of government. A well-publicized love for baseball, poker, and fishing created an aura of sound Americanism that suggested to the voters an opposition to radical innovations. See Bascom N. Timmons, *Garner of Texas: A Personal History* (1948).

JOHN S. EZELL

GARRISON, William Lloyd (b. Newburyport, Mass., Dec. 10, 1805; d. New York, N.Y., May 24, 1879), REFORMER, was trained as a printer. In 1826 he became the editor of the Newburyport *Free Press*, which soon failed. He moved to Boston in 1828 and joined Nathaniel H. White as coeditor of the *National Philanthropist*, a paper devoted to the suppression "of intemperance and its kindred vices." In 1829 he joined **Benjamin Lundy,** an antislavery journalist, in editing the abolitionist *Genius of Universal Emancipation.*

On January 1, 1831, Garrison published the first issue of the *Liberator,* which for thirty-five years was the leading abolitionist newspaper. He helped form the New England Anti-Slavery Society (1831), and in 1833 the American Anti-Slavery Society (president, 1843–65). Garrison favored immediate emancipation. His *Thoughts on African Colonization* (1832) attacked the work of the American Colonization Society.

Resentment against the abolitionists soon became widespread, and Garrison was almost killed in 1835 by a Boston mob. He believed in nonresistance and was even unwilling to employ political methods to end slavery. He also spoke against capital punishment and imprisonment for debt and in favor of woman's rights. He refused to participate in the proceedings of the World Anti-Slavery Convention in London (1840) when he learned that women were excluded from the meeting.

Garrison believed that the North should secede from the Union because it tolerated slavery. He opposed the annexation of Texas and the Mexican War, and objected to the Compromise of 1850 because it sanctioned slavery. On July 4, 1854, at Framingham, Massachusetts, Garrison burned the Constitution, proclaiming, "So perish all compromises with tyranny."

Because of ill health and financial difficulties, Garrison was relatively inactive during the five years preceding the Civil War. The outbreak of the Civil War led to a fundamental transformation of his views: repudiating his philosophy of nonresistance, he supported the emancipation of the slaves that the Civil War promised. He supported Abraham Lincoln's Emancipation Proclamation, and in 1865 he proposed that the Anti-Slavery Society be dissolved on the ground that the Thirteenth Amendment freeing the slaves had ended all need for the organization. However, he continued to be active in movements for woman's rights, prohibition, and justice for Native Americans.

Uniting a radical religious vision, social conservatism, and a humanitarian sympathy for the oppressed, William Lloyd Garrison provided Americans in the three decades before the Civil War with a prototype of the moral reformer. A spiritual child of the second Great Awakening who served his apprenticeship in the evangelical crusade for a Christian America, Garrison brought to the antislavery movement both the conviction that slavery was a "damning crime" and an equally strong urge to testify against it. Out of his hatred for the institution, which sustained his thirty-five-year campaign for emancipation, came his version of "immediatism," the belief that slavery could be abolished through moral suasion and an appeal to a national sense of guilt. The doctrine of immediate emancipation, as he and his abolitionist followers interpreted it, rested on the assumption that slavery was a sin that could be eradicated only by an unrelenting assault on the consciences of Americans who could be compelled to admit their complicity, to repent, and then to abolish it. Such a strategy meant that problems of method and timing mattered less to Garrison than questions of principle. Once the American people stood convicted in their own eyes of the crime of slavery, he believed, they would easily find a way to destroy it. Garrison saw his own role in this drama of mass conversion with single-minded clarity—he would play Isaiah to the nation, indicting slaveholders and an indifferent northern public until he forced them through his rhetoric of attrition to recognize the slave's claim to freedom and equality. "I *will be* as harsh as truth, and as uncompromising as justice," he promised in his first editorial for the *Liberator* in 1831. "On this subject, I do not wish to think, or speak, or write, with moderation."

Moral suasion as a tactic dictated an intensely personal style of agitation that Garrison practiced steadily until the Civil War came. When in the wake of northern reaction to the abolitionist movement in the 1830s he became convinced that church and state were hopelessly corrupted by their connection with slavery, he proposed that abolitionists "come out from among them" and withdraw all support from the government. The political version of this come-outerism he expounded as "No Union with Slaveholders," a combination of Christian nonresistance and northern secession. Increasingly after the Schism of 1840 he demanded absolute fidelity to his scheme for peaceful disunion as the only sure means to emancipation. While political abolitionists in the 1850s organized for a party struggle with the South, Garrison continued to preach his doctrine of peaceful secession to a dwindling number of supporters. When the Civil War came, however, he reluctantly discarded his pacifist principles and accepted force as the solution to the problem of emancipation.

Thus it was as a symbol rather than as a leader—a voice rather than a political presence— that Garrison figured in the minds of Americans both before and after the Civil War. The personal cost of his doctrinal purity was always high and sometimes prohibitive: his editorial career was studded with disputes over principle, personal quarrels, and broken friendships. The moral absolutism which characterized his indictment of slavery was reflective of a temperament that seemed to thrive on adversity. As he once admitted, he made greatest headway "against wind and tide." Austere, humorless, unreflective, a stickler for principle, he often appeared, even to his abolitionist friends, a contradiction in terms—the belligerent pacifist, the autocratic nonresistant. Yet his brand of instinctive moralism, as he occasionally realized, had its tactical uses in goading Americans into facing the moral issue of slavery at a time when a majority of them, whatever doubts they might have entertained concerning its benevolence, were not prepared to admit its enormity. More clearly than most of the abolitionists, he realized the psychological damage done by the institution to both blacks and whites and the importance of personal testimony in discrediting it. As a strict egalitarian in an age of pervasive racism, Garrison was unable to convert Americans to his vision of equality, but as an Old Testament prophet he succeeded, perhaps more effectively than any other single abolitionist, in bringing the country to the point of moral confrontation. See John L. Thomas, *The Liberator: William Lloyd Garrison* (1963).

JOHN L. THOMAS

GARVEY, Marcus Moziah (b. St. Ann's Bay, Jamaica, Aug. 17, 1887; d. London, Eng., June 10, 1940), BLACK NATIONALIST, was educated at local elementary schools until family financial problems forced him to work as a printer's apprentice. Moving to Kingston in 1904, he worked for a printer and helped to lead an unsuccessful printers' strike in 1907. He worked and traveled from 1909 to 1911 in Costa Rica, Panama, and other Central American countries where he became interested in the harsh treatment of black workers. He went to London in 1912 to study.

Returning to Jamaica in 1914, Garvey organized the Universal Negro Improvement Association, a black self-help organization. He moved to New York in 1916 and opened a Harlem branch. By 1919 the UNIA had organiza-

tions in most large American cities, and during the 1920s it enrolled almost a million blacks. Garvey began publishing a weekly newspaper, the *Negro World,* in 1918. He launched the Black Star Line in 1919 to provide steamship transportation to Africa and to connect black business throughout the world. In the same year he founded the Negro Factories Corp., a cooperative of black businesses. In 1920 he presided over the first of several international conventions of the UNIA, and in 1924 he founded the Negro Political Union.

Garvey advocated black unity and black pride. He opposed white colonialism in Africa and tried to unite black communities throughout the world for mutual aid and—the central task—the liberation of Africa. However, the Black Star Line suspended operations in 1922, and Garvey was convicted of fraud in 1923. He launched another steamship line, the Black Cross Navigation and Trading Co., which collapsed in 1925, before he entered the federal penitentiary in Atlanta (1925) to serve a five-year sentence. President Calvin Coolidge commuted the sentence in 1927, but Garvey was deported to Jamaica. He presided over another international convention in Jamaica in 1930, but his movement soon declined. Garvey moved to London in 1934, where he published a magazine, *Black Man,* until his death.

In his short career in the United States, Marcus Garvey, energetic, aggressive, and proud, transformed aspirations for a black community into the largest secular organization in African-American history. Garvey's personal magnetism was vital to his organizing success. A short, powerfully built man, Garvey communicated best when addressing public audiences, a major means of attracting and keeping his followers. As a leader he could be autocratic and uncharitable to those who differed with him. As an administrator he was inattentive to the details of overseeing a large organization. Yet his verbal talents and flair for the dramatic, best expressed in the UNIA's annual conventions and parades, dramatically re-created both the injustices inflicted on black men and the possibilities of present unity and future achievement.

Garvey respected the power and organization of Western nations, yet believed that the "Anglo-Saxons left the masses of the human race ... dissatisfied and discontented." Both to end their oppression and to create a new civilization, which would combine the technological advances of Western culture and popular freedom, Garvey called upon black men "to evolve a national ideal," a goal sought by other contemporary African and African-American intellectuals.

The establishment of an independent black nation or nations in colonial Africa was a prerequisite for the new black civilization. Although Garvey did not define clearly its institutional basis, he believed a black nation-state would finally destroy white beliefs of black inferiority, restore black pride, and protect black citizens of non-African nations. But "to fight for African redemption does not mean we must give up our domestic fights for political justice and industrial rights," he said.

In the United States, Garvey perceived that the black migration from the South to the North during and after World War I had created the social basis for his movement. The new black communities in New York, Chicago, and other cities would provide the wealth and unity both to redeem Africa and to secure the rights of American citizenship. For this reason he opposed the NAACP, which he thought reflected the desires of the bourgeoisie to win social acceptance from whites and therefore encourage participation in existing white institutions at a time when blacks needed to create their own communities.

Internal conflicts based on ideology, priorities, and personalities weakened the UNIA. An important part of the black bourgeoisie was committed to existing racial or interracial institutions, and Garvey could not produce the tangible success to win their allegiance. The Black Star Line, the most ambitious of his business projects, failed in competition with the large, established steamship lines, while Garvey's attempts to

establish UNIA branches in Africa met the active opposition of European nations and some African leaders.

But by viewing the African-American condition as one variant of the condition of all blacks, Garvey was able to tap that part of the experience of blacks in the United States which was colonial and sought outlets in an autonomous community. An end to the black man's oppression seemed possible because of the crisis in Western civilization and capitalism, revealed in the labor and anticolonial struggles of the World War I era. In the United States this world phenomenon produced a militant black bourgeoisie and an aroused mass base. Garvey, proclaiming the unity of black people but permitting the expression of various ideologies, sought to channel this ferment into one organization that could overcome the class and national divisions of his people. See Judith Stein, *The World of Marcus Garvey: Race and Class in Modern Society* (1986).

JUDITH STEIN

GARY, Elbert Henry (b. Wheaton, Ill., Oct. 8, 1846; d. New York, N.Y., Aug. 15, 1927), INDUSTRIALIST, studied law in Illinois and soon had a lucrative corporate practice. He was appointed to the boards of numerous railroad and industrial concerns. In 1898 when **J. P. Morgan** assembled the Federal Steel Co., the first integrated producer in the United States, he selected Gary to manage it. When the United States Steel Corp. was created (1901), Gary was Morgan's choice to head the concern, which at that time controlled almost 70 percent of the country's steelmaking capacity. The greater part of the work involved in arranging the amalgamation had been performed by Gary. Following the merger, Gary followed a policy of circumspection in business dealings and sought to cooperate with the government to avoid an antitrust suit.

During the brief but sharp business recession of 1907, Gary invited the leaders of the independent steel companies to a dinner at which he strongly urged them not to cut prices. The "Gary dinners" became a regular event, the industrialist arguing just as fervently that prices not be raised when prosperity returned. Stability of prices over the long run was his objective. The idea of exchanging views on matters common to an industry developed into the trade association movement of the 1920s. Another of Gary's economic innovations was "Pittsburgh-plus," a system of pricing in which all steel companies quoted a delivered price as though the material had come from Pittsburgh. A powerful stabilizing force in the early days, the system was eventually abandoned under the pressure of competition and public opinion.

Gary's policies bore fruit, however, when the Supreme Court ruled in 1920 that United States Steel was not a combination in restraint of trade. But the previous year Gary's antiunion labor policy culminated in a long and bitter strike in which the union movement in steel was broken. United States Steel preserved the open shop until the 1930s.

From 1901 to 1927 Gary was one of the dozen best-known businessmen in the nation, and thus he serves as a striking example of a number of general trends. His career represents an early instance of the rise of the corporation lawyer to the top ranks of business—a pattern that was to be more and more encouraged by corporate complexity and government regulation. While no extensive studies have been published, probably few of these lawyers were "self-made men." A person starting in a family law firm either near or in a major city and then moving into corporation work in the metropolitan center no doubt followed a normal progression. In the confusing world of the new corporation—of trusts, holding companies, leases, liens, and mergers—lawyers were necessary additions to boards of directors, for only they could guide bankers and industrialists through the dark areas of corporate finance.

In one sense Gary was both representative of the highest achievement and yet unfortunate. When he and other leading attorneys aided investment bankers in merging big competing firms into near-monopolies, it appeared from previous Supreme Court decisions that from the standpoint of the Sherman Anti-Trust Law a monopoly of manufacture was not an illegal conspiracy in restraint of trade. Within a few years new personnel and political pressures on the Court had led to a reversal of this attitude, and the "Steel Trust" was legally vulnerable. This meant that instead of being able to pursue a policy of using the "economies of scale" available to the company to expand and further eliminate competition, Gary had to walk a tightrope, trying to avoid actions that would lead to successful government prosecution and still maintain a secure position in the market. That he was not quite able to do the latter in the face of competitors who could operate more freely did not indicate weak management.

While Gary was unquestionably overly serious, pompous, and restricted in imagination, he tried to be a progressive business leader: giving the stockholders an unusual amount of information in annual reports; assuming responsibility for price leadership and orderly practices of competition; and sponsoring conservative technological progress. That he bitterly opposed labor unions, and seemed to have no conception of the hardships of the seventy-two-hour week, at a time when prices could readily have been readjusted to cover higher labor costs, does not distinguish him from other leaders of big business and finance who believed that wages and hours were controlled by the laws of the market. Ultimately, after defeating a long and violent strike in 1919, he voluntarily corrected the worst hardships in the plants, and the company wage scales were in keeping with or a little better than those generally prevailing. In all, Gary's policies exemplify the proper role of the chief executive of the large corporation as seen by the more conscientious business leaders of the first decades of the century. See Ida M. Tarbell, *The Life of Elbert H. Gary* (1925).

THOMAS C. COCHRAN

GEHRY, Frank Owen (b. Toronto, Ontario, Feb. 28, 1929), ARCHITECT, graduated from the School of Architecture at the University of

Southern California in 1954. He worked for several Los Angeles architectural firms before entering the Harvard Graduate School of Design where he studied city planning. In 1957 he returned to Los Angeles and took a job with the architectural firm of Victor Gruen Associates. In 1962 he founded his own firm, Frank O. Gehry Associates.

At first his work showed the influence of **Frank Lloyd Wright**. With his building, the *Danziger Studio* (1965), he entered a short minimalist period, but by the 1970s he had adopted a style that can only be labeled "expressionist." It incorporated cheap plywood, corrugated metal, and his (by now) famous chain-link fence. He also designed a line of cardboard furniture and dabbled in sculpture. Some of his best work was in creating environments for shows at the Los Angeles County Museum of Art. Among his many awards from his peers, in 1989 he received the Pritzker Architecture Prize, probably the architectural profession's highest honor.

———

Early in his career when Gehry was working as a draftsman in a Los Angeles architectural office, he discovered the slapdash methods of the Southern California construction industry. He detested their sloppy work but decided to make the best of it. "Well," he is supposed to have said, "if you can't beat 'em, join 'em. If that's what you're going to get, then turn it into a virtue." Perhaps having Simon Rodia's towers in Watts in mind, he continued, "You accept the junk of the culture and turn it into art." It should be added that when one of his colleagues heard this remark, he protested: "But when Frank said that, we were short on commissions. He loves all architectural materials, including marble." Indeed, Gehry does employ all the latest engineering devices in order to craft his buildings.

A spirit of adventure infuses all his work. For his own house in Santa Monica (1978), he took a poor, innocent little Dutch Colonial Revival bungalow and transformed it into a wild display of odd forms and unlikely materials. His wonderful design for the new Disney Philharmonic Hall in Los Angeles, which may or may not be realized,

is so expressionistic that one critic has suggested it looks as if the Big One had already come.

Although he emphatically rejects any references to his being the father of a school, he has been an inspiration to many younger architects. He is probably the finest American architect working today. See Peter Arnell and Ted Bickford, eds., *Frank Gehry: Buildings and Projects* (1985).

ROBERT W. WINTER

GEISEL, Theodor Seuss (Dr. Seuss) (b. Springfield, Mass., Mar. 2, 1904; d. La Jolla, Calif., Sept. 25, 1991), AUTHOR, ILLUSTRATOR, graduated from Dartmouth College in 1922 and studied literature briefly at Oxford and the Sorbonne. After college he supported himself as a freelance cartoonist, contributing to such magazines as *Judge, Vanity Fair,* and *Liberty*, and as a magazine illustrator. From 1928 to 1941 he created a famous advertising campaign for Standard Oil's insecticide Flit, making their slogan "Quick, Henry! The Flit!" a part of the language. From 1940 to 1941 he was an editorial cartoonist for the New York City liberal newspaper *P.M.*, and during World War II he made documentary films for the army.

Geisel wrote his first children's book, *And to Think That I Saw It on Mulberry Street*, in 1937 under the pseudonym Dr. Seuss. Its combination of fantasy, doggerel, and whimsical illustration was such a success that he stayed with that formula and pen name for over fifty years. His primer, *The Cat in the Hat* (1957), changed the style of reading primers in American publishing and launched Random House's series Beginner Books, of which Geisel was founder and president. His lifetime output of forty-eight children's books accounted for sales of more than 200 million volumes in twenty languages.

———

Theodor Seuss Geisel had modest success in what he considered his "serious" work as an editorial cartoonist, advertising artist, and screenwriter, all done under his real name; but it was his children's books, written and drawn by Dr. Seuss, that earned him the largest readership in the history of the medium. His combination of goofy illustration, abundant wordplay, free-wheeling rhyme, and anarchic humor appealed to both children and the adults who bought books for them.

Geisel, who had no formal art education, always insisted that he could not draw, and the grotesque human figures and fanciful animals he created never had any pretension to realism or even plausibility. Indeed, their fey appeal lies precisely in their playful distortion. His antic art perfectly complements the zany stories and out-landish rhymes of his text. His cartoonlike illus-trations began to appear around the same time as the first comic books and have much of the same dynamic energy.

Geisel broke the sentimental and didactic mold of American children's fiction by introduc-ing a note of chaos into his stories. His madcap plots often reflect a child's aggressive impulses toward adults, and the author clearly sides with the children. The moral points Geisel sometimes unobtrusively makes—on minority rights in *Horton Hears a Who!* (1954), holiday commercial-ism in *How the Grinch Stole Christmas* (1957), and environmentalism in *The Lorax* (1971), for exam-ple—never seem like preaching.

The Cat in the Hat (1957) sparked a revolution in reading instruction in America; avoiding the stilted prose and bland tone of typical first read-ers, it tells a wild and somewhat subversive story using only 223 different words and proves that learning to read can be fun. Dr. Seuss's feeling for the fantastic inner life of children enabled him to see the world as they see it, even up to his last book, written when he was 87. See Barbara Bader, *American Picturebooks from Noah's Ark to the Beast Within* (1976).

DENNIS WEPMAN

GENET, Edmond Charles (b. Versailles, France, Jan. 8, 1763; d. Schodack, N.Y., July 14, 1834), DIPLOMAT, was educated by private tutors. In 1777 he became secretary to his father, who was head of the Bureau of Interpreters of the Ministry of Foreign Affairs in Versailles. Here he translat-ed many documents relating to the American Revolution. Briefly attached to the French lega-tions in Berlin (1780) and Vienna (1781), he returned to France in 1781 to head the Bureau of Interpreters after his father's death. In 1787, Genet was appointed secretary of the legation in Russia and two years later chargé d'affaires. In 1792, Catherine the Great expelled him from Russia as an indication of her disapproval of the French Revolution. Upon his return to France the Girondists appointed him minister plenipoten-tiary to the United States.

Arriving in April 1793 in Charleston, South Carolina, instead of the capital in Philadelphia, Genet began outfitting privateers to harass and capture British shipping under the Franco-American Treaty of 1778. He also tried to recruit expeditions to conquer Spanish Florida and Louisiana. He then journeyed to Philadelphia by way of Camden, South Carolina; Salisbury, North Carolina; Richmond, Virginia; and Baltimore, Maryland. He was warmly greeted in Philadelphia but soon angered many people when he disregarded President George Washington's orders to cease outfitting priva-teers. Washington and Secretary of State Thomas Jefferson grew particularly angry when the *Little Sarah*, a captured British vessel in Philadelphia, was dispatched by Genet as a French privateer although he had promised not to do so.

Washington asked the French government to recall Genet in August 1793. When his successor, Jean Fauchet, arrived in 1794, Genet settled on a small farm on Long Island, New York, rather than return to France and face possible execution by the Jacobins. He married the daughter of New York's governor **George Clinton** in 1794, moved to a larger farm in Rensselaer County, New York in 1800, and became an American citizen in 1804. In the years that followed, besides farming, Genet promoted a project for hauling canal boats up an inclined plane by using a hydrogen-filled tube in a silo-shaped building, and a second pro-ject involving the propulsion of a hydrogen diri-gible by use of a treadmill powered by a horse. His proposals were published in 1825 in a book, *The Upward Force of Fluids*, which was reprinted in 1861 and is regarded as the first book published in America on the subject of aeronautics.

—⚬∞⚬—

Although Genet owed his appointment as the first minister sent to the United States by the French Republic largely to his devotion to the Revolution, everything about him promised a successful outcome for his mission. Passionately admiring everything American, he was a personally attractive figure, a witty and charming conversationalist with a broad scientific interest, and a talented linguist who spoke fluent English. His failure can be attributed to his impulsiveness, his poor judgment and lack of understanding of the character of American political institutions, as well as the unattainable objectives of his mission, which conflicted with the policy of strict neutrality adopted by the Washington administration. When Washington refused substantial advances on the debt owed to France and forbade the outfitting of privateers, Genet considered the plight of France so desperate that he threatened to appeal to the people to override administration policies. He mistakenly assumed that the American government, like that of France, was directly subject to popular control and that the reception given him on his arrival indicated that the people were committed to the cause of France. He also believed that by rallying public support behind him he could bring the Republicans to power and thus secure an administration friendly to France. His project miscarried, for Washington's prestige was so great that Genet's recall was approved without protest. Even his Republican friends condemned him. Although repudiated by his government, Genet's conviction that France's interest lay in promoting a Republican victory in the United States influenced French policy until Napoleon seized power. See Greville Bathe, *Citizen Genet: Diplomat and Inventor* (1946), and Harry Ammon, *The Genet Mission* (1973).

HARRY AMMON

GEORGE, Henry (b. Philadelphia, Pa., Sept. 2, 1839; d. New York, N.Y., Oct. 29, 1897), JOURNALIST, REFORMER, left school at 14 and went to sea in 1855, sailing to Melbourne and Calcutta. Returning to Philadelphia in 1856, he worked as a typesetter. In 1857 he sailed to San Francisco. After joining the gold rush to British Columbia in 1859 and clerking in a store, he held a succession of newspaper jobs in San Francisco and Sacramento. During the winter of 1868–69, while in New York City on a business trip, he noticed "the shocking contrast between monstrous wealth and debasing want." This experience, added to his growing concern over monopolies, especially monopolies on land, moved him to undertake a study of economic conditions in the United States. In 1871 he published *Our Land and Land Policy*. Although he did not attack private ownership of land, he argued that it was unjust for men to pay landlords a rent for the privilege of applying their own labor to land. George was the editor of the San Francisco *Daily Evening Post from* 1871 to 1875 and served as California inspector of gas meters from 1876 to 1879.

Greatly disturbed by the continued accumulation of land by speculators and by the depressed economic conditions that were accentuated by the panic of 1873, George began to work on a study of the most dramatic paradox of the period: Why was there so much want and suffering amid so much wealth? His answer to this and other questions appeared in *Progress and Poverty* (1879). After asserting that labor was the only true source of capital since it produced capital, he analyzed labor's relation to land. Rising land values, he argued, were a product of social evolution and could not be attributable to the personal qualities of landlords. The rent that landlords charged was, moreover, "a toll levied upon labor constantly and continuously." Since rising rents were a by-product of social evolution, the "unearned increment" that was falling into the hands of the landlords should revert to the public. This could be accomplished by means of a "single tax" on land values. Such a tax, he argued, would yield enough revenue to permit the government to abolish all other forms of taxation. George further claimed that the tax would ameliorate economic conditions and simplify the role of government. His followers, however, made far more of the single tax idea than he himself had done. George also denounced all forms of monopoly and advocated ownership and operation by the federal government of all public utilities. Although George dealt with a technical subject, his passionate sincerity and his analogies to commonplace things humanized his message. His book was an immediate success. He was called upon to lecture, and numerous "single tax" movements sprang up throughout the nation.

George moved to New York City in 1880. Following his publication of *The Irish Land Question* (1881), he went to Ireland as a correspondent for the New York *Irish World*. In 1884 he lectured in Great Britain. Always an ardent free-trade advocate, he summarized his views in *Protection or Free Trade* (1886). In that same year he was the Liberal and Labor Party candidate for mayor of New York City. While he outpolled Theodore Roosevelt, the Republican nominee, he was defeated by **Abram S. Hewitt,** the Democratic candidate. Between 1888 and 1890 he lectured in Britain and Australia. In 1896 he supported **William Jennings Bryan,** the Democrat-Populist candidate for president. In 1897, while again running for mayor of New York City (as an Independent Democrat), he died.

Henry George exerted an enormous influence on the age in which he lived. *Progress and Poverty* outsold any previous work in political economy. More than 2 million copies were sold in America alone, and in the slums of Liverpool and Moscow, and on the banks of the Ganges and Yangtze, poor men, it has been said, painfully spelled out the message of the book in order to grasp a new vision of human society. And not only the poor: men so diverse in the range of their intellectual interests and life styles as George Bernard Shaw and Sun Yat-sen, **John Dewey** and Leo Tolstoy, Sidney Webb and H. G. Wells fell under its influence. The book supplied intellectual and moral inspiration to a whole generation of American progressives, including such

leading figures as **Clarence Darrow, Hamlin Garland,** Tom Johnson, and Brand Whitlock. Some scholars believe that it exercised an unprecedented effect on the American labor movement; others point out that the book, together with **Edward Bellamy**'s *Looking Backward,* launched a whole generation of economic and social reform.

Indeed, George and his work are best seen as the reformist culmination of an era of intensive economic development resulting in the birth of the modern industrial economy. That economy, George knew, had been built by steam and machinery. Steam power applied to vessels and railroads was bringing about a transportation revolution. In 1860 only 30,000 miles of railroad track had been in operation; by 1873 there were 70,000 miles, and by the end of the 1880s, 160,000 miles. The continent had first been spanned by rails in 1869; other transcontinentals were soon built, and as they were pushed to completion, railroad construction and integration went on elsewhere. In the decade between 1869 and the appearance of *Progress and Poverty* the value—in dollars of constant value—of railroad track, bridges, stations, shops, locomotives, and freight cars rose from $1,741 million to $3,297 million. Ten years later the figure reached $6,474 million.

The rise of a national railroad network had important consequences for both agriculture and manufacturing. Railroads help account for the astonishing fact that farmers in the 50 years following the Civil War occupied more land than in the previous 250-year history of America. Between 1860 and 1910 the number of farms in the nation more than tripled, with acreage in farmland leaping from 407 million to about 879 million. In the 1890s, the final decade of George's life, some 200 million acres were added to the agricultural domain—an area larger than France and Germany combined. The railroad also encouraged the spread of the factory. Before 1850 the factory, with its power-driven machinery and labor force performing routine tasks, was still a rarity outside the textile and related industries. By 1879, the year that saw the publication of *Progress and Poverty,* four-fifths of the 3 million workers in mechanized industry labored in factories. In the 1850s the industrial output of the United States was below that of England. By 1894 the value of American products almost equaled the value of the combined output of the United Kingdom, France, and Germany. Annual output per capita had averaged 1.3 percent between 1790 and 1860; in the decades following the Civil War the percentage rose to 1.8 percent. And since income and output are reverse sides of the same coin, average income per capita also rose during those decades. Such figures tell us nothing, however, about the way in which the national income was distributed in the population. George was deeply convinced that wealth was unequally distributed, and he attributed this to the private ownership of land.

George saw the transforming developments of his age with a clear eye, but he did not disapprove of them. Indeed, he attributed the rise of large cities and factories to what he called the "law of concentration." To successfully resist this law, he wrote, "we must throttle steam and discharge electricity from human service." While he castigated monopoly and advocated government ownership of natural monopolies (public utilities), he deeply distrusted governmental authority and wished to preserve laissez-faire capitalism with its freedom of opportunity. That freedom would be the greater, he believed, if the rental value of land were expropriated from the greatest of all monopolists, the landlord.

A century after his death a number of fiscal experts see merit in the idea that land, especially unproductive or underutilized land, ought to be taxed more heavily than structures and other improvements. They hope thus to arrest the deterioration of urban centers and, in developing economies throughout the world, to encourage productive capital formation. Yet George was not primarily an economist and has never been regarded as one by economic scholars. He was primarily a moral philosopher, a deeply religious man with a passionate commitment to social justice. His confidence in his own rightness was supreme, however, and he was capable of telling Pope Leo XIII, "You do not see even fundamen-

tals." His great influence owed much to his self-confidence, to his conviction that his own "law of rent" was God's law—men tend to flock to the standard of such leaders as John Calvin, Karl Marx, Adolf Hitler, and Henry George, who are convinced of the inevitable triumph of their views—and to the purity and sincerity of both his personal life and style of writing. Few books in English are as beautifully composed as *Progress and Poverty*. See Charles A. Barker, *Henry George* (1955).

STUART BRUCHEY

GERONIMO (b. southern Ariz., June 1829; d. Fort Sill, Okla., Feb. 17, 1909), NATIVE AMERICAN LEADER, was a war shaman of the Chiricahua Apaches. His real name was Goyathlay, meaning "one who yawns." Geronimo, his more common name, was given to him by the Mexicans, whom he raided after they had killed his family (1858). As a youth he participated in a number of attacks against white settlers.

When the U.S. army forced Geronimo's people to move to San Carlos, New Mexico, from southern Arizona in 1876, he and a number of followers fled to Mexico and carried out numerous sorties across the border. Shortly thereafter, however, he returned to his people in New Mexico and took up farming. In the early 1880s he commenced a series of raids on white communities, culminating in an all-out campaign in May 1885 against settlements in New Mexico and southern Arizona. Pursued for ten months by General George Crook, Geronimo surrendered in March 1886 but slipped away again shortly thereafter. Captured near the Bavispe River, Mexico (Aug. 1886), by Captain H. W. Lawton, Geronimo formally surrendered to General Nelson Miles at Camp Bowie, Arizona, on September 4, 1886, and after being transferred to a number of prisons, was finally allowed to settle at Fort Sill, Oklahoma. Turning to farming once more, Geronimo converted to Christianity; in the summer of 1903 he joined the Dutch Reformed Church. A legendary figure during his last years,

Geronimo was a popular attraction at several fairs and expositions, and marched in President Theodore Roosevelt's 1905 inaugural procession. In 1906 he dictated his autobiography, *Geronimo's Story of His Life.*

———※———

In the full context of the long interracial conflict by which Native American tribes were dispossessed of almost all the land of the present-day United States, the brief struggle of Geronimo and his handful of Chiricahua Apache followers was little more than a final footnote. But symbolically it was also an exclamation point to all that had gone before, summing up in one last dramatic confrontation with whites the desperate bravery with which all Native Americans fought to remain free.

"Once I moved about like the wind. Now I surrender to you and that is all," said Geronimo when he gave himself up in March 1886. As the last of all the Native American patriots who had led their people everywhere on the continent in war against the whites, he spoke, in effect, for each of them who had earlier surrendered or died fighting.

Geronimo was not a hereditary Apache chief, but he was the personification of the Chiricahua Apache way of life. Living close to nature, able almost to melt into and become a part of the natural landscape of the mountains and deserts of the Southwest, the Apaches were raiders and warriors whose enemies included both the white intruders and other tribes. Dearest to them were their freedom and their attachment to their land. White Americans, moving aggressively into their country, could not coexist with such a society. Geronimo's ability as a guerrilla fighter, his uncompromising enmity toward the whites, and his devotion to his homeland and freedom drew followers to him, and the band he led held out the longest. His efforts to evade capture won increasing attention from the white man's press, and when he finally surrendered, his name was a household word. Increasingly, his determined attempt to remain a free man has come to dramatize and symbolize the brave efforts of all Native Americans who fought for their country and lib-

erty. See *Geronimo: His Own Story,* ed. by S. M. Barrett, Introduction and Notes by Frederick W. Turner III (1970).

ALVIN M. JOSEPHY, JR.

GERRY, Elbridge (b. Marblehead, Mass., July 17, 1744; d. Washington, D.C., Nov. 23, 1814), POLITICAL LEADER, graduated from Harvard (1762) and entered his father's mercantile business. Elected to the Massachusetts General Court in 1772, Gerry became a member of its committee of correspondence (1773). In 1774 he was elected to the first Provincial Congress and served on the executive committee of safety. He was reelected in 1775. During the Revolution he served in the Continental Congress (1776–81, 1782–85), where he was a member of the Treasury board that supervised finance. He was also a signer of the Declaration of Independence and of the Articles of Confederation.

In 1786, Gerry was elected to the Massachusetts house of representatives. In 1787 he was a delegate to the Federal Convention in Philadelphia, where he served as chairman of the committee that presented the "great compromise," settling the controversy over the representation of large and small states. However, he personally disliked this compromise. Although he favored strengthening the central government, he did not support the ratification of the Constitution because he could not reconcile it with his own view of republicanism.

Gerry was elected to the first Congress in 1789. Although he believed that the treasury department should be put under the supervision of a commission, arguing that it was unsafe for a single secretary to control so much money, his belief in "energetic government" led him to support **Alexander Hamilton**'s fiscal program. He left Congress in 1793, convinced that the Federalists were undermining the Republic by seeking an alliance with the British. In 1797, with **John Marshall** and C. C. Pinckney, Gerry was sent by President John Adams to France to negotiate a settlement of Franco-American problems. When the French agents refused to negotiate unless they received a bribe, Marshall and Pinckney returned home. Gerry remained, still hoping to negotiate a treaty, but when Adams published the "XYZ dispatches," relating the bribery incident and precipitating a war scare, Gerry was recalled.

After failing four times to win election as governor of Massachusetts, Gerry was finally elected in 1810 (reelected 1811). His administration is best remembered for the "Gerrymander bill" (1812), which redistricted the state in such a way as to give the Republican Party more seats in the state senate than their actual numbers warranted.

In 1812, Gerry was elected vice president, running on the ticket with James Madison. In the controversy over neutral rights during the Napoleonic Wars, Gerry's attitude toward the British and the Federalists became increasingly bellicose, and he urged President Madison to take action against the Massachusetts Federalists, who he felt were pro-British to the point of treason.

―――∞∞――――

Elbridge Gerry, the Marblehead merchant who spurned the Federalism common to his class and region and became the first Republican governor of Massachusetts and then James Madison's vice president, began his public career forty years earlier as a protégé of **Samuel Adams** in the Massachusetts Revolutionary movement. Rising swiftly to a position of leadership, he, along with John and Samuel Adams and **John Hancock,** became a power in the Second Continental Congress. He was an administrative workhorse in the Congress during the Revolution, making a substantial contribution to the war effort.

During the late 1780s when Gerry resumed cultivating his personal fortune, he grew to believe in reform of the national government so as to increase the power of the central government. To this end, at the Constitutional Convention he was an early advocate of the Virginia Plan. By the time the convention ended, however, Gerry viewed its product as dangerous to republicanism because of what seemed to him its *excessive* centralization, and so he became one

of the few delegates to campaign against ratification. Reversing his field again in the early 1790s, he supported Hamilton's financial programs in Congress. After he left the House of Representatives in 1793, however, he became increasingly hostile to the Federalist tendency toward rapprochement with Britain, preferring to support revolutionary France. From this point onward he moved steadily into the Jeffersonian camp, severing his Federalist ties as a consequence of his inept personal diplomacy during the XYZ Affair.

As a Republican in Federalist Massachusetts, Gerry pursued an independent course. Surviving his Massachusetts colleagues of Revolution days, he cultivated their Old Whig principles and the image of America as a republican Sparta. Yet when he returned to power on the eve of the War of 1812, he soon distinguished himself for bellicose partisanship. After he died it was for these qualities that he was remembered rather than his long years of service to the Revolution and republican principles. See James T. Austin, *The Life of Elbridge Gerry* (2 vols., 1828–29).

RICHARD D. BROWN

GERSHWIN, George (b. Brooklyn, N.Y., Sept. 26, 1898; d. Beverly Hills, Calif., July 11, 1937), COMPOSER, was the son of Russian Jewish immigrants. George, who gradually dropped his original name, Jacob, and his older brother Ira grew up on Manhattan's Lower East Side. His introduction to music was extremely casual; in a penny arcade in Harlem he was fascinated by a coin-operated player piano that ground out Anton Rubinstein's "Melody in F." At about the same time he discovered jazz, which he listened to outside the doors of cabarets in Harlem. A friend, Max Rosen, later a successful concert violinist, introduced him to serious music. In 1910 he began to study the piano under Charles Hambitzer, who encouraged him to attend concerts and to study harmony under Edward Kilenyi.

In 1913 he left high school to take a job as a staff pianist for Remick, popular music publishers in "Tin Pan Alley." He also worked as a rehearsal pianist for Victor Herbert and as accompanist for Louise Dresser and Nora Bayes. After one of his songs was used in a Broadway revue and published (1916), Max Dreyfus of Harms and Co. offered him a regular salary to compose songs. In 1919, Al Jolson sang a Gershwin song, "Swanee," at the Winter Garden, and it was a sensation. Later he interpolated it into *Sinbad*. The same year Gershwin's first complete musical, *La, La, Lucille,* was a mild success. For the next five years he wrote all of the music for George White's *Scandals*. There followed an unbroken succession of hits for which he wrote the music: *Lady, Be Good!* (1924), *Tip Toes* (1925), *Oh, Kay!* (1926), *Funny Face* (1927), *Strike Up the Band* (1929), *Girl Crazy* (1930), and *Of Thee I Sing* (1931), for which he received a Pulitzer Prize. His brother Ira was his principal lyricist (with only minor exceptions for unimportant shows).

Serious musicians noted Gershwin's talents early in his career. Eva Gauthier had included in a recital four of his songs, which a critic called the beginning of sophisticated jazz. His first attempt at opera, the one-act *Blue Monday* (retitled *135th Street*), was too off-beat for the revue into which it had been inserted, but in a concert in 1924, Paul Whiteman played a symphonic jazz piece by Gershwin, *Rhapsody in Blue*. It was an overwhelming success and made Gershwin rich. The *Rhapsody* inaugurated an eager experimentation with jazz ideas by many serious composers, including William Walton, Maurice Ravel, Kurt Weill, and **Aaron Copland.** In 1925, Walter Damrosch conducted the New York Symphony in Gershwin's *Concerto in F,* with the composer at the piano, and in 1928 led the New York Philharmonic in his *American in Paris.* Serge Koussevitzky and the Boston Symphony performed his *Second Rhapsody* in 1932. Gershwin's masterpiece, considered by many the first American opera, is *Porgy and Bess*, with a libretto by DuBose Heyward, based on his novel. A fair success when it first opened in 1935, its revival on Broadway in 1942 achieved the longest run of any musical production up to that time. It was warmly received throughout the world, including the Soviet Union, during a tour sponsored by the State Department in 1952, and since then has been produced by many major opera companies in Europe and the Near East. Gershwin spent his last years in California where he had gone to write music for motion pictures.

George Gershwin was a composer with a creative mission. This is the hallmark of his genius. Consciously and unhesitantly he proceeded to the goal he had set for himself from his boyhood days—always refusing to be deflected from his destiny by money, personal glory, or the kudos of critics. When he was 16 (in 1914) he already knew where his destiny lay. He was studying the piano with Charles Hambitzer, who gave him a thorough training in serious music, at which Gershwin proved remarkably adept. But even then he realized (and said so to Hambitzer) that his own destiny lay in popular music and in giving it artistic status. This is the reason he took a job in Tin Pan Alley: to learn everything he could about popular music at its source. From then on he was driven by two objectives. One was to carry into the American popular song the fullest technical resources of serious music and to make it the American equivalent of the German *Lied.* The other was to write ambitious concert works that would become thoroughly American through the process of absorbing the rhythms, syncopations, accentuations, and blues harmonies of popular music. He died prematurely but not before he had achieved his destiny.

He was a man of extraordinary dynamism, energy, and enthusiasms. He had many extramusical interests and diversions (most significantly painting, for which he revealed a remarkable gift). But in the end it was music—and his own music in particular—that was the be-all and end-all of his existence. He was always playing his music for friends at his home, at their homes, and at parties. And when he was not playing his music, he was talking about it. This was not a manifestation of egomania, as some suspected at the time. It was the parental pride and faith of a genius who knew with finality that his creative brain-children would grow up into influential citizens. See David Ewen, *George Gershwin: His Journey to Greatness* (1970).

DAVID EWEN

GETTY, Jean Paul (b. Minneapolis, Minn., Dec. 15, 1892; d. London, Eng., June 6, 1976), BUSINESSMAN, studied at the University of Southern California, Berkeley, and Oxford University. He first entered the oil business in his early twenties; after an initial failure he made $250,000 in his first two years as an oilman. He then "retired" for three years but reentered the oil business in 1919. In 1930 his father, a successful oilman and founder of the George F. Getty Co., died, leaving him an estate exceeding $15 million. In 1932 he bought control of the Pacific Western Oil Co. and merged it with his father's companies to form the Getty Oil Co., which eventually controlled more than sixty subsidiaries, including the Tidewater ("Flying A") Oil Co. and the Skelly Oil Co., both acquired in the 1930s. In 1966 he reorganized Tidewater and began to dispose of its marketing organization. After 1967 he focused on producing properties. His oil holdings include some of the most important in the Middle East as well as in the United States.

Both in 1957 and in 1968, *Fortune* magazine identified Getty as the richest living American, and at the latter date attributed to him an accumulated personal wealth exceeding $1 billion. His holdings include the Minnehoma Financial Corporation (formerly the Spartan Aircraft Co.) and the Mission Corp. He was the owner of an art collection of more than six hundred items valued at several million dollars and the author of several books, including a history of the Getty family oil company and an autobiography.

At his request he was buried near his home in Malibu, California. He left the bulk of his estate to the J. Paul Getty Museum there. With an initial bequest of $800 million from his estate, it instantly became the richest art museum in the world.

⁓⁓⁓

J. Paul Getty was an enigma in the American business world during the second half of the 20th century because he was a crass individualist in an age of giant corporate enterprise. A colorful owner-manager rather than the typical faceless corporation executive, Getty was cast in the mold of 19th-century entrepreneurs like **John D. Rockefeller** rather than in the image of a 20th-century oil company executive.

Getty's individualism was reflected in his business philosophy, whether in regard to ends or to means. Inheriting the family oil business from his father in 1930, Getty undertook shrewd acquisitions of both producing and marketing properties in the hope of building a large integrated oil firm. This goal eluded him in the 1960s partly because federal restrictions on oil imports into the United States prevented him from marketing all of his Middle Eastern production there. So instead of pursuing further expansion to achieve integration, after 1967 Getty consolidated his varied holdings, revealing great skill and generalship in disposing of as well as acquiring properties.

Getty also revealed himself to be an able, if unorthodox, administrator of the more than one hundred companies under his supervision. Unlike other large petroleum companies that were managed by groups of professional executives, Getty's somewhat uncoordinated oil conglomerate had only one undisputed boss. He managed his vast holdings from Sutton Place, his headquarters in a seventy-three-room 15th-century English manor house in Surrey, near London, which he refurbished in the 1960s. There he worked leisurely in sitting rooms in an atmosphere of elegant gentility. Although delegating many responsibilities to subordinates who often reported to him in person at Sutton Place, Getty made most major policy decisions himself. Business planning, he once noted, was akin to the formulation of military strategy. Groups were not as likely to make as effective decisions as a single individual. He himself preferred a Napoleon to a committee, the entrepreneur to the manager. Certainly, in an industry dominated by corporate giants, Getty's individualistic style was unique for his times. See J. Paul Getty (written with B. W. von Block), *My Life and Fortunes* (1963).

GERALD D. NASH

GIBBONS, James (b. Baltimore, Md., July 23, 1834; d. Baltimore, Md., Mar. 24, 1921), RELIGIOUS LEADER, spent part of his childhood in Ireland but returned to the United States in 1853 to live in New Orleans. He entered St. Charles College near Baltimore in 1855 and St. Mary's Seminary in Baltimore in 1858. He was ordained in 1861 and assigned as an assistant priest of St. Patrick's Church in Baltimore. Gibbons rose rapidly, becoming in 1861 pastor of St. Bridget's Church in the Baltimore suburb of Canton. The Civil War bitterly divided Maryland, but Gibbons remained neutral, giving aid and comfort to both Union and Confederate soldiers in military hospitals. Archbishop Martin J. Spaulding of Baltimore made Gibbons his private secretary in 1865 and assistant chancellor of the Second Plenary Council of Baltimore the following year. In 1868, Gibbons became vicar apostolic of the new Vicariate Apostolic of North Carolina, and in 1872 was named bishop of Richmond. During this period he published his most famous book, *The Faith of Our Fathers* (1876), an exposition of Catholic doctrine. Archbishop James Roosevelt Bayley of Baltimore sought and secured the appointment of Gibbons as his coadjutor with the right of succession in 1877, and upon Bayley's death in October of the same year Gibbons became head of the oldest archdiocese in the United States.

In his capacity as apostolic delegate of the Holy See, Gibbons presided over the Third Plenary Council of Baltimore in 1884, the 319 decrees of which guided American Catholics until the promulgation of the Universal Church's Code of Canon Law in 1918. At the council Gibbons also appointed a committee of bishops to found a Catholic university, and as a consequence the Catholic University of America was opened in Washington, D.C., in 1889 with Gibbons as the first chancellor. Upon the death of Cardinal McCloskey of New York in 1885, Pope Leo XIII named Gibbons the second cardinal in American history. He received the insignia of his office on March 17, 1887. Gibbons was a friend of a number of presidents and was on especially cordial terms with Theodore Roosevelt and William Howard Taft. A strong supporter of the rights of workingmen, he succeeded in 1887 in forestalling a condemnation of the Knights of Labor as a forbidden society by the Holy See. He believed in the separation of church and state, a subject that was the most notable feature of his sermon on taking possession of his titular church in Rome as a new cardinal, Santa Maria in Trastevere, on March 25, 1887. The cardinal also advocated the rapid Americanization of immigrants. He supported American entry into World War I and helped to promote war-bond drives. In his last years Gibbons supported the League of Nations, and it was under his auspices that the American hierarchy established the National Catholic War Council (1917), which later became the National Catholic Welfare Conference, and since 1966 has been called the United States Catholic Conference.

❦

Cardinal Gibbons's extraordinary influence in his dual role as a Catholic churchman and American citizen may be said to have been captured to a certain degree in two statements. In the introduction to his most famous book, *The Faith of Our Fathers,* he wrote, "Should the perusal of this book bring one soul to the knowledge of the Church, my labor will be amply rewarded." The chief aim of the book, as he declared, had been "to bring home the truths of the Catholic faith to our separated brethren." The inspiration for the simple explanation of Catholic doctrine that the book contained had been found while Gibbons was traversing the thoroughly Protestant regions of North Carolina and Virginia, where he spent the first nine years of his episcopacy. The success of his efforts can be measured by the sale of more than 2 million copies of the volume; it broke all records for Catholic apologetical literature and won numerous readers among Americans of every and of no religious persuasion by its irenic tone, clarity of view, and simplicity of language. For countless Americans, Gibbons's book became a vade mecum for an understanding of Catholicism even when they were not converted to that faith.

The second statement, not unrelated to the

first, was contained in a letter of early 1917 when former President Theodore Roosevelt told the cardinal, "Taking your life as a whole, I think you now occupy the position of being the most respected, and venerated, and useful citizen of our country." The usefulness of Gibbons's career as a citizen was preeminently that of a reconciler of religious differences between Americans. In his personal life he was an exemplar, both to his co-religionists and to those outside his church, of what a model citizen should be by way of support to good public causes, as a critic of political and social ills, and as a sincere upholder of national institutions and principles such as separation of church and state. Gibbons was also a prudent counselor of statesmen; for example, at the close of the Spanish-American War he responded to President William McKinley's request for his opinion on whether or not the United States should retain the Philippine Islands: "Mr. President, it would be a good thing for the Catholic Church," he replied, "but, I fear, a bad one for the United States."

Cardinal Gibbons had an almost uncanny ability for cutting through the entanglements around a complicated issue and arriving at a practical judgment that won widespread acceptance from those concerned, a quality best exemplified in his forceful defense of the Knights of Labor in February 1887 when he won a stay of action at Rome by those disposed to condemn the American labor organization as a group that came within the category of the secret societies banned by the Holy See. And in the course of that controversy he demonstrated his benign attitude toward the exercise of authority by those in high position when he told William Henry Elder, archbishop of Cincinnati, in regard to the Knights of Labor that "a masterly inactivity and a vigilant eye on their proceedings is perhaps the best thing to be done in the present junction."

Yet Cardinal Gibbons was singularly unoriginal, having been responsible for beginning nothing of note. Once a problem had been created, however, such as the conviction of many bishops that they needed another plenary council or the increasing call for a national university for the

Catholics, he accepted the responsibility of leadership that was his as occupant of the premier see of the country and led his fellow bishops with superb tact and discretion until the enterprise had been brought to a successful conclusion. His love of country, plus his consciousness of the traditional suspicion and fear of his church among Americans generally, caused him at times to agree too readily perhaps with national policy. Moreover, Gibbons's desire to please others prompted him on occasion to put an interpretation on events that the hard facts would not always warrant, as was true of his letter to Pope Leo XIII of January 30, 1893, expressing joy at the establishment of an apostolic delegation at Washington when in truth Gibbons and most of the bishops had been opposed to the measure.

Allowing for these defects, Cardinal Gibbons could be said to have served as no other Catholic churchman of this country before or since has done, as one who successfully explained the Church of Rome to the United States and the United States to the Church of Rome. See John Tracy Ellis, *The Life of James Cardinal Gibbons, Archbishop of Baltimore* (1952).

JOHN TRACY ELLIS

GIBBS, Josiah Willard (b. New Haven, Conn., Feb. 11, 1839; d. New Haven, Conn., Apr. 28, 1903), SCIENTIST, graduated from Yale in 1858, having won prizes in mathematics and Latin. He received his PhD from Yale in 1863 and served there as a tutor in Latin for two years and in natural philosophy for a third year. He spent the next three years studying at the universities of Paris, Berlin, and Heidelberg. In 1871 he was appointed professor of mathematical physics at Yale.

During the next two decades he devoted most of his attention to thermodynamics, a branch of physics dealing with the mechanical action of heat. His earliest work dealt with the application of graphical methods of analysis to thermodynamics. His greatest achievement, however, came with the publication of his memoir *On the Equilibrium of Heterogeneous Substances* (1876–78) in which he applied the principles of thermodynamics already developed for homogeneous substances (those with a single uniform structure) to substances differing in chemical makeup as well as in physical state. This work laid the theoretical groundwork for the field of physical chemistry. During 1880–84 he developed a modified system of vector analysis, a branch of mathematics dealing with quantities having both magnitude and direction. Mathematical physicists used his system in the computation of planetary orbits and the study of crystals. Gibbs's other major project in the 1880s was the formulation of an electrical theory of optics, which he set forth in several articles published between 1882 and 1889. His final work was in the field of statistical mechanics, culminating in the publication of his *Elementary Principles in Statistical Mechanics* (1902).

The work of Josiah Willard Gibbs has an integrity in method and focus unusual even in theoretical physics. In thermodynamics and in statistical mechanics he took principles established by others (Rudolf Clausius in the case of thermodynamics, Ludwig Boltzmann in statistical mechanics) and wielded them into systems of scope and power never realized by their creators. He therefore changed the direction of development of both disciplines. In method Gibbs stands apart from his contemporaries in his disregard of models of molecules and the inner structure of the ether. His physics was based on accepted general statements of the behavior of matter in mathematical form. From this he developed the mathematical (usually geometrical) properties of those relationships and hence the physical implications of thermodynamics and statistical mechanics in totally new directions—thermodynamics, for example, into the domain of chemistry. James Clerk Maxwell saw the importance of this development (1876), but Gibbs's international reputation dates from the recognition given him by the German chemist Wilhelm Ostwald with his development of physical chemistry. Gibbs's independent approach to thermodynamics led him to focus on the problem of equilibrium and its characteristics when the mechanical, chemical, or electrical properties of a substance are changed.

The same focus is in Gibbs's *Elementary Principles in Statistical Mechanics*, written with the intention of putting thermodynamics on the firm foundation of mechanics through the statistical approach. Again using a very general method and without invoking any special properties for matter, he drew statistical analogues to all his previously developed thermodynamic concepts, including the important relations defining equilibrium under various conditions. His thermodynamics and statistical mechanics survived the quantum revolution intact and needed only extensions into those areas immediately dependent on quantum ideas. Many of Gibbs's thermodynamical concepts were not explored until this century, and they still remain a vital part of the education of physical chemists and chemical engineers. Physicists, while admiring the craftsmanship of his thermodynamics, make practical use of his statistical methods.

Gibbs's papers themselves are models of scientific style. There are no wasted assumptions, words, or phrases; each sentence is significant, and the logic of his argument develops without a break. Quiet independence marked Gibbs's life as well as his work. He was seemingly undisturbed by the turmoil of the Civil War. In 1880, Johns Hopkins offered him a professorship with a salary, as yet not forthcoming from Yale. Only then did Gibbs remind Yale of his years of service and receive a regular salary. He was a reticent man with few close friends and few students. Even his professional reputation was built through the efforts of others (although he saw to it that physicists with the same interests received copies of his monographs). His small private income allowed him to choose the quiet life of a bachelor scholar living with his family. He has left no evidence of spiritual or emotional turmoil. This placid exterior yielded to only a few, yet he had very warm relationships with his sister's children and both privately and professionally with her husband.

This quiet, undisturbed external existence gave Gibbs the opportunity to concentrate on some very subtle and deep problems affecting physics in the 19th century. One can now wonder at the initial confusions over concepts and methods in statistical mechanics and thermodynamics; their clarity and completeness was Gibbs's invaluable legacy to 20th-century physics. See Lynde Phelps Wheeler, *Josiah Willard Gibbs* (1951).

ELIZABETH GARBER

GILMAN, Daniel Coit (b. Norwich, Conn., July 6, 1831; d. Norwich, Conn., Oct. 13, 1908), EDUCATOR, attended the Norwich Academy and graduated from Yale in 1852. Having developed a strong interest in geography, Gilman went to St. Petersburg, Russia, as attaché to the American embassy. He then studied for a season at the University of Berlin. Returning to the United States in 1855, Gilman began a seventeen-year stay at Yale where he helped reorganize the scientific activities of the university as the Sheffield Scientific School and served for a time as librarian. In 1872 he accepted the presidency of the University of California.

Three years later Gilman became president of the new Johns Hopkins University in Baltimore, Maryland, which pioneered in professional graduate training in America on the model of German universities. At Johns Hopkins he emphasized the importance of a first-rate, well-paid faculty and the need for combining teaching with research. He also integrated the new Johns Hopkins Hospital, which the philanthropist had endowed at the same time, into the life of the university. Gilman insisted that the teaching of doctors should be carried on by the university in a separate medical school, while the healing of the sick was the province of the directors of the hospital. A decline in income during the financial troubles of the Baltimore and Ohio Railroad, in which most of the university's endowment was invested, delayed the opening of the hospital until 1889 and of the medical school until 1893, but the Johns Hopkins plan became the general pattern in the rapid development of American medical education thereafter. The medical school was the first to limit admission to students with four years of undergraduate study.

Gilman was a member of the commission that investigated the Venezuela—British Guiana border dispute (1896–97); a supporter of civil service reform; and a trustee of the Russell Sage Foundation. He served as the first president (1902–4) of the Carnegie Institution. His experiences at Johns Hopkins are recorded in *The Launching of a University* (1906).

❧

Born into a strong New England Congregational heritage, Gilman forsook an inclination toward the ministry for the burgeoning field of higher education. Although not a scientist and scarcely a scholar, he learned from his colleagues at Sheffield the importance of science as both a method of inquiry and a source rich in ultimate utilities. He helped bring Darwinian ideas into the American intellectual mainstream, insisting that religion had nothing to fear from science.

A doer from childhood, Gilman enjoyed detail and organizational problems. His many tasks at Yale suggested dilettantism, but in the newly specialized role of university president he found the place for his broad interests and administrative talents. At California, damaging political and religious controversies intensified Gilman's natural tendency to caution, a trait that occasionally qualified his good record in supporting academic freedom.

With a fine touch for personal and public relations, "Oily Dan" made Baltimore, a somewhat unpromising locale, the seat of the nation's first major graduate school and a path-breaking medical school. He could recognize promise in young men and knew how to nurture it. His primary test for faculty and graduate fellows was the production of original work in a specialty. Largely at his instigation Johns Hopkins became the cradle of the scholarly periodical in America.

Not limiting himself to higher education, Gilman helped reform public schools in Connecticut, California, and Maryland, although he declined the superintendency of the New York City schools in 1896. After his nationally acclaimed success at Johns Hopkins he found himself hamstrung as president of the Carnegie

Institution, which he had helped design. But this post, dedicated to support of high scholarship, reinforced his connection with the research ideal, whose advancement was his chief contribution to American life. See Fabian Franklin, *The Life of Daniel Coit Gilman* (1910).

HUGH HAWKINS

GINGRICH, Newton Leroy (b. Hummelstown, Penn., June 17, 1943), POLITI-CAL LEADER, born Newton Leroy McPherson, at the age of 3 received his stepfather's surname when his mother remarried. The stepson of a career army officer, Gingrich was always on the move as a youngster. When he was 10, the family left Hummelstown to live at several military bases both in the United States and overseas. The family finally settled at Fort Benning, Georgia, where Gingrich met his first wife, his high school geometry teacher, Jacqueline Battley. They married in 1962, a year after he graduated. Gingrich received a BA from Emory University (1965) and an MA (1968) and PhD (1971) in history from Tulane University. Proclaiming his research specialties to be "Futurism; process of change; management and communications," Gingrich got a job in 1970 as assistant professor and coordinator of environmental studies at West Georgia College, a position he held until 1978. That year, after unsuccessful efforts in 1974 and 1976, Gingrich, a Republican, won a seat in the U.S. House of Representatives. Two years later he divorced his wife and in 1981 married Marianne Ginther, a government administrator in Ohio. In 1989, Gingrich won the hotly contested post of Republican minority whip by one vote and put himself on the path to the Republican minority leadership. In early 1994, Repubican leader Robert Michel announced his retirement, and in the 1994 Congressional elections the GOP captured the House by twelve seats. These events brought Gingrich to the speakership, the first Republican to head the chamber in forty-five years.

Newt Gingrich is a man of strong opinions and a willingness to voice those opinions in the most strident language. The key to understanding the source of his opinions is Gingrich's enmity toward the counterculture of the 1960s. Many students of his generation (e.g., Bill Clinton) were demonstrating against American involvement in the Vietnam War, experimenting with recreational drugs, questioning traditional middle-class values, and delaying marriage. Much of this protest generation eventually entered traditional politics with a commitment to using an activist government to expand opportunities for all Americans. Gingrich's 1960s experience was different. He supported the war (although he took a family deferment to avoid service), opposed recreational drugs (although he admits to marijuana use in graduate school), gave verbal support to traditional values (although not denying adultery), and married at 19. Gingrich now argues that the philosophy of people such as President Clinton have brought about a decline of values that threatens American society. He says that government has become an enemy of "normal Americans." While Gingrich's critics, comparing his rhetoric with the reality of his own life, find hypocrisy, his supporters see inspirational leadership.

The other key to Newt Gingrich is his rejection of Republican Minority Leader Robert Michel's advice in 1989. When Gingrich won the Republican whip position, Michel advised him always to behave as a gentleman and to work with Democrats for the good of the country. Michel's view was that members of Congress should leave campaign rhetoric behind after election day and cooperate with the other party to fashion good public policy. In contrast, Gingrich has argued that to win a majority Republicans should take every opportunity to use the media to differentiate themselves from Democrats, especially on the most emotional, potentially divisive issues. While he was still new to the House, Gringrich stood out for his uncompromising, strident assaults on his Democratic "enemies" across the aisle. He instinctively rejected the notion that to rise in the House, "to get along," as legendary Speaker **Sam Rayburn** used to put it, "you must go along." To Gingrich this was a formula for Republicans remaining a perpetual minority. Accordingly, Gingrich brilliantly exploited the new possibilities opened up by the House allowing its proceedings to be televised, especially on C-SPAN. To reach a wide if anonymous audience he and relays of Republicans mobilized and organized by him attacked the Democrats relentlessly, often before an empty chamber but in front of that all-seeing TV camera. Those incessant attacks on House Democrats as "corrupt" had an inevitable effect in undermining their standing before the public. The Democrats helped reinforce Gingrich's tactics with scandals that drove one of their Speakers, Jim Wright of Texas, out of office and caused the House leadership to close the House bank that many members were misusing as a source of no-interest loans through the device of bounced checks. All of this led to the GOP sweep in 1994 and Gingrich's ascension to the Speaker's chair. But this deliberate assault on the collegiality that generally prevailed in the House before Gingrich began to wage war on the "go along" policy of Michel has been costly. The House over which the Speaker now presides is more partisan and its atmosphere more poisonous than at any time since the 19th century. The Democrats, now employing the Speaker's tactics themselves, are hurling ethics charges against him, charges that are being investigated by the House Ethics Committee. As Speaker, Gingrich has succeeded in pushing through the Republician Party's "Contract with America" and has begun the process of dismantling many social programs dating back to the New Deal. He has demonstrated in his first years in the speakership remarkable qualities of legislative leadership. But he has not significantly modified the ascerbic and confrontational style that got him there, and many believe it might one day prove to be his undoing. See Hendrick Hertzberg, "Cookie Monster: Newt Gingrich's Book to Renew America" *The New Yorker* (July 17, 1995); "Next Captain in Cyberspace," *The New Yorker* (Aug. 7, 1995); John B. Judis, "Newt's Not-So-Weird-Gurus," *The New Republic* (Oct. 9, 1995).

ROBERT O'CONNOR

GINSBERG, Allen (b. Newark, N.J., June 3, 1926), POET, graduated from Columbia College (1948). He met **Jack Kerouac,** whose New York apartment was a gathering place for young intellectuals including William S. Burroughs and Herbert Huncke, in 1948. In that year Ginsberg experienced a series of mystical visions while reading William Blake's poetry and underwent psychoanalysis, including eight months spent in Rockland (New York) State Hospital for psychoanalysis and therapy. He worked as a market research consultant in New York (1951) and San Francisco (1953).

Ginsberg was a poet of the Beat Generation, a movement of the mid-fifties that sought to challenge American middle-class values and traditional literary forms. His earliest poems (1947–52) were published in *Empty Mirror* in 1962. In 1957 a San Francisco court found him not guilty of obscenity for *Howl and Other Poems* (1956), which indicts American society for destroying what is best in human nature. Autobiographical like his other works, "Kaddish" (*Kaddish and Other Poems,* 1960) is a mourner's prayer and elegy for his deceased mother.

Ginsberg has continuously been associated with movements challenging contemporary American values. In 1960, under Timothy Leary's guidance, he experimented with LSD, the consciousness-expanding drug, but after a tour of India and the Far East with Peter Orlovsky (1962–63) he turned from drugs to yoga and meditation. This shift was the occasion for his poem "The Change," written in 1963. In 1965 he visited Communist Cuba but was forced to leave when he criticized the persecution of homosexuals at Havana University. On a tour of Eastern Europe he was expelled from Czechoslovakia after being declared King of the May by Prague students. In 1965–66 he received a Guggenheim fellowship in poetry, and in 1967 he helped organize the Human Be-In in San Francisco's Golden Gate Park, the first of the large-scale hippie gatherings. At the 1968 Democratic national convention in Chicago, Ginsberg took part in the Festival of Life planned by Abbie Hoffman, Jerry Rubin, and others. While "yippies" (Youth International Party) and police were battling in Lincoln Park, Ginsberg chanted "om," a poetic word from Indian yoga, in order to calm the crowd. At the December 1969 trial of those arrested at the convention (the Chicago Seven) Ginsberg testified as a defense witness. Ginsberg has read his poetry in art galleries, coffee shops, and universities. He has appeared in *Pull My Daisy,* a film about the Beat Generation written by Kerouac. He has also written *T.V. Baby Poems* (1968); *Planet News,* poems that focus on news of the planet as well as himself (1968); *Ankor Wat,* inspired by a visit to the Cambodian ruins (1969); and *Indian Journals* (1969). He received the National Book Award in 1974 for *The Fall of America: Poems of These States, 1965–1971.* In 1971, Ginsberg was made director of the Committee on Poetry Foundation in New York and the Kerouac School of Poetics in Colorado. He has continued to write poetry but no longer roams the country, guru-like, in sandals and finger symbols preaching a "merry doctrine" of pan-sexual free love, mind-expanding drugs, and Eastern mysticism. Instead, dressed in conservative blue three-button suits, pin-striped shirts, and with a Mont Blanc pen tucked in his breast pocket, he meets regularly scheduled classes at Brooklyn College of the City University of New York where, in 1986, he was appointed Distinguished Professor of English, a tenured position he presently holds.

Published in the year of President Dwight D. Eisenhower's reelection, *Howl and Other Poems* was a harbinger of poetic and political radicalism. In the visionary title poem, Ginsberg's best as well as his most famous work, the "angel-headed hipsters" who "coughed on the sixth floor of Harlem crowned with flame under the tubercular sky surrounded by orange crates of theology" are commemorated by fifty-nine other clauses that begin with "who" in a sentence that runs for eight pages. The second and third sections are built mainly of repetitions of single words or phrases. Influenced by **William Carlos Williams**'s theory of prosody, he attempts in the

long sentences to match the rhythm of his breathing. Throughout this and later poems, images from diverse realms of experience are juxtaposed in frequently startling combinations. Themes are as radical as techniques. Ginsberg's howl is a conscious variant of **Walt Whitman**'s "barbaric yawp." His reiterated references to conventionally unmentioned parts of his own body echo Whitman's insistence that he was the poet of the Body as well as of the Soul. Ginsberg's later poems experiment with shorter lines but show no less concern for spontaneity, immediacy, and sincerity.

Ginsberg's politics are as radical as his poetics. "Howl" begins with his angry assertion that the best minds of his generation were "destroyed by madness, starving hysterical naked,/dragging themselves through the negro streets at dawn looking for an angry fix." Although reared in the Marxist milieu re-created in "Kaddish," Ginsberg rejects ideology and fuses his instinctive romantic anarchism with bits and pieces of Zen Buddhism and Hindu mysticism. Conceiving of life and art as a unity, he has become the best known of nonacademic poets, a public figure, a political activist, and the hero of a cult. See Barry Miles, *Ginsberg: A Biography* (1989).

ALLEN GUTTMANN

GIRARD, Stephen (b. Bordeaux, France, May 20, 1750; d. Philadelphia, Pa., Dec. 26, 1831), MERCHANT, BANKER, received little formal education. He went to sea in 1764 as a cabin boy in the French merchant marine. In 1773 he was licensed as a master or pilot and made his first independent voyage as captain of a French merchant ship from Bordeaux to Port-au-Prince in 1774. After falling into debt he joined a New York shipping firm in 1775. Having made several voyages and accumulated some capital, he settled in Philadelphia in 1776 and opened a dry-goods store. When the British occupied Philadelphia in 1777, he moved to Mount Holly, New Jersey, where he set up a business of importing, bottling, and selling French brandies, but he returned to the city when the British left (1778) and thereafter developed a large fleet of merchant ships. He amassed a large fortune despite French and English harassment of American shipping during the wars of the French Revolution. He was also active in philanthropic works, organizing relief measures during Philadelphia's yellow fever epidemics of 1793 and 1797 and aiding many French refugees who fled France during the Reign of Terror.

At the turn of the century Girard began to devote much attention to real estate, insurance, and banking. After Congress refused to extend the charter of the first Bank of the United States, Girard (1811) bought the bank's Philadelphia building and founded the Bank of Stephen Girard. He helped avert a financial crisis during the War of 1812 by underwriting with the aid of **John Jacob Astor** and David Parish most of a government war loan of 1813. Girard vigorously supported the establishment of the second Bank of the United States and became a government director when it was chartered in 1816. He spent his later years on his farm in south Philadelphia planning the distribution of his estate. He also made investments in transportation improvements such as canals and turnpikes. When he died he left endowments to Philadelphia and Pennsylvania for municipal improvements and for the establishment of a school for orphaned white boys (Girard College), which opened in 1848.

———— ✦ ————

Girard is significant primarily as a bridge between the commercial entrepreneur of the 18th and early 19th centuries and the industrial entrepreneur of the late 19th century. Beginning his career as captain of a ship in which he had a financial interest, he followed a long-established pattern of entrepreneurial behavior. He was able to make the bulk of his large fortune of $6 million by deftly utilizing the opportunities for extraordinary profits opened to American neutral traders by the wars of the French Revolution.

The shift of his capital from overseas trade to banking reflected the familiar course of an 18th-century career. But participation in the syndicate that underwrote a large portion of the government loan of 1813 made Girard one of the nation's first investment bankers. During the final period of his life his interest in transportation improvement and large-scale philanthropy also foreshadowed the orientation of later generations of entrepreneurs.

Girard did not have a pleasant personality. He was cold and forbidding, and his business ethics where government regulations were concerned were lax even for the times. Like other commercial entrepreneurs of his generation he could afford to be an individualist, showing little of the interest in business organization and management that is characteristic of entrepreneurs of the late 19th and early 20th centuries. See Harry Emerson Wildes, *Lonely Midas: The Story of Stephen Girard* (1943).

ELISHA P. DOUGLASS

GLADDEN, Solomon Washington (b. Pottsgrove, Pa., Feb. 11, 1836; d. Columbus, Ohio, July 2, 1918), RELIGIOUS LEADER, worked for the Owego (N.Y.) *Gazette* and studied at the Owego Academy. After earning an AB from Williams College (1859) and briefly teaching school, he was licensed to preach by the Susquehanna Association of Congregational Ministers and became pastor of the First Congregational Methodist Church of Brooklyn in 1860; he later had congregations in Morrisania, New York (1861–66); North Adams, Massachusetts (1866–71); and Springfield, Massachusetts (1875–82). Gladden was on the editorial staff of the New York *Independent* (1871–74) where he wrote on ecclesiastical affairs and on the implications of Darwinism for theology. In 1882 he became minister of the First Congregational Church of Columbus, Ohio, a position he held until his death. Here, Gladden became recognized as one of the leading popularizers of the Social Gospel, an attempt to apply Christian principles to social problems. Through his writings, speeches, and actions Gladden became a harsh critic of sweatshops, child labor, and other evils of the industrial system. He was one of the first clergymen to support labor's right to organize, and he advocated government ownership of public utilities.

Gladden was a charter member of the American Economic Association (1885), an organization founded by economists unhappy with the prevalent school of classical economics. He served on the city council of Columbus (1900–2) where he fought for municipal reform. He served as moderator of the National Council of Congregational Churches (1904–7). During this time Gladden received national attention when he proposed rejecting a gift of $100,000 by **John D. Rockefeller,** president of Standard Oil Co., to the American Board of Commissioners for Foreign Missions. Gladden argued that the gift was "tainted money" because it had been earned by corrupt and predatory means. Although Gladden had supported the American war against Spain in 1898 and the suppression of Filipino insurgency thereafter, he opposed the pre–World War I preparedness campaign. Nevertheless, he backed America's entry into the war, hoping that this intervention would indeed make the world "safe for Democracy." Some of Gladden's many books include *Applied Christianity* (1887), *The Church and Modern Life* (1908), and *Recollections* (1909), his autobiography.

Solomon Washington Gladden's general significance stems from the pragmatism and tough-minded realism that he brought to his interlaced careers as clergyman and social reformer. Although imbued with an idealistic vision of the Kingdom of God on earth, he was no dreamy utopian. In seeking Christian social justice in industrial America, he shaped his objectives according to his perceptions of the realities of power and mastered the skills necessary to effect institutional action. On each issue that he confronted, he displayed an expertise derived from his omnivorous reading in contemporary social science and from his grass-roots activism, which involved him in founding a settlement house, trying to mediate strikes, inspecting local hous-

ing, serving on the city council, and reorganizing local charities.

Open to novelty and unthreatened by change, he grew more radical with age. For example, he espoused individualistic self-help to industrial workers in the 1870s but after 1900 came to endorse virtually the whole program of the American Federation of Labor. Similarly, he moved from the racial philosophy of **Booker T. Washington** to the greater militancy of **W. E. B. Du Bois,** and he abandoned a lifelong loyalty to the Republican Party to support Theodore Roosevelt in 1912 and Woodrow Wilson in 1916.

A scholarly man by instinct and reserved in his demeanor, Gladden had two great passions: to reconcile Christian theology and Darwinism, the higher criticism of the Bible, and the study of comparative religions; and to bring Christian ethical perspectives to bear on social problems. His efforts toward these ends reflect the gifts of a popularizer rather than of an original thinker. See Jacob H. Dorn, *Washington Gladden: Prophet of the Social Gospel* (1968).

JACOB H. DORN

GLASS, Carter (b. Lynchburg, Va., Jan. 4, 1858; d. Lynchburg, Va., May 28, 1946), POLITICAL LEADER, left school at the age of 14 and became a journeyman printer. After a period in Petersburg, Virginia, where his father published a newspaper, he returned to Lynchburg (c. 1877). In 1880 he became a reporter for the Lynchburg *Daily News.* He rose to editor (1887) and purchased the paper in 1888. In 1895 he acquired the Lynchburg *Advance.* As editor he was an influential voice in Democratic politics and was elected to the Virginia senate in 1898. He attended the Virginia Constitutional Convention of 1901, where he sponsored successful poll tax and literacy test provisions. In 1902 he was elected to the U.S. House of Representatives, serving until 1918. At the Democratic national convention of 1912 his delivery of the entire Virginia delegation (despite internal dissension) to Woodrow Wilson made him an important figure. In 1912 he became chairman of the House Committee on Banking and Currency.

Glass was coauthor (with economist H. Parker Willis) of the bill that became the Federal Reserve Act of 1913. Although Glass favored banker participation on the proposed supervisory board, President Woodrow Wilson and the liberal Democrats favored independent government control, but the final measure embodied the Glass-Willis idea of twelve privately controlled Federal Reserve banks supervised by a public Federal Reserve Board.

Wilson appointed Glass secretary of the Treasury in 1918, but he resigned in 1920 to serve out an unexpired term as senator from Virginia. He was elected senator in 1924 and served until his death. In 1928, Glass, unlike most southern Democrats, campaigned for **Alfred E. Smith** for president. He strongly opposed the fiscal policies of President Herbert Hoover. At the Democratic convention of 1932, Glass contributed the "sound money" plank of the platform. One New Deal measure, the Glass-Steagall Banking Act of 1933, which separated commercial from investment banking and provided federal insurance of bank deposits, is credited to Glass, although he originally opposed deposit insurance. He soon found himself opposing the deficit financing and heavy government spending of President Franklin D. Roosevelt's administration. However, he supported Roosevelt's foreign policy of aid to the Allies in World War II.

Short, red-haired, and chronically ill, Glass was often a stormy individual. When aroused he was prone to rhetorical flourishes with both tongue and pen that delighted his friends and dismayed his opponents. Impeccably honest and possessing an analytical and critical mind, he despised sham and tended to judge harshly the motives and actions of those with whom he disagreed. He cared little about the normal amenities and won few friends except by the force of his intellect. A political colleague once remarked that Glass could benefit from developing a little hypocrisy in his personality.

In political philosophy he was schooled in the Jeffersonian-Jacksonian ideals of the Democratic Party. The materialism and power dislocations of post–Civil War industrialization were so offensive to him that he joined in leading state reform movements to restrain corporate power, obtain pure food and drug laws, improve education and working conditions, and purify politics. Although the latter effort was marred by racial disfranchisement, Glass personally wanted to eliminate ignorant and venal voters of both races in order to return to the kind of high-minded politics that he believed typified earlier contests.

Glass was always suspicious of politicians and the exercise of governmental power. Won over to free silver in the 1890s by emotional and moral factors, he soon retreated to a more orthodox Jeffersonian position from which he could seldom be dislodged except to attack the overweening power of corporate enterprise. Even as a Wilsonian reformer he resisted efforts to enlarge governmental power at the expense of private enterprise operating in the public interest. Thus the ideals that made him a reformer before the Harding era drew him into conservative ranks after 1920 and ultimately led him to reject the leadership of Franklin D. Roosevelt on constitutional grounds. See Rixey Smith and Norman Beasley, *Carter Glass: A Biography* (1939).

HARRY E. POINDEXTER

GODDARD, Robert Hutchings (b. Worcester, Mass., Oct. 5, 1882; d. Baltimore, Md., Aug. 10, 1945), PHYSICIST, received a BS from Worcester Polytechnic Institute (1908) where he showed an interest in radio physics and rocketry, and his MA (1910) and PhD (1911) from Clark University. He was an instructor at Worcester Polytechnic Institute (1909–11) and spent a year at Princeton (1912–13). In 1914 he returned to Clark, remaining, with various interruptions, until 1942. During World War I, Goddard served as rocket research director for the U.S. Signal Corps. In 1919 the Smithsonian Institution published his pioneering *A Method of Reaching Extreme Altitudes* and provided funds for his rocket research.

During the 1920s Goddard turned his research interests from solid to liquid propellants; in 1926 he launched his first liquid-fuel rocket. Under grants from the Guggenheim Foundation, Goddard took a leave of absence from Clark (1934–42) to continue his experiments at a desert site near Roswell, New Mexico. He discovered ways of ensuring a continuous flow of power in a rocket instead of merely an initial explosion; he demonstrated that rockets operated in a vacuum better than in atmosphere; and he devised means for steering their ascent and parachutes for their descent. Also, he developed the theory of clustered and step rockets, systems of parallel or serial rocket stages as methods for reaching the moon. Goddard was probably first to install a gyroscopic steering mechanism on rockets and succeeded in shooting rockets across the New Mexico desert at speeds of more than 700 miles per hour.

During World War II, the U.S. Navy employed Goddard as a director of research in the Bureau of Aeronautics where he worked on rocket motors and jet-assisted takeoff devices for aircraft. The Nazis used many of his ideas in their V–1 and V–2 rockets. In 1962 the National Aeronautics and Space Administration dedicated the Goddard Space Flight Center (Greenbelt, Md.) in his honor.

───────

In the wake of manned space flight and lunar exploration, three scientist-engineers of the early 20th century—the Russian schoolteacher K. E. Tsiolkovsky, the American professor of physics R. H. Goddard, and the Romanian rocket theoretician H. Oberth—gained worldwide recognition as independent intellectual fathers of space travel. Only Goddard, however, carried through a lifelong program of experimental testing in rocketry as well as concurrent theoretical studies of the possibilities for penetrating "extreme altitudes." Only Goddard personally directed progressive demonstrations of the feasibility of technical ideas at the vanguard among enthusiasts for space flight.

Goddard came from an old-line New England family and was thoroughly imbued with the work ethic and the Yankee ingenuity ethos.

Although plagued by intermittent respiratory illness throughout his life, he believed in indefinite technological and spiritual progress and became dedicated in his midteens to advancing the science of rocketry and space travel. By advancing through physics up the academic ladder, Goddard soon discovered that the dignity of science would not allow speculation to outrun solidly based experimentation and extrapolation. After some unfortunate early publicity that threatened to link his name to "crackpot" ideas for lunar or planetary probes and travel, Goddard became very reticent about his work. While taking advantage of every opportunity to gain financial support from private institutions, foundations, and the government, Goddard nevertheless steadfastly refused to become a team researcher. He maintained a small staff of craftsmen while advancing liquid-fueled rocketry in Massachusetts and New Mexico during the period between the world wars, but he refused to join the teams of Theodore von Karman and William F. Durand, who were projecting similar work in California.

Conscious of his place in history as well as of his patent interests, Goddard persevered through many disappointing test flights to prove the physical principles that he assiduously applied to rocket propulsion, to guidance and control, and for payload purposes. From 1914 through 1944 he was preoccupied with the theory of jet propulsion and the development of progressively more sophisticated experimental rockets. During World War I he demonstrated the practicality of tube-launched solid-fueled projectiles for the army; during World War II he worked for the navy in perfecting jet-assisted takeoff techniques. He lived to see the German V–2 rockets, whose engines were based on his own designs, outstrip the records he set in the late 1930s: speeds of 700 miles per hour and 8,000–9,000-foot altitudes. Thus before his death Goddard's hopes of achieving escape velocities by rocket, ironically through Hitler's vengeance weapons, appeared on the verge of realization.

Temperamentally a lone dreamer with a lively sense of destiny, Goddard the space physicist became overwhelmed by Goddard the rocket engineer as he tried, alone or with a few skilled machinists, to conquer all the technological problems of liquid-fuel rocketry. His legacy of 214 patents shows his achievement, but his private papers (recently published) show his aspirations—boundless, like space itself. See Milton Lehman, *This High Man* (1963).

LLOYD S. SWENSON, JR.

GODKIN, Edwin Lawrence (b. Moyne, Co. Wicklow, Ire., Oct. 2, 1831; d. Brixham, Eng., May 21, 1902), JOURNALIST, graduated from Queen's College, Belfast, Ireland (1851). After briefly studying law in London he turned to journalism. In 1853 he published *The History of Hungary and the Magyars*, a sympathetic account of the Hungarian revolutionary movement under the leadership of Lajos Kossuth. He covered the Crimean War as a correspondent for the New York *Times* and the London *Daily News* (1853–55). Thereafter he lectured on the war and worked for the Belfast *Northern Whig*.

In 1856, Godkin emigrated to the United States, settling in New York City. There he studied law under David Dudley Field and was admitted to the bar in 1858. During the Civil War he again served as a correspondent for the London *Daily News*.

In July 1865, Godkin launched the *Nation*, which soon became one of the country's most influential weeklies. As its editor (1865–99) Godkin took a moderate stand on Reconstruction, supporting the interests of the freedmen but vigorously opposing the carpetbaggers; attacked the corruption in the Grant administration; supported civil service reform; criticized the speculative mania that permeated the Gilded Age; favored free trade; viewed all inflationary schemes, particularly the coinage of silver, with contempt; and bitterly opposed all expansionist ventures. Originally a Republican in politics, he was one of the leaders of the Liberal-Republican movement that tried to unseat Ulysses S. Grant in 1872. However, when the Liberal-Republicans nominated **Horace Greeley,** editor of the New York *Tribune,* Godkin gave Grant his tacit support.

In 1881, Godkin sold the *Nation* to **Henry Villard,** the owner of the New York *Evening Post* but remained its editor. In 1883, with the retirement of **Carl Schurz,** Godkin became editor in chief of the *Post* (to 1900). When the Republican Party nominated **James G. Blaine** for the presidency in 1884, Godkin became one of the leaders of the "Mugwumps," a group of Republicans who left the GOP to back Grover Cleveland, the Democratic presidential candidate.

During his final years Godkin published a number of works on American society, including *Reflections and Comments* (1896), *Problems of Modern Democracy* (1896), and *Unforeseen Tendencies of Democracy* (1898).

⁕

"Publicist, Economist, Moralist," as his epitaph reads, Godkin was one of the most important social critics of his day. Master of a distinguished literary style, he brought to the craft of journalism a broad intelligence, keen wit, and sensitive moral conscience. A brilliant polemicist, he had as well the gift for making dull subjects lively and commonplace thinking memorable. If only because of the considerable stylistic influence he exerted on a generation of young newsmen and editors, Godkin ranks among the great American journalists.

Godkin the publicist conceived of the *Nation* as an American counterpart of the weekly nonpartisan reviews in England, whose trenchant commentary on public issues often changed the thinking of politicians. No question of the day escaped the *Nation*'s attention, and during the first three decades of the journal's existence, almost everything its pages carried bore the imprint of Godkin's pen or authority. If the *Nation* never quite matched its English forebears in political influence, it yet became an acknowledged molder of public opinion, for many of its readers were themselves editors and professors who spread Godkin's views in their own writings and lectures.

As an economist Godkin was the foremost disciple in the United States of English liberalism. Like many disciples, he outdid his masters in espousing their cause, ultimately reducing their political economy to a handful of simple maxims about society and the economy. Few other followers of Smith and Bentham ever construed laissez-faire in more explicit terms or placed narrower restrictions on even the negative functions of the state. Godkin deplored the excesses of the urban industrial society in which he lived, and often his prose quickened the consciences of his readers to its grossest faults. But Godkin failed to comprehend the dynamic nature of industrial capitalism and never came to grips with the fundamental social and economic problems it raised. No dialectical process cluttered his ordered thinking; he remained ever convinced that the "natural laws" of political economy were fixed forever, beyond the reach of man or history.

At heart and always, Godkin was a moralist. Fiercely independent, he judged men and issues unsparingly by his own high standards of moral conduct. At a time when many good men feared for the survival of any standards whatsoever, his attempt to maintain settled rules of decency determined his role as a social critic. Indeed, it made him the preeminent spokesman for liberal reform, that movement of the genteel, educated elite to improve the moral tone of business and politics in post–Civil War America. As their efforts produced few positive results, both Godkin and the movement suffered the same tragic fate of succumbing to unreasoning fear of the democratic masses and deep pessimism about the future of civilization. By the end of the century the once hopeful pundit had become a disillusioned censor. Godkin's mordant commentaries on democracy, a product of his later years, reveal a man grown old in an age he condemned. He died convinced that imperialism doomed the United States to a slavish repetition of the European experience. See John G. Sproat, *"The Best Men": Liberal Reformers in the Gilded Age* (1968).

JOHN G. SPROAT

GOETHALS, George Washington (b. Brooklyn, N.Y., June 29, 1858; d. New York, N.Y., Jan. 21, 1928), ENGINEER, completed four years at the City College of New York (1872–76) and then was appointed to the U.S. Military Academy at West Point, graduating in 1880. Assigned to the Army Engineer Corps, he served in the Department of the Columbia in Washington Territory (1882–84); the Muscle Shoals lock project (1889–94); as chief engineer of the First Army Corps; and as a member of the Army General Staff (1903–7).

During 1907–14 Goethals directed the successful construction of the Panama Canal; in 1908, President Theodore Roosevelt transferred the executive powers of the Isthmian Canal Commission, which was rent with friction, to its chairman, Goethals, who now completely dominated the seven-man Commission. The Commission remained in being and disputes continued to rage, but Goethals received the powers he needed to ensure the canal's completion. Besides dealing with the engineering difficulties involved, Goethals also had charge of maintaining more than thirty thousand workers of varied nationalities, and he established a judicial system in the Canal Zone.

The canal was opened in 1914, and Goethals remained as governor of the Canal Zone until 1916. In 1917, after retiring from the army, he worked briefly as New Jersey state engineer but was soon recalled to duty as acting quartermaster general for the American forces in World War I (1917–18). During 1919–23 he headed G. W. Goethals and Co., consulting engineers for such projects as the Inner Harbor Navigation Canal at New Orleans and the Columbia Basin Irrigation Project. He also served until 1928 as consulting engineer for the Port of New York Authority.

⸺⸺⸺

Although he was a competent and sound engineer, Goethals's primary talent lay in his outstanding ability to manage and lead men. His early work with the Corps of Engineers developed his talents and provided him with the varied engineering and administrative experience that qualified him so superbly for the leadership of the vast Panama Canal project. In dealing with workers, the "genius of the Panama Canal" possessed an uncanny knack for inspiring loyalty, confidence, dedication, and a cooperative spirit that promoted tremendous economy and efficiency. Part of this ability resulted from a phenomenal capacity to master all the details and workings of the projects he directed. This, coupled with his commitment and ability to treat and judge men patiently, considerately, and justly, enabled Goethals to play the role of benevolent despot with astounding success. He expounded a philosophy of management which held that boards are "long, narrow, and wooden," and succeeded most when he alone had complete and unchallenged responsibility and authority, as may be seen from his achievements with the Panama Canal and the Quartermaster Corps, and from his frustrations with government bureaucrats during World War I.

Stern, inflexible once committed, with a tendency to assess things in extremes of right or wrong, Goethals tempered his personal relations with humor and a sense of proportion. He gave himself unstintingly to the tasks he had assumed, although he was averse to public life and social engagements, preferring instead privacy and family life. Paradoxically autocratic yet popular, dynamic yet dignified, he was unreservedly patriotic, devoting his life in major part to public service and to living up to the motto of his alma mater, "Duty, honor, country." His strong sense of ethics led him to reject many opportunities to amass wealth, both during and after his military career. Goethals's effectiveness and national popularity owed much to his exemplary fusion of the sometimes conflicting American values of principle and pragmatism. See J. B. and F. Bishop, *Goethals: Genius of the Panama Canal* (1930).

DONALD DE B. BEAVER

GOLDMAN, Emma (b. Kovno, Russia, June 27, 1869; d. Toronto, Can., May 14, 1940), REVOLUTIONARY, spent her early life in Königsberg, East Prussia, before moving with her family to St. Petersburg in 1882. She arrived in the United States in 1885 with her half-sister and settled in Rochester, New York. After briefly working in a

clothing factory, Goldman moved to New Haven, Connecticut, and worked in a corset factory. Deeply impressed by the trial of the Chicago Haymarket Square anarchists in 1886–87, she began attending meetings with socialists and anarchists. By 1889 she was converted to anarchism and moved to New York City to participate in radical activities. She worked with Russian anarchist Alexander Berkman and helped plan his attempted assassination of United States Steel head **Henry Clay Frick** during the Homestead steel strike in Pittsburgh, for which Berkman was sent to prison in 1892. She was arrested herself in New York in 1893 for inciting to riot and spent one year in prison. After her release she went to Europe (1895) where she studied nursing. Upon her return to the United States she continued her radical activities. She toured Europe again in 1899 but then dropped out of the spotlight for a time because of the attempt to implicate her in President William McKinley's assassination, despite the fact that Leon Czolgosz, the demented killer, insisted to the end that she "didn't tell me to do it."

Beginning in 1906, Goldman edited an anarchist monthly journal, *Mother Earth,* in which she preached the abolition of all government and its replacement by voluntary cooperation. In addition to anarchy, Goldman advocated a number of social reforms, including birth control. She was also a literary critic, publishing *The Social Significance of Modern Drama* in 1914. She attacked the institution of marriage and contemporary child-rearing practices, arguing that they reduced women to the role of inferior dependents. She advocated a fuller sexual life for women as a means of winning their freedom. In 1917 she was arrested for obstructing the military draft after having opposed U.S. entry into World War I. Goldman spent two years in prison in Jefferson City, Missouri, and upon her release was deported to Russia during the 1919 "Red Scare." At first sympathetic to the Soviet Union, she grew disillusioned with the despotism of Lenin and Trotsky. She left the U.S.S.R. in 1921 and then wrote *My Disillusionment in Russia* (1923). Goldman lived in many countries in the following years, including England, Canada, and France. She became deeply involved in the Spanish civil war and toured England and Canada speaking for the anti-Franco revolutionists. Goldman published her autobiography, *Living My Life* (1931), and wrote many essays on anarchy, feminism, and "institutionalized violence."

In Toronto a "draft dodger" is photographed holding a biography of Emma Goldman before his face to hide his identity; at a demonstration in New York the Emma Goldman Brigade of radical feminists marches boldly down Fifth Avenue behind a red-and-black banner bearing her name; in Buffalo a $100-a-plate dinner, featuring the Republican national chairman speaking in defense of the Indochina war, is interrupted by an angry young woman, identified as another Emma Goldman by a GOP spokesman, who cries out: "American ideals? America is based on genocide!"

So Red Emma is once again at large. The resurgence of interest in her and her ideas is demonstrable. Her books are back in print, most of them in paper covers. She has become a counterculture heroine. Why?

She speaks directly to those who are sick of a time filled with lies, language of overkill, apologies for genocide at swank dinners. She has meaning for all those who would seize control of their lives in an attempt to escape a world ruled by enormously powerful, deadly, seemingly anonymous forces. They draw hope from the example of her insurrectionary thrust toward individual freedom.

Her startling contemporaneity derives in large part from the nature of her impact on her own times. Throughout her life in America she drew in countless young people, influenced many of them deeply, and sent them off to act out her fundamental message: Be yourself. The flavor of their response can be sampled through the comments of Adelaide Schulkind, the accomplished woman who over the decades became the mainstay of the League for Mutual Aid: "Can you imagine the effect she had on an East Side girl of

seventeen who knew nothing of the world of culture? I used to travel clear across town on Sunday nights to hear her lecture on literature, birth control, and women." Not in fact a "distinguished critic of the drama," as the New York *Times* once named her, she was rather an extraordinary popularizer of insurgent ideas and one of the most effective, magnetic speakers in American history. She was a pioneer of the birth control movement. She challenged the beliefs of orthodox radicals, especially their faith in the omnicompetent state, with such effectiveness that the Socialist Party once forbade its members to debate her publicly. She aroused the ire of conservatives so effectively that she was subject to ferocious vigilante and police efforts to shut her up. Perhaps the bench mark of her impact in this area came in 1936 when **J. Edgar Hoover** testified before the Senate subcommittee for appropriations. Pressed by the unfriendly questioning of Senator Kenneth D. McKellar to relate what he *personally* had done to apprehend criminals and subversives, Hoover could think of only three cases, beginning with Emma: "I handled the investigation of Emma Goldman and prosecuted that case before the immigration authorities up to the secretary of labor." Seventeen years after the event and a decade after he had taken over as head of the FBI, Hoover still considered the deportation of Emma Goldman his leading achievement. The nation's foremost authority on dangerous ideas therewith underscored, however unwittingly and ironically, the words of civil libertarian Roger Baldwin: "For the cause of free speech in the United States Emma Goldman fought battles unmatched by the labors of any organization."

Though not remarkable for originality of thought, she was phenomenal in meaning what she said: "Revolution is but thought carried into action." Always acting what she believed, she upset city fathers, presidents, both Hoover and Lenin. Men could cease being cannon fodder, she said, and pawns in someone else's political and economic games. Women could be persons, she asserted, and cease being objects and breeders. Like **Margaret Fuller** she dared lay claim to her own body, and unlike contemporary suffragettes she boldly went on to celebrate its sexuality.

She could be unreasonable, short-tempered, even exasperatingly inconsiderate of the feelings of others, for she had a full complement of emotions, temperament, ego. But for the revolution to have her support it had to mean an extension of the range of possibilities for being human. She took her place beside the wretched of the earth and never budged. Beyond doubt the mountain of integrity Rebecca West saw in her, she was also an eruption of novelty in history: though not the American Virgin who **Henry Adams** said would never dare command, she had claims on being the American Venus he declared "would never dare exist." Emma Goldman dared. See Richard Drinnon, *Rebel in Paradise: A Biography of Emma Goldman* (1970).

RICHARD DRINNON

GOLDMARK, Josephine Clara (b. Brooklyn, N.Y., Oct. 13, 1877; d. Hartsdale, N.Y., Dec. 15, 1950), REFORMER, graduated from Bryn Mawr College in 1898. She then became research director for the newly organized National Consumers' League in New York City. She gathered data for the Brandeis brief in *Muller v. Oregon* (1908). In 1909 she assisted **Felix Frankfurter,** then a National Consumers' League lawyer, in the preparation of briefs to support the Illinois ten-hour law. She next undertook a study of fatigue in factory work with **Louis D. Brandeis,** which was published by the Russell Sage Foundation as *Fatigue and Efficiency* (1912). This work described the nature and effects of fatigue on workers; it became an important influence in the movement to reduce hours in factories. Goldmark viewed regular, continuous labor as necessary for the maintenance of the workers' physical and moral condition; what she attacked was the pattern of excessive hours of labor that injured workers' health and lowered their efficiency.

During 1912–14 she served, along with **Alfred E. Smith, Frances Perkins,** and **Robert Wagner,** on the investigating committee that reported on the 1911 Triangle Shirtwaist Co. fire. In 1914 she aided Felix Frankfurter in a successful test case of

the New York law against night work for women, and in 1916 she and Frankfurter published *The Case for the Shorter Workday* and *Women in Industry* in support of the Oregon ten-hour law. Thereafter she retired from public life. Goldmark completed her study *Nursing and Nursing Education in the United States* for the Rockefeller Foundation in 1923. She also wrote *Pilgrims of '48: One Man's Part in the Austrian Revolution of 1848, and a Family's Migration to America* (1930), based on her parents' experiences, and a biography of her friend **Florence Kelley**, *Impatient Crusader* (1953).

———— ⟨∞⟩ ————

A member of a notable family, Josephine Goldmark made her contributions primarily through research and writing on social issues. She was equally adept at the gathering of empirical field data on the consequences of industrial exploitation and at setting forth her findings in direct and forceful prose. A friend and associate of other reformers—Florence Kelley, **Jane Addams,** Julia Lathrop, the Abbott sisters, and others—Josephine and her sister Pauline moved in intellectual, social, and political circles of significant influence. Her detailed research into the consequences of extended hours of labor for women workers formed the factual basis for the famous Brandeis brief and thereby helped establish the constitutionality of state legislation to regulate the hours and conditions of employment. Like many reformers of the Progressive era, she was concerned for the individual health and well-being of the individual, for the efficiency of American industry, and for the larger welfare of the whole society. With them she also placed her faith in the efficacy of enlightened public opinion, believing devoutly in the capacity of informed citizens to shape a better society. Her analysis of the woeful inadequacy of nursing education in the early decades of the 20th century led in the 1920s to the upgrading of nurses' training and the establishment of higher professional standards in health services throughout the country.

Josephine Goldmark did not seek public attention or notoriety; she was content to work behind the scenes and to make her influence felt through her research and writing. Her critical and analytical mind was moved by humane concern for those disadvantaged persons who could not by their own actions secure more equitable conditions of life and labor. Retiring in her private life, she made many contributions to public health, education, and welfare. See Clarke A. Chambers, *Seedtime of Reform* (1963).

CLARKE A. CHAMBERS

GOLDWATER, Barry Morris (b. Phoenix, Ariz., Jan. 1, 1909), POLITICAL LEADER, attended Staunton Military Academy in Virginia (1924–28), then studied at the University of Arizona until the death of his father forced him to enter the family's department store business. He became company president in 1937. In 1941 he joined the Army Air Corps, serving as a pilot on supply missions. He was discharged in 1945 as a lieutenant colonel and returned to the management of Goldwater's department stores. He organized the Arizona air national guard, leading a fight to desegregate the force in 1946.

Goldwater entered politics by successfully campaigning for a "right to work" law (prohibiting union shops) in Arizona, and in 1949 he was elected to the Phoenix city council as a Republican. In 1952 he was elected a U.S. senator. Campaigning on a conservative platform, he opposed the expanded role of the federal government in American life, objected to the United Nations and foreign aid programs, and favored strong military forces.

As senator, Goldwater served on the Senate Labor Committee, opposed the Senate's censure of **Joseph R. McCarthy,** and in 1955 was appointed chairman of the Senate Republican Campaign Committee. In 1957–58 he emerged as the leader of Senate conservative Republicans. He was reelected to the Senate in 1958. In 1960 he published *The Conscience of a Conservative,* setting forth his views in detail. Defeat of Republican presidential nominee Richard M. Nixon by John F. Kennedy in 1960 left reorganization of the party in Goldwater's hands as head of the Republican Campaign Committee. He had received some backing in the 1960 Republican presidential nominating convention, and during the next four years he organized support for his nomination in 1964, which he obtained despite the efforts of liberal Republicans **Nelson Rockefeller** and William Scranton. Goldwater campaigned intensively but was defeated for the presidency by Democratic incumbent Lyndon B. Johnson, by the largest margin in any presidential election until that time (61 percent of the popular vote). Having resigned his Senate seat to seek the presidency, Goldwater returned to private life but was reelected to the Senate in 1968 and served until he retired in 1987. During that period Goldwater played a crucial role in persuading President Richard Nixon to resign in 1974, following the release of the tape that provided the "smoking gun." Disillusioned by the fact that Nixon had lied to him about his role in the Watergate cover-up, he convinced Nixon he would be impeached if he did not voluntarily give up his office. With fellow conservative Ronald Reagan in the White House in the 1980s and the GOP with a majority in the Senate, Goldwater chaired the Senate Armed Services Committee (1981–83). Following his retirement from the Senate, Goldwater continued to speak out on topics dear to conservatives. But he shocked many of them by refusing to support their anti-free choice position on the abortion issue, arguing that this was a private decision between a woman, her conscience, and her doctor and not one the government should meddle in. Similarly, in 1993 he threw his support behind those who advocated the right of homosexuals to be members of the Armed Forces. Some conservatives called for Goldwater's expulsion from the party and movement he once led, but he held fast to his views and denounced their authoritarian tendencies, claiming that they augured ill for the future of the Republican Party and the country.

———— ✦ ————

Goldwater is notable more for what he symbolized and for the movement he gave his name to than for what he accomplished. With his exhortations for a return to the moralities and traditions of an earlier, simpler America, the Republican senator appealed strongly to citizens frustrated by New Deal–style liberalism and cold war containment policies. Handsome, personable, and respected for his personal integrity, Goldwater emotionally articulated his faith in free enterprise and rugged individualism while bitterly condemning the expanding power of the federal government and the menace of international communism.

His influence peaked during the early 1960s. Conservative Republicans argued that their party's presidential nominees from 1940 through 1960 differed little from Democratic candidates. Disgusted with "me-tooism," the conservatives organized a shrewd grass-roots campaign in 1964, won control of the party machinery, and nominated Goldwater as a candidate offering "a choice, not an echo."

The Arizonian refused to woo his party's disgruntled liberals and moderates. He chose another avowed conservative as his running mate and in his acceptance speech bluntly declared: "Extremism in the defense of liberty is no vice!… Moderation in the pursuit of justice is no virtue!" Campaigning, Goldwater was similarly outspoken but often confusing and contradictory. His statements, suggesting recklessness in foreign affairs and callousness toward domestic problems, badly frightened many Americans. Goldwater's crushing defeat in the election significantly damaged both his prestige and his personal brand of conservatism. The belief that millions of silent conservative voters existed proved to be a myth at the time, and the Republican Party edged quickly back toward the hazy but safer middle of the political spectrum in the person of Richard Nixon. But Goldwater has lived to see a surge in conservative voters nationwide, a tide that eventually carried his middle-aged supporter, Ronald Reagan, to the White House in the 1980s, and a young southern Republican of the 1960s generation, **Newt Gingrich** of Georgia, to the speakership of the House of Representatives in the 1990s. It is clear, however, that Goldwater is not entirely satisfied with the direction the movement he helped found is taking at the close of the century. Still an apostle of rugged individualism, the present trend among Christian Right

conservatives to employ the coercive power of the state to impose their personal moral and religious values is worrisome to him. The great irony for Goldwater is that he now perceives the emerging conservative hegemony in the Republican Party as a greater threat to the individual liberties he championed than the liberals and moderates he once railed against. See Robert Alan Goldberg, *Barry Goldwater* (1995).

JIM F. HEATH

GOLDWYN, Samuel (b. Warsaw, Poland, July 1879; d. Los Angeles, Calif., Jan. 31, 1974), was born Schmuel Gelbfisz, the eldest child of a poor peddler. He received an orthodox Jewish education and in 1895, after his father's death, made his way alone first to Germany, then to Great Britain, and in December 1898 to the United States where he took the name Samuel Goldfish. Penniless, he found work as an apprentice glove maker in Gloversville, N.Y., for $3 a week. He studied English at the Gloversville Business College at night, became an expert glove cutter, and in time was a top glove salesman.

In 1912 hard times hit the glove manufacturing industry, and Goldfish entered show business with his brother-in-law, producer and performer Jesse L. Lasky. A year later they formed the Jesse L. Lasky Feature Play Company and hired **Cecil B. DeMille** to direct motion pictures. The business grew but so did tensions within the company, and Goldfish, tired of the corporate infighting, sold out in 1916 and set up an independent motion picture production company in alliance with Broadway producers Arch and Edgar Selwyn. The enterprise was called "Goldwyn"— a combination of Goldfish and Selwyn. Goldfish liked the "Goldwyn" name so much that he legally became Samuel Goldwyn.

But corporate infighting continued to haunt him. In 1922 he was edged out of Goldwyn Pictures and joined United Artists. For the next thirty years Goldwyn produced popular motion pictures. He made purely popular fare—detective films such as *Bulldog Drummond* (1929) and musicals such as *Palmy Days* (1931). He frequently took inspiration from popular Broadway plays and acclaimed novels as in *Dodsworth* (1936) and *The Little Foxes* (1941). But for every heralded serious drama, such as *Dead End* (1937) and *Wuthering Heights* (1939), Goldwyn mixed in emotional and simplistic melodramas starring Anna Sten and fluff musicals starring Eddie Cantor and the "Goldwyn Girls." He reached the apex of his career with *The Best Years of Our Lives,* which earned a number of awards in 1946. Samuel Goldwyn's final film was the Gershwin folk opera *Porgy and Bess* (1959); indeed, during the later years of his career he specialized in musicals, typified by *Hans Christian Anderson* (1952) and *Guys and Dolls* (1955).

———— ∞∞∞ ————

Sam Goldwyn was a true Hollywood pioneer. By joining forces with Jesse L. Laskey and later with Adolph Zukor, he helped found Famous Players-Lasky. Later renamed Paramount, Famous Players-Lasky pioneered basic Hollywood business principles and set in motion the studio system and star system. It showed how to distribute motion pictures worldwide. Recognizing that not all theaters were equal, the company charged more for showings at new, larger movie palaces. It was the first to tap Wall Street for the financing of feature films and later the construction of its own chain of movie palaces. Through these and other innovations Goldwyn helped craft a film industry that came to dominate the world by 1925 and still does three-quarters of a century later.

Like many Hollywood pioneers, Goldwyn was not raised or trained to become a movie mogul. He was reared in poverty as an Orthodox Jew in a world that simply wanted to be rid of Jewish people. It was only by journeying halfway around the world, to the United States, that he found the opportunity to create such a vast and influential institution as Hollywood.

But one would never know from Goldwyn's films that he grew up with little wealth. Goldwyn played the Hollywood game to the hilt, living a lavish lifestyle and hiring (and firing) the leading stars and writers in the movie capital with aban-

don. If his films possess a common theme, it is that they address elite concerns. He wanted his films to be viewed by upper-class America as high-quality productions of intelligence and refinement.

Samuel Goldwyn did learn something from his days struggling to move ahead in the glove industry. Throughout his Hollywood career he refused to remain a faceless producer taking orders from some studio executive. Goldwyn was proud to be independent and always took his latest production on the road "to hawk his wares directly to the public." In seeking to turn every Goldwyn production into a blockbuster, he was ahead of his time.

All these elements of Goldwyn's life came together with his heralded tale of World War II vets trying to adjust to civilian life, *The Best Years of Our Lives.* Working with top director William Wyler and ace cinematographer Gregg Toland, Goldwyn successfully adapted a best-selling MacKinlay Kantor novel to the screen. Goldwyn the immigrant loved this timely drama of three servicemen struggling to fit into a society that seemed so different from what it had been when they went off to war. *The Best Years of Our Lives* dramatized real concerns to create an honest and moving work of charm, richness, and beauty, and rightly earned seven Academy Awards and praise from filmmakers around the world.

Over a fifty-year moviemaking career Samuel Goldwyn discovered many noted stars: Eddie Cantor, Ronald Colman, Gary Cooper, Danny Kaye, Merle Oberon, and Teresa Wright, among others. He also brought more than his share of prestigious writers west, including Ben Hecht, **Lillian Hellman**, and **Sinclair Lewis**. Goldwyn's *The Westerner* (1940), *Ball of Fire* (1941), *The Bishop's Wife* (1947), and *Guys and Dolls* (1955) all rank among Hollywood's most popular films. He may be too often remembered for his Goldwynisms—such as "A verbal contract isn't worth the paper it's written on" and "Include me out"—but behind that mask Samuel Goldwyn was as shrewd and creative a movie producer as was ever let loose in Hollywood. See A. Scott Berg, *Goldwyn* (1989)

DOUGLAS GOMERY

GOMPERS, Samuel (b. London, Eng., Jan. 27, 1850; d. San Antonio, Tex., Dec. 13, 1924), LABOR LEADER, emigrated to the United States with his family in 1863. He joined the Cigarmakers Union (1864) and became its president in 1877. He was instrumental in establishing the Federation of Organized Trades and Labor Unions of the United States and Canada in 1881, which was reorganized in 1886 as the American Federation of Labor, with Gompers as president.

Gompers's belief in the principles of craft and business unionism and economic rather than political action, which became the fundamental policies of the AFL, was developed during the struggles of the cigarmakers in the 1870s. These struggles led him to conclude that American unions could not withstand the shock of depressions or lost strikes unless they were cohesive, financially stable organizations. The AFL under Gompers opposed the ideas of the Knights of Labor, the Socialist Party, and later the IWW.

Gompers opposed many of the post–World War I strikes and organizing efforts and was unsympathetic to radical political ideas. In his later years he became an important public figure: during World War I, President Woodrow Wilson appointed him to the Council on National Defense, where he helped mobilize labor support for the war, and to the Commission on International Labor Legislation at the Versailles Peace Conference. His conservative yet worker-oriented position earned him the title "Labor Statesman." His autobiography, *Seventy Years of Life and Labor* (1925), is an important account of the rise and growth of American trade unionism.

Samuel Gompers served as president of the American Federation of Labor from its inception until his death nearly forty years later. Such an association would naturally define the significance of a man's life but rarely to the extent that it did for Gompers. Putting to the side family and personal fortune, he gave himself up to the labor movement. It was entirely characteristic that, fatally ill and barely able to walk, Gompers traveled to El Paso, Texas, to preside over his last AFL convention in 1924 and then went on to represent American labor at political ceremonies in Mexico City; he died in San Antonio on the trip back. On the other hand, no one was more instrumental than Gompers in providing direction for American trade unionism as it came to maturity. Neither man nor movement can be understood apart.

When Gompers became active in labor affairs as a New York cigarmaker in the 1870s, the labor movement had not yet chosen between its two historic tendencies—labor reform and economic unionism. Gompers committed himself to the latter and, together with other pioneers, formulated the ideas that made trade unionism effective and gave it institutional form. His second great contribution was to attach pure-and-simple unionism (as those ideas became known) to the emergent labor movement. His third, the task to which he devoted his career as AFL president, was to serve as guardian and interpreter of the pure-and-simple doctrine within the labor movement. To do so, ironically, Gompers had to deny himself access to the real functions (as he himself defined them) of trade unionism. If these were, first, to carry on collective bargaining and, second, to exert economic power, by AFL law Gompers could do neither. These rested wholly with the member national unions. It was a special genius of his that, as ambitious and energetic as he was, Gompers always punctiliously respected the rules protecting the autonomy of the national unions. Needless to say, Gompers did take immense pride in the roles he played—as labor's conscience and ideologue, as mediator and chairman in its internal affairs, as its voice before the nation and the world.

Gompers's vast influence within the labor movement, rather than the result of any hold on the levers of power, derived partly from his very identification with its basic principles and partly from his personality. Short and heavyset, with a massive head and pockmarked and expressive face, Gompers invariably impressed observers as a man of immense force and purpose. In public he exuded dignity as befitted the national spokesman for American labor. Among his labor cronies Gompers was a good fellow, a natural joiner (an avid Elk and Mason), a lover of food, drink, and good times. This mixture of qualities, intellectual and personal, gave Gompers his unique place in the labor movement.

The thrust of Gompers's leadership was profoundly conservative. Pure-and-simple unionism operated within the existing economic system and explicitly resisted any influence that might turn it away from the focus on day-to-day improvement of the workingman's lot. Gompers was, moreover, the very antithesis of the alienated man. He identified deeply with his adopted country and in his later years grew inclined toward superpatriotism and incipient nativism. Yet it is important to recognize that these views were an outgrowth, more than a rejection, of his early radicalism. During the 1870s, Gompers had attached himself to the socialist wing that considered trade unionism (and, in fact, coined the phrase "pure-and-simple") the essential mechanism for bringing about revolution, the means for teaching American workers class-consciousness and developing their strength. To accomplish this, Gompers felt, the labor movement had to study and conform to the characteristics of the social order. Hence both Gompers's trade unionism and his Americanism derived from an early radical base. Trade unionism, Gompers had insisted from the start, concerned itself only with the present; the future would take care of itself. Gompers never repudiated this ambiguous radicalism. See Bernard Mandel, *Samuel Gompers: A Biography* (1963).

DAVID BRODY

GOODMAN, Benjamin David (b. Chicago, Ill., May 30, 1909; d. New York, N.Y., June 13, 1986), MUSICIAN, began playing the clarinet in 1919. He studied with his synagogue orchestra and also at Chicago's Hull House with Franz Schoepp of the Chicago Symphony Orchestra. Goodman entered the Lewis Institute in Chicago in 1923 but left later that year to play at Guyon's Paradise, a Chicago dance hall. Quickly establishing himself, he joined Ben Pollack's touring band in 1926 at

Los Angeles. He also made his first solo recording that year. In 1930 he left Pollack's band to freelance.

In 1933, Goodman met John Henry Hammond, Jr., a jazz enthusiast, who helped him organize a jazz band in 1934. After opening at Billy Rose's New York theater-restaurant, the Music Hall, in 1934, this group made an unsuccessful cross-country tour (1934–35) but was well received at the Palomar Ballroom in Los Angeles (1935). Goodman gave Chicago its first jazz concert in 1935 and played to full audiences at New York's Paramount theater in 1937. His famous jazz concert at Carnegie Hall in New York in 1938 featured solo performances by Gene Krupa, Harry James, and Lionel Hampton. Shortly thereafter he became the first band leader to employ black along with white musicians. An accomplished classical clarinetist, Goodman recorded much classical music in this period, most notably Mozart's Concerto in A Major for clarinet (1941). His group disbanded after World War II, but he reformed it in 1955 to supply the music for *The Benny Goodman Story* (1956), a movie based on his life. The band toured the Far East (1956–57) for the State Department, played at the Brussels World Fair (1958), and toured Western Europe (1959). Goodman toured the Soviet Union in 1962 under the State Department's Cultural Exchange Program, playing before Premier Nikita Khrushchev in Moscow. He performed in many places, including a tour of fourteen Western European cities with seventeen British musicians in 1970. Intermittently, through the 1970s and early 1980s Goodman formed small groups and big bands that toured the country giving concerts before large, and generally youthful, audiences, based on the music he became renowned for in the Swing Era. In this way he introduced a whole new generation to jazz and helped promote its revival.

Goodman happened to be a musician with the right background (a decade of jazz jam sessions, playing with jazz-influenced bands and in commercial studio groups) and with exceptional virtuoso skills who was urged at just the right time to become a bandleader and to use arrangements and an arranging talent (Fletcher Henderson) that had been proved during the previous ten years. Under these circumstances he was able to transfer to a white band a swinging attack that had been heard previously only in black orchestras such as Henderson's, and to bring it to a mass white audience that was largely unaware of the foundation on which Goodman built. For this audience Goodman's music was an electrifying and revealing experience. As an apparent innovator, he became the King of Swing. Although much of the consequent furor about swing was essentially press agentry, Goodman was worthy of his stature (unlike the completely misleading labeling of Paul Whiteman as the King of Jazz). He was a dyed-in-the-wool Chicago jazzman whose roots were very evident in his early playing and were later refined, without being lost, in what became a readily identifiable Goodman style. Even without the publicity attendant on his success as a bandleader, he would have ranked as one of the major jazz musicians of his generation.

Despite the seeming breadth of Goodman's musical interests, as evidenced by his performance of classical clarinet works, his jazz interests did not extend beyond the jazz styles that had been developed before World War II. His ventures into bebop in the late forties were unsuccessful largely because he could find nothing of interest in this jazz style. From then on he was content to live on his musical capital, playing his old arrangements when he was leading a big band or jamming on the old standard tunes of the twenties and thirties with small groups. See D. Russell Connor and Warren W. Hicks, *BG on the Record: A Bio-Discography of Benny Goodman* (1958).

JOHN S. WILSON

GOODYEAR, Charles (b. New Haven, Conn., Dec. 29, 1800; d. New York, N.Y., July 1, 1860), INVENTOR, was educated in the New Haven public schools. He worked as a clerk in the Philadelphia hardware firm of Rogers Brothers, a large retail, wholesale, and import house, and in 1821 entered into partnership with his father, Amasa Goodyear, who manufactured farm implements in New Haven. Charles established a retail outlet of A. Goodyear and Son in Philadelphia in 1826. The firm collapsed in 1829, however, and he was thrown in debtors' prison on several occasions before settling the firm's accounts in 1836.

In 1834, Goodyear began to experiment with improvements in rubber-curing processes. Although his "acid gas" process of 1837 improved the surface texture of rubber, the product could not withstand summer heat. In 1837, John Haskins of the Roxbury India Rubber Co. began to support Goodyear's experiments in Roxbury, Massachusetts. Acquiring Nathaniel M. Hayward's patent for a sulfur-turpentine process in 1839, Goodyear experimented with various sulfuric solutions. In Woburn, Massachusetts, that year he hit upon the "vulcanization" process of heating a rubber-sulfur mixture for several hours; and after perfecting it, he received a patent in 1844.

Goodyear personally failed to reap much financial reward from his invention. Under the pressure of heavy debts (nearly $200,000 at his death), he sold licenses on his patent at low royalty rates. However, he did receive immense acclaim at international exhibitions in London in 1851 and Paris in 1855. He published a two-volume study, *Gum Elastic and Its Varieties*, in 1853–55.

The Goodyear family also failed to profit from the "vulcanization" process. The government denied a request for renewal of the Goodyear patent, which expired in 1865. The Goodyear Rubber Co. founded by Frank Seiberling in 1898 bore no affiliation to the inventor's family.

⸻

Charles Goodyear's obsession with rubber seized him suddenly and with an intensity and persistence unusual even among inventors. It is not enough to point out that he followed his Connecticut Yankee father's bent for invention or that the premature rubber industry of the 1830s had shown before its failure what riches awaited the man who could "cure" rubber. Goodyear fell back on supernatural agency to explain the effect on him of a chance introduction to the subject. "A strong and abiding impression" came instantly upon him that he could achieve "an object so desirable and important, and so necessary to man's comfort." It was a "presentiment of which he could not divest himself under the most trying adversity." He ascribed it to "the Great Creator," who chose him as an instrument for the material advancement of mankind.

On this supposition Goodyear may be viewed as not only a fanatic but also a certifiable martyr. In debtors' prison he began many months of experiments, none of which showed a gleam of promise. He persisted despite chronic sickness, abject poverty, and complete ignorance of the scientific principles involved in the process, an ignorance (universal then and even now not entirely surmounted) that left him no course but random trial and error. Faith alone supported his belief that what he sought was possible at all. There were times when debtors' prison seemed as bearable as home to him, and not just through familiarity. Over the years of destitution and deferred hope, six of his twelve children died. Hardships and disappointments may have contributed to his wife's relatively early death (and certainly did to Goodyear's at 59). His kinder friends eventually came to ignore his recurrent predictions of imminent success; others mocked them. For months after he actually achieved his goal, he suffered from the reasonable fear that he would die before anyone took him seriously.

Yet amid all this, Goodyear's honesty made him refuse a French offer to buy his acid gas process; he explained to the bidders that his new vulcanization process would presently supersede it. He repeatedly chose imprisonment for debt over what he considered the dishonorable alternative of pleading bankruptcy. His dedication to improving the lot of mankind persuaded him to forgo a fortune as a manufacturer of rubber goods in order to develop still more for others to exploit, products for every conceivable use except, strangely enough, pneumatic tires,

although these had already been experimented with in England.

The moral that Goodyear himself drew from his astonishing life story was the age-old one of perseverance against odds. But many other persevering inventors, some perhaps as recklessly obsessed as he (though surely none more so), found only disaster and oblivion. Mindful of such unrecorded failures, we may also infer from Goodyear's story the price of technological progress even in its gestation. See Ralph F. Wolf, *India Rubber Man: The Story of Charles Goodyear* (1939).

ROBERT V. BRUCE

GOTTLIEB, Adolph (b. New York, N.Y., Mar. 14, 1903; d. New York, N.Y., Mar. 4, 1974), ARTIST, left high school in 1920 to study with **Robert Henri** and **John Sloan** at the Art Students League. He went to Europe (1921–22) to study art in Paris and to visit museums in Berlin and Munich. Gottlieb then returned to New York to finish high school; he also continued studying art at the Art Students League, the Parsons School of Design, and the Educational Alliance Art School. In 1929 he shared the Dudensing Galleries (N.Y.) National Competition Award for some expressionist landscapes and figures, which were displayed at that gallery in 1930. A founding member of a group of expressionist and abstract painters known as "The Ten," Gottlieb exhibited with this group annually between 1935 and 1940. In 1936 he joined the WPA Federal Art Project and in 1939 won the U.S. Treasury's national competition for a mural for a new post office in Yerrington, Nevada.

With *Eyes of Oedipus* (1941, Mrs. Adolph Gottlieb Collection) Gottlieb introduced his pictographic art—semiabstract symbolic forms presented segmentally. The themes were most often myths and fables. *Voyager's Return* (1946, Museum of Modern Art, N.Y.) is quite representative of this genre. Gottlieb later turned to a fully abstract-expressionist art with *The Frozen Sounds* (1951, Whitney Museum, N.Y.). In 1952 he designed the 1,300-square-foot stained glass façade of the Milton Steinberg Memorial Center in New York; his work consisted of abstract compositions based on Jewish themes. Some of his many other paintings are *Pictograph Symbol* (1942, Mrs. Adolph Gottlieb Collection) and *Red, Blue, Yellow* (1966, Marlborough-Gerson Gallery, N.Y.).

Gottlieb's work represented an important and unique stream in Abstract Expressionism, the clear and sometimes solitary image in a large field of color. In his early work the images are based on tribal signs of Native Americans or of antiquity, which are refined, simplified, and organized into elemental, subtly balanced compositions. While the original meaning of the signs has of course been left behind, a trace of their emotional power and universal import is still conveyed in Gottlieb's simplifications. He stated this as "the simple expression of the complex thought." Along with **Mark Rothko** and **Barnett Newman** he developed an art of meditation and suggestion, although he was more indebted to the Surrealist obsession with specific images and their associated meanings. This group can be clearly distinguished from the other mainstream, the "gesture" or "action" painters—**Jackson Pollock, Willem de Kooning,** and **Franz Kline**—whose work includes a strong element of Surrealist automatism and hence is based more on impulse and chance. Although Gottlieb's images do not readily lend themselves to conceptualization, his influence has been extended by his talent and interest in teaching and by his participation in the numerous artists' sessions that from 1948 drew the New York painters together. In these he was concerned more with attitudes of the artist than with styles.

Gottlieb painted representational pictures for the WPA art project in the middle 1930s in which the clear, rational structures of Henri Matisse are recalled, but by the middle 1940s he had developed his "pictographic" style, which retained the gridlike structures but included simple images suggesting motifs from ancient sources and evoking an exotic mythology. In the 1950s an increasing simplification cast off these echoes of antique

sources together with any traces of tribal myths and tended toward an opposition of only two unlike forms, often like sun and earth, and eloquently balanced in a color field of great richness. See Robert Doty and Diane Waldman, *Adolph Gottlieb* (1968).

HERSCHEL B. CHIPP

GOULD, Jay (b. Roxbury, N.Y., May 27, 1836; d. New York, N.Y., Dec. 2, 1892), RAILROAD MAGNATE, FINANCIER, after studying for a year at the Hobart Academy became a clerk in a general store in 1852 and served as a surveyor's assistant for several months in 1853. Forming his own survey company in 1853, he produced maps of Albany and Ulster counties. He also wrote *A History of Delaware County*, and *Border Wars of New York* (1856).

In 1856, Gould founded a tanning factory in Pennsylvania in partnership with Zadoc Pratt. He invested a large share of the firm's profits in personal banking and real estate ventures. When Pratt discovered this, he sold his interest in the tannery, and Gould formed a new partnership with Charles M. Leupp and David W. Lee (1857). He continued to embezzle funds and speculated heavily with Leupp's notes. His partners discovered these frauds when the panic of 1857 forced Leupp into bankruptcy. Although Leupp committed suicide, Lee pressed for control of the tannery. Gould armed the workers to expel his partner's agents from the factory in 1860. By the time Lee won control of the tannery through legal action in 1861, Gould had siphoned off the bulk of its resources.

Gould purchased the Rutland and Washington Railroad for ten cents on the dollar during the panic of 1857. By improving the facilities and manipulating stock prices he was able to sell the line at a large profit to the Rensselaer and Saratoga Railroad in 1858. He used the proceeds to buy the Cleveland and Pittsburgh Railroad, which he promptly sold at a profit to the Pennsylvania Railroad (1859). Forming the Wall Street brokerage house of Smith, Gould and Martin in 1860, he speculated in stock and gold during the Civil War.

In 1867, Daniel Drew put Gould and **Jim Fisk** on the board of directors of the Erie Railroad. Beginning in March 1868 the three engaged in a lively contest with **Cornelius Vanderbilt** for control of the Erie Railroad. They issued $8 million in watered stock despite a judicial restraining order. When Vanderbilt obtained a contempt-of-court ruling in New York, the three defendants established another office for the Erie in Jersey City. In April, Gould and Fisk dispensed more than $1 million in bribes to obtain a New York law that authorized the stock issue. Although they apparently had won, Daniel Drew resolved the affair amicably by retracting the $8 million of watered stock. Drew and Vanderbilt withdrew from the Erie management, Gould becoming president and treasurer and Fisk general manager and controller. The new directors had issued $23 million in watered stock by October 1868. Drew and other stockholders secured an injunction, but another judge placed the Erie under the receivership of Gould and Fisk.

Gould and Fisk conspired with Abel R. Corbin, the brother-in-law of President Ulysses S. Grant, to corner the gold market in the autumn of 1869. When Grant belatedly released the federal gold reserves on "Black Friday," September 24, 1869, Gould and Fisk sold short, making a profit estimated at $11 million. They continued to pillage the Erie for two more years, but the Erie stockholders finally managed to oust Gould from the board of directors in March 1872.

Gould gained control of the Union Pacific Railroad in 1874 and served as director until 1878. He transferred his interests to the Kansas Pacific Railroad in 1879. By threatening to engage in transcontinental competition, he forced the Union Pacific to consolidate at par with the dilapidated Kansas Pacific in 1880. He subsequently purchased the Missouri Pacific, the Texas and Pacific, and other southwestern railroads. He also acquired other enterprises including the New York *World*, the Western Union Telegraph Co., and the New York Elevated Railroad Co.

In 1883, Jay Gould appeared before a Senate committee investigating the relations between labor and capital; after listening to a portion of his testimony, the committee's chairman announced it was a story that would do the American people "no harm to hear." This might have been a derisory comment if the history had not illustrated the American myth—that of a poor boy making good. At the age of 14, Jay Gould left his father's home to step out for himself. "I did not make very much at farming while I was at it, and I thought I could succeed better at something else." Naturally Gould did not believe that his youthful activities were fraudulent or just plain unedifying. In his own words, the narrative of his early years involved a lot of "silly stuff." Years later a historian, bent on discrediting Gould, had to admit that "little today can be learned" of his early business capers.

Be that as it may, Gould's career continued the pattern of the American story. In 1860 he moved to New York City and became a partner in a brokerage house. At the time of his death, roughly thirty years later, he was one of the best-known and most execrated capitalists in this country. He left a fortune of $77 million. In his congressional testimony Gould said he was "not exactly" a "self-made" man, for the country had grown and he and others had "grown up with it." From the Civil War on, the economic growth of the country had certainly been spectacular. Central to all this expansion were bankers and brokers who created and channelized credit. Fortunes could be made by saving, investing in, and managing properties. This was prosaic and slow. It was more rapidly profitable to buy and sell opportunities for moneymaking, to speculate on the future. "A broker is almost by nature a gambler," wrote a contemporary.

Railroads, said Gould, were his "hobby." In 1868 and 1869 two "raids," as they were then called, demonstrated the methods of his "ring." Both episodes involved, directly or indirectly, the Erie Railroad. This road followed a route from the Hudson to Lake Erie through the southern counties of New York State. Since it was to recompense these districts for the state's earlier choice of a more northern route for the life-giving

Erie Canal, the state helped finance the Erie Railroad. So did counties and municipalities. Individuals, many of whom were English, also invested in it. In 1868, Gould and his allies battled Commodore Vanderbilt, the commander of the New York Central Railroad, for control of the Erie; although this "mixed enterprise" earned little money, it was a dangerous competitor, if extended, for the rich traffic pouring between the Lakes and New York City. This particular struggle was a stand-off. The next year Gould concocted a scheme to make money from the instability of the American currency following the Civil War. He would corner the market in gold. The government had a gold supply, and Gould counted on his influence with the Grant administration to keep this out of the free market where the price of gold fluctuated. As a sort of side effect, Gould expected a successful corner would stimulate the export of wheat, and the Erie and some western roads in which Gould was interested would have larger freights to the port of New York. Gould guessed wrong, for the U.S. Treasury sold gold.

Whatever the financial gains and losses, these episodes had an unforeseen result. They furnished the grist that the **Adams** brothers, **Charles F., Jr.,** and **Henry,** used in their literary exposé of Wall Street and business management. Nearly forty years before the era of the muckrakers, the Adamses spread in magazines the record of Gould's misdeeds. "There was a reminiscence of the spider in his nature.... It is scarcely necessary to say that he had not a conception of a moral principle.... He was an uncommonly fine and unscrupulous intriguer, passably indifferent to the praise and censure of society." The magisterial air and icy contempt of these articles has fixed once and for all the reputation of Gould—at least in the eyes of historians. But Gould had followers as well as detractors. Some of these, like Russell Sage, who appreciated Gould's cunning use of the corporate form, his daring, and his lack of scruples, made fortunes; others, like **Cyrus Field,** lost everything.

In those days American culture, it is claimed, took wealth alone as a measure of merit and power. It is somewhat surprising to discover, therefore, that conservative New York society never accepted Jay Gould. The exclusive New York Yacht Club blackballed him; Mrs. William Astor did not include him among her four hundred. Conceivably the explanation may have been, as Henry Adams wrote, that Gould had a "trace of Jewish origin." The balance of evidence is against this surmise. Actually Gould did not interest Society. He was a homebody and not a woman chaser; he was not a sportsman; he did not maintain a racing stable but cultivated orchids. Physically he was not prepossessing— short, shy, sallow, silent. But he was enough of a realist to feel anguish that his children—four boys and two girls—would eventually "dissipate their fortunes." That inheritance, though it never amounted to the "hundreds of millions" a socialist writer asserted, went to support lifestyles that Gould would hardly have approved. One daughter dispensed personal charities; another ran through two marriages to foreigners of title, ending as the Duchesse de Talleyrand; the boys allowed a railroad empire to crumble while they Americanized polo or sailed away to live abroad or build casinos on the Mediterranean Riviera. Eventually a quarrel over the division of the estate broke out and the courts took over. Gould might have condoned the gambling. He would surely have been at ease in the litigations, for he lived surrounded by injunctions and other writs all his life. See Maury Klein, *The Life and Legend of Jay Gould* (1986).

EDWARD C. KIRKLAND

GRADY, Henry Woodfin (b. Athens, Ga., May 24, 1850; d. Atlanta, Ga., Dec. 23, 1889), JOURNALIST, graduated from the University of Georgia in 1868. After studying law at the University of Virginia (1868–69), he decided on a career in journalism. He wrote some pieces for the Atlanta *Constitution* and in 1871 became editor of the Rome (Ga.) *Courier*. Later that year he bought two rival newspapers and combined them as the *Daily-Commercial*, but the new paper soon failed. In 1872 he founded the Atlanta *Herald*, but it, too, folded (1876). He wrote as a freelancer for the Atlanta *Constitution* and Augusta *Chronicle,* and then went to New York City to write for the New York *Herald.* He returned to Atlanta as the *Herald'*s special correspondent in 1876–77.

In 1879, with $20,000 lent him by **Cyrus W. Field,** Grady purchased a quarter interest in the Atlanta *Constitution,* serving thereafter as managing editor of the paper until his death. Through his writings in the *Constitution* Grady emerged as a leading spokesman for the post–Civil War South. He urged conciliation and a lessening of animosities between the North and the South. An advocate of laissez-faire capitalism and freedom of restraints on business, he vigorously backed crop diversification for the South, the development of local resources, and especially the growth of southern manufacturing and industry. An apologist for southern racism and an outspoken critic of such liberals as George Washington Cable, Grady expounded gradualism, believing the South should be left alone to solve the race problem, a solution that included education and training for blacks before they could become full citizens. Speaking at the New England Club in New York City in 1886, Grady popularized the term "the New South" to typify southern modernism. He became a popular and sought-after orator, making such speeches as "The South and Her Problems" (Dallas, 1887) and "The Race Problem in the South" (Boston, 1889).

The source of Grady's effectiveness was in the ebullient directness of his thought and personality. His mind turned on a few forcefully enunciated ideas, the chief one being that the South needed to grow and prosper through laissez-faire capitalism. The means were at hand: great natural and human resources, a newfound fondness for work—the plantation's leisurely pace was out of step in the world of profits and losses—and the South's readiness to cooperate with northern financiers. In place of an Old South of slavery and sectionalism would be a New South of factories and national markets. In 1880, **Mark Twain** found men of Grady's style everywhere in Dixie: "Brisk men, energetic of movement and speech; the dollar their god, how to get it their religion." For Grady the desire was only incidentally for personal riches or self-aggrandizement; he luxuriated in helping his region. The brisk hum and buzz of the editorial room invigorated him; his own staccatolike editorials in praise of Bourbon Democrats—he was fiercely partisan—reflected the whirling dervish of southern politics of the 1880s. His words were a soothing balm for a war-torn nation, but his solutions were mortgaged to the continued smooth workings of white racial dominance. He was eager to believe that southern race relations were harmonious and cherished by both races; and while he did on occasion criticize lynchings and cautiously defend black suffrage against belligerent racists, on balance his words were aimed at romanticizing racial realities to allay northern misgivings about abetting racism. His own death in 1889 removed him from the scene as two decades of racial violence exploded his mythical views of racial innocence and drove many of his class to acquiesce in the brutalities of white supremacy. See Raymond B. Nixon, *Henry W. Grady: Spokesman of the New South* (1943).

BRUCE CLAYTON

GRAHAM, Martha (b. Pittsburgh, Pa., May 11, 1894 [?]; d. New York, N.Y., Apr. 1, 1991), DANCER, moved with her family to California when she was 10. After the death of her father, a staunch Presbyterian who had attempted to stifle her early interest in the dance, she entered the Denishawn School in Los Angeles in 1916. She came east as a student-teacher when the school moved to New York in 1920 and made her initial professional appearance that year, dancing the leading female role in Ted Shawn's *Xochitl.* In 1923 she was employed by John Murray Anderson as a solo dancer for his *Greenwich Village Follies* but left two years later to embark on her career in modern dance.

Despite early difficulties Graham was chosen by Léonide Massine and Leopold Stokowski in 1930 to dance the feminine lead in the New York premier of **Igor Stravinsky**'s *Le Sacre du*

Printemps. That same year she founded her Dance Repertory Theater in New York and began to attract an increasing number of talented pupils. For many years she presented and participated in a yearly recital with her students. In 1932 she became the first dancer ever to receive a Guggenheim fellowship. In 1935 she helped found the school of modern dance at Bennington College in Vermont. At the Bennington dance festival in 1940 she staged *Letter to the World,* a work portraying the life of **Emily Dickinson** through a combination of dances and poetic recitations.

Over the years Graham choreographed more than 140 major dances. Many well-known composers wrote music especially for her, including **Aaron Copland** (*Appalachian Spring,* 1944, and *Dithyrambic,* 1931), Samuel Barber (*Cave of the Heart,* 1946), and Gian-Carlo Menotti (*Errand into the Maze,* 1947). She traveled under the State Department's International Exchange Program with her dance troupe in Europe (1945) and in the Near and Far East (1955–56). In 1957 she performed *Judith,* a solo work she created in 1950 to music by **William Schuman,** at the dedication of the Benjamin Franklin Congress Hall in Berlin. She has drawn inspiration from numerous sources, including American history (*Frontier,* 1935), biblical stories (*Embattled Garden,* 1958), and Greek drama, which inspired her most ambitious work, *Clytemnestra* (1958), an evening-length dance. She also collaborated with ballet choreographer **George Balanchine** in 1959 to produce *Episodes,* a two-part ballet set to the music of Anton Webern. A noted lecturer on the dance, she headed the Martha Graham School of Contemporary Dance in New York since its establishment in 1926, and the Martha Graham Foundation, founded in 1949, which became the Martha Graham Center in 1968. She produced a documentary film on the dance, inspired by her popular lecture-demonstrations, entitled *A Dancer's World* (1957), which won a Peabody Award. Graham made her final public performance in 1969, but she continued as a teacher and choreographer until she was well into her mid-nineties. In 1975, just before Rudolph Nureyev and Dame Margot Fonteyn danced as guests in her company, Graham pronounced, "The war has ended," which many interpreted as meaning that the perceived conflict between classical ballet and modern dance was over. This declaration was reinforced by the appearance of the classical ballet star Mikhail Baryshnikov with her troupe from 1987 to 1989.

⁂

Martha Graham felt deeply the influences of contemporary life—its music, its art, its dance. Although influenced by **Isadora Duncan** and other innovators, as a choreographer-dramatist she stood supremely alone. Originality was her gift, portrayal of emotion her obsession, dance-drama her medium for communication. In her long productive period she used the dance not only to entertain and delight but to present emotions and stir the soul—to dramatize life. Her dances were intense expressions of inner feelings. She combined pure dance with a commentary on life, using rapid, angular movements in percussive impulses of energy, blazingly and frighteningly alive.

For her dance-dramas she often used seemingly harsh music and classically economical stage decor, not realistic in form but expressionistic. She stripped the stage of recognizable things which then to photographic eyes became distortions. Yet to artistic eyes they were faithful to the mood and aesthetic purpose of the dance. Through use of symbol her stage props contributed to depth of feeling. For example, in *Night Journey,* the story of Jocasta and Oedipus, Jocasta carried a coiled rope, a suggestion of suicide, which later changed to represent the umbilical cord by which she and Oedipus were tied, and finally was altered to represent the tangled web of their fate.

As a director she was always considerate and cordial toward her hardworking company, yet not familiar. As a teacher she was exacting and uncompromising. She accepted praise and applause humbly, and in face of strain or imminent failure she grew in strength and power. A certain reserve and aloofness made closest friends often feel neglected.

Martha Graham's works are her spiritual testament. They are her declaration that paradoxically it is only through one's willingness to be the instrument of higher powers that one achieves individuality and wholeness. See Leroy Leatherman, *Martha Graham* (1966).

THOMAS E. CHENEY

GRAHAM, William ("Billy") Franklin (b. Charlotte, N.C., Nov. 7, 1918), RELIGIOUS LEADER, attended Bob Jones University (1936) and the Florida Bible Institute (now Trinity College) from 1937 to 1940, and graduated from Wheaton College in 1943. Having been ordained a Southern Baptist minister while in Florida in 1939, Graham became pastor of the First Baptist Church in Western Springs, Illinois, a Chicago suburb, in 1943. In 1944 he preached at open-air meetings for returning servicemen in Chicago, and later that year he became the preacher for Youth for Christ, a national crusade that Chicago pastor and religious radio broadcaster Torrey Johnson had founded. During 1945–47 he and Johnson held prayer meetings throughout the United States and Great Britain. In 1947, Graham became president of Northwestern Schools, a religious college in Minneapolis, a post he held until 1952. Rapidly becoming a major personality in the postwar period, he held an eight-week Christ for Greater Los Angeles crusade in 1949, drawing a total audience of 350,000. He obtained spectacular and well-publicized conversions, and won favorable coverage from the Hearst newspapers. After successful crusades around the United States in 1950, Graham formed the Billy Graham Evangelistic Association in Minneapolis to handle his schedules, correspondence, publicity, and finances. In 1950 he began preaching on ABC's radio program *The Hour of Decision,* and in 1951 he formed World Wide pictures, which has since made some three dozen films for Graham. In 1952 he resigned from Northwestern Schools and moved his home to Montreat, North Carolina. He also preached before troops in Korea and in Japan. In 1953, President Dwight D. Eisenhower sought his advice for the inaugural prayer, and during 1954–55, Graham held cru-

sades in Germany, Scandinavia, and Great Britain, where Queen Elizabeth II and Prime Minister Winston Churchill received him. In the years that followed, Graham toured India (1956), held his first New York City rally (1957), went to Australia and New Zealand (1959), held Crusade for Christ rallies in Latin America (1959), visited Africa (1960), returned to England (1960), and that same year pitched his revival tent in divided Berlin at the Brandenburg Gate. In 1967 he went to Yugoslavia, and he has preached (in English) before a Russian Baptist congregation in Moscow. Before the fall of the Soviet Union he returned there many times.

As an antidote to liberal Protestantism's influential journal *Christian Century,* Graham played a major role in founding the conservative evangelical weekly *Christianity Today.* When speaking out on political and social issues, Graham opposed the banning of prayer in schools, and he attacked the Supreme Court for being too permissive with criminals. However, a year prior to the Supreme Court's school desegregation decision, he was preaching to racially integrated audiences in the South—a policy he has continued successfully against considerable southern white opposition. A fervent foe of Communism, he supported American involvement in Vietnam and visited American troops there in 1966. Known as the "friend of presidents," Graham gave an invocation at President Lyndon B. Johnson's inauguration in 1965 and preached at President Richard M. Nixon's White House Sunday services in 1969. It has become almost obligatory for every American president to be seen as least once in his presence, though with Republicans like Gerald Ford, Ronald Reagan, and George Bush the number of visits invariably increase. Graham counseled and prayed with Nixon before and during the Watergate scandal (1972–74) that drove him from office. Recently published diaries (1994) of H. R. Haldeman, Nixon's chief of staff, reveal that Graham shared many of Nixon's deep resentments toward eastern intellectuals, especially Jews, blaming them for the growing opposition to Nixon and his Vietnam War policy. Graham was quoted in the diaries as making blatantly anti-Semitic comments, revealing religious prejudices and ethnic biases he has always been extremely careful never to display in public.

Between the 1970s and 1990s Graham continued his crusades worldwide, and although he has not lost his personal magnetism, their impact on the Christian faithful has diminished because other evangelists, utilizing the modern communications networks on cable television, have siphoned off a good deal of his audience. However, his organization, Billy Graham Evangelistic Association, and the various enterprises that he heads still generate $88 million a year in revenues and contributions and remain a model for modern evangelical crusaders. Graham presently suffers from Parkinson's disease and announced in November 1995 that although he will remain chairman of his organization, his son Franklin Graham will have the right of succession should he become incapacitated. Among Graham's many books are *Peace with God* (1953), *The Secret of Happiness* (1955), *My Answer* (1960), and *World Aflame* (1965).

What Billy Graham may have revived in modern times, above all, is revivalism itself. When he appeared on the national scene at the end of World War II, Graham's style of evangelism—fervent, vivid, biblical—was widely believed to be a quaint survival of folk religion soon destined to disappear. Graham has quite clearly shown otherwise.

He began his ministry in an era of concentration camps and atomic bombs, and continued it into decades of moral unrest and public violence—events that seemed to refute previously held liberal and rationalist optimism about the future. With this dark historical backdrop Billy Graham revived the kind of message that had long ago been preached by **Charles Finney, Dwight L. Moody,** and Billy Sunday, cutting through all social and intellectual complexities to offer his hearers a simple demand for a personal "decision." He also revived and extended his predecessors' organizational methods: advance work to prepare a city for one of his "crusades," coop-

eration with its local clergy, follow-up work with converts in the manner of Moody's "inquiry rooms," and highly professional use of the communications media of his day. Billy Sunday did not have television available, and Moody did not know radio; Graham used—and mastered—both.

Less doctrinaire than some fundamentalist leaders, Graham has been able to work with liberal "mainstream" Protestants in setting up his urban crusades. He has also challenged traditional Protestant antipathies by his platform appearances with such Catholic leaders as Richard Cardinal Cushing and Bishop Fulton J. Sheen in his early days, and numerous others since. See John Pollock, *Billy Graham* (1966).

PAUL A. CARTER

GRANT, Ulysses Simpson (b. Point Pleasant, Ohio, Apr. 27, 1822; d. near Saratoga, N.Y., July 23, 1885), PRESIDENT, graduated from the U.S. Military Academy in 1843. He served under Zachary Taylor and **Winfield Scott** in the Mexican War (1845–48) and was made a captain after the battle of Chapultepec (1847). He later served in California and Oregon but resigned from the army in 1854.

When the Civil War broke out, Grant was commissioned a colonel and was soon raised to brigadier general. Assigned to the western theater, with the aid of armored gunboats he captured Fort Henry and Fort Donelson on the Tennessee and Cumberland rivers. He became a major general in 1862 but was relieved of his command after the battle of Shiloh, in which, although victorious, he suffered heavy casualties. However, Abraham Lincoln restored him to his post, and in July 1863 he won a major victory at Vicksburg, Mississippi, which enabled Union forces to control the Mississippi River. Another victory at Chattanooga cleared the way for an invasion of Georgia. Lincoln then made Grant a lieutenant general and put him in command of all Union forces (1864).

Grant's major objective was to destroy **Robert E. Lee**'s army and capture Richmond. At the battles of the Wilderness, Spotsylvania Court House, and Cold Harbor, his army suffered heavy losses but gradually drove Lee's troops back. Capturing Petersburg, Virginia, below Richmond, after a long siege, he finally broke Lee's lines and forced him to surrender at Appomattox Court House (April 9, 1865), thus ending the war.

After serving as secretary of war under President Andrew Johnson, Grant was elected president in 1868 as a Republican, defeating Horatio Seymour, 214 electoral votes to 80. Grant's administration was marked by scandals in which cabinet members and close associates of the president were implicated. He was reelected in 1872, however, winning 286 electoral votes and defeating **Horace Greeley.** A hard-money man, Grant approved of the demonetization of silver (1873) and the resumption of specie payments. Grant's administration settled the *Alabama* Claims by the Treaty of Washington (1871), Great Britain agreeing to pay for damages inflicted by Confederate warships built in English shipyards. Grant sought to annex Santo Domingo (1870), but the Senate would not ratify the treaty. After retiring, Grant went on a world tour. In 1880 he almost succeeded in winning a third nomination for president on the Republican ticket. Shortly before his death of cancer he completed his *Personal Memoirs* (1885), an account of his military career.

───※───

Few 19th-century government institutions of any nation suffered such sharp oscillations in dignity, power, and effectiveness as the American presidency during the Buchanan-Lincoln-Johnson-Grant years. Grant earned the nomination and election in 1868 because of his forthright wartime leadership and his overtly neutral stand in the postwar duel that Johnson fought with congressional Republicans. But to the surprise of many contemporaries and subsequent commentators who anticipated vigorous behavior by Grant as president, once in the White House he happily accepted congressional preeminence in the national tripartite structure.

A scholarly consensus developed that Grant's lack of leadership, substandard appointments to high office, and admiration of entrepreneurial

leaders reflected simple weakness of character and intellect on his part. Assertions are common that Grant lacked awareness of America's urgent priorities, especially the preservation of natural resources and protection of the freedmen.

Grant was not insensitive, stupid (anyone who has read his *Personal Memoirs* knows better), or weak. Instead, his presidential behavior was the product of considered, thoughtful decisions based on his military career, his insight into American governmental processes, and his understanding of America's actual alternatives and priorities.

First to Grant's experiences and insights into government's workings. Except for the unhappy civilian interlude of the fifties, Grant had been a career army officer. Soldiers respected each president as ceremonial commander in chief, but presidents came and went. Long-service officers looked for career interests to Capitol Hill friends among Congress's appropriations and military affairs committeemen, who decided army budgets, promotions, and assignments.

During the war Grant observed carefully the shrewd way Lincoln cooperated with his Congresses. Grant's swift ascent to highest command derived from his courage and talent, but also from his harmonious obedience to presidential and congressional orders on such tender matters as emancipation and employment of black combat troops, both anathema to the McClellans of the Union galaxy. Then post-Appomattox developments taught Grant to keep tight the army's links with Congress, because Johnson's Reconstruction policy made the army a pawn in political power plays, involving awful risks to the not yet reunited Union of states. Becoming president, Grant acknowledged congressional leadership as a preexisting fact. This was not the self-immobilizing Congress of Buchanan's years. It was capable of creating policies appropriate to the national temper and purposes.

Herein was the key to the Grant of the seventies. His and the nation's priorities did not involve high-visibility national government, creation or maintenance of large-scale coercive bureaucracies for any purposes, or specially protected statuses in constitutional law for America's blacks. On the last point, our own time responds to differing drums. But a century ago, with ratification of the Fifteenth Amendment, an overwhelming assumption obtained in white America even among Negrophiles that no more need be done. The postwar amendments did not increase national power. Instead, very narrow bands of official state action concerning race were circumscribed. Congress's successive enforcement acts placed almost total enforcement responsibility in the national courts. Like congressional aids to railroads and to states' institutions of higher learning, the nation's concerns about intrastate racial decency were satisfied with almost no supervision or coercion.

Grant had no reason to quarrel with these alternatives or priorities. His presidential posture was not insensitively retrogressive or immobile. He sought stability on the White House—Capitol Hill front as well as the North-South racial salient. Measured by alternatives and priorities dominating his time, Grant's achievement was the ability to turn over to his successor an office that he had never let descend to the Buchanan-Johnson depths; a nation that held together despite the crisis of the 1876 disputed election returns. To the generation that had experienced 1860 and its costly aftermath, his success was symbolized not in Reconstruction's abandonment in 1876–77 but in the 1876 centennial celebration of American national existence. See William S. McFeely, *Grant: A Biography* (1974).

HAROLD M. HYMAN

GRAY, Asa (b. Paris, N.Y., Nov. 18, 1810; d. Cambridge, Mass., Jan. 30, 1888), SCIENTIST, received his MD from Fairfield (N.Y.) Medical School in 1831. He briefly practiced medicine, then turned to botany. His *North American Gramineae and Cyperaceae* (1834–35) described two hundred species and was illustrated with dried specimens. Meanwhile, he developed a close friendship with another botanist, John Torrey. He moved to New York City where he became curator of the Lyceum of Natural History in 1836. In

that year his *Elements of Botany* was published.

Gray and Torrey were among the first American botanists to classify plant species on the basis of natural affinity, and together they brought out two volumes of *The Flora of North America* (1838, 1843). In 1842 the first edition of Gray's *Botanical Text-Book,* which helped establish standard botanical terminology in English-speaking countries, was published. That same year he accepted the Fisher professorship in natural history at Harvard University. He directed the Harvard Botanic Garden and developed a herbarium and botanical library there that became the most valuable in America. He produced several important textbooks on various aspects of botany, including his *Manual of Botany* (1848). He was also a pioneer in the field of plant geography. He was a frequent contributor to numerous periodicals, and his book reviews on natural history were often considered to have literary and scientific significance in and of themselves.

Gray was a longtime friend of Charles Darwin. His botanical work influenced Darwin, and Gray in turn became one of the leading exponents of Darwin's theories of evolution as outlined in his *Origin of Species* (1859). Gray, however, maintained that an argument inferring Providence from design found in nature was not damaged by Darwin's ideas. He came into conflict with his staunchly antievolutionist friend and colleague at Harvard, **Louis Agassiz.** Though by no means a completely convinced advocate of all of Darwin's evolutionary theories, Gray was most concerned with giving them widespread American exposure to allow for a fair hearing and appraisal. In his view Agassiz was appealing to an incompetent tribunal in presenting his idealistic natural history to popular audiences. He tried to convince Agassiz by arguing from data he accumulated in a comparative study of Japanese and American flora but never succeeded in repairing completely the intellectual rift. After Agassiz's death in 1873, Gray replaced him as a regent of the Smithsonian Institution.

The basic program of Asa Gray's career as a botanist, lasting from 1825 to 1888, stemmed both from the development of biological sciences in the transatlantic world and from the expansion of the United States both in North America and overseas. By the time he became a partner of John Torrey on the *Flora of North America* in the late 1830s he had assumed the role of gathering botanical information in the form of dried specimens largely collected by others and, after processing it into publications, sending it into the stream of scientific literature abroad. The plants from the Wilkes Expedition of 1838–42 came eventually to him, as did many of the collections made by army expeditions in the trans-Mississippi West during the Mexican War and afterward. The opening of Japan by the Matthew C. Perry expedition and its successors immediately gave Gray materials with which to make comparisons between East Asia and eastern North America. After his retirement from teaching in 1873 he devoted his remaining years to a *Synoptical Flora of North America;* even after the labor of his whole career, it remained unfinished at his death.

The task of Gray, as an institution builder and educator, was also assigned by the American experience in his decades. In the 1820s and 1830s when there was no settled professional role for a botanist, he recapitulated the experience of the previous half-century by being a physician, a high school teacher, a naturalist collector, a member of the corps of an exploring expedition, a librarian to the New York Lyceum of Natural History, a traveler to the scientific centers of Europe, and a textbook writer before he achieved the Fisher professorship at Harvard. For the rest of his career he kept a full line of botanical textbooks and manuals supplied to every level of American education, in the process shaping the study of plant physiology as well as taxonomy. At Harvard, although he found the garden a burden and could get beyond elementary recitations with only a few students during the thirty years he provided the total curriculum in botany, he established the foundations of an international scientific center. On his retirement in 1873 his

duties fell to four different men who carried on not only a specialized department with laboratories but a museum, herbariums, the garden, and the unique Arnold Arboretum. Beyond Harvard he shaped the growth of the botanical profession well into the 1880s, an era of nascent universities from coast to coast.

Gray reached the height of his powers just as Charles Darwin published the *Origin of Species.* In spite of his heavy routine program both taxonomically and institutionally, Gray took a spirited part in the theorizing that went into the Darwinian synthesis. Darwin wrote Gray in 1855 a series of questions that led first to a statistical analysis of the flora of North America and then the comparison between Japan and the eastern United States. From the latter Gray deduced that closely related species in the two areas had descended with modification from a common ancestor, making him a Darwinian before the *Origin.* In addition to his judicious reviews of *Origin,* Gray attempted a reconciliation of the Darwinian position with the argument from design, which Darwin briefly considered as a strategy under the motto "Natural Selection not inconsistent with Natural Theology." Although he followed T. H. Huxley in rejecting this route to a theological accommodation, Darwin continued to rely on Gray for advice concerning his extensive experiments on plants that were an important part of his later career. Gray thus has a place in the history of 19th-century biology as a member of the Darwinian circle to add to his more mundane but solid accomplishments. See A. Hunter Dupree, *Asa Gray* (1959).

A. HUNTER DUPREE

GRAYSON, David. See Baker, Roy Stannard.

GREELEY, Horace (b. Amherst, N.H., Feb. 3, 1811; d. Pleasantville, N.Y., Nov. 29, 1872), JOURNALIST, was apprenticed to Amos Bliss, editor of the *Northern Spectator* at East Poultney, Vermont, during 1826–30. He moved to New York in 1831 and with Jonas Winchester founded and edited *The New Yorker,* a weekly, nonpolitical journal (1834–41). Meanwhile, he also contributed articles to the *Daily Whig* and began a political association with Whig leaders **Thurlow Weed** and **William Seward,** editing Whig campaign weeklies in 1838 (the *Jeffersonian*) and 1840 (the *Log Cabin*). In 1841 he founded the New York *Tribune,* which he edited until his death. He used the *Tribune* as a vehicle for championing a variety of educational and social reforms and a high protective tariff. In the 1840s he was an active supporter of utopian socialist communities. Under his editorship the *Tribune* set high intellectual and news-gathering standards and greatly expanded its circulation. His moral and political influence in both the urban and the rural North was very great.

In addition to his journalistic activities, Greeley made a series of unsuccessful tries for political office on both state and national levels. He served in Congress for three months (Dec. 1848—Mar. 1849). Although he worked closely with Thurlow Weed and William Seward in the 1840s, he resented their political realism and their failure to support his political ambitions. He was an early convert to the new Republican Party in 1854. An ardent opponent of slavery, he nevertheless rejected **William Lloyd Garrison**'s radical views. Denied a place on the New York delegation to the 1860 Republican convention, he served as a delegate from Oregon and helped to defeat Seward for the presidential nomination, thus precipitating a feud with Weed. During the Civil War, Greeley was torn between his belief in emancipation and a hatred of war. In 1864 he urged restoration of the "Union as it was" and engaged in futile peace negotiations with Confederate representatives in Canada. His reconstruction views were a mixture of "Universal Amnesty and Impartial Suffrage." Although he supported the Fourteenth and Fifteenth Amendments and the impeachment of President Andrew Johnson, he favored a conciliatory policy toward the South. He was sharply criticized in the North for signing **Jefferson Davis**'s bail bond in 1867, an act that ended the previous popularity of his Civil War history, *The American Conflict.* In 1872 he broke away from the Republican Party and accepted the presidential nominations of the Liberal Republican and Democratic parties on a platform calling for universal amnesty and civil service reform. He was decisively defeated by President Ulysses S. Grant. He died less than a month after the election.

※

Although he spent two-thirds of his life as one of the best-known New York City editors, Horace Greeley always remained a countryman at heart. As soon as he could afford it, he bought a farm in Westchester County where he could practice his agricultural theories. In appearance he was almost a cartoon figure of the rustic eccentric loose in the big city—his moon-shaped face, fringed with an uneven white beard, spectacles perched on his nose, poorly fitting white coats and flopping trousers, broad-brimmed hats, squeaky voice, and illegible handwriting delighted humorists and cartoonists. Yet exactly this ability to remain outwardly and at heart a lover of the countryside while operating at the center of national politics and journalism helps explain his effectiveness in winning the respect and affection of thousands of readers in a predominantly agricultural nation.

Although politics was Greeley's first love, his political influence was limited by his erratic course, in and out of parties, for or against various leading politicians. His true significance lay in his editorial work. He created in the New York *Tribune* a journal of opinion so widely and carefully read throughout the North, especially in its weekly editions, that by the early 1850s a shrewd observer reported, "The *Tribune* comes next to the Bible all through the West."

Greeley recruited a talented staff for his paper. Charles A. Dana and George Ripley, philosophically acute supporters of communitarian socialism, agricultural reformer Solon Robinson, composer William Fry, and poet Bayard Taylor all held full-time editorial posts. Occasional works appeared from intellectuals as diverse as **Margaret Fuller** and Karl Marx. Through their contributions Greeley offered his readers a wide range of information and opinion on current social, political, technological, religious, and cultural events.

Even more influential were Greeley's own editorials and articles. Always vividly written, whether supporting one of his continuous stream of reform crusades or ardently campaigning for a Whig or Republican presidential candidate, or even contradicting what he had written the previous week, his writings strove to arouse his readers and stimulate them to thought and action. Some might complain that his editorial views colored his news columns, for Greeley always believed in giving the reader more than just the facts. But thousands went on reading him as he promoted conservative Whiggism and communitarian socialism in quick succession, supported a protective tariff, praised labor unions, called for free homesteads for settlers, explored vegetarianism, pacifism, spiritualism, and abolitionism. He had little sense of discretion and never worried that he might make himself look absurd; as a result he was continually interesting. One could never tell what Uncle Horace might be up to in the next issue.

His political career grievously disappointed him, but his work on the *Tribune* made him not merely an outstanding journalist but perhaps the most influential popular educator of his day. See Glyndon G. Van Deusen, *Horace Greeley: Nineteenth-Century Crusader* (1953).

MILTON BERMAN

GREENBERG, Clement (b. New York, N.Y., 1909; d. New York, N.Y., May 7, 1994), ART CRITIC, attended the Art Students League in New York City (1924–25) and graduated from Syracuse University (1930). He worked as a clerk for the Civil Service Commission (1936–37) and with the Customs Service (1937–42). About 1940 he began to contribute articles on art, literature, and politics to a variety of magazines and newspapers, including the *Nation*, *The Saturday Evening Post*, *Arts*, and the New York *Times*. From 1940 to 1943 he was an editor of the *Partisan Review*, and from 1944 to 1945 he edited the *Contemporary Jewish Review*. He also served as art critic for the *Nation* (1940–50) and as associate editor of *Commentary* (1950–57).

Greenberg was an influential art critic, championing modernism in a stream of articles and reviews. His books include *Jean Miro* (1948), *Matisse* (1953), *Art and Culture: Critical Essays* (1961), and *Hans Hoffman* (1961). His *Collected Essays and Criticism (1987, 1993)* reprinted his writings from 1939 to 1969 in four volumes.

***

Clement Greenberg was a controversial figure, but even his opponents agreed that he was the most influential art critic in American history. Like John Ruskin, the 19th-century English critic with whom he has been compared for his effect on critical taste, he was a powerful spokesman for the new art of his time.

A prominent figure among New York intellectuals in the 1940s, Greenberg first attracted attention with his 1939 *Partisan Review* article "Avant Garde and Kitsch." This article added the word *kitsch* to the critical vocabulary and established Greenberg's devotion to "serious" art over trashy popular taste. A relentless foe of pretension, he continued his assault on the inauthentic in art for three decades, establishing himself in many eyes as the supreme arbiter of aesthetics in America and the one person who could, with a good or bad review, make or break artistic careers. Attacked by some as elitist and dogmatic, he wrote extensively on what he viewed as the mutual antagonism between art and the masses. He was widely respected and somewhat feared as a cultural historian (*Life* magazine described him as "formidably highbrow"), but he was never a popular tastemaker. His influence was rather on the critical, curatorial, and academic communities.

Greenberg's most important impact on critical thinking derived from his vigorous championing of the "New York School," to whose style he gave the name Abstract Expressionism. He wrote admiringly of the drip-and-spatter paintings of **Jackson Pollock** and the geometrical abstractions of sculptor **David Smith**. A dedicated formalist, Greenberg rejected all social and political criteria in favor of aesthetic standards in art.

An international influence, Greenberg's support of American modernism played an important role in shifting the world center of art from Paris to New York. See Clement Greenberg, *Collected Essays and Criticism* (1987, 1993).

DENNIS WEPMAN

GREENE, Nathanael (b. Potowomut [now Warwick], R.I., July 27, 1742; d. near Savannah, Ga., June 19, 1786), MILITARY LEADER, worked at his father's iron foundry, then moved to Coventry, Rhode Island (1770) to manage the family forge there. He served in the Rhode Island General Assembly (1770–72; 1774–75).

Although born a Quaker, Greene helped raise a militia company, and in May 1775, Rhode Island named him brigadier general of militia. The next month he was appointed brigadier general in the Continental army and participated in the American siege of Boston. When the British evacuated Boston (Mar. 1776), Greene was put in command of the city. In April he led his troops to New York and received the command of Long Island, but a fever prevented his presence during the battle of Long Island. In August he was made a major general and given command of the troops in New Jersey. After attacking the British at Staten Island, he was recalled to his headquarters when General Richard Howe landed at Throgs Neck. It was primarily Greene who persuaded George Washington to attempt to hold Fort Washington on Manhattan Island, with disastrous results when the British attacked on November 16. Four days later Greene was also forced to abandon Fort Lee across the Hudson River; in these two defeats the Americans lost nearly irreplaceable supplies.

When General Washington crossed the Delaware on Christmas Eve, 1776, to engage the British at Trenton, Greene led the left column, playing a conspicuous part in the victory. Washington later sent Greene to represent him at Philadelphia when the Continental Congress was questioning some of Washington's actions. With the army again, Greene helped save the retreat from the British turning movement at

Brandywine (1777), led the left column at Germantown, and spent the winter of 1777–78 at Valley Forge. In March 1778, Congress appointed him quartermaster general, and he helped establish a system of supply depots. He served in the battle of Monmouth (1778) and later helped drive the British from Rhode Island. He resigned as quartermaster general in 1780 after quarreling with the Continental Congress, and in September 1780, when Washington left his headquarters on the Hudson to confer with the French at Hartford, Connecticut, Greene was placed in command of the area around the Hudson. When **Benedict Arnold**'s plot to surrender West Point to the British was discovered soon thereafter, Greene succeeded Arnold in command of West Point. He presided over the military tribunal that condemned British spy John André to death.

After General Horatio Gates was defeated by the British at Camden, South Carolina, Washington gave Greene command of Gates's troops. Greene reorganized the southern army, and after his subordinate Daniel Morgan won the battle of the Cowpens in January 1871, Greene nearly exhausted Cornwallis's British army by leading it on a winter chase across North Carolina to the Dan River in Virginia. At Guilford Court House, North Carolina, in March and Hobkirk's Hill, South Carolina, in April, the British won Pyrrhic victories over him. Greene then forced them to evacuate Camden, and after winning another Pyrrhic victory at Eutaw Springs, South Carolina (Sept. 1781), the British withdrew to Charleston. After the war the people of Georgia voted to give Greene a plantation. He had pledged his personal fortune to endorse the paper of a war contractor who went bankrupt, and he spent the remainder of his life moving back and forth between Georgia and Rhode Island trying to restore his finances.

——— ∞∞∞ ———

"You see that we must again resume the partisan war," Nathanael Greene wrote after losing the battle of Hobkirk's Hill. Greene was probably the most skillful practitioner of "partisan war" in American military history, and since the term indicated what we call unconventional war or guerrilla war, he commands new attention in the late 20th century. He has long been regarded as second in ability only to Washington among the generals of the American Revolution, if not as Washington's superior as a strategist; the methods of Greene's strategy make him of special interest in the age of Mao Tse-tung and Ho Chi Minh. For Greene's southern campaign of 1781 seems designed to illustrate such Maoist principles as: "The ability to run away is the very characteristic of the guerrilla," and "Enemy advances, we retreat; enemy halts, we harass; enemy tires, we attack; enemy retreats, we pursue." Greene came to the command of the Southern Department when the Revolutionary army there had been ruined by Benjamin Lincoln's surrender of Charleston and Gates's defeat at Camden. Unable to field an army that could match Cornwallis's British army in open combat, Greene instead made his force the center of hit-and-run harassing operations by forces that modern terminology would call "guerrillas," under Thomas Sumter, Francis Marion, Andrew Pickens, and Light-Horse Harry Lee. The presence of Greene's army prevented the enemy from dividing his own field army enough to cope with the guerrillas. Cornwallis therefore attempted to strike at and destroy Greene's army, but Greene first led the British on an exhausting chase—the "race to the Dan"—and then when Cornwallis was debilitated enough to permit Greene to fight him, gave battle at Guilford Court House. Cornwallis won possession of the field, but he suffered such heavy losses that he abandoned the campaign. Greene then repeated the process of hitting, running, and fighting against subsequent British commanders until he completed the reconquest of the South. His tactics on the battlefield were consistently faulty, which helps explain his losing every pitched battle; but in strategy he displayed an ability unmatched by any other American soldier to weave irregular operations together with those of a field army into a coherent and victorious whole. See Theodore Thayer,

Nathanael Greene: Strategist of the American Revolution (1960).

RUSSELL F. WEIGLEY

GREW, Joseph Clark (b. Boston, Mass., May 27, 1880; d. Manchester, Mass., May 25, 1965), DIPLOMAT, graduated from Harvard in 1902. In 1904 he obtained a clerkship in the U.S. consulate in Cairo and then served with diplomatic missions in Mexico City (1906), St. Petersburg (1907), Berlin (1908), Vienna (1911), and again in Berlin (1912). He became counselor to the embassy in Berlin in 1917, and after a brief stint as chargé in Vienna, upon America's entrance into World War I, was named acting chief of the State Department's Division of Western European Affairs. After serving as secretary of the U.S. peace commission at Versailles (1919), Grew was appointed counselor to the embassy in Paris. This was followed by ministries in Denmark (1920) and Switzerland (1921). At the 1923 Lausanne conference Grew negotiated an American treaty with Turkey, which the Senate rejected. The following year he returned to Washington as undersecretary of state. Appointed chairman of foreign service personnel in 1924, Grew played a prominent role in that capacity in helping to further the professionalization of the service. After serving as ambassador to Turkey (1927–32), he was appointed ambassador to Japan in 1932.

During the next ten years he tried to bring about an American-Japanese understanding with moods alternating between hope and frustration. In January 1941 he informed Secretary of State **Cordell Hull** of a rumor current in Tokyo that in the event of war the Japanese would make a surprise attack on Pearl Harbor. At the outbreak of World War II, Grew was interned with the embassy staff but after six months was exchanged for Japanese diplomats. In August 1942 he was appointed special assistant to the secretary of state and two years later became director of the office of Far Eastern Affairs. He served as undersecretary of state from December 1944 until he retired in August 1945.

In retirement Grew served as chairman of the

board of the Free Europe Committee (the organizational sponsor of Radio Free Europe), as vice chairman of the National Security Committee, as a member of the Board of Review of the Atomic Energy Commission, and as honorary co-chairman of the Committee of One Million Against the Admission of Communist China to the U.N. He published *Sport and Travel in the Far East* (1910), *Report from Tokyo—A Message to the American People* (1942), *Ten Years in Japan* (1944), and *Turbulent Era: A Diplomatic Record of Forty Years* (1952).

⁕

Tall, handsome, athletic, urbane, Grew was one of a group of "Ivy Leaguers" who typified the subministerial ranks of the diplomatic service in the early years of the 20th century. A Republican in politics, he survived a succession of party changes in Washington through a combination of demonstrated ability and influential friends. He had served with distinction both in Washington and abroad before being named ambassador to Turkey. The qualities that he showed in five successful years at that post—tact with firmness, personal friendliness, an understanding of the problems of the other side, above all, a belief in diplomacy as a road to harmony and peace—characterized also his most important mission: his ten years in Japan. There, despite unfamiliarity with the language and a hearing difficulty that had plagued him from childhood, he made many warm personal friendships. His hope of finding a peaceful solution for the differences that divided the two nations persisted to the eve of Pearl Harbor, though by the fall of 1940 Japan's alignment with Germany and Italy had convinced him that stern measures to halt Japanese expansion were justified. In September 1941 he urged acceptance of Premier Fumimaro Konoye's proposal for a summit meeting with Franklin Roosevelt, which he continued to believe might have averted war in the Pacific. As special assistant to the secretary of state in wartime and as again undersecretary, he advocated a tolerable peace for the Japanese people and successfully opposed treating the emperor as a war criminal. He thus helped prepare the way for the lenient peace terms that Japan enjoyed and for her friendly postwar relations with the United States. See Waldo H. Heinrichs, Jr., *American Ambassador: Joseph C. Grew and the Development of the United States Diplomatic Tradition* (1966).

JULIUS W. PRATT

GRIFFITH, David Lewelyn Wark (b. La Grange, Ky., Jan. 22, 1875; d. Hollywood, Calif., July 23, 1948), MOTION PICTURE DIRECTOR, was educated in public schools. He held several jobs in the Louisville area, including that of a correspondent for the Louisville *Courier-Journal* (1891), before becoming an actor with the Mefert stock company in 1897. In 1907 he sold his first play, *A Fool and a Girl*, which failed. Turning to motion pictures, he played the leading role in *Rescued from the Eagle's Nest* (1907), which was filmed at the Edison studios. The next year he directed his first film, *The Adventures of Dollie* (1908). In 1913 he became associated with Mutual Films and in 1915 released *The Birth of a Nation*, which he adapted from a novel, *The Clansman*, by Thomas Dixon, Jr. The film, which dealt with the Civil War and the Reconstruction era, was the first "epic" movie with a large cast, spectacular battle scenes, and a high budget. It was enormously successful, earning more than $48 million during Griffith's lifetime. Despite its blatant racism, widely criticized at the time and since, it was regarded as a cinematic masterpiece.

Griffith made about five hundred films throughout his career, among them *Intolerance* (1916), an epic in which sixteen thousand "extras" were used in one scene. Many of Griffith's films dealt with important social questions. He originated and improved many filmmaking techniques, such as the close-up, backlighting, fade-in, fade-out, and night photography, and also the moving camera. In 1919, with **Charlie Chaplin**, Douglas Fairbanks, and Mary Pickford, Griffith founded the United Artists Corp. Less successful in making talking pictures, Griffith retired from filmmaking in 1932. He sold his partnership in United Artists in 1933 and lived in retirement and solitude for the rest of his life. Some of his major films include *Broken Blossoms* (1919), *True Heart Susie* (1919), *Way Down East* (1920), *Orphans of the Storm* (1922), and *America* (1924).

The debt that all filmmakers owe to D. W. Griffith defies calculation. Very early in his career he mastered most of the technical vocabulary of the cinema and then proceeded to simplify his vocabulary for the sake of greater psychological penetration of the dramatic issues that concerned him. Hence, what seemed like a precipitous decline in the early thirties with *Abraham Lincoln* (1930) and *The Struggle* (1931) was in reality a precious distillation of what had been achieved in earlier films.

Even before *The Birth of a Nation*, Griffith had managed to synthesize the dramatic and documentary elements of the modern feature film. One can already see the distinct outlines of *Birth of a Nation* and *Intolerance* in the consummately composed spatial adventures of audience-involving characters in *Musketeers of Pig Alley* (1912) and *The Battle of Elderbush Gulch* (1913). He traced the paths of his players across natural landscapes without the slightest intimation of incongruity. Indeed, the rural countryside of *True Heart Susie* and *The White Rose* is in complete harmony with the careless rapture of Lillian Gish and Mae Marsh. For Griffith, a tree was more than a tree; its strength and swaying vulnerability expressed metaphorically the emotional life of his heroines.

Much has been written of Griffith's Victorian heroines and their obsolescence in the supposedly Roaring Twenties. Where Griffith miscalculated, at least with his public, was in not realizing that film itself had made audiences self-conscious about the depiction of family feelings on the screen. Whereas Griffith tended more and more to use the screen to project his own particular emotional memories, his audiences began to demand that the screen mirror their own cooler fantasies. Unlike Chaplin, however, Griffith was never able to find a consistently viable form with which to express his emotional vulnerability.

The issue of Griffith's bigotry (toward Native Americans and Asians as well as blacks) cannot be swept aside with the broom of aesthetics. At the very least this bigotry, like Shakespeare's, reflects the attitudes of the artist's society. Classic or not, *Birth of a Nation* has long been one of the embarrassments of film scholarship. A frequent academic solution is to honor Griffith's stylistic contributions with a screening of *Intolerance*, itself an act of alleged atonement on Griffith's part for any bad impressions fostered by *Birth of a Nation*.

Curiously, *Birth of a Nation* has become more ambiguous over the years than its blatant bias would indicate. Flora Cameron, played by Mae Marsh, in particular seems more than the conventional victim of black lust. Even by Griffith's outraged Victorian moral standards, Flora's fierce virgin overreacts hysterically to every emotional challenge until, finally, she is doomed not so much by the relatively restrained black-faced pursuer who keeps insisting that he merely wants to talk to her as by her own increasing inability to cope with all the demands made on her feelings. Mae Marsh and Lillian Gish were brilliantly directed by Griffith because he believed in all their Victorian-American manifestations of white womanhood, and he could not bear to see them buffeted about by the disorder represented by Reconstruction. His small-town—agrarian vision of the world is intellectually inadequate by any standard, but of his emotional sincerity there can be no doubt.

Griffith devised a grammar of emotions through his expressive editing. The focal length of his lens became a function of feeling. Close-ups not only intensified an emotion, they shifted characters from the objective republic of prose to the subjective kingdom of poetry. Griffith's privileged moments are still among the most beautiful in all cinema. They belong to him alone since they are beyond mere technique. Griffith invented this "mere" technique, but he also transcended it. See Robert M. Henderson, *D. W. Griffith: His Life and Work* (1972).

ANDREW SARRIS

GRIFFITH, John. See London, Jack.

GRIMKÉ, Angelina Emily (b. Charleston, S.C., Feb. 20, 1805; d. Hyde Park, Mass., Oct. 26, 1879), and **Sarah Moore** (b. Charleston, S.C., Nov. 26, 1792; d. Hyde Park, Mass., Dec. 23, 1873), REFORMERS, daughters of a judge and slave-owner, were educated at home. Unable to tolerate life in a slave society, Sarah Grimké moved to Philadelphia in 1821 and two years later joined the Society of Friends. Following her example, Angelina Grimké began to attend Quaker meetings at Charleston and, failing in her efforts to convert her family and friends to her antislavery ideas, in 1829 joined her sister in voluntary "exile." She, too, became a member of the Philadelphia Society of Friends in 1831 and was gradually drawn toward abolitionism. In 1835, when **William Lloyd Garrison** published in the *Liberator* a letter she had written him in sympathy with his views, she became publicly linked to the abolitionist cause. Her *Appeal to the Christian Women of the South* (1836)and *Appeal to the Women of the Nominally Free States* (1837) were widely distributed by the American Anti-Slavery Society.

Sarah Grimké, converted by her sister to organized abolitionism, wrote a refutation of the pro-slavery Bible argument, *Epistle to the Clergy of the Southern States* (1836). Both sisters defied the opposition of the Philadelphia Friends to their antislavery activities, moved to New York City, and early in 1837 began to lecture to "mixed" audiences of men and women. Volunteering their services as the first female "agents" of the American Anti-Slavery Society, they undertook a New England lecture tour in the summer and fall of 1837. Attacked in the press and pulpit and by a "Pastoral Letter" of the Congregational ministerial association of Massachusetts, they persisted in their activities and asserted the rights of women in two vigorous pamphlets, Angelina Grimké's *Letters to Catherine Beecher* and Sarah Grimké's *Letters on the Equality of the Sexes, and the Condition of Women* (both 1838). The culmination of the speaking tour was Angelina Grimké's testimony before the Massachusetts legislature concerning antislavery petitions early in 1838. Her marriage to the abolitionist **Theodore Weld,** a Presbyterian, and her sister's attendance at the wedding on May 14, 1838, was the formal cause of their dismissal from the Society of Friends. The Welds and Sarah Grimké, who made her home with them for the rest of her life, first lived in Fort Lee, New Jersey, and later in Raritan Bay Union at Belleville, New Jersey, a communal settlement where they founded and ran a school. Both sisters taught school and shared in raising the Welds' three children. After the Civil War they moved to Hyde Park, Massachusetts, where they taught in Dio Lewis's progressive school until their retirement in 1867. They maintained an active interest and limited participation in antislavery and woman's rights activities until their deaths.

⁂

Angelina and Sarah Grimké had a unique role in the antislavery movement as the only white southern women to become leading abolitionists. Their firsthand knowledge of conditions within a slave society made their antislavery testimony particularly effective. Their lifelong struggle against race prejudice and their often expressed conviction that such prejudice was the mainstay of the slavery system placed them far in advance of many white abolitionists, whose concern for the slave was tinged by patronizing paternalism. Their deep political commitment on this issue found expression in their personal lives when, after the Civil War, they discovered the existence of two black nephews, sons of their brother Henry and one of his slaves. The sisters publicly acknowledged the relationship, accepted the young men as part of their family, and helped send them both through college.

Contemporaries acclaimed them primarily as abolitionists. Their early pamphlets were widely circulated; Angelina Grimké's *Appeal to the Christian Women of the South* stands alone in its indictment of slavery from a southern woman's point of view and in its direct appeal to women to defy the slave laws. The sisters' New England speaking tour enabled thousands of listeners to hear their antislavery message. Their pamphlet *American Slavery as It Is: Testimony of a Thousand Witnesses*, which they compiled from southern newspapers and which Theodore Weld edited, was the most widely circulated antislavery publication until the appearance of **Harriet Beecher Stowe**'s *Uncle Tom's Cabin*, for which it served as a source. Angelina Grimké was the first woman ever to testify before the Massachusetts legislature and can claim the distinction of silencing a riotous mob in her speech at Pennsylvania Hall on May 16, 1838, hours before the hall was burned to the ground.

Historically, the Grimké sisters' greatest significance lies in their pioneering feminism. As the first American-born women to make a public speaking tour, they opened the way for women to take part in public affairs. As the first female antislavery agents, they early saw the connection between civil rights for black Americans and civil rights for women. In the face of attacks and criticism by the public, by ministers and even by male abolitionists, they stood their ground, defended their position, and advanced to demanding full equality for women in all spheres of life. Sarah Grimké's pamphlet, *The Equality of the Sexes, and the Condition of Women*, represents the first serious discussion of women's rights by an American woman. They early recognized that the "woman question," which appeared to male abolitionists as a divisive issue, would serve to free the energies of thousands of women and join them to the abolitionist cause. The spectacular growth of female antislavery societies following upon their tour found its full organizational expression in the subsequent antislavery petition campaigns. Moreover, the sisters influenced directly many of the women who would later raise feminism to national and eventually international significance. In their writings and in their persons, the Grimké sisters embodied the fusion of abolition and women's rights, which characterized pre–Civil War reform. See Gerda Lerner, *The Grimké Sisters from South Carolina* (1967).

GERDA LERNER

GRONLUND, Laurence (b. Copenhagen, Denmark, July 13, 1846; d. New York, N.Y., Oct. 15, 1899), REFORMER, was educated at the University of Copenhagen, where, after an interruption during the Danish-German War (1864), he received an MA in 1865. He began to study law, and after migrating to the United States in 1867, he continued his studies while working as a teacher of German in Milwaukee's public schools. In 1869 he was admitted to the Illinois bar and then practiced in Chicago for a number of years. He soon became convinced of the desirability of socialism and in 1878 published *The Coming Revolution: Its Principles*, written in the form of a dialogue. In 1884 he published his major work, *The Co-operative Commonwealth*. Influenced by Karl Marx's theories, Gronlund held that the capitalist class was unjust and exploitative and that revolution was inevitable. He opposed reforms that would strengthen capitalism and postpone revolution. Also influenced by Herbert Spencer, he viewed socialist society as a living organism with each part contributing to the welfare of the whole, replacing individualism with interdependence. However, Gronlund rewrote later editions of *Co-operative Commonwealth* to eliminate his disapproval of reform and emphasize moral and religious solidarity rather than economic factors in bringing about the socialist transformation.

The success of this book led Gronlund to undertake lecture tours throughout the country. In 1887 he published *Ça Ira! or Danton in the French Revolution* and a tract, *An Answer to Henry George*. He worked briefly under **Carroll D. Wright**, U.S. commissioner of labor statistics, in Washington, D.C., but soon returned to lecturing. In 1888 he was elected a member of the executive committee of the Socialist Labor Party. During the 1890s he published *Our Destiny: Influence of Nationalism on Morals and Religion* (1891) and *Socializing a State* (1898). His *New Economy: A Peaceable Solution of the Social Problem* (1898) rejected class struggle and revolution in favor of gradual reform leading to collectivism. In 1899 he was briefly in charge of the labor department of the New York *Journal*.

Gronlund prided himself on thinking and writing in the American idiom. It was appropriate, therefore, that as a pioneer American Marxism his career and ideas should epitomize the drift of native radicalism toward revisionism and nondoctrinaire reformism. Although he endorsed the Marxist theory of historical dynamics arising out of class struggle, he minimized the revolutionary role of the industrial proletariat under capitalism, emphasizing instead the leadership to be furnished by intelligent men and women of all classes who would be sensitive to the injustices and inhumanity of the capitalist order and who would know how to guide the revolution to constructive ends.

On the difficult problem of "immediate demands"—reforms in the existing capitalistic system which if successful would tend to strengthen the system and defer the revolution—Gronlund at first temporized but later endorsed such reforms heartily as he gained a greater appreciation of the potentially revolutionary role of the state in transferring power through legislation. This entailed abandonment of the traditional Marxist doctrine of the state as a committee of the bourgeoisie. Gronlund's uncertainty on the revolutionary role of organized labor was characteristic of American radicalism. He had much in common with **Edward Bellamy,** whose utopian romance *Looking Backward* (1888) precipitated the Nationalist movement with which Gronlund identified himself. In the end, the concept of the nation became the receptacle for the social idealism that was presumed to have been the shaping force of American historical experience. Gronlund's ultimate position was closer to the New Left than to the Old. See Solomon Gemorah, "Laurence Gronlund—Utopian or Reformer?" *Science and Society,* 33 (1969), 446–58.

STOW PERSONS

GROSS, Samuel David (b. near Easton, Pa., July 8, 1805; d. Philadelphia, Pa., May 6, 1884), SUR-GEON, graduated in 1828 from the Jefferson Medical College, recently founded in Philadelphia by Dr. George McClellan. Gross then worked in McClellan's dispensary and published a number of translations of French and German medical texts. In 1830 he published *Treatise on the Anatomy, Physiology, and Diseases and Injuries of the Bones and Joints,* but because his Philadelphia practice was not very large, he moved in 1830 to Easton, Pennsylvania. In 1833 he was appointed a demonstrator of anatomy at the Medical College of Ohio in Cincinnati, serving until 1835.

Gross was appointed professor of pathological anatomy in the Medical Department of Cincinnati College (1835); professor of surgery at the University of Louisville (1840); and professor of surgery at the Jefferson Medical College (1856). He also served for a year (1850–51) at the University of the City of New York. Although active as both a teacher and a surgeon, Gross also published extensively. Among his publications were *Elements of Pathological Anatomy* (1839), *A Practical Treatise on the Diseases and Injuries of the Urinary Bladder, the Prostate Gland, and the Urethra* (1851), and *A System of Surgery, Pathological, Diagnostic, Therapeutic and Operative* (2 vols., 1859), all of which became standard works. At the request of the federal government he also wrote *A Manual of Military Surgery* (1861) for the use of army surgeons.

Samuel D. Gross is perhaps most remembered as the central figure in **Thomas Eakins**'s painting *The Gross Clinic* (1875), but he was one of the most successful and best-known physicians in 19th-century America. He began to practice before the introduction of anesthesia in 1846, and his career spanned the emergence of Joseph Lister's principle of antisepsis, which made surgery not only painless but much safer and more efficacious as well.

Early in the century it was unusual for American physicians to translate European works, much less write their own books. Gross's *Elements of Pathological Anatomy,* the first on this subject in English, hence brought additional credit to its author. The book was generally recognized as one of the significant accomplishments of American medicine.

While always an active medical practitioner, busy teacher, and spokesman for the profession, Gross continued throughout his career to be a prolific writer. He edited a medical journal and authored one of the most widely used textbooks of surgery, which went through six editions between 1859 and 1882. He was also a historian of note, being one of the first to call attention to the ovarian surgery performed by Ephraim McDowell in 1809. In 1861 he edited *The Lives of Eminent American Physicians and Surgeons,* and shortly after his death, his sons published his two-volume *Autobiography,* rich in details of 19th-century medicine.

Gross favored a conservative approach to medicine and surgery. He claimed, for instance, that when Lister's somewhat complicated system of antisepsis was first being widely discussed around 1870, American surgeons had little need for it because their rate of postoperative infection was already low. So, too, he was a great proponent of so-called conservative surgery, by which the surgeon attempted to save limbs rather than amputate. "Comparatively few knivesmen … exist among us," he said in 1876.

Gross's major contribution was in teaching the broad principles of surgery. That these were as well taught in this country as anywhere in the world was in no small measure owing to his untiring efforts. See Samuel D. Gross, *Autobiography* (2 vols., 1887).

GERT H. BRIEGER

GUGGENHEIM, Daniel (b. Philadelphia, Pa., July 9, 1856; d. near Port Washington, N.Y., Sept. 28, 1930), INDUSTRIALIST, completed one year of high school before going to Switzerland in 1873 to help manage an embroidery factory owned by his father, Meyer Guggenheim. He returned to the United States in 1884 to head the family's lace importing business. With his brothers he sold the business to assist his father in the development of a silver and lead mining and smelting business. (Meyer Guggenheim had purchased silver mines in Colorado in 1881 and constructed a smelting plant there in 1889.) In 1891 the family also acquired ore deposits and built two smelting plants in Mexico. When rival firms organized the American Smelting and Refining Co. in 1899, the Guggenheims entered a price war against the combine, and by 1901 they forced their competitors to reorganize American Smelting and Refining under Guggenheim control.

As director of the American Smelting and Refining Co., Daniel Guggenheim developed efficient integration of mining, smelting, and refining in the United States. The company acquired large interests outside lead and silver. It bought copper mines and gold fields in Chile, tin mines in Bolivia, and rubber plantations and diamond mines in the Congo and Angola. Guggenheim also directed the operation of such subsidiary firms as the Guggenheim Exploration Co., the American Smelters Security Co., the Chile Copper Co., and the Utah Copper Co. He retired from the company in 1919.

Guggenheim was an important figure in the Ballinger-Pinchot conservation dispute of 1909–10. Forming a syndicate with **J. P. Morgan** in 1906, he purchased vast mineral deposits in Alaska. In 1907, Richard A. Ballinger, then a commissioner of the General Land Office, approved the sale of extensive coal fields to the Cunningham syndicate, which was secretly affiliated with the Guggenheim-Morgan concern. When Ballinger became secretary of the interior under President William H. Taft in 1909, he terminated an inquiry into the Cunningham claims and discharged the investigator, Louis R. Glavis. **Gifford Pinchot,** chief of the U.S. Forest Service, and other government officials who remained loyal to former President Theodore Roosevelt publicly attacked Ballinger's conservation policies, including his decision about the Cunningham claims. Although adverse publicity induced Ballinger to resign in 1911, the Taft administration declined to invalidate any sales of government mineral deposits to the Guggenheim-Morgan interests.

American Smelting became embroiled in political controversy during the Mexican Revolution of 1910–20 as owners of large mining and smelting operations in Mexico. During the Revolution the mines worked only fitfully. Since major American Smelting holdings were in northwest Mexico, occupied by Pancho Villa's forces, a working arrangement was negotiated: coal was supplied for Villa's locomotives in return for protection. American Smelting switched its support to Venustiano Carranza after Villa suffered decisive military defeats in 1916.

Guggenheim was an active philanthropist throughout his life. In addition to sponsoring free band concerts in Central Park in New York City, he also established the Daniel and Florence Guggenheim Foundation and the Daniel Guggenheim Fund for the Promotion of Aeronautics.

It is impossible to discuss Daniel Guggenheim without discussing the Guggenheims. Meyer Guggenheim—of whose seven sons Daniel was the second—insisted that his boys "be as one." Five of his sons—Isaac, Daniel, Murry, Solomon, and Simon—took his advice and stuck together, constantly conferring, discussing, and bickering but always coming to a unanimous decision. Still, as *primus inter pares,* Daniel was acknowledged as "head" of the House of Guggenheim.

The strong domineering patriarch Meyer arrived at Philadelphia from Switzerland in 1847. Starting as a journeyman tailor and peddler, by 1880 he was able to turn over to his sons his large lace and embroidery business and dabble in stock speculation and private loans. A "flyer" in mines near Leadville, Colorado, turned up a bonanza in 1881, and Meyer saw larger horizons. With a characteristic decisiveness he had his sons abandon the lace business to run his newly built smelter at Pueblo, Colorado, in 1890.

From the first the Guggenheims followed the practice of hiring the best talent available, no matter what the cost, to make up for their own mediocrity in metallurgy and smelter management. This rule paid off handsomely, for their profitable and efficient workings gave the family a strong platform for their forte: corporate finance and metal marketing. While one family member usually inspected most propositions, and the family made a team decision, expert advice was always sought and never dismissed for frivolous reasons.

Daniel, in charge of the New York office and supervisor of all company operations of M. Guggenheim's Sons, became the family leader as their interests spread to Mexico, to copper mines, and to the Perth Amboy, New Jersey, copper refinery. Having avoided joining H. H. Rogers's "smelting trust," the American Smelting and Refining Co., because of their belief that it was poorly financed and would be inefficiently run, the Guggenheims, owning a relatively small operation, were able to take over ASARCO in 1901 as the price of bailing it out. Daniel, who did the negotiating, took control of ASARCO for the family, becoming a director, chairman of the board, and chairman of the executive committee; Murry and Solomon became directors and members of the executive committee, later joined by Isaac and Simon. In 1905, Daniel became president of the company and, ex officio, a member of the finance committee.

A private staircase connected the brothers' offices, and each morning they met in Daniel's office to talk over the day's problems. There was a common saying, "Wherever Daniel sits is the head of the table." Stocky, jovial, and ebullient, with a head full of ideas that his restless energy could transmute into money, Daniel was truly a bold and dynamic figure in mine finance. His was the driving force that made ASARCO the dominant firm in world nonferrous metal mining. Daniel impressed all who saw him. The official company history quotes the lawyer William D. Guthrie as telling Francis Brownell, "You can see brains sticking out all over Daniel Guggenheim's face."

Under Daniel's leadership ASARCO became involved in numerous copper enterprises ranging from the huge open-pit copper mine at Bingham Canyon, Utah, a pioneering achievement, to the immense Chuquicamata copper undertaking in Chile. ASARCO's characteristic mark was the large project. Daniel's retirement was forced by recurrent heart trouble, and for the last decade of his life he had little to do with business. See Harvey O'Connor, *The Guggenheims: The Making of an American Dynasty* (1937).

MARVIN D. BERNSTEIN

GUTHRIE, Woodrow Wilson ("Woody") (b. Okemah, Okla., July 14, 1912; d. New York, N.Y., Oct. 3, 1967), COMPOSER, SINGER, attended schools in Okemah. In 1927 an uncle taught him to play the guitar and fiddle, and he began composing and singing folk songs. In 1937, Guthrie moved to California where he continued writing and singing songs dealing with the Dust Bowl conditions of Oklahoma and Texas and with the life of migrant workers and farm laborers. He performed on station KFVD in Los Angeles in 1938, and after a brief time performing in Mexico, obtained his own show at KFVD the following year.

Moving to New York City in 1940, he recorded *Dust Bowl Ballads* for Victor Records, including the songs "Hard Traveling," "Death Valley Scotty," and "The Talkin' Dustbowl Blues." In 1940 he toured the Southwest and South with Pete Seeger, appearing in migrant labor camps and at union meetings. Guthrie performed on such New York radio programs as *Pursuit of Happiness* and *Cavalcade of America* and on WNYC. He joined the newly formed Almanac Singers in New York with Seeger, Lee Hays, and Millard Lampell; the group sang to union and farm workers across the country in 1941 and again in 1945. His autobiography, together with a few of his songs, appeared as *Bound for Glory* (1943). In 1943–44 he served in the U.S. merchant marines. He also wrote such patriotic songs as "Reuben James" (1943), in collaboration with the Almanac Singers, and "Round, Round Hitler's Grave" (1943). Guthrie helped Seeger and Hays form People's Song, which booked folk song concerts through its agency, People's Artist Bureau, and published new songs in its *People's Song Bulletin*. He also recorded for Moses Asch's Folkways Records in 1945, and his output included the popular "This Land Is Your Land" (1940).

A collection of thirty songs and sketches appeared as *American Folksong* (1947), and this was followed by *Born to Win* (1965), a collection of stories, letters, poems, and essays, edited by Robert Shelton. Afflicted by a hereditary illness, Huntington's disease, Guthrie spent all of his life after 1955 in a hospital.

※

Woody Guthrie's fame rests on his decisive influence on our popular culture as expressed in his many songs (he claimed one thousand) and writings. He was a nonconformist in the best American tradition. In the 1940s, uniting grassroots music with contemporary content, Woody and his close friends Leadbelly and Pete Seeger generated a vital new popular music. Since then a steady stream of old-time ballads and blues, gospel, and breakdowns has invaded our cities from coast to coast.

In the 1960s this country-inspired music, played on guitars, harmonicas, fiddles, and banjos, burst into full bloom, first as a protest song movement and later as folk-rock. To **Bob Dylan** and many others, Woody's songs of the industrial unemployed, the migrants, and the landless farmers of the Dust Bowl represented the real America. In revolt against their own middle-class backgrounds, these younger songwriters were drawn to him as a symbol of integrity, social concern, and personal freedom. Woody became their hero.

Like many leading artists, writers, and musicians, Guthrie was part of the radical movement of the Depression years. Never a doctrinaire propagandist for the causes he espoused, he wrote of the human condition prodigiously and with incomparable country wit, humor, and compassion. "I hate a song that makes you think you are not any good!" he once wrote. "I am out to sing songs that will prove to you that this is your world … no matter how hard it's run you down and rolled over you.… I am out to sing the songs that make you take pride in yourself and in your work." See Henrietta Yurchenco, *Hard Traveling: The Life of Woody Guthrie* (1970).

HENRIETTA YURCHENCO

HALAS, George Stanley (b. Chicago, Ill., Feb. 2, 1895; d. Chicago, Ill., Oct. 31, 1983), SPORTS FIGURE, was graduated in 1918 from the University of Illinois, where he played three varsity sports. During World War I he served as an ensign in the navy. He then worked as an engineer for the Burlington Railroad (1919–20). He briefly played baseball for the New York Yankees (1919), but a hip injury ended his career. In 1921, with the aid of A. J. Staley, a manufacturer, Halas founded a professional football team, the Decatur (Ill.) Staleys. He moved the team to Chicago in 1921 to join the new National Football League and renamed the team the Chicago Bears in 1922. Halas played end for the team until 1929; he was also owner, president, and coach.

By signing University of Illinois all-American "Red" Grange to play for the Bears in 1925, Halas won publicity, prestige, and money for professional football. As a coach he developed the T-formation, the man-in-motion play, and the use of spread receivers. By using more passing and wide-open offenses, he helped make pro football more popular.

In 1942, Halas left the Bears to serve as a captain in the naval reserve. He returned to Chicago in 1946 and, except for a brief retirement (1955–57), remained coach until the end of the 1967 season. His son succeeded him as president of the Bears in 1964, but Halas remained chairman of the board until 1968. During his career Halas led his teams to eight divisional titles and six NFL championships. His teams won 321 games, lost 142, and tied 31. In 1963, Halas became one of the charter members of the National Football League Hall of Fame in Canton, Ohio. In 1970, Halas was elected president of the National Conference of the NFL, a position he held until 1982. He also continued to run the Bears' operations with a firm hand from the front office throughout the 1970s.

The expansion of American sporting frontiers during the 1920s afforded lucrative opportunities for zealous promoters like George Stanley Halas. The third son of an immigrant tailor, Halas grew up convinced that sports and formal education were the surest routes to economic success. While at the University of Illinois the earthy, six-foot, square-jawed Halas won letters in baseball, football, and basketball—destined to capture armies of fans whose support would enrich many a promoter willing to risk capital and skill.

In 1920 baseball already provided a model of a successful venture. After an abortive attempt at a major-league baseball career, Halas in 1921 turned his attention to football, becoming a pioneer organizer of the National Football League while also securing a Chicago franchise for himself. As owner, coach, and player for his Chicago Bears, Halas drew inspiration from his former coach Robert Zuppke's observation that collegiate football afforded a reservoir of talent for a professional league. For the next twenty years Halas nursed the floundering NFL through adversities such as low profits, failing franchises, public apathy, and continuing competition from rival spectacles including rival promoters of professional football.

Halas consistently wrung profits for his Bears by such devices as hiring charismatic stars like "Red" Grange and by renting the spacious Wrigley Field baseball facility to accommodate crowds. His influence reached into all areas of professional football promotion. A tireless worker, he often labored eighteen hours a day during a playing season. He employed daily practices, training films, and talented assistants to improve his teams, but this achievement was overshadowed by his legendary reputation as an offensive genius: his development by 1940 of the T-formation provided the sport with an awesome offensive weapon. Although Halas's innovation owed much to subordinates like Clark Shaughnessy, the T-formation did become the basic offensive weapon in football, and its adoption signaled the coming of age for the NFL. From 1940 to this day most strategic and stylistic innovations in American football come from the professional camps.

George Halas also played a major role in the successful commercialization of football. With his owner allies and talented assistants he led the NFL through a tough developmental phase. But after 1940, Halas's fate, like that of Connie Mack in baseball, was that of the pioneer innovator who stayed too long and failed to assess his waning energies and influence. By the late 1950s Halas's era was over and the NFL faced new problems, including those of growth and expansion, of coping with a rival major league, of handling an "athletic revolution" that included player unionization, and above all the mighty influence of television interests. Yet Halas stubbornly clung to the controls of the Bears until 1968 when old age and arthritis forced him to the press box; his carping presence afforded local color for journalists who sometimes ridiculed him as an albatross around the necks of Chicago fans and of NFL leaders. But Halas's consolation came via profits that made him a millionaire and from the honor of being voted a charter member of professional football's Hall of Fame, established at Canton, Ohio, on the site where Halas had participated in the organization of the NFL. See George Vass, *George Halas and the Chicago Bears* (1971).

DAVID Q. VOIGT

HALE, George Ellery (b. Chicago, Ill., June 29, 1868; d. Pasadena, Calif., Feb. 21, 1938), ASTRONOMER, graduated from the Massachusetts Institute of Technology in 1890. While a student there he invented a spectroheliograph, a device used to photograph the sun and analyze its composition. During 1890–96 he directed the Kenwood Astrophysical Laboratory in Chicago, which his father had built for him, and in 1891 he took the first photographs of sunspots. He was appointed associate professor of astrophysics at the University of Chicago in 1892. After having served as editor of *Astronomy and Astrophysics,* Hale in 1895 founded the *Astrophysical Journal*, which he edited for the next forty-five years. In 1895 he also took charge of constructing the Yerkes Observatory at Lake Geneva, Wisconsin, which contained the world's

largest refracting telescope. He was director from its completion in 1897 to 1905. Hale supervised the construction of the Mount Wilson Observatory in Pasadena, California. As its director (1904–23) he did research into sunspots and discovered solar magnetism, double stars, and distant nebulae. Besides being responsible for the founding of the National Academy of Science's National Research Council in 1916, which promoted cooperation between scientists and the armed forces during World War I, Hale organized the International Astronomical Union in 1919. In 1928 he became supervisor of the projected Mount Palomar Observatory in California. Among his many books are *The Study of Stellar Evolution* (1908), *The Depths of the Universe* (1924), *Beyond the Milky Way* (1926), *Signals from the Stars* (1931), and *The New Heavens* (1932).

⊕

Hale's far-reaching influence on American astronomy was the result of his ability to grasp the most important astronomical problems of the time, to recognize which instrumental developments would be required for their solution, and to convince others that his projects deserved the support needed for their realization.

After having designed and supervised the construction of the Yerkes Observatory with its 40-inch refracting telescope, he realized the need for locating future larger instruments on sites of superior atmospheric stability and transparency. His search for these brought him to Mount Wilson, where, supported by **Andrew Carnegie,** he founded an observatory with 60-inch and 100-inch reflecting telescopes that for a long time remained unsurpassed elsewhere. Soon thereafter he began the planning for the 200-inch reflector of Mount Palomar. The preeminence of the western United States in optical astronomy that has lasted until the present is in no small measure due to Hale's foresight.

Among his own scientific researches probably the discovery of magnetic fields on the sun ranks highest. Hale also played an important role in the organization of science: the *Astrophysical Journal* that he founded is still the leading journal in astronomy, while several important scientific organizations have been influenced by him. See Helen Wright, *Explorer of the Universe: A Biography of George Ellery Hale* (1966).

LODEWYK WOLTJER

HALE, Sarah Josepha Buell (b. Newport, N.H., Oct. 24, 1788; d. Philadelphia, Pa., Apr. 30, 1879), JOURNALIST, was educated at home. She conducted a private school in Newport, New Hampshire, during 1806–11. In 1813 she married, but after her husband died (1822), she opened a millinery shop. She had previously written articles and fiction for local newspapers and in 1823 published a poetry collection, *The Genius of Oblivion*. The *Boston Spectator and Ladies' Album* awarded her a poetry prize in 1826. In 1827 her *Northwood, A Tale of New England* was published. She became editor of *Ladies' Magazine* in 1828, using its columns to campaign for women's education. She did not challenge the belief in women's intellectual inferiority to men but held that educated women would make better mates.

In 1830, Hale published *Poems for Our Children* (which included "Mary Had a Little Lamb"), and in 1833 she helped organize the Seamen's Aid Society. In 1837, Louis Godey of Philadelphia bought the *Ladies' Magazine*, incorporated it into his *Lady's Book*, and hired Hale as literary editor. *Godey's Lady's Book* carried articles on woman's rights, fashion, cookery, and etiquette, as well as poetry and fiction by **Edgar Allan Poe, Harriet Beecher Stowe, Henry Wadsworth Longfellow, Oliver Wendell Holmes,** and **Nathaniel Hawthorne.** Hale published more American and less British literature, and urged women to favor American over European fashions, which she considered too ornate and burdensome for physically active women. Among other feminist activities, she supported **Emma Willard**'s school in Troy, New York, and Vassar College, and she defended **Elizabeth Blackwell**'s right to become a doctor. But she was not a woman suffragist. In 1851 she organized the Ladies' Medical Missionary Society, and the following year she started a shopping service in Godey's *Ladies'*

Magazine. Besides numerous articles Sarah Hale also wrote *Women's Record,* a collection of one thousand biographies of famous women.

❦

Sarah Hale is best described as a great natural force. She was a feminist in a broad sense, though the term might have surprised her. Most of her contemporaries viewed her as well within the bounds of propriety—almost as a conservative. Her emphasis on convention together with her acceptance of a special and separate if not inferior role for women made her anathema to many suffragists of her day. She and *Godey's Lady's Book* were enthusiastically received in circles that shrank from **Elizabeth Cady Stanton** and Lucy Stone. Hale was a traditionalist and possibly a shrewd businesswoman in stressing the differences between the sexes and in helping to maintain strict standards of feminine conduct. At the same time she vigorously promoted women's education and in some instances women in the professions. At the opening of Vassar College she strongly urged women as instructors and administrators. She was interested in training women as physicians. She did her best to discourage the word "female" as applied to women. Her use of feminine efforts to complete the Bunker Hill Monument and to further other causes markedly increased women's opportunities in organizations and in public matters. Hale nonetheless clearly preferred to work within the established framework of society.

Her contributions to public taste were extensive whether for good or for ill. She published stories by many leading authors of the day, especially by women writers. Her editorial policy probably did more for the moral tone of her readers than for their literary judgment. Her own career, however, served amply to promote women's causes. See Ruth E. Finley, *The Lady of Godey's: Sarah Josepha Hale* (1931).

MARY S. BENSON

HALL, Granville Stanley (b. Ashfield, Mass., Feb. 1, 1846; d. Worcester, Mass., Apr. 24, 1924),

SOCIAL SCIENTIST, EDUCATOR, graduated from Williams College and entered Union Theological Seminary in 1867. In 1868 he went to Germany where he studied philosophy for two years at the University of Bonn. Returning to America in 1871, he completed his course at Union and accepted a teaching post in literature and philosophy at Antioch College in 1872. The publication of Wilhelm Wundt's *Foundations of Physical Psychology* stimulated his interest in the new science, and in 1876 he entered Harvard, receiving a PhD in 1878. Two more years of study in Germany followed.

After Hall's return to Harvard in 1880, President **Daniel Coit Gilman** of Johns Hopkins University appointed him professor of psychology and pedagogics, with charge of a research laboratory and a number of young associates, including **John Dewey** (1882). Hall published *The Contents of Children's Minds* (1883), became a leading commentator on educational methods, and in 1887 founded the *American Journal of Psychology*. In 1889 he took over the presidency of Clark University at Worcester, Massachusetts, then newly formed by the philanthropist Jonas Gilman Clark. Hall persuaded Clark, who had planned a conventional men's college, to follow the Hopkins pattern. The philanthropist repeatedly interfered with Hall's work, however, and urged a reversion to the plan for a college.

In 1893, Hall returned to research and writing. In 1904 he published *Adolescence,* which was condensed and republished in 1906 as *Youth.* Hall, whose philosophy leaned toward that of Herbert Spencer and Auguste Comte rather than Georg Hegel, also published *Founders of Modern Psychology* in 1912 and *Jesus, the Christ, in the Light of Psychology* in 1917.

Hall persuaded Sigmund Freud to come to the United States in 1909 to deliver a series of lectures at Clark, which was the first university to confer an honorary degree on the Viennese psychologist.

———

The euphoria induced by a zestful drive for exploring and encompassing all life in the raw and the unrelenting sublimation in scientific labors of the pain and pleasure encountered along the way give us the key to this scholar who treasured as one of his fondest memories the day when he was introduced as the Charles Darwin of the mind. If the recapitulation of the genetic experience of the animal and human world was his doctrine, the most extensive exposure of the scientist as observer and recorder of such experience was his practice. Hall's writings are a treasure chest of unrelated and often contradictory observations and insights. He claimed for himself the accomplishments, honors, and rewards of specialized scholarship, yet he worshiped youth, health, nature, and animal vigor and distrusted the intellect and rational rigor. He inspected everything from prizefights and revivals to morgues and meetings of revolutionaries, yet he frequently did so surreptitiously and for the most part remained aloof from the life he worshiped. An assessment of Hall's contributions must highlight his role as catalyst in getting under way graduate work in psychology, child study, and the study of adolescence. It must also acknowledge that subsequent experimental research has bypassed many of his findings and that our experience with 20th-century social movements has made us wary of his writings on youth, nature, and heredity. Hall, the scholar-aristocrat, was right even in retrospect when he wrote, "The dominantly sad note of my life may be designated by one word, isolation." See Charles E. Strickland and Charles Burgess, eds., *Health, Growth, and Heredity: G. Stanley Hall on Natural Education* (1965).

JURGEN HERBST

HALLECK, Henry Wager (b. Westernville, N.Y., Jan. 16, 1815; d. Louisville, Ky., Jan. 9, 1872), MILITARY LEADER, studied at Union College (AB, 1837) before his admission to the U.S. Military Academy in 1835. He graduated from West Point and was commissioned a second lieutenant of engineers in 1839. He next taught engineering and chemistry at West Point (1839–40) and served with the board of engineers in

Washington, D.C., before being assigned to work on fortifications in New York Harbor (1840–44). Halleck toured Europe in 1844 to study fortifications, after which he delivered a series of lectures at Boston's Lowell Institute in 1845, published as *Elements of Military Art and Science* (1846).

At the outbreak of the Mexican War in 1846 he was sent to Monterey, California, where he served as staff officer and then secretary of state in the military government of California. He also attended the California constitutional convention in 1849. He was promoted to captain of engineers in 1853 but resigned from the army in 1854. Having read law early in his army career, he helped found the San Francisco law firm of Halleck, Peachy and Billings in 1849 and became head of that firm in 1854. He also was president of the Pacific & Atlantic Railroad and director-general of the New Almaden quicksilver mine (1854–60). He wrote *A Collection of Mining Laws of Spain and Mexico* (1859) and *International Law, or Rules Regulating the Intercourse of States in Peace and War* (1861), a popular textbook in its field.

At the outbreak of the Civil War in 1861, Halleck was commissioned a major general in the regular army. He succeeded General **John Frémont** on November 18, 1861, as officer in charge of the Department of Missouri at St. Louis, a command that eventually (1862) included the entire western theater (Department of Mississippi). Halleck cleaned up much of the graft and corruption in this department and personally directed the seizure of Corinth, Mississippi (1862). In July of that year he was named general in chief and commander of all land forces of the United States. Although a capable administrator, Halleck was criticized as a poor strategist and indirectly blamed for Union reverses in Virginia and for General **George Meade**'s failure to pursue **Robert E. Lee** after Gettysburg (1863). When Ulysses S. Grant was appointed to head the Army of the Potomac in 1864, Halleck became chief of staff of the army, under the direction of the secretary of war **Edwin Stanton** and the lieutenant general commanding (Grant), with headquarters in Washington, a position he held until he became commander of the military division of the James

with headquarters in Richmond in 1865. After the Civil War, Halleck commanded the military division of the Pacific in San Francisco (1865) and the division of the South in Louisville (1869).

⸎

One quality that distinguishes great commanders is ruthlessness, an instinct for the jugular. Henry W. Halleck appreciated the need for ruthlessness and knew how to organize and deploy armies for the conduct of total war, but when given responsibility for the execution of strategy, his nerve frequently failed. Halleck's distaste for decisive bloodletting was reinforced by his familiarity with the tactics of Henri Jomini, a complex of recipes for the conduct of war that envisioned armed conflict as a game of maneuver and finesse. In both respects, moral and intellectual, Halleck was in step with most of his military contemporaries; he was as shy of killing as **George McClellan** and as well versed in Jomini as Braxton Bragg—in short, a typical, undistinguished Civil War battlefield general. His glacial progress during the Corinth campaign earned him the sobriquet "Old Brains," bestowed on him by impatient Billy Yanks, who wished he would think less and fight more.

Halleck brought his dislike for taking risks with him when he went to Washington. He opposed **William T. Sherman**'s scheme to plow a furrow through Georgia and opposed the appointment of a volatile upstart like **Philip Sheridan** to command in the Shenandoah. His reputation has also suffered from Lincoln's off-hand remark that Halleck was "little more than a first-rate clerk" and from Grant's postwar enmity, caused by his belated discovery that Halleck had once instigated his brief suspension from command. Then, too, Halleck was not the most charismatic figure in wartime Washington society: stiff and stuffy, too squat and too portly to be cast in heroic proportions, with a quizzical countenance and an exaggerated slouch concealing an excess of self-righteous certitude. Halleck was probably the only prominent Civil War general who betrayed his concern for status and dignity by buttoning every button on his uniform coat.

Yet his contribution to the Union victory should not be underestimated. As general in chief he kept the federal war effort focused on primary objectives, discouraging wasteful sideshows like Nathaniel Banks's grandiose designs for the conquest of Texas, and he forestalled political interference with the authority or autonomy of successful field commanders, neatly eviscerating John McClernand's ambition to complicate Grant's Vicksburg operation. Further, it is no small compliment to say that Halleck was a good administrator; if the Confederacy had enjoyed the services of an equally competent counterpart, Confederate grand strategy might not have been reduced to muddling chaos. In 1864, when demoted to the position of Grant's chief of staff, Halleck finally found his proper place. He relieved Lincoln, Stanton, and Grant of the details of running a war and displayed a rare genius for comprehending both the military and the political dimensions of wartime policy-making. He knew how to translate the government's wishes into a soldier's language. He could explain to Grant why prominent incompetents like **Benjamin Butler** had to be entrusted with high military rank, and explain to the politicians what Grant was doing. Grant's communications with seventeen army and area commanders also filtered through Halleck; it was he who fleshed out Grant's inspirations with operational and logistical directives, and he who sifted reality from the subordinate generals' rhetoric. Whatever his defects, Henry W. Halleck invented the modern office of the chief of staff, a key element in Helmuth Von Moltke's concept of the general staff system. See Stephen E. Ambrose, *Halleck: Lincoln's Chief of Staff* (1962).

ROBERT L. KERBY

HALSTED, William Stewart (b. New York, N.Y., Sept. 23, 1852; d. Baltimore, Md., Sept. 7, 1922), SURGEON, graduated from Yale University in 1874 and received his MD from the College of Physicians and Surgeons, New York, in 1877. He interned at Bellevue Hospital, New York, then studied in Vienna, Leipzig, and Würzburg (1878–80).

Between 1881 and 1886 Halsted was an attending physician at Charity Hospital in New York City; demonstrator of anatomy at Columbia University; chief of surgery at Emigrants' Hospital; associate surgeon at Roosevelt Hospital, New York; and an attending surgeon at Bellevue and Presbyterian hospitals. During this period he developed and perfected new operating procedures that minimized tissue damage, and he discovered the nerve mechanism that accounts for cocaine's painkilling properties (1884–85). In 1886 he moved to Baltimore to work in **William H. Welch**'s laboratory, where he developed new methods of intestinal suture and made studies of gallstones and of the thyroid and parathyroid glands. In 1889 he became acting surgeon and head of the outpatient clinic at the newly opened Johns Hopkins Hospital and developed new methods of hernia repair and new techniques for breast cancer removal. In 1890 he was appointed professor of surgery at Johns Hopkins University Medical School. He investigated arterial surgery, tuberculosis, and gallstones during the 1890s. In the early 1900s he resumed study of the thyroid gland, and he further developed breast cancer surgery (1912–22). He introduced several technical improvements, including the use of rubber gloves by operative personnel. Halsted's *Surgical Papers* was published in 1924.

———⚬⚬⚬———

Halsted started life as a *bon vivant* college athlete from a family with no financial worries. In New York at Bellevue Hospital and as house physician at New York Hospital he came under the aegis of some of the best physicians in the country, including two who were just beginning to experiment with antiseptic surgery. Many of these medical men were also full of enthusiasm for the experimental and clinically advanced approaches that they had seen in Germany. As a postdoctoral student himself in Europe, Halsted worked with an incredibly eminent array of physicians, particularly in Vienna. He returned to an exciting, innovative practice in New York, and he spent an important segment of his energy conducting an influential "quiz" for medical students.

In his New York years Halsted became a critical influence in introducing Listerism into the United States by his emphasis on the principles (rather than techniques) involved. An elegant operator, his work on the reaction of tissues during surgical interventions began a lifelong concern that he passed on to the many students who trained with him. His technical contributions to surgery put him on a par with leading European surgeons, especially after his move to Johns Hopkins gave him the benefit of extensive animal experimentation. With William H. Welch, Howard A. Kelly, and William Osler he was one of the four great founders of the Hopkins medical tradition and was particularly influential in introducing residency training.

During Halsted's extensive pioneer experiments with cocaine he learned with others only too late the addictive nature of the substance, for in using himself as a guinea pig he became dependent on it. Between 1885 and 1888 he was completely incapacitated for long periods of time, but he became a folk hero in that he was finally able to control the habit and continue a remarkably creative career. See W. G. MacCallum, *William Stewart Halsted, Surgeon* (1930).

J. C. Burnham

HAMILTON, Alexander (b. Nevis, British West Indies, Jan. 11, 1755; d. New York, N.Y., July 12, 1804), POLITICAL LEADER, emigrated to New York in 1773 and entered King's College (now Columbia University), where he wrote pamphlets defending the Patriot cause. When the Revolutionary War broke out, he enlisted in the Continental army, and in 1777 he became General George Washington's aide-de-camp with the rank of lieutenant colonel. At Yorktown (1781), Hamilton led a line regiment.

After serving a term in the Continental Congress (1782–83), Hamilton returned to New York City where he practiced law. Convinced that the Articles of Confederation were too weak, as a

delegate to the Annapolis Convention (1786) he suggested a meeting the following year at Philadelphia to amend the Articles. At the Federal Convention (1787), Hamilton was an ardent supporter of a strong centralized government. His major work in support of the new Constitution, however, was done outside the Convention; with **John Jay** and James Madison he wrote the *Federalist Papers* (1788), a collection of essays supporting the new charter. At the New York Convention called to ratify the Constitution, Hamilton took the lead in persuading anti-Federalists to support the charter, which was ratified by a vote of 30 to 27.

In 1789, Hamilton became the first secretary of the Treasury. Instructed by the House to devise a means of retiring the Revolutionary War debts and establishing public credit, early in 1790 he produced his "Report on the Public Credit." In this and three subsequent reports he advocated using the fiscal power of the federal government to establish a stable but flexible monetary system and promote a growing economy. A deal with Secretary of State Thomas Jefferson (to locate the permanent national capital on the Potomac) overcame southern "Republican" opposition to his plan to fund the national debt and assume payment of the state war debts. Hamilton also obtained, again over southern agrarian opposition, passage of a bill chartering a national bank that would serve as a depository for government funds, perform fiscal services for the government, and, most important, facilitate the monetization of the public debt by using it as a basis for a uniform and elastic currency. Jefferson held that the bank was unconstitutional because the Constitution did not specifically authorize Congress to create a bank. Hamilton, however, argued that the authority was an "implied power," incidental to the power to collect taxes and regulate trade. Congress, President Washington, and (in time) the Supreme Court accepted Hamilton's reasoning, and the bank became reality. As to sources of federal revenue, Hamilton relied mainly on import duties, but at James Madison's suggestion he also requested and got an excise tax on whiskey (1791). Finally, in his "Report on Manufacturers" (1791), Hamilton proposed high tariffs to protect industries, bounties for agriculture, and federal internal improvements. Congress failed to act on this report. Another reversal came in 1794 when farmers in western Pennsylvania protested against the excise tax on whiskey (Whiskey Rebellion). Hamilton helped persuade Washington to call out federal troops to crush the rebellion.

When the wars of the French Revolution began, Hamilton insisted that revenue from continued trade with Britain was essential to his financial system and thus to the stability of the U.S. government. Thus he approved Washington's Neutrality Proclamation of 1793. Although Jay's Treaty with Great Britain (1795) failed to guarantee America's rights as a neutral on the high seas or to open trade with the British West Indies, Hamilton, in his "Camillus" letters, supported the treaty. Following the XYZ Affair with France (1798), Hamilton joined President John Adams in a militant anti-French position. Hamilton became actual commander of the armed forces (under Washington's nominal command). Subsequently, Adams, over the objection of Hamilton, sent a new commission to France (1800) and averted war. This intraparty struggle between Hamilton and Adams split the Federalist Party.

In the presidential election of 1800, Jefferson and **Aaron Burr** each received 73 electoral votes, throwing the election into the House of Representatives. Although Hamilton disliked Jefferson, he distrusted Burr and tried (in vain) to persuade Federalist electors to vote for Jefferson. Moreover, when Burr ran for governor of New York in 1804, Hamilton campaigned against him, and he continued to attack Burr's character after the election. Burr then challenged him to a duel. The two met at Weehawken, New Jersey, where Hamilton was mortally wounded.

———∞———

Hamilton has always been among the least understood and appreciated of the founding fathers. His historical image has been that of the patron saint of capitalistic, nationalistic, and aris-

tocratic traditions in America, all of which declined in popular favor—though not in vitality—during the century after Hamilton's death. In the first third of the 20th century he regained some popularity for the capitalistic and nationalistic aspects of his image, but in the 1930s and thereafter he was subordinated to Jefferson. Since then, inaccurately but almost universally, he has been regarded as the champion of the rich against the poor, the elite against the masses, the aristocrat against the democrat.

The lack of appreciation is not difficult to explain despite the greatness of Hamilton's achievements. Actually, he trusted neither elite nor mass. "Give all power to the many," said he, and "they will oppress the few. Give all power to the few, they will oppress the many. Both therefore ought to have power, that each may defend itself against the other." Moreover, Hamilton believed that all men were ruled by the baser passions rather than reason, and especially by ambition and avarice—by an aggressive desire for status and property. Hamilton's entire philosophy and work as a statesman was based on this "pessimistic" view of mankind. He also believed, however, that public institutions, properly organized, would allow for individual wickedness and channel it, on the average, into collective good. In the broad range these views were contrary to a rising tide of rationalism and faith in individual goodness, as represented in America by Hamilton's contemporary enemies— Jefferson, Madison, Burr, **George Clinton**, and **John Randolph**—most of whom were aristocrats whose public posture was in favor of republicanism if indeed not democracy.

Various personal attributes won Hamilton other upper-class enemies as well. He devoutly craved fame, the secularized variation of Christian immortality, and expected to gain it from his peers, but such was not to be. Southern aristocrats deplored his commercial spirit, his acceptance of corruption as a ruling force in matters of state, and, above all, his opposition to slavery. Northern aristocrats admired his policies and his élan, his sense of honor, and his romanticism; but although he aristocratically forswore ambition and avarice on his own account, and cultivated the finest manners, he had about him an arrogance and lack of natural grace that marked him as a man of inferior origins.

Hamilton's foreign policies, often condemned by Jefferson-oriented modern historians, want special notice. Specifically, historians have criticized Hamilton's pro-British stance despite Britain's belligerent maritime policies and the fact that revolutionary and republican America was bound to revolutionary and republican France by a treaty and by ties of professed principle. In the early 1790s Hamilton insisted on friendly relations with Britain because revenues from British trade were essential to his financial system, and that system was, in turn, the most important adhesive of national union. Later (from 1796 onward) Hamilton was instrumental in having the United States join Great Britain in support of the black revolution in Santo Domingo—a policy that horrified the aristocratic slave-owning "republicans" south of the Mason-Dixon line. Then in 1798–1800 Hamilton favored ground-force military preparedness against France, over the opposition of Federalist president John Adams as well as southern Republicans. For years historians regarded Hamilton's insistence on a large army, with himself at the head, as mere megalomania. Only recently has it become clear that Hamilton was right: that France had definite designs on North America and but for chance might well have succeeded in restoring the French empire in America.

Thus Hamilton remains one of the most elusive of great Americans. To dislike him personally is easy, and to object to his view of man is equally so; but to challenge his deeds and policy positions is a monumental and perilous undertaking. See John C. Miller, *Alexander Hamilton: Portrait in Paradox* (1959).

FORREST MCDONALD

HAMILTON, Alice (b. New York, N.Y., Feb. 27, 1869; d. Hadlyme, Conn., Sept. 22, 1970), PHYSICIAN, received her MD from the University of Michigan in 1893. She studied bacteriology in Munich, Germany, in 1895 and pathological anatomy at Johns Hopkins the next year. In 1897 she moved to **Jane Addams**'s Hull House settlement in Chicago, living and working there for nearly twenty years, supporting herself at first as professor of pathology at the Women's Medical School of Northwestern University. In 1902 she returned for some years to bacteriological research under pathologist Ludvig Hektoen at Rush Medical School. In 1910, Hamilton was appointed medical investigator of the Illinois Commission on Occupational Diseases. The same year she was sent by the Commission to Brussels as U.S. representative to the International Congress on Occupational Accidents and Diseases. When the U.S. Department of Labor was established in 1913, she joined its staff, working on problems involving chemical poisoning in lead smelting, paint manufacture, printing, pottery, and copper and mercury mining. During World War I she was in charge of toxicological investigations of the munitions industry. In 1919 she became Harvard's first woman professor. She taught industrial medicine at the School of Public Health until her retirement in 1935. Remaining active after her retirement, she studied poisoning in the rayon industry (1937–38) and silicosis among miners (1940).

Hamilton was a delegate to the 1915 peace meeting of the International Congress of Women and the 1919 Congress that denounced the Versailles Treaty. She was a representative to the League of Nations Health Committee (1924–30) and served on the Hoover Commission on Social Trends (1930–33). Hamilton published *Industrial Poisoning in the U.S.* (1925), *Industrial Toxicology* (1934), and an autobiography, *Exploring the Dangerous Trades* (1943).

⸺⸺

Alice Hamilton was a slim, gentle, but determined lady. Underlying warmth and humor tempered what almost seemed austerity to those who did not know her. A career in industrial medicine might sound hard to mix with concerns for the poor in Chicago's South Side, peace efforts, starving Germans, defense of Sacco and Vanzetti, and other "radical" causes later recognized as right and necessary. The paradox dissolves when one recalls that she went into medicine "because as a doctor I could ... be quite sure that I could be of use anywhere." This purpose bound together all her varied interests. Her family had taught her a strong sense of duty, emphasized classics, the Bible, and languages, and encouraged her, with remarkable freedom, to make her own evaluations and decisions. In industrial investigations she insisted on interviewing and examining workers, often in their homes; studying workplaces, from ladders and catwalks if necessary; and trying to understand each problem through those closest to it. A commitment to help workers never impeded clear, fair appraisals of management requirements. As a result her objectivity was awesome. Fortunately, her personality helped her to persuade. She said of herself: "Employers and doctors both appeared more willing to listen to me as I told them their duty toward their employees and patients than they would have if I had been a man. It seemed natural and right that a woman should put the care of the producing workman ahead of the value of the thing he was producing." See Madeleine P. Grant, *Pioneer Doctor in Industrial Medicine* (1967).

J. WISTER MEIGS

HAMILTON, Edith (b. Dresden, Ger., Aug. 12, 1867; d. Washington, D.C., May 31, 1963), CLASSICIST, graduated from Bryn Mawr College in 1894. She held a Bryn Mawr fellowship (1894–95), then attended the University of Leipzig and the University of Munich (1895–96); at the latter she was the first woman student. In 1896, Hamilton became headmistress of the Bryn Mawr School in Baltimore, where she remained until retirement in 1922. She then devoted her time to research and writing. Her first book, *The Greek Way* (1930), discussed Periclean drama. She followed this with *The Roman Way* (1932) and then wrote *The Prophets of Israel* in 1936. In 1937, Hamilton published her translations of Euripides' *The Trojan Women* and Aeschylus' *Prometheus Bound* and *Agamemnon*, in

Three Greek Plays. Her later works include *Mythology* (1942), *Witness to the Truth: Christ and His Interpreters* (1949), *Introduction to Plutarch, Selected Lives and Essays* (1951), *The Echo of Greece* (1957), *The Collected Dialogues of Plato* (1961), with Huntington Cairns, and *The Ever Present Past* (1964). In 1957 she was made an honorary citizen of Athens.

Edith Hamilton wrote and lived as a great lady. Able and brilliant student though she was, she was famous less for profundity of scholarship than for her remarkable ability to interpret another age for her own. For her, ancient Athens lived, and as her friend and biographer Doris Reid said, she brought its "mind and spirit, intellect and art" to the 20th century. The concept of a nearly forgotten time touched her readers deeply. Miss Hamilton's grace and clarity in writing and her sense of the significance of the past led many people to an understanding of Greek thought they had hitherto missed. This was true of all her books and especially of *The Greek Way*. Any lasting effects of Hamilton's work for classical scholarship remain perhaps beside the point.

Her other great impact on her time came through personal associations in which she reached not only her own circle but those who knew her only through her writings or her speeches. Her years as headmistress were remarkable for her influence on the individual development of her students as well as for the opening of "the excitement of intellectual life" to a number of them. Later, Hamilton's charm, grace, and vivacity, and her very longevity and remarkable success in her second career, brought almost a cult of personality. She had virtually a salon about her and an international reputation. She proved that one's later years might be productive. Although she was no feminist, she did much by example to improve the status of women. She remains very much an individual somewhat apart from her time. See Doris Fielding Reid, *Edith Hamilton: An Intimate Portrait* (1967).

MARY S. BENSON

HAMMETT, Dashiell (Samuel) (b. St. Mary's County, Md., May 27, 1894; d. New York, N.Y., Jan. 10, 1961), WRITER, was educated at the Baltimore Polytechnic Institute but left at about age 17 to work as a newsboy, stevedore, freight clerk, and advertising manager. He became an "operative" for the Pinkerton Detective Agency, then served in World War I as a sergeant in the Motor Ambulance Corps. During the 1920s Hammett worked as a detective, but he also wrote magazine articles and pulp stories until 1929 when he published the highly successful novels *Red Harvest* and *The Dain Curse.* His most famous novel, *The Maltese Falcon* (1930), followed, then *The Glass Key* (1931), *Creeps by Night* (1931), and *The Thin Man* (1934). All sold outstandingly well and in all media—motion pictures, radio, comics, and later television.

Hammett served for two years with the Signal Corps in the Aleutian Islands during World War II. Afterward he was under attack as a left-wing intellectual and invoked the Fifth Amendment when asked by Senator **Joseph R. McCarthy** if he was a Communist and, as a trustee for a "Communist front" bail fund, refused to give up a list of its contributors. As a result he served six months in the federal Correctional Institute in Kentucky. His novels were removed from government libraries abroad but were replaced when President Dwight D. Eisenhower expressed disagreement with this policy.

Dashiell Hammett acquired a remarkable reputation, first as the "dean" of "tough guy" detective-story writers, next as an individual whose life endorsed his art. Finally, he was viewed as evoking comparison with **Ernest Hemingway** for economy of style, character, and dialogue. Hammett had a sharp sense of irony, as illustrated by his *Smart Set* (Mar. 1923) notes from his detective experiences. He was skeptical about detective fiction's keen-eyed sleuths and unique clues. As he wrote, "I know a man who once stole a Ferris wheel."

Nevertheless, his own fiction was replete with more multiple murders than ordinarily accompa-nied a crime and involved highly complex principals and activities, all explained with pyrotechnical skill. It was only when seen as fables that such unlikely events as he created could be credited, as they were by such artists as André Gide and Hemingway himself. Another critic found the key to Hammett in his lack of sentiment and rejection of the fear of death. He noted that Hemingway's characters wore hard masks but revealed sensibility beneath. Hammett's masks were never lifted. Hammett's detective in *The Maltese Falcon,* the memorable Sam Spade, at one point "stared ahead at nothing," symbolically defining his vision of life and Hammett's. He thus expressed a post–World War I mood which tallied with that of other disillusioned writers, and comparisons were often made between his and Hemingway's war experiences and the effect on their writing. Hammett, a tall, spare, gray-haired man, supplemented his outlook on the world with a private code of generosity, hatred of bullies, and a belief that his social views constituted true patriotism. The playwright **Lillian Hellman,** with whom he long maintained a close relationship, saw him as "very involved in America." Critics agreed that his fiction was likely to be read for a long time, but there were differences as to whether it satisfied high culture needs or the less-demanding criteria of popular literature. See Lillian Hellman, *An Unfinished Woman* (1969).

LOUIS FILLER

HAMMOND, James Henry (b. near Newberry, S.C., Nov. 15, 1807; d. Beech Island, S.C., Nov. 13, 1864), POLITICAL LEADER, graduated from South Carolina College in 1825 and briefly taught school before studying law. He was admitted to the bar in 1828. His practice flourished, and he soon turned to politics, establishing the Columbia *Southern Times* to attack the protective tariff. During the nullification controversy he advocated radical states' rights action and received appointment as a military aide to the governor in anticipation of conflict with the national government. Elected to Congress in 1834, Hammond fought to bar abolitionist petitions from the House. As governor of South Carolina (1842–44) he helped establish the Citadel, the state military academy, promoted scientific agriculture, and reformed the state bank. In national affairs he led the extremist Bluffton movement, an effort to eliminate protective tariffs and promote expansion of slave territory into Texas. Hammond sought election to the U.S. Senate but was denied the office for many years mainly because of a personal scandal. Meanwhile, he operated along the Savannah River some of the most diversified and efficient plantations in the region, becoming a friend and leading supporter of Virginia agricultural reformer **Edmund Ruffin.**

Finally elected to the Senate as a Democrat in 1857, Hammond quickly achieved recognition as a spokesman for southern sectionalism. In response to New York Senator **William H. Seward**'s prediction of an "irrepressible conflict" between the sections, Hammond replied (Mar. 4, 1858) in a speech defending the South and slavery, and containing his famous warning, "You dare not make war upon cotton.... Cotton is King." Although an opponent of separate state secession, he acquiesced in the action of his own state, resigning his Senate seat (Nov. 1860). Highly critical of **Jefferson Davis** and his policies, and in declining health, Hammond was not active in the politics of the Confederacy. However, he was influential in establishing the policy of preserving stocks of cotton as a means of maintaining the credit of the government.

———

Hammond was in most respects representative of the planter elite, defending the interests of his adopted class with ardency and skill. A proud, intensely ambitious, and handsome man, of strong intellect, mordant wit, and compelling literary style, Hammond had all the tools needed for political achievement. Yet that potential was never fulfilled, as repeatedly, in critical moments of involvement in public affairs, Hammond experienced lapses of judgment and determination. Weaknesses of the flesh, in the forms of overindulgence, sexual indiscretion, morbid hypochondria, and genuine physical disability, prevented Hammond from ever fully assuming the mantle of leadership laid down by his idol **John Calhoun.**

His contributions to the defense of slavery and the South were nonetheless important. Hammond's widely reprinted letters to the English abolitionist Thomas Clarkson represented a subtle and forceful statement of the pro-slavery position. Himself a wealthy owner of land and slaves, his writings rarely strayed from the twin themes of slavery and democracy: the first, the bulwark of white supremacy and physical security, a "mudsill" or foundation for the southern way of life; the second, a more insidious menace to order and rightful elitist social control. Hammond was never a mere polemicist, and his public career was bound up with the birth and death of the idea of southern nationalism. It was ironic that this lifelong disunionist was shunted aside in the secession crisis, and with characteristic bitterness he wrote in 1861, "A Southern Confederacy has been the cherishing dream of my life. Yet it has been accomplished without apparent agency of mine." But for thirty years Hammond had stood forth as a powerful spokesman for the planter aristocracy he had embraced so completely. See Clement Eaton, *The Mind of the Old South* (1964).

STEVEN A. CHANNING

HAMPTON, Wade (b. Charleston, S.C., Mar. 28, 1818; d. Columbia, S.C., Apr. 11, 1902), POLITICAL and MILITARY LEADER, came from a family of large South Carolina landholders. He graduated from South Carolina College in 1836 and studied law. Never intending to practice, however, he devoted himself to the management of his father's large cotton plantation in Mississippi. He served in the Mississippi legislature (1852–61), incurring strong criticism from Radicals for his opposition to attempts to reopen the slave trade. By 1860, Hampton doubted that slavery would continue to be economically feasible. Although he maintained the constitutional right of a state to secede, he held that there was no need for secession. Nevertheless he was one of the most enthusiastic and effective supporters of the Confederacy. Raising a cavalry unit at his own expense, he saw action at the first battle of Manassas and was wounded at Seven Pines. Promoted to brigadier general, he participated in most of **J.E.B. Stuart**'s cavalry activities and was again wounded at Gettysburg. He then led a number of successful raids on his own, was made major general, and assumed command of the dead Stuart's forces. He was promoted to lieutenant general (Feb. 1865). After the war Hampton at first intended to flee the country but decided instead to return to South Carolina.

Hampton initially remained in the background of South Carolina Reconstruction politics but became a strong opponent of black Reconstruction. In 1876 he was elected governor. Reelected in 1878, he was chosen U.S. senator shortly thereafter, serving until 1891. Although he opposed the Force Bill in 1890, which would have put elections under federal control, politics in South Carolina was changing rapidly and Hampton was defeated for reelection by the followers of Benjamin R. Tillman. His last active years were spent as commissioner of Pacific Railways.

Wade Hampton fits perfectly into **Henry Adams**'s mold for the aristocratic southerner—emotion and instinct, not intellect, governed his life. Nothing suggests that he ever seriously questioned the values of the civilization that produced him. Hampton was born into one of the great planting and slave-owning families of the antebellum South, and his touchstone was duty to that world—South Carolina chiefly, then the South. He played no prominent public role before 1860, but when he felt his world endangered, he offered his person and purse. Raising and equipping the Hampton Legion, he led it to war and for four years he fought courageously, though not brilliantly, for his cause.

In defeat Hampton's loyalty to the South never wavered. Refusing to lead an exodus of former Confederates to Brazil, he admonished them that duty required their services. The South

could not be abandoned in her dark hour.

In the fight to end Reconstruction in South Carolina, Hampton entered battle again because his state had called him. And this time he won. His regime secured the white supremacy of which he approved. But always the confident paternalist, he never indulged in race baiting; he advocated decent treatment of a race that he felt must remain subordinate.

The politics of the Gilded Age did not attract Hampton, whose vision was riveted to the past. For him triumph in 1876 meant restoring an idealized past. Clinging passionately to his vision, he opposed young agrarians assaulting his restoration—to no avail. He lived on past the century's turn, but as he said, "Life seems closed for me." See Manly Wade Wellman, *Giant in Gray: A Biography of Wade Hampton of South Carolina* (1949).

WILLIAM J. COOPER, JR.

HANCOCK, John (b. North Braintree, Mass., Jan. 12, 1737; d. North Braintree [now Quincy], Mass., Oct. 8, 1793), POLITICAL LEADER, MERCHANT, graduated from Harvard (1754) and entered the mercantile firm of his uncle Thomas Hancock. In 1760 he went to London to learn the English side of the business. He was made a partner in the firm in 1763, and when Thomas Hancock died (1764), he inherited it. He opposed the Stamp Act (1765) and other British commercial policies; in 1768 he was defended by John Adams when charged with smuggling in his sloop the *Liberty*.

Hancock was elected to the Massachusetts general court in 1769, where his anti-British sentiments soon marked him as a leading patriot. He played a leading role in the publication of the "Hutchinson Letters" (1773), which were written by Massachusetts governor **Thomas Hutchinson,** a supporter of the Crown. When the Massachusetts general court transformed itself into a provincial congress (1774), Hancock was chosen president and made chairman of the Committee of Safety.

A delegate to the second Continental Congress (1775), Hancock was elected president of the

Congress. He was the first delegate to sign the Declaration of Independence (1776). In 1780 he was elected the first governor of the state of Massachusetts. He resigned in 1785 but was again elected in 1787 (serving until his death). Hancock presided over the Massachusetts convention to ratify the new Constitution (1788), which he supported.

⸺⸎⸺

John Hancock, who became by inheritance the richest Bostonian of his generation while still in his twenties, was remarkable for his deliberate decision to build a public career based on popularity. Introduced to Revolutionary politics by **Samuel Adams,** Hancock swiftly developed a province-wide following of his own owing to the *"Liberty* incident" of 1768 and Hancock's subsequent career in the general court. Hancock, moreover, created a solid political base, both in Boston among his own employees and in the countryside where his gifts of Bibles to impoverished congregations earned him lasting gratitude.

Except where his own pride was involved, Hancock was never doctrinaire but consistently displayed a flexibility and realism that made him a suitable choice as titular leader of the Massachusetts Whigs in 1774 and later as president of the Continental Congress. After his desire to lead the Continental army was thwarted by the election of George Washington, Hancock turned again to Massachusetts politics, where he cultivated a broad constituency ranging from dirt farmers and stevedores to wealthy merchants and Loyalist sympathizers. His reward was an unbreakable lifetime hold on the governorship, which he carried annually with 70 to 90 percent of the vote.

Hancock did not impress other political leaders as being notably able or principled, and their judgment that his primary aim was popular applause is supported by Hancock's indecisiveness at three controversial junctures: independence, Shays' Rebellion, and the ratification of the Constitution. Throughout his long and successful political career Hancock made certain to see which way the tide was running before plunging in. See Herbert S. Allan, *John Hancock, Patriot in Blue* (1948).

RICHARD D. BROWN

HAND, Learned Billings (b. Albany, N.Y., Jan. 27, 1872; d. New York, N.Y., Aug. 18, 1961), JURIST, received both his BA (1893) and MA (1894) from Harvard, and his LLB (1896) from Harvard Law School. Admitted to the New York bar in 1897, he practiced law in Albany before moving to New York City in 1902.

In 1909, President William H. Taft appointed Hand U.S. district judge for the southern district of New York (1909–24). Hand did notsupport Taft in the presidential election of 1912, however, endorsing instead Theodore Roosevelt, the Progressive candidate. In 1913, Hand ran as a Progressive for the position of chief justice of the New York court of appeals but was defeated.

Hand early enunciated his belief that the courts were to serve as an umpire between the federal government, the states, and the individual, and to see that none of them exceeded constitutional boundaries. During World War I when the postmaster general of the United States wanted to curtail the mailing of *The Masses,* an antiwar, radical periodical, Hand held that such an action did not come under the purview of the Espionage Act (1917) and was a violation of the right of free speech.

In 1924, President Calvin Coolidge appointed Hand to the court of appeals for the second judicial circuit, encompassing New York, Connecticut, and Vermont. With Hand as its senior judge, and in time its chief judge by act of Congress, this court came to be the best-known and most highly respected appellate court in the country. During his service on it (he retired in 1951) and in the last decade of his life, during which he continued to sit with the court, he carried a heavy load. His career total of written opinions came to nearly three thousand. These included *Sheldon* v. *Metro-Goldwyn-Mayer Pictures* (1936), one of the most widely known and highly regarded opinions in all copyright law, in which Hand ruled that the movie studio had infringed on an author's novel and play; his 1943 ruling in an antitrust suit against the Associated Press; and his 1945 ruling in the Alcoa antitrust case. In his antitrust decisions Hand established standards for determining monopolistic practices, which the Supreme Court came to adopt. His publicized influence on the Supreme Court was evident in the Dennis case (1951), where the Court, in sustaining conviction of certain Communist leaders for advocating violent overthrow of the government, employed Hand's reconstruction of Oliver Wendell Holmes's "clear and present danger rule," in which he substituted the concept of probability for that of proximity or remoteness in the Holmes formulation. The ruling was reflective of Hand's commitment to judicial restraint, which he elaborated in his 1958 lectures at Harvard Law School, *The Bill of Rights* (1958). Much of his off-the-bench writing and speaking is included in *The Spirit of Liberty* (1952).

—∞∞∞—

Around Hand, a vigorous but unpretentious man of disarming humility, there arose a legend that even his bitterest critics had difficulty cutting through. Hailed early by Holmes and **Felix Frankfurter** as one of America's great justices, he was widely acknowledged, as his career closed, to be "the greatest living judge in the English-speaking world." His reputation for well-written, carefully reasoned, soundly constructed opinions was such that no lower court judge was so often cited by name in opinions of the Supreme Court of the United States or in academic publications. He was put forward on several occasions for membership on the high bench, but timing and geography consistently blocked him even though the press frequently spoke of him as the "tenth Justice of the Supreme Court."

Whether Hand deserved such accolades was a question raised by both contemporaries and latter-day scholars. Certainly his judicial career was commendable. He carried a heavy workload even in official retirement and steered the talented second circuit court of appeals through an annual docket which far exceeded that of the Supreme Court. As the top U.S. commercial court, the C.A.2 decided to a large degree the business law of the country, handing down seldom-appealed rulings on admiralty law, patent and trademark law, bankruptcy, negligence, and agency, and not infrequently important rulings in civil liberties cases. On the bench Hand quickly built a reputation for terrorizing ill-prepared and pompous lawyers who relied on broad generalizations and "eternal principles." He was a legal perfectionist who frequently checked the facts of the case himself, and few things irritated him more than the "meadows of easy assumptions." Firm but fair with his law clerks, he himself exerted a great self-discipline and devotion to work, seldom content with his own finished product. Filled with self-doubt, he once stated that "skepticism is my only gospel, but I don't want to make a dogma out of it."

Yet this very eschewing of legal certainty opened his career to strong criticism. A pragmatist in feeling that courts must continually apply old law to new problems, he saw the judge's role in such a process as one of noninvolvement and neutrality. This meant remaining detached not merely from immediate partisanship but also from any ultimate passion for reform. Such abstinence he regarded as the only condition on which appointed judges could be properly tolerated in a democracy.

In application such a judicial philosophy led him to a posture of restraint far more advanced than either Holmes or his contemporary Felix Frankfurter. When the Supreme Court embraced his position in the famed Dennis case (a step that critics charged was taken to capitalize more on Hand's reputation than his legal ideas) the wrath of liberal activists fell on Hand, and serious questions were raised as to the legitimacy of his claim to the mantle of being a strong civil libertarian. Such criticism surfaced again when in his 1958 Holmes lectures he used the same restraint scale to criticize the **Earl Warren** Court's rulings in civil liberties and segregation cases. Yet it was easy to misread his personal commitments on these bases. Greatly concerned about the "Red Scare" following World War I, he was equally appalled by the excesses of McCarthyism. Yet to Hand, whose Lincolnesque 1944 speech "The

Spirit of Liberty" had moved a nation, the remedy for such anti–civil libertarian activities could not come from courts. As he stated in that address: "I often wonder whether we do not rest our hopes too much upon constitutions, upon laws, and upon courts. These are false hopes.... Liberty lies in the hearts of men and women; when it dies there, no constitution, no law, no court can save it. While it lies there it needs no constitution, no law, no court to save it." To his critics such a posture was an example of needless judicial self-denial and waived aside too rapidly a highly traditional role for courts that had always emphasized their importance in preserving fundamental rights.

Hand's great reputation tended to rest much more firmly on his legal philosophy and public image than on his opinions. As an intermediate appellate judge he was often isolated from the final determination of the great political and constitutional issues of his times. Yet his ability to articulate the importance of the public's finding ways through government to preserve basic American values has remained. And Hand's ability to ask the right and difficult question in order to alert judges as well as the public to the danger to the moral force of court decisions from noncompliance afforded a thoughtful foundation for restraint philosophy. See Gerald Gunther, *Learned Hand: The Man and the Judge* (1994).

PAUL L. MURPHY

HANDY, William Christopher (b. Florence, Ala., Nov. 16, 1873; d. New York, N.Y., Mar. 28, 1958), MUSICIAN, displayed an early aptitude for music against the objections of his father, a minister, who wanted him to become a clergyman. At 19 he left home in search of a position teaching school in Birmingham, but he was to spend the next four years traveling, doing odd jobs, and playing in bands. In 1896 he joined Mahara's Minstrels as cornetist and later became bandmaster, touring the United States, Canada, and Cuba. He taught music (1900–2) at the Agriculture and Mining College in Normal, Alabama, then returned briefly to the Mahara troupe before accepting an offer to direct a band at Clarksdale, Mississippi, in 1903. By 1905, Handy was in Memphis where he organized a band of his own. It was here that he began to write down and arrange some of the music he had heard from the poor blacks of the Mississippi delta country. Popularly known as "the blues," this music reflected the hardship of the black man's lot in America and the tough-minded humor with which he adjusted to it.

Handy received widespread attention when he wrote a campaign song for E. H. Crump of Memphis called "Mr. Crump" (1909), which he published as "Memphis Blues" (1912). He composed numerous other "blues" works, such as "Yellow Dog Blues" (1914), "Beale Street Blues" (1916), and the famous "St. Louis Blues" (1914). In 1913 he founded his own music publishing company. In 1918 he transferred the business to New York, where it was named the Handy Brothers Music Co. During the 1920s Handy and his music became extremely popular. In 1926 he published *Blues: An Anthology*, and in 1928 he conducted a special concert at Carnegie Hall that depicted the musical history of the African-American in the United States. He continued composing during the 1930s. He played before large crowds at the 1939 New York World's Fair and published his autobiography, *Father of the Blues* (1941). In 1943, as a result of an accident, Handy lost his sight. Thereafter he was forced to dictate his compositions.

In his later years he published *Negro Authors and Composers of the United States* (1941), *Negro Music and Musicians* (1944), and *A Treasury of the Blues* (1949), a reprint of his 1926 *Anthology*. Shortly before his death he established the Handy Foundation for the Blind.

⸺⸺❧⸺⸺

W. C. Handy was the first to recognize commercial potential in the unprepossessing tradition of rural black folk music known as blues. In his autobiography he tells of his astonishment when, one night in Cleveland, Mississippi (1903), he saw his well-drilled dance orchestra upstaged by a ragtag local blues band. As "dollars, quarters, halves" showered down on his rivals, Handy had a revelation. "That night a composer was born, an *American* composer," he later wrote. "My idea of what constitutes music was changed by the sight of that silver money cascading around the splay feet of a Mississippi string band."

Handy was suited by talent and temperament for his role as middleman between southern black oral tradition and Tin Pan Alley. His musical roots lay in the South. As he freely admitted, he drew some of the music for his own blues compositions from folk sources. At the same time he was a firm and experienced leader and a keen entrepreneur. These traits, taken together with his posture of upright moral integrity, made him acceptable generally to both black musicians and the white musical establishment.

Handy was more trouper than artist. Though accepting the title "Father of the Blues," he remained skeptical of the musical worth of blues, by his own admission being most deeply moved by such pieces as Malotte's "The Lord's Prayer," Sullivan's "The Lost Chord," and **Irvin Berlin's** "God Bless America." He lived to see himself honored as an exemplar of the black race in America, a role he assumed gracefully and without a trace of uneasiness. See W. C. Handy, *Father of the Blues* (1970).

RICHARD CRAWFORD

HANNA, Marcus Alonzo (b. New Lisbon, Ohio, Sept. 24, 1837; d. Washington, D.C., Feb. 15, 1904), POLITICAL LEADER, MANUFACTURER, became a partner in the family wholesale grocery business in Cleveland after his father's death in 1862. In 1864 he married the daughter of Daniel P. Rhodes, a coal and iron magnate, and later joined his firm, which in 1885 was reorganized as M. A. Hanna and Co. His other Cleveland interests included a bank, a newspaper, the Opera House, and the street railway system.

Hanna's contributions to the 1880 presidential campaign earned him membership on the Republican State Committee. He and Congressman Joseph B. Foraker became leading supporters of Senator **John Sherman** for the presidency in 1884, but when Foraker switched to **James G. Blaine,** Hanna broke with him. Hanna then turned to another fellow Ohioan who had remained loyal to Sherman, Congressman William McKinley. He supported McKinley's protectionist Tariff of 1890 and helped him win the Ohio governorship in 1891. Hanna then organized a McKinley-for-president drive, which culminated in McKinley's winning the Republican nomination in 1896. Hanna contacted many business and political leaders and supplied most of the preconvention expenses. Following McKinley's nomination, Hanna, as Republican National Committee chairman, managed the campaign.

Having rejected a cabinet post, Hanna was appointed U.S. senator from Ohio in 1897 to replace John Sherman, who became McKinley's secretary of state. He was elected to a full term in 1898. As senator, Hanna was a critic of interventionism and imperialism but subsequently was converted to both. He championed big-business interests, was an opponent of civil service reform, and sponsored an unsuccessful ship subsidy bill to restore the declining merchant marine. He was also an advocate of the Panama Canal, and he continued his organizing work in the elections of 1898 and 1900.

After the assassination of McKinley (1901), President Theodore Roosevelt retained Hanna as an adviser. He was chosen chairman of the National Civic Federation in 1901. His pressure on recalcitrant employers to come to terms was important in settling the anthracite strike of 1902. Hanna accepted labor organization as necessary for rapid and efficient settlement of industrial disputes.

⁂

An expansive, gregarious man of striking forcefulness, Hanna was more dominating than domineering. As one of his biographers writes, "He had the gift of refusing requests without incurring enmity, of smoothing over disagreements, of conciliating his opponents, of retaining his friends without necessarily doing too much for them." He shared McKinley's belief that large-scale production was both inevitable and desirable and that tariff protection was in the common interest of workers and manufacturers. He himself was a generous employer in the paternalistic tradition, and though he opposed labor unions during his early business career, he came in time to accept them. As he expostulated in 1902 when management refused to accede to the demands of the United Mine Workers, "Well! They will not only strike, but they will get ten percent increase before they settle."

Hanna was less interested in the formal trappings of power than in shaping policy; in whatever council, his voice was influential if not always decisive. He perceived the potential business base of Republican politics, and in 1896 he devised a system of corporate assessment for campaign funds. Successful to a degree never before equaled, he then adapted the merchandising techniques of business to the campaign itself.

Hanna recognized that the new president's constituency and interests were necessarily broader than his own, and he never dominated McKinley during his presidency; neither did he ever dominate the United States Senate, control of which was exercised by **Nelson W. Aldrich,** Orville H. Platt, John Spooner, and **William B. Allison.** Yet Hanna remained one of McKinley's most important advisers and closest confidants. Partly because he believed that subordinates should not be independent of their superiors, he helped persuade McKinley not to push civil service reform.

Hanna opposed the movement for war against Spain in the winter of 1898 but eventually deferred to the overwhelming popular sentiment for hostilities. He also held out for a while against acquisition of the Philippines, only to submit to the pressure of the GOP's China-oriented business element. "If it is commercialism to want possession of a strategic point giving ... a foothold in the markets of the great Eastern country," he finally declared, "for God's sake let's have commercialism." Unable to prevent the nomination of Theodore Roosevelt for vice president in 1900, Hanna maintained a tenuous but cordial relationship with Roosevelt after McKinley's assassination.

Many business leaders wanted Hanna to challenge Roosevelt for the presidential nomination in 1904. "Stop making presidents and become one yourself," a group of railroad executives urged. Although Hanna did not aspire to the office, he drove for control of the party in order to make Roosevelt beholden to him and the GOP's conservative wing. The drive was thwarted even before Hanna died, five months before the national convention. See Herbert Croly, *Marcus Alonzo Hanna: His Life and Work* (1912).

WILLIAM H. HARBAUGH

HANSEN, Alvin Harvey (b. Viborg, S.D., Aug. 23, 1887; d. Alexandria, Va., June 6, 1975), ECONOMIST, graduated from Yankton (S.D.) College in 1910. After serving as a high school principal (1910–12) and superintendent (1912–13) of the Lake Preston, South Dakota, school system, he entered the University of Wisconsin, receiving an MA in economics in 1915. He was assistant instructor of economics there (1915–16) and at Brown University (1916–19). He received a PhD from Wisconsin in 1918, taught economics at the University of Minnesota (1919–37), and was then appointed Lucius N. Littauer professor of political economy at Harvard. He was also research director and secretary to the Commission of Inquiry on International Economic Relations (1933–34); member of the Columbia University Commission on Economic Recovery (1934); economist for the State Department (1934–35); economic adviser on the Prairie Provinces to the Canadian Royal Commission on Dominion-Provincial Relations (1937–38); member of the Advisory Council on Social Security (1937–38); chairman of the Economic Advisory Council, National Industrial Conference Board (1938–39); special economic adviser to the Federal Reserve Board (1940–45); and chairman of the U.S.-Canadian Joint Economic Commission (1943–45).

Through his students and books Hansen influenced the economic policies of President Franklin Roosevelt. However, his writing during the thirties and forties—*Economic Stabilization in an Unbalanced World* (1932), *A New Plan for*

Unemployment Reserves (1933), *Full Recovery or Stagnation?* (1938), and *Fiscal Policy and Business Cycles* (1941)—sometimes criticized the Roosevelt administration. Hansen's pamphlet "After the War—Full Employment" (1942) advocated prevention of postwar depression through increased taxes, public works and housing programs, and international cooperation to secure full employment. This program became the basis of the unsuccessful Murray-Wagner-O'Mahoney full employment bill of 1945. His *America's Role in the World Economy* (1945) set forth economic and financial policies that he viewed as complementary to the new international political organization of the United Nations. Hansen's later books include *Economic Policy and Full Employment* (with **Paul A. Samuelson**, 1947), *Monetary Theory and Fiscal Policy* (1948), *A Guide to Keynes* (1953), *The American Economy* (1957), *Economic Issues of the 1960's* (1960), and *The Dollar and the International Monetary System* (1965).

Alvin Hansen's signal contribution to economics was the refinement and popularization of the theories of John Maynard Keynes.

Keynes's revolutionary *General Theory of Employment, Interest and Money* challenged the most basic tenets of doctrine on how to increase employment and national income in times of depression. But his work was little understood outside Cambridge University in the 1930s; President Roosevelt totally rebuffed Keynes's one attempt to counsel American policymakers during the period.

Hence the importance of Harvard professor and government adviser Hansen's 1941 book, *Fiscal Policy and Business Cycles.* In rather dull and pedantic fashion *Fiscal Policy* presented the Keynesian schema at a level easily understood by professional economists. Hansen not only supported Keynes's view that the Great Depression could have been quickly ended by massive government intervention but advocated a policy of continuous fiscal "fine-tuning" to maintain full employment over the natural business cycle.

Perhaps as significant, Hansen was largely

responsible for training the first generation of New Economists, both directly (his graduate seminar in fiscal policy included Paul Samuelson and James Tobin) and indirectly (his *Guide to Keynes* laid out the framework for a still larger audience). One might also note that Samuelson's 1948 textbook, written shortly after he received his PhD from Harvard, cemented the academic triumph of Keynesian economics by making it intelligible to students at the introductory level.

Hansen's other contributions to the post-depression renaissance of economics included a mathematical synthesis of Keynes and more traditional theories of national income determination, a synthesis that today forms the core of macroeconomics. His other major work—the so-called Stagnation Thesis—extended the Keynesian approach by arguing that mature industrial economies could avoid depression only through increasing levels of government stimulation. See William Breit and Roger Ransom, *The Academic Scribblers: American Economists in Collision* (1971).

PETER PASSELL

HARDING, Warren Gamaliel (b. Corsica, Ohio, Nov. 2, 1865; d. San Francisco, Calif., Aug. 2, 1923), PRESIDENT, attended Ohio Central College (1879–82) and after a brief attempt at teaching and at selling real estate became owner-editor of the Marion *Star* (1884). He was a Republican member of the Ohio state senate (1900–4) and lieutenant governor (1904–6), but lost the 1910 Ohio gubernatorial election. He was elected to the U.S. Senate in 1914. As senator he was generally conservative. He voted against the confirmation of Associate Justice **Louis Brandeis** to the Supreme Court, attacked President Woodrow Wilson's Mexican policy, but supported the declaration of war against Germany. He favored protective tariffs, opposed high taxes on war profits, and voted to return the railroads to their private owners after World War I.

In 1920, on the tenth ballot, he was nominated as the Republican presidential candidate. Conducting a "front porch campaign," he equivocated on the League of Nations and pledged a return to "normalcy." He easily defeated Democrat James M. Cox, 404 electoral votes to 127, receiving 61 percent of the popular vote. As president, on domestic issues he was basically pro-business and followed a conservative line, supporting a return to laissez-faire, lower taxes on high incomes, a higher tariff (the Fordney-McCumber Act of 1922), and retrenchment on government spending through the creation of the Bureau of the Budget. In foreign affairs he championed the peace treaties ending the war with the Central Powers and convened the Washington Disarmament Conference of 1921–22.

When Harding entered the White House, he brought with him a number of friends who came to be known (somewhat erroneously) as the "Ohio Gang." Included among these were **Harry Daugherty,** the U.S. attorney general; Charles R. Forbes, head of the Veterans' Bureau; and **Albert B. Fall,** secretary of the interior. These men were later found to have engaged in corrupt activities. Daugherty was dismissed by President Calvin Coolidge (1924) for improprieties in office; Forbes was found guilty of embezzlement; and Fall was fined and imprisoned for leasing the government oil reserves at Elk Hills and Teapot Dome to private interests for a bribe. Harding died of a heart attack after a trip to Alaska, before these scandals became public knowledge.

Because of the scandals and also because of rumors surrounding his private life, Harding's personal reputation and his historical significance have remained clouded. Evidence of extramarital affairs as well as myths concerning his sudden death conspired to create the picture of an irresolute man who indulged in dissipated and vulgar habits, who never took his presidential job seriously, and who was constantly manipulated by others.

Harding did have many weaknesses. He had a compulsive desire to be liked and carried friendships beyond the point of reason. In him such normally laudatory traits as loyalty, kindness, and gentleness became destructive. He was not always a good judge of men and selected his close associates poorly. While he possessed a good native intelligence, it was not reinforced by mental discipline or a first-class education. He often arrived at decisions intuitively. When in doubt he sought the path of least resistance and was attracted by the lure of expediency. When facing an extremely difficult decision he was inclined to temporize and hope that time would intervene to solve the problem.

Yet Harding maintained an uncanny rapport with public opinion and was a highly successful politician. In part this success rested on a golden voice and a distinguished bearing—tall, large-framed, square-jawed, silver-haired. In part it rested on his amazing ability to pacify and compromise. But more important, it rested on a careful analysis of the political climate and a strict adherence to the wishes of his Ohio constituents. Rather than being manipulated by others, Harding was always firmly in control of his own political career. He was not a member of the Old Guard, not because of either coercion or complacency but by choice and because of Ohio political realities. In making plans for his presidential candidacy he shrewdly sensed that his own conservative views, those of his Ohio constituents, and those of the national electorate were merging. In 1920, Harding was not a "dark horse," nominated by a Senate cabal, nor was he elected on a fluke. More than almost any other president he represented the mood of the nation at the time of his election. In the universal reaction against the haughty and intellectual Wilson, he was indeed Main Street come to Washington. His remark that he and his wife were "just folks" struck as sympathetic a chord in the nation's breast as did his call for a "return to normalcy."

It is in this area that Harding's major significance lies, not in the scandals or in the sensational aspects of his private life. Both symbolically and actually he served as the bridge between the last acrimonious years of Wilson's second administration and the years of ballyhoo and peace. As a pacifier, as a mediator, and as an emollient Harding was unexcelled. The net effect was restorative for the nation and, despite the scandals (which the nation quickly forgot), beneficial for the Republican Party. To the extent that the Harding policies were followed for the rest of the decade, the 1920s as a whole might be called the Harding era.

Contrary to myth, Harding was an extremely hardworking president and grew in the job as time passed. Typically, he surrounded himself with both the best and the worst that American politics had to offer. It was a strange mixture that saw men such as **Charles E. Hughes,** Hoover, **Andrew Mellon,** Daugherty, and Fall in the same cabinet. Interestingly, Harding, while president, took advice more readily from the first three than from the last two. In the foreign area he remained consistently sympathetic to Hughes's ideas, and his administration not only liquidated the holdover peacemaking problems of the Wilson administration but undertook welcomed departures in policies, especially toward Latin America. Already holding similar views as Mellon on monetary policy, Harding presided not only over a sharp reduction in government debt and expenditures but the transition from postwar depression to economic recovery. Harding considered Hoover the smartest man in his cabinet and allowed him great latitude in initiating business reforms that fed the later Coolidge boom. Still, if Harding can rightly claim a measure of success through the efforts of these men, he must also share the failure of the others. His crucial mistake was in not publicizing the indiscretions of such friends as Daugherty and Fall once they became known to him. Because of his inaction he forfeited whatever chance he had to save himself and his administration from the onus history has placed on it.

It is to Harding's credit that he had no illusions about himself. He knew he had a weakness for friends and once remarked that if he were a girl he would be in a family way all the time; he simply could not say "No." He knew his intellectual talents were not outstanding and once commented: "I know my limitations; I know how far removed from greatness I am." He also knew that he was an avowed conservative whose political values came from an unbridled individualism that prompted him to exhort one audience to "think more of what

you can do for your government than what your government can do for you." Such laudable frankness, of course, cannot be accepted as a substitute for high ability, nor can it compensate for errors made or opportunities lost. Yet Harding was not, as one New York editor once called him, "an indistinguishable unit in the ruck of Republican Senators," and as president he was certainly the equal of a Franklin Pierce, an Andrew Johnson, a Benjamin Harrison, or even a Calvin Coolidge. See Robert K. Murray, *The Harding Era* (1969).

ROBERT K. MURRAY

HARLAN, John Marshall (b. Boyle County, Ky., June 1, 1833; d. Washington, D.C., Oct. 14, 1911), JURIST, graduated from Centre College (1850), studied law at Transylvania University, and then served as adjutant general of Kentucky (1851) and county court judge of Franklin County (1858). In the 1850s Harlan supported the Native-American, or Know-Nothing Party. In 1859 he ran unsuccessfully for a seat in the U.S. House of Representatives. In 1860 he supported John Bell, the Constitutional Union Party candidate for president. When the Civil War broke out he entered the Union army as a colonel but resigned his commission in 1863 to become attorney general of Kentucky. Because Harlan believed that the Thirteenth Amendment abolishing slavery was "a flagrant invasion of the rights of self-government," he supported **George C. McClellan** against Abraham Lincoln in the 1864 presidential contest. After the war he accepted the "war amendments" as a necessary result of the Union victory, and he became a Republican.

Defeated in races for the governorship of Kentucky in 1871 and 1875, Harlan headed his state's delegation to the Republican presidential convention of 1876 and threw his state's support to the successful candidate, Rutherford B. Hayes. In April 1877, following Hayes's election, the president appointed him to a commission established to settle the Louisiana gubernatorial election controversy; in October 1877, Hayes named him to the Supreme Court.

While on the Court Harlan became noted for

his dissents in cases bearing on state and federal regulation of business and for his strong advocacy of black rights. A believer in government regulation of industry, he objected to the Court's decision in the *E. C. Knight* case (1895), which emasculated the Sherman Antitrust Act (1890). He also dissented in *Pollack* v. *Farmer's Loan and Trust Co.* (1895), in which the Court invalidated the income tax. He argued that justices should not abuse their power of judicial review nor base their decisions on natural law. Therefore, when the Court read the word "unreasonable" into the Sherman Antitrust Act so that it could dissolve the Standard Oil and American Tobacco Companies (1911), he dissented.

In the civil liberty controversies of the period—when the Court ruled in the "Civil Rights Cases" of 1883, for example, that equality of rights in public accommodations was not enforceable under either the Fourteenth or Fifteenth Amendments, and in *Plessy* v. *Ferguson* (1896) that "separate but equal accommodations" were in accordance with the Fourteenth Amendment—Harlan dissented. While on the bench Harlan also served as an American representative at the Bering Sea boundary discussions with Great Britain (1892) and lectured at Columbia University (now George Washington University).

If John Marshall Harlan had never written anything but the single sentence in his dissent in *Plessy* v. *Ferguson,* "Our Constitution is colorblind and neither knows nor tolerates classes among citizens," he would still deserve an honored place in our history. At that time this view of the race question was a minority opinion, on the Court and among the white population at large, but neither the opinion nor the underlying moral principle it enunciated could be eradicated, and with the burgeoning of the civil rights movement after World War II, it finally prevailed. Harlan, however, did have a great deal more to say during his thirty-four years on the Supreme Court, and much of it is of equal relevance to our own times. During a period when the Court was checking legislative attempts to control big busi-

ness, he was notable for his powerful statements in defense of the right of regulation. "We must have corporations," he wrote in 1905, "but we must see that they do not corrupt our government.... We [have] reached that point in the management of politics when educated men ... [are] willing to receive from officers of corporations money for political purposes." Yet Harlan was not antibusiness. Government interference with property rights exercised him as much as violations of civil rights.

But what is most remarkable about Harlan is not the contemporary relevance of so many of his ideas. He is a shining example of that rare type of person who can reason through and then rise above his emotional prejudices. Born into a slaveowning family, first achieving political fame as an opponent of freedom, he was nevertheless able, after the Civil War, to confront the new reality and change himself in order to conform to it. He was no mere officeseeker shifting to accommodate to new political winds. Rather, he reexamined his beliefs and reached a new understanding of the public interest. His actions on the Court show clearly the profundity and sincerity of his new convictions. This was his greatness. Our current veneration of his ideas and his courage is in a sense mere chance. Surely it would have pleased him, but his career demonstrates that he did not need popular approval to sustain him. See Tinsley E. Yarbrough, *Judicial Enigma: The First Justice Harlan* (1994).

JOHN A. GARRATY

HARPER, James (b. Newtown, N.Y., Apr. 13, 1795; d. New York, N.Y., Mar. 27, 1869), PUBLISHER, was apprenticed at the age of 15 to the printing house of Paul and Thomas in New York City. In 1817, after his younger brother John had finished a similar apprenticeship, the two Harpers set up their own printing business as J. and J. Harper. Among their first major efforts was a two-thousand-copy edition of *Seneca's Morals*. In 1818 the brothers ventured into publishing, producing under their own imprint an edition of John Locke's *Essay upon the Human Understanding.*

The concern, after taking in as partners Joseph Wesley Harper in 1823 and Fletcher Harper in 1825, changed its name to Harper and Brothers in 1833. In the decades before the Civil War the house prospered and achieved great prestige. Joseph Wesley Harper served as chief literary editor, John was in charge of composition and proofreading, and Fletcher was an innovator and administrator. James, as foreman, kept the house abreast of such technological advances as steam-run presses and electrotyping. He is also believed to have inspired the founding of *Harper's New Monthly* in 1850, one of four periodicals produced by the firm in the 19th century.

In 1844, Harper was elected mayor of New York City on a Protestant-nativist reform ticket, although he did not himself express nativist positions. In 1845, declining to campaign, he was narrowly defeated for reelection by the Democratic candidate William F. Havemeyer. He died after a fall from a carriage.

⸺⸺

James Harper's life was in the classic American pattern of the farm boy who came to the city and found his fortune; it was considerably more industrious than adventurous. As his grandnephew J. Henry Harper wrote, "James Harper's life was not an eventful one. A plain man, devoted to business, shunning official station, and caring little for society, he passed modestly through a long and prosperous career." He gave his life to the enterprise that he and his three younger brothers guided for more than half a century. The Harpers entered the printing business at the dawn of the age of mass production for a mass audience. At the same time that the penny press was transforming journalism, the Harpers were helping to create an expanded readership for books, especially popular novels. Under James Harper's guidance the house learned to perform near-miracles in feeding reader appetites—for example, seizing a new English novel off an incoming boat and having an edition on the street less than twenty-four hours later. With numerous series, such as the 187-volume Harper Family Library, the company anticipated

20th-century book club merchandising. Further, Harper and Brothers' exploitation of the new reading market helped attract the talent that led to New York's reign as the American literary capital; one notable early publication, for example, was the first edition of **Herman Melville**'s *Moby Dick* (1851). The institution that the brothers founded proved enduring, but the next generations of the family proved unable to duplicate the founders' success, and family control ended at the turn of the century. See J. Henry Harper, *The House of Harper* (1912).

JAMES BOYLAN

HARPER, William Rainey (b. New Concord, Ohio, July 26, 1856; d. Chicago, Ill., Jan. 10, 1906), EDUCATOR, graduated from Muskingum College (1870) and received a PhD in biblical studies from Yale (1874). He briefly taught at Masonic College, Macon, Tennessee (1875), and Denison College, Granville, Ohio (1876–79), before joining the faculty of the Baptist Union Theological Seminary in Chicago as a professor of Semitic languages and literature (1879–86). During this period he founded and edited two journals, *Hebrew Student* (later *Biblical World*) and *Hebraica* (later *American Journal of Semitic Languages and Literature*). During 1886–91 he taught at Yale. Beginning in 1885 he became active in the Chautauqua movement, lecturing in the summers.

In 1891, Harper became the first president of the University of Chicago. An advocate of academic freedom and nonsectarian education, he also greatly valued graduate study and research. With financial assistance from **John D. Rockefeller**, Harper assembled some of the nation's best minds at the University of Chicago. During his presidency he instituted a university press, a junior college, university affiliations, the division of the school year into four quarters, and an extension program. Some of his books include *The Priestly Element in the Old Testament* (1902), *Religion and the Higher Life* (1904), *The Trend in Higher Education* (1905), *The Prophetic Element in the Old Testament* (1905), and *Critical and Exegetical Commentary on Amos and Hosea* (1905).

∽∽∽

Many of his contemporaries saw William Rainey Harper as a genius, a *Wunderkind* of American higher education: college graduate at 14, PhD at 18, full professor by the age of 30, and president of a great new university at 35. A person of seemingly inexhaustible energy, he was able to cram into a relatively short life not one but several notable careers. He was a superb college teacher, an industrious if not surpassingly original Old Testament scholar, a dynamic Chautauqua lecturer, the successful promoter of dozens of correspondence and seminary courses on Hebrew and the Bible, a busy editor of both erudite and popular publications, and the chief planner, organizer, fund-raiser, and administrator of America's greatest educational "trust" of the late 19th century—the University of Chicago.

Harper stood alone among the presidents of large modern universities in his insistence on teaching full-time as chairman of his own department (Semitic languages). He also immensely enjoyed planning and launching new educational programs, overseeing important enterprises, getting things done. His infectious enthusiasm enabled him to carry people along with him to achieve whatever goals he wished to attain, whether they were the more effective teaching of Hebrew or the attraction of large donations to a promising new university.

As a university president, Harper was frankly an empire builder, not unlike the transcontinental railroad promoters and corporation executives of his day. Despite his assertion that the University of Chicago in 1891-92 was unique among institutions of higher education, few of its projected features were original. However, Harper's grandiose combination of a multitude of preexisting programs and proposals in one comprehensive, minutely detailed, carefully articulated structure was undeniably significant in its own right. Chicago was America's first true "multiversity"; it was promptly labeled "Harper's Bazaar" by the irreverent. Critics complained that the university was overorganized, yet as long as Harper remained at its helm (with **Thorstein Veblen, John Dewey,** Robert Herrick, and William Vaughn Moody on its faculty), it was one of the most lively and creative centers of thought in the history of American education. See "Memorials of William Rainey Harper," *The Biblical World,* 27 (Mar. 1906), 165–219.

WILLIS RUDY

HARRIMAN, Edward Henry (b. Hempstead, L.I., N.Y., Feb. 20, 1848; d. Orange Co., N.Y., Sept. 9, 1909), RAILROAD MAGNATE, FINANCIER, was educated at Trinity School in New York City and became an office boy in the Wall Street brokerage house of D. C. Hays in 1862. He borrowed $3,000 from his uncle Oliver Harriman in 1870 to purchase a seat on the New York Stock Exchange. In 1879 he married Mary Williamson Averell, the daughter of William J. Averell, a banker from Ogdensburg, New York, and president of the Ogdensburg and Lake Champlain Railroad. Through his connection with the Averell family he gained control of the Lake Ontario Southern Railroad in 1881. Organizing the management and renovating the track and rolling stock, he sold the line at a large profit to the Pennsylvania Railroad in 1883.

Forming an alliance with Stuyvesant Fish, Harriman joined the board of directors of the Illinois Central Railroad in 1883, becoming vice president in 1887. Favoring an expansionist policy, the new directorate outmaneuvered **J. P. Morgan** in a contest to gain control of the Dubuque and Sioux City Railroad in 1887. Fish and Harriman extended the Illinois Central southward to New Orleans by 1892. Placed on a sound financial base by Harriman, the Illinois Central weathered the panic of 1893 that drove many other railroads into bankruptcy.

In 1898, Harriman became chairman of the executive committee of the Union Pacific Railroad. In alliance with the Wall Street firm of Kuhn, Loeb, and Co., he directed the reorganization of this bankrupt line. By 1901 he had placed the Union Pacific on a sound financial basis. Under his management the Union Pacific absorbed the Kansas Pacific, Denver Pacific, and the Oregon Short Line in 1898, and acquired the vast Southern Pacific system in 1901. When **James J. Hill** and J. P. Morgan blocked Harriman's attempt to acquire the strategically situated Chicago, Burlington, and Quincy Railroad road, he engaged in a contest for control of Hill's Northern Pacific Railroad. In a titanic battle the two groups forced the price of Northern Pacific stock up to $1,000 a share, ruining many speculators and precipitating a financial panic (May 1901). The Harriman interests controlled the preferred stock, the Hill-Morgan interests the common. The two groups reached a compromise by forming the giant Northern Securities Co. to coordinate control of the Great Northern, the Northern Pacific, and the Chicago, Burlington, and Quincy. However, when the United States Supreme Court dissolved this combination in 1904, Hill managed to exclude Harriman from control of the three constituent companies.

Harriman became a member of the board of directors of the Baltimore and Ohio Railroad in 1899 and the Erie Railroad in 1903. He gained control of the Equitable Life Insurance Society in a controversial transaction in 1905. Acquiring the Pacific Mail Steamship Co. along with the Southern Pacific Railroad in 1901, he engaged in trade with China and Japan. However, his plans for a trans-Asian railroad fell through under pressure from the Japanese government in 1905.

Financing the Tompkins Square Boys Club in 1876, Harriman participated in the affairs of this organization throughout his life. He organized a scientific expedition to Alaska in 1899. The findings appeared in the *Harriman Alaska Series* (14 vols., 1902–14). He also donated $1 million and ten thousand acres of land for a public park on the Hudson River in 1909.

—❧—

Harriman's rise to a commanding position in the world of American finance capitalism was like an extension of pure will. That his burning ambition to shape great ends found its expression in railroading, the principal industry of 19th-century America, was an accident of time. In anoth-

er epoch he might well have been a military commander or a planter of new colonies. He could do anything, he declared, "if I put my mind on it." This assertion was validated by many episodes in his career, particularly his encounters with J. P. Morgan, from which Harriman usually emerged with enhanced prestige for his intelligent strategy and fearless tactics.

To a business generation that made a cult of Napoleon, the dark-complexioned Harriman, a man of slight physique with deep and piercing eyes set below a powerful brow, inevitably summoned up the visage of the French emperor, but it was his indomitable will, his quick and decisive movements, and his incredibly swift mental processes that made Harriman seem the very essence of Napoleonic energy. His almost legendary courage underscored the resemblance. At one point during his Alaskan expedition, when the ship's captain refused to negotiate a dangerous night passage through the uncharted, glacier-infested waters of a fiord, Harriman himself seized the helm and guided the vessel safely over the risky course.

His career illuminates the transition of the American economy from industrial to financial capitalism between 1885 and 1910. His years as a Wall Street broker dealing mostly in railroad investments gave him a priceless working knowledge of the securities market that later served him well in winning management control of various roads. His brokerage experience also brought him into contact with private bankers whose support he sometimes elicited by bold but effective means. In one crucial respect, however, he was different from the fabricators of paper mergers and the cormorants of speculative finance who milked the American railroad system for its profits at the cost of proper maintenance and left the roads burdened with a massive debt structure they never shook off. To Harriman, stocks and bonds were more than just paper certificates; even as a broker he sensed the sheer physical presence of the tangible assets—locomotives, freight cars, bridges, terminals, and the like—that lay behind the steel-engraved paper.

His first venture in railroading, which saw

him transform a small rundown line into a profitable enterprise, reflected this attitude, as it did his matchless ability to identify and exploit opportunities generally overlooked by others. Speaking years afterward of his acquisition of the Lake Ontario Southern, Harriman said: "This property had great strategic value which nobody seemed to recognize. I knew that if I put it into good physical condition, so it could handle and develop traffic, the Pennsylvania Railroad would jump at a chance to buy it, in order to get an outlet to [Lake Ontario]; and that the New York Central would be equally anxious to buy it, in order to keep its rival out. My experience with this railroad taught me a lesson with respect to the importance of proper physical condition in a transportation property which I have never forgotten." That lesson was: "The only way to make a good property valuable is to put it in the best possible condition to do business."

This was the rule Harriman applied in his most spectacular undertaking, the Union Pacific. His first move was to make a personal survey of its dilapidated main line. For this he used a special train with an observation car in front. Traveling only in daylight, he examined the road down to the smallest detail ("He saw every poor tie, blistered rail, and loose bolt on my division," said one superintendent). He spent huge sums on reconstruction, virtually rebuilding the main line between 1898 and 1901. This was followed by an even more ambitious program of capital spending on new construction and heavier equipment. The resulting economies in operating costs, combined with the growing volume of traffic that accompanied the resumption of farm prosperity after 1897, made the UP enormously profitable.

Harriman's substantial holdings in UP stock became the foundation of his vast fortune. The Wall Street expert John Moody estimated that the purchaser of 100 shares of UP common in 1898 for $1,600 had within eight and a half years garnered a return of $21,900 in dividends and appreciated value. Harriman, however, never prized wealth for its own sake. For him it was a lever for expanding the scope of his will. As he told his friend, the naturalist **John Muir**: "I never cared for money except as power for work. What I most enjoy is the power of creation." His last major project, never realized, was a round-the-world transportation line under single control. Pushing himself to the end, he died of gastric ulcers brought on by overwork and nervous strain. See George Kennan, *E. H. Harriman* (2 vols., 1922).

WILLIAM GREENLEAF

HARRIMAN, William Averell (b. New York, N.Y., Nov. 15, 1891; Yorktown Heights, N.Y., July 26, 1986), DIPLOMAT, heir of railroad magnate **Edward Henry Harriman,** received his BA from Yale in 1913. After becoming vice president in charge of purchases and supplies of the Union Pacific Railroad (1915–17), Harriman bought a small shipyard that built the world's first partly prefabricated ships. This venture became the prosperous Merchant Shipping Corporation, which Harriman headed from 1917 to 1925. He was criticized in 1920 for attempting to evade the excess-profits tax when he bought up the vessels of another firm. The federal government seized the money paid for the ships but then let the matter drop. In 1920, Harriman established a private bank, of which he was chairman of the board until 1931 when he merged it with Brown Brothers. He became chairman of the board of the Union Pacific Railroad in 1932; during the Depression the road remained profitable because Harriman invested in improved rolling stock and services. During the 1920s his business interests brought him in contact with Russian leaders for the first time.

Upon **Harry Hopkins's** recommendation, President Franklin Roosevelt appointed Harriman administrator of Division II of the National Recovery Administration (Jan. 1934); he became NRA administrative officer in October 1934 after Hugh Johnson's resignation, serving until the abolition of the NRA in 1935. Having been a member since 1933, Harriman was chairman of the Business Advisory Council of the Department of Commerce (1937–40), which worked to promote cooperation between government and business. He was appointed chief of the raw materials branch, Office of Production

Management, in 1941, coordinating Lend-Lease aid to Britain and the U.S.S.R. and attending major Allied consultations. As ambassador to the Soviet Union (1943–46), Harriman continued to work on American aid to the U.S.S.R. In March 1946, President Harry S. Truman appointed him ambassador to Great Britain; he returned to the United States seven months later to serve as Truman's secretary of commerce (1946–48). He then became director of economic aid to Europe under the Marshall Plan (1948–50) originated by **George C. Marshall**; special assistant to the president (1950–51); American representative on the North Atlantic Treaty Organization commission to study Western defenses (1951); and director of the Mutual Security Agency (1951–53).

Harriman was elected governor of New York in 1954 but was defeated for reelection by **Nelson A. Rockefeller** in 1958. His gubernatorial accomplishments included middle-income housing and highway construction programs, an active antidiscrimination commission, the first state consumer protection agency, and a call for a war on poverty. President John F. Kennedy appointed Harriman "ambassador at large" in 1961; he was assistant secretary of state for Far Eastern affairs (1961–63) and undersecretary of state for political affairs (1963–65), negotiating the 1962 Laos Accord and 1963 Nuclear Test Ban Treaty. In 1965, President Johnson again appointed him "ambassador at large." He served until 1968 when he was appointed to head the U.S. delegation at the Paris peace talks on Vietnam. He strove for accommodation but found it difficult to achieve partly because of North Vietnamese intransigence and partly because of the inflexible position of the South Vietnamese. With Richard Nixon's election to the presidency in 1968, he stepped down in 1969. He was among those who felt that the Nixon administration gave the South Vietnamese too great a say in the peace negotiations, thus prolonging the war. Those views made him acceptable and even popular to the growing peace movement and helped put pressure on the Nixon administration to end the conflict.

Though he was in private life in the 1970s and 1980s, Harriman remained deeply interested and active in foreign affairs. In 1983 he went to Moscow to meet the new Soviet leader, Yuri Andropov, and reported back to the president the substance of their conversation. Worried about the decline of interest in Soviet studies on the university level, Harriman donated $10 million to the Russian Institute at Columbia University to promote American studies of the Soviet Union. The family's Gladys and Roland Harriman Foundation contributed $1.5 million more for that purpose. Later, Columbia renamed the institute the W. Averell Harriman Institute for the Advanced Study of the Soviet Union. Harriman also donated his country estate in Harriman, N.Y., Arden House, and ten thousand acres to Columbia.

Averell Harriman linked American expansion of the nineteenth century, which his father represented, to that of the twentieth. He inherited wealth and power from his father, E. H. Harriman, and as a young man moved up in his father's world of railroads and finance, operating on a global scale. Wanting more—higher status, new opportunities for action, more power—he shifted his focus from Wall Street to Washington, doing so in an era of state building, the years of the New Deal and World War II.

Harriman had great confidence in himself and could be charming; he was often outspoken, quick to respond, and sharp and penetrating in his criticisms. Those he did not try to charm frequently found him cold, vain, and arrogant. Fascinated by international problems and turning his attention to them during World War II, he could be calm, patient, flexible, and tough. Although elected governor of New York in 1954, he was not reelected and failed in two bids for the presidency. He was more attractive to the leaders with whom he dealt face to face than to the average American voter.

In four Democratic administrations, beginning with Franklin Roosevelt and ending with Lyndon Johnson, Harriman served in a multitude of posts on the secondary level and below. In doing so he championed the development and use of

American power, both economic and military, and helped shape the vast expansion of American efforts in international affairs in the 1940s. Convinced that conflict between the Soviet Union and the United States could not be avoided and taking advantage of the substitution of Harry Truman for Franklin Roosevelt in 1945, he pressed for a "tougher" policy. Only American power, he maintained, could check Soviet ambition for territorial expansion. In the 1960s he became a negotiator, for the Soviet Union's conflict with China and apparent eagerness to avoid atomic war and cut military costs appeared to open opportunities in some areas. Yet he did not discard his assumptions about the global range of Communist ambitions or the importance of American power. In his last years he had little patience with those who blamed the United States for the cold war and objected to the large American role in the world. See Rudy Abramson, *Spanning the Century: The Life of W. Averell Harriman, 1891–1986* (1992).

RICHARD S. KIRKENDALL

HARRINGTON, Edward Michael (b. St. Louis, Mo., Feb. 24, 1928; d. Larchmont, N.Y., July 31, 1989), REFORMER, graduated from Holy Cross College, Worcester, Massachusetts, in 1947. After spending the next year at Yale Law School, he studied English literature at the University of Chicago, receiving his MA in 1949. He did social work in St. Louis before moving to New York City in 1951 to join the Catholic Worker, a Catholic social agency, and to coedit its publication, the *Catholic Worker*. A conscientious objector during the Korean War, Harrington became increasingly involved in Socialist Party politics, serving as organizational secretary of the Workers' Defense League in 1953 and also as a college campus organizer and lecturer for the Young Socialist League. In 1960 he joined the national executive committee of the Socialist Party.

During the 1950s Harrington wrote many articles on social problems for such magazines as *Commonweal* and *Dissent*. He was editor of *New America*, official organ of the Socialist Party

(1961–62). Long interested in the problem of poverty in affluent America, Harrington wrote *The Other America: Poverty in the United States* (1962), which described the poor as demoralized and trapped in a self-perpetuating way of life, "invisible" to the rest of society. This book helped bring the poverty problem national attention. Elected chairman of the board of the League for Industrial Democracy in 1964, Harrington wrote *The Accidental Century* (1965), a defense of socialism, and *Toward a Democratic Left* (1968), which called for socialistic solutions to America's many domestic problems while criticizing U.S. involvement in Vietnam and Southeast Asia. He was elected national chairman of the Socialist Party in 1968. In 1972, Harrington was appointed professor of political science at Queens College, City University of New York, and was given a Distinguished Professorship in 1988. He served as chairman of the League for Industrial Democracy in 1974 and became chairman of the newly formed Democratic Socialists of America in 1982. Harrington contributed many articles to such magazines as *New Republic, Nation,* and *Atlantic*. His other books include *Labor in a Free Society* (1959), edited with Paul Jacobs, *The Retail Clerks* (1962), *Socialism* (1970), *Fragments of the Century* (1974), an autobiography, *The Long Distance Runner* (1988), and *Socialism: Past and Future* (1989).

⸺⸺⸺

Michael Harrington served his world in many ways: as critic, activist, philosopher, and, above all, as apostle of hope. Fired with a passion to place ideas in humanity's service, he consistently challenged the common wisdom—regardless of source. In 1962 *The Other America* achieved national recognition with its challenge to America's affluent self-image. Later, he contested the validity of Communism's claim of being the true interpreter of Karl Marx while simultaneously confronting capitalism with the competing ideal of a yet to be realized democratic socialist utopia. Faithful always to his party, he always spoke his own mind. He combined warnings to party leaders against subservience to the views of labor's leadership with reminders to middle-class reformers and youthful radicals that union labor was an essential component of the democratic left. While ever remaining radical in his call for fundamental structural changes in American society, he yet always worked energetically for the limited changes that seemed possible. In the disputes of the 1960s between the Old and the New Left he was identified with the former for his concern with "mundane" issues—jobs, housing, medical care—and his continued loyalty to the trade union movement, civil rights, the democratic process, economic planning, and the desirability of enhanced federal power. As an activist, philosopher, and socialist visionary, his intellect was moved by compassion and his message was one of hope. Hope was conveyed in many ways: in choosing to live among the poor and defeated of the city; in insisting to demoralized liberals and radicals of the late 1960s that a new democratic left was a possibility; and, finally, in his belief that a revitalized democratic socialism could harness technology to humane ends and that our society had the abundance to make a peaceful transition to a noncompetitive social order. Ideologically rooted but not rigidly dogmatic, Michael Harrington spoke from deep conviction that the ultimate questions were moral and ethical questions and that the ultimate value was man. See Robert A. Gorman, *Michael Harrington: Speaking American* (1995).

ROBERT A. HUFF

HARRIS, Joel Chandler (b. near Eatonton, Ga., Dec. 9, 1848; d. Atlanta, Ga., July 3, 1908), WRITER, served as a "printer's devil" for Joseph Addison Turner's *Countryman* and, after working for a number of newspapers, established himself as a writer for the Savannah *Morning News* and then the Atlanta *Constitution*.

He gradually began to write poems and to put into print plantation tales that he had learned from African-Americans. In 1879 he wrote his first "Uncle Remus" story for the *Constitution*. Harris tried to recapture the Georgian black dialect and the setting of that dialect. He soon collected a number of black legends, folk tales, proverbs, and "sayings," and published them under the title *Uncle Remus: His Songs and Sayings* (1880). In *Nights with Uncle Remus* (1883) he introduced the character of "Daddy Jake," who spoke in the dialect of the South Carolina rice plantations. These stories were an immediate success. Harris published *Uncle Remus and Br'er Rabbit* in 1906. He also wrote children's stories, articles, and poems for the *Saturday Evening Post*. In 1907 he became editor of *Uncle Remus's Magazine*. Some of his other works include *Mingo and Other Sketches in Black and White* (1884) and *Free Joe and Other Georgian Sketches* (1887).

───── ∞ ─────

Harris, a shy, quiet, unpretentious man, never thought of himself as an intellectual or man of letters; he preferred the simpler labels of newspaperman and storyteller. Yet his essays in social criticism and his short stories and novels (as distinct from his well-known dialect tales) make him a pioneer in the early development of critical thinking and realistic fiction in the postbellum South. In measured, loving tones Harris attacked his region's emotional and ancient attachment to sectionalism, sentimentality, religiosity, and romantic literature. Such values were anachronistic in the modern world, Harris said; worse yet, they choked off the truly creative spirit who prizes his region's special qualities more because he feels free to criticize them and because he shares the national vision and strives to measure up to national standards. Less talented hands served up "local color" with an array of literary stereotypes, particularly racial stereotypes, and Harris himself succumbed to this tendency in some of his black characters. But Harris also explored, in a manner quite uncommon for his time, the darker side of the South's past. His plantation stories strip away age-old layers of sham and pretense and sensitively portray the plight of poor whites, mulattoes, free blacks, and cruel and indifferent masters. In all things, however, whether in his personal life or in his art, Harris remained a complex but exceedingly gentle man who lacked the passionate anger necessary to become a radical critic like his contemporary George Washington Cable or the demonic intensity of feeling and imagination necessary for plumbing the depths of man's existence as **William Faulkner** would decades later. Harris's sense of tragedy was tempered by good manners and a genuine fondness for the southern people, white and black. See Paul M. Cousins, *Joel Chandler Harris: A Biography* (1968).

BRUCE CLAYTON

HARRIS, Townsend (b. Sandy Hill, N.Y., Oct. 3, 1804; d. New York, N.Y., Feb. 25, 1878), DIPLOMAT, EDUCATOR, worked in a dry-goods store before he joined his father and brother as a partner in a firm that imported china and earthenware. After serving as school trustee in the ninth ward of New York City, he was elected as a Democrat to the Board of Education (1846) and served as its president. During his tenure he successfully sponsored legislation establishing the New York Free Academy (now the College of the City of New York), which opened in 1847. When his partnership was dissolved after his father's death (1847), he traveled to California and then embarked on a trading voyage to Malaya, India, and China, which proved to be unprofitable. In 1853, Commodore **Matthew C. Perry** declined his offer to serve on Perry's Japan expedition. Following Perry's treaty opening up trade with Japan, however, Harris was named first consul there. En route to his post he negotiated a commercial treaty with Siam (1856). After negotiations (June 1857 and July 1858) he arranged the first treaty between Japan and a Western nation for diplomatic exchange, trade rights, tariffs, and the right of extraterritoriality. In 1859 he was appointed minister resident and consul general, the first Westerner to hold that rank in Japan. After Abraham Lincoln's election, Harris, a Democrat, resigned; however, he supported Lincoln's policies during the Civil War. He spent the rest of his life in New York City, where he engaged in temperance reform and church and missionary activities.

Townsend Harris came from old New England stock but out of very modest circumstances that forced him to leave school at the age of 13. This combination of factors uniquely animated his career. Driven by the Yankee impulse to work hard and save, Harris—in company with his father and brother—became moderately successful in the business of importing chinaware. Until he was in his forties he was a stay-at-home, the beneficiary of the widening economic opportunity opened up by the rising tide of merchant capitalism, and witness to the lengthening reach of the Western nations toward overseas markets.

A confirmed bachelor, Harris was deeply attached to his mother, with whom he lived. He cultivated his mind generously and studied foreign languages as a dilettante. When his mother died in 1847, the wrench led him to drink heavily for a time, but he brought himself under control and soon gave rein to creative energies apparently released by the emotional shock he had suffered. His single-minded crusade for free higher education that led to the establishment of what became the College of the City of New York both reflected and contributed to strengthening the tenet that universal education is the firmest bulwark of democracy. In the field of diplomacy his stunning triumph among the Japanese was also personal as he broke fresh ground in helping to set Americans on the rocky road to living at peace with peoples of other cultures. See Mario E. Cozenza, *The Establishment of the College of the City of New York* (1925), and Oliver Statler, *Shimoda Story* (1969).

HENRY F. GRAFF

HARRIS, William Torrey (b. near North Killingly, Conn., Sept. 10, 1835; d. Providence, R.I., Nov. 5, 1909), EDUCATOR, after brief attendance at several New England academies, entered Yale in 1857, only to leave in the middle of his junior year. After unsuccessfully trying to establish himself in business in St. Louis, he began (1858) teaching in the public school system. He soon became principal of the new Clay School, then assistant superintendent of schools in 1867, and superintendent the following year.

Harris introduced art, music, science, and manual arts into the curriculum, worked to extend the public high schools, and along with Susan E. Blow, he integrated kindergarten into the system. A prodigious writer on education, his thirteen annual reports (1868–80) as superintendent of schools enjoyed an international reputation. A bibliography of Harris's publications, mostly journal articles, would run to almost five hundred titles. He also edited *Johnson's New Universal Encyclopedia,* a new edition of *Webster's New International Dictionary,* and almost threescore books in Appleton's International Education series. In 1889 he was appointed U.S. commissioner of education, serving until 1906.

Harris gained considerable prominence as a philosopher, but his major preoccupation was German literature and philosophy. By the turn of the century he was generally acknowledged the foremost American authority on Hegel. In his writings he sought to relate Hegelian principles to education. He championed Hegel's doctrines of the solidarity of the individual with the state and of the importance of the state, and eschewed the nascent interest in certain contemporary educational circles in "child study" and empirical psychology. In 1867 he founded the *Journal of Speculative Philosophy.* In 1880 he helped establish the Concord School of Philosophy at Concord, Massachusetts, but Hegelian idealism was then on the wane, and he had little success with this project. His representative books include *An Introduction to the Study of Philosophy* (1889), *Hegel's Logic* (1890), and *The Psychologic Foundations of Education* (1898).

education as the process through which man becomes ethical: by nature man is a mere animal; education provides the tools—mainly literacy and self-discipline—which help man ascend from savagery to civilization and culture. For Harris the role of the school was to preserve and transmit the hard-won heritage of humanity, "the wisdom of race," its culture and system of ethics. The discipline, the liberal arts curriculum, and the texts of the school were the means; the end product was the moral, self-directed, self-controlled individual, able to use independently the tools of thought.

No American educator was more widely acclaimed or quoted in his own time; he was the most influential American educator between **Horace Mann** and **John Dewey.** But he is little known or read today. Harris thought he spoke for a new age in American education; in retrospect, it is clear that he ushered out the old. He failed to reckon with the rapid and extensive social changes going on about him: urbanization, industrialization, immigration. A new generation of educators, led by John Dewey, rectified his omissions.

Harris merits the sobriquet "the Conservator." But at a time of lost bearings in American education, his brand of conservatism seems radical. To read Harris is to discern the chaos and poverty implicit in contemporary debates over education. One may disagree with him, but he challenged in fundamental ways the conventional wisdom and can still provoke fruitful discussion. See John S. Roberts, *William Torrey Harris: A Critical Study of His Educational and Related Philosophical Views* (1927).

SOL COHEN

Tall, spare, sharp-featured, Harris appeared to many contemporaries "a needle that could prick keenly and deeply into things." In reality he was a good but dull man who impressed more by his evident virtue than by force of intellect.

It is as a philosopher of education that he is best remembered. Often obscured or muddled by his addiction to Hegelian jargon, Harris stands as the great American exponent of educational conservatism. He adopted the Hegelian definition of

HARRISON, Benjamin (b. North Bend, Ohio, Aug. 20, 1833; d. Indianapolis, Ind., Mar. 13, 1901), PRESIDENT, grandson of President William Henry Harrison and son of Congressman John Scott Harrison. He graduated from Miami University in 1852. Admitted to the bar (1853), he moved to Indianapolis, joined the new Republican Party, campaigned for **John C. Frémont** (1856), won the post of city attorney (1857), and was elected reporter for the Indiana supreme court. During two war-interrupted terms (1861–62; 1865–69) he edited ten volumes of *Reports*. In the Civil War he raised and commanded the Seventieth Indiana Volunteer Regiment through the Atlanta campaign and rose to brevet brigadier general. He was defeated for the Indiana governorship in 1876. After refusing a place in President James Garfield's cabinet, he served as U.S. senator (1881—87). As senator, he opposed President Grover Cleveland's vetoes of veterans' pension bills and supported a protective tariff and the building of a modern navy.

In 1888, Harrison was elected president. Although he trailed Cleveland in the popular vote by more than 90,000, he carried the electoral college, 233 to 168. During his term he suggested and signed into law four major bills, the first two sponsored by **John Sherman:** (1) the Sherman Anti-Trust Act, outlawing trusts and monopolies that restrained trade; (2) the Sherman Silver Purchase Act, which, by increasing government coinage of silver, aimed at arresting deflation of the currency; (3) the McKinley Tariff Act, setting tariffs at record highs to protect American manufacturers; (4) the Dependent Pension Bill, benefiting all veterans unable to work.

During his administration six new states were admitted to the Union. Harrison supported the first Pan-American Conference held in Washington, D.C., and negotiated reciprocal trade treaties with Latin American countries. Many voters turned against him, however, because of his failure to annex Hawaii (1892–93), his inability to settle labor and farm problems, and the heavy expenditures of the "billion-dollar" 51st Congress. Although he appointed Theodore Roosevelt civil service commissioner and classified more positions than Cleveland, civil service reformers also opposed him. He lost the 1892 election to Cleveland (277 electoral votes to 145), trailing by more than 350,000 popular votes. Harrison then returned to his law practice, wrote extensively, stumped for the election of President McKinley, and served as Venezuela's chief counsel in the boundary dispute over British Guiana that was settled by a five-man arbitral court in Paris (1899).

"March King" **John Philip Sousa** once said, "Few intellectual giants have graced the presidency, but General Harrison was one of them." He was a studious, disciplined man of rather exceptional intellect who also had character. Harrison, though never gregarious, was an able politician, a top-flight orator, a sincere Presbyterian, and a keen student of history who had a talent for law. He knew political, legal, and financial successes along with some sobering failures. A good law practice coupled with modest but wise investments afforded him and his family a comfortable income without resort to chicanery in the Gilded Age. He inherited a love of politics from a great-grandfather who signed the Declaration of Independence, from "Old Tippecanoe," his grandfather president, and from his father, a member of Congress who warned that "none but knaves should ever enter the political arena." Short of stature and styled "Little Ben" by his strictly disciplined regiment, he managed to combine compassion with firmness. Though he taught Sunday school and passed the collection plate regularly, he drank, smoked, hunted, fished, and spun yarns with the boys. Initially short on social graces, he learned quickly and well from his gifted wife Carrie Scott.

Protection to industry and trade expansion in the Pacific and with Central and South America fundamentally stamped Harrison's politics. Proponent of a modern, two-ocean navy, he searched for a constructive rather than a negative hemispheric policy. Trade expansionism, he once told Secretary of State **James G. Blaine,** did not mean colonialism. "You know that I am not much of an annexationist, though I do feel that in some directions, as to naval stations and points of influence, we must look forward to a departure from the too conservative opinions … held heretofore." With a limited, albeit vigorous, belief in Manifest Destiny, he did not oppose union with Canada, control of the Caribbean, or dominance in the Pacific that might come naturally or by trade.

Because he was discretion personified, Harrison eschewed chauvinistic conquest. Friendly trade, he felt, would suffice to bring Latin Americans and Hawaiians under U.S. influence.

Forceful, clear-headed, and loyal to his close associates (including Theodore Roosevelt and William Howard Taft, whom he brought to Washington), he seized the reins of presidential power, thus bringing a touch of professionalism to the White House. Compared to Presidents Andrew Jackson, Abraham Lincoln, Theodore Roosevelt, and Franklin Roosevelt, however, he seems to emerge greater as a man than as president. For his era, though, Harrison compiled a strong record of constitutional government that enabled the country to approach the threshold of world power with prudence and caution. As much as any other president he wrestled mightily with the black question. He had the wisdom to discern the developments that have since come about in the affairs of the world and the necessity to make the nation a world power. See H. J. Sievers, *Benjamin Harrison* (3 vols., 1952–68).

HARRY J. SIEVERS

HARRISON, William Henry (b. Berkeley, Charles City Co., Va., Feb. 9, 1773; d. Washington, D.C., Apr. 4, 1841), PRESIDENT, was the son of Benjamin Harrison, a signer of the Declaration of Independence. He attended Hampden-Sidney College (1787–90) and entered the army as an ensign in 1791, rising to captain. In 1798 he became secretary of the Northwest Territory. As the Northwest Territory's first delegate to Congress (1799), he drafted the Land Act of 1800, which provided for the sale of land in tracts of 320 acres or more at a minimum price of $2 an acre. First governor of the Indiana Territory (1801–12), he negotiated several boundary treaties with Native Americans. But as settlers continued to occupy their land, **Tecumseh,** a Shawnee chief, and his brother, known as "the Prophet," tried to unite the tribes east of the Mississippi to stop further encroachment. At the battle of Tippecanoe (1811) Harrison defeated the Indians, destroying their confederation. During

the War of 1812 he defeated the British and the Indians at the battle of the Thames (1813).

A U.S. congressman (1816–19), state senator (1819–21), and U.S. senator (1825–28) from Ohio, he opposed the second Bank of the United States, supported the protective tariff, but was mainly identified with his anti–Native American views. He was U.S. minister to Colombia from 1828 to 1829. One of three Whig candidates for the presidency in 1836, he was defeated by Martin Van Buren. Running again in 1840 on his military record and his supposed humble way of life (the log cabin and cider barrel were his campaign symbols), he defeated Van Buren, 234 electoral votes to 60.

Believing that President Andrew Jackson had exceeded his authority, Harrison hoped to restore the balance of power between the executive and legislative branches of the government. However, one month after his inauguration, he died of pneumonia.

※

William Henry Harrison was a pleasant man, tall and soldierly in bearing and amiable in countenance. As an Indian fighter he perhaps won more credit than was his due for his qualified victory over the Shawnees at Tippecanoe, although he served effectively in the War of 1812. He was also an inveterate officeholder—secretary of the Northwest Territory, delegate to Congress, territorial governor, congressman, state senator, U.S. senator, minister to Colombia, and, finally, clerk of the county court at North Bend, Ohio. There he might have rusticated indefinitely if the emerging Whig Party had not perceived his possibilities as a plainfolks candidate for the presidency.

It was his political "availability" rather than innate ability that led the Whig managers to Harrison. From 1828 through 1832, Andrew Jackson and the Democrats had swept all before them, easily defeating such old-style presidential rivals as John Quincy Adams and **Henry Clay.** Jackson's triumphs were based in part on his reputation as a military hero and his role as spokesman for the common man. By the mid–1830s, several leaders among the conglomerate Whig opposition saw Harrison as a substitute for Jackson who could be presented as a popular hero of their own: as voters had once rallied to "Old Hickory," now they might go for "Old Tippecanoe." Indeed, Harrison showed promise as a challenger against Martin Van Buren in 1836, running well ahead of two other Whig entries with 37 percent of the total popular vote to Van Buren's 51 percent. Soon after Van Buren took office, the nation suffered a severe economic depression, and it looked like 1840 might be a Whig year. Planning ahead, such new-style Whig managers as **Thurlow Weed** of New York and **Thaddeus Stevens** of Pennsylvania did everything they could to make it so. Clear-eyed, hard-boiled, professional, and determined to win, the new breed of Whig politicians passed over Clay and made Harrison their nominee.

An unprecedented campaign followed. Every lever of organization and publicity was brought to bear, every device was employed to mobilize the voters, and the whole campaign was built around the homespun figure of Harrison-hero. Huge rallies and massive parades sold the "log cabin and hard cider" candidate, and songs and jingles extolled his virtues: "To guide the ship, we'll try Old Tip"; "Farewell, dear Van, you're not our man"; "Tippecanoe and Tyler too, Tippecanoe and Tyler too!" (John Tyler of Virginia, the vice presidential candidate.) And so it went, song after song, rhyme after easy rhyme. Meanwhile, Harrison made twenty-three campaign speeches to crowds of fifty thousand or more; it was the first time a presidential candidate had stumped the country in his own behalf. It was also the first great "image campaign," and it brought out an unprecedented 80 percent of the eligible voters. In the end, "Old Tip" triumphed over "Little Van" by 53 percent of the popular vote, and the Whigs carried both houses of Congress for the first time.

Ironically, the object of so much attention died a month after he took office, the first president to do so. Yet the great Harrison campaign set a lasting precedent: professional organization and mass participation were to remain the distinguishing features of national elections for decades to come. Scarcely a dominant figure,

"Old Tip" had helped fix the pattern of popular politics in the American scene. See D. B. Goebel, *William Henry Harrison* (1926).

WILLIAM N. CHAMBERS

HASTIE, William Henry (b. Knoxville, Tenn., Nov. 17, 1904; d. East Norriton, Pa., Apr. 14, 1976), JURIST, graduated from Amherst College in 1925. After teaching at Bordentown (N.J.) Manual Training School (1925–27), he earned a law degree at Harvard (1930). After brief service on the faculty of the Howard University School of Law, he entered private practice in Washington, D.C., in 1931. He received his doctor of jurisprudence degree from Harvard in 1933.

Hastie served as assistant solicitor of the U.S. Department of the Interior from 1933 to 1937 when he was appointed judge of the district court of the U.S. for the Virgin Islands. After his term expired, Hastie returned to Howard as dean and professor of law. In 1940 he became civilian aide to the secretary of war to advise on racial questions and work for equal treatment of blacks in the armed forces. Believing that desegregation was proceeding too slowly, he resigned in protest in 1943 and returned to Howard.

Hastie was appointed governor of the Virgin Islands by President Harry S. Truman, serving from 1946 until 1949 when Truman, whom he had vigorously supported in the 1948 presidential election, appointed him judge of the U.S. circuit court of appeals, third circuit, in Philadelphia, the highest legal post attained up to that time by an African-American. He served twenty-one years on the appellate court, three of them as chief judge. On his retirement in 1971 he received the title of senior judge.

Considered a militant on racial issues during his youth, Hastie had a philosophy that is probably best summed up by a comment he made in 1960. The scholarly, calm, almost aloof jurist declared, "The judge is in the middle. In fact, he belongs there, for that is his assigned post. His basic responsibility is to maintain neutrality while giving the best objective judgment of a contest between adversaries."

Coming from an elite black family that included his cousin Charles H. Houston, the first director-counsel of the NAACP and Hastie's future law partner as well as predecessor as dean of Howard University Law School, Hastie represented the integrationist who viewed the law as chief vehicle for achieving his goal. "The Negro lawyer has played, and continues to play, a very important role in the American Negro's struggle for equality," he observed. In accord with this philosophy, while dean of Howard's Law School, Hastie employed his legal skills to win several civil rights victories before the U.S. Supreme Court. These included decisions in the cases of *Smith* v. *Allwright,* which outlawed the "white primary," and *Morgan* v. *Virginia,* which prohibited the segregation of interstate passengers.

Hastie's legalistic temperament, however, was frequently tried. He took part in demonstrations and picketed against Jim Crow before it was fashionable to do so. When he resigned as an aide on racial matters to Secretary of War **Henry L. Stimson** in 1943, African-American newspapers quoted Hastie as citing "reactionary policies and discriminatory practices of the Army and Air Forces in matters affecting Negroes" as the reason for submitting his resignation.

Widely respected as a judge, as much for his dissenting opinions—such as his opposition to the conviction of five Communist leaders under the Smith Act in 1955—as for his majority holdings, Hastie was often mentioned as a possibility for the first black to sit on the Supreme Court. Although this distinction went instead to **Thurgood Marshall,** Hastie's career was nevertheless one of significance both for American jurisprudence and for his race. See Richard Bardolph, *The Negro Vanguard* (1959).

BRUCE M. STAVE

HAVEMEYER, Henry Osborne (b. New York, N.Y., Oct. 18, 1847; d. Commack, L.I., N.Y., Dec. 4, 1907), MANUFACTURER, improved and expanded the sugar refining properties that had been in the family since their immigration to America from Germany in the early 1800s. Inheriting extensive refining properties in Brooklyn with his brother, Havemeyer developed a thorough knowledge of the refining process, which was being rapidly improved in those years, and of the buying and selling aspects of the business as well. The Havemeyers enjoyed a strong position in the industry, and considerable financial resources. Thus they were able in 1887 to take a leading role in the organization of most of the nation's refiners into a trust, the Sugar Refineries Co. This aggregation of fifteen plants was declared illegal by the New York court of appeals in 1890, but Havemeyer, like **John D. Rockefeller** later on, placed the properties in a holding company, the American Sugar Refining Co., chartered under the laws of New Jersey. Following its acquisition of the Spreckels Sugar Refining Co. and other Philadelphia firms in 1892, it controlled about 90 percent of the nation's sugar refining capacity. Its position was confirmed by the Supreme Court in the E. C. Knight case (1895), which held that the trust did not violate the Sherman Act. Havemeyer continued as its head until his death.

In his later years Havemeyer and his wife assembled a notable collection of paintings and other art, which she bequeathed to the Metropolitan Museum of Art in the 1920s.

Though he initially opposed the consolidation of the sugar refining industry in 1887, Henry Havemeyer soon came to dominate the business. In part, this was because he brought into the consolidation the largest and most efficient sugar refinery in the country, the Havemeyer and Elder plant in Brooklyn, capable of supplying nearly a third of the industry's output. The refinery had been built only four years earlier after fire destroyed the firm's previous plant. So great was Havemeyer's determination to recover from the loss that virtually all the family fortune was committed to the enterprise.

But the more important reason that Havemeyer came to dominate the American Sugar Refining Company was his personality. He was both autocratic and willing to take large risks, and he was a master of the mercantile facets of the sugar business. Perhaps no incident better reveals these aspects of the Havemeyer character than the way he beat back the challenge to his control of the sugar trust in the fall of 1890.

Havemeyer, expecting that the trust would be declared illegal, had disposed of all but a handful of the trust certificates he had received in exchange for his equity holdings in sugar refining companies. The trust in the fall of 1890 was engaged in a price war with Claus Spreckels, the leading West Coast refiner, who had built a refinery in Philadelphia to invade the East Coast market. Francis O. Matthiessen, a member of the trust, wanted to see the price war ended. When Havemeyer refused, Matthiessen bought enough trust certificates on the open market to establish legal control, but when Havemeyer threatened to build a refinery of his own if he were not allowed to have his way, Matthiessen backed down, surrendering de facto control to Havemeyer. Havemeyer later admitted that he had been bluffing, that he had had no intention of building a competing refinery. It was the last real challenge to Havemeyer's authority.

The same combination of single-minded determination and audacity enabled Havemeyer to lead the American Sugar Refining Company to extraordinary growth. By 1907 it was the sixth largest industrial corporation in the United States. It was he who devised the means of forcing wholesalers not to deal with "unfriendly" refiners and of compelling railroads to grant rebates so that the entry of new firms into the industry was made extremely difficult. It was he who, despite hints of bribery and scandal, helped persuade Congress not to lower the high tariff on refined sugar. It was he who met the challenge posed by the emerging beet sugar industry by providing the capital to develop the industry and thereby control it. It was he who arranged for the American Sugar Refining Company's principal competitors to merge and form the National Sugar Refining Company, with the American in secret control. And finally it was he who oversaw virtually every detail of the marketing of sugar throughout the country, not only of

his own but of every other producer. Those who opposed Havemeyer were apt to find themselves faced with a price war, like the one that nearly destroyed John Arbuckle in 1900 when he sought to duplicate in sugar refining his success in coffee roasting.

But the same character traits that enabled Havemeyer to dominate the sugar industry were also the source of his undoing. His way of doing things became more and more anachronistic. By 1907 the American Sugar Refining Company had been found guilty of accepting illegal railroad rebates, the company faced an antitrust suit, and its treasury had been weakened both by the price war with Arbuckle and by unprofitable investments in sugar beets. On November 20, 1907, federal agents swooped down on the Havemeyer and Elder docks in Brooklyn and found evidence of systematic cheating on customs duties. After his death, stockholders in the company discovered that the Havemeyer family owned less than a thousand of the 900,000 shares outstanding. See Alfred S. Eichner, *The Emergence of Oligopoly: Sugar Refining as a Case Study* (1969).

ALFRED S. EICHNER

HAWTHORNE, Nathaniel (b. Salem, Mass., July 4, 1804; d. Plymouth, N.H., May 19, 1864), WRITER, came of old Puritan stock, one of his ancestors having been a judge at the Salem witchcraft trials in 1692–93. He graduated from Bowdoin College in 1825.

During the next decade of his life, which he devoted to learning the craft of writing fiction, he lived in his mother's home in Salem, published one novel, *Fanshawe* (1828), and began to publish short stories in newspapers and magazines. From 1836, when he edited the *American Magazine of Useful and Entertaining Knowledge,* almost to the end of his life, he engaged in various kinds of literary activity to support himself, including retelling Greek myths for children, the editing of *Peter Parley's Universal History,* and the publishing of children's books such as *Grandfather's Chair* (1841).

In 1837, Hawthorne published his first mature

collection of short stories, *Twice-Told Tales,* which was followed by an expanded edition in 1842, another collection, *Mosses from an Old Manse* (1846), and a final group of stories, *The Snow-Image and Other Twice-Told Tales* (1851). Along with the work of **Washington Irving** and **Edgar Allan Poe,** these stories form the first substantial body of short fiction in America.

To support himself and his family, Hawthorne also found it necessary to take a series of government jobs. He was measurer in the Boston custom house in 1839, "surveyor" of the Salem custom house (1846–49), and, finally, U.S. consul in Liverpool, England (1853–57), a position to which he was appointed by a Bowdoin classmate, Franklin Pierce, after he had helped Pierce's candidacy for president by writing his campaign biography.

After a three-year engagement he married Sophia Peabody in 1842. Some of the love letters he wrote to her during the six months of 1841 in which he resided at Brook Farm, a communal project run by Transcendentalists, are moving testaments of romantic love. Their married life was characterized by rootlessness. He lived in various places, including two famous houses in Concord—the Old Manse and the Wayside, where he associated with **Ralph Waldo Emerson, Henry David Thoreau,** and other Transcendentalists—in the Berkshires (where he met **Herman Melville,** who dedicated *Moby Dick* to him), England, and Italy.

Hawthorne published only four complete novels. The first, *The Scarlet Letter* (1850), was controversial because of its treatment of adultery, but it firmly established his reputation. He himself thought the book too gloomy. His favorite was *The House of the Seven Gables* (1851). *The Blithedale Romance* (1852) was based on his experience at Brook Farm, and his final complete work, *The Marble Faun* (1860), used the Italian background with which he had become familiar to explore the theme of "the Fall of Man," a myth that had been a pervasive subject in his fiction from the beginning.

Nathaniel Hawthorne's fiction veils a sensibility that was deeply divided. When he was a young man, he thought of himself as a struggling, sensitive writer seeking fame, self-discovery, and the creation of a then nonexistent American literature out of New England materials. After the publication of *The Scarlet Letter* and its immediate recognition as a "classic," he worked hard at projecting an image of himself as a New England Victorian man of letters. But he never lost his early romantic concerns. "My father," wrote his son Julian, "was two men, one sympathetic and intuitional, the other critical and logical; together they formed a combination that could not be thrown off its feet."

Although his sense of life was deeply tragic, Hawthorne wanted to be optimistic. He was attracted to the romantic world of dream and reverie but felt strongly that the actual world could come to seem unreal in a dangerous way if that bent were indulged. Sometimes he felt that the artist's duty was to present a balanced view of life. When this Victorian desire for balance was joined to the optimistic idea of treating only those emotions approved by his age, his work appears excessively even-tempered and bland. Writing of this sort, more than half his total output, includes such sentimental sketches as "Little Annie's Ramble," moralistic tales like "The Grey Champion," and parts of novels such as the happy ending of *The House of the Seven Gables.* It reflects such 19th-century pieties as a generalized love of nature and faith in evolution.

But at his greatest the divisions of his temperament and his tragic sense of life were allied with the conviction, based both on his Calvinist heritage and on his observation of experience, that the world was too mysterious to be clearly understood and often too impenetrably obscure to be clearly perceived. The fiction writer's role then was to explore those truths of human nature and experience that would, for lack of insight and honesty, remain hidden. The result in his fiction was tension that produced dispassionate representations of the complex psychological lives of characters torn by the opposing claims of faith and doubt, reason and emotion, the need to rebel against and the need to acquiesce in the restrictions of society. This tension expressed itself, too, in his favorite rhetorical device of providing multiple explanations for events, and in such symbolism as the complex interplay of images of light and darkness or the use of clothing to both shield people from society and draw them closer to it.

In his greatest fiction he creates characters who are conscious of their isolation from other people and those systems of values or institutions that seem to make life worth living. Hawthorne's exploration of the inward lives of these characters, their subjectively felt reactions to their actions, is his great subject. This psychological probing is inextricably bound to moral and historical frameworks, but the typical movement of his fiction is from the time-bound framework, perceived as complex and ambiguous, toward consideration of perennial human problems. Thus, in *The Scarlet Letter* he uses Puritan history to explore the relationship between love, justice, and power in society, as this relationship is perceived by characters of all types. And in *The House of the Seven Gables* he uses Salem witchcraft to explore universal problems of idealistic and materialistic approaches to existence.

In his treatment of these themes and others, such as the consequences of self-concern strong enough to overcome normal human feelings of brotherhood ("Ethan Brand") and the difficulty of self-realization in a society engaged in revolutionary modes of social change ("My Kinsman Major Molineaux"), Hawthorne established a tradition in American writing, continued by such major figures as **Henry James, William Faulkner,** and Robert Penn Warren, that explores the tragic aspects of American and, by implication, all life. His great fiction moves beyond criticism of such abstract romantic ideals as the perfectibility of man, the virtues of self-reliance, and the morality of nature to become a poetic and rich consideration of what it means to be a complex person in a problematic world. See Hyatt H. Waggoner, *Hawthorne: A Critical Study* (1963).

ELY STOCK

HAY, John Milton (b. Salem, Ind., Oct. 8, 1838; d. Lake Sunapee, N.H., July 1, 1905), DIPLOMAT, WRITER, graduated from Brown University (1856) and entered his uncle's law firm in Springfield, Illinois (1859), where he first met Abraham Lincoln. A Republican in politics, Hay became President Lincoln's assistant private secretary in 1861. In 1864 he was made an assistant adjutant general in the army, rising to the rank of colonel, detailed to the White House. Following Lincoln's assassination he served successively as first secretary of the American legation at Paris (1865–67), chargé d'affaires at Vienna (1867–68), and first secretary at Madrid (1868–70). Returning to the United States in 1870, Hay worked for the next five years on the editorial board of the New York *Tribune.* In 1871 he published *Pike County Ballads and Other Pieces,* a book of poems.

During the administration of Rutherford B. Hayes, Hay served as assistant secretary of state (1879–81). Between 1881, when he replaced **Whitelaw Reid** as editor of the New York *Tribune,* and 1896 he traveled extensively and published a number of books, including *The Bread-Winners,* an antilabor novel (anonymously, 1884), and (with John G. Nicolay) *Abraham Lincoln: A History* (10 vols., 1890).

In 1897, President William McKinley appointed Hay ambassador to Great Britain. Sharing the views of such expansionists as **Henry Cabot Lodge, Alfred Thayer Mahan,** and Theodore Roosevelt, Hay supported American entry into the Spanish-American War in 1898. Regarding the annexation of the Philippine Islands, Hay originally agreed with McKinley (June–July 1898), believing that the United States should retain only a part of the Philippines and that U.S. approval should be required before any third power could lease any portion of the islands. Hay soon reversed his position, however, and supported total cession.

Hay served as secretary of state from 1898 until his death. In this position he issued two "Open Door" notes (1899, 1900) calling for equal rights for all powers in the China trade and respect for China's "territorial integrity." In 1900 when the Chinese rebelled against foreign influences (Boxer Rebellion), Hay was influential in keeping China from being partitioned.

A firm advocate of the construction of an interoceanic canal, Hay negotiated the Hay-Pauncefote agreement with Great Britain (1901), abrogating the Clayton-Bulwer Treaty of 1850, which had barred the United States from building a canal on its own. In January 1903, Hay negotiated a treaty with Tomás Herrán, the Colombian chargé in Washington, whereby the United States agreed to pay Colombia $10 million and an annual rental of $250,000 in return for a ninety-nine-year lease on a zone across Panama. The Colombia senate rejected this offer, but in November 1903, following the Panamanian revolution against Colombia, Hay and the new Panamanian minister, Bunau-Varilla, concluded a treaty granting the United States rights to the Canal Zone in perpetuity.

⁂

John Milton Hay represented a central theme of 19th-century American life, for he believed in the efficacy of the marketplace whether that marketplace dealt in political, economic, or intellectual goods, and was confident that through its workings a natural aristocracy would rise to lead the republic or, in diplomacy, the world. Raised in a small town on the Mississippi River, he was sent to college at Brown. His talents gained him entry into some of the more sophisticated salons in the East. He was never again satisfied with either the Midwest ("a dreary waste") or with American mass society ("barefoot democracy from the heads of the hollows"). Only a chance encounter with Abraham Lincoln when both were lawyers in Springfield in 1859, and then service with the president during the Civil War, saved Hay from possible inundation by his dilettantism, condescension, and reserve.

During the 1870s he attempted to escape Grant Republicanism by recapturing the best memories of his youth in *Pike County Ballads*. This volume established him as a minor American poet but raised protests because it criticized religious and social institutions that, in Hay's view,

prevented heroic deeds. This theme and an equal amount of debate also marked the publication of *The Bread-Winners*. Written under the influence of the terrible economic upheavals of the 1870s, the novel equated trade unionism with a leveling socialism. Hay, moreover, tried to use the novel to educate his aristocracy in regard to its own political responsibilities.

Sharing the pessimism of his close friend **Henry Adams** concerning the downhill plunge of American society, Hay could not accept Adams's passivity. Believing in the beneficence of the marketplace, he thought the competitive victory must go not to unions or irresponsible rich but to men of learning, travel, political experience, and taste such as himself. In 1874, Hay married the daughter of the Cleveland railroad builder Amasa Stone. When the 1870s depression nearly ruined Stone, his new son-in-law entered the business, helped rebuild the family fortunes, and later assumed Stone's important directorships. During the 1880s Hay continued to prosper even after he moved to Washington and spent increasing time in the glittering intellectual company of the Adamses, naturalist Clarence King, and sculptor **Augustus Saint-Gaudens.**

The worsening economic crisis of the 1890s sharpened and expanded his views, leading Hay after 1897 to place at the center of his diplomacy the arrangement of a proper world marketplace. This policy pivoted on China, the largest yet most precarious of all national markets, and depended on close informal ties with England, the country Hay most trusted because its views on markets and culture resembled his own. The war against Spain and annexation of the Philippines opened the opportunity. Fearing in 1898 that there was "an understanding between Russia, France, and Germany to exclude as far as possible the trade of England and America from the Far East, and to divide and reduce China to a system of tributary provinces," Hay in diplomatic notes of 1899 and again in 1900 asked these powers and Japan to pledge the maintenance of an "Open Door" into an undivided China. The responses were not fully satisfactory, but no power could afford at the time to counter Hay's initiative. With this stroke he apparently had obtained the promise of the powers to maintain what he termed a "fair field and no favor" in the race for the China market.

He clearly understood "the inherent weakness of our position," as he noted privately in September 1900. "We do not want to rob China ourselves, and our public opinion will not permit us to interfere with an army to prevent others from robbing her. Besides, we have no army. The talk of the papers about 'our pre-eminent moral position giving us the authority to dictate to the world' is mere flapdoodle." With Roosevelt's mind on domestic and European affairs, Hay largely determined policies toward Asia until late 1904. Then chronic illness weakened him, but more important, Japan, on whom Hay was depending to block Russia from China's province of Northern Manchuria, defeated the Russians and then established Japanese hegemony in Korea and Southern Manchuria. The door began closing in these areas to American trade. Hay died at that point when Americans began to face the first of several such decisions they confronted in the 20th century: whether to abandon the attempt to restructure the Asian marketplace or to build and commit military force to keep "a fair field and no favor" in the area. That dilemma was John Hay's historical legacy. See Tyler Dennett, *John Hay* (1933).

WALTER LAFEBER

HAYES, Helen (b. Washington, D.C., Oct. 10, 1900; d. Nyack, N.Y., Mar. 17, 1993), ACTRESS, began acting in school at the age of 5, continued as a mime in dance recitals, and made her professional debut in Washington stock companies in 1909. She also made her Broadway debut that year with Lew Fields in *Old Dutch*, and there followied almost continuous appearances in Washington and New York. Her education continued erratically and by correspondence through high school. She appeared with John Drew in *The Prodigal Husband* (1914) and with William Gillette in *Dear Brutus* (1918). She then appeared on Broadway or on tour almost every season through the 1920s and 1930s, playing flappers and then young matrons in scripts some-times tailored to her talents. Among the plays were *Bab, The Wren, We Moderns, She Stoops to Conquer, Dancing Mothers, Quarantine, What Every Woman Knows,* and *Coquette*. After playing in George Bernard Shaw's *Caesar and Cleopatra* (1925), she reached the pinnacle of her career in the 1930s with electrifying royal portraits in the title roles of *Mary of Scotland* (1933) and *Victoria Regina* (1935), shows in which she toured and reprised extensively. She subsequently appeared in *The Merchant of Venice, Twelfth Night, Candle in the Wind, Harriet, Alice-Sit-by-the-Fire, Happy Birthday, The Glass Menagerie, Mrs. McThing, The Wisteria Trees, The Skin of Our Teeth, A Touch of the Poet, Long Day's Journey into Night,* and others. She ultimately played in more than one hundred stage productions in New York and elsewhere. In Hollywood she garnered an Academy Award for her first motion picture, *The Sin of Medelon Claudet,* with a screenplay polished by her husband, journalist-playwright Charles MacArthur. She made a score of films, playing opposite Hollywood leading men including **John Barrymore**, Clark Gable, Ronald Colman, and Gary Cooper. Simultaneously, she pursued a thriving career in radio, starring in her own series and making numerous guest appearances. Retiring from the stage in 1971 due to an allergy to "backstage dust," she appeared occasionaly in film and on television for almost twenty more years. Later films included *Anastasia, Airport* (for which she again received an Academy Award), and several Walt Disney comedies. She coauthored eight books and undertook a lifelong schedule of personal appearances for humanitarian causes.

————

Although only five feet tall, Helen Hayes commanded the stage, the cinema, radio, and television with grandeur, charm, wit, and warmth. Her meticulously devised characterizations combined monumental integrity and awe-inspiring dignity with a down-home familiarity and brilliant comic timing. Enormous innate charisma and talent, boundless energy, good health, solid stage discipline, and unrelenting work gained her stardom in all the entertainment media. Willing and prudent cooperation with the press as well as constant public appearances kept her in the public view. She earned respect as a person of exceptional good will and generosity, giving her time and attention to a myriad of worthy causes. She was notably accessible to fans, signing autographs happily and legibly from her first appearances to the end of her life. The graceful stoicism with which she responded to the untimely deaths of her teenage daughter and her husband endeared her to the public. Later revelations of her forced accommodation to the alcoholism of her mother and husband added further to the admiration of her character. Her adopted son, James MacArthur, became a successful television actor. Ultimately, Hayes became a public figure respected for her inspirational comments and homey wisdom on many topics and for many causes. She was enormously revered and popularly acclaimed for decades as the "First Lady of the American Theater." See Donn B. Murphy, *Helen Hayes* (1993).

DONN B. MURPHY

HAYES, Rutherford Birchard (b. Delaware, Ohio, Oct. 4, 1822; d. Fremont, Ohio, Jan. 17, 1893), PRESIDENT, graduated from Kenyon College (1842) and Harvard Law School (1845). Settling in Cincinnati, he was city solicitor from 1856 to 1861. When the Civil War broke out, he quickly volunteered, rising from captain to major general. He was wounded at South Mountain and served under General **Philip Sheridan** in the Shenandoah Valley (1864).

Hayes served in the House of Representatives (1865–67) and was three times elected governor of Ohio (1868–72 and 1876–77). In 1876 he was the Republican presidential candidate. Although **Samuel J. Tilden** (Democrat) won in the popular vote, the Republicans' claim to the electoral votes of Florida, Louisiana, and South Carolina gave Hayes an electoral college majority, 185 to 184. The Democrats, however, refused to accept the count in these states. The issue was turned over to a special electoral commission that awarded

Hayes all the disputed votes and thus the presidency. Hayes's election was supported by southern Democrats, who were promised that federal troops would be withdrawn from the South and that southerners would receive federal appropriations for internal improvements. They agreed in turn to respect the rights of southern blacks. Hayes was soon complaining, however, about the South's failure to deal fairly with the blacks.

In 1877, when a series of railroad strikes broke out, Hayes sent federal troops to various cities to prevent violence. A hard-money advocate, he vetoed the Bland-Allison Act (1878), which provided for government purchase of $2 million to $4 million worth of silver monthly. He also attempted to reform the civil service. He did not seek reelection to a second term.

⁂

There is irony in the fact that Hayes became president after what may have been the most corrupt election in American history, with both Democratic and Republican parties guilty of wrongdoing. For Hayes himself was not only a man of unquestioned honesty but a political leader who truly believed that honesty in politics *was* the best policy. "He serves his party best who serves his country best," he said in his inaugural address, and the statement was not mere rhetoric with him but the expression of a deep conviction. He was an ambitious man in politics, though not power-hungry, for his ambition was as much to win respect for his integrity as it was to win office. His main aim was to have his name associated with good works. He knew how to "play" politics but did so always with the aura of an amateur, presenting the image at all times of a model "gentleman in politics."

During the time he served as president, political opponents, both in his own party and in the opposition Democratic Party, and cynical commentators tended to sneer at Hayes's stance of honesty. They jeered also at Hayes because liquor was not served at White House social affairs during his administration. Mrs. Hayes was tagged "Lemonade Lucy." All this was reflected for many years in histories and textbooks that tended to downgrade Hayes as a mediocrity who became president through "a bargain" with southern leaders by which Reconstruction following the Civil War was to be ended in the South. But later historians have come to view Hayes in a better light, rating him as a better-than-average president, one who strengthened respect for the presidency after the excesses of the preceding Ulysses S. Grant administrations.

It is now recognized that Reconstruction had been all but ended anyway under President Grant, before Hayes became president, and that Hayes had merely confirmed what was inevitable. The fact was that there was no disposition in the North for continuing Reconstruction.

Hayes's southern policy was recognition of that fact. As a congressman and as governor of Ohio he had supported Reconstruction. As a lawyer he had defended fugitive slaves. He was a founder of the Republican Party, motivated largely by opposition to slavery. But as president he reflected the temper of the country, which wanted the wounds of the war to be healed. He believed that only if they became educated would the freed blacks attain full rights and opportunities as citizens. Both while president and afterward he worked for improved schooling for black Americans in the South as well as in the North.

As he himself once said, Hayes was not "liked" as president by important leaders of his own party. In large part this was because Hayes took the first positive steps of any president toward establishing a merit system for appointment to federal offices. He stood for an end to the system whereby in effect members of Congress did most of the appointing. His withdrawing from congressmen the power of patronage understandably made many enemies for him among those congressmen, notably Senator **Roscoe Conkling** of New York and Representative **Benjamin F. Butler** of Massachusetts. But Hayes was content to be judged by the enemies he made in that connection. He wanted to be liked—which can be said of most men in politics —but not at the expense of his standards of decent politics. See Harry Barnard, *Rutherford B. Hayes and His America*

(1954), and Ari Hoogenboom, *Rutherford B. Hayes: Warrior and President* (1995).

HARRY BARNARD

HAYWOOD, William Dudley (b. Salt Lake City, Utah, Feb. 4, 1869; d. Moscow, U.S.S.R., May 18, 1928), LABOR LEADER, had an irregular schooling and worked at various jobs. In 1884 he became a miner at Eagle Canyon, Nevada, but soon left, it is alleged, to become a homesteader and cowboy. He returned to mining in Silver City, Idaho, in 1894. Becoming interested in the labor movement, Haywood joined the Western Federation of Miners as a charter member of the Silver City local in 1896; three years later he became a member of the national executive board. Haywood was elected national secretary treasurer in 1900 and moved to Denver; he joined the Socialist Party in 1901. Opposed to the exclusive craft unionism of the American Federation of Labor, Haywood presided over a Chicago convention in 1905 that gave birth to the Industrial Workers of the World. The "Wobblies," as they became known, wanted to unify all labor and place all production in the hands of the workers; they advocated strikes, resistance, and even violence if needed to attain these goals.

In 1906, Haywood was arrested for complicity in the assassination of former governor Frank R. Steunenberg of Idaho. Summarily extradited from Denver to Boise, his trial attracted national attention. Defended by **Clarence Darrow,** he was acquitted in 1907. Differences within the Western Federation of Miners led him to be ousted from that union in 1908; in the years following he devoted his time and energies first to the Socialist Party of America and after 1912 to the IWW. Elected to the national executive board of the Socialist Party in 1908, Haywood was recalled in 1913 because he advocated the use of sabotage. He continued as virtual leader of the IWW from 1915 until his arrest in 1917 under the wartime Espionage Act for conspiracy and interference with conscription. Haywood, who had refused to support U.S. entry into World War I, and other IWW members were convicted in 1918 and sentenced to twenty years in jail and a $10,000 fine. While awaiting the results of an appeal for a new trial, Haywood jumped bail and fled to the Soviet Union (1921). He made several speaking tours in the U.S.S.R. for the Communists' International Society for the Relief of Workers in Prisons Abroad and worked on his autobiography, *Bill Haywood's Book* (1929), published posthumously.

William Dudley Haywood's life and career are shrouded in mystery. Unlike the typical labor leader who, over the course of his lifetime, traveled from radicalism to conservatism, Haywood's career trajectory carried him from moderation to militant radicalism. Commonly associated with acts of labor violence, he successfully and regularly advised strikers to practice passive resistance. A proven success as a trade-union administrator and at times even an adept bureaucrat, Haywood nevertheless impressed many of his contemporaries with his frequent outbursts of anarchistic, even nihilistic, rhetoric. Able to appeal forcefully and effectively to rugged migratory workers and immigrant industrial laborers, he also attracted the sympathetic attention of the pre–World War I generation of Greenwich Village intellectuals and bohemians. A man immensely proud of his family's colonial American origins and himself a promoter of the frontier-cowboy myth, Haywood fought in America for a form of syndicalist trade unionism and a revolutionary general strike more commonly associated with French, Italian, and other Latin labor radicals. Unable to promote revolution in the land of his birth, he attempted to build utopia in the country of his exile; but Soviet Russia proved equally unreceptive to Haywood's notions of revolution. What is one to make of such an inconsistent life?

Haywood's life was indeed tragic. One of the few American labor leaders admired by both workers and intellectuals, he led a labor organization (IWW) with few permanent members and disappointed many intellectuals by preferring flight abroad to martyrdom at home. The man the *Nation* described in a poignant 1928 obituary as most at home "standing up before a mass of unskilled workers, preaching the eternal irreconcilability of employer and employed with one breath and the brotherhood of man with the next, denouncing craft unionism and race distinctions," spent his last years lonely, ill, and confined to a hotel in Moscow. Haywood's life and career illustrated the indigenous roots of American working-class radicalism as well as the repression America's rulers reserved for native-born radicals. See Joseph R. Conlin, *Big Bill Haywood and the Radical Union Movement* (1969).

MELVIN DUBOFSKY

HEARN, Lafcadio (b. Santa Maura Island, Greece, June 27, 1850; d. Tokyo, Japan, Sept. 26, 1904), WRITER, was raised in Dublin by his great-aunt and educated in Catholic schools in France and England. Blinded in one eye by a childhood accident, he seriously impaired his vision in the other by overstrain. In 1869, Hearn emigrated to the United States. He first settled in Cincinnati, Ohio, where he learned the printer's trade and in 1872 became an assistant editor of the Cincinnati *Trade List*, a weekly. Later the same year he joined the Cincinnati *Enquirer* and then in 1875 changed to the Cincinnati *Commercial*. While serving his apprenticeship in journalism, he began to translate Théophile Gautier and other French writers.

His two-pronged activities in journalism and literature continued after he moved to New Orleans in 1877. Once on the staff of the *Item* and later the *Times-Democrat*, he wrote editorials, essays, reviews, sketches, and stories, and also regularly contributed translations from French and Spanish writers. *One of Cleopatra's Nights*, his translation of six Gautier stories, appeared in 1882. It was followed by *Stray Leaves from Strange Literatures* (1884), a collection of legends and fables; *Gombo Zhèbes* (1885), a collection of Creole proverbs of Louisiana and the West Indies; and *Some Chinese Ghosts* (1887), a collection of Asian legends—all reflective of his growing interest in things exotic and fantastic. His first original work, *Chita*, a novel depicting the tidal destruction of Last Island off the Louisiana coast, was published in *Harper's Monthly* in 1888 and in book form the following year.

In 1887, Hearn made an arrangement with *Harper's* to go to the West Indies and do sketches on French Creole life. He spent two years mainly in Martinique, an experience that provided him with material for *Two Years in the French West Indies* (1890) and *Youma* (1890), a novel about a slave rebellion.

While back in the United States arranging a similar trip to Japan with *Harper's*, Hearn wrote "Karma," a tale of love and expiation, and translated Anatole France's *Le Crime de Sylvestre Bonnard* (1890). Upon arrival in Japan in April 1890, however, he broke off with *Harper's* and turned to teaching English, first in Matsue and then in Kumamoto. While in Matsue he married Setsuko Koizumi, the daughter of an impoverished samurai family, and in 1895 became a Japanese subject, adopting the name Yakumo Koizumi. After working as editor of the *Kobe Chronicle,* he was appointed a professor of English literature at the Tokyo Imperial University, a post he held until 1903. During these years of teaching (his university lectures on English and American literature were posthumously collected in several volumes), Hearn continued writing a series of books dealing with many aspects of Japanese life and culture: *Glimpses of Unfamiliar Japan* (1894), *Out of the East* (1895), *Kokoro* (1896), *Gleanings in Buddha Fields* (1897), *Exotics and Retrospectives* (1898), *In Ghostly Japan* (1899), *Shadowings* (1900), *A Japanese Miscellany* (1901), *Kottō* (1902), *Kwaidan* (1904), *Japan: An Attempt at Interpretation* (1904), and *The Romance of the Milky Way and Other Studies and Stories* (1905).

Early separated from his ill-matched parents and then forsaken by his bigoted guardian, Hearn was, as it were, marked out to be a victim of life's whims and caprices, as was further confirmed by other events such as the childhood accident that left him defaced and semiblind, his brief marriage to a mulatto that cost him more than a reportorial job in Cincinnati, and his alleged infatuation with Japan that damned him as a traitor to his own color, race, and religion—in a word, an enemy of the West. Small of stature, shy, and sensitive, proud, fastidious, and suspicious, he could easily have been a failure but for his inborn twin passions: namely, his Celtic love of the dreamy, spiritual, and mysterious, and his Hellenic love of the sensual, natural, and beautiful. (After all, these were his birthright as son of an Irish father and a Greek mother.) As much maligned as adored (out of proportion to his marginal status in American literature), he had a complex personality that has somehow eluded his many biographers.

Hearn's image as a rootless cosmopolite was partly his own making. From the outset in his career he resolved to dedicate himself to the cult of "the Odd, the Queer, the Strange, the Exotic, the Monstrous." Yet as a journalist with literary aspirations he had to be a representative of his generation, in courting his poetic Muse by way of journalism; challenging the postbellum South to rise above its chronic self-pity, parochialism, and mediocrity, especially in the department of literature; introducing contemporary French writings to the long English-oriented, New England–centered American literature; and embracing Spencerian Evolutionism with a religious fervor.

All the same, Hearn was a great exotic, perhaps the greatest in American literature. His career, checkered with a succession of wanderings—European, American, West Indian, and Japanese—may superficially suggest a lifelong flight from society and civilization. But he was a "civilized nomad," to use his own words, "whose wanderings [were] not prompted by hope of gain, nor determined by pleasure, but simply compelled by certain necessities of his being." Viewed in this light, his was no mere flight from his own world but in reality an existential quest, search, and pilgrimage. No ordinary escapist or primitivist, he could not long remain content in the tropics and returned to civilization, even though it turned out to be the Orient.

Hearn's complex mind is nowhere more manifest than in his response to Japan. There are two Hearns: if one Hearn often exclaimed, "The East has opened my eyes," the other deplored the apparent smallness of the Japanese, desperately longed for his own world, and resignedly called himself "a caged cicada." There is little that indicates he was an uncritical lover of Japan. By contrasting the faults of the New Japan and the virtues of the Old, he repeatedly urged the iconoclastic Japanese to cherish their cultural identity. At the same time he reminded his own West of its obsessive sexualism, unbridled individualism, and religious dogmatism. And thereupon he called for the reintegration of East and West by way of Buddhism and Evolutionism, or religion and science, and ultimately the reintegration of man through his recovery of faith. Although acutely aware of the enormous cultural difference between East and West, he was nonetheless convinced of the possibility and indeed the necessity of their reunion.

It was in Japan that Hearn finally realized his dream of becoming a "literary Columbus." Now freed of his youthful ambition to create a poetic style, he developed into a consummate artist capable of commanding four literary forms: essays, sketches, legends, and prose poems. Hearn's Japanese books can still be read with profit and delight, and their value remains untarnished despite the passage of time because of his pure, graceful, and mature style; because of his approach, which anticipates that of modern folklore, mythology, and cultural anthropology; and because of his singular faculty as translator, his so-called soul sympathy, which enabled him to enter into his subject, the Japanese in this instance—a feat all the more remarkable considering his severely limited knowledge of their language. See Beongcheon Yu, *An Ape of Gods: The Art and Thought of Lafcadio Hearn* (1964).

BEONGCHEON YU

HEARST, George (b. Franklin Co., Mo., Sept. 3, 1820; d. Washington, D.C., Feb. 28, 1891), BUSINESSMAN, POLITICAL LEADER, attended the Franklin County Mining School. He inherited the family farm at his father's death in 1846 but in 1850 moved to California. For nine years he was engaged in gold mining but with little success. In 1859, however, he struck it rich in western Nevada. He made other valuable strikes there and in Mexico, Montana, and South Dakota, his most notable properties being the Ophir mine in Nevada, Homestake in South Dakota, and Anaconda in Montana. Despite severe financial reverses in 1866 and 1874, by the end of the seventies he was a multimillionaire.

Hearst, who had previously served in the California assembly (1865–66), devoted the rest of his life to politics. Denied the Democratic nomination for governor of California in 1882 despite the support of the San Francisco *Daily Examiner* (which he had bought a short time before), he continued to court the Democratic Party leaders. He was nominated for U.S. senator in 1884 but was defeated by **Leland Stanford.** In 1886 the governor appointed him to complete the unexpired term of Senator John T. Miller, and two years later he was elected for a full term. In the Senate, Hearst worked to further the mining and agricultural interests of his state and to reduce the influence of the railroads. His only child, **William Randolph Hearst,** greatly expanded the family's newspaper holdings.

⊷

George Hearst's career was filled with contradictions. Although he died a mining millionaire whose name had become a symbol for wealth, he had little money in 1849–50 when he quit the Missouri lead mines in order to join in the gold rush to California, and he was no better off when he left California for the Comstock Lode in 1859 after a varied experience in the quartz and placer mines. For half a dozen years prosperity favored him on the Comstock Lode, but then his principal investment there (the Ophir mine) failed. Yet in the 1870s and 1880s this self-taught mining man, whose formal education was limited to two years in country schools in Missouri, was guiding the decisions of sophisticated financial promoters who were risking large sums on Hearst's judgment of new mining properties—and this in a period in which the university-trained mining engineer was rising to dominance.

By the 1870s Hearst was known for shrewdness, good judgment, and knowledge of mines and the ways of miners. He preferred to deal in mining properties and to give advice or direction to others rather than to manage mines himself. His greatest successes came when he won the backing of the noted San Francisco partnership of James Ben Ali Haggin and Lloyd Tevis, whose funds he steered, along with his own, into what proved to be three of the West's richest mines: the Ontario, Homestake, and Anaconda.

Contradictions dominated other aspects of his life also. To the end of his days Hearst remained a picturesque, bearded, tobacco-chewing product of farm and mining camp whose speech and appearance proclaimed his simple origins, at a time when his remarkable wife was bestowing the Hearst name on cultural and social undertakings. See Cora M. Older, *George Hearst: California Pioneer* (1966).

RODMAN W. PAUL

HEARST, William Randolph (b. San Francisco, Calif., Apr. 29, 1863; d. Beverly Hills, Calif., Aug. 14, 1951), JOURNALIST, son of millionaire miner and rancher **George Hearst,** led a sheltered childhood. He enrolled at Harvard in 1882 but was expelled in 1885. Refusing management of his father's mines or ranches, he assumed instead the editorship of George Hearst's San Francisco *Examiner* in 1887. Patterning the *Examiner* after **Joseph Pulitzer**'s New York *World,* Hearst infused it with a blend of sensationalism and idealism, stressing scandals and murders but exposing injustice and corruption as well. He assembled a talented and highly paid staff, and after going into debt by some $800,000, finally began to show a profit in 1890. After receiving $5 million from his mother, he acquired the New York *Journal* and engaged in a circulation war with Pulitzer's *World.* He reduced the price of the *Journal* to one cent, running deficits of $100,000 a month but swiftly raising the *Journal's* circulation to 150,000. Combined with the new *Evening Journal,* the paper claimed a circulation of 700,000 by 1897. Hearst's crusade against Spanish rule in Cuba, which was related to his circulation war

with Pulitzer, was widely believed to have created public sentiment for war with Spain.

After the war, while acquiring a large chain of newspapers, Hearst served two terms in the House of Representatives as a Democrat (1903–7); in 1904 he made an unsuccessful bid for his party's presidential nomination. As an Independent, he narrowly lost the New York City mayoralty campaign in 1905, and in 1906 lost a close race for governor as a Democrat. His Independence Party polled only 87,000 votes in the 1908 presidential campaign, and in 1909 he again lost a bid to become mayor of New York as an Independent.

In 1917, Hearst met the actress Marion Davies, beginning a famous affair that lasted until Hearst's death. With $11 million inherited from his mother in 1919, he began a thirty-year, $30 million project to build a castle at San Simeon, California, and continually bought expensive art objects to fill it. He continued his behind-the-scenes maneuvering in both the Democratic and the Republican parties, and in 1932 "delivered" votes that helped Franklin D. Roosevelt win the Democratic presidential nomination.

Throughout the 1920s Hearst's papers steadily lost readership to newer publications. During the 1930s he grew increasingly conservative and turned against Roosevelt. His newspapers were strongly anti-Communist. By 1937 his heavy spending, estimated at $15 million a year, brought his twenty-seven-thousand-employee empire to the brink of bankruptcy, and he was forced to liquidate much of his property and sell numerous art objects. Hearst spent the last four years of his life in seclusion in Beverly Hills. He left a personal estate valued at $59.5 million plus a publishing organization—which included eighteen newspapers and nine magazines—with assets of $160 million. In 1957 the state of California accepted the San Simeon castle as a gift, incorporating it into the state park system.

When "Willie" Hearst exploded into the world of sensational journalism with the San Francisco *Examiner* in 1887, he began a public career of nearly fifty years that made him one of the best-known, best-hated, and most thoroughly publicized figures in the land. Yet he left no durable journalistic legacy. His monument is not the remnant of his newspaper and magazine empire but his gaudy California castle. He died as he lived, essentially a showman.

Hearst was no innovator. Stunts, crusades, exposures, scandalmongering, and entertainment for the many had been part of popular newspaperdom since the 1830s. But Hearst rode two waves that crested as he reached his manhood. First, there was a technological revolution in journalism. Telephones, cables, cameras, rapid presses, cheap paper, improved photoengraving, color printing, and better sorting and folding machines all were developed by the early 1900s to a point that made it possible to print thousands of papers daily, bedeck them with cartoons and banner headlines, cram them with "ads," features, and latebreaking stories, and sell them cheaply to the semiliterate urban masses whose numbers swelled with each census. Second, these very marvels relentlessly raised fixed costs so that mass circulation and production economies became crucial. Thus, business logic not only dictated savage newspaper rivalries but seemed to underlie Hearst's steady acquisition of newspapers through his inherited millions. While the chainmaking process owed much to his personal imperialism, it seemed a natural step in the age of corporate conglomeration to broaden markets and cut costs through integration. The ultimate logic of the process would have been to have two or three supercombines controlling all the nation's daily journals. But that pattern somehow was reserved for broadcast journalism.

Hearst lived to see his organization succumb to obsolescence in a generation. Sensationalism as a means of mass entertainment was challenged by such rivals as movies (into which he briefly ventured) and radio (with TV just beginning to grow at his death). And the chains—Hearst's and others still in existence—proved that they, too, could be as vulnerable as single papers to mismanagement and economic shocks on the order of the Depression.

Yet Hearst's business setbacks may have galled him less than his political failures. In youth he courted the "workingman" with antiplutocratic crusades in simpleminded words and drawings. Yet his combination of paternalism and populism was never translated into ballot-box strength that professional political managers respected. His inability to win nomination or election as president, mayor, and governor doubtless embittered him and nourished his elderly archconservatism. True, he was a power in national Democratic politics, but more as a millionaire than as an opinion-maker, and certainly less influential than demagogues of stump or microphone like **Huey Long** or **Charles Coughlin.** America, as some may have feared at the height of Hearst's career, would not be governed by a publishing plutocracy.

His life nonetheless remains strong in interest. His obvious enjoyment of his power, his free and unwise spending, his art collections and major love affair, his tantrums and bullying of subordinates, all mark him as belonging to the age of overnight millionaires like his miner father. He was one of the last nabobs of the Gilded Age, living a life that was itself as much a work of public exposure as any of his celebrated, multicolored, screaming front pages. See W. A. Swanberg, *Citizen Hearst* (1961).

BERNARD A. WEISBERGER

HEFNER, Hugh Marston (b. Chicago, Ill., Apr. 9, 1926), MAGAZINE PUBLISHER, the son of strict Methodist parents, grew up in a puritanical household that permitted no smoking, drinking, or swearing. After graduating from the University of Illinois in 1949, Hefner worked for *Esquire*, an experience that helped give birth to the idea for a new type of men's magazine. Inspired by the *Kinsey Report* (1948), Hefner wanted to challenge repressive sexual mores. Supporting himself as circulation manager for *Children's Activities* magazine, Hefner financed the first issue of *Playboy* (1953) with $600 of his own money and $10,000 raised from friends.

From 1953 until 1990, Hefner was the owner and editor in chief of *Playboy*. By 1960 he was selling a million copies a month of *Playboy* and was trying (and failing) with two other magazine ventures: *Show Business Illustrated* and *Trump*, a humor magazine similir to *Mad*. Hefner did far better with his Playboy Clubs (500,000 Playboy Club Key Holder members by 1967), Playboy Press, and Playboy Products spin-off division.

Playboy's circulation peaked at 7 million issues sold in the month of September 1972. A decade later it seemed under attack from all quarters. Attorney General Edwin Meese's Commission on Pornography intimidated the 7-Eleven chain, and it stopped carrying *Playboy*. For the first time serious competition arose in the form of Bob Guccione's *Penthouse*. Hefner closed his casinos, theaters, film, book, and record divisions. He returned magazine publishing to the center of his operations.

In April 1982, Hefner appointed his 30-year-old daughter Christie company president. Through the 1980s she took more and more control. In July 1989, in a highly publicized affair, America's most famous bachelor (he had divorced his first wife in 1959) married Kimberly Conrad, the 1989 *Playboy* "Playmate of the Year." The following year Hefner became chairman emeritus while still owning nearly three-quarters of the company stock. Since then, Christie Hefner has run the magazine and related activities.

———— ❧ ————

By creating one of the biggest success stories in American magazine publishing history, entrepreneur and editor Hugh Hefner wielded a major influence on both the magazine industry and the mores of the United States. In particular Hefner targeted the males of the baby boom generation, born between 1946 and 1964. He appealed to all who, like him, were frustrated by the Victorian values of their parents. Hefner campaigned for a more open sexuality, celebrating the nude female form. "Hef's" hip attitude heralded that sex should not cause shame but should be openly enjoyed. His "good life" proclaimed that sexual fantasies were good for young males, at least in the form Hefner envisioned.

But Hefner's influence would have been insignificant had he not had *Playboy* as a forum.

Playboy ranks among the most successful magazine publishing ventures of the last half of the 20th century. The first issue of *Playboy*, featuring a now celebrated nude calendar of **Marilyn Monroe**, reached the newsstands in December 1953 containing only forty-eight pages and no advertising. A decade later Hefner was turning away advertisers and counting himself among the richest of young Americans.

Through the supposed "radical" 1960s, Hugh Hefner sucessfully and profitably linked sexual pursuit by males with a quest for moving up the capitalist ladder. He was inspired by magazines of the past. Hefner successfully combined the wit and humor of *Esquire* with the pictorial lushness of *Life* with the explicit photographs of *Modern Sunbathing*. He was the master promoter of anything and everything connected to *Playboy*.

But with fame and riches Hefner also wanted respectability. His pioneering issues of *Playboy* contained short stories and nonfiction, tidbits of humor, and advice to fun-loving young urban males as well as celebrated nude images. Hefner bought published articles and stories by big names, including **John Steinbeck** and Somerset Maugham. Ray Bradbury's celebrated *Fahrenheit 451* was serialized in three early issues of *Playboy*. As he made money he commissioned original short stories by **Vladimir Nabokov**, **James Baldwin**, P. G. Wodehouse, and **Isaac Singer**. "Hef" tendered columns on how to buy the best wine, in-depth interviews with noted celebrities, and serious discussions of the raging controversies of the day. He advised the males of the baby boom generation how best to give a party, how to appreciate fine art and music, how to make the most of their sexual pursuits. He told true believers to work hard, play hard, and enjoy the good life.

But the baby boom grew up, and Hefner's empire started winding down. His influence is now associated with the past. It will long be debated how much Hefner really changed American mores, but we can surely and safely place Hugh Hefner within the pantheon of magazine entrepreneurs. See Russell Miller, *Bunny: The Real Story of Playboy* (1985).

DOUGLAS GOMERY

HELLMAN, Lillian (b. New Orleans, La., June 20, 1905; d. Martha's Vineyard, Mass., June 30, 1984), PLAYWRIGHT, attended New York University (1922–24) and Columbia. She then worked for the Horace Liveright publishing company, reviewed books for the New York *Herald Tribune,* and acted as a press agent. After working as a script reader for MGM in California (1930–32), she returned to New York, where she collaborated with Louis Kronenberger on an unproduced farce, *Dear Queen.* At the suggestion of detective-writer **Dashiell Hammett,** with whom she established an enduring relationship, she turned to a 19th-century Scottish law case for the inspiration for her first stage success, *The Children's Hour* (1934), the story of a neurotic child's lies about the relations of two female teachers. The play created a sensation and ran for eighty-six weeks on Broadway. *Days to Come* (1936), a social document about labor strife, was not a success. Hellman traveled to the Soviet Union and Western Europe in 1936. Her play *The Little Foxes,* a scathing indictment of the greed and materialism of a southern family, opened on Broadway in 1939, was adapted by Hellman as a film starring Bette Davis in 1941, and became the basis of Marc Blitzstein's opera *Regina* in 1949.

During World War II, Hellman expressed her loathing of Fascism and of initial American apathy toward it in such wartime dramas as *Watch on the Rhine* (1941), winner of the Critics Circle Award that year, and *The Searching Wind* (1944). In 1944 she was invited to Moscow on a cultural mission in connection with Russian productions of two of her plays, and formed a close friendship with film-maker Sergei Eisenstein. Her experiences in Moscow and on the Russian front are vividly recalled in her autobiography, *An Unfinished Woman* (1969). After the war came *Another Part of the Forest* (1946), which revisits her "little foxes" twenty years earlier, and *Montserrat* (1949), an adaptation of Emmanuel Robles's novel. Other Hellman adaptations included her version of Jean Anouilh's *The Lark* (1955) and the book for *Candide* (1956), a comic operetta based on Voltaire's satire. *The Autumn Garden,* a Chekhovian study of the decay of human decency, was a commercial failure on Broadway in 1951.

The following year she was subpoenaed to appear before the House Committee on Un-American Activities. She offered to testify freely about herself provided she was not asked questions about the political activities of other people. The committee refused, and her rejoinder—"I can't cut my conscience to fit this year's fashions"—became proverbial. Hellman's later plays included *Toys in the Attic* (1960), a disturbing tale of two possessive spinster sisters and the brother they dominate, and *My Mother, My Father and Me* (1963), a stylized adaptation of Burt Blechman's satire *How Much? Pentimento,* a continuation of her autobiography, was published in 1973.

In the 1970s and 1980s Hellman occasionally taught classes in writing at Harvard, Yale, and the City University of New York. She also edited the letters of Chekov, stories by Hammett, and worked on completing her autobiography. *Scoundrel Time* (1976), which dealt with her experiences during the McCarthy era, became a best-seller but created much bitterness toward her because of her sharp denunciation of liberals whom she alleged remained silent or supported the anti-Communist witch-hunters. Other controversies dogged Hellman until her death, particularly because of a law suit she brought for slander against Mary McCarthy, the writer, when McCarthy characterized Hellman on the Dick Cavett show on TV in 1979 as "a dishonest writer" whose every word, "including 'and' and 'the' was "a lie." Another dispute involving Hellman's honesty as a writer erupted over the story of "Julia," an anti-Fascist member of the Austrian underground and a central character in *Pentimento,* which later was an Academy Award movie starring Jane Fonda in the title role. Hellman claimed she befriended Julia and smuggled money to her at the outbreak of World World II. In 1983 a memoir was published by Muriel Gardiner, a psychoanalyst active in the underground in Austria at the same time, which strongly suggested that Hellman had used her life as a model for Julia. Hellman vigorously denied the charges, but dispassionate observers evaluating the evidence agreed that her denials were very suspect. Evidence has also emerged since Hellman's death that contrary to her denials she did become a member of the Communist Party in the 1930s and 1940s, which probably accounted for her repeated refusal to denounce Stalinism during those years.

"I do regret that I have spent too much of my life trying to find what I called 'truth,' trying to find what I called 'sense.' I never knew what I meant by truth, never made the sense I hoped for. All I mean is that I left too much of me unfinished because I wasted too much time. However." These self-questioning lines from the conclusion of Lillian Hellman's fine autobiography *An Unfinished Woman* reflected the fierce moral and social determination that pervades her plays, but they tend to obscure the remarkable record of one of the contemporary American theater's most invigorating practitioners. Few modern American dramatists could rival her popular as well as critical success.

"Sharp, severe, and as keen-minded as she was keen-spirited" was how John Gassner remembered her in the strenuous thirties when she emerged as an outstanding playwright. From the moment the malicious 14-year-old monster Mary Tilford took the stage in *The Children's Hour*, the Hellman knack for drawing chilling portraits of evil was established. "Characters etched in hatred" was one reviewer's assessment of the gouging, predatory Hubbards in her best-known work, *The Little Foxes*, and Tallulah Bankhead's Regina became one of Broadway's most unforgettable embodiments of unredeemed badness. "Sometimes I think it ain't right to stand by and watch them do it," remarks one character about such despoilers of the earth, and there was no toleration of apathy or compromise in the harsh Hellman canon. Although shrill political fervor might occasionally lead her astray in a play like *The Searching Wind* ("more windy than searching," noted critic Stark Young), the unyielding sense of commitment she imparted to the anti-Fascist freedom fighter Kurt Müller (memorably

acted by Paul Lukas) made *Watch on the Rhine* the most powerful anti-Nazi drama of the war years.

When asked by the *Paris Review* whether her kind of play—the taut, suspenseful, situation-oriented "well-made play, one which runs the honest risk of melodrama for a purpose"—would survive, she replied that "survival won't have anything to do with well-made or not well-made, or words like melodrama.… If you can break into a new pattern along the way, and it opens things up and allows you more freedom, that's something. But not everything, maybe not even very much. Take any form, and if you're good—" Although she tried freer and more experimental forms of dramaturgy in later works like *The Autumn Garden* or *My Mother, My Father and Me*, the strength of her playwriting remained her Ibsenian capacity for creating strong characters and strong situations. At its best her drama was a drama of high tension that threatened to erupt into violence, unsentimental, distrustful of rhetoric, harrowing in its logic, and incandescent in its indictment of the dark side of humanity. Its vigorous craftmanship made Lillian Hellman's voice one of the most persuasive in the modern American theater. See Richard Moody, *Lillian Hellman, Playwright* (1972).

FREDERICK J. MARKER

HELPER, Hinton Rowan (b. Rowan [now Davie] Co., N.C., Dec. 27, 1829; d. Washington, D.C., Mar. 8, 1909), WRITER, son of a yeoman farmer, grew up in relative poverty. After graduating from the Mocksville (N.C.) Academy in 1848, he worked in Salisbury, North Carolina, as an apprentice in a store. He moved to New York City in 1850, but failing to make his fortune, he joined the gold rush to California. He returned to Salisbury in 1854 and published an account of his experiences, *The Land of Gold: Reality versus Fiction* (1855), which revealed him as already a man of deep ethnocentric prejudices. He then turned to writing *The Impending Crisis of the South: How to Meet It* (1857), which eventually brought him national recognition.

Spurning moral appeals, Helper attacked the institution of slavery not because it exploited blacks but because it victimized nonslaveholding whites and retarded southern prosperity. The book was violently condemned throughout the South but well received by many in the North, where a fund was raised by Republicans in 1859 to print 100,000 copies of an abbreviated Compendium for wider distribution. Helper achieved his greatest notice in the aftermath of **John Brown's** raid when *The Impending Crisis* became embroiled in the controversy over election for Speaker of the House of Representatives.

During the Civil War, Helper served as consul to Buenos Aires, Argentina (1861–66), where he successfully maintained amicable relations under difficult circumstances. After returning to the United States, Helper, fiercely opposed to radical Reconstruction and black equality, published three racist books: *Nojoque: A Question for a Continent* (1867), *The Negroes in Negroland* (1868), and *Noonday Exigencies in America* (1871). These attacked blacks as a menace to the nation and called for their deportation to Africa or Latin America. Helper also became involved in the northern labor movement, drafting a suggested platform for the National Labor Convention meeting in Philadelphia (1869). He later devoted great energy to promoting an Isthmian canal, along with a grand scheme to build a Pan-American railroad spanning the hemisphere; these plans were designed to encourage trade and to purify and uplift South America with white immigrants and northern capital. Despite extensive travel between the Americas to drum up support for his schemes, he received little encouragement. After spending his last years in poverty and frustration, Helper committed suicide.

❦

Helper, a propagandist with the intellectual and literary tools to achieve real influence, unfortunately turned his considerable energies toward goals that were consistently premature, misguided, or vicious. He was driven by a compulsive sense of personal grievance over his failure to gain wealth, power, and prestige, and his writings and career were characterized by excess in language and behavior. Helper's greatest signifi-

cance was as spokesman and symbol for class disharmony within the South. So apprehensive was the planter elite over the potential disloyalty of the yeoman class that *The Impending Crisis* was thoroughly suppressed, barely reaching nonslaveholding whites. Indeed, the very class of people Helper sought to awaken to a sense of oppression was persuaded to help burn his book and lynch those caught distributing it.

Students of Helper have each emerged marked by a sense of exhaustion and bewilderment over the intensity of their subject's racism. And yet, while Helper never again rose to the level of recognition and influence he had achieved before secession, he was nevertheless potentially a powerful advocate of class revolution. There was a unity in his entire career, for he was devoted to exposing a self-conceived conspiracy of the moneyed class (planters and industrialists) and blacks who were allied to oppress the white working class, whether southern yeoman or northern proletariat. Helper's appeal was, in short, the antithesis of **John Calhoun's** dream of slaveholders and northern capitalists joined in alliance to suppress an imminent class war. Helper's powers of social analysis and persuasion were finally mutilated by a hatred of blacks and all non-Caucasians that was actually symptomatic of a general social pathology in the mind of white America. See Hugh C. Bailey, *Hinton Rowan Helper: Abolitionist-Racist* (1965).

STEVEN A. CHANNING

HEMINGWAY, Ernest Miller (b. Oak Park, Ill., July 21, 1899; d. Ketchum, Idaho, July 2, 1961), WRITER, did not attend college. He worked as a cub reporter for the Kansas City *Star* and during World War I served as an ambulance driver attached to the Italian infantry. After being severely wounded, Hemingway returned to the United States. In 1921 he went to France as foreign correspondent for the Toronto *Star*. In France he met James Joyce, **Gertrude Stein,** and other writers. A collection of his short stories, *In Our Time* (1925), introduced the character Nick Adams. His first major success was *The Sun Also*

Rises (1926), a story of American expatriates in Europe. He returned to the United States in 1928 and completed *A Farewell to Arms* (1929), a tragic story of two lovers during World War I.

Hemingway's *Death in the Afternoon* (1932) popularized his interest in bullfighting, and *The Green Hills of Africa* (1935) described his interest in big-game hunting. He covered the Spanish Civil War for the North American Newspaper Alliance (1936–37), and his *For Whom the Bell Tolls* (1940) was a product of that experience. He also published *To Have and Have Not* (1937) in this period. At the outbreak of World War II, Hemingway, who was then living in Cuba, became a war correspondent in Europe. He was with the first Americans who liberated Paris, winning the Bronze Star for his semimilitary service. After the war he wrote *Across the River and into the Trees* (1950), and he won a Pulitzer Prize in 1953 for his short novel *The Old Man and the Sea* (1952), the story of an aged Cuban fisherman's struggle against a huge fish. Like all his works, the novel dealt with violence, heroism, and courage. In 1954, Hemingway won the Nobel Prize for literature. Later that year he was seriously injured in a plane crash in Africa. In his last years Hemingway suffered from periods of depression; eventually he shot himself. *A Moveable Feast* (1964), sketches of his early life in Paris (1921–26), appeared posthumously. *Islands in the Stream,* a novel, was published in 1970.

Probably no writer of the early 20th century has been more influential than Ernest Hemingway. His stoic insistence on avoiding emotion, his refusal to participate except as a dispassionate observer, his espousal of a code which says that death is inevitable and that each man is to be measured by the manner in which he meets it, his avowal of simplicity in word and deed, his substitution of controlled action for thought—all of these became part of a pattern which seemed to offer protection against a world that suddenly in the 1920s loomed immensely large and incomprehensible. Hemingway's creed, which avoids explosive complications caused by emotion

through allegiance to the regulated violence of big-game hunting, bullfighting, or guerrilla warfare, and the satisfactions derived from simple physical appetites for women and wine, and the companionship of compatible friends, seemed as much a way of life as a view of the world, so that Hemingway became in person a model for his time much as Lord Byron had been a model for his. People tried not only to write like Hemingway but to live like Hemingway, carefully, conscious of wounds, but conscious also that each mastered a manner of confronting the world which was clean and decent because it remained within limits that were small and manageable, and that were respectworthy because they offered stoic preparation for the final inevitability, which is death.

Central to Hemingway's writing is a three-part theme which says, first, that man, born in innocence, is wounded in acquiring knowledge of the world. He then meets a tutor who informs him that man's single chance for salvation is in withdrawal, the making of a "separate peace"—as Nick Adams does in *In Our Time* and as Frederick Henry does in *A Farewell to Arms*—and the espousal of a life which is regulated by expert knowledge of such small skills as how to fish or hunt or cleanly kill a bull, how to drink wine from a goatskin, write controlled and honest prose, or make love honestly, with restraint—ritualized actions that provide anesthetic against thinking too much or feeling too much, providing a shell of form to protect against excesses of mind or body. And, finally, the young man either accepts the limitations of the wound and the code—as Jake Barnes does in *The Sun Also Rises*—or he refuses the code and is mastered by life rather than becoming its master.

Hemingway's prose style was appropriate to his theme, its bareness underlining the bareness of the life presented. The style is harsh and clear, concentrated and controlled, almost completely unemotional, colloquial, and without literary flourish. What happens is presented without comment, for Hemingway was convinced that if "the sequence of motion and fact" was honestly presented, then the emotions would take care of themselves. "I found," he once wrote, "the greatest difficulty, aside from knowing truly what you felt, rather than what you were supposed to feel, and had been taught to feel, was to put down what really happened ... what the actual things were that produced the emotion." His aim was to remain objective, uninvolved, and dispassionately in control of his craft. His typical sentence is a simple sentence, or two or more simple sentences joined conjunctively, with emphasis on sequence rather than causality, more often joined by *and* than by *but, then,* or *because.* What adjectives appear are usually adjectives that have been worn flat with repetition, words like *nice* or *pretty* or *awful* which evoke minimal emotional response. He strove for what he called an honest prose, simple in diction and syntax. It was more difficult to write, he said, than poetry. It must be written "without tricks and without cheating. With nothing that will go wrong afterwards."

Mastering this prose, Hemingway wrote some of the most distinctive and distinguished stories of his time. His style and attitude seem to have been better suited to shorter fiction, the novella or short story, like *The Sun Also Rises* and *A Farewell to Arms* or "The Snows of Kilimanjaro" and "The Short Happy Life of Francis Macomber." In longer fiction, like *For Whom the Bell Tolls* and *Islands in the Stream,* sentiment or authorial guidance sometimes intrudes. But he remained remarkably consistent in technique and attitude, and in sensitivity to the spirit of his time, so that it seems likely he will be remembered as one of its most significant spokesmen. See Carlos Baker, *Ernest Hemingway: A Life Story* (1969).

LEWIS LEARY

HENRI, Robert (b. Cincinnati, Ohio, June 24, 1865; d. New York, N.Y., July 12, 1929), ARTIST, studied with Thomas Anschutz at the Pennsylvania Academy of Fine Arts (1886–88) in Philadelphia. In 1888 he enrolled in the Julian Academy, then the Ecole des Beaux-Arts, Paris, and also studied independently in Brittany, Italy, and Spain. Returning to Philadelphia in 1891, he became an instructor in the Women's School of Design. Four years later he returned to Paris to teach (1895–97). In 1899 he exhibited a painting at the Paris Salon, *La Neige* (Collection Musée de Luxembourg, Paris), which was purchased by the French government.

Between 1902 and 1914, Henri exhibited widely and taught at the New York School of Art. He painted mainly portraits and character studies. *Willie Gee* (Newark Museum), a black boy, and *Diegito* (Museum of New Mexico, Santa Fe), a picture of a Native American, are examples of his style. In 1908, Henri formed a group of artists known as "The Eight" for the purpose of holding exhibitions. He also helped organize the famous New York Armory Show (1913) of modern art and was a leading member of the Society of Independent Artists. Off and on during 1915–23, Henri taught and lectured at the Art Students League in New York and in 1923 published *The Art Spirit*, a collection of his essays, classroom notes, and theories on the teaching of art. In his later years he spent much time painting in Spain and in Ireland. Some of his best-known canvases are *Young Woman in Black* (1904, Chicago Art Institute), *Spanish Gypsy* (1908, Metropolitan Museum of Art, N.Y.), and *Wee Woman* (1927, private collection, Dayton, Ohio).

⁂

Robert Henri grew up in Nebraska where his father founded the town of Cozad. Owing perhaps to the influence of his youth in the West (as well as to his compulsion to investigate everything), he was more open to new ideas than most other American painters of his day. He admired greatly the work of **Thomas Eakins** long before it was generally appreciated, and when he served on juries of the National Academy of Design, he fought for stronger, more vital work than that popular with most other members. Gradually he gathered around him a group of strong young artists, some friends, mostly pupils, the most important of whom was **George Bellows.** Frequently they all exhibited together, and their shows created a sensation. It all caused a breeze to blow through the art world, and American painting has never been the same since. The introduction of the work of the new European artists at the Armory Show (far more advanced than that of Henri or his followers) was to a considerable extent his doing.

In *The Art Spirit,* Henri tells the student to study to see the wonder and beauty of the world around him; the artist will paint his best when he is inspired by what he sees. "There are moments in our lives, there are moments in a day, when we seem to see beyond the usual. Such are the moments of our greatest happiness. Such are the moments of our greatest wisdom." The artist should not care whether his work is modern or conservative or done in some peculiar technique, Henri believed. The important thing is that his canvas show something fine he has discovered about his model, something we might not otherwise have seen. See William Homer, *Robert Henri and His Circle* (1969).

MARGERY A. RYERSON

HENRY, Joseph (b. Albany, N.Y., Dec. 17, 1797; d. Washington, D.C., May 13, 1878), SCIENTIST, was the son of a day laborer. After drifting from job to job he became interested in science and gained admission to the Albany Academy (1823–24) where he prepared himself for a career in medicine. He was appointed professor of mathematics and natural philosophy at the academy in 1826 and began research on the relation of electrical currents to magnetism. His discoveries mark the first period of sustained physical investigations by a scientist in America. His earliest success was an improved electromagnet (1829–30) that employed layers of insulated coils around an iron core in place of a single spiral of wire. Independently of the Englishman Michael Faraday, in 1830 Henry discovered the principle of induction, or induced current: the unit of induction was named the henry in his honor. In 1832 he was the first to describe and build an electric motor using electromagnets. By 1832 he had constructed the first electromagnetic telegraph, showing that magnetic action can be transmitted over long distances, and employed the first electromagnetic relay.

In 1832, Henry became a professor at the College of New Jersey (now Princeton) where he continued his experiments. He developed the electromagnetic relay (1835) and the principle of the modern transformer (1838–42), which can step electric current up or down. His study (1842) of inductive discharges of electricity over long distances had an important bearing on the later development of radio.

In 1846, Henry became the first secretary of the Smithsonian Institution, a post he held until his death. He viewed the Smithsonian's function chiefly as support of original research and opposed the use of Smithsonian funds for a museum, art gallery, and library. Henry helped organize the American Association for the Advancement of Science and was elected its first president in 1849. He also assisted in the founding of the Philosophical Society of Washington in 1871.

⸺∞∞∞⸺

Joseph Henry was the first American scientist since **Benjamin Franklin** to make such fundamental contributions to physical theory as to gain international recognition. Working in the same field (electricity), both men combined experimental skill and great deductive powers which they applied to problems not yet completely dominated by mathematics. Both men also suffered the handicap of working in America, far from the libraries, laboratories, and colleagues that made European capitals the centers of scientific advancement. As a college teacher Henry was obliged to give first priority to the instruction of undergraduates, and he made himself available to local manufacturers who sought his expert advice in solving industrial problems. In a democracy the usefulness of science militated against its theoretical advancement.

Henry's contributions to American science were perhaps even greater after he became the first head of the Smithsonian Institution. Located at the seat of government in Washington, D.C., he successfully built the kind of research-oriented institution that America so conspicuously lacked at mid-century. With a private endowment (from the English scientist James Smithson) but a public board of regents, Henry was able to offer aid and encouragement to many of the nation's scientists over the next generation. Although he resisted waste of the funds of the Smithsonian in mere cultural uplift, he put the facilities and prestige of the institution behind a wide range of scientific enterprises from western exploration to the building of new astronomical observatories. Being in Washington, he was also able to encourage the growth of scientific bureaus in the government and to act as a central clearinghouse for the emerging scientific profession in the country. See Thomas Coulson, *Joseph Henry: His Life and Work* (1950).

CARROLL PURSELL

HENRY, Patrick (b. Hanover Co., Va., May 29, 1736; d. Charlotte Co., Va., June 6, 1799), POLITICAL LEADER, grew up in moderately prosperous circumstances in a part of Virginia where the established Episcopal church was declining under the influence of the "New Light" preachers. After running a country store and farming, he read law briefly and was admitted to the bar. He quickly displayed a skill in courtroom argument that transcended conventional legal erudition. In 1763, Henry became embroiled in the "Parson's Cause," one of several suits stemming from the British Crown's disallowance of a Virginia law that altered the mode of paying the Anglican clergy. The Reverend James Maury won his suit for back salary, but after Henry made an impassioned speech, the jury awarded the parson only nominal pay. The essence of Henry's argument was that by overturning a law passed by the Virginia assembly the king had broken the compact between the ruler and the ruled. This radical concept of government—which could be used to justify revolution—made Henry a popular hero.

Henry was elected to the Virginia House of Burgesses in 1765, and his oratory soon won him a position of influence. When news of the Stamp Act reached Virginia, Henry presented to the House seven resolutions, the most radical of which claimed total legislative independence for the colony. Defending his resolves on May 29, 1765, he declared, "Caesar had his Brutus, Charles the first his Cromwell—and George the third—may profit by their example." At that point he was interrupted by cries of "treason," and allegedly he replied, "If this be treason, make the most of it."

Over the next decade Henry assumed leadership of the radical group in the House of Burgesses; among his allies were **Richard Henry Lee** and Thomas Jefferson. When Governor Dunmore dissolved the colonial assembly in 1774, Henry presided over a rump session at Raleigh Tavern that issued a call for a constitutional convention for Virginia and a continental congress. He was a delegate to the First and Second Continental Congresses (1774–75). In March 1775 he presented resolutions for arming the militia to Virginia's revolutionary convention on the grounds that war was inevitable, and he declared, "I know not what cause others may take, but as for me, give me liberty or give me death!" He served briefly as a commander in chief of Virginia's armed forces, was a delegate to the Virginia convention of 1776, and was elected the first governor of the state later that year. Succeeded by Thomas Jefferson in 1779, Henry returned to the governor's mansion in 1784 and served until 1786. An Antifederalist, Henry led those in Virginia opposed to the ratification of the federal Constitution. He felt it gave too much power to a remote central authority, and he particularly objected to the lack of specific guarantees for the rights of citizens.

Toward the end of George Washington's administration the Federalists courted Henry in order to broaden the basis of their support in Virginia. Henry rejected all offers of a post in the government, but in 1799 he did agree to run for a seat in the state senate as a Federalist. He was elected but died before he could take office.

———— ⊸∞⊷ ————

Patrick Henry is one of America's foremost heroes. His name is familiar to nearly all Americans, and many can even recall something he said. Strangely enough, though, few Americans—even among the most educated— are able to recollect anything he *did*.

Opportunities for fame abounded in those exciting times when Americans were conducting a war for independence, establishing republican governments, and proclaiming the eternal rights of mankind. And Patrick Henry was at the vortex of the political maelstrom most of his life. Before the Revolution he was the acknowledged leader of the radical element in the Virginia House of Burgesses. During the war he served in the Continental Congress, as governor, and in the assembly. After the federal government was established, President Washington at one time or another offered him a place in the cabinet, on the Supreme Court, or on a foreign mission (all of which Henry refused). Yet in this long record of public prominence, during some of the most critical moments of history, there is not a single statute, treaty, battle, or declaration of human rights that can be attributed to him.

Part of the difficulty in evaluating Henry is the lack of documentary evidence. In contrast to the more than fifty thousand items that make up the papers of Thomas Jefferson, Henry's letters number only a few hundred. As a result, historians have to rely on estimates by Henry's contemporaries, and many of these were unfriendly. Jefferson, though an ally of Henry's early in his political career, subsequently concluded that Henry was nothing but a country demagogue with scant knowledge of law or statesmanship. Henry's staunchest defender was William Wirt, a Richmond lawyer who spent many years collecting anecdotal material for a biography that he finally published in 1817. But even Wirt often did more harm than good. Lacking any exact rendition of many of Henry's speeches—since debates in the Virginia assembly were not recorded—Wirt invented his own. On the occasion of the Stamp Act resolves, for instance, the splendid retort, "If this be treason, make the most of it!" is Wirt, not Henry. Yet Wirt meticulously consulted those who were in the hall that day, and there is no doubt that Henry made a memorable speech. Thomas Jefferson, then a student at the College of William and Mary, was standing at the door and later admitted, "He appeared to me to speak as Homer wrote."

Therein, no doubt, was the secret of Patrick Henry's fame. He had an extraordinary gift for oratory in an age that was accustomed to acquiring its information by the spoken, rather than the written, word. He was a giant among men who approached the novel task of creating a republic with no fixed ideas on the subject, men who were willing to listen and be persuaded. And to his credit Henry was as effective among sophisticated legislators as he was among the small farmers south of the James River. Five times he was elected governor of Virginia by the assembly, and his Prince Edward constituents sent him to the House of Delegates whenever he wished to serve. Moreover, he consistently championed the interests of the common man. In the postwar depression years he advocated tax reduction, debtor relief, and an expansion of the money supply to aid the poor. Yet he also opposed the measures sponsored by Jefferson and Madison for reform of the law code and disestablishment of the Church of England. A curious adherence to the status quo induced him first to oppose the federal Constitution and then to support the Washington administration even after it fell under the influence of northern commercial interests loyal to **Alexander Hamilton.** After the Revolution he was never really in step with the times.

Rare is the individual who can both initiate a revolution and erect a new regime. Tearing down a government requires one kind of temperament; creating one takes quite another. Patrick Henry seemed to have a talent only for the former. See Robert D. Meade, *Patrick Henry: Patriot in the Making* (1957) and *Practical Revolutionary* (1969).

NORMAN K. RISJORD

HENSON, James Maury (b. Greenville, Miss., Sept. 24, 1936; d. New York, N.Y., May 16, 1990), PUPPETEER, a member of a puppet club in high school, he took a job in Washington, D.C., with the local NBC station, WRC-TV, the summer before entering the University of Maryland. He did a five-minute program called *Sam and His Friends*, featuring the innovative combination of puppets and marionettes he called "Muppets." The series lasted through his college years, winning him an Emmy in 1958 for best local entertainment show. In 1959, Henson graduated from the University of Maryland with a degree in theater.

After graduation Henson made spot television commercials for several years, and in the early 1960s one of his Muppet creations, Rowlf the Dog, designed by his assistant Don Sahlin, became so popular that it began to appear on network television shows as an independent character. Operated by Henson, Rowlf was a regular guest on the *Jimmy Dean Show* for three seasons, and Henson appeared with Rowlf and other Muppets on the *Ed Sullivan Show* and the *Tonight Show*.

Beginning in 1969, Henson's Muppets became a central part of the public television series *Sesame Street*, produced by the Children's Television workshop. They were largely responsible for making that show the first educational television feature to become popular with the general television audience. His creations, Big Bird, Cookie Monster, and especially Kermit the Frog and Miss Piggy, were among the best-loved characters on the television screen among preschoolers and brought him Emmy Awards for outstanding achievement in children's programming in 1974 and 1976. From 1976 to 1981, Henson had his own weekly half-hour TV series, *The Muppet Show*, for which he won three awards. Other Henson television series included *The Muppet Babies*, winner of four awards, *The Storyteller*, and on Home Box Office, *Fraggle Rock*, the first pay-TV children's program.

Henson was always interested in making movies. In 1965 he received an Academy Award nomination for *Timepiece*, a non-puppet film that he wrote, produced, directed, and starred in. He also produced *Youth '68* (1968) and produced, directed, and cowrote *The Cube* (1969), using human actors. But he achieved his greatest success on the silver screen with three movies he made with his popular hand-operated creations: *The Muppet Movie* (1979), the *Great Muppet Caper (1981)*, and *The Muppets Take Manhattan* (1984). He also created the fantasy films *The Dark Crystal* (1983) and *Labyrinth* (1986), and designed the computerized masks for *Teenage Mutant Ninja Turtles* (1988). Jim Henson Productions leased the rights to some of its characters (for a reported $100–$150 million) to the Walt Disney Company, but they remain in the hands of their creator's five children.

Jim Henson brought a fresh vision to children's television and single-handedly (in a literal as well as a figurative sense) revolutionized the art of puppetry. The simple foam-rubber dolls he created had an amazing range of expression on their flexible, cartoonlike faces and delivered their lines in a contemporary comedic style that both children and adults found irresistible. A self-taught puppeteer, he recognized that television called for something more personal than the mechanical movements and painted faces of traditional marionettes. From the first public appearances of the innovative figures for whom he coined the word "Muppets," which he presented on television while still in his teens, Henson revealed a profound sensitivity to both the requirements of the new medium and the tastes of his youthful audience. He used the full television screen as his stage rather than working from within a conventional theatrical set and incorporated slapstick humor into his fast-paced material. His twenty-one-year run on *Sesame Street*, aimed at three- to five-year-olds, mixed educational entertainment in so merry a blend that learning to read, count, and recognize geometrical shapes became a game that toddlers loved. Live performers interacted with his Muppets so convincingly that it was difficult to distinguish the two.

Henson brought his engaging characters to an adult TV audience with *The Muppet Show* in 1976. The show was rejected by all the major American networks because of its spoofs of television and advertising, and because the Muppets were associated so closely with children that no one believed they would have an adult market. But it was picked up by the independent British producer Lew Grade and proved a great international success. Described as "one of the first truly global television programs," *The Muppet Show* developed an audience of over 250 million people of all ages in more than a hundred countries.

By the time of Henson's sudden death at 53, Kermit the Frog, the ambitious and amorous Miss Piggy, and a half-dozen other Muppet characters had become integral parts of American culture. See David Owens, "Looking Out for Kermit," *The New Yorker*, August 16, 1993.

DENNIS WEPMAN

HERSKOVITS, Melville Jean (b. Bellefontaine, Ohio, Sept. 10, 1895; d. Evanston, Ill., Feb. 25, 1963), ANTHROPOLOGIST, entered the Hebrew Union College and the University of Cincinnati in 1915, but his studies were interrupted by service as an army private in France during World War I. Following his discharge he studied briefly at the University of Poitiers (1919). He received his BA from the University of Chicago in 1920 and his MA (1921) and PhD (1923) from Columbia, where he studied under **Franz Boas.**

During 1924–27, Herskovits was a lecturer at Columbia. A grant from the National Research Council enabled him to pursue studies on the African-American and to spend a year teaching and researching at Howard University (1925). In 1927 he joined the faculty of Northwestern University as an assistant professor (associate professor, 1931; full professor, 1935). At Northwestern he established the first program of African studies in the United States. In 1928 he published *The American Negro: A Study in Racial Crossing,* in which he argued that the African-American represented a mixture of black, Caucasian, and Native American heredity and that he must be accepted as part of a homogeneous population group.

Herskovits believed that the study of the African-American required knowledge of the African background of his slave ancestors. He did extensive fieldwork in West Africa, the West Indies, and South America. In 1928–29, in Dutch Guiana, he studied the parallel development of the Saromacca tribe of Bush blacks and the blacks of the Surinam coastal region. *Anthropometry of the American Negro* (1930) elaborated on this research. In 1931 he worked in Dahomey in West Africa, in 1934 in Haiti. The results of his findings were published in *Outline of Dahomean Religious Belief* (1933; in collaboration with his wife Frances); *Rebel Destiny* (1934; also with his wife), a study of the Bush blacks of Guiana; and *Life in a Haitian Village* (1937), which attempted to describe the Haitian peasant. *Dahomey* (2 vols.) appeared in 1938.

In 1938, Herskovits was appointed chairman of the anthropology department at Northwestern. He participated in a Carnegie Corporation study of the African-American under the direction of Gunnar Myrdal of the University of Stockholm; his contribution was *The Myth of the Negro Past* (1941), in which he sought to trace the survival of African culture in contemporary African-American customs.

During World War II, Herskovits worked for a number of governmental agencies, including the Department of Agriculture (1939–45), the State Department (1940–43), and the Board of Economic Warfare (1942–43). He also led an expedition to Brazil (1941–42). In 1948 he published *Man and His Works,* a survey of cultural anthropology that described how man has tried to adapt to his environment. *Dahomean Narrative: A Cross-Cultural Analysis* (written with his wife) appeared in 1958. In 1963 he published *The Human Factor in Changing Africa,* which focused on the African's reaction to various situations and on the interplay of cultural forces in African life. Some of his other works include *The Economic Life of Primitive Peoples* (1940), revised as *Economic Anthropology* (1952), and *Trinidad Village* (1947; with his wife).

Although he had wider interests, Melville J. Herskovits will be remembered for his contributions to three areas of cultural anthropology: the role of the individual in culture, cultural relativism, and African and African-American ethnology.

While other anthropologists' interests in the individual led to the development of the culture and personality field, Herskovits stressed—some would say overstressed—the innovative roles of the individual. His concern with the cultural manifestations of human creativity distinguished him as an anthropologist of the arts. He was a scientist among humanists and a humanist among scientists. (He enjoyed paradoxes and used them as pedagogic devices.)

Herskovits, who enjoyed debate, reacted sharply against the implicit and explicit ethnocentrism of his time and phrased his counterattack in terms of cultural relativism, a concept he acquired from his teacher Franz Boas. As critics have indicated, his formulation lacked philosophic sophistication, a feature that has almost obscured the simple lesson he sought to state: the standards of judgment that humans so heedlessly use are culturally based—and biased.

As the premier American Africanist of his time, Herskovits stimulated research into a variety of African societies and cultures. This has constituted a significant contribution to anthropology and indirectly changed many popular stereotypes of Africa. His attempts to show African cultural retentions in the New World met with opposition, much of it influenced by the unfavorable stereotypes he fought. Largely as a consequence of his leadership, knowledge of Africa expanded, and he lived to see a measure of acceptance of his hypotheses of African influences in African-American culture. See Melville T. Herskovits, *Man and His Works* (1948).

JAMES H. VAUGHAN

HEWITT, Abram Stevens (b. Haverstraw, N.Y., July 31, 1822; d. New York, N.Y., Jan. 18, 1903), MANUFACTURER, POLITICAL LEADER, was the son of a successful ironmaster who helped build one of the first steam engines in America. Hewitt attended Columbia College on a scholarship and graduated in 1842. He then read law and was admitted to the bar, but an eye defect prevented his going into practice. After Edward Cooper, son of the ironmaster Peter, became Hewitt's close friend, **Peter Cooper** turned his Trenton Iron Works over to the two

young men in 1845. Eventually employing three thousand men, the firm produced wrought-iron girders and beams for the multistory fireproof buildings that were then being built in New York City. In 1862, Hewitt brought a process from England for making gunbarrel iron, and throughout the Civil War he manufactured barrels for the Union army at cost. The first mass-produced steel in America came from a Martin-Siemens open-hearth plant installed by Hewitt in 1868. He also took an active part in the direction of several railroads, notably the Erie.

In 1871, Hewitt and Edward Cooper were associated with **Samuel J. Tilden** in prosecuting **William M. Tweed** and the New York City "Tweed Ring." Their success propelled Hewitt and Tilden to the national level in Democratic politics. Between 1874 and 1886, Hewitt, a Democrat, served in every Congress except one. During the disputed presidential election of 1876 he drafted an aggressive declaration of victory, but Tilden, the Democratic candidate, declined to issue it. When Tilden acquiesced in the establishment of the commission that awarded the election to the Republican candidate, Rutherford B. Hayes, Hewitt reluctantly went along. In Congress, Hewitt took an active role in the tariff reform movement and in defending the gold standard.

In the hotly contested New York mayoralty election of 1886, Hewitt, running as a Democrat reform candidate, defeated both Theodore Roosevelt, the Republican candidate, and **Henry George,** who ran on a labor ticket. While mayor, Hewitt supported municipal ownership of one of the rapid transit lines. After one term he retired from politics.

Hewitt played an important part in realizing Peter Cooper's plans for a free technical and art school, Cooper Union, and administered its financial affairs. He was also a trustee of Columbia University and Barnard College, and an original trustee and first chairman of the Carnegie Institution.

After witnessing Abram S. Hewitt's restless

energy and active temperament in Congress, **Henry Adams** called him "the most useful public man in Washington." Hewitt developed his guiding principles of order and efficiency in a business career that ranged from western cattle to New Jersey steel mills. Receptive to technological change as an entrepreneur, he showed a similar taste for innovation in his advocacy of arbitration of labor disputes and employee ownership of stock. His sympathy for unions did not extend, however, to the closed shop, and he criticized the miners in the 1902 anthracite coal strike.

In politics these business precepts set the boundaries of Hewitt's reform impulse. He wanted social change but only from above. Believing that inefficient government should exercise only a minimal role in the economy, he supported Democrats like Tilden who shared his commitment to genteel leadership and negativism. Close relations with Tilden enabled Hewitt to play a leading part in resolving the disputed election of 1876. Hewitt opposed the tariff both as a clumsy interference with business and for its harmful effects on his personal interests. When Grover Cleveland moved slowly toward tariff reform after 1885 and took mild action against some of Hewitt's business ventures, he broke with the president. Elected mayor as the conservative alternative to Henry George, Hewitt sought administrative rationality and system, but his disdain for partisanship and hostility toward New York's ethnic minorities turned the Democrats against him. His achievements as an industrialist and philanthropist were substantial, but Hewitt also reflected the limitations of the "businessman in politics" in the Gilded Age. See Allan Nevins, *Abram S. Hewitt* (1935).

LEWIS L. GOULD

HILL, James Jerome (b. Rockwood, Ont., Canada, Sept. 16, 1838; d. St. Paul, Minn., May 29, 1916), RAILROAD MAGNATE, left school in 1852 to work as a clerk in a grocery store. In 1856 he settled in St. Paul, Minnesota, where he worked as a clerk for the commission merchants J. W. Bass and Co. In 1865 he formed his own commission merchants firm, becoming the local agent for the Northwestern Packet Co. (1865) and the St. Paul and Pacific Railroad (1867). In 1870 he organized the Red River Transportation Co. to ship goods by steamboat from St. Paul to the new settlement of Winnipeg, Canada, and in 1875 he formed the Northwest Fuel Co. to supply coal to the St. Paul and Pacific and other Minnesota railroads.

In 1878, Hill formed a syndicate to purchase the St. Paul and Pacific Railroad, which had been bankrupt since the panic of 1873. After transforming the existing facilities into a profitable operation, he extended the line westward to Great Falls (1887) and finally to Seattle (1893). He reorganized the various divisions of his railway holdings into the Great Northern Railroad in 1890. Although he received no government land grants or other subsidies, his corporation became the only transcontinental line to avoid bankruptcy during the late 19th century. In 1901, Hill, **J. P. Morgan,** and their associates formed the Northern Securities Co. to coordinate control of the combined interests of the Great Northern, the Northern Pacific, and the Chicago, Burlington, and Quincy railroads. However, in 1904 the Supreme Court dissolved this holding company under the Sherman Anti-Trust Act (Northern Securities case).

Hill also contributed to Canadian railroad development. Joining the board of directors of the Canadian Pacific Railroad in 1880, he helped extend this line from Winnipeg to Vancouver by 1885. Since the Canadian Pacific met the Great Northern at Manitoba, he held a uniquely profitable position in Canadian-American exchange as well as transcontinental trade. After accumulating a fortune in railroad enterprises, Hill invested more than $4 million in the Mesabi iron-ore range and became involved in finance, including associations with Chase National Bank in New York, Illinois Trust and Savings in Chicago, and First National Bank in St. Paul.

Hill also campaigned for the conservation of natural resources. His major speeches and writings on this subject were compiled in *Highways of Progress* (1910). He participated actively in civic, religious, and philanthropic affairs. In St. Paul he founded the Hill Reference Library and endowed a Roman Catholic seminary.

Hill was a combination of an operating man who early demonstrated his understanding of the business details of shipping and transportation, and a student and practitioner of corporate finance, able favorably to impress remote bankers. The fact that he could get money from Canadian financial centers in the depressed year of 1878 to reorganize the bankrupt St. Paul and Pacific Railroad indicates the confidence his smaller operations in Minnesota transportation had inspired. His "shaking off" of the railroad's Dutch bondholders at a low cost was an example of his ability to manipulate corporation finance— a relatively new science, unhampered by modern accounting practices.

A return to bumper, exportable wheat crops in the Red River Valley and adjacent northern areas in 1878 and 1879 endowed early investments in the westward extension of the railroad, now the Great Northern, with unexpected success. But Hill was a careful manager who personally inspected what went on and properly inspired trust in his financial backers. Perhaps other transcontinental railroad promoters would have better served their stockholders if they had spent as much time as Hill on the line of the road.

Hill's reputation for both imagination in developing the area served by the road and attention to the details of railroad operation, plus the strong position of the Great Northern during the financial troubles of the middle nineties, led J. P. Morgan to choose him as an operating ally in seeking to end railroad competition in the Northwest. Their opponents, who had the same ambition, were railroad man **E. H. Harriman** and the financial house of Kuhn, Loeb and Company. In the latter part of the struggle, 1902–4, the attorney general of the United States became a third party seeking to prevent the success of either of the others, but when the dust of battle had subsided, the Hill-Morgan forces were in control of the field and a de facto community of interest had been established between the Great Northern, the Northern Pacific, and the Chicago, Burlington, and Quincy.

The financial and legal drama and the gigantic stature of the contestants made the struggle a heroic climax to the Railroad Age. Very soon, overbuilding of competitive lines to the Pacific coast and completion of the Panama Canal were to make the results seem far less important. A generation later continuing federal regulation and the motor vehicle had reduced giant railroad companies from monopolists threatening to rob shippers to supplicants for permission to merge in order to remain profitable at all. Thus Hill and his rival Harriman may be looked upon as the last of the great railway barons. But whereas Harriman was an aloof financial man from a socially recognized New York family, Hill, even when a great financier, preserved the image of a working railroad man at home with his employees along the tracks. See Albro Martin, *James J. Hill and the Opening of the Northwest* (1976).

THOMAS C. COCHRAN

HILLMAN, Sidney (b. Zagare, Lithuania, Mar. 23, 1887; d. Point Lookout, L.I., N.Y., July 10, 1946), LABOR LEADER, studied to be a rabbi before he moved to Kovno, Russia, where he was arrested in 1905 for demonstrating against the czar. He spent about eight months in jail and upon his release fled to Manchester, England. In 1907 he emigrated to the United States and settled in Chicago where he worked as a clerk. In 1909, Hillman became a garment cutter for Chicago's Hart, Schaffner, and Marx clothing firm. He joined a strike against the company in 1910 and soon became the strike leader. In 1914 he was invited to become chief clerk of the Cloakmakers' Union in New York. That same year he led a revolt against the leadership of the United Garment Workers and helped found the Amalgamated Clothing Workers of America. He became its first president in 1915, serving until his death.

As president, Hillman organized men's clothing workers in all major American cities and enlarged his union's membership. He ran the union in a democratic style and advanced the idea of "constructive cooperation" between business and labor. Hillman and his union founded two banks during the 1920s that helped finance new clothing factories. He also started an unemployment compensation program for union members and a low-cost housing program. A fervent New Dealer, Hillman was a member of the Labor Advisory Board of the NRA (1933), the National Industrial Recovery Board (1935), and the advisory board of the National Youth Administration (1935). Hillman's union joined the AFL in 1933, but in 1935 helped form the new Committee on Industrial Organization and within two years severed all ties with the Federation. Hillman became first vice president of the CIO in 1937 and was largely responsible for its efforts to organize the textile industry. In 1940, President Franklin D. Roosevelt appointed Hillman to the National Defense Advisory Commission and a year later associate director of the Office of Production Management. He became director of the labor division for the War Production Board in 1942 but left the government in 1943 to become chairman of the CIO Political Action Committee. In this position Hillman actively supported the candidacy of Roosevelt in 1944.

⸺ ✧ ⸺

By the time Sidney Hillman emerged as a labor leader just before World War I, American labor had already committed itself permanently to conservative, job-oriented unionism. The significance of Hillman's career, as it unfolded, was above all in the broadening influence that it exerted on the narrow business unionism of the American movement. The relationship cut both ways, of course. Hillman quickly discarded his youthful radicalism. Eminently realistic, impatient with ideology, eager for tangible results, and inclined always to the reasonable and practical, Hillman deliberately tailored his efforts to fit the conditions that he found on the American scene. By the time he assumed a commanding national role during the 1930s, he was very much in the movement's mainstream. But in two important ways that course had been shifted by Hillman's influence.

The first had to do with widening the responsibility of trade unions to their immediate constituencies. Under Hillman's leadership the Amalgamated Clothing Workers became an active industrial partner, not only stressing arbitration and cooperative relations but also striving to maintain the economic health of the clothing industry. For its own members the ACW went much beyond the limited job concerns of other trade unions, providing banking services, building low-cost housing, pioneering in unemployment insurance, even engaging in educational and social activities. This "New Unionism," as it was called in the 1920s, sprang from specific conditions—the instability of the clothing trade, the ethnic composition (especially the Jewish) of both labor and management, and a continuing strain of idealism. But the example thus set had a profound long-term influence on the entire movement, and Hillman's broader perspective accounted largely for his leading part in forming the CIO and organizing the great new mass-production unions.

Hillman also played a signal role in breaking down labor's relative isolation from the political world. Unlike the AFL, the Clothing Workers had from the first taken an active part in partisan politics. During the 1930s the radical cast to this policy was largely shed (as Hillman himself had long advocated), but not the policy itself. Hillman saw in the New Deal great opportunities for his own union and for the entire labor movement, and especially beginning with the 1936 campaign, he rose swiftly in Democratic politics. As the influence of **John L. Lewis** waned, Hillman established himself as the preeminent labor man in American political life. The political activism and the unabashed partisanship of the modern labor movement can be traced more to Sidney Hillman than to any other man. See Mathew Josephson, *Sidney Hillman* (1952).

DAVID BRODY

HINES, Earl Kenneth (b. Duquesne, Pa., Dec. 28, 1905; d. Oakland, Calif., Apr. 22, 1983), MUSICIAN, played trumpet and then piano as a youth. He began his professional career as a musician while still in high school and took his first permanent job in 1922 as pianist for band-leader-singer L. B. Deppe in Pittsburgh. After leading his own band at the Grape Arbor in the same city, Hines went to Chicago in 1924 to play at the Elite No. 2 Club. He then made a nation-wide tour as a member of Carroll Dickerson's band, and on returning to Chicago joined **Louis Armstrong** as musical director at the Sunset café in 1927. Later that year he joined clarinetist Jimmie Noone at the Apex Club. During this period he played on such classic jazz recordings as Noone's "Sweet Sue" and "Apex Blues," and Armstrong's "West End Blues" and "Save It, Pretty Mama." In December 1928, Hines began a twelve-year run at Chicago's Grand Terrace nightclub, where his band was to become famous throughout the country via nightly broadcasts. Among the famous "discoveries" he presented there were Billy Eckstine and Sarah Vaughan, and of the band's many recordings two of the most successful were "Boogie Woogie on St. Louis Blues" and "Jelly Jelly" (1940).

Because of the economic problems that faced "big" bands in the 1940s, Hines dissolved his in 1948 and joined Louis Armstrong's All-Stars, with whom he toured Europe (1948 and 1949). After leaving Armstrong in 1951 and leading small groups on the West Coast, he made his home in Oakland, California. In 1955 he took over leadership of the small band at San Francisco's Hangover Club for a long engage-ment, and apart from a European tour with Jack Teagarden in 1957, he was not much in the public eye until he gave a concert in New York's Little Theater (1964) where he received a rapturous reception. The following years he toured the United States, Canada, and Europe with great success at the head of a quartet. In 1966 he went to the Soviet Union with a sextet in the State Department's Cultural Exchange program and played to enormous, enthusiastic audiences. He toured South America in 1969, Japan and Australia in 1972. He continued to tour the United States and Europe through the 1970s and 1980s. He appeared in New York in 1982 and in San Francisco less than a week before his death.

His best-known compositions are "Rosetta," "My Monday Date," "You Can Depend on Me," and "Blues in Thirds."

⁂

For much of his career Earl Hines was known as "the father of modern jazz piano," because he ("Fatha") more than anyone else emancipated it from the lingering restrictions of ragtime thought and principle. This was particularly evident in the freedom he brought to the role of the left hand, but more important in its entirety was the new style he invented, one that simulated the phrase-ology and vibrato of such trumpet players as Joe Smith and Louis Armstrong by means of an inci-sive attack and tremolos. For this reason he was often referred to as playing "trumpet-style piano." When he became leader of a big band in 1928, before electrical amplification was in use, he also developed a method of playing in octaves in the treble that enabled him to be heard above and through the sound of a brassy ensemble.

Hines was one of the most exciting jazz impro-visers in jazz history, and his energy and powers of invention remained miraculously unimpaired through more than sixty years of professional activity. During the 1930s he was widely imitated by most jazz pianists—Teddy Wilson, Jess Stacy, Nat Cole, and Art Tatum being among those who acknowledged his influence—while subsequent newcomers were frequently inspired by his unique approach to the keyboard. As a band-leader he was one of the more successful during the Swing Era, his flair for talent leading to the discovery of many young musicians who later became internationally famous. His 1943 band was known as the "incubator" of the musical rev-olutionaries responsible for bebop, an idiom that to a considerable extent transformed jazz. See John S. Wilson, "Earl Hines," in Nat Hentoff and Nat Shapiro, eds., *The Jazz Makers* (1957).

STANLEY DANCE

HISS, Alger (b. Baltimore, Md., Nov. 11, 1904), DIPLOMAT, received a BA from Johns Hopkins in 1926 and an LLB from Harvard in 1929. After serving as a law clerk for Justice **Oliver Wendell Holmes, Jr.,** he practiced law in Boston and New York City (1930–33). He was on the Department of Agriculture's legal staff (1933–35) and legal assistant for Senator **Gerald Nye**'s investigation of the armaments industry (1934–35). After serving as a special attorney for the Department of Justice (1935–36), he joined the Department of State as a member of Assistant Secretary Francis B. Sayre's staff. In 1939, Hiss was assistant to the State Department's adviser on Far Eastern political relations, and in 1943 he was special assistant to the director of the newly established Office of Far Eastern Affairs, which developed and coordinated American policy respecting the United Nations. Hiss was executive secretary of the Dumbarton Oaks U.N. Conference (1944) and in 1945 was promoted to deputy director of the Office of Special Political Affairs. After serving on President Franklin D. Roosevelt's staff at the Yalta Conference, Hiss became director of the Office of Special Political Affairs (Mar. 1945). The following month he was elected temporary secretary general of the United Nations at the San Francisco Conference that drew up the U.N. Charter. In the first three months of 1946, Hiss was a principal adviser to the American delegation at the U.N. In December 1946 he was elected president of the Carnegie Endowment for International Peace, serving until 1949.

In 1948 ex-Communist Whittaker Chambers charged before the House Un-American Activities Committee that Hiss had been a member of the Communist Party from 1934 to 1938 and that Hiss had belonged to a spy ring and had copied secret State Department documents, which he gave to Chambers to convey to Soviet officials. Hiss denied the charges before a New York grand jury, but in December 1948 it indicted him for perjury (the statute of limitations prevented an espionage indictment). Hiss's trials attracted international attention: the first (1949) resulted in a hung jury; the second (1950) brought conviction. Appeals having been unsuccessful, Hiss entered the federal penitentiary at Lewisburg, Pennsylvania, in March 1951. He was released in December 1954. Hiss has maintained his innocence but since his release has generally remained out of public view. He has published his own version of his case and lectured occasionally on the New Deal and other subjects. Debate over his guilt or innocence has continued unabated, however. In the early 1990s, after the collapse of Communism in the Soviet Union and Eastern Europe, transcripts of interrogations of Noel Field, a close friend of Hiss, were discovered in the archives of the Hungarian secret police. Although attacked as unreliable by Hiss partisans, those transcripts and other newly unearthed evidence strongly indicate that Hiss did indeed belong to a spy ring that supplied secret State Department materials to the Soviet Union.

In his years of rising fortunes, Alger Hiss was both attractive and ambitious. His intellect impressed the people who came in contact with him, including some very prominent Americans; many also found him calm under fire, courteous, and charming, although reserved. At the same time he seemed eager to move up in American life and did so for a decade and a half before Chambers leveled his charges. By 1948, at 43, Hiss appeared proud of his accomplishments and confident that his progress would continue.

These years formed a still-unclear prelude to the very significant years from 1948 to 1950 and beyond. During that period Hiss became both a symbol and a force. He became a symbol in the hot battles between conservatives and liberals. Many of the former saw him as the major piece of evidence in support of their theory that recent history had been shaped by Communist conspirators, while many of the latter viewed him as the innocent victim of efforts to discredit the domestic and foreign policies of the Roosevelt and Truman administrations. He also became a symbol in controversies among liberal intellectuals concerning their own relations with Communism.

While he had not had a forceful impact earlier, his case stimulated the development of the "Red Scare," helping it become a major feature of American life in the early 1950s. His conviction was followed quickly by Senator **Joseph R.**

McCarthy's anti-Communist crusade and contributed immensely to the atmosphere that the senator exploited so effectively. See Allen Weinstein, *Perjury: The Hiss-Chambers Case* (1978)

RICHARD S. KIRKENDALL

HOAR, George Frisbie (b. Concord, Mass., Aug. 29, 1826; d. Worcester, Mass., Sept. 30, 1904), POLITICAL LEADER, graduated from Harvard College (1846) and Harvard Law School (1849). He then practiced law in Worcester, Massachusetts. Elected to the state legislature in 1852, Hoar soon transferred his support of the Free Soil movement to the new Republican Party, which he joined officially in 1856. In 1868 he was elected to the House of Representatives, serving until 1877 when he became a senator. He was reelected to the Senate four times.

Hoar's work in Congress was chiefly concerned with undramatic administrative and procedural matters. As a member of the judiciary committee of the House he pressed for the impeachment of William Belknap, Ulysses S. Grant's secretary of war, even though the accused had resigned. He served on the Hayes-Tilden electoral commission of 1877. As a member of the Senate committees on claims, on privileges and elections, and on the judiciary, Hoar helped settle numerous Civil War claims, and he fought to preserve the independence of regulatory commissions from politics by opposing the appointment of former senators. Hoar energetically pressed for the independence of Cuba, and after the Spanish-American War, he was a leader in the anti-imperialist movement. He bitterly opposed American annexation of the Philippines. Although his stand against "imperialism" and his unconcealed contempt for nativist movements were unpopular, they did not harm him politically. Despite offers of judicial appointments and of diplomatic posts, Hoar remained at his post in the Senate until his death.

George Frisbie Hoar sought to reconcile the social harmonies of the past with the needs of corporate industrial expansion, and his political creed was correspondingly ambivalent. A dedicated believer in the value of the two-party system, he saw the Republican Party as the sole repository of political virtue. A nationalist in his interpretation of the Constitution and the power of Congress to secure the rights of blacks in the South, he was strong in his sectional loyalty to New England and its economic needs. Although renowned for his political independence on issues of principle, he upheld party regularity and excoriated the Mugwumps. An early advocate of labor reform and woman's rights, he was suspicious of constitutional innovation and accepted the prevailing social and economic order. A firm opponent of insular expansion, he advocated the extension of American markets. A champion of the industrial progress of his adopted city of Worcester, he chose to be buried in Concord, the home of "simple living and high thinking." The mixed goals and inspirations that marked Hoar's career were in measure a reflection of those of the Republican "Half-Breeds" with whom Hoar was early identified.

In his private as in his public life, Hoar prized righteous conduct and was occasionally self-righteous. Provincial in his tastes, he judged prejudice to be a sin, and as a son of the Puritans knew sin to be the enemy. He possessed little understanding of any cultural values outside those of New England, but he championed the rights of Native Americans, Chinese immigrants, southern blacks, and Filipino insurgents. See R. E. Welch, Jr., *George F. Hoar and the Half-Breed Republicans* (1971).

R. E. WELCH, JR.

HOFFA, James Riddle (b. Brazil, Ind., Feb. 14, 1913; d. Detroit, Mich., Jan. 30, 1975), UNION LEADER, attended the Neinas Intermediate School in Detroit until the ninth grade when he left for a job as a stockboy in a department store. At 17 he became a freight handler for the Kroger Grocery and Baking Company and led four coworkers in a successful strike against the company soon after taking the job. In 1931 he helped organize a union at Kroger but left the next year for a job as organizer with the Detroit unit of the International Brotherhood of Teamsters. In 1935 he was president of Detroit teamsters local 299, which became the linchpin of his union power, and helped establish the teamsters' Central State Council. In 1940 he became the Council's chairman and its vice president the following year. In 1953 he took over the presidency of the Central Conference of Teamsters, which was responsible for negotiating contracts for all cartage drivers in twenty midwestern and southern states.

As he rose to power Hoffa came under increasing attack for alleged underworld ties. In 1957 he faced federal charges of taking payoffs from trucking companies in return for labor peace; he was acquitted. That same year he was elected international president of the teamsters union. The Department of Justice continued to investigate Hoffa, and in 1964, under Attorney General **Robert Kennedy,** who became his personal nemesis, succeeded in convicting him for jury tampering, mail fraud, and misappropriation of union funds. He was sentenced to thirteen years in prison and was eventually forced to resign his union presidency, leaving it in the hands of his longtime associate Frank Fitzsimmons. He began his sentence in 1967 but was released from prison in 1971 after receiving executive clemency from President Richard Nixon with the condition that he not resume any union activites or seek office before 1980. Although prohibited from direct participation, he remained a power in the union by playing a significant backstage role. He disappeared in January 1975, and his remains have never been found. Authorities believe he was murdered by members of the Mafia in a struggle for control of the teamsters and its huge pension funds.

———— ⧐∞⧐ ————

Jimmy Hoffa organized a strike while still in his teens and went on to become perhaps the most powerful figure in American labor. He advanced rapidly in the organized labor movement, securing an American Federation of Labor charter for the warehouse where he worked at the age of 18 and becoming president of the Detroit local of the teamsters union at 22. By shrewd manipulation and personal charisma he succeeded during the next twenty years in unifying many smaller unions into the largest, richest, and perhaps most powerful labor union in the United States, the International Brotherhood of Teamsters, Chauffeurs, Warehousemen, and Helpers of America, with some 2 million members.

Hoffa survived the bitter opposition of companies he sought to unionize, suffering twenty-four beatings in his first year as business agent for the Detroit teamsters local. He consolidated his power during the 1950s, often by striking deals with organized crime, pressuring trucking companies to sell out to his associates, and intimidating and strong-arming rivals and critics. By the time the teamsters union was expelled from the AFL-CIO for corruption in 1957, he had absorbed or formed alliances with enough other unions to create the strongest single labor organization in the country. The federal government tried to curb his power and break the hold organized crime had in the union. Attorney General Robert Kennedy, especially, viewed Hoffa as a corrupt blot on the organized labor movement who had to be removed because of his corrosive influence. Finally convicted of various charges in 1964, Hoffa, ever popular with the rank and file whose wages and working conditions improved significantly during his tenure, continued to serve as president of the union even after entering prison and resigned in favor of Fitzsimmons only when it became one of the conditions for his release in 1971. But Hoffa never accepted these or any other conditions that would bar him from the union, and he sought to return to power. This eventually led to his murder.

Variously seen as a martyred champion of the working class and as a ruthless, corrupt powerbroker, Hoffa has left a mixed legacy of accomplishment and betrayal to the American labor movement. He did help create the most influential labor union in America, which brought substantial economic gains to its members. But he also entered into a Faustian bargain with organized crime that seriously eroded public support for organized labor and ultimately weakened and tarnished the very union he served. See Arthur A. Sloane, *Hoffa* (1991).

DENNIS WEPMAN

HOFSTADTER, Richard (b. Buffalo, N.Y., Aug. 6, 1916; d. New York, N.Y., Oct. 24, 1970), HISTORIAN, graduated from the University of Buffalo in 1937, where he had studied American history under Julius W. Pratt. After briefly attending law school in 1937, he decided to specialize in American history and received his MA degree from Columbia in 1938. He was an instructor at Brooklyn College (1940–41) and at the College of the City of New York (1941). He won a William Bayard Cutting traveling fellowship (1941–42) and received his PhD from Columbia in 1942, publishing his dissertation, *Social Darwinism in American Thought, 1860–1915*, in 1944. He was assistant professor of history at the University of Maryland (1942–46). He then returned to Columbia as assistant professor in 1946 and became an associate professor in 1950, full professor in 1952, and De Witt Clinton Professor of American History at Columbia in 1959, a position he held until his death.

An Alfred A. Knopf fellowship in history in 1945 led to *The American Political Tradition: And the Men Who Made It* (1948), a collection of twelve interpretive essays of such famous Americans as Thomas Jefferson, Abraham Lincoln, Theodore Roosevelt, and Franklin D. Roosevelt. He worked with C. De Witt Hardy on *The Development and Scope of Higher Education in the United States* (1955) for the Commission on Financing Higher Education. His *Age of Reform* (1955), a study of the Populist, Progressive, and New Deal reform movements in the United States, won the 1956 Pulitzer Prize in history. Hofstadter and Walter P. Metzger prepared a study, *The Development of Academic Freedom in the United States* (1955), for the American Academic Freedom Project at Columbia, and he held the Pitt chair in American history and institutions at Cambridge University, England, in 1958–59. His *Anti-Intellectualism in American Life* (1963) won the 1964 Pulitzer Prize

for general nonfiction. His Jefferson Memorial lectures at the University of California at Berkeley in 1966 led to *The Idea of a Party System* (1969). A 1966–67 Guggenheim fellowship resulted in *The Progressive Historians* (1968). Some of his other works include *The Paranoid Style in American Politics* (1965), *Sociology and History: Methods* (1968, with Seymour Martin Lipset), a textbook, *The American Republic* (1959, with William Miller and Daniel Aaron), and *American Violence: A Documentary History* (1970), edited with Michael Wallace. *America at 1750: A Social History* (1971) appeared posthumously.

⁂

Richard Hofstadter neatly defined his historical interests as "marginal to both political historians and to practitioners of the history of ideas," situated "between the two fields, at the intersection of their perimeters." His masters were Sigmund Freud and Karl Mannheim; his own witty style had much of Freud's elegance and none of Mannheim's jargon. Hofstadter's approach to American history, a field he traversed from the mid–18th to the mid–20th centuries, was similarly defined by two distinct, though to him compatible, ideals: professional detachment and political engagement. While his books responded to the political situation, they were essays in historical discovery more than exercises in cultural self-criticism. We can read *The American Political Tradition* as a debunking of smug self-congratulation, *The Age of Reform* as a critique of progressive movements by a critic who shared the ideology he analyzed, and *Anti-Intellectualism in American Life* as a despairing anatomy of a pervasive trait in the American character. But what gives them their lasting importance is their revisions of accepted interpretations. These and other works concentrated on the nonrational components of social behavior; in this respect, two essays, *The Pseudo-Conservative Revolt* (1954), written at the height of the **Joseph McCarthy** era, and *The Paranoid Style in American Politics*, written in 1963, after its demise, are typical of his psychosocial perception of history, which has been influential but controversial. In *The Progressive Historians* Hofstadter rebutted the charge that his historical style supported "consensus history." But his intensely personal vision makes applicable to him Jacob Burckhardt's remark about himself: he did not found a school. See Stanley Elkins and Eric McKitrick, eds., *The Hofstadter Aegis* (1973).

PETER GAY

HOLMES, Oliver Wendell (b. Cambridge, Mass., Aug. 29, 1809; d. Boston, Mass., Oct. 7, 1894), PHYSICIAN, WRITER, graduated from Harvard in 1829. In 1830 he published "Old Ironsides," a poem protesting the scrapping of the frigate *Constitution*. His famous "The Autocrat at the Breakfast Table," a series of urbane conversation pieces ("table talk"), was first serialized in the *New England Magazine* (1831–32). After briefly studying law at Harvard, he turned to the study of medicine, first in Paris (1833–35) and then at Harvard, where he received his MD in 1836. Holmes published his first volume of *Poems* in 1836 and won the Boylston medical prize for his essay "Direct Explorations," in which he argued that the stethoscope should be employed more frequently. In 1837 he again received Boylston prizes for his essays on neuralgia and malaria.

Holmes became professor of anatomy at Dartmouth College in 1838. Returning to Boston in 1840, he set up his own practice and published a number of important medical papers, including *Homeopathy and Its Kindred Delusions* (1842), an attack on medical quackery, and *The Contagiousness of Puerperal Fever* (1843), in which he used statistics to prove that disease is spread by contagion. He was Parkman professor of anatomy and physiology at Harvard (1847–82) and dean of its medical school (1847–53). His essay "A Report on Medical Literature," which he prepared for the American Medical Association (1848), urged American physicians to produce original works and not rely so heavily on English texts. His "Currents and Counter-Currents in Medical Science" (1860) was extremely influential in the profession.

In 1857, Holmes became a regular contributor to the newly created *Atlantic Monthly* magazine. After a twenty-five-year lapse he again began serializing his "Autocrat" essays. These were collected and published in book form in 1858. *The Professor at the Breakfast Table,* a sequel to the *Autocrat,* was published in 1860. In 1861 he published his first novel, *Elsie Venner.* In this work, as in *The Guardian Angel* (1887) and *A Mortal Antipathy* (1885), Holmes attacked the New England Calvinist and Unitarian traditions, arguing that human behavior must be judged from a psychological rather than from a religious standpoint. "Mechanism in Thought and Morals" (1870) and "Crime and Automatism" (1875) further developed his psychiatric theory. *The Poet at the Breakfast Table,* another "table talk" work, was issued in 1872.

Some of Holmes's collections of verse include *Poetical Works* (1852), *Songs in Many Keys* (1862), *Songs of Many Seasons* (1875), and *The Iron Gate, and Other Poems* (1880). *Our Hundred Days in Europe* (1887) contains his observations on Europe. *Over the Teacups* (1891) is another conversation book. He also published three biographies: *John Lothrop Motley* (1879), *Ralph Waldo Emerson* (1885), and *Henry Jacob Biglow* (1891).

There are several Holmeses. There is Holmes the conservative, aristocratic Boston Brahmin (a term he coined) who was "politically for equality, socially for *the* quality"; the popular after-dinner speaker, essayist, and poet; the perennial alumnus who at 71 still proudly called himself "a Harvard boy." There is Holmes the scientist and lecturer whose pioneer work in medicine and psychology earned him a secure place in medical history. There is also Holmes the social reformer whose essays on criminal psychology and mental health furnished a sound base for others' work to come; and Holmes the liberal thinker whose disagreements with the orthodox Calvinism of his fathers earned him for a time the name of "moral parricide." Oliver Wendell Holmes, Sr., was not a simple man; the key to his personality lies in no one place but rather in the sum of a complex life.

The center of that life lay in medicine.

Whatever the popularity of his poetry and essays, literature to Holmes was never more than a sideline. His medical papers (and he published many over a forty-year span) were important contributions to his profession and sometimes make better reading than his literary essays. His approach to medical science was enlightened and open-minded; he advocated the use in medical research of all the discoveries in new or auxiliary fields like chemistry, biology, botany, and bacteriology, and he was a constant supporter of the original and experimental. A powerfully effective teacher, his wit and deft use of analogy made facts stick in the mind for years, and he was regarded by generations of medical students with loyalty and affection. The period of his lifetime was one of great changes in medicine—antisepsis, anesthesia, aseptic surgery, psychiatry—and Holmes was always at the forefront of the field.

A sociable and gregarious man, Holmes regarded his poetry and essays as extensions of conversations one might have at a Boston gentlemen's club; his "medicated" novels, however, as he called them, were serious explorations of the problem of moral responsibility and the effects of heredity and environment on individual action. His essays, on which much of his literary reputation rested, would have found an appreciative audience in the coffeehouses of Queen Anne's London. Unlike **Ralph Waldo Emerson, Henry David Thoreau,** or **James Russell Lowell,** who dealt with issues and problems of contemporary concern, Holmes's essays were sparkling table talk, like Joseph Addison's and **Washington Irving**'s before him, which commented in bright, graceful prose on the "fads, follies, and fashions of the day." A man to whom everything was interesting, Holmes found the neoclassic essay form exactly tailored to his talents. He had a gift for the quick shift of idea, a knack of surprising and amusing his reader with information about wine or horse racing or tobacco or universities or whatever caught his eye. He sprinkled his pages with pithy Yankee apothegms that stayed with the reader: "Put not your trust in money, but your money in trust"; "Sin has many tools, but a lie is the handle that fits them all."

Holmes read Horace, admired Pope, and wrote a great many polished Augustan-style verses. Except for a few "serious" poems (among them the famed "Chambered Nautilus"), the bulk of his verse was "occasion" poetry, written for presentation at banquets, dedications, and other public events. Much of it could be quickly forgotten, but within his limited range he was an expert craftsman whose metrical skill and incisive wit were too often underrated. Poems like "The Deacon's Masterpiece, or the Wonderful One-Hoss Shay" or "The Ballad of the Oysterman" were known far and wide, but Holmes also had a wide sentimental streak that appeared in others such as "The Last Leaf" and "The Boys," his class reunion poem at Harvard.

In religion, although the descendant of generations of Calvinists, Holmes believed in and practiced a liberal, creedless, personalized Christianity. His faith was summarized, he said, in the first two words of the Lord's Prayer: "Our Father"; he went to a Unitarian church, but he would be equally at home, he said, in any other. His attacks on traditional New England Calvinism derived from objections to what he considered its rigid view of human nature—religion must "have its creed in the heart, and not in the head."

Holmes's life revolved about Boston, which he named "the hub of the universe," and its "Brahmin caste," of which he was a most distinguished example. The New England mind raised to its highest degree, he represented the lucid, sophisticated, Federal intelligence as it had developed over two centuries in its parochial surroundings. The face he presented to the public, of the Boston court jester and clever commentator on his times, is not his only or true one. His son said of him that "he had the most penetrating mind of all that lot," which is still perhaps the most accurate judgment. See Eleanor Tilton, *Amiable Autocrat: A Biography of Dr. Oliver Wendell Holmes* (1947).

RUSSEL B. NYE

HOLMES, Oliver Wendell, Jr. (b. Boston, Mass., March 8, 1841; d. Washington, D.C., March 6,

1935), JURIST, the son of **Oliver Wendell Holmes,** graduated from Harvard in 1861. As a second lieutenant in the Union army he participated in the battles of Ball's Bluff (1861), Antietam (1862), and Fredericksburg (1863). After having been seriously wounded, he left the army in July 1864 as a captain.

In 1866, Holmes received his LLB from Harvard Law School. He practiced law in Boston and lectured at Harvard Law School (1870–71). He edited the *American Law Review* (1870–73); in 1873 he edited the twelfth edition of **Kent's** *Commentaries;* and in 1881 he published *The Common Law,* in which he argued that laws should evolve as society changed and that economic and social realities must take precedence over legal theories. "The life of the law has not been logic; it has been experience."

In January 1882, Holmes became Weld professor of law at Harvard, but in December 1882 he was appointed to the supreme judicial court of Massachusetts, serving from 1883 to 1902 (chief justice, 1899–1902). During his tenure on the Massachusetts bench he handed down nearly 1,300 opinions.

In 1902, President Theodore Roosevelt appointed Holmes associate justice of the Supreme Court. In 1904, however, he irritated Roosevelt (who was in the midst of his "trust-busting" campaign) when he dissented in the Northern Securities case in which the Court applied the moribund Sherman Anti-Trust Act (1890) to break up a railroad holding company. Holmes argued that the Court was not interpreting the act correctly. But in the Swift and Co. case (1905) in which the Court unanimously upheld the antitrust prosecution of the so-called Beef Trust, Holmes expounded the "stream of commerce" doctrine whereby certain local firms are considered an integral part of interstate commerce.

In *Lochner* v. *N.Y.* (1905), in which the Court invalidated a maximum hours law, Holmes handed down one of his most famous dissents, arguing that if the New York legislature believed that the health of the public was endangered by bakers working long hours, it was not proper for the Court to overrule it. When the Court invalidated a federal law which held that railroad employers could not stop their employees from joining unions on the ground that it violated the Fifth Amendment, Holmes dissented (*Adair* v. *United States,* 1908). In *Hammer* v. *Dagenhart* (1918), in which the Court declared unconstitutional an act that outlawed the interstate shipment of products manufactured by children, Holmes dissented, asserting that Congress's right to regulate interstate commerce was not limited.

In 1919, in *Schenck* v. *United States,* Holmes tried to draw a line between free speech that must be protected and speech that must of necessity be classified as dangerous to the welfare of the state. Speaking for the Court, he upheld the wartime Espionage Act (1917) and established the "clear and present danger" test for free speech, stating: "The most stringent protection of free speech would not protect a man in falsely shouting fire in a theater and causing panic." However, in *Abrams* v. *United States* (1919), in which the Court upheld the conviction of a group of Russian emigrants who were distributing literature opposing American intervention in Russia, Holmes dissented, pointing out that the specific statements made by the defendants did not constitute a real threat to the United States, nor was the war against Germany affected.

In *Adkins* v. *Children's Hospital* (1923) the Court invalidated a law fixing minimum wage rates for women in Washington, D.C., as an infringement on the Fifth Amendment. Holmes again dissented, arguing that "the criterion of constitutionality is not whether we believe the law to be for the public good."

Holmes retired from the Court in January 1932.

─────

The legendary reputation of Oliver Wendell Holmes, Jr., as a giant of the law rests on two principal pillars: his early achievements as a legal scholar and the subsequent eminence he won as a judge, in particular after his appointment to the Supreme Court of the United States.

Holmes's great essay, *The Common Law,* was

virtually the first attempt to subject the Anglo-American legal heritage to systematic historical and philosophical analysis. The work is characterized above all by an intense pragmatism and by a concomitant refusal to accept the legal theories of earlier writers, both German and English, who had treated law as a carefully integrated logical structure resting on clearly defined ethical and metaphysical foundations. To Holmes, the common law reflected not any precise order like that of "a book of mathematics" but rather "the story of man's development through many centuries." Implicit in the work also was something like a Darwinian theory of ethics; the genius of the common law, Holmes argued, lay precisely in its acceptance of the idea of "justifiable self-interest" as the foundation stone of organized society.

For a time in the 1920s Holmes won something of a reputation as an outstanding liberal, principally because of the frequency with which he joined Justice **Louis D. Brandeis** in dissenting from the more reactionary decisions of the conservative majority that dominated the Court during that decade. But the notion that Holmes was a progressive humanitarian liberal will not bear careful scrutiny. His commitment to Darwinian social theory left him coldly skeptical that "tinkering with the system," as he put it, could work any very substantial improvement in the lot of the downtrodden, and on only a few occasions did he express anything like a sense of sympathy for the country's poor, oppressed, or unfortunate. In short, Holmes's liberalism, if it may be called that, was derived from David Ricardo, Thomas R. Malthus, and Charles Darwin, and had very little to do with the American humanitarian reformist tradition.

Above all, Holmes was a social and economic conservative who nonetheless entertained a radical theory of judicial self-restraint. He believed that the Court should pass very narrowly on the constitutional issues presented to it and that the justices properly should refrain from injecting their own social values into constitutional law. This meant in turn that he repeatedly gave his approval to reformist social legislation, not because he approved of its objectives but because he thought it no part of the Court's function to act

as a "negative legislature." This is the meaning of his celebrated dissent in the Lochner case in which he accused the majority justices of reading Herbert Spencer's social theories into constitutional law, as well as of his later dissent in the Adkins case where he joined with Brandeis in castigating the majority's abuse of the idea of freedom of contract. At the time such a conception of the limited scope of judicial review was little short of revolutionary.

Again, in his treatment of the commerce clause Holmes demonstrated an imaginative nationalism quite at odds with the rather narrow judicial conservatism which very often prevailed at that time. The "stream of commerce" doctrine that he expounded in the *Swift* v. *United States* case was destined after 1933 to become the principal constitutional device whereby the federal government was enabled to bring the American economic order under something like effective national control. And his masterful dissent in the first child labor case illustrated not only his willingness to allow the commerce power to be used for federal "police" purposes but also his oft-stated objection to the intrusion of the justices' personal social ideas into constitutional law.

Finally, Holmes in his Schenck and Abrams opinions during World War I laid the foundations for a modern theory of First Amendment freedoms. The "clear and present danger" doctrine that he expounded in the Schenck case is largely outmoded today, but at the time it was an immense advance on the earlier idea that the First Amendment prohibited merely prior government controls on publication. And Holmes's dissent in the Abrams case, in which he castigated the Court majority for its espousal of a policy of repression reminiscent of that maintained under the discredited Sedition Act of 1798, is a great masterpiece of English prose, rivaled in its magnificent defense of freedom of utterance only by John Milton's celebrated *Areopagitica*. The Abrams dissent alone, in fact, would be sufficient to confirm Holmes's stature as one of the grand classic figures in the Anglo-American legal heritage. See Mark De Wolfe Howe, *Justice Holmes* (2 vols.; 1957, 1963).

ALFRED H. KELLY

HOMER, Winslow (b. Boston, Mass., Feb. 24, 1836; d. Scarboro, Maine, Sept. 29, 1910), PAINTER, was apprenticed at the age of 19 to a Boston lithographer. Soon thereafter he opened his own studio and took commissions for illustrations that appeared in *Ballou's Pictorial* and *Harper's Weekly*. In 1859 he moved to New York City where he attended night classes at the National Academy of Design. In 1861 *Harper's* sent him to Washington as its artist in residence. There he recorded Abraham Lincoln's inaugural and scenes of the Peninsular campaign. Two of his Civil War pictures were displayed at the National Academy in 1863; and his most famous painting of this period, *Prisoners from the Front,* was hung at the Paris International Exposition of 1867. After a trip to Paris that same year, Homer returned to America and for a ten-year period concentrated on painting rustic scenes and landscapes, and perfecting his watercolor techniques. His *Snap the Whip,* a picture of boys playing the game during recess at a country school, dates from this time and was one of the outstanding successes of the Philadelphia Centennial in 1876.

Two trips to Tynemouth, on the North Sea coast of England, in 1881–82 were decisive for Homer's future development. There he became deeply interested in seascapes, shipwrecks, fisher-folk, and coast guardsmen. Returning to America, he left New York permanently behind him and in 1884 settled on Prout's Neck (Scarboro Township) in Maine where he lived in almost complete isolation, deeply engrossed in his work. But because he spent his winters in Florida or Bermuda, his seascapes, for which he is most famous, range in subject matter from the rugged New England coast to the blue waters of the Caribbean. *The Life Line* (1884) reveals Homer at his best as a storyteller. *Eight Bells* (1885) and *Lost on the Grand Banks* (1886), the latter tense with the anxiety of fishermen alone in a dory as a fog rolls in unexpectedly, are of like character. And so is *The Gulf Stream* (1886) in which a giant black man is caught adrift on a brokenmasted schooner while hungry sharks swim alongside.

In his last year, when he found the labor of arranging models too great, Homer painted only watercolors.

———— ∞∞∞ ————

Winslow Homer's seascape *Northeaster* (1895) is deservedly well known. It is a favorite of visitors to New York's Metropolitan Museum, its owner since 1910; is familiar to many a child through reproductions that abound in our schools; is regularly illustrated in publications and lately has been disseminated through the mails as a postage stamp miniature. The canvas represents the artist at his magnificent best, transfixing the heave and crash of surf on rock in a design so boldly simplified that it registers as a Homer even when seen from a considerable distance. Nevertheless the very popularity of this work and others like it has helped to categorize Homer in the mind's eye of the public as a "marine painter" and thereby has diverted attention from his broader capacities and achievements.

Had he lived but half his full number of years he would have figured prominently in the annals of American art as an outstanding illustrator. Among the works of artist-correspondents who contributed voluminously to the press through the years preceding and following the Civil War, the cuts after Homer stand out for their clarity and directness of statement, and for an unsentimentalized naturalism exceptional for the times. Numbers of them enrich the files of *Harper's Weekly* between 1858 and 1875. In choosing subjects he avoided the sensational, picturing people at their normal occupations, at play, or at war, reporting events with characteristic objectivity. There is in his early work no foreshadowing of a partiality for maritime drama—it was enough to capture the charm of feminine promenaders at a seaside resort.

Homer's development from illustrator into painter was a slow, deliberate process of self-advancement, an acquisition of skills and change of viewpoint that prepared him for the transforming visits to Tynemouth on the coast of England in the early eighties, when his affinity with the sea and seafaring became fixed. And when shortly thereafter he moved into the studio-home on rocky Prout's Neck, the maturing of his art was evident in its new sobriety, concentration, and a greatly enriched style of execution. A quarter-century of his best oil painting still lay ahead.

Meanwhile, he was mastering another painting medium. Even more clearly than in his oils, the artistic evolution of Homer is recorded in his watercolors in an astounding mutation from the colored drawings of his illustrator period into the fluently and luminously washed papers of his maturity. He gave new stature to the medium while finding in it for himself an unwonted freedom of expression. Because the equipment required was easily transportable, he turned to watercolor especially when traveling, on sporting excursions into the north country, and on winter sojourns in Florida and the Bahamas. Lloyd Goodrich finds in these aquarelles "the essence of his genius," and Homer himself could fancy that "I will live by my watercolors."

Among American artists of repute, the self-trained Homer was notably independent of trends and fashions. Participating little in art activities and unimpressed by reputations, he could advise: "If a man wants to become an artist, he should never look at paintings." If there appear in his work what seem to be parallels to Gustave Courbet's realism or the Impressionists' conquest of light, it is only because, living in the same age, he sometimes on his own account pursued ends similar to those of his European contemporaries.

Thoroughly normal in temperament, esteeming privacy in his everyday life, habitually neat and systematic, he lived to enjoy material success in a profession not always so rewarding to its major practitioners. See Lloyd Goodrich, *Winslow Homer* (1959).

HAROLD E. DICKSON

HOOK, Sidney (b. New York, N.Y., Dec. 20, 1902; d. Stanford, Calif., July 12, 1989), PHILOSOPHER, grew up in Brooklyn, New York. At the age of 13, already interested in poli-

tics, Hook joined the Socialist Party. In 1919 he entered the City College of New York where he studied philosophy under Morris R. Cohen and developed his zest for intellectual battle and the rigorous logical analysis that became his principal rhetorical weapon. After graduating in 1923 he taught in public school and entered Columbia University graduate school where he studied philosophy under **John Dewey**. They developed a lifelong friendship, and Hook became Dewey's best-known interpreter, publishing his first discussion of Deweyan pragmatism in *The Metaphysics of Pragmatism* (1927). Hook received his PhD in 1927 and obtained a position at New York University. In 1948 he became chairman of the philosophy department and remained there until his retirement in 1969.

In the 1930s Hook turned to Marxism and provided a democratic interpretation of Marx in *Towards the Understanding of Karl Marx* (1933). Infatuated with Communism early in his career, Hook eventually broke all connections with it during World War II and became its implacable critic. His later assessment of Marx appeared in *Reason, Social Myths, and Democracy* (1940) and *Marxism and Beyond* (1980). In *Education for Modern Man* (1946) Hook defended a pragmatic educational philosophy; in *The Quest for Being* (1961) he applied his formidable analytical skills in refuting theological arguments; and in *American Freedom and Academic Anarchy* (1970) he responded to the student unrest of the 1960s. This was followed in 1974 by *Pragmatism and the Tragic Sense of Life*, a further defense of pragmatism. Until his death Hook, who was a fellow at the Hoover Institution at Stanford University, remained an active writer and commentator on public issues.

———— ✦ ————

Hook was best known during his lifetime as a pugnacious polemicist on behalf of liberal values, secular humanism, and pragmatism. His disagreements with the Communist Party, the Catholic Church, Mortimer Adler, **Noam Chomsky**, and **Reinhold Niebuhr**, among others, proved that intellectual combat, no less than physical, could be waged with vigor and zest. As Dewey's intellectual heir, Hook brought clarity and a hard edge to his interpretation of Dewey's philosophy. For Hook, as for Dewey, the truth of an idea is warranted by the consequences of actions inspired by that idea rather than prior absolute principles. Because the pragmatist makes choices based on an assessment of probable consequences rather than by coercion or authoritarian fiat, Hook believed pragmatism to be the only philosophy compatible with the democratic ideal of an autonomous citizenry. Arguing that such a citizenry must utilize the scientific method of inquiry and its own intelligence, Hook acknowledged that dependency on the uncertain agency of human intelligence always entails the risk of poor choice. The existence of evil, which he often defined as the failure to use intelligence, notwithstanding, Hook regarded the risk involved in choice as a necessary condition of the fully autonomous life. Unlike Dewey, however, Hook was not sanguine about human prospects under conditions of autonomy. Bleakly aware that wrong choices have been and will be made, Hook argued that pragmatism, grounded in the scientific method and faith in human intelligence, at least increased the probability of successful choice. Acknowledging the rules of logic as its only metaphysical support, Hook's philosophy met life as he did, with a gambler's cool assessment of the odds and a street tough's love of the fight. See Sidney Hook, *Out of Step* (1987).

FRANCES O'NEILL

HOOKER, Thomas (b. Marfield, Leicestershire, Eng., 1586; d. Hartford, Conn., July 7, 1647), RELIGIOUS LEADER, graduated from Cambridge (AB, 1608; AM, 1611) and was a fellow of Emmanuel College (1609–18). In 1620 he became the rector of Esher in Surrey, and in 1626 he was the "lecturer" at St. Mary's Church, Chelmsford, in Essex.

A devout Puritan, Hooker refused to conform to the liturgy of the Church of England. Archbishop Laud forced his retirement, but he opened a school at Little Baddow, where he was assisted by **John Eliot.** When Hooker was summoned to appear before the Court of High Commission (1630), he fled to Holland. He served as the assistant to a minister of a nonconformist church at Delft, and at Rotterdam he was associated with Hugh Peter and with William Ames, one of the leading Puritan theologians.

In 1633, Hooker emigrated to Massachusetts Bay where he became the "teacher" of the church at New Towne and established himself as one of the colony's spiritual leaders. As an orthodox Calvinist he accepted the doctrine of predestination, but he believed that all men must "prepare" themselves for salvation by perfecting their behavior on earth so that their souls could receive God if they were among the elect (saved).

In 1636, Hooker and his congregation founded Hartford, Connecticut, but retained fellowship with the Bay colony despite strained relations. He helped draft the "Fundamental Orders of Connecticut" (1639), which created a government for the Connecticut Valley towns. Around 1645–46 he wrote his famous *Survey of the Summe of Church Discipline*, an explanation of the Congregational churches' polity.

⎯⎯∞⎯⎯

To his own generation Hooker was remarkable not for his politics but for evangelical preaching and careful exposition of Congregational polity. These contributions have been obscured by the continuing debate over Hooker as "democrat." A combination of filiopietists and critics of Puritanism, looking at Hooker's role in the founding of Connecticut and the drafting of the "Fundamental Orders," attempted to transform him into a prophet of Jeffersonian democracy. The characterization ill suits the man who became an eloquent spokesman for the New England Way and served as moderator for New England's first two synods. Primarily it was neither theological nor political orthodoxy that distinguished Hooker from his contemporaries; his uniqueness lay in his rare ability to explain and generate experiential religion. In far too many instances the ordered Puritan communities of New England had worked to dull the cutting edge of a preaching style that had once transformed the English towns. Hooker's continued success is partly attributable to his brilliant use of a language rich with vivid yet homely metaphors. Partly it stemmed from a compassionate personality that avoided strife and sought peace within church and commonwealth. But most important was his careful nurturing of faith. Although he never softened the harsh Calvinist decrees of God's sovereignty and man's depravity, he encouraged, cajoled, and led men to recognize and develop the tiniest seeds of grace. Hooker found grounds for hope where other ministers despaired. **Cotton Mather**'s description, "Piscator Evangelicus," describes the essential Hooker. See Perry Miller, "Thomas Hooker and the Democracy of Connecticut," *Errand into the Wilderness* (1956).

ROBERT G. POPE

HOOVER, Herbert Clark (b. West Branch, Iowa, Aug. 10, 1874; d. New York, N.Y., Oct. 20, 1964), PRESIDENT, graduated from Stanford University (1895). He soon became a mining engineer for a London-based firm, Bewick, Moreing and Co., working first in Australia and later in China and throughout the world. In 1907, Hoover resigned from his position as a partner in the firm and became involved in a profitable venture in Burmese tin and with Russian petroleum interests. When World War I broke out, he became head of relief efforts in London and helped rescue American tourists stranded in Europe. In 1915 he was designated chairman of the Commission for Relief in Belgium. In 1917, President Woodrow Wilson appointed him chairman of the Food Administration Board in Washington, D.C.; in this position Hoover helped encourage agricultural production and persuaded consumers voluntarily to conserve food. At the end of the war he again took charge of economic relief for Europe. In 1921, President Warren Harding appointed Hoover secretary of commerce. Throughout the decade he encouraged foreign sales by American corporations and

supported the trade association movement, believing that the formation of voluntary organizations to exchange information and discuss prices would benefit the entire economy.

In 1928, Hoover defeated the Democratic candidate for president, **Alfred E. Smith,** by 444 electoral votes to 87. Hoover supported the disarmament agreements that the major powers reached at the London Naval Conference (1930). Because of the worldwide Depression, in 1931 he proposed a one-year moratorium on the payment of war debts and reparations. When the Japanese attacked Manchuria in the same year, Hoover refused to cooperate with the League of Nations, believing that economic and military sanctions against Japan might draw the United States into a war. Although Japanese aggression continued, Secretary of State **Henry Stimson** could not persuade Hoover to modify his position, leading Stimson to issue a "Non-Recognition Doctrine" (1932) which stated that the United States should not recognize territorial seizures made in violation of America's treaty rights in the Far East.

After the 1929 stock market crash, Hoover sought to spur private groups to act to restore the slumping economy. He believed that the Depression was a temporary aberration; prosperity was "just around the corner." He argued that wages and prices be maintained; that the federal government encourage the Federal Reserve Board to lower its interest rates to stimulate borrowing for industrial expansion; and that taxes be lowered so that people could purchase more consumer goods. However, he reluctantly signed the protective Hawley-Smoot Tariff of 1930.

While Hoover tried to get the states to expand their relief programs, his belief in voluntarism and individualism led him to resist giving federal relief funds to state and local governments. He approved of aid to tottering financial institutions, however, arguing that this money would be put to productive use and would be repaid. Early in 1932 he supported the creation of the Reconstruction Finance Corporation to make loans to banks, railroads, and insurance companies. When army veterans marched on Washington that summer demanding early payment of World War I bonuses, Hoover called in federal troops; and General **Douglas MacArthur,** disobeying the president's distinct orders, evicted the squatters from their shanty homes on Anacostia flats.

Hoover was defeated for reelection in 1932 by Franklin D. Roosevelt, 472 electoral votes to 59. He then retired from politics but remained somewhat influential in the Republican Party. His interest soon turned to foreign policy and isolationism. As chairman of the Commissions on Organization of the Executive Branch of the Government ("Hoover Commissions"; 1947–49, 1953–55), he helped reorganize the executive department. He also published three volumes of *Memoirs* (1951–52).

The career of Herbert Hoover relates itself to a number of major economic and administrative crises. As food administrator in the United States and director of European relief programs he discovered some of the threats and opportunities a representative government encounters under stress of war. And Hoover's wartime experience together with his repudiation of laissez-faire as secretary of commerce in the 1920s prepared his response to broader problems of economic depression he had to cope with during his presidency. His career illustrates the range of alternatives open to America in wartime and depression, and the extent to which these may be closed by pressures of tradition and politics.

Like **Frederick Winslow Taylor** and other great technicians of his day, Hoover was a practitioner of industrial rationalization. He was often successful in working rational order on large segments of the industrial economy. As secretary of commerce he set out to harmonize the operations not of a single plant but of an entire technical economy, and his accomplishment was considerable. Closely allied was his concept of economic organization, in which he blended a taste for voluntarism and individual decision with a commitment to collective effort; and so he proceeded, always precariously close to contradicting himself, to nurture into existence great cooperative

units that would receive their energies from the bottom up but their efficiency from the top down.

Hoover's reputation for being a Great Engineer was tarnished in the 1930s because the Democratic Party portrayed him as personally responsible for the Great Depression. And in some textbooks he still is put among the conservative Republican presidents of the twenties. But most writers have set him above Warren Harding and Calvin Coolidge. While such portraits do not generally depict Hoover as a modern liberal, he frequently emerges as an intelligent conservative sensitive to the large patterns of events and history.

In domestic affairs it is Hoover's moralism and emphasis on the responsibilities of groups that are sometimes found attractive. As secretary of commerce he worked toward a rationale for business—or for America itself, which was deriving so many of its material and psychological symbols from business. In his *American Individualism* (1922), for example, he called upon business "pioneers" to invade "continents of human welfare of which we have penetrated only the coastal plain." Another side of Hoover's social philosophy is revealed in his response to the Depression, which was both cautious and venturesome. He distrusted bureaucracy and was determined to rely on individual and corporate charity wherever possible. The failure of cooperative efforts on the part of agriculture and business—the selfishness and narrowness of many Americans—was his bitterest disappointment.

Hoover's refusal to become embroiled in foreign disputes has won him the admiration of later critics of American diplomacy. His administration initiated the Good Neighbor approach to Latin America, and he specifically rejected "dollar diplomacy." Indeed, he thought that the government should control the lending of money to foreign countries, for such commitments might bring political entanglements. In Asia he merely deplored the Japanese invasion of Manchuria, believing that in time the Japanese would be either expelled from the mainland or assimilated by its culture.

We may, however, credit Hoover with more

vision than he had. He could be intolerably stubborn even in the face of stark human problems. He possessed insufficient ability to compromise or to delegate work. He lacked the personality, so perfectly embodied in Franklin Roosevelt, necessary to keep the nation from surrendering to fear. And his own written statements very imperfectly suggest his high serious purpose and the complex career that had much of greatness to it and, at its best, a fine generosity. See David Burner, *Herbert Hoover: A Public Life* (1979).

DAVID BURNER

HOOVER, John Edgar (b. Washington, D.C., Jan. 1, 1895; d. Washington, D.C., May 2, 1972), GOVERNMENT OFFICIAL, received an LLB from George Washington University Law School in 1916. Upon admission to the bar in 1917 he became a clerk in the Department of Justice, that same year being placed in charge of the Enemy Alien Registration Section of the Bureau of Investigation (created 1908; renamed Federal Bureau of Investigation in 1935). During the "Red Scare" of 1919–20, Attorney General **A. Mitchell Palmer** appointed Hoover head of the Justice Department's General Intelligence Division, which was authorized to conduct investigations of radicals. Hoover's work led to government deportation proceedings against (among others) the anarchists **Emma Goldman** and Alexander Berkman in 1919. Hoover was appointed assistant director of the Bureau of Investigation in 1921 and continued to direct the GID until its abolition in 1924. Following exposures of corruption and political influence in the Bureau of Investigation during the administration of President Harding, Attorney General **Harlan F. Stone** appointed Hoover director of the Bureau in 1924. He accepted that position on the condition that he would be free to appoint Bureau agents on the basis of merit, remove the Bureau from political influence, and establish procedures for monitoring the agents' performance.

The Bureau was little publicized during the later twenties. In the thirties, however, Hoover gained for it and for himself a national reputation for toughness and daring in well-advertised manhunts and captures of such gangsters as John Dillinger, Alvin Karpis, and "Machine Gun" Kelly. FBI activity was intensified under legislation of 1934 that placed more crimes under federal jurisdiction. The Bureau established a huge fingerprint collection, developed laboratory methods of detection, and created the National Police Academy to train local police officers in scientific procedures. During World War II the FBI broke up Nazi spy rings both in the United States and in South America. A believer in the conspiratorial nature of international Communism, Hoover directed the FBI's energies after the war largely to investigations of suspected Russian spies. The FBI played an important role in the **Alger Hiss,** Julius and Ethel Rosenberg, and Judith Coplon cases of the late forties and early fifties. Many people charged that the Bureau was lax in investigating civil rights cases, but in the early sixties, responding to directions from Attorney General **Robert F. Kennedy,** the FBI began to enlarge its surveillance of the Ku Klux Klan and other right-wing organizations. The Bureau also investigated the assassination of **Martin Luther King, Jr.** (1968). In recent years, the FBI has returned to its earlier emphasis on investigation of radicals, concentrating on non-Communist black and white radical groups. In his last years Hoover was a national spokesman for Americans who believed that radical political activity was a conspiracy threatening the whole society.

───⊗∞⊗───

J. Edgar Hoover enjoyed a position unparalleled in American public life—that of the indispensable man. Two presidents asked him to stay on as head of the FBI beyond mandatory retirement, an indication of his powerful hold on the American imagination. Most of the public saw him as the strong-jawed defender of America's internal security against gangsters and subversives who would otherwise have worked incalculable damage. There were never any doubts about his rectitude. The bachelor Hoover had no vices beyond incessant hard work (and the lack of a sense of humor) except, perhaps, for a passion for horse racing, led a spartan regimen, and remained incorruptible over a lifetime of contact with politicians and criminal enterprises. Under his leadership the FBI evolved from a small and incompetent bureau into a respected national institution with the highest standards of professionalism. The agency pioneered in scientific police work, establishing a crime laboratory, a central fingerprint file, an academy to train local police officers, and an annual report on crime statistics.

Yet the critics had much to say on the other side, especially in Hoover's last years. They argued that the FBI preferred tasks of high visibility and low political risk, mounting major efforts against kidnappers and Communists while remaining complacent about white-collar crime, the Cosa Nostra and other "organized" criminal elements, or violations of civil liberties. Hoover's chief involvement in the civil rights struggle was his longstanding hostility to black leader Martin Luther King, Jr., which led him to wiretap his telephone and to leak news of his private life to various government officials. Critics complained also of Hoover's tendency to see a Communist threat in virtually all internal disorders and radical political groups, and of his maintenance of a secret file of data on millions of citizens who were not aware they were under surveillance. In his lifetime Hoover, with one or two exceptions, made no use of this information to injure any legal political movement or person, but there was understandable concern that the FBI itself had become a menace to American liberties in its zeal to guard against subversion.

But the significance of Hoover's life is obscured by the extremes of veneration and abuse that his activities produced. He should be seen, as Joseph Kraft has said, as the Compleat Bureaucrat, the archetypal version of a breed that has profoundly altered American life, public and private. Son of a government employee, Hoover grew up and attended college in Washington, took his first job with the federal government, and died in the capital. Over his lifetime the number of government employees grew from 240,000 to 13 million; among them, Hoover was the preeminent bureaucrat, the agency head without peer.

Everything he did had as its aim the growth and enhancement of the FBI. These ends he accomplished through rigorous professionalism, resourceful technical innovation, careful attention to public relations, and the selection of enemies so as to produce minimal political complications and maximum public attention. After the celebrated gangster captures of the 1930s, Hoover's budget was never cut. A superior policeman, he was an invincible bureaucrat, the nation's most successful civil servant. This was his not only because he possessed unusual qualities of mind and temperament but because his social views were so closely attuned to the conservative, lawyer-dominated Congress, and behind it the voting public, which he served for more than half a century. See Richard Powers, *Secrecy and Power: The Life of J. Edgar Hoover* (1983).

OTIS L. GRAHAM, JR.

HOPKINS, Harry Lloyd (b. Sioux City, Iowa, Aug. 17, 1890; d. New York, N.Y., Jan. 29, 1946), REFORMER, POLITICAL LEADER, graduated from Grinnell College (Iowa) in 1912. He then worked for Christadora House, a New York City settlement house, and for the Association for Improving the Condition of the Poor. In 1914 he became executive secretary of the New York City Board of Child Welfare. He served with the Red Cross (1917–21), becoming director of the organization's southeastern region. Next he directed a study of urban health conditions for the New York Association for Improving the Condition of the Poor (1921–24). He was executive director of the New York Tuberculosis Association (1929–32).

In 1931, Hopkins was appointed deputy director of New York Governor Franklin D. Roosevelt's Temporary Emergency Relief Administration. When Roosevelt was elected president, Hopkins became Federal Emergency Relief administrator (1932). He headed the Civil Works Administration (1933–34) and the Works Progress Administration (1935–38), and served as secretary of commerce (1938–40).

Hopkins had become President Roosevelt's

close friend and adviser during the New Deal years. In 1941 he traveled to England and the Soviet Union as the president's personal representative to implement the Lend-Lease Act. During World War II he was adviser and representative at all the diplomatic conferences and military planning sessions, including the Roosevelt-Churchill Atlantic Conference (1941), which set forth the "Four Freedoms"; the Arcadia Conference in Washington (1942), which laid plans for the future United Nations; the planning for the Allied invasion of France; and the Yalta Conference (1945), which discussed Russian entry into the war against the Japanese and the future of postwar Europe. The cancer that had weakened Hopkins for many years forced his resignation in 1945. From September 1945 until his death he was impartial chairman (head of a board to arbitrate labor disputes) of the cloak and suit industry in New York City.

Hopkins stressed the need for the maintenance of self-respect and self-reliance as well as the physical preservation of human beings. Although direct-cash relief (the "dole") or market-basket relief would have been cheaper, he emphasized work relief and the creation of projects, such as the controversial artists' and writers' programs, that utilized persons' special skills. Capitalistic assumptions underlay the New Deal work relief program. Roosevelt and Hopkins viewed it as a stopgap measure that reflected the condition of the economic system and would end with the recovery of private enterprise. Hopkins, moreover, was an "unconscious Keynesian" who saw stimulation of the economy as a secondary effect of relief expenditures. Beginning in 1935 he became increasingly involved in politics—partly to protect and promote relief and partly to foster his own ambitions. The dynamic, inspiring, determined, loyal, shrewd, creative, tough-minded but idealistic, sarcastic and cynical but sentimental Hopkins played the leading role, under presidential aegis, in winning support in the 1930s for federal relief and work relief and in keeping the unemployed loyal to democracy. His programs have at least two lessons to offer for today: the permanently unemployable and the victims of structural unemployment in better times require aid different from that given to the victims of massive cyclical unemployment; advocates of the "new federalism" and revenue sharing who want to "bring government closer to the people" should consider the WPA experience in which inability, waste, corruption, and harmful political influence were evident not in Washington but at the state and local levels. See Searle F. Charles, *Minister of Relief: Harry Hopkins and the Depression* (1963).

BERNARD STEARNSHER

HOPPER, Edward (b. Nyack, N.Y., July 22, 1882; d. New York, N.Y., May 15, 1967), ARTIST, was trained as a commercial illustrator in New York City (1899–1900). He then attended the New York School of Art (1901–6), studying painting under **Robert Henri** and Kenneth Hayes Miller. Between 1906 and 1910, Hopper made three trips to Europe, spending most of his time in Paris and Spain. In 1908 he had his first showing along with other Henri students at the Harmonie Club in New York. He sold his first painting at the Armory Show (N.Y.) of 1913. From 1915 to 1923, Hopper concentrated on etchings and (briefly) watercolors. He returned to oils in 1924 and achieved national recognition when New York's Museum of Modern Art gave him a one-man retrospective show in 1933.

Hopper was acclaimed for his realistic painting of such "unpaintable" American scenes as cafeterias, movie lobbies, and gloomy apartment houses. Although a disciple of Henri, founder of the "Ashcan" school, Hopper's paintings were unique for their harsh, silhouetting light. *Night Hawks* (1942, Art Institute of Chicago) is representative of his style. While emphasizing the loneliness and emptiness of modern life, he also portrayed the beauty of ordinary things. Hopper received numerous awards throughout his career, including gold medals from the National Institute of Arts and Letters (1955) and the

American Academy of Arts and Letters (1955). A retrospective exhibition at the Whitney Museum (N.Y.) in 1964 covered fifty-five years of Hopper's painting. Some of his best-known works are: *Lighthouse at Two Lights* (1929, private collection, N.Y.), *Room in Brooklyn* (1932, Museum of Fine Arts, Boston), and *Second-Story Sunlight* (1960, Whitney Museum, N.Y.).

Considered the finest American realistic painter of the 20th century, Hopper fused an excellent sense of abstract design with a profound understanding of modern man's alienation from himself and his society, which he often illuminated by a harsh and abruptly changing light. In his art, form and content are intricately united in ways rarely seen among American artists.

A painter of clearly recognizable images, he nevertheless encased these in abstract formats so that human and inanimate shapes were often incorporated into areas of light and dark colors or into sections of larger masses. Since Hopper, by these devices, literally locked his human figures into separate abstract patterns within the same painting, his forms appear to be isolated from each other. Thus, his manipulation of forms became a way to project a sense of loneliness.

This quality is heightened by the lack of action and the inactivity of the figures. They seem uninvolved in their own lives. They lack assurance and preserve their identity only by isolating themselves from the experiences of others. They reflect that sense of modern despair in which endurance, not progress, characterizes the course of their lives.

As taciturn as his quiet buildings and silent people, Hopper understood and lived a type of urban isolation unknown to the "Ashcan" school painters, whose city views were personal, intimate, and full of village neighborliness. Historically, Hopper belongs to the generation of T. S. Eliot's hollow men who never fully recovered from the effects of World War I. Aesthetically, the quality of his work surmounts the period, and his paintings speak to all those who bear quiet witness to the passing of life. See Gail Levin, *Edward Hopper: An Intimate Biography* (1995).

MATTHEW BAIGELL

HORNEY, KAREN (**Danielson**) (b. Hamburg, Ger., Sept. 16, 1885; d. New York, N.Y., Dec. 4, 1952) PSYCHOANALYST, child of a Dutch mother and a Norwegian father. A sea captain, her father disapproved of her desire to become a doctor, feeling it was not a suitable profession for women. In 1909, Karen married Oscar Horney, a lawyer whom she had met in college, and pursued her dreams even while bringing up three daughters. She entered the medical school of the University of Berlin and received her MD in 1912. During her training she developed an interest in the budding field of psychoanalysis, studying under Karl Abraham, who had been a student of Sigmund Freud. She underwent analysis with him. She practiced in a psychiatric hospital in Berlin (1915–18), developed her own private practice, and taught at the Berlin Psychoanalytic Institute from 1920 to 1931.

Horney, separated from her husband, emigrated from Germany to the United States in 1932 to take a position in Chicago as assistant director of the Institute for Psychoanalysis. In 1934 she moved to New York City where she lived the rest of her life, teaching at the New School for Social Research and the New York Psychoanalytic Institute, writing, and treating patients. In 1941 the Psychoanalytic Institute dismissed her because her ideas had begun to diverge from the standard Freudian doctrine. With **Eric Fromm,** Clara Thompson, and other like-minded psychoanalysts, she helped found the Association for the Advancement of Psycholanalysis (1941), remaining with that organization until her death. It established its own clinical training institute and journal.

Although she had profound respect for Freud's work, Horney expanded his original theory of personality development. She felt that social and cultural factors were as crucial as an individual's inner conflicts. She also challenged Freud's view of women as neurotically obsessed by "penis envy." More important, she argued, was the frustrating role of women in a male-dominated society. As a teacher and writer, and in her work with patients, she expressed these sometimes controversial ideas. She presented them in *The Neurotic Personality of Our Time* (1937), *New Ways of Psychoanalysis* (1939), *Our Inner Conflicts* (1945), and *Neurosis and Inner Growth* (1950).

"We believe that mankind is inherently constructive and capable of creating an environment in which the potentialities of each individual may be encouraged to unfold." This philosophy, expressed in the charter of the Association for the Advancement of Psychoanalysis, embodies Karen Horney's deepest principles. She was an optimist, believing that every individual yearned for happiness and fulfillment. While Freud saw human beings as struggling against their destructive impulses, Karen Horney felt that the human spirit was intrinsically positive. The child developed neurotic defenses not to control his or her rampant drives but as protection against real or perceived dangers.

Karen Horney acknowledged that she "could not have made a step without Freud." She felt that Freud's theories should be the foundation of psychoanalysis but that they should never be taken as absolute truth. Psychotherapy was a new and evolving field, and no one had all the answers.

As a teacher and lecturer Horney was warm and informal, her voice tinged with a faint German accent. A student once remarked that "she smiles with her whole face." During her nearly two decades in New York she lived in an apartment overlooking Central Park. A reporter described it as "like her—warm, strong colors; furniture luxuriously comfortable but austere in design; no gadgets to distract you or make you ill at ease."

Horney's warmth and optimism are revealed through her interest in self-analysis. She was intrigued by the possibility that, even without professional help, women and men could work toward greater self-knowledge, freeing themselves to reach their fullest potential. As she once explained, she hoped "to encourage people to make the attempt to do something with their own problems, at any rate to give up that paralyzing attitude of helplessness, as if one couldn't do anything about one's problems oneself, and as if one were entirely dependent on the help of a specialist." See Bernard J. Paris, *Karen Horney: A Psychoanalyst's Search for Understanding* (1994).

DEBORAH KENT

HOUSE, Edward Mandell (b. Houston, Texas, July 26, 1858; d. New York, N.Y., Mar. 28, 1938), DIPLOMAT, attended schools in Bath, England, and New Haven, Connecticut, before entering Cornell in 1878. Forced to return to Texas before he could graduate, he managed his father's cotton plantations and banking interests for ten years. Becoming interested in politics, he managed the successful reelection campaign of Governor James Hogg of Texas in 1892. (Hogg rewarded House by making him an adviser and honorary colonel, a title that remained with him for the rest of his life.) House successfully managed the campaigns of Texas governors in 1894, 1898, and 1902, becoming a power in Texas politics. In 1911 he supported the governor of New Jersey, Woodrow Wilson, for president.

House became a close adviser of Wilson's, and they soon developed an intimate friendship. House concentrated on foreign affairs. After the outbreak of World War I he was sent on peace missions to London, Paris, and Berlin. With the British foreign secretary, Sir Edward Grey, he initiated a memorandum in 1916 that called for American mediation and looked toward armed assistance to the Allies if Germany refused. After the United States entered the war in 1917, House served on the Supreme War Council and helped negotiate the armistice ending the war in 1918.

House was a U.S. commissioner at the Paris peace conference in 1919, but President Wilson lost faith in him because House differed with him over the terms of the peace treaty and over tactics in the fight for the treaty in the Senate. He returned to private life but briefly resumed his interest in politics in 1932 when he worked for the election of Franklin D. Roosevelt.

The importance of Colonel House, as he was known, is clearly his influence on President Wilson, and since publication of part of House's huge and intimate diary in Charles Seymour's four-volume account (*The Intimate Papers of Colonel House*), and particularly since the opening of unpublished parts of the diary in the Yale University Library, it has become possible to measure this influence fairly precisely. House was an individual of general good judgment, and he was helpful to Wilson, who needed someone with whom he could talk over the business of government, national and international. While House carefully flattered the president, using what he considered psychology (the science then was in its infancy, and House was a psychology buff), his desire to remain close to a man of major political power seems to have made him almost too pliant, too concerned with what Wilson wanted. His advice was disinterested; House had no basis for personal political power and wished the best for his president and country; and yet he was so careful in giving advice that it does not seem to have departed far from what Wilson wanted. House was able to recommend friends for appointment to cabinet and diplomatic posts, and these nominations were his chief influence on the president and American politics. In diplomacy his influence may well have been negative, for he delighted in undercutting resident ambassadors or else substituting himself for them, and his view of European politics was no better than naïve. In the Supreme War Council he ably represented Wilson's Fourteen Points and forced the Allies to give in to all but two of them. At the Paris Peace Conference he miffed Wilson by proving willing to compromise. Once the treaty was in trouble in the Senate, he again advised compromise, but by this time the friendship with the president had come to an end. See A. L. and J. L. George, *Woodrow Wilson and Colonel House: A Personality Study* (1956).

ROBERT H. FERRELL

HOUSTON, Sam (b. Rockbridge Co., Va., Mar. 2, 1793; d. Huntsville, Tex., July 26, 1863), POLITICAL LEADER, worked in a general store in Blount County, Tennessee, and attended school intermittently, often evading such responsibilities by running off and living with the Cherokees. In March 1813, during the War of 1812, he enlisted as a private in the 39th Infantry, attaining the rank of ensign in July and third lieutenant in December. After being severely wounded at the Battle of Horseshoe Bend in March 1814, he was promoted by General Andrew Jackson to second lieutenant and then in 1817 to first lieutenant. He was appointed subagent to the Cherokees but resigned his commission in 1818 because of altercations with Secretary of War **John C. Calhoun.** Soon thereafter he passed the Tennessee bar exam and began to practice law in Lebanon. He served briefly as district attorney of the Nashville district, as adjutant general of the state militia (with the rank of colonel), and as a Democratic congressman from the ninth Tennessee district. In 1827 he was elected governor but resigned in April 1829. For the next three years he lived with the Cherokees near Fort Gibson in Indian Territory, often in a state of dissolution. Because of congressional charges of fraud leveled against him, he stayed in Washington with his friend President Andrew Jackson during the summer of 1832. After acquittal of the charges he set out for Texas, specifically directed by the War Department to hold parleys with nomadic tribes. Upon arrival at Nacogdoches he was elected a delegate to the Convention of 1833 at San Felipe de Austin, which petitioned Mexico for redress of grievances; thereafter, while carrying out his assignment for the War Department, he became deeply involved in Texas politics. With the advent of the Texas revolution in 1835, he participated in several temporary governments before signing the Declaration of Independence on March 2, 1836, and being chosen commander in chief of the Texas army. After the fall of the Alamo he retreated eastward across Texas, pursued by Mexican dictator Antonio López de Santa Anna. At the Battle of San Jacinto on April 21, 1836, he won a resounding victory, captured

Santa Anna, and forced him to declare Texas independent.

A few months later Houston was elected the first president of the Texas Republic. Unable to succeed himself in 1838, he became a congressman in order to check the administrative activities of political opponent President Mirabeau B. Lamar. In 1841 he was reelected president. With the advent of statehood in 1846 he was elected U.S. senator, serving for thirteen years. In 1857 he suffered his first political setback in the state gubernatorial election against southern firebrand Hardin R. Runnels, but two years later he was again elected governor. In 1860, as governor, he obeyed the order of the legislature to submit the question of secession to the electorate, but he refused to recognize the secession convention that met at the capital in January 1861. On February 23, after Texas voted to secede from the Union, he declared that the state owed no allegiance to the Confederacy but had reverted to the status of an independent republic. The secession convention then declared the office of governor vacant and replaced him with Lieutenant Governor Edward Clark. Rather than accept Union army support in reestablishing his position, Houston retired to his farm near Huntsville.

———oↄoↄo———

A well-built man, over six feet in height, Houston was a commanding, magnetic personality who sparked both loyalty and controversy. Although Texans would always revere him as the "Hero of San Jacinto," his loyalty to the Union diminished his popularity at times. While in the U.S. Senate he became an increasingly lonely figure, alienating himself from his southern colleagues through such unpopular stands as voting to organize Oregon as a territory under the Ordinance of 1787 and approving every section of the Compromise of 1850. During the Kansas-Nebraska debates in 1854 he and John Bell of Tennessee were the only southern senators to vote against the repeal of the Missouri Compromise, which was, he proudly announced, "the wisest and most patriotic" decision of his life.

While necessarily focusing on Houston's

stand to maintain the Union, Texas historians have sometimes neglected his role as president of the republic. Yet his contributions were quite remarkable. Between 1836 and 1838 he established a workable government, avoided continual warfare with Native Americans through treaties and decisive military action, and achieved recognition of Texas from President Jackson. During his second term, however, Houston was truly outstanding. Almost immediately he reversed the policies of the Lamar administration, wisely cutting governmental expenses to "the bare bone," instituting a more humane policy concerning Native Americans, and maintaining peace with Mexico. But most important, Houston cunningly and with tremendous diplomatic skill initiated and brought almost to fruition the annexation of Texas to the United States, leaving to his successor Anson Jones merely the final negotiations. See Llerena Friend, *Sam Houston: The Great Designer* (1954).

BEN PROCTER

HOWARD, Oliver Otis (b. Leeds, Maine, Nov. 8, 1830; d. Burlington, Vt., Oct. 26, 1909), MILITARY LEADER, graduated from Bowdoin College (1850) and from the U.S. Military Academy (1854). He served in the Seminole War before returning to West Point in 1857 as an instructor in mathematics. Howard resigned this post in 1861 to become a colonel in the Maine Volunteer Regiment. He participated in many major battles of the Civil War, including Antietam, Chancellorsville, and Gettysburg. He was wounded, losing his right arm, at Fair Oaks in the Peninsular campaign of 1862. Howard was ordered to Tennessee in 1863 and participated in the battles around Chattanooga. As commander of the Army of the Tennessee (1864–65), he participated in **William T. Sherman**'s Atlanta campaign, the March to the Sea, and the Carolina campaign.

In 1865, President Andrew Johnson appointed Howard commissioner of the Bureau of Refugees, Freedmen, and Abandoned Lands, known as the Freedmen's Bureau. Howard's responsibility was to provide for black southerners freed in the war. He often clashed with Johnson, who wanted to restore power to southern whites even if it meant depriving the freedmen of rights. Howard helped establish schools and colleges for former slaves, and he participated in the founding of Howard University (Washington, D.C., 1867), which was named in his honor. He was president of the university from 1869 to 1873. In 1872, Howard was peace commissioner to the Apache Indians and concluded a treaty with Cochise. He became commander of the army in the Pacific Northwest in 1874 and led military expeditions against the Nez Percé, Bannock, and Paiute Indians (1877–78). He served as superintendent of West Point (1881–82) and held commands of the Departments of the Platte (Omaha), Pacific (San Francisco), and Atlantic (New York). At his retirement he held the rank of major general in the regular army. He lived the rest of his life in Burlington, Vermont. In 1895 he helped establish the Lincoln Memorial University in Cumberland Gap, Tennessee. A popular lecturer and author, Howard wrote several books and articles on military history and a two-volume *Autobiography* (1907).

The Civil War over, Howard, known as the Christian General for his piety, was assigned to provide for a peaceful role in the society for 4 million freed slaves. For his model he took the independent farms operated on the Sea Islands by freedmen working lands abandoned by planters who fled Union forces. The 1865 legislation creating the Freedmen's Bureau required him to divide all such abandoned lands into forty-acre farms for freedmen, but President Johnson countermanded the redistribution policy and ordered the lands restored to pardoned former landowners. Howard went south to attempt to persuade the disappointed freedmen to work instead under the contract labor system. This required labor in field gangs, as under slavery, with the promise, often unmet, of wages.

Howard's agency attempted to enforce civil rights, but armed resistance to the blacks' upward mobility caused Congress to embark on radical Reconstruction. The Freedmen's Bureau lost its power as a federal agency with goals of economic and social justice. Thereafter Howard concentrated on assisting the formation of valuable black colleges for the freedmen.

In dealing with Native Americans, the government depended on Howard's reputation for fairness to convince militant leaders to end their resistance. In 1872 he negotiated with Cochise and, after leading an almost exterminative war against the Nez Percé, accepted Chief Joseph's surrender—"I will fight no more forever"—and promised land and fair treatment to the survivors. The Native Americans learned, as had the freedmen, that Howard's paternalistic good intentions would not be sustained by government action. See William S. McFeely, *Yankee Stepfather: General O. O. Howard and the Freedmen* (1968).

WILLIAM S. MCFEELY

HOWE, Elias (b. Spencer, Mass., July 9, 1819; d. Brooklyn, N.Y., Oct. 3, 1867), INVENTOR, was apprenticed in a Lowell, Massachusetts, cotton factory (1835). After the panic of 1837 he worked in machine shops in Cambridge and Boston, where he designed and constructed a sewing machine, perfected during the winter of 1844–45. Although the device was capable of sewing 250 stitches a minute, it did not win immediate success.

In October 1846, Howe sent his brother Amasa to England to sell his sewing machine. Rights were purchased by William Thomas, a corset manufacturer, and Elias Howe went to London to work for Thomas. The two men soon quarreled, however, and in order to obtain enough money to return home, Elias had to sell the English patent rights on his machine.

Upon his return to the United States, he discovered that his machine had gained sudden popularity and that it had been duplicated. He instituted several lawsuits (1849–54) against those who had pirated his invention. After the courts decided in his favor, he received royalties on all machines that infringed on his patent.

When the Civil War broke out, Howe supported the Union, organizing and equipping a Connecticut infantry regiment. In 1865 he established the Howe Machine Co. of Bridgeport, Connecticut. During these years his royalties often amounted to $4,000 per week. In 1867 his machine won the gold medal at the Paris Exhibition.

Far from being "the" inventor of the sewing machine, Elias Howe was not even first with any of its basic elements. The eye-pointed needle and the horizontal fabric support appeared in 18th-century England. In 1830 the French tailor Barthélemy Thimonnier patented a chain-stitch machine so workable as to be suppressed by a mob of other tailors. The first American sewing machine patent, on John J. Greenough's running-stitch machine of 1842, included a feeding mechanism for the cloth and tension controls for the thread. And between 1832 and 1834 the prolific but unworldly inventor Walter Hunt built a machine incorporating the heart of the ultimate invention: an eye-pointed needle used with a thread-carrying shuttle to sew a lock stitch. Whether from reluctance to throw seamstresses out of work or from mere offhandedness, he did not patent it. If he had, Elias Howe would now be forgotten, for Howe's title to fame rests on his being the first American patentee of such a machine. Howe's intellectual limitation was his practical strength: he stuck to a single quarry instead of going after a multitude of notions as Hunt did.

By Howe's account it was an economic lure that engaged him so singlemindedly, an overheard remark that a fortune awaited the inventor of a practical sewing machine. Howe insisted that he arrived independently—through a dream, he said—at the eye-pointed needle. An account of Hunt's machine had already been published, however, so Howe's word must be taken on less than presumptive evidence. In any case he did not officially claim the eye-pointed needle in itself but only in combination with a shuttle to form a lock stitch (as in Hunt's machine).

But to do him justice, there is no positive evidence that Howe had known of Hunt's work; he certainly patented and promoted his machine, whereas Hunt abandoned his in its infancy; and if hard work, constancy, sacrifice, and suffering deserve earthly reward, Howe earned the fortune that at last came his way. In chronic ill health, he persisted through years of privation, craft opposition, business indifference, and the chicanery of an English associate before encountering the first prospects of return for his troubles, and—bitterest of all—saw his wife die before she could share even that belated comfort. More than half the term of his patent went by before it produced much revenue. A seven-year extension of it in 1860, however, helped make him a millionaire before he died; and though he did little manufacturing himself, his brother's successful Howe Sewing Machine Company and the acknowledgments of his patent inscribed on several makes for which he granted licenses contributed to making his name literally a household word in 19th-century America. See Grace Rogers Cooper, *The Invention of the Sewing Machine* (1968).

ROBERT V. BRUCE

HOWE, Julia Ward (b. New York, N.Y., May 27, 1819; d. Newport, R.I., Oct. 17, 1910), REFORMER, was educated by private tutors. In 1843 she married **Samuel Gridley Howe,** a Boston reformer, philanthropist, and teacher of the blind. After spending a year traveling through Europe they settled in Boston. She published her first volume of poems, *Passion Flowers* (1854), and followed it with *Words for the Hour* (1857) and *A Trip to Cuba* (1860). At the same time both Howe and her husband became quite active in the anti-slavery movement and edited a Free Soil newspaper, the Boston *Commonwealth*. While visiting a Union army camp near Washington, D.C., in 1862, Julia Ward Howe was inspired to write a poem, "The Battle Hymn of the Republic," to the music of "John Brown's Body," a popular song. Published in the *Atlantic Monthly* in 1862, the song quickly attained national popularity.

After the Civil War, Howe devoted her time to reform movements, particularly woman's rights.

She participated in the founding of the New England Woman's Club in 1868, became president in 1871, and served until her death. This organization worked for equal educational, professional, and business opportunities for women. She was a founder and president of the New England Woman Suffrage Association in 1868; the following year she attended a Cleveland convention that established the American Woman's Suffrage Association. She formed the American branch of the Woman's International Peace Association in 1871 and served as its first president. However, an attempt in 1872 to assemble an international Women's Peace Congress in London failed. She served as president of the Association for the Advancement of Women (1878–88) and organized the women's department of the Cotton Centennial Exhibition at New Orleans (1885–86). Known for her witty and convincing lectures, she published some of them in *Modern Society* (1881) and *Is Polite Society Polite?* (1895). She wrote two autobiographical works, *Reminiscences* (1899) and *At Sunset* (1910). She was the first woman elected to the American Academy of Arts and Letters.

Julia Ward Howe, though a writer of limited talent, was an important spokeswoman for woman's rights and other reform causes. Except for her contributions to those causes, her one claim to fame was setting the words of her poem "Battle Hymn of the Republic" to the tune then known as "John Brown's Body." The stirring hymn provided a musical call to arms to the North during the Civil War and has lived on as a folk national anthem.

Howe was intelligent and strong-willed, and though deeply devoted to her husband, she insisted on continuing both her intellectual development and her literary career. She published her first book of poetry anonymously, although her authorship was soon known and made her a figure of attention and controversy. Those writers whose opinions she most cherished praised the work. "It was a timid performance upon a slender reed," she commented

years later, "but the great performers in the noble orchestra of writers answered its appeal, which won me a seat in their ranks."

In addition to poetry she wrote essays and plays, and presented some of her works on the stage in the form of readings. Her husband strenuously objected to her public career, and differences over this and other matters nearly destroyed their marriage. On her twentieth wedding anniversary Julia Howe recorded in her journal: "I have never known my husband to approve of any act of mine which I myself valued. Books—poems—essays—everything has been contemptible in his eyes because not his way of doing things." Only her own tact and diplomacy and the fact that Samuel Gridley Howe mellowed with age enabled the family to hold together.

Despite her husband's opposition—or perhaps because of it—Howe became increasingly active in women's rights in the years after the Civil War. World peace, prison reform, and coeducation also enjoyed her support. In later years she frequently preached in Unitarian churches, and she also pursued her lifelong interests in music, drama, and travel. Nevertheless, it remained her Civil War poem that attracted thousands to see her and to hear her recite its powerful words. It was "Battle Hymn of the Republic" that lent weight to her endorsement of any cause. See Laura E. Richards and Maud Howe Elliott, assisted by Florence Howe Hall, *Julia Ward Howe 1819–1910* (2 vols., 1916).

LARRY GARA

HOWE, Samuel Gridley (b. Boston, Mass., Nov. 10, 1801; d. Boston, Mass., Jan. 9, 1876), REFORMER, graduated from Brown (1821) and received an MD from Harvard (1824). After serving as a combat officer (1824–30) and surgeon in the Greek Revolution, he opened a school for the blind in Massachusetts. He returned to Europe to study techniques for educating the blind and, while in Paris (1831), helped organize the American-Polish committee for Polish political refugees. Imprisoned by the Prussian government for six weeks for his pro-Polish activities, he returned to America on his release to found the New England Asylum for the Blind (1832), renamed the Perkins Institution and Massachusetts Asylum (1839), and remained its head until 1876.

Howe pioneered in the printing of books with raised type, and in 1841–42, utilizing this method, he published the Bible in eight volumes. One of the triumphs of Howe's educational techniques was his success in reaching a blind deaf-mute (Laura Dewey Bridgman) after others had failed in similar cases. Howe also worked for prison reform and aid to discharged convicts, and improved methods of instructing the deaf.

An active abolitionist, Howe was defeated as a Conscience Whig candidate for Congress in 1846. Together with his wife, **Julia Ward Howe,** he was one of the founders and editors of the abolitionist journal *Commonwealth* (1851). Howe supported the Free Soilers in Kansas, and though linked with **John Brown**'s activities, he disclaimed any foreknowledge of the raid on Harpers Ferry (1859).

During the Civil War, Howe served on the Sanitary Commission and the American Freedmen's Inquiry Commission. After the war he served on a three-man committee that recommended the annexation of Santo Domingo (1871). He published *Historical Sketch of the Greek Revolution* (1828) and various textbooks for the blind.

Samuel Gridley Howe's significance is as a pioneer in social reform, particularly in the education of the handicapped. In this work he largely followed trial-and-error methods. He never hesitated to acknowledge his mistakes and to change whenever he felt it was warranted. His achievements were many. He was the first person to show that it was possible to teach a person who was deaf and blind. His efforts to teach the feebleminded attracted much praise. In his day the Perkins Institution was the outstanding school for the blind, and he was the leading authority. His prestige was so great that his endorsement was sought for many movements

outside his own specialty. He led the floor fight in the Massachusetts House of Representatives for the passage of **Dorothea Dix**'s *Memorial,* on the treatment of the insane, during the session of 1843. **Horace Mann** found him a powerful ally in the fight for public education; he ran for election to the School Committee in the fall of 1844, specifically to assist Mann. His term on the committee during 1845 was tempestuous, but Mann's program was sustained. In the antislavery movement he played a respectable although not particularly prominent role.

As a person Howe was a man of great vigor and very strong opinions. Because he was always so convinced of the rectitude of his cause, he tended to question the integrity of any who disagreed with him and was occasionally unjust. (This seems to have been a characteristic of many of Boston's social reformers.) See Harold Schwartz, *Samuel Gridley Howe, Social Reformer, 1801–1876* (1956).

HAROLD SCHWARTZ

HOWELLS, William Dean (b. Martins Ferry, Ohio, Mar. 1, 1837; d. New York, N.Y., May 11, 1920), WRITER, ended his formal schooling at 11 and went to work as a typesetter in his father's printing office. Later he served as a political correspondent on the *Ohio State Journal* and contributed poems to the *National Era* and other publications. A Republican in politics, Howells turned out a campaign biography for Abraham Lincoln in 1860. Following Lincoln's election, Howells was appointed U.S. consul to Venice (1861–65). He published two travel books, *Venetian Life* (1866) and *Italian Journeys* (1867), based on this experience.

Upon his return to the United States in 1865, Howells worked briefly for the New York *Nation* under the editorship of **E. L. Godkin.** In 1866 he moved to Boston where he became subeditor of the *Atlantic Monthly* (1866–71; editor, 1871–81). He lectured at Harvard on Italian literature (1869–71). *Their Wedding Journey* (1872), his first novel, was followed by a number of works on manners and morals: *A Chance Acquaintance*

(1873), *A Foregone Conclusion* (1874), *The Lady of Aroostook* (1879), and *Dr. Breen's Practice* (1881).

Howells soon became the major proponent of literary realism in the United States. By "realism" Howells meant "the truthful treatment of commonplace material." He criticized the romantic and sentimental writers of the period severely, arguing that they distorted life and undermined the taste of the public. In *A Modern Instance* (1882) he dealt with such topics as divorce and the low ethics of journalism in Boston. This was followed by *The Rise of Silas Lapham* (1885), an anti-romantic study of Boston society in the 1870s that dealt with such questions as status in society and morality in business.

With the passage of time Howells became an outspoken critic of American society. He was especially repelled by the events that followed the Haymarket bombing in Chicago (1886), after which seven anarchists were sentenced to death. He pleaded for the commutation of the death sentence, arguing that there was no evidence that these radicals were guilty of the bombing. Howells soon began to support the ideas of the Christian Socialists, who believed that the welfare of the nation could be advanced only if the government followed the principles of Christian ethics.

Howells had his own column, "Editor's Study," in *Harper's Monthly* (1886–91). Besides reviewing books he also helped introduce the works of many foreign writers to America. In 1888 he published *Annie Kilburn,* a story of a New England town beset by industrial unrest. His next major work was *A Hazard of New Fortunes* (1890) in which he continued his assault on the values of industrial America and portrayed the whole panorama of urban life in New York City.

In the nineties Howells shifted his residence more or less permanently to New York City. In 1892 he edited *Cosmopolitan* magazine. In 1894 he published *A Traveler from Altruria,* a utopian work in which he discussed his socialistic ideas. From 1900 until his death he wrote the "Easy Chair" column for *Harper's* magazine. During this period he also encouraged many young writers, such as **Stephen Crane, Frank Norris,** and **Hamlin**

Garland. In 1907, Howells published *Through the Eye of the Needle,* a work about a modern ideal commonwealth.

In 1908, Howells was elected the first president of the American Academy of Arts and Letters. In 1909 he helped establish the NACP. Long a close friend of **Mark Twain,** Howells published *My Mark Twain* in 1910. His last novel was *The Leatherwood God* (1916).

⸎

Ever since **H. L. Mencken** scorned him as the "Dean" of American letters, the popular impression of Howells has been that he was a stuffed shirt who wrote emotionally shallow novels about the "smiling aspects" of American life, and who as editor of the *Atlantic Monthly* sacrificed critical integrity in order to win the approbation of **James Russell Lowell, Oliver Wendell Holmes,** and other members of the Brahmin Establishment. Yet if Howells was a clubbable man who manifestly enjoyed his association with the great and near-great of literary Boston, he was also a deeply neurotic personality who was tortured all his life by a startling variety of fears and anxieties. Thus his childhood years in Ohio were in some ways as exhilaratingly free as Huckleberry Finn's, but they climaxed in a series of nervous breakdowns that flooded his soul with rage and despair. Similarly, Howells's happy marriage to the vivacious, artistic Elinor Mead was shadowed not only by his own precarious mental health but by his wife's neurasthenia as well.

In Boston after the Civil War the young outlander from Ohio rose with spectacular speed to the editorship of the *Atlantic.* Nevertheless, Howells did not feel completely at home in Boston. This was partly because of the snobbery of the Brahmins, who condescended to the Ohioan even though they had admitted him to their clubs, arranged to give him an honorary degree at Harvard, and showered other tribal honors upon him. But Howells's insecurity partly stemmed from his own ineradicable nervousness. A further turn of the psychological screw was supplied by his guilty feeling that in becoming a man of letters in Boston he was playing a role—a role that was not merely unnatural but fraudulent. That Howells's two closest friends, Mark Twain and **Henry James,** also had—in their very different ways—extremely ambivalent feelings about the New England cultural scene did nothing to assuage Howells's guilt.

Given his extraordinarily nervous temperament, it is no wonder, then, that in his early novels Howells was concerned with personal relationships and problems of self-consciousness—what he called "the sin and suffering and shame" that flowed "from one to another one, and oftener still from one to one's self." In *The Rise of Silas Lapham,* his best-known comedy of manners, he developed the contrast between Silas the self-made millionaire and the Brahmin dilettante Bromfield Corey with a brilliant and impartial irony. The dinner party scene in which Lapham gets drunk because he is nervous and unaccustomed to wine is justly famous.

At the same time that he was making psychologically shrewd and humorously delightful fictions out of the uneasy confrontation between innocent and sophisticated personalities (as in Henry James's novels and stories, this confrontation most often involved an unsophisticated but morally spontaneous American girl and a well-educated but irresolute young man), Howells was racking up a brilliant record as a magazine editor. When he took over full editorial control of the *Atlantic* in 1871, it was a very influential but exceedingly provincial magazine. When he resigned a decade later, he had given the *Atlantic* a truly national identity. Whether he published their stories or wrote favorable reviews of their books, or both, Howells made Edward Eggleston, Mark Twain, Charles Egbert Craddock, George Washington Cable, and other southern and western writers feel as welcome in the magazine as he did the old-guard New England writers.

A less complex man would have taken enormous satisfaction from such an achievement, but in the climactic psychological breakdown he suffered in 1885, Howells realized in pain and bitterness that his novelistic concern with personal relationships did not enable him to make as sweeping or as harsh an indictment of his society

as he now wished to put forward. Like his father before him, who had been a disciple of Robert Owen's New Harmony, Howells was deeply responsive to utopian visions, and in a decade of rising social unrest he dedicated his art to the dream of a better America. The precise moment of dedication came in late 1885 when as a psychological convalescent he came upon the novels and other writings of Tolstoy, all of which hit him with the force of religious revelation. Thereafter, in such novels as *Annie Kilburn* and *A Hazard of New Fortunes,* he attempted to measure in terms of human suffering what industrial capitalism had cost America, while in *A Traveler from Altruria* and other utopian fictions he attempted to define the benefits of life in a more communal world. He also took a stand—a lonely stand—against the execution of the Haymarket anarchists, thereby reviving the tradition, which had become lost in Gilded Age America, of the socially engagé writer who is willing to speak out on the great issues of the day. See Kenneth S. Lynn, *William Dean Howells: An American Life* (1971).

KENNETH S. LYNN

HUDSON, Henry (b. [?]; d. sometime after June 22, 1611), EXPLORER. Little is known about his life before May 1607 when he set sail on an expedition for the English Muscovy Co. on the *Hopewell* in search of a northeast passage to the Orient. Sailing along the east coast of Greenland, he found it impossible to penetrate the ice packs. He sailed to Spitzbergen (June) and returned to England in September 1607. In April 1608 he again set sail in the *Hopewell* with the objective of finding either a passage between Spitzbergen and Novaya Zamlya or a strait leading to the east coast of Novaya Zamlya. After sighting Novaya Zamlya in June, he was again blocked by ice, which forced him to return to Gravesend in August 1608.

In 1609, Hudson entered into an agreement with the Dutch East India Co. whereby he would again search for a northeast passage. Leaving Amsterdam on the *Halve Maen* (Half Moon) in April 1609, he reached the northern cape of

Norway in May before continuing on for Novaya Zamlya. Again obstructed by icebergs, he altered his course. After encountering further difficulties, he decided to seek a northwest passage around North America. Relying on a map that his friend **John Smith** had furnished him, he sailed south as far as Virginia. On August 28 he entered Delaware Bay and sailed up the Delaware River. Then, after coasting the shores of New Jersey, he discovered New York Harbor (Sept. 12). He sailed up the Hudson River, anchoring below present-day Albany (Sept. 19). After exploring the region he returned to England, whereupon the British government forbade him to work for foreign governments.

Hudson's fourth and final voyage was undertaken in behalf of a group of English adventurers. Sailing aboard the *Discovery,* he left London on April 17, 1610. On June 4 he sighted the coast of Greenland, and on August 2 he passed through Hudson Strait; after exploring Hudson Bay, in November he took his ship into James Bay where he spent the winter. With food supplies low and scurvy becoming more rampant, Hudson's crew became increasingly restive. They mutinied, setting him afloat without supplies on June 22, and then sailed back to England.

———— ∞ ————

Henry Hudson was one of many explorers who searched for northeast and northwest passages to the Far East. Though little is known about the man, Hudson was a good sailor and made use of the best information available. Earlier voyages by other explorers and the most up-to-date cartographic knowledge had convinced him that a northwest passage existed and could be found.

Though hired by the Dutch East India Co. to sail northeast, after doing so he crossed the Atlantic and along the coast of North America northward from Virginia. His sail up the Hudson River to Albany was the only "new" discovery of his voyage. He landed in England and, after difficulties with the authorities, finally reported to his Dutch masters.

Hudson's final voyage was English-financed.

The trip showed again that Hudson was an expert sailor and as good a navigator as most of the explorers of the time. The winter was passed in the New World, and when spring came, Hudson wanted to sail on to the west. But he was not a good captain. Records of his earlier voyages report problems with the crews, which now recurred. A mutiny put Hudson, his son, and some of the crew adrift in a small boat. Hudson's failure as a captain of men cost him his life; the mutineers were not punished upon their return to England.

Although he was unsuccessful in his quest for a sea passage to Asia and not really a "discoverer," Hudson's two voyages to the New World made possible a Dutch West India Co. claim to the New Netherlands after 1621, and an English claim to the Hudson Bay area. See Philip Vail, *The Magnificent Adventures of Henry Hudson* (1965).

BRUCE B. SOLNICK

HUGHES, Charles Evans (b. Glens Falls, N.Y., Apr. 11, 1862; d. Osterville, Mass., Aug. 27, 1948), POLITICAL LEADER, JURIST, briefly attended Madison College (now Colgate) and graduated from Brown University (1881). After teaching at Delhi, New York, he entered Columbia Law School, receiving his LLB in 1884. He practiced law in New York City and lectured at Cornell Law School (1891–93).

In 1905, Hughes was the counsel for the Stevens Gas Commission investigating the gas and electric lighting utilities in New York City. The following year he was retained by the Armstrong Commission to investigate corruption in New York–based life insurance companies. As a result of his investigations the state made comprehensive changes in its insurance laws. Hughes was elected governor of New York as a Republican in 1906 (reelected 1908). As governor he backed progressive labor and welfare legislation, instituted administrative reforms, enforced the constitutional prohibition against racetrack gambling, and sought to regulate utility and insurance companies and to institute a direct primary.

In 1910, President William H. Taft appointed

Hughes associate justice of the Supreme Court. In 1916, however, Hughes left the bench to accept the Republican nomination for the presidency (also getting the endorsement of the Progressive Party). After a campaign during which he was accused by critics of equivocation and political ineptitude, he was narrowly defeated by Woodrow Wilson, 277 electoral votes to 254. In 1917, Hughes served as chairman of the New York City draft appeals board, and in 1918 he investigated the aircraft industry as a special assistant to the U.S. attorney general. During the "Red Scare" of 1919–20 he spoke out in behalf of five Socialists who were denied their seats in the New York legislature because of their beliefs (1920).

Hughes was secretary of state under Presidents Harding and Coolidge (1921–25). As secretary he urged American entry into the League of Nations with reservations and also American membership in the World Court, both without success. In 1921 he was the chief organizer of the Washington Armament Conference. At the conference he proposed that the major powers end their naval race by scrapping ships already built or under construction and agreeing to limit their capital ships to a fixed ratio. In addition to doing so in the five-power treaty, the powers negotiated the four-power treaty, whereby the Anglo-Japanese alliance of 1902 was abrogated and the signatories agreed to respect each other's interests in the Pacific and to consult one another in case of a threat from an aggressive power; and the nine-power treaty, by which they agreed to respect China's territorial integrity and to honor the "Open Door" principle in China. In 1924 when France occupied the Ruhr after Germany stopped paying war reparations to the Allies, Hughes helped develop the **Dawes** Plan whereby private U.S. bankers lent money to Germany to reorganize its finances and to resume reparations payments.

In 1925, Hughes returned to private law practice in New York City. In 1928 he was chairman of the U.S. delegation to the Pan-American Conference in Havana, and in 1929 he became a judge on the Permanent Court of International Justice at The Hague.

In 1930, President Herbert Hoover appointed Hughes chief justice of the Supreme Court. During the New Deal period, the Court was divided into fairly consistent liberal-conservative blocs. Hughes, who was basically a moderate, was often the "swing man" in 5–4 decisions. In 1934 he voted to sustain a law allowing courts to postpone mortgage foreclosures during an economic crisis (*Home Building and Loan Assoc.* v. *Blaisdell*). He spoke for the entire Court when it invalidated the National Industrial Recovery Act of 1933 (*Schecter* v. *United States,* 1935) on the ground that it sought to regulate intrastate as well as interstate commerce. However, in *Retirement Board* v. *Alton Railroad Co.* (1935), in which the Court invalidated the Railroad Retirement Act as violating the due process clause of the Fifth Amendment, Hughes joined the liberals in dissent, arguing that the commerce clause authorized Congress to pass such legislation. In 1936, in *United States* v. *Butler,* he sided with the majority when it nullified the first Agricultural Adjustment Act because of a processing tax that sought to regulate agricultural production.

When President Roosevelt tried to "pack" the Supreme Court with supporters of his New Deal legislation (1937), Hughes was one of the most eloquent opponents of his plan. But he voted with the majority to uphold a Washington State minimum wage law (*West Coast Hotel Co.* v. *Parrish,* 1937), the National Labor Relations Act of 1935 (*NLRB* v. *Jones and Laughlin Steel Corp.*), and other important New Deal legislation.

Hughes retired from the Supreme Court in 1941. Some of his published works include *The Pathway of Peace* (1925), *The Supreme Court of the United States* (1928), and *Pan American Peace Plans* (1929).

❦

Charles Evans Hughes, the son of an abolitionist minister and his devout commonsense wife, early revealed a self-reliant, disciplined, and pragmatic personality. From his parents and environment he derived a firm belief in a divinely directed universe, the inevitability of gradual historical progress, and the role of reason in harmonizing individual, community, and international interests. A highly intelligent and hardworking man, Hughes carefully weighed his decisions and was remarkably confident in the correctness of the actions that he chose. Outwardly reserved and of dignified appearance, he enjoyed social life and was an effective speaker.

Hughes's political philosophy defies neat labels. A conservative in his belief in the business system and in the virtues of American democracy, with its constitutional checks and balances, especially law and the courts, he was liberal in recognizing that abuses must be remedied and society adjusted to the demands of an industrial age. Hughes, as governor of New York and as associate justice of the Supreme Court, accepted the necessity of increased governmental regulation of the private economy and the adoption of social legislation. He was guided by a nondoctrinaire pragmatism that sought to preserve as much of the past as possible by adjusting to the needs of the present. His record as a reform governor and jurist was notable in an age of progressivism. Hughes's great strength as a public leader was in efficient administration rather than bold innovation, and he lacked certain basic political skills, as the 1916 presidential election indicated.

Hughes's practicality was revealed in his foreign policies as secretary of state. He recognized that isolationism was no longer feasible, yet he shared with his fellow citizens a belief in the wisdom of nonentanglement and the preservation of diplomatic freedom. Although he personally favored entering the League of Nations with reservations, he rejected Wilsonian collective security and relied on world law and conciliation to preserve a stable and peaceful international order. Facing a jealous Senate and powerful isolationists in Congress and the public, Hughes quickly abandoned the League issue and concluded a separate peace with Germany. Always pragmatic, Hughes had settled for the obtainable rather than the ideal. Thereafter he sought to promote world stability without the assumption of any binding obligations. He played a statesman-like role in ending the naval arms race in 1921–22 and the reparations crisis in 1924. He failed to see, however, the difficulty of collecting the war debts owed by the Allies or the impediment of the American high tariff to a healthy world economy. His greatest success, the Washington Conference treaties, grew out of the manifest unwillingness of Congress and the public to expend large sums on naval construction versus the desire to preserve U.S. interests in China against an expansionist Japan. His pacts managed to stabilize the naval balance of power in the Pacific and the Far East for a decade. Their collapse in the thirties cannot in fairness be attributed to Hughes—the fault lay elsewhere, and particularly in an American people and Congress that failed to keep the navy up to treaty limits. Yet Hughes's secretaryship fell short of the highest statesmanship because of the limitations of his times and his own lack of boldness and imaginative vision.

Returning to the Supreme Court as chief justice during the difficult years of the Great Depression, Hughes again followed an essentially moderate course. He was inclined to uphold extensions of federal authority to cope with the economic debacle, and as before was committed to the defense of civil and minority rights. Aware that a divided Court risked a public loss of confidence, he was unable to close the gap between his more conservative and his more liberal colleagues. He worked successfully to improve the administrative machinery of the judiciary. Although President Franklin D. Roosevelt and other critics railed at the Court's decisions, especially the 5–4 ones, overturning important New Deal measures, some of these laws were so loosely drafted that the entire Court joined in their invalidation. Hughes was deeply disturbed by FDR's attack on the Court and helped defeat the "packing" scheme by a vigorous letter refuting charges that the Court was lagging in its work. It is noteworthy, however, that thereafter the Court underwent a seeming reversal and began to uphold major New Deal measures. Quite possibly Hughes helped bring about that change. See Dexter Perkins, *Charles Evans Hughes and American Democratic Statesmanship* (1956).

DANIEL M. SMITH

HUGHES, Howard Robard (b. Houston, Tex., Dec. 24, 1905; d. Houston, Texas, Apr. 5, 1976), MANUFACTURER, attended Rice Institute before inheriting his father's multimillion-dollar oil drilling tool business. At 20 he turned to film-making and produced *Hell's Angels* and *Scarface,* which introduced Jean Harlow and Paul Muni, respectively. His other early films included *The Front Page, The Sky Devils, The Racket,* and *Two Arabian Knights.* Hughes founded the Hughes Aircraft Co. in 1935 and undertook a series of flights to illustrate the advantages of his designs. In 1935 he set a speed record of 352 miles per hour; in 1936 he lowered the transcontinental record to nine hours and twenty-five minutes; and in 1938 he set a new round-the-world time of three days, nineteen hours, and eight minutes. In 1937, Hughes obtained control of Trans-World Airlines, which he developed into the first inter-continental carrier. He devoted his attention to the Hughes Tool Co. again (1938–40), then returned to Hollywood, where he became embroiled in controversy over *The Outlaw* (1943), which he directed. Censors forced him to alter sequences which they felt emphasized too much of Jane Russell's bust. In 1947 a Senate Investigating Committee examined his compa-ny's World War II airplane contracts, but the investigation was dropped. In 1948, Hughes bought a controlling interest in RKO Radio Pictures.

Hughes came into public view again when he raised the issue of alleged Communist influence in the film industry after World War II, but in 1952 he began to shun all publicity. In 1966, after an extended legal battle, he was forced to sell his controlling interest in TWA when other stockbro-kers won a suit charging that Hughes had illegal-ly used the airline to finance other investments. Subsequently he established the Howard Hughes Medical Institute and became both a pioneer in the electronics revolution and a powerful force in the Nevada gambling and real estate businesses. In 1967 he bought the Desert Inn complex, part of which he used as a modern-day fortress to hide his business operations from public scrutiny, the Sands Hotel, and the Frontier Hotel. Hughes also purchased Las Vegas station KLAS-TV, Alamo Airways, and numerous other properties in and around the city. His wealth, the ease with which he acquired gambling and broadcasting licenses, and the character of his employees raised many questions concerning his role in Nevada affairs. In 1968, when Hughes tried to purchase another gambling house, the Justice Department made preliminary investigations into possible antitrust violations, and Hughes withdrew his purchase offer. In 1969 he began buying Nevada mineral lands and became involved in controversy with the federal government stemming from his oppo-sition to nuclear testing in Nevada. Rumors cir-culated that Hughes had dealings with crime syndicates and that he was actually dead, while his organization used his name for its business activities. *Fortune* magazine in May 1968 estimat-ed Hughes to be worth between $985,500,000 and $1,373,000,000, which would have ranked him near **J. Paul Getty** as the wealthiest American. In 1972–73 he was much in the news, first in con-nection with a spurious autobiography concoct-ed by Clifford Irving, then when it was revealed that he had secretly contributed $100,000 to President Richard Nixon's campaign for reelec-tion. In his last years Hughes was a drug-addict-ed recluse, living in "germ-free" hotel suites in Las Vegas and Mexico, surrounded by loyal aides drawn from the Mormon Church who responded to his every whim. Gaunt, emaciated, and report-ed to be in periodic drug-induced stupors in the years before his death, he refused to allow his knee-length hair to be cut and his foot-long fin-gernails to be trimmed. He died somewhere over Texas on an airplane flying him from Mexico to a Houston hospital.

Howard Hughes's cultivation of his deepest interest, airplanes, was made possible, ironically, by the automobile. The patent drilling bit that his father innovated unlocked the oil wealth of the world, and through good times and bad, under management that varied from miserably inefficient to pretty good, Hughes Tool Co. pro-vided all the money that was needed, and much more besides. Although little is likely ever to be known of Hughes's formative years, a dim picture emerges of a lonely boy whose impatience to prove that he could be somebody in his own right ruled out patient preparation and the decisiveness that great schemes require. His most youthful decision was perhaps his best: he aggressively bought out the other heirs to "Toolco," thereby saving it from internal dissension, a fate that has befallen many a thriving business after the sudden death of its chief protagonist. He seldom went near the plant, but those who ran it were never allowed to forget for whose benefit it existed. After the post–World War II boom began, Hughes relaxed his control enough to permit others to install more efficient methods. Meanwhile Hughes doggedly played the main role that he had set for himself as innovator and supplier of risk capital. His motion picture production methods were wasteful, and his films were so devoid of style that they are of little interest today (his longtime aide Noah Dietrich said Hughes had a fatal taste for "corn"), but *Hell's Angels* and the new faces he introduced were significant achievements. His flying records gave the feeble aviation industry a powerful psychological boost during the depth of the Depression, and his money made of TWA a demonstration project that set the pattern for the emergence of modern commercial aviation. Although the stream of electronic marvels that flowed from Hughes Aircraft as the United States moved from cold war to Korea to the space age was almost entirely the work of men who soon left to capitalize their reputations, the creator, in the economic sense, was Howard Hughes.

In an age of almost compulsive exhibitionism and bad taste in the squandering of inherited wealth, Hughes tried desperately to leave his mark on the world. In his prime he could be something of a hero. Haggard from his round-the-world flight or righteous in the indignation with which he faced a questioning senator, Howard Hughes outdid all the dissolute playboys and pallid patrons of the arts. He was what was left of the myth of the rugged individualist.

See Noah Dietrich, *Howard—the Amazing Mr. Hughes* (1972).

ALBRO MARTIN

HUGHES, James Langston (b. Joplin, Mo., Feb. 1, 1902; d. New York, N.Y., May 22, 1967), WRITER, graduated from a Cleveland high school and attended Columbia College (1921–22). After working as a steward on a freighter in 1923, Hughes won the *Opportunity* magazine poetry prize for poems later published as *Weary Blues* (1926). Thereafter he won the Witter Bynner undergraduate poetry award and a scholarship to Lincoln University (Oxford, Pennsylvania). He continued writing poetry, publishing *Fine Clothes to the Jew* (1927) and, in 1930, his first prose work, *Not Without Laughter*. He also published a collection of short stories, *The Ways of White Folks* (1934).

Hughes spent 1932 in the Soviet Union and wrote many articles for newspapers and magazines. He covered the Spanish Civil War for the Baltimore *Afro-American* in 1937. In columns for the Chicago *Defender* and the New York *Post* he created the character of Jesse B. Semple, known as Simple. He also translated poems of black writers in Cuba and Haiti.

In the 1950s Hughes wrote many books dealing with black history and the contribution of blacks to American society. *The First Book of Negroes* (1952) and *Famous American Negroes* (1954) were highly praised, and Hughes won the Anisfield-Wolf award for the best book on race relations. His *Fight for Freedom* (1962) told the story of the NAACP. Some of his other works include *Shakespeare in Harlem* (1942), *Simple Speaks His Mind* (1950), and two autobiographical volumes, *The Big Sea* (1940) and *I Wonder as I Wander* (1956).

At 18, Langston Hughes published his first poem, "The Negro Speaks of Rivers," beginning a prolific literary career lasting more than forty-five years. While Hughes's poetry echoed the tradition of **Walt Whitman** and **Carl Sandburg,** his greatest influence was the African-American musical and oral traditions. He saw in the African-American's spontaneous expression a distinctive artistic and cultural source. Beginning with *Weary Blues*, Hughes converted the black musical idiom into poetry, reflecting the various vogues: blues, "swing," "bebop." One of the stars of the Harlem Renaissance (c. 1925–30), Hughes differed from his contemporaries in that he subordinated orthodox standards of literary judgment to welcome the fresh and immediate African-American expression, giving his work a folk quality.

Besides his poetry, Langston Hughes worked widely in other literary fields. He translated poetry from the Spanish. He adapted his satirical "Jesse P. Semple" character into the successful Broadway play *Simply Heavenly* (1957). Indeed, some of Hughes's most important work was done for the stage. From his early collaborations on plays with the folklorist-novelist Zora Neale Hurston, he went on to write the libretto for Elmer Rice's *Street Scene* (1947). His most powerful theatrical efforts, however, resulted from his combining the black gospel and spiritual traditions into stage productions: *Tambourines to Glory* (1959), *Black Nativity* (1961), and *The Prodigal Son* (1964).

Langston Hughes's consistent reliance on the voices and idiom of black people has kept his work popular among African-Americans throughout many changes in vogues of ideology. See Milton Meltzer, *Langston Hughes: A Biography* (1968).

NATHAN T. HUGGINS

HULL, Cordell (b. Overton Co., Tenn., Oct. 2, 1871; d. Bethesda, Md., July 23, 1955), DIPLOMAT, POLITICAL LEADER, graduated from Cumberland University Law School (Lebanon, Tenn.) in 1891 and was admitted to the bar that same year. He was elected as a Democrat to the Tennessee house of representatives in 1892, serving until 1897. When the Spanish-American War broke out, Hull raised a contingent of Tennesseans but saw no combat. He served as

judge of the fifth judicial circuit of Tennessee (1903–7) and was elected to the U.S. House of Representatives in 1906. In Congress, Hull helped draft the income tax act of 1913. He served as chairman of the Democratic National Committee (1921–24) but returned to the House in 1923. Hull was elected to the Senate in 1932 but did not serve, being appointed secretary of state by President Franklin Roosevelt in 1933.

Hull was secretary of state for nearly twelve years, longer than any other secretary. He headed the American delegation to the London Economic Conference in 1933. A fervent supporter of low tariffs, Hull campaigned for the passage of the Reciprocal Trade Program, enacted in 1934, which gave the president power to enter into trade agreements with other nations with broad flexibility to set tariff rates. Hull also supported the Good Neighbor Policy toward Latin America. He attended Pan-American conferences in Montevideo (1933), Buenos Aires (1936), and Lima (1938), and a special foreign ministers' conference at Havana (1940). Hull favored a firm stand against Japanese aggression in Asia. He was rebuking the Japanese envoys in his office as Pearl Harbor was being bombed (Dec. 7, 1941). During World War II he worked for a nonpartisan foreign policy. He participated in the Moscow conference of foreign ministers in 1943 and the Dumbarton Oaks conference for planning the United Nations. He resigned as secretary in 1944 but accepted a last assignment as a delegate to the U.N. conference at San Francisco in 1945. He won the Nobel Peace Prize that same year for his role in creating the U.N. After his retirement, Hull wrote his *Memoirs* (1948).

※

Even though he occupied the post longer than any man before or since, Cordell Hull has not usually been regarded as a "strong" secretary of state. The judgment rests on President Roosevelt's own activism in the foreign policy area, his seeming preference for a succession of personal advisers in the White House, and his failure to include Hull among those who accompanied him to wartime Big Three conferences.

Not a few of the secretary's subordinates in the State Department were amazed that he put up with this treatment for so long.

But put up with it he did. And although he occasionally "flew off the handle," the secretary kept his eye fixed on certain objectives—which he achieved. "The camel is not too bright, is slow moving and ruminating," he once remarked to an aide, "but after all—it carried a greater burden than a whole group of asses." Hull's main objective before the war was to convince Roosevelt and the nation not to abandon economic multilateralism in its trade relations; during the war his objective became the establishment of an international security organization which would extend that principle to the world. As he would put it time and again, economic and political security were indivisible.

In the original New Deal coalition, Hull was numbered among the president's conservative advisers. He was an unhappy conservative, more than half convinced that Roosevelt himself shared the "socialist-nationalist" views attributed to his extreme advisers. With the passage of the Reciprocal Trade Agreements Act, however, he relaxed. Roosevelt might not always agree with him, but they were both traveling in the same direction. "Two years ago," Hull congratulated the president in 1935, "the American people were overwhelmingly in a state of mind to try almost anything in the way of governmental plans or devices or expedients to deal with the horribly dislocated financial and economic conditions." But Roosevelt's "comprehensive economic program" had saved the country from fascism or socialism.

For the next six years Hull tried to make the other major powers see it that way. He concentrated on Germany, Japan, and Great Britain, all of whom had adopted nationalistic economic policies at home and abroad. Fearful of the other two, Great Britain did agree to sign a reciprocal trade agreement with the United States in 1938. The secretary later asserted that if this pact had been one of the first, instead of one of the last, before the war, the conflict might have been avoided. Anyway, he argued, "The political line-up followed the economic line-up."

Once the war began, Hull built outward from that agreement, securing Winston Churchill's reluctant commitment to an article in the Lend-Lease protocol pledging British cooperation in a postwar effort to reduce or eliminate trade discriminations. The campaign he had begun in 1933, first against New Deal nationalism, had been crowned with success: "The foundation was now laid for all our later postwar policy in the economic field." Hull's successors completed the structure. See Julius W. Pratt, *Cordell Hull* (1964).

LLOYD C. GARDNER

HUMPHREY, Hubert Horatio, Jr. (b. Wallace, S.D., May 27, 1911; d. Waverly, Minn., Jan. 13, 1978), POLITICAL LEADER, entered the University of Minnesota in 1929 but had to leave to help in his father's drugstore in Huron, South Dakota. After taking an accelerated course at the Denver (Colo.) School of Pharmacy (1932–33), Humphrey returned to Huron and worked as a registered pharmacist. In 1937 he returned to the University of Minnesota and earned his BA in 1939. He received his MA in political science from Louisiana State University in 1940 and then returned to the University of Minnesota to work for his PhD. Financial problems again forced him to leave school, and after being rejected by the armed forces in World War II, he became state director for War Production Training (1942). He was assistant director of the state War Manpower Commission in 1943. He then taught (1943–44) at Macalester College in St. Paul. A Democrat, Humphrey ran for mayor of Minneapolis in 1943 but was defeated; in 1944 he directed the Minnesota campaign for the reelection of President Franklin D. Roosevelt. He helped initiate the merger of the Minnesota Democratic and Farmer-Labor parties and was elected mayor of Minneapolis in 1945. As mayor he inaugurated housing and welfare programs, and a fair employment practices commission. He helped found the liberal pressure group Americans for Democratic Action in 1947 and received national attention when he fought strenuously for a strong civil rights plank at the 1948 Democratic national convention in Philadelphia.

Elected to the U.S. Senate in 1948, Humphrey made civil rights legislation his specialty. Among the bills he sponsored were measures to obtain equal voting rights, lower taxes for poor people, urban renewal, an increased minimum wage, and expanded social security and welfare benefits. Reelected senator in 1954 and 1960, Humphrey emerged as one of the leaders of the Democratic Party. He made an unsuccessful bid for the 1960 Democratic presidential nomination. In 1961 he became assistant majority leader of the Senate. In that post he helped steer the 1963 Nuclear Test Ban Treaty through the Senate and was floor manager during the passage of the 1964 Civil Rights Act. He was elected vice president on the Democratic ticket with Lyndon B. Johnson in 1964 and nominated for the presidency at the tumultuous Democratic convention in Chicago in 1968. In the election he was narrowly defeated by Richard Nixon, gaining 191 electoral votes to Nixon's 301 and **George Wallace**'s 46. Humphrey had 31.2 million or 42.7 percent of the popular vote, while Nixon polled 31.7 million (43.4 percent) and Wallace 9.9 million (13.5 percent). After teaching at the University of Minnesota and Macalester College, Humphrey was again elected to the U.S. Senate in 1970 and served until his death. Some of his books include *The Cause in Mankind* (1964) and *One Man, One World* (1970).

———— ∞ ————

The son of an ardent follower of **William Jennings Bryan** and **Woodrow Wilson**, Humphrey never questioned his family's allegiance to the Democratic Party, social reform, and small-scale capitalism. The Great Depression, a personally traumatic and impoverishing experience, reinforced his faith. He conceived of liberalism from the New Deal to the Great Society as a "vital center" between socialism and unregulated capitalism, between the extremes of left and right. Essentially a believer in the American success ethic, he wanted to humanize capitalist society and equalize opportunities for advancement in it.

A sincere liberal actively involved in a score of

causes, Humphrey was a hardworking and innovative senator. His ambition led him to seek understandings with the political establishment, but he did so without seriously compromising his reformism. His vice presidency, however, was an unhappy period that brought him abuse from both antiwar liberals and the president whose policies he defended.

Humphrey's own attempts at the White House failed in large part from his inability to secure the financing and organization that a national candidacy requires. But his public image also hurt him. His exuberance, his eagerness to speak with machine-gun rapidity on almost any subject, his frequent betrayals of an inner uncertainty—all offended a generation that sought "coolness" in its political leaders and caused him to be unfairly typed as glib, superficial, and impulsive. In 1972 his attempt to rally the old New Deal coalition could not overcome the challenge of the "new politics," and his defeat for the Democratic nomination signaled the waning of a venerable liberal tradition. See Carl Solberg, *Hubert Humphrey: A Biography* (1984).

ALONZO L. HAMBY

HUNT, Haroldson Lafayette (b. Vandalia, Ill., Feb. 17, 1889; d. Dallas, Tex., Jan. 29, 1974), BUSINESSMAN, spent most of his childhood working on his father's farm and left public school after the fifth grade. Leaving home at the age of 16, he worked for a while as a ranch hand and lumberjack, and upon his father's death in 1911 began using his modest inheritance of about $5,000 to speculate in cotton and timber lands. In 1920, hearing rumors of an oil strike in El Dorado, Arkansas, he borrowed $50, went to El Dorado, and began trading in leases. He soon accumulated enough money to lease an acre of his own and struck oil on his first try. He quickly expanded his holdings, sold a 50 percent interest in forty of his wells for $600,000 in 1924, and by 1930 owned one hundred oil-producing wells throughout the South and Southwest. In 1937 he founded the Hunt Oil Co., which eventually became the largest independent producer of oil and natural gas in the United States. In addition, he was once the leading pecan grower in the nation and had vast real estate holdings. His income was estimated at over a million dollars a week. The most tangible manifestation of his wealth was his mammoth estate on the outskirts of Dallas, Texas, modeled on George Washington's Mount Vernon but several times larger. In the 1960s and 1970s he became concerned with questions of diet and health, and his diversified HLH Products Co. began to produce health foods.

Hunt gained considerable notoriety as a result of his ultraconservative political views and activities. In 1951 he founded "Facts Forum," later to be called "Life Line," which produced and disseminated daily fifteen-minute radio programs which expressed his fear that free enterprise and individual freedom were steadily losing ground to ever expanding Communist influences in America. In 1967 it was broadcast on 541 radio stations reaching 4–6 million people daily. He also directed the Youth Freedom Speakers, a group of twenty thousand young people concentrated mainly in the Southwest who carried his message of support for "God, Country, Christianity, and Freedom" to schools and civic organizations. In addition, in 1964, Hunt started his own weekly newspaper column, "Hunt for Truth," which at its peak was carried by more than eighty daily and weekly papers. Hunt, who was notoriously parsimonious, never established a foundation or gave money of any consequence to charity. He believed that rich men who did so were extremely ill-advised and merely attracted unwanted attention to themselves. Hunt wrote several books and many pamplets expressing his quirky ideas, including *Alpaca* (1960), a utopian novel wherein he describes a mythical state that has a laissez-faire economy and a suffrage system under which citizens have votes in proportion to the amount of taxes they pay.

———

Haroldson Lafayette Hunt vied with **J. Paul Getty** for the title of wealthiest American. Born in modest circumstances, he parlayed his small inheritance into millions until his worth was estimated (in the loose way that the wealthy treat such matters) at between $2 billion and $3 billion. In the 1950s he moved into foreign operations and in the 1960s discovered a Libyan oil field with estimated reserves of more than 6 billion barrels. In June 1973 the Libyan government, which had been sharing equally in the income, announced its nationalization of the Hunt operation.

In some ways Hunt was even better known for his politics than for his business activities, although his astronomical income was of no small assistance in propagating his ideas. All his intimates, and even a few reporters and critics, described him as simple, shy, frugal, unassuming, and absolutely without ego. Certainly some of these qualities were well documented. He drove old, cheap cars, took his lunch to work, and wore clothes that looked as if they had been bought at the local Junior League Thrift Shop. Whether a man who broadcast his opinions to 6 million people daily and wrote a novel describing his idea of a perfect world lacked ego is arguable. Once a big gambler in horses, cards, and sports events, regularly making bets at $25,000 to $50,000, he quit that activity and in 1957, at 68 years of age, joined the Baptist Church. Hunt never wavered on his political opinions, and in his "Life Line" broadcasts and his newspaper column, *Hunt for Truth*, told how he felt about politicians from Franklin D. Roosevelt to Richard M. Nixon, "a bad egg." In 1960 he put $50,000 behind Lyndon B. Johnson's attempt to obtain the Democratic presidential nomination, but then during Johnson's vice presidential and presidential years claimed that Johnson did everything wrong. **Douglas MacArthur** might have suited him. In 1969, despite his Baptist adherence, he talked of joining with the Vatican in pursuing a Youth Freedom Speakers crusade to South America to combat the spread of Communism.

Hunt was certainly likable and could almost be dismissed as a quaint eccentric. The quality that made him sinister in many minds was his extreme wealth and his energy in exporting his ideas well beyond his adopted city of Dallas. These ideas saw leftist plots in everything with which he disagreed. He quietly and effectively promoted the Twenty-second Amendment to get even with the Eisenhower administration, which he looked on as a total disaster. He was on record for believing that the CIA was Communist-dominated and that people should not be permitted to vote. See Ardes Burst, *The Three Families of H. L. Hunt* (1988).

JOE B. FRANTZ

HUNTINGTON, Collis Potter (b. Harwinton, Conn., Oct. 22, 1821; d. near Raquette Lake, N.Y., Aug. 13, 1900), RAILROAD MAGNATE, FINANCIER, after finishing grammar school (1834) became a clerk in the grocery store of Phineas W. Noble. Securing credit from Noble, he began to peddle watches in New York City in 1836. During the next six years he extended his peddling business into most of the states along the eastern seaboard, and in 1842 he established a general merchandise firm with his brother Solon in Oneonta, New York. Although this business flourished, he moved to Sacramento during the California gold rush of 1849 and established another profitable general merchandise firm. Huntington formed a partnership with Mark Hopkins in 1855. Their company rapidly developed into one of the leading retail-wholesale firms in California.

Huntington, Hopkins, **Leland Stanford,** and Charles Crocker formed the Central Pacific Railroad Co. in 1861, with Stanford as president and Huntington as vice president. Since they lacked sufficient capital to construct a transcontinental railroad, the Central Pacific's "Big Four" used patriotic arguments—and lavish bribes—to secure federal subsidies. Under the Pacific Railway Act (1862) the transcontinental companies received five square miles of public land on each side of the line for every mile of track laid, as well as government bonds that ranged in value from $16,000 to $48,000 depending on the difficulty of the terrain.

In 1863 the Central Pacific Railroad began construction eastward from Sacramento, while the Union Pacific built westward from Omaha. The Central Pacific imported Chinese workers to lower the costs of labor. Since the government subsidies were based on mileage, the Central Pacific crews worked all winter to cut a pass through the Sierras, reaching the Great Plains by 1866, where construction costs amounted to only half the federal grants. When the two lines met at Promontory Point, Utah, on May 10, 1869, the Union Pacific had built 1,086 miles of track, the Central Pacific 689. Although the Central Pacific's books were later burned, Huntington and his associates apparently reaped immense profits from the construction.

In 1865, Huntington, Stanford, Crocker, and Hopkins formed the Southern Pacific Railroad Co. Securing federal land and bond subsidies, they completed a line from San Francisco to Los Angeles in 1876. By 1884 they had extended the Southern Pacific to New Orleans without government subsidies. Huntington and his associates then organized the Southern Pacific Co. to coordinate control over the Union Pacific and Southern Pacific lines. Stanford served as president and Huntington as vice president.

Huntington spent much of the 1870s in Washington as a lobbyist. He had gained control of the Chesapeake and Ohio Railroad in 1869. He also acquired the Pacific Mail Steamship Co., the Mexican International Railway Co., the Market Street Railway Co. of San Francisco, and sundry other enterprises. In 1890 he replaced Stanford as president of the Southern Pacific after the two partners quarreled over politics and business.

⎯⎯⎯ ✸ ⎯⎯⎯

Crafty, ruthless, and indefatigable, Huntington was the most astute of that band of "robber barons" known as the "Big Four." The acid-tongued **Ambrose Bierce** said of him: "Of the modern Forty Thieves, Mr. Huntington is the surviving thirty-six." Actually, Huntington was totally amoral in his business dealings and in his cynical manipulation of legislators whose votes he bought with timely bribes. To vast enterprises of public scope he brought the hot and urgent imperatives of an economic individualism that unfailingly set the claims of private property far above those of the common welfare and civic trust. His concentration on the ultimate goal of business power flowed from an imperious ambition that brooked no obstacles. This trait gave Huntington the dimensions of a character drawn by Honoré de Balzac or **Theodore Dreiser.** One observer, in reviewing Huntington's activities, said: "He was always on the scent, incapable of fatigue, delighting in his strength and the use of it, and full of the love of combat.… If the Great Wall of China were put in his path, he would attack it with his nails."

It was a stroke of luck, and one quite in keeping with the other providential turning points which dot his career, that by the time of the Civil War Huntington was in a position to ride the crest of two fundamental forces in the America of his day: the westward movement and the Industrial Revolution. When Huntington arrived in California in 1849, he had all of the shrewd instincts of one who from early youth had been self-reliant and independent, and who as a Connecticut Yankee peddler had learned the arts of calculation and accumulation. Huntington's own comment on his first years as a merchant in the booming economy of the California mining frontier is illuminating: "I kept my warehouse full when prices were low, and when they went up, I sold out." His relentless drive toward acquisition made him a powerful and much-hated man in the last two decades of his life when he became a butt of the antimonopoly movement. Yet even his most determined foes conceded that Huntington never tried to soften or disguise with pious hypocrisy the well-publicized disclosures of unethical business conduct that became familiar after the highly damaging "Colton letters" were published in 1883.

In his rise to business power, Huntington epitomized the rags-to-riches legend, and he later attributed much of his success to having started out in life with no advantages (the section of Harwinton where he was born was called Poverty Hollow, and his family life under a curmudgeonly father was harsh). Although the industrial elite in post–Civil War America were generally recruited from the top social layer, the business leaders who made revolutionary innovations in the economy, excelled in entrepreneurial grasp, or challenged the established business community were "outsiders" drawn from the lower rungs of farm and village society. Huntington was an example of this type, as were the elder **John D. Rockefeller** and **Jay Gould,** among others.

Huntington was a bluff, hearty giant of a man who weighed well over two hundred pounds and in his later years covered his massive domed head with a black silk skullcap because he was self-conscious about his baldness. Compulsively frugal, he once scolded an employee who dropped a four-penny nail and failed to pick it up. His mode of living was fairly modest until he married his second wife, Arabella, in 1884. A lively, socially ambitious woman, she built a Fifth Avenue mansion that cost $2,500,000, took five years to construct, and was crammed with art treasures. She also built a family mausoleum modeled after a Roman temple. See Cerinda W. Evans, *Collis Potter Huntington* (1954).

WILLIAM GREENLEAF

HUTCHINS, Robert Maynard (b. Brooklyn, N.Y., Jan. 17, 1899; d. Santa Barbara, Calif., May 14, 1977), EDUCATOR, attended Oberlin College (1915–17) where his father was a professor in the school of theology. He enlisted in the U.S. ambulance service at the outbreak of World War I, serving in Italy. Upon his return he attended Yale and graduated in 1921. He spent the next two years teaching history and English at the Lake Placid School in New York. While a student at Yale Law School he concurrently served as college secretary (1923–27). He received his LLB in 1925 and taught at Yale from 1925 to 1927, became full professor and acting dean of the law school in 1927, and dean in 1928. In this capacity he expanded the law curriculum to include the social sciences and organized the Yale Institute of Human Relations. In 1929, Hutchins was chosen president of the University of Chicago.

Hutchins saw American education drifting toward overspecialization, scientism, presentism, and pragmatism, trends he opposed. He believed that the undergraduate should have a general education designed to teach him to think in broad, philosophical terms. To carry out these ideas Hutchins developed the "Chicago Plan"— reorganizing the curriculum of the college of the university around the "great ideas" of man as seen in classical writing and allowing the student to move through it at an accelerated rate. The student could enter Chicago after his sophomore year in high school, and the program ended at the end of the traditional sophomore year of college. Hutchins restructured the rest of the university proper into four divisions: the humanities, the social sciences, the biological sciences, and the physical sciences; and he urged the professional schools to stress fundamental principles rather than narrow professional techniques. The law school, for instance, moved away from preparing students to practice law in a direct sense and instead devoted more emphasis to the philosophy of law. Believing that colleges should not emphasize athletics, he dropped intercollegiate football at Chicago in 1939, an action that generated severe criticism from alumni.

A member of the America First Committee, Hutchins opposed U.S. intervention in World War II but backed the war effort after Pearl Harbor. During World War II he authorized the use of University of Chicago scientists and facilities on the project that developed the atomic bomb. Following the war he actively backed the establishment of and American participation in the United Nations and spoke out in favor of international control of atomic energy. He was president of the Committee to Frame a World Constitution in 1945. Moving from president of the University of Chicago in 1945 to chancellor, he continued his leadership of the university until his resignation in 1951. He took a leave of absence in 1946 to devote time to the *Encyclopaedia Britannica*, whose chairman he had become in 1943. A strong advocate of academic freedom, Hutchins headed the Commission on Freedom of the Press in 1947 and strongly opposed loyalty oaths for Chicago professors proposed toward the end of his term as chancellor.

He served as an associate director of the Ford Foundation from 1951 to 1954 when he became president of the Fund for the Republic, created by the Ford Foundation. From 1959 to 1974 he was president of the Center for the Study of Democratic Institutions in Santa Barbara, California, a body established by the fund; he became its board chairman in 1962 and a life senior fellow in 1974. From 1952 on he served as editor in chief of *Encyclopaedia Britannica*'s Great Books of the Western World and in 1963 became coeditor of its annual *Great Ideas Today* with Mortimer Adler. In addition, he published many books, including *The Higher Learning in America* (1936), *The University of Utopia* (1953), *The Conflict in Education* (1953), and *The Learning Society* (1968).

Throughout his long career Hutchins maintained that the primary problems facing America were of a moral, intellectual, and spiritual—not material—nature. The university could alleviate these by adhering to its proper functions: the discovery of the philosophical principles governing the national and social worlds, and the cultivation of the student's intellect to enable him to grasp them. He directed his energies at Chicago toward moving not only the University of Chicago but all the nation's colleges and universities away from empirical, operationally oriented research and teaching toward these goals.

When Hutchins assumed the presidency of the University of Chicago, it was one of the two greatest universities of the country. When he resigned, it had become simply one among many prominent universities. Two decades of turmoil and disruption had seriously damaged it. Many faculty members had found his educational policies inimical to their interests. Although usually charming and gracious, this tall, handsome man occasionally seemed caustic and hostile; and he alienated not only many faculty members but also many wealthy donors. The contributions that continued to come in usually went to the professional schools, not the college. A dedicated advocate of civil rights, Hutchins could not persuade his own board and those responsible for the policies of the city of Chicago to rebuild the city's slums that were blighting the university. He could design a constitution for world government, but Hyde Park lay disintegrating at his doorstep.

Hutchins eventually lost hope in being able to transform American higher education. Thus he turned to other institutions. Both through the Fund for the Republic and through the Center for the Study of Democratic Institutions he hoped to contribute to the shaping of a truly democratic society by supporting the basic thinking and reflective, integrative dialogues that American universities ought to encourage but in his opinion were not.

Hutchins recognized that ends beyond means are needed. Modern Western civilization has developed wonderful techniques to get places and has given the ordinary man a freedom unknown in all previous history. Yet it has not arrived at any consensus of where man ought to be going with his great technical power, nor has it decided what man should do with freedom once he has it. General aimlessness and dismay indeed seem to permeate modern society. Hutchins had the perception and courage rare among leaders of major organizations to move to meet this fundamental crisis. The magnitude of the task he took on gives reason for charity in judging his accomplishments. See Michael R. Harris, "Robert Maynard Hutchins," in *Five Counterrevolutionists in Higher Education* (1970), pp. 133–62.

MICHAEL R. HARRIS

HUTCHINSON, Anne Marbury (b. Alford, Lincolnshire, Eng., 1591; d. Eastchester, N.Y., Aug./Sept. 1643), RELIGIOUS LEADER, in 1634 emigrated with her husband, William Hutchinson, and children to Massachusetts Bay. She admired the preaching of **John Cotton** and soon began to hold informal meetings in her own home, where she "interpreted" his sermons. She believed that only John Cotton (and later John Wheelwright) preached a "covenant of grace," which held that salvation came principally through the individual's own personal awareness of God's divine grace and love, as opposed to a "covenant of works," which held that salvation was impossible without obedience to the laws of the church and state.

The orthodox clergy and the secular leaders of the colony first urged Hutchinson to change her views, but when in a meeting with the general court in November 1637 she argued that grace was a mystical experience which preceded any moral effort and that personal revelation (Antinomianism) absolved from all sin those who had received grace, she was banished from the colony. She was subsequently (Mar. 1638) excommunicated by the Boston church. She moved to **Roger Williams**'s settlement at Narragansett Bay, and in 1642, after the death of her husband, to Long Island, New York. She was killed in an Indian massacre.

The so-called Antinomian controversy with which Anne Hutchinson was intimately connected was the major public incident of the early years of the founding of the colony of Massachusetts Bay. The controversy was a complicated one that involved important doctrinal, political, and social issues in the formative years of the colony.

While at one time it was fashionable to deprecate the theological matters debated in the controversy, most modern commentators would put them to the forefront. Indeed, some scholars have argued that in the eyes of the clergy and magistrates, Anne Hutchinson merely served as a stalking horse for John Cotton, whom she always considered her mentor. Since he was too prestigious to be confronted directly, Cotton's theological views were attacked and criticized indirectly through her. The issue, put very simply, was over the relative importance of the mystery of grace and of outward conformity to the moral implications of the covenant that God had made with the Puritan state and church. Cotton and his opponents agreed that both grace and conformity to the covenant were essential for saintship, but his critics suspected that Cotton's emphasis on grace could lead—as in the case of Hutchinson—to a position outside both church and state.

The political implications of the controversy were many. The colony's very existence was justified in terms of the covenants God had made with man, and to argue that possession of true grace absolved the individual from obedience to the laws of God as interpreted by man in church and state was to destroy the social contract and legitimize all manner of dissent. The question became intertwined with power struggles in the infant colony between those like Roger Williams and Governor Henry Vane who put spiritual principles over all others and leaders like **John Winthrop** who attempted to reconcile spiritual principles with the accepted social and political beliefs of the 17th century.

One social assumption which Hutchinson clearly challenged was that the place of woman was in the home. No one could question the legitimacy of the informal meetings she held in her house as long as only women were present, but she had extended her circle to include many of the male inhabitants of Boston. Since women traditionally were not supposed to be preachers, such meetings came suspiciously close to violating the law. Moreover, Hutchinson had several times questioned the spiritual state and place of the clergy in the colony. At the same time that most of her opponents objected to her pretensions as unwarranted from one of her sex, Hutchinson's exclusion from political and spiritual responsibility because she was a woman undoubtedly accounted for the tortuousness of the proceedings that finally banished her from the colony. The authorities simply did not know precisely how to deal with her; only her voluntary statement of personal revelations in her general court appearance after she had successfully parried all accusations against her gave them legitimate grounds for the banishment that all parties undoubtedly felt was inevitable. See Emery Battis, *Saints and Sectaries: Anne Hutchinson and the Antinomian Controversy in the Massachusetts Bay Colony* (1962).

J. M. BUMSTED

HUTCHINSON, Thomas (b. Boston, Mass., Sept. 9, 1711; d. Brompton, Eng., June 3, 1780), POLITICAL LEADER, graduated from Harvard (BA, 1727; MA, 1730) and entered his father's commercial house. He was elected to the Massachusetts house of representatives in 1737, serving until 1749 (speaker, 1746–48). He opposed the Massachusetts Land Bank, and when the bills of credit that the Massachusetts legislature had issued decreased in value, he proposed the redemption of the outstanding bills of credit at an 11-to-1 ratio. His hard-money stand cost him his seat in 1749, but he was chosen to serve on the Council (1749–66). In 1752 he was appointed judge of probate and justice of common pleas in Suffolk County. He represented Massachusetts at the Albany Congress (1754) and supported **Benjamin Franklin**'s plan for uniting the colonies. Hutchinson was appointed lieutenant governor in 1758 and chief justice in 1760. At first he opposed the issuance of "writs of assistance" (general search warrants) by the governor, but when he learned that such writs were issued in England, he accepted their legality.

He disapproved of the Sugar Act (1764) and the Stamp Act (1765), which he believed would injure Anglo-American trade. However, he never questioned Parliament's authority to tax the colonies. His pro-British position made him the symbol of the "court party," and in 1765 a mob destroyed his home. This action intensified his conviction that Parliament must establish its supremacy over the colonies.

In 1770 he was appointed governor of Massachusetts. After Parliament repealed the Townshend Acts in 1770, it appeared as though tensions might be allayed. But Hutchinson's controversies with the Massachusetts legislature over technical points played into the hands of the radicals. In 1773, **Samuel Adams** published the "Hutchinson Letters," in which Hutchinson had asserted Parliament's supremacy. When the British East India Co. was given a monopoly on the sale of tea in the colonies (1773), Hutchinson's efforts to enforce the law led the patriots to dump British tea into Boston Harbor (Boston Tea Party, 1773).

In 1774, Hutchinson went to England, where, in a personal interview, he described the colonial situation to George III. Although he loved New England, he never returned. Hutchinson was also an accomplished historian, his major work being *History of the Colony of Massachusetts Bay* (3 vols., 1764–1828).

Thomas Hutchinson, the last civilian governor of provincial Massachusetts, was a complex and most unusual man. As a Harvard student he was noted for aiming at perfection, even when cribbing. His mentors expected success from this eager and calculating young man who started to trade while yet a student and kept track of every penny he spent. In maturity he was an emotional partisan but also a loyalist bound to his concept of the "supreme power" of a British imperium.

Hutchinson's impeccable family connections easily qualified him for a political career. While working with a number of governors he built up his own power base, careful in public to mollify the opposition and telling his allies, "We don't live in Plato's Commonwealth, and when we can't have perfection, we ought to comply with the measure that is least remote from it." As was the custom of his times, he proceeded to collect a host of offices from judge of probate to lieutenant governor and chief justice. His outstanding success in this endeavor and the prominence of his Oliver relatives convinced the Otis clan—no mean collectors of posts themselves—and their allies that Hutchinson desired to form an oligarchy.

What is important about these factional maneuverings and bickerings is that British designs to regulate the empire after victory in the French and Indian War transformed the factions into political parties. And Hutchinson, the brains of the "court" party, could not help but be connected with unpopular British measures. Moreover, the opposition "country" party insisted that he was conspiring with Britain to limit colonial autonomy. It is true that he was privy to the information that Britain after 1763 intended to enact sugar and stamp taxes to pay the cost of victory. And he wrote Israel Williams, "This I would not have mentioned [as coming] from me." Yet Hutchinson was correct in claiming that he opposed the Sugar Act, the Stamp Act, and the Townshend duties. And he stated that if the British had paid as heavy taxes as the people of Massachusetts, there would be no debt to be paid. He thus agreed with the substance of colonial protests against British taxation but not with the principle of protest. Hutchinson's enemies believed that he was plotting against their New England liberties; he believed that the opposition to British taxation came from such professional agitators as Sam Adams and **James Otis** and their "plebian party in the town of Boston," which had intimidated the General Court. He wrote the second volume of his *History* to back his version of imperial authority. "I am told it will be of service in the present state of affairs," he said. In 1767 he declared that it was unconstitutional for Great Britain to tax the colonies, but if Parliament did so, "it is more advisable to Submit to it, than by resistance to break of the Connection." He maintained this position while governor and on into exile. See Bernard Bailyn, *Thomas Hutchinson* (1974).

JOHN J. WATERS

ICKES, Harold Le Claire (b. Frankstown Township, Pa., Mar. 15, 1874; d. Washington, D.C., Feb. 3, 1952), POLITICAL LEADER, received a BA from the University of Chicago in 1897 and a JD in 1907. He was a reporter for the Chicago *Record* (1897–1900) and an active supporter of the municipal reform movement in Chicago. He managed the independent Republican John M. Harlan's mayoralty campaign (1905), the unsuccessful mayoralty effort of Republican **Charles E. Merriam** (1911), and in his law practice, which commenced in 1907, often took civil liberties cases without pay. He supported Theodore Roosevelt's Progressive Party in 1912, serving on city, state, and national committees of the party. In 1916, Ickes backed Republican **Charles Evans Hughes**'s campaign for the presidency against Woodrow Wilson. During World War I he worked with the YMCA in France (1918–19). Having opposed the nomination of Warren G. Harding for president at the Republican convention of 1920, Ickes supported the Democratic candidate James M. Cox. In 1924 he managed Republican **Hiram Johnson**'s unsuccessful preconvention presidential campaign. In 1932, Ickes backed Franklin D. Roosevelt for the presidency, organizing support among midwestern liberal Republicans.

Ickes was appointed secretary of the interior by Roosevelt (1933), remaining in that position until 1946. As secretary he headed the Public Works Administration (1933–39), gaining a reputation for honest and careful spending of the huge sums spent on PWA projects. His advocacy of large-scale projects with heavy capital investment conflicted with the views of **Harry Hopkins,** head of the Works Progress Administration (1935–38), who favored immediate relief to the unemployed through small-scale government-funded projects. Although President Roosevelt supported Hopkins in this dispute, Ickes was close to the president and was an articulate spokesman for New Deal philosophy. He played a vital role in the management of the 1940 Democratic convention, which nominated Roosevelt for a third term, and in the election campaign of that year.

During World War II, Ickes administered important wartime agencies (solid fuels, petroleum, fisheries, coal mines). He wrote several books, including *The New Democracy* (1934), *Autobiography of a Curmudgeon* (1943), and *My Twelve Years with F.D.R.* (1948). His *Diary* is a major source for the New Deal years.

Ickes was one of the most colorful, controversial, and significant members of Franklin Roosevelt's administration. A short, heavy man with a jutting jaw, he seemed equipped for the role on the front lines that delighted him. He battled with almost everyone worth taking on except President Roosevelt. (After Roosevelt, he battled with President Harry S. Truman and resigned with a blast.) He found many of his foes inside the administration, enjoyed combat on the public platform even more, and campaigned with gusto, aiming verbal blows at Republican challengers.

Ickes's instinct for combat was part of the baggage he brought with him to Washington. It had been shaped by participation in the Progressive movement in Chicago and the nation. He was one of the New Deal's major links with that movement.

Ickes's progressivism was a curious blend of distrust and confidence. His distrust of businessmen was obvious in Chicago, where he contested with those who sought privileges from city hall, and appeared again in the 1930s, for he was one of the New Deal's leading critics of business power. His distrust of people generally was also apparent in his administration of the Interior Department and PWA, for he spied on his subordinates, looked skeptically at proposals that politicians brought to him, and examined proposed projects with great care, convinced that the forces of corruption were very strong and that the Department of Interior, the department of Richard A. Ballinger and **Albert B. Fall,** was especially vulnerable. While improving the reputation of the department, his doubts hampered the PWA as an agency of recovery, for it pumped money into the economy more slowly than the situation demanded.

At the same time Ickes believed that government could make positive contributions. He was one of the influential advocates of action in the administration. Self-confident and always eager to expand his own power, he enlarged his department and tried to make it even larger, hoping it would become the Department of Conservation. Theodore Roosevelt and **Gifford Pinchot** had helped to interest him in conservation, but he moved beyond them to pay more attention to aesthetic considerations. Using the powers of his department and of the PWA, he enlarged conservation programs, developed public electrical power, initiated experiments in public housing and slum clearance, constructed many other valuable projects, both civilian and military, and pressed for broad federal authority over oil. He also did what he could to improve race relations.

Ickes was also an advocate of action in foreign affairs. Once an isolationist, he was converted by the behavior of Mussolini, Hitler, Franco, and Tojo, and moved to an advanced position in the administration, criticizing the aggressors and calling for American efforts to restrain them. And during the war he became a key man in the economy, developing and administering important programs, often in cooperation with business leaders, and supplying electrical power, petroleum, and other resources needed to win the war.

Impossible to ignore, Ickes was a major figure in the 1930s and 1940s. See T. H. Watkins, *Righteous Pilgrim: The Life and Times of Harold L. Ickes, 1874–1952* (1990).

RICHARD S. KIRKENDALL

INGERSOLL, Robert Green (b. Dresden, N.Y., Aug. 11, 1833; d. Dobbs Ferry, N.Y., July 21, 1899), POLITICAL LEADER, attended Greenville Academy in Illinois (1851–52), clerked in a Marion, Illinois, law office (1852–53), and taught school in Waverly, Tennessee (1853–54). He returned to Marion and was admitted to the bar in 1854, practicing law there from 1855 to 1858 when he moved his office to Peoria, Illinois. In 1860, Ingersoll was defeated when he ran for Congress as an antislavery Democrat on a platform of no federal control over state and territorial institutions. In 1861, after the outbreak of the Civil War, he recruited and organized three Union regiments. Appointed a colonel by General **John C. Frémont** in spring 1862, he

fought at Shiloh, Tennessee, and Corinth, Mississippi. He was captured in Tennessee in 1862 by Confederate General Nathan B. Forrest. Paroled shortly afterward, he resigned from the army in June 1863 and resumed his law practice in Peoria. He also made speeches in favor of abolition and the colonization of freed slaves. When his brother Clark ran for Congress as a Republican in 1864 and 1868, he managed his campaigns. In 1867 he was appointed Illinois attorney general, and a year later he campaigned for Ulysses S. Grant.

A convinced agnostic, in 1869 Ingersoll began to make speeches urging people to resolve religious and ethical questions for themselves rather than seek guidance from organized religion. He soon became known in Illinois as an "infidel." He supported woman suffrage and was elected a delegate to the 1870 American Woman Franchise Association's national convention. In 1870 he also became a director of the Peoria and Springfield Railroad.

During the Republican convention of 1876, Ingersoll made the nominating speech for presidential aspirant **James G. Blaine,** dubbing him the "Plumed Knight." When Blaine lost the nomination to Rutherford B. Hayes, Ingersoll campaigned for Hayes. Through the 1870s he continued to lecture on rationalism, Voltaire, free thought, and religious freedom, while attacking the Bible, Christianity, and the Church. In 1877 he was elected vice president of the National Liberal League, an organization dedicated to the total secularization of public life, free universal education, and the defense of persons charged with violating the Comstock laws by sending purported obscene material through the mails. Ingersoll resigned from the National Liberal League in 1880, taking issue with its involvement in the Comstock law cases.

In 1883, Ingersoll argued what was considered his most important case, successfully defending Stephen Dorsey against charges of defrauding the U.S. mail. In 1884–85 he lectured throughout the United States and Europe, and in 1885 was elected president of the American Secular Union. From 1885 to 1889 he was engaged in litigation against **Jay Gould** involving financial malpractice. Meanwhile, he continued on the lecture circuit, attacking organized religion. He debated William E. Gladstone on evolution and religion in the *North American Review* in 1887, and closed his career by speaking for the gold standard—but not directly supporting William McKinley—in 1896.

"I want to do what little I can to make my country truly free," Robert Ingersoll once declared. "Freedom" was the keynote of Ingersoll's anticlerical appeal: freedom for the school, for the scientific investigator, for the politician, even for the clergyman. He found no inconsistency between his agnosticism and his own partisan affiliation with the Republican Party and its dogmas. It is a comment on his times that that party and candidate James G. Blaine did not disown his allegiance; even today it would be scarcely conceivable for a serious presidential contender to be placed in nomination by an avowed free-thinker. (On the whole, however, the nominator's historical reputation has fared better than that of the nominee.)

During an age that relished oratory, Ingersoll employed all the rhetorical weapons of the platform: sarcasm, pathos, vivid metaphor, moral appeal, and an insistence that one take a stand. "The agnostic does not simply say, 'I do not know,'" Ingersoll explained. "He goes another step, and he says, with great emphasis, that you do not know." It is this emphasis that distinguishes "the Great Infidel," as Ingersoll's contemporaries called him, from the casual nonchurchgoer of the present century. Paradoxically, Ingersoll's commitment to unbelief was deeply religious, and his speeches against orthodoxy were as much "sermons" as were **Dwight L. Moody**'s conventional evangelistic appeals. "They may say I will be damned if I do not believe that," said Ingersoll, referring to the tale of Joshua making the sun stand still, "and I tell them I will if I do." See Orvin Larson, *American Infidel: Robert G. Ingersoll* (1962).

PAUL A. CARTER

INSULL, Samuel (b. London, Eng., Nov. 11, 1859; d. Paris, France, July 16, 1938), BUSINESSMAN, studied stenography and bookkeeping, and became private secretary to Colonel George E. Gouraud, London agent for **Thomas A. Edison,** in 1879. In 1881 he emigrated to the United States to be Edison's private secretary, becoming Edison's constant companion and business manager. He rose to vice president of the newly consolidated Edison General Electric Corp. at Schenectady, New York, in 1889, and following an 1892 merger, he became vice president of the new General Electric Co. That same year, however, he was appointed president of the Chicago Edison Co., which under his leadership became the sole supplier of electricity to the city of Chicago. By 1917, Chicago Edison was serving most of Illinois and had extended into several neighboring states. In 1912, Insull formed his first electrical holding company, Middle West Utilities.

During World War I, Insull served as chairman of the Illinois State Council of Defense. He then conceived the idea of promoting the public sale of utility company stocks, which brought phenomenal growth to his utility companies in the 1920s. The Great Depression dealt his companies a severe blow, however, and his inability to secure desperately needed financing from New York banks resulted in his forced resignation in 1932. Of some $3.5 billion in securities of his various companies, 21 percent became worthless. In his retirement in Europe, he learned of his indictment on charges of fraud, embezzlement, and violation of federal bankruptcy laws. Returned for trial in 1934, he was acquitted on all counts. He never recovered financially, however, and the general hostility toward him by the American public that had lost millions when his empire collapsed was never fully abated.

Insull's virtually unparalleled success as a business innovator before 1930, and his failure and demonetization later, arose from the same personal attributes: a compulsion to run things and an amazing gift for doing so. The compulsion stemmed largely from family relationships; the gift is less readily described. Possessed of inexhaustible energy—he worked more than sixteen hours a day even in his seventies—he nonetheless learned early to render everything he dealt with orderly and efficient, and thereby more easily manageable. Habitually attentive to details, he almost instinctively synthesized them into fundamental business principles. From Edison he learned a passion for innovation ("In my business," Insull said, "the best asset is a first-class junk pile," and he referred to ideas as well as machines). From experience he developed a keen sense of business ecology, an understanding that anything done in any aspect of a big business—and especially one serving a large modern city—must inevitably affect all other aspects and the whole.

Such attributes, in a society become nearly chaotic through the ordeal of industrialization, thrust Insull to the pinnacle of the business world. They also won him enemies among those with the greatest stake in the established order of things; among bankers in general, in the House of Morgan in particular, and among the aristocrats of Chicago's Gold Coast, he was as feared and detested as Napoleon was among the crowned heads of Europe.

When his mistakes provided the opportunity, these enemies forced him out of business. Time, circumstance, and the New Deal destroyed all he had left—his once-great reputation. See Forrest McDonald, *Insull* (1962).

FORREST McDONALD

IRVING, Washington (b. New York, N.Y., Apr. 3, 1783; d. "Sunnyside," near Tarrytown, N.Y., Nov. 28, 1859), WRITER, practiced law briefly, also wrote articles for his brother's newspaper, the *Morning Chronicle*. He spent two years (1804–06) traveling in Europe; after returning to New York, he published, with others, the *Salmagundi Papers* (1807–08), essays on New York life. His comic Diedrich Knickerbocker's *History of New York* (1809) was a popular success. After the War of 1812 he returned to England to work

in a business owned by his family. The business soon failed, but he remained in Europe.

Becoming interested in legendary themes, Irving wrote the essays collected in his *Sketch Book* (1819–20), which included his famous story "Rip Van Winkle." This book won him an international reputation, which was increased by his *Bracebridge Hall* (1822). He spent most of the next three years in Germany and France, and in 1826 moved to Madrid. In Spain he wrote a biography of **Christopher Columbus** (1828) and *The Conquest of Granada* (1829). While living in Granada in 1829 he wrote *The Alhambra* (1832). This collection of stories was an enormous success in both Spain and America. In the fall of 1829 he became secretary of the U.S. legation in London.

Irving returned to the United States in 1832. He then traveled to the western part of the country and published several books based on his experiences, the best-known being *Astoria* (1836). In 1842 he returned to Spain as U.S. minister, serving until 1846. His major work after returning to America was his *Life of Washington* (5 vols.; completed in 1859).

⁂

No other American writer of his time matched Washington Irving in parlaying a modest talent into a major reputation. His foreign fans ranged from Walter Scott to Charles Dickens; at home he was hailed as the man who had first given the lie to Sydney Smith's embarrassing taunt, "Who reads an American book?" But if the accolades showered on him now seem immoderate, Irving himself remained moderate in his tastes. In an era when romantics often strove for grand effects, Irving clung to the commonplace, the comfortable, the familiar. As he wrote in *Bracebridge Hall*: "My only aim is to paint characters and manners. I am no politician.... I shall continue on, therefore, in the course I have hitherto pursued; looking at things poetically, rather than politically; describing them as they are, rather than pretending to point out how they should be; and endeavoring to see the world in as pleasant a light as circumstances will permit."

This strategy assured for Irving a grateful

audience, but opting for gentility shut off a voice that originally had been racier, more critical, more "American" than the Europeanized prose of which his countrymen boasted. In his *Salmagundi Papers* and the first version of Knickerbocker's *History of New York,* his humor had been lusty and his wit vigorously iconoclastic. By the time of the *Sketch Book,* the crusty Diedrich only occasionally intruded on the dreamy mood of Geoffrey Crayon, the reassuringly amateur artist who limned cottages and landscapes but "not a single glacier or volcano." Nostalgia, sentimental humor, placid reverie better suited the gentle Geoffrey. Irving was not conspicuously more intellectual in his later romantic histories. The chronicles of Granada and the lives of Columbus and other explorers revealed a pleasant talent for revivifying historical characters but no genius for illuminating history.

Irving's writings filled twenty-one volumes in the edition of 1860–61. Present-day anthologists are more rigorously selective: portions of Knickerbocker's *History,* a handful of tales and sketches, a bit of *The Alhambra,* perhaps *A Tour on the Prairies.* Above all, two American tales—"The Legend of Sleepy Hollow" and "Rip Van Winkle"—are singled out as his most imaginative contribution to our letters and our legends. In the former he gave us our first Connecticut Yankee in Ichabod Crane and a foreshadowing of the rough-riding frontiersman in Brom Bones. In "Rip Van Winkle" he produced a parable of the passage of America from colony to nation with overtones that probably were deeper than he realized.

Irving was America's first real man of letters, a founding father of a literature that in his own lifetime would outstrip him in both vigor and subtlety. It is easy to fault him: a long shelf of dusty volumes stands as mute accuser of a man who wrote much but dared little. And yet in his best tales he created a handful of mythical characters who entered into the general American consciousness. Not every writer of genius greater than Irving's has managed to do as much. See William L. Hedges, *Washington Irving: An American Study* (1965).

J. V. RIDGELY

IVES, Charles Edward (b. Danbury, Conn., Oct. 20, 1874; d. New York, N.Y., May 19, 1954), COMPOSER, first studied composition and orchestration with his father, a bandmaster and music teacher. A competent church organist at 14, he continued to study music at Yale with Horatio W. Parker. Graduating in 1898, he decided that he had no interest in playing the kind of music that would give him a livelihood, and he became an insurance company clerk in New York. In 1906 he opened his own agency and in 1909 organized Ives and Myrick, general agents for the Mutual Life Insurance Co. Ives and his associates were responsible for a number of innovations in life insurance, notably the first training school for agents and the concepts of educational plans for children and "key executive" coverage for corporations.

Ives worked, however, at his avocation, musical composition, throughout his business career. As a youth he had been intrigued by his father's experiments with dissonances, which, whether produced inadvertently by a country band or deliberately by a square-dance fiddler, the bandmaster felt were among the natural structural elements of music. Like many musicians before and since, both Iveses were fascinated by the phenomenon of harmonious and dissonant combinations of tones. They experimented with instruments that would produce quarter tones (the semitone interval being the smallest that can be produced on the piano and the smallest that traditional Western music embraces) and with exotic chords, which they felt had greater strength than conventional harmonies. Only Charles Ives's wife, who removed every possible obstacle from his composing, encouraged him, however, and as the years passed and unperformed scores piled up in his barn, Ives began to compose less and less. By 1917, when two recitalists gave the first public performance of some of his music in New York, his rate of composition had already slowed down. After 1930 he produced nothing. Exceedingly shy and reluctant to expose himself or his music to criticism, he refused to let it be published except in two instances when he paid the costs himself and distributed the works only to his intimates. In 1925 three of his quarter-tone pieces were played in Town Hall in New York City, and in 1927, Eugene Goossens conducted the *Symphony for Orchestra and Pianos* (now a part of the Fourth Symphony). The Chamber Orchestra of Boston gave the first performance of his best-known orchestral piece, *Three Places in New England,* in 1930. Public acceptance, however, did not begin until about 1939 when the pianist John Kirkpatrick played the *Concord Sonata* (Sonata No. 2) at Town Hall. Enthusiastically received, it was recorded by Columbia Records. In 1951 **Leonard Bernstein** led the New York Philharmonic in the first performance of the Second Symphony, and three years later **George Balanchine** choreographed "Ivesiana" for the New York City Ballet from six Ives pieces. Recipient of the Pulitzer Prize for music for his Symphony No. 3 in 1947, Ives lived to see his work widely performed and acclaimed, in America and Europe.

When Charles Ives was a boy, his father used to play for his son on the piano two different melodies, each in a different key. "You have to learn to stretch your ears," the father insisted. Ives learned how to stretch his ears. Almost from the beginnings of his career as a composer, Ives favored sounds and idioms, forbidden by the textbook and the classroom, with which he tried to free music from subservience to rule and tradition. "I heard something else," is the way he explained it. Beauty of sound as such did not interest him. He was concerned that music express human experiences and musical truth. To do so he had to invent his own vocabulary. He employed polytonality, tone clusters, polyrhythm, polymeters, unresolved discords, microtonal music, and other advanced methods. That his most important compositions came between 1901 and 1916 means that he anticipated, sometimes by a decade or more, modern idioms that other composers have been credited with devising.

Thus Ives must be regarded as the first of the 20th-century modernists. But more significant still is the fact that he was the first composer to realize successfully an authentic indigenous American musical art. In his music he was stimulated by American history, backgrounds, culture, geography, and customs. He frequently quoted American national and popular tunes and hymns—though he enjoyed disfiguring and distorting them, or combining them discordantly. A childhood musical experience he never forgot was the sound of two bands marching into town from different directions, each playing a different melody. The discord when the two melodies met delighted him no end. Again and again he simulated this effect in his orchestral music.

His American nationalism, his pioneer work in creating a modern vocabulary, language, and style for music, and the fact that his works generate such power and extraordinary invention as well as originality are what endow him with his importance and greatness.

He was as unique a man as he was a composer: a thorough individualist who lived the way he wrote, for his convenience alone and without the slightest regard for the opinion of others. As a composer he completely ignored the marketplace. He never submitted a composition to performers or publishers, fame and recognition meaning nothing to him. Combined with this sublime lack of concern for an audience was a charming whimsy that frequently intrudes into his compositions.

In fame (at the end of his life) as in obscurity he remained himself. After his retirement from business he lived on his farm in Connecticut, always dressed in the shabby outfit of an impoverished farmer. He refused access to interviewers, photographers, or those who came to do him homage. He would not even attend any performances of his compositions, which grew increasingly frequent in his last years. He was an individualist through and through, both as a human being and as a musician.

It took the music world almost half a generation to recognize that in Ives it possessed not only a one-of-a-kind but also one of its most important composers, whose best works are enduring monuments in American music. See Henry and Sidney Cowell, *Charles Ives and His Music* (1955).

DAVID EWEN

JACKSON, Andrew (b. Waxhaw, S.C., Mar. 15, 1767; d. near Nashville, Tenn., June 8, 1845), PRESIDENT, served in the Revolutionary army as a youth and was admitted to the bar in 1787. He moved to Nashville, Tennessee, when he was a member of the state constitutional convention (1796). He was elected to the U.S. Congress (1796) and Senate (1797) but resigned to become a judge of the Tennessee supreme court. A major general in the War of 1812, he came into national prominence when his forces defeated the British at the Battle of New Orleans (1815) after the treaty ending the war had been signed. In 1818 he created an international crisis by pursuing Seminole Indians into Spanish Florida, capturing two Spanish forts, and executing two British subjects for inciting the Indians. He was appointed military governor of Florida in 1821 and was again elected to the U.S. Senate in 1823.

In 1824, Jackson ran for the presidency. Although he received more electoral votes than any other candidate, he lacked a majority; the election was thrown into the House of Representatives, where **Henry Clay**'s influence led to John Quincy Adams's victory. When Adams nominated Clay as secretary of state, the Jacksonians maintained that Adams and Clay had entered into a "corrupt bargain" and immediately began preparing for the election of 1828, in which Jackson defeated Adams, 178 electoral votes to 83.

Although Jackson did not make sweeping removals of officeholders as president, the "spoils system" was associated with his name. Convinced that the duties of all public officers were simple, he supported the principle of "rotation of office." For advice he tended to turn to his "kitchen cabinet," an unofficial group of advisers. He did not oppose federal internal improvements, but he vetoed the Mayesville Road Bill (1830) on the ground that it favored local rather than national interests. In his annual message of 1830, Jackson defended the high Tariff of 1828 ("Tariff of Abominations"). Later, however, he

supported downward revision to conciliate the South, but while the Tariff of 1832 reduced duties, it was still protectionist. When a South Carolina convention passed a "nullification" ordinance prohibiting the collection of tariff duties in the state, Congress passed a Force Bill (1833) giving the president authority to enforce the tariff. A compromise tariff formulated by Henry Clay (1833) led to repeal of the nullification ordinance, thus averting a conflict.

A hard-money man who disliked commercial banks, Jackson questioned the constitutionality of the United States Bank, whose charter was due to expire in 1836. Fearful that Jackson would not recharter the bank, **Nicholas Biddle,** the bank's president, applied for immediate renewal, forcing Jackson to take a stand before the 1832 election. Biddle's bill passed the House and Senate but was vetoed by Jackson, who stated that the bank was both unconstitutional and a monopoly. He made the bank the major issue of the campaign and easily defeated Henry Clay, 219 electoral votes to 49. He interpreted his victory as a popular mandate to destroy the bank and ordered all public funds removed from the bank, placing them instead in "pet" state banks. After the United States Bank charter expired, state banks increased the creation of paper money. Seeking to check widespread speculation in public lands, which easy money encouraged, Jackson issued his Specie Circular (1836), which required that only gold and silver be accepted by the government as payment for public lands.

After the election of 1836, Jackson retired to his home, the Hermitage. Although he had refused to approve the annexation of Texas while president, he supported annexation during the campaign of 1844.

As much as any authentic American hero, Andrew Jackson has provoked wildly disparate reactions from those who have sought to take his measure. Hailed by his admirers as the exemplar, if not the progenitor, of a new democratic age, he has been condemned by his detractors as a barbarous military chieftain who, as the tool of others or through his own misguided ambitions, imperiled the stability of the republic. As a national figure he was, in fact, a new type who broke the continuity of the tradition established by the Virginia dynasty and the Adamses. He represented some of the best, as well as some of the ugliest, features of the developing American character.

Proud, courageous, self-willed, and intensely ambitious, he was also domineering, savage in his hatreds, prone to violence, and primitive in his intellectual outlook. His conduct was shaped by the crude code of honor of the southern frontier and by his aggressive determination to acquire wealth and high status. Shrewdly cautious in planning large measures, he was bold and terrifyingly determined to bring them to fruition. His favorite roles were those of commander and patriarch.

In his public life his deepest commitments flowed from his fervent patriotism. "Our Federal Union, it must be preserved," was not only his challenge to **John C. Calhoun** but his often proclaimed creed. Coming to the presidency when ominous strains increasingly threatened the Union, he projected an appeal that transcended sectional boundaries, and around his charismatic figure the first broadly national party formed. He constantly directed his efforts toward compromising or eliminating those issues that were sectionally divisive and exhorted his fellow countrymen to maintain their "blessed Union."

He was a strong president, but his strength was exerted not to aggrandize the federal government but to reduce greatly its sphere of activity. "The successful operation of the federal system can only be preserved by confining it to the few and simple, but yet important, objects for which it was designed," was his dogma. He sensed that the young, sprawling, discordant Union was not prepared to accept vigorous assertions of federal authority.

In the presidency he saw himself as the tribune of the people. He did not claim to represent the "common man" but rather all the people, with the exception of the "moneyed aristocrats" and the "traitorous disorganizers" against whom he railed. He offered the people not specific programs to benefit their lot but freedom from interference and equality of treatment. He had no sympathy for the burgeoning reform movements of the era. He gave his protection to slavery against the assaults of the abolitionists and carried out ruthlessly the removal of the Indian tribes from the Southwest.

The climax of his administration was the bank war. He approached the conflict cautiously, but when the gauntlet was thrown, in the form of the recharter bill, he reacted with characteristic determination. It was thoroughly congruent with his character that he succeeded in utterly destroying the bank and that he failed to devise a satisfactory alternative.

Despite his nationalistic fervor and his propensity for military glory, Jackson was less prone to embrace an expansionist foreign policy than any of his predecessors. Especially remarkable was the restraint he exercised toward Texas. He adopted a position of correct neutrality while Texas fought for its independence, and he made no move toward annexation. He perceived that the Texas issue could imperil the Union.

Jackson is revered as the founder of the Democratic Party, but his attitude toward parties was, at best, ambiguous. The brand of politics he had mastered in Tennessee was a politics of factions and personalities, and prior to his election to the presidency he had frequently expressed opposition to parties. He was always more insistent on personal than on party loyalty among his followers. Nevertheless, he inspired a new style of mass politics and defined the platform on which Democrats were to stand for decades.

A towering personality, Andrew Jackson was an American original who altered the flow of constitutional and political development, redefined the nation's public agenda, and became the potent symbol of the democratic ethos. See Robert Remini, *Andrew Jackson and the Course of American Empire* (1977).

RICHARD P. McCORMICK

JACKSON, Helen Maria Fiske Hunt (b. Amherst, Mass., Oct. 15, 1830; d. San Francisco, Calif., Aug. 12, 1885), WRITER, REFORMER, was educated at Ipswich (Mass.) Female Academy and the Abbott Brothers School in New York. She published her first poem in the *Nation* (1865) and her first prose work in the New York *Independent* the following year. Subsequently, she wrote numerous articles, book reviews, and romantic poems for *Hearth and Home, Scribner's*, the *Atlantic*, the *Century*, and other journals. *Verses* appeared in 1870 and *The Story of Boon*, a poem, in 1874; *Mercy Philbrick's Choice*, a novel reputedly based on the life of her friend **Emily Dickinson**, came out in 1876.

In 1879, while visiting friends in Massachusetts, she heard at firsthand a recital of the injustices suffered by the Ponca Indian tribe and was swept, along with Boston's leading humanitarians, into a zealous crusade for Indian rights that would dominate the remainder of her life. Frustrated by Secretary of the Interior **Carl Schurz**'s apparent lack of humanitarianism in the Ponca removal case, she wrote *A Century of Dishonor* (1881), a critical history of U.S. Indian policy. The following year she and Albert Kinney of Louisiana were appointed special commissioners to investigate the conditions and needs of the Mission Indians of California. Hoping to reach a wider audience than she had been able to do with *A Century of Dishonor* and "do for the Indians a thousandth part of what *Uncle Tom's Cabin* did for the Negro," she turned to fiction. Her romantic novel *Ramona* (1884) depicted the disintegration of the Mission Indian culture under the relentless wave of Anglo-Saxon civilization. Jackson's *Sonnets and Lyrics* (1886), *Glimpses of Three Coasts*, reminiscences of travels in Europe and America (1886), and *Between Whiles* (1887), a collection of short stories, were published posthumously.

———

Like her father, a professor of literature and languages at Amherst, Helen Hunt Jackson possessed a brilliant mind, a ready wit, and a gifted pen. Unable fully to accept the devout orthodoxy of her parents, her doubts made her a religious seeker who hovered uncertainly between Calvinism and Unitarianism. This, and a lively curiosity, attracted her to spiritualism and the supernatural, colored her writings, and eventually helped guide her into humanitarian reform.

Jackson's moral indignation often boiled over when she was confronted with injustices to others, but she gave her attention to a successful writing career and avoided involvement in the multitude of 19th-century reform causes until 1879. Warm and friendly to those of whom she approved, she could be merciless to those she believed were evildoers. She was sometimes too quick to condemn and too impatient to see justice done, traits that lost some support for her Indian rights work and made personal enemies, but none that knew her well could deny her deep sincerity.

From the standpoint of literary quality her poetry would rank higher than her prose, although she would be best remembered for *Ramona* and *A Century of Dishonor*. Both books provided an important stimulus to the flagging policy reform movement concerned with Native Americans, and she believed that they were the most significant of all her writings. Jackson was a latecomer to the ranks of those who labored for the rights of Native Americans, and she regretted that she had not entered the movement earlier. But the nearly seven years she devoted to the cause helped bring favorable legislation for the Poncas and the California Mission tribes and made her name a symbol of the post–Civil War crusade for the rights of Native Americans. See Ruth Odell, *Helen Hunt Jackson* (1939).

ROBERT W. MARDOCK

JACKSON, Jesse Louis (b. Greenville, S.C., Oct. 8, 1941), REFORMER, POLITICAL LEADER, spent his childhood and adolescence in a secure, comfortable environment provided by his mother, Helen Burns Jackson, and his stepfather, Charles Jackson, a sharecropper and minor league baseball player who formally adopted Jesse in 1957 when he was 16. Jackson's biological father, Noah Louis Robinson, Sr., who was married and the stepfather of three children when Jesse was conceived, never denied his paternity but never contributed to his son's upbringing. Jackson graduated from Greenville's Sterling High School in 1959. Active in high school politics, he also earned athletic letters in baseball and basketball and was the school's star quarterback. In 1959 he turned down an offer from the Chicago White Sox because a white Greenville player received more money. He accepted a football scholarship from the University of Illinois but left after his freshman year because he was slotted for a running back position and not quarterback. In 1960, Jackson transferred to the mostly black Agricultural and Technical College of Greensboro, South Carolina, where he met and married Jacqueline Lavina Davis (1962). He participated in athletics, joined various civil rights organizations, and became a student activist, leading lunch counter sit-ins that forced Greensboro to integrate theaters and restaurants. In 1964, Jackson entered the Chicago Theological Seminary on a Rockefeller Foundation grant to train for the ministry. He was ordained a Baptist minister in 1968. Three years earlier, having joined the Reverend **Martin Luther King**'s Southern Christian Leadership Conference, Jackson was put in charge of the organization's Operation Breadbasket in Chicago. He became its national head in 1967 and under his leadership more than nine hundred jobs were provided blacks in white-owned dairies, soft-drink companies, and retail grocery chains—jobs that had previously been denied African-Americans. Jackson was with King in Memphis, Tennessee, when he was assassinated (1968), though his role right after the murder caused controversy among King's associates. Contrary to the facts, Jackson claimed that he was so close to King when he was slain that he was spattered with the martyred civil rights leader's blood. Jackson, hoping to be King's immediate heir, had a falling-out with the SCLC leadership and was removed from Operation Breadbasket (1971). That year he established his own organization, Operation PUSH (People United to Save Humanity), which contained most of Breadbasket's personnel (including Jackson's stepbrother, Noah Robinson, Jr., a

University of Pennsylvania MBA). The PUSH platform became a national and international showcase for stimulating black youths to achieve, pursue education and "be somebody."

Jackson increasingly became a national figure, appearing on the cover of *Time* magazine at the age of 27, and he began to transfer his energies to the political arena. In 1972 he headed a group of Chicago Democrats who succeeded in challenging Mayor **Richard A. Daley**'s slate of delegates at the Democratic national convention. He organized what he called the "Rainbow Coalition" as a springboard to enter the Democratic primary campaigns of 1984 and 1988. Both times he gained enough support in the primaries to play a significant role in shaping the Democratic platform, particularly on issues of concern to the black community. Jackson also became a presence on the international scene. In 1979 he made trips to South Africa, and on a whirlwind tour of the Middle East he was photographed embracing PLO leader Yasir Arafat, a picture that caused great pain in the Jewish community. When he was quoted during the 1988 campaign referring to New York City as "Hymietown," his relations with the Jewish community deteriorated further despite his later apology for those remarks. In 1990, Jackson, now a resident of Washington D.C., was elected one of the senators-at-large from the District and is engaged in a campaign for statehood for the residents of the Capitol.

Philosophic, sometimes poetic, Jesse Jackson played a prominent role in defining political and social reform agendas of the 1980s, just as Martin Luther King, Jr., did in the 1960s. Jackson, who once said that he must "march to the beat that he hears," viewed himself as the drum major of the downtrodden. Jackson has placed the spotlight on problems of black unemployment, inadequate health care, juvenile delinquency, teenage pregnancies, declining levels of education, lack of gun controls, and the misplacement of racism's causes. His chant, "I am somebody," and the statement, "Anyone 16 or 32 can become a father, but it takes a real man to become a dad," favorably influenced thousands of teenagers. His slogan, "Keep hope alive," encouraged young and old, black and white.

Jackson embodied within himself all the contradictions of American racial politics over the last quarter-century. He had his feet planted firmly in both traditions of the black movement of the 1960s: the integrationist wing that sought coalitions across racial lines and the separatist wing that saw black solidarity and confrontation with whites as the major avenue to black advancement. At times Jackson's central message to blacks was self-reliance—their need to advance themselves as individuals through education, self-discipline, and self-achievement. At other times his rhetoric stressed the theme of blacks being victims of implacable American racism.

The rise and decline of Jackson's popularity within the white community was related almost exclusively to which side of his message he was emphasizing at a particular time. Jackson the integrationist who preached self-reliance was immensely popular with whites, but Jackson the separatist who preached anger was immensely unpopular with whites. The Jackson who was seen embracing King's legacy was admired; the Jackson who was seen as allied with Louis Farrakhan was loathed and feared. Within the black community Jackson's ambiguity allowed him to win support from both wings. His black supporters ranged from the moderate, conciliatory older supporters of King to the angry militants who shared Farrakhan's mistrust of white society. Jackson's ambiguity limited his appeal to whites; they wanted the unifying Jackson but were never quite sure at any given time which Jackson they would get.

A high point of Jackson's career came during the Democratic primaries of 1988. His triumphant tours through several states conveyed the sense of a nation trying to heal racial wounds. Throngs came to greet Jackson in a number of towns and cities. Some of the crowds were virtually all white; many had voted for Ronald Reagan in 1984. Yet they cheered Jackson's defense of average people, his proclamations that what unified blacks and average whites was far more

important than what divided them. He called for a rainbow coalition of working people united against special interests. In Jackson's formulation, whites of modest means were no less victims of injustice than blacks. Racism, he argued, was not a sin of the white masses but a technique used by white elites to divide the natural coalition of the downtrodden.

The response to Jackson in many of these towns and cities was overwhelming. Many hands rose to touch him. For at least a fleeting moment an unusual number of white Americans took seriously the possibility of a black man becoming the president of the United States.

Although it is highly likely that no more than a minority of whites actually approved of Jackson, his popularity grew during the 1988 primary campaigns as he spoke out for racial harmony and biracial coalition politics. Most of the time during the primaries it was the conciliatory Jackson who was on display, and his unifying message dominated the Democratic campaigns. Indeed, to a considerable degree the message the Democratic Party was sending to the nation was more Jackson's than Michael Dukakis's, the eventual Democratic nominee. It remains to be seen which Jackson will appear in the future: the legatee of Martin Luther King, Jr., or the ally of Louis Farrakhan. Jackson's choice will determine his place in history. See Barbara A. Reynolds, *Jesse Jackson: America's David* (1985).

MELVIN R. WILLIAMS

JACKSON, Robert Houghwout (b. Spring Creek, Pa., Feb. 13, 1892; d. Washington, D.C., Oct. 9, 1954), JURIST, entered Albany Law School in 1912 and was admitted to the bar in 1913. In 1918 he became corporation counsel for the city of Jamestown and later general counsel for the Jamestown Street Railway Co. and the local telephone company. After serving on Governor Franklin D. Roosevelt's commission examining New York's state judicial system, Jackson took an active part in Roosevelt's 1932 presidential campaign. In 1934, Roosevelt appointed him general counsel for the Bureau of Internal Revenue.

Shortly thereafter he won an income tax evasion case against former Secretary of the Treasury **Andrew Mellon,** who was forced to pay a fine of $750,000. Jackson became special counsel for the new Securities and Exchange Commission (1935), assistant attorney general for the tax division of the Justice Department (1936), and assistant attorney general to head the antitrust division (1937).

After becoming U.S. solicitor general in 1938, Jackson won thirty-eight of forty-four cases before the Supreme Court, most of them concerning the constitutionality of such New Deal legislation as the Social Security Act and laws regulating the stock exchange and public utility holding companies. He became attorney general in 1940 and in that position helped negotiate the destroyers-for-bases deal with Great Britain. In 1941, Roosevelt named Jackson associate justice of the Supreme Court.

After World War II, President Harry S. Truman appointed Jackson to the War Crimes Commission. He served as chief U.S. prosecutor at the Nuremberg war crimes trials. Jackson played a prominent part in the London conference of 1945 that set up the International Military Tribunal and procedures for the trials; he then delivered the indictments and prosecuted the leading Nazi war criminals. In 1946, Jackson returned to the Supreme Court. Although he concurred in the conviction of eleven Communists for violation of the Smith Act (1951) and in the ruling that President Truman's seizure of the steel industry was illegal (1952), he was generally considered part of the Court's liberal wing. Some of his numerous books include *The Nürnberg Case* (1947) and *The Supreme Court in the American System of Government* (1955), published posthumously.

———— ∞ ————

Robert H. Jackson served the New Deal brilliantly and militantly in a succession of tax and antitrust administrative posts, drafted a considerable segment of the Roosevelt legislation, served formidably as U.S. solicitor general (a post in which he won a legendary number of his cases) and then as attorney general (his legal memorandum supporting the destroyer bases deal drew world attention), testified in favor of Roosevelt's court-packing plan, wrote a book highly critical of the expanding judicial power (*The Struggle for Judicial Supremacy,* 1941), and in 1941 was appointed to the U.S. Supreme Court.

Up to that point he seemed the very model of what a justice in the Roosevelt Court should be: he was Populist and antimonopoly and antiholding company in his economic thinking; he had moved with meteoric brilliance through a number of major New Deal posts; he was a superb legislative draftsman; he was canny about all the dodges of interpretation that judges had used for clothing the interests of the dominant economic class with judicial sanction. Yet he surprised everyone by turning out a very different kind of judge. At heart he was a maverick rebel who refused to do the expected. He broke away from the **Hugo Black-William O. Douglas** influence on the Roosevelt Court, mocking the new thrust of rewriting a good many past precedents in the image of liberal philosophy. He became an opponent of the judicial activism of some of his colleagues, whether in the area of property rights or personal freedoms. In his philosophy of "judicial restraint" he was closer to Justice **Felix Frankfurter,** and they shared a continuing feud with Black and Douglas, yet he could also mock Frankfurter's sometimes long-winded attitudinizing. On a Court full of individualists, he was the supreme one. He was the best stylist of them all, and the ironic smile that played around his lips and seemed settled there was translated into dissenting and concurring opinions that had a cutting edge of contempt for the rhetoric of judicial self-righteousness.

It would be useless to sum up his constitutional views as either liberal or conservative since he felt that both labels had lost much of their meaning. He could take sharp positions against the anti-Communist oath in the Taft-Hartley Act, in support of the "right of irreligion" as well as of religion (in the "released time" cases), in support of rape defendants who had been convicted by press headlines before their Court conviction. He spoke out with a canny realism against illegal searches and police lawlessness. But in the Rosenberg espionage case and in the Smith Act convictions of top Communist leaders he took the hard-nosed view that the Constitution was not intended as a suicide pact.

He was moved more than anything by a passionate commitment to the role of law as setting limits—around swollen economic power, swollen governmental and even judicial power, swollen dehumanized nationalisms. It was the last of these that may have led him to fly to Nuremberg in 1945 and set the frame for the prosecution of Nazi war leaders, thereby bringing closer the idea of an emerging world law representing the conscience of mankind. He was moved, at least in part, by a feeling of restlessness on the Court. He had a sense of himself as an icon-smasher, and his political hero was another Jackson—Andrew—who had brought a frontier vigor into the White House. In 1937 there had been a boomlet for him as governor of New York, but nothing came of it. He was generally recognized as Roosevelt's own choice to succeed him in the presidency, but when Roosevelt moved to a third term, nothing came of that either. Jackson later felt that Hugo Black had stopped a movement to appoint him chief justice. Out of this sense of frustration came his ill-conceived cable from Nuremberg with a bitter blast at Black, whom he accused of organizing a cabal against him.

He returned to the Court to serve under Chief Justice Fred M. Vinson and later under **Earl Warren.** His last two years were marred by illness, but while he had doubts about judicial lawmaking, he insisted on sitting with his colleagues to dramatize the Court's unanimity in the Brown desegregation decision in May 1954, several months before his death. Almost two decades later, during the hearings on the appointment of Justice William H. Rehnquist who had been Jackson's law clerk, a 1952 memo initialed by Rehnquist turned up, taking a negative view of what became the Court's reasoning in the case. Rehnquist recalled that he had summarized Jackson's views, not his own. The style was caustic and epigrammatic, and could have been either's. The issue was never resolved. See

Eugene C. Gerhart, *America's Advocate: Robert H. Jackson* (1958).

MAX LERNER

JACKSON, Thomas Jonathan ("Stonewall")

(b. Clarksburg, Va. [now W. Va.], Jan. 21, 1824; d. Guiney's Station, Va., May 10, 1863), MILITARY LEADER, graduated from the U.S. Military Academy (1846) and fought in the Mexican War at the battles of Veracruz, Cerro Gordo, and Chapultepec, rising to the rank of major. In 1851 he became a professor of artillery tactics and natural philosophy at the Virginia Military Institute in Lexington, Virginia, and a year later resigned from the army. At the hanging of **John Brown** (Dec. 2, 1859), Jackson commanded a corps of VMI cadets. When the Civil War broke out, he joined the Confederate army as a colonel and soon became a brigadier general (1861). He earned his nickname "Stonewall" by holding off a strong Union attack at First Bull Run (July 1861). Brevetted major general (Oct. 1861), Jackson took command of the Confederate army in the Shenandoah Valley. Forced to abandon Winchester when Confederate General **J. E. Johnston** evacuated Manassas, Jackson turned down the valley (north) to attack his pursuer, Major General James Shields. Called reckless by some, this daring maneuver forced the Union army to maintain troops in northern and western Virginia that would have been better used to help General **George McClellan** attack Richmond.

Confederate General **Robert E. Lee,** hoping to prevent the dispatch of troops to McClellan at Richmond, now sent Jackson against Brigadier General N. P. Banks at Fort Royal. In the ensuing battle and victory Jackson drove Banks through Winchester to the Potomac (May 1862), forcing General McDowell to suspend his march to McClellan at Richmond in order to protect Washington. Through swift infantry clashes Jackson sought to prevent the dispatch of Union troops from northern Virginia to the Richmond front.

In the midst of these maneuvers Jackson was ordered to Richmond but was delayed. His late entry on the scene at White Oak Swamp hurt Lee's plan to surround McClellan. After destroying a Union base at Manassas Junction (Aug. 1862), Jackson helped defeat General John Pope at Second Bull Run (Aug. 1862). Promoted to lieutenant general after the Battle of Antietam (Sept. 1862), Jackson fought at Fredericksburg (Dec. 1862) but was mortally wounded by his own men during the confusion of the Battle of Chancellorsville (May 1863).

Ungainly and rumpled atop his dumpy Little Sorrel, Stonewall Jackson sucked a mysterious lemon and rewrote the texts of war. Eyes flashing in a long, biblically bearded face, he comes to history a caricature, a man of distorted virtues—diet faddist, religious zealot, a dour and secretive martinet. Sometimes in battle he raised an arm and men believed he called on God for help, but in reality he sought to balance his body's blood supply. He prayed openly, often, and urged his men to similar profession. Some subordinates, notably dyspeptic General Richard Stoddert Ewell, believed him "mad" and likely to issue orders to assault the North Pole at any time. And some of the orders issued by Thomas Jonathan Jackson, VMI's strange professor of natural philosophy and artillery tactics, did ring reckless and alarming.

Men could not do the tasks he set, could not march so far so fast each day, then deploy and fight against desperate odds and win. But Jackson's men did. They did because he cared about them, about their physical condition, their small creature comforts (dry socks, for instance), about wasting in battles without purpose.

During the spring and early summer of 1862, Jackson turned the Shenandoah Valley of Virginia into a magical grid of war. Up and down that 150-mile stretch of lovely, bounteous farmland—the "granary" of Virginia—he threw his small "Army of the Valley District" into a campaign that etched his name forever in the annals of lightning maneuver. His "Valley Campaign" showed him a master of objective, surprise, concentration; a skillful tactician, a fearsome fighter,

and an administrator of growing ability. A tough disciplinarian, he created a hard-hitting, devoted army that he took to Richmond when General Lee called for aid against General McClellan's glacial advance up the Virginia Peninsula.

Subordination sat uncomfortably on Jackson's rising ambition. In the different climes of the Chickahominy bottomlands, in low and swampy ground alien to his Valley men and strange to his taste, Jackson fumbled awkwardly toward battle. During the Seven Days battles around Richmond his men languished strangely at the Grapevine Bridge, and in the fetid clutches of the White Oak Swamp they rested within sound of furious fire. What caused these lapses in Jackson's vaunted energy? One is clearly excusable: the stay at Grapevine Bridge was ordered by army headquarters. The curious lingering at White Oak Swamp can be explained only by fatigue, by that kind of twilight consciousness that numbs the mind and muffles the ear. But once out of boggy ground, "Old Jack's" men hit hard against Malvern Hill, and when Lee reorganized the Army of Northern Virginia for the summer campaign, he recognized Jackson's independent talent and detached him to operate against General Pope. After the Battle of Cedar Mountain—saved by Jackson's daring personal example—Lee combined Jackson's and General **James Longstreet**'s "wings" of the army for the Battle of Second Manassas and the Maryland invasion that culminated in the fighting at Sharpsburg along Antietam Creek in September 1862. There Jackson stood again like a "stone wall" to anchor Lee's left flank.

After his promotion to lieutenant general and command of the Second Corps, Jackson stubbornly contested the Federal advance at Fredericksburg in December. In May 1863, Lee picked him to meet General Joseph Hooker's flanking march near Chancellorsville. Jackson would command more than half the available Confederate strength on a vital detached mission. Lee naturally turned to Jackson for independent duty. They had become model partners in the skills of war—Lee the planner, Jackson the agent. They knew each other's ways and strengths. Lee appreciated Jackson's careful audacity, knew that he always grasped the objective, would do everything to secure it with economy of force and an eye to any advantage.

Wounded at Chancellorsville, Jackson rested calm in Christian certitude when death was imminent. His devoted wife Mary Anna heard his expectations of "translation," helped sing a favorite hymn—"Amazing Grace"—and listened to the last wish of a soldier concerned for his men: "Let us cross over the river and rest in the shade of the trees."

He might have thought then of the Potomac as well as the Jordan, for he was of Joshua's mold and forged with Ireton's mettle. Complex he seemed to many in his combination of iron and prayer; complex he was not to those who knew and followed him. Victory came to the faithful who strove mightily and well. See Frank E. Vandiver, *Mighty Stonewall* (1957).

FRANK E. VANDIVER

JAMES, Henry (b. New York, N.Y., Apr. 15, 1843; d. London, Eng., Feb. 28, 1916), WRITER, brother of **William James,** was educated in New York and abroad before entering Harvard Law School in 1862. He left law school after one semester, however, to pursue a literary career. His early stories appeared in the *Atlantic Monthly;* his early reviews in the *North American Review* and the *Nation.* After two visits to Europe (1869, 1872) he settled in Paris in 1875 and in London in 1876.

James was primarily concerned with the study of Americans abroad and the psychology of human relations. His human drama represented American innocence in conflict with European corruption. His career as a novelist can be divided roughly into three phases. First, the period from the Civil War to the end of the 1870s when he dealt with American characters in both European and American settings. Works during this period include *Roderick Hudson* (1876), a study of an American artist in Rome; *The American* (1877), a novel about an American businessman in Paris; and *The Portrait of a Lady* (1881), a study of an American girl's innocence in con-

fronting European subtleties and her corrupt American expatriate husband.

During the second phase of his career (1880s–1890s), James wrote naturalistic novels such as *The Bostonians* (1886) and *The Princess Casamassima* (1886), one dealing with feminism and the other with anarchism. During the 1890s James sought and failed in the theater. His final or "major" phase was distinctly experimental and was marked by innovations in the novel form and in narrative techniques. Two important works of this period are *The Ambassadors* (1903), a study of American provincialism as reflected in Lambert Strether and his growing awareness that life is meant to be lived to the fullest; *The Wings of the Dove* (1902), a study of a doomed American heiress; and *The Golden Bowl* (1904), the study of an innocent wealthy American girl's marriage to an Italian prince.

In 1915, in World War I, James became a British subject.

Henry James's uniqueness resides in his having been the only major American writer to devote himself for half a century exclusively—and with great power—to his art. He was a supreme artist of the novel. He invented new techniques and created new forms. He converted fiction in English from simple and often rambling storytelling into narratives possessing architecture, symmetry, and high dramatic intensity. Emerging from a half-formed America, a belated child of the Enlightenment, he traveled abroad in search of intellectual and artistic nourishment for his craft. A new civilization, he felt, might be developing some substance but it possessed neither the forms nor the structures required in art. James's entire career was concerned with man's capacity to order his life and create living myths. His quest was for creation, style, and beauty. He moved through the cities of Europe and studied their long past, having experienced in depth the newer cities of America. He remained always observant, sentient, distant; he was an artist who regarded politics, organization, and business as ephemeral forms of life. Only art endured. His world was narrow—but he mined its depths.

Henry James has reached an ever widening audience since his death in 1916. This has been due in part to the enduring force of his highly individual and idiosyncratic style, and the intellectual power he brought to his inventions. Above all he was a profound psychologist of human relations. He understood these long before the modern study of them begun by William James in America and by Sigmund Freud. His rendering of the subjective world of civilized man, the phantasmagoric states of the imagination, his grasp of certain kinds of abnormal psychology, anticipated the stream-of-consciousness movement in the novel; in that sense he was a precursor of James Joyce, **William Faulkner,** and Virginia Woolf. In the fashioning of his career and his legendary expatriation, he ultimately proved to be an archetypal American "culture hero," the prototype of the disinterested American artist.

As with the greatest artists, he did his best work at the end of his life. Had he died in 1889 he would be remembered as a superior craftsman and distinguished storyteller. But through the 1890s he began the writing of a series of experimental novels in which he tested ways of rendering man's observation of the world, and the disparity between "reality" and what the mind imagines. In this he came closer than any of the English novelists to projecting himself into the points of view of his characters. These experiments led to his writing his three final novels, large-scale studies of existential man: *The Ambassadors, The Wings of the Dove,* and *The Golden Bowl.* Rich in their allusive imagery and symbolism, their sense of the meaning of civilization, they are at once visionary dramas of man's quest for modes of life and "philosophical" in their probing of illusion and dream, the question of freedom, the need for order, the uses of myth.

Early hostility in the United States to James because of his expatriation and his abandonment during World War I of his citizenship has largely disappeared. There exists now general agreement that James was that rare figure in letters, the artist who at the same time possessed a rare critical faculty. Out of his workshop came important manifestos on the art of fiction; he created twenty novels, more than a hundred tales, a dozen plays. His letters belong to literature. His influence on modern novelists and critics has been profound. His contemporaries called him "Master," and his posthumous reputation has confirmed this large feeling for him.

A veritable library has formed around James's reputation. His works have been discussed individually in full-length books, and his table talk, when recorded, has served in the writing of many memoirs and reminiscences. More than a hundred studies of him have been published during the past forty years. His letters are legion, and it is estimated that some fifteen thousand survive. He was a master of ironic statement. His themes embraced not only what he called the "Americano-European" legend—that is, the return of prosperous Americans to Europe in quest of art and civilization—but represent a continuing examination of American forms of life. A section of his work is devoted to childhood and the failure of society to educate its young for the realities they must confront. He was a master also of the horror tale, his stories of the supernatural constituting a large volume in which the best-known of his ghost stories, "The Turn of the Screw," is to be found. Modern dramatists have quarried many successful plays out of his works—notably *The Heiress,* taken from *Washington Square; The Innocents,* based on "The Turn of the Screw"; and such successes as *Berkeley Square,* derived from an unfinished James novel and "The Aspern Papers."

James led a private life; an aura of mystery surrounded him wherever he went. And yet he was gregarious, voluble, and friendly; no other writer of his time knew so many of his fellow craftsmen. In his younger years he frequented Ivan Turgenev, Gustave Flaubert, Emile Zola, Léon Daudet, Guy de Maupassant, and Paul Bourget on the Continent. He was the friend of **William Dean Howells, Henry Adams, John Hay, Edith Wharton,** and **Stephen Crane,** among Americans; and in England he consorted with Edmund W. Gosse, Leslie Stephen, Robert L. Stevenson, H. G. Wells, George Meredith, and earlier, George Eliot, Anthony Trollope, and other eminent Victorians. *The American Scene* (1904–5), written on his return to the United States, remains one of the most poetically searching appraisals of the American civilization. See Leon Edel, *Henry James* (5 vols., 1953–72).

LEON EDEL

JAMES, William (b. New York, N.Y., Jan. 11, 1842; d. Chocorua, N.H., Aug. 26, 1910), PSYCHOLOGIST, PHILOSOPHER, was the son of a religious writer and lecturer, and the brother of **Henry James,** the novelist. The family traveled extensively throughout Europe and the United States; thus William received little formal education. After giving up plans to become an artist he entered the Lawrence Scientific School at Harvard in 1861 and the Harvard Medical School in 1864. He received his MD in 1869 after having interrupted his studies for a zoological expedition to the Amazon and a trip to Europe. Poor health and mental depression caused James to spend the next few years as a semi-invalid. But in 1872 he became instructor of physiology at Harvard and remained on its faculty in various departments until his retirement in 1907. James became interested in the new science of psychology and established the first American psychology laboratory in 1876 at Harvard, helping to gain recognition for the discipline as a separate laboratory science rather than a branch of philosophy. He attracted many followers and participated in the formation of the American Society for Psychical Research (1884). The culmination of his work in this area was *The Principles of Psychology* (1890).

In the 1890s James turned his attention to philosophy. *The Will to Believe* (1897), a collection of essays, dealt with the philosophy of religion and other topics. He also condemned the brutality of war in his writings and was an outspoken critic of the Spanish-American War and of imperialism. His *Varieties of Religious Experience* (1902) was a pioneering study of the psychology of religion. With the publication of *Pragmatism* (1907) James became recognized as a leading exponent of the pragmatist school of philosophy, which argued that the meaning of any idea rests with the particular consequences of that idea.

James transcended the aristocratic milieu in which he lived and worked. Spontaneous, warmhearted, energetic, and compassionate, he early freed himself from the social and intellectual conventionalities of his class. His instincts were democratic and his mind lively and far-ranging. He chided his associates for their parochial social sympathies; he also remonstrated with them for their absorption in abstractions remote from daily living. His adventure in ideas began at the family dining room table, where his father encouraged vigorous discussions at mealtimes. An emotional crisis as a young man from which he extricated himself by an existential act of faith in freedom played some part in his liberation. His exposure to Darwinism, which was agitating the intellectual community when he was a student, furthered his emancipation. An America in rapid change after the Civil War also reinforced his growing conviction that the fixities and finalities of traditional Western thought were no longer adequate for grasping reality. James was one of the first American—and Western—thinkers to Darwinize psychology and philosophy. His pragmatism, radical empiricism, and pluralism were thoroughly informed by the evolutionary point of view and foreshadowed 20th-century existentialism, phenomenology, and experimental naturalism.

Change, chance, individuality, and novelty were at the heart of James's universe. In an ever-changing universe, James declared, man was continually confronted with problems of comprehension and adjustment, and his mind was a crucial instrument of adaptation and survival. James's pragmatism held that ideas were hypotheses, tools, and plans of action for dealing with concrete experience and that the test of their validity was their adequacy in solving problems (theoretical, moral, aesthetic, practical) and in putting people into a satisfactory relation with experience. James did not deny the indispensability of abstract concepts in enabling the mind to leap over vast stretches of space and time and to hold huge masses of empirical data in its grasp. He asserted only that concrete experience was the *terminus a quo* and *terminus ad quem* of abstractions. He also declared that ideas were not eternal entities but dynamic, living formulas that continually developed in meaning with the growth of knowledge and experience. An idea put to work in the world was inevitably modified during the course of its application; at the same time, setting an idea to work produced some modification of the world itself. Thought and action were thus closely related, and it was by acting on the ideas he formulated that man contributed creatively to the ongoing processes of the universe.

As a radical empiricist James criticized classical British empiricism for cutting the stream of experience up into a series of simple and discrete ideas that the mind presumably linked together again by mechanical laws of association. Experience as we immediately know it, James insisted, is continuous, not atomistic, and the relations between things—temporal, spatial, causal, conjunctive, disjunctive—are as much a part of our direct experience as the things related. Conceptually, we do not see how Achilles can overtake the tortoise because we divide the distance between the two into an infinite number of points that Achilles can never traverse. Empirically, however, we perceive that Achilles does in fact overtake the tortoise. We should take our immediate experience at face value, James suggested, for it may yield insights into the universe in its deeper reaches that concepts (manmade extracts from the temporal flux) somehow miss. At the perceptual level of experience, freedom, chance, novelty, and creativity are living realities.

James rejected block universes; the monistic vision of creation as a neatly tied-together closed system had no appeal for him. The universe as we experience it directly, he said, is a loose-jointed, strung-along, untidy, Gothic sort of affair. In James's pluralistic universe, men could formulate many truths with a high degree of probability, but they could never reach absolute certainty

or final conclusions. "What has concluded," James liked to ask, "that we may conclude in regard to it?" In his philosophy, universal determinism (of either the optimistic Hegelian variety or the pessimistic Schopenhauerian form) had no place; man was free to some degree to shape his destiny. James called himself a meliorist. Meliorism, he said, held that the world "may be saved, on condition that its parts shall do their best." See Ralph Barton Perry, *The Thought and Character of William James* (2 vols., 1935).

PAUL F. BOLLER, JR.

JAY, John (b. New York, N.Y., Dec. 12, 1745; d. Bedford, N.Y., May 17, 1829), POLITICAL LEADER, JURIST, graduated from King's College (now Columbia University) in 1764, and was admitted to the New York bar in 1768. He was a delegate to both Continental Congresses (1774–75). He opposed the Declaration of Independence, believing that it would be followed by mob rule, but once the Declaration was adopted (1776), he supported the Patriot cause. As a member of the New York provincial congress (1776–77), he helped draft the state constitution. He then served as chief justice of New York (1777–79).

Jay returned to the Continental Congress in 1778 and was elected its president. In 1779 he was appointed minister plenipotentiary to Spain but was unsuccessful in his attempts to get both aid and diplomatic recognition for the United States. In 1782 he joined **Benjamin Franklin** and John Adams in Paris to negotiate a peace treaty with Great Britain. Jay suspected the motives of French minister Charles Vergennes and convinced Franklin that America should negotiate unilaterally with Great Britain. In the fall of 1782, after illness forced Franklin out of the negotiations, Jay withdrew America's demand for the cession of Canada in order to get the Mississippi River as the western boundary of the United States.

In 1784, Congress appointed Jay secretary of foreign affairs. In this position he tried to get the British to withdraw from their northwest posts and to make the Spanish leave the east bank of the Mississippi River. With **Alexander Hamilton** and James Madison, Jay wrote the *Federalist Papers* (1788), a collection of essays urging the adoption of the federal Constitution.

In 1789, Jay was named first chief justice of the Supreme Court. His most important decision was handed down in *Chisholm v. Ga.* (1793), in which he argued that a state could be sued by a citizen of another state. In 1794 he was sent to England to discuss British evacuation of the northwest posts, debts owed by both governments to private citizens, impressment of seamen, and trading privileges. The resulting Jay Treaty did not guarantee America's rights as a neutral on the high seas, failed to obtain trading rights in the British West Indies for American ships, and left other important issues to arbitration commissions. (The justification for this unfavorable treaty was that it guaranteed peace and trade with Britain, which were necessary if the new Federal Union was to establish itself.) The treaty was unpopular in America but was ratified by the Senate because of President George Washington's influence (1795). Jay resigned as chief justice in 1795 and was elected governor of New York as a Federalist (serving 1795–1801). Throughout his career Jay had opposed slavery, and as governor he signed an act abolishing slavery in New York.

———⁂———

Historians in seeking to understand John Jay have been content to follow in the moralistic and pietistic footsteps of 19th-century scholarship, which had as one of its purposes the creation of a roster of "useful" American national heroes. John Jay could be shown to have supported the right positions: independence from Britain, the need to replace a weak confederation with a strong new federal Constitution, the value of judicial review, the sanctity of debts and all property, and the evil of slavery. Moreover, with the victory of the North over the South in the Civil War, Jay became the far-seeing prophet whose great vision of an all-powerful centralistic Union was now confirmed. In this century this tradition has been

continued by S. F. Bemis in his *Jay's Treaty* (1923) with its pro-Federalist bias, and by Frank Monaghan's *John Jay* (1935), which while outdated in its narrative concern with great events is still the best treatment we have of Jay's life.

It is true that the picture presented by John Jay of his conduct, and propagated by his descendants who have written two apologetic biographies and until the sixties monopolized the Jay Manuscripts, stressed his rectitude, learning, and sagacity, his legal and diplomatic accomplishments, his obvious nationalism, and his strong antislavery position. The **Gilbert Stuart** portrait of Jay as chief justice brilliantly mirrors this image of a learned, logical, and impartial judge, and pillar of the Republic. The great weakness in the historiography of John Jay is its implicit belief that this image is correct and that Jay's actions and personality consistently conformed to this virtuous and static Roman ideal.

The views of Jay's contemporaries, friends as well as enemies, are in overwhelming agreement that this humorless man was absolutely honest in fiscal matters; they also show him more of a hater, more suspicious, more pro-British, and a good deal less logical and consistent than his authorized portrait. They saw the anomalies in his career. Jay started as a reluctant revolutionary driven to Independence by the more radical Whigs. As a lawyer he found no fault with English precedents no matter how archaic; as a revolutionist drawing up New York's 1777 constitution he wrote that suffrage ought to be limited to those who paid taxes; and his kind of federalism so favored the central executive, judiciary, and army as to see the states in the role of dependent corporations. Moreover, Jay the stickler for law and order violated his instructions as peace commissioner by entering into direct negotiations with the British rather than being guided by the French. Jay observed that it was to the "obvious interest of Britain immediately to cut the cords which tied us to France" and thought that America ought to be guided by her own best interest. He distrusted the French and held that the states "have no rational dependence except on God and ourselves." While historians support

Jay's independent action in negotiating the 1783 Treaty of Paris, the point is that John Jay selected those orders he would obey.

In 1782, Sir William Jay remarked that his brother "John has always been opposed to the independence of the United States. He hated France as much as his ancestors who were Huguenots, and if he could he would procure a reconciliation between England and her old colonies in America and baffle all the expectations of France by an alliance between the two countries." While there is animus in this fraternal statement, it does touch on the wellspring of Jay's Anglophilia, with which his need to believe in rational order went hand in hand. When Britain refused in 1785 to turn over the western forts because the United States had not removed legal impediments on debt recovery by British nationals, Jay accepted this excuse at face value; moreover, he proceeded to undermine his own government by divulging to Sir John Temple the contents of Jay's confidential report, which agreed with Britain and which had been submitted to Congress meeting in secret session. Furthermore, in negotiating the Jay Treaty this chief justice violated his stated belief in separation of powers—for judges ought not to serve in executive functions—and agreed that a joint commission could hear appeals from his own Supreme Court, thus undermining a jurisdiction he had championed at home. In fact, Jay had little faith in the Court's future and resigned in 1795. His final public service before his retirement in 1801 was as New York's governor. Almost alone of the founding fathers he had not been called to serve at the Constitutional Convention, nor had his countrymen vested him with the federal presidency. Personally, he abhorred the give and take involved in party politics. Behind Jay's profession of logic his career was marked by an urgent, irrational need for established authority, order, and correctness. His countrymen knew his accomplishments and saw his inconsistencies, which is something his biographers have yet to do. See Richard B. Morris, *John Jay, the Nation, and the Court* (1967).

JOHN J. WATERS

JEFFERSON, Thomas (b. Shadwell, Albemarle Co., Va., Apr. 13, 1743; d. Monticello, Va., July 4, 1826), PRESIDENT, attended the College of William and Mary (1760–62) and was admitted to the Virginia bar in 1767. He served in the Virginia House of Burgesses (1769–75), where he adopted an anti-British position in the controversies of those years. His work, A *Summary View of the Rights of British America* (1774), denying Parliament's authority over the colonists, marked him as a leading patriot. A delegate to the Continental Congress (1775–76), he drafted the Declaration of Independence. During the Revolution he worked to reform Virginia's laws. His Statute for Religious Freedom (1786) was a legislative landmark. He was governor of Virginia (1779–81) during the critical period of British invasion. Again elected to the Continental Congress (1783), he drafted the first ordinance (1784) for governing the West—precursor of the Northwest Ordinance of 1787—and devised the decimal monetary system. While minister to France (1785–89), he published his *Notes on Virginia* (1785), a natural and civil history of his native state. Although critical of some of its aspects, he supported the new Constitution and in 1790 became secretary of state in Washington's first cabinet. Issues of both foreign and domestic policy brought him into increasing conflict with **Alexander Hamilton,** secretary of the Treasury. Although he approved funding of the public debt, he considered the Bank of the United States unconstitutional and opposed the centralizing tendencies of Hamilton's fiscal system. When war broke out between France and Britain in 1793, Jefferson acquiesced in official American neutrality but sided with France, while Hamilton sided with Britain. These divisions within Washington's administration contributed to the formation of the opposition Republican Party. Jefferson resigned his post at the end of 1793 and went into retirement at his Virginia home, Monticello.

The Republicans ran him for president in 1796, but he was defeated by John Adams. As runner-up he became vice president. The president's warlike posture following the XYZ Affair, the creation of a standing army, and the Alien and Sedition Acts (1798) strained his long friendship with Adams. In 1798 he drafted the Kentucky Resolutions, which argued that the Sedition Act was unconstitutional and that a state could, in effect, nullify any unconstitutional measures passed by Congress. He defeated Adams in the election of 1800, but he and his running mate **Aaron Burr** each received 73 electoral votes, throwing the election into the House of Representatives where the Federalists backed Burr and threatened a constitutional crisis. But Jefferson was finally elected on the thirty-sixth ballot.

Jefferson's inaugural address was both a bid for political conciliation and a summation of Republican principles. His administration (1801–9) was marked by simplicity and economy. Internal taxes were abolished, but the national debt was reduced from $83 million to $59 million. When France regained possession of Louisiana from Spain, the threat to western commerce led Jefferson to try to buy New Orleans. He got more than he bargained for. The Louisiana Purchase (1803), negotiated by James Monroe and **Robert R. Livingston,** nearly doubled the land area of the United States at a cost of $11,250,000. Jefferson then sent **Meriwether Lewis** and **William Clark** on an expedition (1803–6) to explore this trans-Mississippi domain.

Jefferson hoped to preserve America's neutrality during the Napoleonic Wars, but Anglo-French violations of neutral rights made this increasingly difficult. Finally, after new belligerent decrees virtually closed the Atlantic to neutral commerce, he persuaded Congress to pass the Embargo Act (1807), prohibiting all exports to foreign ports. The embargo proved costly everywhere and unpopular especially in New England. It also failed as a measure of "peaceable coercion" on the European powers. Congress repealed the embargo in the waning hours of Jefferson's presidency.

In retirement Jefferson founded the University of Virginia (1819) and endeavored once again to achieve democratic reform of Virginia laws. He conducted an extensive correspondence and entertained at his home a steady stream of distinguished visitors from all over America and Europe.

Of the revolutionary founders of the United States, Thomas Jefferson was perhaps the most philosophical. He firmly believed that reason and inquiry might lead men away from whatever was false or twisted in human affairs toward the truth inherent in the nature of things; and the realization of this hope of the Enlightenment became linked in his mind with the promise of America. His intellectual range was very wide, encompassing such fields as architecture, linguistics, and paleontology, as well as those of law and politics, to which he was destined by the events of his time. He often complained of this fate and yearned for the tranquil life of his books and his family. Deeply serious, high-minded, and reserved in his intercourse with the world, he was seldom a happy political warrior. Yet he became the first hero of American democracy because his convictions went along with the spirit of the people and because of the power of his ideas and the public trust he inspired.

For Jefferson, as for Enlightenment thinkers generally, ideas were meant to act on the world. What was particularly original about the Declaration of Independence was not the ideas themselves but the determination to embody them in the foundations of government. Jefferson himself at once took up the task in Virginia. He achieved important reforms, for example, the abolition of entail and primogeniture, but failed in others, such as his plan of public education, which he thought essential for republican government. To make the laws reasonable and humane, to reduce privileges and equalize opportunities, to free the mind for inquiry, and to expand the bounds of popular authority—this was the dominant tendency of Jefferson's work throughout his life, and although he was often disappointed, he was never disillusioned. The individualism of his political creed, soundly based in the natural rights philosophy, was never fully reconciled with its democracy. Distrusting all government, he cherished the people less as rulers than as guardians of a free constitution. Fundamentally, his faith was in what free individuals could do for themselves, not in what government could do for them. It was the authentic democratic faith of a bounteous and open society.

Two sets of values converged in Jefferson, and the tension between them helps to explain the characteristic duality of his thought and politics. On the one hand he was a partisan of "nature" against "civilization": simple farmers were "the chosen people of God," cities were dens of iniquity, commerce was an expression of greed, and wealth was a corruption of virtue. In this and much more Jefferson stood in a venerable humanistic tradition. On the other hand he was a realist and a modernist: nature was to be conquered, the Indians were to be "civilized," the Americans elevated by the arts, science and technology encouraged, and foreign commerce—the contagion of civilization—liberated. Jefferson's ambivalent response to Europe epitomized the conflict. He admired the arts and civilities of the Old World but deplored its aristocratic conceits, luxuries, and oppressions, all so much beneath the natural simplicity and equality of the New World.

The famous quarrel between Jefferson and Hamilton turned on qualitatively different conceptions of the new nation. Both wished a strong Union, but Jefferson sought its strength in the trust of the people and the states, Hamilton in the energies of the central government. One viewed the Constitution as a superintending rule of political action, the other as a point of departure for vigorous statesmanship. One feared oppression, the other anarchy. Jefferson, envisioning a growing community of free nations, championed the French Revolution; Hamilton adhered to realpolitik and sided with Britain. The Hamiltonian alliance between government and speculative capitalism repelled Jefferson. Private interest corrupted public virtue; government was founded on opinion, not money and credit; and no good could come to a society floated on the artificial values of paper and stock. In 1798, doubling as vice president and leader of the opposition party, Jefferson became convinced that Adams and the Federalists aimed at war against France and annihilation of the Republicans. The Alien and Sedition Laws unleashed a virtual "reign of terror." The only salvation, he concluded, lay in the political intervention of the states. Thus it was that he drafted the Kentucky Resolutions, which not only contributed to the Republican victory of 1800 but implicated the defense of civil liberties in the resistance of states' rights with momentous consequences for the American polity.

Jefferson was a strong and, on balance, an effective president. Steering a middle course between the extremes of left and right, he tried to allay raging partisanship and bring about a "perfect consolidation" of political sentiment. The reformation of government was bottomed on fiscal policy. Internal taxes were abolished, the army and navy reduced, and the debt put on the course of extinction. Jefferson faced two great crises in foreign affairs. The first, with France on the Mississippi, led to the Louisiana Purchase—a triumphant conclusion to his vision of continental empire. The second, in which Britain was the principal aggressor, involved American peace, commerce, and neutral rights on the seas. Jefferson had long believed that the withholding of American trade could be a powerful force in international disputes, and he now determined to put this theory of "peaceable coercion" to the test. But the Embargo Act proved to be a costly experiment at home and failed to bring Britain to justice. Repealed after a trial of fifteen months, it would have succeeded, Jefferson always insisted, and saved the country from all the calamities that followed had it been continued a little longer.

Jefferson enjoyed a long and active retirement at Monticello, the Virginia home that was both a superb expression of his genius and a monument of his concern for the quality of life in America. The best fruit of these ripe years was the University of Virginia. From the grounds and buildings to the curriculum and faculty and governance, the university was his creation and the final testament of his faith in "the illimitable freedom of the human mind." See Dumas Malone, *Jefferson and His Times* (6 vols., 1948–81).

MERRILL D. PETERSON

JOBS, Steven (b. Los Altos, Calif., Feb. 24, 1955), BUSINESSMAN, was adopted shortly after his birth by Paul and Clara Jobs. He graduated from Homestead High School in Los Altos in 1972 and attended Reed College in Portland, Oregon, for one semester. He then hung around the campus, took a couple of philosophy courses, became a vegetarian, and experimented with LSD. In 1974 he worked as a video game designer for the Atari Company but stayed only long enough to save money for a trip to India. With a shaved head and a backpack he traveled through India in search of a spiritual leader. When his pilgrimage ended, he drifted back to California and his first love: tinkering with electronic gadgets.

While working on a frequency counter for a high school project, he needed a spare part and boldly telephoned William Hewlett, cofounder of the electronics giant Hewlett-Packard. The contact led to a part-time job with the company, where Jobs met Stephen Wozniak, a gifted technician who was five years his senior. Wozniak and Jobs eventually decided to work together developing new electronic products. Their first joint venture produced "blue boxes," outlaw devices used to make free long-distance telephone calls. But soon they began to dream of bigger—and more legitimate—enterprises. During the early 1970s computers were large and expensive contraptions, built mainly for large businesses. Jobs and Wozniak planned something different: an affordable computer intended for home use. Working out of a garage, the partners developed the Apple I, a computer about the size of a typewriter (minus the screen) that sold for the bargain price of $700. From the beginning Wozniak did the nuts-and-bolts work of creating computer hardware, while Jobs concentrated on organizing and financing a new company. To generate funds Jobs sold his treasured VW Microbus and borrowed to his limits. In this manner Apple Computers was born in 1977 with Jobs as chairman. Its skyrocket success became the stuff of corporate legends. Less than four years after its founding, Apple was a $1.3 billion corporation, introducing a succession of increasingly advanced computers, the Macintosh line,

admired for its "user friendliness." In 1985, Jobs left Apple after losing a bitter power struggle with John Scully, whom he recruited to help him run the company. That year he started a new firm, NeXt Computers, which was backed in part by **H. Ross Perot**. Though it brought to market highly sophisticated machines, NeXt simply could not compete with Apple and the plethora of IBM clones that came to dominate the personal computer business. In 1986, Jobs also purchased Pixar, a small computer animation technology company, from Lucasfilm for $60 million. Nine years later the Walt Disney Company distributed *Toy Story*, the first full-length computer-animated film using Pixar's technology; it became an instant box office hit. Pixar offered its stock to the public in November 1995, and in a speculative frenzy Jobs's $60 million investment was bid up to a price that returned him over $1 billion on paper, more than the value of Apple stock during the period he managed the company.

For Steven Jobs computers were an extension of his boyhood curiosity in electronics. He looked upon them as a new toy, and his knowledge of them was almost entirely self-taught. Given the hippie adventures of his youth and his California background, one might think Jobs would be a laid-back sort of individual. In fact, he once said, "I'm just a guy who probably should have been a semi-talented poet on the Left Bank." But in the office he is a lion. He works sixteen-hour days and expects the same marathon pace from his middle managers. In 1993, *Fortune* magazine listed him as one of America's toughest bosses. Said *Fortune*, "His drive for perfection is so strong that employees who don't meet his expectations … face blistering verbal attacks that can eventually burn out even the most motivated." He delivered a legendary tongue-lashing in the late 1980s to a group of NeXt engineers who had been working night and day—including over the Christmas vacation—to develop a revolutionary computer chip. Their toil and sacrifice did not please their boss, however. At a meeting before the entire company he berated the engineers, accusing them of laziness. Humiliated, several of them quit the firm.

Why is Jobs such a tyrant to work for? To begin with he is very bright and possesses a relentless desire to be number one in the very competitive computer industry. Few people he hires can keep up with him, a genius on a mission. But there is a deeper, almost spiritual force behind his driving personality. Having helped create a revolutionary product, the personal computer, and a multibillion-dollar industry, Jobs genuinely believes the revolution he helped initiate is a movement sweeping the minds of men and women like a new religion. He sees himself as an apostle of that religion. Jobs once told *Newsweek,* "There's something going on in here [in the computer business], there's something that's changing the world, and this is the epicenter."

In his teens Jobs was a loner. Now as a powerful entrepreneur he admits to having difficulty communicating with subordinates. Jobs is called both the *wunderkind* and the *enfant terrible* of the computer industry. Still, investors and job seekers line up hoping to attach themselves to his star. At Apple he made at least three hundred shareholders millionaires. In 1995, Jobs, who at one time was referred to as "the kid" by rival corporate executives, celebrated his fortieth birthday. The NeXt company has not enjoyed the dizzying ride to riches that Apple experienced, but many experts believe the Jobs success story is far from over. It is simply entering its next chapter with Pixar. See Jeffrey Young, *Steve Jobs: The Journey Is the Reward* (1988).

R. CONRAD STEIN

JOHNS, Jasper (b. Augusta, Ga., May 15, 1930), ARTIST, attended the University of South Carolina from 1947 to 1948 and then served in the U.S. army. Moving to New York City in 1952 to take up art, Johns worked as a commercial artist designing window displays for New York department stores, painting in his spare time. He held his first one-man show at the Leo Castelli Gallery in New York in 1958. Although not a pure abstract expressionist, Johns's work combines abstraction and even super realism with "pop art" influences. *Construction with Toy Piano* (1954, private collection, New York) and *Figure 5* (1955, artist's collection) are samples of his earlier work. *Painted Bronze* (1960, private collection, New York), with two Ballantine beer cans, shows the pop influence. Johns made many collages and graphics and later nailed objects, even a broom, directly onto the canvas, as in *Fool's House* (1962, private collection, New York). Johns usually exhibits at the Castelli Gallery but had a special one-man show in the Whitechapel Gallery in London in 1964. The Jewish Museum in New York held a ten-year retrospective showing in 1964. Johns has continued to produce original works in his very personal style well into the 1990s. Some of his well-known works include *According to What* (1964, private collection, Los Angeles) and *Passage II* (1966, private collection, New York).

In his remarkable series of flag and target paintings exhibited in 1958, the painter Jasper Johns put forward an artistic microcosm that included the germ of almost every major facet of 1960s American painting. Greeted immediately as the postulation of an alternative to the reigning abstract expressionist style, these paintings consisted of two-dimensional emblems—flags, targets, stenciled numbers—that filled the entire canvas area, forgoing traditional figure-ground relationships and forcing the spectator into intense confrontation with the image. Johns selected his flags and targets because they were "things which are seen but not looked at," and because they were symbols bound so intimately to their utilitarian functions that an entirely new set of conceptual relationships had to be invented for them when they surfaced in an alien context. Like tiddlywinks on a chessboard, images defined by the rules of one "game" were being forced to play another; painted on a canvas, numbers became something to look at, became "art."

Because he obviously utilizes visual imagery

as commentary on art-historical preconceptions, Johns has been frequently labeled "Neo-Dadaist." Despite the undeniable influence of Marcel Duchamp, however, Johns's combined debt to the philosopher Ludwig Wittgenstein, to the artist René Magritte's fracturing of the known and the seen, and to the composer **John Cage**'s aesthetics clearly cost him a Dadaist's career. In contradistinction to Duchamp, Johns makes art, not anti-art, with numbers and beer cans; in his paintings, furthermore, he is always as much artist as thinker, as much magician as logician, as much poet as plainspeaker. He is the sort of artist for whom new categories must be devised and new forms of criticism invented, and with whom we mark a major turning point in contemporary art history. See Max Kozloff, *Jasper Johns* (1969).

PATRICIA FAILING

JOHNSON, Alvin Saunders (b. Homer, Neb., Dec. 18, 1874; d. Upper Nyack, N.Y., June 7, 1971), EDUCATOR, graduated from the University of Nebraska in 1897 (MA, 1898). During the Spanish-American War he served at an army camp at Chickamauga, Georgia. After his discharge he went to New York City to study political science and economics at Columbia (1899–1901) where he worked under **John Bates Clark** and Edwin R. A. Seligman. He was a reader in economics at Bryn Mawr (Pa.) College from 1901 to 1902 and received his PhD from Columbia in 1902. His dissertation, *Rent in Modern Economic Theory,* was published in 1903. Johnson was a tutor and instructor of economics at Columbia (1902–6), also serving as editor of the *Political Science Quarterly.* Between 1906 and 1916 he taught at the University of Nebraska, the University of Chicago, and Cornell. During this period he wrote a textbook, *Introduction to Economics* (1909), and a novel, *The Professor and the Petticoat* (1914). In 1917 he returned to New York City to become editor of the *New Republic* (1917–23). *John Stuyvesant, Ancestor, and Other People* (1919) was a collection of his *New Republic* writings.

In 1919 Johnson joined **Charles A. Beard,** James Harvey Robinson, **Thorstein Veblen,** and other academics in founding the New School for Social Research in New York, an adult education school emphasizing the social sciences. In 1923 he became president of the school and greatly expanded its curriculum to include courses in drama, music, and dancing. He secured funds for a new building for the New School on West 12th Street, which opened in 1930. During the 1930s Johnson obtained funds from the Rockefeller Foundation to bring anti-Fascist German and Italian scholars to the United States, and he found places for many of them at the Graduate Faculty of Political and Social Science (founded 1933) of the New School. After the outbreak of World War II he helped French and Norwegian scholars come to the United States.

Johnson became associate editor of the *Encyclopedia of the Social Sciences* with Edwin Seligman in 1929. He wrote another novel, *Spring Storm* (1936), and *The Public Library—a People's University* (1938), a book dealing with adult education and public libraries. He was president of the American Economic Association in 1936 and president of the American Association of Adult Education in 1939. He retired from the New School in 1945 but remained active in the school's affairs until his death. He also published his autobiography, *Pioneer's Progress* (1952), and such books as *The Clock of History* (1946), *A Touch of Colors, and Other Tales* (1936), and *New World for Old* (1965).

"Middle-western crossed with the classics" was Alvin Johnson's own characteristic description of his antecedents. Born of strong, independent Danish parents, he became even in his childhood a deep student of the ancient languages and literature. Yet, never certain that he was constituted for a life of scholarship, he hungered persistently for action. In retrospect, his career was supremely that of the activist educator.

A multifarious man—classicist, economist, editor, novelist, short-story writer, administrator and champion of public libraries and of adult education—he was always eager for new horizons. His breadth of learning was extraordinary.

"He was the last man who knew everything there was to know," said Max Lerner, "and he carried it so lightly that you never felt that you were walking in his shadow." His colorful conversation, his wisdom, experience, and love of people revealed an unfailing humanism.

"A.J.," as his New School colleagues fondly called him, displayed an ontological optimism toward life and an unshakable faith in man. Knowing the harsh face of discrimination in his own early life and appreciating, too, the international character of scholarship, he was providentially qualified to rescue many eminent foreign scholars from Fascist persecution and death. He played a notable part in the adoption of the New York State fair employment practices law—the first of its kind in the United States. At the New School for Social Research he not only pioneered in the unexplored field of adult education but by establishing the "University in Exile" he opened a historic, intellectual window to Europe. His life was rich in accomplishment and honors. Its inspiration lives on in the character and genius of innumerable others. See Alvin Johnson, *Pioneer's Progress* (1952).

CHARLES H. HESSION

JOHNSON, Andrew (b. Raleigh, N.C., Dec. 29, 1808; d. Carter Station, Tenn., July 31, 1875), PRESIDENT, entered Tennessee politics as a Democrat. He served as mayor of Greenville (1830–33) and was later a member of the Tennessee lower house (1835–37, 1839–41). As a U.S. congressman (1843–53), governor of Tennessee (1853–57), and U.S. senator (1857–62), Johnson worked for the interests of the small farmer, advocating public education, free homesteads, and social equality. He was the only southern senator to support the Union after 1861 and was elected vice president in 1864 on a Union-Republican ticket with Lincoln.

After Lincoln's assassination, Johnson sought to bring the southern states back into the Union as quickly as possible. His policies not only discriminated against freedmen and southern white Unionists but isolated blacks from the law's responsibilities as well as privileges. In 1866, Johnson vetoed the Civil Rights Bill on constitutional grounds, but Congress overrode his veto and in 1867 passed the first Reconstruction Act, which divided the South into five military districts subject to martial law, enfranchised freedmen, and disfranchised ex-Confederates. Congress also tried to restrict Johnson's executive authority by passing the Tenure of Office Act (1867), prohibiting the president from removing officials appointed with the advice and consent of the Senate. When Johnson nevertheless removed Secretary of War **Edwin M. Stanton,** the House of Representatives instituted impeachment proceedings, but in Johnson's trial before the Senate the necessary two-thirds vote for impeachment failed by one. Returning to Tennessee in 1869, Johnson reentered politics and in 1874 was again elected to the U.S. Senate.

Until recently scholars accepted Andrew Johnson's own estimations concerning the meaning of his White House career. He had cast his opposition to substantial post-Appomattox national thrusts within the crumpled Confederate states as noble Jeffersonian defenses of Americans' civil rights and of states' rights against the Republicans' industrial-military establishment. But significant reconsiderations of Reconstruction's actual alternatives, especially with respect to constitutional, political, and race relationships, have restored respect for Johnson's contemporary critics.

The new consensus is that his defectively limited capacity to grow and his Negrophobic emotional commitments underlay the states' rights constitutionalism that endeared him to the most conservative elements of the 1860s. Stated another way, Johnson wished change—history—to halt at Appomattox. He insisted that the Civil War's impact was to be only the Union's restoration and slavery's formal extirpation. But when proofs multiplied that hangover incidents of slavery, including exclusions of blacks from testifying in litigation and from contractual rights and responsibilities, persisted by reason of statutes and custom in the recent-rebel states, Johnson stood fast against the nation's playing any further intrastate role.

Standing fast was the hallmark of his prewar career. Johnson had bootstrapped himself into successively higher elective offices by parlaying his plebeian origins, semifrontier ruggedness in manner and speech, and stubborn dedication to positions once adopted. Adequate to bring him into the United States Senate, these characteristics proved wholly inadequate to evoke from Johnson distinguished service in that forum or in the wartime executive offices to which chance called him. As Tennessee's military governor and as vice president–become-president of the United States, Johnson was unable to work harmoniously with many of the men and institutions that were coping with the war's complex work. Instead of adapting to shifts in the currents of popular temper, as military governor and as president Johnson convinced himself that certain alterations required his unyielding opposition, that his opposition was the only principled course open to honest men, and that therefore only villains held contrary courses. Had he not become president of the United States owing to Lincoln's assassination, these personality characteristics would deserve no place in history. But by the end of 1865, many northern whites were caught up in a profound if ultimately temporary shift in views concerning federalism and civil rights. Johnson was repelled particularly because for the first time in America's history, a preponderant political voice called for nationally defined and enforced intrastate practices with respect to workaday civil rights practices. The president could not comprehend that many northern whites who were not Negrophiles believed that the nation's debts for meritorious wartime Unionism were far higher to the South's blacks than to the southern states. Other northern whites worried that freedmen would descend into anarchy and disrupt social order nationwide if they were less than wholly and equally responsible in their states' legal codes. Either way, decent biracial coexistence on terms other than master-slave (now obliterated) required national

intervention, according to the broadening, non-conspiratorial, thoughtful agreement northward.

But the president looked backward, not forward. He yearned for the amorphousness of prewar America when, according to Thomas Carlyle, government consisted of "anarchy plus a street constable." By sharp contrast, for a few years at least the Civil War and Reconstruction lifted the Age of Lincoln near to modern times. Republicans and their constituents edged toward shores dimly seen where successful advances in the substance of civil rights practices are national political concerns because they are the bare minimums of decent biracial coexistence and the best security for stable social order.

Incapable of achieving such an armed vision, Johnson cut himself off from all but the most conservative Republican-Unionists. His efforts failed to create a conservative national political coalition based on lily-white southern constituencies, on urban machines of northern cities, and on black-shy states of the Old Northwest. Johnson's increasingly obstructive course with respect to Congress dragged the presidency from Lincolnian heights of constructive leadership to the depths of the nation's first impeachment.

Escaping conviction by only one vote, Johnson completed his presidential term without testing again the constitutional and political limits of his office. His 1868 yearnings for a vindicative Democratic nomination and election of himself for a full presidential term went unsatisfied.

Fatefully, Johnson's White House career lowered the presidency to the Buchanan followership level with respect to Congress and to the national Supreme Court. Johnson's return to the Senate in 1874 was sentimental but otherwise insignificant. See Hans L. Trefousse, *Andrew Johnson: A Biography* (1989).

HAROLD M. HYMAN

JOHNSON, Charles Spurgeon (b. Bristol, Va., July 24, 1893; d. Louisville, Ky., Oct. 27, 1956), SOCIAL SCIENTIST, graduated from Virginia Union University in 1916. He earned his PhD at the University of Chicago in 1917 and enlisted in the army a year later, serving in France. After returning to Chicago he was wounded in that city's race riot of 1919. Johnson became an aide to the governor's committee to investigate the causes of the riot and helped write the commission's report, *The Negro in Chicago* (1922). He served as executive secretary of the Chicago Commission on Race Relations (1919–21) before moving to New York City to become director of research for the National Urban League (1921–23). He founded and edited the League's journal, *Opportunity* (1923–29). From 1923 to 1929, Johnson was associate executive director of the Chicago Commission on Human Relations. In 1928 he became chairman of the social sciences department and professor of sociology at Fisk University in Nashville, Tennessee.

While at Fisk, Johnson wrote extensively on the role of blacks in American society and on race relations. Some of his works include *Negro Housing* (1932), *Economic Status of the Negro* (1933), *Shadow of the Plantation* (1934), and *Growing Up in the Black Belt* (1941). He served on a three-man League of Nations commission investigating charges of slavery in Liberia in 1930, and on President Herbert Hoover's Conference on Home Building and Home Ownership as a specialist on black housing in 1931. He was a member of the TVA's sociology committee in 1934. He was named co-director of the racial relations program of the Julius Rosenwald Fund in 1942 and director the following year. Appointed president of Fisk University in 1946, he held that position until his death. In that post he helped develop a tutorial system for poorly prepared students and introduced the use of closed-circuit television as a teaching aid. Johnson served on an education mission to Japan in 1946 and was a delegate to a UNESCO meeting in Paris that same year. Some of his many other books include *To Stem This Tide* (1943), *Culture and the Educational Process* (1943), *Into the Mainstream* (1947), and *Education and the Cultural Crisis* (1951).

Charles Spurgeon Johnson's work as one of the pioneers in applying sociological research to the field of race relations earned him a place in the first rank of American social scientists. He was a member of that generation of black scholars and leaders who came to maturity during the years of transition in African-American thought following the death of **Booker T. Washington** and during the social and racial ferment of the World War I period. He was shaped by the events and mood of this era, as well as by his family and educational background. Growing up in a home environment that provided him with internal security and that prepared him for the world outside, Johnson developed a social philosophy based on a belief in the "improvability of man and of human nature." Another component of his social philosophy was his conviction that "no man can be justly judged until you have looked at the world through his eyes." Johnson credited Robert E. Park, his mentor at the University of Chicago, with helping him link his concern for humanity with science.

Johnson was interested in using social science research to effect social change. Edwin R. Embree called him a "physician to the body politic, carefully diagnosing social ills so that he can cure them and prevent them." His studies of black migration, racial violence, and urban and rural problems were made in this spirit. Johnson's critics maintained, however, that he remained too much the dispassionate scholar in viewing the social ills his research revealed.

As founder and editor of the National Urban League's magazine, *Opportunity,* Johnson made a significant contribution to the black cultural awakening of the 1920s. Along with **Alain Locke, W. E. B. Du Bois, James Weldon Johnson,** and others, he has been called one of the "nursemaids" of the Harlem Renaissance, for *Opportunity* was a medium of expression for young creative artists such as Countee Cullen, Eric D. Walrond, Jean Toomer, and **Langston Hughes.** Johnson viewed art, as he did social science, as a means toward solving the race problem. See Edwin R. Embree, *13 Against the Odds* (1944).

ARVARH E. STRICKLAND

JOHNSON, Hiram Warren (b. Sacramento, Calif., Sept. 2, 1866; d. Bethesda, Md., Aug. 6, 1945), POLITICAL LEADER, left the University of California in his junior year to work as a short-hand reporter in his father's law office. He was admitted to the bar in 1888, but his disapproval of his father's activities as a machine politician and counsel for the Southern Pacific Railroad led to a break between the two in 1904. Johnson first became well known as prosecutor in the bizarre Collins bigamy case. As special prosecutor in the San Francisco graft trials of 1907, he took over from prosecutor Francis J. Heney, who had been shot in court by a spectator, and secured the conviction of boss Abraham Ruef. His resultant popularity led to Johnson's election as governor on the Republican reform ticket in 1910. Reelected in 1914, he introduced many reforms including the direct primary, initiative, referendum, recall, woman suffrage, workmen's compensation, and limitation of hours of work for women and children.

When Theodore Roosevelt ran unsuccessfully for president on the Bull Moose ticket in 1912, Johnson was his running mate. But he returned to the Republican fold as an energetic supporter of **Charles Evans Hughes** in 1916. An apparent snub of Johnson by Hughes during a campaign swing through California, many claimed, cost Hughes the state by a small margin, and thereby the election. Nevertheless, Johnson himself was elected to the U.S. Senate, where he served for twenty-eight years. Johnson was a strong isolationist. He opposed U.S. participation in the League of Nations, international arbitration and arms limitations arrangements, repeal of the Neutrality Act in 1939, the sale of surplus warships to Britain and the Lend-Lease Act in 1941, the Bretton Woods international monetary agreement, and ratification of the United Nations charter. A supporter of Franklin D. Roosevelt in 1932, he opposed the president over the World Court and then in 1940 on the issue of a third term.

———— ◆◆◆ ————

There was something ironic about the fact that American newspapers published their accounts of the atomic bombing of Hiroshima at the same time and on the same pages on which they published the obituary of Hiram Johnson. The Washington *Post* for that day considered him a museum piece, and perhaps he was. He assuredly was the last of the great isolationists, the last survivor among the major opponents of the Treaty of Versailles. He was not, however, the greatest of American Bourbons, as the *Post* also described him, for he had been a Theodore Roosevelt Progressive whose fervor never waned, who all his life fought the battle for good government, attempting to write for other places and times, national and international, the democratic, humane principles he had written into California law during his years as governor of that state.

The roster of the things he opposed was, like that of his colleague in the Senate, **William E. Borah,** far longer than the list of the things he advocated. And on the national and international scene, as in the career of Borah, it was difficult to see much that he pushed to completion. He was another of the negative political leaders of the 20th century. He voted for American entrance into World War I and World War II, but he opposed the major legislative results of both wars—the Treaty of Versailles and the United Nations Charter. His dedication to the anti-League position became legendary, and he was a member of the so-called truth squad that followed President Woodrow Wilson across the country in the autumn of 1919, correcting Wilson's pro-League assertions, pointing out his supposed deceptions and other errors. As for the U.N. Charter, a few days before his death he sent word to the Senate that if he had been present at the voting on the charter, he would have voted in the negative.

Governor **Earl Warren** of California said after Johnson's death that "win or lose" the late senator had "fought what he conceived to be the good fight," and thus delicately stated the reason for Johnson's failure in national politics. He was in essence a loner. If only he had seen his way in 1920 to accept the vice presidential nomination on the Republican ticket with Warren G. Harding, he would have become president. His position in national politics would have been far stronger if while in the Senate he had not opposed, for his own good reasons, sooner or later, every president from Wilson through Franklin D. Roosevelt. His influence was therefore local or, at best, regional. Well before his death his reputation in national politics had disappeared. See Spencer C. Olin, *California's Prodigal Sons: Hiram Johnson and the Progressives, 1911–1917* (1968).

ROBERT H. FERRELL

JOHNSON, James Weldon (b. Jacksonville, Fla., June 17, 1871; d. Wiscasset, Maine, June 26, 1938), WRITER, REFORMER, was educated at segregated public schools in Jacksonville and at Atlanta University, receiving a BA in 1894 and an MA in 1904. In 1894 he became principal of a black elementary school in Jacksonville, which he expanded into a high school. He also edited a short-lived newspaper, the *Daily American,* and read law in his spare time. In 1897, Johnson became the first African-American admitted to the bar in Jacksonville; he practiced law until 1901 when he moved to New York with his brother to pursue a theatrical career.

The Johnson brothers formed an act with entertainer Bob Cole and toured the United States. and Europe. They wrote several songs including "Lift Every Voice and Sing" (1900), to many blacks a national hymn. Johnson campaigned for Theodore Roosevelt in 1904. He served as U.S. consul at Puerto Cabello, Venezuela (1906–8), and Corinto, Nicaragua (1909–12). Resigning from the consular service in 1912, Johnson returned to New York to take up writing. *The Autobiography of an Ex-Colored Man* (1912) told the gripping story of a black man who passed for white. Johnson published *Fifty Years and Other Poems* (1917) and was editor of a black newspaper, the New York *Age*.

In 1916, Johnson became field secretary of the NAACP. He organized the 1917 silent protest parade in New York City condemning the massacre of blacks in East St. Louis and fought for passage of the 1921 Dyer Anti-Lynching bill. He retired from the NAACP in 1930 and again turned to writing while serving as professor of creative literature at Fisk University (1930–34) and visiting professor at New York University (1934–38). During this time Johnson wrote *Black Manhattan* (1930); his autobiography, *Along This Way* (1933); and *Negro Americans, What Now?* (1934).

———⬥———

A man of remarkable versatility, Johnson made significant contributions to black cultural life and to the development of the black protest movement. In both roles he was a transitional figure—a moderate standing between two divergent camps. As a poet and novelist Johnson shared with the bourgeois writers of the late 19th century the view that to be "serious," literature must be genteel and respectable. Yet, like the younger artists of the Harlem Renaissance, he recognized the vitality of the black folk tradition and hoped to erect a "superstructure of conscious art" on the base of creative folk art. His best-known works reflect this vision. In *God's Trombones* (1927), for instance, he employs the cadence and style of traditional black sermons but converts them into "high art" by imposing on them a formal poetic structure.

As a social thinker Johnson was also a man in the middle, straddling the line between the cautious leadership of **Booker T. Washington** and the more militant approach of **W. E. B. Du Bois** and the NAACP. An early advocate of Washington's self-help philosophy, Johnson never accepted Washington's accommodationism, and he supported the NAACP's frontal attacks on segregation and discrimination. His appointment as field secretary of the NAACP was conceived as a move toward unity within the black movement, and one of his major contributions as an organizational leader was to help end the internecine warfare between conservative and radical camps. His leadership reflected his belief that militant protest against discrimination and the development of black-controlled institutions were not mutually exclusive. Personally, Johnson was a courtly and gracious man whose tact served him well in his role as a moderator and conciliator during a difficult and often stormy period in African-American history. See Johnson's autobiography, *Along This Way* (1933).

ALLAN H. SPEAR

JOHNSON, John Harold (b. Arkansas City, Ark., Jan. 19, 1918), PUBLISHER, worked for the Supreme Liberty Life Insurance Co. while attending the University of Chicago part-time (1936–38). He later took night courses at Northwestern's School of Commerce in Chicago (1938–40). As publicity director of Supreme Life, Johnson became interested in a journalism geared for blacks. After borrowing $500 he published the first edition of *Negro Digest* (Nov. 1942). Modeled after the *Reader's Digest*, this magazine was so successful that Johnson left his job with Supreme Life in 1943 to devote himself full-time to Johnson Publishing Co. (which he had founded in 1942).

The first issue of *Ebony*, a picture and feature story magazine modeled after *Life*, appeared in November 1945, and by 1967 its circulation had passed one million. (In 1973 it spawned an offshoot, *Ebony, Jr.*, directed to the children's market.) In 1950, Johnson also started *Tan*, now called *Black Stars*, a women's magazine, and in 1951, *Jet*, a sensationalist periodical. Johnson suspended *Negro Digest* in 1951 but resumed its publication in 1961 as a clearinghouse for aspiring black poets and writers. It is now called *Black World*. The Johnson Publishing Co. began publishing books in 1962 with a novel, *Burn, Killer, Burn* (1962), by Paul Crump, and a popular historical account of blacks in America, *Before the Mayflower* (1962), by Lerone Bennett, Jr. Having gradually accumulated considerable stock in Supreme Life, Johnson became its president and chief executive officer in 1964. He also owns a cosmetic company and a radio station. An activist in the civil rights movement, Johnson joined the board of directors of the Urban League in 1958. He received the Spingarn medal of the NAACP in 1966. President Lyndon B. Johnson appointed him to the National Advisory Council of the Office of Economic Opportunity in 1965. Today, Johnson's corporate interests have clearly made him the wealthiest and most influential African-American businessman in America.

⸎

Johnson's rise from a penniless Arkansas boy into the ranks of American millionaires is a success story in the well-known tradition. His publishing empire was well under way before he was 30 years old, and he had made his mark in other businesses long before he was 50. Interviewers have described Johnson as mild-mannered, affable, earthy, plainspoken, and a man of boundless energy. He neither drinks nor smokes. His folksy humor and unsophisticated characteristics of speech and gestures may disarm the unwary. Business associates and employees have found that beneath these surface traits Johnson is a shrewd and knowledgeable businessman. Some even characterize his business methods as "arrogant" and "ruthless."

One key to the success of Johnson's publishing enterprise has been his ability to assess and cater to the changing mood and thought of masses of black Americans. Concerning his magazines' stand on civil rights, Johnson once said: "We were moderate when the Negro population was moderate, and we became militant when our readers became more militant." Even so, Johnson's publications fulfill important needs for black Americans. *Ebony* is especially significant as a medium for the recognition of black American achievements and for articulating the hopes, ideals, and aspirations of black people. *Black World* is important as an outlet for the works of black writers.

Johnson's success was assured when he was able to persuade white advertisers that they could reach black consumers through his publications. *Ebony*, designed to appeal to the growing urban and middle-class black population, was important in this undertaking. In 1946, Johnson convinced three major national corporations to sign contracts to advertise in *Ebony*. Since that time Johnson has received millions of dollars annually in advertising revenue from national corporations. By 1972 the Johnson Publishing Co.

ranked second in earnings among black businesses. See Louis Robinson, Jr., *The Black Millionaires* (1972).

Arvarh E. Strickland

JOHNSON, Lyndon Baines (b. Stonewall, Tex., Aug. 27, 1908; d. Stonewall, Tex., Jan. 22, 1973), PRESIDENT, graduated from Southwest Texas State Teachers College (1930) and then taught in the Houston public schools (1930–32). During 1935–37 he was state director of the National Youth Administration, a New Deal agency that provided work for young people. He served in the U.S. House of Representatives as a Democrat from 1937 to 1949 except for a leave of absence (1941–42) for naval duty during World War II. While in the House he opposed a federal anti-lynching bill, the outlawing of state poll taxes, and the establishment of a Fair Employment Practices Commission. As a member of the U.S. Senate (1949–61), he was Democratic minority leader (1953–55) and then majority leader (1955–61), working closely with the Republican Eisenhower administration.

In 1960 he was elected vice president. He served as chairman of President John F. Kennedy's Committee on Equal Opportunity, which attempted to stop discrimination by corporations holding contracts with the federal government. When Kennedy was assassinated (Nov. 22, 1963), Johnson became president. In 1964 he pushed through a tax reduction and a Civil Rights Act outlawing discrimination in public accommodations. Johnson was reelected president in 1964, defeating **Barry Goldwater,** 486 electoral votes to 52, and receiving 61 percent of the popular vote. The large Democratic majorities in Congress after the 1964 election permitted him to obtain passage of his "Great Society" measures, including the Medicare Act (a form of hospital and medical insurance for persons over 65) and a $1.3 billion program for education and urban renewal.

Johnson's major problem in office was the war. After North Vietnam ships allegedly shelled American ships in the Gulf of Tonkin, off the North Vietnam coast (Aug. 1964), Johnson ordered air attacks on North Vietnam, and Congress approved the "Gulf of Tonkin Resolution" giving the president power to take "all necessary measures" to repel North Vietnamese attacks against U.S. troops stationed in South Vietnam. Johnson thereafter committed more and more men and arms against North Vietnam. This "escalation" of the war resulted in heavy criticism, especially by such members of his own party as Senator Eugene McCarthy of Minnesota, who announced himself a candidate for president in the 1968 election. When the primaries revealed the extent of the opposition to his war policies, Johnson withdrew as a candidate, throwing his support to **Hubert Humphrey,** his vice president. Johnson spent his remaining years at his Texas ranch, closely supervising the development of the Johnson presidential library in Austin.

Lyndon Johnson was a new type of man in the presidency, for he was fundamentally a cowboy in politics, exhibiting many of the characteristics associated in the popular mind with that species. He was shrewd, earthy, and often scatalogical in his conversation, generous to friends, unforgiving of enemies. He saw the world as divided between "good guys" and "bad guys," yet he was a natural conciliator—as he amply demonstrated when he was the Senate majority leader. He was also "quick on the draw," as his interventions in Vietnam and the Dominican Republic seemed to show.

Johnson was an admirer of the Texas ranchers amid whom he was reared. He grew up in modest—though never impoverished—circumstances: his father experienced a lifetime of ups and downs as a small-scale cattle speculator. Johnson felt deeply devoted to the people he grew up with—rich and poor alike—but he envied the successful men he saw around him and made them his models. As the years passed, his political climb helped make him a lordly benefactor of his neighbors in the "hill country."

Johnson early moved beyond the world of the Perdinales, although he never left it behind. His hand-tailored suits and his lucrative financial investments gave him the outward manner of a business tycoon—at home in the executive suite no less than astride a horse. But he never overcame a sense of inferiority in relation to the representatives of eastern culture—who happened also to symbolize the Kennedy administration. Often he expressed his feelings plaintively: "I come from the wrong part of the country."

Even as Johnson grew in power and prestige, however, he never lost his awareness of what economic insecurity felt like, for he had once known it well. Moreover, the struggle for equality and opportunity waged by America's minorities during his presidency seems to have drawn upon the deep well of sympathy for blacks and Chicanos that he had developed when he was growing up. The presidency gave him a chance to be at the head of the line in devising remedies for racial injustice. Still he took his place there without patronizing the people he was trying to help, with the keen satisfaction that the caprice of history had made a southerner "the Civil Rights President."

A comparable humanity undergirded Johnson's "war on poverty." And in supporting financial aid to education, he reflected his conviction that self-improvement was the principal way for poor young people to rise out of their condition. His own ambivalence as a youth about going to college, which he finally resolved in a decision to attend that brought so much pleasure to his mother whom he adored, may have been a powerful dynamic in his determination to be remembered also as "the Education President."

Johnson was not a reader of books. He learned most, he liked to say, from the great men he had known personally. As a congressman he adopted Speaker **Sam Rayburn** as his surrogate father; as president, he made Franklin Roosevelt's career "a book to be read and reread." But his Herculean labors in the White House, considered as a whole, completed an era rather than commenced a new one. They never aroused the people's enthusiasm, and Johnson, consequently, never had the people's adulation or affection—a frustration that he took to the grave.

In confronting the tragedy of Vietnam,

Johnson also took lessons from FDR and his era. He showed in word and deed that he had been indelibly stamped by his recollection of what the appeasement of Hitler at Munich had done to the world. Johnson was convinced that he must do what he was sure the democracies should have done in the 1930s in order to halt aggression. That the Munich analogy was false, that Ho Chi Minh was not Hitler, and that the rising nationalism of the so-called Third World could not be defeated even by the most advanced military technology were facts that did not enter Johnson's consciousness soon enough. When they finally broke in on him, the shape of his presidential reputation had been cast: he was a man schooled by the events of the 1930s and 1940s wrestling valiantly with new and unwelcome forces. His proud role in helping to prepare the nation for its stunning enterprises in outer space never mitigated the public's dismay over the intractable Vietnam War.

Johnson spent all his waking hours at politics, and he demanded as much of the people around him. He also demanded unswerving devotion and support. In return he offered his own Texas-size loyalty, which paid him rich political dividends. Yet he had an irrepressible fondness for secrecy in his dealings which gave him a reputation for lacking candor that he never fully dispelled.

The long and costly war in Vietnam that Johnson had not avoided, could not win, and did not end will long remain the dark shadow on his record. The domestic legislation and the generous spirit that actuated it will be his shining monument when and if a longer perspective reduces at last the size of that shadow. See Robert J. Dallek, *Lone Star Rising: Lyndon Johnson and His Times, 1908–1960* (1991), and Robert A. Divine, *The Johnson Years, Volume Three: LBJ at Home and Abroad* (1993).

HENRY F. GRAFF

JOHNSON, Philip Cortelyou (b. Cleveland, Ohio, July 8, 1906), ARCHITECT, graduated from Harvard in 1926, where he majored in philosophy. However, he was discouraged by his famous teacher, **Alfred North Whitehead,** from continuing his studies in that subject. He thus turned to his other great interest, architecture. He was particularly drawn to the Modern Movement that he had encountered on his trips to Europe, and through his friendship with Alfred Barr, the first director of New York's Museum of Modern Art who had similar interests, Johnson was chosen to found the museum's architecture department. He and a friend, the architectural historian Henry-Russell Hitchcock, organized a show (1932) whose catalog entitled *The International Style* (the term was apparently Barr's) gave the popular name to the Modern Movement and introduced Americans to the architectural avant-garde.

The exhibition stimulated Johnson's interest in becoming an architect, and he returned to Harvard to get a degree in architecture (1943). After service in World War II he rejoined MoMA and at the same time began his architectural practice. Though he studied with Walter Gropius and Marcel Breuer in the early 1940s, he was most strongly influenced by the great German-born American architect **Ludwig Mies van der Rohe**. Indeed, Johnson applied Mies's doctrine, "less is more," to the design of his own Glass House (1949) near New Canaan, Connecticut.

Johnson was closely associated with Mies in the design of the Seagram Building (1956) in New York City. It was therefore surprising that in his own practice he began to veer away from the International Style that he helped advance. He started to apply Asian, Middle Eastern, Gothic, and even Beaux Arts ideas in his work and thus allied himself with the critics of the machine esthetic.

Perhaps the key to unraveling the mystery of this eccentric man is his frequent assertion that architecture should be art and not a social program. Early and late he sided with Mies and his pure esthetics and against Walter Gropius "who wasn't an artist." In taking this stand he was able to defend himself for going from one style to another, something that all his critics have noted. His study of the history of architecture taught him that it was a parade of style and that archi-

tects have the freedom to draw from the various styles to advance their art. It followed that Johnson was an activist in the preservation movement, though he insisted that he was not a revivalist and that he was merely a borrower seeking to move architecture onward. To defend his eccclecticism, Johnson pointed to the fact that the pavilions he built on his 1949 estate reflect his changing point of view and show his debt to architectural styles as widely separated in time and attitude as those of Hadrian, Sir John Soane, Robert Adam, **Frank Lloyd Wright,** and **Frank Gehry,** as well as Mies. Johnson delighted in these references but played tricks with their scale and proportion. In fact, so plausible was his analysis of his work and so candid his admission of error in the progress of his art that one cannot help suspecting him of playing games with architecture as well as words. At bottom, it would appear that Johnson's personality is greater than his architecture. See Franz Schulze, *Philip Johnson: Life and Work* (1994).

ROBERT W. WINTER

JOHNSON, Virginia Eshelman. See Masters, William.

JOHNSON, William (b. Smithtown, Co. Meath, Ire., 1715; d. Johnstown, N.Y., July 4 or 11, 1774), MILITARY LEADER, DIPLOMAT, arrived in America in 1737 or 1738, to manage an estate on the Mohawk River owned by his uncle, Vice Admiral Sir Peter Warren. Some years later he established his own estate north of the river, near present-day Amsterdam, New York. His relations with Native Americans, among whom he often lived, were exceptionally good. He engaged in a lucrative fur trade with them and in 1746 assumed responsibility for administering the affairs of the Six Nations, but he resigned in 1750 when the colonial government failed to reimburse him for his expenses. In 1754 he was a prominent member of the Albany Congress, which met to discuss, among other things, possible federation for protection against the French.

In 1775, during the French and Indian War, General Edward Braddock gave Johnson command of the forces directed against the French at Crown Point. His victory at Lake George (Sept. 8, 1755), in the light of the defeats suffered by other British forces, made him a hero, and a baronet. He then was named the sole agent for those comprising the Six Nations. Johnson led the forces that captured Niagara on July 25, 1759, and was with General Jeffrey Amherst at the capture of Montreal in 1760.

Johnson favored a consolidated policy on Native American affairs, but in 1768 responsibility for relations with them regarding the fur trade was restored to the individual colonies. He also favored a policy limiting westward settlement, and this was embodied in the Treaty of Fort Stanwix (1768). Johnson continued to work with Native Americans, traveling almost continuously, and apparently used his good relations with them to secure large grants of land. On his estate near Johnstown, New York, which he founded, he introduced sheep raising and made other agricultural innovations. His house was frequently the scene of conferences with Native Americans.

William Johnson's colorful career dramatized two fundamental conflicts: a clash of cultures and of loyalties. The first he resolved in a practical, unorthodox way; the second was more complex and only partially resolved. Johnson was no theorist or philosopher. He handled obvious loyalty conflicts expediently but was unaware of the long-range conflict between his personal and official career and his loyalty to the Six Nations.

Johnson, a poor Irish immigrant, confronted the Native American culture on the Mohawk frontier. Energetic, flexible, and ambitious, he learned the language of the Mohawks and adapted to their life as few settlers did. His fur trade prospered, and he acquired immense land cessions aided by Native American friendships. Johnson's fair trading and integrity earned him the Mohawks' trust, and they made him a chief. He ruled the Mohawk Valley, presiding over Johnson Hall like an English lord, yet sometimes

living among Native Americans or leading them in attack, stripped, feathered, and body-painted.

When Johnson's loyalty to Native Americans collided with Crown interests, he trusted his judgment and acted pragmatically. His controversial Fort Stanwix Treaty ignored Crown boundary instructions but acquired for England present-day Kentucky and large portions of the Ohio Valley watershed. It attested to his power and practicality. He negotiated skillfully, reconciling diverse interests, and expected the treaty to be honored.

Ironically, Johnson, friend of Native Americans, was an unwitting but powerful threat to the future security of the Six Nations. He opened the Mohawk Valley to white Anglo-Saxon settlement, and his Fort Stanwix Treaty ultimately opened the Ohio Valley. His personal and diplomatic successes altered tragically the subsequent history of his Native American allies. See James T. Flexner, *Mohawk Baronet: Sir William Johnson of New York* (1959).

ANNE ZIMMER

JOHNSTON, Joseph Eggleston (b. near Farmville, Va., Feb. 3, 1807; d. Washington, D.C., Mar. 21, 1891), MILITARY LEADER, graduated from West Point in 1829 as a second lieutenant of artillery. He saw action in the Black Hawk expedition (1832), was promoted to first lieutenant (1836), but resigned to become a civil engineer. In 1838 he was recommissioned first lieutenant in the Topographical Engineers and served in the Second Seminole War, where he was brevetted a captain for gallantry. During the Mexican War he was wounded at Cerro Gordo (Apr. 1847), fought through **Winfield Scott**'s campaign, and was brevetted a colonel. After attaining the rank of brigadier general and the post of quartermaster general in June 1860, Johnston resigned from the army (Apr. 1861) and was appointed brigadier general in the Confederate army. Following the Confederate retreat from Harpers Ferry, Johnston took command at Bull Run, organized the southern counterattack (July), and was soon designated the fourth-ranking Confederate general. The next spring he retreated before **George McClellan**'s forces, skirmished near Williamsburg (May 5, 1862), and won a local battle at Seven Pines (May 31), where he was twice wounded. In November 1862 he took command of Confederate armies in Tennessee and Mississippi. In May 1863 he unsuccessfully tried to reinforce Vicksburg before that city fell to Ulysses S. Grant. In December, Johnston was assigned to the Army of the Tennessee with orders to stop **William T. Sherman.** He failed to do so and was replaced in July 1864 by General Hood. Assigned in February 1865 to command the troops being assembled to resist Sherman's march northward through the Carolinas, he failed, far more overmatched in numbers than before. On April 18 he signed an armistice with Sherman and surrendered soon afterward.

After the war Johnston became president of a railroad company in Atlanta (1866–69) and entered the insurance business in Savannah (1868–69). Moving to Richmond, Virginia, in 1877, he was elected to the 46th Congress as a Democrat from Virginia (1879–81). He served as U.S. Commissioner of Railroads (1887–91). Johnston wrote several articles on Civil War themes as well as a *Narrative of Military Operations* (1874).

In his memoirs Ulysses S. Grant wrote of Joe Johnston that he believed Johnston's "policy was the best one that could have been pursued by the whole South—protract the war, which was all that was necessary to enable them to gain recognition in the end." Grant was referring specifically to Johnston's Atlanta campaign of 1864 against the Union armies commanded by Sherman. In that campaign Johnston skillfully employed a Fabian strategy, conserving his own limited strength, using his inferior forces to harass Sherman's detachments, never standing to fight unless he could be reasonably sure of imposing disproportionately high losses on the enemy. Grant thought that Johnston's strategy was much better suited to the Confederacy's resources than **Robert E. Lee's** large expenditure of lives in tactical and strategic offensives. Unfortunately, Johnston's strategy demanded space into which to retreat, and by 1864 the Confederacy was run-

ning out of space; Johnston was removed from his command when his strategy seemed about to yield Atlanta without a serious fight. More unfortunately for both of them, neither the Confederacy nor Johnston had gotten around to a consistent attempt at the possibly effective Fabian strategy earlier in the war when space was available and the chances for success were much better. Except for the 1864 campaign, Johnston's record as a Confederate general is a great puzzle. With evident large abilities and much expected of him, Johnston on every other occasion dissipated his talents in quarrelsomeness, in an unwillingness to cooperate with the War Department and **Jefferson Davis,** and when he was a theater commander over much of the Confederate West during the Vicksburg campaign, in irresolution and timidity. See Gilbert E. Govan and James W. Livingood, *A Different Valor: The Story of Joseph E. Johnston, C.S.A.* (1956).

RUSSELL F. WEIGLEY

JONES, John Paul (b. Kirkbean, Kirkcudbrightshire, Scot., July 6, 1747; d. Paris, France, July 18, 1792), NAVAL OFFICER, born John Paul, served on English ships engaged in the slave trade and rose to the command of a merchant ship in the West Indies (1769–70). In 1773 he emigrated to Fredericksburg, Virginia, and added "Jones" to his name. Commissioned a lieutenant by the Continental Congress in 1775, Jones, as commander of the *Providence,* captured sixteen enemy ships. He was made a captain in 1776. In 1777, commanding the *Ranger,* he carried out raids on British shipping.

In 1779, Jones remodeled an old French ship, the *Duc de Duras,* renaming it *Bonhomme Richard.* In September 1779 the *Bonhomme Richard* met the more powerful British ship *Serapis* off the east coast of England. After hours of heavy fighting at close quarters *Bonhomme Richard* captured the *Serapis* but was herself so damaged that she sank two days later. Jones apparently never said in this battle, "I have not yet begun to fight," but the victory was largely due to his courage and daring.

In 1783, Jones traveled to Paris to arrange a

settlement of the question of prize money for ships he had captured in European waters. An agreement on this question was reached on February 1, 1784, but payment was delayed. Congress acknowledged his service to the nation in 1787 and awarded him a gold medal. The following year he accepted a commission as rear admiral in the Russian navy and saw action against the Turks. He resigned this commission in 1789, however, and went to Paris (1790), where he lived for the rest of his life. In 1905 what were claimed to be his remains were transferred to the U.S. Naval Academy at Annapolis. There is some doubt, however, about their authenticity.

———❧———

No other officer in the American naval service matched the record of John Paul Jones as a fighting sailor during the Revolutionary War. It is true that his successes in single-ship engagements and commerce destruction had no bearing on the strategic situation, but this was no fault of his in view of the immense superiority of the Royal Navy in the western Atlantic. There is good reason to believe that, given the opportunity to engage in complicated fleet actions, Jones would have performed effectively at that level of naval combat.

Not that his qualities as an officer endeared him to his colleagues. A self-educated alien of unimpressive size and appearance, he proved unpopular among his fellows, who were doubtless jealous of his expertise and resentful of the support he created for himself in high places. Jones's boundless ambition prompted him to seek rank and prestige by any means at hand and to quibble over the amount of prize money he considered due him.

The man's private life provides a study in contrast. He openly sneered at wealth and social position, yet he pursued both assiduously. By the same token he posed as a champion of equality and freedom, although he detested the French Revolution and served briefly with flag rank in the navy of the despotic Catherine the Great.

Gentle and urbane in his behavior toward women, Jones had numerous love affairs despite his less than handsome physique. His passionate nature was not confined to the boudoir, however; it brought on outbursts of violence that in two instances resulted in accusations of murder, and in a third a charge of rape.

In sum, Jones was a sailor of indomitable courage, of strong will, and of great ability in his chosen career. On the other side of the coin it must be admitted that he was also a hypocrite, a brawler, a rake, and a professional and social climber. Although these elements of his character do not detract from his feats at sea, they do perhaps cast in doubt his eligibility for a prominent place in the ranks of America's immortals. See S. E. Morison, *John Paul Jones: A Sailor's Biography* (1959).

WALTER R. HERRICK, JR.

JONES, Mary Harris ("Mother") (b. Cork, Ire., May 1, 1830; d. Silver Spring, Md., Nov. 30, 1930), LABOR LEADER, emigrated in 1835 to Toronto, where she was raised and educated. After teaching in a Monroe, Michigan, convent she became a dressmaker in Chicago. Sometime prior to 1861 she moved to Memphis, Tennessee, where she taught school and married. The 1867 yellow fever epidemic killed her family, and she moved back to Chicago and worked as a seamstress until fire destroyed her shop in 1871. She was incensed by the harsh working conditions and poverty she experienced during those years, and, according to her *Autobiography*, witnessed the 1877 Pittsburgh railroad strike, the 1886 Haymarket bombing, and the 1894 American Railway Union strike in Birmingham. She developed a hatred for the increasing power of industrialists and their political allies, and called for direct action by workers to better their conditions. However, she warned against doctrinaire radicals and theoretical panaceas. In 1900 she became an organizer for the United Mine Workers in West Virginia, where during the next two years she took an active role in the strikes that racked the area.

In 1902, Mother Jones, as she became affectionately known, led a children's march from Kensington, Pennsylvania, to President Theodore Roosevelt's Oyster Bay, Long Island, estate to protest child labor, and she organized striking

Pennsylvania miners' wives in picketing and taunting scabs. In 1903 the UMW sent her to organize a strike in Colorado, but when it was called off, she resigned from the union, feeling that it had become subservient to management. In 1906, by raising money and speaking in their behalf, she aided the successful defense of Charles Moyer, **Bill Haywood,** and George Pettibone against the charge of murdering Idaho Governor Steunenberg. In 1911 she returned to the UMW as strike organizer in West Virginia. Two years later she returned to Colorado to assist strikers against the Rockefeller-owned mines in the Trinidad district. Wherever she was she held rallies and raised funds, but her forte was setting a militant example. She often directly confronted management, risking jail and physical danger. In 1915–16, Mother Jones supported striking garment and streetcar workers in New York. She joined the Pittsburgh steel strike of 1919 against the United States Steel Corp. Her *Autobiography of Mother Jones* was published in 1925.

⁕

Mother Jones's life and career seem at first glance incredible. For almost seventy years she lived away from the public spotlight. Then, suddenly, in her eighth and ninth decades she flashed across the American labor firmament, an aging but still brilliant meteor. The influences and events that transformed Mary Harris Jones from a commonplace woman into a militant agitator remain shrouded in mystery partly of her own creation. For two decades (1900–20) Mother Jones agitated among coal miners, participated in bitter strikes, and endured imprisonment in the cause of union organization.

Yet many questions arise concerning the career of Mother Jones; indeed, her renown as a radical rests on a shaky historical foundation. A woman who publicly accused UMW officials of selling out their followers to the capitalist class, she negotiated amicably with John D. Rockefeller, Jr., in the aftermath of the 1914 Ludlow massacre. A militant strike agitator who often advised miners to arm themselves and, if necessary, to use violence, Mother Jones nevertheless observed in her auto-

biography: "Whenever things go wrong, I generally head for the National Government with my grievances. I do not find it hard to get redress." Famous for enlisting workers' wives in the labor struggle, she opposed woman suffrage and insisted that woman's place was in the home. On occasion the United States had no greater champion of the cult of domesticity than Mother Jones. Despite her appearance on the platform of the 1905 founding convention of the Industrial Workers of the World, she never thereafter supported the "Wobblies," and she apparently admired American socialists less than Woodrow Wilson. She was simply and essentially an individualist, one who chose to devote the last thirty years of a long life to the cause of the working class. Her influence on the American labor movement was, however, largely symbolic: the image of a grandmotherly, staidly dressed, slightly built woman unfazed by hostile employers, their hired gunmen, or antilabor public officials intensified the militancy of workers who saw her or who heard of her deeds. There is no sound study of Mother Jones's life, but see McAlister Coleman's revealing but journalistic *Men and Coal* (1943).

MELVIN DUBOFSKY

JOPLIN, Scott (b. Northeastern Texas, 1867 or 1868; d. New York, N.Y., Apr. 1, 1917), COMPOSER, the son of a former slave and a freeborn black woman. Joplin was raised in Texarkana, Texas, and as a child received music instruction from an interested German immigrant, possibly Julius Weiss. In 1896 he attended George R. Smith College in Sedalia, Missouri, to study music and improve his skills. He worked in a variety of saloons and dives as an itinerant musician, playing piano and other instruments, and singing. His first publications were in 1895. They brought him some money and recognition. But it was his "Maple Leaf Rag" (1899), published by John S. Stark of Sedalia while Joplin was living there, that brought him national prominence. He toured the Midwest, billed as the "King of Ragtime," playing dozens of his original ragtimes on the piano, among them "The Easy

Winners" (1901) and "The Entertainer" (1902). After living in St. Louis he settled in Harlem, New York, where he continued to write ragtime but in a more "elevated" or refined style. In all, almost seventy of his piano and vocal compositions were published, including two operas: *A Guest of Honor* (1903) and *Treemonisha* (1911), an ambitious work drawing on folk music themes. *A Guest of Honor* was abandoned after a few performances in 1903 and is now lost. *Treemonisha*, which Joplin published himself, had no complete performances until fifty-five years after his death. Joplin's *Complete Works* were published by the New York Public Library (1971, 1981).

Scott Joplin is valued primarily for his piano ragtime pieces, of which more than forty survive. These are the most sophisticated examples of the style, are crafted with imagination and skill, and are characterized by strong harmonic and rhythmic drive and attractive melodies. Aside from "Maple Leaf Rag," outstanding pieces include "The Entertainer" (1902), "The Ragtime Dance" (1902), "The Chrysanthemum" (1904), "Heliotrope Bouquet" (1907), "Pine Apple Rag" (1908), and "Scott Joplin's New Rag" (1912).

Viewed widely as an African-American form, ragtime was scorned by many. Joplin, however, was intent on winning respect for himself as a serious artist and for his music, which he called "classic ragtime." Neither goal was realized during his lifetime but was fulfilled beyond expectations in the 1970s when several of his ragtime works served as the soundtrack for the highly successful Hollywood movie *The Sting*. This led to a much deserved revival of interest in the man and his music. See Edward A. Berlin, *King of Ragtime: Scott Joplin and His Era* (1994).

EDWARD A. BERLIN

JOSEPH, Chief (b. Wallowa Valley, Ore., 1840; d. Colville Indian Reservation, Wash., Sept. 21, 1904), INDIAN LEADER, was originally called Hinmatonyalakit (Thunder Rolling in the Mountains), but his father renamed him Joseph.

Chief Joseph was the leader of the Nez Percé tribe that once lived in Oregon. Joseph assumed power after his father, the previous chief, died in 1873. At the time a crisis gripped the Nez Percé people. For generations the tribe had lived in the well-watered and fertile Wallowa Valley of eastern Oregon, but starting in the 1860s the land was coveted by whites—first by gold seekers and then by powerful cattle barons. Skirmishes broke out between pioneers and bands of Nez Percé. The army sent a large cavalry force to the region, and full-scale warfare erupted in 1877.

Unwilling to engage powerful cavalry units in open warfare, Chief Joseph led his people on a desperate march over tangled mountains and through uncharted forests toward Canada where he hoped to join with the exiled Sioux leader **Sitting Bull**. During the 1,700-mile trek Chief Joseph masterfully dodged the U.S. Cavalry while, like Moses, delivering his people to a better land. Following his surrender at Bear Paw Mountain, Montana, in October 1877, he was sent to Indian Territory (Oklahoma) but was allowed to return to the Pacific northwest in 1885. There, on the Colville Indian Reservation, he urged his followers not to drink or gamble but to educate themselves. His nobility in waging war and in accepting final defeat made him a hero in his times and a legend in American history.

"I love this land more than all the world," said Chief Joseph about his ancestral home in Oregon. But the chief was a wily political leader who, when war broke out, decided to take his people on what he hoped would be a life-saving retreat rather than stage a suicidal last stand against the U.S. army. In the spring of 1877, Chief Joseph and his tribe began their march toward Canada. He commanded four hundred to five hundred people, including children and the elderly. Only about two hundred of his band were effective warriors. He plotted a zigzag course, one not easily followed by pursuing horse soldiers. The path led through four states, twice over the Rocky Mountains, and across the newly opened Yellowstone National Park where the ragged travelers terrified tourists who were picnicking on the grounds.

During the march Chief Joseph fought only when he was cornered. Some seven hundred mounted troops hounded the tribe, but each time army officers thought they had them trapped, Chief Joseph and his followers melted into the forests and then struck out again in a new direction designed to confound their hunters. In one daring night raid on an army camp, Nez Percé warriors immobilized the cavalry by chasing off their horses. The officers, knowing they were being outfoxed and outgeneraled, developed a grudging admiration for Chief Joseph. One cavalry leader dubbed him the "Red Napoleon."

When forced to fight, Chief Joseph waged a brand of warfare unknown between Native Americans and whites in the west. He forbade his warriors to take scalps. Women who were captured were routinely released. White settlers in his path were generally left unharmed. The drama of his march seized the imagination of the country. Many people in the East, far removed from the "Indian menace," cheered as they read newspaper accounts of the great escape. Like a horse race, drawn out over months, the easterners avidly followed the tribe's progress toward refuge in Canada.

The saga of the Nez Percé ended in early October 1877. On a snow-swept peak in Montana's Bear Paw Mountains, Chief Joseph was finally surrounded and forced to surrender. The tribe was little more than a day's march from the Canadian border. In almost four months the Indians had traveled more than 1,700 miles and fought at least a dozen battles with the army. Fewer than one hundred Nez Percé fighting men remained alive.

But final defeat only enhanced the Chief Joseph legend. Witnessing the scene was a young lieutenant, Charles Wood, who wrote down the chief's surrender statement. It became one of the most famous speeches in Native American literature: "My people ask me for food, and I have none to give. It is cold and we have no blankets, no wood. My people are starving to death.... Hear me, my chiefs. I have fought; but from where the sun now stands, Joseph will fight no more forever."

Chief Joseph and his band were first sent to Indian Territory (Oklahoma), and in 1885 they were relocated to the Colville Indian Reservation where he died. He was buried not far from the Wallowa Valley, the land he loved. See Alvin Josephy, *The Nez Percé Indians and the Opening of the Northwest* (1971).

R. CONRAD STEIN

KAHN, Louis Isadore (b. Osel, Estonia, Feb. 20, 1901; d. New York, N.Y., Mar. 17, 1974), ARCHITECT, was brought to America in 1905. He graduated from the school of architecture at the University of Pennsylvania in 1924 and for the next year worked as a designer in the office of the city architect of Philadelphia. He then served as chief designer for the Philadelphia Sesqui-Centennial Exposition, and in 1928–29 he studied in Europe. He worked as an architect in Philadelphia from 1929 to 1933. He then served on the Philadelphia City Planning Commission, a WPA project (1933–35), and designed for various New Deal agencies (1935–39). In World War II he worked on a number of housing projects and from 1945 to 1953 he engaged in private practice in Philadelphia, except for a year (1950–51) at the American Academy in Rome. He was professor of architecture at Yale from 1952 to 1957 and thereafter professor at the University of Pennsylvania.

Kahn's most important work was done in the last decades of his life. The most highly regarded of his buildings are the Yale Art Gallery (1951), the Richards Medical Laboratories at the University of Pennsylvania (1960), the Salk Institute (1965), the Phillips Exeter Library (1972), and the Kimbell Art Museum in Fort Worth, Texas (1972). He received the gold medal of the American Institute of Architects and many other awards. With Oscar Stonorov he wrote *Why City Planning Is Your Responsibility* (1943) and *You and Your Neighborhood* (1944).

⁂

Louis Kahn's rise to prominence came late; it was not until 1951, with the design of the Yale Art Gallery, that he made his first major statement. The gallery, completed in 1953, was clearly a modern building but one that did not fit into the "organic" school of **Frank Lloyd Wright** or the cleaner, purer European modernist school of **Mies van der Rohe** or early Le Corbusier. Instead, it began to develop the design hallmarks that would emerge as uniquely Kahn's and influence a generation of younger architects: strong, simple geometric forms, basic materials such as brick and concrete, and the absence of many neat "finishing" details that would remove surface imperfections or cover mechanical equipment.

Much of Kahn's work was an attempt to express the essentials of architecture in a building. He believed that neat, false finishing both violated a building's essential purity and destroyed the natural beauty of the materials. The Yale Art Gallery's ceiling of exposed concrete in tetrahedronal patterns with air and heating ducts exposed was at first criticized as raw; later it came to be accepted as a means of enhancing both the natural qualities of the materials and the functions of the building.

Kahn liked to differentiate between what he called "servant" spaces, the mechanical innards of a building, and "served" spaces, the parts that were used by people. The major expression of this concept was in the Richards Medical Laboratories at the University of Pennsylvania, a grouping of seven-story towers of brick that contain stairwells, elevators, and exhaust systems, with the "served" laboratories of glass interspersed around the "servant" towers.

After the Richards Laboratories, **Dr. Jonas Salk**, discoverer of the polio vaccine, offered Kahn the commission for what came to be one of his most acclaimed buildings, the wood-and-concrete laboratory for the Institute of Biological Studies at La Jolla, California. Kahn's work was, as Ada Louise Huxtable has said, both "timeless" and "daringly contemporary." He was probably the most influential American architect of his day, both as a designer and as a trainer of students. See Vincent Scully, Jr., *Louis I. Kahn* (1962).

PAUL GOLDBERGER

KAISER, Henry J. (b. Sprout Brook, N.Y., May 9, 1882; d. Honolulu, Hawaii, Aug. 24, 1967), MANUFACTURER, left school at the age of 13. He held various jobs before becoming a junior partner in the photographic concern of Brownell and Kaiser at Lake Placid, New York, in 1904. Within a year he had purchased the business. He moved to Spokane, Washington, in 1906 and joined a construction company there in 1912. In 1914 he established the Henry J. Kaiser Co. and for the next sixteen years concentrated on highway construction in the Pacific Northwest, California, and Cuba. In 1931 he became head of Six Companies, Inc., a partnership of six contracting firms, which constructed the Hoover (Boulder) Dam on the Colorado River. Thereafter during the 1930s he headed such companies as Bridge Builders, Inc., erectors of the piers for the San Francisco—Oakland bridge; the Columbia Construction Co., builders of the Bonneville Dam in Oregon; and Consolidated Builders, Inc., constructors of the Grand Coulee Dam in Washington. During World War II, Kaiser gained wide attention through his successful management of shipyards in California and Oregon. Although a newcomer to this industry, Kaiser perfected special methods of prefabrication and construction, which enabled him to produce a 10,500-ton freighter in less than five days. His operations turned out about one-third of the entire U.S. merchant shipping built during the war.

Not content to draw upon others for the raw materials needed in his construction projects,

Kaiser engaged in the production of such raw materials as cement, magnesium, and steel. He founded the world's largest cement plant at Permamente, California, and a huge steel plant at Fontana, California. After the war he expanded his industrial empire into the production of aluminum and automobiles. His billion-dollar Kaiser Industries Corporation was producing some three hundred different products at the time of his death. He was also noted for such philanthropic activities as the Kaiser Foundation Medical Care Program, which builds self-sustaining hospitals on the West Coast to provide treatment by independent partnerships of doctors through a prepayment health plan.

———

Kaiser was an entrepreneur in the 19th-century tradition. He combined broad vision, supreme self-confidence, hard work, and ability in the classic proportions. Unlike his earlier counterparts, however, he found many of his opportunities created by depression and war, with government as his principal customer. The giant public works projects of the 1930s and then the wartime challenge of mass-producing ships gave ample scope for his restless imagination and innovative abilities. His drive and enthusiasms, though sometimes excessive, produced solid achievements that made him the industrial hero of World War II.

A strong advocate of free enterprise, Kaiser was aided in his postwar strategy by governmental policy with respect to encouraging production and competition in basic metals for the fast-growing Pacific coast area. Kaiser surrounded himself with able lieutenants who built up a strong organization to manage the multifaceted operations that his appetite for new challenges brought into the Kaiser fold. Although his venture into the passenger car business ended disappointingly, Kaiser Aluminum developed into a major success, as did other Kaiser enterprises.

Even in his last years, when developing a Hawaiian resort complex, Kaiser showed the same drive and imagination that had made him a major figure in American industry. At the age of 81 he was still active, looking ahead to how the nation might meet its needs in the 21st century and urging all who would listen that nothing was impossible. Perhaps his distinguishing characteristic, however, was his concern for people and his belief in testing and developing their potential to the fullest. In this respect his innovative approach to providing medical care for his workers, which became a model for the delivery of such services, will be his most lasting memorial. See Kaiser Industries Corporation, *The Kaiser Story* (1968).

ARTHUR M. JOHNSON

KEFAUVER, Carey Estes (b. Madisonville, Tenn., July 26, 1903; d. Bethesda, Md., Aug. 10, 1963), POLITICAL LEADER, graduated from the University of Tennessee at Knoxville (1924), where he excelled in athletics and campus politics. He taught school for a year in Hot Springs, Arkansas, before entering Yale Law School. After his graduation in 1927 he practiced in Chattanooga and soon became a prosperous corporation and banking attorney. In 1939, after a narrow defeat for the state legislature as a reform leader in Chattanooga, Kefauver, a Democrat, was appointed commissioner of finance and taxation for Tennessee. Later that year he won a special election to fill a vacancy in the U.S. House of Representatives, serving until his election to the Senate in 1948. In the House, Kefauver supported Franklin D. Roosevelt's and Harry S. Truman's foreign and domestic policies and was particularly concerned with economic concentration within the American business community; he also established a reputation as an advocate of modernizing congressional machinery. His views on congressional reform were expounded in *A Twentieth Century Congress* (1947). As a congressman, Kefauver opposed the 1947 Taft-Hartley Act, was critical of the House Un-American Activities Committee, and favored federal aid to public schools. Unlike most southern congressmen, he favored anti-poll tax legislation and was only mildly opposed to stronger civil rights legislation.

In 1948, despite (or perhaps because of) the

vigorous opposition of Tennessee Democratic boss Ed Crump of Memphis, Kefauver donned a coonskin cap and was elected to the Senate in an antibossism crusade that also saw the Crump-backed candidate for governor go down to defeat. Kefauver was reelected in 1954 and 1960.

Less than two years after entering the Senate, Kefauver, as chairman of a Senate Committee to Investigate Organized Crime in Interstate Commerce, led an extensive investigation of organized crime in the United States from 1950 to 1951. Many of the hearings were televised, and as a result of phenomenal public interest in the new medium, Kefauver and his committee became overnight heroes across the nation. The investigation, which exposed corruption in New York's Tammany Hall and gambling rings throughout the country, won widespread acclaim. Kefauver published an account of the investigation, *Crime in America* (1951), and emerged from the investigation as a leading contender for the 1952 Democratic presidential nomination. Although sweeping most of the presidential primaries, he lost the nomination to **Adlai Stevenson;** four years later, after another unsuccessful campaign for the Democratic nomination, Kefauver gained the vice presidential nomination by defeating Senator John F. Kennedy of Massachusetts in a dramatic floor fight. However, Kefauver and Stevenson, who was again the Democratic presidential candidate, lost to Dwight D. Eisenhower and Richard M. Nixon by an electoral vote of 457 to 73. During the remainder of his career Kefauver concentrated primarily on the Senate Subcommittee on Antitrust and Monopoly, which he chaired. He investigated monopoly pricing in major industries, including the drug, steel, and electrical machinery industries. By the time of his death he was generally regarded as the champion of consumer interests in the U.S. Congress.

⁂

Estes Kefauver was one of the great enigmas of American politics in the middle third of the 20th century. Although he was an unflagging champion of civil liberties, the basically conservative Tennessee electorate nevertheless first sent him to the Senate during the postwar anti-Communist hysteria and reelected him six years later in the midst of the **Joseph McCarthy** era. A gentle persuader on behalf of civil rights, he was a three-time winner of segregationist Tennessee's endorsement in periods when concern over black progress was especially aroused. A persistent advocate of consumer protection, he carried on a lonely battle against monopoly at a time when traditional ideals of free competition were considered increasingly anachronistic, especially by the powerful corporate interests that came to look upon him as perhaps the most dangerous threat to their profitable neomonopolistic practices. Finally, in an era in which sheer numbers made a truly personal approach to politics difficult, Kefauver maintained, not only in his Senate and presidential campaigns but also in his day-to-day public service, a unique interest in the individual citizen, both in Tennessee and across the country. In the process he many times bypassed and thus alienated the professional politicians who valued above all the team player sensitive to the interests of the organization, even when there was conflict between those interests and a conscientious concern for the public interest.

An understanding of what Kefauver stood for and fought for furnishes only part of the explanation of his success as a political figure. Equally important is the recognition that he possessed a special kind of charisma—dramatically enhanced, of course, by his appeal to the traditional American sympathy for the underdog, whether fighting organized crime, political bosses, or corporation presidents—but founded ultimately on Kefauver's uncanny ability to make an incredible number of his fellow citizens feel that something very personal was at stake when his career was on the line. It was a talent that almost defies objective analysis and certainly cannot be explained simply in terms of hands shaken, letters written, speeches made, or favors done in response to the avalanche of requests for aid and assistance that flooded his Washington office. It was a gift that perhaps found its most objective expression in a tone of voice that communicated a combination of concern, fairness, integrity, understanding, and, to a surprising degree, help-lessness—not in a personal sense but in a politi-cal sense, as if the success or failure of the imme-diate cause rested in the hands of each and every individual who was exposed to Kefauver's appeal. It is therefore easy to see how the quali-ties that led to Kefauver's success with the "peo-ple" contributed to his problems with the profes-sional politicians, who respect political strength, not weakness. He was the rarest of political ani-mals—a very successful political leader who was never a true politician but, rather, an advocate for his own legislative objectives. These, however, bore a striking similarity to the public interest. His was an approach to issues that left little room for negotiation and compromise. See Joseph Bruce Gorman, *Kefauver: A Political Biography* (1971).

JOSEPH BRUCE GORMAN

KELLEY, Florence (b. Philadelphia, Pa., Sept. 12, 1859; d. Germantown, Pa., Feb. 17, 1932), REFORMER, was the daughter of William D. ("Pig Iron") Kelley, a Democratic congressman from Pennsylvania. She graduated from Cornell University in 1882. Refused permission to study law at the University of Pennsylvania because of her sex, she took courses in law and economics at the University of Zurich (1883–85). She also made a study of Swiss social legislation. While abroad she translated Friedrich Engels's *Condition of the Working Class in England in 1844* (1887), joined the Socialist Party, married, and then went to New York with her husband and son. During 1891–99 she worked at Hull House, the famous Chicago settlement house.

In 1892, Kelley was asked by U.S. Commissioner of Labor **Carroll D. Wright** to supervise an investigation of slum conditions in Chicago, a study that resulted in the *Hull House Maps and Papers* (1895). In 1893–97 she investigat-ed tenement workshops as Governor **John Peter Altgeld**'s appointee to the position of chief Illinois factory inspector, the first woman ever to hold that post. At the same time she studied law at Northwestern University, gaining her degree

in 1895. Kelley also succeeded in having an "Anti-Sweatshop Bill" with an eight-hour clause passed by the Illinois state legislature (1893). In 1899 she went to New York as general secretary of the National Consumers' League and lived at the Henry Street Settlement House in New York City. She lobbied for legal protection of women workers against long hours and unhealthy condi-tions of work and night work and for the U.S. Children's Bureau, which was established in 1912. In 1910 she became one of the founding members of the National Association for the Advancement of Colored People. In 1917–18 she was secretary of the U.S. Board of Control for Labor Standards for Army Clothing. In 1919 she was a delegate to the International Congress of Women for Permanent Peace at Zurich, and in 1921 she attended and addressed a Pan-African Congress in London. In the late 1920s she suc-ceeded in having radium poisoning listed as a compensable disease under the Workmen's Compensation Act. Besides many articles, Kelley wrote four *Annual Reports of the Factory Inspectors of Illinois* (1894–97) and a *Special Report on Smallpox* (1894), *Some Ethical Gains Through Legislation* (1905), and *Modern Industry* (1913).

―――

When Florence Kelley began her fight first to protect and then to "abolish" the working child, she confronted a climate of opinion that accepted as inevitable the miseries attendant on post–Civil War industrialization.

She came into battle well prepared. A father who early instilled in her an awareness of eco-nomic and social injustice, and a Quaker grand-aunt who made conscience the arbiter of action, set her firmly on the road of reform. A socialist outlook, acquired during her student days in Zurich, gave new depth to her belief in the need for social change.

Her campaigns to effect change were based on her confidence that once people knew the facts they would act. From tenement sweatshop and dingy factory, from coal mine and cotton mill, she gathered her facts and fashioned them into an irresistible demand for legislation mandating cleaner workrooms, shorter hours, and compulsory education for children to age 16. Carrying the struggle into almost every state in the Union, she organized some sixty local Consumers' Leagues with members pledged not to buy from manufacturers who employed child labor. And always she emphasized: "It is boys and girls who are being maimed, not statistics."

Peace, woman suffrage, the rights of black people, education, the labor movement, all claimed her energies and her devotion. Few could listen to this woman—dressed in sober black and arguing so earnestly and cogently—and not be moved to take a second look at their own predilections and prejudices.

It is not without reason that Justice **Felix Frankfurter** called her "a woman who had probably the largest single share in shaping the social history of the United States during the first thirty years of the century." See Dorothy Rose Blumberg, *Florence Kelley: The Making of a Social Pioneer* (1966).

DOROTHY ROSE BLUMBERG

KELLOGG, Frank Billings (b. Potsdam, N.Y., Dec. 22, 1856; d. St. Paul, Minn., Dec. 21, 1937), POLITICAL LEADER, moved to southern Minnesota in 1865. He studied law in Rochester, Minnesota, and was admitted to the bar in 1877. After ten years of practice, Kellogg joined the firm of his cousin, Cushman Kellogg Davis, and established connections with railroads and iron interests, amassing a modest fortune.

Kellogg supported President Theodore Roosevelt's trust-busting activities. His prosecution of the Standard Oil Trust made him nationally known. He was elected president of the American Bar Association in 1912. Always active in the Republican Party, he was elected to the Senate from Minnesota in 1916. He supported American entry into World War I and was a "mild revisionist" on the peace treaty ratification issue, breaking with Republican Senate leader **Henry Cabot Lodge.** After losing his Senate seat in 1922, Kellogg returned to his law practice in St. Paul. President Warren Harding named Kellogg a delegate to the Pan-American Conference of 1923 in Santiago, Chile, and in 1924 he became ambassador to Great Britain. In 1925, President Calvin Coolidge appointed him secretary of state.

As secretary, Kellogg encountered difficulties with Mexico over subsoil rights and other problems. He made preparations for the Geneva Naval Disarmament Conference of 1927, although he did not attend, and he actively negotiated the Kellogg-Briand Pact of 1928. The pact, eventually signed by sixty-four nations, outlawed war as an instrument of foreign policy. For this work Kellogg gained the Nobel Peace Prize for 1929. After retiring as secretary of state, he was elected to a seat on the Permanent Court of International Justice (1930), serving until declining health forced his resignation in 1935.

⁕

Kellogg's place in American political history has seemed uncertain to recent scholars, partly because the 1920s have begun to appear as an era of lost opportunities in both domestic and foreign policy, partly because Kellogg's principal claim to fame, the Kellogg-Briand Pact, became a dead letter and even an embarrassment in view of the rise of the dictators and World War II and the enormously complicated international politics of the post–1945 period. While in office as secretary of state Kellogg seemed a kind of fuddy-duddy type—Nervous Nelly, he was called. He seemed to be a querulous elderly man who had obtained his position because when he was a senator he had been kind to President Coolidge, who at that time was a not highly regarded vice president. Kellogg's legal talents were formidable, however, and his work years before as a trust buster (he became known in the Taft administration as *the* trust buster) showed his qualities: he possessed a clear mind and was a hard worker. He prepared his case carefully against the lawyers of Standard Oil, and he won. In the Senate he stood against the conservative, traditional outlook of his own party's manager, Lodge, and had there been more such independent-minded senators in 1919, the Treaty of Versailles would have passed. His work in the State Department was not nearly as inadequate as his critics have contended, for his Latin

American policy was successful, thanks in part to Dwight W. Morrow. In retrospect the Kellogg-Briand Pact was a mistake, but its enthusiastic reception in 1928 showed that many Americans shared its author's enthusiasm. Kellogg was at least sensitive to the problems of Europe, even if—like Europeans themselves—he could not resolve them. His years in the State Department, 1925–29, were generally peaceful years and did not seem to require heroic solutions. See L. Ethan Ellis, *Frank B. Kellogg and American Foreign Relations* (1961).

ROBERT H. FERRELL

KELLOGG, Will Keith (b. Battle Creek, Mich., Apr. 7, 1860; d. Battle Creek, Mich., Oct. 6, 1951), BUSINESSMAN, was the seventh son of Seventh-Day Adventists Ann Janette Kellogg and John Preston Kellogg. Willie Keith Kellogg (he changed his name to Will in 1938) attended public schools briefly and, at the age of 15, began work as a salesman for his father's broom company. He married Ella Davis in 1880, and in 1881 he enrolled in a three-month's course at Parson's Business College in Kalamazoo, Michigan. Thus armed, he took a job as assistant to his flamboyant brother, Dr. John Harvey Kellogg, a health-food crusader, at the new Battle Creek Sanitarium. Functioning as bookkeeper, cashier, shipping clerk, and troubleshooter, he helped his brother bring the sanitarium to national prominence. Supporting his brother's work as a health-food reformer, he honed his business skills by running a subscription service for his brother's health books and by managing the Sanitas Nut Food Company, which developed the first patent process for making a cooked, flaked wheat cereal. In 1906 he launched his own business, initially a subsidiary of his brother's company, the Battle Creek Toasted Corn Flake Company. Employing an extensive newspaper and advertising campaign, Kellogg built the company into a national corporation. After a series of bitter legal battles between 1908 and 1920, Kellogg won the rights to the corporate name and full independence from his brother. Kellogg retired from business in 1937. Blind for the last ten years of his life, he lived on his Arabian horse ranch in Pomona, California, or in his houses in Palm Beach and Battle Creek.

⁂

A driven and domineering man with a shy, withdrawn personality and a determination never to be second best, W. K. Kellogg was difficult to work with. In 1925, after he fired his second son, John L., who in his seventeen years with the company—starting as plant superintendent and developing along the way the waxtite packaging system and patenting more than two hundred processes—he groomed his grandson, John L. Kellogg, Jr., for the presidency, only to become displeased with the young man and demoting him. John Jr., in turn, quit and eventually committed suicide.

Kellogg's stern relationships with his family and associates were counterbalanced by considerable interest in social issues. In addition to numerous gifts to the city of Battle Creek in the form of schools, nurseries, junior high schools, swimming pools, bird sanctuaries, and experimental farms, Kellogg founded the W. K. Kellogg Child Welfare Foundation for physically and mentally handicapped children and eventually increased its funding by $50 million.

Thus, although he broke from his parents' religion early in life, in many ways Kellogg carried over the characteristic behaviors of his Seventh-Day Adventist faith into his business and philanthropic endeavors: hard work, a missionary zeal for whatever he did, a concern for the future, an intolerance for those who did not see the world the way he did, and a concern to help people. Kellogg disliked the limelight and had few friends, but he nevertheless created one of the most successful cereal companies in the country and established one of the largest philanthropic foundations in the nation. See Horace B. Powell, *W. K. Kellogg, A Biography* (1956).

CLIFFORD CLARK

KELLY, William (b. Pittsburgh, Pa., Aug. 21, 1811; d. Louisville, Ky., Feb. 11, 1888), INVEN-

TOR, entered the forwarding and commission business in Pennsylvania and by 1846 was the junior partner of the dry-goods firm of McShane and Kelly. He then purchased iron-ore lands in Kentucky and developed the Suwanee Iron Works and Union Forge. While running the iron-works, Kelly discovered that the slow, costly process of burning out carbon from crude pig iron could be supplanted by air-boiling or forcing a blast of air through the molten metal. Between 1851 and 1856 he built several experimental "con-verters," using the new process. In 1857 he won a U.S. patent for his air-boiling method of refining iron, claiming that he had invented it several years before the Englishman Henry Bessemer. Kelly went bankrupt in the panic of 1857, howev-er, and moved to Johnstown, Pennsylvania, where he installed an experimental converter uti-lizing the new air-boiling process at the Cambria Iron Works in 1859. After five years he returned to Louisville, Kentucky, where he founded an ax manufacturing business.

Kelly's refining patents were controlled by a syndicate that also controlled the patents to other important innovations in the business. Steel was produced under his patents (but with Bessemer equipment) in 1864 by the newly formed Kelly Pneumatic Process Co., at a foundry in Wyandotte, Michigan. However, the syndicate lacked the patent rights to this Bessemer machin-ery and was forced to merge with a syndicate controlling Bessemer's U.S. patents, which thus gained a controlling interest in the new firm. As a result it was Bessemer rather than Kelly who drew most of the fame and profits, and to this day this vital technique of steel production is known as the Bessemer process.

———————

William Kelly was both the victim and the beneficiary of one of those common occurrences in the history of technology—simultaneous dis-covery. He was a victim because the work of Sir Henry Bessemer in England so overshadowed his own and claimed the largest share of financial reward for the new process. He was beneficiary because without the work of Bessemer, it appears

unlikely that Kelly's experiments would have been recognized or brought to some fruition.

He was apparently a mild-mannered man, not particularly forceful or successful in the realm of business. His most sustained and successful enterprise was the battle to realize the benefits of his original patent, which culminated in its exten-sion in 1871.

Kelly's claim to have "invented" the Bessemer process of making cheap steel is in serious doubt. He appears not to have been trying to make steel at all, and there is little evidence that his experi-ments were successful. He played only a small part in establishing the steel industry in the United States, an accomplishment that was achieved without use of his equipment. His chief claim to an American patent was that he was an American ironmaster, and its chief value was as a bargaining tool used against the English Bessemer interests.

Kelly was said to have been modest, honest, and somewhat withdrawn. Perhaps he himself had doubts about the priority or success of his invention. Such personal attributes certainly would have severely handicapped him in the arena of mid–19th-century American business. See Philip W. Bishop, "The Beginnings of Cheap Steel," United States National Museum, *Bulletin 218* (1959), pp. 27–47.

CARROLL PURSELL

KENDALL, Amos (b. Dunstable, Mass., Aug. 16, 1789; d. Washington, D.C., Nov. 12, 1869), JOURNALIST, POLITICAL LEADER, graduated from Dartmouth College at the head of his class in 1811. In 1814 he moved to Kentucky where he became a tutor in the family of **Henry Clay.** In 1816 he took over the *Argus of Western America* in Frankfort. His editorials generally supported the policies of Clay. Kendall broke with Clay in 1826, however, and helped carry the state for Andrew Jackson in 1828. Jackson made Kendall auditor of the Treasury and postmaster general, but his unofficial role as a member of the "kitchen cabi-net" was more important. He played a major part in the "war" against the second Bank of the

United States and wrote the message in which Jackson vetoed the bill renewing its charter. He also wrote a number of annual messages for the president and helped organize the *Globe,* the powerful administration newspaper. An excellent administrator, Kendall thoroughly reformed the Treasury and the post office. He was severely criticized, however, for excluding abolitionist tracts and pamphlets from the southern mails.

Until the end of Martin Van Buren's administration in 1841, Kendall remained active in government affairs. He then tried to publish his own newspaper, but poor health and lawsuits stemming from his days as postmaster general brought failure. In 1845, **Samuel F. B. Morse,** inventor of the telegraph, retained Kendall as his business manager, and by 1859 he had become a wealthy man.

Strongly pro-Union during the Civil War, Kendall opposed the Clement L. Vallandigham "Copperhead" wing of the Democratic Party. Toward the end of his life he was interested in several charities, notably the founding of a school for the deaf in the capital.

Amos Kendall was a versatile man whose success in a variety of careers demonstrated the opportunities afforded by the comparatively open society of antebellum America to a man of his keen and flexible intelligence. While Kendall is thus a striking example of the man on the make using his native wit brilliantly to exploit personal opportunities, his historical importance rests on his unique contributions to American politics. That Kendall has been given high grades even by scholarly critics of Jacksonian Democracy for his performance in the offices he held testifies to his ability. His claim to fame, however, derives not from the quality of his actions as officeholder but from the quality of the political advice he gave to Old Hickory—advice that the president was wise enough to act on. Probably the most influential man in the famed "kitchen cabinet," Kendall was widely regarded as America's "gray eminence" during the years of Jackson's administrations. In her visit to the United States during the 1830s, the sensible Harriet Martineau described her great curiosity about this shrewd political manipulator who operated behind the scenes, concerned not with public acclaim but rather with privately influencing the charismatic man who basked in that acclaim. Kendall was at the president's elbow during the dramatic Bank War, first preparing the marvelously effective Bank Veto message, then taking charge of the plans to replace the second Bank of the United States with state or "pet banks" as repositories of government funds. Kendall's own views—they can hardly be called convictions—on banking and other significant issues had regularly shifted: a recent biographer likens him to a chameleon. All the more remarkable was his ability to imbue what was actually a prosaic financial policy of arguable merit and no discernible effect on the nation's great social problems with the aura of a populistic crusade against bloated Wealth and Aristocracy. See *The Autobiography of Amos Kendall* (1872).

EDWARD PESSEN

KENNAN, George Frost (b. Milwaukee, Wis., Feb. 16, 1904), DIPLOMAT, graduated from Princeton in 1925 and entered the foreign service the following year. He served in Geneva and Hamburg in 1927 and in Berlin and Tallin (Estonia) in 1928. He was third secretary in Riga (Latvia), Kaunas (Lithuania), and Tallin in 1929.

In anticipation of eventual diplomatic recognition of Communist Russia, the State Department sent Kennan to the University of Berlin for two years (1929–31) to study Russian language, history, and culture. When the Soviet Union was recognized in 1933, Kennan accompanied the first American ambassador, William C. Bullitt, to Moscow, becoming third secretary. He was later stationed in Prague (1938–39) and Berlin, where he remained until he was interned by the Nazis in 1941. Released in 1942, Kennan spent a year as counselor in Lisbon before becoming counselor of the American delegation to the European Advisory Commission (1943–44). He then returned to Moscow as minister-counselor (1944–46).

From Moscow in February 1946, Kennan sent his famous cablegram on American postwar foreign policy, which suggested a policy of containment of the Soviet Union, the direct application of counterpressure wherever the Communists threatened to expand. As a result of this cablegram, Kennan was named director of the policy planning staff of the State Department. His article in *Foreign Affairs* magazine (July 1947), written under the name "X," articulated the containment policy. Secretary of State **Dean Acheson** appointed Kennan counselor of the department in 1949, but he left in 1950 to accept an appointment at the Institute of Advanced Study at Princeton. In 1952, Kennan became ambassador to the U.S.S.R. but was declared *persona non grata* by the Russians because of his criticisms of Russian treatment of Western diplomats. He retired from the foreign service and became a member of the Institute for Advanced Study at Princeton (professor, 1956).

Kennan served as ambassador to Yugoslavia (1961–63) and then returned to the Institute where he remained until he retired in the late 1980s. Besides wide traveling, lecturing, and continuing to write extensively, Kennan has campaigned actively to convince "the nuclear powers to abandon the whole wretched preoccupation with nuclear weaponry." This made him somewhat of a heroic elder statesman to the antinuclear movement in the 1970s and 1980s. Similarly, his writings have been acclaimed by critics for their scholarship and literary qualities. He won a Pulitzer Prize for *Russia Leaves the War* (1956) and *Memoirs, 1925–1950* (1967). Other books include *American Diplomacy 1900–1950* (1951), *Realities of American Foreign Policy* (1954), and *Sketches from a Life* (1989), which became a best-seller.

Perhaps George Frost Kennan was the only American to be both a foreign service officer and a member of the American Academy of Arts and Letters, and his two careers were mutually reinforcing. His histories reveal a romanticism and intense commitment to order hidden behind the diplomat's austerity. Both careers, however,

revealed a fear of Soviet power and ideology; an affection for Germany; a very low priority for Asian, especially Vietnamese, affairs, with the exception of Japan's development; a commitment to elite policymaking; and an alienation from, if not sometimes a misunderstanding of, American society. His histories condemned Woodrow Wilson and Franklin D. Roosevelt for legalistic-moralistic diplomacy but displayed little understanding of the presidents' domestic difficulties. He bitterly resented obstacles thrown before the State Department by the Senate, and in 1963 resigned as ambassador to Yugoslavia after Congress restricted trade with that country.

Consequently, whether analyzing American politics, Soviet policies, or student radicalism (as he did unsympathetically during the late 1960s), Kennan cared about methods, for these, unlike objectives, were "real.... I found myself concerned less with what people thought they were striving for than the manner in which they strove for it." This comment helps explain his mistrust of Russia. In the late 1930s he condemned Nazism, but: "Never—neither then nor at any later date—did I consider the Soviet Union a fit ally or associate, actual or potential." In 1945 Kennan unsuccessfully advised allowing Russia its de facto political sphere in Eastern Europe rather than entering into negotiations which in any way would lend respectability to Soviet claims.

Brought back from Moscow to Washington in 1946 by Secretary of the Navy **James Forrestal,** probably the most adamant anti-Soviet member of Harry S. Truman's cabinet, Kennan, under Forrestal's aegis, wrote the Mr. "X" article. The author later lamented that although the essay emphasized tactics, American officials unfortunately soon elevated it to rigid dogma. The essay's analysis of Soviet motivation can indeed be read as dogma, but in 1949, Kennan personally began splitting from Secretary of State Dean Acheson's determination to tighten containment by accelerating military alliances and rearming Germany. Kennan instead urged that soft-pedaling military alliances while using the mere threat of German rearmament in formal Russian-American negotiations could result in a Central

European neutral zone, consequent Russian military retreat, and thus a breakup of the Soviet bloc. Reiterating this approach in 1957, Kennan was publicly attacked by Acheson for not understanding "the realities of power."

In 1967, Kennan "emphatically" denied the application of "the containment doctrine today in situations to which it has, and can have, no proper relevance." After Russia invaded Czechoslovakia in 1968, he nevertheless denied ever having "understood this talk about détente" and urged stationing 100,000 more American troops in West Germany until the Russians left Czechoslovakia. Although the means varied according to Kennan's perception of the circumstances between 1933 and 1968, his object as both diplomat and historian had apparently always been, in the words of the "X" article, the "breakup or the gradual mellowing of Soviet power," a policy that he has lived to see validated by history. See Walter Hixon, *George F. Kennan* (1989).

WALTER LaFEBER

KENNEDY, John Fitzgerald (b. Brookline, Mass., May 29, 1917; d. Dallas, Tex., Nov. 22, 1963), PRESIDENT, graduated from Harvard in 1940, after spending six months during his junior year in London as assistant to his father, Ambassador Joseph Kennedy. His stay in London led to *Why England Slept* (1940), a study of English appeasement of fascism. During World War II he commanded a PT boat in the Pacific.

Kennedy served as a Democrat in the U.S. House of Representatives (1947–53), and in 1952 was elected to the U.S. Senate, defeating Henry Cabot Lodge, Jr. In 1956, while recovering from a back operation, he wrote *Profiles in Courage,* which won a Pulitzer Prize for biography (1957). He was reelected to the Senate in 1958, and in 1960 defeated Richard M. Nixon for the presidency, 303 electoral votes to 219, becoming the first Catholic to win that office. Kennedy's plurality, however, was a mere 118,000 votes.

Believing that economic aid to Latin America would accomplish little unless accompanied by internal reforms, he organized the Alliance for Progress. He also formed the Peace Corps to send volunteers to work on needed public projects in underdeveloped nations.

Kennedy authorized the continuation of a CIA plan to arm Cuban exiles who planned to overthrow the Communist government of Fidel Castro. At the Bay of Pigs invasion, however, the exiles were crushed by Castro's forces (Apr. 17, 1961). In June 1961, Kennedy met Soviet Premier Nikita Khrushchev in Vienna. Khrushchev believed that Kennedy would not resist cold war pressures actively and proceeded to erect the Berlin Wall and to test nuclear weapons.

In 1962, after the discovery that Russia was building missile bases in Cuba, Kennedy demanded that it dismantle these bases; he ordered the navy to stop and search all Soviet vessels headed for Cuba and to turn back those containing "offensive" weapons. When Khrushchev backed down, a possible nuclear war was avoided.

In 1962, Kennedy used presidential pressure to stop a proposed increase in the price of steel, forcing the steel corporations to rescind the increase. He called out the Mississippi national guard to enforce the integration of the University of Mississippi. But plans for federal aid to education, new civil rights laws, medical care for the aged, and a tax cut designed to stimulate economic growth were blocked by Congress. While visiting Dallas, Texas, Kennedy was assassinated by Lee Harvey Oswald.

❧

Kennedy, the youngest man as well as the first Roman Catholic elected to the presidency, was also the first American president born in the 20th century. As he put it in his inaugural address, he was one of "a new generation of Americans— born in this century, tempered in war, disciplined by a hard and bitter peace." His private self-description—an "idealist without illusions"— suggested the combination of high purpose with an ironic, often self-mocking tone that was characteristic of the war generation and, distilled in Kennedy, came to be known as the Kennedy style.

A war hero and a Pulitzer Prize historian, handsome and graceful, son of a rich man and husband of a beautiful woman, he possessed advantages that provoked both admiration and envy. Lucid in his play of mind, formidable in his command of fact, activist by temperament and by philosophy, he had a Rooseveltian view of presidential powers and a wide sense of America's national and world responsibilities. He was a gifted politician but also hoped, in the manner of Franklin D. Roosevelt, to release impulses of idealism he believed had been too long suppressed in American society. He attracted and sought out intellectuals and academics, who entered his administration in unprecedented numbers.

In foreign policy Kennedy was a transitional president. Though a child of the cold war, he saw it not as a religious but as a power conflict. His inaugural address, an overreaction to a truculent speech delivered two weeks earlier by Khrushchev in Moscow, contained much grandiloquent language: "Let every nation know … that we shall pay any price, bear any burden, meet any hardship, support any friend, oppose any foe, in order to assure the survival and the success of liberty." But in another speech nine months later Kennedy, offering what proved to be a truer expression of his idea of America's world role, called on the American people to "face the fact that the United States is neither omnipotent nor omniscient—that we are only 6 percent of the world's population—that we cannot impose our will upon the other 94 percent of mankind—that we cannot right every wrong or reverse each adversity—and that therefore there cannot be an American solution to every world problem." His essential belief was in a world of diversity and self-determination where, "within the framework of international cooperation, every country can solve its own problems according to its own traditions and ideals."

The confrontations of the cold war often obstructed the quest for diversity. When Kennedy approved a CIA-organized invasion by Cuban exiles of their homeland in 1961, a project that was inherited from the administration of Dwight D. Eisenhower, he went on to disaster at the Bay of Pigs. In that year also he blocked Khrushchev's effort to drive the western allies out of Berlin and began to enlarge the American involvement in Vietnam. At the same time Kennedy abandoned the opposition of the Eisenhower administration to neutralism, cultivated the new independent states of Africa, and sought to make American economic aid, as through the Alliance for Progress for Latin America, a means of internal democratization and structural reform.

The cold war reached its sharpest point in 1962 when Khrushchev tried to upset the military and political balance between the two superpowers by secretly installing nuclear missiles in Cuba. Kennedy, resisting the advice of his own military that he should go to war, succeeded in bringing about the peaceful removal of the missiles. He followed this by pressing for a détente with the Soviet Union, especially in his noted American University speech of July 1963, described by Khrushchev as "the greatest speech by any American president since Roosevelt." The first fruit of this effort was the limited nuclear test ban treaty of 1963.

In domestic affairs Kennedy's effort to redeem his campaign promise of "getting America moving again" was complicated by the narrowness of his 1960 victory and by the strength of the conservative coalition between Republicans and southern Democrats in the House of Representatives. Still, as the first Keynesian president, he steadily pursued expansionist policies that, carried further by a tax reduction bill introduced in his administration and passed after his death, helped produce the longest peacetime period of sustained growth in American history. In the area of civil rights, Kennedy, underestimating at first the intensity of the black revolution, concentrated on executive rather than legislative action. In October 1962 he sent federal troops into Oxford, Mississippi, to protect the admission of a black student to the University of Mississippi. In 1963, pronouncing racial justice "a moral issue … as old as the scriptures and … as clear as the American Constitution," he launched a fight for new and sweeping civil rights legislation; this, too, was enacted after his death.

In the White House, Kennedy's directness and openness of mind, his faith in reason, and his compassionate vision of American life helped break the intellectual as well as the political crust that had settled over the country in the fifties. In particular, he communicated not only an insistence on personal excellence but a skepticism about conventional ideas and institutions, and thereby encouraged a great discharge of critical energy throughout American society. He also communicated concern for the less fortunate and sympathy with the frustrations and hopes of the young. If his actual achievements in office were limited, the promise of his presidency seemed almost unlimited; and his murder in Dallas in November 1963 sent a wave of incredulity, shame, and grief not only across the United States but around the planet. See Herbert Parmet, *JFK: The Presidency of John F. Kennedy* (1983).

ARTHUR M. SCHLESINGER, JR.

KENNEDY, Robert Francis (b. Brookline, Mass., Nov. 20, 1925; d. Los Angeles, Calif., June 6, 1968), POLITICAL LEADER, left Harvard after a year to join the navy as a seaman (1944) following his oldest brother Joseph's death in the war. Discharged in 1946, he graduated from Harvard in 1948 and served for a year as a correspondent in Palestine for the Boston *Post.* He received his LLB from the University of Virginia and entered government service in 1951 as an attorney for the Criminal Division of the Department of Justice. He resigned in 1952 to manage his brother John F. Kennedy's successful senatorial campaign, resuming legal work in 1953 as an assistant counsel for the Senate Permanent Subcommittee on Investigations, chaired by Senator **Joseph McCarthy.** He left this position after a few months, joining the walkout of Democratic members of the committee to protest McCarthy's methods, but he returned to the committee as chief counsel when Democrat John McClellan became chairman (1955–57). From 1957 to 1959 he was chief counsel of McClellan's Senate Rackets Committee, attaining national prominence through his investigations of Teamsters

Union leaders **James R. Hoffa** and David Beck. After John F. Kennedy's election to the presidency he was appointed (1961) attorney general of the United States.

As attorney general, Kennedy's major efforts came in the field of civil rights: he implemented the desegregation of interstate transportation terminals, supported the admission of a black, James Meredith, into the University of Mississippi (1961), and strictly enforced the Civil Rights Act of 1963, which strengthened voting rights protection and sought to eliminate segregation in public accommodations. Kennedy also continued his investigations of James Hoffa, who in 1963 was convicted for corrupting the jury that had acquitted him of graft charges in 1962.

Robert Kennedy was his brother John's closest adviser, particularly during the crisis created by the anti-Castroite invasion of Cuba (Bay of Pigs, 1961), the Cuban missile crisis (1962), and the successful efforts to obtain the Nuclear Test Ban Treaty of 1963.

After his brother's assassination (1963), Kennedy resigned as attorney general to run for U.S. senator from New York and was elected in 1964. In the Senate, Kennedy criticized the policy of Lyndon B. Johnson's administration of increasing military involvement in Vietnam and sought legislation to better the life of the urban poor. In March 1968 he announced his candidacy for the 1968 Democratic presidential nomination. He carried the Indiana, Nebraska, and California primaries, but after delivering his victory speech after the California vote, he was fatally shot by Sirhan Sirhan, a Palestinian angered by Kennedy's support for Israel.

Although Robert Kennedy held only one elective office (as senator from New York) and was cut down before he could complete his bid for the 1968 presidential nomination, he was the most dramatic American political figure of the scarred decade of the 1960s. His brief span in the national limelight, roughly from 1958 to 1968, was marked by war, tensions, and violence. Understandably the debate over his image polarized both loyalties and hatreds. But it also evoked an intensity of response from the most alienated elements of the society—the blacks, the poor, the young—that defines his "New Politics" as the politics of hope for those groups.

Like his brothers, his heritage was that of the Gracchi, who were the darlings of Roman aristocratic birth, wealth, and privilege, and made a career of championing the underprivileged. All the Kennedy brothers (he was the third of four, and was called "the runt") grew up encased in the agony of competitiveness that their "founding father," Joseph P. Kennedy, set up for them. With such a father and with two charismatic older brothers to emulate, the strain of growing up was unremitting.

He learned the Kennedy political pragmatism in the campaign field with his brother, as government lawyer (especially in the Hoffa prosecution), and as attorney general. The danger for Robert Kennedy was that of always operating in his brother's shadow and of remaining primarily a brilliant political technician. He escaped this by growing and deepening in every task. This was true in his civil rights encounters as attorney general, which developed his sensibility and his passion for justice. It was true of his role as head of ExCom (the Executive Committee) in the Cuban missile encounter when he learned and showed the arts of swift and prudent judgment in high decisions.

Thus he passed through an extraordinary apprenticeship. When he failed to maneuver Lyndon Johnson into accepting him as a vice presidential running mate in 1964, he decided to use the Senate route to the White House. But he held back from a direct challenge until Johnson's withdrawal from the 1968 campaign forced him in. His entrance split the antiwar forces between him and Senator Eugene McCarthy, but Kennedy clearly had the better chance for the nomination and election.

The key to his appeal lay in the "New Politics," which in turn was a rationalization of the kind of popular appeal he had. It was not only to the blacks, the poor, the young, the rising class of professionals in the knowledge industries but also to the "white ethnics" and the blue-collar workers and middle class. Both the Indiana and the California primaries reflected this extraordinary capacity to stress both the principle of equal access and the role of law in gaining social cohesion. Had he lived, Kennedy might have put together again something like Franklin Roosevelt's "Great Coalition"—except for the South.

The bullet that ended his life on the night of his California triumph ended that possibility. A Robert Kennedy presidency proved the road closed off from history. He would have encountered difficulties, especially since the "politics of promise" (Henry Fairlie's term for the Kennedys) generated greater claims and expectations than it could fulfill. There was more fire of social passion, more of the Savonarola, in Robert Kennedy than in all the other Kennedys put together. It might have prolonged the revolutionary social tensions of the sixties well into the seventies.

But in the Robert Kennedy amalgam there was also the pragmatic political streak and that of prudent decision, and the added skein of the tragic that ran through his life. It was a powerful amalgam and would have fashioned an American civilization very different from that of Richard Nixon. See Arthur Schlesinger, Jr., *Robert F. Kennedy and His Times* (1978).

MAX LERNER

KENT, James (b. Fredericksburgh, N.Y., July 31, 1763; d. New York, N.Y., Dec. 12, 1847), JURIST, graduated from Yale (1781) and read law in the office of Egbert Benson, attorney general of New York. Admitted to the bar in 1785, he practiced law in Poughkeepsie (1785–93). After being defeated in his bid for a seat in the U.S. Congress, he moved to New York City (1793) where he was elected to three successive terms in the New York assembly as a Federalist (1793–96). He became a professor of law at Columbia University (1793–98).

In 1796, Governor **John Jay** of New York named Kent master in chancery, and a year later he became recorder of the city of New York. Appointed a judge of the New York supreme court in 1798, Kent rose to chief judge in 1804. In this post he established the precedent of handing down written opinions. Kent served as chancellor of the New York court of chancery (1814–23), where he was instrumental in laying the foundation for equity jurisprudence.

A staunch conservative, Kent spoke out vigorously against universal suffrage at the New York constitutional convention (1821), arguing that it would "jeopardize the right of property and the principles of liberty." After retiring from the bench in 1823, Kent returned to Columbia (1824) and wrote his *Commentaries on American Law* (4 vols., 1826–30).

⸻

Nurtured by Presbyterianism, classical education, and revolution, James Kent approached the law in late-18th-century America with many of the values that were to be challenged in the next century as a young nation grew. Federalist by choice, conservative by nature, and Anglophile by inclination, Kent incorporated all these perceptions of society into his role as both judge at law and chancellor in equity. Essentially fairminded as a finder of facts, Kent nonetheless never abandoned in the decision-making process his conception of the ultimate responsibility and role of the law. Steadfast in his determination to implant his views into the law, Kent, from his earliest pronouncements from the bench, disputed the emerging notions of first Jeffersonian and then Jacksonian, democracy and economy.

Supporting the cause of individually acquired property, Kent labored to protect that property and ensure that it remain vested. He therefore defended state-granted monopolies, franchises, and privileges. By enforcing the legislative will in this efficacious fashion, Kent often limited or precluded subsequent venturers into the growing economic system either from realizing substantial return on their investment or, indeed, from receiving sufficient encouragement to risk whatever capital they had previously accumulated. Focusing on promoting the first developer to the detriment of those unfortunate enough to desire subsequent interests, Kent clearly believed that encouraging monopolistic practices or restricting

competition would benefit the community or public more than allowing unrestrained competition. He always had the public interest in mind, however, whether it was in deciding litigation broadening the rights of a free press, which he helped accomplish, or the concerns of private or corporate parties. But what Kent and many lawyers of his generation failed to recognize was that the spirit of entrepreneurship in America in the first half of the 19th century did not pose a threat to the community. Rather, this movement was to foster economic development and lead the United States toward the fulfillment of its vast potential. The tension between those who had already established their financial position in the community and those who wished to share in the gathering wealth often found its temporary resolution in the courts. And when James Kent was asked to decide, he invariably opted for the vested interests as opposed to the rising interests.

Kent's concerns in the legal arena were consistent with his fears that the uneducated masses would dominate American government. He opposed loosening the prerequisites for suffrage because he believed that property best qualifies a man to have a voice in the ordering of his government's affairs. So in principle he opposed allowing men to choose their representatives unless they were properly qualified by property ownership. Yet he was seemingly quite willing to severely limit by judicial decision an individual's effort to attain the legitimate goal of property acquisition or suffrage qualification. Kent erected legal barriers to endeavors to enter the system, and in the process reinforced his political views by judicial application.

Exclusive privileges were often defended with English precedents—frequently exhaustive and always relevant. A legal system based on precedent offered stability to both business and government. Kent built a system (particularly in equity) that drew heavily on its English example. In his quest to define fundamental principles peculiarly suited to an American legal system, Kent often relied on the historical and traditional foundation that both English common law and equity conveniently provided.

Confronting radical beliefs that he deemed dangerous to American society, Kent viewed the judiciary and ultimately the law as the final protector of the public interest. He opposed the emerging economic and political forces, and applied his powerful intellect to hamper them. But all his powers of reason and logic were to no avail. Forced to retire from the bench, he turned his exploring and experienced mind to preparing a set of *Commentaries on American Law.* The *Commentaries* had two important effects—one intended and one probably fortuitous. First, and ultimately most significant, the volumes helped educate succeeding generations of American lawyers in a recast body of common law. Second, the *Commentaries,* along with **Joseph Story**'s writings, helped frustrate the codification movement in the United States that was an intellectual offspring of radical democracy. By making American law accessible and relatively concise, Kent partially eliminated the need for exhaustive codifiers seeking to reduce the flexible and extensive common law to a manageable and understandable mass. This inadvertent and indirect effect on codification would have pleased Kent, who was concerned enough with the tenor of popular democracy to welcome any influence that might weaken it. In the final analysis, Kent's legacy must be measured by what he did not accomplish—by the ideology he formulated and propounded that sought to postpone inevitable change and development. See John T. Horton, *James Kent: A Study in Conservatism* (1939).

ALFRED S. KONEFSKY

KEROUAC, Jack (b. Lowell, Mass., Mar. 12, 1922; d. St. Petersburg, Fla., Oct. 21, 1969), WRITER, entered Columbia University (1940) but left in 1941 and subsequently enlisted in the U.S. Navy. Discharged after two months of service, he did odd jobs, served in the merchant marine in the North Atlantic, and then returned briefly to Columbia in 1942. Kerouac's apartment near Columbia became a gathering place for young intellectuals, including **Allen Ginsberg,**

William S. Burroughs, and Herbert Huncke. During 1943–50 Kerouac traveled throughout the United States with Neil Cassidy and other friends, served again in the merchant marine, was a forest lookout in Mount Baker National Forest in Washington, and lived in Lowell, Massachusetts, where he wrote *The Town and the City* (1950), a novel based on his boyhood.

Kerouac coined the term "beat generation," which came to signify that movement of the mid–1950s opposed to contemporary American values and time-honored art forms. He sometimes claimed that "beat" derived from "beatific"; on other occasions he said it meant the despair of being poor, sad, and down and out, a state that compelled a search for new experience. Whereas his first work was written in a traditional literary style and took him three years to complete, his second novel, *On the Road* (1957), was typed in three weeks in 1951 on a continuous roll of paper. A spontaneous personal narrative, it relates the adventurous travels throughout the United States of Kerouac (Sal Paradise), Ginsberg (Carlo Marx), Cassidy (Dean Moriarty), and others. *The Dharma Bums* (1958), which reflects Kerouac's interest in Eastern thought and Buddhism, is the account of cross-country journeys or religious wanderings of Roy Smith, who turns to Buddhism under the influence of Japhy Ryder (modeled on Gary Snyder).

Kerouac considered his novels part of one long work. *Subterraneans* (1958), made into a movie in 1959, concerns one of his love affairs, and *Doctor Sax* (1959) and its sequel, *Maggie Cassidy* (1959), are based on his Lowell boyhood. Kerouac's other novels include *Tristessa* (1960); *Lonesome Traveler* (1960), a book of autobiographical short pieces; *Big Sur* (1962); *Visions of Gerard* (1963); *Desolation Angels* (1965); *Satori in Paris* (1966); *Vanity of Duluoz* (1968); *Pic* (1971); and *Visions of Cody* (1972). He ad-libbed the narrative for *Pull My Daisy* (1961), a film about the beat generation made in a Bowery loft in which Kerouac appeared with Allen Ginsberg and Peter Orlovsky. His poetry includes: *Mexico City Blues* (1959), *Rimbaud* (1960), and the *Scriptures of the Golden Eternity* (1960).

No writer better than Jack Kerouac personified and projected the restless spirit of young Americans of the post–World War II years. Yet at the same time no writer has produced a body of work that would be more difficult to evaluate on a purely literary basis. He wrote most of his books literally at top speed in the sincere belief that when he worked "without consciousness" or reflection, he was able to produce a more aesthetically valid prose. As a result, even his most successful novels—*On the Road, Dharma Bums, Desolation Angels,* and *Big Sur*—are patched with uninspired, slapdash, and sometimes slightly unintelligible passages. But at his best there was a beauty, urgency, and energy to his style that was altogether new to American writing. It did much to inspire those of his own beat generation of the fifties but ultimately had an even greater impact on the New Journalists and young novelists of the next decade. Politically, Kerouac was, if anything, a libertarian rather than a radical, and although his novels had helped shape some of the attitudes and enthusiasms of the turbulent sixties, he himself was repelled by the turn toward a political style that he considered un-American. He felt that what he had written had been twisted by some and misunderstood by others, and so he gradually withdrew into a state of comparative isolation during the latter years of the decade. He continued writing, although with flagging enthusiasm, about his adventures of the years before. See Ann Charters, *Kerouac* (1972).

BRUCE COOK

KEY, Francis Scott (b. Frederick, Md., Aug. 1, 1779; d. Baltimore, Md., Jan. 11, 1843), LAWYER, graduated from St. John's College in Annapolis in 1796 and then studied law. In 1801 he opened a practice in Frederick (now Carroll Co.), Maryland, but moved to Georgetown (D.C.) in 1805 to enter a partnership with his uncle Philip Barton Key. Because he was an influential Washington attorney, Key was asked to obtain the release of his friend William Beanes, a Maryland physician who had been captured by the British during the War of 1812 and retained on a warship in Chesapeake Bay. Key secured the prisoner's release but was forced to remain on board ship on the night of September 13–14, 1814, while the British bombarded Fort McHenry in preparation for an attack on Baltimore. In the morning, when he saw the American flag still flying, he wrote a poem, "The Star-Spangled Banner," expressing his great joy at the sight. The poem, written to the tune of a popular English drinking song, "To Anacreon in Heaven," was published in the Baltimore *American* on September 21, 1814, and in several other periodicals. It was soon sung in many Baltimore taverns and, gaining wide popularity, became the national anthem.

Besides conducting his Washington law practice, Key served as a delegate to the general conventions of the Episcopal Church (1814–26) and wrote many religious hymns. He was U.S. attorney for the District of Columbia (1833–41) and was sent by President Andrew Jackson in 1833 to seek a settlement between state and federal governments over Creek Indian lands in Alabama. *Poems of the Late Francis S. Key, Esq.* (1857) was published posthumously.

Except for "The Star-Spangled Banner," Francis Scott Key's achievements were prosaic. Friends knew Frank Key as a handsome, pleasant fellow who always hurried. Key's local renown as an attorney was due mostly to association with a brilliant uncle and a distinguished brother-in-law, **Roger B. Taney.** Descriptions of Key as a lawyer usually mention an attractive presence, but also a hackneyed style and a characteristic lack of preparation.

Key wished for more than a colorless, if prosperous, legal practice. His constant haste may have covered an urge to outdistance limited ability. Despite the kindly disposition of friends, however, Key's political hopes had to settle for gratification at Taney's triumphs. Literary effort never lifted Key beyond the album versifier. Public acknowledgment of his 1814 verses did little more in his lifetime than make him a curiosity. All this might explain his avowed regret at not choosing the church as a profession. He had to struggle to keep his religious zeal from invading other lives.

It was in a personal sense that Key triumphed. All accounts agree that he was an admirable citizen and human being. His famed effort to rescue Dr. Beanes was part of a customary generosity toward family and community. While torn between town and country, world and spirit, poet's corner and forum, Key nevertheless hastened through life to the considerable benefit of all around him. Yet he was always restless and uneasy. Perhaps in this way the author of America's national anthem may best have captured his country's spirit. See Victor Weybright, *Spangled Banner* (1935).

PAUL C. NAGEL

KING, Ernest Joseph (b. Lorain, Ohio, Nov. 23, 1878; d. Portsmouth, N.H., June 25, 1956), NAVAL OFFICER, graduated from the U.S. Naval Academy at Annapolis in 1901, after having served during his plebe year on the U.S.S. *San Francisco* on Atlantic coastal duty during the Spanish-American War. He graduated fourth in his class.

King, by then a commander, served during World War I as assistant chief of staff to Admiral Henry Thomas Mayo, commander in chief of the Atlantic Fleet. Following the war he served first as supervisor for the reopening of the postgraduate school at the Naval Academy. Then, as commander of a submarine base at New London, Connecticut, he won both a Distinguished Service Medal for his successful salvaging of sunken submarines in 1926 and 1928. He soon became interested in aviation, however, and after qualifying as a naval aviator at Pensacola, Florida, he was appointed assistant chief of the Navy Bureau of Aeronautics (1929–30) and then captain of the aircraft carrier *Lexington* (1930–33). He served as chief of the Navy Bureau of Aeronautics (1933–36), inspector of potential naval base sites in the Aleutians (1937–38), and then vice admiral in command of the Aircraft

Battle Force, which consisted of five aircraft carriers. In this post he worked to improve the coordination between the carriers and other types of combat vessels.

In 1940, in a general reorganization that divided the navy into three major striking forces, King was named a full admiral in charge of the Atlantic Fleet. In December 1941 he was named commander in chief of the U.S. Naval Fleet when Admiral Husband E. Kimmel was relieved of his command in the aftermath of the Japanese attack on Pearl Harbor. Later in the war he was raised to the rank of fleet admiral. From 1942 until his retirement in 1945, he was chief of Naval Operations as well as naval commander in chief. It was thus his responsibility to both plan long-range strategy and supervise its execution. During these years King shifted the emphasis within the navy from the battleship toward reliance on aircraft carriers. He also stressed cooperation with land-based army aircraft, a tactic that played an especially effective role at the battle of Midway. King accompanied Presidents Franklin D. Roosevelt and Harry S. Truman to the conferences at Tehran, Cairo, Yalta, and Potsdam. After his retirement in 1945, King served as an adviser to the secretary of defense and to the president. However, he opposed government policies in 1947, when he testified against plans to unify the armed services, and in 1953, when he called for a naval blockade of the coast of Communist China.

❧

Admiral King was a man of high ability with a single-minded devotion to his profession. Known for his determination and toughness, he was a "driver" (to use his own term) both of himself and of others. Taking as his ideal the Earl of St. Vincent, the taut British disciplinarian, King was "more feared than loved." Yet he inspired devotion and loyalty among those who became sufficiently intimate to penetrate his shell.

King was uniquely qualified for his wartime role. His broad experience with submarines, surface vessels, and aircraft had convinced him of the necessity for the balanced use of all arms. His work with carriers and their tactics had given him a profound understanding of the new type of naval warfare. He had the ability to reduce a problem to its essentials, and he entrusted the execution of plans to his subordinates without interference.

He was recognized as a superb tactician, and Lord Alanbrooke considered him "the ablest strategist on the American Chiefs of Staff." Some two months after Pearl Harbor, perceiving the threat to communications with Australia, King wrote a memorandum outlining the strategy of advancing through the Solomons against Rabaul, thus anticipating the course of the war to the fall of 1943.

Although King never disagreed with the decision that gave primacy to the European theater, he insisted before the combined chiefs and at international conferences that the Japanese should not be allowed to consolidate their gains and that resources needed in the Pacific should not lie idle in Europe. His firmness on this point undoubtedly shortened the Pacific war. See Ernest J. King and Walter Muir Whitehill, *Fleet Admiral King: A Naval Record* (1952).

WINSTON B. LEWIS

KING, Martin Luther, Jr. (b. Atlanta, Ga., Jan. 15, 1929; d. Memphis, Tenn., Apr. 4, 1968), REFORMER, graduated from Morehouse College in 1948. He obtained his BD degree from the Crozer Theological Seminary in Chester, Pennsylvania, in 1951 and then went on to Boston University on a fellowship, where he earned his PhD in systematic theology in 1955. In 1954 he became pastor of the Dexter Avenue Baptist Church in Montgomery, Alabama. On December 1, 1955, Rosa Parks, a black woman, was arrested for breaking the "Jim Crow" bus laws of Alabama, and this set off a boycott of the buses by the blacks of the city. King was asked to head the Montgomery Improvement Association, which had organized the boycott, and even though his house was bombed in January 1956, King continued to lead the boycott in the passive resistance spirit of Gandhi. Finally, in November 1956, the Supreme Court ruled that the Jim Crow

laws were unconstitutional.

In 1957 the Southern Christian Leadership Conference was formed in Atlanta to coordinate civil rights efforts, and King was elected its president. He became co-pastor with his father of the Ebenezer Baptist Church in Atlanta in 1959. While autographing copies of his book on the Montgomery bus boycott, *Stride Toward Freedom* (1958), in a Harlem bookstore he was stabbed by a deranged black woman.

King's prominence increased swiftly. He was active in promoting lunch counter sit-ins throughout the South in 1960, advised "freedom riders" to break interstate bus travel segregation laws in 1961, but was unsuccessful in a similar campaign in Albany, Georgia, in 1962. King launched a major campaign against segregation in Birmingham, Alabama, in 1963 but he met fierce opposition from the city's police commissioner, Eugene "Bull" Connor, who used police dogs and water cannon to quell demonstrations. Arrested and put in jail for eight days, King wrote his famous letter, addressed to white moderates who had urged him to give in, in which he defended the demonstrations and civil disobedience. Later in 1963 King keynoted the March on Washington for Jobs and Freedom with his "I have a dream" speech. He received the Nobel Peace Prize in 1964, the youngest man in history to do so.

After conducting a voter registration drive in Alabama in 1965 and leading a protest march from Selma to Montgomery, King extended his civil rights activities to the North. He lived in a Chicago slum in 1966 and tried to organize tenants into ending de facto segregation in housing. He served a five-day sentence in Birmingham in 1967 for contempt of court in violating a 1963 injunction prohibiting demonstrations. By this time more dramatic black organizations, such as the Black Panthers and the Student Nonviolent Coordinating Committee (SNCC), began to compete for black support, and around 1967 King began to criticize the Vietnam War on moral grounds and also because it was draining many billions of dollars from antipoverty programs which he felt deserved higher priority. Later in

1967 he went to Memphis, Tennessee, to aid sanitation workers, predominantly blacks, in their struggle for better wages and working conditions. While there, in 1968, he was assassinated from ambush, and on March 10, 1969, James Earl Ray, a white man, pleaded guilty to the murder and was sentenced to ninety-nine years in prison.

Martin Luther King, Jr., was the most eloquent and popular voice of the black protest movement between 1956, the year he led the Montgomery bus boycott, and 1968, when he was assassinated. There were black leaders more militant than King or more shrewd or better organizers. But no one could arouse his listeners—whether black or white—as he did, to indignation against injustice, to marches and demonstrations at the risk of facing policemen's clubs, to faith in the inevitable triumph of love over hate, brotherhood over persecution.

King's physical appearance was not distinctive: he was short, stocky, brown-skinned, with a mustache, hair cut close to his head, a roundish face with soft, full features. But when he began to speak—typically, in a crowded, sweating southern church, after singing and handclapping and a day of trouble—there was a magnificence to him, an enormous dignity. His voice was rich and resonant, his articulation both precise and deliberate, his consonants soft, his vowels full and southern. His sentences had a rhythm charged with feeling, and even when, as happened, the substance of his speech was shallow or vague, his rhetoric evoked whatever was profoundly felt or thought among his listeners, in that joint performance by speaker and hearer that great orators achieve.

He was more than an orator; he was a leader of marches, sit-ins, boycotts, and demonstrations, at the start of that new period of mass action (of blacks, students, women, antiwar protesters) that followed the long silence of the forties and fifties. To the southern black man and woman, waiting so long for the slightest hint that change might be possible, King was the son of the local Baptist preacher, still speaking in a familiar accent, but returned from college and divinity school, edu-

cated, confident, bold, commanding the attention of people all over America and the world. Even in the midst of growing doubts about his effectiveness, especially in King's later years, blacks felt affection and pride for him as for no other black leader in this century.

King expressed a philosophy that seemed to fit exactly the capabilities and needs of American blacks in the late fifties and early sixties. He rejected the idea that progress could come through negotiations or favors or the use of courts, and urged direct action by masses of people. But he insisted that this action, although it would bring tension (he used the term "creative tension") and possibly violence, should itself be nonviolent.

He had been influenced by **Henry David Thoreau**'s willingness to disobey the law to support a moral principle, and Gandhi's idea that the force of truth, acted out in massive disobedience, could win against the force of arms. He had also been troubled by the thought of **Reinhold Niebuhr,** of the existence of sin and evil in men, and the idea that love alone was not enough in the real world of power and wealth and malice. King was often torn between his rhetoric of "love your enemy" and his observation that the enemy was halted not by love but by pressure (as in a boycott) or embarrassment (as in a demonstration) or threat (as when the U.S. Army protected King and those who joined him in the 1965 march from Selma to Montgomery).

Segregationists deplored King's aims, and liberal moderates were offended by his tactics. But there was more valid criticism from people who cared for him. The young black militants in the Student Nonviolent Coordinating Committee saw King as a speechmaker and grandstander who flew into the southern towns where they had organized and suffered, who led marches and spent a few ceremonial days in jail, and then left without digging in to help create a continuing grass-roots organization. King was too susceptible to the blandishments of the mighty—not from corruption but from naïveté: a phone call from the Kennedys, a compromise proposal from **Roy Wilkins.** He did not seem to see the limits of his hit-and-run techniques. They were adequate for desegregating lunch counters but not for combating the combined power of giant corporations and a military state that used arms and the laws to keep intact the exploitation of the poor at home and abroad, a power that could play with racism, letting it in or out as a fisherman plays with his catch. Where rule by race was intertwined with rule by class, it would take a revolution, not just new signs at bus terminals.

King's intelligence was keen, however, and his soul sensitive, and he had the courage to break with enticing attachments. Thus, in 1967 and 1968, watching the black riots all over America and the slaughter of the Vietnamese by American technology, and listening to the increasingly popular calls for Black Power by young, angry ghetto dwellers, he moved ahead. Encouraged by the strong antiwar feelings of his wife, Coretta Scott, he thundered against the war in Vietnam, ignoring the advice of those black leaders who lived in timorous alliance with the Democratic administration. He began to see—even his fumbling forays in Chicago and Memphis showed this—that the urban poor would have to be organized in a long struggle to redistribute the wealth of the country. In the midst of this rethinking, and at the start of new plans, he was cut down. See Taylor Branch, *Parting the Waters* (1985).

HOWARD ZINN

KINSEY, Alfred Charles (b. Hoboken, N.J., June 23, 1894; d. Bloomington, Ind., Aug. 25, 1956), SCIENTIST, graduated from Bowdoin College in 1916. He was an assistant in zoology at Harvard (1917–18), a Sheldon traveling fellow (1919–20), and received his DSc in biology from Harvard in 1920. That year he was appointed assistant professor of zoology at Indiana University; he became an associate professor in 1922 and full professor in 1929. During the 1920s and early 1930s Kinsey concentrated on entomology and taxonomy, studying the gall wasp (*cynipidae*). Studies like *The Gall Wasp Genus Neuroterus* (1923) and *The Gall Wasp Genus Cynips: A Study in the Origin of Species* (1930) established his reputation as an expert in the field. He also wrote *An Introduction to Biology* (1926) and *Workbook in Biology* (1934), and directed biological explorations in Mexico and Central America in 1931–32 and 1935–36.

During the late 1930s, having become interested in human sexual behavior and impressed by the lack of information in the field, Kinsey began interviewing people about their sexual experiences. With the backing of the National Research Council, the Rockefeller Foundation, and Indiana University, he expanded his staff, establishing the Institute of Sex Research at Bloomington, Indiana, which was formally incorporated in 1947. Together with Wardell Pomeroy and Clyde Martin, Kinsey published his first findings as *Sexual Behavior of the Human Male* (1948), a statistical survey based on 5,300 personal interviews. Popularly known as the Kinsey Report, this book sold over 500,000 copies. Kinsey next completed a companion volume, *Sexual Behavior of the Human Female* (1953). Both works discussed the practical aspects of human sexuality, which had never before been subjected to scientific study and analysis. They both indicated and documented the existence of wide variations in human sexual behavior. They were criticized by some authorities for the sampling techniques used and for the supposed unreliability of personal responses by interviewees. After Kinsey's death the Institute continued his research, publishing *Pregnancy, Birth and Abortion* (1958) and *Sex Offenders: An Analysis of Types* (1965).

⸺◦≈◦⸺

Kinsey was the first investigator in sex research in America to have a large-scale, popular impact. Having been trained in the tradition of Anglo-American biological science, he applied the empirical techniques that he had used in his work on gall wasps to the study of human sexual behavior. These techniques called for the collection of large masses of data through personal interviews in the field—the field being as much of America as he could get to and as many kinds or groups of Americans as he could identify and question. Then the data was elaborately classified, in terms of both the persons interviewed and the behavior they reported. Finally the classified data was subjected to statistical analysis, and these findings were then summarized.

What resulted, in the *Male* and *Female* volumes, was the first fundamentally reliable survey of the range, frequency, distribution, and variety of human sexual behavior; this was widely considered Kinsey's contribution to knowledge. That consideration remains in force today. There were, however, a number of important reservations, apart from purely technical matters, that attached to his work. First, Kinsey resolutely insisted on treating behavior in isolation; in other words he paid little or no attention to the meanings such behavior had for the persons involved. Such an omission limited the significance of some of his findings or rendered those findings incomplete. Allied to this limitation was the fact that Kinsey was unable to supply a theoretical structure for, or give a theoretical account of, the vast quantity of data he had amassed. His contribution remained within the empirical tradition to which he was unwaveringly loyal.

Nevertheless, Kinsey's work had a widespread effect on American and Western European society. Its disclosures contributed substantially to the general liberalization of attitudes toward sexuality during the last twenty years. It also prepared the way for the even more radical researches into sexual behavior that have been conducted by **Masters and Johnson,** Kinsey's most important successors.

That all this should have emanated from an expert on entomology who was something of a puritan in his own life and habits of work is only one of the many paradoxes of Kinsey's career. That career is representative of some of the unexpected ways in which science and society continue to be related in the modern world. See Wardell B. Pomeroy, *Dr. Kinsey and the Institute for Sex Research* (1972).

STEVEN MARCUS

KISSINGER, Henry Alfred (b. Fürth, Ger., May 23, 1923), DIPLOMAT, POLITICAL SCIENTIST, fled Germany with his family in 1938 to escape the Nazi persecution of Jews. He attended the City College of New York (1940) and was drafted into the army after Pearl Harbor, becoming a citizen in 1943. Kissinger served with the Eighth Army Intelligence Division in Europe during and after World War II. He left the army in 1947 to enter Harvard University. He graduated from Harvard in 1950 and remained there to complete a PhD in Political Science in 1954. His doctoral dissertation on the aftermath of the Napoleonic Wars, published as *A World Restored: Metternich, Castlereagh and the Problems of Peace, 1812–1822* (1957), praised Austrian Chancellor Klemens von Metternich, the conservative statesman, for preserving world order in a revolutionary period by deft manipulations of the balance of power.

Kissinger remained at Harvard as an instructor and director of the university's International Seminar and edited its publication, *Confluence* (1951–58). He headed a special studies project for the Rockefeller Brothers Fund (1956–58) and then became director of Harvard's Defense Studies Program (1958–69). After overseeing a nuclear weapons and foreign policy project for the Council on Foreign Relations, Kissinger published *Nuclear Weapons and Foreign Policy* (1957), in which he argued that these new, destructive tools of warfare had not made traditional diplomacy obsolete. He became a consultant to the National Security Council and also to the Operations Research Office and Weapons Systems Evaluation Group of the Joint Chiefs of Staff. Kissinger was appointed lecturer in the government department at Harvard in 1957, rising to associate professor in 1959, and professor of government at Harvard's Center for International Affairs in 1962.

Kissinger supported New York Republican Governor **Nelson Rockefeller**'s bid for the 1960 Republican presidential nomination. After the election of Democrat John F. Kennedy to the presidency, Kissinger served as a part-time foreign policy consultant to the White House. He provided information about the policies of French President Charles de Gaulle and West German Chancellor Ludwig Erhard. Under President Lyndon B. Johnson he served as a consultant to the White House and State Department (1965–69) and visited South Vietnam on diplomatic missions for the president in 1965 and 1966. In 1967 he opened secret negotiations, code-named Pennsylvania, aimed at ending the war in Vietnam.

President Richard M. Nixon appointed Kissinger special assistant for national security affairs in 1969. He advocated a phased withdrawal of U.S. ground forces from Vietnam, an initiative designed to reduce domestic concerns over the war. He counseled an escalation in the air war over Vietnam and neighboring Cambodia. He also pursued détente with the Soviet Union and new ties with the People's Republic of China, laying the groundwork for Nixon's visits to both countries in 1972. At the same time he conducted negotiations with the North Vietnamese in Paris designed to end the war in Vietnam, culminating in the signing of a cease-fire in January 1973; for his work in this endeavor, he and North Vietnam's Le Duc Tho received a Nobel Peace Prize in October 1973. Kissinger also tried to resolve problems created by the Arab-Israeli October war of 1973. In September 1973, Nixon appointed him secretary of state, and from late 1973 to the middle of 1975, Kissinger shuttled repeatedly to Cairo, Damascus, and Jerusalem, negotiating disengagement agreements between Israeli and Egyptian armies near the Suez Canal and between Israeli and Syrian forces on the Golan Heights.

Kissinger remained secretary of state in the administration of Gerald Ford, but his reputation suffered. The victory of the Communist forces in Vietnam undermined his achievement in the cease-fire negotiations of 1972–73. During the election campaign of 1976 both Democrats and Republicans assailed his policy of détente with the Soviet Union.

Kissinger continued to influence foreign affairs after he left public office in January 1977. Kissinger Associates, his private consulting firm, offered business clients advice on current affairs. Republican presidents Ronald Reagan and George Bush sought his advice on Central American policy, the end of the cold war, and

relations with the Soviet Union and the new Russia. Republican Speaker of the House **Newt Gingrich** also relies heavily on Kissinger's counsel. Some of Kissinger's many books include *The Necessity for Choice: Prospects of American Foreign Policy* (1961), *The Troubled Partnership: A Reappraisal of the Atlantic Alliance* (1965), *American Foreign Policy: Three Essays* (1969), two volumes of memoirs, *White House Years* (1979) and *Years of Upheaval* (1982), and a vast survey of modern statecraft, *Diplomacy* (1994).

———❧———

During his long career as an interpreter and practitioner of foreign affairs, Kissinger won praise for his intellectual prowess and his dramatic and unexpected initiatives. The way in which he fostered détente with the Soviet Union reduced the dangers of nuclear war. His secret diplomacy opening relations with China was a major diplomatic triumph. His shuttle diplomacy between Israel and its neighbors set the stage for the eventual resolution of the Arab-Israeli dispute. Yet for all of his very real achievements, both the content and the style of his diplomacy had serious shortcomings. During his academic career in the 1950s Kissinger promoted the theory of political realism—a concentration on the role of power in international relations. His commitment to realism often gave his foreign policy an old-fashioned flavor. He ignored economics and often appeared indifferent to the human rights of people in other nations. While he directed foreign policy in the Nixon and Ford administrations, Kissinger was often secretive and manipulative in his dealings with other officials.

Kissinger's early experiences as a Jew growing up in Nazi Germany profoundly affected his political and personal outlook. He feared disorder, distrusted intense popular emotions, and exhibited a deep longing for acceptance. The domestic turmoil created by the Vietnam War represented for Kissinger a dangerous threat to social stability. When Nixon appointed him national security adviser, the two men discovered a shared distrust of rivals and a desire to control the foreign policy apparatus of the United

States. The domestic controversy over the conduct of the war in Vietnam had taken a heavy toll on the bipartisan foreign policy consensus that had existed in the United States since 1947. Together Nixon and Kissinger concentrated foreign policy decision-making power within the White House staff to restore the power and prestige of the president in foreign affairs. Kissinger used secret lines of communications to establish détente between the United States and the Soviet Union, and to open relations between the United States and the People's Republic of China.

Kissinger became an accomplished leaker of information to the press and his former academic colleagues. He falsely intimated to these contacts that he favored a more moderate course of action in Vietnam than the one advocated by President Nixon. Kissinger gained extraordinary celebrity in the aftermath of his trip to China in July 1971, as journalists praised him as a strategic genius. Kissinger's reputation continued to grow in 1972 and 1973 as he arranged a cease-fire in Vietnam. Indeed, Nixon became jealous that his aide's prestige might eclipse his own. Nixon's involvement in the growing Watergate scandal only heightened Kissinger's reputation. Reports that Kissinger had instructed agents of the Federal Bureau of Investigation to tap the telephones of his subordinates on the National Security Council staff heightened public awareness of his bureaucratic cunning and manipulations. His standing also suffered from revelations that he had supported the military coup in 1973 that toppled Chile's democratically elected Marxist president Salvador Allende. In 1975 and 1976 liberal critics of his conduct of relations with the Soviet Union argued that détente did not go far enough in checking the arms race and too far in undermining Third World nationalism.

Kissinger's foreign policy became a major issue in the presidential election of 1976. Republican challenger Ronald Reagan said that détente had left the United States militarily vulnerable. Equally critical of Kissinger's approach was Democratic candidate Jimmy Carter, who charged that Kissinger's secrecy and his indifference to human rights abuses in the Communist bloc and in authoritarian regimes allied to America was immoral.

Throughout his career Kissinger sought to bring a European-style perspective to the conduct of U.S. foreign relations. He often criticized American diplomats for moralizing and for having an insufficient awareness of the importance of power in international affairs. Kissinger was enormously intelligent, highly industrious, and knowledgeable, and had few peers as a negotiator. But his distrust for others, his manipulations of subordinates, and his lack of concern for advancing human rights abroad diminished his achievements. His essentially conservative approach to international relations made him a much better analyst of diplomatic history than an interpreter of changes in the international environment. See Robert D. Schulzinger, *Henry Kissinger: Doctor of Diplomacy* (1989), and Walter Isaacson, *Kissinger: A Biography* (1992).

ROBERT D. SCHULZINGER

KLINE, Franz Josef (b. Wilkes-Barre, Pa., May 23, 1910; d. New York, N.Y., May 13, 1962), ARTIST, attended Philadelphia's Girard College (a high school for orphan boys) and then Boston University's School of Fine and Applied Art (1931–35). After studying at the Art Students League of Boston, Kline went to London to study at Heatherley's Art School (1937–38). He settled in New York City in 1938. In 1950 he held his first one-man show at the Charles Egan Gallery, New York.

Kline became known for strongly personal "action" painting. His stark, startling abstractions were characterized by bold strokes of black in irregular grid patterns on white backgrounds. *Black, White, Gray* (1959, private collection) is an excellent example of his style. Kline's paintings were shown with those of other American abstract expressionists at the Tate Gallery, London (1956), and at the São Paulo International Art Exhibition (1957). They were also included in the Museum of Modern Art's important show, "The New American Painting," which toured eight cities during 1958–59. In 1960, Kline exhibited in the Venice International art show and won the

Venice Biennial award. He taught art at various schools, including Black Mountain College, North Carolina (1952), Pratt Institute, Brooklyn (1953), and the Philadelphia Museum Art School (1954). Some of his most representative works are *New York* (1953, Albright-Knox Art Gallery, Buffalo), *Siegfried* (1958, Carnegie Institute, Pittsburgh), and *New Year Wall Night* (1960, private collection).

───※───

Franz Kline came out of a repressive Pennsylvania coal-town childhood (dark, grim, and poor, and he had rheumatic fever), and after schooling in England, he went to New York and developed a style of painting in small, brilliantly colored mystic city scenes that held a dark and flagrant combination of Soutine, Goya, and **Albert P. Ryder;** he also drew sketches of objects and cartoon portraits that he loved drawing. Then, in an intuitive breakthrough, he actualized the structures of painted and drawn domestic scenes and objects: rocking chair, cat, table, wife in rocking chair. Around 1949 he broke into the black and white paintings that made him famous. The paintings were large and as violent as the Continental Drift, loaded with identity, conflicting action—opposites in collision—and language. His paint had the monosyllabic sound of smashing rocks. Or one roar. All energy.

But he was a deeply divided man, and his personal life became the violence of the opposites in collision that he painted. All energy. He was a vertical, spatial man, not horizontal and temporal. **Willem De Kooning** rightly said that Kline used black and white like color; he could see, for example, the deep blue in black, and the black in red. Around 1957 he began to use this approach toward all color. He made color synonymous with energy. Near the end of his life, as he approached this third (volatile, dangerous) major direction, his paintings had a spiritual quality. He kept his proud, generous anger and warmth, identity and language, but he wanted the whole canvas in color, and *of* color. After his second heart attack, too weak to lift those big house-painter's brushes he favored, he sat and stared into his projected, admittedly ruthless color

walls, all color of color where he had not yet gone, where he had touched but not gone. He died on that threshold, just as his friend **Jackson Pollock** had. See Fielding Dawson, *Emotional Memoir of Franz Kline* (1967).

FIELDING DAWSON

KNUDSEN, William S. (b. Copenhagen, Den., Mar. 25, 1879; d. Detroit, Mich., Apr. 27, 1948), MANUFACTURER, emigrated to the United States in 1899, worked in New York shipyards, and in 1902 moved to Buffalo, where he became a mechanic in John R. Keims Mills, a bicycle factory. By 1906 he was assistant superintendent of the factory. In 1911, when **Henry Ford** bought the plant, which had previously converted to auto parts, Ford hired Knudsen. In 1913, Ford moved Knudsen to Detroit and placed him in charge of the twenty-seven Ford assembly plants. During World War I he was head of production and responsible for the Model T.

Knudsen resigned because of differences with Ford in 1921, and General Motors hired him to run its Chevrolet division. Knudsen increased Chevrolet production from 76,000 automobiles in 1921 to 1,180,000 in 1927. In 1933 he became executive vice president of GM, and in 1937, president. In May 1940, President Franklin D. Roosevelt appointed Knudsen to the Advisory Commission of the Council of National Defense. When Roosevelt created the Office of Production Management in January 1941, he appointed Knudsen its director and allotted him the task of assisting industry to meet war production demands. Knudsen resigned this position in June 1945, and in July he returned to General Motors as a member of the board of directors.

───※───

If any American industrialist in the 20th century personified the **Horatio Alger** myth, it was William S. Knudsen. Arriving in the United States in 1899, an obscure immigrant boy, he rose by dint of hard work and extraordinary talent to be president of General Motors, which he helped build into one of the largest corporations in the world.

In personality as well as in philosophy Knudsen was a latter-day **Benjamin Franklin.** A large and jovial man, six feet three inches tall, he was genial with people from all walks of life. Even as a boy in his native Denmark he loved to tinker with his hands, building the first tandem bicycle seen in Copenhagen. He liked sports and music, played the accordion, and loved dancing parties. A many-sided extrovert, Knudsen was generally soft-spoken but could swear as profusely as any of his men.

Knudsen's philosophy was intensely practical. Although largely self-educated, he early showed himself to be a production genius. A foremost advocate of industrial efficiency, he instituted many labor-saving policies in the automobile industry and was remarkably perceptive in applying new technology. He was also a superb organizer and administrator. One of his contributions at General Motors was to decentralize its plants. His genius was revealed in marketing as well. After establishing a mass market for the Model T in the United States, he broke with Ford in 1921 and then developed Chevrolet into America's sales leader. He made both Ford and General Motors multinational corporations.

As **Andrew Carnegie** personified creative entrepreneurship in the United States during the 19th century, so Knudsen represented the creative corporate manager in the first half of the 20th century. See the New York *Times*, April 28, 1948.

GERALD D. NASH

KROC, Raymond Albert (b. Oak Park, Ill., Oct. 5, 1902; d. San Diego, Calif., Jan. 14, 1984) BUSINESSMAN, dropped out of high school at age 15 to join the Red Cross Ambulance Corps in World War I. After the war he worked as a jazz pianist, a real estate salesman in Florida during the 1920s, and midwestern sales manager for the Lily Tulip Cup Co. In 1941 he founded a company to market Multi-A-Mixers, a machine that made five milkshakes at once.

Noticing that a small hamburger restaurant in San Bernardino, California, ordered eight of his mixers in 1954, he investigated and discovered that its owners, Richard and Maurice McDonald, had developed a highly successful format for fast-food service. He convinced the McDonald brothers to franchise their operation in order to increase his mixer business, and by 1960 owned 228 restaurants with profits of $37 million. He sold his Multi-A-Mixer company and in 1961 bought out the McDonalds for $2.7 million.

Over the next twenty years, Kroc built the McDonald's chain into the largest food service organization in America, with over 7,500 outlets in the United States and thirty-one other countries. He established Hamburger University in Elk Grove, Ill., and required that all franchisees attend in order to learn how to run the business and prepare the food so there would be complete uniformity throughout the chain. As the business prospered, he branched into sports, and in 1974 he bought the San Francisco Padres baseball team. He operated the Padres until 1979 when he turned it over to his son-in-law. A major contributor to charities, he founded the Kroc Foundation in 1969. In 1974 he built the first of a series of Ronald McDonald Houses at children's hospitals to provide temporary lodging for families of seriously ill children.

—⊗⊗⊗—

In building an international restaurant chain and amassing a personal fortune estimated at over $500 million, Ray Kroc fulfilled the American dream of success through vision and dedication, and in the process he virtually revolutionized the restaurant industry. After a late start—he discovered the formula for success with his first McDonald's in 1955, at the age of 53—and a variety of dead-end jobs, Kroc found his niche in fast food retailing. A perceptive analysis of the industry led him to target the middle-class family market, building and licensing outlets in the rapidly expanding suburbs rather than in urban centers, and to choose and train his licensees carefully.

By the use of automation and assembly-line methods of preparation, Kroc was able to maintain uniform standards and provide rapid service at low prices. He monitored the operation of his restaurants closely, rigorously enforcing his motto, "Quality, Service, Cleanliness." Determined to keep every McDonald's "a dignified, clean place with a wholesome atmosphere," he instituted an employee dress code and forbade cigarette machines, newspaper racks, and even pay telephones.

Although praised for his extensive philanthropy, Kroc was accused of exploiting his youthful employees by paying them minimum wages, and the nutritional makeup of the McDonald's menu has been criticized for containing too little fiber and too much fat. Nevertheless, the network of restaurants Kroc created and the marketing and operational procedures he pioneered continue to influence the eating habits of the world. See Max Boas and Steve Chain, *Big Mac: The Unauthorized Story of McDonald's* (1976).

DENNIS WEPMAN

KUZNETS, Simon Smith (b. Kharkov, Ukraine, Apr. 30, 1901; d. Cambridge, Mass., July 8, 1985), ECONOMIST, studied economics in Kharkov before he emigrated to the United States in 1922. In that year he was admitted to Columbia University with advanced standing and received his BS in 1923 and his MA in 1924. He was a Social Science Research Council fellow from 1925 to 1927 and received his PhD in economics from Columbia in 1926; his dissertation, *Cyclical Fluctuations,* dealt with business cycles. In 1927 he joined the National Bureau of Economic Research, founded by his mentor at Columbia, **Wesley Clair Mitchell.** While working with the bureau Kuznets made many innovations in the field of quantitative analysis in economics. He became assistant professor of economic statistics at the University of Pennsylvania in 1930, associate professor in 1934, and professor of economics in 1935.

Kuznets worked on the problem of measuring national income, as seen in his two-volume *National Income and Its Composition, 1919–1938* (1941). This work eventually led to the concept of the gross national product. He also studied economic growth in both developed and underde-

veloped nations, publishing *National Product Since 1869* (1947), *Postwar Economic Growth: Four Lectures* (1964), *Modern Economic Growth: Rate, Structure, and Spread* (1966), *Economic Growth of Nations: Total Output and Production Structure* (1971), and *Quantitative Economic Trends and Problems* (1972).

Kuznets was associate director of the Bureau of Planning and Statistics of the War Production Board from 1942 to 1944 and served as president of the American Statistical Association (1949) and American Economic Association (1954). He became professor of economics at Johns Hopkins University in 1954 and then professor at Harvard in 1960. He retired in 1971 and received the Nobel Prize for economics that same year.

⸙

Slight in stature, personally shy and reserved, Simon Kuznets always dominated a situation, not by force of personality but by force of intellect. In discussion he was tough-minded, a steadfast, tireless, and objective seeker for truth. While students may have grumbled that his lectures were barely audible, few denied the wealth of original insights contained in them. His peers may have complained with some reason that he treated them like students, but they readily acknowledged his towering intellect.

Though one of the first Nobel Prize winners in economics, Kuznets was in several aspects a maverick. In a discipline where deductive analysis is the hallmark of accomplishment, Kuznets, though himself a creative and original thinker, was noted for his insistence on facts and measurement. Indeed, his happiest moments were probably those frequent mornings spent over a calculator, bending the diverse facts of reality to manageable size. In a field that prides itself on being the "queen of the social sciences," Kuznets reached out to other disciplines both in his teaching and research. At bottom this reflected his awareness of the limited ability of economic theory to comprehend reality, and especially the subject that came to be his main interest: the worldwide spread of economic development in the modern period. His work in conceptualizing this phenomenon and establishing its quantitative dimensions will stand as a major pioneering achievement in the history of social science. See

Simon Kuznets, *Economic Growth and Structure: Selected Essays* (1965).

RICHARD A. EASTERLIN

LA FARGE, John (b. New York, N.Y., Mar. 31, 1835; d. Providence, R.I., Nov. 14, 1910), PAINTER, received his first art training from his maternal grandfather, Binsse de Saint Victor, a miniaturist. He attended St. John's College (now part of Fordham University) and Mount St. Mary's College, graduating in 1853. During 1856–58 he lived in Europe. In Paris, through his maternal granduncle, Jacques de Saint Victor, author and editor, he was introduced to the conservative stream of French art, while his cousin Paul de Saint Victor kindled his enthusiasm for contemporary intellectual and artistic currents. As yet unconvinced of the merits of a career in art, he studied briefly under Thomas Couture but spent most of his time in Europe working independently in art galleries.

On his return to New York in 1858, La Farge resumed the study of law that he had begun two years earlier but soon moved to Newport, Rhode Island, to study painting under William Morris Hunt, who had been a pupil of Couture's. Concentrating mainly on landscapes and flower studies, he undertook an extensive investigation of light and color. In the 1870s he began to paint murals and was commissioned to decorate Trinity Church in Boston, Massachusetts (1876). He subsequently painted murals in the Church of the Incarnation and in the Church of the Ascension in New York City. He also developed an interest in stained glass, and his invention of opalescent glass, which produces a play of milky tints as in the opal, together with his skillful designing helped bring about a revival of that art form in America and earned him an international reputation.

La Farge also lectured and wrote on art. His books include *Considerations on Painting* (1895) and *Gospel Story in Art* (1913). He traveled extensively, frequently with his close friend **Henry Adams,** particularly in the South Seas where he painted a series of watercolors in the 1890s and about which he wrote *Reminiscences of the South Seas* (1912). He toured Japan (1886) and was one of the first to introduce the American public to Japanese art in such works as *An Artist's Letters from Japan* (1897) and a study of the Japanese artist Hokusai (1897).

Through the circumstances of his birth and early education, through his sensitivity to an immense range of artistic influences, John La Farge was uniquely qualified to respond to and guide the new cosmopolitan taste that arose in the United States in the prosperous decades following the Civil War. From the beginning of his career he engaged in a creative exploration of foreign artistic precedents in search of an art related to traditional iconography and styles and suited to modern American needs. In his work he combined allusions to world history, religion, and mythology with the traditional American respect for objective realism, enhanced by scientific analysis of optical laws, to produce a highly personal fusion of ideal and real elements. His receptivity to a variety of styles was accompanied by a lively curiosity regarding the technical means of their expression. His experiments led to the introduction of the durable encaustic medium for large-scale murals and to the application of opalescent glass to windows, an innovation that inspired numerous competitors, including **Louis Comfort Tiffany.**

La Farge's desire to make the past meaningful for the present, to educate public taste so that he might satisfy it, is manifest in his ambitious works in mural painting and stained glass, his participation in numerous professional organizations, and his publication of extensive art criticism. His efforts to bring America into the mainstream of world art are certainly no less notable than the efforts of his closest friends, Henry Adams, **Henry James, H. H. Richardson,** and **Augustus Saint-Gaudens,** to seek a reconciliation between the European and the American traditions in history, literature, architecture, and sculpture. See Royal Cortissoz, *John La Farge, a Memoir and a Study* (1911).

HELENE BARBARA WEINBERG

LA FOLLETTE, Robert Marion (b. Primrose Township, Dane Co., Wis., June 14, 1855; d. Washington, D.C., June 18, 1925), POLITICAL LEADER, graduated from the University of Wisconsin (1879) and was admitted to the bar in 1880. He practiced law in Madison, Wisconsin, and in 1880 was elected district attorney for Dane County. In 1884 he was elected to the U.S. House of Representatives as a Republican (serving 1885–91).

La Follette came into conflict in Wisconsin politics with Senator Philetus Sawyer who controlled the state Republican organization. He failed to get the Republican gubernatorial nomination in 1896 and 1898, but received the nomination in 1900 and was elected. As governor (1901–6) he opposed corruption and business control of politics. His administration established a direct primary system for nominating candidates and passed a corrupt practices act and laws limiting campaign expenditures. Believing that certain state functions called for technical knowledge, he called in experts to sit on special commissions and agencies to administer law dealing with railroad regulation, conservation, highway construction, and tax assessments. This procedure became known as the "Wisconsin Idea."

In 1905, La Follette was elected to the U.S. Senate (serving 1906–25), where he established himself as a leading progressive. He favored the Payne tariff bill of 1909 and joined the "insurgents" who opposed the higher rates added to it in the Senate. In 1909 he established *La Follette's Weekly Magazine,* which became the organ for his ideas.

In 1911, La Follette helped organize the National Progressive Republican League. He was the favorite presidential candidate of this group until Theodore Roosevelt entered the race. When Roosevelt ran on the third-party Progressive ticket in 1912 against President William H. Taft, La Follette refused to support him or any other candidate.

After the election, La Follette backed much of President Woodrow Wilson's "New Freedom" legislation. In 1915 he sponsored the Seaman's Act, designed to improve working conditions aboard merchant ships.

La Follette opposed American entry into World War I, which he thought would only benefit profiteers. His outspoken opposition to the war was severely criticized, and the faculty of the University of Wisconsin voted to censure him. Following the war he was one of the Senate "irreconcilables" who categorically opposed American entry into the League of Nations or the World Court.

In 1924, La Follette was endorsed for president by the Conference for Progressive Political Action. Supported by the Socialist Party, the American Federation of Labor, and other liberal groups, he ran on a platform advocating the nationalization of railroads, the direct election of the president, the right of labor to bargain collectively with management, and an end to monopoly. He carried only Wisconsin in the electoral college. His *Autobiography* was published in 1913.

Few senators, after their lives are spent, remain in the nation's memory. Among those who have remained, however, is Robert M. La Follette, partly because he lived up to his sobriquet of "Fighting Bob" and partly because of what he fought for and against. As a result of his family's hardships, he was as a young man prepared for struggle. La Follette entered Republican politics after working his way through college and law study. He early developed a dynamic, personal approach to campaigning, and his widespread acquaintanceship with voters and recruitment of political workers from among University of Wisconsin people were to be the hallmarks of his election campaigns.

La Follette became a reformer only after his defeat for reelection to Congress in the Democratic landslide of 1890. Subsequently blocked from influence in the regular Republican machine, he became an apostle of party primaries. His combative and suspicious nature emerged in his long but successful fight during the 1890s to dislodge the venal machine. As governor he developed the "Wisconsin Idea" of combining the political talents of the statehouse with the expertise of the university. That unprecedented alliance led to a spectacular reshaping of Wisconsin government, including establishment of primary election laws, increased regulation of corporations, expansion of educational opportunities, a forestry board, a civil service commission, and a tax commission to put taxation on an equitable basis. The "Wisconsin Idea" dominated the state until World War I. Thanks to La Follette and his supporters, Wisconsin became the pioneer not only in progressive state action but also in drawing upon the resources of the intellectual community.

After taking his seat in the U.S. Senate in 1906, La Follette quickly established himself as that body's leading progressive member. Again his aggressive tactics were strongly in evidence as he sought to combat the power of giant economic interests in America. He employed his rhetorical brilliance both on the Senate floor and around the country to enlist substantial support for progressive legislation. Not only did La Follette tirelessly press for reform measures and strenuously expose the flaws in his opponents' records, but he acted as the conscience for progressivism at all levels of government. His charm and sense of humor were usually left at home during his crusades against privilege.

His record of legislative success is impressive. He was instrumental in the passage of laws to protect the rights of civil servants, to restrict the working hours of railway workers, and to stop the exploitation of merchant seamen. He was also a leader in the successful battles to reform railroad ratemaking, to curb excesses in campaign finances, to extend suffrage to women, and to investigate the Teapot Dome oil leases. No American officeholder was involved so deeply and so consistently as La Follette in the struggle for social justice and democracy in America. But La Follette's record was also one of stirring opposition to what he thought was wrong. This was seen in his attempts to defeat the Payne-Aldrich Tariff, to prevent President Taft's renomination, and to keep the United States out of World War I and out of the League of Nations, which he believed was "an instrument to enforce an unjust peace which could only lead to future wars."

La Follette remained "Fighting Bob" to the end, as was seen in his presidential campaign the year before his death. His platform called for government encouragement of cooperatives, further restriction of capitalism's power, international action to outlaw war and imperialism, and public works programs to combat economic depressions. Although he lost the election, his 1924 platform served as something of a bridge between progressivism and the New Deal.

In retrospect, it is clear that La Follette was too much the advocate of the small town and the farmer in a society rapidly becoming urbanized and industrialized. Moreover, he did not fully see the ramifications of a mass-production-consumption economy and of the revolutionary impact on relations among nations by new economic, transportation, and communications developments. He plainly saw, however, the need in a stable society for social justice and honest government. For those he battled ceaselessly, as he did for perfection of democratic institutions, education of voters, and individual rights in an increasingly organized society. Both as a moral force and as a successful political tactician, La Follette was equaled by few Americans during the 20th century. See David P. Thelen, *Robert M. La Follette and the Insurgent Spirit* (1976).

DONALD R. McCOY

LA FOLLETTE, Robert Marion, Jr. (b. Madison, Wis., Feb. 6, 1895; d. Washington, D.C., Feb. 24, 1953), POLITICAL LEADER, attended public schools in Madison while his father was governor of Wisconsin and also in Washington, D.C., while his father was senator. He attended the University of Wisconsin (Madison) from 1913 to 1915 but had to leave when he became seriously ill. After his recovery from a second and even more severe illness, La Follette became his father's secretary (1919) and helped manage his unsuccessful bid for the presidency in 1924 as the Progressive Party candidate. Upon his father's death in 1925, La Follette was elected to fill his Senate seat as a Republican. He championed labor legislation, farm relief, unemployment compensation, and a St. Lawrence seaway. Elected to a full Senate term in 1928, La Follette attacked President Herbert Hoover's depression policies, particularly when his La Follette–Costigan bill for unemployment relief was opposed and defeated by the administration.

La Follette generally supported Franklin D. Roosevelt's New Deal; he urged expansion of the PWA and Work Relief Bill, and was the key figure in the 1935 tax reform. Revitalizing the Progressive Party in Wisconsin with his brother Philip in 1934, La Follette won reelection to the Senate in 1934 and 1940. He urged the Roosevelt administration to back government ownership of the railroads, munitions plants, electric power facilities, and a central bank. Beginning in 1936, as chairman of the Senate Civil Liberties Committee, La Follette conducted a four-year investigation of antiunion tactics, wages and living standards, and working conditions throughout the country.

An isolationist in foreign affairs, La Follette opposed U.S. participation in the World Court and repeal of the neutrality laws in the 1930s and the Lend-Lease Act. After World War II, however, he supported the United Nations (although with certain reservations as to American involvement). La Follette drafted the congressional reorganization bill to streamline the legislative process, which became law in 1946. After the Progressive Party disintegrated, La Follette lost the 1946

Republican Senate primary to **Joseph R. McCarthy.** He remained in Washington as an economic consultant to such firms as United Fruit Co. and served on the board of Sears, Roebuck and Co. As vice president of the Sears Foundation he administered funds for many philanthropic causes. He committed suicide in 1953.

La Follette began his career in the Senate as his father's heir. He acquired his deep and abiding commitment to progressive principles through close association with his father and exposure to his father's friends. The elder La Follette's activities and concerns were regular topics for family discussion, and his two sons were frequently included in conferences between their father and even his most illustrious visitors. Young Robert was also aware of the vilification his father experienced during World War I, and that experience probably strengthened his own antiwar feelings. He differed from his father in being more cautious and reflective, which may have been due in part to his two long and painful illnesses.

Although elected to the Senate as his father's successor, young Robert soon won recognition in his own right, and his importance grew in the more friendly climate of the New Deal until he became one of the Senate's most influential members. For the most part he worked harmoniously with Roosevelt, but he also played an important role as progressive critic of the New Deal. Much of the legislation of the period bore his stamp, especially in the areas of relief and public works, tax-reform, and labor relations. His Civil Liberties Committee investigation was one of the period's major accomplishments.

La Follette's opposition to World War II tended to undercut his influence, which steadily waned after 1940. He became increasingly divorced from his constituency, allowed his political organization in Wisconsin to crumble, and was defeated in the 1946 primary. Under more favorable circumstances, he (and Philip) might have had a more lasting influence on the political scene, but the New Deal destroyed third-party prospects. Alternatively he might have joined the

Democratic Party and made it a viable force in Wisconsin. He was deterred from doing so partly by the nature of Wisconsin politics and partly by loyalty to Philip. See Roger T. Johnson, *Robert M. La Follette, Jr., and the Decline of the Progressive Party in Wisconsin* (1964).

VAN L. PERKINS

LAGUARDIA, Fiorello Henry (b. New York, N.Y., Dec. 11, 1882; d. New York, N.Y., Dec. 20, 1947), POLITICAL LEADER, received his early education in Arizona, where his father, an army musician, was stationed. After working for the Phoenix *Morning Courier,* he was a correspondent for the St. Louis *Post Dispatch* in Florida. Following his father's death, LaGuardia's family moved to Hungary, where (1901–6) he was a U.S. consul in Budapest and Fiume, and an interpreter.

In 1906, LaGuardia returned to New York City, where he studied law at New York University (LLB, 1910) and worked as an interpreter on Ellis Island (1907–10). In 1914 he was an unsuccessful candidate for the U.S. Congress. In 1915 he was appointed deputy attorney general for New York. Unwilling to cooperate with the Democratic bosses of Tammany Hall, LaGuardia was elected to Congress as a Republican in 1916. In Congress (1917–19) he worked to liberalize the House rules and voted for President Woodrow Wilson's declaration of war (1917). During the war he served in Italy as an air force captain.

Following the war LaGuardia opposed postwar loans to the Allies and vigorously excoriated U.S. Attorney General **A. Mitchell Palmer**'s use of the Espionage Act (1917) to attack aliens. In 1921–23 he served as president of the New York City board of aldermen. In 1922 he was again elected to Congress (serving 1923–33), where he supported old-age pensions, employment insurance, and employers' liability bills. In 1932 he co-sponsored the Norris–LaGuardia Act, which limited the power of the federal courts to issue injunctions against unions engaged in peaceful strikes, and outlawed "yellow-dog" contracts, which required workers to promise not to join unions.

In 1934, LaGuardia was elected mayor of New York City on a Fusion Party ticket (serving until 1945). His administration was marked by its pro-labor attitude and by an intensification of public works projects. He served as president of the U.S. Conference of Mayors (1936–45), and in 1938 he helped push through a new charter for New York City.

When the United States entered World War II, LaGuardia became director of the Office of Civilian Defense (1941–42) and coordinator of the U.S.-Canadian Joint Defense Committee (1940–46). In 1946 he was named special ambassador to Brazil and was later appointed director general of the U.N. Relief and Rehabilitation Administration (1946). His *Autobiography* was published posthumously (1948; ed., M. L. Werner).

Schooled in Manhattan's political jungle as a Republican district leader, LaGuardia could have turned out to be another tough, big-city, small-minded politician. Instead, he involved himself in the great issues and major forces of his society—immigration, the emergence of the United States as a world power, and the evolution of the modern liberal state. But however representative of his times, the ambitious little man who kept a bust of Napoleon on his desk was a very special kind of man.

Raised in Arizona as an Episcopalian by an agnostic father from Italy and a Jewish mother from Austria, LaGuardia was first married to a Trieste-born Catholic and then, after her death, to a Lutheran of German parentage. There were still other reasons that Mayor Jimmy Walker called the Little Flower "the cosmopolite of this most cosmopolitan city." As a result of his consular service in the Balkans, he could campaign, depending on the constituency, in Italian, Serbo-Croatian, Hungarian, Yiddish, or German. And although a lifelong Republican, he ran for office with the endorsement, at one time or another, of the Bull Moose, La Follette Progressive, Socialist, City Fusion, and American Labor parties.

But his first political base rested on a personal

machine in New York City's Italian colony. As East Harlem's congressman in the 1920s, he struggled to enlarge the welfare functions of the federal government, and also fought against Yankee imperialism, the cult of big business, prohibition, and the Nordic nonsense that resulted in immigration restriction. A New York tabloid celebrated him as "America's Most Liberal Congressman." But the gadfly of the Harding-Coolidge era won few victories in Congress, and in 1927 he said, "I am doomed to live in a hopeless minority for most of my legislative days."

He fully came into his own only after the Crash. The Anti-Injunction Act, for which he and Senator **George Norris** had agitated throughout the age of normalcy, was suddenly passed in 1932. More important, the next year LaGuardia was elected mayor of New York City, an office for which he had been twice defeated in the 1920s.

Unlike his upper-class reform predecessors in City Hall, LaGuardia succeeded himself in office, in 1937 and again in 1941. The local coalition that voted for the Democratic Roosevelt was more or less the same coalition that retained the Republican LaGuardia in power for twelve years. The mayor gave the city its own New Deal, and what is equally important, he dramatized himself and the issues so vividly that he made progressive government in New York synonymous with his own name.

When World War II broke out, the mayor, for whom World War I had been a romantic highlight, wanted desperately to be commissioned an army general. The president seemed to be sympathetic, and LaGuardia ordered his uniform. But Secretary of War **Henry L. Stimson** blocked the commission, reasoning that there were generals enough but that only LaGuardia could command the nation's most important home front. When he took over as civilian general of UNRRA after the war, LaGuardia's international reputation as an American liberal leader was exceeded in his generation only by Franklin D. Roosevelt's.

He once boasted to a campaign manager that he could "outdemagogue the best of demagogues," but on another occasion he pleaded for "government with a heart." Therein lies the uniqueness of this extraordinary hybrid in American politics. Part professional politician and part progressive reformer, LaGuardia pursued power cunningly but applied it humanely. See Arthur Mann, *LaGuardia* (1965).

ARTHUR MANN

LAND, Edwin Herbert (b. Bridgeport, Conn., May 7, 1909; d. Cambridge, Mass., Mar. 1, 1991), SCIENTIST, entered Harvard in 1930 but took a leave of absence while still a freshman to work independently on the problem of light polarization and did not return. In 1932 he announced the discovery of what was termed Polaroid—a substance that allowed light to pass through it while permitting objects to be seen without glare. He patented the first Polaroid sheets in 1934. Together with Harvard physicist George Wheelwright III, Land established the Land-Wheelwright Laboratories in Boston in 1932 as general physics consultants. They began manufacturing Polaroid in camera filters to eliminate reflections in 1935, and in 1936 the American Optical Co. began to use Polaroid lenses in sunglasses. In 1937 the Polaroid Corporation was established in Cambridge, Massachusetts, with Land as president, chairman of the board, and director of research, the job to which he devoted most of his time. He developed a film for three-dimensional pictures in 1941 and headed research teams on infrared searchlights and gun sights during World War II. He was also a consultant to Division Five of the National Research Council on guided missiles.

In 1947, Land announced the invention of "one-step" photography, a camera that took and developed pictures within seconds. Marketed in 1948, the camera netted more than $5 million its first year. Also in 1948, Land developed the color translation microscope to observe living and diseased cells in color. His self-developing photographic dosimeter, invented in 1950, measured amounts of exposure to atomic radiation. Polaroid Corporation also made several million dollars manufacturing glasses for viewing three-dimensional movies starting in 1953. Land was visiting institute professor at the Massachusetts Institute of Technology in 1956 while a fellow at its School for Advanced Study. In 1959 he announced development of one-step color photography, marketing the necessary camera and color film in 1963. A member of the President's Science Advisory Committee, Land was awarded the Presidential Medal of Freedom by Lyndon B. Johnson in 1963. He held 533 patents in the areas of light polarization and photography when he retired. In 1972 Land invented the pocket-size Polaroid color self-developing camera and film.

The company ran into problems in the mid–1970s, however, many of them involving the technically sophisticated SX–70, an instant camera with complex optics. At first, with the expectation on Wall Street that the company would generate explosive profits, the stock soared to $149.50 a share in May 1972. But when Wall Street's expectations did not pan out, by July 1974 the stock plummeted to $14.13 a share. The SX–70 was followed by the Polavision instant movie system, which proved to be a flop and was pulled from the market in 1979. Kodak, which brought out an instant camera of its own, began to undermine Polaroid's dominance. But Polaroid sued Kodak for patent infringement, and in 1985 Kodak lost and pulled out of the instant camera market. A federal judge ordered it to pay Polaroid $909.4 million, a sum later reduced by an appeals court to $36 million. Land retired from Polaroid in 1982.

———— ✆ ————

Edwin H. Land can be considered the **Thomas A. Edison** of his time. In an era of specialization he successfully combined the roles of scientist, inventor, and businessman. At a time when intellectuals such as C. P. Snow were lamenting the fragmentation of life, Land was one of those rare individuals who transcended the two cultures of science and government as well as science and the business world. He was as much at home as a professor in the classrooms and laboratories of the Massachusetts Institute of Technology as in the executive offices of the Polaroid Corporation. Scientists, government officials, and business-

men regarded him as one of the most talented and distinguished applied physicists of his day.

Land's success was the result not only of his striking talents but of two significant trends in American life: involvement of the United States in World War II and intensive American concern in the ensuing two decades with national security during the cold war did much to accelerate research and development in applied physics and optics. Moreover, the emergence of an affluent society in the United States between 1945 and 1970, and the growth of consumer and leisure-oriented mass markets opened up vast new opportunities for the camera and related industries. It was a tribute to Land's business acumen that he perceived these opportunities early and capitalized on them brilliantly. In the process he built one of the most innovative and creative large American corporations to emerge during the second half of the 20th century. See Peter C. Wensberg, *Land's Polaroid: A Company and the Man Who Invented It* (1987).

GERALD D. NASH

LANDIS, Kenesaw Mountain (b. Millville, Ohio, Nov. 20, 1866; d. Chicago, Ill., Nov. 25, 1944), JURIST, BASEBALL COMMISSIONER, was the son of a physician who was wounded at the Battle of Kennesaw Mountain, Georgia, during the Civil War and who named his son accordingly but dropped one of the *n*'s. He grew up in Logansport, Indiana, where he quit high school to become a court reporter for the Logansport *Journal*. In 1883, Landis became an official court stenographer in Logansport, a job that stimulated an interest in the law. He attended Union College but did not graduate. After taking YMCA law courses, he was admitted to the Illinois bar in 1891. He served two years (1893–95) as private secretary to Secretary of State Walter Q. Gresham in the Cleveland administration, after which he returned to his Chicago law practice. Originally a Democrat, he switched to the Republican Party in the late 1890s, and in 1905, President Theodore Roosevelt appointed him to the U.S. district court of northern Illinois. Two years later Landis attracted national attention when he fined

Standard Oil Co. of Indiana more than $29 million for accepting freight rebates. The decision, however, was reversed by higher courts. During World War I, Landis received further publicity when he presided over the sedition trials of Socialists and leaders of the International Workers of the World. He sentenced the men to maximum terms, but in 1927 his decision on the Socialists was reversed by the Supreme Court, which cited him for prejudice.

In 1920, in the wake of the "Black Sox scandal" involving the "fixing" of the 1919 World Series, Landis, who had played semiprofessional baseball while working in Logansport, was named organized baseball's first high commissioner. He served both as commissioner and as judge before he was forced to resign from the bench in 1922. Landis remained commissioner until his death and sought to rule baseball with an iron hand, cracking down especially hard on gambling. But some of his decisions, such as his attempt to keep the minor leagues independent of major-league control, were reversed by major-league owners. During World War II he labored successfully to keep baseball alive through the use of older and physically deferred players.

———— ∞ ————

As commissioner of American baseball from 1920 to 1944, Landis earned the reputation of being the game's puritanical "czar" who had saved baseball from the taint of corruption. Ensconced in his spartan Chicago headquarters with *baseball* lettered in black on the door to his office, the white-maned judge made telling use of "a piercing eye, a scowl, and a rasping voice" to foster his own image of the game's "Integrity Mountain." Determined to erase the stain of baseball's "Black Sox scandal," he flailed away at all appearances of corruption by cracking down on suspected players, threatening players and owners engaged in suspicious activities, personally supervising the collecting and disbursing of World Series receipts, and negotiating baseball's first World Series radio broadcasting contracts. Landis's zealous and widely publicized efforts restored an honest image to professional baseball

and won for him a legendary reputation as one of the giant figures in the game's history.

But Landis's overall impact on baseball is more controversial. As self-styled czar he quarreled with club owners who opposed his desire to prevent major-league control of the minor leagues. And on this issue Landis was badly beaten. Meanwhile players, resenting his disregard for their civil rights, were moving to organize themselves to prevent further encroachments. In 1932 a cabal of owners nearly denied his reelection to a seven-year term. His death in 1944 prompted owners to weaken the powers of the commissioner post, a trend that organized players and owners continue to this day. Because of Landis's theatrical high-handedness, the post of baseball commissioner grew increasingly ornamental. Today power and decision-making in the sport are determined far more by the interplay of owner and player interests with those of the communications industry. See David Quentin Voigt, *American Baseball: From the Commissioners to Continental Expansion* (1970).

DAVID QUENTIN VOIGT

LANDON, Alfred Mossman (b. West Middlesex, Pa., Sept. 9, 1887; d. Topeka, Kans., Oct. 12, 1987), POLITICAL LEADER, graduated from the University of Kansas (1908). He became an independent oil operator. He worked for the Progressive Party in 1912 and 1914, and in 1922 became secretary to Governor Henry Allen of Kansas. He was Republican state chairman from 1928 to 1930.

Landon was elected governor of Kansas in 1932. His administration (1933–37) reorganized the state government, reformed state and local finances, started a water conservation program, and instituted effective utility rate regulation. Landon won the Republican presidential nomination in 1936. Although his campaign emphasized governmental efficiency and economy, his views on labor and relief were moderate, on agriculture and conservation distinctly liberal. He carried only Maine and Vermont in the electoral college. After the election he supported President Theodore Roosevelt in the *Panay* controversy (1937) and was vice chairman of the American delegation to the Lima Inter-American Conference (1938). Although he favored developing national defenses and giving some aid to the Allies, Landon vigorously opposed American entry into World War II. He took an independent position after the war, advocating moderation in domestic affairs and seeking liberalized foreign trade and recognition of Communist China. In 1988 his younger daughter, Nancy Landon Kassebaum, was elected to the first of several terms in the United States Senate.

Alfred Landon is best remembered for his landslide defeat in the 1936 presidential election. There is more than that, however, to his place in history. He was strongly influenced by his father's political independence and by his own need for independent action as a freelance oilman. He learned early how to negotiate between conflicting interests and, in case of failure, to pursue what he thought would achieve justice. This led him twice to bolt the Republican Party, as a Theodore Roosevelt Progressive and as a leader in **William Allen White**'s 1924 independent gubernatorial campaign.

Landon had actively opposed the Ku Klux Klan, fought major oil and utility companies, advocated conservation, and been a successful reform governor. As Republican presidential nominee, titular party head, and elder statesman, he endeavored to reconstruct his party into a moderate instead of a conservative force. He urged Republicans, with some success, to recognize labor's interests, regulate capitalism's excesses, support essential welfare services, champion civil liberties, and seek world peace while maintaining adequate national defenses.

Although Landon was charming with small groups, in major appearances he occasionally seemed cranky because of his independence and sometimes dull because of his imperfect oratory. It is ironic that a man who was a splendid executive should spend most of his political life as a critic, for which he was not greatly suited rhetorically. Nevertheless, he contributed substantially throughout his life to the debates within his party

and between parties, which helped to keep vibrant two-party democracy and the freedoms underlying it. See Donald R. McCoy, *Landon of Kansas* (1966).

DONALD R. MCCOY

LANGMUIR, Irving (b. Brooklyn, N.Y., Jan. 31, 1881; d. Schenectady, N.Y., Aug. 16, 1957), CHEMIST, graduated from the School of Mines of Columbia University in 1903, after which he studied at the University of Göttingen, receiving his PhD in 1906. He was an instructor in chemistry at the Stevens Institute of Technology, Hoboken, New Jersey (1906–09). He then joined the General Electric Research Laboratory in Schenectady, New York, serving as assistant (1909–32) and as associate director (1932–50). His first work at the laboratory involved the investigation of gases produced when tungsten filaments were heated in a vacuum—a study related to the rapid deterioration of the filaments used in G.E. electric light bulbs.

In 1912, Langmuir discovered that the use of nitrogen or argon to fill the bulb would retard this deterioration. During World War I he worked at the Naval Experimental Station at Nahant, Massachusetts, on submarine detection devices. In 1928 he invented the atomic hydrogen welding torch. He also did important studies of gas reactions at low pressures, and of the vapor pressures of metals. A collection of some of his scientific papers was published in 1950 as *Phenomena, Atoms, and Molecules: An Attempt to Interpret Phenomena in Terms of Mechanisms of Atomic and Molecular Interaction*. In 1932, Langmuir was awarded the Nobel Prize in chemistry for his work in the field of surface chemistry.

Irving Langmuir's prolific output of high-quality scientific work—more than 200 significant scientific papers—spanned physics, chemistry, and electrical technology. His trademark was the ability to illuminate subtle and sophisticated phenomena through the performance and explanation of simple experiments. His tools were a film of oil upon water in a tray or common gases within an incandescent bulb. To them he brought what a colleague called "the ability to think vividly in atomic terms." Austere, cold, absentminded, and aloof to those who did not know him, Langmuir nonetheless inspired a series of brilliant collaborators—Coolidge, Hull, Kingdon, Blodgett, Schaeffer, and many more. If he was sometimes intolerant of the scientific errors of others or oblivious to his surroundings, it was out of absorption with the problem at hand, not out of deliberate ill will. His scientific intensity might then be discharged in outdoor recreation such as hiking, skiing, and flying.

Langmuir was temperamentally unsuited to teaching. The industrial laboratory was his habitat. He was conscious that in the end a corporate industrial laboratory was judged not by its scientific output but by the products it launched. To this end he contributed the gas-filled lamp, the pure electron discharge tube (in the process verifying and extending O. W. Richardson's physics of thermionic emission), and hydrogen arc welding. His work had limits—he respected the quantum theory but did not venture into it. But inside these limits he boldly subjected a wide range of subjects—from protein structure to rain-making—to his vivid, searching (and usually successful) powers of analysis. See C. Guy Suits and Harold E. Way, eds., *The Collected Works of Irving Langmuir* (12 vols., 1962), esp. Vol. 12, "Langmuir, the Man and the Scientist."

GEORGE WISE

LANSING, Robert (b. Watertown, N.Y., Oct. 17, 1864; d. Washington, D.C., Oct. 30, 1928), DIPLOMAT, graduated from Amherst College in 1886. He was admitted to the bar in 1889, entering his father's law firm. His marriage to Eleanor Foster, daughter of President William H. Harrison's secretary of state John Foster, kindled Lansing's interest in international law and gave him many connections. In 1892 he was associate counsel for the United States in the Bering Sea fur-seal arbitration. He participated in the founding of the American Society of International Law (1905) and helped establish the *American Journal of International Law.*

Lansing represented the United States before many international arbitration tribunals and practiced international law until his appointment as counselor of the State Department in 1914. Upon the resignation of Secretary **William Jennings Bryan** in 1915 during the *Lusitania* crisis, Lansing became secretary of state.

As secretary, Lansing worked for stability and security in the Caribbean and peace with Mexico. He drafted notes of protest to the British for their abuses of neutrals on the high seas but urged a policy of friendship toward England instead of Germany. Lansing helped negotiate the purchase of the Danish Virgin Islands and signed the Lansing-Ishii Agreement (1917) with Japan, which called for the "Open Door" for China but recognized Japan's special interests in that country. After U.S. entry in World War I, he helped persuade Wilson to intervene in Russia and to encourage dismemberment of Austria-Hungary.

Lansing accompanied Woodrow Wilson to the Paris Peace Conference after the war, but the two men broke over several issues concerning the peace treaty. This breach was revealed by William C. Bullitt in his testimony before the Senate Foreign Relations Committee as well as by Lansing's own feeble testimony before that committee. In 1920 the president demanded Lansing's resignation on the ground that he had undermined the president's power by calling unauthorized cabinet meetings during Wilson's illness. Lansing returned to his private law practice in Washington and wrote a number of books, including *The Peace Conference: A Personal Narrative* (1921). He also served as vice president and trustee of the Carnegie Endowment for International Peace.

Despite his abilities and his service during one of the great crises of the 20th century, the importance of Lansing's role has only recently received recognition. A reserved and withdrawn individual, conservative in tastes and views, Lansing was overshadowed by the dynamic president and his well-publicized intimate adviser, Colonel **E. M. House.** Far from being the mere clerk previously assumed, however, Lansing had a vital part in Wilsonian diplomacy. Realistically inclined in foreign affairs, though sharing the American faith in the superiority and destiny of democracy, Lansing viewed a victorious Germany as endangering America's national interests in terms of security, economics, and ideology. Therefore he joined House in urging war against Germany. Thereafter he sought a peace that would preclude imperialism by absorbing Japan and defeated Germany within a stable world order, while countering the revolutionary drive of Bolshevism. Yet while Lansing was entitled to high rank among heads of the State Department, his secretaryship fell short of greatness. His conservative and realistic views on foreign policy and his personality prevented him from establishing a good working relationship with the more idealistic and far-visioned Wilson. Lansing was unable to subordinate his judgments to the president or to give him the uncritical flattery that Wilson found congenial. Moreover, on traditional and realistic grounds, Lansing questioned the soundness of the collective security scheme on which Wilson had set his heart. The real cause for Lansing's dismissal in 1920 was not the "unauthorized" cabinet meetings he called but Wilson's view of him as personally disloyal at Paris and during the struggle for ratification of the Versailles Treaty. See Daniel M. Smith, "Robert Lansing, 1915–1920," in Norman Graebner, ed., *An Uncertain Tradition: American Secretaries of State in the Twentieth Century* (1961), pp. 101–27.

DANIEL M. SMITH

LATROBE, Benjamin Henry Boneval (b. Fulneck, Eng., May 1, 1764; d. New Orleans, La., Sept. 3, 1820), ARCHITECT, grew up in England but was educated at German Moravian schools in Silesia and Saxony and at the University of Leipzig. He returned to study engineering with John Smeaton (1786–88) and then architecture with Greek revivalist Samuel Pepys Cockerell (1788–89). Latrobe designed several homes in England and worked on a canal in Surrey, but after the death of his first wife in 1793, he emi-

grated to Virginia in 1796. He worked as a consultant on projects for improving navigation of the Appomattox and James rivers and in 1797 designed a penitentiary in Richmond where convicts could be held in solitary confinement. He completed the façade of the Virginia State Capitol (1798), designed by Thomas Jefferson, and then moved to Philadelphia in 1799 to work on the Bank of Pennsylvania, the first Greek Revival, Ionic structure in the United States. From 1799 to 1801, Latrobe designed the Philadelphia water supply system, using steam engines to pump water to the city from the Schuylkill River. This plan was described in *View of the Practicability and Means of Supplying the City of Philadelphia with Wholesome Water* (1799).

In 1803, President Jefferson appointed Latrobe surveyor of the public buildings in Washington, D.C., in which post he built the south wing of the Capitol for the House of Representatives, the Senate wing having been completed by architect William Thornton. (The two men had clashed over revised plans for the Capitol, but Jefferson backed Latrobe's ideas.) In 1804, Latrobe designed the Baltimore Cathedral for Bishop John Carroll in Gothic Revival style. He designed the Pennsylvania Academy of Fine Arts in Philadelphia (1805), the Bank of Philadelphia (1807), the Marine Hospital in Washington (1812), and numerous private homes. In 1812, Latrobe formed a partnership with **Robert Fulton, Robert Livingston,** and Nicholas J. Roosevelt to build and adapt steamboats for the Ohio River, but the plan collapsed with the death of Fulton in 1815. After the British burned Washington during the War of 1812, Latrobe was put in charge of rebuilding the Capitol; he designed new Senate and House chambers. Retiring from federal service in 1817, Latrobe advised Jefferson on the designs of several buildings for the University of Virginia. Latrobe went to New Orleans in 1818 to complete the waterworks started by his son Henry, who had died of yellow fever.

———✦———

Combining a learned admiration for antique forms with an engineer's awareness of functional requirements, Latrobe produced an architecture that was highly responsive to both the philosophical aspirations and the practical needs of the young American republic. Hoping to revive "the days of Greece … in the woods of America," to make Philadelphia "the Athens of the Western world," Latrobe would apply the Ionic order of the Erechtheum to the porticoes of the Bank of Pennsylvania and recall the dignity of the Parthenon in his competition design for the second Bank of the United States. He would, however, never sacrifice the necessities of use to the beauty of these borrowings or permit literal replicas of antique buildings to confine or darken his banking halls, counting rooms, or offices. The general character of Greek architecture was thoroughly consistent with his personal aesthetic, and it was this general character that he exploited. When, during his tenure as superintendent of Philadelphia's water supply, he designed the Center Square Pump House, a building for which no classical prototype existed, he produced a work whose massiveness and bold juxtaposition of solids and voids are related at once to the essential breadth of Greek architecture and to the functional forms of modern technology.

Although the major part of his work reflects his preference for Greek forms and looks forward to the Greek Revival that was to dominate American architecture from 1820 to 1860, Latrobe could also experiment with borrowings from other stylistic traditions. Along with the design adapted from the Propylaea which was accepted for the new Catholic Cathedral in Baltimore, Latrobe also submitted a Gothic design, thereby anticipating the second key revival movement in mid–19th-century American architecture.

A bold and innovative designer, Latrobe was unfortunately subject to a series of professional and financial disasters: dismissal from his most prestigious architectural position, the superintendence of the project for rebuilding the U.S. Capitol after the War of 1812, and successive bankruptcies resulting from various engineering schemes. He died penniless. See Talbot Hamlin, *Benjamin Henry Latrobe* (1955).

HELENE BARBARA WEINBERG

LAWRENCE, Amos (b. Groton, Mass., Apr. 22, 1786; d. Boston, Mass., Dec. 31, 1852), MERCHANT, attended Groton Academy before being apprenticed to a merchant in Dunstable, Massachusetts, in 1799. After finishing his apprenticeship in 1807 he went to Boston where he worked as a clerk in a merchant's house before opening his own store later that year. He took in his younger brother Abbott as an apprentice in 1808 and made him a partner in 1814. The firm of A. and A. Lawrence soon became a prosperous commercial house, dealing in imported goods. Lawrence expanded his mercantile activities, invested in banks, and gained a personal fortune estimated at $1 million at his death. In 1830 he established a cotton factory at Lowell, Massachusetts, which grew into one of the largest enterprises in New England. He later expanded into the manufacture of woolens. A Federalist turned Whig, Lawrence served one term in the Massachusetts house of representatives (1821–22) and was a Whig presidential elector.

Declining health forced him to retire as head of his firm in 1831, and Lawrence devoted the rest of his life to philanthropy. He contributed to many schools, including Kenyon College, Wabash College, Williams College, and Groton, which changed its name to the Lawrence Academy in 1846. Lawrence also contributed to the erection of the Bunker Hill Monument, which was completed in 1843. He aided many libraries and contributed heavily to Boston hospitals and aid societies. After his death his sons collected his letters and memoirs, publishing them as *Extracts from the Diary and Correspondence of the Late Amos Lawrence* (1855).

⬥

The career of Amos Lawrence illustrates an important aspect of American economic history—the transfer of capital from the older mercantile sector of the economy to the more rapidly expanding manufacturing sector. Through the 1820s Lawrence's business activities were typical of the many seaboard merchants who built substantial fortunes through trade, primarily through wholesaling. From colonial days into the first half of the 19th century these middlemen—

including such famous examples as **Stephen Girard,** the Hancocks of Boston, the Browns of Rhode Island, **John Jacob Astor,** and others— were the most important and wealthiest businessmen in America. When the Industrial Revolution developed in the United States, many of them invested their mercantile profits in factories like the textile mills that Amos Lawrence backed. Such businessmen provided the support that made a reality of **Alexander Hamilton**'s vision of an industrialized America.

Amos Lawrence embodied the usual array of business virtues of his time (hard work, caution, thrift), but he was also interested in things other than profits. His philanthropic and political endeavors, as well as the very human quality of his diary and letters, marked him as a man concerned with many aspects of life. He was not a pioneering entrepreneur; his mercantile career was like that of many others before him, and he did not enter textile manufacturing until almost two decades after other New England merchants had demonstrated in 1813 the success of factory production of textiles in the path-breaking Waltham mill of the Boston Manufacturing Co. Nevertheless, Lawrence's career earned the admiration of his contemporaries and contributed to the nation's growth. See Freeman Hunt, ed., *Lives of American Merchants,* II (1858), pp. 223–30.

GLENN PORTER

LAWRENCE, Ernest Orlando (b. Canton, S.D., Aug. 8, 1901; d. Palo Alto, Calif., Aug. 27, 1958), SCIENTIST, graduated from the University of South Dakota in 1922 and received his MA from the University of Minnesota in 1923. He then studied physics at the University of Chicago (1923–24) before moving to Yale where he received his doctorate in physics in 1925. After a two-year postdoctoral fellowship from the National Research Council at Yale he became assistant professor of physics there in 1927. He was appointed associate professor of physics at the University of California at Berkeley in 1928 (full professor in 1930), remaining there until his death.

In 1929, Lawrence conceived the idea of a cyclotron, a device that would use an electromagnetic field to hold fundamental nuclear particles in a series of circular orbits so that they could be accelerated to successively higher energies on each orbit within the vacuum chamber. In an experimental cyclotron four and one-half inches in diameter, which he built with M. Stanley Livingston in 1930, Lawrence was able to accelerate hydrogen ions to 80,000 electron volts with less than 1,000 volts on the accelerating electrodes. Five cyclotrons and nine years later Lawrence and his associates could accelerate similar particles to 16 million electron volts in a sixty-inch cyclotron.

These achievements led to the establishment of the Radiation Laboratory at the University of California in 1932, to Lawrence's appointment as director of the independent laboratory in 1936, and to the award of a Nobel Prize in 1939. Ever more powerful cyclotrons permitted the laboratory to play a leading role in the worldwide effort to produce and study scores of artificially created radioisotopes and eventually to create and identify new man-made elements heavier than uranium. Working with his brother John, Lawrence also made important contributions in medical applications of the radiation sources created by the cyclotron.

In World War II, Lawrence played a major role in the Manhattan Project, which produced the atomic bomb. He applied the principles of cyclotron technology in developing the mass spectrograph, or electromagnetic method, for separating the 235 isotope from natural uranium. After the war the Radiation Laboratory under Lawrence's direction developed new types of accelerators, principally the synchro-cyclotron and the proton synchrotron, which made it possible to extend particle energies above 1 billion electron volts and led to the discovery of mesons and other subnuclear particles. In the late 1940s and the 1950s Lawrence received virtually every award that could come to a physicist and engineer. As director of the Radiation Laboratory and as adviser to the Atomic Energy Commission and the Department of Defense, he helped formulate national policy on the development of nuclear weapons—especially the hydrogen bomb, the production of special nuclear materials, the development of nuclear power for civilian purposes, and the design of sophisticated weapons systems for national defense. At the time of his death he was serving as a member of a three-man committee of experts exploring with Soviet representatives at Geneva the possible suspension of nuclear weapon tests.

In many respects the career of Ernest Lawrence closely paralleled the development of American physics after World War I. Through his training at the University of Chicago and at Yale, Lawrence was able to attach himself, at least indirectly, to the then essential European base of modern physics, but he was never fully captivated by the European tradition and in 1928 staked his future on the fledgling physics department at the University of California in Berkeley. There he quickly demonstrated the American predilection for experimental physics. His conception of the cyclotron provided the fundamental tool for the extraordinary developments that occurred in nuclear physics in the next two decades. Lawrence's buoyant self-confidence and enthusiasm attracted to the Berkeley laboratory scores of exceptional students and princely grants from private foundations. He took a decidedly pragmatic approach to developing the hardware of modern physics and finding practical applications in both engineering and medicine for the laboratory's accomplishments.

By the time World War II broke out in 1939, Lawrence had won a Nobel Prize and had gained an international reputation. His eagerness to apply the newly discovered phenomenon of nuclear fission to the war effort was an important contribution to the establishment of the Manhattan Project. Lawrence's energy and creativity, which were so valuable to the project in the beginning, eventually led the American project into what was probably overcommitment to Lawrence's method of producing material for the bomb, but most of the uranium 235 in the

Hiroshima explosion came from this process.

After the war Lawrence used his enormous prestige to make the Berkeley laboratory the world center for high-energy physics, now supported by the largesse of the Atomic Energy Commission rather than by university or private funds. The gathering of Nobel laureates at Berkeley was dramatic evidence that the world looked to America instead of Europe for new trends in research.

During these same postwar years Lawrence continued to support efforts by the American government to develop new military applications of modern physics. As an influential adviser to both the Atomic Energy Commission and the Department of Defense, he promoted the development of the hydrogen bomb and a variety of weapons systems. He also helped establish the new branch of the laboratory devoted to weapons research at Livermore, California.

In the middle fifties, after the **Julius R. Oppenheimer** security hearings, Lawrence was a spokesman for that group of conservative scientists of the World War II generation who felt few moral pangs about helping to build the awesome arsenal of nuclear weapons for national defense during the cold war years. But by the time of his death in 1958, a new social consciousness among younger American scientists and the maturing of institutional structures were already tempering the unrestrained exuberance of the Lawrence tradition. See Herbert Childs, *An American Genius: The Life of Ernest Orlando Lawrence* (1968).

RICHARD G. HEWLETT

LAZARSFELD, Paul Felix (b. Vienna, Austria, Feb. 13, 1901; d. New York, N.Y. Aug. 30, 1976), SOCIAL SCIENTIST, received his PhD in mathematics from the University of Vienna in 1924 and taught mathematics before turning to applied psychology. He became an instructor at the Psychological Institute of the University of Vienna in 1929 and director of its Division of Applied Psychology. He published *Die Arbeitslosen von Marienthal,* a study of unemployment in an Austrian village, in 1933. He arrived in the United States in 1933 on a grant from the Rockefeller Foundation for study in psychology but decided to remain permanently. Becoming director of the Foundation's Office of Radio Research in 1937, Lazarsfeld conducted a study of the influence of radio on public opinion. When the project moved to New York City in 1940 Lazarsfeld joined the sociology department at Columbia. He published *Radio and the Printed Page* (1940) and, with Frank Stanton, *Radio Research, 1941* (1941) and *Radio Research, 1942–43* (1944). During World War II, Lazarsfeld served as a consultant to the Office of War Information, the War Production Board, and the War Department.

During the 1940s Lazarsfeld turned his attention to studying voting patterns. As director of Columbia's Bureau of Applied Social Research he published *The People's Choice* (1944) and later another study, *Voting* (1954). Lazarsfeld stepped down as bureau director in 1949 to become chairman of the sociology department at Columbia, and in 1963 he became Quetelet Professor of Social Science. In 1970 Lazarsfeld was given the title of Distinguished Professor at the University of Pittsburgh, where he taught until his death. He served as president of the American Sociological Association in 1961. Lazarsfeld was coauthor of *The Academic Mind* (1958) and *Continuities in Social Research* (1950). A collection of essays, *Mathematical Thinking in the Social Sciences* (1954), demonstrated the use of mathematics in solving behavioral problems. Some of his other works include *Organizing Educational Research* (1964) and *The Uses of Sociology* (1968).

―――――

When European sociologists speak of "American sociology," they mean the empirical, quantitative, survey-research sociology that Paul Lazarsfeld, a transplanted European, brought into being. Beginning with radio audiences, shifting to the study of audience behavior generally, consumer behavior, and voting behavior, Lazarsfeld literally invented modern survey research. In all this he was driven by the aim of knowing why and how individuals made the decisions that taken together shaped the mass media, the mar-

kets, and the politics of a massive society. He searched for causal relationships rather than mere descriptions of attitude or behavior distributions, and in the search became one of the originators of "panel studies" that extended survey research through multiple waves of interviews with the same sample of persons.

The combination of this search with his earlier training in mathematics led him around 1950 to push in still another direction, opening and giving focus to the field of mathematical sociology. The force of his energy and his personality, the problems he posed, and his own contributions to their solution initiated a body of work that has been central to mathematical sociology since its inception.

The importance of Lazarsfeld to sociology from the 1940s on cannot be seen from his published work alone. He began the Bureau of Applied Social Research at Columbia as almost his personal instrument, and it became the prototype for applied social research organizations throughout the country. He attracted faculty and students around him at the Bureau and in Columbia's sociology department. He dominated whatever environment he was in and transmitted his energy to a host of students. No one around him at Columbia could be neutral to him or to the sociology he practiced; he generated controversy, he made enemies, he created new directions, and he altogether invigorated the social sciences. See Paul Lazarsfeld, *Qualitative Analysis* (1972).

JAMES COLEMAN

LEDERBERG, Joshua (b. Montclair, N.J., May 23, 1925), GENETICIST, graduated from Columbia in 1944, studied medicine at the College of Physicians and Surgeons, Columbia University, 1944–46, and received a PhD in microbiology from Yale in 1947. During 1947–58 he was on the faculty of the University of Wisconsin, becoming professor of genetics in 1954. In 1957 he established the Department of Medical Genetics at Wisconsin. In 1958 he was appointed chairman of the Department of Genetics at the Stanford University School of Medicine. He shared the 1958 Nobel Prize in medicine and physiology with Edward Tatum of the Rockefeller Institute and George Beadle of the California Institute of Technology for his work on the genetics of bacteria. He discovered a method of artificially introducing new genes into bacteria. By this breeding of bacteria he gave new insights into their genetic mechanism, thereby making the study of hereditary substances easier. In 1961 he was named a member of the President's Panel on Mental Retardation. In 1962 he became the director of Stanford University's Lieutenant Joseph P. Kennedy, Jr., Laboratories for Molecular Medicine, and a member of the Panel on Scientific Information of the President's Science Advisory Committee. In 1971 he was named a member of the Institute of Medicine of the National Academy of Science. In the 1970s and 1980s Lederberg was a consultant to NASA, and he wrote extensively on issues dealing with the environment, evolution, and the future of mankind. In the 1990s he appeared as a host on a Public Television program on science.

Through articles, testimony before federal committees, the science column of the Washington *Post*, and public television, Joshua Lederberg became a major spokesman for the scientific community. Eclectic in his interests, the balding, heavyset professor warned of microorganic contamination from space probes, argued for further examination of fluoridation effects, discussed the cost-benefit of peaceful nuclear energy, suggested missile-test monitors as a means to arms control, called for a national board to direct genetics research, and denounced biological warfare.

His most significant contribution, however, was his research in genetics, which strikes at the essence of life itself. Lederberg's work on bacteria, which won the Nobel Prize, demonstrates the sexual nature of bacterial recombination and illustrates the hitherto ignored complexity of such small organisms. It indicates that initial life must have been of a much simpler nature.

Beyond that his study touches the explosive issue of genetic manipulation. But except for prenatal medical use, he rejected both positive and negative eugenics as futile because all humans carry faulty genes. Feasible, however, is clonal propagation, which would duplicate the genetic composition of a living individual. According to Lederberg this would be an "evolutionary cul-de-sac" but would have the advantage of testing environmental against hereditary factors in human development.

On such possibilities, however, his thought reflects an acute appreciation for democratic decisions, common sense, and the need to consider the broad ramifications of genetic tinkering. "The penultimate crime," Lederberg has written of a eutechnical society, "may become to introduce any technological innovation as a subsystem benefit without analyzing its impact on the whole future of man." Worse would be the constraint of earth's most valuable asset—human intellect. See Joshua Lederberg, "Eutechnics—Motif for New Technology," *Technology Week*, XX (Jan. 23, 1967), 49–50 ff.

DAVID McCOMB

LEE, Ann (b. Manchester, Eng., Feb. 29, 1736; d. Watervliet, N.Y., Sept. 8, 1784), RELIGIOUS LEADER, received no schooling and worked in factories during early adolescence. In 1747 her family and other Quakers who believed the Second Coming was imminent followed James Wardley into the Shaker Society. At 26 she unwillingly married Abraham Stanley, and in the next four years bore four children; all died in infancy.

Ann Lee, like other Shakers, was punished for enthusiastic, physical religious practices that were held to profane the Sabbath. While in prison in 1770 she received a vision convincing her that human iniquity derived from sexual intercourse. She subsequently claimed to be the female aspect of God, the woman mentioned in the Bible in Revelation 12 as having the power of grace. She preached against procreation, and in 1774, while imprisoned again, received a vision telling her to go to America. With her husband and a small group of Shakers, Mother Ann sailed for New

York and remained there for two years. Her belief in celibacy heightened tensions in her marriage, and in 1776 she left her husband and joined other Shakers in a community in Watervliet, New York. Economic survival of the settlement was her concern for the next four years. Through visions and prophecies, she continued to teach the progressive development of the kingdom of heaven on earth. In July 1780, during the Revolution, she and the Watervliet elders were imprisoned for treason because they preached against war, but they were released five months later by Governor **George Clinton's** order. That year, New Lebanon, New Light Baptists—then questioning their Baptist affiliation because of visions of the Second Coming—accepted Mother Ann, thereby becoming the second American Shaker community. She traveled through southern New England from 1781 to 1783, meeting frequent mob hostility. She nevertheless established Shaker groups in Enfield, Connecticut, and Harvard, Shirley, Hancock, and Tyringham, Massachusetts. Following her death the Shakers spread through New York and New England, and into the West, under Joseph Meacham.

Ann Lee's teaching of celibacy may have had early psychological determinants. According to Shaker reports, she urged her mother to resist her father's "lust" and gained her mother's protection against her father's whip. The death of her babies and her mother deepened her abhorrence of lust. Because she grew up in the same crowded factory towns which later convinced some economists that overpopulation doomed laborers to degradation, her teachings may be interpreted as a religious response to the Industrial Revolution. In Christian thought, furthermore, saintliness had recurrently been identified with sexual abstinence. This idea had obvious attractions to a movement seeking the liberation of female believers and the reunification of mankind in larger, holier "families." Celibacy promised a perfect escape from sinful competition and an undivided loyalty to the kingdom of God.

Mother Ann Lee taught her disciples to be gentle toward children and to share earthly goods equally with the poor among them. She possessed great serenity and self-confidence. She was especially effective in personal encounters with converts, who were moved by her courage in facing persecution and her humility in answering their doubts. Ann Lee, though celibate, became "Mother" to a family of disciples, on whom she often waited, we are told, like a servant. Her disciples won many new converts during the religious revivals of early-19th-century America; and Shaker communities, based on the common ownership of property, gained worldwide attention. The teachings of this illiterate emigrant from England's "dark satanic mills" have thus been hailed as important precursors of modern socialism. See Henri Desroche, *The American Shakers from Neo-Christianity to Presocialism,* tr. John K. Savacool (1971).

LEWIS PERRY

LEE, Charles (b. Dernhall, Eng., 1731; d. Philadelphia, Pa., Oct. 2, 1782), MILITARY LEADER, was educated at Bury St. Edmunds and later in Switzerland. Commissioned an ensign in his father's regiment, the 44th Grenadiers, at the age of 16, he became a lieutenant in the regiment in May 1751. During the French and Indian War he saw action with General James Braddock's expedition to western Pennsylvania (1755), was wounded in the unsuccessful attack on Fort Ticonderoga (1758), and aided in the capture of Fort Niagara and Montreal (1760). In 1761, while serving as a major in General John Burgoyne's expedition against the Spanish in Portugal, he distinguished himself at the battle at Villa Velha. Later, in 1765, he served in the army of King Stanislaus Poniatowski of Poland as an aide-de-camp and major general. He was Polish minister to Constantinople, Turkey, in 1766, spent the next two years in England, and when a civil war broke out against Poniatowski's rule in 1769, he accompanied the king's forces in Moldavia to put down the rebellion. Returning to England in 1771, he issued some pamphlets attacking King George III and the Tories and professed a love for a not very sharply defined "liberty." Two years later he returned to America, purchased an estate in Berkeley County, Virginia (now W. Va.), and became a warm opponent of British policy toward America. He published a pamphlet (1774) telling Americans they could stand against British troops. (This work, directed against that of Dr. Myles Cooper, bore the title *Strictures on a Pamphlet, Entitled, "A Friendly Address to All Reasonable Americans."*) In June 1775 he was commissioned a major general in the Continental army, having renounced his half-pay pension from the British army. Upon the retirement of Major General Artemas Ward he became second in command of the army to George Washington.

Lee strengthened the defenses of Newport and New York (Jan. 1776), and Williamsburg and Norfolk (Mar.–May 1776). He became critical of Washington's military ability after the fall of Fort Washington and addressed letters to that effect to Joseph Reed and Horatio Gates (Dec. 1776). He was deliberately slow in withdrawing to join Washington's main body in New Jersey from Philipsburg, New York, maintaining that he preferred to harass the British flank. He now argued that Americans could *not* stand up to the British in a major battle and believed in guerrilla warfare for the Continentals. After finally reaching New Jersey, Lee was captured by the English (Dec. 13, 1776) and spent the next eighteen months as a prisoner in New York. While held by the British he prepared a memorandum for General Howe (which came to light in 1858) that has led some to believe he planned to aid British victory. Released by the British in an exchange for General John Sullivan in April 1778, he went to York, Pennsylvania, where he lobbied in Congress on behalf of his own promotion. He returned to the army at Valley Forge in May. He took command of the American advance attack on General Henry Clinton's army at Monmouth (June 28, 1778) but inexplicably retreated. Court-martialed for disobedience to orders, "misbehavior before the enemy … making an unnecessary, disorderly and shameful … retreat," and disrespect to the commander in chief, he was found guilty on all counts and suspended from the army for a year (Aug. 12, 1778). He published a "Vindication" (1778) in the *Pennsylvania Packet* that was extremely hostile to Washington. Henry Laurens challenged him to a duel for his remarks and wounded him in the fight. After an arrogant letter to the Congress, Lee was dismissed from the army in January 1780.

⁂

Lee came from a system in which an officer needed money, connections, or a patron in order to rise. Having none, he was pushy and took care to advertise his own deeds, which were taken at his own evaluation by the Americans. Thus a vain, intelligent, unstable soldier of fortune very early achieved second rank in the Continental army. With some effort he could be persuasive with people who could help him, and he was willing to help himself by undercutting his superiors as a way of building politically on a military reputation.

His physique was odd and gangling. He was said to be usually dirty and threadbare, and never without dogs, of whom he was quoted as saying they were better than people. He was quarrelsome in voice and with pen, but could make loyal friends. He was often generous. A cruel and much reprinted caricature of the time was said by those who knew him to be not a bad portrait. To attract attention he liked to shock a theistic age by irreverent remarks.

At Monmouth he bungled a battle through lack of confidence in the American forces. There is no proof of treason. Rather, he seems to have lost faith in the possibility of a rebel victory by the end of 1776, and perhaps he saw himself as fated to play the glorious role of peacemaker. In fairness it must be noted that British descriptions of Monmouth reported it as a hard and difficult fight. But after Monmouth, Lee had no doubt he was right but had no reason to think he was right.

Lee did not take a direct part in any important Continental victory, nor did he share the severe hardships of the troops. His professional competence may have been overrated, since he neglected the drudging details of security, reconnaissance, and operational planning. His underestimation of the recuperative qualities of the Continentals shows that he simply did not believe the evidence of his senses on that point. He was, above all, imprudent. This was shown most notably in his demand for a showdown with Washington, which he could not possibly win. He sketched himself with true self-knowledge in a letter to the Congress after he left the army in 1780: "If I have ... been guilty of any treason it has been against myself alone, in not once from the beginning of the contest to this day consulting common prudence with respect to my own affairs." See John R. Alden, *Charles Lee, Traitor or Patriot?* (1951).

MARSHALL SMELSER

LEE, Ivy Ledbetter (b. Cedartown, Ga., July 16, 1877; d. New York, N.Y., Nov. 9, 1934), BUSINESSMAN, PUBLICIST, attended Emory College (Atlanta) but transferred to Princeton in 1896 and graduated in 1898. He briefly attended Harvard Law School (1899), but when his money ran out, he went to New York City to work as a reporter for the *Morning Journal.* Between 1899 and 1903 he worked for the *Journal,* New York *Times,* and the New York *World* while studying English at Columbia. In 1903, Lee left newspaper work and became publicity manager for the Citizens' Union, which was backing Seth Low for mayor of New York against George B. McClellan, Jr. He then opened his own publicity firm, serving the Democratic National Committee in 1904 and many large corporations, including the Pennsylvania Railroad. He spent two years in Europe (1910–12) managing a New York banking firm and lecturing at the London School of Economics. He then returned to New York as executive assistant to the Pennsylvania Railroad but was "loaned" by that company to the Rockefeller family in 1914.

His prestige enhanced by the connection with the Rockefellers, Lee opened his own public relations firm in 1916. Besides continuing work for the Rockefeller family and various corporate clients, he served as publicity director and assistant to the chairman of the American Red Cross

during World War I. In the 1920s he prospered as the public relations consultant of trade associations and such large companies as Bethlehem Steel, Armour, and Chrysler. He served as an American delegate to conferences of the Institute of Pacific Relations in 1927 and 1929, and he favored U.S. diplomatic recognition of the U.S.S.R. In 1934, Lee was investigated by the House Un-American Activities Committee for his ties with I. G. Farben but was cleared of charges that he was a propaganda agent for the Nazi government. His books include *Human Nature and Railroads* (1915), *Publicity—Some of the Things It Is and Is Not* (1925), and *Present-Day Russia* (1928).

Lee's basic commitment to the business system was shaped by his family contacts in Atlanta. There he was exposed to the paternalism and enterprise of the class that promoted industry for the "New South." Serious, hardworking, and ambitious, even as a youth he admired and sought contact with famous men. First as a newspaper reporter and then as a pioneer public relations specialist, he impressed business leaders with his understanding of their complex political and economic problems and with his courtly formal manners, which fit the corporate image they desired.

Although his first opportunities came from businessmen's needs to answer muckraking critics of "heartless corporations," Lee insisted that he was not merely a glorified press agent. Beyond publicity he aspired to managerial status as a high-level policy adviser to business and government. Promoting the New Era philosophy of "welfare capitalism," he claimed that competition undermined efficiency and profits and thereby opened the way for chaos and dangerous collectivism. American business could better meet its obligation of public service by improving the world materially and spiritually through cooperation at home and abroad.

Despite the assertion that he was a professional counsel concerned with the total policies and activities of clients, Lee's approach was severely limited. Lacking adequate appreciation of substantive issues, he tended to regard economic or international conflict as essentially the result of faulty communication, which experts like himself could correct. Nothing better revealed that inadequacy than his brief and apparently innocent efforts on behalf of the Nazi-controlled I. G. Farben. See Ray E. Hiebert, *Courtier to the Crowd* (1966).

ALAN RAUCHER

LEE, Richard Henry (b. Westmoreland Co., Va., Jan. 20, 1732; d. Westmoreland Co., Va., June 19, 1794), POLITICAL LEADER, graduated from the Academy of Wakefield in Yorkshire, England (1751). He returned to America in 1752. In 1758 he was elected to the Virginia House of Burgesses where he supported legislation to check the growth of slavery and to investigate the allocation of state treasury funds. When Parliament passed the Sugar Act (1764) and the Stamp Act (1765), Lee organized the Westmoreland Association, a nonimportation league. In 1773, with Thomas Jefferson and **Patrick Henry,** he initiated a proposal for intercolonial committees of correspondence to plan joint action.

As a delegate to the first Continental Congress (1774), Lee supported nonimportation measures. At the second Continental Congress he introduced a resolution (June 7, 1776) calling for a declaration of independence, a confederation of the states, and foreign alliances. During the debates over the Articles of Confederation, Lee urged the Virginia assembly to give up its claims to western lands. Giving most of his time in Congress to foreign affairs, he and **Samuel Adams** led the "eastern faction" opposed to French domination of American peacemaking efforts.

Lee served in the Continental Congress (1784–87; president, 1784–85). He refused to attend the Federal Convention at Philadelphia (1787), and in his *Letters of the Federal Farmer* (1787), he criticized the new Constitution, arguing that the Convention had been authorized only to amend the Articles of Confederation and that the new charter lacked a bill of rights. Nevertheless, Lee was elected to the U.S. Senate (serving 1789–92).

Lee's motion for independence appropriately climaxed a decade of aggressive and confident opposition to British imperial policy. Unfortunately, the fame he achieved at this moment has overshadowed his steady contributions to the creation of the American republic over a thirty-year period. His polished, terse speeches led contemporaries to dub him the Virginia Cicero, but too few samples of his oratory have survived to ensure him a place among great American political orators. Lee and his brothers (William, Francis Lightfoot, Arthur) formed the most significant family group of the Revolution. Despite their importance, they have not received the attention given some lesser men. Yet historians rightfully acknowledge the central political role of Richard Henry Lee.

Beyond Lee's influence on events, his life tells us much concerning the Revolutionary generation. He opposed slavery while he held more than three dozen slaves. He called politics the "Science of fraud" but practiced it to perfection. While advocating the harmonious union of the colonies, he divided Congress and much of the new nation in defense of his brother Arthur. Known all his political life as a relentless partisan with a talent for detecting wrongdoing in opponents, his popular *Letters* against the Constitution were marked by fairmindedness and dispassion. An aristocrat, he used the argument that "supreme power is in the people" to oppose ratification of the Constitution. Though coming from one of Virginia's most notable families, he worked most closely in Congress with New Englanders and once expressed a desire to spend his last days in Massachusetts. See Oliver Chitwood, *Richard Henry Lee* (1967).

CHARLES W. AKERS

LEE, Robert Edward (b. Stratford, Va., Jan. 19, 1807; d. Lexington, Va., Oct. 12, 1870), MILITARY LEADER, graduated from the U.S. Military Academy (1829) and served in the engineer corps, rising to captain in 1838. During the Mexican War he fought at Buena Vista, Veracruz, Cerro Gordo, and Chapultepec, where he was wounded. During 1852–53 he was superintendent of West Point, supervising reform of the curriculum. He was made a lieutenant colonel of cavalry in 1855 and served in Texas. In 1859 his troops helped suppress **John Brown**'s raid on Harpers Ferry.

Although Lee opposed secession, after Virginia left the Union he resigned from the army (Apr. 1861) and accepted the command of Virginia's military forces. After General **J. E. Johnston** was wounded, Lee was given command of the Confederate Army of Northern Virginia, with the rank of general. In the Seven Days' Campaign (June 26–July 2, 1862), Lee defended Richmond against General **George B. McClellan.** Although the battle was indecisive, McClellan's procrastination enabled Lee to check the attack. After defeating General Pope at Second Bull Run (1862), he marched into Maryland but was checked at Antietam by Union forces. He then crossed the Potomac back into Virginia.

Lee defeated General Ambrose Burnside at Fredericksburg (Dec. 1862), and at Chancellorsville (May 1863) he overwhelmed another Union army under General Joseph Hooker. In June 1863, Lee decided to take the offensive and carry the war into the North. On July 1 he took control of the town of Gettysburg, Pennsylvania. His troops then occupied Seminary Ridge, while the Union army, under General **George Meade,** took its position on Cemetery Ridge, a mile to the west. Despite days of heavy fighting, the Confederate army failed to penetrate the Union lines. However, Meade's failure to attack enabled Lee to retreat to safety.

In May 1864, General Ulysses S. Grant began to advance against Lee's forces in Virginia. He was checked at the Battle of the Wilderness (May 5–6), suffering heavy casualties, but moved southeast in a flanking action. The armies clashed again around Spotsylvania Court House (May 8–12). In a five-day attack Grant again lost heavily but, believing that Lee could be defeated only in a battle of attrition, continued to advance. On June 3 he attacked at Cold Harbor, nine miles

from Richmond, again suffering heavy losses. When Grant then attacked Petersburg, Lee dug in to defend that city. Gradually surrounded, he finally tried to retreat to the Richmond and Danville Railroad. Richmond fell on April 3, 1865, and Lee, with fewer than 30,000 able-bodied men at his disposal to Grant's 115,000, surrendered to Grant at Appomattox Court House (Apr. 9), thus ending the war.

After the war Lee became president of Washington College (1865), which was renamed Washington and Lee University in his honor (1871).

Great soldiers often have something odd about them. Lee's superb corps commander **Stonewall Jackson** struck those who knew him at the beginning of the Civil War as schoolmasterish and cranky. Of Lee's chief adversaries, Grant in 1861 was a seedy failure who had resigned his commission years before; and **William T. Sherman,** also out of the army, was a man subject to fits of acute self-doubt. Of the other, more obviously soldierly candidates for high rank on either side—McClellan, **Pierre G. Beauregard,** Joseph E. Johnston—none quite lived up to expectation. Perhaps men who look the part are apt to be too vain, too concerned with appearances, too anxious to go by the book. Robert E. Lee is a rare example of a man who looked like a perfect soldier, and was. His father had been a cavalry hero of the American Revolution and a devoted friend of George Washington. Lee's wife was the great-granddaughter of Martha Washington. He graduated from West Point with a spotless record. His subsequent career was one of steady excellence. In 1861 Lincoln's general in chief, **Winfield Scott,** was ready to offer Lee the field command of the Union forces. Other Virginians, including Scott and **George H. Thomas,** stayed with the Union. Lee no longer owned any slaves, nor was he stirred by the vision of a new southern nation committed to the maintenance of slavery. He fought with the Confederacy not because he loved warfare but for Virginia and for the abstract principle of states' rights. As such he might have been expected to be a little lukewarm in his loyalty to the Stars and Bars or to his new master, President **Jefferson Davis,** who was not an easy person to serve. Or his more than thirty years in the old army, with its humdrum routines, might have made him hidebound and timid. After all, he had never handled as much as a whole regiment, let alone an army; the peacetime army was an affair of isolated fragments, and the Mexican War a fading memory. From the time he became head of the Army of Northern Virginia until the surrender at Appomattox nearly three years later, he was always outnumbered by the enemy and usually short of food, equipment, and ammunition. What then is the secret of Lee's extraordinary performance?

The morale of his men, the genius of Jackson, and the mistakes of his opponents were of course significant factors. But Lee's own qualities are not to be slighted. It was his leadership that sustained the morale of his ragged army and unnerved the Union generals who preceded Grant. One possibly important point is that Lee was in fact fighting in and for his beloved Virginia through most of the war. His initial assignment as military adviser to Jefferson Davis lasted only a few months, and by February 1865, when he was promoted to the supreme field command of all the Confederate armies, it was too late in the day for him to contemplate grand strategy. He was able without strain to equate the effort for the Confederacy with the effort for Virginia. A second point to stress is that sheer necessity encouraged him to be audacious. He knew that he had to offset inferiority in numbers and weapons with superiority in generalship. He had to be nimbler than his opponents in avoiding a battle (when the conditions were unfavorable for him) and in bringing one on as soon as the moment was right (for example, when he had a chance to strike at a detached portion of the Union army instead of having to face its whole strength). He had to rely on his intuitive sense of what the enemy was going to do and to build on his hunches. Conversely, he had to be bold to the edge of recklessness at certain moments, so as to seize the initiative and knock his opponents off balance.

Historians have suggested that even Lee revealed occasional weaknesses or made occasional errors of judgment. A common observation is that he left a little too much discretion to his corps commanders. This was understandable in the case of Jackson, with whom he had an ideal rapport. Perhaps it was less wise with a subordinate like **James Longstreet,** whose reluctance to press the Union forces in the opening stages of Gettysburg had serious consequences. It is also arguable that Lee erred in going over to the offensive so soon after Chancellorsville, when Jackson had been mortally wounded and he had just altered his army's organization. But part of Lee's magic for his officers and men lay in their knowledge that he trusted them and that if things turned out badly, he would not lose his head or his temper. As for Gettysburg, it was a giant raid rather than a full-scale offensive, and as such it certainly had the electrifying effect, North and South, that Lee desired. In sum he was a marvelous soldier—cool, quick, decisive, resourceful, amazingly tactful in dealing with Jefferson Davis and, when defeat eventually faced him, a beautiful loser. See Douglas S. Freeman, *Robert E. Lee* (4 vols., 1934–35).

MARCUS CUNLIFFE

LEIDY, Joseph (b. Philadelphia, Pa., Sept. 9, 1823; d. Philadelphia, Pa., Apr. 30, 1891), SCIENTIST, left school at the age of 16 to work in a drugstore but soon began to study anatomy with a private instructor, Dr. James McClintock. In 1841, Leidy entered the University of Pennsylvania, where he studied under Dr. Paul B. Goddard. Receiving his MD in 1844, his thesis was on "The Comparative Anatomy of the Eye in Vertebrated Animals." During 1844–46, Leidy practiced medicine in Philadelphia. At the same time he continued studying comparative anatomy, publishing reports on fossil shells from New Jersey and on the anatomy of the snail. In 1845 he was elected to membership in the Academy of Natural Sciences in Philadelphia and the Boston

Society of Natural History. Also in 1845 he determined that pork was a prime source of trichinosis in humans. From 1846 until his death he served as chairman of the board of curators of the Academy of Natural Sciences. During 1847–48 he served as demonstrator of anatomy at the Franklin Medical College in Philadelphia and published several essays on parasitology and on vertebrate paleontology. He then moved to the University of Pennsylvania, where he acted as assistant to Dr. William Horner, professor of anatomy. He accompanied Horner on a tour through Europe in 1848. In 1849 he was elected to membership in the American Philosophical Society in Philadelphia.

In 1850, Leidy became assistant to Dr. George B. Wood, professor of the practice and theory of medicine at the University of Pennsylvania. In 1853 he was appointed professor of anatomy at the Medical School of the university, a position he held until his death. During the Civil War he served as surgeon at Salterlee Military Hospital in Philadelphia. When the National Academy of Sciences was founded in 1863, Leidy was one of its charter members. He was also professor of natural history at Swarthmore College (1870–84) and professor of zoology and comparative anatomy as well as director of the newly organized department of biology at the University of Pennsylvania (1884–91). He was president of the Academy of Natural Sciences from 1881 until his death. In addition to his teaching and frequent research trips, Leidy wrote prolifically. He had more than five hundred titles to his credit, some of the more important being *Flora and Fauna Within Living Animals* (1853), *Extinct Mammalian Fauna of Nebraska and Dakota* (1869), *Fresh-Water Rhizopods of North America* (1879), and *Elementary Treatise of Human Anatomy* (1861). In 1884, Leidy won the Lyell Medal from the Geological Society of London, and in 1888 the Cuvier Medal from the Academy of Sciences of Paris.

※

Joseph Leidy was one of the most distinguished descriptive natural historians in 19th-century America. He observed nature with the keen eye of a scientific artist. The precision of his descriptions and his illustrations of fossils and living organisms has never been surpassed. He was respected and admired greatly by his students because of his kindness to them, the clarity of his lectures, and his precise and accurate drawings. It was with their support, as well as that of the medical faculty, that he was appointed professor of anatomy at the age of 30.

The range of his scientific studies was very broad; parasitology in the United States was founded by him, and he was North America's greatest paleontologist. His many studies of fossil mammals and reptiles are basic to this science. Included in his discoveries are the American origin of the horse as well as studies of the fossil remains of the North American camel, sloth, and dinosaur. In later life he became the outstanding contributor to our knowledge of one-celled animals (protozoa).

Though Leidy was primarily a descriptive natural historian, in a paper prepared in 1851 (published 1853) he clearly outlined the basic doctrine of evolution, for he described the disappearance of species, their replacement in time, and the role of the environment in speciation. This is of particular interest because after Darwin published in 1858–59, Leidy rarely discussed evolution even though his own research contributed much to its study. Also, ten years before Pasteur published on spontaneous generation, Leidy clearly denied the possibility of it.

A quiet man, he had great vigor and enormous productivity. His students and young associates all spoke of his kindness and willingness to offer advice, his generosity, and his avoidance of scientific quarrels in a period when such quarrels were common to American science. Leidy had confidence in his stature as a scientist and saw to it that the University of Pennsylvania adequately supported his position and his department. Not as well known to the public as **Asa Gray** or **Louis Agassiz,** his impact on 19th-century American science is unsurpassed, and many of his published scientific works are still of major importance today. See Henry C. Chapman, "Memoir of Joseph Leidy," Academy of Natural Sciences *Proceedings* (1891).

DAVID R. GODDARD AND BEVERLY H. ORLOVE

L'ENFANT, Pierre Charles (b. Paris, Fra., Aug. 2, 1754; d. Prince Georges Co., Md., June 14, 1825), ENGINEER, SOLDIER, son of a court painter, was trained in engineering and architecture. In 1777 he arrived in America to take part in the American Revolution, joining the Continental army. He fought at Savannah (Oct. 1799), was captured in 1779 at Charleston (released in 1782), and was promoted to major in the engineers in 1783. After a brief visit to France he settled in New York City in 1784. There he designed a number of residences and, in 1789, converted the old City Hall into Federal Hall, the first center for a new national government. (The building was much more elaborate and costly than anticipated, and L'Enfant declined the payment offered—ten acres of land and later $750—because he felt he deserved more.) This work brought him to the attention of George Washington, who asked him to survey and design the proposed federal city in the District of Columbia. L'Enfant's designs, based partly on the construction of Versailles, envisioned a much larger and more complex city than had originally been intended. He utilized a combination of gridiron street patterns and long radial avenues to set off his proposal for monumental public structures and extensive parks. His unwillingness to accept the advice of the commissioners of the Federal District, as well as his secrecy about the specifics of his designs, led to his removal from his post in 1792.

During the following year, through **Alexander Hamilton**'s influence, L'Enfant worked on plans for a proposed industrial city near the present Paterson, New Jersey, but once again the grandiose nature of his designs and his unwillingness to share authority ended his employment. He later designed a number of private residences, including a palatial home for **Robert Morris** (1793) that was never finished because it became too costly. In 1784, L'Enfant was appointed temporary engineer to improve the defenses of Fort Mifflin on the Delaware River, but again little work was actually done.

He received $600 plus expenses for his work on the design of the federal city but demanded (1800) $95,500. In 1810 he settled for $1,394.20

and cancellation of $200 due on a lot in Washington. His last public employment (1812) was a commission to strengthen Fort Washington on the Potomac, also never completed because of his extravagant plans.

⸻

Though L'Enfant led a long and moderately active life, his claim to fame is actually based on a single year's work—from March 1, 1791, when Washington commissioned him to "survey the ground" for the new federal city, until February 27, 1792, when Jefferson curtly dismissed him. L'Enfant's accomplishments during that one year were of such a magnitude as to warrant his position in the history of American urbanism. In that brief period he surveyed the terrain, a wilderness of swamp and forest; designed the full armature of a great capital city; outlined a program for its most expeditious development; and set in motion a process of construction that has continued, with some interruptions, for 180-odd years.

L'Enfant's work has been fogged in rumors of arrogance and incompetence from the very beginning, and a fully detailed analysis of it remains to be done. But the documents themselves establish the astonishing prescience of his planning, which envisioned a brand-new city more complete in its amenities than any in the world, including czarist Petrograd. His development proposal envisioned the completion of the entire armature of squares and boulevards in one great effort, with private and public construction being carefully concentrated around these nodes rather than being thinly spread on a hit-or-miss basis. He challenged the financing method (i.e., sale of lots on a first-come, first-served basis), urging that long-range borrowing would permit more rapid and orderly development. And his first work program, for the 1792 season, giving detailed quantities of man-hours, materials, and equipment, shows him a complete master of the actual construction process.

Unhappily, the same documents show how he was defeated in the triangular crossfire between the commissioners (who represented the interests of local landowners); Secretary of State Jefferson (who for all his "Roman" passion was inexplicably cool toward L'Enfant's grand plan); and Washington (who supported L'Enfant most consistently but ultimately surrendered him to bureaucratic exigencies). See H. Paul Caemmerer, *The Life of Pierre Charles L'Enfant, Planner of the City Beautiful, the City of Washington* (1950).

JAMES MARSTON FITCH

LEWIS, Harry Sinclair (b. Sauk Centre, Minn., Feb. 7, 1885; d. Rome, Italy, Jan. 10, 1951), WRITER, graduated from Yale in 1908 and became a reporter and freelance writer. In the years that followed he traveled from New York to California, taking many writing jobs. He published his first novel, *Our Mr. Wrenn*, in 1914. Although he had considerable financial success writing for such popular magazines as the *Saturday Evening Post* and *Cosmopolitan*, he did not win literary acclaim until he published *Main Street* in 1920. The story, set in a small Minnesota town, satirized the narrowness and provincialism of middle America. Lewis followed this success with *Babbitt* (1922), the story of a midwestern businessman, and *Arrowsmith* (1925), an attack on the stifling intellectual atmosphere of the medical profession. Lewis refused to accept the 1926 Pulitzer Prize for *Arrowsmith*. He published *Elmer Gantry* (1927) and *Dodsworth* (1929) before going to Stockholm to accept the 1930 Nobel Prize for literature.

During the later period of his life, Lewis lived in both the United States and Europe. He published ten more novels, many of them commercially very successful and a few concerned with serious subject matter, notably *It Can't Happen Here* (1935), which dealt with the threat of fascism in the United States, and *Kingsblood Royal* (1947), about racial prejudice. But critics considered most of the late novels thin and bloodless.

Sinclair Lewis enjoyed one decade of genuine triumph interspersed between nearly a decade of slow beginning and two decades of protracted deterioration. The years of the 1920s, when he published five novels that established his reputation, made him seem to many to be the greatest of living American novelists. That period of greatness ended with three events that, in retrospect, have symbolic weight: the final collapse of his first marriage and the beginning of his short-lived second to **Dorothy Thompson;** his widely publicized break with Harcourt, Brace, the publisher of those five novels; and his selection as the first American to win the Nobel Prize in literature. After that, everything was downhill, in morale no less than in imaginative achievement.

As sharply set off as the achievement of that one decade may be from what came before and after, the total body of work nevertheless has genuine consistency. The satiric strain in Lewis's work was always there, for example. If it began rather archly and ended sentimentally, its objects were nevertheless constant. It chiefly directs itself against the provincialism of American life, especially in the Midwest—its smugness, hypocrisy, chauvinism, gross materialism, commercial spirit, and moral cant. But there is an opposite object as well, and that is any spirit of snobbery that condescends to what is good in American life—candor, kindliness, hard work, decent thrift, common sense. Often his attack on the second led critics to believe that he was in fact defending the first, and in a few instances (most notably *The Prodigal Parents,* 1938) perhaps he was; but basically his defense was of what he conceived to be the best qualities in a life of freedom. The American defection from the American potentiality for individual freedom is the large subject of Lewis's satire. When he scolded his fellows or laughed at them, it was because they would not be free, and he attacked all the sources by means of which they betrayed themselves into slavery: business organization, intellectual rigidity, theological dogma, legal repression, class convention, social timidity or affectation (either one), complacency, and pomposity.

The plots in novel after novel rest essentially on these two impulses: the individual impulse to freedom and the social impulse to restrict it. In almost all of Lewis's novels, then, there is basically a single theme: the impulse to escape the conventions of class or stultifying routine; an attempt at flight; a partial success and a probably necessary compromise. The theme represents the positive, even the idealistic element in his largely negative presentation of American life. Into that idealism it was not difficult to weave a certain optimism, the happy belief that the little man, the obscure man, the middle-class man, the outsider like the young Lewis himself, could break into a euphoric freedom. This was the motive of Lewis's life no less than of his work. Under his impulsive and erratic social behavior, under his eruptive personal relations, even under the alcoholism that plagued him, just as under the satire of social surfaces in his fiction, lay this ambition and this yearning.

One should observe, too, at least three constants of literary technique. Lewis had an extraordinary eye for physical detail, and he pursued a method of research very nearly like a sociologist's in recording it. If sometimes his fiction bogs down under the weight of his observations, it is nevertheless the sharply observed physical detail that gives his work its body. He had, too, an extraordinarily sharp ear for the peculiar accents of American speech, for the curious lingo that we tend to make of the English language; and again, if sometimes his fiction is overburdened by the cluttered argot, it nevertheless helped to create nearly archetypal characters, such as George F. Babbitt, who transcend their fictions and take a place in American mythology.

Finally, it should be said that he had no great gift for novelistic construction. His books are loosely episodic chronicles, often, like *Babbitt* and *Elmer Gantry*, falling into separate parts, each nearly independent of the others. Both his structures and his prose style suggest that in any strict literary sense he was not a great writer, yet perhaps no other American novelist has documented for such an enormous audience the crass as well as the aspiring character of a people and a class. See Mark Schorer, *Sinclair Lewis: An American Life* (1961).

MARK SCHORER

LEWIS, John Llewellyn (b. Lucas, Iowa, Feb. 12, 1880; d. Washington, D.C., June 11, 1969), LABOR LEADER, the son of a Welsh coal miner, began work in the mines at age 16. His success in winning workmen's compensation and mine safety laws as Illinois legislative agent for the United Mine Workers (1909–11) led to his appointment in 1911 as field and legislative representative for the AFL. Beginning as a protégé of **Samuel Gompers,** Lewis split with the AFL in 1935 over its craft ideology and its shunning of political action. As president of the United Mine Workers of America (1920–60) Lewis built a political machine that enabled him to dominate the organization.

After their experiences had convinced them that workers could not maintain high wages and working conditions while most industries remained unorganized, Lewis and seven other union presidents, including **Sidney Hillman, David Dubinsky,** and Charles P. Howard, formed a Committee of Industrial Organization in 1935 within the AFL. Suspended in 1936, the Committee was reorganized in 1938 as the Congress of Industrial Organizations with Lewis as president. Under his leadership the CIO began to organize mass-production industries, winning union recognition from such former bastions of the open shop as General Motors and United States Steel.

In 1936, Lewis and Hillman founded Labor's Non-Partisan League, which supported President Franklin D. Roosevelt's reelection. But Lewis broke with Roosevelt over his nonsupport of labor during the little steel strike of 1937 and tried to rally labor against FDR's third-term bid in 1940. When Roosevelt was reelected, Lewis resigned as president of the CIO. In 1942, Lewis broke with his successor **Philip Murray** and took the Mine Workers out of the CIO.

Wartime coal strikes led Roosevelt to seize the mines in 1943 and to threaten to draft strikers. In a 1946 coal dispute President Harry S. Truman also seized the mines. These strikes helped precipitate the Smith-Connally Act of 1943 and the Taft-Hartley Act of 1947.

Lewis's national power and influence began to

wane after 1943. As in 1935 when he engineered the passage of the Guffey Coal Act to stabilize coal prices, Lewis again became concerned with the economic position of the industry. He began to cooperate with the mine owners in the 1950s, helping them to automate and agreeing to the closing of inefficient mines in return for high wages in the efficient ones. During his tenure as mineworkers' president he won periodic wage increases, vacation pay, pensions, pay for underground travel time, and improved mine safety through federal inspection of the mines.

∝∝∝

John L. Lewis was, by all odds, the most important figure produced by the American labor movement in the 20th century. His was the dominant voice shaping the labor relations of coal mining during its years of decline from a primary to a secondary place in the American economy. More important, Lewis was the key figure in the labor split during the 1930s that led to the formation of the CIO and the organization of the mass-production sector of the economy. Besides his tangible achievements in these two areas, John L. Lewis acted as a national force during the New Deal, World War II, and the early Truman years. He exerted a powerful influence (intended and unintended) on public policy and served as the visible symbol of the new power of American labor.

Two ingredients combined to produce this remarkable career. The first was rooted in conventional American trade unionism. In his rise to power within the UMWA, Lewis adhered firmly to the "pure-and-simple" doctrines of Samuel Gompers and believed faithfully in the free play of economic forces (as spelled out in his *Miners Fight for American Standards*, 1925). In his relentless struggle to drive out all opposition and gain absolute mastery over the UMWA, Lewis was likewise acting in the mold of business-union leader. But Lewis pursued his conventional goals with exceptional vigor and imagination. The man's personality constituted the second element in the making of his career. There was, to begin with, the physical presence that grew more striking with age—the mass of reddish hair and

heavy brows, graying eventually into pure white, the startling ice-blue eyes, the body that was at once bulky and nimble. Not given to reflection or theorizing, Lewis possessed an agile and retentive mind; his knowledge of the coal trade was unexcelled. A consummate politician, Lewis had a superb sense of time, limitless capacity for manipulation, and a marvelous dramatic instinct. Boundless ambition and lust for power propelled him to supremacy within his union. There was a final, indispensable ingredient: an ability to identify himself with the movement. Born and bred a coal miner, Lewis never put those early days in the pits behind him. "I am one of them," he said of the miners. This sense saved him, however ill-conceived or mean-spirited his actions, from ever degenerating into sheer self-seeking. He was, by his own admission, "something of a man."

But Lewis was not one to surmount his situation. On the contrary, adversity diminished him. Fighting for personal supremacy and against economic odds in the 1920s, he spent himself in sterile, even destructive, battles. Under his leadership the UMWA fell from half a million in 1920 to hardly a hundred thousand in 1930. The coming of the New Deal saved the union. Gambling on the labor guarantees in Section 7(a) of the Recovery Act, Lewis threw everything he had left into a drive to reorganize the miners. He won. Within weeks the union regained the losses of a decade, and soon he was able to establish collective bargaining for almost the entire industry. Buoyed up by this triumph and by the power that it meant, Lewis seemed almost visibly to expand in stature. He quickly took up the cause of the unorganized mass-production workers, and after trying and failing to get the AFL to adopt an effective organizing program, he and his supporters struck off on their own to get the job done. In the formative period of the CIO, and in the dramatic organizing struggles that followed, he performed at the top of his powers. But he had not broken from his past. Both the logic of his efforts and the objectives he had in mind were understandable in strictly trade-union terms.

However, his momentum did lead him on in two significant ways. First, there was a political change. A lifelong Republican, he allied himself with Roosevelt and even toyed with the idea of a labor party. His experience with the New Deal, moreover, showed him the new importance of politics for the labor movement. The other change involved Lewis's personal perspective. His ambitions, hitherto limited to his role as union leader, leaped ahead even of his immense accomplishments. He evidently did not rule out even the White House. These changes proved Lewis's undoing. Disappointed in the return on his political investment on behalf of the New Deal and frustrated in his personal expectations from both politics and organized labor, Lewis broke with Roosevelt and then in 1942 with the industrial-union movement that he had created. Thereafter, he devoted himself to his own UMWA, over which his hold was absolute, and with a vengeance applied to its problems the principles of pure-and-simple unionism. If there is an answer to the enigma of the career of John L. Lewis, possibly it lies in the fact that Lewis was too big a man for the conservative labor movement but not big enough either to transcend it or to remake it to accord with a larger vision (which he himself lacked). See Saul Alinsky, *John L. Lewis: An Unauthorized Biography* (1949).

DAVID BRODY

LEWIS, Meriwether (b. Albemarle Co., Va., Aug. 18, 1774; d. near Nashville, Tenn., Oct. 11, 1809), EXPLORER, moved with his family to a Georgia plantation in 1784. He returned to Virginia in 1787, where he studied with the Rev. Matthew Maury and other private tutors for the next five years. Following his stepfather's death he took over the family estate, but when the Whiskey Rebellion broke out in western Pennsylvania (1794), he joined the Virginia militia. He was commissioned in the army as a lieutenant (1799) and became a captain in 1800.

In 1801, President Thomas Jefferson appointed Lewis his personal secretary. In this capacity Lewis read Jefferson's state of the union message to Congress (Dec. 1801). Lewis and Jefferson had long been interested in exploring the West. In January 1803, Jefferson got an appropriation of $2,500 from Congress to explore an overland route to the Pacific Ocean and placed Lewis in charge of the expedition.

During the winter of 1803–4, Lewis and his men trained at Camp Dubois, Illinois. At St. Charles, Missouri, Lewis was joined by his close friend William Clark, who became co-leader of the expedition. In the spring of 1804, Lewis and Clark and their party set out following the Missouri River, and by fall they reached the Mandan Villages in North Dakota, a 1,600-mile journey. After spending the winter at Fort Mandan, north of present-day Bismarck, North Dakota, they resumed their journey, taking with them a French-Canadian guide and his Shoshone wife, Sacagawea. After reaching the mouth of the Yellowstone (Apr.), passing the Great Falls of the Missouri (July), and descending the Columbia River (Oct.), they reached the Pacific Ocean (Nov.). In the spring of 1806 they began their return trip, during which Lewis was accidentally wounded. Returning to St. Louis in September 1806, they brought back with them a great deal of information about the West and its resources. Their journals became a major source for scientists and future explorers.

In 1806, Jefferson appointed Lewis territorial governor of Louisiana. In this position he negotiated treaties with the Indians, organized the militia, and codified the law. In 1809 he traveled to Washington on official business, stopping off in central Tennessee where he died suddenly.

———

Meriwether Lewis was the product of his boyhood environment in rural Piedmont, Virginia, of his border warfare experiences beyond the Alleghenies, and of Thomas Jefferson's discreet guidance in the nation's capital. Albemarle County, Virginia, habituated him to life in the woods and sharpened his innate love of plants and animals. Fortunes of border warfare provided him with a familiarity of the character and custom of Native Americans and taught the lessons of overcoming hardship and of survival in a hostile land. Jefferson ripened him as a naturalist, heightened the qualities of inquiry and observation, and refined inborn abilities of perseverance and command.

From these unconventional "schoolrooms" Lewis emerged a dreamer, intent, reserved, finedrawn, unwavering. And it was a combination of these and other attributes that came to the fore in 1804–6 to ensure the fortunate outcome of his extraordinary traverse of the trans-Mississippi West.

Accomplishments of the expedition defy recapitulation in a short space. However, briefly as possible, Lewis and Clark introduced new approaches to exploration and fashioned a template for future explorers by systematically recording abundant data on such subjects as weather, fauna, flora, geography, and Native Americans. Their topographic discoveries and resultant maps became prime foundation stones on which Americans built their claim to Oregon and, by extension, to other parts of the Far West. Their reports on the abundance of beaver and other fur-bearing animals resulted in the development of the American fur trade in these parts and of the early opening of the West to settlement. More than that, their achievements led to America's discovery of the corn fields of Iowa, Missouri, Kansas, and Nebraska, the great wheat country of the Dakotas, the gold and silver of Montana and Idaho, the tremendous evergreen forests of Oregon and Washington, and the unexcelled scenic splendors of the Northwest.

The successful transit of the West by Lewis and Clark stands incomparably as the transcendent achievement of its kind in this hemisphere, if not in the entire world. Whereas Louisiana Territory had been "an area of rumor, guess, and fantasy," now that Lewis and Clark had revealed it, it was a focus of reality.

Regretfully, Lewis did not live to receive anything like full recognition for his accomplishments. He died just three years after achieving fame through completing the traverse. Though some will disagree, Jefferson and others of his time held no doubt that Lewis died a victim of his own hand, and today's leading scholars of the expedition incline to the same opinion. When Jefferson was apprised of the tragedy, he wrote:

"Lewis had from early life been subject to hypochondriac affections. It was a constitutional disposition in all the nearer branches of the family." So it would seem fair to say that Lewis was a product of his inheritance as well as environment. See Bernard de Voto, ed., *The Journals of Lewis and Clark* (1953), and Richard Dillon, *Meriwether Lewis* (1965).

PAUL R. CUTRIGHT

LIEBER, Francis (b. Berlin, Germany, Mar. 18, 1800; d. New York, N.Y., Oct. 2, 1872), POLITICAL SCIENTIST, received his early education as a student of Friedrich Ludwig Jahn, a noted founder of modern gymnastics whose schools were also considered training grounds for radicals. After fighting in the Prussian army in 1815 at Waterloo and the Battle of Namur, Lieber continued his studies at the University of Jena (1819–20) because the government had forbidden him, as one of Jahn's students, to study in Berlin. In 1820 he received his PhD in mathematics, which he hoped to teach. He was unsuccessful in obtaining a post because he was suspected of belonging to secret societies plotting to overthrow the French and Prussian governments.

In 1822–23, Lieber was a tutor in Rome for the son of the German ambassador, the historian Barthold G. Niebuhr. In 1823 he returned to Berlin and Halle to study mathematics, although he became more and more interested in government and literary studies. He was arrested in 1824 when the Prussian government sought to eliminate "liberal conspiracies," and in 1826 he fled to England. After working for a year as a language teacher, he left for the United States, where he had been appointed head of a new gymnasium and swimming school in Boston. There he edited the *Encyclopedia Americana* (13 vols., 1829–33). This work, modeled on the German *Conversations Lexikon* and intended to fill a gap between newspapers and massive, expensive encyclopedias, was an immediate success and brought Lieber much acclaim.

After moving to Philadelphia in 1834, he was elected to a chair of history and political economy at the South Carolina College (1835–56). While in Charleston he produced his best-known works, *Manual of Political Ethics* (2 vols., 1838–39) and *On Civil Liberty and Self-Government* (2 vols., 1853). In these books Lieber provided the first systematic studies of the theory and philosophy of the state written in America since the founding of the nation. They analyzed the elements and dimensions of freedom in contrast to a mere recitation of the relevant terms of the Constitution. They also provided an analysis of the citizen's many relationships to the government and of his various obligations to society. Lieber praised limited government and the checks-and-balances system, and warned of the need to limit "democratic absolutism" through the operation of judicial review. Although active as a writer and teacher, Lieber was often unhappy in the South since he opposed states' rights and secessionist ideas so prevalent in that region after the Mexican War. In 1855, after failing to obtain the presidency of South Carolina College, he resigned; he moved in 1857 to New York City where he became professor of history and political economy at Columbia College. From 1865 to his death he taught at Columbia Law School. During the Civil War he was often consulted by the federal government. He wrote *Guerrilla Parties Considered with Reference to the Laws and Usages of War* (1862) and *A Code for the Government of Armies* (1863). These remained the legal basis for international conduct of war well into the 20th century.

Francis Lieber made friends and enemies with equal ease. Physically he was unimposing, of medium height, stout but muscular, possessed of abundant energy. Intellectually he was awesome. His breadth of knowledge, conversational charm, wit (and his fondness for flattering and flirting with attractive young ladies) made him the center of attention in his social circles. Lieber's thirty-year quest to obtain a university post in the North and his ambition led him to cultivate the rich, the well-placed, and the influential public figures of his times. His self-assurance and intellectual arrogance alienated many, as did his willingness to abandon friends in his opportunistic climb toward financial security and public acclaim. The young man who dreamed of assassinating Napoleon matured into a frustrated professor who felt that the world never quite paid him his due. To some he was a scholarly genius, to others the most conceited man in America.

In the loose 19th-century meaning of "a writer on current issues," particularly those of a political nature, Lieber regarded himself a publicist. He aired his views on every public issue, the important and trivial alike. There was one notable exception: to retain his post at South Carolina College he refrained from publicly voicing his growing distaste for slavery. Some of his publishing schemes—such as a multiauthor textbook series for public schools and his pastepot ancient history text *Great Events Described by Distinguished Historians, Chroniclers, and Other Writers* (1840)—earned him the label "hack." Other works like the *Encyclopedia Americana*, although designed to gain fame and profit, also added to the available fund of knowledge. Still others, including his treatises on political theory, his *A Popular Essay on Penal Law* (1838), and his *Essays on Property and Labour* (1841), signaled his desire to contribute reasoned judgment to public debates over questions vital to the nation. These writings remain among a handful of works that serve as a touchstone for midcentury "liberal" thought.

Not surprisingly, Lieber's views on public issues shifted over time and in response to self-interest. By the standards of his day, however, he was an economic liberal and a social conservative. He believed in the marketplace of Adam Smith and David Ricardo, considered himself a friend of labor while denouncing unionism and professing inability to understand the "labor theory of value," and vigorously supported the rising capitalist class.

He opposed the communitarians, the socialists, and those who, like Orestes Brownson, attacked private property. He labored diligently for prison reform, but as he aged he began to oppose other social reform efforts. He spoke of his "inmost aversion to all humbug, flummery, chicken-philanthropy, wishy-washy politics, and all that sort of thing." He urged immigration restriction of nonwhites, derided woman suffrage, castigated the prohibitionists, vilified Mormons and Roman Catholics. Although he despised slavery, he despised even more the "Sumner-Howe" abolitionists. He rejected pacifism, and in the name of nationalism argued that the country stood above the Constitution. He gleefully welcomed the Civil War even though it meant sacrificing the legal precepts of his *Civil Liberty* and dividing his family. One of his three sons enlisted in the Confederate army, the others in the Union forces. During Reconstruction he first championed the congressional radicals but turned against them when they did not accept all his suggestions. He ended his days an anomaly, a free-trade Republican.

Throughout his life, despite his contributions to political theory and international law, he remained true to one constant—himself. Yet few contemporaries better reflect the evolving shape of economic and political nationalism in mid–19th-century America. See Frank Freidel, *Francis Lieber: Nineteenth-Century Liberal* (1947).

STANLEY K. SCHULTZ

LILIENTHAL, David Eli (b. Morton, Ill., July 8, 1899; d. New York, N.Y., Jan. 15, 1981), ADMINISTRATOR, graduated from DePauw University in 1920, received his LLB from Harvard Law School, and was admitted to the Illinois bar in 1923. He was a member of Donald Richberg's Chicago law firm (1923–26) and then started his own practice. During this period he contributed articles to the *Nation* and the *New Outlook* and edited *Public Utilities and Careers Service* for Chicago's Commerce Clearing House (1926–31). In 1931, Governor Philip La Follette appointed Lilienthal to Wisconsin's Public Service Commission, where he helped reorganize and rewrite the state's public utility statutes. President Franklin D. Roosevelt appointed Lilienthal a director of the new Tennessee Valley Authority in 1933. Together with co-directors Arthur E. Morgan and Harcourt Alexander

Morgan, Lilienthal helped draw up plans for dams for hydroelectric power, flood control, and improved river navigation. He proved to be an effective public relations expert, selling the concepts of regional planning to the people of the region.

Lilienthal believed that TVA was a business, a business owned and managed by all the people of the region, an idea he called "grass-roots democracy." He became chairman of the board of directors of the Authority in 1941. His book *TVA—Democracy on the March* (1944) described the work of the TVA.

In 1946, Lilienthal and **Dean Acheson** drew up a plan for an International Atomic Development Authority to control the raw materials, stages of production, and supervision of all atomic weapons. This plan was later incorporated into the **Bernard Baruch** plan for the international control of nuclear arms that was submitted to the U.N. Security Council in 1946 but not adopted. Lilienthal served as chairman of the State Department Board of Consultants on International Control of Atomic Energy in 1946. Later that year he left the TVA when President Harry S. Truman appointed him chairman of the U.S. Atomic Energy Commission, a body maintaining civilian control and government monopoly of atomic energy. He left the AEC in 1950 to enter business in New York City. In 1955 he founded the Development and Resources Corp., a private company organized to provide technical assistance and help in organization, management, and long-range planning for underdeveloped nations. The firm undertook such projects as flood control, industrial site planning, highways, ports, and housing projects in such countries as Iran, Italy, Colombia, and Nigeria. In 1967–69, Lilienthal was co-chairman of the Joint Postwar Development Group for Vietnam. The Development and Resources Corp. was dissolved in the late 1970s. A prolific writer, he published five volumes of memoirs: *The Journals of David E. Lilienthal* (1964–71). Some of his other books include *This I Do Believe* (1949), *Change, Hope and the Bomb* (1963), *Management: A Humanist Art* (1967), and Atomic Energy, a New Start (1980).

David E. Lilienthal participated in four major developments of 20th-century America: the regulation of business by commissions, the Tennessee Valley Authority, the control of atomic energy, and the art of professional management. To each of the four he made outstanding contributions. A superb speaker and a vivid writer, he excelled in analyzing and making intelligible the government's interaction with private entrepreneurship. With an acute sense of the public interest and an energy seldom exhibited by public officials who do not hold elective office, he aggressively pursued policies he believed essential to the operation of the American system. He began his career determined to soften the impact of industrialization on American labor. After the reforms of the New Deal, he began in the 1940s to acquire a deeper appreciation of American business and a more sympathetic stance toward it. The intellectual distance he traveled can be measured by comparing his antibusiness rhetoric of the 1920s and 1930s with his book *Big Business: A New Era*, published in 1953.

A figure neither of the second nor of the very first rank, Lilienthal fits somewhere in between. He exemplified that small group of professional managers charged with making decisions of major importance and sensitivity. In this role he invites comparison with **Robert McNamara**, but Lilienthal had a better sense of history and of proportion. By avoiding pomposity and by familiarizing himself with both the broad contours and the small details of his projects, he helped define the fundamental principles of managing great organizations. He ardently advocated techniques of decentralized management like those he brought to the TVA.

Both his assignments and his combative temperament frequently cast him in controversial roles—as the target of abuse from regulated business interests in Wisconsin and the Tennessee Valley, as a foe of visionary social planners in the New Deal, and as an ill-chosen victim of witch hunters in the hysteria of the early cold war.

Introspective without being introverted, he engaged in constant examination of himself and his work, a process recorded in his voluminous *Journals*. These books provide a unique chronicle of a public servant's evolution from shrewd, ambitious *Wunderkind* to mellowed elder statesman and millionaire. See *The Journals of David E. Lilienthal* (5 vols., 1964–71).

THOMAS K. McCRAW

LINCOLN, Abraham (b. Hardin, Ky., Feb. 12, 1809; d. Washington, D.C., Apr. 15, 1865), PRESIDENT, spent his early years in Kentucky, Indiana, and Illinois. He became postmaster of New Salem, Illinois (1833–36), where he also studied law. He was admitted to the bar in 1836. After service as a Whig state legislator (1834–42), he was elected to a single term in Congress in 1846. Thereafter he returned to his law practice. Opposed to the further extension of slavery, he denounced the Kansas-Nebraska Act (1854), which repealed the Missouri Compromise of 1820, but he recognized the southern states' constitutional right to slavery and supported the fugitive slave laws. Joining the Republican Party in 1856, he was the party's candidate for senator from Illinois in 1858. Accepting the nomination with his "a house divided" speech, he challenged **Stephen A. Douglas** (the Democratic incumbent) to a series of debates. The most famous of these seven contests was at Freeport, where Lincoln asked Douglas how, considering the **Dred Scott** decision (1857), the inhabitants of a territory could exclude slavery before the territory became a state. Douglas replied that slavery could not be maintained without the protection of local laws. Douglas was elected senator, but the debates won Lincoln a national reputation.

Lincoln was the Republican presidential candidate in 1860 and defeated **John C. Breckinridge** (Democrat), John C. Bell (Constitutional Union Party), and Stephen A. Douglas (Democrat) in the election, winning 180 electoral votes but receiving only about 40 percent of the popular vote. Believing that Lincoln would be hostile to the South, by March 4, 1861, seven southern states had seceded and formed the Confederate States of

America. When Lincoln sent a relief expedition to Fort Sumter in Charleston Harbor, the fort was attacked (Apr. 12, 1861) by the Confederates. Lincoln called for seventy-five thousand volunteers to subdue the rebellion, which caused Virginia, North Carolina, Arkansas, and Tennessee to secede. During the Civil War, Lincoln, without congressional authorization, expanded the army, declared martial law, and suspended the writ of habeas corpus. His famous Emancipation Proclamation, effective January 1, 1863, declared that all slaves in the area in rebellion were free. After trying a number of other generals without much success, in 1864 Lincoln appointed Ulysses S. Grant supreme commander of the Union army.

Lincoln defeated General **George B. McClellan** (Democrat) in the 1864 presidential election, 212 electoral votes to 21, and in his second inaugural address stated that the Union must be restored without malice. After the Confederate surrender at Appomattox (Apr. 9, 1865), he hoped to pursue a policy of conciliation toward the South. He based his right to control the South's reentry to the Union on the president's pardoning power. As early as 1863 he had proposed that with the exception of high Confederate officials and a few others, southerners could be readmitted to citizenship by taking a loyalty oath. Under his plan, as soon as 10 percent of a state's registered voters in the 1860 election had taken the oath, that state could set up a government. Radical Republicans countered with the Wade-Davis Bill (1864), which stated that only after a majority of the voters of a southern state took the oath could a constitutional convention be called, and that all those who had fought against the Union should be barred from participation. Lincoln killed this bill by a pocket veto.

On April 14, 1865, while attending a play at Ford's theater in Washington, Lincoln was assassinated by **John Wilkes Booth,** a mentally unstable actor.

———— ✀ ————

In spite of all that has been written about him, the real Lincoln remains something of an enigma. Not a man who easily revealed his inner self, he also has been partly hidden in an enveloping legend. The Lincoln legend is by no means fictional but is rather an amplification of actual characteristics and achievements. It comprises a set of heroic images, notably the young backwoodsman splitting fence rails; the self-made man who studied by firelight; the political gladiator locked in combat with the Little Giant; the wise and patient "Father Abraham" of the war years; the Great Emancipator striking the chains from a whole people; and the fallen leader, martyred on Good Friday and swiftly apotheosized. But there is also a counter-legend depicting a shrewd politician, well intentioned but habitually governed by considerations of expediency. This Lincoln was at best a lukewarm opponent of slavery and no great friend of black people. Complacently sharing the dominant belief in white supremacy, he never came to grips with the underlying problem of American racism.

The idealized portrait belongs to the tradition of romantic nationalism, while the counter-legend reflects a latter-day disenchantment with the American past as well as a tendency to measure historical figures against the standards and needs of the modern world. Lincoln was, in fact, very much a man of his own times and could never have been elected president if he had been a century ahead of them. Growing up in the crude and isolated society of frontier agriculture, he escaped from it by force of will. His pioneering experience remained ever visible in the Lincolnian style, but he had none of his father's westering spirit. At the first opportunity he turned from farming to a townsman's career in law and politics. He was soon moderately successful in both professions. His manner and good sense inspired confidence; he worked hard even on inconsequential cases; and he had a rare capacity for going to the heart of a matter. Above all, Lincoln was a self-made man in his mastery of the English language, increasingly visible in a lean but moving eloquence that contrasted sharply with the florid oratory of the age. It was primarily his mobilization of language that lifted him into contention for the presidency even though he had held no public office for a dozen years and had been defeated twice as a senatorial candidate. He profited also, however, from his frontier background, from the stirring contest with Douglas, and from having found the issue that perfectly suited him.

Lincoln was not a reformer by nature. Hating slavery but seeing no way of abolishing it under the Constitution, he was prepared to settle for a national policy that treated the institution as an evil, prevented its expansion, and pointed toward a day of "ultimate extinction." As president, his first duty was to save the Union. He had no right to convert the war into a crusade against slavery that might alienate too many Americans needed in the battle for the Union. Thus the Emancipation Proclamation, for both constitutional and political reasons, had to be cast as a purely military measure. It nevertheless made the war a social revolution and confronted the nation with the problem of racial adjustment that is still largely unsolved. Lincoln's generation lacked the knowledge and moral resources for providing a solution. The problem baffled him, and his reconstruction program gave it too little attention. He had insisted that blacks were entitled to all the rights guaranteed by the Declaration of Independence. He tried to calm the racial fears of white Americans, and at his death he was beginning to urge that the freedman be given a place in the political system. Yet, knowing the limitations of his countrymen, he remained somewhat pessimistic about the future of the United States as a biracial society. He was probably right in his judgment that the problem of slavery could be dealt with more effectively if it were kept separate from the even more difficult problem of racial adjustment. And slavery, for Lincoln and most of his contemporaries, was always the paramount issue. See David Herbert Donald, *Lincoln* (1995).

DON E. FEHRENBACHER

LINCOLN, Robert Todd (b. Springfield, Ill., Aug. 1, 1843; d. Manchester, Vt., July 26, 1926), BUSINESSMAN, the eldest son of President Abraham Lincoln, graduated from Harvard in 1864. He spent four months at Harvard Law School, was commissioned captain on the staff of General Ulysses S. Grant, and was present at the surrender at Appomattox. He was in Ford's theater when his father was shot.

Taking up the practice of law in Chicago in 1867, Lincoln prospered, numbering among his clients the Pullman Palace Car Co. A Republican, Lincoln served from 1881 to 1885 as secretary of war under Presidents James A. Garfield and Chester A. Arthur. Appointed minister to Britain by Benjamin Harrison (serving 1889–93), he was involved in the Bering Sea controversy and the Alaska boundary dispute.

Upon **George Pullman**'s death in 1897 Lincoln became president of the Pullman Co. He resigned that post in 1911 but remained chairman of the board. Lincoln was also a director of the Commonwealth Edison Co., the Continental and Commercial National Bank, the Chicago Telephone Co., and the Pullman Trust and Savings Bank. He deposited his father's papers in the Library of Congress but ordered that they be sealed for twenty-one years after his own death.

⸻

For several reasons Robert Todd Lincoln can be considered a particularly unfortunate, even tragic, figure. Like many children of famous men, he lacked a strong sense of personal identity. Poignantly he once told a friend: "No one wanted me for Secretary of War ... for minister to England ... for president of the Pullman Company; they wanted Abraham Lincoln's son." R. T. Lincoln was also well acquainted with grief. All three of his younger brothers died before reaching manhood; his father was murdered when Robert was 21; his mother, never emotionally stable, grew especially neurotic after her husband's assassination. His only son died at 16; his daughter married a man of whom he did not approve. Thus **Ida Tarbell** was justifiably surprised to find in R. T. Lincoln "the admirable social poise of the man who has seen the world's greatest and has come to be sure of himself ... in spite of such buffeting as few men have had."

Lincoln did not suffer materially, however. A

millionaire lawyer and businessman, he could well afford to gratify his fondness for comfortable living: Rolls-Royces, elegant dress, golf, and the other pleasures of the wealthy, conventional, conservative Victorian gentleman that he was.

He did not resemble his celebrated father personally or politically. Whereas Abraham Lincoln was warm, humorous, and unpretentious, his son was cold, stuffy, and aloof. A regular supporter of the standpat wing of the Republican Party, Lincoln also lacked his father's concern for liberty and justice. He found public life unappealing. Truly Robert Todd Lincoln was "all Todd," that is to say, he took after his mother's family, among the most proud, eminent, and proper members of Kentucky society. See Ruth Painter Randall, *Lincoln's Sons* (1955).

MICHAEL A. BURLINGAME

LINDBERGH, Charles Augustus, Jr. (b. Detroit, Mich., Feb. 4, 1902; d. Kipahulu Maui, Hawaii, Aug. 26, 1974), AVIATOR, attended the University of Wisconsin (1920–22) but left college to make a career in aviation. After learning to fly at a school in Lincoln, Nebraska, he became a stunt pilot and barnstormed across the country. He was an airmail service pilot on the St. Louis-Chicago route in 1926 when he began to lay plans for making a nonstop flight from New York to Paris to gain a $25,000 prize offered by hotel owner Raymond B. Orteig for the first transatlantic flight. Backed by several St. Louis bankers and civic leaders, Lindbergh's monoplane, *The Spirit of St. Louis,* was designed by Donald Hall and built by Ryan Airlines in San Diego. After flying from San Diego to New York, Lindbergh took off from Roosevelt Field, Long Island, on May 20, 1927, and 33½ hours later landed at Le Bourget airport in Paris, an international hero. Later that same year he made the first nonstop flight from Washington, D.C., to Mexico City. There he met Anne Morrow, daughter of American ambassador Dwight Morrow, and they were married in 1929. In the years following they embarked together on numerous flights and trips of exploration. In 1929, Lindbergh became associated with the Transcontinental Air Transport Co. and Pan American Airways as a technical consultant.

In 1932 the Lindberghs' two-year-old son was kidnapped and murdered by Bruno Hauptmann, an itinerant carpenter. The publicity resulting from the crime and the trial that followed was so intense that Lindbergh went to live in England in 1935 to escape it. In 1936 he visited Nazi Germany, which impressed him with its growing air power. He also made surveys of the Russian, French, and English air forces but found these much inferior to the Luftwaffe. During a second visit to Germany in 1938, Lindbergh was awarded the Service Cross of the German Eagle by the Nazis at the same time that Hitler stepped up his persecution of the Jews. This presentation produced an angry reaction in Great Britain, France, and the United States, and Secretary of the Interior **Harold Ickes** attacked Lindbergh for accepting the medal. Returning to the United States in 1939, Lindbergh went on duty with the Army Air Corps as a colonel. When World War II broke out, he became active in the America First Committee and toured the country declaiming against any American involvement in the conflict. In one speech, at Des Moines, Iowa, on September 11, 1941, he accused the British government, the Roosevelt administration, and the Jews of pushing the United States toward war.

Lindbergh resigned his Air Corps Reserve commission in 1941, but during the war he served as a consultant with the United Aircraft and Ford Motor companies (1943) and as a civilian technician attached to the Army Air Corps in the Pacific theater of operations (1944). Following the Japanese surrender Lindbergh wrote *Of Flight and Life* (1948) and *The Spirit of St. Louis* (1953), which won a Pulitzer Prize for biography. President Dwight D. Eisenhower appointed him a brigadier general in the Air Force Reserve in 1954 and to the board of visitors of the U.S. Air Force Academy (Colorado Springs) in 1956. A frequent adviser to the Defense Department on aviation matters, Lindbergh in his later years also contributed importantly to natural resource conservation. He published his wartime diaries, *Wartime Journals of Charles A. Lindbergh,* in 1970.

———∞∞∞———

Lindbergh's flight had a stimulating if quantitatively indeterminable effect on the growth of American aviation. But far more important and interesting to the historian and psychologist is the mass hero worship that focused on him and the response he made to it in a time of deepening world crisis. A clean-cut, handsome young man with an engaging grin, superbly skilled in his profession, he seemed to care nothing for crowd adulation while obviously caring greatly for his personal privacy. He neither drank nor smoked. His heroism was unquestionably authentic. He refused to "cash in" on his fame in any cheap, obvious way. And this sufficed to elevate him to the status of a god before a public that sickened of political scandal, of blatant commercialism, of the cynical ballyhoo and sensationalism characteristic of the "Jazz Age."

Alas, in a sick time there was much that was morbid in Lindbergh's fame. For one thing, it was monstrously excessive. He could not appear on the street or in any public place without being mobbed; at a picnic in a St. Louis park, well-dressed women fought for possession of a corncob from which he had eaten. And he was ill-equipped by temperament or education to cope with this. He was by nature solitary. When growing up as the only child of a broken home (his parents were never legally divorced but lived apart), he was far more at ease with machinery than with people. Hence the kind of fame he had now to endure was peculiarly galling to him, and he was less able to understand it sympathetically, in historical perspective, than he might have been had he possessed more general cultural information. (He had little more than a high school education when he made the Paris flight, though he subsequently overcame this deficiency through serious reading.)

It is small wonder, then, that Lindbergh reacted against his fame in a way that increased its most unpleasant manifestations. Instead of providing the public with that full exposure of himself that would soon have satiated it, he withdrew and became something of a recluse and man of mystery, and this of course whetted the public's morbid curiosity, especially since he continued to perform spectacular publicity-breeding deeds. Simultaneously he developed a species of contempt for "common people," which in turn bred in him increasing doubts about democracy—attitudes confirmed in him by the kidnap-murder of his son and the ghastly publicity surrounding it. He became easy prey for such totalitarian minds as Dr. Alexis Carrell of the Rockefeller Institute, with whom he worked on scientific medical projects in New York and Europe. He was predisposed to admire the "virility" and "efficiency" of Nazi Germany as contrasted with the "impotence," the "degeneracy," of England and other democracies.

On the evidence, it was this rather than an expert objective analysis of available data that caused him to overestimate hugely Germany's actual and potential air strength (he deemed it greater than that of Czechoslovakia, Russia, France, and Britain combined) during the Munich crisis, and to do so in ways calculated to influence British, French, and American policy. He then entered upon the phase of his career that remains historically the most important: he led a crusade against America's aid to Britain and entry into the war that did not end until Pearl Harbor.

Writing of Lindbergh's historical significance, a biographer has said he "is amazingly symptomatic of certain dominant moods in recent Western culture, and his life describes a remarkably pure symbolic curve across the turbulence of our times." See Kenneth S. Davis, *The Hero: Charles A. Lindbergh and the American Dream* (1959).

KENNETH S. DAVIS

LINDSEY, Benjamin Barr (b. Jackson, Tenn., Nov. 25, 1869; d. Los Angeles, Calif., Mar. 26, 1943), REFORMER, moved to Denver, Colorado, with his family in 1879 and worked at various jobs to help support them after his father's death. He read law in his spare time and was admitted to the bar in 1894. He practiced in Denver and in 1899 was appointed public guardian and administrator of orphaned children. In this position Lindsey developed a strong interest in the plight of underprivileged children. Appointed in 1900 to finish out an unexpired term of county judge, he was elected to that position a year later and soon gained a national reputation for the way he handled juvenile delinquents. He imaginatively used an 1899 school attendance law to create a juvenile court and subsequently drafted legislation to institutionalize the Juvenile and Family Court of Denver. Believing that juvenile offenders should be wards of the court and under the protection of the state, and that treatment rather than punishment should be the aim of incarceration, he sent many boys to the Industrial School at Golden, Colorado, where an honor system was put into effect.

Although regularly reelected to the bench, Lindsey made many enemies through his reformist zeal and was ousted from the bench in 1927. He moved to California in 1931, where he practiced law in Los Angeles. A prolific writer, his *Companionate Marriage* (1927, with Wainwright Evans) expounded his idea of a couple's marrying but not having children until the marriage was solidly established on an emotional level so that the children would grow up in a healthy family situation. Lindsey's views were often confused with Bertrand Russell's "trial marriage" idea, which he opposed. In 1930 he was arrested but released for interrupting a sermon by Episcopal Bishop William Manning in New York, who had attacked him from the pulpit. He was elected a judge of the superior court of California in 1934 and reelected in 1940. In 1939 he wrote the California Children's Court of Conciliation Law and served as the first appointee to the bench of that new court from 1939 to his death. Some of his books include *The Beast* (1910, with Harvey O'Higgins), *The Doughboy's Religion* (1920, with Harvey O'Higgins), *The Revolt of Modern Youth* (1925, with Wainwright Evans), and his autobiography, *The Dangerous Life* (1931, with Rube Borough).

In a manuscript he was preparing for *McClure's*, **Lincoln Steffens** described Ben

Lindsey as a politician. Although Lindsey successfully implored Steffens not to use the term because it might be "misunderstood," it was an apt characterization. The judge was indefatigable in finding journalistic outlets for publicizing anecdotes from his courtroom experiences that appealed to wide audiences by combining two major themes: a humanitarian appeal on behalf of underprivileged children and a condemnation of political and economic wickedness, which he considered the prime cause of juvenile delinquency. Lindsey was not the originator of the juvenile court movement, but in a period of less than five years he became the best-known juvenile court judge in the country and was often erroneously called "the founder of the juvenile court system."

In the public mind Lindsey's secondary identification was with the "sexual revolution" of the 1920s. His writings in that period also derive their chief interest from their anecdotal content and crusading zeal rather than any profound analysis. The "little judge" (so-called because he was slightly less than five feet five inches in height) relished playing the part of St. George battling the dragon of American puritanism.

A pugnacious activist whose causes covered the gamut of American reform movements, Lindsey made his most solid contributions in the pre–1914 years when he drafted juvenile court legislation in Colorado and made personal appearances on behalf of reform legislation in many parts of the country. His real achievements were often overshadowed by his egoism and an almost insatiable craving for public attention. See Charles E. Larsen, *The Good Fight: The Life and Times of Ben B. Lindsey* (1972).

CHARLES E. LARSEN

LIPPMANN, Walter (b. New York, N.Y., Sept. 23, 1889; d. New York, N.Y. Dec. 14, 1974), JOURNALIST, graduated from Harvard in 1910. While still a student he worked as a reporter for the Boston *Common* and served as a teaching assistant to **George Santayana** (1910). He then went to work for **Lincoln Steffens,** preparing articles on municipal and corporate corruption for *Everybody's Magazine* (1911). In 1912 he became executive secretary to the Reverend George R. Lunn, Socialist mayor of Schenectady, New York, but resigned after four months to write *A Preface to Politics* (1913).

In 1914, Lippmann published *Drift and Mastery* and became an associate editor of the fledgling *New Republic.* Three years later he was appointed an assistant to Secretary of War **Newton Baker,** specializing in labor matters. After a brief stint with military intelligence on the Western Front during World War I, Lippmann became secretary and White House liaison of Colonel **Edward M. House**'s Inquiry Commission, a group to which President Woodrow Wilson turned for information and recommendations regarding American peace aims. Lippmann's services with the Inquiry included preparing the official text of thirteen of the Fourteen Points that Wilson approved for dispatch to Lloyd George and Vittorio Orlando.

Lippmann became disillusioned with the Versailles negotiations, however, and soon rejoined the *New Republic.* In 1921 he resigned to write, among other books and articles, *Public Opinion,* a discussion of the citizenry's relative ignorance of public affairs (1922). He then joined the editorial page staff of the New York *World* and in 1923 succeeded Frank Cobb as editor. In 1931, after the demise of the *World,* he moved to the *Herald Tribune* to write a column entitled "Today and Tomorrow." Although Lippmann shared President Franklin D. Roosevelt's opposition to retaining the gold standard, he was never a great admirer of FDR or the New Deal and supported **Alf Landon** in 1936. Lippmann also supported **Thomas E. Dewey** in 1948 and Dwight D. Eisenhower in 1952 before realigning himself with the Democrats in 1956 and 1960. Notable works that reflect shifts in his views on domestic affairs over the years are *A Preface to Morals* (1929), *The Good Society* (1937), and *The Public Philosophy* (1954). He opposed postwar isolationism in *United States Foreign Policy: Shield of the Republic* (1943) and *United States War Aims* (1944). Discussions he had with Soviet leader Nikita Khrushchev formed the basis for *The Communist World and Ours* (1959) and *The Coming Tests with Russia* (1961).

During 1963–68, Lippmann was a fortnightly columnist for *Newsweek.* He was a member of the National Institute of Arts and Letters, which honored him in 1965, and of the American Academy of Arts and Letters. He won a Pulitzer Prize citation (1958) and the Pulitzer Prize (1962) for his "Today and Tomorrow" column.

For some forty years of a career in journalism that spanned more than sixty years, Walter Lippmann's major contribution to his field was his world-famous newspaper column "Today and Tomorrow." During most of those years Lippmann, a small, slender man with a round face, large eyes, and a peckish nose, made Washington, D.C., his home. The study in his house near the Washington Cathedral was designed to allow the most intense cerebration. Even its chimney, a friend of Lippmann's once recorded, was "padded to muffle ... a noisy mocking bird." The column, first published in the New York *Herald Tribune* and then widely syndicated, was, on a schedule that ranged over the years from five to two essays a week, invariably ready to go to press at 12:30 p.m. During the years of such methodical work, the writer had over his desk a cartoon by James Thurber portraying that humorist's man and woman, the latter saying, "Lippmann scares me this morning." While the presence of the drawing suggests a sense of humor and capacity for self-deprecation that only close friends knew in the journalist, no regular reader of the column could ever believe Lippmann to be frightening—or frightened. He was invariably bland, absolutely imperturbable, and omniscient. His genius as a journalist—perhaps the major source of his wide appeal—was an indefatigable capacity to infuse calm order into a world of disordered and usually appalling fact.

In one of his earliest and most brilliant books, *Public Opinion,* Lippmann recognized more clearly than most the fantasy involved in a journalist's power. Repute for influence among pundits usually rests on their access to men of power. By such a measure Lippmann deserves to go down in history as the most powerful political journalist of the 20th century. In his younger days he rather cockily pressed his advice on former President Theodore Roosevelt and President Woodrow Wilson. Almost all American presidents since (Franklin D. Roosevelt, whom Lippmann opposed, was a notable exception) found it politic to seek Lippmann's counsel. Even Calvin Coolidge, not one to curry favor lightly with anyone, had a regular weekly lunch meeting with the journalist. Beyond presidents, there have been few major leaders throughout the world, including Nikita Khrushchev, who did not find cause to grant an audience to the publicist.

In a way rivaled by no other American columnist of the century, Lippmann also, in a half-dozen books from *A Preface to Politics* to *The Public Philosophy,* established a reputation as a political philosopher. A close student of these works hailed Lippmann as "the most sensitive, the most wide-ranging, and in some respects the most impressive" political thinker of the century. Impressive, yes; each of Lippmann's books was a gem of the genre. Yet, beyond the concept of an "Atlantic Community" in his foreign policy works, none of Lippmann's philosophical writings made any perceptible impress on the social thought of its time. His views moved from an early hopeful radicalism to an almost dispairing conservatism, but the main theme of his philosophy, whether radical or reactionary, was its distrust of popular democracy. In *The Public Philosophy* the philosopher proposed that all major national decisions relating to finance, foreign policy, and defense be removed from control by either Congress or the people. In light of such views, perhaps the climactic irony of Lippmann's career was the popular adulation he received in the late sixties and seventies for his staunch opposition to the Vietnam War. See Ronald Steel, *Walter Lippmann and the American Century* (1980).

CHARLES FORCEY

LITTLE, Malcolm. See Malcolm X.

LIVINGSTON, Robert R. (b. New York, N.Y., Nov. 27, 1746; d. Clermont, N.Y., Feb. 25, 1813), POLITICAL LEADER, graduated from King's College (now Columbia University) in 1765 and admitted to the bar in 1768. He briefly practiced law with **John Jay.** As a member of the Continental Congress (1775–76, 1779–81, 1784–85), Livingston served on the committee to draft the Declaration of Independence (1776), although he personally believed that such a statement was not yet necessary. With John Jay and **Gouverneur Morris** he helped draft the New York state constitution (1777).

Congress appointed Livingston secretary of foreign affairs (1781–83). He supported the Federal Constitution and served as chancellor of New York (1777–1801), administering the oath of office to President George Washington in 1789. Livingston soon became critical of the Federalists, however, opposing **Alexander Hamilton**'s fiscal program and denouncing the Jay Treaty (1795) in a number of letters signed "Cato." He ran for governor of New York in 1798 but was defeated by John Jay.

In 1801, Thomas Jefferson appointed Livingston minister to France. When Jefferson learned that Spain had transferred Louisiana to France, he urged Livingston to get France to agree to respect America's right of deposit in New Orleans and to try to purchase West Florida if Spain had given that to France, too. In 1802, Jefferson authorized Livingston to purchase New Orleans and Florida. With James Monroe, Livingston was able to negotiate the purchase of all of the Louisiana Territory (1803) for $15 million. Livingston resigned as minister to France in 1804 and returned to New York.

Long interested in steam navigation, Livingston obtained a state monopoly for the operation of steamboats in New York waters in 1798. With Livingston's assistance, **Robert Fulton** designed the *Clermont,* the first successful steamboat (1807). After their initial successes the two men extended their operations to the Mississippi.

A landed aristocrat, Livingston remained throughout life strongly influenced by a privileged upbringing, family status, and landholding. He supported the Revolution but could never come to accept it as revolutionary. He entered into the political life of the new nation, but he could never become a politician. He had a distaste for rustic lawmakers and for catering to the masses; he was never popular. He was a first-class administrator as secretary of foreign affairs under the Confederation, but he was distressed by his lack of authority and status.

Livingston had a quick, able mind and self-assurance; well read, endlessly curious about the physical world, he was a born improver—among other things a promoter of scientific farming. His ambition repeatedly drew him away from Clermont, but his land and status as chancellor exerted a strong homeward pull. Holding the chancery court at Clermont, Livingston may have been most content as judge and landlord.

While clinging to an aristocratic past and driven by an innate conservatism, Livingston ended up generally on the side of progress. He supported the Constitution and early became a supporter of Jeffersonian republicanism. His nationalism was related to his landholding; his republicanism was imbued with deep-seated agrarian prejudices.

As minister to France, Livingston was shrewd enough to grasp the opportunity that led to the Louisiana Purchase. His contribution in influencing Napoleon's decision and in preparing the ground for the triumph, which he was obliged to share with James Monroe, has rarely been adequately recognized. So also has Livingston's role as the partner of Robert Fulton been overshadowed by the more famous inventor, but Livingston's vision of the uses of steam power on American rivers and his commitment of his financial resources to the venture played a critical role in Fulton's success. See George Dangerfield, *Chancellor Robert R. Livingston of New York, 1746–1813* (1960).

NOBLE E. CUNNINGHAM, JR.

LLOYD, Henry Demarest (b. New York, N.Y., May 1, 1847; d. Chicago, Ill., Sept. 28, 1903), PUBLICIST, REFORMER, graduated from Columbia University in 1869 and was admitted to the New York bar the same year. He became active in the American Free Trade League, and at the Liberal-Republican presidential convention in 1872 he tried to prevent the nomination of **Horace Greeley,** the protectionist editor of the New York *Herald Tribune.*

In 1872, Lloyd moved to Chicago. As financial editor and chief editorial writer of the Chicago *Tribune* (1874–75), he became one of the nation's leading liberal publicists, attacking classical economic theory with its emphasis on competition and focusing attention on the social problems that were plaguing American society. After traveling to Europe to study social conditions abroad (1885), he engaged in two years' study of philosophy and social theory, which led to the formulation of a welfare theory of reform. Following the Haymarket riot in Chicago (May 1886), in which five policemen were killed by a bomb, Lloyd was one of the few prominent Americans who asked for a commutation of the death sentence meted out to the seven anarchists convicted of the crime. In 1890 he published his first book, *A Strike of Millionaires Against Miners,* an exposé of the Spring Valley Co.

In 1894, an active year for Lloyd, he championed **Eugene V. Debs** and other American Railway Union officials who were held in contempt of court for tying up the trunk lines running in and out of Chicago during the Pullman strike; he ran unsuccessfully for Congress on the National People's Party ticket on a platform demanding "The Cooperative Commonwealth," and he published *Wealth Against Commonwealth,* an attack on monopolies in general and the Standard Oil Co. in particular. Based on long study (he published his first indictment against Standard Oil in the *Atlantic Monthly* in 1881), it attracted wide attention. Arguing also that the Darwinian and Spencerian philosophies of survival of the fittest and laissez-faire led directly to monopolies, Lloyd advocated public ownership of all monopolies. He persuaded the Populist St.

Louis Conference of 1894 to adopt this proposal. When the Populists joined with the Democratic Party and subordinated all reform issues to the free coinage of silver in the 1896 election, Lloyd became disillusioned with politics.

During 1897–1901, Lloyd traveled abroad, again studying social conditions. In 1898 he published *Labour Copartnership,* a study of producers cooperatives in England. *A Country Without Strikes* (1900) was a study of compulsory arbitration of industrial disputes in New Zealand. *Newest England* (1900) presents an analysis of progressive democracy in Australasia.

In 1902–3, Lloyd helped present the case of the Pennsylvania miners during the anthracite coal strike arbitration. *Man, the Social Creator* (1906), which presents Lloyd's welfare philosophy, and *A Sovereign People* (1907), a study of all aspects of Swiss democracy, were both published posthumously.

Henry Demarest Lloyd was a man of great personal charm, keen intellectuality, and extraordinary moral courage. Together these made him a major historical force. He led in the reorientation of American democracy from laissez-faire individualism to the positive fostering of the general welfare as the major objective of capitalism and government guided by conceptions of social justice and a positive social ethic. Lloyd's initial formulation of "The Progressive Mind" and later of a social welfare philosophy placed him among his era's leading reformers. His journalistic campaign against industrial abuses and monopoly, for national railroad regulation, and for state regulation of the Chicago Board of Trade were extremely influential. His most important work was *Wealth Against Commonwealth,* which developed the theoretical position broached by his magazine articles of the early eighties. His information bureau and the hospitality that he and his wife extended to socially minded intellectuals, clergymen, social settlement workers, labor leaders, and reformers of all types helped develop an esprit de corps among social critics that stimulated a pluralistic attack on abuses.

In his later years, as the dean of the reform movement in the United States, Lloyd championed compulsory arbitration of strikes, cooperatives, and social security together with an enlightened policy toward the labor movement. He did much to guide the clerical leaders of the Social Gospel movement in Protestant and Catholic churches to a constructive confrontation with contemporary economic and social evils. He was a pioneer muckraker and the leading antimonopolist of his day—the exponent of a far-reaching welfare philosophy from which 20th-century American democracy has drawn heavily.

Lloyd also exerted significant influence on the English Fabians and on William T. Stead, London advocate of a new liberalism. Beginning his career as a Cobdenite liberal, Lloyd advanced to new-liberal "Progressivism," then to a non-Marxian, radical Liberal Socialism attuned to the problems and aspirations of both the American middle class and the trade union movement. His reports on British cooperatives, Antipodean progressive democracy, and Swiss direct democracy contributed to the agenda of the Progressive era and formulated conceptions of social security that bore fruit during the New Deal. Much of Lloyd's impact on his and succeeding generations was made via numerous disciples. See C. M. Destler, *Henry Demarest Lloyd and the Empire of Reform* (1963).

CHESTER M. DESTLER

LOCKE, Alain LeRoy (b. Philadelphia, Pa., Sept. 13, 1886; d. New York, N.Y., June 9, 1954), PHILOSOPHER, attended Harvard (1904–7), and won a Rhodes scholarship for study at Oxford University in England (1907–10), the first black ever to gain this honor. After studying philosophy at the University of Berlin (1910–11), Locke returned to the United States in 1912 to become assistant professor of philosophy and education at Howard University in Washington, D.C. Locke earned his PhD in philosophy from Harvard with his dissertation *The Problem of Classification in Theory of Value* (1918). In 1917 he became chairman of the philosophy department at Howard, a position he held until his retirement in 1953.

With the publication of *The New Negro* (1925), a collection of essays describing the aims of the New Negro movement, or Harlem Renaissance, Locke emerged as a leading spokesman of intellectual blacks. As such he championed many black artists in literature, art, and drama. His book *The Negro in Art* (1941) is a record of the black artist and black themes in art. Locke also wrote on the problem of race relations and coedited *When People Meet: A Study of Race and Culture Contacts* (1942). His last work, *The Negro in American Culture* (1956), was published posthumously. Some of his many other writings include *The Negro in America* (1933) and *The Negro and His Music* (1936).

———

In the black renaissance of the 1920s black artists joined the general revolt against 19th-century certainties but also attacked the ethnic group certainties supported by such myths as the "black Christ." The iconoclasm was liberating but opened the void in which the Lost Generation floundered, and swept away ego defense mechanisms that blacks had used for generations. To this problem Alain Locke, philosophical spokesman for the black artists, addressed himself. Locke was as much attuned to Western artistic and philosophical thought as to black protest, and his answers marked a departure from narrowly defined militancy. For him the crucial thing was the individual's inner life. Confronted by a "cultural wasteland," Locke joined the white Little Renaissance to demand of the artist the re-creation of a sense of the sacred. As to the problem of blasted self-esteem, Locke joined his friend, sociologist **Charles S. Johnson,** in suggesting that the beauty in the black American's experience be built on, thereby also advancing the cause of cultural pluralism and the liberation of all Americans from the "tyranny of the average and mediocre."

Too often, perhaps, Locke's call for a cultural ideal seemed to hint of a new edition of the old myths ("patience, adaptability, loyalty, and smiling humility") or, conversely, of an exotic primitivism. Perhaps his counsels added confusion to an already chaotic movement that ranged from cynical opportunism to poetic mysticism. But the renaissance did ultimately follow his intended road to the masses, once the singers of the spirituals, now the singers of the blues. See D. K. Stafford, "Alain Locke: The Child, the Man, and the People," *Journal of Negro History* (1961).

S. P. FULLINWIDER

LODGE, Henry Cabot (b. Boston, Mass., May 12, 1850; d. Cambridge, Mass., Nov. 9, 1924), POLITICAL LEADER, received his BA (1871) and LLB (1874) from Harvard, and was admitted to the bar in 1875. During 1873–76 he was assistant editor of the *North American Review,* and in 1876 he received a PhD from Harvard, after which he taught American history there (1878–79).

Although originally an independent in politics, in 1878 Lodge was elected to the Massachusetts house of representatives as a Republican. His support of Republican **James G. Blaine** in the presidential election of 1884 established him as a party regular. After two unsuccessful attempts (1882, 1884), Lodge was elected to the U.S. Congress in 1886 (serving 1887–93). In 1890 he introduced the "Force Bill," providing for the supervision of federal elections by the national government in order to protect the voting rights of southern blacks, but the bill was defeated in the Senate.

In 1893, Lodge was elected to the U.S. Senate. He supported the protective tariff, hard money, immigration restriction, and a large navy. He became one of the Senate's leading spokesmen for expansion, attacking President Grover Cleveland for not annexing Hawaii. Lodge also wrote many articles in which he supported the ideas of **Alfred Thayer Mahan,** calling for the acquisition of outlying naval bases to facilitate commercial expansion. He supported the Spanish-American War and the annexation of the Philippines.

During Theodore Roosevelt's administration, Lodge, who was his close friend, backed the president's attempts to build an isthmian canal (1903). In 1903 he served on the commission to settle the Alaskan boundary dispute with Great Britain and Canada.

Lodge opposed such measures as the direct election of senators and woman suffrage. When Theodore Roosevelt ran for the presidency on the Progressive ticket in 1912, Lodge supported the Republican incumbent, William Howard Taft.

When World War I broke out in Europe, Lodge advocated preparedness programs; after the *Lusitania* was sunk (1915), he demanded that President Woodrow Wilson call for a declaration of war. With Theodore Roosevelt, Lodge became one of the most outspoken critics of the Wilson administration, but after the American declaration of war against Germany in April 1917, he supported administration war measures.

Lodge led the senatorial opposition to Wilson's plan to include the League of Nations in the peace settlement after the war. As chairman of the Foreign Relations Committee he obtained the signatures of thirty-six senators to a "Round Robin" (Mar. 1919), objecting to Wilson's League and urging that the question of an international organization be discussed only after a peace treaty with Germany had been negotiated. But he was not an outright opponent of American membership in any international organization. During the Senate debate on the peace treaty he presented fourteen "Lodge Reservations." The most important "reservation" applied to Article X of the League Covenant, which committed the signatories to guarantee the political independence and territorial integrity of member nations. Lodge's reservation provided that Article X should not be binding on the United States unless Congress so voted in a particular case. However, Wilson insisted that the peace treaty be accepted as it stood. When the Senate voted on the treaty with the Lodge reservations, it failed to get the necessary two-thirds vote (1919). Reconsideration in March 1920 produced substantially similar results.

In 1921, Lodge was a delegate to the Washington Disarmament Conference, which established a limitation on the number of battleships of the major powers, abrogated the Anglo-Japanese alliance, provided for consultation in the event of belligerent action in the Pacific (Four-Power Treaty), guaranteed China's territo-

rial integrity, and reaffirmed the "Open Door" principle (Nine-Power Treaty).

Lodge was also a prolific historian and essayist. His works include *Alexander Hamilton* (1882), *Daniel Webster* (1882), *George Washington* (2 vols., 1888), *Selections from the Correspondence of Theodore Roosevelt and Henry Cabot Lodge* (ed., 2 vols., 1925, posthumously), and *The Senate and the League of Nations* (1925, posthumously).

⁂

In his own day Lodge was known as "the scholar in politics," and indeed, since he held one of the first PhD's in history granted by an American university, it was an accurate enough description. The title also identified correctly the relative importance of his two careers. He was a scholar—his books were elegantly written and by the standards of his day respectable historical works—but he was *in* politics. And few more skillful professional politicians ever lived.

Crucial to the development of Lodge's political career was the presidential race of 1884 between Grover Cleveland and James G. Blaine, or better, the way the society Lodge cared about most reacted to his support of Blaine. Lodge began his career as a liberal independent in a solidly Republican state. The Brahmin world of which he was a part approved such a stance, but it was far too small a world to control elections. When Lodge, seeking a seat in the House of Representatives, obtained the Republican nomination and—holding his nose—campaigned for the corrupt Blaine, his peers denounced him as a traitor. In response he burned all his bridges with independency and became totally committed to party loyalty.

In Congress, Lodge generally voted on the conservative side, but he was not a reactionary. Like his great predecessor **Daniel Webster,** he defended the economic interests of Massachusetts and New England, but those interests never held him in their pocket as they had Webster. Partly because he was independently wealthy—and scornful of the grubby business tycoons of his day—he was scrupulously honest and careful to avoid even indirect conflicts of interest. In matters concerning foreign policy he was an expansionist but also an internationalist. He saw the United States as a great power with a major role to play in the world, not as an isolated bastion, remote from the affairs of other states.

In the climactic crisis of his career, the fight over ratification of the Versailles Treaty, he seems in retrospect to have been right in arguing that Article X of the League of Nations Covenant was unrealistic in its assumption that any nation would go to war to defend the integrity of another unless it saw its own interests at stake, and that the article, therefore, was not merely unenforceable but dangerous. Throughout his life he consistently held that international agreements, to be effective, must be based on the practical realities of national self-interest. Yet it is also clear that his dislike of Wilson, which developed out of Wilson's handling of Mexican—American relations and the president's neutrality policy between 1914 and 1917, had much to do with Lodge's tactics as Senate majority leader during the fight over ratification of the treaty. He allowed his personal feelings and his partisanship to influence his activities in a most unstatesmanlike way. Considering the enormous importance of the question, he behaved reprehensibly.

Many of his contemporaries cordially disliked Lodge, and not merely those who favored America's joining the League of Nations. He had a haughty, supercilious quality and a rasping voice that raised many hackles. Yet he made many deep and abiding friendships in politics. His relationship with Theodore Roosevelt, which to Lodge's credit survived both the transition from sponsor to follower that occurred when Roosevelt was catapulted into the White House by the assassination of William McKinley and Roosevelt's sharp shift to the left in 1912, was only one example of this quality. Lodge was also a good public servant. Despite his wealth and social position he abhorred dilettantism. Few senators worked so hard both at the routine of politics and at the study of public issues. See John A. Garraty, *Henry Cabot Lodge: A Biography* (1953).

JOHN A. GARRATY

LOEB, Jacques (b. Mayen, Prussia, Apr. 7, 1859; d. Bermuda, Feb. 11, 1924), SCIENTIST, received his higher education at the universities of Berlin, Munich, and Strassburg, obtaining his medical degree from Strassburg in 1884. During the remainder of the 1880s he was a research assistant in physiology at Würzburg and Strassburg. In 1891 he emigrated to America to become a professor at Bryn Mawr College; in 1892 he went to the University of Chicago, in 1902 to the University of California, and in 1910 he joined the Rockefeller Institute for Medical Research, where he remained until his death.

Loeb's original interest was philosophy, particularly the question of freedom of the human will, but he found philosophical discussions of the issue too abstract. Wanting to test freedom of the will experimentally, he studied (1888–98) tropisms, the mechanical reactions of plants and animals to external stimuli. From his experiments, which revealed that microorganisms normally indifferent to light would swim toward light if carbonic acid were added to the water, Loeb concluded that certain psychological reactions in higher organisms might be reducible to a physicochemical basis; e.g., secretions of a gland may be the source of sexual behavior. Experiments on tropisms formed the basis of Loeb's mechanistic view of life, which he applied to the realm of ethics: instincts such as motherly love or altruism are inherited; ignorance or superstition may warp these instincts; "mutants" may be produced, too many of which would lower the ethics of a community.

From the end of the 1890s forward, Loeb conducted experiments that sought to control life processes from conception to death. In 1899 he succeeded in inducing artificial parthenogenesis in sea urchins—i.e., the production of larvae from unfertilized eggs placed in a salt-water solution. Loeb also studied the phenomena of regeneration of lost organs in certain lower animals and evolutionary adaptations, both of which he argued could be explained by physicochemical processes. Loeb's studies of death revealed that in certain animals, death could be postponed by keeping body temperature sufficiently low, thereby slow-ing down chemical reactions that occur in the process of dying. He concluded that length of life is the time required for completion of a series of chemical reactions.

Seeking to establish a philosophy free from mysticism, Loeb was a pioneer in the use of physics and chemistry in physiology. His important books in English include *Studies in General Physiology* (1905), *The Mechanistic Conception of Life* (1912), *The Organism as a Whole* (1916), and *Regeneration* (1924).

⎯⎯∞⎯⎯

When Jacques Loeb migrated to the United States at the age of 32, he brought with him the aspiration to combine the roles of philosopher, reformer, and scientist. He was a materialist in philosophy, a mechanist in science, and a socialist in politics. He saw these as interlocking commitments—only a mechanistic investigator could realize the full potentialities of biological science, only a socialist would apply them to the welfare of the masses, only a materialist would focus single-mindedly upon improving the material conditions of life.

Such views soon made Loeb one of the best-known iconoclasts in the United States, for no scheme of values could have been more alien to the vast majority of Americans in the 1890s. The principal contemporary deduction from science was the Social Darwinian commendation of rugged individualism, at the polar extreme from Loeb's socialism. His doctrinaire espousal of materialism was, if anything, even more shocking. There had long been a genial conspiracy, initiated by **Asa Gray,** to suppress the conflict between science and religion by proclaiming the neutrality of science toward religious faith and spiritual values. Now Loeb refused to honor the truce and undertook to extirpate spirituality from its last lurking places.

One of his prime targets was the modern theories of instinctual behavior that implied an inbuilt capacity in biological organisms for resisting external stimuli. Loeb regarded all such theories as a thinly veiled rehabilitation of the doctrine of the freedom of the individual will that he

had been trying to demolish since his early manhood. In this context he performed the famous experiments subsumed under the doctrine of "animal tropisms"—identically orienting entire collections of intact organisms by applying a common physical or chemical stimulus to them.

The concept of animal tropisms was severely criticized in Loeb's own lifetime, chiefly by the American biologist Herbert Spencer Jennings. Jennings did not deny that some examples of tropistic behavior occurred. But he showed that even in bacteria and other lower organisms, by far the commonest phenomenon was learning by trial and error how to respond to a stimulus advantageously. In the beginning was spontaneity, and that was anathema to Loeb.

The paradox was that Jennings always insisted on his own indebtedness to Loeb as the great pioneer in the objective analysis of behavior, the man who first made the study of behavior a rigorously experimental science. The firebrand who turned these developments into a scientific revolution was the founder of behaviorism, **John B. Watson.** Watson was a graduate student at the University of Chicago while Loeb was a professor there, and Loeb was his first choice for a thesis director. Watson let himself be dissuaded by other professors who told him Loeb was not "safe" for a student to work with. But it is a fair inference that Loeb had already infected him with a latent virus of hostility toward subjective modes of analysis in psychology. That was the nub of behaviorism, and Loeb was Watson's greatest precursor in exemplifying and proselytizing for this attitude.

Apart from his work on tropisms, the researches by Loeb that had the greatest reverberations in the world at large were his experiments on the fertilization of eggs, culminating in the legendary feat of inducing viable larvae of the sea urchin to develop from unfertilized eggs immersed in salt water. Loeb regarded artificial parthenogenesis as the ideal means of studying and controlling the physical and chemical changes accompanying early stages of development in the fertilized egg. This was the identical spirit in which Gregory Pincus and M. C. Chang embarked on demonstrations of artificial parthenogenesis in mammals from the 1930s forward. It is no accident that they were the men who developed the contraceptive pill. Loeb had nothing to do with the pill as such, but it was the product of men who shared his resolve to bring all aspects of fertilization under scientific control and actually began their endeavors by resuming a line of research indelibly associated with Loeb. See Jacques Loeb, *The Mechanistic Conception of Life*, ed. Donald Fleming (1964).

DONALD FLEMING

LOEB, Sophie Irene Simon (b. Rovno, Russia, July 4, 1876; d. New York, N.Y., Jan. 18, 1929), SOCIAL WORKER, was brought to the U.S. at age 6 and grew up in McKeesport, Pennsylvania. After briefly teaching in the local high school and working for a Pittsburgh newspaper, Loeb went to New York in 1910, where she became a reporter for the *Evening World*. Her *World* articles about slum children helped gain support for the idea of state aid to dependent children as a replacement for orphanages. In 1913 she was appointed to the New York State Commission for the Relief of Widowed Mothers. The Commission sent her abroad to study European child-care methods, and when she returned to the United States, she organized support for establishing the New York State Welfare Board (1915) and for the Mothers' Pension Act (1915).

As president of the Welfare Board (1915–22) Loeb managed to obtain an increase in state welfare aid from $100,000 to $5 million. During the same period she also worked for legislation establishing housing relief, maternity care, public baths, school lunch programs, and play streets. In 1920, Governor **Alfred E. Smith** named her to a commission to systematize New York's welfare laws, and in 1924, she became the first president of the Child Welfare Committee of America, which she had founded to agitate for child welfare programs in other states. Loeb was adviser on child care to the League of Nations and wrote *Epigrams of Eve* (1913), *Everyman's Child* (1920), and *Palestine Awake* (1926).

Sophie Loeb was responsible for directly securing more constructive welfare legislation than any woman in America. She was no lady bountiful or settlement house matron committed to institutional reform for the poor. Left fatherless at 16, with an adored mother and five younger brothers and sisters to support, she cherished her family all the more passionately and dedicated her life to keeping families like her own together. Denied the joys of marriage and parenthood herself, this dynamic little woman came to mother millions. She barely took time to eat or to sleep in her drive to give dignity and pride to every mother and a chance to every child of the tenements. Her capacity for indignation, her gift for organizing public affairs, and her talent for household management were welded into a massive and concerted public effort to gain a hearing for those she loved. In her column in the *Evening World* and on the radio she shrewdly argued their case by demonstrating that allowances that held families together would prove more economical than institutional care. New York's First Lady of social welfare, she declined to run for public office and refused compensation for time devoted to public service. Her motto, "Not charity, but a chance for every child," was inscribed on the monument of this woman devoted to liberty for mothers and children as well as for men and single women. See Ellen Malino James, "Sophie Loeb," *Notable American Women, 1607–1950: A Biographical Dictionary*, II (1971), 416–17.

MOSES RISCHIN

LOEWY, Raymond Fernand (b. Paris, France, Nov. 5, 1893; d. Monte Carlo, Monaco, July 14, 1986), INDUSTRIAL DESIGNER, studied electrical engineering at Paris University and advanced engineering at the Ecole de Laneau. Graduating in 1919 (after an interruption for service with the French army's engineering corps), he emigrated to the United States where he worked for a time on the art staff of *Vogue* and later became a freelance fashion illustrator and window-display artist for Saks Fifth Avenue and Macy's, among others. In 1927 he formed a private industrial design firm that became Raymond Loewy Associates in 1930 and Raymond Loewy International in 1961. In 1938, Loewy became an American citizen.

Loewy's dedication to streamlined, functional styling had its first major success in 1934 with his design for Sears Roebuck's Coldspot refrigerator, which won first prize at the Paris International Exposition and the first Lord and Taylor American Design Award. As a consultant to more than one hundred firms worldwide, he designed products ranging from toothbrushes and ball-point pens to automobiles, airplanes, and ocean liners. In 1937 his design of an electric locomotive for the Pennsylvania Railroad Company received the Paris Fair's gold medal in the transportation field. In the 1950s he added trademark and logo design to his repertoire, creating the well-known symbols of Shell Oil and Exxon and the stylized eagle of the U.S. Postal Service.

───────

No designer of the 20th century has had so pervasive an impact on American visual taste as Raymond Loewy. With a solid background in engineering, he built the largest industrial design firm in the world and changed the look of commercial products from lipsticks to locomotives.

Loewy summarized his professional creed of efficiency, economy, and beauty in his statement, "Good design keeps the user happier, the manufacturer in the black, and the aesthete unoffended." Regarded as the father of modern industrial design, he put his stamp of elegant simplicity and functional styling on toys, furniture, dinnerware, the interiors of Gimbels and the Lever Building in New York City, and a community in Brazil. His 1937 design of the first all-welded locomotive established his reputation as the leader of the streamlining movement. Counting the United States government among his most frequent clients, he redesigned President John F. Kennedy's plane, Air Force One, and was a frequent consultant to the U.S. National Aeronautics and Space Administration.

Among Loewy's most influential vehicular designs was the body of the Studebaker Starliner

(1953), regarded as the most svelte American automobile since World War II and described by one critic as "the top car of all time." The clean look and aerodynamic efficiency of the Starliner was controversial in an industry whose products still looked, as Loewy said in 1979, "like chrome-plated barges," but the Starliner was to be the forerunner of the lightweight, compact cars of the future. See Raymond Fernand Loewy, *Never Leave Well Enough Alone* (1951).

DENNIS WEPMAN

LOGAN, George (b. Germantown, Pa., Sept. 9, 1753; d. Germantown, Pa., Apr. 9, 1821), POLITICAL LEADER, received a strict Quaker upbringing, attending the Friends School in Philadelphia and finishing his education in English schools. Upon his return to Philadelphia in 1770 he was apprenticed to a Quaker merchant, but he went back to England in 1775 and studied medicine at the University of Edinburgh (1776–79). Logan returned to the United States in 1780 and took up farming at his father's estate. He developed an interest in agricultural improvements, publishing several papers on that subject and founding the Philadelphia Society for the Promotion of Agriculture in 1785. He served in the Pennsylvania assembly (1785–89, 1796–1801). A fervent Jeffersonian republican, Logan advocated public education, elimination of the national debt, and the dominance of agriculture over industry.

In 1798, Logan, a pacifist and conscientious objector, undertook a private mission to France to end the undeclared naval war between that country and the United States. He talked with foreign minister Charles Talleyrand, head of the Directory, Philippe-Antoine Merlin, and other officials, and succeeded in securing the release of imprisoned American sailors and in lifting the French embargo on American shipping. His unofficial messages from Talleyrand to President John Adams helped clear the way for an eventual settlement between the two nations. His work, however, angered the Federalists in Congress, who passed the "Logan Act" (1799) forbidding private citizens from engaging in diplomacy without official sanction. Logan was elected to the U.S. Senate in 1801, where he ardently supported President Thomas Jefferson, including his Louisiana Purchase. He retired from the Senate in 1807 but conducted another private mission to London in 1810 to try to settle the differences between the United States and Great Britain that eventually led to the War of 1812.

⸺ ⸺

Logan's success in ignoring the punitive Logan Act underscores American acceptance of a role for private missions in the conduct of foreign affairs. From George Logan to Cyrus Eaton prominent individuals have been tempted without serious challenge to initiate personal approaches in diplomacy that bypassed conventional channels. Despite government opposition they believed they were performing an enormous public service—and frequently their beliefs were justified.

Logan's own altruism was converted to partisan ends by his political friends and enemies. Angry Federalists interpreted his ingenuous efforts to end the quasi-war with France as a species of treason. But it is worth noting that his reports reinforced Adams's recognition of France's desire for a détente, which the president had gathered from other sources. Whether or not Logan's intervention was the critical factor in freeing American sailors in France, he served both French and American interests as a conduit for the termination of hostilities.

More than ten years later, his Quaker pacifist passions still alive, Logan undertook another private mission to Europe, this time to London where he hoped to patch up differences between the United States and Great Britain that threatened to end in war. He was convinced in 1810 that France under Napoleon was a greater threat to liberty than her enemy. His account of the merits of Britain's position had less effect on Madison's conduct than his earlier activity in France had had on Adams. The Logan Act held no more significance for him in 1810 than it held for the American public at any time. See

Frederick B. Tolles, *George Logan of Philadelphia* (1953).

LAWRENCE S. KAPLAN

LONDON, Jack (pseudonym of John Griffith) (b. San Francisco, Calif., Jan. 12, 1876; d. Sonoma County, Calif., Nov. 22, 1916), WRITER, grew up in the waterfront district of Oakland. After an intermittent education he delivered newspapers, was an oyster pirate, and worked as a pinboy before signing on in 1893 with a sealing vessel bound for the Siberian coast. For a few months in 1897 he attended the University of California at Berkeley. During this period he attended Socialist Labor Party meetings in San Francisco. In 1897 he joined the gold rush to Klondike, Alaska, but returned in 1898, having decided to become a writer. In 1899 the *Overland Monthly* published his short story, "To the Man on Trail." During the next four years London published numerous short stories, including a widely acclaimed collection, *The Son of the Wolf* (1900). He also published two novels, *A Daughter of the Snows* (1902) and *The Call of the Wild* (1903), which were based in part on his Alaskan experiences and travels. The latter work—the story of how a dog, Buck, learned to rely on cunning and strength to survive in the Alaskan wilds— brought London international popularity.

In 1902 he set out to cover the Boer War for the American Press Association. When he was informed in London that the assignment had been canceled, he remained in that city, studying slum districts. *The People of the Abyss* (1903) was based on this experience. He then returned to California where he continued to write about the northern wilds as well as about the South Pacific in such novels as *The Sea Wolf* (1904). *The Road* (1907), *Martin Eden* (1909), and *The Cruise of the Snark* (1911) are autobiographical. In all his work London emphasized his belief that man's survival depended on primitive, instinctual qualities rather than on the specialized skills of civilization. London was a Socialist who believed that class struggle would lead to emancipation, but he resigned from the Socialist Labor Party in 1916 because he felt

American Socialism was compromising itself. *War of the Classes* (1904) was a collection of his revolutionary lectures and essays. *The Iron Heel* (1907), a novel, depicted a powerful exploitative capitalist regime of the future, which he called The Obligarchy. His descriptions of extraordinary human strength under adverse conditions helped make his work popular in the Soviet Union.

The work of Jack London appears at a nexus of new ideas and old forms. It stands as a tribute to the truth that art develops styles and conventions which constitute the inertia and the momentum of its expression. The spinning flywheel is not to be diverted from its form and movement, although its energy is available. The artist is subject to the conventions that he works with. Without them he can do nothing; with them he is limited to the expression they make possible. First among these is, of course, language. The "Connecticut Wits" attempted, after the Revolution, to write American epics; but they could write only conventional 18th-century English couplets made of quaint charm and poetic diction; in spite of themselves they described English scenes. Jack London, a century later, inherited the rather syrupy forms—in language, plot, and sentiment—of 19th-century popular fiction. With these he attempted to dramatize the New Science and the new social thinking that it inspired; and withal he was personally drawn to the notion of the Superman in its American avatar—a creature compounded of colossal intelligence, brute strength, eagle-eyed discernment, and heroic fortitude bursting its heart against the brazen anvil of middle-class Mammon.

Thus every story and novel reveals the struggle of these rather incompatible elements. The most sentimental Victorian morality, the plots setting virtue and faith against greed, venality, and treachery—these astonishingly drew their vigor from the popular ideas of struggle for existence, atavism, and survival of the fittest that had been tossed out by the New Science/Philosophy of Evolution which dominated popular thought at the turn of the century.

London, who grows older and more supermanly from year to year as the writer ages, is the obvious if unacknowledged hero of nearly every story. Martin Eden masters the typewriter in a day and confounds the university's leading scientist in debate. The sentimental vanity of such presentation is embarrassing, if not ludicrous; but it is still easy to see why the conflict of ideas fascinated contemporary readers of his work. Two wonderful animal stories stand out as exceptions to these weaknesses: *White Fang* and *The Call of the Wild* will be read as long as boys read, and they will not permit London soon to be forgotten. See Richard O'Connor, *Jack London: A Biography* (1964).

CHARLES CHILD WALCUTT

LONG, Huey Pierce (b. near Winnfield, La., Aug. 30, 1893; d. Baton Rouge, La., Sept. 10, 1935), POLITICAL LEADER, briefly studied law at Tulane University (1914) and was admitted to the Louisiana bar in 1915. He served on Louisiana's railroad commission (later the Public Service Commission) during 1918–28 (chairman, 1922–26). In 1924, Long ran for governor of Louisiana as a Democrat and lost, but was elected in 1928. Having based his appeal to rural voters on a tax-the-rich program, he succeeded in obtaining a constitutional amendment aimed at increasing the taxes paid by oil interests and directing revenues into highway construction and public education. Impeached for bribery and misconduct in 1929, Long escaped conviction. He instituted many needed reforms and construction projects, such as the abolition of the poll tax and the enlargement of the state university (LSU), and he built such a machine that eventually he controlled all branches of the state government.

Elected to the U.S. Senate in 1930, Long did not take his seat until 1932 (serving to 1935) because he wanted to arrange a satisfactory succession to the governorship. At the 1932 Democratic presidential convention in Chicago, Long supported Franklin D. Roosevelt. But shortly after Roosevelt's inauguration, Long broke with the president and began to criticize him severely as an instrument of the plutocratic ruling class. Early in 1934, Long founded an organization whose slogan was "Share Our Wealth." He proposed to liquidate all personal fortunes above a certain sum; to give every family enough money to have a home, a car, and a radio; to grant pensions to the old; to guarantee college educations to the young; to institute a public works program; to have a national minimum wage and a shorter work week; and to give veterans cash bonuses.

This program gained wide popularity, and Long began to be spoken of as a possible presidential candidate in 1936. Indeed, he had made it quite clear that the presidency was his goal; in 1935 he wrote *My First Years in the White House*. In September 1935, however, while supervising a special legislative session at the Louisiana state capital in Baton Rouge, Long was assassinated by Dr. Carl A. Weiss, the son-in-law of a political enemy.

Huey Long once broke up an argument among a group of reporters who were trying to classify him as a political leader. "Oh, hell," he snorted, "say that I'm *sui generis* and let it go at that." Debate over what kind of leader Long was began and raged in his own time and has continued since. Probably more hostile labels have been applied to him than to any other American politician. He has been called democrat but also demagogue, the first great native fascist, an American counterpart of Hitler and Mussolini, the lone man in our history who possessed the capacity to become dictator. It is understandable that he has evoked such reactions. He was a politician but not completely a normal one. In significant ways he shattered the pattern of the democratic leader. He was *sui generis*.

Long grew up in an almost unique political environment. His parish (county) of Winn had a tradition of dissent. In the sectional crisis of 1861 its people had opposed secession, and when war came they gave the coolest of support to the Confederacy. During the 1890s Winn was the center of Populist strength in Louisiana, and after Populism disappeared, a vigorous though minority Socialist Party flourished in the parish. The

young Long absorbed and accepted the ideas of this rural radicalism. The program he would advocate when he entered politics was a version of Populism enlarged to meet the needs of a more modern economy and embellished with ideas gathered from his reading.

He introduced his program for Louisiana when he became governor in 1928. Liberal or progressive in the context of the time, it encountered fierce opposition from conservatives. At one point they tried to remove him from office by impeachment. He defeated the attempt by persuading fifteen senators, two more than one-third of the senate, to sign a "round robin" that they would not vote to convict him. The experience hardened him, made him more ruthless.

Long had an unusual sense of destiny. He had said as a youth that someday he would be president, and when he went to the U.S. Senate in 1932, he used that body as a forum to advance his ambition. In fiery speeches he proposed his program for the nation, Share Our Wealth. It was authentic radicalism, was, as he frankly said, of the "left." Mixed in with his ambition was a real concern for poor people. He once said that his voice would not be stilled until the lives of the poor were made "decent and respectable." With a realism rare in a southern politician, he included blacks as recipients of his benefits.

He attracted a large popular following, and President Roosevelt believed that if the New Deal failed to solve the Depression, there might be a violent reaction from the left led by Long, culminating in a dictatorship. Roosevelt and other liberals feared him because of his methods in Louisiana. There, even though a senator, he was still supreme and determined to extend his program. He almost dispensed with the substance of democracy. Through his machine he controlled the executive, legislative, and judicial branches. He drove laws through the legislature with little regard for parliamentary procedures. "The end justifies the means," he once offered in explanation.

In 1936, Long planned to run a third-party candidate for president. This man would take enough votes away from Roosevelt to throw the election to the Republicans. They would do an even worse job of handling the Depression than the Democrats. Then in 1940 the country would cry for a strong man to save it, would cry for Huey Long. No one can say whether he would have reached his ambition or what kind of president he would have been had not assassination removed him from the scene. He could have become a great president. Or he might have become a great dictator. See T. Harry Williams, *Huey Long* (1969).

T. HARRY WILLIAMS

LONGFELLOW, Henry Wadsworth (b. Portland, Maine, Feb. 27, 1807; d. Cambridge, Mass., Mar. 24, 1882), POET, graduated from Bowdoin College in 1825. From 1826 to 1829 he studied in Europe. He returned to become professor of modern languages at Bowdoin, serving from 1829 to 1835. He was then named professor of modern languages at Harvard, but before assuming his duties he spent a year studying German and the Scandinavian languages abroad. He was professor at Harvard from 1836 to 1854.

Longfellow was an extremely prolific and popular poet. Among his best-known works are "The Village Blacksmith" (1840), *Poems on Slavery* (1842), *Evangeline* (1847), *The Golden Legend* (1851), *The Song of Hiawatha* (1855), *The Courtship of Miles Standish* (1858), *Tales of a Wayside Inn* (1863), and *The Divine Tragedy* (1871). He also published a three-volume translation of Dante's *Divine Comedy* (1865–67). His later work was less popular than the poems of the pre–Civil War period but is more highly regarded by most modern critics.

—————

For more than forty years "Longfellow" and "poet" were synonyms to most American readers. He strove to be the bard of the people, and his public joyfully repaid his efforts; he became the first native author to earn a living solely from the writing of verse. But the very traits that endeared him to his age have made him an embarrassment to a later period distrustful of simplistic pieties.

The pejorative adjectives come easily to the modern critic: Longfellow was clear, decent, patriotic, uncritical, retrospective, sentimental, cozy, and—above all else—moralistic. He was not, of course, unique in his view that literature should be uplifting—what **Edgar Allan Poe** scornfully called "the heresy of the didactic." But the appended lesson now is seen as fatally subversive of his often skillful versifying. These were homilies for the fireside circle; the deeper political and social problems of his day rarely intruded on his pleasantly memorizable lines. Moreover, despite his translations from foreign tongues, he remained essentially parochial; he spoke not from Parnassus but from Bunker Hill. Certainly his contemporaries prized him highly for his attempts to give legendary status to John Alden and Priscilla, **Paul Revere,** Evangeline—and that sanitized savage, Hiawatha. Present-day critics prefer those works least characteristic of this public voice: "The Jewish Cemetery at Newport," the Dante sonnets, a few songs. Longfellow continues to deserve recognition in the history of American popular culture; but the intellectual flaccidity of his verse has undercut any hope he ever held of remaining a living force. See Newton Arvin, *Longfellow: His Life and Work* (1963).

J. V. RIDGELY

LONGSTREET, James (b. Edgefield District, S.C., June 8, 1821; d. Gainesville, Ga., Jan. 2, 1904), MILITARY LEADER, graduated from West Point in 1842 and served as second lieutenant with the Fourth Infantry in Missouri and Louisiana and with the Eighth Infantry in Texas. During the Mexican War he saw action at Palo Alto, Resaca de la Palma, Monterey, the siege of Vera Cruz, Cerro Gordo, Churubusco, and Molino del Rey (1846–47). He was breveted captain after the engagement at Churubusco and major after Molino del Rey (Sept. 1847). Following the war he was assigned to frontier duty and during 1858–61 was a major in the paymaster's department.

Resigning from the federal army in 1861, Longstreet was commissioned brigadier general in the Confederate army. He was promoted to major general after his performance at Bull Run (July 1861). He served under General **J. E. Johnston** at Yorktown (Apr. 1862), at Williamsburg (May 5), and at the defeat at Seven Pines (May 31). After seeing action in the Seven Days battles around Richmond, he was sent to reinforce General **"Stonewall" Jackson** at Orange Court House and routed the Federals at Second Manassas (Aug. 30). His conduct at Antietam won him a promotion to lieutenant general. He then led the Confederate left at Fredericksburg (Dec. 13) and fought in the Suffolk campaign. Although he commanded the Confederate right flank at Gettysburg (July 1863), he opposed **Robert E. Lee**'s plans for a charge up Cemetery Ridge. After Gettysburg he joined General Braxton Bragg's Army of the Tennessee (Sept.) and led the assault on Snodgrass Hill at Chickamauga. He then saw action at Knoxville (Nov. 29, 1863), in the Battle of the Wilderness (May 6, 1864), where he was critically wounded, and, until the war's end, in the defense of Richmond.

After the war Longstreet headed an insurance company and prospered as a cotton factor in New Orleans. He joined the Republican Party and held numerous political offices between 1869 and 1904, including adjutant general for Louisiana (1870), minister to Turkey (1880–81), U.S. marshal of Georgia (1881–94), and U.S. commissioner of the Pacific Railroads (1897–1904). He wrote several articles on Civil War themes as well as a military autobiography, *From Manassas to Appomattox* (1896).

James Longstreet looked like what he was—a fierce and determined fighter. Slightly under six feet tall, heavyset, with cold bluish eyes and a thick, untrimmed brown beard, he habitually wore weathered clothes, dirty boots, and a black hat. Men who knew Longstreet described him as dignified and impressive. His manner was usually taciturn and undemonstrative, but he was proud and combative; at any imagined slight his temper flared. In battle he often exposed himself recklessly, sometimes leading a charge, hat in hand, in front of everybody.

Self-control and endurance enhanced his ability to command; he needed little food or sleep. In times of crisis he always seemed calm; he whittled on a stick or—as at Gettysburg—after posting his troops he found a comfortable spot and took a nap before the action started. When disaster threatened he maintained his poise, tenacity, and blunt sense of humor. And English Colonel James A. L. Fremantle observed that difficulties only made Longstreet "a little more savage."

Although not brilliant in either thought or conversation, he was dependable and systematic, admired for his tactical and administrative skill by his subordinates as well as by General Robert E. Lee, who called Longstreet "my old War Horse." His major weakness as a soldier was the mistaken belief that he was a great strategist, capable of independent command. Given a chance to direct his own army in east Tennessee, Longstreet failed. Gradually he became embittered and lost faith in Confederate victory, but he remained devoted to Lee. At Appomattox, Longstreet said to Lee: "General, unless Grant offers us honorable terms, come back and let us fight it out." See Donald Bridgman Sanger and Thomas Robson Hay, *James Longstreet* (1952).

GRADY MCWHINEY

LOUIS, Joe (b. Chambers County, Ala., May 13, 1914; d. Las Vegas, Nev., Apr. 12, 1981), BOXER, was born Joseph Louis Barrow, the son of a poor sharecropper. In 1921 he moved to Detroit, where he briefly attended school. In 1930 he began boxing in Detroit while also holding down a job at the Ford auto plant in River Rouge. He won the 1934 National AAU light-heavyweight title and then turned professional. Fighting under the name of Joe Louis and coached by trainer Jack Blackburn, he won twenty-two straight fights and acquired the nickname "the Brown Bomber of Detroit." He defeated Primo Carnera (1935), Max Baer (1935), and Charley Retzloff (1935) before losing to the German Max Schmeling in 1936. Louis then defeated Jack Sharkey (1936), Eddie Simms (1936), and Bob Pastor (1936), and on June 22, 1937, he won the heavyweight championship from James J. Braddock in Chicago.

Louis held the title for twelve years and defended it twenty-five times, fighting, among others, Tommy Farr (1937), Schmeling (1938), Tony Galento (1939), Arturo Godoy (1940), and "Jersey Joe" Walcott (1947, 1948). During World War II, Louis fought exhibition matches while in the army and received the Legion of Merit medal for his work. He retired as undefeated champion in 1949 but returned to the ring in 1950, only to lose to the new champion, Ezzard Charles, in a fifteen-round decision. He fought eight more fights but retired after losing to Rocky Marciano on October 25, 1951. He was elected to the boxing Hall of Fame in 1954. Louis tried many business ventures after his retirement, including an attempt to be a boxing promoter in 1969, but he lost most of his once great fortune and experienced a series of difficulties with the federal government over his income taxes. For many years he worked as a greeter and host in Las Vegas gambling casinos. He suffered a nervous breakdown in 1970. A benefit for him held in Detroit that year was attended by about eight thousand people. Louis's health throughout the seventies was precarious at best, and he was confined to a wheelchair after 1977.

Because he had as much style and grace and true sportsmanship in his makeup as he had punching power in his fists, Joe Louis, an Alabama sharecropper's son, advanced the cause of black people everywhere as no sports figure had done before.

Louis was one of the outstanding boxer-punchers of any time in the history of prizefighting, but he had even more significant inner qualities that made him acceptable from the moment it became evident that he might become world heavyweight champion. Even when he made a record twenty-five successful title defenses, the expression "white hope" was never spoken as it had been so often during Jack Johnson's tenure as champion. Louis not only broke barriers of racism but became the sports idol of millions,

and in retirement he remained a beloved American folk hero almost without parallel.

In the early days of World War II, Louis became a soldier in the army of the United States, donated the purses of two title defenses to army and navy relief societies, and, in the middle of Madison Square Garden's ring, told a capacity crowd, "We'll win this war because we're on God's side." Somebody may have written that line for Joe, but it nevertheless became almost unforgettable because it so typified the beloved Brown Bomber. Even in the bitter aftermath of his matchless ring career, a sorry phase that was not of his own doing, Louis steadfastly continued to be a model of sportsmanship. He was as loved at the end of his life as much as on that memorable June night in 1938 when he destroyed Max Schmeling in the first round.

This was a status that Joe Louis enjoyed only partly because he was an unbeatable fighter in his prime. Perhaps, even more so, it was for the reason that he always wore his mantle like a king born to the throne. See Joe Louis, *My Life Story* (1947).

WILLIAM J. LEE

LOVEJOY, Elijah Parish (b. Albion, Maine, Nov. 9, 1802; d. Alton, Ill., Nov. 7, 1837), REFORMER, graduated from Waterville (now Colby) College in 1826. He taught in Missouri until 1827 and then became the editor of the St. Louis *Times*, a Whig paper. Converted at a revival in 1832, Lovejoy attended Princeton Theological Seminary and in 1834 received a license to preach. He returned to St. Louis where he edited the weekly Presbyterian St. Louis *Observer* (1833–36) and took up the banners of reform. He attacked "popery"—though St. Louis had a large Catholic population—and promulgated a moderate antislavery line. His position in St. Louis became untenable after he labeled Judge Luke Lawless an "Irish papist" for not prosecuting a mob that had lynched a black person (June 1836), but before he could move to Alton, Illinois, most of his printing equipment was destroyed by indignant citizens. What remained of his press was thrown into the river at Alton in July.

Lovejoy soon raised money for a new press, however, and in September he published the first issue of the Alton *Observer*.

Lovejoy saw his paper's circulation double during his first year in Alton. He soon adopted a strong abolitionist line and on July 6, 1837, he called for the formation of an Illinois antislavery society. Ordered at a public meeting five days later to cease his "incendiary publications," he refused to do so. On August 21 a mob unsuccessfully attempted to tar and feather him, but it did succeed in destroying his press. When a new press arrived on September 21, persons unknown threw it into the Mississippi.

On October 26, Lovejoy participated in the convention that formed the Illinois Anti-Slavery Society, and the following week a meeting of citizens demanded that he resign his editorship. Lovejoy's fourth press arrived on November 6 and was placed in a warehouse, protected by an armed guard. The following night, as Lovejoy attempted to prevent a mob from setting the warehouse on fire, he was shot and killed.

Lovejoy came from an old Calvinist family and spent all his life in a religious atmosphere. His father, a farmer and Congregational preacher, inculcated in him a Calvinist sense of mission to stamp out sin, to rectify the wrongs of others, to stand up boldly against injustice. It was this sense of mission—for Lovejoy embodied "the Puritan spirit in its most tenacious form"—that brought him west to Missouri, where he carried on a one-man campaign to win the frontier for the Lord. An evangelist in journalism, he exploded against anything he considered godless and unjust: he attacked the Catholic Church as despotic and immoral; he upbraided his St. Louis neighbors for their idolatrous love of money, liquor, and the pleasures of the flesh. Pugnacious, inflexible, and self-righteous, Lovejoy was nevertheless a brave and deeply principled humanitarian who could not abide man's cruelty to his fellow man. Inevitably he became an abolitionist, announcing that he, too, regarded slavery as America's cruelest, most abominable social evil.

Initially he supported colonization as the best solution to the slavery problem, but by 1835 he agreed with **William Lloyd Garrison** that the slaves must be immediately emancipated and assimilated into America's social order.

But it was not as an abolitionist that Lovejoy gained recognition, for he remained a cranky nonconformist in that movement. Rather, Lovejoy's significance lay in his courageous fight for freedom of speech and the press—for the right of the individual in a democracy to give his opinions on controversial issues even if those opinions do not accord with popular will. Ironically, though, it was in his death, not his life, that Lovejoy achieved lasting significance. For when a racist, anti-abolitionist mob killed him because he had dared to speak out for an unpopular cause, he became abolitionism's first martyr. Even his brother Owen announced that Elijah was more important to the movement dead than he had been alive. And in the years that followed, the abolitionists used Lovejoy's name to help identify their movement with freedom of speech as well as black rights, thus giving them a broader hearing in the racially troubled North than had been possible before. See Merton L. Dillon, *Elijah P. Lovejoy, Abolitionist Editor* (1961).

STEPHEN B. OATES

LOWELL, Abbott Lawrence (b. Boston, Mass., Dec. 13, 1856; d. Boston, Mass., Jan. 6, 1943), EDUCATOR, received his AB from Harvard (1877). In 1880 he received his LLB from the Harvard Law School and was admitted to the Massachusetts bar. After practicing law for seventeen years in partnership with Francis Cabot Lowell, a relative, he was appointed a lecturer in government at Harvard in 1897. In 1900 he became professor of the science of government, in 1903 Eaton professor, and in 1909 the 24th president of Harvard, serving until 1933.

Maintaining in his inaugural address that students lacked guidance and intellectual and social cohesion, Lowell replaced the system of free electives instituted by his immediate predecessor, **Charles W. Eliot,** with a program of "concentration and distribution" in which students chose courses in one field as well as exploratory electives (1910). He instituted a tutorial system and general divisional examinations, and made language examinations required for promotion to the junior class. Under Lowell's "house plan," an effort to restore social cohesion among students, the college was subdivided into seven houses for upperclassmen (1930–31), each a complete unit. Freshmen were required to live in a freshman residence. Despite criticism, in the 1920s Lowell proposed a quota for Jewish students—which was subsequently defeated by the board of overseers—and placed African-Americans in a separate residence. He also sought to reorganize graduate education, suggesting that the MA program be devoted to teaching and the PhD to scholarship, but was largely unsuccessful. In 1933, Lowell established the Harvard Society of Fellows, which provided postgraduate fellowships.

Although he was a Republican, Lowell supported Woodrow Wilson's bid for the presidency in 1912 and later Wilson's plan for the League of Nations. He was chairman of the Committee on Platform of the League to Support Peace (1915–21). In his first radio speech (1937) he urged that the United States join the League of Nations in its economic boycott protesting Japan's invasion of China. In 1927, at the request of the governor of Massachusetts, Alvan T. Fuller, Lowell served on an advisory committee that investigated the trial of Nicola Sacco and Bartolomeo Vanzetti, radicals convicted of murdering a paymaster. He wrote the committee's report that upheld the conviction, finding the trial fair and the jury impartial.

From 1900 on, Lowell was sole trustee of the Lowell Institute of Boston, which sponsored lectures and classes, administering the institute and managing it financially. He also wrote extensively on the history and science of government, of which he was considered a leading authority, and on his academic experiences. His works include *Essays on Government* (1889), *Governments and Parties in Continental Europe* (1895), *The Government of England* (1908), *Public Opinion and Popular Government* (1913), *The Governments of France, Italy, and Germany* (1914), *At War with Academic Traditions* (1934), and *What a College President Has Learned* (1938).

⸺⧫⸺

Lowell possessed a directness, an abhorrence of subterfuge, that is to be found only in the fully self-contained. It was his great personal strength and public flaw. A prominent ancestry, inherited wealth, an internalized religious faith, and success both as a student and as an athlete all contributed to his positive sense of self. But so did his incapacity to entertain the proposition that he might be wrong. Few men with his training and connections could have spent so long at the Boston bar with so little to show for it and then abandoned the profession at 44 with self-confidence intact. Once setting his sights on the Harvard presidency, he proceeded to challenge openly the incumbent in precisely those areas (e.g., the elective system, three-year AB) that formed the core of his administration. Whereas Eliot spent his forty-year tenure transforming the Cambridge school from "a social moratorium" for the Boston gentry into a research-oriented university with a national clientele and international reputation, Lowell announced himself twenty years before his inauguration in 1909 as committed to the old Harvard. Unable to dismantle Eliot's university (although his Society of Fellows was intended to subvert what **William James** called "the PhD Octopus"), so well had it been administratively secured, he spent his twenty-three years as president devoting his awesome energies to rescuing the college from those who conceived of it as merely a way station between high school and graduate studies. Those sharing his vision of a homogeneous Harvard applauded his efforts; those who did not grumbled about the university's presumed declining eminence in the world of research. Lowell's efforts on behalf of peace and his ringing defense of academic freedom in 1917 are fine examples of his forthrightness in matters transcending the university; less commendable but equally in character was his willingness to air his prejudices against immigrants, blacks, and Jews. Only in the titling of his last book, *What a College President Has Learned*, is there a trace of disingenuousness: Lowell never learned anything; he knew all along. See Henry A. Yeomans, *Abbott Lawrence Lowell 1856–1943* (1948).

ROBERT A. MCCAUGHEY

LOWELL, Amy (b. Brookline, Mass., Feb. 9, 1874; d. Brookline, Mass., May 12, 1925), POET, CRITIC, was educated in private schools, supplemented by training at home from her mother, an accomplished musician and linguist. After extensive travel in Europe, Egypt, and California (1896–99), she settled in Brookline (1900) where she was active in local educational and library work. In 1902 she began a systematic study of poetic forms and techniques. Her first published work appeared in 1910 in the *Atlantic Monthly* and was followed in 1912 by her first full volume of poems, *A Dome of Many-Coloured Glass.*

In 1913, Lowell returned to Europe where she met **Ezra Pound** and became a sponsor of the "Imagist" poets. The tenets of this group—the use of the language of common speech, and of free verse, or as Lowell called it, "unrhymed cadence"—were evident in her contribution to the anthology *Des Imagistes* (1914) and in her *Sword Blades and Poppy Seed* (1914). In 1918 she published *Can Grande's Castle*, which included four long poems in "polyphonic prose," a style that employed the rhythms, rhymes, and alliterations of conventional poetry but that was arranged into paragraph form. Among her other works were *Fir-Flower Tablets* (1921, with Florence Ayscough), *East Wind* (1926), and *What's O'Clock* (1925), for which she was awarded a Pulitzer Prize. Lowell also wrote criticism, publishing such works as *Six French Poets: Studies in Contemporary Literature* (1915) and *John Keats* (2 vols., 1925). She also gave many public lectures, including a famous series presented at the Brooklyn Institute of Arts and Sciences (1917–18).

───────

A forceful and somewhat outlandish presence, an influential literary practitioner who was often a successful literary politician, Amy Lowell was an appealing mixture of toughness and vulnerability. Her family tree embraced generations of New England Lowells and Lawrences, and her life, deeply rooted in the values of Boston society, was marked by a fundamental loyalty to that tradition. Although her literary bent asserted itself while she was still in her teens, her awareness of her artistic needs and talents ripened later than is usual with writers of her stature. Only when she was 28 and came under the charismatic influence of Eleanora Duse did she discover her identity as a poet, and not until her mid-thirties did this discovery allow her to relinquish her image as a civic leader. Indeed, her gifts did not finally mature until her second volume of verse, published when she was 40.

This fulfillment resulted from her involvement with Ezra Pound and the Imagist poets, who were part of the growing modernist rebellion against established literary conventions. She confidently assumed the generalship of this movement, and despite subsequent differences with Pound, she steadily commanded the loyalty and participation of others in her literary enterprises. About Amy Lowell's poetry the writer Winifred Bryher has said: "The curves of her cadences are sharp with truth, with sensitiveness to the irony of existence which yet believes in adventure and resistance." These words might be equally descriptive of the poet's life. She could be "sharp with truth" in her dealings with others, whether bargaining with publishers or assaulting audiences with her vigorous readings, and she honestly indulged her eccentricities—smoking cigars and traveling like a literary potentate. Yet the "irony of existence" was daily evident to one whose large inherited fortune supported a style of life intended to protect her from painful self-doubts and harsh realities. For, while usually generous toward other writers, she was herself driven by insecurities about the value of her own work and the embarrassments of her extreme corpulence. What finally explains her ability to absorb this irony is the spirit of "adventure" that made possible both her promotion of the New Poetry and her colorful "resistance" to its enemies. See S. Foster Damon, *Amy Lowell: A Chronicle, with Extracts from her Correspondence* (1935).

ANNETTE K. BAXTER

LOWELL, Francis Cabot (b. Newburyport, Mass., Apr. 7, 1775; d. Boston, Mass., Aug. 10, 1817), INDUSTRIALIST, INVENTOR, graduated from Harvard College in 1793. He entered the export-import business and accumulated a fortune during the Napoleonic wars. Lowell's health had never been good, and in 1810 he sought a cure in a prolonged trip to England. While visiting the spinning and weaving mills of Lancashire, he was deeply impressed by their efficiency; he committed as much as he could of their design and layout to memory and made rough sketches of them.

Returning to America in 1813, after trade with Europe had been virtually destroyed by the outbreak of the War of 1812, Lowell organized the Boston Associates and built a textile factory at Waltham, Massachusetts. Aided by Paul Moody, an expert mechanic, he designed and built a spinning frame and a power loom. These machines, which had a number of superior features, were installed in what was the first factory anywhere to combine under one roof all the operations in the manufacture of cotton cloth. Lowell could not compete, however, with the cheap cloth that England dumped on America after the war ended. He and others went to Washington where they persuaded Senators Lowndes and **John C. Calhoun** of the merits of a protective tariff for cotton goods. The result was the Tariff of 1816, the first clearly protective tariff in American history.

Lowell employed young, unmarried farm girls to operate his machines, housing them in boardinghouses in which their personal lives and social activities were carefully sheltered. His employee policies set a standard for New England manufacturers for many years. In 1823 the company moved to a site on the Merrimack River, north of Boston, where superior water power resources existed. When the new town was incorporated in 1826, it was named for Lowell.

━━━⊗⊗⊗━━━

The name of Lowell will always be associated with the beginnings of the factory system in the United States. Until about 1820 goods had been manufactured in urban craft shops and in farmhouses under the so-called putting-out system. Merchants supplied wool, for example, to farm families, or to once-independent master craftsmen and their journeymen and apprentices in the towns, and had them spin it into yarn. They then put out the yarn to be woven into cloth, and after collecting it up had it dyed and finished by mill workers before selling it. The essential characteristics of production under this system were its decentralized nature, use of hand tools, small scale, and wastefulness. The factory system, in contrast, permitted these processes to be centralized: workers were brought together in a single workplace where their tasks could be better organized and supervised, where all processes of production, from raw materials to finished goods, could take place, and where production was geared to power-driven machinery. By integrating and standardizing the entire process of cotton cloth manufacture the factory system made mass production possible.

Obviously the amount of capital required for factory production was far larger than that needed under the older methods. When Lowell incorporated his Boston Manufacturing Co. in 1813, he capitalized it at $300,000. Soon this sum was doubled, and eventually it reached $1 million. Even $300,000 was a great sum to risk in an untried venture, especially in view of the extent to which most American families resorted to homespun for their clothes or relied on cloth imports from England. But Lowell and his Boston associates had become used to highly risky ventures in shipping and foreign trade during the period of the Napoleonic wars. Furthermore, they and some of the other entrepreneurs who soon followed their path possessed an almost messianic belief in the cause of American manufacturing independence from Europe. Highly nationalistic and not a little puritanical, attributes that are commonly found among the elites of underdeveloped nations on the threshold of modernization, they contrasted the degradation of factory labor abroad with the ennobling effects of industrialization on the domestic labor force. Looking upon themselves as servants of the Lord whose destiny was to bring the blessings of manufacturing to the United States, they were often generous in encouraging the establishment of rival factories.

The mass-production system inaugurated by Lowell and his associates made its way slowly among the growing industries of America, encountering ignorance, defense of familiar techniques, and production problems differing from those in cloth manufacturing. Factory methods made very rapid progress in carpet manufacturing in the 1820s, in the iron industry of eastern Pennsylvania and western New Jersey in the 1840s, and, although less completely, in the manufacture of boots and shoes by the eve of the Civil War. In the 1850s, a decade that probably saw a doubling of the number of incorporated manufacturing establishments, the factory system made very rapid gains. In nearly every industry mechanization progressed at an unprecedented rate. Some scholars hold that on the eve of the Civil War, the United States was an industrial power second only to England.

As had been true in England, so, too, in the United States, the Industrial Revolution was clearly no overnight affair. The slow and uneven movement of modern processes of manufacturing under a free market economy helps account for the fact that the rate of economic growth, as measured by real output per person, achieved an annual average of only 1.3 percent in the antebellum United States. The rise of this rate to an annual average of 1.8 percent after the Civil War provides eloquent evidence of the degree to which the methods pioneered by Lowell and improved by others had succeeded in permeating the industrial structure of the nation. See Caroline F. Ware, *Early New England Cotton Manufacture* (1966).

STUART BRUCHEY

LOWELL, James Russell (b. Cambridge, Mass., Feb. 22, 1819; d. Cambridge, Mass., Aug. 12, 1891), POET, graduated from Harvard College in 1838. He received his LLB from Harvard Law School in 1840 but did not practice. In 1841 he published a collection of poems, *A Year's Life,* and in 1843 began a literary journal, the *Pioneer,* publishing his own works as well as those of **Nathaniel Hawthorne, John Greenleaf Whittier,** and **Edgar Allan Poe.** Another collection of his verse, *Poems,* appeared in 1844. Turning to the study of early poetry and literature, he published *Conversations on Some of the Old Poets* in 1845.

Partly influenced by the strong antislavery position of his wife, Maria White Lowell, Lowell frequently contributed to abolitionist journals, including the *National Anti-Slavery Standard,* which he served briefly as corresponding editor in 1848. In 1846 he created in the Boston *Courier* the first letters from Ezekiel Biglow and poems of Ezekiel's son Hosea, beginning a long, popular series of humorous, often satirical, patriotic, and antislavery poems and letters in Yankee dialect. The first series, critical of the Mexican War and the extension of slavery, was published in 1848 as *The Biglow Papers;* the second series, which criticized the Civil War, appeared in 1868. In 1848 he also published *The Vision of Sir Launfal* and *A Fable for Critics,* which included a satirical self-portrait, and in 1849 a third collection of *Poems.*

In 1844, Lowell succeeded **Henry Wadsworth Longfellow** as Smith professor of French and Spanish languages and literature and professor of belles-lettres at Harvard. After two trips to Europe (1851–52, 1855–56), Lowell turned to literary criticism, editing the new *Atlantic Monthly* (1857–61), which published such New England writers as Hawthorne, Whittier, Longfellow, **Ralph Waldo Emerson,** and **Oliver Wendell Holmes.** From 1864 to 1872 Lowell edited the *North American Review,* in which his *Political Essays* (1888) and the second series of *The Biglow Papers,* both reflecting his continuing interest in contemporary American events, initially appeared. Publications of his poetry include *Under the Willows* (1868), *The Cathedral* (1870), *Three Memorial Poems* (1877), and *Heartsease and Rue* (1888). Significant prose volumes at this time were *Fireside Travels* (1864), *Among My*

Books (1870), *My Study Windows* (1871), *Among My Books* (2d ser., 1876).

Having supported Rutherford B. Hayes in the Republican national convention, Lowell was appointed U.S. minister to Spain in 1877 and then minister to Great Britain (1880–85). His more important speeches from this period are collected in *Democracy and Other Addresses* (1887). His last years were spent speaking and writing on public affairs and collecting and editing his work, some of which was published posthumously.

───── ∞ ─────

To **William Dean Howells,** who met Lowell in 1860, the elder man had an instant charm and a voice "that made our rough English come from his tongue as music such as I should never hear again." At this date Lowell was 41. When Agnes Repplier met him twenty-seven years later, she found him "a man … flawlessly urbane." These qualities made Lowell a success on the lecture platform, in the classroom at Harvard, in the diplomatic worlds of Madrid and the Court of St. James's, and at the Saturday Club. They shine from his pages of poetry and prose, together with so much more. For Lowell knew tragic suffering in the loss—within the short span of six years—of two infant daughters, his only son, his mother, and his wife.

He richly deserves his title as America's foremost man of letters, in the fullest sense of that designation, for his work found expression in distinguished poetry and prose. He stands out, with Poe, as the molder of American criticism. Even more than Poe, he saved us from chauvinism. He possessed the rare ability to judge all his contemporaries with the discerning objectivity of a later critic, and his opinions are those of today.

Another manifestation of Lowell's versatility is in the volumes of essays, both literary and political. Above all, through his skill in the use of Yankee dialect in the two series of *Biglow Papers,* he created a vernacular poetry that has rare distinction. See Martin Duberman, *James Russell Lowell* (1966).

CLAIRE MCGLINCHEE

LOWELL, Robert Traill Spence, Jr. (b. Boston, Mass., Mar. 1, 1917; d. New York, N.Y., Sept. 12, 1977), POET, entered Harvard in 1935 but transferred to Kenyon College (Gambier, Ohio) in 1937 in order to study under the poet John Crowe Ransom. Lowell received his BA from Kenyon in 1940. After briefly studying at Louisiana State University, he became an editorial assistant at the publishing firm of Sheed & Ward in New York City (1941–42). Lowell was drafted for military service in 1943 but refused to serve because of his opposition to Allied bombing of civilians. He was convicted in 1943 and served six months of a one-year sentence.

Lowell published his first collection of poems, *Land of Unlikeness* (1944), and followed this with *Lord Weary's Castle* (1946), which won the 1947 Pulitzer Prize for poetry. Lowell's poems in these collections dealt with New England subjects and the themes of alienation, antiwar feeling, and conviction in religion. Lowell won a Guggenheim fellowship (1947–48) and also served as poetry adviser to the Library of Congress. His *Life Studies* (1959) won the National Book award for poetry, and his play, *The Old Glory* (1965), won an Obie award for the best off-Broadway production of that year. While living in New York City in the early 1960s, Lowell commuted to Harvard to conduct seminars. In 1965 he refused to participate in President Lyndon B. Johnson's White House Festival of the Arts because of his opposition to the Vietnam War. He was professor of literature at the University of Essex in England from 1970 to 1972. In 1973 he published three major works, *History, For Lizzie and Harriet*, and *The Dolphins*, which included almost four hundred poems. Some of his other poetry collections included *The Mills of the Kavanaughs* (1951), *For the Union Dead* (1964), *Near the Ocean* (1967), and *Notebook of a Year, 1967–68* (1969).

───── ∞ ─────

Lowell has gradually come to be considered the foremost American poet of the post–World War II era. His early poems are at once quite formal and rebellious. Highly compressed, intense, and intricate in their symbolism, they contain a deep and passionate protest against the spiritual bankruptcy of the times. In 1940 he married the novelist Jean Stafford and converted to Roman Catholicism. At 29 he won a Pulitzer for his second book of poems, but neither the honors nor the marriage nor even his new religion could relieve the suffering of his tortured mind. He left church and wife in 1948 and the next year married the writer Elizabeth Hardwick. In 1954 the Lowells moved to Boston, hoping to recapture his roots. An amazing transformation took place; he wrote his autobiography, and in the process of seeing his own background and his immediate chaotic mental condition within the larger chaos of the world, he wrote his first "confessional" poems. Breaking out of the old tight forms with their emphasis on craft and skill, he moved to a looser, more open line. These poems appeared in his major work, *Life Studies* (1959), and they signaled a return to traditional plain speech; this volume had an enormous influence on American poetry, especially Sylvia Plath's. While digging deeply into the privacy of his own psyche, Lowell developed as a public poet of great conscience, lending his name and his presence to antiwar efforts. In 1974 he received his second Pulitzer Prize for poetry. See Hugh B. Staples, *Robert Lowell: The First Twenty Years* (1962).

FRANCES MONSON

LUCE, Clare Boothe (b. New York, N.Y., Mar. 10, 1903; d. Washington, D.C., Oct. 9, 1987) WRITER, PUBLIC FIGURE, experienced a difficult childhood marked by financial distress and the breakup of her parents' marriage. Despite these adversities she made important social contacts that led to her marriage in 1924 to George Tuttle Brokaw, a rich New York alcoholic playboy. They divorced six years later, leaving Clare Brokaw with a comfortable financial settlement and a daughter. That same year she began a career as a journalist, working first for *Vogue* and then for *Vanity Fair*, where she became managing editor. She quit *Vanity Fair* in 1934 to write plays, two of which—*The Women* (1936) and *Kiss the Boys Goodbye* (1938)—enjoyed success. More signifi-

cant was her marriage in 1935 to **Henry R. Luce**, publisher of *Time*, *Fortune*, and, beginning the following year, *Life*. During World War II, Clare Boothe Luce served as a wartime correspondent for *Life* and won two elections (1942 and 1944) as a Republican congresswoman from Connecticut. After the war she converted to Roman Catholicism, largely as a result of her young daughter's accidental death a few years earlier. She remained highly active in public life as a spokeswoman whose views were widely solicited. President Dwight D. Eisenhower appointed her ambassador to Italy in 1953 and four years later as ambassador to Brazil, a position from which she resigned before assuming her duties. She reduced but did not end her role in public life after her husband's death in 1967. She served on the President's Foreign Intelligence Advisory Board under both Presidents Richard M. Nixon and Ronald Reagan.

———

With the exception of Eleanor Roosevelt, no American woman serving in public affairs during the middle decades of the 20th century received more renown than did Clare Boothe Luce. Overcoming her disadvantaged youth, she employed her keen mind, stimulating personality, and physical charms to forge friendships, amorous and otherwise, with a host of powerful men who enthusiastically abetted her career—or, rather, "careers," for she managed to enjoy several of them: playwright, journalist, politician, publicist. Strong-willed and consistently outspoken, she was never the subordinate partner in her internationally famous though troubled marriage to Henry Luce. Indeed, her various successes, including becoming the first female American ambassador to a major country, served as models for midcentury women who aspired to careers outside the home.

Yet she was hardly a radical feminist or any kind of radical for that matter. Her lifestyle was luxurious, her political preferences solidly Republican and anti-Communist. Like Henry Luce she was committed to Nationalist China and to waging the cold war. More conservative at times than her mate, she strongly voiced support

713

for Senator **Joseph R. McCarthy** during the red scare of the early 1950s and, to the chagrin of liberal and moderate Republicans, for the presidential candidacy of Senator **Barry Goldwater** in 1964. At various times she found herself suggested for the U.S. Senate and even the vice presidency. Despite disappointments and personal tragedy, it is difficult not to conclude that Clare Boothe Luce, *mutatis mutandis*, was something of a 20th-century Horatio Alger, although far more determined to succeed than the fictional hero. See Ralph G. Martin, *Henry and Clare: An Intimate Portrait of the Luces* (1991).

ROBERT MUCCIGROSSO

LUCE, Henry Robinson (b. Tengchow, Shantung Province, China, Apr. 3, 1898; d. Phoenix, Ariz., Feb. 28, 1967), PUBLISHER, was educated at the Chefoo School, a British boarding school in northern China, and at Hotchkiss School in Lakeville, Connecticut. In 1916 he enrolled in Yale College, where he edited the *Yale Daily News*. In 1918 he served briefly with the Yale Student Army Training Corps at Camp Jackson, South Carolina, where he earned a commission as a second lieutenant. He graduated from Yale in 1920. After a year of study at Oxford, he became a reporter for the Chicago *Daily News* and then for the Baltimore *News*.

In 1922, with Briton Hadden, fellow reporter and a friend from Yale, he founded "a weekly news-magazine, aimed to serve the modern necessity of keeping people informed." In March 1923 the first issue of *Time* was published, with a circulation of 12,000. The magazine had tough going for four or five years, but its circulation began a steady rise that eventually reached 2.5 million copies in 1960. In 1930, Hadden and Luce began to publish *Fortune*, a deluxe business periodical that caught on quickly in spite of its coming out during the Great Depression. In 1932, Luce purchased the *Architectural Forum* (divided in 1952 into *Architectural Forum* and *House and Home*). He moved into the field of photo-journalism with *Life* in 1936, and in 1954 he founded *Sports Illustrated*.

Luce remained editor in chief of all his publications until 1964, presiding over a communications empire that extended far beyond the printed page. Purchasing radio and television stations, he produced movies and radio and TV programs, the best known of which was the *March of Time* series (1928–43). He also published many Time-Life books.

Luce played a major role in shaping the content and form of all his productions. Among his innovations were the idea of covering business events as a continuous story; the creation of a writing style peculiar to *Time* magazine; the development of pictorial reporting; and the introduction—implicitly and oftentimes explicitly—of judgments into news columns. These judgments, primarily Luce's own, reflected an aggressive anti-Communism, an unrelenting antagonism to Red China, a faith in free enterprise, and a steady support of the Republican Party.

⁂

Remnants of a childhood stammer made Luce speak in sharp machine-gun bursts that, combined with his tremendous energy, impatience, and Calvinist devotion to work and duty, made him a formidable taskmaster. Aggressive by nature, he conquered his impediment, became an effective public speaker, and at times contemplated seeking high public office. He saw life as a competitive struggle in which diligence and foresight assured success, and failure usually signified a lack of these qualities. His faith in free enterprise—a favorite phrase—reinforced his religious and patriotic conviction that the "American way" should be spread abroad. Believing America to be divinely ordained as a model for all peoples, he pushed his crusade for the nation's world destiny with the zeal of his missionary parents.

His divorce and remarriage to the playwright **Clare Boothe Brokaw (Luce)** was a sensation of the thirties. His editors thereafter had the sometimes ticklish duty of reviewing her plays and commenting on her later political career without causing offense.

Until the advent of *Time*, the ideal of objectivity had become widely accepted in a general journalistic effort to separate news and opinion. Luce rejected this. Objectivity, he said, was not only a myth impossible of achievement but was an evasion of what he regarded as the journalist's duty to explain and interpret the news. Always an internationalist, fascinated by politics and power, he was attracted for a time by qualities of efficiency and inspiration he thought he saw in Mussolini's Fascism. His admiration for outstanding performance in all fields resulted not only in *Time*'s weekly cover personality but in Lucean efforts to meet and speak with these people, which caused him to travel the world extensively. If generals and prime ministers were more glamorous, it was American businessmen who employed labor and led the world in enterprise who had a special place in his esteem. He was one himself, a shrewd entrepreneur as well as a discerning editor, a promoter and salesman of muscular drive. He watched the gross national product as a barometer of American strength. His magazines, with their enormous circulation, carried the world's most profitable bulk of advertising while their text matter extolled the "good life," the American prosperity that enabled more people to buy more products and create still more prosperity. Indeed, there was criticism that the Luce press was excessively materialistic, influencing the public toward a preoccupation with automobiles rather than art, the shallow rather than the sublime. Aware of the danger, Luce sought to educate his middle-class readers with articles about cultural matters as well as politics and the duties of citizenship.

Here his "interpretation" of the news—always suspect to purists of the objective school—was attacked especially by liberals who viewed him as a reactionary propagandist. *Time*, billed as a news magazine rather than an organ of opinion, included deft descriptive and adjectival touches designed to affect the political attitudes of its readers. The Luce press pushed the cold war uncompromisingly and found near-treason in America's failure to prevent the defeat of Chiang Kai-shek. Its heroic view of Dwight D. Eisenhower, coupled with its subtle denigration of his Democratic opponent, **Adlai Stevenson,** caused some journalistic investigators to undertake analyses of the magazine's partisan use of adjectives and anecdotes. But few questioned Luce's inherent news sense even if the news did receive some manipulation at his hands. See W. A. Swanberg, *Luce and His Empire* (1972).

W. A. SWANBERG

LUNDY, Benjamin (b. Greenville, N.J., Jan. 4, 1789; d. Hennepin, Ill., Aug. 22, 1839), REFORMER, was raised on a farm in a Quaker household. He received little formal education. In 1808 he became an apprentice saddlemaker in Wheeling, Virginia (now W. Va.), where he first came into contact with slavery and quickly grew to hate the institution. Moving to St. Clairsville, Ohio, in 1815, Lundy organized an antislavery group, the Union Humane Society. He spent the next few years organizing several antislavery clubs and planning a national structure supported by a system of correspondence and cooperative efforts. Lundy also contributed articles to the *Philanthropist,* a newspaper published by antislavery advocate Charles Osborn at Mount Pleasant, Ohio. After spending two years in St. Louis liquidating his business and helping to organize antislavery clubs, Lundy returned to St. Clairsville in 1821, moved to Mount Pleasant, and began publication of a new paper, the *Genius of Universal Emancipation.* He published the paper in Greenville, Tennessee (1821–24), before bringing it to Baltimore in 1824.

While editing the *Genius* and organizing antislavery groups from Baltimore to Canada, Lundy became interested in the African colonization movement as a possible solution to the race question. He visited Haiti (1825, 1829), the Wilberforce colonization project in Canada (1832), and Texas (1830–31, 1833–34, and 1834–35) in pursuit of this interest. While on a lecture tour of the North in 1828, Lundy met **William Lloyd Garrison** and persuaded him to go to Baltimore in 1829 as associate editor of the *Genius.* The two separated, however, in 1830. Lundy moved the paper to Washington, D.C., that same year because of increasing hostility in Baltimore, and then to Philadelphia. After 1835, publication of the *Genius* was intermittent. Lundy began publishing a new antislavery newspaper in Philadelphia in 1836, the *National Enquirer and Constitutional Advocate of Universal Liberty,* which attacked the annexation of Texas as a plot of slaveowners to gain more power. He published a pamphlet, *The War in Texas* (1836), and supplied John Quincy Adams with information for his antiannexation speeches in Congress. Declining health forced Lundy to sell the *National Enquirer* in 1838 to **John Greenleaf Whittier,** who renamed it the *Pennsylvania Freeman.* Lundy moved to Illinois and labored to advance the antislavery cause there until his death.

Lundy did not plan to antagonize the South but to win it over to programs for emancipating slaves. He hoped to build up antislavery societies in the slaveholding areas and thus erode slavery as an institution from within. Lundy was not diffident in his criticisms of slavery or slaveholders. In 1827, in Baltimore, as a result of his published accusations, he was personally attacked by an enraged Maryland slavetrader. Yet there were differences between him and William Lloyd Garrison that quickly separated them. Garrison meant to draw a line between himself and slaveholders, and held all who did not join with him as implicated in the sin of slavery.

Lundy, on the other hand, expected to rally increased numbers of antislavery partisans of every kind to his cause. His work had quiet but effective results. Thus, colonization as an instrument of abolition was discredited in that era by radicals who held that its sole purpose was to drain out of the country blacks who were already free and whose presence in the United States was in itself a criticism of slavery. Lundy's colonization efforts were generally recognized as more positive in purpose. Especially fruitful were his efforts to establish a free-labor colony in Mexico, even though none materialized. His pamphlet *The War in Texas* impressed John Quincy Adams, then

in Congress, furnishing him with ideas and information that he utilized in his campaign against the annexation of Texas to the United States. Lundy and Adams, working closely, helped consolidate a pro-northern view in Congress, which ensured that the vast Texas terrain could never be divided into the seven or eight slaveholding states of which some southern leaders dreamed.

Harmful to Lundy's fame was the loss in 1838 of his private papers. He had lodged them in Pennsylvania Hall, built in Philadelphia to house reformers. It was destroyed by fires set by rioters during dedicatory ceremonies. See Merton L. Dillon, *Benjamin Lundy and the Struggle for Negro Freedom* (1966).

Louis Filler

LYON, Mary Mason (b. Buckland, Mass., Feb. 28, 1797; d. South Hadley, Mass., Mar. 5, 1849), EDUCATOR, studied at academies in Ashfield and Amherst, Massachusetts, and at the Reverend Joseph Emerson's seminary in Byfield, Massachusetts (1821). During 1821–24 she taught in Ashfield and then was hired by Zilpah Grant to teach at her academy, first in Londonderry, New Hampshire (1824–27), and then in Ipswich, Massachusetts (1828–34). During this period Lyon gradually decided that the crucial need in women's higher education in America was for the establishment of a school that would offer middle-class as well as wealthy girls an advanced curriculum arranged in a systematic, three-year program.

Recognizing the need for a financial endowment sufficient to establish her proposed school on a permanent basis, Lyon spent three years (1834–37) raising the necessary funds. Finally, in November 1837, Mount Holyoke Seminary was opened in South Hadley, Massachusetts, with Lyon as principal. Under her leadership Mount Holyoke's enrollment grew, the physical plant was expanded, and such subjects as modern languages and music were added to the original curriculum of mathematics, English, science, philosophy, and Latin.

Devout, practical-minded, and firm in her commitment to the educational orthodoxies of her day, Mary Lyon was nonetheless a person whose adaptability and adventurousness explain her success in launching an institution that pioneered in the higher education of women. The product of a modest New England upbringing, she learned self-sufficiency at an early age and made service to others the motivating force of her educational endeavors. Indeed, these principles became essential ingredients in the early philosophy of Mount Holyoke Seminary. The requirement of domestic work by students helped reduce costs, but it also instilled responsibility. The disciplined attention to study was relieved by Lyon's encouragement of her students' involvement in the missionary field.

Lyon's own powers as a teacher were early evident, and they were enhanced by her association with Zilpah Grant, a contemporary educator from whom she acquired such techniques as the "self-reporting" system that was the basis of Mount Holyoke's disciplinary code. Lyon's pedagogical approach stressed gradualism: she did not burden her students beyond their capacities, nor did she seek to overwhelm them with her own erudition. Yet her standard of achievement for her students was high: the admission requirements and curriculum of Mount Holyoke Seminary were not far behind those of the leading men's colleges.

With her energetic, compassionate, and engaging personality, Lyon won the affection of faculty, students, and friends of the seminary. Always averse to self-indulgence, she was economical in her personal style as well as in her living habits: she "never used words when an action would do instead." Though her own experience was narrow, her ambitions for other women were not. She was among the first fully to appreciate the importance of providing women with the quality of education that would give them confidence in their powers and thus assist them in becoming more independent and resourceful. See Beth Bradford Gilchrist, *The Life of Mary Lyon* (1910).

ANNETTE K. BAXTER

McADOO, William Gibbs (b. near Marietta, Ga., Oct. 31, 1863; d. Washington, D.C., Feb. 1, 1941), POLITICAL LEADER, BUSINESSMAN, attended the University of Tennessee but left without a degree. Appointed deputy clerk to the U.S. circuit court in 1882 and admitted to the bar in 1885, he practiced law in Chattanooga, Tennessee, before moving to New York City in 1892. There he became president of the Hudson and Manhattan Railroad Co., which opened the first tunnels under the Hudson River between New York and New Jersey (1904–8). A Democrat, McAdoo became a leading figure in Woodrow Wilson's 1912 presidential campaign, later marrying his daughter.

McAdoo became Wilson's secretary of the treasury in 1913. After passage of the Federal Reserve Act that year, he supervised establishment of the Federal Reserve system. During 1914 McAdoo's management of foreign exchange and agricultural support policies helped prevent a depression that threatened because of the withdrawal of European investments following the outbreak of World War I. He also established a system of government insurance of cargoes shipped to war zones. After American entry into the war McAdoo directed the Liberty Bond campaigns and the program of war loans to the Allies and, as director general of railroads (1917–19), managed the entire railroad network of the U.S.

McAdoo was frequently mentioned as a possible Democratic presidential candidate in 1920; he actively sought the nomination in 1924. Supported by the rural, Protestant, prohibitionist wing of the party, he battled with **Alfred E. Smith,** representative of urban, Catholic, "wet" Democrats, until the deadlock was broken on the 103d ballot by nomination of "dark horse" **John W. Davis.** At the 1932 Democratic convention he helped to secure the nomination for Franklin D. Roosevelt. Elected U.S. senator from California in 1932, he supported the New Deal, but he was defeated for reelection in 1938.

McAdoo's sharply cut features hinted at the enthusiasm and energy which made him one of the ablest public figures of his time. Tall and wiry, he had an uncomplex, magnetic personality: exuberant, persuasive, optimistic, humane, and self-assured. Early in the 20th century, as a maverick promoter and businessman, he showed an unusual willingness to support the causes of antitrust and social justice. He contributed one of the great cabinet performances of American history by applying his restless drive and promotional impulses to government. Even before World War I, which drastically expanded its role, McAdoo's Treasury Department was conducting farm and foreign policies all its own. Politically identified with rural America in the early 1920s, McAdoo saw his presidential aspirations thwarted; but he survived to become one of a handful of men who successfully made the transition from active Wilsonian to active New Dealer. In his Treasury years McAdoo had helped to lay some of the foundations of the modern welfare state, and the changes of the thirties came easily to him. He was the epitome of ideological flexibility, unencumbered by class bias or by any deeply inhibiting set of general convictions. During the generation that McAdoo stood near the center of the political stage, he customarily approached issues with a strong commitment to the practical and an impatient suspicion of the conventional. A man of action and tenacity, he liked change, especially when he could take a hand in engineering it. See John J. Broesamle, *William Gibbs McAdoo: A Passion for Change, 1863–1917* (1973).

JOHN J. BROESAMLE

MacARTHUR, Douglas (b. Little Rock, Ark., Jan. 26, 1880; d. Washington, D.C., April 5, 1964), MILITARY LEADER, was the son of Lieutenant General Arthur MacArthur, the army's senior ranking officer in 1906–9. He graduated first in his class at West Point (1903) and became a second lieutenant in the Corps of Engineers, stationed in the Philippines. In 1905–6 he was aide-de-camp to his father, who was on a special reconnaissance mission in East and South Asia. He then served as President Theodore Roosevelt's aide (1906–7), a junior engineering officer at various posts (1907–12), an intelligence officer in the expedition to Veracruz (1914), and a member of the War Department General Staff (1913–17). He was promoted to captain in 1908, major in 1915, and colonel in 1917. In August 1917 he helped organize the 42d "Rainbow" Division, a national guard unit. After a stint as its chief of staff, he commanded the 84th Brigade in France, where he earned the Distinguished Service Medal, Distinguished Service Cross, seven Silver Stars, and many other combat decorations for his roles in the Aisne-Marne, St. Mihiel, and Meuse-Argonne offensives. He also served briefly as commander of the 42d Division in France. After the war he became superintendent of West Point (1919–22), broadening the curriculum and raising academic standards.

Between 1922 and 1930, MacArthur alternated between posts in the Philippines and at home; in 1925 he sat on the court-martial board of Brigadier General **William Mitchell.** He rose to brigadier general (1920), major general (1925), and brevet general in 1930 when President Hoover appointed him chief of staff. He was widely criticized for ordering army troops to drive the "Bonus Army" from Washington (July 1932). After five years as chief of staff, MacArthur was appointed military adviser to the Philippines in late 1935. In August 1936 President Manuel Quezon appointed him field marshal of the Philippine army; he retired from the U.S. army in December 1937.

In July 1941 MacArthur was recalled to active duty in the U.S. army, at which time President Franklin D. Roosevelt gave him command of all

U.S. Army forces in the Far East. Following the Japanese landings in the Philippines in December 1941, MacArthur retreated to Bataan Peninsula and the island fortress of Corregidor. He was ordered by President Roosevelt to Australia in March 1942 to take command of all Allied forces in the Southwest Pacific. For his actions in the Philippines he was awarded the Congressional Medal of Honor (March 1942).

From the fall of 1942 to mid-1944 MacArthur directed American and Australian forces in a series of campaigns which drove the Japanese out of their major strongholds in New Guinea and several nearby islands. After securing Morotai a month earlier, on October 20, 1944, he led the return of American forces to Leyte, in the central Philippines. In December of that year, shortly after capturing Mindoro, he was promoted to the new rank of general of the army. From January to August 1945, his forces fought numerous campaigns in the reconquest of Luzon, the southern Philippines, and Borneo. In April he became commander of all army forces in the Pacific and was scheduled to command the ground invasion of Japan. On September 2, 1945, he accepted the Japanese surrender in ceremonies held on the battleship *Missouri* in Tokyo Bay.

Appointed supreme commander of the Allied occupation forces in Japan, MacArthur prosecuted some Japanese leaders for war crimes. In the next five years he also attempted to alter many aspects of Japanese political, economic, and social life by inaugurating, among other reforms, a new constitution with liberal features, land redistribution, and demilitarization. Following the North Korean invasion of South Korea (June 1950) MacArthur was ordered by President Truman to send ground forces from Japan to the Korean peninsula and was named (July 8) commander of United Nations forces in the conflict. After a series of setbacks he landed American troops at Inchon on September 15, 1950, and routed the North Koreans. He then marched through North Korea toward the Chinese border, but after the Chinese Communists sent large forces into the conflict in November 1950, his forces were pushed steadily back until they established new positions below the 38th parallel. By late January 1951, his army was on the counteroffensive, moving into North Korea again. In spite of orders from President Truman, MacArthur insisted that the U.S. should blockade the Chinese coast, bombard Chinese bases in Manchuria, and support an invasion of the mainland by Chiang Kai-shek's Nationalist forces on Formosa. In March 1951, MacArthur sent a letter to Joseph W. Martin, Jr., Republican minority leader in the House, calling for a broad war to defeat communism in the Far East. In April 1951, President Truman relieved MacArthur of his command. When he returned to the U.S., MacArthur received tumultuous receptions. He addressed a joint session of Congress (April 19, 1951), where he reiterated his demands for massive action against China, as part of an effort to combat the "global" communist threat. Congress investigated MacArthur's removal and the administration's general policies in the Far East during lengthy hearings (May 3–June 25, 1951).

MacArthur served as chairman of the board of the Remington Rand, later Sperry-Rand, Corporation (1952–64). He delivered the keynote address at the 1952 Republican convention. In 1944, 1948, and 1952 some conservative Republican groups tried without success to obtain MacArthur's nomination for the presidency.

General Douglas MacArthur was an immensely complex person, one of the most controversial and colorful military leaders of this century. He often manifested contradictory traits. While some contemporaries called him egotistical, arrogant, aloof, and pretentious, others described him as self-sacrificing, humble, charming, and modest. In part because his personal papers are few and unrevealing, MacArthur the man may always remain an enigma.

MacArthur could inspire loyalty and dedication in subordinates, and most officers who worked closely with him were convinced of his charismatic attraction. His harshest critics were invariably persons with whom he had little or no personal contact. The elusiveness of his personality was compounded by his mastery of role playing. Depending on the occasion, he could appear distant or gracious, austere or extravagant, reticent or flamboyant. He most consistently appeared as the gentleman-aristocrat. Possessed of solemn dignity and keen sensitivity to personal honor, he placed great stress on his distinguished family heritage. Even his detractors generally admitted that he had a brilliant mind and a versatility of knowledge rare among military men. His command of English and speaking ability were superior, although often marked by clichés and verbosity. His conduct was governed by the strictest rules of ethics and etiquette. Like that of a privileged gentleman, his attitude toward others was usually one of noblesse oblige.

His philosophy was a simplistic mixture of the individualism of Herbert Hoover and the nativism of some of his close military colleagues, especially Generals George Moseley and Courtney Whitney. MacArthur's value judgments were decidedly without qualification. He gradually became convinced that America was menaced by an internal conspiracy of liberals and communists and that, partly because of them, Asia, the area of greatest future threat to America, was not receiving adequate national attention. Throughout his long career he exhibited a zealous devotion to the principles of duty, honor, and country.

MacArthur ranks high as a strategist, notably for his operations in the reconquest of New Guinea and the Philippines in World War II and the Inchon landing during the Korean War. Most of his Southwest Pacific operations were conducted with extraordinarily small American casualties because of shrewd strategical planning. Yet he also bore responsibility in large measure for the victories of Japan in the first Philippine campaign and of Communist China in late 1950.

MacArthur showed unusual ability as an administrator, particularly during his West Point superintendency and as a wartime theater commander. In the Japanese and Korean conflicts he operated his headquarters with great efficiency and success despite serious problems. As the administrator of the Japanese occupation, he presided over a host of reform programs which, coinciding with changes evolving in Japanese society, markedly influenced the contemporary transformation of that nation. Although accounts of his bravery and prowess as a combat leader originated as early as World War I, MacArthur in time may be appreciated more as an administrator than as a warrior. See D. Clayton James, *The Years of MacArthur* (3 vols., 1970–1985).

D. CLAYTON JAMES

McCARTHY, Joseph Raymond (b. Grand Chute, Wis., Nov. 14, 1908; d. Bethesda, Md., May 2, 1957), POLITICAL LEADER, graduated from Marquette University (1935) and was admitted to the bar in that year. He was elected circuit court judge of the tenth judicial circuit of Wisconsin in 1939. McCarthy enlisted in the Marines at the outbreak of World War II and served in the South Pacific. In 1944, while still in the service, he ran in the Republican primary for the U.S. Senate but was defeated by the incumbent Alexander Wiley. In 1945 he was reelected to the circuit court.

In 1946 McCarthy defeated **Robert La Follette, Jr.,** for the Republican senatorial nomination and was elected senator. He was involved in several dubious and widely publicized episodes early in his senatorial career: his support of the Pepsi Cola Co. led him to be known as the "Pepsi Cola Kid"; he worked for real estate interests by opposing public housing projects; he engaged in a number of public squabbles with fellow senators.

McCarthy exploded into national prominence in February 1950 when he delivered a Lincoln's Day speech at Wheeling, West Virginia, charging that the State Department was "infested" with communists. As "proof" of his assertions he waved aloft a list which he claimed contained the names of supposed communists. McCarthy's allegations were investigated by a special committee headed by Senator Millard Tydings of Maryland. In its majority report the committee stated that McCarthy's charges represented "the most nefarious campaign of half-truths and untruth in the history of the Republic." McCarthy retaliated by campaigning against Tydings during the 1950 congressional elections. His charge that Tydings was friendly with communists was believed to have contributed to Tydings's defeat. In 1952 McCarthy campaigned against Senator William Benton of Connecticut, who had introduced a resolution for McCarthy's expulsion from the Senate, with the same result.

McCarthy proceeded to attack many of the nation's leading public figures, among them General **George C. Marshall,** who, according to McCarthy, was involved in a "conspiracy" to betray the country to the communists. McCarthy's invectives against such organizations as the Voice of America led to the removal of controversial books from that organization's overseas libraries.

As chairman of the Senate Committee on Government Operations, McCarthy built that hitherto innocuous post into a powerful platform for attracting attention. He quickly became a force which no senator could ignore. In 1953, for example, his opposition to the confirmation of Charles E. Bohlen as U.S. ambassador to Russia, while unsuccessful, led Senator **Robert A. Taft,** the Republican majority leader, to tell President Eisenhower that in the future he would refuse to back any appointments that McCarthy would not consent to.

In 1954 McCarthy accused Secretary of the Army Robert T. Stevens of concealing evidence of espionage activities at Fort Monmouth, New Jersey. The army then proceeded to accuse McCarthy and his legal counsel, Roy Cohn, of seeking preferential treatment for G. David Schine, a McCarthy aide. This charge led to the Army-McCarthy hearings, which were televised nationally. Although the issues were never completely resolved, McCarthy's popularity both within and without the Senate began to slip because of this affair. In December 1954 the Senate voted to censure him, 67 to 22.

—∞∞∞—

Joe McCarthy was not, as one journalist has called him, America's "most gifted" and success-

ful demagogue; but he was surely a character of extraordinary proportion. Painfully shy as a child, he later submerged his fears and insecurities beneath a façade of bluff aggressiveness and relentless energy. It was these qualities which allowed him to capture the communist issue as his own and ride it into national prominence. What McCarthy said at Wheeling and in the years that followed was not very new. The Truman administration had for some time been emphasizing the dangers of communism at home and abroad in its campaign for containment, while Republican politicians had sought to advance their own fortunes by charging that the Democrats were "soft on Communism." McCarthy's importance thus lay in the fact that he brought to a conventional political issue his own highly unconventional personal qualities—a flair for self-dramatization, a superb sense of press agentry, and a stubborn unwillingness to back down. "One should play poker with him to really know him," wrote a friend. "He raises on the poor hands and always comes out the winner."

His power, however, rested from the very outset on the issue of communism in government. Conservatives gladly supported his free-swinging attacks on the Truman administration, while liberals, fearful of being labeled pro-communist themselves, often sought to outdo their opponents in the sponsorship of repression. After 1953 support for McCarthy became increasingly inexpedient and his power steadily waned. Even in condemning him, however, the Senate circumspectly avoided the issues on which he had built his career, choosing instead to censure him for conduct "contrary to senatorial traditions." His legacy, and the legacy of those who supported him or acquiesced in his abuse of power, included the restriction of dissent at home and a policy of reflexive anticommunism abroad. See Robert Griffith, *The Politics of Fear: Joseph R. McCarthy and the Senate* (1970).

ROBERT GRIFFITH

McCLELLAN, George Brinton (b. Philadelphia, Pa., Dec. 3, 1826; d. Orange, N.J.,

Oct. 29, 1885), MILITARY and POLITICAL LEADER, graduated from the U.S. Military Academy in 1846. During the Mexican War he fought in the battles of Contreras, Churubusco, and Chapultepec. After serving as an instructor in engineering at West Point and participating in an exploration of the sources of the Red River he was sent to Europe to study military organization and tactics, and witnessed the siege of Sevastopol (1855) during the Crimean War. McClellan resigned from the army in 1857 and became the chief engineer of the Illinois Central Railroad; in 1860 he became the president of the Ohio and Mississippi Railroad.

When the Civil War erupted, McClellan joined the Union army and was commissioned a major general of the Ohio volunteers; in May 1861 he was appointed a major general in the regular army, and commander of the Department of Ohio. After clearing western Virginia of Confederate troops (thereby opening the way for the admission of West Virginia as a separate state), he was given command of the Division of the Potomac (July 1861) and appointed commanding general of the Union army in November. He organized and trained the Union armies, especially in the East, but his slowness in taking the offensive led to his removal as chief of all the armies in March 1862. Retaining the Army of the Potomac, McClellan believed that if he could capture Richmond, the Confederate capital, the South would concede defeat. He floated his army down the Potomac to Fort Monroe, on the tip of the peninsula formed by the York and James rivers. After capturing Yorktown, he pushed forward cautiously, enabling the Confederates to regroup and engage a part of his force at the battle of Seven Pines, and later in what has been called the Seven Days battles (June 26–July 1, 1862). **Robert E. Lee's** army suffered heavy casualties which severely hampered its effectiveness, but McClellan refused to move swiftly to the offensive. At odds with McClellan because of these cautious tactics, President Lincoln decided to reduce some of his powers by appointing General **Halleck** to the vacant post of commanding general, U.S. army. But Lincoln was forced to rely upon McClellan once again following General Pope's defeat at Second Bull Run (1862).

McClellan next met Lee at Sharpsburg, Maryland, between the Potomac and Antietam Creek (Sept. 1862). Although the battle was indecisive, Lee's troops were thoroughly exhausted; but McClellan refused to pursue Lee, thus enabling the Confederates to withdraw across the Potomac into Virginia. Following this action, Lincoln dismissed McClellan (Nov. 1862) and gave the Army of the Potomac to General Burnside.

In 1864, running on a peace platform, McClellan became the Democratic presidential nominee. He lost to Lincoln, 21 electoral votes to 212. After the election he traveled to Europe, returning to the U.S. in 1868. He served as chief engineer of the Department of the Docks of New York City (1870–72), and was governor of New Jersey (1878–81).

Abraham Lincoln himself said repeatedly during the early years of the Civil War that to return the South to the Union, the federal government must conciliate as well as conquer, and that caution must be observed to prevent the war from degenerating into "remorseless revolutionary struggle." None of Lincoln's generals more clearly recognized this conciliatory aspect of the Union's task than George B. McClellan. While McClellan commanded Union armies, he sought to fight the war in such a way that he would minimize both property loss and casualties on both sides, and thus prepare for the restoration of the Union. McClellan has not always received due credit for this farsighted aspect of his generalship. Unfortunately, he lacked the ability to hew to his conception of the war and still win victories. He organized and trained armies skillfully but consumed so much time at it that he diluted the benefits. When at last he campaigned, his plans were too elaborate to be likely to work well, and in battle he lacked the resolution to endure casualties and push home to victory. These military shortcomings alone eventually would have compelled Lincoln to dismiss him; to the military shortcomings McClellan added a fatal egotism which impaired understanding between him and the civil government and tempted him to blur the soldier's role by flirting with the Democratic opposition party. After losing confidence in McClellan once, Lincoln returned him to responsibility to meet the Confederate invasion of Maryland; but while McClellan used superior numbers to turn the enemy back, his handling of the battle of Antietam was a model of how not to fight a battle—with piecemeal attacks that always gave the enemy a chance to recover. Thereafter McClellan drifted into the political career which culminated in his presidential candidacy and in which he allowed his own resentment over military failure and imagined injustices to embitter further the national political life in which he had once sought to be a bearer of conciliation. See Warren W. Hassler, Jr., *General George B. McClellan: Shield of the Union* (1957).

RUSSELL F. WEIGLEY

McCLURE, Samuel Sidney (b. Frocess, County Antrim, Ire., Feb. 17, 1857; d. New York, N.Y., March 21, 1949), JOURNALIST, was brought to America in 1866 by his widowed mother and grew up in poverty in Indiana. After working his way through Knox College, Galesburg, Illinois (BA, 1882), he moved to Boston to become editor and manager of the *Wheelman,* a magazine for cyclists (1882–84). He then worked for the De Vinne Press in New York (1884), but left after four months to found the McClure Syndicate, the first successful literary syndicate in America.

Among McClure's first writers was Sarah Orne Jewett; he subsequently presented such writers as **Mark Twain, William Dean Howells,** and **Joel Chandler Harris,** and introduced, among others, Rudyard Kipling and Robert Louis Stevenson to American readers. In 1893 he founded *McClure's* magazine, with John Sanborn Phillips as his partner. By June 1898 the low-priced literary journal had attained a circulation of 400,000. It launched in January 1903 the "muckraking" crusade

against large corporations and municipal corruption. *McClure's* staff included **Ida Tarbell, Ray Stannard Baker, Lincoln Steffens,** and the previously unknown **Willa Cather.** McClure lost control of his magazine and syndicate interests in 1912, but he found associates who were able to repurchase the magazine in 1922 and to restore him to nominal control during its short-lived revival. In the meantime he had been editor of the New York *Evening Mail* for two years.

McClure sailed on **Henry Ford's** Peace Ship in 1915, but left the group, disillusioned. During his long retirement he studied fascism in Italy for two years and wrote tracts on government and political theory. His *Autobiography* (1914) was in fact written by Willa Cather from interviews with McClure.

⁂

As a publisher S. S. McClure was one of the greatest instinctive editors ever to function in the U.S., and one of the most wretched businessmen. The contrast was reflected in his career, which had the exhilarating upward soar and sickening downward swoop of a roller coaster; the roots of the contrast can be traced to his personality, which psychiatrists would today likely diagnose as manic-depressive. His estimable characteristics were enthusiasm, pertinacity, and an astonishing talent for sensing in advance what the unpredictable public would find interesting. He burst out of the Midwest to challenge the hegemony of the small group of genteel, cultivated literary folk of New York and Boston, and quite soon was standing sponsor to a growing number of talented young writers—**Theodore Dreiser,** O. Henry, **Frank Norris, Stephen Crane, Jack London, William Allen White,** Booth Tarkington—many of them, like him, from the West. As editor, McClure was always on the wing, sniffing out the nation's concerns, talking with newspaper editors, listening to everybody, and stuffing his pockets with notes. Back in New York he had the staff writers to take hold of his ideas, develop them, document them, and clothe them in lively, accurate prose. This procedure led to his greatest editorial triumph, the several

series of so-called muckraking articles that resulted in far-reaching political and social reforms in
the early years of the century. With his success,
McClure's more trying characteristics—impetuosity, instability, and a hair-trigger impatience—
sorely disaffected his closest associates. Several
of them deserted him in 1906. He published an
excellent magazine for another half-dozen years,
but without a faithful business manager he was
obliged to sell first his book publishing house,
then his syndicate, and at last his magazine.
There were left only his name and his reputation,
both of which were exploited by others during
the last 35 years of his long life, without benefit to
him. See Peter Lyon, *Success Story: The Life and
Times of S. S. McClure* (1963).

PETER LYON

McCOLLUM, Elmer Verner (b. near Fort Scott,
Kansas, March 3, 1879; d. Baltimore, Md., Nov. 15,
1967), BIOCHEMIST, received his BA in 1903 and
MS in 1904 from the University of Kansas, before
entering the Sheffield Scientific School, Yale
University (1904), where he received his PhD
(1906). The following year was spent there as a
postdoctoral fellow. From 1907 to 1917 he worked
at the Wisconsin College of Agriculture, Madison,
passing through the ranks to full professor in six
years. By 1917 his experimental work on cattle
feeding and on rats was widely known and he was
invited to become professor of chemistry and the
first chairman of the Department of Chemistry at
the newly created Johns Hopkins School of
Hygiene and Public Health. Later that same year
President Herbert Hoover appointed him to the
U.S. Food Administration Advisory Committee.
At Hoover's request McCollum traveled throughout the U.S. lecturing on nutrition. His experimental work on rickets began in 1918 and he later did
extensive work on other deficiency diseases.

McCollum's growing reputation led to many
honors. In 1922 he helped set up the Merrill-
Palmer School in Detroit, and from 1923 to 1948
he frequently wrote on nutrition for *McCall's*
magazine. From 1928 to 1937 he was consultant
to the U.S. Dept. of Agriculture, Bureau of

Animal Husbandry, and he served as a member
of the U.S. Pharmacopoecial Revision Board,
1932–49. He also served as a member of the
National Advisory Health Council, 1933–37, and
in 1941 he became a member of both the Food
and Nutrition boards of the National Research
Council and also the U.S. Advisory Committee of
the Coordinator of Information on Food and
Nutrition. He received eleven medals of honor,
and was elected a foreign member of the Royal
Society of London. Although he retired in 1946
from his position at Johns Hopkins, he continued
to work until the end of his life. In 1948 the
McCollum-Pratt Institute at Johns Hopkins was
named after him. Perhaps his most important
book was the classic *The Newer Knowledge of
Nutrition* (1918; fifth ed. 1939). He also wrote *A
History of Nutrition* (1957) and a revealing autobiography, *From Kansas Farm Boy to Scientist* (1964).

Elmer McCollum played a fundamental role in
developing knowledge of nutrition early in this
century. Indeed, his basic research in the first few
decades marked the beginning of the modern age
of the science. It had become clear that chemical
analysis alone could not adequately explain the
nutritional value of foods. By devising scientific
diets which he then fed to rats (whose omnivorous
feeding habits he had observed as a child),
McCollum brought order to a new and chaotic
province of knowledge. By itself, his standardization of the white albino rat as a primary lab animal
was a major contribution to the study of nutrition,
perhaps even greater than the use of fruit flies in
genetics at about the same time. Biological analysis thus succeeded the inadequate, previously
used chemical method of analysis.

Many important discoveries followed his earliest experiments on rats, beginning in January
1908. By 1912 he and his lab assistant had discovered the first vitamin (vitamin A), which they
announced in 1913. Other experiments conducted while at Wisconsin demonstrated the existence of what he called "watersoluble B," thus
continuing the alphabetical designation of the
vitamins. He subsequently had the distinction in

1922 of discovering vitamin D. In more than three hundred articles in popular (particularly *McCall's*) and professional journals, McCollum presented many other important discoveries on vitamins and vital trace elements, specifically potassium, manganese, magnesium, zinc, iron, sodium, chlorine, and aluminum. His work on the effect of diet on dental health also had a broad and significant impact. Perhaps the most appropriate summary of McCollum's brilliant career has been made by the distinguished biomedical scholar Edwards A. Park, who has observed about his career: "I can think of no one in his generation whose record has been quite equal to his." See *Biographical Memoirs of Fellows of the Royal Society,* 15 (1969), 159–171.

H. Lewis McKinney

McCORMICK, Cyrus Hall (b. Rockridge County, Va., Feb. 15, 1809; d. Chicago, Ill., May 13, 1884), INVENTOR, MANUFACTURER, after a grammar school education, assisted his father in the operation of a 1,200-acre grain and livestock farm, and in such auxiliary business ventures as a whiskey distillery and a small farm implement shop. (His father invented and manufactured hemp breaks, reapers, and hydraulic machinery, but none of these devices was commercially successful.) In 1831 Cyrus invented a hillside plow and his famous reaper. Upon learning that Obed Hussey had invented a similar device in 1833, McCormick patented his invention in 1834. Although he continued to perfect his reaper during the next decade, he produced only a handful of the machines at his father's workshop. He farmed a 500-acre tract which his father had given him in 1835, and he and his father purchased the Cotopaxi ironworks in 1836. The panic of 1837 drove them into bankruptcy, and they spent the next seven years paying off their debts.

In 1843 McCormick began to concentrate on the production of his reaper, securing orders for it during a tour of the Midwest with his invention in 1844. In 1847 he established a factory in Chicago, the city which soon became the center of American agricultural trade. Though failing to secure a patent renewal in 1848, McCormick gained a competitive advantage in reaper production through innovations in manufacturing and sales. He organized a mass-production system in his factory and invested heavily in labor-saving machinery; he introduced deferred payments and money-back guarantees, advertised extensively, and conducted on-the-site demonstrations of his reaper. He also established a research department which systematically developed improvements in his products.

In 1851 McCormick displayed his reaper in England, where it was awarded a Council Medal. Although he never managed to develop a major market in western Europe, he won medals at various world fairs and exhibitions after 1851. This acclaim, as utilized in advertising campaigns, helped sales in the U.S. By 1856 he had accumulated more than $1 million and was earning yearly profits in excess of $300,000. During the depression of 1857–60 he purchased large tracts of Chicago real estate and invested heavily in the Merchants Saving, Loan and Trust Co. in Chicago.

McCormick accrued immense gains during the Civil War. Crop failures in Europe and the war at home increased the demand for grain, while the mobilization of troops produced labor shortages. McCormick sold over 250,000 reapers and mowers. After the war he invested heavily in the Union Pacific Railroad and Crédit Mobilier, and in copper, gold, and silver mines in South America.

In 1864 McCormick ran unsuccessfully for Congress on the Democratic ticket, and he served on the central committee of the Democratic party in Illinois (1872–76). After the Civil War he helped to organize the Mississippi Valley Society, which promoted European trade through the southern ports of Mobile and New Orleans. He supported the effort to build an interoceanic canal through Nicaragua, as well as the movement to annex Santo Domingo to the U.S. Throughout his life he contributed to the evangelical efforts of the Presbyterian Church, including large donations to the Union Theological Seminary of Virginia.

Those who maintain that capitalism was built by Calvinist virtues can point to no stronger evidence than the life of Cyrus H. McCormick. First as a farmer in a remote valley of Virginia and later as a millionaire of world fame, he practiced the strict self-discipline taught by the Presbyterian Church of his youth. His farm life was work from dawn to dark interrupted only by church on Sunday and prayer meeting Wednesday evening. His later wealth did not weaken his self-discipline with indulgence but was used without restraint to promote his causes. He never took a trip for pleasure. He did not marry until he was 49. In his factory he paid high wages and was a pioneer in recognizing and negotiating with the labor unions. He bought two Chicago newspapers and imported pro-slavery ministers to sell his southern viewpoint to Chicago prior to the Civil War. He contributed liberally to the McCormick Presbyterian Seminary in Chicago. His chief relaxation was to discuss theological questions with Presbyterian clergymen.

His resource and capital was his own drive and hard work. He discovered no oil wells, acquired no virgin forests, despoiled no natural resources except the prairie sod which was replaced by wheat, thanks to his reaper, which he invented in six weeks at the age of 22. Fortunately, he had indomitable faith in the reaper and a fierce pride in his role as its inventor, for it required 17 years to perfect the machine, demonstrate its feasibility, and get financial backing for its manufacture. When the reaper factory was finally in operation he was seldom seen in the shops or offices, but drove the company with a long, though nonetheless tight rein from New York, Washington, and Europe. He entrusted the direct superintendency to his mechanically gifted brother Leander and business administration to his brother William, while he continued to be a fighter for causes, both personal and public. He fought to protect his invention through innumerable patent suits in the U.S. courts and even through legislation in Congress, and he fought to preserve slavery and the South at the time of the Civil War.

McCormick viewed Lincoln's possible election as a catastrophe and considered **Stephen Douglas** an unprincipled compromiser. His own views were close to those of **John Cabell Breckinridge,** but he hoped to persuade both Douglas and Breckinridge to withdraw in favor of a third candidate. He was opposed to secession but tried to avoid it by having the North make concessions. Through his two newspapers and clergymen friends he relentlessly bombarded Chicagoans with his pro-southern ideas until he became a very unpopular figure in that pro-Lincoln city. This was a factor in his spending 1862–64 in England and on the Continent. When he thought Lincoln could be defeated, he returned in 1864 to run for Congress on the Democratic ticket on a "stop the war" platform. Up to the moment of **Robert E. Lee's** surrender, he believed the South was invincible. Ironically his own reaper, by increasing wheat production while freeing men for the northern armies, was one of the important foundations of the North's victory. In a larger sense, the reaper made possible the great increase in food production that sustained the vast industrialization of the Western world.

McCormick was frugal in his personal living, but lavish in support of his beliefs such as the South and the Presbyterian Church. His fierce pride led him into interminable lawsuits, generally over patent matters but occasionally prompted by personal pique. For example, at a Philadelphia station in 1862 he ordered his family's nine trunks removed from the train to avoid a baggage overcharge of $8.70. Since there was not time to do this before the train departed, the bags went on to Chicago, where four of them subsequently were destroyed by lightning. There began a legal battle between McCormick and the president of the Pennsylvania Railroad. The finest legal minds of the country were engaged by both sides. The case was appealed from court to court; three times it reached the U.S. Supreme Court. The final ruling, a McCormick victory, came twenty-three years after the event and one year after his death. See William T. Hutchinson, *Cyrus Hall McCormick* (1935).

ROBERT OZANNE

MACDONALD, Dwight (b. New York, N.Y., March 24, 1906; d. New York, N.Y., Dec. 17, 1982) CRITIC, POLITICAL ACTIVIST, graduated from Phillips Exeter Academy in 1924, and Yale University in 1928. There he served as an editor of several university publications, won literary prizes, and was named class poet. After a brief stint in Macy's executive training program he became a staff writer for *Fortune*, where he worked from 1929 to 1936. He left because of a dispute over a radical critique of the United States Steel Corporation. In 1937 he became a founding editor, along with Philip Rahv and William Phillips, of the revived *Partisan Review*. In 1937 he became a fellow traveller of the Trotskyist movement, writing for their publications and finally joining their party in 1939. He resigned in 1941. He left his editorship of the *Partisan Review* in 1943 because of his refusal to support the war effort during World War II and established in 1944 his own anarcho/pacifist journal, *Politics*. He edited *Politics* until 1949 and worked as a freelance journalist until 1951. That year he took a job as staff writer for the *New Yorker*, where he remained until 1964. In 1957 he was a visiting editor of *Encounter* in London, where he was one of the first to suspect the alleged influence of the Central Intelligence Agency (CIA) on supposedly independent journals. In the early 1960s, Macdonald was the movie critic for *Esquire* magazine and in 1967–68 he contributed a monthly column, "Politics." From the late 1950s until his death, Macdonald was a frequent lecturer and visiting professor at scores of universities and colleges nationwide.

In the 1960s Macdonald returned to activist dissenting politics, participating in several anti–Vietnam War groups, practicing civil disobedience as well as raising money for the Students for a Democratic Society. He also took part in the Counter Commencement at Columbia University after the student rebellion of 1968. Macdonald

was lecturing at Yale University when he fell ill and died. A prolific writer, his principal works were: *Henry Wallace: The Man and Myth* (1948); *The Root Is Man: Two Essays in Politics* (1950); *The Ford Foundation: The Men and the Millions* (1956); *Memoirs of a Revolutionist* (1957); ed., *Parodies: An Anthology from Chaucer to Beerbohm* (1960); *Against the American Grain* (1962); ed., *Poems of Edgar Allan Poe* (1965); *Dwight Macdonald on Movies* (1969); ed., *My Past and Thoughts: The Memoirs of Alexander Herzen* (1973).

⁓

Dwight Macdonald marched to a different drummer, always intent on exposing the hypocrisy of the prevailing wisdom. Macdonald held a unique place in our intellectual history. Daniel Bell thought his journal, *Politics*, the only magazine that kept calling attention to the changes that were taking place in moral temper. Czeslaw Milosz described Macdonald as a "totally American phenomenon ... the completely free man, capable of making decisions at all times about all things strictly according to his moral judgments."

Macdonald was determined to be a writer as an adolescent. His youthful resistance to pretension foreshadowed his later polemics and candid literary criticism. When a freshman at Yale he denounced compulsory chapel because a sermon was full of "puerile and stupid twaddle" and "an insult to the students' intelligence."

After college Macdonald joined **Henry Luce**'s *Fortune* magazine. Ironically, *Fortune* played a part in his radicalization. He found the members of the corporate community "stupid and scared people." When *Fortune* editors emasculated his study of the steel industry he abruptly quit, leaving a $10,000 a year job in the midst of the depression. He became a leading journalist in the Trotskyist movement, carrying on extensive debates with Max Shactman and the "old man," Leon Trotsky. Macdonald frequently repeated Trotsky's acid observation that "every man has a right to be stupid on occasion but Comrade Macdonald abuses it." Macdonald left the Trotskyist movement in 1941 because of its ideological rigidity. During these years Macdonald served as the most energetic editor of the *Partisan Review*. His antiwar stance led to a break with his coeditors, and he and his wife, Nancy, founded the extraordinary journal, *Politics*. It developed an international reputation for its lively, unorthodox position. Macdonald had an instinct for recruiting talent. He introduced Simone Weil, Bruno Bettelheim, George Woodcock, Albert Camus, Nicola Chiaromonte, and C. Wright Mills to American readers.

In the 1950s Macdonald turned his attention to the quality of American life and its culture. He fashioned the concepts of "masscult" and "midcult," helping to shape the dimensions of the debate concerning mass culture and its relationship to 20th century totalitarianism. As a *New Yorker* staff writer, Macdonald wrote scathing attacks on the banality he found corrupting American literary standards. Robert Hutchins and Mortimer Adler's *Great Books*, *The Revised Standard Version of the Bible*, and *Webster's New International Dictionary* (1961), were among his victims. In the 1960s he was the acerbic film critic for *Esquire*. He remained an outspoken American critic in the defense of tradition, often speaking in the language of classic conservatism. Like George Orwell, with whom he has been compared, Macdonald feared the corruption of culture by commercialism as much as he had feared the corruption of politics by Stalinism.

After the period of cultural crusading but relative political passivity, Macdonald became an opponent of the Vietnam War and an active supporter of draft resistance and civil disobedience. He was always his own man. Macdonald's participation in American intellectual life illuminates American intellectual history from the 1920s to the 1980s. See Michael Wreszin, *A Rebel in Defense of Tradition: The Life and Politics of Dwight Macdonald* (1994).

MICHAEL WRESZIN

MacDOWELL, Edward Alexander (b. New York, N.Y., Dec. 18, 1861; d. New York, N.Y., Jan. 23, 1908), COMPOSER, was educated in the New York public schools through the tenth grade, meanwhile studying the piano. He then went to France to continue his musical training. After three years at the Paris Conservatory, where Debussy was a fellow student, he went to Germany. While at Wiesbaden in 1878–79, he was recommended to head the piano department at the Frankfurt Conservatory by the retiring teacher, Carl Heymann, but was turned down because of his youth. MacDowell had begun to compose seriously, and as a result of a visit to Franz Liszt at Weimar in 1882, was invited to give the first professional performance of a work of his, the *First Modern Suite* (Opus 10).

MacDowell returned to the U.S. in 1888, and for the next eight years lived in Boston, where he taught, composed, and gave recitals. When he played at the French Exposition in 1889, he was enthusiastically received by Europeans, who considered him a leading American composer and pianist. It was during these years that he wrote the *Woodland Sketches*, perhaps his best-known work. In 1896 he accepted the first professorship of music at Columbia University. In his eight years at Columbia, MacDowell converted the college glee club into the first serious male chorus in America, and organized concerts and recitals. But he came to believe that Columbia had little interest in serious music, and in 1904, despondent, he resigned. (He apparently suffered from a brain condition which has never been publicly revealed.) In 1905, he completely collapsed in body and mind.

———

MacDowell, the most well-known American composer abroad, was the envy of his musical contemporaries. George Chadwick, a dean of American music himself, explained MacDowell's early success by recalling that when most American composers were involved with school or sports, MacDowell was practicing the piano and studying harmony and counterpoint. Two reasons may account for the fact that he was never a member of any "school" or identified with any particular philosophy of music. First, he was by nature solitary. Second, his formative years had been spent in Europe under the watchful eye of his mother, a guardianship assumed later by a devoted wife who after his premature death had much to do with the preservation of his memory and his image as a moody genius.

One talent that placed MacDowell in his special niche was his virtuosity as a pianist. For he was able to enhance the effect of his music by performing it before large, adoring audiences. Certainly his demeanor, his expressive face, and his artistry set him apart. Unlike many of the school of American composers centered in Boston, MacDowell eschewed the clean-cut look of the businessman and affected the sartorial and tonsorial fashions of the European artist. But it was the unique magic of MacDowell's music, his individualistic sense of harmony and melody at a time when it was difficult to avoid cliché, that accounts for his high reputation.

In spite of his virtuosity as a pianist and his originality, he was not versatile as a composer. Actually, his fame is based on a few compositions and, at that, works largely limited to the piano. There are no MacDowell symphonies, string quartets, or operas in the repertory. More than any other American composer, he may be called a Romantic. For not only as a man but as an artist he expressed the major concerns of romanticism: passion, the love of nature, and ethnocentricity. One need only hear the first few measures of the *Second Concerto for Piano and Orchestra,* the *Sea Pieces,* and the *Keltic Sonata* to verify this stylistic judgment. Moreover, he was, despite his cosmopolitan, temperamental nature, a musical American who could stimulate the love of native melody among even the most ordinary of his compatriots, as in his simple piano sketch *To a Wild Rose.* Today, some 70 years after his passing, his works are still widely performed and recorded, a fact which cannot be said about any other American composer of his vintage. See Lawrence Gilman, *Edward MacDowell* (1931).

VICTOR FELL YELLIN

McGUFFEY, William Holmes (b. Claysville, Washington Co., Pa., Sept. 23, 1800; d. Charlottesville, Va., May 4, 1873), EDUCATOR, graduated from Washington College (now Washington and Jefferson) in 1826. During 1826–36 he was a professor of philosophy and languages at Miami University in Oxford, Ohio. In 1829 he was licensed to preach in the Presbyterian Church, but he never held a regular ministerial appointment. In 1836 he was appointed president of Cincinnati College, serving until 1839. While president, he helped organize the common school system of Ohio.

In 1836 he published the first of his six *Eclectic Readers,* known more commonly as *McGuffey's Readers,* for elementary school use. Containing selections from English authors, and providing moral and patriotic lessons, these *Readers* (which went through numerous editions) are estimated to have sold about 122 million copies.

McGuffey was president of Ohio University (1839–43), taught at Woodward College (1843–45), then joined the faculty of the University of Virginia as a professor of moral philosophy (1845–73).

⸎

For fifty years after 1836 William McGuffey was enormously influential in shaping American literary taste and moral attitudes, particularly in the Middle West. His *Eclectic Readers* introduced millions of children to good British and American writing in an era when few schools had adequate libraries. McGuffey, like **Horace Mann,** his contemporary, was an eloquent and effective advocate of free public elementary education. "The child," he said, "needs more help than the boy, and the boy more than the man; hence the primary school requires the best, the most philosophic instructors." A learned exponent of Christian and classical disciplines, McGuffey opposed Darwinian theories and decried "materialistic social philosophy." In the judgment of one critic (Richard Mosier), McGuffey's books were "solidly enlisted on the conservative side in the recurrent feud between Hamiltonians and Jeffersonians." H. S. Commager remarked that the *Readers* became "the darling of conservatives who found in them the very symbol and citadel of traditionalism." The pious proverbs and homely aphorisms that McGuffey published

729

derived more from **Benjamin Franklin**'s rules of prudent deportment than from the Puritan austerities of **Jonathan Edwards.** Sympathetic observers like **Hamlin Garland** and Mark Sullivan, strongly influenced by childhood exposure to the *Readers,* rightly stress McGuffey's role as a judicious and beneficent anthologist, who brought to areas of literary impoverishment examples of good writing and provided a valuable common reservoir of literary references. See Harvey C. Minnich, *William Holmes McGuffey and His Readers* (1936).

WILLIAM MCCANN

McKAY, Donald (b. Shelburne, Nova Scotia, Sept. 4, 1810; d. Hamilton, Mass., Sept. 20, 1880), SHIPBUILDER, received a common school education. He moved to New York City in 1827 to become a ship-carpenter apprentice. After finishing this apprenticeship he worked as a shipwright in New York City and Wiscasset, Maine, and in Newburyport, Massachusetts, where he formed a partnership as master shipbuilder with William Currier in 1841. He built two packet ships and then formed a new partnership with William Pickett in 1844 to build the packet ship *Joshua Bates* for the Boston-Liverpool line. Later that year McKay started his own shipyard in East Boston, Massachusetts.

McKay spent the next five years building packets. In 1850 he designed his first clipper ship, the *Stag Hound.* He followed this with the *Flying Cloud* in 1851 and the *Sovereign of the Seas* in 1852. Built for speed rather than for a maximum cargo capacity, these exceptionally fast sailing vessels soon became the most famous merchant ships of their day. His *Great Republic* (1853) was the largest clipper ship of the time, while the *Lightning,* completed for the Liverpool-Australia line in 1855, sailed at a record speed of 21 knots.

During the panic of 1857 and the subsequent depression the demand for clipper ships fell off and McKay's business declined. He spent 1859–60 in Europe visiting dockyards and studying European shipbuilding techniques. When the Civil War broke out he tried to convince the North to construct ironclads instead of relying on wooden ships. His warship designs, however, were rejected. He returned to England and worked for the Admiralty (1861–63), but in 1864–65 he built the monitor *Nausett* and three other naval ships for the Union navy. McKay sold his shipyard in 1869, but continued building steamers and sailing ships, including the *Glory of the Seas* (1869), which continued in service until 1923. Declining health forced him to retire to his estate in Hamilton, Massachusetts, in 1877, where he engaged in scientific farming until his death.

Probably the finest naval architect of his generation, McKay was most notable as an innovator in ship design and shipyard methods. Historically, innovations have come very slowly in the design and construction of sailing vessels, but beginning in the early 19th century a new set of commercial conditions created a need for new types of ships. The burgeoning tide of immigration from Europe to America called the packet ship into being—a relatively small, fast ship equipped to carry large numbers of passengers. Rapid increase in the Far Eastern trade created a need for larger cargo capacity and greater speed. The demand for speed was underscored again by the California gold rush.

McKay met the challenges created by these new conditions in brilliant fashion by the design of his packets and clippers. He also revolutionized shipyard methods by separating and specializing yard work and by introducing steam-powered construction machinery. Unfortunately, he was not as good a businessman as he was a designer. Well on his way to making a fortune by the early 1850s, he failed in 1856 because of an unwise choice of individuals handling his finances. Maintenance and operating costs of his clippers were so high that orders for them ceased after the fifties. Outside circumstances also contributed to his weakening financial condition. The panic of 1857 brought shipbuilding almost to a halt, and Confederate raiders struck blows at American shipping during the Civil War from which it never really recovered. Finally, commercial capital after the Civil War went increasingly into industry and the building of the West, and the United States lost its position as a leading maritime nation. The beckoning opportunities for innovative shipbuilders of the 1840s and 1850s were sharply curtailed by the 1870s, thereby bringing an end to McKay's career. See John Robinson and George Francis Bow, *The Sailing Ships of New England, Series Two* (1924).

ELISHA P. DOUGLASS

McKINLEY, William (b. Niles, Ohio, Jan. 29, 1843; d. Buffalo, N.Y., Sept. 14, 1901), PRESIDENT, studied at Allegheny College. He joined the Union army when the Civil War broke out, rising to major (1865). He fought at South Mountain, Antietam, Winchester, and Cedar Creek. He was admitted to the Ohio bar in 1867, and was prosecuting attorney of Stark County (1869–71). A Republican member of the House of Representatives (1877–91, except for part of 1884), he drafted the high McKinley Tariff of 1890, arguing that American wage levels required protection against "cheap" competition. During 1892–96, he was governor of Ohio.

With the aid of **Mark Hanna,** an Ohio businessman, McKinley won the Republican presidential nomination in 1896. **William Jennings Bryan** was his Democratic opponent. The key issue was the free coinage of silver at a ratio of 16:1 with gold, which McKinley and the Republicans categorically opposed. McKinley conducted a "front-porch campaign" in Canton, Ohio, while Bryan toured the country extensively. In an election marked by sharp sectional divisions McKinley triumphed, 271 electoral votes to 176.

As president, McKinley approved the Dingley Tariff (1897), the highest in U.S. history, and the Gold Currency Act (1900), placing all forms of currency on a parity with gold. In foreign affairs, McKinley sought to avoid involvement in the Cuban revolution against Spain, but popular support of Cuba reinforced his desire to settle the vexing question. The inability of Spain and the U.S. to find a compromise settlement guaranteeing Cuban autonomy forced him (April 1898) to call for a declaration of war against Spain. Victory in the Spanish-American War made the U.S. a world power, and resulted in the acquisition of Puerto Rico, Guam, and the Philippines. But McKinley approved of the annexation of the Philippines only reluctantly.

In September 1901, while attending a public reception at the Pan-American Exposition in Buffalo, New York, McKinley was assassinated by Leon Czolgosz, an anarchist.

⁂

William McKinley was an active politician during a period of rapid growth and change in all aspects of American life. Coming from the expanding Midwest, he was conscious of a changing electorate that registered the challenges and opportunities of a new industrial system. He became a moderate on most issues, as befitted a man representing diverse economic, ethnic, and social interests in Ohio. He gained national fame as an exponent of tariff protection, a policy that unified his diverse constituency, and in whose merits he firmly believed.

McKinley's personal talents matched his view of the nation and of the political process. Like most national politicians, he understood that the era needed unifying, responsible parties more than dramatic spokesmen. It was a time of congressional rather than executive authority, and McKinley always used quiet compromise and indirect methods to obtain his ends. He was an excellent committee worker as a congressman, and a realistic chief executive who seldom if ever penalized men he could not persuade to do his bidding. Reliance on indirection sometimes made McKinley seem weak, yet he could not advertise these methods without weakening their effect.

McKinley had little time for systematic analysis of American society. Yet he perceived that an essentially rural society and an individualistic people must cope with industrialism's tendencies toward concentrated power and social change. Like most Americans, he saw politics as a way to satisfy group needs, while enhancing the individual voter's sense of participation in public affairs. McKinley was a man of his time, confident that expanding opportunity and individual material security promoted social balance. As a strong nationalist, he supported Republican efforts to underwrite, and to regulate, an economy in which every man might work out his talents.

McKinley was preeminently a politician; he traveled widely throughout his career and knew the details of political life in most states. As a candidate in 1896, and as president after 1897, he firmly controlled the Republican party organization, while successfully harmonizing its major factions. He genuinely liked people, and was accessible to a variety of visitors, who were assured of a sympathetic hearing if not always of a positive answer for their pleas. A man of great personal charm, noted for his devotion to an invalid wife, McKinley enjoyed wide popularity before his death.

The dramatic events of his administration often contrasted sharply with McKinley's genial manner and love of indirection. Overseas expansion was the most controversial issue of his presidency. He accepted the specific responsibilities of preparing Cuba for self-rule, and of acquiring the Philippines. In a larger sense, he hoped to make the United States a Pacific power by entering the China trade, acquiring Hawaii, and planning an Isthmian canal. But his expansionism was limited. He did not desire territory as much as a new American presence that he hoped would gain material self-interest, and that would also help stabilize and liberalize existing world order.

McKinley was one of the few presidents to maintain harmonious and productive relations with Congress. He was equally skillful at explaining new departures to the people. And he chose many able subordinates like **John Hay, Elihu Root,** and William Howard Taft. His methods helped reduce tensions that arose around divisive new questions. He enhanced presidential authority within the limits of his situation, yet may be more important historically as a party leader than as a president. His most important general achievement was intangible, helping to develop a party coalition that permitted responsible government and that also enhanced a sense of national unity after a generation of unprecedented change. See H. Wayne Morgan, *William McKinley and His America* (1963).

H. WAYNE MORGAN

McNAMARA, Robert Strange (b. San Francisco, Calif., June 9, 1916), BUSINESSMAN, GOVERNMENT ADMINISTRATOR, graduated from the University of California at Berkeley in 1937 and, in 1939, from the Harvard Graduate School of Business. After working for an accounting firm he returned to Harvard in 1940 as an assistant professor in the business school. During World War II he was involved in devising statistical controls for the air force. Sent to England to train officers in these new management techniques, he was commissioned a captain. At the end of the war he was discharged as a lieutenant colonel in the Air Force Reserve, with the Legion of Merit.

In 1945, McNamara and nine other former air force officers formed a management consulting firm. One of their first clients was the deeply troubled Ford Motor Co., which had just passed under the leadership of young **Henry Ford II.** By 1949 McNamara was controller of the company, whose management had been dramatically reformed in the interim. As assistant general manager of the Ford division after 1953, McNamara worked chiefly in the marketing side of the corporation. His suggestions that the Ford car be upgraded to appeal to more affluent families, that the experimental Thunderbird sports car be enlarged to seat four, and that the company develop a compact car (the Falcon) all led to increased sales. Late in 1960, Henry Ford named him president of the company.

In 1961 McNamara was appointed secretary of defense by President Kennedy. In the sprawling Defense Department, he concentrated on efficiency, setting up a forward planning organization and a single military intelligence arm for the three services. He closed numerous redundant military installations. He played a major policy-making role, assigning responsibility for military space projects to the air force while pushing the missile program and the navy's Polaris atomic submarine project. In *The Essence of Security* (1968) McNamara estimated that the department had saved $14 billion in a five-year period of operation under his programming procedures. He also noted that open housing for all races had been achieved at military posts. After Kennedy's assassination, President Johnson retained McNamara as secretary of defense.

As the Vietnam war escalated after 1964, McNamara increasingly became the day-to-day spokesman for the government on military operations. He was responsible for the preparation of the so-called Pentagon Papers study of American decisionmaking during the war. Increasingly, McNamara was becoming disillusioned about the progress of the war and began to have strong doubts that it was winnable. He kept these doubts largely to himself, however, but the strain showed.

On President Johnson's initiative, the directors of the International Bank for Reconstruction and Development elected McNamara as bank president on November 30, 1967. To this day, McNamara doesn't know whether he was fired or left the Pentagon voluntarily. He stayed on at the Pentagon, however, to assist in the preparation of the budget until the end of February 1968, and took office at the Bank in April 1968, remaining there until 1981. In 1995 MacNamara came out with his memoirs, *In Retrospect: The Tragedy and Lessons of Vietnam*, an apologia for his role as Secretary of Defense during the Vietnam buildup. Admitting that the war was a mistake, "we were wrong," he wrote, "terribly wrong," he tried to explain why he and other policymakers were so wrong in pursuing the conflict. Basically, he argued that he and others had inadequate information and did not fully understand the Vietnamese, North or South, their history or their culture. He claimed to have written his book not to gain sympathy for himself but as a warning to future decisionmakers.

Robert S. McNamara is an accomplished practitioner of a uniquely modern profession: the management of large bureaucracies. Unlike the self-made business entrepreneurs of an earlier era, McNamara and his peers not only come to business and government from universities but also apply abstract concepts, based on a sophisticated knowledge of mathematics, economics, and engineering, to the problems of achieving the maximum results from men and materials.

McNamara, however, is more than a formidable technocrat. A man of skeptical, inquiring mind and humane interests, he has a lively social conscience and deep dedication to the public interest as he understands it. His reputation is clouded and controversial and likely to remain so unless the nation reaches a consensus about the significance of the Vietnam war. An interim judgment is that he was a great defense minister but a less than successful war minister. No one excelled him in preparing the armed forces to fight any of a half dozen conceivable wars varying in size, character, and complexity, but when war came, logic and rationality were not enough to maintain effective control over military operations which developed a logic of their own. A limited war against an ideologically committed foe has political complexities and hidden dimensions with which McNamara was at first unfamiliar.

To appreciate McNamara's achievement at the Pentagon during the first period of his stewardship (1961–64), it is necessary to bear in mind that after years of economizing efforts based on the theory of "a bigger bang for the buck," the Defense Department was ill-prepared to fight any kind of war except a nuclear Armageddon. Also, thoughtful men despaired that any civilian could master the feuds and rivalries of the army, navy, air force, and marine corps.

Relying on a corps of civilian intellectuals (the "whiz kids") and the concept of "cost effectiveness," McNamara quickly dissipated the gathering despair and demonstrated that civilian control of the military could be made a daily, pragmatic reality, at least in peacetime. He introduced the planning-programming-budgeting system in which annual expenditures are related to a five-year cycle and in which the incremental value of proposed programs—whether for an additional division, an improved missile, or a new submarine—could be measured by a common standard. For the first time the military services had to use common terms of reference and to relate their separate functions to the department's major missions.

McNamara's guiding concept was the need to widen the nation's military options beyond mere reliance on the strategic nuclear deterrent, to enable the president, as he put it, "to apply a fly swatter where a fly swatter is a proper weapon, instead of using a sledgehammer." McNamara not only strengthened the nation's strategic nuclear deterrent but also increased by 60 percent the tactical nuclear forces deployed in Western Europe, raised the number of combat-ready army divisions from 11 to 16, increased the number of tactical air squadrons by one-third, doubled the navy's ship conversion and construction program, enlarged the size of the marine corps, and by keen emphasis on airlift capacity greatly enhanced the mobility of all the armed forces.

But beyond increasing this country's range of military options, McNamara had the larger, more inspiring ambition of moving the world away from a doomsday nuclear strategy. Tragically, however, his achievements had another and largely unintended consequence. They enabled President Johnson to intervene in Vietnam in 1965 without mobilizing the national guard or the reserves and therefore without paying an immediate price in popular support. In this fundamental though limited sense, his critics were right that Vietnam was "McNamara's War."

As an adviser on policy, McNamara began the war as a true believer in the importance of holding the line against communism in South Vietnam. He was initially deficient in insight into the politics of Southeast Asia, but he was the first of Johnson's principal advisers to become disenchanted both about the prospects for early victory and about the war's underlying rationale. By the summer of 1966, it was clear to him that bombing would not be decisive and that ground fighting would require larger forces and many more years of involvement. By 1967, he was striving to find a way out of the war. But he lacked the persuasive skills necessary to change Johnson's mind and succeeded only in losing the president's confidence. McNamara's legacy to the nation as secretary of defense was to order the compilation of the Pentagon Papers in an effort to cast light on how the Vietnam tragedy had evolved.

Kicked upstairs to the World Bank presidency by Johnson in 1967, McNamara devoted himself once more to the productive pursuits of peace. Under his leadership, the World Bank grew in size, increased its lending capacity, and expanded its efforts to make the economic growth of the underdeveloped countries keep pace with their population growth and reduce their poverty. This was obviously the task of several lifetimes, but it was the task by which McNamara may ultimately be judged in history. Rather than the production of automobiles or the renovation of the Pentagon's war-making capacity, economic development is an undertaking which brought together in full harmony the technocratic capacities and humane impulses of Robert McNamara. See David Halberstam, *The Best and the Brightest* (1972), and Robert S. McNamara, *In Retrospect: The Tragedy and Lessons of Vietnam* (1995).

WILLIAM V. SHANNON

MADISON, James (b. Port Conway, Va., March 16, 1751; d. Orange County, Va., June 28, 1836), PRESIDENT, graduated from the College of New Jersey (now Princeton) in 1771. He helped draft the Virginia Constitution (1776), served in the Continental Congress (1780–83), and was a member of the Virginia House of Delegates (1784–86). He attended the Annapolis Convention of 1786, called to discuss interstate commercial affairs, and the Philadelphia Convention of 1787, which drafted the Constitution. His notes on the proceedings at Philadelphia are the most important records of the deliberations of the delegates. With **Alexander Hamilton** and **John Jay,** Madison wrote *The Federalist,* a collection of essays describing the inadequacy of the Confederation and defending the new charter.

As a member of the House of Representatives (1789–97), Madison was critical of Hamilton's fiscal program, believing that original holders of federal securities who sold them to speculators at a loss should be compensated, and disapproving of the assumption of state debts. He opposed the Bank of the U.S. on constitutional grounds. He soon became the leader of the anti-Federalists in Congress. When the Alien and Sedition Acts were passed (1798), Madison wrote the Virginia Resolutions, which argued that unconstitutional acts could be nullified by the state legislatures.

Madison was Jefferson's secretary of state (1801–9). Elected president in 1808, he inherited the diplomatic difficulties of the Jefferson administration. Congress replaced the ineffective and difficult-to-enforce Non-Intercourse Act (1809) with Macon's Bill No. 2 (1810), which removed restrictions on commerce with Britain and France but continued to bar Anglo-French warships from U.S. waters. The bill also authorized the president to reapply trade restrictions to either Britain or France if the other power accepted America's definition of neutral rights. When Napoleon agreed to this, Madison invoked the act, which indirectly precipitated the War of 1812 with Great Britain.

Originally opposed to the U.S. Bank, Madison was gradually persuaded that only a national bank could preserve a uniform national currency. In 1816, after the War of 1812, he signed a bill chartering a new Bank for twenty years. He also accepted the Tariff of 1816, designed to protect "infant industries." He did, however, retain his constitutional scruples about the use of federal funds for roads and canals, and vetoed efforts for such expenditures.

After his retirement from the presidency in 1817, Madison participated in the Virginia Constitutional Convention in 1829, and was rector of the University of Virginia (1826–34). In his last years he prepared for publication his notes on the Constitutional Convention.

———

Few among the founding generation played a more important role in the establishment of the American republic than James Madison. He lacked most of the traits that are usually associated with successful politicians. Diminutive in stature—he stood only 5 feet 6 inches and weighed but about 130 pounds—Madison possessed neither an imposing physique nor a strong speaking voice. And yet he more than made up for these shortcomings in other ways. Most importantly, both for his historical reputation and for his standing among his contemporaries, Madison had one of the most careful and yet creative political minds of the time. Remarkably well read in history, political philosophy, and constitutional thought, he was equally at home in theoretical debate and in the designing of specific constitutional forms. At a time when problems of political and governmental reconstruction were foremost in American minds, these skills proved of inestimable value.

Madison was skilled as well in the ways of practical politics, especially as it was carried on during the late 18th century. Although the experience of making a revolution and getting new republican governments under way did much to open up the American political system and broaden its membership, political life was still organized around a fairly coherent community of political notables—men such as Washington, Madison, Jefferson, **Albert Gallatin,** and others. Political influence did not yet depend upon either popular oratory or the organization of mass electorates, but upon one's ability to be persuasive within the community of notables. And for this task, Madison was well suited.

The high point of Madison's career came during the last decade and a half of the 18th century. At the Philadelphia Convention he labored with incredible energy and skill to secure the passage of a strong constitution. His note-taking alone, including reports on all but a few of the speeches, would have exhausted many men. But Madison found the strength as well to speak frequently and play a leading role in caucuses in which many of the crucial decisions were made. A firm believer in the principles of republicanism with their emphasis on government by consent and the dangers of irresponsible power, Madison nonetheless believed that an "efficient" national government was essential if the country was to survive its perilous first years. Breaking with the classic assumption that republics were unsuited to large areas or diverse populations because of their vulnerability to factional discord, he theorized that the danger of factions combining into a tyrannical majority was actually lessened as the number of interests within the society increased. Madison broke new ground as well in elaborating theories of federalism in which both state and national governments would receive authority from the people and share in its use. More creatively than anyone else, he found ways of adapting revolutionary republicanism to the needs of a developing nation.

During the 1790s Madison emerged with Thomas Jefferson as one of the leading organizers of political opposition to Federalist policy. The Federalists, Madison argued, seemed determined to expand the national government's powers far beyond what most persons expected. And when criticism of Federalist policies increased, as during the war scare with France in 1798–99, the Federalists showed their readiness to crush it by infringing on the opposition's rights of free speech and association. With Jefferson as the visible party head, Madison worked skillfully in the Congress and among state political leaders to fashion a coherent party force. His efforts were instrumental in the Jeffersonian victory of 1800.

Madison's terms as president failed to measure up to his earlier successes. In part this was because the national Jeffersonian coalition that he headed was disintegrating, thus reducing greatly the possibilities of effective governance. Madison was caught as well in a difficult foreign policy situation, with England putting pressures on the young republic and the American people unable to agree on a common response. But Madison's troubles were of his own making too, for he seemed unable either to develop a consistent foreign policy or to provide effective leadership once the war had begun. Most seriously, he left the War Department to falter under an incompetent secretary and failed to unite the country on a clear definition of the war's purposes. For the

broader and more demanding tasks of continuing executive leadership, Madison proved unsuited. See Irving Brant, *The Life of James Madison* (6 vols., 1948–61), and Brant's briefer *The Fourth President* (1970).

JOHN HOWE

MAHAN, Alfred Thayer (b. West Point, N.Y., Sept. 27, 1840; d. Quogue, L.I., N.Y., Dec. 1, 1914), NAVAL OFFICER, HISTORIAN, graduated from the U.S. Naval Academy in 1859, and served in the U.S. navy until 1896, retiring as a rear admiral. When the Civil War broke out in 1861 he was made a lieutenant and, with the exception of a few months at the Naval Academy, served on blockade duty along the Atlantic coast. In 1865 he was promoted to lieutenant commander. His *The Gulf and Inland Waters,* a naval history of the Civil War, was published in 1883. In 1885 he was promoted to captain.

In 1886 Mahan began a series of lectures at the newly established Naval War College in Newport, Rhode Island. These were later published as *The Influence of Sea Power upon History, 1660–1783* (1890), which argued that a nation with a powerful modern navy with overseas bases would be invincible in war and prosperous in peace.

While president of the War College (1886–89, 1892–93), Mahan published *The Influence of Sea Power upon the French Revolution and Empire, 1793–1812* (2 vols., 1892). In this work he argued that British sea power had offset Napoleon's strength on the Continent. An expansionist, Mahan believed that since the U.S. had already expanded to its continental limits, it must now construct a strong navy and expand outward; America should annex Hawaii, build an isthmian canal, and obtain coaling stations. Mahan's theories, which were published in a number of magazine articles, were collected under the title *The Interest of America in Sea Power* (1897). His views greatly influenced such men as Theodore Roosevelt, Senator **Henry Cabot Lodge,** and Kaiser Wilhelm II of Germany.

Mahan served on the naval board of strategy

when the Spanish-American War broke out (1898) and was a U.S. delegate to the first Hague Peace Conference (1899). *From Sail to Steam,* his reminiscences, was published in 1907. At the time of his death, Mahan was working on a study of American expansion and its relation to sea power.

Mahan's impact on the building of the modern American fleet has perhaps been overestimated. His influence upon naval strategies and American diplomacy after 1890, however, was great. This austere, bookish officer revised naval strategy in the Western world by showing historically how large concentrations of warships triumphed over single, small commerce-destroyers.

His strategy rested on the insight that war is not fighting, but "business"; that is, it could be made systematic and used to advance the national interest. Mahan defined that interest as economic and spiritual. He deprecated socialism, concluding that the American system therefore must be preserved and extended, and that war on behalf of such a system was beneficial for man's individual and social development. He believed the American future lay in Asia, where the United States, allied with such sea powers as Japan and England, would defeat the Russian land forces. His advice, coinciding with the American industrial drive for Asian markets, affected the policies of presidents McKinley and Theodore Roosevelt. After Japan joined with Russia in 1910 to close off parts of Manchuria, Mahan advised an American retreat to the eastern Pacific. He died before World War I might have revised his faith in both the ability to control force rationally and the spiritual qualities arising from war.

Lionized in England and Germany, Mahan was also a prophet with honor at home, a counselor of statesmen, widely read author, president of the American Historical Association, and an influence on post–1945 American military and diplomatic concepts. See William E. Livezey, *Mahan on Sea Power* (1947).

WALTER LaFEBER

MAILER, Norman (b. Long Branch, N.J., Jan. 31, 1923), WRITER, graduated from Harvard with a BS in aeronautical engineering in 1943. Drafted into the army, he served in the Pacific theater until 1946, returning from his war experiences to write an ambitious and hugely successful war novel, *The Naked and the Dead* (1948). The novels that followed, *Barbary Shore* (1951), *The Deer Park* (1955), *An American Dream* (1965), and *Why Are We in Vietnam?* (1967), like the first, focused dramatically on the contradictions inherent in some key aspects of the American experience at mid-century—politics, Hollywood, war, the mores of sex and marriage.

Beginning in the early 1950s and continuing to the present, Mailer's intellectualism and combative temperament drew him increasingly into journalism. His short pieces appeared in a wide variety of periodicals, from such journals as the *Village Voice, Dissent,* and *Commentary* to wider-circulation magazines like *Harper's, Esquire,* and *Life.* He wrote such books of semificationalized commentary, confession, and polemic as *Advertisements for Myself* (1959), *The Presidential Papers* (1963), *Cannibals and Christians* (1966), *The Armies of the Night* (1968), *Miami and the Siege of Chicago* (1968), *Of a Fire on the Moon* (1970), and *The Prisoner of Sex* (1971).

Among several other volumes of Mailer's work, some of them published only in paperback, *Deaths for the Ladies* (*and Other Disasters*) (1962), a book of poems; *The Deer Park, a Play* (1967), the published version of Mailer's successfully produced stage version of his novel; *Maidstone* (1971), the record of the production of Mailer's third film; and *Marilyn* (1973), a pictorial biography of **Marilyn Monroe**, have special interest. In recent years, Mailer has been busy as ever, producing and directing forgettable movies and publishing articles and novels. His latest novels, *Ancient Evenings* (1984) and *Harlot's Ghost* (1991) were big, powerfully written books but got mixed reviews. In 1995, he came out with an account about **Lee Harvey Oswald**, *Oswald's Tale: An American Mystery,* a pastiche of fact and speculation about the assassin of John F. Kennedy. It concluded that he was indeed the murderer as charged. Again, his effort left many reviewers cold.

———∞∞∞———

The dust jacket of Norman Mailer's first book, his best-selling novel about World War II, carried **Sinclair Lewis**'s judgment that Mailer was "the greatest writer to come out of his generation." The critical and popular success of *The Naked and the Dead* seemed to justify this enthusiastic estimate. But Mailer's next two novels, both of which were ventures into fresh imaginative and intellectual territories for their author, were marked failures. Stung by the attacks of critics and the disinterest of the great public, Mailer responded, just over a decade after the great success of his first book, with *Advertisements for Myself,* a mosaic of several years of his work in several genres—stories; fragments of novels in progress; essays on varied political, social, and psychological subjects; interviews—all of these disparate elements tied together by the author's pained and self-defensive autobiographical analysis of a decade's living and writing by Norman Mailer.

Advertisements for Myself was the breakthrough work which was to give Mailer his special identity in American literature of the 1960s and 1970s. Mailer continued to be, of course, a writer. But unlike most of his contemporaries he also turned into a "personage." As a consequence, his life and career very quickly became a visible pattern in the fabric of the public life of his time as he lived out the substance of books that he would later write—books like *The Armies of the Night,* the philosophized narrative of Mailer's seriocomic participation in the great Washington demonstrations against the Vietnam War. (Mailer chose, significantly, to subtitle *Armies* "History as a Novel, the Novel as History.")

In the late 1960s Mailer directed, produced, edited, and acted in three films of his own devising—films "existential" in their realization in that they were unscripted and depended for their dramatic development on the spontaneous interactions of the players within the prescribed situation. They were films about roleplaying aspects of "Mailer," the ambiguous hero of *The Armies of the Night, The Presidential Papers,* and *Advertisements for Myself.* It may be that Mailer's purest creative achievement along these lines, a kind of *nouvelle concrète* in itself, was his 1969 campaign—unsuccessful—to be elected mayor of New York on a statehood-for-New-York-City platform.

But because Norman Mailer's basic medium is always and finally the word, whether or not written down or printed, he will surely be remembered as part of the literature of America. If he is aligned with some identifiable strain in American literature, it seems likely that Mailer will stand with **Emerson, Walt Whitman, F. Scott Fitzgerald,** and others who took the professed idealism of America's middle-class culture as their main subject matter. It is as a prophet of the best ideals of that culture, and as a loving critic of it, that Mailer emerges as a distinctive voice in American literature of the mid–20th century. See Robert F. Lucid, ed., *Norman Mailer: The Man and His Work* (1971); Leo Brandy, ed., *Mailer: A Collection of Critical Essays* (1972).

RICHARD FOSTER

MALCOLM X (b. Omaha, Neb., May 19, 1925; d. New York, N.Y., Feb. 21, 1965), REFORMER, was the son of a Baptist minister who was an organizer for **Marcus Garvey**'s Universal Negro Improvement Association. After growing up in Lansing and Mason, Michigan, Malcolm Little, as he was named at birth, moved (1941) to live with a half-sister in Roxbury, Massachusetts. During the next five years (1941–46) he worked for brief periods as a shoe shiner in the Roseland Ballroom in Boston and as a dining-car worker, but soon became a hustler, operating mainly in Harlem and dealing in drugs, prostitution, and robbery. In 1946 he was sentenced in Boston to a ten-year term for burglary and larceny. While in prison, Little corresponded with **Elijah Muhammad**, the leader of the Nation of Islam—the sect known popularly as the Black Muslims. In 1952, upon his release from the Charlestown, Massachusetts, prison, he went to Detroit, where he joined the sect and took the name Malcolm X. He quickly became a successful recruiter for the Muslims, establishing new Muslim temples in many major American cities. His success, however, led to reported jealousy within the movement's hierarchy. In November 1963, when he referred to President Kennedy's assassination as "chickens coming home to roost," Elijah Muhammad suspended him from the movement.

In March 1964, Malcolm X announced the formation of a new organization, the Muslim Mosque, Inc., in New York City, and urged blacks to arm and form rifle clubs. In June 1964, after the first of two trips to the Middle East and Africa, he proclaimed the creation of an Organization of Afro-American Unity. He began to release stories of immorality and peculations among the Black Muslim leadership. By late 1964, *Muhammad Speaks*, the official Muslim paper, had declared that "only those who wish to be led to hell, or to their doom, will follow Malcolm." In February 1965 fire bombs gutted Malcolm X's home in East Elmhurst, New York. Finally, on February 21, 1965, while addressing four hundred people in the Audubon Ballroom in New York, he was assassinated. Two known Black Muslims, Norman 3X Butler and Thomas 15X Johnson, and a third man identified by the police as a Muslim, Talmadge Hayer, alias Thomas Hagan, were convicted of the murder in 1966. At the trial, the prosecution suggested but did not offer direct evidence that the murder was plotted within the Muslim sect "as an object lesson to Malcolm's followers."

"I am a field Negro," Malcolm X liked to say, and that was precisely his role in the black movement of the 1950s and 1960s: to give voice to the discontents of the grandsons and granddaughters of field slaves in the backstreet ghettos of urban America. Malcolm was a tall, lean, coppery-colored man, oddly formal-looking in half-rimmed glasses and three-piece suits and very nearly priestly in his bearing and his private life. Away from the podium and the television cameras, he was witty, charming, even elegant—a born aristocrat who had re-created himself out of the ashes of his young manhood and who bore little resemblance to his cartoon press reputation as an apostle of hate and violence. But on stage he was a pitiless, merciless witness for the prosecution against white America for its treatment of black people through more than three centuries. He scolded and accused; he ridiculed the orthodox civil rights leadership, **Martin Luther King, Jr.**, most of all; he attacked integration and intermarriage as bitterly as any southern segregationist; he rejoiced at storms, plane crashes, even the Kennedy assassination—anything that caused white people grief or pain. "Whatever I say, I'm justified," he told an interviewer once; it was a charter he exercised for a dozen years with unremitting fury.

Malcolm was a Black Muslim for most of that time and so believed and preached as literal truth that white people were devils; that Allah was about to visit a terrible vengeance on them; that blacks must accordingly separate from them, to Africa or a partitioned-off part of the United States. His gifts as an advocate and his intuitive genius for the mass media helped transform the Muslims from a storefront sect of perhaps four hundred souls to a small but thriving nation of ten thousand signed-up members and many more sympathizers who saw no relevance to their own lives in the struggle against southern-style segregation. Yet a split became inevitable as Malcolm's fame grew and as his increasing worldliness led him further and further from the cultish beliefs of the Nation of Islam.

Once outside, he made the hajj (or pilgrimage) to Mecca, began a conversion to orthodox Islam, and moderated his views about the inherent evil of whites—though never about what seemed to him the inherent racism of white American society. He spent much of his last year trying to "internationalize" the black American struggle by bringing it before the United Nations; he was brilliantly received on his travels in Africa, but the effort ended in disappointment. His political and religious views were still changing rapidly at his death: he incorporated elements of black nationalism, pan-Africanism, Third World socialism, and Sunni Muslim religious belief into an improvisational mix he summed up in the slogan "freedom *by any means necessary.*"

Malcolm sought but never quite achieved respectability during his lifetime; he was attacked in the press, spurned by the established civil rights movement, and generally written off by most whites and many blacks as a kind of spiritual outlaw. But his reputation and his influence grew enormously after the publication of his brilliant posthumous *Autobiography*. He is widely recognized now as having been the harbinger of a new black consciousness in America—the proud, bold, assertive sense of racial identity that was to flower in the Black Power movement of the latter 1960s. His ministry revealed, to many Americans for the first time, the depths of rage among those of the big-city black poor for whom the white man was the oppressor, integration a trick, nonviolence a deathtrap, and violence of speech and action a legitimate last recourse. "When I speak," Malcolm said, "I speak as a *victim* of America's so-called democracy." He did not create the ghetto's antipathy to whites, nor did he practice violence. But he recognized both undercurrents and saw their explosive potential, and the mission he set for himself was to make America see them, too. See Malcolm X (with Alex Haley), *The Autobiography of Malcolm X* (1965) and Peter Goldman, *Malcolm X* (1972).

PETER GOLDMAN

MANN, Horace (b. Franklin, Mass., May 4, 1796; d. Yellow Springs, Ohio, Aug. 2, 1859), EDUCATOR, REFORMER, was raised in relative poverty, and until the age of sixteen never attended school for more than eight or ten weeks in any one year. In 1816, after a six-month preparation, he entered Brown University, graduating in 1819. He then worked briefly in a law office in Wrentham, Massachusetts, before returning to Brown as a tutor in Latin and Greek (1819–21).

In 1821 Mann entered the Litchfield (Conn.) Law School, and was admitted to the bar in 1823. During 1823–37 he practiced law in Dedham and Boston. He also served in the Massachusetts house (1827–33) and senate (1833–37; president, 1835–37), where he advocated state hospitals for the insane, the restriction of slavery, regulation of liquor sales, and educational reforms. In April 1837 he helped secure passage of an educational bill which provided for the creation of a state board of education; he then served as the board's secretary (1837–48). Under his leadership the powers of the secretary were expanded and numerous reforms instituted. In 1838 he launched the *Common School Journal*, a semi-monthly magazine (editor, 1838–48). The following year he won his fight to have the minimum school year attendance requirement extended to six months.

Believing that schools must be staffed by highly qualified personnel, Mann advocated the establishment of teachers' institutes. In 1839 the first public normal school in the U.S. was opened in Lexington, Massachusetts. He was also a leader in the fight for nonsectarian education. In his annual reports he discussed new teaching methods and described educational practices abroad. By 1848, when he resigned, state appropriations for education had more than doubled, approximately fifty new public schools had been established in Massachusetts, teachers' salaries had been substantially increased, local schools had been put under the control of a central board, and the school curriculum had been greatly modified.

In 1848 Mann, an antislavery Whig, entered the U.S. Congress to occupy the seat left vacant by the death of John Quincy Adams. He served until 1853. In 1852, running on the Free Soil ticket, he was defeated for governor of Massachusetts. From 1853 until his death he was the president of Antioch College. In 1854 he published *Lectures on Education*.

As Homer provided the definitive statement of myths by which the Greeks defined their fundamental assumptions and ideals, so Horace Mann codified the myth for American public schools. More than a century after 1840 those who promoted the public school echoed the voice of Horace Mann, consciously or not. Mann did not originate the myth; he did provide its definitive statement. From a ritualistic standpoint he was perceived as the "founding father" *par excel-*

lence. In these ways he made a forceful impact on American history.

As secretary of the Massachusetts Board of Education, and adviser to educators and legislators in many states, Mann also helped to shape modes of organizing, supporting, controlling, and teaching in elementary and secondary schools. The normal schools he promoted and nurtured have a continuing influence on teacher preparation throughout the nation. Yet important as Mann's contributions were in these matters, he was not clearly exceptional among the promoters and shapers of American public education. **Henry Barnard,** for example, may have had much greater impact. It is as a symbol and rhetorician that Mann stands above others.

Mann's fame as an educator tended, and tends, to blind people to his long and effective career as a leader in the Massachusetts Whig party and, particularly, as a spokesman for the antislavery wing of that party. He brought to the antislavery political wars the same fierce determination and singleness of purpose that characterized his career as educator.

The concept of the public school as the "great balance wheel" of society was central in Mann's argument. Potentially destructive social conflict could, he argued, be prevented by schools which, on the one hand, provided equality of opportunity and social mobility and, on the other hand, indoctrinated all children in a common public faith.

On pedagogical matters Mann was convinced that human nature is highly malleable and that, unless socially corrupted, the impulses of the child tend toward growth in intellectual power and in beneficence toward other human beings. Given these assumptions, he argued, coercive discipline in schools was unnecessary and positively dysfunctional.

Although his overt commitments were those of a humane, 19th-century liberal Christian, Mann was nonetheless a zealot. He talked and behaved as if he both expected and desired martyrdom. Occasionally maudlin, often arrogant, he invested incredible time and energy in what he apparently perceived as an unending war of attrition between himself and social evil. He was among those people who wear themselves out rather than aging and dying gracefully.

Perhaps the key to his personality lies in his relations to 18th-century New England Calvinism. Both his grandfather and the most powerful figure in the community of his childhood were traditional Calvinist ministers, deeply impressed with the sinfulness of mankind. On an intellectual level Horace Mann vigorously rejected Calvinist theology and sought a secular function and philosophy. Nevertheless, he behaved as one with a sacred calling and as one who half-believed himself deserving of damnation. See Jonathan Messerli, *Horace Mann: A Biography* (1972).

MERLE L. BORROWMAN

MARCUSE, Herbert (b. Berlin, Germany, July 19, 1898; d. Starnberg, Germany, July 29, 1979), PHILOSOPHER, was educated at the University of Berlin, and received his PhD in philosophy from the University of Freiburg in 1922. After doing postgraduate work there Marcuse joined the Institute of Social Research, an affiliate of the University of Frankfurt which had been founded in 1923 by Theodor Adorno and Max Horkheimer. He published his first major book, *Hegel's Ontology* (1932), a study of the meaning of some Hegelian concepts. The Institute was shut down in 1933 because of Nazi pressure and Marcuse reopened it in Geneva. In 1934 he then moved the Institute to Columbia University in New York City where he also served as a lecturer; he became an American citizen in 1940. After publishing *Reason and Revolution* (1941), which introduced Hegelian concepts to American audiences, Marcuse joined the Office of Strategic Services and then the State Department's Office of Intelligence Research, where he served as its chief of the Central Europe section until 1950, establishing himself as an expert on Russian affairs. He was a research fellow with the Russian Institute at Columbia from 1951 to 1953 and also lectured in the Russian Research Center at Harvard (1952–53).

In 1954 Marcuse became professor of politics and philosophy at Brandeis University. He wrote *Eros and Civilization* (1954), a Freudian view of social and political repression, *Soviet Marxism* (1958), a largely critical view of Soviet communism, and *One-Dimensional Man* (1965), an application of *Eros* ideas to American society. He became professor of political philosophy at the University of California at San Diego in La Jolla, California, in 1965. While lecturing in Europe in 1967–68 Marcuse consulted with many student leaders of the radical New Left movement, including German Rudolf ("Red Rudi") Dutschke. Upon his return, the citizens of La Jolla tried to have him dismissed for his alleged radical connections and a threat was made on his life. The university, however, backed Marcuse. As the social unrest of the sixties faded into history, Marcuse, sometimes called the "Father of the New Left" faded out of the public spotlight. He retired in La Jolla and continued to lecture in the United States and overseas. But he was no longer the darling of the campuses and in 1971, in Germany, he was shouted down while lecturing to a student audience. But Marcuse never became disillusioned by the conservative tendencies of the 70s. He regarded the hippies and yippies as true "heroes," who did their thing and helped change society. But, he said, "we have moved into a different period, a higher period in terms of historical sequence. We are now in the midst of the organized counterrevolution. You cannot have fun with fascism." Some of Marcuse's writings included *Negations* (1968), a series of essays, *An Essay on Liberation* (1969), *Five Lectures* (1970), *Counter-revolution and Revolt* (1972), and *Studies in Critical Philosophy* (1973).

———— ❧ ————

As a philosopher and social critic, Herbert Marcuse belonged initially to the émigré Frankfurt School, whose most prominent figure was Theodor W. Adorno. Like Adorno and his colleagues, Marcuse's style of thought was Hegelian and deeply influenced by both Marx and Freud. He was distinguished, however, from the other members of the school by his greater fidelity to Hegel (his *Reason and Revolution* remains a basic work on this philosopher); by the fact that he chose to stay in America rather than to return to Germany after World War II; and by his effort to envision what a "nonrepressive" society would look like. This last point of distinction—the utopian or even anarchist strain in Marcuse's writing—helps to explain his polemical stance from the late 1960s on, more particularly his militant opposition to "neocolonialism," which won him the admiration of the student left.

Although *One-Dimensional Man* was the book that offered his fullest critique of contemporary industrial civilization—a critique focused on the "flattening out" of values and the narrowing of meaningful choices—*Eros and Civilization* ranks as his most original work. In it, he applied to Freud the same technique he had earlier used on Hegel: he transformed both into revolutionaries. In the case of Freud, this interpretation entailed coining two new psychoanalytic terms: "surplus repression" and the "performance principle." Marcuse reversed Freud's own pessimistic assessment of the psychic cost of civilization by asserting that under contemporary conditions society demanded far more instinctual repression than was materially or morally necessary. In so doing, Marcuse became a leading exponent of the "Freudian Left" and adopted as his own the slogan of the young militants: "Make love, not war." See Alasdair MacIntyre, *Herbert Marcuse: An Exposition and a Polemic* (1970).

H. STUART HUGHES

MARIN, John Cheri, III (b. Rutherford, N.J., Dec. 23, 1870; d. Addison, Maine, Oct. 1, 1953), ARTIST, grew up in Weehawken, New Jersey. After several years in architects' offices, he practiced architecture briefly and unsatisfactorily, then drew and painted until the end of the century, often on trips that extended as far as the Mississippi Valley. After cursory attendance at the Pennsylvania Academy of the Fine Arts in Philadelphia (1899–1901) and the Art Students League in New York (1901–3), he went abroad in

1905, working independently in etching and watercolor. In 1909 a one-man show was given him by the photographer and art patron **Alfred Stieglitz** at the Photo-Secession Gallery in New York. Marin exhibited there annually until the gallery closed in 1917. Returning permanently to America in 1911, he entered ten works in the Armory Show of 1913, and by the end of that decade was established as an avant-garde painter specializing in watercolors. Later he worked increasingly in oils. In any of the media his mature style was a terse, semiabstract, and dynamic expression of natural forms and their inherent rhythms. His subjects consisted mainly of Manhattan cityscapes (1922, *Red Sun, Brooklyn Bridge*, watercolor, Art Institute of Chicago), landscapes (1945, *Tunk Mountains, Autumn, Maine*, oil, Phillips Memorial Gallery, Washington, D.C.), and seascapes (1935, *Cape Split, Maine*, watercolor, Marlborough Gallery, N.Y.).

From 1916 Marin lived atop the Palisades at Cliffside, New Jersey, but spent his summers in the country or at the seashore, the latter especially after his acquisition in 1934 of a house on Pleasant Bay, Cape Split, Maine. In addition to yearly shows under the auspices of Stieglitz, whose An American Place opened in 1930, Marin exhibited widely, and in 1936 was honored by a major retrospective exhibition at the New York Museum of Modern Art. He is extensively represented in American public and private collections.

As he neared eighty John Marin found himself widely regarded—statistically rated, indeed, in a poll of our art cognoscenti—as the foremost living American painter.

To the artist himself this probably seemed pleasant but rather stuffy. He shied away from Importance, preferred Simplicity: his basic desiderata were health, sanity, and a continuing buoyant delight in a living world that he found "beautiful." Confessing to "a Spleen" about certain notions encountered in art circles, he specified "the non objective approach," the "Exaltation of torture," the "great moral lesson"; and in general he had no stomach for "that deadly humor-lacking/that deadly fun and play lacking/Those who would Start Symphonies early in life/those who would Startle the world. …" He could sincerely refer to his own exciting creations as "my playthings."

Marin had been leisurely enough in his own beginnings—"I was a boy until I was thirty"—and displayed no salient indications of genius before arriving in Europe in 1905 (that momentous year of les Fauves in Paris and die Brücke in Dresden). Even then he was slower than some of his compatriots in converting to a modern idiom, turning rather to masters such as **Whistler,** Méryon, and Rembrandt for guidance in the etching medium that then attracted him.

But soon his prints and watercolors gave evidence of the impact of Cubist and Expressionist developments. When in 1911 he came home to stay, he had gathered all that he needed for a quick and henceforth undeviating advancement into work that in concept and execution was exclusively his own—and, most would say, essentially American.

He made his personal discovery of Manhattan Island, sensed the dynamics of its streets, buildings, bridges, and harbors; however, his inherent affinity was for the natural scene, for landscape and seascape. Magnetically, it would seem, he was drawn northeastward, up the coast, until for the final two decades of his life he lived (except during the winters) on Maine's Cape Split—as far Down East as one can get without leaving the country, and as intimate with the ever active ocean as **Winslow Homer**'s Prout's Neck.

Marin's earliest and greatest acclaim was for his work in watercolor, a medium suited to his procedure, the rapid notation of an empathic reaction to something seen—skyscraper, mountain, choppy sea, rarely the human figure. On paper, drawing with pencil, charcoal, or brush, washing with entrancing color, always conscious of relating to the flat surface, he depicted a contained action—"a jolly good fight"—of symbols abstracted from his subject. A result for the observer is the transmission of a stimulating visual experience.

For a while the éclat of the watercolors impeded the public acceptance of Marin's painting in oils, but with true feeling for this weightier medium he turned to it increasingly during his advancing career. In the forties, while what he called "the noise" was being made by abstract expressionists in New York, Marin in retreat on Cape Split, aging in years yet young in spirit, detachedly explored new ways of "using paint as paint" and engendering movement on the pictorial surface.

"As for painting," he then wrote teasingly to his also aging friend Stieglitz, "I've given that up—I just tie a brush to my fingers and let that old silly brush do that painting." And that brush kept at it, like the apprentice's broom, until in his case death broke the spell. See Clive Gray, ed., *John Marin* (1970).

HAROLD E. DICKSON

MARKHAM, Edwin (b. Oregon City, Ore., April 23, 1852; d. Staten Island, N.Y., March 7, 1940), POET, REFORMER, grew up on a ranch in Lagoon Valley, near San Francisco. He spent an unhappy childhood dominated by his bitter, eccentric mother, who had separated from his father. Graduating from Christian College, Santa Rosa, in 1873, he taught school at Coloma, California. Restless and ambitious, he studied socialism and wrote poetry. During the 1880s he succeeded in publishing poems in various magazines, including *Scribner's* and the *Century.* On January 15, 1899, the San Francisco *Examiner* published his "The Man with the Hoe," inspired by Millet's painting, which made Markham world famous. The poem was eventually translated into forty languages. He then moved to New York, where in 1900 his poem "Lincoln" won him further renown. A leading figure in the Progressive Era, Markham contributed to it his 1906 child labor series in *Cosmopolitan,* "The Hoe-man in the Making." He became a kind of national institution, although his verse made less impression as time passed. His masterpiece, "The Ballad of the Gallows-Bird," was published in **H. L. Mencken**'s *American Mercury,* August 1926, but little noted.

Much identified with the Poetry Society of America, Markham lectured frequently.

Although Markham came to be known as "the dean of American poets," it was evident through most of his public life that the mainstream of American poetry had passed him by. His birthday became a national event, eliciting telegrams from notables and newspaper commentary. Nevertheless, his death put an instant quietus on his memory: evidence of unresolved aspects in Markham's life and work. These doubtful matters were partly of his own making. In his early years he became a dreamer capable of vivid fantasies, the first being that his parents were not divorced, but that his father had died; and that his youth had been a fruitful time, rather than one of constant harassment by a bleak and disturbed mother. Markham also kept obscure his long commitment to the transcendentalist views of the communal experimenter Thomas Lake Harris, and even the evidence of his early marriages. Thus he created a serene image of a species of civilized **Walt Whitman** which pleased the women's clubs, but blurred examination of his vision and philosophy.

"The Man with the Hoe" set up an image of Markham as a reformer which seemed increasingly innocuous, and nullified his religious quest without consolidating his place in reform. "The Hoe-man in the Making," published with additions by others in 1914 as *Children in Bondage,* is one of the era's notable reform writings. Markham undoubtedly dissipated many of his opportunities, being tempted by easy acclaim, which included a year of constant adulation during California's 1915 Panama-Pacific Exposition and his reading of the Lincoln poem at the dedication of the Lincoln Memorial in 1922. A residue of his strongest verse and strongest prose—including letters still uncollected—offers a sense of his numerous significant contacts and associates. See Louis Filler, *The Unknown Edwin Markham* (1966).

LOUIS FILLER

MARSH, George Perkins (b. Woodstock, Vt., March 15, 1801; d. Vallombrosa, Italy, July 23, 1882), SCIENTIST, DIPLOMAT, graduated from Dartmouth College in 1820, was admitted to the bar in 1825, and practiced law in Burlington, Vermont, 1825–34. In 1834 he was elected to the Vermont legislature; in 1835 he was named to the state's supreme executive council, and in 1842 he was elected to Congress as a Whig. He served in Congress until 1849, supporting protective tariffs and opposing the extension of slavery and the Mexican War. As a philologist, Marsh in this period wrote *A Compendious Grammar of the Old-Northern or Icelandic Language* (1838) and *The Goths in New England* (1843), a celebration of Teutonic influences on English language and literature.

In 1849 President Taylor appointed Marsh minister to Turkey. He helped Kossuth and other refugees seek political asylum following the 1848 revolutions, and in 1852 he secured the release from prison in Greece of the American missionary Jonas King. He was recalled in 1854. During 1855 he lectured on English philology and etymology at Columbia. In 1856 he published *The Camel: His Organization, Habits, and Uses, Considered with Reference to His Introduction into the U.S.,* and in 1857–59 served as Vermont state railroad commissioner. He lectured again in 1860–61 at Lowell Institute. Marsh joined the Republican party in 1856, and in 1861 Lincoln appointed him minister to the kingdom of Italy, in which post he remained until his death. While in Italy he wrote *The Origin and History of the English Language* (1862) and *Man and Nature, or Physical Geography as Modified by Human Action* (1864).

———— ∞ ————

For most of his history man simply accepted the environment into which he was born as a fact of life—a "given" he neither created nor controlled. The greatest achievement in the multifaceted career of Marsh was to understand and publicize the fact that the condition of the environment was as much a product of man as of nature. On his travels in the Mediterranean region, in connection with his ministries to Turkey and Italy, Marsh saw land that centuries of careless exploitation had reduced to barren dust. Part of the reason Rome and other empires fell, it occurred to him, might have been the exhaustion of their environment's supporting ability. In particular Marsh bemoaned the loss of the forests surrounding the Mediterranean and the consequent cycle of drought, flood, and erosion. Back in the United States, he saw widespread evidence of the same practices that had wasted parts of Europe and the Near East. His most important book, *Man and Nature,* was intended to warn his countrymen that man's power to transform the environment must entail a commensurate sense of responsibility or civilization itself would be imperiled. A massive tome, the book reflected Marsh's painstaking abilities as scientist and researcher as well as his lawyer's skill at persuasive argument.

One of the first Americans to grasp the meaning of and necessity for stewardship of the earth, Marsh deeply influenced leaders of the early conservation movement such as **Gifford Pinchot,** who read *Man and Nature* as a college student. And Marsh's concept of "geographical regeneration" was a harbinger of regional reclamation efforts such as that involving the Tennessee Valley. In retrospect Marsh's contributions to awakening American concern for the environment overshadow his considerable accomplishments in philology, government, and diplomacy. See David Lowenthal, *George Perkins Marsh: Versatile Vermonter* (1958).

RODERICK NASH

MARSH, Othniel Charles (b. Lockport, N.Y., Oct. 29, 1831; d. New Haven, Conn., March 18, 1899), PALEONTOLOGIST, graduated from Yale (1860) and then attended the universities in Berlin, Breslau, and Heidelberg, Germany (1862–65). In 1866 he was appointed professor of paleontology at Yale, the first such position in this country, and he served until his death.

In 1870 Marsh organized his first Yale scientific expedition. In this and numerous later expeditions, he explored Mesozoic and Tertiary deposits throughout the western U.S. Until 1880, Marsh financed these expeditions privately, but in 1882 he received government support, being appointed vertebrate paleontologist of the U.S. Geological Survey, which he helped to establish. In these expeditions, he discovered more than one thousand new fossil vertebrates, including the first pterodactyl in America (1871) and the first American Jurassic mammals (1878). Of these, he described more than five hundred in numerous papers in the *American Journal of Science,* and in such books as *Odontornithes: A Monograph on the Extinct Toothed Birds of North America* (1880), *Dinocerata: A Monograph on an Extinct Order of Gigantic Mammals* (1884), *Introduction and Succession of Vertebrate Life in America* (1877), and *Dinosaurs of North America* (1896).

Marsh played a leading role in revealing the widespread corruption within the Bureau of Indian Affairs (the Red Cloud Affair, 1874–75) by showing President Grant the moldy flour and beef that the Bureau was providing dependent Native Americans. He also served as president of the National Academy of Sciences (1883–95).

— ⚒ —

During his lifetime Marsh was one of the most influential scientists in the New World, and his reputation was well known internationally. As the first professor of paleontology in America, at a time when natural sciences were flourishing, Marsh quickly gained prominence as a consequence of the large collections of new and strange vertebrate fossils that his expeditions recovered from the western wilderness. The fossils themselves generated much public interest, but they stimulated greater excitement within the scientific community and were heralded by all the eminent scientists of the day, including such notables as Alexander Agassiz, James Dwight Dana, Charles Darwin, Thomas Huxley, and Sir Richard Owen. Darwin himself wrote to Marsh, praising him for his work on the fossil animals of North America that "has afforded the best support to the theory of evolution, which has appeared within the last 20 years." Huxley visit-

ed Marsh at Yale specifically to study these collections, and especially those of fossil horses. This last, very celebrated, collection is the basis of the first evolutionary lineage to be established on fossil evidence, and its recognition and publication by Marsh brought him much acclaim. Marsh's contributions to the knowledge of ancient and extinct life covers most of the vertebrate spectrum, but he is perhaps best known for his enormous collections of dinosaurs that now occupy the galleries of the National Museum of Natural History in Washington, D.C., and the Peabody Museum of Natural History at Yale University. Other major contributions are the precious collections of Jurassic mammals from Wyoming, the Cretaceous toothed birds from Kansas, and a broad spectrum of archaic, primitive mammals from the Tertiary deposits of South Dakota, Nebraska, Wyoming, and Colorado.

Marsh was a man of strong personality and will, rather stern and formal in appearance, and of stiff and sometimes pompous bearing. His stubborn and combative nature is well evidenced by his highly publicized, stormy encounters during the Red Cloud controversy and his long-term running feud with another government scientist, E. D. Cope. Marsh was a proud and jealous man, a man possessed of great energy and drive, strong determination, and an obsession to collect objects of natural science. He thrived on public attention and acclaim, yet he seems to have been aloof and remote except with his closest friends.

One of America's first and most outspoken exponents of the Darwinian theory of evolution by natural selection, Marsh published a large number of scientific papers and described and named hundreds of new species of ancient organisms. But his greatest monument is the large fossil collections at Yale and the National Museum that even today have not yet been completely studied. See Charles Schuchert and C. M. LaVene, *Othniel C. Marsh: Pioneer in Paleontology* (1940).

JOHN H. OSTROM

MARSHALL, George Catlett, Jr. (b. Uniontown, Pa., Dec. 31, 1880; d. Washington,

D.C., Oct. 16, 1959), MILITARY LEADER, DIPLOMAT, graduated from Virginia Military Institute (1901) and entered the army in 1902 as a second lieutenant. He served in the Philippines (1902–3) and in the Oklahoma Territory and Texas (1903–6). In 1906–7 he attended the Infantry-Cavalry School at Fort Leavenworth, Kansas, and graduated from the School of the Line (forerunner of the Command and General Staff School) at Leavenworth the following year. He was an instructor at the school (1908–10) and then served as inspector-instructor of the Massachusetts state militia (1911–12). Following another tour of the Philippines (1913–16), where he served as aide-de-camp to generals J. Franklin Bell and Hunter Liggett, he returned as Bell's aide in San Francisco and on Governors Island, New York (1916–17). He served with the 1st Division in France after the U.S. entered World War I, helping to train its troops and plan operations. Later he helped plan the St. Mihiel offensive (Sept. 1918) and, as chief of operations of the First Army, helped prepare the Meuse-Argonne offensive (Sept.–Nov. 1918).

After serving as General **Pershing**'s aide-de-camp (1919–24), Marshall served three years in Tientsin, China (1924–27) and at the Infantry School, Fort Benning, Georgia (1927–32). As assistant commandant in charge of instruction at Benning, he influenced many future World War II commanders—generals **Omar Bradley, Joseph Stilwell,** J. Lawton Collins, Walter Bedell Smith, and many others. During the thirties he worked with the Civilian Conservation Corps in Georgia, South Carolina, Oregon, and Washington. He was also senior instructor of the Illinois National Guard (1933–36). He became a brigadier general and commander of the 5th Infantry Brigade at Vancouver Barracks, Washington in 1936. In 1938 Marshall was appointed chief of the War Department's War Plans Division and became deputy chief of staff of the army a few months later. He became chief of staff in September 1939.

After the outbreak of World War II, Marshall urged military preparedness, a peacetime draft, and the federalizing of the National Guard for one year's training. He attended all of the key international war conferences from Argentina (1941) through Casablanca (1943), Tehran-Cairo (1943), Yalta (1945), to Potsdam (1945). His influence was crucial in the adoption of the cross-Channel invasion route over Churchill's Mediterranean strategy. Because Franklin D. Roosevelt felt Marshall was too valuable in his post as chief of staff, he was not appointed supreme commander of the invasion—as the president had initially intended. Instead his protégé, General Dwight D. Eisenhower, was selected for the post. At the end of 1944, Marshall was named general of the army with rank over all other five-star generals and admirals except Admiral Leahy. In November 1945 he resigned as chief of staff; soon thereafter he was appointed to head the mission to China with orders to seek a reconciliation between the Nationalists and Communists. In January 1947 he became secretary of state.

During his early months in the State Department, the Truman Doctrine to aid Greece and Turkey was outlined and the European Recovery Program to help in the reconstruction of war-torn European nations (Marshall Plan) was announced (in a speech by Marshall at Harvard on June 5, 1947). He attended the Inter-American conference at Brazil in 1948 which drew up the Western Hemisphere Defense Pact. He resigned as secretary early the following year. Shortly after the outbreak of war in Korea in 1950, he became secretary of defense and served one year. He pushed for the rebuilding of the army and for a plan of universal military service. He oversaw some of the early operations of the Korean conflict and supported Truman's decision to remove General **Douglas MacArthur** in 1951. Senator **Joseph McCarthy** attacked Marshall in 1951, charging that he headed a "conspiracy" to give the Far East to the communists during Truman's administration. Marshall won the Nobel Peace Prize in 1953.

Few men in American history so well deserved the title "soldier statesman" as did General of the Army George C. Marshall, the only career soldier to win the Nobel Prize for peace. He combined more than forty years of service as a superb professional soldier with outstanding service in positions normally held by civilians (mission to China, secretary of state, head of the American Red Cross, and secretary of defense). Although a dedicated soldier, he firmly held that the military should be subject to civilian authority. In accord with this view, he backed President Truman's decision to remove General MacArthur from his Far East command in 1951.

Although not descended from a military family, Marshall developed an interest in a soldierly career before entering the Virginia Military Institute. The outbreak of the Spanish-American War while he was in school helped to strengthen his inclinations—which were not shared by his parents. A western Pennsylvania boyhood, spent near areas closely associated with George Washington's early military exploits, and his exposure to the traditions of **Robert E. Lee** and **Stonewall Jackson** while a cadet at VMI undoubtedly were of great importance in his final decision.

Aloof, self-disciplined, a man with a fiery temper usually under rigid control, decisive, he was a splendid staff officer and an outstanding administrator. At the War and Defense departments and in the Department of State, he instituted striking reforms to get better long-range planning, clearer channels of command, and greater simplicity of operations.

Tall, erect, quietly self-confident, he impressed his associates by his air of command. In the conferences of the Combined Chiefs of Staff, he took the lead in pressing for cross-Channel versus Mediterranean strategy. Although vigorous in his championing of his cause, he helped solve many deadlocks by searching for possible compromise solutions. His quiet authority, capacity to see the global picture, and understanding of the army's needs made him the one American officer capable of dealing with strong-minded commanders in farflung theaters of operations in World War II—a fact which led President Roosevelt to decide at the end of 1943 that he could not spare him from Washington.

As chief of staff of the United States Army,

Marshall was the only one of the top American and British top-level military and political leaders to hold his post from the day the war opened in Europe until after the surrender of Japan. Under his command the U.S. army and the U.S. army air forces grew from some 200,000 to 8,300,000. Recalling the general's role in raising and training a superb fighting force, selecting outstanding officers, and procuring the equipment and weapons necessary for the war effort, Winston Churchill called him "the true organizer of victory."

An effective impromptu speaker and powerful witness before congressional committees, General Marshall won strong bipartisan backing in Congress and from the nation's press. His insistence on staying clear of politics served him well when he led the fight for the passage of legislation providing for the European Recovery program.

The last years of his life, while somewhat overshadowed by bitter criticisms of his China mission and the MacArthur removal, were brightened by expressions of national and international recognition of his contributions. These included, in addition to the Nobel Peace Prize, his appointment by President Eisenhower to head the mission which represented the United States at the coronation of Elizabeth II, the tributes of countries receiving Marshall Plan aid, and the beginning of a campaign, instigated by President Truman and supported strongly by President Eisenhower, to build a George C. Marshall Research Library at Lexington, Virginia. See Forrest C. Pogue, *George C. Marshall* (4 vols., 1963–1987).

FORREST C. POGUE

MARSHALL, John (b. Germantown [now Midland], Va., Sept. 24, 1755; d. Philadelphia, Pa., July 6, 1835), JURIST, served in the Virginia militia (1775), and entered the Continental army when the Revolutionary War broke out, rising from lieutenant to captain. In 1780, after brief study at the College of William and Mary, he was admitted to the bar. He was elected to the Virginia state assembly in 1782, and was made recorder of Fauquier County in 1785.

Marshall was a delegate to the Virginia convention to ratify the Constitution (1788), where he supported the Charter. President John Adams appointed him (with C. C. Pinckney and **Elbridge Gerry)** to a commission to negotiate a treaty of amity with France (1797), but when the French ministers refused to negotiate unless they were given a bribe (XYZ Affair), the Americans returned home. President Adams offered Marshall a seat on the Supreme Court in 1798, but he declined it. In 1799 he was elected to Congress as a Federalist. The next year Adams appointed him secretary of state, and in 1801 the president named Marshall chief justice of the Supreme Court.

In his first major decision as chief justice, Marshall established the power of the Supreme Court (*Marbury* v. *Madison*, 1803) to invalidate a law of Congress. In *Fletcher* v. *Peck* (1810), he held that the constitutional guarantee of the sanctity of contracts prohibited a state (Georgia) from rescinding a grant of public land, despite the fact that the grant was obtained by dubious means. He reinforced this principle in *Dartmouth College* v. *Woodward* (1819), decreeing that the New Hampshire legislature could not alter Dartmouth's charter without the consent of all parties concerned. In *McCulloch* v. *Maryland* (1819), Marshall established the constitutionality of the Bank of the U.S. and denied the states the right to tax a federal institution. In *Gibbons* v. *Ogden* (1824), he broke a state-granted monopoly of steam navigation between New York and New Jersey, broadly defining the federal government's power to regulate interstate commerce. While he was chief justice, Marshall also wrote a *Life of George Washington* (5 vols., 1804–7).

Marshall, who by common consent is recognized as the undisputed colossus of American constitutional law, was both a classic 18th-century liberal and a devotee of Federalist party nationalism. As a follower of John Locke, William Blackstone, and Emmerich Vattel, he believed that the purpose of government and organized society was the protection of man's intrinsic prepolitical rights—life, liberty, and property—to the end of stability, order, and progress. As a Federalist nationalist he was imbued not only with a profound sense of patriotism and love of country but also with the conviction that the great fundamental objectives of government could be secured only by the establishment of an effective national government endowed with adequate sovereign powers.

Marshall's judicial opinions are concerned above all with three or four fundamental constitutional ideas. Most important is the doctrine of national supremacy, which holds that the United States is a nation and not a mere league of sovereign states, that within its sphere of delegated powers the national government possesses full sovereignty, and that in conflicts between federal sovereignty, properly exercised, and that of the states, federal sovereignty must always prevail. Thus in *Cohens* v. *Virginia* (1821), in which Marshall upheld the right of the Supreme Court, pursuant to Section 25 of the Judiciary Act of 1789, to hear appeals on constitutional questions from the various state judiciaries, he declared in a moving passage that for "many purposes" the United States "form … a single nation," and that in many fundamental respects "the American people are one." The right of appeal he defended as intrinsic to the maintenance of federal sovereignty and as implicit in the language of the Constitution itself.

Of almost equal importance was Marshall's exposition of the classic doctrine of broad construction of delegated federal powers. In *McCulloch* v. *Maryland,* Marshall and the Court upheld the constitutionality of the act chartering the Second Bank of the United States, although power to establish such an institution was nowhere mentioned in the Constitution. "Let the end be legitimate," Marshall declared, "let it be within the scope of the Constitution, and all means which are appropriate, which are plainly adapted to that end, and which are not prohibited, are constitutional." Again, in *Gibbons* v. *Ogden*, Marshall, in striking down a New York steamboat monopoly grant as an interference with the federal commerce power, found occasion to define that power in the broadest possible terms. "Commerce," he declared, "undoubtedly, is traffic, but it is something more; it is intercourse." Here was language broad enough to enable Court and Congress at a later date to bring the entire national economy within the sweep of federal sovereignty.

Marshall's concern for property and for vested rights, which he saw ultimately as a means to the protection of liberty, individualism, and social progress, found expression in his expansive exposition of the clause in Article I, Section 10, which prohibits the states from enacting any "law impairing the obligation of contracts." In *Fletcher* v. *Peck* he applied the contracts clause to invalidate a Georgia statute which had rescinded a tainted legislative grant to a private land company. Thereby he brought contracts to which the state itself was a party within the sweep of the clause, although this interpretation was historically questionable. And in *Dartmouth College* v. *Woodward*, he declared that a state charter granted to a private corporation also constituted a contract within the meaning of the Constitution. Marshall's dictum, which amounted to a kind of bill of immunity for private business corporations against governmental interference, is still good law although greatly hedged about by subsequent decisions protecting state police power.

Finally, the doctrine of judicial supremacy, which holds that the Court by means of its review of both federal and state legislation should act as the final expositor of the constitutional system, permeates most of Marshall's decisions. In *Marbury* v. *Madison*, he used his brilliant capacity for syllogistic logic to uphold the Court's right to declare void an act of Congress. But it was through his consistent exercise of the Court's asserted power to review state legislation that Marshall established most firmly the role of the Court as "the balance wheel" of the Constitution. He successfully expounded the principles of federal sovereignty which were to be confirmed later by the Civil War, and which are today the very foundation of American nationhood. See Robert K. Faulkner, *The*

Jurisprudence of John Marshall (1968), and Leonard Baker, *John Marshall: A Life in Law* (1974).

ALFRED H. KELLY

MARSHALL, Thurgood (b. Baltimore, Md., July 2, 1908; d. Bethesda, Md., Jan. 24, 1993), JURIST, graduated from Lincoln University (1930), received an LLB from Howard University (1933). After practicing law in Baltimore, he joined the NAACP (1936), becoming head of its legal staff in 1938. During the next two decades he argued a number of important civil rights cases before the Supreme Court. In 1944, in *Smith* v. *Allwright*, he won for African-Americans in Texas the right to vote in Democratic primaries. In *Morgan* v. *Va.* (1946), he argued that the Virginia law segregating buses involved in interstate commerce was unconstitutional. In *Shelley* v. *Kraemer* (1948), he insisted that racially restrictive housing covenants violated the equal protection clause of the Fourteenth Amendment.

In 1950 Marshall argued two important school cases before the Supreme Court. In *Sweatt* v. *Painter*, he helped end segregation in the University of Texas Law School. The Supreme Court ruled that the school must admit all African-American students who met the academic qualifications. On the same day, the Court also handed down a ruling in *McLaurin* v. *Oklahoma State Regents*, stating that once a school admitted an African-American to graduate school it could not segregate him within the school. The culmination of the effort to end school segregation occurred with the decision handed down in the 1954 *Brown* v. *Board of Education* case which Marshall also handled for the NAACP. Challenging the "separate but equal" doctrine of *Plessy* v. *Ferguson* (1896), Marshall submitted sociological and psychological evidence that segregation made "equal" education impossible, and that separate accommodations had a harmful effect on both black and white children. The Court sustained Marshall's argument in a unanimous decision.

In 1957, when Arkansas governor Orval E. Faubus tried to prevent African-American children from entering schools in Little Rock, Marshall again appeared before the Supreme Court (*Cooper* v. *Aaron*, 1958). While President Eisenhower opened the schools by sending in federal troops and national guardsmen, the Court again asserted that the African-Americans could not be deprived "of their constitutional rights."

In 1961 President Kennedy appointed Marshall judge of the U.S. circuit court of appeals in New York, and from 1965 to 1967 he served as solicitor general of the U.S. In 1967 President Johnson appointed Marshall to the Supreme Court, thus making Marshall the first African-American ever to sit on that bench. The expectations that Marshall would join the activist wing of the Court were generally borne out. Starting with an opinion extending the right to counsel in 1967, he wrote rulings invalidating censorship statutes and expanding protection from libel suits, nationalizing the double jeopardy provision of the Fifth Amendment, and upholding picketing in shopping centers. He was less of an activist in dealing with draftee problems, however, and in *Gillette* v. *U.S.* (1971) denied the principle of selective conscientious objection. His concurring opinion in the Pentagon Papers case (*New York Times Co.* v. *U.S.,* 1971) was a clear statement of his strong belief in separation of powers, and the need of the separate branches to use power within proper spheres. As the Court became increasingly conservative in the 1970s and 1980s Marshall, along with **Justice Brennan**, became a lonely minority on the bench. He was soon accorded the title of "The Great Dissenter." One of his most famous dissents was in *San Antonio School District* v. *Rodriguez* (1973), a sixty-three page opinion sharply criticizing the majority position of the Court that the Constitution's guarantee of equal protection was not violated by the property tax method of financing public education by Texas and most other states. Marshall argued that the right to an education was "fundamental," and that funding schools with property taxes had the effect of discriminating on the basis of wealth. In 1978, Marshall strongly dissented in the *Bakke* case, when the Court majority found it unconstitutional for a state-run medical school to reserve sixteen of one hundred places in the entering class for black and other minority students. In his separate sixteen page opinion, Marshall provided a history of blacks in America, and said that in the light of that sad history the state had an obligation to do everything in its power, provided it was constitutional, to bring African-Americans into the mainstream of American life. Marshall's belief that affirmative action was a valid and necessary constitutional remedy for past racial discrimination also animated his dissent in *City of Richmond* v. *Croson* (1989), in which the majority declared unconstitutional a municipal ordinance setting aside 30 percent of public contracting funds for minority owned companies. On other issues before the Court, particularly the constitutionality of the death penalty, Marshall was unequivocal: it was unconstitutional in all cases. He wrote over 150 dissenting opinions in cases in which the court refused to hear death penalty appeals.

In his last years on the Court, Marshall, increasingly frustrated by the conservative direction of American society, began to make harsh personal comments in public about Republican presidents Reagan and Bush and other public figures he disagreed with. "I wouldn't do the job of dogcatcher for Ronald Reagan," he said in 1989. When asked in a television interview in 1990 what he thought of President Bush, he responded: "It's said that if you can't say something good about a dead person, don't say it. Well, I consider him dead." In July 1991, a few days before his 83d birthday, Marshall announced his retirement from the Court.

Marshall illustrated the dilemma of the professionally skilled black leader. Praised for years by white liberals and blacks generally, while damned by white conservatives, he attained the zenith of his career just at a time when the Black Power movement was challenging most sharply the value to blacks of integration and questioning whether the whole civil rights crusade had not constituted a naïve over-reliance upon law to upgrade the status of black America. Further, to the degree that the civil rights movement, successful or not, was over by 1967, the talents which Marshall had so carefully developed had limited meaning for his immediate Supreme Court career. Thus, despite his thoroughly competent performance as a Supreme Court justice after 1967, most analysts agree that his major contributions were made between 1938 and 1967. That career, however, was in many ways remarkable.

Prior to the time that Marshall as a young attorney began to move into a leadership role in the NAACP's campaign for legal justice in the late 1930s, that organization's strategy had largely been geared to achieving victories in random areas where it was felt the Supreme Court might be solicitous. Marshall early urged the development of a broader plan of legal action, pushing for quick follow-through on the legal committee's agreed-upon strategy in 1934, saying that "it should be made clear that the campaign is a carefully planned one to secure decisions, rulings and public opinion on the broad principles." Extending further the important early work of Charles H. Huston, the first NAACP special counsel in New York, Marshall, as the Legal Defense Fund's director-counsel, quickly became the field general for lawyers in the civil rights movement from the late 1930s to the Kennedy years. He coordinated attacks on discrimination in schooling, voting, housing, recreation, public accommodations and facilities, and criminal justice; traveled thousands of miles to appear in court-rooms all over the South; and lent his presence to isolated and harassed civil rights lawyers in these regions. Although he held strategy conferences and attempted to reach consensus among lawyers involved in key cases, Marshall at all times made the final decisions, going on to accept full responsibility for their ultimate implementation. Further, he saw such cases through. He was on the brief of almost all major civil rights cases in the Supreme Court, and frequently sat alongside others who handled the argument. His style, while earnest and persuasive, was deferential and respectful. He obediently used segregated facilities where the law had not desegregated them, partly out of a "respect for law," but primarily to preserve the Fund's resources for planned legal battles. His oral advocacy record was thirty-two cases argued, twenty-nine won. As a lower court judge and as solicitor general his record was equally impressive. None of the more than 150 opinions which he wrote while a member of the circuit court was reversed, while several of his dissents became the basis for Supreme Court reversal. As the government's attorney he successfully argued fourteen of nineteen cases in areas ranging from antitrust law to further civil rights litigation.

In some ways his most highly publicized action came in the case of *Brown* v. *Board of Education,* in which Marshall not only mustered the many forces determined to outlaw segregated public education generally but responded persuasively to the Court's continued questioning as to whether a ruling of this nature would not be a useless act in the face of southern resistance. In many ways, the historic victory of May 17, 1954, was the ultimate vindication of the civil rights strategy of the postwar decade, and a monument to the wisdom of Marshall's approach and the skill of his advocacy generally.

Authorities differ on Marshall's overall legal contributions. Although critics contend that he was not a competent legal scholar, they acknowledge that his meticulous attention to detail and plainspoken delineation of the moral issues involved enabled him to build up an enviable record, while champions claimed at the time of his elevation to the Supreme Court that "in three decades he had probably done as much to transform the life of his people as any Negro alive today." Both agreed that his zesty earthiness and overall charisma enabled him to draw widely divergent elements behind his positions and that his record as the nation's leading civil rights attorney will not soon be surpassed. See J. P. MacKenzie, "Thurgood Marshall," in L. Friedman and F. Israel, *The Justices of the United States Supreme Court,* vol. 4 (1969), and Roger L. Goldman, *Thurgood Marshall: Justice for All* (1992).

PAUL L. MURPHY

MARX, Groucho, Harpo, Chico, etc. COME-DIANS, Leonard, known as Chico (b. March 22, 1887; New York, N.Y.; d. Hollywood, Calif., Oct. 12, 1961); Adolf (or Arthur), known as Harpo (b. New York, N.Y., Nov. 23, 1888; d. Hollywood, Calif., Sept. 28, 1964); Julius, or Groucho (b. New York, N.Y., Oct. 2, 1890; d. Aug. 19, 1977, Los Angeles, Calif.); Milton, or Gummo (b. New York, N.Y., [?] 1897; d. April 21, 1977, Palm Springs, Calif.), and Herbert, or Zeppo (b. New York, N.Y., Feb. 25, 1901; d. Palm Springs, Calif., Nov. 30, 1979), all grew up on the Lower East Side of New York City. Their parents were of French-German Jewish ancestry. With little formal schooling, the Marx brothers were inspired by an uncle, Al Shean, of the vaudeville act Gallagher & Shean, to enter show business. They began in vaudeville in the early 1900s, when Groucho and Gummo formed an act, managed by their mother, a sister of Al Shean, called the Nightingales. When Harpo joined them in 1908 and Chico in 1912, the Marx Brothers were born. By the time they moved from vaudeville to the legitimate stage in the early 1920s, Gummo had dropped out, to be replaced ultimately by Zeppo. From then until 1933, the act would consist of four of the brothers; after 1933, when Zeppo retired from performing, there would be only three. In *The Cocoanuts* (1925), a satire on the Florida land boom, with a book by George S. Kaufmann and music by **Irving Berlin**, they truly arrived, with a comic style that was at once zany and improvisational. This musical became their first film (1929), and it was in the medium of film that the true greatness of the Marx Brothers was fully realized.

Their second film, *Animal Crackers* (1930), was also based on a stage show (with a book by Kaufmann and Morrie Ryskind and music by Bert Kalmar and Harry Ruby). It was followed in rapid succession by a series of great screen comedies: *Monkey Business* (1931), *Horsefeathers* (1932), *Duck Soup* (1933) (considered their most inspired film), *A Night at the Opera* (1935), and *A Day at the Races* (1937). Although the Marx Brothers continued making films until 1949, none of their later work reached the heights of the 1930s and only Groucho managed to move

successfully from making films to radio and then television, where he became well known to a whole new generation as the wisecracking host of *You Bet Your Life*.

———❧———

The comic style of the Marx Brothers—based on a lightning-fast combination of verbal and visual humor—was ideally suited to the sound film. The great comedians of the silent screen—**Charlie Chaplin** and Buster Keaton—never quite made the transition to sound. Indeed, Chaplin's sound films are actually silent films with only small passages of dialogue whenever absolutely necessary. Their comedy belonged to a different era than that of the Marx Brothers, whose stage careers—first in vaudeville, then on the legitimate stage—gave them what they needed to excel in the new sound movie medium. Moreover, their comedy, like Chaplin's, appealed to a broad audience. Intellectuals saw analogies between their comic routines and such movements in the arts as dada and surrealism; the ordinary filmgoer, on the other hand, could appreciate their antics as amusing for their own sake. With the props and mannerisms for which they became famous—the sarcastic Groucho, with his mustache, long cigar, and funny walk; Harpo, with his fright wig, his musical instrument, and his perpetual silence; and Chico, the ultimate stage Italian, with his curly hair, peaked cap, and constant misunderstanding of English—they amused a whole generation of people with their special brand of humor. See Joe Adamson, *Groucho, Harpo, Chico, and sometimes Zeppo* (1973).

ARCHIE K. LOSS

MASON, George (b. Fairfax County, Va., 1725; d. Fairfax County, Va., Oct. 7, 1792), POLITICAL LEADER, was educated by private tutors and studied law informally. He was elected to the Virginia house of burgesses (1758), but he tired of the routine after serving two terms. As a private citizen Mason opposed the Sugar Act (1764) and the Stamp Act (1765). Following the passage of the Townshend Acts (1767), he helped draft a nonimportation resolution which George Washington presented to the dissolved house of burgesses. After Parliament passed the Coercive Acts (1774), Mason drafted the "Fairfax Resolves," which restated the constitutional position of the colonies vis-à-vis Great Britain. In 1776 he framed the Virginia Declaration of Rights, and was instrumental in drafting the Virginia constitution. In 1777–78 Mason served on a committee that authorized **George Rogers Clark**'s expedition into the Northwest Territory.

Mason was a delegate to the Federal Convention (1787), but refused to sign the new Constitution because it seemed to place the agrarian South at a disadvantage and had no bill of rights. He was also a critic of provisions permitting continuance of the slave trade until 1808.

A disdain for the tedious committee work of legislative service and an impatience with men given to talk rather than action caused George Mason to avoid a larger role in both fomenting and carrying through the Revolution. Even so, he deserves the status of a founding father because of his activities in 1774–76, his persistent effort to give the Revolution a moral tone, and his role at the 1787 Federal Convention.

Mason conducted his plantation affairs astutely and avoided the heavy debt that plagued so many of his contemporaries. His neighbors—including George Washington—admired his financial skill and his intellectual capabilities; and there is abundant evidence that the master of Mount Vernon often asked for (and received) both loans and advice on political affairs after 1765. Infuriated by the Stamp Act, Mason sent a warning to London merchants that Americans had "tasted the Sweets of Liberty" and would not be denied their claim to "the Liberty & Privileges of Englishmen, in the same Degree, as if we had still continued among our Brethren in Great Britain." When his advice went unheeded, Mason fell in with the militant Virginians who considered the Boston Port Bill a threat to all Americans. Thereafter, he was a leader in trans-

forming Virginia from a dutiful royal colony into a belligerent commonwealth.

Mason might have become an even more active revolutionary but for the death of his wife, after she had borne twelve children, in her thirty-ninth year. Left with nine surviving offspring, Mason never concealed his concern for their welfare and often used the family—along with his hereditary enemy, the gout—as an excuse for hurried retirement from public business. Clearly he preferred life at his country seat, Gunston Hall, where he enjoyed good wine and frequent readings of Virgil, Sallust, Plutarch, and the political philosophers of the 17th century, to any honor which either the state or nation might bestow. He twice refused a place in the Continental Congress. As **Edmund Randolph** recalled, Mason's draft of the Virginia Declaration of Rights was so attuned to the sentiments of the 1776 Convention that it "swallowed up all the rest," and his perceptive views on what Virginians wanted in their local government led him to shape a constitution that survived efforts by Jefferson, Madison, and others who wanted to abandon Mason's plan by 1783. Despite such powerful opposition, Mason's ideas remained the bedrock of Virginia government until 1829.

Although chiefly remembered for his major accomplishment in drafting the first American bill of rights, Mason also saw the dangers of denying human rights to slaves and repeatedly sought ways to stifle the traffic in blacks. His earliest political writing (1765) began with an indictment of the effect of slavery "upon the Morals & Manners of our People." Few Virginians supported Mason in his vision of an agrarian society based on freeholders alone, and when he was still inveighing against slavery in the Federal Convention few delegates were inclined to listen. Except for **Patrick Henry** he was perhaps the most influential public man in Virginia between 1775 and 1787, a position recognized by Jefferson's posthumous assessment of Mason as a Virginian "of the first order of greatness." See Robert A. Rutland, *George Mason, Reluctant Statesman* (1961).

ROBERT A. RUTLAND

MASTERS, William (b. Cleveland, Ohio, Dec. 27, 1915), and **JOHNSON, Virginia Eshelman** (b. Springfield, Mo., Feb. 11, 1925), SCIENTISTS. Masters graduated from Hamilton College in 1938 and received his MD from the University of Rochester Medical School in 1943. He was interested in sex research, but on the advice of one of his professors, Dr. George Corner, he first took an internship in obstetrics and gynecology and then taught at Barnes Hospital in the medical school of Washington University in St. Louis. In 1954, after publishing some twenty-five articles in medical journals, he began to study actual human sexual responses. Through the university placement office he obtained the services of a female interviewer, Virginia Johnson, in 1955.

Virginia Eshelman studied music at Drury College and attended the University of Missouri (1944–47) but did not graduate. After separating from her husband, she sought work and this led to her association with Masters. Their research was conducted at the Washington University School of Medicine until 1964 and thereafter at Masters's Reproductive Biology Research Foundation, later renamed the Masters and Johnson Institute, also in St. Louis. The results of their research were published as *Human Sexual Response* (1966) and *Human Sexual Inadequacy* (1970). Although designed to be medical textbooks, each sold more than 250,000 copies. Masters and Johnson also conducted two-week clinical programs for the treatment of sexual inadequacy. In 1971 they married. In the early 1970s they began writing an advice column for *Redbook* magazine, did research on sexual orientations, and trained other therapists in their techniques. The results of their research was *Homosexuality in Perspective* (1979) which proved almost as controversial as their earlier books. More and more, the Masters and Johnson Institute concentrated on treating dysfunctional sexual partners and training therapists. In 1992, Masters and Johnson divorced but continued to work together at their Institute.

———— ◆◆◆ ————

Although Americans in the middle of the 20th century confidently believed they had put Victorian mores on sexuality behind them, ignorance of some of the most basic facts of human sexuality was widespread not only in the general public but also in the medical profession. Research into sexual practices had begun here in the 1920s, chiefly through the efforts of gynecologist Robert Dickinson. By the 1950s, the results of the extensive questionnaires composed and tabulated by **Alfred Kinsey** were well known. But not until William Masters and Virginia Johnson did anyone bring sex into the laboratory to measure and analyze with precision physiological reactions to sexual stimulation.

Where ignorance was so prevalent, myth predominated. What passed for informed opinion reflected an essentially Freudian perspective, particularly as defined in the writings of Helene Deutsch. Male and female sexualities, Deutsch insisted, were fundamentally different, and indeed determined other respective functioning in society. The male was aggressive, dominant, and active in sexual terms, and hence in social ones as well. The female, defining her lack of a penis as a defect, tried to substitute clitoral satisfaction; but the effort at compensation did not work. The clitoris, Deutsch argued, was a stunted penis, "so rudimentary that it can barely be considered an organ." Since it could not satisfy "the active and aggressive instinctual impulses," women abdicated these roles, adopting instead passive, receptive, essentially masochistic ones. Or put more simply, in Deutsch's view they became feminine. The aggressive woman was neurotic and ultimately homosexual. The well-adjusted one was at peace with her biology.

Rather than engage these views in a theoretical debate, Masters and Johnson turned to live subjects, sensing devices, and cameras. First they measured and photographed the physiological changes that occurred during sexual stimulation in normal and well-functioning men and women. Next they turned their attention to the problem of sexual inadequacy, exploring the causes and treatment of impotence. Now they are at work on the issue of sexual orientation, essentially male and female homosexuality. The results of this carefully designed research sequence, from normality to subnormality to abnormality, have in effect contradicted almost all traditional viewpoints on sexuality.

At a minimum, Masters and Johnson have supplied practicing physicians with data necessary for accurate medical counseling. Not until their findings were published did heart specialists, for example, have exact knowledge of changes in heartbeat and blood pressure during sexual intercourse. But the contribution of Masters and Johnson went far beyond that. The very title of their first book, *Human Sexual Response,* conveyed one revolutionary finding: similarity, not differences, marked the anatomy and physiology of sexuality. "Direct parallels in human sexual response … exist to a degree never previously appreciated." Moreover, there was no distinction between a clitoral and vaginal orgasm, and women's sexual responses were at least as intense as men's, perhaps more so. A normally functioning woman, Masters and Johnson reported, "will in most instances be capable of having a second, third, fourth, and even fifth and sixth orgasm before she is fully satisfied." In light of this evidence, it was patently absurd to describe the clitoris as an inadequate penis, or to define men as sexually active and women as sexually inactive. Hence, to understand why men dominated in the marketplace while women passively remained at home, one would have to give up biological or sexual explanations and turn to social ones.

Masters and Johnson not only helped to free women from confining definitions but also the aged of both sexes. While noting that physiological changes occur over time, they demonstrated that "there is no time limit drawn by advancing years to female sexuality," or to male sexuality either. In a similar spirit, their findings extended the definition of normal sexual behavior. A surprisingly wide variety of stimuli produced intense and pleasurable sexual responses.

Finally, Masters and Johnson demonstrated the efficacy of rapid and comparatively simple therapeutic techniques to solve problems of sexual inadequacy. Focusing on the symptom, rather than on underlying psychological dynamics, they achieved dramatically high rates of success with their patients.

The research of Masters and Johnson has been a genuinely liberating force in American society. It may well take several decades for social practices to become consistent with all the implications of their findings. See Nat Lehrman, *Masters and Johnson Explained* (1971).

SHEILA M. ROTHMAN

MATHER, Cotton (b. Boston, Mass., Feb. 12, 1663; d. Boston, Mass., Feb. 13, 1728), RELIGIOUS LEADER, son of **Increase Mather,** grandson of Richard Mather and **John Cotton,** graduated from Harvard (BA, 1678; MA, 1681), and was ordained in 1685 at his father's Second Church of Boston. In 1689, following the news of the overthrow of King James II, Mather supported an uprising against the royal governor, **Edmund Andros,** who had established an Anglican church in Boston.

Like most Puritans, Mather believed in supernatural phenomena. During the Salem witchcraft trials (1692–93), he urged harsh punishments for those who were found guilty of "conspiring" with the devil. In 1693, at the request of the Salem court, he wrote *Wonders of the Invisible World,* describing the Salem trials.

In 1703 the Massachusetts lower house, made up primarily of religious conservatives, chose Mather to be the new president of Harvard. However, they were overruled by the more liberal upper house, who had long resented the Mather family. Mather thereupon resigned his Harvard fellowship and lent his support to the establishment of Yale, which he hoped would preserve the Puritan tradition. An avid scientist, in 1713 he was elected to the British Royal Society. During the Boston smallpox epidemic of 1721 he took the lead in urging inoculations.

The most famous of Mather's many literary productions was his massive *Magnalia Christi Americana* (1702), an ecclesiastical history of New England.

Cotton Mather, frequently scorned and mocked by his contemporaries, has suffered similar judgments ever since. Though he stands as a major transitional figure for New England, he is too often and too easily dismissed either as a psychotic or as an anachronistic conservator of the Puritan legacy. But in the published and unpublished writings he prepared so compulsively, Mather reveals a personality and a career too complex to justify caricatures.

The profundity of his internal religious experience is unquestioned, but from it flowed the excesses that many have found unpalatable. Yet in that Puritan divine, prostrate on the floor of his study pleading his own vileness, lies the core of the man. Despite pastoral and family cares that engrossed his time, he established an extraordinary religious regimen. Six times daily he interrupted his affairs for worship and meditation; twice each month he forced himself through a sleepless vigil of self-examination; fasting became a routine part of his religious observations. This inner life laid the foundation of a faith in God's sovereignty and saving grace which he never tired of trying to impart to others. He drew from this brooding introspection to create the new pietism he increasingly endorsed after 1710 and made explicit in *Bonifacius*. Pietism became his vehicle for revitalizing New England's religious life: it offered men an affective belief in Christ, it cut through sectarian divisions, and it countered the Arminian drift of the times. Mather's pietistic organization would engage men against the evils of society and accomplish the reformation which two generations of New England clergy had unsuccessfully sought.

But Mather's introspection had a second, darker side. The hours of contemplation and self-abasement produced swoonings, groanings, and illuminations which many have condemned. They also produced the guilt and the terror, the sense of his own evil, that made him suspect the worst of himself—and of others. In his diaries he examined himself as few men dare; he never ceased condemning his enormous self-esteem, yet he knew he never conquered that awesome pride. Although he saw through many of his self-deceptions, he often turned this introspection into self-indulgence. And Cotton Mather, like Luther before him, felt himself plagued by the demonic. Tormented by trials and afflictions, he envisioned a Satan with limitless power directed against him; his fears of the demonic frequently bordered on the irrational.

Externally Mather subdued this internal torment. With his father, Increase, he served one of Boston's largest churches, where he acquired a reputation for pastoral care, particularly in his ability to help troubled adolescents. He became an intelligent bibliophile, a discriminating reader, and a prolific, if pedantic, author. Out of his observations of the natural world around him he developed a correspondence with some of Europe's leading men of science and began to articulate a system of divine order and regularity in the universe quite distinct from the providential world of his father. Publicly, Mather was "a cultivated man with a good mind." Privately he oscillated between conventional piety and direct, emotional encounters with the Holy Spirit. See Robert Middlekauff, *The Mathers: Three Generations of Puritan Intellectuals* (1971).

ROBERT G. POPE

MATHER, Increase (b. Dorchester, Mass., June 21, 1639; d. Boston, Mass., Aug. 23, 1723), RELIGIOUS LEADER, graduated from Harvard College in 1656. Mather first preached from his father's pulpit in 1657 but went to England and Ireland later that year, earning an MA degree from Trinity College, Dublin, in 1658. He spent the next few years organizing Congregational churches in England and as chaplain to the garrison on the island of Guernsey before returning to Massachusetts in 1661. Mather was a minister at the Second Church of Boston from 1664 until his death. He became a fellow of Harvard College in 1674, acting president in 1685, and president in 1686. During his tenure he encouraged the study of science.

In 1683 Mather took the lead in opposing Charles II's order that the Massachusetts colonists surrender their original charter which allowed them to elect their own governor. A critic of the Dominion of New England and its governor, **Edmund Andros,** he traveled to London in 1688 to plead the colonists' case. After Boston revolted against Andros in 1689, Mather (1690) became an official representative of the colony. In this capacity he approved the new charter issued by William III in 1691—all attempts to regain the old one had failed—and managed to have his choice, Sir William Phips, nominated as royal governor. Mather returned to Boston in 1692, but his influence soon waned as Phips and the new charter became unpopular. He was forced to resign as president of Harvard in 1701. He remained active in Congregational councils, writing, preaching, and supporting the work of his son **Cotton Mather.** He spoke out against the Salem witchcraft trials (1692), and his tract *Cases of Conscience* (1693) helped persuade Governor Phips to halt the execution of convicted "witches." He was a prolific writer on theology, history, and other subjects. Some of his works include *Brief History of the War with the Indians* (1676), *A Relation of the Troubles ...* (1677), and *Remarkable Providences* (1684).

Increase Mather's vision of New England and of his role in fulfilling its purpose dominated his life—it shaped his career, his theology, and his personality. It gave him the extraordinary power and sense of invulnerability that made him the major clerical figure of his generation.

In his eagerness to succeed, to uphold the family name, to get his way for New England, Mather demonstrated a self-righteousness, a lack of charity, and a literalness that made him harsh and unyielding. His intense piety, born of a deathbed promise to a mother he worshiped, drove him by the end of his life toward an obsession with death and an alienation from ordinary life.

Within the Second Church he defined his role almost exclusively as a preaching ministry and delegated to his son Cotton the burdensome pastoral care. As often as three times weekly and to as many as 1,500 persons, he preached sermons which wove together the themes of human pride, divine sovereignty, and New England's mission.

His increasingly effective style worked as a bridge between the "plaine style" of his father's generation and the evangelical preaching of the Great Awakening.

Although the parish was never totally subservient to him, clearly it represented but one part of his larger mission to make New England a place of God which would fulfill its destiny at the end of history. And he, like most of his generation, despaired its failings and canonized its founders. The conflicts and rebuffs—over the new charter, Stoddardeanism, Harvard—sharpened his feeling that New England was following Israel's road to destruction with dreadful faithfulness, and that only in a remarkable resurgence of personal piety could it be redeemed. See Robert Middlekauff, *The Mathers* (1971).

ROBERT G. POPE

MAURY, Matthew Fontaine (b. near Fredericksburg, Va., Jan. 14, 1806; d. Lexington, Va., Feb. 1, 1873), NAVAL OFFICER and SCIENTIST, became a midshipman in the U.S. Navy in 1825, and served at sea 1825–34; his duty included a voyage around the world. After returning to the U.S. in 1834 he took a leave of absence from the navy and in 1836 published *A New Theoretical and Practical Treatise on Navigation,* which he had begun during his last voyage, and in the same year was promoted to lieutenant. In the following year he studied astronomy. He was appointed astronomer to the navy's exploring expedition to the South Seas, but because of a change in command, he did not go on the expedition. He was then assigned to surveying duties along the southeast coast of the U.S. Between 1838 and 1841 he published a number of articles on the inefficiency of the navy and the need for a naval academy to train officers, which appeared in the Richmond *Whig and Public Advertiser* and the *Southern Literary Messenger.* These were widely circulated among naval officers. In 1839 Maury was injured in a stagecoach accident, becoming permanently lame.

In 1842 Maury was appointed superintendent of the Depot of Charts and Instruments of the navy, which was merged with the U.S. Naval Observatory when the latter was completed in 1844, Maury becoming superintendent of the whole. Soon after this appointment he began research on winds and currents, publishing his *Wind and Current Chart of the North Atlantic* in 1847. This was followed by a work on sailing directions: *Abstract Log for the Use of American Navigators* (1848; reissued in 1850 and 1851 under new titles).

In 1853 Maury represented the U.S. at the Brussels International Meteorological Congress, of which he was the chief organizer. The conference established a uniform system of recording meteorological data for naval vessels and merchant ships. With the aid of this new data, Maury charted a new route that, according to him, reduced the time of passage by ship from New York to San Francisco by about forty-seven days (1855). In 1855 Maury issued *The Physical Geography of the Sea*, the first U.S. textbook on oceanography. He also supported the idea of laying a cable under the Atlantic, and was consulted by **Cyrus Field,** the promotor of the first transatlantic cable (1858).

In 1858 Maury was appointed a commander on the navy's active list, retroactive to 1855. In April 1861, however, after Virginia seceded from the Union, he resigned. He offered his services to his native state and became a commander in the Confederate navy and was sent to England to obtain vessels. After the war he went to Mexico. He then returned to England (1866), where he wrote *First Lessons in Geography* and *The World We Live In* (1868). He returned to the U.S. in 1868 as professor of meteorology at Virginia Military Institute and superintendent of the Physical Survey of Virginia. His other published works include *Physical Survey of Virginia, No. 1* (1868), and *Manual of Geography* (1870).

Maury was first and foremost a naval officer. Unfitted for life at sea by an accident in his early thirties, he made a major contribution to the United States Navy by promoting the reforms of 1842. Rewarded for this effort with a major shore billet, he turned his organizational and promo-

tional talents to science. But the science Maury pioneered was purely empirical, since he was less interested in knowledge for its own sake than in its application to practical problems of seafaring. Though he spent sixteen years directing one of the world's major astronomical observatories, Maury failed to gain a significant reputation as an astronomer.

His major achievement lay elsewhere: the bringing together of vast numbers of observations of winds and currents made at sea. From them Maury constructed charts that presented a climatic picture of the surface winds and currents for all the oceans, and he accompanied his charts with sailing directions to help mariners reduce the duration of their voyages. Maury was the leading developer of the "software" of sail in the age of the clipper ship. His scientific writings on the ocean, drawn mostly from the *Sailing Directions* that accompanied his charts, were brought together in *The Physical Geography of the Sea*, one of the most popular books on science ever published.

Maury's disinterest in pure science and his aggressive promotion of his own activities led to a conflict with the leaders of the embryonic American scientific community that was exacerbated by the rivalry between north and south. His attempt to organize worldwide weather reporting at the Brussels Congress in 1853 was thwarted by Alexander Dallas Bache of the U.S. Coast and Geodetic Survey, **Joseph Henry** of the Smithsonian Institution, and their British allies; Maury's system was accepted for marine observations only. As the Civil War approached, his rivals forced an increasing isolation upon him in the name of a science that demanded objectivity and eschewed supernatural and anthropomorphic explanations of the natural world. In scientific circles Maury's purple prose and his devotion to the navy and the slavocracy were no assets, and his departure for the South in 1861 brought his scientific career to an end.

In his lifetime Maury was widely honored as one of those who refilled the storehouse of facts about nature; his failure either to theorize successfully about these facts or to assist those who could was overlooked. His modern reputation derives from a concerted 20th-century effort by southerners to find heroes in the antebellum past. See Frances Leigh Williams, *Matthew Fontaine Maury: Scientist of the Sea* (1962).

HAROLD L. BURSTYN

MAYER, Louis Burt (b. Minsk, Russ., July 4, 1885; d. Los Angeles, Calif., Oct. 29, 1957), MOVIE PRODUCER, emigrated with his parents to St. John, New Brunswick, in 1888, briefly attended public schools, then entered his father's ship-salvaging and scrap-iron business as a junior partner. He made frequent business trips to the U.S. and finally settled near Boston in 1907. The following year he bought an old burlesque theater in Haverhill, Massachusetts, and made it into a popular attraction by alternating movies with live shows. He soon acquired all the theaters in Haverhill and went into a partnership controlling a chain of New England theaters. In 1914 he founded a film distribution agency and made a small fortune by obtaining the New England rights to the epic movie *The Birth of a Nation* (1915).

Mayer moved to Los Angeles in 1918 to concentrate on film production. He founded the Louis B. Mayer Picture Corporation and released through First National and, subsequently, Metro Pictures Corporation. Highly successful in this enterprise, he was persuaded by theater owner Marcus Loew to combine his operations with those of film producer **Samuel Goldwyn**. Together, in 1924, they formed the Metro-Goldwyn-Mayer Corporation with Mayer as vice president in charge of production. Goldwyn soon sold his interests and formed his own company, although his name remained as part of Metro-Goldwyn-Mayer.

Mayer built MGM into the largest filmmaking enterprise in the world. He discovered such stars as Greta Garbo, Clark Gable, Judy Garland, Robert Taylor, and Joan Crawford while producing many popular, mass-entertainment movies. Mayer served as president of the Association of Motion Picture Producers (1931–36). He commanded a salary exceeding $1 million a year at MGM. A delegate to the 1928 and 1932 Republican national conventions, Mayer supported Herbert Hoover, and he served as vice-chairman of the California Republican State Central Committee.

Growing friction at MGM during the 1940s caused Mayer to resign in 1951. He became chairman of the board of Cinerama Productions Corporation in 1952 but never made any films and sold his shares in 1954. Mayer, nevertheless, remained an active force in the movie world until his death.

⚬⚬⚬

Rightly called the "Czar of Hollywood," Louis B. Mayer ruled the American film industry for three decades, raised the prestige of his studio, MGM, to dizzying heights, and proved himself the greatest star-maker of them all. A supreme dictator in a world ruled by moguls, he swept ruthlessly to power, making and destroying careers as well as people who antagonized him, stubbornly devoted to the rule that the motion picture should represent, first and foremost, clean entertainment. It did not matter that the public might have preferred films with some hint of contemporary social consciousness; they got from Mayer only the world as he idealized it, a world that never existed save in his own mind: motherhood was always sacrosanct for him; the traditional, nuclear American family was supreme; virtue never failed to triumph; the unhappy ending was to be avoided, for did not everything happen for the best in this best of all possible worlds?

Today the pictures made at MGM under Mayer's leadership remain the most glittering, the best produced—and the emptiest. Through them the great stars of the day move gloriously, shining like true superstars in a glossy, tinseled, unreal world.

It was next to impossible for any real creator to work closely with Mayer. His best coexecutive, Irving Thalberg, opposed him constantly, but Thalberg, who represented an innate good taste which Mayer never knew, died too early. Nor could David O. Selznick, Mayer's own son-in-law, produce pictures for any length of time under his father-in-law's aegis; Selznick soon had to strike out on his own.

Mayer was hated, feared, and unloved by most of his contract people, although he insisted that he only wanted to be loved. Forced to resign soon after he brought the socially conscious Dore Schary into the studio as his partner, he could only complain with bitter, childish vindictiveness, "I was a sheep who invited a hungry wolf to dinner."

At Mayer's funeral, Rabbi Edgar Magnin stated significantly, "This is the end of a volume, not a chapter." Certainly nothing could be added to the role of the Hollywood producer after Mayer's long reign. The empire had fallen long before Mayer, its deposed Caesar, fell, a victim to dread leukemia. See Bosley Crowther, *Hollywood Rajah: The Life and Times of Louis B. Mayer* (1960).

DEWITT BODEEN

MAYO, William James (b. Le Sueur, Minn., June 29, 1861; d. Rochester, Minn., July 28, 1939), and **MAYO, Charles Horace** (b. Rochester, Minn., July 19, 1865; d. Chicago, Ill., May 26, 1939), PHYSICIANS, earned their MD degrees respectively from the University of Michigan in 1883 and from Northwestern in 1888. Both did postgraduate work at the New York Medical School and at the New York Polyclinic. Along with their doctor father, the Mayo brothers headed the small, newly opened St. Mary's Hospital at Rochester, Minnesota, beginning in 1889. Both brothers were surgeons, and they performed all the surgery at St. Mary's Hospital until about 1905. From this surgical partnership, the cooperative group clinic later called the Mayo Clinic evolved. The group was small at the beginning, but in the early 1900s, with the addition of many young physicians in the various fields of medicine, it began to grow both in size and in reputation.

The clinic proved a great financial success, although from the start its official policy was to charge the patient only as much as he could afford. The Mayos donated $1.5 million for the establishment of the Mayo Foundation of Medical Education and Research at the graduate school of the University of Minnesota. In 1919 they formed the Mayo Properties Association, a charitable and educational corporation, which transformed the clinic from a partnership to a voluntary association of physicians and specialists in allied fields. They served as associate chiefs of staff at the clinic until their retirement in 1933.

The Mayo brothers also gained distinction for their individual talents as physicians. William specialized in stomach surgery, operating on ulcers. Charles, who was skilled in goiter surgery, succeeded in reducing the death rate from goiter by 50 percent; he was also a professor of surgery at both the Medical School and the Mayo Foundation of the University of Minnesota. During World War I, the Mayos alternated as chief consultants for all surgical services in the U.S. army, with colonel's rank, and after the war both were commissioned as brigadier generals in the Medical Corps Reserve.

The Mayos established their reputations in the period 1890–1910 when surgical intervention was becoming dramatically effective in many parts of medical practice, and their success was in part the success of medicine. In the 1910s and 1920s, as a new medical practice based on physiology developed, the Mayos increased the proportion and importance of that type of work in their clinic. Their fame grew not so much out of innovation as out of their knowledge—and popularization among other practitioners—of the best of contemporary medical work.

William and Charles Mayo helped give substance to a part of the American dream. By establishing in a small Minnesota town a medical practice second to none in the world, they suggested that the miracles that were transforming medicine in their day could be made available to all Americans, even those distant from Europe and the seaboard cities. The press discovered them, and by the World War I era the Mayo Clinic had become symbolic of the idea that medical excellence might become available to anyone.

The Mayos' organization of practice was widely praised and copied, envied even in Boston and New York. In their private group practice they achieved a solution to the growing problem of the fragmentation of medical practice into specialties. Like others, they used expertise; but the Mayos' coordination of the work of one specialist with another was unique. Their ability to provide health care efficiently was an inspiration to generations of medical reformers. The success of the clinic was largely, as William Mayo recognized, a result of "the transformation in medical conditions rather than personal attributes." The successful organization of the specialists, however, was at least in part a reflection of the sensitive way in which the two brothers themselves worked together. See Helen Clapesattle, *The Doctors Mayo* (1941).

J. C. BURNHAM

MEAD, Margaret (b. Philadelphia, Pa., Dec. 16, 1901; d. New York, N.Y., Nov. 15, 1978), ANTHROPOLOGIST, entered DePauw University (Greencastle, Ind.) in 1919 but transferred to Barnard College in New York City in 1920, receiving a BA in 1923. She earned an MA in psychology from Columbia the following year and a PhD in anthropology in 1929 from Columbia. A 1925–26 field trip to the Samoan Islands under a fellowship from the National Research Council led to *Coming of Age in Samoa* (1928), which enjoyed great popular success and established her reputation as an expert on primitive cultures. In 1926 she became assistant curator of ethnology of New York's American Museum of Natural History, being promoted to associate curator in 1942, and curator in 1964. A field trip to the Admiralty Islands in the West Pacific (1928–29) resulted in *Growing up in New Guinea* (1930). Another field trip in 1931–33 to study adolescent and sexual behavior among primitive tribes led to *Sex and Temperament in Three Primitive Societies* (1935). She did further work in New Guinea and Bali in 1936–39, and in 1967.

From 1939 to 1941 Mead was visiting lecturer at Vassar College. She served as executive secretary on the National Research Council's commission on food habits (1942–45) and was a visiting lecturer at Teachers College of Columbia University (1947–51). *Male and Female: A Study of the Sexes in a Changing World* (1949) was widely acclaimed by critics. In 1954 she became adjunct professor of anthropology at Columbia. She served as president of the World Federation for Mental Health (1956–57) and president of the American Anthropological Association (1960). She was named chairman of Fordham University's social science division in 1968. In 1971, she was elected president of the American Association for the Advancement of Science, only the second woman to head the group. A frequent popular lecturer, Mead caused much controversy by defending marijuana users and the new sexual morality among youth in the sixties and seventies. Her *Culture and Commitment* (1970) was a study of contemporary youth and the generation gap. Some of her many other works included: *And Keep Your Powder Dry* (1942), *People and Places* (1959), *Continuities in Cultural Evolution* (1964), and *The Family* (1965).

Margaret Mead was probably the most widely known anthropologist in history. Thousands of students became acquainted with and interested in the field through her works, both professional and popular, and she was the only anthropologist millions of laymen could name. This fame tended to obscure her contributions to the field and evoked the envy of more pedantic colleagues.

Mead was one of the founders of psychological anthropology. She demonstrated the multiple influences of culture upon personality and the advantages of psychological perspectives in the study of culture and thereby significantly drew the fields of anthropology, psychology, and psychiatry closer together. Typical of the cumulative nature of science, her contributions tended to be surpassed and even forgotten with the accumulation of new data and shifts to new modes of analysis. But this was not the case with regard to one of her methodological achievements, for her advocacy of the uses of photography has yet to be fully realized in the profession. Finally, like her teachers **Franz Boas** and **Ruth Fulton Benedict,** she consistently championed anthropology as a human science, one both reflective and relevant. She spoke to issues such as warfare, human rights, man's use of his environment, and the roles of youth and the aged in a changing society. Her conclusions were not always popular, either inside or outside the profession, but the important point was not whether her ideas were popular: it was that she, more than any other anthropologist, tried to bring the conclusions of her profession to bear upon the problems of mankind. See Margaret Mead, *Blackberry Winter: A Memoir* (1972).

JAMES H. VAUGHAN

MEADE, George Gordon (b. Cadiz, Spain, Dec. 31, 1815; d. Philadelphia, Pa., Nov. 6, 1872), MILITARY LEADER, entered West Point in 1831, not so much in hopes of a military career, but more as an inexpensive way to continue his education in light of his family's failing finances. After graduating in 1835 he served his required year of duty in Florida, seeing action against the Seminoles. In 1836 he resigned and took up civil engineering and surveying work.

Meade rejoined the army in 1842, serving under Generals Zachary Taylor and **Winfield Scott** in the Mexican War (1846–48). Thereafter he was a member of the Topographical Engineers, a small, elite branch of the service which maintained its independence from the Corps of Engineers until 1862. At the outbreak of the Civil War, he was in charge of the Northern Lakes Surveys. He was then made brigadier general of volunteers, and assigned to building the defenses of Washington. In 1862 he led troops at Mechanicsville, Gaines' Mill, Glendale (where he was severely wounded), the Second Battle of Bull Run, South Mountain, Antietam, Fredericksburg, and (May 1863) at Chancellorsville.

On June 28, 1863, during General **Robert E. Lee's** invasion of the North, President Lincoln put Meade in command of the Army of the Potomac. Accepting reluctantly, Meade succeeded in halting Lee's advance at Gettysburg (July 1–3). Although criticized for allowing Lee to retreat without a further battle, he was nevertheless promoted to brigadier general in the regular army in recognition of his victory. He was made major general in 1864 (along with **William T. Sherman,** he was one of two men personally recommended by Grant for promotion to that rank in the regular army), continuing as commander of the Army of the Potomac. He was, however, subordinate to Grant after Grant was made lieutenant general in command of all Union forces (1864). Meade participated in the Wilderness, Spotsylvania, and Cold Harbor battles and in the siege of Petersburg (1864–65). After Appomattox, he settled in Philadelphia, heading the Military Division of the Atlantic until his death, except for a year (1868) at Atlanta, Georgia, where he commanded the 3d Military District of the Department of the South under the Reconstruction Acts.

In 1863, at the pinnacle of his career, Meade looked "more like a learned pundit than a soldier." Balding, bearded, with a prominent nose and sad, sunken eyes, he dressed casually and slouched ungracefully but maintained an air of dignified reserve. Ordinarily a gentle man of calm and pleasant conversation, he was both capable of uninhibited merriment and the victim of nervousness, anxiety, insecurity, and a viciously explosive temper. As an officer, he was generally respected for his undemonstrative courage and businesslike competence, although radicals in the army and the Congress mistrusted his professional detachment from political abolitionism, and Lincoln lamented his professional disinclination to acknowledge the harsh implications of modern total war. Meade's conventional training, his experience as a subordinate field commander, and his engineer's eye for terrain combined to make him a superior tactician, but he lacked a strategist's foresight, boldness, and ruthless nerve. As Grant noted, Meade's "first idea was to take advantage of the lay of the ground, sometimes without reference to the direction we wanted to move afterwards." At Gettysburg, where the only decisions left to Meade were tactical, his performance was exemplary; only after the battle and the initiative were won did his shortcomings as a strategist become evident. Cautious irresolution then plagued Meade's operations until Grant assumed personal command in Virginia. Somewhat embittered by the ambiguity surrounding his subordination to Grant, the testy Meade nonetheless served creditably as Grant's lieutenant for the remainder of the war, proving himself one of the Union's better second-echelon combat leaders. See George Meade, *Life and Letters of George Gordon Meade* (2 vols., 1913).

ROBERT L. KERBY

MEANY, George (b. New York, N.Y., Aug. 16, 1894; d. Washington, D. C., Jan. 10, 1980), LABOR LEADER, became a plumber's apprentice in 1910 and a journeyman plumber in 1915. He joined the plumbers' union that same year and soon became active in the labor movement. Elected business agent of the Plumbers' Union Local 463 in 1922, he served in that post until 1934 when he became president of the New York State Federation of Labor. During the late thirties he was also a member of the New York State Industrial Council and the State Advisory Council on Unemployment Insurance. He also worked for reform legislation in Albany. In 1939 Meany was elected general secretary-treasurer of the American Federation of Labor. During World War II he served on the National Defense Mediation Board (1941) and the National War Labor Board (1942–45); he was on the National Advisory Board on Mobilization Policy during the Korean conflict. In 1951 he helped create and became an executive board member of the International Confederation of Free Trade Unions, organized to combat the Communist-controlled World Federation of Trade Unions. Upon the death of William Green in 1952, Meany became acting president of the AFL. He was elected permanent president the following year.

One of Meany's first actions as president was to expel the International Longshoremen's Association for corruption. Always interested in achieving a rapprochement between the AFL and the CIO, he helped bring about their merger in 1955 and was elected the first president of the new organization. Meany continued to battle union corruption by enforcing ethical-practice codes for union leaders, and promoted the AFL-CIO's international crusade against Communist infiltration of the Western world's labor movement. Meany backed Democratic presidential candidates **Adlai Stevenson** (1956), John F. Kennedy (1960), Lyndon Johnson (1964), and **Hubert Humphrey** (1968) and emerged as labor's staunchest defender of President Johnson's Vietnam policies. An increasingly bitter quarrel between Meany and Vice President **Walter P. Reuther** over policy led the United Auto Workers to withdraw from the AFL-CIO in 1969 to form a more activist and reformist-oriented labor organization, the Alliance for Labor Action. In the 1972 presidential election, Meany, who invariably supported Democratic candidates, favored Richard M. Nixon over George McGovern, and used his influence to keep the AFL neutral. During the late 1970s he was a sharp critic of President Carter because he felt his administration ignored the advice and needs of organized labor. In poor health for several years, Meany retired as president of the AFL in November 1979. He was named president emeritus, retaining his salary. Lane Kirkland, his long time close aid and the union's secretary treasurer, succeeded him.

⸎

In his career, and in the brand of leadership he gave to organized labor since he replaced William Green in 1952, George Meany exemplified the evolution of conservative American trade unionism into its modern form. Meany grew up wholly within the tight tradition of craft-oriented business unionism that dominated the labor movement since the late 19th century. His steady advancement, first within the plumbers' union and then in the larger movement, depended on his possession of the qualities prized by American craft unionists—a workingman's background including actual journeyman's experience; a shrewd, realistic intelligence in carrying on union affairs; and an unassailable loyalty to the principles and internal rules of the labor movement. These qualities Meany carried with him for more than thirty years in Washington as a national spokesman for labor. A blunt, cigarchewing, heavyset man, Meany always aggressively defended labor's prerogatives and interests as these were understood by conservative business unionism.

Yet the times changed profoundly for the AFL since Meany became a national leader at the end of the 1930s. And Meany's success owed as much to his ability to respond to the new as to adhere to the old. He advocated an accommodation with the CIO once it demonstrated the viability of industrial unionism, and was instrumental in bringing about the merger in 1955. He instituted internal reforms (when the times called for them) to deal with union corruption and to end discrimination against blacks. He used labor's political muscle in Washington to advance a host of liberal causes, not those of labor alone. He involved the AFL-CIO in foreign affairs to a degree unprecedented in American labor history. And he helped to make organized labor a powerful political force in the country.

In all of this, Meany somehow managed a unique blend of old and new. If he took the labor movement into foreign affairs, it was to advance cold war policies, not disengagement. If he was in politics, it was to support the Humphrey wing of the Democratic party, not the advocates of a new politics. Consistently, Meany's leadership managed to satisfy labor's old guard while breaking new ground. Meany's mixture of old and new—the despair of many outside the movement—probably represented the maximum progress for the united labor movement, and will stand as a monument to his particular genius. See John Corry, "The Many-Sided Mr. Meany," *Harper's* (March 1970), pp. 52–58.

DAVID BRODY

MELLON, Andrew William (b. Pittsburgh, Pa., March 24, 1855; d. Southampton, L.I., N.Y., Aug. 26, 1937), FINANCIER, attended the Western University of Pennsylvania (now University of Pittsburgh) but left in 1872 to start a lumber business near Mansfield, Pennsylvania. In 1874 he entered his father's bank. His father transferred ownership of T. Mellon and Sons to him in 1882. After his father retired (1886), Andrew Mellon took in his brother Richard as a partner (1887). He backed the chemist Charles Hall in establishing the Aluminum Co. of America (Alcoa) in 1890 and became a partner of Edward Goodrich Acheson in the Carborundum Co. in 1896. He helped found Gulf Oil Corporation in 1901 and also the Union Steel Co., Standard Steel Car Co., Pittsburgh Coal Co., and many other firms in this period. Together with **Henry Clay Frick,** Mellon founded the Union Trust Co. of Pittsburgh in 1899. In 1902 T. Mellon and Sons was incorporated as the Mellon National Bank with Mellon serving as its president until 1921. He and his brother established the Mellon Institute of Industrial Research at the University of Pittsburgh in 1913.

Becoming active behind the scenes in Pennsylvania politics just prior to 1920, Mellon became friendly with Old Guard Republican Senator Philander C. Knox. At Knox's suggestion, President Harding appointed Mellon as his secretary of the treasury (1921). As secretary under Harding and Coolidge, Mellon sought to reduce the national debt; between 1921 and 1929, it fell from $24 billion to $16.2 billion. He also believed that taxes on high incomes should be reduced so that the wealthy could invest their money in productive enterprises, and he persuaded Congress to lower tax rates in various revenue measures passed during his tenure. He opposed veterans' bonus bills and the McNary-Haugen farm-relief proposals, but approved of the Agricultural Credit acts in 1921 and 1923, which provided for farm loans.

President Hoover retained Mellon as treasury secretary. During the Great Depression his conservative policies were increasingly attacked, and he lost much of his earlier prestige and popularity. After a 1931 trip to Europe he helped persuade Hoover to declare a moratorium on international war debts. In 1932 Hoover appointed Mellon ambassador to Great Britain, but he resigned when President Franklin D. Roosevelt took office in March 1933. In 1934 he was involved in an income tax evasion case, but a grand jury failed to indict him for lack of evidence. The Board of Tax Appeals in a decision after his death cleared him of any wrongdoing. In 1937 Mellon gave his huge private art collection to the federal government, along with money to build the museum which became the National Gallery of Art in Washington, D.C.

When first appointed secretary of the treasury, Mellon was already sixty-five and one of the three wealthiest men in the nation, the archetype of the modern finance capitalist. He then began a new career which ultimately made him one of the most influential political personalities in the period immediately preceding the New Deal. Although he was never popular with the general public, Mellon was regarded with awe and with great fascination by friend and foe alike, often serving as the center for political controversy and imparting to Republican administrations a "big business" bias. His tax policies unquestionably disproportionately aided the upper-middle and wealthy elements in society and helped set the stage for both the Coolidge boom and the ensuing stock market crash. In the early thirties Mellon became, with some validity, a scapegoat for the Depression.

His personality and his conservative economic ideas did tend to support his critics' charges of short-sightedness and self-interest rather than his friends' claims of wisdom and altruism. Mellon was not an imposing figure like **J. P. Morgan.** On the contrary, he seemed shy, ill at ease, and strangely diffident. One reporter put it this way: "If Mr. Mellon were unjustly accused of crime he would hang himself by appearing in his own defense." Physically Mellon was frail and slight; he usually wore dark clothes, a black tie, and drooping black socks, and always kept his coat buttoned. He smoked small black-paper cigarettes, gingerly puffing on them until there was not so much as an eighth of an inch left. In manner, he was always

serious. A smile rarely crossed his face. He had an odd little hesitation in his speech and was usually so quiet as to appear inarticulate. He shook hands only with the tips of his fingers. Considering his great wealth, the total effect was somewhat disconcerting. As one shocked reporter once claimed after meeting him for the first time: Mellon looked like "a tired double-entry bookkeeper who is afraid of losing his job." Another said that Mellon reminded him of "a dried up dollar bill that any wind might whisk away."

These appearances were, of course, deceiving. Throughout the 1920s presidents and cabinets alike looked to Mellon for guidance and direction in domestic and international financial policy. Harding eagerly sought his advice and took it without question; Coolidge thought of him as his most valued and trusted adviser; and even Hoover, who sometimes had crossed swords with Mellon while a fellow cabinet member, found it impossible to operate without his support. Charges and countercharges notwithstanding, Mellon's importance in the 1921–30 period was summed up best (although somewhat facetiously) by one contemporary who remarked that Mellon was the only cabinet member in American history to have had three presidents serve under him. A new biography of Mellon needs to be written. The best currently available is the outdated and biased Harvey O'Connor, *Mellon's Millions: The Biography of a Fortune* (1933).

Robert K. Murray

MELVILLE, Herman (b. New York, N.Y., Aug. 1, 1819; d. New York, N.Y., Sept. 28, 1891), WRITER. In 1830 his family moved to Albany, where two years later his father died, deeply in debt. Thereafter his mother, a member of the distinguished Gansevoort family, secured the dominant role in her son's life and imagination. After very limited formal schooling, Melville was forced by the large family's financial woes to work during the 1830s as a clerk, a common seaman, and a country schoolteacher. In January 1841 he joined the crew on the whaler *Acushnet*, bound for the South Seas. He deserted in the

Marquesas islands (July 1842) and lived briefly with a cannibal tribe before escaping on an Australian whaler, which he abandoned at Tahiti. At Tahiti he worked as a field laborer, then in 1843 he enlisted as a seaman on an American man-of-war bound for the U.S. In October 1844 he was discharged.

Melville became a prolific writer. *Typee* (1846) and *Omoo* (1847) were romantic narratives of life in the South Seas. Because Melville was one of the first white men to journey to—and write about—this part of the world, the works became popular. His next book, *Mardi* (1849), which also was set in the South Seas, was more complex. Beginning as another South Seas romance, the novel described an allegorical voyage in which the hero sought to find out the "truth about life." In 1849 Melville also published *Redburn*, based on his first voyage to Liverpool, a study of a man's initiation into the world of evil, of innocence confronted with reality. This work was followed by *White-Jacket* (1850), in which Melville sought to give some idea of the interior life in a man-of-war, based on his experience as a seaman returning from Honolulu aboard the U.S. frigate *United States* in 1844.

In 1850 Melville bought a farm near Pittsfield, Massachusetts, where he met **Nathaniel Hawthorne,** whose outlook he felt he shared. In 1851 he published *Moby Dick.* Set against the background of a whaling voyage, the novel treated such themes as good and evil, cowardice and courage, faith and pride. Melville also created in *Moby Dick* some of the most memorable figures in all of American literature, including Ishmael, the youth who goes to sea to understand the meaning of life, and Captain Ahab, who loses his humanity in his quest for the white whale.

Because of its complexity, *Moby Dick* was not understood by most readers. Moreover, as Melville's writing became more allegorical and experimental, his popularity declined. In 1852 he published *Pierre,* which dealt with such controversial matters as incest, suicide, the Oedipal theme, and the love triangle. This was followed by *Israel Potter* (1855), a story of the American Revolution; *The Piazza Tales* (1856), a collection of short stories;

and *The Confidence-Man* (1857), an allegory that takes place aboard a Mississippi riverboat and which further reveals Melville's dark view of man.

In 1856 Melville took a tour of the Holy Land. When he returned he lectured on Italian statuary and the South Seas (1857–60). During the Civil War he visited the battlefields in Virginia, and in 1866 he published *Battle-Pieces,* a collection of poems about the war. From 1866 to 1885 he was a customs inspector in New York City. In 1876 he published *Clarel,* a narrative poem based on his voyage to the Holy Land. *John Marr and Other Sailors* (1888) and *Timoleon* (1891), both works of poetry, were published privately. He worked on the manuscript of *Billy Budd* in 1891, but this story of an innocent youth aboard a man-of-war was not published until 1924.

⁂

With the exception of *Mardi,* in which Melville attempted unsuccessfully to combine romantic adventure and philosophic and political allegory, all of Melville's works before *Moby Dick* took the form of fictionalized autobiography of a kind well suited to please without challenging the taste of the rapidly growing reading public of the day. He himself later belittled them, as the author of *Moby Dick* had every right to.

What *Moby Dick* would have been like had Melville not met Hawthorne and discovered his tales in the summer of 1850 in the Berkshires must remain a matter for speculation, but the evidence suggests that it might well have been more like the earlier *White-Jacket,* which depicted life on board a naval vessel, than the great symbolic romance-epic we know today. Melville found himself immensely impressed by both Hawthorne the writer and Hawthorne the man. His review-article "Hawthorne and His Mosses" expressed with unrestrained enthusiasm his sense that he had at last discovered an American writer who was a kindred spirit, comparing him with Shakespeare in the ability to plumb the depths of experience and praising him for probing "the blackness of darkness" in an age of too easy affirmations. He would have to reread these tales that were sometimes "deep as Dante," he knew, to appreciate their full import, "but already I feel that this Hawthorne has dropped germinous seeds into my soul."

Melville was apparently well into the writing of *Moby Dick* when he discovered Hawthorne, decided to settle near him, and began to cultivate his friendship with an ardor that the contemporary reader may sometimes find embarrassing in the letters he wrote to Hawthorne between visits. But the "germinous seeds" dropped by the older writer sprouted and bore fruit: the period during which the two men were neighbors while Melville was working on *Moby Dick* and Hawthorne was writing *The House of the Seven Gables* was probably the happiest in Melville's life and certainly the period of greatest creative energy and imaginative growth. How much Melville as a writer was indebted to Hawthorne's example is suggested by Melville's dedication of his book to his friend and by much of the imagery and some of the themes of the work but is even more clearly evident in many of the shorter pieces later collected as *The Piazza Tales*. It seems clear that Hawthorne was at least partially responsible for the great creative leap between the thin and clumsy traditional allegory of *Mardi* and the symbolic richness of suggestion of *Moby Dick,* which raises the whaling industry and monomaniac Captain Ahab to epic and mythic proportions reminiscent of both Prometheus and Job.

When Hawthorne decided to move, Melville felt betrayed and suffered a series of nervous illnesses. *Pierre,* his tragic romance of an idealist's betrayal by life, is like *Moby Dick* in its use of symbolic effects and mythic overtones but lacks the control and aesthetic distance of the masterpiece. *The Confidence-Man* pictures life itself as a kind of "confidence game" in which we are all "taken in." When Melville came to write an introductory essay for *The Piazza Tales,* he turned back to Hawthorne's *Mosses,* which he had once so extravagantly admired, and in effect rewrote in his introductory sketch "The Piazza" Hawthorne's introductory essay, "The Old Manse," turning the themes and some of the symbolic images of his model upside down, as it were, to make his own piece a critique of what

had come to seem to him Hawthorne's unrealistic "idealism" and confidence.

After *Moby Dick* only a few of the tales—chiefly "Benito Cereno," "Bartleby the Scrivener," and perhaps *Billy Budd,* which he left unfinished at his death—can bear comparison with the masterwork. With the exception of a handful of poems, chiefly in *Battle-Pieces,* a poetic record of the Civil War, the poetry to which Melville devoted his writing time for some thirty years was unsuccessful, retaining what interest it has despite its awkwardness chiefly for the evidence in it of a keen mind at work on subtle problems. *Billy Budd* has sometimes been interpreted as a "testament of acceptance" of man's fate, but it perhaps might better be read as an allegory of stoic resignation. See Newton Arvin, *Herman Melville* (1950).

HYATT H. WAGGONER

MENCKEN, Henry Louis (b. Baltimore, Md., Sept. 12, 1880; d. Baltimore, Md., Jan. 29, 1956), JOURNALIST, became a police reporter for the Baltimore *Morning Herald* in 1899 and rose to city editor (1903–5). He was briefly (1905) managing editor of the *Evening Herald* before joining the staff of the Baltimore *Sun* in 1906, the paper with which he was associated in various capacities for the rest of his life. In 1908 he became literary critic for the *Smart Set* magazine, and he served as coeditor (1914–23) of that monthly with his close literary associate, drama critic George Jean Nathan. In 1924 Mencken and Nathan left *Smart Set* to found the *American Mercury* with financial backing from publisher Alfred A. Knopf. A year later Nathan ended their coeditorship, Mencken continuing as sole editor until 1933. During the 1920s he was also a contributing editor to *The Nation.*

In 1919 Mencken published *The American Language,* a study of the national vernacular which, in three enlarged editions and supplements (the last in 1948), gained worldwide recognition as a definitive work of philological scholarship. For many years he issued annual collections of his best articles (e.g., the six-volume

Prejudices series, 1919–27) and polemical essays in social philosophy such as *Notes on Democracy* (1926), *Treatise on the Gods* (1930), and *Treatise on Right and Wrong* (1934). He later turned to autobiography, producing three volumes of widely admired reminiscences (*The Days of H. L. Mencken: Happy Days, Newspaper Days, Heathen Days*, 1941–47).

Mencken tried his hand at almost every genre of belles-lettres and journalism, publishing more than thirty books of his own, contributing to scores of others, and, in his active years, writing an average of ten thousand words each week for publication. As a literary critic who attacked popular authors and established literary taste while championing the work of such newcomers as **Theodore Dreiser, Eugene O'Neill, F. Scott Fitzgerald,** and **Sinclair Lewis,** and as a social commentator who mounted sharp attacks on evangelical religion, censorship, super-patriotism, prohibition, Rotarianism, and the American bourgeoisie (whom he dubbed "booboisie"), Mencken was a highly controversial figure who was idolized by the "Young Intellectuals" of the post–World War I era. His influence declined rapidly, however, in the depression-wracked 1930s when he took an anti–New Deal stance, and thereafter he went into virtual retirement.

———— ❧ ————

Mencken came to national prominence in a time of literary burgeoning in America, when enormous growth of literacy and important technological advances in publishing, advertising, and mass circulation had created a huge popular demand for ephemeral literature and had provided a means for inexpensively satisfying that demand. Within a few years the cinema and, still later, radio and television would capture large segments of the great audience that, on the eve of World War I, found diversions on the newsstands and in bookstores in a body of popular writing that was unbelievably cheap, tawdry, and sentimental, supported by criticism that, guided by the principle "if you can't praise, don't dispraise," was either defensively parochial or pedantic. In the face of this, Mencken rightly saw

his mission as that of a destructive critic, cleansing the temple of its false gods and heralding the good, true, and beautiful creations of a neophyte generation. For a brief period, circa 1918–25, he was undoubtedly the most powerful and widely influential literary and social critic the United States has ever had. On the *Smart Set,* his position as critic was reinforced by that as partner in a raucously iconoclastic editorship that, making a virtue of economic necessity, took paternal interest in young writers and espoused experimentalism of at least a cautious sort, thus occupying an important middle ground between the avant-garde and the mass-circulation and literary periodicals.

But the secret of Mencken's power in and out of literary criticism lay in his virtually inimitable style. It was at once abrasive and beguiling, colloquial and learned, slack and aphoristic, full of barnyard wit and recondite allusions. His astonishing, freewheeling vocabulary ranged from slang and deliberate solecisms to the choicest Latin and German phrases. If the Menckenian style masks with skillful rhetoric a certain intellectual thinness and superficiality, it yet succeeds in flattering the reader's sense of superiority as a member of a "civilized minority" without obvious appeals to snobbery. At its worst, Mencken's prose is never ponderous or dull; at its best, it exhibits one of America's most polished satiric styles, observable in such frequently anthologized essays of Mencken as "On Being American," "Puritanism as a Literary Force," and his mock obituary of **William Jennings Bryan,** "In Memoriam: W.J.B." The stamp of **Mark Twain,** whom Mencken revered, is unmistakably on this style, as is that of Thomas Henry Huxley, another of Mencken's youthful idols.

Mencken looked upon literary criticism as but a branch of social and cultural criticism, and it was inevitable that he should move from the smaller to the larger area of critical concern, as he did in the *American Mercury.* Here, as the 1920s waned, he gained his largest popular following, as a "sage" to campus rebels, heterodox Rotarians, and village intelligentsia of the American hinterlands who applauded his rhetorical onslaughts on southern and midwestern religious fundamentalism ("the Bible Belt" was a Mencken coinage), on Puritanism (a term he loosely applied to everything from the quasi-official censorship of "smuthounds" to prohibition), on boosterism and other forms of commercial hypocrisy, and on democracy itself—"the theory that the common people know what they want and deserve to get it, good and hard." In the era of flappers and flivvers, of bootleggers and "tin-horn messiahs," Mencken was lucky in his targets, but he made the most of his opportunities and helped heap laughter on much that needed reforming or was long outmoded. He saw clearly, as but few others had, the paradoxes and contradictions in our national life and its democratic pretensions and, like **James Fenimore Cooper,** John Jay Chapman, and Charles A. Dana before him, he did not hesitate to point out the warts, moles, and blemishes on the face of America, perhaps more successfully than his predecessors had done.

Yet, for all his attractive punditry, Mencken was a tory radical, a man increasingly out of step with his time. Most of his intellectual commitments were made well before 1908 under the influence of Friedrich Nietzsche and other aesthetic philosophers of the *fin de siècle.* His ideal world was a composite of Wilhelmine Germany and his native Baltimore of the 1880s. Thus oriented, Mencken found it difficult to accept the accelerating changes in America after World War I, to comprehend the dangers in the rise of fascism, or to understand the sobering economic realities of the 1930s. The ultimate irony of Mencken's career is that the writer who had once fought so valiantly for freedom of expression and emancipated thought in America ended as the darling of reactionaries. See Douglas C. Stenerson, *H. L. Mencken: Iconoclast from Baltimore* (1971).

CARL DOLMETSCH

MERGENTHALER, Ottmar (b. Hachtel, Ger., May 11, 1854; d. Baltimore, Md., Oct. 28, 1899), INVENTOR, was apprenticed at the age of fourteen to a watchmaker in Bietigheim, Germany,

and emigrated to the U.S. in 1872. He settled in Washington, D.C., where he worked in a scientific instrument shop (1872–76). When this shop was transferred to Baltimore (1876), he moved to that city.

While working in Baltimore, Mergenthaler was called upon to correct the defects in a new printing machine that was planned by James O. Clephane and devised by Charles Moore. The purpose of this machine was to produce print by typewriting and to reproduce the work by means of a lithographic process. After working on this and a related invention for a number of years, however, Mergenthaler abandoned them (1879).

In 1883 Mergenthaler opened up his own instrument shop in Baltimore, and shortly thereafter Clephane asked him to construct a typesetting machine which would produce a papier-mâché matrix from which type could be cast. In July 1884 Mergenthaler perfected the first linotype machine, which was capable of casting type slugs directly from metal matrices. His invention greatly reduced the cost of printing and speeded up newspaper production. With Clephane, he set up the National Typographic Co. of West Virginia to manufacture the machine. In 1885 they established the Mergenthaler Printing Co. During the remaining years of his life Mergenthaler continued to make improvements on the basic device.

———※———

By the 1880s the expense of setting type had become the chief remaining impediment to the flood of information which has since deluged and come near to drowning the modern mind. In their decades-long struggle to mechanize the compositor's work, some men literally went insane. Others such as James Paige, who cost **Mark Twain** a fortune, produced machines of such staggering complexity as to require book-length patent specifications. Yet Mergenthaler's fundamental insight—to cast a line of type directly from metal matrices mechanically positioned by a keyboard, instead of using such matrices for an intermediary papier-mâché mold—seemed so thunderously obvious once stated that Mergenthaler had to reassure his backers with the story of

Columbus's egg. "When I set about the problem," he later explained, "I studied it carefully and chose the best method of attack, without regard for those used by others. I ... intended not to follow them to bankruptcy and ruin."

To carry his idea through, however, Mergenthaler drew upon still other abilities than that of seeing to the simple heart of a complex problem. When the estimated expense of sufficiently precise matrices threatened to block commercial success, he summoned up the energy and confidence that had brought him to the New World, the feeling for precision and complex mechanical harmonies instilled by his watchmaker's training, the versatility of his early American years of making patent models, and the characteristic doggedness of the inventor, and proceeded to build thirty special machines for his own successful matrix factory. His love for his great invention led him to keep improving it even after he sold the basic rights; notwithstanding that quixotic compulsion, the practicality which went with his other traits brought him fame and fortune before his relatively early death. See Willi Mengel, *Ottmar Mergenthaler and the Printing Revolution* (1954).

ROBERT V. BRUCE

MERRIAM, Charles Edward, Jr. (b. Hopkinton, Iowa, Nov. 15, 1874; d. Washington, D.C., Jan. 8, 1953), POLITICAL SCIENTIST, graduated from Lenox College, Hopkinton, and studied briefly at the Law School of the University of Iowa. He took his doctorate at Columbia University (1900) under the direction of William A. Dunning. After a year at the University of Berlin, he joined the faculty of the University of Chicago, where he remained until his retirement. Between 1903 and 1920 his involvement first in Chicago politics and then in the national Progressive party earned him the reputation of scholar-politician, "the Woodrow Wilson of the West"; but a succession of abortive attempts to become mayor of Chicago combined with the decline of progressive politics to end that career. During 1920–30 he worked to broaden the interests of American social scientists through helping to found the Social Science Research Council, the Public Administration Clearing House, and the Local Community Research Committee of the University of Chicago. His presidency of the American Political Science Association in 1925 marked the modernization of that profession's commitment to research in political behavior. His students continued to dominate the profession into the 1960s as products of the group which came to be known as "the Chicago School." Merriam's participation in the federal government's emerging concern with the social sciences came through his membership on the President's Research Committee on Social Trends, appointed by Herbert Hoover in 1929. President Roosevelt appointed him to the planning group which ultimately became the National Resources Planning Board. He was a member of the President's Committee on Administrative Management (1939). His extensive publications ranged from the succession of historical studies of American political theory which grew out of his training under Dunning to the hortatory essays of the 1920s and 1930s, of which *New Aspects of Politics* (1925) is the best example. Of his later efforts to undertake the development of a new American political theory, *Political Power* (1934) was the most influential.

⚬⚬⚬

Merriam's career is a model for the development of the modern academic as a force in American social and political life. Both his political and his academic activities were built on promotion: of the private and public associations which organize reform; of social research; of the application of social research to public needs; of an interest in social research on the part of those who finance it as well as on the part of those responsible for public management. He believed that relationships among universities, philanthropists, and governments at all levels had to be formulated in ways which emphasized their increased dependence on one another. Merriam's point of view originated in his initial concern with American political theory. From his earliest writings he sought to define political thought in terms of the behavior that the practitioners of politics engaged in, and the justifications they gave in political argument for that behavior, rather than through the traditional treatises on which political philosophy had been based. His behaviorism was thus an outgrowth of the pragmatism which had culminated in the writing of **John Dewey.**

But Merriam extended the intellectual and educational base of Dewey's instrumentalism beyond its emphasis on knowledge and ideas to encompass all the processes on which American politics was built: among others, parties, voting behavior, and the practice of administration. Merriam rejected the socioeconomic emphasis which **Charles Beard** and, in his later years, Dewey himself saw at the root of the processes of American politics. Politics was the chief among the sciences of society, he insisted. It was served, but only served, by psychology, history, law, sociology, and economics, in approximately that order. Man's capacity for making moral choices was the key to his political motivation, not economic class. It was the function of social science to analyze that capacity, to inform it, to reshape it. For much of his career, Merriam's political science was an effort to correct the assumptions and refine the instruments of his earlier progressivism. If by the end of his career that progressivism was no longer identifiable in his viewpoint, that itself was an accurate measure of the degree to which progressivism had been transformed. Progressivism's essential failure, to Merriam's generation, was its lack of foundation in the scientific approach to which its adherents gave such lip service. The social science of the twenties and thirties was to be their response. Unmoved by the threats of socialism, communism, or fascism which critics familiar with world trends of the period saw in their involvement in government policy, Merriam and other social scientists of his persuasion sought a definition of social planning which would organize for social research not just experts in government, business, or the universities but all of American society. Democratic planning—planning consis-

tent with the traditional structure of American government—was what Merriam sought. The National Resources Planning Board stands as a monument to his efforts to attain that goal. See Barry D. Karl, *Charles E. Merriam and the Study of Politics* (1974).

BARRY D. KARL

MERTON, Robert King (b. Philadelphia, Pa., July 5, 1910), SOCIOLOGIST, graduated from Temple University in 1931. He received his graduate training in sociology at Harvard (MA, 1932; PhD, 1936). After working as an assistant and tutor (1934–36) and then as instructor of sociology (1936–39) at Harvard, Merton accepted a post at Tulane University, where he was associate professor (1939–40) and then professor and chairman of the department of sociology (1940–41). In 1941 Merton moved to Columbia University as an assistant professor. He was named Giddings Professor of Sociology in 1963 and held that chair until he retired in 1979. He also served from 1942 to 1971 as associate director of the Bureau for Applied Social Research, New York City. He was a Guggenheim fellow (1962–63), and the 1962 Daniel Coit Gilman lecturer at Johns Hopkins University.

Merton has been a prolific and influential writer and theorist. In 1938 the *American Sociological Review* published his "Social Structure and Anomie," while in the same year his book *Science, Technology, and Society in Seventeenth-Century England* appeared. In this latter work, an outgrowth of his doctoral dissertation, Merton sought to elucidate links between technological progress and changing social conditions, basing his work especially on an examination of the careers of persons listed in the *Dictionary of National Biography. Mass Persuasion* (1946) employed content analysis, interviews, and questionnaires to study the impact of a radio appeal made by Kate Smith in support of the Third War Loan program during World War II. In *Student Physicians* (1957), Merton used diaries, observational studies, and questionnaires to examine the attitudes and relationships of medical students at Cornell, Western Reserve, and the University of

Pennsylvania. His major theoretical works are *Social Theory and Social Structure* (1949) and *On Theoretical Sociology* (1968). In these books, Merton has rejected both all-inclusive theoretical systems and mere consideration and summarization of empirical data. Instead, he has fashioned "middle-range theories" which seek to systematize the empirical data relating to a limited range of phenomena. He is perhaps best known as an exponent of the "functional" school of sociology, which studies social phenomena as effects of specific social arrangements such as class or kinship systems. He has sought especially to codify and make explicit the difference between "manifest" and "latent" functions. Among his other works, he coedited a *Reader in Bureaucracy* (1952) with A. P. Gray, B. Hockey, and H. C. Selvin, *Sociology Today* (1959), with Leonard Broom and Leonard S. Cottrell, and *Contemporary Social Problems* (1961) with Robert A. Nisbet.

─── ∞∞∞ ───

Robert King Merton is one of those rare scholars who has exercised almost as great an influence on his discipline by his performance as a lecturer and classroom teacher as by his published writings. Years before the term "charismatic" had diffused far beyond the ranks of academic social scientists to become a journalistic cliché, Merton's students were applying the word to him to explain the powerful attraction he exercised over them as a lecturer, and as a scholar exemplifying the most ambitious hopes of sociology. Tall, straight, youthful, with eyes that seemed to pierce and gleam, his elegant yet precise mode of discourse and the sense of controlled intellectual intensity underlying it entranced his audiences. Many were inspired by him as by no other teacher to pursue careers as academic sociologists, among them Digby Baltzell, Peter Blau, Lewis Coser, Alvin Gouldner, and Philip Selznick to mention only the most eminent.

Yet the very luminosity of Merton's intellectual gifts discouraged some students, an effect that was enhanced by a certain lack of personal warmth behind his almost courtly manners and by his tendency to manipulate his students in a highly controlled kind of Socratic dialogue in the classroom. In contrast to many sociologists who are notorious for their clumsy and jargon-ridden prose, Merton wrote with a graceful and individual style, but his manner of expression often seemed contrived and artificial, excessively patterned on 18th-century prose models. Indeed as a playful venture he wrote and published a book, *On the Shoulders of Giants* (1965), parodying 18th-century humanistic scholarship.

What Merton seemed to embody in the late forties and early fifties was the promise of a truly scientific sociology that might match the natural sciences and the more developed social sciences in precision of results, logical rigor, and significant scope. He projected what might be called the *mystique* of sociology as a social science, probing behind the appearances of social life with a scalpel-like conceptual precision to uncover hidden truths accessible in no other way. Yet the "unity of theory and research" at the level of "middle-range" inquiry that Merton advocated came under attack in the late fifties, notably by the late **C. Wright Mills**, his Columbia colleague, for its avoidance of the most significant and live social and political issues and for its commitment to a narrow view based on natural science models that ignored the distinctive qualities of human experience.

This critique in a variety of different guises spread in the sixties, particularly among younger sociologists, by no means all of them political activists on the left, with the result that Merton's programmatic goals for sociology and the power of his personal example lost influence. Merton increasingly in his own research and teaching turned away from the major issues in sociological theory and method back to his own original field of research, the sociology of science, in which he has continued to inspire a small but energetic group of students. Yet owing to his enormous influence as a teacher on people of very diverse sociological and ideological persuasions, he has managed to escape the extreme censure to which his own teacher, **Talcott Parsons,** has been subjected as the paragon of so-called establishment sociology. In recent years he has worn with grace and good nature the mantle of "elder statesman" in the discipline, even if he can no longer be accurately described as "Mr. Sociology," an epithet once applied to him by the author of a *New Yorker* profile. See M. M. Hunt, "Robert K. Merton," *The New Yorker*, Vol. XXXVI (Jan. 28, 1961).

DENNIS H. WRONG

MICHELSON, Albert Abraham (b. Strelno, Prussia, Dec. 19, 1852; d. Pasadena, Calif., May 9, 1931), PHYSICIST, was brought to the United States in 1854, where his parents established a dry goods store in Murphy's Camp, California. After high school graduation he tried to gain an appointment to the U.S. Naval Academy by competitive exam, but failed. He then went to Washington, where he induced President Grant to give him a presidential appointment to the academy. He received his commission in 1873, served as instructor of physics and chemistry at Annapolis (1875–79), then studied in Germany and France (1880–82). Resigning from the navy and returning to the U.S. in 1883, he served until 1889 as professor of physics at Case School of Applied Science in Cleveland. He then taught at Clark University until 1892. Upon the founding of the University of Chicago, he was chosen head of its physics department, a post he held until his retirement in 1931.

Michelson's experiments, summed up in seventy-eight published papers beginning in 1878, were mainly in the field of optics. His major work was to determine accurately the velocity of light and to study optical interference. His finding in 1879 that the speed of light is $299,910 \pm 50$ kilometers per second was accepted until Michelson himself determined a more precise figure in 1927. One of his objectives was to detect, if possible, the absolute motion of the earth as it moves through space. In common with scientific opinion of the day, Michelson believed that light consisted of an electromagnetic wave motion carried through a stationary ether, against which cosmic motion might be measured. His experiments with light beams, however, showed that no such stationary ether existed. Thus Newtonian assumptions about absolute motion were called into serious question. In 1887, in cooperation with Edward W. Morley, he conducted the famous Michelson-Morley experiments, which investigated the effect of earth's orbital motion on the speed of light. The results showed that the velocity of light is constant, irrespective of the motion of the source of light and of the motion of the observer. This finding and Michelson's preceding investigations of the ether heavily influenced theorists like H. A. Lorrentz and later became cornerstones for **Albert Einstein**'s two theories of relativity.

Michelson also contributed to the theory of spectroscopy, linking molecular motion with temperature. In metrology he reduced the standard meter bar in Paris to an exact number of wavelengths of cadmium radiation. Largely for this achievement and for his innovative instruments in spectroscopy, in 1907 Michelson became the first American to receive a Nobel Prize for physics.

Michelson, a master of measurement in experimental physics, was so good at his profession that he was acknowledged by **George E. Hale** and Albert Einstein, among others, as a master artist of science. His combination of talents, skill, and aesthetic sense led to early and permanent recognition, giving Michelson a commanding position in American science by the turn of the century.

Although generally typical of the Victorian generation of physicists, Michelson raised himself far above mediocrity by his passion for exact measurement, his instinct for truly fundamental work, and his quests for beautiful patterns within precision. Philosophically he was a rather stern Newtonian who believed mostly (except for the ether behind the wave theory of light) in whatever he could measure. Professionally he supported the growing super-specialization of the exact sciences and worked hard all his life to protect and promote the purity and practice of academic physics. Politically conservative as befitted a successful self-made scientist, he nevertheless championed the cause of faculty self-determination while building three departments. Physics in the United States after 1880 owed much of its character and most of its reputation to a handful of leaders like Michelson.

As a champion of the sixth or nth decimal place, Michelson had few peers worldwide in designing and manipulating precision optical devices. His standards for accuracy in spectroscopy, interferometry, metrology, and polarimetry attracted graduate students and colleagues from afar. His family and undergraduates sometimes suffered from his dedication to the research laboratory and from military habits instilled at Annapolis. But Michelson mellowed with age. He took zestful pleasure in billiards, tennis, watercolor painting, and professional politics. At the University of Chicago after 1895 his life became more tranquil, especially after a second marriage. Soon thereafter, as this nation's first Nobel Prize–winning scientist, his status was permanently assured.

Michelson was short in stature, handsome, possessed of a dry wit, and was always careful of appearances. His vision was excellent, his gait energetic, and his brain fertile with testable ideas. Although he was never a charismatic teacher or prolific in his writings, he worked well alone yet became a good administrator. As the epitome of the *experimental* as opposed to the theoretical physicist, Michelson remained somewhat skeptical of the relativity and quantum revolutions, but until death he never lost faith in his "beloved" ether or in using light waves as probes of "the infinite and the infinitesimal." See D. T. McAllister, *Albert Abraham Michelson: The Man Who Taught a World to Measure* (1970).

LOYD S. SWENSON, JR.

MIES VAN DER ROHE, Ludwig (b. Aachen, Ger., March 27, 1886; d. Chicago, Ill., Aug. 17, 1969), ARCHITECT, attended the Cathedral School in Aachen (1897–99) and then a local trade school (1900–1902). He spent the next few years as an apprentice and draftsman for local architects. In 1905 he moved to Berlin, where he was apprenticed to furniture designer Bruno Paul. In 1907 Mies built his first house as an independent architect; the following year he joined architect Peter Behrens, whose office was a training ground for modern architecture, as a draftsman. He left in 1911 and went to The Hague to design the abstractly classical Kröller House. It was never built, however, and he returned to Berlin in 1912 to start his own architectural office. He served in the German army during World War I in the Balkans and on the eastern front (1914–18).

After returning to Berlin in 1919, Mies drew plans for several prophetically modern structures, mostly in glass and steel, which were published but not constructed. He promoted modern art and architecture by financing an avant-garde magazine, *G*, and directed architectural exhibitions for the Novembergruppe, an organization of modern artists (1921–25). Finally, in the mid-1920s, he built several important residences whose textured brick surfaces complemented their otherwise austere façades (Wolf House, Guben, 1926; the Lange and Esters houses, Krefeld, 1928). In the same years, he built workers' apartments (1925) and the Liebknecht-Luxemburg Monument (1926) in Berlin. He also designed the "MR" chair in 1927 and other innovative furniture using metal and leather. He served as first vice president of the Deutscher Werkbund, an organization to promote high standards of applied design (1926–32) and was in charge of the Werkbund's exposition of modern houses designed by architects from all over the world at the Weissenhofsiedlung, Stuttgart, in 1927. His German Pavilion building at the 1929 International Exposition at Barcelona was crisply abstract. His "Barcelona chair" became internationally popular. He designed the Tugendhat house and furniture in Brno, Czechoslovakia, in 1930. Also that year he succeeded Gropius as director of the Bauhaus school of modern design in Dessau. But he was forced to close this "radical" school by the Nazis in 1933.

After visiting the U.S. in 1937, Mies became professor and director of architectural studies at the Armour Institute of Technology in Chicago in 1938; when that school merged with Lewis

Institute in 1940 to become the Illinois Institute of Technology, Mies retained his position. Starting in the early 1940s, he designed and supervised construction of an entirely new campus for the school. He also designed the glass and concrete Promontory Apartments (1948–49) and glass and steel 860 Lake Shore Drive Apartments (1950–51), both in Chicago. He retired from IIT in 1958 and thereafter devoted his time to his Chicago architecture office, designing such buildings as the Seagram Building in New York City (1958), the Chicago Federal Center (1963–68), and the National Gallery in Berlin (1968). He received numerous awards for his work, including the Presidential Medal of Freedom presented by Lyndon B. Johnson in 1963.

Of all the giants of modern architecture, Mies best achieved, in his sublimely stark, elegantly simple compositions, the ultimate in architectural purity and precision. His early abstractions of neoclassical motifs echoed the example of his fellow countryman, the early 19th-century architect Karl Friedrich Schinkel. Yet his greatest and most direct debts were to Bruno Paul, from whom he imbibed a taste for Japanese design, and Peter Behrens, in whose Berlin office he worked along with fellow apprentices Gropius and Le Corbusier. Like most young European architects, before and after World War I, he was also influenced by the work of **Frank Lloyd Wright,** published in 1910 by the German house of Wasmuth. Partially because the original "Wasmuth Folio" presented Wright's buildings via hard-edged line drawings, conveying a sharper, cooler, crisper image than did the later photographs of these warmly textured buildings, the unfolding work of Wright's European admirers resulted in harder, more abstract compositions. Mies was also stimulated by developments in other areas of design, especially the *De Still* paintings of van Doesburg and Mondrian in Holland. Yet besides drawing ideas from the other visual arts, he influenced these as well. Beneath the subtly proportioned post and beam serenity of most Miesian façades, there often lay, especially in the early buildings, a complex and dynamic articulation of space. One such creation, the Barcelona Pavilion, became one of the most celebrated influences in the history of modern design, not only for its spatial and structural effects, but for the quality of its famous furniture. Yet, like his earlier cubistic monument to the German Communists Liebknecht and Luxemburg (subsequently destroyed by the Nazis), the temporary Barcelona exposition building has been seen and admired chiefly through photographs.

Forced by political events to leave Nazi Germany in 1937, this strong, stoic, quietly sensitive man resettled in Chicago and soon felt at home in that fountainhead of modern architecture. In the city that produced the steel frame and the curtain wall, Mies reared his monumental structures of both horizontal and vertical orientations (IIT and Lake Shore Towers, respectively), spawning, in effect, a "Second Chicago School." He also moved outward to produce great buildings for the midwestern countryside and for other American cities. His steel and glass Farnsworth House, Plano, Illinois (1950), demonstrated his continuing sensitivity in the residential idiom, while his New York Seagram Building (1958) utilized the same materials in an exhilarating paradigm of the modern skyscraper form. Mies not only designed the campus and the major buildings at IIT, but he also proved his talents there as an influential teacher. He was served in this regard by the very teachable and communicable nature of his architecture, which by the 1960s had come to dominate the urban skyline. While legitimately and successfully repeatable in the hands of his better followers (Philip Johnson, Skidmore, Owings and Merrill), other examples of the ubiquitous glass tower have been frequently duller and less successful because their builders failed to understand the subtle and complicated elements of Miesian scale and proportion. For in his ordered and deceptively simple forms, one senses an architecture of rational genius and poetry. "Less is more" was his own cryptic motto—and his buildings everywhere reflect that message. See Arthur Drexler, *Ludwig Mies van der Rohe* (1960).

THOMAS S. HINES

MILKEN, Michael (b. Encino, Calif., July 4, 1946), FINANCIER, graduated from the University of California, Berkeley (1968), and received an MA from the University of Pennsylvania (1970), after which he went to work as director of research for low rated bonds at what then was to become Drexel Burnham Lambert (1970).

At the time the bond business was in the doldrums, and it was particularly difficult to sell issues of low rated bonds. With Milken's guidance, Drexel entered the new issue "junk bond" market in 1977. From then to 1983, it underwrote 276 junk issues worth $14.6 billion in principal amount.

Opportunities for immense profits were present, and this induced some within the industry to use their positions for illicit gain. In 1986 Drexel banker Dennis Levine was arrested on charges of insider trading. Promised leniency, he informed on speculator Ivan Boesky, who in turn accepted and was granted leniency for informing on others. Milken was one of those Boesky implicated. After much sparring, in 1990 Milken pleaded guilty to six felonies, none of which involved insider trading, and was sentenced to ten years in prison. He was released in 1993. Since his release, barred from the securities industry, Milken has kept a low profile but in 1995 he received a $50,000,000 commission from **Ted Turner** for advising him during the takeover negotiations of Turner Broadcasting by Time-Warner. Milken, who discovered he had prostate cancer while in prison, has devoted much of his energies in the last several years to setting up a foundation to fund research into the disease. He has poured millions of dollars of his estimated $1 billion fortune into this project.

Milken concentrated on medium-size businesses in new industries for whom markets generally would have been closed. In this period he helped finance such companies as MCI, Turner Broadcasting, and Kindercare.

By the 1980s corporate takeovers by "raiders" had become increasingly common. Drexel was issuing junk bonds used in takeovers by such men as Carl Icahn, T. Boone Pickens, and Ron Perelman. Milken had a network comprised of customers (insurance companies, savings and loans, mutual funds) and clients, like the young companies and takeover practitioners. He came to be seen as the most brilliant and innovative financier of his time by defenders, and a master criminal by those who believed him and his financial methods to be a destructive influence. See Robert Sobel, *Dangerous Dreamers* (1993).

ROBERT SOBEL

MILLER, Arthur (b. Oct. 17, 1915, New York, N.Y.), WRITER, graduated from the University of Michigan in 1938. While at Michigan, he served as night editor of the student paper, the Michigan *Daily,* and wrote a number of plays, one of which, *The Grass Still Grows* (1936), was awarded a Theatre Guild National Award (1938). In that year Miller returned to New York to join the Federal Theatre Project. After funds for this program were curtailed, he became a scriptwriter for such radio programs as "Columbia Workshops" (CBS) and "Cavalcade of America" (NBC). In 1944, after visiting army camps for Lester Cowan, a motion picture producer, to collect background material for a filming of Ernie Pyle's *Story of G.I. Joe,* Miller published a book, *Situation Normal,* based on his findings.

In 1945, he published *Focus,* a novel about anti-Semitism. In November 1944 his play, *The Man Who Had All the Luck,* opened on Broadway. The plot of this work dealt with the efforts of a successful small-town businessman, David Frieber, to test his conviction in the inevitability of disaster in life by launching a mink breeding project. This play closed quickly, but in 1947 Miller's *All My Sons* was awarded the New York Drama Critics' Circle Award as the best American play of that season. In this work, which dealt with the family of Joe Keller, and the exposure of Keller's complicity in the wartime sale of defective airplane parts, Miller treated the conflict between those who seek to evade the truth and those committed to unearthing it. In 1949 came *Death of a Salesman,* a play about a traveling salesman, Willy Loman, and his battle with the loneliness and disappointment of his life on the road. This work was awarded a Pulitzer Prize for drama. Miller followed this success with *The Crucible* (1953), *A Memory of Two Mondays* (1955), and *A View From the Bridge* (1955).

There then followed a long hiatus in his productions for the theater. In 1954 he was refused a passport as a person "believed to be supporting the Communist movement," and in 1956, having been called to testify before the House Un-American Activities Committee, he was cited for contempt of Congress, but given a suspended sentence, for refusing to reveal the names of persons he had seen at meetings of Communist front groups during the 1940s. His main publication during this period was *The Misfits* (1961), a novel based in Reno, Nevada, dealing with the search for a liberated existence by four characters unwilling to accept conventional social roles. This work was later made into a movie. In 1962, Miller completed *After the Fall,* which was the first production of the Lincoln Center repertory company in New York City. This was followed by *Incident at Vichy* (1965), and *The Price* (1968). From the 1970s through the 1990s, Miller's works have been performed in translation all over the world, including China, where a production of *Death of a Salesman* in Chinese received a tumultuous reception. His later plays, including *The American Clock* (1980), have generally received mixed reviews from the critics if not from most audiences who flock to any new play he is associated with.

There are two quite different patterns of concern in what Arthur Miller has written thus far. The first dominates the plays included in *The Collected Plays,* and the second emerged in *The Misfits* and has become increasingly manifest in his latter works.

The central conflict in the plays of Miller's first period grows out of a crisis of identity. Each of the protagonists is confronted with a situation which he is incapable of meeting and which eventually puts his "name" in jeopardy. In the ensuing struggle his inability to answer the question "Who am

I?" produces his downfall. Each of these plays is a judgment of a man's failure to maintain a viable connection with his society because he does not know himself, and the verdict of guilty is based upon Miller's belief that if man faced up to the truth about himself he could be fulfilled as an individual and still live within the restrictions of society.

His second period is concerned with the implications of "otherness" in both the private and public levels of experience. In these plays Miller is dealing with the effect his protagonist has had on the lives of others and his capacity to accept full responsibility for what he has done. But otherness is an ambiguous reality. Unless we can accept a person as another we can never really touch him; yet since we can never really know another, he will always be the stranger—and hence our enemy. This is an absurd contradiction, and for Miller any attempt to live in relationship is to make the Kierkegaardian leap.

Miller described one of his characters as "a lover of things, of people, of sheer living ... [one who] will not compromise for less than God's own share of the world." While he has no such Promethean ambitions Miller might be describing himself. Certainly no living American playwright writes with such moral earnestness and has a greater sense of social responsibility. See Leonard Moss, *Arthur Miller* (1968).

ROBERT W. CORRIGAN

MILLER, Kelly (b. Winnsboro, S.C., July 23, 1863; d. Washington, D.C., Dec. 29, 1939), EDUCATOR, SOCIOLOGIST, was the son of a free African-American tenant farmer who had served in the Confederate army. He showed an early aptitude in mathematics, and in 1878 was admitted to the Fairfield Institute in Winnsboro. He gained a scholarship to Howard University (Washington, D.C.) two years later, and received a BA in 1886 and MA in 1901. Miller also attended the Graduate School of Mathematics and Physics at Johns Hopkins University (1887–89). After briefly teaching high school in Washington (1889), he became professor of sociology at Howard in 1890, a position he held until his retirement in 1934. As dean of Howard's College of Arts and Sciences (1907–18), Miller did much to build up the college and broaden its curriculum.

Deeply interested in the role of the black man in American society, Miller eventually turned from science to the problem of race. An activist in the civil rights movement, he tried to unite all African-American organizations in the U.S. into one front in 1924, but failed. He began writing on sociology while helping **W. E. B. Du Bois** edit *Crisis* magazine. He believed that the race problem was part of the larger problem of all men living together, and hoped that reason and conscience might solve the problems of racism. Some of his many works include: *Race Adjustment* (1908), *Out of the House of Bondage* (1917), and *The Everlasting Stain* (1924).

———— ✦ ————

Kelly Miller was professor of sociology at Howard University for thirty-nine years. His was a sociology which, having just emerged from the womb of moral philosophy, had yet to learn scientific detachment. The sociology he taught from 1890 to 1934 was a blend of traditions: the tradition of humanistic letters, brought south by northern schoolteachers, and the evangelical tradition of soul saving. The resulting educational theory sought exposure to the sunshine of Western culture, with emphasis on the classics, but it also emphasized the student's moral superiority as a black man and his mission to uplift white civilization from its enslavement to greed. The deep ambivalences harbored by Miller's sociology toward both races are obvious. During the great debate between the **Booker T. Washington** forces of assimilation and adjustment and the W. E. B. Du Bois forces of separatism, Miller tried unsuccessfully to act as mediator. Compromisers usually satisfy nobody, but it is possible that Miller's understanding was the more intellectually honest one, with its recognition of the white reality as well as the need for black cultural dignity to cope with that reality. Miller's 1934 retirement coincided with the rise of a new sociology in the black colleges, a myth-blasting social science that rejected the idea of a black cultural tradition in

America; a sociology that permitted scientific detachment from the kind of dilemmas Miller tried to face. The whole of Miller's work, from his famous "open letters" of racial issues to **Thomas E. Watson,** Woodrow Wilson, and Warren G. Harding to his classroom instruction, testify to his deep and lasting involvement. See S. P. Fullinwider, *Mind and Mood of Black America: 20th Century Thought* (1969).

S. P. FULLINWIDER

MILLER, Perry Gilbert Eddy (b. Chicago, Ill., Feb. 25, 1905; d. Cambridge, Mass., Dec. 9, 1963), HISTORIAN, entered the University of Chicago in 1922, but left soon after for several years of wandering in Colorado, in Paterson, New Jersey, as a member of Southern and Marlowe's Shakespearean troupe, as a seaman on a tanker, and as a worker for an oil company in the Belgian Congo. He returned to the University of Chicago in 1926, earning both his PhB (1928) and his PhD (1931) in the field of English. He became an instructor at Harvard, where he worked with Kenneth B. Murdock and **Samuel Eliot Morison,** in 1931; in 1939 he was appointed associate professor of English.

His first book, *Orthodoxy in Massachusetts* (1933), was followed by an anthology, *The Puritans* (1938), with T. H. Johnson, and *The New England Mind: The Seventeenth Century* (1939). The three works served to establish Miller's early reputation of a reinterpreter of American Puritanism. During World War II Miller served as captain and major (1942–45) with the OSS in London. In 1946 he became professor of English at Harvard. He was a fellow at Princeton's Institute for Advanced Studies in 1953–54. In 1960 he was named the first Powell M. Cabot Professor of American Literature at Harvard. He published intellectual biographies of **Jonathan Edwards** (1949) and **Roger Williams** (1953) and, in 1953, what is generally acknowledged to be his greatest book, *The New England Mind: From Colony to Province*. Concurrently, he began an exploration of American romanticism through such works as *The Transcendentalists* (an anthology, 1950), *The Raven and the Whale* (1956), and essays on **Emerson, Thoreau,** and **Margaret Fuller.** In 1956 he published a collection of essays, *Errand into the Wilderness,* selected and arranged to establish the continuity and coherence of his studies in many periods of American thought. Another collection of essays, *Nature's Nation,* was published posthumously, as was his last work, *The Life of the Mind in America from the Revolution to the Civil War* (1965), the two completed sections of an unfinished nine-part, multivolume intellectual history of the early United States, which won a Pulitzer Prize.

Perry Miller's writings of the 1930s served to establish his primary reputation as a reinterpreter of Puritanism or as a "historian of New England" or as a "historian of American religion." Quite undeservedly this reputation came to a degree to be fixed, despite Miller's working well beyond the colonial period into post–Civil War America and even the 20th century, and despite his considerable corpus of writings on American literature, particularly the literature of the romantic period. Moreover, such categorizations of Miller confused his "materials," as he himself put it, with his "subject" and, even, his "subject" with his "theme."

In the larger sense Miller was concerned with "the life of the mind," not in America merely, but (to quote his own self-assessment in *Errand into the Wilderness*) as the "basic factor in human history." Miller's earlier writing challenged the suppositions of social and economic historians, but increasingly he turned to criticism of other would-be "intellectual historians" who, as he once complained, had "taken unto themselves the prerogative of chronicling the life of the mind without themselves distinguishing between the mind and the marketplace." Behind this criticism lay his conviction that both in the history of the human mind and in the writing of history, "form" controls, and must control, matter. The entire body of his writing is a monument to his conviction that historians must come to terms with the "controlling concepts" of any past society—as the forms within which its experience was both understood and responded to in action.

In the years after World War II, Miller became intrigued by what he felt was an even grander theme: America's unending effort to redefine its national "meaning." His sensitivity to the nuances and the ironies of this effort represented something of an extension of his personal conviction that the "liberal" intellectual is called to a kind of "perpetual suicide," being pledged to question and assail all "previous forms of thought," including his own. The spirit of eternal seeking that underlay Miller's work seemed often masked in his writing, in his teaching, and in his personal relationships by what struck many as an intense intellectual arrogance. Yet Miller, driven by his own mode of Augustinian piety, was as unsparing in his judgments of himself as of others, and his manner, like his matter, was part of his preaching a sustained "jeremiad" against all forms of 20th-century intellectual complacency. See Robert Middlekauff, "Perry Miller," in Marcus Cunliffe and Robin W. Winks, eds., *Pastmasters* (1969), pp. 167–90.

ALAN HEIMERT

MILLIKAN, Robert Andrews (b. Morrison, Ill., March 22, 1868; d. San Marino, Calif., Dec. 19, 1953), SCIENTIST, graduated from Oberlin College in 1891. After serving two years as a physics tutor, he studied physics at Columbia (PhD, 1895) and then at the universities of Berlin and Göttingen. In 1896 Millikan joined the faculty of the University of Chicago, becoming a full professor in 1910. At Chicago Millikan wrote several physics textbooks. In the laboratory he isolated the electron and proved that it had a definite constant charge. He received the Comstock prize of the National Academy of Sciences in 1913 for this research. In 1916 he verified **Albert Einstein**'s photoelectric equation and also evaluated Planck's constant, h, the elementary quantum of action. During World War I he served as chief of the science and research division of the U.S. Signal Corps, and worked closely with the U.S. Navy Special Board on antisubmarine devices.

In 1921 Millikan left Chicago to become director of the Norman Bridge Laboratory of Physics and chairman of the executive council at the California Institute of Technology in Pasadena. He was largely responsible for building the Institute into a great scientific institution. Millikan represented the U.S. for ten years (1922–32) on the League of Nation's Committee on Intellectual Cooperation. In 1923 he was awarded the Nobel Prize in physics for his work in isolating and measuring the charge of the electron and for studies of light and electricity (the photoelectric effect). While in California Millikan also pursued the study of cosmic rays (superpenetrating radiation). After his retirement from Caltech in 1946 Millikan served as chairman of the board of directors of the Huntington Library and Art Gallery (San Marino, Calif.).

Taught as a child to fear God, respect hard work, and improve his mind, Millikan was an energetic, self-confident bundle of Protestant ethic who had a knack for choosing research problems of striking significance. His demonstration that all electrons were particles of identical charge and mass helped pave the way for the nuclear model of the atom. His measurements of the electronic charge and Planck's constant served the world of physics for a generation. His conclusive proof that the penetrating radiation in the atmosphere came from the heavens established cosmic rays as a fecund field for the study of high-energy particles.

Millikan hypothesized about the origin of cosmic rays and found proof that the Creator was "continually on His job." An outspoken theological modernist, he always insisted, sometimes sanctimoniously, upon the reconcilability of science and religion. Controversial and widely popularized, his arguments helped make him the most famous American scientist of his day.

So did his espousal of conservative Republicanism. During the Depression, Millikan repeatedly contended that the promotion of science, because it led ultimately to new industries and jobs, was a much sounder way to achieve economic recovery than the New Deal. Simultaneously strong-minded about international affairs, he vigorously advocated military preparedness and collective security. A towering public figure, director of military research in World War I, consultant to corporations, member of numerous scientific boards, and leader of Caltech, Millikan personified the increasing linkage of academic, industrial, and governmental science and their mushrooming importance in national affairs. See Daniel J. Kevles, "Robert A. Millikan," *Dictionary of Scientific Biography* (1970).

DANIEL J. KEVLES

MILLS, Charles Wright (b. Waco, Texas, Aug. 28, 1916; d. Nyack, N.Y., March 20, 1962), SOCIAL SCIENTIST, received his BA and MA from the University of Texas, and PhD in sociology and anthropology from the University of Wisconsin (1941). He taught sociology at the University of Maryland, and was a Guggenheim fellow in 1945. In 1945 he also was appointed assistant professor of sociology at Columbia (professor, 1956). Out of his research while director of the labor research division of Columbia's Bureau of Applied Social Research (1945–48) came two studies, *The New Men of Power* (1948) and *The Puerto Rican Journey* (1950).

Mills's books were both scholarly and popular. Considered a rebel in the profession, he attacked established views and ideas. His *White Collar* (1950), a detailed analysis of the American middle class, was translated into several languages. *The Power Elite* (1956) probed the American ruling class. Mills believed that intellectuals, and especially social scientists, had an obligation to be socially concerned, and he was outspoken in his criticism of colleagues who thought otherwise. He died shortly after finishing *The Marxists* (1963). Some of his other volumes include: *The Causes of World War III* (1958), *The Sociological Imagination* (1959), and *Listen, Yankee: The Revolution in Cuba* (1960), a controversial presentation of Cuban views on U.S. policies.

Tall, heavyset, combative, C. Wright Mills allowed his colleagues in the sociology profession to torment him about as much as he tormented them. His irritation was rarely expressed in intimate, face-to-face relations; indeed, his professional associations with colleagues and students were virtually nonexistent. But—following *The New Men of Power* and *The Puerto Rican Journey,* both written while he was still working in the tradition of Columbia University's Bureau of Applied Social Research—Mills belabored his academic colleagues with a series of publications designed to show what was for him their theoretical conservatism, their methodological narrowness, and, above all, their moral bankruptcy. He considered Karl Marx and Max Weber the great social theorists, and he saw himself as following in their tradition of analysis of social change and, at the same time, of participation in it. *White Collar* and *The Power Elite* departed sharply from the then dominant mode of sociological research: they contained a sprinkling of statistics but were clearly qualitative, rather than quantitative, studies. They focused on problems of contemporary American society with a directness and specificity uncommon in sociological writing; and above all, they breathed a spirit of moral indignation that his colleagues found incompatible with scholarship but which he found requisite to it. In three books written shortly before his death—*The Causes of World War III, The Sociological Imagination,* and *Listen, Yankee*—not even a pretense remains of normal scholarly activity: there is no systematic collection of data, no presentation of evidence, no vestige of research designs. There is, however, a series of polemical essays in which Mills presents his views of recent historical changes, views which, though they still owe much to Marx and Weber, show some discomfort with Marxist society (as distinct from Marxist theory) and the narrowness of economic determinism, and also some restlessness with Weber's notions of scholarly objectivity. What blazes in all Mills's books is his concern that scholars come to grips with the problems of their time, and his contempt for those whose commitment was to other concerns. See Herbert Aptheker, *The World of C. Wright Mills* (1960).

SIGMUND DIAMOND

MITCHELL, John (b. Braidwood, Ill., Feb. 4, 1870; d. New York, N.Y., Sept. 9, 1919), LABOR LEADER, was raised by his stepmother after his father was killed in a mining accident. He went to work in the coal mines at the age of twelve. In 1885 he joined the Knights of Labor; shortly afterward depression in the coal industry forced him to travel west in search of work. He returned to Illinois in 1888 and two years later joined the local branch of the new United Mine Workers of America. He participated in the union's unsuccessful national strike in 1894 and was subsequently discharged from his job. The following year he became secretary-treasurer of his northern Illinois subdivision and in 1897 a member of the UMW's state executive board. He took an active part in the UMW's first victorious national strike in 1897 and was elected national vice president in 1898. Mitchell stepped into the vacant presidency that same year and became permanent president in 1899. He also served in the AFL as fourth vice president (1898–1900) and second vice president (1900–14).

Mitchell achieved national prominence in 1902 when he organized Pennsylvania anthracite coal miners, mostly recent immigrants, and won a five-month strike. After the intervention of President Theodore Roosevelt, the union gained a 10 percent wage increase, a nine-hour day, and a conciliation and arbitration board to handle future disputes. Although Mitchell won considerable prestige for his union he failed to get official recognition. The UMW's failures in West Virginia and Colorado bituminous coal strikes brought him under attack by socialists and other union rivals. Their assaults, together with his declining health, led to his resignation from the UMW presidency in 1908. He served as chairman of the National Civic Federation's trade-agreement department (1908–11), a position that caused his opponents in the labor movement to continue their attacks on him as a class collaborationist. He left the NCF in

1911 after the UMW adopted a resolution forbidding union members to belong to it. Believing that industrial peace and a reconciliation of business and labor would bring progress to both sides, Mitchell lectured and wrote widely, expounding his commitment to business unionism. Mitchell was a member of the New York State Industrial Commission from 1915 until his death. During his last decade he grew wealthy through investments in coal, railroads, and steel. Mitchell wrote two books on trade unionism, *Organized Labor* (1903) and *The Wage Earner and His Problems* (1913).

———⚬⚬⚬———

Paradox characterized John Mitchell's life. A business unionist *par excellence,* his caution and cultivation of public figures infuriated radicals. Yet he used these tactics to lead the mineworkers, who were to provide American labor with most of whatever militance and aggressiveness it could claim for the first forty years of the century, to significant early victories. Although he publicly doubted the élan and steadfastness of eastern and southern European workers, he achieved victory with them in 1902, and they in turn revered him. Lionized by a public impressed with his restraint and conservatism, he was a brilliant success at thirty-two. Before turning forty, however, he fell victim to illness, drink, and the attacks of union rivals; after 1908 he was never again a union leader. During his last decade he amassed a small fortune and associated principally with businessmen, and yet his public utterances and writings during this period reflect a sharper and more explicit class consciousness than he ever revealed as an officer of the UMW. Superficially, Mitchell's is a classic story of upward mobility, but the price of his wealth and social elevation was the growing skepticism of many laborites of his commitment to and sacrifices for the working class. Yet despite his condemnation by militants in the UMW, the anthracite miners continued to honor him. This, together with his financial success, may have sustained him as he contemplated the distance he had traveled from bleak Braidwood's mines to the suburban prosperity of his last years. See

Elsie Glück, *John Mitchell, Miner: Labor's Bargain with the Gilded Age* (1929).

ROBERT H. ZIEGER

MITCHELL, Maria (b. Nantucket, Mass., Aug. 1, 1818; d. Lynn, Mass., June 28, 1889), ASTRONOMER, was educated in her father's school and in that of Cyrus Peirce on Nantucket. In 1835–36 she ran a school for girls there. During 1836–56 she was the librarian of the Nantucket Atheneum and in those years taught herself astronomy and mathematics by reading works in French, German, and Latin. In 1847 she discovered a telescopic comet for which she won a Danish Royal Medal. In 1848 she was elected to the American Academy of Arts and Sciences, the first woman to be so honored. She also became the first woman member of the American Association for the Advancement of Science (1850). In the 1840s and 1850s she made astronomical observations with her father for the U.S. Coast Survey, and during 1849–68 she worked for the *American Ephemeris and Nautical Almanac*. She undertook astronomical research with a five-inch telescope given to her by Elizabeth Peabody in 1858, the gift "representing the women of America." Mitchell became professor of astronomy at newly established Vassar College in 1861, and also director of the observatory, equipped with a 12-inch telescope, then the third-largest in the U.S. She pioneered in the photographic study of sunspots and in the observation of Jupiter, Saturn, and their satellites. In 1869 she was elected to the American Philosophical Society. During 1873 she traveled throughout Europe and helped to found the Association for the Advancement of Women, later serving as its president (1875–76). She retired from Vassar and returned to Lynn in 1888. In 1905 she was elected to the Hall of Fame.

———⚬⚬⚬———

When Maria Mitchell, the first woman astronomer in America, was born on the Quaker island of Nantucket it was the greatest whaling port in the world. From childhood, she helped her father rate the whalers' chronometers and, in time, gained a worldwide reputation as a keen and skill-ful observer of planets, nebulae, and comets. In 1865, when this independent, unorthodox Nantucketer was asked to go to Vassar College, she accepted this opportunity to prove the Friends' belief that women are capable of doing any intel-lectual work that men can do, and to disprove the prevalent belief that too much study might dam-age a woman's brain. Her success as a teacher proved remarkable. As she carried on her research on the sun and planets, she shared it with her stu-dents, who learned to observe and experiment for themselves and to accept nothing without ques-tioning. "We especially need imagination in sci-ence," she insisted. "It is not all mathematics, nor all logic, it is somewhat beauty and poetry." Many, inspired by her example, carved out notable careers: twenty-five of her students were eventual-ly included in *Who's Who in America*. Meanwhile, in countless other ways, beyond the college walls, Maria Mitchell worked for the advancement of women's education and freedom, saying, "When the American girl carries her energy into the great questions of humanity, into the practical problems of life, when she takes to heart the interests of edu-cation, of government, and of religion, what may we not hope for our country!" See Helen Wright, *Sweeper in the Sky: The Life of Maria Mitchell, First Woman Astronomer in America* (1949).

HELEN WRIGHT

MITCHELL, Wesley Clair (b. Rushville, Ill., Aug. 5, 1874; d. New York, N.Y., Oct. 29, 1948), ECONOMIST, received his training at the University of Chicago (AB, 1896; PhD, 1899), and at the universities of Halle and Vienna (1897–98). After finishing his doctorate, he worked for a year (1899–1900) in the Census Office in Washington, D.C., then became an instructor of economics at the University of Chicago (1900–1902). He taught at the University of California as assistant profes-sor of commerce (1902–8) and professor of politi-cal economy (1909–12), and at Columbia University, where he served as lecturer (1913–14) and professor of economics (1914–19, 1922–44).

While active in teaching, Mitchell also had a

long career in public service and research: he was head of the price section of the War Industries Board (1918–19); chairman of the President's Research Committee on Social Trends (1929–33); a member of the National Planning Board, Federal Emergency Administration of Public Works (1933); and a member of the National Resources Board (1934–35). He also served as chairman of the Social Science Research Council (1927–30), and as director of research (1920–45) of the National Bureau of Economic Research, of which he was one of the founders. Besides his teaching and gov-ernment work, Mitchell was also a prolific writer. Among his most important works were *A History of the Greenbacks* (1903), *Business Cycles: The Problem and Its Setting* (1927), and especially, *Business Cycles* (1913). While earlier theories, based upon limited data, had attributed business fluctuations to a few, "key," outside disturbing factors, Mitchell viewed the business cycle as a function of the exi-gencies of business enterprise in the modern econ-omy. His works, based on extensive, detailed, sta-tistical inquiries, indicated that business cycle fluc-tuations were diffused throughout the economy, and caused other economists to see the cycle as neither minor nor accidental to modern economic organization. In *Measuring Business Cycles* (1946), which Mitchell wrote with Arthur F. Burns, the authors described the range of observations need-ed to test for a business cycle and gave criteria for the identification of the cycle.

Though he was a middle westerner by birth, a New England strain was always discernible in the thought and life of Wesley Mitchell. Whether he was making strawberry boxes as in his youth, producing a fine cabinet, or lucidly expounding an esoteric economic theory, he displayed a char-acteristic style of professional workmanship and an amazing capacity for painstaking detail. Notwithstanding his absorption in his work, he was a man of personal warmth, courtesy, and deep concern for others.

While Mitchell was profoundly influenced by **Thorstein Veblen** and **John Dewey,** he pursued his own vision of economics as an empirical science of human behavior. In the Progressive tradition, he endeavored to harness creative intelligence in the service of rational social reorganization. Thus, he studied business cycles from an instrumentalist point of view, hoping to provide indicators (in the various lags and leads among statistical series) that would facilitate the social control of booms and depressions. Critics of his empiricism complain that it resulted in "measurement without theory" and that his self-generating theory of fluctuations failed to explain the causes of cyclical change.

Creative intelligence explains too his participation in the formation of the National Bureau of Economic Research, the New School of Social Research, the Social Science Research Council, and service in innumerable government agencies. The seminal studies of national income by the NBER contributed importantly to the gross national product approach in analyzing the economic process. Mitchell's persuasive efforts for quantitative economics, interdisciplinary research, and economic planning identify him as a master social scientist whose vision blazed new paths to the future. See A. F. Burns, ed., *Wesley Clair Mitchell: The Economic Scientist* (1952).

CHARLES H. HESSION

MITCHELL, William (b. Nice, France, Dec. 29, 1879; d. New York, N.Y., Feb. 19, 1936), MILITARY LEADER, son of U.S. Senator John Lendrum Mitchell, attended the Racine (Wis.) College preparatory school and Columbian Preparatory (later George Washington University) in Washington, D.C. At the outbreak of the Spanish-American War, he left school to join the army. Commissioned a second lieutenant in a volunteer signal company, he served in the postwar occupation of Cuba and fought in the Philippine insurrection. Returning to the U.S. in 1901, he accepted a regular army commission as first lieutenant in the signal corps and spent the next few years in Alaska and at various army posts and staff schools. After another tour in the Philippines, he joined the General Staff in Washington in 1912. After being assigned to the aviation section of the signal corps, in 1916 Mitchell learned to fly. He observed air warfare in Europe in 1917 and arrived in Paris four days after the U.S. entered World War I. As lieutenant colonel, he helped General **John J. Pershing** form the American Expeditionary Forces' aviation program; as colonel, he led U.S. and allied air forces in the St. Mihiel and Meuse-Argonne offensives. "Billy," as he became known to the public, received tremendous publicity and returned home in 1919 with the temporary rank of brigadier general.

Becoming assistant chief of the Air Service, Mitchell launched an energetic campaign for air power and an independent air force. He believed in the offensive potential of airplanes and thus the necessity for air superiority. Mitchell attacked the role of the navy in national defense, claiming battleships were vulnerable to air attack; in tests, he demonstrated this point by using planes to sink several captured German and obsolete American warships (1921–22). Inspection tours of Europe (1921–22) and the Far East (1923–24) confirmed his beliefs, particularly of the vulnerability of the U.S. to attack from Japan. Mitchell wrote two books expounding his views, *Our Air Force* (1921) and *Winged Defense* (1925), and became increasingly critical of his superiors. Transferred from Washington to San Antonio, Texas, with his permanent rank of colonel (1925), Mitchell publicly blamed navy and War Department incompetence for the apparent loss of a naval seaplane and the dirigible *Shenandoah* in a storm. He was court-martialed by the army for this action and convicted in December 1925. Suspended from duty and pay for five years, he resigned from the army early in 1926. He spent the rest of his life farming and writing on the importance of air power and the dangers that Japan posed to the United States.

⸻

As the leading national spokesman for "air power," especially in the years 1919–26, Billy Mitchell epitomized the sensationalism and hero worship of the 1920s. His desire to excel through physical prowess led him to pursue such outdoor pastimes as hunting and horsemanship and to seek military service. And when he fully embraced aviation by learning to fly (at his own expense), he performed courageously and well as a combat pilot. Combined with his handsomeness and social charm, flair for wearing nonregulation uniforms, and unorthodox methods, he had all the markings of a modern American folk hero.

Mitchell's sensational methods, however, became his trademark within the service and out, as he championed the causes of strategic aviation and military preparedness amid service conservativism, general public apathy, and governmental economy-mindedness. Motivated to match the achievements of his railroad tycoon grandfather Alexander Mitchell and his politician father, he often sought financial help and political influence from his family to gain promotion. His service in wartime France, however, and his education in the advanced air theories of the Briton Trenchard and the Italians Caproni and Douhet converted him into a zealous crusader whose personal ambition was subordinated to the more important goal of his new cause. When, for instance, he saw his military career and future possibilities for advancement about to end, he risked court-martial to publicize his theories.

Mitchell thought as boldly as he acted, often overstating his ideas for effect but to his ultimate detriment. From 1917, he angered both his military superiors and the civilian government (and even his wife, whom he divorced in 1922), to the delight of the popular press and public opinion. Yet his excesses hurt him from 1924 on, when his outright emphasis on controversy led him to accuse his superiors of "incompetency, criminal negligence, and almost treasonable" misadministration. After his court-martial, his general credibility waned because of his progressively more radical and uncompromising statements. He was a prophet in his vision of a future war with Japan, the ultimate role and capability of the strategic bomber, and the need for an independent air force. But he erred in stressing the key role of Alaska in modern war, in promoting the dirigible, and in ultimately rejecting the aircraft carrier.

Mitchell's overall contribution to the cause of military aviation must be measured by the response of the government to his crusade at the time. He did not gain his extreme and unrealistic goals, but he served as a catalyst to stimulate aviation reforms within the army and navy. His methodical contemporaries Major Generals Mason Patrick and Benjamin Foulois and Rear Admiral **William A. Moffett** thoroughly outclassed Mitchell in a quiet crusade to win congressional appropriations for naval aviation. His legacy remains that of an outspoken martyr, symbolized by the special medal awarded him posthumously by Congress in 1946, a man impatient with the limitations of the technology and popular attitudes of his own time. See A. F. Hurley, *Billy Mitchell: Crusader for Air Power* (1964).

CLARK G. REYNOLDS

MOFFETT, William Adger (b. Charleston, S.C., Oct. 31, 1869; d. at sea April 4, 1933), NAVAL LEADER, graduated from the U.S. Naval Academy in 1890 near the bottom of his class. Commissioned ensign in 1892, he served in South American waters (1890–92), and on the European station (1893–95). During the Spanish-American War he participated in the investment of Manila aboard the cruiser *Charleston.* Promoted to lieutenant in 1899, he saw duty in the battleships *Kentucky* and *Maine* as well as other vessels before becoming commandant of the naval station at Guantánamo Bay, Cuba (1904–6). After two years' shore duty in San Francisco, Moffett in 1912 was appointed executive officer of the new battleship *Arkansas.* As commanding officer of the scout cruiser *Chester,* he engaged Mexican forces at Veracruz during the diplomatic crisis with Mexico in 1914.

Moffett became commandant of the Naval Training Station at Great Lakes, Illinois, in August, 1914. While organizing that base for possible wartime expansion over the next few years, during which he was promoted to captain (1916), Moffett and his staff converted the place into the navy's major training center when the U.S. entered the war in April 1917. Along with turning out nearly 100,000 enlisted men for the wartime fleet, Moffett directed new aviation and radio communication programs there. His reward for service in this crucial post was command of the "superdreadnought" *Mississippi* late in 1918.

Long interested in the rapidly maturing element of naval aviation, Moffett in 1921 was appointed chief of the new Bureau of Aeronautics with the rank of rear admiral. His enthusiasm for aviation, plus his qualification as a naval aviation observer (one hundred hours of flight training), earned him and naval aviation in general great respect throughout the fleet. Because of the open hostility of army aviation zealots led by General **"Billy" Mitchell** and by battleship-oriented admirals within the navy, Moffett rejected more prestigious posts and further promotion in order to superintend personally the growth of the navy's air arm. He developed the policy and technical aspects of the aircraft carrier and supported the tactical innovations at sea of Admiral Joseph Mason Reeves. Between them, Moffett and Reeves created the nucleus of the World War II carrier force.

Also a proponent of the use of rigid airships in naval operations, Moffett was killed in the crash of the dirigible *Akron* off Barnegat Inlet, New Jersey.

Admiral Moffett deserved the distinction of being the "father of naval aviation," for almost singlehandedly he waged a quiet crusade for the development of American naval air power. A mild-mannered, handsome, erect, distinguished-looking, and energetic man, gifted with a political sense uncommon in the naval officers of his day, he applied his keen administrative skills to develop carrier aviation and other naval air activities in the face of much public and professional doubt and opposition. Astute and diplomatic, he succeeded in gaining appropriations from Congress and in laying the organizational foundation for American naval aviation that would reach fruition in World War II. His low-keyed tact further deterred his critics, the most outspoken of whom, General Mitchell, was court-martialed when he assailed the civilian secretaries and Moffett's program in 1925.

The high morale, deep respect, and even love that Moffett engendered in all his commands endeared him to generations of naval officers from the last sailing days to the nuclear age. So farsighted were Moffett's ideas about modern naval warfare that other navies, notably Great Britain's, beset with interservice strife and doctrinal short-sightedness, looked to Moffett's accomplishments with envy. In only one area, lighter-than-air craft, was Moffett wrong, an error that literally led to his death in the line of duty. Relatively unknown by the public in his unglamorous chores within the governmental bureaucracy, Moffett was nevertheless honored in his own time by his peers, superiors, and subordinates. By serving as chief of the Bureau of Aeronautics for an unparalleled tenure of twelve years, he succeeded where Mitchell had failed. The generation of naval aviators he tutored carried his work forward to the final victory in the Pacific and the multitudinous tasks that faced American naval aviation in the postwar world. See Edward Arpee, *From Frigates to Flat-tops: The Story of the Life and Achievements of Rear Admiral William Adger Moffett, USN* (1953).

CLARK G. REYNOLDS

MONROE, James (b. Westmoreland Co., Va., April 28, 1758; d. New York, N.Y., July 4, 1831), PRESIDENT, left the College of William and Mary in 1776 to join the Continental army. He was elected to the Virginia house of delegates in 1782, and during 1783–86 he served in the Continental Congress. At the Virginia Convention (1788) he opposed the ratification of the Constitution because of doubts about concentration of power in the executive branch. As a U.S. senator (1791–94), he opposed the Bank of the U.S. on constitutional grounds. He was minister to France (1794–96) and governor of Virginia (1799–1802). In 1803, Jefferson appointed him envoy extraordinary to France, where he assisted **Robert R. Livingston** in arranging the purchase of Louisiana. During 1803–6 he was minister to England, negotiating a treaty which Jefferson did not submit for ratification. He was again elected governor of Virginia in 1811, but resigned to become Madison's secretary of state (1811–17), also serving as secretary of war (1814–15).

Monroe was elected president in 1816. His two terms are often referred to as the "era of good feelings," because Federalist-Republican tensions had by then almost disappeared. Opposed to federally sponsored internal improvements, Monroe vetoed the Cumberland Road Bill (1822), but recommended a constitutional amendment to authorize a national system of internal improvements. He accepted the Missouri Compromise (1820), banning slavery north of latitude 36°30′, although he questioned Congress's right to restrict slavery in the territories.

During Monroe's administration, the Rush-Bagot agreement between the U.S. and England provided for the disarmament of the Great Lakes. The Convention of 1818 (in London) settled the Canadian boundary beyond the Lakes at the 49th parallel. In the Transcontinental Treaty (1819), Spain ceded Florida and all claim to the Pacific Northwest to the U.S., while America renounced its claims to Texas.

In 1822, Great Britain, desirous of keeping Spain from regaining control of its former Latin American colonies, proposed an Anglo-American statement opposing European intervention in Latin America. Monroe, with the advice of Secretary of State J. Q. Adams, decided to act unilaterally, issuing his famous Monroe Doctrine (1823), which asserted that the American continent was no longer open for European colonization, and that any attempt to extend European power in the western hemisphere would be considered an unfriendly act by the U.S. Furthermore, the U.S. would not interfere in European affairs.

———— ✦ ————

The last of the Revolutionary generation to occupy the presidency, Monroe had a career closely linked with those of his most intimate friends, Thomas Jefferson and James Madison, whose ideals he fully shared. Throughout his life Monroe worked to make republican institutions both secure and viable, and to set the nation on a course which would fulfill the conviction of his age that a special destiny awaited the United States once it

had shaped a course free from the habits of the Old World. Monroe was less gifted intellectually than Jefferson or Madison; his bent lay in the practical implementation of broad political goals. While his contemporaries did not regard him as possessing a first-rate mind, he won their respect and trust because of the soundness of his judgment and selfless devotion to the demands of public life. Although formal and reserved in public, he was neither cold nor aloof; indeed, the warmth of his personality and the generosity of his spirit were universally praised. Rarely did he cherish a grudge, and he had an unusual ability to work harmoniously with difficult personalities. In appearance he was tall (slightly over six feet), large-framed, and raw-boned; his features were massive, with a large nose and widely set gray eyes.

Monroe had been an active figure among the nationalists during the Confederation, but he did not emerge as a major leader until he joined Jefferson and Madison in opposing **Alexander Hamilton**'s policies, which they considered detrimental to the agricultural community and destructive of republican institutions. His activities as an organizer of the Republican party were interrupted in 1793 when President Washington named him minister to France, a post he took at the urging of his friends, who felt that only a committed republican could prevent a rupture with France by counteracting the impression of **John Jay**'s mission to Great Britain. As much the spokesman of his party as the diplomatic representative of the Washington administration, whose policies he condemned, Monroe's measures to preserve France's friendship, while not overtly improper, led Washington to recall him.

On his return from France he was again active as a party leader, entering the governorship of Virginia to help organize Jefferson's victory. During Jefferson's presidency, Monroe's diplomatic career, which began so auspiciously with the Louisiana Purchase, ended unhappily in 1807 when Jefferson refused to submit for ratification the treaty which he and William Pinkney had negotiated with Great Britain. Neither Monroe nor special envoy Pinkney realized the stress placed by the administration on impressment and had concluded a treaty without obtaining a ban on it. Offended by the rejection of the treaty, Monroe remained out of politics until 1811 when Madison named him secretary of state in an effort to strengthen the administration, which was exposed not only to Federalist attacks but to internal dissension within the Republican party. Monroe's presence gave greater firmness to Madison's policies, for the younger generation of political leaders (especially the "War Hawks") had a high regard for Monroe's practical abilities. During the war Monroe made a notable contribution as secretary of war, bringing to that office an energy and administrative ability lacking among his predecessors.

As president, Monroe considered himself the head of a nation and not the chief of a party, and, short of appointing Federalists to high office, he consciously worked to foster a new epoch free of party animosity. He was a moderate nationalist, accepting the tariff and the Bank of the United States as essential to the well-being of the nation. Only on internal improvements did he adhere to the traditional strict constructionism of his party, insisting that a constitutional amendment was necessary for a federal program. Repudiating party loyalty as a means of executive leadership, Monroe sought to execute his policies by relying on the substantial congressional followings of three members of his cabinet: John Quincy Adams (state), **William H. Crawford** (treasury), and **John C. Calhoun** (war). His relations with Adams were particularly close, for they shared a common nationalist point of view. They sought to develop a foreign policy which would not only be appropriate for a republic and realize America's national interests but also obtain from the European powers a degree of respect previously denied the United States. Hence their decision in 1823 not to cooperate with Great Britain on a common Latin American policy.

During his second term, as the conflict over the presidential succession erupted, Monroe could no longer count on congressional support. Many of his most favored projects, such as his plans to construct stronger coastal defenses and the Anglo-American Treaty of 1823 to prohibit the international slave trade, fell victims of presidential political rivalries. His last years after retirement were clouded by financial difficulties resulting from a burden of debt contracted during his long public career. He had to sell his plantation (Oak Hill near Leesburg, Virginia) and seek a congressional grant, technically a reimbursement for expenses contracted as far back as his first French mission. See Harry Ammon, *James Monroe: The Quest for National Identity* (1971).

HARRY AMMON

MONROE, Marilyn (b. Los Angeles, Calif., June 1, 1926; d. Hollywood, Calif., Aug. 5, 1962) ACTRESS, born Norma Jean Mortensen, she lived with various foster parents during the years her mother was in mental hospitals. Her surname was of the man who fathered her. She later used her mother's surname, Baker. She attended Van Nuys High School in the San Fernando Valley, but left in 1942 to marry James Dougherty, an aircraft worker. They divorced in 1946.

She worked as a parachute inspector and as a paint sprayer in a Los Angeles aircraft factory when she was discovered by an army photographer in the factory. She turned to modeling and appearances on the covers of men's magazines. This led to a one-year contract with Twentieth Century Fox (1946) and a brief role—later edited out—in *Scudda Hoo, Scudda Hay* (1947). After her contract was not renewed she appeared briefly in Columbia Pictures' *Ladies of the Chorus* (1948). A passing but widely noticed role in John Huston's *Asphalt Jungle* (1950) resulted in a part in *All About Eve* (1950) which attracted a growing number of fans. Twentieth Century Fox, now recognizing her appeal, put her under contract again and embarked on a massive campaign to turn her into a sex goddess. In 1952 she shared star billing in *Don't Bother to Knock, Full House, Clash by Night, We're Not Married,* and *Monkey Business.* A nude calendar she had earlier posed for appeared that same year in *Playboy* and the resulting scandal added to her sex appeal. Stardom accompanied the release of *Niagara* (1953), in which she uncharacteristically played a femme fatale. Major roles as sex symbol and comedienne followed in *Gentlemen Prefer Blondes* (1953) and *How to Marry a Millionaire* (1953), with this phase of her career culminating in her portrayal of "The Girl" in *The Seven Year Itch* (1955). Her popularity received a boost from her marriage to baseball great **Joe DiMaggio** (1954) and from her honeymoon trip to Japan and to Korea, where she entertained American troops.

Divorced from DiMaggio after nine months of marriage, and dissatisfied with the roles that forced her to caricature previous performances, Monroe left Hollywood for New York, studied at the Actor's Studio with the celebrated Lee Strasberg and triumphantly resumed her career with a beautifully nuanced portrayal of a singer and aspiring actress in *Bus Stop* (1956). Subsequent roles in the *Prince and the Showgirl* (1957) and *Some Like It Hot* (1959) extended her comedic range. *The Misfits* (1960), provided a dramatic role specifically written for her by playwright **Arthur Miller**, whom she married in 1956 and divorced in 1961.

Monroe's final years, dogged by ill-health and frustration with conventional starring roles, ended in suicide from an overdose of sleeping pills, though there has been much unsubstantiated speculation suggesting she was murdered because of affairs with President Kennedy, his brother **Robert**, and involvement with underworld figures.

※

Marilyn Monroe has become much more than a movie star and sex symbol, more than a cultural figure of the 1950s, having fashioned out of her relationships with DiMaggio, Miller, and the Kennedys an image of herself as a national icon, the focus of various conspiracy theories that make her out to be a victim not merely of the Hollywood exploitation of women but of the machinations of politicians and organized crime. As **Norman Mailer** put it, she is the "magnified mirror of ourselves," a myth around whom the contraditions of the national psyche coalesce.

Yet Monroe's talent should not be discounted. Several actors and actresses have paid tribute to her genius, and a close examination of her films

shows her remarkable gift for comedy and her ability to find expressive life in roles with narrow emotional ranges, roles that defeated lesser actresses who imitated but could not equal her wit and extraordinary timing. See Carl Rollyson, *Marilyn Monroe: A Life of the Actress* (1986).

CARL ROLLYSON

MOODY, Dwight Lyman (b. Northfield, Mass., Feb. 5, 1837; d. Northfield, Mass, Dec. 22, 1899), RELIGIOUS LEADER, received only a limited education. Originally a Unitarian, after he moved to Boston in 1854 he soon became a Congregationalist. In 1856 he settled in Chicago, where he worked in the boot and shoe business, but devoted a great deal of time to religious activities. He organized the North Market Sabbath School in 1858, which became a center for evangelistic services.

In 1860 Moody gave up his lucrative business to devote his life to religion. He became an independent city missionary. During the Civil War he worked with troops through the Chicago Young Men's Christian Association and United States Christian Commission, erecting prayer tents and nursing the sick. In 1864 he founded the Illinois Street Church, a nondenominational "mission" church which reflected the concern of both Moody and the evangelical churches with the problems of the urban poor. During 1865–69 he was president of the Chicago YMCA.

Moody's trip to Great Britain with singer Ira D. Sankey in 1873 marked the beginning of his long career as a popular revivalist. The English warmly received Moody and admired his rapid, dynamic speaking style. He preached a revivalism of friendship, kindness, and forgiveness rather than of hellfire and condemnation. Returning to the U.S. in 1875, he settled in Northfield, Massachusetts, but devoted the rest of his life to extensive speaking tours throughout the U.S. and Canada. He founded the Northfield Seminary for Girls in 1879, Mt. Hermon School for boys in 1881, and the Moody Bible Institute in Chicago in 1889. He conducted annual Bible conferences at Northfield to encourage young people to pursue a life of religion. He was suspicious of the Social Gospel movement, believing that social problems had to be solved primarily by divine regeneration of individuals. He rejected the theory of evolution and preached a literal interpretation of the Bible. Moody died a layman, never having sought ordination.

⁂

Speaking before thousands in a dark business suit, bearded, rotund Dwight L. Moody seemed the epitome of the "businessman in clerical garb" who typified popular religion in late 19th-century America. Less well understood, however, was Moody's sense of humor and love of practical jokes, or the influence a shy, retiring wife exerted on her husband. Earthy, unlettered, a dynamo of energy, the revivalist was very much a man of his times, but perhaps a more sympathetic person than usually depicted in the textbooks.

Moody adapted revivalism, one of the major institutions of evangelical Protestantism, to the urban context. He was ideally suited for the task. His early career as a young businessman in Boston and Chicago, his experience in nondenominational circles through his work with the Chicago YMCA, and his organizational ability, demonstrated in the great revivals he conducted in England, combined to fashion his spectacular career as the creator of modern mass revivalism. Innovative in technique, Moody's *message* looked to the past. On questions of biblical criticism he was a literalist. By the end of his life his closest associates were men soon to be in the front ranks of fundamentalism (although personal breadth of spirit caused him to retain the friendship of more liberal churchmen throughout his life). Conservative socioeconomic views were a factor in his efforts to found Moody Bible Institute in Chicago. Dissatisfied with the decline in influence of revivalism, deeply disturbed by the growing conflict within the church occasioned by science and industrialism, in his last years Moody searched for alternatives to mass evangelism to keep his beloved church abreast of the times. His failure was but one reflection of the general disintegration of the evangelical Protestant world view that was occurring in both England and America in the last third of the 19th

century. See J. F. Findlay, *Dwight L. Moody: American Evangelist, 1837–1899* (1969).

JAMES F. FINDLAY

MOORE, Charles Williard (b. Benton Harbor, Mich., Oct. 31, 1925; d. Austin, Texas, Dec. 16, 1993), ARCHITECT, graduated the University of Michigan in 1947, and received a PhD in architectural history from Princeton in 1957. At one time or another he taught at and was head of the architectural schools at Princeton, the University of California, Berkeley and the University of Texas at Austin, and most notably at Yale (1965–1975), and the University of California at Los Angeles (1975–1985). He had architectural offices on both the east and west coasts and many partners and associates. One of the more important partnerships was Moore Lyndon Turnbull Whitaker (1962–1970). A restless man, he was almost always planning a trip to some part of the world, even claiming to enjoy jet lag.

Moore's oeuvre was large. Although he received commissions in a variety of building types, his heart was in housing, both single family dwellings and multiple housing units. Significantly, his first really extensively published project was the design and construction of a so-called "Condominium I" (1965) at Sea Ranch, a housing development planned by Oceanic Properties, Inc., that is 110 miles north of San Francisco. Here he and his partners, William Turnbull, Jr., Donlyn Lyndon and Richard Whitaker, chose simple, barnlike forms and created exciting spaces and rooflines that seemed to fit well into the lush landscape. Shortly afterwards, he began to chair the architectural school at Yale. From then on, Moore was a celebrity and commissions poured in. Yet, in spite of his peripatetic habits and his heavy workload, he was a distinguished teacher and contributed much to the Yale architectural school's reputation.

⁂

Moore is usually considered to be postmodernist—that is, an architect who understoood the principles of the modernist school of Walter

Gropius, Le Corbusier and **Ludwig Mies van der Rohe** but who essentially objected to its dogma. Naturally, considering his education in architectural history, he objected to the ahistorical approach of the modernists. In answer to their notion that "ornament is crime," he designed his Piazza d'Italia (1975–78) in New Orleans to incorporate segmental arches from Hadrian's Villa at Tivoli (about which he had written a scholarly article) along with neon signage, a cascade that washed down a contoured map of Italy, and even included (à la Ghiberti) two small sculptures of his own head whose mouth gushed water. He believed that architecture can stand a few jokes, especially when the whole assemblage was paid for with taxpayers money.

But there was another side to his work. He once told an architectural critic that "To make a place is to make a domain that helps people know where they are and, by extension, know who they are." At first glance, this remark appears as inscrutable as many of the sayings of his teacher, **Louis Kahn**. But it is made clear when it is applied to his buildings. For example, St. Matthew's Episcopal Church in Pacific Palisades, California, and the First Church of Christ, Scientist in Glendale, California, both show signs of Moore's whimsey as well as his rich understanding of the style of worship and social outlook of these very different denominations. In accordance with his principles, both churches were designed after long discussions between Moore and their congregations. He followed the same policy at Dartmouth College, New Hampshire, where a series of conversations with students, faculty, members of the administration and representatitve townspeople resulted in the Hood Museum, recognized as one of the loveliest small art galleries in the nation. This was obviously what Moore meant by making a "domain that helps people know where they are and … who they are." In his architecture Moore succeeded in doing this brilliantly. See David Littlejohn, *Architect: The Life and Work of Charles W. Moore* (1984).

ROBERT W. WINTER

MOORE, Marianne Craig (b. Kirkwood, Mo., Nov. 15, 1887; d. Brooklyn, N.Y., Feb. 5, 1972), POET, graduated from Bryn Mawr College in 1909. In 1910 she graduated from Carlisle (Pa.) Commercial College and after a summer in Europe taught stenography and other commercial subjects at the U.S. Indian School in Carlisle (1911–15). Moore moved with her mother to Chatham, New Jersey, in 1916 to keep house for her brother John, a Presbyterian minister. After her brother joined the navy as a chaplain she moved with her mother to Greenwich Village in New York City in 1918. While teaching at a New York private school and working as an assistant at the Hudson Park public library she became part of a literary circle which included William Carlos Williams and **Wallace Stevens.** T. S. Eliot had published some of her poems in London's *Egoist* in 1915, but her first poetry collection appeared (without her knowledge) in 1921, published by the Egoist Press. This collection (with additions) was published in the U.S. as *Observations* (1924) and won the Dial Award. In 1925 Moore became acting editor, then editor, of the *Dial*, a literary magazine. She held this position until the magazine ceased publication in 1929.

When her brother was assigned to the Brooklyn Navy Yard, Moore moved to that city in 1929. Her *Selected Poems* (1935) was received with enthusiasm and she received a number of literary awards and prizes, including the Shelley Award in 1940, and a Guggenheim fellowship in 1945. In 1947 she was elected to the National Institute of Arts and Letters. *Collected Poems* (1951) won a Pulitzer Prize, a National Book Award, and the Bollingen Prize. She translated the *Fables of La Fontaine* (1954) and collected her critical essays in a volume entitled *Predilections* (1955). Some of her volumes which followed were: *O to Be a Dragon* (1959), *The Arctic Ox* (1964), *Tell Me, Tell Me: Granite, Steel and Other Topics* (1966), and *The Complete Poems of Marianne Moore* (1967).

Long before her death Marianne Moore had become a celebrity identified with the spirit of poetry. Her tricorn hat and full-length cape seemed to capture for her fans (as one of the most famous Brooklyn Dodgers' rooters in the world she would not find the word disrespectful) the poet's prerogative for eccentricity in a look-alike world. What other modern poet has been asked to name a new car? The Ford Motor Company finally settled upon the "Edsel," but not before her last of many suggestions—"Utopian Turtletop"—had been given due consideration. Miss Moore charmed everyone who encountered her, but the price she paid for her engaging manner and civility was a kind of "lax adulation," and as a result her reputation in the last twenty years has suffered. She has become identified as a poet of brilliant surfaces, an admired technician who has nothing to say, a poet devoted to counting syllables and keeping up elegant appearances but whose substance is as evanescent as cotton candy. The praise of critics in the fifties was a far cry from that of her earliest admirers, who saw her as an "exacting moralist," a "painfully sharp observer of animals, persons and ideas." Eliot said that her verse was an established part of "the small body of durable poetry written in our time," and Yvor Winters commented that she was a poet whose "mastery of phrase and cadence" never failed to "overwhelm" him. But "overwhelming" hardly seems to be the word most critics would now use to describe Moore's poetry. Her precisionist verse, all that attention to prepositions and conjunctions, the impersonal voice and exotic vocabulary, the careful account of her syllables, and the avoidance of anything "stirring" (to use R. P. Blackmur's word) seem totally at odds with contemporary exposures of the self.

But if Miss Moore's poetry has surface brilliance, her most acute critics have always seen beneath the appearances subterranean feelings of confusion and terror that complex surfaces protect and arrange but do not hide. "Only the wildest animals," Donald Hall has observed, "need cages so carefully made." Blackmur, one of her finest critics, comments that **Poe, Hawthorne, Melville, Dickinson,** and **Henry James** "all— like Miss Moore—shared an excessive sophistication of surfaces and a passionate predilection for the genuine—though Poe was perhaps not interested in too much of the genuine; and all contrived to present the conviction of reality best by making it, in most readers' eyes, remote." See Donald Hall, *Marianne Moore: The Cage and the Animal* (1970).

FRANCIS MURPHY

MORGAN, John Pierpont (b. Hartford, Conn., April 17, 1837; d. Rome, Italy, March 31, 1913), FINANCIER, attended a finishing school in Vevy, Switzerland, and studied mathematics for two years at the University of Göttingen in Germany. In 1857 he became a junior accountant with the Wall Street firm of Duncan, Sherman and Co., and in 1860, the New York agent for his father's London-based Junius S. Morgan and Co.

Morgan became involved in a major scandal during the Civil War. In 1861 he loaned $20,000 to Simon Stevens, who purchased obsolete Hall carbines from the War Department at $3.50 and resold them to the government for $22. Although Morgan was officially exonerated, his enemies never allowed the public to forget the "Hall Carbine affair." He also participated in gold speculation schemes during the Civil War, but abandoned such ventures after forming a partnership with Charles C. Dabney in 1864.

In 1869 Morgan gained prominence in business circles in the so-called Susquehanna War, when, as agent for the Albany and Susquehanna Railroad, he blocked a drive by **Jay Gould** and **Jim Fisk** to annex the line to the Erie system. Forming a partnership with Anthony Drexel in 1872, he quickly emerged as the leading dealer in federal securities through his affiliation with J. S. Morgan and Co. in London and Drexel, Harjes and Co. in Paris.

In the 1880s Morgan reorganized a number of major railroads through a process termed "Morganization." Inefficient management, inflated security structures, and unrestrained competition put many railway corporations in shaky financial condition, and bondholders and other creditors turned to Morgan for help. He provided new capital and reduced fixed costs by reissuing the securities at lower interest rates or converting bonds into stock; and in the process he placed himself or a partner on the railroad's board of directors and sometimes appointed new executive officers. He thereby protected his bond-buying clients by ensuring that future management would be competent and honest, and also guaranteed that his firm would control future financing. He neither sought nor obtained ownership or "control" of the companies he reorganized; he preferred to stick with his own line of business, banking and financial reorganization. The profits of doing so were far greater than the profits of running a railroad.

Moreover, in the 1890s the profits of investment banking skyrocketed. Many major railroads collapsed financially in the early nineties and were reorganized, in the midst of a severe depression, with bonds bearing 8 to 10 percent interest. After 1897 interest rates fell to 3 and 4 percent, necessitating still another round of reorganizations, to take advantage of the cheaper money. The total capital involved was close to $15 billion each time, and the net profits to investment bankers were astronomical. By 1895, however, Morgan was receiving stiff competition from the investment banking house headed by **Jacob Schiff,** and in 1901, after a celebrated battle over control of the Northern Pacific, Schiff became the dominant force in railroad finance.

Morgan had meanwhile moved into the reorganization and consolidation of industrial corporations. Between 1892 and 1902, he put together General Electric, American Telephone and Telegraph, International Harvester, and the first billion-dollar corporation, U.S. Steel. He continued to effect such combinations on a large scale until his death.

Morgan was also involved deeply in government finance. After a run on federal gold reserves in 1895, President Cleveland was forced to call upon him to float a $60 million loan abroad, and during the panic of 1907 the New York financiers were forced to obey his directives for stabilizing the stock market. As the personification of the "Money Trust," he became the star witness in the Pujo investigations into monopoly finance in 1912.

Throughout his life Morgan participated in civic, religious, and philanthropic affairs. A leading art collector, he donated his collection of paintings and sculptures to the Metropolitan Museum of Art, and he left a massive accumulation of rare books and manuscripts. These were donated to the Morgan Library, which was founded by his family in New York City in 1924.

J. P. Morgan was a legend and a symbol in his own time and for decades afterward—the personification of the Wall Street "establishment." He was supposedly as wealthy as Croesus. (A new millionaire, admiring Morgan's yacht *Corsair,* asked how much a ship like that cost. "If you have to ask," Morgan snorted, "you can't afford it.") He was also reputedly the most powerful man in America and most influential banker in the world. (A young man, son of a deceased friend of Morgan's, requested a loan for a questionable venture; Morgan refused but said, "I'll let you be seen walking down the street with me on my way to lunch." That was enough to ensure the young man's credit anywhere.)

The myth was overblown; **John D. Rockefeller** was many times as wealthy, and Jacob Schiff was a more powerful and resourceful banker. But Morgan's deeds were in fact of larger-than-life proportions, and so, in their way, were his public services, especially in consolidating and rationalizing industrial corporations. The technological and industrial revolution of the late 19th century had made the economy a jungle, in which predators thrived by devouring the weak; and Morgan did more to restore order than did any lawmaker or administrator in the land.

He did not, however, do so in the efficiency-worshiping spirit of early 20th-century America. Partly his move into industrial consolidation was dictated by necessity: the Jewish financial community headed by Schiff had, by 1900, won an outsized share of the most lucrative bond business, that of the railroads, and Morgan had no other area into which he could expand. But there was more to it than that. Morgan was an aristocrat with a deep-seated aversion to corruption and waste, to the new-rich manufacturers and financial buccaneers who plagued the nation throughout his adult life, to unrestrained competition and the anonymous corporation. Thus he longed for a return to the aristocratic values of the 18th-century sedentary merchant, or those of the merchant princes who reigned in New York, Philadelphia, and London before the Civil War.

In keeping with this attitude, he conducted his business on the basis of personal credit—as a function of character and connections—rather than on the modern basis of money and collateral. He told a disbelieving congressman, at the Pujo Committee hearings, that he would not accept a million-dollar cash deposit from the congressman himself, because he knew nothing of the man's character. He assured the same committee that he would not lend money to a man or a company he did not trust, even if the collateral were "all the bonds in Christendom." And he would not manage the finances of a corporation, no matter how profitable the arrangement, unless he or a trusted associate sat on its board to guarantee its honesty.

But the cost of Morgan's benefactions was often high. For one thing, within the limits imposed by his aristocratic concept of banking, Morgan exacted enormous profits from his operations, including his "rescues" of the Treasury in 1895 and 1907. For another, in the process of reorganizing companies he often sacrificed creativity for the sake of order, and sometimes (because of his insistence on personal familiarity with those he dealt with) he replaced good management with bad. For still another, his sagacity and financial statesmanship declined appreciably after 1900, even as his prestige was reaching a peak. The principal reason for this decline was the death of his most conservative and able partners. He became, in a sense, the victim of the myth of his greatness: younger partners like **George Perkins** were brilliant at executing his decisions, and outside allies like George Baker and James Stillman could lend him support, but no one could really influence his decisions as his earlier partners had been able to do. Thus, for example,

most of the consolidations he effected after 1902 were poorly conceived, unsuccessful, or downright calamitous.

Ironically, it was during these years that the Morgan legend became enshrined in national mythology. He played to the hilt the role of master banker, apparently enjoyed it, and even looked the part. A big and robust man, impeccably dressed and stately of bearing, his walrus mustache, bulbous nose, and shrewd, piercing, hyperthyroid eyes became veritable caricatures of Wall Street power. See Vincent P. Carosso, *The Morgans: Private International Bankers, 1854–1913* (1987).

FORREST MCDONALD

MORGAN, John Pierpont, Jr. (b. Irvington, N.Y., Sept. 7, 1867; d. Boca Grande, Fla., March 13, 1943), FINANCIER, graduated from Harvard in 1889 and in 1891 was made a partner of the House of Morgan. When his father died in 1913, J. P. Morgan, Jr., assumed control of the firm. During World War I he handled French, British, and Russian loans in the U.S., organizing a 2,200-bank syndicate for this purpose; he also acted as the British government's business representative in America.

Following the war Morgan served on an unofficial international bankers' committee on German reparations, which helped draft the Dawes Plan (1924), as a part of which the House of Morgan loaned a total of $1.7 billion to twelve nations. Under the Young Plan (1929), the House of Morgan provided $18,250,000 in additional international loans. Morgan also participated as a private banker in designing the Bank of International Settlements (1929). During the Depression of the 1930s the House of Morgan was subject to several congressional investigations. The Senate Banking Committee revealed in 1933 that neither Morgan nor his partners had paid income tax in 1931 and 1932. In 1936 the Nye Committee on munitions manufacture claimed that Morgan's loans had influenced Wilson's decision to enter World War I on the Allied side, but Morgan denied this interpretation. The 1933

Banking Act forced the firm to separate its security financing from its private banking, and as a result, J. P. Morgan and Co. became a state-chartered commercial bank. Morgan opposed such control, believing that professional ethics was a better regulator than legislation. Morgan was a director of U.S. Steel, the Pullman Corporation, the Discount Corporation of America, and other companies.

J. P. Morgan, Jr., was twenty-four years old when he was made a partner in his father's private banking firm. A tall, broad-shouldered man, with thick black eyebrows, young Morgan not only resembled his father physically, but was like him in other ways as well. Both men had a commanding manner, disliked publicity, and adhered to a high code of business ethics, which young Morgan expressed in these words: "Do your work; be honest; keep your word; help when you can; be fair." In 1913, when he succeeded his father as head of the firm, the House of Morgan was the most important and influential private banking partnership in the country. Jack Morgan continued the policies and traditions established earlier. Under his leadership, the firm functioned much as it had in the past; it dealt in foreign exchange and letters of credit and provided both commercial and investment banking services to a select clientele, mostly large domestic corporations and foreign governments. But whereas the elder Morgan had established himself as the foremost specialist in refinancing tottering railroads and launching giant industrial consolidations such as United States Steel, Jack Morgan earned his reputation financing European governments. During the 1920s the firm achieved a preeminent position in both domestic and international finance, which it held until June 1934, when, in compliance with the provisions of the Banking Act of 1933, it was forced to choose between commercial and investment banking. Morgan opted for deposit banking and ceased underwriting securities, the business which had earned the firm its reputation and influence. From then until his death he headed the bank that bore his and his father's name, but the institution, greatly restricted in its activities, ceased to occupy the commanding position it once had held. The era of the great private banker, epitomized by Morgan and his father, had come to a close. See Ron Chernow, *The House of Morgan: An American Banking Dynasty and the Rise of Modern Finance* (1990).

VINCENT P. CAROSSO

MORGAN, Lewis Henry (b. near Aurora, N.Y., Nov. 21, 1818; d. Rochester, N.Y., Dec. 17, 1881), ANTHROPOLOGIST, received a BA from Union College in 1840, studied law, and was admitted to the bar in 1844. In 1855 he acquired a financial interest in a railroad of which he was legal adviser. He was an active Republican, serving in the New York assembly 1861–68 and the New York senate 1869–70. He was defeated for renomination in 1870.

While in college Morgan and his classmates founded a secret society, later to become "the Grand Order of the Iroquois," and patterned after the Iroquois Confederacy. The society's object was the study of Native American lore and the education of Native Americans into "civilized" ways. This early interest led Morgan to his life's work of Native American studies and later broader anthropological research. In 1846 he presented his first (unpublished) paper on the government of the Six Nations. That same year he was adopted into the Seneca tribe because he had defended the Native Americans against a fraudulent land cession treaty. In 1851 he published what is considered the first scientific account of a Native American tribe, *League of the Ho-dé-no-sau-nee, or Iroquois.* While still practicing law Morgan published a study of Iroquois laws of kinship and descent (1858) and in 1859–62 broadened his Native American studies by traveling to upper Michigan, Kansas, Nebraska, and the Dakotas. He concluded that all North American Indian kinship systems were similar to that of the Iroquois. This finding led him to the general study of primitive kinship throughout the world. In 1860 he had the Smithsonian Institution circulate a questionnaire on primitive kinship systems to its foreign correspondents. His conclusions, published in 1868 and 1871, led to his most important work, *Ancient Society, or Researches in the Lines of Human Progress* (1877). It argued the common origin of all human races and their common passage through stages of savagery, barbarism, and civilization, and postulated that the nuclear family evolved from an original state of group marriage. Though criticized by contemporary and modern anthropologists, Morgan's work influenced such theorists as Karl Marx and Friedrich Engels. During the 1870s Morgan continued his Native American studies, including architecture, history, and migrations. His last work, published shortly before his death, was *Houses and House-Life of the American Aborigines* (1881). He was also interested in the mental processes of lower animals, publishing a study of the beaver in 1868.

———⚮———

In many ways Morgan's life was similar to that of other businessmen of the latter 19th century. The railroad and industrial boom spanning his adult life gave him moderate wealth and unbounded confidence in the future progress of the nation. Most of his colleagues and neighbors knew Morgan as a conservative gentleman, a temperate, parsimonious man, devoted to his family. In matters of religion he seemed entirely guided by the stern Presbyterianism of his wife, and of his pastor and close friend, the Reverend Joshua McIlvaine. To almost all who knew him in Rochester, Morgan's writings seemed an admirable product of his leisure hours, but of no great consequence.

Only a handful of correspondents around the world understood, by 1868, that Morgan was making singular discoveries. A strong classical education, a mastery of inheritance and property laws, combined with an unparalleled knowledge of Native American customs, enabled him to propose a series of brilliant hypotheses in the realm of comparative anthropology: that a universal matrilineal system of kinship preceded the modern monogamous family; that this system corresponded to a stage of social development free of

private property and personal inheritance; and that the origins of patriarchal monogamy lay in the progress of technology and in private claims on economic surpluses.

As an anthropologist Morgan achieved considerable stature among American, English, and German scholars before he died in 1881. But he was propelled to fame posthumously when, in 1884, Friedrich Engels published *The Origin of the Family, Private Property and the State*, a Marxist classic subtitled, "In the Light of the Researches of Lewis Henry Morgan." This book generated interest in the American lawyer's ideas that was to spread around the globe. In 1973, in its first significant exchange of books with the United States, the National Library in Peking requested the works of Lewis Morgan, and none other. See Carl Resek, *Lewis Henry Morgan: American Scholar* (1960).

CARL RESEK

MORGAN, Thomas Hunt (b. Lexington, Ky., Sept. 25, 1866; d. Pasadena, Calif., Dec. 4, 1945), GENETICIST, received his BS in 1886 and MS in 1888 from the University of Kentucky. After earning a PhD in zoology at Johns Hopkins University in 1890, he was appointed a Bruce fellow at Johns Hopkins for the following year. He went to Bryn Mawr College in 1891 to teach biology, and while there began research in embryology and heredity. He wrote *The Development of the Frog's Egg* in 1897, *Regeneration* in 1901, and *Evolution and Adaptation* in 1903. In 1897 Woods Hole Marine Biology Laboratory in Massachusetts made him a trustee, and in 1904 Columbia University appointed him professor of zoology. Morgan began to use the "fruit fly" drosophila for genetic research in 1907, and by 1911 he had discovered the existence of genes and chromosomes, the process of genetic mutation, and the role of chromosomes in sex differentiation. He described his discoveries in *Heredity and Sex* (1913), and translated Mendelian heredity into the terms of the chromosome theory of inheritance in *The Mechanism of Mendelian Heredity* (1915), written with A. H. Sturtevant, H. J. Muller, and C. B. Bridges. He then expanded the application of his theory in *Criticism of the Theory of Evolution* (1916), *The Physical Basis of Heredity* (1919), *Evolution and Genetics* (1925), and *The Theory of the Gene* (1926).

Morgan left Columbia University in 1928 to become director of the William G. Kerckhoff Laboratories of Biological Sciences at the California Institute of Technology. After having served as president of the National Academy of Science (1927–31), Morgan became president of the International Congress of Genetics in 1932. A year later he won the Nobel Prize in physiology and medicine for his work in heredity. He remained at California Institute of Technology until his death. Among his other writings are: *What Is Darwinism?* (1929), *The Scientific Basis of Evolution* (1932), and *Embryology and Genetics* (1933).

Morgan was an outgoing, energetic, generous, and intellectually vibrant personality; he could not abide pomposity or imprecision. He was also the epitome of the experimental scientist, holding that science and philosophy were separate intellectual entities. He thus attacked evolution as an as yet unproved doctrine of overly theoretical and imprecise character. To him, mechanistic, experimental science was solely concerned with observable phenomena that were testable and quantifiable. He was a careful worker who experimented by techniques at once simple and orthodox.

Morgan's scientific achievements were of the highest rank. He studied more than fifty kinds of animals and plants in the realms of embryology, cytology, regeneration, and heredity. His most notable contributions were in the elaboration of facts and mechanisms for the transmission of sexually linked characteristics, thereby providing the basis for modern genetics. His introduction to this field came originally through familiarity with the work of Hugo de Vries. In his inquisitive mind the data and concept of genetics flowered as he saw in this realm a new outlook different from what he thought were the sterile pathways of evolutionists and descriptive biologists.

In 1909, Morgan began his famous studies

with *Drosophila melanogaster,* the quickly multiplying and readily mutating "fruit fly." He published his results in pathmarking papers during the years 1910–16 and, in 1915, elaborated this data into the remarkable monograph *The Mechanism of Mendelian Heredity,* whose coauthors were his Columbia and Woods Hole colleagues. The drosophila studies were unique and elegant quantitative works in the history of sexually transmitted characteristics. Morgan showed how the fruit fly mutated in ways that demonstrated beyond question that transformation in species was sex-linked, with traits of the parents transmitted through chromosome chains from parents to offspring. His experiments thus clarified the patterning in chromosomatic linkage that determined the nature of the offspring. In sum, between 1909 and 1916 Morgan placed biology on a basis as exact and experimentally demonstrable as physics. The drosophila studies demonstrated how certain traits (such as white eyes or rudimentary wings) were sexually linked because of their proximity in the chromosome chain. Inheritance, therefore, was the result of exchanges of "genes" representing traits in male and female that would produce (or fail to produce) qualities in succeeding generations. This work established the causal character of inheritance through chromosomatic character. In 1926, Morgan's *The Theory of the Gene* was an even greater advance, in placing genetics on a completely modern basis by defining the gene as the basis for all human heredity. See Alfred H. Sturtevant, "Thomas Hunt Morgan," National Academy of Sciences, *Biographical Memoirs,* XXXIII (1959), 383–99.

EDWARD LURIE

MORGENTHAU, Henry, Jr. (b. New York, N.Y., May 11, 1891; d. Poughkeepsie, N.Y., Feb. 6, 1967), CABINET OFFICER, entered Cornell University to study architecture in 1909 but left after a brief stay. He worked at miscellaneous jobs and in the family business until 1913, when he returned to Cornell to study agriculture. However, he again left without a degree to run a Hudson Valley farm purchased by his father. A "gentleman farmer," he lived near Franklin D. Roosevelt, with whom he became a friend and political associate in 1915. During World War I he was a lieutenant in the navy for two months and worked with Herbert Hoover's U.S. Food Commission. In 1922 Morgenthau purchased the *American Agriculturalist,* which he edited until 1933.

Morgenthau was business manager of Franklin Roosevelt's 1928 New York gubernatorial campaign. After Roosevelt's election he became chairman of the New York Agricultural Advisory Commission and of a commission which drew up a comprehensive program of farm relief. As commissioner of conservation (1930–33) he played an important part in New York's reforestation program.

After Roosevelt became president he appointed Morgenthau chairman of the Federal Farm Board. Morgenthau consolidated various agricultural credit agencies into the Farm Credit Administration, directed a program of farm mortgage relief, and became a spokesman for New Deal agricultural policies. Having played a role in development of trade with the Soviet Union and in the administration's gold purchase policy, Morgenthau was appointed acting secretary of the treasury in 1933, and secretary in 1934. During the early stages of World War ll he coordinated the programs of aid to the Allies and later promoted War Bond sales. Morgenthau resigned his position in 1945 under criticism by President Truman for his plan to subdivide Germany into a number of small states as well as to dismantle Germany's industry and convert it into an agricultural nation (the Morgenthau Plan). From 1947 to 1954 he was chairman of various Jewish philanthropic organizations.

Henry Morgenthau, Jr., owes his significance in American history almost solely to his relationship with Franklin Delano Roosevelt. His influence on events invariably rested upon Roosevelt's ability to shape those events, and his friendship with Roosevelt was what placed Morgenthau in positions of importance. A successful professional public official by any standard, Morgenthau exhibited no real ambitions for himself; rather he devoted most of his adult life to faithfully serving his friend. Time and again during their thirty years together, Roosevelt entrusted Morgenthau with critically important and difficult tasks—not because of the latter's expertise or intellectual capabilities, but rather because of his common sense, unswerving loyalty, and administrative ability. The intuitive guess was Morgenthau's greatest asset, a talent characterized by a subordinate who said that Morgenthau could be right more often for the wrong reasons than any other man he knew. Morgenthau never confused loyalty with sycophancy. He and the president argued often and heatedly, although once Roosevelt made a decision Morgenthau carried it out in both letter and spirit, regardless of his own views. Fully confident that he held Roosevelt's friendship and respect, Morgenthau willingly permitted the president to use him privately while denying him publicly.

Overall evaluations of Henry Morgenthau have traditionally emphasized his supposed mistakes. Economists still argue over the efficacy of the gold games played by Roosevelt and Morgenthau during the early New Deal, but the Morgenthau Plan for Germany—once ridiculed as the understandable but revengeful product of a Jewish background—ironically seemed to have been carried out before Germany was reunified in 1989 (though not in such small pieces as Morgenthau planned), and much of Germany was deindustrialized in an attempt by the Allies, particularly France and Russia, to obtain reparations. Some historians of the cold war even began to look at the neutralization of Germany, which would have come out of the Morgenthau Plan, as one of the missed opportunities for the partial defusing of the cold war before it subsided.

Those two well-known episodes unfortunately have overshadowed Morgenthau's admirable role in two areas of American foreign policy: the aid-to-Britain program from 1938 through 1941, and assistance to Jewish refugees during World War II. Morgenthau was among the first in

Roosevelt's cabinet to warn of the threat posed to America and the world at large by Nazi Germany, and given his loyalty and administrative skills was a natural choice to coordinate the aid-to-the-Allies program which began in December 1938. From that time until after the passage of the Lend-Lease Act (which was written in the Treasury Department) Morgenthau pushed, cajoled, and encouraged the development of meaningful financial and military aid to the foes of Hitler. Working with Roosevelt's strong if only privately expressed support, the treasury secretary rationalized the purchasing operations of the British and French, squeezed out of the British financial data which proved indispensable in convincing Congress of the need for Lend-Lease, and effectively prevented American manufacturers from exploiting the hardpressed French and British. Morgenthau's support of European Jewish refugees was, for the most part, a lonely and unsuccessful battle. Aided by only a few lesser bureaucrats, he fought the State Department for the entire wartime period in his attempts to increase American assistance in terms of both providing a refuge and applying pressure for other nations to do the same. Although he was an anti-Zionist most of his life, Morgenthau's unhappy experience with the Jewish refugee question probably accounts for his staunch support of Israel in the late 1940s.

Henry Morgenthau, Jr., lacked the charisma or power to make a permanent personal mark on American history—but his humaneness, honesty, and loyalty provided a bench mark for those bureaucrats who keep a government functioning. See John Morton Blum, *From the Morgenthau Diaries* (3 vols., 1959–67).

WARREN F. KIMBALL

MORISON, Samuel Eliot (b. Boston, Mass., July 9, 1887; d. Boston, Mass., May 15, 1976), HISTORIAN, received a BA (1908), MA (1909), and PhD (1912) from Harvard. His doctoral dissertation was *The Life and Letters of Harrison Gray Otis, Federalist, 1765–1848* (1913). In 1914 he briefly taught at the University of California before joining the Harvard faculty, where he remained until his retirement in 1955 (full professor in 1925; Jonathan Trumbull professor of American history, 1941–55).

During World War I Morison served as a private. At the Paris Peace Conference at Versailles, he was attached to the American delegation, but resigned in 1919, believing that the Treaty of Versailles was unjust. Returning to Harvard, in 1921 he published *The Maritime History of Massachusetts, 1783–1860*. The following year he was appointed the first Harmsworth professor of American history at Oxford University (1922–25). His *Oxford History of the United States, 1793–1917* (1927) was written while at Oxford. In 1926 he was appointed official historian for the 300th anniversary of Harvard College. He had already published *The Tercentennial History of Harvard University* (4 vols., 1930–36); *Three Centuries of Harvard* (1936) is a convenient summary. In 1936 he also published *The Puritan Pronaos* (reissued in 1956 under the title *The Intellectual Life of Colonial New England*).

Morison, an ardent sailor, personally retraced **Christopher Columbus**'s voyages in preparing the biography *Admiral of the Ocean Sea* (2 vols., 1942), which won a Pulitzer Prize. In 1942 Morison was appointed a lieutenant commander in the U.S. naval reserve with the title Historian of Naval Operations. During the war he served on eleven ships and received seven battle stars. *The History of the U.S. Naval Operations in World War II* (15 vols., 1947–62) was the result of this appointment. *The Two–Ocean War* (1963) is a shorter edition of this work. In 1951 he was promoted to rear admiral. Morison was awarded another Pulitzer Prize for his biography of **John Paul Jones** (1959). Some of his other works include *Builders of the Bay Colony* (1930); *By Land and by Sea* (1953), a collection of essays and addresses; *The Oxford History of the American People* (1965), *"Old Bruin:" Commodore Matthew Calbraith Perry* (1967); and two volumes on the explorers of the New World.

———

"The great historians, with few exceptions, are those who have not merely studied, but lived; and whose studies have ranged over a much wider field than the period or subject of which they write." These opinions, quoted here from his essay "History as a Literary Art," are themes which Admiral Morison sounded repeatedly and which his career as a historian exemplified. He always insisted that at the very least, his students should visit and savor the places about which they write. From the experiences he gained through his love of sailing and the sea, he drew the perceptions which enriched his *Maritime History of Massachusetts* and his "sailor's biography" of Columbus, and then went on to lay his unique foundation for writing the history of the navy in World War II, his roving among the ships of the wartime fleet to observe a variety of the dimensions of naval war at first hand. Not only his studies but his writings themselves ranged over a much wider field than most modern academic historians dared to attempt. In fact, he did not fit the mold of the academic historian. He remained in many ways closer to the older tradition of literary history, the tradition of **Francis Parkman,** whose works he edited into a one-volume reader. He insisted that good history must be good literature. He insisted also on retaining personal, idiosyncratic, and even somewhat arrogant judgments; it was significant of his attitudes toward modernity in several senses that his naval history was marred by his giving too short shrift to the aircraft carrier (the one major warship type on which he never served) and the fast carrier task forces. Along with these qualities, however, went a stout integrity and an insistence upon the quest for truth as the historian's task. Morison aimed devastating salvos at "History through a Beard"—the **Charles A. Beard** kind of history which called upon the historian to acknowledge the relativism of historical truth, the historian's inability to escape his parochial frame of reference. "… if I were to sum up my credo in a single word," said Morison in his presidential address to the American Historical Association, "it would be that proud motto of Fustel de Coulanges: *Quæro*—I seek to learn." See Samuel Eliot Morison, *By Land and by Sea: Essays and Addresses* (1953).

RUSSELL F. WEIGLEY

MORRILL, Justin Smith (b. Strafford, Vt., April 14, 1810; d. Washington, D.C., Dec. 28, 1898), POLITICAL LEADER, attended the Thetford and Randolph academies before becoming a clerk in a general store in 1825. He then worked in another general store in Portland, Maine (1828–31). Returning to Strafford in 1831, he operated his own store until 1848. Morrill was a delegate to the 1852 Whig party convention, and was elected to the House of Representatives in 1854 as an antislavery Whig. In 1855 he helped organize the Republican party in Vermont.

In the House, Morrill specialized in tariff and financial legislation. A protectionist, he was largely responsible for passage of the Morrill Tariff Act of 1861. During the Civil War he advocated strict economy in government and "sound currency." He therefore opposed issuing "greenback" currency during and after the Civil War. He also sponsored the Morrill Land Grant College Act, which was vetoed by President Buchanan in 1859 but signed by President Lincoln in 1862. He served as chairman of the House Ways and Means Committee from 1865 to 1867.

Morrill was elected to the U.S. Senate in 1866. In the upper house he continued to specialize in financial matters, advocating a return to specie payments. He served frequently as chairman of the Senate Finance Committee (1877–79, 1881–93, 1895–98) and vigorously opposed the free coinage of silver. In 1890 he was influential in passing the second Morrill Act, which gave $25,000 of federal money annually to each of the land grant colleges. As chairman of the Senate Committee on Building and Grounds he helped oversee the completion of the Washington Monument in 1885 and the expansion of the Library of Congress building. An anti-imperialist, he opposed the Spanish-American War and annexation of the Philippines. Morrill wrote *Self-Consciousness of Noted Persons* (1882) and numerous articles on finance and other topics for *Forum* magazine in the late 1880s and 1890s.

Morrill was one of the most prominent public figures of the post–Civil War generation. He enjoyed a prestige and eminence seldom rivaled in American political life. With the general public and his congressional colleagues his reputation rested solidly upon his being the high priest of protection, the defender of sound currency, the father of the land grant colleges, and the member of the House and Senate whose term of office exceeded that of any other person in American legislative history until that time. In addition to the prestige of office and the esteem of many friends, Morrill possessed a modest fortune and domestic happiness. He was among the fortunate as well as the eminent men of his time.

Morrill was a skillful, learned, and painstaking legislator who could read trade reports and account sheets and write tax laws. He was also able to remove the dullness from the debates on tax and tariff bills with flashes of humor and wit. And he had the ability to penetrate to the heart of a financial matter. Banking and finance were the subjects of his mature years in Congress, and he brought to them a mind trained in practical affairs.

Belonging to the older and more conservative wing of the Republican party, Morrill opposed new ideas of finance and sovereignty advanced in his day. He was an unwavering supporter of the doctrine of protection, and did not welcome efforts to revise tariffs downward. But he did say on one occasion, "I suppose that if the Bible has to be revised from time to time, the tariff may have to be." Although many and great questions came up for consideration during his years in the Senate, he set forth few solutions and proposed few policies that departed from the political and financial creed he had worked out in his early years.

Prominent in senatorial politics during a period when national political power was largely vested in Congress and when the office of president was at low ebb in power and prestige, Morrill viewed the Senate as the ultimate political institution, saying on one occasion in declining a cabinet post, "There is no gift, no office to which I could be appointed, that I would accept in preference to a seat in the United States Senate. I consider that the highest honor that could be bestowed on me, and [its duties] the highest functions I could perform." Most of Morrill's contemporaries would have agreed with him. See William Belmont Parker, *The Life and Public Services of William Justin Morrill* (1924).

VINCENT P. DeSANTIS

MORRIS, Gouverneur (b. Morrisania, N.Y., Jan. 31, 1752; d. Morrisania, N.Y., Nov. 6, 1816), POLITICAL LEADER, graduated from King's College (now Columbia University) in 1768, and was admitted to the bar in 1771. During the crisis leading to the Revolution, he favored conciliation with Great Britain, but after the battle of Lexington (1775), he supported the patriot cause. He represented Westchester County in the N.Y. provincial congress (1775–77), where he backed the actions of the Continental Congress in Philadelphia. With **John Jay** and **Robert R. Livingston,** he helped draft the New York state constitution (1776–77).

Morris became a member of the Continental Congress in 1778, but was not returned in 1779 because of his outspoken opposition to the policies of Governor **George Clinton** of New York, especially those relating to claims to land in Vermont. Subsequently Morris lived in Pennsylvania for several years, where (1781–85) he was assistant to Superintendent of Finance **Robert Morris** (no kin).

As a delegate from Pennsylvania to the Federal Convention (1787), Morris favored a strong central government with both the president and the Senate having lifetime tenure. He disapproved of the equal representation of the states in the Senate and the three-fifths compromise, whereby five slaves were counted as three white men for purposes of representation and taxation. However, he voted for the final charter.

In 1789 Morris went to Europe on private business, as agent for Robert Morris, remaining there (mostly in France) until 1798. From time to time during those years he also served as an official of the U.S. government. His diary remains one of the major sources for the study of the French Revolution and its aftermath.

Morris was elected to the U.S. Senate as a Federalist in 1800 (serving until 1803). He became canal commissioner of New York (1810–13) and supported the construction of the Erie Canal. During his later years he denounced Thomas Jefferson's and James Madison's nonimportation measures, condemned the War of 1812, and supported the antiwar states' rights Hartford Convention (1814–15).

***

Morris was one of the most colorful and dashing nonmilitary figures of the Revolutionary and early national period. Among his contemporaries he was noted for three main attributes—personal vanity and a corresponding attachment to the ladies, a frank and bold manner that bordered on the audacious, and skill with the pen that bordered on the poetic.

As to the first, he was tall, broad-shouldered, and slim-hipped in an age when most Americans were short and fat; one of his prides in life was that he modeled, as a stand-in, for a statue of Washington. He had, however, only one leg, having lost the other (according to legend) in an accident while fleeing an irate husband whose wife he had seduced. The loss of the limb cooled neither his ardor for romantic attachments nor his appeal to the opposite sex. He remained in Paris during and after the Reign of Terror, for example, mainly because of a torrid love affair with the erstwhile mistress of Talleyrand. When Morris finally married, he was nearly fifty-eight.

His audacity and frankness both delighted and embarrassed other people. Once, on a bet, he threw his arm around the austere Washington and greeted him with intimate language, only to be cut down by an icy glare. In the Constitutional Convention he helped break some deadlocks—but helped cause others—by the way he got to the heart of matters and spoke out boldly. During the dispute over the basis of representation, he sent a chill through the Convention by remarking that if persuasion could not unite the country, "the sword will." Defending his proposal to make the Senate extremely aristocratic, he candidly admitted that "the Rich will strive to establish their dominion and enslave the rest. They always did. They always will." His remedy was to set the rich apart in a separate branch of government, which the popular branches could watch and control. Regarding the problem of obtaining ratification of the Constitution, he foresaw opposition by popular leaders and observed that "loaves and fishes" would be necessary to "bribe the demagogues." Such language, in a world in which formality, politeness, and indirection were the norm, was both shocking and titillating; but Morris had the wit, charm, and aristocratic bearing to use it effectively.

Morris's great gift as a writer was what won him immortality. At the Constitutional Convention he was entrusted with chairmanship of the Committee on Style, which meant that he actually wrote the final draft of the Constitution. The lean, crisp prose of the document attests to his skill; less obvious are liberties he took with the text. Ostensibly in the interest of good style, he deliberately made the language ambiguous at key points, thus allowing for considerable latitude of interpretation; he introduced several minor departures from the intentions of the Convention; and in at least one instance he slipped in an important feature (the contract clause) that had been expressly voted down by the members. See Max Mintz, *Gouverneur Morris and the American Revolution* (1970).

FORREST MCDONALD

MORRIS, Robert (b. at or near Liverpool, Eng., Jan. 31, 1734; d. Philadelphia, Pa., May 8, 1806), FINANCIER, emigrated to America in 1747 and settled in Oxford, Maryland. He joined the shipping house of Charles Willing in Philadelphia, and in 1754 he became a partner in the firm. In 1765 he signed a nonimportation agreement to resist the Stamp Act. A leading patriot, in 1775 Morris was a member of Pennsylvania's council of safety and committee of correspondence. As a delegate to the second Continental Congress (1776–78), he served on two of its leading committees, one to correspond with U.S. diplomats abroad and the second to obtain munitions. He originally opposed the Declaration of Independence because he still hoped for a rapprochement with England, but he signed the Declaration in August 1776, and supported the Revolution.

While in Congress, Morris helped purchase war supplies. He was defeated for reelection in 1779 after opponents accused him of using his office for personal financial benefit. But he was appointed superintendent of finance in 1781 by the Continental Congress, which was desperately in need of a sound fiscal policy. As superintendent, he worked to fund the debt, obtain money from the states, negotiate a loan with France, and run the government frugally. Through his efforts Congress was able to finance the Yorktown campaign (1781), which ended the war, and to establish the Bank of North America (1782). When the states failed to cooperate with Morris's plans, he resigned (1784).

Morris was a delegate to the Annapolis Convention (1786) and to the Federal Convention (1787), where he supported the new Constitution. He served in the U.S. Senate as a Federalist (1789–95) and was a leading supporter of **Alexander Hamilton**'s programs. But he lost his fortune in land speculation and was confined to debtors' prison (1798–1801).

Robert Morris was a man who would surely have been assigned a place in the American pantheon of first-rank statesmen comparable in stature to that of Washington, Madison, Jefferson, and Hamilton except for the fact that he died bankrupt, an unforgivable sin for American heroes. Morris's formal education was scanty, but his native intelligence and imagination, as well as his demonstrated managerial, political, and financial talents, enabled him to rise from an apprentice in a mercantile firm to the acknowledged Prince of Merchants. In many respects he was a man who lived before his time. When most entrepreneurs thought in terms of a provincial economy, he thought of a vigorous national one. When many Revolutionary leaders shunned

innovative political experiment, he used financial means to strengthen the national government under the Articles of Confederation. When many patriots thought of the past, he struck out boldly for the future.

Morris became a leading figure in the Continental Congress in 1776–77 when the British were having the best of it. His service on two of the Congress's key committees, the Secret Committee of Commerce and the Committee of Secret Correspondence, made him a national figure. Even today his full and descriptive letters dating from this period are alive with energy, action, and hope in those distressing times when **Thomas Paine** was writing bitterly of summer soldiers.

Morris's greatest contribution to the American Revolution came when he was unanimously elected by the Continental Congress to be superintendent of finance in 1781, at a time when Congress and the country were deep in a financial crisis. He introduced a sweeping program of financial reform. He established a completely new form of currency called "Morris Notes" to replace the defunct continental currency; he took steps to bring order out of the chaos involving the national debts; he argued for a national revenue to repay those debts; he instituted a new system of supplying the military forces more efficiently at less expense; and he established the Bank of North America, the first national bank in the history of the United States. Except for the system of national revenue, his measures were successful. Morris regarded these financial measures as a means to an end, to strengthen the Confederation government. His program duplicated precisely that proposed by Hamilton a decade later under the Federalists; yet Morris is little known.

Morris was elected a senator in the new federal government under the Constitution, but his energies were directed principally to entrepreneurial activities. They became so widespread and complex that he overextended himself, especially in landholdings; and when a depression developed, he had ample assets but was short on liquidity. He was unable to weather the crisis, and he filed for bankruptcy. Had he survived this temporary financial depression, he would have become the wealthiest man in America.

To this day a cloud hangs over Morris's reputation, specifically that he used public monies for personal transactions. It is a charge that has never been proven. Scholars familiar with the trading and financial institutions of the period can find no evidence to adjudge him guilty. What happened is that the growing economy of the United States outstripped the existing financial institutions and practices, especially in accounting. Records are imprecise when a handshake or a man's reputation, the practice of the day, constituted his bond. Morris made his great fortune, in the main, after the Revolutionary War, not during it, and much evidence exists to support the theory that inattention to his private affairs while in public service was at the base of his business failure. Robert Morris was one of the nation's first modern businessmen, an unswerving patriot for independence once the Declaration of Independence was adopted, and as significant a figure in the struggle to win independence as any other man of his time, save Washington. See Clarence L. Ver Steeg, *Robert Morris: Revolutionary Financier* (1954).

Clarence L. Ver Steeg

MORRISON, Toni (b. Lorain, Ohio, Feb. 18, 1931), WRITER, CRITIC, born Cloe Anthony Wofford, the second of four children. After graduating from Lorain High School, she attended Howard University (BA, 1953), and later Cornell University (MA, 1955). She taught English at Texas Southern University (1955–57), and Howard University (1957–64). She married Harold Morrison in 1958 and they divorced in 1964. In 1965, she became a literary editor for Random House, in New York City, and eventually rose to senior editor (1969). She remained at Random House for twenty years.

Her first novel, *The Bluest Eye* (1970), received wide acclaim and marked her as a major new figure on the literary scene. It was followed by *Sula*

(1973), nominated in 1975 for the National Book Critics' Circle Award. *Song of Solomon* (1977) was at its publication the most successful of her works and brought her wide national and international fame. It was followed by *Tar Baby* (1981), *Beloved* (1987), and *Jazz* (1992). In 1984 Morrison left Random House to accept the Albert Schweitzer Professorship of the Humanities at the State University of New York at Albany. Thereafter, she taught briefly at Rutgers University and in 1989 went to Princeton University, where she was named the Robert F. Goheen Professor of the Humanities. In 1993 she received the Nobel Prize for literature. Two recent publications have seen her move beyond fiction into literary and social criticism: *Playing in the Dark: Whiteness and the Literary Imagination* (1992); and *Race-ing Justice, En-gendering Power: Essays on Anita Hill, Clarence Thomas and the Construction of Social Reality*, a volume she edited. Recently the *New York Times Book Review* called her "the closest thing the country has to a national writer."

Though America has produced many fine writers in recent times, Toni Morrison has brought special qualities to the novel since the publication of her first, *The Bluest Eye*. Though not herself an avowed feminist, she writes about the world primarily from the point of view of women, especially black women. Special qualities of her work stem from her capacity to write about women in general, black women in particular, men in general, black men in particular, and people in general at one and the same time. Hence, race and gender have a prominent place in her work, but they do not receive single-minded, overriding emphasis. Characters in her work are not good or evil *because* of race, though whatever they are may be influenced, as in life, by racial factors. These factors as well as an astounding sensitivity to language and an uncanny ability to say the right thing in just exactly the right way create a body of work that is dazzling in its interest and complexity.

As a black woman writer, Morrison took the next step in the African-American novelist tradition following **Frederick Douglass**, **William Wells Brown**, Charles Chesnutt, **James Weldon Johnson**, Nella Larsen, Zora Hurston, and **Richard Wright** and **Ralph Ellison**, by writing about African-American experience from inside, imagining her audience not to be a mainstream audience but other African-Americans. Hence she is not a protest writer as such but protest is as natural to her vision as awareness of the racial element is to African-Americans.

Toni Morrison's acclaim has by no means been confined to fiction or to the United States where her books have frequently been on best-seller lists, and her work is probably taught in more college classrooms than that of any living writer. That she received the Nobel Prize for literature in 1993 attests to her international fame and stature. See Toni Morrison, *Playing in the Dark: Whiteness and the Literary Imagination* (1990).

DONALD GIBSON

MORSE, Samuel Finley Breese (b. Charlestown, Mass., April 27, 1791; d. New York, N.Y., April 2, 1872), ARTIST, INVENTOR, graduated from Yale College in 1810. In 1811 he accompanied the portrait painter Washington Allston on a voyage to England, where he studied under Allston and **Benjamin West** at the Royal Academy. He returned to America in 1815 and opened a studio in Boston. Turning to portrait painting, he traveled around New England to obtain commissions during the next several years. From 1818 to 1821 he spent winters painting portraits in Charleston, South Carolina. Settling in New York City in 1823, he continued to paint for another decade. His two well-known portraits of Lafayette were done in 1825. In 1826 he became involved with the formation of the National Academy of Design, serving as president until 1842 and leading an aggressive campaign against the conservative practices of the older American Academy of Fine Arts. He spent the years 1829–32 studying and painting in France and Italy.

Morse returned to New York City in 1832 and was appointed professor of painting and sculpture at the University of the City of New York (later New York University). He also became active in the anti-Catholic movement and ran for mayor on the Native American "Know-Nothing" ticket in 1836. Failing to obtain many commissions for portraits after 1832, he began to concentrate on the invention of the telegraph. He developed the finger-key transmitter, the embossing stylus and sounder receivers, and the Morse code by 1836. After applying for a patent in 1837, he formed a partnership with Alfred Vail, who supplied the capital for the promotion and improvement of the telegraph. In 1843 Congress appropriated $30,000 to construct an experimental telegraph line from Washington to Baltimore. On May 24, 1844, Morse transmitted over this line the message: "What hath God wrought!" When the federal government declined to purchase his invention for $100,000 in 1844, he formed a partnership with **Amos Kendall** to promote the telegraph as a private business venture. Several telegraph companies rapidly constructed a national communications network which was consolidated into the Western Union Co. in 1866.

Morse assisted **Cyrus W. Field** in the laying of the first transatlantic cable and designed the insulation for the second line. An advocate of higher education for women, Morse was a founder of Vassar College in 1865, and of Douglas College in 1871.

⸺⸙⸺

Samuel F. B. Morse was in many ways typical of the mid-19th-century American inventor. He came to the telegraph from another field (painting), lacked capital, influence, and price knowledge of the state of the art, but was endowed with an unshakable conviction of the ultimate worth of his innovation. It was once remarked of him that he had "the faculty of seeing the value of corner lots when other men were lost in contemplation of the surrounding scenery." He had the personal qualities necessary for the task: he was intelligent, persistent, and combative.

Morse "invented" his telegraphic system in three stages, each of which called for different talents. In 1832 he sketched simple and effective mechanisms for sending, transmitting, and recording messages. From 1836 to 1838 he improved the mechanisms by drawing upon the scientific knowledge of Professor Leonard D. Gale and **Joseph Henry,** as well as the mechanical ingenuity of Alfred Vail. After 1838 the problems of the telegraph were primarily financial, political, and managerial. In these areas too he was fortunate in being able to surround himself with men more accomplished than himself.

Predictably, with any device as complicated and widely discussed as the electric telegraph system, involving men of such sanguine temperament as Morse and some of his adversaries, the credit for invention was long and angrily disputed. The least necessary and most ignoble of his disputes was with the dean of American scientists, Joseph Henry. As a college physics teacher, Henry had carried on research in the field of electromagnetism, and had even built an experimental telegraph in his classroom. Although he was aware of and encouraged the practical application of his work, he believed that as a scientist his task was to increase knowledge rather than monopolize it. On several important occasions he shared his knowledge with Morse and publicly endorsed his efforts to perfect the telegraph.

Henry accurately summed matters up by stating that Morse's merit lay in "the invention of a particular instrument and process for telegraphic purposes," rather than any "single original discovery" in science. Accurate though the distinction was, Morse was not of a temperament to take it kindly. With the validity of his valuable patent and no small amount of pride riding on the exact definition of his achievement, Morse could not let the matter pass. In the passion of combat he was less than generous to the real aid Henry had given him.

Morse was well into his forties when he took out his patent for the telegraph, and behind him lay enough professional disappointment and personal tragedy to mar several lives. The deaths of loved ones, an artistic career which never really fulfilled its early promise, abortive forays into nativist politics, and the frustrations of trying to perfect a difficult and sensitive mechanical device made him jealous of reputation and impatient for success. By mid-century both were assured, and the Morse telegraph was internationally recognized as a masterpiece of mechanical invention. See Carleton Mabee, *The American Leonardo: A Life of Samuel F. B. Morse* (1943).

CARROLL PURSELL

MOSES, Robert (b. New Haven, Conn., Dec. 18, 1888; d. West Islip, L.I., July 29, 1981), GOVERNMENT OFFICIAL, graduated from Yale (1909) and earned an MA at Oxford (1913) and a PhD in political science at Columbia (1914). After spending several years on civil-service reform and state reorganization issues, he served as an aide to New York's governor, **Alfred E. Smith**, and devised a plan for state parks. In 1924 Smith appointed Moses to head the Council on State Parks, and during the next four decades, Moses led the effort which greatly expanded the state's park system and forest preserve, including large areas in the Adirondacks and Catskills. In 1924 he also began a thirty-nine-year tenure as head of the Long Island State Park Commission, where he developed and carried out plans for 115 miles of parkways and created Jones Beach.

In 1934 newly elected Mayor **Fiorello LaGuardia** named Moses to be New York City's Park Commissioner; he then appointed Moses to head the Triborough Bridge Authority (1936) and the New York City Parkway Authority (1938). In the 1940s and 1950s, New York's several mayors appointed Moses to an array of other posts, including membership on the City Planning Commission (1942), Construction Coordinator (1946), and chairman of the Slum Clearance Committee (1948); and in 1954 the governor named him to chair the State Power Authority. He held most of these positions into the 1960s and used his interrelated powers to add dozens of parks in the City and across the State, ensure the construction of the United Nations buildings, Lincoln Center for the Performing Arts, and Shea Stadium. His multiple positions also enabled him to take the leading role in the building of several large housing projects in New York City and major power projects in the St. Lawrence/Niagara region, and construct a series of impressive river crossings, beginning with the Triborough and Bronx-Whitestone bridges in the 1930s and ending with the Throgs Neck and Verrazano-Narrows spans in the 1960s. In 1968, at the age of seventy-nine, Moses resigned from his last major post, chairman of the Triborough Bridge and Tunnel Authority; during the next ten years he devoted his energies to advocating the creation of three gigantic spans across Long Island Sound, which he viewed as "vital" projects which would permit Long Island traffic to escape to the mainland without adding to burdensome congestion on New York City's roadways.

Few men in public life have aroused as much intensity of feeling, coupled with sharply divergent assessments of their work, as Robert Moses. In his early years, working with Governor Smith and Mayor LaGuardia on administrative reform, the creation of new parks, and the development of Long Island beaches, Moses was widely applauded for his creative vision, his ability to carry out complex tasks, and his tireless energy in the service of great public needs. By the late 1930s, when he turned his sharp wit against "long-haired planners" who raised questions about his projects, and defended the right of a public-housing sponsor he had wooed to exclude African-Americans from Stuyvesant Town in Manhattan, criticism of his values and of his "self-confidence to the point of arrogance" began to emerge.

Moses's willingness in the 1940s and 1950s to use aggressive tactics to remove tenants in the path of his highway and slum-clearance projects added to the array of critics, who by the 1960s carried a quite different vision of urban society, one which sought to preserve neighborhoods and local social networks and therefore opposed large-scale demolition and monumental construction projects. Moses was a leading member of the now disparaged class. Robert Caro's Pulitzer Prize–winning book, *The Power Broker* (1974), carried this sharply critical view to a new

level of rich detail. Readers found there a Moses who seemed to be "inhuman, inhumane in the way he swept whole neighborhoods and landscapes aside for highways and ill-conceived housing," and who in his later years had an "ever deepening and disfiguring addiction to success" regardless of the cost to the social fabric.

For those who worked closely with Moses, however, and for many who enjoyed the results of his labors, he was "New York's great builder" and "the single-minded genius who molded New York City into a twentieth century metropolis." He had created a marvelous parkway system on Long Island; and the "grandeur of Jones Beach, both in its man-made sweep and its splendid detail," attracted stunned attention in the 1990s as it had for seventy years past. He had made a signal contribution to the environmental movement in his early, successful effort to preserve Jamaica Bay and create a wildlife refuge there, against the pressures to use the Bay as a city garbage dump. The Niagara water-power system was praised as an "outstanding engineering achievement" and Moses's crucial role proclaimed by naming it the Robert Moses Niagara Power Plant.

Moses was not only our last builder of great urban structures but, to his admirers, a "genius at public relations," a public official who could marshal public support for large ideas, in contrast to the "niggardly privatism" that seemed to cramp the spirit of the average citizen and many public officials in the final decades of the 20th century. The greatest of his works were compared to the vast contructions of the Roman Empire, and Moses was seen as the modern caesar. And beneath a "prickly exterior," those who knew him well found a "warm and generous nature."

There is much truth in both perspectives. In his creative energy, his constructive use of political coalitions, his sometimes faulty vision of progress, and his abuse of citizens who opposed him, Moses offers a broad lesson in the opportunities and dangers of concentrated power.

Moses wrote dozens of essays, many of them memorable in their insights both into their author's passion and into the values of three generations of Americans who sought progress through large-scale projects. Some of these writings are excerpted in his compilation, *Public Works: A Dangerous Trade* (1970). See Jameson W. Doig and A. Koziak, eds., *Robert Moses as Skylark and Mole* (1996).

JAMESON W. DOIG

MOTHERWELL, Robert Burns, III (b. Aberdeen, Wash., Jan. 24, 1915; d. Cape Cod, Mass., July 16, 1991), ARTIST, studied painting at the Otis Art Institute, Los Angeles (1926–27) and graduated from Stanford University in 1936. He did graduate work in philosophy at Harvard (1937–38) before going to Europe in 1938 to study art. Returning to the U.S. a year later, he taught art at the University of Oregon before enrolling at the Columbia University Graduate School of Architecture. At Columbia, Motherwell became interested in surrealist and abstract art. He had his first one-man show at Peggy Guggenheim's Art of This Century Gallery (N.Y.) in 1944, and soon became recognized as a leading abstract expressionist. *Pancho Villa, Dead and Alive* (1943, Museum of Modern Art, N.Y.) is representative of his work. *The French Line* (1960, private collection, N.Y.) shows Motherwell's mastery of collage. In 1965, the Museum of Modern Art organized a retrospective of Motherwell's works that traveled to major European cities. Since the mid-1970s he had major exhibitions in Stockholm, Vienna, Paris, Edinburgh, London, Barcelona, Mexico City, and Madrid. In 1982, a permanent Motherwell Gallery was installed at the Bavarian State Museum of Modern Art in Munich, the only gallery for a living artist among those museums devoted to modern art. A retrospective was organized by the Albert-Knox Gallery in Buffalo in 1983 to celebrate forty years of Motherwell's art, and it traveled to five other galleries across the United States before opening at the Guggenheim Museum in New York City for the 1984–85 art season.

In addition to his painting, Motherwell, who was an associate professor of art at Hunter College, CUNY (1951–1958), lectured and taught at many schools and wrote widely on art. Some of his better-known paintings are: *The Homely Protestant* (1948, artist's collection), *The Voyage* (1949, Museum of Modern Art, N.Y.), and *Elegy to the Spanish Republic C* (1963, Marlborough-Gerson Gallery, N.Y.).

Youngest of the original abstract expressionists, Robert Motherwell played a pivotal role in the development of an intellectual and philosophical background for this new form of painting. Bringing to bear ideas from Freud, from Kierkegaard's existentialism, and from French symbolist and surrealist aesthetics, Motherwell formulated an account of the new painting which stressed as essential its universal, supranational character. "Beyond national differences there are human similarities more consequential," he said. "To be merely an American or French artist is to be nothing; to fail to overcome one's initial environment is never to reach the human."

In addition to his role as internationalist, however, Motherwell became a spokesman for those impressed by the merits of plastic automatism as an inventive technique, and for those who valued painting as a source of pleasure. In his own painting, he manifested his convictions through manipulation of the structure, placement, and proportions of a small repertoire of elementary forms which, despite their painterly execution, afforded the impression of solidity and weight. Approaching these shapes as symbolic, evocative schemata, he transformed them into an expressive yet nondescriptive commentary upon, for example, the conflict of Eros and Thanatos, the life-death struggle which fascinated Freud and inspired many of Motherwell's most influential works.

A self-taught painter who evidenced both purposefulness and individuality early in his career, Robert Motherwell became an inspired writer and teacher who spoke openly and voluminously about his ideas and ideals. Motherwell's intellectual concerns, however, were clearly subordinate in his own work to a sensual involvement with materials, an involvement which led him naturally to the medium of collage. As do his paintings, these collages afford a unique synthesis of sensual, emotional, and intellectual pleasures, demonstrating forcefully his own conclusions regarding the value of painting. See Frank O'Hara, *Robert Motherwell* (1965).

PATRICIA FAILING

MOTT, Lucretia Coffin (b. Nantucket, Mass., Jan. 3, 1793; d. Abington, Pa., Nov. 11, 1880), REFORMER, entered the Nine Partners Boarding School, a Quaker academy near Poughkeepsie, New York, in 1806. A student there for two years and then a teacher, her interest in woman's rights was stimulated by the equal tuition but unequal salary accorded females by the school.

Mott began speaking at Quaker meetings in 1818 and was designated a minister in the Society of Friends in 1821. With the great Quaker split of 1827, she reluctantly sided with the liberal Elias Hicks and thereafter remained a champion of intellectual freedom and practical righteousness. She also displayed an early interest in educational reform, the problems of the working class and the poor, and the antislavery movement. In 1833 she was the only woman to participate in the proceedings of the national antislavery convention at Philadelphia. That same year she led in founding the Philadelphia Female Anti-Slavery Society and remained a member of its executive board for most of its existence. She was a major leader of several antislavery conventions of American women and, following the full admission of women, active in the Pennsylvania Anti-Slavery Society. She was also one of the three original female members of the executive committee of the American Anti-Slavery Society and a delegate of that society to the 1840 world antislavery convention in London, where, like other women delegates, she was refused a seat.

By this time Lucretia Mott had become a noted figure in reform circles. She was the only woman very active in the proceedings of the New England Non-Resistance Society, and in the 1840s she led in founding the Philadelphia Association for the Relief and Employment of Poor Women

and served as its president for many years. In 1848 she joined **Elizabeth Cady Stanton** in organizing the first woman's rights convention at Seneca Falls, New York, and was probably the most popular and influential figure of the woman's rights movement of her day.

In the 1850s the Mott home became a sanctuary for runaway slaves and a major center of reform activity of many types. Despite her pacifism, Mrs. Mott supported the Union during the Civil War. At the conclusion of that war she campaigned against racism and for both equality and aid for the freedmen. She presided at the initial Equal Rights Convention of 1866. The following year she helped found the Free Religious Association. In her later years she continued to work for liberal religious causes, temperance, woman's rights, and world peace.

⸻

Lucretia Mott embodied much of the spirit and content of radical, humanitarian reform in the 19th-century United States. Drawing from Quakerism, Transcendentalism, and Unitarianism, her religious teaching stressed the central importance to human progress of the inner light or divinity within each person together with the expression of that divinity through individual reason in an atmosphere of complete freedom and mutual respect. She had little use for theology, an open contempt for dogma and arbitrary authority, and an abiding faith in the people and the possibility of practical righteousness. Her primary goals were broad rather than specific, especially encompassing the concepts of freedom, justice, and brotherly love, and her tactics were those of moral and intellectual persuasion. Perhaps the most important female abolitionist, she helped shape and stood with the Garrisonian movement, and she was the foremost figure in the early woman's rights movement.

Mott brought to the reformers sixty years of activity as well as an unusually sharp intellect, a capability for persuasive public speaking, a calm determination, and a winning personality and manner. Comely and erect, attired in simple Quaker garb, always considerate of her opponents, she spoke with clarity and simplicity and had a talent for defining issues clearly. She was vigorous and effective in her reformism, but remarkably dignified, friendly, and principled in her personal life and behavior, thus bringing not only strength but much dignity and respect to the cause of reform. Although her modesty and reserve lessened her official prominence among reformers, she had few peers as activist, thinker, or platform speaker. An exemplary wife, housekeeper, and hostess, she was blessed with a happy marriage to a like-minded reformer, and the Mott home was a constant social center for East Coast reform activities. Lucretia Mott was sprightly, impulsive, cheerful, and energetic. Her honesty and dedication, her sincere concern and open friendship with white and black, with rich and poor, and her constant efforts represented the very best of the reform currents of her day. See Otelia Cromwell, *Lucretia Mott* (1958).

OTTO H. OLSEN

MOUNT, William Sidney (b. Setauket, N.Y., Nov. 26, 1807; d. Setauket, N.Y., Nov. 19, 1868), ARTIST, grew up in Stony Brook, Long Island. In 1824 he moved to New York City to become an apprentice to his brother Henry, a sign painter. He studied briefly at the National Academy of Design in New York (1826), but poor health forced him to return to Stony Brook the following year. He returned to New York in 1829, where he opened a portrait studio. He became an associate member of the Academy in 1831 and a full member the following year.

Spending most of his time after 1837 in Stony Brook, Mount achieved renown for his genre paintings of rural Long Island life. Such paintings as *Bargaining for a Horse* (1835, New York Historical Society) and *Eel Spearing at Setauket* (1845, New York State Historical Association, Cooperstown) are well-known examples of this style. In 1859 he constructed a portable studio on wheels which attracted much attention. He painted very little in his last ten years because of declining health. Some of his major works include *Dregs in the Cup (Fortune Telling)* (1838,

New York Historical Society) and *Farmers Nooning* (1836, Suffolk Museum and Carriage House, Stony Brook, N.Y.).

To acknowledge William Sidney Mount merely as a recorder of rural scenes and activities is to vastly underestimate the profundity of his artistic concerns, his efforts to reconcile the ideal tradition of European art with American realist interests, and his significance as a representative of one of the most vital trends in 19th-century American painting, luminism. Although Mount rejected European travel and study, fearing "to tarry too long, and thus lose my nationality," he was far from ignorant of the techniques of the European masters. He gleaned from their writings, from prints and descriptions of their works, and from the few examples of their painting available in New York exhibitions an appreciation and understanding of their formulas for color and compositional organization. To a desire to emulate the principles which he admired in traditional art, he added a notable ability to observe and record the appearance of his own surroundings, to capture the nuances of time of day and weather and their effect upon natural forms. Asher B. Durand, **Winslow Homer,** and the French impressionists were to share Mount's interest in the guides to optical laws published by Chevreul and to emulate his devotion to *plein air* painting. Mount's best and most characteristic works, based on careful perspectival arrangements, are organized in the tradition of the masters whom he had studied: Raphael, Veronese, Poussin. The classic calm of these paintings is emphasized by the skill with which Mount captures light and atmosphere, fixing the moment of each scene for eternity. Effacing his own presence from the enameled surfaces of his scenes, Mount, the luminist, permits the viewer to confront the monumental and the eternal, not the merely anecdotal.

Mount's artistic vision, while complex, was far less enigmatic than his personality. His voluminous diaries, journals, and letters reveal him as an ardent Democrat and anti-abolitionist, despite the fact that he was the first American artist to dignify the black man, and as a devotee of spiritualism, despite his concern with recording the observable world in measured, factual terms. See Alfred Frankenstein, *Painter of Rural America: William Sidney Mount* (1968).

HELEN BARBARA WEINBERG

MUHAMMAD, Elijah (b. Sandersville, Ga., Oct. 7, 1897; Chicago, Ill., March 25, 1975), RELIGIOUS LEADER, was raised on a tenant farm. After working as a field hand and railroad laborer, he moved in 1923 to Detroit, where he worked (1923–29) in a Chevrolet plant. In Detroit he became the assistant of W. D. Fard, who, claiming to be a messenger from Allah to American blacks, had established a Temple of Islam. It was at this time that he changed his name from Elijah Poole to Elijah Muhammad. He gradually assumed the leadership of the Detroit temple, but upon the disappearance of Fard in 1934, a rift in the movement's leadership forced Muhammad to move to Chicago. There he assumed the title of "Prophet," and established a new Black Muslim temple, which he headed until 1942, when he was convicted of counseling draft evasion. In 1946, upon his release from the federal prison in Milan, Michigan, Muhammad resumed his active leadership of the Muslims.

In his teachings, he contended that white men were the oppressors of all nonwhite peoples. He demanded that his followers dress conservatively and refrain from using tobacco, narcotics, and alcohol. Under Muhammad's leadership, a variety of Black Muslim business establishments were opened, a "University of Islam" was established, with branches in Chicago and Detroit, and the movement was expanded throughout the nation. In 1959, with two of his sons, he traveled to several Muslim countries in Africa and the Near East, and made the traditional Muslim pilgrimage to Mecca. There is mounting evidence to suggest that Muhammad or his closest associates ordered the assassination of **Malcolm X** (1965) who had broken with the organization and had become a power center in his own right. Before Muhammad's death a struggle for control of the Nation of Islam developed between Muhammad's sons and some of his followers. Eventually, the National of Islam was taken over by Louis Farrakhan who presently leads it.

⁂

Through his organization—the Nation of Islam—Muhammad had a profound effect on the rise of black nationalist sentiment in the United States since the 1950s. As a sharp critic of integrationism and a strong advocate of black separatism, he attracted the attention of many young ghetto blacks who found the nonviolent, interracial approach of the civil rights movement unrealistic and irrelevant to their immediate needs. Muhammad was at the height of his influence in the early 1960s when his organization received widespread publicity and won many converts, particularly among black prison inmates. While his message included religious and moral teachings—which were only vaguely related to orthodox Islam—Muhammad made his greatest impact with his insistence that blacks should withdraw from white society and develop their own nation where they could control their own destinies. Although denounced as a racist and demagogue by most whites and by many black leaders, Muhammad insisted that he was problack rather than antiwhite and that by instilling pride and self-respect in his followers, he had transformed many of them from criminals, alcoholics, and addicts into productive, self-disciplined members of the community.

Despite the vigor and appeal of his message, Muhammad was himself an unimposing man. Small of stature and a poor speaker, in personal appearances he frequently failed to impress any but the firmly committed. In the early 1960s he was overshadowed within the Muslim movement by **Malcolm X,** who, despite his professed loyalty to Muhammad, soon developed an independent following. Friction between the two men led to Malcolm's suspension in late 1963 and his resignation from the Muslims in 1964. Malcolm accused Muhammad of sexual immorality, and Malcolm's assassination a year later was charged to supporters of Muhammad. Since 1965, as other organizations have developed the nationalist message in new directions, the Muslim movement declined. Muhammad's advanced age and failing health, together with continuing dissension within his organization, diminished his influence. But though the number of members who belong to the Nation of Islam has always been a tightly held secret, the organization Muhammad founded began to revive under his successor, Louis Farrakhan. See E. U. Essien-Udom, *Black Nationalism* (1962).

ALLAN H. SPEAR

MUIR, John (b. Dunbar, Scotland, April 21, 1838; d. Los Angeles, Calif., Dec. 24, 1914), NATURALIST. Muir, who emigrated with his family from Scotland to a frontier farm near Portage, Wisconsin in 1849, spent his youth in rigorous physical labor on the family farm. He began keeping journals of his walks through the woods when quite young. In 1861, he was admitted to the University of Wisconsin at Madison (1859–63) where he studied geology, chemistry, Latin and Greek, but he disliked the restrictions imposed by academic life and left the university without a degree. He hiked north into Canada, then south to Indiana, doing odd jobs for meals. He settled briefly in Indianapolis, working in a factory that produced spokes and hubs for carriage wheels until an accident in 1867 temporarily cost him his sight. He then walked to the Gulf of Mexico, keeping a journal, and spent a month in Cuba, where he contracted malaria and typhus. In 1868 he settled in California's Yosemite Valley, where he ran a sawmill and worked as a guide.

Through his friendship with Mrs. Jeanne Carr, the wife of one of his professors in Wisconsin who had moved to San Francisco, Muir met many scientists, artists, and writers, including, in 1871, **Ralph Waldo Emerson**. Muir's nature articles appeared in the *Overland Monthly*, *Atlantic*, and *Scribner's Monthly*.

Muir's interest in glaciers took him to Alaska in 1879, 1880 and again in 1881. He discovered several glaciers in Alaska, one of which is named for him. In 1880 he married Louise Wanda Strentzel, the daughter of a California fruit rancher, and settled on the Strentzel farm. He was so successful at horticulture that he was able to retire in 1890 and devote himself entirely to his travels, which included, before his death, Europe, South America, Africa, and Australia.

Muir's articles decrying the damage done to the Yosemite region by loggers and sheepherders were instrumental in getting the area increased protection as a national park in 1890. A meeting between Muir and President Theodore Roosevelt in 1903 is credited with turning the president wholeheartedly to the cause of conservation. Muir's books include *The Mountains of California* (1894), *Our National Parks* (1901) and *Story of My Boyhood and Youth* (1913). His journals fill several volumes.

⁂

The importance of John Muir has increased since his death, as the urgency of his message has become more apparent. A pioneer of the conservation movement, Muir sounded an alarm that has echoed down the years with ever clearer resonance.

Muir's crusade to safeguard the wilderness was ahead of his time and, in some measure, remains in the vanguard. Writing during a period of vigorous expansionism and exploitation of the environment, he argued for ecological protection on non-utilitarian grounds, foreshadowing the so-called "deep" or "radical" environmentalism of a century later. Although he never used the modern terms "ecology" or "environmental ethics," he shared with such late-twentieth century thinkers as Aldo Leopold a passionate belief in the intrinsic value of nature and its moral right to exist undefiled by man.

The son of a Christian fundamentalist against whose tyrannical religiosity he rebelled, Muir came to embrace a theist position in which the presence of a deity permeated all nature. He was not a scientist by either temperament or training, and although he prepared the way for the scientific environmentalism which was to emerge some years later, his contributions to the technical understanding of the mountains and glaciers he so loved was incidental and, in some cases, erroneous. He overestimated the depth of glacial erosion, for example, and seldom pursued his observations with rigorous investigation. His philosophy was rather a spiritual and aesthetic one that defined nature as "the unspeakably beautiful work of a loving creator."

In his writings Muir deplored the utilitarianism of believing that nature exists for man's use—"sheep for his clothing, oil to light his dark ways, lead for his bullets"—and the meanness of its defilement, calling men "blind to the beauty they desecrate, utterly deaf in their immorality to the celestial love-music of nature." His own feeling for wilderness was so rapturous that, according to his journal, if it had not been for the need of bread he would have readily abandoned civilization for the forests.

Muir's elevated literary style, clearly derived from such sources as the Bible, Milton, and Shakespeare, has withstood the changes of taste less well than that of his mentors, Emerson and **Thoreau**, but in his time it was very effective. His numerous magazine articles campaigning for wilderness protection, published during the 1870s and 1880s in *Scribner's Monthly* and the *Century*, so galvanized public sentiment that the government initiated the National Park System with the passage of the Yosemite National Park bill in 1890 and, in 1891, an act giving the president power to create forest preserves. The next year, Muir called for the creation of an organization to support the exploration and preservation of the Sierra Nevada, and thus originated the influential Sierra Club.

But though Muir's reputation as a naturalist has diminished and his prose has come to seem rather overblown, his stature as an apostle of nature has grown. An activist of singular intelligence, energy, and dedication, he succeeded in influencing not only the laws of the nation but the consciousness of its citizens. See Michael P. Cohen, *The Pathless Way: John Muir and American Wilderness* (1984).

DENNIS WEPMAN

MUMFORD, Lewis (b. Flushing, N.Y., Oct. 19, 1895; d. Jan. 26, 1990, Amenia, New York),

WRITER, REFORMER, attended (1912–18) a number of universities in New York City, but never took a degree. He worked in New York as an investigator in the dress industry (1916) and laboratory assistant with the U.S. Bureau of Standards (1917) before serving as a radio electrician in the U.S. Navy (1917–18). He became associate editor of the *Dial,* a literary magazine, in 1919 and went to London in 1920 to be acting editor of the *Sociological Review.*

Upon his return to New York in 1921, Mumford took up his career as a writer. His contributions to such journals as the *American Mercury, New Republic,* and *Harper's* soon gained him a reputation as a leading architectural critic and expert on cities. His *Sticks and Stones* (1924) related American architecture to social conditions, and *The Golden Day* (1926) took a broader look at American culture. Mumford was also a charter member of the Regional Planning Association of America (1923) and a special investigator for the New York Housing and Planning Commission in 1924.

Intrigued by the problem of how technology can be directed to meet the needs of society, Mumford wrote *Technics and Civilization* (1934), the first of a four-volume study called *The Renewal of Life.* He completed this work with *The Culture of Cities* (1938), *The Condition of Man* (1944), and *The Conduct of Life* (1951). During the 1930s he was the architectural critic for the *New Yorker.* Mumford was a member of New York City's Board of Higher Education (1935–37) and then served on the American Council on Education's Commission on Teacher Education (1938–44). With the rise of fascism in Europe, Mumford called for military resistance to totalitarian governments, and his *Men Must Act* (1939) advocated military preparedness for the U.S.

After World War II Mumford expressed concern over the danger of nuclear weapons and man's capacity to destroy himself, as expressed in *In the Name of Sanity* (1954). He became increasingly concerned with environmental problems; in 1955 he served as cochairman of the Wenner-Gren Foundation Conference on Man's Role in Changing the Face of the Earth. He was visiting professor of land and city planning at the University of Pennsylvania (1952–59), Ford research professor there (1959–61), visiting professor at the Massachusetts Institute of Technology (1957–60), at the University of California at Berkeley (1961–62), and a fellow at the Center for Advanced Studies, Wesleyan University (1963–64). Mumford received a 1962 National Book Award for *The City in History*. He served as president of the American Academy of Arts and Letters from 1963 to 1965. In 1964 he received the Presidential Medal of Freedom. In July 1986 President Reagan awarded him the National Medal of Arts for his lifetime contribution to American culture. A two-part work,*The Myth of the Machine (Technics and Human Development*, 1967, and *The Pentagon of Power*, 1970), also dealt with technology and the needs of civilization. Some of his other books include *Herman Melville* (1929), *The Brown Decades* (1931), and *Green Memories* (1947).

———— ✺ ————

On December 13, 1972, Lewis Mumford attended a ceremony in New York City at which he was presented the National Medal for Literature, an honor he considered "in many ways the climax of my life." But the occasion was marred for him. "I look at the faces, and the buildings, I see nothing but decay and corruption," he reflected. Looking at the metropolis long celebrated as the vibrant, cosmopolitan exemplar of American growth and progress, he saw only "necropolis"—the city of the dead— epitomizing "the rapid downhill pace of our whole civilization." Mumford's total alienation from "our sterile mechanistic culture" and his persistent and uncompromising attacks on the potentially cataclysmic consequences of unbridled technological expansion, uncontrolled urban growth, ecologically suicidal assaults on the environment, and an insane nuclear arms race in an age of "overkill" and "mega-deaths" marked him as perhaps the most passionate and eloquent critic of the dehumanizing tendencies of modern civilization. His critique of American culture was in the tradition of **Emerson,**

Thoreau, Melville, and **Henry Adams,** and he perpetuated the classical American humanistic tradition as faithfully as any modern social philosopher. "To starve the eye, the ear, the skin, the nose is just as much to court death," he once observed, "as to withhold food from the stomach."

Preeminently a visionary and a prophet, Mumford was a prime representative of the Anglo-American prophetic tradition. His writings reflected a kind of Emersonian hope that through adoption of a "new set of habits" and a "fresh scale of values" mankind will be able to achieve a recovery of purpose and "renewal of life" in a reconstructed world. Although he partially subscribed to the idea of an "organic," pre-capitalist, medieval "golden age," he virtually never lapsed into the nostalgic wistfulness about the Middle Ages one encounters in the writings of T. S. Eliot and in Henry Adams's *Mont-Saint-Michel and Chartres*. "It is better to face chaos courageously than to cherish the dream of returning to an outworn synthesis," he once asserted. "The future of our civilization," he wrote in *Sticks and Stones* in 1924, "depends upon our ability to select and control our heritage from the past, to alter our present attitudes and habits, and to project fresh forms into which our energies may be freely poured."

Mumford consistently scorned as futile the piecemeal approach to urban problems marked by such efforts as slum clearance, urban renewal, and model housing. For Mumford considered slums, blight, congestion, pollution, and the entire gamut of ills that afflict our cities not merely as "problems" but rather as "symptoms" of a basic weakness in the ethos and organization of industrial society itself. The ideological roots sustaining this position originated in the mid-19th-century protests of socially conscious intellectuals which reached their highest pitch in Engels's savage indictment of *The Condition of the Working Class in England in 1844,* and Charles Booth's classic studies of life and labor in London. Mumford consistently advocated a non-metropolitan-centered regionalism in which cities would be maintained within "human scale" and in which human needs would take precedence over and control the mechanical means of production. Although he depicted and pointed the way toward a new social order, Mumford unfortunately failed to outline the essentially hard political steps necessary to get there, reminding one of Arthur Koestler's observation that the trouble with the Marxist analysis was that while it created an economic substructure and an intellectual superstructure, there were no stairs leading from the basement to the attic. The problem of means confronted Mumford with a fundamental conflict of values, for his political socialism, rejection of Marxism, condemnation of modern totalitarianism, and belief in the ideal of the democratic community clashed with his admiration for and idealization of cities built for maximum beauty and utility under essentially authoritarian and elitist systems, particularly the towns of medieval Europe and the Dutch and Italian cities of the Renaissance.

Alienated from modern culture and convinced that not since the century of the Black Death had the outlook for humanity been so dismal, Lewis Mumford throughout his literary career published what amounted to periodic and usually adverse minority reports on the condition of the planet. His critics alleged he was merely a pessimistic naysayer and "prophet of doom"—a gloomy Cassandra characterized by *Time* in 1961 as a "raging Jeremiah." It is interesting to note, however, that during the 1920s, and particularly during the 1930s against the backdrop of international economic chaos and the rise of Nazism, Mumford was seen more as an Isaiah, whose "rational idealism" was applauded and whom *Time* then hailed as "a new type of public figure." Although the past decades have all too often verified Mumford's ominous prophecies, and although he basically accepted Oswald Spengler's notion of decline, Lewis Mumford remained a dreamer and a poet with an enduring faith "that in deepest winter, the buds of spring have already emerged and await only the first warm sun." See Donald L. Miller, *Lewis Mumford: A Life* (1989).

ALLEN J. SHARE

MUNSEY, Frank Andrew (b. Mercer, Maine, Aug. 21, 1854; d. New York, N.Y., Dec. 22, 1925), PUBLISHER, FINANCIER, began work at thirteen as a clerk in a store in Lisbon Falls, Maine. After a brief career as a telegraph operator and later as manager of the Augusta telegraph office, and after several months' study at Poughkeepsie Business College, he moved in 1882 to New York City to launch a children's magazine, the *Golden Argosy*, which later became the *Argosy*, for adults. *Munsey's Weekly*, which he founded in 1889, was renamed *Munsey's Magazine* in 1891.

Munsey purchased his first newspaper, the New York *Star*, in 1891, renaming it the *Daily Continent*. However, it failed the same year. He began to acquire newspapers extensively in 1901 and during the next twenty-three years bought and then discontinued, merged, or sold a large number of newspapers, including seven New York dailies. By 1925, however, Munsey owned only the *Sun* and the *Evening Telegram*. He also bought, and then destroyed, merged, or renamed eleven magazines, and at his death owned *Flynn's Weekly Detective Fiction, All Story Weekly, Argosy,* and *Munsey's*. His other investments included the Mohican chain of New England grocery stores, the Mohican hotel and the Plant Building in New London, Connecticut, and the Munsey Trust Co. and Munsey Building in Washington, D.C.

Although he was a lifelong Republican, Munsey supported Theodore Roosevelt's Progressive party in 1912. After World War I he was attacked as a speculator and war profiteer, but he vigorously repudiated the charge. Munsey's charitable contributions included $100,000 each to the Cathedral Fund of St. John the Divine and Bowdoin College. He left the bulk of his $19.7 million estate to the New York Metropolitan Museum of Art.

⚬⚬⚬

Frank A. Munsey has not fared well at the hands of journalistic historians. In his last years he offended the sentiments of newspapermen by weeding out weak and failing newspapers—some of them famous—from an overcrowded field in New York, thereby initiating a trend which has become dominant in American journalism. "The same law of economics applies in the newspaper business that operates in all important business today," he said. "Small units in any line are no longer competitive...."

Emphasis upon this aspect of Munsey's life has tended to obscure his earlier career, which was marked by boldness and inspiration. Beginning as publisher of the *Golden Argosy,* a magazine for juveniles featuring stories by **Horatio Alger** and others, in the 1890s Munsey turned to the publication of popular periodicals for adults. When he reduced the price of *Munsey's Magazine* from twenty-five to ten cents, he inaugurated the era of mass circulation for such publications. For the most part Munsey's newspapers and magazines were uncritical admirers of American capitalism, as a eulogistic series entitled "Our American Millionaires" in *Munsey's Magazine* attests. He had little use for the muckrakers of the same period, declaring, "Muck-raking is one thing, and progress is another."

Despite his support of Roosevelt in 1912, Munsey had little sympathy for progressive reformers. Instead he devoted much space in his publications to convincing businessmen that the Progressive party was not really a threat to the great corporations. Roosevelt would not tamper with the tariff, he maintained, and would seek to regulate corporations only to preserve competition. Munsey was essentially a businessman himself, and he was inordinately proud that his own life exemplified the Horatio Alger success story. See George Britt, *Forty Years—Forty Millions: The Career of Frank A. Munsey* (1935).

JULIAN S. RAMMELKAMP

MURPHY, Frank (b. Harbor Beach, Mich., April 13, 1890; d. Detroit, Mich., July 19, 1949), JURIST, POLITICAL LEADER, graduated from the University of Michigan (1912) and received his LLB from Michigan in 1914. For the next three years he was a law clerk for the firm of Monaghan and Monaghan in Detroit (1914–17). After serving as a captain in the AEF during World War I, he spent brief periods as a law student at Lincoln's Inn, London, and at Trinity College in Dublin (1918–19). He was chief assistant U.S. attorney, Eastern District of Michigan (1919–20), and engaged in private practice in Detroit (1920–23). He also offered night classes in criminal law at the University of Detroit (1922–27).

In 1923, Murphy was elected a judge of the recorder's court in Detroit, a post he held until 1930, when he was elected mayor of Detroit. Although nominally a nonpartisan mayor, Murphy had long been an active Democrat, and had been a strong partisan of **Alfred E. Smith** in 1928. As mayor, he established a relief program that led the nation in the percentage of funds drawn from municipal taxes while encouraging every form of private contribution. By 1932, however, sharp reductions in Detroit's tax revenues forced him to reduce relief expenditures. During 1931–32, as a ranking Democrat in a generally Republican state, he paid a series of visits to other party leaders and became a supporter of Franklin D. Roosevelt. In 1933, Murphy resigned as mayor to become governor general of the Philippines (1933–35). After the islands were granted commonwealth status, he was the first U.S. high commissioner to the Philippines (1935–36). In the islands, he established central control over the government's expenditures, extended public health and low-cost public housing, and worked to smooth frictions which arose during this period of transition toward independence.

In 1936, Murphy returned to Michigan, where he was elected governor (1936–38). As governor, he became particularly prominent through his efforts to promote agreement between General Motors and the United Automobile Workers union to end the automotive workers' sit-down strikes of 1937. In 1939, having been defeated in his bid for reelection, Murphy was appointed by President Roosevelt as attorney general of the U.S. In his brief term (1939–40), Murphy was active in prosecuting antitrust violations, in establishing a "civil liberties" unit in the Department of Justice, and in leading investigations of official corruption which led to the imprisonment of "Boss" Tom Pendergast of Kansas City, and Justice Martin T. Manton of the circuit court of appeals of New York. In 1940, Roosevelt appointed Murphy associate justice of the Supreme Court. On the Court, where he remained until his death, he joined with Justices **Hugo Black, William O. Douglas,** and Wiley Rutledge in forming the "liberal" bloc. He was particularly active in efforts to expand Bill of Rights guarantees pertaining to civil liberties. Among his notable opinions was his vigorous dissent in *Korematsu* v. *U.S.* (1944), in which the majority on the Court upheld the internment of Japanese-Americans during World War II.

Red-haired and blue-eyed, Frank Murphy took deep pride in his Irish rebel ancestors, in his church, in his ascetic refusal to smoke or drink, and in his lifelong defense of the downtrodden. A bachelor, he squired the daughters of society to evening galas after berating their fathers by day for their indifference to hardship. On the bench and in public office, he tempered legality with justice, justice with equity, equity with mercy. Christened Francis William, the soft-spoken Murphy seemed to some a veritable saint with a red halo.

Few served the New Deal so outspokenly in so many official roles. To Depression-paralyzed Detroit he promised "the dew and sunshine of a new morning," but he fed the unemployed while almost bankrupting the city, and he defended the rights of Communists to criticize both the system and the mayor. As governor of strike-torn Michigan, he protected sit-downers and supported their families, insisting that if workingmen were mistaken, they could be taught "without writing the lesson in blood." Respect for government, Murphy warned, is a fragile thing that can crumble if the poor feel neglected, if minorities feel oppressed.

On the Supreme Court, his red hair graying and his presidential ambitions cooling, Murphy missed no opportunity to defend persons whose humanity had been outraged and to reproach colleagues who acquiesced in such outrages. He was the conscience of the Court. "The law knows no finer hour than when it cuts through formal concepts and transitory emotions to protect unpopular citizens against discrimination and persecution," he wrote in one of his dissenting opinions. The best of his opinions became milestones in the progress of civil liberties, ones from which the Vinson Court would retreat, but to which Justice **Earl Warren**'s Supreme Court would return.

Each righteous defense of a minority offended members of some majority. They objected to Murphy's moralizing, to his impassioned rhetoric addressing audiences beyond the courtroom, to the reasoning that drew as much from natural law and Jefferson as from judicial precedent and Blackstone. They complained of "justice tempered with Murphy"; but that sort of justice was basic to his drive and the key to his influence. See J. Woodford Howard, Jr., *Mr. Justice Murphy: A Political Biography* (1968).

MADISON KUHN

MURRAY, Philip (b. Blantyre, Scot., May 25, 1886; d. San Francisco, Calif., Nov. 9, 1952), LABOR LEADER, was the son of a coal miner and local union leader. He went to work in the mines at age ten, but emigrated to the U.S. with his family in 1903, settling near Pittsburgh, where he again became a miner. In 1904 he was discharged for hitting a company weighman, and his fellow workers struck in sympathy. Although the strike was broken, Murray was elected president of the local union. He was elected to the executive board of the United Mine Workers of America in 1912, and became president of the UMW District 5 (Pittsburgh) in 1916. In 1919 he was elected international vice president of the union under **John L. Lewis.** During World War I President Wilson appointed Murray to the Pennsylvania Regional War Labor Board and the National Bituminous Coal Production Committee.

In 1935 President Franklin Roosevelt appointed Murray to the Labor and Industry Advisory Board of the NRA. The following year, Murray helped Lewis, **Sidney Hillman,** and other AFL dissidents form the Committee on Industrial Organization to promote industrial, rather than craft, unionism. He became vice president of the CIO in 1936 and was placed in charge of its Steel Workers Organizing Committee, which succeeded in organizing steelworkers and also auto, textile, and rubber industry workers. When Lewis resigned the presidency of the CIO in 1940 Murray succeeded him. Two years later Lewis, after an unsuccessful attempt to regain power, pulled the UMW out of the CIO. In 1942 Murray was elected president of the United Steel Workers, but continued to serve as CIO president. He was a member of the National Defense Mediation Board during World War II. Although opposed to anti-strike legislation, he pledged a no-strike policy for steelworkers and vigorously supported the war effort. After the war he led the steelworkers to victorious strikes (1945 and 1946) for higher wages. He opposed the 1947 Taft-Hartley Act and backed Harry Truman for president in 1948 and **Adlai Stevenson** in 1952. Murray supported the Korean War and took the initiative in expelling Communists from the CIO. In 1952 he led his last strike against the steel industry after President Truman's seizure was declared unconstitutional.

If John L. Lewis was the creator of the industrial-union movement, Philip Murray was the man who fashioned it into a stable and permanent entity. Wrapped up in that achievement was a story of genuine personal anguish. Murray had built his career as second in command to Lewis in the United Mine Workers. All through the 1920s and early 1930s, while Lewis had waged unrelenting war against progressives and rivals within the UMW, Murray had remained steadfast and loyal; more than any other man of any consequence, he was trusted by Lewis. When Lewis ordered Murray into the steel organizing drive in 1936, he gave Murray the chance to build an independent base of support. Murray did a brilliant organizing job in a field that had hitherto defied trade unionism—a signal contribution to the industrial-union cause—and took permanent command of the new

steel union. When Lewis resigned the CIO chairmanship in 1940, making good his bravado pledge to do so if Roosevelt was reelected president, he handed the reins over to the reluctant Murray. Within two years, Lewis turned furiously against his former lieutenant, and personally drummed him out of the UMW in an agonizing ceremony. If the break caused Murray deep sorrow, it also liberated him from Lewis's influence (although already Murray had revealed a stubborn streak of independence that probably made Lewis's animus inevitable) and enabled him to give the CIO a steady mainstream direction.

Quiet and unassuming, a pious Catholic, a man who never erased the stamp of his early years in the mines, Murray had a capacity for leadership very different from that of the flamboyant and ruthless Lewis: Murray gained men's loyalty through his humaneness and sincerity. Through the stormy 1940s his steady hand fended off inner turmoil within the CIO, managing even to defuse the explosive issue of communist penetration until it was safe to handle at the end of the decade. While Lewis turned against FDR, Murray and the CIO remained steadfastly with the New Deal. While Lewis became an isolationist, Murray and the CIO supported internationalism and then full cooperation in the war effort. The CIO that merged with the AFL in 1955 was far more Murray's legacy than it was Lewis's. See A. H. Raskin, "Philip Murray," *New York Times Magazine* (July 20, 1952), pp. 12 ff.

DAVID BRODY

MURROW, Edward Roscoe (b. Greensboro, N.C., April 25, 1908; d. Pawling, N.Y., April 27, 1965), JOURNALIST, graduated from Washington State College in 1930. He became president of the National Student Federation in 1930 and traveled extensively throughout the U.S. and Europe. In 1932 he was appointed an assistant director of the Institute of International Education, and as secretary of its Emergency Commission for the Aid of Displaced German Scholars (1933–35), he helped to resettle many German anti-Nazi intellectuals. In 1935 Murrow joined the Columbia

Broadcasting System as director of its educational programs. He was sent to London in 1937 to take charge of CBS's European Bureau, and while in Europe covered the 1938 Nazi occupation of Austria. After World War II began, he reported on the blitz of London, often flying with RAF pilots. Murrow reported from London during the war, where he established a reputation for accuracy and objectivity. He published a collection of these broadcasts, *This Is London* (1941), and later reported war news from North Africa and the European continent.

Returning to the U.S. in 1946, Murrow became CBS vice president in charge of news, education, and discussion programs. He left this position in 1947, however, to resume his evening radio news broadcasts. The next year Murrow joined CBS executive Fred W. Friendly in producing a popular news show, *Hear It Now;* this program was adapted for television in 1951 as *See It Now,* a show dealing with politics, the Korean War, and other news topics that set a new style for television news programs. A 1954 program attacked Senator **Joseph McCarthy** as a threat to American civil liberties and helped bring about the senator's downfall. Murrow in 1953 also created *Person-to-Person,* a popular interview program in which he took television cameras into the homes of celebrities. *See It Now* was converted to *CBS Reports* in 1958, and Murrow also started another news show, *Small World.* He took a leave of absence from CBS in 1959 for a world trip and finally left the network in 1961 to become director of the U.S. Information Agency, where he insisted upon dealing with the facts about all of America's problems, including racial tensions. Murrow resigned early in 1964 because of declining health and was subsequently awarded the Medal of Freedom by President Johnson.

"The fault, dear Brutus, is not in our stars, but in ourselves." With this Shakespearean judgment, Edward R. Murrow ended his famed *See It Now* program launching the attack on Joseph McCarthy—an attack that placed the Wisconsin senator on the defensive by displaying his dubious tactics and by juxtaposing vivid images of McCarthy in action with the facts he was ignoring or perverting for his own purposes. The program and its concluding words epitomized Murrow's attitudes about the proper role of journalism: if Americans were presented with the facts about injustice in their society, they would follow their good sense and fundamental decency and act upon them. It was the role of journalists and the media to bring these facts to their attention. This premise provided the raison d'être for the McCarthy program and such other highlights of Murrow's years with CBS as "Harvest of Shame," his classic documentary on the plight of the then invisible migrant worker. Murrow fought for such programming despite personal threats and the opposition of many people in an industry that considered noncontroversial entertainment its main function. Murrow fared less well as director of the United States Information Agency, not because of any personal failings, but rather because of the congenital problems of America's information agencies which presidents invariably enjoy using for overt propagandistic purposes. During his tenure he did, however, elevate the prestige and morale of the USIA to the highest level it had ever attained. But Murrow's chief accomplishment remains the standard of responsibility he laid down for radio and then television—a standard lacking before his time and seldom measured up to since. See Alexander Kendrick, *Prime Time* (1969).

SYDNEY WEINBERG

NABOKOV, Vladimir Vladimirovich (b. St. Petersburg, Russia, April 23, 1899; d. Lausanne, Switzerland, July 2,1977), WRITER, was educated by private tutors before attending the Tenishev School in St. Petersburg. Exiled following the Russian Revolution, he moved to England (1919) and was graduated from Cambridge University with honors in 1922. That year he moved to Berlin, where he published his first, Russian, novels. Recognized early by the Russian émigré community as an important artist, but earning little money from writing, Nabokov gave English lessons, tennis lessons, and occasionally appeared as an extra in silent movies. In 1925 he married Vera Slonim, who was Jewish. They had one son, Dimitri. With the rise of the Nazis, the Nabokovs left Berlin for Paris where Nabokov decided that he had to make himself over into an English novelist, writing *The Real World of Sebastian Knight*. Then, in 1940, just as the invading Germans neared Paris, the Nabokovs escaped to the United States.

In the United States, he taught at Stanford University in the summer of 1941 and at Wellesley (1941–1948). An expert in the science of lepidopterology, the study of butterflies, he became a research fellow in entomology at Harvard's Museum of Comparative Zoology (1942–59). From 1948 until 1959, he taught Russian literature at Cornell and elsewhere, studied butterflies, and continued to publish novels, poetry, and criticism in English. In 1945 he became an American citizen. In 1955 he published *Lolita* in Paris. Three years later, the American edition became a best-seller and Nabokov quit teaching, moving in 1960 to Lausanne, Switzerland, where he would remain until his death, although he never gave up his American citizenship.

Nabokov has been criticized as being concerned only with himself and/or with the aesthetic; indeed, he himself professed himself as uninterested in the moral and political implications of literature. But, although Nabokov's life was intensely important to his writing, at the same moment his novels were hardly autobiographical. What he did was to use his life and his learning in order to discover and to create structures, to give meaningful shape both to life and to art; in brief, to find and to make order. His first novel, *Mary*, is a recovery of the past, but its essence is to show how the past is transmuted into art. And *The Gift*, seemingly autobiographical, is really about the process of artistic creation.

Moreover, art is not escape: if the world is problematic, there are nevertheless absolute values. Most of Nabokov's work was an examination and criticism of society, profoundly moral and indeed humanitarian. Art is related to the individual and to the external world. And so there was an implicit political comment; he was opposed to the Bolshevik regime not because it had deprived him of his money, but because it was anti-art and basically inhumane. The first novel he wrote in America, *Bend Sinister*, was explicitly political, a criticism of both Nazi and Communist dictatorships. *Lolita*, misinterpreted by many as pornography, is rather a denunciation of moral monsters as well as a celebration of life.

Still, for Nabokov, politics were not primary; art is an experience of language, of lived experience, not a philosophical or political experience, although it is also complexly related to those experiences. His formal experiments were ways of showing the problematics of being in the world, and of art's relation to the world. For instance, *Pnin* is the sad-comic tale of a man who loses his language and so is forever at a loss in his new world. And *Pale Fire*, examining the way the world impinges upon us, at the same moment demonstrates how language and art both undermine and create order for us. See Lawrence L. Lee, *Vladimir Nabokov* (1976).

Lawrence L. Lee

NADER, Ralph (b. Winsted, Conn., Feb. 27, 1934), REFORMER, graduated from Princeton in 1955 and received his LLB from Harvard Law School in 1958. He then served six months in the army and traveled throughout Europe and Africa before opening a private law practice in Hartford, Connecticut, in 1959. While at Harvard, Nader had become interested in auto safety, believing that part of the cause of most accidents was unsafe vehicle design. He testified before Massachusetts and Connecticut state legislative committees on the subject, but soon became convinced that action on the federal level was necessary. In 1964 he moved to Washington, D.C., as an aide to Assistant Secretary of Labor Daniel P. Moynihan, working on the auto safety problem. He left the government in 1965 to write a book on auto safety, *Unsafe at Any Speed,* which was published later that year. The book criticized the auto industry for emphasizing profits and style instead of safety. Particularly it condemned General Motors' Chevrolet Corvair as an unsafe car. *Unsafe at Any Speed* became a best-seller.

In 1966 Nader received much publicity when he filed a $26 million suit against General Motors for invasion of privacy and harassment, charging that GM detectives had tried to find evidence that could be used to incriminate him. This action resulted in a public apology by GM president James M. Roche and an out-of-court settlement of $425,000 in 1970. Meanwhile, Nader's auto-safety campaign contributed to the passage of the National Traffic and Motor Vehicle Safety Act of 1966 which set auto safety regulations for manufacturers. Nader then turned his attention to other consumer causes including safer natural gas pipelines, higher meatpacking standards, and preventing the overuse of insecticides, particularly DDT. His work speeded the passage of such legislation as the 1967 Wholesome Meat Act, which imposed federal inspection standards on slaughterhouses and processing plants; the Natural Gas Pipeline Safety Act (1968); the Wholesale Poultry Products Act (1968); and the Federal Coal Mine Health and Safety Act (1969). In 1969 Nader recruited a group of students and volunteers, known as "Nader's Raiders," to fight

for consumer affairs. Their investigation of the Federal Trade Commission in 1969 recommended a reorganization of that body; they also investigated air and railroad safety, radiation leakage from color television sets, and numerous other areas of interest to the consuming public.

In the 1970s and 1980s Nader established The Center for Responsive Law, Public Citizen, Inc., and other consumer and public interest groups. He and his various organizations have also been active in seeking changes to limit campaign financing by businesses and the wealthy. Nader succeeded in lobbying Congress to pass a law requiring airbags in new cars by 1990, but in the early 1990s he lobbied vigorously but unsuccessfully against ratification of the General Agreement on Trade and Tariffs (GATT) with Mexico. He argued that because of these and other allegedly one-sided trade agreements American businesses could avoid compliance with tough United States environmental and consumer legislation. These measures, he contended, would also induce businesses to move jobs overseas and south of the border to take advantage of the Third World's low wages, resulting in growing unemployment in the United States with an inevitable decline in its standard of living. In 1992 Nader made a brief run for president as a write-in candidate, and, in the mid-1990s, is spending much of his energies battling against Republican-sponsored tort reform legislation that would place caps on the punitive damages awarded by juries for perceived wrongs in civil liability cases, like those contending that products have dangerous defects. Should such a measure pass, Nader believes it would be the biggest disappointment of his 30-year crusade against abuses by Big Business.

⁓

Ralph Nader is probably the best living example of the type of reformer—the abolitionist **William Lloyd Garrison** is the most famous example of the genre—who, seeing most social issues and economic problems as simple questions of right and wrong, insists on rooting out evil totally. He is also a reformer in the Progressive tradition best typified by the elder

Robert La Follette. He believes in competition as the safest and truest way to protect the public against corporate exploitation, and he has an unshakable faith in both the good intentions of the mass of ordinary citizens and in their power, when properly informed, to achieve orderly social change. He is also personally a kind of secular saint. He is not merely incorruptible—as General Motors learned to its consternation—he is also extremely ascetic in his personal life. Material goods mean nothing to him—he is said to have only two suits, both gray; lives in a simple apartment; does not use a computer; does not own a car nor have a credit card. Perhaps he is so obsessed by the desire to remain aloof from the corporate giants he seeks to reform that he disdains the use of their products.

At the practical level Nader's originality lies in his development of new techniques and tools for achieving his goals. He has created a kind of Rand Corporation for consumer protection, conducting research and organizing study groups to discover and publicize the facts. He has also made brilliant use of class-action suits and other legal devices. But above all, he is a complete believer in the powers of the organized and informed individual citizen. At first he eschewed grants from foundations and other organizations and relied entirely upon individual contributions, which he obtained in astonishing numbers; speaking fees; and sales from reports and publications. But he has become an institutionalized reformer and no longer a one-person operation, creating over the years a network of over 60 groups that have employed thousands of people. Accordingly, he now accepts foundation grants and donations from the wealthy and, claim a number of critics, funding from some vested interests, such as trial lawyers associations, which support his opposition to tort reform legislation. Unlike earlier reformers, Nader generally distrusts the government as the protector of the public; he would abolish some Progressive and New Deal Era regulatory agencies on the ground that they are mere lobbyists for the industries they are supposed to control. But he is not an ideologue on this issue. There are some

agencies he would strengthen, like the Environmental Protection Agency (EPA) and the Food and Drug Administration (FDA). The fact that Nader stresses the role of the activist citizen and his own total commitment to reform have won him the support of many young idealists— the "Nader's Raiders"—who do much of the burrowing and researching for which he is famous.

Nader is not, however, a saint. His research is at times superficial and his conclusions slanted. There is an element of the fanatic in his makeup and he appears stuck in the anti-Big Business rhetoric of Progressive Era reformers. He may also be criticized for having no constructive theory of politics and for too often refusing to accept half a loaf. Yet on balance he has been a constructive force in our modern, technological society, a symbol of hope and a reminder of how important individual commitment is if reform is to be accomplished. See Charles McCarey, *Citizen Nader* (1972).

JEROME L. STERNSTEIN AND JOHN A. GARRATY

NAST, Thomas (b. Landau, Ger., Sept. 27, 1840; d. Guayaquil, Ecuador, Dec. 7, 1902), ARTIST, migrated to New York in 1846. He studied at the Academy of Design, and in 1855 became a draftsman for *Frank Leslie's Illustrated Newspaper*. In 1859 he began to contribute illustrations to the recently inaugurated *Harper's Weekly*. The following year, he traveled to England to cover a boxing match for the New York *Illustrated News*, and to Italy to cover Garibaldi for several publications. With the outbreak of the Civil War, he went to Washington, D.C., and Baltimore, and contributed sketches to *Harper's* and the New York *Illustrated News*. He became a staff artist for *Harper's* in 1862, and shifted from the simple illustration of events to political commentary, quickly gaining a reputation with cartoons attacking northerners opposed to the vigorous prosecution of the war. During Reconstruction, he aimed equally caustic pictorial barbs at President Andrew Johnson and northern proponents of a conciliatory southern policy. His greatest fame came when he launched a campaign in 1869 to expose the corrupt Tweed Ring which ran New York City. Such cartoons as "The Tammany Tiger Loose" (Nov. 11, 1871) and "Who Stole the People's Money?" (Aug. 19, 1871) made **William "Boss" Tweed**'s face known throughout the world, and aided in his eventual arrest in 1876. Nast's association with *Harper's* ended in 1886. Thereafter he contributed to several journals and briefly edited *Nast's Weekly* (1892–93). In 1902 President Theodore Roosevelt appointed him consul general at Guayaquil, Ecuador.

Nast furthered the development of his genre in America by cutting down on unnecessary pictorial detail and shortening captions. His Christmas cartoons helped form the American notion of the appearance of Santa Claus. He also created such cartoon symbols as the Democratic donkey, Republican elephant, and Tammany tiger.

—————

A short, roly-poly man with a malicious goatee and the self-satisfied air of a respectable German burgher, Nast captivated the genteel reading public of the 1870s with his savage caricatures that kept alive the partisan loyalties of the Civil War years. His prime target was the Democratic party, which he portrayed as a continuing conspiracy of unreconstructed rebels and northern corruptionists—a theme that justified his personal animosity toward Irishmen, Catholics, and southerners. Convinced of the wisdom of radical Reconstruction and the moral superiority of Republican machine politics, he devoted himself to editorial cartooning with a single-minded intensity that aimed, as he once put it, to "hit the enemy between the eyes and knock him down." For all the powerful symbolism of his best drawings, however, he clung to old-fashioned standards of realistic portraiture: working from photographs, he made careful sketches of his subjects' features, altering them only slightly to conform to his polemical design. In his classic cartoon of Boss Tweed, the eyes alone were made smaller and more prominent to suggest the man's insatiable greed. With such colorful personalities as Tweed, **Horace Greeley,**

and **Ben Butler** to work with, Nast was virtually assured of public interest in his work. But by the eighties, as "bloody shirt" oratory declined and politics grew more prosaic, Nast's inventiveness and his audience alike deserted him. Adrift in an industrialized society whose ambiguities confounded him, he ended by venting his spleen upon the Populists and the blacks. At the height of his career, however, he was the acknowledged master of American political cartooning, and did more than any other individual to arouse popular interest in graphic art. See J. Chal Vinson, *Thomas Nast: Political Cartoonist* (1967).

MAXWELL BLOOMFIELD

NEVELSON, Louise (b. Kiev, Russia, Sept. 23, 1899; d. New York, N.Y., April 17, 1988), SCULPTOR, emigrated to America in 1905 and settled in Rockland, Maine. She married Charles Nevelson and moved to New York City in 1920. She studied painting and sculpture at the Art Students League in New York with Kenneth Hayes Miller (1928–30), and with the abstract painter Hans Hofmann in Munich, Germany (1931–32). In 1932 she assisted the Mexican painter Diego Rivera on a mural project in New York City. She began exhibiting her work in New York galleries in 1933 and taught art at the Education Alliance School of Art under the auspices of the Works Progress Administration in New York in 1937. Her first one-woman sculpture show was in Karl Nierendorf's gallery in New York in 1940. Trips she made to Mexico and Central America (1946–47, 1951–52) deeply influenced her later work.

In the early 1950s Nevelson began working in wood, often discards from old tenement houses. Her new style became known as "environmental" sculpture. *Sky Cathedral* (1958, Museum of Modern Art, N.Y.), a wood wall construction painted black, and *Dawn's Wedding Feast* (1959, Martha Jackson Gallery, N.Y.), another wood wall construction painted white, are examples of this work. Nevelson also used other materials in later works, including plexiglass and metal. Her work was shown in the New York Museum of Modern

Art's "Sixteen Americans" exhibition in 1959, and the Whitney Museum in New York staged her first retrospective show in 1967. Commissions started coming her way. These included a work for Princeton University in 1969; a fifty-five-foot wall for Temple Beth-El in Great Neck, L.I. in 1970; and major sculptures in 1973 for Boston, Scottsdale, Ariz, and Binghamton, N.Y. In 1975, she constructed a piece named *Bicentennial Dawn* for the **James A. Byrne** Federal Courthouse in Philadelphia, and a black steel sculture called *Transparent Horizon* for the Massachusetts Institute of Technology. In 1979, the Louise Nevelson Plaza, an entire outdoor environment of her black scuptures on Maiden Lane in lower Manhattan was constructed. Her shows proliferated in the 1970s and 1980s. A large traveling exhibition visited Minneapolis, San Francisco, Dallas, Atlanta, Kansas City, and Cleveland between 1973–75. The U.S. Information Agency organized a show of her work which was seen in India, Iran, and Japan. One of the great works of her career, was her design for the Chapel of the Good Shepherd in St. Peter's Church on Lexington Avenue and 54th Street in New York City which opened in December 1977. Nevelson continued to receive commisions virtually up to her death. Some of her other important sculptures include *Nightscape* (1959, Gimpel and Hanover Galerie, Zurich) and *Homage to 6,000,000* (1964, Israel Museum).

───── ∝∞∝ ─────

Louise Nevelson occupied a crucial position both in American art and within the feminist movement. Since her mature style coalesced in the (and in her) mid-fifties, she was this country's foremost woman sculptor. At that time her natural proclivity for assemblaging "found" objects suddenly burgeoned forth into the construction of wall-size wooden "environments." She worked according to an obsessive, almost automatic, system of proliferation which is diametrically opposed to traditional methods of modeling and carving monolithic forms. Her idiosyncratic working methods, the assertive physicality and frontality of her work, its all-overness, and its

generally large size combined to confirm Nevelson's sculptural equivalence to the pioneering New American Painting. The emotional tenor of her work, on the other hand, shared much with the fantasy world of surrealism. Her highly personal style remained relatively unchanged until her death, and lost none of its power. Aspects of her work—such as its detailed, hand-crafted quality and its clutter of curvilinearity within the architectural confines of stacked, open-fronted rectangular units which carry overtones of doll's houses—feel decidedly "feminine." She said, "My work is the creation of a feminine mind—there is no doubt." Her fierce independence and determination to be an artist despite the pressures of family and friends against this aim, and the ruthless rigor of a lifestyle totally devoted to her work, made her, in light of her great success, an extremely important role model for American women. See Arnold B. Glimcher, *Louise Nevelson* (1972).

APRIL KINGSLEY

NEVINS, Allan (b. Camp Point, Ill., May 20, 1890; d. Menlo Park, Calif., March 5, 1971), JOURNALIST, HISTORIAN, received his BA (1912) and MA (1913) from the University of Illinois. He then served on the staff of the New York *Evening Post* as an editorial writer (1913–23) and also on the editorial staff of the weekly *Nation* (1913–18). In 1914 he published *The Life of Robert Rogers. The Evening Post: A Century of Journalism*, was published in 1922. The following year he edited *American Social History as Recorded by British Travellers* (revised in 1948 as *America Through British Eyes*). This was followed by *The American States During and After the American Revolution* (1924), an economic, social, and political account of the formation of the American states and their early history. During 1924–25 he was literary editor of the New York *Sun*, and in 1925–27 editorial writer for the New York *World*. In 1927 he joined the faculty of Cornell University as an assistant professor of American history. While at Cornell he completed *The Emergence of Modern America* (1927), a survey of the years 1865–78. He was appointed associate professor of history at Columbia University in 1928 and DeWitt Clinton Professor of American History in 1931.

In 1933 Nevins was awarded a Pulitzer Prize for his *Grover Cleveland* (1932). He also edited the *Letters of Grover Cleveland* (1933). In 1937 he was again awarded a Pulitzer Prize for *Hamilton Fish* (1936). In *The Gateway to History* (1938) he discussed the nature of history and analyzed the problems that confront the historian. *Frémont: Pathmarker of the West* (1939) was a biography of the explorer, soldier, and 1856 Republican presidential candidate. In 1939 Nevins helped organize the Society of American Historians to foster the writing of history as literature. In 1954 he was a founder of *American Heritage,* a hardcover historical magazine aimed at the general public. In 1940 Nevins published *John D. Rockefeller* (2 vols.).

In 1940–41 Nevins was Harmsworth Professor of American History at Oxford University. With Henry Steele Commager, he wrote *America, The Story of a Free People* (1942), a survey of American history from its colonization to Pearl Harbor (*A Short History of the U.S.*; 5th ed. rev. and enlarged, 1966). Nevins was a special representative of the Office of War Information in Australia and New Zealand (1943–44). During the summers of 1945–47 he served in the American embassy in London as chief public affairs officer.

In 1947 Nevins published *The Ordeal of the Union* (awarded the Scribner Centennial Gold Medal and a Bancroft Prize), the first two volumes in a study of the U.S. from 1847 to the end of Reconstruction. *The Emergence of Lincoln* (2 vols., 1950) and *The War for the Union* (2 vols., 1959–60) followed. The final two volumes, carrying his account up to 1865 and also titled *The War for the Union,* appeared in 1971. These volumes deal with the complex social, economic, political, and military aspects of this period. Nevins shows how the "failure of American leadership" during the 1850s, the rigidity of the political system, and the "unrealities of passion" exacerbated sectional tensions and led to the Civil War. They won Nevins a posthumous National Book Award in 1972.

While working on this multivolume study, Nevins started the Oral History Research Office at Columbia University (1948). Believing that the recollections of people in public life might be helpful to the historian, he urged the conducting of interviews with participants in a wide variety of fields to build a collection on 20th-century American life. In 1954, with F. E. Hill, he published *Ford: The Times, the Man, the Company,* the first in a three-volume study of **Henry Ford.** *Ford: Expansion and Challenge: 1915–1933* (1957) and *Ford: Decline and Rebirth, 1933–1962* (1963) complete the biography. After retiring from Columbia (1958) Nevins became a senior research fellow at the Huntington Library, San Marino, California.

In 1964 he donated $500,000 to Columbia University to endow a chair in American economic history (later named in his honor). In 1964–65 he was again Harmsworth Professor at Oxford. Some of his other works include *America in World Affairs, 1918–33* (1942), *The New Deal and World Affairs, 1933–45* (1950), and *Herbert Lehman and His Era* (1963). He was also a prolific editor, most notably of the diaries of Philip Hone (1927), John Quincy Adams (1928), James K. Polk (1929), and George Templeton Strong (1952). In 1957 he was awarded the gold medal of the American Academy of Arts and Letters.

Allan Nevins was too modest to permit any publisher to label him "the foremost historian of his time," a garland that Oxford University Press placed upon **Samuel Eliot Morison,** but few scholars would dispute that in American history Nevins stands *among* the foremost, not merely of his own time but of any. Alone among them, he did original research in every period, from Colonial to the recent past. More, his writings commanded audiences that reached far beyond the academic world and brought him more than once to bestsellerdom. Nevins's passionate conviction that history belonged to everyman led him to present it in narrative style; **Francis Parkman,** Prescott, and the great English novelists inspired him more than any contemporary. Academia he accepted with genial tolerance. He never troubled to take his doctorate, and moments before Columbia presented him with an honorary one after he retired, he was found laboring in gown in the library, putting the finishing touches on a book.

Nevins tempered buoyant optimism with an innate judiciousness that gave his work authority and depth. He could interrupt his narrative for the kind of analysis and exposition, as in the closing volumes of *The Ordeal of the Union,* that distinguishes the work of a great scholar. This series of eight volumes on the nation's history from the close of the Mexican War through the Civil War, done on a canvas of breathtaking scope, looms as perhaps his most durable work. Second only to this comes the massive Ford study, a landmark in industrial history, followed by the major biographies.

Two Nevins achievements appear quite as consequential as his writing: the popular magazine of history, *American Heritage,* and the burgeoning oral history movement, which grew out of work he began at Columbia in 1948. (Oral history obtains the memoirs of persons in a wide range of pursuits, by means of recorded interviews which are then transcribed into typescript, edited, and preserved for scholarly use.) A decade before anyone else, Nevins saw the need for both developments, the one to bring history to the millions, the other to compensate for the inroads of technology on letter writing and the diarist, and he brought both to life through his own persistent initiatives.

Much as he relished a walk, a chat, a story, Nevins let nothing compete with work. Friends told of his showing them through his summer home in Vermont, until he reached his library: "And here is where I work," said he, whereupon he sat down at the typewriter and was lost to them. The soul of generosity, he poked fun at his personal thrift. "Come," he greeted his wife and daughters once at the New York Public Library, "I'm going to treat you to dinner on Fifth Avenue!" Thereupon he marched them up to Bickford's cafeteria.

If Nevins's greatest achievement was to so enrich history as to bring Americans to a deeper appreciation of it, he did this not only through his own literary and scholarly abilities but also by inspiring students and associates with his kindly, ebullient spirit, his Illinois farm boy's reverence for hard work, and his broad intellect. He looked upon his students as adopted children, defended them, stirred them by example, on occasion helped them out of pocket. "There will never be another like him" was a common theme in scholarly reviews of his last work. See Nevins's manuscript "Autobiography" (1963), Columbia University Oral History Archives.

LOUIS M. STARR

NEWMAN, Barnett (b. New York, N.Y., Jan. 29, 1905; d. New York, N.Y., July 3, 1970), ARTIST, attended the Art Students League in New York 1922–24 and again in 1929–30. He was graduated from the College of the City of New York in 1927 and entered his father's firm, A. Newman Co., manufacturing men's clothing. The firm, however, had great difficulty during the Depression, and Newman worked as a substitute teacher in the New York public schools (1931–35, 1936–39). He also taught art part-time at the Washington Irving Adult Center (1939–45), and studied botany and ornithology at Cornell University in 1941.

Newman helped pioneer abstract expressionism or "action" painting after World War II. He made surrealist drawings and introduced color into black and white calligraphic pictures. *Gea* (1945, Collection Annalee Newman) and *Genetic Movement* (1947, Collection Annalee Newman) are representative of this work. *Onement, I* (1948, Collection Annalee Newman), the first of several *Onement* paintings, represented a reaction to this surrealism, however, and an interest in chromatic abstractions. Newman held his first one-man show at the Betty Parsons Gallery in New York in 1950. In 1958, with **Robert Motherwell, Mark Rothko,** and others, he founded a new art school in New York, Subjects of the Artist. He led an art workshop at the University of Saskatchewan in 1959 and conducted graduate seminars at the University of Pennsylvania in 1962.

Newman exhibited a series of fourteen paintings he had been working on for several years called *Stations of the Cross* at New York's Guggenheim Museum in 1966. He produced fewer sculptures than paintings, and one of his best-known abstract sculptures is the pyramid-obelisk *Broken Obelisk* (1967, Institute of Religion and Human Development, Houston, Texas).

———

Through a fondness for "raising the issue" (his favorite phrase), Barnett Newman has acquired for much of New York's present population of avant-garde painters the status of radicalism's Old Master. This talent for revolutionary invention accompanied Newman's conviction that in the early 1940s "painting did not really exist" and that painters were obliged to "start from scratch, to paint as if painting had never existed before." For Newman, this act of creation recalled no less than the Book of Genesis and precipitated a series of scholarly investigations into the primitive origins of painting in ritual and magic. His study and meditation ultimately coalesced into ideas about painting prophetic for the next decades—a vision of an artwork as an all-over-whole, a conception of drawing which declares space rather than outlining or shaping it, and a new appreciation of the analogies between extended vertical scale and heroic human height.

These influential formal innovations, however, were subservient in Newman's work to metaphysical ideas. "It is only the pure idea that has meaning," he believed. In order to encourage the survival of ideas within their physical means of expression, Newman limited these means to the most rudimentary essentials; thus, although his art had to do with grand themes, these dramas were played with only the basic characters of rectangle and stripe, and by means of tensions of quantity, scale, and radiance of color. The poetic impact with which he employed these severely restricted means shocked critics and impressed artists, who first recognized Newman's painting as a unique contribution to 20th-century art. See Thomas B. Hess, *Barnett Newman* (1969).

PATRICIA FAILING

NIEBUHR, Reinhold (b. Wright City, Mo., June 21, 1892; d. Stockbridge, Mass., June 1, 1971), RELIGIOUS LEADER, entered Elmhurst College in Illinois in 1910 but transferred to the Eden Theological Seminary in St. Louis in 1913 and then to Yale Divinity School (BD, 1914; MA, 1915). He was ordained by the Evangelical Synod of North America in 1915 and accepted a pulpit at the newly formed Bethel Evangelical Church in Detroit. There he became interested in the plight of organized labor and other social causes, and joined a number of socialist organizations. In 1928 he was named associate professor of philosophy of religion at the Union Theological Seminary in New York City and (1930) professor of applied Christianity (vice-president after 1955). He pioneered the "new theology" or neoorthodoxy, an attempt to restate biblical Christian teaching in a form relevant to the great issues of contemporary life. Along with writing and teaching he maintained his interest in socialism, participating in the founding of the Fellowship of Socialist Christians in 1930. He also joined and later became head of the Fellowship of Reconciliation, a pacifist organization.

With the rise of Hitler, Niebuhr denounced both the dictator's oppression and the isolationism of the United States. After the war, however, he reversed his earlier radicalism and became a vigorous critic of communism and even socialism. He continued writing books and articles and founded the Protestant periodical *Christianity and Crisis* in 1941, editing it until 1966. During the 1950s Niebuhr turned his thinking toward the problem of history and its relation to man, publishing several books on the topic. In 1964 he received the Medal of Freedom from President Johnson. Some of his major works include: *Moral Man and Immoral Society* (1932), *The Nature and Destiny of Man* (2 vols., 1941–43), and *The Structure of Nations and Empires* (1959).

———

Reinhold Niebuhr was the most conspicuous thinker in American Protestantism from the early 1930s to the late 1950s. Reacting against the sentimentality and utopianism of much liberal religion, he reinterpreted such classical theological concepts as God's majesty and human sinfulness in a way that arrested public attention. His profound knowledge of such seminal thinkers as Pascal, Kierkegaard, Marx, and Freud informed his restatements of biblical insights. An indefatigable polemicist, his sharp challenge to liberal theology was a major factor in the decline of that school, while his own work was central not only to the emergence of realistic and neoorthodox theology but also to the general theological renaissance at midcentury. His reputation was international, for he was an active participant in the ecumenical movement and a frequent visitor in Europe. He was a forceful figure in Christian-Jewish and Catholic-Protestant dialogues before they became popular. Despite his attack on liberalism, he remained liberal in spirit. He accepted critical and historical methods, and was thus opposed by conservatives and fundamentalists.

The quality of Niebuhr's thought was widely respected outside the church world. During his active career, he devoted most weekends to extensive lecturing and preaching on university campuses. His comments on domestic politics and foreign policy, poured out in speeches, editorials, articles, and books, were widely followed by many who did not share his religious perspectives. A social philosopher who taught ethics and wrestled with the tensions between the ideal and the real, he was also an activist who played leading roles in the Americans for Democratic Action and in the Liberal party of New York. His political realism was especially influential in the State Department following World War II.

Niebuhr possessed great powers of concentration and analysis; he penetrated to the heart of issues even as he often overstated them. Until illness from which he never fully recovered overtook him in 1952, he enjoyed seemingly endless energy, which enabled him to carry on many activities in religion, education, and politics simultaneously. He was an extempore speaker of compelling magnetism despite awkward gestures and some interminable sentences; the freshness of his thought and the intensity of his convictions riveted attention. He had a sparkling sense of humor, which showed in public address as in informal conversation. His ability skillfully to employ the ideal-typical method and to frame clever epigrams contributed much to his popularity as teacher and writer, but some scholars were troubled by his sweeping generalizations.

He was a man of great personal warmth and generosity of spirit, who gave freely of his time and energies to individuals and to causes. A scintillating conversationalist, he loved company and was a great joiner. In a somewhat paradoxical way, he combined a genuine humility with superb self-confidence, a certain flamboyance with real reserve. Those close to him saw exemplified a quality of grace about which he so often preached. See June Bingham, *Courage to Change: An Introduction to the Life and Thought of Reinhold Niebuhr* (1961), and Ronald H. Stone, *Reinhold Niebuhr: Prophet to Politicians* (1972).

ROBERT T. HANDY

NIMITZ, Chester William (b. Fredericksburg, Tex., Feb. 24, 1885; d. San Francisco, Calif., Feb. 20, 1966), NAVAL OFFICER, was graduated from the U.S. Naval Academy in 1905 and was assigned to the Pacific (1905–8). In 1913 he was given command of the Atlantic Submarine flotilla. During World War I he served as chief of staff to the commander of the Atlantic Submarine Force. In 1918 he was made a full commander and assigned to the office of the chief of Naval Operations in Washington, D.C. In 1919–20 he commanded Submarine Division 14 at Pearl Harbor. He served on the staff of the Naval War College in Newport, Rhode Island (1922–23), and in 1926 established the nation's first Naval Reserve Officers' Training Corps (NROTC) at the University of California.

For several years after 1927, when Nimitz was promoted to captain, he commanded a submarine division. He was then assistant chief of the Bureau of Navigation in Washington (1935–38). Promoted to rear admiral in 1938, he commanded first a cruiser and then a battleship division, and became chief of the Bureau of Navigation in 1939. After the Japanese attack on Pearl Harbor

(Dec. 7, 1941), President Roosevelt appointed Nimitz commander of the Pacific fleet, replacing Admiral H. E. Kimmel.

Given command of the Pacific Ocean Area (General **Douglas MacArthur** commanded the Southwest Pacific), Nimitz set up his headquarters at Pearl Harbor (transferred to Guam in 1944). Using sea, air, and land power, he decisively defeated the Japanese at Guadalcanal (Nov. 1942). His forces won major naval victories at Midway (1942), the Solomons (1942–43), the Gilbert Islands (1943), the Marshalls, Marianas, and Philippines (1944), and Iwo Jima and Okinawa (1945). On September 2, 1945, Nimitz (now a five-star admiral) accepted the Japanese surrender aboard his flagship, the battleship *Missouri,* in Tokyo Bay. In November 1945 he succeeded Admiral **Ernest King** as chief of naval operations (resigning in December 1947).

In March 1949 Nimitz was sent by the U.N. to administer a forthcoming plebiscite in Kashmir, a border state claimed by both India and Pakistan. Although he left this post in July, he continued to work for the U.N. as a public relations consultant. In January 1951 President Truman appointed him chairman of the Commission on Internal Security, but he resigned in October 1951. In 1960, with E. B. Potter, he edited *Sea Power, A Naval History.*

Chester W. Nimitz belied the stereotype of a naval officer. He was mild-mannered, deliberate, and soft-spoken. His demeanor inspired confidence and reflected a keen mind and an iron resolve. His career afloat and ashore provided training and experience, and duty in the Bureau of Navigation brought him in close contact with the highest government officials, who selected him over many senior officers to assume command of the shattered naval forces in the Pacific. Quiet and calm, never given to outbursts or bombast, Nimitz provided the leadership that restored morale and eventually brought about the defeat of Japan. An excellent judge of men, he delegated considerable authority but made the major strategic decisions himself, combining reason and intuition to a remarkable degree. His grasp of the complexities of modern warfare and his mastery of the intricacies of combined operations enabled him to supervise the massive Pacific naval war and resolve the often delicate command relationships among the services. Adept in the art of persuasion, at times he could be firm and uncompromising as he administered innovations in naval strategy such as sophisticated amphibious techniques, the fast carrier task force, and the solution of immense logistics problems. Nimitz was a professional who by his ability and character earned the respect and admiration of his associates, and who enjoyed their loyalty to a degree seldom accorded to other men. His personal life was devoted to his family, and his final years were spent in the San Francisco Bay area that he had come to love. See E. B. Potter, "Chester William Nimitz, 1885–1966," *U.S. Naval Institute Proceedings* (July 1966), pp. 30–55.

RAYMOND G. O'CONNOR

NIXON, Richard Milhous (b. Yorba Linda, Calif., Jan. 9, 1913; d. New York, N.Y., April 22, 1994), PRESIDENT, was graduated from Whittier College in 1934, and from Duke University School of Law (Durham, N.C.) in 1937. He then joined the Whittier law firm of Wingert and Bewley (1937–42), eventually becoming a partner. Nixon moved to Washington, D.C., in 1942 to work for the Office of Price Administration in its tire-rationing section, but left to enter the navy in 1943 as a lieutenant j.g. He served in the Pacific theater as an aviation ground officer. After his discharge in 1946 he returned to California and defeated Democratic U.S. Congressman Jerry Voorhis in a campaign that emphasized a hard line toward communism. Reelected to the House of Representatives in 1948, Nixon served on the Herter Committee on foreign aid, which laid the basis for the Marshall Plan; the House Education and Labor Committee, where he helped formulate the Taft-Hartley Act; and the House Un-American Activities Committee. Here, he achieved national prominence when he pressed for the continued prosecution of former State Department aide **Alger Hiss,** an alleged ex-

Communist who was eventually convicted of perjury. In 1950 Nixon defeated Helen Gahagan Douglas for the U.S. Senate in a bitter campaign in which he tried to link Douglas to Communist groups.

After serving in the U.S. Senate (1951–53), he was elected vice president in 1952, and reelected in 1956. During the 1952 campaign the Democrats accused Nixon of benefiting from a secret "slush fund" provided by California businessmen, but he defended himself on television, winning a vote of confidence from presidential candidate Dwight D. Eisenhower. As vice president, Nixon chaired the president's Commission on Government Contracts, participated in National Security Council and cabinet meetings, and chaired the Cabinet Committee on Price Stability for Economic Growth, from which he helped end the steel strike of 1959. He ran the executive department during Eisenhower's illnesses in 1955, 1956, and 1957. When Eisenhower sent Nixon on a goodwill tour to Latin America in 1958, the trip was marked by violent anti-American demonstrations in Caracas, Venezuela. In 1959 Nixon visited the Soviet Union and engaged in a "debate" over the merits of capitalism with Premier Nikita Khrushchev in Moscow.

Nixon was the Republican presidential candidate in 1960. He defended the Eisenhower administration throughout the campaign. He engaged his Democratic opponent, Senator John F. Kennedy, in four television debates but was defeated by a close popular vote and an electoral vote of 303 to 219. After practicing law in California for the next two years and publishing *Six Crises* (1962), he ran for governor of California but lost to Edmund G. (Pat) Brown. Nixon then moved to New York City (1963) and joined the law firm of Nixon, Mudge, Rose, Guthrie, Alexander, and Mitchell. In addition to his law practice he visited South America, Asia, Africa, and Europe in 1967, speaking on foreign policy. In early 1968 Nixon won the Republican presidential primary in New Hampshire, eventually winning the Republican presidential nomination. Nixon campaigned on a platform promising to end the war in South Vietnam and to attack rising

crime and inflation in America. He defeated his Democratic opponent, Vice President **Hubert Humphrey,** by an electoral vote of 301 to 191.

As President, Nixon supported anticrime legislation, cuts in government spending, and the creation of the Antiballistic Missile System (ABM). Through his policy of Vietnamization (strengthening the South Vietnamese so they could defend themselves), he started withdrawing American troops from that country. He visited South Vietnam and other nations, including Communist Rumania in 1969. In May of 1970 he ordered an invasion of Cambodia to destroy Communist bases supplying the Vietcong in South Vietnam. This caused a wave of antiwar demonstrations throughout the U.S., culminating with the killing of four college students at Kent State (Ohio) University. He replaced the selective service system with a draft lottery and pressed for establishment of an all-volunteer army. In 1971 he imposed a series of economic controls on the nation to fight inflation, including first a wage-price freeze and then a maximum rate of 5½ percent for all price increases. He made trips to the People's Republic of China and the Soviet Union in 1972. Nixon began the process of normalizing relations with China, and he signed the Strategic Arms Limitation Treaty and the Antiballistic Missile Treaty with the Soviets. Nixon was easily reelected over his Democratic opponent, Senator George McGovern of South Dakota, in 1972 by an electoral vote of 521 to 17. In the beginning of 1973 his national security affairs adviser, **Henry Kissinger,** negotiated an end to the Vietnam war, the cease-fire going into effect on January 27, 1973. All American prisoners of war were released by the Communists while all American troops were pulled out of South Vietnam.

Scandal overtook Nixon during his second term. Vice President **Spiro T. Agnew** resigned in October 1973 amid allegations he had accepted bribes from government contractors. Nixon appointed Congressman Gerald R. Ford of Michigan to replace Agnew. Meanwhile, a special prosecutor and a select Senate committee began to uncover evidence of Nixon's involvement in the coverup of a burglary at the Democratic headquarters in Washington's Watergate office complex. In July 1974, the Supreme Court ordered Nixon to surrender to government prosecutors recordings of relevant White House conversations. The Watergate tapes provided clear evidence of Nixon's wrongdoing and led the House Judiciary Committee to recommend his impeachment. Faced with declining congressional and public support, Nixon resigned from office on August 9, 1974.

Twenty-five administration officials went to prison for their role in the Watergate affair and related misconduct, but President Ford pardoned Nixon shortly after taking office. Following a brief self-imposed exile, the controversial former president began to travel widely and to write extensively. By the time he died Nixon had regained a measure of respectability, especially as an authority in foreign affairs.

An anticommunist cold warrior who rose to national prominence during the heyday of McCarthyism, Richard Milhous Nixon was the first president to visit Peking and Moscow. An awkward, insecure introvert, he spent his life in the public spotlight. A prolific writer and a thoughtful student of world affairs, he hated intellectuals as much as they hated him. Reelected president in 1972 in the biggest landslide to that point in American history, less than two years later he became the first president to be forced to resign from office. With a record full of so many apparent contradictions, it is no mystery that writer after writer has tried to uncover the "real" Richard Nixon, or even that Nixon and his handlers seemed to present to the public a succession of "new Nixons," each more mature and statesmanlike than the last.

Yet in a public career spanning the half century from his election to Congress in 1946 to his death in 1994, a few ironies were inevitable. At the same time, some consistent themes run through the Nixon record. If his flexibility helped earn him the nickname "Tricky Dick," philosophically Nixon was a pragmatic centrist, routinely balancing the demands of left and right. Eisenhower accepted the freshman senator as his running mate in 1952 partly because Nixon was palatable to both the GOP's conservative Old Guard, led by Senator **Robert A. Taft** of Ohio, and the party's more liberal eastern wing, then associated with New York Governor **Thomas E. Dewey**. Shy and self-conscious, Nixon's own anxiety about how he appeared to the public contributed to the ambiguity and unease that shrouded his image. Discussing the 1960 presidential debates in *Six Crises*, Nixon wrote, "I knew that what was most important was that *I must be myself.*" He was, he continued, "determined to … convey … sincerity." Critics had to wonder why, for Nixon, looking sincere took such effort.

Nixon had the self-made man's characteristic suspicion of anyone receiving something for nothing—whether it was an inheritance or a welfare check—but he did not share the modern conservative's hostility to most forms of government intervention. In both foreign and domestic policy, Nixon was an activist who accepted the exercise of government power where putatively useful and politically expedient. He prided himself, as a member of Congress and as Vice President on his support of civil rights, and as president he compiled a record of domestic reform that in retrospect was surprisingly progressive. Prodded by the Supreme Court, the Nixon administration presided over the desegregation of the largest number of southern schools in history. The administration expanded the so-called Philadelphia Plan, an experimental program requiring federal construction contractors to hire minority workers, to include all large federal contractors. Nixon signed legislation creating the Environmental Protection Agency and the Occupational Health and Safety Administration, unprecedented expansions of federal power into the areas, respectively, of pollution control and workplace safety. He proposed revamping the welfare system with a Family Assistance Plan, essentially a guaranteed annual income (though, in keeping with his "Tricky Dick" reputation, he did this largely for public relations purposes and to put the Democrats in a bind and ordered the plan to be killed if there was any chance Congress might pass it). When the country was beset by rising inflation, Nixon imposed wage and price controls on the American economy. They proved to be only a temporary palliative; more popular was revenue sharing, a Nixon initiative that sent federal dollars to state and local governments with few strings attached. It survived until 1986.

During his presidency, Nixon received his greatest accolades for his foreign policy achievements. His friendly overtures to China and the Soviet Union surprised those who remembered Nixon as an ally of Senator **Joseph R. McCarthy**, the notorious red-baiter. But Nixon had never been an isolationist or, despite some overheated rhetoric, a foreign policy reactionary. Following what had seemed to be the enlightened opinion of his day, Nixon had supported the Marshall Plan and NATO. By the time of his death, however, scholarly opinion about Nixon's presidential diplomacy had begun to shift. China remained a rogue nation and Nixon's efforts at détente with the Russians had been overshadowed by the collapse of the Soviet Union itself. And if Nixon extricated the United States from Vietnam, it took him four years and 25,000 more American deaths, without preventing an ultimate Communist victory. Less visionary than he appeared at the time, Nixon did not foresee the end of the cold war; he was positioning the United States to continue the struggle in an era of declining American power.

Finally, the Nixon character remained consistent. After slashing campaigns against Jerry Voorhis and Helen Douglas and the fund controversy of 1952, defenders of Nixon's honor would argue simply that he was no worse than the average politician. Above all else, he was a fierce partisan, blindly defending his allies and dismissing his critics as personal enemies. Nixon campaigned doggedly for **Barry Goldwater**, the 1964 Republican presidential nominee, even though he admitted later that the right-wing senator's inflammatory acceptance speech had made him almost physically sick. The exposure of Nixon's efforts to conceal White House involvement in the Watergate break-in revealed the worst side of his own personality. Essentially amoral, Nixon in the White House cared little for legal norms, individual rights, or the other institutions of government. More fundamentally, unlike authentic American icons—unlike Jefferson or Lincoln or even Harry Truman—Nixon lacked faith in the democratic process and in the wisdom of the American people. Ultimately, Nixon was done in by his own cynicism—his belief that politics was a Darwinian struggle for survival, or a game played without any rules. His cynicism was contagious, and it has endured as Nixon's most obvious legacy. The exposure of a strong and popular president as a common criminal left a residue of mistrust among the American people that has yet to disappear. See Stephen E. Ambrose, *Nixon* (3 vols., 1987–1991).

JEFF BROADWATER

NORRIS, Benjamin Franklin (b. Chicago, Ill., March 5, 1870; d. San Francisco, Calif., Oct. 25, 1902), WRITER, displayed artistic talent as a youth and was sent to London and Paris to study art (1887–89). Upon returning to California in 1890, he entered the University of California, where he was deeply influenced by the writings of Emile Zola. After failing to meet the requirements for graduation, he went to Harvard, where he studied English for one year (1894).

In 1895 Norris covered the Boer War in South Africa as a reporter for the San Francisco *Chronicle* and *Collier's*. After returning to San Francisco in the spring of 1896, he wrote for the *Wave*, a literary magazine. He then moved to New York, where he was associated with *McClure's Magazine*. He spent part of 1898 in Cuba covering the Spanish-American War until illness forced him to return. In 1898 he also published his first work of fiction, *Moran of the Lady Letty*, a tale of love and adventure at sea. In 1899 he worked for Doubleday, Page and Co., publishers, in New York.

Norris belonged to the "naturalist" school which believed that novelists should be totally objective. Like a scientist, the novelist should record what he saw, no matter how shocking. The school also maintained that man's fate was determined by internal drives and external forces over which he had no control. Norris particularly liked to describe the clash of titanic forces. In *McTeague* (1899), he told the story of a brutal, self-taught, unlicensed dentist who murdered his miserly wife with his bare fists before he himself was killed in Death Valley. He then began work on his "Epic of the Wheat," a trilogy in which he planned to present an account of the growing, selling, and use of wheat. In *The Octopus* (1901), he gave an account of the struggle between the wheat growers of California and the railroad. *The Pit* (1903, published posthumously) took the story to the Chicago grain market. The final volume, which he planned to title *The Wolf*, was to have shown how the wheat was consumed in a famine-stricken village.

Norris's other works include *Blix* (1899), *A Man's Woman* (1900), *The Responsibilities of the Novelist* (1903), in which he urged authors to avoid commonplace subjects, and *Vandover and the Brute* (1914), which he had written while at Harvard.

Norris shared with his age a mixed bag of Darwinian and Populist doctrines, not always consistently. He was attracted by a literary cult of the brute, derived from the principle that man's bestial instincts, if allowed to run loose without higher controls, would produce degeneracy and animal behavior. Thus violence, war, greed, sex, and murder were his themes. He believed in "life" even more than in technique as the essential element for the novelist. To immerse himself in the workaday life of Polk Street, San Francisco, or in exotic specimens of humanity on the wharfs, or in "the splendid, brutal, bullying instinct" displayed in college football contests—such were his tastes. And to indulge them he needed to rebel against his well-to-do background and his expensive education in Paris and at Harvard and California. Tall, handsome, an all-American boy in appearance, Norris was temperamentally romantic, adventurous, hungry for experience.

His style included both the naturalist's grasp of documentation and circumstantiality and the romantic need for rolling rhetoric and epic effects. The gold-symbolism in *McTeague* is overly insistent and repetitive, but Norris was effective in the localism and realism of lower-middle-class life of the city. In *The Octopus*, bizarre, Dickensian characters play their roles against a background of powerful natural forces and relentless fate. See Larzer Ziff, *The American 1890's: Life and Times of a Lost Generation* (1966), pp. 250–74.

ROBERT FALK

NORRIS, George William (b. Sandusky, Ohio, July 11, 1861; d. McCook, Neb., Sept. 2, 1944), POLITICAL LEADER, won his LLB from Northern Indiana Normal School (now Valparaiso University) in 1883, and was admitted to the Indiana bar that same year. After settling in Nebraska (1885), where he practiced law, he served three terms as prosecuting attorney of Furnas County. He then served as judge of the 14th judicial district of Nebraska (1896–1902).

A Republican, Norris served in the U.S. Congress (1903–13), where he was a leading insurgent, supporting national primaries, the initiative, referendum, and the direct election of U.S. senators, and opposing monopolies. In 1910 he took the lead in the fight to limit the powers of Speaker of the House **Joseph G. Cannon,** and in 1912 backed Theodore Roosevelt, the Progressive party's candidate for the presidency.

Elected to the U.S. Senate in 1912, Norris served until 1943. When World War I broke out in Europe, he staunchly advocated American neutrality, and in 1917 he spoke against a bill to arm merchant ships. One of the few senators who refused to vote for the declaration of war, Norris claimed that the war would only increase the profits of the stockbrokers and munitionmakers who, he said, helped start the conflict. Following the war, he was one of the Senate "irreconcilables" who opposed American entry into the League of Nations.

During the 1920s Norris was one of the nation's most forceful advocates of agricultural relief and the conservation of natural resources. Committed to the public ownership and operation of hydroelectric plants, he tried repeatedly to stop the government from turning over the Muscle Shoals dam in the Tennessee Valley to private industry. His bills in support of government operation of this dam were vetoed, however, by President Coolidge in 1928, and by President Hoover in 1931. In the presidential elections of 1924 and 1928 Norris refused to back the nominees of the Republican party, supporting **Robert La Follette,** a Progressive, in 1924, and **Alfred E. Smith,** a Democrat, in 1928.

In 1932 Norris cosponsored the Norris-LaGuardia Act, which limited the power of the federal courts to issue injunctions against labor unions engaged in peaceful strikes and outlawed "yellow-dog" contracts. In the presidential election of 1932 he supported Franklin D. Roosevelt, the Democratic candidate. In 1933 Norris sponsored the Twentieth, or "Lame Duck," Amendment to the Constitution.

Although Norris supported many of Roosevelt's New Deal measures—including the TVA, which represented a personal victory for his Muscle Shoals policy, and the Rural Electrification Act of 1935—he opposed the National Industrial Recovery Act (1933) because he feared it would encourage monopolies. He assented to Roosevelt's attempt to "pack" the Supreme Court, but with great reluctance.

During the crises leading to World War II, Norris advocated revising America's neutrality acts to permit the president to aid nations whose existence was vital to America's interest. He was defeated for reelection to the Senate in 1942. His autobiographical work, *Fighting Liberal,* was published posthumously (1945).

⁂

The career of George W. Norris, one of the most distinguished in our congressional history, illustrates what one man through ability and persistence can achieve in reforming or changing aspects of American life. His political career, starting in Populistic Nebraska in the 1890s, began and ended with a defeat at the polls. In between,

spanning half a century with forty years of that period on the Washington scene, Norris dealt with problems besetting an increasingly urbanized and industrialized nation groping with the realities of world power. His focus was always from the rural and small-town perspective he knew so well from his experience as a lawyer and district judge in southwestern Nebraska. Starting his career as an avid Republican in a political district engulfed in the enthusiasm of Populism, Norris gradually lost all traces of his partisanship: in part because he rarely received effective party support in his campaigns, and in part because he increasingly disagreed with the programs and policies propounded by his party on the national level. Basically he came to look at issues from the viewpoint of his own conscience and experience rather than from one propounded by the necessities or vagaries of a political context. In 1924 his independence was complete when the Republican party in Nebraska sought him out and allowed him to run for reelection to the United States Senate on his own terms. In 1930 prominent Republicans in Nebraska and elsewhere sought his defeat by supporting a primary opponent, a grocery clerk with his exact name. In his last two campaigns, Norris ran as an independent.

The reforms he sought fall into two categories: those that improved the functioning of the existing political apparatus and those that effectively changed it by establishing new institutions that soon developed histories and loyalties of their own. In the former category can be cited such accomplishments as Norris's role in curbing the power of the speaker of the House of Representatives; the Twentieth, "Lame Duck," Amendment to the Constitution, the only amendment to emanate from a committee other than the Judiciary Committee and largely the work of one man; and legislation curbing the use of injunctions in labor disputes. In addition he supported candidates, regardless of party label, who he thought would better serve the national interest. Thus he was one of three Republicans to support the nomination of **Louis D. Brandeis** to the Supreme Court. In 1926 he stumped the state of Pennsylvania, campaigning against the Republican candidate for senator. Later he endorsed Alfred E. Smith for president. And throughout the New Deal years, he supported Franklin D. Roosevelt in his presidential campaigns, although he disagreed with some of his policies.

In the second and more important category, Norris's chief contribution was his sponsoring of Muscle Shoals legislation which, after a decade-long battle, earned him recognition as the father of the Tennessee Valley Authority. His idea of multiple-purpose river valley development brought him into conflict with utility corporations, which challenged the idea for public generation of hydroelectric power inherent in this proposal. Less well known, but almost as important, was his equally long battle to help establish a "little TVA" in his home state of Nebraska. The Rural Electrification Administration, which Norris sponsored in the Senate, and the Nebraska unicameral legislature for which he vigorously campaigned in 1934 are two further examples of changes in the institutional structure for which he was largely responsible. All of these changes were immediately beneficial to segments of rural America, but the controversy they engendered as well as the implications for further implementation were both national and international.

Slow to anger, modest, simple in his tastes and outlook, respectful of viewpoints other than his own, Norris, by the courage of his convictions and his basic integrity, aided and abetted by a masterful knowledge of parliamentary procedure, was able to convince both colleagues and constituents. During his forty-year tenure in Washington he became one of the most useful legislators in our history, as well as a guide and source of inspiration to innumerable colleagues and to citizens throughout the land who saw in him and his work a symbol of what American democracy at its best could achieve. See Richard Lowitt, *George W. Norris* (1963).

RICHARD LOWITT

NORTON, Charles Eliot (b. Cambridge, Mass., Nov. 16, 1827; d. Cambridge, Mass., Oct. 21, 1908), ART CRITIC, EDUCATOR, was graduated from Harvard in 1846. From 1846 to 1855 he was employed by the Boston importing firm of Bullard and Lee. Concurrently, he directed and taught at the Cambridge Evening School, an adult education school which he founded in 1846. Norton traveled through India, Egypt, and Europe for Bullard and Lee (1849–51). When he returned to Cambridge he wrote a series of articles (1851–54) for the *North American Review* and the *Cambridge Chronicle*, advocating social reform to improve the living conditions of the poor. In 1853 he wrote *Considerations on Some Recent Social Theories*, a plea for those from his social class to involve themselves in a morally inspired movement for gradual social change. After moving to Rome in 1855 for reasons of health, Norton began an in-depth study of art and its relationship to the society that produced it, and wrote *Notes of Travel and Study in Italy* (1860). In 1857, upon his return to the U.S., he joined **James Russell Lowell, Henry Wadsworth Longfellow,** and **Ralph Waldo Emerson** in founding the *Atlantic Monthly*, for which he wrote articles on art and national politics. An early foe of slavery, Norton opposed the "peculiar institution" for moral reasons; he was not, however, in favor of full equality for blacks. He believed the Civil War was inevitable and supported the northern cause. In 1863 Norton became editor of the New England Loyal Publication Society and he was coeditor of the *North American Review* (1864–68) with Lowell. In 1865, after leaving the editorship of the society, Norton helped **E. L. Godkin, F. L. Olmsted,** and J. M. McKim found *The Nation*.

In 1869 Norton again visited Italy primarily to study Dante, and when he returned five years later he was appointed Professor of Art History at Harvard. In his lectures at Harvard he criticized America as culturally barren and contrasted modern societies with the Classical and Renaissance periods, when, he contended, art reflected a higher level of civilization. He often criticized national leaders, especially Grant, for the corruption in his administration. Norton vigorously backed female suffrage and education and the preservation of national scenic wonders.

He saw industrialism as an evil and backed government attempts to curb the power of business. Norton retired from Harvard in 1898. When the U.S. became embroiled in conflict with Spain, he was a leading critic of American expansion abroad. Besides his translation of Dante's *Divine Comedy* (1892), Norton's major works are *Historical Studies of Church Buildings in the Middle Ages* (1880) and the editing of nine volumes of the letters and reminiscences of Thomas Carlyle.

Norton's life exemplifies how traditional Puritanism disappeared from New England. His Eliot ancestors had been ministers and merchants; Norton chose instead to become an art critic and opponent of materialism. The change can be seen in Norton's own career. Before 1870 his life was one of direct action; after that date he immersed himself in culture, giving advice to others in society while assuming the personal role of passive spectator of events. In this respect he was not exceptional. The older Puritan tradition which combined morality with commercial vigor was rapidly giving way in New England to a free-thinking, humanistic cosmopolitanism and ivory-tower social criticism, which contemporaries called "Brahminism" or "Mugwumpery."

It was Norton's later phase as scholar and educator which brought him fame. He was very much a spokesman of late Victorianism, and mirrored the strengths and weaknesses of the period. Like Lord Acton in England, whom he resembled in many ways, Norton was not especially creative and wrote few books. But he possessed to a high degree the educator's capacity for drawing out the best from others more gifted than himself. As a scholar, his career symbolized the shift from academic amateurism to professional competence in late 19th-century higher education. Norton's knowledge of art history was uneven and limited, at best. Yet he turned the subject of art history and criticism from a dilettante's hobby into a university-based field of inquiry.

Norton's transition from Puritan to scholarly humanist was accompanied by growing disillusionment with American intellectual life. Like Henry Adams, he interpreted the United States to his Harvard students as a relatively barbarous western colonial fringe of European civilization, and often seemed to discourage cultural pride or self-reliance among Americans, past or future. See Kermit Vanderbilt, *Charles Eliot Norton: Apostle of Culture in a Democracy* (1959).

FREDERICK D. KERSHNER, JR.

NOYES, John Humphrey (b. Brattleboro, Vt., Sept. 3, 1811; d. Niagara Falls, Can., April 13, 1886), REFORMER, was graduated from Dartmouth in 1830. After studying law at Chesterfield, New Hampshire, he entered the ministry and during 1831–34 attended both the Andover, Massachusetts, Theological Seminary and the theological department at Yale College. While at Yale he came under the influence of the "Finney Revival" and with a group of revivalists organized a free church. In 1834 he first propounded his doctrine of "perfectionism," the belief that it was possible to attain sinlessness in this life. In February 1834, after announcing that he had attained "perfection," he was deprived of his license to preach, forced to withdraw from Yale, and dismissed from the free church.

Noyes then organized a small community at Putney, Vermont, and founded the Bible School (1836). He also established a Society of Bible Communists to promulgate his perfectionist ideas. In the "Battleaxe Letter" (1837) and other statements, he asserted that God was both male and female and that there were no "simple" marriages in heaven. In 1846 he first experimented with a program of "complex" marriages, based on the idea that all members of the group were married to all others. Two years later his "Putney Conservatism" resulted in his arrest. He jumped bail and with a group of his followers founded a new community at Oneida, New York (1848). This community prospered, absorbed other communities, and by 1870 included two hundred members, who jointly owned 664 acres of choice land as well as manufacturing interests valued at more than $200,000. At Oneida, Noyes enforced his programs of complex marriage, birth control, and "stirpiculture," the improvement of the race by selective breeding. The system was finally abandoned in 1879, after Noyes's advanced age had weakened his grip on the community's affairs. He then fled to Canada to escape legal action. Noyes's expositions of his religious and sociological views included *The Berean* (1847), *Bible Communism* (1848), *Male Continence* (1848), *Scientific Propagation* (c. 1873), and *History of American Socialisms* (1870), a study of communistic experiments.

———⁂———

John Humphrey Noyes was a man of unusual zeal and extraordinary determination and forcefulness. Like many who engaged in spiritual and social reform in the mid-19th century, Noyes was a child of New England and its antilatitudinarian moral atmosphere. In common with others who traversed the "psychic highway" binding that area with western New York State, Noyes early set aside profession and thoughts of worldly success for a life dedicated to Christianity. His religious beliefs were unique, combining the view that the "primary resurrection" of Christ had occurred at the time of the destruction of the Temple in Jerusalem with the conviction that a true Christian spirit capable of responding to the next Advent could flourish only in a community guided by the "model exhibited to the world on the day of Pentecost ... that aught of the things which [a man] possessed was his own, but they had all things in common." The Oneida community that Noyes shaped and dominated for a quarter-century after he created it in 1848 was organized on the latter principle.

That Oneida was famous, even notorious, resulted not from its religious principles but its sexual practices. Noyes not only taught his community to practice group marriage; in explicit detail that is charming for its matter-of-factness he outlined the mechanical measures necessary to achieve ecstatic pleasure prior to male withdrawal. Wolves in sheep's clothing who thought that merely by professing Oneida's spiritual ideals they would enjoy its sensual benefits were quickly disabused, booted out by leaders who meant what they said. To Noyes communal liv-

ing arrangements were not an end in themselves but only the milieu that enabled individuals to attain spiritual grace. Socialism or communal work and ownership became Perfectionism only when it was based on and guided by true Christian belief. See John Humphrey Noyes, *History of American Socialisms* (1870).

EDWARD PESSEN

NYE, Gerald Prentice (b. Hortonville, Wis., Dec. 19, 1892; d. Washington, D.C., July 17, 1971), POLITICAL LEADER, son of a La Follette Progressive who edited a country newspaper, was graduated from high school in Wittenberg, Wisconsin (1911) and then returned to Hortonville to become editor of a weekly paper. In the years that followed he owned or edited a variety of newspapers in Wisconsin, Iowa, and North Dakota, where he settled in 1919. A fervent Progressive, Nye backed **Robert M. La Follette** for president in 1924. In 1925 he was appointed to fill a vacant seat in the U.S. Senate from North Dakota and was elected to a full term the following year as an Independent.

In the Senate, Nye soon established a reputation as an advocate of farm relief and as an isolationist. In 1926 he chaired the Senate committee that investigated the Teapot Dome scandal, and he took the lead in opposing U.S. entry into the World Court. Reelected in 1932 to the Senate, he became an arch opponent of the New Deal. He conducted a Senate investigation (1934–36) into the munitions industry which created the impression that American entry into World War I was due to the machinations of munitions makers. An active member of the America First Committee, he attacked Franklin D. Roosevelt's foreign policy in the late 1930s and fought for neutrality legislation geared to keeping the U.S. out of all European conflicts. Gaining a seat on the Senate Foreign Relations Committee in 1940, he fought unsuccessfully to defeat the Lend-Lease Act of 1941. After Pearl Harbor, however, he supported the prosecution of the war. Defeated for reelection in 1944, he became a management consultant in Washington (1946–60). In

1960 he was appointed a special assistant in the Federal Housing Administration but retired soon thereafter.

As a leader of the Senate isolationist bloc in the 1930s, Gerald Nye had an important but limited influence on American foreign policy prior to the outbreak of World War II. A quiet, humorless man, completely lacking in sophistication, Nye entered the Senate in the 1920s as a Progressive Republican in the tradition of Robert La Follette and **George Norris.** He gained a liberal reputation through his devotion to agrarian causes, but he broke sharply with Franklin D. Roosevelt on foreign policy. In 1934, largely at the urging of George Norris, Nye introduced a resolution calling for a probe of the munitions industry. As chairman of the subsequent Senate investigation, he conducted a thorough and revealing exposé of the arms industry, but he gained national fame only when he gave a series of public speeches charging that the "merchants of death" were primarily responsible for American entry into World War I. He played a key role in the adoption of the Neutrality Acts, although this legislation never went as far toward limiting American trade and curtailing presidential power as Nye wished. As the nation turned away from isolationism in the late 1930s, Nye fought a bitter but losing rear-guard action against the Roosevelt administration until he finally adopted an anti-New Deal position on domestic as well as foreign issues. Provincial in outlook and intensely emotional in his public utterances, Nye symbolized the declining influence of agrarianism on American foreign policy in an increasingly industrial age. See Wayne S. Cole, *Senator Gerald P. Nye and American Foreign Relations* (1962).

ROBERT A. DIVINE

OCHS, Adolph Simon (b. Cincinnati, Ohio, March 12, 1858; d. Chattanooga, Tenn., April 8, 1935), PUBLISHER, began his newspaper career at eleven as an office boy on the Knoxville *Chronicle.* He held several other jobs, including work as printer's devil on the *Chronicle* (1872–75) and for the Chattanooga *Dispatch* (1877–78), before purchasing controlling interest in the failing Chattanooga *Times* for $250 in 1878. He quickly improved the paper and purchased the remainder of its stock for $5,500 in 1880. He organized the Southern Associated Press (1891) and was its chairman until it dissolved in 1894. After refusing the job of manager of the moribund New York *Times* for an annual salary of $50,000, Ochs gained control of the *Times* in August 1896 for $75,000. On October 25, 1896, he chose the slogan "All the News That's Fit to Print." Employing a "clear, dignified and trustworthy" format, he steadily boosted the paper's circulation. By 1900 he had stabilized its finances and obtained a majority of its stock. He purchased the Philadelphia *Times* (1901) and the Philadelphia *Public Ledger* (1902), merged the two, and sold them in 1912. He established the 100 Neediest Cases Fund (1912), the *New York Times Index* (1913), *The Annalist,* a weekly financial review, *Current History,* a monthly, and *The Midweek Pictorial,* an illustrated review of the week's news. He served as director and member of the executive committee of the Associated Press from 1900 until his death.

The *Times,* under his direction, was twice awarded the Pulitzer Gold Medal in Journalism (1918, 1931) and received the first annual award of the University of Missouri School of Journalism (1930). Among his other important philanthropies, Ochs donated $500,000 toward the preparation of the *Dictionary of American Biography* and initiated a $5 million endowment fund for Hebrew Union College.

When Adolph Ochs arrived in New York, the phony excitement over Cuba generated by the Pulitzer-Hearst circulation war was at its height. Amid this clamor, Ochs went to work. He aimed to prove that accuracy and thoroughness, presented in an attractive format, could sell newspapers. Typographical perfection, a heritage from his days as a Tennessee printer's devil, became a *Times* trademark.

Within four months, a rival noted Ochs's insistence on quality journalism and concluded: "There is no other journal in the country that approaches more nearly the ideal daily newspaper." That was true by the end of 1896. It remained true throughout Ochs's lifetime. It is still true today.

Adolph Ochs was generous with money almost to a fault, and also lavish in the expenditure of both time and affection on family and associates. He could also be stern, a strict disciplinarian as a father, a hard taskmaster as an employer. Willing, even anxious, to help all who sought his counsel, he expected his advice to be followed.

This was especially true in regard to his desire to make the *Times the* newspaper of record for the United States; and by 1920 it was the paper of record for most of the world in all areas of news coverage. Ochs expanded, and dignified, the sports page. His book review and theater pages became definitive. Under his direction, the *Times* pioneered in the in-depth coverage of science. In the 1920s, the *Times* was first with direct wireless reports from all over the world. It became "an international textbook on contemporary history." Because of the *New York Times Index* it serves as a primary source book for historians of the 20th century.

The documentary presentation of news in print is the most characteristic *Times* institution. Speeches of 11,000 words by dictators, 16,000-word papal encyclicals, and verbatim transcripts of presidential news conferences are all available most readily in the *Times*.

This is the most enduring legacy of Ochs's vision. **Joseph Pulitzer**'s *World,* **William R. Hearst**'s *Journal,* and **Edward Scripps**'s *Telegraph* have all died like the clamor they created. Ochs's *Times,* stressing accuracy and thoroughness, remains. See Meyer Berger, *The Story of the New York Times* (1951).

JUSTIN E. WALSH

O'CONNOR, Sandra Day (b. El Paso, Texas, March 26, 1930), JURIST, was raised on a cattle ranch in Arizona, except for periods when she resided with her grandmother in El Paso, Texas, to get the benefit of urban schools. She graduated from Stanford University with great distinction (1950) and from Stanford Law School (1952), where she ranked third in her class and was an editor of the *Stanford Law Review*, together with her classmate **William H. Rehnquist**.

Despite her outstanding academic achievements, private law firms offered her work only as a legal secretary after her graduation from law school. Discouraged from getting a job as a lawyer in the private sector, she served as a deputy county attorney in California for two years, as a civilian attorney with the United States Army in Germany for three years, and then in occasional private practice in Phoenix, Arizona. This was interrupted by periods as a full-time homemaker raising three sons (1957–65), and by volunteer activity. A Republican, she took part at the local level in **Barry Goldwater**'s 1964 presidential campaign.

In 1965 she was appointed Assistant Attorney General, serving until 1965. That year she was elected to the Arizona Senate and later became Republican majority leader, where she voted against several anti-abortion measures and for Arizona ratification of the Equal Rights Amendment. A decade later, these votes kindled conservative Republican opposition to her nomination to the United States Supreme Court. She resigned from elective office in 1975 to become a judge on the Maricopa County (Arizona) Superior Court, a trial court of general jurisdiction, where she served for four years until her elevation to the Arizona Court of Appeals (1979), an intermediate-level appellate court.

During the 1980 Presidential campaign

Ronald Reagan had promised to appoint a woman to the Supreme Court. Thus, when Justice Potter Stewart resigned in 1981, President Reagan fulfilled that pledge by choosing O'Connor to replace him. Though she expressed personal opposition "to abortion as a method of birth control or otherwise" at her nomination hearings, O'Connor refused to discuss specific precedents such as *Roe* v. *Wade* (1973). That reticence plus her political record in the Arizona Senate provoked conservative resistance to her confirmation. Despite this, she was easily confirmed (1981).

In keeping with the traditional role of Supreme Court Justices, O'Connor terminated her extensive volunteer service upon her confirmation and has avoided public political activity. With the exception of a few law review articles and addresses to legal gatherings, she has confined the expression of her views to opinions she has written as a member of the Court.

∽∞∾

In her earliest major opinion for the Court, *Mississippi University for Women* v. *Hogan* (1982), Justice O'Connor condemned "archaic and stereotypic notions" about gender roles in legislative policy-making. She has not, however, displayed a comparable sensitivity when confronted with state and local efforts to combat racial discrimination through affirmative-action programs, suggesting in an unfortunate passage in *Richmond* v. *J. A. Croson Co.* (1989) that the racial discrimination that has excluded African-Americans from entrepreneurial opportunities may have been due to "both black and white career and entrepreneurial choices," a formalist attitude that ignores social reality. Similarly, in *Lyng* v. *Northwest Indian Cemetery Protective Association* (1988), she permitted federally-sanctioned logging of a sacred site that she conceded could have "devastating effects" on Indian worship.

In the so-called "joint opinion" of *Planned Parenthood of Southeastern Pennsylvania* v. *Casey* (1992), which constitutes her most signal contribution to American jurisprudence to date, Justice O'Connor, together with Justices Anthony Kennedy and David Souter, reemphasized the importance of adherence to *stare decisis* and precedent as essential to "the very concept of the rule of law." *Casey* reaffirmed *Roe* v. *Wade* (1973), the basic abortion decision, but modified its specific doctrine.

Justice O'Connor has revitalized the Tenth Amendment through a vision of federalism that recognizes greater autonomy for the states, holding that Congress may not override "a power [that] is an attribute of state sovereignty reserved by the Tenth Amendment" (*New York* v. *United States*, 1992).

At mid-career, Justice O'Connor has emerged as a prominent member of the centrist bloc on the Supreme Court. Her moderate ideological conservatism has disappointed civil rights advocates and civil libertarians, while her espousal of a feminist approach on issues implicating gender equality has enraged social conservatives. See Harold Woods, *Equal Justice: A Biography of Sandra Day O'Connor* (1985).

WILLIAM M. WIECEK

O'FEARNA, Sean Aloysius. See Ford, John.

O'KEEFFE, Georgia (b. Sun Prairie, Wis., Nov. 15, 1887; d. Santa Fe, New Mexico, Mar. 6, 1986), ARTIST, studied art at the Art Institute of Chicago (1904–5) and at the Art Students League in New York (1907–8). She did freelance commercial art work in Chicago (1909–10) before teaching art in Amarillo, Texas (1912–14). In 1914 O'Keeffe came to New York to study at the Teachers College of Columbia University; she also studied art under Alon Bement and Arthur Wesley Dow. She took a teaching job at West Texas State Normal School (Canyon, Texas) in 1916. After a series of her abstract charcoal drawings was exhibited by **Alfred Stieglitz** at his "291" Gallery in New York, she returned to New York (1918) and devoted herself to painting. She married Stieglitz in 1924.

During the 1920s O'Keeffe did a series of close-up paintings of flowers, including *Black Iris*

(1926, Metropolitan Museum, N.Y.) which earned her recognition as a leading member of the precisionist school. After 1929 she began to spend much time in New Mexico, and her abstract paintings of animal skulls and skeletons set against desert backgrounds (*Cow's Skull: Red, White and Blue,* 1931, Metropolitan Museum, N.Y.) derive from this period. After Stieglitz's death in 1946, O'Keeffe made her permanent home in New Mexico, near Abiquiu. There she continued to paint with the same determination and energy she displayed earlier. But her work, so uniquely her own, did not attract much close attention from New York critics. Then, in 1970, when she was in her early eighties, a retrospective of her work was held at the Whitney Museum of American Art. A whole new generation of art critics and collectors rediscovered her and again her career blossomed. She did not rest on her new laurels, however, but went right on working as hard as ever. She painted new pictures, wrote an autobiography illustrated with her paintings, and cooperated in the production of a film about herself. In 1973, she began a liason with Juan Hamilton, a person who showed up at her doorstep at Abiquiu looking for work. He was twenty-seven years old. He soon made his way up from handyman to secretary to manager of her business affairs to her last love and heir. During her life O'Keefe received many awards, including the Medal of Freedom (1977), the nation's highest civilian award. Some of O'Keefe's major works include: *White Canadian Barn No. 2* (1932, Metropolitan Museum, N.Y.), *Deer's Skull with Pedernal* (1936, William Lane Foundation, Leominster, Mass.), and *Patio with Cloud* (1956, Walker Art Center, Minneapolis).

Georgia O'Keeffe's art was both modern and American as well as mystical and realistic. It recalls and elaborates upon a host of enduring qualities of past and recent art. Her imagery is, generally, easy to identify, but not always understandable. It is a unique distillation of personal feeling encased within a recognizable historical framework.

A mystic who painted with great precision and calculation, her great, sweeping landscapes recall those of the 19th-century Hudson River School, but her simplifications of form, and dry, clean style replaced the transcendental associations of the earlier art with more obscure cosmic overtones. These are often emphasized by the abrupt superimpositions of sharply focused foreground objects upon distant vistas. In the clear distinctions between the near forms—bones, crosses, plants—and the vast landscapes beyond, O'Keeffe seems to be suggesting that allusions to life, death, regeneration, and rebirth must be evaluated against a concept of eternity which has no cycles and which never changes. She poses, either as parallel or as antagonistic forces, the finite with the infinite.

Her flower studies may be viewed in similar fashion. Their various sexual associations, usually feminine, derive strength from the underlying presence of a more all-encompassing sense of nature.

Not all of O'Keeffe's works lend themselves to such exalted interpretation. Her views of New York City, painted in the late 1920s, are, within a Cubist framework, romantic responses to the visual excitement of a big city. In these works, she approached the austerities of **Charles Demuth** and **Charles Sheeler,** with whom she was often associated. But even though she shared with them a concern for hard-edged, precise forms, she preferred to paint the natural rather than the industrial landscape. See Roxana Robinson, *Georgia O'Keefe: A Life* (1989).

MATTHEW BAIGELL

OLMSTED, Frederick Law (b. Hartford, Conn., April 26, 1822; d. Waverly, Mass., Aug. 28, 1903), LANDSCAPE ARCHITECT, traveled widely as a child with his parents in the northeastern states and Canada. He studied engineering privately with Frederick A. Barton for two and a half years, and in his late teens worked in a dry-goods store and spent a year as a sailor on a voyage to China. He attended lectures at Yale (1842–43), and from 1847 to 1857 he ran an experimental farm on

Staten Island, New York. During this period he traveled extensively in the South. His impressions, published in two volumes as *Journeys and Explorations in the Cotton Kingdom* (1861), are noted for their insightful analysis of southern slave society.

After temporarily and unsuccessfully entering the publishing business, in 1857 Olmsted and his friend Calvert Vaux jointly entered a design competition to plan a public park in the center of Manhattan Island, then only dotted with squatters' shacks. In 1858 Olmsted was appointed architect in chief of the project and began to execute the design, which called for an ambitious program of drainage, clearing, and regrading, and the installation of artificial lakes. Political problems added to the difficulties, and Central Park, as it was named, was developed only slowly.

Olmsted moved to Washington in 1861 to organize the U.S. Sanitary Commission. Two years later he went to California to be superintendent of the Fremont Mariposa mining estates. While in California he took the lead in the movement to set aside the Yosemite and Mariposa "big-tree" reservations. After the Civil War he returned to New York and virtually completed Central Park. City politicians who wished to control park jobs finally drove him from his post, but he designed and built Prospect Park in Brooklyn, and also Riverside and Morningside Heights parks in upper Manhattan. In 1875 Olmsted undertook the task of converting the marshes of Back Bay, Boston, into a park—an assignment which grew into a plan for a park system for the entire city. He also designed the Capitol grounds in Washington; the Arnold Arboretum in Brookline, Massachusetts; Mount Royal Park in Montreal; Jackson Park in Chicago; and the scheme for the preservation of Niagara Falls.

Almost eighty parks and thirteen college campuses (including the University of California at Berkeley and Stanford University) were designed by Olmsted. In addition, he was an early town planner, the Chicago suburb of Riverside being his masterpiece. About 1890 he laid out Biltmore, the lavish estate of George Vanderbilt, near Asheville, North Carolina, and in 1893 was among those who designed the World's Columbian Exposition in Chicago.

Like Francis Bacon and Thomas Jefferson, Frederick Law Olmsted was one of those rare individuals whose genius finds expression in several fields. An adventurer and idealist even into old age, he was an enthusiastic and careful experimental farmer, a keen observer, a gifted writer, and an effective administrator. In his capacity as the first director of the U.S. Sanitary Commission, the forerunner of the American Red Cross, Olmsted was the organizing mastermind of medical relief in the Civil War. In later years his interest in preserving the environment led to the establishment of a national park system and the U.S. Forest Service.

After the Civil War, Olmsted became the nation's most prolific and influential landscape architect and an early exponent of suburban living, which he saw not as an escape from the city but as a delicate synthesis of town and wilderness. With Vaux, Olmsted laid out suburbs in several American cities, the most famous of which was Riverside, which opened on the west side of Chicago in 1869. Meticulously planned in every detail, Riverside offered generous lots, curved roadways, and a bucolic setting. Such communities, Olmsted thought, represented "the most attractive, the most refined, and the most soundly wholesome forms of domestic life, and the best application of the arts of civilization to which mankind has yet attained."

Olmsted is best remembered, however, as the father of the urban park movement. In 1857, when his design for New York's Central Park was accepted, no American city provided large open areas for public relaxation, partly because the poor conceived of parks as aristocratic preserves where royalty rode and because the rich thought of parks as refuges for idlers and hobos. To Olmsted, however, a successful social democracy required places where persons of all classes and occupations could come together for enrichment and regeneration. In Manhattan, moreover, where average residential densities exceeded

100,000 per square mile, the need for breathing space was urgent.

Twenty years under construction, Central Park required the labor of 3,800 men to dig out its ponds and to build up its hills. But it was visited by 10 million people even before it opened, and it quickly became renowned as an island of solitude in the midst of a throbbing metropolis. More importantly, Central Park's success and its form—the south end was given over to formal functions like concerts and fountains while the north end was made (not merely kept) as rugged and wild as possible—influenced cities and towns throughout the nation and the world.

Most of Olmsted's parks were more accessible to the middle and upper classes than to the slum families who needed them most. Moreover, he had a forceful personality and an unyielding drive; there was no "user participation" in the design process once Olmsted had decided what he wanted. Yet his parks were important for their demonstration that municipal governments could create public amenities on a grand scale and that much collective community effort was necessary to make cities habitable.

In the late 1870s, Olmsted became increasingly frustrated and disillusioned by politicians, by the rise of big business, and by the degree to which his theories and solutions failed to be accepted. Somewhat in resignation, he retreated for most of the remainder of his life to a private practice for millionaires—the huge Biltmore domain of George Vanderbilt in North Carolina is a good example—in which aesthetic rather than social concerns were emphasized. In the mid-20th century, however, Olmsted has gained wide recognition for his pivotal role as a 19th-century reformer. In 1972, the sesquicentennial of his birth, exhibitions of his papers and his work were held in dozens of cities and institutions as Americans came generally to accept **Lewis Mumford**'s judgment that Frederick Law Olmsted was this nation's "foremost exponent of ecological planning and regional design." See Albert Fein, *Frederick Law Olmsted and the American Environmental Tradition* (1972).

KENNETH T. JACKSON

O'NEILL, Eugene Gladstone (b. New York, N.Y., Oct. 16, 1888; d. Boston, Mass., Nov. 27, 1953), PLAYWRIGHT, was the son of noted actor James O'Neill, whom he accompanied on tours as a child. In 1906 he entered Princeton but left the following year. He traveled extensively the next few years, prospecting for gold in Central America and sailing the Atlantic. In 1912, while working as a reporter for the New London (Conn.) *Telegraph,* he became interested in drama. He took a course in playwriting at Harvard (1914–15) under George Pierce Baker, and after living in New York City for a year, moved to Provincetown, Massachusetts (1916), to join a recently organized little theater group, the Provincetown Players. The Players performed his one-act play *Bound East for Cardiff* in 1916. O'Neill helped manage the group, and when it went to New York's Playwright's theater in the fall of 1916, his play was successfully produced. His full-length play *Beyond the Horizon,* a bitter domestic drama, opened in 1920 and won a Pulitzer Prize. O'Neill won two more Pulitzer Prizes for *Anna Christie* (1922) and *Strange Interlude* (1928), realistic dramas treating disease and insanity. Another tragedy, *Mourning Becomes Electra* (1931), also won widespread critical acclaim. O'Neill followed this with a comedy of first love, *Ah, Wilderness!* (1933). In 1936 he became the second American to win the Nobel Prize for literature.

From 1934 to 1946 O'Neill lived in California, but withheld his new plays from publication. He returned to Broadway with his drama *The Iceman Cometh* (1946). In 1947 O'Neill was stricken with Parkinson's disease. At his death at least three plays were in manuscript form, including his autobiographical *Long Day's Journey into Night* (1956). Some of O'Neill's many other successful plays include: *The Emperor Jones* (1921), *All God's Chillun Got Wings* (1924), and *Desire Under the Elms* (1924).

O'Neill's drama is one of considerable range. His settings are almost uniformly American, but through his long career his technical methods varied greatly. A recurrent feature is his use of personal memories, appearing early in the *Moon of the Caribbees* volume, continuing in *Anna Christie* and in several plays of his early maturity, and culminating in the splendid *The Iceman Cometh* and *Long Day's Journey into Night.* This personal element goes along with a highly self-conscious interest in the art of the theater: writing at first in a realistic manner (modified by a liking for eloquent speech and the verbalized or visual symbol), he moved to a kind of writing, particularly in *The Emperor Jones* and *The Hairy Ape,* which had affinities with the "expressionist" mode of German drama at that time. Later in *Mourning Becomes Electra* he achieved a major success by taking over the plot-outline of the *Oresteia* of Aeschylus, setting it in America just after the Civil War, and giving it a strong infusion of Freudian (or perhaps, rather, Jungian) psychology. Near the end of his career he was planning a series of eleven plays with the general title *A Tale of Possessors Self-Dispossessed,* which was to narrate the fortunes of an Irish family in America from the late 18th to the early 20th centuries: only two of these plays are known to exist.

Often his demands on his audience and on theatrical possibility were extreme. Some of his major plays run to more than four hours in performance, and he could require large casts and imaginatively elaborate settings. To some extent this was in reaction to the popular melodramatic theater with which his father had become particularly associated. At the same time his passion for the theater, his restless desire to find out how much it could do, is to be related to the intimate experience of play-performance that his early circumstances gave him. Also he read avidly in dramatic literature: he admitted the effect that Strindberg and Wedekind had on him; he drew on Maxim Gorky for *The Iceman Cometh* as well as on Aeschylus for *Electra;* he denied that the German expressionists influenced him, but he certainly became conscious of their work. Among nondramatic authors, Nietzsche was of special importance to him, although here the effect was less happy, leading to a straining after impressive effect in some of the plays of O'Neill's middle years.

O'Neill truly belongs to the theater. In reading him we may feel longueurs and may be put off by repeated use of key phrases ("dat ole davil sea" in *Anna Christie,* "pipe-dreams" in *The Iceman*), but in performance his language at its best has a most effective rhetoric. It fits, moreover, with the controlled passion with which he confronts and presents his view of the human condition. He was also a master in the creating of parts for actors, so it is not surprising that his plays are in the repertories of the English-speaking countries and of continental Europe. Many books have been written about his life and his writing, and he takes his place securely as a major dramatist of the 20th century. In giving to American drama a major status in the world, he created an ambience in which his successors could flourish. See John Gassner (ed.), *O'Neill: A Collection of Critical Essays* (1964).

CLIFFORD LEECH

OPPENHEIMER, Julius Robert (b. New York, N.Y., April 22, 1904; d. Princeton, N.J., Feb. 18, 1967), SCIENTIST, graduated from Harvard in 1925 and then attended Cambridge University in England (1925–26). He received his PhD (1927) from the George-August University of Göttingen, Germany, where he studied with physicist Max Born. Oppenheimer held fellowships at Harvard and the California Institute of Technology (1927–28) and studied at the University of Leiden in the Netherlands and the Polytechnic Academy in Zurich (1928–29). Upon his return to the U.S. in 1929, Oppenheimer joined the faculties of both the University of California at Berkeley and the California Institute of Technology. An inspiring teacher, he helped make Berkeley the largest graduate school in theoretical physics in the country. He also did research on the quantum theory, cosmic ray showers, and the theory of nuclear structure. He developed the Oppenheimer-Phillips process to break deuterons from the atom (1935).

Becoming involved in the application of his work to the military use of atomic energy, Oppenheimer joined the atomic bomb production team in 1942 and was named director of the Los Alamos project to build the A-bomb the following year. Organizing and administering this operation, he saw the first A-bomb exploded at Alamogordo, New Mexico, on July 16, 1945. Resigning from the project later that year, Oppenheimer returned to Berkeley and Caltech, but served as a government adviser on the use and control of nuclear weapons. He helped write the Acheson-Lilienthal Report on control of atomic energy and **Bernard Baruch**'s proposal to the United Nations to give nuclear arms and energy control to an international authority (1946). Oppenheimer became director of Princeton's Institute for Advanced Study in 1947 and also chairman of the general advisory committee of the Atomic Energy Commission, which voted against the crash program for a "superbomb" in 1949. In 1952 he stepped down to a consulting role. In 1953, however, the Eisenhower administration revoked his security clearance, and after a 1954 hearing by the Personnel Security Board, Oppenheimer was declared a security risk because of alleged violations of security rules regarding his conduct in relation to the hydrogen bomb program, his personal associations, and supposed "defects in his 'character.'" He was not judged disloyal, and the AEC dropped charges about his "disturbing" conduct regarding the H-bomb, made by the hearing board. He was still debarred from access to government secrets, but two of his judges voted to clear him without prejudice.

Oppenheimer returned to Princeton and taught there until his retirement in 1966. In 1963 the AEC gave him its highest honor, the Fermi Award, for work in theoretical physics and other contributions to science. Some of Oppenheimer's books include *Science and the Common Understanding* (1954) and *Some Reflections on Science and Culture* (1960).

The Oppenheimer case excited international attention because it seemed to dramatize the totalitarian power of a state to sacrifice an individual's reputation to its own definition of truth and morality. Technically, his judges did not quite go so far. They said that they were constrained by the "rigid circumspection" of the rules to make a categorical judgment, and the Atomic Energy Commission dropped the "charge" that Oppenheimer lacked "enthusiastic support" for the H-bomb program. Even so, this pharisaical legalism reflected the climate of appeasement of exaggerated fears about Communist spies, stirred up by demagogues. His left-wing "fellow-traveler" past made him vulnerable to suspicion in the cold war era.

In effect the case ventilated the animosities and prejudices of powerful Air Force spokesmen and their scientific and political allies. Their dogmatic commitment to a strategy of "massive retaliation" made them irrationally suspicious of Oppenheimer's reasoned opposition to the crash program for the "superbomb" and his argument for tactical atomic weapons and continental air defense. No evidence was ever presented that he had not kept the secrets entrusted to him. Early in 1943, however, he had tried to protect a friend and give a disguised tip to security officers at the same time by an improvised embroidered story that he seems not to have fully cleared up until three years later. This lapse gave ammunition to his later judges, and his own mixed feelings about the episode further weakened his armor against a hostile prosecutor's tactics.

By his learning, his administrative experience, and his literary skill Oppenheimer was unusually fitted for interpreting the problems of the nuclear age. Proud, sensitive, and ambitious, he suffered, as two European dramatists have tried to show, the moral dilemmas of a humane man, concerned about the social consequences of "hyperbolic" weapons yet fascinated with their technical possibilities. As his political perspective changed, along with his governmental responsibilities, his relations with former left-wing friends were also troubled.

His successor as chairman of the general advisory committee of the AEC summed up most scientists' view of the case in saying that for the "tremendous achievement" of the atomic program to end in such a humiliating hearing was "a pretty bad show." The presentation of the Fermi

Award was also a symbolic gesture of restitution. See Nuell P. Davis, *Lawrence and Oppenheimer* (1968).

CUSHING STROUT

O'REILLY, John Boyle (b. Castle Dowth, County Meath, Ire., June 28, 1844; d. Hull, Mass., Aug. 10, 1890), REFORMER, served for four years as an apprentice on the Drogheda *Argus* and for three years on the staff of the Preston (Eng.) *Guardian*. Returning to Ireland in 1863, he enlisted in the Royal Hussars. Soon afterward, however, he became active in the Fenian Order, an Irish Republican organization. Discovered in 1866, he was court-martialed by the British and sentenced to death. His sentence was commuted to life imprisonment and was later reduced to twenty years.

In 1867 O'Reilly was deported to western Australia but managed to escape on the American whaler *Gazelle*. He landed in Philadelphia in November 1869. After a stint at lecturing he joined the staff of the influential Irish Boston *Pilot* in 1870. As "war correspondent" of the *Pilot* O'Reilly was highly critical of the Fenian raid from St. Albans into Canada, although he was a firm supporter of Irish home rule. In 1876, together with the Catholic archbishop of Boston, he purchased the *Pilot*, assuming $80,000 of the former owner's debts. His numerous works include *Songs on the Southern Seas* (1873), *Songs, Legends and Ballads* (1878), *Moondyne*, a novel (1879), *In Bohemia* (1886), *Ethics of Boxing and Manly Sport* (1888), and *The King's Men* (1884), a novel written in collaboration with Robert Grant, Frederic J. Stimson, and John T. Wheelwright.

⁂

John O'Reilly may well have been the first Roman Catholic reformer ever to achieve genuine acceptance as an American whose ethnic and religious background really did not matter. Of his early days in Ireland, his biographer has summed up his sunny and attractive character with the words: "Among the things he loved best were a good song and a kind act and a fast and fair fight."

He became so acceptable as an "American" because his past so well summed up what Americans liked to believe their country symbolized. From early youth, he and his family had worked for Irish liberation from England. He early joined the British army the more effectively to betray it, and served miserable years in the worst British prisons and Australian prison farms for his "treason." But his spirit survived, he made a daringly romantic escape from Australia, and when he settled finally in Boston he was soon able to become a spokesman for American freedoms, who only incidentally happened to be a Catholic. He became very popular even while his efforts to mediate between Irish Protestants and Catholics often offended members of both groups. He became a genuine Boston man of letters, and his Papyrus Club was a gathering of literati significant even for Boston, but he was best known for his lectures on democratic themes. Modern Americans can place him handily by remembering that he sought out the friendship of the aging **Wendell Phillips** and became one of the few white Americans beloved in the black community.

His personality appears most clearly in a Boston *Post* column, where he was described as "one whom children would choose for their friend, women for their lover, and men for their hero." His basic attitude was an obvious precursor of modern "melting pot" sociology. As he once told a group of African-Americans: "We must not be Irish or African, or black or white. Not in America. We are gathering here, and boiling down here, all the best blood—the blood of the people—not to build up any petty community, but to make the greatest nation and the strongest brotherhood that God ever smiled upon." Coming from him, the sentiment seemed almost believable. See William G. Schofield, *Seek for a Hero* (1956).

ROBERT M. CRUNDEN

O'SULLIVAN, John Louis (b. Gibraltar, Nov. 1813; d. New York, N.Y., Feb. 24, 1895), JOURNALIST, DIPLOMAT, graduated from Columbia

College (1831) and Columbia Law School (1834). After practicing law for three years he helped found a politico-literary magazine, the *United States Magazine and Democratic Review,* to which **Nathaniel Hawthorne** and other leading writers contributed. In the summer of 1845 O'Sullivan wrote an article urging the aggressive expansion of the United States throughout North America in which the phrase, "manifest destiny" was used for the first time. With **Samuel J. Tilden** he also edited a Democratic newspaper, the New York *Morning News,* from 1844 to 1846. O'Sullivan was active in the struggle to repeal the New York capital punishment law in 1841, but his main interest was in promoting the acquisition of Cuba by the U.S. He supported filibustering activities in Cuba in 1849–51, and was tried and acquitted for violation of the neutrality laws in 1852. The next year President Pierce appointed him chargé d'affaires and later minister to Portugal.

During the Civil War O'Sullivan lived in England, where he worked for the southern cause in the hope that the English would recognize the Confederacy. He returned to America in 1879, living in almost total obscurity, broken only by an invitation to speak at the dedication of the Statue of Liberty in 1886.

O'Sullivan was a man endowed with ability, enormous energy, and an infectious charm that captivated the great and the near-great. Yet, with all these virtues, his career must be accounted a failure. Two fatal flaws in his character negated his obvious talents: a near-classic psychological instability and a total commitment to racism. These failings led him to misread completely the currents of history.

A journalist of the first rank, the equal of his more famous contemporary rivals **Horace Greeley** and **James Gordon Bennett,** O'Sullivan fancied himself to be the voice of the inarticulate yeoman farmer and small businessman. His was a grand if somewhat myopic vision of what the future held in store for the United States. An ardent Jacksonian, he was convinced that agrarian Jacksonian democracy as he understood the

concept held the key to man's happiness. O'Sullivan believed that the virtues of these principles were so obvious that they were destined ultimately to sweep through the world and transform the universe into the American image. For him, developing industrial capitalism was a poison that would corrupt society and ultimately enslave humanity. He was not the first American messianist, but through his influential magazine he became one of this country's most eloquent spokesmen for the agrarian expansionist creed.

O'Sullivan's greater failure, however, was in his blind and obdurate racism. Though a man of great tenderness, who was actively associated with various causes concerned with eliminating a host of societal inequities, he could not recognize the moral worth of black men. Therefore, servility should be their only acceptable status in American society. He preached that slavery was a positive virtue, and the more slave territory incorporated into the Union, the better. O'Sullivan staked his entire career on this doctrine. Thus, this northerner and one-time Free-Soiler volunteered his considerable abilities to the Confederate side. In making this decision he forfeited much of the affection humanitarians had formerly accorded him. See Sheldon H. Harris, "The Public Career of John Louis O'Sullivan," unpublished PhD dissertation (Columbia University, 1958).

SHELDON H. HARRIS

OSWALD, Lee Harvey (b. New Orleans, La., Oct. 18, 1939; d. Dallas, Texas, Nov. 24, 1964), ASSASSIN of John F. Kennedy, born two months after the death of his father, Oswald grew up in a capricious world. Although neither of his siblings were orphans, and his half brother John Pic's father was alive, Oswald's mother, Marguerite Claverie Oswald, placed all three of her sons in a New Orleans orphanage. Her third marriage to the peripatetic Edwin A. Ekdahl, whom Oswald liked, did not last. Troubled in school by dyslexia, by age ten Oswald had attended six schools and, as a Bronx, N.Y. truant, had been recommended for psychiatric treatment, which his mother avoided by moving to New Orleans.

As had his brother and half brother, Oswald fled his mother's home for the U.S. Marines at age seventeen, when he was in the tenth grade. He qualified for sharpshooter in one target test, but then fell back to marksman qualification. Hazed by his fellow Marines during his first year in service, Oswald attempted to wound himself with a mail-order gun and was sentenced to twenty-eight days in the brig.

Lying that his mother needed him, Oswald obtained a hardship discharge in 1959 and then, within weeks, fled the U.S. for the Soviet Union, where he renounced his citizenship. In the U.S.S.R. he married Marina Alexandrovna Medvedeva in 1961, and in 1962 returned with her and their baby to settle in Fort Worth, Texas. In 1963 he moved to Dallas, where he bought a mail-order Mannlicher-Carcano rifle and equipped it with a telescopic sight. He failed to assassinate outspoken right-wing Major General Edwin A. Walker with this gun in March, 1963, and in April moved to New Orleans, where he was jailed for fighting with three anti-Castro exiles. After reading former Vice President Richard Nixon's anti-Castro remarks that month, he told Marina that he was going to assassinate Nixon, but she locked him in the bathroom.

He and Marina, now pregnant, then moved back to Texas, where, after he failed to get a passport to Cuba in a trip to Mexico City, Oswald shot and killed John F. Kennedy on November 22, 1964 from the window of the Texas School Depository, a building in which he was a temporary worker, and which by chance overlooked Kennedy's parade route.

In the opening line of his own unfinished autobiography, Oswald said it all: "Lee Harvey Oswald was born in Oct 1939 in New Orlean, La., the son of an Insuaren Salesman whose early death left a far mean streak of indepence brought on by neglect...." [spelling and capitalization in original]. As a Bronx schoolboy truant, Oswald complained to his social worker that he had to "be his own father."

Oswald's unstable, widowed mother Marguerite, who had lost her own mother at age four, taught him that the world "owed" them, that they were exempt from social norms. Not surprisingly, this angry, fatherless boy grew up fantasizing about killing people and becoming "president of the world."

As a lonely teenager reading in New Orleans public libraries, Oswald found a "father" in Karl Marx, whose vision of a non-exploitative society appealed to him. In the Marines, he boasted of his communist sympathies and hoped to find a new home in the Soviet Union where he would be properly appreciated. After his abortive defection, he came back home to Dallas, where he formed a one-person chapter of the New York-based Fair Play for Cuba Committee, and attempted to appear important to pro-Castroites by attempting to kill a right-wing Texas general. When he found that he was unable to support his Russian wife and daughter, they went to live with a friend in Irving, Texas, while Oswald lived alone with his fantasies in Dallas.

When Fidel Castro alleged the Central Intelligence Agency was attempting to assassinate him, Oswald clipped the press account and seems to have hoped that he could impress "Uncle Fidel," as he called Castro, and win asylum in Cuba, by becoming a pro-Cuban activist or by assassinating Castro's enemies. He suggested to his pregnant wife that their new child be named "Fidel," and he bought two mail-order guns under the alias "Hidell." Denied a visa to Cuba in Mexico City in September, 1963, he became abusive, talked about his "right" to a visa, but left the Cuban Embassy there. He then came back to the United States and announced: "Someone ought to shoot that President Kennedy. Maybe I'll try it."

That November, with two of three shots he fired from his sniper's lair, he assassinated the President of the United States whose motorcade passed by where he worked. Because Oswald was killed by Jack Ruby two days later, many assume incorrectly that Oswald was part of a conspiracy, but, despite uncounted allegations by conspiracy theorists, no other conspirators, guns, cartridges, notes, bullets or bullet holes, have ever been found. Oswald was the lone assassin. See Gerald Posner, *Case Closed: Lee Harvey Oswald and the Assassination of JFK* (1993).

JAMES P. JOHNSON

OTIS, James (b. West Barnstable, Mass., Feb. 5, 1725; d. Andover, Mass., May 23, 1783), POLITICAL LEADER, graduated from Harvard (1743), and was admitted to the bar in 1748. He was appointed king's advocate general of the vice-admiralty court at Boston, but resigned in 1761 to oppose the issuance of writs of assistance, general search warrants. In February 1761 he argued before the superior court that natural law was superior to acts of Parliament. Two months later he was elected to the Massachusetts general court.

Otis soon became a prolific pamphleteer. In 1762 he wrote *A Vindication of the Conduct of the House of Representatives,* a brief exposition of the rights of Englishmen. After Parliament passed the Sugar Act (1764), he issued *The Rights of the British Colonies Asserted and Proved,* in which he argued that man must be "free from all taxes but what he consents to in person, or by his representative." He was a delegate to the Stamp Act Congress (1765), and wrote *A Vindication of the British Colonies,* which advocated colonial representation in Parliament but also accepted Parliament's supremacy.

A moderate in politics, Otis objected to the violence that followed the Townshend Acts (1767). In 1769 he was severely injured during a brawl with John Robinson, an English customs official. Thereafter he played only a minimal role in New England affairs.

———ເ∞∞———

James Otis earned his place in the front rank of American Revolutionary thinkers by asking the right question: Is the power of Parliament limited? His answer, as it evolved through his writings from 1761 to 1766, was so ambiguous, however, that in the long run it satisfied neither Loyalists nor Patriots. His opposition to the writs of assistance in 1761 was later credited by John Adams as the first blaze in the trail that led to the Revolution.

Otis argued that the writs, and the Navigation Acts upon which they stood, were void because they violated a fundamental principle of common law—an individual's "privilege of house."

When passage of the Sugar Act made clear the Grenville ministry's intention to raise a revenue in America, Otis was the first colonial pamphleteer to challenge the new legislation. In his *Rights of the British Colonists,* adopted by the Massachusetts general court in 1764 as their response to the ministry's plans, Otis further developed his views concerning the limitations on Parliament. Misinterpreting a 17th-century precedent, Bonham's Case, Otis asserted that the courts, as guardians of the common law, could declare void all allegedly "unconstitutional" acts of Parliament. He contended that Parliament would then repeal the criticized legislation because, he believed, its members desired to act justly. But such a check on Parliament was hardly realistic in the late 18th century, for by then it wielded supreme authority, and few of its members would have accepted the principle of judicial review. Because of his confidence, however, Otis could charge that parliamentary taxation violated the rights of unrepresented Americans while at the same time he counseled the colonists that "let the Parliament lay what burdens they please on us, we must, it is our duty to submit and patiently bear them, till they will be pleased to relieve us."

Otis was not all words. It was probably his suggestion that the colonies send delegates to a congress to protest the Stamp Act in 1765, and he would have been chosen its presiding officer save for his reputation as an extremist. Only with difficulty, however, could he be persuaded to sign the Congress's resolutions, so strong was his conviction that Parliament alone could regulate its own conduct. No wonder Otis's fellow Patriots found him difficult to understand.

In the next few years Otis suffered increasingly frequent attacks of insanity. Never known for an even temper, he lashed out at friends and foes alike, his political position vacillated more wildly than ever, and he became the butt of tavern jokesters and newspaper scribblers. Although he was several times reelected to positions of importance, his effectiveness as a Patriot leader steadily declined after 1766. His fight with John Robinson in 1769 left no permanent disabilities; his mental decline had already begun. Yet despite the inadequacies and ambiguities of his argument, his assertion that parliamentary acts might be considered unconstitutional served as an important point of departure. Within a decade others would find a simpler answer by declaring that Parliament had no authority over the colonies at all. See Clifford Shipton, *Sibley's Harvard Graduates*, XI (1960), 247–89.

BENJAMIN W. LABAREE

OWENS, Jesse (b. Oakville, Ala., Sept. 12, 1913; d. Tucson, Ariz., March 31, 1980), ATHLETE, born James Cleveland, he was the last of ten children of Alabama sharecroppers Henry and Mary Owens. In 1922, his family moved to Cleveland, Ohio. Owens attended public schools there where he came under the tutelege of coach Charles Riley who helped him develop his abilities as a sprinter and broad (now called long) jumper. Owens, who married Ruth Solomon in 1931, enrolled in Ohio State University in 1933 and became the star of the track team. On May 25, 1935, at the Big Ten Conference championships, he set three new world records and tied another. Owens won an unprecedented four gold medals at the 1936 Berlin Olympic Games. His post-athletic career included show business, sales, sports management, public administration, and public relations. In 1974, President Ford presented Owens a Medal of Freedom, the nation's highest civilian award.

━━━◦◦◦━━━

Like many world class athletes, the high point of Jesse Owens's life came early. He received world acclaim by winning four gold medals at the 1936 Olympics. He led off for the victorious U.S. 400 meter relay team, and set Olympic records for the 200 meters (20.7 seconds) and the broad jump (26' 5½") and tied the world record for the 100 meters (10.3 seconds). The signifi-

cance of this extraordinary achievement was greatly magnified because as a black American his athletic grace and dominance embarrassed Adolph Hitler, who envisioned the Games as a showcase for his racist Nazi ideology. Owens's performance came as no surprise because at the 1935 Big Ten championships he set three new world records and tied another within the space of just forty-five minutes despite a severely strained back muscle. Owens's running style— light and crisp—is still considered to be classic. "He is a floating wonder, just like he has wings," one expert gushed.

Success in athletics, however, did not mean that Owens would enjoy comparable success after his track career ended. Although he returned to Ohio State, he was dismissed for academic reasons in 1941. His marriage lasted until his death, but it was often strained. Strongly motivated to make money because of the poverty he had known as a youth, Owens involved himself in dubious activities, including racing a horse in Havana, awkwardly attempting song and dance routines on the nightclub circuit, doing bit movie parts, and making a series of bad investments which led to a 1939 bankruptcy. In 1966, he barely escaped a jail sentence for failure to file federal income taxes for eight years by pleading *nolo contendere* and securing several prominent character witnesses who reminded the judge of his status as a sports legend.

Owens embraced a conservative political and economic philosophy, endorsing several Republican presidential candidates. Although he often denounced racism, he routinely urged moderation and caution as the civil rights movement developed. In 1968 he was labeled an "Uncle Tom" by militants for his efforts to prevent a "Black Power" protest at the Mexico City Olympics. He published two books on race relations, *Blackthink* (1970) and *I Have Changed* (1972), which reflected ambivalence and confusion on racial issues. Beginning in the late 1950s, Owens gained substantial financial success by giving enthusiastic motivational speeches to conventions and sales meetings in which he emphasized the importance of self-reliance and individual achievement. A multi-pack-a-day cigarette smoker for thiry-five years, he died of lung cancer. See

William J. Baker, *Jesse Owens: An American Life* (1986).

RICHARD O. DAVIES

PAGE, Walter Hines (b. Cary, N.C., Aug. 15, 1855; d. Pinehurst, N.C., Dec. 21, 1918), WRITER, DIPLOMAT, studied at Trinity College (now Duke University), Randolph-Macon College, and Johns Hopkins University (1871–78), but left without taking a degree. He taught English at a Louisville, Kentucky, high school and then worked for the St. Joseph (Mo.) *Gazette* (1880). After touring the South and writing a series of articles depicting southern life, he worked as literary editor for the New York *World* (1882–83). He returned to North Carolina and acquired the Raleigh *State Chronicle*. His editorials crusaded for scientific agriculture, more local industry, and expanded educational facilities for whites and blacks. When the newspaper failed he joined the *Forum* magazine (1887), becoming editor in 1891. In 1895 Page became an adviser for Houghton, Mifflin and Co., publishers, and in 1898, editor of its *Atlantic Monthly* magazine. He then helped found the publishing firm of Doubleday, Page and Co. and *World's Work* magazine, which he edited 1900–13.

Page was an early and strong supporter of Woodrow Wilson, who appointed him ambassador to Great Britain when he became president in 1913. Page strongly urged American aid to the Allies in the early years of World War I, despite Wilson's neutrality policy. However, Page continued to serve as ambassador until declining health forced him to resign in 1918. Page wrote *The Rebuilding of Old Commonwealths* (1902), *A Publisher's Confession* (1905), and *The Southerner* (1909), a novel.

Page resembled many of the persons active in the reformism of the Progressive Era: he was middle-class, energetic, optimistic about life and the future of the United States. A man of at best modest physical appearance—with mustache, receding hairline, heavy-lidded eyes, and an exceptionally large nose—he had a far better than average intellect and talent for clear and lively expression. Frankness and facility with the written word were keynotes of his career. His blunt attacks on intellectual and economic backwardness in the post–Civil War South provoked such opposition that he decided to move north, where he put his literary talents to use in supporting reform of politics, economics, and education. Page's journals were sensible, timely, and good literature.

Thrust with little preparation into the world of international affairs, Page applied his brisk style to the diplomacy of the early 20th century. Convinced of the need for British and American friendship, anxious to see Anglo-American leadership of the world, he believed that coyness, half-truths, and threats—the customary tools of diplomacy—had no place in the dealings between these two natural allies. Anglo-American relations must be warm, honest, straightforward. Hence, when the world war began, Page had no difficulty taking sides. His wartime diplomacy was highlighted by eloquent appeals to President Wilson for policy beneficial to the Allies (beginning in 1915 he urged intervention against Germany) and, when Wilson seemed unresponsive, by brazen advice to the British foreign secretary, Sir Edward Grey, on how best to deal with the United States. While Page's name remains a symbol to groups wishing to promote Anglo-American unity, and while his letters from London represent some of the most moving accounts of World War I, he was not a vital person in the diplomacy of 1914–18. His letters were, if anything, too eloquent, his dedication too obvious and intense for a president anxious to keep his nation at peace. Wilson came to ignore Page, even stopped reading his letters. "Edward Grey's ambassador, not mine," he once remarked about his ambassador in London. See Ross Gregory, *Walter Hines Page: Ambassador to the Court of St. James's* (1970).

ROSS GREGORY

PAINE, Thomas (b. Thetford, Eng., Jan. 29, 1737; d. New York, N.Y., June 8, 1809), POLITICAL LEADER, REFORMER, was apprenticed as a corsetmaker as a youth. During 1757–74 he held a number of odd jobs, and in 1772 published his first pamphlet, *The Case of the Officers of Excise*, in which he argued that excisemen should be paid a living wage. He migrated to Philadelphia in 1774, where he found employment as a journalist. In 1776 he published (anonymously) *Common Sense*, in which he argued that the colonies should declare their independence from Great Britain because the Crown was hampering their economic growth by taxes and trade restrictions, because monarchy was a corrupt form of government, and because it was impractical for an island three thousand miles away to dominate a whole continent. *Common Sense* was an immediate best-seller.

When the Revolution broke out, Paine enlisted in the Continental army. After participating in Washington's retreat across New Jersey (1776), he published the first of his sixteen *Crisis* papers, an eloquent plea for patriotism ("These are the times that try men's souls ..."). In 1777 Congress appointed him secretary of its committee on foreign affairs, but he resigned in 1779 and became clerk of the Pennsylvania Assembly.

Paine returned to Europe in 1787. When Edmund Burke denounced the French Revolution (*Reflections on the French Revolution*), Paine responded with his *Rights of Man* (1791–92), defending the compact theory of government and natural rights, and urging the English people to overthrow the monarchy and set up a republic. Paine was tried for treason and outlawed for this (1792), but France made him an

honorary citizen. He was elected to the French Convention, where he aligned himself with the Girondist party. However, after the fall of the Gironde, Paine was accused of treason and imprisoned (1793–94). While in prison he began to write the *Age of Reason* (1794–96), a defense of deism and rational religion. Paine returned to America, where he spent his remaining years in poverty and obscurity.

Paine stands in history as the prototype of the radical proletarian, one of the first commoners to realize the effectiveness of the press as a tool for political reform. He manipulated the written word with magical success, primarily through appealing to the generally accepted propositions that man is a rational being, that he is fundamentally benevolent but corrupted by society, that each man is politically equal to his neighbor, and that a parallel exists between the laws of science and those of human society. Through Paine's example, the voice of the people emerged as a powerful and decisive force in government. He exposed the inherent weaknesses of hereditary rule and exalted written constitutions over both precedent and arbitrary authority. He demonstrated, moreover, the international character of modern society and the dependence of political justice upon the economic system.

Today Paine is probably better known for his attacks on institutional Christianity than for his contributions to political thought, despite the fact that his deistical writings are far less original than those on society and government. In religion, Paine was much less radical than modern freethinkers, accepting, for example, the concepts of divine justice and immortality.

Both in England and in America, Paine aspired to political and diplomatic leadership, but his personality kept him from positions of influence. Only in France did he ever occupy an elective office; yet he did not know the French language, and the French who elected him to their Constitutional Convention knew him only by his writings. As a person, Paine was vain, opinionated, and hypersensitive, resembling in these traits Rousseau, whom he preferred to Voltaire. See A. Owen Aldridge, *Man of Reason: The Life of Thomas Paine* (1959).

A. OWEN ALDRIDGE

PALEY, William S. (b. Chicago, Ill., Sept. 28, 1901; d. New York, N.Y, Oct. 26, 1990), BUSINESS-MAN, graduated from the Wharton School of Finance at the University of Pennsylvania in 1922. He entered the family business, the Congress Cigar Company, in Philadelphia, and was impressed by the successful results of advertising the company's La Palina cigars on the infant local radio network. He bought the network, the Columbia Phonographic Broadcasting Company, for $300,000 in 1928, renamed it the Columbia Broadcasting System (CBS) and became its president, staying at its helm for the next sixty years. Once in charge, Paley sought areas of broadcasting where CBS might establish its leadership over its rival, the National Broadcasting Company (NBC) under **David Sarnoff.** In 1938, the *CBS World News Roundup* began with extended coverage of the Nazi takeover of Austria. That same year, CBS's broadcast of H. G. Wells's *War of the Worlds*, with **Orson Welles** realistically conveying a Maritian invasion, led to a literal public panic and focused attention on CBS and the power of radio. During World War II, Paley served in the Psychological War Division of the Office of War Information (1943–1945), and in 1951 he was appointed Chairman of the President's Materials Policy Commission.

After the war, Paley presided over CBS's transition from radio to television and the transformation of CBS from a broadcasting company to a multimedia conglomerate with holdings in the music industry (Columbia Records), publishing (Holt, Rinehart and Winston), and sports (the New York Yankees). Paley's greatest contribution to CBS at this time was in the area of programming. In 1948, he lured Jack Benny and other entertainers away from NBC and started a twenty year period of CBS dominance in the ratings. In 1951, CBS launched *I Love Lucy*, and in the 1970s, under Paley's leadership, CBS achieved high ratings and critical praise for introducing

such TV series as *All in the Family, The Mary Tyler Moore Show*, and *M*A*S*H*. In the 1980s Paley began to take a less active role in overseeing the company but he refused to retire. This led to a succession of heir apparents and a sense of corporate instability. Paley continued to devote himself, however, to his charitable activites. Long a member of the Board of Trustees of the Museum of Modern Art and a considerable art collector himself, he served as president of the Board from 1968 to 1972. In 1976, Paley founded the Museum of Broadcasting in New York City and gave it a considerable endowment. Although Paley continued as Chairman of CBS until his death, he effectively ceased to have much power in the company he founded after investor Laurence Tisch took control in 1987.

⎯⎯⎯ ✺ ⎯⎯⎯

William S. Paley is most often compared to another giant of American broadcasting, David Sarnoff. Sarnoff, however, was a visionary whose greatest interest was in technology, whereas Paley was much more pragmatic and more involved in programming. As a result, a more apt comparison might be with Lord John Reith, of the British Broadcasting Company (BBC).

Reith, who was also very involved in programming, set the standard for the BBC as, "taking the lead," or raising cultural levels. In contrast, Paley tried to sum up his broadcasting philosophy by stating that "I am not a highbrow, I do not look down on popular taste. Oftentimes popular taste is my taste." This admission, however, was contradicted by Paley's patrician manner, his collection of Picassos and Matisses, a second wife whose name was usually found at the top of best-dressed lists, and his obvious pleasure in hearing CBS referred to as the "Tiffany network."

Actually, Paley's remarks did not reflect his tastes or lifestyle but his keen understanding as a businessman that in order to survive in commercial broadcasting one had to attract a mass audience and to do that one had to appeal to the lowest common denominator. Hand in hand with that went his awareness that broadcasting was a federally regulated oligopoly where the "public interest" had to be taken into consideration. As a result, for every *Ed Sullivan Show* there was at least one *See It Now*, for every *Beverly Hillbillies* a *M*A*S*H*, and for every *Dallas* a *Playhouse 90*. These choices made Paley one of the most influential figures in American popular culture in the twentieth century. See Sally Bedell Smith, *In All His Glory: The Life of William S. Paley, The Legendary Tycoon and His Brilliant Circle* (1990).

ALBERT AUSTER

PALMER, Alexander Mitchell (b. Moosehead, Pa., May 4, 1872; d. Washington, D.C., May 11, 1936), POLITICAL LEADER, graduated from Swarthmore College in 1891. He then read law while supporting himself as a court reporter, and in 1893 began to practice. An early rebel against the conservative Democrats of his state, Palmer was elected to the U.S. Congress in 1908, 1910, and 1912. He supported advanced progressive measures: wrote a child-labor bill which finally became law in 1916, sponsored woman suffrage legislation and a mine inspection measure, and instigated a federal investigation of the Bethlehem Steel Corporation's labor practices. The AFL gave Palmer its highest endorsement and called him "labor's friend." On the Ways and Means Committee, Palmer drafted the iron and steel sections of the Underwood Tariff of 1913. A strong supporter of Wilson for the presidency, Palmer held the Pennsylvania delegation in line at the 1912 convention which nominated him. He declined Wilson's offer to appoint him secretary of war because of his Quaker scruples, but did accept chairmanship of the Democratic National Committee's key executive committee. He also was elected chairman of the Democratic caucus in the House of Representatives, and he acted as Wilson's liaison man with Democratic progressives. In 1914, having lost a race for U.S. senator which he had entered at Wilson's insistence, he briefly returned to private life. He served as Alien Property custodian (1917–19), and in March 1919 Wilson appointed him attorney general. In this post he helped to force the dissolu-

tion of the meatpacking trust and dealt aggressively, though some felt with doubtful legality, with strikes and postwar profiteering.

His most controversial actions, however, concerned his participation in the so-called Red Scare of 1919–20. Extremist pronouncements by various revolutionary groups, notably anarchists, and a rash of strikes had released a tide of popular fear that the nation was under attack. When, on the evening of June 2, 1919, ten bombs exploded within an hour in eight eastern cities (one at the Washington home of Palmer), the fear of a conspiracy became a widespread conviction. Palmer directed the forces of the Justice Department, which included the newly organized Bureau of Investigation, in raids against thousands of suspected aliens. These raids reached a peak on January 2, 1920, when some seven thousand aliens were arrested, mostly without proper warrants. After investigation of each case by the Labor Department only a few hundred suffered deportation. At the same time organizations such as the Industrial Workers of the World were suppressed. Palmer's activities as Alien Property custodian and attorney general gave rise to numerous congressional investigations, and several grand jury investigations, but no indictments resulted.

After failing to win the 1920 Democratic nomination for president, Palmer retired to private life. He continued to take an interest in Democratic politics, helped write the platform on which Franklin Roosevelt ran in 1932, and was one of Roosevelt's strongest supporters at the 1932 convention.

The career of A. Mitchell Palmer presents an enigma to historians. Somehow the militant reformer of pre-World War I years must be reconciled with the conservative postwar champion of 100 percent Americanism, the seeker of injunctions against labor unions in 1919–20, and the notorious violator of civil liberties who initiated the Palmer Raids in January 1920.

The most obvious explanation for this apparent metamorphosis is a change in the national temper. During the Progressive Era, politicians who supported the powerless and the underprivileged against giant corporations usually won election against defenders of conventional business practices. After World War I, however, a candidate for the presidency—like Palmer—hardly could ignore the popular fear of labor disturbances and Communist-inspired revolution. Nevertheless, Palmer continued until late in the spring of 1920 to urge that President Wilson grant clemency to political prisoners convicted during the war. The attorney general was one of the last in Wilson's cabinet to promise that his office would be used to put down rebellion. He acted against radicals only after the U.S. Senate resolved unanimously that he be required to explain his inactivity. Despite great pressure, then, Palmer did not give up his prewar liberal attitudes easily.

When he finally did adopt repressive policies, Palmer was responding to more than political expediency. He shared many of the racial attitudes that underlay the antipathy displayed by most white native-born Americans toward recent immigrants, blacks, and alien radicals. Furthermore, Palmer seems to have been as affected as most other middle-class Americans by the series of severe societal disturbances that accompanied and followed World War I. His chief advisers appear to have been similarly affected. As attorney general, Palmer was overwhelmed with complicated matters when he attempted, after Wilson fell ill, to take charge of the federal government's attempts to deal with almost all the nation's most severe domestic problems. He was obliged to depend inordinately upon the advice of subordinates. The head of the crucial antiradical intelligence division in Palmer's Bureau of Investigation, **J. Edgar Hoover,** advised drastic action against imminent revolution in 1919, and the overburdened Palmer probably had no way of ascertaining that there was no chance whatever that revolution would occur in the United States at that time. See Stanley Coben, *A. Mitchell Palmer: Politician* (1963).

STANLEY COBEN

PARKER, Theodore (b. Lexington, Mass., Aug. 24, 1810; d. Florence, Italy, May 10, 1860), REFORMER, graduated from Harvard Divinity School in 1836, and became pastor of the Unitarian Church at West Roxbury, Massachusetts. In an article signed "Levi Blodgett" in 1838 he argued against the necessity of miracles, and he openly denied the spiritual authority of the Bible, the supernatural origin of Christianity, and the divine mission of Jesus in a sermon, "The Transient and Permanent in Christianity" (1841). In a series of lectures in Boston, published as *A Discourse of Matters Pertaining to Religion* (1842), he presented a transcendentalist interpretation of Christianity.

Upon returning from a trip to Europe, he published a translation of W. M. L. De Wette's *Einleitung in das Alte Testament,* which caused him to be ostracized by the Boston churches (1844). He resigned his pulpit in West Roxbury in 1845, but was then installed as pastor of the 28th Congregational Society of Boston. In 1848 he published *A Letter to the People of the United States Touching the Matter of Slavery.* He also wrote numerous articles on antislavery themes for the *Massachusetts Quarterly Review* (1847–50).

Active in the rescue of the fugitive slaves William and Ellen Craft (1850), as well as in the abortive attempt to rescue Thomas Sims (1851), Parker also instigated an unsuccessful attempt to free the fugitive slave Anthony Burns from the Boston Court House (1854). Although an indictment brought against him and six others for the attempted rescue was dismissed, Parker nevertheless published a *Defense,* which provided case histories of fugitive slave episodes. Parker was a supporter of the New England Emigrant Aid Society and the Massachusetts-Kansas Committee, and was directly involved in **John Brown's** attempted foray at Harpers Ferry (1859). Parker also published two volumes of sermons, *On Atheism, Deism and the Popular Theology,* and two volumes of *Addresses and Occasional Discourses.*

———— ❧ ————

Theodore Parker was motivated by pride of family and his sense of a noble Puritan heritage.

A grandson of Captain John Parker, who led the Minutemen at Lexington, he kept the Revolution alive in his thoughts. It later furnished rhetoric for comparisons between true patriotic fervor and what he saw as shoddy compromise. His humble rural upbringing gave him a sense of identity with the common people. Parker was much like Orestes A. Brownson in his thirst for knowledge and hunger for religious truth. But where Brownson probed restlessly for light among various sects, before settling into Catholicism and forswearing much of contemporary controversy, Parker, learned and intense, stayed within the confines of Unitarianism while pursuing a quest which all but put him outside of it. He went his own way, determined to keep religion an active factor in American life.

Accordingly, he made of his Music Hall church in Boston a forum which attracted the dissident and humble, as well as some of the most distinguished New England intellectuals. He felt compelled to discuss all issues of the reform era as momentous to the refinement of true religion. Parker's difficult life of work and study left him with few graces of voice or presence, but his moral fervor and clear prose made his sermons and lectures an adventure to auditors and readers. (For this aspect of his achievement, see *Theodore Parker's Experience as a Minister, with Some Account of His Early Life, and Education for the Ministry,* an autobiographical letter addressed to his congregation, published after his death.)

The issue of issues became for Parker the fugitive slave, as it did for many Massachusetts Free-Soilers who had learned to view the debate over slavery from the radical Garrisonian perspective, without feeling free to join these extremists in their repudiation of all churches, their mixture of abolition and woman's rights, and their contempt for the Constitution, among other tenets. The Fugitive Slave Law of 1850, however, seemed to Parker and his coworkers designed to implicate them in support of the slavery system, and to impugn civil rights for all people. Accordingly, they determined to resist the law in any way possible. Parker's major contribution was a passionate eloquence which depicted slave conditions as

wicked, and honored resistance to authority in this connection as necessary to human survival. His interpretation of events traveled far beyond Massachusetts, and probably influenced Abraham Lincoln's thoughts on the issue.

Parker's complicity in the schemes of John Brown was full and direct, though whether he would have admitted responsibility, following Brown's capture at Harpers Ferry, or protested innocence as did Dr. **Samuel G. Howe** and other fiery Free-Soilers, when federal indictments became possible, cannot be known. Suffering illness since 1857, Parker left the country seeking health, January 9, 1859, and his open endorsement of Brown was from abroad, where he died. See Henry Steele Commager, *Theodore Parker* (1936).

LOUIS FILLER

PARKMAN, Francis (b. Boston, Mass., Sept. 16, 1823; d. Jamaica Plain, Mass., Nov. 8, 1893), HISTORIAN, received both BA (1844) and LLB (1846) from Harvard. In 1846–47 he took a trip along the Oregon and Santa Fe trails to recuperate from illness and to study Native American culture. Upon his return to Boston, he suffered a physical breakdown, and for the remainder of his life he was a semi-invalid, suffering from nervous disorders and from poor eyesight bordering on blindness.

While recuperating at Brattleboro, Vermont, Parkman dictated *The California and Oregon Trail,* more popularly called *The Oregon Trail* (1849), to his cousin. In 1851 he published his *History of the Conspiracy of Pontiac,* an account of the 1763–64 Native American uprising which followed the British conquest of North America. This was followed by *Vassall Morton* (1856), a romantic novel. During the Civil War he contributed articles to the Boston *Daily Advertiser.*

In 1865 Parkman published *Pioneers of France in the New World,* the first of seven books in which he traced the struggle between the British and the French for control of North America. The other volumes of this magnum opus are: *The Jesuits in North America* (1867), *La Salle and the Discovery of the Great West* (1869), *The Old Régime in Canada*

(1874), *Count Frontenac and New France under Louis XIV* (1877), *Montcalm and Wolfe* (1884), and *A Half-Century of Conflict* (1892). Employing a sweeping narrative style and relying heavily on primary sources (which often had to be read to him because of his bad eyesight), he traced the Anglo-French rivalry from the early 16th century to the close of the French and Indian War (1763).

Parkman also wrote *The Book of Roses* (1866), a horticultural work. He held a number of positions at Harvard: overseer (1868–71; 1874–76); professor of horticulture (1871–72); and a fellow (1875–88). In 1879 he helped found the Archaeological Institute of America.

Francis Parkman was a handsome man whose large jutting jaw and tight-set lips seemed to bespeak the indomitable will and stubborn determination with which he faced a life filled with physical disabilities, bouts of deep depression, and personal tragedy. Every inch the Boston patrician, he had a disdain for weakness and anything short of excellence, especially in himself. He saw life as a struggle; when not battling what he called the "enemy"—his bad eyesight and poor health—he pitted himself against nature in expeditions through the New England woods, Canada, and the old Northwest, and, of course, along the Oregon Trail, all of which became the basis for his vivid descriptions of physical conditions in the wilderness. Parkman's glorification of the masculine and active life can be seen throughout his histories, especially in such heroic figures as Wolfe and La Salle, who also struggled against tremendous odds.

Parkman's achievement in completing the multivolume narrative of France and England in North America, based on an examination of original sources, was a personal victory made the greater by the fact that his work continues to win readers and accumulates critical acclaim a hundred years after publication. His work is, however, not without flaw, for despite his appetite for original sources, he was preeminently a "literary historian" sharing many of the views and faults of his contemporaries **George Bancroft,** Prescott,

and Motley. The scope of his subject made him a national historian, and his love of the dramatic event and the heroic individual suggests his underlying romanticism. Like his contemporaries he saw human history as the progressive struggle for liberty against tyranny, authoritarianism, and superstitious ignorance. He saw the conflict between England and France for empire in the New World forest in terms of contending forces, personified by his characters. He saw feudalism arrayed against democracy, popery against Protestantism, "the sword against the plowshare," the priest, the soldier, and the noble reigning in Canada over an ignorant, lighthearted peasantry who knew nothing and cared nothing about popular rights and civil liberties, in contrast to Puritan New England, "where the love of liberty and the hatred of power burned with a sevenfold heat." Such a view led him to facile condemnation of Catholics and Catholicism and of monarchist institutions. At times he relied too heavily on paraphrasing weak secondary sources, and the effort to achieve dramatic effect gives too great a role to his particular heroes. Some volumes of his works are better than others. For example, *The Oregon Trail* is unsurpassed as a personal narrative and vivid account of Native American life and habits, particularly of the Sioux, yet Parkman's racial bias shows through in his treatment of Native Americans in *The Conspiracy of Pontiac* and elsewhere. To him the Native American was an uncivilizable savage, treacherous, although usually true to his own sense of honor. His *La Salle and the Discovery of the Great West* is among the great single-volume biographies in the English language. Parkman portrays the heroic and tragic figure of La Salle—who displayed almost superhuman strength and gallantry fighting overwhelming odds—with a sensitivity to the historical sufferings of the explorer that would do credit to the best psychological novelist. *Montcalm and Wolfe* is his best work, because of its dramatic content as the climax of the struggle in the siege and fall of Quebec, his characterization of the warm and homeloving Montcalm, pitted against the poetic Wolfe, both of whom would die on the Plains of Abraham.

Francis Parkman's work generally has survived that of his contemporaries, the "literary historians," not because he was ahead of his time, but simply because he did his job better; and despite his evident shortcomings, one can still read Parkman for his rich description, and exciting portrayal of past events, with the general assurance that the details, if not the interpretation and emphasis, are accurate. See Howard Doughty, *Francis Parkman* (1962).

DAVID D. VAN TASSEL

PARSONS, Talcott (b. Colorado Springs, Col., Dec. 13, 1902; d. Munich, Germany, May 8, 1979), SOCIOLOGIST, graduated from Amherst College (AB, 1924), and attended the London School of Economics (1924–25), where he studied under L. T. Hobhouse, Morris Ginsberg, and Bronislaw Malinowski. He received his PhD from the University of Heidelberg (1927). While in Germany he was introduced to the works of Max Weber, some of whose writings (*The Protestant Ethic and the Spirit of Capitalism*, 1930, and *The Theory of Social and Economic Organization,* 1947) he later translated into English. After leaving Heidelberg, Parsons taught as an instructor in economics at Amherst (1926–27) and at Harvard (1927–31). He soon switched to the sociology department at Harvard, and was promoted to professor of sociology in 1944. In 1946 he became the first chairman of the Department of Social Relations, which he had helped organize, and which combined sociology, psychology, and social anthropology under the aegis of a single department. He retired from Harvard in 1973. He also served as visiting professor at Columbia University (1933, 1935), the University of Chicago (1937), and Cambridge University (1953–54). He was a fellow at the Center for Advanced Study of the Behavioral Sciences (1957–58). Besides his translations of Weber, Parsons published numerous volumes on sociological theory. In these works, his primary concern was to create a single theoretical framework within which both specific and general aspects of society could be systematically classified. As a by-product of this approach,

he eschewed an emphasis on narrow, empirical studies. In the *Structure of Social Action* (1937), he examined, and attempted to merge into a single theoretical system, the works of Alfred Marshall, Emile Durkheim, Vilfredo Pareto, and Max Weber. He theorized that social action was voluntaristic behavior, basing his analysis primarily on a means-ends argument. Parsons's concern with social action was also reflected in his essay "Values, Motives and Systems of Action" (coauthor, Edward A. Shils), which was published in *Toward a General Theory of Action* (1951), a volume which the two scholars coedited. In this essay, Parsons described social action as operating in a frame of reference which included an actor, a situation, and the actor's orientation to the situation. He utilized this analysis to construct theoretical models of "the social system, the personality system, and the cultural system." In these schemes, Parsons emphasized a structural-functional analysis, concentrating on the roles assumed by actors in specific relationships. Among other works, he published *Structure and Process in Modern Societies* (1959), *Social Structure and Personality* (1964), and *Social Theory and Modern Society* (1968).

───※───

When the history of social thought of the 20th century is written, Talcott Parsons will probably be noted as that century's most important sociologist. Not only was he the dominant figure in forging the link between the European and American sociological traditions; he also framed the issues of general sociological theory in such a way that any self-respecting sociologist— whether intellectual friend or foe of Parsons— must face those issues in the terms that Parsons defined them. Parsons's mind was a restless one. He was never content with a theoretical formulation, however final it might seem at a given moment. He was always driven to reformulate, refine, revise, and reach new levels of generalization. As a result, his accumulated thought constitutes a huge architectural structure, layered many times with theoretical building blocks. To many his style was ponderous and impenetrable;

yet those who know his work well are continuously impressed with the lucidity, clarity, and incisiveness of his theoretical and empirical insights. Few have ever been so passionately devoted to the world of ideas as Parsons. Yet this devotion did not produce the expected distance from persons. He developed close relations with more students than any leading sociologist of his time. And while his personal demeanor was marked by shyness and occasional stiffness, he was a gentle and devoted man, who cultivated many deep and lasting friendships among his colleagues and students. See William Mitchell, *Sociological Analysis and Politics: The Theories of Talcott Parsons* (1967).

NEIL J. SMELSER

PARTON, Sara Payson Willis. See Fern, Fanny.

PATTON, George Smith, Jr. (b. San Gabriel, Calif., Nov. 11, 1885; d. Heidelberg, Ger., Dec. 21, 1945), MILITARY LEADER, studied at the Virginia Military Institute for one year before entering the U.S. Military Academy at West Point in 1904. After his graduation in 1909 he served with cavalry units in Illinois, Virginia, and Kansas. He competed in the modern pentathlon events at the 1912 Olympics in Stockholm, Sweden. He served as General **John J. Pershing**'s aide in the 1916 Mexican expedition against Pancho Villa and on Pershing's staff in France when the U.S. entered World War I. In France, Patton organized the American Tank Center at Langres and commanded the 304th Brigade of Tank Corps in the St.-Mihiel and Meuse-Argonne offensives, being seriously wounded in the latter engagement.

After World War I Patton spent twenty years with various cavalry units. In 1940 he returned to tank duty as commander of armored forces at Fort Benning, Georgia, and then at Indio, California. In November 1942, as part of Operation Torch, he headed the task force that landed on the Atlantic coast of French Morocco.

In March 1943, after the disastrous American defeat at the Kasserine Pass, Patton took command of the II U.S. Corps in Tunisia, won the battle of El Guettar, and helped push the Nazis into the showdown battle for North Africa. Relinquishing his command to General **Omar Bradley** in order to plan the attack on Sicily, Patton led the newly formed U.S. Seventh Army in the invasion. He speedily captured Palermo and Messina but fell into disfavor when he slapped two soldiers in a field hospital who were suffering from battle fatigue. However, he apologized to all involved. In the spring of 1944, he took command of the U.S. Third Army in England. After the Normandy invasion (June), he overran Brittany and swept eastward as far as Metz. He circled the Saar basin, crossed the Rhine in March 1945, and drove across central Germany and into Austria and Czechoslovakia by the end of the fighting on May 9, 1945. Promoted to a four-star general, Patton remained with occupation forces in Germany, but was transferred to the Fifteenth Army after his criticism of the Potsdam Conference agreements on denazification and his advocacy of military resistance to Russian expansion in Eastern Europe. He died from injuries received in an auto accident. Extracts from his wartime diary were published posthumously as *War as I Knew It* (1947).

Patton epitomized the fighting soldier in World War II. He exercised unique leadership by his ability to obtain the utmost—some would say more than the maximum—response from American combat troops. Through his charisma, exemplified by a flamboyant and well-publicized image, he stimulated, better than any other high-ranking U.S. army commander, American troops to an aggressive desire to close with and destroy the enemy. He personified the offensive spirit, the ruthless drive, and the will for victory in battle. General Eisenhower characterized Patton's army as "a fighting force that is not excelled in effectiveness by any other of equal size in the world." As the outstanding exponent of combat effectiveness, particularly with respect to the employment of armored forces—that is, the combined use of tanks, motorized infantry, and self-propelled artillery, closely supported by tactical aircraft—Patton brought the blitzkrieg concept to perfection. By the time of his death, he had become a legend.

Patton's profanity, ivory-handled pistols, and apparent egomania were part of the war mask he assumed to impress his soldiers. These highly visible trappings covered a thoroughly professional military man. A distinguished graduate of the Cavalry School, the Command and General Staff College, and the Army War College, he served as a commander at every echelon from platoon to field army and as a staff officer at division, corps, and War Department levels. He studied and worked at his profession harder than most officers. He was widely read in and familiar with the literature of war. He was a thoughtful innovator who believed that the ultimate virtue in warfare was action.

Early in his career he designed the saber adopted by the cavalry and was the army's first Master of the Sword. In Mexico he commanded what was probably the U.S. army's first motorized combat operation, leading his men directly from automobiles to an engagement that killed three prominent Villistas. In World War I he became the U.S. Army's foremost tank expert. Between the wars, he became proficient in amphibious warfare. In World War II he captured the imagination of the world by his successful audacity in battle. When he turned his Third Army 90 degrees in December, 1944, to stick the flank of the German Ardennes counteroffensive forces, a highly difficult but spectacular feat of arms, he demonstrated his technical mastery of the art of war.

Patton consciously modeled himself on General Pershing and insisted on individual physical fitness, extreme neatness in dress, rigorous unit training, sound operational planning, tactical mobility, and boldness in conception and execution. He was a noted horseman, racer, hunter, and polo player, a well-known swordsman, a competent sailor and navigator, an airplane pilot, an amateur poet, and a dedicated athlete and sportsman.

Although impulsive, politically naïve, and autocratic in temperament and outlook, Patton was completely loyal to his superiors and always concerned with the welfare of his subordinates. He was an authentic military genius. See Ladislas Farago, *Patton: Ordeal and Triumph* (1963), and Martin Blumenson, ed., *The Patton Papers* (2 vol., 1972–74).

MARTIN BLUMENSON

PAUL, Alice (b. Jan. 11, 1885, Moorestown, N.J; d. July 9, 1977, Moorestown, N.J.), REFORMER, the child of Quakers, Paul graduated Swarthmore College in 1905 and did graduate work at the New York University School of Social Work. She went to England in 1906, worked in a settlement house in London and was jailed three times for suffragist agitation. While in England she also attended the universities of London and Birmingham. Coming back to the U.S. in 1910, she received a PhD from the University of Pennsylvania (1912). That same year she became chairwoman of the Congressional Committee of the National Woman Suffrage Association. But she found the organization's approach too timid and in 1913 she helped establish the more militant Congressional Union for Woman's Suffrage, which merged in 1917 with the Woman's Party to form the National Woman's Party.

For the next thirty years Paul was a dominant figure in the movement to gain equal rights for women. After women gained the right to vote in 1920 with the passage of the Nineteenth Amendment, Paul became a lawyer in order to fight for woman's rights. She worked to have the first Equal Rights Amendment—the "Lucretia Mott Amendment"—introduced in Congress in 1923. When it failed to pass she turned her attention to championing woman's rights through the League of Nations.

In 1942, Paul was elected chairwoman of the National Woman's Party. Later, in this role, she succeeded in having an affirmation of the equal rights of women and men included in the preamble of the United Nations Charter. She lived to see an Equal Rights Amendment pass

Congress by a two-thirds margin in 1970 and sent to the states for ratification, where it eventually failed.

⁂

Alice Paul was a woman of courage and fortitude, ready and willing to use what many, even in her own movement, believed to be excessive and sometimes outrageous methods in pursuit of her cause. When Paul and her friend, Lucy Burns, returned from England in 1910 they brought with them the more militant methods of the British suffragists.

Paul was a dauntless leader known for her flamboyant, symbolic, publicity-generating methods—large parades, placards intruded into the staid halls of Congress, pickets at the White House, and the specter of women in jail on hunger strikes.

As a leader of the more militant wing of the suffragist movement, she and her tactics became an example for proponents of other political and social causes in the decades to come. She displayed her brilliance in attracting attention to her cause very early in her career when Woodrow Wilson arrived in Washington, D.C. by train for his first inauguration in March, 1913, and found few people to greet him. He was informed that the crowds he had expected were all watching a suffragist parade, guaranteed to be more exciting than seeing a president get off a train. Paul had planned the day perfectly—and typically: huge crowds in the city for the inauguration, plenty of rowdy toughs to harass the marchers undeterred by the police, army troops called out, publicity galore, and indignant Congressmen asking why the police couldn't or wouldn't protect lawful demonstrators.

When many who had been devoted to the woman suffrage movement went back to their everyday lives in 1920, Paul soldiered on because her goals went beyond merely the vote for women. She is remembered as one of feminism's earliest and most radical and intensely committed leaders. See Inez Irwin, *The Story of Alice Paul and the National Woman's Party* (1977).

ROY SORRELS

PAULING, Linus Carl (b. Portland, Ore., Feb. 28, 1901; d. Big Sur, Calif., Aug. 19, 1994), SCIENTIST, REFORMER, graduated from Oregon State College in 1922, and received his PhD in chemistry from the California Institute of Technology in 1925. He studied in Europe on a Guggenheim fellowship (1926–27) before becoming an assistant professor at Caltech in 1927. He became associate professor (1929), professor (1931), and chairman of the division of chemistry and director of the school's Gates and Crellin Laboratories in 1937. Pauling established his reputation as a leading authority in structural chemistry by applying the quantum mechanical concept of resonance to classical structural chemistry. He published *The Nature of the Chemical Bond and the Structure of Molecules and Crystals* in 1939. During World War II he worked in the explosives division and other divisions of the National Research Commission and also with the Medical Research Committee of the Office of Scientific Research and Development. He was a member of the Research Board for National Security (1945–46) and president of the American Chemical Society in 1949. Applying his theories of chemical bonds and molecular structure to the problems of biology as early as 1936, Pauling discovered the structure of several types of protein molecules (1951) and later worked on the relation between molecular abnormalities and such hereditary diseases as sickle-cell anemia. His work also contributed to the solution of problems in such fields as anesthesia and mental disease. In addition, his theoretical studies involved the application of quantum mechanics to the structure of molecules and the nature of the chemical bond, the extension of the theory of valence to include metals and intermetallic compounds, and the development of a theory of the structure of atomic nuclei and the nature of the process of nuclear fission. He was awarded the 1954 Nobel Prize in chemistry.

An early advocate of multilateral disarmament, Pauling warned of the dangers of nuclear fallout and urged an end to nuclear weapons testing. He was denounced, however, by Senator **Joseph R. McCarthy** for being pro-Communist and denied a passport in 1952. In 1957 Pauling circulated a petition signed by some eleven thousand scientists urging a halt to nuclear testing and then wrote a plea for peace, *No More War!* (1958). He received the 1962 Nobel Prize for peace for his activities. In 1963 Pauling left Caltech to join the Center for the Study of Democratic Institutions (Santa Barbara, Calif.) to work for peace and disarmament. He circulated a letter signed by eight Nobel Prize winners in 1965 urging American withdrawal from Vietnam. Pauling became a professor of chemistry at the University of California, San Diego, in 1967 and then at Stanford in 1969. After he retired from Stanford in 1971, he established the Linus Pauling Institute of Science and Medicine. He was joined in this venture by a former student, Dr. Arthur B. Robinson. He soon touched off a scientific controversy with a book, *Vitamin C and the Common Cold* (1970) in which he claimed that large doses of vitamin C would prevent or cure the common cold. He later enlarged his claims for vitamin C's curative powers by saying large doses could prevent cancer. A debate over his theories ensued, with some scientists charging there was no empirical evidence to support the vitamin C hypothesis for either colds or cancer and others urging intensive research into the question. A Mayo Clinic research report in 1979, published in the *New England Journal of Medicine*, found no evidence that patients with advanced cancer benefited from vitamin C. Similarly, many controlled studies found no cold preventive results from large dosages of the vitamin. Other disputes embroiled Pauling at the time. His former student, Dr. Robinson, having been dismissed from the Institute, charged that he, not Pauling, had done all the experimental research on vitamin C and its supposed health benefits. Nevertheless, despite all, Pauling continued to believe in the vitamin's power to prevent colds and cancer until his death. The author of numerous articles and papers, Pauling's books include *Introduction to Quantum Mechanics* (1935) and *General Chemistry* (1947).

Linus Pauling was one of those rare citizens of the world who have contributed to mankind in numerous areas, not only in science but in humanitarian provinces as well. These fundamental contributions were rewarded with Nobel prizes, numerous medals, honorary degrees, and many other expressions of merit. His work in theoretical and experimental chemistry, including applications to biology and medicine, may well be as valuable to the present century as Lavoisier's contributions were to the chemical revolution in the 18th century; moreover, he was to the modern world what Gandhi was to India—appropriately described as a "Supreme Peace Sponsor."

Pauling had to be characterized as mentally audacious, indeed brilliant, energetic, and exceedingly prolific—having produced about five hundred articles and eleven books, some in multiple editions. But to these characteristics must be added unusual perception and tenacity in the face of opposition. An extraordinary amount of his innovative work established the new direction of a particular subject. His ideas on the nature of the chemical bond, for example, were on the very frontiers of knowledge in chemistry, even though his controversial suggestions about the efficacy of vitamin C for the common cold and cancer received little experimental support. As was characteristic of much of his previous scientific work, in this instance some reputable evidence existed before his hypothesis, but it remained for Pauling's creative genius to recognize and refine hidden gold into a cogent argument. Right or wrong, he again stimulated a great deal of valuable research. See Thomas Hager, *Force of Nature: The Life of Linus Pauling* (1995).

H. LEWIS MCKINNEY

PEABODY, George (b. South Danvers [now Peabody], Mass., Feb. 18, 1795; d. London, Eng., Nov. 4, 1869), BUSINESS LEADER, PHILANTHROPIST, was apprenticed to a grocer in Danvers, Massachusetts, at age eleven. Thereafter he worked in Newburyport, Massachusetts, and in Georgetown, where (1814) he became a partner in the wholesale dry-goods house of Riggs and Peabody. In 1815 the firm moved to Baltimore, and in 1829 Peabody became the sole proprietor.

During these years Peabody made a number of business trips to England. In 1835, while in London, he helped negotiate a loan of $8 million for Maryland, which was then on the brink of bankruptcy. In 1836 he was an incorporator and president of the Eastern Railroad. The following year he moved to London and established the banking house of George Peabody & Co. His annual Fourth of July dinners in London became famous social affairs. In 1854 he made Junius Spencer Morgan a partner in his firm.

Throughout his life Peabody took an active interest in education. Some of his more important donations include: $1.5 million for the Peabody Institute in Baltimore; $2.5 million for the Peabody Institute in Peabody, Massachusetts; $1.5 million respectively to Harvard and Yale for museums; $1.4 million for an Academy of Science in Salem, Massachusetts; and $2.5 million to the city of London for the building of workers' housing. In 1867 he gave $3.5 million toward the establishment of the Peabody Education Fund for education in the South.

———

Characteristically, George Peabody made his millions quietly. While contemporary American millionaires were carving out empires in oil, steel, land, and railroads, Peabody cultivated his grocery business. A studious disciple of **Benjamin Franklin,** he blended hard work with frugality and punctuality. Peabody also followed Franklin in his pragmatic approach to business ethics.

Peabody's greatest significance lies in the magnitude of his philanthropy, its objects, and the methods with which he disbursed his wealth. George Peabody was the first large-scale American philanthropist. Anticipating the gifts of **Andrew Carnegie** and **John D. Rockefeller** by a full generation, Peabody also anticipated their philanthropic philosophies. The rich man, he believed, assumed along with his money the responsibility to give it away wisely. In the case

of an unmarried and childless man like Peabody the obligation must have seemed particularly strong.

When it came to selecting an object for his benefactions, Peabody exercised considerable imagination. Remembering his own humble origins, he poured millions into the cause of educating and culturally enriching the lower classes. He gave institutional form to the Jacksonian ideal of equality of opportunity. His giving sought projects such as libraries, schools, museums, and colleges in the attempt to provide people with the opportunities of helping themselves. The concept of a dole to the poor repelled this self-made man as it did Carnegie. Peabody's last great benefaction was to the Peabody Education Fund, which had the object of improving southern common schools. The gift was significant in two respects. First, Peabody gave the money without regard to the race of the beneficiary. Thus he became one of the first northerners to help with the social and cultural reconstruction of the South following the Civil War. The Fund was widely celebrated as a bridge between the former adversaries. It also heralded a new day for southern blacks. The second significance of the Peabody Education Fund was its use of an instrument of giving known today as the philanthropic foundation. Under this arrangement the philanthropist arranges for a board of trustees to dispense and administer a benefaction. In the case of Peabody's foundation, the second president, Jabez Lamar Monroe Curry, became the leading figure in southern education. See Franklin Parker, "George Peabody's Influence on Southern Educational Philanthropy," *Tennessee Historical Quarterly,* XX (1961), 65–74.

RODERICK NASH

PEALE, Charles Willson (b. Queen Anne's Co., Md., April 15, 1741; d. Philadelphia, Pa., Feb. 22, 1827), ARTIST, left school at thirteen and became a saddler. In 1762 Loyalist creditors, incensed at his participation in the Sons of Liberty, forced him out of business. He then took up painting, and artist John Hesselius gave him lessons. He also profited from an acquaintance with **John Singleton Copley,** whom he met while on a trip to New England. Peale had impressed a number of persons with his work, and they financed a trip to England. There he studied for two years (1766–68) with **Benjamin West.** Peale was the first painter to record the features of George Washington when he painted him at Mount Vernon in 1772. (He produced sixty canvases of Washington in all.) By 1776, when he settled in Philadelphia, his services were in great demand, and he painted portraits of a number of the members of the Continental Congress.

When the Revolution broke out, Peale enlisted as a private in the militia. He rose to captain and fought in the battles of Trenton and Princeton; he also was at Valley Forge.

Peale became interested in natural curiosities after the skeleton of a mastodon was found and excavated near his home—an event which he recorded on canvas—and with the help of others founded what eventually became the Philadelphia Museum. There he revolutionized the technique of handling specimens. Not content merely to stuff them, he posed them naturally against a realistic, painted background. In 1795 he was one of the organizers of the short-lived Columbianium, or American Academy of the Fine Arts, in Philadelphia, and in 1805 he helped found the Pennsylvania Academy of the Fine Arts.

―――――

Peale retained all through his long life a primitive strength of character and form, and he became the foremost continuer of the colonial tradition in face painting. In his preference for linear emphasis and literal-mindedness over the technical virtuosity and polite fictions of the British school of painting in which he was trained, he was the last and the greatest of the colonial limners with deep roots in the realism of the native American tradition. The poses of his figures have an underlying archaic stiffness that gives them a particular flavor by which they may be identified today.

Peale's likenesses lack the suavity of the polite neoclassical tradition of the Federal era, and as he advanced in years he became more and more plainly a survivor from an earlier time working within an increasingly antiquated technique. He had a faith in his own competence which was frequently justified by his works (although he is now recognized as one of the most uneven of painters); he was not afraid to exaggerate the ugliest feature in a face if he thought it the most typical. Peale's work was better in its kind than much in the newer way of painting of his day, but not many portrait buyers then thought so. In his technique not only was the color subordinated to line, but the line itself developed relatively little subtlety through the years: the figures it outlined remained inflexible, perhaps a little archaic.

Although Peale continued to paint until the end of his life—despite periodic announcements of his retirement—he gradually began to devote more time to other projects. He was an almost exact contemporary of Thomas Jefferson, with whom he shared many of the same qualities: an amazing versatility and ingenuity, an insatiable curiosity of mind, a dauntless Americanism. He was the Yankee jack-of-all-trades turned 18th-century gentleman, a craftsman so able that he became a universal genius. He left an enduring mark on almost every field he touched, yet never lost the humble directness of the American craft approach.

In addition to being a painter, Peale was a writer, saddler, silversmith, and scientist. He made a series of mezzotints after portraits of historical figures and transparencies for public celebrations, but the principal interest of his later years was a museum in which he attempted, as he wrote, to create "a world in miniature." For it Peale collected a great variety of birds and animals and mounted them in natural attitudes in habitat settings. He made frequent trips to the countryside to collect specimens of plants, minerals, fossils, and other natural curiosities. One of the museum's most popular exhibits was the mastodon which Peale himself helped excavate in Ulster County, New York. This was not the first American museum, but it was the first to be financially successful through three decades. Although Peale's aims were never fully realized—he hoped, for example, that the museum would become a national collection—he did manage to assemble more than 100,000 objects, which he arranged in an unusually orderly fashion for that period. These activities not only supported his family financially but also allayed his artisan need to work with his hands and satisfied his intellectual craving for knowledge.

In his later years Peale also made a number of inventions, including an improved kitchen chimney, a stove that consumed its own smoke, and a steam bath. He improved the polygraph for making copies of documents, made false teeth, and engaged in experimental farming.

Peale may not have been a great painter, because he remained quite content to follow popular taste in America. He could construct anything, mend anything; he was the spirit of the simple folk. That likable humility, that resolute will to adjust himself ungrudgingly to circumstances—these were traits consistently manifested throughout a long life by a man of remarkable goodness. In his own lifetime he had much to do with making and keeping Philadelphia a vigorous center of cultural influence. See Charles Coleman Sellers, *Charles Willson Peale* (1969).

WENDELL GARRETT

PEI, Ieoh Ming (b. Canton, China, April 26, 1917) ARCHITECT, emigrated to the United States to study architecture (1935) and graduated from the Massachusetts Institute of Technology in 1940. He received a Masters in Architecture from Harvard in 1946, studying under Walter Gropius, and went to work with the large contracting firm of Webb and Knapp, as director of architecture (1948–55). In 1955, he founded his own New York firm I. M. Pei & Partners, to be succeeded by Pei Cobb Freed & Partners of New York. Almost from the beginning, Pei designed large-scale, multipurpose projects, often associated with urban revitalization. From among nearly fifty major projects he has designed more than half have won major awards. He is best known for his design of the National Center for Atmospheric Research in Boulder, Colorado (1961–67), the East Building of the National Gallery of Art in

Washington, D.C. (1968–78), and the John F. Kennedy Library, Boston (1965–69). His most recent work includes The Regent Hotel on East 57th Street in Manhattan, the expansion and renovation of the Louvre in Paris, and the Morton H. Meyerson Symphony Center in Dallas. His work in his native China—he is a naturalized American Citizen—includes the Bank of China in Hong Kong as well as the Fragrant Hill Hotel in Beijing.

Arguably the most famous and celebrated architect in the world today, Pei has received almost every honor, award, medal, and prize that can be bestowed on a member of his profession. At last count it was over twenty. He has also been actively engaged as an adviser to foundations, corporations, and governments on matters relating to architecture. Among his many participations on government panels, his membership on the American Institute of Architecture (AIA) Task force on the West Front of the U.S. Capitol may have the most lasting significance.

———— ✑ ————

I.M. Pei's contribution to architecture and to his adopted country is to have defined the facade of The American Empire. It is not inappropriate that the "original" of this face is located not on the fringes of its empire, but near its secluded heart, in Boulder, Colorado. Nor is it odd that the architect is not a native born American, that the "Palace" is a federal research laboratory, that the site is exurban, or that it faces East. This is the National Center for Atmospheric Research (NCAR)—the project Pei most closely identified with. NCAR is a spiritualized physical expression of the Jeffersonian Gridiron's intersection with radial imperialism. It is an intersection in which "rooms" of the building have been inverted into streets—the streets themselves framing views. Thus, the facade of this empire is as much to the air as it is to people on the ground. It is as much an abstraction, a rebus, a puzzle as it is a "statement" to an "actual" viewer. When Pei imported this puzzle-face to Washington, D.C. in the East Building of the National Gallery of Art, his Rubic representation gained common currency. In effect, the East Building turns "art" into a vanguard, an *avant garde*, for the government research, the main body, hidden further West.

Pei sculpts the face of his America to champion architectural art as representation: Representation not only of the patron, the American empire, but of the complex relationships betwen art and the patron. See C. Wiseman, *I. M. Pei* (1990).

JOSEPH B. JUHASZ

PEIRCE, Benjamin (b. Salem, Mass., April 4, 1809; d. Cambridge, Mass., Oct. 6, 1880), MATH-EMATICIAN, ASTRONOMER, graduated from Harvard in 1829. After teaching at the Round Hill School, Northampton, Massachusetts (1829–31), he returned to Harvard as tutor in mathematics (1831–33). He was professor of mathematics and natural philosophy (1833–42) and Perkins Professor of Mathematics and Astronomy (1842–80).

During the 1830s and 1840s, Peirce published a series of textbooks, including *An Elementary Treatise on Plane and Spherical Trigonometry* (1840), *An Elementary Treatise on Algebra* (1837), and an *Elementary Treatise on Curves, Functions, and Forces* (I, 1841; II, 1846). He was also active as an astronomer. He played a major role in the foundation of the Harvard Observatory (1843), and gained his first great renown for his studies of the perturbations in the orbit of Uranus. During 1849–67 he served as consulting astronomer for the *American Nautical Almanac* (after 1860, the *Astronomical Almanac for the Use of Navigators*). He was also active in the U.S. Coast Survey, working as director of longitude determinations (1852–67), as superintendent of the agency (1867–74), succeeding Alexander D. Bache, and as consulting geometer (1874–80). In 1870 he led an expedition to Sicily to study a solar eclipse. Among Peirce's later writings were *System of Analytical Mechanics* (1855) and *Linear Associative Algebra* (1870).

———

Peirce was recognized as an outstanding mathematician, but one of his ability working in the United States in the mid-19th century lacked an audience of equally talented mathematicians with which to interact. Even his greatest work, *Linear Associative Algebra,* used definitions and classifications unknown to the world's mathematics community, which hurt its reception. He championed the theory of quaternions as an analytic tool while most (but not all) European mathematicians supported the use of vector analysis, which eventually was adopted internationally. More interested in science itself than in teaching, Peirce focused his textbooks on mathematics, not instruction, and these books, and his attempts at teaching, were unsuccessful except among the most mathematically inclined students.

Peirce was a major figure in the first community of professional scientists in America, and a leading member of the small, informal group known as the Lazzaroni, who aimed to control American science during the middle of the century. As such, Peirce was involved deeply in such efforts to get major support for science as the establishment of the National Academy of Sciences (1863). Extremely self-confident (his enemies would say arrogant), he assumed that he was the natural leader of the American mathematicians, and he thus alienated many scientists. For example, his theory of Saturn's rings (1851) gave little credit to George P. Bond of the Harvard Observatory, on whose observations Peirce had based his work, and who had developed independently a similar theory. And the controversy he stirred in 1846 and 1847, over what he felt was a misuse of the theory of the perturbations of the orbit of Uranus in the discovery of Neptune, earned him much international notoriety. See Nathan Reingold, ed., *Science in Nineteenth-Century America: A Documentary History* (1964).

MICHAEL M. SOKAL

PEIRCE, Charles Santiago Sanders (b. Cambridge, Mass., Sept. 10, 1839; d. Milford, Pa., April 14, 1914), PHILOSOPHER, graduated from Harvard in 1859 and began working on various projects for the U.S. Coast and Geodetic Survey in 1861. He received his MA from Harvard in

1862 and BSc (in chemistry) in 1863. He lectured at Harvard on the philosophy of science in 1864–65. Interested in mathematics, logic, science, and philosophy, Peirce delivered a paper before the American Academy of Arts and Sciences in 1867 suggesting improvements on George Boole's work on mathematics and logic and published a series of articles for the *Journal of Speculative Philosophy* in 1868. He lectured on philosophy at Harvard (1869–70), and was university lecturer on logic (1870–71). His astronomical observations from 1872 to 1875 were published in *Photometric Researches* (1878), the only book he published during his lifetime. He joined the Coast Survey in 1872 as a physicist and astronomer and was assistant computer for the nautical almanac in charge of gravity investigations in 1873. He was lecturer on logic at Johns Hopkins University during 1879–84.

In an 1878 article in *Popular Science Monthly*, "How to Make Our Ideas Clear," Peirce introduced pragmatism to American philosophy, but he did not approve of all the uses which his friend **William James** made of the ideas appearing in that essay. In 1891 he severed his ties with the Coast Survey so that he could concentrate on his study of logic. He wrote articles and reviews for such magazines as *The Nation* and *North American Review*, but he died impoverished and largely unrecognized. Collections of his many papers appeared posthumously as *The Collected Papers of Charles Sanders Peirce*, edited by Charles Hartshorne and Paul Weiss (vols. 1–6, 1931–35) and by Arthur W. Burks (vols. 7 and 8, 1958).

Peirce (pronounced "purse") was a philosopher's philosopher. James, **Josiah Royce,** and **John Dewey** all learned from him, and professional philosophers still find him suggestive. He was a pioneer in symbolic logic and in the philosophy of science, and he also developed an architectonic system of thought in which chance and probability, as well as regularity and uniformity, were basic constituents of the universe. But he is chiefly remembered for having originated

the pragmatic method that came to be largely identified with James.

Peirce's pragmatism held that the meaning of an idea lay in the idea's practical consequences, and Peirce insisted that this was the view of the scientist working in the laboratory and a scientific application of the biblical statement, "By their fruits ye shall know them." But he was bothered by the interpretation James made of his suggestion, rechristened his own philosophy "pragmaticism," and distinguished it sharply from James's pragmatism. James was too individualistic for Peirce; Peirce's preference, as a scientist, was for the public, objective, and conceptual rather than for the private, subjective, and existential. Whereas James defined ideas by their consequences for particular individuals, Peirce was interested in their consequences for the general public. Whereas James, moreover, tended to stress the particular consequences of ideas, Peirce emphasized the general consequences that give them continuing significance for the community. And whereas James, finally, in Peirce's opinion, overemphasized action when talking of practical consequences, for Peirce the consequences of an idea lay not simply in concrete action but in the general modes of behavior that one can conceive of in connection with that idea and which may be guides for everyone. Peirce hoped the pragmatic view would extend the scientific method into philosophy and eliminate ideas that had no publicly ascertainable significance.

But Peirce was no scientific dogmatist. Scientific formulations, he declared, were only tentatively true, not infallible, and the proper scientific attitude was to acknowledge frankly that human knowledge can never achieve absolute certainty. Peirce took a statistical view of scientific law; the laws of nature, he believed, were approximate, not absolute, regularities and operated with a high degree of probability, not invariantly. This meant that individual facts always departed to some extent from the laws governing their behavior and that chance and novelty played a real part in the universe. As an indeterminist, Peirce argued that mechanical determinism accounted neither for evolutionary development and increasing diversity in the world nor for the spontaneity involved in mental action. He was almost alone in his day in recognizing the statistical character of Darwin's law of natural selection, and he anticipated Heisenberg's principle of indeterminacy, according to which it is possible to generalize about the average behavior of multitudes of subatomic particles but impossible to measure the precise behavior of single particles.

Unlike James and Dewey, Peirce never achieved much public recognition. His style was technical and difficult, he never produced a full-scale exposition of his views, and his acerbic manner and somewhat idiosyncratic behavior prevented him from securing a permanent connection with the academic world. But Peirce's impulses were mainly social, and he never sought personal fame. His chief concern was that ideas he deemed important be given proper attention by scientists and philosophers. After his death his writings became a gold mine, as James predicted they would, for later generations of philosophers. See Joseph Brent, *Charles Sanders Peirce: A Life* (1993).

PAUL F. BOLLER, JR.

PENN, William (b. London, Eng., Oct. 14, 1644; d. Ruscombe, Berkshire, Eng., July 30, 1718), POLITICAL LEADER. Although of a strict parentage, Penn early developed a nonconformist attitude toward religious and social questions. After leaving Oxford in 1662 because of his principles, he was drawn to Quakerism. To broaden his interests, which centered almost entirely on religion, Penn's father sent him to France and Ireland on private business matters. In Ireland he showed considerable aptitude in quelling a local mutiny, and he studied law for a year. Nevertheless, he joined the Society of Friends around 1666. Penn went to prison in Ireland in 1667 and was imprisoned in the Tower of London in 1669 for publishing a nonconformist book, *The Sandy Foundation Shaken* (1668). While in prison he wrote his famous book *No Cross, No Crown* (1669) expounding the Puritan-Quaker morality of humility, nonviolence, and

trust in man. Arrested in 1670 along with fellow Quaker William Mead for preaching in a London street, Penn gained an acquittal by skillfully pleading on the grounds of liberties of person and expression of all Englishmen. A Whig and political liberal, he backed the rights of dissenters, religious toleration, frequent elections, and uncontrolled Parliaments in his speeches and tracts such as *The People's Ancient and Just Liberties Asserted* (1670) and *The Great Case of Liberty of Conscience* (1671). In 1677 he became interested in America while helping arrange the affairs of a Quaker colony in New Jersey, for which he helped draft a charter containing many libertarian provisions. Soon afterward Penn claimed that Charles II granted his wish that a debt which the king owed his father be discharged in the form of an enormous grant of land north of the colony of Maryland. And in 1681 Penn's desire to conduct a "holy experiment" in complete religious freedom was fulfilled when he was made the proprietor of what was to become Pennsylvania. The following year he became proprietor of Delaware as well, given to him by the Duke of York (later James II).

Pennsylvania grew rapidly. When James II sent Penn on a mission to Germany in 1687, he energetically advertised the colony, thus persuading numerous Germans to emigrate to America. Run largely by Quakers, the new colony assured freedom of religious expression, and outlawed capital punishment for all crimes except murder and treason. Especially notable, also, in contrast with other colonies, was Pennsylvania's friendly relations with the Native Americans.

Penn had gone to Pennsylvania in 1682, but in less than two years the political situation in England had deteriorated so badly, and a border dispute with Maryland had become so acute, that he was forced to return to England in 1684. A staunch friend and backer of James II, Penn was undermined by the Revolution of 1688, his loyalty to William and Mary was questioned several times before the Privy Council, and he was deprived of his proprietorship. Nevertheless, he went back to Pennsylvania in 1699. There he found a strong resentment on the part of the legislature against the power of the proprietor and Penn's often inept deputy governors. A new charter of 1701 gave more powers to a single-chamber legislature while reducing the power of the proprietor and his governor to that of owning unclaimed land and a veto, which was subject to coercion by the legislature. He returned to England in 1701 and was sent to debtors' prison for nine months in 1708 because of the corruption of Philip Ford, a former steward who had squandered his money. In 1712, after some years of traveling in Europe as a Quaker missionary, and after unsuccessful efforts to sell his proprietorship to the crown, Penn suffered a stroke which left him incapacitated. Some of his many writings include *An Address to Protestants of All Persuasions* (1679), *A Letter to the Free Society of Traders* (1683), and *An Essay Towards the Present and Future Peace of Europe* (1693).

William Penn's conversion, his conviction that he had a deep communion with the Christ within, gave him a joyfulness, self-confidence, and sense of purpose which he never lost. His conversion was also a statement of political and social protest, of alienation from Restoration society. Penn became a plain Friend in an age when Quakerism and simplicity were rightly understood as revolutionary doctrines. He fought for religious and civil liberties, and held to his belief that the world could be changed for the better, and he could have something to do with changing it.

His politics were at first derived from his desire for religious freedom as a necessary condition for the work of the "light within." A member of the privileged classes, he was perhaps particularly irked by legal restrictions on his freedom to believe, worship, and speak, and in his theoretical writing he identified religious liberty with English civil rights to life, liberty, and property, thus giving a secular thrust to a primarily religious movement. His ideas were not, on the whole, very original. He lived in an era when many sources for a nonconforming politics were available. He was, however, unusually hard-dri-

ving, energetic, sometimes reckless, willing to combine the roles of theoretician and politician. He engaged in a wide variety of political and religious activities, and was missionary, pamphleteer, colonizer, campaigner, lobbyist, courtier, proprietor.

A view of Penn as the complete radical is, however, misleading. He was always anxious to find historical precedents which would fix his conception of religious liberty in a solid English tradition. His services to James II, who seemed to promise religious liberty, suggest that the connection between religious liberty and other civil liberties was not entirely necessary to Penn, and this apparent repudiation of his earlier Whiggism worried his admirers. Despite his participation in the Friends' plain style—in itself, a revolution in manners which had egalitarian implications— Penn could not be called a democrat. He had a lively sense of his own importance, particularly after he became proprietor of Pennsylvania, and was very sensitive to challenges to his position and power.

Penn liked money and although he was certainly sincere about his ambitions for a "holy experiment" in Pennsylvania, he also expected to get rich. He was, however, extravagant, a bad manager and businessman, and not very astute in judging people and making appointments. Philip Ford, his agent, probably defrauded him for years, but Penn had signed so many accounts without study that even after three years in Chancery, nothing was proved.

Penn was gregarious, had many friends, and was good at developing the useful connections which protected him through many crises. Both his marriages were happy, and he would describe himself as a family man, although public affairs took him away from home a great deal and he was disappointed in those children whom he knew as adults. The self-pity which permeates his later correspondence does not completely obscure his essential optimism, nor can the failures in management in his late years obscure his contributions to the development of religious toleration in England and America, and the growth in Pennsylvania of a distinctively heterogeneous and vigorous colonial society. See Catherine Owens Peare, *William Penn: A Biography* (1957).

MARY MAPLES DUNN

PERKINS, Frances (b. Boston, Mass., April 10, 1880; d. New York, N.Y., May 14, 1965), POLITICAL LEADER, REFORMER, waas graduated from Mt. Holyoke College in 1902. After doing social work for the Congregational Church and teaching in a high school, she joined **Jane Addams** briefly at Hull House in the Chicago slums. In 1907 she became secretary of the Philadelphia Research and Protective Association, a group organized to assist immigrant working girls. After further study at the University of Pennsylvania, she received an MA in social economics from Columbia in 1910, and then became executive secretary of the Consumers' League of New York. She also lobbied in the state legislature for social reforms. She served as an investigator for the New York State Factory Committee (1912–13) and as executive secretary of the Committee on Safety (1912–17). During World War I she was director of the New York Council of Organization for War Service. Governor **Alfred E. Smith** appointed her to the New York Industrial Commission in 1919. After serving as director of the Council on Immigrant Education (1921–23), she became a member of the State Industrial Board in 1923 (chairman, 1926). Upon taking office as governor of New York in 1929, Franklin Roosevelt made Perkins state industrial commissioner, and when he became president of the U.S. in 1933, he appointed her secretary of labor, the first woman to serve in the cabinet.

As secretary, Perkins helped draft much New Deal legislation and dealt with many severe labor disputes, such as the 1937 automobile sitdown strike. As chairman of the President's Committee on Economic Security, she helped draft the Social Security Act of 1935. She also worked on the National Labor Relations Act (1935) and the Wages and Hours Act (1938) and helped standardize state industrial legislation. She resigned in 1945 but served as U.S. civil service commissioner until 1953. After lecturing at the University of Illinois (1953) and at Salzburg, Austria (1955), she became a lecturer at the School of Industrial Relations at Cornell in 1956 and remained there until her death. The author of many reports and books, Perkins's writings include: *People at Work* (1934) and *The Roosevelt I Knew* (1946).

Roosevelt's appointment of Frances Perkins as secretary of labor in 1933 was a milestone in the history of women's march toward full citizenship. It was based primarily, however, on his recognition of the ability she had shown as head of the Labor Department in New York State during his governorship and as chairman of the state Industrial Board during the administration of his predecessor, **Alfred E. Smith**.

Along with many distinguished women of her time, Perkins was drawn to social work, applying herself particularly to a study of the living and working conditions of women in the labor force. Her most striking achievement as a lobbyist for the New York Consumers' League was to win passage of a law limiting the working hours of women in industry to fifty-four a week. In that same year, 1911, the Triangle Shirtwaist Company fire, in which 146 persons, most of them young girls, lost their lives, lent special value to her knowledge of hazardous conditions in factory buildings.

As an aftermath of the tragedy the New York state legislature set up a factory investigating committee to look into violations of existing laws and propose more effective legislation, with **Robert F. Wagner,** then state senator, as chairman, and Alfred E. Smith, then speaker of the assembly, as vice chairman. As one of the investigators for the committee, Perkins accompanied Smith on his travels throughout the state in the course of the inquiry, and most of her proposals for fire prevention were incorporated in the remedial measures that Smith and Wagner pushed through the legislature.

It was her association with Smith during this period that led to her appointment as a member of the State Industrial Board when he was elected governor in 1918. Her duties in this post were to formulate codes with regard to factory conditions and to act as referee in workmen's compensation cases, duties which she performed so ably that her rulings were universally upheld in the courts, even when they broke new ground.

Hailed by women's organizations and liberal groups all over the country, her appointment as secretary of labor in Roosevelt's cabinet won only a lukewarm reception from organized labor, whose leaders would have preferred one of their own, and of the male sex, moreover, to hold that office. Nevertheless her achievements, particularly in the early years of the New Deal, were noteworthy. Not only did she help draft some of the more important social legislation of that period, but she also kept the president informed on crucial labor problems, while at the same time strengthening the Bureau of Labor Statistics within her own department, making it one of the more respected branches of the government. On one occasion she won widespread acclaim for her spunk and resourcefulness. While touring western Pennsylvania to obtain information on NRA codes for the steel industry she was denied use of the town hall or a public park for a meeting with steelworkers in Homestead, long a company town and the scene, formerly, of fierce labor disturbances. She thereupon led the way to the United States post office, where as a federal officer she felt free to address the men and listen to their grievances.

With the passage of the new labor laws her role in the Roosevelt administration became a minor one, in part because the labor struggle had moved out of the field of legislation to the plane of union organization, and in part because the new agencies created to adjust labor problems were made independent of her department—much against her will, to be sure. She remained secretary of labor, however, until Roosevelt's death, serving longer than any other member of his cabinet.

The professionals of the trade unions and the political parties were mistakenly suspicious of Frances Perkins as a type of reformer and uplifter. In reality she was a keen administrator with a strongly practical turn of mind, never an idealistic radical. Her objective spirit comes out strongly in her fine memoir, *The Roosevelt I Knew,* one of the most discerning books about him written by that president's intimates. See *Newsweek,* LXV (May 24, 1965), 37.

MATTHEW AND HANNAH JOSEPHSON

PERKINS, George Walbridge (b. Chicago, Ill., Jan. 31, 1862; d. Stamford, Conn., June 18, 1920), BUSINESSMAN, POLITICAL LEADER, had only a grammar school education. In 1877 he began working as a clerk in his father's insurance agency. In 1886, after his father's death, he sold insurance in the West for the New York Life Insurance Co.; achieving an immense and rapid success, he was made a division chief (1887) and then a vice president of New York Life (1892). In the latter capacity he reorganized the agency system of the company and greatly expanded its volume of business.

In 1901 Perkins became a partner in the banking house of J. P. Morgan and Co. He retained his vice presidency of New York Life, serving as chairman of its finance committee. As a result, during the New York Armstrong investigation of the insurance business (1905) he was accused of conflict of interest, since in some transactions he had acted as both buyer and seller of securities. Although he had not profited from these transactions, he was forced to resign from New York Life. While a member of the House of Morgan, Perkins served as chairman of the finance committee of the Morgan-controlled U.S. Steel Corporation. He also engineered the creation of the International Harvester Co. (1902), and he played an important role in **J. P. Morgan**'s successful termination of the bank panic of 1907, and in many other Morgan operations. He was a major figure in the negotiations between U.S. Steel and other Morgan combines and the Bureau of Corporations which led to the Theodore Roosevelt administration's policy of allowing large corporations to avoid antitrust suits by working out agreements (détentes) with the Bureau.

Perkins resigned from the House of Morgan at the end of 1910 to devote himself to publicizing his ideas about industrial cooperation. Bigness was essential, he argued, but large combines should be subject to federal supervision in the public interest. When the Taft administration undertook a series of antitrust suits against U.S. Steel and other corporations, Perkins became active in Theodore Roosevelt's campaign for the 1912 Republican presidential nomination. When this effort failed and Roosevelt formed the Progressive party to contest the election, Perkins became chairman of the party executive committee and contributed large sums to the campaign. After Roosevelt's defeat in the election by the Democratic candidate, Woodrow Wilson, Perkins remained in charge of party affairs, fighting off efforts of the "trust-busting" wing of the Progressives to alter party policy toward corporations. In the 1916 presidential campaign, Perkins supported the Republican, **Charles Evans Hughes,** after Roosevelt refused the Progressive nomination. But Perkins remained in the Progressive party. When the United States entered World War I, he became head of the New York City Food Committee. He also served as chairman of the YMCA finance committee, raising large sums for work among American troops in France. In 1918 he went to France to supervise this work, which was carried out under the auspices of the United War Work Council.

Perkins was prominent in the development of the Palisades Interstate Park, serving on the park commission from 1901 until his death and raising money for its development.

❧

George W. Perkins had three chronologically distinct careers, being first an insurance man, second a banker, and third a political leader. Although he lacked much formal education and began life without either money or high social status, he possessed many remarkable qualities that brought success to almost everything he touched. As an organizer and administrator he had few equals. But he was no bureaucrat; his brilliant balance of imagination and industriousness, of élan and energy, captivated some of the most powerful and individualistic men of his generation—J.P.

Morgan and Theodore Roosevelt to name only the most famous examples. Perkins "inherited" his position in the insurance business. When his father, Ohio agent for the New York Life Insurance Co., died in 1886, Perkins tried to persuade the president of New York Life to let him take over the agency although at that time he was only twenty-five and earning less than $1500 a year. The president, William H. Beers, refused, but commissioned him to sell insurance in Indiana; within a matter of months he had sold so many policies that the company made him a district supervisor, and from there he rose like a rocket and in the process transformed New York Life into the largest insurance company in the country. He replaced the agency system with a network of branch offices, established a pension plan for the salesmen, successfully invaded the European market, and—most important—he began investing the vast sums controlled by the company in the enormously profitable business of underwriting foreign securities.

This last achievement led J. P. Morgan, who preferred to swallow competitors rather than to fight with them, to offer him a partnership. In the House of Morgan Perkins's great achievements were in remodeling the internal structure of Morgan's creation, the United States Steel Corporation, in order to ensure banker control of the business, and in negotiating the mergers that established the International Harvester Co. He was also a pioneer in the movement to rationalize the great corporations by stabilizing prices and wages, avoiding labor-management conflicts through paternalistic policies, and working out both intraindustry agreements to "regulate" competition and détentes with the Justice Department to avoid antitrust suits. He believed firmly that corporate giantism was both inevitable and desirable, but he recognized that the power that accompanied great size must be controlled in the general interest.

This view, of course, was shared by Theodore Roosevelt, and it was Roosevelt's decision in 1912 to form the Progressive party that led Perkins to devote his major attention to politics. While this career made him better known than the earlier two, it was not crowned with the same degree of success, and it brought him almost no personal satisfaction. Indeed, while each stage of his development seemed a step upward toward fortune, influence, and fame, each was progressively less satisfying to him and less significant from the standpoint of history.

Perkins was at heart a reformer. He saw the insurance business as an essentially philanthropic occupation and great corporations as institutions designed to enhance both the material well-being and the security of capitalistic society. And of course he believed that Roosevelt's Bull Moose party stood for reform. The great mistake of his life was probably his decision to join the House of Morgan. It turned him for a season almost exclusively to the making of money, and when he abandoned it for reform politics the "taint" of having been a member of the most powerful private banking firm in the world haunted his every step and burdened the whole Progressive party. Therein lies the closest approach to tragedy in his productive life. See John A. Garraty, *Right-Hand Man: The Life of George W. Perkins* (1960).

JOHN A. GARRATY

PEROT, H. Ross (b. Texarkana, Texas, June 27, 1930), BUSINESSMAN, grew up in east Texas during the Great Depression. He attended Texarkana Junior College before entering the U.S. Naval Academy. He graduated in 1953, and that year married Margor Birmingham. Perot resigned from the Navy as soon as his required tour of duty ended in 1957 and joined International Business Machines (IBM), quickly becoming one of the company's top computer salesmen. When IBM refused to adopt Perot's idea that the company should sell its customers data processing services as well as hardware and software, Perot quit. In 1962, he founded Electronic Data Systems, Inc. (EDS), in Dallas, Texas, to provide software and data processing services for businesses and government agencies handling huge amounts of data. Perot's business grew quickly. Using his skills as a salesman and lobbyist, by the mid-1960s Perot transformed

EDS into the prime Medicare and Medicaid contractor in Texas, California, and other states. In 1965 EDS's profits were $26,000; in 1968 profits amounted to $2.4 million. When Perot took his company public in 1968, he made $200 million overnight and was on his way to becoming a billionaire. In 1984, Perot sold his stock in EDS to General Motors for $2.5 billion, and entered into an alliance with the automaker that ended in acrimony in 1984, with Perot departing with a $700 million settlement. Subsequently, after a period in which he promised not to go into competition with EDS, Perot founded Perot Systems, Inc., as a rival to his old firm.

Perot increasingly became a public figure during the 1970s and not merely because of his great wealth, though that greatly helped. In 1970, he made a highly publicized Christmas flight to Southeast Asia with gifts for American prisoners of war in Vietnam. The North Vietnamese refused to let him fly to Hanoi, but the trip dramatized the plight of the POWs and forever identified Perot with their cause. In 1979, he financed a spectacular secret mission headed by former Colonel Arthur (Bull) Simmons to rescue two EDS employees held in Iranian jails. The mission did not unfold according to plan but the employees slipped out of prison anyway when a mob attacked the place where they were being held. Perot's name and reputation were greatly enhanced by this incident when the author Ken Follett turned it into a best-seller, *On The Wings of Eagles*, starring the Texas billionaire.

In the mid-1980s Texas Democratic Governor Mark White recruited Perot to help overhaul the state public school system. Perot, attracted more and more to public life, used his formidable powers as a salesman to persuade an initially skeptical public to adopt tougher academic standards, especially the "no pass, no play" rule for high school athletes. Other education initiatives did not fare so well. However, Perot's reputation as a no-nonsense businessman willing to make hard decisions was preserved. When he began his bid for the presidency as an independent in 1992, Perot was thus perceived by many, tired with the gridlock of traditional party politics, as a doer, a down-to-earth, nuts and bolts businessman willing both to acknowledge the dreadful shape of the economy and to call for tough reforms that would lower the ever-growing federal budget deficit. By June 1992, Perot, running as a third party candidate, led his rivals, President Bush and Bill Clinton, with 37 percent of the votes in one major poll. But when he unaccountably withdrew from the race in July (for what he cited as threats to his family) his support dropped significantly. When he reentered the race in October he restored some of his stature in the presidential debates that were held between him and the major candidates and finished with a respectable 19 percent of the vote. Perot's personal political organization, United We Stand, into which he has poured millions of dollars, remained in being following the election. Perot used it as a vehicle in his unsuccessful campaign to defeat Senate ratification of the North American Free Trade Agreement (NAFTA) and to defeat other proposals, such as Clinton's failed national medical insurance program. In 1996, Perot appeared to be gearing up either for another third party run at the White House or to shape the agendas of the two major parties without actually entering the race.

⸻

By his ability to win more presidential votes than any other third-party candidate in eighty years, Ross Perot established credibility. He also demonstrated that with enough money a candidate who uses television well can circumvent not only the party system but the need for personal campaigning. Perot's appearances were infrequent in 1992. The hectic city-to-city grind that his Democratic and Republican opponents went through was never his. He was perfectly positioned—and rested—to present his views.

It is impossible to imagine a candidate without the personal fortune of Perot having such media access, but Perot's candidacy was more than a result of the formula which says money plus television equals electoral success. Perot was in essence a suburban populist. He understood that the Wall Street triumphs and the leveraged buyouts of the 1980s had, in fact, left out much of

middle-class America and that deregulation in such areas as the savings and loan industry had been a disaster. Perot was free, in a way that the Republican Party was not, to acknowledge these flaws in the economy.

Perot did not, however, propose a new egalitarianism or a return to an enlarged welfare state. His focus on reducing the debt, on tax breaks for small business, on government-business cooperation rested on faith in the traditional free enterprise system, the same system that made him rich and successful. What he proposed was a return to a business ethic that prized efficiency and personal enterpise and saw large corporations like General Motors and IBM as relics of the past. The poor, under Perot economics, would benefit from an efficient, opportunity economy, not from policies in the New Deal or Great Society tradition.

As a third-party candidate, Perot was never subjected to the close scrutiny that George Bush and Bill Clinton were in 1992. In addition, he was the beneficiary of protest votes that could be cast on his behalf by voters free from the worry that a man who had never been elected to any office and did not have any track record might actually become president.

But there can be little doubt that in a nation in which suburbs now contain the largest bloc of voters the Perot candidacy has enormous promise. It recognizes the deadness of the Reagan conservatism of the 1980s—especially on such personal freedom issues as abortion. And it recognizes the desire for government that is efficient but unburdened by heavy entitlement programs. Perot fills a major niche that at the end of the twentieth century neither major party can fill without alienating its die-hard supporters. See Todd Mason, *Perot: An Unauthorized Biography* (1990).

NICOLAUS MILLS

PERRY, Matthew Calbraith (b. Newport, R.I., April 10, 1794; d. New York, N.Y., March 4, 1858), NAVAL LEADER, entered the navy as a midshipman (1809), serving on the *Revenge*, under the command of his brother, **Oliver Hazard**

Perry. During the War of 1812 he sailed under Commodore John Rodgers in the frigate *President* and was advanced to acting lieutenant (1813). After several leaves, he returned to the navy in 1819 as first lieutenant of the corvette *Cyane*, which escorted the first colony of repatriated American blacks to the west coast of Africa. In 1821 he conveyed the first U.S. commissioner to Liberia in his own first command, the schooner *Shark*. During 1822–27 he was on duty in the West Indies and the Mediterranean, rising to master commandant (1826).

After commanding the sloop *Concord* on a voyage to Russia and in the Mediterranean, in 1833 Perry was appointed second officer of the New York navy yard. He was promoted to captain in 1837, and given command of the *Fulton II*, one of the first steam-powered vessels. In that same year Congress adopted Perry's plan for a naval apprentice system (first formulated in 1824) to help train new men. This system was abandoned, however, after the 1842 mutiny on the schoolship *Somers*. In 1841 he became commandant of the New York navy yard, acquiring the courtesy rank of commodore. He commanded the African squadron (1843–45), the principal duty of which was to suppress the slave trade. When the U.S. Naval Academy at Annapolis was opened (1845), Perry helped prepare its first syllabus.

During the Mexican War Perry became second in command of the Gulf Squadron and then commanded the squadron when it supported General **Winfield Scott**'s attack on Veracruz (March 1847). As vice commodore and commodore he conducted several raids against the Mexican coast from Tampico to Yucatán. During 1848–52 he was on special assignment in New York, where he managed the construction of transatlantic mail steamships.

In 1852 President Fillmore sent Perry to negotiate a commercial treaty with Japan. After opening American relations with Okinawa and visiting the Bonin Islands, in July 1853 his squadron reached Yedo Bay (now Tokyo Bay). Perry impressed the Japanese shogun, who agreed to deliver the president's message to the emperor. Perry then sailed to Macao, but returned in February 1854 with a larger squadron. Following a number of conferences at Yokohama, the U.S. and Japan signed a treaty of peace, amity, and commerce (March 31, 1854), giving the U.S. trading rights at certain ports. Perry is thus said to have "opened up" Japan to American commerce. His report of this expedition is recorded in his *Narrative of the Expedition of an American Squadron to the Chinese Seas and Japan* (3 vols., 1856).

The younger Perry brother is inevitably and rightly best known as the American officer who opened Japan to the commerce of the United States and the world. He was thus the principal instrument of a peculiarly decisive step toward the fateful destiny of the United States as a Pacific Ocean and Asian power. Without Perry as the instrument of this step, furthermore, the destiny might not have turned out quite as it did, for Perry's haughty though amiable firmness and persistence in dealing with the Japanese were probably indispensable to America's being the power that penetrated the isolated island empire. Still, Perry in Japan was an instrument of policy rather than an originator, and thus he remains a secondary historical figure. Since **S. E. Morison** has granted him a far better biography than most secondary figures receive, however, we are well able to judge Perry's other claims to attention. Principal among these was his work as a builder and reformer of the early navy. With foresight and persistence but mixed success, he sought to improve education for officers and training for seamen. More successfully, he helped move the American navy from the age of sail into that of steam. In 1835 he helped persuade the Navy Department to resurrect an 1816 authorization to build a new steam warship, *Fulton II*, to replace the earlier experimental *Demologos* or *Fulton*. He watched over the building of the ship, and although the vessel proved to be badly designed and underpowered, as her captain he got her to perform well enough and publicized her well enough to persuade Congress to authorize three additional steam frigates in 1839. These ships, *Mississippi*, *Missouri*, and *Princeton*, became the nucleus of the steam navy. From the *Mississippi* Perry commanded the Gulf Squadron in the Mexican War, and the same ship formed part of his Japan expedition, which he commanded from the *Susquehanna,* a larger steamer built after the first of the type had proved its utility against Mexico. See Samuel Eliot Morison, *"Old Bruin": Commodore Matthew C. Perry, 1794–1858* (1967).

RUSSELL F. WEIGLEY

PERRY, Oliver Hazard (b. South Kingston, R.I., Aug. 20, 1785; d. near Port of Spain, Trinidad, Aug. 23, 1819), NAVAL LEADER, entered the navy as a midshipman (1799) and served in the West Indies during the naval war with France. During 1802–6 he was stationed in the Mediterranean, and fought in the Tripolitan War, rising to lieutenant in 1807. He next helped construct gunboats in Rhode Island and Connecticut, and commanded a squadron (1807–9) to enforce the Embargo Act. In 1809 he was given command of the *Revenge.* Patrolling the coast of the southern states, he helped recover the *Diana,* an American ship sailing under British colors (1810). Later the *Revenge* ran aground during a fog, but Perry was cleared of negligence (1811).

When the War of 1812 broke out, Perry commanded a small gunboat squadron in Rhode Island waters, with promotion to the rank of master commandant. After several requests for a more active post, early in 1813 he was given command of naval forces on Lake Erie. He spent the spring and summer of 1813 at Presque Isle, the harbor of the modern city of Erie, Pennsylvania, where he built, assembled, equipped, and trained a small fleet. In August 1813 Perry sailed out from Erie harbor to challenge the British Lake Erie squadron under Commander Robert H. Barclay. In September Barclay ventured from his base at Malden (Amherstburg), Ontario, and Perry emerged from Put-in-Bay off the Ohio shore to meet him. After heavy fighting, Perry destroyed the British vessels. This victory gave the U.S. control of Lake Erie and permitted the recapture of the American Northwest from the British. It enabled General William Henry Harrison to foray into upper Canada and win the battle of the Thames there. It was the foundation of the U.S. claim to retain the Northwest at the peace convention at Ghent.

Promoted to captain, in 1816–17 Perry was on duty in the Mediterranean, commanding the *Java.* He was plagued by a controversy with Captain Jesse D. Elliott over credit for the victory at Lake Erie and in 1818 demanded a court-martial of Elliott. When President Monroe suspended the proceedings, Perry decided to resign his commission, but he accepted one more mission. In May 1819 he was given command of a small fleet to visit the republics of Venezuela and Buenos Aires and persuade them to stop countenancing pirates who preyed upon U.S. commerce. In the Orinoco River, Perry contracted yellow fever, of which he died on board his flagship *John Adams.*

Oliver Hazard Perry's place in history depends upon a single event, the battle of Lake Erie; but his fame is well deserved nevertheless, because American retention of the old Northwest turned upon his exploit. In 1813 this region was well on its way to being lost, after the British capture of Detroit and Fort Dearborn at the site of Chicago the previous year and subsequent additional American defeats. The key to reconquering the Northwest and making it secure was naval control of Lake Erie, but at the beginning of 1813 the British held that control with a squadron of six small ships. When Perry arrived at Presque Isle, he first had to build a squadron for himself. Spurring on the shipbuilders Daniel Dobbins and Noah Brown and traveling to Pittsburgh to assure the arrival of essential equipment from there and the East Coast, Perry supervised the construction, with a maximum work force of two hundred men, of two five-hundred-ton brigs and four sixty-ton armed schooners in a few months, a feat which **Samuel Eliot Morison** writes "thrusts into the shade some of the much vaunted feats of World War II shipbuilders." This, and effecting the escape to Presque Isle of five ships bottled up by the British at Black Rock on the Niagara, was Perry's first great accomplishment:

the creation of a fleet. Having done that and having managed to float his brigs into deep water across the shallow bar of Presque Isle harbor by means of an ingenious "camel" arrangement, Perry brought the British to battle and achieved his second major accomplishment: his planning of the battle and carrying through the plan in such a way that he led his ships into action at close quarters, where his superior weight of short-range guns could tell. His third and climactic accomplishment was his inspirational leadership, which survived the loss of his flagship *Lawrence*. Rowed with his flag proclaiming "Don't give up the ship" from *Lawrence* to *Niagara,* he led his squadron to victory from the deck of the latter, and ensured his fame by penning his dramatic dispatch to General Harrison: "We have met the enemy and they are ours." See Charles J. Dutton, *Oliver Hazard Perry* (1935).

RUSSELL F. WEIGLEY

PERSHING, John Joseph (b. near Laclede, Mo., Sept. 13, 1860; d. Washington, D.C., July 15, 1948), MILITARY LEADER, graduated from the U.S. Military Academy (1886), and served with the cavalry as a second lieutenant during the Indian campaigns in the Southwest and South Dakota (1886–90). While assigned as an instructor of military science at the University of Nebraska (1891–95) he earned an LLB (1893). During 1897–1898 he taught military tactics at West Point. In the Spanish-American War he served in Cuba (1898), and during 1898–1903 he organized the Bureau of Insular Affairs and helped suppress the Philippine insurrection. He was a military attaché in Japan in 1905 during the Russo-Japanese War. A year later President Theodore Roosevelt passed over 862 officers to promote Pershing from captain to brigadier general.

In 1906 Pershing returned to the Philippines, remaining there until 1913, at which time he was given command of the 8th Brigade, stationed at the Presidio, San Francisco. Famous for his discipline and stern bearing, he earned the sobriquet "Black Jack" for commanding black troops. Indeed, his real nickname in the old Army was

"Nigger Jack," which the newspapers of the time changed to "Black." When the Mexican rebel "Pancho" Villa raided Columbus, New Mexico (1916), and killed seventeen American citizens, President Wilson sent Pershing in pursuit of him. But under pressure from the Mexican government Wilson ordered his forces recalled after they had broken up Villa's band (1917).

When the U.S. entered World War I in April 1917, Pershing was made commander of the American Expeditionary Force (AEF). Shortly after the AEF reached France (June 1917), it took up positions near Verdun (Oct. 1917). Pershing, now a full general, insisted that the American forces should serve as independent units and not be amalgamated with the French and British. However, during the German offensive of March-June 1918, he released some of his troops to inter-allied commander Ferdinand Foch. And in June 1918 the AEF, under Pershing's command, drove the Germans back from Château-Thiery and Belleau Wood, an action which helped turn the tide of the war. Three months later the AEF and the French defeated the Germans at St. Mihiel (Sept. 1918). Both armies then pushed on into the Argonne Forest and moved against the "Hindenburg Line." On November 1, 1918, they drove through the German center and together with the British, forced the Germans to sue for peace (Nov. 11, 1918).

In 1919 Pershing was awarded the rank of General of the Armies of the U.S. From 1921 until 1924, he served as army chief of staff. His war memoirs, *My Experiences in the World War* (2 vols.), were published in 1931.

⁓

He looms from countless pictures a steeleyed soldier in unruffled tunic, a man aloof and cold. "Lucky," battalions of envious colleagues called Jack Pershing, and indeed this tall, light-haired Missourian did seem fortune's child. In four years at the U.S. Military Academy in the 1880s he achieved scholastic and martial distinction and the coveted rank of cadet "first captain." Frontier service with the Sixth Cavalry taught good soldiering. Special duty with Sioux Scouts and transfer to the crack Negro 10th Cavalry opened a willing heart to the worth of other races. Cadets at the University of Nebraska who took Professor Pershing's classes in military science and tactics taught another lesson—the marvelous military potential of untrained Americans.

In Cuba he showed splendid coolness under fire, sound tactical judgment, and great stamina. As first director of the Bureau of Insular Affairs after the war, he organized America's first major program in foreign military government. And in the Philippines his racial understanding and administrative experience gained him international notice and a citation in one of President Theodore Roosevelt's congressional messages. Moros loved this American who showed mercy to the Prophet's warriors but spoke forcefully of peace. His eye saw a different war as military attaché during the Russo-Japanese War in Manchuria, one of machine guns and forests of barbed wire that shredded men and animals. New wars would be won by men given firepower and trained to use machines. Roosevelt read Pershing's reports with renewed admiration and in 1906 rewarded his enterprising captain in the only way allowed by the strict promotion rules— elevation to the rank of brigadier general.

In 1915, Pershing's wife and three of their four children were burned to death at San Francisco's Presidio. His normal wit and humor chilled, his personality quenched, his discipline stiffened, he led the punitive expedition into Mexico against Pancho Villa with stern competence. Often during a hectic year he disagreed with Wilson's policies, but always he obeyed, winning admiration for constancy and cautious audacity.

Pershing seemed the obvious choice to command the American Expeditionary Force in 1917. In France he brought new vision to an old war. His men came trained for field maneuver, and would know what to do when the blood-caked stalemate broke along the western front. He brought, too, a firm determination to create an American army, a determination that frustrated Allied leaders eager to filter fresh American men into wasted British and French battalions. This man who combined luck, ability, and experience to achieve success accomplished more than his fullest ambition. World adulation, promotion to the unique rank of general of the armies, appointment as chief of staff filled his cup. See F. G. Vandiver, *Black Jack: The Life and Times of John J. Pershing* (1977).

FRANK G. VANDIVER

PHILIP (b. New England, ca. 1639; d. Bristol, R.I., Aug. 12, 1676), NATIVE AMERICAN LEADER, whose given name was Pometacom or Metacomet, became chief or sachem of the Wampanoag tribe of New England in 1662 after the death of his brother, Wamsutta (Alexander). Philip honored his father's treaty with the settlers and tried to remain peaceful but found it increasingly difficult to do so as whites expanded into the Native Americans' hunting grounds. In 1671 he was accused of plotting against the colonists and summoned to Taunton, Massachusetts, where he was fined and forced to surrender part of his tribe's firearms. His regal mannerisms and frequent self-comparisons to his "brother" King Charles II of England caused him to be called "King" Philip by the colonists.

The execution of three warriors in 1675 for the murder of John Sassamon, a Christian Native American who had informed the English of Philip's plans for war, provoked what is known as King Philip's War. Starting in the Narragansett Bay area, the fighting spread throughout the Massachusetts colonies into Connecticut and Rhode Island. The Wampanoags and their Nipmuck allies burned towns and killed many men, women, and children while avoiding a major clash with soldiers. Philip was unable to win the support of the Mohawks, or of the French and Dutch, and the colonial forces finally adopted a strategy of burning Native American crops, capturing their women and children, and offering rewards to Native Americans for deserting Philip. Gradually he lost power, although heavy fighting continued. He took refuge in a swamp in Rhode Island in 1676 but was shot by a Native American traitor.

King Philip seems to fit the mold of the patriot chief. The son of Massassoit, schooled in the necessity for friendship with the white man, yet conscious of the need to maintain the integrity of the tribal order, he finally recognized the threat posed by the Europeans and determined to drive them from the Native American lands. Like Powhatan, **Pontiac,** and **Tecumseh,** he intended to reach across tribal divisions in order to create a pan–Indian alliance against the white man's incursions. And like them, he failed.

Because the story of the destruction of a people lends itself to epic description, this conception of the patriot chief possesses a certain plausibility. In fact, however, recent scholarship offers a more realistic interpretation. Philip emerges less as an epic hero defeated finally by superior force than as an unwitting victim of a cultural process the effects of which he could sense but scarcely understand. He traded with the whites, made alliances with them, and sold them land. But he apparently thought that he could stop short of accepting their religion or abandoning the tribal leadership that was his by right. Despite his efforts to maintain the integrity of native ways, Philip watched the Wampanoags and the surrounding tribes slip under the cultural and political hegemony of the Puritans. He struck at the whites in 1675 because he feared the collapse of his way of life which would entail the loss of his own position of leadership.

His actual role in the conflict belies the image of native leadership attributed to him by the white man. The Wampanoags gained the alliance of only three major tribes, and one of these, the Narragansetts, constituted a frail ally. Most of the Native Americans influenced by Christianity supported the Puritans. Although Philip began the conflict, he lost his position of leadership when the fighting spread outside Plymouth. After the summer of 1675, he took part in none of the great battles. In the end he was shot down by a Native American and his body was quartered by order of Benjamin Church.

King Philip's War took a heavy toll of whites and Native Americans and set back the tide of settlement for twenty-five years. Philip himself, in the words of Douglas Leach, was "more futile than heroic, more misguided than villainous." See Douglas Edward Leach, *Flintlock and Tomahawk: New England in King Philip's War* (1966).

BERNARD W. SHEEHAN

PHILLIPS, Wendell (b. Boston, Mass., Nov. 29, 1811; d. Boston, Mass., Feb. 2, 1884), REFORMER, received BA (1831) and LLB (1834) from Harvard. Following a speech at Faneuil Hall in Boston, in which he condemned the murder of an antislavery newspaper editor, Phillips established himself as a leading abolitionist. In 1840 he attended the World Anti-Slavery Convention in London as a delegate from Massachusetts. Upon his return he became more outspoken in his attacks on slavery and contributed articles to **William Lloyd Garrison**'s abolitionist newspaper, the *Liberator*.

In 1845 Phillips published *Can Abolitionists Vote or Take Office Under the United States Constitution?* in which he denounced the Constitution for condoning slavery and argued that abolitionists should disregard the Constitution. He opposed the annexation of Texas, the Mexican War, and the Compromise of 1850 because they extended and sanctioned slavery.

Unlike Garrison, Phillips did not advocate nonresistance; he argued that laws such as the Fugitive Slave Act should be forcefully resisted. When the Civil War broke out, Phillips placed freeing the slaves above saving the Union. He criticized Lincoln for not immediately freeing the southern blacks, but he approved of the Emancipation Proclamation. He opposed the president's plans for Reconstruction, believing that they would not effectively change the power structure in the South. Phillips insisted that blacks be given free land, an education, and the suffrage.

In 1865 Garrison proposed that the American Anti-Slavery Society be dissolved because the Thirteenth Amendment freeing the slaves had been passed. Phillips, however, insisted that the Society's work had just begun. He was then elected president. He interpreted American history as a series of class struggles, the Civil War as a second revolution. The poor condition of wage earners also preoccupied him. He argued that black labor would not truly be free unless all labor was released from the "slavery" of the wage system. Workers must unite and use the ballot to preserve democracy. In 1870 he ran for governor of Massachusetts on a labor ticket, but was defeated. Phillips supported the eight-hour-day movement, the idea of worker cooperatives, and other reform movements, including the fight for woman's rights.

In his address "The Scholar in a Republic" (1881), Phillips proclaimed the intellectuals' duty to help those less fortunate than themselves and to educate the masses.

———⟨∞⟩———

Wendell Phillips looked like a gentleman and a leader. His aquiline profile, strong jaw, and graceful figure suggested the background of opportunity and power that he had enjoyed. An old family, a Harvard education, legal training, and brilliant oratorical skills all pointed to a public career. Yet the public vocation that Phillips found was unconventional. He became an "agitator"—a professional reformer. His beliefs were far from unusual for the era before the Civil War: a faith in America's national mission, in the moral perfectibility of man, in progress and democracy. Yet Phillips's nationalism led him to denounce slavery as a national sin and to call for disunion. His democracy led to a distrust of politics and an appeal to independent agitation. His belief in progress caused him to fear the effects of industrialism and to become an early patrician champion of the labor movement. His faith in moral perfectibility made him a passionate critic of all around him and at times an uncommonly elegant common scold.

Phillips was the great orator of an age that relished oratory. In thousands of lectures, he exercised his magnificent voice and presence, reveling in his mastery over hecklers and rowdies and proudly contrasting his independence with the cramped and careful mien of ministers, journalists, and politicians. He was direct and precise in a period that usually favored the ornate. The Puritan heritage was as detectable in his plain

style as in his fierce moralism and his penchant for denunciation.

Phillips is best known as an abolitionist, the "golden trumpet" of the Garrisonians. His awareness of the freedmen's needs after emancipation sets him above most of his fellows in that crusade. But his part in creating the role of reformer, of providing the vital link between the transcendental reform impulse of the Age of Jackson and the various movements for the reform of industrial society after the Civil War, is undoubtedly his greatest single contribution to the American spirit. See Irving H. Bartlett, *Wendell Phillips, Brahmin Radical* (1961).

ROBERT D. MARCUS

PICKERING, Timothy (b. Salem, Mass., July 17, 1745; d. Salem, Mass., Jan. 29, 1829), POLITICAL LEADER, graduated from Harvard in 1763 and was admitted to the bar in Salem in 1768. He became active in Salem affairs and a leader of the local militia. During the Revolution he served George Washington as adjutant general and later as quartermaster general. In the latter post he was critical of the lukewarm popular support of the Revolution. He moved to Philadelphia after the Revolution and then went westward, helping to establish the county of Luzerne. As a member of the Pennsylvania delegation to the Constitutional Convention of 1787, he supported a strong central government. In 1791 he was appointed postmaster general in Washington's cabinet. In 1795 he became secretary of war and (later in the year) succeeded **Edmund Randolph** as secretary of state. Pickering, a Federalist, was continued in this office by President John Adams, but by 1800 his extreme anti-French pro-English position (and his intrigues with **Alexander Hamilton** against Adams) led to his dismissal (May 1800).

Pickering moved back to Massachusetts in 1800, settled finally in Wenham, and in 1802 secured an appointment as chief justice of the court of common pleas in Essex County. Elected to the U.S. Senate as a Federalist in 1803, he became a leading opponent of Presidents

Jefferson and Madison. After the purchase of Louisiana (1803) he openly advocated the secession of New England and the formation of a separate northern confederation. Pickering was defeated for reelection to the Senate in 1811, but was elected to the House of Representatives in 1813, serving until 1817. He opposed the War of 1812, and favored, but did not participate in, the deliberations of the Hartford Convention of 1814–15. After leaving public life Pickering spent his last years farming.

In the period of the early republic, Timothy Pickering exemplified both the best and the worst in Federalism. Like many other Federalists who held a place at the helm of government, he exhibited much administrative and executive ability, stern devotion to duty, high personal rectitude, and notable efficiency. In his private life he was an affectionate husband, solicitous of a numerous family, agreeable in his friendships, and devoted to his large farm and commodious house in Wenham, Massachusetts. As a member of the Washington administration he worked loyally to organize and establish the strong national government which the Constitution set forth in blueprint. In this capacity he helped set up the mail system on an effective basis, and served with skill and distinction as a federal commissioner in several important Native American negotiations. In his roles as postmaster general, secretary of war, and secretary of state, he followed high standards of public service and administrative management—a major legacy of the Federalist founders.

But as the Federalist-Republican conflict intensified, Pickering's personality grew narrow and hard. Toward Jefferson and his party he became intolerant, self-righteous, and uncompromising. If advancing years or some emotional defect helped cause this tendency, it was also typical of many other Federalists in this early party age. Unable to distinguish between peaceful opposition politics and sedition, Pickering identified Republicans as dangerous agitators whose threat to the government must be thwarted and crushed. Accordingly, during John Adams's pres-

idency, Pickering was among those "high" Federalists who would stifle Republican criticism through a federal Sedition Law, discredit Republican "Jacobins" and "incendiaries" by exposing their presumably treasonable partiality for France, and escalate the quasi-war with the French Directory to provoke a decisive contest of arms between Republicans and the federal government. Dismissed by Adams for his extremism, Pickering, after the Republican election triumph of 1800, continued his vendetta in the role of a Federalist minority leader. When Jefferson acquired the vast Louisiana territory from France, Pickering hatched an unsuccessful plot to establish a separate Federalist-dominated New England Confederation. Stymied by opposition within his own party, he turned to less blatant methods. He accused the Republicans of playing politics with national security and selling out to Napoleon. The New England states should interpose their authority against the embargo and negate its effect within their jurisdictions. Finally, in the War of 1812, Pickering charged that the Republicans' conduct was unjust, immoral, and based on corrupt political expediency rather than on concern for the national interest. When the Hartford Convention proposed fundamental changes in the Constitution, Pickering endorsed its plan as a step toward final separation. See Gerard H. Clarfield, *Timothy Pickering and American Diplomacy, 1795–1800* (1969), and Hervey P. Prentiss, *Timothy Pickering as the Leader of New England Federalism, 1800–1815* (1934).

ROGER H. BROWN

PIERCE, Franklin (b. Hillsboro, N.H., Nov. 23, 1804; d. Concord, N.H., Oct. 8, 1869), PRESIDENT, graduated from Bowdoin College (1824) and was admitted to the New Hampshire bar in 1827. A state legislator (1829–32; speaker, 1831–32), U.S. representative (1833–37), and U.S. senator (1837–42), he supported many of the policies of the Jacksonians but opposed all internal improvements at federal expense. In the Mexican War, he served as a brigadier under General **Winfield Scott.**

At the 1852 Democratic presidential convention, Pierce was nominated on the 49th ballot. In the election, he defeated the Whig Winfield Scott 254 electoral votes to 42. Pierce tried to ameliorate North-South tensions by maintaining a sectionally balanced cabinet. He approved the Kansas-Nebraska Act (1854), which repealed the Missouri Compromise by establishing the principle of "popular sovereignty," whereby the actual settlers of a territory could determine for themselves whether slavery should be permitted within their borders. During the territorial conflicts in Kansas that followed this act, Pierce, under pro-slavery influence, made no attempt to ensure fair elections, and he condemned radical antislavery groups. The actions of the Pierce administration and other developments led to hostilities in Kansas ("bleeding Kansas") and further exacerbated sectional tensions.

Pierce's administration pursued an active foreign policy: he approved of Commodore **Matthew C. Perry's** mission to Japan, initiated under Millard Fillmore; the Gadsden Purchase (1853), which gave the U.S. 29,000 additional square miles along the Mexican border; and the Canadian Reciprocity Treaty (1854), granting the U.S. fishing privileges in Canadian waters. Pierce also attempted to purchase Hawaii and to get naval bases in Santo Domingo.

During the Civil War, Pierce opposed Lincoln's policies, believing that the president had exceeded his constitutional authority.

—⸎—

The tragedy of Franklin Pierce was personal, familial, and national. The handsome son of a New Hampshire governor, he possessed great charm and endeared himself to friends, including **Nathaniel Hawthorne.** Mrs. Pierce (née Jane Means Appleton) considered her antecedents socially superior to those of her gregarious husband. She detested public life and abhorred the conviviality to which Pierce proved susceptible. In 1842 she was a factor in his resignation from the U.S. Senate at the age of thirty-seven. Ten years afterward, when he became the Democrats' "dark horse" presidential nominee, Mrs. Pierce

appropriately fainted on hearing the announcement of his nomination.

Prior to 1852, Franklin and Jane Pierce had seen two of their little children die. Now one was left, eleven-year-old Benny. Pierce told Mrs. Pierce that the nomination had come unsought, and also that Benny would benefit from being a president's son. Pierce defeated Scott resoundingly; his was the only popular majority after 1840 until 1864. Then, during the interregnum before the inauguration, the three Pierces went riding on a train. An accident occurred. One passenger was killed—11-year-old Benny.

When the bereaved father was inaugurated on March 4, 1853, Mrs. Pierce was not in Washington. Later, when she made the journey, her escort told her that Pierce indeed had sought the nomination. After entering her White House bedroom, she locked the door. No one knows whether grief, anger, or a Puritanical concept of the wrath of God dominated her subsequent moods. But in the circumstances it is scarcely surprising that the saddened, shocked, and all but abandoned president failed to provide strong leadership.

The reason this tragedy had nationwide ramifications is that if Pierce ever was to be a real leader, the time was 1853 when he could point to his vote as a mandate and before the patronage was distributed. Of the presidents serving between late 1850 and early 1861, his was the best leadership opportunity. Pierce allowed the country to drift, called no special session of Congress, and watched the dissipation of the patronage power because—or so it would seem—he was psychologically unequal to the challenge. By early 1854, when Senator **Stephen A. Douglas** and others were debating "the Nebraska question," Pierce had lost advantages accruing to anticipatory White House occupants like Woodrow Wilson, Franklin D. Roosevelt, and Lyndon B. Johnson. While presidential authority oozed away, the well-meaning, polite, and ineffective Pierce appeared ever more pathetic.

James Buchanan, who had been abroad as the Kansas controversy developed, was adjudged more "available" than Pierce for the 1856 presidential palm. Elected that autumn, Buchanan took over in March 1857. Pierce then began the eleven and a half years of retirement that would terminate in his death. Because of his presidential weakness and identification with the doughface image ("northern men with southern principles"), the New Hampshire Democrat never regained his erstwhile popularity. See Roy F. Nichols, *Franklin Pierce: Young Hickory of the Granite Hills* (1958).

HOLMAN HAMILTON

PINCHOT, Gifford (b. Simsbury, Conn., Aug. 11, 1865; d. New York, N.Y., Oct. 4, 1946), POLITICAL LEADER, son of a New York merchant who helped found the Yale School of Forestry. He graduated from Yale in 1889 and after studying forestry abroad (1889–90) became the first professional forester in the U.S., working on the estate of George W. Vanderbilt in Biltmore, North Carolina. After serving as a member of the National Forest Commission (1896) and working for the secretary of the interior (1897), he was appointed chief forester of the U.S. Department of Agriculture in 1898. When responsibility for the nation's forest reserves was transferred from the Department of the Interior to the secretary of agriculture, Pinchot was named chief forester of the U.S. Forest Service.

A prolific writer and frequent speaker, Pinchot served on several conservation commissions and rapidly became one of the nation's leaders in the developing conservation movement. He believed that the nation's natural resources and forest reserves should be managed according to scientific principles and that they should remain under government regulation. In 1909, believing that Secretary of the Interior Richard A. Ballinger's policies were detrimental to conservation, Pinchot accused Ballinger of returning certain water power sites to the public domain, thereby enabling western interests to purchase these sites, and of validating the claims of the Morgan-Guggenheim syndicate to large tracts of coal-rich public land in Alaska. In this "Ballinger-Pinchot controversy" (1909), President Taft supported his secretary of the interior, and when

Pinchot persisted in his attacks, Taft dismissed him. A special congressional committee later cleared Ballinger of Pinchot's charges, but the investigation also revealed that Ballinger was a far from ardent advocate of conservation. Taft's action, together with his handling of other incidents, angered Theodore Roosevelt, a close friend of Pinchot's, and led Roosevelt to seek the 1912 Republican presidential nomination, and that failing, to form the "Bull Moose" Progressive party, which Pinchot supported.

In later years, Pinchot continued to work as a conservationist, serving as state forester of Pennsylvania (1918–20). In 1922 he was elected governor of Pennsylvania. As governor (1923–27, 1933–35) he reorganized and improved the efficiency of the state government, established a budget system, and helped settle the Pennsylvania anthracite coal strike of 1923. During his later years he remained a staunch supporter of conservation.

❦

In the public estimation no name is more closely associated with the early history of conservation in the United States than that of Gifford Pinchot. And in fact no one did more to publicize this cause between 1890 and 1910.

When Pinchot first became interested in responsible environmental management, he stood almost alone in a world of quick-dollar exploitation. Americans of the 1880s, drugged by 250 years of reliance on an undeveloped frontier, simply could not fathom the finitude of natural resources and the consequent necessity of stewardship. Nor did this generation support the idea of government regulation of free enterprise in society's long-term interest. For Pinchot both concepts were essential ingredients of conservation.

Since instruction in forestry was unavailable in the United States in 1889, Pinchot sought it in Germany and France. The experience left a permanent mark on his mind and on the institutions it shaped, such as the U.S. Forest Service. Unlike Americans, Europeans had long accepted the necessity of living within a limited budget of natural resources. Lacking a frontier to bail them out of resource shortages, they learned to manage forests, for instance, as a crop: planting, cultivating, and harvesting in thirty- to eighty-year cycles. The efficiency of these sustained-yield practices made an immense impression on Pinchot. He returned to the United States convinced that scientific management could extract a perennial profit from America's forests.

For a time in the 1890s Pinchot thought that the education and persuasion of private timberland owners would be sufficient to institute forestry in the United States. But most of them continued a cut-out-and-get-out style of lumbering. The answer, in Pinchot's estimation, was National Forests. Under an 1891 act the president had the power to "reserve" forested lands in the public domain. Forests so designated might be leased to private developers, but title and control over lumbering practices resided with the government. In charge of the National Forests after 1898, Pinchot used his power to launch American forestry.

Gifford Pinchot had much in common with Theodore Roosevelt. Both men were products of wealthy, highly placed families and eastern Ivy League colleges. They also shared a driving dedication to the cause of social and economic fair play. Moreover, Pinchot and Roosevelt possessed the enthusiasm, ambition, and self-righteousness that made leadership of the politics of reform highly appealing. Finally, both men enjoyed vigorous outdoor sports and had been friends for a decade before Roosevelt entered the White House.

With Roosevelt occupying the presidency and Pinchot the post of chief forester, Progressive conservation reached full stride. In 1907 Pinchot invented the term "conservation" to describe the scientific management of the total environment for the long-term good of the people. The next year saw the report of the Inland Waterways Commission, the holding of the dramatic White House Conservation Conference, the establishment of the National Conservation Commission with a charge of inventorying the nation's natural resources, and the expansion of the activities of

the Forest Service and the Bureau of Reclamation. Pinchot was the leading figure in most of these undertakings.

To be sure, the Pinchot variety of conservation encountered strong opposition. On the one hand were wilderness enthusiasts such as **John Muir** who prized forests as repositories of beauty and spirituality, not of timber. On the other were business interests, particularly from the western states, who feared that Pinchot intended to "lock up" resources and with them jobs and profits. The strength of this viewpoint in Congress contributed to the withering of support for Progressive conservation once Roosevelt left office in 1909. Frustrated, Pinchot deliberately invited the dismissal he received from President Taft in 1910.

Always hungry for the limelight of public attention and convinced of the justice of his cause (which he increasingly came to see as that of the "people" against "Concentrated Wealth"), Pinchot poured his extraordinary energies after 1910 into the furtherance of Rooseveltian Progressivism. He personally wrote Roosevelt's famous Ossawatomie address of August 31, 1910, which defined the "New Nationalism" and began the Bull Moose bolt from the Republican party. In Pinchot's mind the federal government had to assume sufficient power to check the might of big business. In some instances, such as that of the development of hydroelectric power, the government's control might have to extend to outright ownership. Holding this idea, Pinchot joined the group whose efforts culminated in institutions such as the Tennessee Valley Authority (1933).

For two decades after Roosevelt's unsuccessful political comeback in 1912 Pinchot yearned for personal advancement. His hopes extended to the presidency, and in truth, he was occasionally mentioned as a dark-horse nominee. But his uncompromising, self-righteous manner and his attendant ability to make and hold enemies did not suit the demands of national politics. Still Pinchot twice went to the top of Pennsylvania government, and during the Depression he found an opportunity to implement his big-government philosophy. Indeed Pinchot's Depression leadership of Pennsylvania anticipated many of the relief and recovery programs of President Franklin D. Roosevelt, even earning the name "the little New Deal."

Toward the end of his life Pinchot derived considerable satisfaction from being recognized as the man who made "conservation" a household word in the United States. See M. Nelson McGeary, *Gifford Pinchot: Forester-Politician* (1960).

RODERICK NASH

PINCKNEY, Elizabeth Lucas (b. probably Antigua, West Indies, ca. 1723; d. Philadelphia, Pa., May 26, 1793), AGRICULTURAL INNOVATOR, was educated in England. She came to South Carolina in 1738 when her father, an English army officer, bought Wappoo plantation, near Charleston. Her father returned to Antigua, however, and in 1739 Elizabeth Lucas was left in charge of three plantations. Her problem was to find a crop which could be successfully grown on high land, and which would furnish a staple for export. Using seeds sent by her father, she attempted to grow ginger, cotton, and alfalfa, but by 1742 had decided that indigo offered the greatest potential, though it had not yet been successfully cultivated in South Carolina. By 1747, enough indigo was produced in the colony to merit export to England.

During 1747–53, she lived on her husband Charles Pinckney's plantation Belmont, on Charlestown Neck, where she directed experiments with flax and hemp, and attempted to revive silk cultivation. In 1753 the family moved to London, where Charles Pinckney was to serve as the colony's agent. In 1758, however, while on a visit to South Carolina, Charles died, and Elizabeth Lucas Pinckney once again resumed the task of plantation management.

Elizabeth Lucas Pinckney, often referred to as Eliza Lucas, was energetic, practical, and persistent in her efforts to find an export crop which could be grown profitably on her father's estates in South Carolina. Her efforts in acclimating the indigo plant and producing the dye established the industry in that colony during the 1740s. After she had succeeded in producing indigo, Eliza Lucas raised seed and distributed it among neighboring planters, thus encouraging them to adopt the new crop. This is an interesting example of the dissemination of a new technology. Indigo persisted as an important source of income in the South until after the Revolutionary War. Since indigo was grown and manufactured on plantations, using slave labor, its profitability encouraged the development of the plantation system and slavery.

Pinckney was responsible for plantation management during three different periods of her life. Throughout these times, she experimented with various crops. At the time she established indigo as a productive crop, she also experimented with ginger, cotton, alfalfa, and cassava. Later, she raised flax, hemp, and silk, even making some of her own dresses from the silk she raised. Like many others, she operated her plantations on a largely self-sufficient basis, making cloth, tanning leather and manufacturing harness and shoes, pressing fish oil, constructing barrels, and otherwise keeping a force of carpenters and other artisans busy. Her surviving journal and letters present interesting pictures of plantation life in colonial South Carolina. See Harriet H. Ravenal, *Eliza Pinckney* (1896; reprinted 1967).

WAYNE D. RASMUSSEN

PINKERTON, Allan (b. Glasgow, Scot., Aug. 25, 1819; d. Chicago, Ill., July 1, 1884) DETECTIVE, was apprenticed to a cooper, and became an independent artisan at the age of nineteen. In 1842, after having been active in a Chartist demonstration, Pinkerton fled to America to avoid possible arrest. He worked briefly at a brewery in Chicago (1842–43), but then moved to the Scotch settlement of Dundee near the Fox River in Kane County, Illinois, where he resumed his career as a cooper. His discovery and capture of a counterfeiting gang working on an island in the Fox River soon brought him successive jobs as a private detective, however, and in 1846 he was named deputy sheriff of Kane County. He was soon invited to Cook County to take a comparable post in Chicago and, in 1850, was appointed the sole detective on Chicago's newly organized police force.

In addition to his work with the police, Pinkerton undertook, at the suggestion of local railroad executives, to organize a private detective agency. This agency, one of the first in the nation, began as a partnership with a lawyer, E. G. Rucker. When Rucker left in 1851, Pinkerton resigned from his police post and became a full-time private investigator. Pinkerton's National Detective Agency prospered, particularly after he solved a series of Adams Express robberies (1859–60). In 1861, while working for the Philadelphia, Wilmington, and Baltimore Railroad to counteract threats by southerners against the line's property, Pinkerton's agents learned of a plot, in Baltimore, to assassinate president-elect Abraham Lincoln. Pinkerton therefore arranged with Lincoln's aides to bring the presidential party secretly to Washington, D.C., ahead of schedule. During 1861–62, Pinkerton headed Union secret service operations in the South and directed counterespionage activities in Washington. For the remainder of the war he investigated damage claims against the government. In 1865 he resumed leadership of his agency. The firm opened branches in New York City and Philadelphia; expanded its policy of providing protection for an annual retainer; was called into cases in England and France, notably the 1873 arrest of Bank of England note forgers; and began, in 1877, to provide the antiunion services during labor disputes which would later create much hostility to the firm.

Allan Pinkerton's agency had an important role in breaking up the Mollie Maguires (1875), an organization responsible for numerous murders in Pennsylvania's coal mine regions. He wrote eighteen books on detective experiences, including *The Spy of the Rebellion* (1883), and *Thirty Years a Detective* (1884). These works, which sold in great quantity, were instrumental in spreading the fame of Pinkerton's agency.

It can be said that Allan Pinkerton was the 19th-century prototype of **J. Edgar Hoover** and his private detective organization, an early Federal Bureau of Investigation and Interpol. His story is not just the simple tale of a skillful detective and colorful criminals. He led his operatives, as he called them, on the frontier of the 1850s, chasing, capturing criminals, and solving train and stagecoach robberies. A strong abolitionist, he helped **John Brown** and a number of slaves escape to Canada. During the Civil War he was an imaginative and courageous espionage agent but an incredibly poor military intelligence officer. His courage and ingenuity helped to frustrate an attempt on Lincoln's life in the so-called Baltimore Plot on the eve of Lincoln's first inauguration. In the postwar years he led his men in solving numerous major crimes from murder to robbery.

He was an intense, opinionated, at times unbearably touchy man who had a Bourbon cast of mind. He possessed a venom and a fury that numbed suspected enemies, while his letters reveal he had a shrewd insight into other people's characters and motives. His personal drive and ambition were awesome. He tried to appear self-righteous, but he ruled both his own household and his business with a tyrant's hand. "I am self-willed and obstinate," he once wrote.

But in his lifetime few men peered behind Pinkerton's cold searching eyes to discover the inner complex man, who changed from a violent young radical champion of the exploited workingman to become the protector of big business once he had tasted success and wealth.

He appeared in response to the conditions on the early frontier and changed those conditions, becoming a man of power and influence. In the process he did a great deal of good and evil, yet he influenced historical events during the Civil War and helped to bring law and order to a ruthless frontier. He also left behind a number of methods, tools, and innovations which future generations of urban policemen used to fight national crime. See James D. Horan, *The Pinkertons: The Detective Dynasty That Made History* (1968).

James D. Horan

PINKHAM, Lydia Estes (b. Feb. 9, 1819, Lynn, Mass.; d. May 17, 1883, Lynn. Mass.), BUSINESS-WOMAN, grew up in Lynn, the tenth child of a family of twelve. After graduating from the Lynn Academy, she taught school and joined the Female Antislavery Society. She identified with various causes and reforms, including temperance, Grahamism, and phrenology. In 1843, she married Issac Pinkham. The couple had five children, one of whom died in infancy. Because of her husband's erratic earnings from a series of failed business ventures, she struggled to keep the family together. In the depression of 1873 Issac Pinkham went bankrupt and the family plunged into poverty. Over the years Lydia had earned a reputation for helping sick neighbors by giving them a homemade herbal remedy which she concocted in her cellar. Out of desperation, Lydia's sons William and Daniel suggested she market her remedy. Brewed, bottled, and labeled in the basement kitchen, Lydia E. Pinkham's Vegetable Compound went on sale in Lynn and nearby towns in 1875. The recipe consisted chiefly of two herbs, known locally as pleurisy root and unicorn root. The herbal base was blended with a generous dose of alcohol as a "solvent and preservative." Lydia Pinkham claimed that the concoction was especially valuable in treating "female complaints."

Lydia Pinkham's, as it was commonly known, was a resounding success from the start. Daniel and William were tireless promoters. They advertised in newspapers and magazines, and distributed handbills and pamphlets with glowing testimonials about miracle cures. Mrs. Pinkham's face gazed from the bottle's lable with a reassuring smile. The "vegetable compound" captured a devoted following in New England, and soon caught on in New York City as well.

When Lydia Pinkham died in 1883 the business was grossing $300,000 a year. It continued to flourish, reaching its peak during the 1920s. Generations of American women had unflagging faith in Lydia Pinkham's compound, no matter what their doctors told them. No scientific proof of the remedy's effectiveness has ever been discovered.

Lydia Pinkham's parents were passionate champions of the antislavery movement and other reforms. In her youth Lydia knew such abolitionist leaders as **Frederick Douglass** and **William Lloyd Garrison**. It is little wonder, then, that she marketed her herbal remedy with a reformer's zeal. Lydia E. Pinkham's Vegetable Compound was not only a business; it was a social crusade.

An ardent believer in the powers of her potion, Lydia Pinkham made prodigious promises in her advertisements. A popular song of the time satirized her claims: "Widow Brown, she had no children / Though she loved them very dear / Then she took, she swallowed, she gargled the vegetable compound / Now she has them twice a year."

Like many feminists of a century later, Lydia Pinkham insisted that only a woman could understand female health problems. In an age when sexuality and reproduction were forbidden topics, many women were reluctant to describe their symptoms to male physicians. Thousands wrote to Lydia Pinkham, explaining their "female complaints" in vivid detail. Each letter received a personal reply from her "Department of Advice." She encouraged women to exercise and to practice good hygiene, and of course to take her herbal compound regularly.

Judging from the testimonials, Lydia Pinkham's compound cured a host of ills. Its alcohol content may have dulled the pain for some sufferers. For the most part, the compound probably had a placebo effect. It worked because women were convinced that it would help them. Lydia Pinkham's face, smiling gently from the bottle's label, assured them that everything would be all right, and told them they were not alone. See Jean Burton, *Lydia Pinkham Is Her Name* (1949).

DEBORAH KENT

POCAHONTAS (b. Va., c. 1596; d. Gravesend, Eng., March 1617), NATIVE AMERICAN, was the daughter of Powhatan, the chief of a confederacy of Algonquian tribes in Virginia. As a child she lived north of the York River, near modern Gloucester. According to **John Smith**'s *Generall Historie* (1624), Pocahontas saved his life in 1608 by throwing herself upon him as he was about to be clubbed to death by her father's warriors.

In the spring of 1613, while visiting the chief of the Potomacs, Pocahontas was captured by the English, who planned to exchange her for British prisoners held by the Native Americans. While in Henrico, Virginia, she was instructed in Christianity and baptized Rebecca. There she also met **John Rolfe,** an English gentleman who introduced the cultivation of West Indian tobacco to the colonies. Their marriage (April 1614) established a bond between the Native Americans and the settlers, thereby helping Jamestown to establish itself as a colony.

In 1616 Pocahontas and her husband went to England, where she was presented to King James I and Queen Anne. Before she could return to Virginia she died of either pneumonia or tuberculosis.

───── ∞ ─────

More than most historical characters, Pocahontas has a significance for her own times and a symbolic importance derived from the ways in which Americans have made use of her in literature and in folklore.

For the early history of Virginia, Pocahontas is credited with facilitating relations between the colonists and the Powhatan tribe, with helping John Smith to open trade with the local natives in order to obtain food for the starving settlement, and with establishing peace between the whites and Native Americans after 1614 through her marriage to John Rolfe and conversion to Christianity. Contemporary testimony attests that the Jamestown leadership believed that she played a valuable role in relations between the colonists and the native people. It was precisely this opinion that led Samuel Argall to take her captive in the hope of using her as a pawn in dealing with Powhatan. A period of relative peace (1614–22) did follow, but it can be attrib-

uted with more plausible justification to the developing strength of the colony. With the arrival of Thomas Dale in Jamestown in 1611, an aggressive policy was initiated against the Native Americans. Successful skirmishes were fought, and crops and villages were burned. Powhatan himself moved farther into the forest. Moreover, the establishment of peace coincided with the colonists' discovery of tobacco as a profitable crop. The Virginia settlement after 1614 commanded native respect in a way that it could not in its early years.

As a symbol, Pocahontas represents the reverence for the innocence of primitive life that runs through American literature and thought. As the naked waif who turned cartwheels in the streets of Jamestown, as the Native American "princess" who attended a royal masque in London, and as the subject of sentimental literature and portraiture in the 19th century, she has stood for the purity of life on a continent untouched by civilization. Moreover, her marriage to Rolfe and conversion to Christianity confirmed for white men that civilization would be welcome in primitive America, and that they could expect success for their mission to transform the continent. See Grace Steele Woodward, *Pocahontas* (1970).

BERNARD W. SHEEHAN

POE, Edgar Allan (b. Boston, Mass., Jan. 19, 1809; d. Baltimore, Md., Oct. 7, 1849), WRITER, was orphaned at the age of three and reared by John Allan, a wealthy Richmond, Virginia, tobacco merchant. Poe lived with the Allan family in England (1815–20), and entered the University of Virginia in 1826, but was forced to leave because he had run up debts that Allan was apparently unwilling to pay. In 1827, while living in Boston, Poe published *Tamerlane and Other Poems* anonymously. From 1827 to 1829 he served in the army under an assumed name. In 1829 he went to Baltimore, where he published *Al Aaraaf, Tamerlane and Minor Poems.* He entered West Point in 1830, but was dismissed the following year.

In 1831, Poe, now living in New York, published another book of *Poems*. He moved back to Baltimore in 1831, where his short story "MS. Found in a Bottle," a pseudoscientific tale, was awarded a $50 prize and published in the Baltimore *Saturday Visiter* (1833). As a result of this award, Poe was named assistant editor of the Richmond (Va.) *Southern Literary Messenger* (1835–37). In 1835 he married his cousin Virginia Clemm, who was not quite 14.

In 1838 Poe returned to New York, where he published *The Narrative of Arthur Gordon Pym,* a gloomy and fanciful tale of a shipwreck in the South Seas and the Antarctic region. He next moved to Philadelphia, where he resided until 1844, working as coeditor of *Burton's Gentleman's Magazine* (1839–40) and literary editor of *Graham's Magazine* (1841–42). "The Fall of the House of Usher," a horror story dealing with family decay, was first published in *Burton's* (1839). In 1840 Poe issued *Tales of the Grotesque and Arabesque,* a collection of his short stories, which contained "Ligeia" (his favorite work), a study of psychic survival. "The Murders of the Rue Morgue," the first of Poe's famous "detective stories," in which a clever detective solves crimes by means of his logical reasoning powers, first appeared in *Graham's* (1841). In 1843 Poe was awarded a $100 prize for "The Gold Bug," another detective story published in the Philadelphia *Dollar Newspaper.*

In 1844 Poe again returned to New York, where he briefly served as editor of the *Broadway Journal,* a short-lived weekly. On January 29, 1845, the New York *Mirror* published "The Raven," now Poe's best-known poem. In 1845 Poe also published *Tales* (a collection of short stories which included "The Purloined Letter," another detective story). Some of his other famous short stories include "A Descent into the Maelstrom" (1841) and "The Cask of Amontillado" (1846).

During 1846 Poe edited a gossip column ("Literati of New York") in *Godey's Lady's Book,* and published "The Philosophy of Composition," in which he set down the standards which a "great" poem should meet and demonstrated how "The Raven" met these crite-

ria. "The Poetic Principle" (1848) argued that a poem should not take more than half an hour to read, that it should produce a total effect, and that it must avoid the didactic. In "Eureka" (1848), a long, philosophical prose poem, he claimed to have discovered the key to the universe.

Despite his growing reputation, Poe was often in poverty, and the alcohol and possibly opium in which he now and then sought solace had disastrous effects upon his health.

⁂

We have to reckon with several different versions of Edgar Allan Poe. The first and most damning, that of his severe foster-father and of his malevolent literary executor, Rufus Griswold, is of Poe as a quarrelsome, egotistical, unstable creature, destroyed by alcohol. At the opposite extreme is the French vision of "Edgarpo" developed by Baudelaire and by the Goncourt brothers, who saw him as the creator of "the literature of the twentieth century." To them he was a genius, destroyed by the unsympathetic atmosphere of America; a man born out of and ahead of his time, a romantic and yet possessed of a powerful analytical intellect; a forerunner of the symbolists who perceived the element of perversity in human conduct and who explored the idea of "correspondences" between one sensation of art form and another. Another version, made concrete in **Perry Miller**'s *The Raven and the Whale* (1956), locates Poe in his actual milieu, as an industrious though ill-rewarded littérateur, a "magazinist" (his own word for himself) versed in and immersed in the intellectual and personal controversies of the day. Yet another view is of Poe the southerner—"Our Cousin, Mr. Poe," in the phrase of Allen Tate—who upheld the gentlemanly, idiosyncratic ideal of his region in face of what he took to be the detestable vulgarities of northern democracy, even though he was born in Boston and worked mostly in the North. Finally, there is the Poe who is accorded an honored though not always well-defined place in the literary history of the United States: the nation's first serious critic, seeking to apply the exact categories and ambitious demands of the British critic Samuel Taylor Coleridge to America's emergent literature; a writer who, emphasizing the importance of brevity in fiction and poetry, discerned the trend of the age as being toward "the curt, the condensed, the pointed," and away from "the detailed, the voluminous, the inaccessible"; the author of a handful of haunting little poems, and of others which though of less merit have achieved immortality as anthology pieces; and a brilliant innovator in fiction, a pioneer in and possibly inventor of the art of the detective story, and a master—rivaled in his time only by **Nathaniel Hawthorne**—in the kindred art of the short story as parable, fantasy, conveyor of horror.

All of these versions are true, except that Poe was never a wild bohemian, never a person who needed liquor to prime him, although he did now and then take to the bottle in a vain effort to calm his frantic spirit. But even in the last few years of his short life, when his emotional balance seemed shattered by the death of his wife and by the constant burden of poverty, he managed to write pieces of sustained imaginative and ratiocinative power such as "Eureka." It is impossible to pronounce with finality upon a talent so beset, so haunted, so individual. What if John Allan had treated him more understandingly—and more generously? What if he had been sustained by a private income, of the scale he might well have anticipated from Allan's affluence? Some of his New England contemporaries, like the historian William H. Prescott, are often praised for the heroism of their literary effort in the face of severe physical or psychological handicaps. But their work had a financial underpinning. Poor Poe, in comparison, suffered far worse handicaps. With the sustenance of money he would have been freed from the necessity to churn out reviews that were often inevitably mere hack work. He might have been able to launch the magazine, under his own editorship, of which he dreamed. His editorial labors for other men were highly impressive. What might he not have achieved if he had had a free hand, and no worry about paying the rent, or the doctor's bills for his ailing wife?

Such speculations are of course ultimately futile. Poe's genius derived in part from the very circumstances that crushed him. The literature he created is a literature of frustration, alienation, introversion, revenge, obsession, disaster. Out of his conviction that he had been neglected, wronged, slighted, grew his lyrics of heartbreak, his disdainful dissections of the faults in the writings of his peers (peers? inferiors, as he saw most of them—although he immediately recognized the quality of Hawthorne), and those icy or eerie tales of existence pressing in claustrophobically upon doomed aristocrats whose only weapons—pride, intellect—were inadequate to preserve them from the universal malignance. See Edward Wagenknecht, *Edgar Allan Poe: The Man Behind the Legend* (1963).

MARCUS CUNLIFFE

POLK, James Knox (b. Mecklenberg Co., N.C., Nov. 2, 1795; d. Nashville, Tenn., June 15, 1849), PRESIDENT, graduated from the University of North Carolina (1818) and was admitted to the Tennessee bar in 1820. Active in Democratic politics, he served in the Tennessee state legislature (1823–24) and as U.S. congressman (1825–39), speaker of the House of Representatives (1834–39), and governor of Tennessee (1839–41).

At the Democratic presidential convention of 1844, Polk, a lifelong supporter of Andrew Jackson, was nominated as a "dark horse" on the ninth ballot, after Martin Van Buren failed to get a two-thirds majority because of his opposition to the annexation of Texas. An expansionist, Polk campaigned for "the reoccupation of Oregon and the reannexation of Texas." In the election, he defeated **Henry Clay** 170 electoral votes to 105, his popular plurality being only 38,175.

As president, Polk sought to reduce the tariff, to reestablish Van Buren's independent Treasury, to negotiate a treaty with Great Britain dividing the Oregon Territory at the 49th parallel, and to acquire California. In August 1846 he sent John Slidell to Mexico in the hope of purchasing upper California and New Mexico, and of adjusting the Texas boundary along the Rio Grande. The

Mexican government refused to negotiate with Slidell. On May 11, 1846, after a Mexican force crossed the Rio Grande and attacked American detachments, Congress declared war. Poorly equipped and badly organized, the Mexicans proved no match for the American army. By the Treaty of Guadalupe Hidalgo (1848), Mexico ceded California and New Mexico to the U.S., and the Rio Grande became Texas's southern boundary. Polk served as president from 1845 to 1849. He did not seek reelection.

———— ✸ ————

Polk's prepresidential career was marked by hard work, legislative skill, admiration of Andrew Jackson, and devotion to the Democratic party. A slender man of medium height and undistinguished mien, he lacked charisma and indeed twice failed to be reelected governor of his state. The only speaker of the House to win promotion to the executive mansion, Polk was also the first major-party "dark horse" ever on the presidential track. "Who *is* James K. Polk?" inquired Whigs of 1844 in mock shock or scorn for the Democratic choice. Not only did Polk proceed to beat the long-recognized number one Whig champion, but as president the Tennessean showed very quickly and convincingly that he was a person of remarkable executive efficiency.

The White House record of the eleventh president is a monument to the determination, ardor, and aggressiveness of one who was not merely an expansionist but a continentalist. Only Thomas Jefferson rivaled Polk as a presidential acquirer of land prior to the purchase of Alaska. Any other believer in Manifest Destiny, similarly emphasizing territorial gains, would have been as gratified as Polk regarding his impressive achievements.

Yet the other side of the coin should also be examined. **Ralph Waldo Emerson** said, "Mexico will poison us." By this the New England writer meant that Americans' differences of opinion concerning slavery's extension to western and southwestern soil, acquired from Mexico, would magnify sectional misunderstandings and possibly lead to civil war. By 20th-century standards,

Polk (a slaveholder) was morally obtuse on several counts, one of them being that he considered the antiextension argument irrelevant.

In other areas of accomplishment, Polk—especially in 1845 and 1846—was indubitably dynamic and effective. The low Walker Tariff (1846), sponsored by Polk and Secretary of the Treasury **Robert J. Walker,** was not completely pleasing to all parts of the country and indeed proved unpopular in manufacturing states; nevertheless, it had many supporters, particularly in the South and West, and it remained in force eleven years. High marks have usually been given the independent Treasury, which Polk and the 29th Congress revived. It is doubtful that any U.S. administration, without going to war with Great Britain, could have done better in Oregon from the American viewpoint than to reach agreement with the British on a compromise boundary at 49 degrees.

During the first half of his White House service, Polk had Democratic majorities in Congress. As the results attest, he made the most of this advantage, working in close conjunction with legislative committee chairmen and helping shape bills that he subsequently signed. Whig control of the House of Representatives from 1847 to 1849 stemmed partly from opposition to the Mexican War and partly from the natural midterm reaction (evident in so many administrations) against the party in power. While congressional Whigs checked Polk in some of his moves, he was more embarrassed by a serious error of judgment—letting Antonio López de Santa Anna through the American naval blockade and into Mexico. (Polk thought Santa Anna would stop the fighting; instead, the erstwhile exile accelerated its tempo.) Polk, too, was criticized for transferring most of General Zachary Taylor's seasoned troops to the command of **Winfield Scott,** and for adopting an anomalous attitude toward his treaty negotiator, Nicholas P. Trist.

One of America's few chief executives to keep a diary, Polk dutifully recorded nearly all of what he considered the high points of his administration, together with minute details and numerous nuances of his hopes and thinking. A contribution of the diary is its accurate reflection of social life in the White House circle. Mrs. Polk was resolutely opposed to drinking and dancing but entertained with grace and skill. The Polks had no children. Overall it is doubtful that any other president has been more conscientious, according to his lights, than this emphatic, incredibly industrious, driving, and humorless lieutenant and protégé of "Old Hickory" Jackson. See Charles G. Sellers, *James K. Polk* (2 vols., 1957–66).

HOLMAN HAMILTON

POLLOCK, Jackson (b. Cody, Wyo., Jan. 28, 1912; d. East Hampton, L.I., N.Y., Aug. 11, 1956), ARTIST, grew up in Wyoming, Arizona, and California. After studying under **Thomas Hart Benton** at the Art Students League of New York (1929–31), he traveled through the West for several years. Pollock then settled in New York in 1935. He worked on the WPA's Federal Art Project from 1938 to 1942. Though strongly influenced by Benton's realism, Pollock soon began to evolve a highly abstract style of his own; in 1943 he gave his first one-man show at Peggy Guggenheim's Art of This Century Gallery in New York. *The Sea-Wolf* (1943, Museum of Modern Art, N.Y.), using symbolic motifs, is quite representative of his early abstract work. In 1946 Pollock moved to East Hampton, Long Island, where he continued to develop his technique of dripping and splattering aluminum paint and commercial enamels upon the canvas instead of using a brush. This new style (abstract expressionism), typified by his *Number One* (1948, Museum of Modern Art), emphasized the expressive handling of materials and unarranged pictorial effects which seem to arise spontaneously while the artist worked. It received much attention and criticism, and Pollock emerged as the leader of abstract expressionism or "action" painting.

He was killed in an automobile crash on Long Island. Some of his other works are: *Painting* (1945, Museum of Modern Art, N.Y.), *Eyes in the Heat* (1946, Peggy Guggenheim Collection, N.Y.), and *Blue Poles* (1952, National Gallery, Canberra, Australia).

One of the most original and influential American painters of the 20th century, Jackson Pollock was the artist most identified in public reputation with abstract expressionism. He early turned away from the anecdotal and social reform emphasis of much American painting and struck out in new directions to stress the materials and techniques of visual art. In his major paintings, he customarily poured paint from cans or dripped it from sticks directly onto huge canvases, building up an intricate interlacing of fine lines and interwoven forms alternating with large areas of color. Although the paintings seldom included recognizable symbols, each work usually projected a particular mood of atmosphere. Often Pollock made use of such materials as pebbles, shells, string, or bits of glass, constructing surface textures and stressing tactile qualities as an important aspect of the full meaning of a painting.

Pollock was greatly encouraged and aided by the regionalist Thomas Hart Benton, but he felt that his study with Benton was primarily important "as something against which to react very strongly." By the early 1940s he had developed his characteristic drip painting. Most likely the chief artistic influences on him came from Picasso, Miró, and Kandinsky. Although some critics felt that his paintings were so personal in meaning that they failed to communicate, most enthusiastically hailed Pollock's achievement. By 1948 he was generally recognized as a major American painter, and in 1973 his *Blue Poles* was sold at auction for $2 million, the highest price ever paid for an American painting.

Despite the fact that his principal paintings often give a superficial impression of undisciplined outpouring, the elements of line, color, light, texture, and form are developed with considerable control. Moving away from visual reference to other things, the painting elements become the content of the work. Linearism is especially emphasized. The curling, intertwining lines, together with the spaces in between, commonly provide a sensation of vast continuous space, with forms that emerge and recede. Rich in detail and vigorously rhythmical, these paintings have an exuberant and restless quality that is often lyrical and usually highly evocative.

Although intensely committed to his art and very productive, Pollock often felt deeply troubled about himself and his work. He struck many of those close to him as emotionally unstable. When he was twenty-five he first underwent treatment for acute alcoholism, and until the time of his death he was frequently under psychiatric care. The source of his art was primarily the unconscious, and he indicated that it was "only after a sort of 'get acquainted' period" that he could see what he had been doing. In the process of painting, he became, in a sense, a part of the actual work of art. Usually, he painted with the canvas on the floor and worked on it from all sides. "On the floor I am more at ease. I feel nearer, more a part of the painting since this way I can walk around it, work from four sides and literally be in the painting." Sometimes labeled an "action" painter, Pollock, like other abstract expressionists, emphasized the act of creating an art object as a form of personal commitment and as a move to self-identification. "Painting," he said in 1956, "is a self discovery. Every good artist paints what he is." See Steven Naifeh and Gregory White Smith, *Jackson Pollock: An American Saga* (1990).

PAUL R. BAKER

PONTIAC (b. prob. in Detroit River region, c. 1720; d. Cahokia, Ill., April 20, 1769), NATIVE AMERICAN LEADER. Knowledge of his early life is sketchy. He may have been present when the French and Native Americans defeated General Braddock near Fort Duquesne in 1755; at that time he was chief of the Ottawa tribe and the leader of a loose confederation of other tribes.

After the Treaty of Paris ending the French and Indian War (1763), tensions between the Native Americans and the English mounted. Freed of French competition, the English fur traders cheated the Native Americans, and the British government refused to supply them with food and guns as the French had done. These affronts, added to the threat of a great influx of white settlers into Native American territory, enraged Pontiac. At a conference held near Detroit in April 1763, the Native Americans of the Ohio Valley formed a confederacy under his leadership. His plan to take Detroit ("Pontiac's Conspiracy," May 1763) failed. However, still determined to drive the white man across the mountains, he and his men continued to fight, capturing every English fort west of Fort Niagara except Pittsburgh and ravaging the entire frontier area west of Niagara. He kept up the siege of Fort Detroit during the summer and early fall of 1763. He finally capitulated and withdrew his warriors on October 31, 1763, when he at last realized that the French help he expected would not be forthcoming. By this time a number of tribes in the confederacy had signed peace treaties, but Pontiac moved westward and encouraged the tribes to continued resistance to the British. He finally submitted in 1766, signing a peace pact at Oswego with Sir **William Johnson** in July.

During his remaining years, Pontiac was loyal to the British. While visiting Illinois, he was murdered by a Peoria Native American who was supposedly bribed by an English trader.

⸎

The great Ottawa chieftain was quick to grasp the critical threat that British control of the trans-Appalachian region posed to the continued survival of the Native American nations. A gifted orator and a man of superior intellect and remarkable breadth of vision, Pontiac was able to inspire the tribes to put aside their petty jealousies and rivalries and unite in a war for Native American independence. This was no mean achievement, for these disparate tribes, firmly attached to their own local interests, had had no tradition of acting in unity for a common cause. Pontiac himself had been inspired by the teachings of the Delaware Prophet. This remarkable preacher, who rose to prominence around 1762, taught that the Native Americans would regain their greatness only when they had purified themselves, had destroyed the whites and all the trappings of white culture, and had returned to the simple ways that existed before the Europeans came. Such religious teachings arise only during periods of extreme crisis, when a people feel both culturally and politically threatened. Pontiac was the leader who appeared at just the opportune moment to carry out the Prophet's teachings, which he modified to fit his political ends. Those whites who knew Pontiac at the height of his power testified that he was a man of commanding presence who was highly esteemed by all the tribes and whose word was law. So much the greater was his fall from power, for when he made his peace with the British, he became a figure widely despised among many of his former friends and allies and an exile from his own village. See Howard H. Peckham, *Pontiac and the Indian Uprising* (1947).

BARBARA GRAYMONT

POOR, Henry Varnum (b. East Andover, Maine, Dec. 8, 1812; d. Brookline, Mass., Jan. 4, 1905), BUSINESS LEADER, graduated from Bowdoin College in 1835 and entered his uncle's law office in Bangor, Maine, that same year. Admitted to the bar in 1838, he practiced law in a partnership with his brother John in Bangor until 1848. He also invested heavily in Maine's lumber industry during 1845–47. In 1849 John Poor purchased the *American Railroad Journal* and invited Henry to come to New York City to serve as its editor and business manager. In this capacity, Poor collected, compiled, and published information on railroad development in the U.S. and also on other businesses. Poor also compiled volume one of the *History of the Railroads and Canals of the United States of America* (1860).

Poor left the *Journal* in 1861 to become an editorial writer for the New York *Times* (1861–62). Writing at first on the impact of secession on the economy, he went on to discuss money, banking, public finance, and various economic policies. He strongly favored protective tariffs and internal improvements, especially a transcontinental railroad. In 1862 he became a government commissioner and then the first secretary of the Union Pacific Railroad Co., resigning in 1864. Poor joined his son, Henry William, in 1867 in forming the firm of H. V. and H. W. Poor to import rails and railway supplies. Beginning in 1868 the firm published its *Manual of the Railroads of the United States*, which reviewed railroad progress and published statistics on American railroads; it later provided similar data on industrial and other corporations. Becoming known as *Poor's Manual of Railroads*, the journal was widely used. Poor later edited two other periodicals, *Poor's Directory of Railway Officials* (1886–95) and *Poor's Hand-Book of Investment Securities* (1890–92). He also continued writing on economic questions. *Money and Its Laws* (1887) argued for the gold standard and a central banking system, while his *Twenty-two Years of Protection* (1888) and *The Tariff: Its Bearing upon the Industries and Politics of the United States* (1892) both vigorously advocated protective tariffs.

⬦

Henry V. Poor was one of the very first Americans to make a career of compiling and publishing business information. By effectively serving the business community of his day, he provided invaluable source material on the 19th-century American economy and particularly on its railroads. When Poor became editor of the *American Railroad Journal* in 1849, the nation was on the verge of its first great railroad boom. By 1860 the basic network east of the Mississippi of thirty-thousand miles of track, built and equipped at a cost exceeding a billion dollars, had been completed. To meet the new needs of the railroad industry Poor turned his periodical from engineering to finance. At first he saw himself as the representative of the railroads on Wall Street. As the decade of the 1850s progressed, the *Journal* became increasingly the spokesman for the investor. Poor analyzed and reported on the progress and performance of individual roads and of the American network as a whole. He warned against speculative ventures and pointed to the growing dangers of overconstruction. The recession of 1854 and the sharp depression of 1857, by giving reality to these warnings, enhanced Poor's reputation as a railroad analyst and reformer.

In the *Journal* Poor also included detailed statistical data about individual roads. This information he summarized in the *Journal's* stock and bond list which gave costs, earnings, capital paid in and funded debt, as well as the current prices of securities for all roads whose stocks or bonds were traded on the New York Stock Exchange. In 1854 he increased the accuracy and detail of his list by sending out a long questionnaire to all major roads. The information from these questionnaires and from company and state reports was consolidated into detailed articles on the different roads. These pieces, many of which were published in the *Journal,* provided the basis for the first volume of his history of railroads and canals. The coming of the Civil War turned Poor to writing for the New York *Times* and to serving as secretary of the Union Pacific. Although his second volume never appeared, much of the information prepared for it was printed in the *Journal,* and the data provided a statistical basis for the *Manual of the Railroads of the United States* which Poor and his son began to publish annually after 1867. The *Manual* listed for almost every railroad in the country its physical properties, its officers and directors, and its operating and financial record. In the introduction to the *Manuals,* Poor summarized in tabular form: mileage, capital invested, rolling stock and engines used, miles run, earnings gross and net, dividends, cost per mile, and operating and other ratios for each state, each major region, and the nation as a whole. In addition to these statistical summaries, Poor wrote as introductions to the *Manuals* analytical essays which emphasized the impact of railroads on American farming and industry, and on the business cycle; he pointed out the dangers of competitive construction, stock watering, and misuse of accounts; explained the complexities of railroad economics, and consistently called for publication of railroad accounts and financial statements. In these essays, as in his books on money and on the tariff, Poor spoke for the conservative element in the nation's financial community. See Alfred D. Chandler, Jr., *Henry Varnum Poor: Business Editor, Analyst and Reformer* (1956).

ALFRED D. CHANDLER, JR.

PORTER, Cole Albert (b. Peru, Ind., June 9, 1892; d. Santa Monica, Calif., Oct. 15, 1964), COMPOSER, received an AB from Yale, where he wrote several school songs, in 1913. After attending Harvard Law School for one semester (1914), Porter studied at the Harvard Music School (1915–16). His first musical comedy, *See America First* (1916), was a failure. During World War I he served with the French, and then with the U.S. army. Following the war he wrote the scores and lyrics for two shows, *Kitchy Koo* (1919) and *Greenwich Village Follies* (1924), but from 1924 to 1927 he found it difficult to get his work produced. Finally, Ray Goetz invited him to write the score for a new musical comedy, *Paris* (1928), for which Porter wrote the hit song "Let's Do It." He followed this success with such shows as *Fifty Million Frenchmen* (1929), *The Gay Divorcee* (1932), from which comes his classic "Night and Day," and *Anything Goes* (1934), which included the tune "You're the Top." *Jubilee* (1935) contained "Begin the Beguine," which was made popular in a recording by bandleader Artie Shaw in 1938.

Although severely crippled by a horseback riding accident in 1937, Porter continued writing musical comedies with hardly a letup. *Du Barry Was a Lady* (1939) featured "Do I Love You?" *Kiss Me, Kate* (1948), based on Shakespeare's *The Taming of the Shrew,* became his most popular show with such songs as "Wunderbar" and "So in Love." *Can-Can* (1953) and his last musical comedy, *Silk Stockings* (1955), were also highly successful. Porter wrote the music for many movies, including *Born to Dance* (1936), with the popular "I've Got You under My Skin," *High Society* (1956), and *Les Girls* (1957). Declining health and a leg amputation forced him to live in total seclusion in his New York apartment and his home in Brentwood, California, after 1958. His life story was made into the film *Night and Day* (1948).

Except for *Kiss Me, Kate,* Cole Porter was satisfied to work within the stereotypes and formats of the traditional musical comedy. As a composer and lyricist (and his creative strength is divided equally between the two) he did nothing to extend the horizons of the stage musical as an art form, nor, for that matter, did he make appreciable advances in extending the techniques and structure of songwriting. He was content to write songs following traditional patterns that could fall effortlessly within the slot assigned them in a production, whether they sprang naturally from the text or not, whether or not they helped to enhance dramatic interest or give an insight into characterization. Once again with the exception of *Kiss Me, Kate,* the musicals to which Porter contributed his songs are like museum pieces, even when revived with revised and updated texts. His best songs, however, have become enduring classics.

On each of his little masterpieces the impress of his personality is pronounced. Born a millionaire, and raised from childhood to enjoy the refinements of good living, Porter was the ultrasophisticate who traveled extensively, who played hard at having good times in the fleshpots of Europe, and who, in the process, absorbed a good deal of culture. The wide range of his interests and experiences is reflected in his remarkable lyrics, which cater to adult sophistication in their mastery of versification, their poetic imagery, and their continual urbane references to esoteric, exotic, or erotic themes. And his lyrics find their perfect match in music which, in his ballads, is often characterized by sensuous sweeps of the melody to a thrilling climactic point over a throbbing, irresistible rhythm, or, in his wittier items, by a subtle and at times a rapier-edged sense of humor. See George Eells, *The Life That Late He Led: The Biography of Cole Porter* (1967).

DAVID EWEN

POUND, Ezra Loomis (b. Hailey, Idaho, Oct. 30, 1885; d. Venice, Italy, Nov. 2, 1972), WRITER, entered the University of Pennsylvania in 1900 but transferred to Hamilton College (Clinton, N.Y.), and graduated from there in 1905. He earned his MA in Romance languages and English literature at the University of Pennsylvania (1906). He then studied the work of the Spanish dramatist Lope de Vega in Europe on a fellowship. He taught English at Wabash College (Crawfordsville, Indiana) in 1907 but was dismissed, and settled in London in 1908.

With the publication of *Personae* (1909), a collection of poems, Pound established his literary reputation in both England and the United States. He edited several literary magazines and aided such struggling young writers as T. S. Eliot, Yeats, and Joyce. Pound also began to publish translations from Anglo-Saxon and Provençal poets during this period. After *Homage to Sextus Propertius* (1917) and *Hugh Selwyn Mauberley* (1920), Pound emerged as a moving spirit and innovator of modern English poetry.

Pound lived in Paris (1920–24) before settling in Italy in 1924, where he published the first sections of his epic work, *Cantos* (1925). During the 1930s Pound became concerned about the Great Depression and wrote a series of pamphlets expressing his views on the world economic situation. In 1939 Pound returned to the U.S. for a visit but went back to Italy in 1940. He made a series of broadcasts (1940–45) there—many of them permeated with anti-Semitism—in which he talked not only of literature but of economics. He spoke favorably of fascism and critically of the Roosevelt administration. The American army arrested Pound in Italy in 1945 and jailed him in a cage near Pisa. Out of that experience he wrote *Pisan Cantos* (1948). He was then taken to Washington, D.C., and indicted for treason. After many writers testified in his behalf, Pound was ruled mentally unfit to stand trial and was for ten years remanded to St. Elizabeths Hospital. While at St. Elizabeths he was awarded the prestigious Bollingen poetry prize. Pressure from writers' organizations finally led to his release in 1958. He then returned to Italy. His *Letters* (1950) and *Literary Essays* (1954) reveal much of his complex personality.

———— ✖ ————

Ezra Pound was one of the most highly praised and savagely attacked literary figures of his times. Generous and kind as an individual, his criticism of shoddy work could be scathing. Hated by some and loved by others, he elicited during his life condemnation and defense but little in the way of just appraisal.

Throughout his career, he was an enormously industrious scholar; by the time he was twenty-one, he had mastered Latin, French, Italian, Provençal, Spanish, and Anglo-Saxon. Later on, when he came into possession of the incomplete translations of the orientalist Ernest Fenellosa, he set himself to independent study of Chinese—a study that occupied him for years—in order to finish the translations and be able to read Confucius in the original. Still later, convinced that he had discovered a relationship between economic forces and cultural decline, he turned to history. Concluding that "usury" as practiced by the great international banking houses of Europe and America was ultimately responsible for the sterility of modern life, he propounded his conclusions in pamphlet after pamphlet and allowed his obsession to dominate the historical sections of *The Cantos*.

Though his approach to scholarship was hardly academic and not always systematic, Pound nevertheless saw himself in the role of teacher-scholar. Almost all of his literary commentary, either in handbooks like *The ABC of Reading*, in letters like the notable ones to his former teacher Felix Schelling, or throughout the body of *The Cantos*, is devoted to a persistent reexamination of our basic assumptions as readers and as writers. He wants us to come to terms with the nature of poetry itself: to discover the function of the image, of the juxtaposition of information and poetic invention, and of the subtleties of rhythm that distinguish great poems from mere successions of iambs and anapests. Convinced that all arts are interrelated, Pound attempts to explain poetry in terms of music, painting, and sculpture.

His editorial role is only another manifestation of his role as teacher-scholar. When, as a young man, he succeeded in gaining control of the most significant English and American literary quarterlies—usually calling himself "foreign correspondent" or "European editor"—he began a one-man campaign to transform the literary taste

of his generation. To an extraordinary degree, he succeeded. Almost singlehandedly responsible for making, and keeping, America aware of the work of James Joyce and T. S. Eliot, he was also the most vocal supporter of the early poetry of **Robert Frost,** H. D. (Hilda Doolittle), and **William Carlos Williams**. Frequently at odds with the tastes of the "official" editors of *Poetry, Egoist,* and *The Little Review,* he bludgeoned those good ladies—in letter after threatening letter—into becoming the chief supporters of what he hoped would be a Pound-engineered literary and artistic renaissance.

But that renaissance could not be solidly grounded in America, Pound felt, unless America were made aware of the rich cultural heritage that lay locked up in untranslated or poorly translated European and Asian masterpieces. "Make It New," a motto Pound hung on his wall and chose for the title of one of his books, was the key, he believed, to the revitalization of unavailable works. By showing how ancient Provençal, Anglo-Saxon, and Chinese poetry could be transformed into idiomatic "contemporary" poems, Pound ushered in a totally new breed of translators and adaptors—poets in their own right—who were more concerned with the spirit of the original work than its mechanical form or its line-by-line accuracy. Though critics quibble about the "precision" of Pound's Chinese, no sensitive reader can fail to respond to the moving power of the translations from Li Po: "The River Merchant's Wife," for example, or "Poem by the Bridge at Ten-Shin," or, perhaps greatest of all, "Exile's Letter," a poem that in its last few lines—its emphasis on the silences of old age and death, its emphasis on friendships broken by accidents of time and place—so extraordinarily anticipates Pound's own final years.

According to his detractors, Pound was greater as a literary force than as an original artist, a man who can be pigeon-holed as a kind of 20th-century Dr. Johnson. And certainly by conventional standards, his life-work—the huge, evolving, fragmented, unfinished structure that he called *The Cantos*—seems at best chaotic and at worst impenetrable. His busy life, in contrast, seems vastly "important." And yet if one accepts the notion that a work may indeed exist "in process," if one accepts brokenness, incompleteness, open-endedness as possible "forms," if one—to take an analogy from architecture— accepts as aesthetically satisfying the infinitely complex entanglements of Gaudí's unfinished cathedral at Barcelona, then a different sort of aesthetic has to be invented before "in-process" works (Pound might have called them Vorticist works) can be judged. Perhaps if we see works of this kind as simultaneously representative of form, flux, and disintegration we will come close to an image for what they show us: a universe in which everything is falling apart and being built and in which nothing can or will stand still. Chaos in such art seems always to battle to a draw man's ordering, desperate, formalizing mind. Destructive and synthesizing forces seem endlessly to grapple toward some unresolvable conclusion that cannot by its very nature conclude. In this even battle of making and breaking, of chaos and creation, only the breaking itself and our resistance to it seems to have meaning. From the point of view of a "process" artist, our frantic efforts to rescue from the disappearing past those crucial fragments out of which new life, new art can temporarily be created are the most meaningful gestures that we make. A jumble, a heap of twisted eloquence, an image finally only of itself—or of the process that it represents—*The Cantos* offers us what one man felt worth briefly saving from the silence of lost things. See Charles Norman, *Ezra Pound: A Biography* (1968).

JOHN UNTERECKER

POUND, (Nathan) Roscoe (b. Lincoln, Neb., Oct. 27, 1870; d. Cambridge, Mass., July 1, 1964), LAW PROFESSOR, JURIST, BOTANIST, attended the University of Nebraska, where he received his BA (1888), his MA (1889) and his PhD (1897) in botany. During his early years as a botanist, he discovered a rare lichen thereafter known as "Roscoepoundia." He was a member of the Botanical Survey of Nebraska, and the coauthor of *Phytogeography of Nebraska* (1900), but his inter-

ests increasingly shifted towards the law. After a year at Harvard Law School he returned to Lincoln, was admitted to the Nebraska bar (1890) and began to practice law. In 1901, the State Supreme Court appointed him Commissioner of Appeals. He resigned in 1903 to become Dean of the University of Nebraska Law School. He subsequently took a teaching position at Northwestern (1907–09), spent a year at the University of Chicago (1909–10), and accepted an appointment to the Harvard Law School where he remained for the rest of his career (1910–47) as Dean (1916–36), holder of the fabled Justice Joseph Story Chair and University Professor. In retirement, Pound remained active as a writer, teacher, and consultant both here and abroad. A brilliant legal scholar and prolific author, among his many works are, *Readings on the History and System of the Common Law* (1904), *Law and Morals* (1924), *Justice According to Law* (1951), and *Jurisprudence* (5 vols., 1959).

⁂

Possessed of prodigious learning, an encyclopedic memory, and inexhaustible energy, Roscoe Pound was one of the most original legal theorists in the history of American jurisprudence. Though he did not create sociological jurisprudence and was not the first student of the law to attack court decisions based on dogma, like "liberty of contract," without regard to their practical effect, he was the most provocative and original advocate of that philosophy which stressed the dependence of legal rules on changing social conditions and the most ardent and informed critic of "mechanical jurisprudence." His scholarship encompassed the whole history of American law, uncovered its persistent dependency on outmoded foreign models that dominated legal thought and froze legal progress, and offered a new way of thinking about the law and employing it. As he once superbly put it: "The sociological movement in jurisprudence is a movement for pragmatism as a philosophy of law; for the adjustment of principles and doctrines to the human conditions they are to govern rather than to assume first principles; for putting the human factor in the central place and relegating logic to its true position as an instrument." The law, as he saw it, must take actual societal conditions into account rather than maintaining strict adherence to legal codes.

By 1937, Pound's legal philosophy, eloquently promoted by Justice **Louis Brandeis**, embraced by Justices **Benjamin Cardozo** and **Harlan Fiske Stone**, and given visibility by Justice **Felix Frankfurter**, became the official doctrine of the Supreme Court under President Franklin Roosevelt. But though his ideas were now triumphant on the bench Pound began to have misgivings about how they worked in practice. He began to feel that the New Deal was promoting a welfare or "service state" that boded ill for the future health of the country. A long held but long suppressed conservatism clearly began to reveal itself. *In Justice According to Law* (1951) he set forth his misgivings about what his followers had brought about. He now seemed to argue that society should change itself to conform to legal rules rather than adhere to the sociological jurisprudent philosophy with which his name had become synonymous. Still, whatever his own doubts, he could not undue the legal revolution he had played a major role in unleashing. See David Wigdor, *Roscoe Pound, Philosopher of Law* (1974).

FRED RAGAN

POWDERLY, Terence Vincent (b. Carbondale, Pa., Jan. 22, 1849; d. Washington, D.C., June 24, 1924), LABOR LEADER, became a machinist's apprentice and joined the Machinists and Blacksmith's International Union in 1871. He was elected mayor of Scranton, Pennsylvania, in 1878 on the Greenback Labor ticket and was reelected in 1880 and 1882. In 1879 he became Grand Master Workman of the Knights of Labor. The Knights' program was based on a reformist rather than on a trade-union ideology. It supported boycotts and arbitration, opposed strikes, and advocated producers' and consumers' cooperatives, the regulation of trusts, currency reform, and the abolition of child labor. The Knights hoped to abolish the wage system through edu-

cation rather than economic action, and to replace the existing order with a cooperative society based on the dominance of small producers.

Under Powderly's leadership the Knights was the first industrial union to admit all producers regardless of race or sex. It established hundreds of colored and many integrated locals in the South, and played a role—though not a decisive one—in the passage of the Contract Labor Act (1885). At its height the rank and file successfully challenged monopolies through strikes, boycotts, and political action. Its most dramatic victories were the successful strikes and boycotts against **Jay Gould**'s southwestern railroad system (1885–86).

However, Powderly also helped destroy the Knights. Fearing the rapid growth of the Order after successful strikes, he attempted to limit the number of recruits; ideologically opposed to strikes, he often attempted to prevent or discourage local chapters from using this economic weapon. To appease the Catholic Church after it attacked the Knights as socialist, Powderly tried to make the organization more conservative. He also reversed the Knights' principles of equality, excluded Chinese from membership, and supported the Chinese Exclusion Act (1882).

In 1893 the rural wing of the Knights, supported by the socialists, ousted Powderly. He then became a lawyer and civil servant. He was admitted to the Pennsylvania bar in 1894, and served as commissioner general of immigration (1897–1902). He participated in several business ventures as president of the Black Diamond Coal Co. and as Washington representative of the General Lubricating Co. of Philadelphia (1902–7). He was chief of the Division of Information in the Bureau of Immigration (1907–21), and commissioner of conciliation of the Department of Labor (1924). He wrote *Thirty Years of Labor: 1859–1889* (1889). An autobiography, *The Path I Trod,* a vindication of his public life and work, was published posthumously in 1940.

———◈◈◈———

During the 1880s Powderly was by far the most popular and renowned labor leader in the

United States. His vision of a better world, his voluminous correspondence with the rank and file, his oratorical skills, and his obvious sincerity and sense of mission all contributed to his widespread appeal. It was, in fact, as a publicist and educator that he made his greatest and most enduring contribution to the labor movement. While developing little that was original in the way of organizational techniques or policies, he did help to draw attention to American workers and to make them aware of a growing labor movement.

Powderly's successes in the 1880s were more the result of chance than of design. While he emphasized broad social goals and vague abstractions, many members of the Knights were drawn to that organization because of their concern with higher wages, shorter hours, and job control. This divergence of goals between Powderly and the rank and file resulted in an unbridgeable chasm within the Knights that by the late 1880s had destroyed it as an effective force in the labor movement. In many ways Powderly's character and personal attributes exacerbated organizational tensions within the Knights. More concerned with visions of a better society, he had little patience and few of the characteristics that might have enabled him to transform the Knights into an organization capable of implementing these visions. He saw the Knights as his private domain and often equated disagreement with disloyalty; a number of subordinates who disagreed with some of his policies were expelled. Powderly's feelings of indispensability led him to submit his resignation as head of the Knights more than a dozen times, knowing each time that it would not be accepted.

As an administrator Powderly was unable to delegate responsibility and often insisted upon supervising the most minute details. His relations with his executive board were not close; he remained a hundred miles distant in Scranton even though the board functioned in Philadelphia. Powderly spent much of his time writing letters, many of which expressed dissatisfaction with his heavy burdens. On several occasions he even argued that the president of

the United States had a far lighter task as compared with his own. Moreover, when events moved rapidly, Powderly often proved inflexible and unable to improvise. On a number of key occasions he claimed illness during a time of crisis and offered the poor state of his health as a rationalization for his inaction. By the early 1890s he had so isolated himself that he proved unable to resist a movement to remove him as head of the Knights. Shortly before he was deposed from office, Powderly, in a letter, wrote his own epitaph: "No man in this country has so many domineering bosses as I have, for every member feels it to be his right to sit down and abuse me if he pleases or order me around to do as he likes and not as I think…. On the other hand my relations with my brother officers … are not pleasant…. I who have been preaching independence for others have been the slave of thousands, and as my reward am as little understood by the people I work for as Hoke Smith or Dink Botts." His later career as a federal official was of minor importance. See his autobiography, *The Path I Trod*, which, though highly inaccurate and even misleading, reveals much of his character and personality, and Gerald N. Grob, *Workers and Utopia: A Study of Ideological Conflict in the American Labor Movement 1865–1900* (1961), which deals with Powderly and the Knights in the 1880s.

GERALD N. GROB

POWELL, Adam Clayton, Jr. (b. New Haven, Conn., Nov. 29, 1908; d. Miami, Fla., April 4, 1972), POLITICAL LEADER, came to New York City in 1914 when his father became minister of the Abyssinian Baptist Church in Harlem. After receiving his AB from Colgate in 1930, Powell took an MA from Columbia (1932) and studied for the ministry at Shaw University, where he received his DD in 1935. He became assistant pastor to his father and, upon the latter's retirement in 1937, his successor.

Powell played an active role in the incipient civil rights movement, constantly walking picket lines and demanding that such companies as Con Edison and New York Bell Telephone hire blacks for other than menial work. In 1941 he became the first African-American ever elected to the New York City Council, where he continued to press for the hiring of blacks on public transportation and at the city colleges of New York. In 1942 he founded a militant newspaper, *The People's Voice,* and two years later he was elected to the U.S. House of Representatives after gaining the nominations of the Democratic, Republican, and American Labor parties.

In Congress, Powell served as chairman of the committee on education and labor (1961–66). In this position he was very influential in expediting passage of President Lyndon B. Johnson's "Great Society" antipoverty programs. At the same time Powell fell under increasing criticism for his long absences from Congress, alleged misuse of government money, and failure to pay damages owed because of a 1960 libel suit. In 1967 the House removed him as chairman of his committee, stripped him of his seniority, and refused to seat him. Reelected to Congress in 1968, Powell was finally seated. (The Supreme Court ruled in 1969 that the House had violated the Constitution in refusing to seat Powell.) In 1970 Powell lost the Democratic nomination for his seat in the primary election to Charles Rangel. Powell published many sermons, articles, and books including: *Is This a White Man's War?* (1942) and *Marching Blacks* (1945).

Powell was the first African-American to represent an eastern urban black ghetto in Congress. He differed from his black predecessors in Congress in several crucial respects. Powell came as near to being born with a silver spoon in his mouth as a African-American could in that era; his father was a successful clergyman and built up a small fortune in New York (Harlem) real estate. Adam Clayton Powell, Jr., thus was provided with a college education at an elite institution and seldom suffered privations of any sort. His subsequent political career was affected by this situation.

Having grown up in Harlem, where racial militancy on the part of blacks (especially those of West Indian origin) gained its first major expression—the **Garvey** Movement having originated there around World War I—Powell was not unaware of the political potential of a racial militancy that was wedded to the electoral process. More than any other African-American professional politician in the late 1930s through the 1950s, he transformed racial militancy—popularly called black nationalism—into a reasonably viable political instrument. As early as 1930, he turned his considerable oratorical gifts and skill at popular arousal to the task of mobilizing thousands of Harlem blacks into a direct-action force, directed against the discriminatory practices of Harlem Hospital. The strategy was to create a measure of tension and conflict between blacks and whites that required a concession from the city authorities. The tactic of direct action proved successful, and the Harlem Hospital was forced to alter its discriminatory practices. In 1944, Powell institutionalized this strategy and the tactics associated with it. He directed racial militancy to the electoral process, running for Congress in New York's 21st congressional district. Lacking the support structures of the established political machines, Powell mobilized voting support by politicizing racial perceptions—those of blacks, that is—his main instrument being his charismatic political style. This style also proved invaluable in providing Powell national standing among African-Americans, for he employed it in his daily relationships with white politicians in Congress, differing markedly in this respect from the only other African-American in Congress during Powell's first decade there—William Dawson of Chicago. Rather than compromise with the decisive power formations in Congress when legislation affecting blacks was under consideration—a pattern of compromise that invariably found blacks' needs discarded—Powell aggressively used Congress as a platform for militant defenses of blacks, castigating compromise as betrayal. This tactic was institutionalized from 1961 on when Powell gained the chairmanship of the House Education and Labor Committee; he periodically attached pro-black amendments—popularly called "Powell amendments"—to the crucial legislation from his committee. This caused serious delay in the enactment of such legislation, modification of it, but only seldom its defeat. Powell had no peer as a black politician of enormous national prestige among blacks during his twenty-six years in Congress.

Powell's political style was also compounded of personal ingredients. First, he was a man of more than usual vanity; the demagogic political style—a variant of the charismatic style—was nearly endemic to his character. Thus he considered himself a savior—at least symbolically—to the politically weak, poor, and exploited black populace. In a word, he internalized a messiah complex. Furthermore, he suffered throughout boyhood and young manhood a gnawing urge to realize a sphere of legitimate activity in which he could match the professional success of his father. The resort to politics by such men is not uncommon. As a vocation, politics requires few specialized resources—or as sociologists would say, is functionally diffuse. Thus men with Powell's need to achieve and his charismatic talents pursue politics almost naturally. Powell's thirst for politics was reinforced, moreover, by a rather manic need to deviate from expected behavior. Politics affords more opportunity for fulfillment of such an impulse than other avocations. But Powell misconstrued the limits of politics; he failed to recognize the pitfalls awaiting politicians who use it as outlet for personal impulses but neglect the discipline that the reciprocity of the political process imposes. See Charles Hamilton, *Adam Clayton Powell Jr.: The Political Biography of An American Dilemma* (1991).

MARTIN KILSON

POWELL, John Wesley (b. Mt. Morris, N.Y., March 24, 1834; d. Haven, Maine, Sept. 23, 1902), EXPLORER, SCIENTIST, entered Illinois College in 1855. He also attended Oberlin and Wheaton colleges, but received no degree. When the Civil War broke out, he enlisted in the Union army, rising to the rank of major of artillery. At the battle of Shiloh (1862), he lost his right arm at the elbow. After the war he became professor of geology and curator of the museum at Illinois Wesleyan College. In 1867 he held the same position at Illinois Normal University.

In 1867 and 1868 Powell organized and led a party of naturalists on an expedition to the mountains of Colorado. In 1869, with finances provided by Congress and the Smithsonian Institution, he explored the gorges of the Green and Colorado rivers by boat, a journey of nearly 900 miles, emerging from the mouth of the Grand Canyon in August. During 1871–75 he made three additional western expeditions. His findings were published as *Explorations of the Colorado River of the West and Its Tributaries* (1875; revised and enlarged in 1895 under the title *Canyons of the Colorado*). Powell pointed out that many of the West's canyons were formed as a result of a river's cutting into rocks which were undergoing a process of gradual elevation. This introduced the geological concept of "base level of erosion."

In 1875 Powell became director of the second division of the U.S. Geological and Geographical Survey of the Territories (renamed the Survey of the Rocky Mountain Region in 1877). In 1878 he published his *Report on the Lands of the Arid Region of the United States,* in which he proposed that grazing lands be made available in units of 2,560 acres. In 1879 he took charge of the Smithsonian Institution's anthropological investigations. Long interested in the Native American tribes he had observed during his expeditions, he wrote *Introduction to the Study of American Indian Languages* (1880). Throughout his career he urged Native Americans to accept the values of whites.

During Powell's administration as director of the U.S. Geological Survey (1880–94), the department began to issue bulletins (1883), monograph studies (1890), and folio atlases (1893). In his later years he became interested in philosophical questions, issuing *Truth and Error* in 1898.

⁂

In the late 19th century only a few prophets dared question the prevailing American conception of the proper use of the environment. Powell was one of the most important of the early challengers. His familiarity with the geography of the Far West led him to conclude that the nation's natural resources were not inexhaustible. Beyond the 100th meridian (approximately central Kansas), he pointed out, Americans had to modify their agricultural expectations in view of insufficient rainfall. The West was not the Garden of men's dreams after all. In saying so, Powell underscored the meaning of the vanishing frontier. His realism also helped establish the attitudes that underlay the rise of conservation.

Realistic, sometimes pessimistic, as he was, Powell was still not prepared to accept another popular 19th-century myth—that of the Great American Desert. The Far West might not be a lush garden, but neither was it a sterile and useless wasteland. The arid regions could produce, Powell thought, if the federal government undertook large-scale damming and irrigation projects. Known as "reclamation," Powell's concept and his enormous scientific prestige as head of the U.S. Geological Survey inspired a number of younger colleagues. Their efforts culminated in 1902, the year Powell died, in the passage of the Reclamation Act, which institutionalized many of his suggestions and established the U. S. Bureau of Reclamation. This agency, in turn, helped make water management one of the showpieces of the early conservation movement in the United States. In 1963 the federal government recognized Powell's influence on western water management by naming the 186-mile-long lake behind Glen Canyon Dam on the Colorado River in Utah in his honor.

As an explorer and leader of men, Powell had few peers in American history. His pioneering descent of the Green and Colorado rivers in 1869 with a crew in frail wooden rowboats ranks among the world's greatest expeditions. Symbolically, the only men who died on the trip were three who lost confidence in Powell's leadership and attempted to climb out of the Grand Canyon. See Wallace Stegner, *Beyond the Hundredth Meridian: John Wesley Powell and the Second Opening of the West* (1954).

RODERICK NASH

POWERS, Hiram (b. Woodstock, Vt., July 29, 1805; d. Florence, Italy, June 27, 1873), SCULP-TOR, moved westward with his family to New York and then to Cincinnati in 1819. Upon his father's death he went to work in a Cincinnati clock and organ factory (1822–28). During this period he also began visiting the studio of sculptor Frederick Eckstein, who quickened his interest in art. He then took a job in Dorfeuille's Western Museum in Cincinnati (1829–34), where he sculpted wax figures depicting scenes from Dante's *Inferno*. He also modeled busts of leading local citizens, including Nicholas Longworth, who encouraged him to move to Washington, D.C. late in 1834 to do portraits of famous men. Here he made busts of **John Marshall,** Andrew Jackson, **John C. Calhoun,** and **Daniel Webster,** among others. In 1837 he went to Europe and, after briefly visiting Paris, established a studio in Florence, Italy.

Though Powers received acclaim for his *Eve Before the Fall* (1839), it was his *Greek Slave* (1843, Corcoran Gallery, Washington; copy also at National Collection of Fine Arts, Smithsonian Institution, Washington), a nude female figure, that won him world renown after its showing at the Great Crystal Palace Exhibition in London (1851). Six copies of it were sold by the sculptor. Basically a neoclassicist, Powers was praised on the one hand for his "spirituality" and on the other for his simplicity and precision. His *California* (1858, Metropolitan Museum, N.Y.) and the *Fisher Boy* (1848, Metropolitan Museum) are examples of these two aspects of his work. Powers was invited in 1858 to contribute decorations to the United States Capitol building in Washington and in 1863 produced statues of **Benjamin Franklin** and Thomas Jefferson. Although constantly emphasizing his American origins, Powers never returned to the U.S. after establishing his studio in Florence.

More skilled technically than artistically, Hiram Powers might have become an inventor of note; instead, lured by the profit promised by the popularity of sculpture during the mid-19th century, and without training or imagination, Powers undertook a profession that required both. Moreover, the Italian environment encouraged imitativeness, and the prevailing taste dictated the pursuit of spiritual or didactic themes. Faced with the necessity to produce "sublime" works so uncongenial to his simple and homely Yankee nature, he turned to the Greeks for models. As a result, the greatest part of his career was devoted to turning out mechanically similar cold and precise statues, differentiated only by the trite symbolisms included for narrative purposes. His popular female busts were all *Venus de Medicis* bearing such different titles as *Psyche, Proserpine, Ginevra, Faith,* and *Evangeline;* while his life-sized female figures, like *The Greek Slave, California,* or *America,* are marked by stiff poses, absence of expression, anatomical deficiencies, and artificial composition.

Powers was more successful in his portrait busts of American statesmen. Less self-conscious, and at ease with masculine subject matter as he never was with the female form, he could be more straightforward and realistic. The head of *Daniel Webster* is thoroughly masculine and strongly sculpted. *Andrew Jackson* is a masterpiece of vigorous and lively realism, with its square-cut chin and keenly penetrating eyes. This is perhaps Powers's most forceful work, and one of the best portrait sculptures produced in the United States during this period. In these works, as well as in *John Marshall* and *John C. Calhoun,* Powers's "square, solid, and tangible" personality—these are **Nathaniel Hawthorne**'s words—encountered alive and vital presences; the American realistic tradition took precedence over notions of ideality, and sculpture of permanent interest was created. See Albert Ten Eyck Gardner, *Yankee Stonecutters* (1945).

LILLIAN B. MILLER

PRESLEY, Elvis Aron (b. Tupelo, Miss., Jan. 8, 1935; d. Memphis, Tenn., Aug. 16, 1977), ENTERTAINER, raised in a religious home, Presley was an only child whose twin brothers had died stillborn. He sang as a young boy in an Assembly of God church choir and at revival meetings with his parents. When he was ten, Presley won a singing contest and eventually taught himself how to play the guitar. In 1948, his family moved to Memphis. Presley graduated L. C. Humes High School in Memphis in 1953. He got a job that year as a truck driver and studied evenings to become an electrician. That same year, 1953, he paid $4 to record two songs at the Memphis Sound Studio as a gift for his mother. The following year, the president of Sun Record Company, Sam Phillips, heard the recording and put Presley under contract. In July 1954 Presley produced his first record under the Sun label, "That's All Right, Mama" and "Blue Moon of Kentucky," a combination of country-and-western and rhythm-and-blues that some called "rockabilly." This single created a sensation with local radio listeners who were amazed when they learned he was a white singer. His energetic music caught the ear of "Colonel" Tom Parker, a promoter, who arranged a highly successful concert tour of the South for Presley as the "Hillbilly Cat." In 1955, after releasing Presley's first national hit on the Sun label, Phillips sold his contract to RCA Victor for $35,000, and in January, 1956, the twenty-one-year old singer recorded "Heartbreak Hotel," the first of forty-five Presley singles to sell more than a million copies each. That year also witnessed the release of his hits "Hound Dog," "Don't Be Cruel," "Blue Suede Shoes" and "Love Me Tender."

Shrewdly managed by Parker, Presley was a sensation in live performance and on television. He made his first nationwide television appearance in 1955 on Jackie Gleason's *Stage Show* but it was his appearance in 1956 on Ed Sullivan's *Talk of the Town* that made him the talk of the nation with his aggressive, sexually charged style which angered some adults but captivated a huge youth audience. From 1956 on he made a string of "beach" movies, generally condemned by the critics but hugely successful with the public. Presley's career was interrupted when he went into the Army (1958–60) and was stationed in Germany where he met his future wife, Priscilla. But his fans waited and he returned to his recording and movie careers as if he had never been away. The first superstar of rock 'n' roll, Presley became the highest paid performer in the history of show business in the 1960s. His lifetime total of record sales (over 500 million), top ten hits (39), and consecutive months on the charts (240) remains unchallenged even today.

Though Presley produced his last gold record in 1969, in 1973 his television special, "Elvis: Aloha from Hawaii," captured a worldwide audience estimated at over a billion people. Presley began to appear increasingly on the nightclub circuit, especially in Las Vegas, and he expanded his repetoire beyond rock 'n' roll to include religious and traditional songs. In the 1970s Presley divorced his wife and grew overweight and addicted to drugs. He spent much time at his estate in Memphis, Graceland, surrounded by bodyguards and hangers-on ready to do his bidding no matter how bizzare the request. Bloated and more and more reclusive, Presley died from an overdose of drugs.

With his throaty vocal delivery, arrogant sneer, and sexually suggestive movements, Elvis Presley embodied a new spirit in pop singing that was to focus and express an entire generation's attitude. Though a barely adequate guitarist with an unremarkable voice, his raucous blend of hillbilly, rock 'n' roll, gospel, and rhythm-and-blues singing made him the first international superstar of postwar popular music.

The frank sexuality of his stage manner outraged the parents of his youthful audience—in his appearance on Ed Sullivan's show in 1956, his gyrations were so erotic that he was televised only above the waist—and earned him the nickname "Elvis the Pelvis." That, of course, only added to his appeal for the young. Teenagers found in his raw dynamism an expression of their own rebelliousness, anger, self-pity, and vulnerability. He became a symbol and a hero to the growing subculture of youth, which adopted him as its voice.

Presley's personal magnetism made him a box office attraction, but his success also owed a great deal to astute marketing by his manager, the legendary "Colonel" Tom Parker, who orchestrated his career and rationed his appearances carefully.

Parker skillfully merchandised his commodity and read the market with uncanny accuracy. In the 1960s, when Presley's reign as "the King of rock 'n' roll" had begun to totter after a two-year stint in the army, Parker guided him to a new, less surly and confrontational image and a return to his country-music roots.

The numerous films Presley made from 1956 to 1970 added to his popularity and his fortune, if not to his prestige. Dismissed as shallow personality vehicles, they were nevertheless all financially successful. The soundtracks of several, notably his first, *Love Me Tender* (1956) and what is regarded as his best, *Jailhouse Rock* (1957), generated best-selling albums.

Perhaps the most remarkable thing about the "King" was his seeming imperviousness to age, notwithstanding the effects of an increasingly erratic lifestyle and the vicissitudes of public taste. Corpulent and addicted to drugs, he continued to make films and records with little apparent loss in his following. As his position at the top of the charts was challenged by the Beatles in the mid-1960s, he girded himself in his trademark tight-fitting costumes (now tighter fitting than ever and even somewhat grotesque) and staged a television and concert comeback. It was an extraordinary success. By then more an institution than a performer, he sparked a revival of interest in 1950s rock 'n' roll and filled some of the largest stadiums with rapturous fans. No longer a figure of juvenile revolt, he had become a revered cultural icon for an aging generation.

The impact of Elvis Presley on pop culture has outlived the man. Virtually a cult figure today, he permanently transformed American pop music and with it the popular culture of the world. See Albert Harry Goldman, *Elvis* (1981).

DENNIS WEPMAN

PULITZER, Joseph (b. Mako, Hungary, April 10, 1847; d. Charleston, S.C., Oct. 29, 1911), JOURNALIST, after being rejected as a volunteer by both the Austrian and the French armies in 1864, migrated to America, where he enlisted in the Union army. After serving eight months under

General **Philip Sheridan,** he spent the last few months of the war as an orderly. After the war he went to St. Louis, where under the tutelage of **Carl Schurz** he became a reporter for a German-language daily. The butt of jokes because of his scarecrow figure, hooked nose, and guttural English, Pulitzer nevertheless was a successful reporter. His journalistic reputation (and energetic campaigning) helped elect him to a seat as a Republican in the Missouri legislature, where he served during the 1870 session. A partisan of the Liberal Republican movement, he was named secretary of the Cincinnati convention which nominated **Horace Greeley** for president in 1872. In 1876 he broke with Schurz, joined the Democratic party, and worked for presidential candidate **Samuel J. Tilden** as a public speaker. In 1878 he bought the St. Louis *Dispatch* for $2,500 at public auction, added the St. Louis *Post*, and parlayed sensationalism and crusades for civic reform into annual profits of $85,000 by 1881. Pulitzer bought the New York *World* from **Jay Gould** in 1883 for $346,000, and soon turned it into the leading Democratic daily in the nation. Support of labor, attacks on the trusts, and campaigns for various political reforms, combined with sensationalism and good management, earned Pulitzer $500,000 within three years. He added the *Evening World* in 1887, and by 1896 their combined circulation approached 750,000. In St. Louis the *Post-Dispatch* reached 100,000 in circulation by 1900 with profits in excess of $400,000 by 1908.

Because of frayed nerves, severe physical ailments, and failing eyesight which eventually led to blindness, Pulitzer was forced to give up direct control of his newspapers in 1889, but he continued to oversee his empire while traveling in Europe and the United States.

Beginning in 1896, intense competition from **William Randolph Hearst**'s New York *Journal* sparked a circulation war culminating in the sensationalism that helped whip up sentiment for war against Spain. After the war, Pulitzer strove to bring the *World* back to its previous standards. At his death, Pulitzer left $2 million for the establishment of the nation's first school of journalism at Columbia University, as well as $250,000 for the famed Pulitzer prizes.

———— ❧ ————

More than any other individual, Joseph Pulitzer fashioned the modern American newspaper. Beginning with the *Post-Dispatch*, where he laid the foundations of mass-circulation journalism, a style he subsequently brought to perfection in the *World*, Pulitzer revolutionized newspaper publication to fit the new urban age. In so doing, he combined practices already current, such as **James Gordon Bennett**'s penchant for sensationalism, with a policy of crusading, also borrowed from the past, but with Pulitzer a daily feature. These were united with improvements in mechanical production and a blatant self-advertisement which brought to the publisher a fortune together with a contradictory reputation as an irresponsible purveyor of trash and a highminded journalist devoted to the public interest.

Pulitzer's journalism was, indeed, contradictory. This was deliberate, for, as he said, "I want to talk to a nation, not to a select committee." Consequently, his newspapers, while they by no means ignored matters of significance, indulged in trivialities, "stunts," and, at least initially, in gossipmongering, in addition to promoting entertainment features such as sports, illustrations, comics, and women's fashions. In fact, the development of the daily newspaper as a vehicle of entertainment as well as of genuine information was largely Pulitzer's handiwork. "If a newspaper is to be of real service to the public it must have a big circulation," he said, "first because its news and comment must reach the largest number of people, second, because circulation means advertising, and advertising means money, and money means independence."

Pulitzer valued independence above all, for he conceived the heart of his journalism to be to inform the people on the news pages of imperfections in their society and government by means of crusades of exposure and on the editorial page to goad them into movements of reform. "I hope you will believe me when I say the *World* is to me far more than a property," he remarked once. "I regard it as a public institution, capable of exercising daily influence on public thought, watching and safeguarding public morals and public interests." Pulitzer was a middle-class reformer who sought to make democracy work in the new industrial-urban milieu which arose after the Civil War. His style of multiple crusades, which was a blend of earlier Mugwumpism and later Progressivism and ranged from sustained campaigns against trusts and political bossism to exposure of the plight of the poor in the great cities, was the forerunner in daily journalism of the muckraking press of the early 20th century.

Pulitzer was as contradictory as his journalism. Like some of the more attractive robber barons he attacked, he was a self-made man who became a public benefactor; an advocate of the tenets of democracy, he became a millionaire who gratified aristocratic tastes; a publisher who professed faith in the common man, he ran his newspapers as private satrapies. By turns kindly and tyrannical, he paid his employees well and gave them annual vacations—a rarity at that time. Indeed, more than anyone else he was responsible for raising journalism to the status of a profession. Yet he treated his editors like small boys with an unending stream of directives and lectures. At the same time, he inspired them with a sense of loyalty and pride because, with only occasional lapses (notably the period of "yellow journalism" during the Spanish-American War), he required his newspapers to live up to his ideal that they be disinterested watchdogs of a self-governing society. See W. A. Swanberg, *Pulitzer* (1967).

JULIAN S. RAMMELKAMP

PULLMAN, George Mortimer (b. Brocton, N.Y., March 3, 1831; d. Chicago, Ill., Oct. 19, 1897), INDUSTRIALIST, INVENTOR, after a grade-school education, clerked in a store. On his father's death, which left him the main support of the family, he took over his business of moving buildings along the route of the Erie Canal. Going to Chicago, where the entire business district was being raised to a new street level, he

developed a technique for raising buildings by means of jackscrews which brought him a modest fortune.

Traveling between his old home and Chicago on the Lake Shore Railroad, Pullman had been impressed by the impracticality of the road's fixed-berth sleeping cars. He worked on an upper berth which could be lowered from the ceiling when needed and raised during day travel, and persuaded the Chicago and Alton Railroad to let him convert three day coaches. However, the railroads were reluctant to invest in new equipment during the Civil War, and Pullman went to Colorado to sell supplies to gold miners. When he returned to Chicago in 1863 it was with the plans for a swing-down upper berth and a lower berth which made up from two facing seats. Pullman built a prototype sleeping car with exterior dimensions large enough to accommodate spacious sleeping equipment. The *Pioneer*, as he named it, was too large to clear many of the structures along the railroads, but it was the most luxurious land conveyance in existence, and was finished just in time to carry President Lincoln's body on its journey from Chicago to Springfield. The ensuing publicity was carefully nurtured by Pullman, and the demand for the comforts which the new car could offer on long journeys assured its success. At his death Pullman was a major builder of all types of railroad cars and, having absorbed a number of competitors, the principal operator of sleeping, parlor, and dining cars for the leading American railroads, to whose trains they were coupled. The open-section Pullman "sleeper," its interior essentially unchanged from the original design, was standard equipment on American railroads until after World War II. Many other innovations in car design, notably the enclosed vestibule and improved running gear, originated with Pullman. Comfort, cleanliness, and beautiful surroundings were his primary aims, and his fares were set high enough to assure they would be attained. Pullman engaged briefly in railroad promotion in the 1880s, aiding the West Shore in its unsuccessful attempt to gain some of the New York Central's rich traffic, and was president of

New York's Metropolitan Elevated Railroad.

In 1880 Pullman concentrated his manufacturing activities in a newly laid-out "model" town, named for himself, in what was then a marsh eight miles south of Chicago. He sought to demonstrate that industrialization did not inevitably mean degradation of the workers, or even urbanization, and to provide the company with a steady supply of better than average labor. At first almost unanimous in their praise, students of this experiment in town planning had begun by 1885 to criticize the lack of self-government and the company's strict paternalistic policies. In his last years Pullman's "paternalism" was severely attacked especially after the workers of Pullman struck in 1894 in defiance of wage cuts he had ordered after the onset of the depression. **Eugene V. Debs** and the American Railway Union supported the strike with a refusal to operate any train which carried a Pullman car. When the railroads refused to uncouple the sleepers, a nationwide strike ensued. President Cleveland, determined to move the U.S. mails at any cost, ordered federal troops to Chicago. This broke the strike and Debs's union.

When George Pullman claimed to have "invented railroad comfort," few challenged his statement. To the plaudits of an awed nation he developed and promoted in ten years after 1865 an astonishing succession of new types of cars and services and, as important, pioneered operational innovations in through-travel. In all of this he was guided by the prescient view that middle-class Americans would be pleased to pay for comfort and status. By the 1870s for the first time in history large numbers of people traveled long distances by land for pleasure as well as necessity, and Pullman was famous.

Pullman was not an inventor but an entrepreneur, and his ideas were rarely original; he depended on the inventions of others, which were eagerly sought. His talent and nearly his only interest was business. Aloof and commanding—"a lordly man of lion-like resolve," was **Andrew Carnegie**'s description—Pullman incessantly expanded and improved his company's position. He sought monopoly in the field of car service while probing entry into new areas. In the 1870s his company commenced passenger and freight car production. By the early 1890s it was the largest manufacturing concern in the U.S., and virtually without rival in car operation.

Until 1894 the name Pullman was a byword for efficiency, success, and of course, luxury. But the strike which started in his model town, expanding into perhaps the century's most important labor dispute, challenged his reputation. Indeed the primary historical issue posed by model town and strike has been whether Pullman was an exploiter of labor or a naïve paternalist.

Influenced by a crude environmentalism which gained credence in the second half of the century, George Pullman believed American labor was demoralized by working-class neighborhoods created by industry in large cities. His model town was offered as an alternative. Industry and workers were to be placed in a "wholesome setting" planned on "scientific principles." The town was to be designed by an architect and landscape designer, and its plan included a theater, library, schools, parks, and athletic fields, while bar and brothel were proscribed by fiat. Workers and their families were expected to benefit physically and morally and be elevated into a middle-class respectability. In turn the company would gain contented, responsible workers and a "show-place," while setting rents to receive a reasonable return on the cost of the superior housing and facilities. The scheme's essential premises were that employer and employee shared an identity of interests, and that capital would profit from investing in the welfare of labor.

Pullman refused even after the strike had generally demonstrated the weakness of his scheme to acknowledge the entanglements and responsibilities created by his novel community. "We are landlords and employers, that is all there is of it." During the depression of 1893 Pullman as landlord maintained rents, while as employer he cut wages as his right under the concept of "ordinary contract." These actions are generally offered as the primary cause of the strike. This is an oversimplification, but it is true that the question of rents and wages was seized upon by the men as an issue that could unite them in a union, while serving to win public support for their cause. Another reason for the strike was the inability of the company headquarters at a distance from the town to maintain effective communications with the workers or to control the arbitrary behavior of the plant supervisor and his foremen.

Pullman was neither exploiter nor paternalist in the simple sense of these terms. Though certainly not to be considered a systematic or serious social thinker, Pullman by recognizing employee morale as a principal factor in production provided the 19th century's most extensive and interesting experiment in what later would be known as "welfare capitalism." His behavior offers insight into business and social thought of his day, and the ways the two were influencing each other at a time when industrialization and the rise of big business disrupted older patterns of employer-employee relations. His model town in itself is a significant early instance of modern American town planning. See Stanley Buder, *Pullman: An Experiment in Industrial Order and Community Planning* (1967).

STANLEY BUDER

RABI, Isador Isaac (b. Rymanow, Austria-Hungary, July 29, 1898; d. New York, N.Y., Jan. 11, 1988), SCIENTIST, brought to the United States as a child by his father, an impoverished tailor. His mother soon followed. Rabi went to public schools in Brooklyn, N.Y. and received both his BA (in chemistry) and PhD (in physics) from Cornell University (1927). He then went to Europe (1927–29) for postgraduate work in physics under Niels Bohr, Otto Stern, and Wolfgang Pauli. Rabi, who had tutored at City College of New York (1924–27) while working for his doctorate, was invited to Columbia University in 1929. Rabi remained at Columbia until he retired in 1967.

In 1937, expanding on work he did in Germany under Otto Stern, Rabi developed an atomic and molecular beam resonance method for measuring the magnetic properties of atoms and molecules which helped elucidate atomic and molecular structure. He was awarded the Nobel Prize for physics in 1944 for this method of measuring magnetic properties of atoms, molecules, and atomic nuclei. This work was based on measuring the spin of the protons in the atom's core, a phenomenon known as nuclear magnetic moments.

At the inception of World War II, Rabi refused **J. Robert Oppenheimer**'s invitation to become deputy director of the Manhattan Project to build an atomic bomb. Instead he headed a large team at the Radiation Laboratory of the Massachusetts Institute of Technology (MIT) developing microwave radar. Although he observed the first atomic bomb test in New Mexico in 1945 and contributed ideas to the Manhattan Project he declined to devote himself to making the atom bomb because he believed it might be possible to win the war without the bomb but without radar the war would certainly be lost.

After the war, Rabi served as a science adviser to the United States government and was an outspoken advocate of nuclear arms control. Rabi also was the originator of the idea for the CERN nuclear research center in Geneva (1954) which was crucial to the revival of science in postwar Europe.

Every day when young Isidor came home from school his mother would inquire, "Did you ask any good questions today?" Encouraged by his parents, who ran a small grocery store in Brooklyn, Rabi grew up with an avid interest in everything around him and a love for teaching. Even as a child he organized study and discussion groups in the neighborhood, teaching the other kids how to play chess, build a wireless, repair an automobile. After he earned his undergraduate degree in chemistry he found that, for a young Jewish scientist, jobs were not that easy to be had. He worked computing accounts, and then spent time analyzing the components of furniture polish. One night he went to hear a lecture by **Albert Einstein** and came back to his Brooklyn neighborhood gushing enthusiasm and anxious to pass on what he had learned—and only partly understood—to a study group. Now passionately interested in physics he decided to return to Cornell in 1924 to work for a doctorate.

These years were heady times for physicists, with new ideas filling the air. After getting his PhD and studying under some of the finest scientific minds in Europe, Rabi found himself in some demand and accepted an offer of a lectureship in Columbia University's physics department. He soon established a reputation as an excellent teacher, someone who could make physics enjoyable and understandable to even the dullest undergraduate. But it was as a scientist that he really excelled. His experiments and findings in nuclear physics, quantum mechanics, and magnetism made vitally important contributions to the rapidly growing knowledge of the atom.

Especially important was his Nobel Prize–winning invention in 1937 of the atomic and molecular beam magnetic resonance method of observing atomic spectra. The precise measurements yielded by his method made possible the atomic clock, the maser and the laser, as well as the nuclear magnetic resonance imaging device employed in thousands of hospitals today to diagnose illness. His methods gave scientists the central techniques for virtually all molecular and atomic beam experimentation. For this discovery if for nothing else, Rabi would rank among the great physicists of the modern era. But Rabi was more than a scientist. He was also a

remarkable humanist who worked strenuously to promote the peaceful uses of atomic energy and cared deeply about the social responsibilites of science in an increasingly dangerous world. He set forth his views on these issues in *Science: The Center of Culture* (1970). See John S. Rigden, *Rabi, Scientist and Citizen* (1987).

ROY SORRELS

RAFINESQUE, Constantine Samuel (b. Galata, Turkey, Oct. 22, 1783; d. Philadelphia, Pa., Sept. 18, 1840), SCIENTIST, was educated by private tutors in Marseilles, Pisa, Leghorn (Italy), and Genoa. In 1802 he traveled with his brother to Philadelphia, where he worked in the counting house of Clifford Brothers (1802–4). He also traveled extensively, became friendly with scientists such as **Benjamin Rush** and G. H. E. Muhlenberg, and made detailed studies of the flora of southern New Jersey and of the Dismal Swamp in Virginia. During 1804–15 Rafinesque lived in Palermo, Sicily, where after serving briefly as secretary for the American consul, he became an exporter of medicinal plants. He spent much time there in scientific observation, his special interest being the ichthyology of the surrounding waters. In 1815, upon his return to the U.S., Rafinesque secured a position as tutor at the Livingston manor in Clermont, New York, where he remained until 1818, when he was appointed professor of botany, natural history, and modern languages at Transylvania University, in Lexington, Kentucky. In 1826 he returned to Philadelphia, continuing to do extensive field studies.

Throughout his career Rafinesque was a prolific and wide-ranging writer. Although botany and ichthyology remained his major interests, among his nine hundred publications were such works as *Safe Banking* (1827) and *Pleasure and Duties of Wealth* (1840), as well as studies of the Bible. He also wrote poetry. His major scientific works, such as *American Florist* (1832), *New Flora and Botany of America* (1836), and *Flora Telluriana* (1836–38), although marred by vague and imprecise identifications, provided copious and detailed descriptions of many New World varieties.

A brilliant but erratic naturalist who roamed the American wilderness, Rafinesque has been a controversial figure both with his contemporaries and with historians. Recognized by about 1820 as one of the leading naturalists in America, he lived the remaining two decades of his life in obscurity, scorned by most of the scientific community, and able to publish his works only in his own or other fugitive journals. The eclipse of his reputation was due largely to **Benjamin Silliman,** who after 1818 refused to accept Rafinesque's papers for publication, and to **Asa Gray,** who at Rafinesque's death published a bitterly critical assessment of his later works.

There is no doubt that Rafinesque was often hasty and superficial in his classification; and it is also true that he frequently tried to take credit for the work of others. Yet, the error with which he is most frequently charged—a mania for creating new species—was not a result of superficiality, but of two firmly held beliefs: that species were rapidly transformed into new species, and that because of divergence (although he did not use the term), no plant found in America could possibly be of the same species as a European plant. These two convictions marked Rafinesque as an early adherent of a theory of evolution at a time when such an admission was considered the mark of a madman. It was for his belief in the transformation of species that Asa Gray, later to become a prominent evolutionist, most harshly criticized him.

When one has conceded all of Rafinesque's eccentricity, and has acknowledged that his works were filled with errors of haste, it still remains a fact that he made enormous contributions to the natural history phase of American science: he is credited, for example, with the establishment of thirty-four genera and twenty-one species of American fishes. Innumerable species of American plants also still bear the names he gave them. In many other respects, Rafinesque was ahead of his time. He was, for example, the first in America to campaign for a "natural system" of classification, based on the relations among organisms, to replace the Linnean sexual system. He also utilized advanced teaching methods and gained a reputation as a brilliant teacher at Transylvania University. See T. J. Fitzpatrick, *Rafinesque: A Sketch of His Life with Bibliography* (1911).

GEORGE H. DANIELS

RANDOLPH, Asa Philip (b. Crescent City, Fla., April 15, 1889; d. New York, N.Y., May 16, 1979), LABOR LEADER, grew up in Jacksonville, Florida, then moved to New York City, where he attended the College of the City of New York. In 1917, with the writer Chandler Owen, he founded *The Messenger,* a magazine of black protest. A year later Randolph was arrested in Cleveland for expressing strong opposition to America's entry into World War I. After the war he began to organize black sleeping-car porters. He held the first meeting of his new union in Harlem in 1925 and was elected president. The union affiliated with the American Federation of Labor in 1936. The Pullman Company bitterly fought the sleeping-car porters' union but in 1937 signed a contract with it which provided for wage increases.

Randolph soon became a national figure. In 1935 he served on Mayor **Fiorello LaGuardia**'s Commission on Race in New York City. In 1941 he organized the March on Washington movement, which called for the equal treatment of blacks in obtaining jobs. President Franklin D. Roosevelt, in response, established the wartime Fair Employment Practices Committee. Randolph served as a member of the New York City Housing Authority in 1942, and helped form the League for Nonviolent Civil Disobedience Against Military Segregation. Under pressure from this organization, President Harry S. Truman ordered the end of segregation in the armed forces in 1948. In 1958 Randolph organized a youth march on Washington in support of the Supreme Court's 1954 school desegregation decision. He also participated in the 1963 March on Washington for Jobs and Freedom. Randolph served as vice president of the AFL-CIO in 1957 and was a member of its executive committee. In 1965, the A. Philip Randolph Institute was established with grants from the AFL-CIO and other organizations. Under the leadership of Randolph's protégé, Bayard Rustin, its task was to enlist community leaders for a study of conditions that create entrenched patterns of poverty. Randolph retired as president of the Brotherhood of Sleeping Car Porters in 1968, and became its president emeritus. Eventually, as railroad travel declined, the union merged into the Brotherhood of Railway and Airline Clerks. During the 1970s Randolph withdrew from public view, lived quietly in the Chelsea area of New York, and worked on his autobiography.

———— ∞∞∞ ————

A man with an extraordinary dignity and presence, A. Philip Randolph finished an unparalleled sixty-year career of involvement in every important political and social struggle of America's black people by becoming the acknowledged patriarch among black leaders in the early 1970s, after reaching the age of eighty. Raised in the traditions of the abolitionists by his preacher father, Randolph early displayed unusual oratorical skill and knowledge. Migrating to New York City, he was soon a "City College Socialist." At a time when the black community was divided by the ideas of **Booker T. Washington** and **W. E. B. Du Bois,** Philip Randolph chose an independent viewpoint, that of a radical Socialist. His lifetime belief in unionism and integration flowed from this basic philosophy. His mentor was **Eugene V. Debs,** and his lifelong friend, **Norman Thomas.**

As editor of the Socialist-oriented *Messenger,* Randolph was in the forefront of the black critics of **Marcus Garvey** and the back-to-Africa movement. One victim of the split among black intellectuals and radicals in the early 1920s was *The Messenger.* Randolph then turned to a career as union organizer. The advent of the New Deal and the rise of the CIO industrial unionism enabled his Brotherhood of Sleeping Car Porters to get a charter from the American Federation of Labor and to win a contract from the Pullman Company, but without his organizing work, success would have been impossible.

Randolph emerged as the most outspoken and influential black public figure in the World War II period, when he organized a March on Washington campaign to plan the assembling of 100,000 blacks in the nation's capital to protest racial discrimination in wartime hiring. Failing to dissuade Randolph, President Roosevelt issued Executive Order 8802 to make that practice illegal. After World War II Randolph led the movement to break down discrimination in the armed forces. After a historic confrontation with President Truman, Executive Order 9981 for integration in the armed forces was issued.

When the civil rights movement in the early 1960s assumed massive national proportions, black leaders turned to Randolph to direct another March on Washington. He chose a former critic, but friend, **Bayard Rustin,** to organize that astounding event. Again a president, John F. Kennedy, tried to dissuade Randolph, failed, and then accepted the idea. Randolph was less successful with his union colleague, **George Meany,** president of the AFL-CIO, who refused to support the March on Washington. The gathering of 250,000 people in Washington in 1963 set the stage for the emergence of the Reverend **Martin Luther King, Jr.** as the nation's chief spokesman for the black people.

Randolph still had one major battle to fight: challenging the AFL-CIO to break down discriminatory patterns, especially in the building trades unions. This acerbic conflict between Meany and Randolph ended in compromise. By now age and ill health were taking their toll. Randolph's voice was muted during the Vietnam War, although he told his biographer, Jervis Anderson, that he was opposed to it. See Jervis Anderson, *A. Philip Randolph: A Biographical Portrait* (1973).

B. J. WIDICK

RANDOLPH, Edmund (b. Williamsburg, Va., Aug. 10, 1753; d. Clarke Co., Va., Sept. 12, 1813), POLITICAL LEADER, was educated at the College of William and Mary and studied law under his father, John. When the Revolution approached, the family was badly split. John Randolph, a Loyalist, fled to England, but Edmund remained, residing with his uncle Peyton, a distinguished lawyer. He served as aide-de-camp to General George Washington, was elected mayor of Williamsburg, and at twenty-three was the youngest member of the Virginia Constitutional Convention of 1776. He served as state attorney general, as delegate to the Continental Congress (1779–82), as governor (1787–88), and as a member of the legislature (1788–89). He was a member of the Annapolis Convention of 1786 and of the Constitutional Convention of 1787, to which he presented the Virginia Plan, envisaging a government rather than a revision of the Articles of Confederation. A strong republican, Randolph feared that the office of presidency smacked too much of monarchism, and he withheld his signature from the completed document. Nevertheless, as a member of the Virginia Convention of 1788, he advocated ratification of the Constitution on the ground that it was the only way union could be achieved, and urged that a second constitutional convention be held after a trial period.

Appointed attorney general of the United States in 1789 by President Washington, Randolph attempted to maintain impartiality when he was caught between the contending factions of **Alexander Hamilton** and **Thomas Jefferson**. His difficulties increased when he succeeded Jefferson as secretary of state (1794). Hamilton badly outflanked him during the negotiation of Jay's Treaty. Already more sympathetic to the French than Hamilton and his followers, Randolph feared that too much would be conceded to the English in the treaty negotiations then contemplated. Successfully vetoing Hamilton as special envoy, Randolph only reluctantly consented to **John Jay,** and he opposed granting him power to negotiate a commercial treaty, wishing him to confine himself to England's commitments under the Treaty of 1783. Randolph, however, gave his approval to all of Jay's Treaty except the provisions forbidding certain exports.

Randolph's public career came to an end in 1795 when a letter of Joseph Fauchet, French minister to the U.S., was made public and seemed to implicate Randolph in attempted bribery and treason. He resigned immediately; subsequent denials by both Fauchet and Randolph were insufficient to convince President Washington of Randolph's innocence. Returning to a prosperous law practice, which he followed the rest of his life, Randolph served as **Aaron Burr**'s special counsel in the 1807 conspiracy trial and wrote a manuscript on the history of Virginia. Although he had settled his accounts with the Department of State upon his resignation, a special act of Congress was necessary in 1889 to force the clerk of the State Department to remove the accounts from the books.

Despite the stormy conclusion to his political career, Randolph was a preeminent figure in a great generation of Virginia lawyers, orators, and statesmen. Tall, heavy, and physically handsome, he was noted for his ambition, industry, learning, charm, and dignity. "His whole manner," wrote a contemporary, was "that of an accomplished and engaging gentleman." His legal arguments were scholarly—if at times diffuse—and few men had a more prestigious practice. A renowned speaker, Randolph was occasionally pompous and artificial, but his strong voice, forceful delivery, and intellectual powers often made him both eloquent and persuasive. Inherited debts, personal miscalculations, and the burdens of public office brought chronic financial distress and marred an otherwise exemplary private life.

Randolph's gyrations on the Constitution in 1787–88 tarnished his popularity with charges of inconstancy, which also recurred during his cabinet service. But this should not obscure his major contributions to the document—as seen in his role in the coming of the Philadelphia Convention, his activity there, and especially his hand in Virginia's ratification.

In the cabinet, Randolph was dispassionate, diligent, and competent, but he came increasingly under fire for his political independence. His chief significance—until the Fauchet affair—was in being a gifted, versatile confidant to whom Washington turned for counsel and assistance on a variety of problems. Most historians accept his plea of "not guilty" on the treason, bribery, and defalcation charges but hold him responsible for indiscreet language with Fauchet and for an uncharacteristically clumsy and intemperate defense of his own actions. See M. D. Conway, *Edmund Randolph* (1888).

DANIEL P. JORDAN

RANDOLPH, John (b. Prince George Co., Va., June 2, 1773; d. Philadelphia, Pa., May 24, 1833), POLITICAL LEADER, briefly attended the College of New Jersey (now Princeton) in 1787, studied law in Philadelphia under his cousin, **Edmund Randolph,** and attended the College of William and Mary (1792–93). Randolph served as a Republican in the U.S. Congress from 1799 to 1813, where he was chairman of the Ways and Means Committee (1801–5) and one of the Republican floor leaders. Although an ardent states' rights advocate, he supported the Louisiana Purchase (1803). In 1804 he was one of the managers during the impeachment of Supreme Court Justice Samuel Chase. Randolph broke with the Jefferson administration in 1804–5, when he blocked a bill awarding land grants to certain claimants in what is now Alabama and Mississippi (Yazoo lands). He also opposed Jefferson's attempts to purchase West Florida from Spain (1805), the Embargo Act (1807), the presidential candidacy of James Madison in 1808, and the War of 1812.

Randolph was again elected to Congress in 1815. He voted against both chartering the Second Bank of the U.S. and the protective tariff of 1816 on constitutional grounds. Again a member of Congress (1819–25), he supported Andrew Jackson in the presidential election of 1824. He denounced John Quincy Adams for appointing **Henry Clay** as secretary of state after Clay helped Adams win the election of 1825. As a result, in 1826 Randolph and Clay fought a duel, but neither was injured. Randolph served in the U.S. Senate (1825–27) and again in the House of Representatives (1827–29). At the Virginia Convention of 1829 he aligned himself with the state's conservatives in resisting changes in the state constitution.

In 1830 President Jackson appointed Randolph minister to Russia, but poor health forced him to resign. In 1832 Randolph sided with South Carolina in its dispute with Jackson over the tariff, but he opposed nullification.

―――⁂―――

The Randolph family may not have been the most erratic in Virginia, and John Randolph of Roanoke may not have been the family's most erratic member, but the margin was not great in either instance. Generation after generation, the family had its manic-depressives, schizoids, perverts, sadists, idiots, and geniuses. John, in his own person, combined an equally strange and diverse set of traits. He lived alone on a plantation named Bizarre, never married, never fell in love, and possibly never laughed save in scorn. He regularly withered the House with the most brilliant and corrosive invective it has ever known, self-consciously tilted at windmills, saw devils, experienced prophetic visions. Moreover, throughout his life he fell victim to bouts of extreme and morose drunkenness—which derived from passionate hatreds, irrational fears, bitter rages, and the use of opium as well as alcohol.

But he was more than a mere eccentric aristocrat or a stormy political genius; he was a veritable caricature of the Virginia of his day, a society that stamped its values indelibly upon the American scheme of things. The value system of Virginia Republicanism rested upon an autocratic foundation: vigilant hostility toward any persons or institutions that threatened the tobacco-planting aristocrats in their power over their own domains. Upon this foundation, however, they erected a set of principles that was the antithesis of autocracy, and in defense of these principles Randolph was, within the limits posed by his personal peculiarities, possibly the purest Virginian of them all. The Virginians opposed economic monopolies and religious establishments, and virtually invented the American rhetoric and rituals against these evils; but they believed the greatest menace to human liberty was government, especially government far removed from the people. Accordingly, they favored strict construction of the Constitution, states' rights, legislative power as opposed to executive and judicial authority, militias rather than standing armies, and firm defense of civil liberties. Once they came into power, however, Jefferson and most of his followers found it expedient to compromise these principles, at least in part. Randolph never did. Similarly, the Virginians idealized the agrarian life, reckoned land as the only enduring source of wealth, and opposed commercialism along with all forms of currency based on public debt and on bank credit. In this area, too, most Jeffersonians ultimately compromised; Randolph and his ever diminishing circle of followers did not. Finally— and fatally—the Virginia way rested upon African-American slavery, and though many paid lip service to emancipation, most continued to enjoy the fruits of their slaves' labor. Randolph, with his awesome ability to strip away sham and pretense, squarely identified Virginia-style states' rights Republicanism with the slave power (January 1824), and thus forced the Virginia legacy back to its starting point. In so doing he became, along with Jefferson and **John Calhoun,** one of the crucial links between the Declaration of Independence and Fort Sumter. See Henry Adams, *John Randolph* (1884).

FORREST MCDONALD

RANKIN, Jeanette (b. Missoula, Mont., June 10, 1880; d. Carmel, Calif., May 18, 1973), REFORMER, POLITICAL LEADER, graduated from Montana State University in 1902. Moving to New York City, she became a social worker and studied at the New York School of Philanthropy (1908–9). After doing social work in Seattle in 1909, she took part in campaigns for woman suffrage in Washington, D.C. (1910), California (1911), and Montana (1912–14). She became field secretary of the National American Woman Suffrage Association in 1913 and, as chairman of the Montana State Suffrage

Committee, was influential in gaining the enactment of woman suffrage legislation in Montana in 1914. A Republican, Rankin was elected to the U.S. House of Representatives in 1916 for Montana's at-large seat. She was one of the fifty-six members of Congress who voted against going to war with Germany in 1917.

A convinced pacifist, Rankin became a Washington lobbyist for the National Council for the Prevention of War, the largest peace organization of its time. She was again elected to Congress from Montana in 1940 on a "stay-out-of-war" platform and cast the only vote in Congress against declaring war on Japan after the attack on Pearl Harbor. Defeated for reelection in 1942, she continued her pacifist activities, opposed the Korean War, and renewed her interest in the feminist movement. In 1966 she tried to establish a self-supporting women's commune near her farm in Watkinsville, Georgia, but without success. Rankin opposed President Lyndon Johnson's foreign policy and became an outspoken critic of the Vietnam War. In 1968 she led the ten-thousand-member Jeannette Rankin Brigade's march on Washington to protest American involvement in Southeast Asia.

⸺⸎⸺

Throughout her life Jeanette Rankin espoused two great causes which still profoundly trouble modern society: the liberation of women, and peace. She made them her career, and although she was only partially successful in one, and failed in the other, she has become a symbol of resourcefulness and courage in the pursuit of an ideal through practical politics. As a young woman she championed all the rights women of her generation were demanding, beginning with the right to vote, and when she led the suffrage forces in Montana to victory in 1914, she took the next logical step and put herself forward as a candidate for Congress, to prove that women could and should hold public office.

Then, having won election (she was the first woman elected to Congress), she risked her entire career in an idealistic gesture when she voted against the entry of the United States into World

War I. Politicians wrote her off as a sentimental novice, but as she said at the time, she could not bring herself to send young men to their death in order to win reelection to the House of Representatives. During her short term of office, however, she was extremely active: she brought about reforms in working conditions for women in the Bureau of Printing, took part in mediating a bitter copper strike in Montana, introduced bills to advance the cause of woman suffrage, and cosponsored a bill providing for instruction on female hygiene, including birth control. Not until the advent of Shirley Chisholm and Bella Abzug more than half a century later were women of such reforming zeal seated in Congress.

Between the two world wars and thereafter Rankin gave herself to the peace movement. But unlike other lobbyists, whose efforts were limited to persuading legislators and officeholders to adopt her views, she made a special point of converting their constituents, of urging the voters to put pressure on their representatives. Always concerned with the extension of the democratic process, she waged a campaign for the direct election of the president by preferential voting. This was in line with her belief that wars do not settle disputes between nations, and that if the will of the people were fully exercised, they would find other ways to come to an understanding with their neighbors. See Hannah Josephson, *Jeanette Rankin, First Lady in Congress: A Biography* (1974).

HANNAH JOSEPHSON

RAUSCHENBERG, Robert (b. Port Arthur, Tex., Oct. 22, 1925), ARTIST, was educated in public schools and studied pharmacy at the University of Texas for half a year in 1942 before being drafted into the navy. After his training at Farragut, Iowa, he was stationed as a medical technician at navy hospitals in California. After the war he studied at the Kansas City Art Institute (1946–47), at the Académie Julian in Paris (1947), and then with Josef Albers, an expert on geometric abstraction, at Black Mountain College (1948–49). Moving to New York City in 1949, Rauschenberg studied at the Art Students League with Vaclav Vytacil and Morris Kantor. He had his first one-man show at the Betty Parsons Gallery in New York in 1951.

Rauschenberg did many abstract paintings based on the color red in the early 1950s, such as *Charlene* (1954, Stedelijk Museum, Amsterdam). He also did sculpture, using such items as stuffed birds, buckets, chairs, and Coca-Cola bottles in his work. *Bed* (1955, Collection Mr. and Mrs. Leo Castelli, N.Y.) was made out of a patchwork quilt, a sheet, and a pillow splattered with black paint. *Monogram* (1959, Moderna Museet, Stockholm), a combination painting and sculpture, contained a stuffed goat and an automobile tire on top of a canvas. Rauschenberg toured Europe in 1964 as a set and costume designer, lighting specialist, and stage manager for the Merce Cunningham Dance Company, with which he had been working since 1953. He received the grand prize for painting at the Venice Biennale Exhibition of Art in 1964, awarded to an American for the first time in the Biennale's sixty-nine-year history, and the William A. Clark prize at the Corcoran Gallery Biennial of Contemporary American Painters in 1965 for his oil on canvas *Axle* (1964, artist's collection), which contained an image of John F. Kennedy. In 1967, he and a group of engineers founded Experiments in Art and Technology to experiment with the use of electronics in art. Some of his other important paintings include *Curfew* (1958, Collection Mr. and Mrs. Ben Heller, N.Y.) and *Quote* (1964, artist's collection).

In the 1950s, the aesthetics of abstract expressionism dominated the artistic milieu of New York; less than ten years later, this influence was largely submerged by new forms—happenings, environments, pop art. A significant force behind this change in the artistic climate was Robert Rauschenberg, whom the 1950s regarded as an *enfant terrible* and who, forty years later, is looked upon as an established founding father and pioneer.

Rauschenberg, along with his more intellectually inclined friends **John Cage** and **Jasper Johns,** set out to illustrate that the distinctions between what we call "art" and "real life" are arbitrary and flexible, and that the function of art is not necessarily that of communicating emotions or ideas, or even that of expressing the artist's personality, imagination, or taste. Rauschenberg demonstrated this by incorporating into his painting the anonymous refuse of the city—bottles, stuffed animals, newspapers, old lumber—and by allowing these objects to escape into the spectator's space, rather than safely isolating them behind a frame. Thus the objects, rather than the artist, became dominant: "I'd really like to think that the artist could be just another kind of material in the picture," said Rauschenberg, "working in collaboration with all the other materials."

In 1962 Rauschenberg began working with mass-media images silkscreened onto canvas; here the collaboration is between juxtapositions, separations, bleed-outs, and superimpositions of preexisting imagery, combined to provide maximum sensual profit. In a similar spirit, he began exploring possible interrelations between art and science. In these works, it is the effort of several specialists, rather than that of one individual, which determines the final character of the art. The success of these collaborations, as well as those in the fields of dance and theater, is often due to Rauschenberg's infectious enthusiasm, prodigious energy, and respect for the work of other artists. Being able to accept whatever happens, says Rauschenberg, is "what makes painting an adventure, which is what it is for me." See Andrew Forge, *Rauschenberg* (1969).

PATRICIA FAILING

RAUSCHENBUSCH, Walter (b. Rochester, N.Y., Oct. 4, 1861; d. Rochester, N.Y., July 25, 1918), RELIGIOUS LEADER, grew up in Rochester, but received part of his education in Germany and graduated from the Gymnasium of Gütersloh, Westphalia, in 1883. He received his AB the following year from the University of Rochester (also a DD in 1902) and graduated from the Rochester Theological Seminary in 1886. Being ordained a Baptist, Rauschenbusch accept-

ed a pulpit in the Second German Baptist Church in New York City. Here he became interested in the plight of immigrants and the poor, and in social justice generally. He was influenced by the writings of **Henry George,** whom he supported for mayor of New York in 1886. Rauschenbusch went to Europe for nine months in 1891 to study at the University of Berlin and in England. He met Sidney and Beatrice Webb and became interested in Fabian Socialism, which called for a gradual change to governmental ownership of major industries. He participated in the founding of the Brotherhood of the Kingdom in 1892, an organization of social Christianity. The great depression of 1893 encouraged Rauschenbusch to strive for the Social Gospel, a way to make Christianity more responsive to the suffering of the poor.

Rauschenbusch became professor of New Testament interpretation at the Rochester Theological Seminary in 1897 and professor of church history in 1902, a position he held until his death. He continued his interest in the Social Gospel movement and published *Christianity and the Social Crisis* (1907), which expounded his beliefs. The book was widely read, and was translated into several languages. He was also active in movements seeking honest government and better schools for Rochester.

World War I proved to be a disillusioning experience for Rauschenbusch; he saw nothing in it but a world of militarism and hate. Although not a total pacifist, he opposed American intervention in the war. As a result he was persecuted as pro-German. His major writings include: *Prayers of the Social Awakening* (1910), *Christianizing the Social Order* (1912), *The Social Principles of Jesus* (1916), and *A Theology for the Social Gospel* (1917).

A gifted, industrious, ambitious man, Rauschenbusch combined a devotion to evangelical Protestant piety with commitment to liberal, unitive, social Christianity. Despite deafness that came early in his career, he possessed genuine personal warmth and had a refreshing sense of humor. Idealistic in his philosophical premises and in his hopes for society, he passionately believed that the concept of the coming Kingdom of God on earth provided a way to bring together the best of spiritual religion with the progressive social movements of his day in a living synthesis. Rauschenbusch had a deep compassion for oppressed working men, and supported many of the practical (as opposed to dogmatic) socialistic measures then being advocated. Though his voice was poor, this tall, bearded minister developed an effective platform style, and was widely in demand as a speaker during the last ten years of his life. The books he then wrote made him one of the most influential thinkers of American Protestant history. His contributions were well known abroad. Although conservatives disagreed with him, he ably espoused causes then rising to prominence in the public mind: the Social Gospel, cooperative Christianity, economic justice, municipal reform. His impact on social ethical thought was specifically acknowledged by such prominent figures as Harry Emerson Fosdick, **Reinhold Niebuhr,** and **Martin Luther King, Jr.** The Social Gospel later lost much of the stress on personal, mystical religion so characteristic of him. See Robert T. Handy, ed., *The Social Gospel in America, 1870–1920: Gladden, Ely, Rauschenbusch* (1966).

ROBERT T. HANDY

RAYBURN, Samuel Taliaferro (b. Roane County, Tenn., Jan. 6, 1882; d. Bonham, Tex., Nov. 16, 1961), POLITICAL LEADER, graduated from East Texas Normal College in 1904. He taught school for the next two years to pay off debts and was elected to the Texas state house of representatives in 1906 as a Democrat. Between legislative sessions Rayburn studied at the University of Texas Law School in Austin. He served as speaker of the House from 1911 to 1912, when he was elected to the U.S. House of Representatives. He supported the policies of President Woodrow Wilson and was reelected to the House twenty-five consecutive times. Over the years he became known for his loyalty to Democratic presidents and to the party. In 1931 he became chairman of the House Committee on Interstate and Foreign Commerce. He backed most New Deal legislation, including the Securities and Exchange Act (1934), the Rural Electrification Act (1935), and the Public Utility Holding Company Act (1935), which limited the power of utility trusts. In 1937 Rayburn was elected Democratic majority leader and, upon the death of Speaker William Bankhead in 1940, he became speaker of the House, a position he held longer than any other man in U.S. history.

As speaker, Rayburn was instrumental in gaining extension of the military draft in 1941 and vigorously supported the war effort. After its conclusion he helped push through the Marshall Plan and parts of President Truman's Fair Deal, including the 1949 Housing Act. When the Republican party gained control of the House in 1947 Rayburn yielded the speaker's chair to Representative Joseph Martin; however, he regained it in 1949. Rayburn again lost the chair in 1953 but regained it two years later and did not relinquish it until his death. Although he opposed Truman's civil rights legislation, believing the federal government should leave this matter to the states, Rayburn cooperated with President Eisenhower on passage of the Civil Rights Acts of 1957 and 1960, which protected black voting rights in the South. As speaker, Rayburn relied on persuasion and reason rather than crass power plays to get what he wanted. He served as permanent chairman of the 1948, 1952, and 1956 Democratic national conventions but declined the post in 1960 to act as floor leader of his friend Lyndon B. Johnson's bid for the presidential nomination.

———— ∞ ————

Of the many 20th-century politicians who operated solely within a congressional context, no one ever reached the pinnacle of power and stayed there as long as did Sam Rayburn of Bonham, Texas. As speaker of the House of Representatives, "Mr. Sam" was a public figure recognized by and known to millions of Americans. But because he was a rather taciturn and somewhat remote individual—except in the company of trusted political associates and personal friends like Harry Truman and Lyndon Johnson—Rayburn never established a public identity apart from the institution he served with such devotion. If he lacked color or a beguiling personality, at least he was a man of character, a quality which earned him the lasting respect of his colleagues.

As a leading House Democrat, especially after he became speaker, Rayburn sought to avoid or smooth over dangerous internal conflict (such as in the case of civil rights) that could have threatened the cohesiveness and stability of the *national* Democratic party. And in an attempt to achieve party harmony while promoting ideological moderation, he made the point that "those who go along, get along." Of great importance, also, were Rayburn's efforts to organize a working majority in the House for various foreign policy proposals of Presidents Roosevelt, Truman, Eisenhower, and Kennedy. The support he gave those presidents stemmed from a deep sense of patriotism and a desire to protect the national interest. But, ironically, once the House, with Rayburn's help, began to comply with White House requests in foreign policy matters, it lost, in constitutional terms, a certain autonomy that its speaker had fought so hard to preserve. See C. Dwight Dorough, *Mr. Sam* (1962).

WILLIAM C. BERMAN

REAGAN, Ronald Wilson (b. Tampico, Ill., Feb. 6, 1911), PRESIDENT, ACTOR, graduated from Eureka (Ill.) College in 1932 and became a radio sports announcer that same year in Davenport, Iowa. He also wrote a weekly sports column for a Des Moines newspaper. While covering a sports assignment on Catalina Island near Los Angeles in 1937, Reagan came to the attention of a Warner Bros. agent who gave him a screen test and signed him to a movie contract. Reagan's first movie was *Love Is on the Air* (1937); in the next few years he appeared in numerous pictures including *Knute Rockne–All-American* (1940) and *King's Row* (1941). During World War II Reagan served in the Army Air Corps making training films. He continued his acting career after the war, but also became involved in politics. At first active in many liberal political organizations, such as the Americans for Democratic Action, he soon became fearful of Communist subversion and moved to the right; he testified before the House Un-American Activities Committee in 1947 on Communist influence in the movie industry.

Reagan was a member of the board of directors of the Screen Actors Guild, the AFL-affiliated union of movie actors, serving as president (1949–52, 1959). During 1949 he was chairman of the Motion Picture Industry Council, a body representing labor and management.

From 1954 to 1962 Reagan supervised and performed in the *General Electric Theater*, a weekly television program. He also toured the U.S. for GE, speaking to workers on the merits of free enterprise and the danger of too much government. Reagan was host on television's *Death Valley Days* program (1962–65). Thereafter he devoted full time to politics. By then a fervent conservative, he crusaded for such right-wing organizations as Young Americans for Freedom. He co-chaired the Citizens for **Goldwater**-Miller Committee in 1964 and campaigned for the ticket on national television. In 1966 Reagan defeated Democratic incumbent Edmund G. Brown for governor of California. As governor Reagan tried to cut government spending, dismantle many social welfare programs, and put tight budget limitations on state higher education, and he campaigned against student unrest. He made an unsuccessful bid for the 1968 Republican presidential nomination but was easily reelected governor in 1970. Reagan ran a long, hard, but ultimately futile campaign against Republican incumbent Gerald Ford for the 1976 presidential nomination. In 1980 he captured the Republican nomination and defeated incumbent Democratic Jimmy Carter to become the 40th president. Early in his first term, Reagan survived an assassination attempt by an insane drifter, John Hinckley. The wounded president nevertheless succeeded in convincing Congress to enact most of his proposals, including deep reductions in non-defense spending, lowered tax rates, and great increases in military spending. Ironically, confidence in the federal government increased during President Reagan's first term in office. The irony was that, despite Reagan's railing against the federal government, the American people's trust in that government increased as Reagan seemed to embody a simple honesty and his appointees seemed competent. Although unemployment increased markedly during his first two years in office, by the 1984 election the economy had rebounded and inflation, the bane of the Carter years, was down.

Consequently, Reagan defeated Democrat Walter Mondale handily in 1984. But his second term was less dramatic and far less successful. His administration did pass legislation that simplified the income tax code, but confidence in the federal government and Reagan declined. The customary drop in support for a president in his second term fell even more markedly with the cynicism generated by the Iran arms sale scandal. In 1987 Congress began hearings into actions by White House staff that became known as the Iran-Contra affair. In 1985 and 1986 White House staff members sold sophisticated weapons to Iran, the regime that had held Americans hostage at the American embassy in Teheran in 1979 and 1980. The staff sought Iran's help in obtaining the release of American hostages held in Lebanon. Some money from the sale was diverted by Colonel Oliver North, a member of Reagan's White House staff, to the Nicaraguan contra rebel forces in violation of federal law. President Reagan appeared to be either lying to hide his own complicity or to be out of touch with the activities of close advisers down the hall from his own office. As a result of this scandal, the administration was generally unsuccessful in advancing its conservative agenda. After leaving office in 1989, Reagan began to write his memoirs. Recently, it has been disclosed that the former president is suffering from Alzheimer's Disease.

Ronald Reagan has been a man of contrasts: an ideologue with a pragmatic bent, a fiscal conser-

vative whose administration tripled the national debt, a conservative Republican who used to be a liberal Democrat, and a powerful anti-Communist leader of the free world while supposedly out-of-touch and both dominated and exploited by his staff. His conservative views and policies brought forth both extreme adulation and enmity. History will judge his presidency. We know already that he stands out as a communicator and leader—for better or worse—from other post–World War II occupants of the White House.

Clark Clifford, advisor to Democratic presidents and a keen-eyed observer of the Washington scene since the days of Harry Truman, once privately described Ronald Reagan as an "affable buffoon." Although millions of Americans did not share Clifford's view of Reagan, many political analysts and historians agreed with Clifford. This says much about both Reagan and their own views of how politicians should think about policy and manage the Oval Office.

The "affable" part of the description is important in understanding Reagan and his immense popularity. When Reagan recreated Chicago Cubs baseball games on the radio in the 1930s, there was great competition. Announcer Reagan had to be likeable to listeners who could have heard the Cubs on a different radio frequency. Reagan succeeded in building a persona that worked well in genial roles in the movies and helped him become "the great communicator" as a self-described "citizen-politician." Ronald Reagan the affable fellow who told a good tale was not, however, an actor's deceit. Even his political enemies conceded that Reagan actually was a delightful man who, face-to-face, liked people.

The "buffoon" part of Clifford's comment stemmed from Reagan's way of dealing with issues before him. Intellectuals, the press, and policy analysts generally want political leaders to know the facts, understand the intricacies of policy options, and cite relevant details accurately. Reagan instead started with unalterable assumptions, from which he derived facts. He was an ideologue who knew what he believed and did not feel a need to support his positions by careful logic or presentation of facts. For him an anecdote or two sufficed, like the oft-repeated tale he used to tell of the alleged Chicago "Welfare Queen" who supposedly drove her new Cadillac to the social service office to pick up her monthly check. Whether it was actually true or not did not matter. Reagan thought it was true and that belief reinforced his ingrained hostility to welfare or any form of "dole" which might stimulate dependency. For Ronald Reagan, studies of poverty or the real impact of welfare payments on recipients were unnecessary and critics who reported factual errors in his statements were missing the point. When accused of having simple answers to the world's problems, Reagan agreed and said that social problems did have simple answers. This oft-stated view that there were simple, commonsense answers was a source of popularity for many voters, but also explains why others saw buffoonery and a dangerous anti-intellectualism in his presidency. See Garry Wills, *Reagan's America: Innocents at Home* (1987).

ROBERT E. O'CONNOR

REED, John Silas (b. Portland, Ore., Oct. 20, 1887; d. Moscow, Russ., Oct. 17, 1920), AUTHOR, REVOLUTIONARY, graduated from Harvard in 1910 and settled into Greenwich Village's bohemia. Publishing a variety of poetry, fiction, and reportage, he was attracted by radicalism. He became a contributing editor of the *Masses,* was arrested while covering the IWW Paterson (N.J.) strike, and directed a money-raising labor pageant in Madison Square Garden, New York, on June 7, 1913. His articles on the Mexican Revolution for *Metropolitan* magazine, written after several weeks of riding with Pancho Villa's men, led to his first book, *Insurgent Mexico* (1914). During World War I, which he believed "a trader's war," he covered the western front in 1914 and the eastern front the next year. After several weeks in "barbaric" Russia he wrote *The War in Eastern Europe* (1916). Returning to the U.S., Reed became one of the founders of the Provincetown Players (1916). Even after the U.S. entered the conflict, he remained adamantly opposed to the war and as a consequence was unable to publish in commercial magazines.

Journeying to Russia in the late summer of 1917, Reed became a Bolshevik partisan, witnessed the revolutionary events in Petrograd, and then worked briefly for the Foreign Propaganda Bureau of the Soviet regime. Upon his return to the U.S. he was forced to stand trial for his "seditious" writings and utterances. Early in 1919 he published *Ten Days That Shook the World,* an account of the Bolshevik Revolution. Hoping for a revolution at home, he joined the group that split the Socialist party in 1919, to found the Communist Labor party. As the party's delegate, he returned to Russia, attended the Second Congress of the Communist International in the summer of 1920, and was elected to its Executive Committee, but died a few weeks later of typhus.

To friends and acquaintances Reed was always a little larger than life. Boisterous and brash, he was a culture hero of the new radical bohemians, famed for friendships with the famous and infamous, for stormy love affairs, and for a striking ability to write prose that brought far-off battlefields and revolutions to life. His reporting, always in the first-person singular, helped foster such an image, but the inner Reed was a less confident person than his exterior life indicated.

Sickly as a child (a recurrent kidney ailment ended with a nephrectomy in 1916), Reed retreated into a world of books, internalizing the values of romantic literature, the atmosphere of frontier Oregon and the politics of his Progressive father—who suffered financially for his principled stance. His life became an energetic search for heroism and romance in the modern world. Deciding early to be a poet and novelist, his need for recognition and hunger for experience made him live in an external world far removed from the imaginative core of being. The result was poetry and fiction that were largely traditional and derivative.

Radicalism provided both artistic and personal salvation. Labor struggles at home and revolutions in exotic lands allowed his imagination to take wing and produce some of the most colorful journalism of the day. Like many in prewar Greenwich Village, Reed looked forward to a revolution that would be a broad libertarian advance on economic, political, and artistic fronts. The world war stifled creativity and made it appear as if Western civilization were committing suicide, but revolution in Russia, a combination of pageantry, heroism, and principle, seemed to promise the birth of a new society. Radical politics never proved as satisfying as writing, but the hope and faith kindled in 1917 remained. For Reed, the Bolshevik Revolution turned dreams into a reality, providing a coherent emotional and intellectual structure that gave meaning to both life and death. See Robert A. Rosenstone, *Romantic Revolutionary: A Biography of John Reed* (1975).

ROBERT A. ROSENSTONE

REED, Thomas Brackett (b. Portland, Maine, Oct. 18, 1839; d. Washington, D.C., Dec. 7, 1902), POLITICAL LEADER, graduated from Bowdoin College (1860) and moved to California, where he taught school and gained admittance to the bar (1863). Returning to Portland, Maine, shortly thereafter, he became an acting assistant paymaster in the U.S. Navy. In 1865 he was admitted to the Maine bar. Active in the Republican party, he held a number of offices: state legislator (1867–69); state senator (1869–70); attorney general (1870–72); and city solicitor for Portland (1874–77).

In 1876 Reed was elected to the U.S. Congress. While serving on a committee to investigate the presidential election of 1876, he helped uncover fraudulent actions by the Democrats in Louisiana. A hard-money advocate, Reed voted against the Bland-Allison Act of 1878, which committed the government to buy $2 million to $4 million worth of silver monthly. A strong advocate of protective tariffs, he opposed the Democratic Mills bill (1888), written in response to Grover Cleveland's tariff message (1887),

which called for moderate reductions on a variety of protected products. Reed also favored a strong navy and federally financed internal improvements.

In 1889 Reed was elected speaker of the House. As speaker, he tried to expedite legislative business by coming to grips with the obstructive quorum rule, which held that no measure could be passed unless a quorum (two-thirds) was present *and voting*. A minority could therefore delay legislation by refusing to answer the roll call. Reed broke this legislative roadblock by ordering the clerk to record the names of the silent members as "present and refusing to vote." By such action and other procedural changes Reed earned the sobriquet "Czar." Aided by these changes, the fifty-first Congress enacted a number of bills authorizing large expenditures; it became known as the "billion-dollar Congress." In 1890 the Republicans suffered an overwhelming defeat at the polls, and in 1891 the Democrats took over control of the House. Nevertheless, the Reed rules were kept intact.

In 1893 Reed supported President Cleveland's call for repeal of the Sherman Silver Purchase Act of 1890 in order to stop the drain on the gold reserve. But in 1894, consistent with his protectionist views, he fought doggedly against the Wilson-Gorman Tariff, which reduced duties and put some items on the free list. After the Republicans regained control of the House in 1894, Reed was again elected speaker. He was an unsuccessful candidate for the Republican presidential nomination in 1896.

In the debates over the annexation of Spanish colonies after the Spanish-American War, Reed was an outspoken anti-imperialist. He argued that annexation would be a departure from American traditions and also impractical. Disillusioned by the increasing bellicosity of American public opinion, Reed left the House in 1899, moved to New York City, and practiced law for the rest of his life.

———

Thomas Brackett Reed held office during a period when Maine was unusually important in

American politics. It produced a powerful congressional delegation, and in **James G. Blaine** boasted the era's most popular Republican spokesman. Reed carefully advanced the Pine Tree State's interests, and by 1890 was a national figure.

Though he had a sensitive private side, Reed betrayed no idealism, and accepted men and life as they were. He argued simply that "there are so many people in the world who have to be got into line to make any movement practicable that I am always afraid to undertake too large a program, or to try too much at one time." Maine was safely Republican, and Reed's career was never endangered. This safety enhanced his seniority and power within Congress and allowed him to seem unyielding on many divisive issues. But the lack of abrasion with a changing electorate also reinforced his natural inflexibility and indifference to public opinion.

His suspicion of men's motives, and narrow definition of the ability of politics to change human affairs, produced a desire for order and dispatch, as the Reed Rules of 1890 showed. He was a staunch advocate of tariff protection, gold currency, and partisan government. "The Republican party on the whole represents about that desire for progress, and that element of conservatism which seems to me to embody the most practicable thing we can take hold of," he once said. His Republicanism differed in style, if not in ultimate intent, from that of flexible moderates like William McKinley, who realistically paid close attention to popular support. Always a strong nationalist, Reed opposed innovations in foreign policy, such as tariff reciprocity and Pan-Americanism.

Reed was famous for a caustic humor and quick tongue, and he remained an engaging figure despite the awe and fear he struck in others. He suggested that a statesman was merely a dead politician. When a colleague asked what to say in eulogizing a deceased fellow representative, Reed remarked coolly: "Anything but the truth." Over six feet tall, and weighing some 250 pounds, he loftily reminded one who inquired about his bulk: "No gentleman ever weighed more than 200 pounds."

Though powerful in Congress, Reed never developed a national following. He neither accepted nor understood the changes that overtook late-19th-century American life. The destruction of his presidential ambitions in 1896, and the widespread popularity of President McKinley, whom he disliked, embittered Reed. Rather than accept new policies, especially overseas expansion and a rising sentiment for domestic reform, the "Czar" retired from public life in 1899. His greatest, and much needed, achievement was the rationalization of House rules of procedure in 1890. See William A. Robinson, *Thomas B. Reed, Parliamentarian* (1930).

H. WAYNE MORGAN

REED, Walter (b. Belroi, Va., Sept. 13, 1851; d. Washington, D.C., Nov. 22, 1902), PHYSICIAN, earned MD degrees from the University of Virginia in 1869 and Bellevue Hospital Medical College in 1870. He was commissioned assistant surgeon with lieutenant's rank in the U.S. Army Medical Corps in 1875, and was stationed at Fort Lowell in Arizona during 1876–87. He served as attending surgeon and examiner of recruits at Baltimore during 1890–93. In 1893 he was promoted by the army to full surgeon with major's rank, and became curator of the Army Medical Museum and professor of Bacteriology and Clinical Microscopy at the newly organized Army Medical School in Washington, D.C., a post he held until 1902. He was also (1901–2) professor of pathology and bacteriology at Columbian University in Washington, D.C. Reed made extensive studies of erysipelas (an acute, feverish disease associated with intense skin inflammations) and diphtheria. *The Contagiousness of Erysipelas* was published in 1892. In 1898 he was appointed head of a commission assigned to study the causation and propagation of typhoid fever, which had broken out with epidemic force among American troops fighting in the Spanish-American War in Cuba, and he helped prove that the disease was spread by dust and flies.

Already in 1897, Reed had disproved the theory that yellow fever was caused by a bacillus. As a result, he was made the head of a commission appointed in 1900 to study yellow fever in Cuba. He was led by his observations there to discount the popular idea that yellow fever was transmitted by contact with bedding and clothing of those already infected, and along with James Carroll, Aristides Agramonte, and Jesse Lazear, he proved that it was really caused by a filterable microorganism and transmitted by the anopheles mosquito (*Aëdes aegypti*). This discovery paved the way for the eradication of yellow fever from Cuba by U.S. sanitary engineers led by Major William C. Gorgas in 1902. In recognition of Reed's achievements, the army general hospital in Washington, D.C., is named after him.

———— ∞ ————

Walter Reed's career typifies that of the research-minded physician who spanned two eras—the prebacteriological and the decades after Robert Koch's clear demonstration of the growth and life cycle of the anthrax bacillus in 1876. Not until the 1890s did the germ theory of disease become a major interest for American laboratories. In 1890, Reed went to Baltimore to examine recruits, but of much greater significance was his association during this time with the laboratory of **William H. Welch.** Here he began to work on the basic problems of infectious diseases, learning the proper techniques for isolating and identifying the various known microorganisms causing disease.

The complex problem of yellow fever, with which numbers of investigators had wrestled in the last two decades of the 19th century, remained an enigma until the commission headed by Reed unraveled the complicated epidemiological features of the disease in Cuba in 1900. Reed and his coworkers, using human experimental subjects, tested the passage of the disease from mosquitoes to humans, thereby confirming the necessity of the insect vector. They further showed that only through the bite of a mosquito that had twelve or more days previously fed on a patient sick with yellow fever could the nonimmune individual contract the disease. The resulting immunity conferred by the infection was a long-lasting one.

Together with the elucidation of the basic facts about the passage and the course of the disease, Reed translated the experimental results into practical application. No longer did those who were sick with yellow fever need to be shunned, nor did their belongings or their quarters require burning. Only the proper control of mosquitoes could serve as an effective preventive measure. Not until a quarter-century later did Max Theiler perfect an effective vaccine against the disease. But within about a decade of the Reed Commission's momentous discoveries, his fellow army physician, William C. Gorgas, was able to use effective mosquito abatement to allow the construction of the Panama Canal to proceed without the grave peril of yellow fever. See Howard A. Kelly, *Walter Reed and Yellow Fever* (1906).

GERT H. BRIEGER

REHNQUIST, William (b. Milwaukee, Wisc., Oct. 1, 1924), JURIST, received both has bachelor's and master's degrees from Stanford University in 1948. The following year (1949) he received another master's degree from Harvard, and graduated Stanford Law School three years later (1952). As one of the top law school graduates, he became clerk to Supreme Court Justice **Robert H. Jackson** (1952–53). Following his clerkship, he entered private practice in Phoenix, Arizona. A conservative Republican, Rehnquist was appointed Assistant Attorney General for the Office of Legal Council in 1969. In that position, he promoted a strong anticrime program and issued bitting critiques of proposed civil rights measures. In Oct. 1971, President Richard M. Nixon nominated Rehnquist to be Associate Justice of the Supreme Court. He took his seat in January, 1972. In 1986, President Ronald Reagan named him Chief Justice.

———— ∞ ————

Nixon appointed Rehnquist in pursuance of his goal of placing on the Supreme Court supporters of strict construction of the Constitution, judical restraint, and federalism. Rehnquist has proved more firmly devoted to those principles than probably any other Court appointee since 1937. The framers of the Constitution, he explained in a 1976 speech, intended that Congress and the presidency, rather than the courts, should "furnish the motive power ... for the solution of the numerous and varied problems that the future would bring." But his strongest commitment has been to preserving a broad area of autonomy for the states vis-à-vis the federal government.

Rehnquist has taken a restrictive view of the establishment clause of the First Amendment, seeing its purpose as simply "to prohibit establishment of a national religion, and perhaps to prevent discrimination among sects." He has balked at including so-called commercial speech within the protection of the First Amendment. A strong law-and-order sympathizer, he has stood firm against any further extension of the rights of the criminally accused and even has favored cutting back some of the expansions approved by the **Warren** Court. He has pushed hard to limit federal court interference with the state courts, one of his major goals being to restrict the opportunities for state criminal defendants to challenge their convictions by federal habeas corpus. He would limit the application of the equal protection clause of the Fourteenth Amendment to racial discrimination. Even in such cases, he has taken the position that a plaintiff challenging a government action must show discriminatory intent, not simply discriminatory effects. He has opposed government affirmative action programs as violating the racial neutrality commanded by the Fourteenth Amendment. Averse to recognizing "implied" rights not explicitly found in the constitutional text, he strongly dissented from the acceptance in *Roe* v. *Wade* (1973) of a woman's right to an abortion. He has resisted recognition of any positive or affirmative constitutional rights to governmental assistance.

During his early years on the bench, Rehnquist appeared to occupy an isolated position on the Court's far right. By 1975, however, he had become a major force in the Court's decision-making. His elevation to Chief Justice was wide-

ly perceived—hopefully by some, fearfully by others—as marking the beginning of a period of conservative ascendancy. But the Rehnquist Court has not so far broken sharply with existing precedent. Rehnquist personally remains a controversial figure. No one questions his brilliance; but his constitutional philosophy is the target of liberal hostility. See Sue Davis, *Justice Rehnquist and the Constitution* (1989).

JOHN BRAEMAN

REID, Whitelaw (b. Xenia, Ohio, Oct. 27, 1837; d. London, Eng., Dec. 15, 1912), JOURNALIST, DIPLOMAT, graduated from Miami University (Oxford, Ohio), in 1856. After briefly serving as school superintendent in South Charleston, Ohio, he edited a weekly newspaper, the Xenia *News* (1857–59). Becoming involved in politics, he supported Republican presidential candidate **John C. Frémont** in 1856 and worked for the nomination and election of Abraham Lincoln in 1860. Reid was state legislative reporter for the Cincinnati *Times* in 1860 and also wrote for the Cleveland *Herald* and Cincinnati *Gazette*. He became city editor of the *Gazette* in 1861 but soon moved to Washington, D.C., to be the *Gazette*'s war correspondent. He covered many battles, including Shiloh and Gettysburg. After Appomattox he toured the South and wrote an account of his experiences, *After the War* (1866). He also speculated in Louisiana and Alabama cotton land but lost money. His *Ohio in the War* (1868) was an account of his journalistic work.

In 1868 Reid moved to New York City to join **Horace Greeley**'s New York *Tribune* as an editorial writer; he became managing editor in 1869 and editor in chief upon Greeley's death in 1872. Taking charge of the near-bankrupt *Tribune*, he increased its circulation, improved foreign news service, and added such outstanding contributors as **Mark Twain** and Bret Harte to the staff. An ardent Republican, Reid nevertheless disapproved of President Grant's administration and backed Liberal Republican candidate Greeley in 1872. He returned to the Republican fold, supporting Rutherford B. Hayes and later presidential candidates of the party. President Harrison named him ambassador to France in 1889. Reid returned to the U.S. in 1892 to be Harrison's running mate in the presidential election, but the ticket was defeated.

President McKinley appointed Reid to the commission that negotiated peace with Spain after the Spanish-American War (1898). An advocate of an expansionist foreign policy, Reid favored annexation of the Philippines, expounding his views in *Our New Duties* (1899) and *Problems of Expansion* (1900). A friend and adviser to President Theodore Roosevelt, Reid was appointed special ambassador to the coronation of King Edward VII in 1902 and ambassador to Great Britain in 1905. He relinquished editorship of the *Tribune* that year and continued as ambassador under President Taft.

———— ∞ ————

A skilled reporter, well educated and fervently ambitious, Reid became the nation's leading Republican editor. The crisp objectivity of his Civil War reports won him prominence, and objectivity remained a *Tribune* hallmark. He also had a knack of knowing the right people. Supporting Lincoln against fellow Ohioan **Salmon P. Chase** in 1860, he later cultivated Chase and through him began to build a network of prominent acquaintances that finally included presidents and leading congressmen. In business as in personal life, he knew the value of advertising. The *Tribune* building (1875), capped by a Florentinian tower second in height only to Trinity Church, was a bold bid for much-needed publicity. His pioneering use of the linotype transformed newspaper publishing after 1885. Reversing Greeley's policy, he actively sought college graduates for his staff, the result being a new standard of artistic and literary excellence. Although rivals sometimes pictured Reid as a selfish careerist, notably in slanderous attacks when he took over after Greeley's death, the *Tribune* earned him rightful distinction. While perhaps not the equal in personal force of Charles A. Dana or **Joseph Pulitzer,** he revived and extended the influence of a leading metropolitan daily.

Reid personally shaped *Tribune* editorial policy. Wealthy by marriage, conservative by nature, he instinctively shared the basic values of many businessmen, urging sound currency and low taxes. The *Tribune* on occasion shrilly urged the authorities to meet "every resisting mob with grapeshot," and generally opposed union activities. But Reid, distressed by the clash of labor and capital, believed that the more important problem was how to control the trusts that dominated both. He exhorted the educated classes to assume public responsibility, supported good government and civil service reform, and vigorously exposed the corruption of the Grant era. He was slow in gaining a reputation in foreign affairs, but became a leading spokesman during the 1890s. Although he supported expansion, he also betrayed some ambivalence at the course of events. The war with Spain he pronounced a "great sorrow," urging annexation as the only honorable alternative given the situation. Stressing the need for new markets, he feared expansion that benefited only the trusts. Although Reid's "conservatism" has been criticized then and since, his social views, like his final support of Theodore Roosevelt, underline the complexity of the reform tradition. See Royal Cortissoz, *The Life of Whitelaw Reid* (1921).

ROBERT C. BANNISTER

REMINGTON, Frederic (b. Canton, N.Y., Oct. 4, 1861; d. near Ridgefield, Conn., Dec. 26, 1909), ARTIST, WRITER, attended the Yale School of the Fine Arts (1878–80). After making a tour of the West he returned to New York in 1885 with a portfolio of sketches. He also studied briefly at the Art Students League of New York. He had a painting exhibited at the National Academy in 1886, and quickly gained considerable renown as an accomplished illustrator of western scenes for leading magazines. In 1888 he illustrated a series of articles written for *Century* magazine by Theodore Roosevelt (published later that year in book form as *Ranch Life and the Hunting Trail*). His work helped popularize the original editions of the work of several notable American authors, including **Henry Wadsworth Longfellow**'s *Song of Hiawatha* (1890) and **Francis Parkman**'s *Oregon Trail* (1892).

As an artist, Remington is best known for his documentary-like portrayal of western scenes and figures. He published numerous articles and books on western themes, which served primarily as vehicles for his illustrations. These include *Pony Tracks* (1895), *Crooked Trails* (1898), and *John Ermine of the Yellowstone* (1902), a novel which was adapted for the stage in 1903. He also traveled throughout America, Europe, and Asia, serving as a combination illustrator-correspondent. He was a war correspondent and artist in Cuba during the Spanish-American War, and produced numerous paintings of Cuban scenes. In 1895 he took up sculpture, and in his remaining years, in addition to his large output of paintings and drawings, he produced twenty-five important pieces of sculpture, including his well-known bronze *The Bronco Buster*, considered by many to be the best work of American western art in that medium.

Although Frederic Remington was an easterner and traveled extensively abroad, his great enthusiasm was for the Old West. His early art works were not known for their use of color. Aware of this weakness, the West where the "sun is strong" appealed to him—bright sunshine was just what he needed to improve his color sense. So early in his career he renounced other interests and dedicated himself completely to the West, and he became a very special part of the sagebrush era. He loved the "West of picturesque and stirring events" and was sad as he watched it fade into history. Thus, with keen observation and unusual foresight he sought to record, through various means of art and writing, the true picture of the West. Remington had a great passion for painting cowboys, pioneers, trappers, prospectors, Native Americans, and especially the horse. He caught the important details which most humans miss but which he clearly saw and pictured as few have been able to do. This concern for true visible form made him the world's greatest portrayer of the galloping horse.

Remington never hesitated to go to any means to satisfy himself with his work and always held true to his great passion to portray correctly. Thus, rather late in his career he took up sculpturing, an art which had a great appeal to him. It provided a new means for satisfying his desire for true form; through sculpturing, he believed he would become immortal; all other forms of art might be eaten up by time—not so bronze.

Remington had a most pleasant, warm relationship with great westerners of his day including Theodore Roosevelt and **Owen Wister.** His letters to Owen Wister are a reflection of the good companion and true friend which made up this unconventional man and show the camaraderie of their relationship. See Harold McCracken, *Frederic Remington: Artist of the Old West* (1947).

N. Orwin Rush

REUTHER, Walter Philip (b. Wheeling, W. Va., Sept. 1, 1907; d. Pellston, Mich., May 9, 1970), LABOR LEADER, left high school in 1922 and became an apprentice tool and die maker for the Wheeling Steel Corporation. Discharged for trying to organize a union, he went to Detroit in 1926 and spent the next few years working for the Briggs Manufacturing Co., General Motors, and Ford. He became foreman of a tool and die room at Ford in 1931 but was fired for engaging in union activities in 1933. Reuther and his brother Victor then went on a three-year trip around the world during which time they worked in Russia's Gorki automobile plants and spent time in England, Germany, India, and Japan. Returning to Detroit in 1935, Reuther began to organize autoworkers into the United Auto Workers union, under the auspices of the new Committee on Industrial Organization. He became president of Local 174 (west side of Detroit) and was elected to the UAW executive board in 1936. Reuther participated in most of the UAW's sit-down strikes, including the bloody "Battle of the Over-pass" outside Ford's River Rouge (Mich.) plant in 1937, where he and other union members were beaten by Ford security men. The Ford company finally recognized the

UAW in 1941. Reuther was elected first vice president of the national union in 1942. During World War II he served in the Office of Production Management and on the War Manpower Commission and War Production Board. He developed a plan for mass-producing airplanes in auto factories.

In 1946 Reuther was elected president of the UAW and later that year vice president of the CIO. Though often accused of Communist sympathies, from 1938 on he fought to keep Communists out of the UAW. He also led a series of strikes for higher wages and welfare benefits based on his "wage increases without price increases" theory. Upon the death of **Philip Murray** in 1952, Reuther became president of the CIO. When the AFL-CIO merger took place in 1955, he became vice president of the new organization and head of its Industrial Union Department. In 1961 he served as a chairman of the Tractors for Freedom Committee to obtain the release of Cubans taken prisoner after the Bay of Pigs invasion. Although initially backing AFL-CIO President **George Meany,** especially Meany's opposition to union corruption, Reuther split with Meany in the late 1960s, claiming that the AFL-CIO had become rigid and lifeless. The United Auto Workers withdrew from the AFL-CIO in 1968 and joined with the International Brotherhood of Teamsters a year later to form the Alliance for Labor Action. Reuther was killed in an airplane crash.

Walter Reuther was a strong and aggressive individual, an influential, controversial, and unique kind of American labor leader during his thirty-year career as a prominent national and world figure. He ended his career as he began it: in the role of a maverick. His family heritage, his experiences as a youthful world traveler and as a Depression radical, cast him in the mold of a lifetime social reformer and activist. In marked contrast and conflict with the business union philosophy which permeates most of the trade union hierarchy, Reuther acted the self-conscious role of a "crusader for a better world." With this background, Reuther felt more at home with world leaders like Willy Brandt of Germany, Jawaharlal Nehru of India, and the socialist labor leaders of England and the Scandinavian countries than with his colleagues of the AFL-CIO Executive Council and its president, George Meany. In American politics, his warm friend, confidante, and adviser was **Eleanor Roosevelt.** Both of them sought always to keep alive in their lifetime the New Deal's early sense of social dedication.

Reuther was enormously ambitious and politically skillful, and his rise to union power was swift and sensational. Like many Depression radicals, Reuther worked in the industrial union movement (CIO) directed by **John L. Lewis** as part of a coalition of Communist, socialist, and other CIO forces. But disillusionment with Stalin's Russia, and the machinations of the Communist party in the United States, turned him into a political opponent of Communism. In World War II he reached national stature with his social engineering plans. Reuther's brilliant leadership of the 116-day strike in 1946 against General Motors dazzled the nation and assured him the presidency of the autoworkers union (UAW). He devastated the left-wing coalition competing with him for control of the union. His total victory provided him for the next two decades with an unchallenged base of operations in American society. As the UAW grew to more than 1.5 million members, Reuther's stature increased.

Reuther's flair for publicity and his undeniable public charisma and eloquence soon had him projected as a possible presidential candidate, but the emergence of the cold war and the hysteria of McCarthyism engulfed him and the nation. The voice of the social reformer was muted. Nevertheless, Reuther's talents found ample release in spectacular collective bargaining with the giants of the auto industry: General Motors, Ford, and Chrysler. His innovations included raising the issue of a guaranteed annual wage and pensions for "those too old to work, and too young to die." He expanded two ideas proposed by C. E. Wilson, president of GM: yearly wage increases based on "an annual improvement productivity factor," and a defense against inflation by a cost of living "escalator clause." It was an impressive performance.

In the Kennedy-Johnson era Reuther was very active and influential in the Democratic party and in the campaigns for social legislation. His early commitment to civil rights found him an ardent friend and activist in **Martin Luther King, Jr.** These activities were a major source of Reuther's isolation from his more conservative colleagues in the top leadership of the American trade unions. His willingness to seek new approaches with the U.S.S.R. was another reason why Reuther made an implacable enemy of George Meany, the dominant leader of the AFL-CIO. Reuther also rejected labor's support of the Vietnam War.

Reuther's legacy was clearly visible: a union leadership in the UAW reared in his tradition and with similar experiences, and a union dedicated to social reform, still 1.5 million strong, and recognized as a permanent institution in the auto industry.

Of the many accolades given Reuther after his death by world and American statesmen, the one which most appropriately placed him in historical perspective came from **Henry Ford II,** the grandson of the auto baron who resisted Reuther and the CIO so vigorously until 1941. "Walter Reuther was an extraordinarily effective advocate of labor's interest. His tough-minded dedication, his sense of social concern, his selflessness and his eloquence all make him a central figure in the development of modern industrial history." See Jean Gould and Lorena Hickock, *Walter Reuther, Labor's Rugged Individualist* (1971).

B. J. WIDICK

REVERE, Paul (b. Boston, Mass., Jan. 1, 1735; d. Boston, Mass, May 10, 1818), SILVERSMITH, was already Boston's leading silversmith when he produced an inflammatory engraving of the Boston Massacre in 1770 (copied from Henry Pelham). An early member and messenger of the Sons of Liberty, Revere is said to have participated in the Boston Tea Party (1773) after Parliament gave the East India Co. a monopoly on the sales of tea in the colonies. In 1774 Revere carried the Suffolk Resolves—a series of resolutions adopted by a convention in Suffolk County, Massachusetts, which called for the people of that state to resist the "Intolerable Acts"—to Philadelphia, where the first Continental Congress endorsed them.

Revere then became the Massachusetts provincial assembly's official courier to Congress. When the Boston committee of safety learned that General Gage was going to attack the Concord supply depot, they sent Revere to alert the countryside. He reached Lexington (five miles from Concord), where he warned **Samuel Adams** and **John Hancock** that Gage intended to arrest them, but he was captured before he could reach Concord. However, during the confusing retreat of the British after the battle of Concord bridge, Revere was released.

In 1779 Revere participated in the Penobscot expedition, after which he was accused of being a coward. In order to clear his name he obtained a court-martial which declared his innocence in 1782. Following the Revolutionary War he resumed his career as a craftsman, but maintained his interest in national affairs and was a staunch supporter of the new Constitution. From his copper and brass foundry in Canton, Massachusetts, he supplied materials for the construction of the U.S.S. *Constitution* ("Old Ironsides"), and in 1808–9 he made copper plates for the boilers of Robert Fulton's steamboats.

Though known primarily for his midnight ride, Paul Revere was one of the notable men of his generation in several fields. Creative, ingenious, and versatile, he became a superb silversmith, a key political organizer in Revolutionary Boston, and an innovator in processing bronze and copper. His career, spanning seven decades, illustrates major themes in American development.

Revere learned to work silver with his father, a Huguenot immigrant, and by his twenties he was producing his and America's finest pieces. When the Boston economy went slack in 1764 Revere found time for town politics, where he soon became a leader among the artisans. From the outset he was a Whig, becoming a Son of Liberty in 1765 and a workhorse of the Whig leaders.

During the war Revere was disappointed to remain in Boston commanding a fort. But his thirst for action was more than satisfied by the Penobscot expedition, which ended in retreat and recriminations. Revere never again sought the glories of leadership, and when the war ended he plunged into his work, eager to recoup his finances and ready to remain at the perimeter of politics.

Revere shifted from Rococo to Federal design as easily as he made the transition from being a Whig to a Federalist. Now, in addition to silver, he started a foundry for casting bells and domestic and marine hardware which gradually supplanted silversmithing. This became the Revere copper and brass company. By the War of 1812 his factory was equipped to roll sheet copper to sheathe American ships, and so the artisan who had created ornaments for the colonial elite ended his life as a producer of the hardware of 19th-century commercial and industrial development. See Esther Forbes, *Paul Revere and the World He Lived In* (1942).

RICHARD D. BROWN

Victorian Gothic to that adaptation of French and Spanish Romanesque which came to be known as "Richardsonian." Richardson practiced in New York until 1878, then moved to Boston. In 1876, with **Frederick Law Olmsted** and Leopold Eidlitz, he was commissioned to finish the New York State Capitol at Albany, whose upper floors and interiors show his mark. The ecclesiastical arch, which Richardson adapted to the demands of a variety of buildings, is perhaps his most characteristic feature. Austin Hall (1881) at Harvard is Richardsonianism at the peak of its development.

In the last five or six years of his life Richardson developed a more functional style. His building for **Marshall Field,** Chicago (1885), perhaps his masterpiece, and a series of railroad stations for the Boston and Albany Railroad (1881–85) best display this tendency. Richardsonian design—the characteristic squat arches and roughhewn stone—was widely imitated for about ten years after his death. The "picturesque eclectic" style, of which Richardsonian Romanesque is a leading example, reached the peak of its popularity in such early-nineties buildings as the Pennsylvania Railroad's Broad Street Station in Philadelphia.

RICHARDSON, Henry Hobson (b. St. James Parish, La., Sept. 29, 1838; d. Boston, Mass., April 27, 1886), ARCHITECT, was descended on his mother's side from Joseph Priestley, English chemist and radical. He received his education at public and private schools in New Orleans. Henry Richardson revealed an unusual talent for mathematics and drawing. At Harvard, from which he graduated in 1859, Richardson switched from engineering to architecture. He went to Paris in 1860 to attend the Ecole des Beaux-Arts. He returned to America after the war. His first architectural commission came as a result of a prize competition for a Unitarian church in Springfield, Massachusetts. This building and several more churches, including Boston's Brattle Street Church (1870) and Trinity Church (1872), delineate his development from

Henry Hobson Richardson was beyond question the most important architect of his generation in the United States. He was also the first American architect to have an international reputation, influencing architectural design in Germany, England, and especially Scandinavia. Yet Richardson's preeminence in American architectural history derives from neither any particular originality nor the lasting appeal of his style as such, but from a new approach to architectural design which he more effectively than anyone else introduced and represented in his work.

Richardson was by no means the first or only architect to revive Romanesque forms; as Henry-Russell Hitchcock so well observed, "Richardsonian Romanesque was neither Richardsonian nor Romanesque." And while in the heyday of Richardson's popularity thousands of buildings in his style were erected in every corner of the United States, that heyday lasted only from about 1880 to 1895, and there has never been a hint of any inclination to revive his manner; about most surviving Richardsonian buildings contemporary critics would say what Montgomery Schuyler said of the Glessner house in Richardson's own time: "The building is defensible only in a military sense."

Throughout all previous history, the art of architecture involved making visual metaphors supporting existing institutions of government and religion. Still in the earlier 19th century, state and national capitol buildings in Roman Revival style proclaimed reincarnation of Roman republican ideals in the United States, continuity of British institutions was proclaimed in Gothic Revival parliament buildings, and so on. But the guiding principle of Richardson's Romanesque and "shingle style" alike, honest expression of materials and structure, was fundamentally different, and led directly to the 20th century's "new architecture" of bare steel and glass, raw concrete and wood. It has also led directly to the dilemma that if architecture merely involves expressing materials and structure, with an aesthetic appeal that is entirely subjective, what distinguishes a work of architecture from mere shelter, a cathedral from a cowshed? And what prevents the architectural environment from becoming intolerably mechanical, dehumanized, or barbaric? This unresolved problem is a prime legacy from Henry Hobson Richardson. See Alan Gowans, *Images of American Living* (1964).

ALAN GOWANS

RICKEY, Branch Wesley (b. Stockdale, Ohio, Dec. 20, 1881; d. Columbia, Mo., Dec. 9, 1965), SPORTS FIGURE, joined the Cincinnati Reds in 1904 as a catcher. In 1906 while playing professional baseball and football, he earned a BA from Ohio Wesleyan University. Ending his playing career in 1907, he entered the University of Michigan Law School (LLB, 1911). After a stay at Saranac Lake, New York, to recover from tuberculosis, Rickey opened a law office in Boise,

Idaho. In 1913, however, he joined the American League's St. Louis Browns as a scout; he quickly rose to club secretary, field manager, and finally vice president in 1916. A year later he took over as president of the National League's near-bankrupt St. Louis Cardinals. Following service in the army during World War I as a major in the Chemical Warfare Service, he became field manager of the Cardinals in 1918.

In 1919 Rickey pioneered the "farm system" for developing young players by acquiring partial control of several minor-league teams. Although ridiculed at first, this system was soon adopted by all the major-league teams. Relieved of the duties of president of the Cardinals in 1920 and of manager in 1925, Rickey remained the team's general manager until 1942. During this time he developed the Cardinals into one of baseball's most powerful dynasties through his shrewd trades and keen ability to spot young talent. Under his management the Cardinals won six pennants and four World Series. In 1942 Rickey left the Cardinals to become president and general manager of the Brooklyn Dodgers. Four years later, after an extensive search, he signed **Jackie Robinson** for the Dodgers' Montreal farm team. The Dodgers brought Robinson up in 1947. In 1950 Rickey became general manager of the Pittsburgh Pirates and, five years later, chairman of the board. Hoping to force the major leagues into expansion, Rickey became president of the newly established Continental League in 1959. It went out of existence in 1962 when the major leagues expanded. Rickey then served as a special consultant to the St. Louis Cardinals until 1964.

———

Branch Rickey stands forth as professional baseball's counterpart of that oldest stereotype of American folklore, the shrewd, hardworking, God-fearing Yankee trader. He was also one of baseball's genuine innovators, an administrator who made a lasting imprint upon the industry.

The St. Louis Browns' choice of Rickey, a former college coach, to manage a big-league team was a reversal of the usual practice of enlisting former major-leaguers to coach college teams. Consequently his rule against poker playing, his blackboard talks on baseball theory, and his other teaching innovations—many of them to become standard practice—prompted much scoffing at his "college methods," while his abhorrence of liquor and refusal to manage the team on Sundays provoked sarcasm over his "peculiarities."

Rickey's personal code, stemming from his Methodist upbringing, did not, however, dull his sharpness in the marketplace. It did not preclude his sharing in Sunday gate receipts, or even shifting a weekday game to Sunday so as to create a synthetic doubleheader and thus attract more fans. Neither did his prohibitionist persuasion prevent him from hiring executives, team managers, or players who drank heavily, provided they could benefit his organization. Nor did he shrink from skirting the rules upon occasion by entering into "gentlemen's agreements" with officials of other major-league teams to waive claims on players in order to slip them into minor leagues. Such seeming contradictions between profession and practice, together with his skill in oratorical obfuscation and circumlocution, caused many to regard Rickey as a hypocritical mountebank.

Yet even his detractors acknowledged Rickey's industriousness, organizing genius, and unsurpassed ability to judge the potential of raw recruits. Competitors trading players and players negotiating salaries with Rickey experienced at first hand his sharpness in bargaining. It was said that after dickering with him players came away grateful for a pay cut.

After he joined the St. Louis Cardinals, then a debt-ridden club lacking the means to compete in the player market, Rickey created his "farm system" and thereby revolutionized the economic structure of organized baseball. He did not originate the idea of "farming out" promising young players to lesser leagues to keep them "on ice" for future use, but he carried out the scheme to its logical conclusion, slowly establishing a vertically integrated system that enabled the parent club to maintain and develop a constant flow of cheap, new talent.

Rickey built the Cardinals into a baseball empire that, at its peak, comprised thirty-two clubs, six- or seven-hundred players, and an investment of more than $2 million. The "chain gang," as critics called it, proved a spectacular success. St. Louis won its first National League championship in 1926 and in the next twenty years captured eight more and finished second six times. Even though their paid attendance was much smaller than that of New York, Brooklyn, or Chicago, the Cardinals' profit exceeded that of any other National League club between 1925 and 1950, because Rickey's farm system produced roughly three times the number of players needed, thus enabling him to trade surplus players to other teams for cash. In fact, so successful was the Rickey system that all other major-league teams felt compelled to adopt it in spite of the vehement opposition many of them accorded it at first. As Rickey put it in one of his favorite quotations, "First pity, then endure, then embrace."

During World War II when the military draft dried up the supply of players and the future of professional baseball became uncertain, Rickey, then part owner and general manager of the Brooklyn Dodgers, boldly ordered his scouts to comb the country for prospects below draft age. Thus after the war the Dodgers had engrossed the largest supply of young prospects in the National League. To sort out and classify them, Rickey established a mechanized spring-training complex at Vero Beach, Florida, to house and feed more than six-hundred players during an eight-week period and to process them for distribution among the Dodgers and their network of farm teams. Surplus players were sold to other clubs.

Rickey also realized that the time was opportune to tap the large, cheap, African-American player market, and out of enlightened self-interest succeeded in breaking the longstanding unwritten rule barring blacks from organized baseball by signing Jack Roosevelt Robinson to Brooklyn's Montreal farm team in 1946 and then to the Brooklyn team in 1947. Robinson was not, as is commonly believed, the first black ever to play in organized baseball. That distinction belongs to Moses Fleetwood Walker, who played with Toledo of the American Association, then a major league, in 1884. But the color line had been maintained in baseball for more than a half-century until Rickey made his most important contribution, one that had sociological significance in America that extended beyond professional baseball. See Arthur Mann, *Branch Rickey: American in Action* (1957).

HAROLD SEYMOUR

RICKOVER, Hyman George (b. Makow, Poland, Jan 27, 1900; d. Arlington, Va., July 8, 1986), NAVAL OFFICER, emigrated to the United States with his parents in 1906, and settled in Chicago. A brilliant student, he graduated from the U.S. Naval Academy in 1922. He served aboard battleships and cruisers, earned a Masters in electrical engineering from Columbia University, and qualified for submarine duty in 1930. Owing to a prickly personality, he was exiled from submarines with the result that he spent World War II ashore as chief of the Electrical Division of the navy's Bureau of Ships. In that post, he became convinced that atomic-powered warships were both feasible and necessary. Appointed head of the Nuclear Power Division of the Bureau of Ships, he promoted the development of the submarine *Nautilus* (1954), the first warship propelled by nuclear power. Later, as chief of the Nuclear Reactors Branch of the Atomic Energy Commission he participated in developing an experimental nuclear electric power plant (1956–57). Outspoken and articulate, Rickover was an ardent supporter of educational reforms, especially in the sciences and engineering where he believed America had fallen woefully short. He wrote several books on that subject, including *Education and Freedom* (1959) and *American Education: A National Failure* (1963).

———

Hard work, shameless flattery, and bureaucratic scheming earned Rickover a postwar assignment to the atomic energy complex at Oak Ridge, Tennessee, where he first devised his plan to build and install nuclear reactors in warships. Although he later crafted the myth that navy reactionaries opposed this plan, this was untrue; the Chief of Naval Operations quickly approved it, Rickover participated in the construction of the first prototype reactor, and in 1950 Congress authorized the building of the submarine *Nautilus*, which put to sea four years later. Widely despised by navy men and scheduled to retire in 1953, Rickover, then a captain, waged an unprecedented and ultimately successful public campaign to obtain flag rank of admiral and delay his retirement.

Thereafter, he nurtured close ties with Congress and the Atomic Energy Commission which he used to extend his writ over the navy's nuclear submarine policy as head of the Nuclear Reactions Branch. Critics rightly charged that Rickover's eccentric preferences came to dictate all other features of American submarines, but his innovative safety procedures and preventive maintenance programs eventually spread throughout the navy to the civilian nuclear industry. Owing to the high costs of shipboard reactors, however, Rickover failed to achieve his goal of an "all-nuclear" fleet, and in 1982 was finally forced into a bitter retirement after illegal dealings were uncovered. Acerbic, always shrewd, and ever vengeful, Rickover left a decidedly ambiguous legacy as both the "father of the nuclear navy" and an unbridled expert in the roughest bureaucratic politics. See Heather M. David, *Admiral Rickover and the Nuclear Navy* (1970), and Norman Polmar, *Rickover* (1982).

ROBERT W. LOVE, JR.

RIESMAN, David (b. Philadelphia, Pa., Sept. 22, 1909), SOCIAL SCIENTIST, graduated from Harvard in 1931. After completing Harvard Law School (1934), Riesman served as clerk to Supreme Court Justice **Louis Brandeis** (1934–36). He then became professor of law at the University of Buffalo (1937–41), and visiting research fellow at Columbia Law School (1941–42). He published *The American Constitution and International Labour Legislation* in 1942. Riesman served as deputy assistant district attorney of New York County (1942–43) and then worked for the Sperry Gyroscope Co. (1943–44). He was appointed visiting associate professor at the University of Chicago in 1946 and professor of social sciences the following year.

In the late 1940s Riesman was director of the research project on mass communications for the Yale University Committee on National Policy, out of which came his highly praised *The Lonely Crowd: A Study of the Changing American Character* (1950), an analysis of the emerging American personality in 20th-century urban society. This was followed by *Faces in the Crowd* (1952), a series of interviews and profiles of typical members of American society, and a collection of essays, *Individualism Reconsidered* (1954). Riesman became Henry Ford II Professor of Social Sciences at Harvard in 1958, a position he held until his retirement in 1979. Some of his other works include *Thorstein Veblen* (1953), *Abundance for What? and Other Essays* (1963), *The Academic Revolution* (1968), written with Christopher Jencks, *Academic Values and Mass Education* (1970), written with Joseph Gusfield and Zelda Gamson, and *On Higher Education* (1980).

Few scholars have become as suddenly famous as did David Riesman with the publication in 1950 of *The Lonely Crowd*, written in collaboration with Nathan Glazer and Reuel Denny. Originally published by a university press, it attracted so much attention that it was quickly reissued in a paperback edition and became one of the first "intellectual" paperback best-sellers. Riesman also became the only sociologist to date to be pictured on the front cover of *Time* magazine.

The thesis of *The Lonely Crowd* that accounted for its instant acceptance by so many was that "modern" or "progressive" ideas in morals, education, and management have been so widely diffused by intellectuals and experts through the expanding mass media as to produce a change in American character in the direction of a new, "other-directed" personality type, replacing the "inner-directed" type shaped by the Protestant ethic and the parent-dominated family of the

past. *The Lonely Crowd* both expressed doubts over the human value of the new conformist, group-centered, and anti-individualist ethos and at the same time suggested the obsolescence of older negative images of America as a ruthlessly competitive, predatory society controlled by grasping, philistine businessmen. The latter emphasis was congruent with the reaction against political radicalism in the early years of the cold war. The former view gave rise to a new species of social and cultural, as distinct from political, criticism that became ascendant in the intellectual community during the 1950s and even survived with curious changes of emphasis the revival of radical politics in the 1960s.

Among professional sociologists, however, Riesman was less enthusiastically received. *The Lonely Crowd*, its sequel *Faces in the Crowd*, and his essay collection *Individualism Reconsidered* all appeared at a time when sociologists were primarily concerned with making their discipline more scientific by stressing quantitative research and formal theoretical conceptualization. Riesman's background in law rather than social science, his range of easy cultural reference, his readiness to criticize and make "value judgments" rather than confine himself to analysis, his obvious appeal to literary intellectuals (and, doubtless, his upper-class origins), failed to commend him to his fellow sociologists. He was widely regarded as a maverick. For the minority who favored a "humanistic" or more socially "relevant" (before this term became debased) rather than a scientific sociology, Riesman's work, along with that of **C. Wright Mills,** was an inspiration. In the 1960s when "humanistic" approaches came to the fore, many of Riesman's former students and collaborators at Chicago and Harvard, such as Herbert Gans, Kenneth Keniston, Kai Erikson, and Robert Coles, became influential figures.

Riesman himself by this time ceased to be a prophet without honor in his own field. If none of his other works achieved quite the acclaim of the first, he continued to produce well-regarded essays and books, many of them collaborative. *The Academic Revolution*, coauthored with

Christopher Jencks, was perhaps the most substantial of these, building on a decade or more of research in the development of higher education in the United States, the subject to which Riesman chiefly devoted himself after 1960.

Riesman's influence as a teacher and as a sympathetic participant and adviser to others in a multitude of intellectual and educational enterprises has been almost as great as that of his writings. Although he himself was one of the major students of the trend toward rigorously professionalized education, he has always chosen to reach a wider audience and to address it in a uniquely personal voice rather than as the representative of a discipline. At Harvard he preferred to teach undergraduates. A courtly, gracious, somewhat self-effacing man in personal manner, he rejected professional honors, several times declining nomination for the presidency of the American Sociological Association. See S. M. Lipset and Leo Lowenthal, *Culture and Character: The Work of David Riesman Reviewed* (1961).

DENNIS H. WRONG

RIIS, Jacob August (b. Ribe, Den., May 3, 1849; d. Barre, Mass., May 26, 1914), REFORMER, JOURNALIST, emigrated to the U.S. in 1870. For seven years he wandered about the East, living in semi-poverty, but in 1877 he obtained a job with the New York *Tribune.* One year later he transferred to the *Evening Sun,* where he worked as a police reporter for the next eleven years. As a reporter Riis, whose office was located on Mulberry Street in the heart of the immigrant district, came to know the overcrowded, disease-ridden tenements firsthand. In 1890 he wrote and illustrated with his own photographs *How the Other Half Lives,* a description of the life of the various immigrant groups in the New York slums. The book attracted nationwide attention, and Riis became recognized as an authority on tenement conditions. Shortly after its publication, Riis met Theodore Roosevelt. The two became close friends, and when Roosevelt served as New York City police commissioner (1893–95), Riis often accompanied him on his nocturnal forays into the slums.

After his retirement from the *Sun* in 1899, Riis devoted himself to lecturing and writing. His autobiography, *The Making of an American* (1901), traces his assimilation into American society. He contended that the urban environment polluted the individual and that, with the elimination of the slum, the immigrant would take his place in American society. Housing reform, neighborhood improvement, small parks, and sunshine were the cures to urban ills, Riis maintained. In 1904, when Roosevelt ran for the presidency, Riis published a campaign biography, *Theodore Roosevelt the Citizen.* Among Riis's other important works are *The Children of the Poor* (1892), *The Battle with the Slum* (1902), *Children of the Tenements* (1903), and *The Old Town* (1909), a nostalgic portrait of Ribe, his birthplace.

⁂

Through his vivid writing and his stark photography Jacob Riis helped a generation of Americans to discover the urban slums and the pathos and horror faced every day by the immigrants who lived there. Riis was himself an immigrant, but his life personified American virtues. Ironically the memory of his native Ribe helped reinforce his image of an ideal America where there was family loyalty, community spirit, respect for work and nature, concern for moral development, and love of God. This was the America he dreamed of and that he contrasted to the slums of New York in *How the Other Half Lives* and in his other writing.

Riis's experience with poverty as a young man made him generally sympathetic toward the lot of the poor and perceptive about the conditions underlying poverty. Yet his sympathy had its limits and was circumscribed in part by his own success in rising to the top. In general he accepted the environmental cause of poverty, a theory just beginning to win acceptance in 1890, and he rejected the argument that the poor owed their condition to sinfulness, laziness, or general unfitness. But in discussing certain immigrant groups he wavered—indeed he had a rather stereotyped view of ethnic groups. The

German was most able to advance. "The Italian and the poor Jew rise only by compulsion. The Chinaman does not rise at all; here, as at home, he simply remains stationary." As for blacks, Riis argued that they were "immensely the superior of the lowest of the whites," but he pictured them as childlike and docile by nature, cheerfully accepting the most menial jobs. He reserved his worst invective for the tramp. "The older I get, the more patience I have for the sinner," he wrote, "and the less with the lazy good for nothing who is at the bottom of more than half the share of the world's troubles. Give me the thief if need be, but take the tramp away and lock him up at hard labor until he is willing to fall in line and take up his end. The end he lets lie, someone has got to carry who already has enough."

Riis developed no systematic social theory and offered no overall plan for achieving better housing. His greatest contribution lay in exposing and publicizing the intolerable conditions which existed in the tenements of New York. But he did take part in a great many reform campaigns, joining settlement workers, journalists, and other public-spirited citizens in efforts to improve the schools, build neighborhood parks and playgrounds, and in general make life more pleasant for those who lived in the city. Riis had the optimistic faith of many other reformers in his day that if one could move people from the wretched tenements into decent housing one could improve the character of the people and eventually transform the world. But in part because of his faith in environmental change he broadened the scope of housing reform to include the transformation of the neighborhood. Occasionally he sounded as if he wanted to re-create the small town in the city, and he was an incurable romantic when it came to the beauties of the rural countryside. Yet for all his limitations he left an enduring legacy. He educated a generation of Americans about the dangers of life in the tenements. See Roy Lubove, *The Progressives and the Slums: Tenement House Reform in New York City* (1962).

ALLEN F. DAVIS

RITTENHOUSE, David (b. Paper Mill Run, Pa., April 8, 1732; d. Philadelphia, Pa., June 26, 1796), SCIENTIST, had little formal education. He studied astronomy, mathematics, and optics on his own and opened a clockmaking and instrument shop on his father's farm in Pennsylvania in 1750. After establishing his reputation as a mathematician-instrumentmaker, Rittenhouse surveyed the boundary between Pennsylvania and Maryland for the two states in 1764, using his own instruments. In 1767 he designed an orrery, an instrument representing the motions of the bodies of the solar system and illustrating solar and lunar eclipses. He also invented a pocket metallic thermometer (1767) and experimented with the noncompressibility of water. Rittenhouse presented a paper on the motion of the planet Venus to the American Philosophical Society in Philadelphia in 1769 and, upon his settlement in that city the following year, continued his astronomical work, studying eclipses, the newly discovered planet Uranus, and the transit of Mercury.

When the Revolutionary War began in 1775, Rittenhouse served as an engineer on the Committee of Safety in Philadelphia. He became vice president of the Committee in 1776 and also a member of the Pennsylvania General Assembly and the state constitutional convention. Elected president of the Committee in 1777, he helped in supervising the manufacture of gunpowder and cannon, and worked on rifle improvements. He was treasurer of Pennsylvania (1777–89) and vice-provost and professor of astronomy at the University of Pennsylvania (1779–82). In 1785 he invented the collimating telescope and the following year introduced the use of spider hairlines in the focus of its eyepiece.

President Washington appointed Rittenhouse first director of the U.S. Mint in Philadelphia (1792–95). A longtime member of the American Philosophical Society, Rittenhouse became its president in 1791, succeeding **Benjamin Franklin,** and served until his death. In 1795 he was elected a member of the Royal Society of London.

With the exception of Joseph Priestley, Rittenhouse was probably the greatest scientist resident in late-18th-century America. Even Franklin sought Rittenhouse's advice on scientific matters, while Thomas Jefferson described him as second to no living astronomer, a statement which would have been more accurate had Jefferson confined himself to America. In the breadth of his interests, moreover, Rittenhouse had few peers anywhere, for he made enduring contributions not only to astronomy but to magnetism and optics. Among his contemporaries, only Franklin had a greater transatlantic reputation, and Franklin's reputation, unlike that of Rittenhouse, rested only in part on his scientific achievements.

Despite his eminence, Rittenhouse is difficult to classify. Although he was an ardent patriot, his scientific interests were not distinctively "American." Unlike many of his contemporaries, he did not build his reputation on the classification of New World flora and fauna. Unlike Franklin, he did not concern himself primarily with the practical applications of his discoveries. But neither was he a system builder. Rather, he was content to work within Newton's system, and to delve into problems as they came to his attention. Thus his solution of the cameo-intagho illusion followed but did not grow organically out of his earlier work in astronomy. Born to the plow, he overcame obscure origins to become one of the most honored Americans of his day, but, again unlike Franklin, he drew no moral from his experience, nor did he urge others to emulate him. Although his abilities might have warranted self-promotion, his personality was not of the self-advertising sort. He strongly preferred quiet and privacy, a preference which derived, in part, from his grief over the death first of his wife and later of his two sons-in-law, and, in part, from a prolonged illness, probably caused by an ulcer, which cast the shadow of suffering over his public career.

Rittenhouse's religious and political views resembled those of his friend Thomas Jefferson. In manner and bearing he was an archetype of the 18th-century gentleman and rationalist. See Brooke Hindle, *David Rittenhouse* (1964).

JOSEPH F. KETT

ROBESON, Paul Bustill (b. Princeton, N.J., April 9, 1898; d. Philadelphia, Penn., Jan. 23, 1976), ACTOR, was the son of a runaway slave who became a minister. He graduated from Rutgers, where he excelled in academic and athletic activities, in 1919 (he earned varsity letters in four sports and was named to the All-American football team as an end in 1917 and 1918). After obtaining an LLB from Columbia Law School in 1923, Robeson briefly worked for a law firm, then became an actor. He quickly established a reputation by his work in **Eugene O'Neill**'s *Emperor Jones* (1923) and *All God's Chillun Got Wings* (1924). In 1925 he gave his first concert of African-American spirituals in New York City, and in the years following toured Western Europe and the U.S.S.R., singing and appearing in such plays as *Show Boat* and *Othello*. During the middle 1930s, Robeson returned to the U.S. and starred in such motion pictures as *The Emperor Jones, Sanders of the River,* and *Show Boat,* but he preferred to live in Europe. Deeply impressed by the Soviet Union and especially its seeming lack of racial prejudice, he made frequent trips there.

In 1939 Robeson again returned to the U.S. He supported the American war effort during World War II and campaigned for the sale of war bonds. In 1943 he starred in a New York production of *Othello,* which established the longest Shakespearean run in the U.S. After the war, increasingly disillusioned with the status of blacks in American society, he became outspoken on civil rights issues. Because of his pro-Soviet statements, in 1950 the State Department revoked his passport, charging him with pro-Communist leanings, but in 1958 the Supreme Court upheld his right to go abroad. He then traveled extensively in Europe but came back to the United States in 1963. He lived quietly out of the spotlight in a Harlem apartment until moving to Philadelphia to be with his sister. A recluse during his last years, he did not attend a Carnegie Hall celebration for him on his 75th birthday but sent a telegram of thanks.

Robeson played a formative role in the development of the 20th-century black protest movement. Lionized at an early age as one of the great singers and actors of his time, he became perhaps the best-known black figure in the United States. Yet, highly intelligent and acutely sensitive to racial bigotry, he could not be satisfied merely as a "symbol of Negro achievement." Instead, he determined to use his skills and prestige to fight for the rights of black people, and his refusal to compromise on political and racial issues ultimately ended his career as a commercially successful artist.

As Robeson matured as an artist, he also developed as a social and cultural critic. Early in his career, he accepted stereotyped roles on the stage and in films, believing, as did most black performers, that "what mattered was the opportunity, which came so seldom to our folks, of having a part—any part." Gradually, however, particularly after his stay in Europe, which broadened his political and social vision, he decided that he could not separate his position as an artist from his position as a spokesman for black equality. He became increasingly more selective in the kind of dramatic parts he would play, and he began to use the concert stage as a showcase for African and African-American folk music. Deeply interested in African culture, he mastered several African languages and strove to demonstrate—in his writings and in concert performances—that Africa had made a vital and unique contribution to world civilization. He believed, in particular, that the emotional and intuitive qualities of African culture stood in happy contrast to the overintellectualized art of the West.

Some observers have seen a contradiction between Robeson's advocacy of black cultural uniqueness and his political role as a spokesman for working-class internationalism. Yet he himself maintained that a "belief in the oneness of humankind" could comfortably coexist "side by side with my deep attachment to the cause of my own race." Toward the end of his career, he developed the theory that there is a "world body ... of folk music based upon a universal pentatonic [five-tone] scale"—a notion that clearly flowed out of his belief in the universal solidarity of common people. Still, the destiny of black people remained paramount in his thought, and his defense of Communism and of the Soviet Union was always linked in his mind with his passionate opposition to Western imperialism and racism. Although he never eschewed white allies, he argued in 1958 that "the Negro people's movement must be led by Negroes" and that it must be based on black America's "power of numbers ... power of organization and ... power of spirit."

With his incredibly diverse talents, Robeson came perhaps closer than any 20th-century figure to fitting the Renaissance model of the universal man. He excelled as an athlete, singer, actor, linguist, and cultural theorist. Personally, he was an imposing man, with a large frame and a deep, booming voice, who filled the theater, concert stage, or lecture hall with his presence. Yet his political and racial views caused him to be virtually ignored as a public figure in the United States after 1950. Only since the mid-sixties has his role been reassessed and has he been seen as a "great forerunner" of the black liberation movement. See Paul Robeson, *Here I Stand* (1958) and Martin Duberman, *Paul Robeson* (1988).

ALLAN H. SPEAR

ROBINSON, Edward Arlington (b. Head Tide, Maine, Dec. 22, 1869; d. New York, N.Y., April 6, 1935), POET, was a student at Harvard, 1891–93, but was forced to leave because of financial problems. He published his first collection of poems, *The Torrent and the Night Before* (1896), at his own expense, and followed this with *The Children of the Night* (1897). He returned to Harvard briefly in 1898 and was employed in the office of President **Charles W. Eliot.** Robinson moved to New York a year later. In 1902 two of his friends helped to publish his *Captain Craig.* Robinson was employed in a number of odd jobs including that of a timekeeper at a subway construction site (1904) before President Theodore Roosevelt, who had read *The Children of the Night,* gave him a position in the New York Customs Service in 1905. Robinson left the job in 1909. *The Town*

Down the River (1910) was Robinson's first commercially published volume.

The Man Against the Sky (1916) received favorable criticism, but it was not until the publication of *The Collected Poems* in 1921 that Robinson's literary reputation was secure. He received a Pulitzer Prize for that volume and a second for *The Man Who Died Twice* (1924). A third Pulitzer Prize was awarded to him for *Tristram* (1927). Robinson resided in New York but spent his summers after 1911 at the MacDowell Colony in New Hampshire, where he produced a number of volumes including the psychological narratives *Avon's Harvest* (1921), *Dionysus in Doubt* (1925), *Cavender's House* (1929), and *Matthias at the Door* (1931). Robinson's last work, *King Jasper* (1935), was published posthumously.

It is one of the ironies of Edwin Arlington Robinson's career that after years of almost unbearable loneliness and despair he achieved fame and critical recognition just at the time when most of the influential younger American critics agreed that his usefulness as an example for American poetry was at an end. Poet-critics like T. S. Eliot, R. P. Blackmur, and William Carlos Williams dismissed Robinson as "negligible" and tiresome—and not without cause. While no one could begrudge him his three Pulitzer Prizes, they did come in his most indulgent years and allowed him to publish long psychological narratives which most readers today find unbearable. Robinson will be remembered not for *Tristram* (1927) or *Amaranth* (1934), but for early lyrics like "The Clerks," "For a Dead Lady," "Eros Tyrannos," "The Wandering Jew," "Lost Anchors," and "The Sheaves" and longer meditations such as *Captain Craig* and "Isaac and Archibald." Robinson became a master of conventional forms—the sonnet, the dramatic monologue in blank verse, the lyric in the moral style—in an age of literary experiment. As **Robert Frost** observed, "Robinson stayed content with the old-fashioned way to be new." Of all the major American critics, only Yvor Winters remained steadfast in his praise, but not without

dismissing much of Robinson's later work. Winters admired above all Robinson's impersonal style, the impeccable control of his material, the rational progression of his mind, and the absence of sensual imagery. Though Robinson pondered lives spent in uncertainty and doubt, his tightly controlled and deliberately paced lines seemed to affirm a final order of experience. See Chard Powers Smith, *Where the Light Falls* (1965), and Francis Murphy, ed., *Edwin Arlington Robinson: Twentieth Century Views* (1970).

FRANCIS MURPHY

ROBINSON, Jack Roosevelt (b. Cairo, Ga., Jan. 31, 1919; d. Stamford, Conn., Oct. 24, 1972), ATHLETE, was a star in high school athletics. He attended Pasadena Junior College and entered the University of California at Los Angeles in 1939 on an athletic scholarship. He excelled in baseball and football but left UCLA in 1941 to become assistant athletic director at a National Youth Administration camp. Robinson also played some professional football before being drafted into the army in 1942. He attended officer candidate school and, at the time of his discharge in 1944, was a first lieutenant. After the war, Robinson coached for a semester at the Samuel Houston College for Negroes (Austin, Tex.) and then played for the Kansas City Monarchs of the Negro American Baseball League. While playing for the Monarchs in 1945, Robinson was signed by Brooklyn Dodgers' president **Branch Rickey** and assigned to the Dodgers' Montreal farm team. He thus was heralded as the first black athlete to be under contract to a major league baseball team.

After spending a season with the Montreal Royals in 1946, where he hit .349, Robinson joined the Dodgers in 1947 as the first black player in the major leagues. Voted Rookie of the Year, he led the Dodgers to a National League pennant, batting .297 and playing mostly at second base. He was the Most Valuable Player in the National League in 1949, winning the batting championship with a .342 average. Noted for his hitting, fielding, and baserunning, Robinson helped the Dodgers win five more pennants and the 1955 World Series championship. Traded to the New York Giants in the beginning of the 1957 season, Robinson retired from baseball with a lifetime average of .311. He became vice president of the Chock Full O' Nuts Corporation in New York. A civil rights activist, Robinson served as chairman of the NAACP Fight for Freedom Fund in 1957. In 1962 Robinson was elected to the Baseball Hall of Fame in Cooperstown, New York. He left Chock Full O' Nuts in 1964 to work for Republican **Nelson Rockefeller**'s presidential campaign. He later served as the New York governor's special assistant for community affairs (1966–68). In 1965 he helped found and became chairman of the board of the Freedom National Bank, Harlem's first black chartered and managed commercial bank. He was active in promoting other black capitalism ventures, and on the day of his death planned to participate in a symposium on drug abuse.

That observation which sees each generation rewriting and reinterpreting American history is borne out in the career of Jackie Robinson. It was Robinson's fate and opportunity to be chosen as an experimental test case for the racial integration of major league baseball. Designed by Branch Rickey, the innovative president of the National League Brooklyn Dodgers, the experiment was opposed by powerful, intransigent forces. That Rickey persevered owed as much to his hope of expanding profits as to his sense of social justice. To ensure success, Rickey carefully chose a black player with maximum middle-class credentials who would accept hostility with equanimity. Thus Robinson was drawn into the maelstrom of American race relations and obliged to prove his fitness if he and other blacks were to participate in an all-white sports institution.

At first Robinson silently endured insults and slurs, but soon he was able to talk back and to assert his rights. The rapidity of his postural change mirrored changing patterns of race relations which saw blacks everywhere demanding their legal rights. Thus Robinson, once heralded as the trailblazing hero of 1947, saw his contribution being continually reinterpreted as power relationships between black and white Americans changed.

As a player, Robinson was a good batter, fielder, and baserunner who excelled in aggressive will-to-win and team leadership. A charismatic figure, the well-built six-footer with flashing eyes led the Dodgers to six pennants and two near-misses in a memorable ten-year career.

As a symbol of rising black status, Robinson's success prompted major-league clubs to seek black players, so that by 1960 every club had some black players. This speedy process ended segregated baseball and also destroyed the separatist black major leagues while converting thousands of black Americans into major-league fans.

The same process multiplied problems for black athletes and white owners, as some of the latter, fearful of a black inundation, invoked quotas. Meanwhile black militants saw the death of black leagues as a concession to white racism. To the end of his life Robinson questioned the effect of his personal contribution to racial integration, often expressing disappointment that blacks were not employed as baseball managers or executives.

From the vantage point of the 1970s Robinson's career mirrors the rapidly changing pattern of race relations. Still debated is the question of whether he was the trailblazing hero or the white man's dupe. Certainly he personified the integrationist approach to a racial equilibrium, but the full integration of baseball remains an unresolved issue, as does the integration of other American institutions. See Jules Tygiel, *Baseball's Great Experiment: Jackie Robinson and His Legacy* (1983).

DAVID Q. VOIGT

ROCK, John Swett (b. Salem, N.J., 1825; d. Boston, Mass., Dec. 3, 1866), PHYSICIAN, LAWYER, worked with his parents at menial tasks as a youth, but read avidly in his spare time. In 1844 he became a teacher. He began reading medical books at this time but was turned away from medical schools because he was an African-American. However, he was apprenticed to a local dentist and opened his own office in 1850. He was eventually admitted to the American Medical College in Philadelphia, graduating in 1852. In 1853 he moved to Boston because of "its more liberal atmosphere." There he won a reputation as an abolitionist orator; one of his addresses was given in 1858 at a commemoration of Crispus Attucks and the Boston Massacre.

Bad health made it difficult for him to attend to patients during the cold months, so he began to study law. In 1861 he was admitted to the Massachusetts bar. In 1865, after **Salmon P. Chase** had become chief justice, Rock was admitted to practice before the Supreme Court. The same year, he became the first black man to be received on the floor of the House of Representatives.

———— ∞∞∞ ————

Recent probers into the history of the African-American have discovered many people of interest and importance. The physician John Rock is one of these. He deserves prominence in our national record not only because of his race but also because of his remarkable achievements and his vigorous challenges to white supremacy.

From humble beginnings Rock rose by hard work to positions of recognition in three professions: dentistry, medicine, and law. From 1844 to 1848 he was spending six hours of his day teaching, eight in study, and two in tutoring. This overwork is said to have undermined his health, but he was a tall, handsome man of impressive stature. He was also a gifted public speaker. Before graduation from medical school he had already given an impressive speech at the Twelfth Annual Meeting of the Pennsylvania Anti-Slavery Society at Morristown, New Jersey, and had won a medal for a temperance address. After his move to Boston, he became the most noted black abolitionist of New England. His speeches, polished and delivered in fine oratorical style, were printed in **William L. Garrison**'s *Liberator* as well as in general newspapers. Rock's

sharp thrusts in defense of blacks and his criticism of whites are said to have "enchanted an audience," while also stirring it against slavery. "This estimable lawyer," as **Charles Sumner** referred to him, also broke the color barrier in the Massachusetts courts and in the United States Supreme Court. In his short life, he attacked racial discrimination wherever he saw it. All forms of slavery must, he made clear, be abolished. See William Wells Brown, *The Black Man* (1863).

EUGENE P. LINK

ROCKEFELLER, John Davison (b. Richford, N.Y., July 8, 1839; d. Ormund Beach, Fla., May 23, 1937), INDUSTRIALIST, PHILANTHROPIST, after high school graduation (1855), was employed for four years as bookkeeper-clerk in a commission house in Cleveland, Ohio. In 1858 he formed a similar firm with Maurice B. Clark, and in 1863 the partners invested in another partnership, Andrews, Clark and Co., that built and ran the Excelsior petroleum refinery. Two years later Rockefeller purchased Clark's interest, vested the oil business in Rockefeller and Andrews, retired from the commission house, and concentrated on oil refining. In 1865 he brought his brother William into the firm, then added **Henry M. Flagler** and the funds of Stephen Harkness in 1867. Emphasizing cost saving and expansion, in 1870 the partners organized the Standard Oil Co. (Ohio), a million-dollar corporation, to take over their refineries and several ancillary enterprises.

During the 1870s Rockefeller and a growing number of associates created an alliance of individuals owning forty firms. After voluntary association failed to bring order out of chaos in the oil industry, Ohio Standard and allied firms relied on common ownership of refineries, lubricating oil works, pipelines, cooperage plants, and a series of supporting enterprises. Through cost cutting, favorable railroad rebates, creation of a marketing organization, buying out competitors, occasional price cutting, and other ruthless tactics the Standard Oil group of firms controlled about 90 percent of the petroleum industry by 1881.

In 1882 management of all properties of the forty allied firms was centralized in the trustees of the famous Standard Oil Trust. As *primus inter pares*, Rockefeller captained the team of outstanding executives that administered the Trust until the Ohio supreme court asserted its illegality in 1892. After that date the Standard Oil combination was operated as a community of interest of twenty firms (1892–99), then as a holding company—Standard Oil Co. (New Jersey)—until the separation of thirty-three firms in 1911.

Dismemberment of the combination was strongly supported by widespread criticism of Rockefeller and Standard Oil from the 1870s onward. Critics assailed the Rockefeller-Standard Oil actions in the oil regions, in railroad discriminations, and in large profits. The attacks culminated in **Henry Demarest Lloyd**'s *Wealth Against Commonwealth* (1894) and **Ida Tarbell**'s *History of the Standard Oil Company* (1904).

By then Rockefeller had been devoting almost all his time for ten years to other investments and his philanthropies. Although president of Standard Oil Co. (New Jersey) in name, he ceased active participation in the combination's activities in 1895. In spite of numerous losing ventures, he built a fortune estimated at $200,000,000 in the 1890s to at least $815,648,000 by 1911. Among well-known investments were those in Colorado Fuel and Iron Co., in the development of Everett, Washington, and in Mesabi ore lands, but he also ventured heavily in securities of many other railroads and industrial enterprises.

While accumulating his enormous fortune Rockefeller gave away more than $550 million. In addition to direct individual gifts he endowed four new philanthropic organizations: Rockefeller Institute for Medical Research (1901), General Education Board (1902), Rockefeller Foundation (1913), and Laura Spelman Rockefeller Memorial (1918). Products of his giving still loom important. Among them are the University of Chicago, Rockefeller University, elimination of hookworm and improvement of agriculture in the South, elevation of medical research and standards of medical schools, and strengthening of numerous schools of higher education.

In his personal style Rockefeller was the antithesis of the aggressive business executive. A meditative, reserved man, reticent in public, he was grave in demeanor, never laughed loudly, but enjoyed quiet jokes among intimates. A devoted Baptist all his life, through parental and church training he learned to abhor waste, to be frugal, hard-working, and self-reliant, modest in deportment, quiet in dress, precise and prompt, reliable and scrupulously observant of contracts. Driving and riding horses and gardening provided his relaxation. He had limited taste for music and the theater, and indulged little in reading books; data for decisions came from correspondence and memoranda and by word of mouth from trusted advisers. His business perspective, limited at first to Cleveland and its environs, soon came to encompass the whole world, the market for American petroleum products.

Methodical and systematic by inclination and training, Rockefeller demonstrated a veritable passion for order in all that he attempted. It showed in the careful accounting of his earliest earnings and gifts as well as in laying out and supervising gardens. The chaotic, unrestrained competition in the oil industry during the 1860s appalled him, even though his own enterprise profited steadily. After voluntary associations of refiners and the agency method (South Improvement Company) failed to bring order to the industry, he utilized common ownership of properties as a means to that end. He was the architect of Standard Oil, but many helped him build the combination.

In business Rockefeller accepted the traditions of his occupation. In Standard Oil operations he adhered to secrecy far beyond the time when it was to the best advantage of the firm; he seemingly never realized that by its very size and influence the combination was vested with public interest and that society would insist on making new rules for it. To him the market regulated economic behavior, and monopoly or quasi-monopoly was an inevitable result of competition, the survival of the fittest. Loyal to and tolerant of members of his own group, even suppliers, in order to achieve his economic goals, he authorized and sanctioned tactics of the small businessman that proved ruthless when backed by Standard Oil power. Among such practices, those decried by Ida Tarbell and other critics, were local price cutting to bring pressure on opponents, seeking the ultimate advantage in the rebate system, buying into competing firms for information and influence (Tidewater Oil and Pure Oil), maintaining relatively high prices in some areas while cutting them in others within a state or region, and using bogus (hidden) companies (also in common use by competitors).

As businessman, investor, and philanthropist Rockefeller epitomized the administrator as problem solver through consultation and agreement and the delegation of the implementation of decisions. In his early years he discussed all actions with his partners. As the Standard Oil alliance grew in the 1870s, other names were added to the list of discussants. To assure formerly violent competitors an equal voice in management, under the trust arrangement all decisions were made by an executive committee made up of eight (seven from 1884) of the nine trustees. Rockefeller patiently listened to conflicting views and usually worked out acceptable compromises. He believed in the pooling of knowledge and determination of plans by all participants in the implementation of decisions. To that end decisions of the executive committee were supported by advice from eight other functional committees.

In early investments outside Standard Oil Rockefeller made some mistakes by relying on the advice of friends, but in the 1890s he systematized that activity as he did his philanthropic endeavors. Thereafter he carefully listened to Frederick T. Gates and a sizable group of administrators of his philanthropic organizations, selecting the projects that seemed most fitting to him as steward of the fortune he thought God had bestowed on him. The aim of his giving was expressed in the purpose of the Rockefeller Foundation–"to promote the well-being of mankind throughout the world." See Allan Nevins, *Study in Power* (1953).

RALPH W. HIDY

ROCKEFELLER, Nelson Aldrich (b. Bar Harbor, Maine, July 8, 1908; d. New York, N.Y., Jan. 26, 1979), POLITICAL LEADER, the grandson of **John D. Rockefeller** and Senator **Nelson W. Aldrich,** graduated from Dartmouth College in 1930. He helped manage the family's enterprises, including the Rockefeller Center real estate holdings in New York. He was director of the Creole Petroleum Corporation, the Venezuelan subsidiary of Standard Oil, from 1935 to 1940. He served as coordinator of the Office of Inter-American Affairs (1940–44) under President Franklin D. Roosevelt and then as assistant secretary of state for Latin American Affairs (1944–45). He helped plan the Chapultepec (Mexico) conference of American republics and worked on the planning of the United Nations.

Returning to private life in 1945, Rockefeller organized two foreign aid agencies for Latin America, the International Basic Economy Corporation and the American International Association for Economic and Social Development. In 1950 he became chairman of the Advisory Board on International Development of President Truman's Point Four program, but resigned in 1951. After supporting Dwight D. Eisenhower for president in 1952, Rockefeller was appointed undersecretary of the Department of Health, Education, and Welfare in 1953. He served as special assistant to the president (1954–55) and was chairman of the president's Advisory Committee on Government Organization (1953–58).

In 1958 Rockefeller was elected governor of New York as a Republican. As governor he sought to improve administrative efficiency and worked for civil rights legislation, urban renewal and greatly expanded the state university system. Reelected governor in 1962, 1966, and 1970, he sought the Republican presidential nomination in 1960, 1964, and 1968 but failed all three times. In 1969 he made a fact-finding tour of

Latin America for President Richard Nixon but met hostile crowds and had to cancel parts of the trip. He resigned as governor at the end of 1973 and set up the Commission for Critical Choices. In 1974, after Gerald Ford entered the White House following Nixon's forced resignation during the Watergate scandals, Rockefeller was nominated to be the first appointed Vice President. After extensive Senate Hearings in which Rockefeller released his audited tax returns, confirmation by the Senate followed and Rockefeller was sworn in on Dec. 19, 1974. He served for two years. Returning to private life, Rockefeller concentrated on his enormous collection of modern art to which he was devoted, on preparing a book on his collection, and the establishment of a store in Manhattan to sell reproductions of the artworks he owned. The store opened to great fanfare on Fifth Avenue and 57th Street in New York less than a year before he died. Besides numerous reports that appeared under his name, Rockefeller published *The Future of Federalism* (1962), and *Unity, Peace and Freedom* (1968).

If the public career of Nelson A. Rockefeller had any meaning it suggested one thing about the Republican Party in the second half of the twentieth century: that an enormous personal and family fortune, a famous name, powerful connections, platoons of well-paid public relations consultants and policy advisers, the most up-to-date polling techniques, a lust for power, a shrewd intelligence, and an outgoing personality can effect the capture of a state government and propel one to the forefront of national politics but cannot make a president or even a presidential nominee without the support of ideologically committed conservatives. Unfortunately for Nelson Rockefeller and his ambitions, his ascendancy to the leadership of the moderately progressive wing of the G.O.P. in the late 1950s and early 1960s came at a time when a conservative, grassroots resurgence within the party began to turn it against almost everything he represented—or seemed to represent. Qualities and policies that had made Rockefeller a successful

Republican governor of the polyglot, highly industrialized and urbanized Democratic-leaning state of New York—his commitment to civil rights, his concern for the problems of the cities, his aggressive development of the state university system, his support for social welfare programs, his rapport with blacks, Jews, Italians, and labor leaders—made him anathema to the conservative "heartland" regulars of the **Robert A. Taft** type who had long chafed under the domination of the eastern "liberal" Republican establishment and who, in the 1960s, finally gained control over the party apparatus. To them Rockefeller, like **Wendell Willkie** and **Thomas E. Dewey,** was simply another "metoo" candidate and was thus unacceptable. They yearned for "a choice, not an echo." That he was as much a cold warrior as Richard Nixon, that he was as full-throated an advocate of shaping the federal budget to the demands of the Department of Defense as **Barry Goldwater,** did not alter their perception of him. It now seems clear that his much-vaunted liberalism was, at bottom, little more than an operational strategy designed to win votes, that his objective was to preserve what he called "this wonderful system of ours." But the conservatives erroneously tagged him a "man of the left" and, despite his considerable personal attributes and his virtually unlimited financial resources, they effectively locked him out of the Republican nomination.

Rockefeller's entire career since the late 1960s, therefore, was directed at redefining his image among the party faithful west of the Hudson in the hopes of gaining their support for another run at the White House. His dispatch of state troopers with loaded shotguns to crush the Attica rioters, his imposition of the nation's harshest drug laws, his well-publicized "crackdown" on so-called welfare cheaters, his running battles with liberal Republican Mayor John Lindsay over state aid to the cities—all were calculated gestures to the Republican right wing. As such, they were also loud testimony to his ambitions and the essential superficiality of what was once known as "modern Republicanism." At the end of Rockefeller's political career he did at last sit a heartbeat away from the presidency. But the two year stint he served at vice president could not have offered him much personal satisfaction. After all, he was a man who desperately wanted to be president and that was forever denied him. See Joseph E. Persico, *The Imperial Rockefeller: A Biography of Nelson W. Rockefeller* (1981).

JEROME L. STERNSTEIN

ROCKHILL, William Woodville (b. Philadelphia, Pa., April 1, 1853; d. Honolulu, Hawaii, Dec. 8, 1914), DIPLOMAT, was taken to France at age eleven and received his education at the Collège de France in Paris and at the St. Cyr Military Academy. Upon graduation he served for four years in the French Foreign Legion in Algeria. In 1876 he returned to the U.S., settling in New Mexico, where he started a ranch. He devoted his days to the routine tasks of a cowboy, and in his spare time pursued the interest he had acquired in Asian languages. After three years he returned to Europe, where he started a career of research and writing that led to an international reputation. After service in the U.S. legation in Peking (1885–86) Rockhill went on two expeditions to Tibet. In 1894 he began to work for the Department of State. This led to a career in diplomacy during which he served as assistant secretary (1896–97), minister to Greece (1897–99), director of the Bureau of American Affairs, minister to China (1900–1909), ambassador to Russia (1909–11), and minister to Turkey (1911–13).

Rockhill is best known for his part in the writing of the Open Door Notes of September 1899. In these notes to the major powers having an interest in China, Secretary of State **John Hay** called on these governments to subscribe to the principle of equality of commercial opportunity. They did so but with qualifications. As adviser to Hay and later as minister to China, Rockhill deplored the abuse of the Chinese by foreign powers and urged patience and understanding of the Chinese position. He gave little evidence of concern regarding American business interests in China but, in accordance with his obligations as American minister, defended their treaty rights. Rockhill gave more attention to shifts in the balance of power than he did to purely economic matters. As minister to China during the second term of Theodore Roosevelt he urged restraint, and when younger foreign service officers and consuls pushed for a more aggressive policy, Rockhill did not support them. He served in Russia at the time the Taft administration launched the ill-fated Knox Neutralization proposal, and dutifully sought Russian agreement but met with brusque opposition. Rockhill ranks as one of the first truly professional diplomats in the foreign service of the United States and likewise as one of the first of the important scholars in the field of Chinese history. See Paul A. Varg, *Open Door Diplomat* (1952).

PAUL A. VARG

ROCKWELL, Norman Percival (b. Feb. 3, 1895, New York, N.Y.; d. Nov. 8, 1978, Stockbridge, Mass.), ILLUSTRATOR, began studying art at the Chase School of Fine and Applied Arts in New York City at age fourteen. Two years later he enrolled in the Art Students League of New York City, where he studied with George Bridgman and Thomas Fogarty. He executed his first commission when he was sixteen and illustrated his first book when he was seventeen. At age nineteen he became art director of *Boy's Life*, an association with the Boy Scouts that persisted throughout his life. In the process he did cover artwork for the Boy Scout *Handbook* and did a number of calendars.

Rockwell did his first *Saturday Evening Post* cover when he was twenty-two, the first of 317 he contributed to the magazine during an association that lasted forty-seven years. Rockwell's *Post* covers were a recognition of his talent as an illustrator and guaranteed that for several generations of Americans he would be the nation's best known illustrator. His artwork became so popular that he did every Christmas cover for the *Post* between 1919 and 1943. Finally, in 1963, Rockwell left the *Saturday Evening Post* and went to work for *Look* magazine but in subsequent years he did less and less illustration. His last commission was executed in 1975, concluding a sixty-four-year career.

Rockwell married three times, had three sons, and during his lifetime lived and worked in three communities—New Rochelle, New York; Arlington, Vermont; and Stockbridge, Massachusetts. Models for many of his illustrations were friends and neighbors, particularly when he lived in New England. He initially used posed live models but later relied almost exclusively on photographs he took of posed models.

Among his best known cover illustrations for the *Saturday Evening Post* are "100th Year of Baseball" (July 8, 1939), "Shuffleton's Barber Show" (April 29, 1950), "Rosie the Riveter" (May 29, 1943), the Willie Gillis series during World War II, "Saying Grace" (Nov. 24, 1951), and "Breaking Home Ties" (September 25, 1954). In addition, his Four Freedoms posters—Freedom of Speech, Freedom of Worship, Freedom from Fear, and Freedom from Want—were major artistic contributions to the war effort.

Norman Rockwell's appeal, extending over six decades, stems from his ability to depict fundamental truths and values in a context relevant for the viewer. His early illustrations are scenic tableaus representing a wide variety of lifetime experiences: growing up, young love, leaving home, home and family, working, playing sports, serving the country during wartime, to name a few. These illustrations recreate with simplicity and clarity a world that most have experienced in one form or another. George M. Loring, publisher of the *Saturday Evening Post*, liked Rockwell's covers because he could understand them, and felt that his readers could as well. Rockwell's later illustrations, done after World War II, are visual stories that are more complex, more thoughtful, and more thought-provoking than his earlier work. The illustrations done after leaving the *Saturday Evening Post* are more blatantly political. Beginning with a series of covers for the *Post* featuring the Democratic and Republican candidates in each campaign between 1952 and 1964, Rockwell moved to a series of illustrations for *Look* magazine depicting various aspects of the civil rights struggle, the War on Poverty, and the United Nations. The change in focus was the result of the freedom afforded him by *Look*'s editors and his reactions to the political upheavals of the 1960s.

In addition to being a superb storyteller, Rockwell was a gifted artist, able to translate his ideas into realistic visual images that could be instantly understood. But despite his success Norman Rockwell frequently doubted his ability; in 1932 he took a year off to study in Paris, to learn the latest in artistic styles. But he was never comfortable as anything other than an American Realist, and it was that style that brought him fame and success. See Christopher Finch, *Norman Rockwell's America* (1975), and Susan E. Meyer, *Norman Rockwell's People* (1981).

JAMES J. BEST

RODGERS, Richard (b. Hammels Station, N.Y., June 28, 1902; d. New York, N.Y., Dec. 30, 1979), COMPOSER, began studying piano when he was six and wrote his first song, "Camptown Days," at age twelve. In 1918, a year before he entered Columbia University, Rodgers met lyricist Lorenz Hart, a former Columbia student, with whom he wrote the 1920 Varsity show "Fly with Me." Following two years at Columbia, Rodgers attended the Institute of Musical Art (now Juilliard School of Music) until 1923, and continued writing songs for a traveling musical comedy team. In 1925 he and Hart wrote songs for their first Broadway success, *Garrick Gaieties*, a Theater Guild production. The Rodgers and Hart partnership continued in 1925 with *Dearest Enemy* and in 1926 with five shows, including *The Girl Friend*. In 1927 they did *A Connecticut Yankee*, in 1928 *Present Arms*, and in 1929 *Spring Is Here*. The first phase of Rodgers's film career was 1931–34 when he and Hart created, among other scores for the movies, *Love Me Tonight* (1930), starring Maurice Chevalier. Returning to Broadway from Hollywood, the partners worked together until *By Jupiter* (1942) and an updated revision of *A Connecticut Yankee* (1943). Their productions included *Jumbo* (1935), *On Your Toes* (1936), *I'd Rather Be Right* (1937), and *Pal Joey* (1940).

After Hart's death in 1943, Rodgers wrote musicals with Oscar Hammerstein II, beginning with *Oklahoma!* in 1943, which won a Pulitzer Prize in 1944. In 1945 they did *Carousel*, in 1949 *South Pacific* (winner of a Pulitzer Prize), in 1958 *Flower Drum Song*, and in 1959 *The Sound of Music*. Rodgers and Hammerstein also wrote the words and music for the motion picture *State Fair* (1945, remade in 1962) and a musical for television, *Cinderella* (1957). Rodgers wrote music for *Victory at Sea*, a 1952 NBC television series on the naval battles of World War II, which received the Peabody and Sylvania awards, and *Winston Churchill—The Valiant Years*, a major TV series in 1960. Following the death of Hammerstein, Rodgers wrote the words and music for the stage musical *No Strings* (1962) and the music for *Do I Hear a Waltz?* (1965) and *Two by Two* (1970). Rodgers's autobiography, *Musical Stages*, appeared in 1975.

———— ✿ ————

Richard Rodgers was one of the most significant forces in the evolution of the American musical theater. This statement goes beyond the fact that unquestionably he was the theater's most productive and most important composer. A keen sense for theatrical values combined with a fastidious attention to detail and a restless compulsion for experimentation (qualities which incidentally have made his music what it is) led him, in conjunction with his verbal writing partners, to open up continually new horizons for the musical stage. The music and words team of Rodgers and Hart was responsible for achieving "integration"—not in a racial but in a theatrical sense: to have every element in a musical production subservient to and an inextricable part of the overall subject. Later, Rodgers and Hammerstein transformed musical comedy into musical play, and by the same token from an often stilted and formulistic form of theater into a vibrant art.

As a composer, Rodgers was *sui generis*. As a writer of songs he expanded the boundaries of his work so that some of his numbers have the dimensions of operatic arias (the narratives "Soliloquy" from *Carousel* and "A Puzzlement" from *The King and I*, for example). Through subtle use of modulations, a personal manner of employing chromaticisms, and expressive harmonies, and an uncommon gift to allow a melody to take wing and soar, he produced enduring classics in popular song literature: "My Heart Stood Still," "You'll Never Walk Alone," "Climb Every Mountain," "With a Song in My Heart," "Hello, Young Lovers," "The Sound of Music," are just a few of the hundred or so standards he penned. Time and again he brought to his songwriting a spirituality that led **Cole Porter** to say that it had "a kind of holiness."

His theatrical scores were on a large canvas, including not only songs but also orchestral episodes played under the dialogue, transitions from one piece of stage business to another, mood-setting music. Some of his orchestral writing had symphonic breadth, as is the case with the score for the modernist ballet "Slaughter on Tenth Avenue" in *On Your Toes*, the waltzes played under the opening scene in *Carousel*, or the march of the royal Siamese children in *The King and I*. As far back as 1925 in *Dearest Enemy* Rodgers already proved himself more than the creator of wonderful songs; he was also a musical dramatist. As such his influence upon the younger generation of composers for the musical stage has been incalculable. See David Ewen, *Richard Rodgers* (1957).

DAVID EWEN

ROEBLING, John Augustus (b. Mühlhausen, Prussia, June 12, 1806; d. Brooklyn, N.Y., July 22, 1869), CIVIL ENGINEER, BRIDGE DESIGNER, studied civil engineering at the Royal Polytechnic Institute of Berlin. After graduation, he fulfilled his obligation to work for three years for the Prussian state by building roads. He developed a deep interest in bridges—especially those in which the roadway was suspended from a chain—and, finding few opportunities to practice his profession in Prussia, he emigrated to the U.S. with his brother in 1831. The idea of establishing a German colony in Pennsylvania appealed to them, and upon their arrival they bought seven thousand acres of land near Pittsburgh. Here Roebling farmed for several years, but the land was poor and he returned to professional work. This was the height of canal building and the beginning of the railroad era in Pennsylvania. He was a member of the party which surveyed the route for the Pennsylvania Railroad across the Alleghenies. Bothered by the clumsiness and cost of the thick hemp hawsers required to haul loaded cars up the inclined planes which connected the canal systems, Roebling invented and began manufacturing a smaller but much stronger cable composed of a number of strands of wire. He pioneered in the use of metal cables for bridges as well as the technique of spinning them at the site, and in 1846 he built a highway bridge over the Monongahela at Pittsburgh. In 1848 or 1849 he moved his factory to Trenton, New Jersey. During 1851–55 he constructed a single-span suspension bridge 825 feet across the Niagara River. This was the first cable suspension bridge capable of handling railroad traffic. Several bridges followed, of which the largest was the Cincinnati-Covington bridge across the Ohio.

In 1857 Roebling had suggested to **Abram S. Hewitt,** a leader in New York politics, a plan to link lower Manhattan with Brooklyn with a suspension bridge which would be longer than any yet attempted. Twelve years later work began. But in June 1869 while he was inspecting the pilings on the Brooklyn side a tug bumped them, crushing his foot. An infection set in, and he died of tetanus. His son and chief assistant, Washington A. Roebling, saw the bridge to completion in 1883.

"It is a want of my intellectual nature," wrote John Roebling, "to bring in harmony all that surrounds me." Roebling was driven by an inner need for order. His achievements as engineer, inventor, and industrialist express a man of powerful will and intellectual energy, a man devoted passionately to the ideals of an expanding democratic society. Roebling was not a mere builder. In his youth he had studied with Hegel in Berlin, and throughout his life, in private journals as well as articles, he maintained a constant metaphysical dialogue which reflected upon his physical accomplishments. He saw in America the opportunity for the realization of his ideal of harmony. Valuing inner and external discipline above all else, he imposed great demands upon himself and others, often straining his personal relations (for a long time a barrier of tense silence existed between him and his son, Washington). His commitment to order was foremost. In their technological aspects alone his bridges are milestones in the history of civil engineering; his innovations in the use of caissons, the spinning of wire cables in place, the use of stays as resistance to high winds and earth tremors—these features virtually inaugurated the modern era of the great suspension bridge. But in addition to its technical and practical function the suspension bridge was for Roebling a demonstration of his leading principle: the creation of harmony out of the reconciliation of opposite forces. His noblest monument is Brooklyn Bridge, in which strength combines with lightness, extension into space with compactness, the precision of the steel cables with the aspiring Gothic arches in the stone towers. Roebling, a form maker to his times, created for the emerging urban landscape of the post–Civil War age one of its unique mechanical structures. Brooklyn Bridge testifies to the complexity, the intellectual rigor, the honesty and directness, and the grand scale of his harmonic forms. See Alan Trachtenberg, *Brooklyn Bridge: Fact and Symbol* (1965).

ALAN TRACHTENBERG

ROGERS, William Penn Adair (b. Cologah, Okla., Nov. 4, 1879; d. Point Barrow, Alaska, Aug. 15, 1935), ENTERTAINER, of Native American descent, attended several boarding schools, including the Willow Hassell School in Neosko, Missouri, and the Kemper Military School in Boonville, Missouri. In 1898 he became a cowboy in the Texas panhandle, learning rope twirling and steer roping. He journeyed to Argentina in

1902 and then to South Africa, where he joined a Wild West show. He toured Japan and China before returning to St. Louis in 1904. Rogers made his debut in New York City at Madison Square Garden in 1905, appearing with a Wild West show. He began adding jokes and humorous political commentaries to his rope-twirling act and soon became a popular New York vaudeville entertainer, appearing frequently at Hammerstein's Roof Garden. He played in his first Broadway musical, *The Wall Street Girl*, in 1912, and his performance in *Hands Up* (1915) was a great success. He played in the *Ziegfeld Follies* (1916–18) and appeared in his first movie, *Laughing Bill Hyde*, in 1918. He moved to California in 1919 and appeared in several more films.

Rogers returned to New York in 1922 to play in the current *Ziegfeld Follies* and later that year began writing a series of weekly articles for the New York *Times*. The column, which appeared daily beginning in 1926, established his reputation as a witty but probing critic of contemporary life. It was syndicated and carried by some five hundred newspapers. Rogers toured Europe and the Soviet Union in 1926. *Letters of a Self Made Diplomat to His President* (1926) and *There's Not a Bathing-Suit in Russia* (1927) describe his experiences. He continued to make films, including *A Connecticut Yankee* (1931), *State Fair* (1933), and *David Harum* (1934). An early enthusiast of air travel, Rogers flew around South America in 1931 and in the Far East in 1932. He was killed in a plane crash with pilot Wiley Post. Some of his many books include *Rogersisms—The Cowboy Philosopher on the Peace Conference* (1919), *The Illiterate Digest* (1924), and *Ether and Me* (1929).

In Will Rogers, the 19th-century style of homespun humor encountered the celebrity system and popular mass media of the 20th. The substance and style of his humor—ridicule of politicians, friendly twitting of the famous, commonsensical commentaries on current events, and quasi-rustic writing—were in the direct line from Ike Marvel, Petroleum V. Nasby, and even **Mark Twain.** But Rogers adapted these homely ingredients, with his own personality, to swiftly changing forms of mass entertainment. A son of the last semifrontier, he entered show business via the commercialized packaging of that frontier, the Wild West show. He moved, with seeming ease, from that into vaudeville in its peak years, to silent films, to national syndication in newspapers, to radio, and finally to sound films. Through three decades he maintained the image of cowboy-philosopher almost undimmed, for his commentary remained eventempered and palatable; he never became doctrinaire or strident, even in advocacy. He gradually attained the status of a unique national figure, a statesman without office, known almost equally as a commentator on public affairs and as a performer. His death, while his career still remained at its peak, brought forth the kind of tributes usually reserved for presidents. See Ben Yagoda, *Will Rogers* (1993).

JAMES BOYLAN

ROLFE, John (christened at Heacham, Norfolk, Eng., May 6, 1585; d. Va., 1622), COLONIST, sailed for America in 1609 in the *Sea Adventure*. The vessel was shipwrecked on Bermuda, where the settlers were stranded for several months while building two small craft on which they sailed to Virginia (1610). Shortly thereafter, Rolfe began to grow various kinds of West Indian and South American tobacco, and experimented with new curing techniques that improved the product and expanded the demand for it. Rolfe's English wife having died (c. 1610), he married in 1614 **Pocahontas, John Smith**'s savior and the daughter of Chief Powhatan. This marriage considerably improved relations between Native Americans and colonists during the next eight years. In 1614, upon the departure of Ralph Hann for England, Rolfe was named secretary and recorder of the colony (1614–19). He returned to England in 1616, but rejoined the colony the following year. He was a member of the governor's council (1619) and finally a member of the council of state (1621).

By finding a solution to Virginia's economic plight and by calming Native American–white tensions during the colony's formative period, John Rolfe contributed importantly to the survival of the first permanent British outpost in America. In both cases, Rolfe seems to have been more fortuitous than farsighted. He knew, shortly after his arrival at Jamestown in 1610, that the local variety of tobacco was considered by Europeans to be "poore and weake, and of a byting tast," but his search for a substitute rested principally on the need to make a living. Fortunately for Rolfe and the colony, his importation of seeds from Trinidad and Venezuela and his experimentation with methods of curing resulted in a leaf highly valued in England. Virginia's economy boomed.

Similarly, Rolfe's marriage to Pocahontas, four years after the death of his first wife, appears from his famous letter to Sir Thomas Dale to have stemmed more from human craving than from any awareness of what his marriage to the Native American "nonpareil" would do for racial harmony. Yet relations with the Native Americans, highly volatile from 1607 to 1614, remained peaceful from then until the Massacre of 1622. Despite a persistent tradition that Rolfe fell victim to that bloodbath, the evidence strongly suggests that he died from other causes at about the same time. See P. L. Barbour, *Pocahontas and Her World* (1969).

ALDEN P. VAUGHAN

ROOSEVELT, Anna Eleanor (b. New York, N.Y., Oct. 11, 1884; d. New York, N.Y., Nov. 7, 1962), REFORMER, niece of Theodore Roosevelt, was raised by her grandmother and educated in private schools in the U.S. and abroad. On March 17, 1905 she married Franklin D. Roosevelt, her fifth cousin. During the Progressive Era, she was a supporter of social reform. She also championed the rights of minorities, and was active in numerous consumer, welfare, and charity programs. From 1924 to 1928 she was the finance chairman of the women's division of the Democratic State Committee in New York. In 1928 and 1930 she helped her husband campaign successfully in the state gubernatorial elections; in 1932 she toured the country with him when he campaigned for the presidency.

After Roosevelt's election as president, Eleanor Roosevelt became the most active First Lady in the nation's history. During 1933 alone she traveled about forty thousand miles, seeking to win sympathy for New Deal programs. In 1935 she began writing "My Day," a syndicated newspaper column. She also worked with many reform organizations, especially the NAACP. When the U.S. entered World War II (December 1941), she became assistant director of the Office of Civilian Defense (1941–42), and visited American soldiers in the southwest Pacific (1943) and the Caribbean (1944).

After the death of FDR (April 12, 1945), she accepted an appointment as U.S. delegate to the United Nations. In 1946, as chairman of the Commission on Human Rights, an auxiliary of the Economic and Social Council, she helped draft a universal Declaration of Human Rights. She also remained active in New York and national politics, supporting liberal and reform Democrats. Some of her books include *This Is My Story* (1937) and *This I Remember* (1949).

It is difficult to revive the directness and vitality of Eleanor Roosevelt's impact on the American public during her long career. The influence she wielded over two generations of Americans, which puzzled even her contemporaries, began to decline in the late 1950s.

Eleanor Roosevelt lived many lives; she was a leader of women's movements, a lecturer, a columnist and an author, a fighter for human rights in the United Nations, and an unofficial American ambassador to developing countries. Even some of her admirers accused her of superficiality, believing it humanly impossible to be effectively involved in so many causes simultaneously. To be sure, she was not a professional in any of these roles, but the major thrust of her influence was not as a social philosopher or innovator, although the ideals of a humanistic democracy and a peaceful world order gave unity and consistency to her thought; she was a molder of public opinion. Her basic commitment was to social justice and civil liberties. She perceived herself as a vigilant citizen, performing her civic duties. She held no public office until her appointment to the United Nations late in life and pursued no official political career. As intermediary between the Roosevelt administration and the public, she provided a channel for direct communication. The source of her power was personal rather than institutional. When her access to public power increased, she created new roles for herself and developed a particular style of operating. She thus served as an ombudsman with the increasingly bureaucratized and impersonal government and a symbol of New Deal reform. She became one of the most admired as well as one of the most hated public figures of the 1930s and 1940s.

Eleanor Roosevelt was the first president's wife to develop an independent public career. Singlehandedly she transformed the White House from a genteel mansion into a rallying place for young people, women, farmers, laborers, and blacks. She acted as the voice, the daily agent of reform, as a catalyst, providing a channel for complaints from the dispossessed and underprivileged. The effectiveness of her intervention lay in her willingness to follow up grievances until something was done about them.

In the civil rights area particularly, Eleanor Roosevelt felt less bound by political considerations than the president. Despite the administration's poor record on civil rights, her personal outspokenness rallied African-Americans to the New Deal. Since she did not consciously solicit votes, she mobilized political support in a way politicians were not able to do. After 1945 she continued to serve as the public "conscience," a living link with the Roosevelt era. She helped found Americans for Democratic Action, and was active in New York State and national campaigns. At the same time, she saw herself primarily as a "private citizen" and she directed her energies to the education of the public for social reform, which she believed could best be achieved

through the Democratic party. Her impact outside the United States became most pronounced after 1945. As chairman of the United Nations Commission on Human Rights, she steered the drafting of the Human Rights Declaration through hostile sessions, and after its ratification she devoted the rest of her life to the struggle for its acceptance in the United States and the world.

In historical perspective, Eleanor Roosevelt thus stands out most clearly as an individual reformer who transferred a tradition of personal service and stewardship to the arena of governmental reform. The broad public response that she evoked was not so much because of what she said, and not even because of her power in the White House but because she reached out to groups in American society which had been traditionally overlooked. Unlike **Jane Addams, Florence Kelley,** and other contemporary women who became professional reformers, she functioned within the roles which she had carved out for herself through her husband's career, and never became a representative of the new feminism. She was a devoted fighter for equal opportunity for women, but not an extreme feminist.

Much has been written about the supposed inadequacy of her personal relationship with Franklin Roosevelt. That she had considerable influence on his attitudes toward social reform, both before and after he became president, is clear. That the emotional ties between them had disintegrated long before 1933 is also clear. She was profoundly hurt by his infidelities, although apparently these were neither frequent nor very important to him, and were possibly a response to Eleanor's own sexual problems. These seem to have been produced by her lonely, unhappy childhood—her father was a hopeless alcoholic—by her lack of conventional good looks—she was very tall, toothy, and quite awkward as a young woman—and by the repressive standards of those Victorian times. Whatever the causes, and FDR's insensitivity was surely another, she never solved these sexual problems. This was another of her limitations. Nevertheless, she remains one of the great women, indeed, one of the great human beings, of the 20th century. See J. P. Lash,

Eleanor and Franklin (1971), and *Eleanor: The Years Alone* (1972).

TAMARA K. HAREVEN

ROOSEVELT, Franklin Delano (b. Hyde Park, N.Y., Jan. 30, 1882; d. Warm Springs, Ga., April 12, 1945), PRESIDENT, graduated from Harvard (1904), studied at the Columbia Law School, and was admitted to the bar in 1907. While a Democratic state senator (1911–13), he opposed the political machine of Charles Francis Murphy of New York City. He served as assistant secretary of the navy in the Wilson administration (1913–20) and was the Democratic vice presidential candidate in 1920. In 1921 Roosevelt was stricken with polio, which permanently crippled him but did not prevent him from continuing his political activities. At the 1924 and 1928 Democratic presidential conventions, he nominated Governor **Alfred E. Smith** of New York. Roosevelt was himself elected governor of New York in 1928, and was reelected in 1930. As governor he supported old-age pensions, unemployment insurance, and other social legislation.

In 1932 Roosevelt defeated Herbert Hoover for president, 472 electoral votes to 59. The Great Depression had reached its nadir when he took office in March 1933. He ordered the banks closed and suspended gold transactions. Congress then passed the Emergency Banking Act and the Glass-Steagall Act of 1933, creating the Federal Deposit Insurance Corporation to insure bank deposits and divorcing commercial from investment banking.

Roosevelt's New Deal program was quickly enacted by Congress during the so-called 100 Days. The National Industrial Recovery Act suspended the antitrust laws, thereby permitting industries to draft codes to regulate prices and production. Section 7(a) of this law granted labor the right to bargain collectively. The unemployment problem was attacked in a series of measures: a Civilian Conservation Corps employed males between the ages of eighteen and twenty-five in conservation and road construction projects; the Public Works Administration was estab-

lished to construct roads and public buildings; the Civil Works Administration (1933–34) employed 4 million people in various federal, state, and local projects; and the Works Progress Administration (later Works Projects) was geared toward the employment not only of manual laborers but also of writers, actors, musicians, and other professionals.

Other measures adopted during the 100 Days in 1933 included the Agricultural Adjustment Act, which granted subsidies (paid for by a processing tax) to farmers in return for their taking land out of production; the Tennessee Valley Authority, which built dams and power plants, and developed flood-control and soil conservation projects; and the Home Owners Loan Corporation Act for refinancing mortgages to prevent foreclosures. Later first-term legislation included the Securities and Exchange Commission Act (1934) regulating the stock market, the Wagner National Labor Relations Act (1935), and the Social Security Act (1935), which provided for old-age pensions and unemployment insurance.

In 1936 Roosevelt was easily reelected, defeating **Alfred M. Landon,** 523 electoral votes to 8. Because the Supreme Court had declared the NRA, the AAA, and other important New Deal measures unconstitutional, Roosevelt attempted to "pack" the Court, but the proposal met with great opposition and failed to pass. In 1938 Congress adopted a new agricultural program which permitted the secretary of agriculture to fix marketing quotas, incorporated the "parity" principle, whereby agricultural prices would be placed on a parity with industrial prices, and established an "ever-normal granary" to store surplus crops. Congress later passed the Fair Labor Standards Act (1938), establishing a minimum wage and fixing the standard work week at forty hours.

Although concerned about the aggression of Germany and Italy after 1933, Roosevelt supported the Neutrality Acts of 1935 and 1937. In his "quarantine speech" (1937), however, he argued that the U.S. could not isolate itself from European affairs, and that aggressive nations must be "quarantined" if the health of the international community was to be preserved. After Germany attacked Poland (1939), precipitating World War II, Roosevelt moved toward active support of the Western democracies. The Neutrality Act of 1939 repealed the arms embargo imposed in 1935 and authorized the sale of munitions on a "cash-and-carry" basis. In 1940 Roosevelt, by executive order, traded fifty "over-age" destroyers to Britain for six Caribbean naval bases. He also persuaded Congress to pass the Lend-Lease Act (1941), which supplied munitions to all countries opposing the Axis powers.

Running for a third term in 1940, Roosevelt defeated **Wendell Willkie,** 449 electoral votes to 82. After Japan attacked Pearl Harbor (Dec. 7, 1941), the U.S. became an active belligerent. Throughout the war, Roosevelt took an active part in both military planning and allied diplomacy. At Tehran (1943), he, Churchill, and Stalin agreed to plans for an Anglo-American invasion of Western Europe, and a plan for a postwar international organization (the U.N.) was formulated. In 1944 Roosevelt was elected to a fourth term, defeating **Thomas E. Dewey,** 432 electoral votes to 99. He met again with Churchill and Stalin at Yalta, in the Crimea, in 1945. In exchange for Stalin's pledge to enter the war against Japan, Russia was promised territorial concessions in the Far East. Roosevelt and Churchill also awarded Stalin eastern Poland, in exchange for his promise to allow free elections in Poland and other Soviet-occupied countries. The "Big Three" also continued their work on the formulation of a U.N. charter.

―――∞∞∞―――

When Franklin D. Roosevelt died in 1945 he was universally recognized as one of the major figures of American history and of 20th-century world history. Seen from a national perspective, he had forged an enduring political coalition, won an unprecedented four terms as president, supervised the enactment and administration of reform legislation that changed both federal-state relations and the role of all government in the regulation of the nation's social and economic development, and led the country through the greatest war in history to total victory. Viewed from a worldwide perspective, he symbolized concern for the suffering of the poor in the Great Depression, a willingness to modify existing capitalist institutions in the general interest, and the determination to resist Fascist aggression and to protect individual freedom. He was the preeminent leader of the great coalition that had crushed Germany and Japan and was about to found the United Nations. In both spheres he epitomized the practical reformer—pragmatic yet principled, humane yet toughminded.

Time has modified this evaluation. Today Roosevelt seems less heroic, his achievements more limited, his character somewhat flawed. His domestic New Deal failed to end the Depression of the thirties. Unemployment never fell much below 8 million until 1941, and the widely publicized New Deal programs for industrial and agricultural recovery were at best only partially successful and in some instances were unmitigated disasters. The American economy recovered from the Depression more slowly than that of either Nazi Germany or Great Britain. Furthermore, Roosevelt was a confused and confusing administrator. He lacked deep understanding or even much interest in economic theory. As a defender of freedom and world order he was slow to face the threat of Nazism and less than candid in revealing his plans to the American people when he did decide to face that threat. For at least a year after Pearl Harbor his direction of the war effort left much to be desired, and in the crucial and complex negotiations with the Allies in the late stages of the war he adopted a distressingly simplistic view both of the problems and of his own ability to manipulate other leaders, particularly Joseph Stalin, whom he apparently thought he could beguile or cajole into cooperating with the Western powers. The countless biographies and memoirs of Roosevelt's relatives, friends, and associates have tended to darken his personal portrait, revealing him to have been, despite his many engaging qualities, quite shallow and rather vain and essentially remote, even from those closest to him.

Yet Roosevelt remains a great and admirable

man in the eyes of history. At the very start of the Depression, even while he was governor of New York, he realized that the essential task of government was to help those in need and that this requirement took priority over any ideology or constitutional theory. Unlike his predecessor, Herbert Hoover, he never allowed tradition or a particular political philosophy to stand in the way of action, especially where aid to the unemployed was concerned. He also knew how to *reach* the people: to convince ordinary citizens that he was aware of their problems and would act to solve them. His fireside chats and press conferences and state papers were extraordinarily effective in inspiring mass confidence and patriotism. When he died, millions all over the world felt a profound sense of personal loss. His spirit, fundamentally optimistic even in the darkest times, ended the psychic depression of the thirties and rallied the nation to the grueling struggle of the forties. If his administration was sometimes inefficient it was always energetic. Throughout his presidency, he succeeded in attracting hundreds of intelligent, eager, and imaginative persons into government service. Moreover, if his New Deal failed to restore prosperity, it inaugurated necessary changes in American life—the social security system; banking reform, including the insurance of savings; regional planning; a readjustment of the balance between local and national authority; a new powerful voice for organized labor in its dealings with big business.

In the larger theater of world relations Roosevelt's greatest accomplishment was in rousing the nation to its world responsibilities as a great power. His most imaginative action before the United States entered the war was the lend-lease program. During the conflict he was able, after some hesitation and confusion, to mobilize the economy, check inflation through rationing, price controls, and steep taxation, and rally the people to the war effort without repressing civil liberties or triggering hatreds. In planning for the peace he profited from the mistakes of Woodrow Wilson in World War I (he had observed these errors firsthand as a member of the Wilson administration). He minimized partisan opposition by sharing decision-making with Republican leaders, and he adapted his plan for the United Nations to the realities of world power politics.

Whether Roosevelt's social conscience was purely patrician in origin or whether it resulted from his having been crippled in the prime of life by polio is a moot question. What is certain is that his commitment to social improvement was genuine and profound. This commitment in a man of inherited wealth and social position and also his courage in the face of such a severe physical affliction endeared him to millions. But his finest quality was this: for more than a decade he dominated his countrymen without being domineering. No previous president had held the office so long or exercised so much power, yet Roosevelt remained true to American traditions in this most essential way—he never forgot that he was the repository of power, not its possessor; the representative of the people, not their ruler. See James M. Burns, *Roosevelt: The Lion and the Fox* (1956) and *Roosevelt: The Soldier of Freedom* (1970).

JOHN A. GARRATY

ROOSEVELT, Theodore (b. New York, N.Y., Oct. 27, 1858; d. Oyster Bay, N.Y., Jan. 6, 1919), PRESIDENT, graduated from Harvard (1880), and briefly studied law at Columbia. Devoting considerable time to the writing of history, he produced *The Naval War of 1812* (1882), *The Winning of the West* (1889–96), and several minor works. Meanwhile he served three terms (1882–84) as a Republican in the New York state assembly, where he worked for labor and civil service reform. Although he opposed the nomination of **James G. Blaine** for the presidency by the Republicans in 1884, he angered the Mugwumps, or civil service reformers, by supporting him nominally during the campaign. An unsuccessful candidate for mayor of New York City in 1886, Roosevelt later became U.S. civil service commissioner (1889–95) and president of the board of police commissioners of New York City (1895–97). As assistant secretary of the navy during the McKinley administration (1897–98), he urged war against Spain for both imperialistic and humanitarian reasons. Resigning his assistant secretaryship, he helped organize the "Rough Riders" and covered himself and them with glory as their colonel in the battle for San Juan.

Roosevelt was elected governor of New York in 1898. His support of a tax on corporation franchises, his refusal to serve big business interests, and his failure to cooperate with machine politicians angered Republican party leader Thomas C. Platt. Partly on Platt's insistence, Roosevelt was eased out of New York through the vice presidential nomination in 1900. He became president upon William McKinley's assassination in the fall of 1901.

A conservationist, Roosevelt supported the Newlands Act of 1902, which channeled money received from the sale of western lands into federal irrigation projects. He also settled the anthracite coal strike that same year by threatening to use federal troops to operate the mines if labor and management did not resolve their differences. Under Roosevelt's orders, the Justice Department meanwhile instigated a suit against the Northern Securities Co. (1902), a holding company controlled by **J. Pierpont Morgan** and **E. H. Harriman.** When the Supreme Court ordered this company dissolved (1904), Roosevelt became known as a "trust buster." In 1903 Congress established the Department of Commerce and Labor, which included a Bureau of Corporations empowered to investigate the activities of companies engaged in interstate commerce.

After Roosevelt's victory over Alton B. Parker in the 1904 presidential election, 336 electoral votes to 140, he pressed Congress for further reform legislation. Among the results were the Hepburn Act, permitting the Interstate Commerce Commission to fix railroad rates, and the Pure Food and Drug Act, both of 1906. As his second term progressed, Roosevelt turned increasingly to the left and foreshadowed the "Bull Moose" platform of 1912. In 1908 he advocated a federal income tax and inheritance tax,

greater regulation of corporations engaged in interstate commerce, and reforms to benefit the industrial worker. These recommendations, coupled with Roosevelt's attacks on the courts and the integrity of the "malefactors of great wealth," alienated the Republican Old Guard (conservatives).

Roosevelt was particularly active in foreign affairs. On Colombia's refusal in 1903 to ratify a treaty granting the U.S. a strip of land on the isthmus of Panama for an interoceanic canal, he supported a revolution in Panama in order to acquire the Canal Zone. His desire to protect the canal and his fear that Latin American countries might become European protectorates led him to issue his "Corollary" to the Monroe Doctrine the following year. This asserted that under certain conditions the U.S. would intervene in the internal affairs of Latin American nations in order to prevent European powers from intervening. Then, in 1905, Roosevelt mediated the Russo-Japanese War largely in order to influence the Far Eastern balance of power. For this he was awarded the Nobel Peace Prize. In 1906 he helped arrange the Algerian Conference to discuss European claims to Morocco. And in 1907, after California passed discriminatory legislation against Japanese immigrants, Roosevelt negotiated a "Gentlemen's Agreement" with Japan. It provided that Japan would bar the emigration of Japanese laborers to the U.S. in return for a promise that the Japanese already in America would be treated fairly.

After leaving office (1909), Roosevelt went to Africa on a hunting expedition and then toured Europe. Upon his return in 1910, he became alienated from President Taft, whom he considered too conservative. At Osawatomie, Kansas (1910), in perhaps the most notable speech of his career, he attacked special privilege and advocated a broad program of social reform (the "New Nationalism") to be implemented by an expansion of federal power over the social and economic affairs of the nation. Pressed by Republican progressives to seek the party's nomination in 1912, Roosevelt won most of the primaries. Taft controlled the convention, however, and was renominated. Roosevelt then created the Progressive or "Bull Moose" party and ran for president. He supported the initiative, referendum, and recall, the popular election of U.S. senators, national presidential primaries, the regulation of monopoly rather than the indiscriminate breaking up of large companies, and a virtual panoply of social justice measures. The split within the Republican party assured the victory of the Democrat, Woodrow Wilson, who got 435 electoral votes to Roosevelt's 88 and Taft's 8.

Roosevelt supported the Allies during World War I and was sharply critical of Wilson's neutrality policies. When the U.S. entered the war, Wilson rejected his offer to raise a division. Roosevelt remained critical of the administration and advocated harsh punishment of dissenters at home and unconditional surrender abroad. He also opposed Wilson's version of the League of Nations. He was considered the probable Republican candidate for president in 1920 at the time of his death.

———— ⨯⨯⨯ ————

Theodore Roosevelt remains as controversial now as he was in his lifetime. Some historians continue to view him as a perennial adolescent, protofascist, sheer opportunist, or combination of all three; others insist that he was a sophisticated conservative or a sincere and enlightened progressive. Some argue that he merely mirrored his times; most hold that he had a considerable, if often intangible, impact upon men and events. But virtually all agree that he was a fervent nationalist and a remarkably resourceful president.

A man of surpassing charm, extraordinary charisma, and broad intellectual interests, Roosevelt was a curious compound of realist and idealist, pragmatist and moral absolutist. As a twenty-three-year-old state assemblyman he first began to move beyond the laissez-faire and raw Social Darwinism values inculcated in him at Harvard. By 1899, the year he became governor of New York, he believed that most men were molded by their environment and that it was the manifest duty of the governing classes to reshape

the environment in the public interest. From these reform Darwinian postulates flowed in turn an evolutionary conception of law and a growing conviction that the state should foster distributive justice by regulating working conditions, instituting social security, and imposing heavy taxes on unearned or excessive income.

Yet Roosevelt also felt that not all people could transcend their backgrounds in one generation. So he insisted that blacks should be uplifted before they were integrated, that Filipinos should be trained for self-government before they were given independence, and that the influx of uneducated immigrants should be curbed. For all his pro-labor statements and policies, moreover, Roosevelt was as fearful of the unions' potential power as he was critical of big business's actual power. Like most progressives, Roosevelt also had an abiding faith in scientism, efficiency, and government by experts. His appointment of a spate of factfinding commissions, his insistence that trusts should be regulated rather than dissolved, and his monumental contribution to the conservation movement testify compellingly to this.

In practice, Roosevelt's idealism and intellectualism were diluted by his love of power and urge to achieve hardly less than by the harsh conviction that politics is the art of the possible. He often accepted compromise legislation in the realization that it was all the Republican Old Guard would endorse. On some issues, such as the tariff, he gave up entirely. And on others, notably the regulation of corporations and the abuse of the injunction in labor disputes, he was rebuffed or ignored by Congress. Yet on a few, including conservation, his bold and imaginative use of the executive power carried him through.

Roosevelt's views on foreign policy also changed markedly, though only during his years in the White House. A rank imperialist and uncritical disciple of Captain **Alfred T. Mahan** in the 1890s, he believed that the United States was engaged in a fateful struggle for markets, prestige, and power. Under the sobering responsibilities of office, however, he concluded that the nation's real interests lay in a stable world balance of power rather than in a far-flung colonial empire. As a result, his conduct of foreign policy was restrained and acutely sensitive to the limits of American power and interests. Only the Panama affair, his contempt for China, and the resurgence of his romantic militaristic strain after he left the presidency stained the later record.

In sum, Roosevelt was the first president to understand and respond constructively to both the domestic and the international changes wrought by the industrial and technological revolutions. Failing in his drive to make the Republican party a responsible instrument of reform and adjustment, he succeeded nevertheless in dramatizing the injustice inherent in the existing economic and social system. See William H. Harbaugh, *Power and Responsibility: The Life and Times of Theodore Roosevelt* (1961).

WILLIAM H. HARBAUGH

ROOT, Elihu (b. Clinton, N.Y., Feb. 15, 1845; d. New York, N.Y., Feb. 7, 1937), POLITICAL LEADER, graduated from Hamilton College (1864) and the Law School of the University of the City of New York (1867). Following his admittance to the New York bar in 1867, he specialized in corporation law. He also took an active interest in Republican politics, and President Arthur appointed him U.S. attorney for the southern district of New York (1883–85). A close friend of Theodore Roosevelt's, Root was an adviser to Roosevelt when he ran for mayor of New York City (1886) and when he served as president of the board of police commissioners of New York City (1895–97). In 1894 Root attended the New York state constitutional convention.

During 1899–1904 Root served as secretary of war. During his tenure he reorganized the department to make it more efficient, assisted both in drafting a constitution for the Philippines and in framing the Platt Amendment (1901)—which authorized the U.S. to intervene in Cuba to preserve Cuban independence—and helped found the army college at Fort Leavenworth, Kansas (1901), and the War College in Washington, D.C. (1903). He was a member of the Alaskan Boundary Commission (1903) which set-

tled the boundary between Alaska and Canada. Root served as President Theodore Roosevelt's secretary of state (1905–9). In this position he reorganized the U.S. consular service, made a goodwill tour of Latin America (1906), and negotiated the Root-Takahira Agreement (1908), in which the U.S. and Japan agreed to respect the "Open Door" in China and to maintain the status quo in the Pacific.

Root next served in the U.S. Senate as a Republican from New York (1909–15). In 1910 he represented the U.S. in the Newfoundland Fisheries arbitration at The Hague, which sustained Britain's right to make local fishing regulations and exclude American fishermen from certain bays. During the early years of President Wilson's administration, Root was one of the Senate's most articulate opponents of Wilson's "New Freedom" legislation.

Always actively interested in promoting international arbitration, Root became a member of the Permanent Court of Arbitration at The Hague (1910), and he served as president of the Carnegie Endowment for International Peace (1910–25). In recognition of his work he was awarded the Nobel Peace Prize in 1912.

Root opposed Wilson's neutrality policy during the early stages of World War I. After American entry into the war, Wilson appointed Root ambassador extraordinary to Russia (1917). His mission was to encourage the faltering Kerenski government to carry on the war against the Germans. Although Root supported the principle of a League of Nations, he urged the passage by the Senate of the "Lodge Reservations."

In the 1920s Root continued to work for international harmony. He served on a committee of jurists who formed the Permanent Court of International Justice (1920–21); was a delegate to the Washington Disarmament Conference (1921), where he helped draft the five-power treaty in which the world powers agreed to restrict the use of submarines against merchant ships; and served on a committee to revise the World Court's statute (1929).

Had Elihu Root never held public office, he would still have acquired a durable reputation as one of America's eminent corporation lawyers. However, probably no other American during the first quarter of the 20th century, excepting Theodore Roosevelt and Woodrow Wilson, exercised more influence in projecting the United States toward leadership in world affairs. Historians will long debate the merits of Root's activities and their long-range consequences. As secretary of war, he was instrumental in formulating the legal relationship governing America's newly acquired overseas dependencies: Guam, the Philippines, and Puerto Rico. He was the author of the Platt Amendment to the Army's Appropriation Act of 1901 which, in effect, made Cuba a protectorate of the United States, a model which later served to spread American hegemony like a tent over the Caribbean region. Root introduced the general staff system as an important ingredient toward the modernization of the American military establishment. He pressed hard for an American controlled and fortified transisthmian canal through Panama. In conducting foreign affairs, Root championed the Open Door with its anticipated expansion of the nation's export trade and direct investments, particularly in areas he deemed of vital national interest, like Latin America. As practitioner of realpolitik, Root endeavored to steer American diplomacy into alignment with both Britain and Japan as evidenced by several agreements reached with these countries for the purpose of relaxing tensions and promoting cooperation. No other American statesman in this century worked so assiduously as Root in seeking American participation in arbitration treaties. Through numerous writings and public addresses, he preached the doctrine that obligatory arbitration offered the best means of settling legal disputes between nations—even when national honor itself was at stake. His own presentation of the American argument in the celebrated North Atlantic Fisheries case, successfully settled through arbitration in 1912, illustrated how an international judicial system could serve the cause of peace.

What is perhaps most amazing about Root's long career is not that he made his debut in international politics so late in life; of more significance was the almost complete absence of any previous formal training, experience, and intellectual expertise in military and foreign affairs. These deficiencies were compensated for by an unusual combination of personal and political assets. Root's ability to grasp fundamental issues readily, his talent for administrative organization, and a thorough comprehension of the power structure in government facilitated the development and implementation of his favored programs. His own inclination was to use rhetoric, not lacking in occasional wit, to persuade associates in government of the appropriateness of what he desired. Toward the man in the street he displayed indifference at least in matters of foreign policy. By conscience and preference, Root was and remained a conservative, staunchly loyal to Republicanism. In point of practice, party loyalty became for him an article of faith.

As early as 1915–16, Republicans had founded and assumed leadership of the League to Enforce Peace, a private organization interested in developing postwar international organization, favoring what later came to be known as collective security against aggressor states. Although Root was never himself actively involved in the LEP, he expressed sympathy for the League idea, but proposed modifications calculated to conform to what he believed were American constitutional requirements and national interests. In 1917 Root headed an American fact-finding mission sent by President Wilson to Russia for the purpose of investigating conditions in the wake of the political upheaval which had deposed the czarist regime that spring. The results of the mission were nearly catastrophic. Information brought by the "Root Mission" was of such dubious value that the effort was largely discredited. In spite of this experience and his advanced age, Root was still perceived by political observers to be a logical candidate to serve on the American Commission to Negotiate Peace at the forthcoming peace conference in 1919. Rightly or wrongly, President Wilson distrusted Root's conservatism, his heavy-handed legalist mind, and his seeming rigidity on matters of power politics as well as Root's pronounced Republican loyalties. Later, during the ultimate contest in the Senate over the Versailles Treaty, Root, a moderate and reservationist, joined with **Henry Cabot Lodge** in devising the strategy which ultimately led to America's rejection of the Treaty, thus precluding America's entry into the League of Nations.

To assert that Root's activities during the controversy over the League tainted him with the brush of isolationism would be a serious mistake. Like many reservationists, Root favored American participation in the World Court. He had urged American participation through a treaty in order to guarantee French security in 1919. As a member of President Harding's delegation to the Washington Conference, he displayed an active interest both in naval arms limitation and in reaching a new balance of power in the western Pacific. Here it is important to note that Root continued to place reliance on traditional systems of maintaining world peace. In his world view, collective security offered an untried, utopian, universalist system, an undertaking incurring numerous and unnecessary risks. Instead, he preferred regional spheres of special interests as providing the surest means to preserve peace and acknowledgment of American dominance in the western hemisphere. Adequate military defense serving as a deterrent would offer a better means for maintaining peace than would disarmament. A practitioner of the "Old Diplomacy," Elihu Root had values which survived through a line of protégés, most notably **Henry L. Stimson.** Root strongly believed that statesmanship in the United States was too important to be left in the hands of amateurs and the whims of an uninformed public opinion. His advocacy of a professional diplomatic service reflects better than any other single activity Root's contribution to American leadership in world affairs during this century. See Philip C. Jessup, *Elihu Root* (1937).

LAWRENCE E. GELFAND

ROOT, John Wellborn (b. Lumpkin, Ga., Jan. 10, 1850; d. Chicago, Ill., Jan. 15, 1891), ARCHI-TECT, displayed early talent as both a draftsman and a musician. During the Civil War, his merchant father operated a fleet of blockade runners between English and Southern Confederate ports, and in 1864, after the capture of Atlanta, he sent young John, in the care of friends, to England, where he attended school and studied music with the great organist William Best. With the cessation of hostilities, he returned to New York to study engineering at New York University, graduating with honors in 1869. He then decided to become an architect.

He worked slightly more than a year in the New York office of the neo-Gothicist James Renwick, the builder of St. Patrick's Cathedral, and for a similar period under J. B. Snook, the designer of the old Grand Central Station. In 1872, attracted by the opportunities for rebuilding the recently burned-out city, he moved to Chicago, becoming head draftsman in the firm of Carter, Drake, and Wight. There he met and formed a close friendship with a fellow draftsman, **Daniel H. Burnham,** and the two formed a partnership in 1873. After weathering the depression of 1873, their firm flourished in the late 1870s and became, in the 1880s, one of the most powerful and influential in the country. While Burnham's contributions lay chiefly in administration, public relations, and the conception of internal floor plan arrangement, Root was, by contrast, the firm's chief designer and aesthetic theorist, assimilating and articulating the elements of structure, texture, proportion, color, and ornament to give the buildings their ultimate architectural personality. Throughout the 1870s and 1880s, Burnham and Root produced houses and smaller buildings of quality and historic importance. Yet their major genre was the tall office building, both of the older, wall-bearing mode and of the newer, metal-framed construction, in which the building's weight-bearing responsibilities were transferred from the slightly pyramidal walls to a more even distribution along a stronger, skeletal frame. Their wall-bearing Montauk Block (Chicago, 1881–82) was one of the first buildings to be called a "skyscraper," and their starkly elegant wall-bearing

Monadnock (Chicago, 1889–92) became an important "modern" stylistic reference. Their internally advanced Rookery Building (Chicago, 1885–88) was a mixture of skeletal and wall-bearing construction, but in several completely steel-framed skyscrapers of the late eighties and early nineties, they produced their most characteristic contributions to the "Chicago School of Architecture" (Rand-McNally Building, Chicago, 1888–90; Masonic Temple, Chicago, 1890–91; Mills Building, San Francisco, 1890–91). Root died during the early planning stages of the Chicago World Columbian Exposition (1893), for which he and Burnham were serving as the major architectural consultants.

Despite a steadily growing appreciation of his work, Root has remained an underrated figure in the architectural flowering of the late 19th century, remaining somehow an outside fourth figure in the familiar American triumvirate of **H. H. Richardson, Louis Sullivan,** and **Frank Lloyd Wright.** Obviously influenced by the neo-Romanesque style of the slightly older Richardson, Root, like Richardson, was conscious of the need to imbibe the essence and the spirit of past work while avoiding derivative and academic copying. His occasional penchant for overly exuberant ornamental effect was tempered by the more practical sobriety of his commercially oriented partner to produce, at its best, an architecture of beauty, meaning, and fitness. Indeed much of the success of Burnham and Root resulted from the ability of each partner to work as a team, to recognize and defer to the other's special talents. For while Burnham solved practical problems and represented the firm commercially, the shyer, quieter Root provided its aesthetic rationale, creating in the process an original and influential literature of architectural theory. Long before young Frank Lloyd Wright would claim to have discovered "organic" architecture, Root urged that architects "continually return to nature and to nature's methods...." Nature taught the architect that "no reason is good, no answer worth giving that does not spring from

the present question and is not inherently connected with it." Even before Sullivan developed his credo, "Form follows function," Root wrote that "a building designated for a particular purpose should express that purpose in every part." In fact, he argued, "the force with which that function is expressed measures its value as a work of art." Despite, or indeed because of, such accomplishments, Root's premature death at the age of forty-one occasioned a profound sense of loss and of unfulfilled promise, both from his peers and from succeeding generations. Still, Root made enormous contributions: to the theory and practice of modern building, to the further integration of art and science, and to the cultivation of architecture as both shelter and sustenance. See Harriet Monroe, *John Wellborn Root: His Life and Work* (1896).

THOMAS S. HINES

ROSENWALD, Julius (b. Springfield, Ill., Aug. 12, 1862; d. Chicago, Ill., Jan. 6, 1932), BUSINESS LEADER, PHILANTHROPIST, was educated in the public schools of Springfield, Illinois, then worked for the wholesale clothing firm of Hammerslough Brothers in New York City (1879–85). In 1885 he moved to Chicago, where, with his brother Morris and cousin Julius Weil, he established the clothing firm of Rosenwald and Weil.

In 1895 Rosenwald purchased a one-fourth interest in Sears, Roebuck and Co. Tremendous expansion of the mail-order business in the next two decades turned Rosenwald's original investment of $37,500 into a multimillion-dollar fortune. He was vice president and treasurer of the company (1895–1910), president (1910–25), and chairman of the board (1925–32). A progressive employer, he established one of the country's earliest and most generous employees' profitsharing plans.

Throughout his career Rosenwald took an active interest in philanthropy. His major foundation was the Julius Rosenwald Fund, established in 1917 to work toward the "well-being of mankind." After World War I he pledged $6 million to help settle Russian Jews in agricultural colonies; in 1920 he donated $100,000 to feed children in Germany. His donations helped open YMCA's and YWCA's for blacks in twenty-five cities, and to build more than five thousand public schools for black children in the rural South. As a member of the board of trustees of the University of Chicago, he contributed approximately $5 million to that institution. In 1929 he helped establish the Museum of Science and Industry in Chicago. During his lifetime his donations to humanitarian causes exceeded $63 million.

———∞∞∞———

Rosenwald's donations, large as they were, do not adequately measure his contribution to American philanthropy. He once declared: "It is almost always easier to make a million dollars honestly than to dispose of it wisely." In bestowing his wealth Rosenwald showed as much enterprise and vision as in its accumulation. He regarded his gifts, whether large or small, as social investments, and he sought to make them productive. Instead of attempting to make any field of humanitarian endeavor his special preserve, he used his philanthropic resources to stimulate gifts by other donors and to arouse public authorities to their obligations. Thus the money allocated by the Rosenwald Fund for improvement of African-American education in the South was multiplied six times by appropriations of school boards and gifts of small donors, black and white. Possibly as a result of his association with **Jane Addams** and Judge Julian Mack, Rosenwald came to believe that the major responsibility for social welfare rested with government and that the function of philanthropy was to initiate new projects which, when their value had been demonstrated, should be supported by taxation.

Rosenwald was critical of "the dead hand" in philanthropy and opposed to the establishment of perpetual endowments. He believed surplus wealth should be used to meet present needs rather than stored for future use. When the Rosenwald Fund was reorganized in 1928 he stipulated that all of its money be expended within twenty-five years of his death. In accordance with these instructions, the Fund completed its work on June 30, 1948. See M. R. Werner, *Julius Rosenwald: The Life of a Practical Humanitarian* (1939).

ROBERT H. BREMNER

ROSS, Edward Alsworth (b. Virden, Ill., Dec. 12, 1866; d. Madison, Wis., July 22, 1961), SOCIAL SCIENTIST, graduated from Coe College, Cedar Rapids, Iowa, in 1886. After teaching at a prep school for two years (1886–88) in Fort Dodge, Iowa, he studied at the University of Berlin and also traveled in Europe (1888–89). He then studied economics under **Richard T. Ely** at Johns Hopkins University, receiving his PhD in 1891. After teaching economics at the University of Indiana (1891–92) and Cornell (1892–93), Ross moved to Stanford University in 1893 and began to turn his attention to sociology. He was forced to resign from his post at Stanford in 1900, when Mrs. Leland Stanford made it clear she would no longer tolerate a faculty member who had allegedly maligned her husband's business ethics and who advocated free silver, municipal reform, and restrictions on Japanese immigration to the U.S. Ross taught at the University of Nebraska (1901–6) before becoming professor of sociology at the University of Wisconsin in 1906. He was chairman of Wisconsin's sociology department from 1929 until his retirement in 1937.

Ross's magnum opus, *Social Control* (1901), an effort to explain the sociological concept of order in mass society, established his position among the founding fathers of American sociology. A collection of essays written from 1897 to 1904 and published as *Foundations of Sociology* (1905) helped transform American sociology from a deterministic, "bio-organic," and conservative study to a reformist, environmentalist, and progressive social science. In *Sin and Society* (1907), Ross employed the sociological concept of cultural lag to explain the conservatism of the law and make a plea for sociological jurisprudence. In *Changing America* (1909 and 1912), he advocated a variety of progressive reforms. His popular *Social Psychology*

(1908) was the first American text on that subject. Ross served as president of the American Sociological Society in 1914 and 1915. After visiting Russia in 1917–18 he published *Russia in Upheaval* (1918) and other books on the Soviet Union. In 1920 he published a textbook, *Principles of Sociology,* and further revised it as *New-Age Sociology* in 1940. He was national chairman of the American Civil Liberties Union from 1940 to 1950. Some of his many other books include *What Is America?* (1919), *World Drift* (1928), and his autobiography, *Seventy Years of It* (1936).

———

From the turn of the century, when sociology first began to emerge as a distinct discipline, until the eve of World War II, no sociologist in the United States achieved the prominence enjoyed by Edward Alsworth Ross. Six and one-half feet in height, lean of frame, and frenetically energetic, Ross spent his prime years exposing the inequities of corporate capitalism and injustices perpetrated by big business, proposing a variety of progressive reforms, investigating social conditions and the factors of social change in such faraway places as Soviet Russia, Australia, Latin America, and the Middle East, and investigating slave conditions in Africa, church-state relations in South America, and the future of the foot-binding of women in China. He lectured to thousands on and off the Wisconsin campus, wrote more than two dozen books on scholarly sociological topics, on social reform, and on his travels, hundreds of popular pieces and scholarly monographs, and several highly successful textbooks. In words Billy Herndon used to describe Abraham Lincoln, Ross's "ambition was a little engine that knew no rest."

E. A. Ross can best be understood as a transitional figure; his writings were addressed to a generation which was abandoning the individualistic, agrarian life (what, in *Social Control*, Ross called *community*) for the traumas, exhilaration, and opportunities offered by the industrial metropolis (*society*).

Ross's sociological inquiries, particularly in *Social Control* and in *Social Psychology,* were addressed to the following problem: How can we achieve social stability in a corporate society without abandoning the freedom of the individual? In *Social Control,* Ross cataloged the *formal* restraints he would place on the individual—all of them consonant with his middle-class, progressive ethos: social religion, sociological jurisprudence, and progressive education; in *Social Psychology,* he proposed *informal* controls—including "prophylaxis" against the "mob-mind" and measures through which to enlighten public opinion. In *Foundations of Sociology,* he set forth a sociological system that replaced the deterministic *bio-organicism* of Herbert Spencer with a *social,* nondeterministic definition of institutional change. The result was a "sociology of progressivism"—a melioristic social science.

Ross's proposals for reform were advanced in books such as *Changing America, What Is America?, The Social Trend,* and *Roads to Social Peace.* He demanded greater equity and justice for the common man, a larger role for the government in promoting social welfare, and a smaller role for the businessman in the formulation of national economic and social policy. His most devastating attack came in *Sin and Society,* a slender tract that demonstrated how inadequate were the nation's laws to deal with the new forms of a corporate economy and called for "sociological jurisprudence" to constrain the rapacious businessman.

In addition to liberal reforms, Ross advocated a cluster of nativistic ideas. His "melioristic nativism," in contrast to the conservative variety espoused by Madison Grant and other eastern xenophobes, included advocacy of prohibition, immigration restriction, a quasi-racist variety of eugenics, and restrictions on population growth through birth control. He abandoned some of these nativistic views, however, during the New Deal, when he spoke out often, vigorously, and courageously on behalf of civil liberties, academic freedom, and freedom of the press.

Among sociologists of the post-Progressive Era, Ross's scholarly reputation fell into decline-especially so in the decades following World War II. The image of a facile publicist and textbook writer, popular lecturer, and world traveler over-shadowed Ross's creative contributions to the origins of American sociology. There is no evidence that this would have troubled the Wisconsin sociologist-reformer. The reform of society, according to Ross, not the refinement of "scope and method," was the purpose of sociology. On these terms, Ross admirably fulfilled the role he chose for himself. See Julius Weinberg, *Edward Alsworth Ross and the Sociology of Progressivism* (1972).

JULIUS WEINBERG

ROTHKO, Mark (b. Dvinsk, Russ., Sept. 25, 1903; d. New York, N.Y., Feb. 25, 1970), ARTIST, born Marcus Rothkovich, came to the U.S. in 1913 and settled in Portland, Oregon. He attended public schools in Portland, went to Yale for two years (1921–23), and settled in New York in 1925, where he studied at the Art Students League under Max Weber. This was Rothko's only formal art training; he considered himself largely a self-taught artist. His first one-man shows were held at the Portland Art Museum and the Contemporary Arts Gallery (N.Y.) in 1933. His style at this time was essentially realistic.

Rothko worked on the WPA's Federal Arts Project in New York (1936–37). During the 1940s, greatly influenced by the surrealists, his work became increasingly abstract, and by 1950 he had developed his unique abstract expressionist style. Founded on economical units of form and color, Rothko's art usually contained two or three forceful rectangular shapes and a limited color range, such as *Orange and Yellow* (1956, Albright Art Gallery, Buffalo). Rothko's paintings were included in the XXVIII Venice Biennale (1958) and the New York Museum of Modern Art's European show, "The New American Painting" (1958–59). He was honored by a retrospective exhibition at the Museum of Modern Art in 1961.

Rothko helped found the "Subjects of the Artist" school in New York (1948); he also taught at Brooklyn College (1951–54) and the University of Colorado (1955). A period of deep depression in the 1960s ended with his suicide. Some of his best-known works are: *No. 14* (1949, Betty Parsons Gallery, N.Y.), *Green on Blue* (1956, University of Arizona Art Gallery), and *Number 2* (1962, private collection).

❧

Mark Rothko occupies a foremost position in the history of 20th-century painting. As a dissenter in 1935 to Regionalist domination of the American art scene, he took a leading role in organizing the Europe-oriented group "The Ten." A decade later he was recognized by open-minded critics as one of the significant artists who were creating a new school of painting in this country. His greater claim to significance rests, however, as it must, on the aesthetic quality of his art. Rothko's painting commands awe.

The subject with which he avowedly dealt was the cosmos and man's capacity for intuiting universals. Together with **Jackson Pollock** and others attracted to Jungian concepts, Rothko wanted to find those images that might mediate, like some archetypal myth, between the boundless realm of memory and dream, and the world of humanly perceived phenomena. Stylistically, however, as the avant-garde developed through the 1940s, a division became evident between the gestural painters such as Pollock and the color-field painters among whom Rothko is counted. Color, so physical in essence, so metaphysical in effect, was the vessel he offered those willing to join him in his adventure into the unknown. Repudiating decoration, Rothko spread veils of color across his canvas and conjured luminous rectangles of light that seem to grow in intensity as one gazes. There in his work of the 1950s we see again the *calme, luxe et volupté* of Matisse, who gave visible form to Baudelaire's poetic dream of primeval passion. Now even the canvas support disappears, leaving the viewer with the great apparition before his eyes: disembodied floating rectangles and transparent vibrating color. Surrealism with its search for mythic content is purged of its figurative associations without losing its evocative power or heroic aspirations, and is wholly justified as an aesthetic means. Rothko's part in effecting this transformation adds a final historical importance to his artistic distinction and eminence among the artists who created abstract expressionism, the first international art movement developed in America. See James E. B. Breslin, *Mark Rothko: A Biography* (1993).

IRMA B. JAFFE

ROYALL, Anne Newport (b. Md., June 11, 1769; d. Washington, D.C., Oct. 1, 1854) JOURNALIST, AUTHOR, was raised on the Pennsylvania frontier—rumor said she was a captive of Indians. In 1797 she married William Royall, an educated Virginia gentleman-farmer and Revolutionary veteran, and until his death sixteen years later she lived the life of a well-to-do matron. Although Royall had clearly intended her to be his heiress, ten years of litigation, appealing to archaic law and antifemale prejudice, deprived her of his estate. She then turned to traveling and writing, describing in overhasty but effective prose a fast-changing America. In the process, she ranged through much of its terrain and met innumerable personalities of the time. Best known of her writings was *Sketches of History, Life and Manners in the United States, by a Traveller* (1826); other volumes include *The Black Book* (1828–29), *Mrs. Royall's Pennsylvania* (1829), *Mrs. Royall's Southern Tour* (1830–31), and *Letters from Alabama* (1830). These books first made her famous, but eventually notorious because of her acrimonious tone toward those who rebuffed her in her efforts to secure a Revolutionary widow's pension, who refused the books she hawked, or who scorned her views. Her insistence on separation of church and state earned her clerical hatred which caused her in 1829 to be indicted and convicted in Washington as a "common scold." Her two papers, *Paul Pry* (Dec. 3, 1831–Nov. 19, 1836) and *The Huntress* (Dec. 2, 1836–July 24, 1854), included gossip about notables, reformist views of official American policies, and "pen portraits" of contemporaries.

———— ∞ ————

Anne Royall was not the first female editor, nor was she a woman's rights advocate by later definitions. Moreover, her sharp, individual comment and concern for corruption in government were not unique to her; Democrats and Federalists, and later Whigs, upbraided one another for real or imagined mulcting of government. What distinguished her career—one mainly forced upon her by personal need and circumstances—was its emphasis on human rights. In defending herself, she was defending all widows and females oppressed by inequity; sympathy for them and for children and others requiring, for example, institutional aid was one of the features of her writings. Exposure of corrupt officials in government, demands for better sanitary conditions in the District of Columbia, and similar causes were not undertaken for partisan reasons, but independently and with civic ends in view. Although she followed Andrew Jackson in advocating "sound money," and was Jacksonian in her contempt for abolitionists, she deviated from the party line in her sympathy for Native Americans. Freemasonry was a staff of life to her, but devoid of in-group or conspiratorial features. Accordingly, Heber Blankenhorn's *American Mercury* article in September 1927 correctly perceived her as "The Grandma of the Muckrakers." But, in addition, Royall's insatiable curiosity about people (partly motivated by her search for friends and customers) resulted in an incomparable panorama of personal impressions of the great and near-great of her time over a period of some thirty years. Her eccentricities of person and approach drew brutal rejoinders from foes with little compassion for her age and condition, and no appreciation of her courage and resourcefulness. But though they succeeded in attaching the "common scold" label upon her, it no more than memorialized to posterity their own bigotry and malice. See Sarah Harvey Porter, *The Life and Times of Anne Royall* (1909).

LOUIS FILLER

ROYCE, Josiah (b. Grass Valley, Calif., Nov. 20, 1855; d. Cambridge, Mass., Sept. 14, 1916), PHILOSOPHER, studied at the University of California at Berkeley, where he worked under Joseph Le Conte and the poet and essayist Edward

Rowland Sill. After graduation in 1875, he studied at the universities of Leipzig and Göttingen (1875–76), and then entered Johns Hopkins University, where he became one of the first fellows in the doctoral program. His 1878 PhD dissertation was entitled "On the Interdependence of the Principles of Knowledge." He became an instructor of English at Berkeley in 1878. Three years later, he published a *Primer of Logical Analysis for the Use of Composition Students*. In 1882, at the suggestion of **William James,** Royce joined the Harvard faculty as a visiting substitute for James. He was appointed to the regular staff in 1885, and was named Alford professor of natural religion, moral philosophy, and civil polity in 1914. He also lectured at the University of California (1895), the University of Aberdeen (1899), and Johns Hopkins (1906). In 1885 Royce published the first of his major philosophical works, *The Religious Aspect of Philosophy*. This was followed by many other books, including *The Spirit of Modern Philosophy* (1892), *The Conception of God* (1895), *The World and the Individual* (1899, 1901), and *The Problem of Christianity* (2 vols., 1913). In these works, Royce argued that man could learn truths beyond himself because of his participation in a world-mind; that men's highest development could be achieved only through the life of the community; and that the natural order of the world had also to be a moral order. Through his writings, Royce established his position as a major exponent of post-Kantian idealism in America.

Generally mentioned along with **Charles Peirce,** James, **John Dewey,** and **George Santayana** as one of the "classical" American philosophers, Royce of the five has received the least attention. The underlying reason may well be the peculiar role into which Royce seemed to have been cast: a Hegel in America. Like his incomparably greater German counterpart, Royce knew something about everything, loaded his wideranging essays with experiential content, loved dialectical argument, and was obsessed with systematic completeness. Reason was never so cunning, devious, long-winded, and sophisti-

cal as when Royce was demonstrating the existence of the Absolute from the possibility of error (*The Religious Aspect of Philosophy*), or constructing an Idealist *Weltanschauung* from "the internal meaning of ideas" (*The World and the Individual*). Although Royce the Absolutist metaphysician was not without originality and conceptual power—apocrypha has it that William James required ten years to detect the logical fallacy in one of his friend's God-proofs—metaphysics in the grand style was on its way out. And while Hegel's readers quailed before the master's heady obscurities, Royce's students often agreed with Santayana: "There are moments when Royce is nothing but a hollow-chested parson."

For many, the phenomenological, concrete side of Royce (he wrote both a history and a novel of early California) is the most viable and attractive. From the very first a social philosopher, Royce analyzed and advocated the dialectical interpenetration of self-awareness and social consciousness. A tireless offcampus lecturer, he devoted his last years to articulating "the community of interpretation" (an idea inspired by C. S. Peirce). Here, in the practical sphere, Royce's philosophical virtues—tolerance, liberality, breadth and depth of spirit—were given their freest play. See John J. McDermott, ed., *The Basic Writings of Josiah Royce*, (2 vols., 1969).

PETER FUSS

RUFFIN, Edmund (b. Prince George Co., Va., Jan. 5, 1794; d. Amelia Co., Va., June 18, 1865), AGRICULTURIST, PUBLICIST, was self-educated except for a brief term at William and Mary College. After drilling in the militia for six months in the War of 1812, Ruffin returned to the management of the lands, inherited upon his father's death in 1810, at Coggin's Point, on the James River. His studies and experiments in scientific agriculture were eventually rewarded when he began treating his fields with calcareous earth and marl, both rich sources of calcium carbonate (lime). With corn and wheat yields enhanced by 40 percent, Ruffin began publicizing his findings. A paper on "Calcareous Manures" presented to the Prince George County Agricultural Society in 1818 was expanded and printed three years later in John Skinner's *American Farmer,* the leading agricultural journal of the day. This essay grew into Ruffin's influential book-length *Essay on Calcareous Manures* (1832). For the next ten years he edited and largely wrote a highly regarded journal, the *Farmer's Register.* Ruffin also served as official agricultural surveyor of South Carolina (1842) and as president of the Virginia Agricultural Society (1852).

Throughout this period Ruffin was active in southern politics. During 1823–26 he served in the Virginia senate. During the nullification crisis he emerged as an ardent supporter of states' rights, and for the next three decades he was his state's most militant advocate of secession. He contributed extensively to the pro-slavery literature, upholding the moral superiority of slave over free labor in such widely read pamphlets as *The Political Economy of Slavery* (1857). In 1860 he published *Anticipations of the Future,* an imaginative prophecy of political developments which once again urged secession upon his hesitant fellow southerners. As an honorary member of the South Carolina Palmetto Guard, Ruffin achieved wide notice for firing the first shot at Fort Sumter. Four years later, impoverished, despondent over the death of his two best-loved children, and crushed by the defeat of the Confederacy, Ruffin committed suicide, grandiloquently declaring in a note: "I cannot survive my country's liberty."

⸻

Born into place and power, well married, and possessed of a fine intellect, Edmund Ruffin, the agricultural reformer and southern nationalist, had great impact upon his region. Yet the inner life of this intense man was clearly marked by a sense of frustration. A man whose mother died soon after his birth, whose stepmother had six children of her own, whose father died when he was sixteen, and who was burdened with a family and large plantation before he was eighteen—Ruffin was encumbered for his entire life with an unrealizable desire for attention and approval. Suspicious, vain, and dogmatic, at once envious and bitterly disdainful of popular politicians, he only infrequently achieved the satisfaction and personal tranquillity that his real accomplishments should have brought him.

Ruffin was certainly one of the greatest American agriculturists of the 19th century. He was led by a devotion to his region and a humorless determination to seek solutions to the economic decline of the Atlantic tidewater plantations. From the first he demonstrated an unusual faith that the soils of eastern Virginia, depleted by generations of careless exploitation, could be restored through science. For years he tested with little success the practical proposals in **John Taylor**'s *Arator,* an influential compendium of political philosophy and farming techniques. Fortunately, Ruffin came upon Sir Humphrey Davy's *Elements of Agricultural Chemistry* (1813), for it led him directly to his most important contribution. Ruffin was never truly a scientist, but his careful soil testing and theorizing brought him to the conclusion that "worn-out" lands could be restored to fertility through the application of chemical fertilizers. Most especially, lime was needed to neutralize excess soil acidity. It seems fair to say with his biographer that Ruffin is the father of soil chemistry in America. More important to his fellow farmers, his own practical success and influential preaching launched the great agricultural reform movement and the revival of prosperity in the Chesapeake region which took place in the 1840s.

It also appears fair to say that Ruffin never felt it necessary to test the social and political ideas he had imbibed as a receptive Virginia gentleman from Taylor's *Arator.* He seems never to have doubted the superior virtues of southern agrarian society, and the special fitness to rule of the planter class. Yet he had no firsthand knowledge of any society outside the plantation South, and was astounded when the Civil War evoked widespread denunciations of a "rich man's war" by lower-class whites in his own neighborhood. He embraced racist paternalism without question, believing the African-American biologically devoid of self-control and intelligence; his early advocacy of secession was clearly based on race fear—the conviction that abolition, social and political equality, and bloody race war were inevitable in the Union. Yet all his elaborate agricultural experiments, his advanced six-crop rotation system, and his use of the most modern farm equipment were accomplished with skilled black labor. And when the war came he was uncomprehending when many of these men and women, including his most trusted black overseer, escaped to the Union lines. So thoroughly was his mind locked into the worldview of the planter class that when events destroyed that world he chose also to destroy himself. See Avery O. Craven, *Edmund Ruffin, Southerner* (1932).

STEVEN A. CHANNING

RUMFORD, Count. See Thompson, Benjamin.

RUML, Beardsley (b. Cedar Rapids, Iowa, Nov. 5, 1894; d. Danbury, Conn., April 18, 1960), ECONOMIST, BANKER, BUSINESSMAN, graduated from Dartmouth College in 1915 and received his doctorate in education from the University of Chicago in 1917. From 1917 to 1921 he served as a civilian on the War Department's Committee on Classification of Personnel. He was assistant to James R. Angell, president of the Carnegie Corporation (1921–22), and director of the Laura Spelman Rockefeller Memorial Fund (1922–29), in which post he was influential in changing the fund's emphasis from supporting philanthropic organizations to making grants for social science research. Among other projects, he backed the Public Administration Clearing House in Chicago and made grants to promote better race relations. In 1929 he became a trustee of the Spelman Fund of New York. From 1931 to 1933 he was professor of education and Dean of Social Sciences at the University of Chicago. In 1934, shortly after becoming treasurer of R. H. Macy and Co. (chairman, 1945–49; director from 1951), Ruml invented a new system of accounting (the "Q" system) and devised a cash-time plan that made it possible to buy goods without having to lay out the entire purchase price at once, while allowing Macy's to maintain its policy of "6 percent less for cash."

Ruml served on President Hoover's Committee on Unemployment (1930–31) and helped draft the New Deal "domestic allotment" plan for agricultural relief (1933). After 1935, he served on the National Resources Committee (formerly the PWA National Planning Board). In 1937 he became a director of the Federal Reserve Bank of New York (chairman, 1941–46). In 1943 Congress adopted Ruml's "pay-as-you-go" income tax plan (the withholding tax), and in 1944 he attended the Bretton Woods (N.H.) Conference of monetary experts from forty-one nations, which established the International Monetary Fund and the World Bank. He helped found the businessmen's Committee for Economic Development during World War II. He was a trustee of several other policy research groups, such as the National Planning Association and the National Bureau of Economic Research. He was a director of the liberal *Survey Graphic*. In 1952, during **Adlai Stevenson**'s presidential campaign, he was chairman of the Democratic Party Financial Committee (he was a registered Republican but seldom voted with the party).

In his later years Ruml was active in the National Citizens' Commission for the Public Schools and wrote a number of articles about education, such as "Teaching Salaries Then and Now" (1955) and "Memo to a College Trustee" (1960). He worked for support of education and more direct participation of the president, Congress, and the business community in determining educational policy.

———∞∞∞———

Ruml had both a Falstaffian size and a zest for living. He was an exuberant brainstormer who took delight in proposing plans and ideas for others to carry out. Although **Robert Hutchins** called him "the founder of the social sciences in America" for his efforts at turning philanthropic monies into social science research and for the number of his plans that were adopted in that field, Ruml was not a scholar so much as a business intellectual or an idea man. He was an "elastic conservative," a corporate liberal whose central concern was the anticipated post–World War II stresses on American capitalism. He posed a variant of Keynesian fiscal policy (which he did not label as such) as the key to a prosperous system. In 1938 he had helped convince FDR of the need for deliberate deficit spending. And as a mentor to, and a policy planning expert in, such organizations as the Committee for Economic Development and the National Planning Association, he further developed the idea of compensatory fiscal policy. He urged the use of the federal budget—greatly expanded from New Deal days—to maintain purchasing power and corporate prosperity. But he did not meet the issue head-on. His arguments served to compromise differences more apparent than real between the business and the academic worlds. Taxes could be cut, but only during prosperity; the budget could then be balanced, but it would be continued at a high level. Ruml used similar talents in helping to get banker and congressional consent to the International Monetary Fund, which would help reestablish world trade and advance the American position in the world market. Another important compromising role was performed in helping to get the Murray "full employment" bill passed as the Employment Act of 1946. See Herbert Stein, *The Fiscal Revolution in America* (1969).

DAVID EAKINS

RUSH, Benjamin (b. Byberry, Pa., Dec. 24, 1745; d. Philadelphia, Pa., April 19, 1813), PHYSICIAN, POLITICAL LEADER, REFORMER, graduated from the College of New Jersey (now Princeton) in 1760, studied medicine in Philadelphia (1761–66) and at the University of Edinburgh, where he was awarded his MD in 1768. Rush returned to Philadelphia (1769), practicing medicine there and serving as professor of chemistry at the College of Philadelphia, the first post of its kind in America. His *A Syllabus of a Course of Lectures on Chemistry* (1770) was the premier American text on the subject. In 1772 he pub-

lished *Sermons to Gentlemen upon Temperance and Exercise,* his inaugural tract as a reformer, which led the later American temperance movement to claim him as the founder of its crusade. He soon became associated with many other reform movements and, after publishing an antislavery tract in 1773, dedicated to Anthony Benezet, helped organize the Pennsylvania Society for Promoting the Abolition of Slavery (1774).

Rush was a delegate to the second Continental Congress and a signer of the Declaration of Independence (1776). During the Revolutionary War he was named surgeon general of the Middle Department (1777), but resigned when General Washington did not follow his advice in reforming the medical service.

From 1783 until his death Rush was on the staff of the Pennsylvania Hospital, where, among other innovations, he helped establish the first free public dispensary in the United States (1786). As a member of the Pennsylvania ratifying convention, Rush vigorously supported the new federal Constitution. In 1789 he was appointed to the chair of the theory and practice of medicine at the College of Philadelphia and, after 1792, taught at the New University of Pennsylvania. He soon came to believe that all disease was due to one "proximate" cause: excessive excitability or spasm in the blood vessels; and that disease could be cured by relieving tension through purging and bloodletting. His theories, sometimes known as the "American system of medicine," were published in *Medical Inquiries and Observations* (1789). During the Philadelphia yellow fever epidemic of 1793 Rush used his bloodletting therapy extensively—even indiscriminately, it has been charged—and described his experience in *An Account of the Bilious Remitting Yellow Fever* (1794), still a classic in medical literature. In holding that the epidemic was neither imported nor contagious, but caused by poor sanitation, Rush defied lay and medical opinion.

In 1797 President Adams, despite party objections, appointed Rush treasurer of the U.S. Mint in Philadelphia, a post he held until his death. Later, President Jefferson, a fellow member of the American Philosophical Society, appointed Rush a scientific adviser to the **Meriwether Lewis** and William Clark expedition. Some of Rush's other writings include *Essays, Literary, Moral and Philosophical Lectures upon Animal Life* (1799), a contribution to American philosophical literature, and *Medical Inquiries and Observations upon the Diseases of the Mind* (1812), which in its anticipation of psychoanalysis and other modern developments and improvements in the treatment of the mentally ill earned Rush the title "father of American psychiatry."

———

Apart from his lasting contributions to medicine and social reform, Rush merits recognition for his characteristically bold vision of America's destiny. His ideal conception of the American republic, as the world's first truly Christian commonwealth, which intimate friends like Jefferson and Adams respected, was formed out of the materials of his Great Awakening, Enlightenment, and Revolutionary thought and experience. From the first tradition, that of Gilbert Tennent's, Samuel Finley's, and Samuel Davies's New Light Presbyterianism, at West Nottingham Academy and the College of New Jersey, Rush derived, as it were, his 17th-century *Weltanschauung*. Ultimately, to him, Sir Thomas Browne and not John Locke was the more congenial thinker. In his millennialism, which conceived the Great Awakening and later the founding of the American republic as heralding Christ's Second Coming, Rush invites comparison with **Jonathan Edwards**, although it should be pointed out that Rush's republican "theology" of universal salvation (from, principally, Elhanan Winchester) is anti-Edwardian.

At Edinburgh, a center of Lockean epistemology and psychology, where thinkers like William Cullen, Joseph Black, and, indeed, David Hume were abandoning theological for natural explanations, Rush was introduced to Enlightenment science. This he adopted, however, following the English physico-theologian David Hartley rather than Cullen and Black and turned to his own purposes in, especially, *Three Lectures upon Animal Life*.

At Edinburgh, too, Rush first read Algernon Sidney's Whig classic *Discourses Concerning Government* (1698), whose 17th-century Commonwealth principles Rush used to explain and justify colonial resistance to Parliament and, in 1776, independence itself.

Rush's vision of a revolutionary Christian utopia in America, fulfilling biblical prophecy and world history by natural means, is articulated in his voluminous writings. See N. G. Goodman, *Benjamin Rush: Physician and Citizen, 1746–1813* (1934).

Donald J. D'Elia

RUSK, David Dean (b. Cherokee Co., Ga., Feb. 9, 1909; d. Athens, Geo., Dec. 22, 1994), DIPLOMAT, graduated from Davidson College in North Carolina in 1931. He won a Rhodes Scholarship to Oxford, where he received his MA in 1934, and then joined the political science staff of Mills College (Oakland, Calif.), becoming dean of the faculty in 1938. During World War II he served with the infantry in the China-Burma-India theater and eventually became deputy chief of staff to General **Joseph Stilwell**. After his discharge in 1946, he became assistant chief of the Division of International Security Affairs of the State Department, and later that year special assistant to Secretary of War Robert Patterson. Rusk returned to the State Department as director of the Office of Special Political Affairs in 1947; he became director of the Office of United Nations Affairs in 1948. After serving briefly as first assistant secretary of state for U.N. Affairs (1949) and deputy under-secretary of state (1949–50), he was appointed assistant secretary of state for Far Eastern Affairs (1950–51).

In this position Rusk supported resisting Communist aggression in Korea by force, but also recommended the dismissal of General **Douglas MacArthur** when he sought to expand the war into Red China despite the disapproval of President Truman. Rusk also helped negotiate the Japanese Peace Treaty of 1951. He left the State Department to become president of the Rockefeller Foundation in 1952, expanding the foundation's activities in Asia, Africa, and Latin America. President Kennedy appointed him secretary of state in 1960, in which capacity he dealt with many problems in Cuba, Laos, Berlin, and the Congo. After the assassination of Kennedy, Rusk retained his office under President Johnson until 1969. He helped formulate and implement Johnson's Vietnam policy. Although this policy came under increasing criticism from all segments of American society, Rusk held firm to his beliefs and actively defended the Johnson administration. After leaving office and living for a time in semiretirement, he became Sibley Professor of International Law at the University of Georgia. Always opposed to telling all in his memoirs, he published an "as told to" autobiography of sorts with his son, Richard Rusk, in 1990 called *As I Saw It*.

⁂

Despite the fact that he enjoyed the second-longest tenure of any 20th-century secretary of state, Dean Rusk had remarkably little impact on American foreign policy in the crucial decade of the 1960s. He brought excellent credentials to the post—Rhodes scholar and professor of international relations, high State Department official in the early years of the cold war, nearly a decade as head of the Rockefeller Foundation, with its worldwide activities in science and medicine. Yet lacking a political base of his own, he began his duties with a sense of personal insecurity, fostered by the presence of such Kennedy-appointed subordinates as **Averell Harriman, Adlai Stevenson,** and Chester Bowles, who all had the national prominence and glamour he so conspicuously lacked. By nature a reserved and unassuming man, Rusk stayed quietly in the background, refusing to play the role of advocate in shaping administration policy. His qualities of intelligence, lucid analysis, and judiciousness made him a wise counselor to President Kennedy, but his refusal to assert himself on vital issues, such as the Bay of Pigs and the Cuban missile crisis, weakened the influence of the State Department and left a vacuum which was filled by the Pentagon and members of the White House staff. Rusk's most outstanding trait proved to be his endurance—he outlasted all his

rivals for power within the State Department, and after Johnson became president, Rusk, no doubt aided by rumors that Kennedy had planned to dump him, quickly emerged as one of LBJ's most trusted associates.

Inevitably, Rusk's career as secretary of state became intertwined with the war in Vietnam, and during Johnson's presidency the secretary won prominence as the foremost defender of this controversial policy. Rusk's hawkish views stemmed in part from his penchant for the military. From his high school days in the ROTC through his army service in the China-Burma-India theater under General Stilwell, Rusk formed a keen respect for the military point of view, and his great idol in public life was General **George Marshall.** Equally important, Rusk participated actively in framing the policy of containment after World War II when Marshall brought him from the Pentagon into the State Department. He served with such ardent cold warriors as Robert Lovett and **Dean Acheson,** who both recommended him strongly to Kennedy. Above all, he developed a phobia toward Communist China as a result of his wartime experience and his role in directing American diplomacy as assistant secretary of state for the Far East during the Korean War. In 1951, he delivered a key speech hardening the temporary policy of nonrecognition of the Peking regime into a fixed position, proclaiming that Chiang Kaishek's Nationalists on Formosa represented the only "authentic" Chinese government. Sixteen years later, as secretary of state he asserted that the United States was fighting in Vietnam not only to uphold treaty commitments and the principle of self-determination, but above all to protect Southeast Asia from the future threat of "a billion Chinese on the mainland, armed with nuclear weapons." It was thus appropriate that Rusk spent his last years in office cast in the role of besieged defender, spending long hours before hostile Senate committees attempting to justify a war the nation had come to regret. Johnson appreciated his faithful service, but there is little evidence that the president heeded his advice. As secretary of state, Rusk remained what he had always been, the loyal number two man, the perfect chief of staff, master of detail but utterly lacking in imagination, creativity, or qualities of leadership. Bland and inscrutable behind his round, Buddha-like countenance, Rusk stands as one of the last of the cold warriors, his back turned firmly against the future in a decade that cried out desperately for change in policy. See Warren I. Cohen, *Dean Rusk* (1980).

ROBERT A. DIVINE

RUSSELL, Richard Brevard, Jr. (b. Winder, Ga., Nov. 2, 1897; d. Washington, D.C., Jan. 21, 1971), POLITICAL LEADER, graduated from the Agricultural and Mechanical School at Powder Springs, Georgia (1914), and from the Gordon Institute, Barnesville, Georgia (1915). He received a law degree from the University of Georgia in 1918. After serving a year in the U.S. naval reserve, he opened a law practice in Winder in 1919. A Democrat, he was elected attorney of Barrow County in 1920. Elected to the Georgia house of representatives the following year, he served until 1931 and was speaker from 1927 to 1931, when he became governor of Georgia. As governor, Russell consolidated the state university system and reduced the state debt by cutting spending. Elected in 1932 to fill the unexpired term of U.S. Senator William J. Harris, he was easily reelected to a full term in 1936 and served until his death.

Russell supported such New Deal domestic programs as the National Recovery Act and the Tennessee Valley Authority, but led filibusters against the antilynching laws of 1935 and 1937. As chairman of the Senate Immigration Committee (1945–46) he favored restrictive immigration laws. Although opposing much of President Truman's Fair Deal program, Russell backed Truman for the presidency in 1948 when many southern Democrats bolted the party for the "Dixiecrat" candidate, J. Strom Thurmond of South Carolina. Long a leading member of the "inner circle" of the Senate, Russell became chairman of the Armed Services Committee in 1951. He supported the Korean intervention and won plaudits for his handling of the congressional

investigation of General **Douglas MacArthur's** dismissal as Korean military commander.

Russell sought the 1952 Democratic presidential nomination but lost out to **Adlai Stevenson.** As chairman of the Armed Services Committee, Russell presided over the huge increase of the military establishment during the 1950s and 1960s. He urged President Kennedy to invade Cuba during the 1962 missile crisis and supported President Johnson's intervention into the Dominican Republic in 1965. Although he was initially opposed to American involvement in Southeast Asia, he backed the military effort to the utmost once the commitment was made. A foe of racial integration in any form (he thought integration subversive to the "southern way of life"), Russell led southern senators in filibusters against civil rights legislation. He served on the Warren Commission investigating the assassination of President Kennedy. In 1969 he became chairman of the Senate Appropriations Committee. At his death he was president pro tempore of the Senate.

⸙

Richard B. Russell served in the U.S. Senate for thirty-eight years, and journalists increasingly—and probably accurately—referred to him as the most powerful individual in the Senate. A man of talent and integrity, Russell combined seniority with a profound understanding of congressional functions. Although a leader of senatorial conservatives generally, he was perhaps best known as the leader of the southern delegation in its battle against civil rights legislation. For two decades, Russell marshaled the Dixie bloc in opposition to federal intervention in racial matters. He rested his opposition to minority rights on states' rights and constitutional grounds; however, in matters pertaining to national defense and loyalty-security, Russell favored concentrating authority in the national government at the expense of states' rights and constitutional liberties.

Both by ideology and by instinct, Russell was a conservative. "When I am in doubt about a question," he stated, "I always vote no." He was an advocate of "the spiritual life and simple faith and fullness which sustained our forefathers"; he resisted "new adventures that could lead this country down the road to socialism."

Looking back over his long political career near the end of his life, Russell felt that his support of a strong United States military posture was his major legislative accomplishment. Future historians may well remember him as one of the effective defenders of southern racial practices. In this sense, Russell epitomized the tragedy of southern politics. Much of his formidable ability and energy were channeled into support of white supremacy. See "Richard B. Russell: Champion of a Strong Military," *Congressional Quarterly Weekly Report,* XXIX (Jan. 22, 1971), 195–98.

N. V. BARTLEY

RUSTIN, Bayard (b. West Chester, Pa., March 17, 1910; d. New York, N.Y., Aug. 24, 1987), REFORMER, studied at Wilberforce College, Ohio (1930–31), Cheney State Teachers College, Pennsylvania (1931–33), and the College of the City of New York (1933–35). At CCNY he sang with Josh White and Leadbelly in order to support himself. He joined the Young Communist League in 1938, but left the party in 1941 and became a member of the Fellowship of Reconciliation, an organization of religious pacifists, serving as race relations director (1941–53). In 1941 he became the first field secretary of FOR's offshoot, the Congress of Racial Equality. In that year he also helped **A. Philip Randolph** organize the March on Washington movement to demand better job opportunities for blacks. During World War II he served a prison term (1943–45) as a conscientious objector.

After his release from prison Rustin joined the Free India Committee and later went to India to study nonviolent protest. In 1947 he participated in the first FOR- and CORE-sponsored "Freedom Ride" to challenge the South's Jim Crow laws on public transportation. Arrested in North Carolina and put on a chain gang, Rustin wrote an exposé of his experiences that helped prod the state to reform its prison system. In 1953 Rustin resigned his post with FOR to become executive secretary

of the War Resisters League, a position he held until 1955. An avowed pacifist, he was jailed in France for protesting A-bomb testing in the Sahara, and he took a leading role in mobilizing the Campaign for Nuclear Disarmament's 1959 ban-the-bomb march from Aldermaston to London, England.

His principal concern, however, was civil rights. Rustin helped **Martin Luther King, Jr.,** organize the Montgomery bus boycott in 1955, and for the next five years served as King's special assistant. At King's request he drafted the plan for what became the Southern Christian Leadership Conference in 1957. He organized civil rights demonstrations at the 1960 Democratic and Republican national conventions. Rustin gained national prominence in his own right as chief organizer of the March on Washington for Jobs and Freedom in 1963. A year later he directed the school boycott in New York City. Following King's assassination (April 1968), Rustin organized the march planned by King in behalf of striking sanitation workers. Earlier that year he had helped King chart the strategy for the Poor People's Campaign, but factionalism within SCLC following King's death caused him to resign as national coordinator of the June 19 Poor People's Mobilization in Washington. In 1966 Rustin became executive director and cochairman, with Leon Lynch, of the A. Philip Randolph Institute in New York, an organization working for economic and social reform as a means of promoting racial equality and peace. In the 1970s and 1980s, Rustin continued to press for social and political change on a variety of fronts. He was chairman of the Democratic Socialists U.S.A., a descendant of the Socialist Party of **Eugene V. Debs** and **Norman Thomas**; he was chairman of the executive committee of the Leadership Conference on Civil Rights, and he was the first African-American on the board of trustees of Notre Dame. Shortly before his death, Rustin "came out" and talked openly in an interview about his homosexuality. He believed that prejudice against gays was behind his arrest and subsequent sixty day sentence in 1953 in Pasadena, Calif. on a morals charge. This incident and knowledge he was gay, he asserted, affected his civil rights work and career. "There was considerable prejudice amongst a number of people I worked with," he said, although, he added, they would not admit it.

———— ∞∞∞ ————

From Montgomery to the 1964 Civil Rights Act, Rustin was the chief tactician of the civil rights movement. At first a strategist of nonviolent protest to gain civil rights, he became an advocate of coalition politics as the path to socioeconomic reform. He perceived the problems of blacks as fundamentally economic rather than racial. Civil rights laws were a necessary though intermediate stage in the movement; they failed to improve "the day-to-day lot of the ghetto Negro." To gain better jobs, wages, housing, education, and health services, blacks had to join hands with likeminded white allies—liberals, labor, religious groups, and political leaders—to make the Democratic party an effective instrument of reform. While seeking radical objectives—a fundamental restructuring of the American economy, with a massive war on poverty, unemployment, and slums—Rustin advocated moderate means: nonviolence, legislation, political action.

An elegant, urbane, imposing figure with a trace of a British accent, Rustin was at once the practical organizer and the articulate intellectual of the movement. In the early 1960s he bridged the gap between white labor leaders and young black militants. But his advocacy of coalition politics set him at odds with the exponents of Black Power after 1965. He argued that it was futile for blacks to go it alone; "the racial crisis," he once said, "is not an isolated problem that lends itself to redress by a protesting minority." Alone, blacks lacked the political power to implement their objectives. Black separatism, he pointed out, had always been "indistinguishable from inequality, exploitation, and poverty." At best black capitalism and cultural nationalism were peripheral to black needs; at worst they played into the hands of racial conservatives and perpetuated black inequality. See

Down the Line: The Collected Writings of Bayard Rustin (1971).

NANCY WEISS

RUTH, George Herman (b. Baltimore, Md., Feb. 6, 1895; d. New York, N.Y., Aug. 16, 1948), ATHLETE, received most of his schooling at the Catholic St. Mary's Industrial School in Baltimore. He signed with the minor-league Baltimore Orioles in 1914 (where he acquired the nickname "Babe") as a left-handed pitcher. Baltimore sold his contract almost immediately to the Boston Red Sox. After he spent a year in the minors, the Red Sox brought him up in 1915. He pitched World Series victories over the Brooklyn Dodgers in 1916 and the Chicago Cubs in 1918, setting a record of twenty-nine consecutive scoreless innings in World Series competition, including a fourteen-inning game, against the Cubs. Ruth also had a reputation as a powerful left-handed batter. In 1919 he broke all previous major-league records for home runs in a season. In 1920 the New York Yankees bought him from the Red Sox for about $125,000 plus a $300,000 loan to the Boston owner and stationed him in right field. As an outfielder, he was the American League's Most Valuable Player in 1923 and continued to lead the league in home runs 1919–24 and 1926–31. In 1927 Ruth hit a record sixty home runs during the season. Becoming a tremendous box office attraction, he commanded a salary which rose to $80,000 in 1930. Flamboyant in style, Ruth once during the Depression remarked about his salary when told he was paid more than the president of the United States, "I had a better season than he did."

Ruth, who played in seven World Series as a Yankee, was released in 1935 and signed with the Boston Braves of the National League. Serving as a vice president, assistant manager, and part-time player, he stayed with the Braves for one season. On May 25, 1935, in Pittsburgh, his last game, he hit three consecutive home runs. He spent the 1938 season as a coach for the Brooklyn Dodgers.

In 1936 Ruth was one of the first five players elected to Baseball's Hall of Fame at Cooperstown, New York. His career total of home runs numbered 714, and his lifetime batting average was .342. Declining health limited Ruth's activities after his retirement. He broadcast some New York radio shows (1943–44) and played himself in the movie *Pride of the Yankees* (1942), the story of teammate Lou Gehrig. He established the Babe Ruth Foundation in 1927 to aid underprivileged children.

Babe Ruth's impact on American professional baseball stands unsurpassed by any player. He was its greatest gate attraction and, in terms of purchasing power, its highest-paid player ever. His unprecedented ability to hit home runs and the flair and drama with which he hit them impelled droves of people to come out to watch him wherever he played, whether in major-league cities or in crossroads towns. He became a national figure who, in a twenty-year major-league career, earned about a million dollars in salaries and World Series shares, and as much more from other sources such as endorsements and personal appearances. His matchless gate appeal revived interest in baseball after the dark days of the Black Sox World Series scandal. He created new fans, widened awareness of baseball at home and abroad, raised the general level of player salaries, and made feasible the construction in 1923 of Yankee Stadium, then the largest ballpark and the last one built solely with private capital.

Ruth's batting power was the catalyst for revolutionary change in the style of playing professional baseball. Before he startled the baseball world in 1919, breaking the 1884 home run record of twenty-seven by driving out twenty-nine, baseball was a game of low-score pitching duels and rare home runs. Teams played for one run at a time, a strategy that emphasized the bunt, stolen base, and hit-and-run play. Batters used a short grip—"choked up"—on the bat, striving only to meet the ball and drive it safely past the fielders. Ruth altered all this. In his first season with the New York Yankees (1920) their home attendance alone doubled that of the previous year as Ruth hit a phenomenal fifty-four homers. Baseball club owners responded quickly to the upsurge in gate

receipts engendered by Ruth's long, towering drives. They quietly introduced a livelier ball. Batters began to swing from the end of the bat handle, à la Ruth, and aim for the fences. Teams increasingly abandoned traditional strategy in favor of scoring runs in clusters by means of long hits. Eventually home runs became commonplace, although no one ever equaled Ruth in frequency of production—one for every 11.7 times at bat.

Ruth was an unmistakable figure on the field, standing above six feet and weighing a trim 195 pounds before gluttony expanded his waistline. He had a large head, thick black hair, prominent flat nose, and powerful shoulders, biceps, and wrists, and he walked pigeontoed on slender, ballerinalike legs. At bat he moved a heavy (52-ounce) bat slowly and easily back and forth while awaiting the pitch, and then put his whole body into a quick, rhythmic swing that described a slightly upward arc, the better to lift the ball over the fence.

As a person Ruth was warm, extroverted, uninhibited, and undisciplined. More than once his behavior on the field and his escapades off it brought reprimands, fines, and suspensions from baseball authorities. He was a coarse, hard-drinking, hard-swearing roisterer given to carousing and wenching. Neglectful parents (he was not an orphan, as often claimed) and a squalid childhood doubtless contributed to his unbridled appetites and conduct after his success. Yet the very foibles and flaws in Ruth's character may have contributed to the idolization bestowed on him by adults and youngsters as upon no baseball hero before or since. See Robert W. Creamer, *Babe: The Legend Comes to Life* (1974).

HAROLD SEYMOUR

RYAN, John Augustine (b. Dakota Co., Minn., May 25, 1869; d. St. Paul, Minn., Sept. 16, 1945), RELIGIOUS LEADER, REFORMER, studied at a seminary in St. Paul, Minnesota. Ordained a Roman Catholic priest in 1898, he attended graduate school at the Catholic University of America in Washington (1898–1902). He became professor of moral theology at St. Paul Seminary in 1902, where he was influential in including courses in sociology and economics in the training of priests. Influenced by the social reform ideas of Leo XIII, John A. Hobson, and **Richard T. Ely,** Ryan's STD dissertation, *A Living Wage* (1906), set a theological framework justifying a minimum wage for all workers. The book placed Ryan among the foremost spokesmen in the movement for a minimum wage. In 1909 Ryan designed a comprehensive plan for social reform legislation as an alternative to socialism; it included an eight-hour day, unemployment insurance, taxation of incomes and inheritance, and governmental regulation of monopolies and utilities—ideas that became part of the Progressive party platform in 1912. In 1916 he published an extended justification for this program, *Distributive Justice.*

Ryan was named associate professor of political science at Catholic University in 1915. He switched to the School of Sacred Studies in 1916 and, the following year, became a full professor of theology, a post he retained until his retirement in 1939. He also taught at Trinity College and at the National Catholic School of Social Science. One of the leading social reformers in the Catholic Church, he wrote the "Bishops' Program" for postwar social reconstruction in 1919 and, the following year, became director of the social action department of the newly formed National Catholic Welfare Conference, a post he held until his death. Ryan worked closely with his counterparts in the Federal Council of Churches and the Central Council of American Rabbis and with such secular groups as the American Civil Liberties Union and the Consumers' League to promote social reforms. His suggestion in *The State and the Church* (1922) that the Catholic view on the relations between church and state was at variance with the First Amendment became a hotly debated issue in the election of 1928.

Ryan was an intense partisan of the New Deal. For ten months, 1934–35, he served on the Industrial Appeals Board of the National Recovery Administration. By then a monsignor (1933), he defended Roosevelt against the attacks of Father **Charles E. Coughlin,** and he supported the administration's position on America's entry into and conduct of World War II. His autobiography, *Social Doctrine in Action,* appeared in 1941.

⚬⚬⚬

Monsignor Ryan bridged the gap between Catholic social thought and American reformist traditions. In the early 20th century, Catholic opinion opposed an active state; laws proposing social change loomed as steps toward a godless society. Ryan, reared on the Populism of **Ignatius Donnelly,** inspired by the immense tolerance for public action in Pope Leo's *Rerum novarum* (1891), tutored by Hobson and Ely, acclimated traditional Catholic teaching to the Progressives' view of the state as an instrument of the common good. In a way he was cautious and conservative. He habitually wrote in the idiom of moral theology. He constantly invoked the authority of papal encyclicals. He never soft-pedaled unpopular teachings—those on birth control and on the separation of church and state, for example—even when they excited a furor of reaction. He avoided confrontation with conservative prelates. But, though his language was theological, his agenda came from the Progressive tradition that led into the New Deal. A gruff farm boy, blunt, witty, argumentative, he trained a generation of young priests and social workers to judge the morality of industrial society, and he campaigned indefatigably among Catholics—through lectures, conferences, articles, and books—for social justice in America. The achievements of the New Deal were his triumphs too; the Fair Labor Standards Act (1938) put into law the principle of the "living wage" to which he had devoted thirty years. Honored by both Rome and Washington, he accepted recognition with a not too modest sense that he had changed the mind of the church and possibly even the thrust of the nation. See Francis L. Broderick, *Right Reverend New Dealer* (1963).

FRANCIS L. BRODERICK

RYDER, Albert Pinkham (b. New Bedford, Mass., March 19, 1847; d. Elmhurst, N.Y., March 28, 1917), PAINTER, after moving to New York City in 1868, studied under the painter and engraver William E. Marshall and, beginning in 1871, at the National Academy of Design. Establishing himself in a cluttered studio on 15th Street, he lived the life of a recluse, largely indifferent to the work of other painters as well as to his surroundings. He painted slowly, covering the canvas with layer upon layer of pigment and glaze, thus producing both the luminous quality and the tendency to crack that are characteristic of his work. Despite his lack of interest in worldly affairs, Ryder exhibited regularly and sold a fair proportion of his limited output. His talent was recognized by both conservatives and modernists in the art world; in 1906 he was elected a member of the National Academy, and in 1913 his *Pegasus* was exhibited in the modernist-oriented Armory Show. The year after his death he was honored with a retrospective exhibition at the Metropolitan Museum of Art, New York. Among his most representative canvases, in addition to his characteristic small seascapes (e.g., Museum of Modern Art, New York), are *Macbeth and the Witches* (Phillips Gallery, Washington, D.C.), *Death on a Pale Horse* (Cleveland Museum of Art), and *Jonah and the Whale* (National Gallery, Washington, D.C.).

In his life and in his work Ryder typified the solitary romantic—brooding, eccentric, otherworldly, mystical. Yet he was realistically toughminded, modest, and disciplined as well. His paintings are notable as much for their precision of design and their massive sense of structure as for their poetic visions of nature and the human soul, their ghostly evocations of man's loneliness in the face of the incomprehensibility of the vast universe. To the superficial observer he seemed either a naïf or a neurotic misanthrope, but he was indifferent to material things rather than naïve, eccentric rather than neurotic; in short, simply a man utterly dedicated to his profession. He lived surrounded by filth and litter because he was unconcerned with the routine of life. To him, the beauty of the city rooftops outside his studio window made what was inside totally unimportant. "The artist," he said, "needs but a roof, a crust of bread and his easel, and all the rest God gives in abundance." This attitude made him ignore certain obvious painterly techniques, which explains why his works have deteriorated so rapidly and lost much of the luminous quality his contemporaries admired. "I am trying to find something out there beyond the place on which I have a footing," he once said. This commitment to experimentation, combined with his imagination, his devotion to an ideal, and his innate sense of form made him both great and unique, and a forerunner of 20th-century expressionism. More even than most fine painters, his work is a projection of his particular personality—undefinable yet unmistakably convincing. See Frederick N. Price, *Ryder* (1932).

JOHN A. GARRATY

SAINT-GAUDENS, Augustus (b. Dublin, Ire., March 1, 1848; d. Cornish, N.H., Aug. 3, 1907), SCULPTOR, was brought to New York City as an infant. Apprenticed to a cameo cutter in 1861, he studied art at night at Cooper Union (1864–65), and at the National Academy of Design (1865–66). In 1867 he went to Paris and was admitted to the Ecole des Beaux-Arts the following year. He lived in Rome from 1870 to 1875, and was greatly influenced by the neoclassical mode. After copying famous statues, Saint-Gaudens received a commission to reproduce in marble his first original work, *Hiawatha*, which he had begun modeling in 1870. He returned briefly to New York during the winter of 1872–73 to finish a statue of Senator William Evarts.

In 1876 Saint-Gaudens settled in New York,

where he was to maintain a studio for more than twenty years. He skillfully practiced European neoclassical style but chose American subjects and characterizations. *Admiral Farragut* (1881, Madison Square, N.Y.) and his standing statue of *Lincoln* (1887, Lincoln Park, Chicago) are examples of his work. Saint-Gaudens's memorial to Mrs. Henry Adams, often called *Grief* (1891, Rock Creek Cemetery, Washington, D.C.), is regarded by many as his most important accomplishment. He gave up his New York studio in 1897 and spent the next three years in Europe. He won the Grand Prize of the 1900 Paris Exposition, then returned to the U.S. and settled at his summer home in Cornish, New Hampshire. Despite failing health he continued to sculpt, gaining the special award of the Buffalo Pan American Exposition of 1901. He also designed United States coins, including the $20 gold piece of 1907. Some of his many other statues are: *Amor Caritas* (1887, Luxembourg National Museum, Paris), *Diana* (1891, Philadelphia Museum of Art), and the seated *Lincoln* (1907, Grant Park, Chicago).

A highly personal and characteristically American balance of real and ideal elements distinguishes the sculpture of Augustus Saint-Gaudens. His devotion to naturalism was, perhaps, rooted in his practical training as a craftsman and reinforced by his early studies from the nude at leading art schools in New York and Paris. It was certainly confirmed by his examination of the lively and vigorous works of 15th-century Italian sculptors. Saint-Gaudens consistently tempered this naturalism by a search for expression of the spirit of his subjects. His portraits—and he was essentially a portraitist—are based on faithful study of his models, whether they were common foot soldiers or noted politicians. With a spontaneity and a refinement in modeling, and a superb sense of design, Saint-Gaudens subordinated details of contemporary costume and individual physiognomy to an expression of personality. Even more remarkably, he subordinated personality to the ideal conception, to the immanent spirit of that personality. This potent blend of the real and the ideal yielded a new type of sculptural imagery, a new energy in representations of American heroes. In his *Farragut,* his *Lincoln,* and his *Sherman,* realism is a means to an end, that end being the expression of the confidence and force which guide great men. Even more compelling to modern eyes is his embodiment of an abstract theme, contemplation and acceptance of fate, in his enigmatic *Adams Memorial.* Far more powerful than the dry allegories produced by many of his contemporaries, such a work offers premonitions of 20th-century sculpture in which the abstract concept is the primary vehicle of intellectual and emotional appeal. See Homer Saint-Gaudens, ed., *The Reminiscences of Augustus Saint-Gaudens* (2 vols., 1913).

HELENE BARBARA WEINBERG

SALINGER, Jerome David (b. New York, N.Y., Jan. 1, 1919), WRITER, attended Ursinus College (1938–39) before enrolling in Whit Burnett's short-story class at Columbia University. Burnett published Salinger's first story, "The Young Folks," in his *Story* magazine in 1940, and in 1941 the *New Yorker* bought "Slight Rebellion off Madison," Salinger's first Holden Caulfield story. It was not published, however, until 1946. Salinger entered the U.S. army in 1942, serving until 1945. During these years he attended the Army Signal Corps School, was stationed in Nashville, Tennessee, and received counterintelligence training in Tiverton, England.

During the war Salinger wrote "The Varioni Brothers," which was published in the *Saturday Evening Post* (1943), and "I'm Crazy," which appeared in *Collier's* (1945). From 1945 to 1951 numerous other stories followed, and in 1950 Samuel Goldwyn released a film version of Salinger's "Uncle Wiggily in Connecticut" entitled *My Foolish Heart.* A year later Salinger published *The Catcher in the Rye.* An immediate critical and financial success, it transformed Salinger into American youth's favorite novelist. The book described the story of a sensitive, idealistic boy of sixteen who runs away from a boarding school, and his longing for acceptance into the adult world he hates. *Nine Stories* (1953), also acclaimed by the critics, added to Salinger's reputation. He published *Franny and Zooey* (1961) and *Raise High the Roof Beam, Carpenters, and Seymour: An Introduction* (1963), both dealing with the Glass family of New York. Since 1953 Salinger has lived quietly in Cornish, New Hampshire.

~~~

The line of J. D. Salinger's reputation describes a parabola. For a decade prior to the publication of *The Catcher in the Rye*, his stories appeared in numerous magazines, but his fame, and his chance for a permanent place in American literature, came with that first novel. His subsequent work has been a disappointment. Reevaluations have begun.

Salinger's one great theme is the trauma of the sensitive individual trapped in the middle-class culture of the modern world. Holden Caulfield, adolescent hero of *The Catcher in the Rye*, flees from the "phony bastards" around him, hypocrites who invoke the highest ideals while pursuing the most sordid goals. He rebels against discipline in the name of spontaneity and against society in the name of nature. He dreams that he is the "catcher" of children about to tumble from a cliff, but his dream of saving power merely underlines the fragility of his own psyche. Like Huck Finn, with whom he has marked affinities, he speaks an affecting vernacular language. The cadence of his speech influenced an entire generation's tone of voice.

In "A Perfect Day for Bananafish" (1948), Salinger introduced the Glass family. The story tells of Seymour Glass's suicide. The novellas published in 1961 and 1963 trace moments in the lives of Seymour's siblings as they carry on the struggle against the "phony" in others and in themselves. Ironically, Franny's condemnation of "ego, ego, ego" and Zooey's scorn of the "hairshirty private life of a martyr" are implicit critiques of Salinger's one obsessive theme. Despite the precision of the descriptions and the wit of the dialogue, the episodes seem pointless and repetitive. Salinger had an enormous appeal to several generations of youthful Americans, but

Norman Mailer's harsh judgment, that he is "the greatest mind ever to stay in prep school," cannot be easily dismissed. See Warren French, *J. D. Salinger* (1963).

ALLEN GUTTMANN

SALK, Jonas (b. Oct. 28, 1914, New York, N.Y.; d. June 23, 1995, San Diego, Calif.), SCIENTIST, grew up in the Bronx in a relatively poor family. His father worked in the garment district. An excellent student, Salk attended Townsend Harris High School, a public school for the exceptionally talented. He graduated City College of New York in 1934 and entered New York University Medical School. Following his freshman year, he took a one-year research fellowship to study chemistry. Returning to medical school, he was a research fellow in a virus laboratory, where he first became acquainted with the specialty that would shape his life. In 1939, he earned his medical degree from NYU. That same year he married his first wife and three years later, in 1942, he received a National Research Council Fellowship to study the influenza virus with Dr. Thomas Francis, Jr., an internationally recognized virologist, at the University of Michigan. Together they helped develop commercial vaccines against the flu, a breakthrough that many, remembering the devastation wrought by the great flu pandemic of 1918, considered an important contribution to the war effort. Salk moved to the University of Pittsburgh School of Medicine in 1947 as Associate Professor of Bacteriology. He soon became director of virus research and gradually moved from the study of the influenza virus to focus his attention on the critical need to develop a polio vaccine. Efforts to develop one during the war had failed, causing many to believe the effort was doomed. But polio was on the rise during the postwar period and some means of coping with it was urgently needed. Salk's research produced a promising, if controversial, vaccine, and in 1952 a team began to conduct field tests. Further tests proved successful and, in 1955, his vaccine was released for use in the United States.

Salk continued to do research at the University of Pittsburgh but demands on his time were extraordinary. He had become a national and international scientific hero. For over a decade he had dreamed of establishing a research center where scientists and brilliant minds in other fields could gather and exchange ideas, do uninterrupted research, and work in concert towards goals for the improvement of humanity. In 1963, with the financial support of the March of Dimes, the charity that had contributed so much to Salk's and others' efforts to conquer polio, Salk fulfilled his dream by founding his own research institute in San Diego, California. First called the Institute for Biological Sciences, it was renamed the Salk Institute. There Salk continued doing research, particularly on AIDS, until his death.

⸎

A man of tremendous energy, described by his peers as a scientist of complete devotion and total focus on the task at hand, Salk became during his lifetime an almost mythical representative of the ability of pure science to save thousands of lives. Name a medical researcher? Most people—especially if they were alive in the 1950s—would name Jonas Salk.

It takes nothing away from his accomplishment to say that his burst into public view could hardly have been set up better by a Hollywood scriptwriter. In the early 1950s the world was beset by a particularly ugly and cruel disease. Poliomyelitis, polio for short, was also known as infantile paralysis because it attacked mostly small children. A death-dealing disease would have been bad enough, but this modern-day plague not only killed but often left its victims not dead but cruelly paralyzed, totally dependent for life's breath on a ghastly contraption, the iron lung. The public was horrified by photographs of polio's victims, trapped in a big metal machine with only their heads protruding. Parents were terrified to let their children play with friends, or even to send them to school. In 1952 alone the polio virus struck more than 50,000 in the United States, killing 3,300.

It had been established by Salk and others that there were three distinct strains of the polio virus. Salk discovered that viruses of each strain that had been killed through a process involving formaldehyde could not produce the disease but could produce antibody formation in monkeys.

The first field tests on human subjects in 1952 and again, on a much larger scale, in 1954, proved successful. No introduction of any medical breakthrough ever received the kind of publicity as the Salk vaccine. The nation breathed a collective sigh of relief and Salk became a hero. An opinion poll at the time ranked him as one of the most revered figures in modern history, just between Winston Churchill and Mahatma Gandhi.

Shortly after the polio vaccine was introduced to the public, yet more drama was created by a medical error of huge and fatal proportions. One of the labs producing the vaccine released a batch to be used for innoculation. In this batch the viruses had not been completely inactivated and 80 children became ill, passing the virus on to approximately 120 more victims. In the midst of all the relief and celebrations three-quarters of these children became paralyzed and died.

In 1957, another researcher, Albert Sabin, developed an oral polio vaccine based on a live virus that promised lifetime immunity, while the original Salk vaccine required people to take booster shots periodically. Introduced first on a large scale in the Soviet Union, it was brought to the United States in 1960. Many scientists believed it was superior to the Salk vaccine and it began to be widely employed throughout the world. To this day a debate over the relative merits of the Salk and Sabin vaccine continues. Sabin himself said of Salk's work, "It was pure kitchen science. Salk didn't discover anything." That, of course, was too harsh, and while Sabin's contribution with a live virus was perhaps the more advanced scientific technique, Salk's efforts were truly groundbreaking.

Some scientists, after an accomplishment like the conquest of polio, would have rested on their oars. Not Salk. He developed a flu vaccine that produces immunity for two years which also went into wide use. Working with Alexandra Levine of the University of Southern California and others, he went on to tackle the challenge of AIDS, trying to create a vaccine and also studying ways to stimulate the immune system of those already suffering from the disease. Shortly before his death the March of Dimes and the University of Michigan, where the announcement of the polio vaccine was made in 1955, honored Jonas Salk. When asked about his work on an AIDS vaccine, Salk said, "I am a perennial optimist. We certainly have the knowledge. The question is whether we have the wisdom." See Jonas Salk, *Man Unfolding* (1972); Richard Carter, *Breakthrough: The Saga of Jonas Salk* (1966).

ROY SORRELS

SAMUELSON, Paul Anthony (b. Gary, Ind., May 15, 1915), ECONOMIST, received a BA from the University of Chicago (1935) and MA (1936) and PhD (1941) in economics from Harvard. He was appointed assistant professor of economics at the Massachusetts Institute of Technology (1940), associate professor (1944), Paul Reid professor of economics (1947), and institute professor (1966). He retired from MIT in 1985. In addition, he served as consultant to or member of the National Resources Planning Board (1941–43), the War Production Board (1945), the U.S. Treasury (1945–52), the Rand Corporation (since 1949), the Bureau of the Budget (1952), the President's Commission on National Goals (1959–60), and the National Task Force on Economic Education (1960–61). He was also an adviser to Presidents John F. Kennedy and Lyndon B. Johnson, in which capacity he helped develop the tax legislation and antipoverty programs of their administrations.

Samuelson is known professionally for his clarification of economic analysis by use of mathematical concepts, and for his application of Keynesian theories to current American problems. His PhD dissertation, published in 1947 as *Foundations of Economic Analysis,* was instrumental in laying the mathematical basis for much of modern economic analysis. As a Keynesian, Samuelson argued that government spending is a device to overcome fluctuations between periods of prosperity and depression. Having accumulated budget surpluses during times of prosperity, the government should spend more than its revenue during depressions to finance public works and relief measures to promote full employment. Outside professional circles Samuelson is best known for his textbook *Economics: An Introductory Analysis* (11th ed., 1980), which has familiarized hundreds of thousands of college students in the United States and overseas with Keynesian theory and mathematical analysis. Although the first edition of Samuelson's text (1948) was banned in some parts of the U.S. because of alleged radicalism, his ideas are now firmly established among economists. Samuelson's other publications include numerous coauthored works and *Linear Programming and Economic Analysis* (1958). In 1970 he was awarded the Nobel Prize in economics.

❧

Both those who, since the end of World War II, have learned about economics for the first time and those who, over the same period, have gone on to become professional economists have felt the strong influence of Paul Samuelson—the former through his popular and widely imitated introductory textbook and the latter through his reformulation of most of economic theory in mathematical language. Indeed, the virtues and failings of contemporary economics in the United States are broadly reflected in Samuelson himself.

The first edition of Samuelson's introductory textbook, *Economics,* broke new ground in 1948 by presenting the essence of Keynes's still-novel theories in a manner understandable to beginning students in economics. This blending of the then somewhat radical ideas on how unemployment can be cured with the older tradition in economics that emphasized how prices and various income shares are determined represented a practical synthesis of the old and the new which other textbooks attempted to follow in a vain effort to match the popularity of *Economics.* The MIT professor's impact on the lay audience has been reinforced by his numerous articles, written in the same lively style as *Economics* itself, that have appeared in the popular press and have recommended policies that Democratic administrations, in particular, have tended to follow.

Samuelson's influence on the economics profession, though less generally known—except as it briefly surfaced when he received the Nobel Prize in economics—has been even more substantial. His doctoral dissertation, written before World War II and winner of the David A. Wells prize at Harvard, has become the sourcebook for all recent graduate students seeking to translate economic concepts into precise mathematical terms, either to facilitate an entirely deductive argument or to lay the basis for a statistical investigation. Indeed, the *Foundations of Economic Analysis* is perhaps the single most important reason for the increasing mathematization of economics, not just in the United States but throughout the world. Samuelson followed up his seminal work with a series of scientific papers that now fills two separate volumes. Ironically, these largely mathematical arguments, unlike the ideas of Keynes which Samuelson did so much to disseminate in America, have had little influence on public policy.

For Samuelson's critics, this is seen as no mere coincidence. They point out that the mathematics Samuelson is so wont to rely on is an inappropriate tool for understanding the types of complex social processes reflected in the problems of poverty at home and underdevelopment abroad, problems which deflated the economics profession's hopes and pretensions of the middle 1960s. These same critics also point out that the older theories of how prices and income shares are determined (which Samuelson has insisted on retaining in his grand synthesis) are inappropriate for explaining even the more directly economic factors at work in the inflationary processes that have so bedeviled the efforts since the end of World War II to apply Keynesian insights to the problem of unemployment. If, then, the success of American economics in developing a scientifically respectable body of theory and knowledge can be attributed in no small measure to the intellectual labors of Paul Samuelson, so too can

the failure of American economics to use that theory and knowledge to solve society's most pressing problems. See Ben B. Seligman, *Main Currents in Modern Economics* (1963).

ALFRED S. EICHNER

SANDBURG, Carl August (b. Galesburg, Ill., Jan. 6, 1878; d. Flat Rock, N.C., July 22, 1967), WRITER, enlisted in the infantry during the Spanish-American War and served in Puerto Rico. He attended Lombard College in Galesburg (1898–1902), but left without a degree. After several years of traveling around the country, he settled in Milwaukee in 1907 and became an organizer for the Social Democratic party of Wisconsin. He was secretary to the Socialist mayor of Milwaukee, Emil Seidel, during 1910–12.

Sandburg moved to Chicago in 1913, where he published poems in *Poetry* magazine (1914); they were well-received by the critics and public. He published *Chicago Poems* in 1916, followed by *Cornhuskers* (1918), *Smoke and Steel* (1920), and *Slabs of the Sunburnt West* (1922). Between 1917 and 1928 he worked as a reporter for the Chicago *Daily News*. Settling in Harbert, Michigan, in 1932 (he had bought a house there as a summer residence in 1926), Sandburg also traveled around the country during this period singing and collecting American folk songs; he published a collection called *The American Songbag* (1927). Another collection of poems, *The People, Yes* (1936), paid tribute to the common man in America and expressed Sandburg's faith in democracy. Deeply interested in the life of Abraham Lincoln, Sandburg wrote *Abraham Lincoln: The Prairie Years* (1926), and *Abraham Lincoln: The War Years* (4 vols., 1939), which won the 1940 Pulitzer Prize for history. During World War II Sandburg wrote a syndicated column for the Chicago *Times*. After he had moved to Flat Rock, North Carolina, in 1945, he wrote a novel, *Remembrance Rock* (1948). Sandburg won the 1951 Pulitzer Prize for poetry for *Complete Poems* (1950), a collection of his earlier work. His autobiography, *Always the Young Strangers,* was published in 1959.

The ideological concerns which had led Sandburg to the Wisconsin Social Democrats were reflected as well in many of his poems. Among the themes presented in *Chicago Poems,* for example, were Sandburg's anger at capitalists for encompassing more than their share of American production and his concern for the suffering and deprivation of the poor of Chicago. But his concomitant pride in the satisfactions the workers secured from their lives was also expressed. In his poetry, too, are reflections of his belief in the uselessness and unnecessary suffering of warfare. In spite of this ideology, however, and in contrast to such Socialist leaders as **Bill Haywood,** who sought to hinder the American war effort during World War I, Sandburg decided that once the nation had entered the conflict, it was his duty as a citizen to aid the search for victory. Finally, an enduring concern of Sandburg's was what he viewed as the tendency of the common people to forget past grievances quickly, thus permitting themselves to be deluded and deprived time and again.

⁂

Sandburg's sympathies lay with the common man. The emerging emphasis in his work (poetry, fiction, biography, journalism) was not the elitism of Eliot but the triumph of the "people." His poems are not energized by propaganda, however, but by fellowship, even empathy, and by close and original observation. When he blusters, he is participating in a human feeling for assertiveness and love of life. He balances these extroversions with tenderness and pity.

Sandburg's life followed a route toward the isolation and free time that all writers require. After the socialist involvements of Milwaukee and the journalistic pressures and excitements of Chicago, he betook himself to the lower Michigan shores of Lake Michigan, where, protected by his wife and three daughters, he was able to pursue undistracted his calling as biographer and poet and to sally forth as public reader of his verse and singer of ballads, always with his quiet place to return to. In his role as guitar-strumming, nasal minstrel and people's poet, he cultivated a rather loose-limbed stance, shaggy hair, string ties, and artfully unkempt clothing. When at last he moved to the more temperate climate of a North Carolina farm, with books, family, and herd of goats, he found a nearly ideal haven.

A poet even in his prose, he approached being a successor to **Walt Whitman** in form and material. What he lacked was Whitman's cosmic vision and, even at his best, Whitman's elevation of style and emotion. Sandburg possessed, nevertheless, a profound love for America in all its brashness, sweetness, promise, resilience. He was an articulate and compassionate patriot in the noblest sense. See Richard Crowder, *Carl Sandburg* (1964).

RICHARD CROWDER

SANGER, Margaret Higgins (b. Corning, N.Y., Sept. 14, 1883; d. Tucson, Ariz., Sept. 6, 1966), REFORMER, was educated at Claverack College (Hudson, N.Y.) and studied nursing in the White Plains (N.Y.) Hospital. In 1902 she married William Sanger but was divorced in 1920. Two years later she married industrialist J. N. H. Slee but retained the name of her first husband. Her experience as a nurse in New York's Lower East Side in 1912, her association with radical socialists, Industrial Workers of the World, and anarchists such as **Emma Goldman,** and her contact with pro-Malthusian French syndicalists during a visit to Paris in 1913 prompted her to take up the cause of "birth control," a phrase she coined after her return to the United States in early 1914. She established a monthly magazine, the *Woman Rebel,* which stridently supported woman's liberation, radical politics, and, of course, birth control. The federal government brought several indictments against her and the *Woman Rebel* under the antiobscenity law, or Comstock Act, of 1873. To avoid prosecution she fled to England, where she remained from November 1914 to September 1915. On her return to the U.S. (the government dropped its charges in Feb. 1916) she opened the first birth control clinic in America (Oct. 1916) in Brooklyn, New York. Within weeks the police closed the clinic. She was arrested and sentenced to thirty days in jail.

In late 1916 Sanger founded the *Birth Control Review,* publishing it until 1928. In 1921 she organized the first American Birth Control Conference and at its opening announced the formation of the American Birth Control League, of which she was president until 1928. In 1923 she organized the Clinical Research Bureau in New York to dispense contraceptive services. She quit the League in 1928 and founded the National Committee on Federal Legislation for Birth Control, which lobbied unsuccessfully through the 1930s for changes favorable to birth control in the federal antiobscenity statutes. The National Committee was dissolved in 1937, but in 1938 the American Birth Control League and the Clinical Research Bureau merged to form the Birth Control Federation of America, later called the Planned Parenthood Federation of America. Sanger retired from active leadership in the organization at this time, but continued to speak in the U.S. and abroad in behalf of birth control. She helped organize the International Planned Parenthood Federation after World War II and served as its president in the 1950s. Her books include: *Woman and the New Race* (1920), *The Pivot of Civilization* (1922), and *Margaret Sanger: An Autobiography* (1938).

Margaret Sanger was a striking combination of humanitarian, feminist, egotist, and opportunist. Though she at first regarded birth control as a proletarian weapon in the class struggle, with which the working class could cease to furnish surplus labor and cannon fodder to the capitalists, she soon abandoned her radicalism and instead promoted birth control as an instrument of social control, which would reduce the numbers of the proliferating "unfit." She moved away from her original radical associates like **"Big Bill" Haywood** and Emma Goldman and found, after 1920, that most of her support came from those people alarmed at the swelling numbers of immigrants and potential candidates for the welfare rolls.

Sanger also espoused birth control for purposes of feminine sexual liberation. The fear of pregnancy, she believed, inhibited free sexual expression, and by removing that fear, women would be able to develop their erotic nature, or what she variously called "the absolute, elemental, inner urge of womanhood," the "feminine spirit," or the "intuitive forward urge within." Mrs. Sanger, in short, associated herself with those sexual romantics who insisted that women had a unique sexual nature that deserved cultivation. That insistence marked her ideological distance from feminists such as Charlotte Perkins Gilman who were concerned to minimize, not accentuate, sexual differences. These two themes—social control and erotic liberation—dominated Mrs. Sanger's approach to the question of birth control. She never developed a sophisticated understanding of "the population problem" as we understand it today—as a problem, that is, of balancing human numbers and the earth's resources.

Margaret Sanger all her life delighted in the attitude of the embattled outsider. Alienated from middle-class comforts as a child, she attacked them savagely as a young woman, especially in the *Woman Rebel.* In later years she found it impossible to share power and influence with others interested in the cause, such as physicians, or to effect tactical compromises with her opposition, especially in the Roman Catholic Church. Nevertheless, she remained to the end of her life an extraordinarily energetic and dedicated woman, without whom the worldwide birth control movement would have had a different and less successful history. See David M. Kennedy, *Birth Control in America: The Career of Margaret Sanger* (1970).

DAVID M. KENNEDY

SANTAYANA, George (b. Madrid, Spain, Dec. 16, 1863; d. Rome, Italy, Sept. 26, 1952), PHILOSOPHER, remained a Spanish citizen throughout his life. He came with his family to Boston in 1872 and graduated from Harvard in 1886. He spent the next two years (1886–88) on a fellowship at the University of Berlin. Returning to the U.S., he studied philosophy at Harvard with **William James** and **Josiah Royce** and received his PhD in 1889. That same year he commenced teaching in Harvard's philosophy department; he became a full professor in 1907. He was a popular teacher; among his students were T. S. Eliot, **Walter Lippmann,** and **Felix Frankfurter.**

Santayana published a poetry collection, *Sonnets and Other Verses* (1894), and his first philosophical work, *The Sense of Beauty* (1896), which dealt with aesthetics. He followed this with *Interpretations of Poetry and Religion* (1900) and *The Life of Reason* (1905–6), a five-volume work which traced the development of rationality. In 1910 he published a philosophic study of Lucretius, Dante, and Goethe, entitled *Three Philosophical Poets.* Santayana resigned from Harvard in 1912 and moved to England, never to return to the U.S. He traveled extensively and, after World War I, finally settled in Rome, where he produced some of his most important works. *Realms of Being* was a four-volume study written from 1927 to 1940 dealing with the subjects of essence and spirit. *Turns of Thought in Modern Philosophy* (1933) was a collection of essays on contemporary philosophical problems. His novel *The Last Puritan* (1936) was a satiric look at American life from the vantage point of Boston and Harvard. His autobiography *Persons and Places* appeared in two volumes, *The Background of My Life* (1944) and *The Middle Span* (1945). At the beginning of World War II he moved to a Roman Catholic convent in Rome, where he remained until his death. Some of his many philosophical writings include *Egotism in German Philosophy* (1916), *Scepticism and Animal Faith* (1923), *Dialogues in Limbo* (1926), and *Dominations and Powers: Reflections on Liberty, Society and Government* (1951). A third volume of his autobiography, *My Host the World* (1953), appeared posthumously.

———— ⊗≋⊗ ————

In *The Life of Reason*, Santayana says, "A man's feet must be planted in his country, but his eyes should survey the world." Yet he never planted his feet completely in the United States. He claimed that he was an American only "by long association." However, he also acknowledged that "it has been acquaintance with America and American philosophers that has chiefly contributed to clear and to settle my own mind." Santayana's American experience provided one important perspective from which he surveyed the world philosophically. His vision was penetrating, wide-ranging, and imaginative; his mind was clear and insightful. Although less well known than William James and **John Dewey,** he stands as their equal in American philosophy.

Two qualities dominate Santayana's works. First, there is the beauty of the writing itself. Santayana loved poetry. He studied carefully how art emerges from human life and enriches it. Aiming to make his own philosophy an instance of beauty, Santayana succeeded as few philosophers have. With the possible exception of **Ralph Waldo Emerson,** his style and thought are the most poetic of any American philosopher.

Second, all of Santayana's writings reflect and extend his basic naturalism: everything that we experience and know emerges from nature and has a potential for development toward an ideal end. Thus, whatever Santayana studied (e.g., the life of reason, a nation's culture, or even an individual's personality), he tried both to understand its emergence within nature and to evaluate its present and potential contribution toward beauty and goodness.

One goal of Santayana's analysis was to stimulate men to strive for excellence. He believed that human life occurs within the restrictions of natural boundaries. Nature itself never yields fully to man's reason or desire. However, our challenge—indeed our fulfillment as creatures of nature—is to live so as to make our existence as noble, beautiful, and rational as possible. Santayana's books capture poignantly the limitations and grandeur of the human spirit. With power and emotion, they also reveal nature's order and rich variety, its melancholy, mystery, and magnificence. See George Santayana, *The Life of Reason* (5 vols., 1905–6).

JOHN K. ROTH

SARGENT, John Singer (b. Florence, Italy, Jan. 12, 1856; d. London, England, April 15, 1925), ARTIST, son of an American doctor, traveled extensively in Europe during his childhood. His first lessons in art were at the Academy of Fine Arts, Florence. In 1874 his family settled in Paris so that he could attend the Ecole des Beaux-Arts. He also worked in the studio of Carolus Duran, who considered Velázquez the great ideal. Sargent visited the U.S. for the first time in 1876. The following year, back in Paris, one of his paintings was exhibited in the Salon. In 1879–80 he traveled and painted in Spain and Morocco. His portrait *Madame Gautreau* (Metropolitan Museum of Art, N.Y.) was harshly received when exhibited in France a few years later, and Sargent moved to London. At first English critics condemned his style as severely as had the French, but sitters liked his exotic style of portraiture. Establishing a studio in 1885, Sargent soon earned a widespread reputation, particularly for his portraits of women and children, such as *The Daughters of Edward D. Boit* (1882, Boston Museum of Fine Arts). He was elected to the Royal Academy in 1897.

Sargent came to the U.S. in 1887 to paint portraits, exhibiting that year at the St. Botolph Club in Boston. His success in America, where he painted portraits of Theodore Roosevelt and Woodrow Wilson, was stunning. Around 1890 he painted *Carmencita* (Musée d'art Moderne, Paris), a Spanish dancer, and (perhaps the best example of his intimate portrait style) *Mrs. Edward L. Davis and Son* (Los Angeles County Museum). Thereafter he devoted most of his time to murals for the Boston Public Library, the Boston Art Museum, and the Widener Library at Harvard. The murals completed, he went in 1916 on a trip to the Rocky Mountains and in 1918 was asked by the British to record his impressions of the war. The former trip yielded some landscapes; the latter, marred by illness, was unproductive except for his devastating indictment of modern warfare, *Gassed* (Imperial War Museum, London).

Sargent was a legal resident of Boston after 1900, although he spent part of each year in Europe. He declined a British knighthood in 1907 on the grounds that he was a U.S. citizen.

⸻

John Singer Sargent was the ideal of many painters and critics on both sides of the Atlantic during a productive lifetime. Although personally shy and withdrawn, he moved in exalted circles, painted famous personalities, and caught the external qualities of the era's high society.

Sargent's *portraits d'apparat* of subjects caught in a characteristic moment were famous. He depicted Robert Louis Stevenson slightly off the canvas center, full of nervous energy and apprehension. A portrait of Theodore Roosevelt was more studied, but revealed the president's determination and energy. Sargent progressively wearied of the portraits that made him rich and famous, but at their best they ranked above those of any contemporary except **Thomas Eakins,** whose manner was much more subdued.

Sargent was personally more happy painting religious murals than as a portraitist. His murals for the Boston Public Library revealed both an intricate and satisfying design and rich painting. Those for the Museum of Fine Arts, Boston, and the Widener Library were less effective though appealingly decorative. Sargent also enjoyed the watercolors he did on vacation and while touring the Holy Land. They revealed the same facility that characterized his works in oils, and often seemed to be color abstractions. The more studied watercolors revealed a detachment and solitude that were firmly in the American tradition of a concern for man's relation to a larger natural environment.

Though uninterested in aesthetic theories, Sargent was a friend and admirer of Claude Monet, and helped secure several major impressionist works for American museums. Impressionism influenced Sargent, especially in the 1880s, but like most American painters, he was more concerned with reality than with light. Sargent was not a dazzling colorist, but had a keen sense of painterly values, derived from academic discipline and a love of earlier masters such as Velázquez and the Dutch. Somewhat like **James McNeill Whistler,** he gave an impression of haste when in fact he strived to retain substance while capturing transitory effects.

Sargent's facility made some critics skeptical of his stature, and his huge output was inevitably uneven. Cubism and other abstractionisms made his work seem old-fashioned when he died. Yet the qualities of this "academic impressionist" have become more apparent with the passage of time, and his reputation is rising. In cultural terms, Sargent's life and work revealed the impact of cosmopolitanism on American art. And though he accepted the merits of world tastes and an academic elegance, Sargent retained a historic American concern for external realism, defined space, and individual character that enriched world painting. See Richard Ormond, *John Singer Sargent: Paintings, Drawings, Watercolors* (1970).

H. WAYNE MORGAN

SARNOFF, David (b. Uzlian, Russ., Feb. 27, 1891; d. New York, N.Y., Dec. 12, 1971), BUSINESSMAN, emigrated to New York City in 1900, attended public schools, and became a messenger boy in 1906 for the Commercial Cable Co. He taught himself the Morse code in his spare time and obtained a job with the Marconi Wireless Telegraph Co. of America in 1907 as a junior radio operator, first at Nantucket Island (1908) and then in Brooklyn, New York (1909), where he studied electrical engineering at the Pratt Institute. On April 14, 1912, after stints as a wireless operator on several ships, Sarnoff was in charge of the station on top of **John Wanamaker**'s New York department store when he picked up the first messages from the sinking S.S. *Titanic* and the first list of survivors. Thereafter, rising quickly in American Marconi, he became chief radio inspector (1913), contract manager (1914), assistant traffic manager (1915), and commercial manager (1917).

When the new Radio Corporation of America, headed by Owen D. Young, absorbed American Marconi in 1919, Sarnoff became general manager of the new concern. At American Marconi, he had urged the use of radio for mass entertainment, an idea long advocated by **Lee De Forest**

and others. In 1921, after the spectacularly successful launching of KDKA by Westinghouse, Sarnoff was able to persuade RCA to enter radio broadcasting, and the company soon enjoyed large profits. He was elected vice president of RCA in 1922, and in 1926 helped launch the National Broadcasting Co., organized to sell time for national advertising. In 1929 he went to Europe with Young for the deliberations which led to the Young Plan for German war reparations. The following year he became president of RCA.

Sarnoff took an early interest in the development of television, and was responsible for the NBC television exhibit at the 1939 New York World's Fair and for the founding of a commercial television station, WNBT-TV, in New York in 1941. During World War II he served as General Dwight Eisenhower's communications consultant and was made a brigadier general. In 1947 he retired as president of RCA to become chairman of its board of directors. He successfully petitioned the FCC to grant a competing color television system to CBS's color system in 1953 and then supervised RCA's manufacturing and marketing of color television sets and its programming of color shows. His collection of papers, *Looking Ahead*, appeared in 1968.

Throughout his career Sarnoff was a driving force. He had no childhood and did not seem to miss it. Because his father was fatally ill when mother and children arrived in America, David became family head at ten, keeping things going with a patchwork of earnings—paper route, deliveries for a butcher, job in a synagogue choir. At work he always welcomed added duties. This eager-beaverism earned him scorn, but paid dividends. As Marconi office boy he was given the task of filing letters, and took the trouble to read them all. He understood operations at all levels long before he got there; as office boy, he was already studying presidential prose style. He made himself indispensable and rose rapidly—first at American Marconi, then at RCA.

RCA was for some years controlled by General

Electric, Westinghouse, and AT&T, but antitrust pressures brought a disentangling. It was Sarnoff's detailed knowledge and shrewd, hard bargaining that helped RCA in 1932 to emerge from this process as a potent, independent entity, sole owner of NBC. RCA became virtually a personal Sarnoff empire, ruled firmly from the 53d floor of the RCA Building in Radio City. He tended to become a remote executive. Key division heads addressed him in formal memoranda, on which he scribbled instructions—"???"—"Yes!"—"No!"—"PSM" (meaning "please see me"). An appointment came to have the atmosphere of an audience. When angry, he showed an icy reserve, more feared than an explosion.

RCA was originally formed under navy auspices, and military figures were prominent in its early history. After Sarnoff became a brigadier general, he was always addressed at RCA as "General." He practiced nepotism with an almost religious zeal, juggling executives to fit family plans. While this caused resentment (NBC, in particular, long had serious morale problems), Sarnoff was extraordinarily successful in his relations with the world at large. In patent struggles he was tough and sometimes ruthless. He was ready to venture vast sums to promote television, and later the RCA system of color television. In government relations he was extremely effective. Financially he did not reward himself in baronial style; he worked for the power to control events, identifying himself totally with the great destiny he foresaw for RCA. See John Tebbel, *David Sarnoff: Putting Electrons to Work* (1963), and Erik Barnouw, *A History of Broadcasting in the United States* (1966–70).

ERIK BARNOUW

SCHIFF, Jacob Henry (b. Frankfurt am Main, Ger., Jan. 10, 1847; d. New York, N.Y., Sept. 25, 1920), FINANCIER, was born into a substantial German-Jewish family which apprenticed him, at age fourteen, to a business firm. At eighteen, he emigrated to America, where he became a stockbroker. His firm was dissolved in 1872, however, and he returned to Germany. But after the death of his father (1873), Schiff returned to the U.S. and joined the investment banking house of Kuhn, Loeb and Co. In 1885 he became head of the firm, which he turned into one of the leading underwriters in the financing of railroads, notably the Pennsylvania and the Louisville and Nashville.

Schiff's most celebrated financial undertaking was his role in the formation of the Northern Securities Co., a holding company into which **Edward H. Harriman,** Kuhn, Loeb, **James J. Hill,** and **J. P. Morgan** had placed their stock holdings in the Great Northern, Northern Pacific, and Chicago, Burlington, and Quincy railroads. The combine, attacked by President Theodore Roosevelt in 1902 in his first foray against the trusts, was ordered dissolved by the Supreme Court in 1904. Among many other ventures, Schiff arranged financing for the construction of railroads in Mexico, secured $200 million for the Japanese in 1904 in their war against the Russians, and participated actively in the American banking consortium in China. In politics a Republican, Schiff nevertheless voted for Woodrow Wilson in 1912 and 1916.

Schiff was an active supporter of the American Jewish community and contributed frequently to relief societies. The deplorable conditions under which his co-religionists lived on the Lower East Side of New York always elicited his concern, but he was particularly moved to action by the persecution of Jews in czarist Russia. Because of his feelings on this point, he refused to participate in the Anglo-French loan during World War I. Although Schiff opposed the rise of Jewish nationalism and separatism in America, he believed in the value of preserving Jewish culture, and founded the Semitic Museum at Harvard and the Semitic departments in the New York Public Library and the Congressional Library. Not strictly orthodox, Schiff nevertheless attended the synagogue regularly; and despite the attendant inconvenience in an era when Saturday was a day of business, he always observed the Sabbath.

As a businessman Jacob Schiff was the epitome of success: he married wealth, parlayed his father-in-law's fortune into a gigantic enterprise, challenged and fought to a stalemate no less a man than J. P. Morgan, and emerged as one of America's most powerful financiers. In his broader role as a human being, he failed—but not before he had conceived, and come close to carrying out, a humane dream of awesome magnitude.

By 1901 he was among the richest and most influential Jews in America, commanding resources matching those of the Rothschilds in Europe. But the burden of success weighed heavily upon him: he believed he must do everything in his power for what he called his "co-religionists." The world's Jews, after eons of persecution, now lived with no legal disabilities and with surmountable personal disabilities in Germany, the United States, and Western Europe; and Schiff believed the reason was that Jews had demonstrably become good citizens of nation-states, differing from other citizens only in their religion. Assimilation was therefore the ultimate desideratum, and only two barriers stood in the way: Zionism, which deluded some of the Jews who were already free; and the czarist regime in Russia, which prohibited assimilation in that country (including Poland), wherein nearly half the world's Jews were virtually imprisoned.

Schiff set out to remove both sets of barriers, and seemed to be succeeding until 1914. In the "free" world he fought Zionists and sought to discredit them. He opposed American immigration restrictions, pressuring President Taft in the process; he facilitated Russian-Jewish immigration to Latin America; he sponsored organizations that dispersed Russian-Jewish immigrants throughout the United States, fearing that concentration in New York would arouse xenophobia even among German-American Jews. When hostility erupted between Slavic-Jewish garment workers and German-Jewish manufacturers, Schiff intervened, opposing strikers while secretly supporting their families.

Most of all, he struck at czarist Russia. After the Russo-Japanese War (1905), Schiff was told by Japanese friends that captured Russian officers, if properly indoctrinated, made good revolutionaries. He thereafter, in circuitous fashion, contributed money to revolutionary and other anticzarist activities in Russia. By early 1914 his dream of a free and nationalized world Jewry seemed on the verge of fulfillment.

Then came the Great War, and everything went wrong. Schiff, admiring his German homeland and despising Russia, wanted to help finance the Central Powers. The House of Morgan and other bankers allied to financial houses in Paris and London were loath to lend money to the Central Powers. Through **Robert Lansing**'s influence, President Wilson in 1914 was persuaded to allow the bankers to loan money to the belligerents. When the United States entered the war in 1917, the Morgan group had invested some $3 billion in Britain and France, while Schiff and others of his opinion had invested less than $60 million in Germany. Generally Schiff, as a financier, sat the war out, devoting most of his efforts to large-scale relief of Jewish war refugees, whom the American government and the International Red Cross failed to help.

In 1919, foreseeing that chaos and bloodshed would ensue from a political and economic vacuum in Central Europe, Schiff proposed to **Julius Rosenwald** that they organize what amounted to a Marshall Plan, privately financed. But both men were too old and too tired. Besides, the Russian Revolution had come, deposing the czars but bringing worldwide suspicion of "international Jewry" as Communism's wellspring and persecuting Russian Jews with unremitting vehemence. In a final capitulation to the futility of his grand dream, Schiff joined the Zionist movement. See Cyrus Adler, *Jacob H. Schiff: His Life and Letters* (1929).

FORREST MCDONALD

SCHLESINGER, Arthur Meier, Jr. (b. Columbus, Ohio, Oct. 15, 1917), HISTORIAN, grew up in Cambridge, Massachusetts, where his father taught history at Harvard. He graduated from Harvard summa cum laude in 1938, and spent the next year studying at the University of Cambridge on a fellowship. In 1939 he became a junior fellow at Harvard. During World War II he worked for the Office of War Information and served in the Office of Strategic Services in Europe. After his discharge from the army, Schlesinger published *The Age of Jackson* (1945), which won a Pulitzer Prize. He returned to Harvard to teach history, becoming a full professor in 1954.

Always deeply interested in liberal politics, Schlesinger was one of the founders of the Americans for Democratic Action (1947). In the 1952 and 1956 presidential campaigns he was speechwriter for and adviser to **Adlai Stevenson.** He played the same role for John F. Kennedy in the 1960 presidential campaign and served as special assistant to Presidents Kennedy and Lyndon B. Johnson (1961–64). His account of the Kennedy administration, *A Thousand Days* (1965), won the 1966 Pulitzer Prize for biography. In 1978 he won another Pulitzer Prize for his biography, *Robert F. Kennedy and His Times*. In 1967 Schlesinger became Albert Schweitzer professor of humanities at the City University of New York, retiring in 1992. While at Harvard during the 1950s Schlesinger wrote his *Age of Roosevelt* trilogy: *The Crisis of the Old Order* (1957), *The Coming of the New Deal* (1958), and *The Politics of Upheaval* (1960). A frequent contributor to periodicals, Schlesinger has written several other books including *The Vital Center* (1949), *The Politics of Hope* (1963), *The Crisis of Confidence* (1969), and *The Imperial Presidency* (1974).

As a professional historian Arthur M. Schlesinger, Jr., established an immediate reputation with *The Age of Jackson,* published when he was only twenty-seven. He has since written or edited a substantial number of other books—a longer list than most academics can lay claim to—but he has also been actively involved in current affairs, especially the affairs of the Democratic party, which he has always regarded as the party of hope and reform. Some of his critics say that a historian risks becoming a propagandist through becoming too closely concerned

with politics. Replies to this charge, as put forward in several vigorous essays by Schlesinger, include the view that contemporary history is too important to be left to newscasters; that it is possible to hold firm opinions without surrendering to flagrant bias; and that in fact from Thucydides onward historians have often devoted their energies to interpreting the world about them. One might add that since the New Deal, historians in the United States have usually voted Democratic, and made no secret of their preference.

By the test of his own books Schlesinger is a brilliantly persuasive practitioner of the historical art. His outstanding talent has been for panoramic narrative: that is, telling a clear "story" with emphasis on personality, and yet establishing the social and intellectual climate with a remarkable breadth of reference. His predilections are undisguised but have never been vituperative. He is a defender of liberalism rather than of specific Democratic platforms. As such he has come under fire from radicals as well as conservatives. So far, his writings indicate, American liberalism has historically seemed more long-lasting than its assailants. See Marcus Cunliffe, "Arthur M. Schlesinger, Jr.," in Marcus Cunliffe and Robin Winks, eds., *Pastmasters: Some Essays on American Historians* (1969).

MARCUS CUNLIFFE

SCHOENBERG, Arnold (b. Vienna, Austria, Sept. 13, 1874; d. Los Angeles, Calif., July 13, 1951), COMPOSER, was mostly self-taught in music except for some instruction in counterpoint from Alexander von Zemlinsky, who influenced his early musical development profoundly and whose sister Schoenberg married in 1901. Beginning in 1903 he gathered around him a small group of students (including Alban Berg and Anton von Webern) who became his disciples and who followed his lead in abandoning romanticism for atonality, and then, atonality for the twelve-tone system. As Schoenberg grew increasingly iconoclastic in his writing, the hostile reaction of critics and audiences intensified. The premieres of *Pierrot Lunaire* in Berlin in 1912, and the *Chamber Symphony No. 1* in Vienna in 1913 aroused a furor in the auditorium and vitriolic attacks in the newspapers. All this was just a preview of the scandals that attended the premieres of his later twelve-tone compositions. To insulate himself from this hostility, Schoenberg formed in Vienna the Society for Private Performances dedicated to performances of his own compositions and those of his followers, which denied admission to critics, and was open only to those sympathetic to Schoenberg's ideals.

Between 1918 and 1933 Schoenberg divided his time between his home in a suburb of Vienna and Berlin, where he served as a professor of composition at the Prussian Academy of Art. Though this was a lifetime appointment he was removed in 1933 by the Nazis because he was born a Jew (though early converted to Catholicism). In protest against the rising tide of Nazism, Schoenberg underwent a formal ceremony in Paris in May of 1933 in which he was reinstated into the Jewish faith. Musically, too, he returned to his religion by writing his first work of Hebraic content and interest, the *Kol Nidrei,* for speaker, chorus, and orchestra (1939). After 1933 Schoenberg made his permanent home in the United States. He adopted English as his language, anglicized his name from Schönberg to Schoenberg, and on April 11, 1941, became an American citizen.

Embittered by the past rejections he had suffered from audiences and critics, he ignored or rejected attempts to honor him as, with the passing years, his compositions gained wider circulation and elicited enthusiastic responses. Nevertheless, his seventieth and seventy-fifth birthdays were celebrated throughout the world with commemorative concerts. All his life singularly superstitious, Schoenberg dreaded the number thirteen. When he became seventy-six, he was convinced he would die that year, since the numbers seven and six added up to thirteen. He died, as he had anticipated, in his seventy-sixth year.

During Schoenberg's early years, most of the young composers in Vienna carried the torch of Wagner in their march to "the music of the future." Schoenberg became one of them. In his early works he was a postromantic bearing the ideals and the aesthetics of Wagner. During this phase he completed a monumental cantata, *Gurrelieder* (1901), and *Verklärte Nacht* (1899). The latter is still his most frequently played composition although in its later transcription for chamber orchestra and not in its original version as a string sextet. Then, convinced that postromanticism had run its course, and having become repelled by its structural and emotional excesses, Schoenberg turned to a new direction in his music; away from consonance, formal tonalities, and other long-accepted values, and toward expressionism in which music was reduced to barest essentials, stripped of emotion and human experience, and permitting the musical thought full freedom in expressing itself without regard to rules or traditions.

Three Piano Pieces (1908), *Five Pieces for Orchestra* (1909), and the song cycle, *Pierrot Lunaire* (1912) were the major works of this atonal period. But atonality, Schoenberg discovered, brought not only liberation but anarchy. Feeling the necessity for self-discipline, he sought a new system to replace the ones he had discarded as obsolete. Thus he came upon the twelve-tone system (or dodecaphony), which had been formulated before him by his Viennese contemporary, Josef Mathias Hauer. Here a preconceived row of twelve different notes of the chromatic scale became the spine of a musical work, usable in four different specific ways. For about two decades, Schoenberg used this method with inflexible rigidity in writing works such as the *Third* and *Fourth String Quartet* (1926, 1936), the *Variations for Orchestra* (1928), the opera, *Moses and Aaron,* which he never finished (1932), the *Violin Concerto* (1936) and the *Piano Concerto* (1942). The cerebralism of this music, its stark and forbidding succession of ugly sounds, its strict adherence to a formula repelled much of the general music public. But an entire generation of avant-garde composers found Schoenberg's way of using the twelve-tone system a valuable method with which to avoid personalized emotions.

Following Schoenberg's exile from Germany, and the cataclysmic events that shook him to the very roots of his being, his twelve-tone writing acquired human feeling, emotion, and stirring programmatic subject matter. Compelled to reevaluate his place in society as a result of world-shaking events and to abandon his ivory tower, Schoenberg occasionally made a conscious attempt to preach a gospel, something he had fastidiously avoided before this. *Ode to Napoleon* (1940), based on Byron, was political in its denunciation of autocracy and in its praise of democratic freedom. *A Survivor from Warsaw* (1947), to his own English text, described the heroism and the suffering of the Jews in the Warsaw ghetto in their month-long Herculean resistance to the Nazi war machine. In thus humanizing twelve-tone music (in which he had been anticipated by Alban Berg), Schoenberg finally succeeded in earning the admiration of the general music public which now grew increasingly tolerant of his earlier more abstract and more astringent atonal and twelve-tonal compositions. See H. N. Stuckenschmidt, *Schoenberg* (1959).

DAVID EWEN

SCHOOLCRAFT, Henry Rowe (b. Albany Co., N.Y., March 28, 1793; d. Washington, D.C., Dec. 10, 1864), ETHNOLOGIST, attended Union and Middlebury colleges without obtaining a degree. He then studied his father's trade of glassmaking. Being interested in geology and mineralogy, he explored the lead deposit regions of Missouri and Arkansas (then Native American country) in 1817–18. He published a report on his findings in 1819. Having gained a reputation in geology, Schoolcraft was appointed to General **Lewis Cass**'s expedition to the upper Mississippi and Lake Superior Copper region, and (1822) was appointed U.S. Indian agent for the Lake Superior region. He served in the Michigan territorial legislature (1828–32), and was a founder of the Michigan Historical Society (1828) and the Algic Society of Detroit (1832), which was devoted to Native American researches. After a second exploration (1832) of the upper Mississippi River

(of which he correctly identified the source as Lake Itasca in the present state of Minnesota), Schoolcraft was appointed superintendent of Indian Affairs for Michigan (1836). He negotiated several treaties with the Chippewa tribe, the most important of which ceded Native American–held parts of Michigan to the United States (1836).

In 1839 Schoolcraft published *Algic Researches*, a compilation of Native American allegories and legends, and in 1844–45 *Oneota*, on Native American history and prospects. While a commissioner making a census of New York State Native Americans (1845), he gathered information on the Iroquois and other tribes of the Six Nations, publishing *Notes on the Iroquois,* a popular account, in 1847. That same year Congress authorized a comprehensive collection of information on Native Americans. Headed by Schoolcraft, this project resulted in the massive *Historical and Statistical Information Respecting the History, Condition, and Prospects of the Indian Tribes of the United States* (1851–57). Cessation of government support and developing rheumatism kept Schoolcraft from further work after 1857.

⁂

In the early 19th century, upstate New York contained many rustic places where a sensitive, precocious, and imaginative young person could find solitude. Removed from the boisterous activities of the village youths, Henry Schoolcraft could study, accumulate woods knowledge, or dream. Yet, although he had taught himself German and Hebrew by the age of fifteen, he never earned a college degree.

This is not unusual, for there are many such individuals, brilliant as diamonds in the pursuits of their choice, but lethargic and inefficient away from them. For round-faced, bespectacled Henry, the problem of pursuing the natural sciences as a vocation at a time when they were avocations for most men was compounded by a lack of money or family connections. However, he was, as one of his contemporaries said, self-dependent, self-acting, and self-taught. His abilities attracted the attentions of important men, among them

Senator Lewis Cass of Michigan. With Schoolcraft's appointment as Indian agent of the Lake Superior region, his place in life was established. By his compassion and integrity he became a defender of the Native Americans; with his scholarliness he became America's first social anthropologist and its first field anthropologist; by his tact, courage, and fairness he became a successful negotiator with the tribesmen. He was a man of moderation, a religious man, and with all that, a person without malice. For Henry Schoolcraft, to be given the gift of life was reason enough for an optimistic disposition. See Hoffman R. Hays, *Explorers of Man* (1971).

RICHARD A. BARTLETT

SCHUMAN, William (b. New York, N.Y., Aug. 4, 1910; d. New York, N.Y., Feb. 15, 1992), COMPOSER, received his musical training at the Malkin School of Music in New York and privately with Charles Haubiel and Roy Harris. His first success came in 1939 with the premieres of his *American Festival Overture* and his *Third String Quartet.* His *Symphony No. 3,* first performed in 1941, won wide acclaim, and his cantata, *A Free Song,* won a Pulitzer Prize in 1943, the first time this award was given in music. Since then his work was performed by the most prestigious musical organizations and solo performers of the world. In 1957 he was awarded the Bicentennial Anniversary Medal of Columbia University and the Brandeis University Creative Arts Award in music. His later major works included the ballets *Undertow* (1945) and *Judith* (1949), the *Violin Concerto* (1947), the *New England Triptych* (1956), *Song of Orpheus* (1961), the *Symphony No. 8* (1962), written for the opening of the Lincoln Center of the Performing Arts in New York, and the *Symphony No. 9* (1969). From 1945 to 1962 he was president of the Juilliard School of Music, and for the next six years president of the New Lincoln Center. After resigning the presidency of Lincoln Center, Schuman remained active as the chairman of the executive committee of its Chamber Music Society and as a board member of the center's Film Society. In 1974 he was named chairman of the board of the MacDowell Colony, a summer retreat for creative artists, and was inducted into the American Academy of Arts and Letters.

William Schuman won a permanent place among the leading creative figures in the music of the twentieth century. He enriched the repertory of modern American music with compositions that, while contemporary in their rhythmic and harmonic vocabulary and in their frequent undercurrent of restlessness, maintain a tie with the musical past in their lyricism and their expressive contrapuntal textures. But Schuman's significance to American music lies almost as firmly in his achievements as administrator. As president of Juilliard he revolutionized its curriculum and set a new standard for music education, revitalized the faculty, initiated significant festivals and premieres, and helped to found one of the foremost chamber-music organizations in the world, the Juilliard String Quartet. As president of Lincoln Center, his prestige as a composer and his talent for organization helped to bring the project to full and successful realization.

A man of polyglot interests, Schuman, away from music, was a baseball fan, a voracious reader of literature, a lover of theater and motion pictures, and a swimmer. See F. R. Schreiber and Vincent Persichetti, *William Schuman* (1954).

DAVID EWEN

SCHUMPETER, Joseph Alois (b. Triesch, Moravia, Feb. 8, 1883; d. Taconic, Conn., Jan. 8, 1950), ECONOMIST, grew up in Vienna and graduated from the Theresaianum, a preparatory school for children of aristocrats, in 1901. He received his doctorate in law from the University of Vienna in 1906 and went into private law practice in Cairo, Egypt. But Schumpeter had a keen interest in economics and accepted a professorship in that subject at the University of Gernowitz in 1909. He later became professor of economics at the University of Graz (1911–14), where he published *The Theory of Economic Development* (1912). This work, a study of the process of economic change, introduced many of the ideas that Schumpeter would expand in later writings. After a semester as an exchange professor at Columbia, he returned (1914) to Austria. Following World War I, Schumpeter served briefly as Austrian minister of finance and then became president of Biedermannbank, a private bank in Vienna. When the bank failed in 1924 Schumpeter lost his personal fortune. He returned to academic life in 1925 as professor of public finance at the University of Bonn and in 1932 came to Harvard as professor of economics.

At Bonn and Harvard, Schumpeter published many articles and books on economics. His *Business Cycles* (1939), a massive two-volume study, advanced the theory that cycles were the product of innovation, and explained the relationship of innovation, the chief agent of economic change, to the process of economic development. *Capitalism, Socialism and Democracy* (1942) suggested that both capitalism and communism were heading for a middle course, socialism. Schumpeter stressed the use of mathematics and exact methods in economics. He participated in the founding of the Econometrics Society (mathematical economics) and served as its president from 1939 to 1941. The American Economics Association elected Schumpeter president in 1948, and just before his death he was chosen as the first president of the International Economic Association. His last work, *A History of Economic Analysis* (1954), was completed by his wife.

❦

According to friends, Joseph Schumpeter frequently claimed that his work had not got the attention it deserved. This was true. Most of his life he was a *minoritaire,* frequently swimming against the tide. When, for example, *Business Cycles* appeared, it was largely ignored because economists, preoccupied with the problems of the Great Depression, were more interested in issues raised by the Keynesian revolution. Yet it would be very wrong to conclude that Schumpeter was an economist without influence. His *Theory of Economic Development,* in some ways

his most original contribution, outlined a unique vision of the economic process in which the "entrepreneur-innovator" is cast as the key figure in the dynamics of capitalist society. His essays on imperialism and social class, written in the 1920s, argued that imperialism was not caused by capitalist expansion (as Lenin and J. A. Hobson had claimed) but was the product of precapitalist, feudal, aggressive instincts that had survived into the modern era. His *Capitalism, Socialism, and Democracy* predicted that capitalism was probably doomed and would be succeeded by some form of collectivism. Many of the insights in this work—that capitalism's "demise" was to be the result not of its failures but of its successes, that the romance of business would disappear as it became routinized by bureaucrats, that gilded youth, beneficiaries of capitalist accumulation, would out of ennui turn to radicalism, spouting anticapitalist slogans and heralding the advent of the socialist commonwealth—have proved prophetic indeed.

And his most ambitious project, *Business Cycles,* a veritable tour de force, a mine of knowledge and insights, came into its own after his death. Its stress on the importance of innovation in economic growth had a great vogue in the 1950s. This was a period of celebrating the virtues of private enterprise as an efficient system for allocating resources and assuring progress. Entrepreneurial historians "with a distaste for the impecunious fellow" were refurbishing the image of the robber barons that had been tarnished by the muckrakers. No wonder that in the Eisenhower era, dedicated to the preservation of the status quo, conservatives should have turned to Schumpeter as their economic philosopher.

A stimulating teacher and great raconteur, Schumpeter was fond of reminiscing about his three ambitions as a young man: to be the greatest economist, the greatest lover, and the greatest horseman in Austria. In his old age, however, he said he reluctantly had to confess that he never did become the greatest horseman in Austria. See Seymour E. Harris (ed.), *Schumpeter, Social Scientist* (1951).

WALTER ADAMS AND HERBERT KISCH

SCHURZ, Carl (b. Liblar, near Cologne, Ger., March 2, 1829; d. New York, N.Y., May 14, 1906), POLITICAL LEADER, REFORMER, participated while a student at the University of Bonn in an unsuccessful revolutionary movement (1848–49) and was forced to flee. After three years in Switzerland, France, and England, he migrated to the U.S. (1852), living first in Pennsylvania and then (1856) in Wisconsin. Becoming involved in politics, in 1858 he campaigned for Abraham Lincoln, who was running for the U.S. Senate against **Stephen A. Douglas** in Illinois. During the 1860 Republican presidential convention Schurz was chairman of the Wisconsin delegation which supported **William H. Seward** for the nomination. After Lincoln was nominated, however, Schurz campaigned for him and upon his victory was appointed minister to Spain (1861). He relinquished this post in 1862, and came home to join the Union army as a brigadier general of volunteers. As such he commanded a division at Second Bull Run (Aug. 1862), and was promoted to major general (1863). After taking part in the battles of Chancellorsville, Gettysburg, and Chattanooga, he ended his military career as chief of staff to Major General Slocum.

Following the Civil War, Schurz, at President Johnson's request, made a tour of the South (July–Sept. 1865), producing a very critical report which asserted that the South had an "utter absence of national feeling." He believed that the South should be compelled to accept African-American suffrage before being readmitted into the Union.

He then became Washington correspondent for the New York *Tribune* (1865–66); editor of the Detroit *Post* (1866–67); and coeditor and owner of the St. Louis *Westliche Post* (1867–69). He was the keynote speaker at the 1868 Republican presidential convention, where he took a more conciliatory attitude toward the South.

Schurz was elected U.S. senator from Missouri as a Republican, serving 1869–75. In the Senate he was a strong critic of the Grant administration and helped to organize the Liberal Republican movement (1870–72). He denounced Grant's attempt to annex Santo Domingo (1870), opposed the spoils system, advocated civil service reform with a merit system, and continued to press for conciliation with the South. His opposition to "Grantism" culminated in his support of **Horace Greeley,** the Liberal-Republican-Democratic nominee for the presidency in 1872. Following Rutherford B. Hayes's election as president in 1876, Schurz was appointed secretary of the interior (1877–81). In this post, he favored aid to the Native Americans and conservation, and established a merit system of promotion within his department.

In 1881–83 Schurz was editor of the New York *Evening Post.* In 1884, when the Republicans nominated **James G. Blaine** for the presidency, Schurz and other "Mugwump" reformers left the party to support Grover Cleveland. In the last two decades of his life he was an editorial writer for *Harper's Weekly* (1892–98), and president of the National Civil Service Reform League (1892–1900) and the Civil Service Reform Association of New York (1893–1906). An ardent anti-imperialist, he opposed the Spanish-American War and the annexation of the Philippines. Thus he supported the Democrat **William Jennings Bryan** in the presidential election of 1900. The *Reminiscences of Carl Schurz* (3 vols.) appeared in 1907–8.

⸺

Contempt for anything petty, obsequious, mean-spirited, or selfish marked Carl Schurz's personality and ideology. He was a proud, self-respecting, independent, high-minded man who envisioned the Good Society as one full of people like himself. In Germany and the United States he fought against those principles and institutions which tended to undermine independent character and judgment: autocracy, paternalism, slavery, party despotism, prejudice, and imperialism. His motto might well have been: "Don't tread on me or anyone else."

Schurz's liberalism has been called, with some justice, "aristocratic." Seldom did he express direct concern for the suffering of the downtrodden, nor did he take economic issues very seriously. During the German revolution of 1848 he ignored the workers' movement while championing liberty and democracy. He opposed slavery in America because of its effects on free institutions rather than its effects on the enslaved. Throughout the industrial revolution he focused his attention on the corrupt and degrading spoils system rather than speaking out on the plight of the farmer and the worker.

Schurz believed strongly in the principles of laissez-faire, for he had seen in Germany how debilitating it was for people, as he put it, "to look up to the government as a superior power which, in the order of the universe, was ordained to do everything—or nearly everything—for them, and to whose superhuman wisdom and indisputable authority they had to submit." By practicing local self-government, he felt, people would shed slavishness and become intelligent, resourceful, self-reliant, and self-respecting. Thus Schurz did not share the views of reformers who wished to strengthen the power of the federal government in order to solve social and economic problems.

Schurz was deeply patriotic. Like a prophet or a national conscience, he frequently spoke out, reminding Americans of their best traditions of liberty, justice, tolerance, and equality. What Schurz once said of **Charles Sumner** applies equally well to himself: "He cherished in his mind a high ideal of what this Republic and its Government should be: a Government composed of the best and wisest of the land; animated by none but the highest and most patriotic aspirations; yielding to no selfish impulse; noble in its tone and character; setting its face sternly against all wrong and injustice; presenting in its whole being to the American people a shining example of purity and lofty public spirit.... He felt in himself the whole dignity of the Republic. And when he saw anything that lowered the dignity of the Republic and the character of its government, he felt it as he would have felt a personal offense. He criticized it, he denounced it, he remonstrated against it, for he could not do otherwise." Schurz's most famous aphorism aptly illustrates this idealistic patriotism: "My country, right or wrong; if right, to be kept right; and if wrong, to be set right."

Schurz's political eminence derived from his ability to voice these strong convictions eloquently. Because no other German-American could speak with his power and influence, he rapidly won acknowledgment as the leading spokesman for millions of his fellow countrymen.

While his sincerity and conviction helped make Schurz a great orator, they did not make him an entirely likable human being. Although warm, witty, intelligent, industrious, and able, Schurz could be self-righteous, vain, intolerant of criticism, meddlesome, and presumptuous. He was also an intensely ambitious politician who, while piously protesting his pure motives, fought shamelessly for the offices he won. See Hans L. Trefousse, *Carl Schurz: A Biography* (1982).

MICHAEL BURLINGAME

SCHWAB, Charles Michael (b. Williamsburg, Pa., Feb. 18, 1862; d. New York, N.Y., Sept. 18, 1939), INDUSTRIALIST, was a clerk in a grocery store in the town where **Andrew Carnegie**'s main plant, the **Edgar Thomson** Steel Works, was located. He became acquainted with Captain William R. Jones, the ironmaster, who gave him a job as an engineer's helper. By the age of nineteen he had risen to chief engineer, and by twenty-five to superintendent of the Homestead Works. Named Jones's successor shortly before the Homestead strike of 1892, Schwab assumed the task of repairing the physical and moral damage after the strike was ended. In 1897 he became president of the Carnegie Steel Co. He was influential both in arousing **J. P. Morgan**'s enthusiasm for a consolidation of the steel industry and in persuading Andrew Carnegie to sell out to Morgan. His reward was the presidency of the newly established United States Steel Corp. After clashes with the Morgan faction in the company, headed by **E. H. Gary,** Schwab resigned (1903) and turned his attention to the Bethlehem Steel Co., which he had independently acquired a few years before. He soon made Bethlehem a leading producer of structural steel and armor plate. During World War I he served as director general of the Emergency Fleet Corporation, with the mandate to build a "bridge of ships" between America and Europe.

After Gary's death in 1927 Schwab became the acknowledged "elder statesman" of the steel industry and was president of the American Iron and Steel Institute until the 1930s. He supported Franklin D. Roosevelt for president in 1932, but became disillusioned by the New Deal shortly afterward. A lifetime of expensive living and lavish giving to numerous causes left Schwab at his death with few assets beyond several valuable pieces of real estate.

Of all of Andrew Carnegie's so-called young geniuses, Charlie Schwab was quite clearly his favorite. He was also one of the few among those so grandly labeled by their employer who had some claim to the title. Schwab's genius in steelmaking, however, lay more in his ability to manage men than in his ability to manage dollars. Captain Bill Jones, the true genius of steelmaking in the Carnegie works, who had first hired young Schwab as an engineer's helper, had quite fortuitously discovered this talent when he sent the young man to seek Carnegie's approval for a proposal, and Schwab returned not only with Carnegie's approval but with his enthusiastic praise. From that moment on, Jones arranged for Schwab to see a great deal of Carnegie, an arrangement that the ambitious young man in no way discouraged. The result was Schwab's meteoric rise in the Carnegie hierarchy. When Jones was killed in a blast furnace explosion in 1889, Schwab at twenty-seven was his natural successor to the position of chief superintendent of Edgar Thomson. Three years later, when he stepped into the bitterly tense community that was Homestead after the bloody strike, he got the men back to work and as much as possible assuaged the wounds of labor's defeat by keeping to a minimum recriminations and accusations. His success at Homestead guaranteed his future with Carnegie.

Ebullient and expansive, Schwab had an optimism for the future of steel that surpassed even that of Carnegie. No friend of labor unions, he nevertheless, by the sheer, forceful charm of his personality, was able to convince the laborers that he was their friend and protector. "Genial Charlie" was everyone's friend, but he picked his own friends shrewdly and well. He could communicate with both **Henry C. Frick** and Carnegie, and desperately tried to bridge the chasm that increasingly widened between them. When the final showdown came, however, and Schwab was forced to choose, he had no hesitation in going with the controlling interest, and he was handsomely rewarded for his loyalty. When it came time to sell Carnegie Steel, he was the natural promoter, who with his visionary faith and expansive optimism could charm even the hardheaded J. P. Morgan into climbing Mount Pisgah to view the promised land. Morgan came, saw, and bought at Carnegie's asking price of $480 million. Schwab deserved his title of Star Salesman, and no product was he more successful in selling than himself.

The Morgan syndicate picked him as president of the newly formed United States Steel Corporation, but Schwab was not at his best in directing a finished production. He needed the challenge of competition, the spur of further expansion. He soon retired from United States Steel, and found a challenge appropriate to his restless energy in a small concern, Bethlehem Steel, which within ten years, greatly aided by a booming world militarism, he had built into a competitor to the giant he had earlier helped to create. The war years were Schwab's best years, when once again the demand for steel was unlimited, and Schwab's market had become global.

Schwab always enjoyed the good life to the fullest. As generous to his friends as he was to himself, he traded in futures and lived for the present. It came as no great surprise to his associates that the highest-salaried man in America should die insolvent in 1937. His spectacular career exemplified both the forceful, creative strength and the extravagant, wasteful weakness of American capitalism of the early 20th century. See Robert Hessen, *Steel Man: The Life of Charles M. Schwab* (1975).

JOSEPH FRAZIER WALL

SCOTT, Dred (b. Southampton County, Va., c. 1795; d. St. Louis, Mo., Sept. 17, 1858), SLAVE, was born a slave. When his master, Peter Blow, moved him to St. Louis in 1827, he was assigned to the household of Blow's daughter Elizabeth. In 1833 John Emerson, a U.S. army surgeon, purchased Scott and took him to Illinois and (later) to Wisconsin Territory (now Minnesota). In 1838 Emerson and Scott returned to St. Louis. Upon the surgeon's death, Scott became the property of Mrs. Emerson, who hired him out to various people in the city.

In 1846 Henry T. Blow, son of Scott's former owner, instituted, on Scott's behalf, suits in the Missouri courts to secure his freedom. Blow argued that since Scott had lived in free territory for five years he had become free. Scott was under the control of the St. Louis sheriff while the case was before the courts (1846–52) and was hired out to do various jobs. Finally in 1852, the courts ruled against him. He was then "sold" to John Sanford of New York, who took the case to federal courts. Scott lived in St. Louis virtually a free man while the case lingered in the courts (1854–57). The famous 1857 Supreme Court decision (*Dred Scott* v. *Sanford*) upheld the earlier Missouri decision. Scott, said the Court, being a Negro, was not a citizen and therefore could not institute a suit. Moreover, the Court declared the 1820 Missouri Compromise, which had barred slavery in Wisconsin Territory, unconstitutional. However, Scott was purchased by Taylor Blow in 1857 and given his freedom. He spent the last year of his life as a porter at Barnum's Hotel in St. Louis.

Dred Scott is far better known as a Supreme Court case than as an individual. As sparse as are the known facts of his life, information concerning his personality and character is even rarer. What little is known of him, however, suggests that the opinions of him, publicly expressed by historians, have done him a serious injustice. The views that he was a shiftless slave, and no less so as a freedman during the last year of his life, that in the case which bears his name he was a bewil-

dered creature of circumstance, involved through no fault of his own in a case initiated not by himself but by others, and hardly aware of the value of freedom, does not accord with the little evidence that is available.

At the time of his sale to Dr. John Emerson, he gave evidence of a spirited nature and a desire for freedom: he ran away and hid in the Lucas Swamps, a popular African-American hiding place near St. Louis, where he was subsequently found and returned to his owner. By 1844, he had accumulated savings of $300—no easy task for even the most resourceful and industrious slave—and sought to purchase his freedom and that of his family from Mrs. Emerson, his owner at the time, offering immediate payment of part of the purchase price and security for the remainder. His offer was refused. It was soon thereafter that he petitioned the St. Louis circuit court for the right to institute suit for his freedom, a petition that was granted. In the attempted purchase and in the lawsuit he received encouragement from others, from an unnamed army officer and, later, from members of the Blow family, but it was he who initiated the necessary procedures.

These few facts suggest a sensitive black man who, though unable to read or write, knew the value of freedom and actively sought it for himself and his family. See Vincent C. Hopkins, *Dred Scott's Case* (1967).

LOUIS RUCHAMES

SCOTT, Emmett Jay (b. Houston, Tex., Feb. 13, 1873; d. Washington, D.C., Dec. 12, 1957), EDUCATOR, earned BA (1890) and MA (1901) degrees from Wiley University (Marshall, Texas) while working as a mailman. In 1891 he began working for the Houston *Daily Post* as an assistant janitor and messenger. He became editor of a black newspaper, *Texas Freeman,* in 1894. Three years later Scott became secretary to **Booker T. Washington,** the president of Tuskegee Institute, Alabama. He was elected secretary of the newly formed National Negro Business League in 1900 and served this organization until 1922. President William Howard Taft appointed Scott to the

American Commission to Liberia in 1909, and in 1912 he became executive secretary of Tuskegee.

During World War I, Scott served as special adviser to Secretary of War **Newton D. Baker** on matters affecting black soldiers (1917–19). He wrote a report in 1920 for the Carnegie Endowment for International Peace on African-American migration to the North during World War I, and served as secretary of Howard University (1919–34), where he worked to expand that school's programs. Active in politics, Scott was assistant publicity director of several Republican national conventions. During World War II he was director of personnel for the Sun Ship Co., Chester, Pennsylvania, and continued as a public relations consultant in Washington until his death. Scott was the author of *Tuskegee and Its Peoples* (1910), written with Booker T. Washington; *Booker T. Washington, Builder of a Civilization* (1916), written with Lyman Beecher Stowe; and of *The American Negro in the World War* (1919).

———— ⌇ ————

Scott's position as secretary and press coordinator to Booker T. Washington brought him into contact with many of the nation's leaders. But while his close association with Washington gives the impression that he might have assumed national leadership among blacks upon Washington's death, Scott failed to do so. By the mid-1920s Scott actually had little voice outside black education circles. His decline in stature came at a time when the African-American had been almost eliminated from the political scene. And it was accelerated by Scott's own endorsement of Washington's accommodation philosophy, unacceptable to **W. E. B. Du Bois** and other militant blacks. Scott opposed the National Negro Committee, forerunner to the NAACP, and as late as 1919 he refused to give his personal approval for a national antilynching conference. As assistant to Secretary Baker during World War I, Scott did receive favorable notice for his attempts to lessen racial tension caused by the presence of greater numbers of black troops in the military (those encamped near large cities

in particular), and even Du Bois admitted that Scott had performed these duties well. Nevertheless, Scott's statement that winning the war should take priority over solving racial problems and his apparent lack of concern about prejudice met by African-American troops in Europe only further reduced any claim he may have had to leadership in the black community.

Always publicly optimistic, Scott continued to work for the Republican party and served on a special committee organized to lure African-American votes. Slowly, however, pessimism began to creep into his thinking, and he was to come to acknowledge some validity in **Marcus Garvey**'s contention that black men could not expect any semblance of equality from white Americans. Scott most clearly reveals this new attitude in his book *Negro Migration During the War*, which concludes with extensive statements culled from southern black newspapers, all demanding impartial justice for the African-American.

During his lifetime Scott was both feared and admired. After his death in 1957 and the new militancy in the civil rights movement, his name became relegated to a role of lesser importance. See August Meier, *Negro Thought in America* (1963), and Elliott Rudwick, *W. E. B. Du Bois* (1960).

EUGENE H. BERWANGER

SCOTT, Thomas Alexander (b. Fort Loudon, Pa., Dec. 28, 1823; d. Darby, Pa., May 21, 1881), BUSINESSMAN, began work at the age of eleven and in 1841 became a clerk in the office of his brother-in-law, who was toll collector at Columbia, Pennsylvania. He remained in the state's employ until 1845, and after two years in private business, he became chief clerk in the office of the collector of tolls at Philadelphia. In 1849 he returned to Columbia to work for the transporting firm of Leech and Co., and a year later became station agent for the Pennsylvania Railroad at Duncansville.

Thereafter Scott rose rapidly to the posts of third assistant superintendent in charge of the railroad's division from Altoona (1852), general superintendent (1858), and finally first vice president of the railroad (1860). At the outset of the Civil War he supplied railroad cars and locomotives to open communications between Washington and Annapolis, and he came to Washington on the plea of Secretary of War **Simon Cameron** to administer the transporting of men and munitions from Harrisburg to Annapolis by the North Central Railroad. In August 1861 he was designated assistant secretary of war in charge of railways and transportation. He resigned in June 1862, but returned to the War Department in September 1863.

After the war, when the Pennsylvania Co. was organized to consolidate and operate all roads owned or leased by the Pennsylvania west of Pittsburgh, Scott was named its president (1871–80). While in that post he also obtained a controlling interest in the Southern Railway Security Co. (1871), an early holding company dominating 2,131 miles of southern roads, the Atlantic and Pacific Railroad, the Union Pacific (1871), the Panhandle Route (1871), and the Texas and Pacific Railway (1872).

Having already sold the Union Pacific to the **Vanderbilt** interests in 1872, Scott was forced by the panic of 1873 to abandon plans for linking the Pennsylvania's southern interests with the Memphis and Charleston Railroad. Nevertheless, by 1874, when he became president of the Pennsylvania Railroad, it was the largest railroad system under one management in the world. His principal independent venture was to create a transcontinental line by promoting the Texas and Pacific Railroad, but the effort was hindered by the panic of 1873 and consequent financial problems. Scott suffered a paralytic stroke in 1878. Although he returned to work, he resigned the presidency of the Pennsylvania in 1880 and sold the Texas and Pacific Railroad to **Jay Gould** the following year.

Tom Scott's bold vision of a truly intercontinental railroad system carried him to the threshold of greatness only to abandon him at the critical hour. Had his plans succeeded he would have been remembered as perhaps the most powerful and talented transportation magnate of his era. But he had the misfortune to be in the right place at the wrong time. As president of the nation's largest and richest railroad corporation he could not have occupied a better position for realizing his vast dream. However, the depression after 1873 shattered his hopes and indirectly his health. Within seven years he had dismantled his properties, resigned his presidency, and died.

Scott was uniquely equipped to undertake so grand a scheme. Handsome, personable, and gregarious, he won loyalty and trust from subordinates and rivals alike. Yet he did not rely on charm alone to gain what he needed from politicians and businessmen. Scott was both clever and resourceful; it was talent no less than personal attractiveness that took him to the Pennsylvania's presidency. He was an able administrator, a skilled negotiator, and an imaginative promoter. Above all he was indefatigable. **Collis Huntington** once remarked that Scott seemed to turn night into day and day into night. He threw his enormous energy into every project and may well have worked himself to death.

If Scott had a serious weakness, it was that he was too much of a plunger, sometimes pushing his boldness to the point of recklessness. Grand visions demanded great risks, and Scott did not hesitate to incur them. But the times ran against him. He assumed the Pennsylvania's presidency during an era of contraction and caution, one that demanded restraint rather than expansion. To his credit Scott served the Pennsylvania well, pursuing careful policies. But his own fortunes did not fare so well. His rail empire foundered beneath the weight of depressed times and left Scott awash among those entrepreneurs remembered more for their visions than for their accomplishments. See Samuel Kamm, *The Civil War Career of Thomas A. Scott* (1940).

MAURY KLEIN

SCOTT, Winfield (b. near Petersburg, Va., June 13, 1786; d. West Point, N.Y., May 29, 1866),

MILITARY LEADER, briefly attended the College of William and Mary (1805), studied law, and enlisted in the army. Appointed to the rank of captain in 1808, he was shortly afterward suspended for accusing General **James Wilkinson,** one of his superiors, of being a traitor. After being reinstated, Scott served in the War of 1812 in the battles of Chippewa and Lundy's Lane, and attained the rank of brigadier general (1814). Following the war, Scott helped modernize the army's administrative system and worked to improve the professional training of officers.

Scott participated in the Black Hawk War (1832) and was sent by President Jackson to South Carolina during the nullification crisis. In 1835 he fought against the Seminole and Creek tribes in Florida. Charged with failing to prosecute the campaign with vigor, he was brought before a court of inquiry but exonerated.

In 1841 Scott was made general in chief of the army. During the Mexican War he commanded an amphibious campaign against Veracruz and captured the city (March 1847). He then advanced with more than 10,000 men over the mountains toward Mexico City, winning battles at Cerro Gordo, Churubusco, Molino del Rey, and Chapultepec. In September 1847 he captured Mexico City. Scott's relations with President Polk were never good, and they reached their nadir in quarrels over the peace negotiations and the allocation of credit for victory between Scott's and Polk's friends. Relieved of command in Mexico, Scott returned to the U.S. to follow a court of inquiry investigating the latter issue, which delivered an ambiguous verdict. Nevertheless, in 1852 Scott was rewarded for his Mexican victories with the brevet rank of lieutenant general.

Scott was the Whig candidate for the presidency in 1852, but lost to Franklin Pierce, the Democratic nominee, 254 electoral votes to 42. Following Lincoln's election as president (1860), Scott, still general in chief of the army, urged President Buchanan to reinforce the southern ports and armories. He had little success, however. After Lincoln's inauguration and Fort Sumter, Scott helped establish the strategy of the Civil War by advocating his "Anaconda plan" of blockading the Confederacy. Because of increasing infirmity he retired from the army in November 1861.

⸻

Quixotic, quarrelsome, vain, egotistical, blustering, eventually fat and gouty, addicted to malapropisms like his complaint that President Polk had opened "a fire upon my rear"—"Old Fuss and Feathers" Winfield Scott was all of these. He was also a superb soldier, worthy of being the only officer of the U.S. army to attain the rank of lieutenant general between George Washington and U. S. Grant.

Scott made himself the link between the untrained amateur American soldiers of the Revolutionary War and the first prototypes of the modern professional officer. An amateur soldier himself at first, he read widely in all the available military literature to make himself a master of his work (in a typical episode utilizing to that end the year's enforced leave after he was court-martialed for his intemperate abuse of his superior General Wilkinson). By self-education he became virtually a professional, and then throughout his career as a ranking officer of the army he promoted West Point as a school for a professional officer corps and cultivated the careers of outstanding Military Academy graduates such as **R. E. Lee.** He did much to ensure the permanence of West Point with his famous tribute to its graduates as the authors of rapid American success in the Mexican War.

He earned as much credit as anyone could in the bungled campaigns of Queenston in 1812 and Fort George and the St. Lawrence in 1813, and early in 1814 became a brigadier in charge of a force of newly created regular regiments assembling around Buffalo. Predictably, he had military textbooks in his baggage, from which he trained the troops in standard battlefield evolutions, British mastery and American ignorance of which did much to explain the hitherto unhappy course of the war. As drillmaster and then a brigade commander in the army that General Jacob Brown led across the Niagara frontier in July, Scott laid the foundations for the American successes at Chippewa and Lundy's Lane, where for the first time in the war American troops matched or bettered the skill of British veterans in stand-up fighting in the open field. Chippewa and Lundy's Lane in turn led directly to a new emphasis on the regular army, rather than militia, as the foundation of American military policy after the war, exemplified in the messages of Secretary of War **John C. Calhoun.**

Scott was perhaps too much a professional soldier, in the sense that he had become too much a European-style soldier, to fare well in his Florida campaign against the Seminoles. His overly elaborate, Napoleonic maneuvers put him among the first of a long parade of American commanders to meet frustration against the unfamiliar guerrilla tactics of the Seminoles. He was more comfortable again in his campaign in Mexico in 1847. His march from Veracruz to Mexico City was especially daring in that Scott cut himself off from reliable communication and supply when he hurried away from Veracruz to spare his troops exposure to yellow fever; the Duke of Wellington may well have remarked, as it was reported, that now Scott was lost. The campaign was distinguished also by the adroitness with which Scott maneuvered his way into Mexico City, in general avoiding battles and bloodshed, reaching his objectives by outwitting the enemy rather than by fighting him, and proceeding on the principle, as he once wrote to his rival General Santa Anna, that "too much blood has already been shed in this unnatural war."

His humaneness testified that Scott was a great man as well as a great general, despite the pettiness with which after the Mexican War he resumed his customary quarrels over the dignities and prerogatives to which he felt entitled. When the Civil War came, he still possessed a good military mind, as his sponsorship of the "Anaconda policy" shows; but his equal in petty jealousy, though not in generalship, **George B. McClellan,** pushed him into retirement at last. See Charles Winslow Elliott, *Winfield Scott, the Soldier and the Man* (1937).

RUSSELL F. WEIGLEY

SCRIPPS, Edward Wyllis (b. Rushville, Ill., June 18, 1854; d. Monrovia Bay, Liberia, March 12, 1926), JOURNALIST, became an office boy at seventeen for the Detroit *Tribune,* which was managed by his half-brother James. Later, he joined the staff of the Detroit *Evening News,* a pioneering two-cent paper founded by James, eventually becoming city editor. In 1878, with family financial backing, he became editor of the new Cleveland *Penny Press.* Over the next two years, the Scripps brothers purchased papers in Buffalo, St. Louis, and Cincinnati, forming the first chain of daily newspapers in the country. Financial disagreements, however, caused a split among the brothers, and in 1883 Edward relinquished control of all but the Cincinnati *Penny Post.* After a brief reconciliation in 1888, Edward and James made a final separation two years later. Edward retained control of the Cincinnati and St. Louis papers. Joined by Milton A. McRae, his business manager, he christened this organization the Scripps-McRae League. In 1892 Scripps's half-brother George broke with James and brought the Cleveland *Press* into the League (in 1895 Edward, George, and McRae formed a new partnership). In 1892 Edward acquired the San Diego *Sun,* the first of a separate chain of Scripps newspapers on the West Coast. Scripps and McRae now founded their own independent newsgathering agency, which they developed into the United Press Association (1907). The Newspaper Enterprise Association, which supplied Scripps's and other papers with cartoons, illustrations, and feature articles, was also organized in this period (1902). In 1920 Scripps founded the Science Service to furnish newspapers with descriptions of current scientific research written in popular language.

Scripps's newspapers, although independently edited, generally bore the stamp of his views, and sought to appeal to the "95 per cent," or common men, with liberal pro-labor and politically independent views. Scripps retired because of failing health in 1908, but a conflict over editorial policy with his son James, who used his stock holdings to remove the five West Coast papers and the Dallas *Dispatch* from the Scripps chain, forced him to come out of retirement in 1920 and form a new newspaper combination, the Scripps-Howard chain. In his later years, Scripps engaged along with his sister Ellen B. Scripps in several philanthropic activities, including the foundation of the Scripps Institution for Biological Research at La Jolla, California.

Building on the ideas of his half-brother, James, Edward W. Scripps helped to introduce penny journalism into the growing cities of the Middle West in the eighteen-seventies and eighties and, in the process, created the first important chain of newspapers in the country. In the fashion of the so-called new journalism which revolutionized daily publication in this period, Scripps sought to appeal to the middle and lower classes who had not been attracted to the old-style political journals. Scripps not only sold his papers for a penny or two, but vigorously espoused popular causes. Saying in his direct way, "God damn the rich, God help the poor," he particularly crusaded in behalf of union labor, a distinctly radical position for the time. After the turn of the century, again characteristic of many journals of the new style, Scripps's papers joined the Progressive movement. Scripps himself tended to become conservative after World War I, but his papers retained their tradition of crusading in the public interest.

In constructing his chain, Scripps pursued the practice of establishing dailies in cities of middling size in the Midwest, Far West, and South. Not until his retirement did the League, now under the leadership of Roy W. Howard, invade the eastern metropolitan centers by purchasing such papers as the Pittsburgh *Press* and the New York *Telegram*. Scripps habitually paid low salaries when he established a paper, but he encouraged maximum effort from his subordinates by permitting them to acquire a minority stock interest; if the enterprise succeeded, they would profit.

Scripps was a cantankerous, moody man who preferred to work behind the scenes. While first McRae and later Howard actively managed the League, he lived in seclusion at Miramar, an estate near San Diego. In his last years he wandered across the world aboard his yacht, the *Ohio*. See Oliver Knight, ed., *I Protest: Selected Disquisitions of E. W. Scripps* (1966).

JULIAN S. RAMMELKAMP

SEABURY, Samuel (b. Groton, Conn., Nov. 30, 1729; d. New London, Conn., Feb. 25, 1796), LOYALIST, RELIGIOUS LEADER, received a BA from Yale in 1748, completed medical training with a year's study at the University of Edinburgh in 1752–53, was ordained in 1753, and in the same year was appointed by the Society for the Propagation of the Gospel as missionary at New Brunswick, New Jersey. There he became involved in political controversy as a supporter of Anglican control over the proposed King's College, New York. In 1757 he moved to Jamaica, Long Island, where he was both SPG missionary and rector of a parish. In 1766 he accepted identical posts at Westchester, New York.

In 1774–75 Seabury, generally writing under the name A.W(estchester). Farmer, produced pamphlets opposing the measures of the first Continental Congress. This defiance of the Patriot party, plus a variety of other Loyalist activities, led to his arrest and brief imprisonment at New Haven at the end of 1775. With the start of the British Long Island campaign in the late summer of 1776, he fled for safety within the British lines, supplying General Howe's army with valuable logistical information. A resident of British-controlled New York City throughout the remainder of the war, he practiced medicine, wrote political essays, held a number of clerical appointments (mainly sinecures), and with the ending of hostilities superintended the Loyalist exodus to Nova Scotia. In 1783 the Connecticut Anglican clergy elected Seabury bishop, and he sailed for England seeking consecration. The English bishops refused to grant his request because of the cabinet's position that such action would be regarded by the U.S. as interference in their affairs. However, he received consecration from the Scottish Episcopal Church. Returning to New London as rector of St. James's Church, as bishop of Connecticut (and, from 1790, of the few Rhode Island Anglicans), he organized a diocese and in 1789 joined in forming a nationwide Protestant Episcopal Church. In 1793 Seabury published *Discourses on Several Subjects*. In 1798 a second collection of his sermons, *Discourses on Several Important Subjects,* was issued.

The Revolution and its disruption of colonial Anglicanism largely account for Samuel Seabury's public career. Prior to that cataclysm, a lack of personal ambition had prevented his achieving a prominent position among the Anglican clergy of the northern colonies, despite their leaders' recognition of his talents as a polemicist and repeated, but indifferently successful, attempts to draw him firmly within the leadership circle. With few exceptions—most notably his part in the "American Whig" controversy of 1768–69—Samuel Seabury's life until 1774 was that of the rural pastor-physician, in which role he displayed energy, devotion to duty, jealousy of his good name, and—in his own opinion—only modest achievements.

The assembling of the first Continental Congress interrupted Seabury's routine, forced him into the larger world. Sensing a move toward independence and fearing independence as signaling an assault on the Anglican churches, he strove mightily to maintain the political tie with Britain. Direct political activity—on a scale at least equal to that of any other New York Loyalist—he reinforced with the terse, witty, deliberately colloquial prose of his pamphlets. In these productions he eschewed elaborate ideological arguments and appealed to the self-interest of his province's farmers and merchants and to the *amourpropre* of its assembly. Independence, Seabury ultimately realized, held a more subtle threat than that he had envisioned: the gradual disintegration of Anglican congregations deprived of ties with a historic episcopate. This consideration led him, first, to accept the episcopal office and later, Loyalism notwithstanding, to defy the British government that had refused him consecration.

As bishop of Connecticut, Seabury functioned as principal leader of an indigenous New England Anglicanism—High in its theology, Evangelical in its preaching, and reminiscent in certain structures of its Congregational background. This distinctive churchmanship, dating from the decade of his birth, had molded him from his earliest years. He reflected its preoccupation with the bishop's active and central role, and he sought to make that conception a reality. A hard-working administrator, he held regular visitations of his parishes, preaching, consecrating new churches that testified to Connecticut Anglicanism's continued vitality and growth, and confirming more than ten thousand persons. Operating on the premises that laymen had no authority in church councils (except as regarded "temporal" matters) but that, at the same time, a bishop could take no important action without his pastors' consent, he made a clerical convocation the chief governing organ of his diocese—a unique arrangement in the Protestant Episcopal Church.

In the negotiations which produced that nationally organized body, Seabury exhibited the New England churchman's traditional suspicion of the orthodoxy of brethren from Pennsylvania southward and championed Connecticut's chosen polity forcefully and, indeed, abrasively. Unsuccessful in efforts to exclude the laity from the General Convention, or from the conventions of other states, he nevertheless did secure an organization within which his version of Anglicanism might flourish. He likewise obtained a revision of the communion office in line with the nonjuring theology of his Scottish consecrators. Their eucharistic teaching he vigorously promoted in published writings throughout the period of his episcopate. He thus enriched as well as preserved New England's High Church tradition, providing native precedents for the American Oxford Movement of the 19th century and the Anglo-Catholicism of the present day. See Bruce E. Steiner, *Samuel Seabury 1729–1796: A Study in the High Church Tradition* (1972).

BRUCE E. STEINER

SERRA, Junípero (b. Petra, Majorca, Nov. 24, 1713; d. Carmel, Calif., Aug. 28, 1784), RELIGIOUS LEADER, born Miguel José Serra, entered the Franciscan Order at Palma on the Mediterranean island of Majorca in 1730, changing his name to Junípero. He became a preacher and then professor of philosophy at the Palma convent in 1738, earning his doctor of theology degree at Spain's Lullian University around 1743. In 1749 he joined a group of Franciscans going to Mexico City's Apostolic College of San Fernando, arriving there the following year. From 1750 to 1758, Serra was a field missionary to the Indians of Sierra Gorda. He was recalled in the latter year to be sent to Texas, but owing to unrest among the Indians, he was retained in Mexico City as a circuit missionary for southcentral Mexico (1760–67). He became president of the missions of Lower (Baja) California in 1768 when the Franciscans replaced the banished Jesuits.

In 1769 Serra accompanied the Spanish military expedition under Gaspar de Portolá, which was occupying Upper California, in order to establish a group of missions. The first such mission was founded in San Diego on July 16, 1769. Serra then proceeded to Monterey to establish the San Carlos mission (1770). This mission was moved to Carmel in 1771 and became Serra's headquarters. Serra also founded the missions of San Antonio (1771) and San Gabriel (1771) near modern Los Angeles; San Luis Obispo (1772); San Francisco de Assisi within the limits of modern San Francisco (1776); San Juan Capistrano (1776); Santa Clara (1777); and San Buenaventura (1782) in modern Ventura. In addition to introducing cattle, sheep, grains, and food products from Mexico, Serra converted many Native Americans and helped them settle in agricultural communities around the missions.

Without minimizing the combined efforts of the Spanish state, the armed forces, and the early settlers, it is Junípero Serra, who towers most prominently in the founding of European civilization and Christianity in California. He organized the mission system along traditional lines among the coastal Native Americans living in Stone Age conditions and since classified by anthropologists as lower nomads. Despite ill health from the beginning of his New World apostolate, he was fundamentally rugged and died in his seventy-first year, still working. By nature he was optimistic, zealous, and dynamic. In his personal life he was strongly ascetic and in his missionary endeavors tireless. Totally dedicated, he eschewed frequent correspondence of a social nature with his native Spain. He returned to Mexico only once from California and then on mission business, for which he won the support and sympathy of the viceroy, Antonio María Bucareli. In an age when a close relationship between church and state prevailed, he battled with the civil and military authorities in defense of the Native Americans, whom he genuinely loved, as his letters reveal. This made him a controversial figure.

His correspondence, now published in Spanish and English in four volumes of 1,855 pages, shows Serra to have been an able administrator and shrewd in business matters. In him were combined realism and idealism. In the beginning of his missionary career he chose as his motto: "Always go forward and never turn back." In his declining days he penned what had been his ideal in controversy and frustration: "Let what we are doing be done well." Monuments have been erected to him in Spain, Mexico, Puerto Rico, and the United States. A rich nomenclature recalls his memory from San Diego to Sacramento. Serra was raised to sainthood by the Catholic Church in 1988. See Maynard J. Geiger, *The Life and Times of Junípero Serra, or The Man Who Never Turned Back* (1959).

MAYNARD J. GEIGER

SEWALL, Samuel (b. Bishopstoke, Eng., March 28, 1652; d. Boston, Mass., Jan. 1, 1730), JURIST, WRITER, came to Boston with his family in 1661 and graduated from Harvard College in 1671. He became a resident fellow in divinity at Harvard and earned his MA degree there in 1674. He left Harvard to become manager of the colony's printing press (1681–84), and in 1683 he was selected to the Massachusetts general court from Westfield, Hampden County. In 1684 he became a member of the Governor's Council. He spent 1688 in England supporting **Increase Mather**'s attempts to regain the colony's old charter. Returning to Boston in 1689, Sewall resumed his seat on the council and was named a councilor in the new charter issued by William III in 1691; he served in this position until 1725.

In 1692 Sewall was appointed to a special commission to try the witchcraft cases at Salem and eventually sentenced nineteen persons to death. He publicly confessed the injustice of this decision in 1697 at the Old South Church in Boston, the only Salem judge to do so. He was appointed associate justice of the Massachusetts superior court of judicature in 1692.

Sewall was made a commissioner of the Society for the Propagation of the Gospel in New England in 1699 and became secretary-treasurer the following year. In this capacity he advocated establishing separate reservations for Native Americans where they could learn the language and customs of the whites. He also published one of the first antislavery tracts in the colonies, *The Selling of Joseph* (1700). In 1715 he became judge of probate for Suffolk County, Massachusetts, and in 1718 chief justice of the superior court of judicature, serving until 1728. A prolific writer of verse and political tracts, Sewall is best known for his diary, kept from 1674 to 1729, but not published until 1878, in which he described both contemporary events and the Puritan character and customs of the time. Some of his other works include *The Revolution of New England Justified* (1691) and *A Memorial Relating to the Kennebeck Indians* (1721).

———— ∞ ————

As a high-ranking magistrate, prominent churchman, jurist, and merchant, and as one of the two or three wealthiest New Englanders of his time, Sewall had scarcely a representative life. But it was a symptomatic and a revealing life because it touched upon, or was touched by, most of the major events of the second and third generations of colonial society in Massachusetts. Moreover, by faithfully keeping a diary for more than half a century, Sewall immortalized himself as well as his society, with its anxieties, aspirations and nuances of behavior. Despite his involvement in many significant episodes, his ultimate importance lies not in what he did or who he was, but in his steady sensibility and his *furor scribendi* as a compulsive barometer of daily moods and minor events.

His life was filled with fascinating contradictions, and in that respect, perhaps, may be considered characteristically colonial: an austere man of indulgent girth, round face, sagging jowls, several chins, and flowing white hair; a relatively leisured man in a nonleisured society; a conservative revolutionary; a traditionalist who managed to move with the times, its growing prosperity and changing imperatives; a jurist who was not always judicious; an unoriginal mind, yet an incisive one; a public figure whose family life and courtships, as revealed by his diary, are of more enduring interest. He was, in the final analysis, a secularized Puritan, a man of dignity and decency who sporadically prodded the tagging conscience of New England through efforts to achieve justice for deceased witches, African-American slaves, anglicized Native Americans, and wayward saints. See Ola Elizabeth Winslow, *Samuel Sewall of Boston* (1964).

MICHAEL KAMMEN

SEWARD, William Henry (b. Florida, Orange Co., N.Y., May 16, 1801; d. Auburn, N.Y., Oct. 10, 1872), POLITICAL LEADER, graduated from Union College (1820), and was admitted to the bar in 1822. Elected to the New York state assembly as an Anti-Mason in 1830, Seward advocated internal improvements and supported President Jackson in his controversies over nullification with the South Carolina legislature. He was the Whig candidate for governor of New York in 1834, but was defeated. In 1838, however, he was elected governor. In office he championed internal improvements. He also recommended that the children in the New York public schools should be "instructed by teachers speaking the same language with themselves and professing the same faith." When Virginia demanded the extradition of three sailors who had convinced a fugitive slave to escape to New York, Seward, an opponent of slavery, refused to release them. He did not seek reelection in 1842, and returned to his law practice.

In 1848 Seward was elected to the U.S. Senate (serving 1849–61). He was an outspoken critic of the Compromise of 1850. He favored the admission of California as a free state, but condemned the Fugitive Slave Act, arguing that a "higher law" than the Constitution, the law of God, made slavery immoral. However, when Senator **Charles Sumner** introduced a bill in 1852 repealing the Fugitive Slave Act, Seward did not vote on the measure. His antagonism to the idea of "popular sovereignty," which permitted the actual settlers of a territory to determine whether it should be slave or free, caused him to denounce the Kansas-Nebraska Act (1854), and in 1856 to support the admission of Kansas as a free state under the antislavery Topeka Constitution. Seward denounced the **Dred Scott** decision (1857), which permitted slavery in the territories, as a conspiracy. In 1858 he stated in a speech at Rochester, New York, that the sectional controversy over slavery represented an "irrepressible conflict."

Seward was a leading candidate at the Republican presidential convention of 1860 but lost the nomination to Abraham Lincoln. When Lincoln assumed the presidency (1861), he appointed Seward secretary of state. Determined to take control of the nation's foreign policy, Seward, shortly before the firing on Fort Sumter in April 1861, presented Lincoln with "Some Thoughts for the President's Consideration," in which he advocated an aggressive foreign policy against Spain, France, Britain, and Russia as a means to unite the nation. Lincoln did not act on this proposal.

During the Civil War Seward's policy was to keep the European powers neutral. When the U.S.S. *San Jacinto* stopped the British steamer *Trent* (1861) and removed John Slidell and James M. Mason, Confederate emissaries to England, Seward ordered their release, fearing that

England might declare war. When Lincoln was assassinated by **John Wilkes Booth** (April 14, 1865), Seward was wounded by Lewis Powell, a coconspirator. Following the war, Seward supported a conciliatory attitude toward the South.

Partly as a result of the pressure exerted by Seward, by March 1867 Napoleon III removed the French troops that had occupied Mexico. An expansionist, Seward obtained Alaska from Russia for $7.2 million (1867), and engineered the annexation of Midway Island (1867). He tried to purchase the Danish West Indies and Santo Domingo; demonstrated interest in acquiring Cuba; and advocated the annexation of Hawaii. He also began negotiations to settle the *Alabama* Claims dispute (resolved in 1871), in which Great Britain agreed to pay for damages inflicted on U.S. ships by British-built Confederate boats.

Seward had many of the qualities that make for political leadership. He possessed superior mental equipment, great vitality, and an enormous capacity for hard labor. He was witty and sociable, with a great fund of stories derived from his experiences on the hustings. His devotion to the game of politics impressed his peers, and his oracular utterances dazzled the hoi polloi. Politics was indeed his passion (his marriage and family took second place), and the presidency was his lodestar during practically all of his public career.

This little Auburn lawyer whose gaze was fixed on the nation's capital had large defects of mind and character. His excessive vanity offended not a few, and his penchant for loquacity more than once produced embarrassing results. He also made bad errors of judgment. His decision to withdraw his name from consideration for the 1856 Republican presidential nomination in all probability cost him the nomination in 1860. In the crucial winter of 1860–61 he persistently underestimated the strength of the secession movement. His belief that the seceding states could be brought back into the Union by a bellicose foreign policy amounted almost to an obsession. Coupled with his conviction that Lincoln was unequal to the tasks of leadership, it prompted his "Thoughts for the President's Consideration," one of the most extraordinary state papers of all time. Although he was well disposed toward the blacks and saw the need for black male suffrage, his belief that they were fundamentally inferior to whites was a barrier to his evolving a constructive program for solving the problems of Reconstruction. Worst of all, perhaps, was his passion for what **Horace Greeley** scornfully termed "dexterity in politics," a love of subtlety that led men to wonder if he had convictions and that at times verged on duplicity. These shortcomings were overlooked or minimized by his admirers, who were many, but they cost him support that was sometimes crucial, and raised up enemies who thwarted his constructive efforts.

Seward himself could perceive some of the results of his own defects. It was not entirely whimsy that led him to conclude a letter to his counselor **Thurlow Weed,** "your unfortunate friend, who has faith in everybody and enjoys the confidence of nobody." But there was another and brighter side to his personality. It was a tribute to him that, long before the Civil War was over, Lincoln had come to place a high value on the services of his secretary of state and to treat him as an intimate friend. As Lincoln said of him, he was "a man without gall," one in whose scheme of life personal enmities were never allowed to shape policy. In the State Department he demonstrated an increasing capacity for meeting difficult responsibilities, and he developed a superb sense of timing in handling the country's relations with Britain and with France. The courtesy and aplomb that he displayed toward difficult personalities such as **Thaddeus Stevens** and Charles Sumner enabled him to enlist their services at critical points in the country's diplomatic relations. Most important of all was his vision of the nation's future as a world power. Although many of his efforts to build for this future were unavailing, his marking out of the path the country was to take, signalized by the purchase of Alaska, constitutes one of his chief claims to high rank as a statesman. See G. G. Van Deusen, *William Henry Seward* (1967).

GLYNDON G. VAN DEUSEN

SHAHN, Ben (b. Kovno, Lithuania, Sept. 12, 1898; d. Roosevelt, N.J., March 14, 1969), ARTIST, emigrated to the U.S. in 1906. He became an apprentice lithographer in 1913, and worked his way through high school and college (City College of N.Y., 1922) as a lithographer. He also attended the National Academy of Design (1922) and then studied and traveled in Europe, Japan, and North Africa (1925, 1927–29). His first one-man show was in New York City (1930); it consisted largely of sketches and watercolors of African subjects. In 1931–32, Shahn painted twenty-three gouaches about the Sacco-Vanzetti trial, and fifteen more in 1932–33 on the trial of labor leader Thomas Mooney. These were the first of numerous works showing his concern with social issues.

On the strength of the Sacco-Vanzetti paintings, Shahn was hired by Diego Rivera to assist in the fresco *Man at the Crossroads* for the RCA building (1932). He was commissioned by the PWA to paint eight tempera panels on prohibition (1933–34) and was a photographer and designer for the Farm Security Administration (1935–38). He also executed a mural for the garment workers' resettlement project in Roosevelt, New Jersey, where he lived after 1937. During 1938–42 he did panels for several public buildings, including the Bronx Central Annex Post Office (1938–39), the Jamaica, New York, Post Office (on the Four Freedoms), and the Social Security Building (now the Department of Health, Education, and Welfare), in 1942. He created posters for the Office of War Information (1942–43), and was chief artist of the Political Action Committee of the CIO (1944–46).

In 1947–48, a retrospective exhibition of his works was shown at the Museum of Modern Art, New York City. He created posters and campaign material for **Henry Wallace**'s campaign for the presidency (1948). From 1949 to 1951, Shahn taught art: at the University of Wisconsin (1949); the summer session at the University of Colorado (1950); and the Brooklyn Museum Art School (1951). In 1956–57 he was Charles Eliot Norton Professor of Poetry at Harvard. He wrote *The*

Shape of Content at Harvard; in 1963 he wrote *Love and Joy About Letters;* and in 1965–66 he painted a large mural on the Sacco-Vanzetti trial for Syracuse University.

Shahn also designed stage sets and illustrated a series of religious works, books of poetry, and documentary articles on pressing social questions. His satirical portraits of well-known figures like **Thomas Dewey,** Father **Charles Coughlin,** Adolf Hitler, and Benito Mussolini were widely published. Exhibitions of his works appeared in many parts of the world, and he won many awards, among them two Pennell Memorial Medals (1939, 1953) and the Joseph E. Temple Gold Medal (1956).

———— ∞ ————

Ben Shahn's paintings indicating the treatment of Sacco and Vanzetti, the Italian-born anarchists executed for armed robbery and murder after a trial which was the cause célèbre of American intellectuals in the 1920s and also his series on the trial and imprisonment of the labor leader Tom Mooney made him by far the best-known social realist of the 1930s. His belief that the artist should play an active role in politics was again brought into focus when he and photographers Margaret Bourke-White and Paul Strand founded the Artists' Congress which dedicated itself to spreading antifascist propaganda. By the mid-1930s Shahn was equally known as a photographer. His photographs of Depression-era subjects provided him with material for many of his well-known paintings. He was also renowned as a muralist. This triad of talents reinforced his position as most typical American artist of the WPA period. After the 1940s, Ben Shahn's impact came more from his work as an illustrator, graphic designer, printmaker, and calligrapher. For some years he was probably the most widely imitated of all artists working in that shadowy area separating the "fine" from the "commercial" arts in America. But from a long-range, stylistic point of view, his use of letters and numbers in his paintings and drawings taught the public to "read" as well as to "see" his works, and relate him to such diverse artists as

Reginald Marsh and **Stuart Davis.** He was always more of a draftsman than a painter. In one of his own statements he spoke of "pouncing" his drawing back into a painting when the drawing became obliterated—"pouncing" being a Renaissance technique he learned from working with Diego Rivera on the fresco *Man at the Crossroads* commissioned for the RCA building in Rockefeller Center in New York—later destroyed as the result of political censorship. Ben Shahn's early drawing had a harsh, linear, almost primitive quality. It became gentler, softer, and more ornamental in his later career. See James Thrall Soby, *Ben Shahn: His Graphic Art* (1957).

LAWRENCE CAMPBELL

SHAPLEY, Harlow (b. Nashville, Mo., Nov. 2, 1885; d. Boulder, Colo., Oct. 20, 1971), ASTRONOMER, received a BA in 1910 and MA in 1911 from the University of Missouri, and his doctorate from Princeton in 1913. During 1914–21 he studied the shape and size of the galaxy at Mount Wilson Observatory, California, and in 1921 became professor of practical astronomy at Harvard and also the director of the Harvard Observatory; there, besides continuing his work on galaxies, he investigated the chemical composition of stars and conducted a star census.

In 1926 Shapley lectured in Belgium, in 1928 at Oxford, and in 1934 before the Royal Astronomical Society. During 1941–45 he was a member of the federal Office of Scientific Research and Development. In 1945 he worked for UNESCO and visited the U.S.S.R. to attend the Soviet Academy of Science Jubilee. In 1947 he criticized President Truman's policies toward Greece and Turkey (the Truman Doctrine) as anti-Soviet, and in 1949 he was the chairman of the National Council of the Arts, Sciences and Professions which held the Cultural and Scientific Conference for World Peace. These and other activities caused Shapley to be investigated by the House Committee on Un-American Activities in 1946. In 1950 Senator **Joseph McCarthy** called him a Communist, but shortly afterward, Senator Tydings's Foreign Relations Subcommittee exonerated him of this charge. In 1947 Shapley was elected president of the American Association for the Advancement of Science, and in 1952, one year after his retirement from Harvard, he became a Princeton and an MIT trustee. Among his many scientific works are *Flights from Chaos* (1930) and *Galaxies* (1943).

From humble beginnings as a farm boy in the Midwest, Shapley became one of the foremost astronomers of this century and one of the most influential intellectuals in the world. For his epic-making research on the location of the sun in the galaxy, many writers have referred to Shapley as a modern Copernicus. But besides his scientific accomplishments, he was a humanitarian, a scholar of broad interests, and a gregarious, and sometimes egotistical, spokesman for academia.

Shapley's early education in Missouri was not entirely formal, and his career included a brief early phase as a newspaper reporter. His flair with words was an obvious attribute, later aiding him in his enormously successful public speaking and popular writings. His career was also greatly assisted by some of his undergraduate and graduate professors, particularly his PhD adviser, H. N. Russell.

Shapley's main contributions to research occurred in the decade or so following his doctorate, primarily while he was at the Mount Wilson Observatory. His heavy flow of imaginative and significant research papers in the *Astrophysical Journal* and other similar publications led him to the famous Great Debate in 1920 with H. D. Curtis over the scale of the universe.

After becoming director of the Harvard Observatory, Shapley remained active in research, but administrative pressures began to tell upon him. From the early 1920s to the 1950s, under Shapley's able direction the observatory became well established as a world center; and during that era Harvard probably produced more truly outstanding astronomers than have come from any other institution in a comparable period of time.

Shapley was interested in multitudinous enterprises, including ardent support of Science Service, UNESCO, the National Science Foundation, and other such organizations. He also maintained an active hobby in the study and collection of ants.

Although he was occasionally immodest or arrogant, he was one of the nation's most popular and famous scientists, being constantly in demand for both technical and nontechnical talks. He was a warm, witty, benevolent man, who contributed as much to humanitarian causes as to science. See Owen Gingerich, "Harlow Shapley," in *The Dictionary of Scientific Biography*.

RICHARD BERENDZEN

SHAW, Lemuel (b. Barnstable, Mass., Jan. 9, 1781; d. Boston, Mass., March 30, 1861), JURIST, graduated from Harvard in 1800. He taught in a Boston school for a year (1800–1801) while writing articles for the Boston *Gazette,* a Federalist newspaper. In 1801 he began studying law as an apprentice and was admitted to the bar in 1804. Opening a practice in Boston, he prospered as the lawyer for many of the city's leading merchants. A Federalist, he represented Boston in the Massachusetts state legislature in 1811–14, 1820, and 1829. During his tenure he vigorously opposed the War of 1812. Shaw also served as a state senator (1821–22) and as a member of the Massachusetts constitutional convention (1820). He drew up the first city charter of Boston in 1822, which lasted until 1913. In 1830 he was appointed chief justice of the supreme judicial court of Massachusetts by Governor Levi Lincoln.

As chief justice, Shaw handed down more than 2,200 decisions and became known for his thoughtful, well-reasoned opinions. In *Farwell* v. *Boston & Worcester Railroad* (1842) he upheld the fellow-servant rule, which meant that an employee injured on the job, through no fault of his own, by the negligence of a fellow employee could not make a claim for damages against his employer. However, in *Commonwealth* v. *Hunt* (1842), he ruled that workers could strike whenever an employer hired nonunion labor. Opposed to slavery, Shaw freed all nonfugitive slaves who reached Massachusetts, but refused to release fugitive slaves. In 1849 in *Roberts* v. *Boston* he upheld racial segregation in Boston public schools. He received tremendous publicity presiding over the case in which Professor John W. Webster of Harvard was convicted in 1850 of murdering Dr. George Parkman, a prominent Boston citizen. Shaw resigned from the bench in 1860.

Shaw had the power of a crag vitalized by the human spirit. A formidable-looking man with coarse features, a shaggy mane, and austere manners, he inspired a contemporary to exclaim that people regarded him as the Indian did his totem, feeling that he was ugly but knowing that he was great. Shaw dominated his court. In his record number of opinions over three decades, only one was a dissent, and rarely did his associates disagree with him. His judicial energies were so prodigious that **Daniel Webster** claimed that Shaw could "do the work of ten men and at night eat ham enough to raise the market price." Shaw's opinions were comprehensive, ponderous, and analytical. Even in a simple case he had to "unlimber the heavy artillery of his mind, go down to the roots of the question, consider the matter in all possible relations, and deal with it as if he were besieging a fortress." Often explaining legal principles in terms of policy or social advantage, he placed his decisions on the broadest grounds. From the bench he was one of the nation's foremost teachers of law. Justice **Oliver Wendell Holmes, Jr.,** attributing Shaw's greatness to his "accurate appreciation of the requirements of the community," thought that "few have lived who were his equals in their understanding of the grounds of public policy to which all laws must be ultimately referred. It was this which made him ... the greatest magistrate which this country has produced."

At the time of his appointment to the bench, American law was still in its formative period. Whole areas of the law were unknown, many unsettled. The strategy of time and place presented an unrivaled opportunity for a judge of

Shaw's strength and vision to mold the law. His domain was the whole field of law excepting admiralty. No other state judge in our history through his opinions alone had so great an influence on the course of American law. At a time when other judges sought doctrines of vested rights, he was a champion of the power of government to promote and regulate the economy in the public interest. The foremost advocate of the "police power"—the state's authority to trench on the profitable use of private property for the common good—he laid the legal foundations for the emerging law of public utilities. Committed to judicial self-restraint, he voided legislative enactments in only nine reported cases, most often to protect the rights of the criminally accused.

In the absence of governmental action, Shaw's conservatism displayed itself. He construed the law to minimize the legal liabilities of business so that corporate interests, especially railroads, prevailed. His opinions, like the one establishing the fellow-servant rule, accentuated the inhumanity of the common law and spurred capitalist enterprise. His conservatism also manifested itself in cases involving notable social issues of his time. He handed down the leading opinion on the constitutionality of the Fugitive Slave Act of 1850; he originated the "separate but equal" doctrine that became the legal linchpin of racial segregation; and he sustained a conviction for blasphemy in an opinion that abridged religious liberty.

Yet his mind was open to many of the liberal currents of his time. Witness his support of the free public education movement, his liberating all sojourner slaves, his opinion on the criminal responsibility of the insane, his public-interest doctrines, and his defense of trade unions. His opinion in *Commonwealth* v. *Hunt* was labor's Magna Charta, unshackling unions from the old doctrine of criminal conspiracy. He held that a combination of workers to establish a closed shop by peaceable coercion is not a crime even if injuring the employer. Nor did he see anything illegal in a strike to raise wages. Perhaps his chief contribution was his day-to-day domestication of the common law, making it plastic to serve the shifting imperatives of American life. See Leonard W. Levy, *The Law of the Commonwealth and Chief Justice Shaw* (1957).

L. W. LEVY

SHAW, Robert Gould (b. Boston, Mass., Oct. 10, 1837; d. Fort Wagner, S.C., July 18, 1863), REFORMER, entered Harvard in 1856, but withdrew in 1859. When the Civil War broke out he enlisted in the Union army as a private in the 7th New York Regiment (April 1861). Promoted to second lieutenant of the 2d Massachusetts Regiment in May, he rose to first lieutenant in July and to captain thirteen months later.

In April 1863 Shaw was named colonel of the 54th Massachusetts Regiment, the first black regiment from the North to fight in the war. On July 18, 1863, he was killed while leading a charge on Fort Wagner, near Charleston, South Carolina.

An officer meeting his death while storming an enemy battery was a Civil War occurrence hardly so unusual as to evoke a widespread response on the home front. Robert Gould Shaw, however, was a young colonel who would not fade from memory with the sounding of taps. His distinction came from his character and from the character of the troops he commanded on the July evening he fell in battle. Coming from a family that took its social obligations seriously, Shaw, idealistic and high-principled, showed a particular interest in the abolitionist crusade. In 1860 he welcomed the election of Abraham Lincoln as a step to halt slavery. Early in 1863 when the Union army began to enlist black soldiers, Shaw accepted a commission in a newly formed regiment in order to demonstrate "that a Negro can be made a good soldier," as he put it. Shaw proved his point at Battery Wagner, his men fighting to the death as valiantly as he. Shaw was buried in a trench along with some of his black soldiers. Shaw's father, in a gesture the son would have approved, requested that no effort be made to recover the body to rebury it elsewhere. Shaw's brief career had been an exhibition of a deepseated sense of duty, a family trait. He personified the

moral fervor and sacrificial devotion that saw in the Civil War an opportunity to make a better America, ridding it of human bondage and improving the lot of the free black. See Peter Burchard, *One Gallant Rush: Robert Gould Shaw and His Brave Black Regiment* (1965).

BENJAMIN QUARLES

SHAYS, Daniel (b. Hopkinton, Mass., 1747; d. Sparta, N.Y., Sept. 29, 1825), REFORMER, was reared in poverty and worked as a hired man in Brookfield, Massachusetts. At the outbreak of the Revolution he fought at Lexington, was promoted to the rank of ensign, and fought at Bunker Hill, Ticonderoga, Saratoga, and Stony Point. In 1779 he was appointed captain of the 5th Massachusetts Regiment. Severely criticized for selling a sword that Lafayette had given him, he resigned from the army in 1780. He then moved to Pelham, Massachusetts, where over the next few years he held several town offices.

During the postwar depression the Massachusetts legislature refused to heed the demands of farmers for paper money issues and other laws to prevent the foreclosure of their lands. Mob action soon followed. After an initial period of hesitation, Shays took charge of the insurgents at Springfield (Sept. 26–27, 1786) and forced the state supreme court to adjourn. When the legislature took no action on the farmers' grievances Shays stopped the sitting of another court at Springfield on December 26. A month later he and Luke Day planned an attack on the Springfield arsenal, but a letter from Day postponing the rendezvous was intercepted by Major General William Shepherd's Hampshire Militia, and Shays was routed when he attacked with more than 1,200 men (Jan. 25, 1787). He retreated to Chicopee, where he joined forces with Eli Parsons; they then retreated to South Hadley, Amherst, and Pelham. Shays offered to lay down his arms if a general pardon were granted and if General Benjamin Lincoln's forces, mobilized by the state government to put down the insurrection, returned to Boston. This was refused, however, and Lincoln defeated the insurgents at Petersham (Feb. 4), capturing 150 men. With a reward of £150 on his head, Shays fled to Vermont, and then to Canada before returning again to Vermont. He was one of the fourteen men excluded from the general pardon of June 1787 and was sentenced to death in absentia by the Supreme Court. However, his petition for a pardon was granted in June 1788. After a short stay in Pelham, he settled in Sparta, New York. In his old age he received a federal pension for service in the Revolution.

———— ✺ ————

In many respects the political demise of the war hero Daniel Shays illustrates the limitations of the democratic movement within the American Revolution. A poor man in an era when leadership was normally reserved for men of means and leisure, barely literate in a state where Harvard and Yale degrees conferred automatic legitimacy and respect, Daniel Shays was capable of leading men into battle and attracting the loyalty of impoverished subsistence farmers, but when it came to state politics he was a naïve, inept outsider. A stranger to the men controlling the state government and as mistrustful of their intentions as they were of his, Shays was unable to organize any durable political movement, and so led his followers to inexorable military defeat.

In Shays's view the grievances of indebted farmers were sufficiently compelling to justify armed rebellion, even though the government they attacked was operating according to republican principles and representatives of his own constituency had participated in making the objectionable policies. As leader of an outvoted minority, Shays rejected majority rule in favor of a higher law of individual judgment of natural rights. Nobly standing in defense of these God-given rights and the material interests of his constituents, he failed to appreciate why self-conscious republicans took such a decided stand against his coercive tactics on both pragmatic and ideological grounds. By choosing to lead an army of irate farmers rather than building an organization to manipulate electoral politics, as the Democratic-Republicans would later do, Shays provided an expressive but ineffectual outlet for widespread and profound economic and political grievances. See David Szatmary, *Shays' Rebellion: The Making of an Agrarian Insurrection* (1980).

RICHARD D. BROWN

SHEELER, Charles (b. Philadelphia, Pa., July 16, 1883; d. Dobbs Ferry, N.Y., May 7, 1965), ARTIST, attended the School of Industrial Art in Philadelphia (1900–1903) and then studied at the Pennsylvania Academy of Fine Arts (1903–6) under William Merritt Chase. He traveled through Europe with Chase in 1904 and 1905 and then by himself in 1909. He settled in Philadelphia in 1910, and he contributed six paintings to the famous New York Armory Show of 1913, which presented modern paintings to the American public for the first time. These works demonstrated Sheeler's talents in Cubism and Precision art. *Landscape* (1915, William Lane Foundation, Leominster, Mass.) is another example. In 1912 Sheeler had taken up photography to support himself, and in 1918 he held a one-man photography show at New York's Modern (De Zayas) Gallery. He also did a series of photographs of African tribal masks that same year.

Moving to New York in 1919, Sheeler collaborated with Paul Strand on a motion picture, *Manhatta*, in 1920. He joined **Edward Steichen** in 1923 to make fashion photographs for *Vogue* magazine and was commissioned by **Henry Ford** in 1927 to do a series of photographs of the Ford plants at River Rouge. In 1929 he did a series of photographs of the Chartres Cathedral in France. Sheeler also did such paintings as *Bucks County Barn* (1923, Whitney Museum, N.Y.) and *Upper Deck* (1929, Fogg Art Museum, Cambridge, Mass.) in the 1920s. He began specializing in painting factories, machines, and industrial forms in the 1930s. *River Rouge Plant* (1932, Whitney Museum, N.Y.) and *City Interior* (1936, Worcester Art Museum, Mass.) are examples. In 1939 the Museum of Modern Art in New York gave him a one-man show. His later paintings included *Incantation* (1946, Brooklyn Museum, N.Y.), *Architectural Cadences* (1954, Whitney Museum, N.Y.), and *Golden Gate* (1955, National

Gallery of Art, Washington, D.C.). A stroke suffered in 1959 limited his painting, but in 1962 the American Academy of Arts and Letters presented him its Award of Merit.

In providing a detached, unsentimental view of architectural forms and especially of the industrial-urban landscape of the United States in the 20th century, the paintings of Charles Sheeler have delineated perhaps most fully in modern American art the visual organization of the man-made environment of the contemporary world. Sometimes characterized as a "Precisionist" or an "Immaculate," Sheeler focused in his work on the precise, carefully constructed, lucid detail, with a direct, unsparing realism. Although he was influenced considerably in his style and attitude toward painting by Cézanne and by Picasso and the Cubists, Sheeler dealt with American subject matter and essentially American forms—austere interiors, barns, simple wooden churches and houses, complex machines and factories, and skyscrapers. His interest was in the man-made environmental scene itself, void of people. Both in his paintings of an almost photographic realism and in his more abstract works, Sheeler displayed a remarkable feeling for the ordering of shapes and structures. The images delineate solid basic forms; they frequently have the tangible materiality of architecture, with an interplay of volume, surface, texture, line, and light. His later more abstract pictures often made use of a multiple-image style, with the rhythm of line and shape reinforcing the primary focus on form. In his photography, Sheeler was influenced by the course of his own painting. His photographs again commonly emphasized basic forms through direct, sharply focused, and unsentimental recordings of architectural, urban, and industrial scenes. His work has had considerable impact on the development of photographic art in America. Ultimately, Sheeler was always concerned with illuminating essential visual meanings, bringing to his work a poetic sense of the integrity, harmony, and wholeness of things. See

Constance Rourke, *Charles Sheeler: Artist in the American Tradition* (1969).

PAUL R. BAKER

SHERIDAN, Philip Henry (b. Albany, N.Y., March 6, 1831; d. Nonquitt, Mass., Aug. 5, 1888), MILITARY LEADER, graduated from the U.S. Military Academy (1853). He served along the Rio Grande and in the Northwest and was promoted to captain in 1861. When the Civil War broke out he became the quartermaster of Union troops in southwest Missouri, and served under General **Henry Halleck** during the Corinth campaign. In May 1862 he was promoted to colonel of the 2d Michigan Cavalry. He commanded a brigade at Booneville, Missouri, and following his victory there was promoted to brigadier general commanding divisions in the armies of the Ohio and the Cumberland.

In January 1863 Sheridan was made a major general of volunteers and given command of the 20th Corps of the Army of the Cumberland. After fighting at Chickamauga, he distinguished himself in the assault on Missionary Ridge at Chattanooga (1863). Grant then gave Sheridan command of the cavalry of the Army of the Potomac. He fought in the battles of the Wilderness, Todd's Tavern, and Cold Harbor (1864).

In August 1864 Sheridan took command of the Army of the Shenandoah, with orders to drive off the enemy and destroy supplies in the Shenandoah Valley. He won major battles at Winchester, Fisher's Hill, and Cedar Creek. In November 1864 he was made a major general in the regular army. After destroying the remnants of General Early's army at Waynesboro, he methodically destroyed provisions in the Shenandoah Valley. Rejoining Grant's army, he then harassed **Robert E. Lee**'s railroad communications with the rest of the South. In April 1865, after Lee evacuated Petersburg, Sheridan attacked him at Five Forks and continued to engage Confederate forces until the surrender at Appomattox.

Following the war Sheridan commanded a military division along the Mexican border. Under the Reconstruction Act of 1867 he served as military governor of Louisiana and Texas, with headquarters at New Orleans. His strict enforcement of the Reconstruction Act, however, annoyed President Andrew Johnson, who had him transferred to Missouri, where he participated in Indian wars and forced the hostile Native Americans to settle on reservations. In March 1869 he was made a lieutenant general.

In 1884 Sheridan succeeded **William T. Sherman** as commander in chief of the army, and in 1888 he was promoted to general. His *Personal Memoirs* (2 vols.) was published in 1888.

When he assumed command in the Shenandoah Valley, Philip Sheridan was still a young man of thirty-three. Small in stature, wiry, supple, and bandy-legged, but graced with broad shoulders and a youth's firm physique, Sheridan was born to be a horseman. His ruddy complexion, straggling mustache, and lighthearted Irish laughter added color to his image as a dashing cavalier, while his cold eyes, his fabled bravery, and the finesse with which he manipulated and inspired troops marked him as a man called to command.

"This Sheridan is a little Irishman," Lincoln once observed, "but he is a big fighter." From Corinth to Chattanooga the little Irishman fought his way from a captaincy to the rank of major general, and when, in 1864, Halleck and Grant looked about for the right man to reinvigorate the Army of the Potomac's disreputable cavalry corps, both generals automatically nominated Sheridan. Within weeks, Sheridan transformed the cavalry into an effective combat arm, capable of decisive maneuver both as an independent strike force and in combined operations with cooperating infantry, a model for the future evolution of armor. As a strategist schooled in the brutal western campaigns, Sheridan appreciated that modern total war demanded the ruthless demolition of the enemy's capacity to resist. Once given command in the Shenandoah, Lee's quondam breadbasket, Sheridan shattered Early's rebels and then proceeded, quite methodically, to peel away the Valley's skin of vegetation and civilization, leav-

ing behind a raw scar of blasted desolation. Like Grant and Sherman, Sheridan understood that war was no longer a game with rules. See Philip H. Sheridan, *Personal Memoirs of P. H. Sheridan, General United States Army,* (2 vols., 1888).

ROBERT L. KERBY

SHERMAN, John (b. Lancaster, Ohio, May 10, 1823; d. Washington, D.C., Oct. 22, 1900), POLITICAL LEADER, worked on canal and construction projects, then studied law, and was admitted to the bar in 1844. Settling in Cleveland in 1853, he was elected to the U.S. House of Representatives as a Whig (serving 1855–61). As a member of the Ways and Means Committee, he helped pass the Morrill Tariff (1861).

Sherman entered the U.S. Senate from Ohio as a Republican in 1861. During the Civil War he reluctantly supported the issuance of "greenbacks" as legal tender. Although he took a moderate stand on Reconstruction and sympathized with President Johnson, he voted for impeachment of the president in 1868 for partisan reasons. His main political interest as senator was in finance. He supported the Funding Act (1870) to help restore the national credit. In 1873 he voted for a bill to end the coinage of silver dollars (the "Crime of '73"), and in 1875 he backed the Resumption Act, providing for the return of specie payments and the reduction of the number of greenbacks in circulation.

Sherman was secretary of the treasury under President Hayes (1877–81). He was again elected to the Senate in 1881, remaining until 1897. Throughout the 1880s, he was a prominent contender for the Republican presidential nomination. In the Senate, Sherman supported the regulation of interstate commerce, but questioned the government's right to establish maximum and minimum rates and opposed the outlawing of pools. In 1890 he sponsored two important acts: the Sherman Anti-Trust Act, which sought to restore competition by breaking up combinations in restraint of trade; and the Sherman Silver Purchase Act, which committed the government to purchase 4.5 million ounces of silver monthly.

In 1897 President McKinley appointed Sherman secretary of state. However, Sherman's opposition to the Spanish-American War and to the annexation of foreign territory led him to resign the next year. He published his political memoirs, *Recollections of Forty Years in the House, Senate, and Cabinet* (2 vols.), in 1895.

John Sherman attained prominence as a financial statesman, and helped to establish a national banking system and to finance the Civil War. A strong Unionist, he supported efforts to grant the freed African-American civil rights, but like most moderates concluded that only sectional harmony and economic progress might possibly develop equal rights. Sherman's attitudes essentially grew from small-town origins. He was an individualist in economic affairs, but believed that the government should both promote and regulate national economic enterprises that assisted individuals in utilizing their talents. The Republican party was the mainspring of national development, and he supported tariff protection, "sound currency" that avoided inflation, and internal improvements. Well informed, and wise in the ways of Congress, Sherman became famous for the ability to compromise volatile issues that threatened his party's unity. He was never safe in Ohio's turbulent politics, which fortified a personal bent toward caution and indirection. Despite his power in Congress and party stature, Sherman never won the Republican presidential nomination, on which his heart was set.

Sherman remained masked behind a beard, and was formidable for his achievements and experience rather than for personal appeal. Critics called him "the Ohio Icicle." He once avoided comment on the political implications in a trip home by saying that he merely wished to "mend some fences" at his farm in Mansfield, a phrase that entered common parlance.

Sherman's achievements were no less important for being unspectacular. He was a stabilizing force in the GOP as it sought a national majority. And he shaped important fiscal legislation, including the antitrust and silver purchase acts of 1890 that bore his name. See Winfield S. Kerr, *John Sherman: His Life and Public Service* (2 vols., 1907).

H. WAYNE MORGAN

SHERMAN, Roger (b. Newton, Mass., April 19, 1721; d. New Haven, Conn., July 23, 1793), POLITICAL LEADER, followed his father's trade of cobbling and became a largely self-educated jack-of-all-trades. Moving to New Milford, Connecticut, in 1743, he continued to work as a cobbler, opened a small store, and also served as county surveyor until 1758. In this period he acquired large amounts of land. He was admitted to the bar in 1754, and was elected to the Connecticut General Assembly in 1755. In 1761 he moved to New Haven, where he became a retail merchant, and (1764–66) a local representative for the Connecticut Assembly. Sherman was a lukewarm supporter of the Sons of Liberty, but by 1774, as a member of the Continental Congress, he took a position denying Parliament's right to legislate for the colonies. Serving in the Congress until 1784, he helped draft the Declaration of Independence and proposed a plan of union while the Articles of Confederation were being considered. Despite heavy pressures from within the state, he agreed to the cession of Connecticut's claims to western lands. In 1783 Sherman helped codify the laws of Connecticut.

At the Constitutional Convention of 1787, Sherman presented the "Connecticut Compromise," which embodied his earlier idea of a dual system of representation as a balance between large and small states. In the convention he advocated indirect election of the members of both houses of Congress. Although he had counseled that popular ratification of the Constitution was unnecessary, he led the fight for ratification in his state in 1788.

Sherman served in the House of Representatives during the first Congress and in 1791 moved to the Senate, frequently warning against excessive democratic tendencies. He was a strong supporter of the Hamiltonian fiscal program, and a firm Federalist. A devout "Puritan" member of the

Congregational Church throughout his life, Sherman took much pride in being the only person to sign the four most important Revolutionary documents: the Articles of Association of 1774, the Declaration of Independence, the Articles of Confederation, and the Constitution.

———— ∞∞ ————

Sherman was the epitome of the canny 18th-century New England politician. Gnarled, wizened, given to speaking in a rapid nasal cant, he appeared superficially to be some sort of evil gnome; yet he combined these physical traits with an innocence of eye and sweetness of manner, convincing most observers that he was honest, frank, and totally lacking in guile. Actually he was one of the shrewdest backstage dealers of his time, and his deals resulted in a number of crucial permanent features of the American system of government.

As befits such an operator, some of his most important transactions remain shrouded in mystery. As indicated, he engineered Connecticut's cession of western land claims and sponsored the Connecticut Compromise. There is evidence—though not quite enough to be conclusive—that these two events, seemingly unrelated, were in fact intimately connected, yielded considerable profits to Connecticut land speculators, and gave final shape to the legislative and judicial branches of the federal government. Later as a representative, Sherman joined forces with his fellow Connecticuter, Senator **Oliver Ellsworth** (who had participated in Sherman's deals in the Constitutional Convention), to draft the celebrated Judiciary Act of 1789. That act established the federal court system essentially as it exists today, and for practical purposes forms a part of the Constitution. Once again, inconclusive evidence suggests that the act was part of a larger scheme in behalf of Connecticut land interests. In sum, Sherman's career seems to support the Federalist maxim that the public good is generally served by individuals pursuing their private interests. See Roger S. Boardman, *Roger Sherman: Signer and Statesman* (1938).

FORREST MCDONALD

SHERMAN, William Tecumseh (b. Lancaster, Ohio, Feb. 8, 1820; d. New York, N.Y., Feb. 14, 1891), MILITARY LEADER, graduated from the U.S. Military Academy (1840). During the Mexican War he held a number of administrative offices. After serving as a captain in the commissary department of the army, he resigned to join a San Francisco bank (1853). When the bank failed (1857), he entered business in Leavenworth, Kansas. During 1859–61 he was the superintendent of a new military college in Alexandria, Louisiana (now LSU), but resigned when Louisiana seceded from the Union.

In 1861 Sherman was appointed colonel of the 13th U.S. Infantry. He commanded a brigade in General McDowell's army at the Battle of Bull Run (July 1861). In August 1861 he was made a brigadier general of volunteers and assigned to the western theater of operations. In May 1862, following the Battle of Shiloh, he was promoted to major general of volunteers. General Grant then sent him to Memphis, where he suppressed Confederate guerrillas and established a civil government. Although Grant reorganized the Army of the Tennessee, Sherman retained the 15th Corps, and he conducted operations that contributed to the capture of Vicksburg (July 1863). After he was made a brigadier general in the regular army, he participated in the Battle of Chattanooga (Nov. 1863).

When Grant became supreme commander of the Union forces, Sherman was put in charge of the Army of the Tennessee. He invaded Georgia. After successful campaigns against Generals **Joseph Johnston** and John Hood, he captured Atlanta (1864) and began his "march through Georgia," laying waste to the countryside. After reaching Savannah in December, he advanced northward through the Carolinas. He accepted General Johnston's surrender at Durham, North Carolina (April 1865).

After the war, Sherman commanded the Division of the Missouri, with headquarters in St. Louis (1865–69). During this period he aided in the construction of the transcontinental railway by suppressing numerous Native American attacks. In 1866 he was made a lieutenant general, and in 1869 he succeeded Grant as commander of the army, a position he held until his retirement in 1883. In 1884 he was considered to be a prominent candidate for the Republican presidential nomination, but he categorically opposed a draft.

❈

William Tecumseh Sherman's extremely complex personality contained traits which warred within him, forging a moody, restless, highly intelligent, ambitious military leader. Although harsh and ruthless in his prosecution of the Civil War, he tried to procure a generous peace for the defeated Confederacy at the end of hostilities. Warm and deeply devoted to his family, his opposition to his son's entry into the Roman Catholic priesthood almost destroyed his relationship with his wife. His attitude toward the African-American and the Native American reflected his 19th-century southern Ohio background. He regarded the blacks as inferior and saw the Native Americans as an obstacle to westward expansion. He was uncompromising in his belief in law and order and he highly valued personal integrity.

After a mediocre career in the army during the 1840s, he resigned his commission to enter business. In California he failed as a banker; in New York he failed as a banker; in Kansas he failed as a businessman. In a desperate search for security he accepted the superintendency of the Louisiana State Military Academy, but after the lower tier of southern states seceded from the Union, he returned to his native Ohio, still a failure in his own eyes.

During the first year of the Civil War, he failed as a field commander in Kentucky, suffering a severe breakdown. Returned to health and buoyed by the support of General **Henry W. Halleck,** Sherman became a topflight field commander. By mid-1862 he had evolved his theory of total war. He faulted the hostile southern civilian population for supporting the Confederate armies and dealt harshly with this opposition, believing that it prolonged the conflict. "The entire South, man, woman, and child," he warned, "is against us, armed and determined."

As a military strategist Sherman cast aside orthodox methods, which called for the defeat of the enemy's armies before invasion. His march through Georgia places Sherman among the top-ranking tacticians in the annals of military history.

The Civil War was the first conflict between modern democracies. Sherman clearly saw that the resisting power of a democracy depended as much upon the will of its people as upon its military strength. More than any other Union field commander he realized that strategy dictated the destruction of the enemy's ability to supply its armies, thereby destroying civilian and military morale. President Lincoln was fortunate in discovering Sherman and Grant, who between them decimated Confederate armies, demolished war matériel, and raised Union hopes by victories which simultaneously demoralized the entire Confederacy. See James M. Merrill, *William Tecumseh Sherman* (1971).

JAMES M. MERRILL

SHOCKLEY, William Bradford (b. London, Eng., Feb. 13, 1910; d. Stanford, Calif., Aug. 12, 1989), SCIENTIST, received his BS degree in 1932 from the California Institute of Technology. He then became a teaching fellow at the Massachusetts Institute of Technology, where he studied under J. C. Slater and received his PhD in physics in 1936. Joining the Bell Telephone laboratories that same year as a researcher, he worked on semiconductors and the principles of electrical conduction in solids as a member of a group headed by physicist C. J. Davisson. Shockley began to experiment with solid-state amplifiers in 1938, but his research was interrupted by the war, during which he did antisubmarine warfare studies for the navy at Columbia University. He also served in the office of the secretary of war as a consultant.

After the war, Shockley returned to Bell as director of a research program on semiconductor physics. His group, which included John Bardeen and Walter H. Brattain, announced the invention of the point-contact transistor in 1948 and the junction transistor in 1949, a tiny but highly efficient replacement for the vacuum tube in such electrical devices as computers, hearing aids, and radios. Shockley left the Bell System in 1955 to become director of the semiconductor laboratory of the Beekman Instruments Co. He shared the 1956 Nobel Prize for physics with Bardeen and Brattain for their work on transistors. In 1958 Shockley became a lecturer at Stanford and also president of the Shockley Transistor Corporation, which was absorbed by the Clevite Corporation in 1960. He was director of the Shockley Transistor Unit of the Clevite Corporation in Palo Alto, California (1960–63), and became professor of engineering science at Stanford (1963–1975). He was appointed to the President's Scientific Advisory Committee in 1962. Shockley wrote *Electrons and Holes in Semiconductors* (1950) and *Mechanics* (1966).

In 1965 Shockley became a focal point of controversy because of his persistent attempts to persuade the National Academy of Science to sponsor an investigation of his genetic deterioration hypothesis and his concept of "retrogressive evolution." His theory postulated that intelligence was genetically transmitted, and blacks were genetically inferior to whites and unable to achieve their intellectual level. As a corollary, he suggested that blacks were reproducing faster than whites, hence the retrogression in human evolution. His theory was subscribed to by very few social scientists and it earned him the enmity of many. But Shockley was undeterred from presenting his views. Indeed, according to his colleagues at Stanford, he regarded his work on race more important than his discovery of the transistor and was doing research and writing papers on the issue virtually till the day he died.

———— ❧ ————

Shockley's career illustrated very well the extraordinary impact which the creation of large industrial research laboratories had on science, technology, and society in this century. It also demonstrated the great effect which the winning of a Nobel Prize may have on the recipient's subsequent career by making him an immediate "elder states-man" of science and a public figure. The solid-state amplifier known as the transistor may now be seen as having launched a revolutionary new era in electronics technology which has already made possible remarkable achievements in such areas as computers, satellite communications, and terrestrial communications systems. The role of Shockley's group in bringing about this breakthrough was frequently cited as a justification for substantial support of organized mission-oriented research by industry and government. Shockley frequently stressed that his interest in solid-state research was strongly motivated by the utilitarian goal of supplanting electromechanical switches by all-electronic devices and that it was quite undesirable to draw an invidious distinction between basic and applied science.

Shockley's persistent efforts to promote research in dysgenics caused him to be criticized for holding racist beliefs and conduct unbecoming to a Nobel laureate. A secondary complaint was that he was encroaching on fields of science such as sociology and genetics in which his competence was suspect. Like another eminent Nobel Prize recipient, **Linus Pauling,** Shockley refused to permit himself to be placed on a pedestal and behave in the normative manner expected of an anointed "hero of science." The original stimulus for his interest in dysgenics is not entirely clear but may have developed as a by-product of some studies which he made of individual productivity in research laboratories. Although he believed his last research interest had profound societal implications, it seems quite certain that the impetus which he gave to the coming of the solid-state electronics era will have a far larger effect on social change and the lives of us all. See *Nobel Lectures Including Presentation Speeches and Laureate's Biographies Physics, 1942–1962* (1964).

JAMES G. BRITTAIN

SHUBERT, Levi (Szemanski) (b. Russian Poland, ca. 1875; d. New York, N.Y., Dec. 25, 1953); **SHUBERT, Samuel (Szemanski)** (b. Russian Poland, ca. 1876; d. Harrisburg, Pa., May 12, 1905); **SHUBERT, Jacob (Szemanski)** (b.

Russian Poland, ca. 1880; d. New York, N.Y., Dec. 26, 1963), THEATRICAL PRODUCERS, forced to support themselves at a very early age, Lee (Levi) and Sam (Samuel) had no formal education before entering the theater business, where they began by organizing stock companies for Syracuse's Bastable theater. In 1900 they all came to New York City, where Sam managed the Herald Square theater; they soon acquired theaters in New York, Boston, New Haven, and Kansas City. By 1906 they owned thirteen theaters. In 1905 Sam was killed in a train wreck near Harrisburg, Pennsylvania, and Lee took charge of operations. He combined with producer **David Belasco** in 1905 to form the Shubert Theatrical Corporation with Lee as president and J. J. (Jacob) as vice president. During the 1910s the new concern battled the powerful theater syndicate owned by Marc Klaw and Abraham Lincoln Erlanger and eventually won out. The Shuberts opened or gained control of theaters in such cities as Philadelphia, Cincinnati, Baltimore, and Buffalo and operated New York's popular Hippodrome and Winter Garden theaters. Lee built the Sam Shubert Memorial theater in New York in 1913 directly behind the old Astor hotel. The alley between became known as Shubert's Alley. Featuring such stars as Eddie Foy, Al Jolson, and Eddie Cantor, Shubert shows enjoyed enormous popularity, especially *Sinbad* (1919) and *The Student Prince* (1924).

During the 1920s the Shuberts went into vaudeville; by 1924 they controlled 75 percent of all theaters in the country, and they produced 25 percent of all plays. The Depression forced their corporation into receivership in 1933, but they soon recovered and produced a new version of the Ziegfeld Follies in 1936 starring Fanny Brice, Bob Hope, and Gypsy Rose Lee. During the 1940s the brothers became less active as producers, but still had such hit shows as *Ten Little Indians* (1944) and *Under the Counter* (1947). In 1950 they were taken to court by the federal government for alleged monopolistic practices. After Lee died in 1953 J. J. took over as head of the family enterprises, but a 1955 Supreme Court ruling that they were subject to antitrust laws forced him to sell

twelve theaters in six cities and to give up the booking share of the business.

⁂

The theater has been called many things; temple, shrine, literature, poetry, the noblest art of man.

It is also a business, and no one in the history of the theater grasped that fact better than the Shuberts. Even as they waged their successful war against the Syndicate, they were constructing a more ruthless Shubert monopoly.

With the death of Sam, the one creative Shubert, Lee, with J. J. as his sullen partner, carved out the most successful theatrical empire in history. From coast to coast the Shuberts became the dominant force in determining what plays would be seen, at what prices and when and where.

There is irony here. The form which was born with Aeschylus and which boasts the genius of Shakespeare, Sophocles, Euripides, Ben Jonson, Goethe, Heine, Byron, and a hundred other titans—the form which has given birth to some of the most enduring words of man—was controlled for almost three decades by men who were semiliterate.

Crude, often vulgar, uneducated, they made a personal monopoly of the theater, amassing millions upon millions in the process. When the Great Depression erased their corporate empire, they could have retired, individually wealthy and secure.

Instead, they came to an inexplicable decision. They determined to keep the theater alive. They poured their own money into the gamble. Almost alone the Shuberts kept the marquee lights of the United States burning; two stubborn men fought to save the stage.

Why? Perhaps because in these two men, who could barely read the plays they mounted, there was a passion for the form they never really comprehended. Somehow, they reacted to the beauty, the poetry, the art. They may not have understood, but they loved.

There is paradox in their passion. But the Shuberts were exceedingly complex robber barons, and one of the great anomalies in the

American saga. See Jerry Stagg, *The Brothers Shubert* (1968).

JERRY STAGG

SILLIMAN, Benjamin, Sr. (b. North Stratford [now Trumbull], Conn., Aug. 8, 1779; d. New Haven, Conn., Nov. 24, 1864), SCIENTIST, graduated from Yale College (AB, 1796). He taught at a private school in Wethersfield, Connecticut (1796–98), but then returned to New Haven, where he studied law. He was admitted to the bar in 1802, but in the same year was appointed to a newly created chair in chemistry and natural history at Yale, where he served until 1853. The terms of the appointment included time for Silliman to prepare himself in these fields, which he did at the School of Medicine of the University of Pennsylvania (1802–4), where he studied with Dr. James Woodhouse, and at the University of Edinburgh (1805–6), then a leading center for training in chemistry and geology. He also visited London, where he purchased books and equipment for the college and met such scientists as Sir Humphrey Davy and Sir Joseph Banks.

Following his return to Yale in 1806, Silliman lectured on chemistry and soon added lectures on geology and mineralogy. In 1811 he secured for Yale the famous mineral collection of Colonel George Gibbs of Newport, Rhode Island. He also was active in securing a charter for a Yale School of Medicine (1813), and in 1847 he persuaded Yale to establish a Department of Philosophy and the Arts, from which grew the Sheffield Scientific School and the Graduate School. Silliman also gave public lectures in cities from Boston to St. Louis and New Orleans. He was the founder (1818) and first editor of the *American Journal of Science,* which rapidly gained acclaim as the leading American journal in the natural and physical sciences. He was an active writer, publishing a *Journal of Travels in England, Holland, and Scotland* (1810), *Elements of Chemistry* (1830–31), and *A Visit to Europe in 1851* (1853), as well as numerous scientific articles. He pioneered as a consulting chemist and geologist.

Benjamin Silliman's original contributions to science, comprising about sixty articles and notices published chiefly in his own *Journal,* were very modest. His lasting influence on American science is not to be found in them but rather in his teaching, his educational statesmanship, his catholicity and judgment as an editor, his patriotic zeal for everything that could promote the development of American science and industry, and his fervent conviction that science was the handmaid, not the enemy, of the Christian religion. In Silliman the scientist and the Puritan gentleman were indissolubly united.

After grounding himself thoroughly in chemistry, mineralogy, and geology during his studies at Philadelphia and Edinburgh, Silliman undertook to make Yale the leading institution in the United States for training in these subjects, which up to this time had been taught chiefly in medical schools rather than in liberal arts colleges. In rapid succession he established a well-equipped chemical laboratory, acquired notable mineral collections, edited several American editions of foreign textbooks on chemistry and geology, and produced an excellent chemical textbook of his own.

A born teacher, Silliman soon became famous for the precision and brilliance of his experimental demonstrations in the classroom. Between 1810 and 1845 he trained a generation of American chemists, mineralogists and geologists. By the middle of the century, Silliman had become an institution at Yale: "... his noble countenance and commanding figure [he was nearly six feet in height with a well-built frame] often called forth, as he entered the lecture hall, the involuntary applause of his audience."

But Silliman's energies and influence were not confined to the halls of Yale College. He carried the cause of science, especially chemistry and geology, to the American public in person, lecturing to overflowing audiences all across the country. Of the influence of these lectures Sir Charles Lyell wrote to Silliman: "Now that I have travelled from Niagara to Georgia, and have met a great number of your countrymen on the Continent of Europe, and heard the manner in which they ascribe the taste they have for science to your tuition, I may congratulate you, for I never heard as many of the rising generation in England refer as often to any one individual teacher as having given a direction to their taste." In his lectures, both at Yale and elsewhere, he went out of his way to demonstrate the harmony of science and religion. Everything he did, whether as a teacher, a public speaker, an editor, or a consulting chemist and geologist, was infused with a vigorous Christian faith grounded in the Bible and Christian doctrine as they had been expounded to him by his revered mentor **Timothy Dwight.** See John F. Fulton and Elizabeth H. Thomson, *Benjamin Silliman, 1779–1864: Pathfinder in American Science* (1947).

JOHN C. GREENE

SIMS, William Sowden (b. Port Hope, Ont., Can., Oct. 15, 1858; d. Boston, Mass., Sept. 28, 1936), NAVAL OFFICER, graduated from the U.S. Naval Academy in 1880. After sea duty in the Atlantic and Pacific, he served as a naval attaché in Paris and Leningrad (1897–1900). While an aide to the commander in chief of the Asiatic fleet (1901–2) he devised improved techniques of gunnery practice. During 1902–9 he was the inspector of target practice for the navy, and in 1908–9 naval aide to President Theodore Roosevelt. In 1909–11 he was captain of the battleship *Minnesota,* the only time in history that a commander had charge of a capital ship. He commanded the *Nevada* (1909–11), was on the staff of the Naval War College in Newport, Rhode Island (1911–13), and commanded the Atlantic torpedo boat flotilla (1913–15).

In 1916 Sims was appointed commandant of the naval station at Narragansett Bay and president of the Naval War College. Promoted to rear admiral in January 1917, he was sent to London as a special representative shortly before the U.S. entered World War I. After the declaration of war in April 1917, Sims was appointed commander of U.S. forces operating in European waters. In this post he promoted the adoption of the convoy sys-

tem for protecting merchant ships against submarine attack. In April 1918 he was made a temporary full admiral.

In 1919 Sims returned to the Naval War College as a rear admiral. The following year, in a report to a U.S. Senate subcommittee, he asserted that the U.S. victory at sea had been delayed for about one year because of grave administrative errors. With B. J. Hendrick, Sims wrote *The Victory at Sea* (1920), which won a Pulitzer Prize. He retired in 1922.

When Admiral Sims died in 1939 the New York *Herald Tribune* said "that he influenced our naval course more than any other man who ever wore the uniform." It was a large claim that seemed then, and still seems, wholly justified. In the course of his long career he was a powerful influence on the development of a more sensible education for naval officers, of a more effective means for the selection and promotion of able officers, of a more responsive administrative machinery for the direction of an armed force in a republic. He also was a prime mover in the introduction of the all-big-gun battleship—the capital ship that dominated naval strategy for thirty years. He was, in addition, the father of the destroyer tactics that remained in force until the end of World War II. Finally and above all he was "the man who taught the Navy how to shoot."

These imposing contributions were the product of a discerning mind, remarkable administrative skills, and an extraordinary personal force. Working throughout his career in a complicated, inefficient, and resistant bureaucracy, he achieved his ends by winning the allegiance of younger men, by obtaining the support of the highest authorities, like President Roosevelt, and, ultimately, by the soundness of his own proposals.

His place as a naval officer is secure. In the long list of great captains from **John Paul Jones** to **Ernest Joseph King,** who served with him as a junior officer, he must remain as one of the very few at the very top. Beyond the service he can stand as an enduring example, useful perhaps especially today, of what one man who is willing to work hard, exert his will, and accept real risks can do to move and shake and improve the bureaucratic process. See Elting E. Morison, *Admiral Sims and the Modern American Navy* (1942).

ELTING E. MORISON

SINATRA, Frank (Francis) Albert (b. Hoboken, N.J., Dec. 12, 1917), SINGER, ACTOR, first sang commercially in 1936 as a local Hoboken entertainer while also working as copy boy for the *Jersey Observer.* In 1937 he joined an amateur hour's road company after he and his band won the show's first prize. He then sang on local New Jersey radio until bandleader Harry James hired him in 1939. Sinatra left James's band later that year to join Tommy Dorsey, with whom he performed until 1942. Touring singly as a "star" in his own right, Sinatra sang at the Paramount theater in New York City and in 1943 on the radio show *Your Hit Parade.* He made his first musical film, *Higher and Higher,* in 1943. By 1945 he had become an idol of teenagers and had made six more films.

Sinatra supported Franklin D. Roosevelt's fourth-term candidacy and during the mid-1940s took well-received public stands against racial and ethnic discrimination. He made an antidiscrimination film short with Albert Maltz, *The House I Live In,* for which he won a 1946 Oscar. In 1950–52 and again in 1957–58 he had his own television program. He also played in numerous films including: *From Here to Eternity* (1953), his first nonsinging role, which won him an Academy Award for the best supporting actor; *Guys and Dolls* (1956); *Man with the Golden Arm* (1956); *Pal Joey* (1957); *Can-Can* (1960); *The Manchurian Candidate* (1962); and *The Detective* (1968). He has invested his song and film earnings in restaurants and hotels in Beverly Hills and Las Vegas, music publishing, and film producing. In 1960 he campaigned for John F. Kennedy and sang at Kennedy's inauguration. In 1963 the state gaming commission barred Sinatra from the Nevada gambling industry because of his alleged links to organized crime. Even before these events, Sinatra's relations with the Kennedys'

soured as did his political support for the Democratic Party. In the 1970s and 1980s, Sinatra increasingly appeared at Republican Party events and beside Republican Party senatorial and presidential candidates. Sinatra announced his retirement in 1971, but shortly afterwards he returned for usually sold-out concerts and big city tours. He has appeared regularly in nightclubs in Las Vegas, where he was "Chairman of the Board" of the so-called "Rat Pack," a group of close friends in the entertainment industry that included Sammy Davis, Jr., and Dean Martin. Though almost an octogenarian, Sinatra continues to sing and continues to draw packed audiences for his concert appearances.

⸺⸻⸺

Frank Sinatra was not only the first genuine American teen idol; he was also the first American teen idol to carry his audience with him into middle age. Sinatra grew out of swing, but eventually he epitomized it when he returned to it in the fifties. Meanwhile he was straight, alcoholic, compensatory, lithe, neurotic, masculine, childlike, petulant, and romantic. He sang about the wee small hours, and he walked down lonely streets after a rain. He was a focus for a period in American cultural history that connected a sad-farawayness with guts. He was the kind of man who had been through hell, who tells his story to you, and transforms you into the ever patient waitress who gives him another cup of coffee on the house. It makes everyone listening seem more real. He could be feisty and gentle, yet small and mean and quick-tempered. Which added up to the fact that he was the first pop singer who was also an excellent actor; in fact he paved the way for **Elvis Presley**'s rather unfortunate movie career. Sinatra's performance in *From Here to Eternity* established him as someone who could take it and dish it out without ever losing his feelings. He became the kid who was growing up before our very eyes. Sinatra made the most of the media available to him, and he became one of the most visible of the new pop wealthy: he was envied, his position aspired to and yet fearsome, awesome: to an America that needed heroes and idols he was the King. Even his toupee became famous, and of course it, too, became part of the symbol of the man who let everything show, or at least put up a damn good front of letting everything show. And his career never faded, and in some respects his name became connected with the loves and romances of a new middle class that would see in him the quintessence of style. Yet Sinatra was never style for itself, even though he was, like all pop idols, the creature of the media, the extension of our common myths. He was America grappling with what it thought of as the most profound of quandaries, and somehow it was great to watch ourselves in his struggle. See Steven Petkkov and Leonard Mustazza, eds., *The Frank Sinatra Reader* (1995), and Will Friedwald, *Sinatra! The Song is You: A Singer's Art* (1995).

JONATHAN EISEN

SINCLAIR, Upton Beall, Jr. (b. Baltimore, Md., Sept. 20, 1878; d. Bound Brook, N.J., Nov. 25, 1968), WRITER, REFORMER, graduated from the College of the City of New York in 1897, supporting himself while a student by writing for comic papers and adventure magazines such as *Argosy.* After briefly attending graduate school at Columbia, he moved to Quebec in 1900, where he wrote his first novel, *Springtime and Harvest* (1901, republished as *King Midas*). He joined the Socialist party in 1902 and with the novelist **Jack London** helped found the Intercollegiate Socialist Society in 1905. He moved to Princeton, New Jersey, in 1903, and in 1906 unsuccessfully ran as a Socialist candidate for Congress.

A seven-week visit to Chicago in 1904 led Sinclair to write *The Jungle* (1906), which vividly described unsanitary conditions and the desperate plight of the immigrant workers in Chicago's meatpacking industry. This book made Sinclair a national figure; President Theodore Roosevelt invited him to the White House and passage of a federal Meat Inspection Act promptly followed. Sinclair wrote several other muckraking novels in this period, including *The Industrial Republic* (1907) and *The Metropolis* (1908). He founded a

cooperative community, the Helicon Home Colony, near Englewood, New Jersey, in 1906, but it was destroyed by fire the following year. He lived in a single-tax colony in Arden, Delaware (1909–12), and traveled in Europe (1912–13). During the Colorado coal miners' strike of 1914, he was arrested for picketing the New York offices of the Rockefeller-controlled mining company involved in the strike.

In 1915 Sinclair settled in California. He left the Socialist party in 1917 because of its antiwar stand, believing German militarism a threat to civilization. He published a journal, *Upton Sinclair's Journal* (1918–19), to support U.S. participation in World War I. He rejoined the Socialist party after the war, however, and ran as a candidate for the House of Representatives from California in 1920, for the Senate in 1922, and for governor in 1926 and 1930. He wrote many studies of American life, including *The Brass Check* (1919), *The Goose-Step* (1923), and *The Goslings* (1924). His muckraking novels continued, with *King Coal* (1917), *Oil!* (1927), and *Boston* (1929), dealing with the Sacco-Vanzetti trial. In 1934 he left the Socialist party again, and ran as the Democratic candidate for governor of California, narrowly losing to Republican incumbent Frank Merriam. Sinclair's platform "End Poverty in California" (EPIC) called for government-owned factories and elaborate pension plans. Sinclair wrote an eleven-novel series revolving around a journalist, Lanny Budd, starting with *World's End* (1940). One of the series, *Dragon's Teeth* (1942), which dealt with the rise of Hitler, won the 1943 Pulitzer Prize for fiction. Some of Sinclair's later works included *A Personal Jesus* (1952), *What Didymus Did* (1955), *My Lifetime in Letters* (1960), a collection of letters written to him, and the *Autobiography of Upton Sinclair* (1962).

<hr />

Although Upton Sinclair is generally labeled a muckraker, it is of some interest to try to place him among the broader literary categories of his time. Is he naturalist, realist, or romantic?

Perhaps the safest and most comprehensive way to distinguish between realism and naturalism is to look at the treatment of the forces among which the characters work out their destinies—or have them worked out for them. By and large, a realistic novel acknowledges and delineates a full complex of forces among which the characters live. They are social, hereditary, and economic; they cover or include the whole gamut from early family to later manners and social pressures. Among these forces, fully acknowledged, the characters exercise what freedom is available to the human condition. They do choose, and their choices are what make them take shape as characters.

At the opposite pole, the naturalistic novel greatly simplifies the forces, and it takes the further step of making the forces rather than the people the main actors in the novel. Whether it is a disease, a mania, a hereditary lesion, or a controlling economic pattern, the simplified force is presented as triumphantly dominant in human affairs. *This,* the author shouts, is what really makes things happen! Of course, a novel still has to be about people, and we still find the naturalistic novelist somehow in league with humanity and unable to free himself from a concern for the people he lets his terrible forces destroy. There is, then, an ambiguous imbalance between the scientific display of forces, knowledge of which will liberate mankind from their domination, and the inescapable devotion of the novelist to the plight of the suffering creatures, who have always suffered their tragic human destinies, whether embattled by Fate, ignorance, poverty, or some congenital frailty.

Between these modern poles we find the writings of Upton Sinclair. He is realistic in that his characters are *free,* but he is naturalistic in that their motives are wondrously simplified—simplified to the point where his people become walking automatons of greed, robots of corruption, zombies of political intrigue, all representing one or another reprehensible aspect of commercial, industrial, financial, or institutional rapacity. Thus the characters are transformed into two-dimensional forces: instead of being prey of such naturalistic forces, they become them. And thus the muckraking novel (like the novel of ideas on another level) hovers midway

between realism and naturalism. It is concerned with forces, like the naturalistic novel, but it is intensely moral and primarily always eager to assign moral responsibility for the troubles of society. Both the naturalistic and the muckraking novel try to search out the forces, whether in society, nature, or the hearts of men, that we must understand if we are to correct the evils man suffers. The realistic novel, on the other hand, explores the conditions within which men discover and express themselves.

These remarks are not entirely true of the later Sinclair, particularly in the Lanny Budd series, for these books are panoramic rather than muckrakingly indignant. They paint a broad and simple canvas of 20th-century power politics in action over the Western world, but they do not assign blame so fiercely. They acknowledge what Joyce might have jokingly called "the ineluctable modality of the historical." See Floyd Dell, *Upton Sinclair: A Study in Social Protest* (1970).

CHARLES CHILD WALCUTT

SINGER, Isaac Bashevis (b. Radzymin, Poland, July 14, 1904; d. Surfside, Fla., July 24, 1991), WRITER, studied at the Tachkemoni Rabbinical Seminary, in Warsaw (1920–27). The son and grandson of orthodox rabbis, he abandoned a religious career to become a writer and worked as a proofreader and translator for various Hebrew and Yiddish newspapers in Warsaw from 1923 to 1935. Shortly after publishing his first novel, *Satan in Goray* (1935), he followed his novelist brother Israel to the United States. Singer became an American citizen in 1943.

In New York City he wrote for the Yiddish-language newspaper the *Jewish Daily Forward,* publishing his fiction as Isaac Bashevis and his journalism as Isaac Warshofsky ("the man from Warsaw"). He attracted little attention until **Saul Bellow**'s English translation of his short story "Gimpel the Fool," published in the *Partisan Review* in 1953 and as the title story of a collection in 1957.

Singer wrote more than thirty novels, collections of short stories, and memoirs, mostly recalling Jewish life in rural Poland and originally published in the *Forward* and other Yiddish periodicals. English translations spread his reputation after 1960, and in 1966 he found a new and enthusiastic audience with children's books. Regarded as the leading Yiddish-language writer of his time, Singer received many awards, including two National Book Awards. In 1978 he won the Nobel Prize for literature.

⁂

Isaac Bashevis Singer was a paradox. He wrote in a dying language and used the narrative devices of the traditional folk tale but displayed a contemporary sensibility, rejecting his ancestor's faith in an ultimately benevolent universe and sharing the 20th-century's preoccupation with sexuality, alienation, and existential dislocation. Although his work grew out of an isolated tradition and a vanishing culture, it illuminates universal and timeless aspects of the human situation.

Singer traced the duality in his outlook to his parents' uneasy blend of mysticism and rationalism. His shorter fiction generally depends heavily on the supernatural, but always presents it in a calm, matter-of-fact way, describing demons, witchcraft, and miracles with a serene, unquestioning acceptance of the irrational. The realism of Singer's description of pacts with the devil, the dead dancing among the living, and similar folk motifs enables him to examine the dilemma of modern man under the comfortable guise of legend and fantasy.

Although he spent more than half his life in the United States and spoke English well, Singer wrote exclusively in Yiddish until his last years, defending the practice with the wry observation that a dying language was appropriate to writing about ghosts. In fact, the expressive resources of irony and despair in Yiddish made it the ideal medium for his dark and ambiguous vision. With it he was able to transcend the narrow cultural boundaries of Eastern European village Jewry to create a richly comic and profoundly tragic world outside of time and space. See Paul Kersh, *Isaac Bashevis Singer, The Magician of West 86th Street* (1979).

DENNIS WEPMAN

SITTING BULL (b. Grand River, S.D., ca. 1834; d. Grand River, S.D., Dec. 15, 1890), NATIVE AMERICAN LEADER, was a chief of the Sioux tribe. As a young man he earned a reputation as a warrior and political leader. The Sioux were angered by the large influx of prospectors after gold was discovered in the Dakota Black Hills in 1874, and by the encroachment of railroad crews on their land. In 1875 Sitting Bull became head of the war council to resist the whites. The U.S. army sent Colonel **George A. Custer** to locate the Native Americans' camp (which had moved into the buffalo country) and to block their escape routes. Custer, with a force of only 264 men, underestimated the number of Native Americans opposing him. At the Little Big Horn in southern Montana, Native Americans under Sitting Bull, Crazy Horse, and Rain-in-the-Face annihilated Custer's men (June 25–26, 1876). Despite this victory, Sitting Bull's men were forced to scatter because of a shortage of food and ammunition. In May 1877 he took his braves into Canada, only to return in 1881 when faced with starvation. He surrendered to U.S. troops at Fort Buford, July 19, 1881. After two years at Fort Randall, Sitting Bull was settled on the Standing Rock reservation in the Dakotas. In 1889 adverse economic conditions on the reservation caused unrest and led to the adoption of the ghost dance. While Sitting Bull was not a believer in this new religion, the dancers gathered near his cabin on Grand River, and it was feared that the chief might lead another uprising. A group of Native American policemen were sent to arrest him, and when one of these policemen was shot by one of the chief's followers, others killed Sitting Bull.

⁂

There are at least two prevailing opinions about the ability and character of Sitting Bull. Major James McLaughlin, the agent at Standing Rock, called him "an Indian of very mediocre ability, rather dull, and much the inferior of Gall and others of his lieutenants in intelligence." In this view Sitting Bull achieved prominence by "sheer obstinacy and stubborn tenacity" and by being "pompous, vain and boastful." E. A. Allison, the army scout who escorted the Hunkpapa chief to Fort Buford in July 1881, characterized him as constitutionally a coward whose main concern was his own personal safety and his exalted position as a patriarch of the "greatest nation on earth."

A very different portrait is sketched by the historian Stanley Vestal, according to whom there is no evidence that the Sioux chief ever "lied, or stole, or committed any crime whatever, other than self-defense when attacked." Sitting Bull gained his fame in the white community in the aftermath of the annihilation of Custer's battalion by eluding the army and escaping into Canada. At that time General John Gibbon referred to him as "a rather notorious Sioux who prided himself greatly upon standing aloof from the whites, never going to an agency and never trading with one personally, although he was not averse to trading … through others." As the Sioux leader most difficult to apprehend, Sitting Bull was blamed for depredations committed by others; only starvation compelled him to submit to white control.

The greatness of Sitting Bull is underscored by the fact that he held out to the bitter end against impossible odds. Even in defeat he refused to compromise Native American customs and values. His detractors were those who were charged with the responsibility of ending the nomadic life of the Sioux and of opening their lands to white occupation. He was a practical man of superior intelligence and thus able to react appropriately to any challenge in the best interest of his people. He signed no treaties depriving Native Americans of their lands and rights, advising his followers to hold on to their land. He proposed stock raising instead of farming as the best occupation for the Sioux. In this he was no doubt influenced by a desire to remain as close to the traditional ways as possible.

Those who argue that Sitting Bull was a medicine man are mistaken; he was a political leader of unusual force and persuasive skill. He was nevertheless a man of deep religious conviction and of human sensitivity—like most Native American people, a believer in the world of nature. He never really committed himself to the ghost dance, but given the cultural crisis and economic difficulties among the Sioux at the end of the 1880s he went along with this religious expression of nostalgia for a doomed way of life. See Stanley Vestal, *Sitting Bull* (1932).

HENRY E. FRITZ

SKINNER, Burrhus Frederic (b. Susquehanna, Pa., March 20, 1904; d. Cambridge, Mass., Aug. 18, 1990), PSYCHOLOGIST, graduated from Hamilton College (1926) and received a PhD from Harvard (1931). In 1936 he was appointed an instructor of psychology at the University of Minnesota (assistant professor, 1937–39; associate professor, 1939–45).

As a psychologist, Skinner was a member of the behaviorist school, which argues that human behavior can best be explained in terms of physiological responses to environmental stimuli, and that abstract theories must be subordinated to observable facts. It distinguishes between two kinds of behavior, "respondent" and "operant." Respondent behavior is elicited by a specific stimulus; operant behavior, which Skinner believed to be more common, appears to occur spontaneously, but can, through "operant conditioning," be brought under the control of "reinforcing stimuli." The reinforcing stimulus serves as a "reward," thereby strengthening the response. Working in this tradition, Skinner invented the Skinner Box, a mechanism used for observing and measuring changes in animal behavior. In 1938 he published his findings under the title *The Behavior of Organisms.*

During World War II Skinner did research for the Office of Scientific Research and Development on a missile-guiding system which, through operant conditioning, would be controlled by electric impulses generated by the pecking of pigeons.

During 1945–48 Skinner was a professor of psychology at Indiana University. During this period he developed his Air-Crib, an air-conditioned, soundproof, germ-free box with a sliding window of safety glass designed to provide an optimum environment for a growing baby. In 1948 he published *Walden Two,* a novel about a utopian community operated on his conditioning principles.

In 1948 Skinner became a professor at Harvard University. *Science and Human Behavior,* a survey of his views on learning and behavioralism, was published in 1953. In 1954 he began developing programmed learning "teaching machines," based on the principle of operant conditioning. The student is called upon to fill in a blank statement and is then permitted to see the correct answer. If he is right, his correct answer, according to Skinner, became his reinforcement stimulus (his reward), thus urging him to go on. If his answer was incorrect, he studied the correct answer, thereby increasing his chances of being correct in the next question.

In 1958 Skinner was named Edgar Pierce professor of psychology at Harvard. Skinner officially retired from Harvard in 1974, but he continued to walk the two miles to his office every day, to lecture, to direct graduate students, and to conduct experiments virtually until his last days. Among Skinner's many books were *Verbal Behavior* (1957), *The Technology of Teaching* (1968), *Beyond Freedom and Dignity* (1971), *About Behaviorism* (1974), and *Recent Issues in the Analysis of Behavior* (1989).

One of the best-known of modern psychologists, B. F. Skinner achieved prominence by translating theories of behaviorism into social psychology. Tracing the origins of his own theories back to Darwin, Freud, **Edward L. Thorndike,** and the behaviorist **John B. Watson,** Skinner wrote works ranging from descriptions of animal learning to considerations of metaphysics. Nonetheless, it was as social critic that he seemed most at home. This work was grounded in his belief, as he wrote, that "all behavior is basically unconscious," and acquired either by "aversive stimulation" (punishment) or by "operant reinforcement" (a positive accompaniment to an action). Since in both cases behavior is uncon-

scious, Skinner rejected the ordinary language available to describe intention and experience, calling it historically derived, unscientific, and determined by the "verbal community."

Carrying such ideas one step further in social theory, Skinner insisted that traditional notions of self-consciousness were misleading and that rationalism or free will was an invalid description of behavior. This position led him to doubt that freedom and democracy, as conscious goals, were within the reach of man's best intentions. They may be achieved, but only through social manipulation based upon operant reinforcement. Undoubtedly, here in his separation of behavior from intention, Skinner found his most telling criticism of traditional social psychology. But he was also faced with the dilemma of proposing a positive program of behaviorism. His most interesting attempt to sketch the outlines of a new behavioral society was described in his utopian novel *Walden Two,* published after World War II. A less comprehensive but practical development was the Air-Crib, created to aid parents in raising their children, although the experiment seemed designed more to relieve parents of some of the early burdens of child rearing than to solve problems of child psychology. Despite his interest in a wide range of social problems, Skinner's work in proposing positive forms of social control fell short of his ambitious criticism of traditional assumptions about behavior. For a selection of works which sampled his activities as critic and social engineer see B. F. Skinner, *Cumulative Record* (1959).

JAMES B. GILBERT

SLATER, Samuel (b. Belper, Derbyshire, Eng., June 9, 1768; d. Webster, Mass., April 21, 1835), MANUFACTURER, became an apprentice to Jedediah Strutt, a partner of the textile manufacturer Richard Arkwright, in 1783. Having attained an expert knowledge of the construction and operation of the latest cotton-spinning machinery, Slater decided (1789) to emigrate to the U.S. British law prohibited the export of machinery plans, but he memorized the

Arkwright blueprints. At the port of embarkation he classified himself "farm laborer" to avoid the ban on the migration of mechanics.

Following his arrival in America, he formed a partnership with **Moses Brown** and William Almy of Providence, Rhode Island, in 1790. Constructing Arkwright-type machinery, Slater established the nation's first cotton-spinning mill at Pawtucket, Rhode Island, in 1791. Almy, Brown, and Slater constructed a larger mill in 1793. Forming Samuel Slater and Co. (1798), Slater built mills near Pawtucket in 1799, in Smithfield (later Slatersville), Rhode Island, in 1806, and in Webster, Massachusetts, in 1812. He also invested in various other textile enterprises and served as president of the Manufacturers' Bank in Pawtucket.

Not an inventor himself but rather a highly skilled machinist and an able businessman, Slater nevertheless played a part of great importance in the industrialization and economic growth of the United States. Underlying conditions set the stage for him. The demand for cotton goods and other products increased enormously as the country's population rose and moved westward over turnpikes, canals, and other improved means of transportation. Yet the supply of labor was inadequate to permit these demands to be met. The situation cried out for mechanization of the methods by which self-sufficient farm families had for so long produced the goods required for the sustenance of life. But machinery was expensive, supplies of capital scarce, educational institutions underdeveloped, and engineers few and not well trained. In these circumstances the technological knowledge required for mechanization had to be supplied by more advanced industrial nations. Slater's migration to the United States may be regarded as an export of highly trained human capital from a nation in which supplies of this capital were plentiful to one in which supplies were scarce and dear. **Francis Cabot Lowell**'s later memorization of the secret of the power loom while on a visit to England was a similar instance of technological

borrowing. Together, these innovations made it possible to inaugurate the first modern American factory at Waltham, Massachusetts, in 1813. Machinists, managers, and other skilled operatives trained at Slater's spinning mills and at Waltham gradually transformed manufacturing methods in other industries as well, thus paving the way for the American industrial revolution. See Edward H. Cameron, *Samuel Slater: Father of American Manufactures* (1960).

STUART BRUCHEY

SLOAN, Alfred Pritchard (b. New Haven, Conn., May 23, 1875; d. New York, N.Y., Feb. 17, 1966), BUSINESSMAN, graduated from the Massachusetts Institute of Technology (1895) with a degree in electrical engineering. He was the youngest member of his class, having completed the normal four year program in three. After graduation, Sloan went to work as a draftsman for the Hyatt Roller Bearing Company in Harrison, N.J., which made a special kind of roller bearing designed by John Wesley Hyatt, the inventor of celluloid. He soon left for a two-year stint with a household electric refrigerator firm, but returned to Hyatt after his father and a business associate invested $5,000 in the faltering company and gave Sloan six months to put it in shape. At the end of the six months, Sloan in partnership with Peter Steenstrup, the Hyatt bookkeeper, could show a $12,000 profit. Sloan was made General Manager, Steenstrup Sales Manager. By 1915 Hyatt was providing roller bearings for a number of automobile manufacturers and was having difficulty keeping up with orders.

In 1916, colorful GM and Chevrolet founder **William C. Durant** brought Hyatt into his newly-formed United Motors Corporation—a combination of parts and accessories manufacturers that included Charles F. Kettering's Dayton Engineering Laboratories Company (DELCO), the Harrison Radiator Company, the Klaxon Company, the New Departure (ball bearing) Manufacturing Company, the Perlman Rim Corporation, and the Remy Electric Company. Sloan exchanged Hyatt for $13.5 million in

United Motors stock and became the United Motors president.

When in 1918 a new General Motors Corporation, an operating company, replaced the General Motors Company, a holding company, through an exchange of GM Company, Chevrolet, and United Motors stock, Sloan moved up to become a vice president and director of the General Motors Corporation. Then with Durant's ouster from GM by the du Pont and Morgan interests in 1920, Sloan became executive vice president under interim president **Pierre S. du Pont**. He immediately began to implement an organizational plan, a set of financial controls, and a marketing strategy that would result in GM's outselling Ford by the late 1920s and make the giant corporation the leading automobile manufacturer and most successful industrial corporation in the world into the 1980s. In 1923 Sloan moved up to the GM presidency and in 1937 to chairman of the GM board of directors. He was honorary GM chairman from his retirement in 1956 to his death a decade later. During those years he concentrated on philanthropic work through the Alfred P. Sloan Jr. Foundation, which donated large sums for cancer research and education. The Sloan-Kettering Institute for Cancer Research is one byproduct of the Foundation's grants.

❦

Sloan was the automobile industry's first "gray man." First, last, and always an organization man, he abhorred the autocratic rule of colorful "personal" entrepreneurs such as **Henry Ford** and Billy Durant. Under his leadership General Motors became the archetype of the depersonalized, decentralized corporation run by an anonymous technostructure.

In the "multidivisional structure" that Sloan introduced at GM, strategic decisions affecting the setting of corporate goals and the long-term allocation of resources were centralized in executive and finance committees, while tactical decisions on the day-to-day utilization of these resources were decentralized in the firm's various operating divisions. At du Pont this had resolved problems stemming from a lack of over-

all cooperation and coordination among operating divisions making very different products. At GM the structure had the opposite function of decentralizing operating decisions down to an appropriate level in a formerly too-centralized firm in which the divisions made essentially the same product. For still different reasons, the multidivisional structure was adopted as well in the 1920s at Standard Oil of New Jersey and at Sears, Roebuck. It was at GM under Sloan, however, that the financial controls and coordination of operations that the structure engendered underwent the most refinement and formalization and were most publicized.

Control in the corporation under Sloan passed from engineers like Kettering to cost-cutting accountants. Donaldson Brown, the GM vice president for finance, worked out with Albert Bradley a system of financial controls. They set a 20 percent return on investment as the corporation's expectation. And GM became insulated from the adverse effects of short-term fluctuations in the market for cars by basing unit cost estimates (hence car prices) on a conservative assessment of how many cars GM could expect to sell over a period of years at given prices and average utilization of plant capacity. When demand exceeded these expectations, GM would gain windfall profits, because unit prices had been set on the basis of a lower and consequently costlier level of production. This was called "standard volume pricing." The system of controls called for only a conservative amount of actual profits to be reinvested in expansion of the business, including research and development. It was thus a strategy geared not for producing a technologically superior product at a lower price, but for guaranteeing the safety of invested capital and ensuring high rates of return in a market assumed to be both saturated and technologically mature.

What Sloan chose to call "constant upgrading of product" is more accurately described as planned obsolescence through cosmetic changes. In diametric opposition to the Ford Model T product philosophy of a single, static mode at an ever decreasing unit price, GM attempted to produce "a car for every purse and purpose." Sloanism called for blanketing the market with a car at the top of every price range and encouraging the consumer to trade up from Chevrolet to Cadillac via Pontiac, Oldsmobile, or Buick. Sloanism also called for stimulating sagging sales in a replacement market by inducing the consumer, long before his present car's useful life was over, to trade it in for a newer and higher-priced one. Consumer dissatisfaction with today's car was stimulated by the innovation of the annual model change, which called for major styling revisions every three years, functional or not, with minor annual faceliftings in between. The three-year styling cycle was geared to die life, so that retooling costs would not be excessive. The trick here was to maintain an overall GM product identity while differentiating GM car lines from one another and the GM car models in a given line from year to year. GM initiated bringing out annual models in 1923. But the concept evolved gradually and was not fully formalized and regularized until the 1930s. Sloan intended that this product philosophy would result in GM's gaining each year a larger share of the consumer's dollar. Emulated by Ford and Chrysler, this became the predominant marketing strategy in the automobile industry until outmoded by Japanese practices in the 1980s. See Alfred P. Sloan, Jr., *My Years with General Motors* (1964).

JAMES J. FLINK

SLOAN, John French (b. Lock Haven, Pa., Aug. 2, 1871; d. Hanover, N.H., Sept. 8, 1951), ARTIST, attended schools in Lock Haven and Philadelphia and then worked as a newspaper artist in Philadelphia while studying at night with Thomas Anschutz and **Robert Henri** at the Pennsylvania Academy of Fine Arts. In 1904 he moved to Greenwich Village, in New York City, and began etching, illustrating, and painting. He exhibited at the Macbeth Gallery in 1908 with a group of artists known as "The Eight," the "Ashcan School." The ashcan artists realistically portrayed urban life, as seen in Sloan's *Scrubwomen in the Old Astor Library*

(1910, Munson-Williams-Proctor Institute, Utica, N.Y.), *McSorley's Back Room* (1912, Dartmouth College), and *Six O'clock Winter* (1912, Phillips Collection, Washington, D.C.). Sloan helped organize and exhibited two paintings and five etchings at the famous New York Armory Show of 1913, which introduced modern European art to the United States.

Sloan taught at the Art Students League of New York from 1914 to 1938 and served as its president in 1931. He helped found the Society of Independent Artists in New York in 1917 and became its president the following year. In his later years he turned to painting landscapes, portraits, and nudes. He also published *The Gist of Art* (1939), an autobiographical work. Sloan won the distinguished service gold medal from the American Academy of Arts and Letters in 1950 and received a posthumous retrospective exhibition at the Whitney Museum of American Art in 1952. Some of his other ashcan works include *Sunset, West Twenty-Third Street* (1906, Joslyn Art Museum, Omaha) and *Dust Storm, Fifth Avenue* (1906, Metropolitan Museum of Art, New York).

⁂

Of the group of friends and students who encircled the influential teacher and painter Robert Henri, the one to become most exemplary of their inclinations was the painter and graphic artist John Sloan. Like others in the Ashcan School as Henri's group was baptized, Sloan was seized by the fascination with the big city which affected American painters, writers, and even presidents at the turn of the century. "What infinite use Dante would have made of the Bowery," opined Theodore Roosevelt, articulating a view of art-life relationships which dominated the aesthetics of the Ashcan School and inspired John Sloan's paintings.

For Sloan, the city was above all a human environment, its architecture, forces, and moods acquiring significance as settings for the contrasting lifestyles of diverse urban populations. Mobilizing a real feeling for aphorism, a talent for effective characterization, and a practiced habit of detailed reporting, Sloan recorded the humor and variety of city life with an unsentimentalized warmth. This distinguished his work from that of his contemporaries.

Prior to his association with Henri, Sloan's craftsmanship and flair for creative composition won him recognition as one of the leading artists of the mid-1890s poster style, an American version of Art Nouveau which Sloan adapted uniquely for use in daily newspapers. Abandoning completely this decorative style, Sloan again drew national attention to his graphic work when, in 1912, he became an art editor of the *Masses* magazine and revolutionized in style and format the role of magazine illustration.

Despite his progressive political views, his rebellious disposition and sharp tongue, Sloan's true allegiance was always to his art. A devoted and persuasive teacher, his influence has been recorded by three generations of American artists. See Van Wyck Brooks, *John Sloan: A Painter's Life* (1955).

PATRICIA FAILING

SMITH, Alfred Emanuel (b. New York, N.Y., Dec. 30, 1873; d. New York, N.Y., Oct. 4, 1944), POLITICAL LEADER, left school at the age of eleven. In 1895 he became an investigator in the office of the city commissioner of jurors, and in 1903 he was elected to the New York State Assembly as a Democrat (serving 1904–15; speaker, 1913–15). Following the Triangle fire (1911), in which 146 women workers in a shirtwaist factory died, he served on a commission to investigate New York factory conditions, and was a leader in the passage of remedial legislation. He was a delegate to the New York state constitutional convention (1915). For two years he held the lucrative position of sheriff of New York County (1915–17), and in 1917 he became president of the New York City board of aldermen.

In 1918 Smith was elected governor of New York (reelected 1922, 1924, 1926; served 1919–21, 1923–28). His administrations were marked by an increase in social welfare legislation and by an intensification of public works projects, as well as

by a broad program of administrative reforms. Smith was a leading contender for the Democratic presidential nomination in 1924, but his Catholicism and his antiprohibition stand led to his rejection by the convention. In 1928, however, Smith won the nomination and ran on a conservative platform. In the election, Smith was defeated by Herbert Hoover, 444 electoral votes to 87. In 1932 he was an unsuccessful contender for another nomination, but supported Franklin D. Roosevelt in the campaign.

During 1932–34, while editor of the *New Outlook,* Smith became increasingly conservative, refusing to support New Deal measures. In 1934 he became one of the leaders of the anti–New Deal American Liberty League, and he backed the Republican presidential candidates in 1936, 1940, and 1944.

⸎

Alfred E. Smith, four times elected governor of New York State, and unsuccessful candidate for the presidency in 1928, was one of the ablest political leaders of his time, and was credited by many of his admirers with a kind of genius for democratic politics. Under his guidance the affairs of the Empire State were well and honestly administered and reform laws were enacted that opened a window toward the social welfare legislation now so familiar to present-day Americans.

Though he had little formal education, Al Smith, child of Irish-Italian-German immigrant stock, had an aptitude for learning quickly what he needed to know. His "universities," as he used to say, were those sidewalks of New York that later became the theme of his campaign songs, the local Tammany clubs, but above all the state assembly at Albany where he studied and mastered every aspect of the state government for thirteen years, even while serving as a loyal follower of Boss Charles Murphy. As speaker of the assembly he emerged as the real party leader of the New York Democrats.

The Triangle Shirtwaist Company fire in 1911 made for a turning point in Smith's career: the machine politician, serving as vice chairman of the Factory Investigating Commission to study fire hazard and health conditions, was converted into an ardent social reformer. Joining forces with a group of intellectuals and social workers, of whom some of the more outstanding were women such as Belle Moskowitz and **Frances Perkins,** Smith forged a unique coalition of reformers and machine politicians that made his gubernatorial regime at Albany memorable. Skill in practical politics combined with the social vision of Smith's expert advisers to help carry out far-reaching reforms in the condition of workers as well as in governmental administration. Much of the social legislation sponsored by Smith was copied by other states, and its humane vision was incorporated in the New Deal administration of Franklin Roosevelt at federal levels.

An intuitive master of the art of popular rule, Smith knew how to "go to the people" via the forum, the press, or even the newfangled radio. He was also a good teacher of his craft; Franklin Roosevelt acknowledged himself one of Smith's disciples, and served willingly as his lieutenant in the party hierarchy, until Smith chose him as his successor in the governor's chair. Later, as president, Roosevelt employed the radio, as Smith had done earlier, to go to the people with his message, or to put pressure on a recalcitrant Congress. The New Deal, moreover, was an alliance of reformers and professional politicians, quite like Smith's original model; it even drew for its brain trust on several of the men and women Smith had brought into his "kitchen cabinet."

Smith's image as a public figure has been (somewhat unjustly) diminished by two events belonging to his later career: his defeat in the race for the presidency, and his subsequent turn to conservative politics. Although he was decisively beaten by Hoover, he called forth the largest Democratic vote in U.S. history to that date; and, in the tabulations of Samuel Lubell, converted the Democratic party into the party of the big-city masses and the ethnic-religious minority groups who were destined to become more numerous in the country. The very nomination of Smith for president, a Roman Catholic and product of the more recent immigrant strains, was something

unprecedented. United States history has largely been the story of the prolonged struggle of successive groups of immigrants and other disadvantaged minorities against the intolerance of the descendants of earlier immigrants. As **Walter Lippmann** wrote at the time, the choice of Smith to head the Democrats represented the first bid for power by millions of half-enfranchised Americans. Despite strong manifestations of religious bigotry in the South and West, he waged his campaign on high ground, in the spirit of the "Happy Warrior," as Franklin Roosevelt had named him. The boom times of 1928, along with the strong prohibition sentiment in the country, contributed to his defeat by the Republicans; yet it may be said that his campaign shamed the bigots and paved the way for the eventual victory of John F. Kennedy.

Smith's disciple, Roosevelt, whose sun rose as Smith's sank, proved ungrateful to his former teacher, pointedly ignoring both his help and his advice. In 1928 Smith had turned to wealthy supporters like business executive John J. Raskob for the large campaign funds needed, and he stayed with them loyally after being brusquely eliminated from public life following a quarter-century of devoted public service. And when he joined the faction of the Liberty League in opposition to the New Deal, he aroused deep disappointment in many of his former followers.

A defeated presidential candidate, removed from his habitual employment, is a tragic figure. The wasting of his eminent skills for public service, the emptiness of his functions as "janitor" of the Empire State Building, as he himself called it, contributed in later years to the dimming image of one of the best loved of America's regional leaders. In his heyday he was acclaimed by millions as the "Abe Lincoln of the tenement people." For all his whiskey baritone and East Side twang, the informed persons who worked with him for years over the complex affairs of the nation's most populous state always held that a public servant of great stature was lost. See Matthew and Hannah Josephson, *Al Smith: Hero of the Cities* (1969).

MATTHEW AND HANNAH JOSEPHSON

SMITH, David (b. Decatur, Ind., March 9, 1906; d. near Bennington, Vt., May 23, 1965), SCULPTOR, studied art at Ohio University in 1924 but dropped out a year later to work as a welder at the Studebaker plant in South Bend, Indiana. He attended George Washington University in 1925–26, then went to New York City, where he studied painting with **John Sloan** at the Art Students League (1926–28). In the early 1930s he began welding sculptures in an abstract and semi-abstract style using scrap metal, iron, steel, and old tools. From 1934 to 1940 he worked in his studio in the Terminal Iron Works in Brooklyn and, later, at his home at Bolton's Landing, New York.

During 1935–36 Smith traveled to London, Paris, Greece, and Soviet Russia. In 1937 he worked on the Federal Arts Project. His series *Medals for Dishonor* (1937–40), bronze plaques, was inspired by the atrocities of the Spanish Civil War. The East River Gallery in New York was the scene of his first one-man show (1938). During World War II Smith worked in a tank factory in Schenectady, New York, as a welder.

After the war Smith's work became increasingly abstract and increasingly popular. Some of his best-known sculptures during this period are: *Australia* (1951, William Rubin, N.Y.), *Hudson River Landscape* (1951, Whitney Museum of American Art, N.Y.), and *The Hero* (1951–52, Brooklyn Museum, N.Y.). He taught sculpture at Sarah Lawrence College, Bronxville, New York (1948–50), the University of Arkansas, Fayetteville (1953), and Indiana University (1954–55). He was a Guggenheim fellow in 1950–52. In 1965, shortly before his death in an automobile accident, he was appointed by President Johnson to the National Council on the Arts. Some of Smith's best-known late works include *Tank Totem X* (1960, Dr. Friedrich Moeller, Paris), *Zig IV* (1961, Lincoln Center for the Performing Arts, N.Y.), and *Cubi XVII* (1963, Dallas Museum of Fine Arts).

———— ∞ ————

Today David Smith is considered by artists and critics to be the outstanding American sculptor of the 20th century. He worked unceasingly as a sculptor for thirty years (he also made more than three hundred drawings a year), and his work reflects great strength, clarity, and inventiveness. He had tremendous energy, a powerful, uncompromising, and, on occasion, explosive personality. His interests were extremely diverse—he worked as a logger and welder, lived like a hermit in the mountains, yet was a gourmet cook and lover of fine wines. He was a friendly but lonesome man—his closest friends were artists, mostly painters.

His sculptural style continues in the tradition of open welded sculpture that was invented in the early thirties by Picasso and Gonzalez. Like them, in his early works Smith made use of open forms and "found" materials. But like his American contemporaries, he drew heavily on surrealist symbolic imagery like totems, insectoid birds, and dream relics. Coming out of his interest in surrealism was, perhaps, his most daring stylistic innovation—"aerial drawing" in steel (the counterpart of **Jackson Pollock**'s automatism in painting). Works like *Hudson River Landscape* established Smith as the first sculptor to draw on the pictorial (two-dimensional) tradition to make viable sculpture. This pictorial form reached its peak in the Becca series, in which huge, thin sheets of stainless steel are overlapped to make sculptures which are almost flat. Simultaneously, his forms became more geometric, his art more abstract and more impersonal. In his final and most famous series, the Cubis, Smith stacked and welded hollow steel boxes in arbitrary arrangements that are especially handsome.

In attempts to evaluate Smith's stylistic innovations, questions are still being raised as to whether he went beyond cubist space. Questioned also are anthropomorphic references that never disappear from his work, although his degree of abstraction goes beyond the cubists. Less discussed, but important to note, are his technical innovations. He was the first American sculptor to work consistently in welded metals. He broke with the cubists' found object by using geometric shapes and industrially fabricated units. In the Becca series, he discovered the potentialities of buffed stainless steel sheets as a source of reflection. He invented the hollow steel box for the Cubis. His feeling for materials was superb—the nature of his welds, the way his shapes stamped themselves out, their look, gutsy or refined as the individual piece dictated.

Although hard to measure at this time, Smith's influence should be far-reaching. He has already been a source of inspiration to the minimalist sculptors in his use of reductive, boxlike shapes. He has left his mark on Anthony Caro, the leading exponent of open, welded sculpture in England, and a great number of young American sculptors who are presently exploring its possibilities. See Edward F. Fry, *David Smith* (1969).

Jeanne Siegel

SMITH, John (b. Willoughby, Lincolnshire, Eng., 1579 or 1580; d. London, Eng., June 21, 1631), ADVENTURER, EXPLORER, received a grammar school education and was apprenticed to a merchant, but soon became a soldier of fortune on the Continent. There he traveled widely and served with Eastern European forces which were fighting off the Turkish invasion; in later life his recollection of this adventure included bizarre tales of capture, escape, and wandering in Turkey and Eastern Europe. About 1604 Smith returned to England. An enthusiastic promoter of the Virginia Company, he set out in 1606 for America with its first group of settlers. Unprepared for serious colonizing and short of provisions, the group might have been wiped out but for Smith's expeditions to bargain with the Native Americans for food. Once, while exploring, he was captured by Powhatan's braves, who, according to Smith, would have executed him had not the chief's daughter, **Pocahontas,** intervened. Rival leaders bitterly opposed Smith, and he was sentenced to death for losing two of his men on this venture. He was saved, however, by the arrival of a ship from England bearing a higher authority who restored him to the colonial council. Smith later served a year as president of the council and put the settlers to work at constructive tasks. But after incessant wrangling and a gunpowder explosion in which he was injured, he returned to England in 1609.

In 1614 Smith explored "New" England, as he named the area. His next and last voyage, begun in 1615, ended abruptly when he was captured by pirates. In his remaining years he failed to gain support for new expeditions but wrote accounts of his explorations and adventures. The Pilgrims received valuable guidance from Smith's books, maps, and advice, but did not invite him to lead them.

———— ❧ ————

Short in stature, of modest birth and education, Smith was nevertheless vigorous, bold, and supremely confident. A pious bachelor and pre-eminently a man of action, he avoided "wine, tobacco, debts, dice ... [and] oaths" and preferred giving orders to taking them. His obvious talents, blatant ambition, and complex, assertive personality made him controversial in his day and with generations of scholars afterward.

Smith's early quest for military glory carried him through a series of virtually unbelievable perils and developed his leadership ability. Only twenty-seven years old when he arrived in Virginia, he was already a tough and seasoned captain. Amid Jamestown's confusion and miseries, he emerged by force of character as *the* dominant figure. He brought to the tasks at hand energy and determination, cleverness and courage. He successfully contained the Native Americans, procured food for starving settlers, explored and mapped much of the territory, and, most importantly, gave a central direction and discipline to the struggling colony itself. For the moment he was an indispensable man.

Smith's later colonial schemes were undermined by niggardly support and plain bad luck. His prodigious writings about the New World combined his own memoirs with other contemporary narratives; they inspired colonists at the time by advertising America's manifold opportunities. Although egocentric and in places exaggerated and overly dramatic, Smith's works are now regarded as basically sound, indeed invaluable collections of firsthand information; his maps are remarkably accurate.

His deeds and words were self-serving, but they also served his native land—and America as well. See P. L. Barbour, *Three Worlds of Captain John Smith* (1964).

DANIEL P. JORDAN

SMITH, Joseph (b. Sharon, Vt., Dec. 23, 1805; d. Carthage, Ill., June 27, 1844), RELIGIOUS LEADER, received no formal education. His family settled in Palmyra, New York, in 1816, and in 1820 he experienced the first of many "visions," claiming to have been selected by the voice of this vision to restore the church of Christ to mankind. Instructed, Smith said, to uncover certain plates of gold containing the story of how the Native Americans, descendants from the ancient Hebrews, came to the New World, he translated the plates from an ancient Egyptian writing. He published the work as *The Book of Mormon* (1830).

In 1830 Smith and his two brothers founded the Church of Jesus Christ of Latter-Day Saints in Fayette, New York. The group of believers soon developed into a cooperative society ruled by an ecclesiastical oligarchy. The church moved to Kirtland, Ohio, in 1831, but a bank failure forced Smith to move his congregation to Jackson County, Missouri, in 1838. Continued persecution caused the Mormons to move about in Missouri until they settled in Commerce, Illinois, in 1839. Here Smith and his followers enjoyed five years of peace and prosperity. Illinois authorities gave Smith a large amount of autonomy, and he became the virtual one-man ruler of the city. Among other things, he revived the ancient Hebrew practice of polygamy and took about forty wives. Many converts came to Commerce (renamed Nauvoo) to live and practice the new faith. Smith's prestige was great, but opposition to his dictatorial rule and to his people's practice of polygamy soon developed. After Mormons burned down a Nauvoo newspaper which had criticized Smith in 1844, he was arrested along with his brother Hyrum and taken to Carthage, Illinois, where both men were shot by an angry mob of non-Mormons.

In an age of many self-anointed prophets, Joseph Smith was by far the most successful of the lot, and at least a portion of this success was attributable to his appearance and to his personality. Extremely handsome and well built, he fit perfectly the image of a prophet. Smith, moreover, went out of his way to give his followers the impression that although he was God's anointed he possessed human qualities. He continually bragged, for example, about his prowess as a wrestler. Smith was almost always friendly, gregarious, and charming, and he displayed an enormous zest for living. All of these qualities were reflected in his religion, which completely discarded the austerities of Calvinism and ingeniously blended supernaturalism and materialism. Heaven, as Smith and his successor, **Brigham Young,** envisioned it, was a place in which the righteous would forever indulge in the earthly pleasures—family life, sex, comfort, and glory.

Smith was able to convince his followers—as well as himself—that he had great powers. He constantly asserted that God had commissioned him to save a world headed for destruction, and he preached that he alone would determine who was to enter heaven. Both he and his followers boldly maintained that they were empowered to perform miracles and that they could heal the sick by a simple act, such as placing a holy handkerchief or a cloak on a bed. From the beginning Smith molded Mormonism as the Catholicism of the future. In an age of turmoil he offered bold, exact, positive answers to ancient questions about God and man. Mormonism's dogmatism attracted those who otherwise might have succumbed to the disorders and fears of the pre–Civil War period.

In establishing his church Smith wisely endowed it with unique ingredients that practically ensured its survival. First, he gave Mormonism a written document, *The Book of Mormon,* that immediately set it above the other new sects of the day. Most important of all, Smith made every loyal adult white male a priest. Uniquely, his church had no laity, each man having the authority to speak and to act for God. Smith thus brought into service not just a few dedicated workers called clergymen but a vast, unpaid, ever increasing body of men who yearned for the privilege of serving God.

But if Smith possessed great strengths, he was also plagued by numerous weaknesses. His desire for beautiful women was notorious. For a half-century after his death many of those who had known him asserted that he had concocted polygamy not in obedience to God but to satisfy his own desires. Smith's first wife, Emma, ceaselessly raged about her husband's numerous love affairs. Smith's incompetence in money matters was also well known. In Kirtland he was involved in a bank fraud, and in Nauvoo he engaged in land speculation on a grand scale. Such activities led his enemies to label him a money digger. And although most of his military endeavors turned into fiascos, Smith was obsessed with the notion that he was a great soldier. At Nauvoo he loved to dress in fancy uniforms, and he took great pride in describing himself as the commander of the Nauvoo Legion, the Mormon militia, and consequently the highest-ranking military officer in the United States. Finally, Smith was an extremely emotional man. Unlike Young, who was cold and calculating, Smith often trusted false friends, such as those who, just before he was murdered, assured him he would be safe in Carthage jail. For a prophet Smith seems in retrospect all too human. See Fawn Brodie, *No Man Knows My History: The Life of Joseph Smith, the Mormon Prophet* (1971).

STANLEY P. HIRSHSON

SONDHEIM, Joshua Stephen (b. New York, N.Y., March 22, 1930), COMPOSER, LYRICIST, born into a comfortable, upper-middle class family. A precocious child, his destiny was determined when his parents divorced and he and his mother moved to Doylestown, Pennsylvania. Among his mother's new acquantances was the renowned lyricist, Oscar Hammerstein. Sondheim soon became friends with one of Hammerstein's sons, Jimmy. But it was the father who was to

have the most profound influence on the young boy. Inspired and encouraged by Hammerstein, Sondheim, age fifteen, wrote his first musical, *By George*. This adolescent attempt was presented with pride to his mentor. Hammerstein proceeded to analyze the piece in meticulous detail. He was ruthless, but his analysis provided Sondheim with a foundation for what was to become his life's work. Sondheim graduated from Williams College in Massachusetts and proceeded to use the Hutchinson Prize, a two year fellowship, to study with avant-garde composer, Milton Babbitt. After a brief stint as a writer for the television series *Topper*, Sondheim returned to New York, and was commissioned by set designer/producer Lemuel Ayers to write a musical. The result, *Saturday Night* never reached the stage because of Ayers's untimely death. Sondheim's next commission was to launch him into Broadway history. He became the lyricist for **Leonard Bernstein**'s and Arthur Laurents's *West Side Story* (1957). The success of this work established Sondheim's reputation as America's foremost lyricist, but Sondheim was not content. He wanted to provide both music and lyrics. Although he was to work as lyricist with two of the theater's most distinguished composers, Jules Styne and **Richard Rodgers**, in *Gypsy* (1959), and *Do I Hear a Waltz* (1965), he was frustrated. Finally, in 1962, Sondheim's first work as both composer and lyricist opened on Broadway. Although *A Funny Thing Happened on the Way to the Forum* was a critical success, winning a number of Tony Awards, including Best Musical, Sondheim's work was largely ignored. His next musical, *Anyone Can Whistle* was panned and closed after nine performances. In 1970, however, with the opening of *Company*, Sondheim was finally recognized as the most innovative voice in the American theater.

———— ❦ ————

Prior to Sondheim, it was accepted that musicals were the escapist entertainment of the middle classes. They evoked a larger-than-life world in which emotion was expressed in melody and ultimate happiness was guaranteed. The optimism of post–World War II America was reflected in them. The serene values of the Eisenhower era reigned over the musical stage. After the social and artistic upheavals of the sixties, however, Sondheim and his primary collaborator, director Harold Prince, could not simply churn out this kind of escapist entertainment. They chose instead to confront the tired suburban businessman and his wife with the very issues they had gone to the theater to escape. This was an audacious course to follow. Sondheim was flouting convention and this alienated much of his audience. But he and his many collaborators have blazed a trail of creativity on Broadway. They have chosen *the* populist form of theater and invested it with a truth and seriousness of purpose rarely associated with the Broadway musical. This choice has robbed Sondheim of the kind of commercial success gained by other contemporary composers, but has endowed his work with a theatrical exhilaration and intellectual veracity.

Sondheim's innovation is not limited to his choice of subject matter. His musicals are more closely related to avant-garde non-musical theater than to conventional realist theater. He abandons logical development, employing instead associated structures in which time and space are fragmented. During the 1940s and '50s, the so-called Golden Age of musical comedy, musicals were built around their plots. The integration of song, dance and dialogue became mandatory. The book structure of these pieces meant there must be a story line. The basic structure that informs a Sondheim musical, however, is the *idea*. Music, lyric, dance, dialogue, design and direction fuse to support a focal thought. A central metaphor shapes the entire production. Content and form cannot be separated; the one dictates and is dependent on the other. For this reason each of Sondheim's works is unique. Sondheim's music and lyrics grow out of the dramatic idea inherent in the show's concept. They become part of the drama that previous theater songs would only reflect.

Since *Company*, Sondheim has managed to produce a new musical almost every three years. His work includes *Follies* (1971), *A Little Night Music* (1973), *Pacific Overtures* (1976), *Sweeney Todd* (1979), *Merrily We Roll Along* (1981), *Sunday in the Park with George* (1984), *Into the Woods* (1987), and *Assassins* (1991). With each new work, Sondheim redefines the parameters of musical theater. Despite numerous Tony awards, accolades and a Pulitzer Prize (1985), Sondheim's work remains controversial because it is not easy, and audiences of the musical theater do not expect to be challenged or provoked. Yet Sondheim's prolific output continues unabated. His work now provides the defining standard by which all other musicals are assessed. See Joanne Gordon, *Art Isn't Easy: The Achievement of Stephen Sondheim* (1990).

JOANNE GORDON

SOUSA John Philip (b. Washington, D.C., Nov. 6, 1854; d. Reading, Pa., March 6, 1932), BANDMASTER, COMPOSER, entered the musical conservatory of John Esputa in Washington in 1861, where he learned to play a variety of band instruments. During 1868–72, he was a member of the U.S. Marine Band. He then studied violin, theory, and harmony with George F. Benkert. In 1872 he also conducted an orchestra at Kernan's Theatre Comique, a Washington, D.C., variety house, and played the violin in the orchestra of Ford's Opera House. From 1874 to 1876 Sousa served briefly as orchestra conductor on tour for the Milton Nobles Comedy Co.; orchestra conductor for the Mathew S. Morgan Living Pictures Co.; and violinist for Jacques Offenbach's orchestra at the Philadelphia Centennial Exhibition. During 1876–79 he resided in Philadelphia, where he played for the Chestnut Street and Arch Street theaters, and conducted the Philadelphia Church Choir Co., for which he composed his first comic opera, *The Smugglers*. He then became conductor of the U.S. Marine Band (1880–92), which he reorganized. He composed marches for band, such as "The Washington Post March" (1889), "Semper Fidelis" (1888), "Liberty Bell" (1893), and "Stars and Stripes Forever" (1897). In 1892, Sousa left the Marine Band to form his own band, which gave its first concert in Plainfield, New Jersey, in

September 1892, and which he led until his death. The band toured the U.S. numerous times, made four trips to Europe, and one around the world (1910–12). During the Spanish-American War, Sousa was musical director for the Sixth Army Corps; during World War I, he served as director of navy bands and toured with the Great Lakes Naval Training Station Band to raise money for Liberty Loan drives. In all, he composed more than one hundred marches, ten comic operas, more than fifty songs, and twelve suites.

Sousa was a resolutely public musician. His declared goal was to entertain his audiences; the skill through which he reached that goal he called "showmanship." Sousa's band embodied his showmanly instincts. Dressed in uniform, playing with military precision under the leader's firm direction, commanding a wide range of nuance and impressive virtuosity, the Sousa band was a well-drilled mechanism which impressed even the tone-deaf. In his autobiography, Sousa explained that one important reason he had decided to become a bandmaster was that the medium carried no set repertory or tradition which might encumber him. He prized his "freedom to be absolutely eclectic" in programming and exercised that freedom widely. Sousa's programs were calculated to arouse, amuse, and edify his audience in turn, through juxtaposing widely varying musical selections. Through some four decades of touring and several hundred phonograph recordings the Sousa band was one of the most important dispensers of music in America, introducing audiences to a repertory ranging from Wagner and Chopin to patriotic songs, ragtime, and the leader's own inimitable marches.

Sousa was a confident, witty, physically vigorous man. Chosen in his mid-twenties to conduct the Marine Band, the president's personal musical ensemble, he was a public figure for more than half a century, apparently equally comfortable in the company of royalty and working people. The wide range of Sousa's personal interests corresponded to his musical eclecticism. He

wrote novels and verse as well as music, and he was also an accomplished horseman and an expert trapshooter. See John Philip Sousa, *Marching Along* (1928).

RICHARD CRAWFORD

SPARKS, Jared (b. Willington, Conn., May 10, 1789; d. Cambridge, Mass., March 14, 1866), HISTORIAN, graduated from Harvard College in 1815. He continued his studies at the Harvard Divinity School for three years, during which time he also served briefly as the editor of the *North American Review* (1817–18). Upon graduating with a master's degree, Sparks entered the Unitarian ministry. In 1819 he was installed as pastor of the First Independent Church, Baltimore, Maryland. He was also chaplain of the U.S. House of Representatives (1821–23). In 1823 Sparks left the ministry and bought the *North American Review* which, under his editorship (1823–29), became one of the most important American periodicals.

Sparks's greatest interest, however, was in the study of history. In 1829 he sold the *North American Review* in order to devote all his time to research on the American Revolution. He was a pioneer purchaser and collector of manuscripts dealing with American history, and his exhaustive researches into manuscript collection in both North America and Europe relating to the Revolutionary period laid the groundwork for much subsequent work on the subject. He is most noted for his massive twelve-volume edition of *The Writing of George Washington* (1834–37). He also published *The Life of John Ledyard* (1828); *The Works of Benjamin Franklin* (10 vols., 1836–40); *The Life of Gouverneur Morris* (3 vols., 1832); and *The Diplomatic Correspondence of the American Revolution* (12 vols., 1829–30). In addition he edited the twenty-five-volume *Library of American Biography* (1838–44, 1844–47), and wrote seven of the sixty biographies himself.

Sparks was a member of the Massachusetts Board of Education (1837–40). While McLean professor of ancient and modern history at Harvard (1839–49), the first professor of nonecclesiastical history in the U.S., he organized the history department at Harvard. From 1849 to 1853 he served as president of Harvard University. He encouraged the greater use of lectures in instruction, a return to compulsory courses, and the furtherance of the Harvard Observatory, then the university's only research unit. He resigned in 1853 and devoted most of the remainder of his life to collecting material for his projected but never to be published history of the American Revolution.

———— ✤ ————

Jared Sparks was unquestionably an important intellectual leader in his own time. A tall, handsome man with sad and brooding eyes, his geniality concealed a humorless drive, a genius for organization combined with an enormous capacity for work, which resulted in a great deal of writing, although he did not write well. His prose was pedantic, pompous, and dull.

Sparks's current reputation rests upon two events. The first was his installation as a Unitarian minister in Baltimore, an event which furnished the occasion for William Ellery Channing's epochal sermon "Unitarian Christianity." The other event was an international controversy over Sparks's editorial practices, touched off by the charge of Lord Mahon, the British historian, that Sparks had "greatly altered … corrected and embellished" Washington's correspondence. The charge was generally true and affected all of Sparks's work, because he believed that national heroes should serve as models of national ideals; therefore, he sought to present them in their most impeccable dress. For example, when Washington wrote familiarly, "Old Put," Sparks substituted "General Putnam," or when Washington referred to the miserliness of one small congressional appropriation as "but a flea bite at present," Sparks refined it to read "totally inadequate to our demands at this time." National history and biography were meant to unify, not divide, Sparks believed; therefore, almost all of Washington's animadversions toward New Englanders, Scots, and even the English are deleted.

All of Sparks's writings have been superseded by the works of subsequent historians and edi-

tors, but his significance lies in the attention he focused on American history and the importance of preserving its documentation through his own enormous collecting, editing, and publication efforts. See Herbert Baxter Adams, *The Life and Writings of Jared Sparks* (2 vols., 1893).

DAVID D. VAN TASSEL

SPELLMAN, Francis Joseph (b. Whitman, Mass., May 4, 1889; d. New York, N.Y., Dec. 2, 1967), RELIGIOUS LEADER, graduated from Fordham University in 1911, attended the North American College in Rome (1911–16), and after being ordained in 1916, became a curate in Roxbury, Massachusetts. During 1918–22 he was director of literature for the Boston diocese and editor of the diocesan newspaper *The Pilot*, and in 1922–25, vice-chancellor of the diocese. In 1925 Spellman was appointed the first American attaché to the Vatican secretary, Cardinal Gasparri; he was the official English translator for Pius XI, and was chosen to deliver the pope's 1931 encyclical to the Associated Press in Paris. Made a monsignor in 1926, he returned to the U.S. in 1932 to serve as the auxiliary bishop to Cardinal O'Connell of Boston. In 1939, upon the death of Cardinal Hayes, Pius XII appointed Spellman archbishop of New York and military vicar of the U.S. Armed Forces. In the latter role Spellman visited the troops in England, the Middle East, and Africa in 1943; in 1944 he followed the Allied invasion of Europe and held mass for soldiers on the battlefields. In 1945 he followed U.S. troops into Tokyo.

Spellman was made cardinal of the New York diocese in 1945. He controlled his diocese closely and kept on friendly terms with New York politicians. In 1947 he started a $25-million school, hospital, and church building drive in New York and also endeavored to help the city's Puerto Rican minority attain educational and religious advancement. In 1949 Spellman became involved in a dispute with **Eleanor Roosevelt,** who in her newspaper column criticized his stand favoring federal grants to parochial schools for nonreligious textbooks, bus transportation, and health aids. In an open letter Spellman charged her with being anti-Catholic, but later apologized. In addition to arguing for federal aid to parochial schools, Spellman favored censorship of movies, upheld strict morality, and was firmly against divorce and religious intermarriage. But he fought racial discrimination in New York housing and favored close cooperation among different religions. A fervent anticommunist, he led American Catholics in protesting the persecution of Eastern European Catholics by the Communists during the early 1950s. He backed Senator **Joseph McCarthy**'s anticommunist campaign and was outspoken in supporting United States involvement in Vietnam as necessary to halt Communist expansion. He spent the Christmases of 1964 and 1965 in Vietnam. Spellman wrote *The Road to Victory* (1942), *Action This Day* (1943), on his first European tour, *The Risen Soldier* (1944), *No Greater Love* (1945), and *Prayers and Poems* (1946).

The strengths and weaknesses of American Catholicism in the middle of the 20th century were summed up in the life and work of New York's Francis Cardinal Spellman. As a churchman, Spellman was the foremost example of the skilled administrator and fund raiser so typical of America's episcopate. His diocese, with its extensive programs of education and charity, was a training ground for large numbers of bishops in the postwar years. His influence on such appointments also manifested his role in the church universal, for his friendship with Pope Pius XII, stemming from his years of service in Rome, together with his role as America's most powerful Catholic leader in the years of postwar reconstruction, gave him great power and influence at the Vatican. The circumstances of postwar Europe made the Vatican an important factor in world affairs, so that American presidents and diplomats found it useful to maintain close contacts with the New York cardinal. The nation's Catholics appreciated the sense of status and respectability which Spellman's well-publicized tours of American forces abroad and meetings with national officials symbolized. Most Catholics shared Spellman's vigorous opposition to Communism, and like him, they regarded a militant anticommunist foreign policy as both a religious and a patriotic obligation. Accordingly they were inclined as he was to view opposition to such a policy as un-American and a slight upon the church and its members. Similarly, Spellman's demands for public assistance for Catholic education and his outspoken opposition to pornography and birth control manifested the newfound sense of status and power which suffused the Catholic population. (In the years following World War II, Catholics for the first time began to leave working-class neighborhoods for middle-class suburbs in large numbers and to play significant roles in society.) In the 1960s the death of Pope Pius XII and the calling of an ecumenical council marked a shift in interest for the Vatican, while the election of President John F. Kennedy ended the intense minority-consciousness long characteristic of American Catholics. Spellman's influence abroad declined, while new leaders, attuned to the issues raised by the council and by the tumultuous events in national life, received greater attention. The widespread criticism which greeted Spellman's enthusiastic endorsement of the Vietnam War revealed that a new era had arrived for the American church. Francis Cardinal Spellman had played an important role in national life, but his attitudes did not keep up with the pace of change. See John Cooney, *The American Pope: Francis Cardinal Spellman, 1889–1967* (1984).

DAVID J. O'BRIEN

SPERRY, Elmer Ambrose (b. near Cortland, N.Y., Oct. 21, 1860; d. Brooklyn, N.Y., June 16, 1930), INVENTOR, ENGINEER, attended the Cortland Normal School (1877–80) and heard lectures at nearby Cornell University, where William A. Anthony, a physics professor, lectured on electrical science and technology. Sperry built a dynamo to light the streets of Cortland in 1881, and after moving to Chicago in 1882, he opened the Sperry Electric Light, Motor, and Car Brake

Co. to make dynamos and arc lamps. In 1889 he opened the Sperry Electric Mining Machine Co. to make electrified coal mining equipment of his own design, including mine cars. From mine cars, Sperry changed to street railways: in 1892 he formed the Sperry Electric Railway Co. in Cleveland. The company was sold to General Electric in 1895, and Sperry began experimenting with electrically powered automobiles, and then with diesel combustion engines. In 1900 he was briefly associated with the National Battery Co. of Buffalo, and later set up a laboratory with Charles Townsend in Washington, D.C. They jointly developed the Townsend process for caustic soda and chlorine manufacture. Beginning in 1907, Sperry developed a gyroscopic stabilizer and gyroscopic compass for ships, and in 1910 opened the Sperry Gyroscope Co. in Brooklyn to manufacture them. In 1914 he and his oldest son, Lawrence, demonstrated a gyro-stabilizer for aircraft, and in 1915 he became a member of the U.S. Naval Consulting Board. During the war his company developed naval gunfire controls, searchlights, aircraft instruments, and a flying torpedo.

In 1922 Sperry introduced the automatic ship pilot ("Metal Mike") and in 1928 a rail flaw detector for railroads. He supplied **Albert A. Michelson** with precision devices to determine the speed of light. In 1928 Sperry sold the Sperry Gyroscope Co. to North American Aviation. He was president of the American Society of Mechanical Engineers, a member of the National Academy of Sciences, organizer of the World Engineering Congress held in Japan in 1929, and winner of the prestigious John Fritz Medal. He left the YMCA $1 million.

Elmer Sperry, a prolific inventor and resourceful engineer, contributed substantially to the development of electric light and power and industrial chemistry, which were the leading technologies of the period, but he is best remembered for his gyroscopic devices applied to the automatic guidance and control of ships and aircraft. His interest in technology was intensified by its obvious ability to save labor and raise living standards in an environment where natural forces had been harsh and demanding.

Having embarked upon the difficult career of an independent inventor, Sperry demonstrated a technique for survival. He shifted his concentration from electric light and power to mining machinery, automobiles, electrochemistry, and other fields, as he found critical technological problems to solve that demanded his particular expertise and promised to attract supportive capital. During his career he received 350 patents. He organized several companies to manufacture his inventions, but he also sold his patents after developing them. By 1910 a particularly strong inventive characteristic of his was emerging: although his fields of inventive concentration seemed disparate, many of his works involved automatic feedback controls, devices later categorized as cybernetic.

His ability with these controls enticed him in 1907 into a new field, gyroscope applications. Within five years he had created an outstanding gyro ship stabilizer, a gyrocompass, patents for a gyro airplane stabilizer, and the Sperry Gyroscope Company, which became known throughout the world for the resourcefulness of its enthusiastic young engineers, recruited by Sperry, and for the excellence of its precision-manufactured instruments and devices.

Sperry and his company contributed greatly to America's effort during World War I through gyro applications. Later, Secretary of the Navy Charles Francis Adams observed that no other American had contributed so much to naval technology. Recognized by his peers for his engineering excellence and inventive imagination, Sperry held responsible professional positions and won outstanding honors. Perhaps one of his most revealing remarks was that he never thought of himself in the romantic image of the lone inventor, but as a man who saw problems and tried to solve them. He also said he preferred the difficult problems, for these removed him from vulgar competition. See Thomas Parke Hughes, *Elmer Ambrose Sperry, Inventor and Engineer* (1971).

THOMAS PARKE HUGHES

SPINGARN, Joel Elias (b. New York, N.Y., May 17, 1875; d. New York, N.Y., July 26, 1939), EDU-CATOR, REFORMER, received both his BA (1895) and PhD (1899) from Columbia University. In 1899 he was appointed assistant professor of comparative literature at Columbia. An exponent of the aesthetic school of literary criticism (formulated by Benedetto Croce, an Italian philosopher and critic), Spingarn argued that a literary work should be judged on its own aesthetic qualities rather than by any moral values or predetermined set of rules. In 1899 he published *A History of Literary Criticism in the Renaissance.*

In 1908 Spingarn ran for Congress as a Progressive Republican, but was defeated. In 1911 he was dismissed by Columbia as the result of a controversy over academic freedom. In 1912 he was a delegate to the Progressive party's convention at Chicago.

In 1910 Spingarn joined the board of the National Association for the Advancement of Colored People (chairman, 1913; president, 1930–39). In 1914 he established the Spingarn Medal, which is awarded annually to an American of African extraction for outstanding achievement. He represented the NAACP at the Progressive party convention in Chicago in 1916, and in 1936 he campaigned for Franklin D. Roosevelt for president.

During World War I, Spingarn commanded an infantry battalion and led a movement that resulted in the first officers' training program for African-Americans. In 1919 he was named vice president of Harcourt, Brace and Co., and he edited the publishing house's European Library (1920–24). His other works include *The New Criticism* (1911), *Creative Criticism* (1917; rev. ed., 1931), and *Poems* (1924).

Spingarn's life was one of continual protest and rebellion. First, he rebelled against the "genteel tradition" in American literature and its exponents. The opening round of what developed into a long and bitter controversy began with his public lecture at Columbia entitled "The New Criticism," which was published in 1911. In this contentious discourse he revealed the zeal of the reformer, rejecting most of the criteria of academic criticism. To Spingarn the new criticism would bring one closer to the artist's act of creation, in order to fully perceive its meaning and nature. At about the same time he rebelled against the administration at Columbia, in a controversy over what he considered to be the unjust and high-handed dismissal of classical philologist Harry Thurston Peck. Spingarn also revolted against the status quo in race relations in the United States. His entry into the National Association for the Advancement of Colored People was a protest against racism and injustice.

After his dismissal from Columbia, Spingarn retired to his country estate, Troutbeck, at Amenia, New York. He enjoyed the life of a gentleman farmer enlarging and improving his estate. He took great pride in his prizes and medals for his work with clematis. His published articles identifying more than two hundred varieties of this plant established his reputation as a horticulturist.

Spingarn also used Troutbeck as the site of two conferences of major importance to the civil rights movement in the United States. The first Amenia Conference of 1916 was held following the death of **Booker T. Washington,** and though not officially sponsored by the NAACP was organized by Spingarn and **W. E. B. Du Bois.** Its aim was to bring about a reconciliation between the NAACP and the followers of Washington, to unite their efforts to end lynching and mob violence, and to secure passage and enforcement of laws to protect civil liberties. The conference was largely successful in attaining its goals, and **James Weldon Johnson,** poet and author, a former supporter of Washington, was engaged as field secretary for the NAACP.

A second Amenia Conference was held in the summer of 1933 and resulted from the realization that the New Deal was largely ineffectual as far as blacks were concerned. Moreover, younger black leaders and intellectuals such as **Ralph Bunche,** Abram Harris, and John P. Davis were critical of what they considered to be the outmoded strategy and tactics of the NAACP, with its emphasis on civil and political liberties. This conference was only partially successful. The established leaders were not willing to abandon the interracial character of the NAACP for a program of black nationalism. They also considered the proposal for biracial unionism to be unrealistic, as they had already been repulsed in their overtures to organized labor. However, the conference did lay a new emphasis on political strength to come from bloc voting, and there also emerged the broad outlines for a new economic emphasis and strategy which the Association began to implement after the failure of the national recovery program.

Spingarn also sought to implement his philosophy of politics. To him politics was "a spiritual act" in the world of reality comparable to that of poetry in the sphere of speculative thought. He held that the true politician accepts the world of reality and deals with it in order to transform it. On the other hand he believed that politics is equally important to the poet, in that it gives him a grasp of the world of reality. In 1912, as a delegate to the Progressive Republican party's convention in Chicago, he worked in vain with **Jane Addams** and others for the inclusion of a plank calling for the repeal of discriminatory laws against African-Americans. At the annual meeting of the NAACP in 1916 he urged that the power of a state be curtailed if it denied the franchise to any of its male citizens. Spingarn believed that the Association should also take into account disfranchisement based on sex. He held that before blacks could be fully enfranchised, the women of America would have to secure the vote by constitutional amendment.

During World War I, Spingarn served as a major of infantry. Serious illness led to his transfer to the Department of Intelligence in Washington, D.C., where part of his duty was to deal with black restlessness and discontent. His plan called for securing cooperation from black college students and the black community. He proposed unsuccessfully that W. E. B. Du Bois, editor of the *Crisis,* the official organ of the NAACP, be commissioned a captain in military intelligence, and also agitated for a separate training camp for black officers. This issue sharply divided the NAACP and the black press and brought to the fore a perpetual dilemma. On the one hand was the insult of a separate camp and on the other the irreparable injury that would be done to blacks in their struggle for the rights and duties of full citizenship if they were denied positions of military authority because of the lack of separate camps for officers' training. A black officers' training camp was finally opened at Des Moines, Iowa, and by October 1917, 608 black officers had been commissioned.

Spingarn worked hard for the NAACP. In the early days of the Association he made two extensive trips into the Midwest at his own expense to organize branches and to speak for civil rights. From time to time he provided modest emergency aid. He and Mrs. Spingarn gave prize money to be awarded by the *Crisis* to talented young black writers, poets, and dramatists, and thus fostered the Harlem Renaissance. During the 1920s when he served as treasurer and chairman of the NAACP Investment Committee he expanded the resources of the Association. But even more important was the leadership he gave the Association in its formative years. He was an obstinate man once convinced of the rightness of his cause, and invariably he forced the board to yield to his strongly held convictions. The most important of these for the NAACP was his philosophy of noneconomic liberalism. See B. Joyce Ross, *J. E. Spingarn and the Rise of the NAACP* (1972).

CHARLES FLINT KELLOGG

SPOCK, Benjamin McLane (b. New Haven, Conn., May 2, 1903), PHYSICIAN, graduated from Yale in 1925, and then studied at the Yale Medical School and at the Columbia College of Physicians and Surgeons, receiving his MD in 1929. He interned at Presbyterian Hospital in New York, and completed residencies in pediatrics at the New York Nursery and Child's Hospital (1931–32), and in psychiatry at New York Hospital (1932–33). He also trained for six years in his spare time at the New York Psychoanalytical Institute. From 1933 until 1944, he engaged in the private practice of pediatrics, and gained a reputation for his ability to handle children and put them completely at ease. At the same time, he taught pediatrics at the Cornell University Medical College, was on the pediatric staff of New York Hospital, and served as pediatric consultant to the New York City Department of Health and the Institute on Personality Development.

In 1944 he became a psychiatrist in the Medical Corps of the U.S. Naval reserve, and rose to the rank of lieutenant commander by the time of his discharge in 1946. During this period he wrote *Baby and Child Care* (originally published as *The Common Sense Book of Baby and Child Care* in 1946), a book that became the pediatric bible of a generation of parents, supplanting the then standard authority on child rearing, *Psychological Care of Infant and Child* (1928), by Dr. **John B. Watson.** In contrast to Watson's approach, which tended to foster stern and inflexible parental attitudes, Spock, in a deliberate attempt to counteract the rigidities of the pediatric tradition, adopted a less harsh, more reassuring method. He stressed the importance of flexibility in dealing with the wide range of differences between individual infants and children. Spock clarified his position in later revised editions by counseling parents to temper flexibility by setting firm but reasonable standards of discipline. *Baby and Child Care* has sold well over 20 million copies, and has been translated into many languages.

In 1947, Spock moved to Minnesota, where he taught psychiatry at the University of Minnesota and served as a psychiatric consultant to the Mayo Clinic. In 1951 he became professor of child development at the University of Pittsburgh, then in 1955 transferred to a similar position at Western Reserve University, where he remained until his retirement in 1967.

Spock first became politically active in 1962, when his dismay with President John F. Kennedy's announcement of the resumption of nuclear testing in the atmosphere led him to support the National Committee for a Sane Nuclear Policy (SANE) through a full-page advertisement in the New York *Times.* He joined the organization's national board, and became cochairman in

1963. In the 1964 presidential campaign he supported President Lyndon Johnson because of his seeming pro-peace stance but turned against Johnson after the president "escalated" the war in Vietnam in 1965. At first a reluctant demonstrator, Spock became increasingly more involved in the peace movement. He became cochairman in 1967 of the National Conference for a New Politics, a loose confederation of diverse New Left groups, while resigning as cochairman of SANE, the majority of whose board members were displeased with his "ecumenical promiscuity." He also became a strong supporter of the draft-resistance movement, and his activities in that cause led to his indictment in 1968, along with four others, for conspiracy to aid and abet violation of the Selective Service Act. He was convicted in a federal district court in Boston, sentenced to two years in prison, and fined $5,000. But the conviction was overturned by the U.S. court of appeals for the first circuit in 1969. In 1972 Spock was the pacifist People's Party candidate for president. Spock formally retired from medical practice in 1967, and moved to Maine. During the seventies and eighties, he has kept himself busy sailing and rethinking his theories of child rearing. In 1992, he endorsed a theory that cows' milk was bad for children, and in 1994 he seemed to agree with some earlier critics that a few of his child rearing concepts did not work as effectively as he hoped they would. He also stressed the importance of mothers staying home to rear and nurture their children at an early age and not going off to pursue careers, pronouncements which many in the women's movement denounced as archaic.

❧

There is a humanitarian tradition in American medicine that runs from **Benjamin Rush,** the physician who signed the Declaration of Independence, down to Benjamin Spock, the pediatrician who believed that modern warfare was a serious public health problem. Spock was reared an Episcopalian and marked somewhat by an aristocratic education. Nevertheless he has been strongly democratic and humanitarian in action as well as in word throughout his life. Concern for others has been his hallmark. He felt the aloof intellectual would not stop war; he had to be "humanitarianized," by direct experience and empathy with the sufferings of people everywhere, in the slums as well as in Southeast Asia. This social-minded physician believed furthermore that a medical man also should be made more sensitive to the needs of the less fortunate. Spock combined this humanitarian concern with a strong sense of moral and spiritual values which he has felt should be practiced by educators and parents and taught in schools and homes. In the evenings, from 1943 to 1946, after a full day with child patients, he wrote *Baby and Child Care.* This famous, widely read book has given rise to the phrase "Spock-reared babies" and the false charge that it engendered permissiveness. Spock has always upheld the need for moral guidelines in the school and ethical principles in the home. The 1957 edition especially stressed the need for parents to give positive leadership to their children. Basically, his position is that "you can be both firm and friendly."

Dr. Spock has been described as being solicitous and engaging in all his contacts. His warm, clear speech, spiced here and there with a dash of humor, is still remembered by colleagues at Western Reserve's Children's Clinic, who recall the tall pediatrician sauntering down the hall holding two children by their hands.

Since his retirement from medical practice Spock has written other books and led peace movements; he has joined a select but distinguished company of predecessors who ministered to the body politic as well as to the body physical. See Jessica Mitford, *The Trial of Dr. Spock* (1969).

EUGENE P. LINK

SPOTSWOOD, Alexander (b. Tangier, Africa, 1676; d. Annapolis, Md., June 7, 1740), POLITICAL LEADER, was commissioned in the Earl of Bath's British regiment in 1693. He was stationed in Ireland (1698–1703), and served under the Duke of Marlborough (1703–9) in the War of Spanish Succession, rising to the rank of lieutenant colonel. In 1710 he assumed office as lieutenant governor of Virginia, being in effect the governor, since Governor George Hamilton, the Earl of Orkney, never visited the colony. Spotswood established the Virginia Indian Co. at Fort Christianna in 1714 to regulate the fur trade and develop a more enlightened policy toward the Native Americans; he believed in religious education and fair treatment for the natives. These actions, along with his law requiring the inspection of tobacco destined for export or for use as legal tender, brought him into controversy in 1715 with the members of the Virginia house of burgesses, who felt he was usurping their power. The ill will thus generated continued even after the Crown repealed the law. However, burgesses and council were reconciled in 1720 to a plan brought from England by **William Byrd.**

Besides taking aggressive action against pirates along Virginia's coast (Edward Teach, "Blackbeard," was killed in 1718), Spotswood led an expedition exploring the Shenandoah Valley (1716). He urged the construction of a system of forts and a series of settlements by friendly Native Americans to resist attacks by the hostile Iroquois. In 1722 he concluded a treaty with the Iroquois keeping them north of the Potomac and west of the Blue Ridge Mountains. During his tenure he acquired large personal landholdings in the colony.

Spotswood was removed from office in 1722 because the English government felt he was siding too often with the colonists. He spent the next two years at his ironworks at Germanna in Spotsylvania County, operated by a community of Germans he had brought over in 1714. He went to England in 1724 to adjust his land titles and returned to Virginia in 1730 as deputy postmaster general for the American colonies. In this position he extended regular postal service as far south as Williamsburg. He was also responsible for the appointment of **Benjamin Franklin** as postmaster of Philadelphia in 1737. At the outbreak of war with Spain in 1739 (War of Jenkins' Ear) Spotswood was made a colonel in charge of recruiting a colonial regiment. At his death he held the rank of general.

⎯⎯∞⎯⎯

Alexander Spotswood was one of the most notable governors of Virginia during the colonial period. A military man and an aristocrat, he proved dynamic and efficient, but showed little regard for the "vulgar people." In politics, his aim was to better the colony in dealing with three essential elements in Virginia life: land, tobacco, and Native Americans. He tried to regulate land transactions, to standardize the quality of tobacco, and to improve the condition of the tributary Native Americans while taking steps to educate and Christianize them. But his autocratic disposition brought him into frequent conflict with both burgesses and council, which undoubtedly hampered his action. He explored and opened up the west of Virginia, organized the fight against pirates off the Virginia coast, and contributed to the development of Williamsburg into a real capital with a number of substantial public buildings, setting a new architectural standard in the colony with the Governor's Palace and the Wren Building of the College of William and Mary. Under his governorship, Virginia was thus turned from a narrow strip of coastland with a few scattered plantations into a wider and more civilized country. While trying to reconcile the diverging interests of the king (that is, in fact, the Board of Trade and the English merchants) and of the colonists, he did not always make sufficient allowance for the proud and independent spirit of the planters. Yet in later years he came to be accepted as one of them. He was one of the few men in the colonial era who left their mark on Virginia. See Leonidas Dodson, *Alexander Spotswood, Governor of Colonial Virginia, 1710–1722* (1932).

PIERRE MARAMBAUD

SPRAGUE, Frank Julian (b. Milford, Conn., July 25, 1857; d. New York, N.Y., Oct. 25, 1934), INVENTOR, graduated with high honors from the U.S. Naval Academy in 1878, and then spent two years on duty in the Orient, where he also served as a special correspondent for the Boston *Herald*. After having failed in an attempt to design a system to illuminate warships by electricity rather than oil, he resigned from the navy (1883) and became technical assistant to **Thomas Alva Edison.** He left Edison in 1884 to form the Sprague Electric Railway and Motor Co., for which he developed the first constant-speed electric motor. His company was the first to engage in the general manufacture of industrial electric motors. Next, he turned his attention to railway electrification, culminating in the installation of the first electrical trolley line of any size at Richmond, Virginia, in 1887. More than one hundred other such systems were set up in the next two years. In 1892 he formed the Sprague Electric Elevator Co. and did pioneering work on the development of multiple floor control and automatic elevators, forerunners of modern signal-controlled elevators. Later in life, he invented a system for running two elevators on a common rail in the same shaft. In 1895 he created the multiple unit system for electrical railways, which made it possible to set up and control a train of any number of cars with a single master switch, a process vital to the operation of modern rapid-transit systems. He also founded the Sprague Safety Control and Signal Corporation, which produced many safety devices, such as a danger signal system for the immediate detection of faulty rails. During World War I he served as chairman of the U.S. Naval Consulting Board, and helped develop fuses and air depth bombs. His many inventions earned him the title "Father of Electrical Traction."

⎯⎯∞⎯⎯

Looking back from his seventy-fifth birthday, Frank Sprague ascribed his success to his physical toughness, which "apparently I inherited," to his view of a challenge as "a tempting invitation," and to the fact that "after reaching a decision, following full analysis, I have never hesitated to back it without limit of endeavor or financial risk." All these traits he surely had and needed, but there were more. There was the luck that brought him to the Naval Academy, which gave him the best education in electrical science then available. There was his vision of what electricity might do for American life. There was his grasp of the manifold technical requirements—many yet to be invented—for a profitable electric urban transit system. There was the amazing confidence in his own ability and knowledge which led him twice to commit himself beyond retreat to the immediate technical and material creation of such systems. And there was the ability to vindicate that self-confidence, to carry through what even in retrospect seem impossible undertakings. By fulfilling his Richmond contract of 1887 he converted urban surface transit at a blow from horsecars to trolleys and thus raised urbanization to a new order of magnitude. Ten years later, in his multiple unit system for the Chicago elevated railway, he paralleled his earlier feat in all respects. Not only was he, more than any other, entitled to be called the father of electrical traction; he was also, by virtue of that fact, one of the founding fathers of the urban age in America. See Harold C. Passer, "Frank Julian Sprague," in William Miller, ed., *Men in Business* (1952).

ROBERT V. BRUCE

SPRECKELS, Rudolph (b. San Francisco, Calif., Jan. 1, 1872; d. San Francisco, Calif., Oct. 4, 1958), MANUFACTURER, REFORMER, son of Claus Spreckels, a wealthy West Coast sugar refiner, was sickly and asthmatic as a youth. At seventeen he began work in a new plant which his father had built in Philadelphia to compete with **Henry O. Havemeyer**'s sugar trust. By the time he was twenty-two he had made the plant such a formidable competitor that the trust bought it out. Spreckels then turned his attention to his father's Hawaiian sugar-growing interests, which were not prospering. Within a short time he had put them on a paying basis. But Claus Spreckels and two of his other sons were reluctant to allow Rudolph and another brother who was associated with him to have an entirely free hand running the properties. There followed a struggle in which Rudolph gained control of the Hawaiian operations, but at the cost of a family feud which was not settled until 1905.

Spreckels often asserted that his ambition was financial independence, and having achieved it by the age of twenty-six, he retired. But he was soon drawn back into the sugar business and many other activities as well. In 1900 he got control of the corrupt San Francisco Gas Co. and reorganized it. The First National Bank and the First Federal Trust Co. were also organized by him. In civic affairs he took a leading role in the fight to end the domination of state and city government by such corporations as the Southern Pacific Railroad. He played a large role in the destruction of the corrupt San Francisco political machine of Abraham Ruef. He figured prominently in the relief and reconstruction work which followed the San Francisco earthquake and fire of 1906. Later he was active in electrical utilities and radio manufacturing.

Spreckels steadfastly refused to accept a direct role in politics and government, declining a nomination for the U.S. Senate and, it is said, an offer to make him ambassador to Germany. A progressive Republican and strong admirer of Theodore Roosevelt, he nevertheless supported Woodrow Wilson in the 1912 presidential election. He was reportedly worth $30 million in 1929, but the Great Depression wiped out most of his fortune, and he died in modest circumstances.

⸺⸺

Spreckels had qualities of genius, courage, and imagination that were apparently inherited or learned from his father; but vindictiveness and jealousy combined with the more admirable family traits to make up the aggressiveness and vigor with which he threw himself into a series of battles in both business and politics. Probably his most valuable single contribution to political reform was his personal gift of about a quarter of a million dollars to pay the special expenses of the San Francisco graft prosecution of 1906 to 1909. Along with his public-spirited desire to root out political corruption in general, he felt a strong personal hostility toward several public utility corporation executives, whom he believed to be in corrupt alliance with politicians. For example, when Patrick Calhoun, president of the United

Railroads of San Francisco, proposed to replace cable car lines with overhead trolley wires on many streets, including the one in front of Spreckels's mansion on Pacific Heights, Spreckels urged the substitution of underground electric conduits, which would be less unsightly. Calhoun insisted on trolleys because they were less expensive; and Spreckels was delighted when the graft prosecution proved, as he had suspected, that the United Railroads had secured approval of the trolleys by paying a huge "attorney's fee" to city boss Abraham Ruef.

In the 1920s Spreckels made important financial contributions to the repeated but unsuccessful campaigns for a California state water and power project, which would have put the state into the electric power and light business in competition with the monopolistic Pacific Gas and Electric Co., several of whose executives Spreckels deeply disliked. See Lincoln Steffens, "Rudolph Spreckels, a Business Man Fighting for His City," *American Magazine*, 65 (Feb. 1908), 390–402.

WALTON BEAN

STANFORD, Leland (b. Watervliet, N.Y., March 9, 1824; d. Palo Alto, Calif., June 21, 1893), RAILROAD BUILDER, was educated at the Clinton Liberal Institute and the Cazenovia Seminary in New York. He entered the law office of Wheaton, Doolittle and Hadley at Albany in 1845 and was admitted to the bar in 1848. He then established a law practice in Port Washington, Wisconsin, but after a fire destroyed his office in 1852, he joined his younger brothers in California. In partnership with Nicholas T. Smith, he opened general merchandise stores in Cold Springs in 1852 and Michigan Bluff in 1853. He joined his brothers in a retail enterprise in Sacramento in 1856. Becoming active in the formation of the California Republican party, he ran unsuccessfully for state treasurer in 1857 and for governor in 1859. Following a split in the Democratic party over secession, he won the gubernatorial election of 1861 by a plurality (serving until 1863).

Meanwhile he had become involved with the promotion of a transcontinental railroad. He,

Collis P. Huntington, Charles Crocker, and Mark Hopkins formed the Central Pacific Co. in 1861 with Stanford as president. In 1862 the Central Pacific was designated the western half of the first transcontinental railroad and for this purpose received generous federal subsidies: grants of land on either side of the right of way and loans in the form of government bonds. Other public subscriptions of local origin facilitated the work in California.

In 1863 the Central Pacific Railroad began to construct a line eastward from Sacramento, while the Union Pacific began to build a line westward from Omaha. The Central Pacific encouraged the immigration of Chinese workers to increase the supply and lower the cost of its labor. Since the government subsidies were based on mileage, the company kept its construction crews at work in the high Sierras through the hard winters of 1866–67 and 1867–68 in order to reach the relatively flat country of Nevada and Utah before the Union Pacific. When the two lines met at Promontory Point, Utah, on May 10, 1869, the Union Pacific had built 1,086 miles of track, and the Central Pacific 689. Although the Central Pacific's books were later burned, Stanford and his associates obviously reaped immense profits from the construction.

With the completion of the Central Pacific, Stanford and his associates proceeded to develop other rail and water transportation properties in California. Their Southern Pacific Railroad, incorporated in 1870, acquired and constructed lines running both north and south from San Francisco and ultimately put together a second transcontinental railroad from southern California to New Orleans. In spite of continual hostility from rival commercial interests in the state, the "Big Four" established a practical monopoly of transportation facilities in California. In 1884 their holdings were reorganized under a new Southern Pacific charter granted by the state of Kentucky. Stanford continued to serve as president until 1890 when a quarrel with Huntington over political and business matters led to his resignation.

Elected to the U.S. Senate in 1885, Stanford represented California until his death. He founded Stanford University in 1885 in memory of his son, Leland, Jr., who died in 1884. He bequeathed the bulk of his fortune to the university.

———— ∞∞ ————

The Big Four created one of the classic examples of monopoly in the age of the robber barons. With little knowledge of railroading and little capital to contribute at the outset, four Sacramento merchants parlayed the opportunities of the California frontier into an industrial empire. Stanford's part in the undertaking was largely political—he was the "front man" in California—but the Central Pacific–Southern Pacific empire rested on a political foundation and owed much to Stanford's ability and influence. Like his three associates, Stanford was an opportunist: ambitious, courageous, well suited to the rough and tumble of California politics. He was powerfully built, ruggedly handsome, with an effective if somewhat ponderous style of public address. Although not particularly gifted intellectually, he had an inquiring mind, respect for scholarship, and genuine interest in the sciences.

Politics rather than business brought the Big Four together. They were members of the new Republican party and advocates of its program, including a transcontinental railroad. As governor of California Stanford promoted the Central Pacific (in which he and his associates had acquired a financial interest) as the western link of this grand design; his contacts with the Republican administration (and Huntington's effective lobbying in Congress) made possible the essential federal grants and loans. Operating almost entirely with borrowed money and government subsidies, the four associates were able to complete the project despite public apathy but at frightful cost in human labor and life. Construction companies owned by the Big Four built the line and indirectly received most of the public largess. The owners took their payment in the form of CP stock which proved unsalable on the open market, and when the line was completed the company belonged to them. Convinced that profitable operation would be possible only if they retained their monopoly of rail traffic in California, the associates adopted a

policy of aggressive defense, systematically preempting the other routes of entry into the state and buying control of important river and ocean shipping lines. Their domination was virtually unchallenged until the 1890s.

Although president of the various companies, Stanford found little pleasure in business routine and had little talent for it. Huntington emerged as the true leader of the group. After 1870 Stanford devoted less and less time to railroading, more and more time to his farms and trotting horses at Palo Alto, his experiments in the study of animal locomotion, and his vineyards in the Sacramento Valley. The education of his son, Leland, Jr., became a matter of increasing pleasure, and after the death of the precocious youngster, the building of Stanford University as a memorial became his main interest. He continued to handle relations with western state governments and led the companies' fights against public regulation. In spite of earlier dependence upon government support, he advanced the most extreme claims to private rights in business, opposing even the mild Interstate Commerce Act of 1887. His relations with labor, meanwhile, remained cordial, and as senator he supported such "popular" causes as Chinese exclusion, industrial co-ops, and soft money. For all the hostility toward the Southern Pacific "octopus," Stanford retained the respect of the people of California. See G. T. Clark, *Leland Stanford* (1931).

GEORGE H. MILLER

STANTON, Edwin McMasters (b. Steubenville, Ohio, Dec. 19, 1814; d. Washington, D.C., Dec. 24, 1869), POLITICAL LEADER, attended Kenyon College for three years, and then read law and was admitted to the bar in 1836. After practicing at Steubenville and Pittsburgh, Pennsylvania, he moved to Washington in 1856, where he argued many cases before the Supreme Court. A skilled criminal lawyer, Stanton successfully defended Daniel E. Sickles against the charge of murdering his wife and her lover. His most important cases involved the defense of the state of California against fraudulent land claims arising from the transfer of the territory from Mexico to the U.S., in which he won a series of notable victories. A Democrat, Stanton entered President James Buchanan's cabinet as attorney general in December 1860. Although he supported **John C. Breckinridge** for president in 1860 and advocated the enforcement of all laws regarding fugitive slaves, Stanton strongly advocated resistance to secession and condemned the surrender of Fort Sumter.

Despite the fact he had expressed contempt for Abraham Lincoln, the president, recognizing Stanton's administrative skill, appointed him to succeed **Simon Cameron** as secretary of war in 1862. Almost immediately, he improved the efficiency of the department, and consequently of the Union army and developed good relations with the congressional Committee on the Conduct of the War.

Two years after Lincoln's assassination Stanton broke with President Johnson over Reconstruction policy. In August 1867 the president demanded his resignation and, failing to get it, dismissed him on February 21, 1868. But Stanton, claiming protection under the Tenure of Office Act, blockaded himself in the War Department, giving in only when the impeachment of Johnson failed (May 26, 1868).

Stanton was nominated to the Supreme Court by President Grant and confirmed by the Senate on December 20, 1869, but died before he could take his seat.

Edwin McMasters Stanton has a significant place in America's political history only because his talents meshed precisely with what the nation needed in order to survive secession and Civil War, and because he was willing to spend himself in the nation's service. Stanton was an early example of the organization man enlisted for high-level wartime administrative work. He spanned effectively the gap between the haphazardly individualistic Age of Jackson and the efficient corporate associationism displayed during the Gilded Age by captains of industry and barons of finance. Ironically, though Stanton was

closer to **Andrew Carnegie** than **John C. Calhoun** in spirit, drive, and aspirations, he became Lincoln's enormously effective war secretary because he was also idealistic and loyal. Becoming wholly dedicated to success for Lincoln, the Union army, and the Republican party—which were in fact an indivisible trinity—Stanton's wartime self-education converted the erstwhile Buchanan-Breckinridge Democrat into an ardent emancipationist. His influence was a major factor leading Lincoln toward the Emancipation Proclamation and the recruitment of black soldiers. Simultaneously Stanton rationalized as much as possible the War Department's logistical procedures, made more efficient and humane the internal security arrangements he inherited, and improved civilian controls over the military.

Stanton's troubled post-Appomattox course is understood best in reference to the idealism that the Civil War evoked from him and from so many contemporaries. Odds are that had wartime labors not weakened Stanton so that death came just when he was readying to begin new public service as a Supreme Court justice, Stanton would have supplied useful insights into newer problems of American democracy, including industrialization, urbanization, federalism, and racial justice. See Harold M. Hyman, *Stanton* (1962).

HAROLD M. HYMAN

STANTON, Elizabeth Cady (b. Johnstown, N.Y., Nov. 12, 1815; d. New York, N.Y., Oct. 26, 1902), REFORMER, studied at the Johnstown Academy and attended **Emma Willard**'s Troy (N.Y.) Female Seminary (1830–32). She briefly studied law with her father but soon became interested in reform, especially the elimination of injustices to women. After her marriage to Henry Brewster Stanton, an abolitionist, she attended the London world antislavery convention of 1840, but along with other women delegates, she was denied recognition because of her sex. In the following years she worked for abolition and temperance. A married woman's property law in New York which she supported was enacted in 1848.

That same year she joined **Lucretia Mott** in issuing the call for a woman's rights convention in Seneca Falls, New York, which launched the woman's rights movement in the United States. In 1851 Stanton met **Susan B. Anthony,** and the two started a partnership which lasted until Stanton's death. They convened the first Woman's State Temperance Convention in Rochester, New York, in 1852, and the New York State Suffrage Society in 1854, with Stanton being elected president.

Although a pacifist, Stanton felt the Civil War was necessary in order to end slavery and formed the Women's Loyal League in 1863 to support the Union. After the war, she turned her attention once more to the woman suffrage movement, and in 1868 founded *The Revolution,* a weekly periodical devoted to that cause. Chosen first president of the National Woman Suffrage Association in 1869, she spent the next several years lobbying for a constitutional amendment. She also lectured extensively from 1869 to 1881 on family life and child rearing. In 1888 she organized the International Council of Women in Washington, D.C. When the National and American Woman Suffrage associations merged in 1890, she was elected first president, and served until 1892. A prolific writer, she produced the first three volumes of *History of Woman Suffrage* (1881–86) with Susan B. Anthony and Matilda Gage, and was largely responsible for *Woman's Bible* (1895, 1898). Her reminiscences, *Eighty Years and More,* were published in 1898.

Elizabeth Cady Stanton was notable among feminists both for her radicalism and her brilliance. She was an able speaker and, when she wished to be, an ironic, forceful, and sometimes elegant writer. She was radical, not only on the woman question, but on slavery, religion, and marriage. She was an abolitionist when few dared to be, a skeptic at a time when religious devotion was mandatory for women, a champion of votes for women three-quarters of a century too soon, and doubtful about marriage when it was most sacrosanct. Except for slavery, which she did not know of directly, her views were

formed by experience. Her feminism stemmed from the childhood experience of having her talents dismissed because as a girl she would never be able to make use of them. She turned against religion after being terrified by a revivalist while a schoolgirl.

All her positions were controversial, but her stand on marriage especially so. Though her own marriage was successful in most respects, she wrote later that for her, life began at fifty when she was at last free of domestic responsibilities and able to work full time on her causes. She was an early advocate of free divorce, not for her own sake, but as a first step toward reforming marriage itself. This was a dangerous area to work in, as events demonstrated. Stanton befriended Victoria Woodhull, notorious for her unconventional opinions and behavior, and refused to disown her when Woodhull publicly endorsed free love. The resulting scandals helped divide the woman's movement for years and made it impossible for respectable feminists to raise the marriage question again. Stanton retreated, but never stopped condemning the prudish attitudes that she was certain held women back.

Her religious views were nearly as troublesome for Victorians. Stanton blamed organized religion for discriminating against women, and for doctrines that proclaimed woman's inferiority to man. She and her friends wrote the *Woman's Bible* to cleanse the scriptures of male chauvinism. It was thought so compromising that her own organization, the National Association of Woman Suffrage, repudiated it. She went on attacking "priestcraft and superstition" all the same.

Stanton was a professional agitator, like **Wendell Phillips** and **William Lloyd Garrison.** Careers such as theirs are hard to evaluate. They do not typically enact laws, or write great books, or leave behind monuments to their greatness. Yet we think them great anyway, because they fought for unpopular ideas later accepted, and because they moved people in their time. So it was with Stanton. She left a more imposing physical corpus behind her than most agitators. Her memoirs, and some of her letters and essays, have great distinction and are a pleasure to read even today. But mostly we know Stanton was great from the evidence of her own life and the testimony of those who knew her.

Though at least as important as Susan B. Anthony, Stanton is not so well known today because of her radicalism, which kept her from being made a national institution. It was safe to revere Anthony in her old age as she had grown more conservative. Elizabeth Cady Stanton never did. She was sometimes wrong but never weak. Bold, witty, and eloquent, she shook the complacent, challenged orthodoxies, and was a power for justice all her long life. See Alma Lutz, *Created Equal: A Biography of Elizabeth Cady Stanton* (1940).

WILLIAM L. O'NEILL

STEFFENS, Joseph Lincoln (b. San Francisco, Calif., April 6, 1866; d. Carmel, Calif., Aug. 9, 1936), JOURNALIST, REFORMER, graduated from the University of California at Berkeley (1889). He then spent three years in Europe studying at the Universities of Berlin, Heidelberg, Munich, Leipzig, and Paris. In 1892 he became a reporter on the New York *Evening Post,* and during his five-year tenure there he specialized in financial and police news, covering, among other major stories, the panic of 1893 on Wall Street, Dr. Charles H. Parkhurst's "crusade" against vice and corruption, and the subsequent Lexow investigations. After serving as city editor of the *Commercial Advertiser* (1897–1901) and trying his hand at fiction, Steffens embarked on a meteoric career in magazine journalism. He became an editor and staff writer on *McClure's* (1901–6), *American Magazine* (1906–8), and *Everybody's.* His pioneering work as a muckraker—a series of articles dealing with municipal corruption, later published in book form as *The Shame of the Cities* (1904)—appeared in *McClure's* in 1902 and 1903. Two other books grew out of similar inquiries: *The Struggle for Self-Government* (1906) dealt with corruption on the state level; *Upbuilders* (1909) studied the achievement of five leading reformers of the era of Theodore Roosevelt.

Steffens was also an activist. He attempted to draw up a long-range reform plan for Boston and to work out a just (in his terms, Christian) settlement in the case of labor organizers implicated in the 1910 dynamiting of the Los Angeles *Times* building. In 1914 he made the first of several visits to Mexico to cover the revolution and civil war there; he favored, and to a certain extent advised, the Carranza government. He was in Russia early in 1917, soon after the czar was deposed, and as a student of revolution and a Bolshevik sympathizer, he returned in 1919 as an unofficial member of the secret Bullitt mission, and again in 1923. He stated his theory of revolution in *Moses in Red* (1926). Steffens returned to the U.S. in 1927, took up residence in Carmel, and in 1931 published his widely acclaimed *Autobiography.* He was conspicuous as a lecturer until incapacitated by illness in 1933, and thereafter, through his articles, letters, and conversations with a stream of visitors, he continued to disseminate radical views in general and his admiration for the Soviet Union in particular. A posthumous collection of his articles and comments, *Lincoln Steffens Speaking,* was published in 1936; his *Letters,* edited by Ella Winter and Granville Hicks, were published in 1938.

⁂

Lincoln Steffens's life encapsulates and in turn illuminates the adventures of American liberalism in the period between the waning of the Gilded Age and the bottoming of the Great Depression. He represents in his own way—as **Mark Twain** and **Ezra Pound** do in theirs—a native tradition of grassroots, pragmatic dissent, a homegrown radicalism originating in personality and experience rather than in ideology. Despite Steffens's excursions into the arena of action, he remained primarily an observer and interpreter of his times. Despite his avowed disrespect for liberals and intellectuals—especially toward the end of his life, when he became not a Communist but a publicist for the party line—he remained at heart a liberal and an intellectual.

Steffens's mind was more lively than it was profound, more inquisitive than searching, more reportorial than philosophic, more informed than richly furnished, and when hardpressed by personal and public issues he showed a tendency to seek refuge in paradox. But he displayed a degree of sophistication and originality, personal courage and artistic flair, which set him apart from other journalists and reformers of his period. His work and career as a whole are so powerfully marked by qualities of ethical fervor, compassion, generosity, and good hope tempered by shrewd realism that he remains, and deserves to remain, an emblematic figure in the American consciousness.

He was, indeed, one of its shapers. Steffens's achievements as a muckraker set the pattern for investigative and advocacy journalism in general and confirmed the aptness of the adversary mode for dealing with political and corporate reality in America. His statement, in *The Shame of the Cities* and the other work of his muckraking phase, of the integrality of corruption and the shaping role of interest groups is still impressive and timely—so is the clarity of his analysis, the drama and elegance of his proofs. For a while, during muckraking's ascendancy (roughly 1902–8), Steffens was a commanding figure who stood in the forefront of a band of reformers and visionary (if politically muscular) mayors. Together they proclaimed the belief that the American city could yet be "the hope of democracy" instead of its most "conspicuous failure." But having quickly demonstrated to his own satisfaction that corruption under capitalism was everywhere the same, from the common council of St. Louis to the United States Senate and from the corner saloon to the giant trust, Steffens decided that muckraking and reformism had gone as far as they could, and just as he had come to them early he left them early in search of more structural, more radical approaches.

His success in finding solutions in the single tax, socialism, anarchism, literal Christianity, and the Golden Rule was limited at best, but he conducted his search on a consistently high level of moral commitment: he served a Socratic function by tilting against the conventional wisdom; in the dark and repressive time that followed America's entrance into World War I he remained, along

with **Randolph Bourne,** one of the few uncompromised spokesmen for democratic values and urgent issues of conscience; and he became the champion of desperate and pariah causes. **Walt Whitman**'s lines have a poignant applicability to Steffens's role: "I also say it is good to fail, battles are lost in the same spirit in which they are won."

Steffens never achieved the certainty he sought—the very notion of certainty runs contrary to the fundamentally free-ranging, antidogmatic, and quizzical style of his thought—but he came as close to certainty as he ever would in Russia under the Bolsheviks. He returned from his second visit with a celebrated declaration ("I have been over into the future, and it works") which, like his *Autobiography,* helped turn a generation leftward. He wrote with a vividness and penetration, with a faith in the new and in the intelligence of the young, which established him as a tutelary hero and his book as a controlling document of the Depression era. He was so native to America, as he showed in his book, that he was able to impart to the young radicals who looked up to him a historical legitimacy that went back not only to the sunnier days of reform but to the era of wagon trains and the country's great westward expansion. "Radical," after all, has to do with roots. See Justin Kaplan, *Lincoln Steffens* (1974).

JUSTIN KAPLAN

STEICHEN, Edward Jean (b. Luxembourg, March 27, 1879; d. West Redding, Conn., March 26, 1973), PHOTOGRAPHER, came to the U.S. in 1882 and settled in Hancock, Michigan. In 1888 he became an apprentice designer in a Milwaukee lithographic firm. He was interested in photography and was soon making advertising posters for his firm. In 1900 while on his way to Europe to study painting he met photographer **Alfred Stieglitz** who was struggling to make photography recognized as an art in New York City. While studying in Paris and London, Steichen continued to pursue his interest in photography, and upon his return to New York in 1902 he began photographing such famous people as **J. P. Morgan.** In 1905 he joined Stieglitz in establishing the Photo-Secession Gallery, which exhibited all forms of art, including photography. He returned to France in 1906 and during World War I had charge of aerial photography for the American Expeditionary Force. He returned to New York in 1923.

There Steichen pursued photography exclusively. He joined Condé Nast Publications (*Vanity Fair* and *Vogue*), did advertising and promotional work, and became highly successful. However, in 1938 Steichen closed his New York studio to devote himself to crossbreeding plants at his farm in West Redding, Connecticut. During World War II Steichen served as director of photography for Naval aviation. In 1947 he became head of the department of photography at New York's Museum of Modern Art, where he sponsored many photographic exhibitions. Retiring in 1962, he published his autobiography, *A Life in Photography,* a year later.

––––––⚉––––––

Steichen's earliest works reflect an international trend toward self-conscious aestheticism. His muted, moody paintings belong in the tonal tradition of **James Whistler**'s nocturnes and the later work of George Inness, while his soft-focus portrait and landscape photographs at the turn of the century are key American examples of the movement, called Pictorialism, which sought to establish photography as a fine art in the public mind. Beginning in 1900, his long and fruitful association with the older photographer Alfred Stieglitz provided Steichen with encouragement and support, a place to exhibit his photographs, and an important cause—the promotion of avant-garde art and photography in the United States.

After a period of intensive study and experimentation (1917–22), Steichen gave up painting altogether in order to concentrate entirely on his career in "straight" (sharp-focus) photography of man-made and living things. His advertising and fashion pictures of the 1920s and early 1930s reveal a master's sureness of touch, and his later work as a photomuralist (George Washington Bridge, 1932) and as an organizer of photograph-

ic exhibitions (especially *The Family of Man*, 1955) gained a still wider audience for the art of photography.

Admirers, such as **Carl Sandburg,** have described Steichen as a large healthy man with gifted hands, a winning way with animals and children, a solemn spiritual quality at times, and above all an unquenchable enthusiasm for life. See Edward Steichen, *A Life in Photography* (1963).

ELLWOOD C. PARRY, III

STEIN, Gertrude (b. Allegheny, Pa., Feb. 3, 1874; d. Paris, France, July 27, 1946), WRITER, studied philosophy and psychology at Harvard Annex (now Radcliffe College) under **William James** and Hugo Münsterberg (1893–97), and received her AB magna cum laude in 1898. She attended Johns Hopkins Medical School (1897–1901), but lost interest in taking a degree, remaining, however, for another year in Baltimore doing brain research. In 1903 Stein went to Paris, where she resided for the rest of her life. Independently wealthy, she and her brothers Leo and Michael became influential art patrons, and befriended such young artists as Pablo Picasso and Juan Gris. Her interests turned to literature, and by 1906 she had finished her second novel, *Three Lives* (published 1909). She soon emerged as a leader of the avant-garde literary experimenters of the 1920s. Her *The Making of Americans* (1925) won critical acclaim both in Europe and in the U.S. From her Paris apartment, Stein influenced and encouraged such American writers as **Ernest Hemingway, Ezra Pound,** Sherwood Anderson, and **Thornton Wilder.**

During the 1930s Stein wrote two autobiographical works, *The Autobiography of Alice B. Toklas* (1933), her most popular book, and *Everybody's Autobiography* (1937). In 1934 she returned to the U.S. for the production of her opera libretto, *Four Saints in Three Acts* (1934), written in collaboration with **Virgil Thomson,** and for a lecture tour. She went back to Paris in 1935 and remained there during the Nazi occupation. *Wars I Have Seen* (1945) and *Brewsie and Willie* (1946) reflect her wartime experiences and her conversations with American soldiers. Some of her other writings are *Tender Buttons* (1914), *Portraits and Prayers* (1934), *Lectures in America* (1935), and *Ida, a Novel* (1941).

———∞∞∞———

Gertrude Stein had perhaps the most powerfully original mind of her literary generation. Capable of the severest abstract thought and the most intense subjectivity, of both scientific concision and the most private irrationality, she managed to cast spells over some of the most daring and original writers and artists of her day. Her gift for epigram is memorialized in her most famous phrase, "You are all a lost generation." But she had besides an extraordinary talent for original ways of seeing and understanding, and this is what appealed to other innovative and creative people. She once observed that "in the United States there is more space where nobody is than where anybody is. This is what makes America what it is." She liked to explain narration as "the thing seen by every one living in the living they are doing, they are the composing of the composition that at the time they are living is the composition of the time in which they are living." Her portraits of writers (Sherwood Anderson, **Henry James**) and artists (Matisse, Lipchitz) are remarkable imitations of abstract painting and sculpture in their indifference to meanings. She puzzled and aggravated many of her readers by forcing attention entirely on the way she wrote: on the sounds and mysterious shapes of words, on the rhythm of phrases and sentences, on the "stream of consciousness" (a phrase she learned from William James), and on the elusive reality that language can never fix. Her notorious phrase, "A rose is a rose is a rose," is only the most famous of thousands of attempts to destroy traditional word values in order to reach a fresher, purer reality. And often the language itself, rather than anything it pointed to, was that reality.

Stein's reputation has diminished since her death, and she is no longer thought to have had extraordinary or pervasive influence. Yet she is undeniably one of our great primitive originals,

and much of her voluminous writing has continued to be found popular and historically significant: *Three Lives,* for its experimentation in stream-of-consciousness methods; *Tender Buttons* for its innovations in using collage, cubism, and expressionism; *The Autobiography of Alice B. Toklas* for its wit and oblique self-revelation. Her personality was marked by an incisive wit and a great gift for theatric gesture, but overriding these was her nearly belligerent individuality. Through it she conveyed not crankiness or mere eccentricity, but the charm and mystery of an oracular voice. She became the Sphinx of her generation. See Richard Bridgman, *Gertrude Stein in Pieces* (1970).

DEAN FLOWER

STEINBECK, John Ernst (b. Salinas, Calif., Feb. 27, 1902; d. New York, N.Y., Dec. 20, 1968), WRITER, attended Stanford University, but did not obtain a degree. Moving to New York City in 1925, he worked as a reporter and as a bricklayer before returning to California in 1927. He published his first novel, *Cup of Gold,* in 1929. Two other books followed in quick succession before *Tortilla Flat* (1935) brought Steinbeck popular and critical acclaim and established him as the champion of the poor and downtrodden. *In Dubious Battle* (1936) and *Of Mice and Men* (1937), which was adapted for the stage, were also well received. In 1940 he received the Pulitzer Prize for his novel *The Grapes of Wrath* (1939), a story of an Oklahoma migrant farm family's experiences in California during the depression.

During World War II Steinbeck was a correspondent for the New York *Herald Tribune* in North Africa and Italy. After the war he wrote *The Pearl* (1947), *The Wayward Bus* (1947), and *East of Eden* (1952). He also turned out several screenplays for motion pictures, including *Viva Zapata!* (1952). Several of his later works (*Sweet Thursday,* 1954; *Travels with Charley,* 1962) were light pieces harking back to the comedy of *Cannery Row* (1945), but in *The Winter of Our Discontent* (1961) he composed a full-scale attack on the corruption of American society. In 1962 Steinbeck was awarded the Nobel Prize for literature. After a

1968 trip to South Vietnam, he announced his support of the American military effort there, a stance which alienated many of his readers and friends. Some of Steinbeck's many other works include a collection of stories, *The Long Valley* (1938), *Sea of Cortez* (1941), an account of his explorations off the coast of Baja California with Ed Ricketts, and *A Russian Journal* (1948).

———❧———

Ever since the late 1930s, John Steinbeck's reputation has been threatened and questioned by critics, but it has always been reaffirmed by his large popular audience. The most influential criticism, **Edmund Wilson**'s 1941 treatment of Steinbeck as a mechanistic biologist and sentimentalist, has often been rejected by Steinbeck admirers, but the doubts and questions it raises have continued to plague his claim to greatness. Steinbeck hated sophistication and loved the common people. In book after book he presented a reverence for life unspoiled by money and institutions. His **Walt Whitman**-like sympathy for the poor, the ignorant, and the social outcast makes him, after **Thomas Wolfe,** the chief romantic writer of his era. The very qualities which have won large audiences for Steinbeck's works have impelled critics to question their literary merit. There is undeniable power and memorability in his best novels and stories, but also an erratic taste, a childish rhetoric, and a tendentious anti-intellectualism. Puzzled and hurt by criticism, Steinbeck wrote in 1955, "A man's writing is himself. A kind man writes kindly. A mean man writes meanly. A sick man writes sickly. And a wise man writes wisely." It never occurred to him that the opposites could be just as true, and he spent his career believing that honesty and sincerity of heart would lead him to the truth. Characteristically, in his Nobel Prize acceptance speech, he began by doubting that he deserved the award, went on to sneer at "a pale and emasculated critical priesthood," rejected "the tin-horn mendicants of low-calorie despair," and concluded with statements about "the perfectibility of man" and "humanity's long, proud history of standing firm against natural enemies."

Steinbeck's importance today lies in his capacity to transform social fact into narrative; he should be judged alongside the literary naturalism of **John Dos Passos, James T. Farrell,** and Thomas Wolfe. His finest work, it has become clear, can be found in the short span of years from *In Dubious Battle* in 1936 and *The Long Valley* in 1938 to his undoubted masterpiece, *The Grapes of Wrath* in 1939, and *Sea of Cortez* in 1941. At his best, Steinbeck rivals **Theodore Dreiser** in his cumulative documentary power and intuitive grasp of society's crushing force. But Steinbeck is more satirical than Dreiser, more stridently rhetorical, and more deliberately artificial. He struggled to transform himself from a Salinas Valley farmhand into a visionary social prophet, who could be the nation's conscience. Only a few times did the transformation succeed. See Peter Lisca, *The Wide World of John Steinbeck* (1958).

DEAN FLOWER

STEINEM, Gloria (b. Toledo, Ohio, March 25, 1934) REFORMER, graduated from Smith College in 1956, and spent the next two years in India on a research fellowship, writing articles and a guidebook. After returning to the United States, she worked for the Independent Research Service (1958–1960). Always interested in journalism, she became a freelance writer and attracted much notice with her expose, "I Was a Playboy Bunny," describing her experience working undercover as one of that breed in a New York City Playboy Club. Soon, in the early 1960s, her articles appeared in *Esquire, Vogue, Glamour, McCall's,* and *Cosmopolitan.* As a newly installed member of New York's glitzy intellectual set, most of her early writing described life among the Beautiful People, of which she was clearly one with her flashing blue eyes and long blondish hair. At the same time Steinem tried her hand at writing comedy material for television and accepted an invitation to start a column "The City Politic," (1968) for the recently founded magazine *New York.*

Also in the late 1960s, Steinem became closely identified with the burgeoning women's movement. After attending hearings on New York's abortion law in 1968, she published her first strongly feminist essay, "After Black Power, Women's Liberation." In 1971, she conceived the idea of a new magazine by and for women which would focus on feminist issues. With Gloria Steinem as one of its founding editors, *Ms.* magazine hit the newsstands in January, 1972. It became an instant success, and was long regarded as a major vehicle of the women's movement.

Through the 1970s, Gloria Steinem had a high profile on the lecture and talk show circuits. She helped found several activist groups including Voters for Choice, the Coalition of Labor Union Women, and Women USA. A collection of her writings, *Outrageous Acts and Everyday Rebellions*, was published in 1983.

In 1993, after two decades with *Ms.*, Steinem turned from social change to personal growth in *Revolution Within: A Book of Self-Esteem*. Her 1994 essay collection, *Moving Beyond Words*, returned to more familiar political themes. Still serving as a consulting editor for *Ms.*, Steinem maintains her tireless commitment to a new order that will free both women and men from ancient stereotypes and will allow them truly to live as equals.

Gloria Steinem spent her early childhood moving from place to place as her father shifted from one ill-fated get rich scheme to another. When she was twelve her parents divorced. She spent the next four years tending to her chronically depressed mother in a rat-infested Toledo apartment. Decades later Steinem reflected that this early experience prepared her for a life of caring for the world as a crusader for social justice.

At the start of her career, Steinem bore little resemblance to a crusader. Once described as "the pin-up girl of the New York intelligentsia," she basked in the company of actors, producers, and politicians. Yet as early as 1962 she showed startling insight into society's perception of women. In an article for *Esquire*, she warned that the contraceptive revolution might alter women's role without any corresponding change in men's attitudes.

The abortion-rights issue swept Steinem into the woman's movement in 1968. She went public with her own abortion story, and found a vital bond with others who shared that once unspeakable experience. In the following years, Steinem earned a reputation as a powerful feminist organizer. Always attractive and charming, she made the women's movement seem less threatening to the unconverted. However, she was sometimes criticized as "bourgeois" by radical feminists.

Overall, Steinem's approach is one of optimism. She spreads the message that feminism will ultimately liberate men as well as women. It will enable women to be more assertive and ambitious, and allow men to become gentler and more compassionate. "We're not trading places," she explained in an interview. "We're just completing ourselves." See Carolyn Heilbrun, *The Education of a Woman: A Life of Gloria Steinem* (1995).

DEBORAH KENT

STEINMETZ, Charles Proteus (b. Breslau, Ger., April 9, 1865; d. Schenectady, N.Y., Oct. 26, 1923), PHYSICIST, ELECTRICAL ENGINEER, attended the University of Breslau, 1882–88, where he joined the Student Socialist Society and became editor of the radical weekly *The People's Voice* in 1884. Threatened with arrest for his political activities in 1888, Steinmetz fled to Zürich, Switzerland, and briefly attended the Zürich Polytechnical Institute. He emigrated to the U.S. in 1889. Settling in New York City, Steinmetz became a draftsman for Eickemeyer and Osterheld, Yonkers, New York, manufacturers of hatmaking machinery and electric motors. Shortly thereafter, Eickemeyer assigned Steinmetz the task of developing a commercial alternating-current motor. His related studies led to his proposed 1.6-power law of magnetic hysteresis, published in the *Electrical Engineer* in 1890. Steinmetz's hysteresis equation was initially based on some experimental data already published by the British physicist J. A. Ewing, but the equation was more convenient for engineering purposes than the graphical integration methods used by Ewing. Steinmetz presented two very comprehensive papers dealing with both the theory and the design implications of hysteresis and eddy currents before the American Institute of Electrical Engineers in 1892. He also published a paper on hysteresis in the *Electrical Engineer* in 1892. Following the acquisition of the Eickemeyer and Osterheld Co. by the newly formed General Electric Co., Steinmetz was transferred to General Electric's calculating department in Lynn, Massachusetts, early in 1893. The same year, he read a major paper dealing with the application of the algebra of complex numbers in alternating-current circuit analysis at the International Electrical Congress in Chicago. This provided the basis for a textbook which he produced with Ernst J. Berg, *Alternating Current* (1897), as well as several later books. Steinmetz was moved to the General Electric facility in Schenectady, New York, in 1894. After 1895 he increasingly devoted his time to consulting, teaching, and professional activities. He was elected president of the American Institute of Electrical Engineers in 1901. Appointed professor of electrical engineering at Union College in 1903, Steinmetz remained at GE, where he investigated the problems of long-distance electric power transmission (1905–10) and in 1907 began studying high-voltage discharges. In 1910 he was placed in charge of GE's consulting engineering department, and in 1913 was made professor of electrophysics at Union College, where he taught until his death.

Always actively concerned with social problems, Steinmetz was appointed president of the Board of Education in 1911 by the socialist mayor of Schenectady, George R. Lunn. He held that post through the remainder of his life. Also, from 1916 to 1918, he was the chairman of the City Planning and Park Commission of the Schenectady Common Council. In *America and the New Epoch* (1916) Steinmetz, a moderate socialist, expressed his view that private ownership would eventually yield to government ownership under private management. In 1922 he ran unsuccessfully as Socialist party candidate for New York State engineer. Among his many writings are *Theoretical Elements of Electrical Engineering* (1901) and *Engineering Mathematics* (1911).

Steinmetz is perhaps the most beloved pioneer among American electrical engineers and has become a symbol of the fruitful interaction of mathematical physics and electrical technology. This came about as a result of both his concrete contributions to the fundamental principles of electrical engineering and an understandable sympathy for his unfortunate physical deformity. As the first member of the American electrical engineering profession to carry out investigations comparable in quality to the best in Europe, Steinmetz served an important function in a professional society which was still somewhat defensive concerning the alleged derivative nature of American engineering practice. He also possessed a significant advantage over most of his professional associates because of his superior training in mathematics and science.

Perhaps because of his early experiences in Germany and his physical affliction—he was no more than four feet tall, with a disproportionately large head—Steinmetz was a very compassionate man, at his best with young engineers and their children. He always enjoyed good rapport with his audiences at professional meetings. His remarks were often greeted by friendly laughter or even applause, particularly on occasions when he debated professional issues with such well-known protagonists as Professor M. I. Pupin of Columbia University. Steinmetz was notorious for his omnipresent cigar and for the pranks and practical jokes directed at guests at his fishing camp on the Mohawk River. His reputation served to attract other gifted men, such as the radio pioneer E. F. W. Alexanderson, to come to America in the hope of working with Steinmetz. Alexanderson, who became Steinmetz's successor in the Consulting Laboratory, attributed American preeminence in radio as well as his own success to the systematic application of Steinmetz's methods to problems in radiotechnology. See John Winthrop Hammond, *Charles Proteus Steinmetz: A Biography* (1924).

JAMES E. BRITTAIN

STEINWAY, William (b. Seesen, Ger., March 5, 1835; d. New York, N.Y., Nov. 30, 1896), INDUSTRIALIST, studied at the Jacobsohn College in Seesen before emigrating with his family to New York City in 1850. He was apprenticed to a leading piano manufacturer, William Nunns and Co., in New York in 1851 and joined his father's piano manufacturing firm, Steinway and Sons, in 1853. In 1865 he took full charge of the commercial department of the firm, his brother Theodore handling the technical and scientific ends. In 1867 Steinway persuaded his father to build Steinway Hall in New York in order to stimulate American interest in music and sell more pianos. He also encouraged such great foreign musicians as Anton Rubinstein and Fritz Kreisler to give concerts at Steinway Hall and to tour the United States.

When his father died in 1871, Steinway took charge of the firm, and when it was incorporated in 1876, he became president. The combination of Theodore's technical improvements and William's extensive advertising and shrewd business manipulations enabled the firm to prosper, and its pianos became internationally famous. Steinway opened a Steinway Hall in London in 1876 and established a factory in Hamburg, Germany, in 1880 to help meet the European demand for his pianos. He also bought land on Long Island in that year and established the factory town of Steinway, where his pianos were manufactured. Always active in civic affairs and Democratic party politics, he attended the Democratic national convention of 1888 as a delegate and supported Grover Cleveland. He was the first chairman of the Rapid Transit Commission of New York City, which planned the city's first subway in 1891.

The career of the Steinway family and of William Steinway illustrates a rather rare but very effective pattern of business success. Shortly after emigrating to the United States the family divided up among its members the developing specialties in piano manufacturing—research, design, production, finance, and promotion— and became a business unit. Working together amicably, maintaining a lifelong commitment to the business, bringing talented outsiders into the family group through marriage, the group standardized the product, greatly expanded production, and seized a large segment of a rapidly expanding market. In somewhat the same way, the family of Alexander Brown started what became an international banking firm and the family of **Daniel Guggenheim** made a great business success in mining and smelting. Both families, like the Steinways, were sired by European immigrants.

While the technical problems of pianomaking were being worked out by Theodore Steinway, his brother William was drawn increasingly into advertising and promotional work, again illustrating a pattern of development of family businesses. The building of Steinway Hall and the sponsorship of musical artists were brilliant steps in this direction, identifying Steinway pianos with the cultural life of the nation. As the firm outgrew family management during the 1880s William then devoted himself to a wide range of business, philanthropic, and political activities. The same pattern of development, with variations, can be seen in the careers of **Abram Hewitt, Andrew Carnegie,** and the original partners of **John D. Rockefeller**. Personally William Steinway was gregarious, outgoing, and warm-hearted—a man of imagination and broad cultural and social interests. See Theodore E. Steinway, *People and Pianos: A Century of Service to Music* (1953).

ELISHA P. DOUGLASS

STELLA, Frank Philip (b. Malden, Mass., May 12, 1936), ARTIST, graduated from Princeton University in 1958, where he studied painting with Stephen Greene and William Seitz, then went to New York City, where he supported himself as a housepainter while finding his mode as an artist. Moving away from the then dominant abstract expressionist school, Stella painted his Black series, including *The Marriage of Reason and Squalor* (1959, Museum of Modern Art, N.Y.) and

Tuxedo Park (1960, Stedelijk van Abbemuseum, Eindhoven, Netherlands). These paintings consisted of concentric bands of black paint with interstices that functioned as lines. The Black series was exhibited at the Museum of Modern Art's "Sixteen Americans" exhibition in 1959 and brought Stella widespread recognition. In 1960 his Aluminum series, painted in metallic paint, was exhibited at his first one-man show at the Leo Castelli Gallery in New York. They were his first Shaped Canvases.

Stella's Copper series that followed (1960–61) displayed the most radical shapes, while his Benjamin Moore series returned to simple square ones. While artist in residence at Dartmouth College in 1963 he did his Dartmouth series. *Leo Castelli* (1963, Collection Mr. and Mrs. Peter Brant, N.Y.), from his Purple series, and *Fez* (1964, Albright-Knox Art Gallery, Buffalo, N.Y.), from the Moroccan series, show his new interest in the exploration of color. *The Irregular Polygons,* painted in Day-Glo color, followed one year later. Stella taught at the University of Saskatchewan in 1967 and at Brandeis University in 1969. In those years he completed and exhibited the Protractor and Saskatchewan series. The Museum of Modern Art honored him with a retrospective exhibition in 1970. Since then he has shown a group of Constructions in relief at both the Castelli and the Lawrence Rubin galleries. Good examples of his large sculptural wall reliefs are *The Indian Bird Series* (1977–78). Later, his work went further in that direction, becoming three dimensional.

———— ∞∞∞ ————

Since its inception, Stella's art has concerned itself with concepts of geometry and architecture. Composed out of right angles, triangles, polygons, and circles, it is ordered and generally symmetrical. It is an art of shape, line, and dimension. It makes extensive use of repetition. Its intellectual, systemic approach is, in part, a reaction to the abstract expressionist art that immediately preceded it. Stella, like many young painters in the early sixties, admired abstract expressionism but wanted to break with its passion and mindlessness, its heroic content, as well as the illusionistic space and tactile surfaces that characterized its style. He became a key figure in the shift to a cooler art.

His personality is undoubtedly reflected in this more structured approach to making art. A bright, thoughtful man with a thorough academic background in art history (his particular interests have been in Hiberno-Saxon manuscripts and Islamic art), he sees painting as "problem solving." Beyond the painting itself, he has retained tight control over the distribution and promotion of his work.

The vehicle for the expression of Stella's ideas has been the Shaped Canvas. He was a pioneer in and is the leading exponent of this form. Through first notching and then angling the stretchers which determine the outer shape of the painting, and by using lines that parallel these edges for his internal composition, he has developed a form that relates the internal or depicted shape to the literal shape of the support. By doing this he has restored shape to painting without falling back on three-dimensional form or illusionistic space. In two of the finest series, the Irregular Polygons and the Protractor paintings, he explored interpenetration and interlacing of shapes.

Stella's paintings are generally judged solely in formal terms, but the early, monochromatic Black paintings, which are full of mystery, and the more recent Protractor paintings, which are highly decorative, transcend these aspects. Beyond this, his desire for clarity and immediacy, that is, to have the viewer see the whole idea without any confusion, plus his use of repetition of units and geometric shapes, has had a strong influence on Minimal sculpture.

Since 1963 Stella has been engaged in exploring color. His primacy as a colorist is not as certain as his contribution to structure. However, if nothing further evolves of an innovative nature, Stella's historical place is assured for his explication of structure and shape in the decade when the characteristics inherent in the medium were considered the primary grounds for major art. See William S. Rubin, *Frank Stella* (1970).

JEANNE SIEGEL

STEPHENS, Alexander Hamilton (b. Wilkes [now Taliaferro] Co., Ga., Feb. 11, 1812; d. Atlanta, Ga., March 4, 1883), POLITICAL LEADER, graduated from the University of Georgia (1832), briefly taught school, and was admitted to the bar in 1834. Active in politics, he disapproved of nullification, but upheld the right of secession as a valuable check against the expanding powers of the federal government. He was elected to the Georgia state legislature in 1836, where he advocated the construction of a railroad to link Georgia with the grain regions of the Northwest. Elected to the U.S. House of Representatives as a Whig in 1843, Stephens served until 1859, when he resigned. He approved the annexation of Texas as essential for the preservation of "a proper balance between the different sections of the country." Although he opposed the Mexican War, he denounced (on principle) the Wilmot Proviso (1846), which would have banned slavery from all territory acquired from Mexico.

In 1852 Stephens became a Democrat when the Whig party nominated **Winfield Scott,** a Free-Soiler, for the presidency. In 1854 he approved of the Kansas-Nebraska Act, which opened these territories to slavery under the system of popular sovereignty. Stephens defended slavery on biblical grounds, and by 1859 he was willing to consider the possibility of reopening the African slave trade. He supported **Stephen A. Douglas** in the presidential election of 1860. When Lincoln was elected, Stephens called for a conference of all the southern states. He was reluctant to see the South leave the Union, but agreed to go along with secession if it was agreed upon by the gathering. He was a delegate to the convention at Montgomery which was called to form a union of the seceded states, and was elected vice president of the Confederate States of America. In his "corner-stone" speech at Savannah, Georgia (March 21, 1861), he again defended slavery, asserting that the black man was not the equal of the white man.

Stephens disapproved of many of the actions of **Jefferson Davis** as president of the Confederacy. He objected to conscription laws,

the suspension of habeas corpus, and the establishment of local military governments, which he considered invasions of states' rights. He also sought a conciliation with the North. He was on the commission that met with Lincoln at Hampton Roads (Feb. 3, 1865) to discuss peace terms, but when the South insisted on independence, the conference ended.

After the war, Stephens was imprisoned at Fort Warren in Boston Harbor, but later released without trial. Elected to the U.S. Senate in 1866, he was not allowed to take his seat. He was willing to accept emancipation, but was opposed to giving African-Americans the vote. In 1871 he became part owner of the *Southern Sun,* an Atlanta newspaper. He served in the House of Representatives 1873–82, and in 1882 he was elected governor of Georgia. In his *A Constitutional View of the Late War Between the States* (2 vols., 1867–70), he attempted to justify the South's path toward secession, and its course of action through the war. He answered the critics of these volumes in *The Reviewers Reviewed* (1872).

—◦◦◦—

Alexander Hamilton Stephens stands as an important public man of the 19th-century South. A native of the plantation section of east-central Georgia, Stephens, though not of a planting family, became a planter and slave owner and articulated the goals, hopes, and fears of the cotton South.

Two characteristics marked both his public career and his personality. From youth illnesses wracked his tall, frail frame (he weighed less than one hundred pounds). Typically he spent his first week as a congressman in bed under a doctor's care. But chronic and constant illness seemed to spur his activity in the larger world. During half a century as a public man Stephens took many positions on issues; yet throughout his career runs the theme of total devotion to his conception of principle. And his principle involved a complex combination: legalism, states' rights, and defense of the South.

From his first public address in the 1830s until his death in 1883 Stephens spoke constantly of the South and states' rights. He belonged to the States Rights party in Georgia; and when that party went into the Whig party, he moved with it. For Stephens, Whiggery and loyalty to the South became common signposts, with the latter as first principle. As a good Whig he refrained from jingoism on expansion; at the same time he made clear his conviction that the South and slavery had equal rights in the territories. When a Whig president, Zachary Taylor, announced he would support slavery restriction, Stephens turned away from his political home toward the home of his heart, the South. He defended southernism by constant appeal to states' rights and strict construction. He proudly guided the Kansas-Nebraska bill through the House of Representatives and supported the Lecompton Constitution, even though he believed Kansas could never be a slave state. For Stephens the issue was relatively simple—the South needed and deserved Kansas.

As an opponent of secession in 1860–61, Stephens by his actions seemed to contradict his earlier career. However, he was a practical man, and it seems that the fear of what might follow secession caused him to back away. Standing on his commitment to legalism, he argued that the victorious Republicans had not yet committed an illegal act and for that act the South should wait. His leaving Congress in 1859 also seems uncharacteristic and has not yet been satisfactorily explained.

Although against secession, he accepted the position of vice president of the Confederate States of America. In this post he opposed the administration and efforts of Jefferson Davis with the ardor of an ideologue. Davis concentrated on building a nation while Stephens's vision was fixed on his galaxy of states' rights, legalism, and strict construction.

Stephens remained loyal to that vision. His political contribution after 1865 pales beside that of an earlier time. But his principles he entombed in *A Constitutional View of the Late War Between the States*. See Rudolph Von Abele, *Alexander H. Stephens: A Biography* (1946).

WILLIAM J. COOPER, JR.

STETTINIUS, Edward Reilly, Jr. (b. Chicago, Oct. 22, 1900; d. Greenwich, Conn., Oct. 31, 1949), DIPLOMAT, BUSINESSMAN, entered the University of Virginia in 1919 intending to become a clergyman, but left the university in 1924 without a degree. After working as a stock clerk and as the employment manager of a roller-bearing factory, Stettinius became assistant to one of the General Motors Co.'s vice presidents in 1926. In 1931 he became General Motors' vice president in charge of industrial and public relations. In 1934 he was appointed vice-chairman of the finance committee of U.S. Steel. Stettinius became chairman of the board of U.S. Steel in 1938.

In 1939 President Franklin Roosevelt appointed Stettinius chairman of the War Resources Board, and a year later to the National Defense Advisory Commission. Having resigned his business positions, Stettinius became director of priorities, Office of Production Management, in 1941. He successfully argued for the implemented development of synthetic rubber production. In the fall of 1941 Stettinius took over administration of the Lend-Lease program of aid to the Allies, personally selected for that post by **Harry Hopkins,** who was too ill to continue as Lend-Lease administrator. He was appointed undersecretary of state in 1943, and replaced **Cordell Hull** as secretary of state in late 1944. He achieved a closer liaison between the State Department and the president than had existed previously. Convinced that the U.S. would have to lead postwar efforts to form an international organization, Stettinius, as undersecretary of state, had played an important role at the Dumbarton Oaks Conference (1944), which laid the groundwork for the United Nations. He headed the American delegation at the San Francisco Conference of 1945, which drafted the U.N. Charter. He remained as secretary of state until June 1945, when he became America's first representative to the United Nations. However, he resigned as U.N. delegate in 1946 because of disagreements over policy with Secretary of State **James F. Byrnes.** He was one of Roosevelt's advisers at the Yalta Conference (1945), and published *Roosevelt and the Russians: The Yalta Conference* (1949).

Strikingly handsome, and blessed with an affable manner to match, Stettinius looked every inch the model of an American secretary of state. He was valued primarily as an administrator, however, and FDR did not expect him to innovate new foreign policies. (Roosevelt may have intended his appointment only as an interim assignment to help him over the final hump of wartime diplomacy and peacemaking; in any event, the White House seldom asked Stettinius for opinions on policy matters.)

But the secretary's close ties with the business community were especially useful to Roosevelt in his quest for American participation in a world security organization. Like Cordell Hull, Stettinius was convinced that such a body was the only hope for lasting peace. He had a perfect reply to critics of New Deal "internationalism." "Once in a while one of my business friends speaks to me of government planning as if it were either ridiculous or dangerous," he told a Chicago business audience. "I reply that when I was in business planning was fundamental to successful management and I don't suppose things have changed since." That point settled, the secretary waxed eloquent on administration hopes for the postwar world: "The core of our whole postwar economic program is the expansion of private trade and the encouragement of private enterprise, with such assistance as is required from the government to maintain high levels of production and employment."

Stettinius was also known for his blunt opposition to British efforts to establish a "spheres-of-influence" approach to the peace. He and Prime Minister Winston S. Churchill engaged in a brief but pointed exchange on this issue at the Yalta Conference when Stettinius introduced the American plan for a United Nations trusteeship system. "Never, never, never," growled Churchill. "Under no circumstances would [I] ever consent to forty or fifty nations thrusting interfering fingers into the life's existence of the British Empire." The secretary assured him that he was not referring to the Empire, but it took some doing to smooth over the ruffled prime minister.

Roosevelt's death left Stettinius next in line for the presidency, a situation that no one had intended, and which Truman took immediate steps to correct by appointing James F. Byrnes secretary of state. See Richard L. Walker, "Edward R. Stettinius, Jr.," R. H. Ferrell, ed., *American Secretaries of State and Their Diplomacy*, Vol. XIV (1965).

LLOYD C. GARDNER

STEVENS, Thaddeus (b. Danville, Vt., April 4, 1792; d. Washington, D.C., Aug. 11, 1868), POLITICAL LEADER, graduated from Dartmouth College in 1814. He was handicapped by a clubfoot, which gave him a special sympathy for others crippled by an accident of birth and apparently led him to be a champion of minorities, especially blacks. He practiced law in Lancaster and Gettysburg, Pennsylvania, and defended many fugitive slaves without fee. Elected to the Pennsylvania house of representatives as an Anti-Mason, and then as a Whig, he served 1833–42. He supported free schools, the U.S. Bank, and railroad legislation. In 1838 he refused to sign the Pennsylvania constitution which restricted suffrage to white men, and was denounced as an abolitionist.

Despite his reputation for political agitation, and scandals in his private life, including the rumor that his African-American housekeeper, Lydia Smith, was his mistress, he was elected repeatedly to Congress. Entering as a Whig in 1849, he fought against slavery extension and opposed the Compromise of 1850, predicting that it would become "the fruitful mother of future rebellion, disunion and civil war." Thanks partly to his defense of fugitive slaves in the so-called Christiana Riot of 1851, he lost his seat in 1852 and briefly abandoned politics. He won reelection in 1858 as a Republican.

Stevens opposed President Buchanan's proslavery stand on Kansas, and the **Dred Scott** decision. After Lincoln's election as president, Stevens was one of the few northern congressmen who argued that attempts to conciliate the South were futile, and he urged the use of force to retake the federal forts and arsenals seized by southern insurgents. During the war, as chairman of the House Ways and Means Committee, which handled appropriations and taxes, he vigorously supported Lincoln's war measures. Because of his great parliamentary skill he came to be known as "the old Commoner," leader of leaders. Respectful of Lincoln, but not an intimate friend, he served as a powerful but demanding ally, constantly urging him toward emancipation. Later he led the difficult fight for the Thirteenth Amendment and inaugurated much civil rights legislation for freed blacks.

His disagreement with Lincoln concerned Reconstruction plans for the South, Lincoln favoring a speedy return of the seceded states, and Stevens preferring that they be treated like conquered provinces and not admitted until the blacks were guaranteed political and civil rights. He urged confiscation of the property of Confederate leaders, and division of the plantations into forty-acre plots for the newly freed slaves. After Lincoln's death Stevens became the acknowledged leader of the radical Republicans. Appalled by the new "black codes," which reduced the former slaves, to peonage, and by massacres and widespread lynchings of blacks throughout the South, Stevens helped formulate the Fourteenth Amendment, fathered the Reconstruction Acts of 1867, which subjected the Confederate states to military rule and imposed universal male suffrage, and then laid the groundwork for the Fifteenth Amendment. When Andrew Johnson repeatedly vetoed civil rights legislation for blacks and opposed the Fourteenth Amendment, Stevens considered him a betrayer of the social revolution wrought by the war. Their quarrel became public, with Johnson denouncing Stevens as a traitor as deserving of hanging as **Jefferson Davis,** and Stevens demanding the impeachment of the president as "a moral necessity." Though old and ill, Stevens succeeded in forcing the impeachment proceed-

ings, and he became one of the impeachment managers. Efforts to convict Johnson failed for lack of a single vote. In his last years Stevens was profoundly pessimistic about the burgeoning counterrevolution in the South and the rise of the Ku Klux Klan.

Thaddeus Stevens was one of the most revolutionary and controversial of all American statesmen. His impact on the nation was more profound than that of any of his contemporaries save Lincoln. He has been denounced as a fanatic and Jacobin, called "the Evil Genius of the Republican Party," the Marat and Robespierre of the Second American Revolution. Still hated by most southern whites, he is nevertheless revered by blacks everywhere as their uncompromising champion, and in recent years historians generally have come to recognize the excellence of much of his legislation and the complicated nature of his political genius.

He was deeply scarred by his crippled foot and poverty-ridden childhood. Though denounced as an atheist, he never completely rejected Calvinism, and found it impossible to accept the notion, popular among many of his contemporary New England reformers, that man is capable of perfectibility. His fathomless pessimism had a special impact on the nature of his legislation, for he believed that guarantees must be written into law to prevent man's ineradicable impulse to degrade his fellows.

Stevens's character and history were full of paradoxes and contradictions. He was a man of boundless private charities and vindictive public hates; a Calvinist, convinced that all men are vile, who nonetheless cherished a vision of the Promised Land where all men would be equal before the law; a revolutionary who would carve up the estates of the "bloated aristocrats" of the South, but who would also offer to defend Jefferson Davis in his trial for treason. An economic heretic within his own party, he could support conventional tariff legislation, but enrage Republican bankers and industrialists by agitation for federal controls to prevent wartime profiteering and railroad peculations.

He saw slavery for the horror it was and had no illusions that education and persuasion would ever bring about its disappearance, intertwined as it was with the southerner's economic and caste traditions. He saw with special clarity, like Lincoln, that the prewar compromises with slavery were almost certain guarantees of its expansion. And when the war came he saw, too, that it would be a grim and bloody agony lasting three or four years.

Stevens had no faith in gradualism, and perhaps too much faith in the omnipotence of legislation over human conduct. Although he was resolute, incorruptible, and a great foe of bigotry, he was flawed by a compulsion to punish, which prompted his confiscation schemes, and his unfortunate insistence in bringing Andrew Johnson to impeachment. Although he was fanatical in the pursuit of principle, it should be remembered that he was fanatical for free schools and universal suffrage at a time when opposition fanatics stood for caste and ignorance. If he contributed to the rapacious tariff interests, he also contributed enormously to the spread of democracy by extending suffrage to millions of blacks and poor whites.

By pushing for consolidation of the federal power, he helped transform a sprawling, invertebrate country into a unified nation. His assault on Johnson was not an attack on the executive power as such but on a man who he believed was betraying the principle of equality which dated back to the Declaration of Independence. Stevens's greatest legislation, the Fourteenth Amendment, a bulwark against the tyranny of the state, could never have passed without his leadership, and without the Reconstruction legislation which ensured its ratification. And while this amendment, and the Fifteenth, for which he laid the preparation, were abused and neglected for generations, in the second half of the 20th century they have become what he had intended them to be from the beginning, weapons against bigotry and injustice. See Fawn M. Brodie, *Thaddeus Stevens: Scourge of the South* (1959).

FAWN M. BRODIE

STEVENS, Wallace (b. Reading, Pa., Oct. 2, 1879; d. Hartford, Conn., Aug. 2, 1955), POET, enrolled as a special student in an English program at Harvard in 1897. After graduating from this course in 1900, he moved to New York, where he began working for the New York *Tribune* and *The World's Work*. The following year he entered the New York Law School and in 1904 was admitted to the New York State bar. Stevens published his first poem in 1915. A year later he joined the legal staff of the New York branch of the Hartford Accident and Indemnity Company, but transferred to Hartford where he lived for the rest of his life. *Harmonium,* his first book of poems, was published in 1923, gaining some critical praise but selling fewer than one hundred copies. A dozen years were to pass before his second volume of poems, *Ideas of Order,* appeared. Meanwhile his business career prospered, and in 1934 he became a vice president of the insurance company. The last twenty years of Stevens's life were his most artistically productive ones, witnessing the publication of four volumes of poetry, a volume of essays, and then *The Collected Poems.* He was elected a member of the National Institute of Arts and Letters in 1946, awarded the Bollingen prize in 1950, a National Book Award in 1951, and in 1955, both a Pulitzer Prize and a second National Book Award. In 1957 his last work, *Opus Posthumous,* appeared.

Wallace Stevens is a striking example of the artist who enjoys a delayed but fertile coming of age. Though his first volume of poetry was not published until he was forty-four, he was to become one of the most prominent and influential of all 20th-century American poets.

The overarching concern of Stevens's work, which reflects the influences of the imagist and symbolist movements, is its attempt to harmonize the tensions between existence and consciousness of that existence. In some of his earlier poems—"Sunday Morning," for example—there was a marked tendency to celebrate hedonistically the joys of almost pure sensuous experience. In later works, however, Stevens became increasingly concerned with the interplay between quotidian life and the imagination. This resulted in a shift of emphasis from the physical to the metaphysical. Or, as he wrote in "Men Made Out of Words": "Life consists / Of propositions about life." The shift, of course, was never total. In all his poems—early, middle, and late—there is a persistent attempt to deal with the changing ambiguities existing between polar opposites: imagination and reality, chaos and order, change and permanence. Process or becoming fascinated him more than any quixotic quest for a fixed order. "Final belief," he argued in "Asides on an Oboe," "must be in a fiction."

While Stevens is undoubtedly a major poet, he has not been an especially popular one. Obscure and sometimes nearly unintelligible, his poems require great patience and concentration. Moreover, they tend to be highly abstract, impersonal, and lacking in the drama of vital human relationships. For all these weaknesses, they are compelling. Filled with striking metaphors and analogies, constructed with dazzling rhetoric, they carefully explore in constantly fresh ways the complex ties between art and experience. They seem, in short, to underscore Stevens's contention that "The whole race is a poet that writes down / The eccentric propositions of its fate." See Marie Borroff, ed., *Wallace Stevens: A Collection of Critical Essays* (1963).

ROBERT MUCCIGROSSO

STEVENSON, Adlai Ewing (b. Los Angeles, Calif., Feb. 5, 1900; d. London, Eng., July 14, 1965), POLITICAL LEADER, graduated from Princeton in 1922. After two years at the Harvard Law School, he worked for his family's newspaper, the Bloomington, Ill., *Daily Pantagraph.* After receiving his law degree from Northwestern University in 1926, Stevenson practiced law in Chicago until 1933, when he was named special counsel to the New Deal Agricultural Adjustment Administration. He returned to his law practice in 1934, but was also active in the Chicago Bar Association, the Council on Foreign Relations, and the Committee to Defend America by Aiding the Allies. In 1941 Stevenson was appointed special assistant to Secretary of the Navy Frank Knox, and four years later he became personal assistant to Secretary of State **Edward Stettinius.** He headed the U.S. delegation to the Preparatory Commission of the United Nations in London in the fall of 1945, and served as senior adviser to the U.S. delegation to the first session of the U.N. General Assembly in London (1946). He was an alternate delegate to the second and third sessions in New York (1946–47).

In 1948 Colonel Jacob Arvey, a power in Illinois Democratic politics, tapped Stevenson for the Democratic gubernatorial nomination. Although little known, he won a landslide victory. Taking over a scandal-ridden government, he reformed the state police by substituting a merit system for political appointments, and attacked organized gambling interests. His administration doubled state aid to local schools, improved mental hospitals, and built new highways. At the 1952 Democratic national convention, Stevenson was drafted against his wishes as the party's presidential candidate. In a campaign noted for his eloquent campaign speeches, Stevenson proposed to continue the New Deal and Fair Deal policies at home and abroad, and scathingly attacked McCarthyism as a threat to civil liberties. He was defeated by Dwight D. Eisenhower by 442 to 89 electoral votes. Running again in 1956, Stevenson campaigned for an end to nuclear testing in the atmosphere but again lost to Eisenhower by an electoral vote of 457 to 73; he then returned to law practice. In 1957 he took the leadership in founding the Democratic Advisory Council, which through its policy statements prepared the way for the New Frontier. He was an unsuccessful candidate for the Democratic presidential nomination in 1960.

President Kennedy appointed Stevenson U.S. ambassador to the United Nations in 1961. Because of his prominence he had more influence than his predecessors in this post, and participated in some of the deliberations of the National Security Council, especially during the Cuban missile crisis of 1962. Stevenson was a member of the U.S. delegation which signed the 1963 U.S.-

Soviet treaty banning all but underground nuclear arms testing. He remained U.N. ambassador until his death. His many books include: *Major Campaign Speeches of Adlai E. Stevenson* (1953), *Call to Greatness* (1954), and *Looking Outward: Years of Crisis at the United Nations* (1963).

Stevenson developed a distinguished writing and speaking style—witty, pungent, and rational. During the decade of the 1950s he tried to shake the complacency of the public and alert the nation to such serious problems as poverty amid affluence, civil rights, conservation, aid to under-developed nations, and a relaxation of tensions with the Soviet Union. He became the "Conscience in Politics." He constantly urged young people to enter public life and through his two presidential campaigns involved many new people in politics. The campaign of 1952 with the theme "Let's talk sense to the American people" and the 1956 campaign with the theme "The New America" articulated issues in such a way that Stevenson was the spiritual godfather of John F. Kennedy's New Frontier.

He was noted for his charm and wit. In addition he had a zest for life and a probing curiosity to educate himself about the world in which he lived. He traveled widely—through Asia, the Middle East, and Europe in 1953; Africa in 1955 and 1957; the Soviet Union in 1958; and Latin America in 1960—and wrote many articles about what he had learned. He was a popular and reassuring figure abroad, since he advocated that American power be used generously, reasonably, and with a scrupulous concern for peace. He stood for the America dedicated to the proposition of liberty and equality of opportunity. To him America was "the last best hope" for a decent society for the whole human experiment. See John Bartlow Martin, *Adlai Stevenson and the World: The Life of Adlai E. Stevenson* (1977).

WALTER JOHNSON

STEWARD, Ira (b. New London, Conn., March 10, 1831; d. Plano, Ill., March 13, 1883), LABOR LEADER, served his apprenticeship in a Providence, Rhode Island, machine shop. Dismissed in 1851 because he agitated for shorter hours and other labor reforms, he moved to Boston, where he worked as a machinist while continuing his union activities. As a delegate to the 1863 convention of the International Union of Machinists and Blacksmiths in Boston, he secured a resolution demanding an eight-hour day, the first such union resolution in America. He published a pamphlet, *A Reduction of Hours, an Increase of Wages* (1865), which argued that shorter hours, resulting in more leisure time, would increase consumer spending and create more jobs and higher wages. He spent the next few years lobbying in vain in the Massachusetts legislature for eight-hour laws. In 1869 he helped establish the Massachusetts Bureau of Labor Statistics, the first such body in the U.S. In 1874 he influenced the passage of Massachusetts' first effective ten-hour law for women and children.

Although opposed to a separate labor party, Steward, a socialist, believed in the necessity of labor solidarity. In 1878 he and his followers joined with American members of the Marxist International Workingmen's Association to form the International Labor Union, which sought to organize unskilled workers. Distraught by his wife's death in 1878, Steward spent the next two years living with friends and working on a book to be titled "The Political Economy of Eight Hours," of which he left only fragments.

A whole generation of American trade unionists fed on the economic doctrines of Ira Steward. The aspiration to free their lives from the twin burdens of incessant toil and sporadic unemployment prompted industrial workers to make the eight-hour working day their foremost demand from the time of the National Labor Union to that of the American Federation of Labor. In support of this demand Steward and his colleagues lobbied for legislation and organized strikes, including one of some 100,000 workers in New York City in 1872. They also spread their gospel through books and pamphlets and in the press. Among those who drew explicitly on their doctrines were labor leaders as different from each other as **Samuel Gompers** and **Terence V. Powderly.**

Steward saw in the poverty of workers both a necessary condition of the rapid economic growth which was enriching the country and generating great movements of social uplift and reform, and an insuperable obstacle to the diffusion of the new wealth and the success of those movements. The wealth of the few had productivity utility only because the poverty of the many made them available for hire, he argued, but that same poverty both limited the potential market for the goods labor produced and kept the workers in a state of stupefaction. Under such circumstances, the relentless toil of the poor served only to increase employers' wealth and generate depressions.

Only by a protracted struggle could the workers emancipate society from such contradictions, Steward held. The starting point of that effort had to be the eight-hour day, which would generate a revolution of rising expectations. As workers became more accustomed to leisure and the good things of life, they would themselves devour the fruits of their expanding productivity. Eventually employers would be driven from the industrial field. "The republicanization of labor," an economic counterpart of a "republicanization of government," would follow. See David Montgomery, *Beyond Equality: Labor and the Radical Republicans, 1862–1872* (1967).

DAVID MONTGOMERY

STIEGLITZ, Alfred (b. Hoboken, N.J., Jan. 1, 1864; d. New York, N.Y., July 13, 1946), PHOTOGRAPHER, studied engineering at the College of the City of New York (1879–81) and then at the Berlin Polytechnic (1882), where he became interested in photography. He traveled through Europe photographing for the next few years and won first prize at a London amateur photography exhibition in 1887. Returning to New York in 1890, he bought the Heliochrome Engraving Co., and experimented with three-color work. A pioneer in color photography, Stieglitz was able to photograph rain, snow, and night scenes before the invention of fast lenses and plates. He edited the *American Amateur Photography* magazine (1892–96) and then gave up his business in 1896 to publish and edit *Camera Notes* (1897–1903) and *Camera Work* (1903–17), which was expanded to include art as well as photography. Through these periodicals Stieglitz sought to make photography accepted as a form of creative expression.

In 1902 Stieglitz founded an organization of avant-garde photographers called the Photo-Secession Group and in 1905 opened the Photo-Secession Gallery at 291 Fifth Avenue in New York. The "291," as it became known, soon began displaying modern art as well as photography. This gallery exhibited Rodin and Matisse drawings in 1907 and also works by Toulouse-Lautrec (1909), Cézanne (1910–11), and Picasso (1911). Between 1907 and 1917 Stieglitz exhibited works by young American modern artists like **John Marin, Charles Demuth,** Arthur Dove, and **Georgia O'Keeffe** (whom he married in 1924). After "291" closed in 1917, Stieglitz devoted himself to photography. He specialized in airplanes, clouds, and especially the skyscrapers and people of New York. In 1925 he opened the Intimate Gallery and in 1929 An American Place gallery.

***

The New York *Times* quoted Alfred Stieglitz in 1934 as having said: "Personally I like my photography straight, unmanipulated, devoid of all tricks; a print not looking like anything but a photograph, living through its own inherent qualities and revealing its own spirit." The same newspaper, in reporting the death of **Edward Steichen** in 1973—with Stieglitz and Edward Weston, the dominant figure in American photography of the 20th century—made the claim that Steichen, rather than Stieglitz, had made of photography an art form, apparently because Steichen had experimented with out-of-focus photography, which produced prints which superficially suggested impressionist paintings. Actually the reverse was true. Stieglitz was always better at photographic art, since he consistently avoided making photographs which might be confused with anything else. And as an influence and propagandist he was preeminent; out of what the painter Marsden Hartley called "the largest small room of its kind in the world"—the attic of 291 Fifth Avenue in New York—he directed the Photo-Secession Gallery. Beginning in 1907 when he expanded his exhibitions to include paintings, he offered a steady stream of European and American avant-garde exhibitions. It was he, rather than **Robert Henri, John Sloan,** and Arthur B. Davies, in the 1913 Armory Show, who was the first to introduce modern art to Americans. But to Henri, Stieglitz was "ultramodernist" and faddish, and, consequently, unintelligible to the majority. To Stieglitz, Henri and his associates were conventional and retarded. Interestingly enough, in his emphasis on social themes in his own work as a photographer, his career ran directly parallel to the efforts of the Henri group in their exhibition at the Macbeth Gallery in 1908. It was only in his later work that his photography began to emphasize other more modern concerns such as formal, abstract values. See Barbara Rose, *American Art since 1900* (1967).

LAWRENCE CAMPBELL

STILWELL, Joseph Warren (b. Palatka, Fla., March 19, 1883; d. San Francisco, Calif., Oct. 12, 1946), MILITARY LEADER, graduated in 1904 from the U.S. Military Academy. After serving as a second lieutenant in the Philippines (1904–6) he was assigned to the Military Academy as a language instructor in French and Spanish, remaining there until 1910. Following another tour in the Philippines (1911–12) Stilwell, now a first lieutenant, was stationed at the Presidio, Monterey, California (1912–13). He returned to West Point as a language instructor in 1913. In December 1917 he was sent to France with the American Expeditionary Force. He served with various units including the AEF General Headquarters and participated in the Battle of St. Mihiel (Sept. 1918).

After the war Stilwell was sent (1919) to the University of California at Berkeley to study Chinese. He was promoted to major in 1920 and assigned to Peking, where he continued to study Chinese, eventually becoming fluent in several dialects. In 1924 he graduated from Fort Benning, Georgia, Infantry School, and taught there the following year before returning to China, where he was battalion commander and the first regimental officer in Tientsin (1925–28) and later chief of staff of American forces in China (1928–29). Promoted to lieutenant colonel in 1929, he was assigned to the Infantry School at Fort Benning as an instructor of tactics, and during 1930–33 was chief of the tactical section there. He served with the Organized Reserves in San Diego, California (1933–35) and as U.S. military attaché to China and Siam (1935–39). In the latter post he was sent in 1936 to Shensi province, China, to protect resident Americans during a rebellion.

Appointed brigadier general in 1939, Stilwell was given command of the 3d Infantry Brigade at Fort Sam Houston, Texas. Other commands shortly followed: the 7th Division in 1940, and the III Army Corps, Fort Ord, California, in 1941. In 1942 he was sent to China to take charge of the U.S. army in that theater, which included India and Burma. Stilwell's forces, which consisted basically of the 5th and 6th Chinese Army Corps, aided in the British defense of Toungoo, Burma (April 1942), during the Japanese conquest of the Burma Road supply line to China. Following that campaign he retreated through 140 miles of Burmese jungles with his Chinese and American forces into India (May 3–23, 1942), establishing his headquarters in New Delhi. There, later in 1942, he retrained and reorganized the Chinese army with General Claire Chennault, directing air attacks on Japanese bases. In November 1943, Stilwell began a counterattack against the Japanese, and in August 1944 defeated them at Myitkyina, Burma, thereby gaining northern Burma and opening the Ledo Road to the Burma Road. By the time he was promoted to full general in 1944, Stilwell was not only commander of U.S. forces in the China-Burma-India theater but also chief of staff of the Chinese army, deputy commander of the Southeast Asia Command, Lend-Lease administrator to China, and chief of the Chinese Training and Combat Command.

Stilwell came into conflict with Generalissimo Chiang Kai-shek when he criticized Chiang for inefficiency, aggressiveness, dictatorial rule, corruption, and failure to cooperate with the Chinese Communists in fighting the Japanese. In October 1944 President Franklin D. Roosevelt recalled Stilwell at Chiang's request. Stilwell then served about six months as commander of the U.S. Army Ground Forces. In June 1945 he was given command of the Tenth Army in Okinawa, where he directed final American operations until the war ended in September 1945. His last post was head of the Sixth Army at the Presidio, San Francisco, California, in 1946.

During the two decades prior to 1941 Joseph W. Stilwell built a reputation as one of the U.S. Army's most hard-driving and promising officers and also as one of the few Americans experienced in Chinese military affairs. Therefore his selection in 1942 to command American forces in CBI operations was a natural one, and his two years of leadership in that theater were marked by ingenuity and courage under complex, trying conditions. His problems were manifold and stemmed not merely from personal conflicts with Chiang Kai-shek ("The Peanut" was Stilwell's nickname for him) and other allied commanders but principally from differing Chinese, British, and American governmental views of the objectives of that theater. His difficulties were compounded by trying to hold five major command positions simultaneously, in which he was responsible to different authorities whose aims were rarely coordinated. Although he succeeded in returning to Burma and defeating the Japanese army there, Stilwell was thwarted in his efforts to transform the Chinese army into an effective fighting force united against the Japanese.

Lean and wiry, with short-cropped hair and a hard, decisive face, Stilwell was a born fighter and a strict commander with high standards.

Popular with his troops, "Vinegar Joe" was often seen at the front wearing his World War I campaign hat, a nonregulation sweater, and no insignia. His sarcasm, impatience, tactlessness, and cantankerousness, together with an open disgust for pretentious persons of high rank, contributed to his friction with military and political leaders in the CBI theater. See Barbara W. Tuchman, *Stilwell and the American Experience in China: 1911–45* (1971).

D. CLAYTON JAMES

STIMSON, Henry Louis (b. New York, N.Y., Sept. 21, 1867; d. Huntington, N.Y., Oct. 20, 1950), POLITICAL LEADER, received a BA (1888) from Yale, and MA (1889) and LLB (1890) from Harvard. He was admitted to the New York bar in 1891, and joined **Elihu Root**'s law firm (Root and Clarke) in 1893, becoming a partner in 1897. Active in Republican politics, in 1906 Stimson was appointed U.S. attorney for the southern district of New York by President Theodore Roosevelt. In 1910 he was the unsuccessful Republican candidate for governor of New York.

In 1911–13 Stimson was secretary of war under President Taft. During World War I he served in France as a colonel in the 31st Field Artillery. He opposed President Wilson's plan for a League of Nations, arguing that the League would overcommit the U.S. abroad. In 1927 President Coolidge sent him to Nicaragua, where he managed to get the incumbent government and the rebel faction to agree to let the U.S. supervise the 1928 elections. Stimson's impression of American-Nicaraguan relations is discussed in his *American Policy in Nicaragua* (1927). He was then appointed governor general of the Philippines, serving to 1929. Although not favorably disposed toward Philippine independence, he worked to make the islands "self-governing possessions or colonies."

Stimson next served as secretary of state in the Hoover administration (1929–33). He headed the U.S. delegation to the London Naval Conference of 1930, where he sought to maintain the moratorium on the construction of capital ships among the major naval powers. The conference agreed to maintain the status quo on capital ship construction, limit the tonnage of cruisers, destroyers, and submarines, and establish rules prohibiting unrestricted submarine warfare.

When the Japanese invaded Manchuria (1931), Stimson tried unsuccessfully to persuade President Hoover to take a firmer stand against aggression. He then issued his "Non-Recognition Doctrine" (Jan. 1932), which stated that the U.S. would not recognize any seizures that were made in violation of America's treaty rights in the Far East. Before leaving the State Department (1933), Stimson won the support of Hoover and president-elect Franklin D. Roosevelt for his proposal permitting the president to issue an arms embargo against belligerent nations. The proposal, however, was not acted upon by Congress.

In 1933 Stimson resumed his legal practice. He soon became one of the leading exponents of the idea of "collective security," asserting that the peace of the world could best be maintained if the U.S. supported the League of Nations and the Western democracies. He also advised Secretary of State **Cordell Hull** on foreign policy, urging that the U.S. boycott Japanese silk and place an embargo on oil and scrap iron shipments to Japan (1939). In 1940 President Roosevelt appointed Stimson secretary of war. Hoping to aid the Allies militarily, Stimson worked for the repeal of the Neutrality Acts and came out in favor of using the American fleet to convoy munitions to Britain. He convinced Roosevelt and General **George C. Marshall** to institute a conscription program. Stimson also played an important role as an adviser on atomic policy, and was placed in charge of the Manhattan Project to develop an atomic bomb. When Roosevelt died in 1945, it was Stimson who told President Truman about the development of an atomic bomb. Moreover, Stimson helped influence Truman's decision to drop the bomb on Japan, arguing that it would help shorten the war and save many lives.

Stimson left the War Department in 1945. During the debates over the feasibility of a United Nations organization, Stimson warned that such an organization could succeed only if the major powers could adjust their outstanding problems before entering the organization. Stimson's career is covered in *On Active Service in Peace and War,* which he wrote with **McGeorge Bundy** (1948).

⸎

Stimson was turning sixty when he began the career that was to give him a place in history. He did not look his years, what with his trim body, his square shoulders, and only a hint of gray in his black hair and mustache. Long a horseman, sportsman, and big-game hunter, he was proud of his physical fitness, though in later years the infirmities of age, such as high blood pressure and lumbago, were to give him trouble. Fond of punctilio and protocol, he generally was cold, reserved, and dignified, yet he had a hot temper that occasionally flared up, especially in his dealings with subordinates. He was known for his "tenacity of purpose," which was reflected in his firm lips and hard-set jaw, as well as in his slow and deliberate speech. His sense of rectitude bordered on self-righteousness.

The Stimsons had been one of the more illustrious families of New York, and from them he inherited a soldierly tradition, a feeling of kinship with the great, and a consciousness that he was born to govern. As a boy, he was rather sickly and sober, haunted by a vague feeling that his somewhat detached and distant father blamed him for his mother's death. No wonder the boy became the man he did, humorless, imperious, and self-conscious about his own and others' honor. No wonder he grew up to be as determined an advocate of "the strenuous life" as his friend Theodore Roosevelt. Like Roosevelt, he accepted war as a not altogether disagreeable fact of international life, and he was never so "wonderfully happy" as when he saw a bit of action in World War I. Even in civilian pursuits he always thought of himself as a soldier, "on active service," and in matters of law and government he prided himself on what he called his "combat psychology."

Though there were twists and turns in his public career, it eventually developed a basic consistency. At the end he stood out as the great exponent of a widely accepted complex of ideas, though he was not the originator of any of them. This concept, often referred to as "collective security," assumes a rather clear-cut distinction between "peace-loving" and "aggressor" nations. It implies an obligation, on the part of the peace lovers, to "punish" the aggressors and thus to deter them and other potential evildoers. That is to say, it entails upon certain governments the duty of policing the world and making others behave. Its logical consequence is war to end or prevent war.

For more than twenty years after Stimson's death, one American administration after another persisted in carrying on that kind of policy. The involvement in Vietnam, for example, was repeatedly justified in Stimsonian terms, although it presented the gruesome paradox of enforcing morality by killing or maiming women, old men, and children and leaving countless civilians homeless and impoverished. With regard to Stimson's influence on his own and later times, there will ultimately be at least two possible verdicts. Either he helped to lay the legal and moral foundations of an international society—as his admirers maintain—or, insofar as he influenced events, he contributed to the tensions and instabilities of the world, to the onset of a never-ending crisis. See Richard N. Current, *Secretary Stimson: A Study in Statecraft* (1970), and Elting E. Morison, *Turmoil and Tradition: A Study of the Life and Times of Henry L. Stimson* (1960).

RICHARD N. CURRENT

STONE, Harlan Fiske (b. Chesterfield, N.H., Oct. 11, 1872; d. Washington, D.C., April 22, 1946), JURIST, graduated from Amherst (1894), and received his LLB from Columbia Law School (1898). During 1899–1923 he practiced law in New York City and taught at Columbia Law School (dean, 1910–23). In 1924 President Coolidge, a college friend, appointed him attorney general of the U.S. Stone promptly helped reorganize the Federal Bureau of Investigation, confining it to nonpolitical activities. In 1925

Coolidge nominated Stone to the Supreme Court as an associate justice (chief justice, 1940).

On the Court, Stone early displayed his conservatism with an opinion in the Maple Flooring case (1925) favorable to business consolidation. As time went on, however, he came more under the influence of **Oliver Wendell Holmes, Jr.** and **Louis D. Brandeis,** emerging as a vigorous dissenter in numerous cases voiding regulation of property. (By the end of his career more of his dissenting opinions and positions had become the law of the Court than those of any justice in history.) In the 1930s, especially, he developed a reputation for judicial objectivity. Although personally disapproving of both the federal government's decision to refuse to redeem government bonds in gold and the Agricultural Adjustment Act of 1933, he conceded that Congress's constitutional power to regulate money also affected government bonds (*Perry* v. *U.S.*, 1935, one of the "gold clause" cases); and he dissented bitterly when the Court ruled the AAA unconstitutional (*U.S.* v. *Butler*, 1936). In the latter case, he deplored the Court's setting its own view of proper federal economic power above that of Congress, arguing that the Court was "not the only agency of government that must be assumed to have the capacity to govern."

In the late 1930s Stone was instrumental in conceptualizing a new civil libertarian role for the Court. As the lone dissenter in *Minersville School District* v. *Gobitis* (1940), he expressed disappointment that his brethren would not agree that a compulsory flag salute, imposed upon children of a religious minority, was a form of unwarranted public coercion. His reasoning in the Gobitis case was vindicated in *West Virginia Board of Education* v. *Barnette* (1943). Earlier, he had persuaded the Court to uphold the federal government's power to regulate a state (La.) primary when such an election contest was an integral part of a process that involved choosing a candidate for a federal office. During World War II, however, Stone upheld the government's right to establish military curfew regulations on the West Coast (*Hirabayashi* v. *U.S.*, 1943), and to exclude Japanese from the West Coast (*Korematsu*

v. *U.S.*, 1944), under the war powers. His final opinion (*Girouard* v. *U.S.*, 1946) reversed an earlier position of his own (that pacifist religious convictions should be no bar to naturalization, *U.S.* v. *Macintosh*, 1931). The congressional act involved, he argued, should be respected as a correct interpretation of Congress's aims. While reading this dissent, he collapsed in his chair, and died later that day.

———⁂———

Stone, a resolute but congenial Yankee, cultivated a posture of disinterestedness in terms of his own commitments and their relation to public policy from his first ventures into public life. Basically conservative and property-oriented (his lectures on the *Law and Its Administration* at the Columbia Law School in 1915 read like a traditional businessman's defense of the business community), he nonetheless saw a public servant's role as carrying responsibilities different from those of a private citizen. From the outset of his attorney-generalship, he set out to divest those governmental agencies over which he had authority from powers which would enable them to behave in a partisan fashion. On ascending the Supreme Court bench, he was able to carry that philosophy into a different field. Finding himself most comfortable with Holmes and Brandeis, and later **Cardozo,** he early came to share their concerns regarding the Taft Court's penchant for denying the states effective control over economic activity. In a case in 1927 (*DiSanto* v. *Pennsylvania*) he registered a vigorous dissent, contending that before the Court used rigid and archaic formulas to tell a state that it could not regulate intrastate commerce, it had an obligation to do extensive and objective research on the actual positive and negative impact of such regulations. As the Hughes Court moved to embrace a position of restraint regarding the states' economic power, Stone more and more found himself in a majority position, although he was careful to draw a line between judicial restraint and judicial self-abnegation, and insisted that deference to legislative judgment should not come automatically, but only after the Court had satis-

fied itself that the legislative action did not unduly imperil the national interest.

By the 1930s, the issue had shifted to one of federal power and the vast authority of the federal government in the economic area. Although he joined the majority in negating the NIRA, his sharp dissent in the Butler case, voiding the AAA of 1933, drew national attention to his self-restraint views and gave Roosevelt and New Dealers a ray of hope that despite the bitter hostility of the "Four Horsemen," it might be possible to move the Court to a more sanguine position regarding federal economic activity. In many respects, then, the Court's shift to an expansive view of the commerce and taxing power following the "court-packing" episode represented a triumph not only for Roosevelt but for Stone's views, a triumph which to a large degree culminated in *U.S.* v. *Darby* in 1941. There Stone put the *coup de grace* upon the use of the Tenth Amendment to block the federal wage and hour law, and completed the process of taking the Supreme Court generally out of the business of evaluating the constitutionality of such measures once enacted.

Yet Stone's willingness to allow the popular majority to control man's economic activity did not automatically extend to a similar control over matters affecting conscience and expression. With dictatorship growing in the late 1930s, he proclaimed publicly in 1938, through his famous Carolene footnote, the need for evaluating legislation which curtailed personal freedom on a different scale. Making clear that to him the most basic freedom was the freedom to influence political action, he reiterated in his aroused dissent in the first of the flag-salute cases, and in his careful majority opinion in *U.S.* v. *Classic*, the obligation of the Court to protect the civil and political rights of minorities from the abuse of both public and private power. Such a posture made his capitulation to governmental power in the Japanese relocation cases all the more disillusioning to civil libertarians. Yet he pegged his position here again to self-restraint, capitalizing upon the importance of the Supreme Court's standing aside in a period of national emergency when other branches of the government, charged with coping with national interests, had determined a policy they felt was essential to national survival.

Stone's importance was both actual and symbolic. Clearly his actions in 1936 and 1937 were useful to Roosevelt, and were a factor in Stone's ultimate elevation to the chief justiceship. Similarly his role in shifting the Court's image from that of a selfish, property-oriented conservative body to that of a publicly aware, solicitous agency concerned with human rights did much to resuscitate its authority and prestige. But the image frequently did not match the performance. Tolerant and permissive in dealing with colleagues, Stone as chief justice had great difficulty in "massing" the Court, with the result that it got behind in its agenda, and that the bitter hostilities which erupted among its new members made it the most frequently divided, and most openly quarrelsome, in history. It thus left no clear civil liberties or civil rights heritage. Only with the ascendancy of **Earl Warren** did it again regain a firm leadership role in the body politic. See A. T. Mason, *Harlan Fiske Stone: Pillar of the Law* (1956).

PAUL L. MURPHY

STONE, Isidor Feinstein (b. Philadelphia, Pa., Dec. 24, 1907; d. Boston, Mass., June 18, 1988), JOURNALIST, grew up in Haddonfield, N.J., the son of Russian Jewish immigrants. Stone attended the University of Pennsylvania, but left school in 1927 before graduating. As a student, he worked for the Camden (New Jersey) *Evening Courier* and the Philadelphia *Inquirer.* In 1931, Stone became an editorial writer for J. David Stern's Philadelphia *Record.* Two years later, Stone joined Stern's New York *Post.* In 1938, Stone became Washington editor of the *The Nation.* A political maverick and an outspoken civil libertarian, Stone worked in the 1940s for a succession of liberal plublications owned by Ralph Ingersoll—*PM*, the New York *Star*, and the *Daily Compass.* After the *Compass* folded in 1952, Stone launched *I. F. Stone's Weekly,* a left-leaning, one-man newsletter which he published for nineteen years. A prolific writer, Stone, after retiring from the *Weekly*, continued to contribute articles to the New York *Review of Books.* He published several books during his career, including *The Hidden History of the Korean War* (1951). A self-taught classicist, Stone's last book was *The Trial of Socrates* (1982), a popular best-seller.

———

I.F. Stone began his career in journalism at age fourteen, when he wrote and published three issues of the *Monthly Progress.* It foreshadowed the liberal sentiments Stone would display for the rest of his life; he called for independence for India, cancellation of World War I war debts, and a twenty-five year moratorium on the manufacture of new weapons. A voracious reader but a poor student, Stone, under parental pressure, discontinued the *Progress*, but he was soon working as a cub reporter on a local newspaper.

Stone joined the Socialist Party in the 1920s, and through the 1940s, he worked for a series of progressive publications. But Stone was too much the iconoclast to enjoy party politics, or to be content working for anyone but himself. In the early 1950s, Stone launched *I. F. Stone's Weekly.* His initial list of subscribers included **Eleanor Roosevelt, Albert Einstein**, and Bertrand Russell, but his readership remained small until the 1960s, when his opposition to the Vietnam War attracted a wide audience, especially among liberal intellectuals. By 1971, his readership reached seventy thousand.

Partial deafness forced Stone to forego press conferences and formal briefings. For stories Stone turned a skeptical eye to official documents. "The bureaucracies put out so much," he once said, "that they cannot help letting the truth slip from time to time." Stone published several books in addition to a plethora of articles and essays, but he lacked the traditional scholarly credentials, and he won little more than grudging acceptance from academic historians. Nevertheless, Stone's relentless criticisms of what he saw as America's obsessive anticommunism anticipated much of the revisionist scholarship of later years. See Robert C. Cottrell, *Izzy: A Biography of I. F. Stone* (1992).

JEFF BROADWATER

STONE, Melville Elijah (b. Hudson, Ill., Aug. 22, 1848; d. New York, N.Y., Feb. 15, 1929), JOURNALIST, attended public schools in Chicago. He became a newspaper reporter for the Chicago *Republican* in 1867 but left two years later to run an iron foundry and machine shop. When his business was destroyed by the great Chicago fire of 1871 he went back to newspaper work, serving as editor of various Chicago dailies. In 1875 he organized the first penny daily in the U.S., the Chicago *Daily News*. He started a morning edition with his partner Victor Lawson in 1881 but sold out all his interests in 1888. After spending the next two years traveling in Europe, he returned to Chicago and became president of the Globe National Bank in 1892. He also served as treasurer of the Chicago Drainage Canal Co.

In 1893 Stone was invited to become general manager of the Associated Press of Illinois, which had merged with the Western Association Press when it was not taken into the reorganized United Press. Moving the headquarters from Chicago to New York City to compete with the UP, Stone built the AP into a great news agency. He contracted with the Reuter Telegram Co. of Great Britain for exclusive use of their news in the U.S. (1893), fostered close cooperation between agencies in the system, endeavored to gather and report the news free of partisanship, and tried to avoid sensationalism. In 1904 he succeeded in convincing Czar Nicholas to lift press censorship during the Russo-Japanese War, but his enthusiasm for America's entry into World War I made him an ardent supporter of censorship during that conflict.

In 1918 he won a great legal victory when the Supreme Court ruled that news reports were property and therefore subject to copyright laws. Although he retired as general manager in 1921, Stone remained active as a counselor to the AP until his death. His autobiography, *Fifty Years a Journalist*, appeared in 1921.

⁓

A skilled organizer, Stone set new standards of objectivity and public responsibility in American journalism. The Chicago *Daily News*, one of several mass-circulation dailies to appear in the post–Civil War years, was notably free of political control and impartial in its reporting. Always lively, sometimes saucy, it was sensational only in practicing a "detective journalism" that resulted in the arrest and imprisonment of a number of criminals. Stressing items of substantial public concern, the *News* showed, as Stone later noted, that success did not demand "silly so-called 'human interest stories' of cats born with two heads." A shrewd promoter, Stone imported barrels of pennies from the Philadelphia mint to overcome a local shortage, and encouraged merchants to mark goods 99¢ so the penny change might purchase his paper. Plagued by theft of news items by the McMullen brothers' *Post* and *Mail,* Stone invented an account of famine in Serbia that concluded with a mayor's lament: "Er us siht la Etsll iws nel lum cmeht (The municipality cannot aid)." To his delight his rivals purloined the story before realizing that the Serbian when reversed read: "The McMullens will steal this sure."

Politically moderate, Stone supported civil service reform, savings bank regulation, and various humanitarian ventures. The *Daily News's* even-handed reporting of labor-capital clashes, first apparent in the railroad strike of 1877, continued during the troubled nineties. Copying English practice, Stone hired various experts to write editorials, and also boasted a regular staff that included Eugene Field, **Finley Peter Dunne,** and George Ade, all later contributors to the "Chicago Renaissance."

Overseeing a vast expansion of the AP, Stone extended his principles of public service and impartiality to most leading American newspapers. Coordinating European and domestic newsgathering, he traveled abroad frequently, met leading statesmen, and indirectly influenced events. His greatest triumph came in 1905 when he was instrumental in keeping afloat the peace negotiations that settled the Russo-Japanese War. After urging censorship in World War I, he criticized the appointment of George Creel and many policies of the Committee on Public Information, one result being a near-complete break with

President Wilson. See Melville E. Stone, *Fifty Years a Journalist* (1921).

ROBERT C. BANNISTER

STOREY, Moorfield (b. Roxbury, Mass., March 19, 1845; d. Lincoln, Mass., Oct. 24, 1929), LAWYER, REFORMER, graduated from Harvard in 1866. After a year at Harvard Law School, he accepted a position as clerk of the U.S. Senate Committee on Foreign Relations, serving as personal secretary to its chairman, **Charles Sumner.** In 1869 Storey returned to Boston; after his admission to the bar later that year, he served as assistant district attorney of Suffolk County. In 1873 he joined the firm of Brooks and Ball, specializing in commercial and international law. During 1873–79 he was editor of the *American Law Review.* In 1877 he was appointed to the Harvard Board of Overseers (serving to 1888 and again 1892–1910). He was elected president of the American Bar Association in 1896.

Storey showed an early interest in reform activities and was a leader (1869–97) in the movement to establish a classified civil service and to defeat candidates deemed to be corrupt, regardless of party. In 1884 he joined other dissident reformers ("Mugwumps") in rejecting the Republican presidential candidate, **James G. Blaine,** and supporting the Democrat, Grover Cleveland. Following the Spanish-American War (1898) Storey helped form the Anti-Imperialist League, an organization opposing American annexation of the Philippines, and assumed its presidency in 1905. Though the League declined in importance, he continued to champion Philippine independence, and also to attack American intervention in the Caribbean, until his death. Storey was also deeply concerned with the problems of racial discrimination, suffered most notably by African-Americans. His major work in the field of civil rights came in 1909 when he became the first president of the newly organized National Association for the Advancement of Colored People. Thereafter he played a major role in NAACP litigation before the Supreme Court, winning notable victories in decisions striking down the "grandfather clause" (*Guinn* v. *U.S.,* 1915), prohibiting statutory segregation of residential areas (*Buchanan* v. *Warley,* 1917), and protecting criminal trials against mob intimidation (*Moore* v. *Dempsey,* 1923).

In addition to numerous pamphlets and articles, his published works include *Charles Sumner* (1900), *Ebenezer Rockwood Hoar* (1911, with E. W. Emerson), *The Reform of Legal Procedure* (1911), *Problems of Today* (1920), and *The Conquest of the Philippines* (1926, with Marcial P. Lichauco).

⊗∞∞

An eminent and prosperous lawyer, moving in the most distinguished circles of his time, Storey would seem to be the very model of the proper Bostonian. Sociable and unfailingly cheerful—"There was no better dinner-table comrade in town," one of his friends recalled—he retained the affection of men of widely varying persuasions. Yet his passionate immersion in the causes in which he believed led him in independent, isolated, and—to many of these same men—eccentric directions. That a man of his respectability could see himself as an agitator and identify with the abolitionists of his childhood is less surprising than it might seem, and was made possible by two developments during his lifetime.

Disciple of the antislavery politicians who founded the Republican party, Storey had expected that he too would hold public office; yet so swift were the changes in American politics that by the time he was embarking on his career many of these men were ending their lives in political isolation. Thus, in order to defend the values in which he has been raised, he joined with others to work outside both major political parties in an "independent movement" which emphasized "good government" and laissez-faire.

The values in which Storey had been raised, however, also included anti-imperialism and racial egalitarianism; and those values were threatened at the end of the 19th century, both by the heightened discrimination against black Americans and by the creation of an American empire. Thereafter he devoted his public career to confronting racism and imperialism; and while he never completely abandoned the laissez-faire convictions of his youth, he showed a surprising capacity for intellectual growth when dealing with the problems which concerned him. In the area of civil rights, for example, he began by attacking obvious cases of governmental discrimination but then moved on to broader critiques of legally imposed segregation, and ended his career by challenging areas of discrimination (such as restrictive covenants) long considered beyond the reach of the Fourteenth Amendment. Similarly, in the area of foreign policy, he began by opposing the formal annexation of the Philippines; then he extended his attack by opposing military intervention in the Caribbean; and he concluded by opposing economic exploitation, defining "imperialism" and "self-determination" more broadly than any but a few contemporaries.

Aided by his superior forensic and intellectual abilities and sustained by an invincible optimism, Storey spent much of his life fighting for the values in which he believed and died confident that "the tide of freedom is irresistible." Too often remembered as another of the genteel reformers of the Gilded Age, he deserves to be regarded as one of the pioneers of the civil rights and anti-imperialist movements of the 20th century. See William B. Hixson, Jr., *Moorfield Storey and the Abolitionist Tradition* (1972).

WILLIAM B. HIXSON, JR.

STORY, Joseph (b. Marblehead, Mass., Sept. 18, 1779; d. Cambridge, Mass., Sept. 10, 1845), JURIST, graduated from Harvard in 1798 and was admitted to the bar in 1801. He served in the Massachusetts state legislature (1805–8) and in the U.S. House of Representatives (1808–9). In Congress, although a Jeffersonian Republican, he advocated the repeal of Jefferson's Embargo Act. In 1811 he returned to the Massachusetts legislature, but later that year he was appointed an associate justice of the Supreme Court by President Madison.

On the Court, Story was an ardent nationalist. In the case of *Martin* v. *Hunter's Lessee* (1816), he argued that the Supreme Court had the authority to reverse the decisions of the state courts when a constitutional question was involved. In *Martin* v. *Mott* (1827), he opined that a state had to transfer its power over its militia to the federal government if the president ordered it to do so. Following Chief Justice **John Marshall**'s death (1835), Story became the Court's leading spokesman for a broad interpretation of the Constitution. In the Charles River Bridge case (1837), in which the question before the Court was whether or not rights not explicitly granted by a contract could be inferred from the language of the contract, he dissented from the Court's ruling that contracts must be interpreted narrowly.

Story's opposition to slavery is evidenced in the Amistad case (1819), in which he freed and ordered returned to Africa a number of blacks who had murdered the officers of a slave-running ship. In 1842 he drew up rules providing for equity jurisdiction for the Supreme Court and the circuit courts.

From 1829 until his death, Story was Dane professor of law at Columbia University, where he wrote his *Commentaries on the Constitution of the United States* (3 vols., 1833).

⤬

Kindly, warm, talkative, immensely industrious, Joseph Story labored prodigiously in the formative years of American law to provide firm constitutional doctrines for the new nation and a reliable heritage of private law principles for its inhabitants. Weaned on a Harvard education he revered, fancying himself for a while a poet, and additionally, while still young, adroitly maneuvering on a political tightrope between Republicanism and Federalism, Story was in later years to continue to live a multifaceted life—but one distinctly immersed in the legal culture of the period. First lawyer, then judge, and concurrently to be author and teacher, Story had a unique chance to influence both the era he lived in and the generations that followed.

As Supreme Court justice, Story aligned himself essentially with the established order, whether national in scope or mercantile in nature. His judicial opinions reflect a deference for stable notions of government and law, yet he believed in flexible, timely reform though not radical change. Fulfilling his Supreme Court duties as a traveling circuit court judge, Story was faced with intricate questions of private law. He brought erudition to his task, but his written opinions reveal a pragmatic understanding of the real world that reduced the highly technical rule to a workable standard. As a legal treatise writer, Story reduced narrow categories of law to a manageable system that helped lay the foundation for American variations and nuances. In the process he became an American codifier of sorts, though not in the sense that some Jacksonians would have wished. And finally as teacher, Story played a pivotal role in the transformation of American legal education. By the force of his personality, intellectual capacity, and reputation, he helped summon the educative process out of the drab lawyer's office and into the university classroom, where the study of law became a discipline and not just a poorly supervised foray into complex and often outdated formulas. In all his roles, Joseph Story was a guiding influence in the Americanization of the legal process in the young republic. See Gerald T. Dunne, *Justice Joseph Story and the Rise of the Supreme Court* (1971).

ALFRED S. KONEFSKY

STOWE, Harriet Elizabeth Beecher (b. Litchfield, Conn., June 14, 1811; d. Hartford, Conn., July 1, 1896), WRITER, REFORMER, attended schools in Litchfield and Hartford, Connecticut, before moving to Cincinnati in 1832, where her father was president of Lane Theological Seminary. In 1836 she married Calvin E. Stowe, a professor of biblical literature at Lane. During this time she also wrote sketches for the *Western Monthly Magazine.*

In 1850 she and her husband returned to New England when he became a professor at Bowdoin College. Although she was never an abolitionist, the passage of the Fugitive Slave Act (1850), which she called an "abomination," infuriated her. She published a number of serialized stories (1851–52) in the *National Era*, an antislavery

newspaper located in Washington, D.C. These were collected and published in 1852 under the title *Uncle Tom's Cabin*. The work was an immediate success: 300,000 copies were sold in a year, and it was translated into many languages. Although she had little firsthand knowledge of slavery or the South, her portrayal of Uncle Tom appealed to the humanitarian and romantic tastes of the period. She did not hurl invectives at the South, but attacked slavery as an institution. Her southerners were kind, whereas the villain (Simon Legree) was northern-born.

Uncle Tom's Cabin was severely criticized by southerners, who argued that Stowe had distorted plantation life. She responded to her critics in *A Key to Uncle Tom's Cabin* (1853), much of the material for which was inspired by **T. D. Weld**'s *American Slavery as It Is* (1839). She then traveled to England, where she was warmly greeted. In 1856 she published another antislavery novel, *Dred: A Tale of the Great Dismal Swamp.*

Following the Civil War Stowe published many short sketches for the *Atlantic Monthly*, the New York *Independent*, and the *Christian Union*. Her story "The True Story of Lady Byron's Life," published in the September 1869 issue of the *Atlantic Monthly*, caused an international furor when she charged Lord Byron with having had a love affair with his sister. In *Lady Byron Vindicated* (1870), she renewed her charge and added that a child was born as a result of this incestuous affair. Some of her other works include *The Minister's Wooing* (1859), *The Pearl of Orr's Island* (1862), and *Oldtown Folks* (1869), all of which have a New England background.

⁕⁕⁕

Harriet Beecher Stowe was influenced by social and family factors to write the work that shook the country, as well as other writings which *Uncle Tom's Cabin* overshadowed. Her father's hearty Calvinism and her husband's thoughtful religious learning created in her a seamless fabric of Puritan duty and morality impressive to her readers. Her warm personal odyssey as daughter and wife filled her with anecdotes, nuances of language and deportment, scenes, and concerns absorbing to the common man and woman. It is too rarely noted that Stowe not only treated African-American characters as human beings, but treated men and women with democratic impartiality. She had, indeed, little experience with slavery. The main events influencing her were a brief visit to a Kentucky plantation, and her beloved brother **Henry Ward Beecher**'s visit to New Orleans and to the Red River. But she grew with the subject as did her contemporaries, picking up their discriminations and translating them into scenes which agitated northern and southern readers. Richard Hildreth preceded her in antislavery fiction with his *The Slave; or Memoirs of Archy Moore* (1836), but though it was esteemed by abolitionists, it lacked the vivid portrayals and human crises which Stowe's epochal novel attained. There can be no doubt that fugitive slave times and gathering tension contributed to *Uncle Tom's Cabin's* compulsive success, but these facts do not wholly explain why all her fiction has received admiring analyses.

The stroke of genius which impelled Stowe to paint friendly pictures of southern slaveholders, and to make Simon Legree a degraded offspring of Puritanism, has often been noted. Her natural ability to limn types and their relationships requires emphasis. Although she did not begin serious authorship until she was past forty, her letters reveal her strong and ready grasp of persons and events. The ease with which she reproduced conversations and noted individual peccadilloes gave some of her correspondence the character of fiction. Awareness of her talent caused her husband and relatives to encourage her writing. The intense feeling created in the North as a result of the Fugitive Slave Law released her pen and resulted in a novel which, although it roused tears and anger because of the fate of Uncle Tom and other ill-used blacks, unconsciously reassured sympathetic readers by proposing African colonization for blacks. Her 1856 novel *Dred*, also successful, further reflected the gathering antisouthern feeling of the North by treating black insurrectionists as justified in their appeal to arms.

Much comment respecting these works centered on the question of whether or not they were tracts or literature. It aids perspective to perceive Stowe as a pioneer of and significant figure in the local-color school of literature. Her fiction ranged in time from colonial scenes to the then present, and in substance from theological controversies to the homeliest of her recollections or knowledge of the towns and characters of changing America. Although Stowe's world renown doubtless aided their circulation, the response of readers was that accorded such other local-color artists as **John Greenleaf Whittier,** Mary N. Murfree, and Sarah O. Jewett. It has been conjectured that the international storm over *Lady Byron Vindicated* damaged Stowe's reputation, but it probably did no more than deprive her of the special status given her for *Uncle Tom's Cabin*. See Joan D. Hedrick, *Harriet Beecher Stowe: A Life* (1995).

LOUIS FILLER

STRAUSS, Levi (b. Buttenheim, Bavaria, Feb. 26, 1829; d. San Francisco, Calif., Sept. 26, 1902), BUSINESS LEADER, immigrated to the United States in 1847. He became a notions peddler in Lexingon, Kentucky, and in 1848 joined his two brothers in New York City. In 1853, Strauss moved to San Francisco, California, to join his brother-in-law, David Stern, who had established a dry goods business there in 1850. In the flourishing gold-rush economy of the West, Strauss developed a thriving trade in a wide range of clothing.

Approached by Nevada tailor Jacob W. Davis with an idea for riveting the pocket corners of pants for extra strengh, Strauss patented the process with Davis in 1873. The name "Levi's" and the double bow pattern stitched on the hip pockets were copyrighted the same year.

Levi Strauss & Co. became one of the principal clothing manufacturers in the country, with sales of over $2 million even during the depression of 1873. Strauss, who never married, eventually turned the business over to two nephews but he remained active in municipal and philanthropic activities. He served as a director of the

California Immigrant Union, the Nevada Bank, the San Francisco Gas Co., and the Union Trust. He contributed to the Eureka Benevolent Society, established twenty-eight scholarships at the University of California, and provided support to Jewish, Protestant, and Roman Catholic orphanages. At his death, he left over $6 million, much of it to charity, and was described in San Francisco obituaries as "a pioneer merchant and philanthropist."

—◦◦◦—

Levi Strauss was a prime example of the opportunity America offered enterprising Europeans at the turn of the century. A Jewish immigrant at seventeen with no trade and almost no English, he was to become a merchant prince and an honored philanthropist.

Strauss carried canvas to sell for tents and Conestoga wagon covers when he left New York for San Francisco in 1853, and, observing the need for sturdy work pants among the miners, he had a tailor make some from this fabric. These prototypes of modern jeans were so popular that Strauss soon exhausted his stock of canvas, and he turned to denim and duck cloth. When he added copper rivets to reinforce the pocket corners in 1873, the garment became the most popular work pants in the West among miners, teamsters, cowboys, and lumberjacks.

During the next three decades Levi Strauss & Co. abandoned retailing and focused on wholesaling and manufacture, offering a range of dry goods but focusing on its line of indigo-dyed, riveted denim work clothes. Known for his generous treatment of employees, as well for his extensive personal charities, Strauss was one of the most respected and beloved merchants in the West as well as one of the most properous. The firm he started was and continues to be a pioneer in equal opportunity employment.

Strauss promoted and popularized a style which was to revolutionize men's work and leisure wear. In addition to the world's most widely known style of trousers, he provided a model of personal initiative, merchandising vision, and social responsibility. See Ed Cray,

Levi's: The Shrink-to-Fit Business that Stretched to Cover the World (1978).

DENNIS WEPMAN

STRAVINSKY, Igor (b. Oranienbaum, Russia, June 17, 1882; d. New York, N.Y., April 6, 1971), COMPOSER, was the son of the leading basso of the St. Petersburg opera. Though he early revealed talent for music, Igor was directed to law study, but while attending the University of St. Petersburg he was encouraged by Rimsky-Korsakov to pursue his musical education with private tutors and self-study. Under Rimsky-Korsakov's influence and direction, Stravinsky completed his first symphony, and a song cycle for mezzo soprano and orchestra (*Le Faune et la Bergère*), publicly performed in St. Petersburg on February 29, 1908. Meanwhile, in 1905, he decided to concentrate exclusively on composition, though he had already completed law study. Two orchestral works, *Scherzo Fantastique* (1908) and *Feu d'artifice* (1908), performed in St. Petersburg on February 6, 1909, attracted the interest of Serge Diaghilev, a promoter of the arts who was then planning the founding of the Ballet Russe. Diaghilev drew Stravinsky into his artistic orbit, and had him prepare music for productions by the Ballet Russe which first brought Stravinsky world fame: *L'Oiseau de feu* (1910), *Petrouchka* (1911), and *Le Sacre du Printemps* (1913).

In 1919 Stravinsky left Russia. He lived in Paris for the next two decades, and became a French citizen. Subjected to the influence of French culture, he sought greater clarity, objectivity, precision, and refinement in his writing. In 1939 Stravinsky abandoned France to establish permanent residence in Hollywood, California; he became an American citizen in 1945. In America his French manner of writing was replaced by expressionism and abstraction. Most of Stravinsky's major works, beginning with the *Canticum Sacrum ad Honorem Sancti Marci Nominis* (1956), were based on either religious or biblical subjects and were in a serial technique. Now a world figure, he was the recipient of numerous honors, including the gold medal of the Royal Philharmonic in London in

1954, the Sibelius gold medal in 1955, the Sonning Foundation of Denmark international award in 1960, and the international Sibelius award in 1963. Stravinsky combined his career as composer with a highly successful one as conductor, principally of his own compositions.

Stravinsky was an omnivorous reader of literature, a devotee of art, and was passionately concerned with science, politics, and philology. A precisionist, his life was meticulously ordered, with set times for composing, relaxation, entertaining friends and visitors, attending to his business affairs, doing physical exercises, and going daily to his doctor. Though sick and old, he left California in 1970, embittered that Los Angeles had never given him the tribute he felt he deserved, but died in New York only one week after arriving there.

———— ∞ ————

No composer so dominated the world of 20th-century music as did Igor Stravinsky for more than fifty years, and few composers have so deeply influenced their contemporaries. Three times in his career Stravinsky embarked on a new phase of creativity, and in each instance (though more forcefully in the first two than in the third) his impact upon younger composers was cataclysmic. After his apprentice years, when he had been tied ideologically and stylistically to the Russian schools of Rimsky-Korsakov and Tchaikovsky, he struck a path of his own by initiating the neoprimitive movement that radically changed the course of music. This neoprimitive phase included, together with his three ballets for Diaghilev already mentioned, *Le Chant du Rossignol*—which exists in three versions, as an opera (1914), a ballet (1914), and a tone poem (1917)—and the cantata, *Les Noces* (1917). During this period of his career, Stravinsky rejected postromanticism for music in which the dynamic, elemental forces of primitive music were combined with sophisticated structures. Rhythm displaced melody as a basic element, with changing meters, polymeters, polyrhythms, and displaced accents predominating, and with percussion instruments given prominence. Melodic lines

were built from fragments, often consisting of a few repeated notes producing a hypnotic effect. Emphasis was placed on contrasting dynamics and sonorities. Discords and polytonality injected brutal strength.

At first, the world of music was horrified; audiences and critics were vituperative; the premiere of *Le Sacre du Printemps* caused one of the greatest scandals in the history of musical performances. The power and originality of this music demanded familiarity, and familiarity brought admiration, then adulation and imitation. Then, after settling in Paris, Stravinsky once again caused a major upheaval in music by abandoning the style that had made him the most provocative and influential composer of his time for another that was in direct opposition to it. Turning away from his former concern with complex rhythmic and metrical structures, orgiastic sounds, discords, and pulverized melodic materials within spacious structures, Stravinsky embarked upon neoclassicism in which he reverted to the structures of the baroque era without abandoning 20th-century vocabulary. Within such formal designs as the symphony, the concerto, the concerto grosso, the sonata, the oratorio, the mass, and the opera buffa, his writing became lean and spare, more concerned with contrapuntal procedures than with rhythmic ones, and with replacing pictorial or programmatic writing with abstract music. After the *Octet* (1923), with which he entered upon neoclassicism, his principal works in this style included the *Piano Concerto* (1924), the opera-oratorio, *Oedipus Rex* (1927), the ballet, *Apollon Musagète* (1928), the *Symphony of Psalms* (1930), the *Violin Concerto* (1931), the melodrama, *Perséphone* (1934), *Dumbarton Oaks*, a concerto for sixteen instruments (1938), the *Symphony in C* (1940), the *Symphony in Three Movements* (1945), the *Mass* (1948) and the opera buffa, *The Rake's Progress* (1951).

The Rake's Progress, modeled after Mozart, was Stravinsky's last work in the neoclassic style. Beginning with the *Cantata on Four Poems by Anonymous English Poets* (1952) and continuing with the *Septet* (1952), he adopted the twelve-tone technique developed by **Arnold Schoenberg,** from which he progressed to serialism, an extension of the twelve-tone technique. To that idiom he remained faithful for the rest of his life. This radical change of course was dictated by the conviction that he had exhausted all the potential of neoclassicism and now had to adopt a new set of musical principles. Strangely, all his life Stravinsky had expressed opposition to Schoenberg and the twelve-tone system. Now, past seventy, he embraced dodecaphony passionately, a change that caused as much shock in the music world as when in the early 1920s he had left neoprimitivism for neoclassicism. Among his last works were the ballet *Agon* (1957), the choral works *Threni* (1958), *Abraham and Isaac* (1963), and the *Requiem Canticles* (1966), and the *Variations for Orchestra* (1965). Whether one accepts the artistic validity of Stravinsky's last works or not, and many do not, he remained a highly influential figure, with many of the younger composers ready and willing to follow his lead. See Arnold Dobrin, *Igor Stravinsky; His Life and Times* (1969).

DAVID EWEN

STRONG, Benjamin (b. Fishkill-on-Hudson, N.Y., Dec. 22, 1872; d. New York, N.Y., Oct. 16, 1928), BANKER, graduated from high school in 1891 and went to work as a clerk for Jesup, Paton and Co., private bankers in New York City. Soon he was managing the investments of the firm's British clients. In 1900 he became assistant secretary of the Atlantic Trust Co., and in 1904, secretary of the recently organized Bankers' Trust Co. During the panic of 1907, when **J. P. Morgan** worked to solve the crisis, Strong headed the subcommittee which determined which banks and trust companies could be saved.

Strong became vice president of Bankers' Trust in 1909, and played a role in promoting Senator **Nelson W. Aldrich**'s plan for a National Reserve Association. In 1914, despite his earlier opposition to some provisions of the Federal Reserve Act, he was elected the first governor of the Federal Reserve Bank of New York. Although there was some question about who should be superior, the chairman or the governor, Strong quickly emerged as the chief executive officer. During his tenure as governor (1914–28), he initiated open market operations as a means of regulating the volume of credit. He formed and headed the governors' investment committee that was established in 1922 to centralize open market operations. He also was active in the international money market. He worked closely with Montagu Norman, governor of the Bank of England, and conferred frequently with the heads of the Bank of France and the German Reichsbank. In 1924 and again in 1927, Strong lent his support to easy money policies in the U.S. in order to help restore and maintain Great Britain's gold standard.

❦

Benjamin Strong was the most innovative central banker in American history, rivaled in importance only by **Nicholas Biddle.** His energy, knowledge of banking, and willingness to change his ideas and opinions in the light of experience explain his distinguished banking career. His position as governor of the New York Bank and the open market committee and his powerful personality enabled him to dominate the Federal Reserve System from 1914 until shortly before his death from tuberculosis.

Strong was active in international money management, but his principal accomplishments were his innovations in Federal Reserve philosophy and objectives. Originally the System was designed to prevent banking crises. Its creators believed that the economy would act well if the world adhered to the gold standard and if the commercial banks confined their activities to making short-term, self-liquidating, commercial loans. Central banks should merely provide liquidity for the commercial banks, and raise or lower rediscount rates when gold flowed out and in. It never occurred to the founders of the System to try to influence the level of business activity, income, and prices.

At first, Strong followed the orthodox testament, but in the early twenties he became convinced that it could no longer work because the world was no longer willing to accept its basic premises. Under his guidance, the System abandoned its reliance on the reserve ratio as a policy guide and shifted to reliance on indexes of business activity, interest rates, the extent of speculative activity, and such. Thus discretionary judgment replaced the rules of orthodox central banking. As time passed, a further change apparently occurred in Strong's thinking. He appeared to pay more attention to the desirability of a steadily increasing money supply. He certainly came to believe that the Federal Reserve, by judicious use of open market policy, could stop any panic and prevent any serious depression.

Strong often disagreed with the Treasury and with politicians who knew less about banking than they thought they knew, and he was often in conflict with members of the Federal Reserve Board who resented his dominance. His philosophy and objectives also presented problems. A thriving domestic economy took top priority, but he also wanted international monetary stability and an absence of domestic speculation. Thus he was confronted by the conflicts of interest that have continually plagued central bank policy. It is impossible to encourage business while discouraging speculation, and attempts to maintain international monetary stability often result in undesired domestic inflation or deflation.

But when decisions had to be made, Strong acted to maintain domestic prosperity. In the opinion of many scholars, the Depression of the 1930s would have been little more than a 1927-type recession if Strong had been able to maintain his health through 1929. See Lester V. Chandler, *Benjamin Strong: Central Banking* (1958).

HERMAN E. KROOSS

STRONG, Josiah (b. Naperville, Ill., Jan. 19, 1847; d. New York, N.Y., April 28, 1916), RELIGIOUS LEADER, graduated from Western Reserve College in 1869, then studied at Lane Theological Seminary in Cincinnati. He was ordained a Congregationalist minister and took his first pulpit in Cheyenne, Wyoming, in 1871. In 1873 he returned to Western Reserve as chaplain and instructor of theology; in 1876 he accept-

ed a pastorate in Sandusky, Ohio; in 1881 he became secretary of the Congregational Home Missionary Society for Ohio and other states; and in 1884 he was appointed minister of the Central Congregational Church in Cincinnati.

In 1885 Strong published his famous book *Our Country*, which mirrored the thoughts and ideology of late 19th-century American Protestantism. This book stressed the missionary duty of the American people to "purify" their own country and then to spread this zeal throughout the world. It advocated many Social Darwinist ideas and implied the superiority of the Anglo-Saxon race over all others. It also anticipated **Frederick Jackson Turner**'s ideas about the impact of the closing American frontier on American life. *Our Country*, which sold half a million copies in twenty years, earned Strong a DD from Lane Seminary and a job as general secretary of the American Evangelical Alliance in New York City. He hoped to use this position to advance the Social Gospel, a belief which, stressing the social and pragmatic implications of Christianity, called for good works and social reform.

Strong resigned from the Evangelical Alliance in 1898 and founded the League for Social Service, reorganized in 1902 as the American Institute of Social Service. As president of this organization, he lectured, wrote, and traveled extensively. His other publications include: *The Twentieth Century City* (1898), *The Next Great Awakening* (1902), and *Our World: The New World Life* (1913).

⁂

Strong's restless energy found fulfillment best in his later career as an evangelical reformer and popular author. Although an early exponent of the Social Gospel, he was not as radical as those clergymen like W. D. P. Bliss and **Walter Rauschenbusch** who espoused a complete Christian Socialism. Historically Strong was most significant for his ardent, often jingoistic, support of American expansionism. He was confident that the Anglo-Saxon race, the divine depository of the principles of Christianity and civil liberty, was destined to spread over the earth. As the principal home of this race, the center of its coming power and influence, the United States had the responsibility to assume leadership in the competition of races for world supremacy.

Although Strong's vision was utopian, his catalog of evils to be eliminated, and remedies to be imposed if the United States was to achieve its goal, was more sober and specific. The chief dangers to the nation's future stemmed from unrestricted mass immigration, Catholicism, Mormonism, intemperance, socialism, urbanism, excessive wealth, and materialism. The missionary movement, for which he constantly appealed for additional funds, had the function to correct or alleviate these ills. Only then could the country begin to cope with the problems raised by the close of the frontier and rise of the city. A tireless advocate of his ideas, Strong expressed the optimism characteristic of the Progressive Era. The racial and religious bigotry implied by his old-line Protestant hostility to Roman Catholic and immigrant influences, though tempered by Christian ethics, remained nevertheless the foundation of his messianic belief in the world wide expansion of American civilization. See Jurgen Herbst, Editor's Introduction to Strong's *Our Country* (1963).

ARTHUR A. EKIRCH

STUART, Gilbert (b. North Kingstown, R.I., Dec. 3, 1755; d. Boston, Mass., July 9, 1828), ARTIST, demonstrated a talent for drawing early in life. His first formal instruction in painting came from an itinerant painter, Cosmo Alexander, who persuaded the boy to return to Edinburgh with him. After Alexander's death in 1772, Stuart returned to America, but in 1775 went back to England, where **Benjamin West,** a celebrated portraitist and painter of historical subjects, took him into his home as a pupil and assistant for five years. While a member of the West household, Stuart received a request for a portrait from one William Grant, a young man with political ambitions. On the day of Grant's sitting the weather was so cold that the two impulsively decided to go ice skating. When they returned Stuart began to paint, and the resulting *Portrait of a Gentleman Skating,* exhibited in 1782,

was a popular success. For several years thereafter he painted fashionable people for high fees and exhibited regularly at the Royal Academy, but his lavish living style left him in poor financial condition. In 1778 he moved to Ireland, but did not change his ways; by 1792 his financial situation was desperate. In that year he returned to America for the express purpose of painting and selling as many pictures as possible of George Washington, the national hero and first president of the new federal government.

It is as Washington's portraitist that Stuart is best known. He received during his life a total of thirty-nine requests for copies of his first Washington painting (the "Vaughan" type), done in 1795. The second was a life-size, standing portrait of Washington (the "Lansdowne" portrait). About the same time Stuart painted a bust portrait of the left side of Washington's face (the "Atheneum" type), eyes facing front, which Stuart apparently liked so much that he deliberately left the stock and coat unfinished so that he would not have to deliver it. Still among the painter's effects at his death, it is the most famous of all of Stuart's paintings of Washington, and one of the most frequently reproduced paintings of all time.

The Washington portraits had been painted in Philadelphia, the interim capital, and in Germantown, Pennsylvania. In 1803 Stuart moved to Washington, the new capital, where in two years he painted a considerable gallery of portraits of the leaders of the new nation, most notably of Jefferson, Madison, and Monroe. In 1805 he returned to Boston, where he lived the rest of his life. His financial improvidence continued, however, and he died insolvent.

⁂

In London, the center of the art world for colonial Americans seriously interested in learning to paint, Gilbert Stuart discarded his early, wooden, provincial style as he acquired a far more fashionable, brilliant, almost magic touch in portraiture. Beneath the flashy brushwork, however, his head-and-shoulder likenesses remain as solid and dignified as neoclassical portrait busts in marble, although his style of painting and use of color always give his subjects greater warmth and life.

What distinguished Stuart from his older countrymen in London, Benjamin West and **John Singleton Copley,** was the fact that he never desired to paint "history pictures" in the grand tradition of the artist-as-a-philosopher. Instead, he admitted to being merely a face painter. Untroubled by higher ambitions, Stuart obviously loved the basic challenge of portraiture—to capture on canvas the essential characteristics of a sitter as quickly and as accurately as possible. Once the face was well painted, however, Stuart rapidly lost interest in what he considered the more menial tasks of finishing the costume and the background surrounding the likeness. For this reason full-length portraits are relatively rare in his oeuvre, and a number of his smaller canvases were left unfinished.

Money was a constant concern for Stuart, since he liked to live above his means. In moving to Ireland for a period of five years and then in returning to the United States, he may have kept a step or two ahead of his creditors, but he was also opening up new territories in which he would be the finest and most sought after portraitist available. His income did not suffer from competition with less talented artists.

With his initial portraits and then numerous copies of *George Washington,* Stuart became the closest thing in America to a court painter. He actually followed the seat of the new government from New York, to Philadelphia, to Washington, D.C., serving as the chief portrait painter for the Federalist aristocracy and thereby leaving a social chronicle of the age in his pictures.

As a man, Stuart was always extremely generous with others and sometimes overindulgent with himself. He liked to wear fine clothes and to entertain lavishly. His astonishing gifts as a painter were matched by his natural talents as a raconteur. He sometimes stretched the truth beyond the point of recognition in telling or retelling a story about himself, but to hear his brilliant and charming conversation was one of the keenest pleasures of sitting for a portrait by Stuart.

As an artist, Gilbert Stuart had a significant effect on American art well into the 19th century. The example of his international success was another proof that the young Republic could produce artists of the highest caliber, and the technical brilliance of his pictures served as a source of inspiration for younger men to copy. Stuart's willingness to give sound and patient advice to all those who sought his aid made him the patriarch of American painting until his death in 1828, and his influence lived on in his pupils. See William T. Whitley, *Gilbert Stuart* (1932).

ELLWOOD C. PARRY III

STUART, James Ewell Brown (b. Patrick Co., Va., Feb. 6, 1833; d. Richmond, Va., May 12, 1864), MILITARY LEADER, attended Emory and Henry College (1848–50) before entering the U.S. Military Academy in 1850. After graduating in 1854, he was commissioned a second lieutenant. In March 1855 he was transferred to the 1st Cavalry and spent the next six years in Kansas (first lieutenant, 1855). He served as **Robert E. Lee**'s aide at Harpers Ferry in the suppression of **John Brown** and his followers (1859). Following Virginia's secession from the Union, Stuart resigned from the U.S. army to join the Confederacy.

Stuart was commissioned a lieutenant colonel of the Virginia infantry and a captain of the Confederate cavalry (1861). At the First Battle of Bull Run (1861) he protected the Confederate left, contributing to the Confederate victory with a well-timed charge. In September 1861 he was promoted to brigadier general. After participating in the Confederate withdrawal to the Chickahominy, Stuart was sent on a reconnaissance mission by General Lee to locate the right flank of **George B. McClellan**'s army (1862). During the battle of Second Bull Run (Aug. 1862), he raided General Pope's headquarters and brought back documents which enabled Lee to discover the position and strength of the Union forces. During the Maryland campaign (Sept. 1862), Stuart, now a major general, defended one of the passes at South Mountain, thus enabling

Lee to concentrate on McClellan's forces. At Fredericksburg (Dec. 1862), he helped check an attack on **Thomas "Stonewall" Jackson**'s forces. After Jackson was killed at Chancellorsville (May 1863), Stuart temporarily took command of the 2d Corps. However, hoping to interpose his cavalry between the Union army and Washington, D.C. before joining General Lee in Pennsylvania, Stuart was delayed for a number of days. This delay had an adverse effect on Lee's movement at Gettysburg (July 1863), since it deprived Lee of information on Union troop movements. When General **Philip H. Sheridan,** commander of the cavalry of the Army of the Potomac, headed for Richmond (May 9, 1864), Stuart was fatally wounded at the battle of Yellow Tavern (May 11).

"Jeb" Stuart looked best on a horse. Nearly 6 feet tall, he weighed 180 pounds. A flaring brown beard and mustache covered much of his face. Dressed in white buckskin gauntlets, a silk saber sash, gold spurs, with an ostrich feather in his hat, and a scarlet-lined cloak, he was an impressive figure. "I was much amused to see Stuart pass ... with a large cavalcade of staff and couriers and two bugles blowing most furiously," wrote an officer. Stuart was always on parade. "It was impossible to take him all in," noted an observer. Between battles Stuart liked gaiety, beautiful girls, and dances. He wore a red rose in his jacket and covered his horse with garlands of flowers. Practical jokes delighted him; he laughed much, enjoyed singing, and wrote execrable poetry. About him gathered an entourage of oddities, including Sweeny, his banjo player, and the giant Prussian Heros von Borcke.

Critics denounced Stuart as a vain and reckless exhibitionist. He was that and more. Ostentatious and boyish in his need for praise, he was nevertheless an outstanding raider and reconnaissance officer. As the "eyes and ears" of Lee's army, Stuart had the difficult task of screening the Confederates while he located enemy forces and determined their movements. This he usually did well, for he was a good observer with tremendous energy and endurance. Most of his

mistakes were the results of his boldness. His absence from the main army on a raid during much of the Gettysburg campaign forced Lee to fight blindly. Perhaps Lee, who understood his cavalry chief's character, should have given Stuart fewer discretionary orders. That "zealous, ardent, brave & devoted soldier," as Lee called Stuart, needed from his superiors both praise and control. See Burke Davis, *Jeb Stuart, the Last Cavalier* (1957).

GRADY MCWHINEY

STUYVESANT, Peter (b. Friesland, Neth., c. 1600; d. New York, N.Y., Feb. 1672), POLITICAL LEADER, studied for a short time at the University of Franeker. After several years in the service of the Dutch West India Co., including a tour of duty in Brazil in 1635, he went to the Leeward Islands as governor of Curaçao. While leading a military force against the Island of St. Martin in 1644, Stuyvesant was shot in the right leg, which had to be amputated. He was fitted with an artificial leg which, with its silver ornaments, became his most familiar feature. In 1646 Stuyvesant was appointed director-general of the colony of New Netherland. Arriving in May 1647, he began an energetic policy of strengthening the settlement's defenses, expelling Spanish trespassers, driving the Swedes from the Delaware (1655) and annexing that territory, and concluding the Treaty of Hartford (1650) with the English, which established the boundary between the Dutch colony and Connecticut. At the same time Stuyvesant, a member of the Dutch Reformed Church, sought to enforce the strict observance of the Sabbath and to forbid the sale of liquor after 9 P.M. He also tried to suppress the Lutheran Church and to withhold civil rights from Jews. In 1650 he bought the Bouwerie, a farm along the East River.

Stuyvesant's policies produced growing dissent. Although he appointed a Board of Nine to deliberate the affairs of the colony in 1647, by 1649 the residents were demanding an independent municipal form of government. Their demands were granted for New Amsterdam in

1653. The English occupied the colony in 1664, and Stuyvesant, who had surrendered New Netherland without a fight, felt called upon to go to the Netherlands in 1665 to defend his actions. Returning to America in 1667, he spent the rest of his life quietly on his farm.

———— ✺ ————

Peter Stuyvesant was essentially a difficult man thrust into a difficult position. Quick-tempered, self-confident, and authoritarian, he was determined as governor, or director-general, of New Netherland to rule firmly and to repair the fortunes of the company. The company, however, had run the colony solely for trade profits, with scant attention to encouraging immigration and developing local government. Stuyvesant's predecessors in office had been dishonest or, at best, inept, so there was no tradition of respect and support for the governorship on which he could build. Furthermore, the colonists were vocal and quick to challenge authority. Stuyvesant's very industriousness and identity with the interests of the company set him at odds with the inhabitants almost from the start. Throughout his administration there were constant complaints to the company of his tyrannical acts and pressure for more local self-government. On the other hand, although he had broad executive powers, he could be overruled by the directors of the company in Amsterdam and hence was in the middle. His religious intolerance also exacerbated relations with the colonists, most of whom did not share his narrow outlook.

The colony's external problems were no less a difficult inheritance. The most fundamental of these was the Anglo-Dutch rivalry over trade. Then there were the almost constant difficulties with Native Americans and with the boundaries of neighboring colonies. New Netherland was actually a series of little posts all spread out, with no exact boundaries. Chronically underpopulated, it was very difficult to defend. The conflicting territorial claims of Sweden were triumphantly erased by Stuyvesant in his most successful diplomatic venture. Relations with Connecticut, however, proved much more difficult. Both Connecticut and New Netherland claimed land in the Connecticut Valley, and English settlers from Connecticut ignored Dutch claims and settled there and on Long Island, which the Dutch West India Company had bought from the Native Americans. Even the Treaty of Hartford, by which Stuyvesant gave up effective claim to the Connecticut Valley and accepted merely a modest portion of Long Island, did not end the problem. Connecticut eventually ignored the treaty, and English settlers within Dutch boundaries agitated against Stuyvesant's rule. Finally in 1664 England decided to take over New Netherland. Stuyvesant's surrender, which came only because the colonists refused to fight, epitomized the twofold problem of the colony: domestic dissatisfaction and overwhelming external pressures. Although he ruled for seventeen years with seriousness of purpose and considerable administrative ability, Peter Stuyvesant survives only as a symbol of impatience, violent language, and imperiousness. See H. H. Kessler and E. Rachlis, *Peter Stuyvesant and His New York* (1959).

ELEANOR BRUCHEY

SULLIVAN, Harry Stack (b. Norwich, N.Y., Feb. 21, 1892; d. Paris, France, Jan. 14, 1949), PSYCHIATRIST, graduated from the Chicago College of Medicine and Surgery (MD) in 1917. During World War I he served on the Board of Examiners for the Medical Corps of the Sixth Service Command Area. In 1919 he became assistant medical officer in the Eighth District headquarters of the Rehabilitation Division of the Federal Board for Vocational Education; he came to Washington, D.C., in 1920 to be chief executive officer of that division. After briefly returning to Chicago, Sullivan began psychiatric study at Washington's St. Elizabeths Hospital under Dr. William A. White (1922). He did clinical research at the Sheppard and Enoch Pratt Hospital, Towson, Maryland (1923–30), becoming director of clinical research there in 1925. In 1931 he entered private practice in New York City and devoted himself to teaching, writing, and studying psychiatry. He helped establish the William Alanson White Psychiatric Foundation (1933) and the Washington School of Psychiatry, an enterprise of the Foundation (1936). During 1940–41 he was a consultant in psychiatry for the Selective Service System.

While doing research at the Pratt Hospital, Sullivan developed his concept of psychiatry as the study of interpersonal relations. His ideas aroused much debate in psychiatric circles and stimulated many new studies of the relation between social processes and psychiatric disorders. At Pratt, he established what became a celebrated special ward for the treatment of schizophrenics by means of group therapy. He was widely recognized by his colleagues as having removed schizophrenia from the list of "incurable" mental disorders.

Sullivan viewed personality characteristics and psychiatric disorders as interpersonal phenomena, insisting that the notion of a unique, individually formed personality was a myth: each personality was molded by its contact with other personalities throughout life. Similarly, he conceived of infant anxiety as resulting from disturbances in the child's relations with the mother figure; children develop in response to this a "self-dynamism" which serves to guide their future behavior in a manner calculated to avoid further disturbances and thus reduce anxiety. He also asserted that such anxiety tends to retard or preclude tendencies toward social integration or close interpersonal relations. He devoted the last years of his life to applying his theories of interpersonal relations to the study of tensions in international relations.

―――∞∞∞―――

Sullivan grew up as a lonely farm boy, and his sense of isolation was underlined in his own mind by his belonging, as he recalled, to the only Roman Catholic family in the community. In his later work, and as symbolic leader of a large group of thinkers concerned with the interactions of one person with another, he more than made up for his youthful failure to establish normal peer group relationships. Throughout his career, however, and despite his wit and considerable charm, Sullivan was often in contention with professional colleagues. His persuasiveness grew out of his almost uncanny sense of how to handle a patient, especially a psychotic patient. This practical clinical prescience won him great influence among many colleagues, and his writings on technique were of particular value to a large number of beginners in psychiatry.

The growth of Sullivan's influence involved particularly four developments of the 1930s and 1940s. First, he was the most eloquent protagonist of the view that even the very gravely afflicted mentally ill can be treated by psychotherapy. Since psychoanalysis was becoming increasingly successful for neuroses, and since no other therapy except shock treatments had shown up for psychoses, Sullivan and other psychotherapists seemed to offer the only hope that psychiatry might be able to cope further with this terrible social problem. Second, a general emphasis on social (as opposed to biological) factors and social environment was growing in science and even in general American culture. Sullivan reflected and in turn validated this social emphasis. Third, mainline American psychiatrists did not get involved in the World War II defense effort early, and for some time Sullivan led the only progressive psychiatric forces trying to make inroads upon military medicine. As psychiatric services grew spectacularly in and after the war, Sullivan and the Sullivanians therefore had disproportionate influence. Finally, Sullivan represented humane, as opposed to hard, science. He utilized facts that everyone knew—such as that an infant and its mother communicate with each other without words—even though no scientific or measurable evidence of the facts existed. This antireductionist element in particular was appealing to both humanistically inclined psychotherapists and colleagues who found the essence of modern science to be complexity and obscurity rather than simplicity and clarity. Sullivan's theoretical statements were in fact not systematic or consistent, but they were often illustrated with clinical material, and thus convincing not only to clinicians but to sociologists and psychologists also. See Clara Thompson, "Introduction," in Harry Stack Sullivan, *Schizophrenia as a Human Process* (1962).

J. C. BURNHAM

SULLIVAN, Louis Henri (b. Boston, Mass., Sept. 3, 1856; d. Chicago, Ill., April 14, 1924), ARCHITECT, was the son of an Irish immigrant who ran a dancing academy in Boston. Entering the Massachusetts Institute of Technology in 1872, he quickly became bored with the formal study of architecture as it was taught by a faculty heavily influenced by the French Ecole des Beaux-Arts. Nevertheless, after working in Chicago with William Le B. Jenney (who designed the first tall steel-skeleton structure), he went to Paris in 1874 and enrolled at the Ecole. Although he appreciated the rational precision of the solutions produced by the Beaux-Arts system, he objected to the nature of the problems being studied and left Paris after a year.

In 1879 Sullivan formed a partnership with Dankmar Adler, a successful Chicago architect. At this time he was seeking a universal law of architecture, one that would allow him to combine delicate, even profuse, ornamentation with a functional design. The largest single commission of Adler and Sullivan was the Auditorium complex, Chicago (1886–89), consisting of an opera house, hotel, and office building. The exterior owes much to the Richardsonian Romanesque style. Sullivan's search for a way to fuse ornamentation and functionalism continued in the Wainwright Building, St. Louis (1891), while his stubborn rejection of the classic revival was dramatically revealed in his Transportation Building at the 1893 Chicago Fair.

The yearning for monumental buildings which produced the classic revival, and the urgent need for a solution to the new problems posed by urban growth and development of new building materials, were irreconcilable. As one of the few architects who realized this (another was a young student of Sullivan's, **Frank Lloyd Wright**), Sullivan found the field of tall building design perfectly attuned to his theories. His most notable results were the Wainwright Building, the Gage Building (1896–99) in Chicago, the Guaranty Building (1894–95) in Buffalo, and the structure for what is now the Carson, Pirie, Scott Co., Chicago (1899–1904).

After Adler broke up their partnership in 1895

(he died in 1900) Sullivan found commissions increasingly difficult to obtain. He leaned heavily on an assistant, George Elmslie, for ideas and work. His fame in these latter years rests primarily on a series of small bank buildings in the Midwest, most notably the National Farmers' Bank, Owatonna, Minnesota (1907–8). In his *The Autobiography of an Idea* (1924), the story of his life and the ideals that guided it, Sullivan summed up this theory of architecture in a simple dictum: "… the function of a building … must predetermine and organize its form."

The significance of Louis Sullivan for American architecture lies primarily in his philosophy and in the pattern of his career. After achieving major success as a designer of commercial buildings in the booming Chicago of the 1880s and 1890s, he was reduced, in the last twenty-four years of his life, to a meager handful of minor commissions. There were complex reasons for this neglect; among them may be mentioned Sullivan's personal arrogance, alcoholism, a disastrous marriage, and the fact that American taste was, in fact, moving in a neoclassic direction with which he had no sympathy whatever. Through these bitter years Sullivan stubbornly maintained his integrity and gave expression to his architectural philosophy in a remarkable series of writings, the most important of which was *Kindergarten Chats* (1905). His vision of architecture was essentially poetic and religious. Part of the irony of his story is that in an age of commercial materialism he saw architecture as an embodiment of man's highest aspirations. His life was therefore both a reproach to his own contemporaries and a stimulus to future generations.

As an architect Sullivan's major achievement was in giving form to the skyscraper. More than any of his contemporaries he understood that the problem of the tall building was to make it *look* tall; his major office buildings of the 1890s are solutions to this easily phrased but extremely difficult problem, and the best of them, such as the Guaranty Building in Buffalo, are remarkable anticipations of 20th-century form. He also understood that the new system of steel cage construction demanded an entirely new architectural expression. In his analysis of the curtain wall, which he saw as the necessary expression of the skeleton frame, he achieved possibly his finest result in the Schlesinger-Mayer Building, now Carson, Pirie, Scott. A structure of almost overwhelming emotional impact, it is still classified by critics as one of the key buildings of the entire modern movement. Though much smaller, some of the late works, notably the Owatonna bank, have much the same quality.

Sullivan's famous motto "Form Follows Function" has been greatly misunderstood. In using this phrase he did not refer to the simplified kind of engineering functionalism advocated by the machine-inspired architects of the 1920s. He meant a spiritual and religious function analogous to that claimed by **Walt Whitman** for his poetry; Sullivan was, in fact, a great admirer of Whitman and for a time corresponded with him. In Sullivan's buildings the imagery is always organic, not mechanistic. Thus the ornament was intended to represent the flowering of the structure, like the blossoms of a plant. Frequently the sources of this ornament may be found in books on botany. Ornamentation was also, especially in Sullivan's late years, an area of personal expression for him. He sensed that the entire process of building was becoming dehumanized, and ornament was for him a kind of signature, a means by which the architect could assert his precious individuality.

The history of Sullivan's reputation is a clue to his importance for American culture. At the time of his death in a third-rate Chicago hotel room, he was poverty-stricken and dependent on the charity of a few close friends and loyal disciples. For the next decade his name was almost forgotten, and the cause for which he had fought appeared lost. Then, in 1935 Hugh Morrison's biography stimulated much interest, and after the hiatus of World War II, there was a spate of publications. In 1952 the American Institute of Architects honored Sullivan with a posthumous gold medal, and in 1956, his centennial year, the Chicago Art Institute staged a major exhibition in his honor. Today he is a kind of folk hero in American architecture, and it is clear that, as Morrison wrote, the lost cause is, in fact, triumphant. See Hugh Morrison, *Louis Sullivan: Prophet of Modern Architecture* (1935).

LEONARD K. EATON

SULLY, Thomas (b. Horncastle, Lincolnshire, Eng., June 8, 1783; d. Philadelphia, Pa., Nov. 5, 1872), ARTIST, came to the U.S. in 1792 and settled in Charleston, South Carolina. Although placed with an insurance broker in order to pursue a business career, he soon showed an interest in art. Encouraged by an older brother, in 1799 Sully moved to Richmond, Virginia, to live with him, and in 1801 they moved to Norfolk, where he painted his first miniature portrait from life (1801). He continued painting in Richmond and Norfolk until 1806, when he moved to New York City. There he painted many influential people. He also met **Gilbert Stuart** and studied with him at his Boston studio (1807). In 1808 Sully settled in Philadelphia.

Financed by a group of merchants, Sully studied in England under **Benjamin West** and the English portrait painter Sir Thomas Lawrence. Upon his return to Philadelphia in 1810 he emerged as one of the most highly regarded American artists of his day. In 1837 he again visited England, commissioned by Philadelphia's Society of the Sons of St. George to paint a full-length portrait of the young Queen Victoria.

At the time of his death, Sully had produced about 2,600 paintings, mostly portraits. A few of his better-known portraits are *Lady with a Harp: Eliza Ridgely* (1818, National Gallery of Art, Washington, D.C.), *Mother and Son* (1840, Metropolitan Museum of Art, N.Y.), and *Marquis de Lafayette* (1824, Independence Hall, Philadelphia). Aside from formal portraiture, his best-known work is the large (12 by 17 feet) *Passage of the Delaware* (1819, Boston Museum of Fine Arts), a "historical portrait" of George Washington, originally commissioned for the North Carolina Capitol but rejected because of its excessive size.

Among American painters of his time, Thomas Sully must be ranked second only to Gilbert Stuart (twenty-eight years his senior) as a practitioner and disseminator of the painterly technique of the contemporary English school. His fluent brushwork and clear color are as characterful as handwriting on the canvas. But the most personal ingredient of his portraiture is a feeling for graceful posturing and romantic idealization of the subject. He was early renowned as *par excellence* the painter of American womanhood (of childhood, too); but also in his best portraits of men he succeeds brilliantly in blending naturalistic vision with an air of "genteel carriage"—as in the handsome full-length *Dr. Samuel Coates* (1812; a gift of the artist to the Pennsylvania Hospital, Philadelphia). However, when carried to extremes, as can happen, his graces become saccharine and his forms insubstantial: a fellow artist, C. R. Leslie, observed, when pressed for criticism, "Your pictures look as if you could blow them away."

Sully's extensive influence as a painter has sometimes been understated. Members of his large family (eight others of the name are listed in Groce and Wallace, *Dictionary of Artists in America*), especially his talented son-in-law John Neagle, and numbers of lesser craftsmen benefited from his personal instruction and from the study of his works.

"A perfect gentleman, a thoroughly pure, good, noble man" (thus feelingly described in a friend's diary), he was one of the most beloved Philadelphians: toward the end of his life the city deferred a street operation to avoid evicting the Sullys from their longtime home at 11 South Fifth Street, just off Chestnut. See Edward Biddle and Mantle Fielding, *The Life and Works of Thomas Sully* (1921).

HAROLD E. DICKSON

SUMNER, Charles (b. Boston, Mass., Jan. 6, 1811; d. Washington, D.C., March 11, 1874), POLITICAL LEADER, received his BA (1830) and LLB (1833) from Harvard. After serving as the reporter of the U.S. circuit court, he lectured at the Harvard Law School (1835–37) and traveled abroad (1837–40). Returning to the U.S., he practiced law and became active in many reforms, including the abolition of slavery, prison reform, and international peace movements. His opposition to the Mexican War led him to help organize the Free-Soil party (1848).

In 1851 Sumner was elected to the U.S. Senate on a Free-Soil–Democratic coalition ticket. He opposed the Fugitive Slave Act of 1850, and in 1852 he introduced a bill to repeal it. Believing also that the Kansas-Nebraska Act (1854) which established the principle of "popular sovereignty" in the territories was immoral (he called Senator **Stephen A. Douglas** of Illinois, the author of the act, the "Sancho Panza" of slavery, "ready to do its humiliating offices"), on May 19, 1856, Sumner made his famous "Crime against Kansas" speech, in which he sharply denounced Senator Andrew P. Butler of South Carolina for his support of slavery. Three days later, Representative Preston Brooks, a kinsman of Butler's, beat Sumner badly with a cane in the Senate chamber, after which Sumner did not return to the Senate until 1859.

After the Civil War broke out, Sumner urged President Lincoln to emancipate the slaves immediately, believing that such a move would end the war. He also argued that the Confederate states had "committed suicide" by seceding, and had forfeited their constitutional rights. While Sumner and Lincoln had many disagreements as to how the war should be prosecuted, they remained friends throughout the conflict; and Sumner was often called to the White House for consultations with the president.

During the Reconstruction period, Sumner was one of the leading Radical Republicans in the Senate. As such he demanded that the freedmen be granted their civil rights before the South could reenter the Union. He also supported the impeachment of President Johnson, asserting that the president was an "enormous criminal" and a menace to the Union. In 1870 Sumner tried to strengthen the Civil Rights Act of 1866 by guaranteeing African-Americans equal rights in places of public accommodation. By 1872 Sumner had modified his views on Reconstruction, and introduced a bill to end the listing of battles between U.S. citizens in the Army Register. The Massachusetts legislature, however, characterized Sumner's bill as "an insult to the loyal soldiers of the nation."

As chairman of the Senate Foreign Relations Committee, Sumner came into conflict with President Grant and his secretary of state, **Hamilton Fish,** by demanding large reparations for damages inflicted on Union vessels by British-built Confederate ships (*Alabama* claims dispute). He also refused to support Grant's attempts to annex Santo Domingo (1870). His friction with Grant led Sumner to support **Horace Greeley,** the Liberal Republican candidate, for the presidency in 1872. In that same year, he was removed as chairman of the Foreign Relations Committee, but he continued serving in the Senate until his death.

———— ∞ ————

In many ways Sumner appeared to be marked for greatness. He was an impressive figure, six feet, two inches tall, and his frame was broad and massive in proportion. His handsome face, with its olive complexion and dark brown eyes, surmounted by long brown locks that slowly turned to iron gray, made him a center of attention at any public spectacle. In addition to these attributes, he was blessed with a thunderous voice and a marvelous memory, an orator in an era when oratory was highly prized. Ambitious, industrious, endowed with a capacity for immense enthusiasms, he made friends easily, being generous in performing services for valued acquaintances on both sides of the Atlantic. Active in the antislavery movement, in efforts to improve prison discipline in Massachusetts, and in the cause of international peace, he was a reformer in an age when, and in a region where, reform had great appeal. During the pre–Civil War era he was a successful politician, utilizing his activities in these good causes to ensure his elevation to the U.S. Senate. There he speedily became a leader of the antislavery members of Congress and a founder of the Republican party.

But not all the omens were favorable for Sumner's continued rise to greatness. His sense of humor was rudimentary, and it early became apparent that his passion for praise was practically without limits. He equated opposition with persecution, and by the time he was thirty it was evident that he was prone to make extreme statements and to abuse those who differed with him. The attack by Preston Brooks accentuated these unfortunate tendencies, for from then on he regarded himself as a martyr in the cause of righteousness, without stain and without reproach.

Sumner found it more and more agreeable to put on the armor of righteousness during the years of the Civil War and Reconstruction. He at first professed to be the real guide of the Lincoln administration in foreign policy, but his extreme antislavery views soon made him dissatisfied with the president and hostile to Secretary of State **William H. Seward.** He accepted the Emancipation Proclamation more because to do so helped his reelection to the Senate than because it was a great step in the destruction of slavery. As chairman of the Senate Committee on Foreign Relations he occasionally exercised considerable influence on governmental policy, but his tactics alienated not only Republican politicians in Congress but also intellectuals and reformers in the country at large. He had some influence on public opinion but had little to do with the actual enactment of the laws that concerned emancipation, civil rights, and the reconstruction of the Union. During the Grant administration he sought to dominate Secretary of State Hamilton Fish in the conduct of foreign policy and became hopelessly at odds with President Grant. Sumner's faults threw his virtues in the shade, but in one respect he outshone practically all his contemporaries. His high-minded views on desegregation and complete civil and political equality for the blacks were not put to the test of practice, but represented ideals that were far in advance of his time. They are his chief claim to fame. See David Donald, *Charles Sumner and the Coming of the Civil War* (1960), and *Charles Sumner and the Rights of Man* (1970).

GLYNDON G. VAN DEUSEN

SUMNER, William Graham (b. Paterson, N.J., Oct. 30, 1840; d. Englewood, N.J., April 12, 1910), SOCIAL SCIENTIST, graduated from Yale in 1863. He then studied in Geneva, Göttingen, and Oxford. He returned to Yale in 1866 as a tutor but decided to become a clergyman. In 1869 he became assistant minister in the Calvary Church of New York, and in 1870 rector of the Church of the Redeemer, Morristown, New Jersey. In 1872 he accepted the newly created chair of political and social science at Yale.

Sumner was a popular teacher and a strong supporter of academic freedom and innovative methods of teaching and study. He divided his scholarship between economics and sociology. As an economist he advocated sound money and free trade. Believing in the sanctity of individual initiative and liberty, Sumner opposed any form of government intervention in business. He believed all life was governed by natural laws; government intervention would only upset nature. As a sociologist Sumner was recognized as one of the leading Social Darwinists of his day. Strongly influenced by the works of Herbert Spencer, he accepted competition for social status and wealth as beneficial, arguing that it led to the elimination of the weak and the preservation of racial soundness. In *The Forgotten Man and Other Essays* (1883) he criticized welfare-state proposals because they imposed burdens on the "forgotten man," the individual who quietly went about his business and asked for no help. Sumner culminated his scholarly work in *Folkways* (1907), which examined social mores and behavior. He was elected president of the American Sociological Society in 1909. His other publications include: *A History of American Currency* (1874), *Protectionism* (1885), and *The Financier and Finances of the Revolution* (1892).

A teacher, scholar, and essayist of uncommon force, Sumner schooled a long generation of Americans in the stern lessons of Social Darwinism. More skillfully than any contemporary, he tied evolutionary imperatives back into the durable fabric of Yankee puritanism, until the struggle of fit men to survive acquired for his audience all the moral drama of a quest for secular salvation, and the poverty of the unfit became a penalty for lack of diligence. Launching his career at a time when social science was still enmeshed in the precepts of moral philosophy, he not only sought to vindicate the truths of classical economics but did much to shape the early structure of sociology as an academic discipline. Dour, righteous, and dogmatic, he was ever scornful of soft euphemisms and wishful thinking, among which he included the doctrines of the natural rights tradition and the notion that all men were created equal. Inequality, expressed in the ability of some men to accumulate substantial wealth by frugal living and hard work, was for him the mainspring of material progress in a society of open competition. His essays championed the autonomous individual, whether personified in the gilded millionaire or in Sumner's long-suffering hero, the Forgotten Man, a figure apparently modeled after his own father. He was caustic in denouncing political measures which promised to damage the integrity of private property and the family, the twin values of an achieving middle class. He assailed socialism, plutocracy, tariff protection, and imperialism as looming threats to his vision of sane government. No flabby apologist for the status quo, Sumner never resolved the tension between his scholarly determinism and his bent for moral polemics. To a society on the make, he offered harsh and rigorous prescriptions. See Harris E. Starr, *William Graham Sumner* (1925).

GEOFFREY BLODGETT

SWIFT, Gustavus Franklin (b. Sandwich, Mass., June 24, 1839; d. Chicago, Ill., March, 29, 1903), BUSINESS LEADER, left the family farm to become a butcher. Buying live cattle was the most important phase of a butcher's work in the days of locally slaughtered meat, and Swift developed exceptional skill in judging beef cattle. By 1875 he was operating a cattle-buying firm in Chicago, from which the animals were shipped live to eastern markets. Realizing the inefficiencies of this method, Swift determined to ship dressed beef. At first such shipments, made in ordinary boxcars, were restricted to the winter months. But Swift hired an engineer to design a car in which low temperatures could be maintained by means of air circulating over bunkers of ice. Trouble, however, came from public prejudice against meat dressed at a distance, and from the railroads, which had substantial investments in stock cars, pens, and other handling facilities. Swift solved the first problem by going into partnership with local butchers. The second was met by shipping over the Grand Trunk Railway, a traffic-hungry line which had never had much live-cattle business. The economies of shipping dressed beef were enormous, and Swift prospered. In the merger wave of the early 1900s the properties of Swift and his two principal competitors, J. O. Armour and Edward Morris, were combined in the National Packing Co., the so-called Beef Trust.

———

Like most of the great industrial capitalists of his generation, Swift early displayed an entrepreneurial flair for turning a profit. He started out on his own at the age of sixteen, when he borrowed $25 from his father, bought and slaughtered a heifer, sold the dressed beef to neighbors, and netted $10 on the deal. From that time his business ambition knew no rest, and his drive toward expansion was so intense that Swift was chronically short of working capital even after becoming a giant of the meatpacking industry. Although he went into the panic of 1893 owing $10 million to bankers, he weathered the financial storm by promptly converting all his inventory into cash, and emerged from the long depression of the nineties stronger than ever.

His genius for systematic organization raised labor productivity to new heights, but his workers, like those of Armour and other leading packers, were driven men. Donning cowhide top boots, he frequently left his office to visit the packing-house floor, where his vigilant eye soon detected inefficiency and waste. Tall, stooped, and bearded, this laconic Cape Cod Yankee habitually wore an expression of thoughtful repose that lent him the appearance of a poet or scholar, but no man was more preoccupied with profit or better personified the axiom that "time is money." His passion for statistics put him ahead of his time. Swift insisted on detailed weekly reports which at a glance enabled him to place his finger on trouble spots. "You've got to know how you stand every week," he said. "If you wait a month maybe you're broke."

His contribution to a national market for fresh dressed beef made Swift a prime mover of the tide of urbanization that swept over America in the late 19th century. His deepest commitment, however, was to the Puritan work ethic. He exalted self-reliance, perhaps to an extreme. One wintry morning, as he was driving his carriage to work, his horse slipped on the icy ground. Some passersby rushed forward to aid the fallen animal. "Let him alone," barked Swift. "If he can't get himself up, I don't want him." See R. A. Clemen, *The American Livestock and Meat Industry* (1923).

WILLIAM GREENLEAF

———

TAFT, Robert Alphonso (b. Cincinnati, Ohio, Sept. 8, 1889; d. Washington, D.C., July 31, 1953), POLITICAL LEADER, son of William Howard Taft, graduated from Yale College (1910) and Harvard Law School (1913). During World War I he served as assistant counsel for the U.S. Food

Administration, under Herbert Hoover (1917–18). In 1919 he worked for the American Relief Administration in Europe. He was a member of the Ohio house of representatives as a Republican (1921–26), serving as majority leader (1925) and speaker (1926). Elected to the Ohio senate in 1930, he was defeated for reelection in 1932 and returned to his law practice.

In 1938 Taft was elected to the U.S. Senate (serving until his death). A staunch conservative who always placed frugality high on his list of priorities, Taft regarded the New Deal with great distaste and voted against most of Roosevelt's domestic programs. In foreign affairs, Taft opposed American involvement in the European war. The Lend-Lease Act (1941), which permitted the president to supply or lease arms to any country whose defense he deemed vital to the U.S., received Taft's condemnation because, he said, it would "give the President power to carry on a kind of undeclared war." Following the attack on Pearl Harbor, however, Taft supported the declaration of war.

Throughout his career Taft supported civil rights measures, favoring a federal law against lynching and the abolition of poll taxes. But except for his sponsorship of public housing legislation and of federal aid to education (a position he shifted on during World War II), his conservative tenets never deserted him, and he continued to attack what he regarded as "socialistic trends." Always an advocate of free collective bargaining, he believed that the National Labor Relations Board (created under the Wagner Act, 1935) sanctioned unfair union practices, especially the closed shop and the secondary boycott. Taft, in an effort to curb these practices without endangering the right to strike, helped frame and pilot through Congress the Taft-Hartley Act (1947), which banned the closed shop, permitted employers to sue unions for breaking contracts and for damages inflicted during a jurisdictional strike or secondary boycott, and required an eighty-day "cooling off" period before unions could strike.

During the postwar years Taft remained an anti-interventionist and nationalist. He was one of the most articulate critics of NATO. He backed the Truman Doctrine (1947) to aid Greece and Turkey against possible Communist aggression, and, although he opposed what he regarded as the excessive expenditures proposed under the Marshall Plan (1947) because it struck him as too much like "a European TVA," the Plan finally elicited his support. Always a strong anticommunist, he severely criticized the Democratic China policy (constantly calling for Secretary of State **Dean Acheson** to resign from the Truman cabinet) and what he called the general Democratic "softness" toward Communism. As a result, he condoned Senator **Joseph McCarthy**'s campaign to root out purported Communists in government.

Repeatedly a leading candidate for the Republican presidential nomination, Taft was defeated by **Wendell Willkie** in 1940, by **Thomas E. Dewey** in 1948, and by Dwight D. Eisenhower in 1952 in a bitter convention battle. However, following Eisenhower's victory and the election of a Republican Senate, Taft became Eisenhower's trusted majority leader.

───※───

Taft's upbringing seems to have profoundly affected his personality and political philosophy. His father imparted to him the family heritage of devotion to public service, of respect for the law, of adhering to one's beliefs even if they occasionally proved vulnerable politically. His mother, Helen Herron Taft, was cool, intelligent, ambitious. Friends of the family always believed that Taft developed his sense of duty from his father and his impersonality—some said his coldness—from his mother.

It was partly because of these traits that Taft failed to receive the Republican presidential nominations in 1940, 1948, and 1952. His philosophy on domestic issues, while flexible enough to embrace public housing and federal aid to education, too often struck people as narrowly frugal, excessively partisan, more concerned with individual freedom than with the problems of the masses. His nationalistic approach to foreign affairs seemed unduly pessimistic about the potential of American presence abroad, too budget-conscious to understand the desire of other nations for American dollars, too pacifistic to sense the threat of fascism. In the Truman years it also seemed so inconsistent that he simultaneously opposed extensive American military commitments in Europe while criticizing American "softness" in Asia. Like his father, Taft seemed too much the advocate of a strict construction of the Constitution to accept the dramatic expansion of the federal government under Presidents Roosevelt and Truman. Unlike his father, he lacked the verve, the color, the public image of joviality which Republicans deemed necessary in a successful presidential candidate.

Taft's three abortive efforts for the presidency obscured his greater historical significance. Taft was the most consistent Republican foe of Truman and Roosevelt between 1939 and 1953. Coolly intelligent, exceptionally hard-working, wholly free of cant, Taft impressed his colleagues as unusually courageous politically. He not only led the powerful bipartisan coalition in the Senate against many New Deal–Fair Deal measures but emerged as the favorite of millions of Americans who yearned for a more limited national government. By the sheer force of his intellect and the strength of his will he dominated his Republican colleagues as have few senators in American history.

Taft's chief legislative accomplishment was the Taft-Hartley Act. Attacked by many labor unions as the "slave labor act," it proved in fact a moderate law which subsequent Congresses failed to repeal. In the Truman years Taft also led successful moves to limit spending, to soften price controls, to cut taxes, and to prevent enactment of national health insurance. His legacy to his party or to American political ideas was less certain. For all his dominance over Republican senators during his lifetime, he proved too progressive on public housing and aid to education to serve as a model for subsequent Republicans, and he seemed too much of an anti-interventionist in foreign policy to satisfy later Republican defenders of an active American policy in Korea or Vietnam. On the other hand, his insistence on limiting presidential prerogatives and on circum-scribing American commitments abroad led some observers during the years of the Vietnam conflict to regard him with renewed respect. Taft, it seemed, was too colorless to provide mass leadership, too attached to precedent to move at ease with his times. But these very traits modeled a sober, industrious and consistent public servant of uncommon influence. Few American politicians have been more forthright and responsible. See James T. Patterson, *Mr. Republican* (1972).

JAMES T. PATTERSON

TAFT, William Howard (b. Cincinnati, Ohio, Sept. 15, 1857; d. Washington, D.C., March 8, 1930), PRESIDENT, JURIST, graduated from Yale College (1878), and the Cincinnati Law College (1880). He was assistant prosecuting attorney of Hamilton County, Ohio (1881–82), collector of internal revenue for Ohio's first district (1882–83), assistant solicitor of Hamilton County (1885–87), and superior court judge (1887–90).

President Benjamin Harrison appointed Taft solicitor general of the U.S. in 1890, and from 1892 to 1900 he was a federal circuit court judge. President McKinley appointed him president of the Philippine Commission in 1900, and in 1901 he became civil governor of the Philippines. President Roosevelt made him secretary of war in 1904, and in 1908, as Roosevelt's personal choice, Taft won the Republican presidential nomination. He defeated **William Jennings Bryan** in the 1908 election, 321 electoral votes to 162.

Taft's first act as president was to call Congress into special session to revise the tariff. He approved the reduction contained in the Payne Bill (1909), but when the Senate emasculated the measure he failed to resist, thus alienating Republican insurgents. He backed the Mann-Elkins Act (1910), which placed the telephone, cable, and wireless companies under the jurisdiction of the Interstate Commerce Commission and gave the Commission authority to suspend railroad rate increases, and also supported a postal savings system (1910) and a commission on efficiency and economy to investigate federal expenditures. He enforced the Sherman Anti-Trust Act

(1890) vigorously; under his administration, the Standard Oil and American Tobacco company trusts were dissolved.

When congressional Progressives tried to reduce the power of Speaker **Joseph Cannon** (1910), Taft sided with Cannon. In 1910 he backed his secretary of the interior, Richard A. Ballinger, in his controversy over Alaskan mineral resources with chief forester **Gifford A. Pinchot.** When Pinchot refused to back down, Taft removed him.

Taft's foreign policy of "dollar diplomacy" sought to extend America's economic influence into underdeveloped areas as a substitute for military intervention. In 1909 he personally appealed to the Chinese regent to permit U.S. financiers to enter a four-power consortium to finance a railroad in China. He also supported economic intervention in Latin America.

Taft's domestic policies angered Roosevelt, who, urged on by progressive Republicans, decided to oppose Taft for the presidential nomination in 1912. Taft's control of the party machinery won him the nomination, whereupon Roosevelt broke with the party and ran for president on a new Progressive party ticket. The Democrat, Woodrow Wilson, won the election with 435 electoral votes to Roosevelt's 88, and Taft's 8.

Taft then accepted a post as professor of law at Yale (1913–21). He supported Wilson's League of Nations proposal after World War I. Appointed chief justice of the Supreme Court in 1921 by President Harding, Taft tried to unite the Court so as to reduce the number of dissents that were issued, and to make it more efficient. In *Bailey* v. *Drexel Furniture Co.* (1922), he argued that a federal tax levied on products manufactured by child labor in interstate commerce was unconstitutional. He issued one of his few dissents in *Adkins* v. *Children's Hospital* (1923), when he supported an act fixing minimum wages for women on the ground that low wages affect health and morals just as much as long hours.

Throughout most of his life both preferment and attainment in public affairs came easily to William Howard Taft. Except for the Yale period of teaching he held one appointive public office after another, from the age of twenty-four to the last year of his life. Only during the four years of the presidency did he occupy an elected position. A politically influential and wealthy family, a first-class if conventional mind, an obviously tolerant and affable spirit, and an easy facility for making and keeping friends account for his impressive career. The triumphs of his younger life as well as a lack of a burning sense of ambition may have also limited his later achievements. He showed neither the frenetic energy of Theodore Roosevelt nor the almost messianic urge of Woodrow Wilson, and his lifelong inclination to procrastinate when confronted by important but laborious tasks was to cost him dearly at times. Aside from the pleasures of the table (his weight ranged from 250 to more than 300 pounds), conversations with his many friends, politics, and the law, Taft had few other absorbing interests. His letters and court decisions, while clearly styled, are largely innocent of elegant passages, memorable phrases, or allusions to literature and the fine arts.

Taft's political philosophy, stemming mostly from the 19th century, was in part inherited from his family, in part influenced by the teachings of **William Graham Sumner** of Yale, and in part shaped by his career on the bench. While this rigorous creed was positioned on individualism and the economic doctrines of the classical English liberals, its more harsh aspects were softened by Taft's essentially humane spirit and his upper-class concern for the underprivileged. Taft disliked concentrated economic power and especially resented the attempts of either organized capital or labor to obtain favors from government. He recognized the right of labor unions to exist, but throughout his life he opposed their use of force to obtain concessions from employers. Although a democrat by persuasion, Taft was also an elitist who believed in the necessity of restraining the mass will through representative institutions and constitutional checks. Although occasionally forced to violate his Whig precepts during his term of office, Taft viewed the presidency as largely an administrative office and not as a dominating force in either judicial or administrative matters.

As an administrator Taft was so successful that he became Theodore Roosevelt's chief emissary abroad for the solving of difficult problems. Once a presidential policy decision was made, Taft had the ability to implement it with a minimum of friction and opposition.

As a politician Taft was something less than a star; not caring for the game, he played it poorly. Both his training on the bench and his personal inclinations prevented him from using the manifold wiles of the craft. He was too honest to wheedle votes from a crowd by conventional subterfuges or to win over a senator by flattery; too much of a judge either to be an intense partisan or to be many things to many men. He did succeed in doing what he had promised—carrying out much of the unfinished legislative business of the Roosevelt years—but in the process Taft lost the control of his party, the defeat of which in the congressional elections of 1910 led to the agonizing personal schism with Roosevelt and to his own defeat two years later.

Taft had grave doubts about running for the presidency, and unquestionably the unhappiest period of his entire public career was related to the four years of his incumbency. After his appointment to the federal circuit court in 1892, his persistent ambition in life was to be a Supreme Court justice. He was never more content than when on the bench, and his 1921 appointment as chief justice of the high court was, he felt, a satisfying culmination to his career.

Taft was not a great or a creative jurist either in his younger days or as a member of the Supreme Court. As a young judge, during the troublesome nineties, he is best remembered for his decisions, circumscribing the rights of labor. He was appointed to the Supreme Court, he wrote to a friend, "to reverse some [liberal] decisions" of the Wilson years. His subsequent career did not disappoint that expectation. As a conservative and a strict constructionist, he consistently sided with the majority of the Court which, except for the added powers needed to enforce the prohibi-

tion amendment and to uphold action against political subversives, whittled away at existing federal regulatory powers, some of them established by precedent as early as 1904. But pointing up the chief justice's qualities as a person was his fondness and admiration for Justice **Oliver Wendell Holmes, Jr.,** who together with **Louis D. Brandeis** inspired most of the many minority decisions registered during the Taft years.

Taft would have been an adornment to the presidency and to the Supreme Court in a more stable age. His unquestioned administrative skills, his obvious integrity, and his all-around ability would have placed him far above the ordinary run of presidents and chief justices. But the 20th century was running too fast for a 19th-century conservative even to keep abreast of it. Thus this able, kindly, and honest man is perhaps remembered more for his negative positions rather than for his positive accomplishments. See Henry F. Pringle, *The Life and Times of William Howard Taft* (1939).

GEORGE E. MAURY

TANEY, Roger Brooke (b. Calvert Co., Md., March 17, 1777; d. Washington, D.C., Oct. 12, 1864), JURIST, POLITICAL LEADER, graduated from Dickinson College (1795), and was admitted to the bar in 1799. He served in the Maryland state legislature as a Federalist (1799–1800), but later broke with the party because it opposed the War of 1812. During 1810–15 he was the director of a branch of the Maryland state bank. He served in the Maryland senate (1816–21) and was director of the Frederick County Bank (1818–23). A hard money advocate, Taney favored laws to prevent excessive issue of paper money.

In 1824 Taney supported Andrew Jackson for the presidency. Following Jackson's defeat, he became chairman of the Maryland state Democratic central committee. After serving as district attorney of Maryland (1827–31), he became President Jackson's attorney general (1831) following Jackson's 1828 election victory. Like Jackson, he believed that the second Bank of the U.S. was too powerful, and that it should not be rechartered. In July 1832 he helped draft Jackson's bank veto message. After Secretary of the Treasury William J. Duane refused to remove the federal deposits from the Bank, Jackson made Taney secretary (1833), and Taney proceeded with the removal. When Congress convened in 1834, the Senate refused to confirm Taney's appointment. The Senate also rejected his nomination as associate justice of the Supreme Court in 1835.

Later in 1835 Jackson appointed Taney chief justice of the Supreme Court. In the Charles River Bridge case (1837), concerning whether or not rights not explicitly stated in a charter could be inferred from the language of the document, Taney announced that contracts must be construed narrowly, and that ambiguous clauses must operate against corporations and in favor of the public.

Taney's states' rights views directly affected his most famous decision: the Dred Scott case (1857). **Dred Scott,** a slave, sued for his liberty on the ground that his owner had taken him into a free state (Ill.) and into a free territory (Wis.). Although five separate decisions were written, Taney's was universally regarded as the majority opinion. He ruled that blacks were not citizens of the U.S. and therefore could not bring suit in a federal court. In an obiter dictum, he added that since Congress had no power to deprive any person of his property it could not prohibit slavery in the territories. Thus, the Missouri Compromise (1820) banning slavery north of latitude 36° 30' was unconstitutional. It had been repealed already by the Kansas-Nebraska Act (1854).

When the Civil War broke out, Taney objected to Lincoln's suspension of the writ of habeas corpus (*Ex parte Merryman,* 1861) and to many other efforts to preserve the Union. His rulings, however, had little effect on Lincoln or the conduct of the war.

If Taney—the name is pronounced "Tawney"—had died in 1855 when he lost his wife and daughter to yellow fever, his eminence on the Supreme Court would be undisputed.

Instead, he survived nine years longer to become known for generations as the judge who denied Congress's authority to prevent the spread of slavery into the territories (Dred Scott), and who impeded Lincoln's efforts to preserve the Union. He held the heretical view, safe only in peacetime, that civil liberties transcend military necessity. When Taney died, an anonymous pamphleteer (probably Senator **Charles Sumner**) described him as second only to Pontius Pilate in judicial infamy; and a U.S. district judge (David McDonald, Indiana) rejoiced: "Shame will forever roll its burning fires over his memory; and such a consummation is justly his due."

Yet those who knew him personally respected him, and many loved him. His long political and judicial career was characterized by gentleness, sensitivity, and intelligence. He was uniquely qualified, both temperamentally and philosophically, to guide the Supreme Court toward judicial self-restraint. Taney and the other Jacksonians who dominated the Court accepted precedents established by **John Marshall,** but qualified them to meet a new age, rather than pursuing them relentlessly to their natural conclusions as Associate Justice **Joseph Story** demanded. The legislative power preserved for state governments by Taney was essential in an era when Congress refused to exercise the power which Marshall sought to give it. Taney sought grounds to uphold state legislation, rather than seeking to overrule it. Even the disastrous Dred Scott decision, in which significant federal legislation was for the first time ruled invalid by the Supreme Court, was in part a manifestation of judicial restraint; it left the decision regarding slavery to the individual states. But it was totally and disastrously out of character for the Taney Court to have attempted to solve an insoluble political question which had been beyond the capacities of Congress and the president.

Taney's upper-class, landholding background in a border state was an influence on his public career. It led him into the Federalist party as a youth; it persuaded him to support local banks but to oppose banking monopoly; it encouraged him to protect local governments against the central government and, in particular, against the burgeoning and dangerous North; finally, it forced him to protect slavery, even though he personally disapproved of it.

Sympathetic biographers insist that Taney was not really as homely as his portraits imply. But even with a liberal allowance for unflattering portraiture, Taney remains a remarkably unattractive chief justice. He was tall and gaunt with a flat chest and stooped shoulders; his long, lean face featured a wide mouth with poor teeth and, usually, a cigar; his voice was low and flat, and he spoke (and wrote his opinions) directly and earnestly, shunning the oratorical flourishes characteristic of his time. For many of his eighty-seven years, Taney anticipated that each year might be his last. He was the star patient in an otherwise female family of semi-invalids. See Walker Lewis, *Without Fear or Favor: A Biography of Chief Justice Roger Brooke Taney* (1965).

DONALD O. DEWEY

TANNER, Henry Ossawa (b. Pittsburgh, Pa., June 21, 1859; d. Paris, France, May 24, 1937), ARTIST, studied under **Thomas Eakins** at the Pennsylvania Academy of the Fine Arts in 1880, and taught art himself briefly in 1890 at Clark University in Atlanta, where he enjoyed the friendship and patronage of Bishop Hartzell. In 1891 Tanner went to Paris to study; at the Académie Julian he began painting biblical scenes, his major theme. In 1896 Rodman Wanamaker supported Tanner's first painting trip to Palestine, and in 1898 and 1899 he finished the *Annunciation* (Philadelphia Museum) and *Christ and Nicodemus* (Pennsylvania Academy), both of which were immediately bought for Philadelphia museums. Tanner again tried living in America for a time in 1902, but quickly decided to return to France, dividing the year between Paris and a summer home at Trépied. At his first one-man show in New York in 1908, his work was praised for its depth of emotion. Tanner continued showing his prizewinning paintings in Paris and in the United States until his death.

As a black man with light skin, an artist's sensitivity, and deep religious convictions, Tanner faced countless obstacles at the start of his career. While studying painting in Philadelphia, he belonged to neither world; on the street he was taunted by other African-Americans for having white friends and white ambitions, and in the Pennsylvania Academy the uncomfortable fact of his presence was tolerated only so long. One day his fellow students carried him out into Broad Street and left him there, firmly tied to his easel. No wonder that Tanner found Paris, the international center of the art world at the turn of the century, a far more congenial city in which to work! There his considerable talent, his warm though rather quiet personality, and his dedication to his art could be appreciated without racial bias.

To the modern charge that Tanner did little to improve the social condition of the African-American there is no answer. Two quiet but deeply moving genre paintings of 1893–94—*The Banjo Lesson* (Hampton Institute) and *The Thankful Poor* (Pennsylvania School for the Deaf)—show what he might have contributed to this cause, but it was impossible for him to work effectively in the United States. At the annual Paris Salons Tanner's passionate yet restrained biblical subjects, painted in a rather conservative style, unaffected by more modern art movements, won him many awards, including chevalier of the Legion of Honor (1923). In America his famous example, if not the content of his work, became a source of inspiration for younger black artists. See Marcia M. Mathews, *Henry Ossawa Tanner, American Artist* (1969).

ELLWOOD C. PARRY III

TARBELL, Ida Minerva (b. Erie County, Pa., Nov. 5, 1857; d. Bridgeport, Conn., Jan. 6, 1944), JOURNALIST, HISTORIAN, graduated from Allegheny College (1880), taught school in Poland, Ohio, then returned to Allegheny College (MA, 1883). After working for the *Chautauquan*, a Meadville (Pa.) magazine, until 1891, she spent three years studying in Paris at the Sorbonne and the Collège de France. While in

Paris she wrote a series of articles on Napoleon Bonaparte for *McClure's* magazine, later published as *Life of Napoleon* (1895). Upon her return to the U.S. in 1894 she joined *McClure's* as associate editor and staff writer. During this period she wrote several books on Abraham Lincoln, including *Early Life of Abraham Lincoln* (1896) and *Life of Abraham Lincoln* (1900). She received national attention when she published her *History of the Standard Oil Company* in nineteen installments in *McClure's* in 1902 (published as book, 1904).

In 1906 Tarbell left *McClure's* to join **Ray Stannard Baker** and other muckrakers in purchasing the *American* magazine; she remained associate editor until 1915, campaigning for honest government, an end to business abuses, and the breaking up of "bad" trusts. She also supported low tariffs: *The Tariff in Our Times* (1911) expounded her views. After World War I she was a member of President Wilson's Industrial Conference (1919) and President Harding's Unemployment Conference. As she grew older she became less critical of big business, publishing two friendly biographies of business leaders, *Life of Elbert H. Gary* (1925) and *Owen D. Young* (1932), and a history, *The Nationalizing of Business: 1878–98* (1936). Active in the woman's rights movement after 1919, she was a member of the National Women's Mobilization Committee for Human Needs (1933–38). Tarbell published her autobiography, *All in the Day's Work* (1939), and did her last writing while serving as consulting editor of a Tucson (Ariz.) magazine, *Letter,* in 1943–44.

Ida Tarbell was the most eminent woman active in the muckraking movement, and one of the most respected business historians of her generation. Like many progressive intellectuals, she came from a strict Protestant background, lost much of this faith when she discovered scientific and humanistic ideas, and yet always seemed to retain a Christian serenity and optimism that apparently never left her. Ray Stannard Baker, her friend and associate for four decades, summed up the feeling many progressives had for her when he wrote in his diary in 1937: "She lives so warmly in the hearts of her friends that they take new courage in a discordant universe; are reestablished in their faith in the human race, learning anew what it can be, at its best."

Her family background also marked her writing. Her father had been a carpenter working at building wooden tanks in the western Pennsylvania oil boom, and she was convinced that the Standard Oil Company had not only caused him to fail in business but had also driven his partner to suicide. She was also influenced by **Henry Demarest Lloyd**'s *Wealth Against Commonwealth,* and this background helps explain the hostility of her work on Standard Oil. When her own memories were less involved, in her later books on business and businessmen, she was friendlier—to the dismay of those who interpreted her earlier criticisms as an expression of basic anticapitalism instead of mildly concealed personal revenge.

Certainly her personality was quite different from what her earliest readers imagined. Mr. Dooley expressed the public view with his comment, "Idarem's a lady but she has the punch!" **Lincoln Steffens,** however, knew her better; to him she was an almost maternal conciliator, "sensible, capable, and very affectionate." By succeeding in those most male of worlds, journalism and business analysis, she proved as well that these "feminine" qualities were not necessarily disqualifications in the pursuit of the world's affairs. See Mary E. Tomkins, *Ida M. Tarbell* (1974).

ROBERT M. CRUNDEN

TAYLOR, Frederick Winslow (b. Germantown, Pa., March 20, 1856; d. Philadelphia, Pa., March 21, 1915), MANUFACTURER, SOCIAL SCIENTIST, attended Phillips Exeter Academy (1872–74), and then became an apprentice in the shops of the Enterprise Hydraulic Works in Philadelphia. In 1883 he earned an ME from Stevens Institute of Technology. In 1878 he joined the Midvale Steel Co., where he remained until 1889, rising to the position of chief engineer. At Midvale, Taylor formulated his ideas of scientific management. He believed that by detailed analysis of the steps of production of any operation the capacities of both worker and machine could be exactly determined. Hence, production could be altered accordingly to increase efficiency and output.

After serving as general manager of the Manufacturing Investment Co. of Philadelphia (1890–93), Taylor founded his own consulting firm. The Bethlehem Steel Co. retained him as exclusive consultant in 1898; there Taylor developed, with Maunsel White, the Taylor-White process for the heat treatment of steel, which increased metal-cutting capacities by 200 to 300 percent. Taylor received a gold medal at the Paris Exposition (1900) for this work. In 1901 he left Bethlehem Steel to focus on his interest in scientific management. He served as president of the American Society of Mechanical Engineers (1906) and wrote widely on management, including *The Principles of Scientific Management* (1911). Taylor received about one hundred patents for his inventions by the time of his death, and his system of management has been adopted by many large industrial establishments.

———

Taylor was a member of the generation of upper-middle-class easterners who experienced a profound identity crisis in the 1880s. Like his contemporaries Theodore Roosevelt, **Henry Cabot Lodge,** and **Owen Wister,** he felt a strong sense of cultural decadence. These men from well-to-do families, educated in the best private schools, believed that their fathers were being displaced as the economic and political leaders of America because they lacked the vitality to adjust to changing social and economic circumstances. And now these young eastern aristocrats wanted to find new ways of reasserting their control over the novel patterns of the emerging urban-industrial nation.

Taylor, like Roosevelt, thought that his class had lost the will to work hard, the will to achieve success. He developed psychosomatic eye troubles so that he could not go to college. For Taylor, classical education could lead only to greater decadence. He chose then to work in family fac-

tories where he could master the forces of industrialism. This was a rejection of his father, whom he saw as an effete engaged in the irrelevant pursuit of writing poetry. His commitment to the development of a theory of industrial efficiency offered him a way to escape the decadence of his father's class. And he regained his health as he worked with machines.

Taylor's concept of scientific management as a way of putting the new forces of industrialism under rational control had a parallel in the academic world in the writings of the economist **Thorstein Veblen,** and in the business world in the philosophy of **Henry Ford.** Many of the political theorists and political scientists of the Progressive movement tried to apply Taylor's ideas to politics. When **Herbert Croly** founded the *New Republic* magazine in 1914, he hoped to make American politics more rational by spreading Taylor's theories. And professors **Charles Beard** and Frank Goodnow hoped to make Taylor's ideas central to the National Voters League and the Bureau of Municipal Research. See Samuel Haber, *Efficiency and Uplift: Scientific Management in the Progressive Era, 1890–1920* (1964).

DAVID W. NOBLE

TAYLOR, John (b. in or near Caroline Co., Va., Dec. 19, 1753; d. Caroline Co., Va., Aug. 21, 1824), POLITICAL LEADER, POLITICAL PHILOSOPHER, attended the College of William and Mary (1770–72) before reading law in his uncle's office; he was licensed to practice in 1774, and the same year was elected a delegate to the Continental Congress. Joining the Continental army at the outbreak of the Revolutionary War, Taylor served in New York, Pennsylvania, and Virginia, rising to the rank of major, before resigning in 1779. That year he was elected to the Virginia House of Delegates and served, with the exception of the 1781–82 term, until 1785. He was extraordinarily active in these sessions, a leader in the movements for religious disestablishment, land reform, and arming the state. After the war he practiced law and made his home at his plantation, Hazelwood, where he engaged in agricultural experiments later published as *The Arator* (1813). In 1789 Taylor joined **George Mason** and others in opposing the new Constitution because it lacked a bill of rights. Rigidly Jeffersonian in outlook, he served in the U.S. Senate from 1792 to 1794. He favored a wider franchise, fairer representation and taxation, and strict construction of the Constitution, being an early exponent of states' rights and southern consciousness. He attacked **Alexander Hamilton**'s financial system in two influential pamphlets, *A Definition of Parties* (1794), and *An Enquiry into the Principles and Tendencies of Certain Public Measures* (1794), charging that the program would create a new moneyed aristocracy which would threaten popular democracy.

Taylor again served in the Virginia legislature from 1796 to 1800 and helped draft and introduce James Madison and Thomas Jefferson's resolutions in 1798 condemning the Alien and Sedition Acts and asserting the state's right to interpose itself against legislation which overextended federal authority. He was a staunch supporter of Jefferson for president in 1800, backed his actions including the Louisiana Purchase, and played an important role in passage of the Twelfth Amendment. He spent 1803 in the U.S. Senate finishing the term of the late Stevens Monroe. In 1808 Taylor joined "Tertium Quid" Republicans in backing James Monroe rather than James Madison for president, and he later opposed the War of 1812 as an abuse of federal power. He spent much of his later life writing such political tracts as *An Inquiry into the Principles and Policy of the Government of the United States* (1814), which criticized excessive federal and executive power, and *Tyranny Unmasked* (1822), which attacked the protective tariff system. Taylor disapproved of the Missouri Compromise in *Construction Construed and Constitutions Vindicated* (1820), believing Congress had no right to interfere with the expansion of slavery into the territories. He served again in the Senate from 1822 to 1824, filling another vacant seat.

It is difficult to study the career of John Taylor without gaining a sense of the paradoxes involved in his writings and the causes he espoused. He is, for example, remembered for *The Arator,* a widely read discussion of farming techniques, which marks him as the foremost advocate of agricultural reform in the early national period. Yet his specific suggestions were generally abandoned, even by such reverent students as **Edmund Ruffin.** In fact, Taylor's agricultural writings stemmed much more from his political convictions than his scientific interests. Few if any men exceeded Taylor's devotion to the principles of Physiocracy and localism. His writings in defense of the agrarian interest and state and individual rights, against the alleged onslaught of consolidating mercantile capitalism, placed him in the vanguard of the anti-Hamiltonian party movement. Yet this great enemy of "paper wealth" amassed his own considerable fortune by inheritance, marriage, and a successful law practice. Furthermore, throughout his long career, Taylor articulated an intense sensitivity over infringements to individual and community rights and freedom of action, while at the same time vigorously defending the enslavement of blacks, and denouncing all plans and activities of the nonplanting classes.

Above all, Taylor's writings embody the fundamentally conflicting tendencies inherent in American political thought of the period, tendencies which would first be transformed into action by such men as Andrew Jackson and **John C. Calhoun,** and later by Abraham Lincoln and **Jefferson Davis.** An ardent spokesman for civil liberties, a broad suffrage, and rotation in office, Taylor logically also defended the paramountcy of local interests, states' rights, and the validity of secession. John Taylor of Caroline epitomizes the essential continuity in outlook of the southern planter class which carried it from the heights of colonial revolution and constitution building, to the disruption of the Union. See Eugene Mudge, *The Social Philosophy of John Taylor* (1939).

STEVEN CHANNING

TAYLOR, Zachary (b. Orange County, Va., Nov. 24, 1784; d. Washington, D.C., July 9, 1850), MILITARY LEADER, PRESIDENT, served in the army—with the exception of a single year—from 1808, when he was commissioned first lieutenant, to 1849, when he was a major general. He defended Fort Harrison, Indiana Territory (1812); fought Native Americans in the Black Hawk (1832) and Second Seminole wars (1837); had charge of all troops in Florida (1838–40), and commanded the Army of Occupation on the Mexican border (1845–46). When Mexicans attacked a Taylor patrol near the Rio Grande opposite Matamoros, Congress declared war. From beginning to end of the Mexican War, "Old Rough and Ready" loomed as a hero. He was victorious at Palo Alto, Resaca de la Palma, Monterrey (all 1846), and Buena Vista (1847), where he took the measure of Antonio López de Santa Anna.

Hoping to capitalize on Taylor's popularity, the Whigs nominated him for the presidency in 1848. He defeated **Lewis Cass** (the Democratic nominee), 163 electoral votes to 127. Although a slaveholder, Taylor believed that California and New Mexico should determine for themselves whether they would be free or slave states. When Californians ratified a constitution prohibiting slavery, Taylor recommended immediate statehood. He opposed the Compromise of 1850, but died while it was being debated. During his administration, the Clayton-Bulwer isthmian canal treaty was signed with Great Britain (1850).

As a general, Zachary Taylor is one of the important secondary figures in American military history. Intensely patriotic and well regarded by his troops, he was brave, straightforward, devoted to duty, and almost invariably fortunate in battle. During most of his forty army years, he served as a protector of the frontier in or near the Indian country in fourteen states and future states. With hazel eyes, Roman nose, deeply lined cheeks, and iron-gray hair, Taylor—when he emerged as a public personality—seemed to be and was a strong and stocky leader, utterly informal, unpretending in manner, and attractive in a natural, earthy way.

Fame came to the veteran officer late in life, mainly because of a favorable reputation gained in the Second Seminole War. Lacking the flair of Andrew Jackson and the strategic ingenuity of **Winfield Scott,** Taylor showed to best advantage at Buena Vista, where the confidence he inspired in green volunteer soldiers turned the tide against Santa Anna. There the Mexicans lost after two days of fighting, although "Old Zack" had fewer than five hundred regulars and his army was outnumbered four to one.

In the White House, Taylor was a more significant president than has usually been realized. The major question of the day was whether slavery should be extended into, or excluded from, the vast western and southwestern area acquired by the Treaty of Guadalupe Hidalgo. In 1850, a year of crisis, civil war was a possibility as many southerners resented the prospect of federal containment of their "peculiar institution." Taylor's objections to compromise proposals stemmed chiefly from his belief that sectional agitation could best be reduced by admitting California and New Mexico into the Union with free-state constitutions. Intertwined with this big issue lay other provocative ones, including a sizzling dispute over Texas's western boundary. When reports reached Washington that Texas militiamen might move against U.S. troops at Santa Fe, Taylor made no secret of his determination to quell that or any similar rising.

Why would a president who owned slaves and planted cotton take an adamant stand against slavery's expansion? The explanation is found in the fact that Taylor long had been a nationalist. He had lived in the Northwest as long as in the Southwest, was essentially western more than southern, and behaved much as "Old Hickory" Jackson—likewise a slaveholder and a westerner—had behaved in 1832. Taylor saw no contradiction in (1) continuing slavery in states where it was legal and (2) concurrently refusing to extend it. Opposed by nearly all southern congressmen, the "President's Plan" won the support of every northern Whig senator except two, and of numerous northern representatives. As a general, Taylor was admired by **Jefferson Davis** and Ulysses S. Grant; as a president, by Abraham Lincoln. In the South, however, he was widely considered a southern man with northern principles. When Taylor died, his successor, Millard Fillmore, favored the Compromise of 1850, which was enacted under the guidance of Illinois Democrat **Stephen A. Douglas.** See Holman Hamilton, *Zachary Taylor* (1966).

HOLMAN HAMILTON

TECUMSEH (b. near Springfield, Ohio, March 1768; d. near Thamesville, Ont., Can., Oct. 5, 1813), NATIVE AMERICAN LEADER, was a chief of the Shawnees. In 1808 he settled in the present state of Indiana, where the Tippecanoe Creek joins the Wabash. Troubled by the continued influx of white settlers into Native American territory, he sought to resist further expansion. With his brother Tenskwatawa, better known as the Prophet, he planned to unite the tribes east of the Mississippi into a confederacy and to make them proud of their Native American heritage.

By 1811 thousands of Native Americans were organizing under Tecumseh's leadership at what became known as Prophet's Town. The white settlers called on General William Henry Harrison, governor of the Indiana Territory, to destroy Tecumseh's camp. In September 1811 Harrison set out from Vincennes, and after a long march his troops camped about a mile from the Native American village. During this time Tecumseh was traveling in the Southeast, seeking to recruit more tribes for his confederacy. The Prophet, however, believing that he could destroy Harrison with his magic, attacked Harrison's camp, whereupon Harrison's men beat back the Native Americans and destroyed their village (battle of Tippecanoe). While the battle itself was indecisive, it was instrumental in scattering the Native Americans and destroying the confederacy.

When the War of 1812 broke out, Tecumseh joined the British army and fought with them on the Canadian border. At the battle of the Thames, the Americans, again under the leadership of Harrison, defeated the British, and Tecumseh was killed in the fighting.

Tecumseh and his brother the Prophet envisaged an Native American alliance to save their lands. Their roles were complementary: Tecumseh was the warrior-diplomat; the Prophet was the mystic. The mysticism of the Prophet restored the Native Americans' faith in their traditional culture and advocated severance of Native American dependence on white men for arms, clothing, and artifacts. Tecumseh witnessed the cession of land by chiefs manipulated by United States agents led by his adversary William Henry Harrison. Corrupted by gifts and liquor, the old chiefs were selling the Native Americans' landed heritage. He insisted that the land belonged to all tribes; therefore no tribe or its leaders could cede land. Assassination and coercion reinforced the Prophet's teachings until hundreds of warriors left the tribes of the Old Northwest, including the Potowatomi, Kickapoo, Winnebago and others, to join the Shawnees and the brothers.

Twice Tecumseh took his message south. Among the southern Native Americans he found in 1811 and 1812 some sympathetic response, but again he encountered opposition from tribal leaders. Totally unable to unify the Native Americans east of the Mississippi River, Tecumseh joined the British in the War of 1812. His vision of Native American unity failed because of intertribal distrust, a Native American tendency against comprehensive alliances, and the reluctance of established chiefs to relinquish power to a challenger. Even if Tecumseh had provided unity, Native American strength had declined too far. American frontiersmen were too numerous, powerful, and determined to be checked by Tecumseh's time. See Glenn Tucker, *Tecumseh: Vision of Glory* (1956).

DONALD J. BERTHRONG

TELLER, Edward (b. Budapest, Hungary, Jan. 15, 1908), SCIENTIST, studied at Karlsruhe, Munich, and at Leipzig, winning his PhD with a dissertation on the hydrogen molecule in 1930. He was then a research associate at the University of Göttingen (1931–33). After the Nazis seized power in Germany, he studied under Niels Bohr in Copenhagen on a Rockefeller fellowship and then served as a lecturer at the University of London. In 1935 he came to George Washington University, Washington, D.C., as a professor of physics. Four years later Teller was one of the scientists who persuaded **Albert Einstein** to write President Franklin D. Roosevelt on the possibilities of building an atomic bomb. He went to Columbia University in 1941 to do atomic energy research with **Enrico Fermi** and continued work on the project when it was transferred to the University of Chicago in 1942. Teller subsequently worked at the Los Alamos (N.M.) Laboratory which produced the first A-bomb in 1945. Unable to obtain strong backing for exploration of the possibility of a hydrogen bomb, Teller left Los Alamos in 1946 to become a professor of physics at the University of Chicago. He supported **Bernard M. Baruch**'s plan for international control of atomic power. But after the Russians exploded their A-bomb in 1949, he again urged development of the H-bomb. Teller returned to Los Alamos to work on the H-bomb (1949–51), taught again at the University of Chicago (1951–52), and then went to the Atomic Energy Commission's new weapons laboratory at Livermore, California. His work contributed significantly to the explosion of the first H-bomb in the Marshall Islands in November 1952. He became professor of physics at the University of California at Berkeley in 1953, associate director of its Lawrence Radiation Laboratory in 1954, and professor of physics at large in 1960, retiring in 1975. He won the AEC's Enrico Fermi Award in 1962. A firm believer in maintaining nuclear superiority in the cold war, Teller testified against the nuclear test ban treaty in 1963 and spoke in favor of the antiballistic missile system in 1969. Teller became convinced in the 1970s that it was technically and theoretically feasible to build a space-based antiballistic system that could protect the United States from a possible nuclear attack from the Soviet Union. All we lacked, he believed, was

the political will to go ahead with it. Teller lobbied ardently for this system, which he personally proposed to President Ronald Reagan early in his first term, assuring him that "strategic defense was feasible." Reagan found Teller's arguments stimulating, and, after the president gave a televised address to the nation championing the system's potential to shield America from nuclear devastation, the spaced-based antiballistic project, now dubbed "Star Wars," began to receive billions of dollars of appropriations which are still in the pipeline today though at reduced levels of funding. Among Teller's many publications are *The Structure of Matter* (1949), with Francis O. Rice, and *The Legacy of Hiroshima* (1962), with Allen Brown.

⸺⸺⸺

Since the Soviet Union tested its first A-bomb, Teller has been without peer among American scientists as a promoter of the arms race. Not only has he contributed directly to the pace of weapons development, but he has also lobbied for nuclear superiority with enthusiasm and persistence. His efforts, motivated both by love of technological progress and by a deep fear of Soviet aggressiveness, have been rewarded with considerable success, most recently on the issue of "Star Wars." Thanks to Teller, America probably developed the H-bomb a couple of years sooner than it would otherwise have done. Thanks to Teller, America built not just one but two nuclear weapons laboratories whose friendly rivalry has done much to increase the variety of its arsenal. Thanks largely to Teller, America carried out more than twice as many nuclear tests as the Soviet Union in the fifties and early sixties. These achievements have brought him fame—e.g., a portrait on the cover of *Time* (1957)—and notoriety—e.g., the "Dr. Strangelove Award" (1970).

Teller makes a strong impression. He has intense eyes under bushy brows, a quick sense of humor, and, until opposed, a warm and open manner. Though he has been branded a "stooge" and "flunky," he is really in the mold of a 19th-century liberal who believes in individualism, capitalism, and progress. It will be interesting to see how the demise of the Soviet Union affects Teller's approach to questions of national defense in the future. See Edward Teller, *The Legacy of Hiroshima* (1962), and Stanley A. Blumberg and Louis G. Panos, *Edward Teller: Giant of the Golden Age of Physics* (1990).

KARL HUFBAUER

THOMAS, George Henry (b. Southampton Co., Va., July 31, 1816; d. San Francisco, Calif., March 28, 1870), MILITARY LEADER, graduated from the U.S. Military Academy in 1840, then was stationed in the South (1840–44). He fought in the Mexican War, participating in the battles of Monterrey and Buena Vista, and won brevets for gallantry. During 1851–54 he was an artillery and cavalry instructor at West Point. In 1855 he was commissioned major in the largely southern-officered 2d Cavalry, under A. S. Johnston and **R. E. Lee.**

When the Civil War broke out, Thomas, despite his southern background, supported the Union. After being promoted to colonel and commanding brigades in the Department of Pennsylvania and the Shenandoah Valley, he was commissioned a brigadier general of volunteers (Aug. 1861). He assumed command of the 1st Division of the Army of the Ohio and won a victory at Mill Springs, Kentucky (Jan. 19, 1862). He was made a major general of volunteers in April 1862, and commanded the right wing of General Halleck's army in the capture of Corinth. He was second in command of the Army of the Ohio at Perryville. Thomas commanded the XIV Corps of the Army of the Cumberland at Stones River (Dec. 31–Jan. 2, 1862/63) and in the Tullahoma campaign (June–July, 1863), which forced General Bragg out of Tennessee. His ability to withstand the Confederates at Chickamauga (Sept. 1863) earned him the name "the Rock of Chickamauga." In October 1863 he was promoted to brigadier general in the regular army.

Thomas replaced General Rosecrans as commander of the Army of the Cumberland, and was ordered to hold Chattanooga. At the battle of Chattanooga (Nov. 1863) his troops played the principal role in capturing Missionary Ridge. During **William T. Sherman**'s Atlanta campaign (1864), the Army of the Cumberland represented more than half of Sherman's forces. Thomas later commanded a new force that defeated General Hood at Nashville (Dec. 1864). For this victory he was commissioned major general in the regular army. After the war he commanded the military division of the Pacific, with headquarters in San Francisco.

⎯⎯ ⚬⚬⚬ ⎯⎯

George H. Thomas's nickname "Slow Trot" suggests, along with his southern birth, why he did not reach a high independent command in the Union army until nearly the end of the Civil War. He gave a personal impression of ponderosity, and he moved his troops with such elaborate preparations and apparent ponderousness that his superiors never quite trusted him to act rapidly enough; even after he received his independent command, Grant almost removed him because he seemed to take too long in preparing the defenses of Nashville. But unlike some other commanders who have prepared for battle laboriously, Thomas could put his preparations to good effect and fight aggressively once battle was joined. His smallscale victory at Mill Springs was one of the most complete tactical triumphs of the war and helped assure the retention of Kentucky for the Union. Under commanders of lesser strength of character, Buell and Rosecrans, Thomas was long a principal source of moral resolution in the Army of the Ohio, which became the Army of the Cumberland, especially in sustaining Rosecrans's decision not to retreat after the costly first day at Stones River. His resoluteness brought him one of his finest hours as "the Rock of Chickamauga," holding his XIV Corps and the Reserve Corps solid against repeated Confederate assaults after the rest of the army and its commander, Rosecrans, had fled the field. He performed capably as commander of the Army of the Cumberland during Grant's Chattanooga and Sherman's Atlanta campaigns, though he was not a warm friend of either Grant or Sherman, and this and his reputation for slowness helped prevent either from giving him large opportunities to show his full capacity. Awarded an independent command at last, as the army assembled to counter Hood's thrust toward Nashville, Thomas ended the war as he had begun it: his battle of Nashville, like Mill Springs, was one of the most complete tactical triumphs of the war, and it ended the career of the Confederate Army of the Tennessee. If his opportunities had been larger, he might have emerged as unquestionably one of the greatest soldiers of the war. No general more consistently rose to every opportunity given him. See Freeman Cleaves, *Rock of Chickamauga: The Life of General George H. Thomas* (1948).

RUSSELL F. WEIGLEY

THOMAS, Martha Carey (b. Baltimore, Md., Jan. 2, 1857; d. Philadelphia, Penn., Dec. 2, 1935), EDUCATOR, reared in a Quaker household where her parents encouraged independent thinking and religious leadership. While attending Howland Institute (1872–1874), a Quaker boarding school, she was encouraged by one of her teachers, Jeannie Slocum, to transfer to a coeducational institution and not a woman's college for further education. She entered Cornell University as a junior and graduated two years later. She then attempted to get a second degree at Johns Hopkins University but since women were then denied full access to the university she was accepted under the condition she work independently. Unhappy at Johns Hopkins, she withdrew after a year (Oct. 1878) but had nevertheless made lasting friendships with women there that became instrumental in later helping her organize and promote Bryn Mawr.

Thomas traveled to Europe in 1879 to study. She became the first woman to receive a PhD from the University of Zurich (1882). During this period, Joseph Wright Taylor, a physician interested in educating Quaker women, established and endowed Bryn Mawr College. With a PhD in hand, Thomas sought the post of president of Bryn Mawr and campaigned for it among members of the college's executive board, several of whom were relatives, including her father and

uncle. They chose James E. Rhoades instead but appointed Thomas professor of English and Dean of the Faculty (1884). In that role she implemented the college's curriculum. Thomas also played a significant part in helping to found the Johns Hopkins Medical School. In 1894, Thomas succeeded Rhoades as president of Bryn Mawr, a position she held until retiring in 1922.

M. (she did not use her first name) Carey Thomas was a woman of strong convictions and a perfectionist in everything she attempted. From an early age she abhorred the exclusion of women from higher education and set out to prove that women were as capable as men in virtually every field of endeavor. But, she believed, in order for women to compete professionally and economically with men, they must have unlimited access to education.

Although she rejected the religious tenets of her Quaker upbringing, the sect's openness towards women in church affairs and its belief in equal educational opportunities for women gave Thomas the foundation she needed to pursue her goals. Her greatest achievements for women in higher education took place at Bryn Mawr. There, as Dean of Faculty, she hired women professors and structured the curriculum on demanding European models and on those offered by leading American universities. She continued to follow that course of action as president of the college.

As president Thomas was a powerful advocate for woman's rights but she also displayed less admirable traits, especially elitist and racist attitudes. She focused her attention only on the problems of middle- and upper-class women and only they benefited from a Bryn Mawr education. On one occasion, rather than admit a qualified black woman, she steered her to Cornell instead, seeing to it that she received a scholarship to go there. She was not above using deceitful and duplicitous tactics if she felt the end warranted it. An autocratic and controlling administratior, her domineering style triggered a long simmering faculty revolt in 1915 that prompted the college's executive board to give the faculty more say in running Bryn Mawr. This experience proved painful for Thomas but she soon put it behind her because her overriding concern was always the betterment of the institution she headed.

Through her writings, commencement addresses, and public debates Thomas articulated the cause of women's education with a power and passion few could equal. The example she established at Bryn Mawr, with its rigorous academic standards and its top-notch faculty, not only debunked the myth that women's schools were inferior institutions of learning but also helped raise the standards of higher education for women, and men, nationwide. See Helen Lefkowitz Horowitz, *The Power and Passion of M. Carey Thomas* (1994).

CANDACE COOK VAN DALL

THOMAS, Norman Mattoon (b. Marion, Ohio, Nov. 20, 1884; d. Huntington, N.Y., Dec. 19, 1968), REFORMER, graduated from Princeton in 1905. He worked at the Spring Street Presbyterian Church and Settlement House (1905–7), took a trip around the world (1907), and then returned to New York as an assistant to the pastor at Christ Church (1908–10). He was associate minister of the Brick Presbyterian Church in New York (1910–11) while he attended the Union Theological Seminary. He received his BD degree in 1911 and was ordained a Presbyterian minister that same year. (He resigned from the ministry in 1931.) Thomas became pastor of the East Harlem Presbyterian Church in 1911 and also chairman of the American Parish, a nearby settlement house. He joined the Fellowship of Reconciliation, an organization of religious pacifists, in 1916, and founded and edited its official journal, *The World Tomorrow* (1918–21). Vigorously opposed to American entry into World War I, Thomas joined Roger Baldwin in founding the American Civil Liberties Union in 1917 to aid conscientious objectors avoiding military service.

After supporting New York Socialist mayoralty candidate Morris Hillquit in 1917, Thomas left his church and joined the Socialist party in 1918. He favored public ownership and democratic management of the nation's industries, natural resources, and transportation. After serving as associate editor of *The Nation* (1921–22), Thomas became codirector of the League for Industrial Democracy, the education arm of the Socialist party (1922–37). He ran for governor of New York on Socialist and Progressive party tickets in 1924 and was the Socialist candidate for mayor of New York City in 1925 and again in 1929. Upon the death of **Eugene V. Debs** in 1926 Thomas became head of the Socialist party. He ran for president on the Socialist ticket six times (1928–48), doing best in 1932, when he received 884,781 votes. During the Depression he advocated public works, slum clearance, a five-day work week, a minimum wage, and numerous other reforms. He criticized the New Deal and President Franklin D. Roosevelt for not nationalizing major industries and natural resources. Although he had serious criticisms of Stalin's rule in the Soviet Union, he believed until the mid-thirties that Russia's economic system was progressive. His visit to the Soviet Union in 1937 further disillusioned him with Communism and Stalin's dictatorial rule. He organized the Keep America Out of War Committee in 1938 to prevent American involvement in World War II. After Pearl Harbor he supported the war effort, but continued to criticize government policies. He vigorously protested the internment of Japanese Americans on the West Coast and denounced the A-bombing of Hiroshima and Nagasaki in 1945.

Thomas lost leadership of the Socialist party at its 1950 convention when he advocated changing the party into an educational body instead of running candidates for offices. Nevertheless, he remained the unofficial spokesman of the party. Thomas spent his later years working for international peace and nuclear disarmament. Some of his many books include *Human Exploitation* (1934), *A Socialist's Faith* (1951), *The Prerequisites for Peace* (1959), and *Socialism Reexamined* (1963).

In his private life, Thomas reflected his Protestant-Victorian upbringing. He neither smoked nor drank, and he prided himself on the absence of divorce in his children's marriages. His tastes in literature and art were equally conventional. But his politics were unconventional, and if he won acceptance in his old age as a "respectable radical," it was a personal testimony to the man and not from the acceptance of his ideas. Next to Eugene Debs, Thomas was the most important American socialist in the 20th century. His power as a socialist leader came neither from his theoretical formulations nor from his organizational abilities, but from his ability to project into the cause of socialism (and the subsidiary individual causes for which he fought) democratic ideals, an evangelical fervor, and the power of his personal integrity. Thomas was not a systematic thinker. He wrote perceptive books and articles stating socialist beliefs and analyzing problems facing socialists, but he never attempted to be, nor pretended to be, an original socialist thinker. His ideas were eclectic: they derived in part from his Social Gospel background, in part from Marxian concepts, but mostly from his experience with capitalist war and injustice. As the emerging leader of the Socialist party in the late twenties and early thirties, he was able through tireless effort and his ability to attract energetic youthful followers to breathe new life into a moribund party. But internal quarrels, the New Deal, and Thomas's opposition to aid to the Allies before Pearl Harbor decimated the party. Thereafter, whatever abilities Thomas had as an organizer or party builder were academic. Thomas's failure to end the Socialist party's isolation from the pragmatic mainstream of American life has led numerous commentators to conclude that his weakness lay in not recognizing that politics was the "art of the possible." But, rather than being a weakness, this was central to his strength as a great political leader. It was his ability to keep open an alternative way of organizing the economy, to not rest content with the "given," that gave socialism and Thomas their relevance. It was also his "alternative vision" that gave him the ability to carry on his lifetime struggle for civil liberties, for labor's rights, and against war, without floundering in a pessimism

that could easily have resulted from the often unsuccessful results of his efforts. Thomas's attitudes toward certain issues did change in his lifetime: his criticism of Russia increased in the late thirties, and after World War II he was willing to graft more aspects of the "mixed economy" onto his socialism. But his essential beliefs remained unchanged from the twenties until his death. During the **McCarthy** period, he struggled for the civil rights of Communists, whom he had opposed politically for years, and his last years were spent speaking out against the insanity of the arms race and the American involvement in Vietnam. When Norman Thomas died, columnist Murray Kempton wrote that there always exists "some lonely, unfashionable place where only he would stand." It was a fitting tribute to Thomas's great strength: his willingness to stand steadfastly for an ideal or a cause—and alone, if necessary. See Harry Fleischman, *Norman Thomas* (1964).

FRANK A. WARREN

THOMPSON, Benjamin (Count Rumford) (b. Woburn, Mass., March 26, 1753; d. Paris, France, Aug. 21, 1814), SCIENTIST, LOYALIST, began his career as a merchant's apprentice and medical student, and at nineteen married the wealthy Sarah Rolfe and was appointed a major in the newly formed Second New Hampshire Provincial Regiment. In 1774 a Concord, New Hampshire, committee tried him for informing for the British and being "unfriendly to American liberty" but dismissed the charge for lack of evidence. He was, however, further harassed, and returned to Woburn.

After 1776, when Thompson went to London and obtained a secretaryship of the province of Georgia, he devoted his major efforts to experiments on the velocities of projectiles, recoil, and cohesion. He presented a paper on cohesion, and was elected to the Royal Society in 1779. Two years later he was commissioned lieutenant colonel in the British army and was sent to Long Island to form a regiment of the various Loyalist bands operating there. In 1784 he accepted an appointment in the Bavarian administration, rising to lieutenant general, minister of war, and minister of police. In Munich he reformed the army and the poor aid system, and built a municipal garden and park. For these services the Bavarian elector made Thompson a count of the Holy Roman Empire. He was knighted in 1784 by George III of Great Britain.

In 1795 Thompson returned to England and resumed research on gunpowder, heat transmission, and moisture absorption. He demonstrated heat loss by radiation, and presented his kinetic theory of heat—that heat is a form of motion. The prevailing caloric theory, however, held sway until the 1860s. In 1796 he published his first collection of writings: *Essays Political, Economical, and Philosophical.* For the next four years, he designed heating and cooking facilities for public buildings and private homes, organized the Royal Institution, and helped establish the Bavarian Academy of Arts and Sciences. In 1802 he left England to travel on the Continent, where he remained, continuing research until his death.

Benjamin Thompson was a controversial figure. Throughout his life he displayed ambivalent and contradictory qualities of personality and character. This first became apparent during the pre-Revolutionary crisis of 1774–75. Ambitious and opportunistic, he equivocated initially, consulting his interest, then nominally espoused the American cause for some months. However, new evidence in British official papers makes clear his early commitment to the Crown. He was in fact a secret agent, apprehending deserters for Gage, while his espionage reports to Gage and Howe won him commendation to Lord Germain. Meanwhile, he displayed remarkable intrepidity under American committee investigations, even petitioning Congress for review of his case.

The same ambivalence was apparent in his work as a scientist and inventor. Thompson was no Archimedes, but he showed some creativity in original research, particularly in heat and in the theory of light. At the same time his interest in the practical applications of his scientific work, wherein he resembled **Benjamin Franklin,** often

put him at odds with other physicists of his time. His talent for invention is indisputable: the Rumford stove and fireplace, his combustion calorimeter, photometer, steam radiator, and pressure cooker, and nutrition inquiries prove his abilities.

Thompson was something of a philanthropist and humanitarian, initiating plans to educate soldiers and inform artisans, and advocating extensive reform in poor relief. Cuvier called him "a defender of the human race against its two greatest enemies, hunger and cold." But his biographers agree that in fact he had little love for humanity. Dictatorial and arrogant with both subordinates and equals, he was essentially aristocratic in temperament and impatient with democracy. His ruling passion, at last, was not humanitarianism, but efficiency. He worshiped order; it governed his personal life and inspired all his work. See W. J. Sparrow, *Knight of the White Eagle: A Biography of Sir Benjamin Thompson, Count Rumford* (1964).

ANNE ZIMMER

THOMPSON, Dorothy (b. Lancaster, N.Y., July 9, 1894; d. Lisbon, Portugal, Jan. 30, 1961), JOURNALIST, graduated from Syracuse University in 1914. She had already become active in the woman's rights movement and after graduation worked in the Buffalo area for the New York State Suffrage Association. From 1917 to 1920, she worked with the Social Unit, an urban philanthropic project, in Cincinnati and New York. Beginning in 1920, she traveled and wrote freelance foreign correspondence in Europe, finally settling in Vienna as a correspondent for the Philadelphia *Public Ledger.* In 1925, she became head of the Berlin bureau for the *Ledger* and the New York *Evening Post,* both owned by Cyrus H. K. Curtis; she was the first woman to head a major American overseas news bureau. After divorcing her first husband, Josef Bard, in 1927, she left her Berlin job and married the novelist **Sinclair Lewis.** They returned to the U.S. and bought a farm in Barnard, Vermont.

Thompson continued freelance journalism

and lecturing during her marriage to Lewis. She traveled frequently to Europe, and in 1931 interviewed Adolf Hitler, who, she believed erroneously, would be unable to rule Germany; her account was published as a book, *I Saw Hitler!* (1932). In 1934 the Nazis expelled her from Berlin because of her writings about their regime. Two years later, at the urging of Helen Rogers Reid, wife of the publisher of the New York *Herald Tribune,* she undertook the column that made her a national figure. "On the Record," a thriceweekly essay on foreign or domestic affairs, not only appeared in the *Herald Tribune* but was widely syndicated. She began to write a monthly article as well for the *Ladies' Home Journal* and to broadcast weekly network-radio commentaries. In these years, she concentrated on attacking Hitlerism and aiding its victims. She created a well-publicized incident in 1939 by ridiculing a German-American Bund rally in New York. In 1940 she proposed a coalition national ticket of Franklin D. Roosevelt and **Wendell L. Willkie.** She supported Willkie when he became the Republican nominee, but ultimately endorsed Roosevelt for a third term. These shifts led the Republican *Herald Tribune* to drop her contract; in 1941 she moved her column to the Bell Syndicate.

After World War II, the column's popularity declined as she became involved in Middle Eastern issues. She served as president of American Friends of the Middle East, an organization that urged United States impartiality between Israel and Arab nations. Her books included *The New Russia* (1928), *Refugees: Anarchy or Organization?* (1938), *Dorothy Thompson's Political Guide* (1938), *Let the Record Speak* (1939), *Listen, Hans!* (1942), and *The Courage to Be Happy* (1957); all were based on her journalism.

———— ∞ ————

The daughter of a minister, Dorothy Thompson always remained something of an evangelist, although not in overtly religious terms. Her first cause was woman's rights; she found her second, opposition to totalitarianism, during her extraordinary career as a journalist. While still under thirty, she became a member of a generation of American journalist-celebrities—among them, John Gunther, Vincent Sheehan (her good friend), and Negley Farson—who rose to fame in Europe's turmoil between the world wars. Basking in a glamour new to their calling, they produced a journalism often richer in individual exploit and personal observation than in depth; Thompson's *I Saw Hitler!* was characteristic. Yet she and her colleagues aided in alerting the United States to the new danger abroad. This became even more her role when she became a national newspaper and radio commentator. Nor did she rely on quiet persuasion; her column was always outspoken, sometimes producing the effect, in the words of the critic Charles Poore, "of having someone bellow in your ear." Nonetheless, she commanded attention to a degree that the State Department considered her the major opponent of its inert refugee policy, and, in 1940 the president invited her to a personal conference (which led to her endorsement of him for a third term).

Once the United States was fully engaged against the Axis, she became almost a crusader without a cause. Her interest in domestic affairs remained tepid, and after the war, she chose to concentrate on the Israeli-Arab conflict. But where she had tapped a vein of favorable public response before World War II, her neutral position on Israel ran head-on into American friendliness toward the Israelis. She was aware of the adverse effects on her popularity; in outlining her autobiography (never written), she noted the year 1949 as the beginning of her "decline." She remained in her final years an unremittingly hard worker, a domineering conversationalist, and the sponsor of many modest personal philanthropies. Despite the considerable disappointments in her private life, she was not basically a bitter or vengeful person, as could be seen in her tribute to Sinclair Lewis, from whom she was divorced in 1942, in the year before her death. See Marion K. Sanders, *Dorothy Thompson: A Legend in Her Time* (1973).

JAMES BOYLAN

THOMSON, John Edgar (b. Springfield Township, Pa., Feb. 10, 1808; d. Philadelphia, Pa., May 27, 1874), FINANCIER, RAILROAD LEADER, was trained by his father, a civil engineer. He participated in the preliminary surveys for the Philadelphia and Columbia Railroad under Major John Wilson (1827). Three years later, now an assistant state engineer, he had charge of surveys on the Camden and Amboy Railroad's eastern division. Shortly afterward, he went to Europe to study English railroad engineering techniques and upon his return (1832) became chief engineer of the Georgia Railroad, in charge of completing the line between Augusta and Atlanta. He later was business manager of the road. In 1847 he was appointed chief engineer of the Pennsylvania Railroad to supervise construction of the Harrisburg–Pittsburgh line, completed in 1854. In 1852 he became president of the Pennsylvania Railroad Co. Thomson advocated the extension of the road westward beyond Pittsburgh, and in 1856 several lines were consolidated into the Pittsburgh, Fort Wayne and Chicago Railway, with Thomson a director, later (1858) chief engineer, and briefly president (until 1860) of the company. In 1870 the line became part of the Pennsylvania system.

During the 1860s, the Pennsylvania set high standards of railroad operating practices and was a pioneer in the development of new devices and equipment. Under Thomson's direction it established a connection between Pittsburgh and Cincinnati (1869), organized the American Steamship Co. connecting Philadelphia with Liverpool and Antwerp (1870), leased the rail and canal properties of the United Companies of New Jersey for 999 years (1871) and purchased a one-sixth share in the Southern Railway Security Co. with links to all major points of the South (1873). Thomson also established holdings in the Texas and California Railroad and the Atlantic and Pacific Co., as well as in several minor lines.

In 1832 when J. Edgar Thomson became the chief engineer of the Georgia Railroad and Banking Company, railroading in the United States was in its infancy. Few engineers were acquainted with the actual construction and practical operation of railroads, and consequently railroad promoters felt they were lucky to employ or get on loan from the national government someone trained at the Military Academy at West Point. This was a limited group, and the Georgia Railroad failed to get such leadership. Thomson, on the other hand, had been instructed by his father in civil engineering, had visited England—as did many aspirant engineers—to view the railroad works in the nation that had invented them, and had served on railroad surveys in Pennsylvania and New Jersey. The Georgia Railroad, where Thomson began his major career, was a local road filling the gap in a through route from Charleston and Savannah to the Mississippi River, the first transectional road in the South.

When he moved northward in 1847 to a better job on the Pennsylvania Railroad, Thomson was still serving a trunk line, but on a larger scale. The established Atlantic ports in the Northeast—Boston, New York, Baltimore, and Philadelphia—were all striving for improved communication with the interior of the country. New York, with the Hudson River, the Erie Canal, and the Great Lakes, seized a head start. In Pennsylvania the State's Public Works, a sequence of short railroads and canals, connected Philadelphia and Pittsburgh over the Appalachian Mountains, but that was about all. Since the passage of these works was slow and expensive, Philadelphia secured the charter of the Pennsylvania Railroad in 1846 and made a large stock subscription to it. Thomson's chief task was to find and construct a route over the mountains between Harrisburg and Pittsburgh. By 1854 he had solved his problem. The State's Public Works could not compete with the newcomer.

After the road reached Pittsburgh, Thomson became president. Already he had become the apostle of expansion through the Midwest over lines which the Pennsylvania or its stockholders financed or controlled. During the fifties the Pennsylvania and other trunk lines reached the Chicago and St. Louis gateways. Most eastern railroad executives then paused to consider whether they should control their own communications beyond the Mississippi. Thomson in company with a few other rich men, like **Thomas Scott** and **Andrew Carnegie,** undertook such expansion for the Pennsylvania. These imperial outthrusts came to grief, and the panic of 1873 put a further damper on such visions. By coincidence the first tremor of this "railroad panic" had induced the directors of the Pennsylvania to investigate the recent history of their enterprise. They found a system whose technical excellence had reached a high level and which paid a gratifying 10 percent per annum. The "master mind" of President Thomson was one explanation for this happy outcome. Nonetheless the directors acknowledged a certain uneasiness at the imperiousness or impetuousness of their leader, who in making decisions had brushed aside the technicalities of charters and the customary way of doing corporation business. Recommending a more conservative policy, they thought the presidency was "beyond the mental or physical power of one man to handle" and an "incompetent or dishonest president" could cause "a havoc and destruction of values." See G. H. Burgess and M. C. Kennedy, *Centennial History of the Pennsylvania Railroad Company, 1846–1946* (1949).

EDWARD C. KIRKLAND

THOMSON, Virgil Garnett (b. Kansas City, Mo., Nov. 25, 1896; d. New York, N.Y., Sept. 30, 1989), COMPOSER, attended the Kansas City Polytechnic Institute and Junior College from 1914 to 1917 but left to enlist in the army. Although commissioned a second lieutenant in the Military Aviation Corps he never served overseas. He entered Harvard in 1919. As a student he traveled extensively in Europe with the Harvard Glee Club, and also studied with Nadia Boulanger in Paris. After graduating from Harvard in 1923, he studied for a year at the David Mannes School of Music in New York before returning to Harvard as an assistant instructor (1924–25). In 1925 he settled in Paris, where he was influenced by early 20th-century French composers. *Sonata da Chiesa* (1926), and

his first symphonies, *Symphony on a Hymn Tune* (1928) and *Symphony Number* 2 (1931), based on American folk material, were written in this period. He collaborated with the writer **Gertrude Stein** on a burlesque opera, *Four Saints in Three Acts,* which was produced in the U.S. in 1934. Thomson also wrote music for New York productions of *Macbeth* (1936), *Hamlet* (1936), and *Androcles and the Lion* (1938).

After the Nazi occupation of Paris in 1940, Thomson returned to the United States, settling in New York. He was music critic for the New York *Herald Tribune* (1940–54). In 1946–47 he again collaborated with Stein on an opera, *The Mother of Us All,* based on the life of feminist **Susan B. Anthony.** He composed symphonic poems dedicated to Paris, *The Seine at Night* (1947), and to his native Missouri, *Wheat Field at Noon* (1948). His motion picture score for *Louisiana Story* (1948) won a Pulitzer Prize. Thomson wrote a cello concerto in 1950, a flute concerto in 1954, and *Missa Pro Defunctis* (1960), which he conducted himself at its New York premiere. His conducting in later years ended because of increasing deafness. He won the Gold Medal of the National Institute of Arts and Letters in 1966. A collection of his writings, *The Virgil Thomson Reader* won the National Book Circle award for criticism in 1981. In addition to his autobiography, *Virgil Thomson* (1966), Thomson wrote many books on music, including *The Musical Scene* (1945), *Music Reviewed, 1940–54* (1967), and *American Music Since 1910* (1971). His *Selected Letters* appeared in 1988.

⬥⬥⬥

As a creative artist and as a man Thomson demonstrated a sense of security and self-awareness seldom found among American composers buffeted by the great social and stylistic upheavals of the 20th century. An inner serenity always seemed to protect him from the pitfalls of fashion in modern music as it shifted from the historical eclecticism of **Igor Stravinsky** to **Arnold Schoenberg**'s numerical predestination. Early in his career he recognized that his talent for vocal composition and his roots in a melodic tradition from Elizabethan madrigals to Missouri folk songs and hymns could form the basis for a personal yet communicative style. And he bolstered this foundation by gaining professional experience as an organist, by his academic sojourn at Harvard, and later, by expanding his social and intellectual horizons in the salons of Paris during the 1920s and 1930s, especially in the circle of Gertrude Stein and her friends. But while Stein provided him with librettos for his two landmark operas, *Four Saints in Three Acts* and *The Mother of Us All,* and consequently was seized upon by some as the main reason for his success, in reality it was his genius that transformed these blueprints into works of art. He imposed large-scale musical logic on Stein's verbal whimsies. But even more significant, he provided a classic model of musical declamation for her American speech. He thus reoriented serious American opera by divorcing it from the imitation of foreign language, from a preoccupation with 19th-century dramaturgy, and from the affectation of grandiose symphonic gestures. See Kathleen Hoover and John Cage, *Virgil Thomson: His Life and Music* (1959).

VICTOR FELL YELLIN

THOREAU, Henry David (b. Concord, Mass., July 12, 1817; d. Concord, Mass., May 6, 1862), WRITER, graduated from Harvard (1837), briefly taught school in Concord, then worked as a pencilmaker and a surveyor (1837–38). He and his brother John ran a tutoring school (1838–41). While Thoreau lived with **Ralph Waldo Emerson,** 1841–43, he published essays in the *Dial,* the transcendentalist magazine.

From July 4, 1845, to September 6, 1847, Thoreau lived in solitude at Walden Pond, on a plot of land given to him by Emerson. He did not isolate himself entirely (he made many trips to Emerson's home in Concord), but sought to prove that he could exist in the woods without the products of industrial civilization. During this period he was arrested for his refusal to pay a poll tax to support the Mexican War, which he considered a Southern conspiracy to extend slavery. Although he spent only one night in jail, the experience led to his essay "Civil Disobedience," in which he criticized centralized government and argued that the individual should resist the state if it required him "to be an agent of injustice to another."

When Thoreau returned to Concord in 1847 he pursued a career as a lecturer. In 1849 he published *A Week on the Concord and Merrimack Rivers,* based on a journey he had taken with his brother in 1839. Thoreau used the book as a vehicle for the discussion of his ideas on literature, life, and religion.

In *Walden* (1854), Thoreau urged men to "simplify" their lives, arguing that the new industrial economy, with its emphasis on wealth, was hindering spiritual development. He also stressed the beauty of nature and of contemplation. *Walden* reveals Thoreau's wide reading in the Hindu and Chinese classics and in Greek and Roman mythology.

Although not active in reform movements, Thoreau supported the abolitionist cause. Following **John Brown**'s raid on the arsenal at Harpers Ferry (1859), he made many speeches in Brown's behalf. His other works, which were published posthumously, include: *Excursions* (1863), *The Maine Woods* (1864), *Cape Cod* (1865), and *A Yankee in Canada* (1866). *The Writings of Henry David Thoreau* (20 vols.), which also contains the *Journals* he began keeping in 1834, was published in 1906.

Thoreau in his writings and in his life epitomizes a major strain in American culture: the passionate yearning for absolute self-determination, self-definition, self-realization. He lived in a time and milieu when such a quest would not seem implausible. The presuppositions and the institutions of Western European life had been markedly weakened when whites emigrated to what they increasingly regarded as a "new world," and the moral force of all traditions had been eroded by a political revolution which culminated not in a Thermidor but a Bill of Rights and a steady evolution toward egalitarianism. It had proved possible to subsist economically without desperate, all-consuming struggles with an unfriendly environment, or without enslaving oneself to a landlord or a machine or a commune. Perhaps most important, the influence of the Enlightenment in America was not to replace one dogmatic cast of thought with another, but to free those who were so inclined to create their own view of the past, present, and future—their own sense of the world and the individual. To the young Thoreau it was an exhilarating prospect.

Although he was exposed to the traditional education offered at Harvard, Thoreau was not ensnared by it. He much preferred to read widely and unsystematically in those ancient and modern writers who appealed to him; he was especially drawn to contemporary English, French, and German romantics, and to Asian philosophers, all of whom seemed to encourage individual inquiry and untrammeled speculation. Formal religion seemed irrelevant. If the Unitarianism to which he was early indebted seemed a radical departure from the faith of his fathers, Thoreau could readily have stigmatized it, as did his friend Emerson, as "corpse-cold." Neither Concord, in which he lived most of his life, nor his family were tightknit organisms; it was appealingly easy to walk purposefully or aimlessly in and out without sanction or censure. Probably few men have been as free to explore what it meant to be free. The only compulsion he seems consciously to have acknowledged was to write down, perhaps first for himself, but also for the enlightenment of others, what was possible and what was demanded of one who would be free.

After a week's trip down the Concord and Merrimack rivers in the company of his brother, Thoreau published a remarkable journal. Although it is studded with observations of how to manage a rowboat, and where it is comfortable to camp, it is not a handbook for outdoor living; although it includes many observations of the farms and small towns through which they passed, it is not a sociology of rural culture. Rather it is a narrative of what he did, saw, was reminded of, and thought about—an artful account of the clues this passage through time and space yielded him about the possibility of a self-realized life. He was disappointed, but probably not surprised, that few copies of his book were sold in his lifetime.

His sojourn for more than a year in a cabin he built for himself near Walden Pond resulted in a far more powerful book. Some of its strength derives from the discipline of style and organization he imposed upon his prose; its language is the language of experience, not of imperfectly forgotten literary traditions; it does not ramble from thought to thought; there is little sense of randomness in its sequence. It is strong also because he more explicitly contrasts what he is searching for with the "lives of quiet desperation" he declares most other men lead. It is also more candid in its acknowledgment that, worthy as this quest supremely is, there is always risk of monomania.

Something of the same eloquence and balance informed Thoreau's famous essay "Civil Disobedience." It is hard, from the perspective of the 20th century, to regard the state of that day as pervasively coercive. Yet it did levy taxes, which were in part used to sustain the institution of slavery and to support wars against Mexicans and shameful policies toward Native Americans. Thoreau makes a powerful case for the duty of an individual not to violate his own convictions by acquiescence; there are times when the individual must not only say no but act on his refusal. He warns against transforming a decision not to comply into a dogmatic, organized effort to resist the state in its every act; it may be only a minor nuisance, or even a helpful recourse at times. And he shared Emerson's horror of becoming embroiled in mass crusades, however elevated the avowed purpose. Yet when the state, or any part of it, commits what a man deeply believes is absolute wrong, Thoreau would sanction any form of resistance, civil or violent; hence his passionate defense of John Brown, who had not hesitated to kill in an attempt to wipe out state-supported slavery.

Thoreau's later years, however, were preoccupied not with the individual's relationship to state and society, but with an attempt to define the individual self. In that attempt, he determinedly eschews even latently familial, sexual, or neighborly contact with human beings. He seeks to contour his self through an increasingly direct interpenetration of nature. As the *Journals* make clear, the nature he wants to come to terms with is not the grand system of order that entranced the Enlightenment, or even the "spirit" that inspired Wordsworth and infused transcendentalism. It is the specific natural object that he inspects, pores over, meditates upon. With increasing ruthlessness, he rejects any easy moralizing, any consoling aestheticism, any disposition to "contribute to science." As a result, while the *Week* is redolent with an optimistic expectancy, and *Walden* with a largely confident sense of accomplishment, the *Journals* are a poignant record of the psychological costs paid by such a relentlessly uncompromising seeker.

Thoreau's life concludes, then, in pathos, if not tragedy. But his life and his writings, taken in the whole, remain an unmatched symbol, not just of the profoundly individualizing tendency in American culture, but of an uncompromising courage. His rejection of all the institutional and psychological props which shore up, as they limit, most men, may seem perverse, but it was beyond cavil authentic. If the experience which he determined to make his only guide seems to most of us a horribly straitened experience, it was his determination, and he lived and died by it. See H. S. Canby, *Thoreau* (1939).

ROBERT D. CROSS

THORNDIKE, Edward Lee (b. Williamsburg, Mass., Aug. 31, 1874; d. Montrose, N.Y., Aug. 9, 1949), PSYCHOLOGIST, LEXICOGRAPHER, graduated from Wesleyan (1895), and received his MA (1896) and PhD in psychology from Harvard (1898). In 1898–99 he taught psychology at Western Reserve University. Thorndike was a pioneer in experimental animal psychology, taking animals into the laboratory and observing how they solved problems he presented to them. According to Thorndike, animals did not solve problems by reasoning or instinct, but by learning the correct responses through trial and error.

Animal Intelligence (1898) is an account of his findings.

From 1899 until 1940 Thorndike taught at Columbia University's Teachers College (professor from 1904; director of the Institute of Educational Research from 1922). While at Teachers College he devised tests to distinguish between the ability to learn and already acquired intelligence, and used statistics to measure test results.

Thorndike was a "reinforcement" theorist, believing that responses to stimuli could be conditioned. His "law of exercise" stated that bonds are strengthened if the response occurs in the presence of a stimulus. His "law of effect" argued that the consequences of an activity determine whether or not it will be learned. If the stimulus is followed by a response and then a "satisfier," the stimulus-response connection is strengthened; if followed by an "annoyer," it is weakened. His theories were elaborated in *Educational Psychology* (1903), *Mental and Social Measurements* (1904), and *The Psychology of Learning* (1913).

During World War I Thorndike was chairman of a committee that helped classify personnel for the army. In 1926 he published *The Measurement of Intelligence*. He also produced two dictionaries: *The Thorndike Century Junior Dictionary* (1935) and *The Century Beginning Dictionary* (1945).

Thorndike's widespread influence in furthering the functional and behavioristic tendencies in American psychology and in promoting professionalism and efficiency in education was not the result of a charismatic personality. Except in his family circle and among friends, he was introspective, reserved and self-sufficient despite his comment that his lifework resulted not from an inner drive but from his responses to opportunities and to educational needs. He did not exploit or publicize his kindness to others, his subtle sense of humor, or his capacity to make provocative statements. Highly intelligent (he estimated his IQ at 175), tough-minded but tolerant, hardworking to an amazing degree, Thorndike was a man of great integrity completely dedicated to his values. These derived less from the religion of his parents than from 19th-century ethical naturalism. He set great store in the work ethic, efficiency, individual initiative, perseverance despite obstacles, and an optimistic faith in science and its utilitarian application to both personal and social life. Challenged by the growing complexity of a technological culture, these values needed to be reinforced by specific applications of this theory to the tasks at hand: showing how the individual could be fitted to the work for which he was best suited, how he could maximize his inherited intelligence through utilizing his capacity to learn and to develop his character. Thorndike seemed to provide answers to emerging individual and social needs. Specifically, his contributions lay in devising tests, measurements, and achievement scales, in standardizing these statistically, and in giving greater emphasis to the practical content of the school curriculum and in taking account of individual differences in the classroom. The tests and measurements he devised for the selection of personnel in industry and in the armed forces similarly answered social needs.

Thorndike was a true empiricist in the tradition of the British associationists and Darwinian evolutionists. He revised his laws of learning as a result of continuing experiments. Nevertheless, methodological criticisms from behavioral scientists and substantive objections from the Gestaltists did not shake his belief that learning is not instinctive, cognitive, rational, or insightful. He continued to hold it to be the result of trial and error and reinforcement in problem-solving situations. Neural bonds or connections between the stimulating situation and the response are the key to learning. His theories, though modified and supplemented, have provided the frame within which subsequent investigations of learning have taken place.

Thorndike's efforts in his later years to apply his psychology to social issues in general and to communities in particular reflected his distrust of sentimental compassion, his conviction that "nature" is more important than "nurture." He was committed to the statistical treatment of social science data that in his view stemmed from knowledge about behavior. His applications also reflected his belief that insofar as the world can be improved, the way is through education, defined as the finding of more precise and verifiable conditions under which learning can take place. Social improvement might also be advanced, he held, through the promotion of mutual aid, the recognition of the need of a natural aristocracy and the illusory character of the "democratic dream," and, especially, through the continuing application of scientific methods and findings to social engineering. See Geraldine Joncich, *The Sane Positivist: A Biography of Edward L. Thorndike* (1968).

MERLE CURTI

THORPE, Jim (b. Keokuk Falls, near present-day Prague, Okla., May 28, 1888; d. Lomita, Calif., Mar. 28, 1953), ATHLETE, was also given the Sac and Fox name Wo-Tho-Huck (Bright Path). From 1903 to 1912 he attended the Carlisle Indian School in Pennsylvania, interrupting his studies to work on farms and to play semipro baseball. He first achieved national notice when the Carlisle football team defeated Harvard in 1907. In 1911 and 1912 Thorpe was named to Walter Camp's All-America football teams.

At the 1912 Olympic games at Stockholm, Thorpe won the decathlon and pentathlon events, but was later forced to return his medals when it was discovered that he had played baseball for money. He then played major league baseball for the New York Giants and the Boston Braves (1913–19). From 1917 to 1929 he played professional football for a number of teams, including the Canton, Ohio, Bulldogs, the New York Giants, and the Chicago Cardinals. After retiring from football, he played bit parts in western films. In the late 1930s, living in Oklahoma, he became active in Native American affairs, and in 1940 he made a nationwide tour lecturing on this subject and on sports. He served in the merchant marine in 1945, then settled in California. He was a technical adviser for the film, *Jim Thorpe: All-American,* starring Burt Lancaster, in 1951.

———— ∞∞ ————

In the early years of the 20th century American spectator sports were expanding and diversifying, moving in the direction of a seasonal equilibrium wherein the sports year came to be shared in turn by baseball, football, basketball, and track and field. Among these, football and track and field grew rapidly in popularity, challenging the dominant position of baseball, a surge that owed much to the charismatic presence of Jim Thorpe. His brilliant achievements in intercollegiate and professional football and his spectacular performance in the 1912 Olympic track and field events presented American sports fans with a superhero of extraordinary versatility. Seemingly Thorpe's feats counteracted a societal trend that was ever in the direction of more narrow specialization.

Born of parents of predominantly Sac and Fox heritage, Thorpe was raised as a Sac and Fox Native American. Six feet tall and handsomely sturdy, with a heroic face topped by a bold shock of black hair, he was an All-American halfback renowned for his brilliant passing, running and kicking. But he was even more skilled in track and field. He put America on the international sporting map by winning the revived Olympic decathlon and pentathlon events at Stockholm with record performances that won him the worship of a generation of nationalistic American sports fans who saw in the handsome Native American a super athlete. Nor was Thorpe's reputation significantly challenged when in 1913 he was obliged to return his Olympic medals after it was revealed he had played professional baseball in North Carolina prior to his Olympic performance.

If Thorpe's baseball performance was modest, his impact on professional football was not. His brilliant play aside, he was an innovative force behind the rising National Football League. He also mastered a variety of other team and participation sports. His effortless grace enhanced his heroic mystique. In 1950 an Associated Press panel voted Thorpe the "Greatest Athlete of the Century" and in 1951 a movie biography of his life appeared.

His death in 1953 triggered further acclaim and prompted promises of a memorial center first to be located in his native state of Oklahoma, and later when that failed in Mauch Chunk, Pennsylvania. A group of promoters in 1954 succeeded in moving Thorpe's body to Mauch Chunk, which was renamed Jim Thorpe. See Gene Schoor, *The Jim Thorpe Story* (1951), and David P. Willoughby, *The Super Athletes* (1970).

DAVID Q. VOIGT

THURBER, James Grover (b. Columbus, Ohio, Dec. 8, 1894; d. New York, N.Y., Oct. 4, 1961), WRITER, CARTOONIST, attended Ohio State University but left without obtaining a degree (1918). He worked on the college magazine and newspaper, then as a reporter for the *Columbus Dispatch* (1920–21). A freelance writer and reporter, with stints of regular employment at the Chicago *Tribune* and New York *Evening Post*, he was hired in 1927 by *New Yorker* editor Harold Ross to write the "Talk of the Town" section. Soon his comic sketches, stories, and cartoons—famous for their whimsical and fablelike quality—made him one of the most enjoyable and popular writers of his generation. *My Life and Hard Times* (1933), and *The Thurber Carnival* (1945) secured his reputation. His selected letters were published in 1981.

———— ∞∞ ————

Thurber's classic story, "The Secret Life of Walter Mitty," epitomizes his appeal, for it captures the ordinary man's capacity to dream great things, to suppose that he will conquer the world, even though his triumph will be purely an imaginative one. Thurber makes the discrepancy between illusion and reality amusing, if faintly sad and certainly outrageous. Yet the human spirit persists in his work, which features fantastic people and animals, misshapen and repressed, yet dogged in the face of incredible upsets, so that they elicit empathy.

Thurber cannot be bettered for explaining his approach: "Humor is a kind of emotional chaos told about calmly and quietly in retrospect." He takes the same tack in his memoir, *The Years with*

Ross (1959), which turns Thurber's years at the *New Yorker* into a Thurber story, exaggerating his triumph over his anarchic editor's regime.

Thurber is one of the major delineators of modern marriage. His cartoons and stories of husbands and wives have left a memorable impression, encapsulating moments of marital discord in inimitable spare line drawings and deadpan prose. Sardonic and psychologically perceptive, with an unerring eye for every human frailty, he spoofed and satirized domestic life, joshing Americans with the absurd little dramas of their days at home—often in the bedroom. But his criticism has warmth and engagement; he wrote and drew from within these familial situations, and indeed their success seems to derive from his familiarity with his material and a sense that his skewering of his characters originates in his own mundane follies. See Neil S. Grauer, *Remember Laughter: A Life of James Thurber* (1994).

CARL ROLLYSON

TIFFANY, Louis Comfort (b. New York, N.Y., Feb. 18, 1848; d. New York, N.Y., Jan. 17, 1933), ARTIST, son of the founder of Tiffany and Co., studied art with George Inness in New York City (1866–68), and with Léon Bailly in Paris (1868–69). He then traveled in North Africa with artist Samuel Colman (1869). Returning to New York, he established his reputation as a painter, mainly of landscapes and oriental scenes in both oil and watercolor. He was made an associate member of the National Academy of Design in 1871, joined **John La Farge, Augustus Saint-Gaudens,** and others in 1877 to organize the Society of American Artists, became that organization's treasurer the following year, and in 1880 he was elected to the National Academy.

Tiffany began experimenting with stained glass in 1875. His patents of 1881 covered several new methods for using glass in tiles and windows. He established his own plant for producing both window and blown glass at Corona, Long Island, in 1892, using the name "Favrile" as his trademark. He also designed textiles and rugs, and founded a company to decorate homes and buildings. In 1882 President Arthur commissioned him to redecorate the reception rooms of the White House, a task he completed the next year. His work, especially his glass, enjoyed great popularity. He won numerous prizes, including the Grand Prix at the 1900 Paris Exhibition. His glass mosaic curtain at the Palacio de Bellas Artes in Mexico City (1911) won international acclaim. Upon his father's death in 1902 Tiffany became vice president of Tiffany and Co. In 1918 he established the Louis Comfort Tiffany Foundation for artists at Oyster Bay, Long Island. He spent his later years teaching art students.

⸎

Louis Comfort Tiffany wrote in 1916, "I have always striven to fix beauty in wood or stone, or glass or pottery, in oil or watercolor, by using whatever seemed fittest for the expression of beauty." The primary source for the beauty he sought was the flora and fauna of North America. His forms express the continuity of growth. His unconventional creative originality makes him one of the first modern artists. He was prolific, energetic, and ambitious. Self-conscious about his lack of formal education, he surrounded himself with trained professionals. At the peak of his career he employed several hundred people. A kind and generous boss, he was admired, even loved, by most of his workers. But he succeeded in directing them according to his wishes; the many thousands of objects produced under his supervision all bear the stamp of his personal style.

Tiffany was one of the creators and leading proponents of Art Nouveau. In interiors he completed before 1880 there are elements that foreshadow forms used later by **Louis Henri Sullivan** and **Frank Lloyd Wright.** When S. Bing opened the Salon de l'Art Nouveau in Paris in 1895, Tiffany's work was featured. He collaborated with Toulouse-Lautrec, Bonnard, and Mucha. By 1900 he had achieved international fame as a designer and craftsman.

The two homes that he designed for himself and his family, in New York City in 1885 and in Oyster Bay in 1902, were among America's finest mansions. See Robert Koch, *Louis C. Tiffany, Rebel in Glass* (1964).

ROBERT KOCH

TILDEN, Samuel Jones (b. New Lebanon, N.Y., Feb. 9, 1814; d. Yonkers, N.Y., Aug. 4, 1886), POLITICAL LEADER, studied briefly at Yale College, but left after one term because of poor health. He published several political essays while still in his twenties and began to study law in 1838 at what is now New York University; he was admitted to the New York bar in 1841.

Tilden combined a highly successful law practice with an active political career. He became a prominent trial lawyer and a corporation lawyer specializing in reorganizing and refinancing railroads. More than half the railroads located between the Hudson, Ohio, and Missouri rivers engaged Tilden's services at some point in his career. He augmented his fortune by shrewd investments in railroads, Michigan iron mines, and New York real estate. A staunch Democrat, he served in the state legislature in 1846 and as a member of the New York constitutional conventions of 1846 and 1867. Long identified with the "Barnburner" faction of the Democratic party, Tilden nevertheless refused to follow its Free Soil members into the Republican party, which he regarded as sectional and divisive, an attempt to shut the South out of the national government. Thus he opposed Lincoln's election, and although he advocated whatever measures were required to crush the rebellion, he played no role in the conduct of the Civil War.

As chairman of the New York State Democratic Committee (1866–74), Tilden worked in harmony with **William "Boss" Tweed** until the latter exploited the home rule features in the 1870 charter for New York City. Tilden's role in exposing the "Tweed Ring" in 1871–73 and his activities in restructuring the New York judiciary brought him national fame, and in 1874 he was elected governor of New York. As such he proceeded to break up the "Canal Ring," which fed on graft from funds appropriated to rebuild state canals. He was the Democratic candidate for president in

1876. In the election Tilden received a national majority of 250,000 votes, but the Republicans challenged enough electoral votes to give the presidency to Rutherford B. Hayes, 185 to 184, after a prolonged and tense constitutional crisis marked by an electoral commission and a complicated sectional compromise. Tilden accepted the outcome in the interests of national harmony, but always insisted that he had been legally elected president. After his defeat, Tilden was plagued by investigations of his tax returns and of the "Cipher Despatches"—these concerned dubious negotiations by Democratic politicians for disputed electoral votes—about which Tilden claimed to be ignorant. Although many Democrats wanted to nominate Tilden for president in 1880 and again in 1884, he refused to run and retired to his Yonkers estate, Greystone, where he devoted himself to accumulating a library.

By his will, Tilden, a bachelor, directed that the bulk of his estate ($5,229,000 at the time of his death but more than $6 million by 1890) go to the Tilden Trust to establish a great public library in New York City. Although the will was broken by disgruntled relatives, the trust eventually received about $2,250,000 as well as Tilden's large private library, which when combined with the Astor and Lenox libraries, in 1901 formed the New York Public Library.

⁂

Tilden is remembered as the reforming Democrat whom Republicans "counted out" of the presidency despite his apparent majority in the electoral college. For many that loss coupled with Tilden's earlier successes in fighting the Tweed and Canal rings symbolizes the defeat and frustration of heroic virtue in the Gilded Age. Whatever he may symbolize, Tilden was not heroic. His loss of the presidency climaxed a long career in which his ambitions suppressed his reform impulses and his indecisiveness frustrated his ambitions.

Tilden's reaction to slavery illustrates his tentative commitment to reform. He was an ardent Jacksonian in the 1830s, a reform Barnburner in the 1840s, and a delegate to the 1848 national

Free-Soil party convention, where he declared that to extend the "blighting presence" of slavery "would be the greatest opprobrium of our age." Significantly, however, Tilden opposed slavery extension on political and economic grounds. Growing wealthy and conservative by the 1850s, he returned to the Democratic party, dismissed his antislavery statements as juvenile utterances, and in 1860, lest the Union be disrupted and war engulf the nation, passionately opposed Lincoln and the Republican program to limit slavery geographically. During the war Tilden feared the tyranny of a powerful central government more than either the destruction of the Union or the evils of slavery; and after the war he denounced Radical Republican attempts to secure racial justice.

Not only was Tilden indifferent to the African-American, he also let partisanship inhibit his reform impulses. As the shrewd and knowledgeable chairman of the State Democratic Committee, Tilden for years cordially cooperated with William Marcy Tweed and was slow to attack his corrupt ring. Although the New York *Times* had published evidence damning the Tweed Ring by July 1871, Tilden moved cautiously and delayed joining the nonpartisan, anti-Tweed, proreform Committee of Seventy established in September 1871. By October, however, it was obvious that the *Times* had mortally wounded the Tweed Ring, and Tilden suddenly, if belatedly, administered the *coup de grâce.* Joining Tammany's rival, the Apollo Hall Democracy, which reformers had established in 1870, Tilden uncovered and examined bank accounts proving that Tweed and his friends had stolen from the city and swore out the affidavit that led to their arrest. Characteristically, however, he voted with most Democrats to defeat the Apollo Hall–backed reform charter which the Committee of Seventy had proposed for New York City. Having jailed Tammany's leaders, Tilden himself helped fill the vacuum. Abandoning Apollo Hall, he became a Tammany sachem on April 15, 1872. Tilden's reform reputation gave Tammany the gloss that it needed, while Tammany gave Tilden the broad base that

he needed to further his political ambition.

The stratagem worked. In 1874 the Democratic party nominated the partisan while the people elected the reformer governor of New York. Proving himself a meticulous administrator, Tilden reduced expenditures and taxes by introducing economies and added to the substance of his reform reputation by destroying the bipartisan Canal Ring. His excellent gubernatorial record earned Tilden the Democratic presidential nomination in 1876, but the bitter campaign and its aftermath besmirched his name. He was accused of being disloyal during the Civil War and of filing fraudulent income tax returns for 1862 and 1863 and no returns from 1864 to 1871. Republicans also stressed his connection with powerful railroad corporations and his frail health. Indeed sickness, his absorption with his gubernatorial duties, and his secretive and aloof nature convinced his campaign committee that he was indifferent; and his slight build, boyish face, weak voice, and nervous actions were not assets. Nevertheless Tilden's intellect and reform reputation inspired a majority of voters; he evidently won the election but was timid, dilatory, and noncommittal in its disputed aftermath. Claiming victory, audacious Republicans successfully wooed southern Democrats from Tilden with promises of political and economic advantages if Hayes were elected. Investigations of Tilden's tax returns and of the "Cipher Despatches" later tarnished Tilden's image as a reformer, and in 1880 his vacillating before deciding not to run again hurt his party.

Though at times Tilden effectively fought slavery, as well as the Tweed and Canal rings, his ambition and partisanship, his lack of conviction and nerve, prevented him from realizing his potential as a reformer, politician, and statesman. See Alexander Clarence Flick, *Samuel J. Tilden: A Study in Political Sagacity* (1939).

ARI HOOGENBOOM

TILLICH, Paul Johannes (b. Starzeddel, Brandenburg, Germany, Aug. 20, 1886; d. Chicago, Ill., Oct. 22, 1965), PHILOSOPHER, attended the universities of Berlin (1904–05, 1908), Tübingen (1905), and Halle (1905–07). He received his PhD in the philosophy of religion from the University of Breslau in 1911 and his degree of licentiate of theology from Halle the following year. He was ordained as a minister in the Evangelical Lutheran Church in 1912 and served as a chaplain in the German Army 1914–18. He was a *Privatdozent,* or freelance teacher, at the University of Berlin from 1919 to 1924 before serving as professor of theology at the universities of Marburg (1924–25), Dresden (1925–29), and Leipzig (1928–29). During this time Tillich wrote several theological works, including *Die religiose Lage der Gegenwart* in 1926 (translated into English as *The Religious Situation* in 1932). He became professor of philosophy at the University of Frankfurt-am-Main in 1929 but lost the chair in 1933 because of his anti-Nazi views.

Upon the invitation of **Reinhold Niebuhr,** Tillich came to the U.S. in 1933 as professor of philosophical theology at the Union Theological Seminary in New York City. Here Tillich began writing his many works which attempted to correlate Christian faith to challenges from psychology, existentialism, and socialism. He rapidly emerged as one of the leading exponents of Protestant faith. His major book was the three-volume *Systemic Theology* (1951–63); others include *The Protestant Era* (1948), *The Courage to Be* (1952), and *Biblical Religion and the Search for Ultimate Reality* (1955). Tillich became an American citizen in 1940. He aided central European refugees during World War II as chairman of the Committee on Self-Help for Refugees. He retired from the Union Seminary in 1955 and then lectured at the Harvard University Divinity School until 1962, when he became Nuveen professor of theology at the divinity school of the University of Chicago. He was a minister of the Evangelical and Reformed Church in America. Tillich's collections of sermons include *The New Being* (1955) and *The Eternal Now* (1963). Several collections of lectures, sermons, and essays were published posthumously, including *Political Expectation* (1971).

Paul Tillich ranks as the greatest American systematic theologian of modern times—indeed, the only recent American theologian to attempt a really massive systematic statement of Christian theology. Of course, he was already middle-aged when he came to the United States, and his formation had been entirely European. He introduced to the American theological scene a whole new style of thought, derived from existentialism, from the insights of depth psychology, and from the whole German idealist tradition. Although native American theology has generally been more tentative and pragmatic, the great range and depth of Tillich's treatment won him a respectful hearing, and he is assured of a permanent place in the history of American religious thought.

His new style of theology was matched by a new vocabulary which helped to refurbish faded theological ideas. Many of the expressions he used have passed into the common theological parlance. Sin was expressed as "estrangement," a word borrowed from existentialism and depth psychology. The latter of these provided the word "acceptance," which gave a new relevance to the old theological idea of justification. God was related to man's "ultimate concern" while salvation was seen as the "new being." In all of this, Tillich saw himself as building bridges between Christianity and modern culture. His work could in fact be described as a theology of culture. As he saw it, the motivation for theology arises out of the culture. The human situation at any given time raises questions of a more or less ultimate nature, and it is the business of theology to try to answer these questions out of the resources of a spiritual tradition. As a theologian of culture, Tillich tends to belong to the liberal tradition, though in his early days he had been associated with Barth and others in the revolt against liberalism.

He was more successful in relating to some aspects of culture than to others. He had a deep understanding of art, literature, and continental philosophy, but was much less at home with the natural sciences and remained quite antipathetic to Anglo-Saxon analytic philosophy. Practitioners of the latter criticized the imprecision of his language, and especially such expressions as "ground of being." On the other hand, Tillich had a good understanding of Eastern religions and often engaged in exchanges, especially with Japanese Buddhists, who found his ideas congenial.

Because of the strictly academic character of his theology, Tillich has sometimes been unfairly represented as an aloof person with little interest in human affairs or the practical applications of Christianity. This is quite wrong, and overlooks his long association with Christian Socialism in Germany and the fact that he was considered so dangerous by the Nazis that he was expelled from the country. He was, however, for most of the time a reserved man and even at the height of his career he remained very sensitive to criticism. But many students found his teaching had almost the quality of revelation. See Rollo May, *Paulus: Reminiscences of a Friendship* (1973), and Carl J. Armbruster, *The Vision of Paul Tillich* (1967).

JOHN MACQUARRIE

TROTTER, William Monroe (b. Springfield Township, Ohio, April 7, 1872; d. Boston, Mass., April 7, 1934), JOURNALIST, graduated magna cum laude from Harvard in 1895 and received his MA there the following year. For a time he worked as a real estate and mortgage broker in Boston, but concerned about the plight of blacks in the U.S., he established with George Forbes a weekly newspaper, the Boston *Guardian*, in 1901 to fight racial discrimination and crusade for full equality for all Americans. He stridently opposed **Booker T. Washington**'s conciliation ideas and served a month in jail for disrupting a speech by Washington in Boston in 1903. Trotter collaborated with **W.E.B. Du Bois** in organizing the Niagara Movement for civil rights in 1905 but later refused to join forces with the National Association for the Advancement of Colored People because he mistrusted the intentions of the whites involved.

In 1913 and 1914 Trotter led delegations of the National Equal Rights League, which he had helped found in 1908, to protest to President Woodrow Wilson against the federal government's discriminatory practices. In 1915 he was arrested for picketing the film *Birth of a Nation* in Boston but was acquitted. He also went to the 1919 peace conference at Versailles as a delegate of the National Equal Rights League. He led several other delegations to the White House for the National Equal Rights League in the 1920s. He continued editing the *Guardian* until his death.

———⬥———

Monroe Trotter of Boston was the 20th century's first important black leader in the militant tradition. He is best known as the fearless editor who stirred up a hornet's nest within the race by spearheading the attack against the racial leadership of Booker T. Washington. Briefly he joined forces with W. E. B. Du Bois in the Niagara Movement; after their estrangement Trotter's role as the main advocate of protest among middle-class blacks was gradually assumed by Du Bois and the NAACP. Once into middle-age Trotter made his mark only in occasional episodes. Essentially he was, like his revered father, a black Mugwump who felt obliged to "set an example." After his early successes he seemed old-fashioned in his own time, but from some modern perspectives he is greatly admired.

His strongly felt Christian gentleman's concept of duty and service was the major factor in his most crucial decision, to give up a promising business career and life among Boston's black elite and to assume a precarious existence in journalism and racial organizing. But this change of career occurred slowly, during several years when his business was having its "ups and downs," as he said. At the same time, his overnight notoriety brought some rewards which he could not get in his business. Those considerations aside, he did spend more than thirty rather thankless years in what he called "the stern path of duty," right down to his death, an apparent suicide, on his 62d birthday. See Stephen R. Fox,

The Guardian of Boston: William Monroe Trotter (1970).

STEPHEN R. FOX

TRUMAN, Harry S. (b. Lamar, Mo., May 8, 1884; d. Kansas City, Mo., Dec. 26, 1972), PRESIDENT, managed the family farm near Kansas City, Missouri, and participated in unsuccessful business ventures before serving as an artillery captain in France during World War I. He attended night classes at the Kansas City School of Law (1923–25). With the support of the Democratic Pendergast machine, he was elected judge of the Jackson County court (1922–24), presiding judge (1926–34), and U.S. senator (1934–44). He became nationally prominent during World War II as chairman of a Senate "watchdog" committee investigating the national defense program. Elected vice president in 1944, he succeeded to the presidency upon the death of Franklin D. Roosevelt (1945).

In the last stages of the war, Truman authorized the use of the atomic bomb at Hiroshima (Aug. 6, 1945) and Nagasaki (Aug. 9, 1945). A rift had already developed with the Soviet Union over Russian ambitions in Eastern Europe and the Middle East. The Potsdam Conference (July 1945), at which Truman represented the United States, divided Germany into occupation zones but failed to solve fundamental East-West difficulties. In 1946, a "cold war" began to develop as the U.S. pursued a "hard line" against the U.S.S.R. In early 1947 Great Britain announced that it could no longer aid Greek anticommunists. Truman requested $400 million in military and economic assistance for Greece and Turkey and proclaimed the Truman Doctrine, which committed the U.S. to aid nations threatened by external subversion. Shortly afterward, the United States instituted **George C. Marshall**'s European Recovery Program (the Marshall Plan) to rebuild the war-shattered European economy and thereby ward off Communist revolutions.

In 1948 the U.S.S.R. attempted to disrupt plans for the creation of a West German republic by cutting off access to the western zones of Berlin.

Truman ordered an airlift which flew supplies over the Soviet blockade and forced its termination after almost a year. He obtained Senate ratification of the North Atlantic Treaty (1949), a mutual defense pact between the U.S. and the non-Communist nations of Europe.

In 1950, pursuant to a United Nations resolution, Truman ordered U.S. troops to South Korea to repel an invasion from the Communist North. The U.N. allies, under General **Douglas MacArthur,** took the offensive and moved to occupy North Korea. The Communist Chinese thereupon entered the war and inflicted a devastating defeat upon the U.N. The president wanted to limit the war to Korea, and when MacArthur publicly demanded authority to bomb China, Truman dismissed him for insubordination (April 1951).

Truman's domestic program, the Fair Deal, carried on the tradition of the New Deal. It included national medical insurance, federal aid to education, civil rights legislation, and public housing. In 1949 Truman advocated a new farm program, the Brannan Plan, which would have allowed food prices to fall while compensating family farms with direct payments. Most of the Fair Deal was blocked by conservative Republicans and Democrats in Congress. The president did secure a National Housing Act (1949), but it was poorly funded and administered. Truman also obtained major increases in such New Deal programs as public power, social security, and the Fair Labor Standards Act.

Truman was unable to effect a stable economic reconversion after World War II. Congress failed to heed his request for extension of strong wartime price controls, and serious inflation followed. In May 1946 he broke with labor and requested authority to conscript striking railway workers. His unsuccessful veto of the Taft-Hartley Act (1947), which placed several restrictions upon unions, brought labor back behind him. In the 1948 presidential election, he conducted an intensive "whistle-stop" campaign and won a surprise victory over **Thomas E. Dewey,** 303 electoral votes to 189.

After a serious initial spurt of inflation,

Truman was able to stabilize the economy during the Korean War. In April 1952 he attempted to avert a steel strike by seizing the mills, but the Supreme Court declared his action unconstitutional. Throughout his second term, Truman was harassed by charges of pro-Communism, although he had established a stringent government loyalty program (1947). He unsuccessfully vetoed the McCarran Internal Security Act (1951), charging that it was unconstitutionally repressive. He did not run for reelection in 1952. His *Memoirs* (2 vols.) appeared in 1955–56.

Truman's character was shaped by his strong-willed mother, who pushed him toward books and the piano; by his myopic eyesight, which inhibited his childhood; and by his father, whose aggressive, profane masculinity he idealized. He seemed impetuous and quicktempered but actually gave careful thought to important matters and was capable of great patience when necessary. His political outlook was a "persuasion" rather than a systematic philosophy and grew out of personal experience. His family impressed upon him a fervent sense of loyalty to the Democratic party. Both he and his father were unsuccessful in business, and he developed the viewpoint of a midwestern small businessman who felt victimized by restrictive government economic policies and eastern financiers. His alliance with the Pendergast machine taught him how to deal with the urban democracy—the immigrant groups, the African-Americans, and the labor unions. The New Deal taught him the political appeal of welfare-state liberalism.

As a county administrator, Truman carried out a substantial road-building and construction program with honesty and efficiency. As a senator, he supported the New Deal and was especially vocal in his distrust of monopoly and eastern financial interests. However, he cultivated friendships in all wings of the party and was considered a machine politician rather than an independent progressive. He gained great prestige as head of the war investigating committee, and his acceptability to all Democratic factions made him a logical "unity candidate" for vice president in 1944.

He ascended to the White House at a difficult time. He had to manage a fundamental realignment of international power, deal with the social-economic problems the war had caused at home, hold his badly divided party together, and establish a political identity of his own. After some initial fumblings, which culminated in the Democratic loss of Congress in the 1946 elections, Truman perceived that the coalition of voters which had supported the New Deal still constituted a solid majority. He aligned himself with the liberal tradition, added new programs to it, and succeeded in depicting himself as a scrappy little fighter battling to preserve the New Deal from the forces of reaction. It was this appeal which enabled him to prevail in 1948 despite defections from the right and left wings of the Democratic party. His failure to obtain enactment of most Fair Deal programs in 1949–50 indicated, however, that many of the people who voted for him did so primarily out of a desire to conserve past reforms, not enact new ones.

Wholly inexperienced in international relations, Truman was never comfortable with foreign policy. He vaguely but firmly believed that the United States had a divinely ordained mission of world leadership, he tended to personalize complex diplomatic problems, and he took a moralistic-legalistic attitude toward most international issues. He detested Communism and did not shrink from tough rhetoric. But he also chose his advisers well and drew upon an inner restraint and balance which belied his aggressive exterior. Favoring positive economic solutions to foreign problems, he enthusiastically advocated the Marshall Plan and called for large-scale technical assistance to the underdeveloped areas of the world. His most serious mistake came when he countenanced the effort to occupy North Korea, but the coolness and resolution with which he rejected MacArthur's demands demonstrated his desire for peace.

Truman carefully created an image of himself as the epitome of the common man; it was both a political strength and a weakness. At times he achieved a valuable sense of identity with the ordinary American, but he could not project the commanding personality which is the hallmark of great democratic leadership. A skilled professional politician working in trying circumstances, he served his country well by defending the liberal tradition and meeting the Soviet challenge with intelligence and moderation. See Alonzo L. Hamby, *Man of the People: A Life of Harry S. Truman* (1995).

ALONZO L. HAMBY

TRUMBULL, John (b. Lebanon, Conn., June 6, 1756; d. New York, N.Y., Nov. 10, 1843), ARTIST, the son of Connecticut Governor Jonathan Trumbull, graduated from Harvard (1773), then taught school (1773–75). He served in the Revolutionary War as an aide to General George Washington, utilizing his cartographic ability, and to General Horatio Gates at the battle of Ticonderoga (1776). Resigning his commission as deputy adjutant general with the rank of colonel in 1777, Trumbull spent 1778 and 1779 painting. In 1780 he went to London to study under **Benjamin West.** There, he was arrested in reprisal for the execution of British spy John André in 1780 and spent seven months in prison. After his release, Trumbull continued his studies under West (1782–85). In 1786, with encouragement from Thomas Jefferson, he began a series of historical canvases. Painted in neoclassical style, his illustrations of the American Revolution were noted for their liveliness and bravura. *The Battle of Bunker Hill* (1786, Yale Art Gallery, New Haven) and *The Death of General Montgomery in the Attack on Quebec* (1788, Yale Art Gallery) are good examples of this work.

Trumbull traveled extensively throughout the U.S. from 1789 to 1794 collecting portrait studies and data for future paintings. He returned to London in 1794 as a secretary to **John Jay**'s mission and remained there until 1804, implementing the Jay Treaty and conducting his own business ventures. After four years in New York (1804–8) Trumbull returned to London for the last time in 1808. He returned to New York in 1815 (maintaining a studio there until 1837). In 1817 Trumbull was commissioned to paint four large pictures for the rotunda of the Capitol in Washington, D.C.: *The Declaration of Independence, The Surrender of General Burgoyne at Saratoga, The Surrender of Lord Cornwallis at Yorktown,* and *The Resignation of General Washington at Annapolis, Maryland,* all completed by 1824. Trumbull served as president of the American Academy of Fine Arts in New York (1817–36). In 1831, in return for a $1,000 annuity from Yale, he consigned to the university his collection of his own paintings and designed the gallery to house them, the oldest art museum connected with an educational institution in the United States. Trumbull lived in New Haven from 1837 to 1841 while working on his *Autobiography, Letters, and Reminiscences of John Trumbull, 1756–1841* (1841). He spent his remaining years in New York.

Trumbull painted best during his thirties, when his work was infused with a freshness and technical verve that he seldom afterward attained. Theodore Sizer pinpointed the artist's thirtieth year, 1786, as "the high point, esthetically speaking, of the long career of JT...." From that year came *The Battle of Bunker Hill,* followed promptly by *The Death of General Montgomery* and the composition (portraits to be inserted) of *The Declaration of Independence,* these the first executed subjects in a projected sequence of scenes, to be engraved, from the American Revolution, in which the artist followed the lead of his compatriots West and **John S. Copley** and their innovative painting of contemporary history.

There were then too few subscribers to Trumbull's proposed series of engravings to warrant its continuance; but soon after the War of 1812 the resuscitated "national enterprise," as he termed it, rewarded him with the unprecedented $32,000 congressional commission for four mural-size historical pictures for the new rotunda of the U.S. Capitol; he profited also from engravings and from exhibiting the canvases before their permanent installation. There were many at the time, however, who observed that the quality of his earlier works had slackened in these, and the murals are now generally regarded as rather dull paintings. Yet Trumbull remains securely implanted as *"par excellence, the documentary recorder of the Revolutionary War."*

If recognition of his historical painting has always exceeded that given to his portraits, it is in good part because the latter with too few exceptions are unexciting, less interesting than those of **Gilbert Stuart** and several other American portraitists of the time. The effects of some years' exposure to contemporary French painting can be discerned in portraits executed after 1800, such as *John Vernet and Family* (Yale University) of 1806.

There were in Trumbull's character elements of vanity, hauteur, and a disdain for democratic ideology that especially in his later years generated enmities. When in 1834 William Dunlap's *Arts of Design,* the first actual survey of the arts in America, came out with its overtly critical essay on Trumbull, the painter, verging on eighty, was impelled to write the self-justifying *Autobiography* (1841) that happens also to be the first full account of an American artist published in the United States. See Theodore Sizer, ed., *The Autobiography of Colonel John Trumbull, Patriot-Artist, 1756–1843* (1953), and Sizer's *The Works of Colonel John Trumbull, Artist of the American Revolution* (1950).

HAROLD E. DICKSON

TRUTH, Sojourner (b. Ulster County, N.Y., ca. 1797; d. Battle Creek, Mich., Nov. 26, 1883), ABOLITIONIST, was born a slave on the farm of Colonel Johannes Hardenbergh, where she was given the name Isabella. Between 1797 and 1810 she belonged to a number of masters, including Hardenbergh's son Charles, John Neely of Ulster County, and Martin Scriver of Kingston, New York. During 1810–26, she worked on the farm of John J. Dumont, of New Paltz, New York. In 1827, after Dumont broke a pledge to release her a year before New York State's mandated emancipation date, she fled from his farm to that of Isaac Van Wagenen, who purchased her services from Dumont. In 1827 she successfully sued to force the return and emancipation of her son Peter, who had been illegally sold to a planter from Alabama.

In that year too, under the provisions of a New York statute of 1817, she became legally free and adopted the name of Isabella Van Wagenen. During 1829–43, she lived in New York City, where she joined a variety of religious groups and worked as a house servant. In 1843 she left the city and took the name Sojourner Truth. She explained her actions as a response to a divine inspiration to travel to the east and to show people their sins. After speaking at revival meetings throughout Long Island, New York, she moved on through Connecticut, and into Massachusetts, where in 1847 she settled in Northampton. There she met such noted abolitionists as **William Lloyd Garrison** and **Frederick Douglass.** Her biography, *The Narrative of Sojourner Truth* (1850), was prepared by Olive Gilbert. During the 1850s, she lectured on the evils of slavery throughout the eastern states and the Midwest.

In 1864 Truth was received by President Lincoln in Washington. After the Civil War, she sought to aid the southern freedmen—first by investigating conditions in the South, and then through a lecture tour by which she sought, unsuccessfully, to gain support for a federal grant of western lands for settlement by the freedmen.

———— ⌘ ————

Among the ex-slaves who traveled the abolition circuit in the 1840s and 1850s, Sojourner Truth was unique. As a woman she advocated woman's rights as well as abolition. While other black abolitionists became increasingly militant, she continued to rely on God's providence in bringing about a peaceful end to slavery. She felt a compulsion to lecture, explaining, "The Lord has made me a sign unto this nation, an' I go round a-testifyin', an' showin' on 'em their sins agin my people." She never failed to make a profound impression on her listeners. To see and hear her was, to use the 19th-century term, an immensely "affecting" experience. Her tall, spare frame clothed in simple, Quaker-like dress, her turbaned head, her captivating dialect, even her name, with its evocation of the age-old quest—all conspired to create an awesome figure on the podium. All of her lectures testified to what one observer called "her deep religious and trustful nature."

Perhaps **Harriet Beecher Stowe** offered the most perceptive observation as to Sojourner Truth's appeal, saying, "I do not recollect ever to have been conversant with any one who had more of that silent and subtle power which we call personal presence than this woman." Indeed, for Stowe, as for many other Americans, Sojourner Truth must have appeared as the female flesh-and-blood counterpart of the fictional hero in Stowe's famous novel. As such she could not help but have a considerable impact on romantic, evangelical-minded Americans. See Arthur H. Fauset, *Sojourner Truth, God's Faithful Pilgrim* (1938).

ANNE C. LOVELAND

TUBMAN, Harriet Ross (b. Dorchester City, Md., c. 1821; d. Auburn, N.Y., March 10, 1913), REFORMER, was born of slave parents. She worked as a field hand on a large Maryland plantation and received no schooling. In 1844 she was forced to marry John Tubman, but they soon separated. When her owner died in 1849 and it appeared that she would be sold in the Deep South, she escaped to Philadelphia and became active in the underground railroad, working as a cook to raise money to aid the fugitives. In 1857 she rescued her parents and settled them in Auburn, New York, in a house purchased from **William H. Seward.** An outspoken abolitionist, Tubman was also an advocate of woman's rights and often touched on that subject during her travels throughout the United States.

During the Civil War, Tubman attached herself to the Union army in South Carolina as a laundress, cook, and nurse. She frequently acted as a scout for Union soldiers and as a spy behind Confederate lines. In 1869 she married Nelson Davis, a war veteran, and worked to establish schools for freedmen in North Carolina. Sarah Bradford wrote her biography, *Scenes in the Life of Harriet Tubman* (1869), later revised as *Harriet, the Moses of Her People* (1886). The proceeds of this book were used to establish the Harriet Tubman

Home for indigent blacks in Auburn. Tubman spent her later years in poverty, although she earned numerous honors and tributes, including a medal from Queen Victoria of England.

Harriet Tubman became a legend of resourcefulness in devising means for rescuing harassed blacks and plotting insurrection. She was first of all an activist, who boldly entered the slavery domain to bring out runaways and lead them into the free states and Canada. Since her work was undercover, many of the details of her exploits were necessarily lost and became subject to embroidery and sentimental fancies. Nevertheless, enough is known to sketch an active and courageous life, which may have resulted in some two to three hundred slave rescues, and which certainly inspired other runaways and substantial slave unrest in the Maryland area and beyond. Her most public action, that of rescuing the fugitive mulatto Charles Nalle, April 27, 1860, from prison officials and federal commissioners at Troy, New York, gave ample proof of her reckless courage and inspiring presence, and threw light on her methods of operating under desperate conditions.

Her role as an insurrectionary is more controversial. All her fame here lies in her unfulfilled connection with **John Brown,** who dubbed her "General" Tubman, and remarked, arrestingly, that she was "the most of a man, naturally, that I ever met with." This admiration Tubman reciprocated. She would certainly have followed Brown to Harpers Ferry had sickness not intervened. Her sole contribution to the Brown effort lies in the conjecture it arouses as to how she might have comported herself in that crisis. It is difficult to believe she would have permitted herself to be penned up in the arsenal, as Brown was, and subjected to military assault and trial. See Earl Conrad, *Harriet Tubman* (1943).

LOUIS FILLER

TUGWELL, Rexford Guy (b. Sinclairville, N.Y., July 10, 1891; d. Santa Barbara, Calif., July 21,

1979), ECONOMIST, studied at the Wharton School of Finance and Commerce, University of Pennsylvania (BS in economics, 1915; MA, 1917; PhD, 1922). After having served as instructor of economics at the University of Pennsylvania (1915–17) and as an assistant professor at the University of Washington (1917–18), he joined the economics faculty of Columbia University, where he remained until 1937. Beginning with his thesis, *The Economic Basis of Public Interest* (1922), Tugwell produced a series of books, including *The Trend of Economics* (1924) and *Industry's Coming of Age* (1927), in which he criticized laissez-faire economic thought and called for increased use of economic planning and government regulation of business. In 1927 he visited the Soviet Union with a delegation of trade unionists, after which he edited and contributed a chapter on Russian agriculture to *Soviet Russia in the Second Decade* (1928). In 1928 he made a survey of American agriculture and its problems for Governor **Alfred E. Smith** of New York. He served in the Roosevelt administration, working as assistant secretary (1933) and then undersecretary (1934–36) of the Department of Agriculture, where he was active in efforts to alleviate the lot of sharecroppers, tenant farmers, and farm laborers. In 1935 he was appointed head of the new Resettlement Administration, which sought to move farmers from submarginal land to better soil and created three "greenbelt" towns— new communities near sources of employment yet surrounded by countryside. Tugwell's views on industrial growth and development, and particularly his support of national economic planning helped shape early New Deal industrial legislation, such as the National Industrial Recovery Act (1933).

In 1938 Tugwell worked on the New York City Planning Commission, after which he was appointed chancellor of the University of Puerto Rico (1941) and then governor of Puerto Rico (1941–46). In 1947 he published *The Stricken Land*, regarding his tenure as governor. During 1946–57, he was a member of the political science faculty at the University of Chicago. He was a senior fellow, then associate, of The Center for the Study of Democratic Institutions in Santa Barbara

(1964–79). Tugwell wrote *The Democratic Roosevelt* (1957) a prize-winning biography, and several other books reflecting on Roosevelt and the New Deal, including the *The Brains Trust* (1968) and *In Search of Roosevelt* (1972). A three-volume autobiography was completed with the posthumous publication of *To the Lesser Heights of Morningside* in 1982.

———◆———

The career of Tugwell as a New Dealer is a case study in the eternal clash between intellectuals and politicians. As a systematic thinker among practical men, he supplied ideas, exciting Roosevelt's imagination, and stayed out of politics. Loyal but no yes-man, he was aware of intellectual limitations—especially Roosevelt's orthodox economic thought—and political constraints on "making America over." Tugwell, however, felt frustrated when it became clear that reconstruction in the United States did not take the form of great coordinated movements forward, that when politicians treated intellectuals as expendable commodities, they were simply practicing their profession. This complicated experience was undergone by a complicated man: a pessimistic optimist, impatient evolutionary, pragmatic ideologist, realistic romantic, indignant despairer, stand-offish democrat, flippant foe and warm friend, tactless gentleman, and pro-business antagonist of the titans of business. Tugwell saw corporations as good servants, but as bad masters when they made economic decisions beyond the control of the democratic political state and without regard to social result. Another Brain Truster, **Adolf A. Berle,** later claimed that the New Deal had made the corporation responsible to the political state. Tugwell discerned the distortion of original intentions through the regulation by the regulated by the regulators. Tugwell's earlier writings on Roosevelt and the New Deal emphasized missed opportunities for more substantial change, but he later concluded that FDR had accomplished about as much as could be reasonably expected in the face of formidable ideological, political, and institutional obstacles to reform. Tugwell's death in 1979 occurred on the eve of an era in which America moved further from the kind of nation he envisioned in a proposed revision of the U.S. Constitution (1967) that provided for regional governments and a fourth, planning branch. See Bernard Sternsher, *Rexford Tugwell and the New Deal* (1964), and Otis L. Graham, Jr., Epilogue to *The Lesser Heights of Morningside* (1982).

BERNARD STERNSHER

TURNER, Frederick Jackson (b. Portage, Wis., Nov. 14, 1861; d. Pasadena, Calif., March 14, 1932), HISTORIAN, received his BA (1884) and MA (1888) from the University of Wisconsin, and PhD from Johns Hopkins (1890), where he studied under **Herbert Baxter Adams.** While teaching at the University of Wisconsin (1888–1910), Turner presented his influential paper "The Significance of the Frontier in American History" at a meeting of the American Historical Association in 1893. The history of America, he argued, was to a large extent the history of the colonization of the West. Now, however (citing a recent bulletin issued by the superintendent of the census), the western frontier had disappeared, thus marking "the closing of a historic movement." He believed that the availability of land had lured men westward and affected their thinking and the structure of their political institutions. The isolation of the frontier forced each wave of western pioneers to contend with "primitive conditions." The necessity for creating civilization anew, Turner suggested, developed many of the distinctive features of the American people, including democracy and individualism. Since Turner believed that the West was a salient agency through which the immigrant was Americanized and democracy developed, he modified the ubiquitous germ theory of political institutions—that democracy was developed in the German forests, brought to America, and matured in an American environment—arguing instead that the uniqueness of the American frontier had developed democracy. Above all, Turner believed that the frontier promoted mobility and opportunity ("safety-valve" theory): "So

long as free land exists, the opportunity for a competency exists, and economic power secures political power."

Turner's essay marked a major turning point in American historiography, focusing attention on a relatively unexplored area. In his seminars at the University of Wisconsin, Turner encouraged his students to apply interdisciplinary techniques to the study of history ("History is the biography of society in all its departments").

In 1906 Turner published *The Rise of the New West,* which covered the period 1819–29. In 1910 he became professor of history at Harvard, where he taught until 1924. From 1924 until his death he was at the Huntington Library in Pasadena, California. Turner published one other book, *The Significance of the Frontier in American History* (1920), a collection of essays. Two other works were published posthumously: *The Significance of Sections in American History* (1932, awarded a Pulitzer Prize), and *The United States 1830–1850* (1935).

—∞∞∞—

Among the eminent historians of United States history who are known at home and abroad for their originality and contributions to historical thought, Frederick Jackson Turner continues to be a popular and a controversial figure. The decade of criticism of Turner's writings in the 1930s widened into an era of some thirty additional years of searching analysis of the frontier-sectional theory. Not the least of Turner's contributions to the writing of history has been the legacy of controversy that he left. This involved historians in a debate on the wide-ranging implications of the frontier theory. At the same time it is possible to argue that his insistence on a more disciplined, more scientific and interdisciplinary approach to historical research was even more enduring than his provocative theorizing. Turner himself, looking back on a lifetime of work in an autobiographical letter, went so far as to state that he did not think of himself as a historian of the West: "Although my work has laid stress on two aspects of American history—the frontier and the sections ... I do not think of myself as primarily either a western historian or a human geographer. I have stressed these two factors, because it seemed to me that they had been neglected, but fundamentally I have been interested in the inter-relations of economics, politics, sociology, culture in general, with the geographical factors, in explaining the United States of today by means of its history thus broadly taken. Perhaps this is one of the reasons I have not been more voluminous!" We have here a key to understanding Turner, the wise teacher and probing investigator whose limited publications were based on a complex formula of historical research. His reputation does not rest on his published writings alone but also on his very shrewd concept of what was actually involved in writing history. His fundamental concern was with the historical origins of modern American society with all its problems. He discarded the old barriers separating the disciplines and declined to confine himself to conventional methods of study. His papers preserved at the Huntington Library today reveal that he devoted much of his time to analysis of such problems as the exhaustion of resources, population explosions, and the prospect of a great international war involving the use of a dreaded "chemist's bomb." Indeed, Turner was vitally interested in what he called "a strategy of peace." In several of his unpublished essays he attempted to apply his theory of sections to Europe's problems. He reasoned that if America's sections could be restrained by political parties from allowing rivalries to mushroom into armed conflict, perhaps international political parties in a world government might cut across national boundaries and play a similar kind of binding role. It is no accident that Turner became a controversial figure, for he believed in the uses of history. He was convinced that the past can illuminate the present and help us to prepare for the future. See Wilbur R. Jacobs, *The Historical World of Frederick Jackson Turner* (1968).

WILBUR R. JACOBS

TURNER, Henry McNeal (b. Abbeville, S.C., Feb. 1, 1834; d. Windsor, Ontario, Can., May 8, 1915), RELIGIOUS LEADER, was born a freeman, but worked as a youth in cotton fields with slaves. Later, while working as a janitor in an Abbeville law office, he was taught to read and write by the firm's clerks. In 1848 he joined the Methodist Episcopal Church and was licensed to preach in 1853. He preached throughout the South until 1858, when he joined the African Methodist Episcopal Church (bishop, 1880), and was then transferred to a Baltimore training mission. After studying Latin, Greek, and Hebrew at Trinity College, he became pastor of the Israel Church in Washington, D.C., in 1862 and was appointed army chaplain by President Lincoln in 1863, becoming the first black to hold such a position.

After the Civil War, President Andrew Johnson appointed Turner a chaplain in the regular army and assigned him to the Georgia office of the Freedman's Bureau. Turner soon resigned, however, and turned to recruitment for the African M.E. Church in Georgia. He was also an active Republican party organizer in that state. He was a delegate to the 1868 Georgia constitutional convention, and was elected to the state legislature in 1868 and 1870. In 1869 President Grant appointed Turner postmaster in Macon, Georgia, and in the years following he also served as a customs inspector in Savannah. In 1876 Turner became manager of African M.E. publications in Philadelphia and was elected bishop by the 1880 general conference in St. Louis. He served as bishop for his church in Georgia (1880–92) and chancellor of Morris Brown College in Atlanta.

Because Turner had become convinced that African-Americans had no chance for equality in the U.S., he advocated for their return to Africa, and sponsored an ill-fated colonization attempt to Liberia in 1878. Beginning in 1868, pan-African nationalism was his major interest. He founded several magazines, *The Southern Christian Recorder* (1889), *The Voice of Missions* (1892), and *The Voice of the People* (1901), and wrote a number of books, including *The Genius and Theory of Methodist Polity* (1885) and *The Black Man's Doom* (1896), a criticism of Supreme Court civil rights decisions. He visited Africa four times in the 1890s to generate interest in black emigration to that continent.

───✦───

Turner's life exemplified the dilemmas of blacks in 19th-century America. In a slave society, he was neither slave nor white. Eager to take advantage of his freedom, he could not get a formal education. A politician by nature, he had to be satisfied during most of his life with churchmanship. Proclaiming that Africa was the true home of African-Americans, he could neither persuade many to emigrate nor extract himself from the web of American life. Within his church he gave vigorous leadership, especially in the years just after the Civil War, but he could not convert educated blacks to black nationalism.

Despite these handicaps Turner rose to prominence and power by sheer force of personality. He was a gifted orator and an energetic worker, and his leadership was based on a blunt, astringent style that thrived on controversy. His harsh criticism of American racism won him the admiration of many blacks who were afraid to speak their own minds. Most of his following was among the unlettered rural blacks of the South, attracted by his too-simple African emigration scheme and his blistering verbal assaults on middle-class blacks who disagreed with his ideas. But with a politician's instinct for survival, he stayed on good terms with many leading southern whites.

Turner's active life spanned both the heady years of emancipation and Reconstruction and the long decline of race relations that followed. **Booker T. Washington,** the apostle of accommodation, emerged as the black spokesman for the time, but Turner persisted in both his strong criticism of American racism and his call for black separatism. Had Turner lived to see those themes rise again in the 1920s and 1960s he would have been a strong ally of **Marcus Garvey** and **Malcolm X.** See Edwin S. Redkey, *Black Exodus: Black Nationalist and Back to Africa Movements, 1890–1910* (1969).

EDWIN S. REDKEY

TURNER, Nat (b. Southampton Co., Va., Oct. 2, 1800; d. Jerusalem, Va., Nov. 11, 1831), REVOLUTIONARY, was born a slave on the plantation of Benjamin Turner, and subsequently passed into the ownership of Joseph Travis. Claiming to see visions and hear divine voices, he developed a religious and mystical fanaticism early in his career. He soon came to believe that he was divinely ordained to lead his fellow slaves to freedom. Beginning in about 1828 he urged blacks in Southampton County, Virginia, to rise up and slay their white enemies when a sign appeared. Following the solar eclipse of February 1831, Turner planned his slave uprising for July, but later postponed it until August.

On Sunday, August 21, 1831, Turner and about seven followers murdered Turner's master and five members of his family. With his band increased to more than seventy, Turner went on a rampage through the countryside, killing some fifty-seven men, women, and children in what was the bloodiest slave uprising of the antebellum South. Although his followers were dispersed and captured by August 25, Turner was not found until October 30. With about twenty other slaves, he was sentenced to death. As a direct result of his uprising, southern slave codes were made stricter, sectional tensions were exacerbated, and southern manumission societies suffered a serious setback.

───✦───

Occasionally a historical figure is rescued from obscurity through a work of fiction—a classic example is Robert Rogers, hero of Kenneth Roberts's *Northwest Passage*. In *The Confessions of Nat Turner,* William Styron has done the same for the leader of the bloodiest slave rebellion in the United States. Styron's "meditation on history" caused an angry and far-reaching literary controversy: a dozen or more black critics assailed his portrayal of Nat Turner as a celibate "hired nigger," claiming it bore little resemblance to the courageous insurrectionist committed to the freedom of his people. Defenders have argued for the validity of the Styronic portrayal.

The truth is that we know very little about

Turner. Thomas R. Gray, a white lawyer, interviewed Turner at the time of his apprehension and obtained his confession. This remarkable document is virtually our sole source for information about Turner's religious convictions and his motivation to rebellion. Nothing in the narrative contradicts the known facts of the rebellion. Styron, among others, contends, however, that Gray tampered with Turner's words, using them to illustrate for his white audience the wickedness and needlessness of Turner's "atrocious and heart-rending deeds."

It is certain that Nat Turner was reared in a genuinely religious atmosphere and from an early age believed that he "was ordained for some great purpose by the Almighty." He had no formal education, but Gray believed that in natural intelligence and quickness of apprehension he was surpassed by few men. In the year 1825 he experienced a vision of white and black spirits engaged in battle; in 1828 the Holy Spirit told him to prepare himself for a sign to arise and slay his enemies with their own weapons. When it first appeared in February 1831 (a solar eclipse), Turner set July 4 as his starting date, but fell sick from his great agitation. When the sign reappeared in August, he steeled himself to begin the bloody uprising that sent waves of panic throughout the South. After his capture he faced death with calm and deliberate composure; when asked if he realized the mistake he had made, Turner responded: "Was not Christ crucified?" See John B. Duff and Peter M. Mitchell, *The Nat Turner Rebellion: The Historical Event and the Modern Controversy* (1971).

JOHN B. DUFF

TURNER, Ted (Robert Edward III) (b. Cincinnati, Ohio, Nov. 19, 1938), BUSINESS LEADER, grew up mainly in Atlanta, Georgia, where his father, Ed Turner, owned an advertising business. He attended Brown Univesity but was expelled in 1960 before receiving a degree. Plagued by business reversals, his father committed suicide in 1963, and twenty-four-year-old Ted Turner inherited the firm. He built the company, which consisted primarily of highway billboards,

into a communications giant. A pioneer invester in cable and satellite networks, in 1970 he bought an independent Atlanta UHF station and turned it into the first transmitted superstation. From that beginning, he founded the Cable News Network (CNN), the Turner Broadcasting System (TBS), and Turner Network Television (TNT). Branching into movies, Turner bought Castle Rock Entertainment and New Line Cinema in 1993. In 1994, *U.S. News and World Report* estimated his holdings in television alone to total $1.8 billion. After long and difficult negotiations, in the fall of 1995 Turner sold his media holdings in a stock swap to Time-Warner Communications, a deal that made Turner hundreds of millions of dollars and turned Time-Warner into the largest media giant in the world. Turner, besides being a major stockholder in Time-Warner, still owns the Atlanta Braves baseball team and the Atlanta Hawks basketball squad.

⸎

Turner said that as a boy his father used to beat him with a wire hanger in order to "get my attention." The floggings failed to turn Ted Turner into a model child. He attended the military-oriented McCallie School in Chattanooga, Tennessee, where he was dubbed "Terrible Ted" because of his constant pranks, one of which included bringing live snakes into the dorm. At Brown University he was booted out of his fraternity after he burned down the school's homecoming display. He finally left Brown in 1960 after a second suspension, this time for having a female guest in his room. But aside from dormitory rebellions, Turner still achieved bursts of academic success. He won the Tennessee State high school debating contest, and at Brown he plunged into an independent study of ancient Greek culture.

Turner's life took a horrific turn when his father killed himself with a pistol. For years afterward, Turner hinted to friends that some day he too might take his own life. However in business he enjoyed a string of steady successes, despite a penchant for roll-of-the-dice investments. In 1980 he gambled (and won) public acceptance of

CNN, an all news TV network. The CNN format, which earned the company a huge international audience because of its prize-winning in-depth coverage of Iraq and Operation Desert Storm in 1990–91, is now imitated by TV companies throughout the world. Observers claim Turner approaches each new undertaking in the communications industry with a supreme air of confidence. It is as if he views movie studios and television stations as cards in a monopoly game—a game he knows he will eventually win.

Trim and athletic, Turner pursues a vigorous personal life. Long an active man-about-town, he has been married three times. He is now married to actress and environmental activist Jane Fonda. A superb yachtsman, he won the coveted America's Cup award in 1977. He is often seen in the stands, cheering for his Atlanta Braves baseball team. Shortly after he bought the Braves, he entertained the fans by pushing a baseball from first base to home plate with his nose. It is no wonder people still call him "Terrible Ted." See Porter Bibb, *It Isn't As Easy As It Looks: Ted Turner's Amazing Story* (1993).

R. CONRAD STEIN

TWAIN, Mark. See Clemens, Samuel Langhorne.

TWEED, William Marcy (b. New York, N.Y., April 3, 1823; d. New York, N.Y., April 12, 1878), POLITICAL LEADER, left school at eleven, becoming a chairmaker and then a saddler. Having studied bookkeeping, he became a clerk. In 1851 he was elected New York City alderman on the Democratic ticket. He served in the U.S. House of Representatives (1853–55), then returned to the aldermanic council. Gradually he became the leader of the Tammany Hall political machine. Through his law office Tweed extorted bribes in the guise of fees from the Erie Railroad and others for whom he secured city favors, and many city franchises, such as the right to operate ferry boats. Concerns in which he was interested sold building materials to the new county courthouse behind City Hall; it ultimately cost $12 million, three times as much as was justified.

By 1868 Tweed controlled the New York State Democratic machine and was grand sachem of Tammany Hall. Aided by a city charter which Tammany had bribed through the legislature, the "Tweed Ring" placed graft on a businesslike basis, padding all bills by a fixed amount and dividing the spoils according to an established formula in which Tweed's share was one-fifth. By 1870 he was a millionaire. In January of that year *Harper's Weekly* began a series of cartoons by **Thomas Nast** which devastatingly depicted the way Tweed was supposed to have accumulated his fortune. In September the New York *Times* joined the attack, and in July 1871 it published evidence of the corruption of the Ring gathered from discontented city officials. In 1873 Tweed was sentenced to twelve years for graft, but this was reduced on appeal to one year. Two years later, however, he was jailed for inability to pay a large judgment obtained in a civil action. He escaped to Cuba in 1876, but the Spanish government returned him. Hoping to be released from prison, Tweed divulged details of many dishonest dealings, but died in his cell at the Ludlow Street jail.

⎯⎯∞⎯⎯

The concept "Boss" covers a multitude of political styles. The ordinary treatment of Tweed as the archetypical leader of an urban political organization both slanders a great many honest politicians and obscures the special dynamics of his career.

There were three major elements in these dynamics. He occupied, first, a position of central leadership which was repeatedly challenged by ward leaders and reformist committees. His control was insecure, his hegemony—such as it was—short-lived. Second, he achieved power in the midst of a vast wave of urban development, including not simply the infamous courthouse but a revision of the city plan, new roads, parks, boulevards, transit, and facilities construction, and a revision of the municipal charter. Finally, he mobilized support for the developmental program by paying off disparate groups with both cash and construction.

The final element links the first two. The fragmented social structure and communications system of the city made it extremely difficult to command assent and cooperation without immediate payoffs. Later bosses, with more power built on broader consent and organization, could afford to be more honest than Tweed.

This argument does not require proof that Tweed himself had a grand vision of the city and only reluctantly stooped to conquer. He was, undoubtedly, a complete scoundrel who managed, however, to succeed for a while where honest men foundered. See Seymour J. Mandelbaum, *Boss Tweed's New York* (1965).

SEYMOUR J. MANDELBAUM

TYLER, John (b. Greenway, Va., March 29, 1790; d. Richmond, Va., Jan. 18, 1862), PRESIDENT, graduated from the College of William and Mary (1807) and was admitted to the bar in 1809. A Virginia state legislator (1811–16), member of the U.S. House of Representatives (1817–21), governor (1825–27), and U.S. senator (1827–36), Tyler was an ardent states' righter. He opposed the Missouri Compromise (1820), believing that Congress could not restrict slavery in the territories, voted against the high Tariff of 1828, and, disapproving of Andrew Jackson's aggressiveness during the nullification crisis, opposed the Force Bill (1833). In 1836 he resigned his Senate seat rather than honor the Virginia legislature's "instructions" that he support a resolution deleting from the record the Senate's censure of Jackson for his withdrawal of the federal deposits during the U.S. Bank controversy.

Tyler then returned to the Virginia state legislature (1838–40). He was elected vice president on the Whig ticket in 1840. When William Henry Harrison died in office (1841), Tyler became president. He twice vetoed a bill for a U.S. "Fiscal Bank" on constitutional grounds which led to the resignation of all members of the cabinet except **Daniel Webster.** Tyler approved the Preemption Act (1841), legalizing the right of settlers to occupy unsurveyed land and to later buy it at $1.25 an acre, and the Tariff of 1842, which raised duties to the level of the Act of 1832. He favored the annexation of Texas, which was accomplished shortly before the end of his term by a joint resolution of Congress (1845).

In his remaining years, Tyler fought for states' rights principles. Hoping to allay sectional tensions, he presided over the Washington "Peace Convention" (1861). When this failed, he supported secession from the Union, and was elected to the Confederate Congress.

———— ❧ ————

By ordinary standards John Tyler was a most successful man and politician. Of a respected Virginia family that was aristocratic if not of the very first rank, Tyler became a lawyer shortly after graduating from one of the country's most prestigious colleges before he was eighteen years old (albeit such youthful graduation was not uncommon at the time). A state legislator before he was thirty, governor and then U.S. senator from Virginia before forty, Tyler crowned his political career by ascending to the nation's highest office at age fifty, making him the youngest president of the United States up to that time.

Yet it is indisputable that Tyler's presidency was a failure and his historical reputation low. He became the nation's tenth president not because the people wanted him but because he happened to be vice president when for the first time an incumbent died in office. Tyler was thereafter derided as "His Accidency" not by the Democrats alone but by his own party, the Whigs, as well. Credited even by his severest modern critics for political consistency and sincere convictions with regard to states' rights, strict construction, legislative dominance, the limited veto, and other articles of the old Jeffersonian Republican faith, Tyler had no use for the nationalistic and pro-business policies championed by **Henry Clay,** the great leader of the Whig party. For all his courtliness and soft-spokenness, Tyler was a courageous—detractors would say stubborn—man who refused to bend to Clay, and in so doing brought about an anomalous situation in which the chief executive was in effect written out of his party at a time when it was in power. The tragedy stemmed from the fact that Tyler was hardly a Whig at all.

He had been given the second place on that party's ticket not because of his beliefs or his struggles on its behalf but rather because as a former anti-Jackson Democrat and a good southerner he helped balance that ticket. Tyler's major problem was that in an age that rewarded political opportunism and evasiveness, he was adept at neither. He was a man of scruple, who could oppose the Bank of the United States as unconstitutional, yet write a senatorial report conceding the Bank's fitness as a government repository.

Tyler was hardly a large man, however. If as president he was the wrong man at the wrong time, his failure lay only in part to unusual circumstances outside his control. Tyler's greatest weakness was not his determination to resist Clay's program but his inability to mount support or even seriously go about winning support for the presidential position. Great political reputations require better luck than Tyler enjoyed and both sterner and more flexible stuff than he was made of. See Oliver Perry Chitwood, *John Tyler, Champion of the Old South* (1939).

EDWARD PESSEN

UPDIKE, John Hoyer (b. Shillington, Pa., March 18, 1932), WRITER, graduated from Harvard (1954), where he was president of the *Lampoon* magazine. He spent the following year on a Knox fellowship at the Ruskin School of Drawing and Fine Arts at Oxford University. Upon his return to the U.S. in 1955 he joined the staff of the *New Yorker,* writing essays, poems and parodies, and also the magazine's "Talk of the Town" column. Updike left the *New Yorker* in 1957. He published his first poetry collection, *The Carpentered Hen,* in 1958, his first novel, *The Poorhouse Fair,* in 1959, his first short-story collection, *The Same Door,* in 1959. He followed these works with *Rabbit, Run* (1960), *Pigeon Feathers* (1962), and *Telephone Poles and Other Poems* (1963). His novel *The Centaur* (1963) won the 1964 National Book Award for fiction. *Olinger Stories* (1964) was based on life in Shillington, the town of his youth, while *Assorted Prose* (1965) contained parodies, memoirs, and criticism. He wrote a short novel, *Of the Farm* (1965), and a short-story collection, *The Music School* (1966). In his best-selling novel *Couples* (1968), describing with great candor a group of married people in a small suburban community, Updike criticized the emptiness of American middle-class life. For nearly three decades, Updike's writings have been pouring from his

prolific pen—or word processor—like clockwork. By 1990, one critic counted thirty-six books, including novels, short stories, poems, essays, criticism, children's stories, and a play. Among this plethora of works are such notable titles as *Bech: A Book* (1970), *Rabbit Redux* (1971), *Museums and Women and Other Stories* (1972), *Rabbit is Rich* (1981), *The Witches of Eastwick* (1989), and *Rabbit at Rest* (1990). His memoirs, *Self Consciousness,* appeared in 1989.

Precocity, preciosity, virtuosity: these are the labels which critics most frequently have attached to the works of John Updike, at times unfairly blanking out the seriousness and breadth of his creativity. Precocious he certainly was, selling his first short story when he was just twenty-two, and producing two mature novels before he was thirty. Moreover, the characteristic preciosity of his style cannot be denied, particularly the concern for prose rhythms, the sly allusiveness, the startling imagery, the lush metaphor, the delight (especially in his verse) in wit and wordplay. And virtuoso he remains, working with ease in the novel, short story, poem, essay, review, and even minor genres like sketch and parody. Perhaps it is not surprising, then, that critics faced with the prolific display of multiple talents tended to emphasize the manner over the substance, contending that Updike's absorption in the creation of the world of a private sensibility precluded concern for the more general human condition. But Updike's world actually extends far beyond his almost naturalistically realized settings of Pennsylvania countryside, of New York City, or of New England exurb: it is by implication the world of truly fallen post–World War II man, achingly aware of moral ambiguities. This is why religion and marriage (especially its sexual aspect) are obsessive themes, for each involves a reaching out, a quest for some sort of certainty in a climate of disintegration. Updike has not been uniformly successful; the mythological framework of *The Centaur*, for example, smothers what is essentially a simple tale. But as a creator of moral fables which try to see the human world in relation to a spiritual realm, Updike is without real peer among the American writers of his generation. See Alice and Kenneth Hamilton, *The Elements of John Updike* (1970).

JOSEPH V. RIDGELY

VAIL, Theodore Newton (b. Carroll County, Ohio, July 16, 1845; d. Baltimore, Md., April 16, 1920), INDUSTRIALIST, attended the Morristown (N.J.) Academy. After briefly studying medicine with an uncle, he went to New York City in 1864 and became an operator for the Western Union Telegraph Co. After working in Waterloo, Iowa, and Pinebluff, South Dakota, he settled in Omaha, Nebraska, in 1869, where he was employed by the railway mail service as a route agent. While traveling across the country on mail trips, Vail devised many improvements in the operations and routings of the service. In 1873 he was transferred to the Washington, D.C., railway mail service office. He became assistant general superintendent in 1874. After inaugurating Fast Mail service between New York and Chicago, using the New York Central and other railroads (1875), he ws promoted to general superintendent of railway mail service in 1876.

In 1878 President Gardiner Hubbard invited Vail to become general manager of the new Bell Telephone Co. Vail increased telephone sales, extended lines of communication, and consolidated many smaller companies; he incorporated the subsidiary American Telephone and Telegraph Co. and became its first president in 1885. He retired from business in 1887 and spent the next several years on his farm at Lyndonville, Vermont, and traveling in Europe. In 1894 he was asked to work on industrial development in Argentina and between then and 1907 he helped build a water-power plant at Córdoba, a street-railway system in Buenos Aires, and telephone systems in Argentina's large cities. Returning to the U.S. in 1907, Vail was elected president of AT&T. He moved company headquarters from Boston to New York, further consolidated the system, and bought Western Union in 1909. When the federal government charged antitrust violations in 1913, Vail divested AT&T of the telegraph company. In 1915 he participated in opening the first transcontinental telephone line with President Wilson. During World War I he helped build an American telephone system in France. In 1919 Vail retired as president of AT&T to become chairman of its board of directors.

More than anyone else, Theodore Vail was responsible for the structure of the telephone industry. At the time he became manager of the bell Telephone company in 1878, there were many small, local systems in operation, some localities having three or more competing lines. Many used Bell patents, while others utilized patents and equipment developed by other firms. Western Union, far larger than all the telephone companies combined, had employed **Thomas A. Edison** to develop new equipment, and in many ways the Edison versions were superior to those employed by Bell Telephone.

Competition between rival lines meant that interconnected services were out of the question. Long-distance communication by telephone was not even considered; that was the province of Western Union. Subscribers to a system received a list of others on the same line, whom they could call for a fee. That was as far as it went. The telephone was considered not much more than an intriguing toy. Although its promise was evident, without rationalization it would remain a toy.

Vail set out to unite all the lines into one system, thus eliminating duplication and bringing all the telephones in the nation into one network, dominated by Bell. This would make long-distance calls possible, encourage the use of telephones, and so increase the numbers of subscribers. He recognized that his plan would necessitate a creation of a monopoly—he called it a "regulated monopoly"—because in no other way could the industry develop and expand. He eliminated Western Union from the industry, began the process of buying out smaller firms, and obtained the banker **J. P. Morgan's** backing to facilitate expansion. Having created a vehicle for long-distance lines, American Telephone and Telegraph, in 1885, and thus having brought his plan to fruition, he retired in 1887, when only 42.

The company progressed without Vail, but soon was in poor financial shape as a result of heavy expenditures and an insistence on paying large dividends. It almost failed in the panic of 1907, at which time Vail was asked to take charge once again. He returned, with the understanding that he would run the company while J. P. Morgan would have control in financial matters.

In this second stage of his career Vail "reabsorbed" Western Union and tried to create a communications monopoly, but as a result of antitrust action he was obliged to again get rid of the telegraph company. He did manage to gain control of Western Electric, which became Bell's manufacturing arm, while the work in expanding long-distance lines continued. The independent

telephone companies also grew in this period, but the Bell-controlled lines expanded even more rapidly.

At the time of Vail's death in 1920 it seemed evident that American Telephone and Telegraph would dominate the industry, with several medium-sized and a host of small independents tied to the Bell lines. In this respect, Vail's concept of regulated monopoly succeeded, and was accepted by the government. See Albert B. Paine, *Theodore N. Vail: A Biography* (1929).

ROBERT SOBEL

VALLANDIGHAM, Clement Laird (b. New Lisbon, Ohio, July 29, 1820; d. Lebanon, Ohio, June 17, 1871), POLITICAL LEADER, studied at Jefferson College (Cannonsburg, Pa.), but withdrew to study law. Admitted to the bar in 1842, he entered politics, characterizing himself as a Jacksonian Democrat and a states' righter. He served two terms (1845–47) in the lower house of the Ohio legislature, and then edited the Dayton, Ohio, *Western Empire* and practiced law with Thomas J. S. Smith, on Ohio elder statesman. He organized several companies of state militia, becoming a brigadier general in 1857. Defeated for Congress in 1852 and in 1854, he successfully challenged the 1856 returns and was seated by the House of Representatives in 1858.

Vallandigham supported Buchanan for president at the Democratic national convention of 1856. Passing through Harpers Ferry soon after the **John Brown** raid of 1859, he interrogated the wounded prisoner, trying to link "the conspiracy" to Ohio Republicans.

As secretary of the Democratic national committee, he witnessed the breakup of the Charleston convention of 1860, attended the **Douglas**-dominated Baltimore convention, and campaigned energetically for the "Little Giant" and his own successful reelection. After Lincoln's election, Vallandigham supported compromise measures, and after the attack on Fort Sumter he opposed "coercion" of the South, preferring compromise and reunion.

He served as a gadfly in the 37th Congress,

opposing "all abolition measures," arbitrary arrests, and federal conscription. Defeated for reelection in 1862 after the Republican-controlled state legislature had changed the boundaries of his district, he sought his party's gubernatorial nomination, courting arrest and seeking "martyrdom" through his antiwar activities. He was arrested on May 5, 1863, for the "violation of General Orders No. 38," issued earlier by Major General Ambrose E. Burnside, found guilty by a military commission, and ordered "placed in closed confinement in some fortress of the United States." President Lincoln, however, changed the sentence to banishment to the Confederacy.

While an exile in the South, Vallandigham won the Ohio Democratic gubernatorial nomination. Making his way to Canada, he campaigned from Niagara Falls and Windsor. He was defeated for governor by the Republican-Unionist John Brough. In June 1864 he returned to Ohio, but Lincoln chose to ignore him rather than order his rearrest. Elected a delegate to the Democratic presidention convention of 1864, he wrote a controversial peace plank which **McClellan**, the Democratic nominee, later repudiated. After the war, Vallandigham attended the Democratic national convention of 1868 and dreamed futilely of vindication and election to a seat in the U.S. Senate. He accidentally killed himself with a pistol during a trial while demonstrating how a crime had been committed.

———— ❧ ————

In his own day, Clement L. Vallandigham was a most controversial figure. Peace Democrats, called "Copperheads" by Republicans in Civil War days, characterized him as personable, courageous, and possessed of leadership qualities. Republican critics, on the other hand, viewed him as one-minded, self-serving, and impractical. Actually, he misjudged the mind and mood of the South as well as that of his own section; his opposition to the war and his addiction to compromise as a means to end the war made him a dreamer in a realistic world.

Although nationalist historians had a tendency to dismiss Vallandigham as a fanatic and trai-

tor, he was essentially a conservative opposing the changes taking place during the Civil War. His early exposure to Calvinism, his hatred of abolition, and his devotion to Edmund Burke's preachments helped shape his conservatism. He opposed the centralization of power in Washington and the transformation of the federal union into "a new nation." He opposed the ascendancy of industrialism over agriculture. As "a western sectionalist" he resented the Northeast's control of government and business, expressing himself as "inexorably hostile" to "Puritan domination in religion or morals or literature or politics." He also opposed Lincoln's emancipation policy, believing it unconstitutional and irresponsible. He came to believe that the South could not be conquered and that eventually free elections and civil rights would disappear. As the spokesman for Peace Democracy, he helped popularize the slogan: "The Constitution as it is, the Union as it was"—proof that he feared the future and worshiped the past. As a conservative and disciple of Burke, he believed that changes should be "evolutionary rather than revolutionary" and that the deep roots of the past must be cultivated continuously.

Vallandigham's role as gadfly and dissenter during the Civil War has given him his niche in history. His arrest, trial, and exile put his name on every lip. In *Ex parte Vallandigham* (1864), the U.S. Supreme Court avoided a conflict with the military by stating it had no right to review the proceedings of a courtmartial even if a citizen were tried illegally by it. Two years later, however, in *Ex parte Milligan*, the Court reversed itself and enunciated the principle that military trial of civilians, in areas where the civil courts were open and functioning, was both unwarranted and illegal. Vallandigham always believed that the decision in *Ex parte Milligan* had vindicated him and indicted General Burnside and President Lincoln. He always believed that time would vindicate him, but it has vindicated Lincoln instead. See Frank L. Klement, *The Limits of Dissent: Clement L. Vallandigham and the Civil War* (1970).

FRANK L. KLEMENT

VAN BUREN, Martin (b. Kinderhook, N.Y., Dec. 5, 1782; d. there, July 24, 1862), PRESIDENT, was admitted to the bar in 1803. A state senator (1812–20) and attorney general (1816–19) of New York, he was the leader of the "Albany Regency," a political machine. He served in the U.S. Senate (1821–1828) and was elected governor of New York (1828) but resigned in March 1829 to become Andrew Jackson's secretary of state. He soon became one of Jackson's closest advisers and replaced John C. Calhoun as vice-president in Jackson's second term (1833–37). In 1836 he was himself elected president.

During the depression of 1837, Van Buren concerned himself with the finances of the federal government and overlooked the problems of the whole economy. His main occupation was to find a substitute means of handling federal funds after Jackson prevented the recharter of the U.S. Bank. Believing that the government should "divorce" itself from all banking activities, he proposed the Independent Treasury Bill (1837), whereby government-owned vaults would be constructed to store all federal revenues. All payments to the government were to be in hard money. This system was approved by Congress in 1840.

Van Buren was defeated for reelection in 1840 by William Henry Harrison, 234 electoral votes to 60. In 1844 he failed to obtain the Democratic nomination for president because he opposed the annexation of Texas, which he believed would lead to war with Mexico. In the 1848 presidential election he was the candidate of the Free-Soil party opposing the extension of slavery, but was defeated. However, he supported the Compromise of 1850.

Many contemporaries had a rather jaundiced view of Martin Van Buren. They dubbed him "the Little Magician," "the Red Fox of Kinderhook," and "the Master Spirit," in recognition, if not resentment, of his surpassing skills as a political operator. He was indeed a highly professional politician, devoted to the art of politics and acutely sensitive to the nuances of public and individual needs and aspirations. He was instinctively cautious and circumspect, so much so that his politics were labeled "non-committal." His view that the "sober-second thought" of the people could never be wrong expresses precisely his democratic attitude.

Short in stature, fair-complexioned with sandy hair and "small brilliant eyes" under a protruding forehead, Van Buren was one of the most "polished and captivating" men of his age, urbane, courteous, self-assured, and adept at blending dignity with ease and suavity. But what resembled charm and sophistication to some men was interpreted as guile and deviousness by others. During the social feud in Jackson's first cabinet, **Amos Kendall** watched Van Buren maneuver to improve his standing with the president and described him as gliding "along as smoothly as oil and as silently as a cat."

Because of his public reputation Van Buren never attracted a wide popular following. His rise to the presidency was greatly assisted by the favor of Andrew Jackson; nevertheless Van Buren's creative contribution to the political development of the nation was enormous, and as such he earned his way to the presidency. After gaining control of New York's Republican party he organized the Albany Regency to run the state in his absence while he pursued a national career in Washington. The Regency was a governing council in Albany consisting of a group of politically astute and highly intelligent men. It was one of the first statewide political machines in the country whose success resulted from its professional use of patronage, the legislative caucus, and the official party newspaper.

Van Buren arrived in Washington during the so-called Era of Good Feelings, when the party system verged on complete disarray. For the next several years he labored to bring about the reorganization of the Republican party through an alliance between what he called "the planters of the South and the plain Republicans of the North." His efforts resulted in the coalition of the factions supporting Andrew Jackson, John C. Calhoun, and William H. Crawford and eventually emerged as the Democratic party which elected Jackson to the presidency in 1828. This party emphasized the importance of building popular majorities, and it perfected political techniques which would appeal to the masses.

Van Buren was the prototype of the new, highly professional politician who appeared after the War of 1812, and he played a central role in gaining acceptance of the idea that party government is essentially representative government. Heretofore parties were regarded as evils to be tolerated; Van Buren argued that the party system was the most sensible and intelligent way the affairs of the nation could be democratically conducted, a viewpoint that eventually won national approval.

Van Buren's political philosophy was fundamentally a reaffirmation of the Jeffersonian faith, with special emphasis on the importance of the states within the federal system. As president he expressed his liberal views toward labor in an executive order that prohibited anyone from working on federal projects more than ten hours a day. He became increasingly hostile to the expansion of slavery into the territories, and he predicted its eventual demise coupled with a warning that the nation would suffer a frightful bloodbath: "The end of slavery will come—amid terrible convulsions, I fear, but it will come." See Robert V. Remini, *Martin Van Buren and the Making of the Democratic Party* (1959).

ROBERT V. REMINI

VANDENBERG, Arthur Hendrick (b. Grand Rapids, Mich., March 22, 1884; d. Grand Rapids, Mich., April 18, 1951), POLITICAL LEADER, attended the University of Michigan Law School but dropped out in 1902 to join the staff of the Grand Rapids *Herald*. He rose rapidly from copyboy to city political editor to state political editor. His support of the *Herald's* owner for U.S. senator won him the editorship of the paper at age twenty-two (1907). As editor he became influential in Michigan Republican politics.

In 1928 Vandenberg was appointed U.S. senator to fill a vacancy. Elected to a full term later that year, he remained in the Senate until his death. In the area of foreign affairs, he became a leading figure in the Senate. He was originally an isolationist, consistently opposing international involvements. He favored the neutrality legislation of the 1930s and in 1941 opposed the Lend-Lease Act, whereby nations fighting the Axis powers were given access to American supplies. However, he did not try to obstruct the program's implementation.

Like many isolationists, Vandenberg supported President Roosevelt's war measures once the U.S. entered World War II. In January 1945 he renounced isolationism by declaring his backing of the proposed United Nations organization. Roosevelt appointed him U.S. delegate to the San Francisco meeting which drew up the U.N. Charter (1945); and President Truman chose him as delegate to the first and second U.N. General Assemblies (1946). He served as adviser to the secretary of state at the Big Four foreign ministers' meeting (Paris, 1946). Vandenberg was a key supporter of the "Truman Doctrine," the program of economic aid to Greece and Turkey (1947). The Vandenberg amendment to the doctrine strengthened the role of the United Nations by making continuance of aid conditional upon acceptance by a majority of the U.N. Security Council and General Assembly. Vandenberg also supported the Marshall Plan of massive economic aid to Western Europe (1948), and worked with the Truman administration in drafting the proposal for a military alliance between America and Western Europe which in 1949 materialized as the North Atlantic Treaty Organization.

※※※

Although **Dean Acheson** once ranked Arthur Vandenberg with such Senate immortals as **Henry Clay, Daniel Webster,** and **John C. Calhoun,** historians are much more skeptical about his claims to greatness. Vandenberg's major achievement was his support of bipartisanship in the early days of the cold war; as a leading Republican senator and prewar isolationist, he symbolized the willingness of the GOP to support Truman's increasingly tough policy toward Russia in the late 1940s. Working closely with **John Foster Dulles,** he persuaded **Thomas Dewey** not to make foreign policy an issue in the

1948 election, and thus prevented a badly needed public debate over the developing containment policy. At the time, Vandenberg's bipartisanship seemed to serve the national interest by avoiding an isolationist resurgence, yet in a broader perspective he can be charged with failing to provide the responsible opposition that is essential to the formulation of foreign policy in a democracy.

A vain, pompous man, Vandenberg could easily be swayed by flattery and clever management. As secretary of state, Dean Acheson realized Vandenberg's weakness and maneuvered him skillfully, allowing Vandenberg to vent his anger at a new policy in an explosive outburst, then winning him over by allowing the senator to make a minor change and thus convince himself that he had transformed the policy into "true doctrine." In this way Vandenberg, after vigorous initial opposition, came to support the United Nations Charter, the Truman Doctrine, and the Marshall Plan. Yet despite his prominent role in these major policies, Vandenberg never commanded the personal regard that his fellow Republicans held for **Robert Taft,** and he never received serious consideration for the GOP presidential nomination. He thus stands as a minor figure whose contemporary fame has not been able to stand the test of time. See A. H. Vandenberg, Jr., *The Private Papers of Senator Vandenberg* (1952).

ROBERT A. DIVINE

VANDERBILT, Cornelius (b. Staten Island, N.Y., May 27, 1794; d. New York, N.Y., Jan. 4, 1877), RAILROAD PROMOTER, left school in 1805 to work at odd jobs on the waterfront. In 1810 his mother loaned him $100 to purchase a small flat-bottomed sailing vessel in order to enter the ferry trade in New York harbor. In 1814 he secured a profitable three-month government contract to supply the island forts when the British threatened to invade New York during the War of 1812. After the war he expanded his ferry service and engaged in the coastal trade as far south as Charleston, South Carolina. In 1818 he

became captain of Thomas Gibbons's steamship, the *Mouse,* which operated from New Brunswick, New Jersey, to Manhattan. Although their operations proved profitable in spite of legal obstacles, he and Gibbons waged a six-year war of litigation against Aaron Ogden, who had a license from **Robert Livingston,** the holder of a state monopoly for the operation of steam vessels in New York waters. The Supreme Court finally invalidated the monopoly in *Gibbons* v. *Ogden* in 1824.

Vanderbilt had accumulated more than $30,000 by 1828. In 1829 he established his own steamboat company. By successfully engaging in speed contests and price wars, he built a large fleet with numerous lines emanating from New York. Following the discovery of gold in California in 1849, he established steamship service between New York and San Francisco, his Accessory Transit obtaining monopoly rights to the portage across Lake Nicaragua. He reaped immense profits from this enterprise before selling his ships for $1,350,000 in 1852.

In 1853 Vanderbilt embarked upon a highly publicized voyage to Europe in his new $500,000 steam yacht, the *North Star.* However, during the sojourn, his partners, Charles Morgan and Cornelius K. Garrison, ousted him from control of the Accessory Transit Co. and later conspired with William Walker, who became dictator of Nicaragua in a filibustering expedition in 1855, to exclude Vanderbilt enterprises from the portage. Vanderbilt manipulated his wealth to regain control of Accessory and operated steamships below cost to drive the "interlopers" into bankruptcy. He also used his political influence and financial resources to precipitate the downfall of Walker in 1857. He regained control of the Nicaragua system in 1857, but then terminated the service when two Panamanian steamship lines, Pacific Mail and United States Mail, payed him $40,000 a month to abandon competition. These payments, increased to $56,000 a month in 1858, ended in 1859 when the construction of the Panamanian Railroad eliminated the competitive advantage of the Nicaragua route.

Vanderbilt entered transatlantic steamship

competition in 1854, when Britain's Cunard Line temporarily curtailed service in order to transport troops during the Crimean War. Although his elegant vessel *Vanderbilt* set speed records, he failed to reduce costs enough so that his mail subsidy from the U.S. government would warrant year-round scheduled service, competing with the more heavily subsidized Cunard Line. Seeing little future for Americans in transoceanic shipping, he began to invest in railroads with the purchase of a controlling interest in the Harlem Railroad in 1857 and the Hudson River Railroad in 1865. After gaining control of the New York Central in 1867, Vanderbilt consolidated his various holdings into one system which extended from New York City to Buffalo. Although he failed to wrest control of the Erie Railroad from Daniel Drew, **James Fisk,** and **Jay Gould** in 1866, by 1873 he had extended his transportation empire westward to Chicago through the acquisition of the Buffalo and Lake Shore and the Michigan Southern railroads. The New York Central System extended more than 4,500 miles of track in 1877.

With a fortune exceeding $100 million, Vanderbilt did not engage in philanthropy until the last years of his life, when he donated $1 million to found Vanderbilt University.

Only a few businessmen in American history have been both major economic figures and folk heroes. One of these was Cornelius Vanderbilt. In his long working life he spanned the period from small enterprise to large, or from sailing ship to trunk line railroad, and in handling each phase of change he grasped and applied the business principles most important for personal profit. A dictatorial and rather ruthless boss, he nevertheless became a heroic symbol of the common man's shrewdness, disregard for social distinctions, and superior physical strength.

Except for a few letters scattered in many manuscript collections, there is little direct evidence regarding Vanderbilt's personality. The letters show him to be taciturn, ungrammatical, clever, cautious, and forceful. He had the self-confidence that often comes from a commanding presence and great physical strength. As the young owner of a sailing ship he was one of the "strong boys" of the New York City waterfront. All his life he appears to have been a cold, withdrawn calculator who paid attention to material details and possibilities rather than to the sensibilities of those around him. Although at a fairly early age he came, for example, into close association with well-spoken gentlemen like Aaron Ogden, he never adapted his waterfront language to that expected in good society, nor did he ever show much respect for social or legal niceties.

Vanderbilt was first and foremost a businessman, and if seeing all the possibilities of manipulation justifies the term, he was a genius. He had the cautious good judgment not to assume the risks of pioneering, but rather to acquaint himself carefully and patiently with a situation before he took vigorous action. For about a decade he taught himself the details of steam navigation by running ships for Ogden, with an increasing share of the returns, before he branched out for himself in Hudson River navigation. Like the later **J. Pierpont Morgan,** he regarded free competition as ruinous to highly capitalized transportation. The saying "If you can't beat 'em, join 'em" may have originated with the man who was now beginning to be called the Commodore.

His career in deep-water shipping from about 1840 to the beginning of the Civil War was an excellent example of understanding of the business flexibility of seaworthy ships that could move in any direction. Vanderbilt's vessels went where the money was, and he boasted that he could operate 25 percent more cheaply than competitors. Whether or not this was true to the degree he stated, he took maximum risks on undermanning and turnarounds too quick for thorough repairs, and yet avoided serious disaster. In the Nicaraguan Transit battles of the 1850s he showed mature understanding of the nature and possibilities of the corporation, that money could be made equally well from building them up, tearing them down, or blackmailing them. At this period the New York *Times* likened him to the old German robber barons of the Rhine.

In railroads he exercised the same initial caution as in steam navigation, going in gradually and studying the nature of the business operation. With an enormous liquid capital for that day, reputedly as much as $10 million, he became a feared operator in railroad securities before finally committing his interests to the New York Central in 1867. By this time he had learned that the really big money came not from dividends on railroad stock, but from selling or leasing land or equipment to the road and manipulating its securities. It is said that he personally owned all the New York Central bridges from New York to Buffalo and leased them to the company. But unlike most market operators, the old financial pirate ran an efficient moneymaking railroad. Next to the Pennsylvania, it was a model for the country, and when the Commodore was finally forced by death to surrender control to his son, the latter received a financially sound, profitable property. See Wheaton J. Lane, *Commodore Vanderbilt* (1942).

THOMAS C. COCHRAN

VANDERBILT, William Henry (b. New Brunswick, N.J., May 8, 1821; d. New York, N.Y., Dec. 8, 1885), RAILROAD LEADER, eldest son of "Commodore" **Cornelius Vanderbilt.** He attended Columbia College Grammar School, worked in a ship chandler's shop (1838), then became a clerk in the banking house of Drew, Robinson and Co. (1839). In 1857 he was appointed receiver of the moribund Staten Island Railroad and stabilized its finances. When his father acquired the New York and Harlem Railroad he became its vice president (1864) and assumed the same post on the New York and Hudson Railroad, which his father acquired in 1865. Upon his advice his father consolidated the newly purchased New York Central with the Hudson River line for a direct New York–Buffalo link (1867), and the younger Vanderbilt became first vice president and executive officer of the merged road. Again, upon his son's advice his father purchased the Lake Shore and Michigan Southern Railroad (1869) and the Michigan Central Railroad as well as stock in the Canada Southern Railroad.

Upon his father's death (1877), Vanderbilt inherited the bulk of his estate and became president of the New York Central and Hudson River Railroad, which he expanded greatly in the years that followed. Vanderbilt linked the Canada Southern to the New York Central network, combined it with the Michigan Central, and became president of the affiliated corporations. He then acquired control of the Chicago and North Western Railway (1880–83) and purchased a large interest in the Cleveland, Columbus, Cincinnati and Indianapolis line. In 1883 he obtained control of the Nickel Plate (New York, Chicago and St. Louis) Railway, which he turned over to the Lake Shore line. In 1885, at the insistence of **J. P. Morgan,** he leased the New York, West Shore and Buffalo Railway. In 1883 he turned his executive positions over to his sons and son-in-law but remained director and member of the executive committees of all his roads. Vanderbilt donated $450,000 to Vanderbilt University and $500,000 for new buildings for the Columbia University College of Physicians and Surgeons.

William Henry Vanderbilt was, more than his famous and domineering father Cornelius, the builder of one of the world's largest railroad systems, the New York Central. Yet he accepted his role with reluctance. During the mid-1860s he had helped his father shift the family's investment and entrepreneurial activities from steamboats to railroads by obtaining control of the two roads between New York and Albany and then the New York Central between Albany and Buffalo. Neither he nor his father wanted to expand their business empire beyond New York State. The cost was simply too high. However, they were forced in 1869 to obtain control of the Lake Shore to protect themselves from **Jay Gould**'s attempt to capture the Central's major connection to Chicago. During the depression of the 1870s, he was willing to purchase the Michigan Central and Canadian Southern, competitors to the Lake Shore, when they could be had at bargain rates.

Even after his father's death, William Vanderbilt made no attempt to follow the example of the Central's major rival, the Pennsylvania, by building a carefully integrated railroad system. Nor did he imitate the Pennsylvania by providing centralized administrative controls over the roads that he did own. Vanderbilt expected that his lines would provide one another with essential through traffic between New York or Chicago and that the Eastern Trunk Line Association—a carefully organized cartel which he had helped to found in 1877—would assure the stability of rates and traffic in the larger region in which his roads operated.

By 1880, he decided that the earlier Vanderbilt policies had failed. The control of the western lines did not assure through traffic, and the Eastern Trunk Line Association had not been able to maintain stability. Therefore, Vanderbilt moved quickly to build a system comparable to that of the Pennsylvania, obtaining control of roads to Columbus, Cincinnati, Indianapolis, St. Louis, Pittsburgh, Minneapolis, and St. Paul and buying a new competitor to the Lake Shore, the Nickel Plate. In 1883, in anticipation of retirement, Vanderbilt placed each of the constituent roads in the hands of competent professional managers and set up an organization for their overall control. Operations remained quite decentralized. The presidents of the constituent roads met regularly but had not the staff or other institutional means for systematically appraising and planning for the system as a whole. On the other hand, the accounting and financial offices of the roads were consolidated, some being housed in the headquarters of the New York Central. The financial executives reported directly to the chairman of their boards (usually one of Vanderbilt's sons) and to their executive and financial committees. These committees were made up largely of Vanderbilts and their financial allies working closely with the professional managers in determining general policies as to rates, scheduling, and capital investment for the system as a whole. While the governance of the Central was less systematic than that of the Pennsylvania, it won the admiration of J.

Pierpont Morgan, for many years a member of the Central's board and key committees. Morgan in turn used Vanderbilt's method of control in railroad reorganizations in the 1890s and in such industrial consolidations as the United States Steel Corporation. See Edwin P. Hoyt, *The Vanderbilts and Their Fortunes* (1962).

ALFRED D. CHANDLER, JR.

VAN WAGENEN, Isabella. See Truth, Sojourner.

VEBLEN, Thorstein Bunde (b. Manitowoc Co., Wis., July 30, 1857; d. Palo Alto, Calif., Aug. 3, 1929), SOCIAL SCIENTIST, graduated from Carleton College (Northfield, Minn.) in 1880. After teaching at a private school, he studied at Johns Hopkins but left when he failed to get a fellowship. He received a PhD in philosophy in 1884 from Yale. After a period of ill health, he enrolled (1891) at Cornell, studying economics and finance under J. Laurence Laughlin. When Laughlin moved to the University of Chicago in 1892, Veblen became a teaching fellow there, and then an assistant professor of economics. He helped found the *Journal of Political Economy* and served as managing editor from 1896 to 1905. His *The Theory of the Leisure Class* (1899), which criticized business and middle-class values, was followed by *The Theory of Business Enterprise* (1904).

In 1906 Veblen was forced to leave Chicago because of an extramarital affair. He became associate professor of economics at Stanford University but was forced to leave for similar reasons in 1909. Veblen taught at the University of Missouri (1911–18), then he moved to New York to become the first editor of *Dial* magazine. In 1919 he joined the faculty of the newly created New School for Social Research in New York. The American Economic Association offered its presidency to Veblen in 1925, but he refused to accept it. He retired the following year and returned to Palo Alto. At his death he was recognized as one of the leading social critics of his day. Some of his many other books include: *The Instinct of*

Workmanship (1914), *Imperial Germany and the Industrial Revolution* (1915), and *The Higher Learning in America* (1918).

❦

Veblen's heretical and frequently original ideas flowed from a highly idiosyncratic personality. Second-generation Norwegian, with a rural childhood and a strict and demanding father, he seemed bent from youth on protecting himself from emotional involvement with other individuals or through his writings. His decisions to marry, to do graduate work, to teach, and to write were all made without enthusiasm or apparent commitment. He refused to accept or play the conventional roles demanded of faculty politics, teaching, or citizenship. It was never his unorthodox social ideas—he frequently received the enthusiastic endorsement of the most conservative academicians—that endangered his various positions, but a flaunting of the mores and norms of the institutions which employed him. Underneath his protective lifestyle was an extremely shy, sensitive, and troubled man. He complained of ill health, apparently psychosomatic in origin, throughout his life, and saw himself as analogous to "the wandering Jew." His ironic detachment, his brilliant ability to uncover meanings that escaped others, and his creativity arose as much from his personality and his inability to assimilate into American society as they did from the intellectual influences that were exerted upon him. He did experience and was a participant in the widescale revolt against the certainties of 19th-century social thought. Yet his perspective was always fresh, unique, and, unlike the other thinkers of the era, unprogrammatic. Only after World War I, when he was old and increasingly bitter, did he half-seriously suggest any social reforms. By then his gentle irony had become sardonic and vitriolic.

Although Veblen was frequently ambiguous, sometimes contradictory, and always unsystematic, his writings have provided much of the sensitivity, perspective, and vocabulary of 20th-century social thought. His inquiry began with the customs and rituals of economic man rather than the mechanics of how men overcome scarcity. He saw two major tendencies running through modern society: one was toward "useful" production, the other toward wastefulness. Neither trend was completely triumphant, but "wastemanship," which had arisen through cultural evolution, was pervasive. Using his broad understanding of anthropology and psychology, Veblen posited three major cultural stages in the history of man: savagery, barbarism, and the modern pecuniary society. He depicted a romantic savagery that was peaceful, sedentary, and communal. When society accumulated a surplus of commodities, savagery evolved into barbarism which was characterized by warfare, exploitation of the weak, private property, status differentiation, and the appearance of the leisure class. Machine technology ushered in the final stage, the pecuniary culture. Yet cultural change had failed to alter the instinctual equipment that man had inherited from earlier stages. Modern man was relentlessly driven to emulate the leisure class. Some of the most hilarious and yet tragic chapters of American satire can be found in Veblen's telling descriptions of the valiant efforts of the middle and lower classes to ape the leisure class.

The drive to emulate resulted in wasteful production, production not essential to survival. In his typically detached and supposedly objective manner Veblen insisted that his use of the term "waste" did not carry an invidious connotation. To consume ostentatiously or to have large amounts of leisure required pecuniary abundance. Sharp bargaining, manipulation, chicanery, and even the deliberate sabotage of production were more efficient means for obtaining wealth than frugality or industriousness. Thus the leisure class represented the updated predators of the barbaric age. The class was archaic, parasitic, and a barrier to higher levels of useful production. Offsetting somewhat the influence of the pecuniary or business culture was Veblen's "instinct of workmanship." This instinct propelled man toward increased efficiency and output and could give meaning to work. The engineer and the skilled craftsman, interested primarily in quality production and not money rewards, were representatives of the survival of this instinct. In his later works, Veblen hoped that the machine itself would provide the means for men to escape the tyranny of leisure-class mores and rituals. He then even advocated the domination of industrial life by a "soviet of engineers." See Joseph Dorfman, *Thorstein Veblen and His America* (1934), and David Riesman, *Thorstein Veblen: A Critical Interpretation* (1953).

BENJAMIN G. RADER

VENTURI, Robert (b. Philadelphia, Pa., June 25, 1925), ARCHITECT, graduated Princeton University with both an AB (1947) and an MFA (1950) degree. From 1954 to 1956 he was Rome Prize Fellow at the American Academy at Rome. He worked in the offices of the architects Oskar Stonorov, Eero Saarinen and **Louis I. Kahn** before opening his own office in Philadelphia in 1958. Presently, he is associated with his wife, Denise Scott Brown, in the firm of Venturi, Scott Brown Associates.

His best-known works are the much written about house for his mother (1961), the Benjamin Franklin Court (1972), an addition (1973) to the Allen Memorial Art Museum at Oberlin, Ohio, the Seattle Art Museum (1984), and the Sainsbury Wing (1986) of the British National Gallery in London. A recipient of many architectural awards, he received architecture's highest honor, the Pritzker Architecture Prize, in 1991.

Venturi is an influential theoretician as well as architect. His books *Complexity and Contradiction in Architecture* (1966), *Learning from Las Vegas* (1972, coauthored with Denise Scott Brown and Steven Izenour), and *A View from the Campidoglio* (1984, coauthored with Denise Scott Brown), a collection of articles written between 1953 and 1984, are considered classics in the field of architectural theory and are extremely influential.

⁂

Robert Venturi has the distinction of producing buildings and writings that have conspicuous quality and are also very controversial. His first book, *Complexity and Contradiction in Architecture*, shocked many of those in a profession that had been educated on the spartan principles of what was then called "The International Style." Most architectural schools at the time taught that ornament was evil and that modern architecture must express function and eschew style for, as one of its doyens, **Ludwig Mies van der Rohe**, put it, "Less is more." In an erudite, elegant and persuasive argument, Venturi countered that "Less is a bore." He pointed out that the aesthetic of scarcity, far from being functional, was simply symbolic of function, another style, and that historically architecture had been rich in conception and detail. To demonstrate his point he put a picture of Michelangelo's "Porta Pia" on the cover of his book, as well as fully illustrating the point in the pictures that accompanied the text.

In 1972, he followed up this argument in *Learning from Las Vegas* where he observed that the much-maligned architects of that flamboyant and much-maligned city were infinitely more adept at housing functions and pleasing clients and their patrons than the architects of the establishment. *A View from the Campidoglio*, essays written over his entire career, shows him expanding on these same themes. Particularly significant is his attack on "liberals" who rail against billboards, gas stations and utility poles in their efforts to clean up the environment. Why, he asks, do they not spend more time campaigning for better housing for the underprivileged?

Lest Venturi be dismissed as simply otherwise-minded, his own architecture demonstrates his sensitivity and brilliance in incorporating the old with the new. In the Franklin Court, a monument to the great man who lived there, the firm found that, although the foundations of Franklin's house and shop were evident, there were no pictures of the facade to show what might be replicated. The architects decided simply to set up a steel frame on the foundations and let it go at that. When asked to design an addition to the British National Gallery, the Sainsbury Wing, which became a subject of some controversy, the Venturi firm played off its modernist sensibilities against the tired neoclassicism of Sir William Wilkins's old museum. While literally adopting the proportions and details of Wilkins's building, the architects made knowledgable adjustments to them that are recognized immediately by the cognoscenti, who are delighted or repelled by them, but not by the average viewer who tends to see the building as simply a successful essay in contextualism. Venturi's work here and everywhere rests on function but also on wit. See *The Architecture of Robert Venturi* (1989).

ROBERT W. WINTER

VESEY, Denmark (b. St. Thomas, West Indies [?], c. 1767; d. Charleston, S.C., July 2, 1822), REVOLUTIONARY, was sold to Captain John Vesey, a slave trader, in 1781. After winning $1500 in a lottery (1800), Vesey purchased his freedom for $600 and used the rest of his money to open up a carpenter's shop in Charleston, South Carolina.

Disturbed by the enslavement of his several wives and numerous children, and outraged by the stigma of inferiority that was attached to blacks, Vesey, who had somehow learned to read, sought to convince blacks that slavery was immoral and that slave rebellions were sanctioned by the Bible. Spurred on by the success of slave rebellions in South America and the Caribbean, Vesey, with the aid of Gullah Jack, an Angolan "witch doctor," rebuked slaves who endured insults and set out to organize an insurrection among the house servants and artisans in Charleston. It was originally scheduled to take place on July 14, 1822, but Vesey apparently felt forced to move the date up to June 16 after a number of house servants revealed his plans to their masters. However, the insurrection was foiled before any overt act took place. Following his capture on June 22, Vesey was sentenced to death and executed with thirty-five other conspirators. Another thirty-odd followers were deported. As a result of this affair, South Carolina adopted stricter slave codes.

Whether an actual insurrection was imminent or could have materialized in 1822 can never be known, because of the debatable nature of the evidence. But that Vesey and some of his associates were of a revolutionary frame of mind, and willing to lose their lives in an insurrection, seems patent. Moreover, the "conspiracy" exposed the apprehensions of whites and contradicted their allegations respecting their society's stability. They evidently identified with the nearby Santo Domingo whites who had, in 1791–92, suffered slave insurrections and, subsequently, revolution. Many escaped to the mainland, a substantial number to Charleston, which received them sympathetically. As a result of the Vesey effort, white South Carolinians not only restricted slave and freedman opportunities; they transgressed the rights of free black seamen on Massachusetts ships, and even on British vessels, defying Congress, the president, and international treaties. The Vesey affair entered into abolitionist and black lore. Vesey himself was introduced imaginatively into **Harriet Beecher Stowe**'s novel *Dred* (1856) as having a son who portended more insurrections. Although **Nat Turner**'s abortive uprising in 1831 in Virginia received greater attention than Vesey's because of the killing of whites and Turner's widely read "Confession," the earlier event has won a secure place in the history of black unrest. Its reality was contested in Richard Wade's *Slavery in the Cities* (1964), Wade holding it merely involved black discontent and white hysteria; Wade was controverted in Robert S. Starobin, ed., *Denmark Vesey: The Slave Conspiracy of 1822* (1970). See John Lofton, *Insurrection in South Carolina: The Turbulent World of Denmark Vesey* (1964).

LOUIS FILLER

VILLARD, Henry (Ferdinand Heinrich Gustave Hilgard) (b. Speyer, Rhenish Bavaria, April 10, 1835; d. Dobbs Ferry, N.Y., Nov. 12, 1900), FINANCIER, studied at the universities of Munich and Würzburg. He emigrated to the U.S. in 1853, adopted the name Villard, and briefly resided in Cincinnati, Chicago, and Belleville, Indiana (1854–55). After studying law and trying his hand at several jobs with little success, Villard became special correspondent for the New York *Staats-Zeitung* (1858). In 1859 he joined the Cincinnati *Commercial* to report on the gold rush at Pike's Peak County, Colorado, and the following year published a guidebook, *The Past and Present of the Pike's Peak Gold Regions.* He covered the 1860 Republican national convention for the *Commercial,* the *Daily Missouri Democrat* (St. Louis), and the New York *Herald.* During the Civil War he reported on several important battles including Bull Run, Fredericksburg, and the Wilderness, for the *Herald* and later for the New York *Tribune.* In 1865 he became Washington correspondent of the Chicago *Tribune* and covered the 1867 Paris Exposition for that paper.

On a trip to Germany in 1873, Villard joined a committee formed to protect the bondholders of the Oregon and California Railroad. In the course of the next eight years, he gained control of the Oregon Steamship Co. and the Oregon and California Railroad (1874), the Oregon Steam and Navigation Co. (1879), and, through a "blind pool," the Northern Pacific Railroad (1881). Villard also organized the Oregon Railway and Navigation Co. (1879), the Oregon and Transcontinental (1881), a holding company, and the Oregon Improvement Co. He was forced out of the Northern Pacific in 1884, but returned to the board in 1888, becoming chairman the following year. He was again forced out of the Northern Pacific in the panic of 1893.

Villard acquired controlling interest in the New York *Evening Post* and *The Nation* in 1881, but allowed his editors, **E. L. Godkin** and Horace White, to run these enterprises as they saw fit. In 1890 he purchased the Edison Light Co. (Newark, N.J.) and the Edison Machine Works (Schenectady, N.Y.), and organized them as the Edison General Electric Co. (1891), serving as its president for two years.

———

Unusual results could be expected from placing a European Renaissance Man in post–Civil War America. Opportunity was everywhere for one who could be a journalist, a social scientist, a politician, or an entrepreneur, but the big money was in the last, and almost irresistibly the highly astute Henry Villard was pulled toward the world of railroad finance.

To operate effectively in this big league one had to represent capital, and his upper-middle-class German family connections were important. Becoming a representative for German bondholders gave him leverage in the far western railroad bankruptcies of the 1870s, and soon this brilliant forty-year-old foreigner was being made president of reorganized companies. As a receiver for the Kansas Pacific (1879–83), he so impressed **J. Pierpont Morgan** that the latter was prepared to back him in larger operations.

Since Drexel-Morgan were syndicate leaders for an enormous bond issue of the Northern Pacific Railroad and Morgan doubted the good judgment of the existing management, he privately endorsed Villard's takeover by the "blind pool" of 1881. As a railroad president with Morgan's backing, Villard proved to have too much imagination. By the next depression, 1883–86, he had completed the road to a connection with his Oregon properties, but, partly by overadvertising the region in the United States and Europe, he had exhausted the company treasury.

Forced by financial exigencies to resign, he still retained the friendship of the rapidly rising House of Morgan. This led to his return to the Northern Pacific board, and to assistance in combining the Morgan-financed Edison companies into Edison General Electric. But again, Villard's personal charm, intellectual ability, and optimism proved unequal to the periodic pressures of the business cycle, and with the panic of 1893 his active career ended. See James B. Hedges, *Henry Villard and the Railways of the Northwest* (1930).

THOMAS C. COCHRAN

VILLARD, Oswald Garrison (b. Wiesbaden, Ger., March 13, 1872; d. New York, N.Y., Oct. 1, 1949), JOURNALIST, REFORMER, son of **Henry Villard,** owner and publisher of the New York *Evening Post* and railroad magnate. Educated at Harvard (BA, 1893; MA, 1896), he taught American history there (1894–96) before joining the Philadelphia *Press* as a reporter (1896–97). After a stint as editorial writer on the *Evening*

Post he assumed control of that paper as well as *The Nation,* its weekly supplement, in 1898. Villard was one of the founders of the National Association for the Advancement of Colored People (1909). An ardent pacifist, he opposed American entry into both the war with Spain in 1898 and World War I. In 1918 he was forced to sell the *Post* because of his pacifism. He retained control of *The Nation* until 1932, however, and from its columns attacked the Versailles Treaty, the Teapot Dome Affair, and both Communism and Fascism. After retiring as editor in 1932, Villard served as contributing editor until 1940, though he sold his financial interest in 1935. Having left *The Nation* because of its support for Roosevelt's defense policies, Villard was active in the Keep America Out of War Committee (1940–41). During his lifetime he owned *Yachting* magazine, which he founded in 1907, the *Nautical Gazette,* the Fort Montgomery Iron Co., and two realty companies. He wrote numerous volumes on current political issues as well as a biography of **John Brown** (1910) and an autobiography, *Fighting Years: Memoirs of a Liberal Editor* (1939).

───※───

Villard was a prototype of the intransigent liberal reformer during the first half of the 20th century. Grandson of the great abolitionist **William Lloyd Garrison,** he brought to reform journalism the energy and commitment of capitalist expansion and zealous humanitarianism. Like his grandfather he had little respect for men who were incapable of "hot indignation at something or other," and he cherished the charge that he had made "more acres of public men miserable per square unit of circulation than any editor alive."

There were few causes that Villard did not champion in fifty years of active journalism. He fought the civil rights battle for blacks and women long before it was fashionable. He rallied his papers against conscription and in behalf of the conscientious objector and campaigned for Wilson's "Peace without Victory" program. In 1919, when he felt that the president had betrayed the Fourteen Points, Villard took up the

battle against the Treaty as a "Covenant with Death." During the reaction of the twenties he defied 100 percent Americanism by his support of radical dissent and the Russian revolutionary government. He helped organize the Committee of 100 for Irish Independence, was one of the first to denounce Italian Fascism, and as early as 1933 stumped the country decrying Hitler as a threat to the entire world. Despite his inherited belief in laissez-faire and his suspicion of centralized power, Villard supported most of the New Deal legislation. Only when he felt that Roosevelt was drawing America into the European conflict did he turn against the administration and join the pacifist isolationist campaign of the late thirties.

Villard's politics were first and foremost the politics of pacifism. This ultimately led to contradictions with his humanitarianism. In 1940 when he argued that European democracies were obliged to resist fascist terror while denying America the same obligation, he seemed more intent on keeping America out of war than in keeping war out of the world. But Villard never wavered in his belief that war and liberalism were inherently incompatible. Total acceptance of an absolute Christian ethic protected him from the anguished reflection of a man like **Reinhold Niebuhr** who reluctantly concluded that nonresistance could be as lethal and irresponsible as taking up the sword. For Villard there could be no compromise. Recalling the words of **Wendell Phillips,** he responded: "I entrench myself on principles of human liberty and leave the working out of details to almighty God!"

Villard was not a reflective thinker. Most of his ideas were inherited, and he accepted them on faith. His translation of every cause into a moral movement offended the mid-20th-century world of realpolitik. His absolutism frequently seemed to rule out reasoned debate. But despite his intransigence, which on occasion led to failures of insight and analysis, the genuine measure of his integrity and achievement cannot be overlooked. Villard exemplified a tradition which at its best maintained a critical perspective ever sensitive to injustice. It is doubtful that the world can become freer or more humane without the prodding consciences of men like Oswald Garrison Villard. See Michael Wreszin, *Oswald Garrison Villard: Pacifist at War* (1965).

MICHAEL WRESZIN

VON BRAUN, Wernher Magnus Maximilian (b. Wirsitz, Germany, March 23, 1912; d. Alexandria, Va., June 16, 1977), ROCKET SCIENTIST, was a Prussian baron who became enthralled by the dream of spaceflight as a teenager. He joined Weimar Germany's nascent rocket movement and, while an engineering student, participated in amateur experiments in Berlin (1930–32). In late 1932, the German Army hired him for a new, secret liquid-fuel rocket project destined to create the world's first ballistic missile. For his work, von Braun earned a doctorate in physics at the University of Berlin (1934). With the creation of the Peenemünde rocket center in 1937, he became its technical director for development. He joined the Nazi Party (1937) and the SS (1940), and accepted exploitation of slave labor in rocket production. The Gestapo briefly arrested him in 1944 because of SS designs on the program, then under the control of the German Army. The most important product of his work was the V-2 missile, which was launched against Allied cities beginning in September 1944.

On May 2, 1945, von Braun surrendered to the U.S. Army. He came to America in September that year to lead about 120 Peenemünde veterans being assembled at Fort Bliss, Texas. His group moved to the Army's Redstone Arsenal in Huntsville, Ala., in 1950, where they developed nuclear-armed missiles. During the fifties, von Braun became famous through his writings, speeches and television appearances advocating spaceflight. Rockets designed under his leadership put the first U.S. satellite in orbit (1958) and the first U.S. man into space (1961). In 1960, he became Director of the Marshall Space Flight Center when his group was transferred to NASA. Von Braun was a top manager in the Apollo program and his gigantic Saturn V booster put the first humans on the moon in 1969. He moved to Washington, D.C. the following year as Deputy Associate Administrator for Planning at NASA Headquarters, but left two years later to become a Vice President at Fairchild Industries in Germantown, Md. He died not long after receiving a National Medal of Science from President Gerald Ford.

To millions of Americans in the 1950s and 1960s, when the cold war and the space race were at its height, Wernher von Braun was an unqualified hero. His articles in *Colliers* magazine and his appearances on Walt Disney's television program had already made him the country's most successful salesman for space travel. After the Sputnik shock of October 1957, his central role in launching Explorer 1, the first American satellite, cemented his heroic image. Yet doubts were never far below the surface. His skeptics—such as the satirical songwriter Tom Lehrer—criticized him for opportunism and for willful ignorance of the military uses of his work by Nazi Germany and the United States. Yet that criticism seems to have had little effect on his many admirers. It was only late in his life, and in the years after his death, that the biggest scandal in his past began to emerge: his involvement, however tangentially, in the deaths of thousands of slave laborers in V-2 production between 1943 and 1945.

Few engineers and scientists of the twentieth century have embodied the Faustian bargain as clearly as von Braun. There can be no doubt about his lifelong commitment to exploring space, nor can one question his fundamental contributions to technology, his charismatic personality, and his talent for managing engineering organizations. Yet his willingness to labor energetically for Hitler's Third Reich in order to advance the technology he so loved—rocketry—will always leave a stain on his legacy. See Michael J. Neufeld, *The Rocket and the Reich: Peenemünde and the Coming of the Ballistic Missile Era* (1995).

MICHAEL J. NEUFELD

VONNEGUT, Kurt, Jr. (b. Indianapolis, Ind., Nov. 11, 1922), WRITER, studied biochemistry at

Cornell for two years (1940–42), then transferred to Carnegie Institute of Technology, but left to enlist in the army in 1942. Serving as an infantryman in Europe, Vonnegut was captured by the Germans at the Battle of the Bulge (1944) and assigned to a POW work force in Dresden, Germany. On February 13, 1945, he witnessed the British and American firebombing of that city, an event that had a tremendous impact on his life. After the war he studied anthropology at the University of Chicago (1945–47) but took no degree. He worked as a police reporter for the Chicago City News Bureau in 1946 and was a public relations man for General Electric in Schenectady, New York, from 1947 to 1950. In 1950 he moved to a farm on Cape Cod, Massachusetts, to devote himself to writing.

Vonnegut wrote short stories for such magazines as the *Saturday Evening Post, Collier's* and *Cosmopolitan* in this period; he also wrote for science-fiction magazines. His first novel, *Player Piano* (1952), was a satire about engineers rebelling against automation, and he followed this with *The Sirens of Titan* (1959), *Mother Night* (1961), and *Canary in a Cathouse* (1961), a collection of short stories. *Cat's Cradle* (1963), a novel about the conflict of science and religion, first brought him literary recognition. *God Bless You, Mr. Rosewater* (1965) concerned a millionaire philanthropist, and *Welcome to the Monkey House* (1968) was another story collection. *Slaughterhouse Five* (1969) was Vonnegut's account of the Dresden firebombing and its impact on the novel's main character, Billy Pilgrim; the novel was made into a movie in 1972. Vonnegut's play *Happy Birthday, Wanda June* (1970), produced off-Broadway, was so successful it moved to Broadway in December 1970. Vonnegut was a lecturer at the University of Iowa's Writers' Workshop (1965–67) and taught English at Harvard (1970–71). Some of his recent works include *Between Time and Timbuktu, or Prometheus-5* (1972), a play assembled out of a TV script, *Breakfast of Champions* (1973), *Wampeters, Foma & Granfalloons* (1974), *Deadeye Dick* (1983), *Galapágos* (1985), and *Bluebeard* (1987).

In a line of almost apostolic succession, five writers have succeeded each other as the dominant influence on college students over the past generation. The title has passed from **J. D. Salinger** to William Golding (for *Lord of the Flies*) to J. R. R. Tolkien to Hermann Hesse to Kurt Vonnegut. No generally acceptable successor to Vonnegut has yet appeared, though his standing among students has waned considerably in the last two decades. The five have in common primarily their romanticism, in each case taking the form of a rejection of contemporary culture.

Vonnegut is the least favored of the five by serious critics. He offends them by his apparent anti-intellectualism, and by such literary irreverence as claiming that he never knew he was a satirist until he read it in a review of his second book. He is, nevertheless, a major writer.

All his novels except the first employ what can be called a cartoon-strip style—very short chapters, rapid pace, a free use of fantasy, and mostly two- or even one-dimensional characters. In this he most nearly resembles Nathanael West. *God Bless You, Mr. Rosewater,* his best book so far—though *Slaughterhouse Five* is technically more interesting—is a study of the limits of human compassion. So, really, is all his work. Vonnegut succeeds in embracing the dilemma that human beings constantly use each other, and life uses us all, which is tragic—but nevertheless, as Beatrice Rumfoord says in *The Sirens of Titan,* "The worst thing that could possibly happen to anybody would be not to be used for anything by anybody."

Vonnegut, a renegade scientist in the sense that he values meaning above truth, is completely serious in his writing, though most of it comes out wildly funny. (The weakest, chiefly short stories, come out sentimental.) He is also a prophet, even more than most science fiction and anti-science fiction writers. But his prophecies emerge in a cloud of dark (never black) humor, and in this he is unique. See Tony Tanner, "Kurt Vonnegut," in *City of Words* (1971).

NOEL PERRIN

VON NEUMANN, John (b. Budapest, Hung., Dec. 28, 1903; d. Washington, D.C., Feb. 8, 1957), MATHEMATICIAN, studied chemistry at the University of Berlin (1921–23) and graduated from the Federal Institute of Technology in Zürich, Switzerland, in 1925. He received his PhD in mathematics from the University of Budapest the following year. After a year as a fellow at the University of Göttingen, and another as a lecturer in mathematics at the University of Berlin (1927), he became an assistant professor at the University of Hamburg in 1929. The following year von Neumann came to the U.S. to be a lecturer at Princeton. In 1931 he was appointed professor. He joined Princeton's Institute for Advanced Study at its beginning in 1933, and remained with it until his death.

At Princeton, von Neumann worked on pointset theory, theory of continuous groups, theory of rings of operators, and especially his mathematical theory of games. *Theory of Games and Economic Behavior* (1944), written with Oskar Morgenstern, expounded his mathematical approach to games of strategy as well as to economic behavior, social organization, and strategy in war. A consultant to the army, navy, and Office of Scientific Research and Development during World War II, he worked on the Los Alamos (N.M.) project for the development of the atomic bomb, making contributions based on his work in quantum mechanics. In 1945 he became director of the federal electronic computer project at the Institute for Advanced Study and helped develop high-speed computers such as UNIVAC, ENIAC, and ORDVAC. His work on MANIAC (mathematical analyzer, numerical integrater and computer) contributed to the development of the H-bomb in 1952 while his NORC (naval ordinance research computer) predicted weather and tidal changes, and solved logistical problems for the navy. He was appointed to the General Advisory Committee of the Atomic Energy Commission in 1952, and named by President Eisenhower to succeed Eugene M. Zuckert as a member of the five-man AEC in 1954. He received that organization's Enrico Fermi Award in 1956 along with the Presidential Medal of Freedom. Some of his many writings include *Mathematical Foundations of Quantum Mechanics* (1932) and two posthumous works, *Theory of Self-Reproducing Automata* (1966) and *Collected Works* (vols. 1–3, 1961–62; vols. 4–6, 1963).

John von Neumann was the most nearly universal mathematician of his generation, a scientist in the tradition of Gauss, Poincaré, and Hilbert. Like them, he felt keenly that mathematics should maintain close ties with the empirical sciences. Significantly, however, he considered the criteria of success in mathematics, and even in theoretical physics, to be fundamentally aesthetic.

An axiomatic approach was characteristic of much of his work. His formulation of the principles of quantum mechanics first brought him wide recognition. His extensive work in operator theory was motivated by physics, but during the same years he made important contributions to logic, set theory, and measure theory, abstract fields whose empirical roots are more remote. His basic paper on the theory of games was published in the same year (1928) as some of his most intensive work in quantum mechanics.

After 1940 he became increasingly absorbed in the application of scientific ideas. The Manhattan Project and other war-related work occupied much of his time. He played a leading role in the early development of high-speed computers, being commonly credited with having introduced the idea of a stored program, a key notion in computer design which vastly increased their flexibility and power.

Von Neumann was gregarious, witty, and very much in tune with his times. His quick, clear, and penetrating mind was highly respected by the many engineers, physicists, and administrators who sought his advice, but his work was most truly appreciated by the young mathematicians he inspired. Among them he was universally known as "Johnny." See William Poundstone, *Prisoner's Dilemma* (1992), and Norman Macrae, *John von Neuman* (1992).

JOHN C. OXTOBY

WADE, Benjamin Franklin (b. Feeding Hills, Mass., Oct. 27, 1800; d. Jefferson, Ohio, March 2, 1878), POLITICAL LEADER, grew up on a farm and received little formal education. He moved to Andover, Ohio, in 1821, and, after spending the next few years at various jobs, began to study law in an office in Canfield, Ohio (1825). Admitted to the bar in 1828, he joined Joshua Giddings, a noted opponent of slavery, in 1831 to form a lucrative law practice in Jefferson, Ohio. Entering politics, Wade served a term as prosecuting attorney of Ashtabula County (1835–37) before being elected to the Ohio state senate in 1837. Denied reelection in 1839 because of his strong antislavery views, Wade served a second term two years later (1841–43). He was appointed presiding judge of Ohio's third judicial circuit in 1847, supported Zachary Taylor in 1848, and in 1851 was elected to the U.S. Senate as the choice of a Free-Soil–Whig coalition against the Fugitive Slave Law. Becoming a leader of the antislavery faction in Congress, Wade supported a move to repeal the Fugitive Slave Law in 1852 and denounced the Kansas-Nebraska Bill (1854). He helped organize the Republican party in Ohio (1854) and was twice reelected to the Senate as its candidate (1857 and 1863). In the Senate he also supported protective tariffs, internal improvements, and favorable legislation to homesteaders.

A member of the Committee of Thirteen which voted against the compromise Crittenden proposals to prevent southern secession, Wade was a leader of the radical Republicans in Congress, urging swift military action against the Confederacy, emancipation of the slaves, and punishment of the South. He became chairman of the Joint Committee on the Conduct of the War in 1861 and attacked General **George McClellan** for his dilatory tactics. Since he favored the punishment of southern leaders and confiscation of their property, Wade found himself in conflict with President Lincoln's Reconstruction policies. He cosponsored the Wade-Davis Bill (1864), making Reconstruction a congressional concern. When it was pocket-vetoed by Lincoln, Wade, together with Henry Winter Davis, denounced this action in a manifesto published in the New York *Tribune*. Nevertheless, he backed the Republican ticket in 1864. After Lincoln was assassinated, Wade initially supported Andrew Johnson, but broke with him when it became evident that Johnson would continue Lincoln's moderate policies. Elected president pro tem of the Senate in 1867, Wade favored Johnson's impeachment and voted for his conviction. In 1868 Wade, having failed to be reelected to the Senate, lost a bid for the Republican vice presidential nomination under U.S. Grant. He resumed his law practice in Jefferson in 1869, but served as chairman of the Ohio delegation to the 1876 Republican national convention in Cincinnati.

Wade was one of the best-known Radical Republicans during the era of the Civil War and Reconstruction. Blunt, outspoken, and uncompromising, he typified the radicalism that helped bring about the founding of the Republican party, the emancipation of the slaves, and the elevation of the freedmen.

Wade's radicalism was part of his heritage. An impoverished descendant of leading Puritans, he settled on the Western Reserve in Ohio, one of the most progressive regions in the United States. Somewhat narrow and provincial in his outlook, he nevertheless was practical enough to reject chimerical solutions and refused to join any third party until after the collapse of the Whigs. Yet his radicalism was real. He supported not only the crusade against slavery, but also the struggle for free land, woman's rights, and labor reform.

After his entry into the Senate in 1851, Wade became known for his fierce diatribes against slaveholders, his quick rejoinders to opponents, and his willingness to defend himself against physical threats. Together with other radicals, he played a leading role in the founding of the Republican party. Seeking to keep the organization faithful to its early principles, during the secession crisis he took a decided stand against all efforts to make further concessions to the South. When war came, he became one of the most outspoken advocates of emancipation and the vigorous conduct of hostilities. In addition, he was partially responsible for the passage of the Homestead Act.

Even as a Republican, Wade retained the Whigs' distrust of executive power. Frequently clashing with Lincoln about emancipation, the army, and Reconstruction, he finally carried his opposition so far as to sign the ill-considered Wade-Davis Manifesto, an action which proved exceedingly damaging to his reputation.

Wade's distrust of executive power was strengthened by the events of Reconstruction. One of the leaders in the struggle against Andrew Johnson, the senator firmly believed in the necessity of a radical policy in the South. Had the president been convicted, Wade would have succeeded him. But the senator's extreme position in favor of woman suffrage, a new deal for labor, and tariff protection contributed to Johnson's acquittal.

Wade's strong stand against slavery did not mean that he was free from racial prejudice. He admitted this shortcoming himself, but declared that reason rather than prejudice ought to govern political action. His importance lies in the consistency with which he fought for his radical policy. Without the steady pressure exerted by Wade and his colleagues, the great reforms of the period could not have been enacted. See H. L. Trefousse, *Benjamin Franklin Wade: Radical Republican from Ohio* (1963).

Hans L. Trefousse

WAGNER, Robert Ferdinand (b. Nastatten, Hesse-Nassau, Ger., June 8, 1877; d. New York, N.Y., May 4, 1953), POLITICAL LEADER, emigrated to America with his parents at the age of nine and grew up in a New York tenement neighborhood. After receiving his LLB from New York Law School (1900), he practiced law in New York City, soon becoming active in Democratic politics. A Tammany Democrat, loyal to the organiza-

tion throughout his career, he was elected to the New York state assembly in 1904, and in 1908 to the state senate. In 1911 he chaired the New York State Factory Investigating Commission, which produced pioneering legislation regulating industrial working conditions. Wagner remained in the state senate until 1918, having served as acting lieutenant governor in 1914. During 1919–26 he was a justice of the New York state supreme court.

In 1926 Wagner was elected to the U.S. Senate, where he served until 1949. As senator, he pioneered and championed New Deal social legislation, including the Social Security Act of 1935. He also sponsored the National Labor Relations Act of 1935, passed after the National Industrial Relations Act with its Section 7a guaranteeing collective bargaining in labor disputes was voided by the Supreme Court. This "Wagner Act" established a National Labor Relations Board with power to conduct elections for bargaining purposes and to prevent employers from discharging workers because of union membership. Company-controlled unions and other "unfair" labor practices were outlawed. Wagner also gave his name to the Housing Act of 1937 (Wagner-Steagall Act), which created the United States Housing Authority to provide loans for low-cost public housing. He sponsored the Railroad Retirement Act (1934), which established pensions for railway workers, and an unsuccessful antilynching measure (1934). He consistently supported President Franklin D. Roosevelt's domestic and foreign policies. After World War II Wagner worked to expand the social security and housing programs and to establish a system of national health insurance. He supported the Palestine independence movement which resulted in the creation of Israel, and was chairman of the American Palestine Committee until his death.

"Whether you like his laws or deplore them, he has placed on the books legislation more important and far-reaching than any American in history, since the days of the Founding Fathers....

The one real product of life in a modern crowded city in the Senate, the first thoroughly urban member of the Upper House ... Mr. Wagner has succeeded precisely because he has given more study to modern industrial conditions than any other Senator."

In these words journalists of the 1930s succinctly assessed the significance of Robert F. Wagner and his career. His contributions, both in Albany and in Washington, to the construction of the modern American welfare state represented the coming of age of the urban, industrial, largely immigrant-derived element of the population. His progression to prominence—from obscurity as a Tammany ward heeler in New York City at the turn of the century, to statewide reputation as Democratic leader of the Empire State's legislature during the Progressive Era, to national renown and responsibility during the New Deal—paralleled almost exactly the course that the growing influence of his class followed. The emergence of that influence helped produce a revolution in American politics and in American socioeconomic thinking and practice; a revolution that took place at considerable expense to the public treasury, and at considerable expense, also, to the cluster of values that the nation had inherited from its more homogeneous, rural, and agrarian past, when individualism and laissez-faire had been enshrined as cardinal tenets of the old American creed. To conservative critics at the time, the result of Wagner's brand of modern urban liberalism amounted to the conquest of America by alien ideas and ideals, and the nationwide Tammanyizing of the country's governmental and social processes. To Wagner and his allies, on the other hand, the path that American society traveled during his lifetime represented "the next step in the logical unfolding of man's eternal quest for freedom"—the translation of "the virtues, aspirations, and ideals of a rural people so as to serve in the development and progress of an urban people."

Like most of his liberal contemporaries, Wagner assumed that satisfaction of man's basic economic needs—an objective which he felt was well within the capability of a properly orga-

nized and directed American welfare state—would automatically open the way for full development of each individual's best potentialities. Preoccupied with meeting those fundamental needs, which loomed so large during the first half of the 20th century, Wagner and his collaborators devoted little time to contemplating what the next stages in the evolution of the economically satisfied society might concretely be like. Yet even before their mission was fully completed, they have in recent years been accused of fostering bureaucracy, centralization, and a degrading impersonality which actually stifles individual development—surely an outcome different from what Wagner envisaged.

Thus it remains to be seen what Americans will make of the welfare state which is the legacy of Senator Wagner and those like him. In any event, however, it would be well to remember how it all started: with a generous, compassionate impulse. In Senator Bob Wagner that impulse found one of its noblest embodiments. See J. Joseph Huthmacher, *Senator Robert F. Wagner and the Rise of Urban Liberalism* (1968).

J. JOSEPH HUTHMACHER

WAITE, Morrison Remick (b. Lyme, Conn., Nov. 29, 1816; d. Washington, D.C., March 23, 1888), JURIST, graduated from Yale (1837), and was admitted to the bar in 1839. He was an unsuccessful candidate for the U.S. Congress in 1846. In 1849–50 he served in the Ohio state legislature as a Whig. Settling in Toledo, Ohio, in 1850, he established himself as an attorney. He supported the Union in the Civil War, and ran for Congress as a Union Republican, but was again defeated (1862). With Caleb Cushing and William M. Evarts, he served on the Geneva Arbitration Committee that settled the *Alabama* claims dispute (1871), in which Great Britain agreed to pay for damages inflicted by British-built Confederate ships. In 1873 he was president of Ohio's constitutional convention.

In 1874 President Grant appointed Waite chief justice of the U.S. Supreme Court. As chief justice, he believed in not restricting the power of the states. He adopted the philosophy of the Court in the Slaughterhouse cases (1873), in which the justices distinguished between state and national citizenship by holding that the Fourteenth Amendment applied only to a limited category of federal citizenship rights. In the case of *U.S.* v. *Reese* (1876), Waite argued that sections of the Force Act of 1870, which sought to enforce the Fifteenth Amendment in the South, were unconstitutional because the act radically changed state election procedures by substituting broad federal controls. According to Waite, enforcement of the Fifteenth Amendment required carefully limited federal legislation aimed exclusively and explicitly at racial discrimination.

Waite's most famous decisions were handed down in the so-called Granger cases, which arose out of attempts of farmer-dominated state legislatures to regulate railroads and other utilities. In *Munn* v. *Illinois* (1877), which involved an Illinois law (1873) fixing maximum rates for grain storage, Waite, speaking for the Court, asserted, "When … one devotes his property to a use in which the public has an interest, he, in effect, grants to the public an interest in that use, and must submit to be controlled by the public for the common good." He dissented in the Wabash case (1886), in which the Court invalidated an Illinois statute as an infringement on Congress's right to control interstate commerce. In the Railroad Commission cases (1886) he acknowledged the right of "due process of law," but recognized the states' broad powers to regulate business in upholding a Mississippi railroad rate regulation law.

A capable attorney and an occasional participant in Ohio Republican politics, Morrison R. Waite was a political unknown in 1874 when nominated by President Grant. He was also uncontroversial and therefore acceptable to a Senate that had blocked Grant's previous nominations. Dubbed "His Accidency" by one critic, Waite quickly proved to be an effective chief justice. Through hard work, unwavering personal integrity, and an uncanny sense of human rela-

tionships, he managed a tribunal composed of brilliant and often headstrong associate justices. "Mott" Waite modestly believed in "being yourself" but also in taking "the place that belongs to you, not offensively, but let everybody feel that it is yours."

Constitutionally, Waite's judicial opinions were stabilizing influences. He favored a policy of conciliation between North and South, and his opinions recognized a large role for the states, free from much federal interference, in dealing with civil rights issues. In this respect, Waite reaffirmed traditional pre–Civil War constitutional values. He found ample precedence in English law and American traditions for both federal and state legislative regulation of business. His opinions in *Munn* v. *Illinois* and other cases emerging from the Granger movement remain as Waite's major constitutional legacies relevant to the present.

Chief Justice Waite's most enduring contributions are those based on his personal qualities and his determination to separate the judiciary from partisan political involvements. The Gilded Age of the seventies and eighties was a period tarnished by narrow politics and corruption in public office; Waite was a refreshing contrast. He scorned those economic buccaneers who valued "the dollar" too much and "character and humanity too little." When given an opportunity to contest for the presidency in 1876, he removed himself from all consideration by simply declaring that a chief justice "cannot be a candidate for any political office without damaging the place he holds." He helped restore the Supreme Court's prestige as an independent constitutional tribunal and set model standards for the behavior of judges. See C. Peter Magrath, *Morrison R. Waite: The Triumph of Character* (1963).

C. PETER MAGRATH

WALD, Lillian D. (b. Cincinnati, Ohio, March 10, 1867; d. Westport, Conn., Sept. 1, 1940), SOCIAL WORKER, graduated from the New York Hospital Training School for Nurses in 1891, and worked for a year in an orphan asylum, where she came to disapprove of the prevailing manner of institutional care of children.

Following a period of study at the Woman's Medical College, New York, Wald, together with Mary Brewster, moved to the College Settlement on Rivington Street in New York's Lower East Side. She established her own settlement house on Jefferson Street (1893), then, with financial support from **Jacob Schiff,** Solomon Loeb, and others, moved into expanded quarters at 265 Henry Street (1895). There she organized a visiting nurse service and offered classes in art and dance to community residents. In 1902, with Lina Rogers, she set up the world's first public school nursing system. On her suggestion the Metropolitan Life Insurance Co. started a nursing service for policyholders, and she also encouraged the Red Cross to organize its department of home nursing. Wald established a playground on Henry Street, helped reclaim areas for parks, including Seward Park, was active in organizing social halls, and fought for improved child-labor conditions. She was a member of the Mayor's Pushcart Commission (1906) and of the New York State Committee on Immigration (1909). She also lectured at Teachers College and at the New York School of Social Work. She and **Florence Kelley** originated the idea of the U.S. Children's Bureau, which was established in 1912. Wald was a supporter of woman suffrage and a pacifist, helping to organize the Women's Peace Crusade. During World War I, she helped provide nursing care for soldiers and was a member of the Council on National Defense. After the war she represented the U.S. at several international conferences that dealt with medicine and public health. In 1918–19 she organized the fight against the influenza epidemic and chaired the Nurses' Emergency Council. She retired as head worker at Henry Street in 1931 and resigned as president of the Settlement's board of directors in 1937.

———— ∞ ————

Like all the settlement-house leaders, Lillian Wald was a link between immigrants and natives, working class and middle class. In particular she was able to build on the identifications and aspirations of New York Jewry, poor and rich, downtown and uptown. Although she sympathized with exploited workers and the disadvantaged, she rejected dogmatic panaceas and radicalism in favor of neighborly sharing and social service. Her greatest contribution, which brought her international recognition, was to develop the profession of public health nursing. She looked upon it as a mode of education, in addition to its specific medical functions, and a general interest in education underlay other notable ventures that she sponsored in recreation and the arts. She was gifted with unflagging good will, cheerful resourcefulness, and executive ability; these qualities won her continued support despite her interest in many controversial causes, as when she favored neutrality in World War I and prohibition in the 1920s.

The central experience of her life was the daily stream of visitors to the settlement, people of every class and age, race, religion and nation, helped and helpers, enthusiasts and inquirers. These associations confirmed her intuition of the common humanity and individual dignity that underlay all social distinctions, and her conviction that all social groups were interdependent and mutually responsible. She herself visited, not only her neighbors on Henry Street, including the urchins, but also New York governors, British prime ministers, Russian revolutionaries, and Japanese physicians. In years when her country and the world were tragically divided, she made herself a beloved symbol of what is democratic, cosmopolitan, humane, and practical in our tradition. See R. L. Duffus, *Lillian Wald, Neighbor and Crusader* (1938).

JAMES LEIBY

WALKER, Francis Amasa (b. Boston, Mass., July 2, 1840; d. Boston, Mass., Jan. 5, 1897), ECONOMIST, graduated from Amherst College in 1860, worked briefly in a law office, and entered the Union army at the beginning of the Civil War. After the war, in which he rose to the rank of brevet brigadier general, he worked as a journalist and teacher until in 1869 he was appointed head of the Bureau of Statistics of the U.S. Treasury. In this office he supervised the census of 1870. In 1871–72, Walker served as U.S. commissioner of Indian affairs. Appointed professor of political economics and history at Yale in 1872, he inaugurated, in collaboration with **William Graham Sumner,** what was probably the first course in statistics in an American university. He taught briefly at Johns Hopkins University in 1876, and returned to public service to supervise the census of 1880. In 1881 he became president of the Massachusetts Institute of Technology, a position he held until his death. In addition to his writings in economics, statistics, history, education, population, politics, and the Native American problem, he was involved in numerous civic and professional activities, including service as president of the American Statistical Association (1883–97) and of the newly formed American Economic Association (1885–92).

A prolific writer, his most important books include: *The Wages Question* (1876), *Money* (1878), *Political Economy* (1883), *Land and Its Rent* (1893), and *International Bimetalism* (1896).

———— ∞∞∞ ————

Walker achieved his contemporary reputation through textbooks, lectures, popular articles, and more extended treatises, and through service as an organizer. His writings on monetary economics helped to educate American teachers and students about the major concepts then current in that rapidly changing area of economic theory. He played a major role in discrediting the classical wages-fund doctrine, which held that wages were determined by capital accumulated in the past and set aside for labor. According to Walker, wages are paid out of current product. His controversial theory of distribution, constructed after 1883 as an extension of his revision of the wages fund, introduced two original ideas about distributional shares: a "rent" theory of profits and a "residual" theory of wages. Walker's economics stressed the importance of entrepreneurs rather than capitalists in the organization of industry and the creation of wealth. In addition, he was the first economist to develop an explicit

theory of "perfect" competition, a concept he used as a basis for advocating limited state interference in the economy.

Walker's contributions to statistics were both organizational and technical. As director of the census—struggling against congressional indifference, limited funds and authority, and the conventional use of the Bureau of Statistics for purposes of political patronage—he worked to present an accurate description of the condition and development of the nation. One of America's pioneer demographers, he contributed numerous studies and a controversial "displacement" principle, which stated that immigration does not add to the total population because it is offset by the fall in the birth rate of the native population.

Walker was a man of compromise rather than of controversy among men whose livelihoods depended on explaining the rapid changes in American society. As an economist, he was notable less for his originality than his ability to modify received classical doctrines with American ideas and economic experience and newer European theories and methods, and to communicate changes in the state of the economists' art to a broad public. An intellectual statesman, he brought together men of different generations, technical skills, and convictions in two emerging professions: statistics and economics. His administrative career, public and academic, is notable for solid, gradual achievement, incorporating innovation with careful attention to political feasibility.

Two intellectual controversies of his later career are more important as incidents in the history of the social sciences in the United States than for the ideological interest sometimes imputed to them. The debate over Walker's theory of the distribution of wealth was the first major controversy in a professional economics journal in the United States. The displacement theory of immigration is less important for its nativism than as an early example of the effects of confusing correlation with causation. In his politics, as in his technical and administrative career, Walker was a cautious reformer with strong instincts to moderation. He left no disciples, and his most interesting ideas foreshadowed rather than influenced the work of other men. His legacy is his influence on institutions: the social science professions, public administration based on the application of systematic knowledge, and the American university. See Bernard Newton, *The Economics of Francis Amasa Walker: American Economics in Transition* (1968).

DANIEL M. FOX

WALKER, Robert John (b. Northumberland, Pa., July 19, 1801; d. Washington, D.C., Nov. 11, 1869), POLITICAL LEADER, graduated from the University of Pennsylvania in 1819. Admitted to the bar in 1821, he began to practice law in Pittsburgh, where he became an ardent supporter of Andrew Jackson. After joining his brother in a prosperous law practice in Natchez, Mississippi, in 1826, Walker was elected to the U.S. Senate from that state in 1835 as a Democrat. He supported a preemption law and the right of the states to public lands, while opposing protective tariffs, the distribution of the federal surplus, and **Henry Clay**'s "American System." In 1841 he was reelected to the Senate.

An expansionist, Walker drafted the Texas annexation resolution and advocated acquisition of Cuba and Mexico. At the 1844 Democratic convention, he supported James K. Polk over Martin Van Buren and was appointed secretary of the treasury by Polk in 1845. His 1845 report, in which he argued for the principles of free trade, was widely read in America and Europe. He managed the financing of the Mexican War and contributed the import warehousing idea in the handling of customs. In addition, he was influential in the creation of the Department of the Interior. After his retirement in 1849, he was a lawyer in Washington, D.C.

Walker reentered public life in 1856 as a supporter of James Buchanan for the presidency. Buchanan appointed him governor of Kansas Territory in 1857, with the firm understanding that any constitution presented by that future state would reflect the free will of eligible voters. When Buchanan insisted on accepting a constitu-

tion drafted at Lecompton, Kansas, and ratified in December 1857, by a highly undemocratic procedure, Walker resigned, later speaking and writing against the administration's Kansas policy.

Philosophically a Free Soiler (he freed his own slaves in the 1830s), Walker, although a Democrat, supported the Union in the Civil War. He spent two years in England selling government bonds during the conflict. After the war he resumed his career as a Washington lawyer and lobbyist; in the latter role he was active in successfully lobbying the purchase of Alaska.

— ∞ —

Walker was a typical Jacksonian. Ambitious and energetic, he combined pursuit of the main chance with skillful politics. His decision to back Jackson for the presidency was almost visceral in its origin. His commitment was to the man rather than to a program. He candidly admitted that had Jackson decided to recharter the second Bank of the United States he would have supported the decision. A northerner who made his political career in the Deep South, he swallowed his scruples about slavery. Deeply involved in land speculation, he so compromised his integrity that Jackson warned Polk against appointing him secretary of the treasury. Time and again, he became involved in ventures that were to blemish his reputation.

But his career reflected more than an uninhibited entrepreneurship. He vigorously espoused "Manifest Destiny." When he became convinced that Van Buren would oppose the annexation of Texas, he maneuvered his defeat at the Democratic convention of 1844. Rewarded by Polk with the Treasury, he revealed an administrative talent and an innovative spirit that ranks him among the greatest of secretaries of the treasury. Convinced that American economic security depended on foreign markets, he developed free trade arguments that remain classics. When he left the Treasury in 1849, his political career had crested.

The last twenty years of his life testify how thoroughly the Jacksonians failed to resolve the slavery issue. A strong Unionist, he allied himself with those Democrats who sought to achieve a final sectional compromise. It was a fruitless endeavor. He saw more clearly than most northerners that only a bloody, remorseless war would force the South back into the Union. He briefly attempted to check radical Reconstruction and then advised the South to accept the inevitable. A practical and talented politician, prepared to work in an atmosphere of give and take, he was ill-equipped to function within a politics of absolutes, more suited to the ideologue than to the politician. See James P. Shenton, *Robert John Walker: A Politician from Jackson to Lincoln* (1961).

JAMES P. SHENTON

WALLACE, Dewitt (b. Nov. 12, 1889, St. Paul, Minn.; d. Mt. Kisco, N.Y., March 30, 1981), PUBLISHER, attended Macalester College, where his father was the president (1907–9) and the University of California (1909–11). He then worked in the book department of a St. Paul concern issuing farm magazines and high school texts. Next he turned to direct mail advertising, interrupting his work to serve in World War I, during which he was wounded. After the war he became a publicist for Westinghouse Electrical and Manufacturing Company. The postwar depression led him to develop his idea of a digest of articles, with the cooperation of Lila Bell Acheson, whom he married.

The first issue of *Reader's Digest* came out in October 1921 and five thousand copies were printed and sold by subscription. It grew slowly, by 1925 reaching twenty thousand copies. The Wallaces moved to Pleasantville, New York, and by 1929 the magazine was available on the newsstands and selling 109,000 copies. Although some publishers were alarmed by the possibility that the *Digest* might diminish their market, they were reassured that reprints, with credit lines, advertised them and constituted no threat. Wallace constantly added to his program for interest and variety, filling pages with curious or entertaining items, compiling observations or news on single themes, condensing books, and more and more commissioning original articles, which the *Digest* planted elsewhere, then reprinted.

The Wallaces' growth internationally made theirs the largest single publication in the world. Since they accepted no advertising until the 1960s, they published no circulation figures of readership. But as South American, Swedish, and Arabic editions multiplied, their vast audience led public attention to their politics, which were variously criticized as antilabor, anti–New Deal, profascist. The Wallaces firmly denied the imputations, declaring they were pro-America. Living simply in their home not far from the *Digest* complex, they emphasized loyalty, financial scrupulousness, and service. The Wallaces formed the Reader's Digest Association, with Dewitt Wallace receiving 51 percent of the stock and his wife the rest. As the two Association stockholders they became millionaires many times over and founded the Reader's Digest Foundation to dispense much of their money to worthy causes.

⸺⸻⸺

Dewitt Wallace's entire concentration was on what has been called Middle America. For it he developed a three-point program of applicability: (1) involving the reader in the article's message; (2) lasting interest, so that it could be read with satisfaction so much as a year later; and (3) a positive approach, which Wallace clearly saw as good works and avoiding defeatism. Readers responded to his message. They noted, too, that the *Digest* did not rest on its laurels, but thought constantly in terms of new features, new approaches to format and content.

Criticism came mainly from competitors and public personages who were suspicious of its message. It was pointed out, for example, that in November 1939 **Charles A. Lindbergh** had, in the *Digest,* warned about guarding our "heritage" from "inferior blood," that the magazine had in 1943 urged the removal of union restrictions on shipyard production, that it had employed for a while the acknowledged fascist Lawrence Dennis, and otherwise followed a "reactionary" pattern.

Wallace protested that the *Digest* was apolitical, and indeed it could also be noted that it had employed Max Eastman, once famous as a radical intellectual though, to be sure, he had turned against Soviet Russia. The *Digest* also fought to curb syphilis, and printed the pros and cons of birth control. Wallace was unsmiling in his pursuit of what he termed, in capitals, a better America.

Critics, however, observing the *Digest*'s effect on many publications, its advance into motion pictures and other media, and other signs of expansion, feared it as a potential monopoly. Proceedings on that score were seriously considered by government agencies. In February 1944 the *New Yorker* decided to refuse reprint rights to the *Digest* on the ground that it was influencing too high a percentage of American magazine contents. The next month the *New Republic* took a similar position, criticizing the *Digest* as antiliberal. A long concern of *Digest* critics was its bad prose—a consequence of the regular reduction of articles to one-fourth their length, and the still-more drastic truncating of longer writings. But despite such challenging questions, the *Digest*'s continuing success demonstrated that Wallace produced a form that millions of readers wanted and enjoyed. See John Heidenry, *There Was The Kingdom: Lila and DeWitt Wallace and the Story of the Reader's Digest* (1993).

LOUIS FILLER

WALLACE, George Corley (b. Clio, Ala., Aug. 25, 1919), POLITICAL LEADER, graduated from the University of Alabama Law School in 1942, and was admitted to the bar that same year. During World War II he trained as a flyer in the army Air Corps and served as a flight engineer in the Pacific theater. Discharged in 1945, Wallace was appointed an assistant attorney general for Alabama (1946–47) and was elected to the state legislature in 1947. As a member of the Alabama delegation to the Democratic national convention of 1948, Wallace took a strong stand against the civil rights plank in the party platform. However, he did not leave the convention. In 1953 Wallace was elected judge of the third judicial circuit of Alabama, where he gained a reputation as an ardent segregationist, partly because of his defiance of the U.S. Civil Rights Commission. In 1958,

after he lost his bid in the Democratic gubernatorial primary, Wallace returned to private law practice in Clayton, Alabama. Four years later, however, he again ran and was elected.

In his inaugural address Wallace promised to preserve "segregation now, segregation tomorrow, and segregation forever." In 1963 he personally barred two black students from registering at the University of Alabama. He yielded, however, when President John F. Kennedy federalized the National Guard and ordered it to the campus. Although a strong segregationist, Governor Wallace took a liberal tack on economic issues, doubling the state debt by spending money on highways, schools, and mental hospitals. A fervent foe of alcohol, he tightened state liquor control and barred alcohol from the governor's mansion. Prohibited by the state constitution from running for a second consecutive term as governor in 1966, Wallace kept the reins of power in his own hands by engineering the election of his wife, Lurleen. He served as her "chief adviser" until her death in 1968. That same year he ran for president on the American Independent party ticket. He attacked the Supreme Court's decisions "handcuffing" the police, urged a cut in federal government spending and more power to local governments (especially in matters pertaining to racial relations), and promised to listen to the military in formulating his Vietnam War strategy. Although he ran third to Richard Nixon and **Hubert Humphrey,** he won five states (Alabama, Arkansas, Georgia, Louisiana, and Mississippi), garnering more than 9 million votes, 13 percent of those cast. In 1970 Wallace defeated his protégé, Albert Brewer, and was reelected governor of Alabama. In 1972, while campaigning for the Democratic presidential nomination, he was shot in the spine by a would-be assassin. The injury left him paralyzed in his lower body. He withdrew from the presidential race but remained governor of Alabama. Confined to a wheelchair and in almost constant pain, he would serve three more terms as governor (1971–79, 1983–87). Appearing to have mellowed in the last decade, Wallace now expresses repentence for his racist campaigning, arguing that he was merely seeking to uphold states' rights and was never a committed segregationist. Skeptics, however, of whom there are many, refuse to accept this avowal of contrition as genuine.

George C. Wallace emerged during a period of social change to assert that folk customs and traditional modes of behavior are more important than laws, constitutional processes, and intellectual theories. An effective and hard-driving campaigner, Wallace consistently appealed to—and reflected the views of—the common (white) Alabaman. Entering politics as a protégé of economically liberal and racially moderate Governor James E. Folsom, Wallace moved to an ever more racist position as popular hostility toward public school desegregation mounted. In 1958 State Attorney John Patterson defeated Wallace in a Democratic gubernatorial primary campaign that was fraught with anti-black emotionalism. "Patterson out-segged me," Wallace reportedly said, "and I'll never be out-segged again." Opposition to civil rights advances became the focal point of his general defense of rural small-town southern values. During the 1960s he dominated Alabama politics and came to symbolize white resistance to integration nationally. His third-party presidential effort in 1968, however, revealed his limited appeal to the white common "folks" outside the southern region. Wallace ranks among the shrewdest of 20th-century southern demagogues. Truly a political animal, he had few apparent interests other than his profession. Yet as governor of Alabama, he expanded badly needed state services while at the same time exacerbating racial tensions. See Dan T. Carter, *The Politics of Rage: George Wallace, the Origins of the New Conservatism, and the Transformation of American Politics* (1995).

N. V. BARTLEY

WALLACE, Henry Agard (b. Adair Co., Iowa, Oct. 7, 1888; d. Danbury, Conn., Nov. 18, 1965), POLITICAL LEADER, son of a former secretary of agriculture under Presidents Harding and Coolidge, graduated from Iowa State College in 1910 and worked as associate editor of his family's newspaper, *Wallace's Farmer*. He became editor upon his father's death in 1924 and incorporated the paper with the *Iowa Homestead* in 1929. During this period, Wallace formulated many ideas on farm relief, production control, and soil conservation. He also engaged in scientific experiments, developing a high-yield hybrid strain of corn which resulted in major advances in plant genetics.

Although originally a Republican, Wallace supported **Al Smith** for president in 1928 and Franklin D. Roosevelt in 1932. Roosevelt appointed Wallace secretary of agriculture in 1933. He reorganized the department and helped draft the 1933 Agricultural Adjustment Act; he and others later rewrote it after it was declared unconstitutional by the Supreme Court. Although severely criticized for plowing under cotton and slaughtering pigs in 1933 to reduce supplies, the AAA program succeeded in raising farm prices and limiting production. Wallace was elected vice president of the U.S. in 1940, and traveled extensively in Latin America and the Far East while in this office. He also served as chairman of the wartime Supply Priorities and Allocation Board and Board of Economic Warfare. Replaced by Harry Truman on the 1944 Democratic ticket, he became secretary of commerce in 1945. Wallace was compelled to resign by President Truman in 1946 after he made a speech attacking Truman's "get tough" foreign policy toward the Soviet Union. After serving as editor of the *New Republic* magazine (1946–47) Wallace ran for president in 1948 as the Progressive party candidate, but won only 1,138,000 popular and no electoral votes. He then returned to private life and spent most of his time on his farm in South Salem, New York, working on agricultural experiments. He wrote *Sixty Million Jobs* (1945), *The Long Look Ahead* (1960), and numerous other books, pamphlets, and articles on agriculture and politics.

A many-sided and highly controversial man, Henry A. Wallace worked near the center of the national stage for a decade and a half and became the champion of a broad program of reform at home and cooperation abroad. He was an idealist and an intellectual, but he was also a hard-headed administrator and politician. Being guided by political and economic "realities," he was not inflexible.

In his early years, Wallace was interested mainly in agriculture. He came to Washington after a career as an agricultural scientist and economist, farm editor, and "agribusinessman," and he was a very active and constructive secretary of agriculture during the Depression, shaping a complex set of programs designed to make the farm business profitable once again.

During his years in Roosevelt's cabinet, Wallace developed from a mere servant of the nation's commercial farmers to a philosopher and spokesman for the New Deal. He displayed a cautious concern for the rural poor, he made a bolder effort to reform land-use practices, and he became very interested in the expansion of urban purchasing power. The change was so striking that some of his former allies became very critical of him, convinced that he had deserted the farmer for other groups.

As vice president, Wallace's outlook continued to expand. He became more interested in international affairs and became the leading spokesman for American liberalism, building a large following among New Dealers. His liberalism, however, alienated most Democratic politicians in the South and the city machines, and they forced FDR to discard Wallace in 1944 and accept an alternative running mate.

After the war, Wallace was the most prominent critic, on the left, of Truman's "get tough" and "containment" policies, as well as a leading proponent of a full-employment economy and a foe of racial segregation. Convinced that the United States and Russia must cooperate and that all nations must trade with one another, he blamed the new foreign policies on the influence of an economic and military elite, labeled the policies imperialistic, and insisted that they were leading toward atomic war. His critique also emphasized the domestic consequences of international conflict, especially the frustration of reform, and called for reliance on the United Nations for the management of international affairs.

Convinced that Communists and liberals must work together, Wallace joined with Communists and some liberals in a third-party venture in 1948, but he was portrayed as a tool of the Communists, and received only a small vote, in spite of his very strenuous campaign. Thereafter, he played only a small role in politics. See Edward L. and Frederick H. Schapsmeier, *Henry A. Wallace of Iowa: The Agrarian Years, 1910–1940* (1968) and *Prophet in Politics: Henry A. Wallace and the War Years, 1940–1965* (1970).

RICHARD KIRKENDALL

WALLACE, Lewis (b. Brookville, Ind., April 10, 1827; d. Crawfordsville, Ind., Feb. 15, 1905), MILITARY LEADER, WRITER, received little formal schooling. He moved to Indianapolis in 1837 when his lawyer father was elected governor of Indiana as a Whig. After working for the Indianapolis *Daily Journal* (1844–45), Wallace read law in his father's firm. He enlisted in the army during the Mexican War and served as a second lieutenant. Returning to Indiana, he was admitted to the bar in 1849 and began to practice in Indianapolis. In 1850 he moved to Covington, Indiana, and was twice elected prosecuting attorney (1850, 1852). After moving to Crawfordsville, Indiana, in 1853, Wallace was elected to the state senate in 1856. At the outbreak of the Civil War he became adjutant general of Indiana and then colonel of a volunteer regiment. He rose to brigadier general and major general of volunteers (1861–62), at the time the youngest of the latter rank in the Union army. Wallace fought at Shiloh and, as commander of the Middle Division and 8th Army Corps in Baltimore, helped defend Washington against Confederate General Jubal Early (1864). But Grant removed him from command for alleged dilatoriness at Shiloh. Wallace was a member of the court that tried those associated with the assassination of

Abraham Lincoln, and was president of the court-martial that tried Henry Wirz, the commandant of the Andersonville (Ga.) Prison. Leaving the army in 1865, Wallace spent seven months (1866–67) in Mexico helping Juarez raise funds and an army to defeat the French. He then returned to practice law in Crawfordsville.

Wallace was an unsuccessful candidate for Congress as a Republican in 1870, and following his defeat turned his attention to literature. His first novel, *The Fair God* (1873), was a historical romance about the conquest of Mexico. Appointed governor of New Mexico Territory in 1878, Wallace finished writing *Ben-Hur: A Tale of the Christ* (1880) in Santa Fe. This dramatic novel, dealing with the coming of Christ, was enormously popular and was translated into ten languages. A play based on it traversed the country from 1899 to 1920, and two spectacular movies were made of it (1925, 1959). Wallace served as minister to Turkey (1881–85); this mission resulted in *The Prince of India* (1893), another historical romance. *Lew Wallace: An Autobiography* (1906) was completed posthumously by his wife. His other books include *The Life of Benjamin Harrison* (1888) and *The Boyhood of Christ* (1888).

***

It has been claimed that Wallace's *Ben-Hur* broke the dike of village opposition in the United States to the novel. More plausibly the book can be compared with *Paradise Lost:* the folk came to believe that both stories are to be found in the Bible. Just as Milton grafted Homeric machinery, English high policy, and Puritan morality on the Old Testament, Wallace superimposed the American horse race, the global love triangle, and a military triumph on the New.

One cannot discount as inspiration plain Yankee ingenuity in belles-lettres, but perhaps more significant in Wallace's case were particular frustrations. He yearned for glory in the Mexican War; he got disillusionment with Zachary Taylor. He won the highest laurels from Grant in the Civil War, but unsuccessful strategy earned him a reprimand. Dream castles in Mexican silver mines failed to materialize. In New Mexico he

fought crime, corruption, and Native Americans inconclusively. Even as a writer he was ignored by the Brahmins of his generation—**James R. Lowell, Oliver Wendell Holmes,** Thomas B. Aldrich, **William D. Howells.**

"I shall look back upon *Ben-Hur* as my best performance," he wrote his wife in 1885. By 1905 the plaudits of the public had resulted in greater financial returns than had been received for a fictional work by any other author of his generation in the United States. By 1936, when the copyright expired, *Ben-Hur* had drawn the greatest monetary reward meted out to the owners of an American novel. See Irving McKee, *"Ben-Hur" Wallace: The Life of General Lew Wallace* (1947).

IRVING McKEE

WANAMAKER, John (b. Philadelphia, Pa., July 11, 1838; d. Philadelphia, Pa., Dec. 12, 1922), MERCHANT, POLITICAL LEADER, received a grammar school education. In 1852 he began work as a stock boy in the clothing store of Barclay Lippincott. Following a disagreement with his employer over window displays in 1854, he became a stock boy in the rival clothing firm of Tower Hall. There he rapidly advanced to salesman and manager of the men's furnishing department.

Forming a partnership with Nathan Brown, Wanamaker opened a men's clothing shop called Oak Hill in Philadelphia in 1861. Developing new marketing techniques, Wanamaker set a standard price on all goods and offered money-back guarantees. He also advertised extensively in newspapers. By 1868 Oak Hill had become the largest clothing store in the U.S. Wanamaker established John Wanamaker and Co., a luxury clothing store on fashionable Chestnut Street, in 1869, and in 1876 he opened the Grand Depot, a giant department store in a renovated railroad station. In 1896 he also purchased A. T. Stewart's, a large department store in New York City.

Wanamaker became active in politics as a fund raiser for the Republican party during the presidential campaign of 1888; President Harrison appointed him postmaster general in 1889 in reward for his services. Despite the opposition of civil service reformers, Wanamaker continued the traditional "spoils system" of distributing patronage to loyal party members. He organized an insurgent movement against the Quay machine in Pennsylvania during the 1890s, but he failed in his efforts to win the Republican nomination for senator in 1896 and governor in 1898. He was active in YMCA affairs and energetically supported the prohibition movement.

John Wanamaker participated in two stages of the evolution of modern large-scale merchandising. The first of these was the introduction of the large single-line establishments to replace the older general store. A high-volume, single-line store, such as Wanamaker's Oak Hill, had the advantages of economies of scale in financing, advertising, and management. In addition, this type of store could bypass the wholesaler and use its market strength to obtain better-quality merchandise. The success of a high-volume store, however, depended on the existence of a large market area. It was only with urbanization and improved transportation that such stores were possible. Wanamaker's genius was that he saw the new opportunity and acted upon it.

The second development of which Wanamaker was a part, the coming of the department store, was the logical outgrowth of the single-line store. Once you had a large building, once you had established a name through advertising, once you had developed an efficient management system, it was rather easy to add other lines to your merchandise. Whether Wanamaker was the first to introduce the large-scale diversified store is questionable. Macy's and Lord and Taylor in New York were evolving into department stores in the 1870s, and, in fact, at one time Wanamaker cited Macy's as being the earliest.

Although in retrospect Wanamaker appears to have been one of several men who were engaged in adapting the distribution system to the needs of the city, he interpreted his successful rise from obscurity as justification of his value system. Whether through his newspaper advertisements

or from the pulpit of a church, he was always eager to tell how he had made it and how anyone else could. Thus like many other 19th-century entrepreneurs, he sought to be both an economic and a cultural leader of his generation. See Russell H. Conwell, *The Romantic Rise of a Great American* (1924).

ALAN D. ANDERSON

WARBURG, Paul Moritz (b. Hamburg, Ger., Aug. 10, 1868; d. New York, N.Y. Jan. 24, 1932), BANKER, graduated from the Hamburg gymnasium in 1886. He then worked for exporting firms, and in banking houses in London and Paris. In 1895 he was admitted to the banking firm of M. M. Warburg and Sons, which his great-grandfather had founded and of which his father was a member. That same year, he married the daughter of Solomon Loeb of the New York banking firm of Kuhn, Loeb and Co., and came to New York in 1902 to become a member of that firm.

Warburg had studied the central banking systems of the major European nations, particularly his native Germany, and with the coming of the panic of 1907 he was prominent among those who urged fundamental reform of the American banking system. In 1907 he wrote a pamphlet, "A Plan for a Modified Central Bank," and a New York *Times* article, "Defects and Needs of Our Banking System," outlining his views. As a result, Senator **Nelson W. Aldrich,** chairman of the National Monetary Commission, asked him to act as his ex-officio expert consultant in forming a new banking system. The report issued by the Commission in 1911, which ultimately led to the establishment of the Federal Reserve Board in 1913, embodied several of Warburg's key ideas about monetary reform, especially his theory of a modified central banking system with a paper currency backed substantially by commercial acceptances.

Warburg was appointed one of the members of the first Board of Governors of the Federal Reserve System in 1914, and after resigning to avoid the possibility of public hostility to a German-born high public official during World War I, he returned to private banking, opening his

International Acceptance Bank. This bank ultimately failed, however. He was a member of the advisory council of the Federal Reserve Board (1921–26), and director or trustee of many companies and societies. A sharp pre-Depression critic of "orgies" of stock speculation, he warned of the impending crash. His two-volume *The Federal Reserve System: Its Origin and Growth* (1930) described his plans to strengthen the power of the Federal Reserve to curb future economic disasters.

Warburg played an influential and innovative role in reforming American banking at a time when its poor organization and consequent instability adversely affected both domestic and international finance. He found the panic of 1907 especially alarming—a warning that "the financial machinery of Europe may break down some time under our huge weight." Until his death, he worked diligently and with measurable effect to redirect American banking so that it could take the financial responsibilities appropriate to its capacities. But he was never satisfied with the Federal Reserve System because the reforms he advocated were not fully adopted in his lifetime. The System was not centralized until 1935; the acceptance and discount system did not assume the importance in New York that it did in London. The stock market continued to dominate the New York money market, a situation he deplored. Without the System, however, it is doubtful that the United States could have responded as well to the financial demands and opportunities of the war period.

Having left his mark on the logic and organization of the banking system in 1913, Warburg reached a second peak of influence in the post–World War I period. He adapted his talents to an unfavorable situation, showing qualities of financial leadership which had not been so evident before. The rapid transition of the United States from a debtor to a creditor position led him to demand changed financial and fiscal policies. It was no longer sufficient for the United States to carry its own weight and not be a burden to Europe, he insisted. The country must now *support* Europe. He was in the forefront of the effort to apply government finance to the problems of postwar reconstruction. When that failed, he organized the International Acceptance Bank and, in 1924, a consortium of some of the biggest New York banks to finance trade credits to Germany. While both of these efforts must be considered at least short-term successes, Warburg became increasingly pessimistic about the future of the economic system.

Partnership in the second-largest investment banking house in the United States had opened doors to the exercise of Warburg's unusual background in international finance. But as a constructive individual who thought in large terms, he built on these opportunities and, in his own right, made outstanding contributions to his country and to international banking. See Ron Chernow, *The Warburgs: The 20th-Century Odyssey of a Remarkable Jewish Family* (1993).

PAUL P. ABRAHAMS

WARD, Lester Frank (b. Joliet, Ill., June 18, 1841; d. Washington, D.C., April 18, 1913), SOCIAL SCIENTIST, grew up on a farm, where he taught himself Latin, Greek, French, and German. After briefly attending a preparatory school in Pennsylvania he enlisted in the Union army during the Civil War. Seriously wounded at Chancellorsville (1863), he was discharged for physical disability the next year and became a clerk in the Treasury Department. He rose to be chief of the Division of Navigation and Immigration and then librarian of the Bureau of Statistics. While working in Washington, Ward attended Columbian College (later George Washington University), where he earned his AB in 1869, LLB in 1871, and AM (botany) in 1872. In 1881 he joined the U.S. Geological Survey as an assistant geologist. He was promoted to geologist in 1883, and to chief paleontologist in 1892.

During this period Ward carried on extensive research in paleobotany, but he also became increasingly interested in the sociological writings of Auguste Comte and Herbert Spencer. He became convinced that sociology had to be systematically integrated with psychology, biology, and other disciplines, and, after extensive reading, produced *Dynamic Sociology* (2 vols., 1883). This work, sharply critical of laissez-faire, expressed his belief in a functional sociology which could be useful in planning a better society. An advocate of compulsory education, Ward felt that all men and women had equal capacities and needed only equal opportunities to develop them. In 1906 he accepted a position as professor of sociology at Brown, where he remained until his death. He served as president of the Institut International de Sociologie (1900–1903) and was president of the American Sociological Society (1906–7). Some of his many writings include: *Pure Sociology* (1903), *Applied Sociology* (1906), and *Text-Book of Sociology* (1905), written with his friend James Q. Dealey.

Ward has been called a "Yankee Aristotle." Immensely learned, he took all knowledge as his province and attempted to make a grand synthesis of the natural sciences and social studies which would illuminate human behavior. Democratic, humanitarian, and equalitarian in outlook, he called the masses "the fourth estate," insisted that slum children were as promising as children of the rich, and refused to observe the invidious distinctions commonly made between people from different walks of life. Having risen himself from poverty and obscurity to distinction in the world of scholarship, he was anxious for all young men and women to possess by right what he had obtained by hard work and fortunate circumstances: economic and educational opportunities to advance in life. He looked to the newly developing field of sociology to point the way to the Great Society. He was a pioneer sociologist, but also a zealous reformer.

American sociology in Ward's early years was dominated by Herbert Spencer's amalgamation of laissez-faire individualism and organic evolution known as Social Darwinism. The Social Darwinists held that society should, like nature, be governed by the law of the survival of the fittest and that the unregulated competitive-capitalist system, in which social selection automatically weeded out the unfit and rewarded the most deserving, had scientific sanction. Ward called this let-alone philosophy "social Nirvana"; he preferred *faire marcher* to laissez-faire. He was the first scholar to challenge Social Darwinism on scientific grounds. He did so by making a sharp distinction between natural and social evolution. Nature's method is blind, haphazard, and wasteful, he pointed out; it is no model for man's behavior. The appearance of "psychic factors"—reason, imagination, foresight—in human evolution made it possible for man to transcend the blind struggle for existence, interfere with natural processes, and shape his own natural and social environments. Was not civilization itself, asked Ward, "the result of man's *not* letting things alone, and of his *not* letting nature take its course?"

Ward advocated "telesis"—deliberate planning—to improve society. His ultimate goal was a "sociocracy"—a society in which trained sociologists, serving in all levels of government, studied social problems scientifically, proposed solutions to them, and supervised piecemeal experiments for bettering conditions. What Ward called "social engineering" was to be accompanied by the democratization of education and the unleashing through schooling of the vast creative energies which he saw latent in the masses of men.

With the decline of Social Darwinism, much of Ward's work lost its urgency, and by the turn of the century younger sociologists were emphasizing analysis of the actual behavior of men in society rather than social reconstruction. They were also eschewing grand theories of empirical and statistical methods of analysis. They therefore regarded Ward as a social philosopher rather than as a sociologist. Though Ward did grasp some issues of concern to 20th-century sociology, his work today is primarily of interest to historians of social thought rather than to sociologists. See Samuel Chugerman, *Lester F. Ward: The American Aristotle* (1939).

PAUL F. BOLLER, JR.

WARHOL, Andy (b. somewhere in Penn., Aug. 6, 1928; d. New York, N.Y., Feb. 22, 1987), ARTIST, FILMMAKER, born Andrew Warhola, he was the youngest child of a barely literate, working-class Czechoslovakian immigrant family living in Pittsburgh, Pennsylvania. Warhol's father died when he was thirteen years old but left him with a legacy of hard work, a dedication to making money, and a painfully accumulated nest egg so that the already precocious young Andy could get a college education. So provided, Warhol graduated from the Carnegie Institute of Technology in 1949. He moved to New York City, where he worked as a commercial artist for the next several years. He began painting his Campbell soup can series of thirty-two paintings in 1961. In 1962 Warhol was represented in the New Realist exhibition at the Janis Gallery in New York, which established the identity of a new international trend. After his first one-man show at the Stable Gallery he became a recognized leader in the "pop art" movement. *7¢ Airmail Stamp* (1962, Collection Mrs. P. N. Matisse, Santa Monica, Calif.), *Coca-Cola* (1962, Collection Mr. and Mrs. Melvin Hirsh, Beverly Hills, Calif.), and *Campbell's Soup Can* (1965, artist's collection) are examples of this style. Warhol also produced stenciled newspaper pictures of famous people and events, using a silkscreen process. Such works as *Marilyn Monroe* (1962, Collection Galerie Ileana Sonnabend, Paris) and *Jackie* (1964, Leo Castelli Gallery, N.Y.), a portrait of Jacqueline Kennedy Onassis, are examples.

Becoming interested in underground moviemaking, Warhol made several 8-millimeter films, including *Sleep*, which showed a man sleeping for six hours. He then moved into 16-millimeter films and made such features as *Empire* (1965), *Poor Little Rich Girl* (1965), and *The Chelsea Girls* (1966), which enjoyed wide popularity. In 1968 Warhol was shot and severely wounded by an embittered former actress. He published *a*, a series of tape-recorded conversations, in 1969. He presented more films including *Lonesome Cowboys* (1969), *Blue Movie* (1969), *Trash* (1970), *Heat* (1972), and *Frankenstein* (1974). In 1975 Warhol published *The Philosophy of Andy Warhol (From A to B and Back Again)* which contained his contrarian views on diverse subjects in epigramatic form. During the 1980s he took on a host of commissions, one of which was a series of prints—based on animals considered endangered species—which were first shown at the American Museum of Natural History (1983). And in 1985 he exhibited a group of prints of clowns, robots, monkeys, and other images he produced for the children of the Newport (R.I.) Art Museum. During the 1980s, too, Warhol acted as mentor and friend for a whole group of young artists bursting upon the scene, including Keith Haring and Jean-Michel Basquiat.

—————&—————

It is not easy to place the elusive Andy Warhol, who after a successful career in commercial art applied the techniques he had acquired in that field to produce parodies of it—American pop art. After a few dazzling years he more or less abandoned pop (he would later refer to the work he produced as "junk") for a career as a leading underground movie director and producer. The essence of Warhol's personality was to shock and at the same time to intrigue a public much vaster than the art public. These qualities the critic Barbara Rose likened to those of Salvador Dali. But unlike the Spanish surrealist, or his well-known contemporaries in pop art—Roy Lichtenstein, Jim Dine, Claes Oldenburg, James Rosenquist, and Tom Wesselmann—Warhol's contributions were never sentimental or nostalgic. He was always less of a fine artist than they. His attitude was totally uninvolved with any aesthetic. His specialty was sets of images silkscreened to look like enlargements of newspaper photographs. Among the most audacious were the Brillo boxes (1963–64) which could not be opened but otherwise looked exactly like the real thing, and *Cow Wallpaper*—Elsie the Borden cow—which brought his career in pop art to an end in 1966. According to the critic David Antin, Warhol was "the master of a communication game that elicits the false response." For most this response was boredom, and yet boredom was precisely what Warhol spotted as typical of our era. Thus, willy-nilly, he was always a social critic. In Warhol's early films the technique of inducing boredom was deliberately primitivist: a fixed camera, virtually no editing, direction, or story, a kind of flow of events improvised by the actors themselves, who move into and out of range of the camera which functions like a keyhole through which the audience is allowed to peer. After his first real commercial success—*Chelsea Girls*—the films which left his loft studio, known as The Factory, tended to head in the direction of nonart entertainment. *Lonesome Cowboys* was a spoof on Hollywood westerns. Its photography is also more interesting than that in most of his other films. See Parker Tyler, *Underground Film: A Critical History* (1969), and Victor Bockris, *The Life and Death of Andy Warhol* (1989).

LAWRENCE CAMPBELL

WARREN, Earl (b. Los Angeles, Calif., March 19, 1891; d. Washington, D.C., July 9, 1974), POLITICAL LEADER, JURIST, received a BL (1912) and JD (1914) from the University of California. After practicing law in San Francisco and Oakland, he served as clerk for the state legislature (1919), deputy city attorney for Oakland (1919–20), state deputy district attorney (1920–25), district attorney for Alameda County (1925–39), and attorney general of the state (1939–43).

During 1942–53 Warren, a Republican, was governor of California, the first man to be elected governor three times. During his administration both the state debt and tax rates were reduced, while expenditures on education, old age, and unemployment benefits were increased. In 1948, running on the ticket with **Thomas E. Dewey,** he was the unsuccessful Republican candidate for vice president.

In 1953 President Eisenhower appointed Warren chief justice of the United States. In this position he argued that the Court must be guided by economic and social realities and not merely by legal precedents when handing down its decisions, especially in the area of civil rights. In 1954 Warren wrote the opinion in the school desegregation case *Brown* v. *Board of Education of Topeka,* which repudiated the *Plessy* v. *Ferguson* (1896) "separate but equal" doctrine. "We conclude that in the field of public education, the doctrine of 'separate but equal' has no place. Separate educational facilities are inherently unequal." In *Quinn* v. *U.S.* (1955) and *Watkins* v. *U.S.* (1957), the Warren Court protected the rights of witnesses appearing before congressional investigating committees. In *Trop* v. *Dulles* (1958) it invalidated a federal statute revoking the citizenship of military deserters.

Following the assassination of President Kennedy in 1963, President Lyndon Johnson named Warren to head a seven-man committee to investigate the assassination. In September 1964 this committee delivered its "Warren Report," stating that Lee Harvey Oswald was the sole assassin of the president and that there was no evidence of a conspiracy.

In 1964, in *Reynolds* v. *Sims* (commonly referred to as the "one-man, one-vote case"), the Court stated that representation in state legislatures must be apportioned on the basis of population. Warren retired from the Court in 1969.

Like all chief justices of the United States, Earl Warren will go down in history not for his individual deeds but rather because of the accomplishments of the Supreme Court during his tenure as its presiding officer. Warren will, therefore, be acclaimed and damned for decisions in which his role was sometimes necessary but never sufficient to command the result.

Earl Warren was an impressive, hearty, bluff personality. He made friends easily and was an accomplished politician before he ascended the bench. Indeed, it was a deal at the 1952 Republican convention between Warren and Eisenhower that made the one president and the other chief justice of the United States.

As governor, attorney general, and district attorney in California, Warren was anything but an ideologue. That was not the road to political office, which then, as now, demands the capacity of the trimmer. Thus, there is some irony in the judicial record by which Warren will be judged. For once on the Supreme Court, he did become an ideologue committed to an ideology largely created by justices **Hugo Black** and **William Douglas** long before Warren's arrival in Washington.

The irony derives from the fact that the three hallmarks of the Warren Court were, first and foremost, the school desegregation cases, which sparked and supported the civil rights movement of the fifties, sixties, and seventies; second, the extension of an expansive reading of the Bill of Rights of the national Constitution to state criminal processes; third, the judicial intervention into the political scene of legislative apportionment through the creation and application of the requirement of the "one-man, one-vote" rule. But it was Warren as attorney general of California who led the fight for segregation and removal of the Japanese Americans from the West Coast at the time of World War II. It was Warren as a hard-hitting county prosecutor who made his reputation by criminal convictions obtained frequently through evidence that he later outlawed. It was Warren as governor of California who fought a constitutional amendment to reapportion the state legislature in closer conformity to the "one-man, one-vote" standard.

Warren was a political chameleon adapting his colors to his surroundings. It made him an astute politician and an adequate judge. But it was the Court that formed Warren, not Warren who formed the Court.

Warren presided over the Court during the most activist period of its history and will be regarded by history as second only to **John Marshall,** whose Court first helped fuse a nation out of disparate states. Like all its predecessors, the Warren Court will also be noted for its nationalistic bent, assuring the centralization of governmental authority in one or the other of the national branches at the expense of state power. Unlike most of its predecessors, however, the Warren Court was deeply committed to the freedom of the individual—and particularly the political dissenter—from governmental restraints. And, unlike many of its predecessors, the Court put few if any barriers in the way of governmental regulation of economic enterprises. Equality was its lodestar, as it labored mightily, if largely in vain, to fuse the black society with the white, even to the point of justifying compensatory rather than equal treatment of the black minority.

Warren will thus take his place in history beside Marshall as a great chief justice, not because of his great intellect or his capacity to lead, but because, in Justice **Oliver Wendell Holmes, Jr.**'s terms, he "was there" when the Court engaged in its historic battles, and his name will be the symbol by which the efforts of himself and some fifteen other justices framed the Constitution of the period. Whether the Warren Court's construction of that plastic document proves long-lasting or not, and some of its work will surely never be undone, the Court of this era was a more significant factor in the governance of the country than during most of this nation's history. And so, strangely, Earl Warren will be better known to future generations than the persons who bested him in the contest for the presidential nomination and the one who nominated him for the Court, Dwight Eisenhower, whose presidency seems likely to be marked as an interregnum. See John D. Weaver, *Warren: The Man, the Court, the Era* (1967), and G. Edward White, *Earl Warren* (1982).

PHILIP B. KURLAND

WARREN, Mercy Otis (b. Barnstable, Mass., Sept. 14, 1728; d. Plymouth, Mass., Oct. 19, 1814), PLAYWRIGHT, HISTORIAN, lived and was educated at home in Barnstable until she married James Warren and moved to Plymouth, Massachusetts, in 1754. While rearing her family, she wrote poetry for local newspapers. In 1773 she wrote her first play, *The Adulateur*, a satire on Governor **Thomas Hutchinson** and his family, published by the *Massachusetts Spy*. A sequel, *The Defeat*, appeared in the Boston *Gazette* in 1773. In 1775 she wrote *The Group*, a satire on Boston Tories, and in 1776 replied to General Burgoyne's *The Blockade of Boston*, an attack on the colonial army, with *The Blockheads*, a farce about General

Gage's army. She then focused her wit on Boston war profiteers in *The Motley Assembly* (1779), which was published anonymously.

Following Shays's Rebellion, Warren wrote a criticism of the Constitution for lacking a bill of rights, "Observations on the New Constitution and on the Federal Conventions" (1788), which was originally ascribed to **Elbridge Gerry,** who distributed it and provided some of its ideas. In 1790 she wrote two dramas, *The Ladies of Castile,* about a popular uprising similar to the American Revolution, the *The Sack of Rome,* both of which were included in her collection, *Poems, Dramatic and Miscellaneous* (1790). Her last and best-known work, the three-volume *A History of the Rise, Progress, and Termination of the American Revolution,* was published in 1805. In it she defended the Revolution, expressed antiaristocratic leanings, expressed her belated approval of the Constitution, and presented character sketches of leading participants.

Mercy Otis Warren, an able and vigorous person, was fortunate in being more widely read and having through family connections more knowledge of public affairs than most women of her day. The sister of **James Otis** and wife of James Warren, she could hardly have escaped revolutionary fervor. She influenced a select circle of Massachusetts leaders who found her plays valuable propaganda and published them for a wider group. She at first questioned the appropriateness of political writing for her sex, but her friends urged on her the duty of using her talents for the American cause. She yielded readily. Later her interest in political matters and the suggestions of her acquaintances led her naturally into history. She managed the somewhat stilted and romanticized style of the time with reasonable skill. As a historian she used her sources thoroughly, and from her standpoint conscientiously. Her concept of history included the pointing of moral lessons. The plays and the history both reflect her strong partisanship, whether in support of the early patriots against the Hutchinson faction or in criticism of the Federalists. The history remains a useful source for revolutionary attitudes and to a lesser extent as a firsthand account of events.

Was she a feminist? Interpretations vary. Her expressed approach to a woman's position on life was fairly traditional but had overtones of impatience at some of its restrictions. She encouraged women's "literary inquiries" while stressing the cheerful performance of domestic duties. She belongs among those able 18th- and 19th-century women who promoted feminism without fanfare—and possibly without intent. See Katharine Anthony, *First Lady of the Revolution: The Life of Mercy Otis Warren* (1958).

MARY S. BENSON

WASHINGTON, Booker Taliaferro (b. Hale's Ford, Franklin Co., Va., April 5, 1856; d. Tuskegee, Ala., Nov. 14, 1915), EDUCATOR, was the son of a slave and a white father. Shortly after the Civil War his mother moved to Malden, near Charleston, West Virginia. Although illiterate, she was determined that her son be educated. During the day he worked at a salt furnace; at night he was tutored by a teacher in the local black elementary school. In 1862 he enrolled at Hampton Institute in Virginia, a teacher-training school. To earn money for his room and board, he worked as school janitor. During the winter of 1878–79 he attended Wayland Seminary, a black Baptist theological seminary in Washington, D.C.

In 1881 Washington was appointed to head a new black normal school at Tuskegee, Alabama. While this school was supported by some state appropriations, most of the funds for the maintenance of the school were raised in the North. During the thirty-four years of his leadership, Tuskegee grew into an institution with more than 1,500 students and a faculty of nearly 200.

Washington eventually became the most prominent black spokesman in the nation. He believed that African-Americans should give up struggling for political and social equality in return for economic opportunities. After they had improved their economic status, he argued, full rights would eventually follow. Washington presented these ideas most cogently at the

Atlanta Exposition of 1895, where he spoke at the opening ceremonies. His argument that blacks must sacrifice civil rights for economic gain was later attacked by a number of African-American leaders, most notably **W. E. B. Du Bois.** During his day, however, Washington's point of view was accepted, both North and South, as the best hope for the African-American.

As a leader in the field of race relations Washington had a great influence. He advised Presidents Roosevelt and Taft on patronage, racial, and sectional questions; he was active in such groups as the Afro-American Council, the National Negro Business League, and the Committee of Twelve; and he helped allocate the funds of several philanthropic foundations, including the **Julius Rosenwald, Jacob H. Schiff,** and Jeanes funds. He also influenced the donations of **Andrew Carnegie, John D. Rockefeller,** and other wealthy men to a variety of black schools and enterprises. His autobiography, *Up From Slavery,* was published in 1901. Some of his other works include *The Future of the American Negro* (1899) and *Sowing and Reaping* (1900).

Though nominally only the principal of a black vocational school in Tuskegee, Alabama, Booker T. Washington was the most powerful black American of the late 19th and early 20th centuries. Keenly aware of the forces prevailing at this time and disposed toward accomplishing what *could* be done rather than demanding what *should* be done, Washington developed a compromise program that enabled blacks and whites to come together in support of a new trinity: white supremacy, black subordination, and economic development. Yet while Washington was an extraordinarily effective spokesman for the interracial harmony and sectional reconciliation that underlay the economic growth of his age, he was not a theorist but a man of action. Less concerned with ideology than with power, he celebrated the conventional wisdom of his era and in return found his own prestige and influence reinforced by the ruling powers.

At the outset of his career, Washington decided

that an effective black leader would have to win the support of three groups: sympathetic southern whites, well-to-do northerners, and members of his own race. He claimed that no movement for the elevation of African-Americans could succeed without the cooperation of the best southern whites, and hence he emphasized examples of southern white benevolence and deprecated protest and agitation; he knew it was easier to win friends "by giving credit for all the praiseworthy actions performed than by calling attention to the evils done." He also assured the leaders of the post-Reconstruction South that "in all things that are purely social we can be as separate as the fingers," and he preceded the Supreme Court in calling for "equal but separate" accommodations for blacks.

While thus appeasing the white South, Washington called on northern philanthropists to adjust to the reality of Jim Crow segregation. Striving to save black education from total destruction at the hands of white supremacists, he urged northern men of wealth to shift their benefactions away from egalitarian black liberal arts colleges and toward vocational schools that promised not to raise the African-American out of his "place" but to instill the personal habits and traits of character that would make blacks more efficient workers. By concentrating on the elementary lessons of carpentry, gardening, and homemaking, northern philanthropy and black education could survive and prosper even in the heartland of white supremacy.

Washington phrased his program of conciliation and economic service in such an engaging fashion that among whites he undoubtedly became the most popular African-American of his generation. Yet this very popularity with whites inevitably aroused suspicions among blacks, especially among professional men and women who feared that vocational training within the constraints of white supremacy would relegate African-Americans to serfdom. They also believed that submission to white oppression demeaned blacks and led psychologically to loss of pride and self-respect and feelings of helplessness. Black critics, led at first by **Monroe Trotter** of the Boston *Guardian* and later by W. E. B. Du Bois of the NAACP, challenged Washington's hegemony during the first decade of the 20th century and organized a campaign for full citizenship rights. In the last years of his life Washington was increasingly on the defensive, but he always maintained a great measure of influence among those blacks who believed that the Tuskegeean's program was well suited to the harsh, white-supremacist reality of the era. Washington was admittedly not the bearer of glad tidings, but he was a practical statesman who had made a bargain with powerful whites and could deliver tangible benefits in the form of political patronage and foundation grants.

Drawing on his contacts with powerful whites, Washington established a personal political machine that employed spies, secret agents, and provocateurs against his black critics. Leaders of government and business conferred with Washington before giving appointments or promotions to blacks, with the tacit understanding that his approval would be withheld from blacks who threatened the status quo. By ostracizing those who protested against white supremacy and rewarding those who obligingly adapted to their situation, Washington taught blacks to accept what whites were willing to offer. Washington's defenders claim that he made as good a bargain as was possible in an age aptly characterized as "the nadir" for African-Americans, but critics maintain that Washington confused his own personal interest with that of his race, and used his influence to suppress blacks who advocated viewpoints that differed from his own.

An extraordinarily able orator who radiated geniality and good humor, in private Washington was somewhat aloof. Even his closest associates found it impossible to call him by his first name. A reserved man who rarely let down his guard, he never forgot that he was a spokesman for African-Americans and that any breach of decorum on his part would be blamed on his race. In his personal life Washington was the very epitome of Victorian respectability; he practiced all the Sunday school virtues that he preached. See

Louis R. Harlan, *Booker T. Washington: The Making of a Black Leader* (1972), and *Booker T. Washington: The Wizard of Tuskegee, 1901–1915* (1983).

RAYMOND WOLTERS

WASHINGTON, George (b. Bridges Creek, Westmoreland Co., Va., Feb. 22, 1732; d. Mount Vernon, Va., Dec. 14, 1799), PRESIDENT, was educated by his father and half-brother, Lawrence. He was appointed surveyor for Culpeper County, Virginia, in 1749. He eventually inherited Mount Vernon, Lawrence's estate on the Potomac, and lived there from 1752. Commissioned a major in the Virginia militia (1752), he was sent by Governor Dinwiddie (1753) to carry an ultimatum to the French demanding their withdrawal from lands in the Ohio Valley claimed by the British. When the French refused, he was sent back to drive them out, but was defeated, being forced to surrender Fort Necessity (1754). During the French and Indian War he participated in General Braddock's defeat (1755). Later appointed colonel and commander in chief of the Virginia forces, he helped capture Fort Duquesne (1758).

In 1759 Washington was elected to the Virginia House of Burgesses, where he opposed British legislation affecting the colonies. He was a delegate to the First and Second Continental Congresses (1774–75), which chose him commander in chief of the Continental army in the Revolutionary War. He forced the British to evacuate Boston but was defeated in several battles around New York City and forced to retreat to New Jersey. Crossing the Delaware on Christmas Eve, 1776, he defeated the British at Trenton (1776) and Princeton (1777). After the battles of Brandywine and Germantown (1777), he was forced to evacuate Philadelphia, and spent the winter at Valley Forge (1777–78). At the Battle of Yorktown, he defeated Cornwallis, ending the war (1781).

Like many others, Washington believed that the Articles of Confederation governing the states were too weak. He attended the Annapolis Convention (1786), called ostensibly to talk about trade relations between the states but really geared to strengthen national unity. Later he presided over the Philadelphia Constitutional Convention (1787). In 1789 he was unanimously elected the first president of the U.S.

As president, Washington supported Secretary of the Treasury **Alexander Hamilton**'s funding of the foreign and domestic debt at par, government assumption of state debts, and the creation of a national bank. When a federal excise tax on distilled liquor led to the Whiskey Rebellion in western Pennsylvania (1794), Washington called out the army to restore order—though there was no actual fighting.

Washington worked to keep America neutral during the wars of the French Revolution, issuing a Neutrality Proclamation (1793). But when Citizen Genet, the French emissary, sought to enlist American volunteers, Washington demanded his recall. Washington's prestige helped assure passage of the unpopular Anglo-American **Jay**'s Treaty (1795).

Determined not to accept a third term, Washington issued his "Farewell Address" (1796), calling for national unity and warning his countrymen of the dangers of sectional political parties and of "permanent" alliances with foreign powers. Retiring to Mount Vernon, he supported the Federalists but spent the short remainder of his life as a gentleman farmer.

Most historical reputations slide up and down on posterity's stock market: witness those of Thomas Jefferson or Andrew Jackson. None in the United States, not even that of **Benjamin Franklin,** has remained as steady and as high as that of George Washington. It is true that occasional criticism was directed at him while he was alive. During the Revolutionary War, in the period 1777–78 before the French alliance was made known, a few soldiers and a few members of the Continental Congress grumbled that his military performance was uninspiring. During his presidency there was some feeling among the followers of Jefferson and Madison that his style was too regal and that he had lent his name too readily to the support of Federalist policies. In the

decade after his death the same complaint was voiced, and coupled with hints from former associates like John Adams that their old chief had been a slightly cold and wooden personage. But these were muted criticisms, hardly audible amid the universal chorus of acclaim. His life was so full, so fruitful, and so exemplary that he has both inspired and baffled a long succession of biographers. He has become almost synonymous with the very fabric of the Republic, the father figure among the founding fathers. Efforts to debunk him or even to humanize him, once the narrative goes beyond his youthful years, bounce off his invincible righteousness. He is formidable to the point of impenetrability.

The actuality seems to have been that the inner and the outer man, his own inclinations and the needs of his time and his country, were almost perfectly matched, but that he did not sense this and so did not become messianic. He could never conceive of a greater happiness than being the master of Mount Vernon. He suffered some frustration in his early military career: he was obliged to conduct thankless operations with inadequate resources. He revealed the American passion for land speculation. But these fevers had largely burned out in him by the time he became commander in chief. He had become a respected Virginia planter and therefore in the natural course of events a public figure. He had made an excellent match in marrying the wealthy, amiable widow Martha Custis. He was tall, handsome, dignified, active. He conveyed a quality of sober, assured competence that made men ready to follow him; and perhaps they trusted him the more because he was no orator. He was personally brave, and ready to bring on a battle when he thought the conditions were right. Perhaps his main strength as a military leader, though, was sagacity rather than dash. He was an organizer, a chairman of councils of war, a coalition general somewhat on the model of that latter-day Virginian soldier **George C. Marshall.** He kept things going, for more than eight years, most of them bad years.

His presidential record was of the same order. If he was inclined to appear formal and statuesque, in a way that offended the leveling instincts of certain Republican congressmen and journalists, then this austereness was arguably necessary. Feeling his way forward in an unprecedented situation, in his own eyes he was correct to be correct. He was the first incumbent of a new office, the emblematic representative of a new nation—far less than a king and yet far more than a king. His concern was to give tone and credibility to the affairs of government. As a general and as a statesman, it is possible that he made mistakes. Recent historians have suggested that Washington failed to understand the radical aspirations of Americans of the Jeffersonian persuasion. They see him as blind to the embryonic emergence of the American party system—as a Federalist, though admittedly not an ultra-Federalist of the Hamiltonian type, still visualizing himself as an impartial patriot. There may be something in this: he did tend to react with outraged amazement when polemicists such as **Philip M. Freneau** attacked him and his administration. But other American presidents have been at least as rattled by criticism; and after all, the shape of party politics remained obscure for quite a number of years after his death. By the test of comparison—a test employed again and again by admirers throughout the world— George Washington is in fact unique among warrior-statesmen: Caesar, Cromwell, Napoleon, and so on. He was, in other words, a natural leader but not an autocrat, a vigorous man but not a bully, an uncomplicated person but very far from stupid. We have learned to distrust hero worship. Yet in Washington's case the clichés nearly all seem to be true. See James T. Flexner, *George Washington* (4 vols., 1965–72).

MARCUS CUNLIFFE

WATERHOUSE, Benjamin (b. Newport, R.I., March 4, 1754; d. Cambridge, Mass., Oct. 2, 1846), PHYSICIAN, was apprenticed to Dr. John Halliburton of Newport, Rhode Island, in 1770, then studied medicine in London and Edinburgh (1775–78) and Leyden, Holland (1778–81), before returning to Newport in 1782. In 1783 he was appointed professor of physic in the new Harvard Medical School. He also lectured on natural history at Rhode Island College, Providence (now Brown University), in 1786–87 and after that at Harvard. In 1799 John Coakley Lettsom informed him of Edward Jenner's experiments with smallpox vaccination, and in 1800 Waterhouse successfully vaccinated in America. He reported his results in *A Prospect of Exterminating the Small Pox* (Part I, 1800; Part II, 1802). Although he met much personal opposition locally, largely because of his efforts to establish a monopoly, his vigorous advocacy in the press and through correspondence with Thomas Jefferson and others helped significantly to win acceptance for vaccination. In 1805 he warned against the use of alcohol and tobacco in his widely distributed *Cautions to Young Persons Concerning Health,* and in 1811 he published a portion of his natural history lectures as *The Botanist.* Waterhouse was dismissed from Harvard in 1812 after a disagreement over the medical school's move from Cambridge to Boston and other matters. In 1813 President Madison appointed him to the army medical service. He was stationed in the Boston area until he retired in 1821. He published in outline part of his medical lectures in *A Synopsis of a Course of Lectures on the Theory and Practice of Medicine* (1786), wrote *An Essay Concerning Tussis Convulsiva, or Whooping-cough* (1822), prepared for publication *A Journal of a Young Man of Massachusetts* (1816), argued that Pitt was Junius in *An Essay on Junius and His Letters* (1831), and edited John B. Wyeth's *Oregon* (1833).

⁂

Benjamin Waterhouse was both blessed and cursed with unusual educational opportunities for an American physician of his time. After having lived in London and studied at the best medical schools, he was unfitted for the rigors of medical practice in a New England town. These experiences had instilled instead a relish for book learning and a penchant for writing. Never very successful in his practice, he apparently found it galling that others with less learning were preferred. Perhaps this is why, when his opportunity came to promote vaccination, he used it also to promote himself and attempted at first to establish a monopoly for his pecuniary advantage. Later more ethical efforts to encourage the use of vaccination won Waterhouse much support away from his home, and his published accounts of his difficulties, accepted uncritically by biographers, have given him an undeservedly high posthumous reputation. He made no original observations of consequence in science or medicine but rather is remembered for popularizing natural history at Harvard and for promoting the practice of vaccination throughout the country. He is also remembered for his contentious personality and quarrels with colleagues, but his voluminous political writings in opposition to the Federalist establishment are largely forgotten. See J. B. Blake, "Benjamin Waterhouse, Harvard's First Professor of Physic," *Journal of Medical Education*, XXIII (1958), 771–82.

JOHN B. BLAKE

WATSON, James Dewey (b. Chicago, Ill., April 6, 1928), SCIENTIST, received his BS degree from the University of Chicago in 1947. He earned his PhD in biology (genetics) from Indiana University (Bloomington) in 1950. Watson worked at the University of Copenhagen 1950–51 under a National Research Council fellowship before joining Francis H. C. Crick at the Cavendish laboratory at Cambridge University in 1951 where they evolved a structural model of the deoxyribonucleic acid molecule (DNA). The model provided the basis for understanding how this molecule carries genetic specifications. After serving as a research fellow at the National Foundation for Infantile Paralysis (1952–53) and senior research fellow in biology at the California Institute of Technology, Pasadena (1953–55), Watson became assistant professor of biology at Harvard. He again collaborated with Crick in proposing a structure of bacterial viruses in 1957, and became associate professor at Harvard in 1958, professor of biochemistry and molecular biology in 1961, and shared the Nobel Prize for medicine and physiology with Crick and Maurice H. F. Wilkins in 1962. He became director of the Cold Spring Harbor Laboratory in 1968 and a member of the National Cancer Board in 1972. Watson left the Cold Spring Laboratory in 1988 to become director of the National Center for Human Genome Research at the National Institute of Health (1989). Currently, under his direction the center is engaged in trying to map the human genetic structure. Watson has written quite extensively. Among his works are *Molecular Biology of the Gene* (1965), a college textbook, and *The Double Helix* (1968), the story of the discovery of the structure of DNA.

—◦◦◦—

The ultimate goal of most of the laboratory biologists and not a few chemists since at least the middle of the 19th century has been to show how life can be created by man from inorganic materials. In 1953 Watson shared in the most dramatic discovery furthering this ancient quest: demonstrating a molecular structure for the substance involved in the replication of living material. In 1968 he wrote a literate, best-selling account of that discovery showing the researchers involved to have been fully human and foiled as well as brilliant and dedicated. The race for priority of discovery that he described showed that in the middle of the 20th century science was the last refuge of the highly competitive personality.

Watson is a genius for whom life went well, almost according to schedule. He was prepared to be challenged, and to respond. Educated in excellent schools and admitted in the early student program of the University of Chicago, in graduate school he was by chance thrown in with pioneers of molecular biology at work at Indiana University. Supported comfortably by the postwar science establishment, he went to Europe and did his most brilliant work in the Cavendish laboratory at Cambridge. He ended up, no doubt predictably, as a professor at Harvard and pursued, among other lines of research, protein biosynthesis—a persistent problem for reductionistic scientists—and cancer research, an area of possible application of molecular biology.

But Watson took a place in American life

greater than even a Nobel Prize entitled him to. He became one of the new heroes whose creative egoism was mistaken for individualism. He was in fact a part of much collaborative and team research. At a time when cooperative work was dominant in producing results in science, especially in cross-disciplinary areas such as molecular biology, individualism was hardly appropriate—certainly as little as elsewhere in society. When Watson, then, like other romantics of the mid-century era, dramatized the colorful and eccentric, he removed some of the self-righteousness and mystery from the scientists. His irreverent portrayal of researchers' ambitions and zest became a permanent legacy modifying the popular image of the antiseptic laboratory. See James D. Watson, *The Double Helix* (1968).

J. C. BURNHAM

WATSON, John Broadus (b. Greenville, S.C., Jan. 9, 1878; d. New York, N.Y., Sept. 25, 1958), PSYCHOLOGIST, ADVERTISING EXECUTIVE, received his MA from Furman University in 1899, and studied (1900–3) under James Rowland Angell at the University of Chicago (PhD, 1903). He taught experimental psychology at Chicago (1903–8), where he did research on the behavior and neurology of rats, apes, rabbits, and terns. From 1908 to 1920 he was professor of experimental and comparative psychology at Johns Hopkins University and director of the university's psychology laboratory. Beginning in 1907, he developed his theory of behaviorism, described in 1913 in the *Psychological Review,* which he edited 1908–15. Watson's behaviorism emphasized environmental influences and claimed that behavior was the result of training. After becoming acquainted with Pavlov's work before World War I, Watson reconceptualized habit formation in terms of conditioning.

In 1914 Watson wrote *Behavior: An Introduction to Comparative Psychology,* and in 1915 he was elected president of the American Psychological Association. Watson conducted research on human infants beginning in 1917, trying to discover what, if any, instincts children bring into

this world (he found only three primitive reactions). In 1919 he wrote *Psychology from the Standpoint of a Behaviorist.* In 1920 Johns Hopkins forced him to resign because of publicity incident to a divorce suit.

Watson then moved to New York City, where he became an account executive at the J. Walter Thompson Co., a leading advertising agency. He lectured at the New School for Social Research in New York (1922–26), and published an influential child-rearing manual, *The Psychological Care of Infant and Child* (1928). In *Behaviorism* (1925) and other writings of the 1920s he popularized his ideas. He was vice president of J. Walter Thompson Co. (1924–36), and became vice president of another advertising firm, William Esty and Co., in 1936. He retired in 1945.

Watson was a colorful and charismatic leader of a "school" within psychology. Although his popularizing activities of the 1920s diminished his scientific respectability, for many years his work moved younger psychologists in two directions: toward reductionism, by means of employing biological methods for the study of human beings; and toward developing a psychology that could be used in practical ways to influence and shape men's actions. Watson held up as a model for human psychology animal psychology: all that the experimenter knows is the stimulus presented to the animal and the animal's response. Mental contents—processes between stimulus and response—are inaccessible. Moreover, mental contents are irrelevant, for if a pattern of connections can be established between environmental presentations and behavior, then it becomes possible to predict behavior. Furthermore, as in any science, the object of prediction is control. Behaviorism was, then, aimed essentially at controlling human beings. Watson was the prototype of the legendary "rat psychologist" who equates human beings with laboratory animals that are conditioned to react predictably.

The evangelical Baptist tradition within which Watson grew up affected his life deeply. He reacted strongly against the content of his training and spoke out in favor of what his mother would have thought was godlessness. Yet he used the form of religious exhortation and proselytizing for scientific argumentation and, later, flamboyant popularization. His early professional eminence as one of the fathers of modern animal psychology was based largely on his skill as an experimenter. But this poor boy from the South always actively sought the limelight, and in extolling his kind of work, he attracted not only many of his peers in a rapidly expanding profession but other intellectuals as well. Especially through his advocacy of a mechanical and detached method of child rearing did he make a significant and substantive impression on American life in general. Once in advertising, he did little to utilize his psychological training, and his growth as a thinker ended with his departure from academia. See David Bakan, "Behaviorism and American Urbanization," *Journal of the History of the Behavioral Sciences*, II (1966), 5–28.

J. C. BURNHAM

WATSON, Thomas Edward (b. near Thomson, Ga., Sept. 5, 1856; d. Chevy Chase, Md., Sept. 26, 1922), POLITICAL LEADER, attended Mercer College for two years and then studied law while teaching school. In 1876 he began to practice and became a successful criminal lawyer. Championing the small farmers against the bankers and industrialists who controlled the Democratic party, Watson served one term in the Georgia legislature in 1882. With the support of the Farmer's Alliance, he was elected to Congress in 1890, and then became a Populist. However, he was defeated in 1892 and 1894 by the Democratic candidate. The Populists nominated Watson for vice president in 1896, but since the party supported the Democratic presidential candidate, **William Jennings Bryan,** and since the Democrats named their own vice presidential candidate, Watson's position became, as he said, "most humiliating," and he received very few votes.

Watson then retired from politics. For the next eight years he devoted much of his time to writing a history of France and biographies of Napoleon and Thomas Jefferson. (Later he wrote a biography of Andrew Jackson, a novel, and his political memoirs.) In 1904 and again in 1908 Watson ran as the Populist candidate for president. He was more successful as publisher of *Watson's Magazine*, which attacked Catholics, Jews, African-Americans, and socialists and opposed America's entrance into World War I. Watson was a power in Georgia politics after 1908. He was defeated for election to Congress in 1918, but two years later, he was handily elected to the Senate on an anti–League of Nations, prolabor platform.

Tom Watson was a crusader. Whether fighting for (the farmers, the Populists, himself) or against (the banks, the blacks, the Jews), Tom Watson shook the earth in his battles. Some of those campaigns have been deemed noble, others ignoble. But in them all Tom Watson went all the way.

His first crusade and the one he continued longest was the resurrection of the war-devastated Watson family fortunes. Watson's grandfather had been a slaveowner and a planter, one of the ruling group within the antebellum South. But in the shocks that came after 1861 his father had lost both land and status. In time Watson regained it all, and more. He turned to the law so that he might return to the land. He became an enormously successful criminal lawyer and the owner of thousands of acres. Symbolically he announced the return of the Watsons by building a traditional southern-mansion home.

Tom Watson did not spend all of his tremendous energy reclaiming economic and social position. In the 1890s he became a national figure as the incarnation of the radical southern agrarian. As early as the 1880s he embraced the cause of the hard-pressed farmers backed against the wall by declining prices and overproduction. He pressed their case before the Georgia Democratic party. Elected to Congress in 1890 as a member of that party, he soon decided that Democrats were the bondservants of finance capital. Quickly he turned to the fledgling Populist party, whose platform of national ownership of railroads, income taxes, and government assistance to the farmer became his own. His leaving the white man's party, identifying the black as a comember of the exploited masses, and calling for blacks to support Populism brought forth bitter denunciations from Georgia Democrats. And fraud, violence, and bloodshed marked his futile attempts at reelection.

Watson was no "fellow traveler." Populism became his life, and he bitterly opposed fusion between his party and the Democrats in 1896. His cries that Populism would be swallowed up fell on ears attuned to the victory march they thought they heard. His prediction proved correct, and the demise of Populism carried him away from the maelstrom of politics an embittered man.

He returned in 1908 and until his death in 1922 was the arbiter of Georgia politics. Now he left Populism and returned to the Democratic fold. His zeal remained, but his passion turned to power. Moving from one ally to another, he constantly maneuvered so that Tom Watson bossed Georgia.

The crusading did not stop; it merely changed direction. His new causes became, as had the old, extensions of his flamboyant personality. In his books, magazines, and newspapers—and often in strident, vicious language—he denounced not only Wall Street and banks but Roman Catholics, Jews, foreign missions, and blacks. Then when war came, he struck out at conscription and militarism, until his publications were banned from the mails. See C. Vann Woodward, *Tom Watson: Agrarian Rebel* (1938).

WILLIAM J. COOPER, JR.

WATSON, Thomas John, Sr. (b. Campbell, N.Y., Feb. 17, 1874; d. New York, N.Y., June 19, 1956), INDUSTRIALIST, after a year in a business school experimented with several jobs before joining the National Cash Register Co. in 1895. The president, John H. Patterson, selected him in 1903 to lead a fight aimed at stamping out concerns dealing in secondhand machines. Because of the resulting activities, Watson, by then general sales manager, and several associates were convicted in 1913 of criminal violation of the

antitrust law, a verdict subsequently set aside. The same year Watson lost his job with National Cash Register.

When Charles R. Flint, a specialist in mergers and organizer of the U.S. Rubber Co., put together the Computing-Tabulating-Recording Co., Watson joined the new firm. He became president in 1914, and after 1924, as chief executive officer, he concentrated on the company's tabulating equipment, which he believed had a broader application than had been realized. A direct-printing tabulator and key-operated electric card-punching machine were readied for market by 1919. Growth of the company, renamed International Business Machines in 1925, was steady but unspectacular during the 1920s and early 1930s. But Watson pushed the development of an alphabet-printing tabulator, and beginning in 1935, with the advent of the Social Security Administration and its enormous data-processing needs, the demand for IBM equipment increased at an accelerating rate. IBM was also an early developer of equipment and application techniques in electronic data processing.

Watson's enthusiasm for whatever work he was engaged in permeated his entire company. In the slogan, "Think," of which he had already made use at National Cash Register, he preached the need for continual self-improvement, and in his personal deportment he set a strict standard for employees. His mien was closely copied by lesser executives, and his rule against alcohol during the business day or in the company's employee resorts was strictly observed.

After World War II, Watson's interests were concentrated on building up IBM's world trade. He formed a subsidiary through which the company's foreign business was channeled. When the antitrust division attacked the company's rigid policy of leasing, rather than selling, its machines, Watson opposed any compromise, but in 1956 he was persuaded to yield, and the suit was settled.

Until a few weeks before his death Watson continued as the chief executive officer of IBM. By that time his policy of limiting cash dividends and reinvesting most of the profits had made IBM an outstanding "growth" company. Since 1940 the largest office equipment concern in the United States, at Watson's death the company employed 60,000 persons.

⸺⸺⸺

Few leaders of the capital goods industries realized more profoundly than Thomas J. Watson, Sr., that success requires both the development of equipment well engineered for a broad range of applications and the creative sales ability to show a potential customer where an application exists for the equipment in his business. Awareness that the most sophisticated tool is useless unless put to work intelligently came to him early as a star salesman for National Cash Register Co. "Don't talk your machines; talk your prospect's business," he told the men whose job it was to sell John H. Patterson's expensive machines in the sedate days before World War I. It was in the meeting of the engineering genius of a succession of men and the virtuoso salesmanship of Watson that the idea behind IBM was born. When he took over the C-T-R company in 1914 his problem had been too much engineering and almost no salesmanship. The crude tabulating equipment had made great savings in the processing of census data since 1890, but then its inventor, Herman Hollerith, had formed a parental attachment to it which precluded any outside ideas. Watson changed all that. Whether from some sixth sense—certainly not from any great technical knowledge of the data-processing problems of the business world—or through sheer luck, Watson determined that it was in the application of improved tabulating equipment to accounting jobs that he would build the company. Beginning with two engineers and a draftsman in the dingy loft building, IBM never stopped its intensive program of self-improvement. By no means the only supplier of similar equipment, then or later, IBM became almost a generic term for automatic data processing. The gratitude of a growing number of controllers and financial vice presidents who had been shown ways to save money by Watson's salesmen stood behind the company's preeminent image as the years wore on.

Watson's role in IBM was not unlike that of the powerful, ruthless individuals who created the earlier basic industries whose development, in fact, made IBM necessary. The final decade of his leadership was the most hectic, as the giants of the electronics and office equipment world jockeyed for position in the new computer field. On a grander scale than ever, Watson hewed to his policy of selling not hardware but its application, and at his death it was clear that his company would be a winner in the race. Only in his last year, when he steadfastly opposed a rapidly changing public policy in regard to the length of time a company is to be permitted to monopolize its inventions, did Watson appear to have fallen behind the trend.

A hard-driving, demanding leader who had a curious impatience with facts that ran contrary to his desires, Watson infuriated and frustrated many a subordinate, but from those who learned to work his way he exacted fierce loyalty and exceptional accomplishment. The paternalism which he so blatantly imposed on IBM's employees, and especially on the executives who often made ludicrous efforts to follow his example, seemed strangely out of place to many people, but not to Watson. To him one's job and one's life were the same thing. He never thought much about where the one left off and the other began, nor did the men who rose under him to positions of wealth and power in the newest industry of the mid-20th century. Watson's brand of revivalist enthusiasm probably serves a purpose during a critical stage in the history of all kinds of human endeavors. No longer a primary factor at IBM, it is likely to appear in important undertakings in the future. See Thomas G. Belden, *The Lengthening Shadow: The Life of Thomas J. Watson* (1962).

ALBRO MARTIN

WAYNE, Anthony (b. Chester Co., Pa., Jan. 1, 1745; d. Presque Isle [now Erie], Pa., Dec. 15, 1796), MILITARY LEADER, attended an academy in Philadelphia (1761–63), where he learned enough mathematics to work as a surveyor and to serve a Philadelphia land company in 1765 in a survey of 200,000 acres in Nova Scotia. He returned to Pennsylvania the following year.

In 1774–75 Wayne represented Chester County in the Pennsylvania assembly, where he opposed British policies affecting the colonies. He became chairman of the Chester County Committee of Safety and helped prepare the local militia for conflict with the British. In 1776 he was appointed colonel of the 4th Pennsylvania Battalion and sent to Canada to reinforce General **Benedict Arnold**'s troops. After participating in the defeat at Trois Rivières he commanded Fort Ticonderoga. He was promoted to brigadier general in February 1777, and in April he joined General Washington at Morristown, New Jersey. In September he participated in the action at Brandywine as commander of the Pennsylvania Line. He was surprised and his men were badly beaten at the Battle of Paoli (Sept. 21), for which he was charged with negligence, but he immediately demanded a court-martial and was cleared. After leading one of the attacking columns in the Battle of Germantown (Oct. 4), he spent the winter of 1777–78 with Washington's army at Valley Forge. In June 1778 he led an advance attack against the British at the Battle of Monmouth and held the American center in the subsequent defense. In June 1779 Washington ordered him to take command of a brigade of light infantry. On July 16 Wayne captured the British garrison at Stony Point, the northernmost British position on the Hudson. After the dissolution of the picked light infantry command, he returned to the Pennsylvania Line. When Benedict Arnold's plot to surrender West Point was uncovered, Wayne quickly moved his troops to safeguard the fort (Sept. 1780). Accumulated discontents for which he was not responsible led to the mutiny of his Pennsylvania Line, January 1–10, 1781, but he conducted himself well in helping to quiet the mutiny. In 1781 he served in Virginia under Lafayette. After the British surrendered at Yorktown (Oct. 1781), Wayne helped General **Nathanael Greene** subdue the British, Loyalists, and Native Americans in Georgia. In 1782 he

negotiated treaties with the Cherokees and Creeks. He left the army as a brevet major general in 1783.

In 1783 Wayne was elected to the Pennsylvania Council of Censors, and in 1784–85 he again represented Chester County in the Pennsylvania assembly. In 1785 he went to Georgia to work a rice plantation that the state had given him. He subsequently lost the plantation to creditors. He ardently supported the new Constitution at the Pennsylvania ratifying convention (1787). In 1791 he was elected to the U.S. Congress as a delegate from Georgia. The following year, however, his seat was declared vacant because of election and residence irregularities.

In 1792 President Washington commissioned Wayne major general and commander of the U.S. army to subdue the Native American uprisings in the Northwest Territory. On August 20, 1794, at the Battle of Fallen Timbers (near present Toledo, Ohio), he decisively defeated the Native Americans. They formally surrendered at Greenville, Ohio (Aug. 1795), agreeing to abandon their claims to much of the land in the Northwest Territory.

For his accomplishments in the final three years of his life, Anthony Wayne might well be considered the father of the American regular army. Despite the impetuousness implied by his sobriquet, "Mad Anthony," these accomplishments like the other most conspicuous achievements of his career showed him capable of patience, thorough preparations, and taking infinite pains. Earlier, in the Revolution, he redeemed his defeat at Paoli with his victory at Stony Point; the most outstanding characteristic of his attack there was not the boldness of the bayonet charge with weapons unloaded (to avoid forewarning the British), but the care of Wayne's preparations in reconnaissance, secrecy, planning, and the instruction of his troops. In the adversity of the mutiny of the Pennsylvania Line, Wayne also showed patience and calm good judgment belying his nickname. When President Washington appointed him to command the U.S.

army in March 1792, the army was a demoralized wreck, broken by losses in two successive Indian campaigns in 1790 and 1791, and with no important success to its credit since the dissolution of the Continental army of the Revolution. Wayne took advantage of new negotiations with the Native Americans of the Northwest to spend the better part of the next two years diligently training and drilling the remnants of the defeated forces and the recruits sent to him. He combined stern discipline and quick punishment of infractions of his rules with stimulants to morale such as distinctive colored markings for the four sublegions of his "Legion of the United States." He made his army impressive on the parade ground, the better to overawe the Native Americans; proficient in the rapid construction of field fortifications, to protect itself against surprise attack; and steady on the battlefield, as he proved in another bayonet charge after he took the field in the summer of 1794. The army he created and with which he won the Battle of Fallen Timbers was a skillful professional army of a standard that few units of Washington's Continentals had ever attained. He gave the new army of the constitutional republic its first traditions of proficiency and victory. See Charles J. Stillé, *Anthony Wayne and the Pennsylvania Line* (1893).

RUSSELL F. WEIGLEY

WAYNE, John (originally Marion Michael Morrison) (b. Winterset, Iowa, May 26, 1907; d. Los Angeles, Calif., June 11, 1979), MOVIE ACTOR, moved to Lancaster, Calif., at the age of nine where his family took up farming, and then to Glendale, Calif., where his father worked as a druggist. In the sixth grade he acquired the nickname "Duke," after his pet Airedale, and it stuck for the rest of his life. He starred on the Glendale High School football team, graduating in 1925, and received an athletic scholarship to the University of Southern California. He attended USC from 1925 to 1927, dropping out before graduating when he lost his scholarship after being injured. While a student he worked in movies as an on-camera extra, usually as a football player, and upon leaving USC took a job at the William Fox Studios as an assistant prop man. He became friendly with **John Ford**, the director, who gave him bit parts. He worked as a stunt man and played a small role as a sailor in the Ford-directed *Men Without Women* (1930).

He did two more movies as a bit player when he was given a screen test by director Raoul Walsh, who liked his rugged good looks and his rich baritone voice. This led to a starring role as a frontier scout for *The Big Trail* (1930). Walsh and the studio substituted "Wayne" for Morrison, when a book on Revolutionary War hero "Mad" **Anthony Wayne** caught their eye. Wayne did not like Anthony and suggested "John" instead and John Wayne was born. *The Big Trail* flopped but Wayne caught on and for the next nine years appeared in over twenty grade "B" films, mostly westerns and serials.

Wayne's career took off when John Ford cast him in *Stagecoach* (1939) as Ringo Kid, an outlaw seeking to avenge the murder of his father. The movie won three Oscars, elevated westerns to a higher level, and made Wayne a star. During World War II, he starred in action movies, comedies, and also began to produce movies himself. His acting scope developed in the postwar decades as he was cast in more mature, but still dashing and tough, starring roles. In *Red River* (1948), he played a heartless cattle baron, and in *Fort Apache* (1948), *She Wore a Yellow Ribbon* (1949) and *Rio Grande* (1950), he portrayed cavalry officers. In *The Sands of Iwo Jima* (1949), he was a Marine combat sergeant, and in *The Quiet Man* (1952), he was a retired American prizefighter. Other noteworthy parts were a pilot who survived a plane crash in *The High and the Mighty* (1954), a post–Civil War loner in *The Searchers* (1956), navy flyer Frank "Spig" Wead in *The Wings of Eagles* (1957) and a valiant sheriff defending his town singlehandedly in *Rio Bravo* (1959).

In 1960, Wayne invested $1.3 million to make *The Alamo*, in which he starred as **Davy Crockett**. The movie was particularly significant to him for its patriotic content and he was crushed when it failed. But his depression was short-lived and he appeared in a host of successful films, including

The Man Who Shot Liberty Valance (1962), *Hatari* (1962), *The Longest Day* (1962), and *How the West Was Won* (1963).

In 1964, Wayne, a chainsmoker, contracted lung cancer. His left lung was removed, but he recovered and returned to acting as a hired gunfighter in *El Dorado* (1967). In 1968, he played a Green Beret colonel in *The Green Berets*, which aroused a storm of protest from the antiwar movement but was a box-office success. This film was in keeping with his politics, which from the 1940s on had been fervently anticommunist and conservative. He was a founding member of the Motion Picture Alliance for the Preservation of American Ideals, established to counter perceived left-wing influence in Hollywood. He became president of the organization in 1949 and served until 1952. The MPA was accused of naming suspected communists to the House Committee on Un-American Activities, a charge he denied. In later years he supported the presidential candidacies of Republicans **Barry Goldwater**, Richard Nixon, and Ronald Reagan.

In 1970 Wayne won an Oscar for his portrayal of Rooster Cogburn, a disreputable, hard-drinking, one-eyed U.S. Marshal, in *True Grit* (1969). That same year, he starred in his first television special, *Swing Out, Sweet Land,* a patriotic musical comedy salute to the United States. Despite failing health, he continued to make films, among them *Chisum* (1970), *Rio Lobo* (1970), *The Cowboys* (1972), *The Train Robbers* (1973), *Brannigan* (1975), *Rooster Cogburn* (1975) a sequel to *True Grit*, and *The Shootist* (1976), in which he played a gunfighter dying of cancer. It was his last film.

John Wayne was the quintessential Hollywood movie star, making his first (uncredited) walk-on in a silent motion picture and his last in *The Shootist*, nearly fifty years later. From 1950 through 1965 movie theater owners annually voted Wayne the number one male box office attraction.

It took Wayne more than a decade to learn his craft. Through the late 1920s and 1930s he worked in many of Hollywood's worst films, for-gettable "B" westerns. We can now understand that these efforts, in such quickies as *Range Feud* (1931) and *Riders of Destiny* (1933), served him well, as a vital acting apprenticeship.

Wayne made his best films when under the careful eye of a great director. For example, under John Ford, Wayne essayed a remarkable number of performances, from the aging military leader in *She Wore a Yellow Ribbon* (1949) to the psychotic outsider in *The Searchers* (1956) to a self-reflexive examination of his own heroic image in *The Man Who Shot Liberty Valance* (1962).

But to millions John Wayne came to represent more than a popular movie star. In the **McCarthy** days after World War II Wayne led the ultraconservative Motion Picture Alliance for the Preservation of American Ideals. In time, Wayne's controversial right-wing politics, particularly during the Vietnam era, overshadowed any objective analysis of his movemaking contributions.

His private life was also a mess. Tabloids of the day chronicled failed marriages and a lifelong smoking addiction that ultimately led to fatal lung cancer.

All this makes "John Wayne" hard to evaluate. Noted movie critic Andrew Sarris correctly warned that with studies of Wayne we too often simply get "cant that has traditionally inundated the subject when treated by the politically and artistically censorious. [We should stand] off at enough of a disinterested distance to compute the pluses and minuses clearly and coherently." This analysis will take time. We are still trying to assess the contribution of John Wayne to some of the finest Hollywood movies ever made. See Emanuel Levy, *John Wayne: Prophet of the American Way of Life* (1988).

DOUGLAS GOMERY

WEAVER, James Baird (b. Dayton, Ohio, June 12, 1833; d. Des Moines, Iowa, Feb. 6, 1912), POLITICAL LEADER, SOLDIER, was reared on farms in Michigan and Iowa. He carried the rural mail, kept store, and prospected for gold in California before taking up the study of law. After a year at the Cincinnati Law School, he began to practice in Bloomfield, Iowa, in 1856. Originally a Democrat, he joined the newly formed Republican party. In 1861 he volunteered as first lieutenant of the 2d Iowa Infantry. He fought at the battles of Fort Donelson, Shiloh, and Corinth in 1862 and was cited for bravery and initiative under fire. He was eventually promoted to colonel and, in 1865, brigadier general. After the Civil War, Weaver became active in Iowa Republican politics; but by 1874 he had so alienated the party regulars by his prohibitionism, his outspoken opposition to the taking of bribes from the railroads, and his leanings toward inflationary monetary policy that they denied him nomination to Congress. The following year he also lost out in his bid for the gubernatorial nomination. In 1878 he left the GOP and was elected to Congress on the Greenback ticket; two years later, running as that party's presidential candidate, he received 350,000 votes. He was again elected to Congress in 1884 and served until 1889.

As agricultural discontent swept the Plains states in the late eighties, Weaver became active in the Farmers' Alliance movement, and in 1892 he accepted the Populist party's nomination for the presidency. He received twenty-two electoral votes. In 1896 Weaver was influential in getting the Populists to fuse with the Democrats. He returned to his law practice and in 1897 was elected mayor of Colfax, Iowa.

⁂

Weaver was an able, respected, and courageous man who occupied a prominent place in the political reform movement of the late 19th century. His service with the Union forces during the Civil War, his Anglo-Saxon ancestry, and midwestern orientation, his integrity and sense of purpose, figured in winning for him the nomination and election to Congress as a Greenbacker. By helping organize the Populist party in 1892, Weaver once more found himself in the vanguard of a new political alignment that had for its objective the wresting of the control of government from the special interests and returning it to the people. He also has the dubious distinction of winning the presidential nomination of two different minor parties on two different occasions on platforms that gave prominence to the money question.

His defeat for the presidency in 1892, although hardly unexpected, did result in his winning the largest number of popular and electoral votes by a third-party candidate since the Civil War. This achievement served as an inspiration to the independents in the congressional elections of 1894 and again in the presidential campaign of 1896. His advocacy of fusion with the Democrats in 1896 and the defeat of **William Jennings Bryan** that year left him without a party and brought an end to his national political career. This often has been the price that independents have paid for their actions. Nevertheless, Weaver was one of the leading insurgents of his day. See F. E. Haynes, *James Baird Weaver* (1919).

THEODORE SALOUTOS

WEAVER, Robert Clifton (b. Washington, D.C., Dec. 29, 1907), POLITICAL LEADER, graduated from Harvard cum laude in 1929 (MA, 1931). After briefly teaching economics (1931–32) in North Carolina, Weaver returned to Harvard and earned a PhD in economics (1934). In 1933 he went to Washington to work for the New Deal. He spent four years (1933–37) as an adviser on minority-group problems to Secretary of the Interior **Harold L. Ickes** before becoming special assistant to U.S. Housing Authority administrator Nathan Strauss (1938–40). In 1940 Weaver was administrative assistant to **Sidney Hillman** of the National Defense Advisory Commission. During World War II he headed the Negro employment branch of the Office of Production Management (1942), the War Production Board (1942–43), and the Negro Manpower Service of the War Manpower Commission (1943–44). He left the federal government in 1944 to become executive director of the Mayor's Committee on Race Relations in Chicago.

Weaver served as a member of the United Nations Relief and Rehabilitation Administration's mission in the Ukraine, U.S.S.R., in 1946, and as an officer of the

American Council on Race Relations in 1947. He was a visiting professor at Northwestern University (1947), Columbia University (1949), New York University (1948–51), and the New School for Social Research (1949). During 1949–55 he directed the fellowship program of the John Hay Whitney Foundation, resigning to become New York State rent commissioner.

In 1961 President Kennedy appointed Weaver, who then was vice-chairman of the New York City Housing and Redevelopment Board, to head the Federal Housing and Home Finance Agency. Five years later he became the first African-American to hold a cabinet position when President Johnson appointed him secretary of the newly created Department of Housing and Urban Development.

After leaving the cabinet at the end of the Johnson administration, Weaver served as president of Bernard M. Baruch College in New York (1969–70), as distinguished professor of urban affairs at Hunter College (1970–78), as president of the National Commission Against Discrimination in Housing (1973–87), as a member of the Rent Stabilization board in New York City (1974–87), and as a member of the Municipal Assistance Corporation of New York City (1975). Weaver also wrote many articles and books, including *The Negro Ghetto* (1948) and *The Urban Complex* (1964).

Weaver represents the ascendancy of a new type of black political appointee. Whereas several black politicians had been given important patronage appointments prior to the New Deal, President Franklin D. Roosevelt pioneered the practice of appointing expert black *professionals* to combat racial discrimination. As one of FDR's first black appointees, Weaver worked both officially and unofficially to ensure fair treatment for blacks: he pioneered the development of minimum percentage clauses—requiring that public housing contractors pay African-Americans a percentage of the total payroll that was adjusted according to the proportion of black workers in the area—and he used his influence to alert government officials

to the special problems of blacks. Occasionally Weaver employed "direct action" in behalf of black rights, as when he personally conducted a 1934 sit-in that forced the integration of the cafeteria in the Department of the Interior. But essentially Weaver is a black professional, a Harvard-trained economist who has published important scholarly works in the field of urban affairs and has also spent five decades working for government manpower and housing agancies.

Weaver's personal style is that of the successful black middle class that has protested not against the larger culture but against the exclusion of African-Americans from it: he is a shy and fundamentally reticent man who enjoys the theater, savors his stereophonic collection of Liszt and Chopin piano concertos, sips twelve-year-old bourbon when working at home, and dresses in conservative dark suits. When Weaver became director of the Housing and Home Finance Agency he moved into an urban-renewed Washington apartment, but he left within a year for fashionable upper Connecticut Avenue.

Two civil rights organizations, CORE and SNCC, opposed Weaver's 1966 nomination for the cabinet, claiming that he was "too conservative." Given Weaver's long commitment to the struggle for African-American rights, however, it may be that the real objection was to Weaver's acculturated style—his refusal to court popularity by adopting the manners and rhetoric of lower-class, inner-city blacks who are estranged from the larger society and tend toward advocacy of black separatism. Fortunately for Weaver, his rise through the government bureaucracy never depended on political considerations but on the mastery of the complicated problems of urban housing and the respect of professional specialists in that field. See *Time*, March 4, 1966, pp. 29–33; *Ebony*, April 1966, pp. 82–92.

RAYMOND WOLTERS

WEBSTER, Daniel (b. Salisbury, N.H., Jan. 18, 1782; d. Marshfield, Mass., Oct. 24, 1852), POLITICAL LEADER, graduated from Dartmouth (1801), read law in Salisbury and Boston, and was admitted to the bar in 1805. A Federalist, he opposed the Embargo Act (1807) banning foreign commerce in his *Considerations on the Embargo Laws* (1808). His opposition to the War of 1812 helped elect him to the U.S. Congress from Portsmouth, New Hampshire (serving 1813–17). In the House he refused to vote for taxes to support the war, and he opposed conscription, the terms of the charter reestablishing the Bank of the U.S., and the protective Tariff of 1816.

Webster moved to Boston in 1816 and established himself as one of the nation's leading constitutional lawyers. He represented Dartmouth College (*Dartmouth College* v. *Woodward,* 1819), when the New Hampshire legislature tried to transform the college into a public institution in violation of its charter. In *McCulloch* v. *Maryland* (1819) he defended the constitutionality of the U.S. Bank, and argued that a state could not tax a federal instrumentality. In *Gibbons* v. *Ogden* (1824) he opposed the monopoly of interstate navigation that had been granted to Ogden by the state of New York.

Webster was elected to Congress from Massachusetts in 1822 (serving to 1827), becoming chairman of the judiciary committee. He voted against the protective Tariff of 1824, and for John Quincy Adams when the presidential election of 1824 was thrown into the House of Representatives. By the time he was elected to the U.S. Senate in 1827, manufacturing had supplanted shipping in the economy of New England. He supported the Tariff of 1828 because it protected the growing textile industry. In January 1830, when Senator Robert Y. Hayne of South Carolina, a spokesman for Vice President **John C. Calhoun,** suggested that the South and the West enter into an alliance whereby the West would support a low tariff in return for southern votes to make land in the West readily available at low prices, Webster accused Hayne of attempting to exacerbate sectional tensions. Following Hayne's rebuttal, Webster delivered his famous second reply to Hayne, arguing that the Constitution was the expression of the American people, not an agreement between the states, and that Hayne's states' rights theories could lead only to civil war.

When, after the South Carolina legislature had nullified the Tariff of 1832, **Henry Clay** sought to allay sectional tensions by proposing a compromise tariff which reduced rates (1833), Webster denounced the compromise.

In 1836 Webster was one of three Whig candidates for president, but he was defeated, receiving but fourteen electoral votes. The election was won by the Democratic candidate Martin Van Buren. During the Van Buren administration Webster took a partisan Whig position on most measures, opposing, for example, the president's subtreasury proposal. During 1841–43 he was secretary of state under William Henry Harrison and John Tyler. When Tyler vetoed a bill creating a new national bank, the entire cabinet, with the exception of Webster, resigned. Webster remained to negotiate the Webster-Ashburton Treaty (1842), which settled the northeastern boundary dispute with British Canada.

During 1845–50 Webster once again served in the Senate. He opposed the acquisition of Texas (1845) and condemned the Mexican War, but, like many Whigs, he voted for war supplies. He favored banning slavery from the territory acquired from Mexico after the war, but despite his opposition to some of the provisions of the Compromise of 1850, he supported it in his famous "Seventh of March" speech "not as a Massachusetts man, nor as a northern man, but as an American." From July 1850 until his death he served as President Fillmore's secretary of state.

⸺⸎⸺

Daniel Webster was known in his own day as the great defender of the Constitution, and his preeminence as a constitutional lawyer was hardly challenged during the more than thirty years that spanned the period between the Dartmouth College case and his death. The single-minded nationalism he sustained in the Senate and in every act and thought of his public life, against the challenge of Calhoun and the state sovereignty school, was translated into legal terms and had become by Webster's death an enduring gloss upon the Constitution. No man except **John Marshall** himself did more to provide the legal framework within which the economic development of modern America took place.

Webster's conservatism was solidly based on almost reverent respect for property. He believed, with the New England Federalists who were his mentors, that government should not only protect property but should encourage its accumulation. His courtroom skills brought him clients from the business community, and from each case he learned more of the workings of the system. By the 1820s he had become the leading spokesman for business, both in the courts and in the Congress. During the War of 1812 he took a states' rights position because like Jefferson before him he recognized in the states the only effective check upon the federal government. His merchant constituents lost heavily by the interruption of commerce, and he saw no better way to end the war and reopen the seas to shipping. When New England reinvested her idle capital in manufacturing, Webster changed sides. Only the national government could impose and enforce the protective tariffs on which the prosperity of this newborn industry rested, and so, with the Tariff of 1828, Webster became a protectionist.

There was more to it, of course, than this. Webster had come to see through reasoning as Jackson saw by instinct that sovereignty was indivisible. If the nation was to endure, or even to exist under the name, it could have only one source of power. It was this conviction that sparked his debate with Hayne, and the later senatorial battles with Calhoun. The increasingly significant role of the national government was implicit in his arguments dealing with such matters as interstate commerce, banking, and bankruptcy; and in his use of the State Department to promote not only international amity but international trade.

The most critical appraisals of Webster have been in connection with his personal financial activities and in relation to the dominant issue of his time—slavery. There is no doubt that Webster shared the American dream of material success. He admired the rich and strove continuously with indifferent success to achieve wealth for himself. He speculated in western lands, bought and sold shares in business enterprises, and solicited prosperous clients. Many of his activities seem, to a later generation, to involve conflict of interest, but he cannot be singled out in this regard for special censure. His ethical standards were those of his time, shared by his contemporaries. Even his acceptance of money donated by his constituents to keep him in the Senate seemed to him perfectly legitimate. It was no more than an additional source of income, to compensate in part for the concomitant loss of legal fees. Those who raised the money took their chances on getting some return. It was less a bribe than a retainer. There was never any doubt that he would serve the interests of his constituents to the best of his judgment, with or without monetary inducement.

His attitude toward slavery was always compounded of a personal dislike for the institution and a deep respect for the law. He is on record against slavery as early as 1804. He opposed the Missouri Compromise and later the extension of slavery to territories acquired as a result of the war with Mexico. But he opposed equally the activities of the abolitionists, who became thereby implacable political foes. In his famous Seventh of March speech, supporting the Compromise of 1850, he upheld the fugitive slave law in spite of New England's strong feelings against it. The Constitution recognized slaves as property, and sectional peace required that southern property no less than northern be secured. To his abolitionist constituents he had sold out to the "slave power," presumably in return for votes; but to the extent that his efforts passed the Compromise, he secured a ten-year deferment of the Civil War—enough to ensure victory for the free states.

Although he never achieved the presidency, Daniel Webster left a more enduring mark upon American institutions than any man who did hold that office in his time. Of almost equal permanence was his hold on the American imagination. He was a striking figure in his prime—powerfully built, a little under six feet tall, with barrel chest and massive shoulders topped by a great leonine head. His complexion was dark, his over-abundant hair coal black, and his large deep-set eyes, though they could flash with fire on occasion, added to the impression that earned him the nickname "Black Dan." When he rose to speak, the largest audience was instantly hushed, so magnificent was his presence and so towering his reputation. His rhythmic sentences flowed like music as they led up to crashing chords that made the blood boil or tingle at the speaker's will; and when one shook off the spell and read the words in cold print, the reasoning remained as tight and clear and compelling as a lawyer's brief. Such transcendent performances as the Dartmouth College case, the first Bunker Hill oration, and the second reply to Hayne made him a contemporary legend and a folk hero for generations to come. It was his tragedy to enter upon the public stage at a time of great emotional and moral crisis, when no man—not even Daniel Webster—could move impartially between the contending forces without being crushed. He was above all a supremely rational man who believed in every fiber of his being that differences were not resolved by violence but by reason and good will. See Irving H. Bartlett, *Daniel Webster* (1978).

CHARLES M. WILTSE

WEBSTER, Noah (b. West Hartford, Conn., Oct. 16, 1758; d. New Haven, Conn., May 28, 1843), LEXICOGRAPHER, graduated from Yale in 1778. During 1778–81 he taught school while studying law. He was admitted to the bar in 1781. A staunch patriot and nationalist, Webster was disturbed that his countrymen were still relying on British schoolbooks. In 1782, while teaching at Goshen, New York, he prepared an elementary school speller, *A Grammatical Institute of the English Language* (1783), the preface of which urged Americans to be cognizant of their own achievements. This work, Webster's grammar (1784), and his reader (1785) championed all things American. The wide use of these works— many millions were sold—did much to standardize American spelling and pronunciation.

In 1785 Webster published *Sketches of American Policy*, a pamphlet in which he advocated a strong central government, and in 1787 he enthusiastically supported the new Constitution. After briefly editing the *American Magazine* in New York (1787–88), he returned to Hartford, Connecticut, where he practiced law. A Federalist in politics, in 1793 he returned to New York to edit the *Minerva*, a daily, and the *Herald*, a semi-weekly (in 1797 these papers were renamed the *Commercial Advertiser* and *Spectator* respectively).

Beginning in 1803, Webster devoted most of his time to lexicography, and in 1806 he published *A Compendius Dictionary of the English Language*. He moved to Amherst, Massachusetts, in 1812, and in 1821 he helped found Amherst College. After twenty years' work on his *An American Dictionary of the English Language*, it was published in two volumes in 1828.

Noah Webster touched life at almost every point and did much to shape the thinking of Americans in the first years of the young republic. Like so many of his generation, Webster was a man of enormous energy, wideranging interests, and encyclopedic knowledge, but he did not endear himself to everyone. He was a short, vain, intense, and contentious man whose high-pitched voice annoyed critics. Nevertheless, he was effective in politics and in scholarship. It was he who first promoted state and then federal copyright laws. He wrote a standard history of epidemic diseases, and innumerable effective political essays. He was an amateur statistician, climatologist, and historian, as well as a professional teacher, lawyer, politician, and journalist. But above all, he was a nationalist and a lexicographer.

Webster was a Washington Federalist, but, like his contemporary Thomas Jefferson, he saw the connection between popular education and popular sovereignty. He believed the popular will should rule in church and state, and that the popular will be guided by right principles founded on knowledge. He envisioned the citizenry of the new republic equipped with a uniform language and a unique national culture, fostered by a national system of education. Webster, like

Benjamin Franklin, was an advocate of language reform and attempted to promote a phonetic alphabet. But ironically his spelling books and dictionaries succeeded so well in strengthening the grasp of orthographical orthodoxy that they doomed to failure his efforts at language reform and those of all his successors.

Webster's American dictionary was a scholarly achievement of the first rank, winning critical acclaim at home and abroad despite some obvious defects. He established the practice of freely recording nonliterary words—although not all spoken language, as the 20th-century editions of his dictionaries have attempted to do.

Although Noah Webster is remembered only for his dictionary, his contributions to the establishment of a national literary culture and a national system of education place him among the first rank of the fathers of the country. See Harry Warfel, *Noah Webster: School Master to America* (1936).

DAVID D. VAN TASSEL

WEED, Thurlow (b. Greene Co., N.Y., Nov. 15, 1797; d. New York, N.Y., Nov. 22, 1882), JOURNALIST, POLITICAL LEADER, was apprenticed to a printer (1808), and later worked at a succession of printing jobs in central New York. In 1813 he briefly served in the army as a private in a New York contingent stationed on the Canadian frontier. In 1817 he became foreman of the Albany *Register,* writing editorials supporting Governor **DeWitt Clinton**'s plans to construct a canal.

After some unsuccessful attempts to establish newspapers in Norwich and Manlius, Weed moved to Rochester, New York (1822), where he became associated with the *Telegraph*. In 1824 he supported John Quincy Adams for the presidency. The *Telegraph* sent him to Albany to unite the supporters of Adams and **Henry Clay** to oppose the election of William H. Crawford, the presidential candidate of Martin Van Buren, the leader of the Albany Regency, a powerful statewide political machine. His success in this endeavor marked Weed as an astute lobbyist and political manager.

In 1825 Weed was elected to the state legislature as an Anti-Mason. In that same year he purchased the Albany *Telegraph,* which he soon gave up to publish the *Anti-Mason Enquirer*. He then published the Albany *Evening Journal* (1830–63). In 1832 Weed supported William Wirt, the Anti-Masonic presidential candidate.

During the 1830s Weed helped bring many former Anti-Masons into the newly created Whig party. His managerial abilities and his skillful use of patronage enabled him to become one of the nation's most powerful politicians. In 1838 he helped elect **William H. Seward** governor of New York; in 1840 he supported William Henry Harrison's successful presidential campaign; and in 1848 he helped Zachary Taylor win first the Whig nomination over Henry Clay and then the presidency. The following year Weed was instrumental in Seward's election to the U.S. Senate; and after Seward's reelection in 1855 as a Republican, Weed also joined the Republican party.

In 1860 Weed backed Seward for the Republican presidential nomination. After Lincoln's nomination and election, Seward became secretary of state, and following the *Trent Affair* (1861), in which the U.S.S. *San Jacinto* intercepted a British steamer with two Confederate emissaries aboard, Seward sent Weed to London to allay tensions. In 1863 Weed settled in New York City, and in 1867 became editor of the *Commercial Advertiser*. His *Autobiography* was published posthumously (1883).

⸺⸺

Genial, gregarious, always ready to offer a cigar or light up himself, Thurlow Weed of New York was virtually a stereotype of the 19th-century professional politician. It is a stereotype that has begun to fade only in the age of television and the multimedia. Dark, tall, his gangling legs stretched out as he sat in the capitol lobby in Albany, Weed might have been a traveling salesman. Indeed, his foes called him the "Jolly Drummer." But they underestimated him: beneath his easy manner he had a mind and will of steel.

He was a newspaper editor for decades, and

his Albany *Evening Journal* was a bellwether of anti-Jacksonian politics in the Empire State. His most significant role, however, was that of a resourceful, ruthless party manager. Like his longtime rival in New York, Martin Van Buren, he was a master political craftsman. He had convictions, but his basic political pragmatism rose above them. He feared universal suffrage as demoralizing, but in an era of massive voting participation he wooed the voters. He was deep in the Anti-Masonic party, but when it reached a dead end after 1832 he turned to the new Whig force. He believed in **Nicholas Biddle**'s Bank of the United States, but when it was apparent that the issue lost votes he cut the Bank adrift. Looking to the presidential election of 1840, he bluntly informed the brilliant, ever hopeful Henry Clay that he lacked "availability"—Weed wanted the Whigs to *win,* for a change. Indeed, Weed's first, great, representative triumph came in the "Log Cabin," "Tippecanoe and Tyler Too" campaign of 1840, with its strident, plain folks, democratic rhetoric, although William Henry Harrison was not Weed's first choice for the nomination. He helped to establish an informal prototype of a national campaign committee in Washington, raised money, set up **Horace Greeley** as editor of the *Log Cabin,* a campaign paper, and looked after the nuts and bolts of Whig organization in the crucial states. He won again in 1848 with another handpicked military hero, Zachary Taylor.

For years, Weed labored to hold the excessively diverse elements of the Whig coalition together, and he became a Republican only when it was clear that the Whigs were doomed. Meanwhile he had tied his career in New York to the imposing William H. Seward and helped to make him governor, senator, and (missing the presidency) secretary of state.

The second American party system of 1828–54 was a mixture of democratic impulses, all-out appeals to masses of voters, and professional organization and management. In the craft of political management, Weed was one of its leading geniuses. See Glyndon G. Van Deusen, *Thurlow Weed: Wizard of the Lobby* (1947).

WILLIAM NISBET CHAMBERS

WELCH, William Henry (b. Norfolk, Conn., April 8, 1850; d. Baltimore, Md., April 30, 1934), PATHOLOGIST, BACTERIOLOGIST, graduated from Yale College in 1870, taught school for a year, worked as apprentice to his physician-father for a few months, but then returned to formal study at Yale's Sheffield Scientific School. He entered the College of Physicians and Surgeons, New York City, in 1872, receiving an MD in 1875. In 1876 he interned at Bellevue Hospital, New York City, and then pursued medical studies in Germany (1876–78), after which he returned to Bellevue and organized the first teaching laboratory for pathology in the U.S. During 1878–84 he worked there and was also demonstrator of anatomy at Bellevue. In 1884 Welch, after appointment as the first professor in the projected new medical school at Johns Hopkins University, returned to Europe to study bacteriology under Robert Koch. Returning from Europe in 1885, he began research in Baltimore on thrombosis, diphtheria, and pneumonia, and spread Koch's new bacteriological knowledge among medical scientists, including **Walter Reed.** Welch helped to organize the Johns Hopkins University Hospital, which opened in 1889.

In 1891 Welch discovered the bacillus causing gas gangrene, called in his honor *Bacillus welchii.* During 1893–98 he was dean of the Johns Hopkins Medical School, and as professor of pathology he was noted for making biology, chemistry, and physics the basis for teaching medicine. He founded the *Journal of Experimental Medicine* in 1896 and was its editor until 1906. Welch was president of the Maryland State Board of Health (1898–1922), chairman of the Board of Scientific Directors of the Rockefeller Institute of Medical Research (1901–33), chairman of the executive committee of the Carnegie Institution of Washington (1909–16), president of the American Medical Association (1910–11), president of the National Academy of Sciences (1913–16), and first director of the new Johns Hopkins School of Hygiene and Public Health (1918–26). His final role was to serve as first occupant of the William H. Welch professorship of the history of medicine at Johns Hopkins

(1926–31). His *Papers and Addresses,* in three volumes, were published in 1920.

———∞∞∞———

Welch, though not the most distinguished American medical scientist trained in Germany, became the prime agent in the successful transmission of the German research impulse to American medical schools. In the process, he and a handful of contemporaries at Harvard, Pennsylvania, and Johns Hopkins raised the level of the best medical instruction in the United States from among the lowest in the Atlantic community of nations to the highest in the world in one generation—roughly from 1885 to 1915.

Welch played a decisive role in shaping both the Johns Hopkins Hospital and the Johns Hopkins Medical School. He was the source of the unprecedented admission requirements for medical students—a bachelor's degree, with appropriate courses in mathematics and science, plus a knowledge of French and German.

The students who enrolled before World War I included four future Nobel laureates (George H. Whipple, E. Joseph Erlanger, Herbert S. Gasser, Francis Peyton Rous). Welch resisted (in vain) the demand of the female donors to the medical school that it be coeducational, another breach with precedent among American medical schools of the first rank, but he soon acknowledged that he had been wrong. The early women students included **Gertrude Stein** and Florence Sabin (first woman member of the National Academy of Sciences).

Welch was the major figure in recruiting his colleagues on the medical faculty, including anatomist Franklin P. Mall, surgeon **William S. Halsted,** and clinician Sir William Osler. The distinctive note of their teaching was that students should learn by doing, in laboratories and wards, with a prompt initiation into independent research and a minimum of authoritatively imposed instruction. Though this system produced many respected local practitioners, its main impact lay in the scores of professors in medical faculties in the United States and abroad who had been trained at Johns Hopkins—above

all, Welch's own disciples, the famous "Welch rabbits," including the first director of the Rockefeller Institute, Simon Flexner, whose brother, **Abraham Flexner,** in a famous report of 1910 on medical education portrayed Johns Hopkins as the only satisfactory medical school in the country. This report forced all other institutions to approximate to the Hopkins standard or perish.

Beyond the limits of Baltimore, Welch became the most influential scientific statesman of America in the period from 1890 to 1930. From 1901 he was the main scientific adviser to **John D. Rockefeller** in launching his medical philanthropies, the man who gave the signal for creating the Rockefeller Institute in 1904.

In 1908 Welch got Dr. Charles W. Stiles, a lecturer on medical zoology at Johns Hopkins, appointed to Theodore Roosevelt's Country Life Commission. Stiles promptly began to propagandize for a major assault on hookworm disease in the southern states. This enterprise was taken up by the Rockefellers in 1909, when Welch and Stiles were among a small group commissioned to make a plan for spending $1 million over a five-year period to stamp out the disease—the first great public health "demonstration" in history. This brilliantly executed campaign triggered all the subsequent activities of the Rockefeller Foundation in the realm of public health.

The Rockefellers' decision to move in this direction immediately spotlighted the fact that there was no systematic provision of any sort in the United States for training public health workers. Welch insisted over considerable opposition that the very first step had to be the creation of a full-scale university institute committed to fundamental research. The result was the Johns Hopkins Institute of Hygiene and Public Health, inaugurated in 1918 with Welch as director and eventually endowed by the Rockefeller Foundation with $6 million. The Hopkins model was speedily imitated with Rockefeller money in London, Toronto, Copenhagen, São Paulo, Zagreb, Prague, Tokyo, Ankara, and Sofia.

From 1896 on, the progress of experimental medicine in the United States was threatened by projected federal legislation severely restricting experiments on animals. Welch was the moving spirit in several successful campaigns to block such enactments, and the key figure in creating in 1908 the American Medical Association's highly effective Committee for the Protection of Medical Research—the chief lobbying and propaganda organ of the vivisectionists.

With his colleague Osler, Welch took the lead in enlisting laymen in the campaign against tuberculosis—the first time that laymen were treated as equals in an assault upon disease. This innovation deserves to rank with mass conscription, the marketing of government securities to the citizens at large, and the institution of a popular press as a decisive event in the involvement of the general public in the making of their own history. See Donald Fleming, *William H. Welch and the Rise of Modern Medicine* (1954).

DONALD FLEMING

WELD, Theodore Dwight (b. Hampton, Conn., Nov. 23, 1803; d. Hyde Park, Mass., Feb. 3, 1895), REFORMER, entered Hamilton College (1823), but in 1825 joined **Charles G. Finney**'s "holy band" of evangelists and for two years preached in western New York. During this period he also studied for the ministry at Oneida Institute, Whitesboro, New York. Weld was recruited to the antislavery movement by Captain Charles Stuart, principal of the Utica (N.Y.) Academy, who provided for part of Weld's expenses at Oneida. Weld in turn "converted" the Tappan brothers of New York. In 1831 the Tappans commissioned him to find a site in the West for a theological seminary to train Finney's converts for the ministry. Weld selected Lane Seminary, Cincinnati, Ohio, for his project, but he was expelled in 1834 when he founded an antislavery society at the seminary. In 1836 Weld organized a conference to train new agents for the American Anti-Slavery Society. He also took over the Society's publicity and conducted a successful pamphlet campaign in which he anonymously wrote widely distributed essays. During 1841–43 he lobbied in Washington, D.C., for an antislavery faction in the Whig party, but shortly retired from public affairs. He later made a number of personal appearances before antislavery and Republican audiences. During 1854–62 Weld headed the integrated coeducational school, Englewood, near Perth Amboy, New Jersey. In 1864–67 he taught English at the Lexington (Mass.) Women's Seminary. Weld was a town officer in Hyde Park, Massachusetts, a member of the school board, and chairman of the board of the free public library for nine years. During the 1870s he supported the woman suffrage movement, and in his old age he took up the conservationists' cause. He lectured occasionally until the age of ninety. His publications, few of which bore his name, include *Slavery and the Internal Slave Trade in the United States* (1831), *The Power of Congress over Slavery in the District of Columbia* (1836), *The Bible Against Slavery* (1837), *Emancipation in the West Indies* (1837), and the influential compilation of materials, chiefly drawn from southern newspapers, *American Slavery as It Is* (1839).

Weld was peculiarly fitted for the work he accomplished, mainly during the 1830s. He was accustomed to strenuous farm labor, and was of vibrant religious disposition. Humorless and evangelical, he combined pride and devoutness in a fashion which caused him to avoid publicity and publish writings anonymously. His intense early studies hurt his eyes, and his lack of formal education helped preserve the unadorned quality of his exposition, which especially attracted farmers. Weld's course was molded by Finney's evangelicalism, Charles Stuart's mixture of religion and antislavery, and the manual labor program fostered by the Reverend Beriah Green at Oneida Institute. These causes, plus temperance and moral reform, inspired Weld in the 1820s and early 1830s to realize his power over country audiences. Tall, carelessly dressed, with wild hair and magnetic eyes, Weld seemed an apostolic figure, mingling biblical references with moral judgments.

Lane Seminary in Cincinnati was to be a western bastion against Catholicism, but Weld's vision ranged above such parochial goals. He sought in various ways to prove that "in Christ Jesus there is neither Jew nor Greek." Sometime after September 1832 he abandoned colonization as a proper solution to slavery, and in 1834 carried off his first major coup by initiating at Lane a debate on slavery which turned a majority of its spirited, mature students into abolitionists seeking action. The debate split the campus, sending the rebels off to Oberlin College in Ohio's Western Reserve. Weld himself went to New York to join the new American Anti-Slavery Society as an organizer and editor.

There he convened a large group of evangelical abolitionists, some from Lane, and sent them off into the countryside to stir the populace. Their work differed in kind from that being pressed by the talented followers of **William Lloyd Garrison.** Garrisonians upbraided their audiences; the Weld moderates sought to persuade them of their antislavery duty. Both groups were effective in different ways. Weld himself briefly continued to be powerful and dynamic as a speaker. His voice, exhausted from speechmaking, however, failed him in 1836. His major services thereafter were in the production of powerful, factual pamphlets and, in 1841–43, gathering data for antislavery congressmen. His marriage to **Angelina Grimké** in 1838 changed both their lives. She left the fold of Garrisonians, who had supported her pioneer antislavery public speeches. He became increasingly critical of mere enthusiasm which did not touch the root of conduct or devoutness, and found himself without a "call" in antislavery, though urged to continue in the work. In addition, the rapid politicization of the slavery issue by way of the Liberty party, the Texas issue, and fugitive slave controversies in large measure rendered obsolete his brand of evangelical abolitionism. After 1843, Weld was out of public life, bemused by family affairs, farming problems, and schoolteaching. A historian's discovery of Weld's and the Grimké sisters' letters, and the development of a historical viewpoint which honored moderate abolitionists at the expense of Garrisonians, created a place for Weld in scholarship, rumor of which, however,

rarely reached the larger public. See Gilbert H. Barnes and Dwight L. Dumond, eds., *Letters of Theodore Dwight Weld, Angelina Grimké Weld, and Sarah Grimké, 1822–1844* (1934).

LOUIS FILLER

WELLES, (George) Orson (b. Kenosha, Wis., May 6, 1915; d. Los Angeles, Calif., Oct. 10, 1985), ACTOR, DIRECTOR, graduated in 1930 from the Todd School (Woodstock, Ill.), which specialized in dramatics. In 1931 he traveled in Europe and played in *Jud Suss* with the Gate theater in Dublin. Back in the U.S., Guthrie McClintic and Katharine Cornell hired him for secondary roles in their Shakespeare Company chorus, and in 1934 he made his Broadway debut as Tybalt in *Romeo and Juliet.* He then produced his radio show *The March of Time* for NBC and helped organize the WPA federal theater project in New York City, which produced *Macbeth* with an all-black cast, *Dr. Faustus,* and Marc Blitzstein's *The Cradle Will Rock.*

Welles and John Houseman founded the Mercury theater in 1937 and that year put on *Julius Caesar,* in which some actors wore Nazi uniforms. In 1938 the Mercury mounted a production of Shaw's *Heartbreak House* and Buchner's *Danton's Death.* Welles provoked a minor panic in 1938 when the *Mercury Theater of the Air* adapted H. G. Wells's *War of the Worlds* for CBS in the form of a news broadcast of a Martian invasion of the U.S. Welles also directed his first film in 1938.

Welles went to Hollywood in 1939 and signed a contract with RKO. In 1940 he directed, produced, helped write, and acted in *Citizen Kane,* a movie based in part on the life of **William Randolph Hearst.** In 1941, on Broadway, he presented **Richard Wright**'s *Native Son,* and then returned to Hollywood to direct *The Magnificent Ambersons* and *Journey into Fear* in 1942. During World War II he produced a propaganda radio show about Latin America, *Hello Americans, The Mercury Wonder Show* for servicemen, and a political commentary program for ABC. Welles supported Franklin Roosevelt on radio and in his

1942 and 1943 New York *Post* column. In 1946 he put on a Broadway musical for Michael Todd, **Cole Porter**'s version of Jules Verne's *Around the World,* but it was a failure. He also directed *The Stranger* (1946), *The Lady from Shanghai* (1948), *Othello* (1952), *Mr. Arkadin* (1955), *Touch of Evil* (1957), *The Trial* (1962), and other films. Between films Welles returned to the stage and worked with television: in 1953 he produced a television version of *King Lear,* and in 1960 in London, he directed Ionesco's *Rhinoceros.* In the 1970s and 1980s Welles appeared on American television a good deal, as a guest on talk shows but most memorably as a TV pitchman for the Gallo Winery. One of Welles's last films was "F for Fake" (1973).

We find in Orson Welles the classic instance of the artist who is destroyed by self-indulgence, and by a final lack of confidence in the essence of his artistry. We find, too, the classic instance of the artist who, by seeking wealth, fame, and the love of everyone, betrays the very nature of his being. His brilliance lay always in the inspired use of others; when those others no longer adhered to him, he became an artist without materials.

His flamboyance, from the outset, was not a pose but the authentic expression of a personality. In an age of the common man, he inevitably turned into a baroque clown. His art was bizarre, uncommon, romantic, exaggerated, alive with fantastic images which enlarge reality. Hence, he was not adored by the mass public, except as a conjuror and as an agile performer in films and on talk shows. To the public, he was a lovable ham, to the colleges a demigod brought low by the corrupt, to the few who really knew him, a hateful and lovable, irresponsible, extravagant child who received all the gifts that can be bestowed upon a man—looks, a handsome body, the ability to learn fast, talent in a dozen media— and who threw almost all of those gifts away. He was wrecked by impatience and because he lived in an age in which popularization was the fate of the creative he played to the masses. Working in

film and theater, he was cursed by the fact that the first is an art form run by businessmen, and the second is an art no longer commanding, but rather begging, admiration. He should have been born one hundred years earlier, lived as an aristocratic artist of the senses, and addressed himself with thunderous force to the elite. Instead, he had to become meretricious, since specialized talent is of itself suspect. It is significant that his greatest disciple and interpreter was the English theater critic Kenneth Tynan, who like others connected to the high arts had to act the jongleur in order to satisfy a mass-educated public.

Welles was typical of our time in being a physical as well as an intellectual gypsy, with no fixed address. He courted publicity by seeming to avoid it, ate immensely rather than selectively, read widely but not deeply, made films which dazzled at once and continue to dazzle, but rarely explored below the surface of life. He was also utterly modern in that his superficial brightness and laissez-faire concealed boredom, apathy, laziness, irresolution, and a desperate extravagance. He could never have equaled *Citizen Kane* with all of the freedom and all of the budgets in the world, because at twenty-four he reached his emotional peak. Since then, he remained twenty-four, but without the energy.

As he survived into old age, he issued a succession of autobiographical *cris de coeur,* utterly American in their declaration of the fear of old age, together with equally American appearances on the media designed to show that he was forever young. If **F. Scott Fitzgerald**'s career was a tragedy without a third act, then Welles's was a melodrama without a second. See Charles Higham, *The Films of Orson Welles* (1970).

CHARLES HIGHAM

WELLES, Gideon (b. near Glastonbury, Conn., July 1, 1802; d. Hartford, Conn., Feb. 11, 1878), POLITICAL LEADER, attended the Episcopal Academy at Cheshire, Connecticut (1819–21) and the American Literary, Scientific, and Military Academy at Norwich, Vermont, now Norwich University (1823–25). After studying law he became editor of the Hartford *Times* (1826–37). An advocate of Jacksonian democracy, Welles was elected to the Connecticut legislature in 1826. In that post he wrote the Connecticut business incorporation law which became a model for other states. Following an unsuccessful try for Congress in 1834, Welles was elected state controller of public accounts in 1835. He was reelected in 1842 and 1843. He also served as postmaster of Hartford (1836–41) and chief of the Bureau of Provisions and Clothing for the navy (1846–49). In 1850 Welles ran for the U.S. Senate but was defeated.

Around 1854 Welles left the Democratic party largely because of his opposition to slavery and then joined the newly organized Republican party. He helped establish the Republican Hartford *Evening Press* and wrote for many other newspapers. An unsuccessful Republican nominee for governor of Connecticut in 1856, Welles served as a member of the Republican national executive committee and headed the Connecticut delegation to the 1860 Republican national convention. President Lincoln appointed Welles secretary of the navy in 1861. During his tenure he helped develop an ironclad navy and organized the effective naval blockade of the Confederacy. After the war he favored leniency toward the South and a quick restoration of southern states to the Union. He supported President Andrew Johnson's policies and backed the president when he was impeached.

Retiring from the Navy Department in 1869, Welles wrote many articles for *Galaxy* and *Atlantic Monthly* magazines, and a book, *Lincoln and Seward* (1874). He returned to the Democratic party in 1868. His *Diary of Gideon Welles* (3 vols., 1911), edited by his son Edgar T. Welles and later by Howard K. Beale (3 vols., 1960), is a major source for the history of the era.

———

Gideon Welles served his country well as secretary of the navy during the Civil War. He proved to be a competent, tenacious, and thoroughly honest administrator, with a reformer's zeal for method and integrity in the management of departmental affairs. By no means a brilliant man, he applied common sense and realism to the formulation of naval policy. He possessed in addition the ability to judge the characters of those around him with accuracy tempered by kindness. His dedication to the navy was matched only by his devotion to his family.

Despite such worthy traits, Welles became a controversial figure almost as soon as he arrived in Washington. His tactlessness, which his careers in journalism and politics had failed to correct, accounted for some of the clashes he had with his associates, while his oversensitive concern for status led to a lasting feud with Secretary of State **William Seward.** Still another source of irritation to his cabinet mates was the air of serenity he assumed in times of crisis, when they were on the verge of panic. There is little doubt that Welles made as many enemies as friends during his eight years in the Navy Department.

His physique, moreover, impressed people unfavorably. Indeed, his appearance was apt to inspire laughter rather than confidence. His henna-gray wig and massive chin whiskers prompted casual observers to dismiss him as an ineffectual old fogy incapable of discharging his duties properly.

Welles's directions of naval operations in wartime, however, dispelled such misgivings. Largely responsible for the "anaconda policy" of cautious constriction of the South, he overcame major obstacles and opposition to the execution of this policy. His stubborn insistence on establishing and maintaining blockades of the Confederacy's Atlantic and Gulf coasts, and on the naval occupation of the Mississippi River system, isolated the South, cut it in two, and rendered it incapable of continuing the war. See John Niven, *Gideon Welles: Lincoln's Secretary of the Navy* (1973).

WALTER R. HERRICK, JR.

WELLS, David Ames (b. Springfield, Mass., June 17, 1828; d. Norwich, Conn., Nov. 5, 1898), SOCIAL SCIENTIST, graduated from Williams College in 1847 and from the Lawrence Scientific

School at Harvard in 1851, where he then became an assistant professor. With George Bliss, he published *The Annual of Scientific Discovery* during 1850–66. He made several important inventions related to newspaper publishing and the manufacture of textiles. As a partner in G. P. Putnam and Co. (1857–58), he published textbooks on chemistry, geology, and natural philosophy. In 1864 he published his first work in economics, *Our Burden and Our Strength.* This pamphlet was designed to reassure foreign and domestic investors that the United States, with its dynamic economy, could pay off its large Civil War debts. Some 200,000 copies were printed, in many languages. Wells was named chairman of the National Revenue Commission in 1866. He also founded the Bureau of Statistics in the Treasury Department.

While on a trip to Europe in 1867 Wells became converted to free trade, arguing thereafter that American manufacturers had the efficiency to compete effectively in foreign markets. He was also a defender of laissez-faire, and one of the earliest economists to understand the implications of technological developments in lowering the cost of production. He served as president of the American Social Science Association (1875–79) and of the American Free Trade League (1881). He attended many Democratic national conventions and ran (unsuccessfully) for Congress twice. He also advised Presidents Garfield and Cleveland on tariff problems. His other books include: *The Creed of Free Trade* (1875), *Robinson Crusoe's Money* (1876), and *Recent Economic Changes* (1889).

———— ⚬⚬⚬ ————

Wells, who was something of a 19th-century **Benjamin Franklin,** had a New England upbringing, a restless curiosity about all aspects of the universe except the metaphysical, and a genius for resolving practical problems. He was a jack-of-all-trades. By the age of thirty-five he had been a successful chemist, publisher, editor, teacher, and inventor, and had earned a comfortable fortune. Before the Civil War he wrote and edited numerous articles and elementary treatises on a wide variety of scientific subjects. The war stimulated his interest in political economy, a subject to which he devoted most of his later years. Informed by an intimate personal knowledge of industrial processes, his economic investigations and writings dealt mostly with current economic problems. Written in a lucid and vernacular style and studded with statistics, his works reached an unusually large public audience. But his most lasting contribution probably rests on his investigations of the federal and several state revenue systems. He pioneered in the careful gathering and interpretation of concrete economic data and impressed public officials with the need of more factual support for public decisions. Originally a disciple of **Henry C. Carey** and a protectionist, he became an ardent champion of free trade, a proponent of hard money, and successively a Mugwump and a Democrat. He believed that America's technological superiority and skilled labor force placed it in a favorable position to compete successfully in foreign markets. Reducing the tariff, particularly on raw materials, would further increase the advantage of American manufacturers. From the Civil War to his death in 1898 he advised political leaders, but failed on two occasions to win an elective office. Wells did not possess the vivid or colorful personality of a Franklin. See F. B. Joyner, *David Ames Wells: Champion of Free Trade* (1939).

BENJAMIN RADER

WELLS-BARNETT, Ida B. (b. Holly Springs, Miss., July 16, 1862; d. Chicago, Ill., March 25, 1931), REFORMER, born a slave and orphaned at age fourteen, attended Rust College in Holly Springs and then became a teacher in a one-room schoolhouse. In 1883 she moved to Memphis, where she taught and did freelance writing for such newspapers as the Detroit *Plaindealer.* In 1889 she became editor and a part owner of the Memphis *Free Speech,* writing articles exposing the bad conditions under which blacks lived. She was driven out of Memphis in 1892 after she published the details of the lynching of three black grocers by their white competitors. Moving to New York City, Wells became a reporter for **T.**

Thomas Fortune's New York *Age* (1892). She also lectured throughout the Northeast on the evils of lynching and made a highly successful lecture tour of the British Isles in 1893.

In 1893 Wells attended the World Columbian Exposition in Chicago, which became her permanent residence. She joined **Frederick Douglass** and other black leaders in condemning the Exposition's failure to honor the contributions of black Americans. In 1895 she published the first statistical study of lynching, *The Red Record,* which won her an international reputation. She continued working for antilynching legislation and led a delegation to President McKinley in 1898, protesting the lynching of a black postmaster in South Carolina. In 1908 she was an organizer and first president of the Negro Fellowship League in Chicago and the following year helped organize the National Association for the Advancement of Colored People at its Niagara Falls Convention. She founded a settlement house in Chicago in 1913 which assisted migrant blacks from the South in finding jobs and homes, and became a probation officer for the city that same year. An active member of the National Equal Rights League, she was named chairman of the Chicago Equal Rights League in 1915. Wells spent the rest of her life lecturing on the horrors of lynching and participating in various civil rights organizations. She ran as an independent candidate for the Illinois state senate in 1930 but was defeated. Her *Autobiography* was published posthumously in 1970.

The name of Ida B. Wells first came to national attention in 1892 when an editorial she had written for her Memphis black newspaper so enraged local whites that a mob smashed the paper's offices and threatened to burn her at the stake if she ever returned to the city. "Nobody in this section," she had written, "believes the old thread-bare lie that Negro men assault white women." Southern white men were so insistent that interracial sex was justification for lynching that, if they were not more cautious in their assertions, "a conclusion will be reached which will be

very damaging to the moral reputation of their women." During the next forty years, Ida B. Wells-Barnett continued courageously to confront injustice, as an antilynching crusader and investigator of race riots, a militant opponent of **Booker T. Washington**'s accommodationist policies, and a founder of the black women's club movement and advocate of woman suffrage.

Few Americans have equaled Ida B. Wells-Barnett in her fiery denunciation of discrimination, exploitation, and brutality. In her opinion, no just society could permit either race or sex to be an obstacle to the full realization of individual potential. Quite often, however, being determined to move faster and further than her activist colleagues, she found herself on the fringes of the movements for equality for blacks and women. Outspoken, undiplomatic, suspicious of the motives of both friends and enemies, and with a seemingly boundless ego, she had, she once wrote, a vision of a society in which "human beings … pay tribute to what they believe one possesses in the way of qualities of mind and heart, rather than to the color of the skin." To battle for such a society in the United States at the turn of the 20th century, one doubtless had to have an abundance of self-confidence and self-righteousness. And these characteristics, though not always commendable in themselves, she not only had but frequently put to effective use. See Alfreda M. Duster, ed., *Crusade for Justice: The Autobiography of Ida B. Wells* (1970).

WILLIAM M. TUTTLE, JR.

WELTY, Eudora (b. Jackson, Miss., April 13, 1909), WRITER, attended Mississippi State College for Women (1925–27) before graduating from the University of Wisconsin (1929). After a stay at the Columbia University Graduate School of Business (1930–31), she held an advertising job briefly in New York City. She returned to Jackson and worked as a writer for local radio stations and a Memphis, Tennessee, newspaper. This led to a position in the 1930s with the Works Projects Administration (WPA) as a publicity agent and spokesperson. She also lectured at several colleges but soon she turned her full attention to writing fiction.

Welty's first published work, a short story, appeared in the magazine *Manuscript* in 1936. During the following years, her writings appeared frequently in *The Southern Review*, *New Directions*, *The Atlantic Monthly*, and the *New Yorker*. Her first collection of stories, *A Curtain of Green* (1941), with an enthusiastic introduction by Katherine Anne Porter, won wide acclaim for its technical proficiency. That same year she received the O. Henry Award for her short story, "A Worn Part."

Living in Jackson, Miss., with brief interruptions for travel, Welty has produced a stream of short stories and novels, mostly set in her native state and dealing with local types. Expecially praised for her short stories, she has received six O. Henry Awards. In 1955, The American Academy of Arts and Letters presented her the **William Dean Howells** Medal for her short novel *The Ponder Heart*, which was successfully dramatized for the stage the next year. In 1972 Welty was awarded the Pulitzer Prize for her novella *The Optimist's Daughter* (1972). *The Collected Stories of Eudora Welty* appeared in 1980.

From her first publications in small-circulation Southern magazines, Eudora Welty's work has stayed close to her native Mississippi in both setting and characterization, but her distinctively styled and masterfully crafted fiction has transcended the label of regionalism with which she is most often identified. She is not concerned with the larger social issues of her region, but excels at the creation of individual character and the fine shading of Southern rural life. Peopled by often engaging eccentrics, her fiction has a distinct flavor that, although peculiar to the American South, has a resonance which often conveys universal truths.

The tone of Welty's tales ranges from whimsical and droll to dark and almost sinister. But although her characters are often grotesques she never descends to that mannered style known as Southern Gothic. Usually focusing on a decayed aristocracy with a deep sense of proud, if anachronistic, tradition, she develops her characters with both humor and pathos. Her 1946 novel *Delta Wedding*, for example, portrays the sometimes bizzare dynamics of the inbred Fairchild family, as seen obliquely through the eyes of a child. *The Ponder Heart* depicts the simple-minded benevolence of Daniel Ponder, whose impulsively generous heart leads to both his ruin and his salvation.

If Welty's characters are involuted and idiosyncratic, her prose style is lucid and exquisitely modulated. Katherine Anne Porter observed in 1941 that Welty has "an eye and an ear sharp, shrewd and true as a tuning fork." But though her use of Southern vernacular is unerringly accurate, it is at the same time unmistakably her own. Eudora Welty's sensitive portraits of Mississippi life, and the often odd people who live it, stand outside regional literature as a uniquely personal creation. See Ruth M. Vande Kieft, *Eurdora Welty* (1962).

DENNIS WEPMAN

WEST, Benjamin (b. Springfield, Pa., Oct. 10, 1738; d. London, Eng., March 11, 1820), ARTIST, demonstrated an early aptitude for art in sketches and portraits drawn in his father's tavern. He entered the College of Philadelphia (now the University of Pennsylvania) in 1756, but never completed the course of study. Instead he took up portrait painting in Philadelphia, where he came under the influence of William Williams, an itinerant scene painter whose collection of handbooks of painting stimulated the young man to dream of a career in the arts. In 1759 West moved to New York to continue his work; and a year later, with the aid of his patrons in Philadelphia and New York, he traveled to Italy to study in Florence, Bologna, and Venice. Here he was deeply influenced by the then popular neoclassical style. In 1763 West moved to London, where he remained until his death. In London, he quickly established his reputation and emerged as an important figure in English art circles. In 1768 he was introduced to King George III, a meeting which started a long friendship between the two men. Enjoying financial support from the Crown,

West painted many portraits of the royal family and became a charter member of the Royal Academy of Arts in 1768. He later became president, succeeding his close friend Sir Joshua Reynolds in 1792.

Because West had previously painted in the neoclassical mode, his *Death of Wolfe* (c. 1769), which depicted the subject in contemporary dress, was the subject of much controversy at its 1771 showing. However, despite the criticism George III appointed him as the court's historical painter in 1772, a position he held until 1801 when he fell out of favor with the king. West's studio was hospitable to young American artists, among whom **Charles Willson Peale, Gilbert Stuart, John Trumbull,** William Dunlap, Washington Allston, **Thomas Sully,** and **Samuel F. B. Morse** were most important. Some of West's best-known pictures were painted during his later years, including *Christ Healing the Sick in the Temple* (1811, Pennsylvania Hospital, Philadelphia), *Christ Rejected by the Jews* (1814, Pennsylvania Academy of the Fine Arts, Philadelphia), and *Death on the Pale Horse* (1817, Pennsylvania Academy of the Fine Arts, Philadelphia).

West's neoclassicism emphasized moralistic themes derived from religious, mythological, or historical sources, and eclecticism, or the borrowing of styles, furnishings, and groupings from renowned painters of the past, in order to achieve "classic grandeur." As a result, his huge formal pictures—"ten-acre canvases," in Gilbert Stuart's words—appear static and without originality or vitality. Groups are mechanically and melodramatically presented according to precisely defined rules of composition, while characterizations are so generalized that they lose individuality. Many of West's paintings are marred also by poor color and hard drawing. One of the best of the early works, however, is *Penn's Treaty with the Indians* (c. 1771–72, Independence Hall, Philadelphia), which reflects West's familiarity with his native landscape and his interest in contemporary dress. Some of his more romantic later paintings, like

Death on the Pale Horse, reveal an attempt to break away from the constraints of neoclassicism and a consequent loosening of brush and imagination that make them more interesting aesthetically than his more formal history paintings.

Despite his artistic limitations, West's influence on American art was large, through the encouragement he offered to young American artists, his didactic view of art's mission, and his own example. Impressed by their native-born genius, Americans were influenced to consider art more seriously, as a conveyor of moral lessons in patriotism, religion, and social behavior. At a time when art was frequently viewed as frivolous and lascivious, the justification of art as a source of morality was of great importance in the cultural development of the nation. See Grose Evans, *Benjamin West and the Taste of His Times* (1959).

LILLIAN B. MILLER

WESTINGHOUSE, George (b. Central Bridge, N.Y., Oct. 6, 1846; d. New York, N.Y., March 12, 1914), INVENTOR, MANUFACTURER, enlisted in the Union army as a private in 1863. In 1864 he served in the navy as an acting third assistant engineer. In 1865 he received a patent for a rotary steam engine. In 1866, after brief study at Union College, he assisted his father in the operation of a farm implement factory in Schenectady, New York.

In 1869 Westinghouse invented an air brake for railroad cars (later improved by twenty additional patents). Forming the Westinghouse Air Brake Co. at Allegheny, Pennsylvania, he reaped large profits, for the Westinghouse brakes revolutionized the railroad industry by enabling trains to operate safely at much higher speeds. While manufacturing air brakes, he also experimented with the improvement of railroad switches and signals. In 1882, after studying European systems, he organized the Union Switch and Signal Co. to design and install electrically controlled systems. These controls, like the air brake, contributed to the safety and efficiency of railroad transportation. In 1883 he also developed a system for transmitting natural gas over long distances.

Establishing the Westinghouse Electric Co. in 1886, he began to promote the development of alternating-current electrical systems. The Westinghouse research department, led by Nikola Tesla, perfected the two-phase adaptor to power both motors and lights. Although opposed by the Edison interests, Westinghouse eventually established the superiority of alternating current over direct current.

The Westinghouse Electric Co. fell into bankruptcy during the panic of 1907. Although Westinghouse regained control of the company in 1908, he failed to revive the firm's prosperity. In 1911 he retired from active management. However, he continued to conduct experiments with steam turbines and automobile air springs. He secured more than four hundred patents during his career. From 1905 to 1910 he served (with Grover Cleveland and Morgan J. O'Brien) on the board of trustees which supervised the reorganization of the Equitable Life Insurance Co.

⁂

During the last half of the 19th century scientifically uneducated but imaginative mechanics could still create valuable (and patentable) improvements in devices with which they were familiar and earn large financial rewards. After 1900 important improvements generally required more specialized knowledge. One of the greatest of the earlier practical inventors was George Westinghouse.

Like his rival, **Thomas A. Edison**, Westinghouse had a keen eye for what was needed and commercially practical. Born into a successful manufacturing family and, by virtue of the air brake, a businessman in his own right at the age of twenty-three, he made money earlier and played a more active business role than Edison. In the perspective of history his most important activities between 1870 and 1885 were probably his scouting in Europe for mechanical and electrical devices that could successfully be introduced in the United States. In this work he was perceptive, intelligent, and successful. In "transplanting" alternating electric current from English and Central European sources he was the first to see that the ability to reduce high alternating voltages for local use through transformers would be the key to cheap long-distance electrical power transmission.

As innovators he and his coworker, William Stanley, were highly successful. But marketing a system involving voltages so high that contact meant instant death proved more difficult. Westinghouse was determined, aggressive, and resourceful, but like so many Americans of this type, he seldom had sufficient patience and caution. Partly because of strong opposition from Edison, it was harder to market alternating-current systems than Westinghouse supposed, and his electric company, in contrast to the air brake company, did not immediately make large profits. Consequently, it lost out to the Morgan-financed Edison group in the fight to control the chief independent, the Thomson-Houston Electric Company. Up to 1896, when he entered into a patent pool with the Edison General Electric Company, Westinghouse was steadily involved in costly litigation over infringements.

To some extent his relatively moderate success as a businessman in the electrical equipment industry may be blamed on the fact that the perfection of new devices rather than business problems seemed always to dominate his imagination. See Henry G. Prout, *A Life of George Westinghouse* (1922).

THOMAS C. COCHRAN

WESTMORELAND, William Childs (b. Spartanburg County, S.C., March 26, 1914), MILITARY LEADER, studied one year at the Citadel (1931–32), Charleston, South Carolina, before entering the U.S. Military Academy at West Point in 1932. Upon his graduation in 1936 he was commissioned a second lieutenant and sent with the 18th Field Artillery to Fort Sill, Oklahoma. Later that year he joined the 8th Field Artillery in Hawaii and remained there until he became operations officer of the 34th Field Artillery, 9th Infantry Division, at Fort Bragg, North Carolina, in 1942. He saw action with this unit in North

Africa and Sicily and on Utah Beach during the Normandy invasion. Promoted to colonel in 1944, he was chief of staff of the 9th Infantry from 1944 to 1945; he then took command of the 60th Infantry Regiment at the beginning of the German occupation. After completing paratroop and glider training at Fort Benning, Georgia, Westmoreland commanded the 504th Parachute Infantry Regiment (1946–47) and was chief of staff of the 82d Airborne Division at Fort Bragg (1947–50). He taught at the Command and General Staff College at Fort Leavenworth, Kansas, and then at the Army War College there (1950–52). He commanded the 187th Airborne Regiment Combat Team in Korea (1952–53) after being promoted to brigadier general in 1952.

Westmoreland's next assignments included deputy assistant chief of staff (G-1) for manpower control at the Pentagon (1953–54) and secretary to the General Staff in Washington, D.C. (1955–58), during which time he became a major general (1956). He commanded the 101st Airborne Division at Fort Campbell, Kentucky (1958–60), and was superintendent of the Military Academy (1960–63). After serving as commanding general of the XVIII Airborne Corps at Fort Bragg in 1963, Westmoreland was promoted to a four-star general in 1964 and put in command of all U.S. forces in South Vietnam, where he developed and utilized the tactic of massive search-and-destroy missions. President Johnson made Westmoreland chief of staff of the U.S. army in 1968. Upon his retirement in 1972 Westmoreland received the Distinguished Service Medal from President Nixon. In 1974, Westmoreland unsuccessfully sought the Republican gubernatorial nomination for South Carolina. He published his autobiography, *A Soldier Reports* in 1976, in which he blamed America's failure in Vietnam on "the ill-considered" policy of "graduated response" forced on the military by the civilian authorities. He claimed that had the military been allowed to employ its power quickly, decisively, and without strings attached, the Vietnamese would have been defeated. From 1982 to 1985 Westmoreland engaged in a libel suit against CBS News and its program *60 Minutes* for claiming that he had lied

to the Johnson administration by deliberately "cooking the numbers" in overestimating how many enemy soldiers were left on the ground in the South. In the end Westmoreland dropped the suit and CBS publicly stated that it did not intend to cast doubt on Westmoreland's honesty and truthfulness.

⸻

Westmoreland's career was a series of precocious and uninterrupted successes until it foundered in Vietnam. No general could have been in command there during the same years and come home a popular hero, but because he was so conspicuous during the great American buildup and the bloodiest battles of the war, Westmoreland became nearly as provocative a symbol of American involvement in Vietnam as Lyndon Johnson himself.

The very characteristics that brought him so far so fast, that made him an outstanding field-grade officer and might have made him an ideal high-level commander in World War II, were those that proved his undoing in Indochina. Still, he was by no means an outright failure there. Had he been rotated home in 1966, he could have returned in relative triumph.

In the first half of his Vietnam tour, 1964–66, he conducted a rescue operation, starting at a point when the South Vietnamese army and government were on the verge of collapse. Using his talent for moving soldiers fast and decisively, demonstrated earlier in North Africa and Germany, he executed that rescue successfully. To do so he wielded the best weapon at hand, American troops, often airlifting them directly into battle areas from overseas staging points.

But in the second half of his tour, 1966–68, his long hours of work, his faultless military bearing, and his devotion to the offensive were largely irrelevant. His training and inclination enabled him to break down and systematize complex operations, to expedite movement, but often he sought to quantify problems that were too subtle for that approach. His shortcomings were in imagination, in originality beyond tactical innovations.

Hindsight is clear: he should have given higher priority much sooner to shifting the burden of combat onto the South Vietnamese themselves. Instead, he responded to Washington's mounting pressure for quick success by continuing to use that best weapon, American troops, and by asking for more and more of them to complete the job. Thus American casualties rose, and popular support for American involvement largely disappeared. When Westmoreland was transferred home to become chief of staff of the entire army, a position long predicted for him and the peak of any professional soldier's ambition, many countrymen considered it a demotion instead. It was not, for Johnson had decided months earlier to reward him thus. Yet for a man who considered soldiering an almost religious calling and was a textbook example of soldierly conduct and loyalty, it was hardly the shining fulfillment of his youthful dream.

At retirement, after hoping for but not getting some high appointment from President Nixon, Westmoreland's deepest concern was that what happened in Vietnam had tarnished the army he served for thirty-six years. Accordingly, when the CBS television newsmagazine *60 Minutes* carried an investigative piece which accused him of deliberately misleading President Johnson by overestimating the number of enemy soldiers killed and thus painting too rosy a picture of how the war was progressing, he brought a libel suit against the network and its correspondents. See Ernest B. Furgurson, *Westmoreland: The Inevitable General* (1968).

ERNEST B. FURGURSON

WHARTON, Edith Newbold Jones (b. New York, N.Y., Jan. 24, 1862; d. St. Brice-sous-Forêt, France, Aug. 11, 1937), WRITER, was educated at home by private tutors and governesses. She traveled frequently with her family throughout Europe but never attended college. In 1885 she married Edward Wharton, a wealthy Boston banker. In 1907 they established themselves in Paris, where she remained for the rest of her life, making only brief visits to the U.S. She divorced her husband in 1913.

Having published some poems as a youth (*Verses*, 1878), Wharton decided on a literary career. A collection of short stories, *The Greater Inclination*, appeared in 1899, and her first novel, *The Touchstone*, was published in 1900. *The Valley of Decision* (1902) followed, and *The House of Mirth* (1905) established her reputation. Deeply influenced by **Henry James,** Wharton described in a witty, satiric style the aristocratic New York society in which she grew up. The novelette *Ethan Frome* (1911), a tragic love story set on a rustic New England farm, was widely praised. Other novels in this period included *The Reef* (1912), *The Custom of the Country* (1913), and *Summer* (1917), another novelette of New England life.

During World War I, Wharton organized the American Volunteer Motor Ambulance Corps in France and was active in many relief organizations with her friend Walter Berry. She wrote *Fighting France, from Dunkerque to Belfort* (1915) and a war novel, *The Marine* (1918). Wharton won a Pulitzer Prize for her novel *The Age of Innocence* (1920), another story of New York society. Four novelettes of a similar vein appeared as *Old New York* (1924), one of which, *The Old Maid,* was dramatized by Zoë Akins in 1935. Novels in this period included *Twilight Sleep* (1927), *Hudson River Bracketed* (1929) and its sequel, *The Gods Arrive* (1932), and *The Buccaneers* (1938), published posthumously. She wrote a manual, *The Writing of Fiction* (1925), and her autobiography, *A Backward Glance* (1934). *Twelve Poems* appeared in 1926. Her short-story collections include *Xingu* (1916) and *Certain People* (1930).

The great formative influence on Edith Wharton's life and art was the closed aristocratic world of "Old New York" to which she belonged. In the deepest sense, however, she did *not* "belong," and it was this sense of separation that produced the dominant theme of her fiction: society versus the individual. Yet society also had its positive influence: it helped to form her exquisite taste, evident not only in the elegance of her person and the decoration of her houses but also in a writing style of striking purity—concise, controlled, epigrammatic, witty. Most importantly her society provided her with a subject which few other American writers have known from the inside. It is here her real achievement lies, for she made no contribution to technique. Her satiric delineation of the old New York aristocracy and its invasion by the *nouveaux riches*—the industrial barbarians of the seventies who forced their way into "good" society by sheer financial weight and ruthlessness—advanced the novel of manners in America, a debt acknowledged by **Sinclair Lewis** and **F. Scott Fitzgerald**. She had other subjects as well, but the one constant of her work is a profound concern with moral issues, particularly those involving the interaction of society and the individual. Behind this theme is a brooding sense of tragedy and fatalism. Though she never publicly affirmed an orthodox faith, the inscription on her grave, *O Crux Spes Unica*, which she herself chose, suggests that religious hope may have been the bedrock of her life after all. See Marilyn J. Lyde, *Edith Wharton: Convention and Morality in the Work of a Novelist* (1959).

MARILYN J. LYDE

WHISTLER, James Abbott McNeill (b. Lowell, Mass., July 10, 1834; d. London, Eng., July 17, 1903), ARTIST, was the son of an engineer engaged in building locks and canals in Massachusetts. In 1843 the family joined the father in Russia, where he was supervising the building of the St. Petersburg–Moscow railway. They then lived in England from time to time, but after the elder Whistler's death (1849), James entered the U.S. Military Academy in 1851. Dropped from the academy in his third year, Whistler attributed his failure to his weakness in chemistry. "If silicon had been a gas," he said, "I would have been a major general." After his dismissal from West Point he spent a year engraving maps for the Coast Survey and then left for Europe, never to return.

Settling down in Paris, he began to live a bohemian existence. Although never formally trained in art he became a master of the etcher's technique, influenced by the realism of Gustave Courbet. He published a portfolio of etchings in 1858. In 1863 his *White Girl,* which forecast his style of muted coloring, was the sensation of the Salon des Refusés, after it had been rejected by the traditional Salon. Thereafter, he spent more and more of his time in London, where his mother had settled in 1863. In London he painted his best-known canvas, *Portrait of My Mother— Arrangement in Grey and Black* (1872, Louvre). Whistler worked prodigiously, and in many media, including etchings and lithographs. Apart from his portraits, for which he is best known, Whistler painted a number of pictures in which he sought to express his ideas of color harmonies. Called "Nocturnes" and "Symphonies," the most representative is perhaps *Battersea Bridge.*

Whistler's reputation as a pugnacious contender for his ideas was firmly established when he won a libel suit (damages of one farthing were awarded) against the critic John Ruskin, who had bitterly attacked his work. At once a drawing-room idol and one of the most hated men in the artistic and literary world, he served as president of the Society of British Artists in 1886–89. He published a number of volumes of impressions and reminiscences, perhaps the most important of which is *The Gentle Art of Making Enemies* (1890).

⁂

One of the most colorful of American expatriates of the late 19th century, Whistler for many years took a leading part in the artistic life of both London and Paris. Flamboyant in dress, vain, egotistical, willful in his manners and behavior, and witty and acerbic in his conversation, he became well known as a public character and showman, roles he gloried in.

As a painter he early turned away from representing a literal interpretation of what he saw in favor of a flattened perspective and a two-dimensional design. He was greatly influenced by Far Eastern art, and was one of the first Westerners to apply Asian ideas directly in his painting and to introduce a taste for this art into England. In the classic battle between the proponents of drawing and the supporters of color as the critical element in painting—the *ligne ou couleur* tempest—Whistler enthusiastically came out for color. He considered the chief objective in painting to be the achievement of harmony of colors. Foreshadowing aspects of 20th-century painting, Whistler moved in some canvases toward non-representational "impressions" filled with evocative overtones of association and suggestion.

As a leading aesthete and advocate of art for art's sake, he was an aggressive spokesman for the full freedom of the artist. He frequently attacked the dominant artistic standards of his day and was an outspoken critic of bourgeois concerns and of artistic philistinism. His most serious call was for high art as a necessity for a civilized life and the fullest development of the individual. See Horace Gregory, *The World of James McNeill Whistler* (1959).

PAUL R. BAKER

WHITE, Alfred Tredway (b. Brooklyn, N.Y., May 28, 1846; d. Harriman State Park, Orange County, N.Y., June 29, 1921), REFORMER, was educated at the Brooklyn Collegiate and Polytechnic Institute and Rensselaer Polytechnic Institute (Troy, N.Y.), from which he received a degree in civil engineering (1865). He returned to Brooklyn as an apprentice in his father's importing firm, the W. A. and A. M. White Co., and soon became a junior partner. He undertook a study of housing problems and of tenement innovations in London (1872) and in 1877 built a small group of tenements that incorporated English developments, such as providing for windows in every room. He built more tenements in 1878, and in 1890 completed the Riverside Tower and Homes Building. White's housing innovations contributed to the adoption of New York's tenement reform laws, the first of which was passed in 1895.

A director of the Children's Aid Society (1868) and of the Brooklyn Society for the Prevention of Cruelty to Children, White established one of the first summer camps for slum children (1876). He was an organizer of the Brooklyn Bureau of Charities (1879) and served as its president for twenty-five years. During 1893–95 White was commissioner of City Works in Brooklyn, and he later served on the Tenement Housing Commission (1900–1901).

During World War I, White was prominent in the activities of the Brooklyn chapter of the Red Cross and for some time was a member of the national organization's executive committee. He was also a trustee of the Russell Sage Foundation, and was among the incorporators of the Brooklyn Academy of Music. He published *Improved Dwellings for the Laboring Classes* (1879), *Better Homes for Workingmen* (1885), *Sun-Lighted Tenements: Twenty-Five Years as an Owner* (1912), and *Report on Additional Water Supply for Brooklyn*.

———

Alfred White was a businessman and philanthropist who pioneered in the development of the model tenement in the United States. He did not originate the idea, but he certainly was its most enthusiastic and important advocate. Depressed by "the badly constructed, unventilated, dark and foul tenement houses of New York" which he believed spread disease and destruction even in the better neighborhoods, he set out to prove that one could build "well-ventilated, convenient and agreeable" housing for the working class and still make a profit.

White's scheme was immediately dubbed "philanthropy plus 5 percent." It was an essentially conservative reform which sought to combine self-interest and altruism. Each unit was supposed to make a profit so that it would inspire imitators, and of course, it would never do to give the impression that one was giving charity, for if the poor got something for nothing it would weaken their character and self-reliance. The model tenement was supposed to help the poor by providing a decent home at a reasonable rent, thus giving them a chance to help themselves.

White's model tenement scheme won wide acceptance in theory because it offered no challenge to the free enterprise system, but few businessmen were content with 4 or 5 percent in an era of rapid expansion and huge profits. The model tenement did little to improve housing in the United States, but White was one of the first to point out the dangers of overcrowded urban tenements. See Roy Lubove, *The Progressive and the Slums: Tenement House Reform in New York City* (1962).

ALLEN F. DAVIS

WHITE, Andrew Dickson (b. Homer, N.Y., Nov. 7, 1832; d. Ithaca, N.Y., Nov. 4, 1918), EDUCATOR, DIPLOMAT, briefly attended Geneva College (now Hobart), and graduated from Yale in 1853. Thereafter he studied in Europe, and in 1854–55 he served as an attaché to the American legation in St. Petersburg. After returning to the U.S. he received his AM "in course" at Yale (1857), and then became a professor of European history at the University of Michigan (1857–63).

In 1863 White returned to New York. During 1864–67 he served in the state senate as a Republican. As chairman of the committee on education he helped establish the state's first normal schools, and worked to gain support for the founding of a state university. With the help of Ezra Cornell, a charter for a university at Ithaca, New York, was granted in April 1865. Cornell University was opened in 1868, with White its first president.

In 1871 President Grant named White to a commission to study the possibility of annexing Santo Domingo. Following the Panic of 1873, in which Ezra Cornell lost a great deal of his money, White contributed from his own funds to help save the university. In 1876 he published *Paper-Money Inflation in France*, a book on the French Revolution, based on lectures.

In 1878 President Hayes appointed White minister to Germany. In 1884 White helped found the American Historical Association, serving as its first president. During the 1884 presidential election, White, although a civil service reform advocate, supported **James G. Blaine,** refusing to join Republican "Mugwump" reformers who supported Grover Cleveland, the Democratic candidate.

In 1885 White resigned as president of Cornell. In 1892 President Benjamin Harrison appointed him minister to Russia. During the boundary dispute between Venezuela and British Guiana (1895), President Cleveland named him to a commission created to determine the boundary. In 1896 White published *History of the Warfare of Science with Theology in Christiandom* (2 vols.), in which he discussed the controversy between the advocates of Darwin's theory of evolution and those who supported a literal reading of the Bible. During 1897–1902 he was U.S. ambassador to Germany. In 1899 White headed the American delegation to the International Peace Conference at The Hague. White's *Autobiography* (2 vols.) appeared in 1905.

—⁂—

Andrew Dickson White had a profound influence upon American higher education as the intellectual architect and first president of Cornell University. He brought three traits to his executive position unusual for the times: experience as a teacher in the leading state university of the era, extensive European travel and studies, and political sophistication born of service in the New York State legislature. White recognized scholarship when he encountered it and knew how to deal with worldly men. As a result, Cornell from the outset was a model of commitment to high intellectual standards as well as practical knowledge. White supplemented the teaching of his brilliant young faculty with a constant stream of older scholars brought in for visits of a few months. These senior academics, many with international reputations, spread the fame and increased the fortunes of the fledgling institution. Further, White kept in constant contact with old friends such as **Daniel Coit Gilman** (first president of Johns Hopkins University), rarely missing an opportunity to extend Cornell's influence. White and Cornell stood for nonsectarian instruction, coeducation, equality of practical with academic subjects, and freedom for faculty to develop their special areas of scholarship.

Andrew White was an irenic man, a natural diplomat as well as gifted administrator. His academic status combined with his political experience to make him a powerful elder statesman of the Republican party until the end of the 19th century. His talent for conciliation placed him at the center of factions trying to organize the American Historical Association and led to his most significant publication, an effort to resolve the conflicts between traditional religion and Darwinian science. See Glenn Altschuler, *Andrew D. White: Educator, Historian, Diplomat* (1979).

MARK BEACH

WHITE, Edward Douglass (b. Lafourche Parish, La., Nov. 3, 1845; d. Washington, D.C., May 19, 1921), JURIST, left school to enlist in the Confederate army, and was taken prisoner at Port Hudson, Louisiana (1863). Admitted to the Louisiana bar in 1868, he practiced in New Orleans. He served in the state senate as a Democrat (1874–78), and in 1879–80 he was a judge on the state supreme court. White later served in the U.S. Senate (1891–94), where he fought for a protective tariff for sugar. He was named to the Supreme Court in 1894, after President Cleveland had failed to get two previous nominees to the Court confirmed.

As an associate justice (chief justice, 1910–21), White concurred in the *U.S. v. E. C. Knight Co.* decision (1895), which declared that the Sherman Anti-Trust Act did not apply to intrastate manufacturing combinations; and in *In re Debs* (1895), which upheld the right of the federal courts to issue injuctions when strikes affected interstate commerce. He dissented in *Pollock* v. *Farmer's Loan and Trust Co.* (1895), which invalidated federal income taxes unless apportioned among the states according to population.

White's decisions affecting labor were mixed. He dissented in *Lochner* v. *N.Y.* (1905), which invalidated a New York maximum-hour law; he upheld the Adamson Act establishing an eight-hour day for railroad employees (*Wilson* v. *New*, 1916); but he dissented in *Bunting* v. *Oregon* (1917), which upheld an Oregon ten-hour law. In *Adair* v. *U.S.* (1908), he agreed with the majority that employers could not require workers to sign an agreement not to join a union ("yellow-dog" contract) as a prerequisite for employment. His attitude toward the trusts, too, was not fixed. He dissented in the Northern Securities case (1904), which revived the Sherman Anti-Trust Act. But in the Standard Oil and the American Tobacco Co. cases (1911), in which the Court dissolved two large trusts, White was responsible for the "rule of reason" doctrine.

⸺∞⸺

Chief Justice Edward Douglass White is remembered today as among the less able of the fifteen men who have successively occupied the nation's highest judicial office since 1789. In part, White's modest reputation arises from the fact that his opinions all too often were turgid and confused—one critic called them "models of what opinions ought not to be." More serious, White in his quarter-century on the Supreme Court proved unable to develop a clear-cut judicial philosophy to guide him through the bewildering maze of complex social, economic, and political forces which played upon the Court incident to the rise of a nationalized urban industrial society.

On many occasions White's judicial stance appeared to reflect a broad liberal nationalism in the tradition of **John Marshall.** His vigorous dissent in the two Pollock cases, in which he argued cogently that federal income taxes were not direct taxes within the meaning of the Constitution and thus need not be apportioned among the states according to population, was of this kind. So also was his nationalistic opinion in *Wilson* v. *New*, while his successive votes between 1902 and 1916 to accept the new concept of a federal police power to control national social problems, among them lotteries, impure foods and drugs, and traffic in prostitutes, bespoke the same nationalistic conviction. But White also possessed a highly traditional notion of the sanctity of private property and corporate vested interests, which on occasion inspired him to adopt a narrow states' rights view of federal power. It was apparently in this spirit that he concurred in the Knight decision placing the great majority of the gigantic new manufacturing trusts outside the purview of the Sherman Act.

His support for the majority opinion in *Hammer v. Dagenhart* (1918) striking down the First Child Labor Act reflected the same conservative concern for vested rights.

White's vacillation and inconsistency in his approach to due-process cases involving state and federal social regulation almost defies analysis. He could dissent from the narrow and unimaginative "legislative" opinion in the Lochner ten-hour bakeshop law case, vote three years later in *Muller* v. *Oregon* (1908) to uphold Oregon's pioneering ten-hour law for women, and then do an "about-face" and dissent in the Bunting case, in which the Court majority to all intents and purposes overruled the Lochner decision. Again, the explanation for White's dualism appears to lie in the inner conflict he felt between a recognition of the necessity for the regulation of corporate property and his reverence for vested rights.

Notwithstanding his failure to develop a consistent judicial philosophy, White made two major contributions to modern constitutional law: the "rule of reason" in trust prosecutions and the "incorporation doctrine" in the so-called Insular cases. The "rule of reason," which White borrowed in part from English common law, in effect declared that the Sherman Act prohibited only unreasonably restrictive combinations in restraint of trade. Unfortunately, this language not only flew directly in the face of the plain language of the act but also cleared the way for an unprecedented new era of monopolistic combinations in American industry generally. White's "incorporation doctrine" had more fortunate consequences. Here he argued in successive Insular cases that the "Constitution follows the flag" to newly annexed territories overseas only when Congress has by law indicated an intent to incorporate the new possession within the United States. The "incorporation" doctrine proved in practice to be a successful solution to a difficult and complex problem. See James F. Watts, Jr., "Edward Douglass White," in F. L. Israel, ed., *The Justices of the United States Supreme Court* (1951), XIII.

ALFRED H. KELLY

WHITE, Elwyn Brooks (b. Mt. Vernon, N.Y., July 11, 1899; d. North Brooklin, Me., Oct. 30, 1985), WRITER, graduated Cornell University in 1921. He began writing in high school and was editor in chief of the *Cornell Daily Sun*. In 1926, he began his long career at the *New Yorker*, assembling its "Talk of the Town" column; then he turned to prose parodies, humorous sketches, parables, and light verse, coauthoring his first book with **James Thurber**, *Is Sex Necessary? Or, Why You Feel the Way You Do* (1929). He specialized in witty criticisms of modern trends, essays on urban, surburban, and rural life. He published his light verse in *The Lady Is Cold* (1929) and *The Fox of Peapack* (1938); his *New Yorker* editorial essays in *Quo Vadimas or, The Case for the Bicycle* (1939); his sketches of the city in *Here Is New York* (1949). His selected *Poems and Sketches* appeared in 1981. *Charlotte's Web* (1952) is his masterpiece, delighting children and adults alike. His other childrens' books *Stuart Little* (1945) and *The Trumpet of the Swan* (1970) were nearly as successful. An elegant stylist, he revised William Strunk's manual *The Elements of Style* (1959), which has become a classic text. White's collected essays were published in 1977; his letters in 1979.

White's reputation sometimes suffered because he was thought to be an amusing but not a serious writer. James Thurber, White's collaborator and colleague at the *New Yorker*, objected to this patronizing attitude toward humorous writing and sounded what later critics took as the reflective undertones of White's well-turned and seemingly effortless sentences. There was a dark and even depressive side to his writing. In his "Notes and Comments" page in the *New Yorker* he confronted such subjects as the aftermath of World War II, the creation of the United Nations, the dangers of nuclear war, the ruin of the environment, civil rights, and McCarthyism.

White deflected attention from his serious purposes by playing the homespun Yankee. He excelled in prose that was precise, elegant and idiomatic, rhythmic but brief and to the point. His clipped tone became in itself a moral stance, a way of not taking himself or others too seriously. He encoded his points in understatement while satirizing the pretentious and inflated styles of other writers. Like his manual, *The Elements of Style*, his prose and verse is therapeutic, ridding language of its excesses.

White's childrens' books have become his lasting contribution to literature. His evocation of life on a farm and his character's personalities have attracted generations of readers. Adults respond to the elegiac tone of his graceful, unaffected stories; children treasure the picaresque adventures and extraordinary intimacy he establishes between animals and human beings. See Scott Elledge, *E. B. White: A Biography* (1985).

CARL ROLLYSON

WHITE, Stanford (b. New York, N.Y., Nov. 9, 1853; d. New York, N.Y., June 25, 1906), ARCHITECT, was educated in New York private schools. Entering the architectural office of Gambill and Richardson of Boston in 1872 as an apprentice, he worked on **Henry Richardson**'s designs for such buildings as Boston's Trinity Church.

While in Europe (1878–79), White studied with **Augustus Saint-Gaudens** in Paris. In 1879 he joined the New York architectural firm which became known as McKim, Mead and White. Planning many luxurious homes in Newport and New York City, and its surrounding suburbs, White specialized in furniture and interior design. He also designed pedestals for many of Saint-Gaudens's works, including the statue of Admiral Farragut in Madison Square (1880–81). In 1889 White designed Madison Square Garden, becoming a stockholder and organizer of its entertainment programs. He designed the Washington Arch, commemorating the first president's inauguration, in Washington Square (1889–92) and also the Battle Monument at West Point (1896). White planned the restoration of the University of Virginia in 1895, modeled after Thomas Jefferson's original ideas. He worked mainly in the formal, neoclassical tradition; some of his many buildings include New York City's Century Club (1889–91), the Metropolitan Club (1892–94),

the Hall of Fame building of New York University (1896–1900), and the University Club (1896–1900).

White was shot and killed by railroad millionaire Harry Kendall Thaw on the roof garden of Madison Square Garden because of an alleged affair between him and Thaw's wife. His partners finished his last major building, the Pennsylvania Railroad station in Manhattan (1906–10).

The significance of Stanford White lies rather more in the nature of his career than in his actual architectural achievement. From an early age he showed a talent for drawing and sketching. The noted Romanesque revivalist H. H. Richardson considered him one of his most valued assistants. His major work, however, followed his joining forces with Charles Follen McKim and Rutherford B. Mead in what was to become unquestionably the most successful architectural partnership of its time. During the first few years of its existence, the firm produced many brilliant designs in the suburban Richardsonian manner which has since become known as "the Shingle Style"; their masterpiece in this vein was probably the Newport Casino of 1881. Despite their success in this idiom the partners apparently felt that what American architecture needed was a greater degree of discipline than it offered, and in order to supply it they turned in 1882 to the Italian Renaissance manner for a complex of town houses on Fifth Avenue for the railroad promoter **Henry Villard** and four of his friends (Joseph Morrill Wells, a draftsman in the office, may have been important in this design). In the city the effect of this new departure was immediate and overwhelming, and on the national scene it was reinforced by the triumph of neoclassicism at the Chicago World's Fair of 1893. From this time onward commissions poured into the offices of McKim, Mead, and White, and in sheer volume of business the firm was unquestionably the most important on the Eastern Seaboard.

As a principal designer, Stanford White played a major role in all this activity, and in addition was very much a part of the brilliant New York social scene of his day. A man of great personal charm, inexhaustible energy, and undoubted gifts as a designer, he was, on more than one occasion, seduced into the role of exterior decorator rather than architect. At the same time, his best work has an unquestionable authority. For this reason, and because the style in which he worked has been for many years generally discredited, a fair assessment of his historical contribution is difficult. He was undeniably one of the leading architectural personalities of his time, but probably more important as a tastemaker than as an architect. See Charles C. Baldwin, *Stanford White* (1931).

LEONARD K. EATON

WHITE, William Allen (b. Emporia, Kans., Feb. 10, 1868; d. Emporia, Kans., Jan. 29, 1944), JOURNALIST, worked as a typesetter for the El Dorado (Kans.) *Democrat* while attending the College of Emporia. Serving as reporter (1886) and then city editor (1887) of the El Dorado *Daily Republican,* he attended the University of Kansas (1886–90) and concurrently worked as reporter for the Lawrence *Journal.* White left college to become business manager of the *Republican,* worked briefly for the Kansas City *Journal* (1891), and then joined the Kansas City *Star* as an editorial writer. He purchased the Emporia *Daily Gazette* in 1895 and became nationally prominent during the election of 1896, when **Mark Hanna** widely circulated his anti-Populist editorial "What's the Matter with Kansas?" White's first published book, a collection of short stories entitled *The Real Issue,* appeared the same year and also attracted much attention. He became a contributor to numerous magazines, among them *McClure's* and *Harper's Weekly,* and published a succession of novels including *A Certain Rich Man* (1909), which sold more than 250,000 copies. He was active in local Republican affairs. Being a friend and admirer of Theodore Roosevelt, in 1912 he resigned his newly won post of Republican national committeeman for Kansas to become national committeeman and member of the executive committee of Roosevelt's Progressive party. He remained with the Progressives until 1916.

In 1917 White served as a member of a Red Cross mission to Europe. He was also a delegate to the 1919 Prinkipo Conference. In 1923 he won a Pulitzer Prize for his July 23 Emporia *Gazette* editorial on freedom of expression, "To an Anxious Friend." Although he ran unsuccessfully for governor of Kansas on an anti-Klan plank, his campaign helped to discredit the Klan both in Kansas and throughout the nation. White served as a member of the Hoover Commission in Haiti (1930). He founded and chaired the Committee to Defend America by Aiding the Allies (1940). His posthumously published *Autobiography* (1946) was a best-seller.

White had a gregarious temperament and a boundless enthusiasm for the causes and persons dear to him. He was also a hardheaded businessman, a skilled politician, and an intelligent journalist, if not a first-rate intellect. From the early years of the 20th century, he was increasingly regarded as the most articulate representative of midwestern small-town values. The *Gazette,* together with the articles and books which he wrote, provided the vehicles for this role; his prodigious output and the positions he took gave him his influence. His writings mirrored many of the ideals of his readers: the sanctity of the school and the church as pillars of democracy; the commitment to the virtues of the small community in contrast to the impersonality of the city; the need for personal rectitude in public life; the necessity to make politics conform to the norms of fair play and civic righteousness. Normally a loyal Republican, he supported the Progressive party in 1912 partly because he believed that Roosevelt represented the righteous fervor of the nation.

What changed the laissez-faire, anti-Populist conservative of 1896 into an ideological Progressive? Roosevelt's role was certainly crucial. When they met in 1897, Roosevelt, then assistant secretary of the navy, had a charismatic effect on the young editor. But certain factors in White's background probably made him susceptible to Roosevelt's influence. White's father was a freethinker and a moralist, his mother, a zealous if unorthodox Protestant. Both parents were ardent crusaders for prohibition and woman's rights in a state whose moral militancy dated from the Kansas-Nebraska Act and the Civil War. Moreover, White entered a profession which in Kansas was as fervidly moralistic as the state. Kansas journalism was typically evangelical and crusading. Until he met Roosevelt, White's moral indignation was reserved for the Populists, whom he regarded from his solid position in the middle class as failures and crackpots. As the power of Populism waned, Roosevelt converted him to the idea that the enemy of right was privileged "interests." Thus White's family and occupational background made him receptive to the idealism which he thought Roosevelt embodied.

White's brand of Progressivism combined such democratic aspects as support for the initiative and referendum, and workmen's compensation, with a strong streak of elitism. Direct democracy was imperative if the people were to elect the best men, who, aided by a corps of experts, would establish a government with strong regulatory powers. Such a mixture of elitist and democratic sentiments was not uncommon among Progressives. Neither was his dislike of class conflict and his unwillingness to support the political power of labor as an organized group. Here White represented the reliance on middle-class leadership so typical of the Progressive reformer. White also shared the middle-class faith in an enlightened and altruistic public opinion as the major agent of social reform. His optimism, his faith in the powers of political education, and his belief in a God-ordained progress were typical of many of his generation.

After Roosevelt's failure to win the election of 1912, White returned to the Republican fold, but he continued to hope for the emergence of a Progressive leader within the party. During the 1920s he was often critical of Republican conservatism. But like many Progressives who lived to see the depression, White did not approve of the New Deal. He disliked its support for special-interest groups and distrusted its collectivist tendencies. White's position on the New Deal high-lights the ideology and also the limitations of much of Progressive reform. See Walter Johnson, *William Allen White's America* (1947).

JEAN B. QUANDT

WHITEFIELD, George (b. Gloucester, Eng., Dec. 16, 1714; d. Newburyport, Mass., Sept. 30, 1770), RELIGIOUS LEADER, graduated from Oxford University and was admitted to deacon's orders in 1736. While at Oxford he became associated with John and Charles Wesley, leaders of the "Methodist movement," which attacked religious rationalism, formalism, and skepticism. While the Wesleys were in Georgia, he assumed the leadership of the movement. He was ordained as a priest in 1739, but the English clergy refused to let him preach in their churches, thus forcing him to become an itinerant, open-air preacher. In 1739 he came to America (which he had visited briefly the previous year).

Whitefield's American sermons—extemporaneous, simple, but highly emotional—helped produce the "Great Awakening," a major religious revival. He returned to England in 1741 and became the leader of the "Calvinistic Methodist movement." Between 1744 and 1770 he made five additional trips to America.

———❧———

Whitefield's part in the American religious revival of the early 1740s was as a catalyst for a number of scattered currents. Spiritually, he was able to combine an indigenous American thrust for religious revival (associated principally with **Jonathan Edwards** in New England and Gilbert Tennent in the middle colonies) with a broader international upsurge of pietistic concern for an intense personal relationship with God (represented in England by the Wesleys and William Law). Practically, he exploited and perfected a number of new devices for bringing religion to large numbers of people and making it personally meaningful, including itinerancy, the open-air mass meeting, and advance publicity. The Great Awakening was colonial America's first popular or mass movement, and George

Whitefield was its high priest. He is perhaps best understood if seen as a pop cult figure, an 18th-century forerunner of **Elvis Presley** or John Lennon.

The success of Whitefield in his famous American preaching tour of 1739–41 was greatest in the cities, where he was able to use communications facilities and the presence of a potential mass audience to its utmost advantage. His personal appearances were heavily promoted; he had his own publicity man placing stories in local newspapers and seeing that Whitefield's writings—especially his *Journals* of previous successes—were locally published. Criticism and opposition were grist for his mill, since they roused people's curiosity. When Whitefield arrived, what the crowd discovered was a practiced performer. In his youth he had been drawn to the stage, as a preacher he merely shifted from the theater to the church. Some of his most avid fans were themselves performers, such as the Shakespearean actor David Garrick, who once said that he would give one hundred guineas to be able to exclaim "O" as effectively as the preacher. Even the most hostile critic was impressed with Whitefield's abilities to hold a crowd with his presence and delivery.

Never much of a theologian, Whitefield avoided doctrinal complexities. He stressed the need for the "new birth," a crisis conversion experience such as that he himself had experienced. Although nominally an Anglican—Whitefield never broke with the Church of England—his appeal was ecumenical. He left the colonies in 1741 at the height of his success, but at the time of his second American tour in 1745 he came under fierce attack from opponents of revivalism.

The evangelist had little private life. A marriage in 1741 to a Welsh widow was apparently not very happy. One of Whitefield's few close friendships—with John Wesley—ended when the two men split over ecclesiastical and doctrinal issues. Whitefield always remained a public figure; he lived in the constant glare of publicity. See Luke Tyerman, *The Life of the Rev. George Whitefield* (2 vols., 1877).

J. M. BUMSTED

WHITEHEAD, Alfred North (b. Ramsgate, Eng., Feb. 15, 1861; d. Cambridge, Mass., Dec. 30, 1947), MATHEMATICIAN, PHILOSOPHER, graduated from Cambridge University in 1884. Appointed lecturer in mathematics in 1885 at Trinity College, Cambridge, he taught there until 1910. He was awarded the DSc by Cambridge in 1905. He published his first book on mathematics and philosophy, *A Treatise on Universal Algebra*, in 1898, and the three-volume *Principia Mathematica*, which he wrote with Bertrand Russell, was published 1910–13. This work showed that the principle of mathematical induction is analytic in the sense that it reduces problem solving to a principle of pure logic by suitable definitions of the terms involved. In 1911 Whitehead became lecturer of applied mathematics and mechanics and a reader in geometry at University College, London, and in 1914 was named professor of applied mathematics at the Imperial College of Science and Technology, University of London. He served as Tarner lecturer at Trinity College, Cambridge, in 1919. While teaching at the Imperial College he wrote *Concept of Nature* (1920) and *Principle of Relativity* (1922).

In 1924 Whitehead left England to become professor of philosophy at Harvard University. He retired in 1937, and in 1945 received the British Order of Merit award. Whitehead's basic contribution to modern thought is his philosophy of "organism," which was concerned, in his words, "with the becoming, the being, and the relatedness of actual entities." He stated these ideas most fully in his *Process and Reality* (1929). Other important publications of this period are *Science and the Modern World* (1925), *Religion in the Making* (1926), *Symbolism: Its Meaning and Effect* (1927), *The Aims of Education and Other Essays* (1929), and *Adventures of Ideas* (1933).

Whitehead was both a mathematician and a philosopher throughout his career, which began with a series of philosophical works on mathematics and culminated in a metaphysics based upon the conceptual innovations of mathematical physics. He characterized philosophy as "an attempt to express the infinity of the universe in terms of the limitations of language." He brought to that task a profound sense of the history and culture of England, absorbed from the country-side of his childhood home, of his school in Dorsetshire, and of Cambridge. That sense was strengthened and disciplined by his studies in the classics and mathematics. But his traditional side was balanced by an equally strong sense of the present, developed during the period of his direct involvement in the stir of educational inno-vation at the University of London, where urban, technological, and industrial problems were uppermost, in contrast to the more bucolic and theoretical atmosphere of his earlier years.

Whitehead's views on education were as broad as his experience, and he stressed in his writings and his practice the need to break down the barriers between disciplines, to avoid nar-rowness of perspective, and to transmit disci-pline and culture, encompassing both the preci-sion of science and mathematics and the vision of art and philosophy. He continued to spread those educational views when he went to Harvard, where students and colleagues found him a com-manding and inspiring presence in the life of the university. His inquiries into the nature of reality during this period were far over the heads of most of the students there, but his conversations, his informal conferences, and the open houses he and Mrs. Whitehead regularly held provided rich intellectual fare for all who came to him.

A man of great personal kindness and charm, as well as brilliance, Whitehead has left his spe-cial imprint on the theoretic developments in log-ical and mathematical theory of this century, on the theory and practice of education at London and at Harvard, and on both current and future thought in the realm of scientific metaphysics. The extreme terminological and philosophical difficulty of *Process and Reality* make it a formida-ble challenge to scientists and philosophers alike, but the diverse and far-reaching influence of that work already is enough to assure its continuing major significance.

Whitehead asserts that the historical evolution of every school of philosophy requires two stages, the first an analysis that sticks close to experience but is not consistent, the second a reduction of the discoveries of the first stage to a thoroughgoing consistency. He considered his philosophy to be in the first stage, by which he meant that, despite the intricacy of the structure of his thought, his principal interest was in remaining true to the facts rather than in achieving an elegant mathe-matical coherence. His erudition equaled that of any man of his time, yet that erudition remained rooted in the actualities of an industrial world. Whitehead fully realized the validity of the prac-tical emphasis of the pragmatists of his day, but he saw too the necessity to reach beyond the prac-tical in order to understand the universe within which we act. See Paul A. Schilpp, ed., *The Philosophy of Alfred North Whitehead* (1951).

DARNELL RUCKER

WHITMAN, Walt (b. Huntington, L.I., N.Y., March 31, 1819; d. Camden, N.J., March 26, 1892), POET, JOURNALIST, grew up in Brooklyn and left school at thirteen to become a printer's devil. During 1833–41 he taught school intermittently and held a succession of newspaper jobs in the metropolitan area. In 1841–48 he was associated with at least ten newspapers and periodicals, including the Brooklyn *Eagle* and the *Democratic Review,* a literary magazine. In 1842 he published *Franklin Evans,* a temperance novel. Whitman was named editor of the Brooklyn *Eagle* in 1846. An ardent Democrat, he spoke out on the issues of the day. The owner of the paper dismissed him (1848) after Whitman denounced the Democratic party for failing to take a stand against the estab-lishment of slavery in the territories. He then worked briefly for the New Orleans *Crescent.* Returning to New York, he wrote for the *Freemen* (1848–49), an antislavery newspaper. Thereafter he worked in a bookstore, a printing office, and a carpenter's shop.

In 1855 Whitman published (at his own expense) the first of nine editions (1855–92) of *Leaves of Grass,* which showed the influence of **Ralph Waldo Emerson** ("I was simmering, sim-mering, simmering, Emerson brought me to a boil") and of the transcendental belief that man's capacities were virtually unlimited and that nature was the essence of divinity (Whitman believed that one could gain insights into the universe by studying a blade of grass). The first edition consisted of a prose preface and twelve untitled poems. Employing free verse and a colloquial vocabulary, Whitman sought to present himself as the bard of the people. This is most evident in his long poem "Song of Myself" (so titled in the 1881 edition), in which he asserts that he is typical of all mankind. He believed that poetry should be a spontaneous experience. However, his use of foreign phrases (often incorrectly), coinages (intentional misspellings of words), slang and vulgar language, and explicit sexual references led to much criticism. In later editions Whitman continued to praise the entire panorama of American life. He also added many poems that were considered indecent. The third edition of *Leaves of Grass* (1860), for example, included "Children of Adam," which dealt with procreation.

Whitman edited the Brooklyn *Times* (1857–59) and contributed to the Brooklyn *Standard* and New York *Leader*. In December 1862, after receiving word that his brother had been wounded in Virginia, Whitman went to Washington, where he served as a volunteer nurse for the Union army. Following the Civil War he remained in Washington, working for the Department of the Interior. In 1865 he published *Drum Taps*, a collection of poems dealing with the war. After President Lincoln was assassinated in 1865, Whitman wrote "When Lilacs Last in the Dooryard Bloom'd," a classical ode.

When Whitman's superiors in the Department of the Interior learned that he was the author of *Leaves of Grass* (a work they considered "indecent"), he was dismissed. But his friends found him a job in the attorney general's office. Distressed by the materialism of the Gilded Age, Whitman criticized American greed in "Democratic Vistas" (1871). In 1873 he suffered a paralytic stroke and left Washington, settling in Camden, New Jersey. Some of his other works include *Passage to India* (1871), *Specimen Days and Collect* (1882–83), and *Good-bye, My Fancy* (1891).

When Emerson received Whitman's *Leaves of Grass* upon its publication in 1855, though he rubbed his eyes in astonishment, he was not blind. Here at last, he was sure, was the poet and the poetry he had prophesied for America. "I greet you at the beginning of a great career," he immediately wrote the author, "which yet must have had a long foreground somewhere for such a start." Whitman had, of course, had a start. He had worked and read and traveled. And like so many of the great American writers from **Benjamin Franklin** to **Mark Twain** to **Ernest Hemingway,** his apprenticeship as a writer had been served not in the academy but in the exacting discipline of newspaper work.

Yet reading his early work in no way prepares us for the miracle of *Leaves of Grass*. For Whitman's whole aim was to free *himself* and his nation into a democratic form of poetry. In his very first poem he epically announced and pursued his intention to sing *himself* at all cost. What lifted Whitman's radically democratic aim above rhetorical vaunt was his miraculous discovery of a form equal to his vision. Thus, when he declared himself to be the same as all men, he did it in an unrhymed, irregular line which freed him from the traditional hierarchies of meter and rhyme. And when he asserted a radical unity between particular and universal, between art and life, between nature and man, he sought a form which would deny the distinction between poet and reader. Seizing upon the cardinal fact that in the pronominal system of modern English there is no distinction between second person singular and plural, Whitman addressed each reader—and simultaneously all readers—as *you*. And he went even further, proclaiming that by virtue of the created poem the poet would enter into and become its readers—one and all, present and future. Thus, "Song of Myself" (the poem which, then untitled, had opened the first edition of *Leaves of Grass*) when truly read would be both Whitman's song and ours. Here was poetry which truly might be scripture, and it is not surprising that, of all the traditional forms with which Whitman's poetry has been compared in an effort to seek its sources, the poetry of the Bible yields the most compelling resemblances. For Whitman carried the romantic and democratic impulses of 19th-century America to their extremities and in his own way elected himself a Democratic God.

His aim, however, was never to exalt himself at the expense of his subjects (though many a reader has rejected him on just that score). Instead, he sought to equalize body and soul, thought and act, art and nature, poet and reader, through nothing less than the word of his poetry. Such a vision presupposed a great deal of programmatic bombast, of which Whitman had an ample supply, but it also exacted fearful responsibilities. It required Whitman to be at once masculine and feminine, particular and abstract, intimate and public (how else could he speak to both singular and plural you?), secret and open, elusive and direct. To encompass these polarities, Whitman had to envision love with an intensity and pervasiveness which no poetry before him had risked or imagined. How else was he to reach and embrace all those readers without abandoning himself to the most radical exposure of his own person? And how was he to democratize the body without giving every part equal voice—the loins as well as the brain? There was not only love; there was death. For how could Whitman reach his future readers but by dying into them? If he was to be the poet of love and union, he must also be the poet of death and resurrection. Then, too, there was change, growth, for how could Whitman claim that he was his book and that his book itself was nature without literally embodying a principle of organic growth? He accomplished this by holding to his original title, *Leaves of Grass*, and releasing ever new editions (in 1856, 1860, 1867, 1871, 1876, 1881, 1888, and at last, in 1891–92, a "deathbed edition") in which he revised and reordered old poems even as he added and interpolated new ones.

Finally there was time. How could Whitman secure the future without being equal to the present? He was equal to it, proving that his prophetic poetry of 1855 had prepared him to meet the crisis of Civil War as no other writer of his time could imagine meeting it. For Whitman—true poet of love, union, and death— was fully armed to face the inner division of his country. He not only participated in the conflict as a male nurse ministering to the sick and wounded; he loved both northern and southern soldiers with a passionate tenderness which confirmed for some of his contemporaries, as it has confirmed for many later students of Whitman, his homosexuality. If he was a homosexual, and he may have been, he was nonetheless first of all a writer, even to the point of writing letters home for his dear wounded soldiers; and he emerged from the conflict with an elegy for Lincoln's death—"When Lilacs Last in the Dooryard Bloom'd"—equaling the great elegies of world literature. In a certain way it was his own elegy, a fulfillment of his epic promise of 1855. Though he wrote more poems, his poetic energy had largely spent itself.

There remained for him prose, and in "Democratic Vistas" he translated his poetic vision into a curiously tense but expansive prose. Giving voice to his awareness of the utter crassness and vulgarity of American materialism in that remarkable essay, he called for the divine democratic poet who, necessarily transcending the mere imported culture of the past, would give expression to the unborn conscience of democracy. In *Specimen Days*, he sounded a new music—by turns eloquent, acutely critical, reminiscent, and wistful. Made up largely of his notebook jottings during the Civil War, *Specimen Days* remains to this day a magnificent record of Whitman's response to his time—a heartbreaking recognition of the heroism, the sacrifice, the cruelty, and the beauty of war.

When Whitman died in 1892, he had indeed been equal to his time, his century, and his country. More than any poet who has followed him, he was himself the poet he called for in "Democratic Vistas"—the poet who *embodied* the spirit of democracy. See G. W. Allen, *The Solitary Singer* (1955).

JAMES M. COX

WHITNEY, Eli (b. Westboro, Mass., Dec. 8, 1765; d. New Haven, Conn., Jan. 8, 1825), INVENTOR, MANUFACTURER, assisted his father in the operation of a manufacturing shop, where he installed a forge to produce nails during the Revolution. When the resumption of normal trade lowered the price of nails after 1783, he converted this enterprise to the production of hat pins and other items. In 1789 he entered Yale College, graduating in 1793. He then accepted a position as a private tutor in South Carolina. Traveling first to Georgia, he visited a friend, Phineas Miller, who managed the Mulberry Grove plantation of Catherine Greene, widow of General **Nathanael Greene.** There he became interested in designing a device to remove the seeds from cotton. With financial support from Miller, he quickly developed a workable cotton gin, and he and Miller formed a partnership to manufacture his invention. Although he secured a patent in 1794, numerous other entrepreneurs began to copy his machines, and many planters constructed their own gins. His patent was validated by a court decision in 1807, but by then gin manufacturing had become widely dispersed, and Congress refused to renew his patent after it expired in 1812. Thus the cotton gin transformed cotton planting into a profitable enterprise, but Whitney himself failed to reap financial rewards from his invention.

In 1798 Whitney obtained a contract to manufacture ten thousand muskets for the federal government. Purchasing a mill near New Haven (later Whitneysville), he installed an "interchangeable-part" system of manufacturing firearms. Although Simeon North and other entrepreneurs independently introduced "uniformity" systems, Whitney played the leading role in popularizing mass-production methods through his energetic promotional efforts. He obtained additional contracts to produce fifteen thousand guns for the federal and New York State governments during the War of 1812, and eventually established himself as a modestly prosperous manufacturer.

———— ✿ ————

The impress of Whitney, perhaps more than that of any other man, lies across the economic life of the 19th century. Both of his inventions were destined not only deeply to affect American life but also to exert a world impact as well. The gin made possible the rise of the Cotton Kingdom in the American South, gave the declining institution of slavery a new lease on life, and provided the great bulk of the raw material for the new textile machinery that was paving the way for Great Britain's rise to technological and industrial leadership. The technique of manufacturing by means of standardized interchangeable parts, together with **Oliver Evans**'s invention of the system of continuous process manufacturing, lies at the basis of modern methods of mass production. Ironically, Whitney may be said to have enabled the South to rise to a position of power and helped furnish the sinews of its defeat.

Before the final decades of the 18th century, cotton had been cultivated on a small scale in the United States. First to respond to the increased British demand that flowed in the wake of the textile inventions by Kay, Arkwright, Hargreaves, Crompton, and others was a type known as "Sea Island," and by 1805 exports amounted to nearly 9 million pounds. Climatic requirements, however, confined the culture of Sea Island cotton to within a strip thirty or forty miles wide along the coast of South Carolina and Georgia, and in consequence exports never amounted to as much as 16 million pounds in any year prior to 1860. In contrast, "Uplands" cotton would grow anywhere in the South and could be cultivated on a large scale once Whitney's gin abridged the labor cost of separating the sticky short fibers from the green seeds.

The production of short staple cotton moved first into the backcountry of Georgia and soon covered the upland parts of that state and South Carolina. For more than a quarter of a century this was the principal cotton-producing region of the nation. From its original center the cotton belt moved north into North Carolina and Virginia and west over the mountains into Tennessee. Following the War of 1812 the decisive movement was to the Southwest, with the tide of cultivation flowing first into Alabama, Mississippi, and Louisiana, and eventually into Arkansas and Texas. Expressed in terms of changing proportions, the states and territories from Alabama and Tennessee westward increased their share of the nation's total output of cotton from one-sixteenth in 1811 to one-third in 1820, one-half before 1830, nearly two-thirds in 1840, and three-fourths in 1860. It was this decisively westward movement that convinced southern leaders on the eve of the Civil War that slavery must be free to move into the territories if their system was to survive.

Meanwhile cotton exports rose from a mere 2 million pounds in 1794 to 1768 million pounds in 1860, with three-fourths of it going to Great Britain. By then that nation was almost entirely dependent upon the American South for its cotton supply. The economic growth of the United States also owed much to cotton. For the period 1815–60 as a whole cotton alone constituted more than half the total value of domestic exports. These exports provided a main means of paying for imports not only of consumption goods but also of such capital goods as railroad iron and, in addition, of capital funds invested in growing American enterprises.

Whitney's other invention encountered difficult problems at first. As late as the 1840s interchangeability of parts was limited to sets of ten guns at his armory in New Haven. And even this much precision required much hand filing. Gradually milling machines and other machine tools made it possible to achieve true standardization and interchangeability. Until about mid-century, arms production dominated manufacturing by interchangeable parts. After 1850 small steam engines, watches, sewing machines, and machine tools themselves were made with interchangeable parts, with locomotives added around 1860. Manufacture by interchangeable parts was a prior condition for the commercial success of sewing machines, harvesters, typewriters, and a whole series of motors. By mid-century the method had received international recognition as the "American System," and in 1855 even the British government ordered a complete set of machine tools from the United States for the con-

struction of a gun factory near London. By 1880 the compiler of the tenth census could comment, "The general growth of the 'interchangeable system' in manufacturing ... has had an influence in the development of manufacturing, agriculture, and other industries which but few have heretofore appreciated. It may not be too much to say that, in some respects, this system has been one of the chief influences in the rapid increase in national wealth." In sum, it may be said that it is given to few men to cast so long a shadow as Eli Whitney. See Allan Nevins and Jeanette Mirsky, *The World of Eli Whitney* (1952).

STUART BRUCHEY

WHITNEY, William Collins (b. Conway, Mass., July 5, 1841; d. New York, N.Y., Feb. 2, 1904), FINANCIER, POLITICAL LEADER, graduated from Yale (BA, 1863) and the Harvard Law School (1864). After working in the law office of Abraham R. Lawrence he was admitted to the New York bar (1865). In 1871 he helped organize the Young Men's Democratic Club, and the following year he became inspector of schools for New York City. An early opponent of Tammany Hall, Whitney helped organize the County Democracy and, as corporation counsel for New York City, successfully litigated suits that grew out of the **Tweed** Ring's corruption.

In 1884 he joined Thomas Fortune Ryan, W. L. Elkins, P. A. B. Widener, and Anthony Brady to form a syndicate that won control of the New York Metropolitan Traction Co., remaining involved in street railway affairs until the Metropolitan's reorganization in 1902. In 1898 he and Ryan organized the American Tobacco Co., which by 1901 had gained control of 80 percent of the American market.

As a political leader Whitney served as secretary of the navy in Grover Cleveland's first cabinet (1885) and supervised the modernization of the navy. One of Cleveland's closest advisers, he played a major role in Cleveland's nomination and election in 1892, but declined an offer of a cabinet post in the new administration.

A devoted sportsman, Whitney began a racing

stable (1898), was president of the Saratoga Association and charter member of the Jockey Club (1894), and published *The Whitney Stud* (1902).

≈≈≈

The career of William Collins Whitney was unusual and variegated. A complex man, he lived at the heart of a fascinating era. He mirrored most of the strengths of this time and few of its faults—he thus proved to be among the most personally attractive of the late 19th-century capitalistic entrepreneurs.

By combining great ability, boundless energy, charm, and unusual executive skill in planning and managing large and complex projects, Whitney attained leadership in whatever he turned to: the law, politics, public office, business, his racing stable and fine breeding stock, patronage of the arts, and a cultivation and frank gratification of his tastes for the finer things in life. He had a precise, logical mind wedded to the training of a lawyer, he knew exactly what his goals in life were, and he drove relentlessly to reach them.

Consequently, Whitney amassed a tremendous fortune (yet retired in his business prime, at sixty-one, to enjoy his wealth rather than senselessly to continue to earn more). Despite his drive to gain monopoly control through intricate financing, he was no buccaneer—a grand jury exonerated his traction holding company in 1907, after his death, from any corporate or financial wrongdoing—and he probably gave back to the community more than he took. As secretary of the navy in President Cleveland's first cabinet, he overhauled, depoliticized, and revitalized that department, commenced the construction of a modern steel navy, and encouraged American steelmakers to fabricate large-dimensioned products. In the realm of political reform he was one of the founders of the anti-Tammany Apollo Hall and New York County Democracies successively, which were gallant failures; and as one of the astute discoverers of Grover Cleveland, helped to steer him into the executive mansions at Albany and Washington. He managed Cleveland's presidential campaign in 1892 with such consummate artistry as to make it a classic of its kind.

Perhaps his greatest achievement among his many business involvements, even if it ultimately ended in corporate bankruptcy (but not operational failure), was his creation, with associates, of a street railway transit empire throughout Manhattan and the Bronx, offering cheap mass transit that was vital if the city were to grow or even survive. In business and politics, hiding power under velvet, ironhanded on the reins, the eternal strategist, resourceful and nimble-witted but extraordinarily quiet in execution, Whitney could be considered adroit but not sinister, a master of capital but not a predator, and a planner but not a plotter. See Mark D. Hirsch, *William C. Whitney: Modern Warwick* (1969).

MARK D. HIRSCH

WHITTIER, John Greenleaf (b. Haverhill, Mass., Dec. 17, 1807; d. Hampton Falls, N.H., Sept. 7, 1892), POET, had little formal schooling. His first poem, "The Exile's Departure," was published in 1826 in the Newburyport *Free Press,* whose editor was the abolitionist **William Lloyd Garrison.** Encouraged by Garrison, Whittier continued to write poetry, but he turned to journalism in 1829 when Garrison secured for him the editorship of the *American Manufacturer,* which brought him into active participation in the abolitionist movement. He soon became a widely read writer of antislavery material. He edited the *New England Weekly Review* (1830–32), the *Pennsylvania Freeman* (1838–40), and the *Middlesex Standard* (1844–45), and served as corresponding editor of the Washington *National Era* (1847–60). His abolitionist views were reflected in his fiery pamphlet *Justice and Expediency* (1833), and in *Poems Written during the Progress of the Abolition Question in the United States* (1837). He served as secretary of the Anti-Slavery Convention at Philadelphia in 1833 and of the Anti-Slavery Society in 1836. He served a term in the Massachusetts legislature as representative for Haverhill in 1835.

Convinced that the abolitionist cause would be best served by working through regular political channels, Whittier broke with Garrison. He

1220

supported nonabolitionist candidates unfriendly to slavery, including Abraham Lincoln. During these pre–Civil War years, he published eight volumes of poetry and five of prose. Included in this immense output were his *Lays of My Home and Other Poems* (1843), *Leaves from Margaret Smith's Journal* (1849), his only novel, and scores of articles and reviews. As a staunch Quaker, he was committed to nonviolence, which alienated him from more extreme abolitionists. He decried **John Brown**'s raid on Harpers Ferry (1859) as a "dangerous and unjustifiable act," and in his poem "A Word for the Hour" (1861) strongly advocated allowing southern secession rather than resorting to war. After the war, he endorsed Lincoln's offer of a generous peace and deplored the imposition of harsh or revengeful Reconstruction policies upon the southern states.

Whittier is best remembered as a nostalgic poet of serene rural New England. His reputation rests primarily upon a few widely known pastoral poems, particularly "The Barefoot Boy" (1855) and "Snow-Bound" (1866). He infused much of his poetry with eloquent expressions of his deep religious fervor and his dedication to justice and tolerance, and many of his poems are still sung as church hymns by Christian denominations. Among his works are *Legends of New England in Prose and Verse* (1833), *Old Portraits and Modern Sketches* (1850), and *The Pennsylvania Pilgrim and Other Poems* (1872).

Whittier is not usually considered a great poet, or even consistently a good poet, but he was a good man, honest in recognizing his limitations. "I am not a builder," he said, "in the sense of Milton's phrase of one who 'builds a lofty rhyme.' My verses have been of the humbler sort—merely the farm wagons or buckboards of verse." Much that he wrote was household verse, moralistic or sentimental in nostalgia or incitement to better living. His aim was for simplicity: "To paint forgetful of the rules of art, / With pencil dipped alone in colors of the heart." True beauty to him was "the beauty of holiness, of purity, of the inward grace which passeth show."

Most of his early verse rambled discursively, in borrowed phrase and conventional moods guaranteed to attract newspaper audiences. As a journeyman propagandist his verses excoriating slavery are an important part of the history of his time. They may be found important also in Whittier's development as a poet. For using words as weapons, he learned control and concentration, forced by the requirements of debate to relate poetry to reality. "Ichabod," devastating in invective, derives from this period, as does the forthright "Massachusetts to Virginia." But most of Whittier's better poems were written after he had withdrawn from partisan journalism. Among them are the vernacular ballad of "Skipper Ireson's Ride," the New England idyll "Snow-Bound," and "Telling the Bees," a minor masterwork anticipating the rural vignettes of **Robert Frost** and **Edwin Arlington Robinson.** See Lewis Leary, *John Greenleaf Whittier* (1961).

LEWIS LEARY

WIENER, Norbert (b. Columbia, Mo., Nov. 26, 1894; d. Stockholm, Sweden, March 18, 1964), MATHEMATICIAN, the son of a Harvard professor of Slavic languages, graduated from Tufts College in 1909 (AB). He then continued his studies at Harvard (1909, 1911–13 [1910–11 at Cornell]), where he was awarded an MA in 1912 and a PhD and the Bowdoin prize in 1913 for a dissertation in mathematic logic. During 1913–15, Wiener did postgraduate work at Cambridge University, where he studied under Bertrand Russell and G. H. Hardy, at Göttingen University, Germany, and at Columbia University. He was appointed lecturer in mathematics at Harvard (1915–16), and was then instructor of mathematics at the University of Maine (1916–17). In 1917–19 he wrote articles as a staff member of the *Encyclopedia Americana* and worked on the Boston *Herald* and as a civilian computer at the Government Proving Ground at Aberdeen, Maryland.

In 1919 Wiener resumed his teaching career, serving as instructor (1919–24), assistant professor (1924–28), associate professor (1918–32), and finally professor (1932–60) of mathematics at Massachusetts Institute of Technology.

During World War II, Wiener did government research on guided missiles and radar systems. In this work, he became aware of similarities between the operations of complex computers and those of the human nervous system. In 1947 his book *Cybernetics, or Control and Communication in the Animal and the Machine,* based upon these observations, was published in France and a year later in the U.S. Although this was his most famous work, Wiener also published extensively in such diverse topics as probability theory, mathematical logic, and relativity. His last book, *God and Golem, Inc.* (1964), published posthumously, won a National Book Award for science, philosophy, and religion. He also wrote two autobiographical works, *Ex-Prodigy* (1953), and *I Am a Mathematician* (1956).

A child prodigy who knew the alphabet at eighteen months, was ordered by his doctor to give up reading for a half-year to rest his myopic eyes at age eight, and entered college literally wearing knee pants at age eleven, Norbert Wiener, nonetheless, counted with his fingers long after other children, was so physically clumsy in the laboratory that he had to give up graduate study in biology, and developed only indifferent skill at bridge and chess. In his later years, those of his world fame, his short, round figure with his gray hair, mustache, spade beard, cigar, and horn-rimmed glasses gave the misleading appearance of the typical benevolent professor. He was, indeed, absentminded, or preoccupied with questions. Answers sometimes awoke him at three in the morning, and then, frantically, he had to ransack his house for writing materials. His restless mind produced a thousand ideas, but he possessed only limited human energy to pursue them. Wiener, consequently, was at moments irritable, depressed, exhausted, and confused. He had devoted friends, but did not tolerate fools easily. He lacked amiability with strangers, and preferred the company of those who could understand his ideas.

Wiener worked best with small, interdisciplinary science groups, sometimes introducing his thoughts with, "You don't mind my talking science fiction with you, do you?" It was here, within this no man's land between disciplines, that he made his greatest discovery. Wiener was the intellectual catalyst in a mixture of engineering, mathematics, and physiology that produced a new science, and his report on the subject, *Cybernetics,* is one of the great books of the 20th century. Outlining the principle of feedback as the significant dynamic element in purposeful machines and animals, his insight sparked through the intellectual community, setting off conferences, debates, papers, and new subdisciplines.

Since Wiener foresaw cybernetics as a second industrial revolution that would replace man's brain, just as the first had replaced his muscles, popular reporters glimpsed a Frankenstein specter, the "thinking machine" that would make mankind obsolete. Perhaps because of his training in philosophy, or his Unitarian religion, the "father of cybernetics" worried about this possibility, as is apparent in his later publications. He had, ironically, no definite solution for the problem, and at his death left only the legacy that if the machines take over, then it is man's own fault, and that man should be valued not on the basis of what he can do, but, simply, because he is human. See Gordon E. Olson and J. P. Schade, "A Tribute to Norbert Wiener," *Cybernetics of the Nervous System,* ed. by Norbert Wiener and J. P. Schade, XVII (1965), 1–8.

DAVID McCOMB

WILDER, Thornton Niven (b. Madison, Wisc., April 17, 1897; d. Hamden, Conn., Dec. 7, 1975), WRITER, attended Oberlin College (1915–17) and served in the coast guard during World War I. He received his BA from Yale in 1920, studied at the American Academy in Rome (1920–21), and obtained an MA from Princeton in 1926. From 1921 to 1928 he taught French at the Lawrenceville School, in New Jersey. His first popular success as a writer came with the novel, *The Bridge of San Luis Rey* (1927), which won a

Pulitzer Prize. He taught literature at the University of Chicago from 1930 to 1936, also publishing a number of books. His play *Our Town* (1938) was both a critical and popular success and brought him another Pulitzer Prize.

In 1941 Wilder traveled to South America on an educational mission for the State Department. In 1942 another play, *The Skin of Our Teeth* won him his third Pulitzer. During World War II he was an intelligence officer in the U.S. Air Corps. Among his later important works were the novel, *The Ides of March* (1948), the play, *The Matchmaker* (1954), and the musical, *Hello, Dolly!* (1964). His *The Eighth Day* (1967) won a National Book award. Wilder's last, somewhat autobiographic, novel, *Theophilus North*, was published in 1973 to glowing reviews. In 1950–51 he lectured at Harvard on "The American Character in Classic American Literature." He also lectured frequently in Europe, where his works are widely read.

If Thornton Wilder had never written anything except *Our Town* he would still have received the highest respect of the American people. *Our Town* is an inspired allegory of human life—beautiful, merciful, and touching, but also familiar in style and reassuring. "Do any human beings ever realize life while they live it—every, every minute?" one of the chief characters mournfully inquires in the last act. "No," the commentator replies. "The saints and the poets, maybe—they do some." Also Thornton Wilder—he knew the worth of life in 1938—in the middle of the Depression, incidentally.

But he wrote another inspired play in 1942 when World War II was clamoring across the world. *The Skin of Our Teeth*, he called it. Like *Our Town*, which never doubts the worth of life, *The Skin of Our Teeth* reminds us humorously that the world goes on from generation to generation and from crisis to crisis and that the human race steadily acquires more knowledge. "I could go on for seventy years in a cellar and make soup out of grass and bark without ever doubting that the world has work to do and will do it," says the chief female character as she emerges from a war shelter into a world burned and blasted by another war. Wilder was not deliberately optimistic when he wrote these two plays in the middle of anxious periods. His experience, his knowledge, his personal spirit always convinced him that life was creative.

He was a man of modesty and grace who never wrote plays or novels on a routine basis. His first novel, *The Bridge of San Luis Rey* (1927), was—and is—fresh and original. It presides over the destinies of human beings with insight and compassion. A humorous novel, *Heaven's My Destination*, portrayed an exuberant American in the middle of the Depression in 1935. *The Ides of March*, in 1948, *The Eighth Day* in 1967, and *Theophilus North* in 1973 are also original and they are obviously the work of a citizen of faith.

But his dramas are his most significant work, not only because of their belief in people but because of Wilder's impromptu style. He was a sufficiently brilliant intellectual to be able to write simply. *Pullman Car Hiawatha*, *The Happy Journey to Trenton and Camden*, and *The Long Christmas Dinner* (all from 1931 incidentally), show a master craftsman simplifying the form of theater. These brief plays consist of writing and acting and, as in the case of *Our Town*, they make the stories more intimate and affecting. Since he was a believer in life as well as art, comedy was becoming to him. Although the loud and spectacular musical entertainment, *Hello, Dolly!* is twice removed from Wilder's *The Merchant of Yonkers* in 1938, its folksy good humor derives from Wilder's original sources.

He was formidably learned and educated. But he was also civilized. Early in his career he realized that there was nothing more heartening and poignant than, to quote the spokesman for *Our Town*, a simple statement of "the way we were in our growing up and in our marrying and in our doctoring and in our living and in our dying." See Rex Burbank, *Thornton Wilder* (1961).

BROOKS ATKINSON

WILEY, Harvey Washington (b. Kent, Ind., Oct. 18, 1844; d. Washington, D.C., June 30, 1930),

CHEMIST, REFORMER, interrupted his academic career at Hanover College (Hanover, Ind.) to take part in the Civil War as a member of the 137th Indiana Volunteers. Returning to Hanover after being mustered out because of ill health, he completed his studies (BA, 1867; MA, 1870) and taught Greek and Latin at Northwestern Christian University (later Butler College) during 1868–70 while enrolled at Indiana Medical College. He received an MD in 1871. He taught science at an Indianapolis high school (1871), earned a BS from Harvard (1873), and taught chemistry at Butler and at the Medical College of Indiana (1874). He was appointed professor of chemistry at Purdue University as well as chief state chemist of Indiana in 1874. Four years later he went to Germany to study chemistry, physics, pathology, and food adulteration, and in 1879 began investigations at Purdue into food adulteration. His reports to the Indiana Board of Health were among the first of their kind in the United States.

In 1883 Wiley was appointed chief chemist of the U.S. Department of Agriculture. In that post he made important studies of sugarcane and sugar beets, contributed to the development of methods of agricultural chemical analysis, and continued his studies of adulteration, including the testing of food preservatives on his "poison squad" of twelve young men (organized in 1902). More than any other one man, Wiley was responsible for congressional passage of the 1906 Pure Food and Drugs Act. His rigorous efforts to enforce this law involved him in numerous controversies, and President Theodore Roosevelt, who opposed Wiley's campaigns against saccharine and benzoate of soda, successfully curbed his powers over food and drug questions. Wiley resigned from the Department of Agriculture in 1912 amid charges of maladministration which he denied. Thereafter, until his death, he served as director of foods, sanitation, and health for *Good Housekeeping* magazine.

A founder (1884), secretary (1889–1912), and president (1886) of the Association of Official Agricultural Chemists, Wiley was also president of the U.S. Pharmacopoeial Convention (1910–20) and of the American Chemical Society (1893).

During 1899–1914 Wiley was professor of chemistry at George Washington University. His works include: *Principles and Practices of Agricultural Analysis* (3 vols., 1894–97), *Foods and Their Adulteration* (1907), *Health Reader* (1916), *History of a Crime Against the Food Law* (1929), and an *Autobiography* (1930).

⸙

Wiley's historical importance rests on his role as generalissimo of the army-congressmen, responsible food processors, state chemists, physicians, muckraking journalists, women's club members—which won the 1906 law. Massive of stature, with rough-hewn face and penetrating gaze, Wiley had the knack of enlisting tremendous loyalty. An eloquent orator, he possessed both wit and warmth. Long a bachelor, he could move about freely, was an ardent clubman, an eager dinner guest. Reporters liked him, for he made good copy. His correspondence was prodigious. Endowed with great energy, he operated without tiring on many fronts at once. Wiley desired power, needed acclaim.

"What is this great movement for purity of food and drugs?" Wiley asked rhetorically. "Only the application of ethics to digestion and therapeutics." Initially Wiley's sense of righteousness was disturbed only by the dishonesty of adulterators, for he did not believe adulteration posed dangers to health. His "poison squad" experiments persuaded him otherwise. Wiley retained the rural perspective, tended to think nature's ways best, and distrusted the complexity of modern industrialism.

Having won the law, Wiley sought to enforce it to the utmost of its implications. Farmers and food processors thought some of his decisions wrong. Roosevelt, pressed politically, made uneasy by Wiley's extreme stands, turned contested issues over to a blue-ribbon scientific panel which in some cases supported Wiley, in others reversed him. His crusader's temperament could not stand this rebuke. He left office hoping to stir a huge public outcry, but the pure food issue had passed its crest. Wiley did not mellow with age, remaining bitter at his betrayal. His brand of consumerism would in due course rise again. See Oscar E. Anderson, Jr., *The Health of a Nation: Harvey W. Wiley and the Fight for Pure Food* (1958).

JAMES HARVEY YOUNG

WILKINS, Roy (b. St. Louis, Mo., Aug. 30, 1901; d. New York, N.Y., Sept. 8, 1981), REFORMER, was reared by his aunt and uncle in St. Paul, Minnesota, graduated from the University of Minnesota (BA, 1923), where he was night editor of the college newspaper and secretary of the local chapter of the National Association for the Advancement of Colored People. After graduation he worked for the Kansas City (Mo.) *Call,* an African-American weekly, and soon became its managing editor. In 1931 Walter F. White invited Wilkins to become assistant executive secretary of the NAACP. Moving to New York City, he soon became prominent in the civil rights movement and in 1934 succeeded **W. E. B. Du Bois** as editor of the *Crisis,* the official organ of the NAACP, holding that post until 1949.

During World War II Wilkins served as a consultant to the War Department on the training and placement of blacks in the armed forces; he also served as a consultant to the American delegation at the United Nations organization conference in San Francisco (1945). He was acting executive secretary of the NAACP for a year (1949–50) while Walter White was on leave of absence; he then was its administrator for internal affairs (1950–55). Upon White's death in 1955, Wilkins became executive secretary.

Wilkins favored direct action methods of protest and reform. As executive secretary, he worked to implement the 1954 Supreme Court school desegregation decision and also fought for black voting rights. He helped organize the 1963 March on Washington for Jobs and Freedom and was one of its principal speakers. He became executive director of the NAACP in 1964.

⸺◦∞◦⸺

For more than four decades Roy Wilkins worked as an important official in the nation's most effective civil rights organization, the NAACP. He possessed an acute sense of the times in which he lived and of how public opinion could be influenced to facilitate change. Drawing on his background in journalism, Wilkins sought to publicize the essential facts regarding American race relations, in the hope that people of every color could be persuaded to champion the African-American's cause. He believied that the black minority must work with the white majority if progress was to be achieved, and he thought that emphasis on the manner in which the practice of racial discrimination contradicted the egalitarian American creed would galvanize whites into action on behalf of blacks. Much as the muckrakers of the Progressive Era believed that reform could be achieved if men of good will were made aware of the existence of graft and corruption, so Wilkins and the NAACP assumed that Americans would put an end to racial injustice if only they realized the true nature of the prevailing racial oppression.

While emphasizing the need for an interracial coalition of blacks and whites working for equal rights, Wilkins also recognized that the much-discussed managerial revolution has transformed philanthropic organizations as well as business corporations. Joining the NAACP's national office staff during the years of the Great Depression, a time when the Association was split into rival camps revolving around the executive secretary, Walter White, and the editor of the *Crisis,* W. E. B. Du Bois, Wilkins adroitly avoided the infighting. When White finally emerged victorious, Wilkins realized that the Association was dominated by its middle management—though authority formally resided with the board of directors—and he served as White's right-hand man for more than two decades. After becoming executive secretary, he used the powers of this office to repulse those who would have the Association deviate from its goal of equal rights for blacks or its tactic of interracial cooperation.

If there was one thing that Roy Wilkins understood, it was power. But as befit an efficient organization man, he was soft-spoken, meticulously well groomed, and always in control of his emotions. Somewhat shy and aloof, Wilkins had many acquaintances but only a few close friends. An avid worker who generally spent twelve or more hours each day on the affairs of the Association, Wilkins lived quietly and had little time for purely social matters. See Roy Wilkins, *Standing Fast: The Autobiography of Roy Wilkins* (1982), and Martin Arnold, "There Is No Rest for Roy Wilkins," *New York Times Magazine,* Sept. 28, 1969.

RAYMOND WOLTERS

WILKINSON, James (b. Calvert Co., Md., Jan. 1, 1757; d. Mexico City, Mex., Dec. 28, 1825), SOLDIER, in 1775, while a medical student in Philadelphia, joined Thompson's Pennsylvania Rifle Battalion. Later he served on the staffs of **Benedict Arnold** and **Nathanael Greene.** After he was appointed aide to Horatio Gates, he became a lieutenant colonel and then deputy adjutant general of Gates's Northern Department. At the age of twenty he was brevetted brigadier general for his service in the Saratoga campaign. Through Gates he became involved to an extent that is not clear in the movement to unseat Washington known as the Conway Cabal. This made him unpopular with many officers, and after he quarreled with Gates as well, he felt obliged to resign his commission. His departure was followed by a tour as clothier general of the army (1779–81). He took up farming in Bucks County, Pennsylvania, and in 1783 was elected to the state assembly. A year later he moved to Kentucky Territory and was soon intriguing for power by exploiting western discontent over proposed American concessions to the Spanish. Meanwhile he obtained a monopoly of American trade through New Orleans by telling the Spanish governor that he was working for secession of the western territories.

In 1791 Wilkinson rejoined the army as lieutenant colonel of the 2d Infantry, and soon was a brigadier general again. Except during the quasi-war with France, he was the highest-ranking officer in the army from **Anthony Wayne**'s death in 1796 until 1812. Commanding on the southern frontier from 1798, he resisted Spanish and French efforts to persuade him to desert the U.S.

Appointed military governor of Louisiana in 1803 and territorial governor in 1805, Wilkinson became involved in the controversial plans of **Aaron Burr.** Their talks concerned the future of the Louisiana Territory, although whether they intended to turn it over to the Spanish or use it as a springboard for invasion of Spanish territory has never been made clear and may not have been finally decided by the plotters. Jefferson removed him in 1806, at about the same time that word of Burr's conspiracy began to leak out. Wilkinson was the main government witness in Burr's trial for conspiracy, and narrowly avoided indictment himself when a court of inquiry acquitted Burr in 1809 and again in 1811.

Wilkinson served as major general in the War of 1812, taking possession of the Mobile area of west Florida for the U.S., and participating in the campaign of 1813 against Montreal. His remaining years were spent on his plantation below New Orleans, and in Mexico City, where he received a land grant from the Mexican government in what is now Texas. He died before he could lay claim to it.

Frederick Jackson Turner called James Wilkinson "the most consummate artist in treason that the nation ever possessed." A man described in such superlative terms is bound to attract considerable biographical and historical interest, and for a figure of the second rank, Wilkinson has captured more than his share of attention. The importance of his alleged intrigues and the dangers they posed for the development of the West have often been exaggerated. Some recent writers have essayed Wilkinson's rehabilitation, and they have succeeded at least to the extent that Turner's judgment requires qualifying. Wilkinson was not a traitor but merely a rascal. When he was in Spanish pay, though also the ranking general of the U.S. army, he was apparently serving his country by selling the Spanish information available to any knowledgeable observer and thereby deflating their hopes, since the information suggested the West could not be detached from the United States. When he engaged in intrigues with

British officials in Canada, he served them no better than he had the Spanish. When he consorted with Aaron Burr, his consistent intent was not to betray his country—even if his friend Burr ever had such a design, which is doubtful—but merely to betray Burr, which he accomplished by transmitting inflated accounts of Burr's schemes to President Jefferson. Wilkinson had a large capacity for self-dramatization, which he displayed in advertising the Burr affair and his part in it, and which helps account for the frequent historical notice he receives. He also had the considerable intelligence required to play off a multitude of conflicting interests and acquaintances against one another. He possessed much less capacity in his formal profession as a soldier. Carelessness or preoccupation with his own affairs led to the Terre aux Boeufs military tragedy of 1809, in which perhaps a thousand soldiers died in an unhealthful campground which Wilkinson selected along the Mississippi. He was an abysmal failure in the St. Lawrence River campaign of 1813. See Thomas Robson Hay and M. R. Werner, *The Admirable Trumpeter* (1941).

RUSSELL F. WEIGLEY

WILLARD, Emma Hart (b. Berlin, Conn., Feb. 23, 1787; d. Troy, N.Y., April 15, 1870), EDUCATOR, attended local schools and the Berlin Academy (1802–3). She taught briefly at a school in Westfield, Massachusetts (1807), before serving as the head of the Female Academy in Middlebury, Vermont (1807–9). In 1814 she opened the Middlebury Female Academy, which emphasized math, philosophy, and other scholarly subjects instead of the normal female curriculum of sewing, singing, and painting. Willard petitioned Governor **DeWitt Clinton** of New York for state aid for founding girls' schools and campaigned for her *Plan for Improving Female Education* (1819) before the state legislature in Albany. Upon Clinton's invitation she moved her school to Waterford, New York, in 1819. The school was chartered by the legislature but received no funds. She therefore accepted an offer from residents of Troy, New York, to move

the school there and (1821) founded the Troy Female Seminary, the first women's college-level institution in the U.S. Emphasizing history, philosophy, the sciences, and gymnastics, the seminary soon gained a widespread reputation, particularly for producing women schoolteachers. Willard wrote many textbooks on history and geography and also published a collection of poems, *The Fulfillment of a Promise* (1831). In 1832 she vigorously campaigned and raised money for the establishment of a girls' teacher-training school in Athens, Greece.

Willard retired from the Troy Seminary in 1838 to concentrate her efforts on improving public schools in Connecticut and New York. She made a long tour of the South and West (1845–47), where she campaigned for more women teachers, higher salaries, better buildings, and equal education opportunities for women. In 1854, with Connecticut educator **Henry Barnard,** she represented the United States at the World's Educational Convention in London. Upon her return, Willard settled in Troy, but she continued to take an active interest in education. Some of her many books include *Last Leaves of American History* (1849), *Astronography, or Astronomical Geography* (1854), and *Late American History* (1856).

⁂

Emma Willard focused her gifted intelligence, remarkable self-confidence, and driving ambition for power, prestige, and prosperity on securing for women access to the same education as men received. The sixteenth of seventeen children, Emma experienced success after success: as student (she taught herself subjects usually forbidden to women, such as geometry and philosophy); as teacher (she pioneered the use of maps in teaching history and geography); as school administrator (all her schools prospered; the Troy Seminary became the East's most fashionable girls' school). In 1809 she married a wealthy physician (her one child, a son, was born in 1810) but returned to her educational activities when he suffered financial reverses. Her fame, her means (her texts earned large royalties), and her charm and wit won her entrée to the best society.

Her second marriage (1838) to another physician who sought to seize her possessions, saddle her with his gambling debts, and ruin her reputation, shook her confidence. Humiliated and aging, she became a follower rather than a leader, the "grande dame" of the seminary and of women's education, but something of an anachronism. Always vain, regal in appearance, somewhat domineering, she was nevertheless a brilliant and warm teacher.

Emma Willard thought conventionally and conservatively. She avoided the woman's rights movement; she favored colonization of slaves but opposed abolition, even as late as 1862. She argued that higher education for women would train girls to serve society as teachers (who would work more cheaply than men) and mothers of future citizens rather than to gossip of fashion, novels, and dances. Emotionally, she was far less conservative about a woman's rightful aspirations. Beneath her safe rhetoric lay a deep commitment to education for those like herself—the "master-spirits [among women], who must have pre-eminence, at whatever price they acquire it." Her example and her seminary inspired far greater ambitions among women than any she had been able to voice. See Alma Lutz, *Emma Willard: Daughter of Democracy* (1929).

ROBERT L. CHURCH

WILLARD, Frances Elizabeth Caroline (b. Churchville, N.Y., Sept. 28, 1839; d. New York, N.Y., Feb. 18, 1898), REFORMER, studied at the Milwaukee Female College (1857) but transferred to North-Western Female College (Evanston, Ill.) in 1858, graduating the following year. She taught in a country school near Evanston in 1860, and then at several other schools, including Pittsburgh Female College (1863–64) and Genesee Wesleyan Seminary, Lima, New York (1866–67). After spending two years traveling in Europe (1868–70), she accepted the presidency of the new Evanston College for Ladies. When it merged with Northwestern University in 1873, she became dean of women. Meanwhile, she became increasingly interested in the temperance movement. She left Northwestern in 1874 to become president of the Chicago Woman's Christian Temperance Union.

She became next secretary of the Illinois WCTU, then corresponding secretary of the national WCTU, and national president of the organization in 1879, serving until her death. She allied the WCTU with the woman suffrage movement, fought for woman's rights, and worked for improved industrial conditions for women. She helped reorganize the national Prohibition party in 1882, and in 1883 she toured every state and territory crusading for temperance. She became president of the National Council of Women, an organization for general social reform, in 1888 and president of the World WCTU in 1891. She participated in the 1892 Industrial Conference in St. Louis, Missouri, a forerunner of the Populist party. Willard made an extended lecture tour of England in 1892–93. The author of many articles and pamphlets, her books include *Woman and Temperance* (1883) and *Glimpses of Fifty Years* (1889).

Willard was one of the most perceptive, energetic, and charismatic figures of late 19th-century reform. After her death she was virtually deified by the WCTU, and the state of Illinois placed her statue upon a pedestal in the national capitol's Hall of Statuary. This recognition came despite her failure to bring about the change in American society she desired. She failed to unify her fellow reformers, or even to influence significantly the future course of the WCTU. She traced her own discontent to the stereotyped female role into which she had been forced as a young girl; thus she could empathize with the feelings of deprivation shared by other women and voiced by aggrieved farmers and workers. After exposure to **Edward Bellamy**'s *Looking Backward* (1888) and to labor leaders such as **Terence V. Powderly** of the Knights of Labor, she urged cooperation among all reformers so as to realize Bellamy's socialist vision. Yet her strategies for change remained elitist and manipulative. She believed that "to *reform* one must first one's self *conform*." In her numerous portraits, for example, one can find few hints of her strong sympathies for changes in women's dress.

Willard was responsible for drawing thousands of women out of domestic isolation into the manifold activities of the WCTU, but she allowed them (and herself) to believe that through reform they simply extended woman's domestic sphere. She believed that the dissatisfaction with the present order shared by Populists and Prohibitionists would cause them to overlook differences in strategy and achieve unity. It is thus understandable that reformers rejected her proposals for fusion, and that after her death even the WCTU gradually withdrew from the commitment to broad social change in which she had so earnestly believed. See M. Earhart, *Frances Willard: From Prayers to Politics* (1944).

JACK S. BLOCKER, JR.

WILLIAMS, Roger (b. London, Eng., ca. 1603; d. Providence, R.I., 1683), RELIGIOUS and POLITICAL LEADER, was educated at Cambridge (BA, 1627), and took holy orders in the Church of England (1628). In 1631 he emigrated to Massachusetts Bay. Williams was a "Separatist," believing that the Church of England was beyond redemption. He refused to accept a "call" from the Boston Church unless its members renounced the Church of England. He alienated the Puritan clergy when he asserted that the civil magistrates were not authorized to enforce the religious precepts of the Ten Commandments. When he accepted a call from the Salem church, the civil authorities objected, but in 1633, in defiance of the Massachusetts general court, Salem accepted Williams as minister. However, after he had criticized the Crown by insisting that the king had no right to take the lands of the Native Americans without paying for it, he was banished (1635).

In 1636 Williams founded Providence, Rhode Island, where he put his ideas about the separation of church and state, land policy, and friendly relations with the Native Americans into practice. He soon became skeptical of his own earlier religious beliefs, and became a Baptist (1639). Eventually, he refused to accept any specific reli-

gion, although he still accepted the basic tenets of Christianity.

Williams visited England in 1643 and obtained a charter for the Providence plantation (1644). While in England he wrote his *The Bloudy Tenent of Persecution* (1644), a plea for religious liberty. He returned again to England in 1652, and issued his *The Bloudy Tenent Yet More Bloudy*, a direct reply to John Cotton's *The Bloudy Tenent Washed and Made White* (1647). During 1654–57 Williams was president of the colony of Rhode Island.

During his remaining years Williams was active in town affairs. In 1659 he worked to save the land of the Narragansett tribe, and during King **Philip**'s War (1675–76) he helped command the Providence forces.

To the 19th- and 20th-century American, Williams has most often been considered a prophet of modernism in an otherwise archaic age, an irrepressible democrat and an advocate of religious liberty. To the men of his own time, too, he seemed in many respects not to belong. As his mind evolved from an early acceptance of England's Book of Common Prayer, through Separatism and Baptism, to an ultimate position of denying the efficacy of any formal church, as he denounced the conjunction of church and state in an age when the two were considered irrevocably conjoined, denied the validity of oaths when oaths were the most solemn of undertakings, even condemned prayer offered in company with one not of God's Saints, his contemporaries could only gasp. For **Cotton Mather** he was a windmill gone mad; for Quaker George Fox he was a New England "Fire-Brand," and for still another he was a "meer *Weather Cock*, Constant only in Unconstancy."

Yet Williams was entirely a man of his own century. Deeply religious, he viewed the world in terms of the Bible and its divine cosmography, ultimately coming to the conclusion that his own time was that of "dreadful *Apostacy* and *Desolation*," dominated by Antichrist and given over to the noxious and sinful beasts described in the Book of Revelation. Christ's true church—

that of the Apostles—was in the past; the Saints were merely scattered witnesses against rampant falsity; the time of Christ's new church, when the Saints would be gathered together once again, was not yet come. Williams's innate greatness lay in the intellectual stamina which allowed him to hold such a belief and to proceed to its logical conclusions. He would not affiliate with any given church because, while some "come nearer to the *first primitive Churches*" than others, the time was in reality one "of many *Flocks* pretending to be Christ's" but all falsely. And he must stand for freedom of conscience and separation of church and state not to protect the truth or the true church but to allow error and false churches to play their roles. Christ's church, when its time came, would not need the protection of mere men but would appear despite men. He would even refrain from converting the heathen Native American to Christianity because it was not yet time: "Gods great businesse between Christ Jesus the holy Son of God and Antichrist the man of sin and Sonne of perdition, must ... be first over, and *Zion* and *Jerusalem* be rebuilt and re-established, before the Law and word of life be sent forth to the rest of the Nations of the World." Even his lifestyle reflects his thought. He was an occasional witness against error and for Christ (as he would put it)—in Massachusetts in the early 1630s, during his two sojourns to England, against Quaker beliefs in the 1670s, although, of course, he would tolerate Quakers as he would any false church. For the rest, he eschewed the great things of life and gloried in the humble, proclaiming himself content "*to tug at the* Oar, *to dig with the* Spade, *and* Plow" in the rural backwater of Rhode Island.

Ironically, the hyperreligious tone of Williams's writings—symptomatic of the religious root of his thought—worked against his quick canonization into American mythology. George Chalmers, in 1780, identified Williams with "dark fanaticism"; the first American biographical dictionary in 1790 excluded him; and in 1818 a commemorative speaker in New York argued that Williams's religious naïveté should not obscure his greatness. But from **George** Bancroft's 1834 *History* on, historians, by misrepresenting Williams's religious thought, have imbued him with a secular greatness as "the great apostle of civil and religious freedom." Thus Williams became "an integral element in the meaning of American democracy, along with Jefferson and Lincoln." See Edmund S. Morgan, *Roger Williams: The Church and the State* (1967).

DARRETT B. RUTMAN

WILLIAMS, Tennessee (b. Columbus, Miss., March 26, 1911; d. New York, N.Y., Feb. 25, 1983), PLAYWRIGHT, born Thomas Lanier Williams, entered the University of Missouri in 1931 but was forced to drop out. He then spent two years (1933–35) as a clerk for the International Shoe Co. Following a breakdown and a period of recuperation at the home of his grandparents in Memphis, he attended Washington University in St. Louis (1936–37) and transferred to the University of Iowa, where he graduated in 1938. Several of his early plays were produced by local groups, and in 1939 Williams (who had by now adopted the name Tennessee) was awarded a prize by the Group Theatre for a collection of three one-act plays entitled *American Blues*. The following year saw his first professional production, *Battle of Angels* (later rewritten as *Orpheus Descending*), which had a short Boston run. For the next few years he drifted and took odd jobs. As a screenwriter for MGM in Hollywood, he planned a film synopsis called "The Gentleman Caller" which, after its rejection by the studio, became the basis for his first Broadway triumph, *The Glass Menagerie*, starring Laurette Taylor. This autobiographical play won the Critics' Circle Award in 1945. Elia Kazan's production of Williams's masterpiece, *A Streetcar Named Desire*, two years later won the Critics' Circle Award, the Donaldson Award, and the Pulitzer Prize and firmly established its author as one of the world's foremost living dramatists.

The plays that followed *Streetcar* during the late forties and fifties solidified Williams's reputation. *Summer and Smoke*, confronting the sexually repressed Alma Winemiller with the virile Dr.

John Buchanan, ran for only 102 Broadway performances in 1948 but enjoyed a triumphant revival at Circle-in-the-Square four years later. *The Rose Tattoo,* a vigorous, comic "Dionysian paean" to sexual fulfillment set in a Sicilian colony on the Gulf Coast, opened in 1950. *Camino Real* confused its first New York audiences in 1953 with its imaginative expressionist exploration of a wasted world of cruelty, but was successfully revived in 1960 and 1970. Far more popular was *Cat on a Hot Tin Roof,* yet another chronicle of Williams's decadent South with a gallery of despoilers reminiscent of **Lillian Hellman**'s *The Little Foxes. Cat* won the Critics' Circle Award and another Pulitzer Prize in 1955. Williams's next plays were *Suddenly Last Summer* (1958), a psychoanalytic one-acter whose unusual theme—cannibalism—was greatly sensationalized in the Gore Vidal film version, and *Sweet Bird of Youth* (1959, revised 1961), about the relationship of the gigolo Chance Wayne and an aging actress.

The sixties was a period of personal disorientation for Williams. The success of *The Night of the Iguana* (1961), a haunting mood study of loneliness and futility that again won the Critics' Circle Award, was not shared by the allegorical *The Milk Train Doesn't Stop Here Anymore* (1963), the double bill *Slapstick Tragedy* (1965), the perplexing, Pirandellian *Two Character Play* (1967), presented again in New York as *Outcry* in 1971, the three-character tragicomedy *The Seven Descents of Myrtle* (1968), or *In the Bar of a Tokyo Hotel* (1969), autobiographical in its depiction of a famous dying painter whose plight illustrates a recurring Williams theme: the impossibility of crying out for help to loved ones.

Williams followed this play with *Small Craft Warnings,* staged off-Broadway in 1972, *Our Cry,* a quick failure on Broadway in 1973, *The Red Devil Battery Sign,* which closed in Boston but had a run in London, and *Vieux Carre,* which briefly played on Broadway in 1979. The most popular of Williams's later plays was *A Lovely Sunday at Creve Coeur* (1979). His last Broadway play, *Clothes for a Summer Hotel,* a drama about Scott and Zelda **Fitzgerald,** turned out to be one of his greatest

failures. Despite the cool critical and public reception his latter works received, Williams continued turning out plays virtually until his death. In 1981, *Something Cloudy, Something Clear,* opened Off Off Broadway. And in 1982, *A House Not Meant to Stand,* about the physical and emotional breakdown of an elderly married couple in Mississippi, premiered in Chicago and opened subsequently at the New World Festival of the Arts in Miami. Besides his many plays, Williams also wrote a novel, *The Roman Spring of Mrs. Stone* (1950), numerous screenplays, and collections of poetry and short stories.

"I think of myself as a very peculiar and eccentric person, and I don't see how people can relate at all to the characters I create," said Tennessee Williams in Harry Rasky's unique film documentary about the playwright. "I inhabit my own country—it's where my head is, I guess." As deeply subjective as Williams's country, bounded by "the past, the present, and the perhaps," may be, no American dramatist in this century created characters to whom audiences have related more intensely. One explanation for this was Williams's own profound compassion for his characters, creating a tension between the need to condemn and the desire to pardon, which, far from being the weakness some critics have pointed to, remains his abiding strength. In *A Streetcar Named Desire* his ambivalent attitude toward Blanche, the weak, anachronistic embodiment of the old South, and Stanley, the hedonist with (in Kazan's words) "all the confidence of resurgent flesh," was characteristic. Within Blanche there was "something genuine and tender," insisted the playwright, for Blanche and Stanley were "two sides of every human nature. I am both sides." The bothsidedness prevails in his best as well as his lesser plays, from *The Glass Menagerie* to *The Two Character Play* (*Outcry*). One is led, of course, to think of Chekhov, whom Williams described as "the most moving writer who ever lived." Tennessee Williams's South, like Chekhov's Russia, was imbued with romantic melancholy ("never sadness"), inhabited by "weak, beautiful people," and chronicled with unfailing compassion.

Even more central than Chekhov in Williams's literary parentage was the figure of D. H. Lawrence. "Lawrence felt the mystery and power of sex as the primal life urge," proclaimed Williams in the preface to *I Rise in Flame, Cried the Phoenix* (1941), an early, botched play about Lawrence's death, and Matilda in Williams's *You Touched Me*, adapted in 1942 from Lawrence's short story by that name, became the playwright's first, fumbling embodiment of the Lawrentian theme of the awakening of sexual life. The fragile, delicate Laura in *The Glass Menagerie* fails to awaken. In *The Rose Tattoo* Serafina delle Rose, grieved by her husband's death, rejects life until Alvaro Mangiacavallo, displaying "her husband's body with the head of a clown," fills her with life again. Tom and Rosa in these plays are the sympathetic figures of youth reaching out for fulfillment.

Williams's entire production was a lyrical outcry against "the vacuity of life without struggle," against the nullifiers and rejectors of (sexual) life, against needless cruelty toward living things. Yet his vision was seldom unambiguous. "Deliberate cruelty is not forgiveable," declares Blanche, without realizing that she, like Brick in *Cat on a Hot Tin Roof*, is guilty of the rejection and destruction of another desperate human being. At times, as in *Orpheus Descending, Sweet Bird of Youth,* and *Camino Real*, the vision becomes a still more ominous one of a world of universal cruelty and corruption, into which the innocent wanderer "descends" to be ruthlessly destroyed (Val Xavier is lynched with a blowtorch, Chance Wayne is castrated, Kilroy watches his own autopsy in the brutal, squalid inferno of the Camino Real).

Exciting, sometimes shocking plots and vivid characters are enunciated in the best of Tennessee Williams with exceptional theatrical clarity. Insistent that "a play in a book is only the shadow of a play and not even a clear shadow of it," he wrote with a keen awareness of theatrical values, merging poetic concepts and symbolic devices with a suggestive, selective realism.

Convinced from the outset of "the unimportance of the photographic in art," his poetic imagination sought to transform surface realities into the intensified dramatic expression of a mood. In Williams's greatest plays that transformation seemed magical—and, as he said in the Rasky documentary, "magic is the habit of our existence." See Esther M. Jackson, *The Broken World of Tennessee Williams* (1965).

FREDERICK J. MARKER

WILLIAMS, William Carlos (b. Rutherford, N.J., Sept. 17, 1883; d. Rutherford, N.J., March 4, 1963), WRITER, studied in Switzerland and Paris (1897–99) before receiving a medical degree from the University of Pennsylvania (1906). After studying pediatrics at Leipzig, Germany, he became a family doctor in Rutherford, N.J. (1910). His first book of poems was privately printed in 1909. Among his notable collections of poetry are *Kora in Hell* (1920), *Spring and All* (1923), *A Voyage of Pagany* (1928), *Paterson*, a long poem in three parts (1946, 1948, 1949), and *Pictures from Brueghel* (1962). He also published an innovative collection of essays on American History, *In the American Grain* (1925); three important novels, *White Mule* (1937), *In the Money* (1940), and *The Buildup* (1952); a play *Many Loves* (1959); short fiction, *The Farmer's Daughters: The Collected Stories of William Carlos Williams* (1961); and an autobiography, *The Autobiography of William Carlos Williams* (1951).

———

Williams continued the tradition of free verse pioneered by **Walt Whitman**. But instead of emulating Whitman's long, sweeping lines, Williams excelled in the short line, elegantly compressed and yet seemingly casual, almost offhand. A doctor all his working life, he took his subjects from everyday experience, evoking the view outside a hospital window with an economical sensibility that had no time or words to waste. His lines can seem simple and prosaic until their juxtaposition on the page are carefully studied; then their sound, sense, and rhythm move the eye, the mind, and the heart.

Williams wrote about his doctoring experiences in his short fiction. His story, "The Use of Force," has become a much taught classic. His novels form a trilogy about an immigrant family, the Stechers, and are noteworthy for their treatment of children and women. Williams's greatest contribution, however, is to American poetry. His work encouraged generations of American poets to mine their indigenous, daily experiences, and to develop unique forms that seemed proselike but intensified the poet's ability to make an art out of the mundane. Always an experimentalist and iconoclast, Williams had a broad vision of America, best exemplified in *In the American Grain*, where he identifies with and probes all sides of history, from the outcast **Aaron Burr** to the grand but humiliated Montezuma. A poet of contemporary America as well, his epic poem, *Paterson*, about an industrial city in New Jersey, is notable for its re-energizing of urban verse. See Neil Baldwin, *To All Gentleness: William Carlos Williams the Doctor-Poet* (1984).

CARL ROLLYSON

WILLKIE, Wendell Lewis (b. Elwood, Ind., Feb. 18, 1892; d. New York, N.Y., Oct. 8, 1944), BUSINESS and POLITICAL LEADER, obtained his BA (1913) and LLB (1916) from Indiana University, and joined his father's law firm in 1916. After service in World War I as a lieutenant, he became a partner in an Akron, Ohio, law firm (1919–29). In 1929 he was named attorney for Commonwealth and Southern, a large utility holding company, and became its president in 1933.

Since Commonwealth and Southern controlled four electric power companies in the Tennessee Valley, Willkie came into conflict with the Tennessee Valley Authority, the New Deal agency which distributed cheap electric power in the area in competition with private industry. Willkie favored private purchase and distribution of the power produced by TVA, arguing that direct government competition with business hampered economic recovery by discouraging entrepreneurial initiative and investment. After the Supreme Court upheld the constitutionality of TVA, Willkie sold Commonwealth and Southern's Tennessee Valley holdings to the government (1939). This long controversy won him national prominence and the backing of many Republicans despite his lifelong membership in the Democratic party.

Willkie emerged as a "dark horse" contender for the 1940 Republican presidential nomination. He was nominated by the convention on the sixth ballot, defeating **Thomas E. Dewey** and **Robert A. Taft.** Although the Republican party was dominated by isolationists such as Robert A. Taft and **Arthur H. Vandenberg,** Willkie was an internationalist in foreign policy, favoring aid for the Allies. He criticized New Deal policies toward business, but did not attack specific New Deal reforms. Despite an energetic campaign, he lost to President Roosevelt by some 5 million popular votes (Roosevelt, 449 electoral votes; Willkie, 82).

After his defeat Willkie was a leader of the Republican internationalists who supported Roosevelt's preparedness measures and plans for a postwar international organization. He endorsed Lend-Lease aid to Britain (1941) and flew to England to demonstrate American solidarity with that nation. In 1942 he persuaded the Republican National Committee to endorse American cooperation with the Allies to ensure lasting peace, and at President Roosevelt's request made a goodwill tour of many allied nations, including the Soviet Union. His best-selling *One World* (1943), describing this trip, argued that world peace could be achieved only through international cooperation. He enthusiastically supported creation of the United Nations organization.

⸻

Wendell Willkie was a man of considerable ability who, one feels, ought to have made more of a mark than he did. He was gifted with intelligence and dynamism, and managed to retain the unaffected simplicity of the midwestern commoner during the long years in which he ascended the rungs of the capitalist ladder. His instinct for power led him into a profitable Wall Street law practice, and fated him to enter the 1930s as a spokesman for the business community. But for this accident Willkie might well have been a New Dealer—for he had the reformer's restless activism, distaste for dogma, and optimism in the face of social change. But he found himself on the other side, and spent the 1930s fighting a rearguard action for his utility company against TVA. He was actually a Democrat, but he seized the Republican presidential nomination in 1940 simply because he was the most energetic and appealing candidate available to a desperate party. The tides were wrong. Willkie met the master politician of the 20th century, and although he ran more strongly than the previous two Republican nominees, he was barred from public office—permanently, as it turned out. Yet Willkie, frustrated in his hopes for a larger role, seems to have exerted a considerable influence upon his party and his country. Despite lapses during the campaign of 1940, brought on no doubt by fatigue and desperation, Willkie stood for the view that conservatives could accept governmental assurance of minimal economic security and the basic rights of organized labor. Perhaps more important, he helped move his party away from isolationism toward a recognition of America's responsibility to cooperate with the family of nations. This was vision enough for one life, but Willkie went further. His popular book *One World* not only perceived global interrelatedness but urged Americans to respond sympathetically to the coming uprising of colonial and colored peoples. In the last year of his life, Willkie spoke out angrily to condemn American racial discrimination. As his critics pointed out, he left no monuments but words, and his words were neither original nor profound. Yet they were bold enough for their time, especially when we remember that he uttered them in the circles of American conservatism. He wished to lead his country, and he deserves to be remembered not for the defeat of that dream, but for its substantial fulfillment. See Ellsworth Barnard, *Wendell Willkie: Fighter for Freedom* (1966).

OTIS GRAHAM, JR.

WILMOT, David (b. Bethany, Pa., Jan. 20, 1814; d. Towanda, Pa., March 16, 1868), POLITICAL LEADER, studied at the Beech Woods Academy in Bethany, Pennsylvania, and then at the Cayuga Lake Academy in Aurora, New York. In 1832 he entered a Wilkes-Barre, Pennsylvania, firm to read law, and began practicing law in Towanda in 1834. There he became active in politics and was elected to Congress in 1844 as a Jacksonian Democrat. In the House he supported the Mexican War and the Walker Tariff of 1846. However, he opposed the extension of slavery and in 1846 introduced a proviso in the House prohibiting slavery in any territories that might be acquired by the U.S. as a result of the Mexican War. The proviso was adopted in the House but defeated in the Senate.

Wilmot bolted from his party and supported Free-Soil candidate Martin Van Buren for President in 1848. The James Buchanan wing of the Pennsylvania Democratic party blocked Wilmot's reelection to the House in 1850. He became president judge of the 13th judicial district of Pennsylvania in 1851. A founder of the Republican party, which adopted his proviso, Wilmot was the first Republican candidate for governor of Pennsylvania (1857) but was not elected. He was appointed to fill a vacancy in the U.S. Senate in 1861, and became a judge of the reorganized U.S. court of claims in 1863.

———※———

Until August 1846, David Wilmot was one of countless American politicians—a lawyer of some talents and local influence, but with no real prospect of national standing. But when a group of congressmen chose him to introduce a proviso barring slavery from any territory acquired in the Mexican War, Wilmot in one moment made the leap from obscurity to fame. Why Wilmot, who previously had no antislavery record, introduced the measure has long puzzled historians; various interpretations stress his annoyance at patronage snubs by the administration of James K. Polk, and a desire to counterbalance political damage done by his vote in favor of the Walker tariff. Most recently, Wilmot has been viewed as one of a group of congressional followers of Martin Van Buren, who resented southern control of the administration and desired to protect northern Democrats against the Whig charge that the Mexican War was a plot to extend slavery.

From 1846 until his death, Wilmot's name was inextricably identified with the principle of the nonextension of slavery. He defended his proviso in countless speeches, some eloquent, some marred by outright rascism (he called it "the White Man's Proviso" and pledged it would preserve the West for men "of my own race and own color"). Wilmot was considered by some contemporaries undisciplined and lazy, while at the same time filled with political ambition. Throughout the period of his political success, his notoriety rested not on any special talents or original thought, but on the fact that by an accident of history he personified the political antislavery movement. See C. B. Going, *David Wilmot, Free-Soiler* (1924).

ERIC FONER

WILSON, Edmund (b. Red Bank, N.J., May 8, 1895; d. Talcottville, N.Y., June 12, 1972), WRITER, graduated from Princeton University, where he became close friends with fellow student **F. Scott Fitzgerald** in 1916. He worked as a reporter for the New York *Evening Sun* (1916–17) and also studied sociology at Columbia. When the U.S. entered World War I, he enlisted as a private in the U.S. Army. He served in a base hospital unit in France and then with the Intelligence Corps before his discharge in 1919. He was managing editor of *Vanity Fair* literary magazine from 1920 to 1921, but then concentrated on freelance writing. He was coauthor with John Peale Bishop of *The Undertaker's Garland* (1922), a satiric work on death and funerals in poetry and prose. In 1929 he published his only novel, *I Thought of Daisy*, which dealt with life in New York City's Greenwich Village. From 1926 to 1931 he was associate editor of the *New Republic*, specializing in book reviewing.

With the publication of *Axel's Castle: A Study in the Imaginative Literature of 1870–1930* (1931), Wilson established himself as a leading American literary critic. The work dealt with Yeats, Eliot, Valéry, Joyce, and others, in terms of the French symbolist movement. In 1932 Wilson wrote *The American Jitters*, describing conditions in Depression America. In that year he supported Communist party candidate, William Z. Foster, for president. Wilson visited the Soviet Union in 1935 on a Guggenheim fellowship and wrote *Travels in Two Democracies* (1936), contrasting the U.S. and U.S.S.R. *The Triple Thinkers* (1938) criticized 19th-century Russian, English, French, and American literature, while *To the Finland Station* (1940) analyzed the writings of Marx, Stalin, Lenin, and Trotsky in terms of the European revolutionary tradition. *The Wound and the Bow* (1941), a psychological study, dealt with such writers as Dickens, Joyce, and **Ernest Hemingway.** From 1944 to 1948 Wilson was a book reviewer for the *New Yorker.* After visiting postwar Europe, he wrote *Europe Without Baedeker: Sketches Among the Ruins of Italy, Greece, and England* (1947). A collection of six stories treating the spiritual crises of the thirties and forties, *Memoirs of Hecate County* (1946), was banned in New York State as obscene. A play, *The Little Blue Light,* was produced in New York in 1951. In 1950 *Classics and Commercials,* a collection of his many articles written for such magazines as the *New Yorker* and *New Republic*, appeared.

After visiting the site of the Dead Sea Scrolls discovery, Wilson wrote *The Scrolls from the Dead Sea* (1955), a study which many biblical scholars attacked as tendentious. Dividing much of his time between homes in Talcottville, New York, and Cape Cod, Wilson looked back over sixty years of his life in *A Piece of My Mind* (1956) and stripped bare many of the injustices done to the Native American in *Apologies to the Iroquois* (1959). Wilson evaluated the writings of **Harriet Beecher Stowe,** Lincoln, Grant, and others who left records of their Civil War experiences in *Patriotic Gore* (1962). His *The Cold War and Income Tax* (1963) was a scolding assault on government defense spending and the Vietnam War, which he bitterly opposed. Some of his many other writings include *Discordant Encounters* (1926), *Poets, Farewell* (1929), *This Room and This Gin and These*

Sandwiches (1937), *The American Earthquake* (1958), *Bit Between My Teeth: A Literary Chronicle of 1950–65* (1965), and *Upstate: Records and Recollections of Northern New York* (1971), his last published work.

———— ∞ ————

Devotion to literature and the common intellectual life it serves is the primary reason for Edmund Wilson's distinguished place in American criticism. Himself a man of letters, he practiced criticism in the way in which members of his family practiced law and medicine—as a professional in the service of society. Coming from an upper-class family that had lost out in the status revolution that followed the Civil War, he found in literature—in criticism—a way to enter the great world and assume leadership there. His point of view remained that of the class that had experienced the transformation of preindustrial America; it was at once assured yet marginal and limited and sensitive to change and loss, crisis and disorder. His critical method was complementary, attending to the historical and psychological grounds of art, to the intersections of men and history and the relations of art and politics.

In the early decades of his career, his major effort was to introduce avant-garde art to the middle classes and to instruct them in Marxism. After World War II, his effort, though remote from immediate social issues but no less relevant, was to call attention to the precariousness of civilization, the dangers of national myths, and the encroachments on individual liberties by nation-states. His mind was dialogic, seeking in the encounter of ideas the balance amid extremes, and his interest in literature was notable for its gusto, openmindedness, and curiosity. Though he is not to be ranked with those critics who teach us to read literature in new ways, his achievement is equally rare. For more than fifty years he served the republic of letters, never corrupted, always surviving cultural change. During much of this time he provided an indispensable gauge of morale, just as now his work provides one of the indispensable chronicles of our era. Resolutely

Emersonian in his self-reliance and witness, he exemplified his belief in the humane value of literature. See Sherman Paul, *Edmund Wilson: A Study of Literary Vocation in Our Time* (1965).

SHERMAN PAUL

WILSON, James (b. Carskerdo, Scot., Sept. 14, 1742; d. Edenton, N.C., Aug. 21, 1798), JURIST, was educated at Scottish universities before emigrating to America during the Stamp Act crisis of 1765. A Latin tutor at the College of Philadelphia briefly, he then studied law at the office of **John Dickinson** and was admitted to the bar in 1767. He practiced law at Reading, Pennsylvania (1768), before settling in Carlisle, where he specialized in frontier land disputes. In the early 1770s he began a lifelong involvement in land speculation. He headed a Carlisle committee of correspondence in 1774, and was a delegate to the first provincial conference at Philadelphia. His *Considerations on the Nature and Extent of the Legislative Authority of the British Parliament* (1774) denied the power of Parliament over the colonies in all cases, but argued that the colonies should remain loyal to the king. Elected to the Second Continental Congress in May of 1775, he voted for and signed the Declaration of Independence. But opposition to the radical 1776 Pennsylvania Constitution cost him his seat in Congress in 1777. In 1778 he settled in Philadelphia, where he became a leader of the Republican Society and a counsel for loyalists. His house was attacked by a mob in 1779.

During the Confederation period Wilson was active in trade, banking, manufacturing, and land speculation. He was again in Congress, 1785–87, and he participated in the 1787 Constitutional Convention. He was active in the Pennsylvania fight for ratification of the Constitution, and helped draft his state's revised constitution of 1790. He was appointed associate justice of the U.S. Supreme Court in 1789. In a series of lectures at the College of Philadelphia (1789) he outlined a legal theory stressing American nationalism. His belief in the superiority of federal over state sovereignty appears in his 1793 decision in *Chisholm* v. *Georgia,* in which he held that the Constitution gave the Supreme Court the power to decide cases brought against a state by citizens of another state or foreign nation. Unfortunate land speculations brought him financial ruin in the 1790s, and he died deeply in debt.

———— ✦ ————

James Wilson's career illustrates the deceptively small gulf that often separates aspiration from attainment in a lifetime. Well educated in Scotland before his journey to America, Wilson was directed toward the ministry by his parents. Yet on arrival he abandoned theological quests for a career in law. And as a result, he was to emerge as one of the primary constitutional, legal, and political theorists of his generation. Personally ambitious, seeking both respectability and status in the New World, Wilson was frustrated countless times in his endeavors. Ill-fated land speculations and poorly conceived investments deprived him of financial security and left him impoverished and pursued at death; he found the approbation of the people at large withheld because of the aristocratic image created by his monetary and societal entanglements, and yet he was one of the most democratic of thinkers; he unsuccessfully sought from President Washington appointment as the first chief justice of the United States, and an associate justiceship was proffered in its stead. And still despite all these uncomfortable personal annoyances, Wilson remained one of the most original and farsighted planners of the American system. As an architect, drafter, and defender of the federal Constitution, Supreme Court justice, and law lecturer, he articulated distinctly anti-aristocratic notions of democracy that incorporated influential conceptions of sovereignty residing in the people. In addition, he strongly favored the supremacy of the national government under the new constitutional format. Wilson's consciously anti-Blackstonian tone in his law lectures also helped undercut traditional views of the aims of a legal system, and made it more susceptible to American adaptations. James Wilson, then, was a student of political systems—a man capable of formulating innovative intellectual constructs, but tragically plagued by personal misfortune throughout his life. See Charles Page Smith, *James Wilson: Founding Father, 1742–1798* (1956).

ALFRED S. KONEFSKY

WILSON, Thomas Woodrow (b. Staunton, Va., Dec. 28, or 29, 1856; d. Washington, D.C., Feb. 3, 1924), PRESIDENT, graduated from Princeton (1879), studied law at the University of Virginia, and was admitted to the bar in 1882. After briefly practicing law in Atlanta, Georgia, he entered Johns Hopkins University, and received a PhD in political science in 1886. His doctoral dissertation, *Congressional Government* (1885), showed his admiration for the parliamentary system of government and argued that the real authority in Congress lay in congressional committees. He taught at Bryn Mawr (1885–88) and Wesleyan (1888–90) before coming to Princeton in 1890. Appointed president of Princeton in 1902, he instituted reforms of the curriculum and teaching methods. His attempts to institute social changes and to control the policy of the graduate school led to his forced resignation in 1910.

Wilson was elected governor of New Jersey in 1910 on the Democratic ticket. As governor he obtained a variety of progressive reforms, including workmen's compensation, direct primaries, school reforms, and the regulation of public utilities. As the Democratic presidential candidate in 1912, he advocated a "New Freedom," arguing that social justice could best be advanced by abolishing special privileges and restoring competition by strict enforcement of the antitrust law. Because of a split within the Republican party, Wilson was easily elected, receiving 435 electoral votes to Theodore Roosevelt's 88, and William Howard Taft's 8.

Wilson's specific reform proposals, personally presented before Congress, were swiftly enacted. The Underwood Tariff (1913) reduced duties and provided for a graduated income tax on personal incomes. The Federal Reserve Act (1913) created an elastic currency and divided the nation into twelve banking districts. In 1914 Congress established the Federal Trade Commission to investigate the activities of corporations, and a new antitrust law, the Clayton Act, was passed. In 1916 Wilson persuaded Congress to pass the Adamson Act, which provided for an eight-hour day for railroad employees.

Wilson denounced American "dollar diplomacy" and sought to base his foreign policy on firm moral principles. He refused to recognize the reactionary regime of Victoriano Huerta in Mexico, because Huerta came to power by murdering President Francisco Madero. When a number of American troops were arrested at Tampico, Mexico (1914), Wilson demanded an apology. When Huerta refused, Wilson occupied the port of Veracruz. The controversy was settled through the mediation of Argentina, Brazil, and Chile in 1914. In October 1915, Wilson recognized Venustiano Carranza as de facto president of Mexico. When bandits led by Pancho Villa attacked Columbus, New Mexico, Wilson sent General **John J. Pershing** into Mexico to pursue Villa. Although Villa was a rebel, Carranza insisted that the U.S. withdraw its troops, which was finally done in 1917.

When World War I broke out in Europe, Wilson issued a neutrality proclamation. According to international law, neutrals could carry on noncontraband trade with belligerents, and Wilson insisted that this right be respected. The British, however, controlled the North Atlantic, and declared nearly all commodities to be contraband of war. They forced American ships into allied ports, searched them, and often confiscated their cargoes. Wilson protested but took no action. However, when the Germans proclaimed the British Isles a war zone, the U.S. sent a number of diplomatic protests to Germany, warning the Germans that they would be held accountable for the loss of American lives. Following the sinking of the British liner *Lusitania* (1915), by a German submarine, Wilson announced that he would hold the Germans to "strict accountability" for American losses resulting from such attacks.

In 1916 Wilson was reelected, defeating **Charles Evans Hughes,** 277 electoral votes to 254. Revived German U-boat activity in early 1917 led Wilson to conclude that the U.S. must enter the world conflict on the side of the Allies. Proclaiming that "the world must be made safe for democracy," he issued a war message (April 2, 1917), and Congress declared war.

Wilson was an effective wartime leader and administrator. He organized a number of war boards, each with specific responsibilities, and managed to bring order to the mobilization effort. He sought, however, a "peace without victory." On January 8, 1918, he issued his "Fourteen Point" plan for postwar reconstruction which called for an end to secret treaties; freedom of the seas in war and peace; removal of trade barriers; armament reduction; a colonial system that would consider the interests of the native peoples concerned; the evacuation, restoration, and readjustment of certain countries and boundaries (points 6–13); and the creation of a League of Nations to prevent future international conflicts.

After the armistice (Nov. 11, 1918) Wilson attended the Versailles Peace Conference, which drafted a treaty including a League of Nations. But he could not persuade the necessary two-thirds of the Senate to ratify the treaty. The isolationist "irreconcilable" senators opposed it outright, and the "reservationists," led by **Henry Cabot Lodge** of Massachusetts, demanded modifications. Wilson, refusing to compromise, went on a speaking tour in an effort to get public support for the treaty. At Pueblo, Colorado (Sept. 25, 1919), he collapsed and soon suffered a paralytic stroke. Although incapacitated, he remained in office. He continued to oppose all modifications of the treaty, and as a result, the Senate refused to ratify it. After retiring, Wilson remained in Washington, where he formed a law partnership with Bainbridge Colby, but his poor physical condition did not permit him to work actively.

———— ✼ ————

Woodrow Wilson was unique in American history because he had in effect three different careers and made significant contributions to the three separate fields of scholarship in the social sciences, educational administration, and government and diplomacy. Within each of these fields, his contributions were multifaceted.

Trained in the modern social sciences at Johns Hopkins, Wilson was a pioneering political scientist and historian whose work still has considerable impact. His *Congressional Government*, a hardheaded analysis of the way the American national government worked, is still widely read and quoted, as is his later *Constitutional Government in the United States* (1908). His *The State* (1889) was the first textbook in any language in comparative government and dominated the field for more than a quarter of a century. It was most significant for its repudiation of laissez-faire and its call for positive political action to reconstruct the American political economy. Wilson was also the pioneer in the field of public administration in the United States and, as a teacher at Johns Hopkins, had a large hand in training a generation of administrators. As a historian, Wilson had his greatest impact as an analyst and interpreter. In his two major historical works, *Division and Reunion* (1893) and *A History of the American People* (5 vols., 1902), but particularly in numerous articles and essays, he developed interpretations of the significance of the frontier, the nature of Jacksonian democracy, the causes of the Civil War, and the enduring significance of the European connection which fertilized American historical thought and writing in the 1890s and early 1900s.

In the field of education, Wilson made his most enduring impact upon the thousands of students he taught at Bryn Mawr, Wesleyan, and Princeton, in the way in which he inspired them to high ideals of public service. More easily measured, however, is his impact as president of Princeton University from 1902 to 1910. His reorganization of the Princeton curriculum in 1904, to require students to major in a single subject and to follow an integrated course of study, provided the first significant alternative to the chaos of the free elective system then in vogue in American colleges and universities. His institution of the preceptorial system in 1905, providing systematic small-group discussion to supplement lectures, was one

of the most important intellectual breakthroughs in higher education in the 20th century. His proposal for the reconstitution of Princeton into residential colleges, advanced in 1906–7, although rejected by the Princeton trustees, provided the model for the college system at Yale and the house system instituted at Harvard in the 1930s.

Catapulted into the governorship of New Jersey in 1911 and the presidency of the United States in 1913, Wilson was to leave an enduring mark on American political and diplomatic institutions, practices, and traditions. He effected a political revolution in New Jersey not so much by the legislation that he accomplished as by transforming the governorship and proving that bold executive leadership was possible under an antiquated constitution.

Wilson's most significant contribution to national political institutions was his restoration of the presidency to the full power envisaged for that office by the framers of the Constitution. This he did by audacious stimulation and leadership of public opinion, which he used as a spur on Congress; by his initiative in and guidance of legislation; and by his use of moral leadership and patronage to achieve mastery of the Democratic party. His "New Freedom" reform program of tariff, banking, antitrust, and labor welfare legislation substantially reconstructed the American political economy and laid the foundations for the superstructure added in the New Deal era. By eschewing extremes both of the right and of the left, Wilson led the way down the political middle of the road that reform presidents after him would follow.

Wilson's impact on the course of world affairs and American diplomatic traditions during his presidency is too varied to be described in a few words, but he made three contributions of particular moment. First, by shielding the Mexican Revolution from Americans and Europeans who desired to overthrow it, he made it possible for the Mexican people to hew out their own political destiny. Second, his advocacy of a postwar international peace-keeping organization from 1916 to 1919, his authorship of the Covenant of the League of nations, and his strenuous efforts to persuade the American people to accept world leadership in 1919 and 1920 all give him claim to the title of the preeminent champion of international cooperation in modern times. Third, his insistence upon the right of the Russian people to self-determination and his vetoes of numerous Allied proposals for intervention in the Russian Civil War of 1917–20 very substantially guaranteed that the Russians should solve their own problems in their own way.

Wilson combined incisive and quick intelligence with wide reading. Personally open and generous, he was capable of deep friendship and enduring loyalty; at the same time, he was extremely sensitive, proud, and ambitious, almost ruthless at times. The latter traits were magnified following severe strokes in 1906 and 1919. He recovered substantially from the first (although it left enduring marks on his personality) but not from the second. Throughout his life, Wilson was a man of deep Christian faith who tried, however imperfectly, to put his faith into action. See Arthur S. Link, *Wilson* (5 vols., 1947–65).

ARTHUR S. LINK

WINTHROP, John (b. near Groton, Suffolk, Eng., Jan. 22, 1588; d. Boston, Mass., March 26, 1649), POLITICAL LEADER, attended Cambridge (1602–5), and was admitted to Gray's Inn in 1613. In 1619 he became Lord of Groton Manor in Suffolk, the family estate. He was appointed an attorney to the court of wards and liveries in 1626, and was admitted to the Inner Temple in 1628.

Winthrop, a Puritan, was deeply disturbed by the religious and economic conditions in England, and by the religious wars in Europe. When the Massachusetts Bay Company offered to make Winthrop governor of the Massachusetts Bay Colony in America, he accepted. He believed that he had received his "calling" to lead men, and to establish a Bible commonwealth free from the "corruption" of the Church of England.

In 1630 the Puritans left Southampton for America. On board the *Arbella*, Winthrop issued his "Model of Christian Charity," which described the type of stratified society in which the Puritans would live. Winthrop was governor of Massachusetts Bay for ten years, and deputy governor for nine. In 1634 the "freemen" (church members who voted) accused Winthrop of usurping power from the general court, and refused to reelect him governor. He presided over the trial of **Anne Hutchinson** and approved of her banishment in 1637. Following this antinomian crisis, he issued a defense of restricting immigration to those who accepted the Puritan theology. When the New England Confederation was established (1643) to protect the colonists from the Native Americans, Winthrop became its first president. In 1644 he issued a statement on the powers of the magistrates, arguing that magistrates must have wide discretion in applying the law.

During the first two decades of the Massachusetts Bay colony, John Winthrop provided much of its political and moral leadership. As the colony's first resident governor and its leading lay figure until his death, he was not always right—in the eyes of his contemporaries or of later historians—and he was occasionally at odds with factions of his own colony, but it would be difficult to exaggerate the primacy of his influence in shaping early Massachusetts.

In many respects Winthrop epitomized the Puritan outlook he advocated in his "Model of Christian Charity": brotherly love, intensity of religious commitment, and moderation in all worldly matters. In America Winthrop set the example that others should follow, seldom exhibiting rancor or resentment, and generally pursuing matters of state and of religion with tact and forbearance. At the same time, Winthrop kept his eye on the main goal. He and the other founders had left England to create in America a Puritan refuge and an example to all Christians, for "the Eies of all people are uppon us." To allow it to be subverted either by anti-Puritans from without or by dissident factions from within the broad spectrum of reformed Calvinism would be not only to have hazarded their lives and fortunes in vain but more importantly to invite the wrath of God, who had called them to this holy errand.

Despite the overwhelming emphasis on divine mission, Winthrop managed a host of mundane problems. He had to oversee the distribution of land, the creation of towns, the evolution of political practices, and the conduct of quasidiplomatic relations with Anglican England and Catholic Canada. At times he became overbearing, as in 1634 when he appeared to have exceeded the governor's prerogatives. (As one critic observed, Winthrop had "too much forgot & over shott himselfe … [and] hath lost much of that aplaws that he hath had.") Still, the voters of the colony soon returned him to office. There was murmuring again in 1637 when Winthrop took the side of Puritan orthodoxy against Anne Hutchinson, and in the face of the antinomian uprising he perhaps acted his least conciliatory. Yet in the end he led the way to a bloodless solution to the most serious challenge to the Bay colony's theological and social homogeneity.

Winthrop's success stemmed partly from his strength of character, but also from a fortuitous blend of experience and background superbly suited to the task of founding a Puritan state. As a student at Cambridge and at the Inns of Court he had been exposed to the best educational opportunities of his day; as a manor lord and attorney he had had fiscal and administrative experience and had dealt with a wide range of Englishmen; and as a devout Puritan he nicely fused the clerical and secular ingredients of New England colonization. "In my youth," Winthrop wrote in explanation of his decision to join the migration, "I did seariously consecrate my life to the service of the Churche (intendinge the ministry) but was diverted from that course … but it hathe ofte troubled me since, so as I thinke I am the rather bounde to take the opportunitye for spendinge the small remainder of my tyme, to the best service of the Churche which I may." In Massachusetts Winthrop found an opportunity to serve God in a layman's role. See E. S. Morgan, *The Puritan Dilemma: The Story of John Winthrop* (1958).

ALDEN T. VAUGHAN

WISE, Isaac Mayer (b. Steingrub, Bohemia, March 29, 1819; d. Cincinnati, Ohio, March 26, 1900), RELIGIOUS LEADER, received theological training at talmudical academies in Prague and Jenikau (Bohemia), and secular education at the Universities of Prague and Vienna. He was ordained a rabbi in 1842, and accepted a congregation in Radnitz, Bohemia, the following year. Because of government restrictions on Jews and the conservatism of his rabbinical superiors and congregation, Wise emigrated to New York in 1846 and became rabbi of a synagogue in Albany. He introduced far-reaching reforms in the ritual and used the pulpit to expound his philosophy of Reform Judaism. He preached a universalistic interpretation of Judaism which combined Judaism with the free spirit of America. Wise became rabbi of Congregation Bene Yeshurun in Cincinnati, Ohio, in 1854 and quickly made Cincinnati into the center of the American Reform movement in Judaism. He founded a weekly newspaper, the *Israelite,* in 1854 and issued his reform prayer book, *Minhag America,* in 1856.

One of Wise's main goals was to bring about a united American Jewry. He had long deplored the disunity that characterized Jewish religious life in America. By calling a rabbinical synod, by federating all congregations into a single organization, and by establishing a central rabbinical seminary, he hoped to bring unity and direction to the American Jewish community. Thus, in 1873, he organized the Union of American Hebrew Congregations. In 1875 he founded the Hebrew Union College in Cincinnati, serving as its president until his death. The last of Wise's goals was achieved in 1889 with the founding of the Central Conference of American Rabbis. Since he advocated the universalistic approach of Reform Judaism, Wise frowned upon the restoration of a Jewish state and bitterly opposed Zionism. A prolific writer, some of his many works include: *Judaism: Its Doctrines and Duties* (1872), *The Cosmic God* (1876), and *Reminiscences* (1901).

More than a systematic theological thinker, Isaac M. Wise was a religious statesman who was bent upon reshaping Judaism to conform with the philosophic currents of his time. He was preeminently the architect, organizer, and builder of institutions, and as such he gave coherence to the disjointed and often crude efforts of scattered congregations to Americanize their Judaism. He succeeded as well as he did because of his tenacity, his prodigious energy, his gifts as speaker and writer, and, above all, his readiness to forgo doctrinal consistency to achieve as broad a consensus as possible.

Wise arrived in America steeped in the teachings of the 18th-century Enlightenment. To his mind America was the child of the Enlightenment and its ideals corresponded with the enduring component of Judaism, whose "aim and mission are the universal triumph of truth, the sovereign dominion of justice, equity, and freedom." The task at hand, then, was to remove the accretion of religious regulation and custom of pre-Enlightenment times from Judaism: the notion of Jewish nationality, personal messianism, and faith in miracles. It included reforming the liturgy in the direction of briefer, more decorous services with a central place given to the sermon (English replacing much of the Hebrew in the prayers). In brief, it meant reforming Judaism in the institutional mold of liberal Protestantism. The American Jews of German origin, well established in the middle class by the second half of the 19th century, welcomed Wise's efforts to solemnize and formalize the piecemeal changes they, with scant religious training, had been introducing.

Among the Reform rabbis, Wise was under constant attack by the more radical reformers as well as by the conservatives. His intention, which was not realized, was to have the Union of American Congregations include all but the extreme right-wing congregations, and to have the Hebrew Union College serve as a nonsectarian Jewish theological seminary. Striving for broadly based institutions and seeking to mediate between opposing camps, his doctrinal flexibility was criticized as expediency.

Wise, being prepared to accept slavery in the South as the price for preserving the Union, vigorously attacked the abolitionists. Similarly he vehemently criticized the notion that the United States was a "Christian nation." On these questions as in his fulminations against Zionism he gained a reputation as a harsh, unbending polemicist. See James G. Heller, *Isaac M. Wise* (1965).

ARTHUR A. GOREN

WISE, Stephen Samuel (b. Budapest, Hung., March 17, 1874; d. New York, N.Y., April 19, 1949), RELIGIOUS LEADER, came to the U.S. in 1875. He attended the City College of New York (1887–91) and received his AB from Columbia in 1892. Descended from a long line of rabbis, he studied for the rabbinate with his father and returned to Germany to be ordained. His first pulpit was the Madison Avenue Synagogue in New York City, which he held for seven years (1893–1900). He then accepted a congregation in Portland, Oregon.

In Portland, Wise became involved in the Progressive movement. He worked for honest local government and for social reforms such as the abolition of child labor. In 1906 he founded the Free Synagogue of New York, where he remained chief rabbi until his death. In New York, he fought bitterly with the Tammany Hall political machine and sided with the struggling labor movement. He was also concerned with Zionism, the establishment of a Jewish national homeland in Palestine. He founded the Federation of American Zionists in 1897 and became a close friend of Zionist leader Theodore Herzl. Wise represented the Zionist cause at the Versailles Peace Conference of 1919. During the 1930s he devoted much of his time to fighting Nazi anti-Semitism through the American Jewish Congress, serving as its president (1924–49), and the World Jewish Congress, which he founded in 1936. Wise supported America's entry into World War II and urged President Roosevelt to support the establishment of a national homeland for Jews after the war.

Wise's powerful frame, impassioned voice, leonine presence, and limitless energies equipped him splendidly for his unique role as the People's Rabbi. For more than four decades he mesmerized a congregation that reached out from his midtown New York pulpit to embrace Jews of all origins and Americans of all faiths. A latter-day prophet in frock coat and striped trousers, he continually captivated his Sunday morning audiences, first at the Hudson theater and subsequently at Carnegie Hall and at his own Free Synagogue, where he dramatized all liberating causes, denounced all breaches in the moral law, and in thunderously mellifluous tones spared neither persons nor institutions in his stinging indictments. Thriving on controversy and eyecatching headlines, he marched, protested, organized, pleaded, and remonstrated for woman suffrage, African-American rights, Irish freedom, Armenian independence, liberal Judaism, interfaith services, and an end to child labor. Although he refused to run for public office, periodically Wise swooped down on City Hall, on Governor Franklin Roosevelt's New York study, and on the White House. Above all, he was Zionism's great orator. After 1933, his anti-Hitler activities overshadowed all else as he eloquently but vainly expended his failing strength in efforts to rescue doomed Jews. With the unselfconsciousness of a great actor and religious leader who rarely doubted the wisdom of his heart, Wise vividly personified the liberal Jewish democratic ethos of his time. To his detractors he appeared emotional, unctuous, inconsistent, tactless, and pompous. To those who recognized his rare talents and fine instincts, he seemed a bulwark for his harassed people, whose honor he defended and whose soul he laid bare in a world gone mad. See Carl Hermann Voss, *Stephen S. Wise: Servant of the People— Selected Letters* (1969).

MOSES RISCHIN

WISTER, Owen (b. Philadelphia, Pa., July 14, 1860; d. North Kingstown, R.I., July 21, 1938), WRITER, graduated from Harvard in 1882. He then studied music under Ernest Guiraud at the Paris Conservatoire. In 1884 he returned to the U.S., and after working in New York City briefly as a bank clerk, he entered the Harvard Law School in 1885 (LLB, 1888). Admitted to the Philadelphia bar in 1889, he practiced law until 1891, when he decided to devote full time to writing. *Harper's* magazine published two of his short stories, "Hank's Woman," and "How Lin McLean Went East," in 1892. A number of volumes of short stories followed, including *Red Men and White* (1896), *Lin McLean* (1898), and *Jimmyjohn Boss* (1900). In 1902 he published his first novel, *The Virginian*, which brought him immediate and widespread fame. By 1938, sales had exceeded 1.5 million, and the book had been turned into a number of movies as well as a successful play. After 1902, although he continued to write extensively, Wister turned largely away from stories about the West. He produced biographies such as *Roosevelt: The Story of Friendship, 1880–1919* (1930), novels like *Lady Baltimore* (1906), and a trilogy on tensions in Europe, *The Pentecost of Calamity* (1915), *A Straight Deal, or the Ancient Grudge* (1920), and *Neighbors Henceforth* (1922).

———

Throughout his life, whether as lawyer, novelist, or political commentator, Wister remained a gentleman of the Philadelphia Main Line. Yet his values were his own, expressed in a unique way. His devotion to the gentleman's code of his day—family, education, tradition, social order— was infused with ideals of "manliness" which his longtime friend Theodore Roosevelt popularized in the catch phrase "the strenuous life." Like Roosevelt, Wister grew alarmed at the emergence of sprawling cities, industrial blight, financial empires, and labor unions—all were signs of mediocrity and the rise of a mass mind. He himself represented "old money" and status, though before *The Virginian* appeared he had more status than wealth. Wister sniffed at plutocrats and labor leaders: their uncouth grasping and squabbling for riches and power were destroying American ideals. His apprehensions, shored up by the confidence of his class, prompted him to rally behind Rooseveltian Progressivism and to create, in his early writings, legendary portraits of "real men." The Virginian, prototype of the good man, is brave, honest, shrewd, handsome, courtly after his fashion, and moral. Here was the true American—a Virginian, riding the plains of Wyoming, living life with Rooseveltian grace and gusto. Yet Wister's romantic images of virgin prairies and gallant cowboys faded into mirages. Wister's later writing has overtones of disillusionment with his Arcadia, and he could not regain his imaginative vision. At his best Wister wrote excellent "local color," but his later fiction was as out of favor as his scorn for the New Deal. He remained comforted to know that *The Virginian*, having touched some deep longing in the American people, continued in popularity. See G. Edward White, *The Eastern Establishment and the Western Experience* (1968).

BRUCE CLAYTON

WOLFE, Thomas Clayton (b. Asheville, N.C., Oct. 3, 1900; d. Baltimore, Md., Sept. 15, 1938), WRITER, received his BA from the University of North Carolina in 1920. He then studied playwriting under George Pierce Baker at Harvard, where he wrote and produced several plays. After earning an MA in 1922, he accepted a job teaching English at New York University in 1924, a post which he intermittently held until 1930 while he traveled through Europe. In 1926, while returning from a trip to Europe, Wolfe began writing his first novel, *Look Homeward, Angel,* a semiautobiographical account of his youth. This enormously long manuscript was edited and cut down into a workable length together with Maxwell Perkins of Charles Scribner's Sons. Published in 1929, it received wide critical acclaim.

Wolfe left New York University in 1930 and spent the next year on a Guggenheim fellowship in Europe. In the years that followed he wrote *A Portrait of Bascom Hawke* (1932) and *Of Time and the River* (1935), again with the help of Perkins. Wolfe visited Germany in 1936 and, although ambivalent at first, bitterly denounced Nazism in

a 1937 article for the *New Republic,* "I Have a Thing to Tell You." A collection of short stories, *From Death to Morning,* was published in 1935, *The Story of a Novel* in 1936. Three novels, edited by Edward Aswell of Harper's, were published posthumously: *The Web and the Rock* (1939), *You Can't Go Home Again* (1940), and *The Hills Beyond* (1941). Two volumes of Wolfe's letters appeared in 1943 and 1956.

Wolfe's call for largeness of spirit, his certainty that life finally was good and that America, though lost, was rich in promise, and his extravagant outpouring of words differentiate him from those writers of the 1920s who, like **Ernest Hemingway,** wrote with stoic economy of language or emotion or who, like Eliot, found the world a wasted land inhabited by hollow men. Wolfe seemed a harbinger of a kind of spiritual valor which dared reach beyond what it could grasp. With **William Faulkner,** who adventured with better control, he explored man's inevitable conflict between hungers of aspiration and those of inclination, between his dream and his desire. Wolfe's verbal gusto, his exuberant goodwill, his ecstatic delight in sensation, and his enthusiastic acceptance of life as in itself good have made him a perennial favorite among young readers. His fervor is a youthful fervor, his frankness and sincerity are those of a young man, and his melodic paeans to joy or wonder or disenchantment expansively echo what almost any person feels on first confronting the rich confusions of maturity. To older readers, his lyric outbursts often seem finally inchoate. His stature, however, has not been completely measured. When it is, his work may be found not only to reflect the conflicts but also to present an important criticism of his time. See David Herbert Donald, *Look Homeward: A Life of Thomas Wolfe* (1987).

LEWIS LEARY

WOOD, Grant (b. Anamosa, Iowa, Feb. 13, 1891; d. Iowa City, Iowa, Feb. 12, 1942), ARTIST, graduated from Washington High School in

Cedar Rapids, Iowa, in 1910, and attended the Chicago Art Institute, taking courses in the evening (1917). He worked as a housepainter, carpenter, and interior decorator in Cedar Rapids until entering the Army in 1917. After World War I, he taught art in Cedar Rapid's public schools.

Wood traveled to Europe frequently during the 1920s, haunting the museums. He studied at the Academie Julian in Paris (1923) and for a time adopted an impressionistic style in his paintings. But he came to reject modernism under the influence of the medieval German and Flemish art he saw in Munich, Germany.

Returning to Iowa and devoting himself to the American Midwest for subject matter, Wood had his first major success in 1930 with the painting *American Gothic*. It won the Harris Prize and was purchased by the Chicago Art Institute. Now regarded as the leading regionalist painter in the United States, he founded an art colony at Stone City, Iowa, in 1933. The next year, shortly after the New Deal established programs to help unemployed artists, he was appointed state chairman of the Federal Public Works Art Project, supervising twenty-four of the thirty-four Iowa projects, and executed a mural for the Washington, D.C. Post Office Department Building. In 1934 he was also appointed associate professor of art at the University of Iowa in Iowa City. Among Wood's best known paintings are *Daughters of the American Revolution* (1932), *Spring Turning* (1936), and *Parson Weem's Fable* (1939).

———— ⚬⚬⚬ ————

Grant Wood was seen during his lifetime as the most American of painters, the leader of the regionalist movement which rejected foreign styles and subject matter to focus on rural America. He found success with both the public and the critics for meticulously detailed portraits that captured the regional character of his fellow Iowans. When, in 1930, he posed his sister and a Cedar Rapids dentist in front of a farmhouse for *American Gothic*, he created perhaps the best-known image in American art. Open to many interpretations, the careworn, expressionless faces of his subjects have been read both as an ironic comment on Midwestern rural life and as simple local-color realism. Less ambiguous are the explicit satire in Wood's *Daughters of the American Revolution* and the witty commentary on American historical legend in his *Parson Weem's Fable*. Despite his outspoken rejection of modernism, such lyrical landscapes as his *Spring Turning* reduced Midwestern farm scenes to almost abstract compositions.

Wood was associated with artists John Steuart Curry and **Thomas Hart Benton** in the short-lived regionalist movement, and after his death many critics dismissed him as a mere illustrator because of the sharp focus, Art-Nouveau motifs, and narrative content of much of his work. His reputation went into eclipse until a major retrospective of his work at New York's Whitney Museum of American Art in 1983 demonstrated his complex and sophisticated technique and restored him to an important position in the history of American art. See James Dennis, *Grant Wood: A Study in American Art and Culture* (1975).

DENNIS WEPMAN

WOOD, Leonard (b. Winchester, N.H., Oct. 9, 1860; d. Boston, Mass., Aug. 7, 1927), MILITARY LEADER, received his MD from Harvard in 1884. He served briefly as house surgeon at Boston City Hospital and then entered private practice. In 1885 he received an interim appointment as a contract surgeon in the army and he reported to Arizona, where he was commissioned assistant surgeon with the rank of first lieutenant (1886). For his service in the capture of the Native American leader **Geronimo** he was promoted to captain assistant surgeon and awarded the Congressional Medal of Honor (1898). In 1892 Grover Cleveland appointed him physician and aide to the president, and William McKinley retained him in this post. Commissioned colonel of the 1st U.S. Volunteer Cavalry after the outbreak of the Spanish American War (1898), he commanded the Rough Riders at Las Guasimas and San Juan Hill. He was promoted to brigadier general of U.S. Volunteers in July and to major general in December.

In December 1899 he became military governor of Cuba. After introducing many reforms and supporting the physicians who discovered the cause of yellow fever, he transferred the government of Cuba to civilian nationals in May 1902. The following March, Wood, now a brigadier general in the regular army, was transferred to the Philippines and became governor of Moro Province in July 1903. A month later he was promoted to major general. After commanding the Philippine Division (1906–8), Wood headed the Department of the East for two years. He was named army chief of staff in July 1910.

A leading spokesman for the preparedness movement, he organized summer officer training camps for college students at Monterey and Gettysburg (1913) and at four other locations the following year. Reassigned to the Department of the East in 1914, he was not given command of the American Expeditionary Force in 1917 although he was the senior officer in the army. During the war he developed new military training techniques. When President Wilson refused to permit Wood to go to Europe with the 89th Infantry Division, which he had trained, he became the center of a political storm.

A Republican, Wood was a prominent candidate for the GOP presidential nomination in 1920, which eventually went to Warren G. Harding. In 1921, Wood became governor general of the Philippines. A recipient of the Distinguished Service Medal for his efforts during World War I, Wood also received the Roosevelt Medal of Honor (1923) and was decorated by France, Italy, China, and Japan. He wrote several books and articles on military subjects, including *Our Military History: Its Facts and Fallacies* (1916).

———⚬⚬⚬———

"Quick to comprehend and to act," in his biographer's apt phrase, Wood was a man of resolution, wit, and fertility of mind. He shared many of the values, including a romantic view of war, of his friend Theodore Roosevelt, but lacked Roosevelt's depth and breadth. Wood was more concerned with social order than with social justice, and he was clearly out of his element as a political candidate. Within the military, however, he was an exceptional organizer, administrator, and troop commander. The modernization of the army prior to World War I owed much to his efficient and imaginative leadership as chief of staff.

Wood's enthusiasm for preparedness and early American entry into World War I led him to overstep the bounds between military and civilian authority. At the urging of President Wilson, the secretary of war privately reprimanded Wood in December 1914. The administration's fear that Wood would emerge as a "political" general figured importantly in his failure to receive an overseas command during the war.

Following Roosevelt's death in January 1919, Wood inherited Roosevelt's more nationalistic support and seemed destined to win the Republican presidential nomination. As the national convention drew near, however, Wood's ultranationalism, obsession with the "Red Scare," and huge campaign expenditures alienated many progressives. Under pressure to be more specific in his pronouncements, he then destroyed all possibility of nomination as a unity candidate by unveiling a conservative nationalist platform. His convention high of 314 1/2 votes came mainly from conservative easterners. Wood closed out his active career as governor general of the Philippines, where he initiated many reforms but helped defeat independence legislation in 1924. See Hermann Hagedorn, *Leonard Wood* (2 vols., 1931).

WILLIAM H. HARBAUGH

WOODHULL, Victoria Claflin (b. Homer, Ohio, Sept. 23, 1838; d. Worcestershire, England, Sept. 9, 1927), REFORMER, grew up in Ohio, one of ten children of a mother afflicted with mania and a father suspected of pyromania. As a young girl, she and her sister Tennessee toured Ohio as itinerant spiritualists and patent medicine peddlers, offering cures for whatever disease ailed their audience. Among their potions was The Elixer of Life, until one of Tennessee's steady customers died of breast cancer and she was indicted for manslaughter. Victoria married Dr. Canning Woodhull in 1853, and had two children with him. But they divorced in 1866, and she then married Col. James Harvey Blood, a spiritualist. In 1868, a "spirit" told her to move to New York City, and she went there with Col. Blood and Tennessee, now married to a gambler. There the two sisters were discovered by Commodore **Cornelius Vanderbilt**, the aged railroad tycoon, who was especially attracted to Tennessee and her "magnetic healing." He proposed marriage to her but demonstrated his infatuation instead by setting the sisters up as the first "lady brokers" on Wall Street, running Woodhull Claflin & Company. Victoria then came under the sway of Stephen Pearl Andrews, a spelling reformer, faddist, and advocate of free love, and in 1870 she announced her candidacy for President of the United States, the first woman to do so. That same year, both sisters, now prosperous from the brokerage business and good investment tips provided by Vanderbilt, began publishing *The Woodhull & Claflin Weekly*, which appeared for the next six years filled with articles on fads, sexual remedies and advice—"Impregnation," "Sexual Generation," "The Law of Sexual Intercourse"— and articles decrying social injustice. The first English translation of Marx's and Engel's *The Communist Manifesto* appeared in the *Weekly*. Victoria lectured on a variety of social and political issues, particularly the right of women to vote, and she won a wide following among labor and socialists. In 1871, she made such a moving plea in favor of woman suffrage before the House Judiciary Committee that she was asked to sit on a platform beside **Susan B. Anthony** and other suffrage leaders then meeting in convention in the nation's capitol. The Equal Rights Party and her own *Weekly* endorsed her for president and **Frederick Douglass** for vice president in 1872 but she wasn't allowed on the ballot or to vote.

Increasingly, Victoria's main focus became the issue of sexual freedom and she began to advocate the concept of free love. Through friends she learned that the Rev. **Henry Ward Beecher**, one of the most distinguished clergymen in the nation and a symbol to many of moral righteousness,

was having an affair with one of his female parishioners, Mrs. Theodore Tilton. The husband of Mrs. Tilton, who was Rev. Beecher's best friend, complained to Victoria about his wife's affair while they consummated a six-month affair of their own. When **Harriet Beecher Stowe**, the author of *Uncle Tom's Cabin* and the sister of the Rev. Beecher, began to initiate rumors in her circle about the Tilton-Woodhull relationship, Victoria revealed the story of the Beecher-Tilton romance in the Nov. 2, 1872 issue of the *Weekly*. Her explosive allegations, along with other stories, particularly details about how a leading but unnamed New York gentleman had seduced two adolescent virgins, aroused Anthony Comstock, secretary of the Society for the Suppression of Vice and New York's chief moral guardian. He brought charges against the Woodhull sisters of printing and distributing through the mails obscene materials. They were thrown into prison. Released after four weeks, they were later put on trial and acquited (1873). But the scandal left Victoria in financial ruin and earned her the sobriquet of "Mrs. Satan," coined by the cartoonist **Thomas Nast**. The *Weekly* folded and Victoria became the subject of allegations that she used her connections with prostitutes to blackmail their middle-class clients. Denied outlets for her free-love lectures, Victoria, with Tennessee in tow, moved to England in 1877. Victoria toured the lecture circuit there speaking on "The Human Body the Temple of God," and met a proper and very rich English banker, John Martin, whom she married in 1883. Tennessee got married in 1885 to a wealthy English merchant, and when he was made a viscount, she became Lady Cook. Not content to bask in their vastly improved material and social status, Victoria and Tennessee continued to pursue their old causes with undiminished vigor, both in England and on periodic trips back to America, and discovered some brand new ones to promote. Victoria established a periodical *Humanitarian* (1892–1901) devoted to one of them, the new pseudoscience of eugenics. She remained committed to this and various other of her causes and enthusiasms until her death.

Victoria Woodhull, a mesmerizing speaker and a powerful polemicist, perhaps campaigned more ardently for women's sexual freedom than any feminist in the nineteenth century or since. Her New York home was actually more like an eighteeenth century Parisian salon, where she presided over radical activists and politicians who, like her, were seeking to remedy gender, class, and racial injustices. But it was the cause of sexual freedom that really engaged Victoria Woodhull's attention. She advocated loving whom one pleased without governmental sanction or marriage restrictions. This was based on democratic ideals of liberty and equality—women (and men) should not be bound to strict ideas of proper sexual behavior and women should not be "owned" by a husband. According to Woodhull and other proponents of free love, prostitution (which was then legal) would be unnecessary if both men and women could make love in the "purest sense,"—with all whom they loved. To most Americans at the time Woodhull's philosophy of free love was outrageous and dangerously destructive to the stability of the family, the welfare of the nation, and most importantly the well-being and happiness of women who might be tempted to practice it.

Woodhull and other advocates of free love sharply criticized the sexual double standard that allowed men to have affairs or visit prostitutes yet demanded that women remain pure and chaste. When Woodhull found herself isolated by many suffragists because of her radical sexual views and heard her morals denounced by **Harriet Beecher Stowe** and her sister Catherine Beecher, Woodhull felt her only recourse was to expose their hypocrisy by exposing Henry Ward Beecher, that supposed pillar of virtue, as a *de facto* practitioner of free love. Given the rigid rules of sexual behavior that "good" women were subject to in the late nineteenth century it is not surprising that Woodhull was condemned as a prostitute and a publicity-seeking blackmailer who hurt the credibility and standing of the woman suffrage movement to which she belonged. Yet a few reformers, like the suffragist **Elizabeth Cady Stanton**, regarded Woodhull as that rare woman who expressed ideas that other women feared even to think. She performed "a work for Women that none of us could have done," Stanton marvelled. "She ... dared men to call her names that make women shudder." See Johanna Johnston, *Mrs. Satan: The Incredible Saga of Victoria C. Woodhull* (1967).

Susan Gonda

WOODSON, Carter Godwin (b. New Canton, Va., Dec. 19, 1875; d. Washington, D.C., April 3, 1950), HISTORIAN, son of former slaves, taught himself to read and write. In his teens he moved to Huntington, West Virginia, where he attended high school (1895–96) and then studied at Berea College, Kentucky (1896–98), before becoming principal of his old high school in Huntington (1900–3). He spent the next four years traveling in Egypt, Asia, and Europe, where he briefly studied at the Sorbonne in Paris. After returning to the U.S. he earned a BA (1907) and an MA (1908) at the University of Chicago. While teaching in Washington, D.C. high schools (1908–18) he studied summers for his PhD in history at Harvard, receiving the degree in 1912.

Believing that the history and achievements of blacks in America had long been neglected, Woodson founded the Association for the Study of Negro Life and History in 1915 to concentrate on the researching and writing of black history. In 1916 the association launched the *Journal of Negro History,* with Woodson as editor-director. In 1919 Woodson, who was then principal of Armstrong High School in Washington, D.C., became dean of the School of Liberal Arts at Howard University; a year later he took a similar job at West Virginia State College. In 1921 he organized and became president of Associated Publishers, Inc., which devoted itself to books on black history. He retired from teaching in 1922. Thereafter he continued to emphasize the necessity of making whites aware of the black contribution to American history, and in 1937 he founded the *Negro History Bulletin* for this purpose. In addition to editing and publishing the works of others, Woodson wrote many books, including: *A Century of Negro Migration* (1918), *History of the Negro Church* (1921), and *African Heroes and Heroines* (1939).

———— ∞∞∞ ————

Although his leadership was based more on his program than on his personality, Carter G. Woodson was a great organizer and inspirer of others. He viewed his work as a foundation on which others would build, and he helped young scholars acquire formal training at the same time that he sought to build a grassroots base for the promotion of the history of black people. He deeply resented the exaltation of European history and culture and the concomitant denigration of Africa and the history and culture of black, brown, yellow, and red peoples. He stressed the importance of the masses in history, and he did not like the notion that some races, nations, classes, or other human groups are biologically superior to others, or that some have contributed significantly to history while others have made no important contribution. He was convinced that knowledge of the positive contributions of blacks to history and culture was a necessary source of inspiration for his race and a means of gaining respect from the majority group. The textbook which he wrote on African-American history, entitled *The Negro in Our History* (1922), the documents which he published, and such ventures which he launched and promoted as "Negro History Week," the *Negro History Bulletin,* the *Journal of Negro History,* and the annual programs of the Association for the Study of Negro Life and History were very important in leading to the establishment of African-American history as a fully accepted historical field. He initiated the Associated Publishers, the *Journal,* and the *Bulletin* because he believed that nowhere else, in the field of history, was the contribution of blacks respected and appreciated adequately, and nowhere else were blacks consistently a central rather than peripheral concern.

The disfranchisement and oppression of African-Americans and the rise in the United States of the field of professional university-trained historians constitute a part of the background which inspired the work of Carter G. Woodson. The Progressive revolt, which was under way when Woodson's formal academic training was completed, failed to address itself in any major way to the plight of blacks who were suffering from great economic, political, social, and other deprivations. The faith of Social Darwinism which was then in vogue stressed that blacks should look to themselves largely for the means of their uplift. **Booker T. Washington** accepted and preached much of this doctrine. In organizing and promoting the Negro History Movement, at the scholarly and lay levels, Woodson acted on the self-help doctrine. He had great sacrificial love for and dedication to this movement. See Earl E. Thorpe, *Black Historians: A Critique* (1971).

EARL E. THORPE

WOODWARD, Calvin Milton (b. Fitchburg, Mass., Aug. 25, 1837; d. St. Louis, Mo., Jan. 12, 1914), EDUCATOR, graduated from Harvard in 1860, and the same year became principal of the Brown High School in Newburyport, Massachusetts. In 1862 he enlisted as a private in the 48th Massachusetts Volunteers. Rising to the rank of captain, he participated in the capture of Port Hudson, Louisiana (1863). He then returned to his principalship in Newburyport. In 1865 he moved to St. Louis to become vice principal and teacher of mathematics at the Smith Academy of the new Washington University. He was promoted to assistant professor of mathematics at the university in 1867, professor of geometry and topographical drawing in 1869, Thayer Professor of Mathematics and Applied Mechanics in 1870, and dean of the university's polytechnic school in 1871, a position he held until 1896.

In 1879 Woodward formulated the plans and became director of the St. Louis Manual Training School, which opened in 1880 under the auspices of Washington University. Woodward advocated manual education along with traditional academic subjects. The School's students studied metal and woodwork as well as mathematics, science, history, and English; girl students took courses in the domestic sciences as a counterpart to the manual training for boys.

The St. Louis school rapidly became a model for those in other cities, and Woodward became a much sought-after speaker. He delivered a series of lectures on manual education in Manchester, England, in 1886. He was a member of the St. Louis Board of Education from 1877 to 1879 and again from 1897 until his death, serving two terms as president of the board (1899–1900, 1903–4). He served on the board of curators of the University of Missouri (1891–97), was president of the American Association for the Advancement of Science (1905–6), and was dean of the Washington University's school of engineering and architecture (1901–10). Some of his books included *The Manual Training School* (1887), *Manual Training in Education* (1890), and *Rational and Applied Mechanics* (1912).

Woodward was the most important popularizer of manual education in late 19th-century America, and an ardent proponent of the larger movement seeking diversity and relevance in schooling. His advocacy of manual activities raised questions about the function of schools. Initially he sought to make engineering education more practical by exposing his students to the tools of their profession in a workshop setting. He thus allied himself with those seeking to create skilled industrial leaders and technicians for the growing industrial society. Accusing existing schools of excessive bookishness and a neglect of work needs, and confronted by hostility from educators concerned about preparing students for specific vocational roles, Woodward contended that manual training would make education more democratic by keeping children in schools longer and by exposing them to a wider range of occupational choices. Moreover, he claimed, manual activities trained the mind through the hand. In doing so, they inculcated habits and moral values basic to good citizenship and economic success, and were thus necessary for all children. By so justifying the value of hand

learning in traditional terms, Woodward and his supporters were able to gain widespread support for manual education by the beginning of the 20th century. Yet the movement was more important for its transitional role; by asserting the value of vocational utility in schooling, it paved the way for the emergence of vocationalism as an essential feature of the educational system. See Marvin Lazerson and W. Norton Grubb, *Education and Industrialism: Documents in the History of Vocational Education* (1973).

MARVIN LAZERSON

WOOLWORTH, Frank Winfield (b. Rodman, N.Y., April 13, 1852; d. Glen Cove, L.I., N.Y., April 8, 1919), MERCHANT, attended public schools, did farm work, and studied for a brief period at a business college in Watertown, New York. At the age of nineteen he began clerking in local stores, but had little success as a salesman. In 1878, learning of a method of displaying a wide variety of goods at a single low price, he convinced his employers, the Watertown firm of Moore and Smith, to set up a counter filled solely with goods selling for five cents. In 1879 W. H. Moore agreed to back him in setting up a five-cent store in Utica, New York. Though the store closed within three months, Woolworth was convinced that the main cause of his failure was an insufficient variety of merchandise; later that year Moore again backed him, this time in establishing a "five-and-ten-cent" store in Lancaster, Pennsylvania. This venture proved successful, and additional stores were opened in various cities in New York, New Jersey, and Pennsylvania. Soon his brother C. S. Woolworth, his cousin Seymour H. Knox, and his close friends F. M. Kirby and E. P. Charlton joined him in the business, running their stores separately but being careful to avoid competing with one another. In 1912 all these stores, along with two owned by W. H. Moore, were merged into the F. H. Woolworth Co. The following year Woolworth, with his own funds, built the Woolworth Building, at the time the world's tallest skyscraper.

At his death, Woolworth's company owned more than one thousand stores in the United

States and Canada, with a business volume exceeding $100 million. Woolworth's personal fortune was estimated at $65 million.

———∞∞∞———

The career of Frank Woolworth added a new dimension to retailing in the United States and in England. He was the leading pioneer in the creation of the "five-and-ten" variety store, a marketing innovation aimed primarily at the lower-middle classes. By buying direct from manufacturers in high volume and by stocking his stores with a wide range of goods which sold for ten cents or less, Frank Woolworth attracted millions of Americans who had little money to spend but who enjoyed the luxury of choosing among a great many kinds of merchandise. Woolworth's success attracted numerous imitators, some of whom built major chains of retail variety stores, such as the Kress, Kresge, and Newberry stores. The appearance of the five-and-dime store meant a new kind of retail store in small towns, small cities, and giant metropolitan centers across America in the closing decades of the 19th century.

Frank Woolworth was a classic "self-made man" who embodied both the strengths and the weaknesses of that stereotype. He was tough-minded and persevering, believing in the future of the five-and-ten store first in this country and then in England, despite initial hardships and the skepticisms of his acquaintances. He remained insistent on the smallest economies, even long after his businesses were worth millions. Self-confident, egotistical, penurious, and bold, he joined the ranks of the poor boys grown vastly rich in the rise of big business during the decades before World War I. See John K. Winkler, *Five and Ten: The Fabulous Life of F. W. Woolworth* (1940).

GLENN PORTER

WRIGHT, Carroll Davidson (b. Dunbarton, N.H., July 25, 1840; d. Worcester, Mass., Feb. 20, 1909), STATISTICIAN, graduated from Reading (Mass.) High School in 1859. Until 1862 he taught at academies in New Hampshire and Vermont while studying law. He served in the Union army in 1862–65, rising from lieutenant to colonel. After a business failure, he returned to Reading in 1867 and developed a prosperous practice, specializing in patent law. A Republican, he was elected in 1871 and 1872 to the state senate, where he helped draft legislation requiring railroads to run reduced-rate trains for commuters. He also advocated a state fire insurance corporation.

In 1873 Wright was appointed Massachusetts commissioner of labor statistics. In addition to collecting facts about labor, he organized the state census of 1875, the most complete American survey executed to that date. By 1879 his agency had become a model for other states. In 1880 he administered the federal census in Massachusetts. In writings and lectures he discussed the usefulness of statistical inquiries and the methods of conducting them, especially those relating to living and working conditions.

In 1885 he was appointed federal commissioner of labor, in charge of the Bureau of Labor established in 1884 in the Interior Department. He held this position until 1905, under four presidents. (He retained his state post until 1888.) During 1893–97 he supervised publications of the federal census of 1890, and he served on commissions to investigate the Pullman strike of 1894 and the anthracite strike of 1902. In 1902 he became president of Clark College. He lectured at many universities and was on the advisory committee on economics and sociology for the Carnegie Institution of Washington.

———∞∞∞———

Wright's statistical career put him at the heart of the paradox of progress and poverty that puzzled his generation. His census work and many special investigations quantified the dimensions of national growth; he was especially interested in the productivity of the factory system. On the other hand "labor statistics" were a response to the "labor problem" in the new industrial order. Was the "wages system" just? Would a cooperative arrangement or socialism be better? Were long hours of work, child and female labor, high divorce rates, slums, pauperism, strikes, depressions, convict labor, and industrial accidents proper subjects of reform? Bureaus of labor followed Wright's lead in collecting facts on these and related subjects. In investigating such problems, Wright looked upon himself as a vehicle of "the altruistic spirit of the age." He was critical of dogmatic economists, laissez-faire or socialist, and of panaceas such as the movements for an eight-hour work day, a single tax, and currency reform. True to his religious upbringing and interests—the son of a Universalist clergyman, he became president of the American Unitarian Association—he took "an ethical view of the labor question," holding both employer and employee to fairminded and responsible behavior. His administrative ability and his impartial but humanitarian posture, as well as his rather optimistic and conservative conclusions, helped to make him a highly respected authority. He supervised more than a hundred statistical volumes and summarized his findings and opinions in several popular textbooks, among the earliest of their kind. Skeptical about theorizing and increasingly so about the quantifiable aspects of social problems, he made lasting contributions to the practical administration of statistical investigation. See James Leiby, *Carroll Wright and Labor Reform: The Origin of Labor Statistics* (1960).

JAMES LEIBY

WRIGHT, Frances (b. Dundee, Scot., Sept. 6, 1795; d. Cincinnati, Ohio, Dec. 13, 1852), REFORMER, was educated in London. She visited the U.S. in 1818 and, in addition to producing her play *Altorf* (1819) in New York City, mingled with intellectuals and traveled widely. Returning to London in 1820, she published an account of her experiences, *Views of Society and Manners in America* (1821). Becoming friendly with the Marquis de Lafayette, she accompanied him on his triumphant return trip to the U.S. (1824–25) and settled in America. Long interested in the problem of slavery, Wright contributed a large part of her assets to establishing a settlement for slaves in western Tennessee in 1825, which she called Nashoba. She hoped to purchase slaves, resettle them at Nashoba, where they could work

to repay this cost, and then colonize them outside the U.S. Though Nashoba failed, she carried out part of her plan by colonizing a group in Haiti in 1830.

In 1828 Wright joined Robert Dale Owen in editing the *New Harmony Gazette*. She began lecturing throughout the East, attacking religion, slavery, and the institution of marriage, which she wanted to replace with a free union based on moral, not legal, obligations. A frequent target of mobs wherever she lectured, Wright settled in New York City in 1829, where she edited a newspaper, *Free Enquirer*, and published the *Course of Popular Lectures* (1829). She formed the Association for the Protection of Industry and for the Promotion of National Education in 1829 to promote her causes, and "Fanny Wright Clubs" soon sprang up throughout the East. She also joined the Workingmen's party (1829) but resigned when it refused to adopt all of her views. She spent the next six years in Europe and returned to the U.S. in 1835. In 1836 she began a second period as a public lecturer, and spent most of the next three years speaking on "Chartered Monopolies, Slavery, and the 'Nature and History of Human Civilization.'" In addition she contributed articles to the Boston *Investigator*, a reformist paper published by Abner Kneeland, and edited the Philadelphia *Manual of American Principles*. Having spoken out in the past against banking and other monopolies, Wright was an active supporter of President Andrew Jackson's attack on the Second Bank of the United States.

───── ⚭ ─────

Frances Wright had, as she once admitted, an unusually "independent way of walking through the world"—a consequence, she explained, of having "learned, as well to struggle with the elements as any male child of Adam." Yet her apparent infatuation with Lafayette and intellectual dependence upon "her Socrates," Jeremy Bentham, and Robert Dale Owen betray a contrasting side of her character. In her personality as well as her career, she was a study in paradox.

As a reformer, she often undercut her own well-intentioned efforts. The Nashoba enterprise might have succeeded in serving as a practical example of gradual emancipation had Wright not insisted on making it an experiment in communitarianism as well. She further jeopardized the venture by advocating racial amalgamation and criticizing marriage and religion. She spoke on behalf of the case of sexual equality, seeking to persuade her audiences, as much by example as by rhetoric, that "the mind has no sex but what habit and education give it." But unlike other feminists, she seems to have had little sense of sisterhood and never joined any of the organizations campaigning for woman's rights. By discussing such forbidden topics as birth control she further alienated herself from the majority of pre–Civil War feminists.

Frances Wright was a "free enquirer" untrammeled by convention or majority opinion. Yet her radical views were so far in advance of the American people she admired that, as a consequence, she exerted comparatively little influence on them. See A. J. G. Perkins and Theresa Wolfson, *Frances Wright, Free Enquirer: The Study of a Temperament* (1939).

ANNE C. LOVELAND

WRIGHT, Frank Lloyd (b. Richland Center, Wis., June 8, 1869; d. Phoenix, Ariz., April 9, 1959), ARCHITECT, studied geometry and drawing for one year (1886) at the University of Wisconsin before beginning his architectural career in 1887 as a draftsman in Chicago, first for J. L. Silsbee, and then in the office of Dankmar Adler and **Louis Sullivan.** In 1893, having absorbed Sullivan's philosophy and designed several buildings on his own, he began to practice in Oak Park, Illinois. His residence for W. H. Winslow in River Forest, Illinois, expressed Wright's belief that a structure should be human in scale and harmonize with its surroundings. His concept of "organic architecture" led in the early 20th century to the "prairie house"—horizontally oriented buildings with open floor plans, a minimum of applied ornament, and close relationships to site—that won him international acclaim.

In 1909 Wright toured Europe and upon his return established his practice in a new house, which he designed for himself and named "Taliesin" (Welsh, "shining brow"), in Spring Green, Wisconsin. Here he developed an enthusiastic and devoted following of young architectural students, and for the rest of his life combined his practice with an intensive, year-round regimen of teaching. He also lectured and wrote extensively, publishing *An Autobiography* in 1932 (expanded in 1943), followed by numerous other books and articles. In 1930–32 he also proposed "Broadacre City," a model for a decentralized America, and he founded the Taliesin Fellowship, a group of resident student-apprentices. Three buildings in 1936–37 contributed to the resurgence of his practice: the Jacobs House in Madison, Wisconsin, the prototype of his moderately priced "Usonian" home for middle-income families; the Kaufmann House, a luxury weekend retreat cantilevered over a waterfall in Pennsylvania, and the Johnson Wax Administration Building in Racine, Wisconsin, with its huge windowless workspace. From 1936 until his death Wright executed 180 projects; during his entire seventy-two-year career some 300.

Although known primarily as a residence architect, Wright built many impressive public structures, from Unity Temple (1905–6) in Oak Park, to the vast Imperial Hotel (1913–22) in Tokyo, to the spiral Guggenheim Museum (1943–56) in New York. In the 1950s he also produced dozens of spectacular, controversial, and futuristic designs: a mile-high office building with atomic-powered elevators for Chicago, a cultural center with floating gardens for Baghdad, a plexiglass and concrete synagogue forming a Star of David, an entire college campus in Florida, and several civic centers. All these projects enhanced his reputation. He was as prolific an author in his last years as he was an architect, publishing *The Future of Architecture* (1953), *The Natural House* (1954), *A Testament* (1957), *The Living City* (1958), and numerous speeches and articles. At his death he left about fifty buildings in various stages of planning and construction, and a corps of assistants and students eager to carry on his principles.

During the last three decades of his life Wright assumed the role of an iconoclastic genius, claiming that he alone (although sometimes with Louis Sullivan's help) had revived architecture from the doldrums in which it had languished since the Renaissance. He once admitted in a court of law that he was indeed the world's greatest architect. "I was under oath," he explained later with a straight face. He was not much interested in professional organizations, adopting an independent posture which the public interpreted as arrogance, braggadocio, and irreverence for established values. Wright pontificated on a wide range of subjects. Although some of what he said was uninformed bombast—the verbal liberties of a cultural elder statesman—few observers denied that his architecture and many of his ideas were of major importance.

Yet in many ways Wright was a traditionalist. His objective in open-plan residences, for example, was to bring the family together under ideal circumstances, to reaffirm or re-establish ties that had been weakened by the centrifugal demands of urban and suburban living. Similarly, in his public buildings he tried to create an atmosphere of purposeful unity and old-fashioned community, whether in the beautiful, shared workspace at the Johnson Wax Factory or with the rhythmically repetitive articulation of offices at the Marin County Civic Center near San Francisco. He objected to architectural authority symbols from the Old World. Believing the East to be decadent and corrupt, he built mostly in the West and Midwest—the "real America." With **Ralph Waldo Emerson** and **Henry David Thoreau** among his literary heroes and Thomas Jefferson as his most admired statesman, he was in many ways a 19th-century man who believed in the inevitability of human progress, the superiority of American institutions, and the unlimited potential of unrestrained individualism.

But Wright was a radical innovator in architectural technique. The list of present-day commonplaces he experimented with, invented, or popularized is impressively long: corner and casement windows, built-in lighting and furniture, air conditioning and fireproofing, dry wall construction, prefabrication, radiant heating, the elimination of attics and cellars, increased fenestration, cantilevering, overhanging eaves, concrete block construction, horizontal orientation, the open plan, and much more. He influenced the work of contemporary European architects like Peter Behrens. His "prairie" designs before World War I began a midwestern movement in residential architecture toward reduced scale, increased open space, and fenestration which made a permanent impact, and in the 1930s his one-floor Usonian home with carport, open plan, patio, bedroom wing, and glass partitions became the prototype of the ubiquitous postwar American residence—the suburban ranch house. Wright's sculptured forms and his rejection of classically balanced rectangular organization— epitomized late in life by the Guggenheim Museum—encouraged younger practitioners to break other barriers of habit and style. Although his grand manner and his somewhat intangible ideas made him a mediocre pedagogue—no one has really carried on his work—Wright's legacy continues to instruct those willing to shatter precedent and tradition. See Robert C. Twombly, *Frank Lloyd Wright* (1973).

ROBERT C. TWOMBLY

WRIGHT, Orville (b. Dayton, Ohio, Aug. 19, 1871; d. Dayton, Ohio, Jan. 30, 1948), and **WRIGHT, Wilbur** (b. Millville, Ind., April 16, 1867; d. Dayton, Ohio, May 30, 1912), INVENTORS, left high school before graduating and worked as printers. In 1892 they opened a bicycle repair shop in Dayton, Ohio, and in 1895 they began manufacturing their own bicycles. In the early 1890s they became interested in flying after reading of Otto Lilienthal's experiments with gliders, but they did not undertake flying seriously until after Lilienthal's death in a glider accident in 1896. They then proceeded to familiarize themselves with all previous efforts in the field.

In 1899 they built a biplane kite and conducted

two man-carrying glider experiments at Kitty Hawk, North Carolina (1900, 1901). In 1901 they built a wind tunnel, where they tested about two hundred wing and biplane surfaces. They began to build a powered aircraft in October 1902. During their experiments they perfected a system of aileron control, the basic stabilizing mechanism of modern planes, which maintained the plane's equilibrium by shifting the angles of the wings and other parts to balance outside air pressure.

On December 17, 1903, at Kitty Hawk, North Carolina, Orville made the first piloted flight in a powered heavier-than-air plane, remaining aloft for twelve seconds and covering a distance of about 120 feet. The Wrights made four flights during that day, the longest of which was Wilbur's flight of fifty-nine seconds over a distance of 852 feet. In 1905 they flew a plane for thirty-eight minutes covering twenty-four miles around Huffman Field, Dayton, Ohio.

During the next several years, which were marked by both popular skepticism and bitter struggles over patents with American and foreign rivals, the Wrights improved their machine. On September 9, 1908, they demonstrated their plane to the U.S. army at Fort Myer, Virginia. The government awarded the Wrights a contract to manufacture airplanes capable of flying at forty miles per hour (1909). The Wright Co. was then established in Dayton, Ohio. With large-scale plane manufacturing under way, the courts finally decided the airplane patent issue in favor of the Wrights. In 1915, three years after Wilbur's death, Orville sold his patent rights and retired from active manufacturing to devote the rest of his life to experimentation and research.

Man had been experimenting with the problems of flight since the French balloon ascensions of the 1780s. In 1810 the British experimenter Sir George Cayley gave a classic statement of the problem: "to make a surface support a given weight by the application of power to the resistance of air." During the next century a host of balloonists and glider pilots sought to accomplish this. Gradually a body of experimental data was built up, theories to explain the data were put forward, and inventors improved such necessary components as the gasoline-fueled internal combustion engine. The Wright brothers took up the problem at a time when these several factors were beginning to converge, thus joining an international race to be the first to fly.

Although lacking even a high school education, they moved forward in a manner familiar to trained engineers and at times had even to act as scientists. They collected data (corresponding with Samuel P. Langley, secretary of the Smithsonian Institution and a leading expert on flight), tested the efficacy of theories, and conducted careful experiments on their own initiative. Much of their eventual success must be laid to the fact that far from being simple mechanics, they performed as competent and even brilliant engineers.

Their entrepreneurial ability was also marked. They soon realized the value of publicity both at home and in Europe, where Wilbur flew many exhibitions. They also realized that the federal government (and particularly the military) was an important potential patron for the advancement of flight, thus helping to establish a relationship which has continued to be important to the present time. See Fred C. Kelly, *The Wright Brothers* (1943).

CARROLL PURSELL

WRIGHT, Richard (b. near Natchez, Miss., Sept. 4, 1908; d. Paris, France, Nov. 28, 1960), WRITER, was born on a cotton plantation. His sharecropper father deserted the family when Wright was five, and he was raised by his mother with the help of a succession of relatives. At the age of seventeen he moved to Memphis, Tennessee, where he worked as a dishwasher and messenger.

In 1927 Wright moved to Chicago, where he worked as a post office clerk. During the Depression he was employed on the New Deal Federal Writers' Project (1935), and he became a member of the American Communist party, serving as executive secretary of the Chicago John Reed Club and contributing poetry and fiction to such party organs as *Left Front, Anvil,* and the *New Masses.* He also worked on the stories that later became his first book, *Uncle Tom's Children* (1938). In 1937 Wright moved to New York City, where he was the Harlem editor for the *Daily Worker,* and a contributing editor to the *New Masses,* while also being employed on the New York Federal Writers' Project. In 1939 a Guggenheim Fellowship enabled him to devote full-time to the completion of his first novel, *Native Son* (1940). The book was an instant popular success, and was later adapted for both the stage and the screen. *Native Son* was followed by *Twelve Million Black Voices* (1941)—a photographic history of the African-American—and by an autobiography, *Black Boy* (1945).

In 1946 Wright visited Paris at the invitation of the French government. He settled there permanently in 1947. In Paris, Wright was celebrated as a man of letters, invited to lecture, widely quoted by the press, and subjected to frequent interviews and visits from distinguished persons from all over the world. He traveled widely in Africa and Asia during the late 1940s and 1950s and published, as records of these trips, *Black Power* (1954) and *The Color Curtain* (1956). In 1957 he completed *White Man, Listen!,* among other things a summary of his concerns and observations on the colonial revolution taking place in those lands. His other works include the novels *Lawd Today* (1963), *The Outsider* (1953), and *The Long Dream* (1958). In "I Tried to be a Communist" (*Atlantic Monthly,* 1944) he recounted his growing disenchantment with communism (he resigned from the CPA in 1944), which, he became convinced, had little to offer black people in America.

———∞∞∞———

Richard Wright is one of the few politically oriented writers of the thirties whose work is still widely popular. Most writers of his day who felt that literature has a political function are either not read or have changed their conception of the nature and function of literature.

Wright, however, because of historical accident (the black liberation movement of the sixties and the resulting interest in black writers) and his prodigious talent is read. This is not unrelated to the fact that he was throughout his writing career committed to deeply felt but conflicting claims: the notion that the individual through exercise of will determines his own fate; and the notion that society, through its operational mechanisms, determines the fate of the individual. His lack of total commitment to social determinism has probably made his work palatable to modern readers, while most writers committed to social determinism are dismissed or belittled.

All of his fiction from *Lawd Today* (his earliest written but last published novel) to *The Long Dream* reveal this dichotomy. His emphasis changed as his politics changed, but he never totally lost sight of the responsibility of the individual for his fate and at the same time of the impingement on individuals of social necessity. Unlike many of his leftist contemporaries (Stephen Spender for example), Wright never became an apologist for political reaction. His nonfiction bears out the same conclusion. His orientation remained progressive despite his belonging to no political organization. See Constance Webb, *Richard Wright* (1968).

DONALD GIBSON

WRIGHT, Silas (b. Amherst, Mass., May 24, 1795; d. Canton, N.Y., Aug. 27, 1847), POLITICAL LEADER, graduated from Middlebury College in 1815. In 1819 he was admitted to the bar at Canton, New York, which thereafter was his home. He was an admirer of Jefferson and Madison, and was a major factor in the development of Jacksonian democracy in upstate New York. He served in the state senate (1824–27), and was by 1827 one of the leading members of the Albany Regency, which controlled New York state politics in that era. A strong advocate of the "pay-as-you-go" principle in government finance, Wright discouraged the further development of canals in his state by withholding the power to incur long-term debt and by helping to depose **DeWitt Clinton** as Erie Canal commissioner. Wright served in Congress (1827–29), where he initially supported the protective tariff, including the "Tariff of Abominations" of 1828, but later reversed his position. He was comptroller of New York (1829–33), and then replaced **William Marcy** (who had been elected governor of New York) in the U.S. Senate.

Wright enthusiastically supported the financial policies of Jackson and Van Buren, opposing the recharter of the second Bank of the United States, and favored the withdrawal of federal funds from the banking system into an independent treasury, but he opposed distribution of the surplus and the annexation of Texas. Elected to a full term in 1837 and reelected in 1843, he helped secure passage of the Independent Treasury bill in 1840. He worked to renominate Van Buren for president in 1844, and after the Democratic convention chose James K. Polk, he flatly refused the vice presidential nomination. However, he agreed to run for governor of New York, thereby helping to carry the state for Polk. As governor he alienated both the tenants of the great landholders of the Hudson Valley by calling out the militia to restore order during the antirent wars and the landlords by calling for legislation to severely limit their power. He was defeated for reelection in 1846.

Silas Wright was an interesting example of a Jacksonian politician and of the way certain northern Jacksonians reacted to the growing conflict over slavery in the 1840s. He began his career as a thoroughly professional officeholder and party man, convinced of the soundness of William L. Marcy's famous adage: "to the victor belong the spoils." (His own way of putting it was: "When our enemies accuse us of feeding our friends instead of them, never let them lie in telling the story.") Both as a state official under the Albany Regency and as a member of Congress he was a party wheel horse. During the Van Buren administration he became a leading figure in the Senate, chiefly because of his close personal relationship with the president.

However, when the question of annexing Texas became important, he began to act more on principle than for political advantage; he was in a large measure responsible for Van Buren's stand against annexation in 1844. Clearly by this date Wright had come to realize that politics was more than a game and that checking slavery was more important than any electoral victory. After Van Buren lost the Democratic presidential nomination to James K. Polk because of his stand against Texas, the convention actually nominated Wright for vice president. But he refused to accept—the only man in history to turn down a nomination for national office after it had been made.

Although Wright was notable as an extremely heavy drinker even in an age when many politicians consumed enormous amounts of alcohol, he was also widely admired for probity and devotion to duty, as is seen in his sobriquet, "the Cato of the Senate." His last service, as governor of New York, was politically disastrous; he abandoned all efforts at political accommodation, let alone manipulation, and behaved more like a J. Q. Adams, whom in his younger days he considered laughably inept, than like a Jackson or a Van Buren. See John A. Garraty, *Silas Wright* (1949).

JOHN A. GARRATY

WYETH, Andrew Newell (b. Chadds Ford, Pa., July 12, 1917), ARTIST, was the son of the illustrator and mural painter Newell Convers Wyeth. He was educated by private tutors and received all of his art training from his father. Wyeth held his first one-man show in Philadelphia in 1936; he had his second show at the William Macbeth Gallery in New York the following year, and soon won wide acclaim. Working mainly in watercolor and egg tempera, he painted landscapes, and people from all levels of society. Most of his works deal with the Brandywine Valley around his Chadds Ford studio and the area near his summer home in Cushing, Maine, which is the setting for his most famous work, *Christina's World* (1948, Museum of Modern Art, N.Y.). Wyeth has gained numerous honors and prizes throughout his career. He was elected to the National Institute of Arts and Letters in 1945, and is currently a member of the American Academy of Arts and Letters. In 1966 Wyeth won the gold medal of the Pennsylvania Academy of the Fine Arts. Some of his many works include: *That*

Gentleman (1960, Dallas Museum of Fine Arts), *Garret Room* (1962, artist's wife's collection), and *Day of the Fair* (1963, City Art Museum of St. Louis). In 1977, Wyeth was inducted into the French Academy of Fine Arts, the first American since **John Singer Sargent** to be so honored. Similarly, the Soviet Academy of the Arts made him an honorary member in 1978. Since the 1980s, Wyeth has remained generally out of the public spotlight except for his series, *The Helga Pictures* (1971–85), which received a swirl of publicity and public, if not critical, acclaim.

Andrew Wyeth's popularity, extending beyond the outposts of museums and galleries, must have something to do with the kind of people he depicts and their rural surroundings, unquickened by modern life, and in the niceties of his craft with its memories of honest Yankee skills. Most Americans, feeling their rootlessness, yearn after both. There is little difference between Wyeth's nature and the nature painted by mid-19th-century Americans. His program, set forth in 1943, reads like theirs: "… to escape from the medium with which I work. To leave no residue of mannerisms to stand between my expression and the observer. To seek freedom through significant form and design rather than through the diversion of so-called free and accidental brush handling." This desire to paint as though nothing was between him and his vision, to conceive of the outside world of things—the real—as indissolubly connected with the ideal—his idea—is a development of American painting out of **Ralph Waldo Emerson** and the transcendentalists. One aspect of Wyeth, however, belongs to the period since **Winslow Homer** and **Thomas Eakins:** his fondness for presenting his subjects from points of view like the angle shots his public sees daily in magazines and newspapers. Wyeth never indicates any ironic detachment from the bleak coziness he calls nature, and in this respect he is less of his own time than **Edward Hopper,** whose real subject is modern man's alienation from his surroundings. But lack of irony may well be the real secret of his present success, although this mythic primitivism may not guarantee the future of his work. See David McCord, *Andrew Wyeth* (1970).

LAWRENCE CAMPBELL

YOUNG, Brigham (b. Whitingham, Vt., June 1, 1801; d. Salt Lake City, Utah, Aug. 29, 1877), RELIGIOUS LEADER, had only eleven days of formal education. After reading **Joseph Smith**'s *The Book of Mormon* (1830) and a period of study and contemplation he became a member of the Church of Jesus Christ of Latter-Day Saints in 1832. The following year he led a band of converts to Kirtland, Ohio.

Young rapidly rose in the Mormon church hierarchy. He became second in seniority on the newly formed Quorum of the Twelve Apostles in 1835, and in 1838 he became the senior member of that body. He directed the Mormon migration to Nauvoo, Illinois, in 1839 and went to England the following year to do missionary work. Returning a year later, he became the leading fiscal officer of the church. While on a stumping tour for Joseph Smith's presidential campaign in 1844, Young learned of the Mormon leader's murder and returned to Nauvoo, where, after a bitter struggle with several rivals, he took over leadership of the church.

Young decided that Mormons could not live within American society and that western migration was necessary. Becoming president of the church in 1847, he led his followers to Utah in 1848. Settling near the Great Salt Lake, he began irrigation and public works projects, encouraged continued immigration to Utah, and built many schools. After the Utah Territorial Act of 1850, Young became the first governor of the territory.

When President Buchanan asked him to surrender the office in 1857 Young refused, and Buchanan sent troops to Utah under Albert Sidney Johnston. Young was forced to yield in 1858, but retained his position as president of the Mormon church until his death. He was widely criticized not only for his totalitarian authority but for his practice of polygamy. He had perhaps fifty-five wives and fifty-six children.

⁂

Brigham Young was a mass of contradictions. He was, on the one hand, a man of God who professed inspiration from Jesus and in his sermons often cited the Master's doctrines of meekness and nonmaterialism. On the other hand, he was a man of violence who boldly and repeatedly preached holy war against non-Mormons. And, in later life, the quest for material gain and personal pleasure dominated Young's thinking.

The savior of a great religion, Young possessed many admirable qualities. His God imbued him with courage, determination, great organizational skills, and the capacity to inspire and lead men. A practical man of enormous common sense, he marched his people to the Rockies, directed the establishment of more than 325 western towns, built railroads, constructed stores, erected factories, brought to Utah tens of thousands of immigrants, and created the superbly organized and brilliantly administered missionary system that today brings well over one hundred thousand new members into the Mormon church each year.

But only Young's most uncritical admirers considered him a theologian or a deep thinker. He himself frequently bragged about his meager education. His most distinctive and most important contribution to Mormon theology, polygamy for the masses, died a dozen years after he did, in part because the completion of the transcontinental railroad brought new ideas into Utah. But during Young's lifetime polygamy separated the Mormon elite from the rank and file, for only a man with several wives could hope to rise in the church hierarchy. Young himself married at every opportunity. Some of his brides were lonely old women who desired his companionship on earth, but several were young and beautiful girls who were made to believe that their salvation in heaven depended upon following his orders to the letter. A few of his wives left their husbands to join him, and at least three were women whose marriages to other Mormons Young, using one pretext or another, dissolved so that he might take these women for himself.

Young remained handsome and virile throughout most of his long life. He was five-feet ten-inches tall and possessed an unusually powerful frame. (His chest, broadened by the rigors of outdoor life, measured forty-five inches.) Like his predecessor, Joseph Smith, he possessed great personal charm. Women found both men unusually attractive.

Young bequeathed to his followers a mixed legacy. He left a people determined to survive, to prosper, and to spread God's word, but one forever fearful of a monster called Satan and constantly afraid of excommunication and damnation. Questioning church doctrine or authority has remained, as in Young's day, an unpardonable sin that subjects a Mormon to almost immediate excommunication. And Young left a church so rooted in anti-intellectualism that its leaders still remain deeply suspicious of new ideas. But his place in history is secure. Revered by nearly four million Mormons, he will survive as long as the religion he saved endures. See Stanley P. Hirshson, *The Lion of the Lord: A Biography of Brigham Young* (1969).

STANLEY P. HIRSHSON

YOUNG, Whitney Moore, Jr. (b. Lincoln Ridge, Ky., July 31, 1921; d. Lagos, Nigeria, March 11, 1971), REFORMER, graduated from Kentucky State College in 1941. He entered the army the following year and was sent to study engineering at the Massachusetts Institute of Technology. In 1944 he was assigned to a road-building program in Europe with an all-black outfit. Upon his discharge he earned an MA degree in social work from the University of Minnesota (1947). He joined the St. Paul (Minn.) Urban League that same year as director of industrial relations and vocational guidance, and became a lecturer at the College of St. Catherine (St. Paul) in 1949. He moved to Nebraska in 1950 to become executive director of the Omaha Urban League and at the same time taught at the School of Social Work of the University of Nebraska (1950–54) and at Creighton University (1951–52). In 1954 he became dean of the School of Social Work of Atlanta (Ga.) University. He studied at Harvard on a fellowship (1960–61) and then moved to New York City in 1961 to become executive director of the National Urban League.

Taking charge of this biracial social work agency, Young launched new programs to provide equal opportunities for blacks in employment, housing, and education. He lectured widely, and enjoyed the confidence of many white businessmen, whom he often tried to persuade to employ more blacks. He was one of the leaders of the 1963 March on Washington for Jobs and Freedom and in 1964 organized the Community Action Assembly in Washington to fight poverty in black communities. Young worked particularly closely with President Lyndon B. Johnson on civil rights and antipoverty programs, urging a "domestic Marshall Plan" to lift blacks from poverty and make them self-sufficient. In 1967 Young, at President Johnson's request, visited South Vietnam to observe that nation's presidential elections, but later criticized American involvement in Southeast Asia. He served on President Johnson's Committee on Youth Employment and Committee on Equal Opportunity. In addition to writing a national syndicated newspaper column, he published several books, including *To Be Equal* (1964) and *Beyond Racism* (1969).

Whitney Young worked throughout his adult life as an intermediary between blacks and whites. While in Europe as an army engineer during World War II, he was pressed into service working to ameliorate the racial tension that inevitably arose when white officers were placed in charge of segregated and recalcitrant blacks who were poignantly aware of the hypocrisy of the claim that they were fighting for democracy. Young's work as an interracial mediator continued during his more than two decades with the National Urban League, an organization dedicated to the welfare of black workers but financed almost entirely by contributions from whites.

Young possessed an appropriate personality for a power broker with one foot in each racial camp. An extremely gifted speaker who radiated geniality and good humor, he was at once urbane and down-home. He could affect the charm and manners of an aristocrat when he put on his tuxedo and mixed with the ladies and gentlemen of high society. But he could also roll up his sleeves and speak the language of the ghetto in such a way that few doubted he was a real "soul brother." There were some blacks, to be sure, who noted with dismay that Young was never arrested in the civil rights cause and chose to live in a well-to-do white suburb. Yet it is surprising not that Young was subjected to the barbs of a few black radicals (and white standpatters) but that he managed to bring blacks and whites together in times of intense racial suspicions.

Young was one of the most influential of the civil rights leaders. He was consulted in the formulation of President Lyndon B. Johnson's domestic programs and would have joined the cabinet of President Richard M. Nixon had he not feared that "the 'brothers' just would not have understood." Most significantly, Young played a preeminent role in persuading America's corporate elite that it should provide better economic opportunities for African-Americans. Occasionally criticized for his moderation, Whitney Young, perhaps more than any other black leader of the 1960s, worked to channel the nation's racial consciousness so as to provide economic gains for black workers. See Nancy J. Weiss, *Whitney M. Young, Jr., and The Struggle for Civil Rights* (1989).

RAYMOND WALTERS

ZAHARIAS, Mildred Ella "Babe" Didrikson (b. Port Arthur, Texas, June 26, 1911; d. Galveston, Texas, Sept. 27, 1956), ATHLETE, was the sixth of seven children born to Norwegian immigrant parents. She received the nickname "Babe" from her mother's use of the Norwegian "baden" (baby) as well as her self-proclaimed prowess as a baseball player equal to **Babe Ruth**. After a hurricane leveled Port Arthur the family moved to Beumont, Texas, where Didrikson attended Beaumont High School. In 1930, just shy of completing her senior year, she was hired by the Employer's Casualty Insurance Company of Dallas, Texas, to play on their industrial league women's basketball team. Financially strapped because of the Depression, her parents consented. In 1931 and 1932 Didrickson led her team to the national championship. In the off-season, the company started a field and track team to keep her occupied. At the 1932 Amateur Athletic Union track and field Olympic tryouts in Chicago, Didrickson competed as a one-woman team and her multi-event victories catapulted her into the national spotlight. At the 1932 Los Angeles Olympics she won gold medals in the women's javelin (143' 7"), and the 80 meter hurdles (11.7 seconds), and just missed a third gold in the high jump (5'5 1/4") because of her controversial jumping style. As a result of her spectacular performance, she was nationally acclaimed as the "Texas Tomboy."

To earn some money after the Olympics, Didrickson took to the stage on the RKO circuit for a one-week exhibition of her athletic prowess. In the mid 1930s she barnstormed with the all-male, bearded House of David baseball team, sparred with a middleweight boxing champion, and pitched in exhibition baseball games against major league players. Spending lavishly on her family all the while, she was alternately well-off or flat broke.

In 1938, Didrikson met pro wrestler George Zaharias at an amateur golf match in Los Angeles. Dubbed the "Crying Greek from Cripple Creek," his blustery personality and skills at self-promotion equalled hers. After a brief courtship they married that same year. He retired from wrestling to manage her career. Speculation that had persisted for years about her sexual orientation was stilled—though did not entirely stop—by the marriage.

With her husband's support Didrickson attempted to enter tennis but ran afoul of the sport's officialdom who questioned her amateur status. She then devoted herself to perfecting her golf game and won the 1935 women's amateur tournament in Texas. Though shunned by golf's monied elite, who regarded her as uncouth or worse, in the 1940s she began a decade-long domination of women's golf by winning thirteen consecutive amateur tournaments. She became the first American to win the British Women's Amateur Open (1947). That same year, she helped to found the Ladies' Professional Golf Association (LPGA). Though she had a stormy relationship with her peers in the golf world, she was president of the LPGA until just prior to her death and was largely responsible for its growth and development. She was the first woman athlete to earn over $100,000 a year, and many believe she was largely responsible for transforming women's golf into the successful sport it became.

In 1950, Didrikson met Betty Dodd, a young golfer from San Antonio, Texas. Dodd became enamored of Didrickson and devoted herself to her. She lived with the Zahariases from 1950 until Didrickson's death. Never admittedly lesbian, for Didrikson this relationship supplanted her marriage with George as a life-sustaining force. During these years, the Didrikson household was a tempestuous triad. Throughout it all, the press, friends, and family maintained silence as to the nature of the women's bond.

Didrikson was stricken with colon cancer in 1953 but returned to the links a mere fourteen weeks after her operation and quickly regained her championship form. Believing she had beaten cancer, she was one of the first public figures to disclose their disease and present themselves as self-help role models for other cancer victims. She founded the Babe Zaharias Foundation to help others battling cancer and raised money for cancer research and treatment. Her cancer returned in 1955, eventually causing her death.

Throughout her life and afterwards, Didrikson received many commendations, including the Associated Press's Athlete of the half-century award in 1950. In all, Didrikson won nearly four hundred trophies, cups, awards, and medals.

Babe Didrikson Zaharias was undoubtedly the finest athlete of her era, and arguably the best athlete—male or female—in twentieth-century America. She challenged long-held notions of women's physical capabilities, and for a few years in her early twenties delighted in shocking the press and public with her crude and unladylike mannerisms and verbiage. She was charismatic, a formidable foe on or off the field and given a wide berth by some of her peers. Yet those who embraced her idolized her.

Didrikson was average in stature, 5′ 5″ and 145 pounds when competing, although she gained a more womanly physique, topping out at 170 pounds, during her golfing years. She sought acceptance as both an appropriately feminine woman and as one sophisticated enough to ascend social class and hobnob with golf's country-club elite. She "succeeded" only modestly in both endeavors.

Before her marriage, Didrikson was often an object of press speculation about her gender identity and sexual orientation. That speculation ranged from probing to vicious. She was deemed a "muscle moll" and the premiere member of the "third sex"—neither male nor female. This, together with her self-aggrandizing bravado, cast her outside the parameters of acceptable female behavior. Her personality, which was abrasive and self-interested to a fault, made her a dubious teammate and a worrisome enemy.

Her relationship with Betty Dodd was kept private—even rendered invisible—lest innuendos and speculation as to her normalcy which her marriage had quieted somewhat, re-emerge. Understandably, her relationship with George deteriorated badly and, while they discussed divorce, her illnesses precluded it.

Didrickson was clearly the dominant personality behind the formation of the LPGA, although not its most skilled administrator. Her interests were nearly always self-centered. At bottom, she was a hustler, a one-woman band. While she made time for sports reporters despite their unkind remarks about her, she cared little about advancing the "cause" of women's sports beyond how she might personally benefit.

The notable exception to her great egotism was her work on behalf of cancer patients. There she gave herself to others. Most times, however, she was exhalted and fussed over, particularly by her family and her two life mates. Didrikson was a difficult, immensely talented and relentlessly practiced athlete. By her example if for nothing else, her impact on women's sports and cultural beliefs about women athletes, continues to resound in the present. See Susan E. Cayleff, *Babe: The Life and Legend of Babe Didrickson Zaharias* (1995).

SUSAN E. CAYLEFF

ZIEGFELD, Florenz (b. Chicago, Ill., March 21, 1869; d. Hollywood, Calif., July 22, 1932), THEATRICAL PRODUCER, was educated in Chicago's public schools. After a period as treasurer of his father's Chicago Musical College, he was sent by the elder Ziegfeld to Europe to import musicians for a concert hall at the World's Columbian Exposition in 1893. The musicians failed to attract audiences, and instead Ziegfeld brought from the Casino in New York Eugene Sandow, the celebrated strong man. Ziegfeld managed Sandow for three years. In 1896 he and the comedian Charles Evan Evans imported French actress Anna Held to New York, starring her in specialty numbers in Hoyt's *A Parlor Match*. Nationwide ballyhoo resulted in Held's American triumph. Later, Ziegfeld mounted a series of vehicles for the star, whom he passed off as his wife.

Among these shows the best was *Miss Innocence* (1908), a daringly staged production. With his collaborators Harry B. Smith and Julian Mitchell he had also staged *The Parisian Model* (1906).

Abhorring vaudeville, Ziegfeld developed his Follies shows in 1907 with the aid of Harry B. Smith. These were sophisticated, fluid, fast-moving displays of pretty girls, political satire, and "in" Broadway jokes. The 1907 Follies was a moderate success, but by 1910 the Follies had become as important an annual event in New York as the Easter Parade. Ziegfeld promoted and developed **Will Rogers,** W. C. Fields, Leon Errol, Lillian Lorraine, Mae Murray, and Fanny Brice along with scores of other stars. In 1914 his Midnight Frolic began. Ziegfeld produced *Sally* (1920), with Marilyn Miller, and *Show Boat* (1927), and coproduced with the Selwyns *Bitter-Sweet* (1929). **William Randolph Hearst** and Arthur Brisbane allowed him to lease at an unusually low price the handsome Ziegfeld theater, completed in 1927 at a cost of $3 million. Ziegfeld was ruined by gambling debts, gross extravagance, and the stock market crash of 1929, in which he lost more than $2 million.

⌘

Impatient, irascible, overwrought, with a high-pitched, whining voice, Ziegfeld was a misunderstood genius whose arrogance, perfectionism, and unceasing quest for flawless beauty on the stage alienated most of his conservative colleagues in the theater. His private life was squalid and destructive, and his love affairs with Anna Held, Lillian Lorraine, Marilyn Miller, Olive Thomas, and other stars were disfigured by quarrels, scandalous public behavior, and a marked lack of good taste. In the theater, however, Ziegfeld was obsessed with aesthetic balance and harmony, and completely rejected the drab sets, filthy vaudeville routines, and knockabout comedy which marked much of the late-19th-century comedy theater on Broadway. His glorification of the American girl, begun with his shows for Anna Held in which her chorus paraded in beautiful Paris gowns, was not merely devised to excite tired businessmen; it was intended to show how human beings and objects could be combined into moving pictures in a manner not then attainable by the black-and-white screen. He introduced film sequences onto the stage, which he combined with live action as early as 1910; he prepared choreographic ensembles which foreshadowed Busby Berkeley's on the screen; he insisted that no scene take longer than seven minutes, and that no comedian be allowed to hold up the sweep of a show. The result was that those who saw the Ziegfeld Follies were swept into a romantic world of glamour, color, and vivid movement that the American stage has never seen equaled. It became a show for the rich and privileged, put on by the rich and privileged. It was swept away by the advent of talkies and the screen musical Ziegfeld in fact engendered, and by the Depression, which made $5 ticket prices intolerable to the public. After the Crash, Ziegfeld's manic drive worked in a vacuum, and his death at the outset of the 1930s was entirely symbolic. See Charles Higham, *Ziegfeld* (1972).

CHARLES HIGHAM